THE
ALL ENGLAND
LAW REPORTS
1979

Volume 3

Editor
PETER HUTCHESSON LL M
Barrister, New Zealand

Assistant Editor
BROOK WATSON
of Lincoln's Inn, Barrister
and of the New South Wales Bar

Consulting Editor
WENDY SHOCKETT
of Gray's Inn, Barrister

London
BUTTERWORTHS

ENGLAND: Butterworth & Co (Publishers) Ltd
                    London: 88 Kingsway, WC2B 6AB

AUSTRALIA: Butterworths Pty Ltd
                    Sydney: 586 Pacific Highway, Chatswood, NSW 2067
                    Also at Melbourne, Brisbane, Adelaide and Perth

CANADA: Butterworth & Co (Canada) Ltd
                    Toronto: 2265 Midland Avenue, Scarborough, M1P 4S1

NEW ZEALAND: Butterworths of New Zealand Ltd
                    Wellington: T & W Young Building, 77–85 Customhouse Quay

SOUTH AFRICA: Butterworth & Co (South Africa) (Pty) Ltd
                    Durban: 152–154 Gale Street

USA: Butterworth & Co (Publishers) Inc
                    Boston: 10 Tower Office Park, Woburn, Mass 01801

©

Butterworth & Co (Publishers) Ltd

1979

ISBN 0 406 85134 4

Typeset by CCC, printed and bound in Great Britain by William Clowes (Beccles) Limited, Beccles and
London

REPORTERS

House of Lords

Mary Rose Plummer Barrister

Privy Council

Mary Rose Plummer Barrister

Court of Appeal, Civil Division

Mary Rose Plummer Barrister
Sumra Green Barrister
Frances Rustin Barrister
Avtar S Virdi Esq Barrister
J H Fazan Esq Barrister

Court of Appeal, Criminal Division

N P Metcalfe Esq Barrister
Sepala Munasinghe Esq Barrister

Courts-Martial Appeals

N P Metcalfe Esq Barrister

Chancery Division

Jacqueline Metcalfe Barrister
Evelyn M C Budd Barrister
Hazel Hartman Barrister

Queen's Bench Division

Jacqueline Charles Barrister
M Denise Chorlton Barrister
J M Collins Esq Barrister
Janet Harding Barrister
Lea Josse Barrister
Gwynedd Lewis Barrister
Deirdre McKinney Barrister
K Mydeen Esq Barrister

Family Division

Georgina Chambers Barrister

Revenue Cases

Rengan Krishnan Esq Barrister

Admiralty

N P Metcalfe Esq Barrister

Employment Appeal Tribunal

S H J Merali Esq Barrister

MANAGER

John W Wilkes Esq

House of Lords

The Lord High Chancellor: Lord Hailsham of St Marylebone

Lords of Appeal in Ordinary

Lord Wilberforce
Lord Diplock
Viscount Dilhorne
Lord Salmon
Lord Edmund-Davies

Lord Fraser of Tullybelton
Lord Russell of Killowen
Lord Keith of Kinkel
Lord Scarman
Lord Lane
(appointed 28th September 1979)

Court of Appeal

The Lord High Chancellor

The Lord Chief Justice of England: Lord Widgery

The Master of the Rolls: Lord Denning

The President of the Family Division:
Sir George Gillespie Baker (retired 27th September 1979)
Sir John Lewis Arnold (appointed 28th September 1979)

Lords Justices of Appeal

Sir John Megaw
Sir Denys Burton Buckley
Sir John Frederick Eustace Stephenson
Sir Alan Stewart Orr
Sir Eustace Wentworth Roskill
Sir Frederick Horace Lawton
Sir Roger Fray Greenwood Ormrod
Sir Patrick Reginald Evelyn Browne
Sir Geoffrey Dawson Lane
(appointed Lord of Appeal in Ordinary,
28th September 1979)
Sir Reginald William Goff

Sir Nigel Cyprian Bridge
Sir Sebag Shaw
Sir George Stanley Waller
Sir James Roualeyn Hovell-Thurlow
Cumming-Bruce
Sir Edward Walter Eveleigh
Sir Henry Vivian Brandon
Sir Sydney William Templeman
Sir John Francis Donaldson
(appointed 28th September 1979)
Sir John Anson Brightman
(appointed 28th September 1979)

Chancery Division

The Lord High Chancellor

The Vice-Chancellor: Sir Robert Edgar Megarry

Sir John Patrick Graham
Sir Peter Harry Batson Woodroffe Foster
Sir John Norman Keates Whitford
Sir John Anson Brightman
  (appointed Lord Justice of Appeal,
  28th September 1979)
Sir Ernest Irvine Goulding
Sir Raymond Henry Walton

Sir Peter Raymond Oliver
Sir Michael John Fox
Sir Christopher John Slade
Sir Nicolas Christopher Henry Browne-
  Wilkinson
Sir John Evelyn Vinelott
Sir George Brian Hugh Dillon
  (appointed 28th September 1979)

Queen's Bench Division

The Lord Chief Justice of England

Sir Alan Abraham Mocatta
Sir John Thompson
Sir Helenus Patrick Joseph Milmo
Sir Joseph Donaldson Cantley
Sir Hugh Eames Park
Sir Stephen Chapman
Sir John Ramsay Willis
Sir Graham Russell Swanwick
Sir Patrick McCarthy O'Connor
Sir John Francis Donaldson
  (appointed Lord Justice of Appeal,
  28th September 1979)
Sir Bernard Caulfield
Sir Hilary Gwynne Talbot
Sir William Lloyd Mars-Jones
Sir Ralph Kilner Brown
Sir Phillip Wien
Sir Peter Henry Rowley Bristow
Sir Hugh Harry Valentine Forbes
Sir Desmond James Conrad Ackner
Sir William Hugh Griffiths
Sir Robert Hugh Mais
Sir Neil Lawson
Sir David Powell Croom-Johnson
Sir Tasker Watkins VC
Sir John Raymond Phillips

Sir Leslie Kenneth Edward Boreham
Sir John Douglas May
Sir Michael Robert Emanuel Kerr
Sir Alfred William Michael Davies
Sir John Dexter Stocker
Sir Kenneth George Illtyd Jones
Sir Haydn Tudor Evans
Sir Peter Richard Pain
Sir Kenneth Graham Jupp
Sir Robert Lionel Archibald Goff
Sir Stephen Brown
Sir Gordon Slynn
Sir Roger Jocelyn Parker
Sir Ralph Brian Gibson
Sir Walter Derek Thornley Hodgson
Sir James Peter Comyn
  (transferred from Family Division,
  1st October 1979)
Sir Anthony John Leslie Lloyd
Sir Frederick Maurice Drake
Sir Brian Thomas Neill
Sir Roderick Philip Smith
Sir Michael John Mustill
Sir Barry Cross Sheen
Sir David Bruce McNeill
Sir Harry Kenneth Woolf

Family Division

The President of the Family Division

Sir Reginald Withers Payne
  (retired 27th September 1979)
Sir John Brinsmead Latey
Sir Robin Horace Walford Dunn
Sir Alfred Kenneth Hollings
Sir John Lewis Arnold
  (appointed President of the Family Division,
  28th September 1979)
Sir Charles Trevor Reeve
Sir Francis Brooks Purchas
Dame Rose Heilbron
Sir Brian Drex Bush
Sir Alfred John Balcombe

Sir John Kember Wood
Sir James Peter Comyn
  (transferred to Queen's Bench Division,
  1st October 1979)
Sir Ronald Gough Waterhouse
Sir John Gervase Kensington Sheldon
Sir Thomas Michael Eastham
Dame Margaret Myfanwy Wood Booth
Sir Christopher James Saunders French
  (appointed 28th September 1979)
Sir Anthony Leslie Julian Lincoln
  (appointed 28th September 1979)
Dame Ann Elizabeth Oldfield Butler-Sloss
  (appointed 28th September 1979)

CITATION

These reports are cited thus:

[1979] 3 All ER

REFERENCES

These reports contain references, which follow the headnotes, to the following major works of legal reference described in the manner indicated below.

Halsbury's Laws of England

The reference 35 Halsbury's Laws (3rd Edn) 366, para 524, refers to paragraph 524 on page 366 of volume 35 of the third edition, and the reference 26 Halsbury's Laws (4th Edn) para 577 refers to paragraph 577 on page 296 of volume 26 of the fourth edition of Halsbury's Laws of England.

Halsbury's Statutes of England

The reference 5 Halsbury's Statutes (3rd Edn) 302 refers to page 302 of volume 5 of the third edition of Halsbury's Statutes of England.

English and Empire Digest

References are to the replacement volumes (including reissue volumes) of the Digest, and to the continuation volumes of the replacement volumes.

The reference 44 Digest (Repl) 144, *1240*, refers to case number 1240 on page 144 of Digest Replacement Volume 44.

The reference 28(1) Digest (Reissue) 167, *507*, refers to case number 507 on page 167 of Digest Replacement Volume 28(1) Reissue.

The reference Digest (Cont Vol D) 571, *678b*, refers to case number 678b on page 571 of Digest Continuation Volume D.

Halsbury's Statutory Instruments

The reference 12 Halsbury's Statutory Instruments (Third Reissue) 125 refers to page 125 of the third reissue of volume 12 of Halsbury's Statutory Instruments; references to subsequent reissues are similar.

CORRIGENDA

[1979] 2 All ER
p 1204. **R v Stephenson.** Solicitors for the Crown: read *'Drivers*, New Malton' instead of as printed.

[1979] 3 All ER
p 254. **St Catherine's College v Dorling.** Line *g* 2: for 'let as separate dwellings' read 'let as a separate dwelling'.
p 390. **R v Inland Revenue Comrs, ex parte Rossminster Ltd.** Lines *e*1 and 2: for 'his contentions could support' read 'the applicants contend'. Page 391, line *j* 4: for 'treated' read 'tested'. Page 392, line *a* 2: for 'because' read 'on the grounds that'. Page 395, line *h* 3: for 'one document to contain' read 'one document thought to contain'. Page 396, line *e* 3: delete the words ', as I see them, but again' and insert full point in their place.
p 744. **Bocardo SA v S & M Hotels Ltd.** Line *e* 3 and footnote 4: for 'Prideaux's Precedents in Conveyancing' read '11 Encyclopaedia of Forms and Precedents (4th Edn) 321, form 2:27'.

Cases reported in volume 3

Shaw v Shaw

b FAMILY DIVISION
BALCOMBE J
9th FEBRUARY 1979

Constitutional law – Diplomatic privilege – Immunity from legal process – Removal of immunity on cessation of diplomatic function – Divorce proceedings by wife of diplomatic agent – Summons by husband to strike out petition on ground of diplomatic immunity – Husband a diplomatic agent at date of petition and issue of summons but ceasing to be diplomatic agent before summons heard – Whether petition should be struck out – Whether petition rendered void by issue of summons – Diplomatic Privileges Act 1964, Sch 1, art 31(1).

On 19th December 1978 the wife presented a petition for divorce in which she averred that she and the husband had been habitually resident in England throughout the year ending with the date of presentation of the petition. On January 12th 1979 the husband issued a summons to strike out the petition on the ground that he was immune from suit under the Diplomatic Privileges Act 1964. At the date of presentation of the petition and the issue of the summons the husband was a diplomatic agent within the 1964 Act, being the commercial attaché at the United States Embassy, and was therefore entitled to rely on diplomatic immunity as a bar to the petition, under art 31(1) of Sch 1 to the Act. On 25th January, however, his appointment came to an end and he ceased to be a diplomatic agent. Accordingly, when the summons came on for hearing on 9th February he was no longer entitled to immunity from suit. He nevertheless contended that as he had been entitled to immunity from suit at the date of issue of the summons, the petition became null and void from that date and the court should strike it out, even though the wife could present a fresh petition to which the husband could not object on the ground of immunity from suit.

Held – The petition remained a valid petition until it was struck out on the ground of the husband's immunity from suit, notwithstanding the existence of the procedural bar of diplomatic immunity. It therefore remained a valid petition despite the issue of the summons and was valid at the date of the hearing of the summons. Since at the date of the hearing the husband was not entitled to immunity from suit, there was no justification at that date for striking out the petition. It followed that the summons would be dismissed (see p 6 *b* to *f*, post).

Empson v Smith [1965] 2 All ER 881 applied.

Notes
For immunity from jurisdiction of diplomatic agents, see 18 Halsbury's Laws (4th Edn) para 1566, and for cases on the subject, see 11 Digest (Reissue) 733–737, 505–533.

For the Diplomatic Privileges Act 1964, Sch 1, art 31, see 6 Halsbury's Statutes (3rd Edn) 1019.

Cases referred to in judgment
Dickinson v Del Solar [1930] 1 KB 376, [1929] All ER Rep 139, 99 LJKB 162, 142 LT 66, 11 Digest (Reissue) 742, 590.

---

a Article 31, so far as material, is set out at p 3 *c d*, post

Empson v Smith [1965] 2 All ER 881, [1966] 1 QB 426, [1965] 3 WLR 380, CA, 11 Digest
(Reissue) 743, 596.

Musurus Bey v Gadban [1894] 2 QB 352, [1891–4] All ER Rep 761, 63 LJQB 621, 71 LT
51, CA, 11 Digest (Reissue) 736, 517.

R v Madan [1961] 1 All ER 588, [1961] 2 QB 1, [1961] 2 WLR 231, 125 JP 246, 45 Cr App
R 80, CCA, 11 Digest (Reissue) 736, 525.

Suarez, Re, Suarez v Suarez [1918] 1 Ch 176, [1916–17] All ER Rep 641, 87 LJCh 173, 118
LT 279, CA, 11 Digest (Reissue) 742, 589.

Cases also cited

Baccus SRL v Servicio National Del Trigo [1956] 3 All ER 715, [1957] QB 438, CA.
C (infant), Re [1958] 2 All ER 656, [1959] Ch 363.
Ghosh v D'Rozario (or Rosario) [1962] 2 All ER 640, [1963] 1 QB 106, CA.
Rahimtoola v Nizam of Hyderabad [1957] 3 All ER 441, [1958] AC 379, HL.
Zoernsch v Waldock [1964] 2 All ER 256, [1964] 1 WLR 675, CA.

Summons

By a summons dated 12th January 1979, the husband, Charles Marlowe Shaw, applied
for an order that the petition for divorce filed on 19th December, 1978 by his wife,
Christina Maria Shaw, be struck out, set aside or stayed or that such order be made as
regards the continuation of the petition as might be just, on the grounds that the
husband was immune from the jurisdiction of the court by reason of the Diplomatic
Privileges Act 1964. The facts are set out in the judgment.

Alan Ward for the husband.
Eleanor Platt for the wife.

BALCOMBE J. I have before me a summons by a respondent husband that the
petition be struck out or set aside or stayed, or that such order be made as regards the
continuation of the petition as may be just, on the grounds that the husband is immune
from the jurisdiction of the court by reason of the Diplomatic Privileges Act 1964.

This raises a short but by no means uninteresting, and to me at any rate novel, point
of law which arises in these circumstances. On 19th December 1978 the wife presented
a petition for divorce in the Divorce Registry. She avers that she and her husband were
married in 1960 in the United States of America; that they have since lived in London;
that neither party is domiciled in England and Wales, but that both have been habitually
resident in England and Wales throughout the period of one year ending with the date
of presentation of the petition. She then states her occupation, and states that the
husband is a diplomat and civil servant.

He has put in evidence an affidavit, supported by a certificate from the Foreign Office,
that he was at the date in question, 18th January 1979, when he swore the affidavit, the
commercial attaché at the United States Embassy, and as such a member of the diplomatic
staff of the United States mission in this country; and that was the ground on which he
claimed the relief in the summons which I have already mentioned.

However, since the date of the summons and, indeed, since the date of that affidavit,
the husband has ceased to be the commercial attaché at the United States Embassy. His
appointment in that capacity has ended with effect from 25th January 1979, and I am
told that he has now returned to the United States of America. And it is in those
circumstances that this application comes before me.

Counsel, in an able and spirited submission on behalf of the husband, has submitted
to me that the fact that the husband has gone back to the United States of America and
is no longer entitled to diplomatic immunity is neither here nor there, because at the
date of the issue of the summons he was so entitled; therefore, submits counsel, I should
strike out the petition. He accepts that the point is a somewhat technical one in that he
further accepts that it would be possible for the wife to present a fresh petition tomorrow

a to which no such objection could be taken; but, nevertheless, if the point is a good one I must give effect to it.

I turn first to consider the provisions of the Diplomatic Privileges Act 1964, on which the point is based. Section 1 says: 'The following provisions of this Act shall, with respect to the matters dealt with therein, have effect in substitution for any previous enactment or rule of law.' I find that section a somewhat encouraging one because a number of the cases cited to me indicate that the previous law was by no means clear. It then goes on b in s 2 to apply the articles set out in Sch 1 to the 1964 Act (being articles of the Vienna Convention on Diplomatic Relations[1] signed in 1961) to the law of the United Kingdom, and I turn straight away to the schedule. Article 1 is a definition article and defines 'a diplomatic agent' as 'the head of the mission or a member of the diplomatic staff of the mission', and then in turn defines the 'members of the diplomatic staff' as 'members of the staff of the mission having diplomatic rank'.

c On the evidence before me, to which I have already referred, I am satisfied that at the date of the petition, as well as at the date of the summons to strike out, the husband was a diplomatic agent within the meaning of that article. Article 31, para (1), then provides: 'A diplomatic agent shall enjoy immunity from the criminal jurisdiction of the receiving State. [Nothing turns on that in this case. It goes on:] He shall also enjoy immunity from its civil and administrative jurisdiction, except in the case of . . .' and then there are d three exceptions listed, none of which is relevant to the case I have before me. The matrimonial jurisdiction of the High Court is part of the civil jurisdiction of the court and therefore, in my judgment, the husband would be entitled to rely on his diplomatic immunity as a bar to the petition in this case, if it is still available to him.

Finally, I must refer to art 39, which provides by para (2):

e 'When the functions of a person enjoying privileges and immunities have come to an end, such privileges and immunities shall normally cease at the moment when he leaves the country, or on expiry of a reasonable period in which to do so, but shall subsist until that time, even in case of armed conflict. However, with respect to acts performed by such a person in the exercise of his functions as a member of the mission, immunity shall continue to subsist.'

f Now, this petition is not based on any acts performed by the husband in the exercise of his functions as a member of the mission and, as I have already said, counsel for the husband concedes that the husband has now lost his immunity in the sense that any fresh petition launched by the wife could not now be met by any similar plea of diplomatic immunity. And so the short point that I have to decide is this: on the basis, as I have said, that the husband had diplomatic immunity at the date when the petition was launched and at the date when he issued his summons to strike out the petition, but has as of g today's date lost that immunity, what order should I now make?

There have been cited a number of cases on the old law. Some of those cases are very difficult to understand or to reconcile with each other, largely because of the language used in the Diplomatic Privileges Act 1708 which, paraphrased, said that all suits against ambassadors should be utterly null and void to all intents and purposes. And yet there were a number of cases where it was held that suits brought against diplomats in the past h were valid where the immunity had been waived, and much legal ingenuity has been devoted to try and reconcile these apparently contradictory statements. In Re Suarez[2] Scrutton LJ made it clear that he was troubled by this apparent contradiction and said that he desired to reserve his liberty to consider how exactly a writ issued without the consent of an ambassador, and therefore apparently a nullity (and he cited another case in the Court of Appeal which was cited to me, Musurus Bey v Gadban[3]) was made an j effective writ by the consent of the defendant and the extent to which it became effective.

1 Vienna, 8th April 1961, TS 19 (1965), Cmnd 2565
2 [1918] 1 Ch 176 at 200, [1916–17] All ER Rep 641 at 650
3 [1894] 2 QB 352, [1891–4] All ER Rep 761

Fortunately, it seems to me that I am not bound to have to deal with that troublesome point, because of a more recent decision in the Court of Appeal in *Empson v Smith*[1], by which I am bound and whose reasoning I find compelling. In order to understand the reasoning in that case, it is right that I should refer to the headnote which sets out the relevant facts[2]:

> 'On October 17, 1961, the plaintiff let her house in London for one year certain less one day to the defendant, an administrative officer in the employ of the High Commission of Canada in the United Kingdom. A special clause in the tenancy agreement provided, inter alia, that in the event of the tenant being officially ordered by his Government to duty outside London and the landlord being duly notified in writing by the tenant, the agreement should cease and terminate three calendar months after the date of the delivery of such notice to the landlord. In December, 1961, the defendant, who alleged that he had been officially ordered to Europe for duty, gave notice to the plaintiff to terminate the tenancy agreement and left the premises in March, 1962. In March, 1963, the plaintiff began proceedings in the county court for damages for breach of the tenancy agreement. The defendant did not enter an appearance, but a certificate was issued by the Ministry of Commonwealth Relations under section 1(3) of the Diplomatic Immunities (Commonwealth Countries and Republic of Ireland) Act, 1952, certifying that he was a member of the official staff of the High Commissioner. On the basis of that certificate the registrar, on 26th March, 1963 [and I correct the date in the headnote because according to the text the date was 26th April], stayed the action. On July 31, 1964, the Diplomatic Privileges Act, 1964 . . . was passed [and then there is a reference to article 37 (2). The headnote continues:] On August 31 the plaintiff applied for removal of the stay, her application being adjourned. On October 1, 1964 the Diplomatic Privileges Act, 1964, came into force. On November 4, the defendant applied for an order dismissing the action on the ground that it was a nullity. On December 15 both applications were heard together and a certificate, issued under section 4 of the Act of 1964, certifying that the defendant was a member of the administrative staff of the High Commissioner, was before the judge. The judge struck out the action on the ground that the proceedings were a nullity at the time they were begun and were not affected by the Act of 1964.
>
> On Appeal by the plaintiff: *Held*, – (1) that, as the law stood at the time that the proceedings were begun, the defendant was covered by diplomatic immunity, and the proceedings could not be lawfully maintained while that immunity remained; but that the action subsisted until struck out by the judge and the stay imposed by the registrar could have been removed and the action allowed to proceed if the immunity had been lost either by a valid waiver or, in respect of acts done by the defendant in his personal capacity, by the cessation of his diplomatic employment; that a change in the law similarly permitted the action to proceed, if not barred by the Limitation Act, 1939, if it removed the immunity previously enjoyed, which was probably the case here. [And then various cases are cited. Then:] (2) That, since the defendant had not applied to have the action dismissed on the grounds that it was a nullity before the Act of 1964 came into force, he could not now do so, since under the new Act immunity from civil suit of administrative and technical officers had been curtailed, and the defendant's immunity depended on whether the acts done by him in relation to the tenancy were within or outside the course of his duty. Accordingly, the plaintiff was entitled to have her action tried and that issue determined.'

The Court of Appeal was unanimous in allowing the appeal. Sellers LJ gave a short judgment for allowing the appeal, Dankwerts LJ a slightly longer one, in which he ends

---

1 [1965] 2 All ER 881, [1966] 1 QB 426
2 [1966] 1 QB 426 at 427–428

up by saying[1]: 'Some logical difficulties have been suggested in regard to the survival of
a an action which is described as having been a nullity [That is a reference to some of the
earlier cases that I have already mentioned:] but, in my opinion, and in the circumstances
these do not form a useful mental exercise.' Diplock LJ giving, if I may say so with
respect, one of his usual very lucid judgments, really analyses the jurisprudential
problem. After setting out the facts, he says[2]:

b 'When the action was commenced in March, 1963, the defendant was entitled
under s. 1(1) (b) of the Diplomatic Immunities (Commonwealth Countries and
Republic of Ireland) Act, 1952[3] "to the like immunity from suit and legal process as
is accorded to members of the official staff of an envoy of a foreign sovereign Power
accredited to Her Majesty". He was thus entitled so long as he remained en poste to
complete immunity from civil suit in the United Kingdom, both as respects acts
done in his official capacity on behalf of his government and as respects acts done in
c his private capacity. This immunity he could, however, lose at that date in one of
two ways: first, as respects acts done in either capacity if his immunity were waived
by the head of his mission on behalf of the Government of Canada [and then two
cases are cited] or secondly, but only as respects acts done in his personal capacity, if
he should cease to be en poste and a sufficient time had elapsed thereafter for him
to wind up his affairs. [and then other cases are cited, including *Musurus Bey v
d Gadban*[4]. Diplock LJ continues:] If the defendant had applied before the
commencement of the Diplomatic Privileges Act 1964, to have the plaintiff's action
dismissed there would have been no answer to his application, but he delayed until
November, 1964. By that date his right to immunity from civil suit had been
curtailed by that Act, which applies to the United Kingdom the provisions of the
Vienna Convention. [Then he sets out the effect of arts 31 and 37 of the
e Convention. Diplock LJ continues:] It is elementary law that diplomatic immunity
is not immunity from legal liability but immunity from suit. If authority is needed
for this, it is to be found in *Dickinson* v. *Del Solar*[5], which has been cited by
DANKWERTS, L.J. Statutes relating to diplomatic immunity from civil suit are
procedural statutes. The Diplomatic Privileges Act 1964, is in my view clearly
applicable to suits brought after the date on which that statute came into force in
f respect of acts done before that date. [Then he continues and cites various other cases
which had been cited to the judge below. Then:] It follows therefore that until steps
were taken to set it aside or to dismiss the action the plaintiff's plaint was no nullity:
it was a valid plaint. If the defendant had, with the permission of his High
Commissioner, appeared to it before Oct. 1, 1964, the procedural bar to the hearing
would have been removed. So too if the defendant had ceased to be en poste while
g the plaint was still outstanding the action could then have proceeded against him.
I can see no reason in logic or the law of nations why the position should be any
different when the procedural bar has been removed by Act of Parliament –
particularly when that Act of Parliament gives statutory effect to an international
convention . . . In holding, in my view, incorrectly, that the proceedings were a
nullity at the time they were commenced, the deputy county court judge founded
h himself on a passage in the judgment of LORD PARKER, C.J., in *R.* v. *Madan*[6] in which
he referred to the proceedings being "null and void unless and until there is a valid
waiver which, as it were, would bring the proceedings to life and give jurisdiction

---

1   [1965] 2 All ER 881 at 885, [1966] 1 QB 426 at 435
2   [1965] 2 All ER 881 at 885–887, [1966] 1 QB 426 at 437–439
3   Section 1(1) of the 1952 Act was subsequently re-enacted by the Diplomatic Privileges Act 1964,
s 8(4) and Sch 2
4   [1894] 2 QB 352, [1891–4] All ER Rep 761
5   [1930] 1 KB 376, [1929] All ER Rep 139
6   [1961] 1 All ER 588 at 591, [1961] 2 QB 1 at 7

to the court." LORD PARKER was clearly not using the words "null and void" in a
precise sense for what is null and void is not a phoenix, there are no ashes from *a*
which it can be brought to life. In that case he was concerned only with waiver as
removing the procedural bar of diplomatic immunity. His words should not be
read that only waiver can, as it were, bring the proceedings to life. The removal of
the procedural bar from any other cause will have the same effect.'

Faced with that decision counsel for the husband, admittedly pressed by myself, did
not feel able to assert that the petition in this case was null and void ab initio; although *b*
certainly some of the cases he cited to me would only be relevant if that were the case.
What he sought to do was to say that the petition had merely some inchoate existence
and that unless it were brought to life, either by waiver or, possibly, by termination of
the diplomatic immunity by loss of the position, it had no force; and in this case he said
it was not brought to life by the husband departing for the United States on 25th January,
because it had previously been killed stone dead when the summons was issued on 12th *c*
January. I hope I do no injustice to counsel's argument, but that seems to me to be a
summary of it.

I cannot accept that argument. It seems to me from the reasoning of Diplock LJ[1]
which I find compelling, that this petition was a valid petition at the moment of its
issue. The husband himself was entitled, as he did, to claim diplomatic immunity; and
if he had still been entitled to that immunity at the moment when this summons came *d*
to be heard, the court would have struck it out. Similarly, as it appears from the
authorities, if it had come to the attention of the court without direct action on the part
of the husband that he was entitled to diplomatic immunity, the court should of its own
motion have struck it out. But nevertheless, the fact is that by the time the matter has
come before the court the husband is no longer entitled to diplomatic immunity. In
those circumstances, therefore, the procedural bar has gone and I can see no justification, *e*
either as a matter of law nor, I am glad to say, of sense, for striking out a petition when
it is accepted that an identical petition could be issued tomorrow because of the removal
of the bar to proceedings.

I therefore dismiss the husband's summons to have the petition struck out.

Summons dismissed.   *f*

Solicitors: *Davies Arnold & Cooper* (for the husband); *Brecher & Co* (for the wife).

Georgina Chambers   Barrister.

---

1   See *Empson v Smith* [1965] 2 All ER 881 at 885–886, [1966] 1 QB 426 at 437

Pearson and others v Inland Revenue Commissioners

COURT OF APPEAL, CIVIL DIVISION
BUCKLEY, BRIDGE AND TEMPLEMAN LJJ
5th, 6th, 7th, 8th, 11th JUNE 1979

Capital transfer tax – Settlement – Interest in possession – Beneficiary entitled under settlement to income of property subject to trustees' power to accumulate – Whether beneficiary's interest a present interest or an interest in reversion or remainder – Whether beneficiary's interest an interest in possession – Finance Act 1975, Sch 5, para 6(2).

By a settlement dated 30th November 1964, a settlor settled a trust fund during a defined period ('the trust period') on such one or more of his children and their issue as the trustees should appoint. The settlement provided that until and subject to any such appointment the trustees were to 'accumulate so much (if any) of the income of the trust fund as they shall think fit' during a period of 21 years from the date of the settlement. Subject to that the trustees were to hold the capital and income of the trust fund in equal shares absolutely for such of the children of the settlor as attained the age of 21 or married under that age. The settlor had three daughters, all of whom had attained the age of 21 years by the end of February 1974. By a deed of appointment dated 20th March 1976 the trustees, in exercise of their power of appointment, appointed a sum of £16,000 (part of the capital of the trust fund comprised in the settlement) to be held on trust to pay the income to F, one of the settlor's daughters, during her life or the trust period, whichever was the shorter. It was common ground that in consequence of the appointment, F became entitled to an interest in possession in the appointed £16,000. The Crown contended however that prior to the appointment F had no interest in possession in any part of the trust fund, by virtue of the fact that the trustees were under a duty to consider from time to time whether income from the trust fund, as it arose, should be paid to the three daughters in equal shares, be accumulated or be dealt with partly in one way and partly in the other, with the result that when on the execution of the deed of appointment F became entitled to an interest in possession in the £16,000 there was a capital distribution by the trustees, within para 6(2)[a] of Sch 5 to the Finance Act 1975, rendering them liable to capital transfer tax.

Held – A beneficiary's 'interest in possession' under a settlement was an interest which conferred on him a right to the present enjoyment of the subject-matter of the interest, even though it was defeasible by an exercise of one or more of the discretionary powers vested in the trustees, whether the power was one of appointment or of accumulation. Furthermore, the fact that the immediate enjoyment of the income from the trust property might be postponed for a reasonable period to permit the trustees to consider whether to exercise any of the powers vested in them in defeasance of the beneficiary's vested right to the income was not sufficient to deprive the beneficiary's interest of the character of an interest in possession, because in that period the beneficiary would still be entitled to the income, although in the event his right to it might be partially or wholly defeated. It followed, therefore, that at the time of the appointment F was already entitled to an interest in possession in the trust fund and accordingly the appointment did not involve a capital distribution out of the trust fund within the charge to capital transfer tax under para 6(2) of Sch 5 to the 1975 Act (see p 11 e to h, p 12 a, p 14 g h and p 15 c, post).

Decision of Fox J [1979] 1 All ER 273 affirmed.

---

a   Paragraph 6(2) is set out at p 9 *d e*, post

Notes

For the meaning of interest in possession, see 19 Halsbury's Laws (4th Edn) para 636.   *a*
For the Finance Act 1975, Sch 5, para 6, see 45 Halsbury's Statutes (3rd Edn) 1889.

Cases referred to in judgments

Allen-Meyrick's Will Trusts, Re, Mangnall v Allen-Meyrick [1966] 1 All ER 740, [1966] 1
WLR 499, Digest (Cont Vol B) 733, *3435*.
Attorney-General v Power [1906] 2 IR 272, 21 Digest (Repl) 33, *⋆40.*   *b*
Gartside v Inland Revenue Comrs [1968] 1 All ER 121, [1968] AC 553, [1968] 2 WLR 277,
[1967] TR 309, 46 ATC 323, HL, Digest (Cont Vol C) 326, *74b.*
McPhail v Doulton [1970] 2 All ER 228, [1971] AC 424, [1970] 2 WLR 110, HL, Digest
(Cont Vol C) 805, *1324a.*
Jones, Re (1884) 26 Ch D 736, 53 LJ Ch 807, 50 LT 466, CA, 40 Digest (Repl) 797, *2776.*
Morgan, Re (1883) 24 Ch D 114, 53 LJ Ch 85, 48 LT 964, 40 Digest (Repl) 797, *2775.*   *c*

Cases also cited

Aylwin's Trusts, Re (1878) LR 16 Eq 585.
Baird v Lord Advocate [1979] 2 All ER 28, [1979] 2 WLR 369, [1979] STC 229, HL.
Buttle's Will Trusts, Re, Buttle v Inland Revenue Comrs [1977] 3 All ER 1039, [1977] 1 WLR
1200, [1977] STC 459, CA.   *d*
Locker's Settlement Trusts, Re Meachem v Sachs [1978] 1 All ER 216, [1977] 1 WLR 1323.
Master's Settlement, Re, Master v Master [1911] 1 Ch 321.
Rochford's Settlement Trusts [1964] 2 All ER 777, [1965] Ch 111.
Weir's Settlement, Re, McPherson v Inland Revenue Comrs [1970] 1 All ER 297, [1971] Ch
145, CA.

e

Appeal

The Crown appealed against an order of Fox J[1] dated 31st July 1978, granting the
plaintiffs, Clifford Pearson, Arthur Cope Pilkington and John Murray McKenzie ('the
trustees'), a declaration that, for the purposes of Sch 5 to the Finance Act 1975, a
settlement made on 30th November 1964 by the settlor, Sir Richard Pilkington, was
such as to confer on the principal beneficiaries, namely the daughters of the settlor, Fiona   *f*
Pilkington, Victoria Serena Pilkington and Diane Penelope Julia Pilkington, interests,
which on 27th March 1974 were beneficial interests in possession in equal shares in the
trust fund. The facts are set out in the judgment of Templeman LJ.

Martin Nourse QC and *Michael C Hart* for the Crown.
D J Nicholls QC and *C H McCall* for the trustees.   *g*

BUCKLEY LJ. This is an appeal from a decision of Fox J[1], given on 31st July 1978.
The question is whether capital transfer tax became payable under the Finance Act 1975
on 20th March 1976, when the trustees of a settlement made by the late Sir Richard
Pilkington appointed, under a power conferred on them by the settlement, £16,000,
part of the trust fund in favour of one of the settlor's daughters during her life or the   *h*
continuance of a defined trust period, whichever should be the shorter. Fox J[1] decided
that the tax did not become payable, and the Crown appeals.

The judgment of the learned judge is now reported[1]. The facts are clearly and
sufficiently stated in the judgment and I shall not recapitulate them now.

The capital transfer tax was brought into existence by Part III of the 1975 Act. By ss
19 and 20 the tax is charged on any chargeable transfer made after 26th March 1974,   *j*
other than an exempt transfer. A chargeable transfer is any 'transfer of value' as defined
by s 20(2), that is, any disposition made by a person as a result of which the value of his
estate immediately after the disposition is less than it would be but for the disposition.

---

1   [1979] 1 All ER 273, [1979] 2 WLR 353, [1978] STC 627

a So primarily the Act deals with dispositions inter vivos, but by s 22 it is made to apply also to property passing on a death, and s 21 enacts that Sch 5 to the Act shall have effect with respect to settled property.

It is common ground that the property comprised in the settlement in the present case was at all relevant times settled property for the purposes of the 1975 Act. By the date of the appointment, 20th March 1976, which was the first of the four appointments made by the trustees to be made after the commencement of the Act, all the the settlor's

b three daughters had attained 21. So the capital and income of the settled property, so far as not already appointed, was then held on trust for the three daughters in equal shares absolutely, but subject to (a) the power of the trustees to make further appointments in favour of objects of that power, who are defined in cl 1(d) as the discretionary objects, (b) the power of the trustees to accumulate so much of the income as they should think fit during a period ending on 29th November 1985, (c) the power of the trustees under cl

c 21 of the settlement to apply income in payment of taxes etc, (d) a power contained in cl 14 of the settlement (not referred to by Fox J) to lay out capital or income on the management and exploitation of any property comprised in the settlement, and (e) any other powers vested by law in the trustees.

There is no dispute that in these circumstances each daughter had an interest in the trust property. The question which arises is whether that interest was an interest in

d possession within the meaning of the 1975 Act.

Paragraph 6(2) of Sch 5 provides as follows:

'Where a person becomes entitled to an interest in possession in the whole or any part of the property comprised in a settlement at a time when no such interest subsists in the property or that part, a capital distribution shall be treated as being made out of the property or that part of the property; and the amount of the

e distribution shall be taken to be equal to the value at that time of the property or, if the interest is in part only of the property, of that part.'

It is common ground that in consequence of the appointment of 20th March 1976 the settlor's daughter Fiona became entitled to an interest in possession in the appointed £16,000. If that were all, a liability for tax would have arisen under para 6 of the

f schedule, but the trustees contend that para 6(2) does not apply to the present case because at the date of the appointment an interest in possession already subsisted in the £16,000. The Crown, on the other hand, contends that on the true construction of the statute an interest in possession subsists only where the beneficiary is entitled to all the net income of the trust property, or of the relevant part of the trust property, as it accrues. They contend that that is not the case here because none of the three daughters is entitled to any of the income of the unappointed part of the trust property until the

g trustees have had a reasonable time to decide whether to accumulate all or any part of that income, or perhaps to apply it under any other power possessed by the trustees otherwise than by distributing it to the daughters in equal shares. The case turns on the short point whether, within the meaning of the 1975 Act, an interest in possession in the £16,000 subsisted immediately before the appointment of 20th March 1976. It is

h common ground that the presence of the trustees' power of appointment does not affect this question. Before Fox J it was treated as common ground that the expression 'interest in possession' in the 1975 Act has the same meaning as it had in antecedent estate duty legislation, but that is no longer the case.

In this court the Crown has put forward the following submissions: 1. For the purposes of Part III of the 1975 Act there is an interest in possession in settled property

j if the holder of the interest is entitled to the net income (if any) of the property as it arises, but not if the net income is subject to a discretion or power, in whatever form, which can be exercised so as to withold it from him after it has arisen. 2. On 26th March 1974 there was no interest in possession in the settled property in the present case for the following reasons: (1) Under cl 3 of the settlement the trustees' duty from time to time was to consider whether income as it arose should (i) be paid to the three daughters in equal shares under (b), or (ii) be accumulated under (a), or (iii) be dealt with partly in one way and partly in the other. (2) Accordingly, cl 3 was in its practical effect the same as one which (a) conferred power on the trustees for a period of 21 years to pay so much (if any) of the income of the trust fund as they should think fit to the three daughters in equal shares, (b) imposed a trust during the like period to accumulate any income not so paid and, subject as aforesaid, (c) gave the capital of the trust fund to the three daughters in equal shares absolutely. (3) It is clear that under trusts drawn as in (2) there would have been no interest in possession in the settled property and the legislature could not have intended to distinguish between (1) and (2) in a taxing statute. 3. The expression 'interest in possession' in Part III of the 1975 Act does *not* have the same meaning as in the estate duty legislation, entitlement to income as it arises being the hallmark of the former. 4. Alternatively to 3, there would not have been an interest in possession in the present case for the purposes of the estate duty legislation.

In support of his first submission counsel for the Crown has referred to para 3(2), (3) and (5) of Sch 5, all of which refer to a person being entitled to income of trust property. He says that these provisions lay emphasis on the person's entitlement, that is to say, his right to demand payment. He says that in the present case the trustees are bound, before paying any income to the daughters, to consider whether they should accumulate any, and if so how much, of the income and whether they should distribute any, and if so how much; and he says that as a matter of practical reality that problem would arise and would present itself in precisely the same way whether the settlement contained, as it does, a power to accumulate and a trust to distribute whatever is not accumulated, or a power to distribute and a trust to accumulate whatever is not distributed. In neither case could the daughters demand instant payment of any part of the income as it accrued, or object if the trustees were to decide to accumulate all the income. Counsel for the Crown suggest that the legislature would not have intended to draw a distinction between these two cases. Counsel for the Crown distinguishes the effect of a discretionary power, such as a power to accumulate, from a power of appointment on the ground that the latter does not affect the subsisting interests of the beneficiaries down to the date of appointment and only operates on subsequently accruing income, whereas the former deprives the beneficiaries of the right to receive income as it accrues and so operates on income which has already accrued. He referred us to *Gartside v Inland Revenue Comrs*[1] and also to *Attorney-General v Power*[2], a case decided in Ireland in 1906; he also referred us to *Re Allen-Meyrick's Will Trusts*[3] and to *McPhail v Doulton*[4].

Counsel for the trustees, on the other hand, has presented the following submissions: 1. For many years the expression 'interest in possession' has had a well recognised meaning in English law, distinguishing simply such an interest from one in remainder or reversion (or expectancy). 2. In accordance with that well recognised meaning, the existence of a prior power to deal with income does not of itself convert an interest which would otherwise be in possession into one not in possession. This is so, whether the power is one of appointment, or of revocation, or of payment or application to or for the benefit of others, or of accumulation, or of use for capital purposes. 3. Under that well recognised meaning the interest of each of the three daughters in one-third of the settled fund was in possession in March 1974. 4. The estate duty legislation, over many years, repeatedly used the expression 'interest in possession' in its traditional sense, and from the terms of that legislation it is clear that each of the three daughters would have been regarded as having a beneficial interest in possession. 5. There is no context in the capital transfer tax legislation requiring, or permitting, the (undefined) expression 'interest in possession' to be given some meaning other than its traditional one. On the contrary,

1   [1968] 1 All ER 121, [1968] AC 553
2   [1906] 2 IR 272
3   [1966] 1 All ER 740, [1966] 1 WLR 499
4   [1970] 2 All ER 228, [1971] AC 424

there is a strong context requiring the use of the traditional meaning, which is the same meaning as in estate duty, with which capital transfer tax overlapped and interlocked, and on the concepts of which it has drawn to a significant extent.

Counsel for the trustees has referred us to Preston on Estates[1] and to Mr Fearne's famous Essay on Contingent Remainders[2] in support of his submission as to the meaning of the term 'interest in possession'. He has cited Re Morgan[3] and Re Jones[4], a decision in this court, where the same distinction is drawn by distinguished judges between an interest in possession and an interest in expectancy; and he has drawn our attention to numerous statutory contexts where he says that the expression 'interest in possession' is clearly used in the same sense, and in several of which it is so used in contrast with an interest in expectancy. These include several instances in taxing Acts relating to estate duty. These statutory provisions, which I do not propose to deal with individually, seem to me to support the contention that the term 'interest in possession' has been consistently used by the legislature over a long period in the sense given by Preston[1] and Fearne[2].

The question in the present case is, in my opinion, purely one of construction of the 1975 Act. That was an Act of Parliament introducing a quite novel system of taxation, and there is no particular reason, apart from internal evidence in that Act itself, to suppose that it intended to carry over concepts from earlier taxing legislation. Language used in other Acts cannot, in my judgment, assist directly on the question.

The 1975 Act contains no definition of the meaning of 'interest in possession', notwithstanding that, as the learned judge pointed out in his judgment, there are important differences in the fiscal consequences of an interest in possession existing or not existing in various circumstances. In the absence of a statutory definition a term of this kind must, in my opinion, be given its primary meaning, if it has one, unless the context otherwise requires, and the absence of a definition is at least some indication that the legislature did not think that the meaning of the expression called for any explanation. In my judgment the expression 'interest in possession' has a clear, recognised and well-established meaning in our law, indicating an interest which confers a right to present enjoyment of the subject-matter. If one were to ask what interest one of the settlor's daughters had under the settlement as at the first day of a trust year of account next before 26th March 1976 in the unappointed part of the trust fund and its income during the ensuing year, the answer could, in my opinion, only be that she was then entitled to one-third of that income. True, one would have to go on to say that that interest was in certain respects defeasible, but it was a vested interest carrying the right to the enjoyment of the whole one-third of the income unless and until it was defeated, either by an appointment or by an exercise of one or more of the discretionary powers vested in the trustees. The description 'interest in possession' would, in my opinion, fit it perfectly. The fact that the immediate enjoyment of the income might be postponed for a reasonable period to permit the trustees to consider whether to exercise any discretionary power vested in them in defeasance of the lady's vested right to the income is not, in my opinion, sufficient to deprive her interest of the character of an interest in possession. During that period she would be the person entitled to the income, although in the event her right to it might be partially or wholly defeated.

I recognise that, so far as the fiduciary duties of the trustees are concerned, there may be little difference between a power to accumulate coupled with a trust to distribute in a particular manner whatever is not accumulated and a power to distribute in that particular manner coupled with a trust to accumulate whatever is not distributed. The process of weighing the competing claims to consideration of those who will benefit from accumulation against those who will benefit by distribution may be the same in each case; but that cannot entitle one to rewrite either the statute or the settlement.

1   Elementary Treatise on Estates (2nd Edn, 1820)
2   10th Edn (1844), p 2
3   (1883) 24 Ch D 114
4   (1884) 26 Ch D 736

Moreover, a discretion to distribute all or such part of the settled income as the trustees think fit amongst a number of specified beneficiaries in specified shares would, I think, be a strange kind of discretion, for one would expect it to extend to the shares in which the named beneficiaries should take as well as to the amount which they should receive collectively. The ordinary rule applicable to the interpretation of taxing statutes must apply. First, one must endeavour to determine what Parliament has enacted and then one must apply that to the actual facts of the particular case. One can only depart from the primary meaning of what Parliament has said if it produces results which are so bizarre, or so unreasonable, as to convince the mind that Parliament cannot have intended what it appears to have said, and even then one must find some other meaning which the language is reasonably capable of bearing.

In the present case, although it may be possible to find instances in which the 1975 Act will be liable to produce strange, and perhaps not very satisfactory, results if the term 'interest in possession' is construed in what I think is its normal and primary sense, nothing has been said which convinces me that Parliament cannot have meant the term to bear that meaning. Arguments by reference to anomalies in the construction of a statute of this kind do not seem to me to afford any very valuable assistance. The ingenuity of counsel can almost always produce possible anomalies in either direction, and that has been the case in the present matter.

I consequently accept the trustees' construction of the term and reject the Crown's. I agree with the following passage of the judgment of Fox J[1]:

'It seems to me that the essential question is not whether a beneficiary can say of any income as it arises, "That is mine". In all but the simplest cases he will very often not be able to say that because the income will be subject to various administrative powers of the trustees. Nor, it seems to me, is the quantum of income which ultimately reaches the beneficary a material matter. The fundamental question, I think, is whether his entitlement, whatever, if anything, it may turn out to be in terms of quantum, is a present entitlement in right of an interest in the trust property subject only to the proper exercise of the trustees' powers. And, an entitlement is a present entitlement notwithstanding that the trustees have, as they must have, a reasonable time in which to consider what course to adopt as to exercise of powers.'

I also agree with the learned judge's grounds for distinguishing *Attorney-General v Power*[2] and *Gartside v Inland Revenue Comrs*[3] from the present case.

For these reasons I would dismiss this appeal.

BRIDGE LJ. I agree.

TEMPLEMAN LJ. By the Finance Act 1894 estate duty was levied on property, inter alia, when death caused a change of ownership or a change of possession. Estate duty on a change of possession was avoidable by a timely change of possession inter vivos. By s 11 of the Finance Act 1900, replaced by s 43 of the Finance Act 1940, estate duty was levied on the death of a beneficiary formerly entitled to an interest in possession if his interest was determined within a specified period, ultimately extended to seven years, prior to his death. After 1940 estate duty was avoidable by settlements which did not create interests in possession. Property was confided to trustees for the duration of a long perpetuity period on discretionary trusts of capital and income for beneficiaries

---

1   [1979] 1 All ER 273 at 284–285, [1979] 2 WLR 353 at 637, [1978] STC 627 at 638–639
2   [1906] 2 IR 272
3   [1968] 1 All ER 121, [1968] AC 553

who, as mere objects of a discretion, acquired no interest in possession or otherwise: see
a *Gartside v Inland Revenue Comrs*[1].

By the Finance Act 1969 estate duty was levied on the death of a member of a
discretionary class by reference to the benefits received by the beneficiary during the last
seven years of the life of that beneficiary. Estate duty was avoidable by judicious
distributions to those not destined to die within seven years.

By the Finance Act 1975 capital transfer tax was introduced to replace estate duty. In
b the case of discretionary settlements, where and so long as there is no interest in
possession, tax is levied on any distribution or disposition of property in favour of any
beneficiary. Tax is also levied once in every ten years on property which has not been
distributed but remains held on discretionary trusts.

In the case of settlements which create interests in possession, capital transfer tax is
levied on a change of possession whether resulting from death or from some distribution
c or disposition inter vivos. For some mysterious reason Parliament did not impose the tax
on a distribution or disposition of property in favour of a beneficiary who immediately
before the distribution or disposition is entitled to an interest in possession in that
property.

In the present case settled property has been disposed of in favour of a beneficiary. If
that beneficiary was already entitled to an interest in possession in that property, capital
d transfer tax is not payable. If the beneficiary has no such interest then the tax is payable.

By the settlement dated 30th November 1964 a trust fund was settled during a defined
and subsisting perpetuity period on trust for a large class of discretionary objects,
including children of the settlor, as the trustees appoint. Subject to any such appointment
the trust fund was settled during a defined and subsisting accumulation period on trust
to accumulate as an accretion to capital so much of the income of the trust fund as the
e trustees think fit. Subject to the trustees' power of appointment and subject to the
trustees' power of accumulation, the trust fund was settled, in the events which
happened, on trust as to capital and income for the three daughters of the settlor in equal
shares. Each daughter acquired a vested interest in the capital and income of one-third
of the trust fund liable to be divested by an exercise of the trustees' power of
appointment. Each daughter became entitled to one-third of any income which
f devolved in default of and pending any appointment, unless the trustees exercised their
power of accumulation.

By an appointment dated 20th March 1976, the trustees in exercise of their power of
appointment settled £16,000, part of the capital of the trust fund comprised in the
settlement, on trust for the settlor's daughter Fiona for life. We were informed that for
the purposes of this appeal, and this appeal only, we may ignore the fact that Fiona only
g held an interest in one-third of the £16,000 property prior to the appointment.

By para 6(2) of Sch 5 to the 1975 Act, so far as material:

> 'Where a person becomes entitled to an interest in possession in . . . property
> comprised in a settlement at a time when no such interest subsists . . . a capital
> distribution shall be treated as being made . . . equal to the value at that time of the
> property . . .'
h
By para 6(4) capital transfer tax is charged on any such capital distribution.

It is common ground that Fiona became entitled to an interest in possession in the
£16,000 property by virtue of the appointment which conferred on her a life interest in
the £16,000 property and thereby entitled her to enjoy all the income of the £16,000
property thenceforward during the remainder of her life. The Crown concedes that
j immediately before the appointment, the three daughters, including Fiona, held interests
in the property comprised in the settlement, including the £16,000 property. The
Crown claims that the interests of the daughters immediately prior to the appointment
were not interests in possession, on the ground that the daughters were not entitled to

enjoy the income of the property but only to enjoy such part of the income, if any, which the trustees did not decide to accumulate and add to capital. The trustees contend that *a* the daughters had interests in possession because they were entitled in equal shares to the income, if any, available for distribution to them in right of their admitted interests in default of appointment.

The Crown concedes that a present vested interest in capital and income, subject only to, and liable to be divested by, the exercise of a power of appointment, is an interest in possession. The trustees in the present instance could exercise their power of appointment *b* so as to deprive the daughters of their interests. This possibility does not prevent the interests of the daughters from being interests in possession until the power is so exercised. The reason for this concession, says the Crown, is that the power of appointment cannot be exercised to deprive the daughters of income which arises before the power is exercised. The trustees' power of accumulation is, however, a power which, according to the Crown, prevents the daughters' interests in default of appointment from being in possession because the power is exercisable after income arises. The daughters *c* have no present right to enjoy income when it arises, but only a right to enjoy such sums as the trustees fail to accumulate.

In common legal parlance and in trust law an interest is either in possession, when there exists a present right of present enjoyment, or in remainder or expectancy, when there exists a right of future enjoyment. The Crown was not bold enough to claim that *d* a life tenant subject only to a power of accumulation has an interest in reversion, remainder or expectancy. It claims that such a life tenant is entitled to an interest which cannot properly be described by accepted categories of interest, but is distinguished possibly in trust law, possibly in estate duty law but certainly in capital transfer tax law, by the purely negative characteristic of not being an interest in possession.

The trustees contend that the Crown's argument is part fallacy, part wishful *e* thinking. The fallacy lies in the assumption that a life tenant is entitled to enjoy the gross income of a trust fund, whereas in truth he is only entitled to enjoy the income, if any, which remains after the trustees have discharged the responsibilities laid on them by the settlement and by the general law. These responsibilities include decisions, which may be taken at any time, before or after any particular income is received, to employ income for a variety of purposes which may enure for the benefit of the life tenant or the *f* remainderman, or both; for example, expenditure on repairs or improvements. In the present case the trustees' responsibilities extend to a consideration of whether to accumulate in a manner which may benefit the life tenant or remainderman or both, having regard to many factors including the extensive powers of disposition and other powers vested in the trustees and the fiscal effects of any decision.

I agree with the trustees. I can find no relevant distinction in principle between the *g* power of appointment and the power of accumulation. Each power may be exercised so as to defeat the interests of the daughters. Neither power deprives the daughters of the present right of present enjoyment of the income which is not affected by any exercise of the power. The daughters are entitled to the income; it is their income unless and until the trustees devote that income to other authorised purposes.

I find nothing in the 1975 Act which persuades or requires the court to attribute to the *h* expression 'interest in possession' any meaning other than that which trust law ascribes to that expression. I have no doubt that in trust law a life interest subject to a power of accumulation is an interest in possession.

The Crown relies on para 3(2) of Sch 5 to the 1975 Act, which provides that, where—

'a person entitled to an interest in possession in settled property is entitled to part only of the income (if any) of the property, the interest shall be taken to subsist in *j* such part only of the property as bears to the whole thereof the same proportion as the part of the income to which he is entitled bears to the whole of the income.'

But in my judgment this paragraph is not relevant to the question whether a life tenant subject to a power of accumulation is entitled to income. The paragraph is dealing with a case in which a life tenant is not entitled to the whole but is entitled to a specific part of the income.

a

The Crown also argues that there is no material distinction between a discretionary settlement which confers power to distribute to a beneficiary coupled with a trust for accumulation and a strict settlement which confers power to accumulate coupled with a trust to distribute to a beneficiary. In my judgment there is one vital distinction. Under the discretionary settlement the beneficiary has no interest. Under the strict

b

settlement the beneficiary is admitted to possess an interest. The fact that roughly the same result can be achieved by creating or failing to create an interest does not assist in the determination of the question whether an interest which is admitted to have been created is in possession or not.

Fox J[1] considered the authorities which were cited by the Crown, the detailed provisions of the estate duty and capital transfer tax legislation on which the Crown relies, and the anomalies and difficulties which will admittedly arise if the Crown's

c

arguments are accepted. I cannot improve on the judge's analysis and I agree with his conclusions.

For these reasons, and for the reasons given by Fox J and by Buckley LJ, I agree that this appeal must be dismissed.

d

Appeal dismissed. Leave to appeal to the House of Lords refused.

Solicitors: *Solicitor of Inland Revenue ; Alsop, Stevens, Batesons & Co* (for the trustees).

J H Fazan Esq Barrister.

e

Re a debtor (No 13 of 1964), ex parte Official Receiver v The debtor

CHANCERY DIVISION
FOX AND BROWNE-WILKINSON JJ

f 8th, 9th, 21st MAY 1979

Bankruptcy – Discharge – Suspension – Attachment of condition – Condition subsequent to discharge – Debtor discharged from bankruptcy in 1968 on condition that he continue to pay instalments to creditors – 1976 statute providing for absolute discharge of bankrupt in certain circumstances – Person adjudicated bankrupt more than five years before 1st October 1977 and not 'discharged' by that date to be in same position as if he had been granted absolute discharge on

g *1st October 1977 – Full sum not paid by bankrupt to creditors by 1st October 1977 – Whether bankrupt already discharged by 1st October 1977 – Whether conditional order including order where conditions subsequent imposed – Whether bankrupt still liable to pay – Insolvency Act 1976, s 7(4)(5).*

The debtor was adjudicated bankrupt on 3rd April 1964. In 1968 he applied for his

h discharge. On 16th May 1968 the registrar ordered that the discharge be granted but suspended for six months until 16th November 1968, subject to the condition (which was to continue after the date of discharge) that the debtor pay to the Official Receiver for distribution among the creditors in the bankruptcy the sum of £20,000 by instalments of £1,000 every six months, first instalment to be paid on or before 1st June 1968. Thereafter the debtor made regular payments in reduction of his obligations under the

j order. On 1st October 1977 s 7 of the Insolvency Act 1976 came into force. Section 7(4)[a] provided that where a person had been adjudicated bankrupt more than five years before

---

1   [1979] 1 All ER 273, [1979] 2 WLR 353, [1978] STC 627
a   Section 7(4) is set out at p 17 *g*, post

1st October 1977 and had not been discharged before 1st October 1977, he was to be in
the same position as if the court had granted him an absolute order of discharge on 1st
October 1977. Section 7(5)[b] provided that the references to 'discharge' in s 7(4) were to   *a*
include references to discharge 'by the expiration of the period, or satisfaction of any
requirement, specified by a suspended or conditional order'. In 1978 the debtor still had
nearly £7,000 to pay under the 1968 order. He was going to ask for the conditions of
payment to be varied but was advised that he was no longer under any liability to pay the
outstanding balance because he had, by reason of s 7(4) of the 1976 Act, been absolutely   *b*
discharged on 1st October 1977 since, for the purposes of s 7(5), he had not been
'discharged' before that date because he had not fully satisfied the condition as to
payment specified in the 1968 order. The Official Receiver contended that the 1968
order was not a 'conditional order' within the meaning of s 7(5) and that s 7(4) could not
apply. He applied for a review of the 1968 order under s 108 of the Bankruptcy Act
1914. The county court judge held that the debtor had been absolutely discharged by   *c*
reason of s 7(4) of the 1976 Act and dismissed the application without considering the
circumstances of the case. The Official Receiver appealed.

Held – On the true construction of s 7(5) of the 1976 Act, a conditional order was an
order where conditions precedent to discharge were imposed and did not include an
order where conditions subsequent to discharge were imposed. Since the conditions
imposed by the 1968 order were conditions subsequent, the debtor had been discharged   *d*
on 16th November 1968 (ie on the expiry of the six months' period of suspension
provided for in the order) and as he had not been absolutely discharged on 1st October
1977 by virtue of s 7(4) of the 1976 Act, the 1968 order was still open to review.
Accordingly the appeal would be allowed and the Official Receiver's application remitted
to the county court for consideration on its merits (see p 18 *e f*, p 19 *c d h* and p 20 *f g*,
post).   *e*
     Re a Debtor (No 946 of 1926) [1939] 1 All ER 735 and *Re Tabrisky* [1947] 2 All ER 182
applied.

Notes
For discharge from bankruptcy subject to conditions, see 3 Halsbury's Laws (4th Edn)
para 850, and for cases on the subject, see 4 Digest (Reissue) 618–621, 5475–5506.   *f*
     For the Bankruptcy Act 1914, s 108, see 3 Halsbury's Statutes (3rd Edn) 134.
     For the Insolvency Act 1976, s 7, see 46 ibid 157.

Cases referred to in judgment
Debtor (No 946 of 1926), Re a [1939] 1 All ER 735 [1939] Ch 489, 108 LJ Ch 225, 160 LT
     349, [1938–39] B & CR 106, CA, 4 Digest (Reissue) 627, 5545.   *g*
Tabrisky, Re [1947] 2 All ER 182, [1947] Ch 565, [1947] LJR 1372, 177 LT 445, CA, 4
     Digest (Reissue) 621, 5499.

Case also cited
Green v Premier Glynrhonwy Slate Co Ltd [1928] 1 KB 561.

          h
Appeal
This was an appeal by the Official Receiver against an order made by his Honour Judge
Paul Hughes at Nottingham County Court on 16th January 1979, dismissing an
application by the Official Receiver under s 108 of the Bankruptcy Act 1914 for a review
of an order of discharge of the debtor dated 16th May 1968. The facts are set out in the
judgment of Browne-Wilkinson J.   *j*

Michael Crystal for the Official Receiver.
Stephen Lloyd for the debtor.

---

b   Section 7(5) is set out at p 17 *h*, post

Cur adv vult

a 21st May. The following judgment was read.

BROWNE-WILKINSON J delivered the first judgment at the invitation of Fox J. This is an appeal from his Honour Judge Paul Hughes, who dismissed an application by the Official Receiver under s 108(1) of the Bankruptcy Act 1914 to review an order of discharge of the debtor dated 16th May 1968.

The appeal raises a short but difficult point on s 7(4) of the Insolvency Act 1976. The

b relevant facts are that the debtor was adjudicated bankrupt on 3rd April 1964. In 1968 the debtor applied for his discharge, which was granted by an order dated 16th May 1968. That order recites that certain facts of the kind specified in s 26(3) of the Bankruptcy Act 1914 as amended, had been proved, and then continues as follows:

'It is ORDERED that the bankrupt's discharge be granted but suspended for six months and that he be discharged as from the 16th day of November, 1968, subject

c to the following conditions as to his after acquired property estate and earnings which conditions shall operate concurrently with the aforesaid suspension and shall continue to operate, if necessary, after 16th November, 1968, that is to say, the bankrupt shall pay to the Official Receiver and Trustee for distribution among the creditors in the bankruptcy the sum of £20,000 by instalments of not less than £1,000 in each six months period, the first instalment to be paid on or before 1st

d June, 1968.'

It is to be noted that the order both suspends the discharge for a specified time and also imposes conditions which are to continue after the date of discharge.

After a short while the debtor was unable to continue payments at the rate of £1,000 every six months, but, without dissent by the Official Receiver, made payments of £100

e per month. He had paid in all some £12,100. In 1978 the debtor desired to vary the conditions as to payment, saying that his circumstances had changed. He was then advised that by reason of s 7(4) of the 1976 Act he had been absolutely discharged and that the condition as to payments contained in the order of May 1968 was no longer operative. The Official Receiver did not share this view, and made an application for review of the 1968 order. The judge decided that the debtor had been absolutely

f discharged by s 7(4), and, without going into the circumstances of the case, dismissed the Official Receiver's application.

Section 7(4) and (5) of the 1976 Act, which came into force on 1st October 1977, read as follows:

'(4) Where a person has been adjudged bankrupt more than five years before the coming into force of this section and—(a) has not been discharged in respect of the

g adjudication under section 26 of the said Act of 1914 before the relevant date (that is to say, the coming into force of this section or the tenth anniversary of the date of the adjudication, whichever is the later); and (b) the adjudication has not been annulled before the relevant date under section 21(2) or 29 of that Act, the same results shall ensue as if the court had on the relevant date granted him an absolute order of discharge under the said section 26.

h '(5) In subsections . . . (4) (a) above references to discharge are references to discharge by an absolute order of discharge or by the expiration of the period, or satisfaction of any requirement, specified by a suspended or conditional order.'

In the present case the debtor was adjudicated bankrupt more than five years before 1st October 1977. Accordingly, if he was not discharged before 1st October 1977 he will be in the same position as if he had obtained an absolute discharge on 1st October 1977,

j ie from that date onwards the conditions for payment would cease to apply. The only question is whether or not, for the purposes of s 7 of the 1976 Act, the order dated 16th May 1968 is to be treated as having discharged the debtor on 16th November 1968 (ie the expiry of the time suspension) or whether he is to be treated as having remained undischarged on 1st October 1977, the condition as to the payment of £20,000 not having been fully satisfied by that date.

I will first consider the position as it would have been apart from the special definition in s 7(5) of the 1976 Act. Section 26(1) of the 1914 Act provides for a debtor to apply for his discharge. Subsection (2) then provides as follows:

'On the hearing of the application the court shall take into consideration a report of the official receiver as to the bankrupt's conduct and affairs (including a report as to the bankrupt's conduct during the proceedings under his bankruptcy), and may either grant or refuse an absolute order of discharge, or suspend the operation of the order for a specified time, or grant an order of discharge subject to any conditions with respect to any earnings or income which may afterwards become due to the bankrupt, or with respect to his after-acquired property: Provided that where the bankrupt has commited any misdemeanour under this Act, or any enactment repealed by this Act, or any other misdemeanour connected with his bankruptcy, or where in any case any of the facts hereinafter mentioned are proved, the court shall either (i) refuse the discharge; or (ii) suspend the discharge for such period as the court thinks proper; or (iii) suspend the discharge until a dividend of not less than ten shillings in the pound has been paid to the creditors; or (iv) require the bankrupt as a condition of his discharge to consent to judgment being entered against him by the official receiver or trustee for any balance or part of any balance of the debts provable under the bankruptcy which is not satisfied at the date of the discharge ...'

It then continues with certain other detailed provisions. There is a second proviso to sub-s (2), which I need not refer to. Then sub-s (3) sets out the facts which bring into operation the first proviso to sub-s (2).

If one were to read sub-s (2) without reference to authority, there would be much to be said for the view that it only authorises the imposition of conditions as conditions precedent to the discharge, ie if the debtor does a particular act he will thereafter be discharged. But there is a longstanding practice (which the Court of Appeal has considered on at least two occasions) whereby, as in the present case, conditions subsequent are imposed, ie the debtor is discharged on condition that thereafter he does certain things. In my judgment it is established that, under the law applicable before 1976, an order such as that of 16th May 1968 discharges the debtor as from the date on which the order states that he is to be discharged even though the order imposes conditions to be observed thereafter: see *Re a Debtor (No 946 of 1926)*[1]. In that case the Court of Appeal had to consider the validity of a variation of an absolute order for discharge, the variation requiring the debtor to make annual payments. Greene MR said[2]:

'The bankrupt was discharged. His discharge is effective, and he remains discharged. He is no longer an undischarged bankrupt, and there is nothing in this order which puts him back into that condition. The order is entirely without prejudice to the discharge, and merely does what could admittedly, by a proper form of words, have been provided in the original order for discharge. It continues the personal order against the bankrupt in such a way that it operates after his discharge, and imposes upon him liability in respect of after-acquired property which would not vest in his trustee in bankruptcy. Therefore, in my opinion, the suggestion that this in some way interferes with the status of the bankrupt is entirely unjustified.'

See also *Re Tabrisky*[3].

The question, therefore, is whether the special definition in sub-s (5) of s 7 of the 1976 Act requires the word 'discharge' to be given a special meaning. Counsel who argued the

1 [1939] 1 All ER 735, [1939] Ch 489
2 [1939] 1 All ER 735 at 741, [1939] Ch 489 at 500
3 [1947] 2 All ER 182 at 183, [1947] Ch 565 at 567

case most persuasively for the debtor urged that we should give effect to the obvious
a policy of the Act, which he said was to get rid of old bankruptcies and to ensure that the
backlog of undischarged bankruptcies would never be repeated. He pointed out that for
the future sub-ss (1) to (3) of s 7 provide machinery for an automatic discharge after five
years if the court decides to invoke the machinery. In cases in which that machinery is
not invoked s 8 ensures that there will be a review after five years. Then, he said, in
dealing with the past the intention was to wipe the slate clean and give absolute
b discharges in all cases where no such discharge had been obtained before the section came
into force.

Against this background, counsel submitted that the three types of case referred to in
s 7(5) (ie an absolute order, an order suspended for a time, and a conditional order)
corresponded to the same three types of order referred to in s 26(2) of the 1914 Act.
Therefore, he said, if, as in the present case, there is an order which is conditional s 7(5)
c requires one to say that there has been no discharge until that condition has been
satisfied. On this argument the words 'conditional order' in s 7(5) refer to orders
containing conditions subsequent to discharge as well as conditions precedent. Finally,
he says that where a conditional order has been made, for the purposes of s 7(5) no
discharge is to be treated as having occurred until the conditions are fully satisfied, even
though the order itself states that the discharge was to take place at some other time.

d Counsel who argued equally persuasively for the Official Receiver has convinced me
that counsel's arguments for the debtor ought not to be accepted. Counsel for the
Official Receiver submitted, and I accept, that s 7 is designed only get rid of the status of
bankruptcy as such. There is no good reason why the existing rights of creditors under
existing conditional orders should be prejudiced provided that the debtor is no longer
labouring under the stigma and disabilities of being an undischarged bankrupt. In my
e judgment there is no general policy behind the 1976 Act which requires one to treat
someone who had in fact been discharged before 1977 as not having been discharged.

Section 7(5) states that 'reference to discharge are references to discharge' by one of
three methods. The definition by its clear words requires one to find that one or other
of those methods has produced a discharge. Counsel's submission for the debtor really
asks us to overlook this reference to 'a discharge by' certain means, and to read that
f subsection as though it said (in relation to cases involving a conditional discharge)
'references to discharge mean the satisfaction of any requirement specified by a
conditional order'. In my judgment that is not legitimate. Subsection (5) requires one
to find an effect (discharge) produced by specific events: it does not say that the occurrence
of those events is to be treated as producing the effect. One has to ask of each order 'by
what means was a discharge produced? Was it by an absolute order, or by the expiry of
g a time suspension or by the satisfaction of a condition?' In each case one has to look to
see what produced the discharge, not to treat an event which did not in fact produce a
discharge as though it did. If an order has imposed only conditions subsequent, there can
never be an occasion when there has been a discharge by satisfaction of the requirements
of that condition: it is not the satisfaction of the condition that produces the discharge
but some other event. Therefore, in my judgment it is only possible to read the
h references to conditional orders in sub-s (5) as references to cases where the condition was
imposed as a condition precedent to the discharge.

Both sides sought to support their arguments by reference to anomalies which the
opposite view would produce. Counsel for the Official Receiver pointed out that, if the
debtor's submission is correct, there would be a strange distinction between those cases
where, pursuant to the proviso to s 26(2) of the 1914 Act, the court had required the
j debtor to submit to judgment before discharging him and cases such as the present.
There is nothing is s 7 of the 1976 Act to get rid of such a judgment.

On the other side counsel for the debtor points out that the Official Receiver's
construction leaves the good bankrupt (who has obtained his discharge subject to
conditions subsequent) under a continuing obligation, whereas the bad bankrupt (who
has not been able to get a discharge on any terms) gets away free of any obligations since

he gets an absolute discharge on 1st October 1977. This is true, but to my mind not decisive. The bad bankrupt has laboured under his disability for ten years at least: the good bankrupt has enjoyed the period since his discharge free of any disability at the price of submitting to the conditions.

Counsel for the debtor also points out that if there were an order which contained no time suspension, but gave an immediate discharge subject to conditions subsequent, on the Official Receiver's construction the case would not fall within sub-s (5) at all. It would not be a discharge by an absolute order, nor would there ever be a discharge by any other means mentioned in sub-s (5): therefore, it is said, in such a case the statutory absolute discharge would operate. I will assume, without deciding, that this is so. But in my judgment the anomaly would not be sufficient to justify a departure from the clear meaning of the words. We were told that, in practice, conditional orders are not normally made except in cases where the mandatory provisions of the first proviso to s 26(2) apply, ie in cases where the discharge has to be suspended (either for a time or until a condition is satisfied) or the bankrupt has to submit to judgment. Therefore, the anomaly, if it exists, will not be one of common occurrence.

There is one further point which appears to me to support the Official Receiver's argument, but as it was not argued it should be treated with some reserve. The definition in s 7(5) applies not only to sub-s (4) but also to sub-s (2). The scheme for automatic discharge in sub-ss (1) to (3) of s 7 is that at the conclusion of the debtor's examination the court can make an order that sub-s (2) is to apply. If such an order is made, on the fifth anniversary of his adjudication the debtor is automatically discharged if, but only if, before that date the debtor 'is not discharged'. It seems to me that if the construction of counsel for the debtor is correct, where the s 7(2) machinery has been invoked it will be impossible for a court subsequently to grant a discharge subject to effective conditions such as those imposed in this case. Say that an order has been made under sub-s (1), but four years after his adjudication a deserving debtor were to apply for his discharge and be prepared to agree to pay annual sums to the Official Receiver for the benefit of his creditors. If the court were to impose such conditions, and counsel for the debtor's construction is right, the debtor would receive an automatic absolute discharge at the expiry of five years after his adjudication free from the conditions imposed by the conditional discharge. In my judgment the legislature should not be taken to have intended such a result, the effect of which would be to militate against deserving debtors getting an early discharge on terms beneficial both to them and to their creditors.

For these reasons, in my judgment the debtor in this case was discharged on the expiry of the suspension to 16th November 1968 provided for in the order of 16th May 1968. Therefore, he was not absolutely discharged on 1st October 1977, by virtue of s 7(4) of the 1976 Act. Accordingly, the order of 16th May 1968 is still open to review and the application should be remitted to the county court to consider on its merits.

FOX J. I agree.

Appeal allowed. Application remitted to county court.

Solicitors: *Treasury Solicitor ; Law & Co*, Leicester (for the debtor).

Jacqueline Metcalfe   Barrister.

Minister of Home Affairs and another v Fisher and another

PRIVY COUNCIL

LORD WILBERFORCE, LORD HAILSHAM OF ST MARYLEBONE, LORD SALMON, LORD FRASER OF TULLYBELTON AND SIR WILLIAM DOUGLAS

26th, 27th FEBRUARY, 14th MAY 1979

Bermuda – Constitutional law – Construction of Constitution – Protection of freedom of movement – Person deemed to belong to Bermuda – Child – Illegitimate child – Child of person possessing Bermudan status deemed to 'belong to Berumda' – Whether 'child' including illegitimate child – Constitution of Bermuda (SI 1968 No 182, Sch 2), s 11(5)(d).

In 1972 the Jamaican mother of four illegitimate children born in Jamaica married a Bermudan who from the date of the marriage accepted all four children as children of his family. In 1975 the mother and her children took up residence with the husband in Bermuda and soon afterwards all four children were placed in state schools. In October 1976 a government Minister refused permission for the children to reside in Bermuda and ordered that they should leave. The mother and her husband applied to quash the order and for a declaration that the four children were 'deemed to belong to Bermuda' under s 11(5)(d)[a] of Chapter I of the Constitution of Bermuda because they were each a 'child' of a person who possessed Bermudan status, and that their constitutional right of freedom of movement under s 11(1) of that Constitution had been infringed by the Minister. The Supreme Court of Bermuda refused the declaration sought, on the ground that the word 'child' in s 11(5) only referred to legitimate children. The Court of Appeal of Bermuda reversed that decision, holding that the children were deemed to belong to Bermuda within the meaning of s 11(5)(d). The Minister appealed to the Privy Council.

Held – (i) A constitutional instrument was a document sui generis, to be interpreted according to principles suitable to its particular character and not necessarily according to the ordinary rules and presumptions of statutory interpretation (see p 26 c d, post).

(ii) Provisions in a constitutional instrument dealing with individual rights were therefore to be interpreted according to the language used and the traditions and usages which had influenced that language. Having regard to the broad and ample style of Chapter I of the Constitution of Bermuda which laid down principles of width and generality in regard to the protection of fundamental rights and freedoms of the individual, and to the fact that the constitution was influenced by both the United Nations' Universal Declaration of Human Rights and the European Convention for the Protection of Human Rights and Freedoms, the provisions in Chapter I, including s 11, were to be generously interpreted to give full recognition and effect to the fundamental rights and freedoms referred to (see p 25 f to j and p 26 d e, post).

(iii) Accordingly, the question whether the children were each a child which was deemed to belong to Bermuda, notwithstanding that they were illegitimate, was to be approached with an open mind unfettered by presumptions as to legitimacy arising in ordinary legislation dealing with property, succession or citizenship. Since s 11 began with a general declaration of the right of freedom of movement and since s 11(5)(d) in the context in which it appeared clearly recognised the unity of the family as a group and accepted the principle that young children should not be separated from a group which as a whole belonged to Bermuda, both of which factors were consistent with the protection of children under international conventions without discrimination as to birth, the term 'child' in s 11(5)(d) was not restricted to legitimate children. The mother

---

a   Section 11, so far as material, is set out at p 23 h to p 24 a, post

and her husband were therefore entitled to the declaration sought and the appeal would
accordingly be dismissed (see p 26 *e f* and *j* to p 27 *c* and *f*, post).   *a*

Notes
For protection of freedom of movement in Bermuda, see 6 Halsbury's Laws (4th Edn)
para 1024.

Cases referred to in judgment   *b*
Brule v Plummer (23rd January 1973) unreported, Supreme Court of Canada.
Dickinson v North Eastern Railway Co (1863) 2 H & C 735, 3 New Rep 130, 33 LJ Ex 91,
    9 LT 299, 159 ER 304, 32 Digest (Reissue) 36, 238.
Galloway v Galloway [1955] 3 All ER 429, [1956] AC 299, [1955] 3 WLR 723, HL, 27(2)
    Digest (Reissue) 902, 7245.
R v Totley (Inhabitants) (1845) 7 QB 596, 2 New Sess Cas 42, 14 LJMC 138, 5 LTOS 196,   *c*
    9 JP 583, 9 Jur 595, 115 ER 614, 28(2) Digest (Reissue) 663, 3.
Sydall v Castings Ltd [1966] 3 All ER 770, [1967] 1 QB 302, [1966] 3 WLR 1126, CA,
    Digest (Cont Vol B) 454, 3146a.
Woolwich Union v Fulham Union [1906] 2 KB 240, 75 LJKB 675, 70 JP 321, 95 LT 337, 4
    LGR 1021, CA; *affd sub nom Fulham Union v Woolwich Union* [1907] AC 255, 76 LJKB
    739, 71 JP 361, 97 LT 117, 5 LGR 801, HL.   *d*

Appeal
This was an appeal by the Minister of Home Affairs (formerly the Minister of Labour and
Immigration) and the Minister of Education against a decision of the Court of Appeal of
Bermuda (Georges and Duffus JJA, Hogan P dissenting) dated 15th July 1977 which
allowed an appeal by the respondents, Collins MacDonald Fisher and Eunice Carmeta   *e*
Fisher, his wife (claiming as mother and next friend of Cheryl Angela Morgan, Valentine
Denver Morgan, Fitzroy O'Neil Stuart and Samuel Isaiah Tait, her illegitimate children),
from the judgment of Seaton J given on 6th January 1977 in the Supreme Court of
Bermuda and declared that the children were to be deemed to belong to Bermuda within
the meaning of s 11(5)(d) of the Bermuda Constitution Order 1968 with the consequence
that they were entitled to reside in Bermuda by virtue of s 11(1) of that Constitution.   *f*
The facts are set out in the judgment of the Board.

Colin Ross-Munro QC and *Christopher Carling* for the appellants.
Christopher French QC, Julian E S P Hall (of the Bermuda Bar) and *Narinder Hargun* for the
    respondents.

          g
LORD WILBERFORCE. This is an appeal from a judgment of the Court of Appeal
for Bermuda, which by a majority (Georges and Duffus JJA, Hogan P dissenting) allowed
the appeal of the respondents from a judgment of the Supreme Court of Bermuda
(Seaton J) dated 6th January 1977.
    The proceedings relate to the status in Bermuda of four illegitimate children of Mrs
Eunice Carmeta Fisher, all under the age of 18. They were born in Jamaica, as was Mrs   *h*
Fisher herself. In May 1972 Mrs Fisher (then Robinson) married Mr Collins MacDonald
Fisher who possessed Bermudian status. As from the date of the marriage Mr Fisher has
accepted all four children as children of his family. On 31st July 1975 Mrs Fisher came
with the four children to take up residence with Mr Fisher in Bermuda; they were
admitted by the immigration authorities, and soon afterwards were placed in state
schools. Following a routine check carried out in the school year 1976–77 Mr Fisher was   *j*
informed that the Ministry of Labour and Immigration had refused permission for two
of the children to remain at school, and on 22nd October 1976 the Ministry informed
Mrs Fisher that she and the four children must leave Bermuda by 30th October 1976.
    Separate legal proceedings (later consolidated) were then started by both Mr Fisher and
Mrs Fisher seeking to establish (i) under the Bermuda Immigration and Protection Act

1956, s 16(4), that the four children are 'deemed to possess and enjoy Bermudian status'

a and (ii) under s 11(5)(*d*) of the Constitution of Bermuda that they 'belong to Bermuda'. The procedural details of these proceedings are no longer material. At the hearing the Minister of Education gave an undertaking to reinstate the children in recognised schools in Bermuda, and this undertaking has been honoured.

It was decided by Seaton J in the Supreme Court that: (i) the children were not entitled to Bermudian status because, although s16(4) of the 1956 Act applied to stepchildren of

b persons enjoying Bermudian status, and Mr Fisher, whose stepchildren they were, enjoyed that status, the word 'stepchild' did not include an illegitimate child; (ii) that they did not 'belong to Bermuda' because the words 'child' and 'stepchild' in s 11(5) of the Constitution did not include persons who were illegitimate.

On appeal the Court of Appeal unanimously upheld the decision of Seaton J on point (i), namely that the children were not deemed to enjoy Bermudian status. On point (ii)

c the majority held, reversing Seaton J, that the children belonged to Bermuda. There is no appeal against the decision on point (i), and the only question left is whether the four children 'belong to Bermuda' within the meaning of s 11 of the Constitution. The appellants have undertaken in any event to treat the children as if, under s 100(*c*) (as renumbered in 1971) of the 1956 Act, they enjoyed immunity from deportation. The question therefore for decision is whether the word 'child' in s 11(5)(*d*) of the Constitution

d includes an illegitimate child. The clause must first be placed in its context.

The Bermuda Constitution was brought into existence by the Bermuda Constitution Order 1968[1] made under the Bermuda Constitution Act 1967 of the United Kingdom. It opens with Chapter I headed 'Protection of Fundamental Rights and Freedoms of the Individual'. Section 1 reads as follows:

e 'Whereas every person in Bermuda is entitled to the fundamental rights and freedoms of the individual, that is to say, has the right, whatever his race, place of origin, political opinions, colour, creed or sex, but subject to respect for the rights and freedoms of others and for the public interest, to each and all of the following, namely:—(*a*) life, liberty, security of the person and the protection of the law; (*b*) freedom of conscience, of expression and of assembly and association; and (*c*)

f protection for the privacy of his home and other property and from deprivation of property without compensation, the subsequent provisions of this Chapter shall have effect for the purpose of affording protection to the aforesaid rights and freedoms subject to such limitations of that protection as are contained in those provisions, being limitations designed to ensure that the enjoyment of the said rights and freedoms by any individual does not prejudice the rights and freedoms of others or the public interest.'

g Section 11 deals with freedom of movement; the following subsections are relevant:

 '(1) Except with his consent, no person shall be hindered in the enjoyment of his freedom of movement, that is to say, the right to move freely throughout Bermuda, the right to reside in any part thereof, the right to enter Bermuda and immunity from expulsion therefrom.

h '(2) Nothing contained in or done under the authority of any law shall be held to be inconsistent with or in contravention of this section to the extent that the law in question makes provision . . . (*d*) for the imposition of restrictions on the movement or residence within Bermuda of any person who does not belong to Bermuda or the exclusion or expulsion therefrom of any such person . . .

 '(5) For the purposes of this section, a person shall be deemed to belong to

j Bermuda if that person—(*a*) possesses Bermudian status . . . (*c*) is the wife of a person to whom either of the foregoing paragraphs of this subsection applies not living apart from such person under a decree of a court or a deed of separation; or (*d*) is

under the age of eighteen years and is the child, stepchild or child adopted in a
manner recognised by law of a person to whom any of the foregoing paragraphs of
this subsection applies.'

a

Thus fundamental rights and freedoms are stated as the right of every individual, and
s 11 is a provision intended to afford protection to these rights and freedoms, subject to
proper limitations. Section 11 states the general rule of freedom of movement, which is
to include the right to enter and to reside in any part of Bermuda, but it allows, as a
permissible derogation from this right, restrictions in the case of any person who does
not 'belong to Bermuda'. Section 11(5) then defines the classes of persons who 'belong to
Bermuda'. Among these is 'the child ... of a person to whom any of the foregoing
paragraphs of this subsection applies'. One such person is the wife of a person who
possesses Bermudian status. What is meant, in this context, by the word 'child'?

b

The meaning to be given to the word 'child' in Acts of Parliament has been the subject
of consideration in many reported cases. One finds in them a number of general
statements: 'The law does not contemplate illegitimacy. The proper description of a
legitimate child is "child"' (*R v Totley (Inhabitants)*[1] per Lord Denman CJ); '... the word
"child" in the act means legitimate child' (*Dickinson v North Eastern Railway Co*[2] per
Pollock CB). Then, as society and social legislation become more varied, qualifications
come to be made:

c

'It is of course true that that is only prima facie the meaning to be given to the
word, and that a wider meaning may, in the case of some statutes, be given to it, so
as to include an illegitimate child or illegitimate children, where that meaning is
more consonant with the object of the statute.' (*Woolwich Union v Fulham Union*[3] per
Vaughan Williams LJ.)

d

'I do not think it necessary to refer to the authorities which established beyond
question that, prima facie, the words "child" or "children" in an Act of Parliament
mean a legitimate child or legitimate children, and that illegitimate children can
only be included by express words or necessary implication from the context.'
(*Galloway v Galloway*[4] per Lord Tucker.)

e

Founding on these statements, learned counsel for the appellants took as his starting
point the compound proposition: (a) that we are here concerned with the interpretation
of an Act of Parliament; (b) that in all Acts of Parliament the word 'child' prima facie
means 'legitimate child'; (c) that departure from this meaning is only possible on the
basis indicated in the words used by Vaughan Williams LJ or on that indicated in other
words by Lord Tucker. Thus they invited their Lordships to consider the merits of the
two formulae, to prefer that of Lord Tucker, and in any event to say that the preferred
test, or, in the last resort, either alternative test, was not satisfied as regards the
Constitution of Bermuda.

f

g

Their Lordships approach this line of argument in two stages. In the first place they
consider that it involves too great a degree of rigidity to place all Acts of Parliament in
one single class or on the same level. Acts of Parliament, particularly those involving the
use of the word 'child' or 'children', differ greatly in their nature and subject-matter.
Leaving aside those Acts which use the word 'child' apart from any relationship to
anyone (in which cases 'child' means simply a young person) there is a great difference
between Acts concerned with succession to property, with settlement for the purposes of
the Poor Law, with nationality, or with family matters, such as custody of children.

h

In cases concerned with the administration of the Poor Law, recognition is given to the
existence of illegitimate children and to their dependence on their mother. To this

j

1   (1845) 7 QB 596 at 600
2   (1863) 33 LJ Ex 91, similarly in 2 H & C 735 at 736
3   [1906] 2 KB 240 at 246–247
4   [1955] 3 All ER 429 at 439, [1956] AC 299 at 323

extent their Lordships respectfully think that Viscount Simonds may have gone too far
when he described the common law of England as not contemplating illegitimacy and
shutting its eyes to the facts of life (*Galloway v Galloway*[1]). Matrimonial law in England
has increasingly diminished the separation of illegitimate from legitimate children by
the adoption of the concept 'child of the family'. Indeed the Matrimonial Causes Act
1974 (Bermuda), as well as recognising the 'child of the family', contains a definition of
'child', in relation to one or both of the parties to a marriage, as including 'an illegitimate
or adopted child of that party or, as the case may be, of both parties' (s 1(1)). This is, it is
true, by way of express statutory enactment, but the fact that the separation is, for many
purposes, less sharp than it was in the last century enables and requires the courts to
consider, in each context in which the distinction between legitimate and illegitimate is
sought to be made, whether, in that context, policy requires its recognition.

In matters of succession, and the same applies to the interpretation of wills and trust
instruments (see *Sydall v Castings Ltd*[2] per Diplock LJ), the rule that 'child' means
legitimate child is firmly rooted in the common law and in the sources of the laws of
property, so it has always been insisted that clear words are needed if illegitimate, or
adopted, children are to be treated in the same way as legitimate children. Instances of
such clear words are becoming more frequent in modern legislation. But even without
such clear words in a statute, a movement towards a biological interpretation of the word
'child,' even in this context, is appearing (see *Brule v Plummer*[3]).

In nationality Acts, which provide for acquisition of nationality by descent, the
assumption is a strong one that 'child' means legitimate child; the fact that such Acts
often contain a definition to this effect, and provide expressly for exceptions, for example
in favouring legitimated, or illegitimate, children, does not detract from the strength of
this rule. In Bermuda, the Immigration and Protection Act 1956 proceeds on this basis,
referring in certain places (ss 16(4) and 100(*c*)) to legitimated or illegitimate children; and
it was the existence of these express exceptions, coupled with the general rule, that led
both courts below to conclude that 'stepchild', in s 16(4)(*b*), did not include the
illegitimate child of a Bermudian man's wife.

So far the discussion has been related to Acts of Parliament concerned with specific
subjects. Here, however, we are concerned with a Constitution, brought into force
certainly by Act of the United Kingdom Parliament, the Bermuda Constitution Act
1967, but established by a self-contained document set out in Sch 2 to the Bermuda
Constitution Order 1968. It can be seen that this instrument has certain special
characteristics. (1) It is, particularly in Chapter I, drafted in a broad and ample style
which lays down principles of width and generality. (2) Chapter I is headed 'Protection
of Fundamental Rights and Freedoms of the Individual'. It is known that this chapter,
as similar portions of other constitutional instruments drafted in the post-colonial period,
starting with the Constitution of Nigeria[4], and including the constitutions of most
Caribbean territories, was greatly influenced by the European Convention for the
Protection of Human Rights and Fundamental Freedoms[5]. That convention was signed
and ratified by the United Kingdom and applied to dependent territories including
Bermuda. It was in turn influenced by the United Nations Universal Declaration of
Human Rights 1948[6]. These antecedents, and the form of Chapter I itself, call for a
generous interpretation avoiding what has been called 'the austerity of tabulated
legalism', suitable to give to individuals the full measure of the fundamental rights and
freedoms referred to. (3) Section 11 of the Constitution forms part of Chapter I. It is
thus to 'have effect for the purpose of affording protection to the aforesaid rights and

1   [1955] 3 All ER 429 at 431, 432, [1956] AC 299 at 310, 311
2   [1966] 3 All ER 770 at 774 et seq, [1967] 1 QB 302 at 313 et seq
3   (23rd January 1973) unreported
4   SI 1960 No 1652, Sch 2
5   Rome, 4th November 1950, TS 71 (1953), Cmd 8969
6   Paris, 10th December 1948, UN 2 (1949), Cmd 7662

freedoms' subject only to such limitations contained in it 'being limitations designed to ensure that the enjoyment of the said rights and freedoms by any individual does not prejudice . . . the public interest'.

When therefore it becomes necessary to interpret 'the subsequent provisions of' Chapter I (in this case s 11) the question must inevitably be asked whether the appellants' premise, fundamental to their argument, that these provisions are to be construed in the manner and according to the rules which apply to Acts of Parliament, is sound. In their Lordships' view there are two possible answers to this. The first would be to say that, recognising the status of the Constitution as, in effect, an Act of Parliament, there is room for interpreting it with less rigidity, and greater generosity, than other Acts, such as those which are concerned with property, or succession, or citizenship. On the particular question this would require the court to accept as a starting point the general presumption that 'child' means 'legitimate child' but to recognise that this presumption may be more easily displaced. The second would be more radical: it would be to treat a constitutional instrument such as this as sui generis, calling for principles of interpretation of its own, suitable to its character as already described, without necessary acceptance of all the presumptions that are relevant to legislation of private law.

It is possible that, as regards the question now for decision, either method would lead to the same result. But their Lordships prefer the second. This is in no way to say that there are no rules of law which should apply to the interpretation of a constitution. A constitution is a legal instrument giving rise, amongst other things, to individual rights capable of enforcement in a court of law. Respect must be paid to the language which has been used and to the traditions and usages which have given meaning to that language. It is quite consistent with this, and with the recognition that rules of interpretation may apply, to take as a point of departure for the process of interpretation a recognition of the character and origin of the instrument, and to be guided by the principle of giving full recognition and effect to those fundamental rights and freedoms with a statement of which the Constitution commences. In their Lordships' opinion this must mean approaching the question what is meant by 'child' with an open mind.

Prima facie, the stated rights and freedoms are those of 'every person in Bermuda'. This generality underlies the whole of Chapter I which, by contrast with the 1956 Act, contains no reference to legitimacy, or illegitimacy, anywhere in its provisions. When one is considering the permissible limitations on those rights in the public interest, the right question to ask is whether there is any reason to suppose that in this context, exceptionally, matters of birth, in the particular society of which Bermuda consists, are regarded as relevant.

Section 11 opens with a general declaration of the right of freedom of movement, including that of residence, entry and immunity from expulsion. These rights may be limited (s 11(2)(d)) in the case of persons 'not belonging to Bermuda', a test not identical with that of citizenship, but a social test. Then, among those deemed to belong to Bermuda are (s 11(5)) a person who—

'(a) possesses Bermudian status; . . . (c) is the wife of [such a person]; or (d) is under the age of eighteen years and is the child, stepchild, or child adopted in a manner recognised by law of a person to whom any of the foregoing paragraphs of this subsection applies.'

In their Lordships' opinion, para (d) in its context amounts to a clear recognition of the unity of the family as a group and acceptance of the principle that young children should not be separated from a group which as a whole belongs to Bermuda.

This would be fully in line with art 8 of the European Convention for the Protection of Human Rights and Fundamental Freedoms (respect for family life), decisions on which have recognised the family unit and the right to protection of illegitimate children. Moreover the draftsman of the Constitution must have had in mind (a) the

a United Nations' Declaration of the Rights of the Child adopted by resolution[1] on 20th November 1959 which contains the words, in principle 6:

'[the child] shall, wherever possible, grow up in the care and under the responsibility of his parents . . . a child of tender years shall not, save in exceptional circumstances, be separated from his mother,'

b and (b) art 24 of the International Covenant on Civil and Political Rights 1966[2] which guarantees protection to every child without any discrimination as to birth. Though these instruments at the date of the Constitution had no legal force, they can certainly not be disregarded as influences on legislative policy.

Their Lordships consider that the force of these argument, based purely on the Constitution itself, is such as to compel the conclusion that 'child' bears an unrestricted meaning. In theory, the Constitution might contain express words forcing a contrary
c conclusion, though given the manner in which constitutions of this style were enacted and adopted, the possibility seems remote. But, in fact, their Lordships consider it most unlikely that the draftsman being aware, as he must have been, of the provisions of the 1956 Act could have intended a limitation of the word 'child' to legitimate children. In the first place, if he had intended this limitation, he must surely, following the example of the 1956 Act, have felt it necessary to spell it out. In the second place the concept of
d 'belonging' of itself suggests the inclusion of a wider class; yet if the appellants are right, those described under s 11(5)(d) of the Constitution would largely coincide with persons having, or deemed to have, Bermudian status. Thirdly, under s 100 of the 1956 Act, these illegitimate children would enjoy immunity from deportation until they were 21. It seems most unlikely that such children should not be treated as 'belonging to Bermuda' or that a stricter test, in respect of their right to freedom of movement, should
e be imposed on such children under s 11 of the Constitution than is imposed under the earlier Act. Their Lordships fully agree with the majority of the Court of Appeal in regarding these points as significant although they prefer to base their judgment on wider grounds.

Their Lordships are therefore of opinion that the judgments of the majority of the Court of Appeal are right and accordingly they will humbly advise Her Majesty that the
f appeal be dismissed. The appellants must pay the respondents' costs of the appeal.

Appeal dismissed.

Solicitors: *Charles Russell & Co* (for the appellants); *Hewitt Woollacott & Chown* (for the respondents).

g

Mary Rose Plummer   Barrister.

---

1   Resolution 1386 (xiv)
2   New York, 16th December 1966, Misc 4 (1967), Cmnd 3220

Midland Bank Trust Co Ltd and another v Green and others

COURT OF APPEAL, CIVIL DIVISION

LORD DENNING MR, EVELEIGH LJ AND SIR STANLEY REES

12th, 13th, 14th MARCH, 11th APRIL 1979

Land charge – Failure to register – Estate contract – Contract void against purchaser of legal estate for money or money's worth – Purchaser – Sale of land by husband to wife for consideration substantially less than real value of land – Substantial element of gift in transaction – Transaction executed for ulterior motive of defeating option to purchase land – Option not registered – Whether wife a 'purchaser' of the legal estate for money or money's worth – Whether option binding on her estate – Land Charges Act 1925, s 13(2).

In 1961 a father, who was the owner of a 300 acre farm, granted his son, who was the tenant of the farm, an option to purchase it at the price of £75 an acre, the option to be effective for 10 years. The option was not registered under the Land Charges Act 1925. By a conveyance dated 17th August 1967 the father conveyed the legal estate in the farm, then worth some £40,000, to his wife for the sum of £500. The purpose of the conveyance was to defeat the son's option. In October 1967 the son discovered the existence of the conveyance when he gave notice to exercise the option. Neither the father or the mother complied with the son's notice. The mother died in 1968. In 1970 the son commenced an action against his father and the executors of his mother's estate claiming, inter alia, a declaration that the option was binding on his mother's estate and specific performance of the option. The defendants pleaded in their defence that the conveyance was a bona fide sale, that the mother was 'a purchaser of [the] legal estate for money or money's worth' for the purposes of s 13(2)[a] of the 1925 Act, and that therefore the unregistered option was void as against her under s 13(2). The judge held[b] that the conveyance had effected a genuine passing of the legal estate for money or money's worth, notwithstanding either the inadequacy of the consideration or the ulterior motive behind the conveyance, and had therefore rendered the son's option void. On appeal,

Held (Sir Stanley Rees dissenting) – The appeal would be allowed and a declaration for specific performance granted against the executors of the mother's estate, for the following reasons—

(i) (per Lord Denning MR) A purchaser of a legal estate 'for money or money's worth' was not protected by s 13(2) of the 1925 Act against an unregistered land charge if he or she had not paid an adequate sum or a fair and reasonable value by way of consideration. The consideration paid by the mother was grossly inadequate and her estate was not, therefore, entitled to the protection afforded by s 13(2) to a purchaser for money or money's worth. In addition, the conveyance was a fraud, since it was a dishonest transaction done stealthily and speedily in secret for insufficient consideration so as to deprive an innocent person of what was rightfully his (see p 34 c d f g and p 35 a b, post).

(ii) (per Eveleigh LJ) Provided the land had not been dealt with further and no one else had subsequently acquired an interest in it, the court was entitled to look at the reality of the transaction to decide whether the purchaser should be allowed to deal with it as unencumbered land. Since the £500 paid by the mother to the father was for a property worth £40,000, the consideration (although not the conveyance) was a sham; the true transaction was a gift, coupled with a token £500 in an attempt to secure the protection of s 13 of the 1925 Act, and accordingly the mother was not a purchaser for

---

a   Section 13(2) is set out at p. 33 g, post

b   [1978] 3 All ER 555

money or money's worth for the purposes of s 13(2). In addition, the mother had
a induced a breach of contract for which she could be sued by the son and, in the absence
of any adverse claim to the land, the court could restore the status quo existing before the
breach by ordering the mother's estate to convey the land to the son on payment of the
option price (see p 36 d and g to j and p 37 a to d and h to p 38 b, post).

Decision of Oliver J [1978] 3 All ER 555 reversed.

b **Notes**
For the position of purchasers in relation to unregistered pending actions and for the
effect of unregistered estate contracts, see 23 Halsbury's Laws (3rd Edn) 63, 77, paras 118,
160.

For the Land Charges Act 1925, s 13, see 27 Halsbury's Satutes (3rd Edn) 706.

For the Law of Property Act 1925, s 199, see ibid 619.

c **Cases referred to in judgments**
Crofter Hand Woven Harris Tweed Co Ltd v Veitch [1942] 1 All ER 142, [1942] AC 435, 111
LJPC 17, 166 LT 172, HL, 45 Digest (Repl) 534, *1175.*
Hollington Brothers Ltd v Rhodes [1951] 2 All ER 578, 31(1) Digest (Reissue) 181, *1515.*
Hornal v Neuberger Products Ltd [1956] 3 All ER 970, [1957] 1 QB 247, [1956] 3 WLR
d 1034, CA, 22 Digest (Reissue) 47, *268.*
Lazarus Estates Ltd v Beasley [1956] 1 All ER 341, [1956] 1 QB 702, [1956] 2 WLR 502,
CA, 31(2) Digest (Reissue) 1050, *8270.*
Madell v Thomson & Co [1891] 1 QB 230, 60 LJQB 227, 64 LT 9, CA, 7 Digest (Repl) 18,
81.
Midland Bank Trust Co Ltd v Hett, Stubbs & Kemp (a firm) [1978] 3 All ER 571, [1978] 3
e WLR 167.
Miles v Bull [1968] 3 All ER 632, [1969] 1 QB 258, [1968] 3 WLR 1090, 20 P & CR 42,
21(1) Digest (Reissue) 96, *692.*
Mogul Steamship Co Ltd v McGregor, Gow & Co [1892] AC 25, [1891–4] All ER Rep 263,
61 LJQB 295, 66 LT 1, 56 JP 101, 7 Asp MLC 120, HL; *affg* (1889) 23 QBD 598, CA,
45 Digest (Repl) 301, *183.*
f *Monolithic Building Co, Re, Tacon v Monolothic Building Co* [1915] 1 Ch 643, [1914–15] All
ER Rep 249, 84 LJ Ch 441, 112 LT 619, 21 Mans 380, CA, 10 Digest (Reissue) 840,
4842.
Polsky v S & A Services [1951] 1 All ER 185; *affd* [1951] 1 All ER 1062, CA, 7 Digest (Repl)
18, *79.*
Snook v West Riding Investments Ltd [1967] 1 All ER 518, [1967] 2 QB 786, [1967] 2 WLR
g 1020, CA, Digest (Cont Vol C) 56, *86b.*
Stock v Frank Jones (Tipton) Ltd [1978] 1 All ER 948, [1978] 1 WLR 231, [1978] ICR 347,
HL.
Stoneleigh Finance Ltd v Phillips [1965] 1 All ER 513, [1965] 2 QB 537, [1965] 2 WLR 508,
CA, 10 Digest (Reissue) 863, *4977.*
Twyne's Case (1601) 3 Co Rep 80b, 76 ER 809, 7 Digest (Repl) 172, *38.*
h *Watson, Re, ex parte Official Receiver in Bankruptcy* (1890) 25 QBD 27, 59 LJQB 394, 63 LT
209, 7 Morr 155, CA, 7 Digest (Repl) 6, *14.*
Yorkshire Railway Wagon Co v Maclure (1882) 21 Ch D 309, 51 LJ Ch 857, 47 LT 290, CA,
26 Digest (Reissue) 17, *55.*

Cases also cited
j *Amos, Re, Carrier v Price* [1891] 3 Ch 159, [1891–4] All ER Rep 320.
Bolton (HL) Engineering Co Ltd v T J Graham & Sons Ltd [1956] 3 All ER 624, [1957] 1 QB
159, CA.
Fry v Lane, Re Fry, Whittet v Bush (1888) 40 Ch D 312, [1886–90] All ER Rep 1084.
Greene v Church Comrs for England [1974] 3 All ER 609, [1974] Ch 467, CA.
Vartoukian v Daejan Properties Ltd (1969) 20 P & CR 983.

Appeal

By a writ and statement of claim dated 27th January 1970 and subsequently amended the a
plaintiff, Thomas Geoffrey Green, claimed against the defendants, Walter Stanley Green
personally and as executor of his wife, Evelyne Green deceased, and Robert Derek Green
as executor of Evelyne Green deceased, (1) a declaration that an option to purchase a
property known as Gravel Hill Farm, Thorton-le-Moor, Lincolnshire, granted by Walter
Stanley Green to Thomas Geoffrey Green was binding on the estate of Evelyne Green,
(2) specific performance of the contract arising out of the option and the notice exercising b
it dated 6th October 1967, (3) all necessary accounts and enquiries, (4) damages in lieu of
or in addition to specific performance, and (5) damages for conspiracy. On Walter
Stanley Green's death his executrix, Beryl Rosalie Kemp, carried on the action as a
defendant by an order to carry on dated 19th January 1973. On Thomas Geoffrey Green's
death his personal representative, the Midland Bank Trust Co Ltd and Margaret Ann
Green, carried on the action as plaintiffs by an order to carry on dated 16th November c
1973. Following the trial of the action, Oliver J[1] dismissed the claim for a declaration
and specific performance. The plaintiffs appealed. The facts are set out in the judgment
of Lord Denning MR.

Jeremiah Harman QC and *Jonathan Parker* for the plaintiffs.
Leonard Hoffman QC and *Gavin Lightman* for the defendants. d

Cur adv vult

11th April. The following judgments were read.

LORD DENNING MR. The Greens are a Lincolnshire farming family. This story e
might be called the Green Saga. The father and mother were Walter and Evelyne
Green. They had two sons, Geoffrey and Derek, and three daughters. The father Walter
had the freehold of two farms. They were a few miles apart in the northern part of
Lincolnshire called Lindsey. One of 700 acres was called Thoresway, near Market Rasen,
which he farmed himself with his younger son Derek. The other of 300 acres was called
Gravel Hill Farm which he let to his elder son Geoffrey as a tenant ever since he came of f
age.

When father Walter was about 62 years of age, he decided to retire. He let each son
have a farm as his own. Geoffrey was aged about 28 and Derek a year or two younger.
Both married with children. He sold the 700 acre farm to his younger son Derek at £75
an acre. That was well below the market price. But he did not treat Geoffrey, the elder
son, so favourably. He only gave him an option to buy his farm, Gravel Hill Farm, the g
300 acre farm. He gave him an option to buy it. It was to be at the same price as Derek's,
£75 an acre, but it was only an option. The father did this so as to enable him to get out
of death duties. The option was to be effective for ten years. Meanwhile the elder son
Geoffrey was only to be a tenant of his farm.

The option was drawn up by the family solicitor, Mr Stubbs, of Brigg, about seven
miles away. Father and son went tó see him at Brigg. The solicitor wrote it out. Father h
Walter signed it. It figures so largely in this case that I will set it out in full;

> 'To Geoffrey Green, Gravel Hill Farm . . . IN CONSIDERATION of the sum of One
> pound paid by you to me I hereby give you the option of purchasing the Gravel Hill
> Farm now in your occupation at the sum of £75 (Seventy five pounds) per acre.
> This option to remain effective for ten years. Dated this 24th March 1961. W. S.
> Green.' j

The option was signed over a sixpenny stamp and kept by Mr Stubbs in his office at
Brigg. Now Mr Stubbs was a very careful and meticulous solicitor, but strangely enough

---

1   [1978] 3 All ER 555, [1978] 3 WLR 149

he made a serious mistake. He ought to have registered the option as an estate contract under the Land Charges Act 1925. It was the simplest thing in the world to do. But he did not do it. Why he did not, no one knows. It is a mystery. Neither father Walter nor elder son Geoffrey knew of this mistake. They thought everything was in order; and continued for years to think so. The mistake was afterwards to cost everyone dear.

For six years the family lived happily as families do. Father Walter and mother Evelyne retired to the Old Rectory at Croxby near Caistor, three or four miles away. The sons and their wives went over at the weekends to see them, taking the grandchildren with them. Geoffrey wanted to exercise the option. He and his wife Margaret often discussed it with his father and mother. But father said No. He wanted to keep Gravel Hill Farm as an agricultural investment so as to save death duties. Mother Evelyne was there at all these discussions and knew all about them. She knew that Geoffrey wanted to exercise the option.

Then something transpired which was to shake the family to its roots. Father Walter decided to deprive the elder son Geoffrey of the option. He met a lawyer somewhere or other and told him of the option. We do not know who this lawyer was. But he seems to have suggested to the father a way of getting out of the option. This lawyer said to father Walter: 'See if the option has been registered. If it has not been registered as a land charge, you can sell Gravel Hill Farm over the head of Geoffrey and get rid of the option.' That unknown lawyer went further. He seems to have made enquiries at the Registry and found that the option was not registered. He told father Walter. Father Walter told his wife, mother Evelyne. They both told the younger son, Derek. Together the three of them hatched a plot. I call it a plot because it certainly was. It was that father Walter should sell Gravel Hill Farm to mother Evelyne for £500 and convey it to her. It was to be done quickly, without the elder son Geoffrey knowing anything about it. The conveyance was to take place before Geoffrey could exercise the option. Once the conveyance was executed, his option would be defeated.

We would much like to know the reason for this plot: but the court has been left completely in the dark. Father and mother are dead. Geoffrey is dead. Derek, the younger son, probably knows. But he did not give evidence (his lawyers advised him that the reason was not relevant). At any rate Derek took the inititative in carrying out the plot. He telephoned his own separate solicitor, Mr Harrod of Spalding. That was in Holland in the south of the county, 60 miles away from Brigg. He did not telephone the family solicitor, Mr Stubbs, at Brigg because Mr Stubbs knew all about the option and would not of course allow any such plot to go through: so Derek the younger son got his own solicitor Mr Harrod to come over the 50 or 60 miles to his (Derek's) farm: and Derek got his father Walter to meet him there. Father Walter had never met Mr Harrod (Derek's solicitor) before, but he there and then instructed Derek's solicitor. He told him to prepare a conveyance of Gravel Hill Farm from his (Walter's) name into his wife (Evelyne's) name for the sum of £500. That was a grotesquely small sum. It was worth £40,000 or £50,000. Father Walter gave authority to Mr Harrod to collect the title deeds from the bank at Brigg so as to draw up the conveyance. He made it clear that it had to be done as quickly as possible. It had to be done before Geoffrey got to hear of it and before the option was registered.

That meeting at Derek's farm was on 14th August 1967. Mr Harrod, Derek's solicitor, did as he was instructed. Never in the history of conveyancing has anything been done so rapidly. It was all done and completed in three days. A search was requested of the Registry. The reply was got by telephone that no option was registered. Mr Harrod's partner, Mr Jenkinson, went over from Spalding to Brigg (60 miles). He collected the title deed of Gravel Hill Farm from the bank at Brigg. He did not go back to his own office at Spalding to draw up the conveyance. He went to a friendly firm of solicitors at Brigg, borrowed the use of a secretary and office space and prepared the conveyance. He took it over from Briggs to Cleethorpes (about 15 miles) where father Walter was in a nursing home. There it was executed by father Walter and mother Evelyne. Father Walter transferred Gravel Hill Farm to his wife for £500. Mother Evelyne gave the

solicitors a cheque (in their favour) for £500 drawn on her bank account, overdrawn, for
the purpose. The solicitor, Mr Jenkinson, by an error of judgment, certified that the *a*
value of the land did not exceed £5,500. Whereas it was worth at least £40,000: and was
being transferred for £500. Dated the 17th August 1967. All in three days.

The deed was done. This is how Walter himself described it in an affidavit made on
24th June 1970, after his wife's death:

> 'Neither the option nor any estate contract constituted by the option and the
> notice of intention to exercise it had been registered at the Land Charges Registry, *b*
> and the Testatrix and I were advised by our Solicitors that in these circumstances if
> I transferred the farm to a purchaser, the purchaser would take free of Geoffrey's
> rights thereunder. Thereupon in order to defeat Geoffrey's option over the farm, on
> the 17th August, 1967 I sold and conveyed the farm (subject to the tenancy) to the
> testatrix in consideration of the payment by her to me of £500.'
> *c*

As happens in families, one of them could not keep a secret. A rumour reached the
elder son Geoffrey: 'Father has sold your farm to Mother for £500.' At once he went over
to his father and said: 'I want to exercise the option.' Father said: 'I am not going to
discuss it with you.' Geoffrey went off to his solicitors. Then those solicitors did what
they ought to have done six years before. On 5th September 1967 they registered the
option. But it was too late. Three weeks too late. The conveyance had been executed on *d*
17th August 1967. It was, as the judge said, 'a case of bolting the stable after the horse
had gone'. On 6th October 1967 Geoffrey's solicitors gave notice of exercising the
option. But was it any good then? Was it not also too late?

Six months later on 28th March 1968 the mother Evelyne died quite unexpectedly.
She left her property to her husband for life and afterwards for her five children
equally. So if the conveyance of Gravel Hill Farm is valid, it goes to all five children. *e*

Walter and Geoffrey both died in the next year or two. Walter died on 8th February
1972. Geoffrey died on 11th May 1973. His wife and children have remained on at
Gravel Hill Farm, farming it and paying an agreed rent for it. If the conveyance to the
mother was good and free of the option they will have to leave. The farm will have to
be sold and the proceeds divided among the five children of Walter and Evelyne. Only
one-fifth for Geoffrey's widow and children. That does seem most unfair to Geoffrey, his *f*
widow and children, who have farmed it all their lives, and ought in justice to be able to
remain there.

The litigation

Now for the story of the litigation. It bids fair to rival in time and money the story of
Jarndyce v Jarndyce[1].
g

First, Geoffrey, while alive, sued Walter for damages for breach of the option
contract. This took Walter by complete surprise. The unknown lawyer never warned
him that this might happen. He at once got rid of all his assets so as to avoid paying any
damages to Geoffrey. He gave his property at Croxby to the younger son Derek and his
sisters. The judge suggested that he repented of what he had done.

Second, Geoffrey also, while alive, started an action[2] against his mother's estate *h*
represented by her executors (who were his father Walter and his brother Derek). He
claimed that the option was binding on her estate. He also claimed damages for
conspiracy. Then Walter died and his daughter Beryl was added as defendant as his sole
representative: Geoffrey died and his widow and the bank became his executors.

Third, Geoffrey, while alive, started an action against the family solicitors for
negligence in failing to register the option. After his death it was continued by his *j*
executors (see *Midland Bank Trust Co Ltd v Hett, Stubbs & Kemp (a firm)*.[3]).

---

1   See Dickens, Bleak House
2   See [1978] 3 All ER 555, [1978] 3 WLR 149
3   [1978] 3 All ER 571, [1978] 3 WLR 167

All sorts of points have arisen in the course of interlocutory proceedings. At one stage
a Beryl failed to plead plene administravit and may find herself personally liable (see
Midland Bank Trust Co Ltd (No 2)[1]. At another stage there was a prolonged argument
whether there could be a conspiracy between husband and wife (see *Midland Bank Trust
Co Ltd v Green (No 3)*[2]).

It looks to me as if there may be claims against some solicitors or others for negligence
in some stages of this litigation.
b
The one point in the case

Having thus told the story, I come to the one point in this case: is the option binding
on the mother's estate? If it is, Geoffrey's widow is entitled to call for a conveyance to her
of Gravel Hill Farm on payment of £75 an acre, that is £22,500: and all the outstanding
litigation will come to an end, save for endless arguments about the costs involved. If the
c option is not binding on the mother's estate, then Gravel Hill Farm will belong to her
estate: and all the outstanding litigation will continue to vex the courts for years to
come. The value of farming land has gone up so much that it may have reached £1,500
an acre: at which Gravel Hill Farm would be worth about £454,500. A prize worth a
fight.

We have been shown an opinion given by counsel to father Walter on 10th March
d 1970 while father and Geoffrey were still alive. It said:

'I have no doubt that T. G. Green had a good cause of action against his mother
and could have enforced his option against her as soon as he learnt of the sale. The
sale was clearly a sham, and in purpose and effect a gift. Accordingly,
notwithstanding non-registration of the option, the option ran with the land and
bound the mother, for she was not a *bona fide* purchaser for money or money's
e worth.'

But Oliver J in his considered judgment held the contrary. He said[3]: 'I . . . find myself
compelled . . . to hold that Evelyne was a purchaser for money or money's worth of the
legal estate against whom Geoffrey's option was, under the statutory provisions, void.'

f *The statutory provisions*

The option was an 'estate contract' within Class C(iv) as to which s 13(2) of the Land
Charges Act 1925 says:

'A land charge of . . . Class C . . . shall (except as hereinafter provided) *be void as
against a purchaser* of the land charged therewith, or of any interest in such land,
unless the land charge is registered in the appropriate register before the completion
of the purchase: Provided that, as respects . . . an estate contract created or entered
g into after the commencement of this Act, this subsection only applies *in favour of a
purchaser of a legal estate for money or money's worth.*' (Emphasis mine.)

And 'purchaser' is defined in s 20(8) as meaning 'any person (including a mortgagee or
lessee) who, for valuable consideration, takes any interest in land or in a charge on
h land'. But that is 'unless the context otherwise requires'.

To these must be added s 199(1) of the Law of Property Act 1925 which says:

'A purchaser shall not be prejudicially affected by notice of—(i) any instrument
or matter capable of registration under the provisions of the Land Charges Act, 1925
. . . which is void or not enforceable as against him under that Act . . . by reason of
the non-registration thereof . . .'

j
And 'purchaser' there means, by s 205(xxi), 'a purchaser in good faith for valuable

---

1   [1979] 1 All ER 726, [1979] 1 WLR 460
2   [1979] 2 All ER 193, [1979] 2 WLR 594
3   [1978] 3 All ER 555 at 570, [1978] 3 WLR 149 at 166

consideration . . . [and] "purchase" has a meaning corresponding with that of "purchaser"; and "valuable consideration" includes marriage but does not include a nominal consideration in money'.

On reading those various provisions, it is significant that s 13 makes an estate contract void for non-registration except as against 'a purchaser of a legal estate for money or money's worth'. It is significant that this does not include 'in good faith' or 'valuable consideration'. And there is an express provision that such a purchaser in good faith or valuable consideration is not to be prejudicially affected by 'notice' of non-registration. Somehow or other we must reconcile these.

The construction of those sections

To my mind the key words are 'for money or money's worth'. They mean for an adequate sum in money or money's worth. I cannot believe that the legislature intended to protect a purchaser who paid far less than the land was worth in collusion with the vendor. If that were the case, it would open the door to fraud of the worst description. All that a man who had contracted to sell his land would have to do to get out of his bargain would be to convey it to his wife for a very small sum. I know that, in the ordinary law of contract, we never enquire into the adequacy of the consideration. But this is different. 'Money or money's worth' means a fair and reasonable value in money or money's worth: not an undervalue: particularly a gross undervalue as here.

Fraud

Apart from that, I am clearly of opinion that these provisions for protecting a purchaser are of no avail when the sale to him is done in fraud of the holder of the estate contract. This is shown by *Re Monolithic Building Co*[1] where it was held that a purchaser, who paid full value, was protected notwithstanding that he had full notice. But Lord Cozens-Hardy MR expressly said[2]: 'I put aside altogether any question of fraud. The doctrine of the Court in a case of fraud, of course, proceeds upon a different footing, and any security may be postponed if you can find fraud in its inception.'

And Phillimore LJ said[3]: 'Let us not import considerations which may be applicable, or which it might be desirable to make applicable, where there is dolus malus.'

With that encouragement, I am prepared to say as I did in *Lazarus Estates Ltd v Beasley*[4]:

'No court in this land will allow a person to keep an advantage which he has obtained by fraud. No judgment of a court, no order of Minister, can be allowed to stand if it has been obtained by fraud. Fraud unravels everything.'

By fraud here, I do not mean only the sort of fraud which is actionable in deceit. I mean the sort of fraud as was spoken of by Sir Edward Coke when he condemned conveyances made in fraud of creditors: see *Twyne's Case*[5]. Fraud in this context covers any dishonest dealing done so as to deprive unwary innocents of their rightful dues. The marks of it are transactions done stealthily and speedily in secret for no sufficient consideration. All these appear in this conveyance made by Walter to his wife Evelyne.

If the judge had viewed the case in this light he would certainly have decided in favour of Geoffrey's widow. He said[6]: 'The conclusion I have reached therefore is one which I reach with regret, because as it seems to me Geoffrey had a clear legal right which was deliberately frustrated by his parents in breach of the contract created by the option.'

If it were necessary, I should have thought that the agreement between Walter and Evelyne might amount to a conspiracy. The predominant purpose was to damage

---

1   [1915] 1 Ch 643, [1914–15] All ER Rep 249
2   [1915] 1 Ch 643 at 663, [1914–15] All ER Rep 249 at 251
3   [1915] 1 Ch 643 at 670, [1914–15 All ER Rep 249 at 255
4   [1956] 1 All ER 341 at 345, [1956] 1 QB 702 at 712
5   (1601) 3 Co Rep 80b, 76 ER 809
6   [1978] 3 All ER 555 at 570, [1978] 3 WLR 149 at 167

a Geoffrey, see *Crofter Hand Woven Harris Tweed Co Ltd v Veitch*[1]; and I see no reason why, in modern times, husband and wife should not be liable to an action for conspiracy. But it is unnecessary to go so far. Suffice it that in my opinion the agreement was made, and the conveyance executed, deliberately to deprive Geoffrey of the benefit of his option. That was a fraud on Geoffrey. The mother was a party to the fraud. She cannot be allowed to take advantage of it to the prejudice of Geoffrey. Nor can her executors take advantage of it as against his widow and children. The mother's estate took Gravel Hill

b Farm subject to the option, even though it had not been registered at the Land Registry. The option was duly exercised on 6th October 1967. The mother's estate should honour it by transferring Gravel Hill Farm to Geoffrey's estate. I would allow the appeal accordingly.

EVELEIGH LJ. I am left with a very uncomfortable feeling that the court is being
c kept in the dark. Counsel for the defendants has urged the court not to speculate. That is a temptation which is difficult to resist but on the other hand I think it would be wrong to allow speculation to influence one's decision in this case. On the one hand, one might conjure up reasons for criticising Walter's conduct to a greater degree than the facts found by the judge warrant. On the other hand, it is not difficult to think of excuses for him. It may be that we are dealing with a family arrangement which has
d gone wrong. It may be that we are dealing with the case of a man mindful of the interests of his family who is seeking so to arrange his affairs as to avoid greater death duties.

Geoffrey had an option to buy the farm for £75 an acre. The option was not registered. Walter conveyed the farm to his wife and the consideration expressed in the conveyance was £500. The farm was worth at least £40,000. It could be foreseen that
e it would become even more valuable. It is today worth about £400,000. Both Walter and his wife knew of the option and they knew that it was not registered. Walter conveyed to his wife in order to defeat Geoffrey's option.

Section 199 of the Law of Property Act 1925 and s 13 of the Land Charges Act 1925 relate to this transaction. By reference to the respective definition sections and to the wording of the sections themselves one finds that the provisions of s 199 apply to a bona
f fide purchaser for valuable consideration, which includes marriage. The provisions of s 13 of the Land Charges Act 1925 so far as they are relevant apply to a purchaser for valuable consideration in the form of 'money or money's worth'. There is no reference to bona fides.

It is difficult to reconcile the two sections and the view has been put forward that s 199 was really unnecessary in view of the provisions of s 13. It has been said that s 199 might
g have been an oversight.

In such a carefully prepared scheme of legislation as we see in the six Acts of Parliament of 1925, I feel that s 199 was designed to fulfill a void in the picture which would or might have existed if s 13 had stood alone. Seeing that s 199 makes specific reference to the provisions of s 13 I cannot but conclude that s 199 was inserted to be complementary to s 13 for the express purpose of putting the effect of s 13 into perspective. The scheme
h of the Land Charges Act 1925 was to allow the relevant interests in land to be dealt with unencumbered by other interests which were not registered. Thus it is provided that the unregistered estate contract shall be void as against a purchaser for valuable consideration in the form of money or money's worth. It does not make the contract void for all purposes. The intention is that the land or the relevant interest in it shall pass unencumbered. The provisions are designed to preserve priorities and not to rob various
j transactions referred to in s 13 of all effect. Thus, for example, whilst an unregistered prior mortgage may be postponed to a subsequent registered mortgage it would seem that the prior mortgagee could exercise the mortgagor's equity of redemption.

Section 13 does not in as many words deal with the effect on a purchaser of notice of

---

1   [1942] 1 All ER 142 at 149, [1942] AC 435 at 445

the charge. As the contract is void it might be said that notice could not possibly make any difference. On the other hand, it might be said that whilst the purchaser's title was **a** unaffected some residual personal liability lay with him. To induce a vendor to sell when there is knowledge of a binding option given to someone else would on the face of it appear to be the tort of inducing a breach of contract. It might also be said that the transaction could involve a conspiracy. Since the decision of *Crofter Hand Woven Harris Tweed Co Ltd v Veitch*[1] it might be difficult to argue conspiracy where full consideration was given for the property because the predominant object would not be to harm **b** someone else. Other considerations might well arise, as they have done in the present case, when it is claimed that the consideration is wholly inadequate.

It seems to me that the provisions of s 199 might well be invoked as a defence when an essential ingredient in a claim against a purchaser included knowledge of the land charge. But it would only come to the assistance of a bona fide purchaser of the land. I would hesitate long before coming to a firm conclusion as to the purpose of s 199 and it **c** is not necessary for this case that I should do so. I am of the opinion, however, that its careful provisions are quite deliberate and emphasise that the provisions of the Land Charges Act 1925 are designed to protect title to the land itself but not to protect the personal liability of those dealing with it in bad faith in whose hands the land still is. As no one else has yet acquired an interest in the land, I see no obstacle to the court enquiring into the bona fides of the purchaser and consequently the genuineness of the **d** transaction with a view to deciding whether the purchaser should be allowed to deal with the land as unencumbered land.

Section 13(2) of the Land Charges Act 1925 provides:

'A land charge of Class B, Class C or Class D, created or arising after the commencement of this Act, shall (except as hereinafter provided) be void as against a purchaser of the land charged therewith, or of any interest in such land, unless the **e** land charge is registered in the appropriate register before the completion of the purchase: Provided that, as respects a land charge of Class D and an estate contract created or entered into after the commencement of this Act, this subsection only applies in favour of a purchaser of a legal estate for money or money's worth.'

This section is providing that the charge in question shall be void for the purpose of **f** charging the land. It is made void, however, only where there is a purchaser as defined in s 20(8), that is, 'any person (including a mortgagee or lessee) who for valuable consideration takes any interest in land or in a charge on land' and where he takes that interest 'for money or money's worth'. As I read s 13, it applies to a transaction where the money or money's worth provides the reason for the vendor parting with his interest and for the purchaser acquiring his. £500 is money. However, when the estate that is **g** conveyed is worth some £40,000, it seems to me wholly unrealistic to conclude that the transfer was for £500. There are many cases in the law of contract where inadequate valuable consideration has been held to suffice but there the importance of consideration is to provide a test whereby legal relations can be said to have been concluded. It is the hallmark by which we recognise a binding contract. Something more than that, in my opinion, is envisaged by s 13 of the Land Charges Act 1925. In very many cases there **h** will be a deed that of itself will produce a binding legal transaction. I do not think that money or money's worth is to be treated in the same way as valuable consideration is treated in the law of contract. There the adequacy of the consideration is irrelevant. Under s 13 I do not think that this is so. The requirement of a return in money or money's worth goes to the quality of the transaction. It envisages a transaction where the failure to register should not be allowed to prejudice the purchaser. In other words, a **j** transaction where it is right that the land should be free of the charges.

Counsel has argued that it is not permissible to go behind the transaction. This would include the contention that it is not permissible to enquire into the true value of the

---

1   [1942] 1 All ER 142, [1942] AC 435

land. It is said that we are dealing with a genuine conveyance which transfers the legal
a estate and as that is achieved it is wrong to say that the conveyance is a sham. I do not say
that the conveyance is a sham. In my opinion, however, the consideration of £500
expressed in the conveyance is a sham. It is not for £500 that the property was conveyed.
The true transaction, in my opinion, was a gift coupled with a token of £500 sought to
be included to meet the requirements of s 13 of the Land Charges Act 1925. It is not
dissimilar from the giving of a halfpenny when one makes a friend a present of a knife.
b I think that the court is always entitled to look behind the form adopted and ascertain the
true nature of the transaction. The cases where a bill of sale masquerades as a hire
purchase agreement are good examples of this: see *Re Watson, ex parte Official Receiver in
Bankruptcy*[1]. In those cases the whole of the document is treated as being a deceptive
form to cover the real nature of the transaction. In the present case I do not say that the
conveyance was a deceptive form but I do think that the statement of the consideration
c was deceptive. Money would never have passed had it not been thought necessary in
order to satisfy s 13. Its role in this transaction was simply a token. I do not regard the
transaction as a conveyance following a contract of sale of the land. I regard it as a
conveyance giving effect to a gift coupled with the reference to a payment of £500 in an
attempt to secure the advantage of s 13. In my opinion, the court is entitled to ask the
true value of the land in order to discover the true character of the £500.
d   In *Polsky v S & A Services*[2] Lord Goddard CJ said:

> 'The court has to determine whether the transaction in question is a genuine sale
> by the original owner of the chattel to the person who is finding the money and a
> genuine re-letting by the latter to the original owner on hire-purchase terms, or
> whether the transaction, though taking that form, is nothing more than a loan of
> money on the security of the goods'.

e
He went on to say:

> 'The court is not to look merely at the documents. It must discover what the real
> transaction was. As LORD ESHER, M.R., said in *Madell* v. *Thomas & Co*[3]: ". . . the
> court is to look through or behind the documents, and to get at the reality; and, if
> in reality the documents are only given as a security for money, then they are bills
f of sale."'

I test the matter in this way. Let us assume that the law forbids the gift of property
between husband and wife. Could it be said that the payment of £500 robbed the
transaction of its character as a gift and made it a sale? In my opinion it could not.
       When we refer to s 205 of the Law of Property Act 1925, we find that 'purchaser'
g means 'a purchaser in good faith for valuable consideration' and that 'valuable
consideration' includes marriage but does not include a nominal consideration in
money. I do not say that it is permissible to import the definition section from the one
Act into the other, but to refuse to acknowledge that the £500 is money for which the
property was conveyed gives consistency to the scheme to be found in the two Acts.
       If I am wrong in saying that £500 was not valuable consideration in money within the
h meaning of the words in s 13, I think that the case could be approached in another way.
I can assume, contrary to my opinion, that s 13 has made Geoffrey's charge void as against
his mother in so far as it can be said that she holds unencumbered land which another
purchaser can safely take. Nonetheless the mother will have induced a breach of contract
and could be sued for this by Geoffrey. She could not invoke s 199 because she was not
a bona fide purchaser and because (I would be prepared to say) the £500 was only a
j nominal consideration (see s 205(1)(xxi) of the Law of Property Act 1925). If she can be
sued for damages for breach of contract in that she has caused Geoffrey to lose the land,

1   (1890) 25 QBD 27
2   [1951] 1 All ER 185 at 188
3   [1891] 1 QB 230 at 234

it seems to me that the court should be in a position to order her to convey the land to Geoffrey on payment by him of the option price provided that no one else has an adverse *a* claim to the land. There is nothing, as I see it, in such a situation which should prevent the court from restoring the status quo before the breach of contract.

However, I prefer to approach this case on the basis I have first indicated above. At least as long as the land has not been dealt with further, I think that the court can look at the reality of the transaction. I do not regard the sum of £500 as being valuable consideration for which the legal estate was transferred to the wife. *b*

I would therefore allow this appeal.

SIR STANLEY REES. The background of this most unfortunate case and all the relevant facts have been so fully canvassed in the judgment at first instance of Oliver J and in the judgment of Lord Denning MR that I can proceed at once to consider what I regard as the two major issues which confront us. They are, first, whether fraud in *c* relation to the conveyance of Gravel Hill Farm to Evelyne has been established by the evidence against Walter and Evelyne. If it were established then counsel on behalf of the plaintiffs finally claimed a declaration that Evelyne took the farm subject to Geoffrey's option and that accordingly her estate is bound thereby. Alternatively, if fraud were established, the plaintiffs might be entitled to have the conveyance set aside on the principle succinctly encapsulated by Denning LJ in the sentence 'Fraud unravels *d* everything' (see *Lazarus Estates Ltd v Beasley*[1]). Whichever approach is adopted the plaintiffs would be entitled to acquire the freehold subject to payment of the price specified in the option of £75 per acre for 303 acres, namely £22, 725.

The second major issue is whether on the evidence the unregistered option is void (as against the conveyance to Evelyne) pursuant to s 13(2) of the Land Charges Act 1925.

I now turn to deal with the fraud issue. The issue of fraud was pleaded thus in para 9 *e* of the amended statement of claim, of which I cite the relevant parts:

'. . . the said Conveyance was executed pursuant to an agreement or arrangement made between [Walter and Evelyne] whereby they conspired together to defraud and injure [Geoffrey] by completing a sale or what purported to be a sale of Gravel Hill Farm by [Walter to Evelyne] and to deprive [Geoffrey] of the benefit of the said option.' *f*

The statement of claim was originally dated 27th January 1970, and when it came on before Oliver J seven years later in October 1977 the issues before the judge were thus stated by him[2]:

'. . . it is a claim by Geoffrey's executors against Derek, as the sole surviving personal representative of Evelyne, for specific performance of the option and for *g* damages for conspiracy and against Walter's executrix [who is his daughter Beryl] for damages, the latter claim being undefended.'

I add that the claim against Walter's estate was undefended because the defence was struck out for failure to comply with an order for discovery. Oliver J continued[2]:

'What is in issue on the pleadings is the question of whether the conveyance *h* constituted a bona fide sale by a vendor to a purchaser or whether it was, in truth, a fraudulent and colourable transaction or a sham.'

The case strongly presented to us by counsel for the plaintiffs was that Walter and Evelyne were guilty of a fraudulent conspiracy in order to deprive Geoffrey of his option and he argued that certain passages in Oliver J's judgment disclose that the judge had *j* found fraud proved against Walter and Evelyne.

---

1 [1956] 1 All ER 341 at 345, [1956] 1 QB 702 at 712
2 [1978] 3 All ER 555 at 561, [1978] 3 WLR 149 at 156

Accordingly it is necessary to consider at the outset what are the essential ingredients of a fraudulent conspiracy in civil law and what is the onus of proof in relation to it.

As to the essential ingredients of the tort of conspiracy, I go first to *Crofter Hand Woven Harris Tweed Co Ltd v Veitch*[1]. The case is so familiar that I need not recite the facts.

As to the tort of conspiracy in civil law Viscount Simon LC says[2]: 'The appellants, therefore, in order to make out their case, have to establish (*a*) agreement between the two respondents (*b*) to effect an unlawful purpose (*c*) resulting in damage to the appellants.' So the object of the conspiracy must be to effect an unlawful purpose. Viscount Simon LC[3] emphasises the importance of the wrongfulness of the intention by citing and approving a statement of Bowen LJ in *Mogul Steamship Co v McGregor, Gow & Co*[4]: 'An intent to "injure" in strictness means more than an intent to harm. It connotes an intent to do wrongful harm.' On that passage Viscount Simon LC comments[3]: 'A bad motive does not *per se* turn an individual's otherwise lawful act into an unlawful one.'

Viscount Simon LC further points out that even where there is an inducement by one party to procure another to break a contract there may be a justification. As an example, he says this[5]:

'In some cases, however, B may be able to justify his procuring of the breach of contract—e.g., a father may persuade his daughter to break her engagement to marry a scoundrel. (This is not, of course, to say that the scoundrel would not have an action against the daughter for breach.) The father's justification arises from a moral duty to urge [his daughter] that the contract should be repudiated.'

Finally Viscount Simon LC deals with the object or purpose of the persons combining together in this passage[6]:

'It is enough to say that if there is more than one purpose actuating a combination, liability must depend on ascertaining the predominant purpose. If that predominant purpose is to damage another person and damage results, that is tortious conspiracy. If the predominant purpose is the lawful protection or promotion of any lawful interest of the combiners (no illegal means being employed), it is not a tortious conspiracy, even though it causes damage to another person'.

We are reminded of Lord Cozens-Hardy MR's dictum in *Re Monolithic Co*[7]:

'The doctrine of the Court in a case of fraud, of course, proceeds upon a different footing, and any security may be postponed if you can find fraud in its inception. But it is not fraud to take advantage of legal rights, the existence of which may be taken to be known to both parties.'

I have already referred to Denning LJ's sentence as to the effect on a transaction when fraud is proved.

The burden of proof of the allegation of fraud made against Walter and Evelyne, of course, rests on the plaintiffs who allege it. Although fraud is alleged, the standard of proof in civil proceedings is no higher than to establish the allegation on a balance of probabilities. But as Denning LJ said in *Hornal v Neuberg Products Ltd*[8]:

'... the standard of proof depends on the nature of the issue. The more serious

---

1   [1942] 1 All ER 142, [1942] AC 435
2   [1942] 1 All ER 142 at 147, [1942] AC 435 at 440
3   [1942] 1 All ER 142 at 148, [1942] AC 435 at 442
4   (1889) 23 QBD 598 at 612
5   [1942] 1 All ER 142 at 148, [1942] AC 435 at 442–443
6   [1942] AC 435 at 445, cf [1942] 1 All ER 142 at 149
7   [1915] 1 Ch 543 at 563, [1914–15] All ER Rep 249 at 251
8   [1956] 3 All ER 970 at 973, [1957] 1 QB 247 at 258

the allegation the higher the degree of probability that is required; but it need not, in a civil case, reach the very high standard required by the criminal law.'   *a*

In the instant case the plaintiffs are handicapped in that Walter and Evelyne and Geoffrey are dead and therefore were unable to give evidence. Derek was available to give evidence. We were told at the bar that Derek was not called as a witness as the result of counsel's advice. I am not myself prepared to draw any inference hostile to the case of any party to these proceedings as a result of the failure of Derek to give evidence. In particular I think it would be wrong and dangerous to do so in a case involving a charge *b* of fraud alleged against two elderly folk who are dead and have not been able to defend themselves against the serious attack which has been made against their integrity and sense of duty as parents.

It is with the foregoing principles in mind that I turn to consider the evidence in relation to the allegation of fraud made against Walter and Evelyne.

Walter was a generous father to his children as will appear from an examination of the *c* facts. He had two sons, Geoffrey and Derek, as well as three daughters, of whom Beryl is the executrix of his estate. From 1954 he had granted a tenancy of his 303 acre farm called Gravel Hill Farm to Geoffrey at a rent of 30s per acre. At the time of the letting he made a gift to Geoffrey of the live and dead farming stock and of the tenant rights together with a sum of £500. Walter estimates in his affidavit that the value of what he *d* gave Geoffrey at this time was about £15,500. Geoffrey in his affidavit says that the value was less than £4,000. In this way Geoffrey the elder son was set up as a farmer in his own right. Walter farmed the larger farm Thoresway of 700 acres, and in about 1958 he made an arrangement for a joint enterprise between himself and Derek to manage that farm.

In about 1960 Walter decided to retire. He sold Thoresway to Derek at the price of *e* £75 per acre which was well below the market price. Geoffrey wished to buy Gravel Hill Farm at the same price. Walter was unwilling to agree to this because he wished to retain the agriculture land in order to obtain an estate duty advantage. Accordingly he gave Geoffrey an option in writing dated 24th March 1961 whereby for the sum of £1 Geoffrey gained the right to purchase Gravel Hill Farm at the price of £75 per acre. The option was to remain effective for ten years. The fact that Walter wished to retain the *f* farm for an estate duty advantage and that the option was for ten years does give rise to a possible inference that he desired that a benefit should accrue to his family on his death. It was, of course, a family transaction so that the price of £1 was nominal, and Walter says it was neither asked for nor paid though Geoffrey says he did pay the £1. Because it was a family transaction that might possibly explain why the option was overlooked and not registered as an estate contract under s 10(1) of the Land Charges Act 1925. In view of the powerful comments which have so properly been made about the *g* inadequacy of the £500 actually paid by Evelyne for the farm, it is perhaps slightly ironic to observe that for the wholly nominal, and perhaps even illusory, sum of £1 Geoffrey gained an option to buy Gravel Hill Farm for half its true value which was then £40,000 and is now said to be worth ten times that sum. Yet the law of contract in relation to consideration is such that no one has argued that the option was a sham or on any ground *h* unenforceable.

So from 1961 Derek owned and farmed Thoresway and Geoffrey as a tenant farmed Gravel Hill. In 1961 Walter lent Geoffrey £8,000 at 5% interest and made a gift of that sum to him in 1965. In 1966 Geoffrey purchased from Walter a property known as The Poplars for the sum of £43,000. We do not know what the market value of that property was, but it would at least accord with the evidence before us as to Walter's way *j* of dealing with his family for that transaction to embody an element of gift. Out of the price which Walter obtained for The Poplars he gave away £32,000 to Derek and the three daughters. That was £8,000 each because Geoffrey had received his £8,000 as a gift in 1965. So from 1960 Geoffrey owned The Poplars and farmed Gravel Hill as a tenant.

a Oliver J held on the evidence before him including the oral testimony of Geoffrey's widow that Geoffrey's option was often discussed in the presence of Evelyne and Walter. But Walter was unwilling to agree that it should be exercised because he still wanted to retain Gravel Hill Farm as an agricultural investment. There can be no doubt but that Evelyne was fully aware of the family arrangements, including Geoffrey's option.

b In July 1967 Walter became very seriously ill and was taken to hospital. Geoffrey says in his affidavit that 'We in the family all thought my father was going to die'. Shortly after in the middle of August 1967 Walter carried out the conveyance of Gravel Hill Farm to Evelyne despite Geoffrey's option. Since all the family thought that he was going to die in July it is not unreasonable to suppose that Walter (who was about 72 years of age) also contemplated the possibility of death and was giving thought to his and the family's financial arrangements. If this were so, it might explain how Walter came to

c seek legal advice during the period and so learnt that Geoffrey had not registered his option and that it could be avoided by a conveyance for money or money's worth. He must also have learnt that unless Geoffrey were acquiescent then he could defeat the plan by registering the option and/or by exercising it. Walter states in his affidavit that at the time of the conveyance 'and for a few months prior thereto there was and had been a serious quarrel between Geoffrey and Evelyne and himself'. Geoffrey in his affidavit

d states that he had never been on good terms with Evelyne but that there had been no quarrel between himself and Walter until 6th October 1967 when he learnt of the conveyance of Gravel Hill Farm to Evelyne. It is right to add that Geoffrey says that he realised as early as August 1967 that 'something was amiss' because the atmosphere in the family was so bad.

So Walter and Evelyne (who by then was herself in a nursing home) and Derek set to

e work to complete the conveyance of the farm from Walter to Evelyne. Oliver J held on overwhelming evidence that the primary purpose and intent of both Walter and Evelyne in completing the conveyance was to defeat Geoffrey's option. This being the intention of the parties, it is obvious that it had to be carried out swiftly and secretly lest Geoffrey be given the chance to register or to exercise the option and thus defeat his parents' plan. So the transaction was surrounded by what counsel for the plaintiffs called the

f trappings of fraud. These have been fully described and I can deal with the main items very briefly. Walter did not go to his normal solicitor, the transaction was completed in three days between 14th and 17th August, the consideration paid was only £500 which was about one-eightieth of the true value and there was no separate contract of sale. As a result the plan was successful. The conveyance was completed on 17th August 1967 when the £500 was paid by Evelyne to Walter. Geoffrey registered the option on 5th

g September 1967 and exercised it on 6th October 1967.

It is common ground that by October 1967 there was very serious quarrelling and ill-will between Geoffrey and his parents. Nevertheless, on 20th December 1967, that is four months after the conveyance was executed, Evelyne made a will. After some small specific bequests, she left the residue of her estate, including, of course, Gravel Hill Farm on trust for Walter for his life and thereafter to all five children in equal shares. Walter,

h Derek and Geoffrey were appointed executors. The result therefore in broad terms was that each child would receive 20% of the value of Gravel Hill Farm so that Geoffrey's share of the farm was reduced from 100% (less £22,725 which he would have had to pay if he exercised the option) to 20%. Evelyne died shortly afterwards on 28th March 1968 and subsequently Geoffrey started proceedings against Walter and Evelyne's estate.

Now on the whole of the evidence have the plaintiffs discharged the onus of proof so

j as to establish that Walter and Evelyne were guilty of a conspiracy to defraud Geoffrey? They certainly agreed together to complete the conveyance in order to defeat Geoffrey's option and did so swiftly and secretly so as to prevent Geoffrey frustrating their plan. That was as the judge found their primary intention. We know that within four months of the conveyance and subject to Walter's life interest the farm was devised by Evelyne so that Geoffrey's share was greatly reduced and the proceeds were divided equally between all the children including Geoffrey. The evidence gives rise to a strong inference that the reason or motive for defeating Geoffrey's option was to effect a redistribution of the family assets in the way set out in Evelyne's will. Owing to the deaths of Evelyne, Walter and Geoffrey before the hearing of the case and the failure of Derek to give evidence, there is no direct testimony to explain what the motives of the parents were. Walter had been generous to his children, including Geoffrey. Between 1954 and 1967 Geoffrey received from Walter by way of gifts in kind or money's worth £23,000 according to Walter and according to his own evidence about £12,000. Even after the family quarrel he was left 20% of the value of Gravel Hill Farm of which he was tenant. Walter had allowed him to purchase The Poplars in 1966 at a price in respect of which Geoffrey makes no comment or complaint and which may have contained an element of gift.

Counsel for the plaintiffs submitted that Oliver J had made a finding of fraud against Walter and Evelyne. I have been unable to discover any such finding in the judge's most careful judgment. If he had found fraud, he would undoubtedly have stated such a finding explicitly; furthermore it is inconceivable that he would have failed to set aside the conveyance and made such an order as to ensure that Gravel Hill Farm was held subject to the option. What he did was to give judgment against Walter's estate for damages for conspiracy and he held that any claim there might be against Evelyne's estate was statute barred by the provisions of the Law Reform (Miscellaneous Provisions) Act 1934. As we are informed, the judge has recently decided[1] that the tort of conspiracy may be committed by a husband and wife conspiring together. He considered the provisions of s 13(2) of the Land Charges Act 1925 to which I shall refer in a moment and found that the conveyance fell within the ambit of the section and the option was void in relation to the transfer of the farm.

Accordingly, in my judgment, the judge did not find fraud proved, though it is plain that he considered that the merits of the case were all in favour of Geoffrey.

The plaintiffs have clearly established that Walter and Evelyne set out deliberately to defeat Geoffrey's option and carried out the transactions swiftly and secretly so as to prevent Geoffrey from taking steps to protect his option. They have shown that to have been their primary intention. The family background to the case as well as what was done with the farm in my judgment plainly gives rise to an inference that the motive of Walter and Evelyne was to redistribute their assets among the family in a manner which they considered justified in the family interest. Similarly, the evidence does support an inference that Walter and Evelyne were acting spitefully and deceitfully and without any just cause at all to deprive their eldest son Geoffrey of his contractual right in the farm which he had worked since 1954. If the latter inference were established and the former disproved by the plaintiffs, that would clearly justify a finding of fraud. In my judgment, the evidence on a balance of probabilities is in favour of the inference that Walter and Evelyne acting as they believed fairly in the family's interest had just cause to act as they did. What they did would harm Geoffrey by depriving him of his option and was a breach of contract committed by Walter and procured by Evelyne. But, as Viscount Simon LC pointed out, in a family situation there may well be a justification for such action so that it would not amount to fraud. It is not, however, necessary in order to decide the issue of fraud to hold that the inference from the facts against fraud is stronger than the inference in favour of fraud. It is sufficient to say that the plaintiffs have not established their allegation of fraud to the standard required.

Accordingly, in my judgment, Oliver J was correct in not finding fraud proved against Walter and Evelyne. But if, contrary to my view, he did find fraud proved, I should hold that he was not justified in so finding.

I now come to consider the second main issue, namely whether pursuant to s 13(2) of the Land Charges Act 1925 Geoffrey's option is void as against the conveyance executed by Walter and Evelyne. If it is void, then Evelyne's estate is entitled to the unencumbered

---

1 See [1979] 2 All ER 193, [1979] 2 WLR 594

benefit of the farm but if it is not then her estate is subject to the option and Geoffrey's
estate is entitled to recover the farm of 303 acres on payment of £22,725.

a

I approach this aspect of the case on the basis that fraud has not been established against
Walter and Evelyne for the reasons I have already stated.

Lord Denning MR has most helpfully set out the relevant statutory provisions so that
I need not restate them. The central question which remains is whether Evelyne was
within the meaning of the proviso to s 13(2) 'a purchaser of a legal estate for money or
money's worth'.

b

It has been argued by counsel for the plaintiffs that the conveyance was a sham in the
sense that it was not the purchase of a legal estate but merely a gift transaction dressed up
as a sale with the intention of destroying the option. In *Snook v London and West Riding
Investments Ltd*[1] Lord Diplock considers the concept of a sham transaction in a passage
which is in these terms:

c

> 'As regards the contention of the plaintiff that the transactions between himself,
> Auto Finance, Ltd. and the the defendants were a "sham", it is, I think, necessary to
> consider what, if any, legal concept is involved in the use of this popular and
> pejorative word. I apprehend that, if it has any meaning in law, it means acts done
> or documents executed by the parties to the "sham" which are intended by them to
> give to third parties or to the court the appearance of creating between the parties

d

> legal rights and obligations different from the actual legal rights and obligations (if
> any) which the parties intend to create. But one thing I think, is clear in legal
> principle, morality and the authorities (see *Yorkshire Railway Wagon Co. v. Maclure*[2]
> and *Stoneleigh Finance, Ltd. v. Phillips*[3]), that for acts or documents to be a "sham",
> with whatever legal consequences follow from this, all the parties thereto must have
> a common intention that the acts or documents are not to create the legal rights and

e

> obligations which they give the appearance of creating. No unexpressed intentions
> of a "shammer" affect the rights of a party whom he deceived.'

In *Miles v Bull*[4] Megarry J adds these comments about a sham:

> 'On the other hand, a transaction is no sham merely because it is carried out with
> a particular purpose or object. If what is done is genuinely done, it does not remain

f

> undone merely because there is an ulterior purpose in doing it.'

And he adds this experienced comment in relation to the level of prices in family
dealings: '. . . after all some genuine transactions within the family are carried out at low
prices.'

The deed of conveyance dated 17th August 1967 recited that the vendor had agreed to
sell the fee simple of the farm to the purchaser for £500. The deed thereupon conveyed

g

the beneficial interest in the estate to Evelyne.

The £500 was paid by Evelyne to Walter. The parties certainly intended that the farm
should be conveyed from Walter to Evelyne. That the ulterior motive for the transaction
was to defeat Geoffrey's option, that the price was exceedingly low, perhaps only one-
eightieth of the true value of the farm in 1967, and that the normal step of a written
contract preceding the conveyance did not take place; all these factors undoubtedly

h

existed. Nevertheless I respectfully agree with Oliver J's view that the conveyance did
and was intended to convey the estate from Walter to Evelyne. It was not a 'sham' and
cannot in my view be converted into a sham because of the motive or reason for the
transaction, namely because the parties wished to take advantage of the provisions of s
13(2). So no fraud has been proved and the transaction was not a sham. But it remains

j

1   [1967] 1 All ER 518 at 528, [1967] 2 QB 786 at 802
2   (1882) 21 Ch D 309
3   [1965] 1 All ER 513, [1965] 2 QB 537
4   [1968] 3 All ER 632 at 636, [1969] 1 QB 258 at 264

to consider whether Evelyne was a 'purchaser for money or money's worth' within the ambit of the proviso to s 13(2).

There is a powerful argument in support of the view that the phrase 'money or money's worth' does not, or at least cannot be permitted to, bear the ordinary meaning of the words. It is suggested that the phrase should be so construed that 'money or money's worth' means a fair and reasonable value.

The circumstances in which a gloss may properly be placed on the words of a statute has recently been considered by the House of Lords in *Stock v Frank Jones (Tipton) Ltd*[1], and Lord Simon of Glaisdale said this[2]:

> 'All this is not to advocate judicial supineness: it is merely respectfully to command a self-knowledge of judicial limitations, both personal and constitutional. To apply it to the argument on behalf of the appellant based on anomaly, a court would only be justified in departing from the plain words of the statute were it satisfied that: (1) there is clear and gross balance of anomaly; (2) Parliament, the legislative promoters and the draftsman could not have envisaged such anomaly and could not have been prepared to accept it in the interest of a supervening legislative objection; (3) the anomaly can be obviated without detriment to such legislative objective; (4) the language of the statute is susceptible of the modification required to obviate the anomaly.'

In my respectful opinion, the intention of Parliament in this proviso is clear. It was, to adopt the words of Harman J in *Hollington Bros Ltd v Rhodes*[3], 'the policy of the framers of the legislation of 1925 to get rid of equitable rights of this kind unless registered'. The equitable rights to which Harman J was referring were created by an unregistered estate contract.

Further one may assume that the presence in s 3(1) and (3) of the Land Charges Act 1925 itself of the express words 'in good faith' preceding the same phrase for 'money or money's worth' indicate that the omission of any qualifying words in the proviso to s 13(2) was deliberate.

I respectfully agree with the reasoning and the opinion of Oliver J in relation to the arguments advanced by counsel for the plaintiffs on two points. I think that despite the definitions of 'purchaser' in s 20(8) in the Land Charges Act 1925 as a person who takes 'for valuable consideration' and by s 205(i)(xxi) of the Law of Property Act 1925 as a person who acquires 'in good faith for valuable consideration' one must look to the specific and clear definition which is contained in the proviso to s 13(2) and not elsewhere. Nor do I think that one can read s 199(1) of the Law of Property Act 1925 as giving rise to a valid argument that a purchaser who enters into a transaction with the deliberate intention of taking advantage of the provisions of the Land Charges Act 1925 is to be prejudicially affected by an unregistered estate contract.

I recognise that difficulties may arise in cases in which the consideration for a contract for the sale of an estate may be what has been called nominal or illusory in deciding whether in a given case the price is 'nominal' or 'illusory'. Equally there could be difficulty in some cases in deciding what is a valuable consideration agreed in good faith. But I am driven to the conclusion that unless fraud is proved or unless the conveyance is a sham or unless the consideration is nominal or illusory then an unregistered estate contract is void against it. Were this not the case one would be departing from the sound ordinary rule in contract law that the court will not look into the adequacy of consideration and from what seemed to Harman J and seems to me the policy of the Land Charges Act 1925, namely to get rid of the equitable rights arising

---

1   [1978] 1 All ER 948, [1978] 1 WLR 231
2   [1978] 1 All ER 948 at 954, [1978] 1 WLR 231 at 237
3   [1951] 2 All ER 578

from unregistered estate contracts. Nevertheless the protection remains that 'Fraud
a unravels all'.

Accordingly I would dismiss the appeal.

Appeal allowed. Declaration for specific performance. Leave to appeal to the House of Lords.

Solicitors: *Sidney Torrance & Co,* agents for *J Levi & Co,* Leeds (for the plaintiffs);
b Simmons & Simmons, agents for *Roythorne & Co,* Spalding (for the defendants).

Frances Rustin Barrister.

c # Attorney-General v British Broadcasting Corporation

COURT OF APPEAL, CIVIL DIVISION
LORD DENNING MR, EVELEIGH LJ AND SIR STANLEY REES
1st, 2nd, 5th, 6th MARCH, 11th APRIL 1979
d

*Contempt of court – Publications concerning legal proceedings – Court – Inferior court – Local
valuation court – Defendants proposing to broadcast television programme on issue pending
before local valuation court – Plaintiffs seeking injunction to restrain broadcast – Whether local
valuation court 'an inferior court' – Whether contempt of local valuation court punishable by
committal – General Rate Act 1967, s 88 – RSC Ord 52, r 1(2)(a)(iii).*

e
The BBC intended to broadcast a television programme on 19th February 1978 about a
religious sect. The programme was extremely critical of the sect, including the fact that
it was receiving rate relief for its meeting houses. The sect claimed that its meeting
places were 'places of public religious worship' for the purposes of s 39 of the General
Rate Act 1967 and therefore exempt from rates. The sect had applied for rate relief for
f its meeting place at Andover, but the local authority and the valuation officer had both
lodged objections. A hearing of the application before the local valuation court,
constituted under s 88 of the 1967 Act, at Andover was therefore arranged for 10th
March. On hearing of the BBC's proposal to broadcast the programme the sect's solicitors
demanded that it be cancelled because, they said, the programme would be a contempt
of the Andover local valuation court. When the BBC refused, the Attorney-General
g applied for an injunction against the BBC restraining them from showing the
programme. The BBC contended, inter alia, that the local valuation court was not 'an
inferior court' for the purposes of RSC Ord 52, r 1(2)(a)(iii)[a] and therefore the High Court
had no power to punish a contempt committed in connection with the local valuation
court's proceedings. The Divisional Court[b] held that a local valuation court was an
inferior court and in lieu of issuing an injunction accepted an undertaking by the BBC
h not to show the programme. The BBC appealed to the Court of Appeal.

Held (Lord Denning MR dissenting) – A local valuation court constituted under s 88 of
the 1967 Act was an inferior court for the purposes of RSC Ord 52, r 1(2)(a)(iii) and
therefore if a contempt was committed in connection with its proceedings the Divisional
Court of the Queen's Bench Division had power to punish that contempt by committal
j (see p 56 c, p 57 j and p 62 d, post).

---

a   Rule 1(2), so far as material, provides: Where contempt of court—(a) is committed in connection
with . . . (iii) proceedings in an inferior court . . . then . . . an order of committal may be made only
by a Divisional Court of the Queen's Bench Division.'

b   [1978] 2 All ER 731

Per Lord Denning MR and Eveleigh LJ. It is difficult to envisage that a court, whether composed of lawyers or laymen, would be influenced by newspaper publications or *a* television broadcasts (see p 52 *b*, p 55 *a b* and p 56 *e*, post).

Per Lord Denning MR. The immunities and protections which are accorded to the recognised courts of the land should be extended to all tribunals set up by or under the authority of Parliament or of the Crown which exercise equivalent functions by equivalent procedures and are manned by equivalent personnel as those of the recognised courts (see p 53 *c d*, post). *b*

Decision of the Divisional Court of the Queen's Bench Division [1978] 2 All ER 731 affirmed.

Notes

For what constitutes a court, see 10 Halsbury's Laws (4th Edn) paras 701–702, and for cases on the subject, see 16 Digest (Repl) 113–115, 1–20.

For the constitution and procedure of local valuation courts, see 32 Halsbury's Laws *c* (3rd Edn) 122–123, paras 167–168.

For the General Rate Act 1967, ss 39, 88, see 27 Halsbury's Statutes (3rd Edn) 130, 182.

Cases referred to in judgments

Attorney-General v Butterworth [1962] 3 All ER 326, [1963] 1 QB 696, LR 3 RP 327, [1962] *d* 3 WLR 819, CA, Digest (Cont Vol A) 454, 395a.

Attorney-General v Leveller Magazine Ltd [1979] 1 All ER 745, [1979] 2 WLR 247, HL.

Attorney-General v Mulholland, Attorney-General v Foster [1963] 1 All ER 767, [1963] 2 QB 477, [1963] 2 WLR 658, CA, Digest (Cont Vol A) 539, 4460c.

Attorney-General v Times Newspapers Ltd [1973] 1 All ER 815, [1973] QB 710, [1973] 2 WLR 452, CA; *rvsd* [1973] 3 All ER 54, [1974] AC 273, [1973] 3 WLR 298, HL, Digest *e* (Cont Vol D) 254, 204c.

Attwood v Chapman [1914] 3 KB 275, 83 LJKB 1666, 111 LT 726, 79 JP 65, 16 Digest (Repl) 114, 11.

Balogh v Crown Court at St Albans [1974] 3 All ER 283, [1975] QB 73, [1974] 3 WLR 314, 138 JP 703, CA, Digest (Cont Vol D) 253, 92a.

Bonnard v Perryman [1891] 2 Ch 269, [1891–4] All ER Rep 965, 60 LJ Ch 617, 65 LT 506, *f* CA, 32 Digest (Reissue) 323, 2686.

Church of Jesus Christ of Latter Day Saints v Henning [1963] 2 All ER 733, [1964] AC 420, [1963] 3 WLR 88, 127 JP 481, 61 LGR 565, [1963] RVR 422, HL, Digest (Cont Vol A) 1287, 376a.

Collins v Henry Whiteway & Co Ltd [1927] 2 KB 378, 90 LJKB 790, 137 LT 297, 32 Digest (Reissue) 218, 1859.

Dawkins v Lord Rokeby (1875) LR 7 HL 744, 45 LJQB 8, 33 LT 196, 40 JP 20, HL; *affg* LR *g* 8 QB 255, Ex Ch, 16 Digest (Repl) 113, 2.

Fairfax (John) & Sons Pty Ltd v McRae (1955) 93 CLR 351, [1955] ALR 25 (Aust HC).

Gouriet v Union of Post Office Workers [1977] 3 All ER 70, [1978] AC 435, [1977] 3 WLR 300, HL.

Hoffmann-La Roche (F) & Co, Attorney-General v Secretary of State for Trade and Industry *h* [1974] 2 All ER 1128, [1975] AC 295, [1974] 3 WLR 104, HL, Digest (Cont Vol D) 543, 1351a.

Kitcat v Sharp (1882) 52 LJ Ch 134, 48 LT 64, 28(2) Digest (Reissue) 1102, 1011.

Lewis (T D) v British Broadcasting Corpn [1979] Court of Appeal Transcript 193.

Lincoln v Daniels [1961] 3 All ER 740, [1962] 1 QB 237, [1961] 3 WLR 866, CA, Digest (Cont Vol A) 52, 4a.

Mersey Docks and Harbour Board v West Derby Assessment Committee and Bottomley (Revenue *j* *Officer)* [1932] 1 KB 40, [1931] All ER Rep 409, 101 LJKB 8, 145 LT 592, 95 JP 186, 29 LGR 576, CA, 16 Digest (Repl) 114, 12.

Morris v Crown Office [1970] 1 All ER 1079, [1970] 2 QB 114, [1970] 2 WLR 792, CA, Digest (Cont Vol C) 224, 5364hs.

a *R v Clarke, ex parte Crippen* (1910) 103 LT 636, [1908–10] All ER Rep 915, DC, 16 Digest (Repl) 13, 55.

R v Daily Herald, ex parte Bishop of Norwich [1932] 2 KB 402, 101 LJKB 305, 146 LT 485, DC, 16 Digest (Repl) 13, 57.

R v Daily Mail, ex parte Farnsworth [1921] 2 KB 733, 90 LJKB 871, 125 LT 63, DC, 16 Digest (Repl) 13, 56.

b *R v Daily Mirror, ex parte Smith* [1927] 1 KB 845, 96 LJKB 352, 136 LT 539, 28 Cox CC 324, 16 Digest (Repl) 37, 318

R v Davies [1906] 1 KB 32, [1904–7] All ER Rep 60, 75 LJKB 104, 93 LT 772, DC, 16 Digest (Repl) 12, 44.

R v Evening Standard, ex parte Director of Public Prosecutions (1924) 40 TLR 833, DC, 16 Digest (Repl) 25, 194.

c *Rondel v Worsley* [1967] 3 All ER 993, [1969] 1 AC 191, [1967] 3 WLR 1666, HL, Digest (Cont Vol C) 42, 284a.

Royal Aquarium and Summer and Winter Garden Society Ltd v Parkinson [1892] 1 QB 431, [1891–4] All ER Rep 429, 61 LJQB 409, 66 LT 513, 56 JP 404, CA, 16 Digest (Repl) 114, 5.

Sirros v Moore [1974] 3 All ER 776, [1975] QB 118, [1974] 3 WLR 459, 139 JP 29, CA, Digest (Cont Vol D) 736, 572a.

d *Society of Medical Officers of Health v Hope (Valuation Officer)* [1960] 1 All ER 317, [1960] AC 551, [1960] 2 WLR 404, 124 JP 128, 58 LGR 165, 5 RRC 388, HL, 21 Digest (Repl) 249, 333.

Vine Products Ltd v Mackenzie & Co Ltd [1965] 3 All ER 58, sub nom *Vine Products Ltd v Green* [1966] Ch 484, [1965] 3 WLR 791, sub nom *Vine Products Ltd v Daily Telegraph* [1965] RPC 538, Digest (Cont Vol B) 206, 275a.

e *Wallersteiner v Moir, Moir v Wallersteiner* [1974] 3 All ER 217, [1974] 1 WLR 991, CA, Digest (Cont Vol D) 254, 204e.

Cases also cited

Addis v Crocker [1960] 2 All ER 629, [1961] 1 QB 11, CA.

Arsenal Football Club v Smith (Valuation Officer) [1977] 2 All ER 267, [1979] AC 1; *affg* sub
f nom *Arsenal Football Club Ltd v Ende* [1977] 1 All ER 86, [1977] QB 100, CA.

Attorney-General v Blundell, Attorney-General v Glover [1942] NZLR 287.

Attorney-General v Butler [1953] NZLR 944.

Boulter v Kent Justices [1897] AC 556, 77 LT 288, HL.

Gateshead Assessment Committee v Redheugh Colliery Ltd [1925] AC 309, 132 LT 583, HL.

Morecambe and Heysham Corpn v Robinson (Valuation Officer) [1961] 1 All ER 721, [1961]
g 1 WLR 373, CA.

R v City of Westminster Assessment Committee, ex parte Grosvenor House (Park Lane) Ltd [1940] 4 All ER 132, [1941] 1 KB 53, CA.

R v Edwards, ex parte Welsh Church Temporalities Comrs (1933) 49 TLR 383, DC.

R v McKinnon (1911) 30 NZLR 884.

R v St Mary Abbots Assessments Committee, Kensington [1891] 1 QB 378, 64 LT 240, CA.

h *Shell Co of Australia Ltd v Federal Comr of Taxation* [1931] AC 275, [1930] All ER Rep 671, PC.

Soul v Inland Revenue Comrs [1963] 1 All ER 68, [1963] 1 WLR 112, CA.

Appeal

By a summons dated 17th February 1978, the plaintiff, Her Majesty's Attorney-General,
j sought an injunction to restrain the defendants, the British Broadcasting Corporation ('the BBC'), by themselves, their servants or agents or otherwise from broadcasting or causing or authorising to be broadcast a programme dealing with matters relating to the Exclusive Brethren and the matter pending before the local valuation court at Andover. By a summons, also dated 17th February 1978, the plaintiffs, David Roy Dible and Laurence Norton Marsh, two of the Exclusive Brethren, sought an injunction restraining

the BBC from broadcasting on television or otherwise a television broadcast entitled
'Anno Domini—Brethren' previously broadcast on television on or about 26th September
1976 or any part of that television broadcast, and such further or other injunctions as
might be necessary or proper for the purpose of restraining the BBC from committing
any contempt of court in relation to certain proceedings in the Chancery Division of the
High Court of Justice, and in relation to an appeal of the plaintiff David Roy Dible in
respect of hereditaments at East Street, Andover, Hampshire, pending before a local
valuation court intended to meet at Andover. The plaintiffs sought interlocutory
injunctions before Lawson J, sitting as a judge in chambers, and the matter was referred
to and heard by the Divisional Court. On 17th February 1978 the Divisional Court[1]
(Lord Widgery CJ, Wien and Kenneth Jones JJ) gave judgment in favour of the
plaintiffs. The BBC appealed. The facts are set out in the judgment of Lord Denning
MR.

A T Hoolahan QC, Richard Walker and *Harry Sales* for the BBC.
Harry Woolf and *David Latham* for the Attorney-General.

Cur adv vult

11th April. The following judgments were read.

LORD DENNING MR. Although this case is concerned with the British Broadcasting
Corporation, it cannot properly be understood unless you know something of the
'Exclusive Brethren'; and in particular of those of 'the Brethren' who adhere to the
teachings of an American, one James Taylor junior. So I must tell something of their
activities as disclosed in the papers before the court; though it must be taken with reserve
as these activities have not been proved in evidence.
    The Exclusive Brethren are a Christian religious sect. They read the Bible. They sing
hymns. They say prayers. They meet together for religious worship. In buildings with
blank walls and no windows. They keep themselves very much to themselves. They
hold to a doctrine which separates evil from good. They carry it so far that, in their eyes,
everyone who is not one of them is evil. So that, even in a single family, any one of the
family who belongs to the Exclusive Brethren must separate himself from those who do
not. He must dissociate himself from them because they are evil. He must not talk to
them or have meals with them. When a whole family join the Exclusive Brethren, they
must have nothing to do with their neighbours; because they are evil. Everyone is evil
who does not belong to the Exclusive Brethren. They apply this doctrine so strictly that
it has caused much distress and unhappiness among deeply religious people. Families
have been split asunder. Husband from wife. Children from parents. Never seeing
friends or relatives. Such distress that it is said that in Andover it led to two deaths which
the coroner described as murder and suicide.
    This sect claims to be a charitable body and to have all the privileges and exemptions
which attach to charities. It gave the Charity Commissioners so much anxiety that in
1975–76 under their statutory powers (contained in ss 6 and 7 of the Charities Act 1960)
they asked Mr Hugh Francis QC to hold an inquiry into the Exclusive Brethren and to
report on it. It is open to the Charity Commissioners to publish his report but they have
not done so yet. The report is, I gather, very critical of the Exclusive Brethren.
    The sect also claims to be relieved from payment of rates. They rely on the exemption
granted in s 39 of the General Rate Act 1967 to 'places of public religious worship'. We
had to consider that exemption in the case of the Mormon Church (more fully the
Church of Jesus Christ of Latter Day Saints). A Mormon temple was held not to qualify
for relief but their chapels did: see *Church of Jesus Christ of Latter Day Saints v Henning*[2].

---

1 [1978] 2 All ER 731
2 [1963] 2 All ER 733, [1964] AC 420

On 26th September 1976 the BBC showed a television broadcast entitled 'Anno-
Domini—Brethren'. We have been supplied with a transcript of it. It was all about the
a Exclusive Brethren. It was extremely hostile to, and critical of, them. It has been
described by their solicitors as 'defamatory, inaccurate, biased, unfairly prejudicial and
wholly unjustified in its attack on the Brethren and the pro-Taylorites'. It included an
interview with Mr Hugh Francis, in which he expressed the view that—

> 'the doctrine of separation from evil as interpreted and applied under the
> *b* teachings of James Taylor, Junior was detrimental to the true interests of the
> community . . .'

It also included a statement by a lady who said:

> '. . . an awful lot of exclusive Brethren meeting houses up and down the country
> have applied for, and do get, rate relief. Now, one of the conditions of this
> *c* beneficence is that the doors must be open to all members of the public for services
> on meeting days, you know. Well, they aren't at all—they'll keep you out. Now
> that means really that they're not entitled to the rate rebate that a lot of them are
> getting . . .'

In the course of the broadcast, the spokesman said: 'We have given the Brethren the right
d to reply—they haven't chosen to exercise this. And, in the meantime, the tragedies go
on.'

After that broadcast the Exclusive Brethren commenced an action in July 1977 by a
writ entitled *Rule and others v Charity Commissioners and Francis* in which they claimed an
injunction against Mr Francis. They brought into question the entire validity and status
of his report; and sought specific relief in respect of the publication of the report or any
e material derived from it. In addition there are a number of other actions pending in the
High Court which relate to charitable trusts connected with the Exclusive Brethren.

Early in February 1978 the BBC proposed to repeat the showing of their programme
'Annon Domini—Brethren'. It was announced in the Radio Times of Thursday, 9th
February 1978. It said that the programme would be repeated on Sunday 19th February
1978. This gave rise to intense activity by the solicitors for the Exclusive Brethren and
f by the Treasury Solicitor. They asked that the repeat programme should not take
place. They suggested that it would be a contempt of the High Court proceedings.
There were telephone conversations and letters in rapid succession. Mr Hugh Francis
asked that his contribution should not be included in the repeat programme. The BBC
agreed to his request entirely on a 'without prejudice' basis, but refused to withdraw the
rest of the programme. On 14th February 1978 the solicitor for the BBC wrote to the
g Treasury Solicitor that:

> 'After giving the matter full consideration, I have been obliged to advise the
> Corporation that the transmission of the above programme will not constitute a
> contempt of the proceedings in the High Court.'

That matter however, contempt of the High Court, was never resolved. It was because
h someone told that there was to be on Friday, 10th March 1978, a hearing before the local
valuation court at Andover. It appears that there was at Andover a meeting room of the
local assembly of the Exclusive Brethren. The trustees of the meeting room had made
a proposal in writing to the valuation officer that their meeting room should be granted
relief from rates, on the ground that it was a 'place of public religious worship'. The local
authority and its valuation officer had both objected to the proposal. Their objections
j were treated as an appeal to the local valuation court. So the chairman had arranged for
the court to be convened on Friday, 10th March 1978, to hear the appeal.

The London solicitors of the Exclusive Brethren got to know of that rating case on
Wednesday, 15th February 1978. They immediately wrote to the BBC asserting that the
repeat programme, on Sunday 19th February, would be a contempt of the local valuation
court. They said:

'In these circumstances even if there were no question of contempt in respect of the various High Court proceedings, the repetition of the broadcast represents a wholly improper and unwarranted canvassing in public of issues which are to come before a Court consisting of a panel of persons unlikely to have legal qualifications and the hearing is to take place in 3 weeks' time . . . Only the complete cancellation of the proposed broadcast will avoid the risk of grave prejudice to the Appellants in the Andover proceedings and to the Brethren in general and the risk of the Corporation committing a serious contempt.'

Those solicitors on Thursday, 16th February, put the matter urgently before the Attorney-General. He seems to have been persuaded that the showing of the programme would be a contempt. His assistant took immediate steps to apply for an injunction against the BBC. One of his assistant solicitors swore an affidavit saying:

'To the best of my knowledge and belief the members of local Valuation Courts are not legally qualified and as the programme will be broadcast in the Andover area there is every possibility that it may be seen by one or more of the members of the Court and they may be influenced accordingly.'

Everything was done in a great hurry. On Friday morning, 17th February, two writs were issued: one by the Attorney-General against the BBC for contempt in respect of the proceedings before the local valuation court at Andover; the other by two of the Exclusive Brethren against the BBC for contempt in respect of the High Court proceedings and also the local valuation court at Andover. On the same Friday morning they went to the judge in chambers. He referred it to the Divisional Court[1]. They heard it at once. The only issue debated was whether the local valuation court at Andover was or was not an 'inferior court' within RSC Ord 52, r 1(2). The BBC without making any admissions, said that, if it was, they would not proceed to show the programme on the air at all. The court held that it was such an 'inferior court'. So the BBC did not transmit the programme. It was all decided on that one day, Friday, 17th February, because of the programme on the Sunday. It is a pity that it all had to be done so quickly.

There was really no need for it. Because, as it turned out, there never was a hearing of the local valuation court. The Exclusive Brethren were granted rate relief on their hall at Andover without any hearing at all. On that very Thursday, 16th February, the objectors had withdrawn their objections, but that news had not got through to London. So on Friday, 17th February, everything was rushed through in London on the basis that there would be a hearing at Andover, whereas the local valuation court down there knew there would not be a hearing at all.

The position of the Attorney-General

These are proceedings for criminal contempt, in respect of civil proceedings. In *Attorney-General v Times Newspapers Ltd*[2] (the *Thalidomide* case) I suggested that it was desirable for the party to the civil action (who alleged that the trial was being prejudiced) himself to make the application. That used in my early days to be the regular course. And it had the inestimable benefit that, if the party sought an interim injunction, he would have to give an undertaking in damages, so that if the publication was eventually held not to be a contempt, he would have to pay compensation to the publisher. Such an undertaking was, I have no doubt, given in *Kitcat v Sharpe*[3]. So far as I know the first case in which the Attorney-General himself sought an interim injunction was the *Thalidomide* case[4] itself. In the House of Lords it was intimated that in all these cases of contempt the proper person to bring the proceedings was the Attorney-General, and not

1   [1978] 2 All ER 731, [1978] 1 WLR 477
2   [1973] 1 All ER 815 at 820, [1973] QB 710 at 737
3   (1882) 52 LJ Ch 134
4   [1973] 3 All ER 54, [1974] AC 273

the party himself; for the simple reason that contempt (even in respect of a civil action)
is a criminal offence punishable by imprisonment; and the enforcement of the criminal
law (by action in the civil courts) is the peculiar responsibility of the Attorney-General;
see *Gouriet v Union of Post Office Workers*[1]. Lord Diplock made this clear in the *Thalidomide*
case[2] when he said:

> '. . . the Attorney-General accepts the responsibility of receiving complaints of
> alleged contempt of court from parties to litigation and of making an application in
> his official capacity for committal of the offender if he thinks this course to be
> justified in the public interest. He is the appropriate public officer to represent the
> public interest in the administration of justice.'

Lord Diplock went on to stress the serious responsibility thus resting on the Attorney-
General. Especially because an interim injunction is a severe restriction on freedom of
speech and freedom of the Press. To which I would add that, in this type of case, the
Crown would not usually be called on to give an undertaking in damages: see *F Hoffmann-
La Roche & Co AG v Secretary of State for Trade and Industry*[3]. Counsel for the Attorney-
General told us that, in this very case, he would not have given it, even if asked. This
means that, by proceeding as he did in this case, the Attorney-General, with all the
authority of his office, is seeking a 'gagging injunction' at the instance of a party to the
case. To my mind the courts should not award him such an injunction except in a clear
case where there would manifestly be a contempt of court for the publication to take
place. The same reasoning applies here as in the cases where a party seeks to restrain the
publication of a libel. The words of an exceptionally strong Court of Appeal in *Bonnard
v Perryman*[4] apply, not only to libel, but also to contempt of court. Suitably adapted, they
run[5]:

> 'The right of free speech is one which it is for the public interest that individuals
> should possess, and, indeed, that they should exercise without impediment, so long
> as no wrongful act is done . . . the importance of leaving free speech unfettered is a
> strong reason in cases of [contempt of court] for dealing most cautiously and warily
> with the granting of interim injunctions.'

As a result of that decision, an interim injunction is rarely, if ever, granted in cases of
alleged libel where the publisher says the words are true and that he intends to justify
them. Equally it seems to me that, in cases of alleged contempt of court (in respect of a
civil action), an interim injunction should rarely, if ever, be granted where the publisher
says that the words are true in substance and in fact and that the comment is fair
comment on a matter of public interest. It would seem strange to me that a party (who
could not get an interim injunction restraining a libel) could all the same get (by going
to the Attorney-General) an interim injunction restraining a contempt of court.

Take this very case. The Exclusive Brethren could not conceivably get an injunction
to restrain the repetition of the programme on the ground that it was a libel on them.
Nor could they get it on the ground that it was a contempt of their action in the High
Court. That was to be heard by a judge of the Chancery Division. No one can suppose
that he would be influenced by the television programme, even if he watched it. The
position of a High Court judge was well expressed by Buckley LJ in *Vine Products Ltd v
Mackenzie & Co Ltd*[6]:

> 'This is not an action which will be tried by a jury. Although I suppose that there
> might be a case in which the publication was of a kind which might even be

j   1   [1977] 3 All ER 70, [1978] AC 435
    2   [1973] 3 All ER 54 at 74, [1974] AC 273 at 311
    3   [1974] 2 All ER 1128, [1975] AC 295
    4   [1891] 2 Ch 269, [1891–4] All ER Rep 965
    5   [1891] 2 Ch 269 at 284, [1891–4] All ER Rep 965 at 968
    6   [1965] 3 All ER 58 at 62, [1966] 1 Ch 484 at 496

thought capable of influencing the mind of a professional judge, it has generally been accepted that professional judges are sufficiently well equipped by their *a* professional training to be on their guard against allowing any such matter as this to influence them in deciding the case.'

I notice that Professor Borrie in his book on the Law of Contempt[1] rules out any possibility of contempt by publication on the ground that it might influence a professionally trained judge, a view with which I entirely agree. No professionally *b* trained judge would be influenced by anything he read in the newspapers or saw on television. No interim injunction has ever been granted on this ground. Nor should it be started now. No criminal proceedings for any such publication have ever been taken. Nor should they be started now. So no interim injunction could conceivably be granted in respect of the High Court proceedings.

c

What is an inferior court?

What is an 'inferior court'? The discussion before the divisional court was solely whether the local valuation court was an 'inferior court'. The discussion was so confined because the judges have evolved a set of principles which apply to bodies which are 'courts' in the proper sense of the word, but not to bodies which are not 'courts'. To solve the problem, it is as well to recall those principles which apply only to 'courts'. *d*

The object throughout has been to keep the stream of justice pure and clear. It must not be disturbed by stones or polluted with mud. The rulings hitherto have been, for the most part, concerned with the superior courts of law. Recent examples are: the proceedings must not be disrupted by shouts or slogans (*Morris v Crown Office*[2]); or by laughing gas (*Balogh v Crown Court at St Albans*[3]). The judges are granted immunity from suit for anything done in their judicial capacity (*Sirros v Moore*[4]). The advocates are not *e* liable to be sued for the way they conduct their cases in court (*Rondel v Worsley*[5]). The witnesses are given an absolute privilege in respect of anything they say in the witness box. Nor are they to be threatened beforehand or victimised afterwards (*Attorney-General v Butterworth*[6]). The parties are not to be blackmailed or intimidated by publicity in the newspapers (see *Attorney-General v Times Newspapers Ltd*[7]). No case is to be prejudged in the Press or on the media. Nothing must be done to prejudice a fair trial. There must *f* be nothing in the nature of 'trial by newspaper' or 'trial by television'.

How far do these principles apply to the inferior courts? I pause to say that the word 'inferior' is a misdescription. They are not inferior in the doing of justice; nor in the judges who man them; nor in the advocates who plead in them. They are called 'inferior' only because they try cases of a lesser order of importance, as it is thought. But the cases which they try are often of equal concern to the parties and the public. I see no *g* reason whatever why the principles which have been evolved for the superior courts should not apply equally to the inferior courts. The stream of justice should be kept pure and clear in all the courts, superior and inferior alike. That is the way in which the law seems to be developing: as is shown by the cases on contempt of court (see *R v Davies*[8]) and the important judgment of Dixon CJ in (*John Fairfax & Sons Pty Ltd v McRae*[9]); and the cases on the liability of judges (see *Sirros v Moore*[4]); and on absolute privilege of *h*

---

1   G J Borrie and N V Lowe, The Law of Contempt (1973), pp 96–97
2   [1970] 1 All ER 1079, [1970] 2 QB 114
3   [1974] 3 All ER 283, [1975] QB 73
4   [1974] 3 All ER 776, [1975] QB 118
5   [1967] 3 All ER 993, [1969] 1 AC 191
6   [1962] 3 All ER 326, [1963] 1 QB 696
7   [1973] 3 All ER 54, [1974] AC 273
8   [1906] 1 KB 32, [1904–7] All ER Rep 60
9   (1955) 93 CLR 351

j

advocate and witness (see *Lincoln v Daniels*[1] per Devlin LJ). The only qualification is in the
a manner of enforcing those principles. Where there is contempt of court, if it comes to
granting injunctions or inflicting penalties, this is left to the superior courts: see *Attorney-
General v Mulholland, Attorney-General v Foster*[2], and *Attorney-General v Leveller Magazine
Ltd*[3]. But otherwise the principles should be the same for all.

But the principles, which confer immunity and protection, have hitherto been
confined to the well-recognised courts, in which I include, of course, not only the High
b Court, but also the Crown Court, the county courts, the magistrates' courts, the consistory
courts and courts-martial. The principles have not hitherto been extended to the newly
established courts of which we have so many. The answer cannot depend on whether
the word 'court' appears in the title. There are many newly formed bodies which go by
the name of 'tribunal' but which have all the characteristics of the recognised courts: such
as the industrial relations tribunals, and the Solicitors' Disciplinary Tribunal. To my
c mind the immunities and protections which are accorded to the recognised courts of the
land should be extended to all tribunals or bodies which have equivalent characteristics. After all, if the principles are good for the old, so they should be good for the new.
I would therefore be venturesome. I would suggest that the immunities and protections
should be extended to all tribunals set up by or under the authority of Parliament or of
the Crown which exercise equivalent functions by equivalent procedures and are manned
d by equivalent personnel as those of the recognised courts of the land: see the judgment
of Devlin LJ in *Lincoln v Daniels*[1].

Applying this test I would suggest that commercial arbitrations are excluded because
they are not set up by or under the authority of Parliament or of the Crown. Planning
inquiries are excluded because their function is not to hear and determine, but only to
inquire and report. Licensing bodies are excluded because they exercise administrative
e functions and not judicial (see *Attwood v Chapman*[4] and *T D Lewis v British Broadcasting
Corpn*[5]). Assessment committees are excluded because they are manned by laymen and
not by lawyers. And so on.

What then about a local valuation court? It is the successor of the old assessment
committees which were certainly not courts: see *Mersey Docks and Harbour Board v West
Derby Assessment Committee and Bottomley*[6]. But counsel for the Attorney-General set out
f 14 characteristics which he suggested qualified it for inclusion in the list of 'inferior
courts'. They were these: 1. The members are selected from a panel approved by the
Minister. 2. Witnesses can be compelled to attend by subpoena. 3. It sits in public. 4.
It has power to administer oaths. 5. Its decisions are final, subject to appeal. 6. An appeal
is to the Lands Tribunal which hears the case de novo: and the Lands Tribunal is
undoubtedly a 'court'. 7. It has rules of procedure like any court. 8. It deals with matters
g of public interest. 9. It is judicial, not executive or administrative. 10. The proceedings
taken there form a lis. 11. It is named in its title as a 'court'. 12. Although its decisions
are not directly enforceable, they amount to a declaration which is binding on those
concerned. 13. They administer the law. 14. They have exclusive jurisdiction within
their allotted sphere.

Although this is an impressive list, the decision of the House of Lords in *Society of
h Medical Officers of Health v Hope (Valuation Officer)*[7] shows that the local valuation court has
different characteristics from those of a court properly so called. In any case, to my mind
this body lacks one important characteristic of a court: it has no one on it or connected

---

j 1 [1961] 3 All ER 740 at 747–748, [1962] 1 QB 237 at 254–255
2 [1963] 1 All ER 767, [1963] 2 QB 477
3 [1979] 1 All ER 745, [1979] 2 WLR 247
4 [1914] 3 KB 275
5 [1979] Court of Appeal Transcript 193
6 [1932] 1 KB 40, [1931] 1 All ER Rep 409
7 [1960] 1 All ER 317, [1960] AC 551

with it who is legally qualified or experienced. To constitute a court there should be a chairman who is a lawyer or at any rate have at his elbow a clerk or assistant who is a *a* lawyer qualified by examination or by experience, as a justice's clerk is. The reason is that a lawyer is, or should be, by his training and experience better able than others to keep to the relevant and exclude the irrelevant; to decide according to the evidence adduced and not be influenced by outside information; to interpret the words of statutes or regulations as Parliament intended; to have recourse to legal books of reference and be able to consult them; and generally to know how the proceedings of a court should be *b* conducted.

It is for this reason that it is my opinion that the local valuation court is not a court properly so called whereas the Lands Tribunal is a court. It is interesting to notice that the only ground on which it was suggested that the members would be prejudiced by the television programme was that 'the members of local valuation courts are not legally qualified'. It is that very reason which, in my opinion, disqualifies them from being a *c* court properly so called.

Was there a 'contempt of court'?

In case I am wrong on that point, however, I would proceed to consider one further matter: would the publication by the BBC be a contempt of court?

At the outset I would say that we are here concerned not with criminal proceedings *d* but with civil proceedings. So far as criminal proceedings are concerned, when a person is charged with a criminal offence, the courts have always been anxious to prevent any newspaper or the like from publishing any matter which may prejudice the fair trial of the accused person. This was introduced at a time when most criminal cases were tried by jury; and it was thought they might be prejudiced if they had read beforehand in the newspapers of matters which were inadmissible in evidence at the trial, such as his previous convictions or his bad character; or statements made by witnesses not subject to *e* cross-examination and the like. The courts intervened strongly so as to prevent anything in the nature of 'trial by newspaper' or 'trial by television'. It applies not only to the trial court itself, but also to the preliminary proceedings before the magistrates: see *R v Davies*[1], *R v Clarke, ex parte Crippen*[2], *R v Evening Standard, ex parte Director of Public Prosecutions*[3], *R v Daily Mirror, ex parte Smith*[4]. This jurisdiction has been extended to a *f* trial of a soldier for desertion by a court-martial: see *R v Daily Mail, ex parte Farnsworth*[5]. It has also been extended to a trial of a clergyman for immorality by a consistory court: see *R v Daily Herald, ex parte Bishop of Norwich*[6].

It is very different however, or it should be very different, where no one is accused of any offence; and the party concerned has himself instituted a civil action or matter for damages or other relief, be it in the High Court or the county court or any inferior court. He cannot, by so doing, claim to restrain any newspaper or anyone else from *g* publishing criticism of him or his conduct. In former times he often used to issue a writ so as to 'gag' his opponent: a 'gagging writ' as it was called. But this has been stopped for two reasons: first, that in balancing the competing interests the freedom of speech and of the Press has priority over any suggested interference with a fair trial of the civil action (see *Wallersteiner v Moir*[7]); secondly, that the civil action will usually be tried by a *h* professional judge, and that no professional judge would be influenced in the least by any criticism that appeared in the newspapers, even if he read them, or on the television, even if he watched it (see *Vine Products Ltd v Mackenzie & Co Ltd*[8]).

---

1   [1906] 1 KB 32, [1904–7] All ER Rep 60
2   (1910) 103 LT 636, [1908–10] All ER Rep 915
3   (1924) 40 TLR 833
4   [1927] 1 KB 845
5   [1921] 2 KB 733
6   [1932] 2 KB 402
7   [1974] 3 All ER 217, [1974] 1 WLR 991
8   [1965] 3 All ER 58, [1966] 1 Ch 484

If such be the case where the civil case is tried by a professional judge, how stands it when a civil matter is to be decided by laymen? In most cases there is a panel of laymen. It will be easy to assemble enough of them who have not read the newspaper or seen the television. This would be done at a local valuation court just as it would with magistrates. Even if that were not so, it must be remembered that there is an appeal from them to the Lands Tribunal, both on fact and law, a complete rehearing; and the Lands Tribunal is presided over by a professional judge, very nearly of equal standing to a High Court judge. There is no conceivable possibility of the Lands Tribunal being influenced by the newspapers or television. Seeing that there is this safeguard, I would hold that no publicity affecting a local valuation court should be regarded as a contempt of court.

Conclusion

Since the hearing of this case, we have had yet another case in which someone had attempted to stop a BBC programme on the ground of contempt of court, *T D Lewis v British Broadcasting Corpn*[1]. It failed. So should all requests for 'gagging injunctions' which seek to prevent true and fair comment on matters of public interest.

I would, therefore, allow this appeal.

EVELEIGH LJ. We are concerned to determine whether the local valuation court is an 'inferior court'. This is the expression used in RSC Ord 52, r 1, but that order does not create a jurisdiction where none existed before. It uses the expression 'inferior court' to describe the tribunal which the Queen's Bench Divisional Court is concerned to protect from interference by committal for contempt.

Those tribunals are aptly described as inferior courts for the expression contemplates a superior court, namely a court of record. So one looks for a comparable tribunal but at an inferior level, that is, with limited jurisdiction.

What then are the attributes of such a tribunal? In my opinion the first is that it should have been created by the state. At one time courts were created or recognised by the monarch. Now they are created by Parliament. Thus while an arbitration tribunal may contain many of the attributes of a court, it will lack this first essential one. Secondly, it must conduct its procedure in accordance with the rules of natural justice. Thirdly, that procedure will involve a public hearing with the power at least to receive evidence orally, to permit the oral examination and cross-examination of witnesses and to hear argument on the issues before it. Fourthly, it arrives at a decision which is final and binding as long as it stands. Fifthly, there will be two parties at least before it, one of whom may be the Crown, who are interested in the decision. Sixthly, the decision will be concerned with legal rights:

> 'The only kind of rights with which the courts of justice are concerned are legal rights; and a court of civil jurisdiction is concerned with legal rights only when the aid of the court is invoked by one party claiming a right against another party, to protect or enforce the right or to provide a remedy against that other party for infringement of it, or is invoked by either party to settle a dispute between them as to the existence or nature of the right claimed'. (*Gouriet v Union of Post Office Workers*[2] per Lord Diplock.)

A court will also be concerned with criminal matters.

When the valuation officer decides to include a property in the valuation list he is making an administrative decision. He is of course bound to follow the requirements of the law in so doing and to act judicially, but he is not a court. Until he makes his decision no one's right or duty has been affected. When the matter comes before the valuation court, it will determine as between the appellant and the valuation officer whether the

1   [1979] Court of Appeal Transcript 193
2   [1977] 3 All ER 70 at 100, [1978] AC 435 at 501

officer has properly performed his duty and whether the appellant has been denied a
right (in the present case the right to be excluded from the list). The court may decide
that both parties are wrong and announce a decision which is somewhere between the
opposing contentions.

In my opinion, all the requirements of a court exist. It is not necessary that there
should be a lawyer presiding, in my opinion, or indeed that there should be a legally
trained clerk. A coroner's court is a court. It lacks or may lack these attributes when a
doctor presides as he so frequently does. In practice the clerk actually present in the
magistrate's court is not always legally qualified. So too at quarter sessions the chairman
used not to have to be a person with legal training and it was not essential for there to be
present a legally trained clerk.

The Divisional Court in its contempt jurisdiction is concerned to protect those inferior
courts of the land which are designed to enforce the law of the land. Those courts give
to a person or to the state a remedy against one who has acted in violation of another's
rights. As I see it, that is what the valuation court does vis-à-vis the valuation officer. Its
jurisdiction is indeed limited but so is the jurisdiction of many a court and I do not think
that the extremely narrow field of the valuation court's jurisdiction should cause me to
deny its entitlement to the description which Parliament has given it.

The court has the attributes I have referred to above and those listed for us in
argument by counsel for the Attorney-General. Instinctively one has little difficulty in
deciding that the Lands Tribunal is a court. In relation to rating valuation that tribunal
performs the same task as the local valuation court from which it hears appeals and it
proceeds in the same manner. It may be that it has itself some further procedural
powers, for example discovery, but that does not in my opinion differentiate it in
character.

However, I would like to add this. For the reasons given by Lord Denning MR I find
it very hard to envisage a case where I could hold that a court whether composed of
lawyers or laymen would be influenced by newspaper publications or broadcasting.
Nonetheless, on the question before this court whether the valuation court is or is not an
inferior court I would hold that it is, and I would therefore dismiss this appeal.

SIR STANLEY REES. The question which arises for decision by this court is whether
a local valuation court set up under the provisions of the General Rate Act 1967 is an
inferior court within the ambit of RSC Ord 52, r 1. If it is, then the Queen's Bench
Division has power by injunction to restrain contempt by way of publications which
might prejudice pending proceedings before that court. The Queen's Bench Division
may exercise this power at the instance of Her Majesty's Attorney-General as well as at
the instance of any person aggrieved by any such intended publication. In fact
proceedings were started in this case both by the Attorney-General and by persons
aggrieved. But we have been solely concerned with the Attorney-General's action.

A Queen's Bench Divisional Court presided over by Lord Widgery CJ held that the
local valuation court of Andover was an inferior court within RSC Ord 52, r 1.
Accordingly they granted an interim injunction restraining the broadcasting of a
programme dealing with, and commenting on, the central issue in a rating appeal which
was shortly to be heard and decided by the local valuation court.

Neither this court nor the Queen's Bench Divisional Court was addressed nor required
to consider in detail the content of the proposed broadcast. The transcript was available
but was not read by the Queen's Bench Divisional Court owing to lack of time. We have
read it. But as the only issue argued fully before us was whether a local valuation court
was an inferior court I do not, speaking entirely for myself, feel qualified to express any
decided opinion one way or the other whether the facts disclosed in support of the
application would justify granting an injunction. It was conceded on behalf of the BBC
in the court below that if it were decided that the local valuation court at Andover was
an inferior court they would abandon their intention to broadcast the programme.

Accordingly I consider the sole question whether a local valuation court is or is not an

inferior court. This is of considerable public importance. On the one hand, it is vital to
a ensure that the proceedings in any inferior court shall not be prejudiced by publications
of damaging material in any form. On the other hand, it is also vital to ensure that
freedom of expression in the Press and in broadcasting should not be unwarrantably
fettered. It is equally important that the press and the broadcasting authorities should be
able to know in advance what tribunals are inferior courts within the ambit of RSC Ord
52, r 1. There are in existence in modern times a large number of tribunals in respect of
b which a question might arise whether they are or are not inferior courts; for example, 33
tribunals are listed in Sch 1 to the Tribunals and Inquiries Act 1971.

I start by observing that RSC Ord 52, r 1, does not define an 'inferior court', nor is there
to be found in statutes or elsewhere a list of such courts. It is necessary to look to the
common law as enshrined in the decided cases, and this I proceed to do as briefly as may
be.

c   In *Royal Aquarium and Summer and Winter Garden Society Ltd v Parkinson*[1] the Court of
Appeal held that the London County Council meeting to decide whether to grant a
music and dancing licence was not a court so as to confer absolute privilege in respect of
defamatory statements made in the course of proceedings. Lord Esher MR said in
reference to the rule granting absolute immunity[2]:

d   'The ground of that rule is public policy. It is applicable to all kinds of Courts of
justice; but the doctrine has been carried further; and it seems that this immunity
applies wherever there is an authorised inquiry which, though not before a Court
of justice, is before a tribunal which has similar attributes. In the case of *Dawkins* v
Lord Rokeby[3] the doctrine was extended to a military Court of inquiry. It was so
extended on the ground that the case was one of an authorised inquiry before a
tribunal acting judicially, that is to say, in a manner as nearly as possible similar to
e   that in which a Court of justice acts in respect of an inquiry before it. This doctrine
has never been extended further than to Courts of justice and tribunals acting in a
manner similar to that in which such Courts act.'

I add for good measure an extract from the well-known statement of Fry LJ[4]:

f   'It was said that the existence of this immunity is based on considerations of
public policy, and that, as a matter of public policy, wherever a body has to decide
questions, and in so doing has to act judicially, it must be held that there is a judicial
proceeding to which this immunity ought to attach. It seems to me that the sense
in which the word "judicial" is used in that argument is this: it is used as meaning
that the proceedings are such as ought to be conducted with the fairness and
impartiality which characterize proceedings in Courts of justice, and are proper to
g   the functions of a judge, not that the members of the supposed body are members
of a Court. Consider to what lengths the doctrine would extend, if this immunity
were applied to every body which is bound to decide judicially in the sense of
deciding fairly and impartially. It would apply to assessment committees, boards of
guardians, to the Inns of Court when considering the conduct of one of their
members, to the General Medical Council when considering questions affecting the
h   position of a medical man, and to all arbitrators. Is it necessary, on grounds of
public policy, that the doctrine of immunity should be carried as far as this? I say
not. I say that there is ample protection afforded in such cases by the ordinary law
of privilege.'

I apprehend that there can be no doubt but that if a tribunal is protected by absolute
j privilege that is a strong indication that it is an inferior court.

---

1   [1892] 1 QB 431, [1891–4] All ER Rep 429
2   [1892] 1 QB 431 at 442, cf [1891–4] All ER Rep 429 at 432
3   (1875) LR 7 HL 744; *affg* LR 8 QB 255
4   [1892] 1 QB 431 at 447, cf [1891–4] All ER Rep 429 at 434

In *R v Davies*[1] a Divisional Court of the Queen's Bench Division held that a magistrates' court about to engage in committal proceedings in a case which might go for trial to quarter sessions or to the High Court was an inferior court so that a publisher of a newspaper which featured damaging material about the accused could be attached for contempt. Giving the judgment of the court Wills J, after stating the vital importance of preventing interference with, and denigration of judges and courts, said this[2]:

'With a few verbal alterations those eloquent words will apply with at least equal force to writings, the direct tendency of which is to prevent a fair and impartial trial, or at least one that can be so considered, from being had in Courts of inferior jurisdiction which have not the power of protecting themselves from such encroachments upon their independence. The public mischief is identical, and in each instance the undoubted possible recourse to indictment or criminal information is too dilatory and too inconvenient to afford any satisfactory remedy.'

It will be sufficient if I state in summary form the effect of some further reported cases in which tribunals have been held to be inferior courts.

In *R·v Clarke, ex parte Crippen*[3] a coroner's court investigating the death of the victim in the Crippen case was held to be an inferior court so that a prejudicial publication could be restrained. In *R v Daily Mail, ex parte Farnsworth*[4] a court-martial held under the Army Act trying a man for desertion was held to be an inferior court so that a prejudicial publication could be restrained. In *R v Daily Herald, ex parte Bishop of Norwich*[5] an ecclesiastical consistory court dealing with the alleged misconduct of a vicar was held to be an inferior court, and a prejudicial publication could be restrained.

Finally I turn to one case in which a tribunal was held *not* to be an inferior court. In *Collins v Henry Whiteway & Co Ltd*[6] Horridge J held that a court of referees set up under the Unemployment Insurance Act 1920 was not an inferior court so that communications to that court did not enjoy absolute privilege. Horridge J said this[7]:

'Upon the best consideration that I can give to the sections of the Unemployment Insurance Act, 1920, and the regulations thereunder, I think that the result is that by such Act and regulations the Court of Referees was created for the purpose of deciding claims made upon the insurance funds. It is not a body deciding between parties, nor does its decision affect criminally or otherwise the status of an individual. I therefore do not think that I ought to extend the protection given in *Dawkins v Lord Rokeby*[8] to the present case.'

As has been pointed out to us the assessment committees from 1862 to 1948 were the immediate predecessors of the local valuation courts and there have been some decided cases in which serious doubt has been cast on the status as inferior courts of these assessment committees, and in particular the very well-known statement of Scrutton LJ in *Mersey Docks and Harbour Board v West Derby Assessment Committee and Bottomley*[9] which is highly relevant. In that case Scrutton LJ said[10]:

'In my opinion the Assessment Committee could be ordered by mandamus to hear and determine. The prerogative writs will run to a body which is not "a Court," and it may be that like some kinds of Licensing Justices the Assessment

---

1   [1906] 1 KB 32 [1904–7] All ER Rep 60
2   [1906] 1 KB 32 at 41, [1904–7] All ER Rep 60 at 66
3   (1910) 103 LT 636, [1908–10] All ER Rep 915
4   [1921] 2 KB 733
5   [1932] 2 KB 402
6   [1927] 2 KB 378
7   [1927] 2 KB 378 at 383, 137 LT 297 at 299
8   (1875) LR 7 HL 744; *affg* (1873) LR 8 QB 255
9   [1932] 1 KB 40, [1931] All ER Rep 409
10 [1932] 1 KB 40 at 104

a
Committee is not "a Court"; it does not hear evidence on oath and has no particular rules of procedure, though it acts under a statutory duty and authority (see the decision of Avory J. as to Licensing Justices: *Attwood v Chapman*[1]). The proceedings in the Assessment Committee do not appear to be commenced under any Rules of Court, and the provision that the appellant begins in Quarter Session shows that the proceedings have already commenced by a decision against which there is an appeal to Quarter Sessions, and that the hearing in Quarter Sessions is not an original hearing on which there is a first decision.'

b
Lord Widgery CJ in giving judgment in the instant case found support for his view that local valuation courts were inferior courts when he compared their functions and procedure with those so described by Scrutton LJ.

By the Local Government Act 1948 assessment committees were abolished and local valuation courts were provided in their stead. This Act was repealed and replaced by the General Rate Act 1967 which with the Rating Appeals (Local Valuation Courts) Regulations 1956[2] now governs the power and procedure of local valuation courts. I shall attempt to set out in summary form the constitution, powers and procedure of these courts.

The court is constituted by a chairman and two other members drawn from a local valuation panel and supported by a clerk. No legal qualifications are required and the panel are nominees of the local council approved by the Secretary of State. The court is convened as may be required and the date and place of hearing must be advertised by the clerk. As to procedure, the court may sit in public with a discretion for good cause to sit in private. It has no power of itself to summon witnesses. But we are told that the Crown Office will, and does on request, issue witness summonses to compel the attendance of witnesses. The court may administer the oath to witnesses who thereupon give their testimony on oath. All witnesses may be examined and cross-examined. The valuation officer and any party concerned may appear and conduct his or her case in person or by solicitor or by counsel. A party, but not the valuation officer, may also have his or her case conducted 'by any other representative'. The clerk must keep 'minutes' of the proceedings in court.

The function of the court (see reg 3 of the 1956 regulations) is to hear and determine any appeal brought before it and the issue to be decided relates to the manner in which any hereditament shall be treated in the valuation list. Such an issue when disputed between the valuation officer and an aggrieved party may come before the valuation court for a decision. In the instant case the dispute was whether a building used by a religious sect known as the Exclusive Brethren was a place of public worship within the meaning of s 39 of the General Rate Act 1967 and so became entitled to rating relief. It was the case of the valuation officer that it was not and the case on behalf of the sect that it was. This was an issue of mixed fact and law. Having considered the matter, the court is required to put its 'decision' (this is the word used in reg 10 of the 1956 regulations) into writing and cause it to be signed by the chairman and sent to all parties. Then in accordance with its decision the court would give directions as to the manner in which the building was to appear in the valuation list.

There is a right of appeal by any person aggrieved by the decision of the court to the Lands Tribunal. It is the duty of the court to inform every party of this right of appeal when sending a copy of the court's written decision. This appeal is by way of a complete rehearing. There is a right of appeal from the Lands Tribunal to the Court of Appeal on a point of law by way of a case stated. There is also, and somewhat incidentally, a further right of appeal under s 7 of the 1967 Act to quarter sessions (now to the Crown Court) by any person aggrieved by a rate in respect of any matter which could not be dealt with by way of appeal to the Lands Tribunal. It is obvious that the valuation court has a number

---

1   [1914] 3 KB 275
2   SI 1956 No 632

of characteristics of a court, including, though this is of minimal importance, the statutory label of 'court'.

But counsel in his helpful address on behalf of the BBC argued that it lacked a number of important characteristics usually found in courts of law or of justice. It is not presided over by a lawyer or advised by a legally qualified clerk. It has no power of itself to summon witnesses or to compel production of documents. It is not a court of record. It has no power to commit for contempt in the face of the court. It is not bound by the rules of evidence. The members may use their own knowledge in reaching their decision. It has no power to enforce its own orders or to award costs. He also made three submissions which the Attorney-General did not fully accept: (1) that the decisions of a local valuation court are not final nor binding, (2) that there was no true lis between the parties, and (3) that the valuation officer was not in any real sense a party. It was a specific ground of appeal against the decision of the Divisional Court that Lord Widgery CJ had wrongly stated that subject to the appellate system the decisions of a local valuation court 'are final and binding, just like any other court'[1]. On these three controversial submissions assistance is to be found in a decision of the House of Lords in *Society of Medical Officers of Health v Hope (Valuation Officer)*[2].

In that case their Lordships held that a decision of a local valuation court does not create an estoppel per rem judicatam when a valuation list comes to the end of its quinquennial life. For the purposes of deciding the point it was necessary for their Lordships to consider the nature and power of the local valuation court as set up by the provisions of the Local Government Act 1948 which in relevant respects are similar to those of the 1967 Act. A local valuation court on the evidence before it decided in 1951 that the society was entitled to a statutory exemption from rates. The valuation list was amended accordingly. A new valuation list came into force in 1956 and it was contended by the society that in the absence of evidence that there was a change in the society's activities or constitution the valuation officer was estopped from contesting the statutory exemption granted on the same facts by the local valuation court in 1951. As to the binding force of the court's decision Lord Radcliffe said[3]:

'For that limited purpose it is a court with a jurisdiction competent to produce a final decision between the parties before it; but it is not a court of competent jurisdiction to decide general questions of law with that finality which is needed to set up the estoppel per rem judicatam that arises in certain contexts from legal judgments.'

As to the lis and the position of the valuation officer he said[4]:

'Again, the valuation officer is no doubt a party to a controversy between himself and the complainant; but, having regard to his statutory function and duties, including that of preparing the new valuation list, and to the interests of the whole body of ratepayers from time to time in the contents of the list, is this controversy a lis or is he a party for the purpose of the principles of estoppel per rem judicatam?'

Counsel for the BBC placed reliance on the views expressed by Lord Keith of Avonholme which included this passage[5]:

'I find it difficult to equate the procedure followed out under the statute with a proper lis inter partes, though that, of itself, might not be conclusive. Nor do I find it easy to distinguish the functions performed by assessment committees before the coming into operation of the Local Government Act 1948 from those now

1 [1978] 2 All ER 731 at 734, [1978] 1 WLR 477 at 481
2 [1960] 1 All ER 317, [1960] AC 551
3 [1960] 1 All ER 317 at 321, [1960] AC 551 at 563–564
4 [1960] 1 All ER 317 at 320, [1960] AC 551 at 562
5 [1960] 1 All ER 317 at 324, [1960] AC 551 at 567–568

performed by a local valuation court, or to think, because the new body is differently constituted and called a court, that a greater importance and effect should be attached to its decisions.'

It is important to appreciate that in this case their Lordships were not considering or deciding the question which is raised before us, namely whether a local valuation court is an inferior court for the purposes of contempt injunctions to prevent unwarranted interference with its proceedings. They were only considering whether a local valuation court's decision was capable of creating an estoppel per rem judicatam. For this reason the technical point was vital whether there was in strict law a lis inter partes which was conclusively determined by the court's order.

After considering the dicta to which I have referred and the *Hope* case[1], as a whole I conclude that, as the decisions of a local valuation court have only a limited binding force between the parties, there is not a lis inter partes in the fullest sense and that the local valuation officer is not a party to a lis in the strict sense of that phrase.

Counsel for the BBC strongly argued that there were a number of important factors which rendered it against the public interest for this court to extend the contempt jurisdiction beyond the recognised courts of justice and of law and such other tribunals as have been held to be subject to this jurisdiction by existing High Court decisions or by statute, such as ecclesiastical consistory courts and courts-martial. He submitted that if this appeal were allowed it would make the task of the Press and broadcasting authorities extremely difficult to decide which other tribunals were subject to the jurisdiction and which not. A great number of these shared many of the characteristics of a local valuation court. It has already been observed that there are 33 tribunals named in the Tribunals and Inquiries Act 1971 and there are many more including domestic disciplinary tribunals. And there are of course a number of local valuation courts in most counties. The important question therefore is how the Press and the broadcasting authorities could be expected to know whether any item of news is likely to prejudice proceedings which may be pending in such a vast number of minor tribunals. Further it would be open to a person who wished to stop publication of an item of distasteful news about himself to start proceedings in any one of these tribunals and threaten contempt proceedings in order to 'gag' the news media.

Counsel on behalf of the Attorney-General grasped the nettle firmly and submitted that it was in the public interest and in accordance with sound principle that this court should uphold the decision of the Queen's Bench Divisional Court. He reminded us of the two vital but conflicting aspects of public interest involved, namely the public interest on the one hand in protecting courts from unwarranted interference by public discussion of issues to be tried and on the other in the right of freedom of speech. He referred us to *Attorney-General v Times Newspapers Ltd*[2] and to the two well-known extracts from the speeches of Lord Morris of Borth-y-Gest and Lord Diplock. Lord Morris of Borth-y-Gest said[3]:

'In the general interests of the community it is imperative that the authority of the courts should not be imperilled and that recourse to them should not be subject to unjustifiable interference. When such unjustifiable interference is suppressed it is not because those charged with the responsibilities of administering justice are concerned for their own dignity: it is because the very structure of ordered life is at risk if the recognised courts of the land are so flouted that their authority wanes and is supplanted. But as the purpose and existence of courts of law is to preserve freedom within the law for all well disposed members of the community, it is manifest that the courts must never impose any limitations on free speech or free discussion or free criticism beyond those which are absolutely necessary. When

1   [1960] 1 All ER 317, [1960] AC 551
2   [1973] 3 All ER 54, [1974] AC 273
3   [1973] 3 All ER 54 at 66, [1974] AC 273 at 302

therefore a court has to consider the propriety of some conduct or speech or writing, decision will often depend on whether one aspect of the public interest definitely *a* outweighs another aspect of the public interest.'

Lord Diplock said[1]:

'The due administration of justice requires *first* that all citizens should have unhindered access to the constitutionally established courts of criminal or civil jurisdiction for the determination of disputes as to their legal rights and liabilities; *b* *secondly*, that they should be able to rely on obtaining in the courts the arbitrament of a tribunal which is free from bias against any party and whose decision will be based on those facts only that have been proved in evidence adduced before it in accordance with the procedure adopted in courts of law; and *thirdly* that, once the dispute has been submitted to a court of law, they should be able to rely on there being no usurpation by any other person of the function of that court to decide it *c* according to law. Conduct which is calculated to prejudice any of these three requirements or to undermine the public confidence that they will be observed is contempt of court.'

Counsel for the Attorney-General's submissions may, I trust, be fairly summarised thus. There is a vital public interest involved in protecting the administration of public justice from unwarranted interference. All courts should be protected from such *d* interference and it is even more important that inferior courts should be protected than the superior courts. The sole question in this appeal is the definition of an inferior court and this definition should not be a restricted one. There are a number of controls which will prevent abuse if the jurisdiction is extended. The Attorney-General has the right and the duty to decide whether to intervene in proceedings for injunctions and will act responsibly to prevent abuse. The Queen's Bench Division has the supervisory *e* jurisdiction and in every case will ensure that all aspects of the two conflicting public interests are carefully considered and balanced so that publications are only prohibited where there is, or is likely to be, serious and obvious unwarranted interference with a pending trial. There is therefore ample power to deal with frivolous applications or 'gagging writs'. Unless the Queen's Bench Division's supervisory powers to protect inferior courts by contempt proceedings are preserved, there is no other effective means *f* available to do so. As a result the parties concerned and the public at large might lose confidence in, and respect for, inferior courts.

Counsel for the Attorney-General dealt fully with the argument that there was no relevant distinction between the function now performed by local valuation courts and that of the assessment committees by referring in detail to the differences in their constitution and procedure which I need not repeat. He emphasised the importance of *g* the right of appeal by way of complete rehearing to the Lands Tribunal which he submitted is clearly an inferior court subject to the protection of contempt proceedings. He reminded us that in *R v Davies*[2] it was regarded as an important factor, in deciding whether committing magistrates in a criminal case were an inferior court, that the case, if committed for trial, would go either to quarter sessions or to the High Court, both of which were plainly protected by contempt proceedings. *h*

There are obviously strong arguments on both sides in respect of the question which we have to decide which I have tried to summarise in the foregoing part of this judgment and have carefully considered. I think it proper to put into the scales in favour of holding that a local valuation court is an inferior court the opinion of Lord Widgery CJ in the judgment which is the subject of the present appeal. Lord Widgery CJ[3] said this, and two judges of the Queen's Bench Division agreed: 'I am bound to say I think that the local *j*

---

1   [1973] 3 All ER 54 at 72, [1974] AC 273 at 309
2   [1906] 1 KB 32, [1904–7] All ER Rep 60
3   [1978] 2 All ER 731 at 736, [1978] 1 WLR 477 at 483

valuation court is one of the clearest examples of an inferior court that we meet in the field of administrative justice.' Nor do I think that view is invalidated to any substantial respect by the fact that Lord Widgery CJ said earlier in his judgment that the decisions of a local valuation court 'are final, and binding just like any other court', subject to the appellate system. Authorities and arguments presented to us, but not to the Queen's Bench Division, showed that there are limitations on the binding effect of valuation court decisions. Nevertheless the clear impression of all the members of an experienced Queen's Bench Divisional Court adds weight to the conclusion I have reached, namely that a local valuation court is an inferior court within RSC Ord 52, r 1.

I would therefore dismiss the appeal.

Appeal dismissed. Application for leave to appeal to the House of Lords granted.

Solicitors: *E A C Bostock* (for the BBC); *Treasury Solicitor.*

Sumra Green   Barrister.

Note
Warinco AG v Samor PA

HOUSE OF LORDS, APPEAL COMMITTEE
LORD EDMUND-DAVIES, LORD KEITH OF KINKEL AND LORD SCARMAN
27th JUNE 1979

House of Lords – Leave to appeal – Petition – Presentation out of time – Need to comply with Standing Orders – Standing Orders of the House of Lords regulating Judicial Business, SO II.

At the conclusion of the hearing of a petition for leave to appeal by Warinco AG from a decision of the Court of Appeal[1], the chairman of the Appeal Committee, **LORD EDMUND-DAVIES**, said: We have heard this petition for leave to appeal on its merits, and we dismiss it. But I think it is right to point out that it is as a matter of indulgence that we have allowed the merits to be gone into at all, because this is a petition which is 6½ months out of time. A wholly inadequate attempt has been made to explain the delay. The excuses offered, even when taken at their face value, explain some 3½ months only of the delay which has occurred, leaving a substantial period of time wholly unexplained.

Laxity in relation to compliance with Standing Orders[2] is increasing and it must be curbed. Earlier this year, in February, in another case[3] quite unrelated to the present one, the noble and learned Viscount Dilhorne said in words that we respectfully adopt:

'The Standing Orders of this House are meant to be complied with. There are very experienced firms of solicitors acting on both sides, and there is a great deal of money involved. The Standing Orders of this House really cannot be treated as if they meant nothing, so that the parties can ignore them. The fact that there is no excuse for it is a matter we shall have to consider . . .'

We have considered the non-compliance in this case very carefully, and we want it to become known that laxity of this kind will not be tolerated. If it is persisted in, the day will dawn when parties seeking leave to appeal will find that they are out of court for that reason alone, regardless of the merits. Disobedience to the clear rules as to time disorganises business in this House and shows disrespect if non-compliance occurs which is wholly or (as in the present case) largely unexplained. We refuse leave to appeal.

Mary Rose Plummer   Barrister.

---

1 [1979] 1 Lloyd's Rep 450
2 Standing Order II provides: 'ORDERED, that, in all Appeals from the Court of Appeal, the Court of Appeal in Northern Ireland or the Court of Session in Scotland in which the leave of the House is required under the provisions of any Act of Parliament, a Petition for leave to appeal be lodged in the Parliament Office within one month from the date of the last Order or Judgment appealed from, and that such Petition be referred to an Appeal Committee to consider whether such leave should be granted.'
3 *Unitramp Ltd v Garnac Grain Co Inc* (15th February 1979) unreported

a
Pao On and others v Lau Yiu and another

PRIVY COUNCIL
LORD WILBERFORCE, VISCOUNT DILHORNE, LORD SIMON OF GLAISDALE, LORD SALMON AND LORD SCARMAN
15th JANUARY, 9th APRIL 1979

b
Contract – Consideration – Performance of existing contractual duty – Performance to be remunerated by conferment of benefit – Plaintiffs purchasing shares in company of which defendants majority shareholders – Plaintiffs promising not to sell shares for a year – Restriction on sale to be compensated for by defendants guaranteeing price of shares – Subsequent promise by defendants to indemnify plaintiffs against fall in value of shares during year sale restricted – Whether antecedent promise not to sell shares sufficient consideration for subsequent promise of
c
indemnity – Whether consideration for subsequent promise of indemnity invalidated on ground of public policy if promise of indemnity secured by threat to repudiate existing contract or by abuse of dominant bargaining power.

Contract – Duress – Economic duress – What constitutes duress in commercial contract –
d
Whether economic duress recognised by English law.

The plaintiffs owned the issued share capital of a private company ('Shing On') incorporated in Hong Kong. The defendants were the majority shareholders in a public investment company ('Fu Chip') in Hong Kong. Shing On's principal asset was a building. The plaintiffs wished to realise the value of the building by selling the shares
e
of Shing On and the defendants wished to extend the property holding of Fu Chip by acquiring Shing On's shares. Accordingly, on 27th February 1973 two written agreements were entered into. The first ('the main agreement') was a contract for the sale by the plaintiffs of Shing On's shares to Fu Chip. The parties to that agreement were the plaintiffs as vendors, Fu Chip as the purchasers, and Shing On. The price for the Shing On shares was to be satisfied by the allotment to the plaintiffs of 4·2 million ordinary
f
shares of $1 each in Fu Chip. It was provided, for the purpose of the main agreement, that the market value of each Fu Chip share was to be deemed to be $2·50. The plaintiffs gave an undertaking in the main agreement that they would not, before the end of April 1974, sell or transfer 2·5 million of the 4·2 million shares to be allotted to them. That restriction was of great importance to the defendants for heavy selling by the plaintiffs of Fu Chip shares could depress the market and devalue the defendants' shareholding in
g
Fu Chip. The plaintiffs realised that by giving an undertaking to postpone sale of the Fu Chip shares they exposed themselves to the risk that the price of the shares might fall below $2·50 a share during the period of postponement. They therefore sought from the defendants a guarantee against a fall in the price of the shares. Accordingly, by a subsidiary agreement dated 27th February the defendants agreed to buy back from the plaintiffs, on or before 30th April 1974, 2·5 million of the allotted Fu Chip shares at the
h
price of $2·50 a share. Under the two agreements the defendants obtained the better bargain because if, as was generally expected, Fu Chip shares rose in value beyond $2·50 a share, the plaintiffs still remained bound by the subsidiary agreement to sell back 2·5 million of the allotted Fu Chip shares to the defendants at $2·50 a share. The plaintiffs, appreciating they had made a bad bargain, indicated to the defendants that they would not complete the main agreement with Fu Chip unless the subsidiary agreement was
j
cancelled and replaced by a true guarantee by way of indemnity, guaranteeing the price of 2·5 million of the allotted shares at $2·50 a share. The defendants knew that Fu Chip could claim specific performance of the main agreement without cancelling and replacing the subsidiary agreement, but were anxious to complete the transaction for otherwise public confidence in Fu Chip (which had only recently gone public) might be impaired. Thus, having considered the matter, the defendants chose to avoid litigation

and to accede to the cancellation of the subsidiary agreement and its replacement by a
guarantee by way of indemnity. The subsidiary agreement was therefore cancelled and,
on 4th May 1973, the defendants signed a guarantee that the price of the 2·5 million of   *a*
the allotted shares would not be less than $2·50 a share on the marketing day immediately
following 30th April 1974 and that they would indemnify the plaintiffs if the shares fell
below that price. The guarantee referred to the terms of the main agreement (which had
not yet been performed) and stated that the main agreement had been entered into at the
defendants' request. The guarantee, by referring to the terms of the main agreement,   *b*
thereby incorporated as part of the stated consideration for the guarantee the plaintiffs'
promise to Fu Chip in the main agreement not to sell 2·5 million of the allotted shares
before 30th April 1974. Between 4th May and 30th April 1974 share prices slumped and
by 30th April Fu Chip shares had fallen to 36 cents a share. The defendants failed to fulfil
their promise of indemnity under the guarantee of 4th May 1973. The plaintiffs
brought an action against them claiming $5,392,800 due under the guarantee, or   *c*
alternatively specific performance of the guarantee. By their defence the defendants
asserted (i) that no valid consideration for the defendants' promise of indemnity was
expressed in the guarantee, (ii) that extrinsic evidence to prove additional consideration
was inadmissible and (iii) that the guarantee was void on the ground that it was induced
by economic duress on the plaintiffs' part. The judge in the Supreme Court of Hong
Kong gave judgment for the plaintiffs. On the defendants' appeal the judge's decision   *d*
was reversed and the appeal allowed. The plaintiffs appealed to the Judicial Committee
of the Privy Council. All four judges below were agreed that the consideration expressed
in the guarantee was past consideration and therefore incapable of supporting the
defendants' promise of indemnity but held (by a majority) that extrinsic evidence was
admissible to prove additional consideration. All four judges were also agreed that the
facts negatived the defendants' contention that there was economic duress which made   *e*
the guarantee void. The extrinsic evidence showed that the primary consideration for
the defendants' promise of indemnity was the plaintiffs' promise to the defendants to
perform their existing contract with Fu Chip under the main agreement. Before the
Board the plaintiffs contended that the consideration expressed in the guarantee was
sufficient to support the defendants' promise of indemnity. The defendants contended
that the expressed consideration was past consideration, and that the primary   *f*
consideration established by the extrinsic evidence, although otherwise valid, was
invalidated as being against public policy, even if economic duress could not be
established, because the promise of indemnity was secured by the plaintiffs' threat of
repudiation of their pre-existing contract with Fu Chip and by abuse of a dominant
bargaining position.

g

Held – The appeal would be allowed for the following reasons—
   (i) An act done before the giving of a promise to make a payment or to confer some
other benefit could be consideration for the promise where (i) the act was done at the
promisor's request, (ii) the parties understood that the act was to be remunerated either
by payment or the conferment of a benefit, and (iii) the payment or conferment of   *h*
benefit was legally enforceable. Since the consideration expressed in the guarantee
included, by incorporation, the plaintiffs' promise in the main agreement not to sell the
shares for a year, the defendants' promise of indemnity could not be treated as
independant of the plaintiffs' antecedent promise not to sell, because the parties
understood at the time of the main agreement that the restriction on sale was to be
compensated for by the benefit of a guarantee conferred by the defendants against a drop   *j*
in the price of the shares. On that basis, the plaintiffs' promise to Fu Chip in the main
agreement not to sell part of the allotted shares for a year was made at the defendants'
request, the promise of indemnity was given to fulfil that intention, and it was legally
enforceable. It followed that, although the plaintiffs' promise was antecedent to the
guarantee, it was good consideration for the defendants' promise of indemnity (see p 74

b to d and p 75 b to d, post); *Lampleigh v Brathwait* (1615) Hob 105 and dictum of Bowen
LJ in *Re Casey's Patents, Stewart v Casey* [1892] 1 Ch at 115–116 applied.

a
(2) Where the consideration for a promise was an existing contractual duty to a third
party which was otherwise valid consideration, it was not invalidated as being against
public policy (in the absence of proof of duress) merely because the promise had been
secured by a threat to repudiate the existing contract or by unfair use of a dominant
bargaining position. Where businessmen were negotiating at arm's length it was
b unnecessary for the achievement of justice to invoke that principle, for what justice
required was that a businessman be held to his bargain unless his consent to it could be
shown to have been vitiated by fraud, mistake or duress. Accordingly the primary
consideration for the promise of indemnity, established by the extrinsic evidence, was
not invalidated on the ground of public policy (see p 77 d and h to p 78 a, post); *Harris
v Watson* [1775–1802] All ER Rep 493 and *Stilk v Myrick* (1809) 2 Camp 317 explained
c and distinguished.
(3) Nor was the guarantee voidable because of duress on the part of the plaintiffs. To
constitute duress of any kind there had to be coercion of will so as to vitiate consent, and
in relation to a contract commercial pressure alone did not constitute duress. Whether
there had been coercion of will vitiating consent depended on whether the person alleged
to have been coerced did or did not protest, whether he had an alternative course open
d to him (such as an adequate legal remedy) at the time of the alleged coercion, whether he
was independently advised and whether after entering into the contract he had taken
steps to avoid it. On the facts, the Board would not disturb the unanimous finding below
that there had not been coercion of the defendants' will to sign the guarantee (see p 78 f
to j, post); dicta of Lord Wilberforce and Lord Simon of Glaisdale in *Barton v Armstrong*
[1975] 2 All ER at 476, 477 applied; dictum of Kerr J in *The Siboen and The Sibotre* [1976]
e 1 Lloyd's Rep at 336 approved.
Per Curiam. There is nothing contrary to principle in recognising economic duress as
a factor which may render a contract voidable, provided the basis of such recognition is
that the duress must amount to a coercion of will, which vitiates consent. It must be
shown that the payment made or the contract entered into was not a voluntary act (see
p 79 d e, post).

f **Notes**

For past consideration, and for compliance with legal obligations imposed by a contract
with a third party as consideration, see 9 Halsbury's Laws (4th Edn) paras 320, 327, and
for cases on the subject, see 12 Digest (Reissue) 264–268, 1858–1902.

For a contract entered into under duress, see 9 Halsbury's Laws (4th Edn) paras 296,
g 297, and for cases on the subject, see 12 Digest (Reissue) 118–124, 640–679.

Cases referred to in judgment

Astley v Reynolds (1731) 2 Stra 915, 2 Barn KB 40, 93 ER 939, 12 Digest (Reissue) 687,
4951.
Barton v Armstrong [1975] 2 All ER 465, [1976] AC 104, [1975] 2 WLR 1050, 3 ALR 355,
h   [1973] 2 NSWLR 622, PC, Digest (Cont Vol D) 117, *486a.
Casey's Patents, Re, Stewart v Casey [1892] 1 Ch 104, 61 LJ Ch 61, 66 LT 93, 9 RPC 9, CA,
12 Digest (Reissue) 235, 1568.
Harris v Watson (1791) Peake 72, [1775–1802] All ER Rep 493, 170 ER 94, NP, 42 Digest
(Repl) 704, 4561.
Lampleigh v Brathwait (1615) Hob 105, 1 Browne 7, Moore KB 866, 80 ER 255, 12 Digest
j   (Reissue) 267, 1885.
Maskell v Horner [1915] 3 KB 106, [1914–15] All ER Rep 595, 84 LJKB 1752, 113 LT 126,
79 JP 406, 13 LGR 808, 12 Digest (Reissue) 688, 4960.
New Zealand Shipping Co Ltd v A M Satterthwaite & Co Ltd [1974] 1 All ER 1015, [1975]
AC 154, [1974] 2 WLR 865, [1974] 1 Lloyd's Rep 534, [1974] 1 NZLR 505, PC, Digest
(Cont Vol D) 114, *99a.

North Ocean Shipping Co Ltd v Hyundai Construction Co Ltd, The Atlantic Baron [1978] 3 All
ER 1170, [1979] 1 Lloyd's Rep 89.

Scotson v Pegg (1861) 6 H & N 295, 30 LJ Ex 225, 3 LT 753, 158 ER 121, 12 Digest
(Reissue) 261, *1831.*

*Siboen, The, and The Sibotre, Occidental Worldwide Investment Corpn v Skibs A/S Avanti, Skibs
A/S Glarona, Skibs A/S Navalis* [1976] 1 Lloyd's Rep 293.

Skeate v Beale (1840) 11 Ad & El 983, 3 Per & Dav 597, 9 LJQB 233, 4 Jur 766, 113 ER 688,
12 Digest (Reissue) 122, 663.

Stilk v Myrick (1809) 2 Camp 317, 6 Esp 129, 170 ER 1168, NP, 42 Digest (Repl) 704,
4562.

Williams v Williams [1957] 1 All ER 305, [1957] 1 WLR 148, 121 JP 93, CA, 27(1) Digest
(Reissue) 256, *1883.*

Appeal

This was an appeal by the plaintiffs, Pao On, Ho Lei Chun and Pao Lap Chung, against
the judgment of the Court of Appeal of Hong Kong (Leonard and McMullin JJ, Briggs
CJ dissenting) dated 5th November 1976 allowing an appeal by the defendants, Lau Yiu
Long and Benjamin Lau Kam Ching, from the judgment of the Supreme Court of Hong
Kong (Li J) dated 17th February 1976 ordering the defendants to pay the plaintiffs the
sum of $HK 5,392,800 with interest which the judge found to be due to the plaintiffs
under a written agreement dated 4th May 1973. The facts are set out in the judgment
of the Board.

F P Neill QC, Marion Simmons and *Andrew Li* (of the Hong Kong Bar) for the plaintiffs.
Andrew Leggatt QC and *Christopher Swift* for the defendants.

LORD SCARMAN read the following judgment of the board.

The litigation

By a judgment dated and entered 17th February 1976 Li J ordered the defendants, Lau
Yiu Long ('Lau') and his younger brother Benjamin, to pay the plaintiffs, Pao On, his wife
and son $5,392,800 with interest as from 1st May 1974 to the date of judgment. The
judge found the money to be due under a written agreement dated 4th May 1973. It is
convenient to refer to this agreement as 'the guarantee'. It was, in fact, an indemnity.
The defendants appealed. The Court of Appeal, by a majority (Briggs CJ dissenting),
allowed their appeal. The plaintiffs now appeal to Her Majesty in Council.

Two issues are fundamental. Was there consideration for the contract of guarantee?
If there was, was the consent of the defendants vitiated by duress? All the judges below
regarded the consideration appearing on the face of the document of 4th May 1973 as a
past consideration, which, by itself, could not in law support the defendants' promise to
indemnify the plaintiffs against their loss. The trial judge, however, ruled that extrinsic
oral evidence was admissible to prove an additional, but not contradictory, consideration,
found that the evidence did establish the existence of good additional consideration, and
rejected on the facts the defendants' case of duress.

In the Court of Appeal McMullin J was of the opinion that extrinsic evidence to prove
the existence of an additional consideration was in the circumstances of this case
inadmissible, and so was for allowing the appeal. He expressed the opinion that such
consideration as the extrinsic evidence, if admitted, would reveal was bad in law because
it showed the plaintiffs to have obtained the 'guarantee' by dishonest means. 'The
consideration', he declared, 'might be good in a technical or legalistic sense and yet the
bargain based on it be found voidable'. He also 'inclined to the view that the doctrine
[of economic duress] is not appropriate to the circumstances of the parties in the present
case'. Leonard J thought the extrinsic evidence admitted by the trial judge was not
contradictory of the written instrument containing the guarantee, and was, therefore,
admissible to prove an additional consideration. But he held that to regard as valuable

consideration the promise given by the plaintiffs not to break their contract with a third
a party was in the circumstances of this case 'contrary to public policy and contrary to
ordinary justice'. Accordingly he also was for allowing the appeal. He was 'unconvinced'
that there was any evidence of economic duress. Briggs CJ agreed that there was no
evidence of duress. He held that the extrinsic evidence revealed an additional
consideration consistent with that stated in the guarantee. He found the additional
consideration in the 'whole arrangement' to which the parties came on 4th May 1973,
b the date of the guarantee. He was for dismissing the appeal.

There are three significant features in these judgments. First, all four judges are
agreed that the consideration expressed in the written guarantee of 4th May 1973 was a
past consideration not, by itself, capable of supporting the defendants' promise of
indemnity. This, being a question of construction of a written contract, is a decision on
a point of law. It is the subject of a vigorous challenge mounted for the first time in the
c appeal to this Board. Secondly, three of the four judges held the extrinsic evidence
admissible, expressing the opinion that the additional consideration revealed by it was
not inconsistent with the terms of the written guarantee. Two judges, however, held
that it would be contrary to public policy to recognise as valid the consideration revealed
by the extrinsic evidence. Finally, all the judges negatived on the facts the defendants'
case of economic duress.

d

The questions for the Board

Three questions call for decision by their Lordships' Board. (1) Does the guarantee on
its proper construction state a valid consideration for the defendants' promise of
indemnity? (2) Does the extrinsic evidence as to the circumstances in which the
e guarantee was given establish the existence of a valid consideration additional to the
consideration, if any, stated in the agreement? (3) If there be consideration for the
promise of indemnity, is the guarantee nevertheless unenforceable, the consent of the
defendants having been induced by duress? On the third question there are concurrent
findings of fact. It would have to be shown, therefore, that the judges below had
misconceived the relevant law before the Board could reverse their unanimous rejection
f of the defendants' case based on economic duress.

The facts

In February 1973 the plaintiffs ('the Paos') owned the issued share capital of the Tsuen
Wan Shing On Estate Co Ltd, a private company incorporated in Hong Kong. The
defendants ('the Laus') were at that time the majority shareholders in the Fu Chip
g Investment Co Ltd. Fu Chip had been incorporated in January 1973 and 'went public'
on 9th February 1973, when permission to deal in its shares was granted by the Far East
Stock Exchange. The principal asset of the Shing On company was a 21-storey building
under construction ('the Wing On building'). The Paos were keen to realise the value of
the building by selling the shares of the company. The Laus were keen to extend the
property-holding of Fu Chip, an investment company. There were discussions between
h the Paos and the Laus on or about 21st February. On Tuesday, 27th February, all was
settled and two written agreements were signed.

The first (known as 'the main agreement') was a contract for the sale by the Paos of
their shares in the Shing On company to Fu Chip. The parties to the agreement were the
Paos as vendors, Fu Chip as purchasers, and the Shing On company, whose total issued
share capital was to be transferred to Fu Chip. The price payable by Fu Chip was $10·5
j million, and was to be met by the allotment to the Paos of 4·2 million ordinary shares of
$1 each in Fu Chip. It was provided that the market value of a Fu Chip share for the
purpose of the agreement was to be deemed to be $2·50 for each $1 share. Completion
was to be on or before 31st March 1973. It was stipulated that time should 'in every
respect be the essence of this Agreement'. The parties did, however, agree on 28th March
to defer the date for completion to 30th April 1973.

These provisions had the effect that no cash was to pass under the agreement. The whole of the price was to be satisfied by the issue of shares. The Paos gave Fu Chip an undertaking as to the way they would deal with the shares to be allotted to them. They undertook, by cl 4(k) of the agreement, that—

> 'Each of the Vendors shall retain in his own right in Fu Chip 60% of the shares allotted to him under this Agreement and shall not sell or transfer the same on or before the end of April 1974.'

In other words, the Paos gave an undertaking to Fu Chip that they would not sell or transfer before the end of April 1974 2·5 million of the 4·2 million shares to be issued to them in satisfaction of the price of $10·5 million. The restriction was of great importance to the Laus, as majority shareholders in Fu Chip. As Lau said in evidence, the Paos must support the Fu Chip shares. He feared that heavy selling by the Paos could depress the market, and so the value of his shareholding in Fu Chip. Not unreasonably the Paos wanted a measure of protection before agreeing to the restriction. They wanted from the man, for whose benefit the undertaking was given, a guarantee 'against a fall in value of the shares during the year in which they could not sell'. When Mrs Pao asked Lau 'what happened if the shares dropped below $2·50', Lau offered to sign an agreement to buy back the shares at $2·50 after one year. The trial judge said he was 'inclined to believe that the first defendant's [Lau's] account is accurate to the extent that in the course of the discussion the plaintiffs did not object to the first defendant's offer to purchase their retained shares *as a sufficient form of guarantee*' (emphasis mine). This finding is important because of the stress laid by McMullin and Leonard JJ on the dishonesty of Mrs Pao who gave evidence that the parties had orally agreed on a guarantee. The trial judge found that she was genuinely seeking 'a guarantee'. While he rejected her evidence as to the nature of the agreement reached, he did find that the Paos and Lau saw Lau's offer to buy back the shares as a form of guarantee. Indeed, when Lau came to give evidence, he described his offer as 'my guarantee'.

Accordingly, the second agreement ('the subsidiary agreement'), signed also on 27th February 1973, was a contract under which the Paos agreed to sell and Lau agreed to buy on or before 30th April 1974 at a price of $2·50 a share 2·5 million shares in Fu Chip (being 60% of the total allotment made by Fu Chip in satisfaction of the price to be paid for its acquisition from the Paos of the issued share capital of Shing On). The commercial effect of these two agreements was remarkable. Lau had got very much the better bargain, as he himself recognised. No cash was required of him or Fu Chip on completion. If Fu Chip shares fell below $2·50 on 30th April 1974, the Paos would, however, be protected by the obligation on Lau to buy back 60% of the shares at $2·50 a share. They secured, therefore, their 'guarantee' against a fall in the share price. But if the price on that date was higher, the Paos still remained bound to sell back the shares at $2·50. The Paos had elected shares as their price for the issued capital of Shing On because shares could go up in value whereas cash could not, and they expected, as everyone else (including the Laus) did in February 1973, that share values would rise. Yet by the form of guarantee against a fall in the value of the shares which they accepted they deprived themselves, so far as 60% of their holding was concerned, of the very advantage which by taking their price in shares they hoped to gain, and without receiving any other benefit for having to wait a year before they could realise cash on 60% of their price. It is not surprising either that Lau thought he had the better of the bargain or that Mrs Pao became indignant when she appreciated what she and her family had given away by the subsidiary agreement. She and her husband, therefore, made up their minds that they would not complete the main agreement unless they could substitute a guarantee by way of indemnity for the subsidiary agreement.

On 25th April 1973 solicitors, describing themselves as acting for Shing On, wrote a letter to the solicitors for Fu Chip asking them—

a
'to send us on behalf of our clients a guarantee from your clients that the intended allotment of 4·2 m. ordinary shares of your clients would be of the value of the sum $10·5 m.'

The confusions of the letter are remarkable, but irrelevant. It was well understood that the solicitors who wrote the letter also acted for the Paos, that the solicitors who received it also acted for the Laus and that the guarantee was sought in respect of 60% only of the 4·2 million shares allotted in satisfaction of the purchase price under the main

b
agreement. The reply was a denial of any agreement of guarantee, correct no doubt according to the card but not really consistent with Lau's view of the subsidiary agreement as his guarantee of 60% of the price.

The Paos now made clear that they would not complete the main agreement with Fu Chip unless the subsidiary agreement was cancelled and a true guarantee (by way of indemnity) substituted for it. Mr Pao disappeared on a business trip to Taiwan, while

c
Mrs Pao remained in Hong Kong, saying there would be no completion until he had returned and considered the position. Mr Pao returned to Hong Kong on 29th April and immediately made plain to Lau that, as the judge put it—

'unless a guarantee and indemnity for the price of the 2·5 m. Fu Chip shares was given by the defendants the plaintiffs would not complete the main agreement with

d
the Fu Chip.'

This was serious for Lau. Fu Chip had only recently gone public. A public announcement had been made of Fu Chip's acquisition of the Wing On building by its take-over of the share capital of Shing On. If the deal fell through, the public would, Lau thought, lose confidence in Fu Chip shares.

Lau had, therefore, to decide whether to yield to the Paos' demand for the cancellation

e
of the subsidiary agreement and for a guarantee in its place or to stand by the two agreements of 27th February, and have Fu Chip sue for specific performance of the main agreement. The first course would enable completion to take place on or very soon after 30th April; the second course would entail the delays of legal action, though Lau was well aware that there was no defence. Lau's problem is best described in the words of the trial judge. After quoting Lau's evidence that he would lose a lot if Fu Chip failed to take

f
over Shing On, the judge said:

'These words reflect the optimism and hope of the first defendant [Lau] when he yielded to the plaintiffs' demand for a guarantee. At the time the demand was made the first defendant placed the matter in the hands of his solicitors. He had proper legal advice. He knew very well whether he gave the guarantee or not the main

g
agreement between the Fu Chip and the plaintiffs was still valid as a separate document. The Fu Chip could have sued the plaintiffs for specific performance or for damages. Out of the original issued and paid up capital of 12,600,000 shares in the Fu Chip the first defendant owned 6,531,000 shares. In addition he had purchased more since the listing of such shares. His brother, the second defendant, owned 1,500,000 million shares. Between the two of them they owned the controlling interests of the Fu Chip. By then the first defendant had already set

h
himself about in manipulating the price of the Fu Chip shares by buying and selling. If the defendants refused to give the guarantee on the Fu Chip shares, then the Fu Chip shares might drop a few 10 cents in price only if the general condition of the market remained bullish. It would be possible for the first defendant to push the price up again with his manipulation. The Fu Chip, after all, is an investment company. All its assets consist of landed property. So long as the properties in the

j
Fu Chip have been quoted in their true value the success or failure in the taking over of the Shing On could not have affected the true value of the Fu Chip shares. Whatever set back in the market price of the Fu Chip shares could not have sent them below their true value. Even if it did, the defendants might have suffered a temporary paper loss of profit but would not have suffered a financial ruin. The

first defendant did threaten that the Fu Chip would sue the plaintiffs on the main agreement. However, in the end he chose to avoid litigation and yielded to the plaintiffs' demand. The first defendant must have considered the matter thoroughly in the light of the then marketing condition and formed the opinion that the risk in giving the guarantee was more apparent than real. As I have said earlier on, neither party at the time could have foreseen the stock market subsequently slumping in such manner. Had the plaintiffs realised that the prices in general in the stock market would fall to the extent as we now know then they would not even bother to demand for the guarantee. They would be quite satisfied with the subsidiary agreement. Therefore I find as a fact that when the defendants agreed to sign the guarantee neither they nor the plaintiffs envisaged a drastic fall of the market and that the defendants never expected that on the guarantee they might be required to compensate the plaintiffs in terms of millions of dollars. This was an error of judgment in a business deal. The defendants were reluctant to be deprived of a good bargain—the subsidiary agreement. But I find that they were quite prepared to take a calculated risk (which at the time appeared to be very little) in order to pacify the plaintiffs who were adamant. It was in such circumstances that the guarantee was given.'

In the light of these findings it is surprising that the trial judge also found that the cancellation of the subsidiary agreement formed no part of the consideration for the giving of the guarantee on 4th May. The judge found, no doubt correctly, that the Paos wanted the subsidiary agreement cancelled in any event. But the existence of their desire is perfectly consistent with its cancellation and the substitution for it of a guarantee as part and parcel of a comprehensive settlement accepted by Lau as the best and most effective way of securing early completion of the main agreement, which was his objective throughout the negotiations of 4th May.

Their Lordships agree with Briggs CJ's analysis of those negotiations. He said:

'However, the cancellation was part of the arrangement for the completion of the main agreement. It was cancelled by mutual agreement as part and parcel of this: it does not stand alone. The consideration for the guarantee was the whole arrangement for the completion of the main agreement of which the cancellation of the subsidiary agreement formed part. The Judge found that the plaintiffs wanted the subsidiary agreement to be cancelled in any event. But there is no evidence that this was what the defendants wanted. The defendants agreed to the cancellation only as part of the whole arrangement. The cancellation cannot be considered in vacuo.'

This analysis is supported by the evidence of Lau himself. When asked whether the subsidiary agreement was cancelled on the basis that a written guarantee would be executed and would be effective, he replied 'Yes', saying that he was 'forced' to regard the guarantee as a substitute for the subsidiary agreement. He went on to add the significant observation that once he had signed the guarantee he regarded it as binding.

The events of 4th May can be very shortly stated. Lau's legal advisers produced the first draft of a contract of guarantee. It was revised by both parties, and an option inserted to enable Lau to buy back the shares, if they dropped below $2·50, and he chose to do so. According to Lau, the cancellation of the subsidiary agreement was immediately followed by the signing of the guarantee. The judge made no finding as to the sequence of events, but was satisfied that the guarantee was signed to induce the Paos to complete the main agreement. A somewhat angry discussion then ensued in which Lau was seeking some effective safeguard (eg retention of the scrip or share certificates) against the Paos defaulting on their obligation (of great importance to Lau) not to sell before 30th April 1974. The issue was settled by the Paos giving Lau and his brother an indemnity in the event of any breach of their obligation not to sell the shares. The parties then went to the offices of Fu Chip's accountants, where they completed the

<blockquote> a </blockquote>

transaction under the main agreement. There is no suggestion that Lau signed the contract of guarantee under protest. On the contrary, he had present his own legal advisers and, as the trial judge put it, was 'quite prepared to take a calculated risk (which at the time appeared to be very little).'

During the period 4th May 1973 to 30th April 1974 share prices slumped. By 30th April Fu Chip shares had fallen to 36 cents a share. Yet Lau allowed the Paos to continue in the belief that they had their price of $2·50 a share guaranteed by him. Nor has Lau at any time offered to restore the Paos to the 'status quo ante', ie to their position under the subsidiary agreement. Indeed it is his (remarkable) contention that neither the subsidiary agreement nor the guarantee of 4th May has legal effect. The Paos, therefore, having accepted a year's restriction on dealing in 60% of the shares allotted to them, were left, according to his case, by the events of 4th May without any safeguard against a fall in the market, the damaging effects of which they were powerless to forestall or diminish. If the law really compels such a conclusion, one may be forgiven for thinking that the time has come to reconsider it.

The first question

The first question is whether on its true construction the written guarantee of 4th May 1973 states a consideration sufficient in law to support the Laus' promise of indemnity against a fall in value of the Fu Chip shares. The instrument is, so far as relevant, in these terms:

> 'Re: Tsuen Wan Shing On Estate Company Limited
>
> 'IN CONSIDERATION of your having at our request agreed to sell all of your shares of and in the above mentioned Company whose registered office is situate at 274 Sha Tsui Road Ground Floor Tsuen Wan New Territories in the Colony of Hong Kong for the consideration of $10,500,000:00 by the allotment of 4,200,000 ordinary shares of $1·00 each in Fu Chip Investment Company Limited whose registered office is situate at No. 33 Wing Lok Street Victoria in the said Colony of Hong Kong and that the market value for the said ordinary shares of the said Fu Chip Investment Company Limited shall be deemed as $2·50 for each of $1·00 share under an Agreement for sale and purchase made between the parties thereto and dated the 27th day of February 1973, we LAU YIU LONG (   ) of No. 152 Tin Hau Temple Road, Flat C1, Summit Court, 14th floor in the Colony of Hong Kong Merchant and BENJAMIN LAU KAM CHING (   ) of No. 31 Ming Yuen Street West, Basement in the said Colony of Hong Kong Merchant the directors of the said Fu Chip Investment Company Limited HEREBY AGREE AND GUARANTEE the closing market value for 2,520,000 shares (being 60% of the said 4,200,000 ordinary shares) of the said Fu Chip Investment Company Limited shall be at $2·50 per share and that the total value of 2,520,000 shares shall be of the sum of HK$6,300,000:00 on the following marketing date immediately after 30th day of April, 1974 AND WE FURTHER AGREE to indemnify and keep you indemnified against any damages, losses and other expenses which you may incur or sustain in the event of the closing market price for the shares of Fu Chip Investment Company Limited according to The Far East Exchange Limited shall fall short of the sum $2·50 during the said following marketing date immediately after the 30th day of April, 1974 PROVIDED ALWAYS that if we were called upon to indemnify you for the discrepancy between the market value and the said total value of HK$6,300,000:00 we shall have the option of buying from you the said 2,520,000 shares of Fu Chip Investment Company Limited at the price of HK$6,300,000:00 . . .'

Counsel for the plaintiffs before their Lordships' Board but not below contends that the consideration stated in the agreement is not in reality a past one. It is to be noted that the consideration was not on 4th May 1973 a matter of history only. The instrument by its reference to the main agreement with Fu Chip incorporates as part of the stated consideration the Paos' three promises to Fu Chip: to complete the sale of Shing On, to accept shares as the price for the sale, and not to sell 60% of the shares so accepted before *a* 30th April 1974. Thus, on 4th May 1973 the performance of the main agreement still lay in the future. Performance of these promises was of great importance to the Laus, and it is undeniable that, as the instrument declares, the promises were made to Fu Chip at the request of the Laus. It is equally clear that the instrument also includes a promise by the Paos to the Laus to fulfil their earlier promises given to Fu Chip.

The Board agrees with the submission of counsel for the plaintiffs that the consideration *b* expressly stated in the written guarantee is sufficient in law to support the Laus' promise of indemnity. An act done before the giving of a promise to make a payment or to confer some other benefit can sometimes be consideration for the promise. The act must have been done at the promisor's request, the parties must have understood that the act was to be remunerated either by a payment or the conferment of some other benefit, and payment, or the conferment of a benefit, must have been legally enforceable had it been *c* promised in advance. All three features are present in this case. The promise given to Fu Chip under the main agreement not to sell the shares for a year was at Lau's request. The parties understood at the time of the main agreement that the restriction on selling must be compensated for by the benefit of a guarantee against a drop in price: and such a guarantee would be legally enforceable. The agreed cancellation of the subsidiary agreement left, as the parties knew, the Paos unprotected in a respect in which at the *d* time of the main agreement all were agreed they should be protected.

Counsel's submission for the plaintiffs is based on *Lampleigh v Brathwait*[1]. In that case the judges said[2]:

'First . . . a meer voluntary curtesie will not have a consideration to uphold an assumpsit. But if that curtesie were moved by a suit or request of the party that *e* gives the assumpsit, it will bind, for the promise, though it follows, yet it is not naked, but couples it self with the suit before, and the merits of the party procured by that suit, which is the difference.'

The modern statement of the law is in the judgment of Bowen LJ in *Re Casey's Patents, Stewart v Casey*[3]. Bowen LJ said: *f*

'Even if it were true, as some scientific students of law believe, that a past service cannot support a future promise, you must look at the document and see if the promise cannot receive a proper effect in some other way. Now, the fact of a past service raises an implication that at the time it was rendered it was to be paid for, and, if it was a service which was to be paid for, when you get in the subsequent document a promise to pay, that promise may be treated either as an admission *g* which evidences or as a positive bargain which fixes the amount of that reasonable remuneration on the faith of which the service was originally rendered. So that here for past services there is ample justification for the promise to give the third share.'

Conferring a benefit is, of course, an equivalent to payment: see Chitty on Contracts[4]. *h*

Counsel for the defendants does not dispute the existence of the rule but challenges its application to the facts of this case. He submits that it is not a necessary inference or implication from the terms of the written guarantee that any benefit or protection was to be given to the Paos for their acceptance of the restriction on selling their shares. Their Lordships agree that the mere existence or recital of a prior request is not sufficient in itself to convert what is prima facie past consideration into sufficient consideration in law *j*

1 (1615) Hob 105
2 Hob 105 at 106
3 [1892] 1 Ch 104 at 115–116
4 24th Edn (1977), vol 1, para 154

to support a promise: as they have indicated, it is only the first of three necessary
a preconditions. As for the second of those preconditions, whether the act done at the
request of the promisor raises an implication of promised remuneration or other return
is simply one of the construction of the words of the contract in the circumstances of its
making. Once it is recognised, as the Board considers it inevitably must be, that the
expressed consideration includes a reference to the Paos' promise not to sell the shares
before 30th April 1974, a promise to be performed in the future, though given in the
b past, it is not possible to treat the Laus' promise of indemnity as independent of the Paos'
antecedent promise, given at Lau's request, not to sell. The promise of indemnity was
given because at the time of the main agreement the parties intended that Lau should
confer on the Paos the benefit of his protection against a fall in price. When the
subsidiary agreement was cancelled, all were well aware that the Paos were still to have
the benefit of his protection as consideration for the restriction on selling. It matters not
c whether the indemnity thus given be regarded as the best evidence of the benefit
intended to be conferred in return for the promise not to sell, or as the positive bargain
which fixes the benefit on the faith of which the promise was given, though where, as
here, the subject is a written contract, the better analysis is probably that of the 'positive
bargain'. Their Lordships, therefore, accept the submission that the contract itself states
a valid consideration for the promise of indemnity.

d   This being their Lordships' conclusion, it is unnecessary to consider the further
submission of counsel for the plaintiffs (also raised for the first time before the Board)
that the option given the Laus, if called on to fulfil their indemnity, to buy back the
shares at $2·50 a share was itself a sufficient consideration for the promise of
indemnity. But their Lordships see great force in the contention. The Laus promised to
indemnify the plaintiffs if the market price of Fu Chip shares fell below £2·50. However,
e in the event of the Laus being called on to implement this promise they were given an
option to take up the shares themselves at $2·50. This on the face of it imposes on the
plaintiffs in the circumstances envisaged, an obligation to transfer the shares to the Laus
at the price of $2·50 if called on to do so. The concomitant benefit to the Laus could be
a real one, for example, if they thought that the market, after a temporary set-back,
would recover to a price above $2·50. The fact that the option is stated in the form of a
f proviso does not preclude it being a contractual term or one under which consideration
moves.

The second question
     There is no doubt, and it was not challenged, that extrinsic evidence is admissible to
prove the real consideration where: (a) no consideration, or a nominal consideration, is
g expressed in the instrument, or (b) the expressed consideration is in general terms or
ambiguously stated, or (c) a substantial consideration is stated, but an additional
consideration exists. The additional consideration must not, however, be inconsistent
with the terms of the written instrument. Extrinsic evidence is also admissible to prove
the illegality of the consideration. In their Lordships' opinion the law is correctly stated
in Halsbury's Laws of England[1].

h   The extrinsic evidence in this case shows that the consideration for the promise of
indemnity, while it included the cancellation of the subsidiary agreement, was primarily
the promise given by the Paos to the Laus, to perform their contract with Fu Chip, which
included the undertaking not to sell 60% of the shares allotted to them before 30th April
1974. Thus the real consideration for the indemnity was the promise to perform, or the
performance of, the Paos' pre-existing contractual obligations to Fu Chip. This promise
j was perfectly consistent with the consideration stated in the guarantee. Indeed, it
reinforces it by imposing on the Paos an obligation now owed to the Laus to do what, at
Lau's request, they had agreed with Fu Chip to do.

_____

1   12 Halsbury's Laws (4th Edn) para 1487

Their Lordships do not doubt that a promise to perform, or the performance of, a pre-existing contractual obligation to a third party can be valid consideration. In *New*   *a*
Zealand Shipping Co Ltd v A M Satterthwaite & Co Ltd[1] the rule and the reason for the rule
were stated as follows[2]:

> 'An agreement to do an act which the promisor is under an existing obligation to
> a third party to do, may quite well amount to valid consideration: . . . the promisee
> obtains the benefit of a direct obligation . . . This proposition is illustrated and   *b*
> supported by *Scotson v Pegg*[3] which their Lordships consider to be good law.'

Unless, therefore, the guarantee was void as having been made for an illegal consideration
or voidable on the ground of economic duress, the extrinsic evidence establishes that it
was supported by valid consideration.

Counsel for the defendants submits that the consideration is illegal as being against   *c*
public policy. He submits that to secure a party's promise by a threat of repudiation of
a pre-existing contractual obligation owed to another can be, and in the circumstances of
this case was, an abuse of a dominant bargaining position and so contrary to public
policy. This, he submits, is so even though economic duress cannot be proved.

This submission found favour with the majority in the Court of Appeal. Their   *d*
Lordships, however, consider it misconceived. Reliance was placed on the old 'seaman'
cases of *Harris v Watson*[4] and *Stilk v Myrick*[5]. Counsel also referred to certain
developments in American law, which are to be found described in two leading works,
Corbin on Contracts[6] and Williston on Contracts[7]. Their Lordships would make one
general observation on what is revealed by these two distinguished American works.
Where some judges speak of public policy, others speak of economic duress. No clear
line of distinction between the two concepts emerges as settled in the American law.   *e*

In the seaman cases there were only two parties, the seaman and the captain
(representing the owner). In *Harris v Watson*[4] the captain during the voyage, for which
the plaintiff had contracted to serve as a seaman, promised him five guineas over and
above his common wages if he would perform some extra work. Lord Kenyon thought
that if the seaman's claim to be paid the five guineas was supported 'it would materially   *f*
affect the navigation of this kingdom'. He feared the prospect of seamen in times of
danger insisting 'on an extra charge on such a promise', and non-suited the plaintiff. In
Stilk v Myrick[5] Lord Ellenborough also non-suited the seaman. According to the report
in Campbell[8] he said:

> 'I think *Harris* v. *Watson*[4] was rightly decided; but I doubt whether the ground of
> public policy, upon which Lord Kenyon is stated to have proceeded, be the true   *g*
> principle on which the decision is to be supported. Here, I say, the agreement is
> void for want of consideration.'

Espinasse, who appeared as junior counsel for the unsuccessful plaintiff in the case,
reports the case somewhat differently. He reports[9] Lord Ellenborough as saying that   *h*
'. . . he recognised the principle of the case of *Harris v Watson*[4] as founded on just and

1   [1974] 1 All ER 1015, [1975] AC 154
2   [1974] 1 All ER 1015 at 1021, [1975] AC 154 at 168
3   (1861) 6 H & N 295
4   (1791) Peake 72, [1775–1802] All ER Rep 493   *j*
5   (1809) 2 Camp 317, 6 Esp 129
6   (1963), vol 1A, ch 7
7   3rd Edn (1970) vol 13, ch 47
8   2 Camp 317
9   (1809) 6 Esp 129 at 130

proper policy.' But the report continues: 'When the Defendant [sic—but surely the
a plaintiff is meant?] entered on board the ship, he stipulated to do all the work his
situation called upon him to do'. These cases, explicable as they are on the basis of an
absence of fresh consideration for the captain's promise, are an unsure foundation for a
rule of public policy invalidating contracts where, save for the rule, there would be valid
consideration.

When one turns to consider cases where a pre-existing duty imposed by law is alleged
b to be valid consideration for a promise, one finds cases in which public policy has been
held to invalidate the consideration. A promise to pay a sheriff in consideration of his
performing his legal duty, a promise to pay for discharge from illegal arrest, are to be
found in the books as promises which the law will not enforce[1]. Yet such cases are also
explicable on the ground that a person who promises to perform, or performs, a duty
imposed by law provides no consideration. In cases where the discharge of a duty
c imposed by law has been treated as valid consideration, the courts have usually (but not
invariably) found an act over and above, but consistent with, the duty imposed by law:
see *Williams v Williams*[2]. It must be conceded that different judges have adopted differing
approaches to such cases: contrast, for example, Denning LJ[3] with the view of the
majority in *Williams v Williams* case[4].

But, where the pre-existing obligation is a contractual duty owed to a third party, some
d other ground of public policy must be relied on to invalidate the consideration (if
otherwise legal); the defendants submit that the ground can be extortion by the abuse of
a dominant bargaining position to threaten the repudiation of a contractual obligation.
It is this application of public policy which counsel for the defendants submits has been
developed in the American cases. Beginning with the general rule that 'neither the
performance of duty nor the promise to render a performance already required by duty
e is a sufficient consideration' the courts have (according to Corbin on Contracts[5]) advanced
to the view 'that the moral and economic elements in any case that involves the rule
should be weighed by the court, and that the fact of pre-existing legal duty should not be
in itself decisive'.

The American Restatement of the Law of Contracts[6] has declared that performance
(or promise of performance) of a contractual duty owed to a third person is sufficient
f consideration. This view (which accords with the statement of our law in *Satterthwaite's*
case[7]) appears to be generally accepted but only in cases where there is no suggestion of
unfair economic pressure exerted to induce the making of what Corbin[5] calls 'the return
promise'.

Their Lordships' knowledge of this developing branch of American law is necessarily
limited. In their judgment it would be carrying audacity to the point of foolhardiness
g for them to attempt to extract from the American case law a principle to provide an
answer to the question now under consideration. That question, their Lordships repeat,
is whether, in a case where duress is not established, public policy may nevertheless
invalidate the consideration if there has been a threat to repudiate a pre-existing
contractual obligation or an unfair use of a dominating bargaining position.

Their Lordships' conclusion is that where businessmen are negotiating at arm's length
h it is unnecessary for the achievement of justice, and unhelpful in the development of the
law, to invoke such a rule of public policy. It would also create unacceptable anomaly.
It is unnecessary because justice requires that men, who have negotiated at arm's length,

---

j 1 See the cases cited in 9 Halsbury's Laws (4th Edn), para 326, footnote 2
   2 [1957] 1 All ER 305, [1957] 1 WLR 148
   3 [1957] 1 All ER 305 at 306–307, [1957] 1 WLR 148 at 149–151
   4 [1957] 1 All ER 305 at 307–310, [1957] 1 WLR 148 at 151–155
   5 (1963), vol 1A, ch 7, s 171
   6 Para 84(d)
   7 [1974] 1 All ER 1015, [1975] AC 154

be held to their bargains unless it can be shown that their consent was vitiated by fraud, mistake or duress. If a promise is induced by coercion of a man's will, the doctrine of *a* duress suffices to do justice. The party coerced, if he chooses and acts in time, can avoid the contract. If there is no coercion, there can be no reason for avoiding the contract where there is shown to be a real consideration which is otherwise legal.

Such a rule of public policy as is now being considered would be unhelpful because it would render the law uncertain. It would become a question of fact and degree to determine in each case whether there had been, short of duress, an unfair use of a strong *b* bargaining position.

It would create anomaly because, if public policy invalidates the consideration, the effect is to make the contract void. But unless the facts are such as to support a plea of non est factum, which is not suggested in this case, duress does no more than confer on the victim the opportunity, if taken in time, to avoid the contract. It would be strange if conduct less than duress could render a contract void, whereas duress does no more *c* than render a contract voidable. Indeed, it is the Laus' case in this appeal that such an anomaly is the correct result. Their case is that the Paos, having lost by cancellation the safeguard of the subsidiary agreement, are without the safeguard of the guarantee because its consideration is contrary to public policy, and that they are debarred from restoration to their position under the subsidiary agreement because the guarantee is void, not voidable. The logical consequence of counsel's submission for the defendant's *d* is that the safeguard which all were at all times agreed the Paos should have (the safeguard against fall in value of the shares) has been lost by the application of a rule of public policy. The law is not, in their Lordships' judgment, reduced to countenancing such stark injustice: nor is it necessary, when one bears in mind the protection offered otherwise by the law to one who contracts in ignorance of what he is doing or under duress. Accordingly, the submission that the additional consideration established by the *e* extrinsic evidence is invalid on the ground of public policy is rejected.

The third question

Duress, whatever form it takes, is a coercion of the will so as to vitiate consent. Their Lordships agree with the observation of Kerr J in *The Siboen and The Sibotre*[1] that in a contractual situation commercial pressure is not enough. There must be present some *f* factor 'which could in law be regarded as a coercion of his will so as to vitiate his consent'. This conception is in line with what was said in this Board's decision in *Barton v Armstrong*[2] by Lord Wilberforce and Lord Simon of Glaisdale, observations with which the majority judgment appears to be in agreement. In determining whether there was a coercion of will such that there was no true consent, it is material to enquire whether the person alleged to have been coerced did or did not protest; whether, at the time he *g* was allegedly coerced into making the contract, he did or did not have an alternative course open to him such as an adequate legal remedy; whether he was independently advised; and whether after entering the contract he took steps to avoid it. All these matters are, as was recognised in *Maskell v Horner*[3], relevant in determining whether he acted voluntarily or not.

In the present case there is unanimity amongst the judges below that there was no *h* coercion of Lau's will. In the Court of Appeal the trial judge's finding (already quoted) that Lau considered the matter thoroughly, chose to avoid litigation, and formed the opinion that the risk in giving the guarantee was more apparent than real was upheld. In short, there was commercial pressure, but no coercion. Even if this Board was disposed, which it is not, to take a different view, it would not substitute its opinion for that of the judges below on this question of fact.   *j*

1   [1976] 1 Lloyd's Rep 293 at 336
2   [1975] 2 All ER 465 at 476–477, [1976] AC 104 at 121
3   [1915] 3 KB 106, [1914] All ER Rep 595

It is, therefore, unnecessary for the Board to embark on an enquiry into the question
a whether English law recognises a category of duress known as 'economic duress'. But,
since the question has been fully argued in this appeal, their Lordships will indicate very
briefly the view which they have formed. At common law money paid under economic
compulsion could be recovered in an action for money had and received: see *Astley v
Reynolds*[1]. The compulsion had to be such that the party was deprived of 'his freedom of
exercising his will'[2]. It is doubtful, however, whether at common law any duress other
b than duress to the person sufficed to render a contract voidable; see Blackstone's
Commentaries[3] and *Skeate v Beale*[4]. American law (Williston on Contracts[5]) now
recognises that a contract may be avoided on the ground of economic duress. The
commercial pressure alleged to constitute such duress must, however, be such that the
victim must have entered the contract against his will, must have had no alternative
course open to him, and must have been confronted with coercive acts by the party
c exerting the pressure: see Williston on Contracts[6]. American judges pay great attention
to such evidential matters as the effectiveness of the alternative remedy available, the fact
or absence of protest, the availability of independent advice, the benefit received, and the
speed with which the victim has sought to avoid the contract. Recently two English
judges have recognised that commercial pressure may constitute duress the pressure of
which can render a contract voidable: see Kerr J in *The Siboen and The Sibotre*[7] and Mocatta
d J in *North Ocean Shipping Co Ltd v Hyundai Construction Co Ltd*[8]. Both stressed that the
pressure must be such that the victim's consent to the contract was not a voluntary act on
his part. In their Lordship's view, there is nothing contrary to principle in recognising
economic duress as a factor which may render a contract voidable, provided always that
the basis of such recognition is that it must amount to a coercion of will, which vitiates
consent. It must be shown that the payment made or the contract entered into was not
e a voluntary act.

For these reasons their Lordships will humbly advise Her Majesty that the appeal be
allowed and that the judgment of the trial judge be restored with interest up to the date
of Her Majesty's Order in Council disposing of this appeal. The defendants must pay the
plaintiffs' costs here and below.

f *Appeal allowed.*

Solicitors: *Stephenson, Harwood* (for the plaintiffs); *Bower, Cotton & Bower* (for the
defendants).

Mary Rose Plummer   Barrister.

g _____

1   (1731) 2 Stra 915
2   2 Stra 915 at 916
3   12th Edn (1793), vol 1, pp 130–131
4   (1841) 11 Ad & El 983
5   3rd Edn (1970), ch 47
h 6   3rd Edn (1970), ch 47, s 1603
7   [1976] 1 Lloyd's Rep 293
8   [1978] 3 All ER 1170

James Marshall v British Broadcasting Corporation

COURT OF APPEAL, CIVIL DIVISION

LORD DENNING MR, WALLER and CUMMING-BRUCE LJJ

27th APRIL 1979

Elections – Parliamentary – Broadcasting election items – Candidate's consent to broadcast – Candidate who 'takes part in' election item entitled to refuse consent to broadcast – BBC filming candidate while campaigning – Whether candidate taking part in film – Whether candidate entitled to injunction restraining broadcast of film – Representation of the People Act 1969, s 9(1).

A parliamentary candidate who had told the BBC that he did not wish to take part in an election programme they were making for television about his constituency during an election campaign later discovered that the BBC were continuing to film him while campaigning and proposed to include the film in a news broadcast. He sought an injunction against the BBC to restrain them from broadcasting, without his consent, any programme which contained both himself and a particular opposition candidate. He relied on s 9(1)[a] of the Representation of the People Act 1969 which provided that it was not lawful to broadcast an election item if a candidate who 'takes part in' the item refused his consent. The judge granted the injunction and the BBC appealed.

Held – Having regard to the importance of freedom of communication on political matters during an election campaign, s 9(1) of the 1969 Act was to be construed as only conferring a right of veto on a candidate in respect of the broadcasting of an election item if the candidate actively participated in the item, and since the candidate in the present case had merely been shown in, and had not actively participated in, the programme it did not require his consent before it was broadcast. He was not therefore entitled to an injunction, and the BBC's appeal would be allowed (see p 81 f to j and p 82 a to j, post).

Notes

For the Representation of the People Act 1969, s 9(1), see 11 Halsbury's Statutes (3rd Edn) 822.

Appeal

The defendants, the British Broadcasting Corporation ('the BBC') appealed from an order of Lloyd J made on 26th April 1979 granting the plaintiff, James Marshall, the Labour Party candidate for the Leicester South parliamentary constituency, an injunction restraining the BBC by themselves, their servants or agents or otherwise howsoever from broadcasting any item without the plaintiff's consent about the Leicester South parliamentary constituency which contained film of the plaintiff including film made on 25th April 1979 in which item the National Front candidate also took part. The BBC intended to broadcast the item in a news feature in the evening of 27th April. The facts are set out in the judgment of Lord Denning MR.

A T Hoolahan QC and *Andrew Caldecott* for the BBC.

Michael Howard for Mr Marshall.

LORD DENNING MR. This case raises a short point on the interpretation of the Representation of the People Act 1969. Mr James Marshall is the Labour candidate in the

---

a   Section 9, so far as material, is set out at p 81 d, post

constituency of Leicester South. There are three other candidates—Conservative, Liberal, and National Front.

a

On Monday 23rd April 1979 the British Broadcasting Corporation ('the BBC') decided to send out a camera unit to film all the candidates during the course of the election campaign. They told Mr Marshall that they were going to film all the candidates for the purpose of a programme which they were going to broadcast. Mr Marshall said that he would not willingly take part in any such programme.

b

On Wednesday 25th April Mr Marshall was campaigning outside the East Midlands Gas Board in Leicester. He suddenly became aware that he was being filmed by a BBC camera crew. He protested. He said that he had not consented to take part in a programme and that the camera crew were infringing his rights as a candidate. The BBC crew did not accept his protest. They continued to film him.

Thereupon Mr Marshall issued a writ against the BBC. He asked the court for an injunction to restrain them from broadcasting without his consent any item in which he took part in which the National Front candidate also took part. He would not mind the BBC broadcasting a programme which contained himself and the Conservative and Liberal candidates: but he would not consent if it contained the National Front candidate as well. The judge granted an injunction to that effect.

c

The BBC now appeal to this court. They say that Mr Marshall has not a veto of this kind. It all depends on a few words in s 9 of the Representation of the People Act 1969. Subsection (1) of that section provides:

d

> 'Pending a parliamentary or local government election it shall not be lawful for any item about the constituency or electoral area to be broadcast from a television or other wireless transmitting station in the United Kingdom if any of the persons who are for the time being candidates at the election takes part in the item and the broadcast is not made with his consent.'

e

It is said on behalf of Mr Marshall that the words 'takes part in' means if he 'is shown in' the item. He is shown on this film. So he takes part in it.

The BBC say the contrary. They say the words 'takes part in' mean 'actively participating' in the item. It is only if he actively participates in the item that he has a power of veto. That is the contest.

f

Looking at the mischief at which the statute is aimed, it seems to me that it is designed to protect a person who actively participates in a programme—as in the case of a candidate who is sitting on a panel, or is being questioned by an interviewer. A candidate who is being interviewed on television may be cross-examined by the interviewer and forced into a position in which he gives answers which he afterwards regrets. It is only right that he should be protected. The programme should not be transmitted except with his consent. Furthermore all these programmes are edited. The result of the editing may be that an impression is given which is quite unfair to the person who was taking part in that way. That is the mischief at which the subsection is aimed. It is to protect a candidate who is actively participating in a programme if he thinks that it shows him in a bad light.

g

h

But it seems to me that that does not apply to a candidate who has not actively participated in a programme. A candidate who merely acquiesces in a film being taken or in a speech being taped does not actively participate. Nor does a candidate who co-operates by being filmed walking around the constituency. Such candidates cannot object to the broadcast being made.

It is important to observe that the BBC has accepted a duty to be impartial in their programmes. This is especially important during an election campaign. They are not to favour one candidate or party more than another candidate or party. Take this very case. If Mr Marshall is right, he can say: 'Film of the National Front candidate is not to be shown in this review of the constituency at all.' If he can say that about the National Front, he can say it about any other opposing party. He could say to the BBC: 'Either them or me, but you have to choose between us.' If they have to choose between two

j

parties, they are ceasing to be impartial. If Mr Marshall's claim were correct, it would mean that the BBC would no longer be impartial. They would be forced by this veto to become partial.

The words 'takes part in' do not mean 'is shown in'. They do not even go so far as to mean 'co-operates in'. They apply only when the candidate actively participates in the item. If he actively participates in the item, then he has a veto: and the item is not to be shown except with his consent. The BBC should be free to present an impartial account or film of an election campaign—impartially as between the various candidates, whatever colour they might be.

I would allow the appeal and hold that Mr Marshall has not a veto here.

WALLER LJ. I agree. The rival contentions of counsel for the BBC and counsel for Mr Marshall are that counsel for the BBC says that the words 'takes part in the item' mean 'actively participates in the item', whereas counsel on behalf of Mr Marshall submits that 'takes part in' means 'is shown or recorded in the item'.

In my view, prima facie to take part in something does indicate actively doing something and not merely being a part of; and, when one looks at the rest of this very difficult section, there appears a passage which I will quote. It is the second part of sub-s (1), and it includes the passage:

> '. . . and where an item about a constituency or electoral area is so broadcast pending a parliamentary or local government election there, then if the broadcast either is made before the latest time for delivery of nomination papers, or is made after that time but without the consent of any candidate remaining validly nominated, [and here come the important words] any person taking part in the item for the purpose of promoting or procuring his election shall be guilty of an illegal practice, unless the broadcast is so made without his consent.'

As it seems to me, it is quite impossible to take part in an item for the purpose of doing something unless you are taking an active part; and I do not see that it is possible to construe the words 'takes part in' in the first part of the section and the words 'taking part in the item' in the second part of the section so as to give a different meaning to the phrase 'takes part' from 'taking part'. In my view, the only conclusion which can be drawn from that is that 'takes part in' means 'actively participates in', which is more than 'co-operates in'. It requires active participation.

For the reasons also that Lord Denning MR has given about the general policy, I am satisfied, as he has said (it is not an easy question), that the narrower construction of those words should prevail.

CUMMING-BRUCE LJ. I agree. Before s 9(1) of this Act was on the statute book broadcasting authorities had the right freely to photograph or record the appearance or the words of parliamentary candidates during an election, subject to their duty to be fair. By this section that important freedom was cut down.

It is manifest that the freedom of communication about political matters is of the utmost importance during the run up to an election. On the question of construction, looking at the language of the section, what restriction on the previous freedom to report by broadcasting has Parliament enacted? There are two possible constructions. Either the words 'takes part in' mean simply 'is shown or recorded in' or the words may mean 'voluntarily participates in'.

In spite of the fact that the judge took a different view, I think, for the reasons stated by Lord Denning MR and Waller LJ and for the reason that I am reluctant to give a wider meaning to words which cut down an existing freedom than the words compel me to do, that this appeal should be allowed.

Appeal allowed. Injunction refused. Leave to appeal to the House of Lords refused.

a   Solicitors: *E A C Bostock* (for the BBC); *Lewis Silkin & Partners* (for Mr Marshall).

Sumra Green   Barrister.

B v W and others (wardship: appeal)

b   HOUSE OF LORDS

LORD DIPLOCK, VISCOUNT DILHORNE, LORD EDMUND-DAVIES, LORD KEITH OF KINKEL AND LORD SCARMAN

28th FEBRUARY, 5th APRIL 1979

c   *Appeal – Review of exercise of discretion – Duty of appellate court – Infant – Wardship proceedings – Judge hearing applicant and taking all relevant factors into consideration – Court of Appeal taking hostile attitude towards applicant – Whether Court of Appeal justified in varying judge's order.*

d   *Natural justice – Disclosure to parties of information before court – Wardship proceedings – Discretion of court to withhold confidential reports – Letter written by social worker to court registrar not disclosed to applicant – Disclosure not harmful to children – Court relying on letter to reach its conclusions – Whether court in breach of rules of natural justice.*

The appellant and his wife were the grandparents of two wards of court, a boy aged 14 and a girl aged seven who were the children of the appellant's daughter and her *e*   husband. Relations between the daughter and the grandfather had never been good. The grandfather was a wealthy man who had built up a successful business. He was said to be aggressive and domineering and the daughter, who had an assertive personality, resented his interference with the upbringing of her children. The grandfather hoped his grandson would succeed him in the business. After her marriage in 1963 the *f*   daughter's husband had many changes in employment. The children had never had a settled home. In September 1976, at the instance of the grandfather, the children were made wards of court as a result of the parents' decision to remove the boy from the boarding school he was then attending at the grandfather's expense. In December 1976 the judge ordered that until further order the children should remain wards of court in the care of the local authority with staying access to the grandfather. In 1977 the daughter's husband left her and she became a patient at a psychiatric clinic. The children *g*   were received into a children's home. In April 1977 the same judge ordered that the children should be committed to the care of the local authority but directed that they were to live with their mother so long as circumstances permitted and in circumstances of emergency were to be placed in a children's home. The grandfather was granted staying access during weekends and school holidays. In June 1977 the building society foreclosed on the mortgage of the daughter's house and she and the children went to live *h*   with the grandfather. In December 1977 the daughter set fire to the grandfather's business premises which were destroyed and the daughter was imprisoned pending trial despite the grandfather's offer to pay £5,000 bail for her. The grandfather and his wife were devoted to their grandchildren and there was no criticism in any of the welfare reports of the way in which they looked after their well-being while the mother was in prison. On 6th February 1978 the matter came before the court again and the same *j*   judge ordered that the children should remain wards of court in the care and control of the local authority, that if possible they should become weekly boarders at a special school and that the grandfather should have staying access during weekends and school holidays. The grandfather appealed seeking an order granting himself care and control. The Court of Appeal dismissed his appeal but on its own initiative varied the

judge's order by deleting provisions relating to the children's education and giving the
grandparents weekend and school holiday staying access. The court decided that it *a*
should be made 'unequivocally clear to the grandfather that he is not in control of these
children', largely on the basis of a letter sent by a social worker on 10th November 1977
to the registrar of the Family Division which suggested that the grandfather was
'ruthlessly determined to achieve complete control over the children'. The letter was
apparently not placed before the judge and was certainly not disclosed to the grandfather
or his advisers either before the hearing below or before the Court of Appeal hearing. *b*
The grandfather appealed to the House of Lords.

Held – The appeal would be allowed for the following reasons—
    (i) There were no grounds for the Court of Appeal's conclusion that the judge below,
who was familiar with the case and had had the advantage of hearing the grandfather
giving evidence, had erred in the exercise of her discretion. The Court of Appeal's *c*
hostility towards the grandfather was not a sufficient reason for varying the judge's order
(see p 85 *e f*, p 86 *j* to p 87 *e*, p 89 *b* to d *f*, p 91 *d*, p 94 *b c g* and p 95 *b c*, post); dicta of
Viscount Simon LC in *Charles Osenton & Co v Johnston* [1941] 2 All ER at 250 and of Lord
Wright in *Evans v Bartlam* [1937] 2 All ER at 654 applied.
    (ii) Although in wardship proceedings the court had a discretion to withhold *d*
confidential reports from the parties, the Court of Appeal had acted irregularly and in
breach of the rules of natural justice in relying on the social worker's letter of 10th
November 1977 when it had not been disclosed to the grandfather or his advisers, since
disclosure would not have been harmful to the children and other reports had been
disclosed. In the circumstances the judge's order would be restored pending a further
application to the court for the matter to be considered afresh (see p 90 *f g*, p 91 *c d*, p 92
e g h, p 93 *g* to p 94 *c*, p 95 *b c and p* 96 *b*, post). *e*
    Per Curiam. Where there was a serious dispute between parties in cases concerned
with the care and custody of children, it may on occasion be inevitable that an assessment
has to be made of the character of one or more of them from the point of view of
suitability of access to the child. But such an assessment can rarely be made satisfactorily
by anyone who has not heard all relevant evidence and in particular has not had the
opportunity of observing the parties in the witness box. The assessment should always *f*
be expressed in moderate language, lest the dispute be exacerbated and there be
impairment of the prospects of securing that all concerned contribute as much as may be
within their power towards promoting the welfare of the child (see p 85 *e f*, p 91 *h* to p
92 *a*, p 94 *c* to *e* and p 95 *d e*, post).

g

Notes
For appeals from the exercise of a judge's discretion, see 30 Halsbury's Laws (3rd Edn)
452, para 856, and for cases on the subject, see 51 Digest (Repl) 790–791, *3481–3494*.
    For access to minors by grandparents, see 24 Halsbury's Laws (4th Edn) para 547.

h

Cases referred to in opinions
Evans v Bartlam [1937] 2 All ER 646, [1937] AC 473, 106 LJKB 568, 157 LT 311, HL, 50
    Digest (Repl) 401, *1113*.
F (a minor) (wardship: appeal), Re [1976] 1 All ER 417, [1976] Fam 238, [1976] 2 WLR
    189, CA.
K (infants), Re [1962] 3 All ER 179, [1963] Ch 381, [1963] 3 WLR 1517; rvsd [1962] 3 All *j*
    ER 1000, [1963] Ch 381, [1962] 3 WLR 1517, CA, rvsd sub nom *Official Solicitor v K*
    [1963] 3 All ER 191, [1965] AC 201, [1963] 3 WLR 408, HL, 28(2) Digest (Reissue)
    2233.
Onassis and Calogeropoulos v Vergottis [1967] 1 Lloyd's Rep 607; rvsd [1968] 1 Lloyd's Rep
    294, CA; rvsd [1968] 2 Lloyd's Rep 403, HL.

Osenton (Charles) & Co v Johnston [1941] 2 All ER 245, [1942] AC 130, 110 LJKB 420, 165 LT 235, HL, 51 Digest (Repl) 681, 2840.

Appeal

The appellant, the grandfather of two minors who had become wards of court on 9th September 1976, appealed against the judgment of the Court of Appeal (Stamp, Ormrod and Bridge LJJ) dated 16th February 1978 varying an order made by Lane J in the Family Division on 6th February 1978 whereby she ordered that the two minors should remain wards of court in the care of the local authority and made provision granting the appellant and his wife, the children's grandmother, weekend and school holiday staying access. The Court of Appeal varied the order by deleting that part which granted the appellant and his wife staying access. The Official Solicitor acted as the minors' guardian ad litem. The facts are set out in the opinion of Viscount Dilhorne.

Marcel Picard for the appellant.
G Boyd for the mother.
Shirley Anne Ritchie for the Official Solicitor
The father did not appear.

Their Lordships took time for consideration.

5th April. The following opinions were delivered.

LORD DIPLOCK. My Lords, in cases dealing with the custody of children an appellate court ought to be particularly chary of exercising its power to interfere with the way in which a judge of the Family Division of the High Court has exercised his or her discretion. I agree with your Lordships, whose speeches I have had the opportunity of reading in advance, that in the instant case there was no material before the Court of Appeal which could justify it in varying the order of Lane J, or castigating the conduct of the children's grandfather which that very experienced judge, before whom he had given evidence, had deliberately and wisely refrained from criticising.

I would allow the appeal and restore the order of Lane J. However, since circumstances have changed since the date of her order, the matter should now go back to a judge of the Family Division for further consideration in the light of those changes.

VISCOUNT DILHORNE. My Lords, on 16th February 1978 the Court of Appeal (Stamp, Ormrod and Bridge LJJ) varied an order made by Lane J ten days earlier in proceedings relating to two wards of court, the other members of the court agreeing with the judgment delivered by Ormrod LJ. From this decision an Appeal Committee of this House (Lord Wilberforce, Lord Salmon and Lord Fraser of Tullybelton) gave leave to appeal on 27th April 1978. The questions now to be determined are whether the Court of Appeal was entitled to interfere with the exercise of discretion by Lane J and, if they were, whether they were right to alter her order as they did.

In view of a number of observations made by Ormrod LJ in the course of his judgment on which I feel I have no alternative but to comment, I find it necessary to go in some detail into the history of this case.

The appellant and his wife are the grandparents of the two wards of court, one a boy of 14 years of age and the other a girl of seven. They are the children of the appellant's daughter and her husband. The appellant has built up a successful business and is now a wealthy man. He and his wife live in the south of England. His daughter married in July 1963 a man from whom she obtained a divorce on 14th September 1977 on the ground that she could not reasonably be expected to live with him and the marriage had broken down irretrievably. His daughter had not been happy at home before she married or at school. After leaving school she worked for a time in her father's business. She did not enjoy that. On three occasions during her youth she left home and was brought back by the police. When 19 she received a sentence of imprisonment for house-breaking, which she thought was the direct result of her home life. Her husband was a man of limited education from farm working stock. The appellant has a strong *a* personality and there is no doubt that he strenuously seeks to secure that in matters affecting his children and his grandchildren his views prevail. His daughter, it is said, has 'an assertive personality'. She resents his domination and his interference with the upbringing of her children and regards him as seeking to gain control over their upbringing and in particular over that of her son.

After their marriage in 1963, the daughter's husband had many changes of *b* employment, working as a semi-skilled mechanic, a milkman, a driver, on a farm, in timber felling and in his father-in-law's business. These changes of employment meant a series of moves for his family. In 1970 he bought a house. The appellant says that he lent him £1,500 towards the purchase price. In 1973 the daughter had a breakdown and was for some months an in-patient in a mental hospital. In that year the appellant arranged for his grandson to go to a boarding school. The boy's parents acquiesced in *c* this. During the school holidays the boy spent a good deal of time with his grandparents. The appellant paid the school fees.

In the course of his judgment Ormrod LJ said that the husband was—

'a man who has never been able to hold down a job for any length of time but has changed jobs and homes and moved about in a very incompetent way, one could say, although one does not know what pressures have been put on him and his wife *d* by the grandfather.'

The husband says that he only left one job for another to increase his income or because transport became difficult. He left employment as a driver for a brick company he says at the appellant's request and was then employed by the appellant. He hurt his back timber felling after he had left the appellant's employment and the appellant then *e* sought to set him up in the vacuum cleaning business and that when that failed, the appellant again employed him. Apart from his leaving one employment at the request of the appellant, I see nothing in the papers before us, which were before the Court of Appeal, to suggest that his frequent changes of employment should be attributed to pressures put on him or his wife by the appellant.

In 1974 the house was sold and the daughter and her husband went to Wales leaving *f* their children with the grandparents. The daughter and her husband then found a shop and house to rent in the Midlands. The appellant says that he helped his son-in-law to the extent of £1,500 in this venture. They left in February 1976 and then with their children lived with the appellant and his wife until August 1976. They then went away with their children. They decided to take their son away from the boarding school which he had attended for about three years, the daughter saying that they decided to do *g* so as he was not doing well there and was unhappy. The appellant says that he was told this only after his daughter had asked him for a loan of £600 and he had refused it.

The appellant thought that it was undesirable that his grandson's education should be interrupted. No doubt he hoped that in due course his grandson would succeed him in the management of his business and that was one reason why he was prepared to pay for his grandson's education. It was because he believed that the boy should remain at the *h* school that at his instance on 9th September 1976 his grandchildren were made wards of court. He sought an order that the boy should return to the school for at any rate the next term.

At the beginning of his judgment Ormrod LJ said:

'Whenever grandparents find it necessary to make their grandchildren wards of court and to make their own son or daughter a defendant, the situation is one which *j* could scarcely be more difficult or more disadvantageous for the children; litigation between parents and their children is a very unfavourable situation.'

While I entirely agree that litigation between parents and their children is most distasteful and seldom justifiable, if by this passage it was intended to suggest that in this

a   case and in other cases grandparents should not make their grandchildren wards of court, it is a suggestion with which I feel bound to disagree. Where there is serious conflict between grandparents and their children and they are unable to agree as to what will be in the best interests of the grandchildren, the only way to secure a satisfactory solution may be to take that course. I cannot agree that in those circumstances if the children are made wards of court, the situation could scarcely be more disadvantageous for them. In the present case I am not prepared to conclude that that course was not taken for the best

b   of motives or to conclude that the parents' desire to take their son away from his school was not also genuinely thought by them to be in his interests.

Ormrod LJ said that the appellant's reaction to the decision to take the boy away from the school was—

c   'a violent one (perhaps it would be more correct to say, a vehement one); he proceeded to take out an originating summons . . . making these children wards of court and applied to the court for directions as to their education.'

I would not myself think it right to describe the appellant's recourse to the courts as either violent or vehement. If he honestly believed that it was in the boy's interest to remain in the school where he had been for three years and thought that it would be a disaster for him to be taken away, that was the only course he could take, and in the light

d   of what occurred later, it was, I think, fortunate for the children that he did so. I also see no ground for the learned Lord Justice's statement that the appellant's desire that his grandson should succeed him in the conduct of his business 'may have coloured and distorted his judgment in many ways'. That was, I think, a perfectly legitimate desire and that his grandson should have the opportunity of doing so if he wished, can hardly be said not to have been in his interests.

e   The matter came before Lane J on 13th December 1976. In the autumn of that year the daughter and their children were living in the Midlands, the husband being employed as a plant operator at a salary of £66 per week. In October 1976 they bought a house there for £9,495. Lane J ordered that the children should remain wards of court during their minorities or until further order. This she would not have done if she had not thought that it was in their best interests and this is perhaps the best answer that can

f   be made to any criticism of the appellant for applying to make them wards of court. She also ordered that the present arrangements for the education of the boy should be continued. He was then attending a very good school locally. She also ordered that the parents should allow the appellant reasonable access to the children, such access to be agreed between the parties and in default of agreement, she said that application was to be made to the court. Finally she ordered that the children should be under the

g   supervision of the social services department of the local authority.

The appellant then tried to arrange for access. He invited his daughter, her husband and the two children to lunch with him and his wife, as, he says, 'a step to reconciliation'. This invitation was refused, the husband saying that he did not wish to be the appellant's guest and that the hotel suggested was too expensive for him. Failure to obtain access led to another application to the court on 4th February 1977 when

h   Lane J ordered that the parents should allow the appellant staying access to the children for one week during the Easter school holidays, for two weeks during the summer holidays and for one week during the Christmas holidays.

When the supervising officer visited the daughter on 19th January 1977 he found her in a very distressed state and, after consultation with her doctor and a consultant at a local psychiatric clinic, it was agreed with the daughter that she should have a period of in-

j   patient treatment. She was discharged from hospital on 5th February but on 12th February she was again in a distressed state. On that day her marriage broke up, her husband leaving her and going to live with his parents. A woman from the house next door also went to his parents' house. The psychiatric clinic accepted the daughter for a further period of treatment. The children were then received into a children's home. On 15th February the daughter was again discharged. The daughter on 20th March cut

her wrists. She says that it was an attempt to commit suicide. As the injuries she
inflicted on herself were very minor, this was described by the supervising officer as a
suicide gesture. The daughter was again admitted to the clinic. Throughout most of
this period the children remained at the children's home.

When the husband left his wife, the appellant, it is said, made 'his usual moves to fill
the breach' but his daughter felt unable to accept his overtures as she thought that there
would be strings attached. When seen on 16th April the appellant had experienced a
much happier and therefore reassuring meeting with his daughter. While his daughter
was in hospital, he had thought it right to make further enquiries about boarding schools
as it was his view that, having caring grandparents who had met their needs for a long
time, the children should not be occupying places at a children's home which could be
filled by children without other resources.

On 20th April 1977 the matter again came before Lane J. She then ordered that the
children should be committed to the care of the local authority with a direction that (1)
so long as circumstances permitted they were to live with their mother and (2) in
circumstances of emergency the children were to be placed if possible in the children's
home, or, if that was impossible, with the appellant. She also ordered that the appellant
should have staying access for periods during the school holidays.

In June 1977 the building society foreclosed on the mortgage of the house in the
Midlands and the daughter and her children, being without a home, went to live with
the appellant. On 10th November 1977 a social worker wrote to Mr Registrar Tickle of
the Family Division a letter to which I shall have to refer in some detail later, reporting
on the situation at the appellant's home as she then saw it and asking for comments.

On 17th December 1977 the daughter set fire to the appellant's business premises and
they were burnt down. She was taken to Holloway Prison and kept there though the
appellant was willing to put up £5,000 bail for her, and to welcome her back home if bail
had been granted. After the hearing in the Court of Appeal she pleaded guilty to the
charge of arson and was put on probation for three years.

The appellant and the social worker disagreed about whether the children should be
told that their mother was in prison. The appellant had told them that their mother was
ill and in hospital. He thought that if she was found not guilty, it would be unnecessary
for them to know that she had been in prison. The social worker on the other hand,
while recognising that this was a viable point of view, thought that on balance it was
better that the appellant should tell them she was in prison as the boy at least might
know the true facts and she thought that it would be better for the appellant to tell them
than for the children to find out by some unfortunate mischance. Eventually they were
told and they were greatly distressed.

On 26th January 1978 it was ordered that the children should be made defendants in
these proceedings and the Official Solicitor agreed to act as their guardian ad litem.

On 6th February 1978 the matter again came before Lane J. She, of course, was fully
acquainted with the distressing history and after hearing evidence by the appellant, she
made the following order against which the appellant appealed and which the Court of
Appeal varied by the deletion of the words in the first set of brackets:

'It is ordered that the minors ... do remain wards of this court during their
respective minorities or until further order and that until further order do remain
in the care and control of the ... County Council. [And it is directed that if this can
possibly be achieved, each of the said minors becomes a weekly boarder at the ...
School. Transfer to this arrangement to be at the discretion of the ... County
Council in consultation with the Official Solicitor and similarly where the said
minors spend their weekends and holidays to be at the discretion of the ... County
Council in consultation with the Official Solicitor. The present views of the Court
being that some, if not all, weekends pending the discharge of the minors' mother
should be spent with the grandparents as should school holidays following such
discharge. Staying access of appropriate duration to be with the grandparents].

a
Liberty to any party to apply with regard to access AND it is further directed that the said minors be informed of the true whereabouts of their mother, such information desirably to be imparted either by [the social worker] or by a representative of the Official Solicitor. Access to the mother at Holloway Prison, if this cannot be arranged elsewhere, to be at the discretion of the local authority and on the first such access to be supervised desirably by [the social worker].'

b
In his judgment Ormrod LJ said:

'It is plain from Lane J's judgment, which was extremely short, that she knew all about this case and knew all about the personalities involved and all about the interrelation of grandfather and children's mother and *she realised that she was dealing with a man who was utterly rigid, who was not prepared to take advice from anybody about these children and who was determined, as the mother had always thought he was, to take complete control of them away from their parents.'* (Emphasis mine.)

c
I am completely at a loss to know on what grounds these conclusions which I have emphasised were attributed to Lane J. I find no support for that in either her judgment or in anything that she said during the course of the hearing. In her judgment she sensibly refrained from making any criticism of the appellant or of his daughter.

I now come to the question, was the Court of Appeal entitled to vary her order? In
d *Charles Osenton & Co v Johnston*[1] Viscount Simon LC said:

'. . . appellate authorities ought not to reverse the order merely because they would themselves have exercised the original discretion, had it attached to them, in a different way. If, however, the appellate tribunal reaches the clear conclusion that there has been a wrongful exercise of discretion, in that no weight, or no sufficient weight, has been given to relevant considerations . . . then the reversal of the order
e on appeal may be justified.'

He referred to *Evans v Bartlam*[2] where Lord Wright had said that the Court of Appeal should not interfere with the discretion of a judge unless the court is clearly satisfied that he is wrong: see also *Re F (a minor) (wardship: appeal)*[3] per Browne LJ.

I can find no grounds for concluding that such an experienced judge as Lane J, who
f had the advantage of seeing the appellant in the witness box, on the materials before her erred in any way in the exercise of her discretion and consequently, in my opinion, the Court of Appeal should not have varied her order unless the variation was justified on materials which were not before her.

It is apparent from Ormrod LJ's judgment that they varied her order to make it 'unequivocally clear to the grandfather that he is not in control of these children' but that
g was surely made clear by Lane J's order that the children were to remain in the care and control of the local authority. The appellant was appealing to the Court of Appeal against that order and it would have sufficed just to dismiss the appeal.

From his judgment it would appear that Ormrod LJ took a very hostile view of the appellant. That both before and after her marriage there had been much conflict between the daughter and her father is clear beyond doubt. The reason why I have stated
h the past history at such length is that it appears to me to show that the faults were not only on one side and that despite the conflicts the grandfather was always ready to help and did help when the daughter was in difficulties. He arranged for the children to go to the special school, where Lane J thought they should be boarders. It was recognised by the social worker that he and his wife had always been devoted to their grandchildren and that while their mother was in prison they were 'obviously receiving very good care
j from their grandparents'; nor is there in the various social welfare reports any criticism of the way in which the grandparents looked after their material well-being.

1   [1941] 2 All ER 245 at 250, [1942] AC 130 at 138
2   [1937] 2 All ER 646 at 654, [1937] AC 473 at 486
3   [1976] 1 All ER 417 at 432–433, [1976] Fam 238 at 257

Ormrod LJ regarded a letter written by the appellant on 10th February 1978 to his daughter (which cannot have been seen by Lane J) 'quite enough of itself to indicate how totally unsuitable a person he is to have the upbringing of his two grandchildren'. That was a very unpleasant letter, written in reply to one which the appellant described as 'abusive' and which he said had upset his wife. Without seeing the letter to which it was a reply, I find it difficult to reach a conclusion with regard to it and while it reveals the grandfather's feelings towards his daughter at that moment of time, I cannot agree with the statement that it showed him to be totally unsuitable to have the upbringing of his grandchildren.

Great reliance was placed by Ormrod LJ on the letter from the social worker of 10th November 1977 to Mr Registrar Tickle. That letter apparently was on the court file. In it the social worker said that the daughter had had a brief spell in a psychiatric hospital since her return to her parents' home and that she greatly resented her father's arrangements for the children's education at the special school, education for which the appellant was paying. In the course of the letter she said that the appellant was 'ruthlessly determined to achieve complete control over the children', language which one finds repeated in Ormrod LJ's judgment. What were the grounds for this conclusion she does not state. She did not repeat it in the long social welfare report she made on 6th February or in her report of 15th February. Ormrod LJ preferred the letter to the report of 15th February which he said showed 'in a much more muted form the acute difficulties' the social worker was experiencing with the grandfather.

Whether or not Lane J saw this letter, one does not know, but if she did see it and attached importance to it, it is to my mind inconceivable that she would have done so without letting the appellant's advisers know of its contents. What is clear beyond doubt is that this letter was not seen by the appellant or his advisers until after the Court of Appeal hearing for Ormrod LJ said:

'That document [the letter] was not sent to the grandfather or his solicitors; no doubt he may well feel aggrieved at that. My only comment on it is had he seen it at the time he would have been even more infuriated than he is at present and no useful purpose would have been served in letting him see it.'

For a court to act on what it regards as an invaluable report without a party to the case seeing it, or even, it would seem, being aware of its existence, is to me astonishing bearing in mind that it was not suggested and cannot be said that disclosure to the parties would have been harmful to the children and the fact that other social welfare reports were disclosed. Letting the appellant and his advisers see it might in the end have served no useful purpose but they should have had an opportunity of dealing with it. In my opinion in failing to let the appellant and his advisers see a document which the court regarded as of such importance and on which its decision was largely, if not mainly, based, the court failed to meet the requirements of natural justice. And on this ground too I would allow the appeal.

I do not propose to add to the length of this very long speech by dealing in detail with other observations of Ormrod LJ which appear to me to be open to criticism. He said that the court would support the county council in whatever order they might think fit to make. In my opinion he had no power to give any such pledge as to future action. He also said that it would be wrong for the court to judge what is for the immediate benefit of the children. That to my mind is the task and duty of the court and a duty of which it cannot divest itself. He went on to say that if the appellant failed to co-operate with the county council, the court would fully understand a decision by the local authority to cut him off altogether, for the time being at any rate, from these children.

My Lords, there are bound to be occasions when parents, grandparents and social workers do not agree and it is not to be assumed that social workers are always right. If there is failure to co-operate on the part of the appellant, the question is not whether cutting him off from the children is an appropriate punishment for him but what course of action should be taken in the interests of the children. This is a difficult case. The grandfather and his daughter may both be difficult persons. He may be aggressive and domineering. She is said to have an assertive personality. The history that I have detailed shows that the children have not had a settled home of their own. Perhaps their grandparents' home is the nearest thing that they have had to one. At the time of the Court of Appeal hearing the daughter could not provide a home. Perhaps she can now.

In view of the time that has elapsed and the changes that may have taken place, the case must now in my opinion go back to the Family Division for it to be decided what is now the proper order to make. The grandparents love their grandchildren. Their mother loves them. It is regrettable that the children should suffer in consequence of conflict between the appellant and his daughter. It is perhaps too much to hope that now the conflict has died down. If, alas, it continues the governing consideration must be what is best for the children and in deciding that now, no regard should be had to the observations about the appellant in the judgment of the Court of Appeal. There should be a fresh start.

For the reasons stated I would allow this appeal, and restore the deletion made from Lane J's order. There should be a further application to the Family Division for that order to be reviewed.

LORD EDMUND-DAVIES. My Lords, I am obliged to say that I can find no acceptable juridical basis for the course taken by the Court of Appeal in this case. The melancholy facts giving rise to it have already been spaciously related by my noble and learned friend, Viscount Dilhorne, and I shall not repeat any of them. Nor is there any reason to think that Lane J did not have them all in mind when on 6th February 1978 she ordered that two children at the centre of a family situation of Compton-Burnett tortuosity remain wards of court in the care and control of the local authority. She was in truth very familiar with the facts, having dealt with the case on at least two previous occasions, and it is unchallengeable that her order was throughout based on her conclusion that it would advance the children's welfare, that being her first and paramount concern. The Court of Appeal were accordingly right in dismissing the grandfather's appeal from that order.

So far, so good. But what has given rise to the deepest perturbation, certainly in my mind, was the further decision of the Court of Appeal to vary that part of the learned judge's order which granted staying access 'of appropriate duration' to the grandparents. It was not suggested that there had been any material change of circumstances since she dealt with the case ten days earlier. Yet although she had directed that 'some, if not all, weekends pending the discharge of the minors' mother should be spent with the grandparents, as should school holidays', the Court of Appeal ordered the deletion of those words and thereby virtually cut off the children from their grandparents. And this they did despite the absence of any cross-appeal and even though no such variation was suggested by counsel who appeared on behalf of the Official Solicitor to safeguard the minors' welfare. They also did it despite the fact that on two occasions (the second being on the very day when she made her order) Lane J had seen and heard the appellant grandfather giving evidence. Yet the Court of Appeal, who had been denied that advantage, concluded that until further order all access was to be denied.

Why did they adopt such a course? And how came it about that, in striking contrast to the measured language of Lane J's judgment, Ormrod LJ thought fit to speak in terms of unbridled and unrelieved condemnation of the appellant? Questions of access are pre-eminently matters of discretion, to be exercised in the light of the relevant, and admissible, facts. As to matters of fact, a body of case law establishes that the findings of a trial judge who has had the inestimable advantage of seeing and hearing the witnesses should only in exceptional circumstances be upset by an appellate court. No more striking illustration of that proposition could I think, be found than the varying decisions arrived at by successive and ascending courts in *Onassis and Calogeropoulos v Vergottis*[1].

---

1   [1967] 1 Lloyd's Rep 607, Roskill J; [1968] 1 Lloyd's Rep 294, CA; [1968] 2 Lloyd's Rep 403, HL.

And the view formed by a trial judge not only of the credibility but of the whole range of personal attributes of parties is pre-eminently important and frequently crucial in *a* cases concerning the upbringing of minors. For an exercise of discretion is almost invariably involved in such cases, and, as Lord Wright said in *Evans v Bartlam*[1]:

'It is clear that the Court of Appeal should not interfere with the discretion of a judge acting within his jurisdiction, unless the court is clearly satisfied that he was wrong... The court must, if necessary examine anew the relevant facts and circumstances, in order to exercise a discretion by way of review which may reverse *b* or vary the order.'

That, indeed, is what the Court of Appeal proceeded to do in *Re F (a minor) (wardship: appeal)*[2], where the relevant decisions were extensively reviewed.

My Lords, I should accordingly have paused a long time before accepting any submission for the appellant that in the present case the unquestionable advantage of *c* having seen and heard the grandfather must be treated as so considerable that the Court of Appeal were, in effect, powerless to differ from the conclusion of Lane J, though for my part I can see no ground for criticising it in the slightest respect. But no such submission was in fact made, and the task which has concerned your Lordships has been that of ascertaining why it was considered right to vary the order at all. It is a task that has presented no difficulty, for the language of Ormrod LJ's judgment has the merit of *d* complete frankness on the point. It has indeed served to create considerable doubt in my mind that the learned Lord Justice regarded the trial judge as having enjoyed any advantage over the members of the Court of Appeal in forming a view as to the character and personality of the appellant. It has furthermore convinced me that Ormrod LJ was most markedly influenced by material (I studiously avoid the word 'evidence') to which he had no entitlement to pay regard. I refer to the letter sent in November 1977 to the *e* Family Division by the social worker, a children's officer employed by the local authority. Whether Lane J ever saw it remains uncertain, but if she did it is significant that she nevertheless concluded that continued access between grandparents and grandchildren was desirable. What we do know, however, is that, whereas the Court of Appeal saw it, neither the appellant nor his legal advisers ever did. But for the purposes, its nature is sufficiently conveyed by the observation of Ormrod LJ that 'had [the *f* appellant] seen it at the time he would have been even more infuriated than he is at present'. This led the learned Lord Justice to conclude that 'no useful purpose would have been served in letting him see it', and this despite that fact that '... it is an invaluable report from the point of view of the court, because it gives an unvarnished picture of this situation'. We learn further from the judgment that the social worker's later report of 15th May 1978 (that is, after the hearing before Lane J), a copy of which *g* *was* made available to the appellant, dealt 'in a much more muted form' with the difficulties she was apparently experiencing in dealing with the appellant.

My Lords, I have with understandable reluctance to say that, in relying as they clearly did on the 'invaluable' expression of the social worker's views in a document never seen by the person condemned in it or his legal advisers, the Court of Appeal in my judgment acted irregularly and unjustly. I take that view notwithstanding my awareness that, in *h* relation to wards of court the Family Division exercises a paternal jurisdiction and that such proceedings partake of an administrative character and not of a mere conflict between parties. It follows that in such cases the disclosure of confidential reports is a matter of discretion for the judge, and a party is not as of right entitled to see them. But it is equally clear that confidential reports should not be submitted as a matter of routine, but only in exceptional cases when the Official Solicitor believes that the disclosure of *j* certain information might be harmful to the young persons involved. Thus it is that what generally happens when reports are furnished by a court welfare officer is that the

1   [1937] 2 All ER 646 at 654, [1937] AC 473 at 486
2   [1976] 1 All ER 417, [1976] Fam 238

parties are notified and may order copies. *Re K (infants)*[1] was concerned with the non-
disclosure to a mother in wardship proceedings of confidential reports lodged with the
court by the Official Solicitor, the trial judge[2] holding that disclosure need not be made
to the mother of matters thereby made known to the court which it would be contrary
to the infant's welfare to disclose. When the matter reached your Lordships' House, Lord
Hodson said[3]:

> '... this appeal raises an acute conflict between two principles. It is said with
> force, as RUSSELL, L.J., remarked[4], that it is contrary to natural justice that the
> contentions of a party in a judicial proceeding may be overruled by considerations
> in the judicial mind which the party has no opportunity of criticising or
> controverting because he or she does not know what they are: moreover the judge
> may (without the inestimable benefit of critical argument) arrive at a wrong
> conclusion on the undisclosed material, and that even worse, the undisclosed
> evidence may, if subjected to criticism prove to be misconceived or based on false
> premises. On the other hand the substantive law governing proceedings of this
> character is summarised in the Guardianship of Infants Act, 1925, which s. 1 says
> that the first and foremost consideration is the welfare of the infant. How then, it
> is said, can it be right to insist on the application of a view of natural justice over
> procedural law in a manner which in the view of the judge will do harm to the
> infant? ... In the last resort the welfare of the child must dominate and in those
> rare cases, of which this is one, where the judge has found himself unable to
> disregard a secret and unverified report yet has thought the report must not in the
> child's interest be shown to the parents, his view must prevail.'

Lord Devlin in his turn said[5]:

> '... no special privilege attaches to reports from the Official Solicitor. The
> question is whether the judge can have regard to evidence from any source that is
> not also laid before the parties ... The mother ... relies on the fundamental
> principle of justice that the judge should not look at material that the parties before
> him have not seen. The appellant replies that this principle has no application to the
> special jurisdiction in the case of wards which comes from the Crown as parens
> patriae. This is the important issue before the House.'

Your Lordships' House resolved that issue by holding that non-disclosure was permissible,
not as a matter of routine, but (in the words of Lord Devlin[6]) 'only in exceptional cases
when the Official Solicitor believes that the disclosure of certain information may be
harmful to the infant'. But *Re K (infants)*[1] was markedly different from the present
case. There is here no suggestion that the concealment of the social worker's letter from
the appellant sprang from any desire to save the two grandchildren from harm. Non-
disclosure seems, at best, to have been fortuitous, and that is far from rendering it
excusable. What renders it insupportable is that only when judgment was being
delivered did the appellant learn of its existence and have *some* opportunity of surmising
the hostile nature of those 'invaluable' contents which unquestionably played a dominant
part in leading the court to its conclusion that '... this is the end of the road as far as [the
appellant] is concerned.'

My Lords, he would be a very odd sort of suitor who could leave court feeling that he

---

1   [1962] 3 All ER 179, [1963] Ch at 384, Ungoed-Thomas J; [1962] 3 All ER 1000, [1963] Ch 381,
    CA; [1963] 3 All ER 191, [1965] AC 201, HL
2   [1962] 3 All ER 179 at 181, [1963] Ch 381 at 388
3   [1963] 3 All ER 191 at 206–207, [1965] AC 201 at 234
4   [1962] 3 All ER 1000 at 1015, [1963] Ch 381 at 416
5   [1963] 3 All ER 191 at 208, [1965] AC 201 at 237
6   [1963] 3 All ER 191 at 211, [1965] AC 201 at 242

had received justice in such unfortunate circumstances as those of the present case. In the result, I hold that, while the appeal from Lane J was rightly dismissed, the Court of Appeal acted irregularly in varying her order as they did, and, to the extent of holding that their variation should be excised and her original order restored in its fullness, I would allow the appeal.

LORD KEITH OF KINKEL. My Lords, I agree with the speech of my noble and learned friend, Viscount Dilhorne.

I am of opinion that there were no sufficient grounds on which the Court of Appeal could properly have allowed the appellant's appeal to them against that part of Lane J's order which directed that the two children should meantime remain in the care and control of the local authority. But I am of opinion likewise that the Court of Appeal were not entitled to interfere with that part of the order which dealt with ancillary matters, in particular the expression of Lane J's view regarding access to be had by the grandparents.

Any judge with experience of dealing at first instance with cases concerned with the care and custody of children must be well aware of the necessity to treat the matter with the utmost discretion and tact. Where there is a serious dispute between parties involved, it may on occasion be inevitable that an assessment has to be made of the character of one or more of them from the point of view of suitability to have care of or access to a child. But such an assessment can rarely be made satisfactorily by anyone who has not heard all relevant evidence and in particular has not had the opportunity of observing the parties in the witness box. The assessment should always be expressed in moderate language, lest the dispute be exacerbated and there be impairment of the prospect of securing that all concerned contribute as much as may be within their power towards promoting the welfare of the child.

In the present case Lane J, a most experienced judge in this field, who had been concerned with the case over a considerable period, was fully familiar with all the circumstances, and had the opportunity of seeing and hearing the appellant in the witness box, made an order, on a purely interim basis, which in my view was not open to any reasonable criticism. She wisely refrained from saying anything more than was strictly necessary in the circumstances.

The Court of Appeal, however, thought fit to interfere with the order largely on the basis of a letter from a social worker, which it does not appear was intended by the writer to be taken judicially into account at any stage for the purpose of deciding how the welfare of the children could best be promoted, and the existence and terms of which were unknown to the appellant and his advisers. In doing so the Court of Appeal, in my opinion, not only went beyond its proper function but also acted in a heavy-handed manner which was unfair to the appellant and not likely to promote the welfare of the children concerned.

I would allow the appeal to the effect of restoring in full the order of Lane J.

LORD SCARMAN. My Lords, I agree with the speeches delivered by my noble and learned friends, and would allow the appeal to the extent that they propose.

The appellant, who is the grandfather of the two children (a boy now aged 14, and a girl now seven years old), appealed to the Court of Appeal from an order of Lane J committing the care of the children to the local authority. The grandfather was seeking an order granting himself care and control. The Court of Appeal dismissed his appeal, correctly, in my judgment. Lane J (whose knowledge of the case was extensive and included twice seeing and hearing the grandfather give evidence) included in her order detailed provisions granting him (and his wife, the children's grandmother), weekend and school holiday staying access. The Court of Appeal varied this part of the order, leaving the extent of access to the discretion of the local authority. The court varied the access order because of their assessment of the character, attitude and motives of the grandfather. It does not, however, appear that they were asked by any party to the proceedings to make any such variation: nor was there a cross-appeal, though the

children were at all material times separately represented by counsel instructed by the
a Official Solicitor. The court acted on its own initiative. It made its assessment of
the grandfather's character, attitude and motives without having seen or heard him give
evidence and in reliance, to a large extent, on a document not seen by him or his
advisers. The document was a letter written in November 1977 by the social worker
in charge of the case. The Court of Appeal seems to have accepted without question
her opinion. But the judgment of a social worker is as prone to human fallibility as
b that of the rest of us.
     In varying the access order, the Court of Appeal went too far. Of course, the court was
entitled, and indeed bound, to reverse or vary the judge's order, if they thought it plainly
wrong: see *Evans v Bartlam*[1] and *Re F (a minor) (wardship: appeal)*[2]. But, for the reasons
given by my noble and learned friend, Viscount Dilhorne, it is not possible to say that the
judge's access order in favour of the grandparents was wrong. On the contrary it was
c plainly right.
     Lane J was careful to refrain from passing any judgment on the grandfather or his
daughter (the mother of the children) but made an order, the fulfilment of which would
have maintained and encouraged a continuing relationship between the grandchildren
and the grandparents whose help had always been immediately and generously
forthcoming in the various crises into which the breakdown of the marriage between
d their parents had plunged the children from time to time. Where a trial judge, who has
seen and heard the parties in a custody case, refrains from criticising individuals, there is
often very good reason. The present case is a good illustration. Judicial restraint was
needed, if any good was to be done for the children. A swingeing condemnation of
mother or grandfather would only embitter an already distraught family life and might
also influence the social workers who would be exercising the care entrusted to the local
e authority. There was little or no chance of a happy family life for the children, save with
their grandparents, until their mother was sufficiently recovered to have the care of
them. And, when their mother recovers, as it is to be hoped she will, the children and
the mother will need all the support, financial and in terms of loving care, that they can
get from the grandparents. The judge's order, taken as a whole, was designed to help in
the reconstruction of the children's family life. The care order in favour of the local
f authority must be seen as a support in time of trouble, not a preferred alternative. But,
and I greatly regret to have to say it, the terms of the Court of Appeal's judgment and
their order, if left unchallenged, are more likely to destroy than to mend this family
life. Nor am I prepared to assume that what the Court of Appeal has said would not
influence the social workers in exercising their responsibilities under the care order.
     I would mention one further consideration. The grandparents, it is reasonable to
g hope, will live to be available long after the local authority's period of duty of care has
come to an end. The two children's future may be significantly better if their relationship
with their grandparents has been nurtured and developed. In the long term, as well as
the short term, the loving care of one's family is more important than the care, however
dedicated, of a local authority. When Lane J forebore from critical comment, she was
wise and far-seeing.
h The temptation to substitute one's own opinion for that of the trial judge (or to state
an opinion where the judge has preferred silence) is well known to all who have exercised
appellate jurisdiction in custody cases. I would not be so bold as to claim I have always
successfully resisted it. But it must be resisted, if error and injustice are to be avoided.
The Court of Appeal has, broadly speaking, three courses open to it, if it be minded to
reverse or vary a custody order. First, if the evidence is such that it is able to demonstrate
j that the order was wrong, it will allow the appeal and make the appropriate order.
Secondly, if satisfied that the order was wrong but unsure on the evidence what order
ought to be made, the court can remit the case to the judge (or to another judge) with

---

1   [1937] 2 All ER 646, [1937] AC 473
2   [1976] 1 All ER 417, [1976] Fam 238

such directions for the care and control of the child in the meantime as it thinks best in the child's interest. Thirdly, and exceptionally, the court may hear evidence in order to *a* resolve its doubts. But at the end of the day the court may not intervene unless it is satisfied either that the judge exercised his discretion on a wrong principle or that, the judge's decision being so plainly wrong, he must have exercised his discretion wrongly.

Since there is no reason to doubt the wisdom of the judge's order at the time it was made, I would allow the appeal to the extent of restoring the order. It is accepted by all concerned that the family circumstances have changed since the order was made. The *b* proper course is for application to be made to a judge of the Family Division for an order that is now appropriate. Meanwhile the children will remain where they are, and in the care of the local authority.

Appeal allowed.

c

Solicitors: *Chatterton & Co* (for the appellant); *Knapp Fisher & Co* (for the mother); *Official Solicitor.*

Mary Rose Plummer   Barrister.

Church of Scientology of California v Department of Health and Social Security and others.

a

COURT OF APPEAL

b   STEPHENSON, BRANDON AND TEMPLEMAN LJJ
15th, 16th, 17th, 18th, 19th, 22nd JANUARY 1979

Discovery – Production of documents – Confidence – Undertaking not to make improper use of disclosed documents – Court's discretion to restrict production unless undertaking given – Court ordering that discovery of medical records be refused unless to a medical practitioner – Court
c   *further ordering that discovery of other documents be refused unless party's solicitor gave undertaking that documents would not be used for collateral or ulterior purpose – Whether court has inherent jurisdiction to restrict production subject to conditions – RSC Ord 24, r 9.*

By three actions which were consolidated the plaintiffs, a religious sect, sued the Department of Health and Social Security and two of its senior officials for libel in respect of information released to the press by the Minister of Health and letters written by the
d   officials to health authorities in Sweden and Canada which suggested that the plaintiffs were dangerous charlatans who gave inexpert medical treatment to mentally ill people which made their condition worse rather than better. The defendants filed defences alleging justification and fair comment. In the course of mutual discovery in the action the defendants served on the plaintiffs a list of documents in which they objected, on the ground of confidentiality, to unrestricted production of medical records and certain
e   letters from people (including potential witnesses for the defence) who had written to the department complaining about the plaintiffs and their methods. The master made an order in the terms requested by the defendants, excusing them from giving inspection of (i) the medical records except to a medical practitioner nominated by the plaintiffs on his giving an undertaking not to disclose the contents and (ii) the other documents in
f   question unless the plaintiffs' solicitor gave an undertaking that the documents would not be shown nor their contents revealed to anyone other than counsel for the plaintiffs and that the plaintiffs would not use the documents for any purpose collateral or ulterior to the conduct of the action. On appeal by the plaintiffs, the judge affirmed the order. The plaintiffs appealed to the Court of Appeal, contending (i) that the court had no jurisdiction under a general discretion to make the order, or if there was such a discretion there were no grounds for exercising it. There was evidence and material before the
g   court that the plaintiffs had in the past had a policy of harassing critics in order to discourage them from continuing with their criticisms.

Held – (i) Although under RSC Ord 24, r 9[a] a party to litigation normally had the right of unrestricted inspection of those documents disclosed by the other party on discovery
h   and for which privilege was not claimed, the court had, as part of its inherent jurisdiction to ensure that the ambit of discovery was not wider than necessary to dispose fairly of the action or to prevent conduct which might amount to an abuse of the process of the court or a contempt, a general power to impose restrictions on inspection, if for example there was a real risk of the right of inspection being used for a collateral purpose. Such a restriction could be imposed either by refusing an order except on an undertaking being
j   given or by granting an order conditional on an undertaking being given (see p 103 c to e, p 104 e, p 105 e to g, p 106 c to p 107 a, p 112 d e, p 113 h j, p 114 a d e and p 116 d to h, post); *Warner-Lambert Co v Glaxo Laboratories Ltd* [1975] RPC 354, *Alterskye v Scott*

---

a   Rule 9, so far as material, is set out at p 102 g, post

[1948] 1 All ER 469 and *Riddick v Thames Board Mills Ltd* [1977] 3 All ER 677 applied;
McIvor v Southern Health and Social Services Board [1978] 2 All ER 625 distinguished.

    (ii) Because there was a real risk that an unnecessarily wide circulation of information
obtained by the plaintiffs on discovery might lead to harassment of persons who had
written to the department by over-zealous supporters of the plaintiffs either in England
or abroad, some restriction on inspection of the defendants' documents by the plaintiffs
was required. However, the restrictions imposed by the master were too restrictive and
the court would substitute an order in terms agreed by the parties. To that extent the
appeal would be allowed (see p 109 *f g*, p 110 *e*, p 112 *e f*, p 113 *f* to *h*, p 114 *e f*, p 115 *g*
to *f* and p 116 *a*, post).

Notes
For objections to production of documents on discovery, see 13 Halsbury's Laws (4th
Edn), paras 67–95, and for cases on the subject, see 18 Digest 177–122, 902–942.

Cases referred to in judgments
Alterskye v Scott [1948] 1 All ER 469, 18 Digest (Reissue) 62, 426.
Bustros v White (1876) 1 QBD 423, 45 LJQB 642, 34 LT 835, 3 Char Pr Cas 229, CA, 18
    Digest (Reissue) 71, 499.
Coles and Ravenshear, Re [1907] 1 KB1, 76 LJKB 27, 95 LT 750, CA, 51 Digest (Repl) 806,
    3626.
Crompton (Alfred) Amusement Machines Ltd v Customs and Excise Comrs (No 2) [1973] 2 All
    ER 1199, [1974] AC 405, [1973] 3 WLR 268, HL, 18 Digest (Reissue) 102, 756.
D v National Society for the Prevention of Cruelty to Children [1977] 1 All ER 589, [1978] AC
    171, [1977] 2 WLR 201, 76 LGR 5, HL.
Foot v Associated Newspapers Group Ltd (19th January 1977) unreported.
Hope v Brash [1897] 2 QB 188, [1895–9] All ER Rep 343, 66 LJQB 653, 76 LT 823, CA,
    18 Digest (Reissue) 71, 500.
Hubbard v Vosper [1972] 1 All ER 1023, [1972] 2 QB 84, [1972] 2 WLR 389, CA, 13
    Digest (Reissue) 121, 1002.
McIvor v Southern Health and Social Services Board [1978] 2 All ER 625, [1978] 1 WLR 757,
    HL.
Piller (Anton) K G v Manufacturing Processes Ltd [1976] 1 All ER 779, [1976] Ch 55, [1976]
    2 WLR 162, [1976] RPC 719, CA.
Printers and Finishers Ltd v Holloway [1961] RPC 77, CA.
Riddick v Thames Board Mills Ltd [1977] 3 All ER 677, [1977] QB 881, [1977] 3 WLR 63,
    CA.
Science Research Council v Nasse [1978] 3 All ER 1196, [1979] QB 144, [1978] 3 WLR 754,
    [1978] ICR 1124, CA.
Warner-Lambert Co v Glaxo Laboratories Ltd [1975] RPC 354, CA, 36 (2) Digest (Reissue)
    1272, 3621.
Woodworth v Conroy, Conroy v Woodworth [1976] 1 All ER 107, [1976] QB 884, [1976] 2
    WLR 338, CA.

Interlocutory appeal
By writs dated 23rd July, 6th August and 10th September 1974 the plaintiffs, the Church
of Scientology of California, sued the defendants, the Department of Health and Social
Security, George Godber and John Cashman, for damages for libel. By order dated 9th
June 1975 the actions were consolidated. By notice dated 2nd May 1977 the defendants
applied for an order that they be excused from giving inspection of certain documents
unless the plaintiffs, by their solicitor, gave an undertaking within 14 days not to reveal
the contents of the documents to anyone other than the plaintiffs' counsel and not to use
them for any purpose ulterior to the conduct of the action, and that the defendants be
excused from giving inspection of other documents comprising medical records and
hospital notes other than to a registered medical practitioner appointed by the
plaintiffs. On 11th May 1977 Master Lubbock made the order in the terms asked for.

The plaintiffs appealed but on 22nd February 1978 Melford Stevenson J dismissed their
appeal. The facts are set out in the judgments of Stephenson LJ and Templeman LJ.

Benet Hytner QC and *John Hamilton* for the plaintiffs.
Peter Bowsher QC for the defendants.

STEPHENSON LJ. This appeal concerns discovery in three consolidated actions for
libel brought by the Church of Scientology of California, the first action against the
Department of Health and Social Security alone, the second against that department and
its principal medical officer, Sir George Godber, and the third against the department and
an under-secretary in it, Mr John Cashman.

On 11th May 1977 Master Lubbock made an extraordinary order. Paragraph 3, sub-
paras (3) and (4) of that order are as follows:

'(3). The defendants be excused from giving inspection of the documents
numbered 7, 30, 150, 166, 171, 205, 305, 306, 314, 315 and 323 in Part 1 of
Schedule 1 of their List of Documents served on the 26th February 1977, unless
within 14 days the Plaintiffs by their solicitor, Stephen M. Bird, expressly undertake
that the said documents will not be shown nor their contents revealed to anyone
other than Counsel for the Plaintiffs and that the Plaintiffs will not use the said
documents for any purpose collateral to or ulterior to the conduct of this action;

'(4). The Defendants be excused from producing for inspection the documents
numbered 146, 152, 177, 178, 179, 202, 239, 240, 241, and 424 in Part 1 of Schedule
1 of their said List of Documents other than to a registered medical practitioner
appointed by the Plaintiffs for the purpose of these consolidated actions and upon
his expressly undertaking in writing that he will not disclose the contents thereof.'

On 22nd February 1978 Melford Stevenson J affirmed that order by dismissing the
appeal from it.

The writs in these three actions were issued on 23rd July, 6th August and 10th
September 1974. The allegations claimed to be defamatory are in effect that the plaintiffs
are dangerous charlatans who give inexpert medical treatment to mentally sick persons
and make them worse rather than better; and that they are an undesirable and evil
body. Those allegations were made in background notes issued by the Minister of
Health to the press in 1968, the subject of the first action, and in letters in the other two
actions, one by Sir George Godber to a health authority in Sweden, and the other by Mr
Cashman to another health authority in Ontario, Canada.

The defences in all three consolidated actions contain pleas of justification and fair
comment in paras 5 and 6, and annexed to them are particulars referring to ten cases of
mentally sick persons whom they allege to have been so treated, two of whom are now
dead.

In the course of the proceedings, and that course has not been swift or expeditious for
various reasons, the defendants have made and served a list of documents. Paragraphs 2,
3 and 4 of that list are in these terms:

'2. The defendants object to produce the documents numbered 146, 152, 177,
178, 179, 202, 239, 240, 241 and 424 in Part 1 of the said Schedule 1 other than to
the plaintiff's medical adviser on the ground that such documents contain extracts
from patients' medical records or material based thereon and are thus confidential
in nature and ought not otherwise to be disclosed.

'3. The defendants object to produce document numbered 7 in Part 1 of the said
Schedule 1 unless the plaintiff, by its proper officer, gives an undertaking not to use
any of the material contained in the document otherwise than for purposes
reasonably necessary for the conduct of the actions, and not for any collateral or
ulterior purpose. The defendants further object to disclosing any part of the letters
comprising the document which might reveal identifying details of the writer

thereof or the individuals referred to therein. These objections are made to preserve
the necessary relationship of confidence between the Secretary of State for Social   *a*
Services (formerly the Minister) and his Department and those who write to him
regarding matters on which the Secretary of State ought to be informed.

'4. The defendants object to produce the documents numbered 30, 150, 166,
171, 205, 305, 306, 314, 315 and 323 in Part 1 of the said Schedule 1 unless the
plaintiff gives an undertaking in respect thereof in similar fashion to that mentioned
in the preceding paragraph. The defendants further object to disclosing any part of   *b*
the said document which might reveal identifying details of those who corresponded
with the person named in Part 1 of the Schedule in respect of such documents.'

Now the documents referred to in para 2, the first of those three paragraphs, are
hospital notes and medical reports on the ten patients to whom I have referred, and in
that list it is asked that the contents of those documents should only be disclosed to the
plaintiffs' medical adviser and nobody else, and that is the order that has been made by   *c*
the master and affirmed by the judge in respect of those documents.

The second head of documents to which objection to production is made is no 7
referred to in para 3, and that contains 250 letters from some 30 or 40 persons (we are
told) who have given information to the defendants adverse to the plaintiffs. The
documents referred to in the last paragraph are letters passing between a Mr Maurice
Johnson and some six other 'renegades', persons (we are told) who have been scientologists,   *d*
and allegations in the pleadings show that Mr Johnson is also a person who has been
treated by the plaintiffs.

The objection taken in the last two paragraphs of the list of documents which I have
read is to producing those letters, the Maurice Johnson letters or the other informants'
letters, to the plaintiffs unless the plaintiffs, by their proper officer, give the undertaking
which I have read.   *e*

It will be noticed that the order under appeal goes further than that objection because
it forbids production to any proper officer, or an undertaking by any proper officer, other
than Stephen Bird, the plaintiffs' solicitor. The undertaking which he is required to give
on the order, and which the proper officer was requested to give in this list, is an
undertaking which the law implies, as is shown by the case of *Alterskye v Scott*[1]. The way
in which these objections are taken in this list is the same as that in which it was taken   *f*
in that case, and in *Foot v Associated Newspapers Group Ltd*[2], in which the following order
was made on 19th January 1977 by Ackner J, in these terms:

'... there be inspection of documents within 7 days of the service of the
defendants' list. That the plaintiff be excused from giving inspection of the
documents at Item 5 of Schedule 1, Part 1 of the plaintiff's list of documents served   *g*
on 30th March 1976, unless within 14 days the defendants by their solicitors
expressly undertake that the said documents will not be shown to anyone other than
the second defendant, and the legal advisers to the defendants [the Associated
Newspapers Group Ltd and the second defendant] including [and there are named
two persons] and expert medical advisers and that the defendants will not use the
documents for any purpose collateral to or ulterior to the conduct of this action.'   *h*

No claim is made in this list of documents for privilege. Confidentiality, as is
recognised and was declared by the House of Lords in *Alfred Crompton Amusement
Machines Ltd v Customs and Excise Comrs (No 2)*[3], is not a ground of privilege although it
may be relevant to the question of privilege. Counsel appearing for all the defendants,
has affirmed and re-affirmed in this court that he is making and can make no claim to
privilege for any of the documents which are the subject of the order under appeal on the   *j*

1   [1948] 1 All ER 469
2   (19th January 1977) unreported
3   [1973] 2 All ER 1199, [1974] AC 405

grounds of public interest. The only privilege claimed is claimed for certain documents
a in part 2 of the first schedule and those documents are not those with which we are
concerned.

The judge decided to dismiss the appeal and affirm the master's order, after some
argument, on a balance of conflicting interests: the balance of conflicting interests stated
by Lord Denning MR in *Riddick v Thames Board Mills Ltd*[1]. Lord Denning MR referred
to the public interest in discovering truth so that justice may be done between the
b parties, and how that had to be put into the scales against the public interest in preserving
privacy and protecting confidential information. It was in balancing those two public
interests that the judge came to his conclusion that the master's order should stand.

The judge had before him certain evidence, to which I shall be referring. The master
had no evidence, but he had full particulars setting out copious extracts from documents
attributed to the plaintiffs and their founder, Mr Ron Hubbard; and I shall have to refer
c later to the points that were taken before him and the points taken before the judge. At
the moment all I would say is this, that the judge must, by implication (although we are
not told that he did so expressly), have rejected a submission that there was no jurisdiction
in the court to make an order depriving a party of the right to inspect documents which
were not protected by any privilege claimed.

Two questions are raised by the notice of appeal which is put on three grounds:

d   '(i) That save in certain established instances e.g. under the Administration of
      Justice Act 1970 sections 31 or 32 or where trade secrets are involved, there is no
      general discretion in the Court, where a party is not claiming that documents are
      privileged from production, to limit the right of the other party to inspect the
      documents disclosed by the first party; (ii) That if there is such a general discretion
e   the principal consideration which should govern the exercise thereof is that a
      litigant should be able to inspect the document disclosed by his opponent in order
      to prepare his case; (iii) That there were in any event in the instant case no or no
      sufficient grounds advanced or established which could or did derogate from the
      generality of the proposition in (ii) above and that there were no grounds to support
      the manner in which the learned Judge exercised the general discretionary power
f   (if it exists) to limit inspection.'

So the first question this court has to consider is: has the court jurisdiction to restrict
the discovery (production, that is, for inspection) of documents in the way in which it has
been restricted or in some such way, as I have said, the judge must by implication have
held that we have? Clearly if there is no such jurisdiction, the judge went wrong in law
and this court could and should reverse him.

If, however, the answer to the first question is, Yes, and there is such jurisdiction, there
g then arises , subject to a further question of the form of restriction about which I shall
have to say something later, the second question: was there material on which the court
could restrict production and inspection in the way it has been restricted? There, as has
been pointed out by counsel for the defendants, this court, before it can reverse the judge
must, of course, be satisfied that he was plainly wrong in the exercise of his discretion,
h and it has to be shown that in balancing the various factors and conflicting public
interests he did leave out something or put into the scales something which it was wrong
for him in the one case to leave out and in the other to put in; or that from the order
which he did make this court can conclude that he must have given the wrong weight
to some very important factor, a much more difficult operation for an appellant to carry
out.

j   Counsel for the plaintiffs, who has said everything that could be said in support of this
appeal, has conveniently submitted to the court five typed propositions, but I am not
going to read those because to do so I think would be unnecessary and lengthen a
judgment which I am conscious may well be too long without them. But the appeal does

---

1   [1977] 3 All ER 677 at 687, [1977] QB 881 at 895–896

raise important matters so I shall make no further apology for going into them at no little
length.

Nor am I going to read every rule of RSC Ord 24, the order comprising the Rules of
the Supreme Court which now cover discovery and inspection of documents, although
there is also a provision of RSC Ord 77 which must be read, as one of the parties to these
appeals is a government department and these proceedings are therefore civil proceedings
against the Crown, but these rules, except rr 1 and 2, are applied to them by RSC Ord 77,
rr 1 and 12.

The parties to an action are required by RSC Ord 24 to make mutual discovery, first
of all by disclosing what documents are or have been in their possession, custody or
power relating to the matters in question in the action (r 1(1)) and secondly to produce
those documents for inspection. They first of all make that discovery, either with or
without an order under rr 2 and 3, by exchanging a list of documents set out in two
schedules. As is well known, the first schedule contains the documents which are in
their possession, custody or power, and the second schedule those documents which are
no longer in their possession, custody or power. But the form given in Appendix A no
26 makes it plain that the first schedule is divided into two parts: those documents, in the
first part, which the party making discovery does not object to produce for inspection,
and those documents, in the second part, which he does object to produce for inspection.
If the party objects to produce documents for inspection he has to state the grounds. If
the documents have left his possession, custody or power, he has to state when, and what
has become of them, and in whose possession they now are. That is provided for by RSC
Ord 24, r 5(1) and (2). If his objection to production is by a claim of privilege from
production, that claim must be made in the list with a sufficient statement of the
grounds of privilege (r 5(2)). But it is clear from r 13(2) that objection may be made on
another ground than privilege, and that is the position here. Objection has been made
in this list of documents on another ground than privilege.

If a party does not make or serve such a list on the other party, the court may make
orders of different kinds ordering him to do so (that is r 3) but it will only order him to
do so if of opinion that discovery is necessary, or necessary at the stage when applied for,
either for disposing fairly of the cause or matter or for saving costs (that is rr 8 and 13(1):
compare r 2(5), where 'the action' takes the place of 'the cause or matter'). After
discovery of documents by disclosing what documents are or have been in the parties'
possession, custody or power, there comes discovery by producing documents for
inspection, and a party who has served this list, by r 9, a rule of importance in this case
which I therefore quote—

'. . . must allow the other party to inspect the documents referred to in the list (other
than any which he objects to produce) and to take copies thereof and, accordingly,
he must when he serves the list on the other party also serve on him a notice stating
a time within 7 days after the service thereof at which the said documents may be
inspected at a place specified in the notice.'

Those words 'must allow the other party to inspect the documents referred to in the list'
are strongly relied on by counsel for the plaintiffs in this case.

If a party objects to produce any document for inspection the court may, on the
application of the party entitled to inspection, make an order for production of the
documents in question for inspection at such time and place, and in such manner as it
thinks fit, but only again if of the opinion that the order is necessary fairly for disposing
of the cause or matter or for saving costs: that is r 11(1) which is expressly made subject
to r 13(1). There is provision in the rules for the parties agreeing to dispense with or
limit discovery of documents by disclosure, or the court may by order limit discovery to
specified documents or matters or dispense with it if satisfied that discovery is not
necessary, or not necessary at that stage of the cause or matter, either for disposing fairly
of the cause or matter or for saving costs, and that is rr 1(2), 2(5) and 3(3). There is also
provision for the court ordering further discovery under r 7, but none of those rules has

a any application, as I read them, to production of documents for inspection; they relate
only to disclosure of their existence, not of their contents.

Finally, all those are to be 'without prejudice to any rule of law which authorises or
requires the witholding of any document on the ground that the disclosure of it would
be injurious to the public interest': that is r 15 (compare RSC Ord 77, r 12(2)), and r 17
empowers the court to revoke or vary any existing order made under any of these rules
on sufficient cause being shown.

b These rules then require one party to produce to the other for inspection and copying
all the first party's documents relating to matters in question in the action, subject to two
restrictions. The first restriction is that the production of documents is required only if
and in so far as they are necessary for disposing fairly of the cause or matter or for saving
costs: see rr 11 and 13(1) to which I have referred. Secondly, production is not required
of those documents to which valid objection has been taken by a claim of privilege, or on
c any other ground upheld by the court or perhaps taken by the court as by a rule of law
to be witheld in the public interest: see rr 11, 13 and 15 to which I have referred. There
is nothing that I can find *in the rules* which expresses or implies a power in the court to
deny production or inspection to the other party, or to order production to a third person
not authorised by the other party to act as his agent to inspect them or copy them, or to
order production to a third person, whether authorised by the other party or not, with
d a condition that he should not show them to his principal, the other party, or give him
a copy. Nor is there anything in the rules to indicate what other grounds than claim of
privilege may support an objection to production, or whether those grounds go beyond
objections to production as unnecessary for disposing fairly of the cause or matter or for
saving costs, or perhaps as injurious to public interest.

Counsel for the defendants contends that there is jurisdiction, first under RSC Ord 24
e itself and secondly under the court's inherent jurisdiction, to make such orders as have
been made in this case. On the first question whether there is any power in the court,
either under RSC Ord 24 or under its inherent jurisdiction, to prevent a party at any stage
from himself inspecting a document not protected by privilege, or receiving a copy of it,
if he wants to, there seems to be no express authority, or, rather, the point never appears
to have been taken and decided, at least since 1876. The judgment of Lawton LJ, in
f *Woodworth v Conroy*[1] seems equivocal, favouring no discretion in one passage[2] and the
existence of discretion in another[3]. Against any such discretion would appear to be the
language of RSC Ord 24, r 9 and the decision of this court (eight judges strong) in *Bustros
v White*[4] that the predecessor of RSC Ord 24, r 9, though couched in very permissive
terms, perpetuated the old equity practice under the Chancery Procedure Act 1852,
which gave a party inspection as of right and which was by the Supreme Court of
g Judicature Act 1873 to prevail over the common law practice of treating inspection as a
matter of discretion: see Bray on Discovery[5]. In favour of such discretion would appear
to be the language of RSC Ord 24, rr 11 and 13, and the established practice (i) approved
by this court in *Hope v Brash*[6] in actions for libel, of refusing to a plaintiff suing a
newspaper, inspection of a document supplied to the newspaper containing the libel
published in the newspaper but adding nothing to the publication except the name of
h the author, and (ii) in actions for infringement of patents or otherwise concerned with
trade secrets, of restricting inspection of documents containing trade secrets to persons
other than the party concerned, whether an individual or a limited company: see
Warner-Lambert Co v Glaxo Laboratories Ltd[7] and cases there cited.

---

j 1 [1976] 1 All ER 107, [1976] QB 884
2 [1976] 1 All ER 107 at 111, [1976] QB 884 at 890
3 [1976] 1 All ER 107 at 112, [1976] QB 884 at 891
4 (1876) 1 QBD 423
5 The Principles and Practice of Discovery (1885), p 152
6 [1897] 2 QB 188, [1895–9] All ER Rep 343
7 [1975] RPC 354

In none of those cases does the point of jurisdiction appear to have been taken, but the basis of those practices appears to be necessity in the interest of justice. It may have been merely no necessity or no necessity at that stage for fairly disposing of the action, which may or may not be the same thing as necessity in the interests of justice; but though Buckley LJ in *Warner-Lambert Co v Glaxo Laboratories Ltd*[1] talks of unrestricted inspection serving no useful purpose and the judgment of Rigby LJ in *Hope v Brash*[2] struggles to derive the restriction on disclosing documents supplied to a newspaper from similar words to those of RSC Ord 24, r 13(1) in the old rules, I find it difficult to be certain that the restriction is based on that principle or its expression in the language of any such provision in the rules. In the newspaper libel cases the restriction seems to rest on public interest in preserving the anonymity of informants.

I am, however, far from being persuaded by counsel for the plaintiffs that the restrictive practice of discovery where trade secrets are concerned is derived from special statutes or rules or from anything but the necessity to protect one trader from the abuse by another trader of the powerful weapon furnished by discovery where the weapon is particularly liable to such abuse: see Terrell on the Law of Patents[3].

The terms of RSC Ord 103, r 26, on which counsel for the plaintiffs relied, seem to be against him on this point rather than for him; for the exclusion of RSC Ord 24, rr 1 and 2 from applying to proceedings within RSC Ord 103 by r 26(3) in my opinion supports the applicability of the rest of RSC Ord 24 to such cases, as does the judgment of Lord Evershed MR in *Printers and Finishers Ltd v Holloway*[4]. Indeed, I find that the leading judgment of Buckley LJ in the *Warner-Lambert* case[1], which was cited to this court in the most recent case on discovery of *Science Research Council v Nasse*[5], throws much light on our problems and assists us to make the right order in this case.

Counsel for the defendants, on the other hand, has not persuaded me that any of the rules of RSC Ord 24 or any other order entitles the court to deny to a litigating party inspection of an unprivileged document of which inspection by somebody is necessary for fairly disposing of an action. The words of RSC Ord 24, r 9 are mandatory, as I have already stressed. The Rules of the Supreme Court may be the hand-maiden, not the mistress, of the court (see *Re Coles v Ravenshear*[6]) but they are made by the Rules Committee under s 99 of the Supreme Court of Judicature Act 1925 to be obeyed by the parties and enforced by the courts and the courts cannot disobey their own mandatory instructions by re-writing the rules as they may think they should have been written, any more than they can re-write a statute: see *McIvor v Southern Health and Social Services Board*[7]. There the House of Lords held, overruling decisions of this court, that s 32(1) of the Administration of Justice Act 1970 which gave the court power on the application of a party to certain proceedings, to order production to the applicant, did not give the court power to order production to medical advisers nominated by the parties. Nor does the practice approved by this court in *Anton Piller K G v Manufacturing Processes Ltd*[8] suggest any power in the rules to bend the rules. On the contrary it indicates[9] the power in the court to order or permit conduct related to discovery which is not covered by any of the rules, though it may help counsel for the defendants towards establishing the inherent jurisdiction of the court to restrict discovery in an appropriate case.

The object of mutual discovery is to give each party before trial all documentary

1   [1975] RPC 354
2   [1897] 2 QB 188, [1895–9] All ER Rep 343
3   12th Edn (1971), p 350, para 900
4   [1961] RPC 77 at 78
5   [1978] 3 All ER 1196, [1979] QB 144
6   [1907] 1 KB 1 at 4
7   [1978] 2 All ER 625, [1978] 1 WLR 757
8   [1976] 1 All ER 779, [1976] Ch 55
9   See [1976] 1 All ER 779 at 783, [1976] Ch 55 at 61

a material of the other party so that he can consider its effect on his own case and his opponent's case, and decide how to carry on his proceedings or whether to carry them on at all. The sight of one document may lead a plaintiff to abandon his action or a defendant to throw up his defence, or it may lead a party's legal advisers to advise one of those courses but may not deter the client from pursuing his action or his defence against their advice.

b Another object is to enable each party to put before the court all relevant documentary evidence, and it may be oral evidence indicated by documents, so that justice can be done. This object is achieved by each party inspecting all documents disclosed if it wants to. Unless a party is in person, production would ordinarily be by a solicitor to a solicitor. Solicitors are a convenient receptacle or screen, if I may say so without disrespect, for the other side's documents. Some documents' effect on litigation is better judged by legal advisers than by the parties themselves or their agents. Some documents c are better valued or appreciated by experts, eg an accountant or an architect or a doctor. Some documents are better not seen by an individual plaintiff or a defendant, for example in infant cases. In some cases (like this) the party is a body corporate and inspection must be by the eyes of servants or agents.

Can then an individual litigant insist that he or she sees what his or her legal advisers see? Can a litigating company insist on some servant or agent seeing what its legal d advisers see? The answer, I think, must normally be, Yes. If a party objects to the other party inspecting except by an agent can the other party insist on personal inspection, if the party is an individual, or inspection by any particular officer or officers, or servant or agent, if the party is a corporation? Or has the court power under the rules, or outside them by inherent jurisdiction, to deny inspection to a party and restrict it to an appropriate servant or agent approved by the court, or by the other side, or by both, for e instance to its solicitors and to them only, or to its medical advisers and to them only, where (as here) the party is a body corporate?

The authorities seem to me to show that one party can object to a particular agent appointed by the other party to inspect, and the court will uphold the objection and restrict inspection to an agent considered suitable, appropriate or approved. They also show that one party can object to the other party, whether an individual or a corporation, f inspecting, and the court will uphold such objection and control disclosure in the interests of justice and fairness to both parties, and will restrict inspection to an approved agent on his undertaking not to disclose the inspected document or its contents to others, including his own principal, the party concerned himself or itself. This is established in the case of trade secrets and in the case of press informants on the authorities which I have already cited.

g Counsel for the plaintiffs submits that RSC Ord 24, r 9 does not permit the court to deny a party the right to inspect himself or the right to inspect by some agent of his choice, and that applies to a corporation, which has a right to select its own officers or agents for the purpose of inspecting documents produced by the other side for inspection. He submits that the words of RSC Ord 24, r 9 are as clear as the words of ss 31 and 32 of the Administration of Justice Act 1970. Now the only point of jurisdiction h taken in McIvor v Southern Health and Social Services Board[1] was as to the court's jurisdiction under that Act; but there are two illuminating passages in the judgment of Sir Robert Lowry LCJ which were approved by different members of their Lordships' House in that case. Lord Scarman agreed with Sir Robert Lowry LCJ when he said[2]:

'If Parliament had wished to enact provisions for discovery, limited in the ordinary case to medical advisers, it could have done so, instead of using language j importing conventional discovery. It could still enact such provisions but not I hope, before very careful deliberation.'

---

1   [1978] 2 All ER 625, [1978] 1 WLR 757
2   [1978] 2 All ER 625 at 629, [1978] 1 WLR 757 at 763

Lord Russell of Killowen approved this statement by Sir Robert Lowry LCJ[1]:

> 'The High Court has an inherent jurisdiction to attach conditions to most orders **a**
> in the interests of justice, but I do not think it has any jurisdiction to order disclosure
> to the applicant on condition that disclosure is *not* made to the applicant (or to his
> legal advisers).'

It is I think implicit in those speeches and those quotations that conventional discovery
is regarded as ordering production for inspection by a party or his legal advisers, but the **b**
question never arose in that case whether there could be production for inspection by the
legal adviser but not by the party himself. The only issue was between an order for
production for inspection by the party or his legal adviser on the one side and an
inspection by a medical adviser on the other side. So I get no help from that case in
deciding this point, although it does, I think, emphasise what is perhaps obvious that in
the ordinary course inspection must be inspection by the party himself, herself or itself. **c**

What the court is being asked to do, counsel for the plaintiffs submits, is contrary to
r 9 as no privilege is claimed. I am of opinion that, as no privilege is claimed, the court
can only act contrary to the rule if compliance with the rule is unnecessary for fairly
disposing of the action or if the court has inherent jurisdiction to act contrary to the rule.

Counsel for the defendants has not submitted that compliance is not necessary for the
purpose of disposing fairly of the action or of saving costs, and I doubt if such a **d**
submission could be made with success. I am of opinion that counsel for the defendants
is, however, right in submitting that the court has inherent jurisdiction to prevent the
abuse of its own process, or, as it is sometimes termed, 'process of law', and that that
jurisdiction gives it the power which was taken by the master and by the judge in this
case.

The court has always, in my judgment, inherent jurisdiction to prevent abuse of that **e**
process, and indeed must take steps to prevent it of its own motion, as where illegality is
brought to its attention. Discovery, including production of documents for inspection,
is part of its process to enable an action to be carried to a just conclusion. As Lord
Denning MR said in *Riddick's* case[2]: 'A party who seeks discovery of documents gets it
on condition that he will make use of them only for the purposes of that action, and no
other purpose.' To use a document produced for inspection for a collateral or ulterior **f**
purpose is a misuse against which the court will proceed for contempt or by injunction:
see *Alterskye v Scott*[3]. But that proceeding may be after the abuse has taken place. The
court has power to prevent or reduce the chance of such an abuse taking place by an
undertaking. As it seems to me, it can do it in two ways; it can do it either by refusing
an order except on an undertaking or it can do it by giving an order conditional on an
undertaking being given. Which way it does it does not seem to me to matter, and **g**
seems to me a question of form rather than substance, with all respect to counsel for the
plaintiffs' argument.

Furthermore I do not think it matters in most cases whether the object of preventing
an abuse of process is achieved or attempted to be achieved by restricting inspection to
a person other than the party or only by refusing to order any inspection unless the party
undertakes not to misuse the material. In most cases, an undertaking is unnecessary **h**
because it is implied, as was pointed out in *Alterskye v Scott*[3] where an undertaking was
refused. In the remainder, an undertaking by the party himself or by his counsel or
solicitor may be enough; but it seems to me that there is a very small hard core of cases
where the undertaking is not enough and where the court may come to the conclusion
that the party cannot be trusted not to misuse the information and so abuse the process

j

---

1 [1978] 2 All ER 625 at 629, [1978] 1 WLR 757 at 762
2 [1977] 3 All ER 677 at 688, [1977] QB 881 at 896
3 [1948] 1 All ER 469

of discovery. That is really what counsel for the defendants is maintaining in this case in
a support of the order under appeal; and in the form in which it is made, particularly that
which relates to the hospital notes and medical reports, it seems to me that the order
must be justified on that basis, or it must be revoked or modified.

If this is a case of threatened abuse of process, it seems to me unnecessary to decide how
far the broad statement of principle laid down by Lord Denning MR in *D v National
Society for the Prevention of Cruelty to Children*[1] for balancing one public interest against
b another, has survived the pruning it received at the hands of the House of Lords in
reversing the decision of this court. It seems to me only necessary to remember that that
statement was made and modified in a case where it is clear from more than one of the
judgments in both courts that privilege from production was claimed under RSC Ord 24,
r 5(2).

Treating this case as a case of threatened or likely or foreseeable abuse of process, I
c proceed to consider whether the order made can be justified on that ground, or whether
some other order ought to be made of a restrictive character, or whether counsel for the
plaintiffs is right in saying that even if this court has jurisdiction, on the material which
it has it should none the less make an unrestricted order.

On this second question, argument, or at any rate emphasis, has changed, as so often
in this court, from the form or forms which it took in the courts below, largely I think
d in response to indications from the court itself, but partly as a result of the decision in
Riddick's case[2] and, on the other side, the decision in *McIvor's case*[3] which had not been
reported at the time when the master and judge reached their decisions. *Riddick's case*[2]
had been reported and was indeed referred to by the judge, but it to some extent renders
nugatory one of the grounds relied on in argument and in the affidavit by which the
defendants supported the master's order.

e If one looks at the affidavit of Mr Beaven, a senior legal assistant in the office of the
minister of the defendant department, sworn in the consolidated actions, one sees that
the grounds by which he seeks to support the order made by the master are limited. First
of all, in para 3 of his affidavit he deposes that:

f 'The documents referred to in paragraph 2 of the said List comprise extracts from
Hospital Case Notes and confidential medical reports furnished by Hospitals. Such
documents are essentially confidential in nature as they contain, as well as the case
history and diagnosis, personal details of the individuals concerned and the
treatment they received. The items in question were furnished to the Defendant
Department as the responsible Authority in matters concerning health, and it
would be contrary to the interests of the individuals concerned to afford unlimited
g disclosure in respect thereof. For these reasons it is considered that the documents
should not be disclosed other than to the Plaintiff's Medical Adviser, and upon his
expressly undertaking in writing that he will not disclose the contents thereof.'

In other words, it is the interests of the individuals who are the subject of the hospital
notes and confidential medical reports on which the objection is based.

h The next paragraph of his affidavit deals with the 250 items which are contained in
document no 7, and that is this bundle of 250 letters:

'Some letters were received direct from members of the public, others were
received by Members of Parliament from their constituents and subsequently
transmitted to or copies thereof furnished to the Defendant Department and a few
j came into the possession of the Defendant Department from other sources. Many

---

1   [1977] 1 All ER 589, [1978] AC 171
2   [1977] 3 All ER 677, [1977] QB 881
3   [1978] 2 All ER 625, [1978] 1 WLR 757

of the letters were expressed to be confidential and the conditions specified in the said paragraph 3 were imposed to preserve the necessary relationship of confidence between the Secretary of State for Social Services (formerly the Minister of Health) and his Department and those who write to him regarding matters on which the Secretary of State ought to be informed. To this end it is considered that every precaution should be taken to ensure that individuals who wrote letters should not be approached by or on behalf of the Plaintiffs, either personally or by correspondence, and that confidential letters should not be made the subject of public discussion unnecessarily.'

So the claim in respect of the letters from these 30 or 40 informants to protect them from being approached by or on behalf of the plaintiffs and to preserve the necessary relationship of confidence between such persons and the Secretary of State for Social Services, the claim getting near to a claim for Crown privilege and covering, I would have thought not merely, as counsel for the plaintiffs submits, an approach to persons who might be potential witnesses and therefore likely to be diverted or perverted from assisting in doing justice in the action between the parties, but covering also an approach which might endanger them. There is an allegation in the next paragraph that the plaintiffs—

'. . . have commenced numerous legal proceedings for the purpose of intimidating their critics and silencing criticism but have brought very few of such actions to trial, [and the deponent then goes on to refer to various documents and to a list of 43 libel suits referred to in The Toronto Sun and goes on to say:] I verily believe that the Plaintiffs have a propensity to harass individuals with libel actions and at the hearing of the Summons for Directions herein on 11th May 1977 I understood learned counsel for the Plaintiffs to claim the right to sue the authors of defamatory statements if libellous material emerged on discovery in these proceedings.'

The last paragraph, para 6 of the affidavit, deals specifically with the Maurice Johnson letters and it is those letters which it is said are—

'. . . written to and by a witness for the Defendants [that is Mr Maurice Johnson] to correspondents, whose identities are not disclosed in the Defendants' List of Documents but are potential witnesses for the Defendants and who, I would respectfully submit, ought to be protected at this stage in view of the matters referred to in the preceeding paragraph of this my Affidavit.'

Now it was decided by this court in *Riddick's* case[1] that it is an improper or collateral or ulterior use or misuse of a document disclosed in one action to make it the basis of another action for libel and that is the reason for which every member of this court agreed that Mr Riddick's action should be dismissed. So it is said by counsel for the plaintiffs that these individuals writing 250 letters, and Mr Johnson's correspondents, will not be harassed by libel actions because the court will protect them from such harassment, or it may be that bearing in mind the decision in *Riddick's* case[1], writs will never be issued based on any document which discloses their names and what they have said against the plaintiffs. It is also said that such actions would be statute-barred.

The position, in my judgment, is not quite as simple as that, first because it will still be open to the plaintiffs to threaten such individuals with libel actions and require them to go to legal advisers to tell them what the law is and that they have nothing to fear and that they can apply to have those actions stayed, and secondly, as has been pointed out by

---

1   [1977] 3 All ER 677, [1977] QB 881

counsel for the defendants, there is always the possibility of re-publication of a libel and
that might extend the period of limitation so as to remove the protection of these

a individuals from such libel actions. Still the force of that ground of potential harassment
is undoubtedly weakened by the considerations which have been put before us by
counsel for the plaintiffs.

Counsel for the defendants in this court, has transferred the weight of his argument
principally, if not entirely, to harassment—I think of all the persons concerned, whether

b as writers of letters to the defendant department or their MP's, or as the subject of
medical reports, or as possible witnesses, or as corresponding with Mr Maurice Johnson—
to harassment in the sense not of harassment by libel actions, but harassment by
accusations, by threats of blackmail or even by assault, which may prevent them from
giving evidence for the defence, or injure them or upset them whether they are witnesses
or not. Probably not, I think, on the evidence, harassment by anybody in England;

c harassment perhaps here but more probably abroad if such potential victims are to be
found abroad, where the strong arm of Mr Ron Hubbard may be suspected as likely to
pursue against what are termed 'suppressives' the policy of 'fair game', some of the
provisions of which have already been referred to in this court: see the judgment of
Megaw LJ in *Hubbard v Vosper*[1].

I bear in mind the fact that this is a different allegation from what we are told was

d made before the judge. It seems to have figured, to some extent at any rate, before the
master but not before the judge. It would be wrong in my judgment for this court to be
prevented by that circumstance from considering the weight of the evidence, or simply
because it is not stressed or may not even be mentioned in the affidavits to which
documents have been exhibited. Pleadings of course are not evidence, nor is hearsay
even in an affidavit; but the documents set out in the pleadings and the documents

e exhibited to the affidavit are, as it seems to me, evidence and material which the court
is bound to take into account in considering whether the right orders have been made in
this case, whether they can be justified or whether the plaintiffs are entitled to the
unrestricted inspection for which counsel for the plaintiffs asks.

I have carefully considered the documents to which we have been referred and some
to which we have not. I am satisfied by my consideration of the documents that there

f is a real risk that all three categories of documents may be misused, ie not for legitimate
purposes of the action but for harassment of individual patients, informants and
renegades named in them, not only by proceedings for defamation against them but by
threats and blackmail, and that they may be distributed to those in other parts of this
worldwide organisation who may misuse them in the same way.

I am thinking chiefly of the 'fair game law' against suppressive persons expounded in

g the HCO policy letter of 1st March 1965 and referred to in the particulars, and the policy
letter of 21st October 1968 cancelling publication of the policy in the interests of public
relations, but not the policy itself.

I am also impressed by the 'dead file' system set out in the particulars. The history of
Maurice Johnson is not evidence, but it is material which we are entitled to take into
account as likely to be the subject of evidence. I also take into account what is written

h about 'noisy investigations' in HCO executive letter of 5th September 1966 and the
extract in Sir John Foster's report from the HCO policy letter of 15th February 1976,
which is exhibited to the affidavit of Mr Beaven.

Again, I am impressed by Mr Hubbard's statement published in the article in the
Toronto Sun, exhibited to the same affidavit, a document which sets out the purpose of
bringing actions in Mr Hubbard's view, which I will not quote.

j Again, I have considered the affidavit of Mr Bird, the plaintiffs' solicitor, sworn in
another action, which is exhibited to the affidavit of Mr Grant, a solicitor in the office of
the Treasury Solicitor, in which Mr Bird deposes that the writ in the action was issued on

---

1 [1972] 1 All ER 1023 at 1031–1032, [1972] 2 QB 84 at 99

25th July 1974, and would not have been issued if the government had acted on Sir John Foster's report and removed the ban excluding alien scientologists, including Mr *a* Hubbard, from entering this country. I appreciate what has been sworn about that article and the manner in which English actions are conducted by Mr Parselle, the barrister, who claims in his affidavit to have had charge of the legal department of the plaintiffs in these actions since 1968, but who we are now told is in charge of the worldwide legal department also situated at Saint Hill Manor at East Grinstead, but is subject to Mr Tampion who is head of the legal department of the plaintiffs. In addition *b* to the 43 actions brought by the Church of Scientology of California in Toronto, referred to in the article, there are 29 actions brought by the plaintiffs in this country and Mr Grant has sworn that none of them has been settled on terms really favourable to the plaintiffs and only one has been fought, and that has been lost by the plaintiffs.

We have to weigh the claims of Mr Parselle and Mr Bird that the plaintiffs here do not bring proceedings for Mr Hubbard's declared purposes, or conduct them except in *c* accordance with the procedure and directions of the court, against the evidence that the founder is the de facto controller of all the organisations of this church, including the plaintiffs, whatever separation of legal entities there may be.

I am not myself impressed by the defendants' contention that the object of bringing these actions is to remove the ban on Mr Hubbard and other alien scientologists and not, therefore, to clear their name. It seems to me the two purposes very naturally and *d* understandably run together and there is nothing improper in the plaintiffs wishing to clear their name in order to enable them to carry on their work with the assistance of those who are not natives of this country, including their founder. But reading paras 8 to 11 in the particulars of the defence and the further and better particulars given under sub-para 8(a) served on 31st October 1975 and also Mr Hubbard's 1966 note to all staff on corporate status, I would need evidence, which I do not find here, that Mr Hubbard has *e* changed his position since 1966 (or about that time) and that it is now no longer the policy of this church's founder to act and to require subordinates to act and members of his church to act as those documents indicate.

I must not, however, lose sight of the important fact that there is no evidence that the plaintiffs have ever broken the law of this country or disobeyed an order of the courts of this country. Why should the defendants fear, says counsel for the plaintiffs, that the *f* plaintiffs should break the law that a document disclosed in an action cannot be used for any purpose external to the action either by a solicitor of the Supreme Court, who though an 'in-house' solicitor and a scientologist is also an officer of the court and also subject to the discipline of the Law Society? Or by a barrister who is also a scientologist and an 'in-house' lawyer but who though no longer in practice is also subject to the discipline of the judges and the Senate and Bar Council? Or, if a copy of the document *g* is in fact in their hands, by the plaintiffs themselves?

But who are the plaintiffs? A company, like the plaintiffs, must act and inspect through agents and I can see nothing outrageous in requiring some limitation on the dissemination of confidential information to a company. Why should confidential information be disseminated and not restricted to as few persons as possible and as necessary for justice and a fair disposal of the action? *h*

It was with that in mind that the court asked for particulars of the plaintiffs' organisation, and of course we bore in mind RSC Ord 5, r 6(2) (to which Brandon LJ drew attention in the course of the argument) that a body corporate may not begin or carry on proceedings in the High Court otherwise than by a solicitor.

Counsel for the plaintiffs was good enough to give us those particulars; he told us that this Church of Scientology of California is a trustee corporation without shares or share *j* capital incorporated under the non-profit corporation law of the state of California. It has three trustees, Americans, who do not include Mr Hubbard, and those trustees are empowered to elect directors both in the United States of America and here and to remove the directors whom they elect here. Subject to that, the church here, the plaintiffs, is an autonomous body.

a   Counsel gave us the names of three British nationals who are the three directors of the church here at present, and of the registered agent, a British lady appointed by the United Kingdom directors. The organisational head of the plaintiffs in England is Mrs Tampion. There are two legal departments, one of the church in England (the plaintiffs) and one worldwide, and both these legal departments are stationed at Saint Hill Manor, East Grinstead, and the worldwide legal department supervises litigation throughout the world. The head of the English legal department is Mr Tampion, who is not a lawyer;

b   the head of the worldwide legal department is Mr Parselle, whose affidavit is before us and who, as I have already said, is a non practising barrister. Mr Bird, the plaintiffs' solicitor, who has sworn an affidavit, is employed by the worldwide legal department but he also acts for the English legal department. In practice, the conduct of the plaintiffs' action is in the hands of Mr Tampion and he would act in settling the action or making any major decisions with regard to it in conjunction with Mrs Tampion and Mr Parselle

c   and Mr Bird. That information is something which I think we should bear in mind, with all the other circumstances, when we consider what the right order to make in this case is.

However, I find it unnecessary, in view of the order which I propose we should make in this case (if my brethren agree), to take the invidious course of deciding, on I think inadequate material (put bluntly), who among those whose names have been given to us

d   by counsel for the plaintiffs is to be trusted with confidential information. I am glad not to be bound to decide that question. It would be quite wrong however to suppose that I am taking an adverse view of any of those persons whose names have been given to us or whose names I have mentioned.

At a late stage in the argument counsel for the defendants submitted that in any event whatever order we make on this appeal, it would be desirable that it should be conditional

e   on further discovery being made by the plaintiffs. He pointed out that as long ago as 2nd May 1977 the defendants had requested further discovery which had been said to be awaiting counsel's advice as long ago as 1st December 1977, but the request had not yet been complied with. That is a matter which counsel for the plaintiffs said we should certainly not consider in relation to the substance of the order which we make on this appeal, but could take into account in considering whether to make the order subject to

f   that further condition.

There is one more matter:

'To complicate matters further [and here I am quoting from the words of the document itself (counsel for the plaintiffs, for the assistance again of the court and of counsel for the defendants, put in what he called a 'memorandum' of the plaintiffs' documents). That memorandum says:] The plaintiffs may have had in

g   their possession, custody or power documents relating to (a) the medical cases [and then he sets out the ten names of patients to whom I have referred and against which names he has said:] The whereabouts of these persons, and documents which may relate to them are not known at this time. [Then it goes on:] (b) and other scientologists or ex-scientologists named in the defendants pleadings [and a long list of persons is then set out, some with 'USA' against their names and in relation to all

h   these names he says:] The whereabouts of these persons and documents that may relate to them is not known with certainty at this time. [Then at the bottom of the document, one sees:] Any documents pertaining to persons in the United States of America would be outside the possession, custody or power of the plaintiff, being in the possession, custody or power of a separate legal entity. [Then:] To complicate matters further [and here are the words which I have quoted] the relevant functions

j   of the plaintiff are now being performed by the Church of Scientology Religious Education College Inc. The last named Corporation would now have any documents which may have been held by the plaintiffs. As such, these documents would be outside the plaintiffs' possession, custody or power.'

In elaboration of this counsel for the plaintiffs frankly informed us that this education college took over the functions (or some of them) and the documents (that does not mean all the plaintiffs' documents but any of the documents which are referred to in this list) at the end of 1976 or the beginning of 1977 and that this is an education college which has been incorporated in Australia. That information in effect is consistent with what is sworn by Mr Grant in his affidavit, and gives the date of the incorporation of that company, and of its taking over some of the functions of the plaintiffs, as March 1977.

Counsel for the plaintiffs has further told us that the reason why this rough draft further list of documents, which is what it really is, is so vague and says neither that the plaintiffs have in their possession, custody or power or have had in their possession, custody or power, but that they *may have had* in their possession, custody or power certain documents, is two-fold. First of all before this action started there was a bonfire of documents of which some or all of these documents may or may not have been included, and secondly there have been what he called 'periodic clear-outs' of documents which may or may not have included some or all of these documents. I confess that I am troubled by this memorandum, and what counsel for the plaintiffs says about it, in the light of such documentary material as we have; for instance, Mr Hubbard's boasts about case histories, which are contained in the particulars given under para 16 of the defence, and the document which I have referred to about the 'dead file' system.

I hope I have now covered, at too great a length, all the matters which, for my part, I think have to be considered in arriving at the right order to make in this case. (1) I am satisfied that the court has inherent jurisdiction to do what it can to restrain a threatened or likely or foreseeable abuse of the process of the court by misusing the documents which are the subject of the order under appeal for a purpose other than the purposes of this action, and to do that by controlling or restricting production for inspection of documents for which privilege has not been claimed. (2) I am satisfied that on the material which we have in this case some sort of restriction ought to be imposed in the exercise of that jurisdiction. (3) I am of opinion that the restrictions which were imposed, particularly the restriction to a medical officer of the hospital notes and the medical reports, were wrong.

Faced with the possibility of the court taking that view, counsel for the plaintiffs is prepared to submit to an order setting out certain restrictions with which counsel for the defendants is satisfied. That absolved the court, as I see it, from upholding the master's order or from devising an order of its own if, as I think right, it can and should make an order restricting discovery in some way.

The order which I propose we should make is this: that the appeal should be allowed and for the order made by the master and affirmed by the judge, should be substituted this order:

'Upon the plaintiffs by their counsel expressly undertaking that on inspection Mr Bird, their solicitor only will attend and take one copy of each of the documents referred to in this order (hereinafter called the restricted documents) and that Mr Bird shall keep the same confidential to himself and leading and junior counsel save insofar as he be advised in writing to the contrary by counsel. And upon the plaintiffs by their counsel undertaking that Mr Bird will show a copy of this order to every person who is to be supplied with a copy of a restricted document or supplied with information therefrom before the supply of such copy or information with a warning that the document or information is not to be used for any purpose other than a purpose connected with this action. And upon the plaintiffs by their counsel expressly waiving legal or professional privilege in respect of any such written advice relevant to any issue that may be before the court in this consolidated action (whether raised in committal or sequestration proceedings or otherwise) as to whether they have acted wholly or partly in accordance with or contrary to such advice and undertaking to instruct any counsel who may be instructed to give such advice to keep a copy thereof and to be at liberty, in the event of any such issue arising and his being called upon by the court so to do, to lodge such copy with the

court, and further to instruct him to be at liberty, should he entertain any reasonable
apprehension that the plaintiffs are acting or may act otherwise than in accordance
with any such advice, and should he see fit to inform counsel for the defendants of
such apprehension and/or to furnish counsel for the defendants with a copy of the
advice on which such apprehension arises.

'Order, that the defendants do allow Mr Bird, the plaintiffs' solicitor personally to
inspect the documents referred to in sub-paras (3) and (4) of para 3 of the master's
order of 11th May 1977.

'Order, that the plaintiffs do make and serve a further and better list of documents
verified by affidavit of the plaintiffs by their proper officer within 21 days.

'Order, that the defendants be not bound to give inspection of the restricted
documents except on mutual discovery of documents generally after the service of
the said further and better list of documents and the final determination of any
application arising therefrom.'

To that I would add, after discussion with counsel:

'Order, that the defendants do make and serve a further and better list of
documents verified by affidavit of the defendants by the defendant Cashman within
three months.

'Order, that all future interlocutory applications be made to a judge who shall so
far as practicable retain such matters to himself.'

That, subject to the agreement of Brandon and Templeman LJJ and the comments of
counsel, is the order which I would make.

BRANDON LJ. Four questions appear to me to arise on this appeal. First, is it shown
that, if the plaintiffs are given an unrestricted right of inspection of the defendants'
documents, there is a real risk that they would use such right for a collateral and harmful
purpose? Second, if so, does the court have power to impose restrictions on the plaintiffs'
right of inspection in order to prevent or discourage such use? If the court has such
power, third, what kind of restrictions can be imposed? Fourth, what method should
the court use to impose them?

With regard to the first question, there is material to which Stephenson LJ has referred
in detail in his judgment, which shows that it has been the policy of the plaintiffs, in the
past at any rate, to treat their critics as enemies and to use various techniques of
harassment in order to discourage them from pursuing their criticisms. In these
circumstances I consider that, if the plaintiffs are given an unrestricted right of inspection
of such of the defendants' documents as would reveal the identities of persons who have
criticised them, and the nature and extent of their criticisms, there is a real risk (I do not
put it any higher) that the plaintiffs will use such right for a collateral and harmful
purpose in harassing those persons.

With regard to the second question, the principles applicable are, in my view, as
follows. 1. A party to litigation has a prima facie right of unrestricted inspection of the
documents of which discovery has been made by the other party so far as may be
necessary to dispose fairly of the case or for saving costs. 2. A party is not entitled to use
his right of inspection for any collateral purpose. 3. If it is shown that there is a real risk
of a party using his right for a collateral purpose, the court has power to impose
restrictions on such right in order to prevent or discourage him from doing so. I think
that this power is derived from the inherent jurisdiction of the court to prevent abuse of
its process rather than from anything in RSC Ord 24 itself.

But it seems to me that the use of the word 'may' rather than 'shall' in RSC Ord 24, r 11
(1) and (2) has the effect of preserving the power, or else that the power survives despite
the absence of any express words in RSC Ord 24 designed to preserve it. The power in
question appears to have been exercised only, or almost only, in cases involving secret

trade processess or analogous matters: see *Warner-Lambert Co v Glaxo Laboratories Ltd*[1] and the authorities there cited.

In my view, however, the principle on which the power has been exercised in such cases is of general application and applies in particular to a case like the present one where the collateral purpose potentially involved is the harassment of third parties.

With regard to the third question, the authorities on cases involving secret trade processes show that the restrictions which may be imposed include restrictions relating to (a) the person or persons who may inspect and take copies of the documents on behalf of the party concerned; (b) the distribution of copies of documents when taken; and (c) the dissemination of the contents of such documents and copies.

There was argument before us whether the court had power to impose such restrictions on inspection as would prevent a personal litigant from inspecting or taking copies of documents on his own behalf. Since the plaintiffs in the present case are a corporation, which can only inspect and take copies of documents through an agent acting on their behalf, it is not necessary to decide this question on this occasion. My provisional opinion however, based on the cases concerning secret trade processes, is that the court would have power in a proper case to do just that.

With regard to the fourth question, two methods of imposing restrictions were discussed before us: first, by making an order allowing inspection only on terms expressed in such order; second, by making an order allowing inspection only subject to undertakings given by the party concerned.

It was contended for the plaintiffs that the court, assuming it had power to impose restrictions at all, could only proceed by the second method. I do not accept this contention. It appears to me to be inconsistent with authority in cases concerned with secret trade processes. I should, however, be content, on the footing that the plaintiffs are willing to give such undertakings as the court thinks are needed, to use the second method in this case.

On the basis of my answers to the four questions discussed above, I agree that the appeal should be allowed on the ground that the restrictions imposed by the judge went too far. But I think it should only be allowed to the extent of substituting for the restrictions imposed by the judge the different restrictions proposed by Stephenson LJ, and adding the further provisions to the order which he has indicated.

TEMPLEMAN LJ. I agree. The defendants, the Department of Health and Social Security, seek to withhold from certain of the officers of the plaintiffs, the Church of Scientology of California, and from the members of the plaintiffs' church and from other persons, knowledge of the contents of certain documents which are admittedly relevant to this action and which have been disclosed in the department's lists of documents.

The plaintiffs sue for libel and seek to establish that they are a religious and charitable organisation promoting the beliefs of scientology. The department contend, inter alia, that scientology is a system of indoctrination aimed at attracting individuals particularly those who are insecure, disturbed or unhappy, and obtaining their total commitment so that large fees can be extracted from adherents, and that the plaintiffs resort to intimidation and undue influence to attain their ends. That is the department's case as pleaded.

Amongst the documents which appear in the department's list are three categories which the department are only willing to disclose on terms which secure a restricted circulation. The first category consists of medical reports. The second category consist of about 250 letters of complaint about the practice of scientology, some of which are expressed to be confidential. The third category consist of letters to and by a potential witness for the department, namely a Mr Maurice Johnson.

The department do not put forward a claim for privilege for any of these

_____
1 [1975] RPC 354

a documents. The affidavits filed by the department in support of their claim for restricted circulation do not in themselves prove any compelling reason for restriction. The exhibits to the affidavits, which include documents emanating from the plaintiffs, and the particulars of the defence, which include allegations of harassment of Mr Maurice Johnson, do however show cause for anxiety. Stephenson LJ has mentioned in particular the documents which give cause for concern. The flavour of those can be gained from an extract which was a communication from the Hubbard communication office address

b which is now the English address given by the plaintiffs on 5th September 1962, and which referred to an earlier letter which had given details how to go about dealing with attacks on scientology. It was addressed to scientologists, and the subject was:

c   'How to do a noisy investigation. Further to HCO executive letter of 3 August 1966, Cathy Gogerly HCO Area Secretary, Adelaide Australia has given details of how to go about dealing with attackers of scientology... "Here's what you do. Soon as one of these threats starts you get a Scientologist or *Scientologists* to investigate noisily. You find out where he or she works or worked, doctor, dentist, friends, neighbours, anyone and phone 'em up and say, 'I am investigating Mr/Mrs ... for criminal activities and he/she has been trying to prevent Man's freedom and is

d   restricting my religious freedom and that of my friends and children, etc. ...' You say now and then, 'I have already got some *astounding* facts' etc. etc. (*use a generality*) ... It doesn't matter if you don't get much info. just be *noisy*—its very off at first but makes fantastic sense and works.'

e   Counsel for the plaintiffs, submitted that the extracts which I have read and which Stephenson LJ has referred to are from the plaintiffs' past and were culled from a period in the history of the plaintiffs during which the plaintiffs were fighting for survival and were using what counsel described as 'robust American methods of defence'. The plaintiffs' policy and tactics have, he said, since been modified. The plaintiffs are an autonomous body with a legal department whose members are well aware of the

f restrictions imposed in this country on the use of documents revealed on discovery. It is not in the interests of the plaintiffs to countenance any harassment or improper conduct. There is no recorded allegation that, in the course of much litigation in all parts of the world, there has been any harassment of witnesses or disobedience of an order of the court, apart from the instant allegation about Mr Johnson, and those allegations are disputed.

g   I acknowledge the force of these submissions and make no finding and reach no conclusion, tentative or otherwise, adverse to the plaintiffs. Nevertheless, the former policies and tactics of the plaintiffs, as revealed by the extracts which I have read and by other documents, are disturbing. The plaintiffs are a foreign corporation; there is no evidence of their present doctrines, policies or tactics, and the information we have gleaned from counsel of its relations with other sister-organisations and about the persons

h who control the plaintiffs in theory and practice, are not altogether reassuring.
    Moreover it is plain that the plaintiffs, in the course of their activities and as part of the work of scientology, must inevitably assist individuals who have personality problems and whose zeal might outrun their discretion. The possibility has been raised and persists that an unnecessarily wide circulation of information obtained on discovery might result in some harassment in England or abroad even if the plaintiffs themselves

j were not responsible and were themselves prejudiced by an excess of zeal on the part of some supporter.
    In my judgment, the interests of the prudent administration of justice and the interests of the plaintiffs themselves require that reasonable precautions be taken to restrict the circulation of information without hampering or prejudicing the plaintiffs in their pursuit of the remedies they seek in this action.

Counsel for the plaintiffs submitted that the court had no jurisdiction to impose restrictions and that in any event no sufficient case was made out to justify any *a* restrictions, or at any rate to justify the restrictions which were canvassed in argument. For the reasons I have already given, I am of the view that restrictions are desirable if they are lawful and I turn, therefore, to consider the objection of jurisdiction.

RSC Ord 24, r 9 requires the department to allow the plaintiffs to inspect the documents referred in the department's list of documents. This rule will be fully complied with if the plaintiffs' solicitor is allowed to inspect and take copies as the agent *b* of the plaintiffs which, being a corporation, can only act through agents. RSC Ord 24, r 13(1) provides that the court shall only make such order for discovery as is necessary for disposing fairly of the cause or matter.

If a litigant makes use of information obtained on discovery for improper purposes, that is to say otherwise than bona fide in the course of the action, he is guilty of contempt of court: see *Alterskye v Scott*[1]. If he begins an action based on such information his action *c* is liable to be struck out as an abuse of the process of the court: see *Riddick v Thames Board Mills Ltd*[2].

These sanctions are usually sufficient to procure that documents disclosed on discovery are only used for the purpose of the relevant action. But where, as in the present case, misuse whether by parties to the litigation or by other persons is apprehended, then it seems to me that there are three principles which enable the court to impose reasonable *d* restrictions. The first principle is that the court shall not order discovery which is not necessary for the fair disposal of the action. It follows that the court has power to impose restrictions which ensure that the ambit of discovery is not wider than is necessary to dispose fairly of the action. The second principle is that the court may act to prevent any possibility of conduct which might constitute contempt of court. The third principle is that the court may act to prevent what may be an abuse of the process of the court. Of *e* course a strong case must be made out for the court to impose restrictions, and the court will endeavour to ensure that the litigants are not prejudiced by the restrictions in the reasonable prosecution of their claim, but in the unusual circumstances of this case I am satisfied that the court ought to intervene and that there is jurisdiction for the court so to do.

True, a litigant is entitled to inspect documents disclosed on discovery and to take *f* copies: see *McIvor v Southern Health and Social Security Board*[3]. But if there is a danger that inspection and copying in the manner desired by the litigant may lead to misuse of information, the court in the exercise of its power to prevent a possible contempt of court or in the exercise of its power to prevent an abuse of process and in the exercise of its power to confine discovery to the ambit which alone is necessary for the disposal of the action may dictate the manner in which inspection is carried out, whether by an *g* individual litigant or by a corporate litigant, and may regulate the taking and safeguarding of copies, and may impose limitations on the circulation of copies and information.

The powers of the court are explained in the considered judgment of Buckley LJ in *Warner-Lambert Co v Glaxo Laboratories Ltd*[4]. The court imposed restrictions in that case to preserve the secrets of a business. It must be able to act similarly to protect the persons *h* or property or even the peace of mind of individuals. I agree with the order which has been proposed.

Appeal allowed ; order agreed between the parties substituted for order of the master. Leave to appeal to House of Lords refused.

j

---

1   [1948] 1 All ER 469
2   [1977] 3 All ER 677, [1977] QB 881
3   [1978] 2 All ER 625, [1978] 1 WLR 757
4   [1975] RPC 354

Solicitors: *Stephen M Bird*, East Grinstead (for the plaintiffs); *M W M Osmond*, Department
of Health and Social Security (for the defendants).

Elizabeth Hindmarsh   Barrister.

Cedar Holdings Ltd v Green and another

COURT OF APPEAL, CIVIL DIVISION
BUCKLEY, GOFF AND SHAW LJJ
19th, 22nd JANUARY, 9th MARCH 1979

*Joint tenancy – Land held on trust for sale – Severance of joint tenancy – Creation of charge by
joint tenant on property held jointly – Charge effectual to create charge of 'interest in property'
– Whether beneficial interest of joint tenant under statutory trust for sale an 'interest in property'
– Whether joint tenancy severed – Law of Property Act 1925, s 63.*

A husband and wife lived in a freehold house ('the matrimonial home') registered in
their joint names, and of which they were joint beneficial owners. The marriage broke
down and the wife was granted a decree nisi. She continued to live in the matrimonial
home. After the decree nisi the husband approached a bank to obtain a loan and offered
a charge on the matrimonial home as security. The bank required the charge to be
executed by both the husband and wife. The wife was not informed of the transaction
and instead the husband and a woman impersonating the wife attended at the bank's
offices, signed a request for a loan, and agreed to accept it on the terms that it was secured
by a legal charge on the freehold estate in the matrimonial home. Later the husband and
the woman executed the legal charge. The bank subsequently brought an action against
the husband and wife claiming (i) a declaration that the legal charge was valid and
binding on both the husband and the wife; alternatively (ii) a declaration that by
executing the legal charge the husband had charged to the bank all his beneficial interest
in the proceeds of sale of the matrimonial home under the statutory trusts for sale created
by ss 34(2), 35 and 36 of the Law of Property Act 1925. The bank conceded at the trial
that the wife was not in any way bound by the legal charge and that her interest could
not be affected by it. They contended that, either by the legal charge itself or by the pre-
existing contract to create the legal charge arising out of the written application for the
loan and the bank's acceptance of it, the husband had effectively severed the joint tenancy
in the proceeds of sale subsisting under the statutory trusts so as to become entitled to an
undivided half share of the proceeds of sale. They relied (i) on s 63(1)[a] of the 1925 Act,
contending that the husband's interest in the proceeds of sale of the matrimonial home
under the statutory trusts was, within the meaning of s 63(1), an 'interest . . . in . . . the
property conveyed or expressed or intended to be conveyed' by the legal charge and that
the legal charge was accordingly effectual to create a charge of that interest; alternatively
(ii) on the principle that when a vendor contracted to grant a particular interest in
property which was in fact greater than the interest which he was competent to grant,
the purchaser could elect to affirm the contract and compel the vendor to grant such
lesser interest in the property as he was competent to grant.

Held – (i) On the true construction of s 63 of the 1925 Act a beneficial interest in the
proceeds of sale of land held on statutory trusts was not an 'interest in the [land]' within
the meaning of that section and a conveyance of the land did not pass a beneficial interest
in the proceeds of sale. Accordingly the legal charge executed by the husband was not
effectual to charge his beneficial interest in the proceeds of sale of the matrimonial home

---

a   Section 63(1) is set out at p 121 *e*, post

(see p 123 d e, p 127 a to d and p 128 d, post); *Cooper v Critchley* [1955] 1 All ER 520 and
Irani Finance Ltd v Singh [1970] 3 All ER 199 considered.

(ii) As the husband had no legal or equitable interest in the matrimonial home but
merely an interest in one-half of the proceeds of sale and of any rents and profits until
sale, the bank could not demand the grant of that interest, because it had a different
subject-matter from that which the husband had contracted to mortgage, ie the freehold
estate in the matrimonial home (see p 124 c to f, p 127 g and p 128 d, post); *Thelluson v
Liddard* [1900] 3 Ch 635 and *Basma v Weekes* [1950] 2 All ER 146 considered.

Per Goff and Shaw LJJ. In any event the court would not have ordered specific
performance because it would have prejudiced the other co-owner, the wife, because (i)
she had at least an arguable case for saying that the husband had not made a disposition
of his share, so that she could claim protection under s 16 of the Matrimonial Proceedings
and Property Act 1970, and (ii) in any case, irrespective of whether the court would
ultimately order a sale under s 30 of the Law of Property Act 1925, such specific
performance must be prejudicial to her position in proceedings against her under that
section (see p 127 h to p 128 d, post).

Notes

For the severance of joint tenancies, see 32 Halsbury's Laws (3rd Edn) 334–337, paras
522–528, and for cases on the subject, see 38 Digest (Repl) 823–827, 360–395.

For the Law of Property Act 1925, ss 30, 34, 35, 36, 63, see 27 Halsbury's Statutes (3rd
Edn) 385, 389, 391, 393, 441.

For the Matrimonial Proceedings and Property Act 1970, s 16, see 40 Halsbury's
Statutes (3rd Edn) 818.

Cases referred to in judgments

Attorney-General v Day (1749) 1 Ves Sen 218, 27 ER 992, LC, 38 Digest (Repl) 856, *695*.
Basma v Weekes [1950] 2 All ER 146, [1950] AC 441, PC, 40 Digest (Repl) 28, *127*.
Carr Lane (No 39), Acomb, Re, Stevens v Hutchinson [1953] 1 All ER 699, sub nom *Stevens
v Hutchinson* [1953] Ch 299, [1953] 2 WLR 545, 21 Digest (Repl) 781, *2652*.
Cooper v Critchley [1955] 1 All ER 520, [1955] Ch 431, CA, 40 Digest (Repl) 21, *81*.
Fox, Re, Brooks v Marston [1913] 2 Ch 75, 82 LJ Ch 393, 108 LT 948, 32 Digest (Reissue)
604, *4512*.
Hazeldine's Trusts, Re [1908] 1 Ch 34, 77 LJ Ch 97, 97 LT 818, CA, 47 Digest (Repl) 329,
2972.
Horrocks v Rigby (1878) 9 Ch D 180, 47 LJ Ch 800, 38 LT 782, 44 Digest (Repl) 167, *1471*.
Irani Finance Ltd v Singh [1970] 3 All ER 199, [1971] Ch 59, [1970] 3 WLR 330, 21 P&CR
843, CA, Digest (Cont Vol C) 342, *1628Aa*.
Kempthorne, Re, Charles v Kempthorne [1930] 1 Ch 268, [1929] All ER Rep 495, 99 LJ Ch
107, 142 LT 111, CA, 23 Digest (Repl) 545, *6074*.
Mellish, Re (1st July 1927) unreported.
Price, Re [1928] Ch 579, 97 LJ Ch 423, 139 LT 339, 24 Digest (Repl) 935, *9473*.
Thellusson v Liddard [1900] 3 Ch 635, 69 LJ Ch 673, 82 LT 753, 20 Digest (Repl) 532,
2441.
Thomas v Cross (1865) 2 Drew & Sm 423, 6 New Rep 18, 34 LJ Ch 580, 12 LT 293, 11 Jur
NS 384, 62 ER 682, 21 Digest (Repl) 769, *2546*.
Thomas v Dering (1837) 1 Keen 729, [1835–42] All ER Rep 711, 6 LJ Ch 267, 1 Jur 211,
48 ER 488, 12 Digest (Reissue) 105, *554*.
Warren, Re, Warren v Warren [1932] 1 Ch 42, [1931] All ER Rep 702, 101 LJ Ch 85, 146
LT 224, 20 Digest (Repl) 359, *852*.
Williams v Hensman (1861) 1 John & H 546, 30 LJ Ch 878, 5 LT 203, 5 Jur NS 771, 70 ER
862, 28 Digest (Repl) 824, *367*.
Witham, Re, Chadburn v Winfield [1922] 2 Ch 413, 92 LJ Ch 22, 128 LT 272, 32 Digest
(Reissue) 655, *4802*.

Cases also cited

a   *Bird v Syme Thomson* [1978] 3 All ER 1027, [1979] 1 WLR 440.
     Turner (a bankrupt), Re, ex parte the trustee of the bankrupt v Turner [1975] 1 All ER 5,
     [1974] 1 WLR 1556.

Appeal

This was an appeal by the plaintiffs, Cedar Holdings Ltd ('the bank'), against an order of
b   Whitford J dated 28th January 1977 whereby (i) it was ordered that the first defendant,
     Ira Green ('the husband') should pay to the bank the sum of £3,980·69, due under a legal
     charge executed on 3rd December 1971 and securing the property known as 12 Preston
     Road, London ('the matrimonial home') which was jointly owned by the husband and
     the second defendant, Grace Ann Green ('the wife'), together with interest thereon at the
     rate of 9% per annum from the date of the order to the date of payment, (ii) it was
c   declared that the bank was entitled to a lien by subrogation to a legal charge dated 1st
     April 1970 of Pankine Ltd in the sum of £520·16 together with interest thereon at the
     rate of 9% per annum from the date of the order to the date of payment, and (iii) it was
     ordered that on payment by the husband of the sum due to the bank pursuant to the
     above order and declaration, the register of properties should be rectified with regard to
     the matrimonial home having title numbered NGL 51246 by deleting therefrom the
d   legal charge of 3rd December 1971. No order was made against the wife. The facts are
     set out in the judgment of Buckley LJ.

Peter Millett QC and *Denis Levy* for the bank.
Leolin Price QC and *Alastair Norris* for the wife.
The husband did not appear and was not represented.

e
                                                                          Cur adv vult

9th March. The following judgments were read.

BUCKLEY LJ. The first and second defendants were formerly husband and wife.
f   They lived in a freehold house ('the matrimonial home') registered in their joint names,
     of which they were joint beneficial owners. The property was subject to a first registered
     charge in favour of the Greater London Council and to a second registered charge in
     favour of Pankine Ltd. The marriage came to grief and in or shortly before 1971 the
     husband left the matrimonial home. The wife instituted divorce proceedings and
     secured a decree nisi in October 1971, which has since been made absolute. On 13th
g   October 1971 the wife's solicitors intimated to the husband or to his solicitors that the
     wife would apply in the divorce proceedings for a property transfer order extinguishing
     the husband's interest in the matrimonial home. The wife has continued to live and still
     lives there with the four children of the marriage, of whom she has custody, the eldest
     being now aged about 18 years and the youngest, I think, about 11 years.
     After the date of the decree nisi the husband approached the plaintiffs ('the bank') with
h   a view to obtaining a loan from them. He offered by way of security a charge on the
     property. The bank naturally insisted on the charge being executed by both the husband
     and wife. None of this was disclosed to the wife. On 1st November 1971 the husband
     attended at the offices of the bank accompanied by a woman who was not the wife. The
     husband represented to the bank that the woman was his wife and on that date he and
     the woman in question, signing in the name of the wife, signed a request to the bank for
j   an overdraft of £1,500 repayable over 120 months by monthly payments of £26·25
     secured by a second mortgage on the matrimonial home. That document contained a
     paragraph in the following terms:

     'I/we understand that I/we will be bound to accept the advance on the above
     terms upon your posting to me/us notification of approval of my/our application

unless, prior to that time, you have received a written notification from me/us cancelling my application.'

On 3rd December 1971 the husband and the woman referred to earlier, who again signed in the name of the wife, executed a legal charge expressed to be made between the husband and wife (thereinafter called 'the borrower'), in the singular, of the one part and the plaintiff (thereinafter called 'the bank') of the other part. The charge was to secure all moneys due or to become due by the borrower jointly or severally to the bank. Clause 2, so far as material, was in the following terms:

'The Borrower as Beneficial Owner [and I here omit certain words which, as is common ground, were intended to be deleted from the printed form which was used] HEREBY CHARGES by way of legal mortgage ALL THAT the property described in the First Schedule hereto . . . with the payment of the principal money interest and all other monies hereby covenanted to be paid by the Borrower subject only to the prior mortgage particulars of which are set out in the Second Schedule hereto the amount now outstanding on such prior mortgage being as specified therein . . .'

The first schedule to the legal charge is in the following terms:

'ALL THAT Freehold messuage or dwellinghouse and buildings with the land and appurtenances thereof known as [the matrimonial home] being the whole of the land comprised in the title registered at H.M. Land Registry under the Land Registration Acts 1925 to 1966 with absolute title under Title Number NGL 51246.'

The second schedule contained particulars of the Greater London Council first charge, the principal amount secured being stated as £4,500. Pankine Ltd's second charge was paid off by the bank and the amount was debited to the husband's account.

By a writ dated 22nd May 1973 the bank sued the husband and wife for a declaration that the legal charge of 3rd December 1971 was valid and binding on both the husband and wife; alternatively, a declaration that by executing that legal charge the husband had charged to the bank all his beneficial interest in the matrimonial home under the trusts for sale affecting the same; possession, and an order for sale of the property pursuant to s 103 or alternatively s 30 of the Law of Property Act 1925. The bank conceded at the trial that the wife was plainly not bound in any way by the legal charge and that her interest could not be affected by it. The husband took no part in the action. The wife by way of counterclaim claimed a declaration that the property was not subject to nor incumbered by any mortgage or charge in favour of the bank and an order vacating the entry of that charge in the register.

The action came before Whitford J, who on 28th January 1977 entered judgment for the bank against the husband in the sum of £3,980·69 due under the legal charge of 3rd December 1971, with interest thereon at 9% per annum from 28th January 1977 to date of payment and declared that the bank was entitled to a lien by subrogation to the legal charge of Pankine Ltd in a sum of £520·16, together with interest theron at 9% per annum from 28th January 1977 to date of payment. He ordered that on payment of the sum due to the bank pursuant to the beforementioned order and declaration the registration of the legal charge be deleted. In his judgment the judge held that the legal charge was ineffective to effect any severance of the joint beneficial ownership of the husband and wife or to effect any charge on the husband's interest in the proceeds of the sale of the property under the statutory trust for sale affecting it. It seems to me that the order for vacation of the registration of the legal charge is couched in language which does not give due effect to what the judge intended. His decision was to the effect that the only charge which the bank had on the property was a lien by subrogation under the Pankine mortgage. The order should, it seems to me, have directed vacation of the registration of the charge on satisfaction of that lien and on that alone.

The bank appeals against the judge's order, seeking a declaration that by executing the legal charge the husband charged all his beneficial interest under the trust for sale of the

a matrimonial home, an order for possession of the property and an order for sale pursuant to either s 103 or s 30 of the Law of Property Act 1925. Under s 36 of the 1925 Act the legal estate in the matrimonial home was vested in the husband and wife as joint tenants on the statutory trusts set out in s 35. The bank's contention in the present case is that either by the legal charge itself, or by a pre-existing contract to create the legal charge arising out of the written application for a loan and the bank's acceptance of it, the husband effectively severed the joint tenancy in the proceeds

b of sale subsisting under the statutory trusts so as to become entitled to an undivided half share of the proceeds of sale. If the effect of either the legal charge itself or of a contract to create the legal charge was, in the one case, to occasion a disposal by the husband of his beneficial interest under the statutory trust or, in the other, to oblige the husband to dispose of that interest, there can, I think, be no doubt that the legal charge or the contract would have effected a severance of the joint beneficial ownership. The legal

c charge or the contract would constitute an act by one of the joint owners operating on his own share. This would fall within the first of the three methods of severance mentioned by Page Wood V-C in *Williams v Hensman*[1]. The effect of such an act is to destroy the unity of interest theretofore existing between the joint owners and so put an end to the joint ownership.

d Counsel for the bank relies in this respect, first, on s 63 of the 1925 Act and secondly on the principle that where a vendor contracts to grant a particular interest in property which is in fact greater than the interest which he is competent to grant, the purchaser can elect to affirm the contract and compel the vendor to grant such lesser interest in the property as he is competent to grant.

Section 63(1) of the 1925 Act provides:

e 'Every conveyance is effectual to pass all the estate, right, title, interest, claim, and demand which the conveying parties respectively have, in, to, or on the property conveyed, or expressed or intended so to be, or which they respectively have power to convey in, to, or on the same.'

Subsection (2) makes the section applicable only if and as far as a contrary intention is not expressed in the conveyance, and provides that it shall have effect subject to the terms

f of the conveyance and to the provisions contained in it. 'Conveyance' includes in the Law of Property Act 1925 a mortgage or charge (s 205(1)). Counsel for the bank contends that the husband's interest in the proceeds of sale of the matrimonial home under the statutory trusts constituted an interest in the property conveyed or expressed or intended to be conveyed by the legal charge for the purposes of s 63. So, he says, the legal charge was effectual to create a charge of that interest. The property charged or

g expressed to be charged by the legal charge was undoubtedly the freehold estate in the matrimonial home registered with absolute title under title no NGL 51246. Was the husband's beneficial interest under the statutory trusts an interest in that property?

In *Irani Finance Ltd v Singh*[2] this court had to consider whether the beneficial interests of joint tenants under the statutory trust for sale could be the subject-matter of a charging order under s 35 of the Administration of Justice Act 1956 which enables a

h court, for the purpose of enforcing a judgment or order for the payment of money, to impose by order 'on any such land or interest in land' of the debtor as may be specified in the order a charge for securing payment of the moneys due. Cross LJ, delivering the judgment of the court, said[3]:

'No doubt such tenants in common are interested in the land in a general sense, as was remarked by Russell LJ in *Re Kempthorne, Charles v Kempthorne*[4]. But that is

j

1 (1861) 1 John & H 546 at 557
2 [1970] 3 All ER 199, [1971] Ch 59
3 [1970] 3 All ER 199 at 203, [1971] Ch 59 at 79–80
4 [1930] 1 Ch 268 at 292, [1929] All ER Rep 495 at 501

not the same thing as their being owners of equitable interests in the realty. The whole purpose of the trust for sale is to make sure, by shifting the equitable interests away from the land and into the proceeds of sale, that a purchaser of land takes free from equitable interests. To hold these to be equitable interests in the land itself would be to frustrate this purpose. Even to hold that they have equitable interests in the land for a limited period, namely until the land is sold, would, we think, be inconsistent with the trust for sale being an "immediate" trust for sale working an immediate conversion, which is what the Law of Property Act 1925 envisages (see s 205(1)(xxix)); although, of course, it is not in fact only such a limited interest that the plaintiffs are seeking to charge.'

This court held in that case that the interests of the joint beneficial owners under the statutory trusts were not interests in land for the relevant purpose. It is true that in that case the legislative history of the statutory provision in question played a considerable part in the reasoning of the judgment, as also did references to the Land Charges Act 1925 and the Land Registration Act 1925 contained in the section under consideration. Consequently, in my opinion, that case and the authorities referred to in it are not by any means directly in point in the present case.

In *Cooper v Critchley*[1] there are observations in this court which indicate that references to an 'interest in land' may in appropriate circumstances include an interest in the proceeds of sale of land, but there seems to be no judicial authority on the meaning and effect of the expression 'interest in the property conveyed' in s 63. That section replaced s 63 of the Conveyancing Act 1881, which was in identical terms. The purpose of that section was clearly to ensure that a conveyance should operate to convey all that the grantor could convey in relation to the subject-matter, notwithstanding that the language of the conveyance might not be in every respect apt to produce that result, and to eliminate the need for an 'all estate' clause of the kind which conveyancers had previously been accustomed to include in conveyances. It is not surprising that we have not been referred to any pre-1926 decision in which s 63 of the 1881 Act was held to operate in relation to an interest in the proceeds of sale of land held on trust for sale.

The bank says that it would be strange if the effect of s 63, in conjunction with the 1925 reform of real property law was that, whereas a conveyance executed on 31st December 1925 of the whole interest in land of which the sole grantor was one of two or more co-owners would be effectual to pass his undivided share of the property, a similar conveyance executed on 1st January 1926 would not be effectual to pass that which on that date became substituted for his previous undivided share in the land, viz, his undivided share in the proceeds of sale. The wife, on the other hand, contends that the historic function of s 63 and of its predecessor, s 63 of the 1881 Act, is and was connected with the normal operations of conveyancing, and that the section is not, and has never been, designed to deal with matters which have no relation to the title in the subject-matter of a conveyance which the grantee acquires under the conveyance, and in particular with matters which since 1925 are for conveyancing purposes behind the curtain of a trust for sale.

In *Re No 39 Carr Lane, Acomb, Stevens v Hutchinson*[2] Upjohn J had to consider whether the interest of a beneficial tenant in common of land held on the statutory trust for sale was an equitable interest in land within the meaning of s 195 of the Law of Property Act 1925. He said[3]:

'It was conceded that, apart from the definition clause, to which I must refer in a moment, an interest in the proceeds of sale of land is not aptly described as an equitable interest in land, but it is said that the definition to be found in s. 205(1)(x) of the Act of 1925 makes an interest in the proceeds of sale come to be included in

---

1   [1955] 1 All ER 520, [1955] Ch 431
2   [1953] 1 All ER 699, [1953] Ch 299
3   [1953] 1 All ER 699 at 702, [1953] Ch 299 at 306

the definition of an equitable interest in land. [Upjohn J then read s 205(1)(x)] When that definition section is carefully examined, in my judgment, it does not operate so as to make an equitable interest in land include an equitable interest in the proceeds of sale. The definition is not of an "equitable interest in land" but of an "equitable interest", and I can see nothing in para. (x) which makes "interest in the proceeds of sale of land" mean "equitable interest in land". The definition relates to equitable interests. The words in s. 195 (1) refer only to equitable interests in land. Accordingly, in my judgment, s.195 does not create a charge on the proceeds of sale of land.'

In s 63 we are concerned with the expression 'interest in the property conveyed or expressed or intended so to be'. This, as it seems to me, focuses attention on the particular subject-matter conveyed or expressed or intended to be conveyed. If, as in the present case, that subject-matter is land it would seem to me a strong thing to construe the word 'interest' in such a way as to make a conveyance effectual to pass property which is not land in any sense.

The device of the statutory trust for sale in respect of property vested in co-owners must have been very prominent in the minds of those who framed the 1925 property legislation. Had they intended s 63 of the Law of Property Act 1925 to have a different kind of operation from that which s 63 of the Conveyancing Act 1881 had been designed to achieve, I would certainly have expected some indication of this fact in s 63 of the 1925 Act. Instead, s 63 of the 1881 Act was left intact by the amending Act (the Law of Property Act 1922) and was consolidated without any change in its language into the 1925 Act. In my judgment, on the true construction of s 63 of the 1925 Act a beneficial interest in the proceeds of sale of land held on the statutory trusts is not an interest in that land within the meaning of the section and a conveyance of that land is not effectual to pass a beneficial interest in the proceeds of sale. It follows that, in my judgment, in the present case the legal charge executed by the husband was not effectual to charge his beneficial interest in the proceeds of sale of his matrimonial home.

I turn therefore to the other way in which counsel for the bank presents his argument. Where a vendor is unable to make a good title to the whole of what he has contracted to sell, the purchaser may, as a rule, elect to enforce the contract in respect of so much as he can get with an appropriate abatement of the purchase price. Lord St Leonards stated the rule thus[1]: 'A purchaser generally, although not universally, may take what he can get with compensation for what he cannot have.' Mr Cyprian Williams puts the matter thus[2]:

'The purchaser therefore is, as a rule, entitled, if it turns out that there is a mere *deficiency*, whether of area, estate or right, and whether substantial or not, between the property described in the contract and that offered in fulfilment thereof, to enforce the specific performance of the contract, taking such interest in the property sold as the vendor has and receiving compensation for the deficiency.'

Counsel for the bank contends that the husband having contracted to mortgage the freehold interest in the matrimonial home and being unable to do so, the bank can elect to compel him to charge his beneficial interest in the proceeds of sale of the property under the statutory trusts for sale. He referred us to *Basma v Weekes*[3], a case before the Judicial Committee of the Privy Council, in which three tenants in common of two houses contracted to sell them to the plaintiff. One of the vendors was incompetent to enter into the contract. The question arose whether the plaintiff was entitled to have specific performance of the contract against the other two tenants in common in respect of their undivided shares in the houses. The legal position was unaffected by any

1   In Sugden on Vendors and Purchasers (14th Edn, 1862), p 316
2   Williams on Vendor and Purchaser (4th Edn, 1936), p 725
3   [1950] 2 All ER 146, [1950] AC 441

legislation comparable to the Law of Property Act 1925. The Judicial Committee, founding themselves on certain observations by Fry J in *Horrocks v Rigby*[1], and an observation of Lord Hardwicke LC in *Attorney-General v Day*[2], held that the plaintiff was so entitled. Counsel for the bank also referred us to *Thellusson v Liddard*[3] where a purchaser was held entitled to specific performance against a vendor who had contracted to sell the freehold estate in certain houses in which he had no more than an equitable leasehold interest. In each case what was specifically enforced was a sale of an interest in the land, although a less interest than that contracted to be sold. Neither of those decisions was concerned with the problem which arises where a grantor contracts to sell a legal estate in land in circumstances in which he has no estate or interest in the land, legal or equitable, but merely an equitable interest in part of the proceeds of its sale. They consequently do not, in my opinion, carry the bank home in this appeal.

The doctrine in accordance with which those cases were decided is, in my opinion, directed to ensuring that the grantee shall obtain, if he so elects, as much of the subject-matter contracted to be granted as the grantor can convey, whether the deficiency be in respect of the physical extent of the subject-matter or of the estate or interest of the grantor in the subject-matter. It does not enable the grantee to demand a grant of some different subject-matter in lieu of that contracted for.

In the present case the bank contracted for a mortgage of the freehold estate in the matrimonial home. Neither the bank nor the husband contemplated a mortgage of the husband's share of the proceeds of sale of the property. Both the application for a loan and the legal charge itself explicitly refer to the freehold estate in the whole of the property. If the bank had realised that the husband was competent to charge no more than a half share in the proceeds of sale, the transaction would never have taken place. Nevertheless, had the husband been competent to charge some estate or interest in the matrimonial home less than the freehold, such as a leasehold interest, the bank would, I think, have been entitled to elect to claim specific enforcement of the creation of a charge on that lesser interest. The husband, however, has no interest in the matrimonial home; his interest is confined to a half share of the proceeds of sale of the house and of any rents and profits until sale. That interest is, in my opinion, an entirely different subject-matter from that which the husband contracted to mortgage. Accordingly, in my judgment, the principle in accordance with which such cases as *Basma v Weekes*[4] and *Thellusson v Liddard*[3] were decided has no application to the present case.

For these reasons I would dismiss this appeal.

GOFF LJ. Counsel for the bank claims an equitable charge on the husband's beneficial interest, which was a joint interest with his former wife in the proceeds of sale of the matrimonial home under the statutory trusts created by ss 34(2), 35 and 36(1) of the Law of Property Act 1925, although, if the bank be right, the creation of that equitable charge has severed the joint tenancy in equity, so that the husband and wife are now entitled to those proceeds as tenants in common in equal shares subject, as to his half only, to the equitable charge. There could, of course, be no severance of the joint tenancy at law: see s 36(2) of the 1925 Act.

Counsel for the bank presented his case in two alternative ways. First, he submitted that the husband having signed the overdraft agreement whereby he acknowledged that he was bound to accept the advance of £1,500 on the terms therein stated, which included a second mortgage by way of legal charge on the matrimonial home, once the bank accepted that application there was a binding contract by him to give the bank such a security. Further, he could not escape his own liability on that contract, on the ground

1   (1878) 9 Ch D 180 at 182
2   (1749) 1 Ves Sen 218 at 224
3   [1900] 3 Ch 635
4   [1950] 2 All ER 146, [1950] AC 441

that he had no power to deal with the legal estate save with the concurrence of the wife,
a who was not in fact or in law a party to that application or to the purported legal charge
which followed, because she was impersonated by another woman, by whom her
signature was forged, and she knew nothing about the transaction at all.

So much must, I think, be right, and then he argues further that the bank is entitled
to take what it can get from the husband and so to elect to take specific performance
against his beneficial interest in the proceeds of sale under the statutory trusts.

b It is contended by counsel for the wife that even if this argument would have prevailed
before 1925 it cannot do so now, because the statutory trusts have converted the
husband's interest into a personalty interest in proceeds of sale instead of an interest in
land.

Counsel's alternative case for the bank is that the husband's interest is read into the
purported legal charge by virtue of s 63 of the 1925 Act, which is in these terms:

c '(1) Every conveyance is effectual to pass all the estate, right, title, interest, claim,
and demand which the conveying parties respectively have in, to, or on the property
conveyed, or expressed or intended so to be, or which they respectively have power
to convey in, to, or on the same.

'(2) This section applies only if and as far as the contrary intention is not expressed
in the conveyance, and has effect subject to the terms of the conveyance and to the
d provisions therein contained.'

That instrument is, of course, a conveyance within the meaning of the Act: see
s 205(1)(ii).

I was at one time disposed to think that there was no conveyance on which s 63 could
operate, because the only purported conveyance was a charge by way of legal mortgage
on the entirety which the instrument must be wholly inoperative to create, the wife not
e being a party. I am satisfied, however, that that short answer begs the question, for by
s 63, if otherwise applicable, the conveyance is effectual to pass the subject-matter
specified in s 63(1) so that if there be anything comprehended within the words 'estate,
right, title, interest, claim, and demand . . . on the same', the conveyance is by the section
made effectual to that extent.

f This being so, counsel for the bank would in my judgment, prior to 1925, have been
correct in his argument on s 63: see *Thellusson v Liddard*[1] where a party had purported to
convey certain houses by way of mortgage in fee. In fact he had with respect to some of
them a legal mortgage sub term and no more[2], and as to the others only a right to have
a lease which had merged at law kept alive in equity. It was held that those interests
passed under s 63 of the Conveyancing Act 1881, the forerunner of the present s 63 of
g the 1925 Act, and that the grantee was entitled in equity subject to an undertaking to
accept proper legal leases: see also *Basma v Weekes*[3].

Counsel for the wife argues, however, that as the conveyance was a purported charge
by way of legal mortgage, that is to say a conveyance of an estate or interest in land, s 63
can only be used to read into it some other or limited interest in land, and not an interest
in proceeds of sale, which is an interest in personalty and not in land. Therefore, he
h submits it cannot include the husband's share of the proceeds of sale under the statutory
trusts, for they work a conversion in equity.

This is, I think, a very difficult question to decide, for it is clear that a share of the
proceeds of sale of land under the statutory trusts is for some purposes, and even for the
Law of Property Act 1925 itself, to be regarded as an interest in land.

First, this was clearly the view of the whole Court of Appeal in *Cooper v Critchley*[4], with
j regard to s 40 of the 1925 Act, although this was obiter only, since the actual decision was
that there was no concluded contract.

1 [1900] 3 Ch 635
2 See [1900] 3 Ch 635 at 641
3 [1950] 2 All ER 146, [1950] AC 441
4 [1955] 1 All ER 520 at 524, [1955] Ch 431 at 439

Secondly, it has been decided that a share of proceeds of sale under a trust for sale is an interest in land for the purposes of s 34 of the Real Property Limitation Act 1833, and s 8 of the Real Property Limitation Act 1874: see *Re Hazeldine's Trusts*[1],which, although a decision of the Court of Appeal, would not be absolutely binding on us, since the court held the question was res judicata, because it had been determined on an earlier summons, but both Cozens-Hardy MR[2] and Fletcher Moulton LJ[3] went out of their way to say they did not question the correctness of that decision, and Farwell LJ in terms said[4]: 'I am clearly of opinion that the effect of the Act of 1833 was to extinguish the title of the mortgagee in a case like the present': see also *Re Fox*[5] and *Re Witham*[6], where Sargant J felt himself bound by *Re Hazeldine's Trusts*[1], although contrary to his own inclination.

The relevant sections in those cases were governed by a definition which said that the word 'land' should extend to, amongst other things, 'any share, estate or interest' in land 'whether the same shall be of a freehold or chattel interest', but chattel interest could not refer to proceeds of sale, and so the share in the proceeds of sale was held to be a share, estate or interest in land.

On the other hand, although ademption has been avoided where the testator has republished his will after 1st January 1926, and in *Re Mellish*[7] Eve J apparently held that a devise of all the testator's share and interest in an estate known as the Rushall estate was as a matter of construction wide enough to carry his share of the proceeds of sale of that estate arising under the statutory trusts for sale, and in *Re Warren*[8] Maugham J said:

'. . . I attribute weight in these cases to the consideration that the result of the statutory trusts is not wholly to deprive the person previously entitled to an undivided share of all interest in the land . . .'

Yet in *Re Price*[9] and *Re Kempthorne*[10] the statutory trusts were held to cause ademption.

Then in *Irani Finance Ltd v Singh*[11] this court decided that a share of proceeds of sale under the statutory trusts is not an 'interest in land' within the meaning of s 35 of the Administration of Justice Act 1956 so as to enable a charging order to be made on it. That is not absolutely binding in this case, because it was a decision on a different Act[12] and rested in part on the long standing authority of *Thomas v Cross*[13] that proceeds of sale under a trust for sale are not within the words 'lands and hereditaments "of or to which any person was seised, possessed or entitled for any estate or interest[14]"' in that section, now replaced in s 195 of the Law of Property Act 1925 by the words 'every estate or interest (whether legal or equitable) in all land', and in further part to a large degree on the proviso in s 195(3)(i) that a judgment—

'shall not operate as a charge on any interest in land or on the unpaid purchase money for any land unless or until a writ or order, for the purpose of enforcing it, is registered in the register of writs and orders at the Land Registry . . .'

1   [1908] 1 Ch 34
2   [1908] 1 Ch 34 at 38
3   [1908] 1 Ch 34 at 39
4   [1908] 1 Ch 34 at 40
5   [1913] 2 Ch 75 at 78–79
6   [1922] 2 Ch 413 at 423
7   (1st July 1927) unreported; but see *Re Wheeler* [1929] 2 KB 81, [1928] All ER Rep 510
8   [1932] 1 Ch 42 at 50, [1931] All ER Rep 702 at 706
9   [1928] Ch 579
10   [1930] 1 Ch 268, [1929] All ER Rep 495
11   [1970] 3 All ER 199, [1971] Ch 59
12   Judgments Act 1838 (1 & 2 Vict c 110), s 13
13   (1865) 2 Drew & Sm 423
14   See 2 Drew & Sm 423 at 426 per Kindersley V-C

In the *Irani* case[1], however, Cross LJ, delivering the judgment of the court, said:

a   'No doubt such tenants in common are interested in the land in a general sense, as was remarked by Russell LJ in *Re Kempthorne, Charles v Kempthorne*[2]. But that is not the same thing as their being owners of equitable interests in the realty. The whole purpose of the trust for sale is to make sure, by shifting the equitable interests away from the land and into the proceeds of sale, that a purchaser of the land takes free from equitable interests. To hold these to be equitable interests in the land

b   itself would be to frustrate this purpose. Even to hold that they have equitable interests in the land for a limited period, namely, until the land is sold, would, we think, be inconsistent with the trust for sale being an "immediate" trust for sale working an immediate conversion, which is what the Law of Property Act 1925 envisages (see s 205 (1)(xxix)); although of course, it is not in fact only such a limited interest that the plaintiff company is seeking to charge.'

c
Those words seem to me to apply directly to the problem before us, and I have with respect come to the same conclusion as Buckley LJ, though I confess not without some hesitation on the way.

In my judgment, however, even if this be wrong, the result is still the same, because sub-s (2) must exclude the beneficial interest in the proceeds of sale.

d   If this had purported to be a conveyance of the fee simple in exercise of the statutory trusts then it could not have been intended to pass the beneficial interest in the proceeds of sale. The purchaser takes the beneficial as well as the legal interest in the land because the trustees have power to convey both to him, the beneficial interest of the beneficiaries being overreached, that is to say shifted away from, the land and into the proceeds of sale. Accordingly those beneficial interests must be excluded from s 63 of the Law of

e   Property Act 1925 by sub-s (2). Counsel for the bank very rightly conceded that this must be so, and indeed himself advanced this proposition to meet counsel's argument for the wife that otherwise the result would be absurd. Now in such a case the defect in the conveyance due to the fact that one of the trustees was not a party could not alter the construction of s 63. It could, and would, defeat the purported conveyance of the legal estate, but it could not alter the construction or cause to be read in, under s 63, words

f   which would be excluded if the conveyance was good according to its tenor.

We are, of course, dealing not with a conveyance of the fee simple, but with a legal mortgage, but the principle must be exactly the same, since the mortgage was one purporting to be made by the trustees in the exercise of their statutory powers in that behalf.

Having reached this conclusion, I have no hesitation in agreeing respectfully with all

g   that Buckley LJ has said on counsel's other argument for the bank, and I note that in the examples given in the passage cited from Williams on Vendor and Purchaser[3] the following words occur 'or formerly to an undivided moiety only'. It may be said that the learned author was not specifically directing his mind to the problem before us, but at least it does not seem to have occurred to him that the principle in question would still apply, albeit to the proceeds of sale.

h   I think too that counsel's case must fail on another ground, namely that even in the straightforward case where the purchaser has some estate or interest in the land, albeit less than he contracted to give, the court will not order specific performance to the extent of his true estate or interest 'where the alienation of the partial interest of the vendor might prejudice the rights of third persons interested in the estate': see Fry on Specific Performance[4], and *Thomas v Dering*[5] where Lord Langdale MR said:

j
1   [1970] 3 All ER 199 at 203, [1971] Ch 59 at 79–80
2   [1930] 1 Ch 268 at 292, [1929] All ER Rep 495 at 501
3   4th Edn (1936), pp 725–726
4   6th Edn (1921), p 588, para 1270
5   (1837) 1 Keen 729 at 747–748, [1835–42] All ER Rep 711 at 718

'I apprehend that, upon the general principle that the Court will not execute a contract, the performance of which is unreasonable, or would be prejudicial to *a* persons interested in the property, but not parties to the contract, the Court, before directing the partial execution of the contract by ordering the limited interest of the vendor to be conveyed, ought to consider how that proceeding may affect the interests of those who are entitled to the estate, subject to the limited interest of the vendor.'

Such specific performance would, as it seems to me, prejudice the other co-owner, the *b* wife, in two ways. First, whilst the matter remains in contract, she has at least a well arguable case for saying that the husband has not made a disposition of his share, so that she can claim protection under s 16 of the Matrimonial Proceedings and Property Act 1970, notwithstanding s 16(2). It might be different if he had made a contract to charge his share, but his only contract is to charge the entirety, and the court would by its order be 'executing the contract, *cy près*, or rather perhaps carrying into execution a new *c* contract[1]'. In any case whether or not the court would ultimately order a sale under s 30 of the Law of Propery Act 1925, such specific performance must be prejudicial to her position in proceedings against her under that section.

In the circumstances the questions raised under s 30 do not call for decision and I agree that this appeal should be dismissed. *d*

BUCKLEY LJ. Shaw LJ is unfortunately unable to be with us this afternoon, but he authorises me to say that he agrees with both the judgments which have been delivered.

Appeal dismissed. Leave to appeal to House of Lords refused.

Solicitors: *Derrick & Co* (for the bank); *Prestons & Kerlys* (for the wife). *e*

J H Fazan Esq   Barrister.

---

1   See Fry on Specific Performance (6th Edn, 1921), p 587, para 1268

a Attorney-General of Saint Christopher, Nevis and Anguilla v Reynolds

PRIVY COUNCIL

LORD SALMON, LORD SIMON OF GLAISDALE, LORD FRASER OF TULLYBELTON, LORD RUSSELL OF KILLOWEN AND LORD SCARMAN

b 12th, 13th, 14th, 15th MARCH, 25th JUNE 1979

Saint Christopher, Nevis and Anguilla – Constitutional law – Governor's powers – State of emergency – Discretion to detain persons in time of emergency – If the Governor is satisfied – Governor having power to detain persons if satisfied that it was necessary to do so – Whether Governor's power unrestricted – Whether Governor required to be satisfied on reasonable
c *grounds that detention of person reasonably justifiable and necessary – Constitution of Saint Christopher, Nevis and Anguilla (SI 1967 No 228, Sch 2), ss 3(6), 14, 103, 108 – Leeward Islands (Emergency Powers) Order in Council 1959 (SI 1959 No 2206), s 3(1) – Emergency Powers Regulations 1967 (St Christopher, Nevis and Anguilla) reg 3(1).*

The plaintiff, a former police inspector of good character, was a member of an opposition
d party in St Chrisopher, Nevis and Anguilla. On 27th February 1967 the Constitution[a] of the State of St Christopher, Nevis and Anguilla came into force. Section 103[b] of the Constitution provided that 'existing laws shall, as from the commencement of this Constitution, be construed with such modifications, adaptations, qualifications and exceptions as may be necessary to bring them into conformity with ... this Constitution'. By virtue of s 3(1)[c] of the Leeward Islands (Emergency Powers) Order in
e Council 1959[d], which was an 'existing law' for the purposes of s 103 of the Constitution, the Governor of the State had power during a period of emergency to make such laws 'as appear to him to be necessary or expedient for securing the public safety, the defence of [the state] or the maintenance of public order . . .' Under s 108[e] of the Constitution the 1959 order was to cease to have effect as part of the law of the state on 1st September 1967. On 30th May 1967 the Governor declared a state of emergency and made the
f Emergency Powers Regulations 1967 pursuant to the power conferred on him by the 1959 order. Under reg 3(1)[f] of the 1967 regulations a person could be detained without trial 'if the Governor is satisfied' that that person had recently been concerned in acts prejudicial to the public safety and to public order and that 'it is necessary' that he be detained. On 11th June the plaintiff was arrested and detained in prison under a detention order signed by the Deputy Governor. He remained in prison, in insanitary
g and humiliating conditions, until 10th August. In July a tribunal was set up to inquire into the cases of persons detained and at the hearing Crown counsel admitted that he had no evidence against the plaintiff. On his release the plaintiff brought an action against the state claiming damages for false imprisonment, and compensation under s 3(6)[g] of the Constitution for his unlawful arrest and detention. At the trial of the action, where again no justification for the plaintiff's detention was put forward on behalf of the state,
h the judge found the plaintiff's allegations proved and awarded him $5,000 damages. On appeal the West Indies Associated States Court of Appeal, relying on two of its previous decisions, held that s 3 of the 1959 order was so out of conformity with the Constitution that it was impossible to construe it in conformity with it as required by s 103 and that

---

j *a* SI 1967 No 228, Sch 2
   b Section 103, so far as material, is set out at p 134 *j* to p 135 *a*, post
   c Section 3(1) is set out at p 133 *j* to p 134 *a*, post
   d SI 1959 No 2206
   e Section 108 is set out at p 135 *d*, post
   f Regulation 3(1) is set out at p 132 *a b*, post
   g Section 3(6) is set out at p 134 *b c*, post

therefore s 3 of the 1959 order and with it the 1967 regulations made thereunder were invalid. The court increased the damages to $18,000 which included 'a small sum as exemplary damages'. The state appealed to the Privy Council, contending, inter alia, that the effect of s 108 of the Constitution was to preserve the 1959 order and the unrestricted powers it conferred on the Governor unimpaired by the Constitution until 1st September 1967. The state also contended that the Court of Appeal had erred in not quantifying the exemplary damages as a separate item.

Held – (i) Under the provisions of ss 103 and 108 of the Constitution the 1959 order continued to have effect until 1st September 1967 for the purpose of giving the state legislature time in which to pass legislation replacing it, but during the period from 27th February to 1st September the order was to be construed in conformity with the Constitution. The power to arrest and detain contained in the order therefore had to be modified, adapted, qualified or excepted as required by s 103(1) so as to conform generally with the protection of fundamental rights and freedoms contained in the Constitution and in particular with the power contained in s 14[h] to arrest and detain only if it was reasonably justifiable to do so. Accordingly, for the period from 27th February to 1st September the 1959 order was to be construed as empowering the Governor to make emergency laws only to the extent that the measures taken were reasonably justifiable for dealing with the situation which existed during a period of public emergency (see p 135 g to p 136 b, post).

(ii) It followed that the 1967 regulations made under the 1959 order were to be similarly construed in conformity with the Constitution, with the result that the words 'If the Governor is satisfied that . . . it is necessary to exercise control over [a person]' in reg 3(1) thereof did not confer unrestricted power on the Governor but required him to be satisfied on reasonable grounds that it was reasonably justifiable and necessary to exercise control over the person before ordering him to be detained. On that construction, the 1967 regulations were therefore lawful and valid, but equally the detention of the plaintiff was invalid since no justification or ground for detaining him had been given to him or put forward at the 1967 inquiry or the trial of the action (see p 137 b to f, p 140 g h and p 141 d to g, post); dictum of Lord Atkin in *Liversidge v Anderson* [1941] 3 All ER at 356, *Nakkuda Ali v M F de S Jayaratne* [1951] AC 66 and *Secretary of State for Education and Science v Metropolitan Borough of Tameside* [1976] 3 All ER 665 considered.

(iii) When exemplary damages were awarded, the amount of such damages was not required to be specified separately from the amount of compensatory damages awarded. The Board would not therefore interfere with the award of damages to the plaintiff on that ground and there were no other grounds on which the Board was justified in interfering with it. The appeal would accordingly be dismissed (see p 141 j to p 142 a and c to e, post); dictum of Lord Devlin in *Rookes v Barnard* [1964] 1 All ER at 411 explained.

Per Curiam. The West Indies Associated States Court of Appeal is right to consider itself bound, like the English Court of Appeal, by its own previous decisions on a point of law. So long as there is an appeal from a Court of Appeal to the Board or to the House of Lords, the Court of Appeal should follow its own decisions on a point of law and leave it to the final appellate tribunal to correct any error in law which may have crept into any previous decision of the Court of Appeal (see p 139 g and p 140 e to g, post); *Young v Bristol Aeroplane Co Ltd* [1944] 2 All ER 293 approved.

Notes

For the office of Governor in the West Indies Associated States, see 6 Halsbury's Laws (4th Edn) para 1091, and for St Christopher, Nevis and Anguilla, see ibid paras 1079–1100.

Cases referred to in judgment

Australian Agricultural Co v Federated Engine-Drivers and Firemen's Association of Australia (1913) 17 CLR 261, 28(2) Digest (Reissue) 1106, *600.

---

h   Section 14 is set out at p 000, post

Charles v Phillips and Sealey (1967) 10 WIR 423.

a *Farrell v Alexander* [1976] 2 All ER 721, [1977] AC 59, [1976] 3 WLR 145, 32 P & CR 292, HL.

Herbert v Phillips and Sealey (1967) 10 WIR 435.

Liversidge v Anderson [1941] 3 All ER 338, [1942] AC 206, 110 LJKB 724, 166 LT 1, HL, 17 Digest (Reissue) 467, 28.

Minister of Home Affairs v Fisher, p 21, ante, [1979] 2 WLR 889, PC.

b *Nakkuda Ali v MF de S Jayaratne* [1951] AC 66, PC, 8(2) Digest (Reissue) 811, 621.

Ridge v Baldwin [1963] 2 All ER 66, [1964] AC 40, [1963] 2 WLR 935, 127 JP 295, 61 LGR 369, HL, 37 Digest (Repl) 195, 32.

Rookes v Barnard [1964] 1 All ER 367, [1964] AC 1129, [1964] 2 WLR 269, [1964] 1 Lloyd's Rep 28, HL, 17 Digest (Reissue) 81, 14.

Secretary of State for Education and Science v Metropolitan Borough of Tameside [1976] 3 All
c ER 665, [1977] AC 1014, [1976] 3 WLR 641, 75 LGR 190, HL.

Young v Bristol Aeroplane Co Ltd [1944] 2 All ER 293, [1944] KB 718, 113 LJKB 513, 171 LT 113, CA; affd [1946] 1 All ER 98, [1946] AC 163, 115 LJKB 63, 174 LT 39, 79 Ll L Rep 35, HL, 30 Digest (Reissue) 269, 765.

Appeal

d John Joseph Reynolds brought an action against the Attorney-General of St Christopher, Nevis and Anguilla, as representing the State of St Christopher, Nevis and Anguilla, for damages and compensation for assault, battery and false imprisonment. On 15th October 1976 the High Court of St Christopher, Nevis and Anguilla (Glasgow J) awarded Mr Reynolds the sum of $5,000 damages against the Attorney-General. On 28th November 1977 the Court of Appeal of the West Indies Associated States Supreme Court, St Christopher, Nevis, Anguilla, St Christopher Circuit (St Bernard ACJ, Peterkin JA and
e Nedd AJA) dismissed an appeal by the Attorney-General and allowed a cross-appeal by Mr Reynolds by increasing the award of damages to $18,000. By leave granted by the Court of Appeal on 30th November 1977 the Attorney-General appealed to the Judicial Committee of the Privy Council. The facts are set out in the judgment of the Board.

f *The Attorney-General of St Christopher, Nevis and Anguilla (Lee L Moore), Henry L Browne* (Crown Counsel of St Christopher, Nevis and Anguilla), *Richard Fernyhough* and *Delano Bart* with him, in his own behalf.
Jonathan Harvie for Mr Reynolds.

LORD SALMON. Before dealing with the important points of law raised by this
g appeal, it is necessary to set out the relevant facts which were established by uncontradicted and unchallenged evidence called on behalf of Mr John Joseph Reynolds at the trial of an action which he brought against the Attorney-General of the State of St Christopher, Nevis and Anguilla and to which reference will be made later in this judgment.

Mr Reynolds was a member of the Leeward Islands Police Force from 20th October
h 1933 to 31st December 1959 and of the St Christopher, Nevis and Anguilla Police Force from 1st January 1960 until 26th October 1964. Having then reached the age limit, he retired from the force holding the rank of inspector of police. Prior to his retirement he had on at least one occasion acted as assistant superintendent of police and he had received the Police Efficiency Medal and the Police Long Service Medal. He was described by the Chief of Police in his discharge certificate as a 'dependable and
j knowledgeable officer'. Mr Reynolds was a happily married man with four children whose conduct and behaviour reflected 'a good home upbringing'. He had the reputation of being 'a very decent and upright person' and a good churchman. He was also a member of the People's Action Movement, which was a political party in opposition to the party in power in 1967.

On 30th May 1967 the Governor of the State of St Christopher, Nevis and Anguilla (which will be referred to in this judgment as 'the state') made a proclamation declaring that a state of emergency was in existence. On the same day he made and published the Emergency Powers Regulations 1967. The only relevant regulation is reg 3(1), which reads as follows:

> '*Detention of Persons.* If the Governor is satisfied that any person has recently been concerned in acts prejudicial to the public safety, or to public order or in the preparation or instigation of such acts, or in impeding the maintenance of supplies and services essential to the life of the community and that by reason thereof it is necessary to exercise control over him, he may make an order against that person directing that he be detained.'

On 10th June 1967 Mr Reynolds was warned by an anonymous telephone call and by certain acquaintances that he was about to be arrested and imprisoned, and he was advised by his acquaintances to return to Antigua, where he was born. Mr Reynolds replied that he had done nothing wrongful, so he had nothing to fear and would stay where he was. On 11th June 1967 Mr Reynolds was arrested by the police and taken to the prison where he was detained until 10th August 1967 in most insanitary and humiliating conditions. His arrest and detention were carried out under a detention order signed by the Deputy Governor. It reads as follows:

> 'ORDER MADE UNDER THE EMERGENCY POWERS REGULATIONS, 1967
> 'WHEREAS I am satisfied with respect to JOHN REYNOLDS that he has recently been concerned in acts prejudicial to the public safety and to public order, and that by reason thereof it is necessary to exercise control over him:
> 'NOW THEREFORE, in pursuance of the power conferred on me by Regulation 3 of the Emergency Powers Regulations, 1967, and all other powers thereunto enabling me, I DO HEREBY ORDER AND DIRECT that the said JOHN REYNOLDS be detained.
> 'Ordered by me this 10th day of June, 1967
>
> (sgd.) B. F. DIAS
> 'Governor's Deputy.'

On 16th June 1967 the following written statement (supposedly under s 15(1)(a) of the Constitution[1] which is set out later in this judgment) was delivered to Mr Reynolds whilst he was in prison:

> 'That you JOHN REYNOLDS during the year 1967, both within and outside of the State, encouraged civil disobedience throughout the State, thereby endangering the peace, public safety and public order of the State.'

Early in July 1967 a tribunal presided over by a chairman, who later became a Supreme Court judge, inquired into the cases of a number of persons, including Mr Reynolds, then detained in prison. This inquiry was held under s 15(1)(c), (d) and (e) of the Constitution. The hearings lasted about two weeks. The government was represented by senior Crown counsel. Mr Reynolds and the other detainees were also legally represented. During the course of the hearings, the chairman said to Crown counsel: 'You have not led any evidence against John Reynolds [and two other detainees].' To which Crown counsel replied: 'I have no evidence against them.' The chairman said: 'So I can make my recommendation.' Crown counsel replied: 'I will speak to the authorities.' The clear inference from those remarks was that the chairman considered that there were no grounds for detaining Mr Reynolds and that Crown counsel agreed and would report accordingly to the authorities.

It was not, however, until 10th August 1967 that Mr Reynolds was released from detention. This happened to be on the same day as that on which the Court of Appeal gave judgment ordering that Mr Charles and Dr Herbert, who had been arrested and detained at about the same time as Mr Reynolds, should be released on the grounds that

---

1   Saint Christopher, Nevis and Anguilla Constitution Order 1967 (SI 1967 No 228), Sch 2

the Emergency Powers Regulations 1967 contravened the Constitution and were
therefore unlawful, and that, accordingly, the detention orders made under those
regulations were invalid.

a

    Early in February 1968 Mr Reynolds brought an action against the state in the name
of the Attorney-General claiming, amongst other things, damages for false imprisonment
and compensation under s 3(6) of the Constitution on the ground that his detention had
been unlawful. The defence delivered early in March 1968 alleged that Mr Reynolds had
been lawfully arrested and detained and that, in any event, his claim should be 'discharged
and made void' under the state's Idemnity Act 1968. On 28th May 1968 the solicitor
acting for the Attorney-General issued a summons praying that Mr Reynolds's action
should be stayed under the Indemnity Act 1968. After that, nothing happened for about
five years until April 1973, when the Attorney-General's summons for a stay of the action
was heard and dismissed by Glasgow J. After about another three years' delay, the action
finally came on for hearing before Glasgow J towards the end of July 1976. The trial
judge gave judgment for Mr Reynolds, holding that he was bound to find that Mr
Reynolds's arrest and detention were unlawful because of the decisions of the Court of
Appeal in *Charles v Phillips and Sealey*[1] and *Herbert v Phillips and Sealey*[2]. Glasgow J also
found that the Indemnity Act 1968 contravened the Constitution and accordingly was of
no effect, and he gave judgment for Mr Reynolds for the sum of $5,000.

b

c

d

    The Attorney-General appealed from that judgment, and Mr Reynolds cross-appealed
praying that the judgment should be varied by increasing the sum of the damages
awarded. The Court of Appeal dismissed the appeal and allowed the cross-appeal
increasing the damages to $18,000. The Attorney-General now appeals to Her Majesty
the Queen in Council from both those decisions of the Court of Appeal.

    This appeal raises the three following points of law and a fourth point of mixed fact
and law. 1. Were the Emergency Power Regulations 1967 lawful? 2. If they were, was
the detention order made against Mr Reynolds under those regulations lawful? 3. If the
first two points or either of them is decided in favour of Mr Reynolds, does his claim fail
because of the Indemnity Act 1968? 4. If Mr Reynolds' claim succeeds, ought the award
of $18,000 to be reduced?

e

    1. The first is probably the most important point to be decided, namely, whether or
not the Emergency Powers Regulations 1967 were lawful. They purport to be made by
the Governor under the Leeward Islands (Emergency Powers) Order in Council 1959[3]
and s 17(1) of the Constitution.

f

    Section 17(1) of the Constitution empowers the Governor to proclaim a state of
emergency but it gives him no power to make any regulations. Accordingly, the only
source from which the Governor could derive the power to make regulations in a state
of emergency was the Order in Council of 1959.

g

    This Order in Council had originally been made under s 3 of the Leeward Islands Act
1956, which was repealed by the West Indies Act 1962. This latter Act however enabled
the 1959 Order in Council to be kept alive because the West Indies (Dissolution and
Interim Commissioner) Order in Council 1962[4] was made under it. That Order in
Council provided that all laws in force in each territory immediately before the
dissolution of the federation (which included the 1959 Order in Council) should remain
in force. The 1962 Order in Council also amended the 1959 Order in Council by adding
three new subsections to it.

h

    The only relevant section of the 1959 Order in Council is s 3(1) which reads as follows:

       'The Administrator of a Colony to which this Order applies may, during a period
       of emergency in that Colony, make such laws for the Colony as appear to him to be
       necessary or expedient for securing the public safety, the defence of the Colony or

j

1   (1967) 10 WIR 423
2   (1967) 10 WIR 435
3   SI 1959 No 2206
4   SI 1962 No 1084

the maintenance of public order or for maintaining supplies and services essential to the life of the community.'   *a*

In order to decide whether the Emergency Powers Regulations 1967 and the detention order against Mr Reynolds were lawful, it is necessary to examine the following relevant parts of the Constitution.

Section 3:

'(1) No person shall be deprived of his personal liberty save as may be authorised *b* by law in any of the following cases, that is to say:—[none of the cases then recited in this subsection includes regulations made by the Governor]...

'(6) Any person who is unlawfully arrested or detained by any other person shall be entitled to compensation therefor from that other person or from any other person or authority on whose behalf that other person was acting.'   *c*

Section 14:

'Nothing contained in or done under the authority of a law enacted by the Legislature shall be held to be inconsistent with or in contravention of section 3 or section 13 of this Constitution to the extent that the law authorises the taking during any period of public emergency of measures that are reasonably justifiable for dealing with the situation that exists in [the state] during that period.'   *d*

Section 15:

'(1) When a person is detained by virtue of any such law as is referred to in section 14 of this Constitution the following provisions shall apply, that is to say:—(a) he shall as soon as reasonably practicable and in any case not more than seven days after the commencement of his detention be furnished with a statement in writing in a *e* language that he understands specifying in detail the grounds upon which he is detained...'

The rest of this subsection provides, amongst other things, that not more than one month after the commencement of the detention, the detainee's case shall be reviewed by an independent and impartial tribunal, that the detainee shall be allowed to have a *f* lawyer to represent him before the tribunal and that the tribunal may make recommendations to the authority by which the detention was ordered but that authority shall not be obliged to act on such representations.

Section 16:

'(1) If any person alleges that any of the provisions of sections 2 to 15 (inclusive) *g* of this Constitution has been ... contravened in relation to him ... then, without prejudice to any other action with respect to the same matter which is lawfully available, that person ... may apply to the High Court for redress. ...'

Section 35 is the entrenchment section and provides, amongst other things, that the legislature may not alter any of the provisions of the Constitution except by the votes of *h* not less than two-thirds of all the elected members of the House of Assembly, and also provides that a Bill to alter s 35 or Sch 1 to the Constitution, or any of the provisions of the Constitution specified in Part I of that schedule, shall not be submitted to the Governor for assent unless after the Bill has passed the House of Assembly it is approved on a referendum by not less than two-thirds of all the votes validly cast on that referendum. Part I of Sch 1 to the Constitution specifies, inter alia, ss 1 to 18 inclusive *j* of the Constitution.

Section 103:

'(1) The existing laws shall, as from the commencement of this Constitution, be construed with such modifications, adaptations, qualifications and exceptions as may be necessary to bring them into conformity with . . . this Constitution . . .

a   '(2) Where any matter that falls to be prescribed or otherwise provided for under this Constitution by the Legislature or by any other authority or person is prescribed or provided for by or under an existing law . . . that prescription or provision shall, as from the commencement of this Constitution, have effect (with such modifications, adaptations, qualifications and exceptions as may be necessary to bring it into conformity with . . . this Constitution . . .) as if it had been made under

b this Constitution by the Legislature or, as the case may require, by the other authority or person.

'(3) The Governor may by Order made at any time before 1st September 1967 make such amendments to any existing law as may appear to him to be necessary or expedient for bringing that law into conformity with the provisions of . . . this Constitution . . . or otherwise for giving effect or enabling effect to be given to those

c provisions . . .

'(5) For the purposes of this section, the expression "existing law" means any Act, Ordinance, law, rule, regulation, order or other instrument made in pursuance of (or continuing in operation under) . . . the West Indies (Dissolution and Interim Commissioner) Order in Council 1962[1] and having effect as part of the law of [the state] . . . immediately before the commencement of this Constitution.'

d   Section 108:

'The Leeward Islands (Emergency Powers) Order in Council 1959[2] shall cease to have effect as part of the law of [the state] on 1st September 1967 or such earlier date as the Legislature may prescribe.'

Their Lordships consider that s 103(5) makes it plain, beyond doubt, that the 1959

e Order in Council was an 'existing law' immediately before the commencement of the Constitution. The Constitution came into operation on 27th February 1967 (see the Saint Christopher, Nevis and Anguilla Constitution Order 1967[3], s 1(2)). Nor are their Lordships in any doubt that the 1959 Order in Council continued to have effect, with the modifications and adaptations which will presently be described, until 1st September 1967 or such earlier date as the legislature may have prescribed. The legislature certainly

f made no such prescription before 10th August 1967, the date on which Mr Reynolds was released.

The Attorney-General, whose arguments were all most ably presented, contended however that the effect of s 108 of the Constitution was to preserve (for the period specified) the Order in Council in full force and vigour as drafted. He submitted that, by reason of the section, the Constitution left untouched and unimpaired the provisions of

g the Order in Council and the powers it conferred on the Governor. Their Lordships cannot accept this submission. The purpose of s 108 was a limited one, to ensure that powers existed to deal with an emergency, should one arise (as, indeed, happened) before the legislature had enacted appropriate (and constitutional) legislation for dealing with such an event. Their Lordships cannot read the section as limiting the generality of s 103 or protecting the Order in Council from any modifications or adaptations necessary to

h bring it into line with the Constitution.

It seems plain that s 108 intended to give the legislature six months within which to pass an Act replacing the Order in Council. This gave the legislature ample time; and they would surely have passed such an Act within the specified period. Otherwise, in a state of emergency, there would have been no law giving the Governor or any other authority the right to arrest and detain anyone, however reasonably justifiable and

j urgently necessary it may have been to do so. During a period of emergency it may well be urgently necessary, in order to preserve the safety of the state, to detain certain persons

---

1   SI 1962 No 1084
2   SI 1959 No 2206
3   SI 1967 No 228

immediately. If the House of Assembly were not sitting, or even if it were, it might be impossible to get the necessary Act through in time to deal effectively with the danger *a* to the state. Until 1st September 1967, however, but only until such date, the 1959 Order in Council, construed with such modifications, adaptations, qualifications and exceptions as were necessary to bring it into conformity with the Constitution, would be available to preserve the safety of the state if and when a period of emergency came into existence.

In *Charles v Phillips and Sealey*[1] and in *Herbert v Phillips and Sealey*[2] the Court of Appeal *b* held (1) that the provisions of s 3 of the 1959 Order in Council were not in conformity with the Constitution and (2) that they were so much out of conformity, that it was impossible to construe them so as to bring them into conformity with the Constitution, and that, therefore, the Emergency Powers Regulations 1967 which purported to be made under that Order in Council were invalid. Their Lordships agree with the first part of that finding but not with the second. *c*

The law laid down by s 3 of the 1959 Order in Council (as it originally stood) and by s 14 of the Constitution had the same purpose, namely, to ensure that measures could immediately be taken during a state of public emergency, to arrest and detain persons whom it was necessary to arrest and detain in order to secure public safety or public order. The difference between the two laws was that the first law gave an authority absolute discretion, and indeed the power of a dictator, to arrest and detain anyone, *d* whilst s 14 of the Constitution allows a law to be enacted conferring power to arrest and detain only if it was reasonably justifiable to exercise such a power. It is this very real difference which makes the 1959 Order in Council out of tune with the Constitution. If the Court of Appeal were right in concluding that no modification or adaptation or qualification or exception could bring the Order in Council into line with the Constitution, then they would have been plainly right in holding that the Order in *e* Council was nugatory and the Emergency Powers Regulations 1967 invalid. Their Lordships cannot, however, accept that the Constitution would have preserved the life of the 1959 Order in Council for any period if the Order in Council could not be construed under s 103 of the Constitution so as to bring it into conformity with the Constitution. It is inconceivable that a law which gave absolute power to arrest and detain without reasonable justification would be tolerated by a Constitution such as the present, one of *f* the principal purposes of which is to protect fundamental rights and freedoms. Their Lordships do not consider that there is any difficulty in construing the Order in Council by modification, adaptation, qualification or exception so as to bring it into conformity with the Constitution. As stated in the judgment of their Lordships' Board in *Minister of Home Affairs v Fisher*[3], a Constitution should be construed with less rigidity and more generosity than other Acts. Their Lordships are of opinion that the Order in Council *g* should be construed, in accordance with s 103(1) and in the light of s 14 of the Constitution, as follows: 'The Governor of a state may, during a period of public emergency in that state, make such laws for securing the public safety or defence of the state or the maintenance of public order or for maintaining supplies and services essential to the life of the community, to the extent that those laws authorise the taking of measures that are reasonably justifiable for dealing with the situation that exists in the *h* state during any such period of public emergency.'

Having regard to the view which their Lordships take about s 103(1), it is perhaps unnecessary to express any opinion about the rather abstruse sub-s (2) of s 103 of the Constitution. Out of respect, however, for the arguments addressed to their Lordships' Board on this subsection, their Lordships would observe that as the Constitution preserved the life of the 1959 Order in Council for a limited period, it seems to follow *j* that if, during that period, a state of emergency arose, it would fall to be provided for, not

---

1   (1967) 10 WIR 423
2   (1967) 10 WIR 435
3   See p 26, ante

by the legislature, but by an 'existing law', namely the 1959 Order in Council, and that
a that Order in Council, during its life after 'the commencement of [the] Constitution',
would have effect 'with such modifications, adaptations, qualifications and exceptions as
may be necessary to bring it into conformity with [the] Constitution'. If this view is
correct, the Order in Council would have exactly the same effect under s 103(2) as it has
under the construction which their Lordships have given it under s 103(1) of the
Constitution.

b   In these circumstances, the fact that the Governor did not exercise his power under
s 103(3) of the Constitution to amend the 1959 Order in Council so as to bring it into
conformity with the Constitution is irrelevant.

Since this judgment decides that the Order in Council can and should be construed so
as to bring it into conformity with the Constitution, it destroys the basis on which the
Court of Appeal found that the Emergency Powers Regulations 1967, made under that
c Order in Council, were invalid. It does not however necessarily follow that the
Emergency Powers Regulations are therefore valid. Their validity depends on the
proper construction of the following crucial words in reg 3(1): 'If the Governor is
satisfied . . .' These words can and should be given a meaning which is consistent with
ss 3 and 14 of the Constitution and with the construction which their Lordships have put
on the Order in Council under which the regulation was made. Accordingly 'is satisfied',
d which might otherwise mean 'thinks' or 'believes', does mean 'If the Governor is satisfied
satisfied on reasonable grounds that any person has recently been concerned in acts
prejudicial to the public safety, or to public order . . . and that by reason thereof it is
reasonably justifiable and necessary to exercise control over him, he may make an order
against that person directing that he be detained.'

Their Lordships consider that it is impossible that a regulation made on 30th May
e 1967 under an Order in Council which, on its true construction, conformed with the
Constitution on that date, could be properly construed as conferring dictatorial powers
on the Governor; and that is what the regulation would purport to do if the words 'if the
Governor is satisfied' mean 'if the Governor thinks etc'. No doubt Hitler thought that
the measures, even the most atrocious measures, which he took were necessary and
justifiable, but no reasonable man could think any such thing.

f   For these reasons their Lordships consider that reg 3(1) of the Emergency Powers
Regulations 1967, on its true construction, does conform with the Constitution.

Several authorities have been cited in argument which are helpful but none of which
is directly in point. The first is *Liversidge v Anderson*[1]. It concerns the construction of the
Defence (General) Regulations 1939[2], reg 18B (1), which, so far as relevant, read as
follows:

g   'If the Secretary of State has reasonable cause to believe any person to be of hostile
. . . associations . . . and that by reason thereof it is necessary to exercise control over
him, he may make an order against that person directing that he be detained.'

The plaintiff was detained by an order made under reg 18B (1), and he then brought an
action for damages for false imprisonment against the Home Secretary who had made
h the order for his detention. The majority of the House of Lords decided that the words
'If the Secretary of State has reasonable cause to believe' meant 'if the Secretary of State
thinks that he has reasonable cause to believe' providing he acts in good faith. Lord
Atkin, in his celebrated dissenting speech, held that the words 'If the Secretary of State
has reasonable cause to believe' meant what they said, namely that they give only a
conditional authority to the Minister to detain any person without trial, the condition
j being that he has reasonable cause for the belief which leads to the detention order.

The Attorney-General, whilst not relying on the decision in *Liversidge v Anderson*[1]

---

1   [1941] 3 All ER 338, [1942] AC 206
2   SI 1939 No 927

because it was not directly in point, did however rely on the following passage in Lord Atkin's speech[1]:

> '... if there were a certain ambiguity in the words "has reasonable cause to believe" the question would be conclusively settled by the fact that the original form of the regulation issued in Sept., 1939, gave the Secretary of State the complete discretion now contended for ("The Secretary of State is satisfied, etc."). However, it was withdrawn, and was published in Nov. 1939, in its present form ... What is certain is that the legislature intentionally introduced the well-known safeguard by the changed form of words.'

Whilst their Lordships consider it unnecessary, for the reasons given by the Attorney-General, to express any view about what Lord Reid in *Ridge v Baldwin*[2] described as 'the very peculiar decision of this House in *Liversidge* v. *Anderson*[3]', they do consider it necessary to deal with the passage in Lord Atkin's speech on which the Attorney-General did rely. No doubt that passage supports the argument that the words 'The Secretary of State is satisfied, etc' *may* confer an absolute discretion on the Executive. Sometimes they do, but sometimes they do not. In *Secretary of State for Education and Science v Metropolitan Borough of Tameside*[4] the question arose whether s 68 of the Education Act 1944 gave an absolute discretion to the Secretary of State. That section reads as follows:

> 'If the Secretary of State is satisfied ... that any local education authority ... have acted or are proposing to act unreasonably with respect to the exercise of any power conferred or the performance of any duty imposed by ... this Act [on the authority], he may, notwithstanding any enactment rendering the exercise of the power or the performance of the duty contingent upon the opinion of the authority ... give such directions as to the exercise of the power or the performance of the duty as appear to him to be expedient.'

The House of Lords decided that that section's opening words 'If the Secretary of State is satisfied' did not confer an absolute discretion on him, and that accordingly the court should exercise its judgment (a) whether grounds existed which were capable of supporting the Secretary of State's decision and (b) whether he had misdirected himself on the law in arriving at his decision. The House also held[5] that, if no such grounds existed or the Secretary of State had misdirected himself, his decision, however bona fide it was, should be overruled.

The *Tameside* case[4] was exceptional in that the Secretary of State had to be satisfied not that the local authority had made a wrong decision in the exercise of the power conferred on them but that they had made a decision which no reasonable local authority could have made. The decision which the local authority made, that certain grammar schools should continue in existence and should not be turned into comprehensive schools, was a policy decision. It may have been right or wrong but it certainly was not a decision at which no reasonable local authority could have arrived. Similarly, the local authority's decision that there was plenty of time before the beginning of the next term in which to make the necessary arrangements for the grammar schools to continue in existence may have been right or wrong. It was however impossible for the Secretary of State to have been satisfied that no reasonable authority could have come to that decision on the evidence which was before them. Accordingly it followed either that the Secretary of State had misdirected himself as to the true meaning of s 68 of the Education Act 1944 or that no reasonable Secretary of State could have been satisfied that the local authority's decision was a decision at which no reasonable local authority could have arrived.

---

1   [1941] 3 All ER 338 at 356, [1942] AC 206 at 237
2   [1963] 2 All ER 66 at 76, [1964] AC 40 at 73
3   [1941] 3 All ER 338, [1942] AC 206
4   [1976] 3 All ER 665, [1977] AC 1014
5   [1976] 3 All ER 665 at 682, 695, 700, 703, [1977] AC 1014 at 1047, 1064–1065, 1070, 1074

In *Nakkuda Ali v M F de S Jayaratne*[1] their Lordships' Board, on an appeal from the
a Supreme Court of Ceylon, had to consider the meaning of reg 62 of the Defence (Control
of Textiles) Regulations 1945 (Ceylon), which read as follows:

> 'Where the Controller has reasonable grounds to believe that any dealer is unfit
> to be allowed to continue as a dealer, the Controller may cancel the textile licence
> . . . issued to that dealer.'

b Lord Radcliffe, in delivering the judgment of this Board, referred to *Liversidge v
Anderson*[2], and said[3]:

> 'Their Lordships do not adopt a similar construction of the words in reg. 62 . . .
> Indeed, it would be a very unfortunate thing if the decision of *Liversidge's* case[2] came
> to be regarded as laying down any general rule of law as to the construction of such
> phrases when they appear in statutory enactments . . . After all, words such as these
c are commonly found when a . . . law-making authority confers powers on a minister
> or official. However read, they must be intended to serve in some sense as a
> condition limiting the exercise of an otherwise arbitrary power. But if the question
> whether the condition has been satisfied is to be conclusively decided by the man
> who wields the power the value of the intended restraint is in effect nothing . . .
> Their Lordships therefore treat the words in reg. 62 . . . as imposing a condition that
d there must in fact exist such reasonable grounds, known to the Controller, before he
> can validly exercise the power of cancellation.'

The facts and background of the *Tameside* case[4], *Liversidge v Anderson*[2], the *Nakkuda Ali*
case[1] and the present case are, of course, all very different from each other. This is why
their Lordships have reached their conclusion as to the true construction of reg 3(1) of the
e Emergency Powers Regulations 1967, in reliance chiefly on the light shed by the
Constitution, rather than on such light as may be thrown on that regulation by the
authorities to which reference has been made.

Their Lordships have been asked by the Attorney-General to express their opinion
whether the Court of Appeal was right in considering itself to be bound by the two
previous decision of that court in *Charles v Phillips and Sealey*[5] and *Herbert v Phillips and
f Sealey*[6] to hold that reg 3(1) of the Emergency Powers Regulations 1967 was invalid.
Their Lordships consider that the Court of Appeal was right in holding itself to be so
bound, although their Lordships have decided that reg 3(1) was valid for the reasons
stated in this judgment.

Their Lordships agree with the decision in *Young v Bristol Aeroplane Co Ltd*[7] that, save
for three exceptions there stated but which are irrelevant to the present case, the Court
g of Appeal is bound by its own decisions on points of law. The Court of Appeal in
England has never since 1944 departed from that decision and the House of Lords has
frequently endorsed it, firstly in the *Bristol Aeroplane Co* case[8] itself and most recently in
Farrell v Alexander[9].

The opinion of their Lordships' Board and of the House of Lords on this question can

1 [1951] AC 66
2 [1941] 3 All ER 338, [1942] AC 206
3 [1951] AC 66 at 76–77
4 [1976] 3 All ER 665, [1977] AC 1014
5 (1967) 10 WIR 423
6 (1967) 10 WIR 435
7 [1944] 2 All ER 293, [1944] KB 718
8 [1946] 1 All ER 98 at 100, [1946] AC 163 at 169
9 [1976] 2 All ER 721 at 742, 753, [1977] AC 59 at 92, 105. But see also *Davis v Johnson* [1978] 1 All
ER 1132, [1979] AC 264

however be only of persuasive authority. No doubt it would be treated with great respect but it cannot be of binding authority because the point can never come before *a* this Board or the House of Lords for decision. Indeed if a case came before either in which the Court of Appeal had refused to follow one of its own previous decisions on a point of law the appeal would have to be dismissed if the final appellate tribunal concluded that the previous decision was wrong.

The Attorney-General has drawn the attention of this Board to *Australian Agricultural Co v Federated Engine-Drivers and Firemen's Association*[1] and in particular to a passage in the *b* judgment of Isaacs J in that case. That passage reads as follows[2]:

> 'The oath of a Justice of this Court is "to do right to all manner of people *according to law*". Our sworn loyalty is to the law itself, and to the organic law of the Constitution first of all. If, then, we find the law to be plainly in conflict with what we or any of our predecessors erroneously thought it to be, we have, as I conceive, no right to choose between giving effect to the law, and maintaining an incorrect *c* interpretation. It is not, in my opinion, better that the Court should be persistently wrong than that it should be ultimately right . . . In my opinion, where the prior decision is manifestly wrong . . . it is the paramount and sworn duty of this Court to declare the law truly.'

Attractive as this pronouncement may sound and great as is the reputation of Isaacs J, *d* their Lordships cannot agree that the basis on which which he rests his opinion is sound. After all, the judicial oath to which he refers is taken not only by judges of the High Court but by all judges. Accordingly, if any puisne judge sitting at first instance concluded that a judgment of the High Court, or, for that matter, of this Board, was wrong in law, he also would be bound by his oath to disregard that judgment. Their Lordships consider that if this became the accepted practice of the courts the law would *e* become so uncertain that no one could ever know what the law was or where he stood. This would certainly be very much contrary to the public good. So long as there is an appeal from a Court of Appeal to their Lordships' Board or to the House of Lords, the Court of Appeal should follow its own decisions on a point of law and leave it to the final appellate tribunal to correct any error in law which may have crept into any previous decision of the Court of Appeal. Neither their Lordships' Board nor the House of Lords *f* is now bound by its own decisions, and it is for them, in the very exceptional cases in which this Board or the House of Lords has plainly erred in the past, to correct those errors, just as it is for them alone to correct the errors of the Court of Appeal.

In the circumstances such as the present where there is an appeal from the Court of Appeal to their Lordships' Board it is, in their Lordships' view, for the reasons stated, most important in the public interest, that the Court of Appeal should be bound by its *g* own previous decision on questions of law save for the three exceptions specified in the *Bristol Aeroplane Co* case[3].

2. It is now necessary to consider the second question, whether the detention order made against Mr Reynolds was lawful. On the construction which their Lordships put on reg 3(1) of the Emergency Powers Regulations 1967, this question must depend on whether there existed reasonable grounds on which the Governor could be satisfied that *h* Mr Reynolds had been concerned in acts prejudicial to public safety or to public order and that, by reason thereof, it was reasonably justifiable and necessary to detain him.

Neither at the inquiry made early in July 1967 (to which reference has already been made in this judgment) nor at the trial of the present action presided over by Glasgow J nor in the Court of Appeal was there any glimmer of a suggestion put forward by the Governor or by the Attorney-General of any reason, justification or ground on which any *j* reasonable Governor could have been satisfied that Mr Reynolds had been concerned in

---

1   (1913) 17 CLR 261
2   17 CLR 261 at 278–279
3   [1944] 2 All ER 293, [1944] KB 718

acts prejudicial to the public safety or public order. Mr Reynolds gave evidence at the
a trial repeating what in effect he had said in evidence at the inquiry, namely that he had
been warned that he was about to be arrested and advised to leave the state, that he had
done nothing wrong and so he was not afraid and had decided to stay where he was. No
evidence was called by Crown counsel at the inquiry and none by the Attorney-General
during the trial of the action. Had there been any evidence which could have shown that
Mr Reynolds's detention was reasonably justifiable, surely it would have been called on
b both occasions.

Section 15(1) of the Constitution has been set out in full earlier in this judgment. It
provides that anyone in Mr Reynolds's position has to be furnished, not more than seven
days after the commencement of his detention, with a statement in writing specifying
'*in detail*' the grounds on which he was detained. As already mentioned, on the sixth day
after the commencement of his detention he was served with a notice supposed to be in
c accordance with s 15(1). It is very short and its barren words bear repetition:

'That you JOHN REYNOLDS during the year 1967, both within and outside of the
State, encouraged civil disobedience throughout the State, thereby endangering the
peace, public safety and public order of the State.'

d It is difficult to imagine anything more vague and ambiguous or less informative than
the words of this notice. It was indeed a mockery to put it forward as specifying in detail
the grounds on which Mr Reynolds was being detained.

It seems plain to their Lordships that the irresistible inference to be drawn from this
notice is that there were no grounds, far less any justifiable grounds, for detaining Mr
Reynolds. Had there been any such grounds they would surely have been set out in the
e notice. If they were omitted from the notice by accident, which is hardly likely,
evidence on behalf of the Governor could have been called by Crown counsel at the
hearing of the inquiry early in July 1967 or at the trial that took place about nine years
later, showing that his detention was reasonably justifiable. Naturally the Governor
would not have been obliged to furnish anyone with the sources of his information if he
considered that it was contrary to public policy to do so. He could, however, have had
f evidence called on his behalf or given evidence himself to state, with full particularity,
exactly what Mr Reynolds had done to justify his detention, and when and where and
how Mr Reynolds had done it. The fact that no grounds of any kind have been put
forward on behalf of the Governor to justify him making a detention order against Mr
Reynolds, and all the circumstances of the case, raise an irresistible presumption that no
such grounds have ever existed. Accordingly their Lordships have no doubt that the
detention order was invalid and that Mr Reynolds was unlawfully detained.
g
3. The next question concerns the Attorney-General's contention that the Indemnity
Act 1968 affords him complete protection against any such claim as the present. Sections
3 and 5 of that Act have been set out in Peterkin J A's judgment in the Court of Appeal
with which the other judges sitting with him concurred. It is unnecessary to repeat these
sections in this judgment. Their Lordships entirely agree with the Court of Appeal, for
h the reasons which they so clearly give, that 'the Indemnity Act is unconstitutional, null
and void'.

4. The last question that falls to be decided concerns the damages being raised to
$18,000 by the Court of Appeal. Clearly the trial judge, who gave an excellent judgment
on all the issues of law that arose, was in some doubt as to the amount of damages he
should award. He said: 'I am unable to find any similar cased decided in the region or
j elsewhere. They might have assisted me on the question of quantum.'

The Court of Appeal came to the unanimous conclusion that, taking everything into
account, the sum of $5,000 awarded at first instance was wholly inadequate, and they
raised that sum to $18,000. It is not the usual practice of their Lordships' Board to
interfere with the quantum of damages assessed by the Court of Appeal in cases of this
kind, save in exceptional circumstances. Their Lordships cannot find anything on the

facts of the present case which could justify them in interfering with the damages of
$18,000 as assessed by the Court of Appeal.

The Attorney-General relied on the last few words of the judgment which revealed
that the sum awarded included 'a small sum as exemplary damages'. His argument was
that no exemplary damages should have been awarded because compensation alone
could be claimed under s 3(6) of the Constitution. This, no doubt, would be true, but for
s 16(1) of the Constitution, which makes it plain that anyone seeking redress under the
Constitution may do so 'without prejudice to any other action with respect to the same
matter which is lawfully available'; and in the present case, Mr Reynolds claimed (1)
'Damages for . . . false imprisonment' and (2) 'compensation pursuant to the provisions
of section 3(6) of [the Constitution]'.

The Attorney-General did not dispute that, if the Governor had acted unconstitution-
ally, the present case would fall into the first category of the cases which the House of
Lords laid down as justifying an award of exemplary damages, namely, 'oppressive,
arbitrary or unconstitutional action by the servants of the government': see *Rookes v
Barnard*[1]. The Attorney-General did however argue that the Court of Appeal had erred
in not quantifying that part of the $18,000 which represented exemplary damages. The
observations on this topic in *Rookes v Barnard*[2] were confined to trials by jury. Even so,
they do not suggest that if the jury gives exemplary damages it must necessarily specify
the amount of those damages separately from the amount of compensatory damages
which it awards. Their Lordships are satisfied that obviously that judgment does not cast
any such obligation on a trial judge sitting alone or on the Court of Appeal. Accordingly,
their Lordships can find no grounds which could justify them in reducing the award of
$18,000 damages or remitting it for re-assessment.

For these reasons, their Lordships will humbly advise Her Majesty that the appeal be
dismissed with costs.

Appeal dismissed

Solicitors: *Kingsford Dorman & Co* (for the Attorney-General); *Philip Conway Thomas & Co*
(for Mr Reynolds).

Mary Rose Plummer   Barrister.

---

1   [1964] 1 All ER 367 at 410, [1964] AC 1129 at 1226
2   [1964] 1 All ER 367 at 411, [1964] AC 1129 at 1228

Re Attorney-General's References (Nos 1 and 2 of 1979)

COURT OF APPEAL, CRIMINAL DIVISION

ROSKILL LJ, BRISTOW AND MICHAEL DAVIES JJ

18th JUNE 1979

Criminal law – Burglary – Attempted burglary – Entering or attempting to enter a building or part of a building as a trespasser – Mens rea – Intent to steal – Indictment not alleging intention to steal any specific or identified object – Whether entering or attempting to enter building with the intention of stealing anything in building worth stealing sufficient intent to constitute offence – Theft Act 1968, s 9(1)(a).

Indictment – Theft-related offences – Framing of indictment where theft or attempted theft of specific objects not alleged.

Where a person is charged with burglary, contrary to s 9(1)(a)[a] of the Theft Act 1968, the particulars whereof are that that person entered a building or part of a building as a trespasser with the intention to steal therein, but the indictment does not aver an intention to steal any specific or identified object, the necessary intent for conviction is established if it is proved that at the moment of entering the building or a part thereof as a trespasser the accused intended to steal even though there was not in fact anything there worth stealing, for on a charge of burglary it is not necessary to prove that the accused intended to steal a specific object. It follows that the fact that the accused intended to steal only if there was anything worth stealing is not a defence to a charge of burglary where an intention to steal a specific object is not alleged. Similar considerations apply where the charge relates to attempted burglary (see p 144 *j*, p 145 *a*, p 150 *c*, p 151 *g* to p 152 *a* and *e f* and p 153 *c* to *e*, post); dictum of Lord Scarman in *Director of Public Prosecutions v Nock* [1978] 2 All ER at 664 and *R v Walkington* [1979] 2 All ER 716 applied; *R v Easom* [1971] 2 All ER 945, dictum of Lord Scarman in *R v Husseyn* (1977) 67 Cr App R at 132 and *R v Hector* (1978) 67 Cr App R 224 explained.

Where it is undesirable to frame an indictment of a theft-related offence by reference to the theft or attempted theft of specific objects, it is permissible, if the justice of the case so requires, to adopt a less precise method of pleading, by for example pleading in the indictment that the accused entered a building as a trespasser with intent to steal therein or, in relation to attempted theft, by particularising the objects of the attempted theft generically as, for example, some or all of the contents of a car or handbag, so long as the indictment correctly reflects the alleged offence and gives the accused adequate details of what he is alleged to have done (see p 148 *d*, p 152 *g* to p 153 *b*, post).

Notes

For burglary, see 11 Halsbury's Laws (4th Edn) para 1274, and for cases on the intent required for burglary, see 15 Digest (Reissue) 1355–1356, 11,829–11,843.

For the mental element in attempts, see 11 Halsbury's Laws (4th Edn) para 65, and for cases on the subject, see 14(1) Digest (Reissue) 107–109, 723–738.

For the particulars of offence in an indictment, see 11 Halsbury's Laws (4th Edn) para 204.

For the Theft Act 1968, s 9, see 8 Halsbury's Statutes (3rd Edn) 788.

Cases referred to in judgment

Director of Public Prosecutions v Nock [1978] 2 All ER 654, [1978] AC 979, [1978] 3 WLR 57, 67 Cr App R 116, HL.

---

a   Section 9(1), so far as material, is set out at p 145 *b*, post

Haughton v Smith [1973] 3 All ER 1109, [1975] AC 476, [1974] 2 WLR 1, 58 Cr App R
    198, HL, 14(1) Digest (Reissue) 113, 756.

a

Partington v Williams (1975) 62 Cr App R 220, CA, 14(1) Digest (Reissue) 113, 755.

R v Boʒickovic [1978] Crim LR 686, Crown Court at Nottingham.

R v Easom [1971] 2 All ER 945, [1971] 2 QB 315, [1971] 3 WLR 82, 135 JP 477, 55 Cr App
    R 410, CA, 14(1) Digest (Reissue) 112, 754.

R v Hector (1978) 67 Cr App R 224, CA.

R v Husseyn (1977) 67 Cr App R 131, sub nom *R v Hussein* [1978] Crim LR 219, CA.   b

R v M'Pherson (1857) Dears & B 197, 26 LJMC 134, 29 LTOS 129, 21 JP 325, 3 Jur NS 523,
    7 Cox CC 281, CCR, 14(1) Digest (Reissue) 112, 751.

R v Stark (5th October 1967) unreported, CA.

R v Walkington [1979] 2 All ER 716, CA.

Cases also cited

c

R v Bentham [1972] 3 All ER 271, [1973] QB 357, CA.

R v Buckingham (1976) 63 Cr App R 159, CA.

References

These were two references by the Attorney-General under s 36 of the Criminal Justice
Act 1972, asking the Court of Appeal, Criminal Division, to give its opinion on two   d
points of law. The terms of the references are set out in the judgment.

David Tudor Price QC and *Stephen Mitchell* for the Attorney-General.
Simon Brown as amicus curiae.

ROSKILL LJ delivered the following judgment of the court: We have before us two   e
references by Her Majesty's Attorney-General under s 36 of the Criminal Justice Act
1972, those being respectively nos 1 and 2 of 1979.

The matters arising for determination are of wide general importance for the
administration of justice both in the Crown Court and in magistrates' courts. There
appears, from what we have been told by counsel and from an admirable memorandum
prepared by the Law Commission for the assistance of the court on these references, to   f
be a question of law which is causing and has caused considerable confusion, and has led
to what would appear to be unjustified acquittals as a result of circuit judges or their
deputies in the Crown Court and also magistrates' courts acceding to submissions that
there was no case to answer, the submission being based on a single sentence in the
judgment of this court in *R v Husseyn*[1], decided on 8th December 1977, the court
consisting of Viscount Dilhorne, Lord Scarman and Cusack J. The Attorney-General has   g
referred two such cases decided in the Crown Court to this court in order that a decision
may be obtained whether the acquittals with which we are immediately concerned, and
also certain other acquittals of which we have been told, were in fact justified.

The question referred in reference no 1 is:

'Whether a man who has entered a house as a trespasser with the intention of
stealing money therein is entitled to be acquitted of an offence against s 9(1)(a) of   h
the Theft Act 1968 on the grounds that his intention to steal is conditional on his
finding money in the house.'

The answer of this court to this question is No.

In the second reference the question is:

'Whether a man who is attempting to enter a house as a trespasser with the   j
intention of stealing anything of value which he may find therein is entitled to be
acquitted of the offence of attempted burglary on the ground that at the time of the

---

1   (1977) 67 Cr App R 131

a   attempt his said intention was insufficient to amount to "the intention of stealing anything" necessary for conviction under s 9 of the Theft Act 1968.'

The answer of this court to this question is also No.

Since it is essential to have regard to the language of the relevant statute, we begin by reading s 9 of the Theft Act 1968, under the rubric 'Burglary':

b   '(1) A person is guilty of burglary if—(a) he enters any building or part of a building as a trespasser and with intent to commit any such offence as is mentioned in subsection (2) below . . . [I need not read para (b)]

'(2) The offences referred to in subsection (1)(a) above are offences of stealing anything in the building or part of a building in question of inflicting on any person therein any grievous bodily harm or raping any woman therein, and of doing unlawful damage to the building or anything therein.'

c   Now s 9(2) includes a reference to the offence of stealing, and that takes one back to s 1(1) which bears the rubric 'Basic definition of theft' and reads:

'A person is guilty of theft if he dishonestly appropriates property belonging to another with the intention of permanently depriving the other of it; and "thief" and "steal" shall be construed accordingly.'

d   How the present problem arises is told with admirable clarity in the Law Commission's memorandum. There are certain passages which I read in full, because it would be impossible, if I may say so, to improve on them:

'10. In turning to the problems raised by these references, it is desirable to say something about the term "conditional intention". From the letter from counsel
e   for the appellant in the July 1978 issue of the Criminal Law Review[1], it appears that during argument in R. v. Hussein[2] Viscount Dilhorne expressed strong disapproval of the use of "conditional intention". This is certainly understandable. The content of the criminal law should be kept as clear and simple as is consonant with reality and any development which required magistrates to think or Crown Court judges to sum up to juries in terms of all the verbal complexities which such pseudo-
f   philosophical or psychological concepts as conditional intent would involve could only be accepted if no other way could be found of enabling a fair and accurate description of the appropriate mental element in these crimes to be conveyed to those who have to decide such questions of fact. [Thus far this court wholeheartedly and emphatically agrees.] Nevertheless, it is a convenient term in which to describe collectively a variety of mental states in argument before an appellate court, and its
g   use in the text books, in Easom[3] and Hussein[2] and academic discussion of these and subsequent cases and in the present references themselves necessitate the use of this term in this memorandum. "Conditional intent" is used here to describe any state of mind falling short of an intention permanently to deprive a person of property of his, which property at the time of the intention is specific and identifiable in the mind of the accused. It means that the accused does not know what he is going to
h   steal but intends that he will steal whatever he finds of value or worthwhile stealing.'

We respectfully agree with Viscount Dilhorne's stated strong disapproval of the phrase, but if it is to be used, it should only be used for that limited purpose set out in the last sentence which I have read.

j   In para 13 the paper goes on:

_____

1   [1978] Crim LR 444–446
2   (1977) 67 Cr App R 131
3   [1971] 2 All ER 945, [1971] 2 QB 315

'The doctrine finds its first expression in the statement of Lord Scarman in *Hussein*[1] that "it cannot be said that one who has it in mind to steal only if what he finds is worth stealing has a present intention to steal". *Hussein*[2] was a case of attempted theft and, taken literally, the statement means that a conditional intent to steal in the sense of an intention to steal whatever the accused may find worth stealing or of value is insufficient to ground a charge of attempted theft. It follows from this that a charge or indictment for attempted theft must necessarily be quashed as bad in law if it specifies the mental element as "intending, at that time, to steal whatever he might find worth stealing (or of value) therein". Thus, wherever the prosecution has to establish an intention to steal as one of the constituents of a theft-related offence, it must prove a fixed and settled intention, contemporaneous with the act forming the other (actus reus) element of the offence, on the part of the accused, permanently to deprive someone of a specified indentifiable object which either exists or is believed by the accused to exist in or near the scene of his operations (or "the target", as the references aptly describe it). This is self-evident in cases of completed theft or "successful" burglary or robbery where, ex hypothesi, the accused is charged with having appropriated a specific identifiable object. The importance of the doctrine lies in the field of attempted theft or other cases where, although an intention to steal is required, the relevant actus reus does not postulate that anything should necessarily have been appropriated. These offences include burglary, attempted burglary, assault with intent to rob, or, as a suspected person, loitering with intent to steal or rob.'

Thus the so called doctrine of 'conditional intention' is described.

It will be useful to go through some of the cases to show how this so-called doctrine has developed and to explain, as each member of this court is satisfied is the position, that the whole problem arises from a misunderstanding of a crucial sentence in Lord Scarman's judgment[1], which must be read in the context in which it was uttered, namely an indictment which charged an attempt to steal a specific object.

We start with *R v Stark*[3] heard on 5th October 1967 in this court consisting of Edmund Davies LJ, Stephenson and James JJ. That case had been tried at Middlesex Sessions. The charge was larceny under the law as it was before the Theft Act 1968. It was plainly a decision on and only on misdirection. The charge was larceny of a tool kit out of the boot of a car, larceny of a specific object. The chairman at Middlesex Sessions had told the jury:

'The question here, really, is, is it not, and I think one cannot put it better than this: was Stark intending, if he could get away with it, and if it was worth while, to take that tool kit when he lifted it out? If he picked up something saying: "I am sticking to this, if it is worth while", then he would be guilty.'

Edmund Davies LJ went on:

'In the view of this court, that is not the correct way of stating the law; and if one looks at other passages where "if it is worth while" is repeated by the chairman we think it is possible the jury would have the impression that an innocent taking might be converted into a larceny although there was no intention permanently to deprive the owner of the alleged subject of the larceny at the time of taking because subsequently, although it might be quite a short time afterwards, the intention to steal was formed when the condition of worthwhileness had been satisfied.'

That passage lays down the general principle, but is merely a restatement of a proper direction to a jury where the charge was the larceny of a specific object.

---

1 (1977) 67 Cr App R 131 at 132
2 67 Cr App R 131
3 (5th October 1967) unreported

a The next case is *R v Easom*[1]. It is important in *R v Easom*[1] to observe what the indictment charged. It contained a single count[2] alleging that Easom 'stole one handbag, one purse, one notebook, a quantity of tissues, a quantity of cosmetics and one pen, the property of Joyce Crooks'. Once again the charge was of theft of specific objects. It was a typical case of attempted theft in a cinema.

The facts are set out in the judgment of the court, also delivered by Edmund Davies LJ[2]:

b   '. . . Woman Police Sergeant Crooks and other plain-clothes officers went to the Metropole cinema in Victoria. Sergeant Crooks sat in an aisle seat and put her handbag (containing the articles enumerated in the charge) alongside her on the floor. It was attached to her right wrist by a piece of black cotton. Pc Hensman sat next to her on the inside seat. When the house lights came on during an interval, it was seen that the appellant was occupying the aisle seat in the row immediately
c   behind Sergeant Crooks and that the seat next to him was vacant. Within a few minutes of the lights being put out, Sergeant Crooks felt the cotton attached to her wrist tighten. She thereupon gave Pc Hensman a pre-arranged signal. The cotton was again pulled, this time so strongly that she broke it off. Moments later the officers could hear the rustle of tissues and the sound of her handbag being closed. Very shortly afterwards the appellant left his seat and went to the lavatory. The
d   officers then turned round and found Sergeant Crooks's handbag on the floor behind her seat and in front of that which the appellant had vacated. Its contents were intact. When the appellant emerged from the lavatory and seated himself in another part of the cinema, he was approached by the police officers. When the offence of theft was put to him, he denied it.'

e The deputy chairman at London Sessions, like the chairman at Middlesex Sessions in *R v Stark*[3], had misdirected the jury, and in a somewhat similar respect. Edmund Davies LJ, after setting out that misdirection, said[4]:

      'In the respectful view of this court, the jury were misdirected. In every case of theft the appropriation must be accompanied by the intention of permanently depriving the owner of his property. What may be loosely described as a
f   "conditional" appropriation will not do. If the appropriator has it in mind merely to deprive the owner of such of his property as, on examination, proves worth taking and then finding that the booty is valueless to the appropriator, leaves it ready to hand to be repossessed by the owner, the appropriator has not stolen. If a dishonest postal sorter picks up a pile of letters, intending to steal any which are registered but, on finding that none of them are, replaces them, he has stolen
g   nothing, and this is so notwithstanding the provisions of s 6(1) of the Theft Act 1968. In the present case the jury were never invited to consider the possibility that such was the appellant's state of mind or the legal consequences flowing therefrom. Yet the facts are strongly indicative that this was exactly how his mind was working, for he left the handbag and its contents entirely intact and to hand, once he had carried out his exploration. For this reason we hold that conviction of
h   the full offence of theft cannot stand.'

There followed a discussion about attempt. Edmund Davies LJ said[5]:

      'But as to this, all (or, at least, much) depends on the manner in which the charge is framed. Thus: "If you indict a man for stealing your watch, you cannot convict

j ───

1   [1971] 2 All ER 945, [1971] 2 QB 315
2   [1971] 2 All ER 945 at 946, [1971] 2 QB 315 at 318
3   (5th October 1967) unreported
4   [1971] 2 All ER 945 at 947, [1971] 2 QB 315 at 319
5   [1971] 2 All ER 945 at 948–949, [1971] 2 QB 315 at 321

him of attempting to steal your umbrella", per Sir Alexander Cockburn CJ in *R v
M'Pherson*[1], unless, of course, the court of trial has duly exercised the wide powers
of amendment conferred by s 5 of the Indictments Act 1915. In our judgment, this
remains the law and it is unaffected by the provisions of s 6 of the Criminal Law Act
1967. No amendment was sought or effected in the present case, which accordingly
has to be considered in relation to the articles enumerated in the theft charge, and
in relation to nothing else. Furthermore, it is implicit in the concept of an attempt
that the person acting intends to do the act attempted, so that the mens rea of an
attempt is essentially that of the complete crime (see Smith and Hogan, Criminal
Law[2]). That being so, there could be no valid conviction of the appellant of
attempted theft on the present indictment unless it were established that he was
animated by the same intention permanently to deprive the police officer of the
goods enumerated in the particulars of the charge as would be necessary to establish
the full offence. We hope that we have already made sufficiently clear why we
consider that, in the light of the evidence and of the direction given, it is impossible
to uphold the verdict on the basis that such intention was established in this case.
For these reasons, we are compelled to allow the appeal and quash the conviction.'

Two things must be noted: first, the charge in question was not of attempted theft but
of theft, and secondly, the offence charged was theft of the handbag and of a number of
specific identified contents. But there is nothing in this decision which makes it wrong
in such a case to charge an attempt to steal the contents of a handbag, describing the
objects of the alleged attempted theft generically in that way.

The next case is *R v Husseyn*[3], the crucial sentence in the judgment in which has led to
the present controversy. *R v Husseyn*[3] is reported in the Criminal Appeal Reports as a
note to the decision of the House of Lords in *Director of Public Prosecutions v Nock*[4]. In this
and other reports of the decision the indictment is not set out. This omission has led to
much misunderstanding of the background to what Lord Scarman said. The indictment
in *R v Husseyn*[3] (the registrar has supplied the court with copies) was as follows:

'STATEMENT OF OFFENCE
'Attempted Theft.

'PARTICULARS OF OFFENCE
'Ulus Husseyn and Andrew Demetriou on or about the 27th day of February
1976 in Greater London, attempted to steal a quantity of sub-aqua equipment
belonging to David Johnson.'

Here therefore the relevant count was of attempted theft and not of theft, but the
charge related to a specific object. Therefore it was essential, in order to establish guilt
on this charge of attempted theft, that the accused's intention had been to steal, not the
contents of the parked van in question, but the specific object named in the count,
namely the sub-aqua equipment. Lord Scarman's judgment must be understood against
the background of that fundamental fact, which, unfortunately, appears to have been
overlooked until *R v Walkington*[5] came before this court last February.

The facts in *R v Husseyn*[3] were these. The appellant was seen by police officers standing
in the middle of the road, looking up and down. The officers heard an alarm go off and
one of them then noticed that another young man appeared to be tampering with the

1   (1857) Dears & B 197 at 200
2   2nd Edn (1969) p 163; see now 4th Edn (1978) p 247
3   (1977) 67 Cr App R 131
4   (1978) 67 Cr App R 116. *Director of Public Prosecutions v Nock* is also reported, but without a report
    of *R v Husseyn*, at [1978] 2 All ER 654, [1978] AC 979
5   [1979] 2 All ER 716

back door of a van. As the officer approached, the young man who was tampering with
a the back door appeared to close it and both young men, who proved to be the two
appellants, made off at a fast pace.

Lord Scarman dealt with the law relating to attempts and said that in that respect there
was no misdirection by the judge. But his Lordship then went on[1]:

'Very different considerations apply when one comes to consider the way the
learned judge summed up the issue of intention. The learned judge said that the
b jury could infer that what the young men were about was to look into the holdall
and, if its contents were valuable, to steal it. In the view of this Court that was a
misdirection. What has to be established is an intention to steal at the time when
the step is taken, which constitutes, or which is alleged to constitute, the attempt.
Edmund Davies L.J. put the point in EASOM[2]: "In every case of theft the appropriation
must be accompanied by the intention of permanently depriving the owner of his
c property. What may be *loosely* described as a 'conditional' appropriation will not
do. If the appropriator has it in mind merely to deprive the owner of such of his
property as, on examination, proves worth taking and then, finding that the booty
is valueless to the appropriator, leaves it ready to hand to be repossessed by the
owner, the appropriator has not stolen." The direction of the learned judge in this
case is exactly the contrary. It must be wrong, for it cannot be said that one who has
d it in mind to steal only if what he finds is worth stealing has a present intention to
steal.'

We were asked to say that either that last sentence was wrong or that it was obiter. We
are not prepared to do either. If we may say so with the utmost deference to any
statement of law by Lord Scarman, if this sentence be open to criticism, it is because in
e the context it is a little elliptical. If one rewrites that sentence, so that it reads 'It must be
wrong, for it cannot be said that one who has it in mind to steal only if what he finds is
worth stealing has a present intention to steal *the specific item charged*' (our emphasis), then
the difficulties disappear, because, as already stated, what was charged was attempted
theft of a specific object, just as what had been charged in *R v Easom*[3] had been the theft
of a number of specific objects.

f The next case in chronological order is *R v Hector*[4]. With respect to the reporter
concerned, the report of *R v Hector*[4] contains an inaccurate note at the beginning. It
contains the phrase 'Whether Conditional Intention Enough'. No such words or phrase
appear in the judgment of the court delivered by Lawton LJ.

Lawton LJ undoubtedly thought that although this particular conviction for attempted
theft could not be supported because of misdirection, had the appellant been charged
g with an offence under the Vagrancy Act 1824, he would have been liable to be
convicted. Lawton LJ said[5]: 'Up to that point his conduct had provided ample evidence
that he was loitering with intent to steal and that he was going about equipped for theft.'
Later Lawton LJ said[6]:

'It is necessary at this stage to call attention to the exact terms of the indictment.
The particulars of the offence read as follows: "Joseph Hector, on the 18th day of
h November, 1976, attempted to steal a spirometer, a peak flow meter and a clothes
dryer belonging to Susan Brailsford." I stress that it was an allegation of attempting
to steal specific articles.'

---

j 1 (1977) 67 Cr App R 131 at 132
     2 [1971] 2 All ER 945 at 947, [1971] 2 QB 315 at 319
     3 [1971] 2 All ER 945, [1971] 2 QB 315
     4 (1978) 67 Cr App R 224
     5 67 Cr App R 224 at 225
     6 67 Cr App R 224 at 226

Lawton LJ then referred to *R v Easom*[1] and pointed out that the direction given by the
judge was wrong and, as he put it[2]:

> 'The judge's failure to direct the jury on it means that the jury were not given the
> opportunity of considering a possible defence. A judge has a duty to direct the jury
> about any defence which is reasonably open to the accused. His failure to do so, in
> the ordinary way, makes a verdict unsatisfactory.'

So we have these four cases: *R v Stark*[3], *R v Easom*[1], *R v Husseyn*[4] and *R v Hector*[5]. In
each the charge related to specific objects and in each the conviction was quashed because
there had been a misdirection or because the Crown was not in a position to prove that
there was on the part of the accused person or persons at the relevant time an intent to
steal or to attempt to steal the specific objects which were the subject of the charges or for
both those reasons. None of those cases is authority for the proposition that, if a charge
is brought under s 9(1) of entering any building or part of a building as a trespasser with
intent to steal, the accused is entitled to acquittal unless it can be shown that at the time
he entered he had the intention of stealing specific objects.

The last case to which it is necessary to refer is *R v Walkington*[6]. Both counsel agree that
if *R v Walkington*[6] is right, as they submitted and as we think it clearly is, that decision is
conclusive as to the answer in reference no 1, for the reasons given by Geoffrey Lane LJ
in giving the judgment of the court.

R v Walkington[6] came before this court after the acquittals with which we are presently
concerned but before the then Attorney-General referred them to the court. But it is
right to say that when the Attorney-General referred these two cases, it was not known
whether the House of Lords would give leave to appeal in *R v Walkington*[6]. On 3rd May
1979 the Appeal Committee of the House of Lords refused such leave. Accordingly
we proceed on the footing that their Lordships did not consider that the decision in
R v Walkington[6] was open to question.

In *R v Walkington*[6] the indictment was for burglary. At the beginning of his judgment
Geoffrey Lane LJ set out the indictment[7]:

'STATEMENT OF OFFENCE
'Burglary, contrary to section 9(1)(a) of the Theft Act 1968.
'PARTICULARS OF OFFENCE
'Terence Walkington on the 15th day of January 1977 entered as a trespasser part
of a building known as Debenhams Store with intent to steal therein.'

Be it noted there was no averment in those particulars of any intention to steal any
specific or identified objects.

Geoffrey Lane LJ, after dealing with the first point which is presently irrelevant, dealt
with the second and relevant point[7]:

> 'The second ground has given us, if we may say so, rather more trouble. The
> reason why this second ground was not included in the original notice of appeal was
> that it is based on decisions of this court which had not seen the light of day at the
> time when the original notice of appeal was drawn. Consequently we deemed it
> right and fair that counsel for the appellant should have the opportunity of arguing
> the point and accordingly we gave leave. [Geoffrey Lane LJ then set out the

1 [1971] 2 All ER 945, [1971] 2 QB 315
2 (1978) 67 Cr App R 224 at 228
3 (5th October 1967) unreported
4 (1977) 67 Cr App R 131
5 67 Cr App R 224
6 [1979] 2 All ER 716
7 [1979] 2 All ER 716 at 717

additional ground and went on:] These submissions are based on the decision of
a   this court in *R v Husseyn*[1], if we may say so respectfully, a most powerful court,
because it consisted of Viscount Dilhorne, Lord Scarman and Cusack J.'

Geoffrey Lane LJ then read the headnote and the passage in Lord Scarman's judgment[2]
on which we have already commented. Geoffrey Lane LJ continued[3]:

'What counsel for the appellant suggests to us is that that last passage, the last
b   three sentences, meets the situation in this case and that if the facts were that the
appellant in this case had it in mind only to steal if what he found was worth
stealing, then he had no intention to steal. That is the way he put it. First of all we
would like to say that the particulars of offence in *R v Husseyn*[1] were that the two
men "attempted to steal a quantity of sub-aqua equipment". Plainly what
considerations have to be applied to a charge of attempting to steal a specific article
c   are different considerations from those which have to be applied when one is
considering what a person's intent or intention may be under s 9 of the Theft Act
1968. That, we feel, is sufficient to distinguish our case from *R v Husseyn*[1].'

Then Geoffrey Lane LJ read what Lord Scarman himself had said about *R v Husseyn*[1] in
Director of Public Prosecutions v Nock[4] (I will return to this shortly) and said[5]:

d   'In this case there is no doubt that the appellant was not on the evidence in two
minds as to whether to steal or not. He was intending to steal when he went to that
till and it would be totally unreal to ask oneself, or for the jury to ask themselves, the
question, what sort of intent did he have? Was it a conditional intention to steal if
there was money in the till or a conditional intention to steal only if what he found
there was worth stealing? In this case it was a cash till and what plainly he was
e   intending to steal was the contents of the till, which was cash. The mere fact that
the till happened to be empty does not destroy his undoubted intention at the
moment when he crossed the boundary between the legitimate part of the store and
the illegitimate part of the store. The judge's direction which we have cited already
covered that point, and the matter was accurately left to the jury. It has again been
pointed out to us, and it is right that we should make reference to it, that that
f   decision in *R v Husseyn*[1] has apparently been causing some difficulty to judges of the
Crown Court. We would refer to *R v Bozickovic*[6] and another, even more recent,
case, [I will not give its name, because that case is the subject of the first reference].
I will just read the brief report in [that case] which will suffice to demonstrate the
difficulties which have arisen . . .'

After reading that report Geoffrey Lane LJ went on[7]:

g   'A reading of that would make the layman wonder if the law had taken leave of
its senses, because, if that is the proper interpretation to be applied to s 9(1)(a) of the
1968 Act, there will seldom, if ever, be a case in which s 9(1)(a) will bite. It seems
to this court that in the end one simply has to go back to the words of the Act itself
which we have already cited, and if the jury are satisfied, so as to feel sure, that the
h   defendant has entered any building or part of a building as a trespasser, and are

---

j   1 (1977) 67 Cr App R 131
2 67 Cr App R 131 at 132
3 [1979] 2 All ER 716 at 723
4 [1978] 2 All ER 654 at 664, [1978] AC 979 at 1000
5 [1979] 2 All ER 716 at 724
6 [1978] Crim LR 686
7 [1979] 2 All ER 719 at 724–725

satisfied that at the moment of entering he intended to steal anything in the building or that part of it, the fact that there was nothing in the building worth his while to steal seems to us to be immaterial. He nevertheless had the intent to steal. As we see it, to hold otherwise would be to make a nonsense of this part of the Act 1968 and cannot have been the intention of the legislature at the time when the Theft Act was passed. Nearly every prospective burglar could no doubt truthfully say that he only intended to steal if he found something in the building worth stealing. So, whilst acknowledging that these recent decisions do provide difficulties which have been pointed out to us clearly by counsel for the appellant, it seems to us in the end that one must have regard to the wording of the Act. If that is done, the meaning, in our view, is clear.'

I come back to what Lord Scarman himself said in *Director of Public Prosecutions v Nock*[1]. His Lordship, after referring to the decision of the House of Lords in *Haughton v Smith*[2], said[3]:

'We were invited by the Crown to express an opinion as to the correctness or otherwise of three decisions of the Court of Appeal: *R v Easom*[4], *Partington v Williams*[5] and *R v Hussein*[6]. *R v Easom*[4] and *R v Hussein*[6] (to which I was a party) were, I think, correctly decided; but each, like every other criminal appeal, turned on its particular facts and on the way in which the trial judge directed the jury on the law. In *R v Easom*[4] Edmund Davies LJ emphasised that in a case of theft the appropriation must be accompanied by the intention of permanently depriving the owner of his property . This, of course, follows from the definition of theft in s 1(1) of the Theft Act 1968. All that *R v Hussein*[6] decided was that the same intention must be proved when the charge is one of attempted theft. Unfortunately in *R v Hussein*[6] the issue of intention was summed up in such a way as to suggest that theft, or attempted theft, could be committed by a person who had not yet formed the intention which the statute defines as a necessary part of the offence. An intention to steal can exist even though, unknown to the accused, there is nothing to steal; but, if a man be in two minds whether to steal or not, the intention required by the statute is not proved.'

We venture to draw particular attention to the opening part of that last sentence: 'An intention to steal can exist even though, unknown to the accused, there is nothing to steal . . .'

We had an interesting discussion, with the help of counsel, how, in these cases of burglary or theft or attempted burglary or theft, it is in future desirable to frame indictments. Plainly it may be undesirable in some cases to frame indictments by reference to the theft or attempted theft of specific objects. Obviously draftsmen of indictments require the maximum latitude to adapt the particulars charged to the facts of the particular case, but we see no reason in principle why what was described in argument as a more imprecise method of criminal pleading should not be adopted, if the justice of the case requires it, as for example attempting to steal some or all of the

1 [1978] 2 All ER 654 at 663, [1978] AC 979 at 999–1000
2 [1973] 3 All ER 1109, [1975] AC 476
3 [1978] 2 All ER 654 at 663–664, [1978] AC 979 at 1000
4 [1971] 2 All ER 945, [1971] 2 QB 315
5 (1975) 62 Cr App R 220
6 (1977) 67 Cr App R 131

contents of a car or some or all of the contents of a handbag. The indictment in
a R v Walkington[1] is in no way open to objection. There is no purpose in multiplying
further examples. It may be that in some cases further particulars might be asked for
and if so the prosecution could in a proper case no doubt give them without difficulty.
The important point is that the indictment should correctly reflect that which it is
alleged that the accused did, and that the accused should know with adequate detail what
he is alleged to have done.

b   Taking as an example the facts in R v Easom[2], plainly what the accused intended was
to steal some or all of the contents of the handbag if and when he got them into his
possession. It seems clear from the latter part of Edmund Davies LJ's judgment that, if
he had been charged with an attempt to steal some or all the contents of that handbag,
he could properly have been convicted, subject of course to a proper direction to the jury.

It follows that this court respectfully and wholeheartedly adopts Geoffrey Lane LJ's
c judgment on the second question in R v Walkington[1] which, as I have already said, is
conclusive of the answer in the first reference.

So far as the answer in the second reference is concerned, it would, as counsel appearing
as amicus curiae very properly agreed, be very strange if a different answer had to be
given in the second reference, which is concerned with attempted burglary, from that
given in the first reference. In our view it is impossible to justify giving different
d answers according to whether the charge is burglary or attempted burglary, theft or
attempted theft or loitering with intent to commit an arrestable offence, which in most
cases will be theft. In our view both principle and logic require the same answers in all
these cases.

For those reasons the answers in the two references will be, as I have already indicated,
No in the first and No in the second.

e
Opinions accordingly.

Solicitors: *Director of Public Prosecutions; Treasury Solicitor.*

Howard Roberts Esq   Barrister.

f _____

1   [1979] 2 All ER 716
2   [1971] 2 All ER 945, [1971] 2 QB 315

Re W (minors) (wardship: jurisdiction)

COURT OF APPEAL, CIVIL DIVISION
ORMROD, BROWNE AND BRIDGE LJJ
10th OCTOBER 1978

Child – Care – Local authority – Wardship proceedings – Jurisdiction of court to review decisions of local authority – Wardship proceedings by natural parent – Decision of local authority to discontinue parent's access to child – Local authority taking into account future possibility of adoption by foster parents in deciding to discontinue access – Whether jurisdiction to review merits of decision where wardship proceedings invoked by natural parent – Whether natural parent having inalienable right to access to child – Whether local authority misdirecting itself by taking into account future possibility of adoption – Children and Young Persons Act 1969, s 1.

The mother's two infant children were taken into care by the local authority, in 1970 and 1974 respectively, and made the subject of care orders under s 1 of the Children and Young Persons Act 1969, because of the stressful and violent domestic atmosphere in the parents' home. The children were placed with foster parents where the mother visited them. Her visits caused stress to the elder child and the local authority became concerned about the effect on the child of the visits. Accordingly in 1976 the local authority decided that the mother should no longer have access to the children, that long term fostering was inevitable and that it would be in the children's best interests for them to be adopted by the foster parents. The mother was notified of that decision. She issued a wardship summons to have the children made wards of court, for the purpose of seeking a review by the court of the decision to refuse her access to the children. On the hearing of the summons the judge concluded that on the existing authorities he was not entitled to exercise the wardship jurisdiction of the court in order to review the merits of the local authority's decision since it was a decision taken in exercise of the authority's discretion under the 1969 Act. He therefore discharged the wardship. The mother appealed. She did not seek to challenge the propriety of continuing the care orders but contended (i) that where a wardship application was made by a natural parent of a child subject to a care order the court was entitled to exercise the wardship jurisdiction to review the manner in which a local authority was exercising its powers under the 1969 Act, (ii) that a natural parent had an inalienable right of access to her child, and (iii) that the judge was not bound by the authorities because they dealt with wardship applications by foster parents and not by a natural parent. Alternatively, the mother contended that there was jurisdiction to review the local authority's decision on the ground that the authority had misdirected itself in reaching the decision to refuse access by taking into account the future possibility of adoption by the foster parents when that was irrelevant to the question of access.

Held – The appeal would be dismissed for the following reasons—

(i) A natural parent of a child subject to a care order was in the same position as foster parents and had no right to challenge the merits of a local authority's decision in respect of the child, since the exercise by the local authority of its discretionary powers under a care order could not be reviewed by the courts except under the limited supervisory jurisdiction to review administrative decisions which were unlawful. Moreover, a natural parent did not have an inalienable right of access to her child. It followed that the judge had been right to conclude that he was bound to abstain from exercising the wardship jurisdiction invoked by the mother (see p 158 c d and f g, p 160 b to d, p 161 a to c and f g, p 162 d and g h and p 163 c to e, post); *Re M (an infant)* [1961] 1 All ER 788, *Re T (AJJ) (an infant)* [1970] 2 All ER 865 and dictum of Ormrod LJ in *Re H (a minor) (wardship jurisdiction)* [1978] 2 All ER at 908–909 applied.

(ii) In considering what was in the best interests of a child a local authority had to look at the situation in the past and present and also at the future possibilities in relation to the *a* child. Accordingly, if it would be desirable in the future that the child should be adopted by its foster parents, that was a relevant factor to be taken into consideration in deciding whether it was proper to discontinue a parent's access to the child. It followed that the local authority had not misdirected itself in taking into account the possibility of future adoption by the foster parents when deciding whether to discontinue the mother's access to the children. There was no ground, therefore, on which the court could exercise its supervisory jurisdiction (see p 161 c to g and p 163 c to e, post); *Associated Provincial*

b *Picture Houses Ltd v Wednesbury Corpn* [1947] 2 All ER 680 applied.

Notes

For the care of a child by a local authority, see 24 Halsbury's Laws (4th Edn) para 787, for the assumption of parental rights by a local authority, see ibid paras 790–793, and for cases on the subject, see 28(2) Digest (Reissue) 940–943, 2432–2442.

c For wardship jurisdiction, see 24 Halsbury's Laws (4th Edn) paras 576–583, and for cases on the subject, see 28(2) Digest (Reissue) 911–916, 2220–2247.

For the Children and Young Persons Act 1969, s 1, see 40 Halsbury's Statutes (3rd Edn) 849, 882.

Cases referred to in judgments

d *Associated Provincial Picture Houses Ltd v Wednesbury Corpn* [1947] 2 All ER 680, [1948] 1 KB 223, [1948] LJR 190, 177 LT 641, 112 JP 55, 45 LGR 635, CA, 45 Digest (Repl) 215, 189.

H (a minor) (wardship: jurisdiction), Re [1978] 2 All ER 903, [1978] Fam 65, [1978] 2 WLR 608, 76 LGR 254, CA.

J v C [1969] 1 All ER 788, [1970] AC 668, [1969] 2 WLR 540, HL, 28(2) Digest (Reissue)

e 800, 1230.

M (an infant), Re [1961] 1 All ER 788, [1961] Ch 328, [1961] 2 WLR 350, 125 JP 278, 59 LGR 146, CA, 28 (2) Digest (Reissue) 940, 2433.

T (AJJ) (an infant), Re [1970] 2 All ER 865, [1970] Ch 688, [1970] 3 WLR 315, 134 JP 611, CA, 28(2) Digest (Reissue) 913, 2239.

f ### Appeals

The mother appealed from an order of Sheldon J made on 31st July 1978 on the hearing of a wardship summons by her relating to her two infant children whereby he discharged both the wardship and the Official Solicitor who had been appointed guardian ad litem of the children. The facts are set out in the judgment of Bridge LJ.

g *Amanda Barrington-Smythe* for the mother.
Mervyn Roberts for the local authority.
Jonathan Cohen for the guardian ad litem.

BRIDGE LJ delivered the first judgment at the invitation of Ormrod LJ. This is an appeal from an order of Sheldon J made on 31st July 1978, on the hearing of a wardship

h summons relating to two infant children A and E, and I emphasise that it is most undesirable in this case that the identity of any of the parties, or the locality where the parties reside, should be disclosed as a result of this judgment.

The decision of the judge under appeal is a decision to discharge the wardship, and to discharge the Official Solicitor who has been appointed as guardian ad litem of the infant children who were the subject of the summons.

j Very shortly, the point raised in this appeal is this: these two children are the subject of care orders made under s 1 of the Children and Young Persons Act 1969. The local authority in whose care the children are, have in the circumstances which have developed, reached the decision that the mother (who is the plaintiff in the proceedings) should be denied further access to the two children.

On the hearing before the judge, before the merits were gone into, the local authority raised the point that having regard to the decided cases which govern the matter, it would be an improper exercise of the court's wardship jurisdiction to interfere with a decision of the local authority with regard to the day-to-day conduct of the lives of these two little children, for the court to review the local authority's decision on its merits as opposed to deciding whether it was a decision which had been properly taken, and which could be reviewed on the footing that some ministerial or administrative impropriety impugned its validity. The grounds of course on which ministerial or administrative decisions can be reviewed by the courts are very narrow and very well known.

The judge came to the conclusion that on the authorities binding on him, the local authority's preliminary objection to the proposed exercise of the court's wardship jurisdiction to order, contrary to the decision of the local authority, that the mother should have access to the children, would be an improper exercise and one which the authorities do not permit, and it was on that basis that he discharged the wardship and it is against that decision that appeal is now brought.

The factual background of the matter is, if I may say so, quite admirably summarised in a passage from the judge's judgment. I do not intend to take up time in setting out the facts because for the purpose of deciding the point of appeal it is not necessary. Summarising the facts in my own language I will do no more than set out the very barest bones of the matter.

The parents of these two children were married in April 1970 when the mother was already six months pregnant with the child A who is the older child, the subject of the proceedings. It is clear that A's early years passed in an extremely stressful and violent domestic atmosphere, with great disagreements between the parents and there are some indications that she may have been what is known now as a 'battered baby', although any suggestion of violence being used to her by the mother is energetically disputed by the mother. She was eventually taken into care under a local authority place of safety order. The care order, under which the local authority now have her, was made on 9th October 1974.

Another child, C, was born in May 1974, and was found very soon after its birth to be suffering from certain injuries and was also taken into care under a place of safety order, and in due course under a care order, and was really not seen by the mother for any substantial period after that. This second child, C, subsequently died as a consequence of the injuries which she received.

The third child, E, who is a boy, the subject of the present proceedings, was born in, I think, June 1976, and was taken into care pursuant to a place of safety order very shortly after that and made the subject of a s 1 care order, which presently subsists, on 23rd September 1976.

Initially, after A was taken into care, she was placed by the local authority with foster parents in a locality where it was possible for her to be seen regularly by her mother who had regular access to her. But the time came, in circumstances which I need not go into, when the local authority came to the conclusion that that was unsatisfactory, and, when A was removed to foster parents in a remoter locality, the intention was that the mother should not know the whereabouts of those foster parents. We have been told by counsel for the mother that she in fact did get to know and she has not abused that, which is of course to her credit.

The child E shortly after he was taken into care, was also placed with those foster parents. Initially, after the second foster parents had the child A, there was reasonably regular access to the child by the mother, but it became less frequent and the local authority became more concerned about the effect on the child of the mother's visits, and eventually access was terminated altogether, the last visit when the mother had access to either child having been on 7th October 1976.

Finally, in December 1976, the local authority reached a decision in principle that there should be no further access to these children for reasons which again I need not set out in detail. The passage from the affidavit of the social worker/director who is the responsible official of the local authority, which was before the judge reads as follows:

a

'At a further review held in December 1976 when again no progress with the parents could be reported, it was agreed that long term fostering was inevitable for these children, and that it would be in their best interests to be adopted by the foster parents. It was also decided then that there should be no further access to the children for the time being, having regard to the increased stress suffered by [A] as a result of her parent's visits, and to her own expressed wish not to see the mother.'

b

I should add, for completeness, that the father has now disappeared from the picture and, his present whereabouts not being known, he plays no part in the present proceedings.

It is against that decision in December 1976, which was confirmed to the mother in a letter of July 1977 from the local authority, that the present appeal is brought in effect, and it was with a view to overturning that decision and securing the right of access to her children that the mother issued her wardship summons on 20th October last year.

c

The judge held that he was bound by authority to decline to exercise the court's prerogative jurisdiction in wardship by way of review of the merits of the local authority's decision taken in exercise of a statutory discretion conferred on it by the Children and Young Persons Act 1969.

So it is convenient to go straight to the authorities which led the judge to his conclusion. The basic decision was the decision of this court in *Re M (an infant)*[1]. That was the case of a child in care of the local authority under s 1 of the Children Act 1948

d

in relation to whom the local authority had resolved under s 2 of that Act that all the powers of the mother be vested in them. The child had been placed by the local authority with foster parents and in due time, the local authority came to the conclusion that the child should be returned to its natural parents, and in that case it was the foster parents who by way of wardship proceedings sought to challenge and invite the court to review the decision at which the local authority had arrived.

e

In a long and careful judgment with which the two other members of the court agreed, Lord Evershed MR reviewed the statutory provisions under which the local authority exercised jurisdiction in that case, and at the conclusion of that review he said this[2]:

f

'On those premises, that is to say in the absence of any challenge as to the propriety of what the local authority or its officers have done as distinct from their wisdom, I feel compelled, by the clear indication of the language to which I have alluded in the statute, to conclude that this matter of judging the present best interests of the child in the circumstances of this case has been placed by Parliament in the exclusive jurisdiction of the local authority.'

Then a little later on he said[3]:

g

'I confine myself to saying that the state of affairs which is before us is one which is within the strict contemplation and comprehensive provisions of the Act of 1948, as I interpret it, and in the absence of any impeachment of the propriety of what has been done by the local authority or their representatives, the result in this case seems to me to be that the old prerogative jurisdiction must be treated as pro tanto restricted and the proper order to make is that which CROSS, J., made, viz., to declare that the infant should cease to be a ward of court.'

h

The basis of that decision as I understand it is that the court when invited in wardship proceedings to consider a decision of a local authority exercising its statutory discretion over the care of a child pursuant to s 2 of the Children Act 1948 can only exercise a supervisory as opposed to an appellate jurisdiction, in other words, can only review the

j

decision of the local authority to the extent that the court will interfere on well-known

1   [1961] 1 All ER 788, [1961] Ch 328
2   [1961] 1 All ER 788 at 793, [1961] Ch 328 at 342
3   [1961] 1 All ER 788 at 794, [1961] Ch 328 at 343

principles with the exercise of a statutory discretion by some statutory body, as opposed
to reviewing the matter on the merits.   *a*

That case was followed and affirmed by *Re T (AJJ) (an infant)*[1], where again the
plaintiffs and appellants on the wardship summons were seeking to quarrel with and
challenge the wisdom and merits of a local authority's decision, and in this case again
there were foster parents.

The child which was the subject of the dispute in *Re T (AJJ) (an infant)*[1] was a child in
respect of whom a juvenile court had made a fit person order, committing the care of the *b*
child to a local authority pursuant to ss 62(1) and 76(1) of the Children and Young
Persons Act 1933, and it is common ground that this is a binding authority which
determines the relationship of the court in wardship proceedings to the local authority
in respect of a child who is the subject of a care order under s 1 of the Children and Young
Persons Act 1969.

In that case, the court held it was bound by the principle which had been enunciated *c*
in *Re M (an infant)*[2] to conclude that the court had no right to constitute itself an appellate
body to review the merits of the local authority's decision in the exercise of its statutory
discretion as the body to whom the care of a child was committed. Russell LJ, giving the
reserved judgment of the court, said[3]:

> 'In the case of *Re M (an infant)*[2] this court held quite clearly that in wardship *d*
> proceedings the court will not substitute its own view as to the appropriate steps to
> be taken in relation to the care and control of a child, concerning whom the local
> authority has passed a resolution (which has not been objected to) under s 2 of the
> 1948 Act, for that of the local authority, on the ground that the legislature has
> confided all such decisions in the most ample manner to the local authority, and the
> court will accordingly not interfere with any such decision. There is, of course, an *e*
> obvious exception to this, which has been variously expressed, that the courts, and
> not least the Chancery court in wardship proceedings, will interfere with the
> exercise by an administrative body such as a local authority of the exercise of a
> discretion in a field committed to it by the legislature, on well-known principles for
> which we can conveniently and briefly refer to the judgment of Lord Greene MR
> in *Associated Provincial Picture Houses Ltd v Wednesbury Corpn*[4].'   *f*

The latest in the series of authorities on the subject, however, and the only other
authority which it seems to me necessary to refer to is the very recent decision of this
court in *Re H (a minor) (wardship jurisdiction)*[5]. This was an unusual case where a care
order had been made under s 1 of the 1969 Act in favour of the local authority in respect
of a Pakistani child who had suffered non-accidental injuries inferentially at the hands of *g*
the child's parents. The parents were Moslems and there were other children of the
family. The parents, having resided for some time in England, were intending to return
to their native Pakistan. They brought wardship proceedings whereby they sought to
recover care and control of the child, the subject of the care order, so that the child could
accompany them on their return to their native country. Balcombe J acceded to their
application and made an order that the child should remain under the care and control *h*
of the local authority until the parents had made arrangements and were ready to return
home to Pakistan with the child, and he then granted them leave in the event to take the
child out of the jurisdiction.

I need not refer to the judgment that the judge at first instance gave. The matter came
to the Court of Appeal when the whole state of the authorities in this field of law was, if

                                                                                          j

1 [1970] 2 All ER 865, [1970] Ch 688
2 [1961] 1 All ER 788, [1961] Ch 328
3 [1970] 2 All ER 865 at 869, [1970] Ch 688 at 692–693
4 [1947] 2 All ER 680 at 682–683, [1948] 1 KB 223 at 228–229
5 [1978] 2 All ER 903, [1978] Fam 65

I may say so respectfully, most comprehensively reviewed in a reserved judgment given
a by Ormrod LJ. Having recited the substance of the decision in *Re M (an infant)*[1] and *Re
T (AJJ) (an infant)*[2], Ormrod LJ continued[3]:

b 'Two observations may be made about these decisions. In both cases the
applicants were foster-parents, but the effect has been to leave the natural parents
without any means of challenging a local authority's decision, for example, to place
the child with foster-parents a long way away from the parents' home so that
visiting is difficult or impossible, or to deny all access to the child by one or both
parents, or to refuse to disclose to the parents where the child is living. This result
necessarily follows because, although there is a right of appeal to the juvenile court
against the resolution in the one case or to apply to discharge the care order in the
c other, the juvenile court has no power to interfere with the exercise of the local
authority's discretionary powers. It is not clear whether the court in either case had
this consequence in mind. The second also applies to both decisions. No reference
appears to have been made in argument in either case to s 1 of the Guardianship of
Infants Act 1925, and no mention of the welfare of the child as the paramount
consideration is made in the judgments. *Re M (an infant)*[1] was of course decided
d some years before *J v C*[4] and at a time when the significance of this section was
perhaps not fully appreciated. Probably, however, it would not have affected the
court's conclusion, because Lord Evershed MR said[5]: "I feel compelled, by the clear
indication of the language to which I have alluded in the statute to conclude that
this matter of judging the present best interests of the child in the circumstances of
this case has been placed by Parliament in the exclusive jurisdiction of the local
e authority." These observations are not intended to cast doubt on the binding effect
of these decisions on this court at the present time, but they are sufficient to
discourage an extension of the reasoning to cases like the present where the challenge
is directed, not to the exercise of the discretionary power, but to the source of that
power. In this case the parents are not seeking to influence the local authority's
discretion, but to remove the child altogether from the control of the local authority,
f in other words, to supersede the care order of 23rd August 1976 by a new order in
the wardship proceedings.'

These to my mind are the important passages from the three most important cases by
which we are bound in relation to the decision which we are now called on to make.
g Counsel for the mother, who has said everything that could possibly be said on her
behalf, has acknowledged that there can be no challenge here, as there was in *Re H (a
minor) (wardship: jurisdiction)*[6] to the propriety of the continuance of the care order. It is
not the care order itself which is under challenge: it is the manner in which the local
authority's powers under the care order are to be exercised. What we are fairly and
squarely asked to do is to exercise the wardship jurisdiction to overrule the decision of the
h local authority taken as to the manner in which those powers ought to be exercised.
Counsel for the mother has made a courageous attempt to distinguish this case from the
authority of *Re M*[1] and *Re T*[2], and I hope I fairly summarise the effect of her argument,
basically on the single ground that this is an application by a *natural parent*, whereas the
plaintiffs in the wardship proceedings who sought to challenge the decision of the local

j 1   [1961] 1 All ER 788, [1961] Ch 328
     2   [1970] 2 All ER 865, [1970] Ch 688
     3   [1978] 2 All ER 903 at 908–909, [1978] Fam 65 at 75–76
     4   [1969] 1 All ER 788, [1970] AC 668
     5   [1961] 1 All ER 788 at 793, [1961] Ch 328 at 342
     6   [1978] 2 All ER 903, [1978] Fam 65

authorities in both *Re M (an infant)*[1] and *Re T (AJJ) (an infant)*[2] were foster parents. The argument runs that a natural parent has some kind of inalienable right or perhaps, to put it more accurately, the child has the inalienable right of access to the natural parent and ought not to be separated from the natural parent and it is said on that ground the court ought to distinguish this case from *Re M (an infant)*[1] and *Re T (AJJ) (an infant)*[2]. Again it is said if there is no remedy by way of wardship proceedings whereby the decision of the local authority can be brought under review there is no appellate remedy available to the mother at all and that produces an anomalous situation as compared with other situations where the court can give an effective appellate remedy. For my part, sympathetically though I listened to those arguments and much as I appreciate the sense which lies behind them, I am quite unable to say that they are valid arguments when one examines the ratio decidendi both of *Re M (an infant)*[1] and *Re T (AJJ) (an infant)*[2]. The court, as Ormrod LJ observed in *Re H (a minor) (wardship: jurisdiction)*[3], in deciding the cases of *Re M (an infant)*[1] and *Re T (AJJ) (an infant)*[2], may not have appreciated the effect which its decision would have on the rights of natural parents, but I can discover no logical ground whatsoever, when one looks at the basis of the decision, namely that the jurisdiction conferred on the local authority is an exclusive one in which the court can only interfere on a strictly limited ground, on which the present case can be distinguished. The character of the party who invokes the jurisdiction can make no difference whether the plaintiff in the wardship proceedings who invites the court to review the decision of the local authority is a natural parent or a foster parent; I cannot accept that there is any such inalienable right, a right of access of a natural parent to a child, as to found the distinction which counsel for the mother seeks to make.

The other broad line of argument which has been urged on us as a reason for departing from the view taken by the judge was that on the facts of this case there really was a basis on which the court could review the decision of the local authority in the exercise of its supervisory jurisdiction, as I called it earlier in this judgment.

Counsel for the mother has reminded us of the well-known passage from the judgment of Lord Greene MR in the case of *Associated Provincial Picture Houses Ltd v Wednesbury Corpn*[4] where he said:

'I do not wish to repeat what I have said, but it might be useful to summarise once again the principle, which seems to me to be that the court is entitled to investigate the action of the local authority with a view to seeing whether it has taken into account matters which it ought not to take into account, or, conversely, has refused to take into account or neglected to take into account matters which it ought to take into account. Once that question is answered in favour of the local authority, it may still be possible to say that the local authority, nevertheless, have come to a conclusion so unreasonable that no reasonable authority could ever have come to it. In such a case, again, I think the court can interfere. The power of the court to interfere in each case is not that of an appellate authority to override a decision of the local authority, but is that of a judicial authority which is concerned, and concerned only, to see whether the local authority have contravened the law by acting in excess of the powers which Parliament has confided in it.'

First of all it is said that the decision must be suspect because of the measure of antagonism and hostility which throughout the history of this unfortunate matter has

---

1 [1961] 1 All ER 788, [1961] Ch 328
2 [1970] 2 All ER 865, [1970] Ch 688
3 [1978] 2 All ER 903, [1978] Fam 65
4 [1947] 2 All ER 680 at 685, [1948] 1 KB 223 at 233–234

been existing between the mother on the one hand and the officials of the local authority

a on the other. For my part I am satisfied that this ground of attack on the local authority's decision does not come within a mile of bringing the case within the narrow area in which the interference by the court with the decision of a statutory body would be justified. It has often been said, and it is said in another passage from Lord Greene MR's judgment in the case referred to that a party seeking to challenge a ministerial or administrative decision made under statutory powers on the ground that it is unlawful

b has a heavy onus to show that it is so, and we have not been referred to any evidence in the course of the argument which to my mind begins to show that any animosity which there might have been between the officials who had the control of this matter and the unhappy mother has in any way affected their decision or has deflected the local authority from taking a decision in what they believe to be the best interests of the child.

The other ground on which it is suggested that the decision should be impugned

c relates to the reference in the passage already cited from the affidavit of the social worker referring to the desirability of these children being adopted at some future date by the present foster parents. Counsel for the mother has argued vigorously that considerations which would be relevant to the propriety of making an adoption order are quite different considerations from those which are relevant when it comes to a question of considering whether or not the mother should have access to her children, and she has

d suggested that, by looking forward to a future possible adoption as the desirable outcome of this case, the local authority had misdirected itself or, in Lord Greene MR's language, taken into account matters which it ought not to have taken into account.

Again, for my part, I am unable to take that view. The local authority has to look at the overall picture. It has to look at the past, the present and the future in considering what is presently in the best interests of these two children, and, if one of the possibilities

e in the future which the local authority sees as a desirable possibility, one which it may well be appropriate to work towards, is the eventual adoption of these children by the foster parents, I am quite unable to see how it could possibly be said that that was an irrelevant factor and not properly to be taken into account in deciding whether or not it is proper that the mother should have continued access to the children at present.

For these reasons I am quite satisfied that the judge was right to come to the conclusion

f that he was bound by *Re M (an infant)*[1] and *Re T (AJJ) (an infant)*[2] to abstain from exercising the prerogative wardship jurisdiction of the court so as to interfere with the local authority's decision regarding access in this case. The several grounds on which it is proper, notwithstanding these decisions, to interfere with the decisions of local authorities which have been urged on us have no application in the present case. I would dismiss the appeal.

g

BROWNE LJ. I agree that this appeal should be dismissed for the reasons given by Bridge LJ. However, I would like to add a few words in view of the admirable argument which has been presented to us by counsel for the mother.

Sheldon J in his judgment reviewed most or all of the authorities to which we have

h been referred. Then he said this:

'In short, in my opinion, where the court is being asked to exercise its wardship jurisdiction in relation to a child committed to the care of the local authority, it is clear (on *Re M (an infant)*[1], *Re T (AJJ) (an infant)*[2], *Re H (a minor) (wardship: jurisdiction)*[3]

j   and other cases) that, where in effect all that the court is being invited to do is to

---

1 [1961] 1 All ER 788, [1961] Ch 328
2 [1970] 2 All ER 865, [1970] Ch 688
3 [1978] 2 All ER 903, [1978] Fam 65

review or to interfere with the exercise by the local authority of the discretion given
to it by statute, the court will not intervene save at the request or with the consent   *a*
of the authority unless it can be shown that the authority has acted improperly or
in excess of its jurisdiction within the principles laid down by Lord Greene MR in
Associated Provincial Picture Houses Ltd v Wednesbury Corpn[1]. In the words of Russell
LJ in *Re T (AJJ) (an infant)*[2]: "... in wardship proceedings the court will not
substitute its own view as to the appropriate steps to be taken in relation to the care
and control of a child ..." In such cases, to adopt the words of Lord Greene MR in   *b*
Associated Provincial Picture Houses Ltd v Wednesbury Corpn[3]: "The power of the court
to interfere ... is not that of an appellate authority to override the decision of the
local authority, but is that of a judicial authority which is concerned, and concerned
only, to see whether the local authority have contravened the law by acting in excess
of the powers which Parliament has confided in it." In all these circumstances,
formidable though the argument may be for the intervention of the court in this   *c*
case, as there is no escape from the conclusion that all that I am being asked to do is
to exercise the court's powers of control in a sphere of activity which has been
entrusted to the local authority by Acts of Parliament, I am satisfied that it is not
open to me to interfere.'

In my judgment, that judgment of Sheldon J was plainly right. The decision of this   *d*
court in *Re M (an infant)*[4] is of course binding on us and in my judgment it is quite
impossible to distinguish it. The effect of *Re M (an infant)*[4] was stated by Ormrod LJ in
his judgment in *Re H (a minor) (wardship: jurisdiction)*[5] in a passage which was quoted by
Sheldon J. He said this:

'In *Re M (an infant)*[4], the Court of Appeal held that where a local authority has   *e*
passed a resolution assuming parental rights over a child the exercise of the local
authority's statutory powers in relation to the child cannot be challenged in
wardship proceedings because Parliament has entrusted all decisions as to the welfare
of the child to the discretion of the local authority. The court can only interfere if
the local authority has acted improperly or unlawfully, that is, in accordance with
the principles on which the court will review the exercise of ministerial or   *f*
administrative discretions generally ... Where the local authority are acting under
a fit person order or a care order the same reasoning necessarily applies because the
local authority's statutory powers are similar: *Re T (AJJ) (an infant)*[6].'

In *Re H (a minor) (wardship: jurisdiction)*[7] Ormrod LJ recognised, in the passage which   *g*
Bridge LJ has already quoted, that the effects of the decision in *Re M (an infant)*[4] on the
position of real parents as opposed to foster parents might not have been fully considered
there, but nevertheless it is quite clear that that is not a ground for distinguishing *Re M
(an infant)*[4] from *Re H (a minor) (wardship: jurisdiction)*[8], or from the present case. *Re H
(a minor) (wardship: jurisdiction)*[8] was a quite different case from this case as appears from
the passage which has been quoted[9]:   *h*

---

1   [1947] 2 All ER 680, [1948] 1 KB 223
2   [1970] 2 All ER 865 at 869, [1970] Ch 688 at 692
3   [1947] 2 All ER 680 at 685, [1948] 1 KB 223 at 234
4   [1961] 1 All ER 788, [1961] Ch 328   *j*
5   [1978] 2 All ER 903 at 908, [1978] Fam 65 at 75
6   [1970] 2 All ER 865, [1970] Ch 688
7   [1978] 2 All ER 903 at 908–909, [1978] Fam 65 at 75–76
8   [1978] 2 All ER 903, [1978] Fam 65
9   [1978] 2 All ER 903 at 909, [1978] Fam 65 at 76

a   'These observations are not intended to cast doubt on the binding effect of these decisions on this court at the present time, but they are sufficient to discourage an extension of the reasoning to cases like the present where the challenge is directed, not to the exercise of a discretionary power, but to the source of that power.'

So therefore in my judgment *Re H (a minor) (wardship: jurisdiction)*[1] gives the mother no support.

b   It was suggested by counsel for the mother that this was a case in which the decision could be challenged on what I may call the *Wednesbury*[2] basis, but Bridge LJ has already dealt with the two factors which are said to support that view: the antagonism or hostility between the parent and the local authority and the reference in the social worker's affidavit to the future adoption.

I agree with Bridge LJ that this mother cannot begin to make a case for saying that this decision can be attacked on the *Wednesbury*[2] basis, so accordingly for the reasons given by

c   Bridge LJ and for the reasons which I have tried to give, which are exactly the same, I have no hesitation in agreeing that the appeal must be dismissed.

ORMROD LJ. I agree with both judgments which have been delivered and I only add one thing: this case clearly in my judgment cannot be distinguished from *Re M (an infant)*[3] and *Re T (AJJ) (an infant)*[4] for the reasons which were set out in the judgment of

d   this court in *Re H (a minor) (wardship: jurisdiction)*[1]. Counsel for the mother has made a valiant attempt, unsuccessfully, I am sorry to say, to construct a mode of appeal for parents whose children are the subject of care orders and unfortunately it is clear on the authorities that this court cannot act as an appellate court in those circumstances. Whether or not some other statutory form of appeal should be created is a matter which certainly requires consideration although I cannot conceal from myself the difficulties

e   that would be involved. For the reasons set out in the judgment of the court in *Re H (a minor) (wardship: jurisdiction)*[5], there is no doubt that this question is one which requires consideration but I do not pretend to know what the solution is, but consideration it certainly needs. I agree the appeal should be dismissed.

Appeal dismissed. Leave to appeal to the House of Lords refused.

f   Solicitors: *Stollard & Limbrey*, agents for *Jackson, Kent & Hodges*, Littlehampton (for the mother); *Ian Holdsworthy*, Chichester (for the local authority); *Official Solicitor*.

Avtar S Virdi Esq   Barrister.

---

1   [1978] 2 All ER 903, [1978] Fam 65
2   [1947] 2 All ER 680, [1948] 1 KB 223
3   [1961] 1 All ER 788, [1961] Ch 328
4   [1970] 2 All ER 865, [1970] Ch 688
5   [1978] 2 All ER 903 at 909, [1978] Fam 65 at 76

Thorne v Thorne

a

FAMILY DIVISION
COMYN J
8th NOVEMBER 1978

Costs – Taxation – Review of taxation – Certificate of taxation – Finality of certificate – Application for leave to file objections to taxed costs out of time – Delay due to mistake in solicitors' office – Delay a short one – Whether court having power to set aside certificate of taxation and extend time for objections – Whether power should be exercised – RSC Ord 3, r 5, Ord 62, r 33. *b*

On 14th July 1978 the costs to be paid by a husband in divorce proceedings were assessed by a taxing officer at £10,027. The husband and his solicitors thought that the costs should be not more than £7,000. The particular solicitor dealing with the case left the firm and as a result no application for a review of taxation was made within the 14 day period prescribed by RSC Ord 62, r 33[d] (ie by 28th July). On 1st August the taxing officer issued his certificate of taxation for £10,027. Shortly afterwards, when a newly-engaged solicitor was given the papers connected with the husband's case, the solicitors discovered that the objections to taxation had not been lodged in time. On 15th August, which was as soon as practicable, the new solicitor went to the registry to try to get the mistake rectified. The registrar in charge of the matter was by then away on holiday and so a summons, returnable before him on 5th September, was issued for leave to file objections to the taxed costs out of time. The registrar dismissed the summons on the ground that he had no jurisdiction to deal with it because RSC Ord 62, r 33, stated that no application under the rule for review of a decision in respect of any item might be made after the signing of the certificate of taxation dealing finally with that item. The husband appealed against his decision, contending that although the words of RSC Ord 62, r 33, appeared to be mandatory, the court nonetheless had power to set aside a certificate of taxation and, either under RSC Ord 3, r 5[b], or under its inherent jurisdiction, to extend the time for objections. At the hearing of the appeal, the wife submitted that the mandatory words in RSC Ord 62, r 33, could not be overridden by the general words of RSC Ord 3, r 5. *f*

c

d

e

Held – (i) The court had power to set aside a certificate of taxation in proper circumstances, e g where the certificate was obtained by fraud or was granted in circumstances which were contrary to natural justice or where there was a mistake as to any of the vital details or where there was an error and a delay of a short period. Consequently under RSC Ord 3, r 5, and also under its inherent jurisdiction, the court could extend the time for objections to taxed costs (see p 168 *h* and p 169 *a* to *c e* and *g*, post); *Re Furber* (1898) 42 Sol Jo 613, *Brown v Youde* [1967] 3 All ER 1070 and *Maltby v D J Freeman & Co* (1976) 120 Sol Jo 284 applied. *g*

(ii) Since there was a satisfactory explanation of the default on the husband's side (ie the overlooking of the matter by his solicitors) and the delay had been very short, it was proper in the circumstances to order that the certificate of taxation be set aside and the husband be given seven days in which to file objections. Accordingly the appeal would be allowed and the order made (see p 169 *e* to *j*, post). *h*

---

a　Rule 33, so far as material, is set out at p 166 *e*, post

b　Rule 5, so far as material, provides:

'(1) The Court may, on such terms as it thinks just, by order extend or abridge the period within which a person is required or authorised by these rules, or by any judgment, order or direction, to do any act in any proceedings.

'(2) The Court may extend any such period as is referred to in paragraph (1) although the application for extension is not made until after the expiration of that period . . .'

A

Notes

a For review of taxation of costs, see Supplement to 30 Halsbury's Laws (3rd Edn) paras 819–820.

Cases referred to in judgment

Brown v Youde [1967] 3 All ER 1070, [1967] 1 WLR 1544, Digest (Cont Vol C) 1100, 5013 Aa.

b *Furber, Re* (1898) 42 Sol Jo 613, CA, 43 Digest (Repl) 234, 2419.

Maltby v D J Freeman & Co (1976) 120 Sol Jo 284, CA.

R v Kingston-upon-Hull District Registrar, ex parte Norton [1944] 1 All ER 546, DC, 43 Digest (Repl) 232, 2410.

Summons

c On 1st August 1978 a certificate of taxation for £10,027 was issued in relation to divorce proceedings between Doris Winifred Thorne ('the wife') and Alan Arthur Thorne ('the husband'). On 15th August the husband applied for leave to file out of time objections to the taxed costs. On 5th September Mr Registrar Colgate dismissed the application. By a summons dated 8th September the husband (i) applied to have the certificate of taxation of 1st August set aside and (ii) appealed against Mr Registrar Colgate's
d decision. The matter was heard in chambers. The facts are set out in the judgment which is reported by leave of the judge.

Howard Godfrey for the husband.
R Hayward-Smith for the wife.

e **COMYN J.** This case raises an interesting and very important point about the taxation of costs, and the point is one applicable not only to this division of the High Court but the other divisions as well. Application is made on behalf of the husband for two things: (i) to set aside the certificate of taxation which has been made and (ii) to appeal against the decision of Mr Registrar Colgate, who rejected his application to file objections to taxation out of time.

f The short history of the matter on the facts is this. That there were divorce proceedings between the husband and the wife accompanied and followed by ancillary proceedings, and the costs assessed came to a total of £10,027. In due course, as I will show, that is the figure which the taxing officer arrived at as payable by the husband and for which his certificate was given. The dispute arises because the husband and those advising him say that that total is excessive by at least £3,000, and pursuant to that point of view they have
g paid £7,000 on account to the other side, so the amount that I am concerned with is a sum of £3,000 out of a total of about £10,000. What happened was this: the taxation of the costs took place on 14th July 1978 and the husband had 14 days in which to file objections, that is to say by 28th July. He did not do so, and early in the following week, on Tuesday, 1st August, the taxing officer issued his certificate of taxation in the amount I have mentioned.

h The case put forward on behalf of the husband before me today, and which as to its facts is not disputed by the other side, is that the failure to put in objections in time and the failure to do anything after the taxation was due to trouble in the husband's solicitors' office. It was said that the gentleman dealing with the matter, a time-honoured figure in the law, had left, and that it was only a little time later that a newly-engaged solicitor, Miss Hirst, was seised of the matter and found out what had gone wrong. Accordingly,
j on 15th August, as soon as practicable after she had found out about the mistake, she went to the registry to seek to have it rectified. Mr Registrar Colgate, the registrar in charge of the matter, was away on holiday, and accordingly a summons was issued, returnable before him on 5th September, for leave to file objections to the taxed costs out of time. I am aware not only of the decision he made then, but helpfully of the reasoning which led him to it, for there is on my copy of the summons his note: 'No

jurisdiction. Order: Dismiss the summons', and then he ordered the husband to pay the costs of it. There has consequently been an appeal in the form I have indicated to this court, and it will be convenient now if I say a few general words about the problem.

The question of a taxing officer's certificate has figured in the law since at least the Rules of the Supreme Court of 1883. Since then, there have been three main cases on the question of the finality or otherwise of a taxing officer's certificate. There has been a fourth case, peripherally referred to by counsel for the wife, which I will come to in its place, but, unhappily, the three real cases bearing on the point are not very fully reported and leave a lot of question-marks.

The problem can be crystallised as follows. Under the 1883 rules, Ord 65, r 27, had various provisions about the taxation of costs, culminating in sub-r (41), which said:

> 'Any party who may be dissatisfied with the certificate or allocation of the taxing officer as to an item or part of an item, which may have been objected to as aforesaid, may within fourteen days . . .'

go to the judge.

It had in its previous provisions allowed for objections to be made, and it is plainly these objections that sub-r (41) was referring to; in other words, the certificate would go forth with objections attached, and it could then be taken to the judge. There are no time limits in regard to objections or hearings.

But now we come to the present-day rules and the major problem which has arisen here. Under RSC Ord 62, r 33, there is, first of all, a provision that any party to taxation who is dissatisfied may apply for a review, and it says that an application for review may be made at any time within 14 days after that decision. Then occur these very important words:

> 'Provided that no application under this rule for review of a decision in respect of any item may be made after the signing of the taxing officer's certificate dealing finally with that item.'

It next goes on to deal with the question of review and of objections, and gives time limits in regard to them.

What is said here on behalf of the successful claimant, the wife, is that RSC Ord 62, r 33, is absolutely mandatory, and that once there has been a taxing officer's certificate, that, to paraphrase the final words, deals finally with the matter. In one's search through the rules, one finds, amongst others, the often utilised RSC Ord 3, r 5, which gives the court general powers to extend or abridge time; and it is at that early stage in the rules because, as I believe, it is covering all the matters that follow thereafter. But it is said, and said with some force by counsel for the wife, that general words such as contained in RSC Ord 3 cannot override mandatory words such as occur in RSC Ord 62, r 33(2); no application for review of a decision may be made after the signing of the taxing officer's certificate. He says, and again with much force, that, like so much else in legal life and ordinary life, where there is a fixed absolute time limit it is important that it should be obeyed so that people may know where they stand. He further says, again I find impressively, that solicitors have hitherto believed a taxing master's certificate to be final and conclusive, and incapable of being re-opened, and that that enables them to get on, for example, with distribution of money to their client, or, an example which occurred in the course of argument, to give an assurance to a bank or others that their client has so much money freely available.

Now to look at the cases very shortly. The first is Re Furber[1], an appeal to the Court of Appeal from a decision of Kekewich J, which mentions at the beginning Ord 65, r 27, of the 1883 rules which I have already mentioned. I need not read out the facts. I think it is a fair summary to say that the litigation between the solicitor and Miss Watkins in that case to'd and fro'd, with one successful at one moment and one at the next. They were

---

1   (1898) 42 Sol Jo 613

getting near the end of their running dispute when this matter came on, and what
a happened was the solicitor was out of time in regard to the certificate of taxation. He
took out a summons, which would be before a master, and he lost that. He moved the
court to set aside the certificate. Kekewich J made an order setting it aside and directed
it to be re-signed and dated as at a later date in order to allow the solicitor to carry in his
objections. As yet a further round in the battle, Miss Watkins took the matter to the
Court of Appeal, and her case is very briefly but cogently summed up in these words in
b the report[1]:

> 'Miss Watkins, the client, appealed, and urged that as the solicitor did not carry
> in objections to the taxation, the certificate was conclusive, and the taxation could
> not now be reviewed.'

c The judgment of the Court of Appeal as reported[1] is brief in the extreme, and I will read
it in full, conscious that it will not require long to do so:

> 'THE COURT (LINDLEY, M.R., and CHITTY and COLLINS, L.JJ.) dismissed the appeal.
> LINDLEY, M.R., said that the order must be left alone, as it was substantially correct.'

d I confess that I have found it difficult to understand the word 'substantially' in that
context because the order was so far as I can see the whole substance. 'There had
obviously been a blunder [Lindley MR said] and a miscarriage of justice. The appeal
must be dismissed but without costs.'
When I said earlier that the three main cases did not give that full illumination that I
would have hoped, I think I have illustrated by this short reference that there are many
e questions one would have liked to have asked about *Re Furber*[1]; what consideration, for
example, was given to RSC Ord 65, r 27? What was the blunder? Because it appears to
me the blunder was merely the passage of time. And precisely what was the miscarriage
of justice? But, as so often happens, *Re Furber*[1] became the structure on which other cases
built themselves, and *Re Furber*[1] is referred to in the main textbooks as authority for the
proposition that in certain circumstances a taxation certificate can be set aside.
f The next case to refer to is *Brown v Youde*[2] in 1967, a decision of Chapman J given in
chambers but, with his leave, reported. It was a Fatal Accidents Acts 1846 to 1959 and
Law Reform (Miscellaneous Provisions) Act 1934 claim, and what happened was, the
district registrar taxed some costs, and on the same date, without informing the parties
of his intention to do so, signed a certificate of taxation. The defendant took out a
summons to the district registrar for an extension of time. That summons was dismissed
g and the appeal was taken to Chapman J in chambers to set aside the certificate of
taxation. In his judgment he begins by saying[3]:

> 'The proviso to R.S.C., Ord. 62, r. 33(2) [that is the one I am concerned with] is
> mandatory and a certificate of taxation is an absolute bar to a review of taxation
> unless set aside.'

h Then occur these important words:

> 'The proviso does not merely impose a time limit capable of extension under
> R.S.C., Ord. 3, r. 5. As to the application to set aside the certificate of taxation,
> Ord. 62, r. 33, contemplates that an opportunity to apply for a review will be open.
j I find it surprising that the certificate was signed immediately after taxation, which

---

1   (1898) 42 Sol Jo 613
2   [1967] 3 All ER 1070, [1967] 1 WLR 1544
3   [1967] 3 All ER 1070, [1967] 1 WLR 1544 at 1545

is certainly not the practice in London. In my judgment, the district registrar should not do that unless he has made it absolutely clear to the parties that that is   *a* what he is in mind to do . . .'

He then says[1]: 'It is contrary to justice to allow the certificate to stand, and the case falls within the principle laid down in *Re Furber*[2].'

The passage which I reserve for closer attention in a few moments is the passage which says: 'The proviso does not merely impose a time limit capable of extension under   *b* R.S.C., Ord. 3, r. 5.'

The last case to be referred to as a main case on this subject is *Maltby v D J Freeman & Co*[3]. It is a 1976 case, again very shortly reported. There was again a dispute about costs, and the taxing master found a certain sum. Then there was an application and he reduced it, and the plaintiffs, before applying for a review by a judge, had to apply for a statement of reasons from him which 'must be made within 14 days after the review'; that quotes another part of RSC Ord 62[4]. They were out of time for that, and there was   *c* an appeal. The judge upheld the master's decision, and in the Court of Appeal Cairns LJ, again with the brevity that seems to mark these cases, said[3]: 'The rules as to time for stating reasons should be observed and extensions should not be given as a matter of course.'   Then he said the delay was a brief one: 'The judge should have exercised his own discretion anew. The court in exercising its own discretion would allow the appeal and permit time to be extended.'   I said there was a fourth case, and it was relied on by   *d* counsel for the wife. I can deal with it shortly. It is not directly in point, as he immediately acknowledged, but it is called *R v Kingston-upon-Hull District Registrar, ex parte Norton*[5]. The headnote says:

> 'The taxing master's *allocatur* of costs need not be a separate document, but may be indorsed on or written at the foot of the bill of costs provided the bill of costs   *e* together with the *allocatur* contains the name of the cause or matter, the name of the party whose costs are to be taxed, the amount at which the costs are taxed, and the signature of the taxing officer. The *allocatur* is not bad because the taxing fee is not paid before it is given.'

That was a decision of the Divisional Court presided over by Lord Caldecote CJ and the use that is made of it is to say the case would not have gone off that way at all on the question of a document if there had been a power in the court to set aside the certificate.

One of the matters, and I am coming to the heart of this case, which has concerned me since I first read it was the observation of that distinguished judge, Chapman J, in *Brown v Youde*[6], where he said: 'The proviso does not merely impose a time limit capable of   *g* extension under R.S.C., Ord. 3, r. 5.' The decision he reached, it will be recalled, applied the principle of *Re Furber*[2], which is the principle that a taxation certificate can be set   *h* aside. I am not, with respect, altogether clear as to the meaning of that observation in the context, and the result, of that case. If it suggests that the wide extending powers of RSC Ord 3 cannot apply I am constrained to disagree.

My own findings are these. First, that the court has got the power to set aside a certificate of taxation in proper circumstances. Secondly, that consequent on that, and, as I believe, under RSC Ord 3, and under its inherent powers as well, the court has power   *j* to extend the time for objections. In elaboration of these reasons I think it is an unhappy

---

1   [1967] 3 All ER 1070 at 1071, [1967] 1 WLR 1544 at 1545
2   (1898) 42 Sol Jo 613
3   (1976) 120 Sol Jo 284
4   RSC Ord 62, r 34(4)
5   [1944] 1 All ER 546
6   [1967] 3 All ER 1070, [1967] 1 WLR 1544 at 1545

fact that this vitally important part of the rule has hitherto stood on cases very briefly
a reported. That is no criticism of those who reported them; it is simply stating a fact. But
I think the three cases relied on have the effect of giving the court power in a proper case
to set aside a taxation certificate in spite of the apparently mandatory tone of RSC
Ord 62. In my judgment, it is manifest that the court would have power to do so in
many circumstances, which do not, of course, arise here; for example, if there were a
situation where the certificate was obtained by fraud, or if the certificate were granted at
b the registry by mistake. By 'mistake', I mean a mistake in procedure; a mistake in any
of the essential ingredients; a mistake as to date; a mistake as to amount; a mistake as to
any of the vital details. It would further be a case for revoking a certificate if it had been
granted in breach of the rules, or if it had been granted without jurisdiction, or if it had
been granted in circumstances which were contrary to natural justice, which is the
attractive way counsel for the wife has sought to get round *Brown v Youde*[1], in effect
c saying that it is an exceptional decision on its own very special facts and there would have
been a breach of natural justice had the certificate stood.

There are many instances in our law where apparently final orders are capable of
appeal or of postponed or suspended or conditional finality. Every day there are
judgments in all divisions of the High Court in absolute and mandatory terms, and they
take effect unless they are stayed by the court of first instance or the Court of Appeal. So
d in this case the certificate of taxation could have been enforced. But we set pride by our
appeal system that a man or woman shall not be judged, so far as possible, by one person
alone and finally, and, however mandatory the orders of the court are, the everyday run
of order is appealable, it has to be appealed within a set time, in many cases that is usually
28 days, but the time itself is capable of being extended and a court can grant stays.
Extensions and stays can in proper cases extend over long periods.
e I see no difference in principle between the matters which I have just mentioned and
a taxation certificate. I think it is open to the court to set aside a taxation certificate if it
is proper to do so. In this case, I hold that it is proper to do so because (i) there has been
a satisfactory explanation of the default on the husband's side, namely the overlooking
of the matter by his solicitors, and (ii) the delay has been, and was, a very short one. It
will be remembered the certificate was issued on 1st August, and it was on 15th August
f that his solicitor, Miss Hirst, went along to try to have the matter rectified, but finding
that Mr Registrar Colgate was on holiday she then issued the summons of 15th August
which came on in early September and is now under appeal to me.

I think that the circumstances for setting aside a registrar's certificate of taxation have
got to be strong, but they are not to be confined to the heads I have mentioned, such as
fraud or mistake, or breach of natural justice. They are, in my judgment, sufficient to
g cover error and a delay of a short period. In so far as it was suggested that solicitors have
hitherto thought the contrary and that the textbooks with the notes to the Supreme
Court Practice[2] suggest the contrary, I find that I can spell out of the three cases I have
mentioned, with respect to them and the courts that decided them, a rather clearer
principle than they enunciate, and a definite one, that a taxation certificate can be set
aside where the court thinks it right and proper in all the circumstances to do so. With
h no criticism whatever of the learned registrar, because the law has been, to say the least,
rather confused, I think he was wrong to refuse to have this matter re-opened. It will do
no injustice whatever to have it re-opened. It might do injustice to allow it to be
closed. The amount at stake is substantial, it is £3,000 or thereabouts, and it forms a
substantial proportion of the total costs of £10,027. I propose, therefore, to order that
the taxation certificate be set aside, that this appeal be allowed, that the husband do have
j seven days from today to bring in objections to the costs and that the matter proceed
thereafter in the ordinary course of taxation as if there had been no allegedly final
taxation.

---

1   [1967] 3 All ER 1070, [1967] 1 WLR 1544
2   See, e g, 1969 Edn, pp 1022–1023, paras 62/33/1, 62/33/2

The last thing is this. The husband, not personally but through his solicitors, has been the author of all this recent litigation. The delay has been caused in the circumstances that I have mentioned. He must, as the party concerned, in my judgment therefore pay in any event the costs of and occasioned by the application before the registrar and before me and do so on a solicitor and own client basis. Just as this case began about the costs, so it ends with costs. The details and final incidence of the costs of taxation can be dealt with between the husband and his solicitors. They will decide who actually pays them.

Appeal allowed; certificate of taxation set aside. Extension of seven days to bring objections.

Solicitors: *Franks Charlesly* (for the husband); *Gordon Dodds & Co* (for the wife).

Georgina Chambers   Barrister.

Bates v Bulman

QUEEN'S BENCH DIVISION
LORD WIDGERY CJ, CROOM-JOHNSON AND STOCKER JJ
24th MAY 1978

Criminal law – Offensive weapons – Article intended for use for causing injury – Article borrowed for immediate use to cause injury to person defendant assaulting – Article not made or adapted for use as an offensive weapon – Whether defendant 'had with him' an offensive weapon – Prevention of Crime Act 1953, s 1(1).

The appellant assaulted a man in the street ('his opponent') by slapping and punching him. He then requested another man to hand him an unopened clasp knife (which was not made or adapted for use for causing injury) which he intended to use to injure his opponent. The appellant then opened the knife and held it against his opponent's head. An information was preferred against the appellant alleging that he had with him in a public place an offensive weapon, namely a knife, without lawful authority or reasonable excuse, contrary to s 1(1)[a] of the Prevention of Crime Act 1953. The justices convicted the appellant of that offence. He appealed contending that the nature of an offence under s 1(1) was the carrying, and not the use, of a weapon, and accordingly a person who borrowed from another an article not offensive per se, with the immediate intention of using it as an offensive weapon, was not guilty of an offence under s 1(1) for in such a case there was not possession of the weapon for a long enough period to say that the defendant 'had [the weapon] with him' in a public place, within s 1(1).

Held – The real purpose of the 1953 Act was to prevent the carrying of offensive weapons, and therefore a person not previously in possession of an article which was not offensive per se, who acquired it by borrowing it or picking it up in the street with the immediate intention of using it as an offensive weapon, was not guilty of an offence under s 1(1) of that Act. Moreover, the case was indistinguishable from cases where the defendant was already in possession of an article not offensive per se which he was carrying innocently and which he subsequently decided to use for an offensive purpose, which had been held not to constitute an offence under s 1(1). In either case use of the article was better dealt with by charging the defendant with a substantive offence, eg

---

a   Section 1(1), so far as material, is set out at p 172 *h*, post.

assault causing bodily harm. It followed that on the facts the appellant had not
committed an offence under s 1(1). The appeal would therefore be allowed (see p 176 *a*
to *e*, post).

Ohlson v Hylton [1975] 2 All ER 490 and *R v Humphreys* (1977) 68 Cr App R 28 applied.

Notes

For possession of an offensive weapon, see 11 Halsbury's Laws (4th Edn) para 852, and for
cases on the subject, see 15 Digest (Reissue) 900–903, 7758–7777.

For the Prevention of Crime Act 1953, s 1, see 8 Halsbury's Statutes (3rd Edn) 407.

Cases referred to in judgments

Harrison v Thornton [1966] Crim LR 388, DC.
Ohlson v Hylton [1975] 2 All ER 490, [1975] 1 WLR 724, 139 JP 531, DC, 15 Digest
(Reissue) 903, 7776.
R v Dayle [1973] 3 All ER 1151, [1974] 1 WLR 181, 138 JP 65, 58 Cr App R 100, CA, 15
Digest (Reissue) 902, 7771.
R v Humphreys (1977) 68 Cr App R 28, CA.
R v Jura [1954] 1 All ER 696, [1954] 1 QB 503, 118 JP 260, 38 Cr App R 53, CCA, 15
Digest (Reissue) 901, 7765.
Woodward v Koessler [1958] 3 All ER 577, [1958] 1 WLR 1255, 123 JP 14, DC, 15 Digest
(Reissue) 900, 7761.

Case stated

This was an appeal by Barry Steven Bates by way of case stated by the justices for the
County of Lincoln sitting in and for the petty sessional division of West Elloe in respect
of their adjudication as a magistrates' court sitting at the Sessions House, Spalding, on
30th March 1976.

On 25th February 1976 an information was preferred by the respondent against the
appellant that on 23rd February 1976 he had with him in a public place called Westlode
Street, Spalding, an offensive weapon, namely a knife, without lawful authority or
reasonable excuse contrary to s 1 of the Prevention of Crime Act 1953, as amended. On
25th February 1976 informations were preferred by the respondent against the appellant
and Stephen Leonard Bates that each, on 23rd February 1976, in a public place called
Westlode Street, Spalding, used threatening words and behaviour whereby a breach of
the peace was likely to be occasioned contrary to s 5 of the Public Order Act 1936 as
amended. The appellant pleaded guilty and Stephen Leonard Bates pleaded not guilty to
that charge.

It was contended by the appellant in relation to the alleged offence under s 1 of the
1953 Act: (a) that there was no or no sufficient evidence that he had possession of the
knife for a period long enough in terms either of time or of the events which took place
to say that 'he had with him' such knife contrary to s 1 of the 1953 Act as interpreted by
the courts; (b) that there was no or no sufficient evidence of any unlawful intention on
his part sufficient to convert a clasp knife not made or adapted for use for causing injury
to the person into an offensive weapon; (c) that there was no or no sufficient evidence
that he had any intention to use the knife to enable him to cause injury to the person.
It was contended by the respondent: (a) that there was ample evidence that the appellant
had with him a knife in a public place; (b) that the opening of the previously closed clasp
knife in a public place by the appellant and the holding of the same against the head of
Anthony Kevin Rivett was sufficient to convert the clasp knife into an offensive weapon
which he had with him without lawful authority or reasonable excuse in a public place;
(c) that the words 'such use by him' in s 1(4) of the 1953 Act included the use, in the
circumstances of this case, of the knife.

The justices found the following facts in respect of the information against the
appellant under the 1953 Act: (a) the appellant slapped and punched Anthony Kevin
Rivett in Westlode Street, Spalding, on 23rd February 1976; (b) the appellant was then
at his request handed an unopened clasp knife by Stephen Leonard Bates, the appellant

having formed the intention to use the knife to cause injury to Rivett; (c) the appellant opened the clasp knife and held it against Rivett's head; (d) the clasp knife was not made or adapted for use for causing injury to the person.

The justices were of opinion that, on those findings and on consideration of the submissions on behalf of the appellant and the respondent, the appellant had with him in a public place an offensive weapon. Accordingly they convicted the appellant and ordered him to pay a fine of £25, with witness costs of £11·25 and to make a contribution order of £10 towards his legal aid costs.

The questions for the opinion of the High Court were: (a) whether there was evidence on which the justices were entitled to hold that the appellant had with him the clasp knife; (b) whether there was evidence on which the justices were entitled to hold that the appellant intended to cause injury to Rivett; (c) whether on the justices' findings of fact they were entitled to hold that the clasp knife was an offensive weapon as being an 'article . . . intended by the person having it with him for . . . use by him' for causing injury to the person, within s 1(4) of the 1953 Act, so as to entitle the magistrates to convict the appellant.

Nigel Baker for the appellant.
Bernard Livesey for the respondent.

STOCKER J delivered the first judgment at the invitation of Lord Widgery CJ. This is an appeal by Barry Steven Bates, who was convicted of an offence of having with him in a public place an offensive weapon, and is an appeal by way of case stated by the justices for the County of Lincoln acting in and for the petty sessional division of West Elloe in respect of their adjudication on 30th March 1976 as a magistrates' court sitting at the Sessions House, Spalding.

On 25th February 1976 an information was preferred by the respondent against the appellant that he, on 23rd February 1976, did have with him in a certain public place called Westlode Street, Spalding, an offensive weapon, namely a knife, without lawful authority or reasonable excuse, contrary to s 1 of the Prevention of Crime Act 1953.

On the same day a further information was preferred against him of committing an offence of using threatening words and behaviour, contrary to s 5 of the Public Order Act 1936. To that second information the appellant pleaded guilty.

The matters came before the court on 30th March 1976, and the court convicted the appellant of the offence under s 1 of the 1953 Act.

The facts as found by the justices were these. The appellant slapped and punched a man called Anthony Kevin Rivett in Westlode Street, Spalding, on the day in question. The appellant then at his request was handed an unopened clasp knife by another man, the appellant having formed the intention to use that knife to cause injury to Rivett, his opponent. The appellant then opened the clasp knife and held it against Rivett's head. Finally, the justices found that the clasp knife was not made or adapted for use for causing injury to the person.

On those facts the justices were of the opinion that the offence was proved.

It is first necessary, therefore, to look at the terms of s 1 of the 1953 Act. The heading reads: 'Prohibition of the carrying of offensive weapons without lawful authority or reasonable excuse.' Subsection (1) provides:

'Any person who without lawful authority or reasonable excuse, the proof whereof shall lie on him, has with him in any public place any offensive weapon shall be guilty of an offence, and shall be liable [to certain penalties].'

By sub-s (4) of that section 'offensive weapon' is defined as meaning 'any article made or adapted for use for causing injury to the person, or intended by the person having it with him for such use by him'.

So far as this appeal is concerned nothing turns on the definition of 'offensive weapon' in so far as there is a dichotomy between weapons which are offensive per se and weapons which become offensive weapons for the purposes of the 1953 Act by reason of the intention of the person having it with him, and because it is conceded by counsel for the appellant before this court that the finding of the justices that the appellant had formed an intention to use the knife to cause injury precludes that argument being open before this court.

Before the justices the contention of the appellant, so far as is relevant to this appeal, was that there was no sufficient evidence that he had possession of the knife for a period long enough in terms either of time or in the context of the events which took place for it to be said that he 'had it with him' in a public place.

Before this court that submission, though it is basically the one on which this appeal is founded, was put forward in somewhat more detail. First of all, counsel for the appellant referred us to the long title of the 1953 Act, which is an Act described as being: 'An Act to prohibit the carrying of offensive weapons in public places without lawful authority or reasonable excuse.' He draws attention to the fact that the nature of the offence as there described appears to be the carrying of the weapon in contradistinction to its use.

Secondly, counsel for the appellant says, and this is perhaps the argument which he developed in greater detail, that in view of the authorities there could be no distinction between a person who has lawful possession of an article which is not offensive per se and who then uses it, and a third party who had not got possession previously but who borrows such an article in circumstances in which it is subsequently used for offensive purposes.

We have been referred to a number of authorities, some of which on the face of it might appear to be in conflict. Counsel for the appellant relies primarily and in the forefront of his argument on *Ohlson v Hylton*[1]. That was a decision of this court. The facts can be very shortly stated. A man who was by trade a carpenter was returning home and had in his bag the tools of his trade, which included a hammer. It so happened that on the way home, due to some industrial action, transport facilities were extremely crowded, and a fracas resulted between him and the victim of the assault that subsequently occurred. A dispute and acts of physical aggression having been commenced between these two people, the defendant produced the hammer from his bag, which was one of the tools of his trade, and struck the victim with it. Those are the facts, and it is in the context of those facts that the judgments have to be considered.

The first passage which appears to be of relevance is where Lord Widgery CJ, having dealt with the division of weapons into those which are offensive per se and those which are not, said this[2]:

> 'The second category relates to articles not so made or adapted and which have a perfectly innocent and legitimate use but which nevertheless may come into the category of offensive weapons if the person having the weapon with him so has it with an intention to use it for causing injury to the person.'

Then he refers to the arguments between the prosecutor and the defendant in these terms[2]:

> 'It was argued by the prosecutor both here and in the court below that, on a literal reading of the terms of the section, that offence was proved. It is pointed out that at the moment when the defendant seized his hammer he had the intention of using it on the unfortunate Mr Malcolm. Accordingly it is said that there was at all events a short period of time in which the hammer, formerly in the innocent possession of the defendant, became a weapon which he had with him with the intention of using it on Mr Malcolm. Accordingly, counsel for the prosecution

1   [1975] 2 All ER 490, [1975] 1 WLR 724
2   [1975] 2 All ER 490 at 493, [1975] 1 WLR 724 at 727

submits, the offence is established. The defendant's argument, both in this court and in the court below, was that the section did not extend to the seizing and use of *a* a weapon for the purpose of causing injury if the weapon was seized only at the moment when the intention to assault arose, and that the type of activity contemplated by the section is not the use of a weapon for offensive purposes but the premeditated carrying of a weapon for those purposes.'

In a later passage having considered the judgment in *Woodward v Koessler*[1] Lord Widgery *b* CJ continued[2]:

'I accept that it is unnecessary for the prosecution to prove that the relevant intent was formed from the moment when the defendant set out on his expedition. An innocent carrying of, say, a hammer can be converted into an unlawful carrying when the defendant forms the guilty intent, provided, in my view, that the intent is formed before the actual occasion to use violence has arisen.' *c*

Finally, in considering *R v Dayle*[3] and *R v Jura*[4], this was said[5]:

'The real question is whether the offensive use of the weapon is conclusive on the question of whether the defendant "had it with him" within the meaning of the Act. Lord Goddard CJ thought that it was not, and that must now be accepted as correct. Accordingly, no offence is committed under the 1953 Act where an *d* assailant seizes a weapon for instant use on his victim. Here the seizure and use of the weapon are all part and parcel of the assault or attempted assault. To support a conviction under the Act the prosecution must show that the defendant was carrying or otherwise equipped with the weapon, and had the intent to use it offensively before any occasion for its actual use had arisen.'

That case was considered in a later case in the Court of Appeal, *R v Humphreys*[6]. That *e* was a case of a man involved in a fight who managed to extract a penknife from his pocket in the course of that fight. He was convicted of unlawful wounding and having an offensive weapon in a public place. There was an issue of self-defence which does not arise in the case before this court. He appealed. It was held, allowing the appeal and following *Ohlson v Hylton*[7], if a person merely happened to have on him an inoffensive weapon like a penknife and in desperation or in the heat of the moment drew that *f* weapon ad hoc, and used it for injuring a person intending then and there to cause injury to another person, he was not guilty of the offence of having an offensive weapon in a public place, because he had not been carrying in a public place that weapon with the necessary intent to cause injury. His intention was formed, as it might be said, ad hoc.

The court pointed out that it was in those terms that the jury ought to have been directed, and, as they were not, it was a case in which the conviction was quashed. I draw *g* attention to that case not only for its express approval of *Ohlson v Hylton*,[7] but also in the context of its date, which was 1977, and the fact that it is a decision of the Court of Appeal.

Against that proposition put forward by counsel for the appellant, counsel for the respondent says that there is a third category of case not covered by either *Ohlson v Hylton*[7] or *R v Humphreys*[6], and that is where a person selects a weapon, an article which *h*

---

1   [1958] 3 All ER 577, [1958] 1 WLR 1255
2   [1975] 2 All ER 490 at 495, [1975] 1 WLR 724 at 729
3   [1973] 3 All ER 1151, [1974] 1 WLR 181
4   [1954] 1 All ER 693, [1954] 1 QB 503
5   [1975] 2 All ER 490 at 496, [1975] 1 WLR 724 at 730–731
6   (1977) 68 Cr App R 28
7   [1975] 2 All ER 490, [1975] 1 WLR 724

is not an article which is an offensive weapon per se, but selects it, it not having been in his possession before, with the intention of making immediate use of it as an offensive weapon, and that in those circumstances there would be an offence under s 1 of the 1953 Act, accepting that the distinctions in the situation in *Ohlson v Hylton*[1] and *R v Humphreys*[2] would otherwise enable the defendant to be acquitted.

In support of that proposition he relies on *Harrison v Thornton*[3]. That is a case where a defendant and another man with whom he was present had got into a fight with two other men. The police arrived and the defendant at some stage took up a stone and threw it at one of the other two men. He was arrested for being in possession of the stone, which it was said was an offensive weapon. It was held, the justices having convicted him, that they were right because the defendant had made the stone an offensive weapon by his conduct with it.

There is a commentary by the editors of the Criminal Law Review[4], referring to an article in Smith and Hogan[5], drawing attention to the apparent discrepancy between that case and cases like *Ohlson v Hylton*[1] and *R v Humphreys*[2], though they could not be specifically mentioned[6].

Counsel for the respondent relies on that case as supporting his third category of articles which had not previously been carried by the defendant but were either borrowed or fortuitously collected for offensive use, the implication being that in those circumstances the intention at the time of the collection or borrowing renders the article an offensive weapon within the meaning of the 1953 Act.

He also relies on *R v Dayle*[7]. The facts in that case were that the appellant had produced, during a fight, the jack of a motor car and thrown it at his intended victim. Most of the argument in that case, and most of the ratio decidendi of it, turned on a different point with which this court in this appeal is not concerned.

But towards the end of the judgment of the court, which was delivered by Kilner Brown J, the judge made these observations. He said[8]:

'The terms of s 1(1) of the Prevention of Crime Act 1953 are apt to cover the case of a person who goes out with an offensive weapon without lawful authority or reasonable excuse and also the person who deliberately selects an article, such as the stone in *Harrison v Thornton*[3], with the intention of using it as a weapon without such authority or excuse. But, if an article (already possessed lawfully and for good reason) is used offensively to cause injury, such use does not necessarily prove the intent which the Crown must establish in respect of articles which are not offensive weapons per se. Each case must depend on its own facts.'

That expression by the judge in that case would appear not to be direct authority for either proposition, since he is pointing out that each case must depend on its own facts.

Harrison v Thornton[3], which might be apt to support the contention of counsel for the respondent on his third category, is again reported extremely shortly, and for my part it would perhaps be open to question whether the full argument had been produced correctly. It is a Divisional Court case, and, in the view of this court, the more recent

1   [1975] 2 All ER 490, [1975] 1 WLR 724
2   (1977) 68 Cr App R 28
3   [1966] Crim LR 388
4   [1966] Crim LR 389
5   Criminal Law (1st Edn, 1965), p 285
6   The cases had not been decided at the date of the commentary in the Criminal Law Review
7   [1973] 3 All ER 1151, [1974] 1 WLR 181
8   [1973] 3 All ER 1151 at 1154, [1974] 1 WLR 181 at 184

authorities of *Ohlsen v Hylton*[1] and *R v Humphreys*[2], which is an authority of the Court of Appeal, are certainly more apt to cover the facts of the case now before us than any of the others.

In my judgment, the facts of this case cannot be distinguished from those in those two cases without resort to what, in my view, would be a rather academic and over-analytical approach by making a distinction between an innocent weapon subsequently used with the intention of an assault and which is being carried innocently by the defendant in the case, and a similar article which is acquired either by borrowing from somebody else or fortuitously by being picked up in the street.

For my part also, it seems to me that the purport of the 1953 Act, as revealed by its long title, is to cover the situation where an accused person, a defendant, has with him and is carrying an offensive weapon intending that it shall be used, if necessary, for offensive purposes. Where an assault in fact takes place, whether it amounts to an assault causing actual bodily harm or a lesser or greater criminal substantive offence, and the only circumstances in which the weapon used is converted or could be converted into an offensive weapon for the purposes of the definition are its use itself in the assault concerned, then an alternative or second charge under the 1953 Act would be more likely to confuse than to resolve the situation.

Therefore, in my judgment, the real purpose of the 1953 Act is to prevent the carrying of offensive weapons. Their use would almost inevitably be better dealt with by a substantantive offence. For the reasons I have endeavoured to give, for my part I would allow this appeal.

CROOM-JOHNSON J. I agree.

LORD WIDGERY CJ. I agree and the appeal will be allowed and the conviction quashed.

Appeal allowed. Conviction quashed.

Solicitors: *Peter Frost & Co,* Spalding (for the appellant); *Roythorne & Co,* Spalding (for the respondent).

Lea Josse   Barrister.

---

1   [1975] 2 All ER 490, [1975] 1 WLR 724
2   (1977) 68 Cr App R 28

Harmony Shipping Co SA v Davis and others

COURT OF APPEAL, CIVIL DIVISION

LORD DENNING MR, WALLER AND CUMMING-BRUCE LJJ

30th APRIL, 1st, 2nd, 3rd MAY 1979

Evidence – Expert witness – Compellability – Witness giving opinion on facts to one side and thereafter advising other side on same facts – Handwriting expert consulted by plaintiffs on authenticity of document – Expert giving opinion unfavourable to plaintiffs' claim – Expert's practice not to advise both sides in a case – Expert inadvertently advising defendants on authenticity of document – Defendants wanting to call expert to give evidence of his opinion – Defendants issuing subpoena to compel expert to give evidence – Whether expert a compellable witness for defendants – Whether plaintiffs having property in expert's evidence – Whether express or implied contract by expert not to assist defendants on authenticity of document – Whether such a contract contrary to public policy.

A handwriting expert, one of only a few such experts, was approached by the plaintiffs in an action to advise on the authenticity of a document, the genuineness of which was crucial to their case. The expert advised that the document was not genuine. In discussing his fee for the advice the expert stated that it was a rule of his not to give advice to both sides in an action. Subsequently the expert was approached by the defendants to the action to advise them of the document's authenticity. Not realising that he had already advised the plaintiffs on the matter, he advised the defendants that the document was not genuine. He later realised that he had advised both sides and told the defendants that he could accept no further instructions from them. The defendants, who wished the expert to give evidence on their behalf, issued a subpoena ad testificandum requiring him to attend and give such evidence. The plaintiffs applied to the trial judge to set aside the subpoena but the judge ruled that the expert was a compellable witness and ought to give evidence as to his opinion of the document. The plaintiffs appealed, contending that there was a contract, express or implied, between them and the expert that he would not voluntarily assist the defendants on matters on which he had advised them and would use his best endeavours not to appear for both sides.

Held – The appeal would be dismissed for the following reasons—

(i) The principle that no party had any property in the evidence of a witness of fact and that he could be compelled by the court to give evidence applied to an expert witness. The court was therefore entitled to compel an expert witness to give evidence both of the facts he had observed and of his opinion on those facts, subject only to any claim to legal professional privilege by the expert in respect of communications between him and a party's lawyers. Accordingly, on principle the court was entitled to have before it the document in question and the expert's opinion on it and the defendants were therefore entitled to subpoena the expert to give evidence of his opinion on the genuineness of the document. It followed that the judge had been right not to set aside the subpoena (see p 180 *h j*, p 181 *b c e* to *g* and *j*, p 182 *f* to *h* and p 184 *c d* and *j*, post).

(ii) Furthermore, the plaintiffs had failed to establish an express contract in the terms alleged, for the expert's statement that it was his practice when consulted by one side in a case not to assist the other side, did not amount to an express contract to that effect. Nor had the plaintiffs established that it was an implied term of the contract to advise to them that the expert would not assist the defendants (see p 182 *b d* and *g*, p 183 *j*, p 184 *a d* and *h j*, post).

Per Curiam. A contract by which a witness binds himself not to give evidence before the court on a matter on which the judge could compel him to give evidence is contrary to public policy and unenforceable (see p 182 *c d* and *g* and p 184 *d*, post).

Notes

For opinions of experts as evidence, see 17 Halsbury's Laws (4th Edn) para 83.   *a*
For compellability of witnesses, see ibid, para 234.

Cases referred to in judgments

Liverpool City Council v Irwin [1976] 2 All ER 39, [1977] AC 239, [1976] 2 WLR 562, 74
  LGR 392, 32 P & CR 43, HL.
McDonald Construction Co Ltd v Bestway Lathe & Plastering Co Ltd (1972) 27 DLR (3d) 253, *b*
  Digest (Cont Vol D) 327, *3098a.

Cases also cited

Beer v Ward (1821) Jac 77, 37 ER 779.
D v National Society for the Prevention of Cruelty to Children [1977] 1 All ER 589, [1978] AC
  171, HL.   *c*
Lively Ltd v City of Munich [1976] 3 All ER 851, [1976] 1 WLR 1004.
London and Leicester Hosiery Co v Griswold (1886) 3 RPC 251.
Manchester Ship Canal Co v Manchester Racecourse Co [1900] 2 Ch 352.
Morgan v Morgan [1977] 2 All ER 515, [1977] Fam 122.
R v Sang [1979] 2 All ER 46, [1979] 2 WLR 439, CA; *affd* [1979] 2 All ER 1222, HL.
Rowden v Universities Co-operative Association Ltd (1881) 71 LT Jo 373.   *d*
Seyfang v G D Searle & Co [1973] 1 All ER 290, [1973] 1 QB 148.
Tedeschi v Singh [1948] Ch 319.
Weld-Blundell v Stephens [1919] 1 KB 520, CA; *on appeal* [1920] AC 956, [1920] All ER Rep
  32, HL.

Interlocutory appeal   *e*

The plaintiffs, Harmony Shipping Co SA, the owners of a ship, brought an action against
the second defendants ('the defendants'), Saudi Europe Line Ltd and Mohammed A R
Orri trading as Saudi Europe Line, as the charterers of the ship, claiming hire due under
an alleged charterparty between the parties dated 3rd December 1976. The defence to
the action was that the charterparty was a sham and not intended to create legal relations
between the parties. A crucial document in the action was a letter dated 9th February *f*
1977 from the plaintiffs to the captain of the ship which, if genuine, went a long way to
establishing the plaintiffs' claim. The defendants challenged the authenticity of the
letter. During the hearing of the action the plaintiffs' solicitors obtained the opinion of
a handwriting expert, the first defendant, Mr Derek Davis, that the letter was not
genuine. Some weeks later the defendants also consulted Mr Davis on the validity of the
letter and he, not realising he had already advised the plaintiffs, advised the defendants *g*
that the letter was not genuine. The defendants wished to call Mr Davis as an expert
witness in support of their case in the action and served on him a subpoena ad
testificandum. The plaintiffs made an application to the trial judge in the action asking
him to set aside the subpoena and to rule that Mr Davis be excluded from giving
evidence on behalf of the defendants. The plaintiffs also issued a summons against Mr
Davis and the defendants seeking (1) an injunction restraining Mr Davis from disclosing *h*
to the defendants or any legal adviser, servant or agent of theirs (a) the nature or terms
of any instructions given to him by the plaintiffs, their servants or agents, (b) the fact of
or the nature or any terms of any advice given by him to such persons, (c) any information
given to him by such persons for the purpose of or in connection with such advice and
(d) any information obtained by him when acting pursuant to those instructions; (2) an
injunction requiring Mr Davis to apply to the court to set aside the subpoena ad *j*
testificandum served on him by the defendants; (3) an injunction restraining Mr Davis
(a) from appearing voluntarily to testify in the action on behalf of the defendants, (b)
from accepting or continuing to accept instructions from the defendants and (c) from
advising or continuing to advise the defendants; (4) an injunction restraining the
defendants by themselves, their servants or agents from procuring or inducing Mr Davis

to do anything which under paras (1) and (3) the plaintiffs prayed that he should be restrained from doing. (5) Against Mr Davis damages for breach of contract and/or duty. On 11th April 1979 the trial judge, Lloyd J, gave judgment dismissing the application in the action and refusing the injunctions claimed in the summons. The plaintiffs appealed. The facts are set out in the judgment of Lord Denning MR.

Christopher Bathurst QC and *Peter Goldsmith* for the plaintiffs.
J B W McDonnell for Mr Davis.
John Wilmers QC and *Anthony Clarke QC* for the defendants.

Cur adv vult

3rd May. The following judgments were read.

LORD DENNING MR. Mr Davis is an expert in handwriting. He finds himself in an embarrassing position. He has been consulted by both sides in an action. The question is whether he should give evidence for one side without the consent of the other.

Harmony Shipping Co SA, the plaintiffs, own a ship called the Good Helmsman. They allowed a Saudi Arabian company, the defendants, the use of that ship. Hire would be payable to the plaintiffs for the use of that ship during the time the defendants had it. The case involves the question of a charterparty. The defendants, by one of their agents, signed a charterparty for the hire of this vessel, the Good Helmsman. They signed it in December 1976. The plaintiffs sue on that charterparty. They say that the ship was delivered under it and that the defendants are liable for the hire accordingly. But the defendants seek to avoid their obligations under that charterparty. They say: 'It is a sham. It was never intended to be a real charterparty. It was only signed so that it could be taken to the bank in order that the plaintiffs could raise money from the bank on it.' That is not a very laudable defence: but that is what the defendants say.

A question has arisen as to the validity of a particular document which appears to have come into being on 9th February 1977. It is a letter from the plaintiffs to the master of the Good Helmsman. It says:

> 'Re Charter Party Dated December 3rd 1976
> 'Dear Captain
> 'Enclosed please find a copy of charter party dated December 3rd 1976 attached with adendem [sic] dated January 22nd 1977 between Harmony Shipping Co S.A and Saudi Europe Line. Please treat the charterers like owners and offer them the most possible facilities . . .'

If that is a genuine, good, authentic letter, it goes far to show that this was a genuine charterparty, intended to be acted on by the master of the vessel.

The defendants say that that is not a good, valid or genuine document. Only carbon copies were produced of it: and one carbon seems to differ from an earlier one.

In order to prove that the letter was genuine and authentic, a firm of London solicitors, Messrs Holman, Fenwick & Willan, acting for the plaintiffs decided to obtain the services of a handwriting expert. They approached Mr Davis.

Mr Davis is a very busy man. We have been told that he works on about 200 cases at any one time. He always does his best to avoid accepting instructions from more than one side in any particular case. That is one of his professional rules. He maintains a systematic index record of instructions which he has received.

When Messrs Holman, Fenwick & Willan decided to consult Mr Davis, he happened to be engaged in another case in these courts and was waiting to be called as a witness. After communicating with his secretary, it appeared to Mr Davis that he had not been consulted by anyone else in this case. So he saw Mr Robinson of Messrs Holman, Fenwick & Willan on that day (27th February) outside court 26 in this building. At that interview the carbon copies of the letter were produced to Mr Davis. He expressed his opinion as to the genuineness and authenticity of one or other of them. At the same time there was discussion about his fee. There was communication between counsel and Mr Davis. He said that it was not his practice to accept instructions from one side once he had been instructed by the other side. Something was said to the effect that he would give his usual undertaking that he would not accept instructions from the other side.

I think it may be inferred that Mr Davis said that in his opinion the letters were not genuine. So his evidence would not help the plaintiffs, the clients of Messrs Holman, Fenwick & Willan. Therefore they told him that they would not be wanting his assistance again: but, if they did, they would let him know. That was on 27th February. That was all that Mr Davis heard about the matter from the plaintiffs' side.

In April 1979 Mr Davis was being consulted by Messrs Thomas Cooper & Stibbard about another case. Then, on Friday, 6th April, he received a message from Messrs Thomas Cooper & Stibbard asking him whether he could give his opinion on some documents which had been brought in. He said he would. He saw one of the partners from Messrs Thomas Cooper & Stibbard. He examined the documents and gave his opinion of them to the partner concerned. He probably said that they were not genuine. So his evidence would help the defendants, the clients of Thomas Cooper & Stibbard. But in the course of his conversation with the partner from Thomas Cooper & Stibbard something was said as a result of which, for the first time, it occurred to Mr Davis that he had already been consulted by the other side. So he referred to his file and realised it might be the same matter. Immediately he told the partner from Thomas Cooper & Stibbard, 'I cannot accept any further instructions in the matter since I have already been consulted by the other side'.

There it is. On 27th February he had given his opinion on some of the documents to the solicitors for one side and then on 6th April he had given his opinion on like documents to the solicitors for the other side. He had done it quite inadvertently. Having discovered that he had given his opinion to the other side, he said he could go no further.

Messrs Thomas Cooper & Stibbard wanted his evidence because they realised it would be helpful to them. They attended at counsel's chambers. A decision was reached that they would subpoena Mr Davis to give evidence on their behalf. That is what they did. They issued a subpoena ad testificandum on Mr Davis so that he should give evidence in the case as to his opinion on the genuineness of these letters, to the effect that they were not genuine. The plaintiffs took objection. They said that Mr Davis should not have been subpoenaed. They said that the subpoena ought to be set aside because he should not give any evidence as he had already been consulted by them.

The trial has been going on for a long time. Lloyd J has been considering the case for some weeks. He has ruled that Mr Davis is compellable and ought to give evidence as to his opinion of these documents. He said that there was no reason for debarring him from doing so, but, as it was a difficult point which had never arisen before, he adjourned the case pending the decision of the Court of Appeal whether he was right or wrong.

So we have before us a question of principle. If an expert witness has been consulted by one side and has given his opinion to that side, can he thereafter be consulted and subpoenaed by the other side to give his opinion on the facts of the case? That is the issue which this court has to decide.

So far as witnesses of fact are concerned, the law is as plain as can be. There is no property in a witness. The reason is because the court has a right to every man's evidence. Its primary duty is to ascertain the truth. Neither one side nor the other can debar the court from ascertaining the truth either by seeing a witness beforehand or by purchasing his evidence or by making communication to him. In no way can one side prohibit the other side from seeing a witness of fact, from getting the facts from him and from calling him to give evidence or from issuing him with a subpoena. That was laid down by the Law Society in their Guide to the Professional Conduct of Solicitors[1] in

---

1   (1944) 41 LS Gaz 8

1944. It was affirmed and approved in 1963 by Lord Parker CJ and the judges. It is published in the Law Society's Gazette for February 1963. It says[1]:

'. . . the Council have always held the view that there is no property in a witness and that so long as there is no question of tampering with the evidence of witnesses it is open to the solicitor for either party in civil or criminal proceedings to interview and take a statement from any witness or prospective witness at any stage in the proceedings, whether or not that witness has been interviewed or called as a witness by the other party.'

That principle is established in the case of a witness of fact: for the plain, simple reason that the primary duty of the court is to ascertain the truth by the best evidence available. Any witness who has seen the facts or who knows the facts can be compelled to assist the court and should assist the court by giving that evidence.

The question in this case is whether or not that principle applies to expert witnesses. They may have been told the substance of a party's case. They may have been given a great deal of confidential information. On it they may have given advice to the party. Does the rule apply to such a case?

Many of the communications between the solicitor and the expert witness will be privileged. They are protected by legal professional privilege. They cannot be communicated to the court except with the consent of the party concerned. That means that a great deal of the communications between the expert witness and the lawyer cannot be given in evidence to the court. If questions were asked about it, then it would be the duty of the judge to protect the witness (and he would) by disallowing any questions which infringed the rule about legal professional privilege or the rule protecting information given in confidence, unless, of course, it was one of those rare cases which come before the courts from time to time where in spite of privilege or confidence the court does order a witness to give further evidence.

Subject to that qualification, it seems to me that an expert witness falls into the same position as a witness of fact. The court is entitled, in order to ascertain the truth, to have the actual facts which he has observed adduced before it and to have his independent opinion on those facts. It is interesting to see that it was so held in Canada in *MacDonald Construction Co Ltd v Lathe & Plastering Co Ltd*[2]. In this particular case the court is entitled to have before it the documents in question and it is entitled to have the independent opinion of the expert witness on those documents and on those facts, excluding, as I have said, any of the other communications which passed when the expert witness was being instructed or employed by the other side. Subject to that exception, it seems to me (and I would agree with the judge on this) that the expert witness is in the same position when he is speaking as to the facts he has observed and is giving his own independent opinion on them, no matter by which side he is instructed.

In this particular case Mr Davis has been subpoenaed by the defendants. It seems to me that that is very right and proper. It was suggested that the subpoena should be set aside. As far as I know, no subpoena ad testificandum has ever been set aside except at the instance of the witness himself when he has claimed that it would be oppressive to make him answer that subpoena. Otherwise a subpoena as testificandum must be obeyed by the witness. He must come to the court and be ready to give his evidence and answer such questions as the judge permits to be answered. He will be protected in so far as there is any proper claim for legal professional privilege or confidence. So it seems to me on principle that Mr Davis can be subpoenaed. He can be seen beforehand and give a proof on those limited matters I have mentioned, and give evidence accordingly.

Against this argument of principle, counsel for the plaintiffs put forward this argument. He said that in this case there was an express contract: or, alternatively, an

---

1   (1963) 60 LS Gaz 108
2   (1972) 27 DLR (3d) 253

implied contract to the effect that Mr Davis would not voluntarily assist the other side. He analysed the evidence, and submitted that at the conversation, which I have mentioned, on 27th January it was understood that Mr Davis would not accept instructions from the other side, however inadvertently. Counsel for the plaintiffs submitted that Mr Davis recognised this: because as soon as he realised what had happened he said that he could not go on any further in the case at all.

To my mind no such contract, express or implied, is to be found. At most there was a statement by Mr Davis of his practice, namely that, having been instructed by one side, he would not accept instructions from the other. That is a statement of a proper professional practice. It is no doubt very valuable in order to save embarrassment to him and others like him when they are placed in a situation like this: as handwriting experts often are because there are not many of them. But it is not a contract. It is not a binding contract at law, express or implied. But I would go further. If there was a contract by which a witness bound himself not to give evidence before the court on a matter on which the judge said he ought to give evidence, then I say that any such contract would be contrary to public policy and would not be enforced by the court. It is the primary duty of the courts to ascertain the truth: and, when a witness is subpoenaed, he must answer such questions as the court properly asks him. This duty is not to be taken away by some private arrangement or contract by him with one side or the other.

So on those two grounds, (1) that there is no proof of any contract express or implied, and (2) that it is against public policy, I would hold that the point raised by counsel for the plaintiffs in this case is not a good one.

I would add a further consideration of public policy. If an expert could have his hands tied by being instructed by one side, it would be very easy for a rich client to consult each of the acknowledged experts in the field. Each expert might give an opinion adverse to the rich man, yet the rich man could say to each, 'Your mouth is closed and you cannot give evidence in court against me'. We were told that in the Admiralty courts where there are a very limited number of experts, one side may consult every single one of them. Does that mean that the other side is debarred from getting the help of any expert evidence because all the experts have been taken up by the other side? The answer is clearly No. It comes back to the proposition which I stated at the beginning. There is no property in a witness as to fact. There is no property in an expert witness as to the facts he has observed and his own independent opinion on them. There being no such property in a witness, it is the duty of a witness to come to court and give his evidence in so far as he is directed by the judge to do so.

I find myself in general agreement with the judgment of Lloyd J, and would dismiss the appeal.

WALLER LJ. I agree. Mr Davis has found himself in a difficult position in spite of all the steps he has taken to avoid such a position; and his first reaction when he realised what had happened was to say, 'I can take no further part in this matter'. But the field in which he is an expert is one in which there are not very many people of ability. Therefore this situation has arisen where he has been subpoenaed by the defendants to give evidence although he had first been consulted by the plaintiffs.

As Lord Denning MR has said, the general principle must be that no party has any property in a witness; and the argument before us has partly involved a discussion whether there is a difference between a witness of fact and an expert. In my view, there is no difference between those two kinds of witnesses as a matter of general rule. Were it otherwise, as Lord Denning MR has indicated, in a sphere of a small number of specialists it might be possible for one party to buy up all the possible experts, and clearly such a situation is not right. On the other hand, of course, it is clearly undesirable that expert witnesses should be involved with both sides, and Mr Davis has, very properly, a rule of conduct which he adopts for himself to use his very best endeavours to make sure that such a state of affairs does not happen. I say at once that I feel great sympathy with him in this case where his first involvement in this case was in a hurried consultation

during the midday adjournment whilst he was engaged in giving evidence in another
case. That indicates how it was that this accident happened.

The safeguard against an expert witness giving evidence on more than one side is the
existence of professional privilege, and it is clear that there is professional privilege for all
the discussions which took place between Mr Davis and the plaintiffs' advisers outside the
door of the court where the consultation took place; and whether or not Mr Davis is put
in a situation of considerable embarrassment has been a matter for him to consider.

Counsel for Mr Davis on his behalf has explained that, when he was subpoenaed,
consideration was given whether or not he could apply to have the subpoena
discharged. Counsel set out three grounds which might possibly have been grounds for
setting aside the subpoena which he categorised, firstly, as convenience, secondly,
whether it would be very difficult for Mr Davis to disentangle those matters which had
been given to him as a matter of confidence from those which were not and, thirdly,
whether it could be said that for him to give evidence would have been a breach of
contract. Counsel, who very helpfully addressed the court about these matters, said that
Mr Davis had come to the conclusion that it was quite impossible to sustain any of those
grounds.

I need not deal any further with the ground of convenience or breach of contract
because I shall return to contract in a moment, but I will simply deal with the second of
those three, whether or not Mr Davis would be in difficulty in separating out in his mind
anything which had been given to him in confidence during that consultation from the
rest of his evidence.

It is not surprising that Mr Davis is unable to make that objection. What he is
required in the main to give evidence about is the examination of four documents. It has
been agreed that two out of the four are not carbon copies from the other two, and he is
required to express an opinion whether or not it was probable or highly probable, I
suppose, that the two that were not copies of the other two were in fact deliberately
intended to look as if they were copies of the other two. As it seems to me, that is not a
matter which depends on confidential information at all. It depends entirely on an
examination by somebody expert in those matters looking at the documents and
deciding from a number of factors, counsel for the defendants has said that there are 10
or 11 points which indicate deliberation, whether or not it must have been a deliberate
imitation and not an accidental one. So I completely accept that it would be difficult for
Mr Davis to make the case that he was oppressed by being subpoenaed in this case unless,
of course, counsel's argument for the plaintiffs about contract could be established.

Counsel for the plaintiffs has sought to get round the difficulty in this case, the
difficulty I have just mentioned, by submitting that there was a contract either express
or implied that Mr Davis should not voluntarily give assistance to the other side on the
same or related matters and to use his best endeavours not to appear for both sides. Mr
Davis willingly accepts that that is a principle by which he acts but does not accept that
there was any contractual term to that effect. Counsel for Mr Davis, in dealing with the
particular facts of this consultation, posed the question, 'When was the contract made?
Was it made when the telephone conversation making the appointment was made, or
was it made at the moment when the consultation started outside the door of the court,
court 26, or was it made at some later stage?', and arrived at the conclusion that whenever
it was made it was certainly clearly made before Mr Robinson, the instructing solicitor,
had left and before any observation had been made at all by anybody about Mr Davis's
personal rules about trying to avoid being instructed by both sides. So I find no
possibility of establishing that there was an express term in the contractual arrangements
between Mr Davis and the plaintiffs.

Was there then an implied term? Counsel for the defendants has drawn attention to
Liverpool City Council v Irwin[1] where, taking the matter very shortly, both Lord

---

1   [1976] 2 All ER 39, [1977] AC 239

Wilberforce and Lord Cross have indicated that a term should not readily be implied unless it is necessary to imply such a term, and it clearly is not necessary to imply such *a* a term in this case, and I find myself quite unable to give such an indication.

In my view, although it cannot be a general rule and every case must depend on its own facts, in this particular case, Mr Davis, giving evidence of the nature I have indicated, having expressed the view that he does not willingly give evidence, would not be embarrassed in being compelled to give evidence to the court. For the reasons I have given, in my view there is no contract and therefore there would be no oppression on Mr *b* Davis which would make it difficult for him to give evidence.

I should add this. It is significant, having arrived at that conclusion that he cannot sustain such an objection, that the attempt to set aside the subpoena is made by the plaintiffs. I do not find it surprising that there is no such case where the objection is made by somebody other than the person subpoenaed. It seems to me that that is the natural result of the situation, and the case where somebody else can set aside the *c* subpoena must be, if not non-existent, then very, very rare indeed.

I would dismiss this appeal.

d

CUMMING-BRUCE LJ. I agree. I would only add that the different kinds of expert witness are various, and this case is concerned with the particular functions, responsibilities and activities of a handwriting expert, and the problems raised by the case arise from very unusual and peculiar facts.

When Mr Davis was first confronted with the plaintiffs' solicitors it was in the luncheon adjournment at a time when Mr Davis had been giving evidence in court 26 *e* in this building. He was then shown a couple of documents; and the solicitor concerned, having received a reaction from Mr Davis, left after a mere 20 minutes.

Some six weeks later a partner in another firm who had been instructing Mr Davis in an entirely different matter happened to ask him if he would be good enough to give an opinion on some documents to another partner of that firm that same evening if that other partner brought the documents to him that night on his way home. Thus on the *f* telephone, without the faintest idea about any details at all, Mr Davis agreed to do what he was asked to do; and at eight o'clock in the evening the other partner, to whom I have referred, left some documents with him. Mr Davis proceeded to spend a couple of hours or so looking at the documents and thinking about them. Then he telephoned not the partner who first asked him if he would act but that second partner who was concerned in the case and left the documents, and he gave preliminary opinions on the documents *g* to that gentleman. Then, and then only, in the ensuing conversation something was said which enabled Mr Davis to realise that quite inadvertently he had got himself into a situation in which he had given an opinion to the defendants although six weeks earlier he had given advice to the plaintiffs. Mr Davis himself in his affidavit makes it perfectly clear that he is quite unaware of the risk of any disclosure of confidential information received by him from the plaintiffs' solicitors. Thus it will be seen on what very special *h* facts these proceedings involving Mr Davis have reached this court.

For my part, I agree with Lord Denning MR and Waller LJ that the plaintiffs have failed to establish any express contract in the terms that they allege and they have also failed to establish that the implied terms which they seek to set up are necessary to the contract originally made when the plaintiffs' solicitors asked Mr Davis originally to help, as he did, outside court 26.

It is not necessary for the determination of this appeal to consider the situation of any *j* other kind of expert in any other kind of situation; and this court decides only the obligations that arise from the very peculiar facts that have been described in the evidence in this case.

I agree that the appeal should be dismissed.

Appeal dismissed.

Solicitors: *Holman, Fenwick & Willan* (for the plaintiffs); *John Harte & Co* (for Mr Davis); *Thomas Cooper & Stibbard* (for the defendants).

Frances Rustin   Barrister.

Practice Direction

QUEEN'S BENCH DIVISION

Practice – Chambers proceedings – Masters' summonses – Queen's Bench Division – Return date – Expedition – New arrangements.

1. The arrangements for return dates for the hearing of summonses before the Queen's Bench masters in chambers have been revised and the current practice will continue.
2. The Practice Direction[1] (Return Date for Masters' Summonses) is therefore amended by deleting the first three paragraphs and substituting therefor the following paragraphs:

'1. The current practice for the hearing of summonses before the Queen's Bench masters in chambers will continue.

'2. Two masters will sit each day to hear summonses in chambers and they will sit as at present in rooms 95 and 96 at 10.30 am.

'3. The present "Supplementary Lists" on Tuesdays and Thursdays will continue but will be listed for hearing before the master at 2.00 pm, and the master will sit in room 95 or 96, as necessary. If the business before the masters makes it necessary or desirable, the masters may take an occasional "Additional List".'

In all other respects the Practice Direction referred to above will continue to apply.

Sir Jack I H Jacob QC
Senior Master of the Supreme Court.

16th July 1979

1   *Practice Direction* [1977] 3 All ER 943, [1977] 1 WLR 1221, sub nom *Masters' Practice Direction* 16A(1) (*Return date for masters' summonses*) (see the Supreme Court Practice 1979, vol 2, para 917A, p 212)

Antco Shipping Ltd v Seabridge Shipping Ltd
The Furness Bridge

COURT OF APPEAL, CIVIL DIVISION
LORD DENNING MR, LAWTON AND GEOFFREY LANE LJJ
21st, 22nd, 23rd MARCH 1979

Arbitration – Special case – Conditions on stating a case – Discretion of arbitrator to state special case for High Court – Direction by court that special case be stated – Discretion of arbitrator and court to make order as to costs 'or otherwise' – Arbitrators making award on condition that charterers pay amount which was indisputably due – Whether arbitrators or court having power to impose condition on stating of case – Arbitration Act 1950, ss 21(1), 28.

Following the determination of the judge that the charterers were liable in damages to the owners, the question of the quantum of the award was referred to arbitrators. The arbitrators decided that the charterers were liable to the owners in any event to the extent of $475,000, and that dependent on a point of law they could be liable to the extent of a further $70,000 or so. The charterers requested the arbitrators to state a special case for the decision of the High Court, under s 21[a] of the Arbitration Act 1950, but the arbitrators refused to do so unless the charterers agreed to pay into a joint account the $475,000 found inevitably to be due. On the hearing of the special case the charterers took the point that the arbitrators had no power to impose such a condition in agreeing to state a special case. The judge held that the arbitrators had such power, and, in giving the charterers leave to appeal, he also imposed such a condition.

Held – An arbitrator's discretion under s 21(1) of the 1950 Act to state an arbitration award in the form of a special case for the decision of the High Court and the court's power under that section to order an arbitrator to do so, coupled with the power of an arbitrator and the court under s 28[b] to make an order on an award on such terms as to costs 'or otherwise' as they thought fit, included the power to impose a condition on the stating of a case for the payment of any amount which was indisputably due by either party, if it was just to impose such a condition (see p 189 c d and h to p 190 a and g, p 191 a b and d, p 192 a b d e and g h and p 193 c, post).

Halfdan Grieg & Co A/S v Sterling Coal & Navigation Corpn, The Lysland [1973] 2 All ER 1073 distinguished.

Dictum of Brandon J in *The Golden Trader* [1974] 2 All ER at 696 considered.

Notes

For statement of a special case by arbitrators, see 2 Halsbury's Laws (4th Edn) paras 599, 602.

For the Arbitration Act 1950, ss 21, 28, see 2 Halsbury's Statutes (3rd Edn) 450, 457.

As from 1st August 1979 s 21 of the 1950 Act is repealed by the Arbitration Act 1979, ss 1(1), 8(3)(b). For judicial review of arbitration awards on and after that date, see s 1 of the 1979 Act, and for the determination of preliminary points of law by the High Court, see s 2 of that Act.

Cases referred to in judgments

Golden Trader, The, Danemar Scheepvart Maatschappij BV v Owners of the motor vessel Golden Trader [1974] 2 All ER 686, [1975] QB 348, [1974] 3 WLR 16, [1974] 1 Lloyd's Rep 378, Digest (Cont Vol D) 39, 369d.

Granvias Oceanicas Armadora SA v Jibsen Trading Co, The Kavo Peiratis [1977] 2 Lloyd's Rep 344.

---

a   Section 21, so far as material, is set out at p 189 b c, post
b   Section 28 is set out at p 189 d, post

Halfdan Grieg & Co A/S v Sterling Coal & Navigation Corpn, The Lysland [1973] 2 All ER
1073, [1973] QB 843, [1973] 2 WLR 904, [1973] 1 Lloyd's Rep 296, CA, Digest (Cont
Vol D) 42, *1144a*.

Cases also cited

Alexandria Cotton & Trading Co (Sudan) Ltd v Cotton Co of Ethiopia Ltd [1965] 2 Lloyd's Rep
447.
Associated Bulk Carriers Ltd v Koch Shipping Inc, The Fuohsan Maru [1978] 2 All ER 254,
[1978] 1 Lloyd's Rep 24, CA.
Athenee (Owners of cargo ex) v Athenee (1922) 11 Ll L Rep 6, CA.
Atlantic Star, The, The owners of the Atlantic Star v The owners of the Bona Spes [1973] 2 All
ER 175, [1974] AC 436, HL.
Cap Bon, The [1967] 1 Lloyd's Rep 543.
Czarnikow v Roth, Schmidt & Co [1922] 2 KB 478, 28 Com Cas 29, CA.
*Eleftheria, The, Owners of Cargo lately laden on board ship or vessel Eleftheria v Owners of ship
or vessel Eleftheria* [1969] 2 All ER 641, [1970] P 94.
Foresta Romana SA v Georges Mabro (Owners) (1940) 66 Ll L Rep 139.
Knight and Tabernacle Permanent Benefit Building Society, Re [1892] 2 QB 613, CA.

Appeal

This was an appeal, pursuant to leave granted by the judge, by Antco Shipping Ltd ('the
charterers'), the respondents in a pending arbitration, against an order of Donaldson J
dated 2nd March 1979 whereby he ordered that the arbitrators (Messrs John L Potter and
Robert W Reed) in an arbitration between the charterers and Seabridge Shipping Ltd
('the owners'), the claimants in the pending arbitration, be ordered to state an award in
the form of a special case on a question of law, namely, on the true construction of the
charterparty what was the extent of the liability in damages of the charterers to the
owners, provided the charterers paid $US475,000 into a joint account of the solicitors to
the parties within 14 days of the making of the order?

David Johnson QC and *Bernard Eder* for the charterers.
John Hobhouse QC and *Nicholas Legh-Jones* for the owners.

LORD DENNING MR. On 9th October 1973 a charterparty was arranged between
owners and charterers. It was to be a single voyage charter for the carriage of oil to the
Caribbean. The owners were to nominate a ship to perform the carriage. The charterers
contemplated loading the oil in Libya, but in the charterparty the agreed loading ports
were expressed to be 'European Mediterranean and Libya'. The shipowners nominated
a vessel, the Furness Bridge, a huge vessel carrying 154,000 tons, to take the oil in
accordance with the charterparty. But war broke out between Israel and the Arabs.
Libya imposed an embargo on the export of oil from Libya to the Caribbean. The
charterers did not accept the nomination of the vessel. The owners said that the
charterers had repudiated the contract. The charterers relied on the clause about the
restraint of prices. The issue went to arbitration on the question of liability.

It was an Exxonvoy 1969 charter which contained a clause for London arbitration.
After a long hearing, the arbitrators found that the charterers were wrong in repudiating
because they were not bound to ship oil from Libya. There was the possibility that they
might have obtained oil from some other port in the Mediterranean and so fulfilled their
charter. The case is reported in Lloyd's Law Reports[1].

There remained the issue of damages. The freight payable under the charter was fixed
in October 1973 before the war, when rates were high. When the charterers repudiated
the charterparty, the owners chartered the vessel to the big Bunge worldwide

1   *Seabridge Shipping Ltd v Antco Shipping Ltd, The Furness Bridge* [1977] 2 Lloyd's Rep 367

organisation. She was sent over to the Mississippi to fetch grain from there. There was
much trouble with the contract with Bunge. When the vessel arrived at the Mississippi, *a*
she was of such great length that they had trouble getting to the loading berth. All sorts
of troubles arose. That led to another arbitration and a great deal of discussion. I will not
go into details, but that had to be decided before damages could be assessed under the
original charterparty.

Eventually the question fell to be decided: what damages were the owners entitled to
as a result of the original repudiation by the charterers? The measure would be this. *b*
First: calculate the amount of freight which the owners would have received if the
charterparty had been fulfilled by carrying the oil from a Mediterranean port (other than
Libya) to the Caribbean. Second: calculate the credit which the owners should give in
one of two ways: either (i) by the actual amount which the owners made by putting the
vessel to profitable use with the Bunge organisation; or (ii) by taking the market rate of
freight which the owners could have made by letting the vessel out on the market. *c*

The arbitrators heard all the evidence in the matter. When it came to the award, the
charterers asked that it be stated in the form of a special case so that the point of law could
be resolved whether it was the market rate or the actual amount in mitigation of
damages.

That point of law, however, only involved $US70,000. The amount of damages was
bound to be large anyway. If the owners succeeded on the point of law, the figure would *d*
be $US499,400. If the owners failed on the point of law, the figure would be
$US391,958·59. So the point of law involved a difference of only $US70,000. The
charterers were in any case liable for $US391,958·59, plus interest, and so forth, making
a total of $US475,000.

Summarising it quite shortly, the amount involved in the point of law is $US70,000.
If the charterers are right in this point of law, they save $US70,000. If they are wrong, *e*
they will have to pay the $US70,000 extra. In any event, in the opinion of the arbitrators,
the charterers were liable in any case to $US475,000.

Now I come to the point. The charterers wanted the case to be stated on the point of
law which I have mentioned, that only $US70,000 was in dispute. But the arbitrators
said that in any event they should pay the amount they found inevitably to be due, the
sum of $US475,000. The charterers did not agree to that. The arbitrators said they *f*
would state a special case, on condition that $US475,000 was paid. I will read the order
they made at the conclusion of the arbitration hearing on 19th December 1978:

> 'The Tribunal will proceed to an award unless one of two things happen by
> January 10, 1979: (1) The Respondents issue a Summons asking the Commercial
> Court to overrule the Tribunal's decision and order that the Award be stated in the
> form of a Special Case; OR (2) The Respondents pay into a joint account the sum of *g*
> $475,000, in which case (a) the Award will be stated in the form of a Special Case,
> and (b) the Claimants and Respondents to supply the Tribunal with the question of
> law on which the Award is to be stated by not later than 10 days after the payment
> into the joint account of $475,000.'

In other words, they would state a case if the charterers would pay $US475,000 into a *h*
joint account. Otherwise they would not state a case: they would make their award
without stating a case at all.

The point was taken before Donaldson J. It was submitted that the tribunal had no
power to make it a condition of a special case that that $US475,000 should be paid into
a joint account. Donaldson J, after hearing the arguments on both sides, held that he did
have a discretion. He ordered that the arbitrators state a case on the questions set out in *j*
the summons: provided the respondents, ie the charterers, paid the sum of $US475,000
into a joint account in the names of the solicitors to the parties within fourteen days.

Now there is an appeal to this court. Counsel for the charterers has urged before us
that there is no jurisdiction in arbitrators to make such a conditional order. It was
suggested that when the appeal came before Donaldson J he might have said that the

arbitrators should have made an interim award for the sum of $US475,000. Counsel for
a the charterers would not commit himself whether that was possible. He said that it does
not arise now in the circumstances. I would like to say in passing that it seems to me that
the power under the Arbitration Act 1950 is wide enough to include an interim award
of the amount which the arbitrators found to be inevitably due in any case.

But that is by the way. That does not really arise in this case. The whole question is
whether arbitrators can state an award in the form of a special case and attach a condition
b for payment. That depends on the sections of the 1950 Act. There are only two in
question. Section 21(1) provides:

> 'An arbitrator or umpire may, and shall if so directed by the High Court, state—
> (a) any question of law arising in the course of the reference [that is not this case];
> or (b) an award or any part of an award, in the form of a special case for the decision
> of the High Court.'

c
The important word to notice there is 'may'. The word 'may' gives a discretion. Even
if no further words had been said, it seems to me that those words give the arbitrators
power to make any term or condition which in their discretion is proper when stating a
case.

But one need not stop at that. Section 28 provides: 'Any order made under this Part
d of this Act may be made on such terms as to costs or otherwise as the authority making
the order thinks just.' It seems to me that that, coupled with s 21, does give power to
impose conditions on the stating of a case.

On the wording of the sections, it seems to me that the jurisdiction is there. But
counsel for the charterers said that the discretion which had been given by those sections
had been limited by the decision of this court in *Halfdan Grieg & Co A/S v Sterling Coal*
e *& Navigation Corpn, The Lysland* [1], where this court endeavoured to set out guidelines as
to the circumstances in which arbitrators should state a special case. But I would like to
say at once that those guidelines do not apply here. We did not have in mind at all a case
such as the present, where the arbitrators find that a certain sum is undoubtedly and
indisputably due.

There are some observations of Brandon J which help much. It was in *The Golden*
f *Trader, Danemar Scheepvart Maatschappij BV v Owners of the motor vessel Golden Trader* [2].
A ship had been arrested for a debt. The question was whether that ship should be
released pending an arbitration, and whether it could be released on the condition that
security should be given for the amount of the debt due. It was a case of an international
arbitration where the granting of a stay was mandatory. On that account Brandon J held
that the vessel had to be released. He dealt with cases where the granting of a stay is
g discretionary. He said [3]:

> 'In cases where the grant of a stay is discretionary, the court can refuse a stay
> unless alternative security is provided. The defendant then has to choose between
> having a stay subject to a term for the provision of such security, and not having a
> stay at all.'

h Likewise, where the stating of a case is discretionary, it seems to me that the party may
have to choose between having a case stated on condition that he pays a sum into a joint
account or into court, or having no case stated at all.

So here, how should the discretion be exercised? The charterers are a subsidiary of the
great British Petroleum Corporation. There is an amount of $US475,000 which, in the
arbitrators' view, is indisputably payable in any event. The only amount in dispute is an
j additional $US70,000. That is all the case stated deals with. It seems to me very proper
that a condition should be imposed urging the payment of the $US475,000.

1   [1973] 2 All ER 1073, [1973] QB 843
2   [1974] 2 All ER 686, [1975] QB 348
3   [1974] 2 All ER 686 at 696, [1975] QB 348 at 360

So I think that the arbitrators and Donaldson J were quite right. It was within their jurisdiction to make an award stating the special case only on condition that the $US475,000 was paid. That was a legitimate and proper condition to impose. I would dismiss the appeal, accordingly.

LAWTON LJ. The excessive use of remedies often brings about a reaction by both Parliament and the courts. The history of the remedy of certiorari in the hundred years before 1848 is an example of this tendency. In recent years there has been an excessive use of the powers given by s 21 of the Arbitration Act 1950 to have an award stated in the form of a special case: see the comments of Kerr J in *Granvias Oceanicas Armadora SA v Jibsen Trading Co, The Kavo Peiratis*[1]. At the present time there is a Bill before Parliament which to some extent restrains the use of this power[2]. Meanwhile this appeal affords an opportunity to consider whether under the existing law arbitrators and the High Court can ensure that the power is not used in a manner which may bring about injustice.

The possibility, indeed the probability, of injustice being done in this case to the owners seems clear. The charterers have been found liable to the owners on the charterparty. They undoubtedly owe the owners a substantial sum. The arbitrators, who heard all the evidence, found that that sum was no less than $US475,000. The charterers in this court, through counsel, have accepted the sum as being not less than $US300,000. What is in dispute is a sum between $US67,000 and $US90,000. Pending the decision by the High Court on this issue, the charterers say that the owners can be, and should be, kept out of a large sum which they admit the owners are entitled to have. This, in my opinion is an injustice which the judges of the High Court should prevent if they can. The owners, through their counsel, say that the High Court can prevent an injustice of that kind because there are powers in the Arbitration Act 1950 which can be used. The charterers, through their counsel, say that there is no injustice anyway to the owners and that, if there is any, it is to the charterers. But he went on to submit that there are no powers given by the 1950 Act which enable the court to act as the commercial judge Donaldson J acted in this case.

The question in issue here turns on the construction of two sections of the 1950 Act, ss 21 and 28. Section 21(1) is in these terms:

'An arbitrator or umpire may, and shall if so directed by the High Court, state— (*a*) any question of law arising in the course of the reference [that is not applicable here]; or (*b*) an award or any part of an award, in the form of a special case for the decision of the High Court.'

That subsection clearly gives both the arbitrators and the High Court discretion about stating a special case. That discretion is not to be fettered unless the law requires it to be fettered. The problem therefore has been whether there is anything which does fetter the discretion of either the arbitrators or the High Court. Counsel for the charterers says 'Yes; there is something, and it is the decision of this court in *Halfdan Grieg & Co A/S v Sterling Coal & Navigation Corpn, The Lysland*[3]'. He says that what has happened in this case is that the commercial judge took into consideration matters which he ought not to have taken into consideration because they were not matters to which this court referred in *The Lysland*[3]. As Lord Denning MR has pointed out, *The Lysland*[3] was not in any way concerned with the terms on which a special case could be ordered. It was concerned with the identification of a point of law. It follows, in my judgment, that *The Lysland*[3] does not put a fetter of any kind on the discretion which this court is considering in this case.

The next problem is whether there is anything in s 28 of the 1950 Act which puts a

---

1 [1977] 2 Lloyd's Rep 344 at 349
2 See now the Arbitration Act 1979 (assented to 4th April 1979)
3 [1973] 2 All ER 1073, [1973] QB 843

fetter on the exercise of the court's discretion under s 21. The terms of that section are
a as follows: 'Any order made under this Part of this Act may be made on such terms as to
costs or otherwise as the authority making the order thinks just.' Section 21 comes in the
same Part of the Act as s 28. It follows, therefore, that s 28 applies to s 21.

The next problem is what is meant by the word 'otherwise' which appears in s 28? It
is very wide indeed and can clearly cover, in my judgment, the making of conditions
such as were made by Donaldson J in this case.

b It is pertinent to bear in mind, however, that the exercise of powers under s 28 are for
the purpose of making an order which the court thinks just. Only rarely would the
court be justified in making a condition such as was made in this case. The sort of
circumstances in which such a condition might be required are those which have arisen
in this case, viz where clearly there is a considerable sum due to one party and the
amount involved in the dispute is small. On the other hand, it would clearly not be just
c to impose this kind of condition when there is a dispute whether any sum is due; but
even in such a case there might be exceptional circumstances. It follows that great care
will have to be taken both by arbitrators and by the High Court when deciding whether
to make an order of the kind which was made in this case.

For those reasons and the reasons given by Lord Denning MR I too would dismiss this
appeal.

d
GEOFFREY LANE LJ. The arbitrators here had to decide quantum. Liability had
already been determined in favour of the owners by Kerr J on a special case, reported in
Lloyd's Law Reports[1]. There is no doubt that the charterers are liable to pay a substantial
sum to the owners. There has been a good deal of doubt about the precise figure, and
necessarily so, but at the moment it seems that the sum is likely to be in the region of
e $US300,000 plus interest, and it is much more likely to be in excess of $US475,000. But
there is a dispute as to the basis on which the calculation of damages should be made. If
the charterers' contentions on this aspect of the case are ultimately held to be correct, that
success will profit them to the extent of only some $US70,000 at the very most and
probably a good deal less.

The arbitration hearing as to quantum was to all intents and purposes at an end, and
f all that remained in effect was for them to state the figure at which they had arrived. At
that moment the charterers, as they were entitled to do, asked the arbitrators to state the
award in the form of a special case. One of the results of acceding to that request would
be that the charterers would have what amounts to a stay of execution in respect of the
whole of the sum owing, whatever that might be. Accordingly, it is not surprising that
the arbitrators' reaction to the request was, as Lord Denning MR has already said, to
g announce an order as follows:

> 'The Tribunal will proceed to an award unless one of two things happens by
> January 10, 1979: (1) The Respondents issue a Summons asking the Commercial
> Court to overrule the Tribunal's decision and order that the Award be stated in the
> form of a Special Case; OR (2) The Respondents pay into a joint account the sum of
> $475,000, in which case (a) the Award will be stated in the form of a Special
h Case ...'

The matter was then taken before Donaldson J, who in substance upheld that decision of
the arbitrators. The matter now comes before us by way of appeal from Donaldson J.

The charterers contend that there is a question of law which is the proper subject of a
special case, indeed as the judge has found. That being so, submits counsel for the
j charterers, it is improper to make the charterers pay for the privilege of having the
special case stated. The owners, on the other hand, through their counsel, contend that
ss 21 and 28 of the Arbitration Act 1950, either taken singly or in combination, give to
the arbitrators and to the judge power to impose such terms as they think just when they

---

1 [1977] 2 Lloyd's Rep 367

make an order. The owners submit that these terms are eminently proper and just and accordingly the judge's discretion was exercised on proper grounds and should not be disturbed even if the result is open to objection, which they submit it is not.

At the outset I am bound to say that the order of the judge seems to me to be eminently just and sensible; and the suggestion made by counsel for the charterers, albeit faintly, that it was a wrong exercise of his discretion if he had such a discretion, is plainly unsupportable. The parties submit to arbitration in the knowledge that if money is found due from one party to the other it will have to be paid. It should come as no shock to the party in default when the arbitrators or the court say so.

The real and sole question which we have to determine is whether, first, in the light of previous decisions of this court and, secondly, on the wording of the 1950 Act itself, the judge and the arbitrators had the power to make the orders which they made or not.

It is convenient to deal with precedent first. Lord Denning MR and Lawton LJ have already referred to *The Lysland*[1], and there of course the court laid down guidelines as to the circumstances in which arbitrators should accede to a request to state a special case. Counsel for the charterers submits that the case we are dealing with, the instant case, fulfils all the requirements contained in those guidelines and therefore it is quite wrong to impose any fetter or clog on the right to have a special case stated and that it would be flying in the face of that decision if we were to do so.

If the clear point of law here had related to the whole of the damages to be awarded, then there is much to be said for this argument, but the court in that case was not concerned with the situation which faces us here at all, and that decision provides no proper argument against the owners' contention. These charterers, whatever the outcome of the point of law, are going to have to pay $US475,000 or thereabouts; and to require the charterers in these circumstances to pay into a joint account a sum of money which on any view they are going to have to pay to the owners seems to me to be no more than elementary justice, if, and only if, it is permissible under the terms of the statute.

The two sections with which we are concerned primarily are ss 21 and 28. It seems to me unnecessary to go further than s 28, and that reads as follows: 'Any order made under this Part of this Act may be made on such terms as to costs or otherwise as the authority making the order thinks just.' Counsel for the charterers submits that neither the arbitrators nor the judge had made an order. That is not an argument which appeals to me at all. Indeed, one only has to look at the form of document embodied in the judge's decision to read these words: 'Upon hearing Counsel for the Parties and upon reading the Affidavits of Pamela Gai Tetlow and Timothy Charles Maxwell Howard filed herein IT IS ORDERED . . .' That seems to dispose of that particular argument. But the words 'costs or otherwise' appear to me to be amply wide enough to cover the actions both of the arbitrators and of the judge in this case. That is the basis on which the learned judge came to his conclusion. It was to my mind the correct conclusion and the correct basis. True it is a wide power, and care must be taken in its exercise to ensure that there is no suspicion of injustice in the way it is operated. It seems to me, in those circumstances, unnecessary to consider whether any discretion in the circumstances of this case arises under the provisions of s 21.

We were referred to s 12(6)(*f*) of the 1950 Act. The provisions of that subsection, so far as they are relevant, read as follows:

'The High Court shall have, for the purpose of and in relation to a reference, the same power of making orders in respect of . . . (*f*) securing the amount in dispute in the reference . . . as it has for the purpose of and in relation to an action or matter in the High Court. . .'

---

1   [1973] 2 All ER 1073, [1973] QB 843

a It is perhaps fair to say that that provision has a very narrow application indeed, and it has to be read in conjunction with RSC Ord 29, r 2(3), which reads as follows:

'Where the right of any party to a specific fund is in dispute in a cause or matter, the Court may, on the application of a party to the cause of matter, order the fund to be paid into court or otherwise secured.'

b It has no relevance to the present situation and certainly it does not have the effect of providing a form of RSC Ord 14 procedure.

In any event, the whole basis of the judge's order in the present case is that liability was already completely decided and quantum almost completely. The charterers were bound to pay a large sum on any view and can hardly have been surprised at the form of the order.

I would dismiss this appeal accordingly.

c *Appeal dismissed. Leave to appeal to the House of Lords refused.*

Solicitors: *Holman, Fenwick & William* (for the charterers); *Norton Rose, Botterell & Roche* (for the owners).

d Sumra Green   Barrister.

Practice Direction

e QUEEN'S BENCH DIVISION

Practice – Trial – Setting down action – Setting down action for new trial – Queen's Bench Division – Setting down after time ordered has expired – Leave of court or consent of defendant no longer required – RSC Ord 3, r 6, Ord 34, r 2.

f 1. Subject to compliance with RSC Ord 3, r 6 (requirement of service of notice of intention to proceed after a year's delay), where applicable, the plaintiff need not obtain the leave of the court or the consent of the defendant or the defendants, if there are more than one, before setting an action down for trial after the expiry of the period fixed by an order made under RSC Ord 34, r 2(1).

2. The foregoing change in the practice in no way relieves the plaintiff of his obligation to set the action down for trial within the time fixed by the order of the court, and his g failure to do so may entail the dismissal of the action for want of prosecution under RSC Ord 34, r 2(2).

3. The Practice Direction[1] (Setting Actions Down for Trial) dated 30th September 1964 is hereby revoked.

SIR JACK I H JACOB QC
Senior Master of the Supreme Court.

h 16th July 1979

1 [1964] 3 All ER 496, [1964] 1 WLR 1272

Bremer Vulkan Schiffbau Und Maschinenfabrik v South India Shipping Corporation
Gregg and others v Raytheon Ltd

QUEEN'S BENCH DIVISION
DONALDSON J
19th, 20th, 21st, 22nd, 23rd, 26th MARCH, 10th APRIL 1979

Arbitration – Practice – Want of prosecution – Dismissal of claim – Power of arbitrator to dismiss claim for want of prosecution – Whether arbitrator having same power as courts in litigation to dismiss claim for want of prosecution.

Arbitration – Practice – Want of prosecution – Injunction restraining arbitration – Jurisdiction of courts to grant injunction – Conduct of claimant justifying dismissal of claim for want of prosecution constituting repudiatory breach of arbitration agreement entitling respondent to elect to treat agreement as ended – Respondent entitled to apply to court for injunction enjoining claimant from proceeding with arbitration – Whether court entitled to grant injunction on ground agreement to refer being impeached.

Parties who submit disputes to arbitration impliedly clothe the arbitrator with jurisdiction to give effect to their rights and remedies to the same extent and in the same manner as a court (subject only to the well-known exceptions in relation to, eg, the grant by an arbitrator of injunctive orders), for arbitrators, like the courts, are concerned with the administration of justice. There is an obligation on a claimant to pursue his claim with reasonable despatch even though in arbitration there are no rules, like the rules of the Supreme Court applicable in litigation, to provide a basic timetable for taking interlocutory steps. Accordingly, in the absence of agreement by the parties curtailing an arbitrator's jurisdiction, he has the same power as a court to dismiss a claim for want of prosecution in an appropriate case, and in such a case can make an award dismissing a claim on that ground (see p 199 *j* to p 200 *a*, p 201 *a* to *d* and p 204 *a*, post); dictum of Tucker LJ in *Chandris v Isbrandtsen Moller Co Inc* [1950] 2 All ER at 623 applied; *Crawford v A E A Prowting Ltd* [1972] 1 All ER 1199 not followed.

Furthermore, the courts have power to grant an injunction enjoining a claimant from proceeding further with an arbitration where, in litigation, the courts would dismiss the claim for want of prosecution, since conduct of a claimant which justifies dismissal of his claim for want of prosecution constitutes a repudiatory breach of the agreement to refer to arbitration. It is implicit in such an agreement that each party will use his reasonable endeavours to bring the matter to a speedy conclusion, and inordinate and inexcusable delay which causes serious prejudice to the respondent, or is likely to give rise to a substantial risk that a fair trial will not be possible, strikes at the root of the agreement. In such a situation, therefore, the respondent can elect to accept the claimant's conduct as a repudiation terminating the agreement to refer, and can then apply to the court for an injunction enjoining the claimant from proceeding with the arbitration. Since an application for such an injunction involves the impeachment of the agreement to refer, the court has power to grant an injunction (see p 203 *b c* and p 204 *b* to *d*, post); *Kitts v Moore* [1895] 1 QB 253 and dictum of Jessel MR in *Beddow v Beddow* (1878) 9 Ch D at 93 applied; *North London Railway Co v Great Northern Railway Co* (1883) 11 QBD 30 distinguished.

Guidelines on the power to dismiss for want of prosecution in litigation (see p 197 *c* to p 198 *h*, post).

Notes

a For the court's power to restrain arbitration proceedings by injunction, see 2 Halsbury's Laws (4th Edn) para 518, for an arbitrator's powers generally, see ibid, para 577, and for cases on restraint of arbitration by injunction, see 3 Digest (Reissue) 95–98, 484–500.

For dismissal of actions for want of prosecution, see 30 Halsbury's Laws (3rd Edn) 410, para 771.

b **Cases referred to in judgment**

Allen v Sir Alfred McAlpine & Sons Ltd, Bostic v Bermondsey and Southwark Group Hospital Management Committee, Stenberg v Hammond [1968] 1 All ER 543, [1968] 2 QB 229, [1968] 2 WLR 366, CA, Digest (Cont Vol C) 1091, 2262b.

Beddow v Beddow (1878) 9 Ch D 89, 47 LJ Ch 588, 3 Digest (Reissue) 97, 495.

Ben & Co Ltd v Pakistan Edible Oil Corpn Ltd [1978] The Times, 13th July.

c Birkett v James [1977] 2 All ER 801, [1978] AC 297, [1977] 3 WLR 38, HL.

Chandris v Isbrandtsen Moller Co Inc [1950] 2 All ER 618, [1951] 1 KB 240, 3 Digest (Reissue) 202, 1241.

Compagnie Française de Télévision v Thorn Consumer Electronics Ltd [1978] RPC 735, CA.

County and District Properties Ltd v Lyell [1977] Court of Appeal Transcript 314.

Crawford v A E A Prowting Ltd [1972] 1 All ER 1199, [1973] 1 QB 1, [1972] 2 WLR 749,
d   3 Digest (Reissue) 116, 637.

Den of Airlie Steamship Co v Mitsui & Co Ltd and British Oil and Coke Mills Ltd (1912) 106 LT 451, 12 Asp MLC 169, 17 Com Cas 116, CA, 3 Digest (Reissue) 96, 491.

Exormisis Shipping SA v Oonsoo [1975] 1 Lloyd's Rep 432.

Gibraltar, Government of v Kenny [1956] 3 All ER 22, [1956] 2 QB 410, [1956] 3 WLR 466, 3 Digest (Reissue) 23, 104.

e Gouriet v Union of Post Office Workers [1977] 3 All ER 70, [1978] AC 435, [1977] 3 WLR 300, HL.

India, President of v John Shaw & Sons (Salford) Ltd [1977] The Times, 27th October.

Kitts v Moore [1895] 1 QB 253, 64 LJ Ch 152, 74 LT 676, 12 R 43, CA, 3 Digest (Reissue) 96, 488.

London and Blackwall Railway Co v Cross (1886) 31 Ch D 354, 55 LJ Ch 313, 54 LT 309,
f   CA, 3 Digest (Reissue) 96, 486.

Malmesbury Railway Co v Budd (1876) 2 Ch D 113, 45 LJ Ch 271, 3 Digest (Reissue) 97, 494.

Maunsell v Midland Great Western (Ireland) Railway Co (1863) 1 Hem & M 130, 2 New Rep 268, 32 LJ Ch 513, 8 LT 347, 826, 9 Jur NS 660, 71 ER 58, 3 Digest (Reissue) 96, 490.

g Miliangos v George Frank (Textiles) Ltd [1975] 1 All ER 1076, [1975] QB 487, [1975] 2 WLR 555, [1975] 1 Lloyd's Rep 436, 587, CA; affd [1975] 3 All ER 801, [1976] AC 443, [1975] 3 WLR 758, [1976] 1 Lloyd's Rep 201, HL, Digest (Cont Vol D) 691, 64c.

Montgomery v Montgomery [1964] 2 All ER 22, [1965] P 46, [1964] 2 WLR 1036, 27(2) Digest (Reissue) 936, 7555.

North London Railway Co v Great Northern Railway Co (1883) 11 QBD 30, 52 LJQB 380, 48
h   LT 695, CA, 3 Digest (Reissue) 95, 485.

Ramdutt Ramkissen Das v E D Sassoon and Co (1929) 98 LJPC 58, [1929] All ER Rep 225, 140 LT 542, 3 Digest (Reissue) 55, 296.

Rasu Maritima SA v Perusahaan Pertambangan Minyak Dan Gas Bumi Negara (Pertamina) and Government of Indonesia (as interveners) [1977] 3 All ER 324, [1978] QB 644, [1977] 3 WLR 518, [1977] 2 Lloyd's Rep 397, CA.

j Siskina, The, owners of cargo lately laden on board the vessel Siskina v Distos Compania Naviera SA [1977] 3 All ER 803, [1979] AC 210, [1977] 3 WLR 818, [1978] 1 Lloyd's Rep 1, HL.

Sociedade Portuguesa de Navios Tanques Limitada v Hvalfangerselskapet Polaris A/S [1952] 1 Lloyd's Rep 407, CA, 12 Digest (Reissue) 111, 617.

Wood v Leake (1806) 12 Ves 412, 33 ER 156, 3 Digest (Reissue) 161, 948.

Cases also cited

Biss v Lambeth, Southwark and Lewisham Area Health Authority [1978] 2 All ER 125, [1978]   *a*
   1 WLR 382, CA.
Mehta v Adams [1978] Court of Appeal Transcript 348.
Sayers v Collyer (1884) 28 Ch D 103, [1881–5] All ER Rep 385, CA.
Thorne v British Broadcasting Corpn [1967] 2 All ER 1225, [1967] 1 WLR 1104, CA.

Actions   *b*
   Bremer Vulkan Schiffbau Und Maschinenfabrik v South India Shipping Corpn
By a writ issued on 25th April 1977, the plaintiffs, Bremer Vulkan Schiffbau Und
Maschinenfabrik ('the builders'), a body corporate of West Germany, claimed against the
defendants, South India Shipping Corpn Ltd ('the owners'), a body corporate of India, (i)
an injunction restraining the owners by themselves or their agents from proceeding
with, pursuing or taking any further step in a reference to arbitration in which the   *c*
owners were the claimants and the builders were the respondents, commenced pursuant
to an arbitration clause in a contract between the parties dated 6th August 1964 and in
which the Rt Hon Sir Gordon Willmer was appointed sole arbitrator by an agreement
dated January 1972, (ii) alternatively, a declaration that the arbitrator had power to make
and issue a final award in the reference dismissing the owners' claim on the grounds only
that they had failed to prosecute their claims in the reference with diligence and had
been guilty of gross and inexcusable delay causing serious prejudice to the builders   *d*
and/or that the dispute could not fairly be tried at the likely time of the hearing.

Gregg and others v Raytheon Ltd
By a writ issued on 1st December 1978, the plaintiffs, Newton Gregg, Lucile Gregg and
Malcolm Kelly, claimed against the defendants, Raytheon Ltd ('Raytheon'), a body
corporate of Massachusetts, USA, (i) an injunction against the continuance of an   *e*
arbitration commenced by Raytheon against the plaintiffs and another party concerning
disputes arising out of a contract dated 2nd June 1970 between the plaintiffs and the
other party and Raytheon, by reason of Raytheon's inordinate and inexcusable delay in
prosecuting the arbitration, together with the plaintiffs' costs of the arbitration as
damages for breach of contract or under the court's inherent jurisdiction, the costs to be
assessed by a taxing master, and (ii) a declaration that the arbitrators in the arbitration   *f*
had power to strike out Raytheon's claim in the arbitration for want of prosecution. The
facts in each action are set out in the judgment.

Kenneth Rokison QC and *David Grace* for the builders.
Gerald Butler QC and *G Caldin* for the owners.
Mark Waller for the plaintiffs in the second action.
Marcus Jones for Raytheon.   *g*

                                                                               Cur adv vult

10th April.   **DONALDSON J** read the following judgment: These two actions raise
issues of fundamental importance to English arbitration. In each case the plaintiffs are
the respondents in arbitrations initiated by the defendants. The plaintiffs contend that
the conduct of the defendants has been such that, had their claims been the subject-   *h*
matter of litigation, the court would have dismissed the claims for want of prosecution.
They further contend that in such circumstances the court can and should enjoin the
defendants from further proceeding with the arbitrations. Further or alternatively, they
seek a declaration that the arbitrators have power to issue a final award dismissing the
defendants' claims. So far as I or counsel know, the claim for an injunction is completely
novel and the contention that arbitrators have power to dismiss claims for want of   *j*
prosecution has only once been considered by the courts. This occurred in *Crawford v
A E A Prowting Ltd*[1], when Bridge J held that arbitrators had no such power.

---

1   [1972] 1 All ER 1199, [1973] 1 QB 1

I mention this dearth of authority not as casting doubt on the validity of the plaintiffs'
a submissions, but as showing their importance. The novelty of submissions must always
cause a court to consider with particular care whether (a) the contention is so obviously
correct that no one has ever seen fit to challenge it, (b) it is so obviously wrong that no one
has ever before thought to put it forward or (c) it has surfaced for the first time because
the law is in one of its evolutionary stages. But it has no other significance. In the
present case I have little doubt that the explanation is that in this, amongst other fields,
b the law is in a state of active evolution responding to the changing needs of the times.
Let me start by considering the law as it applies to litigation. It has developed
considerably in the last 12 years and the guidelines which are to be applied are now
mainly to be found in two cases: *Birkett v James*[1] and *Allen v Sir Alfred McAlpine & Sons
Ltd*[2]. However, assistance is also to be obtained from *County and District Properties Ltd v
Lyell*[3] and *President of India v John Shaw & Sons (Salford) Ltd*[4]. These guidelines can, I
c think, be summarised as follows:
　1. The power to dismiss for want of prosecution should be exercised only where the
court is satisfied that either: A. the default has been intentional and contumelious, e g
disobedience to a peremptory order of the court or conduct amounting to an abuse of the
process of the court; or B. (i) there has been inordinate and inexcusable delay on the part
of the plaintiff or his lawyers, and (ii) such delay (a) either will give rise to a substantial
d risk that it is not possible to have a fair trial of the issues in the action, or (b) is such as is
likely to cause or to have caused serious prejudice to the defendants either as between
themselves and the plaintiff or between each other or between them and a third party.
　2. Only in exceptional cases should an action be dismissed before the relevant
limitation period has expired, at least if it is likely that the plaintiff will issue a new writ.
　3. As Parliament has conferred a legal right on plaintiffs to institute proceedings at
e any time within the relevant limitation period, the action of a plaintiff in delaying for
almost all or any part of that period cannot be relied on as constituting inordinate or
inexcusable delay. Nor, without more, can the defendant rely on this delay as having
caused him prejudice or as giving rise to a risk that there can be no fair trial. But such
delay is far from being irrelevant. It will have an important bearing on the degree of
expedition which is required of the plaintiff once the proceedings have been instituted,
f although again he will be entitled to the benefit of the timetable provided by the Rules
of the Supreme Court. Delay in the course of the proceedings which would have been
acceptable if they had been begun promptly may become inordinate and inexcusable if
it occurs after a late start. Similarly, whilst the defendant must show prejudice flowing
from delay in the course of the proceedings, the degree of prejudice created by any given
period of delay may be greatly heightened if proceedings were not begun promptly.
g Contrary to legend, it was not the last straw which broke the camel's back. It was the
addition of that straw. The defendant must show that straws of the appropriate kinds
were heaped on his back during the course of the proceedings, but the court must have
regard to the load which he was already carrying when the proceedings began.
　4. Prejudice to the defendant can take many forms. Lapse of time may affect the
ability of the defendant to marshal the evidence which would have been available to him
h at an earlier time. Thus witnesses may die, become untraceable or their recollections
may dim. Again they may retire or leave the defendant's employment, depriving them
of the personal interest which they might otherwise have had in the proceedings and
tending to reduce the enthusiasm with which they search their recollections. But
prejudice is not limited to matters of recollection and evidence. The very fact of having
a large unquantified claim hanging over the head of the defendant for a long period may
j itself be highly prejudicial.

1   [1977] 2 All ER 801, [1978] AC 297
2   [1968] 1 All ER 543, [1968] 2 QB 229
3   [1977] Court of Appeal Transcript 314
4   [1977] The Times, 27th October

5. The defendant will lose his right to have the action dismissed if he induces in the plaintiff a reasonable belief that, notwithstanding the delay, he is willing for the action to proceed and, in consequence, the plaintiff does work or incurs expense in the further prosecution of the action. But the right may be revived by further delay. As Diplock LJ said in *Allen v Sir Alfred McAlpine & Sons Ltd*[1], in such circumstances the defendant cannot obtain dismissal of the action 'unless the plaintiff has thereafter been guilty of further unreasonable delay'. Salmon LJ in the same case said[2] that the defendant 'will be precluded from relying on the previous delay by itself as a ground for dismissing the action'. This had led to an interesting discussion in the present case on whether, following acquiescence in the plaintiff's delay, the defendant can rely on that delay for any purpose. The extreme view is that he cannot. He must show inordinate and inexcusable delay following the acquiescence and must further show prejudice flowing from that delay. I do not think that this is right.

Much will turn on the nature of the acquiescence. For example, if the defendant by words or conduct leads the plaintiff to believe that he is content that matters shall drift on unless and until he indicates that he wishes the dispute to be brought to trial, the plaintiff will be entitled to take his time. It will not then be open to the defendant to complain of subsequent delay until he has given notice to the plaintiff that time is of the essence and thereafter further delay has occurred. But a more usual situation is one in which the defendant shows that he is prepared to overlook previous inordinate and inexcusable delay and any prejudice caused thereby, if the plaintiff will now bring the matter to trial with expedition. If the plaintiff still drags his feet, it may be said that the condition on which the acquiescence is based has not been fulfilled and that the defendant is entitled to rely on all delay and prejudice, whether occurring before or after the acquiescence. An alternative view is that in such circumstances the defendant must show some delay and prejudice following the acquiescence, but that the extent of the delay and prejudice which will give rise to a fresh right to have the action dismissed will be influenced greatly by events prior to the acquiescence.

I doubt whether it is possible to lay down any rule of general application. Acquiescence in delay is not a permanent bar to a subsequent successful application for an order dismissing the action for failure to prosecute it. Each case will have to be considered in the light of its own particular facts, the court asking itself the question: bearing in mind the conduct of the defendant, is it just and equitable in all the circumstances that the plaintiff shall be denied a trial of his action on its merits?

6. Mere inactivity on the part of a defendant is not to be construed as acquiescence in delay by the plaintiff. 'Sleeping dogs, in the form of sleeping plaintiffs, need not be aroused by defendants from their slumbers' (per Roskill LJ in *Compagnie Française de Télévision v Thorn Consumer Electronics Ltd*[3]). The reasons underlying this attitude by the courts were discussed by Diplock LJ in *Allen v Sir Alfred McAlpine & Sons Ltd*[4]. His conclusion was that it was inherent in an adversary system of litigation, which relied exclusively on the parties to an action to take whatever procedural steps appeared to them to be expedient to advance their own case, that a defendant could, with propriety, refrain from spurring the plaintiff to proceed to trial and then, if the facts otherwise justified such a course, apply to have the action struck out for want of prosecution.

I now turn to consider whether these guidelines have any application in the control of arbitration. Whether an arbitrator had power to dismiss a claim for want of prosecution was considered by Bridge J in *Crawford v A E A Prowting Ltd*[5]. It was a small building dispute. The contract to build the house was made in 1960, points of claim were served in May 1966 and discovery was completed in October 1966. The builders sought further

1   [1968] 1 All ER 543 at 556, [1968] 2 QB 229 at 260
2   [1968] 1 All ER 543 at 564, [1968] 2 QB 229 at 272
3   [1978] RPC 735 at 739
4   [1968] 1 All ER 543 at 554–555, [1968] 2 QB 229 at 257–258
5   [1972] 1 All ER 1199, [1973] 1 QB 1

and better particulars of the claim, but in vain.   In January 1968 there was an
a appointment for directions, but the arbitrator 'made no order and it was left to the parties
to arrange a fresh appointment to fix a date for the hearing'. Neither party arranged a
fresh appointment and in November 1970 the builders applied to the arbitrator to
dismiss the claim for want of prosecution. The arbitrator refused this application and
stated a case for the opinion of the court. That special case was in many respects
inadequate, but it was sufficient to raise the issue of principle.
b   Bridge J held that arbitrators had no power to dismiss claims for want of prosecution.
He said[1] that the argument to the contrary rested on the assumption—

> '. . . that in an arbitration, as in proceedings in court, and apart from any express
> obligation being put on him, there is a duty on the claimant to the exclusion of the
> respondent to promote the progress of the arbitration and correspondingly it is
> assumed, as the basis of counsel for the builders' argument, that the respondent to
c   > the arbitration can sit by and do nothing, letting the sleeping claimant dog lie until
> he is ready to wake him up with his application to dismiss for want of prosecution.'

The judge then referred to the remarks of Diplock LJ in *Allen v Sir Alfred McAlpine
& Sons Ltd*[2] and, having said, no doubt correctly, that the court in that case did not have
the conduct of arbitrations in contemplation, expressed the view that 'there is a
d fundamental difference between the nature of the duties on the parties in relation to
interlocutory progress in an action on the one hand and in an arbitration on the
other'[1]. He supported this conclusion by contrasting the position under the Rules of the
Supreme Court, which he said put the onus of keeping the litigation moving fairly and
squarely on the plaintiff, with the position in arbitration where, although there may be
a heavier duty on the claimant to pursue his claim than on the respondent to take steps
e for his part, 'nevertheless it is for both parties, having agreed that the arbitrator shall
resolve their differences, to obtain from the arbitrator such interlocutory directions as are
appropriate to enable the matter to be prepared for trial[3]'. He concluded that the
respondents' remedy lay in seeking an interlocutory order from the arbitrator requiring
the claimant to take some step, such as delivering points of claim, and in default of
compliance, seeking an ex parte hearing of the claim.
f   This decision is not binding on me and, with all respect to the judge, I do not think
that it is right. Arbitrations vary greatly in their character from major proceedings
which are wholly indistinguishable from a heavy High Court action to disputes on the
quality of commodities (the 'look–sniff' arbitration). But so do actions. Actions
prosecuted under the small claims procedures in the county courts are indistinguishable
from similar claims determined by arbitration under the auspices of the motor, building
g or travel industries or by so-called small claims courts, which are in fact not courts but
arbitral bodies. With the sole exception of the look–sniff arbitration, all employ the
adversary system. In saying this, I am not overlooking the fact that s 12(1) of the
Arbitration Act 1950 gives the arbitrator power to examine the parties on oath or
affirmation. This power is essential in any proceedings in which the parties may be
unrepresented and a similar power is, in effect, exercised by county court judges every
h day of the week. Nor is it to be thought that a court is powerless to take the initiative
itself in order to ensure that proceedings make progress. The National Industrial
Relations Court did so frequently and I have recently threatened to list a case of my own
motion, because it is being incorrectly reported in the press that this court is dragging its
feet in fixing a date for the hearing. The only real difference between litigation and
arbitration is that, in the case of litigation, rules of court provide a basic timetable for
j taking interlocutory steps. In the case of arbitration, there is no such basic timetable

---

1   [1972] 1 All ER 1199 at 1203, [1973] 1 QB 1 at 7
2   [1968] 1 All ER 543, [1968] 2 QB 229
3   [1972] 1 All ER 1199 at 1204, [1973] 1 QB 1 at 7

unless it is provided by relevant arbitration rules, by agreement of the parties or by order of the arbitrator. But this does not mean that there is no obligation on the claimant to *a* pursue his claim with reasonable despatch. Indeed, in so far as one of the advantages claimed for arbitration is that it leads to a speedier resolution of disputes, there may well be a heavier onus on the parties to arbitration to use expedition than there is on parties to litigation. And I say 'parties' rather than 'plaintiffs and claimants', because it is not correct that the onus in litigation is always on the plaintiff. There are times, for example, after delivery of a statement of claim, when the onus is on the defendant. The same is *b* true of arbitration.

The suggestion that the respondent's remedy in arbitration lies in obtaining an order for the delivery of points of claim and, in default, seeking an ex parte hearing of the claim seems to me to require careful examination. If there has been inordinate and inexcusable delay which causes serious prejudice to the respondent and a fortiori if it has been such as to render a fair trial impossible, any requirement that before an order is *c* made summarily terminating the proceedings the arbitrator must first make an interlocutory order, such as to deliver points of claim, with which the claimant can comply would, in the words of Salmon LJ in *Allen v Sir Alfred McAlpine & Sons Ltd*[1] 'be an encouragement to the careless and lethargic'. And what happens if the claimant does not comply with the order? It is clear law that the arbitrator can proceed ex parte if one of the parties having been duly summoned does not attend (see *Wood v Leake*[2]). But what *d* if he does attend and wishes to present his case. Can the arbitrator refuse to allow him to do so? Unless there is power to dismiss the claim for want of prosecution I do not think that he could. And if he could not, the respondent would be at a hopeless disadvantage.

The power of the courts derives from statute and their inherent jurisdiction. The power of arbitrators derives from statute and from a consensual conferment of *e* jurisdiction by the parties when agreeing to submit disputes to arbitration. There are at present no statutory provisions which are directly material. The question is therefore what jurisdiction is impliedly conferred by the parties on the arbitrator. This was considered by the Court of Appeal in the context of a power to award interest on damages in *Chandris v Isbrandtsen Moller Co Inc*[3]. The headnote to the report reads[4]:

'. . . the power of an arbitrator to award interest was derived from the submission *f* to him, which impliedly gave him power to decide "all matters in difference" according to the existing law of contract, exercising every right and discretionary remedy given to a court of law.'

Although the decision is in terms limited to the power to award interest, I think that the generality of this part of the headnote is justified. Thus Tucker LJ said[5]: *g*

'I cannot see why any distinction should be drawn between the duty of an arbitrator to give effect to such statutes as the Statute of Limitations and his jurisdiction in his discretion to award interest. An award of interest is only a part of the damages recoverable, and, adapting to the facts of this case the language of LORD SALVESEN in the case to which I have just referred[6]—language which was approved by LORD MAUGHAM—it would read as follows: "Although the Law Reform *h* (Miscellaneous Provisions) Act, 1934, does not in terms apply to arbitrations, I think that in mercantile references of the kind in question it is an implied term of the contract that the arbitrator must decide the dispute according to the existing law of contract, and that every right and discretionary remedy given to a court of law can

1   [1968] 1 All ER 543 at 562, [1968] 2 QB 229 at 270
2   (1806) 12 Ves 412, 33 ER 156
3   [1950] 2 All ER 618, [1951] 1 KB 240
4   [1951] 1 KB 240
5   [1950] 2 All ER 618 at 623, [1951] 1 KB 240 at 261–262
6   *Ramdutt Ramkissen Das v E D Sassoon & Co* (1929) 98 LJPC 58, [1929] All ER Rep 225

j

a be exercised by him." To that there are certain well-known exceptions, such as the right to grant an injunction, which stand on a different footing. One of the reasons why an arbitrator cannot give an injunction is that he has no power to enforce it, but such an objection does not apply to an award of interest.'

Whilst it is always open to the parties to agree to curtail the arbitrator's jurisdiction, other than his power to state an award in the form of a special case for the opinion of the High Court or in any other respects which are contrary to law, if this is not done I think b that an arbitrator has the same power as do the courts to make peremptory orders which provide that, in default of compliance, the claim will be dismissed or, as the case may be, the respondent will be debarred from defending, and also of making orders dismissing a claim for want of prosecution. Courts and arbitrators are in the same business, namely the administration of justice. The only difference is that the courts are in the public and arbitrators are in the private sector of the industry. Their problems are the same and so c should be the solutions which they adopt. In my judgment, parties who submit disputes to arbitration impliedly clothe the arbitrators with jurisdiction to give effect to their rights and remedies to the same extent and in the same manner as a court, subject only to the well-known exception in relation to injunctive orders and the grant of a remedy, such as rectification, which would indirectly extend their own jurisdiction.

d The next question is whether the courts can intervene and enjoin a claimant from further proceeding with an arbitration in a situation in which, if the problem arose in litigation, they would dismiss the claim for want of prosecution. The supervisory jurisdiction of the courts in respect of arbitration is limited. In appropriate cases they can and will require an arbitrator to state a question of law arising in the course of a reference or an award or part of an award for their decision under s 21(1) of the 1950 Act. They can and will remit an award for further consideration by the arbitrator or set it aside under e s 22 or s 23 of the 1950 Act. They can and will give leave to a party to revoke the authority of the arbitrator under s 24 of the 1950 Act. But they will not substitute their discretion for that of the arbitrator, by ordering him to allow amendments to pleadings or otherwise reversing his interlocutory orders (*Exormisis Shipping SA v Oonsoo*[1]).

But there is another class of case in which the courts will intervene in arbitration proceedings. Although they may appear to be exercising a supervisory jurisdiction, that f is not in fact the case. I refer to the jurisdiction to intervene by injunction to prevent a party proceeding with an arbitration where the agreement to refer is itself being impeached. The leading case is *Kitts v Moore*[2] in which the plaintiff was denying that he had ever entered into an arbitration agreement, but the principle applies wherever the agreement is impeached, whether on grounds of fraud, mistake or otherwise (see *Malmesbury Railway Co v Budd*[3] and *Beddow v Beddow*[4]). And it is not infrequently g exercised in the Commercial Court to this day when, for example, a plaintiff alleges that the agent who purported to commit him to a purchase of a commodity under a contract containing an arbitration clause had no authority to act on his behalf or where it is alleged that there is no agreement to arbitrate because the parties were not ad idem on the terms of the alleged contract which contains the arbitration clause (see *Sociedade Portuguesa de Navios Tanques Limitada v Hvalfangerselskapet Polaris A/S*[5], and also Russell h on Arbitration[6]).

It has been objected in the present case that this is contrary to the decisions of the Court of Appeal in *North London Railway Co v Great Northern Railway Co*[7], which was followed

j 1 [1975] 1 Lloyd's Rep 432
2 [1895] 1 QB 253
3 (1876) 2 Ch D 113
4 (1878) 9 Ch D 89
5 [1952] 1 Lloyd's Rep 407
6 18th Edn (1970), pp 79–80
7 (1883) 11 QBD 30

in *London and Blackwall Railway Co v Cross*[1]. I confess that I find these cases difficult to understand, although, for what they may decide, this does not render them any less
 binding on me.

In the earlier case of *Beddow v Beddow*[2] Jessel MR granted an injunction restraining an arbitrator from proceeding with the arbitration on the ground that he was unfit or incompetent to act. He considered the limits of the court's jurisdiction under s 25 of the Supreme Court of Judicature Act 1873 and held that he had[3]—

> 'unlimited power to grant an injunction in any case where it would be right or
> just to do so: and what is right or just must be decided, not by the caprice of the
> Judge, but according to sufficient legal reasons or on settled legal principles.'

In doing so he was affirming his earlier expression of opinion in *Malmesbury Railway Co v Budd*[4]. Both those decisions were considered in the *North London Railway* case[5]. Brett LJ held that the section did no more than extend the jurisdiction of any division of
 the High Court to all divisions. The position had previously been and remained that no court could issue an injunction where there was 'no legal right on the one side or no legal liability on the other at law or in equity'[6]. He agreed with Jessel MR's decisions, because prior to the Judicature Act the common law courts would have removed an arbitrator in such circumstances and the grant of an injunction produced the same result. Cotton LJ[6] expressed the same view. I would only comment that it is in the highest degree
 inconvenient if judges exercising jurisdiction in 1979 have to try to find out what was the extent of the jurisdiction of their predecessors over a century ago.

The next case is *London and Blackwall Railway Co v Cross*[1]. Mr Cross instituted arbitration proceedings under the Lands Clauses Consolidation Act 1845 against the railway company using the name of the Poplar and Greenwich Ferry Co. The railway company sought an injunction to restrain him from carrying on these proceedings on
 the grounds that he had no authority to use the ferry company's name. Chitty J granted the injunction, but his decision was reversed on appeal. Lindley LJ held himself bound[7] by the *North London Railway* case[5], but added that it only decided that the settled practice of the courts as to when injunctions would be granted had not been altered by the Judicature Acts and that there was still no right or jurisdiction to restrain a person from proceeding for compensation under the 1845 Act on the ground that he was not entitled
 to compensation. He added[8]:

> 'The case does not decide that in no case is it right to restrain persons from
> proceeding to arbitration; there are cases in which it is quite right to do so. One of
> such cases came before Vice-Chancellor Wood, *Maunsell* v. *Midland Great Western
> (Ireland) Railway Company*[9]. It was an action by a shareholder on behalf of himself
> and the other shareholders in the company, against the company and its directors
> and another company, to restrain them from proceeding to arbitration under an
> agreement in respect of breaches of clauses which were *ultrà vires*. That case, and
> cases of that kind, are wholly unaffected by the decision to which I am alluding.
> The case must not be supposed to go this length, that there is no authority whatever
> in the Court of Chancery to restrain proceedings before an arbitrator, but I think it

---

1   (1886) 31 Ch D 354
2   (1878) 9 Ch D 89
3   9 Ch D 89 at 93
4   (1876) 2 Ch D 113
5   (1883) 11 QBD 30
6   11 QBD 30 at 38
7   (1886) 31 Ch D 354 at 368
8   31 Ch D 354 at 368–369
9   (1863) 1 Hem & M 130, 71 ER 58

a goes this length, that in all cases under the *Lands Clauses Act* the practice is that the question of right or no right to compensation is to be tried by an action on the award, and not by an action for an injunction in the earlier stage of the proceedings. One can easily see that there are conveniences on the one side and on the other, but in my opinion the balance of convenience is in favour of declining to interfere by injunction.'

b   This brings me to *Kitts v Moore*[1]. Lindley LJ said that before the Judicature Acts, courts of equity had granted injunctions to stay references on the ground that the agreement containing the arbitration clause was impeached. In the *North London Railway* case[2] there was no impeaching of the arbitration agreement and no more ground for stopping the arbitration than for stopping an action because it was a frivolous one. That decision in no way reduced the power of the courts to continue to grant injunctions, where the arbitration clause was impeached.

c   So far as I know, nothing more was heard of the *North London Railway* case[2] until 1911 when it was considered in *Den of Airlie Steamship Co Ltd v Mitsui & Co Ltd and British Oil and Coke Mills Ltd*[3]. There[4] the Court of Appeal affirmed its headnote, namely that:

'... the High Court has no jurisdiction to issue an injunction to restrain a party from proceeding with an arbitration in a matter beyond the agreement to refer,
d although such arbitration proceeding may be futile and vexatious.'[2]

It was two world wars later before this troublesome case reappeared. It was then resurrected (to my personal discomfiture as counsel, because I had failed to find it) in *Government of Gibraltar v Kenny*[5]. Sellers J clearly shared my lack of enthusiasm for the decision and also my inability to overrule it. However, he held, obiter, that it did not restrict the power of the court to grant a declaration. Since then it has been cited in
e *Montgomery v Montgomery*[6], for the unexceptionable proposition that the High Court can enforce any legal right which was capable of being enforced either at law or in equity prior to 1873; in the *Siskina* case[7] for the equally unexceptionable proposition that the High Court has no power to grant an interlocutory injunction except in protection or assertion of some legal or equitable right which it has jurisdiction to enforce by legal judgment; in the *Pertamina* case[8], in which Lord Denning MR[9] and Orr LJ seem to have
f considered that the decision was not binding in so far as it purported to fetter the discretion of the court to grant injunctions 'in any case where it would be right or just to do so'[10]; in *Ben & Co Ltd v Pakistan Edible Oils Corpn Ltd*[11] where Lord Denning MR held that to allege that there was no arbitration agreement was to impeach the alleged agreement and that accordingly the court had jurisdiction to grant an injunction; and in *Gouriet v Union of Post Office Workers*[12] by Lord Edmund-Davies for the proposition that
g it was not 'just' to grant an injunction, save in defence of a legal right recognisable by the courts.

Accordingly, on the authorities, the courts can issue an injunction in cases in which the respondent to an arbitration alleges that there never was an agreement to arbitrate or that the agreement has ceased to bind him, but not where he alleges that the arbitrator

h
1   [1895] 1 QB 253
2   (1883) 11 QBD 30
3   (1912) 106 LT 451
4   106 LT 451 at 453
5   [1956] 3 All ER 22, [1956] 2 QB 410
6   [1964] 2 All ER 22, [1965] P 46
j 7   [1977] 3 All ER 803, [1979] AC 210
8   [1977] 3 All ER 324, [1978] QB 644
9   [1977] 3 All ER 324 at 333, [1978] QB 644 at 660
10   [1977] 3 All ER 324 at 336, [1978] QB 644 at 664
11   [1978] The Times, 13th July
12   [1977] 3 All ER 70 at 113, [1978] AC 435 at 516

!

is about to exceed his jurisdiction or that, whilst he agreed to arbitrate with the claimant, the person using the claimant's name is not authorised to do so. However, in all these *a* cases the courts can give a declaration. This seems to me to be very strange, but that is a matter for the House of Lords and not for me to consider.

I have already said that in my judgment an arbitrator has power in an appropriate case to make an award dismissing a claim for want of prosecution. But I further think that conduct by the claimant which justifies such an order also constitutes a repudiatory breach of the agreement to submit disputes to arbitration. It is implicit in such an *b* agreement that each party will use reasonable endeavours to bring the matter to a speedy conclusion. Any unjustified delay will constitute a breach of that agreement, but one which is inordinate and inexcusable and which further causes serious prejudice to the defendant or is likely to give rise to a substantial risk that it will not be possible to have a fair trial seems to me to be more than a simple breach of contract, it strikes at the root of it. In such a situation the respondent has a choice. He can affirm the agreement to *c* arbitrate by carrying on with the arbitration either generally or in the form of an application to the arbitrator to make an award dismissing the claim for want of prosecution. Alternatively, he can accept the claimant's conduct as a repudiation, thus, if he is right, terminating the agreement to refer and can then apply to the court for injunctive relief. It will be within the court's power to grant such relief, because the issue between the parties will involve the impeachment of the arbitration agreement. *d*

Having considered the matter in terms of general principle, and without regard to the Arbitration Act 1979, which received the Royal Assent on 4th April and is not yet in force[1], I now have to apply those principles to the facts of these two actions.

THE SHIPBUILDING DISPUTE

The plaintiffs ('the builders'), Bremer Vulkan Schiffbau Und Maschinenfabrik, are, as *e* their name implies, German shipbuilders. Equally self-evidently the defendants ('the owners'), South India Shipping Corpn Ltd, are shipowners. In August 1964 the builders agreed to build five bulk carriers for the owners. They were duly built and delivered between 4th November 1965 and 3rd December 1966.

The shipbuilding contract was governed by German law, but it also provided that any disputes should be referred to arbitration in London pursuant to the Arbitration Act *f* 1950. The contract contained a clause whereby the shipbuilders agreed to rectify defects appearing within 12 months of delivery and reserved the right to keep a guarantee engineer on board during this period. This right was exercised. The guarantee periods expired between 4th November 1965 and 3rd December 1967. The shipbuilders have been advised that, subject to any agreement to the contrary, all claims under the contract would become time barred as a matter of substantive German law six months after the *g* end of the guarantee period. On this basis the last date for beginning an arbitration would have been 3rd May 1967. This view of German law is not accepted by the shipowners and, for present purposes, I have to assume that they are right and that the relevant law is English.

The arbitration proceedings in fact began in January 1972, over five years after the last vessel was delivered. Points of claim were served in April 1976, over nine years after that *h* delivery. These proceedings, which were begun a year later in April 1977 have only been heard in March 1979, over 12 years from the delivery of the last vessel and nearly 15 years from the time when the contract was concluded. Clearly some explanation is called for, not only from the parties, but also from the court.

The court's responsibility could not begin until the writ was issued in April 1977, but the nature of the proceedings was such that I should have expected that they would have *j* been heard and determined before the end of July in that year. If one party is alleging that there has been intolerable delay, it is clearly of the greatest importance that no time

---

1   The 1979 Act came into force on 1st August 1979: see SI 1979 No 750

be wasted in deciding whether or not the proceedings shall be allowed to continue. I was, therefore, concerned to find out whether the delay was the responsibility of the court or of the parties. The facts, I think, speak for themselves.

Although the writ was issued in April 1977, it was not until June 1978 that the matter was brought to the attention of the court. There was then an application to fix a date for the hearing and a date in November 1978 was allocated. Taking account of the fact that a five day hearing was involved and that the long vacation was approaching, this was, I think, an excusable delay, although I should have preferred it to have been less. The next event was an application by the parties to vacate the November date. This was done and the case was re-fixed for December 1978. Unfortunately, and exceptionally, the court itself had to vacate this date, because of unexpected congestion in the list. The parties were asked when it would be convenient to fix a new hearing date and they agreed on March 1979. They could have had an earlier date had they wished.

Let me now turn to the chronology which is relevant to my decision in these proceedings. If the relevant limitation period is to be found in English law, the owners had a period of six years from the accrual of the various causes of action in which to begin arbitration proceedings. Sir Gordon Wilmer accepted appointment as sole arbitrator in January 1972. Some complaints relate to the first vessel which was delivered in November 1965. This does not mean that these complaints are time-barred, because there may well be a separate cause of action based on a failure to remedy the defects during or shortly after the expiration of the guarantee period for that vessel in November 1966. Complaints in respect of the other vessels would have arisen later, but the guarantee period on the last vessel to be delivered expired in December 1967, four years before the arbitration proceedings began.

The fact that the arbitration only began in January 1972 cannot be a matter for complaint. The owners were entitled to take as much time as they wished before beginning proceedings, provided only that they did not allow the statutory limitation period to supervene. But their exercise of this right has some bearing on the degree of expedition which they should have shown after the proceedings began.

As was only to be expected, experience during the guarantee periods showed up certain defects. This, after all, is what a guarantee period is for. However, they were, or were thought to be, of such importance that the owners consulted solicitors and their P & I club by as early as August 1966. The builders accepted liability for some, but not all, of these defects in discussions between the parties in August 1966 and August 1967. In October 1967 there was a further meeting at which all the matters then in dispute were discussed and some of these were settled. It was further agreed that (a) on the completion of the guarantee period for the last vessel (December 1967) the owners would send a representative to meet the builders with a view to discussing and settling all claims, and (b) as both parties wished to achieve an amicable settlement, recourse to arbitration would be deferred for the time being, although each party reserved the right to take this course if they wished. This latter agreement was formally recorded on 13th October 1967.

It might have been expected that this projected meeting between the parties would have taken place in early 1968, but this was not to be. The owners lost no time in appointing the well-known consulting surveyors, Casebourne Leach & Co, to advise them. This was done on 7th November 1967. But thereafter the matter appeared to go to sleep. Various claims were notified to the builders, including a claim in respect of cracks in the engine cylinders. In reply to this claim the builders on 3rd September 1969 said that all guarantee claims which had not been raised before the end of the guarantee periods, ie at latest by 3rd December 1967, would be rejected. However, it was not until after this letter was received that the owners' solicitors tried to arrange a meeting between their clients and Casebournes. This meeting in fact took place in March 1970 and immediately thereafter the builders were told that the claims were being collated. Bearing in mind that Casebournes had been appointed in November 1967 and that an early meeting between the builders and the owners was then contemplated, one might

have expected that the owners would have met Casebournes with a view to collating all
claims at the latest in early 1968.

The actual letter of claim was sent on 28th May 1970. It contained 18 heads of claim,
but stated that the list was not exhaustive and that there would, in addition, be claims for
the detention of the vessel and for expenses. I think that the builders are justified in
complaining that it gave no hint of the magnitude of the claims which the owners were
contemplating, or at least of the claims which they are now putting forward. Thus the
only figures mentioned in respect of the crane claim were £30,000 and DM7,000. But
when this was first fully quantified in the points of claim six years later, it had reached
a staggering DM23 million.

The builders replied on 2nd July 1970 rejecting all the claims and pointing out that all
were statute-barred under German law. Whilst drawing attention to the difficulties
created for them by the passage of time, they nevertheless offered to discuss the claim and
suggested a meeting later that month or in August. The owners first suggested a
meeting at the beginning of August, but then postponed it until the end of the month.
The builders could not attend until the end of September and the owners were not free
until November or December. A meeting was in fact arranged for January 1971, but Mr
Dastur of the owners was disturbed to receive reports of a very severe winter in Europe
and suggested a postponement. The builders then suggested a meeting in May, when
the weather would be warmer, adding 'As the settlement of the differences between
Bremer Vulkan and your esteemed company have been pending so long, there is no
hurry to speed up a settlement'. I interpret this as an indication of resignation to, rather
than acquiescence in, the delays which had occurred.

In fact, the meeting took place in April 1971. No progress was made. Immediately
thereafter the owners claimed arbitration and although it took until January 1972 before
the appointment of Sir Gordon Wilmer was perfected, I do not think that either party is
in a position to criticise the other in this respect.

This is the beginning of the critical stage in the chronology. The owners had exercised
their right under the English law to wait for a very long time before beginning the
proceedings. By January 1972 the first ship had been trading for over six years and the
last for over five. The last of the guarantee periods had expired more than four years
before. The owners had been advised by solicitors for over five years and by consulting
surveyors for four years. No complaint can be made that they did not begin the
proceedings earlier, but after so much time had elapsed, I consider that there was a heavy
onus on them to attempt to make speedy progress. They can hardly claim to have done
so.

1972

It was not until April 1972 that the owners' solicitors told the builders' solicitors that
Sir Gordon Wilmer had in fact accepted appointment as arbitrator and they said that
they would deliver a full statement of claim. The builders agreed promptly. But it was
not until November 1972 that counsel was instructed to settle this document.

1973

On 22nd May 1973 the owners' solicitors gave notice that additional stern damage
claims would be included in the points of claim. They added that this would be a rather
formidable document, but that they hoped to be in a position to serve it shortly. The
builders' solicitors replied by return of post saying that:

'Since we had not heard from you since April last year, we rather assumed that in
view of the inordinate delay in bringing this matter before the Arbitrators that it
was going to be abandoned. We note that you have now virtually put yourselves in
a position where you will be able to serve this pleading.'

1974

Only two letters were sent to the builders' solicitors during the course of this year. The
first in March 1974 expressed the hope that it would be possible to deliver the points of

claim 'in the very near future'. The second, in October, said that the particulars which
a   would be delivered with the points of claim were so voluminous in detail that a
considerable time had been incurred in preparing them. However, the pleading was
almost in a state for delivery.

1975
There was a flurry of correspondence in April. The owners' solicitors said that they
had hoped to have delivered the points of claim by then, but that one or two points on
b   the figures were still outstanding. They then reported that an explosion on one of the
vessels had occurred in November 1974. They asked that with a view to saving the extra
cost of beginning a new arbitration a claim in relation to that explosion might be
included in the current arbitration, without prejudice to the question of whether it was
time-barred. The builders' solicitors said that they would take instructions on this
c   suggestion. With regard to the points of claim they said:

> 'We acknowledge receipt of your letter of 8th April and are pleased to note that
> after approximately ten years your Clients are practically in a position to proceed
> with this matter. In view of the very slow progress which this case appears to have
> been making, we have not done any more than indicate to our Clients on an annual
> basis that the matter had not been dropped so far as you were concerned. Since we
d   > ourselves were instructed four years ago, and very little has happened since then, we
> had begun to wonder whether your clients had realized that they did not have a
> justified claim and had given it up.'

Two weeks later the builders' solicitors agreed to the inclusion of the explosion claim
in the current arbitration, but it did not in fact feature in the points of claim as eventually
delivered.
e
1976
On 23rd April the points of claim were delivered and it was indicated that
supplementary points of claim relating to the explosion would follow 'shortly'. The
owners' solicitors also enquired whether the builders' experts could undertake a joint
examination of a cylinder block then being held by the Port of London Authority. The
f   points of claim are a truly formidable document. The main body of the pleading consists
of 15 different claims totalling over DM50 million, ie more than the total cost of two of
the five ships. It was accompanied by two schedules of particulars running to nearly 100
foolscap pages. The builders' solicitors replied promptly by letter dated 26th April as
follows:

> 'It is, to say the least, with immense surprise that we have received these
g   > documents after such an inordinate period of delay. You and we were in
> consultation with each other back in 1971 and although you had indicated from
> time to time that the matter was by no means dead, we must formally protest on
> behalf of our clients that a case which is based on facts going back to as early as 1965
> failed to have been prosecuted with any reasonable despatch. We will have to
> consider most carefully, together with our Counsel, what steps to take to protect our
h   > clients' position in this regard. We note that you say [about inspection of the
> cylinder block] and clearly from a practical point of view what you propose is
> reasonable. However, having not considered this file in detail for over four years we
> cannot be expected to make any comment at this stage. We are sending the Points
> of Claim to our clients who will no doubt consider them and instruct us accordingly.'

j   On 17th June 1976 the owners' solicitors sought an answer concerning the proposed
joint examination of the cylinder block, but the builders' solicitors said that they had no
instructions.

1977
On 21st January 1977 the builders' solicitors wrote to the owners' solicitors as follows:

'We refer to the past correspondence in respect of this matter, which, as you can appreciate, in view of the length of time it has taken to produce the Statement of Claim has caused our Clients considerable difficulties. We have naturally been to Counsel in this regard, and the purpose of writing this letter is to assure you that we have not let the matter rest and it is our intention to apply to the Court for an injunction restraining your Clients from proceeding any further with the case on the grounds that it is now too stale a case and that many of the important witnesses of fact have either died or left our Clients' employ.'

On 31st January 1977 the owners' solicitors forwarded supplements to Schs A and B to the points of claim together with some corrections to the original Sch B and these corrections were themselves corrected by a further letter dated 14th March 1977.

The builders issued their writ on 25th April 1977.

The first matter which I have to consider is whether the delay following the institution of the arbitration proceedings was inordinate and inexcusable. Notice of arbitration had been given in April 1971 and the appointment of the arbitrator was perfected by January 1972. The ships had been delivered between November 1965 and December 1966 and the last guarantee period had ended in December 1967. Consulting surveyors had been appointed by the owners in November 1967. Having had so long to consider and prepare their claim before the arbitration proceedings were begun, the delay thereafter was prima facie inordinate and inexcusable.

Two different explanations are offered. The first rests on the complexity of the claim, the difficulty in arranging meetings with the buildings to discuss a settlement, the other commitments of the owners' solicitors and the limited number of counsel capable of handling such claims. The second rests on an allegation that the builders led the owners to conclude that there was no hurry.

I entirely accept that this was a very heavy claim and that it presented problems both to busy solicitors and to busy counsel. I also accept that, in litigation of this type, solicitors, having once instructed counsel, would find it difficult to 'change horses', especially as there are a very limited number of counsel who are familiar with this sort of work. But counsel were only instructed to settle the points of claim in November 1972 and there was throughout not the slightest sign of any sense of urgency.

This lack of a sense of urgency is virtually admitted and forms the basis of the second explanation. Thus, it is said that the points of claim *could* have been served at latest by early 1975, if the builders or their solicitors had given any indication at any stage that they were concerned that they might be prejudiced by the delay in settling the points of claim. This is the 'sleeping dogs' explanation and I do not accept it. As early as May 1973 the owners' solicitors were saying that the points of claim would be served 'shortly' and the builders' solicitors were talking of 'inordinate' delay saying that they had rather assumed that the proceedings had been abandoned. A year later, in March 1974, the points of claim were to be served 'in the very near future'. After another year, 'one or two points on the figures were still outstanding'. The only conceivable encouragement which the builders' solicitors gave to the owners was in April 1975 when they agreed to the explosion claim being included. They could well have refused and made the present application at that stage. No doubt in fact they applied their minds not to the current arbitration, but to whether the builders ought to insist on separate proceedings in respect of the explosion claim, which incidentally has still not been included. If the points of claim had been delivered shortly thereafter, it might have been said that there was acquiescence, but nothing which was said or done by the builders or their solicitors could have led the owners to think that they could delay delivery of the points of claim for a further year. That delay is said to have been caused by the decision in *Miliangos v George Frank (Textiles) Ltd*[1] and the new possibility of making a claim in Deutschmarks. But this possibility existed in relation to arbitrations long before then and, in any event, the points of claim could have been delivered and subsequently amended.

---

1 [1975] 3 All ER 801, [1976] AC 445

a I am therefore driven to conclude that the delay in delivering the points of claim was both inordinate and inexcusable and, further, that no significant part of the delay was induced by the conduct of the builders. The builders claim that they have thereby suffered serious prejudice in three ways. Two of these I accept.

Destruction of documents

b The builders say that under German law records do not have to be preserved after seven years and that some may have been destroyed. German law does not appear to require the destruction of documents and, if they have been destroyed, the builders have no one to blame but themselves.

Witnesses

c Sixteen senior employees engaged in the design and building of these vessels are now dead, retired or have left the builders' employment. In addition, one of the five guarantee engineers is dead and three left the builders' employment many years ago. The owners say that statements should have been taken from them. There is something in this, but such statements would have been of limited value unless related to the points of claim. The owners also say that in so far as the witnesses are dead, they died before the proceedings could have been heard even if there had been no delay and, further, that in *d* so far as recollections have dimmed, again, they would have dimmed before the hearing in any event. I accept that the hearing might not have taken place before September 1973 when Herr Erlinwein died and would not have taken place before Herr Hofman died in June 1971. But Herr Hofman was an assistant manager in the electric lay-out department and his death made the recollection of Herr Leo, the head of the department, all the more vital. He died in February 1977.

e

Nature of the defence

The owners' claims are based on repair costs, replacement items, port expenses and damages for delay over a period stretching back to 1965–66, including many ship repair firms and many ports. The yard had no opportunity of checking many of them before the points of claim were received and it was then far too late to do so. In addition, and *f* perhaps even more important, assuming that the various breakdowns are proved, the arbitrator will have to decide whether the cause was something for which the builders were responsible or was due to poor seamanship, bad maintenance and abuse of the vessel's machinery. If, and to the extent that, they were not the fault of the builders, I do not see how the builders can hope at this stage to collect the necessary evidence to ensure that justice is done.

g I am satisfied that if the proceedings had been pursued by action, I should have dismissed them for want of prosecution. It follows that the owners' inaction was repudiatory and that, the builders having accepted it as terminating the arbitration agreement, I should grant them an injunction restraining the owners from proceeding further with the arbitration agreement.

h THE SHARE DEAL DISPUTE

In June 1970 the plaintiffs, Newton Gregg, Lucille Gregg, Malcolm Kelly and others, agreed to sell their shareholdings in Gregg International Publishers Ltd. The purchaser was Raytheon Ltd, the defendant ('Raytheon'). The contract contained the usual warranties as to the balance sheet, stock valuation, taxation, book debts, litigation, and so on. By cl 11 it was provided:

j

'In the event that any dispute or controversy shall arise between the parties hereto, the same shall be resolved by arbitration in Geneva, Switzerland, under the rules then prevailing of the International Chamber of Commerce. The laws of England and the laws of the State of Delaware shall be deemed equally applicable to this Agreement and in the event of conflict between the two bodies of law the

Arbitrator shall be free to apply whichever of said laws will in his opinion most
equitably secure the results contemplated herein. The decision of the Arbitrator(s) **a**
shall be final and binding upon both parties and judgment thereon may be entered
in any court of competent jurisdiction.'

Disputes arose after completion and on 28th April 1971 Raytheon wrote to the
plaintiffs and to Mr Teesdale who was another vendor claiming indemnity for losses
consequent on alleged breaches of the warranties. The total amount claimed was about **b**
£500,000 and it was advanced under a number of different heads. The plaintiffs'
solicitors sent a detailed reply denying liability in a letter dated 21st October 1971 and
asked for further details of the claim which were provided in November and December
1971. Correspondence continued between the parties and on 14th April 1972 Raytheon's
solicitor, Mr Leslie Wainstead, asked that the dispute be referred to arbitration. A formal
application for arbitration was made to the International Chamber of Commerce ('the **c**
ICC') by Raytheon in June 1972.

Raytheon had suggested that the venue be changed from Geneva to London and in
July 1972 the ICC confirmed this change and also called on each party to pay a deposit of
$US15,000 to secure the arbitrator's fees and the administration charge. The plaintiffs
failed to pay their deposit and in February 1973 Raytheon paid it in order to get the
proceedings under way. This default by the plaintiffs was a constant source of irritation **d**
to Raytheon, but does not seem to have had any causal connection with the delays which
were later to occur. Exercising hindsight, a more serious problem was created by the
change of venue because Mr Wainstead took the view, which he still maintains, that, save
in so far as the arbitral procedure was prescribed by the ICC rules, the law of Geneva and
not the Arbitration Act 1950 would apply.

The plaintiffs complain of delay during the winter of 1972–73, but I do not think that **e**
this was of any importance. By May 1973 Mr Desmond Miller QC, Mr Michael Mustill
QC and Mr I F H Davison had been appointed as arbitrators. On 2nd May 1973 there
was a meeting for directions. An order was made that points of claim be delivered
within 21 days, unless Raytheon wished to rely on their letters which had already
outlined their claims. In fact, Raytheon relied on the letters. Points of defence were to
be delivered 21 days thereafter and in fact a detailed pleading was delivered on 14th June **f**
1973. Points of reply were ordered for 14 days thereafter with discovery 21 days after
the close of pleadings and inspection 21 days after discovery. The arbitrators also fixed
3rd December 1973 as the date for the hearing.

In July 1973 Raytheon asked for and were granted an extension of time for filing
points of reply. On 5th October 1973 the plaintiffs' solicitors complained of lack of
progress and, in particular, of the fact that discovery would be time consuming and could **g**
not begin before pleadings were closed. They therefore suggested that the date for the
hearing would have to be vacated. On 20th November 1973 the points of reply were
delivered and the arbitrators (a) ordered discovery within a little under four months and
(b) fixed a new date for the hearing in June or July 1974.

Lists of documents were exchanged in May 1974, and at the same time Raytheon
applied for a further short adjournment of the hearing date until August 1974 on the **h**
grounds that two witnesses in the United States were not available in June or July. The
plaintiffs for their part complained that discovery by Raytheon was wholly inadequate.

This led to yet another meeting for directions on 4th June 1974. The second date for
hearing was vacated by consent, but there was considerable discussion about discovery.
On the evidence it is quite clear that Mr Wainstead gave an undertaking to give specific
discovery as set out in a form which appears in the bundle of correspondence, subject to **j**
two minor qualifications contained in a letter from him dated 18th June 1974. The
arbitrators directed that discovery should be completed by the end of August 1974,
notwithstanding that Mr Wainstead had said that in view of 'the formidable nature of
the task' he might not be able to give discovery within this period, although he was
making every effort to do so.

On 1st October 1974 the parties once again appeared before the arbitrators. Mr
a Wainstead said that he had a further 1,000 relevant documents in his possession and that
he had been unable to comply with the timetable. A list would be delivered within a
week. In addition two further files had come to light each containing about 100
documents and a list would be delivered within two weeks. The arbitrators took the
view that no further order could profitably be made until they were satisfied that
discovery was complete and they adjourned until 15th November 1974.
b During October two further lists of documents were served by Mr Wainstead, but by
15th November discovery was still not complete. Various other matters were dealt with
by the arbitrator on that day and, in particular, the hearing was refixed for 29th
September 1975. This was the third date which had been fixed.

In December 1974, 11 supplementary lists of documents were served by Mr
Wainstead. The plaintiffs' solicitors complained in March 1975 that they had been
c unable to relate the lists to the documents disclosed and further complained that there
still had not been full compliance with Mr Wainstead's own undertaking of June 1974.

On 3rd July 1975 the arbitrators met yet again and considered the problem of
discovery. Mr Wainstead said that he had given full disclosure of all documents under
his direct control and that he had asked Raytheon in the USA to make an additional
search for any documents relevant to discovery as understood in English law. He also
d undertook to verify discovery by affidavit. The September hearing date was abandoned
and the arbitrators suggested that they should meet again later in the month to give
further directions. However, after discussions between the plaintiffs' solicitors and Mr
Wainstead, the former decided to seek an order from the High Court concerning
discovery and also the provision by Raytheon of security for costs. Accordingly, by a
letter dated 22nd July 1975 they invited the arbitrators to adjourn the proceedings
e generally with liberty to either party to restore. The arbitrators made an order
accordingly.

On 9th October 1975, before any application had been made to the High Court, Mr
Wainstead told the plaintiffs' solicitors that a bundle of documents was on its way to him
from Raytheon in the USA. The plaintiffs' solicitors replied by letter dated 15th October
1975 that in the circumstances they would wait for Raytheon's next (and sixteenth) list
f of documents before taking the matter any further. They also asked that any new
documents should be identified as such. The documents in fact arrived from the USA on
or about 23rd October 1975.

Apart from a 'without prejudice' meeting in December 1975, it was over three years
before the plaintiffs' solicitors heard anything more from Raytheon or from Mr
Wainstead. On 16th November 1978 they received a letter from Mr Wainstead offering
g inspection of a report by Coopers & Lybrand[1] and of several thousand invoices on which
the report was based. This was apparently relevant to one item of claim, the slow
moving stock item. Mr Wainstead also said that he was preparing a comprehensive
substitute list of documents. This was in fact delivered on 13th December 1978, but
meanwhile the plaintiffs' solicitors had notified him that they proposed to institute the
present proceedings. This was done by a writ issued on 1st December 1978.
h Mr Wainstead has two answers to the plaintiffs' complaint of inordinate and
inexcusable delay. The first is that he is a single-handed practitioner and that early on in
the proceedings it had become apparent to him that he could entrust the task of
discovery to no one else. Accordingly, he could only get on with it 'at such times as I
could spare from any other work'. I am sure that everyone sympathises with the plight
of the one-man firm. But the short answer is that they should not take on work which
j they cannot handle. The second answer is that there was an agreement that the
arbitration should stand adjourned until after an application had been made to the High
Court by the plaintiffs in relation to discovery and security for costs. He says that the
plaintiffs never made any such application and that, therefore, the arbitration still stands

---

1   A firm of accountants

adjourned by consent. This explanation ignores the sensible letter from the plaintiffs' solicitors dated 15th October 1975 telling Mr Wainstead that they would take no further *a* steps until Raytheon's next list of documents was served. I say 'sensible' because that list might have resolved the whole problem of discovery. Security for costs was a quite separate matter, which might not have been worth pursuing by itself, bearing in mind the likelihood of the court taking account of the plaintiffs' failure to contribute their half of the ICC deposit. Furthermore, Mr Wainstead has never suggested that the plaintiffs' failure to seek an order on discovery caused him to abate his efforts to comply with his *b* undertaking given in June 1974. His astonishing lack of progress with discovery was in no way attributable to anything said or done by the plaintiffs' solicitors and, in the light of their letter of 15th October, he had not the slightest reason to think and did not think that the plaintiffs were content that he should do other than comply promptly with his own undertaking.

On these facts I have no doubt that Raytheon's delay in prosecuting the proceedings *c* generally, and in particular in relation to discovery, would, if it had occurred in litigation, have rightly been characterised as inordinate and inexcusable.

I now have to consider whether the plaintiffs have been prejudiced by the delay. As a result of that delay I doubt whether it would have been possible to have arranged for a hearing before the summer of 1979. This would have been nearly nine years after the transaction. Counsel for Raytheon submits that recollections will be irrelevant and that *d* the claim falls to be determined on the basis of contemporary documents and, in particular, the company's accounts. The conflict between the parties will, he says, be as to matters of law and accountancy practice. No doubt he is right, looking at the matter from the point of view of Raytheon. Indeed, this is an important feature of the case. As counsel for the plaintiffs pointed out, delay usually prejudices the claimant as much or more than the respondent. But in this case Raytheon as claimant will have no problem. *e*

But the latter is quite otherwise from the point of view of the plaintiffs as respondents in the arbitration. Their defence rests in most cases on allegations that the matters relied on as constituting breaches of warranty were fully explained to Raytheon at or about the time when the contract was concluded. These explanations were all oral. Furthermore, in the case of one head of claim, there is an issue whether a particular document is a forgery. Personal recollections will be vital to sustain these defences. It may well be that *f* those concerned prepared proofs of evidence when the hearing was first fixed for December 1973, but at that time they had had no discovery. They will now have to check their recollections against discovery (which may still not be complete) and this will be extremely difficult.

The prejudice which the plaintiffs have suffered as a result of Raytheon's delays is, in my judgment, most serious. *g*

In these circumstances, I have no doubt that if the dispute between the parties had been the subject-matter of an action, I should have made an order dismissing Raytheon's claim for want of prosecution. On the view which I take of the law, the plaintiffs could have asked the arbitrators to make an award in similar terms. Instead they have issued their writ and elected to treat Raytheon's conduct as repudiatory. I think that on the facts they were entitled so to do. This terminated the arbitration agreement. As *h* Raytheon do not accept that this is the position, I am entitled to order them to desist from taking any further action in purported pursuance of the arbitration agreement.

Injunctions granted.

Solicitors: *Norton, Rose, Botterell & Roche* (for the builders); *Richards Butler & Co* (for the *i* owners); *Herbert Smith & Co* (for the plaintiffs in the second action); *Leslie Wainstead* (for Raytheon).

K Mydeen Esq   Barrister.

W T Ramsay Ltd v Inland Revenue Commissioners

COURT OF APPEAL, CIVIL DIVISION

LORD SCARMAN, ORMROD AND TEMPLEMAN LJJ

8th, 9th, 24th MAY 1979

Capital gains tax – Disposal of assets – Debt – Debt on a security – Security – Need for document or certificate issued by debtor – Loan by taxpayer company to subsidiary – Loan not secured on assets of subsidiary – Taxpayer company provided with statutory declaration by director of subsidiary recording its acceptance of loan offer – Whether loan a 'debt on a security' – Finance Act 1965, Sch 7, paras 5(3)(b), 11(1).

The taxpayer company, having made a capital gain, wished to create a capital loss to set against it. For that purpose it embarked on a tax avoidance scheme pursuant to which the following transactions were carried out. On 23rd February 1973 the taxpayer company acquired the whole of the issued shares of another company, C Ltd, for £185,034. By a letter of the same date the taxpayer company then offered to make two loans ('loan L1' and 'loan L2') to C Ltd, each of £218,750, repayable at par after 30 and 31 years respectively. C Ltd would be entitled to make earlier repayment, if desired, and was obliged to do so if it went into liquidation; if either loan were repaid before its maturity date, it had to be repaid at par or at its market value, whichever was the higher. Both loans were to carry interest at the rate of 11% per annum but the taxpayer company was to have the right, exercisable on one occasion only, to decrease the interest rate on one of the loans and to increase correspondingly the interest rate on the other. The offer was accepted orally by C Ltd and afterwards the taxpayer company was provided with a statutory declaration, made by one of C Ltd's directors, recording C Ltd's acceptance of the offer. The £437,500 was duly advanced by the taxpayer company to C Ltd. On 2nd March 1973 the taxpayer company reduced the interest on loan L1 to nil and increased the interest rate on loan L2 to 22%, and sold loan L2 to M Ltd for £391,481, which was its approximate market value. The taxpayer company thus made a capital profit of £172,731 by selling loan L2. In due course, after further loan and share transactions, loan L1 was repaid at par and the taxpayer company incurred a capital loss of £175,647 in respect of the sale of shares in C Ltd. In computing its corporation tax for the accounting period ended 31st May 1973 the taxpayer company claimed, inter alia, that loan L2 was not a 'debt on a security' within paras 11(1)[a] and 5(3)(b)[b] of Sch 7 to the Finance Act 1965, because it had not been evidenced in a document as security, and that the capital profit of £172,731 arising on the sale thereof was therefore not a chargeable gain. The Special Commissioners held that loan L2 was 'loan stock or similar security', within Sch 7, para 5(3)(b), that its disposal was therefore a disposal of a 'debt on a security', within para 11(1), and that accordingly the gain arising on its sale was not exempt from liability to tax. The judge[c] allowed an appeal by the taxpayer company on the ground that the essential feature of a security as defined in para 5(3)(b) was a document or certificate issued by a debtor which would represent a marketable security or which would enable it to be dealt with in and if necessary converted into shares or other securities and that, since no such document had been issued by C Ltd to the taxpayer company as security for the loan, the loan was not a 'debt on a security' for the purpose of para 11(1). The Crown appealed.

Held – Loan L2 was a 'debt on a security' within para 11(1) of Sch 7 to the 1965 Act: it was similar to loan stock because it had all the characteristics of loan stock and was

---

a   Paragraph 11(1), so far as material, is set out at p 217 *f*, post
b   Paragraph 5(3), so far as material, is set out at p 218 *e f*, post
c   [1978] 2 All ER 321

evidenced by a document or security (ie the statutory declaration made by the director)
which was similar to the document or security that was usually furnished by a debtor   *a*
company (ie a loan certificate) and adequately fulfilled the functions of such a
certificate. The statutory declaration represented a marketable security and the loan
could, if necessary, be converted into shares. It followed that the gain arising on the
disposal of loan L2 to M Ltd on 2nd March 1973 was not exempt from liability to tax.
The appeal accordingly would be allowed (see p 219 *c d* and *j* to p 220 *b* and *e f*, p 221 *c*
to *e* and *h* to p 222 *a*, post).   *b*

Dictum of Lord Russell of Killowen in *Aberdeen Construction Group Ltd v Inland Revenue
Comrs* [1978] 1 All ER at 975 applied.

Decision of Goulding J [1978] 2 All ER 321 reversed.

Notes

For the treatment of a debt on a security for the purposes of capital gains tax, see 5   *c*
Halsbury's Laws (4th Edn) para 104.

For the Finance Act 1965, Sch 7, paras 5, 11, see 34 Halsbury's Statutes (3rd Edn) 953,
956.

Cases referred to in judgments

Aberdeen Construction Group Ltd v Inland Revenue Comrs [1978] 1 All ER 962, [1978] AC   *d*
885, [1978] 2 WLR 648, [1978] STC 127, HL; *varying* [1977] STC 302, CS.

Agricultural Mortgage Corpn Ltd v Inland Revenue Comrs [1978] 1 All ER 248, [1978] Ch
72, [1978] STC 11, CA.

Cleveleys Investment Trust Co v Inland Revenue Comrs 1971 SC 233, 47 Tax Cas 300, 50 ATC
230, [1971] TR 205, CS.

Floor v Davis [1979] 2 All ER 677, [1979] 2 WLR 830, [1979] STC 379, HL; *affg* [1978]   *e*
2 All ER 1079, [1978] Ch 295, [1978] STC 436, CA.

Appeal

The Crown appealed against an order of Goulding J[1], dated 2nd March 1978, allowing an
appeal by W T Ramsay Ltd ('the taxpayer company') against a decision of the Special
Commissioners, dated 30th January 1976, whereby, on an appeal by the taxpayer   *f*
company against an assessment to corporation tax in the sum of £176,552 for the period
ended 31st May 1973, the commissioners held that a loan made by the taxpayer company
to Caithmead Ltd was a 'debt on a security' within the meaning of the Finance Act 1965,
Sch 7, paras 5(3)(*b*), 11(1), and that a chargeable gain accrued to the taxpayer company
when it disposed of the loan to Masterdene Finance Ltd on 2nd March 1973. The facts
are set out in the judgment of Templeman LJ.   *g*

Brian Davenport for the Crown.
D C Potter QC and *David C Milne* for the taxpayer company.

Cur adv vult

24th May. The following judgments were read.

TEMPLEMAN LJ (delivering the first judgment at the invitation of Lord Scarman).
This is an appeal by the Crown from Goulding J[1]. The facts as set out in the case stated[2]
by the Special Commissioners demonstrate yet another circular game in which the
taxpayer and a few hired performers act out a play; nothing happens save that the
Houdini taxpayer appears to escape from the manacles of tax.

The game is recognisable by four rules. First, the play is devised and scripted prior to

---

1   [1978] 2 All ER 321, [1978] STC 253
2   The case stated is set out at [1978] 2 All ER 322–329

performance. Secondly, real money and real documents are circulated and exchanged.

a Thirdly, the money is returned by the end of the performance. Fourthly, the financial position of the actors is the same at the end as it was in the beginning save that the taxpayer in the course of the performance pays the hired actors for their services. The object of the performance is to create the illusion that something has happened, that Hamlet has been killed and that Bottom did don an asses head so that tax advantages can be claimed as if something had happened.

b The audience are informed that the actors reserve the right to walk out in the middle of the performance but in fact they are the creatures of the consultant who has sold and the taxpayer who has bought the play; the actors are never in a position to make a profit and there is no chance that they will go on strike. The critics are mistakenly informed that the play is based on a classic masterpiece called 'The Duke of Westminster'[1] but in that piece the old retainer entered the theatre with his salary and left with a genuine entitlement to his salary and to an additional annuity.

c The game now under appeal was put on the market by the tax consultants Dovercliffe Consultants Ltd and was bought by the taxpayer company, W T Ramsay Ltd. The taxpayer company arranged to borrow money from the bankers Slater Walker Ltd on terms that the money should be used only for the performance and with safeguards which ensured that the bankers would be reimbursed.

d The taxpayer company and the consultants revolved and exchanged money through companies controlled by them or their directors and thereby at negligible cost to the taxpayer company and without earning a gain or suffering a loss, created for the taxpayer company a claim for a non-taxable gain and for a tax deductible loss, thus achieving no result save a manufactured claim to entitlement to tax relief.

The Crown assumed that the majority decision of this court in *Floor v Davis*[2] was

e indistinguishable and precluded them from relying on the fact that nothing happened in the present case except the manufacture of a tax advantage. They reserve the right to argue otherwise in the House of Lords. Therefore I concentrate on the capital gain as though it was independent of the capital loss and inspired by commerce.

The taxpayer company acquired a company called Caithmead Ltd and provided it with capital of £622,534 consisting of £185,034 subscribed for shares and £437,500 in

f moneys advanced. The moneys advanced were paid in accordance with a written offer dated 23rd February 1973, whereby the taxpayer company wrote to Caithmead as follows:

'Dear Sirs,

'We write to advise you that we are prepared to make two loans to you (hereinafter referred to as "L1" and "L2" respectively) on the terms and conditions set out below:

g (1) Each of L1 and L2 is to be for the sum of £218,750. (2) We shall be entitled to demand repayment of L1 at par 30 years from the date hereof and L2, also at par, 31 years from the date hereof. (3) You shall be at liberty to repay either L1 or L2 at any earlier time than that mentioned in the last preceeding [sic] paragraph and you will be obliged to repay both L1 and L2 if the company goes into liquidation before our right to demand repayment arises. (4) If either L1 or L2 is repaid by you

h prematurely (ie before 30 years from the date hereof in the case of L1 and before 31 years from the date hereof in the case of L2) the amount to be repaid will be whichever is the higher of:—(i) the face value of the loan (£218,750) or (ii) the market value of the loan on the assumption that it would remain outstanding for the full period of 30 or 31 years. (5) Each of L1 and L2 is to carry interest at the rate of 11% per annum payable quarterly on the 1 March, 1 June, 1 September, 1

j December in each year, the first of such payments to be made on March 1st 1973. (6) We reserve unto ourselves the right, exercisable on one occasion only and only

---

1 *Inland Revenue Comrs v Duke of Westminster* [1936] AC 1, [1935] All ER Rep 259
2 [1978] 2 All ER 1079, [1978] Ch 295, [1978] STC 436

while both L1 and L2 remain in our beneficial ownership, to decrease the interest rate on one of the loans and to increase correspondingly the interest rate on the other. If you wish to accept this offer on the terms set out in this letter please signify your acceptance orally to us and upon receipt of your oral acceptance we will arrange for the necessary finance to be made available in order to pay you the amounts due in respect of each of L1 and L2.

'Yours faithfully . . .'

The offer was orally accepted and the sum of £437,500 was duly advanced. The taxpayer company was provided with a statutory declaration or a copy of a statutory declaration in the following terms:

'I George William Livingston of 2 Ash Grove, Gainsborough, Lincs. do solemnly and sincerely declare as follows:—(1) I am a Director of Caithmead Limited (hereinafter called "[Caithmead]"). (2) ON the 23rd day of February 1973 a letter of offer (a copy of which is annexed hereto and marked 'A') addressed by [the taxpayer company] to [Caithmead] and dated the said 23rd day of February 1973 was received by [Caithmead]. [Of course the letter of offer was the letter I have already read.] (3) ON the 23rd day of February 1973 at a Board Meeting at which I was present the Directors of [Caithmead] resolved that the offer contained in such letter should be accepted orally by any one Director. The Board Meeting was then adjourned. (4) ON the said 23rd day of February 1973 I orally informed Mr R. B. Ramsey on behalf of [the taxpayer company] that [Caithmead] accepted the offer. Following such oral communication of acceptance the Board Meeting of [Caithmead] resumed and at such resumed Meeting Mr R. B. Ramsey (who is also a director both of [Caithmead] and [the taxpayer company] was present and he produced a letter to Slater Walker who had agreed to make the necessary finance available to [the taxpayer company] to pay to [Caithmead's] bank account an amount of £437,500 being the amount payable by [the taxpayer company] upon acceptance of its offer. AND I MAKE this solemn Declaration conscientiously believing the same to be true and by virtue of the provisions of the Statutory Declarations Act 1835.'

By a letter dated 2nd March 1973 addressed to Caithmead the taxpayer company altered the rate of interest payable on the loans to Caithmead. The letter reads:

'Dear Sirs,
                                    'Loans L1 and L2.
'Reference is made to our letter of offer relating to L1 and L2 which was orally accepted by you on the 23rd day of February 1973. In exercise of the right which we reserved unto ourselves under paragraph number 6 of our letter we hereby direct that the rate of interest on L1 shall be reduced to nil and that the rate of interest on L2 shall be correspondingly increased to 22%. Kindly acknowledge receipt of this letter and at the same time confirm to us that you will act in accordance with the direction herein contained.

'Yours faithfully . . .'

On the same day Caithmead replied as follows:

'Dear Sirs,
                                    'Loans L1 and L2.
'We acknowledge receipt of your letter to us dated the 2nd day of March 1973 wherein you directed that the rate of interest on L1 should be reduced to nil and that the rate of interest on L2 should be correspondingly increased to 22%. We write to confirm that [Caithmead] will act in accordance with the direction received from you . . .'

On 2nd March 1973 the taxpayer company offered to sell the loan L2 to Masterdene Finance Ltd ('Masterdene'). The offer was in these terms:

'Dear Sirs,

a   'We enclose herewith a copy of [a] Statutory Declaration dated the 2nd day of
March 1973 [that is the one I have read] together with the exhibits "A" "B" "C" and
"D" therein referred to [and those exhibits were copies of all the documents I have
read] and your attention is drawn to exhibit "A" and to the loans therein offered to
be made which are therein and are hereinafter save where the context otherwise
requires referred to as L1 and L2. We are informed that the market value of L2 is
b   £393,750 and we hereby offer to sell to you the benefit of the right to repayment of
L2 at that price less a discount of the aggregate of ·5% thereof and £300. This offer
remains open for acceptance for a period of seven days and thereafter will lapse. L2
is subject to a charge in favour of Slater Walker Limited and we enclose a copy of a
letter from the bank undertaking to release its charge upon payment of the amount
therein specified. We undertake to use so much of the purchase consideration as the
c   mortgagee requires to release L2 from such charge. We declare that nothing herein
contained imposes upon us any obligation to procure the debtor company to repay
L2 to you. If you wish to accept this offer on the terms set out in this letter please
signify your acceptance orally to us and transfer the sum of £391,481 to Slater
Walker Limited for the credit of our account with them.
'Yours faithfully . . .'

d   The offer was accepted and the purchase price paid. The taxpayer company thus made
a capital profit of £172,731 being the difference between the L2 loan of £218,750 and
the purchase price of £391,481 paid by Masterdene. Goulding J held that this capital
profit was not liable to charge under the capital gains provisions of the Finance Act
1965. The Crown appeals to this court.

By s 19 (1) of the Finance Act 1965 tax shall be charged in respect of capital gains, 'that
e   is to say chargeable gains computed in accordance with this Act and accruing to a person
on the disposal of assets'. The taxpayer company disposed of an asset, namely the loan
L2, and made a capital gain. The question is whether it is a chargeable gain. Paragraph
11 of Sch 7 to the Act provides:

'(1) Where a person incurs a debt to another . . . no chargeable gain shall accrue to
f   that (that is the original) creditor on a disposal of the debt, except in the case of the
debt on a security (as defined in paragraph 5 of this Schedule).'

Caithmead incurred the debt L2 to an original creditor, the taxpayer company, who
disposed of the debt to Masterdene. No chargeable gain accrued to the taxpayer company
on that disposal unless L2 was 'the debt on a security'.

The provisions of para 11 of Sch 7 to the Finance Act 1965 which exempt the original
g   creditor from capital gains tax on the disposal of a debt other than the debt on a security
become explicable only in the light of the other provisions of the Act. By s 20 (4) capital
gains tax is charged on the total amount of chargeable gains accruing in a tax year of
assessment after deducting any allowable losses. By s 23 (2) the capital gains provisions
of the Act (including Sch 7) 'which distinguish gains which are chargeable gains from
those which are not apply also to distinguish losses which are allowable losses from those
h   which are not . . .'

An original creditor who lends money repayable by the debtor at any time or on
demand by the creditor can never make a capital gain because in the hands of the original
creditor the debt can never be worth more than the sum advanced. Such a creditor can
however make a loss, particularly if the debtor becomes insolvent. The creditor may
never recover the whole of the debt or may be forced to sell or may choose to sell the debt
j   for less than the sum advanced. Since capital gains tax is calculated on the amount by
which annual chargeable gains exceed chargeable losses it would be illogical to include,
in the ambit of tax, assets the disposition of which can result only in a loss and never in
a gain.

A loan to a corporation may also take the form of a debt in respect of which the original creditor can sustain a loss but cannot earn a capital gain. One example is a bank overdraft repayable on demand. On the other hand there are certain types of loan to a corporation, whether protected by a charge on property or not, which constitute forms of investment and which are capable of being realised by the original creditor at any time either at a profit or at a loss depending on the circumstances at the time of disposal. For example a creditor may lend a limited company £100 and receive a certificate for £100 unsecured loan stock payable in 30 years' time with interest in the meantime at 10% per annum. The original creditor can sell the loan at any time during the 30 years. If the company prospers and the market rate of interest falls to say 5%, the original creditor will be able to sell his stock for more than £100 and thus make a gain. If the company struggles or if the market rate of interest rises to 15%, the original creditor will still be able to sell his loan but only for a sum less than £100 and will thus make a loss.

In order to constitute a coherent system of capital gains taxation it was therefore necessary to exclude the effect of dispositions of debts by owners where the dispositions cannot give rise to a gain but to include dispositions of debts in the form of investments which may result in gains or losses in the same way as dispositions of other investments.

Paragraph 11 of Sch 7 to the Finance Act 1965 affects only an original creditor and not his assignee for value. The original creditor cannot make a gain on a simple debt of £100 but if he assigns the debt for £50 the assignee will make a gain if he recovers or assigns over for more than £50 or a loss if he receives less than £50. Hence the distinction in para 11 between an original creditor and an assignee of the debt for value. Paragraph 11 then provides that even an original creditor shall be deemed to make a chargeable gain or a deductible loss if he disposes of the 'debt on a security'. For the reasons already advanced 'the debt on a security' the disposition of which is thus brought or retained within the ambit of capital gains tax will be a debt which can be disposed of by the original creditor either at a gain or at a loss and which is in the nature of an investment rather than, or as much as, a loan.

The word 'security' is defined for present purposes by para 5(3)(b) of Sch 7 as including 'any loan stock or similar security ... of any company, and whether secured or unsecured'.

A loan which is protected by a fixed or floating charge may be more valuable than a loan which is not so protected but each form of loan may on sale yield a gain or inflict a loss, hence the 'debt on a security' for the purposes of para 11 extends to a debt comprised in a 'security' which does not protect or 'secure' the loan by a fixed or floating charge.

The dispute in the present case is narrowed to the question whether the arrangements made with regard to the loan L2 as between the taxpayer company and Caithmead created, in the light of the provisions and discernible objects of the capital gains tax legislation, a security (not supported by a fixed or floating charge) similar to loan stock.

The terms of the loan L2 are similar in many respects to the terms of issue of loan stock. The terms which are so similar are as follows. First the creditor was not entitled to call in the loan for a long period, in this case 31 years; secondly the debtor company had power to redeem before the end of the 31-year period and was bound to redeem on liquidation; thirdly a premium was payable on early redemption if the market value of the loan at the date of redemption exceeded its face value; fourthly interest was payable; and fifthly the debt was assignable. These terms together created an asset in the form of an investment which the original creditor, the taxpayer company, could sell at any time at a gain or at a loss depending on the fortunes of the debtor company Caithmead and on the prevailing market rates of interest.

There were two unusual features of the loan L2, one of which increased the power of the original creditor to make a capital gain while the other required explanation to the purchaser. The provisions of the loans L1 and L2 which authorised the original creditor to vary the rates of interest as between them enabled the taxpayer company to enhance or diminish the value of either loan and thus to vary the capital gain and the capital loss which could be exacted by the taxpayer company from either loan. In fact when the rate of interest of L2 was increased from 11% to 22% the original creditor was able to sell L2

for a market value which earned for the original creditor a capital gain equal to 80% of
the loan less a small discount. The taxpayer company could hardly argue, and did not
argue, that this unusual feature made L2 so dissimilar to loan stock that the capital gain
was for this reason alone not a chargeable gain. The other unusual feature was the
substitution of a statutory declaration for a loan certificate as evidence of title. It is not
necessary to decide on this appeal whether a debt otherwise similar to loan stock would
qualify as a debt on a security in the absence of any written evidence of the terms of the
debt. It is hardly possible to conceive of such a debt. In any event in the present case the
statutory declaration made by the director of Caithmead contains all the information
which, in slightly less eccentric circumstances, would have been enshrined in a loan
certificate. Of course a purchaser of L2 or any part of L2 would inquire why a statutory
declaration had been substituted for a loan certificate and would make the usual inquiries
from the debtor company to ascertain that the loan was still outstanding and to ascertain
whether the company had received any notices of prior assignments of the whole or part
of the debt. But there was a perfectly satisfactory explanation for the absence of a loan
certificate, as inquiries would have shown, and the substitution of a statutory declaration
for a loan certificate would have been productive perhaps only of some little delay or
hesitation or diminution in purchase price. It does not lie in the mouth of the taxpayer
company, who accepted the statutory declaration in the first place instead of a loan
certificate and who found no difficulty in satisfying the purchaser of L2 or in selling at
a handsome profit, to argue that the statutory declaration was in substance different from
or inferior to a loan certificate as evidence of title or otherwise.

Counsel for the taxpayer company pointed out certain respects in which he said the
loan L2 was not similar to loan stock. The differences which he pointed out are however
differences of form and not of substance and they are due to the fact that there was only
one creditor. A debt on a security which is otherwise similar to loan stock will not be
dissimilar merely because there is only one creditor initially.

The differences on which counsel for the taxpayer company relied are as follows. First
there was no 'subscription'; but a subscription is only an offer to lend and payment
pursuant to that offer, usually by two or more lenders for separate amounts. Secondly
there was no 'issue'; but as Scarman LJ said in *Agricultural Mortgage Corpn Ltd v Inland
Revenue Comrs*[1]:

'... a company proposes to issue loan capital when it offers to accept specified
obligations towards, and to confer corresponding rights on, a person or persons who
advance money for capital purposes. "Issue" consists of the acceptance of the loan or
loans on the terms offered.'

There was therefore an 'issue' in the present case by Caithmead to the taxpayer
company when Caithmead accepted the loans on the terms offered and received the
amounts of the loans. Thirdly there was no 'register'; but a register is only a record of the
identity of lenders and their assignees; and fourthly there was no 'stock'; but loan stock
is only a proportion of an aggregate debt.

In the present case the taxpayer company alone was invited to subscribe, and did
subscribe, for the loans L1 and L2. Therefore Caithmead issued one, and only one,
certificate in the form of a statutory declaration. There was nothing to prevent the
taxpayer company assigning proportions of each loan in specified amounts to several
assignees, thus dividing the loan into separate sums of stock; the assignees would then
have given notice of their acquisitions of stock to the company Caithmead in order that
their entitlement and priority should be established and these notices and the identities
of the holders of stock for the time being would have been registered with the company,
whether in one formal register or not.

To fall within the description of 'the debt on a security' for the purposes of para 11 the

---

1   [1978] 1 All ER 248 at 264, [1978] Ch 72 at 105, [1978] STC 11 at 27

debt need only be comprised in a 'security' which is similar to, but not necessarily identical with, loan stock. The debt L2 displayed all the characteristics of loan stock and was evidenced by a document or security, namely the statutory declaration, which was similar to the document or security which is usually furnished and adequately fulfilled the functions of the document or security which is usually furnished by a debtor company, namely a loan certificate.

Finally counsel for the taxpayer company relied on authority. None of the decided cases deals with a loan transaction on terms evidenced in writing and similar to loan stock in every respect save for the substitution of a statutory declaration for a loan certificate. In *Cleveleys Investment Trust Co v Inland Revenue Comrs*[1] the original creditor advanced to a company £25,000 repayable after not more than six months on the terms of a bill of exchange. Lord Migdale said[2]:

> '"The debt on a security" means debt evidenced in a document as a security. I cannot see any similarity between the letter of acceptance or the bill of exchange in this case and loan stock or, for that matter, an unsecured debenture.'

Lord Cameron said[3]: '. . . the word "security" in para. 11 (1) is a substantive and refers to those securities which are or can be subject to a conversion.'

That case decided that a loan which did not bear any resemblance to the form of loan secured by loan stock does not fall within the expression 'the debt on a security' and, in effect, that a bill of exchange in normal terms is not a certificate of loan stock. If the test of convertibility is to be applied, there is little or no difference between unsecured loan stock on the one hand and deferred redeemable preference stock on the other hand. A simple debt is not in fact converted into shares; it can be notionally repaid, and the sum advanced and repaid can be invested in the purchase of or subscription for shares. Loan stock however can be truly converted in the sense that at any time during the long period for which it is issued it can be exchanged for shares, if the debtor company and the creditor agree, on terms which reflect the current value of the loan stock and the current value of the shares of the company. The loan L2 was similarly convertible and in this respect was identical with loan stock.

In *Aberdeen Construction Group Ltd v Inland Revenue Comrs*[4] a loan of £500,000 made by the original creditor to a company was repayable on demand and not evidenced by any document or certificate. The Court of Session rejected the argument that the loan was 'the debt on a security'. The Lord President (Lord Emslie) said[5] that on the true construction of para 11(1)—

> '. . . what is in contemplation is the issue of a document or certificate by the debtor institution which would represent a marketable security, as that expression is commonly understood, the nature and character of which would remain constant in all transmissions.'

Counsel for the taxpayer company argued that the Lord President in his reference to 'marketable security' had in mind an instrument or loan which would be freely negotiable on the Stock Exchange. The expression 'loan stock' has however a far wider meaning than this, and I do not understand the Lord President to be considering the situation which arises when a private company issues loan stock to one creditor and one creditor alone. Lord Johnston said[6]:

> '. . . what appears to be in contemplation is the issue of a document by the debtor

---

1 1971 SC 233, 47 Tax Cas 300
2 1971 SC 233 at 243, 47 Tax Cas 300 at 315
3 1971 SC 233 at 244, 47 Tax Cas 300 at 318
4 [1977] STC 302
5 [1977] STC 302 at 309
6 [1977] STC 302 at 313

a
which would represent a marketable security. No such document was issued to the taxpayer company ...'

Lord Johnston was not considering the position which now arises when the document issued by the debtor is not a formal certificate but a statutory declaration. In the present case that statutory declaration represents a marketable security in that it enables the debt to be assigned; it is a document which is similar to a loan certificate and the debt is similar to loan stock. The House of Lords upheld the decision of the Court of Session on

b
this point in *Aberdeen Construction Group Ltd v Inland Revenue Comrs*[1]. Lord Wilberforce[2] drew a distinction—

'between a pure unsecured debt as between the original borrower and lender on the one hand and a debt (which may be unsecured) which has, if not a marketable character, at least such characteristics as enable it to be dealt in and if necessary

c
converted into shares or other securities.'

The loan L2 in the present case falls within the latter class. Lord Russell of Killowen said[3] that loan stock—

'suggests to my mind an obligation created by a company of an amount for issue to subscribers for the stock, having ordinary terms for repayment with or without

d
premium and for interest.'

Bearing in mind the fact that there was only one creditor in the present case, the loan L2 falls within the description of a security similar to loan stock as defined by Lord Russell of Killowen.

Goulding J came to the conclusion that he was bound by the decision of the Court of Session in *Aberdeen Construction Group Ltd v Inland Revenue Comrs*[4], to which I have

e
referred, to hold that the loan L2 was not a debt on a security. For the reasons I have endeavoured to explain I am unable to agree with him and I would allow the appeal.

LORD SCARMAN. I agree with the judgment of Templeman LJ and would allow the appeal. In doing so I express the hope that the majority decision of this court in *Floor v Davis*[5] may in the not too distant future be reviewed by the House of Lords. It is a

f
misfortune, though an inevitable casualty of the litigation process which in a system of law based on judicial precedent forges the law, that when *Floor v Davis*[6] reached the House of Lords it was decided on another point.

Approaching this case on the limited premise which Templeman LJ has reluctantly but unavoidably accepted, I reach the same conclusion as he does. The draftsman of the statute was driven by the technical problems which he had to master to use the strange

g
term 'the debt on a security' to distinguish between a loan which could result at best in repayment without a gain and a loan which in the hands of the creditor or his assignee could produce a gain (or a loss). In simple English (not of course appropriate to the complications of a taxing statute) the distinction is between a loan and an investment. In the world of the City the distinction is no longer capable of being thus simply drawn; for some loans are investments in which there is a market where creditors and assignees

h
may make a profit or a loss. I would respectfully agree with Lord Russell of Killowen's description of loan stock in *Aberdeen Construction Group Ltd v Inland Revenue Comrs*[3]. Loan L2 has, for the reasons given by Templeman LJ, the characteristics of loan stock; it falls within the description, therefore, of a 'debt on a security'.

j   1   [1978] 1 All ER 962, [1978] AC 885, [1978] STC 127
    2   [1978] 1 All ER 962 at 968, [1978] AC 885 at 895, [1978] STC 127 at 133
    3   [1978] 1 All ER 962 at 975, [1978] AC 885 at 903, [1978] STC 127 at 140
    4   [1977] STC 302
    5   [1978] 2 All ER 1079, [1978] Ch 295, [1978] STC 436
    6   [1979] 2 All ER 677, [1979] 2 WLR 830, [1979] STC 379

ORMROD LJ. I agree and have nothing I wish to add.

a

Appeal dismissed. Decision of the Special Commissioners declared correct and assessment as determined by them restored. Leave to appeal to the House of Lords granted.

Solicitors: *Slowes* (for the taxpayer company); *Solicitor of Inland Revenue*.

Christine Ivamy Barrister. *b*

Practice Direction

QUEEN'S BENCH DIVISION

c

Practice – Chambers proceedings – Masters' summonses – Adjournment – Restoration – Vacation of appointments.

1. *Summons in the ordinary list*

A summons in the ordinary list may be adjourned or withdrawn or transferred to *d* counsel's list or for a special appointment without reference to a master (a) by consent or (b) if the summons has not been served. In all other cases application must be made to the master to whom the summons has been assigned.

2. A summons may be restored to the ordinary list for hearing (a) without the leave of a master if for any reason the summons has not been heard, or, if heard, has not been fully disposed of, (b) in other cases, by leave of a master. *e*

3. *Special appointments before the masters*

An application for the adjournment of a special appointment given by a master must be made to the master who gave the appointment personally.

4. Where the matter involved in a summons for which a master has given a special appointment has been settled, it is the duty of solicitors for the parties and particularly *f* the solicitor who obtained that appointment to notify that master immediately.

Sir Jack I H Jacob QC
16th July 1979   Senior Master of the Supreme Court.

Engineers' and Managers' Association v Advisory, Conciliation and Arbitration Service and another (No 1)

COURT OF APPEAL, CIVIL DIVISION

LORD DENNING MR, LAWTON AND CUMMING-BRUCE LJJ

11th MAY 1979

Trade union – Legal proceedings – Right of audience in High Court and Court of Appeal – Union an unincorporated body – General rule that unions to be legally represented – Discretion of court to dispense with rule – Dispute between two unions as to recognition by employers – Small union with limited means added as party to proceedings – Application by small union to be represented by deputy general secretary in those proceedings – Only minor matter involved – Whether application should be granted.

UKAPE, a small trade union, which obtained its funds from subscriptions by individual members, was involved in a recognition issue at a factory. It was joined as a party in proceedings in the High Court instituted by EMA, another trade union, which was also involved in a recognition issue at the factory. UKAPE wished to be represented in the court proceedings by H, its deputy general secretary, instead of being legally represented. The only matter on which UKAPE wanted H to speak on its behalf was as to the form of a questionnaire to be submitted to workers at the factory in connection with the recognition issue. UKAPE was not eligible for legal aid. As a trade union it was a legal entity but, by virtue of s 2[a] of the Trade Union and Labour Relations Act 1974, it could not be treated as a body corporate. The judge held that H had no right of audience in the High Court. On appeal,

Held – As a general rule trade unions should be represented by counsel in the High Court and Court of Appeal because the issues involved in proceedings concerning trade unions were normally complicated. The court had, however, a discretion to make exceptions to that rule and would exercise that discretion in favour of UKAPE because it was a small union with limited resources and H merely wanted to put forward a simple point on its behalf. Accordingly he would be permitted to speak on UKAPE's behalf (see p 225 d to j and p 226 d e, post).

Collier v Hicks (1831) 2 B & Ad 663 considered.

Notes

As to the right of audience in the High Court and Court of Appeal, see 3 Halsbury's Laws (4th Edn) para 1158.

For the Trade Union and Labour Relations Act 1974, s 2, see 44 Halsbury's Statutes (3rd Edn) 1823.

Cases referred to in judgments

Bonsor v Musicians' Union [1955] 3 All ER 518, [1956] AC 104, [1955] 3 WLR 788, HL, 30 Digest (Reissue) 209, 314.

Collier v Hicks (1831) 2 B & Ad 663, 9 LJOSMC 138, 109 ER 1290, 3 Digest (Reissue) 762, 4602.

Cases also cited

Kinnell (Charles P) & Co Ltd v Harding, Wace & Co [1918] 1 KB 405, 87 LJKB 342, CA.

Llewellyn v Carrickford [1970] 2 All ER 24, [1970] 1 WLR 1124.

---

a Section 2, so far as material, is set out at p 224 g, post

Ruling on a point of law

Two trade unions, the United Kingdom Association of Professional Engineers ('UKAPE') *a*
and the Engineers' and Managers' Association ('EMA') wanted to be recognised by the
employers, GEC Reactor Equipment Ltd, for collective bargaining purposes. The
Technical, Administrative and Supervisory Section of the Amalgamated Union of
Engineering Workers ('TASS') opposed both claims for recognition. On 9th July 1976
UKAPE applied to the Advisory, Conciliation and Arbitration Service ('ACAS') for
recognition. Before ACAS dealt with UKAPE's application, TASS complained to the *b*
Trades Union Congress ('the TUC') about a recruiting campaign initiated by EMA in aid
of its claim for recognition. On 16th March 1977 a disputes committee appointed by the
TUC made an award in favour of TASS and stated, inter alia, that EMA should not
proceed with its claim for recognition. On 27th April 1977 EMA referred the recognition
issue to ACAS. ACAS prepared a questionnaire for submission to the professional
engineers employed by GEC Reactor Equipment Ltd. The questionnaire was not sent *c*
out because on 13th October 1977 EMA issued a writ against the TUC claiming that the
award of its disputes committee was ultra vires and void, and ACAS decided that in
consequence it could not, for the time being, proceed with UKAPE's and EMA's
references. On 25th January 1978 EMA issued a writ against ACAS claiming a
declaration that ACAS had failed to carry out its statutory duty to investigate and report
on the recognition issue and that it was bound to carry out that duty. On 3rd March *d*
1978 UKAPE was joined as a party to the proceedings. At the trial of the action UKAPE
wanted to be represented by Mr Hickling, its deputy general secretary, instead of being
legally represented. The only matter on which UKAPE wished Mr Hickling to address
the court was as to the form of a questionnaire drafted by ACAS. Oliver J held that Mr
Hickling had no right of audience. On 7th April 1978 Oliver J dismissed EMA's claim
for declaratory relief. EMA appealed to the Court of Appeal[1]. At the hearing of the *e*
appeal, the question arose whether Mr Hickling could make representations to the court
on behalf of UKAPE and the court was invited to give a ruling on the matter.

Simon Goldblatt QC and *Peter C L Clark* for EMA.
Henry Brooke for ACAS.
Simon Brown on behalf of the Attorney-General as amicus curiae.   *f*

LORD DENNING MR. A question has arisen about the position of the United
Kingdom Association of Professional Engineers (UKAPE). It is a trade union. Mr
Hickling, the deputy general secretary, has come before us. He wants to make
representations on its behalf. The judge's view was that Mr Hickling had no right of
audience. The matter is of such importance that we invited the assistance of the
Attorney-General. Counsel on his behalf has given us much help.   *g*

Under s 2 of the Trade Union and Labour Relations Act 1974 a trade union 'shall not
be, or be treated as if it were, a body corporate'. Nevertheless, it is a legal entity (see
Bonsor v Musicians' Union[2]), and it is 'capable of suing and being sued in its own name,
whether in proceedings relating to property or founded on contract or tort or any other
cause of action whatsoever'. How can such a legal entity be represented?

If the trade union had been a body corporate, then under RSC Ord 5, r 6(2) and RSC *h*
Ord 12, r 1, it could not appear or carry on proceedings except through a solicitor. But
as it is not a body corporate it does not come within that prohibition.

If this court had been an employment appeal tribunal, then under Sch 11, para 20, of
the Employment Protection (Consolidation) Act 1978—

> 'Any person may appear before the Appeal Tribunal in person or be represented *j*
> by counsel or by a solicitor or by a representative of a trade union or an employers'
> association or by any other person whom he desires to represent him.'

---

1   See p 227, post
2   [1955] 3 All ER 518, [1956] AC 104

If this court had been a county court, then under s 89 of the County Courts Act 1959—

'In any proceedings in a county court any of the following persons may address the courts, namely—(a) any party to the proceedings; (b) a barrister retained by or on behalf of any party; (c) a solicitor acting generally in the proceedings for a party thereto (in this paragraph referred to as a 'solicitor on the record'), any solicitor employed by a solicitor on the record, any solicitor engaged as an agent by a solicitor on the record and any solicitor employed by a solicitor so engaged; (d) any other person allowed by leave of the court to appear instead of any party.'

I do not think that the High Court or the Court of Appeal should be in any different position.

It is well settled that every court of justice has the power of regulating its own proceedings; and, in doing so, to say whom it will hear as an advocate or representative of a party before it. As Parke J said in *Collier v Hicks*[1]:

'No person has a right to act as an advocate without the leave of the Court, which must of necessity have the power of regulating its own proceedings in all cases when they are not already regulated by ancient usage.'

The general rule in the High Court and the Court of Appeal is that we only hear members of the Bar. But we do allow exceptions when the circumstances make it desirable. Take litigants in person. Sometimes we have heard a husband speaking for his wife: or a son speaking for his mother: and so forth. So also it seems to me that with this new thing, a trade union which is a legal entity but not a body corporate, we can ourselves decide whom we should allow to speak on its behalf.

In the ordinary way I should have thought that a trade union as a legal entity, especially a large trade union with ample funds, on a complicated matter would think it right and proper to employ a solicitor to conduct the proceedings and instruct counsel to appear in the High Court to put its case on its behalf. While that is the general rule, it seems to me it can be subject to exceptions. If the court in its discretion thinks it right to make an exception, then it can do so.

Take, for instance, this particular case. We know that UKAPE is an association of professional engineers. It has a small membership; and it obtains its funds from subscriptions by the individual members. It is not eligible for legal aid. It seems to me that if it desires to put a simple point before the court, it is within the discretion of the court to allow the union to be represented by a secretary or any other officer duly authorised on its behalf. Mr Hickling has come here to put forward a simple point as to the form of a questionnaire, asking that UKAPE's interests should be considered in that regard. It seems to me that that is a perfectly proper and reasonable matter on which he may appear on behalf of the trade union. Although we at first heard him de bene esse, now we have further considered the matter, it seems to me that it is proper that we should hear him and take into consideration the representations he made.

LAWTON LJ. It has been my experience both as a member of the Bar and as a judge that cases in which trade unions are either plaintiffs or defendants are usually of considerable complication and far from easy to elucidate. In those circumstances, in the ordinary way as a matter of policy it would be advisable for courts to have the assistance of counsel on the hearing of any case involving a trade union. There may be exceptional cases, and this is one, where the point involving a union is of such small compass that the employment of counsel to put it is unnecessary. But in general I should have thought that it was necessary.

The history of rights of audience has, I think, to be considered in connection with the problem we have been asked to decide. The history can start for the purposes of this case

---

1   (1831) 2 B & Ad 663 at 672, 109 ER 1290 at 1293

at the beginning of the 19th century.   At that time there was doubt as to whether anyone
appearing at a hearing of an information before magistrates was entitled as of right to be
represented by either an attorney or by counsel.   In *Collier v Hicks*[1] this problem of
representation was considered, and was dealt with in this way.   Lord Tenterden CJ said[2]:

> 'This was undoubtedly an open Court, and the public had a right to be present, as
> in other Courts; but whether *any* persons, and *who* shall be allowed to take part in
> the proceedings, must depend on the discretion of the magistrates; who, like other
> Judges, must have the power to regulate the proceedings of their own Courts.'   (My
> emphasis.)

Parke J, who was sitting with him, said[3]:

> 'No person has a right to act as an advocate without the leave of the Court, which
> must of necessity have the power of regulating its own proceedings in all cases
> where they are not already regulated by ancient usage.   In the Superior Courts, by
> ancient usage, persons of a particular class are allowed to practise as advocates, and
> they could not lawfully be prevented; but justices of the peace, who are not bound
> by such usage, may exercise their discretion whether they will allow any, and what
> persons, to act as advocates before them.'

In 1831 trade unions were unlawful conspiracies.   At that time ancient usage did not
contemplate them at all.   They are not now unlawful conspiracies: they are legal
entities.   The practice of the courts must be adjusted to deal with the rights of audience
of trade unions.   The rules, perhaps by an oversight, do not specifically deal with them;
and, in my judgment, as Lord Denning MR has said, the court should now regulate its
own procedure in the way he has indicated.

CUMMING-BRUCE LJ. I agree.

Solicitors: *Lawford & Co* (for EMA); *Treasury Solicitor*.

Sumra Green   Barrister.

---

1   (1831) 2 B & Ad 663, 109 ER 1290
2   2 B & Ad 663 at 668, 109 ER 1290 at 1292
3   2 B & Ad 663 at 672, 109 ER 1290 at 1293

Engineers' and Managers' Association v Advisory, Conciliation and Arbitration Service and another (No 2)

COURT OF APPEAL, CIVIL DIVISION

LORD DENNING MR, LAWTON AND CUMMING-BRUCE LJJ

8th, 9th, 10th, 11th, 14th MAY 1979

Trade union – Recognition – Reference of recognition issue to Advisory, Conciliation and Arbitration Service – Duty of Service to ascertain opinion of workers to whom issue relates – Whether Service has any discretion to defer making enquiries – Employment Protection Act 1975, ss 12, 14.

In the course of a recognition dispute at an engineering factory where about 300 professional engineers were employed, a professional association ('UKAPE') which was not affiliated to the Trades Union Congress ('the TUC') applied on 9th July 1976 to the Advisory, Conciliation and Arbitration Service ('ACAS') for recognition for the purposes of collective bargaining at the factory. Two unions ('EMA' and 'TASS') which were affiliated to the TUC also wished to represent the professional engineers in collective bargaining at the factory. At the end of 1976 a complaint by TASS to the TUC about EMA's recruiting of new members at the factory was referred to a disputes committee of the TUC in accordance with the TUC's rules. On 16th March 1977 the committee decided that EMA should cease recruiting at the factory, existing EMA members there should transfer to TASS, and EMA should not proceed with any claim for recognition. In defiance of the committee's decision, EMA referred the recognition issue to ACAS on 27th April. ACAS had not at that stage reached a decision on UKAPE's application and was thus faced with two applications for recognition and also the decision of the TUC's disputes committee. It delayed taking any action until June when, under pressure to carry out its duty under ss 12[a] and 14[b] of the Employment Protection Act 1975 to 'ascertain the opinions of workers to whom the [recognition] issue relates', it drafted a questionnaire asking the professional engineers which trade union they wished to represent them. EMA agreed to the form of the questionnaire but UKAPE did not and while that was being discussed EMA issued a writ against the TUC on 13th October claiming, inter alia, that the decision of the disputes committee was ultra vires and invalid. Directions were given for pleadings to be delivered speedily with a view to an early trial. Because of the issue of the writ, ACAS postponed sending out the questionnaire and on 14th December informed EMA and UKAPE that 'for the time being' it could not proceed with its enquiries in relation to the recognition issue. On 25th January 1978 EMA issued a writ against ACAS claiming a declaration that ACAS was in breach of its duties under the Act and that it was bound to investigate and report on the recognition issue. By the time the case came before the judge the progress in relation to EMA's action against the TUC was slower than had been hoped but there was a prospect that trial of the action might take place before the end of 1978. ACAS informed the judge that it had decided on 14th December 1977 to defer its enquiries because the issue of the writ against the TUC had introduced such uncertainty into the recognition issue that no purpose would be served by making the enquiries until the uncertainty had been resolved since until the professional engineers knew whether the disputes committee's decision was valid or not, and whether EMA would be expelled from the TUC for defying the decision, they could not properly answer the questionnaire. On 7th April 1978 the judge held that ACAS had a discretion to postpone

---

a Section 12, so far as material, is set out at p 237 *d*, post

b Section 14, so far as material, is set out at p 234 *e f*, post

the investigations and had not wrongly exercised that discretion. EMA appealed. By the
time the appeal came on for hearing in May 1979 the date for the trial of EMA's action   *a*
against the TUC had been fixed for March 1980. ACAS informed the court that it did
not intend to proceed with its enquiries, unless the court held otherwise, until the
litigation between EMA and the TUC was concluded.

Held – (i) ACAS had a mandatory duty under s 14 of the 1975 Act to ascertain the
opinion of the workers involved but it had a discretion as to the means which it   *b*
employed to do so and the time when it started its enquiries. However, it had to act
within a reasonable time and could not postpone exercising its discretion indefinitely (see
p 234 *f* to *j*, p 237 *d e* and p 239 *j*, post).

(ii) In determining whether ACAS was entitled to defer its enquiries pending the result
of the litigation between EMA and the TUC, the court could not confine itself to
considering the situation as it was on 14th December 1977 but had to look at the   *c*
situation as it was at the date of the hearing of the appeal and give judgment on the basis
of the situation at that time (see p 236 *e f*, p 238 *d e* and p 240 *a*, post); *Attorney-General
v Birmingham, Tame and Rea District Drainage Board* [1911–13] All ER Rep 926, *Curwen v
James* [1963] 2 All ER 619 and *Murphy v Stone Wallwork (Charlton) Ltd* [1969] 2 All ER
949 applied.

(iii) ACAS might have been entitled on 14th December 1977 to postpone making its   *d*
enquiries for a few months but it was not reasonable for it to do so for any longer than
that. The professional engineers were unrepresented for collective bargaining purposes
and ACAS could not delay ascertaining their opinions for several years pending the result
of the litigation merely because it considered that their replies to a questionnaire would
be inconclusive or of little help in deciding whether to recommend recognition. If
ACAS found that the replies suffered from such defects, it could point that out in its   *e*
report. It followed that ACAS had erred in law in deciding to wait until the uncertainty
posed by the disputes committee's decision and the issue of the writ had been resolved
before proceeding with its enquiries. Accordingly the appeal would be allowed and the
declaration granted (see p 234 *j* to p 235 *a* and *j* to p 236 *c*, p 238 *f* to p 239 *b e f* and *j* and
p 240 *a b*, post).

Notes   *f*
For the reference of a recognition issue to the Advisory, Conciliation and Arbitration
Service, see Supplement to 38 Halsbury's Laws (3rd Edn) para 677A, 2.
    For the Employment Protection Act 1975, ss 12, 14, see 45 Halsbury's Statutes (3rd
Edn) 2384, 2386.

Cases referred to in judgments   *g*
Attorney-General v Birmingham, Tame and Rea District Drainage Board [1912] AC 788,
    [1911–13] All ER Rep 926, 82 LJ Ch 45, 107 LT 353, 76 JP 481, 11 LGR, HL, 28 (2)
    Digest (Reissue) 1124, *1233*.
Curwen v James [1963] 2 All ER 619, [1963] 1 WLR 748, CA, Digest (Cont Vol A) 1210,
    1208b, 51 Digest (Repl) 824, *3805*.
Grunwick Processing Laboratories Ltd v Advisory, Conciliation and Arbitration Service [1978]   *h*
    1 All ER 338, [1978] AC 655, [1978] 2 WLR 277, [1978] ICR 231, CA and HL.
Hick v Raymond & Reid [1893] AC 22, [1891–4] All ER Rep 491, 62 LJQB 98, 68 LT 175,
    7 Asp MLC 233, 1 R 125, HL, 12 Digest (Reissue) 377, *2739*.
Murphy v Stone Wallwork (Charlton) Ltd [1969] 2 All ER 949, [1969] 1 WLR 1023, 7 KIR
    203, HL, Digest (Cont Vol C) 1098, *3808b*.
National Employers Life Assurance Co Ltd v Advisory, Conciliation and Arbitration Service and   *j*
    Association of Scientific, Technical and Managerial Staffs (23rd February 1979) unreported.
Powley v Advisory, Conciliation and Arbitration Service [1978] ICR 123, [1977] IRLR 190.
*United Kingdom Association of Professional Engineers v Advisory, Conciliation and Arbitration
    Service* [1979] 2 All ER 478, [1979] 1 WLR 570, CA.

Appeal

By a writ dated 25th January 1978, the plaintiffs, the Engineers' and Managers' Association ('EMA'), brought an action against the first defendants, the Advisory, Conciliation and Arbitration Service ('ACAS'), claiming the following relief: (i) a declaration that ACAS, in refusing and/or failing to investigate and/or report on a recognition issue dated 27th April 1977 concerning all Category 3 and 4 engineers not covered by the Technical, Administrative and Supervisory Section ('TASS') procedural classes at GEC Reactor Equipment Ltd, Whetstone, Leicestershire, referred to it under s 11 of the Employment Protection Act 1975, on the sole ground that the issue was alleged to be the subject-matter of a complaint to the Trades Union Congress ('the TUC') of alleged breaches of the TUC Disputes Principles and Directives ('the Bridlington Agreement'), was acting in breach of its statutory duties and unlawfully, (ii) a declaration that ACAS in refusing and/or failing to investigate and/or report on the recognition issue on the sole ground that the issue was the subject-matter of a complaint to the TUC was acting in breach of its statutory duties and unlawfully; (iii) a declaration that ACAS in refusing or failing to investigate and/or report on the recognition issue on the ground that the issue was the subject of a High Court action between the TUC and EMA concerning the application of the Bridlington Agreement was acting in breach of its statutory duties and unlawfully; (iv) a declaration that ACAS in refusing and/or failing to investigate or report on the recognition issue on the sole ground that the issue had been the subject-matter of a complaint to the TUC and that a disputes committee of the TUC had issued an award thereon was acting in breach of its statutory duties and unlawfully; and (v) a declaration that ACAS was bound in pursuance of its statutory duties under s 12 of the Act of 1975 to investigate or report on the issue which had been referred to it. By notice of motion dated 10th February 1978 EMA applied for declarations in the same terms as those in the writ. On 3rd March 1978 the United Kingdom Association of Professional Engineers ('UKAPE') was joined as second defendant to the proceedings by leave of Templeman J. The parties agreed that the motion should be treated as the trial of the action. On 7th April 1978 Oliver J dismissed the motion. EMA appealed. The facts are set out in the judgment of Lord Denning MR.

Simon Goldblatt QC and *Peter C L Clark* for EMA.
Henry Brooke for ACAS.
Mr C K Hickling, deputy general secretary, for UKAPE.

LORD DENNING MR. In the engineering industry there has for many years been a conflict between the rival unions. In particular between the lower grades of workers (such as manual workers) on the one hand, and the higher grades of professional men (such as university graduates) on the other hand. The lower grades of workers are represented by TASS which is a subsidiary section of a big union (the Amalgamated Union of Engineering Workers). The higher grades of professional men are represented by two independent unions. One of them is called the Engineers' and Managers' Association (EMA). The other is the United Kingdom Association of Professional Engineers (UKAPE). Some professional men belong to EMA. Others belong to UKAPE. Others belong to no union at all. But there is this significant difference. EMA is affiliated to the big organisation of trade unions called the Trades Union Congress (TUC). Whereas UKAPE is not so affiliated. This difference looms large in the present case.

This conflict has led to many battles for power. Recently there was a battle about a factory at Bedford where they manufacture steam turbines. UKAPE sought to obtain recognition for the purpose of collective bargaining. This was vigorously opposed by TASS and its associates. The issue was referred to the Advisory Conciliation and Arbitration Service (ACAS). They refused to recommend recognition. One of the reasons was because ACAS feared that TASS would use its industrial 'muscle' if UKAPE were recognised. This court held that the report of ACAS was invalid[1]. It is under appeal to the House of Lords.

This time it is a battle about a factory at Whetstone near Leicester where the General Electric Company manufacture reactor equipment. Most of the professional engineers desire to be recognised for the purpose of collective bargaining. Either by EMA or UKAPE but not by TASS. This is vigorously opposed by TASS. Again TASS want all the higher grade professional men to join TASS and to exclude EMA and UKAPE altogether. The issues have been referred to ACAS. But everything has become bogged down because ACAS have been marking time. The professional engineers have become very restive about the delay. They have come to the courts asking for a declaration that ACAS should get on with their job. In particular they ask that ACAS should hold a ballot of the professional engineers so as to ascertain their opinions.

But this case differs from all other cases hitherto because there is here another body which claims to have jurisdiction over the dispute. It is the disputes committee of the TUC. This is a domestic body which has no statutory authority whatever. It arose out of a congress of the TUC held at Bridlington as far back as 1939, long before ACAS was thought of. That congress was concerned about disputes between unions which were affiliated to the TUC. It enunciated eight principles. These were to be regarded as morally binding on affiliated unions, but not legally binding. It made regulations to govern the procedure for resolving disputes between unions. In particular they were to be referred to a disputes committee which could give directions to an affiliated union. If those directions were disobeyed, the affiliated union could be suspended or even expelled from membership of the TUC.

The situation at Whetstone

In 1976 at Whetstone the professional men in the higher grades numbered about 300. Out of these some 113, that is more than one-third of them, were members of EMA; some 91, that is nearly one-third, belonged to no union at all. The remaining one-third were about equally divided, some 49 to UKAPE and 40 to TASS. Many of these professional men were anxious to be represented for the purpose of collective bargaining with their employers on such matters as their salaries and conditions of service. The first move was made by UKAPE. On 9th July 1976 they applied to ACAS for recognition for the purpose of collective bargaining with the employers, GEC. This application got held up for a time for one reason or another.

Meanwhile EMA also sought recognition from the employers for the purpose of collective bargaining. In aid of it EMA started a recruiting campaign so as to increase their membership at Whetstone. They already had over 100 out of 300 in the higher grades. They tried to recruit new members from among the 90 or more who had not joined any union at all. TASS strongly objected to this. They wanted to get all the higher grades within their own sheep-fold.

Seeing that EMA were affiliated to the TUC, TASS at the end of 1976 complained to the TUC. They appointed a disputes committee under the terms of the Bridlington congress. On 16th March 1977 this committee made an award in favour of TASS. It found that EMA had infringed the Bridlington principles by recruiting at Whetstone. It awarded that EMA should cease recruiting among the professional engineers. It said that the existing EMA members (over 100 of them) should join TASS. It awarded that EMA should not proceed with its claim for recognition. In short the disputes committee awarded that EMA and its members should be ousted from the Whetstone factory altogether and be replaced by TASS.

EMA challenge the award

This award was a body blow to EMA. They protested at once. They claimed that the

---

1   *United Kingdom Association of Professional Engineers v Advisory, Conciliation and Arbitration Service* [1979] 2 All ER 478, [1979] 1 WLR 570

award was a nullity and void. There was, however, nothing in the TUC rules which
a enabled EMA to appeal against the award. So on 25th April 1977 their secretary wrote
to Mr Len Murray, the General Secretary of the TUC, and said that the award was
perverse. He put their case so forcibly that I would quote it:

> 'I am bound to advise you that my Association can see no way in which it can be
> held to be morally bound by an Award which is so flagrantly at variance with the
> principles which should determine the Award, and so contrary to the evidence
b > which was submitted.
>
> 'Further, if my Association were to comply with the Award it would effectively
> deprive all our members in the engineering industry of their right to representa-
> tion—indeed of their right even to seek recognition. For the tens of thousands of
> staff working at broadly professional and managerial levels in the engineering
> industry who are not members of any union, and therefore quite unrepresented,
c > implementation of the Award would imply in general that they are to be denied the
> opportunity to choose freely even as between affiliated unions, and specifically that
> they are not to be allowed to choose the one affiliated union—my own Association—
> which exists to represent these levels of staff in particular.'

d *EMA apply to ACAS*
Getting no satisfaction from Mr Murray, EMA threw down the gauntlet. In defiance
of the award, they took advantage of the new statute. They made an application to ACAS
for the reference of a recognition issue under s 11 of the Employment Protection Act
1975. It was made on 27th April 1977.
On getting this application, ACAS had to consider seriously the position at
e Whetstone. In particular they had already received an application by UKAPE for
recognition there. It was unlikely that both unions would be recommended. If
recognition were to be afforded to the professional men, it would have to be either
UKAPE or EMA—one or the other—or both jointly. ACAS seemed to be uncertain
what to do. They were faced with the award by the disputes committee of the TUC. The
delay was such that on 16th June 1977 EMA went to their solicitors and threatened
f proceedings against ACAS. Further pressure was brought to bear by the decision of this
court in the *Grunwick* case[1]. It was there declared that the duty imposed on ACAS was
mandatory and not directory.
Under these pressures ACAS got on with their job. They prepared a questionnaire for
submission to the professional men at Whetstone and got it agreed. This was followed
on 20th September 1977 by a meeting of the council of ACAS at which they—

g > 'considered a number of representations with regard to the s. 11 applications
> made by UKAPE and EMA. Its decision was that ACAS had no alternative but to
> exercise its statutory duty to proceed with the enquiry at GEC REL, and the Council
> also agreed the form of questionnaire to be used.'

The agreed form of questionnaire
h The agreed form of questionnaire has assumed such importance that I think it would
be useful to set it out. Each employee was asked:

> '1. What is your present job title?
> '2. In what category are you employed?
> '3. At which location are you employed?
> '4. In which department are you employed?
j > '5. Are you a member of a trade union—if so, which one?

---

1 *Grunwick Processing Laboratories Ltd v Advisory, Conciliation and Arbitration Service* [1978] 1 All ER
338, [1978] AC 655

a

United Kingdom Association of
  Professional Engineers   UKAPE

Engineers' and Managers' Association   EMA

Association of Scientific Technical
  and Managerial Staffs   ASTMS

(AUEW) Technical Administrative and
  Supervisory Section   TASS

b

*Another trade union

Not a member

*If you have ticked 'Another trade union' please write its name here

'6. Do you wish to have your pay and conditions of employment determined by collective bargaining, that is by negotiations between the company and a trade union acting on your behalf?   Yes *c*

No
Don't know

'7. Which trade union, if any, do you wish to represent you in negotiations with the company about pay and conditions of employment?

d

United Kingdom Association of
  Professional Engineers   UKAPE

Engineers' and Managers' Association   EMA

Association of Scientific Technical
  and Managerial Staffs   ASTMS

(AUEW) Technical Administrative and
  Supervisory Section   TASS

e

*Another union

No trade union

Don't know

*If you have ticked 'Another union', please state its name here   *f*

'8. Are there any further comments you would like to make about employee representation in GEC (REL)?'

I pause here to say that UKAPE would have liked a further question: '7A. If you cannot have your first choice, what would be your second choice?' The reason for this further question was because UKAPE anticipated that the decision of the disputes committee might prevail with the result that EMA would withdraw from the Whetstone site. In *g* that event the professional engineers would only have this choice before them: either to become members of TASS or to become members of UKAPE or to be unrepresented. Faced with that choice, UKAPE believed that most of them would choose to belong to UKAPE rather than TASS.

In order to press their claim to this further question, UKAPE at one time contemplated bringing an action against ACAS; and later on have been joined as parties to these *h* proceedings. On their behalf Mr Hickling has asked us to allow that further question to be asked.

The electoral reform ballot

Whilst all this was under discussion EMA felt that they ought themselves to test the opinion of all the professional engineers at Whetstone. They engaged the Electoral *j* Reform Society to hold a secret ballot. The relevant questions were as follows:

'Which Trade Union, if any, would you be prepared to join?
'If you had the deciding of which one Union should be recognized, what would be your order of preference?'

The result was given on 15th October 1977:

'Number of workers balloted   304
Number of responses   225 (75%)

Name of trade union	Would join if recognized		First choice	
ASTMS	12	(5%)	9	(4%)
EMA	168	(75%)	137	(67%)
TASS	25	(11%)	28	(14%)
UKAPE	62	(28%)	30	(15%)
No Union	21	(9%)	—	— '

That ballot showed an overwhelming majority for EMA. It seems pretty clear that most of those who were not already members of EMA would join if it it were recognised. So if ACAS had issued a questionnaire, there is little doubt that EMA would have won handsomely; and it would be difficult for ACAS to refuse to recommend EMA for recognition.

The writ against the TUC

Now I come to an event which led to the questionnaire being postponed indefinitely. On 13th October 1977 EMA issued a writ against the TUC claiming that the award of the disputes committee was invalid; and, in particular, that part of the award which said that EMA should not proceed with its claim for recognition was invalid by reason of s 118(1) of the Employment Protection Act 1975 or contrary to public policy.

In issuing this writ, EMA were on strong ground. Section 118(1) of the Employment Protection Act 1975 provides:

'... any provision in an agreement ... shall be void in so far as it purports—(a) to exclude or limit the operation of any provision of this Act; or (b) to preclude any person from ... making any reference, claim, complaint or application under this Act to [ACAS].'

Supported by that section, EMA moved for an injunction against the TUC, but arrangements were made by consent whereby pending trial EMA indicated that they would not try to recruit new members; and the TUC agreed not to enforce the award of the disputes committee. Directions were given for pleadings to be delivered speedily with a view to an early trial. These directions were not fulfilled by either side. The statement of claim took three months instead of seven days. The defence took two months instead of seven days. Further particulars were asked by both sides. Discovery is a big job. The trial has been fixed, I believe, for March 1980 and is expected to last for 14 days. There may well be an appeal. So it may take two or three years before a decision is come to.

The effect on ACAS

The council of ACAS thought that the issue of the writ was of decisive importance. It decided not to proceed with the reference for recognition. It issued a press notice on 14th December 1977:

'At its meeting today the Council of ACAS reconsidered its position with regard to proceedings on the references for trade union recognition concerning the United Kingdom Association of Professional Engineers (UKAPE), the Engineers' and Managers' Association (EMA) and GEC Reactor Equipment Limited (Whetstone).

'The Council decided that it would not proceed, for the time being, with its enquiries on those references. In reaching its decision, it took particular account of the implications of the writ which has been served on the TUC by EMA, one of the applicant unions. This writ which is still outstanding seeks to challenge an award by a TUC Disputes Committee in respect of a recognition and recruitment issue concerning the group of employees who are the subject of the EMA reference.'

This decision caused much dismay among the professional men at Whetstone. In
December 1977 they drew up a petition which was signed by over 200 out of the 300 of *a*
them and presented it to the chairman of ACAS. It said:

> 'The engineering staff at GEC-REL are concerned at the excessive delays which
> have been incurred in dealing with these references, since throughout these delays
> they are being denied the benefits of collective bargaining which Parliament
> intended should be available to them with the setting-up of the Service. As far as
> these staff are concerned the second round of pay restraint expires in March 1978 *b*
> and time is therefore very short for meaningful negotiations to take place with the
> Company before the subsequent policy becomes established . . . We wish the Service
> to proceed with its enquiry and questionnaire (the format of this latter having been
> circulated in final draft form to interested parties in September 1977) and to make
> a recommendation or otherwise in line with its findings as required by the
> provisions of the Employment Protection Act.'   *c*

The writ against ACAS

Despite this letter and another, ACAS remained adamant. So on 25th January 1978
EMA issued a writ against ACAS asking for a declaration that ACAS had failed to carry
out its statutory duties and was bound to do so. It followed this up by a motion to the
court. On 3rd March 1978 Templeman J allowed UKAPE to be joined as a party. The *d*
parties agreed that the motion should be treated as the trial of the action. On 7th April
1978 Oliver J held that ACAS had a discretion to postpone the investigation and that it
had not been wrongly exercised. EMA appeal to this court.

The law

The legal questions in this case turn on these few words in s 14(1) of the Employment *e*
Protection Act 1975:

> 'In the course of its inquiries into a recognition issue . . . [ACAS] shall ascertain the
> opinions of workers to whom the issue relates by any means it thinks fit . . .'

The two questions of law are: (1) Has ACAS a discretion to defer ascertaining the opinions
of workers? (2) If so, did it have reasonable grounds for deferring it in the present case? *f*

As to the first question, it is clearly established that the requirement (to ascertain the
opinions of workers) is mandatory and not directory. It is not to be cut down by
introducing such words as 'so far as reasonably practicable': see *Grunwick Processing
Laboratories Ltd v Advisory, Conciliation and Arbitration Service*[1] per Lord Diplock and Lord
Salmon. Nor is it to be qualified by introducing such words as 'at such times as it thinks
appropriate', for that too would give too wide a discretion to ACAS. It would enable it *g*
to postpone indefinitely the determination of the issue, contrary to the opinions of the
workers themselves. The discretion is only as to the 'means' to be employed, but not as
to the duty itself. The only implication that can properly be made in the statute is that
the requirement must be fulfilled 'within a reasonable time', similar to the implication
which is made in a contract when no time is expressed for the performance of an
obligation: see *Hick v Raymond & Reid*[2] per Lord Watson. What is a reasonable time *h*
depends, of course, on all the circumstances of the case. It may take a few weeks to draw
up a questionnaire, or to get together a meeting, or use other 'means' of ascertaining the
opinion of the workers. But so long as a fair questionnaire can be drawn up, or opinions
fairly ascertained in some other way, I think ACAS is bound to ascertain the opinions of
workers without delay. It cannot postpone its task simply because it thinks that the
opinions, when ascertained, will be inconclusive or unreliable or uninformed or *j*
misleading or of little help in seeing whether to recommend recognition. If afterwards

1   [1978] 1 All ER 338 at 361, 368, [1978] AC 655 at 691, 699
2   [1893] AC 22 at 32, [1891–4] All ER Rep 491 at 495

a the opinions should be found to be suffering from such defects, ACAS can point them out in their report, but it is not a ground for deferring or delaying their duty of ascertaining the opinions of workers. Nor should ACAS delay overlong on agreement on a questionnaire. If those concerned do not agree, ACAS must take the responsibility themselves of deciding on the questions. So long as it does so fairly, no court will interfere with the way in which the questions are framed: see the recent case of *National Employers Life Assurance Co Ltd v Advisory, Conciliation and Arbitration Service and*
b *Association of Scientific, Technical and Managerial Staffs*[1] decided by Browne-Wilkinson J on 23rd February 1979 in which he explained *Powley's case*[2] as being quite exceptional.

The reasons of ACAS for deferring its enquiries
      It is clear from the evidence that ACAS decided to postpone its enquiries until the pending action of *Engineers' and Managers' Association v Trades Union Congress* was decided. These are some significant passages from the affidavit of Mr Norcross (a director
c of ACAS):
            'The existence of this legal challenge was the most potent factor in influencing the Council of ACAS to defer its inquiries until the validity of the award [of the Disputes Committee] was clarified in the Courts or the writ withdrawn . . .
            'ACAS would like to proceed with the conduct of the references but considers that it would be untimely to do so in the light of the legal action between the EMA and
d   the TUC which is still pending.'
      And before us counsel for ACAS said that his instructions were that ACAS were not going to proceed with their enquiries until the validity of the award was determined.
      The reason for this decision was this: if the award of the disputes committee was *valid*, it would mean that EMA would have to withdraw altogether from the Whetstone plant or be faced with expulsion from the TUC. Alternatively, if the award was *invalid*, EMA
e would be able to recruit new members at Whetstone and remain affiliated to the TUC. In the face of these uncertainties, ACAS thought that the professional men at Whetstone would not be able to form a sound judgment or give suitable answers to a questionnaire. On that account, ACAS thought that the enquiry should be deferred until the uncertainty was resolved. In the words of Mr Norcross, ACAS postponed its duty of ascertaining the opinion of the workers until such time 'as it judges that it is
f likely to obtain a reliable response and that the options available to the workers are clearly defined'.
      In placing such reliance on the award of the disputes committee, ACAS relied on the Code of Practice[3] which says in para 85:
            'Responsibility for avoiding disputes between trade unions about recognition lies principally with the unions themselves and, in the case of affiliated unions, with the
g   Trades Union Congress. Unions concerned should make full use of the available procedures.'
      That Code of Practice was issued long before ACAS came into being. It cannot prevail over the statutory duty of ACAS.
      If I may hazard a guess, however, if the award was held to be valid, ACAS would be
h likely to report in favour of its being implemented, or at any rate recommend against recognition for EMA: whereas, if the award was held to be invalid, ACAS would be likely to report in favour of EMA because of the overwhelming support given by the majority of the workers involved.
      In short, ACAS wanted to know whether the award of the disputes committee was valid or invalid because their report would be largely influenced by the outcome. But
j this seems to me no reason for not ascertaining the opinion of the workers themselves.

1   (23rd February 1979) unreported
2   *Powley v Advisory, Conciliation and Arbitration Service* [1978] ICR 123.
3   Ie the Code of Practice issued by the Secretary of State under the Industrial Relations Act 1971, s 3, and having effect by virtue of the Employment Protection Act 1975, ss 6, 125(2), Sch 17, para 4

Are those reasons reasonable?

If the legal action between EMA and the TUC could have been determined quickly, *a* one way or the other, I think it might well have been useful for ACAS to postpone its enquiry for a short time, because the workers would have made their choice on full information. For instance, if EMA had been expelled from the TUC or was likely to be, some of the professional men might have voted for UKAPE instead of EMA. But, as soon as it appeared that the legal action would take a considerable time to resolve, then I think it was the imperative duty of ACAS to get on with the enquiry; for the plain fact is that *b* these 300 professional men would be left unrepresented at the bargaining table until the issue was resolved. No doubt, pending the litigation, the future of EMA would remain uncertain. But it has been uncertain ever since March 1977 when the disputes committee made its award. That award was challenged immediately by EMA who contended that it was null and void. Even so, ACAS was able to produce a questionnaire which would serve to ascertain the opinion of the workers. The litigation only heightened the *c* uncertainty. It did not create it. Despite the uncertainty, I think it was the bounden duty of ACAS to get on with the enquiry, in justice to the workers, who desired urgently to be represented at the bargaining table by a union of their choice, and not by TASS. The framing of the questionnaire was essentially a matter for ACAS, but I should have thought that the further question desired by UKAPE was quite reasonable and might have been included with advantage. After all these professional men are endowed with *d* considerable intelligence, and may safely be assumed to be able to weigh up the contingencies ahead; especially if they were explained, as they could well be, at a public meeting or a conference convened by ACAS.

Counsel for ACAS urged us to consider this case as at December 1977 when ACAS decided to defer its enquiries 'for the time being' or in February 1978 when arrangements were made for the early trial of the pending action of *Engineers' and Managers' Association* *e* *v Trades Union Congress*. At that time it was anticipated that the litigation would be speedily concluded. The decision of ACAS was right, he said, at that time. It should not be reversed, he said, at this time simply because it now appears that the litigation will not be determined for two or three years. I cannot accede to that argument. It is well settled that on an appeal this court is entitled and ought to rehear the case *as at the time of rehearing*; and ought to give such judgment as ought to be given if the case came *at that* *f* *time* before the court of first instance: see *Attorney-General v Birmingham, Tame and Rea District Drainage Board*[1], *Curwen v James*[2], *Murphy v Stone Wallwork (Charlton) Ltd*[3]. So we have to decide the case as at to-day's date, 14th May 1979.

Conclusion

The arguments presented to us in this case have a parallel to those in the *Grunwick* *g* case[4]. We have heard arguments on behalf of EMA, UKAPE and ACAS. But in the midst of it all the persons who are most concerned of all, the 300 professional men at Whetstone, have not been heard at all. They have been caught in the cross-fire between TASS, EMA and UKAPE. The evidence in this case shows that most of them urgently desire to be represented by some union or other for the purpose of collective bargaining. Every one of them has a right which is recognised by the European Court *h* of Human Rights 'to form and to join trade unions for the protection of their interests'. Yet they are being hindered or prevented from exercising this right by the failure of ACAS to ascertain their opinions—as ACAS is by statute enjoined to do. I am tempted to remind ACAS of the words of Magna Carta: 'To none will we sell, to no one will we delay or deny right or justice'. Let them get on with their appointed task—in justice to the workers themselves.

I would allow this appeal and declare that ACAS are bound to get on with their duties. *j*

1   [1912] AC 788 at 801–802, [1911–13] All ER Rep 926 at 939
2   [1963] 2 All ER 619, [1963] 1 WLR 748
3   [1969] 2 All ER 949, [1969] 1 WLR 1023
4   [1978] 1 All ER 338, [1978] AC 655

a   **LAWTON LJ.** The plaintiffs allege in this appeal that the first defendant, ACAS, has refused or failed to investigate and to report on a recognition issue referred to it pursuant to s 11 of the Employment Protection Act 1975. They ask for a declaration that ACAS is bound by statute to investigate and report on that issue in pursuance of its statutory duty under s 12 of that Act.

     ACAS accepts that it is under a statutory duty to investigate and report, but it has
b   submitted that in the circumstances of this case it was entitled to postpone the enquiries which have to be made before a report can be prepared because of the uncertainties arising from the fact that the plaintiffs on 13th October 1977 issued a writ against the TUC asking for a declaration that an award made by the disputes committee of that body was ultra vires and void.

     This submission involves answering two questions. First, has ACAS any discretion to
c   hold up enquiries. Secondly, if it has, whether it was entitled to do so as from 14th December 1977 and to go on doing so until the final determination of the issues arising between the plaintiffs and the TUC.

     When a recognition issue is referred to ACAS under s 11 of the 1975 Act, s 12 provides that it must deal with it as best it can. When doing so, it 'shall consult all parties who it considers will be affected by the outcome of the reference and shall make such inquiries
d   as it thinks fit'. Enquiries have to be made, but how they are to be made is for ACAS to decide. Making a decision about methods of enquiry will always call for thought and may take time. Even when a decision has been made circumstances may change so as to call for a change of method. Changing the method may require more time. It follows, in my judgment, that the discretion given to ACAS as to what method it uses carries with it some discretion as to when to start enquiries and, if there is a change of circumstances
e   whilst enquiries are being made, a discretion to stop what was being done and to give thought to new ways of making enquiries. This discretion, however, must be limited by what is reasonable. It cannot be used to avoid doing what the Act says shall be done.

     When on 27th April 1977 the plaintiffs referred the recognition issue which is the subject-matter of this appeal, ACAS was faced with a most difficult problem. The disputes committee of the TUC had made an award which manifested disapproval of the
f   plaintiffs' recruiting activities in areas in which a powerful union, TASS, had hopes, largely unfulfilled in the past, of recruiting engineers with professional qualifications. The plaintiffs might defy the TUC, which could, and probably would, lead to their expulsion from that body. TUC disapproval, however, was by itself no good reason in law for refusing the plaintiffs recognition for the purpose of collective bargaining with the employers at the GEC reactor plant at Whetstone; but it was a factor which ACAS was
g   entitled to take into consideration. There was ample evidence that many professionally qualified engineers at that plant, probably most of them, did not want to belong to TASS, whose membership was mostly made up of draughtsmen and technicians. There were two unions which sought the membership of these engineers, the plaintiffs, who were affiliated to the TUC but who might be expelled if they disregarded the disputes committee's award, and a small union known as UKAPE who were not so affiliated.
h   ACAS knew that unions affiliated to the TUC tended to have a more powerful voice in negotiations with employers and with the Government than those which were not. It followed that there was a possibility that some of the professional engineers at the GEC plant who wanted to join the plaintiffs rather than TASS or UKAPE might change their minds if the plaintiffs were expelled from the TUC. How to cope with this factor of uncertainty was one of the problems with which ACAS had to deal once the plaintiffs had
j   made their reference. ACAS appreciated that under the Act it had to do its best to make the necessary enquiries. It prepared a questionnaire to be answered by the professional engineers at the GEC plant. It was sent to the interested unions for comment and agreement. The plaintiffs were satisfied with it: UKAPE were not. Before it was sent out to be answered the plaintiffs issued a writ against the TUC. On 15th December 1977 ACAS wrote to the plaintiffs as follows:

'The Council [that is, the Council of ACAS] met again on 14th December and
... decided that, for the time being, it would not be able to proceed with its
enquiries with regard to the EMA reference at GEC REL. In reaching its decision,
it took particular account of the outstanding writ served by the EMA on the TUC
in respect of the award made by the TUC Disputes Committee.'

Since 14th December 1977 ACAS has done nothing more to examine the recognition
issue referred to it. It has taken no notice of the petition of some 200 professional
engineers at the GEC plant, which was put before it in January 1978 requesting that
enquiries should be made. Counsel on behalf of ACAS told us that it does not intend to
make any enquiries, unless this court adjudges otherwise, until the litigation between
the plaintiffs and the TUC is concluded.

It justifies its decision on two connected grounds: first, that the issues raised by the
writ have introduced such uncertainties into the recognition issue that no useful purpose
would be served by making enquiries until these uncertainties have been cleared up;
and, secondly, that the expert advice available to ACAS and its own experience indicates
that the uncertainties cannot be resolved either by a revised questionnaire or by any other
way of ascertaining the opinions of the professional engineers.

The trial judge was persuaded that the existence of such uncertainties as there were
justified ACAS in deciding as it did. The decision was within the ambit of its
discretion. He considered the problem as it was at the date when the decision was made,
that is on 14th December 1977, and not when the case was before him. In looking back
to December 1977 he was, in my judgment, taking too narrow a view of the case. At all
material times the plaintiffs have been complaining not only about what ACAS refused
to do on 14th December 1977 but about its failure to discharge its statutory duties.
Failure to discharge statutory duties is a continuing wrong which a court seised of such
an issue is entitled to deal with as at the date of hearing, as is shown by the cases to which
Lord Denning MR has referred.

In December 1977 the recognition issue had been complicated by the plaintiffs' issue
of a writ against the TUC. In my judgment ACAS was entitled to halt its enquiries whilst
it considered whether new methods of enquiry would be necessary and what they should
be. What it was not entitled to do was to adjourn the enquiries indefinitely. It claims
not to have done so. Counsel for ACAS submitted that what it anticipated in December
1977 was that the litigation initiated by the writ would be concluded within about a
year. This was thought to be a reasonable time for a halt in enquiries. Anyway, the
plaintiffs themselves were at fault in not pressing on with the litigation against the TUC.
I do not agree that a halt as long as ACAS contemplated was reasonable. As I have already
said, such discretion as ACAS had to halt enquiries was limited and should have been
used to reconsider methods of enquiry and, if necessary, to apply any new methods
which might be decided on. If in any recognition case ACAS finds the going getting
rough, as it did in this case when the TUC became closely involved, it must struggle on.
It cannot become a spectator, looking on from the comfort and security of the equivalent
of winter quarters—and not for one winter but two and probably three. By the date of
the issue of the writ in this case, namely 25th January 1978, ACAS probably had had
enough time to decide what change of method, if any, was required to deal with the
complication brought about by the issue of the writ in the TUC action. In my judgment,
the complication was minor anyway. If the plaintiffs succeeded in their action against
the TUC, the disputes committee's award would be declared void. There would be no
immediate risk of the plaintiffs being expelled from the TUC and their dispute with
TASS might have to go before the disputes committee again. The problem for ACAS
would still have been what it was before the issue of the writ, namely how many of the
professional engineers at the GEC plant wanted to belong to the plaintiff union and
whether they would still want to do so if at any time the plaintiffs were expelled from the
TUC and, if they were so expelled, which union would they want to join. Counsel for
ACAS submitted that putting questions of this kind to those who were involved would

produce unreliable answers which would be useless for reporting purposes. I do not

a agree. In any event, as Lord Denning MR has said, if the results of enquiries were unreliable, this could have been dealt with in the report.

In my judgment ACAS's approach to the problem which it has to solve was wrong. It proceeded on the assumption that it was entitled to wait until the difficulties, which lacked substance anyway, had disappeared. In so waiting, it erred in law.

I would allow the appeal.

b

CUMMING-BRUCE LJ. I have found the problems raised by this appeal more difficult to resolve than Lord Denning MR and Lawton LJ. The difficulty of which I have been most conscious is this, that the proceedings below were primarily concerned with the validity or otherwise of a decision of ACAS dated 14th December 1977 when they decided in the circumstances then prevailing not to proceed to the stage of enquiry.

c The judgment of the judge was given on 7th April 1978; and the judge was clearly addressing his mind largely to the question whether the way in which ACAS had exercised its discretion on 14th December 1977 had been shown to be clearly wrong; and, for the reasons given by the judge, he decided that that onus of proof had not been discharged and that in the circumstances prevailing on 14th December 1977 it was not clearly shown that ACAS was then wrong in holding its hand before proceeding to

d enquiry.

As I read the judgment of the judge, he was also of the view by implication that by April 1978 it was still too early to hold that the events between December 1977 and April 1978 had been such as to make it clearly wrong for ACAS to continue to adopt the stance that it was not immediately proceeding to enquiry.

However, these proceedings in this court, which appear on the face of the notice of

e appeal to challenge the correctness of the trial judge's decision, did not come on for hearing and decision here until May 1979; and much has happened since. If one compares the situation at the time when the judge was deciding the issues before him, although the plaintiffs had been dilatory in the TUC proceedings, yet there was still a prospect that the first instance determination of the proceedings between the plaintiffs and the TUC would happen within a matter of months. Today, however, the situation

f is wholly different. We are told that it is common ground that the most probable date for the trial of the proceedings between the plaintiffs and the TUC is March 1980. On the one hand, counsel for ACAS has submitted that there are indications that the plaintiffs in those proceedings are going as slowly as they can. On the other hand, on behalf of the plaintiffs, it has been submitted that the plaintiffs have been having trouble with discovery against the TUC. We have no information to enable this court to judge

g the validity of either points of view on those matters.

But on any view, if the first instance trial takes place in March 1980, even assuming (which is a very big assumption) that there is no appeal to this court, there then remains before finality on the question of the affiliation of the plaintiffs with the TUC the many steps to be taken—negotiations, consideration by the TUC Council, and probably by the TUC Congress because the jurisdiction of the TUC Council in this regard is extremely

h limited. So that now it does not look as if there is any prospect of the uncertainty arising from the decision of the plaintiffs to claim a declaration against the TUC being resolved certainly for another 18 months, and I would have thought probably for a good deal longer.

So the effect of the decision taken by ACAS in December 1977 is now seen in this court to involve necessarily in the way in which events have proceeded a decision to keep the

j applications for recognition both by EMA and by UKAPE on ice for a period not less than about three years from the date of the applications before even proceeding to enquire of the opinion of workers. I cannot accept that such a long postponement can be regarded as a proper exercise of the undoubted discretion vested in ACAS to determine its manner of proceeding and how to set about finding out the opinion of workers and its undoubted discretion to give itself reasonable time before attempting to proceed to enquiry.

Therefore, although in my view on the facts before him the judge was right in taking the view that it had not then been shown that the discretion vested in ACAS had been *a* wrongly exercised, in my view it is not only open to this court but it is the duty of this court to declare that the situation is now different and—as counsel for ACAS states that it is not the intention of ACAS to proceed to enquiry stage until the uncertainties flowing from the litigation and the dispute between EMA and the TUC have been finally resolved—the interval of time involved and the delay which ACAS has now determined shall necessarily be involved in its course of conduct is shown to be a delay which *b* constitutes a manner of exercising its discretion which is outside the manner of exercising discretion contemplated by the statute.

For those reasons I agree with the order proposed by Lord Denning MR and Lawton LJ.

Appeal allowed. Declaration that ACAS is bound in pursuance of its statutory duties under s 12 *c* *of the Employment Protection Act 1975 to investigate or report on the issue which had been referred to it. Leave to appeal to the House of Lords refused.*

Solicitors: *Lawford & Co* (for EMA); *Treasury Solicitor.*

Sumra Green   Barrister. *d*

a # Zainal bin Hashim v Government of Malaysia

PRIVY COUNCIL

LORD WILBERFORCE, VISCOUNT DILHORNE, LORD EDMUND-DAVIES, LORD RUSSELL OF KILLOWEN
AND LORD KEITH OF KINKEL

30th APRIL, 1st MAY, 19th JULY 1979

b *Statute – Retrospective operation – Pending proceedings – Alteration of law after judgment and before appeal – Dismissal of police constable by chief police officer – Dismissal held to be in contravention of statute – Amendment of statute after judgment and before appeal – Amendment validating dismissal of constables by chief police officers – Whether amendment affecting pending proceedings – Whether dismissal of constable validated retrospectively by amendment – Federal Constitution of Malaysia, art 135(1) proviso.*

c On 16th December 1971 the appellant, a police constable in the Malaysian police force, was convicted of an offence under the Malaysian Penal Code. Article 135(1)[a] of the Federal Constitution of Malaysia provided that no member of the police force should be dismissed by an authority subordinate to that which at the time of the dismissal had power to appoint a member of that service of equal rank. The Malaysian Police Force Commission, under power conferred on it by the Constitution, delegated to chief police
d officers the power to dismiss constables but not the power to appoint them. On 20th January 1972 a chief police officer made an order dismissing the appellant from the police force with effect from the date of his conviction. The appellant brought an action against the Malaysian government claiming a declaration that his dismissal was void and inoperative and an order for an account to be taken of the salary and emoluments due to him from the date of his dismissal. On 21st March 1975 the trial judge gave judgment
e in favour of the appellant on the ground that his dismissal contravened art 135(1) because the chief police officer had no power to appoint constables. On 27th August 1976 art 135(1) was amended by adding a proviso[b] thereto 'that this Clause shall not apply to a case where a member of [the police force] is dismissed . . . by an authority in pursuance of a power delegated to it by [the Police Force Commission], and this proviso shall be deemed to have been an integral part of this Clause as from [31st August 1957]'. The Malaysian
f government, relying on the amendment, appealed against the judge's decision to the Federal Court which allowed the appeal on the ground that the proviso operated to validate the appellant's dismissal and that he was consequently not entitled to the pay and emoluments which would otherwise have been due to him. The appellant appealed to the Judicial Committee of the Privy Council contending that the amendment could not apply as his action had been commenced and judgment given on his claim before the
g amendment came into force.

Held – (i) For pending actions to be affected by retrospective legislation the enactment did not have to state expressly that it applied to such actions but its language had to be such that the only possible conclusion was that the legislature had intended it to so apply (see p 245 c, post); dictum of Evershed MR in *Hutchinson v Jauncey* [1950] 1 All ER at 168
h applied; dictum of Jessel MR in *Re Joseph Suche & Co Ltd* (1875) 1 Ch D at 50 doubted.

(ii) On the true construction of the amendment to art 135(1) of the Constitution, no actions commenced after 31st August 1957, whether proceeding or not commenced when the amendment was made, could succeed on the ground that the power to dismiss had not been exercised by someone with power to appoint. It followed that as a result of the amendment the appellant had been deprived of his right to maintain that his
j dismissal was invalid owing to the omission to delegate to chief police officers the power to appoint constables. Accordingly the appeal would be dismissed (see p 245 f to p 246 a and g, post).

---

a   Article 135(1), so far as material, is set out at p 243 d, post
b   The proviso is set out at p 243 h, post

Notes
For the retrospective effect of statutes generally, see 30 Halsbury's Laws (3rd Edn) 423–428, paras 643–648, and for cases on the subject, see 44 Digest (Repl) 284–287,1132–1167, 294–300, 1236–1300.

Cases referred to in judgment
Attorney-General v Vernazza [1960] 3 All ER 97, [1960] AC 965, [1960] 3 WLR 466, HL, 44 Digest (Repl) 286, *1148*.

Hough v Windus (1884) 12 QBD 224, 53 LJQB 165, 50 LT 312, 1 Morr 1, CA, 44 Digest (Repl) 294, *1240*.

Hutchinson v Jauncey [1950] 1 All ER 165, [1950] 1 KB 574, CA, 44 Digest (Repl) 299, *1293*.

Najar Singh v Government of Malaysia [1976] 1 MLJ 203.

Reid v Reid (1886) 31 Ch D 402, 55 LJ Ch 294, 54 LT 100, CA, 44 Digest (Repl) 284, *1133*.

Suche (Joseph) & Co Ltd, Re (1875) 1 Ch D 48, 45 LJ Ch 12, 33 LT 774, 44 Digest (Repl) 299, *1291*.

Wijesuriya v Amit [1965] 3 All ER 701, [1966] AC 372, [1966] 2 WLR 385, PC, Digest (Cont Vol B) 664, *1688a*.

Young v Adams [1898] AC 469, 67 LJPC 75, 78 LT 506, PC, 44 Digest (Repl) 287, *1167*.

Appeal
Zainal bin Hashim appealed against a judgment of the Federal Court of Malaysia (Suffian LP, Lee Hun Hoe CJ (Borneo) and Wan Suleiman FJ) dated 21st July 1977 allowing an appeal by the respondent, the Malaysian government, against the judgment of Abdul Hamid J in the High Court in Malaya at Kuala Lumpur dated 21st March 1975 granting the appellant a declaration that his dismissal from the Royal Malaysian Police was void and of no effect and that he was still a member of the Royal Malaysian Police, and an order for an account of all salary and emoluments due to him from the date of his purported dismissal, 16th December 1971. The facts are set out in the judgment of the Board.

G T Rajan (advocate and solicitor, Malaysia) for the appellant.
Donald Farquharson QC and *John G C Phillips* for the Malaysian government.

VISCOUNT DILHORNE. The appellant was appointed a police constable in the Royal Malaysian Police Force on 1st March 1962. In 1971 he was charged with an offence under s 353 of the Penal Code of Malaysia. To that charge he pleaded guilty and he was discharged conditionally on his entering into a bond in the sum of $500 for a period of two years. On 22nd December 1971 he received notice by letter dated 20th December that he was suspended from duty with effect from 16th December 1971, the date on which he had pleaded guilty, on account of his conviction on that charge.

On 28th December the chief police officer at Selangor wrote to the appellant saying that he intended to take action to dismiss the appellant from the Royal Malaysian Police on account of his conviction and telling him that he could make any representations with regard thereto in writing within 14 days.

On 30th December the appellant submitted representations and on 20th January 1972 a letter signed by S W Moreira, then deputy chief police officer at Selangor, was sent to him. It contained the following sentence: 'I hereby make an order of "dismissal" with effect from 16.12.71.' The appellant was also told in this letter that he could appeal from this decision within ten days. He did so and submitted written representations to the Inspector-General of Police. On 7th February he was told by letter by the chief police officer that his appeal had been considered by the Inspector-General and dismissed.

On 9th August the appellant started an action against the chief police officer and the government of Malaysia in which he claimed a declaration that his dismissal from the Royal Malaysian Police was void and inoperative and an order that an account be taken of the salary and emoluments due to him from the date of his purported dismissal. Later he discontinued his action against the chief police officer.

In his statement of claim it was alleged that the letter of 20th January dismissing him
a had been signed by S W Moreira 'for and on behalf of the First Defendant', the chief
police officer. It was alleged that the chief police officer had no power to dismiss him and
that his dismissal was contrary to the provisions of the Federal Constitution. It was
asserted that only the Police Force Commission had power to dismiss him and that,
contrary to the requirements of natural justice, he had not had a reasonable opportunity
to defend himself or to make representations with regard to his dismissal.
b   The trial of the action took place in the High Court at Kuala Lumpur before Abdul
Hamid J. The appellant gave evidence and admitted that he had pleaded guilty to the
offence with which he had been charged. He complained that he had not been given an
oral hearing before he was dismissed from the police force. S W Moreira was called as a
witness for the appellant. He said that it was the chief police officer's decision that the
appellant should be dismissed and that the letter of 20th January which he signed was
c written by him for and on behalf of the chief police officer. Despite this evidence and
the allegation in the statement of claim, in the hearing before their Lordships it was
contended that the appellant had been dismissed by S W Moreira and that consequently
his dismissal was invalid. It suffices to say that it is clear beyond all doubt from the
evidence that he was dismissed by the chief police officer.
      Abdul Hamid J gave judgment on 21st March 1975 in favour of the appellant on a
d ground on which, he said, counsel for the appellant had not made any submissions to
him.
      Article 135 (1) of the Federal Constitution provides:

      'No member of any of the services mentioned in paragraphs (b) to (h) of Clause
      (1) of Article 132 [one service mentioned is the police force] shall be dismissed or
      reduced in rank by an authority subordinate to that which, at the time of the
e   dismissal or reduction, has power to appoint a member of that service of equal rank.'

It is obvious that 'authority' in this article must include a person.
      Article 140 of the Constitution provided for the creation of a Police Force Commission
which by art 140(6)(b) had power to delegate its powers and duties 'to any member of the
Commission or the police force'. By an instrument dated 18th August 1971 the
f commission delegated its functions relating to the appointment of constables to the
Inspector-General of Police and its functions relating to the exercise of the power to
award the disciplinary punishment of dismissal to constables to 'a senior police officer of
and above the rank of Senior Assistant Commissioner of Police or a Chief Police Officer'.
      As a chief police officer had no power to appoint constables, dismissal of a constable by
him contravened art 135(1) of the Constitution and it was on this ground that Abdul
g Hamid J found in favour of the appellant.
      The government of Malaysia appealed and in the appeal they sought to rely on an
amendment made to art 135(1) by the Constitution (Amendment) Act which came into
force on 27th August 1976 by the addition to it of the following proviso:

      'And provided further that this Clause shall not apply to a case where a member
      of any of the services mentioned in that Clause is dismissed or reduced in rank by
h   an authority in pursuance of a power delegated to it by a Commission to which this
      Part applies, and this proviso shall be deemed to have been an integral part of this
      Clause as from Merdeka Day[1].'

      The Federal Court, in allowing the government's appeal, held that this proviso operated
to validate the appellant's dismissal. The main question in this appeal is whether they
j were right in so holding.
      At the time he was dismissed, as that was in breach of the Constitution, the appellant
had a right to claim a declaration that he had not been dismissed and that he was entitled
to the pay and emoluments he would have received but for that dismissal. He started

---

1   31st August 1957

proceedings to establish that right. He obtained judgment and but for this amendment of the Constitution, their Lordships think that he would succeed in upholding that judgment.

Now it is contended, as it was in the Federal Court, that his dismissal is validated retrospectively by this amendment and that consequently he is not entitled to the pay and emoluments which otherwise would be due to him.

That the proviso has some retrospective effect cannot be disputed. If the amendment did not cover a case of dismissal wrongful on the instant ground before a declaration had been claimed the reference to Merdeka Day would have no effect at all. In Craies on Statute Law[1] it is said that—

'perhaps no rule of construction is more firmly established than this—that a retrospective operation is not to be given to a statute so as to impair an existing right or obligation otherwise than as regards matter of procedure, unless that effect cannot be avoided without doing violence to the language of the enactment.'

When delivering the judgment of the Board in *Wijesuriya v Amit*[2] Lord Wilberforce said in construing a retrospective Act:

'It must be shown that the enacting words clearly cover the case to which it is sought to apply them. The court will no doubt prefer an interpretation which gives effect to the amending Act, rather than one which denies it any efficacy, but it will not strain the language used, nor will it rewrite or adapt it to cover cases other than those to which it clearly applies.'

It is to be observed that the Board in that case, which was one of an attempted retroactive enactment of a fiscal law, was only able to escape the clear retroactive language by the fact that retroactive effect could not be reconciled with the pre-existing fiscal machinery.

In the present case, in their Lordships' opinion, giving retrospective effect to this amendment made to the Constitution cannot be avoided without doing violence to the language of the amendment, but as Bowen LJ said in *Reid v Reid*[3]:

'. . . you ought not to give a larger retrospective power to a section, even in an Act which is to some extent intended to be retrospective, than you can plainly see the Legislature meant.'

Did the legislature mean by the amendment to the Constitution to go so far as to deprive the appellant of his entitlement to a declaration that his dismissal was void and, consequently, to the pay and emoluments which but for his dismissal he would have received? Recognising that the amendment has a retrospective effect, is it possible and right to draw a distinction between a case where a dismissed constable has such a claim, a case where he has commenced an action to establish his entitlement and a case where he has obtained judgment on the trial of such a claim?

As was said in Craies on Statute Law[4]:

'It is a well "recognised rule that statutes should be interpreted, if possible, so as to respect vested rights"[5] but [quaere 'and'] such a construction should never be adopted if the words are open to another construction.'

And also[6]:

1 7th Edn (1971), p 389
2 [1965] 3 All ER 701 at 703, [1966] AC 372 at 378
3 (1886) 31 Ch D 402 at 409
4 7th Edn (1971), p 398
5 *Hough v Windus* (1884) 12 QBD 224 at 237 per Bowen LJ
6 7th Edn (1971), p 399

a
'Where, however, the necessary intendment of an Act is to affect pending causes of action, the court will give effect to the intention of the legislature even though there is no express reference to pending actions.'

This last citation is based on the observations of Evershed MR in *Hutchinson v Jauncey*[1] where he doubted 'whether the principle ought to be expressed in quite so precise language as Sir George Jessel, M.R., stated it in *Re Joseph Suche & Co., Ltd*.[2]' In that case

b
Jessel MR[3] had said:

'... it is a general rule that when the Legislature alters the rights of parties by taking away or conferring any right of action, its enactments, unless in express terms they apply to pending actions, do not affect them.'

If by his reference to 'express terms' Jessel MR meant that the enactment must state that it applies to pending actions, their Lordships agree with Evershed MR's comment.

c
In their view for pending actions to be affected by retrospective legislation, the language of the enactment must be such that no other conclusion is possible than that that was the intention of the legislature.

On behalf of the appellant reliance was placed on *Young v Adams*[4]. In that case a civil servant in New South Wales brought an action for damages for wrongful dismissal. Five months after he had been dismissed the Public Service Act 1895 was passed. By s 58 it

d
was enacted:

'Nothing in this Act, or in the Civil Service Act of 1884, shall be construed or held to abrogate or restrict the right or power of the Crown as it existed before the passing of the said Civil Service Act, to dispense with the services of any person employed in the Public Service.'

e
Lord Watson[5], delivering the judgment of the Board, said that these words could not—

'be reasonably construed so as to include persons who are not employed in the public service, and who, like the respondent [the plaintiff], had ceased to be so before its power of summary dismissal was given back to the Crown.'

f
The language of s 58 is very different from that of the amendment to the Constitution. That requires art 135(1) to be construed as if from Merdeka Day onwards it had included the proviso added by the amendment. The effect of the amendment was to deprive a constable dismissed for misconduct by a chief police officer, to whom power to dismiss him had been properly delegated, of the right to maintain that his dismissal was invalid owing to the omission to delegate to the chief police officer power to appoint constables. If the appellant had started his action after the operative date of the

g
amendment, their Lordships think that in consequence of the amendment it would have been bound to fail. Otherwise the reference to Merdeka Day would have no legislative content. Can the amendment be construed so that a different result would follow if such an action had been started by a wrongly dismissed constable before the Constitution was amended? In their Lordships' opinion the answer must be in the negative. If this is right, it can make no difference that the action started had got to the stage of judgment being given for the constable and under appeal when the amendment was made. In

h
their Lordships' view the conclusion is inescapable that the legislature intended to secure that no such actions started after Merdeka Day, whether proceeding, or not started, when the amendment was made, should succeed on the ground that the power to dismiss had not been exercised by someone with power to appoint.

j
It follows that in their Lordships' opinion the Federal Court in the exercise of their

1 [1950] 1 All ER 165 at 168, [1950] 1 KB 574 at 579
2 (1875) 1 Ch D 48
3 1 Ch D 48 at 50
4 [1898] AC 469
5 [1898] AC 469 at 475

powers (see *Attorney-General v Vernazza*[1]) rightly allowed the appeal from Abdul Hamid J on this ground.

It was also contended for the appellant that the word 'authority' in the proviso added by the amendment to art 135(1) did not include a person. In support of this contention reference was made to Sch 11 to the Constitution where in the reference to s 29 of the Interpretation and General Clauses Ordinance 1948 the following words appear: 'Where a written law confers upon any person or authority . . .' it is being argued that there was no need to refer to a person if the word 'authority' included a person. If, it was said, the proviso was intended to apply to a person, it would have said 'any person or authority'. In their Lordships' opinion the Federal Court rightly rejected this contention. Article 135(1) in its unamended form refers to an authority and there clearly the word includes a person. It would indeed be odd if the proviso had added the words 'any person'. A person may be an authority within the meaning of that word in the article but not every authority is a person. Indeed if the chief police officer was not an 'authority' what was the relevance of the view that he was unable under the Constitution to dismiss because he was an 'authority' lower in rank that the authority authorised to appoint?

It was also argued that it was contrary to art 135(2) and to natural justice that the appellant was given no opportunity of making oral representations to the chief police officer and to the Inspector-General though he was given the opportunity of making written representations to both of them and did so. A similar contention was advanced in *Najar Singh v Government of Malaysia*[2] and rejected by the Board. For the reasons given in that case, this contention is again rejected.

Regulation 34(1) of the Public Officers (Conduct and Discipline) (General Orders, Chapter D) Regulations 1969, states:

'Where criminal proceedings against an officer result in his conviction, upon receipt of the result of the proceedings, the Head of Department shall apply to the Registrar of the Court in which the proceedings against the officer had taken place for a copy of the record of the said proceedings, i.e., the charge, the notes of evidence and judgment of the Court . . .'

It was contended on behalf of the appellant that, as no such application had been made, the dismissal was void. The chief police officer in evidence admitted that he had not applied and said that he had not done so as he was aware of the facts of the case from the documents in his possession. The respondents contended that the regulation was directory and not mandatory. It does not appear that compliance with it would in this case have served any useful purpose and non-compliance with it would not in their Lordships' opinion render invalid a dismissal otherwise valid.

For these reasons their Lordships will advise His Majesty the Yang di-Pertuan Agong that the appeal be dismissed, that the order as to costs made by the Federal Court should not be disturbed and that the appellant should pay the costs of the appeal to the Privy Council.

Appeal dismissed.

Solicitors: *Philip Conway, Thomas & Co* (for the appellant); *Stephenson Harwood* (for the Malaysian government).

Sumra Green   Barrister.

---

1   [1960] 3 All ER 97, [1960] AC 965
2   [1976] 1 MLJ 203

R v Richardson

a

COURT OF APPEAL, CRIMINAL DIVISION
LORD WIDGERY CJ, SHAW LJ AND MCNEILL J
3rd JULY 1979

b
Jury – Juror – Discharge during trial – Discretion to discharge juror for good reason – Exercise of discretion – Discharge of juror by judge otherwise than in open court – Trial continuing with only 11 jurors – Defendant and counsel unaware of discharge of juror – Whether discharge of juror can take place only in open court – Whether discharge of juror by judge before coming into court a material irregularity in the trial – Juries Act 1974, s 16(1).

c
On the morning of the second day of the appellant's trial in the Crown Court one of the 12 jurors notified the court that she could not attend the trial because her husband had died the previous night. Her explanation was communicated to the trial judge who, before he came into court that morning, discharged the juror. The judge did not inform anyone, when he came into court, that he had discharged the juror and the trial continued with 11 jurors. The appellant, counsel and the judge's associate were unaware that a juror had been discharged. The jury returned a verdict of guilty. The appellant
d
appealed against his conviction on the ground that discharge of a juror otherwise than in open court constituted a material irregularity in the trial.

Held – Under s 16 (1)[a] of the Juries Act 1974 a judge was entitled, if he had good reason to do so, to discharge a juror otherwise than in open court, since a juror in difficulty who sought discharge should not have to come to court to apply there for discharge. Since the
e
discharge of the juror had been for good reason it followed that it was a proper discharge under s 16, even though it had not been done in open court. Accordingly the appeal would be dismissed (see p 249 *e* to *g*, post).

Notes

f
For discharge of individual jurors, see 11 Halsbury's Laws (4th Edn) paras 264–279.
    For the Juries Act 1974, s 16, see 44 Halsbury's Statutes (3rd Edn) 575.

Case referred to in judgment

R v Hambery [1977] 3 All ER 561, [1977] QB 924, [1977] 2 WLR 999, 141 JP 707, 65 Cr
    App R 233, CA.

g ## Cases also cited

R v Browne [1962] 2 All ER 621, [1962] 1 WLR 759, CCA.
R v Dubarry (1976) 64 Cr App R 7, CA.

Appeal

h
Michael Richardson appealed against his conviction on 8th November 1978 in the Crown Court at Kenton Bar, before his Honour Judge Hall and a jury, on three counts of theft and one count of criminal damage. He was sentenced to borstal training. He appealed against his conviction on the ground that there was a material irregularity in the course of the trial, which began on 7th November 1978, because a juror had been discharged otherwise than in open court. The facts are set out in the judgment of the court.

j
Jeremy Hargrove for the appellant.
Duncan Percy for the Crown.

_____

a   Section 16, so far as material, is set out at p 249 *c*, post

LORD WIDGERY CJ delivered the following judgment of the court: In March 1978 at the magistrates' court at Newcastle upon Tyne, the appellant was charged with a *a* number of offences of dishonesty. There was a committal to the Crown Court for sentence. There were on two occasions a deferment of sentence and eventually on 8th November 1978 in the Crown Court at Newcastle upon Tyne the appellant was sentenced to a period of borstal training.

He appeals against that conviction and his appeal is based on one very short, simple and uncommon ground. He says that in the course of his trial the jury of 12 men and *b* women having retired for the day, one of them failed to return the following day, giving the explanation that her husband had died in the night. That explanation was communicated to the judge before he came into court on the morning of the second day. He immediately decided that he would discharge the unfortunate woman and he acted accordingly. He did not say anything to counsel in court when he sat again. It may be he thought that the point having been dealt with in their absence, as it had been, he *c* need not say anything about it. Neither counsel nor the associate was aware of the missing juror, nor any of the jurors themselves. Back they came and answered the question put by the clerk and they returned a verdict of guilty. Still nobody realised that there were only 11 jurors present. Quite shortly after that, after the shorthand writer had gone home, the point was brought to the notice of counsel.

What is the effect of all this? Counsel for the appellant, who has put his argument *d* skilfully, says that the decision of the trial judge to discharge the juror was a decision which could only properly and constitutionally be made in open court in the presence and hearing of the accused, counsel and others concerned.

There is some authority which gets near to it. In *R v Hambery*[1], it was—

'*Held* (1) that although section 16(1) of the Juries Act 1974 did not expressly confer on the trial judge the power to discharge a juror, if such a juror was *e* discharged the jury should be considered as remaining for all purposes of the trial, for ever since 1925 a trial judge had a discretion to discharge a juror without discharging the whole jury; (2) The Court of Appeal, Criminal Division, had power to review the exercise of a judicial discretion to discharge one or more jurors; but as in the present case the trial judge was entitled to infer that it was important that the juror he discharged should go on the holiday on the date she planned, and as there *f* was nothing capricious about the exercise of his discretion, the appeal would be dismissed.'

So the case as put forward by the appellant is that there is a right of appeal. Any matter which is capable of appeal must, it is said, be dealt with in open court as a matter of principle. This was clearly not done in open court. *g*

The case on the other side is put in this way. It is quite clear that there was no power to discharge a juror in this way before 1925. If anything material went wrong with a juror, the whole jury had to be discharged and the trial started again. In 1925 an important amendment to this branch of the law was made by s 15 of the Criminal Justice Act 1925 and the terms of that section were these:

'Where in the course of a criminal trial any member of the jury dies or is *h* discharged by the court as being through illness incapable of continuing to act or for any other reason, the jury shall nevertheless, subject to assent being given in writing by or on behalf of both the prosecutor and the accused and so long as the number of its members is not reduced below ten, be considered as remaining for all the purposes of that trial properly constituted, and the trial shall proceed and a verdict may be given accordingly.' *j*

As we have observed, not only does that section somewhat restrict the circumstances in which it might apply, but it also contains the provision that the parties should

1   (1977) 65 Cr App R 233; cf [1977] 3 All ER 561, [1977] QB 924

consent. Only no doubt after these formalities are complied with can the statute be
a complied with.

The 1925 Act is no longer the ruling provision on this subject. The discharge of jurors
is now in the Juries Act 1974. Before looking at that Act, I refresh my memory about the
position in common law in regard to discharge of jurors. The position is clearly stated in
Archbold[1] in this way:

b   'It is established law that a jury sworn and charged in respect of a defendant may
      be discharged by the judge at the trial, without giving a verdict, if a "necessity," that
      is, a high degree of need, for such discharge is made evident to his mind . . .'

So the power is there and by s 16 of the 1974 Act we are told what is the effect in
modern times, and the present case is that situation. Section 16 provides:

c   '(1) Where in the course of a trial of any person for an offence on indictment any
      member of the jury dies or is discharged by the court whether as being through
      illness incapable of continuing to act or for any other reason, but the number of its
      members is not reduced below nine, the jury shall nevertheless (subject to
      subsections (2) and (3) below) be considered as remaining for all the purposes of that
      trial properly constituted, and the trial shall proceed and a verdict may be given
      accordingly . . .'

d
What it comes to is this: a juror may be discharged for good reason, but the remaining
jurors shall constitute an effective jury and continue to exercise jurisdiction accordingly
provided the number are not reduced to below the statutory minimum.

One turns to apply this subsection to the case before us. The first thing one has to ask
oneself is, was the lady whose husband died properly discharged under s 16 of the 1974
e Act? We have no doubt that she was properly discharged. It is not in our judgment
right to say that the operation of the discharge of a juror can only take place in open
court. All sorts of situations might arise. Jurors who are in considerable difficulties and
who seek a discharge, should not have to come personally to court and make their
applications there. The judge's conclusion in this case to discharge this unfortunate
woman is obviously not open to criticism. In our judgment the fact that it was not done
f in open court is neither here nor there.

That means one has not got to be troubled about the identity of the jury who heard the
case and the jury who returned the verdict, because what the 1974 Act clearly
contemplates is, given an effective discharge of the juror, the remaining jury can
continue. Therefore one does not have to bother about transfer of jurisdiction from one
jury to another. What remains of the original jury can effectively continue to act and
g come to a conclusion.

For all these reasons we do not find that there was any material irregularity in the
proceedings before us and accordingly the appeal is dismissed.

Appeal dismissed.

h Solicitors: *Registrar of Criminal Appeals*; *Williamson & Co*, Newcastle upon Tyne (for the
Crown).

                                                          Lea Josse   Barrister.

───

1   40th Edn (1979), para 437

St Catherine's College v Dorling   *a*

COURT OF APPEAL, CIVIL DIVISION
MEGAW, EVELEIGH AND BRANDON LJJ
23rd, 24th, 25th MAY 1979

Rent restriction – Protected tenancy – Tenancy under which a dwelling-house is let as a separate
dwelling – Premises let to educational institution – Covenant to use premises 'as private residence   *b*
only in the occupation of one person per room' – Covenant to sublet only to person who is pursuing
or intending to pursue course of study provided by institution – Five of institution's students each
taking a room – Each student having exclusive use of own room – Students sharing cooking and
washing facilities – Whether 'dwelling-house let as a separate dwelling' – Rent Act 1977, ss 1, 8.

House owners were reluctant to provide students with rented accommodation because   *c*
of the protection given to tenants by the Rent Acts. To ease the situation Parliament
provided by s 8(1)[a] of the Rent Act 1977 that a tenancy was not a protected tenancy if it
was granted to a person who was pursuing, or intending to pursue, a course of study
provided by a specified educational institution, and was so granted by that institution.
With a view to making accommodation more readily available to undergraduates in
Oxford a firm of estate agents introduced a scheme whereby owners of houses let them   *d*
to colleges which then made them available to undergraduates. In 1978 five
undergraduates applied to the agents for accommodation. The agents found a suitable
house, the owner of which agreed to let it to the undergraduates' college for one year less
seven days at a rent of £224·25 per month. Under the tenancy agreement the college
covenanted not to use the demised premises otherwise than for occupation by a person
or persons who were pursuing or intending to pursue a course of study provided by the   *e*
college, not to assign, sub-let or part with possession or occupation of all or part of the
premises provided that if the tenant was an educational institution and 'either the Tenant
sub-lets only to a person who is pursuing or intending to pursue a course of study
provided by the Tenant or the Tenant grants a licence for the use of the demised premises
to such person' that was not to amount to a breach of the agreement, and to use or permit
the premises to be used 'as private residence only in the occupation of one person   *f*
per room'. The five undergraduates each signed a document entitled 'Agreement and
Indemnity' whereby they agreed that in consideration of the college entering into the
tenancy agreement they would fulfil all the conditions and covenants contained in it and
indemnify the college against all liabilities which might arise under it. The five
undergraduates each took a room equipped for use as a bedroom, study and sittingroom,
and shared the kitchen and bathroom. Each undergraduate gave a cheque for his share   *g*
of the rent. Shortly after signing the tenancy agreement the college applied to the rent
officer for the registration of a fair rent and also applied to the court for a declaration that
the tenancy was a protected tenancy within s 1[b] of the Rent Act 1977, i e that it was 'a
tenancy under which a dwelling-house . . . is let as a separate dwelling'. The county court
judge found that the undergraduates had exclusive use of their own particular rooms and
concluded that the owner and the college intended that to be the arrangement. He   *h*
refused to grant the declaration on the ground that the house was not let as a separate
dwelling within s 1 of the 1977 Act. The college appealed, contending, inter alia, that
the words 'to be used as private residence' in the tenancy agreement meant 'to be used as
a private residence' and furthermore that the wording of the sub-letting clause showed
that it was contemplated that not more than one person pursuing or intending to pursue
a course of study at the college would take but that if more than one did so they would   *j*
take jointly and be responsible for the whole.

---

a   Section 8(1) is set out at p 252 *a*, post
b   Section 1 is set out at p 251 *j*, post

Held – The tenancy was not a protected tenancy within the meaning of s 1 of the 1977

a Act because (i) on the true construction of the tenancy agreement the phrase 'used as private residence' meant 'used for residential purposes' and what was being granted to the college was a tenancy of a building which contained a number of units of habitation and (ii) the arrangement envisaged was inconsistent with the concept of a building which could itself be described as a separate dwelling. It followed that the appeal would be dismissed (see p 254 *b* to *g* and p 255 *g* to p 256 *b* and *f g*, post).

b *Horford Investments Ltd v Lambert* [1974] 1 All ER 131 considered.

Notes

For protected tenancies for the purpose of the Rent Act 1977, see Supplement to 23 Halsbury's Laws (3rd Edn) para 148A.

For the Rent Act 1977, ss 1, 8, see 47 Halsbury's Statutes (3rd Edn) 393, 405.

c **Cases referred to in judgments**

Horford Investments Ltd v Lambert [1974] 1 All ER 131, [1976] Ch 39, [1973] 3 WLR 872, 27 P & CR 88, CA, Digest (Cont Vol D) 593, 8058a.

Ponder v Hillman [1969] 3 All ER 694 [1969] 1 WLR 1261, 31(2) Digest (Reissue) 999, 7973.

Whitty v Scott-Russell [1950] 1 All ER 884, [1950] 2 KB 32, CA, 31(2) Digest (Reissue)

d 1006, 8016.

Wolfe v Hogan [1949] 1 All ER 570, [1949] 2 KB 194, CA, 31(2) Digest (Reissue) 1002, 7988.

Wright v Howell (1947) 204 LT Jo 299, 92 Sol Jo 26, CA, 31(2) Digest (Reissue) 1003, 7992.

Cases also cited

e *Cole v Harris* [1945] 2 All ER 146, [1945] KB 474, CA.

Curl v Angelo [1948] 2 All ER 189, CA.

Feather Supplies Ltd v Ingham [1971] 3 All ER 556, [1971] 2 QB 348, CA.

Goodrich v Paisner [1956] 2 All ER 176, [1957] AC 65, HL.

Langford Property Co Ltd v Goldrich [1949] 1 All ER 402, [1949] 1 KB 511, CA.

Neale v Del Soto [1945] 1 All ER 191, [1945] 1 KB 144, CA.

f **Appeal**

St Catherine's College, Oxford, appealed against an order made by his Honour Judge Clover in the Oxford County Court on 14th March 1979, whereby he dismissed an application by the college for a declaration that the tenancy of the premises known as 208 Headington Road, Oxford granted to the college on 8th July 1978 by the respondent landlord, J A Dorling, was a protected tenancy under s 1 of the Rent Act 1977. The facts

g are set out in the judgment of Eveleigh LJ.

Alan Boyle for the college.
Terence Etherton for the respondent.

h **EVELEIGH LJ** delivered the first judgment at the invitation of Megaw LJ. On 14th March 1979, in the Oxford County Court, his Honour Judge Clover refused to grant a declaration, on the application of St Catherine's College, that the premises 208 Headington Road, Oxford, of which the college was the tenant, were the subject of a protected tenancy under s 1 of the Rent Act 1977. That section provides:

j 'Subject to this Part of this Act, a tenancy under which a dwelling-house (which may be a house or part of a house) is let as a separate dwelling is a protected tenancy for the purposes of this Act.'

As a result of the reluctance of house owners to provide rented accommodation for students, Parliament introduced s 8 of the Rent Act 1977, sub-s (1) of which reads as follows:

'A tenancy is not a protected tenancy if it is granted to a person who is pursuing, or intends to pursue, a course of study provided by a specified educational institution and is so granted either by that institution or by another specified institution or body of persons.'

A firm of estate agents in Oxford, Messrs Runyards, with the co-operation of a large number of Oxford colleges, introduced a scheme by which it was envisaged that accommodation would more readily be made available to undergraduates. They published a booklet giving details of that scheme. The general idea was that the owner of the house would let premises to the college, who would then make the accommodation available to undergraduates. A £50 deposit was taken from undergraduates who had made an application for the accommodation, and that deposit was treated as an application fee, unless the arrangements were finally completed, when it was treated as part-payment of rent. Runyards orally guaranteed to the colleges concerned that every undergraduate would have a separate room.

In so far as 208 Headington Road is concerned, there were four undergraduates of the college who applied to Messrs Runyards for accommodation. They found a suitable house, namely, 208 Headington Road. The college was willing to take those premises under a lease.

On 12th June 1978 the undergraduates signed a document entitled 'Agreement and Indemnity', which stated:

'In consideration of the College, through the Domestic Bursar, entering on my behalf into a Lease of 208 Headington Road, Oxford, from 8th July 1978 for one year less 7 days at a rent of £224.25 per month . . . I hereby agree with the College to fulfil and observe all conditions and covenants contained in their lease and to indemnify the College against all liabilities which it may incur there under.'

That document bears five signatures, for, on discovering that the house would accommodate five, one further undergraduate was found to live there.

It is not alleged in this case that the college took a lease as agent for the undergraduates who signed that indemnity or for any other undergraduate. Indeed, the landlord clearly would not have made a contract with the undergraduates themselves. Nor is it shown that the landlord was aware of the terms of that agreement.

The premises consisted of three rooms upstairs and two rooms downstairs. There was a small kitchen; there was a bathroom; and there were two WCs, one inside and one outside. One of the two downstairs rooms had a dining table and four chairs. There were no locks on the doors of the rooms. Each room was equipped with sufficient furniture for its use as a bedroom and a study and sittingroom. The premises were occupied by the five undergraduates. Each took a room. Each gave a cheque for his share of the total rent; and generally speaking one of them would take all the cheques to Runyards. The dining table was taken from the room where it was when they first occupied the premises and set up in the kitchen. The general practice was for these occupants to cook in relays, providing their own individual food, although on occasions, at weekends in particular, they might eat together around that table.

The question in this case is whether the premises were let as a separate dwelling within the meaning of s 1. The important point in answering that question is to determine the contemplated use of the premises. In *Ponder v Hillman*[1], Goff J referred to *Wolfe v Hagan*[2] and to a particular passage in the judgment of Evershed LJ[3], and then continued:

'He there approved a passage in MEGARRY ON THE RENT ACTS[4] in these terms: "Where the terms of the tenancy provide for or contemplate the use of the premises

1 [1969] 3 All ER 694 at 696, [1969] 1 WLR 1261 at 1263
2 [1949] 1 All ER 570, [1949] 2 KB 194
3 [1949] 1 All ER 570 at 574, [1949] 2 KB 194 at 203
4 4th Edn (1949) p 19

for some particular purpose, that purpose is the essential factor, not the nature of the premises or the actual use made of them. Thus, if the premises are let for business purposes, the tenant cannot claim that they have been converted into a dwelling-house merely because somebody lives on the premises."'

So it follows that one has to consider the terms of the lease and the surrounding circumstances at the time that the lease was granted. It may be that in some cases that assistance can be obtained from the subsequent user of the premises. But in my opinion generally speaking such assistance will be found to be a matter of last resort.

I turn to consider the terms of the tenancy agreement in this case. There is the usual habendum and reddendum, and then I turn to cl 2 (l) (i), in which the tenant covenants:

'Not to use the demised premises otherwise than for occupation by a person or persons who are as specified by Section 8 of the Rent Act 1977 pursuing or intending to pursue a course of study provided by the Tenant whether the said person or persons occupy the demised premises as sub-tenants or licensees.'

Sub-clause (l) (ii) reads:

'Not to assign sub-let part with possession or share possession or occupation of all or part of the demised premises furniture fixtures fittings or effects or any part thereof provided that there shall be no breach of this clause if the Tenant shall be a specified educational institution as defined by Section 8 of the Rent Act 1977 and either the Tenant sub-lets only to a person who is pursuing or intending to pursue a course of study provided by the Tenant or the Tenant grants a licence for the use of the demised premises to such person.'

Then sub-cl. (m), the user clause, reads as follows:

'Not to carry on or permit to be carried on upon the demised premises any profession trade or business whatsoever or let apartments or receive paying guests in the demised premises but to use or permit the same to be used as private residence only in occupation of one person per room and not in any way to contravene the Town and Country Planning Acts and not to exhibit any notice or poster on any portion of the demised premises.'

Counsel for the college has submitted that here a group of students, or undergraduates, intended to occupy the premises as joint occupants of the whole, and that this was the object and purport of the tenancy granted to the college. He particularly relied on sub-cl (m) and invited the court to say that the words 'to be used as private residence only' should be read to include the indefinite article: that is to say, 'to be used as *a* private residence only.'

Counsel for the college then referred the court to *Whitty v Scott-Russell*[1]. There, a house and cottage which were semi-detached were the subject of the letting. There was no internal intercommunication. The tenant covenanted 'to use the premises as and for a private dwelling-house only'. It was held[2] in that case—

'that, notwithstanding that the tenant did not and had never intended to occupy the cottage himself, the house and cottage were, having regard to the terms of the lease and, in particular, the covenant by the tenant to use the demised property as a dwelling-house only, let as a single dwelling and therefore constituted a dwelling-house within the definition'

in the Rent Act, in that case the Rent and Mortgage Interest Restrictions (Amendment) Act 1933.

---

1   [1950] 1 All ER 884, [1950] 2 KB 32
2   [1950] 2 KB 32 at 33

Counsel for the college has argued, by analogy, that if these premises were to be used as *a* private residence, the emphasis being on the indefinite article, it meant that they   *a* were not to be used as a number of different private residences, therefore they were let as a whole, with the object of their being inhabited jointly by the students. He also placed some reliance on the words of sub-cl (l) (ii), where it reads 'either the tenant sublets only to a person who is pursuing' etc. He said it was therefore contemplated that no more than one person would take, or that persons could take jointly being responsible for the whole.   *b*

On the other hand, counsel for the respondent landlord has contended that cl 2(m) comes to his aid. He has invited the court to construe the phrase 'as private residence' as meaning for residential purposes. I would myself accept that submission. One cannot read the words 'as private residence' without reading the words that follow, namely, 'in the occupation of one person per room'. In my opinion it is no accidental omission of the indefinite article. There is an intentional omission; and the phrase 'as private residence'   *c* is used similarly to the expression 'as business premises'. It is descriptive of the user and not of the premises themselves.

When one then sees that what is envisaged is the occupation of one person per room, using that for private purposes, and then turns to the other provision in sub-cl (l) which I have read, one sees that subletting or a licence to use is contemplated, and the words used are 'sublets only to a person'. The importance, to my mind, of the words in that   *d* sub-clause is that they show that a subletting is envisaged. That envisages, as I see it (for one must read this as a whole) that the college is permitted to sublet to a person who is to occupy a single room as a private residence. If the college is to be allowed to 'sublet to a person' (to use the words of the sub-clause) any part of the building, it would follow that it should be allowed to let to more than one person, or the building would otherwise have another part unused. Quite clearly it was never contemplated that the college itself   *e* should occupy or make any particular use of the premises, other, that is to say, than as accommodation for undergraduates. Furthermore, of course, the plural is used in sub-cl (l) (i), where we see the words 'for occupation by a person or persons'.

I therefore read these two sub-clauses as saying that the college shall be in a position to sublet, and shall be in a position to sublet to 'persons'; but they must be persons 'pursuing or intending to pursue a course of study'. The use of the singular in para (ii) is simply   *f* because it is describing the type of person who may be a sub-tenant; and, as the college may sublet to a particular type of sub-tenant and must do so only for occupation of one person per room, it follows, in my opinion, that the purpose of this letting was that the college should be in a position to do just that. In other words, what was being granted to the college here was a tenancy of a building which contained a number of units of habitation, as they have been called. From that interpretation of this lease I would   *g* conclude that the premises were not let as separate dwellings.

In *Horford Investments Ltd v Lambert*[1], a landlord let to a tenant two houses. Those houses had been converted into a number of 'units of accommodation', and at the time of the lease those units were in fact occupied. The question arose in that case whether this was a letting of a dwelling-house, and indeed a separate dwelling-house, so as to attract the protection of the Act. Russell LJ said[2]:   *h*

> 'Accordingly, in my judgment the tenancy of each of the two houses in this case is not within the definition of a protected tenancy because of the plurality of dwellings, or, as I have labelled them, units of habitation, comprised in the premises when let and obliged by the terms of the letting to be so maintained.'

In that case the covenant in regard to one of the two flats, the user clause in the lease, was   *j* in these terms:

1   [1974] 1 All ER 131, [1976] Ch 39
2   [1974] 1 All ER 131 at 136, [1976] Ch 39 at 48

a
'The lessee will not use ... the premises or any part thereof for the purposes of any trade or business nor for any purpose other than residential in multiple occupation.'

In my opinion, cl 2 (m) of the lease which this court has to consider is to the same effect: it is, not to use for any purpose 'other than residential in multiple occupation'.

b
Counsel for the college, however, has argued that the rooms in this house were not dwellings, and consequently *Horford Investments Ltd v Lambert*[1] has no application. He further submitted that there is a distinction in that the individual units were already let in that case. I cannot accept that those arguments prevent, or in any way militate against, the construction of the lease which I have just stated.

Counsel for the college referred the court to *Wright v Howell*[2], where the appellant was the tenant of an unfurnished room in a flat of the respondent landlord. He used as toilet and other facilities those that existed in another flat in the same building which was

c
occupied by the parents-in-law. It was held[3] that, in those circumstances—

'as the room, when let to the tenant, was devoid of cooking arrangements and water supply, and as the word "dwelling" on its true construction included all the major activities of life, particularly sleeping, cooking and feeding, and as one of those activities, sleeping, was at all relevant times no longer being carried on there,

d
the room was not a dwelling and the tenancy was not protected.'

I do not myself see a parallel, on the facts of that case. In the present case the undergraduates were sleeping on the premises; there were facilities provided. It is not necessary, as the many cases under the Rent Acts show, for those facilities to exist in the room itself. Counsel for the college argued that these rooms did not themselves attract the protection of the Rent Acts: as some accommodation was shared they would be

e
outside that protection, and from this he inferred, in what I regard as a non sequitur, that, as they were not themselves protected dwellings, the whole of the house was itself let as a separate individual dwelling. As I say, that to my mind is a non sequitur. The fact (and I would not concede this) that the rooms might not be protected by the Rent Act does not mean that they were not let. There are many cases where accommodation has been let but by virtue of the sharing of other accommodation, essential accommodation,

f
has been held not to come within the terms of the Rent Act because of the words 'let as a separate dwelling'. But that does not in any way deny the finding of the learned judge in this case, on ample evidence to support it, that the undergraduates in fact had the exclusive use of their own particular rooms. Furthermore, on the facts of this case, in my judgment, the learned judge was justified in concluding that it was the intention of the landlord and the tenant college that that should be so.

g
Counsel for the respondent has submitted, and I agree with the submission, that such an arrangement is not consistent, generally speaking anyway, with the conception of 'a dwelling-house let as a separate dwelling'. Generally speaking, 'a dwelling-house let as a separate dwelling' envisages that at least someone, that someone being in most cases the tenant in occupation, will have the right to go to any part of the premises he chooses. It may well be that a tenant who takes a separate dwelling-house will sublet so as to

h
preclude himself, vis-à-vis the sub-lessee, from entering another part of the premises for the period of the subletting; but that is something which occurs after the lease has been entered into and in no way detracts from the right of the tenant vis-à-vis the landlord to go to another room. The existence of someone able to go of his own right to all the rooms of the premises is one of the hallmarks of a dwelling-house. That is completely absent on the findings in this case. That being so, I would agree with counsel for the

j
respondent's submission that the arrangement envisaged in this case was inconsistent

1   [1974] 1 All ER 131, [1976] Ch 39
2   (1947) 204 LT Jo 299
3   204 LT Jo 299 at 300

with the concept of a building which itself could be described as a separate dwelling.
For those reasons I would dismiss this appeal.   *a*

BRANDON LJ. I agree that the appeal should be dismissed, for the reasons given by
Eveleigh LJ in his judgment.

MEGAW LJ. I also agree with the conclusion reached by Eveleigh LJ and with the
reasons given by him.   *b*
   The agreement in this case was made on 8th July 1978. On the face of it, it was agreed
on that day by St Catherine's College that a certain rent should be payable. Five days
later, on 13th July 1978, St Catherine's College, being a party to that agreement, applied
to the rent officer for registration of a fair rent. That is to say, the college sought to
challenge that the rent which they appeared to have agreed five days earlier was a fair
rent, or the rent which in law could be insisted on. There is no doubt that the other party *c*
to that agreement of 8th July 1978, Mr Dorling, through his authorised agents, was
firmly of the opinion that the form of the agreement was such as to take it outside the
scope of the provisions of law which would have enabled the rent to be referred for an
assessment of any rent different from the rent which had been, apparently, agreed. It is
difficult to think that the college, in entering into the agreement on 8th July 1978, was
not aware that that was the view held by the other party to the agreement. But, as   *d*
counsel for the college, in my opinion rightly, submits, whatever view might be taken
of that in other respects, no such view can properly influence the decision as to the legal
effect of the agreement. All that I would say about it, then, is this: it seems to me that
the decision at which this court has arrived is more likely to help the continuance of
schemes of this sort, if schemes of this sort are desirable, than would have been the result
if we had arrived at the contrary conclusion. But, once again, that is not a matter that can *e*
rightly affect our judgment in this matter. If indeed it was the view of St Catherine's
College, when it made this agreement on 8th July 1978, that the figure of rent contained
in that agreement was higher than a fair rent and that therefore the rent which it itself
thereafter required the five undergraduates to pay was higher than the college thought
to be a fair rent, it might be a matter of hope, and expectation, that the college, now that
it has been established that its view of the legal effect of that agreement is not justified, *f*
would feel that it would not be appropriate that the undergraduates should bear the
consequences of the college having seen fit to agree a rent which it believed (if indeed it
did so believe) was a rent higher than a fair rent.
   I agree that the appeal falls to be dismissed.

Appeal dismissed. Leave to appeal to House of Lords refused.   *g*

19th July. The Appeal Committee of the House of Lords (Lord Wilberforce, Lord Russell of
Killowen and Lord Keith of Kinkel) dismissed a petition by the college for leave to appeal.

Solicitors: *Linnell & Murphy*, Oxford (for the college); *Outred & Co*, Weybridge (for the
respondent).   *h*

Mary Rose Plummer   Barrister.

Mutasa v Attorney-General

a

QUEEN'S BENCH DIVISION
BOREHAM J
30th APRIL, 1st, 2nd MAY 1979

b
Crown – Duty – Duty to protect subject – Whether a legal duty enforceable in the courts.

Crown – Proceedings against – Liability of Crown – Liability arising 'otherwise than in respect of Her Majesty's government in the United Kingdom' – Plaintiff seeking declaration against United Kingdom government in respect of his arrest and detention by illegal regime in Rhodesia – Whether Crown's liability for plaintiff's arrest arising otherwise than in respect of United Kingdom government – Southern Rhodesia Act 1965, s 1 – Crown Proceedings Act 1947, s
c *40(2)(b).*

In 1965 the government of the colony of Southern Rhodesia unilaterally declared independence from the United Kingdom and for the purposes of English law became an illegally constituted regime. By virtue of s 1[a] of the Southern Rhodesia Act 1965 it was enacted that the United Kingdom government was to continue to 'have responsibility
d and jurisdiction as heretofore for and in respect of' Southern Rhodesia. The plaintiff, a citizen of Southern Rhodesia and a British subject, resigned from his post in the Southern Rhodesia civil service when the illegal regime declared independence. In 1970 he was arrested and detained in prison without trial by the regime. He was unable to obtain redress or relief in the Rhodesian courts and the British government was unable to secure his release. In 1972 he was released from detention on condition that he immediately
e left the country. He fled to the United Kingdom where he commenced an action seeking inter alia, a declaration that the United Kingdom government had failed in its duty to protect him from unlawful arrest and detention or to secure his early release. At the trial of the action it was contended on behalf of the Crown (i) that although the Crown owed him such a duty, it was only a political or moral duty and not a legal duty enforcable in a court of law, and (ii) that any liability of the Crown was a liability 'arising
f otherwise than in respect of [Her] Majesty's Government in the United Kingdom', which was therefore protected from suit by s 40(2)(b)[b] of the Crown Proceedings Act 1947.

Held – The plaintiff's claim would be dismissed for the following reasons—
(i) The Crown's duty to protect a subject from unlawful arrest and imprisonment was not a legal duty since it could not be enforced in a court of law and breach of the duty did
g not give rise to a cause of action (see p 262 *b c*, p 264 *g h* and p 265 *a*, post); dicta of Brett LJ in *Attorney-General v Tomline* [1874–80] All ER Rep at 985 and of Rowlatt J in *China Navigation Co Ltd v Attorney-General* (1931) 40 Ll LR at 112–113 applied.
(ii) In any event the effect of s 1 of the 1965 Act was that the constitution in force immediately before the unilateral declaration of independance was preserved with such amendments as the new circumstances demanded. It followed that if any liability of the
h Crown arose it arose under that constitution and not in respect of Her Majesty's government in the United Kingdom which was therefore entitled to avail itself of the protection conferred on it by s 40(2)(b) of the 1947 Act (see p 263 *a b f* and p 265 *a*, post).

Notes
For the Crown's duty towards the subject, see 8 Halsbury's Laws (4th Edn) para 861, and
j for cases on the subject, see 11 Digest (Reissue) 658, 5–7.
For the Southern Rhodesia Act 1965, s 1, see 4 Halsbury's Statutes (3rd Edn) 573.
For the Crown Proceedings Act 1947, s 40, see 8 ibid 871.

---

a   Section 1, so far as material, is set out at p 258 *h*, post
b   Section 40(2), so far as material, is set out at p 262 *d*, post

Cases referred to in judgment

Attorney-General v Tomline (1880) 14 Ch D 58, [1874–80] All ER Rep 981, 49 LJ Ch 377,
    42 LT 880, 44 JP 617, CA, 7 Digest (Reissue) 280, *1934*.   a

China Navigation Co Ltd v Attorney-General (1931) 40 Ll LR 110; *affd* [1932] 2 KB 197,
    [1932] All ER Rep 626, 101 LJKB 478, 147 LT 22, 18 Asp MLC 288, CA, 11 Digest
    (Reissue) 658, 7.

Franklin v Attorney-General [1973] 1 All ER 879, [1974] QB 185, [1973] 2 WLR 225,
    Digest (Cont Vol D) 263, 362a.   b

Pyx Granite Co Ltd v Ministry of Housing and Local Government [1958] 1 All ER 625, [1958]
    1 QB 554, [1958] 2 WLR 371, 122 JP 182, 56 LGR 171, 9 P & CR 204, CA; *rvsd* [1959]
    3 All ER 1, [1960] AC 260, [1959] 3 WLR 346, 123 JP 429, 58 LGR 1, 10 P & CR 319,
    HL, 45 Digest (Repl) 336, 37.

Vine v National Dock Labour Board [1956] 3 All ER 939, [1957] AC 488, [1957] 2 WLR 106,
    [1956] 2 Lloyd's Rep 567, HL, Digest (Cont Vol A) 970, 280aa.   c

Action

By a writ dated 7th June 1976 the plaintiff, Didymus Noel Edwin Mutasa, sought (i) a
declaration that his arrest and detention from 18th November 1970 to 27th November
at Sinoia and Salisbury Prisons, Rhodesia, was unlawful, (ii) a declaration that Her
Majesty's government in the United Kingdom had failed in its duty to protect the   d
plaintiff from that unlawful arrest and detention and in its duty to secure his early
release, (iii) a declaration that Her Majesty's government had failed to secure to the
plaintiff the rights and freedoms which he enjoyed under arts 5 and 6 of the European
Convention of Human Rights, and (iv) damages. The defendant was the Attorney-
General. The facts are set out in the judgment.

Sir John Foster QC and *Colonel G Draper* for the plaintiff.   e
L Blom-Cooper QC for the Attorney-General.

Cur adv vult

2nd May. **BOREHAM J** read the following judgment: In this action the plaintiff by his   f
statement of claim claims three declarations and damages in respect of his unlawful
arrest and detention in Rhodesia. No oral evidence has been adduced before this court.
The essential facts on which that claim is based have been agreed.

The plaintiff was born in Southern Rhodesia in 1935. At that time that territory was
a Crown colony, with a substantial measure of self government which had been granted
under the Southern Rhodesian Constitution Letters Patent 1923. This Constitution was
replaced in 1961 by one that was annexed to the Southern Rhodesia Constitution Order   g
in Council 1961[1]. It was under the 1961 constitution that the affairs of Rhodesia were
ordered until the unilateral declaration of independence which was made on 11th
November 1965.

Within a few days of that event, namely on 16th November, there was passed the
Southern Rhodesia Act 1961, by which it was declared, by s 1:   h

'. . . Southern Rhodesia continues to be part of Her Majesty's dominions, and that
the Government and Parliament of the United Kingdom have responsibility and
jurisdiction as heretofore for and in respect of it.'

It is sufficient to say at this stage (for it will be necessary to return to these matters) that
by s 2 wide powers were given to Her Majesty to provide by Order in Council for the   j
future government of the country.

On the same day and in pursuance of those latter powers, the Southern Rhodesia

_____

1   SI 1961 No 2314

a Constitution Order 1965[1] was made; again it will be necessary to refer to some of the terms or to some of the sections of that order at a later stage. At the time of the Declaration of Independence, or UDI as I shall call it for convenience, (and I now quote from the first of the admitted facts):

'The plaintiff was at all material times a citizen of Southern Rhodesia by virtue of the Citizenship of Southern Rhodesia and British Nationality Act No 63 of 1963, and by virtue of such citizenship and of s 1(3), British Nationality Act 1948 was at
b all material times a British subject.'

He remained a British subject thereafter, that is after UDI. By 1965 the plaintiff had become a prominent civil servant in Southern Rhodesia, but on UDI he resigned; thereafter he concerned himself with a multi-racial agricultural community known as the 'Cold Comfort Farm Society', of which he became chairman. It is right to say, in
c view of the events which occurred, that he was known in this country, in Britain, as a man who played an active part in defending the rights of Africans, but he was not regarded in any way as an extremist.

On 13th November 1970, and again I quote from the admitted facts:

'... the plaintiff was arrested in Rusape, Southern Rhodesia ... and thereafter detained in prison (first in Sinoia and then Salisbury, Southern Rhodesia) under
d purported powers of the illegal regime in Southern Rhodesia. The said purported powers were exercised by persons who, having held office as ministers under the Constitution of Southern Rhodesia 1961, were on 11th November 1965 lawfully dismissed by the Governor of Southern Rhodesia, Sir Humphrey Gibbs, and thereafter were suspended from holding office as Ministers under such constitution by virtue of the provisions of s 4(1)(b) of the Southern Rhodesian Constitution Order
e 1965. The persons who exercised those purported powers did not hold office at any material times as Ministers under the lawful constitution of Southern Rhodesia, nor did they lawfully hold any other office under the Crown.'

Thus he was illegally arrested and illegally detained.

It is clear from documents which have been put before me and to which it is
f unnecessary to refer in detail, that the plight of the plaintiff was soon known in Britain, where it invoked very considerable sympathy. No relief, of course, was available to him in the courts of Rhodesia, and for a time the government felt that, in the circumstances, there was nothing they could effectively do to order or secure his release from detention. I say at once that counsel for the plaintiff makes no criticism of the government on that account.

g After prolonged negotiations and pressure and with financial and other assistance from a number of sources the plaintiff was released on 27th November 1972, on condition that he and his family took immediate flight to this country; a condition, I may add, with which he readily complied, and thus they came, he and his family, to this country.

The plaintiff now contends first, that he being a British subject and resident in one of
h Her Majesty's territories at the material time, the Crown was under a legal duty to protect him from unlawful arrest and detention. It may be convenient to say in passing that it was at one time contended on behalf of the plaintiff that that duty, that alleged legal duty, was imposed, or at least reinforced, by arts 5 and 6 of the European Convention of Human Rights[2]. The argument then being that that convention was to be regarded as part of the law of this land. But now, after authorities have been cited to the court, his
j counsel no longer relies on that contention for reasons which, if he will allow me to say so, appear to me to be entirely sound; thus I need not dwell on it.

---

1 SI 1965 No 1952
2 Convention for the Protection of Human Rights and Fundamental Freedoms, Rome, 4th November 1950; TS 71 (1953); Cmd 8969

Secondly, it is contended that the Crown has not carried out that duty. In the statement of claim it is put thus, para 11:

'The plaintiff says that the Government of the United Kingdom has failed in its duty towards him in that: (i) It failed to protect him from illegal arrest and detention; (ii) It failed to do anything to secure his early release after his illegal arrest and detention.'

I have quoted those words again in order to emphasise that counsel for the plaintiff has made it clear that the use of the expression 'failed in their duty' is not to be taken to infer any criticism of the British government in that regard. Rather, it is intended to mean that they have not in fact carried out their duty. Counsel accepts, and I am in no position to judge, for the facts on which I might judge are not before me, that there may very well be perfectly good reasons why nothing effective could be done.

Thirdly, it was argued on behalf of the plaintiff that that legal duty to which I have referred is enforceable, and a breach of it is actionable in this court, and thus the plaintiff is entitled to damages. I am not sure that the plaintiff now relies on that contention. Certainly it is now accepted on his behalf that there is no right to damages or compensation in the circumstances of this case.

Finally, it is contended on his behalf that, whether or not that legal duty is enforceable or justiciable in the courts or this realm, it being a legal duty the plaintiff now is entitled to, or in the court's discretion should be granted, a declaration substantially in the terms of para 2 of the prayer for relief in the statement of claim. That paragraph reads as follows:

'[A claim for] A declaration that Her Majesty's Government of the United Kingdom failed in its duty to protect him from the said unlawful arrest and detention and in its duty to secure his early release.'

In view of what I have already said about the expression 'failed in its duty', counsel for the plaintiff would amend that sought for declaration in order to conform with, if I may say so, the very proper attitude which he has taken so far as the non-fulfilment of that duty is concerned.

On behalf of the Crown, it is conceded that the plaintiff being resident in one of Her Majesty's territories, and being a British subject, the Crown did owe him a duty to protect from unlawful arrest and detention, and that that duty has not been carried out. It is argued, however, first, that what is called by the plaintiff 'a legal duty' is no more (as it is put by counsel for the Attorney-General) than a political or moral duty or obligation; it is not a legal duty. Secondly, that even if it is to be regarded as a legal duty it is not enforceable, nor would its breach be actionable in this court.

Next, it is argued that even if the Attorney-General is wrong in those contentions that the plaintiff is precluded from bringing these particular proceedings by the provisions of s 40(2)(b) of the Crown Proceedings Act 1947.

Finally, it is contended on behalf of the Attorney-General that, even if I am against his, the Attorney-General's, contentions on all other points, the plaintiff is not entitled to, nor in its discretion should the court grant, any declaration in the circumstances of this case.

I turn, therefore, to the first question raised by these contentions, namely whether or not the Crown's duty to protect from unlawful arrest and imprisonment is a legal duty and is a matter which is justiciable in this court. In support of his contention for a legal duty, counsel for the plaintiff relies on a number of citations from well known text books on constitutional and administrative law. It is sufficient if I quote from one, for the others are to the like effect, and I quote from Professor Hood-Phillips's text book on Constitutional and Administrative Law[1], where it is stated:

'"The principal duty of the King is, to govern his people according to law," says Blackstone, quoting Bracton and Fortescue to like effect. Blackstone cites the

_____
1   6th Edn (1978), p 272

a   Coronation Oath but adds that, "doubtless the duty of protection is impliedly as much incumbent on the Sovereign before coronation as after."[1]

To like effect is a quotation from de Smith[2]. Before leaving those text books, it is to be observed that in each case the writer asserts by way of preface to the words already quoted: 'The sovereign in theory has duties, but these are not legally enforceable.'

On behalf of the plaintiff it is argued that that latter assertion as to the non-enforceability of those duties is unsupported by authority, and he says is ill-founded in

b   law. It is true that there is no authority directly in point, but there are authorities which relate to similar duties, and which in my judgment are helpful in this particular context. The first to which I make reference is *Attorney-General v Tomline*[3]. That was a case where the duty was somewhat different from that which is asserted here, though it falls in my view into the same category. There the duty was the duty of the Crown to protect the realm from the inroads of the sea. Brett LJ had no doubt that the duty

c   existed, nor did his brethren (James and Cotton LJJ), and he had this to say[4]:

> 'Now I confess to my mind that is a duty of what is called imperfect obligation. Supposing that the King were to neglect that duty, I know no legal means—that is, no process of law—common law or statute law—by which the Crown could be forced to perform that duty, but there is that duty of imperfect obligation on the
>
> d   part of the Royal authority, and that duty on the part of the King gives a corresponding right to the subject; but inasmuch as the duty of the King seems to me to be a duty of imperfect obligation, the right of the subject is also an imperfect right. It is a right which as against the Crown the subject has no means to enforce: nevertheless the right exists. The right of the subject exists and the duty of the King.'

e   There followed in 1931 *China Navigation Co Ltd v Attorney-General*[5]. There again the duty is somewhat different. The duty alleged in that case, in the court of first instance, was a duty cast on the Crown to protect His Majesty's subjects in British ships on the high seas. In the course of his judgment, Rowlatt J came to the point where he was comparing the duty of officers of the Crown with the duty of the Crown itself; he said[6]:

> f   'It seems to me, as was said in another case, that the analogy fails, because the word "duty" in the two cases is made to describe two totally different things. In the case of the officers they have the duty to perform the duties confided to them by the statutes in question, i.e., duty in the eye of the Courts of law. But in the case of the Crown and the use of its forces, what is called the duty is not that sort of thing at all. It has not any obligation, as I understand it, which comes within the purview
>
> g   of the Courts of law. It is a different sort of thing in a different region altogether. It is merely what I venture to call a political duty, using the word "political" in its proper and original sense. It is what any Government would be expected to do for its people, but the Court cannot examine it. Nobody could come to the Court and say whether the Government of any country did or did not perform its duty in that respect. That confusion with the double use of the word "duty" lies at the bottom
>
> h   of the whole argument in this case. The case for the plaintiffs is on a complete fallacy.'

That decision was tested in the Court of Appeal[7]. There the argument shifted

j   1 1 Bl Com, ch 6
    2 Constitutional and Administrative Law (2nd Edn, 1973), p 126
    3 (1880) 14 Ch D 58, [1874–80] All ER Rep 981
    4 14 Ch D 58 at 66, [1874–80] All ER Rep 981 at 985
    5 (1931) 40 Ll LR 110
    6 40 Ll LR 110 at 112–113
    7 [1932] 2 KB 197, [1932] All ER Rep 626

somewhat; whereas in the court below it had rested on the assertion of an unqualified duty to protect, in the Court of Appeal the shift of emphasis was towards an assertion that the Crown had no right to charge for affording protection. It is sufficient to say that in the judgments, in particular that of Lawrence LJ, the dicta of Brett LJ in the *Tomline* case[1], and the decision of Rowlatt J, on the question of duty and its non-enforceability were completely confirmed.

It seems to me that the principles which are to be gleaned from those authorities apply to the duty here alleged by the plaintiff and conceded by the Attorney-General. In my judgment, therefore, the duty here relied on is not in the proper sense a legal duty, namely one which can be enforced in a court of law or the breach of which would give rise to a cause of action in a court of law. The duty here is one, as Brett LJ said, to protect from arrest and imprisonment, and whatever the extent of that duty may be it is one of imperfect obligation and is not enforceable in this court.

That in my view, is sufficient to dispose of the plaintiff's claim, but other questions, as I have indicated, have been extensively canvassed and I turn to them now. First, the effect of s 40 of the Crown Proceedings Act 1947. As I have indicated, it is counsel's contention for the Attorney-General that that section, and in particular sub-s (2)(*b*), precludes the plaintiff from bringing these proceedings in the present circumstances. The relevant part of para (*b*) of the subsection reads as follows:

'Except as therein otherwise expressly provided, nothing in this Act shall . . . (*b*) authorise proceedings to be taken against the Crown under or in accordance with this Act in respect of any alleged liability of the Crown arising otherwise than in respect of His Majesty's Government in the United Kingdom . . .'

I need read no further.

Counsel's contention for the Attorney-General is short. It is this: that the liability alleged in this case is a liability of the Crown which does arise otherwise than in respect of Her Majesty's Government in the United Kingdom.

As I understand his argument, counsel for the plaintiff accepts that that would be a valid contention if the 1961 constitution of Southern Rhodesia were still in force. But, he contends, first that the Queen of the United Kingdom and the Queen of Southern Rhodesia are one and indivisible; a role, he says, which applies to Her Majesty in respect of all her dependent territories. It is unnecessary for me to dwell on this aspect of the matter, save to say that there are authorities which tend to support the contention made in this regard on behalf of the plaintiff, and there are authorities which, in my judgment, contend against it. It is an interesting proposition and an argument of wider interest, no doubt, of constitutional lawyers. But, for reasons which will appear, it seems to me unnecessary for me to dwell on it, certainly at this stage.

Secondly, counsel for the plaintiff contends that the expression 'His Majesty's Government in the United Kingdom', in para (*b*), indicates no more than the place where the government is to be found, namely the location of the government. It is not to be read as restrictive of that government's sphere of operation.

Finally, to complete his contention, he argues that because of UDI there is now no legal government in Rhodesia, with the result that all executive acts are performed, and I quote the words from para (*b*) again, 'by Her Majesty's Government in the United Kingdom'. In short, perhaps to use a more homely phrase, his contention is that the government in the United Kingdom has now taken over in Rhodesia; at least, it has taken over in law, though in fact, as I have indicated, its effectiveness is virtually non-existent.

In my judgment, therefore, it is necessary to see what has happened to the 1961 constitution. I have already referred to s 1 of the Southern Rhodesia Act 1965, which declared that 'the Government and Parliament of the United Kingdom have responsibility and jurisdiction as heretofore for and in respect of Southern Rhodesia'. The plaintiff says

---

1   (1880) 14 Ch D 58, [1874–80] All ER Rep 981

that the word 'heretofore' in that section does not relate to the situation which obtained
a immediately before UDI. In other words, it does not relate to the 1961 constitution, but
it must take us back to a much further point in time. I say at once that that is an
argument which I cannot accept. As I hope will be demonstrated, it seems to me that the
whole purpose of the 1965 Act and the Order in Council made in pursuance of that Act,
is to preserve the 1961 constitution with only such amendments as the new circumstances
demand.

b Thus I proceed with a short review of the 1965 Act. Section 2(2) makes provision '(*a*)
for suspending, amending, revoking or adding to any of the provisions of the
Constitution of Southern Rhodesia 1961; (*b*) for modifying, extending or suspending the
operation of any enactment . . .' and I need read no further, though other provisions are
made. Section 3 provides for continuing the operation of s 2 from year to year by Order
in Council. It is of interest, if not more, to refer to sub-s (3)(*b*) of s 3, which reads thus:
c 'The expiration of section 2 of this Act shall not affect . . . (*b*) the Constitution of Southern
Rhodesia 1961 as in force immediately before the expiration of that section.'

So far as the order made under s 2 of the 1965 Act was concerned it is to be observed
that, by s 1(2) of the order, the expressions used in the order are to have the same
meaning as they have in the Constitution of Southern Rhodesia 1961. Section 4 deals
first with the governor's powers. Then it orders that ss 43, 44, 45 and 46 of the
d constitution shall not have effect; if I may attempt a paraphrase, ss 43–46 were provisions
relating to the appointment and the obligations of ministers, deputy ministers, and
parliamentary secretaries. Section 4 goes on to provide, in short and in effect, that the
powers hitherto vested in those persons under the consitution shall now be exercised by
one of Her Majesty's Secretaries of State. Of course, the reason for that is manifest. No
longer is there a lawful legislative assembly in Southern Rhodesia; thus there are no
e longer lawfully appointed ministers or deputy ministers or parliamentary secretaries.
Hence the need for provision to be made in their place. It is to be observed, without
going into the details, that many other facets of the constitution are left untouched by
the 1965 order, for instance, matters relating to the judiciary and other important
matters. But I have read enough, at least to have persuaded myself, first that the word
'heretofore' in s 1 of the 1965 Act must refer to the position immediately prior to UDI.
f It refers to the position under the 1961 constitution. Secondly that the 1961 constitution,
amended, as I have said, in order to meet present difficult circumstances, is still lawfully
in force. In those circumstances, in my judgment, it follows that the alleged liability in
this case arises otherwise than in respect of Her Majesty's Government in the United
Kingdom.

Before leaving this particular matter, it is not without interest and is certainly of some
g comfort to me, that in *Franklin v Attorney-General*[1] it was admitted or accepted on both
sides and by Lawson J in the course of his judgment that in the circumstances of that case,
though somewhat different to the present, the liability arose otherwise than in respect of
Her Majesty's Government in the United Kingdom. The circumstances put very shortly
were these. The plaintiff was one of a number of holders of Government of Southern
Rhodesia Trustee Stock, interest on which had been paid half-yearly until UDI. Since
h then no interest had been paid. The government of Southern Rhodesia had failed to put
the Bank of England in funds to pay the interest. In other words, there was a claim in
respect of a default on the part of the government of Southern Rhodesia. As I say, the
circumstances are different. In my judgment, the principle is the same. As I have said,
I take comfort from the fact that in that case it was conceded or accepted on all sides,
without argument let it be said, that there the liability arose otherwise than in respect of
j Her Majesty's Government in the United Kingdom.

In those circumstances, there remains the final question to be dealt with, namely
whether a declaration can or should be granted in the circumstances here. The court's

---

1 [1973] 1 All ER 879, [1974] QB 185

power to make a declaratory judgment is not doubted, but it may be helpful to refer to
RSC Ord 15, r 16, which reads thus: *a*

'No action or other proceeding shall be open to objection on the ground that a
merely declaratory judgment or order is sought thereby, and the court may make
binding declarations of right whether or not any consequential relief is or could be
claimed.'

Counsel for the plaintiff says that the words of that rule are wide enough to justify the   *b*
making of a declaration in present circumstances. He has referred the court to a number
of authorities where declarations have been made in actions in which no right or relief,
other than the declaration itself, has been claimed. It is sufficient, and I trust that I do
justice to his argument, if I limit myself to a citation from one such authority. It comes
from *Pyx Granite Co Ltd v Ministry of Housing and Local Government*[1]. It is unnecessary to
recite the facts of that case. The matter in issue there was a planning matter. It is far   *c*
removed from this case, and thus the facts are not important. Lord Denning has this to
say:

'Counsel for the Minister on this part of the case takes another preliminary
objection. There is nothing here corresponding to s. 17 [of the Town and Country
Planning Act 1914] on which he previously relied. But he relies on the wide
discretion given by s. 14 to the planning authority to impose conditions, and he says   *d*
that this discretion is not open to proceedings for declaration.'

Lord Denning goes on to refer to a citation of authority by counsel which was to the
effect that the remedy by declaration only lies where there is no jurisdiction and not
where it is wrongly exercised. He then continues[2]:

'I do not think that there is any such limit to the remedy by declaration. The   *e*
wide scope of it can be seen from the speech of VISCOUNT KILMUIR, L.C., in *Vine* v.
National Dock Labour Board[3], from which it appears that if a substantial question
exists which one person has an interest to raise, and the other to oppose, then the
court has a discretion to resolve it by a declaration, which it will exercise if there is
good reason for so doing.'   *f*

That, of course, is a dictum which binds me, but in any event it is a dictum which I am
happy to follow. One must observe that Lord Denning there, as were the respective
judges in the other authorities quoted on behalf of the plaintiff, was dealing with matters
which were justiciable by the court. In other words, with rights and liabilities that were
enforceable in the courts. It seems to me that the overwhelming difficulty which lies in
the plaintiff's way in this particular respect is this. If I am correct in holding, as I have,   *g*
that the duty on which the plaintiff relies is not enforceable in this court, then it follows
that his claim must fail; and it fails in limine; thus there is no basis on which a
declaration could be made. It follows, therefore, that having regard to the decision that
I have reached, I have no power to make the declaration which the plaintiff now seeks.
Moreover, the declaration which he does seek, namely that the Crown has a duty to
protect him and has not in fact carried out that duty, would, in my view, serve no useful   *h*
purpose. I appreciate, of course, as was argued by counsel for the plaintiff, that such a
declaration would be welcomed by the plaintiff as a confirmation of his contention that
the Crown owed him a duty. But it would establish or advance no right for him, nor, in
my judgment, could it now relieve him from any liability. In any event, it seems to me
that it would be no more than a reiteration of matters which were agreed at the outset
of this trial and which have formed the agreed basis for this judgment. So it is that even   *j*

---

1   [1958] 1 All ER 625 at 632, [1958] 1 QB 554 at 570
2   [1958] 1 All ER 625 at 632, [1958] 1 QB 554 at 570–571
3   [1956] 3 All ER 939 at 943–944, [1957] AC 488 at 500

a if I felt that there was power to make a declaration now sought, I should in the exercise of my discretion refuse to make it. In those circumstances, the plaintiff's claim must fail.

Declarations refused.

Solicitors: *Peter Kingshill* (for the plaintiff); *Treasury Solicitor.*

b
Janet Harding   Barrister.

Re a debtor (No 44 of 1978), ex parte the
c # debtor v Chantry Mount and Hawthorns Ltd

CHANCERY DIVISION
FOX AND BROWNE-WILKINSON JJ
10th, 11th MAY 1979

d *Bankruptcy – Receiving order – Jurisdiction to make order – Appeal pending against refusal to set aside bankruptcy notice on which petition based – Application to set aside notice heard and determined by registrar – Whether application 'heard' if appeal against registrar's decision pending – Whether even though application 'heard' court will stand over application for receiving order where appeal against registrar's decision bona fide and pursued with diligence – Bankruptcy Rules 1952 (SI 1952 No 2113), r 179.*

e On 13th March 1978 the petitioning creditors obtained judgment against the debtor for non-payment of a debt. The judgment debt remained unsatisfied and on 14th September the petitioning creditors served on the debtor a bankruptcy notice based on the judgment debt. The debtor applied to set aside the bankruptcy notice. On 4th October the registrar heard the application to set aside the notice and ordered that it be dismissed. On 23rd *f* October the debtor lodged a notice of appeal to the Divisional Court against the registrar's refusal to set aside the notice but took no immediate steps to set down the appeal. On 30th October he obtained an extension of 30 days to set down the appeal. On 1st November the petitioning creditors presented a bankruptcy petition based on the debtor's failure to comply with the bankruptcy notice. On 28th November the time within which the debtor was required to set down his appeal was further extended to 21st December. On 15th December, when the debtor's appeal was still outstanding, the *g* registrar made a receiving order against him. On 20th December the debtor obtained yet another extension of time to set down his appeal, this time until 15th January 1979. On 5th January the debtor gave notice of appeal against the receiving order on the ground, inter alia, that in making the receiving order the registrar had failed to take account of the pending appeal against the order of 4th October. By virtue of r 179[a] of the Bankruptcy Rules 1952 a receiving order could not be made against the debtor until the *h* application to set aside the bankruptcy notice had been 'heard', and the question arose whether an application to set aside the notice had been heard if an appeal against the dismissal of the application was outstanding.

Held – Where a registrar had completed the hearing of an application to set aside a bankruptcy notice and given his decision on it, the application had been 'heard' for the *j* purposes of r 179 of the 1952 rules even though an appeal against the decision was pending. Accordingly r 179 did not in itself prevent a receiving order being made where an appeal was pending, although normally the court would stand over the application to

---

a   Rule 179 is set out at p 267 *j* to p 268 *a*, post

make the receiving order where there was a bona fide appeal against refusal to set aside a bankrupcy notice which was being pursued with diligence. Because the debtor had not pursued his appeal against the order of 4th October with diligence and the time for appealing had expired on 15th January 1979, the court would not set aside the receiving order. The appeal would therefore be dismissed (see p 270 c d f to h, p 271 a and p 272 b c, post).

Re a debtor (No 10 of 1953), ex parte the debtor v Ampthill Rural District Council [1953] 2 All ER 561 applied.

Re Marendez (2nd February 1979, unreported) distinguished.

Notes

For a receiving order where the act of bankruptcy is non-compliance with a bankruptcy notice and an appeal is pending from an order setting aside the notice, see 3 Halsbury's Laws (4th Edn) para 356, and for cases on the grounds for refusal of a receiving order, see 4 Digest (Reissue) 176–178, 1573–1599.

For the Bankruptcy Rules 1952, r 179, see 3 Halsbury's Statutory Instruments (3rd Reissue) 244.

Cases referred to in judgments

Debtor (No 10 of 1953), Re a, ex parte the debtor v Ampthill Rural District Council [1953] 2 All ER 561, [1953] 1 WLR 1050, 4 Digest (Reissue) 147, 1292.

Marendez, Re, Re a debtor (No 10 of 1978), ex parte the debtor v Ready Mixed Concrete (Lincolnshire) Ltd (2nd February 1979), unreported, DC.

Appeal

This was an appeal by the debtor from a receiving order made by the registrar of the Bournemouth County Court on 15th December 1978, on the petition of Chantry Mount and Hawthorns Ltd ('the company',). The facts are set out in the judgment of Browne-Wilkinson J.

The debtor appeared in person.

Christopher Brougham for the company.

BROWNE-WILKINSON J delivered the first judgment at the invitation of Fox J. This is an appeal by the debtor from a receiving order made by the registrar of the Bournemouth County Court on 15th December 1978 on the petition of Chantry Mount and Hawthorns Ltd ('the company').

I can state the background very shortly. The debtor and his wife owned and carried on a school which appears to have got into some financial difficulties. In 1975 they entered into an agreement with, amongst other people, the company, under which for a limited time the financial but not the scholastic management of the school was vested in the company as attorneys. Under that agreement, the debtor and his wife bound themselves to pay over to the company all the school fees which were payable, and the company in its turn made various disbursements provided for and entered into certain contracts. The agreement provided that the debtor and his wife would indemnify the company against any liability. For reasons which it is not necessary for me to go into, a disagreement of a serious nature emerged between the debtor and his wife on the one hand and the company on the other. Shortly, it appears that the company had alleged that it was not receiving all fees and in acting under the agreement it had incurred liabilities. The matter culminated in a writ in the Queen's Bench Division, issued on 15th December 1977, under which the company claimed a fixed sum by way of indemnity against liabilities they had incurred. The company proceeded under RSC Ord 14 to obtain judgment, which was obtained after a hearing before the master in the Queen's Bench Division on 13th March 1978, at which both parties were represented by ... The judgment was for the sum of £17,130 odd, but execution on that judgment ... The stay was removed on 4th May 1978. The debtor has told us that during that period he was suffering from severe illness. The judgment remaining unsatisfied,

a on 14th September 1978 the company served a bankruptcy notice based on that judgment and claiming the sum of £10,360·82, being the amount of the judgment plus costs, less two sums which they had received from third parties in reduction of the judgment debt.

On 4th October 1978, the registrar in the Bournemouth County Court refused an application by the debtor to set aside the bankruptcy notice. It is to be noted that there

b was an actual hearing of that application. On 23rd October the debtor gave notice of appeal to this court against the registrar's refusal to set aside the bankruptcy notice, but took no immediate steps to set down that appeal. On 30th October he obtained an extension of time for 30 days for setting down his appeal to the Divisional Court. On 1st November the company presented the petition on which the receiving order was based, relying on failure to comply with the bankruptcy notice. On 28th November the debtor

c obtained a further extension to 21st December for setting down his appeal against the order of 4th October. On both occasions the explanation was that the debtor was applying for legal aid which he expected to get shortly.

On 15th December the receiving order was made by the registrar. On 20th December (that is to say, after the date of the receiving order) the debtor gave notice of appeal against the Ord 14 judgment, being an appeal to the Queen's Bench judge in chambers,

d and on the same date he obtained yet another extension of time for setting down his appeal to this court against the refusal to set aside the bankruptcy notice. That final extension of time expired on 15th January 1979.

On 5th January the debtor gave the notice of appeal against the receiving order which is the appeal before us today. A week later, on 12th January, the Queen's Bench judge in chambers dismissed the debtor's appeal against the Ord 14 judgment. The debtor then

e appealed against the Queen's Bench judge in chambers' order. His appeal was heard on 6th March, and the Court of Appeal dismissed his appeal. Accordingly, the Queen's Bench judgment under the Ord 14 proceedings is final and unappealable.

The notice of appeal given by the debtor states the following grounds for the appeal:

'1. That the Debtor denies he is indebted for £10,360·82p. 2. That the Registrar having been informed by the Debtor that he proposed to Appeal against the

f Judgment of March 13th 1978 on which the Petition Debt was based did not adjourn the Hearing of the Petition in order that that could be done. 3. The Registrar failed to take any or any proper account of the copy of Legal Aid Certificate [which he identifies] to enable the Debtor to prosecute properly for Damages for Breach of Contract and for Negligence against [five persons including the company] or to Councels [sic] Opinion with particular reference to the nature of the

g Proceedings and identity of the Defendants. 4. The Registrar erred in his discretion in failing to give the Debtor an opportunity to file evidence disputing the Petition Debt. 5. The Registrar failed to take any or any proper account of the Debtor's Appeal against the Order of Mr Registrar Wood dated 4th October 1978 whereby he dismissed the Debtor's Application to set aside the Bankruptcy Notice . . .'

h I will deal first with the fifth ground of appeal, because it raises a point which was not apparent to the debtor (who presented his case in person), involving, as it does, a point turning on the construction of the Bankruptcy Rules 1952[1] and two earlier decisions of this court.

It will be noted that when the receiving order was made in this case on 15th December 1978 the debtor's appeal against the registrar's refusal to set aside the bankruptcy notice

j was still outstanding. Rule 179 of the 1952 rules provides as follows:

'Where the act of bankruptcy alleged in the petition is non-compliance with the requirements of a bankruptcy notice, then—(a) if the debtor has applied to set aside

---

1   SI 1952 No 2113

the notice, no receiving order shall be made against him until the application has been heard; and (b) if the notice is set aside or while proceedings are stayed, no *a* receiving order shall be made; and the petition shall be adjourned or dismissed as the court thinks fit.'

In an unreported judgment of this court, *Re Marendez*[1], the reasoning in the judgment of the court suggests that, for the purposes of r 179, the application to set aside the bankruptcy notice may not have been 'heard' within the meaning of that word in the *b* rule so long as an appeal against the registrar's decision is outstanding. It appeared to us that, if the decision in *Re Marendez*[1] covered this present case, the debtor's appeal would be bound to succeed.

In a particularly persuasive argument, counsel for the company has persuaded me that the decision in *Re Marendez*[1] does not in terms cover the present case and that there is an earlier decision of this court which is directly in point which was not cited to the *c* Divisional Court in *Re Marendez*[1].

In order to understand the argument, I must refer to certain other bankruptcy rules. Rules 137 and 138 require a bankruptcy notice to be endorsed with a statement that if the debtor has a counterclaim, set-off or cross-demand which could not have been raised in the original action on which the judgment was founded he must file an affidavit within three days. Rule 139 then reads as follows: *d*

'(1) The filing of the affidavit referred to in Rule 137 shall operate as an application to set aside the bankruptcy notice, and thereupon the Registrar shall, if he is satisfied that sufficient cause is shown, fix a time and place for hearing the application, and shall give not less than three clear days' notice thereof to the debtor, the creditor, and their respective solicitors, if known.   *e*
'(2) If the application cannot be heard before the time specified in the notice for compliance with its requirements, the Registrar shall extend the time, and no act of bankruptcy shall be deemed to have been committed under the notice until the application has been heard and determined.'

In *Re a debtor (No 10 of 1953)*[2] the Divisional Court had to consider the meaning of *f* what is now r 139. The headnote reads as follows[3]:

'On September 10, 1952, the registrar dismissed an application by a debtor to set aside a bankruptcy notice which began to run from that date. On appeal to the Divisional Court the registrar's order was discharged, but on February 10, 1953, the Court of Appeal reversed the decision of the Divisional Court and directed that the *g* registrar's order of September 10, 1952, be restored. On March 10, 1953, a petition was presented, founded on the act of bankruptcy which was complete on September 10, 1952:—*Held*, that, as the time for the validity of the bankruptcy notice (namely, three months), began to run at the latest on September 11, 1952, and the Court of Appeal had reversed the decision of the Divisional Court and restored the registrars' judgment, that judgment accordingly remained standing as from the date when it *h* was given, namely, September 10, 1952, and the petition was out of time and must be dismissed.'

That headnote is not altogether accurate, but for present purposes the point in question is accurately summarised by Harman J, in these terms[4]:

j

---

1   (2nd February 1979) unreported
2   [1953] 2 All ER 561, [1953] 1 WLR 1050
3   ~~WLR 1050~~
      ll ER 561 at 563, [1953] 1 WLR 1050 at 1053

'The second ground taken was that the act of bankruptcy was complete on Sept.
10, 1952, when the registrar made his order, and, therefore, was not available as a
foundation for a petition filed more than three months thereafter, viz., on Mar. 10,
1953 ...'

He then deals with that point where he says this[1]:

'As to the second point, it is enough to remember the two dates appearing on the
face of the receiving order, viz., Aug. 22, 1952 (the date of service of the notice) and
Feb. 10, 1953 (the date of failure to comply) to suggest at once the conclusion that
the interval is too great. The notice in the ordinary course expired on Aug. 29, and
it was admittedly extended by the registrar, under Bankruptcy Rules, 1915, r. 141
to Sept. 10, 1952. On that date, prima facie the act of bankruptcy was complete and
the three months then began to run. It was, however, argued for the respondents
that either the notice of appeal filed by the appellant on Oct. 18, 1952, or the order
of this court on Nov. 10, 1952, discharging the order of Sept. 10, 1952, and setting
aside the bankruptcy notice, in some way suspended the running of time, and that
time remained so suspended until the final determination of the matter by the
Court of Appeal on Feb. 10, 1953. That order allowed the appeal, rescinded the
order of this court of Nov. 10, 1952, and restored the registrar's order, and it is said
that the respondents had three months from that date to enter their petition, and
complied by filing it on Mar. 10, 1953. We are unable to accede to this argument.
In our judgment, it follows from the terms of r. 141 of the rules of 1915 (replaced
now without material alteration in this respect by the Bankruptcy Rules 1952,
r. 139), that the only person who can extend the time for complying with the
bankruptcy notice is the registrar, or, having regard to the definition in r. 3, his
deputy. The rule is directory and compels the registrar to extend it 'until the
application has been heard and determined'. These words can only apply, in our
judgment, to the determination before the registrar of the application to set aside
the bankruptcy notice made by filing the affidavit mentioned in the rule, and
cannot apply to its determination either by this court or by the Court of Appeal. It
seems to us, therefore, that the time began to run at the latest on Sept. 11, 1952.
There were in fact, on any view, two months during which the registrar's order
stood and in which a petition could have been presented. Of course, when this
court set aside the bankruptcy notice it would also have set aside the petition, but
the order of the Court of Appeal would have restored both.'

In my judgment, this is a clear decision that for the purposes of r 139, where there has
been an actual hearing by the registrar of an application to set aside a bankruptcy notice,
that application is 'heard and determined' at the date of the registrar's decision and that
the only power to extend the time for complying with the bankruptcy notice is that
contained in r 139, the maximum period of extension being until the registrar, and not
any appellate court, has heard the application.

In *Re Marendez*[2], the debtor had apparently applied to set aside the bankruptcy notice
by an affidavit as required by r 139. There was no actual hearing of that application,
because the registrar had refused to fix a day for the hearing, presumably on the ground
that no sufficient cause was shown. The debtor appealed to the Divisional Court against
the refusal to set aside the bankruptcy notice, but whilst that appeal was pending a
receiving order was made. The Divisional Court was hearing an appeal against a refusal
to rescind the receiving order, and held that the appeal should be allowed since the
receiving order was made in contravention of r 179. There is no transcript of the
judgment of the Divisional Court before us, but we have a note of the judgment made
by the registrar, which includes the following passage:

1   [1953] 2 All ER 561 at 563–564, [1953] 1 WLR 1050 at 1054–1055
2   (2nd February 1979) unreported

'Rule uses "heard". Literal construction of "heard". "Heard" when heard by
Registrar. Too narrow a construction. Seems that rule prohibits receiving order   *a*
whilst still pending issue as to validity of notice. Counsel argues might enable
debtor to prolong by appeal. Quite true. Might be said. Equally one must consider
injustice suffered by the debtor. Severe injustice if receiving order made because in
the event Registrar might wrongly have refused to set aside. Don't think rule
relates to Registrars only. Rule comprehends whole course of proceedings, statutory
and non-statutory. No reason limiting "hearing" to initial hearing.'   *b*

I have in one respect altered the note to make it read comprehensibly.

The decision in *Re a debtor (No 10 of 1953)*[1] was not drawn to the court's attention in
Re Marendez[2]. Since *Re a debtor (No 10 of 1953)*[1] was concerned with the exact point we
have to decide today, in my judgment it covers the present case, that is, where there has
been an actual hearing by the registrar, the application has been 'heard' for the purposes
of the rule once the registrar has given his decision, notwithstanding that there is an   *c*
appeal pending against that decision. It is true that the decision in *Re a debtor (No 10 of
1953)*[1] was concerned with r 139 and not r 179, which is the rule with which we are
concerned, but unless there is a good reason shown to the contrary in my judgment the
same words appearing in the same set of rules and dealing with the same subject-matter
ought to be given the same meaning.

In *Re Marendez*[2], the court was dealing with a case where there had been no hearing   *d*
at all of the application to set aside the bankruptcy notice. The part of the judgment in
Re Marendez[2] which I have read may suggest that, even where there has been an actual
hearing by the registrar, the matter cannot be treated as having been 'heard' for the
purposes of r 179 if an appeal is pending. In my judgment, if so, the reasoning goes too
far since it is inconsistent with *Re a debtor (No 10 of 1953)*[1]. In my view, if *Re a debtor (No
10 of 1953)*[1] had been before the Divisional Court in *Re Marendez*[2], that would not have   *e*
formed one of the grounds for its decision. But for the present purposes it is sufficient
to say that *Re Marendez*[2] was dealing with a case different from that before us, since in *Re
Marendez*[2] there had not been any hearing of any kind of the application to set aside the
bankruptcy notice.

Although, in my judgment, r 179 does not preclude the making of a receiving order
once the hearing by the registrar to set aside the bankruptcy notice has been completed,   *f*
of course in the ordinary event a court dealing with an application to make a receiving
order will stand over that application until the appeal against the refusal to set aside the
bankruptcy notice has been finally dealt with. But that will only be the case if there is
a bona fide appeal being pursued with due diligence. If there is no bona fide appeal or
there is no diligence in pursuing it, then, in my judgment, r 179 does not preclude a
receiving order from being made. Once it is held that r 179 provided no absolute bar to   *g*
the making of the receiving order in this case, in my judgment the fact that theoretically
there was such an appeal on foot does not provide any ground for overturning the
receiving order in this case. The debtor's appeal against the refusal to set aside the
bankruptcy notice was being pursued with anything but diligence. Moreover, any
possibility of such an appeal now being brought has disappeared since even with the
three extensions of time that he was granted the time for setting down such an appeal   *h*
expired on 15th January 1979.

I turn next to the first and fourth grounds which the debtor has urged for setting aside
the receiving order. These were really the grounds that he developed in argument
before us. He sought to show, by miscellaneous pieces of evidence, that at the date of the
Ord 14 judgment the company held funds belonging to himself and his wife more than
sufficient to offset that amount owed by him to the company. On the view that I take   *j*
of the matter, it is not necessary to go into the details of his submissions on the point. I

---

1   [1953] 2 All ER 561, [1953] 1 WLR 1050
2   (2nd February 1979) unreported

can perhaps illustrate it by reference to one item which he alleges reduced the

a indebtedness due at that date. He says that at that date the company's solicitors were holding a substantial sum of money, which ought to be credited against the liability of himself and his wife to the company. But the company's solicitors state that they were holding no moneys on behalf of the debtor or his wife: what they were holding were moneys paid to them by the debtor in satisfaction of other orders for costs. This illustrates the unsatisfactory nature of the case the debtor is trying to make; he takes the judgment

b debt as the only indebtedness and then says that, by showing that there were other funds available at the time, the whole of that indebtedness has been offset. I am not satisfied that in any case the sum was not due. But in my judgment that is not the point. What the debtor is trying to do is either to show that there was no debt, or to show that he had a set-off which extinguished an existing debt.

To the extent that he is seeking to show that there was no debt, it seems to me

c impossible for this court to entertain such an argument. There is the judgment of the master, the judge in chambers and the Court of Appeal that the debt is due; there is a judgment for that sum. He has shown no grounds for going behind that judgment, save that in one respect he says that the material that he has put before us was not available in his hands until recently. There is no evidence of the date at which the material came to him. Indeed, in relation to the majority of the material, it is quite clear that it has been

d in his hands for a considerable period.

If the debtor is seeking to set up these matters by way of set-off, the set-off plainly arises out of the same transaction, namely the agreement between him and the company, and it could and should have been set up in the action in which the judgment was given. This was not done, though the debtor appears to have been given considerable leeway to put up such a set-off even after the Ord 14 judgment.

e Turning to the third ground of appeal, this appears to be a claim based on a counterclaim. No argument was developed by the debtor before us based on any such counterclaim. No opinion of counsel was produced to us. There is no evidence of any kind to substantiate the existence of such a counterclaim. In any event, for the same reasons that I have given in relation to set-off, the matter should have been raised by way of counterclaim in the original action and is not open as a ground now for attacking the

f receiving order.

As to the second ground of appeal, namely that he proposed to appeal against the judgment of 13th March 1978, in my judgment the registrar was fully at liberty, bearing in mind the time-table I have set out, to disregard that matter. In any event, the appeal has now taken place and the appeal has been dismissed.

Finally, the debtor in his reply (but not to my understanding in the course of his

g opening) put forward some suggestion that the Ord 14 judgment had been obtained either by fraud or by the perjury of deponents to the affidavits which were sworn in support of the Ord 14 summons. Nothing that he has said suggests that he has even a prima facie case of fraud. What he is saying is that he was not indebted in the sum. In any event, having pursued his appeal against the Queen's Bench judgment to the Court of Appeal without previously raising any allegation of fraud, in my judgment he is too

h late to raise that matter now, unless he shows that there is new material which prevented him from raising the point earlier. As I have said, there is no indication that there is such material.

For these reasons, I would myself dismiss the appeal.

FOX J. I add only some observations about *Re Marendez*[1]. In that case, the debtor had

j filed an affidavit under r 137 asserting a counterclaim or a set-off. Under r 139, that operates as an application to set aside the bankruptcy notice, and, under the same rule, the registrar, if satisfied that sufficient cause is shown, is to fix a time and place for hearing the application. In *Re Marendez*[1] the registrar refused to fix the time or place for

---

1   (2nd February 1979) unreported

hearing. The debtor appealed against that. The appeal was not heard until after the receiving order. At the time the receiving order was made therefore, the application to set aside the bankruptcy notice had never been heard at all. The refusal to fix a hearing was effected merely by the registrar endorsing the affidavit 'No cause shown', or some similar words, and without a hearing. Rule 179 prohibits the making of a receiving order until the application to set aside the bankruptcy notice has been heard. As I have said, when the receiving order was made in Re Marendez[1], the application had not been heard, the registrar having refused to fix a date and time for hearing. Thus the issue in Re Marendez[1] was whether the application could be said to have been heard prior to the determination of the appeal by the Divisional Court. That being said, and although we have only a very brief note of the judgment in Re Marendez[1], I think it is very probable that my observations were on any view too widely expressed, having regard in particular to Re a debtor (No 10 of 1953)[2], which was not cited to the court in Re Marendez[1]. I agree with Browne-Wilkinson J that the latter case, Re a debtor (No 10 of 1953)[2], is directly in point in the present case and covers the present point.

In the circumstances, I agree that the appeal must be dismissed.

Appeal dismissed.

Solicitors: *Adlers & Aberstones* (for the company).

Jacqueline Metcalfe   Barrister.

---

1   (2nd February 1979) unreported
2   [1953] 2 All ER 561, [1953] 1 WLR 1050

Bradshaw and another v Pawley

a

CHANCERY DIVISION
SIR ROBERT MEGARRY V-C
5th, 9th APRIL 1979

Landlord and tenant – Lease – Rent – Grant of new lease to existing tenant – New lease
b *increasing rent payable – Time from which new rent operative – Covenant by tenant to pay new*
rent from date before execution of new lease – Whether tenant liable to pay rent at new rate from
prior date or only from date of execution of lease.

The landlords let certain business premises to a tenant for a term of 21 years less a day
from 25th March 1953 at a rent of £312 per annum. The lease contained no provision
for rent reviews. Part II of the Landlord and Tenant Act 1954 applied to the tenancy and
c so it continued after the expiration of the term on 24th March 1974. Pursuant to the Act
the landlords gave the tenant notice on 13th February 1974 to terminate the tenancy on
14th August 1974 and on 12th June 1974 the tenant applied to the county court for the
grant of a new tenancy. Prolonged negotiations followed between those advising the
parties. Finally, on 11th January 1977, a consent order was made in the county court for
d the grant of a new lease for a term of 'Ten years from the 25th March 1974 at a rent of
£1750' a year with provision for 'upward reviews' during the term. By virtue of ss 24
and 64 of the Act the tenancy created by the old lease came to an end on 23rd May
1977. The new lease was not executed until 10th March 1978. It stated that the
premises were let to the tenant by the landlords 'from the 25th day of March 1974 for the
term of ten years [the tenant] Yielding and Paying Therefor during the said term yearly
and proportionately for any fraction of a year' the rents specified in the lease, which were
e 'For the first four and three quarter years of the said term' a rent of £1,750 per annum,
'for the next three years of the said term' a rent determined in accordance with cl 3 of the
lease which contained provisions for rent review, and 'for the remainder of the said term'
a rent determined in accordance with a similar provision. The tenant's covenants were
made 'to the intent that the obligations may continue throughout the said term'. The
first of the covenants was 'to pay during the said term the said reserved rents at the times
f and in [the] manner [specified]'. During the period from 25th March 1974 to 10th
March 1978 the tenant continued to pay rent at the rate of £312 per annum. The
landlords demanded payment of rent at the rate of £1,750 per annum for that period.
The tenant refused to pay the excess, contending that his obligation to pay rent at the
new rate did not arise until the new lease had been executed and that he was only liable
to pay rent at the new rate from 10th March 1978 onwards. The landlords brought an
g action against him claiming, inter alia, a declaration that he was obliged to pay rent at the
rate of £1,750 from 25th March 1974.

Held – (i) Where a lease created a term of years which was expressed to run from some
date earlier than that of the execution of the lease, although the term created did not
commence until the date of execution of the lease and no act or omission prior to that
h date would normally constitute a breach of the obligations of the lease, there was nothing
to prevent the parties from defining the expiration of the term by reference to a date
prior to the execution of the lease or from making contractual provisions which took
effect by reference to such a date (eg by defining the period for the operation of a break
clause or an increase of rent) or to prevent the lease creating obligations in respect of any
period prior to the execution of the lease. Whether in fact such obligations were created
j depended on the construction of the lease (see p 276 j to p 277 c and e to p 278 c g h and
p 279 b to e, post).

(ii) On the true construction of the consent order and the new lease, the rent of £1,750
was to be paid throughout the period of 10 years from 25th March 1974 irrespective of
the date on which the new lease was actually executed. It followed that the tenant was
liable to pay the balance outstanding (see p 276 f g, p 279 f g and p 278 e, post).

Notes

For tenancies to which the Landlord and Tenant Act 1954 applies, see 23 Halsbury's Laws *a*
(3rd Edn) 885, para 1707.

For the Landlord and Tenant Act 1954, Part II, see 18 Halsbury's Statutes (3rd Edn)
554.

Cases referred to in judgment

Bird v Baker (1858) 1 E & E 12, 28 LJQB 7, 32 LTOS 74, 4 Jur NS 1148, 120 ER 812, 31(1)
Digest (Reissue) 153, *1318*.   *b*

Cadogan (Earl) v Guinness [1936] 2 All ER 29, [1936] Ch 515, 105 LJ Ch 255, 155 LT 404,
40 Digest (Repl) 366, *2932*.

M'Leish v Tate (1778) 2 Cowp 781, 98 ER 1359, 31(1) Digest (Reissue) 473, *3876*.

Roberts v Church Comrs for England [1971] 3 All ER 703, [1972] 1 QB 278, [1971] 3 WLR
566, CA, 31(1) Digest (Reissue) 176, *1492*.

Shaw v Kay (1847) 1 Exch 412, 17 LJ Ex 17, 154 ER 175, 17 Digest (Reissue), 438, *1993*.   *c*

Wyburd v Tuck (1799) 1 Bos & P 458, 126 ER 1009, 31(1) Digest (Reissue) 527, *4408*.

Cases also cited

Colton v Becollda Property Investments Ltd [1950] 1 KB 216, CA.

High Road, Kilburn, Re 88, Meakers Ltd v DAW Consolidated Properties Ltd [1959] 1 All ER
527, [1959] 1 WLR 279.   *d*

Tottenham Hotspur Football and Athletic Co Ltd v Princegrove Publishers Ltd [1974] 1 All ER
17, [1974] 1 WLR 113.

Action

By a writ issued on 29th June 1978, the plaintiffs, John Richard Bradshaw and Norman
Frederick Bradshaw ('the landlords'), brought an action against the defendant, Alexander   *e*
Christopher Pawley ('the tenant') claiming (i) a declaration that on the true construction
of a lease dated 10th March 1978 the tenant was obliged to pay rent to the landlords at
the rate of £1,750 per annum from 25th March 1974; (ii) £4,673·50 (being the amount
of rent due at the rate of £1,750 per annum from 25th March 1974 less the amount paid
by the tenant from that date); (iii) interest; (iv) further or other relief. The facts are set
out in the judgment.   *f*

David Hands for the landlords.
Robert Moxon Browne for the tenant.

Cur adv vult

g

9th April.   **SIR ROBERT MEGARRY V-C** read the following judgment: This case
raises a short point of principle on the law of landlord and tenant. The basic question is
whether on the grant of a new lease to an existing lessee a covenant to pay rent at a certain
rate from a date anterior to the date when the lease was executed can make the lessee
liable for rent at that rate from that anterior date or only from the date when the lease
was executed. The question arises in an action brought by the landlords against the   *h*
tenant claiming rent at the agreed rate from the anterior date; and a striking feature is
that the two dates are nearly four years apart.

The relevant facts may be briefly stated. The premises in question are business
premises which the tenant formerly held under a lease for 21 years less a day from 25th
March 1953. The natural expiration of the term was thus on 24th March 1974, but of
course the Landlord and Tenant Act 1954, Part II, applied to the tenancy. The landlords   *j*
accordingly gave a statutory notice on 13th February 1974 to determine the tenancy on
14th August 1974; and on 12th June 1974 the tenant applied to the county court for the
grant of a new tenancy under the Act.

Prolonged negotiations then took place between those advising the parties. From
early on these were on the basis of a new term for ten years, and after a while this

emerged as being ten years from 25th March 1974. Finally, on 11th January 1977, a
a consent order was made in the county court for the grant of a new lease of most of the
premises for a term of 'Ten Years from the 25th March 1974 at a rent of £1750' a year,
with provision for 'upward reviews' during the term. The rent payable under the
previous lease, I may say, was £312 a year, with no provision for rent revision. In each
case there was in addition an insurance rent which does not affect what I have to decide.

It is regrettable that the order does not state on the face of it that it was a consent order,
b as every consent order ought to do; but it is common ground that in fact it was a consent
order. The order also provided that the parties should jointly apply to the court under
s 38(4) of the 1954 Act for an order authorising an agreement to exclude ss 24 to 28 of the
Act in respect of the new lease; and it was agreed that this agreement should be included
in the lease. This, of course, would prevent the new lease from conferring any right to
a new tenancy under the Act when it expired. On 16th May 1977 the court made the
c requisite order to this effect.

A week later, on 23rd May 1977, the tenancy flowing from the combined effect of the
old lease and the 1954 Act came to an end. Section 24(1), when read with s 64, had
prolonged the tenancy until the expiration of three months after the end of the period
of six weeks allowed for an appeal from the order of 11th January 1977. The Supreme
Court of Judicature (Consolidation) Act 1925, s 31(1)(h), does not prohibit appeals from
d consent orders, though it does require leave for such an appeal. The new lease, however,
still had not been executed, for dissension arose on the point now before me for
decision. Finally, on 10th March 1978 the lease was duly executed; and on 29th June
1978 the writ was issued.

It will be seen that there are thus four main periods with which I am concerned.

1. Until 24th March 1974 the old lease was running at a rent of £312 a year; and this
e period is not in issue.

2. From 24th March 1974 until 23rd May 1977 the tenancy created by the old lease
was being continued by force of the 1954 Act. This second period is very much in
issue. The tenant contends that his liability for this period is at the rate of £312 a year,
whereas the landlords contend that it is at the rate of £1,750.

3. From 24th May 1977 until 10th March 1978, the old lease was at an end and the new
f lease had yet to be granted. This third period is also in issue. There is the same dispute
about the amount of the rent, and counsel for the tenant was forced to contend that
either the tenant was holding over during that period, without any lease or tenancy, or
else that he was there by virtue of the agreement for a lease evidenced by the consent
order, on the terms of that order.

4. From 10th March 1978 onwards the new lease was in force, and there is no dispute
g that thereafter the tenant was liable for rent at the rate of £1,750 a year.

Accordingly, what I have to decide is the liability of the tenant during the second and
third periods.

With that, I turn to the provisions of the new lease, which is expressed in terms of 'the
lessor' and 'the lessee'. By the habendum, the premises are demised to the lessee to hold
the same unto the lessee—

h
'from the 25th day of March 1974 for the term of ten years but determinable as
hereinafter provided YIELDING AND PAYING THEREFOR during the said term yearly and
proportionately for any fraction of a year the rents hereunder set out . . .'

There are then specified 'for the first four and three-quarter years of the said term' the
rent of £1,750 a year, and 'for the next three years of the said term' a rent determined in
j accordance with cl 3, which contains provisions for rent review. There is then a similar
provision 'for the remainder of the said term'; and all the rents are to be paid quarterly
in advance on the usual quarter days. The lessee's covenants are made 'to the intent that
the obligations may continue throughout the said term'; and the first of these is 'to pay
during the said term the said reserved rents at the times and in manner aforesaid', and so
on.

In considering the rival contentions, I think that the starting point is to construe the
lease in the ordinary way, before considering whether there is anything in the law to a
modify that construction or to prevent it being effectuated. It seems perfectly clear that
the obligation to pay a rent of £1,750 a year is an obligation to pay that rent for the
period of ten years from 25th March 1974. The reddendum is in terms of paying rent
at that rate 'during the said term', and so is the covenant to pay rent: and there is no term
in the document that can be called the 'said' term except the 'term of ten years' running
'from the 25th day of March 1974'. b

That construction seems to me to be supported (if support be needed) by the
consequences of an answer which counsel for the tenant gave to a question from the
Bench. He was constrained to accept that the time-table for increases of rent for the
specified periods 'of the said term' was to operate during the ten years from 25th March
1974 and not the six years and a few days running from the execution of the lease on
10th March 1978. Accordingly, the revised rent was to run from the expiration of 'the c
first four and three-quarter years of the said term', and so would commence at Christmas
1978, and so on. Counsel for the landlords said that on this footing it was impossible to
see how it could be said that 'the said term' meant one thing for the purpose of laying
down a rent of £1,750 a year and another for the purpose of the time-table of rent
increases, especially when the first 4¾ years of that time-table provided for the rent to be
£1,750 a year. The 'said term' must mean the same term, whether the phrase is 'during d
the said term' or 'of the said term'.

That contention seems to me to be unanswerable. The contentions of counsel for the
tenant reduced him to contending that the obligation to pay £1,750 a year 'during the
said term' really meant not 'during the said term of ten years from 25th March 1974', but
'during so much of the said term of ten years from 25th March 1974 as subsists while the
parties are in the relationship of landlord and tenant under this demise', and so when the e
lease was executed meant during the next six years and a few days. Similarly, the
provision in the consent order for the grant of a new lease 'for a term of Ten Years from
the 25th March 1974 at a rent of £1750' was really an agreement to pay a rent of £1,750
not for ten years but for so much of the then unexpired period of approximately seven
years and two months out of that ten years as still remained unexpired when the lease
was finally executed. As the difference between the two rents is nearly £4 a day, each f
day's delay in executing the lease would save the tenant some £4. As a matter of
construction I cannot accept these contentions. I feel no doubt that on ordinary principles
of construction the true meaning of the consent order and the lease is that a rent of
£1,750 a year was to be paid throughout the period of ten years from 25th March 1974,
irrespective of the date on which the lease was actually executed.

The question, then, is whether there is anything in the law to require the lease to be g
construed differently, or to prevent effect being given to the natural construction of its
language. When asked, counsel for the tenant agreed that on this he relied not on any
provisions of the Act but on the general principles of the law. The only qualification to
this was that he relied to some extent on the provisions of the 1954 Act which prevented
the old tenancy from determining when the old lease expired; and he also contended that
s 24A, when read with s 64, would be pointless if the landlords were right. This latter h
point, however, did not withstand investigation, and I need not pursue it further. In the
main, counsel for the tenant relied on authorities which for the most part are
conveniently collected in *Roberts v Church Comrs for England*[1]. As he contended, there are
indeed some limitations on the effect that can be given to a term expressed to run from
a date prior to the execution of the lease, and I must consider these.

First, it is well settled that a lease cannot retrospectively vest an estate in the lessee. If j
today a lease is granted for seven years from this day a year ago, no term of seven years
is brought into being, but only a term of six years from today. A lease, of course, is more

---

1   [1971] 3 All ER 703, [1972] 1 QB 278

a than a mere contract, for it operates by way of grant to create an estate or interest in the land; and you cannot grant today that X shall have had a term of years vested in him a year ago. Whatever contractual obligations there may be between the parties, no actual term of years can be created until the lease has been executed and so the grant has been made. Thus where the question is what term has actually been created, as where a statute refers to terms of a particular length, the commencement of the term cannot be earlier than the date of the grant of the lease. There is, of course, no objection to a lease defining

b the term by reference to some past date, as in the grant of a term of seven years from this day a year ago; but this merely creates a term of six years from today.

Second, a lease for a term from some past date will not, at any rate normally, make into a breach of covenant that which was not a breach when it was committed. An act or omission by a prospective lessee which would be a contravention of the proposed lease is not turned into a breach of covenant by him merely because he subsequently accepts the

c grant of the lease for a term which is expressed to run from some date anterior to the act or omission. That, I think, follows from *Shaw v Kay*[1]. There, the landlord sued on a repairing covenant in respect of acts done by the tenant before the lease was executed, basing the claim on the lease having been expressed to run from an earlier date. The claim failed, though no reasoned judgments were delivered.

It may be tempting to infer from these two propositions that when a term is expressed

d to run from some date prior to the actual grant of the lease, that prior date can have no function save as a unit of calculation in ascertaining the date on which the term will expire; and in *Shaw v Kay*[2] there is a dictum of Parke B which can be read as indicating this. Whatever the temptation, I think that it would be wrong to draw any such inference. The dictum on which Parke B relied, uttered by Eyre CJ in *Wyburd v Tuck*[3], must be understood in relation to the facts of the case; and what the court was concerned

e with there was a lease of tithes as giving the plaintiff a title to sue for the tithes. As the lease did not vest the term in the tenant before it was executed, he could not sue for tithes due before the date of execution. However, when what is in issue is not title but obligation or liability, I do not see why the parties should not, if they so choose, make the obligation or liability enforceable in respect of such anterior date as they wish. Thus if a lease is granted for a term of 21 years from a date two years prior to the grant of the

f lease, with a provision for determination at the end of the 7th or 14th years of the term, then (in the words of Clauson J[4])—

'it is perfectly easy as a matter of construction of such a document to say that the seven years according to the obvious intention of the parties is not to run as from the date of the execution of the lease but from the moment spoken of, though inaccurately, as the beginning of the term in the document.'

g
Bird v Baker[5] provides an example of this. There, the lease was granted in July 1851 for 14 years from Christmas 1849, with power to break 'at the expiration of the first seven years thereof': and the Court of Queen's Bench held that the break came at Christmas 1856 and not in July 1858.

h I cannot see what there is to stultify an agreement in a lease to make payments in respect of past periods, or to require the court to construe a lease so as to prevent any agreement from relating to past periods unless compelled to it. It is by no means unknown for a lease not to be executed until after the prospective lessee has entered (usually with safeguards for the lessor), and for the lessee then to pay rent and observe the terms of the lease as from a date prior to the execution of the lease. If as a matter of

j
1   (1847) 1 Exch 412
2   1 Exch 412 at 413
3   (1799) 1 Bos & P 458 at 464
4   *Earl Cadogan v Guinness* [1936] Ch 515 at 518, cf [1936] 2 All ER 29 at 32
5   (1858) 1 E & E 12

construction the obligation is to pay rent at a specified rate from some date earlier than
that of the execution of the lease, why should that not be enforceable?

a

I think that some support for this view is provided by a dictum of Pollock CB in *Shaw
v Kay*. The report in the Exchequer Reports[1] that was cited to me omits this, but it is to
be found in the report of the case in the Law Journal Reports, Exchequer[2]. Pollock CB
said:

> 'A party may covenant to indemnify another from what has passed. I may   *b*
> demise premises to-day, and covenant to save my tenant harmless from what has
> happened six months before.'

On the same footing I do not see why, by suitable wording, a lease should not impose on
one of the parties some liability for things past.

Counsel for the tenant stressed that rent was something that had to be paid periodically,   *c*
and so an obligation to pay nearly four years' rent at a blow indicated that what was being
paid could not truly be called rent. However, I do not think that rent becomes denatured
when a sufficiency of gales remain unpaid. Nor do I see why an obligation to pay rent
in respect of periods of occupation by the tenant prior to the grant of the lease should not
be regarded as rent. What must matter, surely, is what the payments are due for, rather
than how and when the payments are in fact made. I would follow Foa's General Law   *d*
of Landlord and Tenant[3] in regarding rent as being prima facie 'the monetary
compensation payable by the tenant in consideration for the grant, however it be
described or allocated', though I think that I would insert the word 'periodical' before the
word 'monetary'. I would also pay more attention to modern than medieval concepts in
considering the nature of rent. If the parties to a lease choose to agree that the lessee shall
pay rent to the lessor in respect of a period prior to the grant of the lease, I do not see why   *e*
this should not be valid and enforceable. So far as it goes, I think that *M'Leish v Tate*[4]
supports the view that rent may still be rent even though it is reserved in respect of the
occupation by a tenant at some time prior to the execution of the instrument which
reserves the rent. Even if this is wrong, and the payments in dispute, though described
as 'rent', are not in law 'rent', strictly so called, I cannot see why the lessors should not
enforce payment. There is nothing to stop a man from being liable on a covenant to pay   *f*
a sum of money in respect of some past period.

Counsel for the tenant relied to some extent on the tenant holding on the terms of the
old lease, as extended by the Act, from 24th March 1974 until 23rd May 1977; this is the
second period that I mentioned earlier. As during this period the tenant held at a rent of
£312 a year, why should he now pay more? The answer, I think, is that he would be
under no obligation to pay more unless he had bound himself to do so; and on the true   *g*
construction of the new lease that is just what he has done. The fact that he need not
have paid more if he had not entered into a new lease, or if instead he had entered into
a differently worded lease, cannot alter the consequences of what he did do. I know of
nothing at common law to prevent a tenant under an existing tenancy from agreeing to
pay a higher rent, or from entering into a new tenancy at a higher rent, in place of his
existing tenancy. Nor can I see any magic in the Act which would make the terms of the   *h*
extended tenancy prevail over those of the new lease. The position of the tenant during
the third period is a fortiori; for his old tenancy had ended and until the new lease was
executed the tenant's only right of occupation was by virtue of the agreement evidenced
by the consent order of 11th January 1977. That agreement, of course, was for the same
rent as the rent under the new lease, namely, £1,750 a year, and so whatever the road, the
terminus is £1,750 a year.

j

1   (1847) 1 Exch 412
2   17 LJ Ex 17 at 18
3   8th Edn (1957), p 101
4   (1778) 2 Cowp 781 at 784

I do not think that any difficulty arises from the payment and acceptance of rent at the rate of £312 a year after 25th March 1974; and, indeed, no difficulty has been suggested. Obviously credit must be given for the payments made against the payments due at the rate of £1,750 a year, and the landlords' claim is, of course, properly made on that basis. Nor, I think, is there any difficulty in the fact that the payments at the higher rate have not been made punctually each quarter day since 25th March 1974. No obligation under the new lease to make these payments could arise until the lease had been executed, and so the omission to make those payments at any earlier date could not constitute a breach of covenant.

In the result, I think that where a lease creates a term of years which is expressed to run from some date earlier than that of the execution of the lease, the relevant law may be summarised as follows:

1. The term created will be a term which commences on the date when the lease is executed, and not the earlier date. 2. No act or omission prior to the date on which the lease is executed will normally constitute a breach of the obligations of the lease. 3. These principles do not prevent the parties from defining the expiration of the term by reference to a date prior to that of the execution of the lease, or from making contractual provisions which take effect by reference to such a date, as by defining the period for the operation of a break clause or an increase of rent. 4. There is nothing in these principles to prevent the lease from creating obligations in respect of any period prior to the execution of the lease. 5. Whether in fact any such obligations have been created depends on the construction of the lease; and there is nothing which requires the lease to be construed in such a way as to avoid, if possible, the creation of such obligations.

On the facts of the case before me, these principles and the other matters that I have discussed point to only one conclusion, namely, that the landlords' claim succeeds. The precise terms of the order are for discussion.

Order accordingly.

Solicitors: *Kingsley, Napley & Co* (for the landlords); *CA Maddin & Co* (for the tenant).

Hazel Hartman   Barrister.

Carvalho v Hull Blyth (Angola) Ltd

COURT OF APPEAL, CIVIL DIVISION
BROWNE AND GEOFFREY LANE LJJ
12th, 13th, 14th JUNE 1979

Conflict of laws – Stay of proceedings – Agreement to refer to foreign court – Action commenced in England – Contract providing for disputes to be decided by foreign court – Revolution in country of foreign court – Country becoming independent under revolutionary government – Law applied by foreign court changing after contract made – Whether foreign court under revolutionary government was the same court contemplated by parties when making contract – Whether English court should exercise discretion to refuse stay of proceedings.

The defendants, a company registered in England, carried on business in Angola through subsidiary companies in which the plaintiff had a 49% shareholding. In 1973 the plaintiff, who was then living in Angola, agreed to sell his shareholding to the defendants for 76 million escudos, payable in four instalments. The contract provided that 'In the case of litigation arising the District Court of Luanda should be considered the sole Court competent to adjudicate to the exclusion of all others'. At the time of the contract Angola was a province of Portugal and part of the Portuguese legal system, there being a right of appeal to the Supreme Court in Lisbon. In 1975 Angola became independent under a revolutionary government. Under the new constitution Portuguese law continued to be applied provided it did not 'conflict with . . . the Angolan Revolutionary Process'. The right of appeal to Lisbon was abolished, and although there continued to be a District Court of Luanda, the judges were appointed on a basis different from that formerly applying. The plaintiff left Angola in 1975, allegedly in fear of his life, and thereafter resided in Portugal. The defendants paid the first three instalments due under the contract but failed to pay the fourth instalment of 20 million escudos due in January 1976. The plaintiff issued a writ in England claiming the amount due or its sterling equivalent (about £300,000). The defendants applied to have the action stayed, relying on the clause in the contract that the District Court at Luanda was to have exclusive jurisdiction in any litigation. The judge dismissed the application, and the defendants appealed.

Held – The appeal would be dismissed for the following reasons—

(i) The defendants could not rely on the clause in the contract giving the District Court at Luanda exclusive jurisdiction, because on the true construction of that clause the court of that name constituted under the revolutionary government was not the court contemplated by the parties when the contract was made, since it was no longer a Portuguese court applying Portuguese municipal law but an Angolan court applying Angolan law. The plaintiff was therefore not bound by the agreement to litigate only in Angola (see p 285 g to p 286 a, p 287 c to e, p 288 h j and p 289 a f g and j, post).

(ii) In any event, the court had a discretion to refuse a stay if the plaintiff proved that it was 'just and proper', or that there was 'strong cause', to do so (those being merely different ways of expressing the same test), and because of the political and legal changes in Angola it was an appropriate case for the exercise of that discretion. The plaintiff would therefore be allowed to continue his action in England (see p 286 b c g h, p 287 b to e and p 289 g to j, post); dicta of Brandon J in *The Eleftheria* [1969] 2 All ER at 645 and of Willmer J in *The Fehmarn* [1957] 2 All ER at 710 applied.

Notes

As to stay of proceedings in England where parties have agreed to submit disputes to a foreign tribunal, see 8 Halsbury's Laws (4th Edn) paras 792–793, and for cases on the subject, see 11 Digest (Reissue) 633, 1690–1691.

Cases referred to in judgments

a *Adolf Warski, The, and the Sniadecki* [1976] 2 Lloyd's Rep 241, CA.

Eleftheria, The, owners of cargo lately laden on board ship or vessel Eleftheria v owners of ship or vessel Eleftheria [1969] 2 All ER 641, [1970] P 94, [1969] 2 WLR 1073, [1969] 1 Lloyd's Rep 237, 11 Digest (Reissue) 633, 1691.

Fehmarn, The [1958] 1 All ER 333, [1958] 1 WLR 159, [1957] 2 Lloyd's Rep 551, CA; *affg* [1957] 2 All ER 707, [1957] 1 WLR 815, [1957] 1 Lloyd's Rep 511, 11 Digest (Reissue)

b 633, 1690.

Makefjell, The [1975] 1 Lloyd's Rep 528; *affd* [1976] 2 Lloyd's Rep 29, CA.

Unterweser Reederei GmbH v Zapata Off-Shore Co, The Chaparral [1968] 2 Lloyd's Rep 158, CA.

Case also cited

c *Ellinger v Guinness, Mahon & Co, Frankfurter Bank AG and Metall Gesellschaft AG* [1939] 4 All ER 16.

Appeal

The defendants, Hull Blyth (Angola) Ltd, an English registered company carrying on business as ships' agents and motor traders in Angola, appealed against the decision of

d Donaldson J on 19th February 1979 refusing the defendants' application for a stay of the proceedings commenced by the plaintiff, Joaquim Carvalho, a resident of Portugal, by writ issued on 29th April 1977 claiming the sum of 20 million escudos or the sterling equivalent thereof alleged to be payable by the defendants to the plaintiff under a contract dated 5th December 1973. The facts are set out in the judgment of Browne LJ.

e *Richard Wood* for the defendants.
Richard Siberry for the plaintiff.

BROWNE LJ. This is an appeal by the defendants from a decision of Donaldson J given on 19th February 1979, when he refused the defendants' application to stay the

f plaintiff's action but gave leave to appeal.

The defendants' application is based on cl 14 of the contract on which the plaintiff's action is based. I quote: 'In the case of litigation arising the District Court of Luanda should be considered the sole Court competent to adjudicate to the exclusion of all others.'

I should like to say at once that this case was extremely well argued on both sides and we are very much obliged to counsel for their help.

g The plaintiff formerly lived in Angola, but left in August 1975 and now lives in Portugal. The defendants are an English registered company, so there is no doubt that the English courts have jurisdiction, but we are told that the defendants have no assets here. They have carried on and still carry on business entirely in Angola. They have carried on business there for 100 years. Their present business is that of ships' agents, and

h they also carry on business as motor traders through subsidiary companies.

In 1970 their motor trading business was reorganised in such a way that there were five subsidiary companies known as the UNAIO Group; in each of these companies the defendants owned 51% of the shares and the plaintiff owned 49%. By a contract dated 5th December 1973, exhibited to Mr Woodhouse's affidavit dated 15th July 1977, the plaintiff agreed to sell and the defendants agreed to buy all his shares in the five

j subsidiary companies for a total price of 76 million escudos. Clause 6 of the contract provided for the payment of the price by four instalments. The first three instalments were paid. The fourth instalment of 20 million escudos (of which the sterling equivalent is about £300,000) should have been paid in January 1976 but has not been paid. On 29th April 1977 the plaintiff issued his writ in this action claiming that sum or its sterling equivalent. I have already quoted cl 14 of the contract.

Counsel for the defendants submits that the proper law of the contract is Angolan law
and tells us that the defence to the plaintiff's claim will be: (1) that, under Angolan law,
the 'economic hardship' suffered by the UNAIO Group as a result of events in Angola
from 1975 onwards would entitle them to a reduction or postponement of the payment
claimed in the action; (2) that, under the Angolan exchange control regulations, the
defendants are precluded from making any payments otherwise than in Angola in the
new currency, known as kwanzas, which has superseded the escudo. Any judgment
obtained by the plaintiff here could not be satisfied by the defendants without a breach
of the Angolan exchange control regulations which might expose them to criminal
sanctions. I need not refer, I think, in detail to the evidence about this, but it is dealt with
in Mr Woodhouse's affidavit of 15th July 1977 and in two letters from a Dr Torres dated
16th March 1976 and 8th August 1977, which deal with the hardship point. I am bound
to say that I find Dr Torres's letters extremely obscure. So far as the exchange control
point is concerned, it is dealt with in Dr Oliveira's affidavit.

Until 1951 Angola was a colony of Portugal. In 1951 it became a province of
Portugal. In January 1975, after a coup d'état in Portugal, the new Portuguese
government announced that Angola would become independent in November 1975. In
1975 civil war broke out in Angola, but on 11th November Angola did become
independent and, in due course, a new constitution was promulgated to which I will
refer in a moment. A party or group known as MPLA assumed power, that being the
Popular Movement for the Liberation of Angola, and Dr Neto became president. Since
then Angola has been recognised by Her Majesty's government, among a number of
other states, and ambassadors have been exchanged between Angola and this country.

The plaintiff, as I have said, left Angola in August 1975. There was before Donaldson
J an affidavit by Mr Englefield, the plaintiff's solicitor, in these terms:

'1. I have the carriage of this action on behalf of the Plaintiff and have spoken to
him on a number of occasions both in this country and in Portugal. The Plaintiff
has informed me that in August, 1975 he was forced to leave Angola with his family
and received threats against his life and the lives of his family. The Plaintiff left
behind in Angola his house, furniture, balance in his Bank Account and four farms
belonging to him. The Plaintiff's property and farms have now been taken over by
officers of the Marxists' Government. 2. The Plaintiff is unwilling to return to
Angola and believes that if he does so he will be liquidated.'

Since the hearing before Donaldson J an affidavit has been sworn by the plaintiff himself,
verifying that affidavit and including a list of the property which he says he left behind
in Angola and which has been confiscated. That affidavit was put before us without
objection from counsel for the defendants.

I should now refer to the constitution, which is exhibited to Dr Almeida's affidavit of
28th October 1977. So far as relevant, it provides:

'Article 1 The People's Republic of Angola is a Sovereign, independent and
democratic State, the foremost objective of which is the total liberation of the
Angolan people from the vestiges of Colonialism and from domination and
aggression by Imperialism and the construction of a prosperous and democratic
country, completely free from any form of exploitation of man by man,
materialising the inspirations of the popular masses.
'Article 2: All sovereignty is vested in the Angolan people. The political,
economic and social guidance of the nation are vested in the MPLA, its lawful
representative, consisting of a wide front which includes all the patriotic forces
engaged in the anti-Imperialist struggle . . .
'Article 7: The People's Republic of Angola is a lay State, there being complete
separation between the State and religious institutions. All religions will be
respected and the State will grant protection for churches, places and objects of
worship, provided that they comply with State laws . . .

'Article 10: The People's Republic of Angola recognises, protects and guarantees private property and activities, even those of foreigners, provided that they are useful to the economy of the country and the interests of the Angolan people . . .

'Article 44: The exercise of the jurisdictional function aimed at the realisation of Democratic justice is exclusively incumbent on the Courts. The organisation, composition and competence of the Courts will be fixed by Law . . .

'Article 45: The Judges will be independent in the exercise of their duties . . .

'Article 58: The Laws and Regulations currently in force will be applicable where not revoked or altered and provided that they do not conflict with the spirit of this Law and the Angolan Revolutionary Process . . .'

The judge also referred to art 54, which dealt with the flag of the new state, but I confess that I cannot see that has any relevance to this appeal.

We have an agreed note of the judgment of Donaldson J, approved by him. He said this:

'Of course, I accept Brandon J's approach as set out in The Eleftheria[1]. These are the sort of matters one would consider in the ordinary case where there has been no political change. However, they are not necessarily applicable. I rely on the rule in Dicey[2]. If I were to decide the matter at my discretion, I would note that the plaintiff left Angola in 1975 at the same time as some 300,000 other people who feared for the future, although they obviously had mixed motives. He left all his property there, and it has been seized. The recent affidavit of Mr Englefield states that the plaintiff would be in fear of his life if he returned to Angola, and also that he might have difficulty in obtaining an entry visa, although any such difficulty might be thought to be inconsistent with his life being at risk. It may be that litigation could proceed in his absence, but in my view if a plaintiff is a party to an action he is entitled to attend the trial, and to consult with his legal advisers. Mr Steyn [who appeared for the plaintiff below] submits that there is some risk that the plaintiff may now be treated as an enemy of the Angolan people. Anyway, whether his reasons are good or bad, the plaintiff is not prepared to risk returning to Angola. Mr Steyn submits that, as to the courts, there is some real doubt as to the quality of the legal representation that is now available. Certainly there has been a change in the judges in that now the appointees do not go up through the legal profession. [I think the judge may have said "judicial profession". However, it appears as "legal profession" in the note. To continue with the judgment:] It does seem to me that you are likely to have an entirely different type of judge; whether they are an improvement would be impertinent for me to say. At any rate, the court in contemplation when the contract was made is now different. A third important matter is the discontinuance of the final right of appeal to Lisbon. I take a broad and common sense view in saying that, at the time the contract was made, the courts in Angola operated under a colonial judicial system whereas now there is an entirely different system, a post-revolution court under a post-revolution constitution. I draw attention to arts 2, 54 and 58 as to the laws. Surely part of the purpose of the revolution was to change the judicial system. Mr Steyn says there has never been a case like this; the nearest similar case is perhaps a contract made in Imperial Russia, and the situation after the 1917 revolution, or, alternatively, a contract made during the Shah's regime in Iran, and being enforced in the present circumstances. I find strong grounds for refusing a stay either as a matter of construction of the clause, or because it would be just and proper to allow the plaintiffs to continue. All the usual reasons for sending the matter back to Angola, including exchange control difficulties, are present, and all the elements here point to allowing the case to go ahead in Angola except the one thing that really matters,

---

1   [1969] 2 All ER 641 at 645, [1970] P 94 at 99
2   Dicey and Morris, The Conflict of Laws (9th Edn, 1973) p 222, r 30

whether it is just and proper to remit the matter to Angola. I refuse to stay. Costs in cause. Leave to appeal.'   *a*

In *The Eleftheria*[1] Brandon J said this, and this is the passage, as I understand it, quoted by Donaldson J:

'The principles established by the authorities can, I think, be summarised as follows: (I) Where plaintiffs sue in England in breach of an agreement to refer disputes to a foreign court, and the defendants apply for a stay, the English court, *b* assuming the claim to be otherwise within its jurisdiction, is not bound to grant a stay but has a discretion whether to do so or not. (II) The discretion should be exercised by granting a stay unless strong cause for not doing so is shown. (III) The burden of proving such strong cause is on the plaintiffs. (IV) In exercising its discretion the court should take into account all the circumstances of the particular case. (V) In particular, but without prejudice to (IV), the following matters, where *c* they arise, may properly be regarded: (a) In what country the evidence on the issues of fact is situated, or more readily available, and the effect of that on the relative convenience and expense of trial as between the English and foreign courts; (b) Whether the law of the foreign court applies and, if so, whether it differs from English law in any material respects; (c) With what country either party is connected, and how closely; (d) Whether the defendants genuinely desire trial in the *d* foreign country, or are only seeking procedural advantages; (e) Whether the plaintiffs would be prejudiced by having to sue in the foreign court because they would (i) be deprived of security for their claim, (ii) be unable to enforce any judgment obtained, (iii) be faced with a time-bar not applicable in England, or (iv) for political, racial, religious or other reasons be unlikely to get a fair trial.'

Rule 30 in Dicey's Conflict of Laws[2], on which the judge also relied, is in these terms: *e*

'Where a contract provides that all disputes between the parties are to be referred to the exclusive jurisdiction of a foreign tribunal, the court will stay proceedings instituted in England in breach of such agreement, unless the plaintiff proves that it is just and proper to allow them to continue.'

Counsel for the defendants relied strongly on the passage from the judgment of *f* Brandon J which I have just quoted, which was approved by the Court of Appeal in two later cases: *The Makefjell*[3] and *The Adolf Warski*[4]. He submitted that the factors set out by Brandon J pointed clearly to a stay here. He rightly accepts, however, that in this court he can only attack Donaldson J's decision on the limited grounds on which a decision made in the exercise of discretion can be attacked on appeal, as is emphasised by the Court of Appeal in the two cases to which I have referred.   *g*

Simply by way of example I refer to what Cairns LJ said in *The Makefjell*[5]. He said this:

'In *The Chaparral*[6] . . . each member of the Court of Appeal (Lord Justice Willmer, Lord Justice Diplock and Lord Justice Widgery) emphasised that this court should not interfere with the exercise of the Judge's discretion on an issue of this kind unless he had gone wrong in law or in the basis on which he exercised his discretion *h* or was plainly wrong in the way in which he exercised it.'

Counsel for the plaintiff did in fact refer us to *The Chaparral*[7] but I do not think I need refer to what was said in that case.

---

1   [1969] 2 All ER 641 at 645, [1970] P 94 at 99
2   Dicey and Morris, The Conflict of Laws (9th Edn, 1973) p 222   *j*
3   [1976] 2 Lloyd's Rep 29
4   [1976] 2 Lloyd's Rep 241
5   [1976] 2 Lloyd's Rep 29 at 35–36
6   [1968] 2 Lloyd's Rep 158 at 163, 164 and 164, respectively
7   [1968] 2 Lloyd's Rep 158

Counsel for the plaintiff says that there were two issues before Donaldson J: (1)
a whether, as a matter of construction of the contract, the parties had agreed that litigation
arising thereunder should be referred to the District Court of Luanda as now constituted
(or, I suppose, strictly as constituted at the time of the commencement of this action)
under the legal system as now prevailing in Angola; (2) whether the judge, in his
discretion, should grant the stay, the question then being, as he accepts, whether there
are strong grounds for allowing the action to proceed here. Donaldson J decided both
b issues in favour of the plaintiff and counsel on his behalf submits that, the first issue
having been decided in favour of the plaintiff, the second issue did not and does not arise.

Donaldson J's judgment was delivered extempore and is, perhaps, not as full and lucid
as most judgments of that judge, but it is clear that he did consider and decide both
issues. As to construction he said in words I have already quoted, but I think it is
convenient to quote them again:

c

'At any rate, the court in contemplation when the contract was made is now
different . . . at the time the contract was made, the courts in Angola operated under
a colonial judicial system whereas now there is an entirely different system, a post-
revolution court under a post-revolution constitution . . . I find strong grounds for
refusing a stay either as a matter of construction of the clause, or because it would
d be just and proper to allow the plaintiffs to continue.'

Counsel for the plaintiff submits that the District Court of Luanda is now a different
court and counsel for the defendants submits that it is not. He says that, although there
are differences, they are not material.

It is clear from the affidavits filed on behalf of the plaintiff, and it is not disputed by the
e defendants, that, when the contract was made in December 1973, Angola was a province
of Portugal. The law applied was Portuguese law and the legal system then in force was
procedurally and substantively Portuguese. The judicial organisation of Portuguese
Angola was part of the judicial system of Portuguese Europe and was in every respect
identical with it. The qualification of judges was the same as in Portugal (see the
affidavits of Dr Almeida, dated 28th October 1977 and of Dr Carvalho for the plaintiff;
f and of Dr Oliveira for the defendants). Angola clearly then had no separate legal system
and there was no such thing as Angolan law except, perhaps, in some native customary
courts. Now Angola is an independent sovereign state with a new constitution. It is true
that it seems, from the affidavits filed on behalf of the defendants, that, in general,
Portuguese law is still applied and that the previous structure of the courts still exists,
except for the abolition of the right of appeal to the Supreme Court in Lisbon. But it
seems to me plain from the constitution that this situation can be changed at any
g moment (see especially arts 44 and 58). It seems, from the proviso to art 58, that,
without any formal change, the previous law will not be applied if it does 'conflict with
the spirit of this Law and the Angolan Revolutionary Process'.

It is also clear from the defendants' evidence that the system for the appointment of
judges has completely changed. According to the evidence filed on behalf of the
h defendants, the District Court of Luanda still exists under the same name but, in my
judgment, the judge was right in holding that it is a different court from the court in
contemplation when the contract was made. It was then a Portuguese court in all the
respects to which I have already referred. It is now an Angolan court operating within
the framework of the Angolan constitution and legal system and applying Angolan law.

One can perhaps test it in this way. If the parties had known in December 1973 what
j the situation would be in Angola now, would they have agreed to include cl 14 in the
contract? I think it is impossible to say that the answer must be Yes. There is a complete
conflict in the affidavit evidence about the present situation as to the administration of
justice in Angola. This court cannot resolve this conflict but, in my view, it is unnecessary
to do so to arrive at the conclusion that the present District Court of Luanda is a different
court from that contemplated by the contract. If my conclusion on the construction

point is right, it is unnecessary to decide the discretion point, but it was fully and ably argued and I think I should deal with it.

Counsel for the defendants' main criticisms of Donaldson J and where he submits he went wrong in principle in exercising his discretion are (i) that he applied the wrong test, and (ii) that he relied essentially on the political changes and changes in the structure of the legal system in Angola since the date of the contract. He submits that these changes, without any finding that the quality of justice had been affected and that it would prejudice the plaintiff's chances of a fair trial, are irrelevant.

So far as the first point is concerned, counsel for the defendants says that Dicey[1] is wrong in saying that the test is 'unless the plaintiff proves that it is just and proper to allow him to continue'; and that the right test is Brandon J's statement that the plaintiff must prove strong cause. Donaldson J, as I have said, quoted both tests, and it seems to me fairly clear that he did not consider that there was any difference between them. In my judgment, there is no real difference between the two phrases.

If one reads the commentary on r 30 in Dicey[2], this is said:

'The court's power to grant a stay under this rule is discretionary but, once the contract has been proved, the onus of inducing it not to do so rests on the plaintiff, and not, as in cases of *lis alibi pendens*, on the defendant. This is because the ground on which the court grants a stay is not that there is vexation and oppression but that the court makes people abide by their contracts.'

Then, a little lower down, the factors stated by Brandon J in *The Eleftheria*[3] are set out and *The Eleftheria*[4] itself is referred to in a footnote.

The 'just and proper test', it seems to me, is taken, among other places, from the judgment of Willmer J in *The Fehmarn*[5] where he says:

'... it is well established that, where there is a provision in a contract providing that disputes are to be referred to a foreign tribunal, then prima facie this court will stay proceedings instituted in this country in breach of such agreement, and will only allow them to proceed when satisfied that it is just and proper to do so. I think that fairly states the principle to be applied.'

That decision was affirmed by the Court of Appeal[6].

As it happens, Sir Gordon Willmer was a party to the decision of this court in *The Makefjell*[7] to which I have already referred. In that case he referred to a number of previous authorities, including *The Eleftheria*[4], and it seems to me clear that he did not consider there was any conflict between what he said in *The Fehmarn*[5] and what Brandon J said in *The Eleftheria*[3].

Counsel for the defendants' criticism of Dicey[1], as I understood it, was that it put the burden on the plaintiff too low and that it did not sufficiently emphasise the importance of holding people to their contracts. But, as I have already quoted from the commentary, Dicey[2] does refer specifically to the importance of making people abide by their contracts and, in my judgment, there is no real difference between the two tests of 'just and proper' and 'strong cause'.

In support of his other point that the judge attached undue importance to the political

---

1   Dicey and Morris, The Conflict of Laws (9th Edn, 1973), p 222, r 30
2   Ibid p 223
3   [1969] 2 All ER 641 at 645, [1970] P 94 at 99
4   [1969] 2 All ER 641, [1970] P 94
5   [1957] 2 All ER 707 at 710, [1957] 1 WLR 815 at 819
6   [1958] 1 All ER 333, [1958] 1 WLR 159
7   [1976] 2 Lloyd's Rep 29

changes, counsel for the defendants emphasises that the judge did not find that the plaintiff could not now get a fair trial in Angola, and there is no respondent's notice. Indeed, he told us that the plaintiff did not make that submission to Donaldson J. He submits that there is a presumption that there would be a fair trial in Angola, citing again Willmer J in *The Fehmarn*[1].

It seems to me that, as I read the judgment, Donaldson J did not hold that the political changes, as such, were enough to justify refusing a stay, and I am not convinced by this argument of counsel for the defendants. Counsel also relied on several of the factors listed by Brandon J as pointing clearly to the grant of a stay in this case. He said that most of the evidence relevant to the defence of economic hardship is in Angola, that is, evidence as to the state of the Angolan economy and its effect on the UNAIO Group. The proper law of the contract is Angolan law, which is different in important respects from English law. The defendants still carry on business in Angola, while the plaintiff has no connection with England. The defendants genuinely desire trial in Angola.

It is, however, clear that Brandon J did not intend his list of factors to be exhaustive. I have already quoted his sub-paras IV and V and need not quote them again.

In this case the matters to which I have referred in dealing with the construction point are also relevant to the discretion point. I do not think it necessary to go through the various relevant factors in detail. Applying the established principle, I can find no sufficient ground for interfering with Donaldson J's exercise of his discretion, even if I am wrong on the construction point.

I would dismiss this appeal.

GEOFFREY LANE LJ. I agree. The defendants complain that the judge was in error in refusing to stay the plaintiff's action in this country. It is said that the plaintiff has expressly agreed that any dispute should be tried in the court in Luanda and that, having made that agreement, he should be held to it. It is said that there are no strong grounds for exercising the court's undoubted discretion to allow this matter to be tried in England.

There are two aspects, therefore, to the appeal. The first one is this: has the plaintiff in fact resiled from any agreement which he made to the effect that the matter should be tried in Luanda? Does cl 14 apply? It says[2]: 'In the event of a dispute supervening, the only court considered competent, with the express elimination of all others, is that of the Municipality of Luanda.'

The second point is this. If that clause does bite, and if the plaintiff is bound by it, are there, nevertheless, strong grounds, to use Brandon J's words in *The Eleftheria*[3], for the court exercising its discretion in favour of the plaintiff and allowing him to proceed in England rather than having to go to Luanda in order to pursue this claim?

The judge decided both points in favour of the plaintiff, and the words he used (there are two passages) are these:

'At any rate, the court in contemplation when the contract was made is now different. A third important matter is the discontinuance of the final right of appeal to Lisbon.'

The second passage in which he deals with it runs as follows: 'I find strong grounds for refusing a stay either as a matter of construction of the clause, or because it would be just and proper to allow the plaintiff to continue.'

This court, as indeed was the judge, has been faced by the difficulty that the two sets of affidavits, those sworn on behalf of the plaintiff and those sworn on behalf of the defendants, are almost totally contradictory in every possible respect. Consequently, it seems to me that, in so far as we have to decide any matters of fact on those totally

1   [1957] 2 All ER 707 at 711, [1957] 1 WLR 815 at 821
2   This translation is taken from an affidavit on behalf of the plaintiff
3   [1969] 2 All ER 641 at 645, [1970] P 94 at 99

contradictory affidavits, the only way in which we can do it is either to take the lowest
common denominator of the affidavits, namely the very few points where they do agree, *a*
or else to accept, for the purposes of argument, the statements contained in the
defendants' affidavit. Of course, the burden of proof lies on the plaintiff. Accordingly,
it seems to me that, in so far as we have to choose one set of affidavits rather than the
other, those must be the defendants'.

The points which counsel for the defendants makes so far as the first aspect of the case
is concerned are these. First of all, he says that the court referred to in cl 14, namely, the *b*
court of the municipality of Luanda in Angola, still exists; and there is no doubt on either
of the sets of affidavits that the court does as a building still physically exist in Luanda.

His next point is that the laws are the same now as they were at the time this contract
was signed. The new revolutionary government in Angola has, he says, at least for the
time being, adopted the laws of Portugal which existed and were in force there before the
coup d'état.   *c*

Counsel for the defendants' third point is that the judges, although they are appointed
apparently on a different basis, are just as competent as, if not more competent than, the
judges who existed before the change of government.

The courts have plenty of time in which to try actions; they are underworked. It
seems the most litigious part of the population has now gone back to Portugal.

The fifth point is that there is no confiscation, except of pre-revolutionary assets. We *d*
had the various articles of the constitution read to us and it seems that the assets of people
who had been absent from Angola at the time of the revolution for 45 days or more
without just cause have had their assets confiscated, and amongst those sufferers is the
plaintiff in this case. But it is said that, so far as the confiscation of future assets is
concerned, and this, of course, comprises also any damages which the plaintiff might
successfully get from the courts in Angola, there is no more danger of those being *e*
confiscated by government decree than there is possibly in any other country.

Finally, it is said that there is no difficulty, as it appears on the affidavits, in employing
or paying an advocate to prosecute his claim in Angola.

Added to these counsel for the defendants makes these supplementary points. First of
all, he submits that it is Angolan law which applies to the contract and it would be proper
for the matter to be tried in Angola. It would be more convenient, he suggests, from a *f*
point of view of witnesses and, finally, much more convenient for the defendants who
would wish to raise a defence which, it is said, is available in Angolan law or Portuguese
law, namely, the defence of economic hardship. That defence was not put forward in
any affidavit but is contained, or the suggestion of it is contained, in two letters from a
Dr Torres, which have been, by agreement, put before us. I must confess that those two
letters seem to me to be obscure to the point of unintelligibility, and I do not think that *g*
any question of defence of economic hardship has been sufficiently raised for us to have
to deal with it.

As against that, what are the facts, which must be undisputed, on the other side of the
picture? They seem to me to be these. First of all, although the court building in the
municipality of Luanda still exists, that is not the meaning of 'court' in these
circumstances. It has an abstract meaning as well as a physical meaning, and it seems to *h*
me that it is the abstract meaning of 'court' which is the important one so far as this
matter is concerned. It seems to me that, so far as the abstract meaning of the word
'court' is concerned, the court now in Luanda is not the court which was in Luanda at the
time this contract was signed. First of all, the judges are different; secondly, it was
certainly Portuguese municipal law which was applicable in this province of Portugal at
the time the contract was signed because it was a province of Portugal. Now, although *j*
for the time being the new revolutionary government has adopted the laws of Portugal,
it is clear from the articles of the constitution that that may be a very short-lived
situation, and what is now applicable in this court in Luanda is plainly Angolan law and
not Portuguese law. One of the more obvious symptoms of that undisputed fact is that
the appeal on a point of law to the Supreme Court in Lisbon is now no longer available,

and that really sets the scene.   So you have got now a court manned by judges selected on
a   a different basis (although, no doubt, just as competent as the earlier judges) operating a
system of law which, at the moment, superficially resembles and in many respects is
precisely similar to the earlier operated Portuguese law.   But it is Angolan law and one
only has to look at one or two of the articles to which Browne LJ has already referred in
the constitution to see what the differences very soon may be.

First of all:

b   'Article 2: The political, economic and social guidance of the nation are vested in
the MPLA, its lawful representative, consisting of a wide front which includes all
the patriotic forces engaged in the anti-Imperialist struggle.'

I select those which seem to be the most relevant to the present consideration.

c   'Article 10: The People's Republic of Angola recognises, protects and guarantees
private property and activities, even those of foreigners, provided that they are
useful to the economy of the country and the interests of the Angolan people.'

It is plain that that article gives a very wide discretion to the MPLA, who are responsible
for the government of the country.   The next article which appears to have some
relevance is:

d   'Article 44: The exercise of the jurisdictional function aimed at the realisation of
Democratic justice is exclusively incumbent on the Courts.   The organisation,
composition and competence of the Courts will be fixed by Law.'

Then:

e   'Article 58: The Laws and Regulations currently in force will be applicable where
not revoked or altered and provided that they do not conflict with the spirit of this
Law and the Angolan Revolutionary Process.'

It seems to me that those articles make it plain that the existing application of
Portuguese law may be very short-lived, and it is impossible to predict what effect those
f   articles, when applied, may have on the present system of law in Angola and on the
contents of the Portuguese laws which are presently administered there.

Accordingly, for those short reasons, it seems to me that the judge was right in
deciding the first point, namely what he called the construction point, in favour of the
plaintiff.   But perhaps more accurately, there was ample ground on which he could come
to the conclusion which he did.

So far as the second point is concerned, namely the discretion point, there it is plain
g   that the same reasoning can be applied.   All those matters which I have endeavoured to
set out provide the basis for saying that there were strong grounds in any event for the
matter being decided in favour of the plaintiff and for no stay being granted.   Here again,
there was ample ground on which the judge could exercise his discretion in the way that
he did and, having said that, that is really enough to dispose of this aspect of the case
h   which is a discretionary one.

I wish to add only this.   One of the matters which the judge did mention was the fact
that the plaintiff was reluctant to return to Angola and, indeed, has declared his intention
of not returning to Angola on the basis that he feared for his life if he were to go back
there.   On all the evidence it seems to me that, plainly, the plaintiff was the sort of person
who would be anathema to the present government in Angola.   That can scarcely be
j   disputed and it seems to me there was a ground for the plaintiff's fear.   However, that is
not a matter on which I would desire to base my decision.

In my view, the judge was right on the first point, the construction, so the second
point, the discretion point, therefore did not strictly arise.   In deference to the arguments
of counsel, to which I would also like to pay tribute, I have mentioned it.   It seems to me
that on all these matters the judge was right and I would dismiss the appeal.

Appeal dismissed.

Solicitors: *Lawrence Jones & Co* (for the defendants); *Boyce, Evans & Sheppard* (for the plaintiff).

Sumra Green   Barrister.

Morris v Beardmore

QUEEN'S BENCH DIVISION

CUMMING-BRUCE LJ AND NEILL J

16th MARCH 1979

Road traffic – Breath test – Accident owing to presence of motor vehicle on road – Arrest – Arrest for failure to provide specimen of breath – Validity – Constable a trespasser at time of request for specimen of breath – Statutory conditions precedent for request of specimen complied with – Whether evidence of events subsequent to time when constable became a trespasser admissible in proceedings for failure to provide specimen – Road Traffic Act 1972, s 8(2)(5).

An accident occurred involving a car driven by the respondent. Police officers in uniform, who knew about the accident, went to the respondent's home to interview him about it. They were let into the house by the respondent's son. The respondent refused five requests by the senior police officer to come down from his bedroom and discuss the accident. He then passed on a message through his son to the police officers that they were trespassers and requested them to leave his house. The officers then went upstairs to the respondent's bedroom and requested him to provide a specimen for a breath test. The respondent refused, was arrested and taken to a police station. There he refused to supply a specimen of breath for a breath test and subsequently a specimen of blood or urine for a laboratory test. He was then charged with contravening ss 8(3)[a] and 9(3)[b] of the Road Traffic Act 1972. The justices dismissed the information, being of opinion that in the circumstances the requirement for a breath test specimen had been made not by a constable but by a trespasser, that the respondent's arrest was accordingly unlawful and that all evidence of matters following that arrest was inadmissible. On appeal by the prosecutor,

Held – The conditions precedent to a valid request for a breath specimen under s 8(2)[c] of the 1972 Act were (a) that there had to have been an accident owing to the presence of a motor vehicle on a road or other public place, (b) that the person requesting the specimen had to be a constable in uniform, and (c) that the constable had to have reasonable cause to believe that the person required to provide the specimen had been driving or attempting to drive the vehicle at the time of the accident; and if those conditions were present, then the constable had the right to require a specimen, and the fact that he was a trespasser at the time of the request could not affect the validity of an arrest under s 8(5)[d], the lawfulness of any subsequent breath test procedure, or the

---

a Section 8(3), so far as material, provides: 'A person who, without reasonable excuse, fails to provide a specimen of breath for a breath test under subsection . . . (2) above shall be guilty of an offence.'

b Section 9(3) provides: 'A person who, without reasonable excuse, fails to provide a specimen for a laboratory test in pursuance of a requirement imposed under this section shall be guilty of an offence.'

c Section 8(2), so far as material, is set out at p 294 g, post.

d Section 8(5), so far as material, provides: 'If a person required by a constable under subsection . . . (2) above to provide a specimen of breath for a breath test fails to do so and the constable has reasonable cause to suspect him of having alcohol in his body, the constable may arrest him without warrant . . .'

admissibility of evidence of events subsequent to the arrest. If the action of the constable *a* was found to be oppressive the court could at most exercise its discretion to exclude the evidence. It followed that the appeal would be allowed and the matter remitted to the justices to continue the hearing (see p 294 *h* to p 295 *a d* to *f* and *j* and p 296 *a*, post).

Per Curiam. In respect of the breath test procedure and arrest the whole procedure and arrest is invalidated if the police fail exactly to comply with all the procedural steps prescribed in the 1972 Act in relation to obtaining specimens of breath or subsequently *b* of breath, blood or urine; and provided those procedural steps are followed the requirement of a specimen of breath, blood or urine and any subsequent arrest do not become unlawful merely because in the course of making the requirement or the arrest the constable does anything which he has not got a lawful right to do (see p 294 *a* to *c* and p 296 *a*, post); *Spicer v Holt* [1976] 3 All ER 71 explained.

c **Notes**
For the power to require a specimen of breath for a breath test and the power of arrest following refusal to provide a specimen, see Supplement to 33 Halsbury's Laws (3rd Edn) para 1061A.3,6.

For the Road Traffic Act 1972, ss 8,9, see 42 Halsbury's Statutes (3rd Edn) 1651, 1655.

d **Case referred to in judgments**
Spicer v Holt [1976] 3 All ER 71, [1977] AC 987, [1976] 3 WLR 398, 140 JP 545, 63 Cr App R 270, [1976] RTR 1, HL.

Cases also cited
Bourlet v Porter [1973] 2 All ER 800, [1973] 1 WLR 866, HL.
e *Cannings v Houghton* [1977] RTR 55, DC.
Davis v Lisle [1936] 2 All ER 213, [1936] 2 KB 434, DC.
Great Central Railway Co v Bates [1921] 3 KB 578, DC.
Jeffrey v Black [1978] 1 All ER 555, [1978] QB 490, DC.
Kuruma, son of Kaniu v R [1955] 1 All ER 236, [1955] AC 197, PC.
R v Burdekin [1976] RTR 27, CA.
f *R v Smith (Benjamin)* [1978] Crim LR 296, Crown Court at Preston.
Sakhuja v Allen [1972] 2 All ER 311, [1973] AC 152, HL.
Scott v Baker [1968] 2 All ER 993, [1969] 1 QB 659, DC.

Case stated
g This was a case stated by justices acting in and for the Petty Sessional Division of Walsall, in respect of their adjudication as a magistrates' court sitting at Walsall on 27th November 1978.

On 1st August 1978 informations were preferred by the appellant, Chief Superintendent of Police Raymond Morris, against the respondent, John Allan Beardmore, that he on 2nd July 1978 at 14 Little Aston Road, Aldridge in the Metropolitan Borough of Walsall, *h* being a person whom a constable in uniform had reasonable cause to believe was driving a certain motor vehicle, namely a motor car, at the time when an accident occurred owing to the presence of that vehicle on a certain road called Chester Road, Brownhills, and having been required by the constable to provide a specimen of breath for a breath test at the place where the requirement was made, namely 14 Little Aston Road, the respondent did without reasonable excuse, fail to do so, contrary to s 8(3) of the Road *j* Traffic Act 1972, and that he, having been arrested under s 8 of the 1972 Act and having been required by Police Sgt Hogg, at Walsall police station, to provide a specimen of blood or urine for a laboratory test on the ground that when given the opportunity to provide a specimen of breath for a breath test, at the station under s 8(7) of the 1978 Act, he failed to do so, did without reasonable excuse fail to provide such a specimen of blood or urine for a laboratory test.

The justices found the following facts. At 10.45 pm on Saturday 1st July 1978 an accident occurred at Chester Road, Brownhills between a motor car being driven by the respondent and a motor car being driven by Ian Michael Darby. At 12.20 am on Sunday 2nd July 1978, Supt Jones, who knew of the accident, accompanied by Insp Adams and Sgt Broadhurst all of whom were in uniform visited the home of the respondent at 14 Little Aston Road, Aldridge and were invited in by Alan Beardmore, the respondent's son. The respondent failed to respond to five requests by the superintendent to descend the stairs and discuss the accident in which he was involved, and passed a message through Alan Beardmore that the police officers were trespassers and that their continued presence in the house was against the respondent's wishes. The police officers ascended the staircase and entered a bedroom where the superintendent explained to the respondent that he had reason to believe the respondent had been involved in an accident whilst driving his car and that he required the respondent to supply a specimen of breath for a breath test. The respondent refused indicating that the police had no right to be there. The superintendent formed the opinion that the respondent had consumed alcohol. The respondent was arrested, taken to a police car and driven to Walsall police station. The respondent refused to supply a specimen of breath following a request at the police station and subsequently refused to supply a specimen of blood or urine for laboratory analysis.

It was contended by the respondent's solicitor that the police officers, having no statutory or common law right to remain on the premises in the circumstances were trespassers from the moment they were requested to leave, and as such ceased to be able to exercise the functions of constables. The subsequent arrest was invalid because (a) the requirement for a specimen of breath was made by a trespasser and not by a constable, and the respondent was therefore under no legal obligation to supply such a specimen and (b) the arrest was made by a person who was not then acting as a constable and in circumstances where a private individual had no power to arrest. It was further contended that the invalidity of the arrest rendered all evidence of subsequent events inadmissible.

It was contended by the appellant's solicitor that the method of obtaining evidence was irrelevant and that the proper approach was to consider whether what was being obtained was relevant.

The justices were of the opinion that in the circumstances the requirement for a breath specimen was not made by a constable, the arrest of the respondent was unlawful and that all evidence on matters following that arrest was inadmissible, and accordingly dismissed the informations and ordered that the appellant pay to the respondent £50 towards his costs.

The prosecutor appealed. The question of law on which the opinion of the High Court was sought was whether a constable in uniform who had been invited into a private house by someone other than the occupier and whose permission to remain therein was subsequently withdrawn by the occupier continued to be a constable in uniform empowered under s 8 of the 1972 Act to require a person in that house, whom he had reasonable cause to believe had been driving or attempting to drive a motor vehicle which had been involved in an accident on a public road, to provide a specimen of breath for a breath test, and in the event of a refusal to provide such a specimen to effect a lawful arrest of that person.

Richard Wakerley for the appellant.
David Latham for the respondent.

CUMMING-BRUCE LJ. This is an appeal by case stated at the instance of the Chief Superintendent of Police of Walsall that arises in the following circumstances.

On 1st August 1978 informations were preferred by the appellant against the respondent alleging that he, on 2nd July 1978 at 14 Little Aston Road in Walsall, being a person whom a constable in uniform had reasonable cause to believe was driving a

certain motor vehicle, namely a motor car, at a time when an accident occurred owing
a to the presence of that vehicle on a certain road, and having been required by the
constable to provide a specimen of breath for a breath test at the place where the
requirement was made, without reasonable excuse failed to do so, contrary to s 8(3) of the
Road Traffic Act 1972.

There was a futher information that, having been arrested under s 8 and carried off to
the police station and having been required by the sergeant to provide a specimen of
b blood or urine for a laboratory test when given the opportunity to provide a specimen for
a breath test, he without reasonable excuse failed to provide such specimen.

The case does raise a very narrow point of some general importance because it affects
the rights and duties which may flow from a situation in which a police constable carries
out, or attempts to carry out, the breathalyser procedure at a time when he, the constable,
is an unwelcome, and indeed prohibited, visitor in the home of the person to whom the
c constable is addressing his attention.

The facts are these. They are quite short. There was an accident between a motor car
and another motor car, and later on that night a superintendent of police, who knew
about the accident, accompanied by a police inspector and a police sergeant, all of whom
were in uniform, visited the home of the respondent. They were invited in by the
respondent's son. The respondent failed to respond to the five requests by the
d superintendent to descend the stairs and discuss the accident in which he was involved
and passed a message through his son that the police officers were trespassers and that
their continued presence in the house was against the respondent's wishes. That, perhaps,
is expressed almost too politely. The police officers ascended the stairs and entered a
bedroom where the superintendent explained to the respondent that he had reason to
believe that the respondent had been involved in an accident while driving his car and
e required the respondent to supply a specimen of breath for a breath test. The respondent
refused, indicating that the police had no right to be there. The superintendent formed
the opinion that the respondent had consumed alcohol. The respondent was arrested,
taken to a police car and driven to the police station. There he refused to supply a
specimen of breath following a request at the police station, and subsequently he refused
to supply a specimen of blood or urine for laboratory analysis.

f When the case came on, the respondent's solicitor took a point of law. He submitted
to the justices that the police officers, having no statutory or common law right to
remain on the premises from the moment that they were requested to leave the
respondent's house, were trespassers and as such ceased to be able to exercise the functions
of constables; and he submitted that the subsequent arrest was invalid because the
requirement for a specimen of breath was made by a trespasser and not by a constable,
g so that the respondent was under no legal obligation to supply a specimen, and the arrest
was made by a person who was not then acting as a constable because he was a
trespasser. Therefore, all subsequent events at the police station were inadmissible.

The justices thought that was right. They expressed an opinion that in the
circumstances the requirement for the breath specimen was not made by a constable, and
the arrest of the respondent was unlawful and everything that followed afterwards was
h inadmissible, not as a matter of discretion but because it was inadmissible. They
dismissed the informations.

The question of law on which they seek this court's opinion is this: whether a
constable in uniform who has been invited into a private house by someone other than
the occupier and whose permission to remain therein is subsequently withdrawn by the
occupier continues to be a constable in uniform empowered under s 8 of the 1972 Act to
j require a person in that house, whom he has reasonable cause to believe was driving or
attempting to drive a motor vehicle which had been involved in an accident on a public
road, to provide a specimen of breath for a breath test, and in the event of a refusal to
provide such a specimen, to effect a lawful arrest of that person.

Counsel for the appellant submits that the answer to that question is that the constable
would not cease to be a constable empowered to require a breath test by reason of the fact

that on notice that the invitation to enter had been withdrawn or cancelled he had become a trespasser.

Counsel's submission is this. There is a familiar line of cases, which eventually reached the House of Lords in *Spicer v Holt*[1], which established that an arrest pursuant to s 8 of the 1972 Act is unlawful if the procedures specified in the section are not strictly complied with, and the same in respect of specimens for laboratory tests under the next section.

Counsel for the appellant submits that it is a misunderstanding of that line of authority to hold that it involves the proposition that, if any constable does anything that he has not got a legal right to do in the course of requiring a specimen of breath or a specimen of urine, thereby the requirements and the arrest become unlawful. Counsel submits that the line of authority to which I have referred establishes a much narrower proposition, and the proposition it does establish is only that in respect of such a breathalyser procedure and arrest the whole procedure and the arrest is invalidated if the police fail exactly to comply with all the procedural steps prescribed in the 1972 Act in relation to obtaining specimens of breath or subsequently breath, blood or urine.

For my part, I think that is right, and the authorities culminating in *Spicer v Holt*[1] established no proposition broader than that described.

The next question is: as a matter of construction of s 8, does the section enact that the right to require a specimen shall be vested only in a constable in uniform, who in every respect at the time of thus requiring the specimen has complied with the whole of his legal duty?

Counsel for the respondent takes up his position on a broad constitutional basis. In this country the subject is protected from the arbitrary invasion of his private property by the police or other representatives of the executive unless the policeman or such other representative of the executive, like a gas man or an electricity man, is armed with the appropriate legal authority to enter. In the case of a police officer such legal authority has to be a warrant to enter premises, and that, counsel submits, is such a fundamental constitutional right of the subject that it is to be assumed that Parliament, when creating a new right of arrest, would intend the ordinary rights of the subject to be protected against arrest within his house without warrant to be protected unless express words appear in the section showing that that constitutional right has been taken away.

Section 8 provides:

'(1) A constable in uniform may require any person driving or attempting to drive a motor vehicle on a road or other public place to provide a specimen of breath for a breath test there or nearby, if the constable has reasonable cause—(a) to suspect him of having alcohol in his body, or (b) to suspect him of having committed a traffic offence while the vehicle was in motion . . .'

That requirement under para (b) has to be made as soon as reasonably practicable after the commission of the traffic offence. Then the section goes on:

'(2) If an accident occurs owing to the presence of a motor vehicle on a road or other public place, a constable in uniform may require any person who he has reasonable cause to believe was driving or attempting to drive the vehicle at the time of the accident to provide a specimen of breath for a breath test . . .'

I need not at this moment read the other words of the subsection.

On the express words of the subsection the conditions that have to be present to arm a constable with power to require someone to provide a specimen of breath are these. There has to have been an accident owing to the presence of a motor vehicle on a road or other public place. Secondly, the person who can require a breath test is a constable in uniform. Thirdly, that constable must have reasonable cause to believe that the person

---

1   [1976] 3 All ER 71, [1977] AC 987

he is going to seek to breathalyse was driving or attempting to drive the vehicle at the
a time of the accident. Those are the express conditions which Parliament has enacted as
the conditions that confer on the said constable in uniform the power to require a
specimen of breath.

Counsel for the respondent submits that, if Parliament had intended to confer the
right on a constable in uniform, all the other conditions being present, in circumstances
wherein the constable in uniform was entitled to invade the privacy of a subject's home
b without invitation or in spite of prohibition, that striking invasion of the subject's
constitutional right would have been expressly stated. As it is not stated, the court
should construe s 8(2) to hold that the unlawfulness of the presence of a constable in a
private house as a trespasser has the effect of invalidating such powers as the constable
would otherwise have to require a breath test. It is suggested he ceases to be a constable
at all; he is not in the execution of his duty, if he is a trespasser.

c   In my view, counsel's submission for the respondent is founded to some degree on the
familiar case which had the effect that an assault on the constable by a man when the
constable was a trespasser in that man's house and was refusing to go was not an assault
on the constable in the execution of the constable's duty. In my view, that is a long way
away from the problem with which this court is faced today. The question is a very
different one from the question that was being considered in the case to which I have just
d referred.

For my part, this being, as has been stated in the House of Lords, a kind of procedure
and a kind of power of arrest which is different from any other power of arrest or any
other procedure that exists at common law or by statute, the right approach is to look at
the words of the section, decide what those clear words mean, and, if on those clear words
the conditions preceding the grant of the power to require a breath test are present, then
e the constable has the right to require a breath test. If, as in this case, on the facts at the
time that he requested a breath test he had become a trespasser, that could not go either
to the validity of the arrest or the lawfulness of the subsequent breathalyser procedure,
or to the admissibility of evidence of events subsequent to the arrest. It would give rise
to the situation that, if the action of the constable had been held to be oppressive, the
court in considering whether admissible evidence as a matter of discretion should be
f admitted would have the right to exclude such evidence as a matter of discretion. But
it is to be expected that, before holding that such admissible evidence should be excluded
on that ground, the court should have clear evidence of substantial oppressive behaviour
on the part of the relevant constable.

As this matter has to go back to the justices, it is probably better for this court to say
no more than that the matter the justices will have now to consider is whether it has been
g shown there is any sufficient ground as a matter of discretion for refusing to admit the
relevant evidence which they wrongly held to be inadmissible. Nothing that has fallen
from me should be interpreted to suggest that it is the view of this court that, if in the
case of pursuit of a suspected person, or pursuit of a person who is reasonably suspected
by the police of being an appropriate subject for a breathalyser test, the police do infringe
the strict rights of privacy of the subject, such infringement is necessarily to be regarded
h as oppressive.

Thus, in the present case, if it be the case (as it appears it was) that the constable refused
to leave the house when he no longer had a legal right to be there, the owner of the house
has an action for trespass against the constable which he is entitled to bring in the county
court or the High Court if he likes to chance his arm there. Whether he would expect
to get damages of more than a shilling is another matter. It would turn on the
j circumstances of the trespass.

For my part, I would allow this appeal and direct that the case go back to the justices
for them to continue the hearing. It will be their duty, amongst other things, to decide
whether they ought to exercise their discretion to exclude admissible and relevant
evidence which they wrongly thought was inadmissible and to proceed appropriately
with the continuation of the case in the ordinary way.

NEILL J. I agree that this appeal should be allowed, and I agree with the order proposed by Cumming-Bruce LJ. I do not think I can usefully add anything.   *a*

Appeal allowed. Case remitted to justices with direction to continue hearing.

The court refused leave to appeal to the House of Lords but certified, under s 1(2) of the Administration of Justice Act 1960 that a point of law of general public importance was involved, namely: whether a constable in uniform who has been invited into a private house by someone other *b* *than the occupier, and whose permission to remain therein is subsequently withdrawn by the occupier, continues to be a constable in uniform empowered under s 8 of the Road Traffic Act 1972 to require a person in that house, who he has reasonable cause to believe was driving or attempting to drive a motor vehicle which had been involved in an accident on a public road, to provide a specimen of breath for a breath test, and in the event of a refusal to provide such a specimen, to effect a lawful arrest of that person.*   *c*

24th May. The Appeal Committee of the House of Lords (Lord Diplock, Lord Russell of Killowen and Lord Scarman) granted leave to appeal.

Solicitors: *Ian S Manson*, Birmingham (for the appellant); *Haden & Stretton*, Walsall (for the respondent).   *d*

N P Metcalfe Esq   Barrister.

Re Camburn Petroleum Products Ltd

CHANCERY DIVISION
SLADE J
11th, 12th, 14th JUNE 1979

Company – Compulsory winding-up – Petition by creditor – Petition opposed by contributory – Creditor's debt and company's inability to pay its debts proved – Contributory applying for adjournment of petition – Contributory alleging indebtedness of company due to fault of another contributory supporting petition and that continuation of company would enable it to pay its debts – Whether court should grant adjournment on application of opposing contributory – Companies Act 1948, ss 225(1), 346(1).

A creditor of a company for a debt which exceeded £300,000 presented a petition to the court for the winding-up of the company. At the date of presentation of the petition the company was, for the purposes of ss 222(e) and 223(d) of the Companies Act 1948, unable to pay its debts. A contributory of the company opposed the petition while another contributory supported it. Both contributories were also directors of the company. The opposing contributory alleged that the company's inability to pay its debts was due substantially to the fault of the supporting contributory and that if the company was allowed to continue operating it could rapidly become solvent again. Accordingly, the opposing contributory applied for an adjournment of the petition. The petitioning creditor opposed an adjournment and sought an immediate winding-up order.

Held – Where a winding-up petition was presented by a creditor who proved that he was unpaid and that the company was unable to pay its debts, he was prima facie entitled to a winding-up order even though the petition was opposed by a contributory of the company, for, although the court had a discretion under ss 225(1)[a] and 346(1)[b] of the 1948 Act to consider the wishes of a contributory, ordinarily it would attach little weight to those wishes in comparison with the wishes of an unpaid creditor. A creditor was entitled to assume, in the absence of notice to the contrary, that a company's affairs were being run in such a way that its debts would be promptly discharged, and internal disputes between directors or contributories of the company were no concern of his. Although, therefore, the court had jurisdiction to adjourn a creditor's winding-up petition at the request of a contributory, it would do so only if it was satisfied that there were exceptional circumstances. On the facts, any injustice caused to the opposing contributory by making an immediate winding-up order would be far outweighed by the injustice that an adjournment would cause to the creditor, and accordingly the court would refuse the application for an adjournment and make the winding-up order (see p 303 c to j and p 304 e to p 305 a, post).

Dictum of Lord Cranworth in *Bowes v Hope Life Insurance and Guarantee Co* (1865) 11 HL Cas at 402 applied.

Re Brighton Hotel Co (1868) LR 6 Eq 339 distinguished.

Notes

For adjournment of a winding-up petition, see 7 Halsbury's Laws (4th Edn) paras 1030, 1033.

For the Companies Act 1948, ss 222, 223, 225, 346, see 5 Halsbury's Statutes (3rd Edn) 289, 292, 295, 369.

Cases referred to in judgment

Bowes v Hope Life Insurance and Guarantee Co (1865) 11 HL Cas 389, 11 ER 1383, sub nom

---

a   Section 225(1), so far as material, is set out at p 302 *d*, post
b   Section 346(1), so far as material, is set out at p 302 *e*, post

Bowes v Hope Mutual Life Assurance Co 35 LJ Ch 574, 12 LT 680, 11 Jur NS 643, HL, 10 Digest (Reissue) 932, 5429.
Brighton Hotel Co, Re (1868) LR 6 Eq 339, 37 LJ Ch 915, 18 LT 741, 10 Digest (Reissue) 965, 5725.

a

Petition

This was a petition presented on 19th March 1979 by Chevron Oil (UK) Ltd ('Chevron'), a creditor of Camburn Petroleum Products Ltd ('the company'), in the sum of £368,821·78 alleged to be due in respect of petroleum products sold and delivered to the company. The petition was supported by Mr Aubrey Kreike, a contributory, but opposed by another contributory, Mr Eric Cooper. Mr Kreike and Mr Cooper were the sole directors of the company. The facts are set out in the judgment.

b

Mary Arden for Chevron.
John Cone for Mr Kreike.
G A Mann for Mr Cooper.

c

SLADE J. This is a creditor's petition presented by Chevron Oil (UK) Ltd ('Chevron'). It seeks the usual compulsory winding-up order in respect of Camburn Petroleum Products Ltd ('the company'). The petition is supported by one contributory, Mr Aubrey Kreike, but is opposed by another contributory, Mr Eric Cooper.

d

Before the company's incorporation Mr Kreike had, since 1964, been a director and shareholder of an oil company called Keburn Oil Distributors Ltd ('Keburn'). Mr Cooper for several years had had an interest in a number of oil companies, in particular two named Baxenden Autopoint Ltd ('Baxenden') and Eccles Autopoint Ltd ('Eccles'), which were not associated or connected with Keburn.

e

Mr Cooper and Mr Kreike had done business together on behalf of their respective companies. In or about 1977 they decided, after some discussion, to form a company which would fill what they regarded as a gap in the oil distribution market, by buying large quantities of petrol from the larger petrol companies and selling on smaller quantities of petrol to retail garages. Accordingly the company was incorporated on 16th March 1978 as a private company limited by shares, with a registered office in Manchester. Shortly after its incorporation, one £1 share was issued and allotted to Mr Kreike, and one £1 share was issued and allotted to Mr Cooper. These remain the only two issued shares. Mr Kreike and Mr Cooper were appointed and still remain the two sole directors of the company. They appointed Mr Stewart Last, an accountant, to be secretary, but he has since resigned.

f

The company began trading in April 1978. The arrangement appears to have been that the day-to-day administration should be left to Messrs Cooper and Last. The company was initially quite successful; Mr Kreike has sworn an affidavit in which he states that from 3rd April 1978 until 31st January 1979 the total turnover of the company was about £500,000, and he estimates that the profit after payment of costs and expenses was £100,000. These figures have not, I think, been challenged by Mr Cooper.

g

Unfortunately, however, from about August 1978 onwards disputes began to arise between Mr Kreike and Mr Cooper as to the manner in which the company was being and should be run. There is a considerable volume of affidavit evidence before me in which the disputes are ventilated, and in which charges and counter-charges are made by each of them against the other. There has, however, been no cross-examination on any of the affidavits before me. On the hearing of this creditor's petition by Chevron, I think it is neither necessary nor appropriate to express even a provisional view as to the rights and wrongs of the various matters in dispute between Mr Kreike and Mr Cooper.

h

j

The further facts material for present purposes in my judgment are the following, which I think are either common ground between the parties or are sufficiently proved by the affidavit evidence before me. For some time prior to January 1979 Chevron had been supplying and delivering to the company petroleum products of very substantial value, which had resulted in corresponding substantial indebtedness of the company to

_a_ Chevron from time to time. On 17th January 1979 the company executed a debenture by way of floating charge on its undertaking and assets in favour of Chevron, to secure the company's present and future indebtedness. This was signed by Mr Kreike and Mr Cooper on behalf of the company. Also on 17th January 1979 Mr Cooper and Mr Last drew a company's cheque for £93,330·41 in favour of Chevron. On 22nd January 1979 Mr Cooper and Mr Last drew two company's cheques respectively for £142,786·84 and

_b_ £112,935·30 in favour of Chevron. These three cheques, totalling £349,052·55, were drawn in respect of moneys due for payment from the company to Chevron on 20th January 1979. Payment of the cheques was, however, countermanded on behalf of the company and none of them was met on presentation. Mr Kreike was the director who effected this countermanding; Mr Cooper's evidence is that it was done without his authority or consent and he suggests that Mr Kreike acted wrongly in doing it. It is,

_c_ however, common ground between Mr Kreike and Mr Cooper that, at the time, the funds in the bank account of the company would not nearly have sufficed to cover the full amount of the three cheques drawn.

In or about the last week of January 1979 an arrangement was made between Chevron and the company that the overnight balances standing to the credit of the company's account at its bank should be transferred direct to the credit of Chevron. Mr Cooper's

_d_ evidence is that five transfers totalling £211,964 were made in this manner between 30th January 1979 and 7th February 1979, which would or should have reduced the indebtedness of the company to Chevron accordingly.

Chevron's evidence, contained in an affidavit sworn on its behalf by Mr P O Marshall on 8th June 1979, is that the credits actually received by Chevron under this arrangement amounted to only £148,074·06, because an aggregate sum of £63,889·94 paid to

_e_ Chevron by the company on 31st January was duly directed by the company to be applied in satisfaction of an account of a company named Koil Oil Products Ltd with Chevron.

There appears on the evidence to be some doubt as to the position in regard to the £63,889·94. Mr Cooper suggests that the direction given by the company to Chevron in this respect was given by Mr Kreike wrongly, and without Mr Cooper's knowledge or

_f_ consent. But I do not think that this is really material for present purposes; for three points are, I think, common ground. First, no further payments have been made in reduction of the company's indebtedness to Chevron since 7th February 1979. Secondly, additional invoices became due for payment by the company on 20th February 1979. Thirdly, at very least the aggregate amount of the debt owed by the company to Chevron on the latter date was £304,931·84, (representing the difference between £368,821·78

_g_ and £63,889·94), and this sum still remains outstanding. If the sum of £63,889·94 is added to £304,931·84 the resulting outstanding aggregate debt is £368,821·78, and this is the debt on which Chevron's petition is now based.

Though this fact has not been admitted by Mr Cooper in his evidence, I think that the affidavit of Mr Marshall, to which I have referred, establishes that demands had in fact been delivered to the company by 31st January 1979, seeking payment of all the debts

_h_ relied on in the petition, though it has not been asserted that these demands entitle the petitioner to rely on s 223(_a_) of the Companies Act 1948.

Reverting to the history of the matter, on 24th January 1979 Mr Last resigned as secretary of the company. On 14th February 1979 Mr Kreike presented a contributory's petition to the Manchester District Registry seeking a compulsory winding-up order in respect of the company, substantially on the grounds of deadlock and Mr Cooper's

_j_ alleged misconduct. The company and Mr Cooper were and are respondents to this petition.

On 22nd February 1979, on Mr Kreike's application, an order was made in the Manchester District Registry appointing one of the official receivers attached to the court to be provisional liquidator of the company until the conclusion of the hearing of the Manchester petition, or further order. The court limited and restricted the powers of the provisional liquidator to taking possession of, collecting and protecting the assets of the company, instituting proceedings for the recovery of its assets, including the collecting of debts and the paying of creditors where appropriate. The official receiver thus appointed has been present in court before me, and has told me that, by a further direction of the court, the only creditors of the company whom he has been authorised to pay are its employees.

On 19th March 1979, Chevron presented the petition which is now before me. I should read paras 5 to 10 of this petition, which summarise its essential case:

'5. The Company is indebted to your Petitioner in the sum of £368,821·78 being the sum due to your Petitioner in respect of petroleum products sold and delivered by your Petitioner to the Company.

'6. On the 17th and 22nd January 1979 the Company drew cheques in favour of your Petitioner for sums amounting to £349,052·55 in the aggregate in respect of part of the monies due to your Petitioner as aforesaid. Payment of the said cheques was thereafter countermanded on behalf of the Company and the said cheques were accordingly not met on presentation.

'7. All monies and liabilities by the Company to your Petitioner are secured by a Debenture created by the Company in favour of your Petitioner and dated 17th January 1979. The said Debenture created a Floating Charge in favour of your Petitioner over the undertaking assets and property whatsoever and wheresoever both present and future of the Company including its uncalled capital for the time being.

'8. Your Petitioner has made application to the Company for payment of the said sum of £368,821·78, but the Company has failed and neglected to pay the said sum or any part thereof.

'9. The Company is insolvent and unable to pay its debts.

'10. In the circumstances it is just and equitable that the Company should be wound up.'

On 13th April 1979 Chevron's petition came before me for first hearing. I was then told of the petition pending in the Manchester District Registry, but was told that, for practical purposes, proceedings under that petition were frozen, owing to industrial troubles in the Manchester District Registry. Counsel for Chevron asked for an order under s 231 of the Companies Act 1948 giving leave to Chevron, so far as leave might be necessary, to proceed with its petition, and also for an appropriate adjournment for the purpose of dealing with evidence. Counsel for Mr Cooper asked for leave to be added to the list of persons who had given notice of their intention to appear on the petition, out of time and on the usual undertaking, and opposed the making of any order under s 231.

After hearing argument I decided, contrary to the submissions made on behalf of Mr Cooper, that there was a sufficient allegation of insolvency in the petition, and that in all the circumstances it was right that Chevron's petition should be allowed to continue. I therefore made the order sought under s 231, and gave certain further directions, to which I need not refer. The Manchester petition has, I understand, now been set down for hearing on 3rd to 7th September 1979.

In regard to the evidence before me, I need only refer to the following further points. Mr Kreike has sworn an affidavit on 27th April 1979 exhibiting a statement of the company as at 22nd February 1979. This statement shows assets of £432,652, comprising:

'Balance at bank	£53,613
'Trade debtors	£347,718
'Loans and Advances	£26,971
'Furniture, Fittings and Utensils	£4,250
'Other property	£100'

It shows as liabilities:

a

'Preferential Creditors	£26,845
'Owed to Debenture Holder	£368,965
'Owed to other creditors	£19,439
'Outstanding expenses	£2,289'

This results in liabilities of £417,538, and would produce an estimated surplus of

b £15,114. This surplus, however, would fail to be reduced by the costs of the provisional liquidation, and could on the figures be reduced to nil, if 5% or more of the trade debts proved to be bad ones.

Mr Cooper has not yet produced a statement of affairs. In his evidence before this court, however, he has given reasons for suggesting that Mr Kreike has underestimated the value of the company's assets by at least £73,723. Thus, at least on the basis of Mr

c Cooper's evidence, the company's assets, when all its book debts were collected, would be likely quite comfortably to exceed its liabilities. The fact remains, however, that Chevron has not been paid any part of the debt exceeding £300,000, which it is admitted on all sides has been owed to it by the company since January or February 1979. Furthermore, there is no immediate prospect of Chevron being paid this large outstanding debt. The official receiver has told me that all the tangible assets of the company have been realised,

d that he has so far collected £161,565 and is in the process of collecting the outstanding book debts which exceed £200,000. He has told me, however, that some of these book debts are due from companies which are controlled by Mr Kreike or by Mr Cooper, and have so far paid nothing. I understand from the affidavit evidence that these companies include Keburn, Baxenden and Eccles, and that the sums involved are substantial. The official receiver has informed me that some of the small book debts are disputed, and that

e since 30th April 1979 only about £19,000 has been collected. The process of collection thus appears at present to be a somewhat slow one.

Against this background, counsel for Chevron has submitted that the position is a simple one. Chevron has been proved to be a creditor for a debt exceeding £300,000, which has not been paid; its demands for payments have not been complied with; cheques given to it in purported payment of debts have been countermanded on

f presentation; and the evidence, she submits, shows that the company is not presently able to pay what is owed to Chevron. Accordingly, in her submission, the only proper course can be for the court to make the usual compulsory winding-up order.

Section 224 of the Companies Act 1948 confers on any creditor such as Chevron the right to petition the court for a winding-up order. Under s 222(e) the court has jurisdiction to wind up the company if 'the company is unable to pay its debts'. Under

g paras (a) and (d) of s 223 a company is deemed to be unable to pay its debts—

'... (a) if a creditor, by assignment or otherwise, to whom the company is indebted in a sum exceeding fifty pounds then due has served on the company, by leaving it at the registered office of the company, a demand under his hand requiring the company to pay the sum so due and the company has for three weeks thereafter neglected to pay the sum or to secure or compound for it to the reasonable

h satisfaction of the creditor; or ... (d) if it is proved to the satisfaction of the court that the company is unable to pay its debts, and, in determining whether a company is unable to pay its debts, the court shall take into account the contingent and prospective liabilities of the company.'

As I have already said no statutory notice under para (a) is relied on in the present case.

j As para (d), however, indicates, neglect on the part of a company to comply with a statutory notice is only one of several methods of proving insolvency. Insolvency may be shown in any way. The law, in my judgment, is correctly stated in two passages in Buckley's Companies Acts[1]:

---

1   13th Edn (1957) p 460

'Thus dishonour of the company's acceptance, or the fact that the company have informed him being a judgment creditor that he had better not levy, for they have no assets, is enough . . . The particular indications of insolvency mentioned in paras (a) (b) and (c) are all instances of commercial insolvency, that is of the company being unable to meet current demands upon it. In such a case it is useless to say that if its assets are realized there will be ample to pay twenty shillings in the pound: this is not the test. A company may be at the same time insolvent and wealthy. It may have wealth locked up in investments not presently realizable; but although this be so, yet if it have not assets available to meet its current liabilities it is commercially insolvent and may be wound up.'

In my judgment, on the facts which I have summarised, the company was, at the date of presentation of Chevron's petition, and is at the present date, manifestly unable to pay its debts, within the meaning of ss 222(e) and 223(d), inasmuch as it did not and does not have assets available for the discharge of all its current liabilities.

Counsel for Chevron, and counsel for Mr Kreike, who supports Chevron's petition, thus affirm and rely on the present inability of the company to pay its debts. Counsel who opposes the petition on behalf of Mr Cooper does not dispute such inability, though he suggests that it is substantially due to the fault of Mr Kreike and could be relatively quickly cured, if the company were allowed to go into active operation again.

Faced with these difficulties, counsel for Mr Cooper, in his excellent argument, has invited me neither to allow nor to dismiss Chevron's petition, but to stand it over until the first petition day of next term, by which time it appears that the Manchester petition would have been heard and disposed of. He has referred me to s 225 of the Companies Act 1948, which gives the court general jurisdiction, on hearing a winding-up petition, to 'dismiss it, or adjourn the hearing conditionally or unconditionally'. He has also referred me to s 346(1), which, so far as material, provides:

'The court may, as to all matters relating to the winding up of a company, have regard to the wishes of the creditors or contributories of the company, as proved to it by any sufficient evidence . . .'

He has also referred me to the decision of Malins V-C in *Re Brighton Hotel Co*[1]. In that case, the petitioner was a creditor of the company in respect of a debenture for £250, and a contributory, inasmuch as he held 20 shares in it. He was the only person before the court who wished to wind up the company, and his petition was opposed by a number of other contributories, together holding 1,450 shares. Malins V-C stood over the petition for some four weeks, because he took the view that there was a hope of some 'reasonable arrangement' being made to enable the company to pay its debts, and he considered that those who desired to make the effort should be given an opportunity of doing so[2]. Counsel for Mr Cooper naturally relied strongly on this decision, because it was a case where the court granted an adjournment of a petition of a creditor at the request of persons who were no more than contributories, and in the face of opposition from the petitioning creditor.

It appears, however, from Malins V-C's judgment that, though he recognised that the petitioner was in fact a creditor, he paid far more regard to his other capacity as a contributory, and treated the petition, on the facts, as being for practical purposes a contributory's petition. Thus he said[2]:

'Although it is very true this gentleman's debenture fell due in April, and no doubt he ought to have had his money, yet I do not think the money is of any very great importance to him, and it is not on account of that that he presses for the order. If I made an order for the immediate winding up of the company that would not give to him his £250. Therefore regarding the interest of every one, except this

---

1   (1868) LR 6 Eq 339
2   LR 6 Eq 339 at 343

Petitioner, I feel bound to give the time asked for, and I am equally clear that it is to the interest of this Petitioner himself that I should give the time asked for.'

Thus I think that *Re Brighton Hotel Co*[1] throws little light on the attitude which the court should generally adopt if faced with a request to make a winding-up order in respect of a company shown to be unable to pay its debts, when that request is made by an undisputed unpaid creditor, but opposing contributories seek an adjournment. Though there are a number of authorities which give guidance as to the attitude of the court where some creditors support the making of an immediate winding-up order and other creditors oppose it, counsel have been unable to find any other authority which gives guidance as to such attitude, where the contest is between a petitioning creditor on the one hand and contributories on the other hand.

I do not, however, feel much doubt in principle as to what that attitude should be. In the case of a creditor's petition not opposed by other creditors, the general approach of the court was expressed by Lord Cranworth in *Bowes v Hope Life Insurance and Guarantee Co*[2] as follows:

'... I agree with what has been said, that it is not a discretionary matter with the Court when a debt is established, and not satisfied, to say whether the company shall be wound up or not; that is to say, if there be a valid debt established, valid both at law and in equity. One does not like to say positively that no case would occur in which it would be right to refuse it; but, ordinarily speaking, it is the duty of the Court to direct the winding up.'

In other words a creditor in the circumstances mentioned is prima facie entitled to his order, and is prima facie not bound to give time to enable the debtor to pay. In my judgment, subject to the discretion given to it by ss 225 and 346 of the 1948 Act, to which I have already referred, the attitude of the court should be, and is, essentially unchanged today. While I recognise that it would have the right under those two sections to pay regard to the wishes of contributories, in deciding whether or not to make a winding-up order on a creditor's petition, or to adjourn the hearing, in my judgment it can, and should, ordinarily attach little weight to the wishes of contributories, in comparison with the weight it attaches to the wishes of any creditor, who proves both that he is unpaid and that the company is 'unable to pay its debts'. A creditor giving credit to a company, after all, cannot ordinarily be expected to know of or ascertain the potential difficulties which may face the company in regard to the discharge of its debts on account of internal disputes between the directors or between the contributories or on account of other internal matters. He is, I think, ordinarily entitled to assume that his debt will be punctually paid by the company as and when it falls due, and to exercise the remedies given to him by s 224 and the following sections of the 1948 Act if it does not. The exercise of such remedies may perhaps in some cases cause a degree of hardship to a contributory, particularly if the failure of the company to pay its debts has arisen on account of neglects or defaults by other contributories or directors, to which the contributory in question has not been a party. This, however, is a type of risk which a contributory inevitably assumes, when he first becomes a contributory of a company. In my judgment a creditor, in advancing money to a company, at least in the absence of notice to the contrary, is ordinarily entitled to assume that its affairs are being run in such a manner as will enable it promptly to discharge its debts when they fall due, and to say to the court, and to other persons, that internal disputes between directors and/or contributories of the company are no concern of his.

For these reasons, while I accept that the court would have jurisdiction to adjourn Chevron's petition, as asked by counsel for Mr Cooper, I think it should only do so if it were satisfied that there were exceptional circumstances that justified this course.

1   (1868) LR 6 Eq 339
2   (1865) 11 HL Cas 389 at 402, 11 ER 1383 at 1389

There are some passages in the affidavits filed on behalf of Mr Cooper which imply that Chevron's petition may have been presented in bad faith and in collusion with Mr Kreike. If this suggestion had been supported by any firm evidence, this might well have constituted an exceptional circumstance sufficient to justify the court in acceding to Mr Cooper's request for an adjournment. The suggestion, however, is not supported by any such firm evidence, and very properly, if I may say so, counsel for Mr Cooper, during the course of his address expressly disclaimed it for the purpose of his argument.

The points on which he relied in support of his application for an adjournment were essentially as follows. He referred to the Manchester petition and pointed out the close links between the events which gave rise to that petition and those which gave rise to Chevron's petition. On the hearing of the Manchester petition, it would be contended that Mr Kreike's unjustified acts were the cause of the company's failure hitherto to discharge the debt due to Chevron. On this petition, counsel for Mr Cooper told me (though this is not formally in evidence) that Mr Cooper would now intend to seek relief under s 210 of the Companies Act 1948 with the object of both preventing a winding-up order and enabling him to resume the company's trading, without interference from Mr Kreike. If this relief were granted to Mr Cooper on the Manchester petition, it would be his hope, I was told, that he would be in a position to pay off the company's creditors sooner than they could ever by paid off by the Official Receiver. Little would be gained, it was submitted, by making an immediate winding-up order; the company is not trading; its assets are not in jeopardy because of the provisional liquidation; it could be that its creditors would in the event be paid off even quicker, if the adjournment sought were granted, than if a winding-up order were made today. The making of such an order today would in the submission of counsel do a substantial injustice to Mr Cooper, because it would deprive him of the opportunity of airing his grievances against Mr Kreike on the Manchester petition.

If this application for an adjournment were not opposed by Chevron, I might well accede to it. It is, however, strongly opposed by Chevron, and in my judgment there are no sufficient reasons why the wishes of Chevron, as the sole creditor appearing before me, and an unpaid creditor for a very large sum, should not prevail. It has been owed over £300,000 by the company since at least February 1979. By October next the debt will have been outstanding for over nine months. Chevron takes the view that the adjournment now sought would be likely to result in at least several further weeks' delay before its debt was discharged. Its prediction cannot, in my view, be regarded as an unreasonable one. Any such delay would be a serious matter in view of the size of the sum involved and the fact that, in the winding-up of an insolvent company, debts carry no interest after presentation of the petition. Every day that passes by, therefore, Chevron runs the risk of being deprived of the further use of its money without compensation.

The situation in the present case seems to be very far removed from that in *Re Brighton Hotel Co*[1], since, unlike Malins V-C in that case, I have no confidence that an adjournment would ultimately benefit the petitioning creditor. I think that an adjournment could well do it a substantial injury; and Chevron, it must be remembered, is not at fault in any way and cannot, in my view, be reasonably expected to suffer because of the unhappy domestic disputes that have arisen between Mr Cooper and Mr Kreike in the running of this company.

In all the circumstances I think that any injustice that might be caused to Mr Cooper by the making of an immediate winding-up order would be far outweighed by the injustice to Chevron that would be caused by the grant of the adjournment sought, in opposition to its wishes. I should point out that if Mr Cooper be right in suggesting that there has been misfeasance on the part of Mr Kreike remedies will be available to Mr Cooper in the winding-up, just as remedies will be available to Mr Kreike himself, in so far as there may have been misfeasance on the part of Mr Cooper. Chevron has, in my

---

1   (1868) LR 6 Eq 339

judgment, established its right to a winding-up order in respect of this company, and,
a subject to the question of costs, I propose to make the usual compulsory winding-up
order.

Order accordingly.

Solicitors: *Addleshaw Sons & Latham*, Manchester (for Chevron); *Bloom, Betesh & Co*,
b Manchester (for Mr Kreike); *Pricketts*, Stockport (for Mr Cooper).

Jacqueline Metcalfe   Barrister.

Alexander and another v Mercouris and another
c

COURT OF APPEAL, CIVIL DIVISION
BUCKLEY, GOFF AND WALLER LJJ
21st, 22nd, 23rd MAY 1979

d
Negligence – Defective premises – Duty to build dwelling properly – Scope of duty – Date for determining whether duty applies – Work taken on before commencement of defective premises legislation – Taking on work – Work completed shortly after commencement of legislation – Whether statutory duty applies – Whether duty to ensure that on completion of work dwelling fit for human habitation provided – Whether duty merely to ensure during carrying out of work that
e *work done in proper manner with proper materials – Defective Premises Act 1972, s 1 (1).*

On 20th November 1972 the defendants entered into an agreement with the plaintiff to
purchase a property for him and arrange for the modernisation and conversion of the
property into flats. Pursuant to the agreement the plaintiff in August 1973 entered into
a further agreement with a firm of builders for work to be done on the property. The
f work was completed on 27th February 1974. Prior to that date, namely on 1st January
1974, the Defective Premises Act 1972 came into force. The plaintiff brought an action
against the defendants claiming damages for breach of the duty imposed by s 1(1)[a] of the
1972 Act, alleging that the defendants had failed to ensure that the work was done in a
professional manner with proper materials and had failed to ensure that the property
would be fit for habitation on completion of the work. A master ordered that a
g preliminary issue be tried whether s 1(1) applied to the agreement of 20th November
1972 and the work done pursuant to it. On the trial of that issue the judge held that the
section did not apply because the relevant date in determining whether the section
applied was the date when the agreement to do the work was entered into, and not the
date when it was completed. He accordingly dismissed the action. The plaintiff
appealed, contending that the duty imposed by s 1(1), being a duty to ensure that the
h work was done in a workmanlike manner with proper materials 'so that as regards that
work the dwelling will be fit for habitation when completed', was a duty to provide a
dwelling fit for human habitation on completion and continued until the work was
completed, and that therefore the section applied because completion took place after the
commencement of the Act.

j **Held** – The duty imposed by s 1(1) of the 1972 Act requiring a person 'taking on work'
in connection with the provision of a dwelling to ensure that the work was done in a
proper manner with proper materials was a duty which arose when the contract to do the
work was entered into or at the latest when the work was commenced and was a duty

---
a Section 1(1) is set out at p 307 *f*, post

required to be performed while the work was being carried out. On that construction, and applying the presumption that the Act was not intended to be retrospective in effect, the duty only applied to work begun after the commencement of the Act and not to work taken on prior to, but completed after, the commencement of the Act. The appeal would therefore be dismissed (see p 308 *f*, p 309 *c f g*, p 310 *b* to *d* and p 311 *c d*, post).

Dictum of Lindley LJ in *Lauri v Renad* [1892] 3 Ch at 421 applied.

Per Curiam. The duty imposed by s 1(1) of the 1972 Act is to ensure that the work is done in a proper manner with proper materials during the carrying on of the work. The reference to the dwelling being 'fit for habitation when completed' merely indicates the intended consequence of the proper performance of the duty and provides a measure of the standard of the requisite work and materials; it does not mean that the duty is such that no relief can be obtained until completion (see p 308 *f* to *h*, p 309 *g h* and p 311 *b d* and *e*, post).

Notes

For the presumption against the retrospective effect of a statute, see 36 Halsbury's Laws (3rd Edn) 423, para 644, and for cases on the subject, see 44 Digest (Repl) 284–289, *1136–1188*.

For the Defective Premises Act 1972, s 1, see 42 Halsbury's Statutes (3rd Edn) 1395.

Cases referred to in judgments

Hancock v B W Brazier (Anerley) Ltd [1966] 2 All ER 901, [1966] 1 WLR 1317, CA, 7 Digest (Reissue) 331, *2231*.

Lauri v Renad [1892] 3 Ch 402, 61 LJ Ch 580, 67 LT 275, CA, 44 Digest (Repl) 287, *1166*.

R v St Mary, Whitechapel (Inhabitants) (1848) 12 QB 120, 3 New Sess Cas 262, 17 LJMC 172, 11 LTOS 473, 116 ER 811, 44 Digest (Repl) 285, *1144*.

Cases also cited

Bagot v Stevens, Scanlan & Co [1964] 3 All ER 577, [1966] 1 QB 197.

Customs and Excise Comrs v Thorn Electrical Industries Ltd [1975] 1 All ER 439, [1975] 1 WLR 437, DC; *affd* [1975] 3 All ER 88, [1975] 1 WLR 1661, HL.

Master Ladies Tailors' Organisation v Minister of Labour and National Service [1950] 2 All ER 525.

Solicitor's Clerk, Re a [1957] 3 All ER 617, [1957] 1 WLR 1219, DC.

Sparham-Souter v Town and Country Developments (Essex) Ltd [1976] 2 All ER 65, [1976] QB 858, CA.

Appeal

By a writ dated 29th December 1975 the plaintiffs, John Alexander and his wife, Eileen Julia Alexander, brought an action against the defendants, Spiro Mercouris and Costas Movrommatis, claiming damages for breach of duty under the Defective Premises Act 1972 in respect of alleged defective work carried out under an agreement dated 20th November 1972. By an order dated 12th May 1978 Master Cholmondeley-Clarke ordered that a preliminary issue be tried whether s 1 of the 1972 Act applied to the agreement and the work carried out under it. For the purposes of that issue the defendants conceded that the agreement dated 20th November 1972 was entered into in the course of a business. On 22nd June 1978 Walton J gave judgment declaring that s 1 of the 1972 Act did not apply to the agreement or to the work carried out under it and dismissed the action. The plaintiffs appealed on the ground that the judge had erred in law in holding that the date of the agreement, 20th November 1972, and not the date when the work was completed, 27th February 1974, was the relevant date in determining whether s 1 of the 1972 Act applied, and accordingly had erred in holding that the section did not apply. The facts are set out in the judgment of Buckley LJ.

Michael Browne QC and *Geoffrey Jaques* for the plaintiffs.
Andrew Bano for the defendants.

BUCKLEY LJ. This is an appeal from a decision of Walton J on 22nd June 1978, on
a preliminary issue arising on the construction and effect of the Defective Premises Act
1972. The relevant facts can be concisely stated.

On 20th November 1972 the first plaintiff, Mr John Alexander, entered into an
agreement with the defendants that they would make the necessary arrangements for
the purchase by the first plaintiff of 96 Palace Gates Road, London N22, for the
modernisation of that property and its conversion into two self-contained flats at a
particular stipulated cost, including all the services there mentioned or in any way
necessary for the completion of that project. The defendants entered into that agreement
in the course of their business, which consisted of, or included, providing or arranging
for the provision of dwellings. They appointed a supervising officer and, in accordance
with arrangements they had made, the first plaintiff entered into a building agreement
with a firm of builders for the completion of the project. It was completed on or about
27th February 1974 when the supervising officer certified that the project was practically
completed.

In the meantime the Defective Premises Act 1972, which had been enacted on 29th
June 1972, came into force on 1st January 1974, that being the commencement date
fixed for the Act by s 7(2). The plaintiffs allege that in breach of a statutory duty imposed
on the defendants by that Act the defendants have failed to see that the work comprised
in the project was done in a professional manner, and that it was done with proper
materials, and that they had failed to see that the premises were handed over in a
condition fit for habitation when the project had been completed.

By an order of 12th May 1978, Master Cholmondeley-Clarke ordered that the
following question be tried as a preliminary issue in the action, that is to say, whether s 1
of the 1972 Act applies to the agreement of 20th November 1972, and the work carried
out thereunder. The defendants concede, for the purposes of that preliminary issue, that
the agreement was entered into in the course of their business. Walton J answered that
question in the negative and dismissed the action.

Section 1(1) of the 1972 Act is in the following terms:

'A person taking on work for or in connection with the provision of a dwelling
(whether the dwelling is provided by the erection or by the conversion or
enlargement of a building) owes a duty—(a) if the dwelling is provided to the order
of any person, to that person; and (b) without prejudice to paragraph (a) above to
every person who acquires an interest (whether legal or equitable) in the dwelling;
to see that the work which he takes on is done in a workmanlike or, as the case may
be, professional manner, with proper materials and so that as regards that work the
dwelling will be fit for habitation when completed.'

The judge took the view that that section applies only in a case in which the person
sought to be made liable had taken on the relevant work after the commencement of the
Act; he regarded the agreement as being the act of taking on the work in the present case
and, since that agreement antedated the commencement of the Act, he held that the Act
did not apply to the defendants.

The plaintiffs appeal on the ground that the judge erred in holding that the date of the
agreement and not the date of the completion of the dwellings was the relevant date for
determining whether the Act applied.

The plaintiffs have contended that the Act creates a single and continuing duty, which
is not either completely performed or breached until the work has been completed. It
is, they say, a duty to provide a dwelling which is fit for habitation by work done in a
workmanlike or professional manner with proper materials. If work taken on is not
completed until after 1st January 1974, the statutory duty becomes enforceable after the
commencement of the Act which, when so construed, does not, the plaintiffs submit,
have a retroactive effect.

The defendants, on the other hand, contend that on the language of s 1(1) the statutory duty arises when a person takes on work for or in connection with the provision of a dwelling and continues throughout the course of the work, so that when the work is *a* completed it will have been done in a workmanlike manner with proper materials and the dwelling will be fit for habitation. They say that the plaintiffs' construction involves giving the Act a retroactive effect and should therefore be discarded.

The Act creates new statutory duties and new statutory rights and obligations. These are quite distinct from rights existing at common law in contract or negligence, although they may in many respects resemble and overlap such common law rights. Moreover, *b* the Act may create such duties, rights and obligations between parties between whom they would not exist at common law: see s 1(1)(*b*), which I have already read, and s 1(4), which provides as follows:

> 'A person who—(*a*) in the course of a business which consists of or includes providing or arranging for the provision of dwellings or installations in dwellings; or (*b*) in the exercise of a power of making such provision or arrangements conferred *c* by or by virtue of any enactment; arranges for another to take on work for or in connection with the provision of a dwelling shall be treated for the purposes of this section as included among the persons who have taken on the work.'

Whenever new rights or obligations are created by statute, anomalies will inevitably arise initially. Whatever date is found to be the earliest date at which the new duties, *d* rights or obligations can arise, it will be possible to suggest instances in which one man will escape liability by a day and another, who has followed an exactly similar course of action but 24 hours later, will find himself liable. In such a case an argument by reference to anomalies is, in my opinion, unlikely to be helpful, and I think the question is purely one of interpretation of the statute.

The Act employs the rather unusual expression 'A person taking on work'. This must, *e* I think, be because it is intended to apply not only to cases in which a contractual obligation to do work exists, but also to cases in which the work may be done without contractual obligation but in circumstances in which he who does the work could claim reward on the basis of a quantum meruit, to cases in which the work is done voluntarily without expectation of a gain and, perhaps most importantly, to cases in which a *f* building owner does the work himself.

It seems to me clear on the language of s 1(1) that the duty is intended to arise when a person takes on the work. The word 'owes' is used in the present tense, and the duty is not to ensure that the work has been done in a workmanlike manner with proper materials so that the dwelling is fit for habitation when completed, but to see that the work *is* done in a workmanlike manner with proper materials, so that the dwelling *will* be fit for habitation when completed. The duty is one to be performed during the *g* carrying on of the work. The reference to the dwelling being fit for habitation indicates the intended consequence of the proper performance of the duty and provides a measure of the standard of the requisite work and materials. It is not, I think, part of the duty itself. If, at an early stage in the provision of the dwelling, for instance, the putting in of the foundations, someone who had taken on that part of the work failed to do it in a workmanlike manner, then in my judgment, assuming that s 1(1) applied, an immediate *h* cause of action would arise. It would not be necessary to await the completion of the dwelling to claim relief on the basis of a breach of statutory duty.

The argument that the duty is a single duty which continues in operation until completion of the dwelling but in respect of which no relief can be obtained until the dwelling is completed, is in my view inconsistent with, or at least accords very ill with, s 1(5), which is in these terms: *j*

> 'Any cause of action in respect of a breach of the duty imposed by this section shall be deemed, for the purposes of the Limitation Act 1939, the Law Reform (Limitation of Actions, etc.) Act 1954 and the Limitation Act 1963, to have accrued at the time when the dwelling was completed, but if after that time a person who

a has done work for or in connection with the provision of the dwelling does further work to rectify the work he has already done, any such cause of action in respect of that further work shall be deemed for those purposes to have accrued at the time when the further work was finished.'

It is true that that subsection could have the effect of making time run from an earlier date than it would run from if the damage did not occur until after completion of the work; but if that were the object of the section, I would have expected it to be in different b language. To enact that any cause of action in respect of this statutory duty shall be deemed to have accrued at the time when the dwelling was completed is a very strange way of putting it if that would be the time at which a cause of action would in fact accrue in a normal case.

If the duty arises, as I think, when the person takes on the work, to treat the section as applicable to any case in which the dwelling is completed after 1st January 1974, c notwithstanding that the person may have taken on the work and have done the greater part of it before 1st January 1974, must, it seems to me, involve giving a retroactive effect to the section. Suppose that A takes on work for providing a dwelling under a contract with B made on 1st January 1973 and does the greater part of the work before 1st January 1974 but does not complete it until some time in January 1974, the plaintiffs' argument would impose on him a statutory duty to B in relation to work done at any time after 1st d January 1973; and moreover, if anyone other than B were to acquire an interest in the dwelling it would impose on A a statutory duty to that other person, to whom he would, apart from the statute, owe no duty at all. In the event of any default by A in performance of the duty at any time in the course of the work, whether before or after 1st January 1974, A would be liable for damages for that breach of duty. Apart from the statute, he could not have been so liable. This clearly attributes to the section a retroactive effect.

e As Lindley LJ said in *Lauri v Renad*[1]: 'It is a fundamental rule of English law that no statute shall be construed so as to have a retrospective operation unless its language is such as plainly to require such a construction ...' This, it seems to me, is a strong argument against the plaintiffs' construction in the present case.

In my judgment, however, the language of s 1 is really not susceptible of supporting that construction. I think it applies only to cases in which the person sought to be f charged took on the relevant work after the commencement of the Act.

Accordingly, I think Walton J reached the right conclusion and I would dismiss this appeal.

GOFF LJ. I agree. Counsel for the plaintiffs argued that 'taking on work' in s 1(1) of the Defective Premises Act 1972 is equivalent to 'doing', that there is only one duty imposed g by the section, namely to provide a dwelling fit for habitation when completed and that, therefore, a breach of the statutory duty occurs when the building is finished and not earlier, so that the Act applies if it comes into force before that happens, even if but very little remains to be done.

This argument could not be sustained without some qualification because the statutory duty must, in my judgment, be broken as soon as bad workmanship, or the use of faulty h materials, takes place. Indeed, as Buckley LJ has pointed out, and I agree, the concluding words of s 1(1) do not state the duty but the measure of the duty imposed by the earlier words, that is to say, to do the work in a workmanlike or, as the case may be, professional manner and to do it with proper materials, so that the result may be produced that the dwelling will be fit for habitation when completed.

Leading counsel for the plaintiffs and his junior, therefore, submitted that the duty j and the breach are continuing ones, so that there is a breach as soon as the Act comes into force, if any defects then existing are not immediately rectified. This, however, with all respect, seems to me to beg the question, for it assumes that the Act will apply as soon as it comes into force, but whether that is true is the very question to be determined.

---

1   [1892] 3 Ch 402 at 421

In support of his argument, counsel for the plaintiffs relied on *Hancock v B W Brazier (Anerley) Ltd*[1]; but in my judgment the judge was right when he distinguished that case, **a** for there the defendant was unquestionably subject to a contractual duty to complete a house in a proper and workmanlike manner and all that was decided was, the house not being in that state when finished, that it was no answer to a claim for breach to say that the defects arose before the contract, for they should have been put right. Here, however, the question is whether the defendants are under the statutory duty at all.

It seems to me that the judge was right to give the words 'taking on work' in s 1(1) **b** their natural meaning, and they clearly point to the beginning of operations and not the end. For my part I cannot read them as equivalent to 'doing', still less to 'having taken on' or 'having done'. Where there is no contract the time when a person takes on work must, I think, be when he starts to do it. Where there is a contract, I would think the time would be when the contract is made; but in any case it cannot be later than when the party starts to perform it.   **c**

The construction for which the plaintiffs contend would, in my judgment, make the operation of the Act truly retrospective, and ought not to be accepted, because there is nothing in the Act to overcome the presumption that legislation is not intended to be retrospective. On the contrary, the language of s 1(1) is consistent with, and supports, that presumption.

In support of this part of his argument counsel for the plaintiffs relied on *R v St Mary,* **d** *Whitechapel (Inhabitants)*[2] and similar cases, which show that where a statute is to operate prospectively the presumption does not apply even although the facts or circumstances which bring the case within the statute arose before it was passed. But in my judgment, if the plaintiffs' arguments were right, this Act would not be operating prospectively, because it would create new rights and duties arising out of the past transaction; that is to say, the contract made, or work undertaken, on the faith of the law as it then stood, **e** particularly in cases coming within s 1 (4) of the Act.

As it seems to me, the matter falls precisely within the principle stated in Craies on Statute Law[3], in these words:

> 'A statute is to be deemed to be retrospective, which takes away or impairs any vested right acquired under existing laws [and then come the important words for present purposes] or creates a new obligation, or imposes a new duty, or attaches a **f** new disability in respect of transactions or considerations already past.'

Moreover, one must not overlook the fact that, as the plaintiffs could not contravert if their argument be right, the Act would apply although the work was taken on before even the Act was passed.

Both sides relied on s 1(5) of the Act, to which Buckley LJ has referred. Counsel for the **g** plaintiffs said that the legislature there showed that it was looking to the completion of the works. Counsel for the defendants, on the other hand, said that if the plaintiffs' argument be right, there would be no need to deem the breach to have arisen on completion.

In my judgment, however, that section does not really help either way. It is dealing with a particular matter only, namely the commencement of time running under the **h** Limitation Acts, and all that it does is to prevent argument whether that should start when the breach occurred by bad workmanship or the use of defective materials, or when the work was finished, or even later, when damage results or the defects are, or ought to have been, discovered.

Counsel for the plaintiffs relied further on s 2(7), which he said shows that the legislature was indeed using the words 'taking on' or 'take on' on the one hand and 'doing' **j** or 'does' on the other as synonymous. For my part, I do not think s 2(7) does show that.

---

1   [1966] 2 All ER 901, [1966] 1 WLR 1317
2   (1848) 12 QB 120 at 127, 116 ER 811 at 814
3   7th Edn (1971), p 387

If anything, I think it distinguishes those expressions, but in any case it is dealing with
a   a very particular matter and in my judgment does not throw any light on the problem
before us.

Finally, the plaintiffs relied on s 4 which deals with repairing convenants in leases.
That section, however, is not directed to 'taking on' work, but to a continuing obligation
to do works if and when they should become necessary, for which special provision was,
in my view, requisite or desirable, if for no other reason, to prevent disputes. I do not see
b   how the plaintiffs can derive any comfort from that section which, to put it at its lowest,
does not proceed on the basis that the Act, on coming into force, would automatically
apply without express provision, and it is carefully worded to make its operation
prospective.

For these reasons I agree with Buckley LJ and with the judge below, and I too would
dismiss this appeal.

c
WALLER LJ. I agree. I would only add that the phrase 'taking on' is an unusual
phrase to find in a statute, and in my opinion would appear to be incapable of being
construed in a manner which is different from the starting of the work or the entering
into of the contract. In other words, the latest time at which 'taking on' could possibly
mean would be the time when the work was started.

d   Counsel's submission for the plaintiffs that the duty was an all-embracing duty
including the completion of the work is, I think, further made difficult by the words
towards the end of s 1(1). The duty is to see that the work which he takes on is done in
a workmanlike manner etc, so that as regards that work the dwelling will be fit for
habitation when completed. As it seems to me, the duty starts when the person takes on
and continues while the work is done, and the test of the manner in which the work is
e   done is that when the building is completed it is fit for human habitation.

Appeal dismissed.

Solicitors: *Lewis & Dick*, agents for *Zabell & Co,* Cheam (for the plaintiffs); *B M Birnberg
& Co* (for the defendants).

f   J H Fazan Esq   Barrister.

Nickerson v Barraclough and others

CHANCERY DIVISION

SIR ROBERT MEGARRY V-C

9th, 10th, 23rd, 24th, 25th, 26th OCTOBER, 21st, 27th NOVEMBER, 18th DECEMBER 1978, 19th MARCH 1979

Easement – Way of necessity – Express term in grant of land excluding right of way – Conveyance of landlocked building land – Whether public policy preventing exclusion of way of necessity for building purposes.

Easement – Right of way – Creation – Right of way to one plot of land as means of access to another plot lying beyond it – Implied grant of right of way – Whether right of way to second plot where right of way to first plot forming actual means of access to second plot or intended to be used as means of access – Law of Property Act 1925, s 62(1).

By a conveyance made in 1906 a plot of building land forming part of a building estate was conveyed by the owners of the estate to X subject to the building regulations set out in a schedule to the conveyance, which were similar to the regulations applicable to other plots on the estate. The plan on the conveyance showed routes for proposed new roads on the estate and included a proposed road along the route of an unmade lane (belonging to the owners of the estate) which adjoined the eastern boundary of the plot conveyed, being separated from it by a dyke. The lane ran into a public highway. It appeared, however, from the plan that the plot conveyed was landlocked and wholly without access to any highway. By para 7 of the schedule to the conveyance it was provided that the vendor 'did not undertake to make any of the proposed new roads shewn on the plan nor did he give any rights of way over the same until the same should (if ever) be made'. There was evidence that from 1908 there was an eight foot wide sleeper bridge over the dyke giving access from the lane onto the plot, through a ten foot gate to the plot, and that from 1921 there was enjoyment of a way over the lane. By a further conveyance made in 1922 the owners of the estate conveyed to X a strip of land adjoining the plot conveyed in 1906, and thereby that plot was enlarged. In 1922 the strip and the rest of the plot were used for cricket and agriculture. The enlarged plot was not built on and remained a field used for cricket and agriculture. The entire plot became vested in the plaintiff. The lane, which remained an unmade road, together with the dyke, became vested in the defendants. From 1973 the defendants, by pulling down the bridge on several occasions, attempted to prevent the plaintiff from exercising a right of way from the plot over the lane to the highway. The plaintiff brought an action against the defendants claiming, inter alia, (i) a declaration that she was entitled to use a right of way of necessity over the lane, on the ground that it was to be implied from the 1906 conveyance that it had been the common intention of the parties to that conveyance that X should have a right of way for building purposes, from the plot thereby conveyed over the lane to the highway, and that public policy prevented the exclusion of that right by any express term in the conveyance such as that contained in the second limb of para 7 of the schedule, (ii) alternatively a declaration that she was entitled to use a right of way over the lane by virtue of the 1922 conveyance and s 62(1)[a] of the Law of Property Act 1925, because by virtue thereof a right of way was created from the lane onto the strip and it could be used as a means of access from the strip to the rest of the plot.

---

a   Section 62(1), so far as material, provides: 'A conveyance of land shall be deemed to include and shall by virtue of this Act operate to convey, with the land, all . . . easements, rights, and advantages . . . appertaining or reputed to appertain to the land, or any part thereof, or, at the time of conveyance, demised, occupied, or enjoyed with or reputed or known as part or parcel of or appurtenant to the land or any part thereof.'

Held – (i) Because it was in the public interest that land should not be made unusable
there was a rule of public policy that a transaction was not, without good reason, to be
a treated as being effective to deprive land of a suitable means of access. Alternatively, any
transaction which without good reason appeared to deprive land of any suitable means
of access was, if it were possible to do so, to be construed so as not to produce that
result. Since the plot conveyed in 1906 was conveyed as building land and no valid
reason had been suggested for leaving it cut off from access to a highway, para 7 of the
b schedule to the 1906 conveyance was to be construed, after giving proper weight to the
doctrine against derogation of grant and to the rule of public policy, as not negating the
implication of a way of necessity over the lane for building purposes, but merely as
freeing the vendor from any obligation to make up the proposed new roads by reason of
any undertaking or which might be implied from the grant of easements of way over the
routes of the proposed roads. If, however, such a construction of para 7 was not
c permissible, public policy required that it was not to have the effect of negativing an
implied grant of a way of necessity over the lane for building purposes, and that such a
way had been created (see p 322 *g h* and p 323 *b* to p 324 *a*, post); dictum of Glynne CJ in
Packer v Wellstead (1658) 2 Sid at 112 applied; *North Sydney Printing Pty Ltd v Sabemo
Investment Corpn Pty Ltd* [1971] 2 NSWR 150 distinguished.

(ii) Although the general rule was that an express grant of a right of way to plot A
d could not be used as a means of access to plot B which lay beyond it, that rule did not
apply where at the time of the grant plot A formed an actual means of access to plot B or,
as between the parties to the transaction, was intended to be used thus, and in such cases
the right of way to plot A could be used as a means of access to plot B. That exception to
the general rule applied not only where there was an express grant of the right of way to
plot A but.also where the grant was implied by s 62(1) of the 1925 Act. It followed that
e as, by virtue of s 62(1), the 1922 conveyance of the strip was deemed to include a right
of way to the strip from the lane for agricultural and sporting purposes because such a
right appertained or was reputed to appertain to the strip, and as the strip formed part of
the rest of the plot conveyed in 1906, the right of way to the strip (implied by s 62) could
be used as a means of access to the rest of the plot but, on the evidence, only for
pedestrians and for vehicles for agricultural and sporting purposes and not for vehicles
f for building purposes (see p 324 *b* to *j*, post); *Harris v Flower* (1904) 74 LJ Ch 127
distinguished.

Notes

For easements of necessity, for non-derogation from grant, for ascertainment of the
extent and nature of an easement and for the effect of s 62 of the Law of Property Act
1925 on conveyances, see 14 Halsbury's Laws (4th Edn) paras 29, 37, 54, 55, and for cases
g on those subjects, see 19 Digest (Repl) 106–110, 114–117, 38–40, 637–674, 708–723,
202–205.

For the Law of Property Act 1925, s 62, see 27 Halsbury's Statutes (3rd Edn) 438.

Cases referred to in judgments

Barry v Hasseldine [1952] 2 All ER 317, [1952] Ch 835, 19 Digest (Repl) 107, 653.
h *Bracewell v Appleby* [1975] 1 All ER 993, [1975] Ch 408, [1975] 2 WLR 282, 29 P & CR
204, Digest (Cont Vol D) 279, 39*a*.
Brown v Burdett (1882) 21 Ch D 667, 52 LJ Ch 52, 47 LT 94, 48 Digest (Repl) 278, 2488.
Dutton v Tayler (1700) 2 Lut 1487, 125 ER 819, 19 Digest (Repl) 107, 654.
Fender v St John Mildmay [1938] AC 1, sub nom *Fender v Mildmay* [1937] 3 All ER 402,
106 LJKB 641, 157 LT 340, HL, 12 Digest (Reissue) 325, 2352.
j *Gayford v Moffat* (1868) 4 Ch App 133, 33 JP 212, LC, 19 Digest (Repl) 47, 249.
Harris v Flower (1904) 74 LJ Ch 127, 91 LT 816, CA, 19 Digest (Repl) 119, 738.
Jones v Pritchard [1908] 1 Ch 630, 77 LJ Ch 405, 98 LT 386, 19 Digest (Repl) 45, 241.
Lyttleton Times Co Ltd v Warners Ltd [1907] AC 476, [1904–7] All ER Rep 200, 76 LJPC
100, 97 LT 496, PC, 12 Digest (Reissue) 747, 5376.
North Sydney Printing Pty Ltd v Sabemo Investments Corpn Pty Ltd [1971] 2 NSWR 150.

Packer v Wellstead (1658) 2 Sid 111, 82 ER 1284, 19 Digest (Repl) 99, 585.
Pwllbach Colliery Co Ltd v Woodman [1915] AC 634, [1914–15] All ER Rep 124, 84 LJKB *a*
874, 113 LT 10, 31 TLR 271, HL, 19 Digest (Repl) 13, 27.
Union Lighterage Co v London Graving Dock Co [1902] 2 Ch 557, [1900–3] All ER Rep 234
71 LJ Ch 791, 87 LT 381, CA, 19 Digest (Repl) 19, 68.
Wong v Beaumont Property Trust Ltd [1964] 2 All ER 119, [1965] 1 QB 173, [1964] 2 WLR
1325, CA, Digest (Cont Vol B) 230, 214*a*.

b

Action
The plaintiff, Mrs Erna Nickerson, was the owner in fee simple of a field ('the pink land')
in the parish of New Waltham, Lincolnshire. The pink land adjoined a ditch which in
turn adjoined a private road both of which were vested in the second and third
defendants, John Letten Mountain and John Thomas Roberts. The second and third
defendants were also the owners of a golf course and club house at the end of the road *c*
which were occupied on their behalf by the first defendant, T A J Barraclough. By a
statement of claim served on 2nd February 1976 the plaintiff claimed against the
defendants, inter alia, (1) a declaration that she was entitled to use a right of way from the
pink land over a bridge crossing the ditch and over the road to the point at which the
road joined a public highway, by virtue of a conveyance dated 28th April 1922 and s 62
of the Law of Property Act 1925, (2) alternatively a declaration that she was entitled to *d*
use the right of way of necessity and/or by implication of law, (3) alternatively, a
declaration that she was entitled to use the right of way as having being enjoyed by her
and the possessors of the pink land through whom she claimed, by virtue of a deed made
by all necessary parties which had been accidentally lost or destroyed, (4) alternatively, a
declaration that the plaintiff was entitled to use the right of way as of legal right under
s 2 of the Prescription Act 1832 and as appertaining to the pink land. The facts are set out *e*
in the judgment.

Spencer G Maurice for the plaintiff.
F M Ferris for the defendants.

Cur adv vult *f*

27th November. **SIR ROBERT MEGARRY V-C** read the following judgment: The
main issue in this case is whether the plaintiff has a right of way for all purposes to her
field over a private road known as Scouts Lane. The field is a few miles south of
Grimsby. It is roughly rectangular in shape and has an area of 3·35 acres. In the *g*
statement of claim it is called the 'pink land' and I shall adopt this description. The pink
land lies immediately to the west of Scouts Lane, and is separated from it by a dyke or
ditch which runs parallel with the lane. In the north-east corner of the field there was
once a little bridge over the dyke. Scouts Lane runs roughly north and south, and if one
proceeds northwards along it from the bridge, one reaches Humberstone Avenue, a
public highway. Numbers 10 and 12 Humberstone Avenue abut on the northern *h*
boundary of the pink land. Number 12, which abuts on the eastern half of the northern
boundary of the pink land, has a return frontage to Scouts Lane, but plays little part in
the case. Number 10, on the other hand, which abuts on the western half of the
northern boundary of the pink land, was at one time in common ownership with the
pink land, and plays a material part in the case.
   Both Scouts Lane and the dyke are vested in the second and third defendants. Scouts *j*
Lane leads to a golf course which lies south-east of the pink land, and this also is vested
in the second and third defendants. The first defendant is manager of the golf course and
club house, and occupies them on behalf of the second and third defendants. It was he
who more than once dismantled the bridge across the dyke over which the plaintiff
claims a right of way. The central question is whether the plaintiff has such a right of

way along the northern half of Scouts Lane and over the bridge into her pink land. The
a pink land was conveyed to her on 12th November 1973.
   The title to the pink land is in two parts, and I shall have to consider that title at some
length. The major part of the pink land is held under a conveyance on sale dated 8th
December 1906 to Mr G L Alward. The residue, consisting of a strip 36 feet wide
running east and west at the north of the pink land, is held under a conveyance on sale
to Mr G L Alward dated 28th April 1922. Apart from a mortgage of this strip in 1922
b which was discharged in the same year, the pink land thereafter devolved as a whole.
The plaintiff's claim to the easement is made under four heads. First, it is based on an
implied grant under the 1906 conveyance. Second, there is a claim by virtue of s 62 of
the Law of Property Act 1925 under the 1922 conveyance of the strip. Third, the
easement is claimed by prescription under the Prescription Act 1832; and fourth, it is
based on prescription under the doctrine of lost modern grant. Apart from the issues of
c fact, there has been a detailed examination of the plaintiff's title, which rests on what
appears to have been some not very expert conveyancing. The defendants' title has not
been the subject of dispute. All that I need say is that by a conveyance dated 6th October
1961, the golf course, Scouts Lane and another strip of land were conveyed to a company
controlled by the first defendant, Mr Barraclough, and on 30th April 1971, that company
conveyed all the land to the second and third defendants to hold on trust for sale on the
d trusts of a settlement.
   The writ was issued on 6th August 1975. Under the statement of claim in its final
form, a variety of declarations and injunctions are claimed, as well as damages. The
whole argument, by counsel for the plaintiff and counsel for the defendants, has been
directed to whether or not there is an easement of way from Humberstone Avenue over
Scouts Lane to the pink land, and, if there is, what is the ambit of that easement. The
e claim is for an easement of way on foot and with animals, carriages and motor vehicles
at all times and for all purposes. I shall leave any question of the appropriate relief for
discussion after I have resolved whether there is any right of way, and if so, what is its
extent.
   [His Lordship found the following facts. The plaintiff's and the defendants' land
originally formed part of the Carrington Settled Estates. On 20th April 1900 part of the
f estate, divided into building lots and described as the Humberstone Building Estate, was
put up for sale by auction. Each lot consisted of about half an acre. The plan on the
auction particulars showed proposed new roads on the building estate which included a
strip of land running parallel to what became Scouts Lane. The particulars described the
lots as valuable freehold building sites and contained a set of building regulations and
general conditions regulating the number of houses, their minimum cost etc. The
g regulations and conditions ended with the words, 'The Vendors do not undertake to
make any of the proposed New Roads shewn on the Plan'. The lotted land included plots
7, 8 and 9 (which fronted the public highway, Humberstone Avenue) and plots 45, 46
and 47 which lay immediately to the south of them. Plot 45 bounded on the west a
proposed road which became Enfield Avenue. The lotted land did not include plots 77
and 78 which lay to the south of plots 45, 46 and 47 and to the south of a 36 foot strip of
h land (proposed as a road to connect the future Enfield Avenue with the future Scouts
Lane) or plot 78A which consisted of the pink land minus its northern strip; that strip was
part of the 36 foot strip proposed as a road. All the foregoing plots together formed an
L-shaped block of land. The pink land formed the eastern part of the foot of the L. By
conveyances dated 1900 and 1901 and by a further transaction Mr G L Alward acquired
plots 7, 8, 9, 45, 46, 47, 77 and 78. By a further conveyance dated 8th December 1906
j he acquired plot 78A. The 1906 conveyance recited the 1900 auction sale, provided that
Mr Alward and his successors should hold plot 78A subject to the general restrictions and
conditions contained in Sch 1 to the 1906 conveyance and contained a covenant by Mr
Alward for himself and his successors to observe and perform the stipulations and
restrictions in Sch 1. Those stipulations and restrictions consisted of building regulations
similar to those contained in the 1900 auction particulars. The 1906 conveyance was not

in evidence, but an abstract of the conveyance was; and para 7 of Sch 1 of the conveyance, as abstracted, provided that 'The Vendor did not undertake to make any of the proposed *a* new roads shown on the [plan on the 1906 conveyance] nor did he give any right of way over the same until the same should (if ever) be made'. It appeared from the 1906 conveyance that plot 78A was landlocked and wholly without access to any highway. By a conveyance dated 28th April 1922 Mr Alward acquired, inter alia, part of the 36 foot strip to the north of plots 77, 78 and 78A proposed as a road. He thereby completed the acquisition of the pink land and the acquisition of the L-shaped block of land. By various *b* subsequent conveyances the plaintiff became the owner of the pink land. His Lordship continued:]

With that I can turn to the four heads of claim. First, there is the claim of an implied grant of the way under the 1906 conveyance. [His Lordship said that the major obstacle in the path of counsel for the plaintiff in respect to that claim was the second half of para 7 of Sch 1 which, referring to the vendor and to the proposed new roads on the plan to *c* the conveyance, read: '. . . nor did he give any rights of way over the same until the same should (if ever) be made.' Counsel for the plaintiff did not rely on a way of necessity based on direct evidence as to the physical state of affairs in 1906, on which no evidence had been called. Instead, he relied on what appeared from the 1906 conveyance construed in its context. His Lordship continued:]

The classic statement of the law on the implication of easements is in the speech of *d* Lord Parker of Waddington in *Pwllbach Colliery Co Ltd v Woodman*[1]. The speech first mentions implied grants of ways of necessity and what are called continuous and apparent easements. It then discusses easements which are implied because the right is necessary for the enjoyment of some right expressly granted, as where a right of way is implied on the grant of an express right to draw water from a spring. The speech then turns to cases where the implication depends not on the terms of the grant itself but on *e* the circumstances under which it was made. Lord Parker says:

'The law will readily imply the grant or reservation of such easements as may be necessary to give effect to the common intention of the parties to a grant of real property, with reference to the manner or purposes in and for which the land granted or some land retained by the grantor is to be used. See *Jones* v. *Pritchard*[2] and *Lyttelton Times Co.* v. *Warners*[3]. But it is essential for this purpose that the parties *f* should intend that the subject of the grant or the land retained by the grantor should be used in some definite and particular manner. It is not enough that the subject of the grant or the land retained should be intended to be used in a manner which may or may not involve this definite and particular use.'

In the present case the land conveyed was plainly intended to be used for building *g* purposes, and of course it plainly needed access for building materials and for the occupants of the houses when constructed: yet there was the express negativing of the grant of any way in the second limb of para 7 of Sch 1, despite the need for some grant of a way that appeared from the surrounding circumstances as disclosed by the conveyance itself. The mere fact that some of the surrounding land belongs to persons other than the grantor is no bar to a way of necessity being implied (*Barry v Hasseldine*[4]), *h* and I think the same must apply where some of the surrounding land belongs to the grantee himself, if he has no right in respect of it which will enable him to have access from a highway to the land being conveyed to him. The essence of necessity is necessity, whatever the cause. I think that there must be a similar approach where the implication is made in order to give effect to the common intention of the parties.

j

1　[1915] AC 634 at 646–647, [1914–15] All ER Rep 124 at 130
2　[1908] 1 Ch 630, [1908–10] All ER Rep 80
3　[1907] AC 476, [1904–7] All ER Rep 200
4　[1952] 2 All ER 317, [1952] Ch 835

I find great difficulty in holding that there has been granted by implication something
that the grant expressly negatives. Of course it may be that the grant could be rectified
so as to exclude the express negative, though at this distance of time that seems highly
improbable. But while the conveyance remains as it is, I find it almost impossible to
imply a grant in the teeth of the express negation of any grant; and the grant of a way of
necessity seems plainly to be one form of implied grant. There is, however, one
consideration that is peculiar to ways of necessity that seems to be in point. During
argument, I was referred to a sentence in Gale on Easements[1] on the subject of ways of
necessity, which runs: 'The principle appears to be based on the idea that the neglect of
agricultural land is contrary to public policy': and for this two old decisions are cited. I
have now looked at these. In *Packer v Wellstead*[2] Glynne CJ referred to a way of necessity
and said this: 'nest solement un private inconvenience, mes est auxy al prejudice del weal
publick que terre gisser fresh & unoccupied.' In *Dutton v Tayler*[3] it was held[4] of a way of
necessity in the Common Bench that 'est pro bono publico que le terre ne serra unoccupy'.
     This seems to be to raise a novel point of some difficulty and importance. Put shortly,
it is whether on a grant of land in circumstances which otherwise would create a way of
necessity, or a way implied from the common intention of the parties based on a
necessity apparent from the deeds, it is open to the parties to negative the creation of such
a way by some express term in the conveyance. I cannot think that the point is in any
way confined to agricultural land: whatever the actual or prospective use of the land, the
question arises whether in the absence of special circumstances public policy will permit
the parties to a conveyance to make land inaccessible save by air transport and thus
unusable. As applied to the present case, the question would be whether the court
should impose on the second limb of para 7 of Sch 1 a qualification which would exclude
from its operation any way required for access for building purposes which would
otherwise be implied. As the evidence stands, apart from para 7 I would have no
hesitation in holding that in the circumstances of the 1906 conveyance there was an
implied grant of a way to plot 78A for building purposes; for the contemplated use of the
plot was for those purposes, and so the extent of the way is to be measured by those
purposes: see *Gayford v Moffat*[5]. As for the line of the way, since no express allocation of
a line by the grantor appears to have been made, I think the tacit allocation of a way over
the future Scouts Lane which has emerged from the user that I shall describe in due
course would suffice as an allocation.
     The point, as I have said, is novel; and although I was referred indirectly to the two old
cases from which I have cited, the point of public policy was not argued out before me.
One case that has since occurred to me is *Brown v Burdett*[6]. That was the case of a devise
of a house on trust to block up nearly all the rooms in it for 20 years. The case was argued
on the footing that this left the house undisposed of for 20 years, and Bacon V-C held that
this was the case. In the Law Times Reports[7] he is reported as saying that the trusts of the
house were 'invalid', and that 'the directions as to the blockade must be treated as
ineffectual'. The books refer to the case under headings such as illegality, and although
there is no explicit mention of public policy, I think that this must have played some part
in the decision. However, in the absence of full argument on the point I do not think
that I ought to decide it; and unless the plaintiff fails on the other bases on which he
claims, I can leave the point undecided. I therefore propose to consider the other bases
on which the plaintiff's claim is made.

---

1   14th Edn (1972), p 117
2   (1658) 2 Sid 111 at 112, 82 ER 1284 at 1285
3   (1700) 2 Lut 1487 at 1489, 125 ER 819 at 821
4   But see p 321 *c*, post
5   (1868) 4 Ch App 133 at 136
6   (1882) 21 Ch D 667
7   47 LT 94 at 96

The other three heads of claim all require an examination of the use made of Scouts Lane, either before or after it acquired that name. For prescription either under the *a* Prescription Act 1832 or under the doctrine of lost modern grant, that user is directly in point; for the Law of Property Act 1925, s 62, in relation to the 1922 conveyance, it is of course relevant in determining what appertained or was reputed to appertain to the 36 foot strip on being added to plot 78A in 1922. I shall therefore turn to the evidence of user. [His Lordship reviewed the evidence and stated it was to be considered on the footing that from 1908 until late 1972 or early 1973 there was a sleeper bridge eight feet *b* wide, across a dyke at the north-east corner of the pink land, which connected Scouts Lane, which lay to the east of the bridge, with the pink land which lay on the west of the bridge, through a ten foot gate opening into the pink land. Furthermore the evidence as a whole established user of Scouts Lane as a means of access to the pink land from at least 1921 until 1972 or 1973, and that from 1921 the pink land had been used for games such as cricket and football and for agricultural purposes. His Lordship continued:]   *c*

I turn to the three remaining heads of claim. First, there is s 62 of the 1925 Act in relation to the 1922 conveyance. This, of course, merely conveyed part of the 36 feet strip of which a segment became the northern part of the enlarged plot 78A. So far as user is concerned, there is little in the evidence before me to support the existence of a right of way over Scouts Lane to reach the strip, as distinct from the rest of plot 78A. On the other hand, there was some sort of visible track down Scouts Lane, and there was the *d* plain and visible sleeper bridge to provide an entrance from Scouts Lane to the strip, without there being any other obvious means of access. When in such circumstances the common owner of both the lane and the strip conveys the strip, I think the court will be ready to treat the access by means of the lane and the bridge as falling within the very wide words of s 62(1) of the Law of Property Act 1925 unless the contrary is made reasonably clear. However, this may not suffice counsel for the plaintiff, since it can be *e* said that a means of access to the strip does not, under the doctrine of *Harris v Flower*[1], operate as a means of access to the rest of the enlarged plot 78A. On this, counsel for the plaintiff said that as there was a common vendor for both the strip and the rest of plot 78A, *Harris v Flower*[1] should in some way be distinguished, since to apply the decision would be ridiculous.

Now the assertion that something is ridiculous is not a very cogent argument unless *f* the ridicule is plain for all to see: if it is not, there must be some process of reasoning which demonstrates why the result said to be ridiculous does not follow. I say what I am about to say with some hesitation as the point was not argued out; indeed, although *Harris v Flower*[1] was mentioned on a number of occasions, the report was never put before me. After looking at the case, together with *Bracewell v Appleby*[2] in which it was recently applied, and some of the earlier cases cited in it, there does seem to me to be an *g* intelligible distinction. If a right of way is granted to go to plot A, then the grantee cannot use the way as a means of access to his adjoining plot B, whether he already owned it when the way was granted to him or whether he acquired it subsequently: for what he was granted was no more than a way to plot A, and it is an excessive user of that way to use it for some purpose not included in the grant. That, as I understand it, is the doctrine of *Harris v Flower*[1]. Where, as in those cases, there is an express grant of the way, it may *h* usually be seen what the dominant tenement was, and what was the extent of the grant. Here, however, I am concerned with the operation of s 62, which, although operating by way of express grant, does so by reference to general rather than specific terms. The question, then, is what grant was made by virtue of s 62 when the strip was conveyed to Mr Alward.

Now at that time the sleeper bridge had for some 14 years been in position, and there *j* had for a long while been some form of track down the future Scouts Lane. The strip

---

1   (1904) 74 LJ Ch 127
2   [1975] 1 All ER 993, [1975] Ch 408

had for long been regarded as the site for a future road, and that future road, being
a contiguous on its south side with the north side of plot 78A, would obviously be regarded
as at least a potential means of access to plot 78A. In 1921, for example, the cricketers
must have gone down the track on the future Scouts Lane, across the sleeper bridge on
to the strip and then on to plot 78A. What the 1922 conveyance did was to give to Mr
Alward the sole ownership of the strip which until then had been a potential (and to
some extent at least an actual) means of access to plot 78A. If he had not bought the strip,
b he could have asserted that the sleeper bridge appeared to be the means of access to plot
78A via some portion of the strip: it would be remarkable if, having bought the strip, he
were to be told that he could use the bridge to get on to the strip but not, now that he
owned the strip, to get on to plot 78A. In other words, where what is being conveyed
forms part of a means of access to a larger plot, I think that the court will find it easy to
treat the grant under s 62 of a right of way to that means of access as including a right of
c way to the larger plot itself. What appertains to that means of access is not a way merely
to that means of access, but a way to what that means of access gives access to. [His
Lordship then considered counsel for the defendants' contention that s 62 did not apply
because a contrary intention appeared from the 1922 conveyance or from the surrounding
circumstances. His Lordship said that s 62(4) required any contrary intention to be
'expressed in the conveyance', so that the surrounding circumstances would not suffice,
d and that in any case he could find no contrary intention either in the conveyance or
outside it. His Lordship continued:]
        Now as I have indicated, my tentative view is that *Harris v Flower*[1] is distinguishable
on the lines that I have stated. My view is tentative because I have not had the advantage
of having the point argued out. On that tentative basis, I would be prepared to hold that
under s 62 a right of way had been granted in 1922 whereby Mr Alward was entitled to
e reach plot 78A over Scouts Lane. At the same time, I can see little evidence to support the
view that the right of way is for all purposes, including vehicles; and in any case I would
make no order on this basis until the parties had had the opportunity of submitting
further arguments. Accordingly, without resolving this point further, I turn to
prescription. [His Lordship then considered the claims to a prescriptive right of user
over Scouts Lane under the Prescription Act 1832 and under the doctrine of lost modern
f grant. His Lordship concluded on the evidence that a right of way over Scouts Lane had
been made out both under the Act and under the doctrine of lost modern grant, but only
for agricultural and sporting purposes for the land in its existing undeveloped state, and
not for the purposes of erecting houses. His Lordship continued:]
        The limited nature and extent of the prescriptive rights that I have held to exist may
not suffice to resolve the matter, and it may be necessary to reach a decision on implied
g grant, and, possibly, on s 62. As I have indicated, I am unwilling to decide these points
without further argument, and so if either side wishes me to decide either point, I shall
restore the case for further argument.
        In leaving matters in that state, I should add that I did of course consider whether it
would not be better to restore the case for further argument generally before delivering
any judgment, rather than delivering a judgment which leaves some points undecided.
h However, I came to the conclusion that it would be likely to assist the parties and save
costs if I at least narrowed the issues by making findings of fact and deciding the claims
based on prescription, and also giving some indication of my provisional views on the
undecided points. I therefore took that course. I propose to direct that no order is to be
drawn up until counsel have been able to consider this judgment and make any
application to me that they may wish.
j   [Subsequently, the case was restored for further argument on whether there was a
right of way of necessity over Scouts Lane, and on the rule in *Harris v Flower*[1].]

---

1   (1904) 74 LJ Ch 127

Cur adv vult

a

19th March. **SIR ROBERT MEGARRY V-C** read the following judgment: In the judgment that I have already delivered in this case, there were two points that I refrained from deciding, though I gave counsel the opportunity, if they wished, to argue these points further in the light of my findings of fact and my comments on those points. Counsel availed themselves of this opportunity, and argued the points for a day and a half towards the end of last term. Put shortly, and in general terms, the points are as b follows. First, if land is conveyed in circumstances which otherwise would create a way of necessity, or a way implied from the common intention of the parties based on a necessity apparent from the deeds, does public policy prevent the creation of such a way from being negatived by an express term in the grant? Second, under what is sometimes called the doctrine of *Harris v Flower*[1], a right of way to plot A cannot be used as a means of access to plot B which lies beyond it. But where plot A itself is, or is intended to be, c a means of access to plot B, does the doctrine apply, or will the grant of such a right by virtue of the Law of Property Act 1925, s 62, confer a right of access over the way to plot B via plot A? So far as I know, both points of law are novel in this country.

I shall take the point on public policy first. This was the subject of an article by Mr E H Bodkin in the Law Quarterly Review[2] which counsel for the plaintiff read to me and adopted as part of his argument. The article observes at the outset that the possible d impact of public policy on agreements purporting to exclude the implication of easements of necessity does not appear to have been considered in any reported case. The view of the author, with his great learning and experience of conveyancing, was that any provision made by a grant of real property (at any rate if it was for value), or expressed or implied in the whole arrangement contained in the grant and any ancillary agreement which was to be read therewith, would be held to be void if it purported to exclude the e implication of a way of necessity, or substantially to limit its extent[3]. Of the authorities which I mentioned in my judgment, the article cites *Packer v Wellstead*[4] and *Brown v Burdett*[5], though not *Dutton v Tayler*[6]. A footnote[7] refers to an Australian decision, *North Sydney Printing Pty Ltd v Sabemo Investments Corpn Pty Ltd*[8], a case that was not cited to me but which I shall have to consider in due course: for brevity I shall call it the *North Sydney* case. f

It seems clear that necessity may be relevant to rights of way in two distinct but overlapping ways. First, there may be a way of necessity, strictly so-called. Here the necessity is that without the way the land would be landlocked, and could not be used at all: see *Union Lighterage Co v London Graving Dock Co*[9]. Second, the way may be necessary (a) for the enjoyment of some right expressly granted by the conveyance (as where the grant of a right to draw water from a spring will imply a right of way to the spring), or g (b) in order to give effect to the common intention of the parties. Under the first head, and also under limb (b) of the second head, easements of way may arise either in favour of the grantor or in favour of the grantee; and both heads are instances of implied grant. See generally *Pwllbach Colliery Co Ltd v Woodman*[10] per Lord Parker of Waddington. The overlapping nature of these two heads is illustrated by *Wong v*

h

---

1   (1904) 74 LJ Ch 127
2   (1973) 89 LQR 87
3   89 LQR 87 at 90
4   (1658) 2 Sid 111 at 112, 82 ER 1284 at 1285
5   (1882) 21 Ch D 667
6   (1700) 2 Lut 1487, 125 ER 819
7   89 LQR 87 at 91
8   [1971] 2 NSWR 150
9   [1902] 2 Ch 557 at 573, [1900–3] All ER Rep 234 at 241
10   [1915] AC 634 at 646–647, [1914–15] All ER Rep 124 at 130

i

j

Beaumont Property Trust Ltd[1]. There, Lord Denning MR[2] spoke of easements of necessity,
a and gave a way to a landlocked close of land as an instance, thus plainly referring to the
first head: but he cited in support only those passages in Lord Parker's speech in the
Pwllbach Colliery case[3] which related to limb (b) of the second head.

Now in this case, as stated in the judgment which I have already delivered, counsel for
the plaintiff disclaimed any intention of relying on any factual evidence of plot 78A being
landlocked in 1906, and said that he relied solely on the 1906 conveyance, construed in
b its context. As I said, apart from public policy, I found great difficulty in holding that
there had been granted by implication something that the grant expressly negatived; the
question for me now, of course, is whether public policy produces any different result.
Packer v Wellstead[4] contains a dictum of Glynne CJ which indicates that it should; and he
added a reference (which must, I think, be to his predecessor in office, Rolle CJ) to a
previous view to the same effect having been expressed on circuit at Winchester. This
c case was cited in *Dutton v Tayler*[5], in which it was said (not 'held', as by a slip appeared in
my previous judgment[6]) that the public good required that land should not be
unoccupied; but this was merely one part of the argument of counsel for the plaintiff,
which in the event failed.

Thus far, such authority as there is supports the existence of this aspect of public
policy. There is *Packer v Wellstead*[7] which seems to be accepted by Gale on Easements[8]
d (with the comment that 'The law on the subject is antiquated and, in some respects, not
fully developed'), and then there is the article in the Law Quarterly Review[9]. But there
is also the *North Sydney* case[10]; and to this I must turn.

The *North Sydney* case[10] was decided in the Supreme Court of New South Wales by
Hope J, sitting in equity. Put very shortly, the facts were that a company sold part of its
land, which abutted on to a street. The retained land had no access to a highway, but the
e company intended subsequently to sell it to the local authority as an addition to a
contiguous car park owned by that authority. The proposed sale to the local authority
went off, and the company was left with its retained land, which was landlocked. The
company then sought a declaration that its retained land had a way of necessity over the
land sold; and this claim failed. Over twenty authorities (half of them English) were
cited in argument, including *Packer v Wellstead*[7] and *Dutton v Tayler*[11].

f The opposing contentions seem to have been pitched high. The company contended
that it was entitled to a way of necessity by virtue of public policy, and that the intention
of the parties was irrelevant. The purchaser contended that public policy was irrelevant,
and that the company was entitled to no right of way, since the intention of the parties
was that the company should have no such right. The issue was thus not whether there
was any rule of public policy on the point, but whether the creation of ways of necessity
g was based on public policy or on intention. The judgment cited a number of English
authorities which rest the doctrine on intention, and, not surprisingly, came to the
conclusion[12] that 'a way of necessity arises in order to give effect to an actual or presumed
intention'. The judge added that no doubt difficulties could arise in some cases because
of differing actual intentions on the part of the parties, though for the way to arise it

h

1   [1964] 2 All ER 119, [1965] 1 QB 173
2   [1964] 2 All ER 119 at 122, [1965] 1 QB 173 at 180
3   [1915] AC 634, [1914–15] All ER Rep 124
4   (1658) 2 Sid 111 at 112, 82 ER 1284 at 1285
5   (1700) 2 Lut 1487 at 1489, 125 ER 819 at 821
6   See p 317 c, ante.
j 7   2 Sid 111, 82 ER 1284
8   14th Edn (1972), p 117
9   (1973) 89 LQR 87
10   [1971] 2 NSWR 150
11   2 Lut 1487, 125 ER 819
12   [1971] 2 NSWR 150 at 160

must at least be possible, in a case such as that before the court, to presume an intention on the part of the grantor that access to the land should be given over the land conveyed. In fact, the company's actual intention was the contrary; its intention was that the land retained should have no access over the land conveyed, but instead should have access over the car park. Furthermore, under town planning legislation the company had at all material times a right to compel the local authority to acquire the retained land; and if this right was exercised, there would be access to the retained land. Accordingly it was held that no way of necessity over the land conveyed had arisen for the benefit of the land retained.

So far as I have been able to ascertain, that is the only case in modern times in which public policy has been considered in relation to ways of necessity. I regret that this case was not cited to me and discussed in argument, and that the footnote in which it appears in Mr Bodkin's article[1] says so little about the case. I must therefore do the best that I can on my own: I do not think that it would be right to restore the case once more for further argument. It will be observed that the *North Sydney* case[2] differed in a number of ways from the case before me. First, the claim to a way of necessity was made by the vendor, and not, as in the present case, by successors in title of the purchaser; and although ways of necessity are in a special position, the law is far more ready to imply the grant of easements than it is to imply their reservation. There is a doctrine against derogating from a grant, but not against derogating from a reservation. Second, the way of necessity was claimed in the teeth of a positive intention by the claimant that access should be by means of a different way over different land; it was not a case of a mere general negation of any rights of way over proposed new roads in general, as in the present case. Third, there was no unqualified necessity for the way. The way that the company intended the land to have over the car park could at all material times have been provided by the company. True, this could be achieved only by the company selling the retained land to the local authority; it could not both retain the land and require the local authority to grant a way over the car park. But at no time was the company unable to prevent the land being landlocked and so unusable. The necessity was at most a qualified necessity.

I cannot see anything in the *North Sydney* case[2] to negate the existence of a head of public policy which requires that land should not be rendered unusable by being landlocked. As I have indicated, the question in that case was whether public policy, rather than intention, was the source of ways of necessity: indeed, it is only on the assumption that there is some rule of public policy to this effect that such a question could arise. I readily accept that the court must be careful not to carry matters of public policy beyond the proper bounds, and I bear in mind the warnings to be found in *Fender v St John-Mildmay*[3] per Lord Atkin, and elsewhere. At the same time, where, as here, the existence of some public policy on a point is no mere novelty but has long had some foundation in the law, and, what is more, is attuned to modern needs, I think the court ought not to shrink from applying that policy. With the vast increases in population in England that have occurred over the last three centuries, I cannot think that today it is any less important than it once was that in the public interest land should not be made unusable.

If such a head of public policy exists, as I think it does, the question is what its bounds are. I do not think it can be said that, whatever the circumstances, a way of necessity will always be implied whenever a close of land is made landlocked. One can conceive of circumstances where there may be good reason why the land should be deprived of all access. The land may contain large quantities of highly toxic substances with a long life; or it may be desired to produce a bird sanctuary that will, as far as possible, be free from any disturbance; or there may be some other good reason, in no way contrary to the

---

1   (1973) 89 LQR 87 at 91
2   [1971] 2 NSWR 150
3   [1937] 3 All ER 402 at 46–407, [1938] AC 1 at 10–12

public interest, why it may be desired that the land should remain inaccessible.
Accordingly, I would not go beyond saying that there is a rule of public policy that no
transaction should, without good reason, be treated as being effectual to deprive any land
of a suitable means of access. Alternatively, the point might be put as a matter of
construction: any transaction which, without good reason, appears to deprive land of any
suitable means of access should, if at all possible, be construed as not producing this
result.

With that, I return to the 1906 conveyance. I can see nothing whatever that could be
described as being a good reason for leaving plot 78A landlocked. The land was sold and
conveyed as building land, and no suggestion has been made of any possible valid reason
for leaving it cut off from any access from any highway. The vendor must not derogate
from his grant, and to sell building land as such and yet to negative any means of access
to it seems to me a plain instance of derogation. If, therefore, the words of negation can
be read in some way so as not to produce any derogation from grant, they should be so
read. The rule of public policy requires the same approach. The question, then, is
whether the words negating any right of way can be construed in such a way as to
produce a sensible result, and to avoid, at least to this extent, stultifying the purpose of
the conveyance.

Now the wording of the clause in question, para 7 of Sch 1 to the 1906 conveyance, as
it appears in the examined abstract and with the contractions expanded, runs as follows:
'The Vendor did not undertake to make any of the proposed new roads shewn on the said
Plan nor did he give any rights of way over the same until the same should (if ever) be
made'. Grammatically, the words 'the same' must mean 'the proposed new roads shown
on the said plan'. This clause of the schedule seems primarily concerned to relieve the
vendor of any obligation to make any of the proposed new roads, in the sense of
constructing roadways over the routes shown on the plan. If one disregards public policy
and the doctrine of derogation from grant, I think the natural meaning of the second
limb of the clause is that until roadways had been constructed on the routes shown on the
plan, the purchaser was to have no right of way over the routes along which those
roadways were to be constructed.

I think, however, that it is also possible, though less natural, to read the second limb
as in effect merely reinforcing the first limb. The first limb simply negatives any
undertaking by the vendor to make up the new roads; the second limb goes on to
prevent the conveyance giving any rights of way over the new roads which might enable
the purchaser to claim that, having been granted a right of way over the new roads he
can, by virtue of that right, require the vendor to construct them. On that footing, the
second limb does not negative any way of necessity over the unmade sites of the proposed
new roads. All that is negatived is any rights of way over the proposed new roads until
they are constructed. It is, of course, obvious that one cannot have a right of way over a
made road until the road has been made: but if a way is granted over a road to be made,
it might be contended that that imposed an obligation to make the road, and so the
glimpse of the obvious in the second limb would, on this construction, perform a useful
purpose for the vendor. In short, the vendor was to be freed altogether from any
obligation to make up the roads, whether by virtue of any undertaking or by virtue of
any implication from the grant of easements of way. Nothing, however, was done to
negative any way of necessity, though the inference would be that the way should be
over some route over the proposed new roads; and there was at least the implication that
when the new roadways, or any of them, were constructed, the purchaser was to have
rights of way over each of them as constructed.

I readily accept that this may be regarded as a somewhat strained interpretation of para
7 of Sch 1; but I do not think that it is so impossible that I must reject it. If, then, in
construing this provision I give proper weight to the doctrine against derogation from
grant and the rule of public policy, I think that I can construe para 7 in this particular
way, and that I ought in fact to do so. If I am wrong in this, then I would hold, though
with some hesitation, that public policy requires that para 7 should not take effect so as

to negative the implied grant of a way of necessity. As I have already held, I think that there has been a tacit allocation by user of a way over what is now Scouts Lane, and that the way granted by implied grant is a way for building purposes. For brevity I have referred simply to a 'way of necessity', though I think the way should be more accurately referred to as a way implied from the common intention of the parties, based on a necessity apparent from the deeds, though disregarding that part of the intention which is contrary to public policy.

  With that, I turn to the second point, the so-called rule in *Harris v Flower*[1]. In my previous judgment I set out the view that I provisionally took, the point not having been argued then. That view was that although the general rule was that the grant of a right of way to reach plot A cannot be used as a means of access to plot B, which lies beyond, this rule would not apply if, at the time of the grant, plot A forms a means of access to plot B. I have not been referred to any authority which seems to me to bear at all directly on the point, and so I have to deal with it as a matter of principle. Let me take as an example a case where plot A consists of a footpath some three feet wide and a hundred yards long, running from land near a public highway up to plot B. If there is an express grant of a right of way to plot A over land which lies between plot A and the highway, it seems to me that the grant would, subject to any language to the contrary, be construed in the light of the nature and user of plot A at the time of the grant. Since that nature and user is as a footpath which constitutes a means of access to plot B, then I would have thought that the grant would be construed as authorising the dominant owner to use the way as a means of access to plot A for the purposes for which plot A is used, namely, as a means of access to plot B. In the result, the way can be used as a means of access to plot B via plot A, notwithstanding *Harris v Flower*[1]. If plot A is not used as an actual means of access to plot B but as between the parties to the transaction it is intended to be used thus, I think that the same rule would apply.

  If that is the rule for an ordinary express grant, then I think that it can be no narrower for an express grant which takes effect by virtue of the words implied by the Law of Property Act 1925, s 62; for these words are both wide and general. Rights which appertain or are reputed to appertain to land are likely to be rights which are less precisely defined than rights which have been defined in conveyancing language in an ordinary express grant. I have heard nothing to disturb the view that I had tentatively formed when I prepared the judgment that I have already delivered. I therefore hold that by virtue of the 1922 conveyance, s 62 created a right of way over Scouts Lane to the sleeper bridge and across it on the strip of land conveyed, and that this way could be used as a means of access not only to the strip conveyed but also to plot 78A. At the same time I can see nothing to justify the contention that this is a way for all purposes, including building purposes. On this, I think counsel for the defendants is right. At the time of the 1922 conveyance the strip and plot 78A had been used for agriculture and cricket, and the access from Scouts Lane was via a gate some ten feet wide and the sleeper bridge, which was some eight feet wide. In those circumstances, I do not see how a way to the land for building purposes could be said to appertain or be reputed to appertain to it. On the other hand, a sleeper bridge some eight feet wide is more than is needed for mere pedestrian access, and agricultural use and cricketing use will normally require the access of at least some vehicles. The evidence of user in and about 1922 is far from detailed; but on the whole, I think that what appertained or was reputed to appertain to the strip was a way for pedestrians and vehicles for agricultural and sporting purposes, though not vehicles for building purposes. In view of what I have already held in relation to prescription and s 62, the details of my decision under this head may well be of no great significance; but however that may be, I think the result is as I have stated.

---

1   (1904) 74 LJ Ch 127

Declarations accordingly.

Solicitors: *Lee Bolton & Lee*, agents for *Roythorne & Co*, Spalding (for the plaintiff); *Sharpe Pritchard & Co*, agents for *Bates Mountain & Co*, Grimsby (for the defendants).

Hazel Hartman   Barrister.

Macarthys Ltd v Smith

COURT OF APPEAL, CIVIL DIVISION
LORD DENNING MR, LAWTON AND CUMMING-BRUCE LJJ
23rd, 24th 25th MAY, 19th, 25th JULY 1979

Employment – Equality of treatment between men and women – Like work – Comparison of woman's work with duties of former male employee – Substantial interval between respective employments – Whether comparison restricted to comparing woman's work with that of man in contemporaneous employment – Equal Pay Act 1970 (as amended by the Sex Discrimination Act 1975), s 1(2)(a)(4) – EEC Treaty, art 119.

The employers employed a man to manage their stockroom and paid him £60 a week. He left their employment and four and a half months later they appointed the applicant, a woman, to manage the stockroom in his place at a wage of only £50 a week. The applicant claimed that she was entitled to equal pay by virtue of s 1(2)(a)(i)[a] of the Equal Pay Act 1970. An industrial tribunal found in her favour on the grounds that she was employed on like or broadly similar work to that of her male predecessor and it was only because she was a woman that she was paid less. The employers appealed to the Employment Appeal Tribunal, contending that her case did not come within the 1970 Act because s 1(2)(a)(i) only applied where a man and a woman were employed by the same employer on like work at the same time. The Employment Appeal Tribunal[b] dismissed the appeal on the grounds that s 1(2)(a)(i) was to be construed so as to give effect to the principle contained in art 119[c] of the EEC Treaty that men and women should receive equal pay for equal work, and that since it was clear from the terms of art 119 that it covered not only cases where a man and a woman were contemporaneously

---

a   Section 1, so far as material provides:
    '(1) If the terms of a contract under which a woman is employed at an establishment in Great Britain do not include (directly or by reference to a collective agreement or otherwise) an equality clause they shall be deemed to include one.
    '(2) An equality clause is a provision which relates to terms (whether concerned with pay or not) of a contract under which a woman is employed (the "woman's contract"), and has the effect that—
    (a) where the woman is employed on like work with a man in the same employment—(i) if (apart from the equality clause) any term of the woman's contract is or becomes less favourable to the woman than a term of a similar kind in the contract under which that man is employed, that term of the woman's contract shall be treated as so modified as not to be less favourable, and (ii) if (apart from the equality clause) at any time the woman's contract does not include a term corresponding to a term benefiting that man included in the contract under which he is employed, the woman's contract shall be treated as including such a term . . .
    '(4) A woman is to be regarded as employed on like work with men if, but only if, her work and theirs is of the same or a broadly similar nature, and the differences (if any) between the things she does and the things they do are not of practical importance in relation to terms and conditions of employment; and accordingly in comparing her work with theirs regard shall be had to the frequency or otherwise with which any such differences occur in practice as well as to the nature and extent of the differences.'
b   [1978] 2 All ER 746
c   Article 119, so far as material, is set out at p 328 c and p 329 h, post.

employed on like work but also cases where a woman was employed on like work in
succession to a man, s 1(2)(a)(i) meant that a woman employee was entitled to make
comparisons with the duties of a former male employee on like or broadly similar
work. The employers appealed. *a*

Held – (i) (Lord Denning MR dissenting) The 1970 Act was to be construed according
to the ordinary canons of construction and since according to its natural and ordinary
meaning s 1(2)(a)(i) was confined to cases where a man and a woman were in the same *b*
employment at the same time the court could not use the terms of art 119 of the EEC
Treaty as an aid to the construction of s 1(2)(a)(i) and thereby give it a meaning other than
its natural and ordinary meaning (see p 332 *c d h* and p 334 to p 335 *a g* and *j*, post).

(ii) (Lord Denning MR dissenting) It was not clear from the wording of art 119
whether it applied only to cases where a man and woman were doing like or broadly
similar work side by side at the same time or whether it extended to cases where a *c*
woman was employed on like work in succession to a man (see p 333 *f* to *j*, p 334 *h* and
p 335 *h j*, post).

(iii) (Lord Denning MR concurring) As there was a doubt as to the ambit of art 119 and
as the court was bound by s 2ᵈ of the European Communities Act 1972 to give effect to
the provisions of the EEC Treaty in priority to a United Kingdom statute, the question
of the true interpretation of art 119 would be referred to the Court of Justice of the *d*
European Communities under art 177 of the Treaty. Pending the decision of that court,
the proceedings would be stayed (see p 331 *g h*, p 333 *j*, p 334 *b c g h*, p 335 *j* and p 336
a b, post).

Notes
For equal treatment of men and women as regards terms and conditions of employment,
see 16 Halsbury's Laws (4th Edn) para 767. *e*

For the Equal Pay Act 1970, s 1 (as amended by the Sex Discrimination Act 1975), see
45 Halsbury's Statutes (3rd Edn) 290.

For the EEC Treaty, art 119, see 42A ibid 779.

For the European Communities Act 1972, s 2, see 42 ibid 80.

Cases referred to in judgments *f*
Amministrazione delle Finanze dello Stato v Simmenthal SpA [1978] ECR 629.
Blackburn v Attorney-General [1971] 2 All ER 1380, [1971] 1 WLR 1037, CA, 11 Digest
(Reissue) 743, 600.
Clay Cross (Quarry Services) Ltd v Fletcher [1979] 1 All ER 474, [1978] 1 WLR 1429, [1979]
ICR 1, CA.
Defrenne (Gabrielle) v Société Anonyme Belge de Navigation Aérienne (SABENA) [1976] ECR *g*
455, [1976] ICR 547, CJEC.
Shields v E Coomes (Holdings) Ltd [1979] 1 All ER 456, [1978] 1 WLR 1408, [1978] ICR
1159, CA.
Snoxell v Vauxhall Motors Ltd, Charles Early & Marriott (Witney) Ltd v Smith [1977] 3 All
ER 770, [1978] QB 11, [1977] 3 WLR 189, [1977] ICR 700, EAT.
Van Duyn v Home Office (No 2) [1975] 3 All ER 190, [1975] Ch 358, [1975] 2 WLR 760, *h*
[1974] ECR 1337, [1975] 1 CMLR 1, CJEC, Digest (Cont Vol D) 317, 4.

Cases also cited
Amies v Inner London Education Authority [1977] 2 All ER 100, [1977] ICR 308, EAT.
Costa v Ente Nazionale per l'Energia Elettrica (ENEL) [1964] ECR 585, [1964] CMLR 425,
CJEC.
Defrenne (Gabrielle) v Belgian State (Reference for a preliminary ruling by the Belgian Conseil *j*
d'État) [1971] ECR 445, [1974] 1 CMLR 494, CJEC.
Defrenne (Gabrielle) v Société Anonyme Belge de Navigation Aérienne Sabena (preliminary ruling

---

d　Section 2, so far as material, is set out at p 334 *f*, post.

requested by the Cour de Cassation, Belgium) [1978] ECR 1365, [1978] 3 CMLR 312,
a   CJEC.
*Enka BV v Inspecteur der Invoerrechten en Accijnzen, Arnhem (preliminary ruling requested by
the Tariefcommissie, Amsterdam)* [1977] ECR 2203.
Hargreaves v Hopper (1875) 1 CPD 195, 33 LT 530.
National Coal Board v Sherwin [1978] ICR 700, EAT.
National Vulcan Engineering Insurance Group Ltd v Wade [1978] 3 All ER 121, [1979] QBD
b   132, CA.
Navy, Army and Air Force Institutes v Varley [1977] 1 All ER 840, [1977] 1 WLR 149, EAT.
Pye v Minister for Lands for New South Wales [1954] 3 All ER 514, [1954] 1 WLR 1410, PC.
R v Chief Immigration Officer, Heathrow Airport, ex parte Salamat Bibi [1976] 3 All ER 843,
[1976] 1 WLR 979, CA.
Siskina, Owners of cargo lately laden on board vessel v Distos Compania Naviera SA, The Siskina
c   [1977] 3 All ER 803, [1977] 3 WLR 532, CA; *rvsd* [1977] 3 All ER 803, [1977] 3 WLR
818, HL.
Sorbie v Trust Houses Forte Hotels Ltd [1977] 2 All ER 155, [1977] QB 931, EAT.
Waddington v Miah [1974] 2 All ER 377, [1974] 1 WLR 683, HL.

Appeal

d   Macarthys Ltd ('the employers') appealed against a decision of the Employment Appeal
Tribunal[1] (Phillips J, Mr E Alderton and Mrs A L Taylor) dated 14th December 1977,
dismissing their appeal against the decision of an industrial tribunal (chairman
Mr H A Harris) sitting at London on 28th April 1977 allowing the complaint of the
employee, Mrs Wendy Smith, that she was entitled to equal pay commensurate with that
paid by the employers to her predecessor, Mr McCullough. The facts are set out in the
e   judgment of Lord Denning MR.

R L Turner for the employers.
Anthony Lester QC and *Charles Welchman* for Mrs Smith.

                                                        Cur adv vult

19th July. The following judgments were read.

f   **LORD DENNING MR.** Macarthys Ltd are wholesale dealers in pharmaceutical
products. They have warehouses in which they keep the goods and send them out to
retailers. Each warehouse is divided into four departments. One of these is the
stockroom. In 1974 the manager of the stockroom was a man named McCullough. He
left on 20th October 1975. For four months the post was not filled. But on 1st March
g   1976 a woman was appointed to be manageress of the stockroom. Her duties were not
quite the same as those of Mr McCullough. For instance she did not know anything
about the maintenance of vehicles whereas he did: but he had assistants to help him
whereas she did not. The tribunal found that her work was of equal value to his. They
said:

'. . . whilst it cannot be said that [Mrs Smith's] work was the same as that of Mr
h   McCullough, it was of a broadly similar nature and we do not think that the
differences between the work of [Mrs Smith] and Mr McCullough were practical
differences to warrant the terms and conditions of the contract being any
different. We accordingly find that [Mrs Smith] was employed on like work with
her immediate predecessor Mr McCullough.'

j   Nevertheless, although they were employed on like work, the employers paid Mrs
Smith only £50 a week whereas they had paid Mr McCullough £60 a week. The
tribunal found that this difference was not due to any material difference other than the
difference of sex. That is, it was due to the difference in sex. In short, because she was

1   [1978] 2 All ER 746, [1978] 1 WLR 849

a woman and he was a man. In these circumstances the industrial tribunal held unanimously that she was entitled to be paid at the same rate as Mr McCullough. She *a*
remained in the employment as manageress from 1st March 1976 to 9th March 1977. The industrial tribunal awarded her extra remuneration accordingly. The Employment Appeal Tribunal affirmed that decision[1]. The employers appeal to this court.

The employers say that this case is not within the Equal Pay Act 1970. In order to be covered by that Act, the employers say that the woman and the man must be employed by the same employer on like work *at the same time*: whereas here Mrs Smith was *b*
employed on like work *in succession* to Mr McCullough and not at the same time as he.

To solve this problem I propose to turn first to the principle of equal pay contained in the EEC Treaty, for that takes priority even over our own statute.

The EEC Treaty
Article 119 of the EEC Treaty says: *c*

'Each Member State shall during the first stage ensure and subsequently maintain the application of the principle that men and women should receive equal pay for equal work . . .'

That principle is part of our English law. It is directly applicable in England. So much so that, even if we had not passed any legislation on the point, our courts would have *d*
been bound to give effect to art 119. If a woman had complained to an industrial tribunal or to the High Court and proved that she was not receiving equal pay with a man for equal work, both the industrial tribunal and the court would have been bound to give her redress: see *Defrenne (Gabrielle) v Société Anonyme Belge de Navigation Aérienne (SABENA)*[2] and *Shields v E Coomes (Holdings) Ltd*[3].

In point of fact, however, the United Kingdom has passed legislation with the intention *e*
of giving effect to the principle of equal pay. It has done it by the Sex Discrimination Act 1975 and in particular by s 8 of that Act amending s 1 of the Equal Pay Act 1970. No doubt the Parliament of the United Kingdom thinks that it has fulfilled its obligations under the Treaty. But the European Commission take a different view. They think that our statutes do not go far enough.

What then is the position? Suppose that England passes legislation which contravenes *f*
the principle contained in the Treaty, or which is inconsistent with it, or fails properly to implement it. There is no doubt that the European Commission can report the United Kingdom to the European Court of Justice; and that court can require the United Kingdom to take the necessary measures to implement art 119. That is shown by arts 169 and 171 of the Treaty.

That is indeed what is happening now. We have been shown a background report of *g*
the European Communities Commission[4] dated 20th April 1979 which says:

'The European Commission recently reported on how the nine member countries of the Community were implementing the Community equal pay policy for men and women. It found that in all countries practice fell short of principle . . .

'*Where national legislation does not comply*. The Commission has written letters to the following governments outlining why it considers that their legislation does not *h*
conform . . .

'*United Kingdom*: the concept of work of equivalent value seems to be given a restrictive interpretation on the basis of the Equal Pay Act . . .

'*The British position*: The government has maintained that the Equal Pay Act 1970 and the Sex Discrimination Act 1975 fully comply with Community legislation against sex discrimination . . .' *j*

1   [1978] 2 All ER 746, [1978] 1 WLR 849
2   [1976] ECR 455, [1976] ICR 547
3   [1979] 1 All ER 456, [1978] 1 WLR 1408
4   European Communities Commission, Background Report, ISEC/B16/79

It is unnecessary, however, for these courts to wait until all that procedure has been

a gone through. Under s 2(1) and (4) of the European Communities Act 1972 the principles laid down in the Treaty are 'without further enactment' to be given legal effect in the United Kingdom; and have priority over 'any enactment passed or to be passed' by our Parliament. So we are entitled and I think bound to look at art 119 of the EEC Treaty because it is directly applicable here; and also any directive which is directly applicable here: see *Van Duyn v Home Office (No 2)*[1]. We should, I think, look to see what those

b provisions require about equal pay for men and women. Then we should look at our own legislation on the point, giving it, of course, full faith and credit, assuming that it does fully comply with the obligations under the Treaty. In construing our statute, we are entitled to look to the Treaty as an aid to its construction; but not only as an aid but as an overriding force. If on close investigation it should appear that our legislation is deficient or is inconsistent with Community law by some oversight of our draftsmen

c then it is our bounden duty to give priority to Community law. Such is the result of s 2(1) and (4) of the European Communities Act 1972.

I pause here, however, to make one observation on a constitutional point. Thus far I have assumed that our Parliament, whenever it passes legislation, intends to fulfil its obligations under the Treaty. If the time should come when our Parliament deliberately passes an Act with the intention of repudiating the Treaty or any provision in it or

d intentionally of acting inconsistently with it and says so in express terms then I should have thought that it would be the duty of our courts to follow the statute of our Parliament. I do not however envisage any such situation. As I said in *Blackburn v Attorney-General*[2]: 'But if Parliament should do so, then I say we will consider that event when it happens.' Unless there is such an intentional and express repudiation of the Treaty, it is our duty to give priority to the Treaty. In the present case I assume that the

e United Kingdom intended to fulfil its obligations under art 119. Has it done so?

Article 119

Article 119 is framed in European fashion. It enunciates a broad general principle and leaves the judges to work out the details. In contrast the Equal Pay Act is framed in English fashion. It states no general principle but lays down detailed specific rules for the

f courts to apply (which, so some hold, the courts must interpret according to the actual language used) without resort to considerations of policy or principle.

Now consider art 119 in the context of our present problem. Take the simple case envisaged by Phillips J. A man who is a skilled technician working single-handed for a firm receives £1·50 an hour for his work. He leaves the employment. On the very next day he is replaced by a woman who is equally capable and who does exactly the same

g work as the man but, because she is a woman, she is only paid £1·25 an hour. That would be a clear case of discrimination on the ground of sex. It would, I think, be an infringement of the principle in art 119 which says 'that men and women should receive equal pay for equal work'. All the more so when you take into account the explanatory sentence in art 119 itself which says:

h '. . . Equal pay without discrimination based on sex means . . . that pay for work at time rates shall be the same for the same job.'

If you go further and consider the Council directive of 10th February 1975[3], it becomes plain beyond question:

j 'The principle of equal pay for men and women outlined in Article 119 of the Treaty, hereinafter called "principle of equal pay," means, for the same work or for work to which equal value is attributed, the elimination of all discrimination on ground of sex with regard to all aspects and conditions of remuneration.'

---

1   [1975] 3 All ER 190, [1975] Ch 358
2   [1971] 2 All ER 1380 at 1383, [1971] 1 WLR 1037 at 1040
3   EEC Council Directive 75/117, art 1

That directive may be directly applicable in England; but, even if it be not, it is
relevant as showing the scope of the principle contained in art 119. It shows that it *a*
applies to the case of the skilled technician (which I have put) and that the difference
between the woman and the man should be eliminated by paying her £1·50 an hour just
like the man.

In my opinion therefore art 119 is reasonably clear on the point; it applies not only to
cases where the woman is employed on like work *at the same time* with a man in the same
employment, but also when she is employed on like work in succession to a man, that is, *b*
in such close succession that it is just and reasonable to make a comparison between
them. So much for art 119.

The Equal Pay Act 1970
Now I turn to our Act to see if that principle has been carried forward into our
legislation. The relevant part of this Act was passed not in 1970 but in 1975 by s 8 of the *c*
Sex Discrimination Act 1975.

Section 1(2)(*a*)(i) of the Equal Pay Act 1970 introduces an 'equality clause' so as to put
a woman on an equality with a man 'where the woman is employed on like work with
a man in the same employment'. The question is whether the words 'at the same time'
are to be read into that subsection so that it is confined to cases where the woman and the
man are employed *at the same time* in the same employment. *d*

Reading that subsection as it stands, it would appear that the draftsman had only in
mind cases where the woman was employed *at the same time* as a man. The use of the
present tense 'is' and of the phrase 'in the same employment' carry the connotation that
the woman and the man are employed on like work *at the same time*.

Section 1(2)(*a*)(i) does not however carry the same connotation. It introduces an
equality clause: '... where the woman is employed on work rated as equivalent with *e*
that of a man in the same employment ...' That subsection looks at the value of the
work done in the job. If the job is rated as equivalent in value, the woman should get the
rate for the job, no matter whether she is employed at the same time as the man or in
succession to him.

Some light is thrown on the problem by reference to the Sex Discrimination Act
1975. It applies to all cases of discrimination against a woman in the employment field: *f*
see ss 1 and 6(1) and (2) except where she is paid less money than the man: see s 6(6).
Now take a case where a man leaves his job and the employer discriminates against an
incoming woman by offering her (not less money) but less benefits than he would offer
a man for the same job: for instance, less holidays or less travelling facilities or the like.
And she accepts them. That would be discrimination against her on the ground of her
sex. It would be unlawful under ss 1 and 6(1) and (2). In such a case you would think *g*
that there should be an 'equality clause' introduced under s 1(2) of the Equal Pay Act: so
that, in regard to her holidays or her travel facilities, she would be put on equal terms
with the man. But in order to achieve that just result, it is necessary to extend s 1(2)(*a*),
so that it extends not only to employment 'at the same time' as the man but also to
employment in succession to a man.

Now stand back and look at the statutes as a single code intended to eliminate *h*
discrimination against women. They should be a harmonious whole. To achieve this
harmony s 1(2)(*a*)(i) of the Equal Pay Act should *not* be read as if it included the words
'at the same time'. It should be interpreted so as to apply to cases where a woman is
employed at the same job doing the same work 'in succession' to a man.

Combining the two provisions   *j*
By so construing the Treaty and the statutes together we reach this very desirable
result: it means that there is no conflict between art 119 of the Treaty and s 1(2) of the
Equal Pay Act; and that this country will have fulfilled its obligations under the Treaty.
This is a consideration which weighed very much with Phillips J in the very important

'red circle' cases: *Snoxell v Vauxhall Motors Ltd, Charles Early & Marriott (Witney) Ltd v*
a *Smith*[1]. In the reserved judgment of much value Phillips J said[2]:

> 'It is important to observe that art 119 establishes a principle, with little or no
> detail of the way in which it is to be applied. It appears to us that the [Sex
> Discrimination Act 1975], and the [Equal Pay Act 1970], must be construed and
> applied subject to, and so as to give effect to, the principle.'

b   In our present case Phillips J[3] quoted that very passage and said:

> 'What has to be given effect to is the *principle* of art 119, and the principle is that
> men and women should receive equal pay for equal work. An Act which permitted
> discrimination [*on succession* of a woman to the same job] would not be a successful
> application of the principle.'

c   So I would hold, in agreement with Phillips J, that both under the Treaty and under
the statutes a woman should receive equal pay for equal work, not only when she is
employed *at the same time* as the man, but also when she is employed at the same job *in*
succession to him, that is, in such close succession that it is just and reasonable to make a
comparison between them.

d *If I am wrong*
     Now my colleagues take a different view. They are of opinion that s 1(2)(*a*)(i) of the
Equal Pay Act should be given its natural and ordinary meaning, and that is, they think,
that it is confined to cases where the woman is employed *at the same time* as a man.
     So on our statute, taken alone, they would allow the appeal and reject Mrs Smith's
claim. My colleagues realise, however, that in this interpretation there may be a conflict
e between our statute and the EEC Treaty. As I understand their judgments, they would
hold that if art 119 was clearly in favour of Mrs Smith it should be given priority over our
own statute and Mrs Smith should succeed. But they feel that art 119 is not clear, and,
being not clear, it is necessary to refer it to the European Court at Luxembourg for
determination under art 177 of the Treaty. If I had had any real doubt about the true
interpretation of art 119, I would have been disposed to agree with my colleagues, and
f refer it to the European Court at Luxembourg for the reasons which Lawton LJ will
give. But I would not put it in the form which he has suggested; it is somewhat loaded.
I would like it to be reviewed after counsel have had an opportunity to consider our
judgments.

Conclusion
     For myself I would be in favour of dismissing the appeal, because I agree with the
g decision of the Employment Appeal Tribunal. I have no doubt about the true
interpretation of art 119.
     But, as my colleagues think that art 119 is not clear on the point, I agree that reference
should be made to the European Court at Luxembourg to resolve the uncertainty in that
article.
     Pending the decision of the European court, all further proceedings in the case will be
h stayed. It will be put in the list again as soon as the ruling of the European Court is
received.

LAWTON LJ. This case started by raising what seemed to the parties to be an issue of
fact, namely whether Mrs Smith had been employed on like work of a broadly similar
nature to that done by her immediate predecessor, a Mr McCullough, in the job of taking
j charge of the employer's stockroom. It will end as a case of historical interest as being the
first to be sent by this court to the Court of Justice of the European Communities

1   [1977] 3 All ER 770, [1978] QB 11
2   [1977] 3 All ER 770 at 777, [1978] QB 11 at 26
3   [1978] 2 All ER 746 at 749, [1978] 1 WLR 849 at 853

(hereinafter referred to as the European Court of Justice) for an opinion on the construction and application of an article of the EEC Treaty. Further it may be of *a* constitutional importance if the opinion when given conflicts with the clear terms of a statute.

As Lord Denning MR has already recounted the history of this case and summarised the submissions made on both sides, I can start with the issues as I see them. They are these: first, is the meaning of the relevant parts of the Equal Pay Act 1970 as amended, (hereinafter referred to as 'the Act') clear? If it is, what is it? Secondly, if it is not clear, *b* how is the Act to be construed? Thirdly, is the meaning of art 119 of the EEC Treaty clear? If it is, what is it? Fourthly, if that clear meaning conflicts with the clear meaning of the relevant parts of the Act, what should this court do? Fifthly, if the meaning of art 119 is not clear, what should this court do?

The Act envisages that women's contracts of employment shall contain an equality clause: see s 1(1). Such a clause is to contain provisions having specified effects: see *c* s 1(2). In my judgment the grammatical construction of s 1(2) is consistent only with a comparison between a woman and a man in the same employment at the same time. The words, by the tenses used, look to the present and the future but not to the past. They are inconsistent with a comparison between a woman and a man, no longer in the same employment, who was doing her job before she got it.

I find in the words used a clear indication of policy, namely that men and women in *d* the same employment doing like work, or work of a broadly similar nature, should be paid the same. Before the Act came into force, which was on 29th December 1975, women were often paid less than men, even though they were working side by side. This was the unfairness which was so obvious, which rankled and had to go. It was of a kind easy to identify. If a job is open, subject to a few statutory exceptions, women should be considered for it as well as men. The Sex Discrimination Act 1975 says so. If *e* a woman is given the job she must be paid the same as any man in the same employment doing the like or broadly similar work. In such a situation there is no scope, nor should there be, for an economic argument: see s 1(3) of the Act and *Clay Cross (Quarry Services) Ltd v Fletcher*[1]. But when a comparison is made between what a woman is being paid in a job with what her male predecessor was paid, the scope of the enquiry may widen. The lower pay of the woman may have been due, not to sex discrimination, but to economic *f* pressures, such as diminishing profits, or to other factors such as a more accurate job evaluation. Some such factor as this may be present even when a woman takes over from a man without any time interval, the situation which troubled Phillips J, and which counsel for Mrs Smith submitted was so anomalous. The employers may have gone on paying the man more than they could afford out of sympathy for his personal position as a long service employee or his family commitments. Phillips J in his judgment *g* accepted that such factors could exist. Parliament may have done so too and have decided to restrict the concept of equal pay to those cases in which men and women were doing side by side like or broadly similar work and not to burden industrial tribunals with the more complicated enquiries which would be required if economic factors had to be considered.

As the meaning of the words used in s 1(2) and (4) is clear, and no ambiguity, whether *h* patent or latent, lurks within them, under our rules for the construction of Acts of Parliament the statutory intention must be found within those words. It is not permissible to read into the statute words which are not there or to look outside the Act, as counsel for Mrs Smith invited us to do and Phillips J did, to read the words used in a sense other than that of their ordinary meaning. Counsel for Mrs Smith submitted that the Act should be read in harmony with the Sex Discrimination Act 1975; but that Act, *j* as s 6(6) expressly provides, 'does not apply to benefits consisting of the payment of money when the provision of those benefits is regulated by the woman's contract of

---

1   [1979] 1 All ER 474, [1978] 1 WLR 1408

employment'. It follows, so it seems to me, to be irrelevant that the Sex Discrimination
a Act 1975 does allow a comparison between the benefits, other than those consisting of
money, which a man got when doing a job and which his successor, a woman, did not
get when doing the same job, whereas under the Act relied on by Mrs Smith in this case
comparison in relation to pay is outside it.

What led Phillips J to construe s 1(2) and (4) of the Act so as to allow such a comparison
were the provisions of art 119 of the EEC Treaty to which Lord Denning MR has referred
b for its full terms. In this court counsel on both sides have submitted that the meaning
of this article is clear; but they have differed as to what that meaning is. Counsel for Mrs
Smith has submitted that under art 119 a woman should receive the same pay as a man
she follows in a job, unless there are factors, other than sex discrimination, which justify
the difference. If this be right, art 119 says something different from what I adjudge to
be the plain, unambiguous meaning of s 1(2) and (4) of the Act. When an Act and an
c article of the EEC Treaty are in conflict, which should this court follow? Counsel for Mrs
Smith says the article, because s 2 of the European Communities Act 1972 so provides,
as does European Community law. Thus in *Amministrazione delle Finanze dello Stato v
Simmenthal SpA*[1] the European Court of Justice adjudged:

> 'A national court which is called upon, within the limits of its jurisdiction, to
> apply provisions of Community law is under a duty to give full effect to those
d > provisions, if necessary refusing of its own motion to apply any conflicting provision
> of national legislation, even if adopted subsequently, and it is not necessary for the
> court to request or await the prior setting aside of such provisions by legislative or
> other constitutional means.'

Counsel for the employers submitted that art 119 envisages that men and women
e working side by side for the same employer and doing like or broadly similar work
should be paid the same. He further submitted that the opening words of the article,
'Each Member State shall . . . ensure and subsequently maintain . . .', envisages that the
member states should enact their own legislation to ensure and maintain the application
of the principle that men and women should receive equal pay for equal work. He
argued that the United Kingdom had done so by amending the Equal Pay Act 1970 and
f that if the Commission of the European Communities ('the EEC Commission') thought
that the United Kingdom had not done enough in this respect, it was not for this court
to ignore what it had done by way of legislation but for the European Court of Justice to
adjudge whether the United Kingdom had discharged its Treaty obligations.

As to the meaning of art 119, in my opinion, counsel for the employers is right in his
submission that it envisages men and women working for the same employer. They are
g to receive 'equal pay' for 'equal work' and 'pay' is defined as what the worker receives
from his employer. It follows that men and women doing 'equal work' are to receive the
same pay from their employer. For this to make sense they must each have the same
employer. This construction is strengthened by the reference to work at 'time rates
[which should] be the same for the same job'. Counsel for the employers submission as
to the meaning of art 119 did not, however, convince me that when construed in
h accordance with the canons of construction as used in our court for finding out the
meaning of statutes and deeds, its ambit was confined to men and women doing like or
broadly similar work side by side at the same time. The part of the article which begins
with the words 'Equal pay without discrimination based on sex' takes in para (*a*) 'the
same work' and in para (*b*) 'the same job' as the bases of comparison. A woman may do
'the same work' or 'the same job' after a man as well as alongside a man. In my opinion
j there is some doubt whether art 119 applies to the facts of this case.

We cannot, as counsel for the employers submitted, ignore art 119 and apply what I
consider to be the plain meaning of the Act. The problem of the implementation of art

---

1   [1978] ECR 629 at 630

119 is not one for the EEC Commission to take up with the government of the United Kingdom and Northern Ireland, as counsel for the employers submitted it was. Article 119 gives rise to individual rights which our courts must protect. The European Court of Justice has already adjudged that this is so: see *Defrenne (Gabriele) v Société Anonyme Belge de Navigation Aérienne (SABENA)*[1]. The doubts which I have about the meaning of art 119 are not dissipated by art 1 of the Council of the European Communities' directive of 10th February 1975[2].

Being in doubt as to the ambit of art 119 and being under an obligation arising both from the decisions of the European Court of Justice in the two cases to which I have referred and s 2 of the European Communities Act 1972 to apply that article in our courts, it seems to me that this is a situation to which art 177 of the EEC Treaty applies. I consider that a decision is necessary as to the construction of art 119 and I would request the European Court of Justice to give a ruling on it. The question which I suggest tentatively should be answered is this: whether art 119 applies to a case in which a woman has claimed that, because of discrimination based on sex, she was paid less than a man whose job she took over $4\frac{1}{2}$ months after he had left it, her work in that job being broadly similar in nature to what he had done.

Before saying au revoir, if not adieu, to this appeal, I would like to set out my reasons for deciding as I have that there should be a reference to the European Court of Justice. First, counsel on both sides persuaded me that it would be more convenient and less expensive to the parties for this court to request the European Court of Justice to give a ruling on the application of art 119 than for the House of Lords to do so. The issue in the appeal is clear, even if by English concepts the construction of art 119 is not. The ruling when given may decide the case; and when the ruling is given, there can be no appeal from it. There seems to be nothing else which would justify an appeal to the House of Lords. Further, I can see nothing in this case which infringes the sovereignty of Parliament. If I thought there were, I should not presume to take any judicial step which it would be more appropriate for the House of Lords, as part of Parliament, to take. Parliament by its own act in the exercise of its sovereign powers has enacted that European Community law shall 'be enforced, allowed and followed' in the United Kingdom of Great Britain and Northern Ireland (see s 2(1) of the European Communities Act 1972) and that 'any enactment passed or to be passed . . . shall be construed and have effect subject to [s 2]' (see s 2(4) of that Act). Parliament's recognition of European Community law and of the jurisdiction of the European Court of Justice by one enactment can be withdrawn by another. There is nothing in the Equal Pay Act 1970 as amended by the Sex Discrimination Act 1975, to indicate that Parliament intended to amend the European Communities Act 1972, or to limit its application. Secondly, as I am in doubt as to what is the right construction of art 119 when our canons of construction are applied and in ignorance as to how the European Court of Justice would construe that article when it applies its own rules of construction, I consider myself under a judicial duty not to guess how that court would construe it but to find out how it does.

CUMMING-BRUCE LJ (read by Lawton LJ). I agree with the reasoning and conclusion of Lawton LJ. The first question is: what does s 1(2)(a)(i) of the Equal Pay Act 1970 as amended by the Sex Discrimination Act 1975 mean? This question has to be answered by applying the ordinary rules of construction which have been established in this country. One such rule is that words in an Act of Parliament have their natural and ordinary meaning unless such a meaning is manifestly inconsistent with the context, or gives rise to such absurdity or injustice that Parliament cannot have intended such meaning.

At first sight s 1(2)(a)(i) contemplates a man and a woman being employed by the same

---

1   [1976] ECR 455, [1976] ICR 647
2   EEC Council Directive 75/117

employer at the same time. The use of the present tense strongly points to that meaning, as both Lord Denning MR and Phillips J accepted. But three grounds are put forward for the contrary view.

(1) The fact that the draftsman in s 1(2)(b)(i) evidently used the term 'is employed on work rated as equivalent with that of a man in the same employment'—in a descriptive sense. In that clause attention is focussed on the rating of the work, and to that issue the time factor is irrelevant. The rating is the same whether the man and woman do the work at the same time or one after the other. As the phrase 'is employed . . . in the same employment' is used in a sense that describes the job and not the time when the job is done, in s 1(2)(b)(i) it is evident that the same words in s 1(2)(a)(i) are not as free from ambiguity as might appear on first impression; and there is sufficient doubt to justify a look at the consequences of the two alternative meanings to see if one produces absurdity or results apparently inconsistent with the general intention of the Act while the other does not.

(2) There are undoubtedly some results of the contemporaneous employment meaning which are odd and inconsistent with an attempt to achieve that any woman employed is paid the same as any man whom she has replaced on like work. Examples cited at the bar include: (a) where there is only one job, in which case the equal pay provision could never apply; (b) where the man and woman have worked together but the man is promoted the day before her claim to be paid as much as him; (c) where the man leaves the job, and the woman succeeds him next day.

But these results are only anomalous or unfair if the intention of Parliament was to deal with situations extending beyond the cases of a man or woman working on like work at the same time. The argument of anomaly is circuitous. If the intention is clear, the anomaly is clear, but as the anomaly is relied on to discover the intention, the reasoning is chasing its own tail. I take the view that a scrutiny of the whole of the Act leads to the conclusion that it is perfectly possible that Parliament was regarding, and only regarding, the mischief of women working beside men for less money. If so, the anomalies relied on are not anomalies at all. And there is what may be described as a practical difficulty, rather than an anomaly, which is inherent in the other meaning. Whenever an employer reduced his wages and a man left because he would not work for lower wages, the employer could only take on a woman as replacement at the risk of a lawsuit. This peril does not exist in the different case of job evaluation where the essence of the matter is the objective evaluation of the job.

(3) It is said that it is absurd that if the battle is about terms and conditions of employment other than pay the Sex Discrimination Act clearly gives the palm to the woman whether she is comparing herself with a previous employee or one with whom she works. The short answer is that s 6(6) of the Sex Discrimination Act 1975 clearly provides that its rules are not to apply to equal pay.

I am left so far wholly unconvinced that there is any reason for giving s 1(2)(a)(i) a meaning other than that which at first impression I thought was the ordinary and natural meaning of the words.

This is what Phillips J thought too. But he thought that the effect of art 119 of the EEC Treaty was clear in the sense that Lord Denning MR has quoted from the judgment of Phillips J, and that it was permissible to use the article as an aid to construction of the English statute. Lord Denning MR agrees with Phillips J on both points. With respect to them both, I take a different view on each point. Like Lawton LJ I do not find it easy to discern the application of art 119 to the circumstances contemplated by s 1(2)(a)(i) of the English statute having regard to my construction thereof. I take the view that art 119, which expresses a general principle, may be perfectly consistent with the English legislation as I construe it. But I am not sure about that, and therefore agree that the court at Luxembourg should give an authoritative answer to that question. Secondly, I do not think that it is permissible, as an aid to construction, to look at the terms of the Treaty. If the terms of the Treaty are adjudged in Luxembourg to be inconsistent with the provisions of the Equal Pay Act 1970, European law will prevail over that municipal legislation. But such a judgment in Luxembourg cannot affect the meaning of the English statute.

For these reasons I agree with the order proposed by Lawton LJ, subject only to an appropriate revision of the question to be put to the European Court after counsel have had the opportunity to consider it.

Order that questions of Community law be referred to Court of Justice of the European Communities, proceedings to be stayed pending determination of question by that court.

25th July. The court ordered that the following questions be referred to the Court of Justice of the European Communities for a preliminary ruling in accordance with art 177 of the EEC Treaty:

(1) Is the principle of equal pay for equal work, contained in art 119 of the EEC Treaty and art 1 of the EEC Council directive of 10th February 1975 (75/117/EEC), confined to situations in which men and women are contemporaneously doing equal work for their employer?

(2) If the answer to question (1) is in the negative, does the principle apply where a worker can show that she receives less pay in respect of her employment from her employer (a) than she would have received if she were a man doing equal work for the employer or (b) than had been received by a male worker who had been employed prior to her period of employment and who had been doing equal work for the employer?

(3) If the answer to question (2)(a) or (b) is in the affirmative, is that answer dependent on the provisions of art 1 of the directive?

(4) If the answer to question (3) is in the affirmative, is art 1 of the directive directly applicable in member states?

Solicitors: *Baileys, Shaw & Gillett* (for the employers); *John L Williams* (for Mrs Smith).

Sumra Green   Barrister.

D v D (nullity)

FAMILY DIVISION AT WINCHESTER
DUNN J
19th, 28th JULY 1978

Nullity – Bar to relief – Approbation of unconsummated marriage – Adoption of children by spouses – Recognition of existence of marriage by petitioner – Common law doctrine of approbation replaced by statutory bar – Whether public policy still a factor to be considered – Nullity of Marriage Act 1971, s 3(1)(4) – Matrimonial Causes Act 1973, s 13(1).

The parties were married in 1966. Despite attempts by the husband the marriage was never consummated because the wife had a physical impediment to consummation. The impediment could have been cured by an operation but the wife refused to undergo one. In 1971 at the request of a children's society the parties agreed to foster two young children and later, at the society's suggestion, they applied to adopt them. At the hearing of the application for adoption the court was not told that there were any difficulties in the marriage. The adoption order was made in 1975. In 1976 the husband left the wife and children and went to live with another woman. He then petitioned for a decree of nullity on the ground of the wife's incapacity or wilful refusal to consummate the marriage. She filed an answer in which she alleged that the husband, knowing that he could apply for a decree of nullity on the ground that the marriage was voidable, had so conducted himself as to lead her to believe that he would not in fact do so and that it would be unjust to her to grant the decree. She subsequently withdrew her answer and the case came on for hearing undefended. The husband admitted that before the adoption order was made he had known that it was open to him to have the marriage avoided. Section 3[a] of the Nullity of Marriage Act 1971 which abrogated the rule of law whereby a decree might be refused by reason of approbation, ratification or lack of sincerity on the part of the petitioner, was replaced by s 13 of the Matrimonial Causes Act 1973 which provided, inter alia, that the court should not grant a decree of nullity on the ground that the marriage was voidable if the respondent satisfied the court, first, that the petitioner, with knowledge that it was open to him to have the marriage avoided, so conducted himself in relation to the respondent as to lead the respondent reasonably to believe that he would not seek to do so, and, second, that it would be unjust to the respondent to grant the decree. There was no reference in either section to the rule which had applied in cases prior to the 1971 Act that the court should have regard to public policy. The question arose whether the court still had to consider that aspect.

Held – (i) In so far as the concept of public policy formed part of the common law rule relating to approbation, ratification and lack of sincerity, it was not, following the abrogation of the rule by s 3(4) of the 1971 Act, a relevant consideration under the statutory bar contained in s 3(1) of that Act, and the replacement of the latter subsection by s 13(1) of the 1973 Act did not revive the rule (see p 343 *a b h* and p 344 *a b*, post); *G v M* [1881–5] All ER Rep 397, *W v W* [1952] 1 All ER 858, *Tindall v Tindall* [1953] 1 All ER 139 and *Slater v Slater* [1953] 1 All ER 246 considered.

(ii) The bar set out in s 13(1) of the 1973 Act, which was absolute and not discretionary, related wholly to conduct inter partes, and the only relevant considerations were the conduct of one party towards the other and the possibility of injustice to the respondent. Those considerations were conjunctive, and therefore, although the husband's conduct in agreeing to the adoption of the children while knowing that he could have the marriage avoided would otherwise have been a bar, there was no injustice to the wife giving rise to a bar, since (a) she was content for the decree of nullity to be

---

a   Section 3, so far as material, is set out at p 342 *g*, post

pronounced and (b) even if a decree was granted, no estoppel could be maintained against
her, other than her wilful refusal to consummate the marriage, in any subsequent
proceedings for custody, financial provision or transfer of property. Accordingly a
decree of nullity would be pronounced (see p 343 *a* and p 344 *b* to *e*, post).

Notes
For voidable marriages celebrated before 1st August 1971, see 13 Halsbury's Laws (4th
Edn) para 539, for bars to relief where a marriage is voidable and proceedings are
instituted after 31st July 1971, see ibid para 536, and for cases on the subject, see 27(1)
Digest (Reissue) 325–327, 2374–2380.
    For the Nullity of Marriage Act 1971, s 3, see 41 Halsbury's Statutes (3rd Edn) 755.
    For the Matrimonial Causes Act 1973, s 13, see 43 ibid 556.

Cases referred to in judgment
Black-Clawson International Ltd v Papierwerke Waldhof-Aschaffenburg AG [1975] 1 All ER
    810, [1975] AC 591, [1975] 2 WLR 513, [1975] 2 Lloyd's Rep 11, Digest (Cont Vol D)
    858, 460b.
G v M (1885) 10 App Cas 171, [1881–5] All ER Rep 397, 53 LT 398, 12 R (Ct of Sess) 36,
    22 Sc LR 461, HL, 27(1) Digest (Reissue) 551, 3983.
Slater v Slater [1953] 1 All ER 246, [1953] P 235, [1953] 2 WLR 170, CA, 27(1) Digest
    (Reissue) 326, 2377.
Tindall v Tindall [1953] 1 All ER 139, [1953] P 63, [1953] 2 WLR 158, CA, 27(1) Digest
    (Reissue) 326, 2378.
W v W [1952] 1 All ER 858, [1952] P 152, CA, 27(1) Digest (Reissue) 326, 2376.

Petition
This was a petition by the husband for a decree of nullity on the grounds of the wife's
wilful refusal, or in the alternative, her incapacity to consummate the marriage. The
wife filed an answer alleging that the marriage had in fact been consummated and
alternatively that the husband knew it was open to him to have the marriage avoided,
but had so conducted himself as to lead her to believe that he would not do so, and it
would be unjust to the wife to grant the decree. The answer was dismissed by consent
leaving the petition to proceed undefended. The facts are set out in the judgment.

Patrick Clarkson for the petitioner.
The respondent did not appear.

Cur adv vult

28th July. **DUNN J** read the following judgment: In this suit, the husband seeks a
decree of nullity on the grounds of wilful refusal or alternatively incapacity. The wife by
her answer alleged that the marriage had in fact been consummated, and also alleged in
the alternative that the husband had knowledge that it was open to him to have the
marriage avoided, but so conducted himself in relation to her as to lead her to believe that
he would not in fact do so, and it would be unjust to the wife to grant the decree.
Furthermore, on 30th June 1978, the wife's solicitors wrote to the court in the following
terms:

    'Following the filing of reports by the medical inspector, negotiations took place
    between the parties and the suit has been compromised on terms that the Answer
    filed on behalf of the Respondent, our Client, be dismissed, leaving the Petitioner to
    proceed on his prayer for nullity undefended and that there be no order for costs
    save for the usual legal aid taxation. Although we had agreed the terms of the order
    to be made with the Petitioner's Solicitors, the Order has not yet been made
    formally and presumably it will not be done before the case comes on for hearing.
    It is clear however that the case will go short as it is to be undefended.'

As a result of that letter, the case came before me undefended, the husband being represented by counsel, the wife being unrepresented.

Although s 1(3) of the Matrimonial Causes Act 1973 placing a duty on the court to enquire into the facts alleged by the petitioner relates only to petitions for divorce, and there are no similar provisions in relation to petitions for nullity, s 15 of that Act gives the court power to direct argument by the Queen's Proctor in nullity cases as well as divorce cases, and I conceive it to be the duty of the court in nullity cases as well as in divorce cases to enquire into the facts as well as to satisfy itself as to the law. I accordingly followed this course.

The marriage in this case was in fact celebrated on 3rd September 1966, the husband being then 21 and the wife being 28 years of age. Having heard the husband's evidence as to non-consummation in camera, according to the normal practice and having read the report of the medical inspector dated 21st March 1978, I was satisfied that the husband was capable of consummating the marriage, that the wife was virgo intacta, and the marriage was never consummated despite attempts by the husband. Evidence showed that the wife had a physical impediment to consummation, which could have been cured by a comparatively common operation. The wife refused to undergo this operation, although requested to do so by the husband. Therefore prima facia the husband is entitled to a decree of nullity on the ground of wilful refusal.

I go on to consider the plea raised by the wife in her answer, to which I have referred. At the time of the marriage the husband was a theological student. Shortly afterwards he became a clerk in holy orders. He was a curate in the South of England and then went on to a second living as a curate. While there, at the end of 1971, the husband and wife were approached by the Church of England Children's Society with a request to foster two children with coloured blood. The children were born respectively in 1968 and 1970. They were both in a hostel, which was closing down, and fostering would give them an opportunity of a normal home life. The alternative would have been for them to go to another hostel, because the older child was something of a problem child, and it was difficult to find foster parents for them. The husband and wife agreed to take the children on a long term fostering basis, and they came into the matrimonial home early in 1972. In October 1973, the husband became a parish priest, and the husband and wife and two foster children moved into the vicarage. The Church of England Children's Society then suggested that the husband and wife should adopt the children. By then there were difficulties in the marriage. The husband was frustrated by the wife's continued refusal to consummate. The husband and wife disagreed on the upbringing of the children. The wife refused to have them baptised. The husband said the wife did not wish to become pregnant and bear children of her own, and in his opinion that was the real reason for her refusal to consummate the marriage. On the other hand, he said she enjoyed bringing the children up, and liked having them round the house. She wished to adopt the children, so the husband agreed. The application for adoption was made. The natural mother gave her consent. The application was heard by Judge Lee in the county court. Neither the guardian ad litem nor Judge Lee was told of the difficulties in the marriage. The husband said in evidence before me that the guardian ad litem was more interested in the welfare of the children than in the state of the marriage. The husband said that he knew before the adoption of his remedy in nullity but that if he took nullity proceedings he would have to give up his ministry, which would have deprived him of his job and his livelihood. He was anxious to salvage his ministry. By adopting the children he did not feel that he was doing anybody any harm. His wife loved them, they loved the husband and the wife, and by agreeing to adopt them he felt that he was giving them security. He accepted in evidence before me that he did mislead Judge Lee, and the adoption order was made on 12th November 1975.

In the summer of 1975 the husband had been suffering from extreme sexual frustration. At that time he committed an isolated and casual act of adultery in London. This was done to prove to himself that he was capable of consummating the

marriage. Subsequently he told his wife about it. At about the same time, he became
very friendly with a married lady. This was one of his parishioners. He fell in love with *a*
her.

Within a fortnight of the adoption, the husband suffered a nervous breakdown. He
told me in evidence that he attributed it to feelings of guilt at having misled Judge Lee
as to the state of the marriage. But I think he also felt guilt at having committed
adultery, and torment of mind at having fallen in love with another married woman.
He went to his general practitioner and then to a psychiatrist, and on the psychiatrist's *b*
advice attended a psychiatric clinic daily for therapy. He consulted his bishop and
archdeacon, and told them the whole story. He received advice from them. He finally
decided to leave his wife and the two foster children, and set up home as man and wife
with the other lady, which he did late in February or early March 1976. They set up
home together with her two children, and they have lived together ever since. She and
her husband were subsequently divorced on the ground of irretrievable breakdown, *c*
evidenced by two years' separation and consent. The husband's licence as a parish priest
was revoked, but he remains a clerk in holy orders. He recognises that if he were to
marry the other lady, he would be breaking canon law. He says that his understanding
is that if he were divorced even on the grounds of a two years' separation and consent, he
would be, as he put it, unfrocked; but he is hopeful that, if he is granted a decree of
nullity, he might be able to continue as a clerk in holy orders, although he recognises that *d*
he cannot in any event continue his ministry in the Church of England.

The case raises fairly and squarely the extent to which the common law doctrine of
approbation has been abolished or modified by s 3 of the Nullity of Marriage Act 1971,
repealed and replaced by s 13 of the Matrimonial Causes Act 1973. So far as I know, there
is no authority on this question. At common law approbation, insincerity or ratification
of marriage as it was variously called, constituted a discretionary bar to relief in respect *e*
of voidable marriages. As this marriage was celebrated before 1971, the grounds for a
decree of nullity are the same as those in common law, and wilful refusal was one such
ground. Non-consummation renders a marriage voidable. The common law doctrine
of approbation as it existed before 1971 was authoritatively stated in *G v M*[1]. Lord
Selborne LC said this:

'... there may be conduct on the part of the person seeking this remedy which *f*
ought to estop that person from having it; as, for instance, any act from which the
inference ought to be drawn that during the antecedent time the party has, with a
knowledge of the facts and of the law, approbated the marriage which he or she
afterwards seeks to get rid of, or has taken advantages and derived benefits from the
matrimonial relation which it would be unfair and inequitable to permit him or
her, after having received them, to treat as if no such relation had ever existed. Well *g*
now, that explanation can be referred to known principles of equitable, and, I may
say, of general, jurisprudence. The circumstances which may justify it are various,
and in cases of this kind, many sorts of conduct might exist, taking pecuniary
benefits for example, living for a long time together in the same house or family
with the status and character of husband and wife, after knowledge of everything
which it is material to know. I do not at all mean to say that there may not be other *h*
circumstances which would produce the same effect; but it appears to me that, in
order to justify any such doctrine as that which has been insisted upon at the bar,
there must be a foundation of substantial justice, depending upon the acts and
conduct of the party sought to be barred.'

Lord Watson said this[2]:

'I agree with the observations which have been made upon the English cases
bearing upon [insincerity] by my noble and learned friend the Lord Chancellor. It

1   (1885) 10 App Cas 171 at 186, [1881–5] All ER Rep 397 at 399
2   10 App Cas 171 at 197–198, [1881–5] All ER Rep 397 at 402

a humbly appears to me that the expression is not a very happy one, and also that it has been used occasionally in circumstances which render it still more inappropriate. I think that when those cases are dissected they do shew the existence of this rule in the law of England, that in a suit for nullity of marriage there may be facts and circumstances proved which so plainly imply, on the part of the complaining spouse, a recognition of the existence and validity of the marriage, as to render it most inequitable and contrary to public policy that he or she should be permitted
b to go on to challenge it with effect.'

That concept of public policy was referred to and followed in a number of succeeding cases. *Tindall v Tindall*[1] was a case in which a wife petitioner for nullity had made application to the justices for a matrimonial order against her husband. Although the justices dismissed the application, in subsequent proceedings which she took for nullity, she was held to have approbated the marriage. Singleton LJ pointed out that when she
c made the application to the justices she clearly knew the facts and the law as to nullity[2]:

'... and with that knowledge she put forward a case before the justices the foundation of which was the marriage, as the complaint shows. She sought to obtain an order against the husband to which she could only be entitled if he was her husband, and she persisted in that claim by way of appeal to the Divisional
d Court, and in three letters, two before and one after those proceedings, she showed the same spirit. I see no answer to this argument. If ever a party to such a suit did approbate the marriage, surely this wife did. It seems to me that her conduct is within the words of LORD SELBORNE[3] which I have read. And, further, if the words "public policy" in LORD WATSON'S[4] speech are to be given their ordinary meaning, they apply in this case. It surely must be contrary to public policy that a spouse
e should be able to go as far as the Divisional Court relying on the validity of the marriage, and thereafter succeed on a petition for nullity if, as in the present case, she had knowledge of the facts and of the law.'

Shortly before *Tindall v Tindall*[1], *W v W*[5] had been decided in the Court of Appeal. *W v W*[5] was a case in which the marriage took place in 1941. The marriage was not consummated owing to the incapacity of the wife. In 1944 the husband and wife
f adopted a child, and in 1945, that child having died, they adopted a second child. The husband left the wife in 1946, and did not return to her. He wrote her thereafter a number of letters in which he never referred to, or complained of the non consummation of the marriage. In October 1950, he presented a petition to have the marriage annulled. The commissioner granted the decree nisi of nullity. On appeal, the Court of Appeal set aside the decree, holding that the marriage had been approbated. In the
g course of his judgment, Evershed MR pointed out first that a decree of nullity did not operate to bastardise the children although the marriage was voidable; but any children, including adopted children, remained legitimate. He also held, although there was no issue, that the husband knew of his remedies in nullity at the date of the adoption. He held that the husband must be taken to have known of his remedy, having regard to all the circumstances. Evershed MR then went on to say this[6]:

h 'In all the circumstances and upon the facts of this case (and I need hardly say that every case of this kind, as every other case, must depend on its own special and particular facts), I think the formula in Lord Selborne L.C.'s speech in *G. v. M.*[3] has

---

1 [1953] 1 All ER 139, [1953] P 63
2 [1953] 1 All ER 139 at 143–144, [1953] P 63 at 72
3 (1885) 10 App Cas 171 at 186, [1881–5] All ER Rep 397 at 399
4 10 App Cas 171 at 197, [1881–5] All ER Rep 397 at 402
5 [1952] 1 All ER 858, [1952] P 152
6 [1952] P 152 at 163, cf [1952] 1 All ER 858 at 863

been satisfied and that the conduct of the husband, taken over the whole period, was consistent and consistent only with such affirmation of the marriage as now to make   *a* it inequitable (that is, unjust as between the two parties to the suit) and also contrary to public policy for this court to grant his prayer.'

W v W[1] was distinguished in *Slater v Slater*[2]. *Slater v Slater*[2] was also a case in which the marriage had never been consummated. The parties adopted a child. Karminski J dismissed the wife's petition for nullity, because he held that by agreeing to adopt the   *b* child, she had approbated the marriage. The Court of Appeal reversed the judge's finding. They held that at the date of the adoption, the wife did not know of her remedy in nullity. She was apparently a sick woman, who had suffered a nervous breakdown. Singleton LJ said this[3]:

'All the circumstances must be examined to determine whether there has been   *c* approbation of the marriage so that it is inequitable or against public policy that the petition should be granted. The matters on which most reliance was placed were the adoption of the child and the artificial insemination treatment of the wife. Both those took place before the wife had knowledge that she had any remedy. So far as I can see, there is nothing which occurred after she had that (somewhat hazy) knowledge which counts either way. True the judge said: "She deliberately chose   *d* to go on with this particular husband and with the adopted child", but I cannot see that a woman who in such circumstances stays in the matrimonial home must thereby be said to have approbated the marriage. There is nothing in her conduct after Nov. 24, 1949, which makes it inequitable that she should be granted relief.'

If the common law doctrine still applied, I would find it very difficult to distinguish   *e* the instant case from *W v W*[1]. As I have said, in *Slater v Slater*[2] that case was distinguished, because the wife did not know of her remedy at the date of the adoption. In *W v W*[1], the husband was taken to have known of his remedy. The instant case seems to me to be a stronger case than *W v W*[1], because the husband in the instant case admitted that he knew of his remedy before the adoption.

At common law too, public policy was a relevant consideration, and if I had been   *f* considering the common law doctrine of approbation, I would have had to consider how far it is in accordance with public policy to allow a petitioner to choose his remedy in circumstances such as this, and I would also have considered whether it is contrary to public policy that a spouse should be able to adopt children relying on the validity of the marriage and then to seek to avoid the marriage in subsequent nullity proceedings. The law was however changed by the Nullity of Marriage Act 1971. Section 3 of that Act is   *g* in the following terms:

'(1) The court shall not, in proceedings instituted after the commencement of this Act, grant a decree of nullity on the ground that a marriage is voidable (whether the marriage took place before or after the commencement of this Act) if the respondent satisfies the court—(*a*) that the petitioner, with knowledge that it was open to him   *h* to have the marriage avoided, so conducted himself in relation to the respondent as to lead the respondent reasonably to believe that he would not seek to do so; and (*b*) that it would be unjust to the respondent to grant the decree . . .

'(4) Subsection (1) of this section replaces, in relation to any decree to which it applies, any rule of law whereby a decree may be refused by reason of approbation, ratification or lack of sincerity on the part of the petitioner or on similar grounds   *j* . . .'

---

1   [1952] 1 All ER 858, [1952] P 152
2   [1953] 1 All ER 246, [1953] P 235
3   [1953] 1 All ER 246 at 248, [1953] P 235 at 244–245

a   I make two observations about s 3 of the Nullity of Marriage Act 1971. The first is that the common law doctrines of approbation, ratification, and lack of sincerity are expressly removed and replaced by the statutory bar in sub-s (1). Secondly, that the new statutory bar is absolute and not discretionary. The question remains, however, how far if at all, does the statutory bar introduced by the 1971 Act, require the court to have regard to considerations of public policy.

b   There is no mention of public policy in the words of the section itself. The common law rules are abrogated and replaced by the statutory bar, and therefore I would be prepared to hold on the ordinary natural meaning of the words of the statute, that public policy has no place in the statutory bar.

c   In *Black-Clawson International Ltd v Papierwerke Waldhof-Aschaffenburg AG*[1] the House of Lords held that where there is ambiguity in the statute the court may have regard to a report of a committee presented to Parliament containing proposals for legislation in order to determine the mischief which the statute was intended to remedy. Although I see no ambiguity in the words of s 3 of the Nullity of Marriage Act 1971, I have looked at and intend to refer to the report of the Law Commission on Nullity of Marriage. The Law Commission report[2], which was laid before Parliament by the Lord Chancellor and ordered by the House of Lords to be printed, contained the following words:

d   'Hence we recommend that the opportunity should be taken to introduce a definite statutory bar replacing the common law doctrine and making it clear that there are no separate doctrines of "lack of sincerity", ratification or the like which have been invoked in some of the cases. We also recommend that it should be so defined as to encourage parties to do their best to overcome their difficulties. If the bar can be too readily invoked they may be discouraged (or their lawyers may discourage them) because of the risk that they will thereby lose any chance of

e   having the marriage annulled should their efforts fail. As stated above, the case law suggests that there must be (a) conduct after full knowledge of the right to relief which (b) plainly implies a recognition of the existence and validity of the marriage, so as (c) to make it unjust between the parties and contrary to public policy to challenge its validity. We are somewhat concerned regarding the inclusion of the reference to public policy. If, as the classical statement in [*G v M*][3] implies, there is

f   approbation only if there is both injustice to the parties *and* conflict with public policy the inclusion is innocuous but, as we see it, redundant. If, as may be intended, "and" should be interpreted as "or", so that a court may hold that a marriage has been approbated because it thinks that some concept of public policy so requires despite the absence of injustice to the parties, we regard the requirement as unfortunate. In our view if there is a defect rendering the marriage voidable

g   either party should be entitled (subject, in certain cases, to the three-year time-limit) to have it annulled unless his conduct after he knew his position has been such as to lead the other party reasonably to believe that he would not seek to have the marriage annulled and it would be unjust to the other for him to do so. Lawyers cannot advise their clients with any certainty if there is a risk of individual notions of public policy being invoked.'

h   That paragraph fortifies my view, based on the ordinary natural meaning of the words used in the statute, that if and in so far as some concept of public policy forms part of the common law rule as to approbation, that concept is no longer a relevant consideration under the statutory bar. This is in accordance with the spirit of the divorce reform legislation of the late 1960s and early 1970s. Parties are to be encouraged to resolve their

j   differences, and, to do that, certainty in the law is a requisite, untrammelled by considerations of public policy which may vary from judge to judge.

---

1   [1975] 1 All ER 810, [1975] AC 591
2   Law Com 33 (1970), para 44
3   (1885) 10 App Cas 171, [1881–5] All ER Rep 397

Section 3 of the Nullity of Marriage Act 1971 was repealed and replaced by s 13 of the
Matrimonial Causes Act 1973. By that time, the common law rules of approbation, *a*
ratification and insincerity had been abrogated. Although they are not expressly referred
to in the 1973 Act, they could not have been revived except by express Parliamentary
enactment, and accordingly, the 1973 Act did not mention them. It simply re-enacted
in respect of proceedings commenced after 1971, the bars set out in the Nullity of
Marriage Act 1971. The bars relate wholly to conduct inter partes, and the only relevant
considerations are (a) the conduct of one party towards the other, and (b) the absence of *b*
injustice to the respondent.

In this case, the husband frankly admitted that he knew before adoption that it was
open to him to have the marriage avoided, and by agreeing to adoption, in my judgment,
so conducted himself in relation to his wife as to lead her to believe that he would not
seek to do so. So I am satisfied as to the first limb of the statutory bar; but I must also be
satisfied as to the second limb, namely that it would be unjust to the wife to grant a *c*
decree. The second limb is conjunctive to the first by reason of the word 'and'. Although
by her answer the wife raised the conduct of the husband towards her, she does not now
seek to pursue it. She is content for the decree of nullity to be pronounced. She has
wilfully refused to consummate this marriage. If a decree of nullity is granted, she has
the same rights to apply for custody, financial provision, and transfer of property, as she
would have on a decree for divorce. In any such subsequent proceedings, no estoppel can *d*
be maintained against her, except that she wilfully refused to consummate the
marriage. If and in so far as the conduct of the husband is relevant to those subsequent
proceedings, the wife will be at liberty to raise it, and rely on it. In my judgment, it
would not, in the circumstances of this case, be unjust to the wife for a decree of nullity
to be granted. Accordingly, there will be a decree nisi of nullity on the ground of her
wilful refusal. *e*

Decree nisi pronounced.

Solicitors: *Robinson, Jarvis & Rolf*, Newport (for the husband).

Georgina Chambers   Barrister. *f*

R v Bristol City Council, ex parte Browne

QUEEN'S BENCH DIVISION *g*
LORD WIDGERY CJ AND LLOYD J
21st JUNE 1979

*Housing – Homeless person – Duty of housing authority to provide accommodation – Applicant
and children leaving matrimonial home in Eire and coming to Bristol to escape violent husband
– Welfare officer in Eire giving Bristol authority assurance that suitable accommodation available* *h*
*for applicant and children in Ireland – Housing authority advising applicant to return to Eire
and obtain accommodation from welfare officer – Whether authority fulfilling statutory duty –
Whether authority required to provide accommodation in Bristol – Housing (Homeless Persons)
Act 1977, ss 5(1)(4), 6(1)(c), 16.*

The applicant and her seven children left the matrimonial home in Tralee, Eire, on *j*
medical advice because of the husband's violence. At first the applicant went to a
women's hostel in Limerick but when the husband discovered she was there, the hostel
arranged for her and the children to go to Bristol. They spent the first night in Bristol in
a local hostel but being unable to stay there any longer, the applicant applied the
following day to the Bristol District Council ('the housing authority') for accommodation

as a homeless person. The housing authority commenced enquiries under the Housing

a (Homeless Persons) Act 1977 and telephoned the community welfare officer in Tralee who was aware of the husband's violence. He gave an assurance to the housing authority that if the applicant and her children were to return to Tralee he would secure suitable accommodation for them on their arrival. From their enquiries the housing authority concluded that the applicant had become homeless unintentionally and had a priority need and, though she had no connection with Bristol and responsibility for her could not

b be transferred to any other authority under the 1977 Act (because she came from Eire), that the authority had a duty under s 4(5)[a] of the Act to secure accommodation for her. Under s 6(1)(c)[b] of the Act the authority could fulfil that duty by giving the applicant 'such advice and assistance' as would secure that she obtained 'accommodation from some other person'. Since the Tralee welfare officer was willing to secure accommodation for the applicant, the authority considered that they could properly carry out their

c statutory duty by advising the applicant to return to Tralee and contact the welfare officer there, and by offering to arrange and pay for her journey. The applicant, who did not wish to return to Tralee, applied for judicial review by way of mandamus requiring the authority to provide accommodation for her and the children in Bristol. She conceded that the authority could fulfil their duty under the 1977 Act by assisting her to go back to Tralee even though it was outside the jurisdiction.

d
Held – The application would be refused for the following reasons—

(i) When giving an applicant advice and assistance for the purpose of carrying out their duty within the terms of s 6(1)(c) of the 1977 Act, a housing authority were not confined to securing that accommodation was obtained from 'some other person' within the authority's area. Accordingly, the housing authority were entitled to carry out and

e thereby fulfil their duty under the Act by advising and assisting the applicant to obtain accommodation from the welfare officer in Tralee (see p 350 e f, p 351 f and p 352 b, post).

(ii) On the assumption that s 5 of the 1977 Act applied to the case and that therefore both the Bristol and Tralee authorities as the notifying and notified authorities respectively had to be satisfied for the purposes of s 5(1) and (4)[c] that the applicant and her children would not 'run the risk of domestic violence' in Tralee, the fact that the

f applicant had previously suffered domestic violence in Tralee did not necessarily mean that she would run the risk of such violence there in the future. Since the Bristol

---

a   Section 4(5) provides: 'Where—(a) [a housing authority] are satisfied—(i) that [a person] is homeless, and (ii) that he has a priority need, but (b) they are not satisfied that he became homeless intentionally, their duty, subject to section 5 below, is to secure that accommodation becomes available for his occupation.'

g b Section 6(1) is set out at p 347 e, post

c   Section 5, so far as material, provides:

'(1) A housing authority are not subject to a duty under section 4(5) above—(a) if they are of the opinion—(i) that . . . the person who applied to them for accommodation or for assistance in obtaining accommodation . . . has a local connection with their area, and (ii) that the person who so applied . . . has a local connection with another housing authority's area, and (iii) that . . . the

h   person who so applied . . . will run the risk of domestic violence in that housing authority's area, and (b) if they notify that authority—(i) that the application has been made, and (ii) that they are of the opinion specified in paragraph (a) above.

'(2) In this Act "notifying authority" means a housing authority who give a notification under subsection (1) above and "notified authority" means a housing authority who receive such a notification.

j   '(3) It shall be the duty of the notified authority to secure that accommodation becomes available for occupation by the person to whom the notification relates if . . . he . . . has a local connection with the area of the notifying authority but the conditions specified in subsection (4) below are satisfied.

'(4) The conditions mentioned in subsection (3) above are—(a) that the person to whom the notification relates . . . has a local connection with the area of the notified authority, and (b) that . . . he . . . will [not] run the risk of domestic violence in that area.'

authority had carefully considered that aspect of the case before deciding that the applicant and her children could be accommodated in Tralee without running the risk of violence, the authority's decision could not be impeached under s 5 (see p 350 *j* to p 351 *b f* and p 352 *b*, post). *a*

(iii) Even though the welfare officer in Tralee had not specified to the Bristol authority a particular house as being available for the applicant, his offer of accommodation in Tralee was 'accommodation available for occupation', within s 16^d of the 1977 Act, since it was sufficient for the housing authority to be satisfied that accommodation would be *b* available if the applicant returned to Tralee (see p 351 *b* to *d f* and p 352 *b*, post).

Notes
For a housing authority's duties to a homeless person, see 22 Halsbury's Laws (4th Edn) paras 513–514.

For the Housing (Homeless Persons) Act 1977, ss 5, 6, 16, see 47 Halsbury's Statutes (3rd Edn) 319, 321, 330. *c*

Cases referred to in judgments
Associated Provincial Picture Houses Ltd v Wednesbury Corpn [1947] 2 All ER 680, [1948] 1 KB 223, [1948] LJR 190, 177 LT 641, 112 JP 55, 45 LGR 635, CA, 45 Digest (Repl) 215, 189.

Secretary of State for Education and Science v Metropolitan Borough of Tameside [1976] 3 All *d* ER 665, [1977] AC 1014, [1976] 3 WLR 641, 75 LGR 190, HL.

Cases also cited
Bristol District Council v Clark [1975] 3 All ER 976, [1975] 1 WLR 1443, CA.
Connelly v Director of Public Prosecutions [1964] 2 All ER 401, [1964] AC 1254, HL.
Cutler v Wandsworth Stadium Ltd [1949] 1 All ER 544, [1949] AC 398, HL.
R v Burnham Justices, ex parte Ansorge [1959] 3 All ER 505, [1959] 1 WLR 1041, DC. *e*
Thornton v Kirklees Metropolitan Borough Council [1979] 2 All ER 349, [1979] 3 WLR 1, CA.
Wear (River) Comrs v Adamson (1877) 2 App Cas 743, [1874–80] All ER Rep 1, HL.

Application for judicial review
This was an application by Eileen Philomenia Browne ('the applicant') for judicial review by way of an order of mandamus directed to the Bristol District Council ('the council') *f* requiring them to provide accommodation for her and her children, and, by way of interlocutory relief, for an order requiring the council to provide temporary accommodation for the applicant and her children until final determination of the application. The grounds on which relief was sought were (i) that the council were the housing authority for the area in which the applicant was residing and were the relevant housing authority for the purpose of the Housing (Homeless Persons) Act 1977, (ii) that *g* the applicant applied to the council on 12th March 1979 for accommodation pursuant to the 1977 Act, (iii) that on 15th March 1979 the council, having carried out the necessary enquiries pursuant to the Act, made written findings that the applicant was homeless, that she had a priority need, that she had not become homeless intentionally, that although the council were satisfied that the applicant did not have any local connection they did not propose to notify any other housing authority that an application for *h* assistance had been made, and that the council were under a duty to secure that accommodation was made available for the occupation of the applicant, and (iv) that the council had refused to provide the applicant with accommodation in spite of those findings. The facts are set out in the judgment of Lloyd J.

R L Denyer for the applicant.
D H Fletcher for the council. *j*

---

d Section 16, so far as material, provides: 'For the purposes of this Act accommodation is only available for a person's occupation if it is available for occupation . . . by him . . . and any reference in this Act to securing accommodation for a person's occupation shall be construed accordingly.'

LLOYD J delivered the first judgment at the invitation of Lord Widgery CJ. This is an
a application for an order of mandamus directed to the Bristol District Council ('the
council') as the housing authority for the City of Bristol. It raises an important point in
relation to the Housing (Homeless Persons) Act 1977. The main provisions of that Act
are becoming well known, but it is convenient to have the scheme of the Act in mind
before coming to the facts of this particular case.

Section 1 of the Act defines what is meant by a homeless person. Section 2 creates a
b particular category of homeless person, namely a homeless person with a priority need
for accommodation, such as a person who has dependent children residing with him or
her. Section 3 then sets out the preliminary duties of the housing authority, that is to say
to make the appropriate enquiries. Section 4 describes the various duties imposed on the
housing authority in relation to homeless persons. Where the homeless person has a
priority need for accommodation and did not become homeless intentionally as defined
c by s 17 of the Act, the duty of the housing authority is to secure that accommodation
becomes available for his occupation. That is a duty imposed by s 4(5), and that is the
relevant duty as will appear later for the purpose of the present application.

The duty under s 4 is, however, subject to s 5 of the Act which provides that the
housing authority shall be under no duty if the homeless person has no local connection
with their area, as defined by s 18 of the Act, and if he has a local connection with some
d other housing authority. In that case the duty to secure that accommodation becomes
available may be transferred to that other housing authority, subject to certain conditions
being fulfilled. Again I will have to return to that matter.

Section 6(1) is important, and I will read it in full:

e 'A housing authority may perform any duty under section 4 or 5 above to secure
that accommodation becomes available for the occupation of a person—(*a*) by
making available accommodation held by them under Part V of the Housing Act
1957 or Part VII of the Housing (Scotland) Act 1966 or under any other enactment,
or (*b*) by securing that he obtains accommodation from some other person, or (*c*) by
giving him such advice and assistance as will secure that he obtains accommodation
from some other person.'

f I can omit any reference to s 7.

Section 8 provides that when a housing authority has completed their enquiries under
s 3 they shall notify the applicant of their decision on the various questions there set out.
I think I can safely pass over the remaining sections of the Act.

I now turn to the facts of this particular case, and it is important that they should be
g stated in some detail. The applicant arrived in this country from Limerick in Eire on
12th March 1979. She was accompanied by her seven children. She is now 29. She was
married in 1967 and lived with her husband at Tralee in County Kerry. According to
her affidavits, of which we have two before us, her husband is a man given to violence.
She refers to a number of incidents of violence culminating in November 1978. As a
result of that incident she was advised by her doctor to leave the matrimonial home and
h go to the Women's Aid Hostel in Limerick where she remained with her children for
some four and a half months. She left that hostel in March 1979, and she says she did so
because her husband had discovered her whereabouts.

At all events, the people who run the hostel in Limerick made arrangements for her
to come to Bristol where they put her in touch with the Bristol Women's Aid office. She
arrived by air in Bristol on 12th March. They had paid her air fare of £152. She was met
j by a representative of Bristol Women's Aid at the airport, and she spent her first night in
England at their hostel.

The next day at 11 am she visited the Bristol Council's housing aid centre, accompanied
by two representatives of Bristol Women's Aid. There she was presented as a homeless
person. She was interviewed by two of the council's officers, Mr Jeremy Ball and Mr Rex
Hodgkinson, and they started enquiries at once as provided by s 3 of the 1977 Act. They

also booked accommodation for her and for her children at a local guest house, initially for one night, while they completed their enquiries.   *a*

There was a further discussion on the afternoon of the same day with representatives of Bristol Women's Aid. Mr Hodgkinson asked why the applicant in this case had been brought to England when they had no accommodation for her. The explanation they gave us was that the accommodation which they hoped to provide for her had been taken up by three emergency admissions over the weekend.

On the next day, 14th March, Mr Ball telephoned a Mr Burke, who is the community   *b* welfare officer in Tralee and is the man responsible for homeless families in that part of Ireland. Mr Burke said that if the applicant were to return to Tralee he would make provision for her and her children.

The next day, 15th March, Mr Hodgkinson spoke to Mr Burke in order to satisfy himself as to what the position was. I think it is best that I should quote from his affidavit in which he describes that conversation. He says: *c*

'Following Mr Ball's telephone conversation with Mr Burke, the community welfare officer in Tralee on 14th March 1979, I subsequently spoke to Mr Burke on 15th March 1979 and he assured me that if the applicant returned to Tralee accommodation would be secured for her and her children upon her arrival. He indicated to me that he was fully aware of the applicant's background and   *d* volunteered information concerning her husband's illegal activities. I again asked for confirmation that should the applicant return to Tralee he would make provision for her, and he confirmed that he would. In the light of this discussion, I concluded that any accommodation which Mr Burke arranged for the appplicant would be arranged in the full knowledge of her husband's violent nature and that Mr Burke would have regard to the possibility of violence in arranging that accommodation.'   *e*

The case was then considered by Mr Martin, the principal assistant in charge of housing aid and information services at Bristol, and the superior of Mr Ball and Mr Hodgkinson. He had in fact been in touch with the case from the start, and, having discussed the matter with Mr Ball and Mr Hodgkinson, he came to the following decisions, which I quote from Mr Martin's affidavit:

'(a) That the applicant was homeless. (b) That the applicant had a priority need.   *f* (c) That the applicant had not become homeless intentionally. (d) That the applicant did not have a local connection with the City of Bristol but that it would not be appropriate to transfer responsibility to another housing authority under section 5 of the Act as there was no relevant housing authority in England, Wales or Scotland.'

He concluded on the basis of those findings that the council were under a duty to   *g* secure that accommodation became available for the applicant. Those findings and that conclusion were subsequently set out in a written notification dated 15th March which was given to the applicant in accordance with s 8 of the 1977 Act.

Mr Martin then gave consideration to the question how the council should perform their duty under the Act. Again it is best to give Mr Martin's reasons in his own words. I quote from his affidavit: *h*

'I concluded that the authorities in Tralee in Eire had with full knowledge of the facts surrounding her case indicated their willingness to accept responsibility for the applicant and that the community welfare officer charged with the responsibility for securing the health and well-being of the inhabitants of the area would not have agreed to the applicant returning if he was not able to make arrangements for the   *j* applicant to be adequately protected against any risk of violence. I therefore concluded that as the primary responsibility for the applicant rested with the Irish authorities in the country from which she had originated, and as the authorities were prepared to take responsibility for the applicant, the city council could properly carry out its duty under the Act by advising the applicant to return to Tralee and to a   contact the community relations officer there and by arranging for travel assistance to be available to enable the applicant to return. I was satisfied that the city council could properly carry out its duties in this way under the provisions of section 6(1)(c) of the Act, i.e. by giving such advice and assistance as would secure the applicant to obtain accommodation from some other person.'

b   Meanwhile, while all this had been going on, the council had arranged to continue to provide accommodation for the applicant and her children at the guest house at a cost, we are told, of about £18 a night.

On 16th March the matter was referred to the housing committee. They had before them a report of the director of housing. The committee determined unanimously, after what appears from the minute of the meeting to have been a full discussion of the question, that the applicant should be assisted to return to Ireland if she wished to take

c   advantage of that assistance.

The minute reads:

'After further debate, it was unanimously agreed that, in view of the assurance of assistance from the community welfare officer in Tralee, Eire, Mrs Browne and her family should return to Eire and that she be assisted in an approach regarding a

d   travel warrant.'

At 5 pm on the same day, Mr Ball told the applicant of the committee's decision. He also told her that an appointment had been made for her to see the Department of Health and Social Security at 10 am on 19th March with a view to their providing her with a travel warrant if she wished to take advantage of the assistance offered by the council to

e   return to Eire. The applicant thereupon said that she had no wish to return to Ireland. Mr Ball also informed her that, if she did not take advantage of the council's offer of assistance, the case would be referred back to the housing committee on 19th March. The applicant failed to attend at the meeting which had been arranged with the Department of Health and Social Security at 10 am on 19th March. She again explained that her reason was that she had no intention of returning to Ireland.

f   The matter then went back to the housing committee on 19th March. There was a further discussion, at the end of which it was decided to continue the provision of accommodation at the guest house until 20th March but not beyond. Thereafter the cost of her accommodation was defrayed jointly by Bristol Women's Aid and by Shelter for a few days until 2nd April, when they declined to help her further.

To complete the history of the matter, on 5th April there was an application to this

g   court for leave to apply for judicial review, which was granted. On 6th April the applicant went back to the housing aid centre in Bristol and again presented herself as a homeless person. She was again interviewed, on this occasion by Mr Hodgkinson. Mr Hodgkinson again discussed the matter with Mr Martin, and it was decided to treat that application as being a fresh application notwithstanding the previous decision. Accordingly, the council prepared a further notification, this time dated 6th

h   April, under s 8 of the Act in identical terms to the previous notification. On the afternoon of 6th April, Mr Hodgkinson informed the applicant of the council's decision. Again I think it is important to quote his precise words. He said:

'I offered to provide the applicant with transport and to make funds available for her in order to purchase train and boat tickets for the return journey to Eire. The

j   applicant told me that she would not require this assistance as she did not wish to return to Eire. I explained that bed and breakfast accommodation would be provided until the morning of Monday 9th April 1979 and that if she had any change of mind over the weekend she should contact me first thing on Monday morning. I advised the applicant that if she did decide to return to Eire then she should contact the community welfare officer in Tralee.'

Mr Hodgkinson also handed the applicant a letter dated 6th April 1979 from the director of housing, which reads as follows:

'With reference to your visit to the Housing Aid centre this morning, I attach herewith the written notification as required under section 8 of the Act. This decision must be regarded by you as a final decision and is made without prejudice to this authority's view that their duty towards you has already been discharged. You have been verbally informed that I am satisfied that accommodation will be made available upon your return to the Republic of Ireland and travel and other relevant details will be provided. However, in view of the particular circumstances of your case this further assistance is being given although the city council does not consider that it is statutorily obliged to do so and no consideration will be given to any further application under the Act.'

Those being the facts of the case, the sole question for our consideration is whether the council have complied with their statutory duty under the 1977 Act. That turns on the language of s 6(1), which I have already read in full and need not read it again. It provides, in effect, that the council can perform their duty either by providing accommodation themselves or by securing that the homeless person obtains accommodation from some other person or by giving such advice and assistance as will secure that he obtains accommodation from some other person.

In the present case, on the facts which I have recited, it is clear beyond any doubt that the council have given such advice and offered such assistance (although it has not been accepted) as would enable the applicant to obtain accommodation from Mr Burke, the community welfare officer in Tralee. It is true that there is no affidavit from Mr Burke himself, but there is no reason why we should not accept what is said by Mr Ball and Mr Hodgkinson in that respect.

Thus the question comes down to this very narrow point: is Mr Burke a 'person' within the meaning of s 6(1)(c) of the 1977 Act? In my judgment, he is. Indeed, counsel, who has appeared on behalf of the applicant, did not suggest the contrary, or at any rate did not suggest it very strenuously. Putting the question of violence on one side, counsel for the applicant accepted that the council could fulfil their duty under the Act by assisting the applicant and her children to go back to Tralee, even though Tralee is outside the jurisdiction. It may well be that in most cases the person referred to in s 6(1)(c) of the Act will be a person within the area of the housing authority in question. But there is nothing in the Act which expressly so confines it; and, as I say, counsel did not strenuously argue that it should be so confined.

The real point which counsel makes is that the applicant should not, on the special facts of this case, be asked to go back to Tralee, because that is the place where she has suffered the domestic violence in the past. In that connection counsel for the applicant referred us to s 5(3) and (4) of the Act, which I should now read in full.

'(3) It shall be the duty of the notified authority to secure that accommodation becomes available for occupation by the person to whom the notification relates if neither he nor any person who might reasonably be expected to reside with him has a local connection with the area of the notifying authority but the conditions specified in subsection (4) below are satisfied.

'(4) The conditions mentioned in subsection (3) above are—(a) that the person to whom the notification relates or some person who might reasonably be expected to reside with him has a local connection with the area of the notified authority, and [this is the important condition] (b) that neither he nor any such person will run the risk of domestic violence in that area.'

It is not of course argued that Tralee is itself a housing authority within the meaning of the 1977 Act; nobody suggests that the conditions set out in s 5(4) apply as such. But what is argued is that s 5(4)(b) can and should be applied, as it were, by analogy.

There is, I think, a short answer to that submission. The fact that Tralee is the place from which the applicant has come and the place where she has suffered violence in the

past does not mean that she would necessarily suffer any risk of violence if she goes
a   back. Obviously she will not go back to the same house; but there is other
accommodation in the same area. The risk involved in her going back was, in my
judgment, a matter for the council to consider together with the community welfare
officer in Tralee. The passages from the affidavits which I have read show that that risk
was considered very carefully by the council. The view which they have formed is quite
clear, namely that accommodation can be provided in Tralee without risk to the applicant
b   or her children. There is no material on which this court can possibly interfere with that
conclusion or say that it was not justified. Counsel's main point, therefore, fails.
  The only other submission which he made was that the accommodation offered by the
community welfare officer in Tralee is not accommodation which is available for
occupation within the definition of s 16 of the 1977 Act because it is not sufficiently
defined or specific. There is nothing in that submission. The council have satisfied
c   themselves that the accommodation will be available if the applicant returns to Ireland.
It was not incumbent on the council to identify the particular house in question which
the community welfare officer in Ireland had in mind.
  I have listened with great care to all that counsel has urged in this anxious case on
behalf of the applicant. On the facts I cannot find that the council have failed in their
statutory duty, and therefore the application for mandamus must fail.
d   That being so, it is not necessary to deal with the various other submissions made by
counsel on behalf of the council, which I mention out of courtesy and out of gratitude for
his helpful argument. Those submissions were, in brief, that a person who has a local
connection outside the United Kingdom but has no local connection within the United
Kingdom is not a person within the meaning of the 1977 Act at all. Secondly, to hold
that such persons are within the Act would lead to absurdity. Thirdly, in any event, the
e   remedy of mandamus does not lie in this case at the instance of an individual, even if it
were established that the council had failed in their statutory duty. Those questions will
have to remain for another day.

LORD WIDGERY CJ. I agree with everything which has fallen from Lloyd J and I
would particularly emphasise that there are many points left undecided on the 1977 Act
and indeed we have a great deal more work to do on it before we have mastered it. I
f   would leave open for another day the interesting argument whether the safeguards of
the 1977 Act are available at all for someone who has no legal connection with this
country and comes, for example, from overseas. I would also leave open for consideration
on another day how far mandamus itself should go in this type of case.
  Counsel for the council argues that the ordinary principles of common law which
apply to this type of case prevent this court from exercising any power to look behind the
g   local authority's decision and reach a different conclusion itself.
  In support of his own contention counsel for the applicant cited from Lord
Wilberforce's speech in *Secretary of State for Education and Science v Metropolitan Borough
of Tameside*[1] where, quoting in fact Lord Denning MR[2], Lord Wilberforce said:

  'The section is framed in a "subjective" form—if the Secretary of State "is
h   satisfied". This form of section is quite well known, and at first sight might seem
to exclude judicial review. Sections in this form may, no doubt, exclude judicial
review on what is or has become a matter of pure judgment. But I do not think that
they go further than that. If a judgment requires, before it can be made, the
existence of some facts, then, although the evaluation of those facts is for the
Secretary of State alone, the court must enquire whether those facts exist, and have
been taken into account, whether the judgment has been made on a proper self
j   direction as to those facts, whether the judgment has not been made on other facts
which ought not to have been taken into account.'

---

1 [1976] 3 All ER 665 at 681–682, [1977] AC 1014 at 1047
2 See *Secretary of State for Employment v Associated Society of Locomotive Engineers and Firemen (No 2)*
[1972] 2 All ER 949 at 967, [1972] 2 QB 455 at 493

The actual language used there is in itself a reference back perhaps to the best known case on this topic, which is *Associated Provincial Picture Houses Ltd v Wednesbury Corpn*[1], where it is laid down that to attack a local authority's exercise of discretion one must normally show that the authority erred in principle, which means either that it took into account a consideration which it should have left out or left out a consideration of which it should have taken account. Once one can be satisfied that the local authority avoided those dangers, then it is not open to the court to interfere.

For those reasons, already covered by Lloyd J's judgment, I agree with what he said, and I agree also that the application should be refused.

Application refused.

Solicitors: *Ward Bowie*, agents for *Galbraith, Quinn & Co*, Bristol (for the applicant); *John A Brown*, Bristol (for the council).

N P Metcalfe Esq   Barrister.

Re Transatlantic Life Assurance Co Ltd

CHANCERY DIVISION
SLADE J
11th, 13th JUNE 1979

Company – Shares – Register – Rectification – Issue of security in breach of exchange control legislation – Shares issued to person resident outside scheduled territories without Treasury permission – Whether issue wholly invalid and void – Whether court should exercise discretion to order rectification – Exchange Control Act 1947, s 8(1) – Companies Act 1948, s 116(1)(a)(2).

In April 1966 a company which was wholly owned by another company ('LACOP') resident outside the scheduled territories issued to LACOP 50,000 ordinary £1 shares in the company and LACOP was entered in the company's register of members as the holder of those shares. Treasury permission required by the Exchange Control Act 1947 was obtained for the transaction. On 12th March 1974 the company made a further issue of 200,000 £1 ordinary shares to LACOP in consideration of the transfer to the company by LACOP of sterling investments to the value of £200,000. LACOP's name was entered in the company's register as the holder of the 200,000 shares. It did not occur to the company or to LACOP that Treasury permission was required for that issue and since such permission had not been obtained the issue was made in breach of s 8(1)[a] of the 1947 Act. In 1977 the company discovered that Treasury permission ought to have been obtained and decided, with LACOP's consent, to put right the error by applying to the court under s 116(1)[b] of the Companies Act 1948 for rectification of its register of members by striking out LACOP's name as the holder of the 200,000 shares and thereafter applying for permission under the 1947 Act to make a new issue of 50,000 shares to LACOP. The company proposed, if the order for rectification were made, to repay £150,000 to LACOP representing the consideration received for the issue of the 200,000 shares, less the sum due to it on the proposed new issue. The question arose whether the court was entitled to order the rectification sought.

Held – (i) On the true construction of s 8(1) of the 1947 Act, read in conjunction with s 18(1)[c] of that Act, the purported issue of a security in a manner prohibited by the 1947

---

1   [1947] 2 All ER 680, [1948] 1 KB 223
a   Section 8(1) is set out at p 354 j, post
b   Section 116 is set out at p 357 b, post
c   Section 18(1) is set out at p 355 d, post

Act rendered the issue wholly invalid and void. The issue of the 200,000 shares was
a therefore void and conferred on LACOP no title whatsoever to the shares. Moreover,
under s 13(a)^d of the 1947 Act the company was prohibited from entering LACOP's
name in the register as the holder of those shares. It followed that LACOP's name had
been entered in the register as the holder of those shares 'without sufficient cause', within
s 116(1)(a) of the 1948 Act, and the court had jurisdiction under s 116(2) to order
rectification of the register by deleting LACOP's name as holder of the 200,000 shares
b (see p 355 *f* to *h* and p 357 *a* and *c* to *e*, post); *Re Fry* (deceased) [1946] 2 All ER 106
applied.

(ii) Although the transaction might appear at first sight to effect a reduction of capital
carried through without the protection provided by ss 66 and 67 of the 1948 Act, it
would not have that effect because the issue of the 200,000 shares having been wholly
void the company's issued share capital was in fact only £50,000, notwithstanding that
c the company and its directors had, albeit innocently, represented that it was £250,000.
The order sought would merely direct that the register be rectified in such manner as to
reflect what had throughout been the true position according to law, and would grant
relief strictly ancillary thereto; it would not include express approval of the company's
proposal to repay the £150,000 to LACOP. The court would therefore, in exercise of its
discretion, make the order sought (see p 357 *g* to p 358 *a c* and *d*, post).

d **Notes**

For rectification of the register of members and for jurisdiction to rectify the register, see
7 Halsbury's Laws (4th Edn) paras 307–308.

For the issue of securities to persons outside the scheduled territories without Treasury
permission, see 27 Halsbury's Laws (3rd Edn) 130, para 211.

For the Exchange Control Act 1947, ss 8, 13, 18 see 22 Halsbury's Statutes (3rd Edn)
e 908, 913, 918.

For the Companies Act 1948, ss 66, 67, 116, see 5 ibid 171, 172, 204.

Case referred to in judgment

Fry (deceased), Re, Chase National Executors and Trustees Corpn v Fry [1946] 2 All ER 106,
[1946] Ch 312, 115 LJ Ch 225, 175 LT 392, 25 Digest (Repl) 582, 226.

f **Case also cited**

Portuguese Consolidated Copper Mines Ltd, Re (1889) 42 Ch D 160, CA.

Motion

By a notice of motion dated 25th April 1979 Transatlantic Life Assurance Co Ltd ('the
company') applied under s 116 of the Companies Act 1948 for rectification of their
g register of members to strike out the name of Life Assurance Co of Pennsylvania
('LACOP'), the respondents to the motion, as the holder of 200,000 ordinary shares of
£1 each in the capital of the company, for authorisation to effect the necessary alterations
in the register and for an order that notice of the rectification be given to the registrar of
companies. The facts are set out in the judgment.

h *Richard Sykes* for the company.
LACOP was not represented.

SLADE J. This is a motion seeking relief under s 116 of the Companies Act 1948 in
somewhat unusual circumstances. By the terms of the notice of motion, Transatlantic
Life Assurance Co Ltd ('the company') seeks—

j   'An Order pursuant to Section 116 of the Companies Act, 1948, that the Register
of Members of the [company] may be rectified by striking out the name of Life
Assurance Company of Pennsylvania as the holder of the 200,000 Ordinary Shares
of £1 each in the capital of the [company] numbered 50,001 to 250,000 inclusive.

---

d   Section 13, so far as material, is set out at p 356 *e*, post

And that the [company] may be authorised to effect the necessary alterations in the said Register for carrying such Order into effect. And that notice of such *a* rectification may be ordered to be given to the Registrar of Companies or that such other Order may be made in the premises as to the Court shall seem meet.'

Life Assurance Company of Pennsylvania ('LACOP') is sole respondent to the motion, but is not represented before me. It is a company resident outside the scheduled territories.

The motion is supported by an affidavit sworn by Mr R J Beard, a director of the *b* company. From this affidavit and the exhibits thereto, the following facts appear. The company is a wholly owned subsidiary of LACOP. It has an authorised capital of £250,000. Its objects include those of carrying on insurance business and it is authorised by the Department of Trade to carry on ordinary long-term insurance business. It was incorporated on 21st March 1966 as a company limited by shares. Following its incorporation, 50,000 ordinary shares of £1 each were issued for cash at par to LACOP. *c* This issue was made on 26th April 1966 pursuant to a permission granted prior to the incorporation of the company under the Exchange Control Act 1947, by the Bank of England on 6th September 1965. The shares were numbered 1 to 50,000. On 5th March 1974 the board of the company resolved that a further issue of 200,000 ordinary shares be made in favour of LACOP. Pursuant to this resolution the issue was made on 12th March 1974 at par, and the shares were numbered 50,001 to 250,000. The *d* consideration was satisfied by the transfer from LACOP to the company of sterling investments having a value of £200,000. It did not occur to any of the persons concerned that any permission under the 1947 Act was required for this last mentioned issue and no such permission was sought. In these circumstances, it is submitted that the issue, constituting (as it did) an infringement of the 1947 Act, was accordingly wholly void.

The company discovered early in 1977 that the requisite exchange control permission *e* had not been obtained for the issue of shares in 1974. An application to the Bank of England for a retrospective permission was then made. Before it was granted, and while the company was still dealing with queries raised by the bank, it was decided by the company and LACOP that, instead of seeking to validate the issue, they would prefer to have the matter set right by rectification of the register of members of the company and then, by means of a new issue of shares with the appropriate permission, to provide the *f* company with the capital required for its business. Accordingly the application for retrospective permission was withdrawn and application for a new permission was made. Permission has in fact been granted to the company to make a new issue of 50,000 ordinary shares of £1 each.

These are the circumstances in which the company makes the application before me. Mr Beard states in his affidavit that LACOP consents to it and that it has agreed, on the *g* register of members of the company being rectified, forthwith to subscribe for 50,000 new ordinary shares of £1 each at par. If the order for rectification is made as sought, the company would intend immediately to repay £150,000 to LACOP, which it would apparently regard as being due to LACOP.

The first question that falls to be considered is whether, as counsel for the company submits, the further issue of 200,000 ordinary shares by the company in March 1974 was *h* wholly void. Section 8(1) of the 1947 Act provides as follows:

'Except with the permission of the Treasury, no person shall in the United Kingdom, issue any security or, whether in the United Kingdom or elsewhere, issue any security which is registered or to be registered in the United Kingdom, unless the following requirements are fulfilled, that is to say—(*a*) neither the person to *j* whom the security is to be issued nor the person, if any, for whom he is to be a nominee is resident outside the scheduled territories; and (*b*) the prescribed evidence is produced to the person issuing the security as to the residence of the person to whom it is to be issued and that of the person, if any, for whom he is to be a nominee.'

a LACOP was a person resident outside the scheduled territories at the relevant time, and the permission of the Treasury was not obtained in respect of the issue of the 200,000 shares. Accordingly, it is clear that this issue did involve a breach of the provisions of s 8(1). Though Sch 5 to the 1947 Act renders certain breaches of the provisions of the Act a punishable offence, the Act appears to contain no further explicit guidance as to the effect in law of issuing securities without Treasury permission in breach of s 8(1). Section 8(2), so far as material for present purposes, provides as follows:

b '   'The subscription of the memorandum of association of a company to be formed under the Companies Act, 1929 . . . by a person resident outside the scheduled territories . . . shall, unless he subscribes the memorandum with the permission of the Treasury, be invalid in so far as it would on registration of the memorandum have the effect of making him a member of or shareholder in the company . . .'

c This subsection therefore expressly provides for the invalidity of the subscription to this extent and in these circumstances. I do not, however, think it throws much light, one way or the other, on the construction of s 8(1).

Far greater assistance, in my judgment, is to be derived from s 18(1), on which counsel for the company principally relied. This section reads:

d '   '(1) The title of any person to a security for which he has given value on a transfer thereof, and the title of all persons claiming through or under him, shall, notwithstanding that the transfer, or any previous transfer, or the issue of the security, was by reason of the residence of any person concerned other than the first-mentioned person prohibited by the provisions of this Act relating to the transfer or issue of securities, be valid unless the first-mentioned person had notice of the facts by reason of which it was prohibited.

e '   '(2) Without prejudice to the provisions of subsection (1) of this section, the Treasury may issue a certificate declaring, in relation to a security, that any acts done before the issue of the certificate purporting to effect the issue or transfer of the security, being acts which were prohibited by this Act, are to be, and are always to have been, as valid as if they had been done with the permission of the Treasury, and the said acts shall have effect accordingly.

f '   '(3) Nothing in this section shall affect the liability of any person to prosecution for any offence against this Act.'

In my judgment counsel for the company is correct in submitting that this section, by necessary inference, presupposes that the purported issue of a security in manner prohibited by the 1947 Act is wholly invalid. Were this not so, I could see no point in the g provisions of s 18(1) which, when applicable, by their terms operate to validate the title to such a security of a person who has given value on taking a transfer thereof. Were this not so, I could likewise see no point in the provisions of s 18(2) which empower the Treasury to issue a certificate, inter alia, retrospectively validating acts purporting to effect the issue of a security in manner prohibited by the 1947 Act. The very use by the legislature of the phrase 'purporting to effect', in s 18(2), in my judgment further h illustrates that the acts which purport to effect the issue in a prohibited manner do not in fact operate to effect that issue ab initio. In these circumstances, on a bare reading of the Act, I would conclude that the purported issue of 200,000 ordinary shares by the company in March 1974 was wholly invalid and void.

Counsel for the company has been unable to refer me to any decided case which touches directly on the construction of s 8 of the 1947 Act, but he has referred me to one j decision which, I think, provides some indirect assistance. In *Re Fry*[1] Romer J had to consider the effect of a transfer of shares by a father in favour of a son, effected in breach of the restrictions imposed on the transfer of securities by para (1) of reg 3A of the

---

1   [1946] 2 All ER 106, [1946] Ch 312

Defence (Finance) Regulations 1939[1]. Paragraph (1), so far as material for present purposes, provided:

'(1) Subject to any exemptions which may be granted by order of the Treasury no person shall . . . transfer . . . otherwise than by operation of law or by inheritance, any securities or any interest in securities, unless the Treasury or persons authorised by or on behalf of the Treasury are satisfied that no person resident outside the sterling area has, immediately before the transfer . . . any interest in the securities: Provided that nothing in this paragraph shall prohibit any . . . transfer . . . which is effected with permission granted by the Treasury or by a person authorised by them or on their behalf.'

Paragraph (4) provided:

'(4) Subject to any exemptions which may be granted by order of the Treasury, no person shall, except with permission granted by the Treasury or by a person authorised by them or on their behalf, enter any transfer of securities in any register or book in which those securities are registered or inscribed unless there has been produced to him such evidence that the transfer does not involve a contravention of this Regulation as may be prescribed by instructions issued by or on behalf of the Treasury.'

This latter provision was to much the same effect as s 13(a) of the 1947 Act, which provides:

'Except with the permission of the Treasury, no person concerned with the keeping of any register in the United Kingdom shall—(a) enter in the register the name of any person in relation to any security unless there has been produced to him the prescribed evidence that the entry does not form part of a transaction which involves the doing of anything prohibited by this Act . . .'

The regulations in that case, like the present, did not expressly state what was to be the effect in law of a purported transfer effected in breach of them. Romer J, in his judgment, first considered the question whether the purported transferees were in a position which entitled them, as against the company, to be put on the register of members and whether everything had been done that was necessary to put them into the position of the transferor. In this context he said[2]:

'Having regard, however, to the Defence (Finance) Regulations, 1939, it is impossible, in my judgment, to answer the questions other than in the negative. The requisite consent of the Treasury to the transactions had not been obtained, and, in the absence of it, the company was prohibited from registering the transfers. In my opinion, accordingly, it is not possible to hold that, at the date of the testator's death, the transferees had either acquired a legal title to the shares in question, or the right, as against all other persons . . . to be clothed with such legal title.'

Romer J then proceeded to consider an argument that at the relevant time a complete equitable assignment had been effected. He rejected this argument on, inter alia, the following grounds[3]:

'The interest in the shares so acquired by the assignees would indubitably be an "interest in securities" within the meaning of reg. 3A; and, inasmuch as they are prohibited from acquiring such an interest except with permission granted by the Treasury, this court cannot recognise a claim to such an interest where the consent of the Treasury was never given to its acquisition.'

---

1   SR & O 1940 No 1254
2   [1946] 2 All ER 106 at 111, [1946] Ch 312 at 316
3   [1946] 2 All ER 106 at 112, [1946] Ch 312 at 318

The reasoning of Romer J in *Re Fry*[1], mutatis mutandis, in my judgment, supports the
conclusions, which I would have reached in its absence, that the relevant issue of the
200,000 shares to LACOP was wholly invalid and void and that it operated to confer on
LACOP no title whatever to any such shares, either at law or in equity.

Section 116 of the Companies Act 1948, provides as follows:

> '(1) If—(*a*) the name of any person is, without sufficient cause, entered in or
> omitted from the register of members of a company; or (*b*) default is made or
> unnecessary delay takes place in entering on the register the fact of any person
> having ceased to be a member; the person aggrieved, or any member of the
> company, or the company, may apply to the court for rectification of the register.
>
> '(2) Where an application is made under this section, the court may either refuse
> the application or may order rectification of the register and payment by the
> company of any damages sustained by any party aggrieved.'

In the circumstances, it seems to me clear that the name of LACOP was entered in the
register of members of the company, as the holder of the relevant 200,000 shares,
'without sufficient cause' within the meaning of s 116(1)(*a*). Indeed by virtue of s 13(*a*)
of the 1947 Act the company was, I think, actually prohibited from making such entry
in the absence of the prescribed evidence that the entry did not form part of a transaction
which involved the doing of anything prohibited by that Act. In my judgment the
wording of s 116 of the Companies Act 1948 is wide enough in its terms to empower the
court to order the rectification of a company's register by deleting a reference to some
only of a registered shareholder's shares. The section can, in my judgment, still operate,
even though the proposed rectification does not involve the entire deletion of the name
of the registered holder concerned as a member of the company concerned, inasmuch as
he, or it, is still properly shown as the holder of other shares, to which the rectification
does not relate. I therefore conclude that the court has jurisdiction to order the
rectification sought in the present case.

Are there then any reasons why the court should, in the exercise of its discretion,
decline to make the order sought? Mr Beard's affidavit contains evidence to the effect
that the company no longer writes new insurance business and its insurance liabilities
would be amply covered by its available assets, without the net amount of £150,000
which it intends to repay to LACOP in the event of the order for rectification sought
being made. This evidence, however, is not very full and is not directed at all to such
liabilities of the company (if any) as are not insurance liabilities; in theory, I suppose,
these liabilities might be substantial. In these circumstances, the point which has
principally troubled me is the position of creditors of the company, none of whom are
represented before me, particularly in the light of the announced intention of the
company to repay the £150,000 to LACOP in the event of the proposed order being
made. The transaction, viewed at first sight, has some flavour of a reduction of capital,
carried through without the protection of the machinery provided for by ss 66 and 67 of
the Companies Act 1948, which is designed in particular to safeguard the interests of
creditors of the company concerned.

I think, however, that there are two answers to any misgivings which may be felt on
this account. First, if I am right in concluding that the issue of the 200,000 shares was
wholly void, then the position must, in my judgment, be that, though the issued capital
of the company was, from March 1974 until at least 1977, thought by all concerned to
be £250,000, it has in truth, at all material times, been only £50,000, so that in truth no
reduction at all is involved by the order which the court is now asked to make. Secondly,
an order in the terms sought would in any event be of only limited scope, inasmuch as
it would embody no more than an order for rectification of the register of members and
relief strictly ancillary to the making of such an order. It would not include express
approval of the company's announced intention of repaying the £150,000 to LACOP

---

1   [1946] 2 All ER 106, [1946] Ch 312

after the order had been made and I do not, as at present minded, propose to give such express approval. The company has apparently been advised that, if and when the order *a* has been made, it will be entitled, and indeed bound, to repay to LACOP the sum of £150,000, representing the consideration which was paid to the company under the unlawful transaction of March 1974 less the £50,000 due to it under the proposed new issue. While not intending to cast any doubt on the correctness of this advice, I express no opinion whether it is correct. This is a question which has been canvassed only very briefly before me. I would merely observe that, if the advice should happen to be *b* incorrect, and were acted on, any remedies which creditors of the company might seek to pursue would, as I see the position, be unaffected by the order which I now propose to make.

The same comment applies to any remedies which creditors of the company might hereafter seek to pursue, arising from the fact that, over a number of years, the company and its directors, albeit apparently quite innocently, have (for example in the company's *c* latest audited accounts as at 31st December 1977) represented to the world that it had an issued share capital of £250,000, while its true issued share capital, according to my judgment, was only £50,000.

In all the circumstances I can see no good reason for declining to make the order sought. The effect of the order will merely be to direct that the register be rectified in such a manner as to reflect what I think has throughout been the true position according *d* to law.

I propose therefore to grant relief in the terms of the notice of motion. This, however, will be subject to an undertaking, which I understand counsel for the company will be prepared to give on behalf of the company, that an affidavit will be sworn on its behalf, by someone who can properly speak to this matter, confirming that LACOP has not executed transfers of any of the 200,000 shares purportedly issued to it in March 1974. *e* I require this undertaking in view of the provisions of s 18(1) of the 1947 Act. My order will also be made subject to an undertaking hereafter being given to the court, on behalf of LACOP, to the effect that it will forthwith subscribe for 50,000 new ordinary shares of £1 each, in the company, at par. This undertaking will be required in order to ensure that the company will hereafter comply with the requirements as to paid up share capital imposed by the Insurance Companies Act 1974. *f*

Order accordingly.

Solicitors: *Lovell, White & King* (for the company).

Jacqueline Metcalfe   Barrister.   *g*

Re Grant's Will Trusts

CHANCERY DIVISION
VINELOTT J
18th, 19th DECEMBER 1978, 16th MARCH 1979

Rule against perpetuities – Unincorporated association – Gift to association – Absolute gift to members on trust for association – Bequest in will – Gift to committee of local political party – Whether bequest a gift to members of association – Whether gift imposing a trust on association – Whether gift void for perpetuity.

The testator was for many years a member of the Labour Party and also the financial secretary to his local constituency party ('the old Chertsey CLP'). In 1959 the old Chertsey CLP bought a property ('the property'). By virtue of the terms of a trust deed the trustees held the property on trust for the old Chertsey CLP absolutely and were bound to deal with it in such manner as the Chertsey CLP general management committee should direct. In the redistribution of the parliamentary constituency boundaries in 1970 the Chertsey constituency ceased to exist but part of it became the Chertsey and Walton constituency. The old Chertsey CLP was dissolved in 1971. Pending resolution of the ownership of the property following the boundary redistribution, the management of the property was placed in the hands of a local property committee comprising delegates from each of the three local Labour parties. After the dissolution of the old Chertsey CLP a new constituency party ('the new Chertsey CLP') was formed and the testator was made its financial secretary. Its headquarters were always at the property, which after the local authority reorganisation remained within the area that was formerly the Chertsey Urban District Council area. The new Chertsey CLP rules provided, inter alia, (i) that the management of the new Chertsey CLP should be placed in the hands of a general committee, (ii) that the general committee should accept and make such changes in the rules as were agreed to by the annual party conference or made by the National Executive Committee ('the NEC') of the Labour Party, (iii) that the general committee should, subject to the approval of the NEC, have power itself to make changes in the rules provided that they did not contravene the spirit or intention of the annual party conference, (iv) that the general committee should, subject to the approval of the NEC, have power to buy land and property, to appoint trustees to hold any land and property so acquired for and on behalf of the new Chertsey CLP, and to define the powers of any trustees so appointed and lay down the manner of exercise of such power. The rules contained no provision as to what was to happen to any land or property purchased by the general committee in the event of the dissolution of the new Chertsey CLP. On 12th May 1975 the testator made a will appointing the trustees of the property as his executors and devising 'all my real and personal estate to the Labour Party Property Committee for the benefit of the Chertsey Headquarters of [the new Chertsey CLP] providing that such Headquarters remain in what was the Chertsey Urban District Council Area (1972), if not, I declare that the foregoing provision shall not take effect and in lieu thereof I give all my said estate to the National Labour Party absolutely'. At the date of the will and the testator's death on 6th June 1975 there was not a body connected with the new Chertsey CLP formally called 'the Labour Party Property Committee' and the question of ownership of the property not having been resolved it was still managed by the local property committee. It was common ground that when the testator referred in his will to 'the Labour Party Property Committee' he must have intended to refer to the local property committee. The trustees of the trust deed applied to the court to determine (i) whether the bequest was a valid gift or was void for uncertainty or for perpetuity or otherwise, and (ii) if it was a valid gift who was entitled to benefit thereunder.

Held – The bequest was not a valid gift, and the testator's estate accordingly devolved as on intestacy, for the following reasons—

(i) The bequest could not be construed as a gift on the trusts of the trust deed and therefore the residuary estate was not an accretion to and did not follow in all respects the devolution of the property or the proceeds of sale thereof because it was clear from the proviso to the will that the testator contemplated that the property might not continue to be the headquarters of the new Chertsey CLP (see p 369 *a* to *e*, post).

(ii) The bequest could not be construed as a gift to the members of the new Chertsey CLP at the date of the testator's death subject to a direction that it be used for headquarters' purposes because the members of the new Chertsey CLP did not control property given by subscription or otherwise to the new Chertsey CLP, they could not alter the rules so as to apply the testator's bequest for some purpose other than that provided by the rules, they could not direct the bequest to be divided amongst themselves beneficially, and in the event of the dissolution of the new Chertsey CLP any remaining fund representing subscriptions would, as the rules stood, be held on a resulting trust for the original subscribers. Furthermore, the gift over to the national Labour Party prevented the bequest from being construed as a gift to those who were members of the national Labour Party at the date of the testator's death subject to a direction not amounting to a trust that the national party permit it to be used by the new Chertsey CLP for headquarters' purposes (see p 371*f* to p 372 *c*, post); *Neville Estates Ltd v Madden* [1961] 3 All ER 769 and *Re Recher's Will Trusts* [1971] 3 All ER 401 applied; *Re Denley's Trust Deed* [1968] 3 All ER 65 distinguished; *Re Drummond* [1914–15] All ER Rep 223 considered.

(iii) Because the bequest was not in terms a gift to the new Chertsey CLP but a gift to the Labour Party Property Committee, who were to hold the property for and on behalf of the Chertsey headquarters of the new Chertsey CLP, the bequest could not be construed as a gift to the members of the association at the date when it took effect but had to be construed as imposing a trust which, being non-charitable, failed because it infringed the rule against perpetuities (see p 366 *h* to p 367 *b* and p 372 *c* to *e*, post); *Re Lipinski's Will Trusts* [1977] 1 All ER 33 distinguished; *Re Price* [1943] 2 All ER 505 and *Leahy v Attorney-General of New South Wales* [1959] 2 All ER 300 considered.

Notes

For gifts for associations and perpetual institutions, see 5 Halsbury's Laws (4th Edn) para 553, and for cases on the subject, see 8(1) Digest (Reissue) 296–298, 389–403.

Cases referred to in judgment

Clarke, Re, Clarke v Clarke [1901] 2 Ch 110, 70 LJ Ch 631, 84 LT 811, 8(1) Digest (Reissue) 298, 400.

Denley's Trust Deed, Re, Holman v H H Martyn & Co Ltd [1968] 3 All ER 65, [1969] 1 Ch 373, [1968] 3 WLR 457, Digest (Cont Vol C) 1039, 423*a*.

Drummond, Re, Ashworth v Drummond [1914] 2 Ch 90, [1914–15] All ER Rep 223, 83 LJ Ch 817, 111 LT 156, 8(1) Digest (Reissue) 300, 419.

Leahy v Attorney-General of New South Wales [1959] 2 All ER 300, [1959] AC 457, [1959] 2 WLR 722, [1959] ALR 869, 33 ALJR 105, PC, 8(1) Digest (Reissue) 376, *535.

Lipinski's Will Trusts, Re, Gosschalk v Levy [1977] 1 All ER 33, [1976] Ch 235, [1976] 3 WLR 522.

Neville Estates Ltd v Madden [1961] 3 All ER 769, [1962] Ch 832, [1961] 3 WLR 999, 8(1) Digest (Reissue) 275, 246.

Price, Re, Midland Bank Executor and Trustee Co v Harwood [1943] 2 All ER 505, [1943] Ch 422, 112 LJ Ch 273, 169 LT 121, 8(1) Digest (Reissue) 260, 135.

Recher's Will Trusts, Re, National Westminster Bank Ltd v National Anti-Vivisection Society Ltd [1971] 3 All ER 401, [1972] Ch 526, [1971] 3 WLR 321, 8(1) Digest (Reissue) 297, 398.

Turkington, Re, Owen v Benson [1937] 4 All ER 501, 8(1) Digest (Reissue) 375, 1032.

Cases also cited

a *Astor's Settlement Trusts, Re, Astor v Scholfield* [1952] 1 All ER 1067, [1952] Ch 534.
Endacott (decd), Re, Corpe v Endacott [1959] 3 All ER 562, [1960] Ch 232, CA.
Macaulay's Estate, Re, Macaulay v O'Donnell [1943] Ch 435.
Ogden, Re, Brydon v Samuel [1933] Ch 678, [1933] All ER Rep 720.

Adjourned summons

b By an originating summons dated 12th July 1977 the plaintiffs, Bertram Henry Harris, Keith Jeffrey Joseph Thompson and Denis Wood, the executors of the will of Wilson Phelps Grant deceased, applied to the court for the determination of the following questions and for the following relief: (1) whether on the true construction of the will and in the events which had happened the expression 'The Labour Party Committee' appearing therein was void for uncertainty, and if it was not void who were the persons *c* constituting the committee; (2) whether on the true construction of the will and in the events which had happened the gift in the will to the Labour Party Property Committee for the benefit of the Chertsey headquarters of the Chertsey and Walton Constituency Labour Party (a) was a valid gift in respect of which the persons constituting the committee or some other and if so what person or persons were able to give the plaintiffs an effective receipt and discharge, (b) was void for uncertainty, want of a beneficiary, *d* perpetuity or some other and if so what reason, or (c) had some other and if so what effect; (3) if the answer to question (2) was in sense (b), whether the gift in the will to the national Labour Party was a valid absolute and beneficial gift to the Labour Party, or the whole estate of the testator was undisposed of and passed as on intestacy; (4) that the third defendant, Margery Godden, might be appointed to represent all those persons entitled to share in so much, if any, of the testator's estate as passed on intestacy; (5) if and so far *e* as necessary, administration of the trusts of the will. The defendants were (1) Anthony Sidney Anderson, a member of the Chertsey and Walton Constituency Labour Party (which claimed to be beneficially interested under the trusts of the will) sued on his own behalf and on behalf of all other members of Chertsey and Walton Constituency Labour Party, (2) Ronald George Hayward, General Secretary of the Labour Party (which claimed that it might be beneficially interested under the trusts of the will) sued on his own *f* behalf and on behalf of all other members of the Labour Party, and (3) Margery Godden, who claimed to be beneficially entitled to share in so much of the testator's estate as passed as on intestacy. The facts are set out in the judgment.

Nicholas Stewart for the plaintiffs.
J H G Sunnucks for the first and second defendants.
Jonathan Simpkiss for the third defendant.

g
Cur adv vult

16th March. **VINELOTT J** read the following judgment: The testator, Wilson Phelps Grant, died on 6th June 1975. By his will dated 12th May 1975 he appointed 'the trustees of 36 Guildford Street, Chertsey, to be the executors of this my Will'. At the date of the will, and of the testator's death, the property, 36 Guildford Street, Chertsey, was *h* the headquarters of the Chertsey and Walton Constituency Labour Party. The plaintiffs were registered as proprietors with an absolute title, and as hereafter appears they held the property as trustees of a trust deed dated 26th June 1959. The plaintiffs duly proved the will, which was never altered or revoked, on 8th December 1975.
After the appointment of the executors, the will continues as follows:

j   'I give all my real and personal estate to the Labour Party Property Committee for the benefit of the Chertsey Headquarters of the Chertsey and Walton Constituency Labour Party providing that such Headquarters remain in what was the Chertsey Urban District Council Area (1972), if not, I declare that the foregoing provision shall not take effect and in lieu thereof I give all my said estate to the National Labour Party absolutely.'

The factual background which forms the context in which these words have to be construed is shortly as follows. The testator was a member of the Labour Party for upwards of 24 years. He played an active part in the affairs of his local constituency party which until shortly before his death was the Chertsey Constituency Labour Party ('the Chertsey CLP'). In the redistribution of Parliamentary constituency boundaries in 1970 the Chertsey constituency ceased to exist; part is now in north-west Surrey, part is in the Chertsey and Walton constituency. The Chertsey CLP was accordingly dissolved. The general management committee of the Chertsey CLP held its last meeting on 29th January 1971. The testator was present. He was the Chertsey CLP's financial secretary. The last sentence of the minutes records '. . . That this meeting dissolves the Chertsey Constituency Labour Party'.

Some time later a new constituency party, the Chertsey and Walton CLP, was formed. Its rules, which are in the form of model rules prescribed by the national Labour Party, were adopted by the general committee of the new CLP on 28th February 1975. I shall have to return to examine these rules in detail later in this judgment. I should mention at this stage that the testator was also the financial secretary of the Chertsey and Walton CLP, an office which he continued to hold until his death.

The property, 36 Guildford Street, was bought by the old Chertsey CLP in 1959. A trust deed was executed on 26th June 1959, the parties being Arthur Imisson and Charles Frederick Huggins as trustees of the one part, and Roy Goodall, vice-chairman of the general management committee of the Chertsey CLP on behalf of himself and all the members of the general management committee, who are named in the first schedule and include the testator, of the other part. The trust deed recites that, by the instrument of transfer specified in the second schedule, the property, 36 Guildford Street, had been transferred to the trustees who had been registered as proprietors with an absolute title. In fact, as appears from subsequent documents, the transfer was not registered until 16th October 1959 and was in favour of Messrs Imisson, Huggins and Goodall. The trust deed recites that the property had been purchased out of moneys provided by the Chertsey CLP, and that under its rules it was provided that the management of the affairs of the Chertsey CLP should be vested in its general management committee. Clause 2 contains a declaration that the trustees—

> '. . . shall hold the said property until the same shall be sold or otherwise disposed of upon trust for the Party absolutely and shall deal with the same as the Committee shall from time to time by resolution direct. [I should mention in passing that 'the Party' is defined as the Chertsey CLP. It continues:] The Trustees shall have full power with the approval of a resolution of the Committee to raise money for any purpose connected with the said property including the provision of the whole or any part of the cost of purchasing the said property, or erecting enlarging or improving any building for the time being thereon.'

Of the remaining provisions of the trust deed only two require to be mentioned. Clause 9 provides:

> 'The Trustees shall until otherwise directed by the Committee hold all trust monies whether income or capital monies and howsoever the same shall arise in the joint names of the Trustees and may invest them or any part of them in any securities authorised by law for the investment of trust funds in the joint names of the Trustees and shall pay the income of such investments and the rent and profits of any hereditaments to the account of the Party with the Bank.'

Clause 15 provides:

> 'If the Party shall cease to exist for any reason the said property shall be held by the Trustees upon trust for the Labour Party absolutely and the National Executive Committee of the Labour Party shall thereafter exercise all the powers now vested in the Committee hereunder.'

The plaintiffs were appointed trustees of the trust deed on 6th April 1975. From then *a* until the testator's death they remained the trustees thereof. They were clearly the persons designated by the phrase '. . . the trustees of 36 Guildford Street' in the testator's will and, as I have said, they duly proved the will.

The property was purchased with the help of a mortgage from a building society, which was discharged on 24th April 1975, very shortly before the date of the will. The testator as financial secretary of the Chertsey CLP and later of the Chertsey and Walton *b* CLP must have been well aware of this history. As I have said, he was a member of the general management committee at the time of the purchase.

There is one other fact which I should mention before I turn to explain what happened to 36 Guildford Street on the reorganisation of the Chertsey CLP. No 36 Guildford Street was in the language of a proviso to the will '. . . in what was the Chertsey Urban District Council Area (1972)'. Since the local authority reorganisation in 1974 it has been within *c* the geographical area of the Runnymede district. It has at all material times been the office, and the only office, of the Chertsey and Walton CLP.

An affidavit has been sworn by the first defendant, who is joined to represent the members of the Chertsey and Walton CLP, and who is an officer and general election agent of the Chertsey and Walton CLP, explaining the arrangements made with regard to the ownership of 36 Guildford Street following the redistribution of parliamentary *d* constituency boundaries in 1970, and the dissolution of the Chertsey CLP on 29th January 1971. It appears that at the time of the redistribution the management of 36 Guildford Street was put into the hands of a property committee consisting of delegates from each of the three local Labour parties, namely, those of Egham, Bagshot and Chertsey. Although the Chertsey CLP was dissolved the local Labour parties did not cease to exist, and of course the plaintiffs continued to hold the property as trustees. This *e* arrangement for managing 36 Guildford Street was intended as a temporary arrangement pending resolution of the ownership of the property. That question remained unresolved at the testator's death, though since his death an arrangement has been made under which the ownership of 36 Guildford Street will pass to the Chertsey and Walton CLP subject to the payment of a sum of £4,000 to the North-West Surrey CLP in recognition of the part played by former members of the Chertsey CLP within the North-West *f* Surrey CLP in the acquisition and maintenance of 36 Guildford Street.

It is common ground that in these circumstances the testator when he spoke of 'the Labour Party Property Committee' must have intended to refer to the property committee formed to manage 36 Guildford Street, after dissolution of the Chertsey CLP and pending resolution of the question of ownership.

The question raised by the summons is whether the gift in the will of the testator's real *g* and personal estate is a valid gift, or is void for uncertainty or for perpetuity or otherwise; and if it is a valid gift who are the persons entitled to benefit thereunder.

Before turning to this question, it will be convenient to explain what are in my judgment the principles which govern the validity of a gift to an unincorporated association. A convenient starting point is a passage in the decision of Cross J in *Neville Estates Ltd v Madden*[1] which is often cited:

h   'The question of the construction and effect of gifts to or in trust for unincorporated associations was recently considered by the Privy Council in *Leahy v. Attorney-General for New South Wales*[2]. The position, as I understand it, is as follows. Such a gift may take effect in one or other of three quite different ways. In the first place, it may, on its true construction, be a gift to the members of the association at the relevant date as joint tenants, so that any member can sever his *j*   share and claim it whether or not he continues to be a member of the association. Secondly, it may be a gift to the existing members not as joint tenants, but subject

---

1   [1962] Ch 832 at 849, cf [1961] 3 All ER 769 at 778–779
2   [1959] 2 All ER 300, [1959] AC 457

to their respective contractual rights and liabilities towards one another as members of the association. In such a case a member cannot sever his share. It will accrue to *a* the other members on his death or resignation, even though such members include persons who became members after the gift took effect. If this is the effect of the gift, it will not be open to objection on the score of perpetuity or uncertainty unless there is something in its terms or circumstances or in the rules of the association which precludes the members at any given time from dividing the subject of the gift between them on the footing that they are solely entitled to it in equity. *b* Thirdly, the terms or circumstances of the gift or the rules of the association may show that the property in question is not to be at the disposal of the members for the time being, but is to be held in trust for or applied for the purposes of the association as a quasi-corporate entity. In this case the gift will fail unless the association is a charitable body. If the gift is of the second class, i.e., one which the members of the association for the time being are entitled to divide among themselves, then, even *c* if the objects of the association are in themselves charitable, the gift would not, I think, be a charitable gift.'

This statement, though it may require amplification in the light of subsequent authorities, is still as I see it an accurate statement of the law.

In a case in the first category, that is a gift which, on its true construction, is a gift to members of an association who take as joint tenants, any member being able to sever his *d* share, the association is used in effect as a convenient label or definition of the class which is intended to take; but, the class being ascertained, each member takes as joint tenant free from any contractual fetter. So, for instance, a testator might give a legacy or share of residue to a dining or social club of which he had been a member with the intention of giving to each of the other members an interest as joint tenant, capable of being severed, in the subject-matter of the gift. Cases within this category are relatively *e* uncommon. A gift to an association will be more frequently found to fall within the second category. There the gift is to members of an association, but the property is given as an accretion to the funds of the association so that the property becomes subject to the contract (normally evidenced by the rules of the association) which governs the rights of the members inter se. Each member is thus in a position to ensure that the subject-matter of the gift is applied in accordance with the rules of the association, in the same *f* way as any other funds of the association. This category is well illustrated by the decision of Brightman J in *Re Recher's Will Trusts*[1]. There a share of residue was given to 'The Anti-Vivisection Society 76 Victoria Street London S.W.1'. The society in fact ceased to exist, being amalgamated with another society, during the testatrix's lifetime. Brightman J first examined whether the gift would have been valid if the society had continued to exist. He said[2]: *g*

'A trust for non-charitable purposes, as distinct from a trust for individuals, is clearly void because there is no beneficiary. It does not, however, follow that persons cannot band themselves together as an association or society, pay subscriptions and validly devote their funds in pursuit of some lawful non-charitable purpose. An obvious example is a members' social club. But it is not essential that *h* the members should only intend to secure direct personal advantage to themselves. The association may be one in which personal advantages to the members are combined with the pursuit of some outside purpose. Or the association may be one which offers no personal benefit at all to the members, the funds of the association being applied exclusively to the pursuit of some outside purpose. Such an association of persons is bound, I would think, to have some sort of constitution; *j* ie the rights and the liabilities of the members of the association will inevitably depend on some form of contract inter se, usually evidenced by a set of rules. In the

1   [1971] 3 All ER 401, [1972] Ch 526
2   [1971] 3 All ER 401 at 407–408, [1972] Ch 526 at 538–539

present case it appears to me clear that the life members, the ordinary members and the associate members of the London and Provincial Society were bound together by a contract inter se. Any such member was entitled to the rights and subject to the liabilities defined by the rules. If the committee acted contrary to the rules, an individual member would be entitled to take proceedings in the courts to compel observance of the rules or to recover damages for any loss he had suffered as a result of the breach of contract. As and when a member paid his subscription to the association, he would be subjecting his money to the disposition and expenditure thereof laid down by the rules. That is to say, the member would be bound to permit, and entitled to require, the honorary trustees and other members of the society to deal with that subscription in accordance with the lawful directions of the committee. Those directions would include the expenditure of that subscription, as part of the general funds of the association, in furthering the objects of the association. The resultant situation, on analysis, is that the London and Provincial Society represented an organisation of individuals bound together by a contract under which their subscriptions became, as it were, mandated towards a certain type of expenditure as adumbrated in r 1. Just as the two parties to a bipartite bargain can vary or terminate their contract by mutual assent, so it must follow that the life members, ordinary members and associate members of the London and Provincial Society could, at any moment of time, by unanimous agreement (or by majority vote if the rules so prescribe), vary or terminate their multi-partite contract. There would be no limit to the type of variation or termination to which all might agree. There is no private trust or trust for charitable purposes or other trust to hinder the process. It follows that if all members agreed, they could decide to wind up the London and Provincial Society and divide the net assets among themselves beneficially. No one would have any locus standi to stop them so doing. The contract is the same as any other contract and concerns only those who are parties to it, that is to say, the members of the society. The funds of such an association may, of course, be derived not only from subscriptions of the contracting parties but also from donations from non-contracting parties and legacies from persons who have died. In the case of a donation which is not accompanied by any words which purport to impose a trust, it seems to me that the gift takes effect in favour of the existing members of the association as an accretion to the funds which are the subject-matter of the contract which such members have made inter se, and falls to be dealt with in precisely the same way as the funds which the members themselves have subscribed. So, in the case of a legacy. In the absence of words which purport to impose a trust, the legacy is a gift to the members beneficially, not as joint tenants or as tenants in common so as to entitle each member to an immediate distributive share, but as an accretion to the funds which are the subject-matter of the contract which the members have made inter se.'

Two points should be noted. First, as Brightman J pointed out, it is immaterial in considering whether a gift falls within this category that the members of an association have not joined together for a social and recreational purpose, or to secure some personal advantage, but in pursuit of some altruistic purpose. The motive which led the testator to make the gift may have been, indeed most frequently will have been, a desire to further that purpose. It may be said that in that sense the gift is made for the furtherance of the purpose. But the testator has chosen as the means of furthering the purpose to make a gift to an association formed for the pursuit of that purpose in the expectation that the subject-matter of the gift will be so used, without imposing or attempting to impose any trust or obligation on the members, or the trustees, or the committee of the association. Indeed, there are cases where the gift has been expressed as a gift for the purposes, or one of the purposes, of the association, and nonetheless has been held not to impose any purported trust. Two examples will suffice. In *Re Turkington*[1] the gift was

1   [1937] 4 All ER 501

expressed as a gift to the Staffordshire Masonic Lodge No 726 as a fund to build a suitable temple in Stafford. Luxmoore J construed the gift as a gift to the members of the lodge *a* and construed the words '. . . to build a suitable temple in Stafford' as, and I cite from his judgment[1], '. . . simply an indication by the testator of the purposes for which he would like the money to be expended, without imposing any trust on the beneficiary'.

In the recent decision of Oliver J in *Re Lipinski*[2] the gift was '. . . for the Hull Judeans (Maccabi) Association in memory of my late wife to be used solely in the work of constructing the new buildings for the association and/or improvements to the said *b* buildings'. Oliver J said[3]:

'If a valid gift may be made to an unincorporated body as a simple accretion to the funds which are the subject-matter of the contract which the members have made inter se, and *Neville Estates Ltd v Madden*[4] and *Re Recher's Will Trusts*[5] show that it may, I do not really see why such a gift, which specifies a purpose which is within the powers of the unincorporated body and of which the members of that body are *c* the beneficiaries, should fail. Why are not the beneficiaries able to enforce the trust or, indeed, in the exercise of their contractual rights, to terminate the trust for their own benefit? Where the donee body is itself the beneficiary of the prescribed purpose, there seems to me to be the strongest argument in common sense for saying that the gift should be construed as an absolute one within the second category, the more so where, if the purpose is carried out, the members can by *d* appropriate action vest the resulting property in themselves, for here the trustees and the beneficiaries are the same persons.'

As I read his judgment, Oliver J construed the gift as one under which the members of the association could have resolved to use the property for some other purpose, or, indeed, have divided it amongst themselves. He said[6]: *e*

'There is an additional factor. This is a case in which, under the constitution of the association, the members could, by the appropriate majority, alter their constitution so as to provide, if they wished, for the division of the association's assets amongst themselves.'

That leads to the second point. It must, as I see it, be a necessary characteristic of any *f* gift within the second category that the members of the association can by an appropriate majority (if the rules so provide), or acting unanimously if they do not, alter their rules so as to provide that the funds, or part of them, shall be applied for some new purpose, or even distributed amongst the members for their own benefit. For the validity of a gift within this category rests essentially on the fact that the testator has set out to further a purpose by making a gift to the members of an association formed for the furtherance *g* of that purpose in the expectation that, although the members at the date when the gift takes effect will be free, by a majority if the rules so provide or acting unanimously if they do not, to dispose of the fund in any way they may think fit, they and any future members of the association will not in fact do so but will employ the property in the furtherance of the purpose of the association and will honour any special condition attached to the gift. *h*

Turning to the third category, the testator may seek to further the purpose by giving a legacy to an association as a quasi-corporate entity, that is to present and future members indefinitely, or by purporting to impose a trust. In the former case the gift will fail for perpetuity, unless confined within an appropriate period; though if it is so

1   [1937] 4 All ER 501 at 504   *j*
2   [1977] 1 All ER 33, [1976] Ch 235
3   [1977] 1 All ER 33 at 43, [1976] Ch 235 at 246–247
4   [1961] 3 All ER 769, [1962] Ch 832
5   [1971] 3 All ER 401, [1972] Ch 526
6   [1977] 1 All ER 33 at 45, [1976] Ch 235 at 249

confined and if the members for the time being within the perpetuity period are free to
a alter the purposes for which the property is to be used and to distribute the income
amongst themselves it will not, as I see it, fail on any other ground. In the latter case, the
gift will fail on the ground that the court cannot compel the use of the property in
furtherance of a stated purpose unless, of course, the purpose is a charitable one. As Lord
Simonds said in *Leahy v Attorney-General for New South Wales*[1]:

b 'If the words "for the general purposes of the association" were held to import a
trust, the question would have to be asked, what is the trust and who are the
beneficiaries? A gift can be made to persons (including a corporation) but it cannot
be made to a purpose or to an object; so, also, a trust may be created for the benefit
of persons as cestuis que trustent, but not for a purpose or object unless the purpose
or object be charitable. For a purpose or object cannot sue, but, if it be charitable,
the Attorney-General can sue to enforce it. (On this point something will be added
c later.) It is, therefore, by disregarding the words "for the general purposes of the
association" (which are assumed not to be charitable purposes) and treating the gift
as an absolute gift to individuals that it can be sustained.'

There are two cases in which, if this analysis is correct, the reasons given for the
decision, though possibly not the decision itself, are not well-founded. First, there is a
decision of Eve J in *Re Drummond*[2], where the testator gave his residuary estate on trust
d for the Old Bradfordians' Club, London, and by a codicil directed that the moneys[3]—

'. . . should be utilized by the club for such purpose as the committee for the time
being might determine, the object and intent of the bequest being to benefit old
boys of the Bradford Grammar School residing in London or members of the club,
and to enable the committee, if possible, to acquire premises to be used as a club-
e house for the use of members, being old boys of Bradford Grammar School, with
power to the committee to make rules and regulations as to residence in or use of
the same, and further that it was the object of the bequest that the moneys should
be utilized in founding scholarships or otherwise in such manner as the committee
for the time being should think best in the interests of the club, or the school.'

f Eve J held that he could not say that the gift was a gift to the members of the club, but
he is reported as having said that[4]:

'There was, in his opinion, a trust, but there was abundant authority for holding
it was not such a trust as would render the legacy void as tending to a perpetuity: *In
re Clarke*[5]. The legacy was not subject to any trust which would prevent the
committee of the club from spending it in any manner they might decide for the
g benefit of the class intended. In his opinion, therefore, there was a valid gift to the
club for such purposes as the committee should determine for the benefit of the old
boys or members of the club.'

The second is *Re Price*[6], where Cohen J held that a gift of a share of residue to the
Anthroposophical Society of Great Britain '. . . to be used at the discretion of the chairman
and executive committee of the society for carrying on the teachings of the founder, Dr.
Rudolf Steiner' was a valid gift. There the only question considered by the judge was
whether the gift tended to a perpetuity, and having held that it did not he held the gift
was a valid gift, without considering whether it was not void as creating a trust for a non-
charitable purpose. There is to be observed that he said[7]: '. . . had it been necessary for

j 1 [1959] 2 All ER 300 at 307, [1959] AC 457 at 478–479
2 [1914] 2 Ch 90, [1914–15] All ER Rep 223
3 [1914] 2 Ch 90 at 91, [1914–15] All ER Rep 223 at 225
4 [1914] 2 Ch 90 at 97–98, cf [1914–15] All ER Rep 223 at 228
5 [1901] 2 Ch 110
6 [1943] 2 All ER 505, [1943] Ch 422
7 [1943] 2 All ER 505 at 511, [1943] Ch 422 at 435

me to deal with the point I should have been inclined to uphold the gift . . . as a valid charitable gift.'

I have also been referred to the recent decision of Goff J in *Re Denley's Trust Deed*[1]. There by cl 2 of a trust deed trustees were given powers of sale over land held by them and were directed to hold the land while unsold during a defined perpetuity period on trust, that[2]—

'. . . [(c)] The said land shall be maintained and used as and for the purpose of a recreation or sports ground primarily for the benefit of the employees of the company and secondarily for the benefit of such other person or persons (if any) as the trustees may allow to use the same with power for the trustees from time to time to make any alterations they shall think proper with regard to the laying out of the ground or the preparation of parts thereof for special purposes or otherwise provided always that the trustees shall not at any time be bound to execute any works in or upon the said land or in or to any buildings erections or works thereon or otherwise to incur any expenses in relation to the said land unless funds shall be provided by the employees of the company or other users of the said land and there shall for the time being be in hand a sum which shall in the opinion of the trustees be available and sufficient to answer the costs of the said works and to meet such expenses . . . [(d)] The trustees shall have power from time to time to make rules and regulations with regard to the times and manner of user of the said land and subject to such rules and regulations as shall from time to time be made by the trustees the employees of the company shall be entitled to the use and enjoyment of the said land . . . [(j)] If at any time the number of employees subscribing shall be less than seventy-five per centum of the total number of employees at any given time (subscribing at the rate of 2d. per week per man) or if the said land shall at any time cease to be required or to be used by the said employees as a sports ground or if the company should go into liquidation then the trustees shall notwithstanding anything that shall or may have been done or partly accomplished and subject to the repayment to the company of the aforesaid sum of £400 with interest thereon convey the said land to the General Hospital Cheltenham or as it shall direct.'

Goff J, having held that the words '. . . secondarily for the benefit of such other person or persons (if any) as the trustees may allow to use the same' conferred on the trustees a power operating in partial defeasance of a trust in favour of the employees, held that the trust deed created a valid trust for the benefit of the employees, the benefit being the right to use the land subject to and in accordance with the rules made by the trustees. That case on a proper analysis, in my judgment, falls altogether outside the categories of gifts to unincorporated associations and purpose trusts. I can see no distinction in principle between a trust to permit a class defined by reference to employment to use and enjoy land in accordance with rules to be made at the discretion of trustees on the one hand, and, on the other hand, a trust to distribute income at the discretion of trustees amongst a class, defined by reference to, for example, relationship to the settlor. In both cases the benefit to be taken by any member of the class is at the discretion of the trustees, but any member of the class can apply to the court to compel the trustees to administer the trust in accordance with its terms. As Goff J pointed out[3]:

'The same kind of problem is equally capable of arising in the case of a trust to permit a number of persons—for example, all the unmarried children of a testator or settlor—to use or occupy a house, or to have the use of certain chattels; nor can I assume that in such cases agreement between the parties concerned would be more likely, even if that be a sufficient distinction, yet no one would suggest, I fancy, that such a trust would be void.'

---

1   [1968] 3 All ER 65, [1969] 1 Ch 373
2   [1968] 3 All ER 65 at 67–68, [1969] 1 Ch 373 at 376
3   [1968] 3 All ER 65 at 72, [1969] 1 Ch 373 at 388

With those principles in mind, I return to the testator's will. Counsel, who appeared
a both for the first defendant (joined to represent the members of the Chertsey and
Walton CLP) and the second defendant (joined to represent all members of the national
Labour Party), argued, first, that the gift should be construed as a gift on the trusts of the
trust deed so that the residuary estate would be an accretion to and follow in all respects
the devolution of 36 Guildford Street or the proceeds of sale thereof. The intention of
the testator in making the gift, said counsel for the first and second defendants, may have
b been to provide a fund which could be used as to both capital and income for the
enlargement, improvement and maintenance of 36 Guildford Street. But the terms of
the proviso seem to me to place an insuperable obstacle in the way of this construction,
for it is clear from the proviso that the testator contemplated that 36 Guildford Street
might not continue to be the headquarters of the Chertsey and Walton CLP. The
residuary estate was, nonetheless, to be held '. . . by the Labour Party Property Committee
c for the benefit of the Chertsey Headquarters of the Chertsey and Walton Constituency
Labour Party provided the Headquarters remained within the geographical limits of the
former Chertsey Urban District Council'. There are two other considerations which also
weigh heavily against this construction. First, although the trustees of 36 Guildford
Street are appointed executors of the will, the gift is for '. . . the Labour Party Property
Committee'. If the testator had intended his residuary estate to be held on the trusts
d applicable to 36 Guildford Street, or the proceeds of sale thereof, one would have
expected the testator to have given it to the trustees of 36 Guildford Street. Secondly, it
is clear from the affidavit of the first defendant, to which I have referred, that the
question as to the ownership and the use of 36 Guildford Street, following the
reorganisation of constituency boundaries, remained unresolved until after the testator's
death.

e   Counsel's second submission for the first and second defendants was that the gift
should be construed by analogy with *Re Lipinski*[1] as a gift to the members of the Chertsey
and Walton CLP, with a superadded direction, not imposing any trust, that it should be
used for what may be broadly expressed as headquarters' purposes rather than general
purposes, which might include, for instance, the cost of an election campaign, but
subject, nevertheless, to a gift to the national Labour Party in defeasance of the prior gift
f in the event that at the testator's death the headquarters of the Chertsey and Walton CLP
should be outside the geographical limits of the old Chertsey Urban District Council. I
observe in passing that, construed as a gift over operating at any time, the gift over would
have been void under the rule against perpetuities, though the initial gift would then
stand free from the proviso.

     Before examining this submission, it is first necessary to look at the rules governing
g the Chertsey and Walton CLP. Those rules, as I have said, were in the form of model
rules prescribed by the national Labour Party. The provisions which appear to be
material are as follows. Clause I defines the Chertsey and Walton CLP as 'This Party'.
Clause II sets out the objects of the party. Sub-clause (1) sets out the familiar objects of
the national Labour Party under the heading 'National'; and under the heading
'Constituency' reads:

h   '(a) To unite the forces of Labour within the constituency and to ensure the
      establishment of, and to keep in active operation, Branches throughout the
      constituency, and to co-ordinate their activities; and (b) To secure the return of
      Labour Representatives to Parliament and Local Government bodies.'

Clause III deals with membership. It provides:

j   '(1) There shall be two classes of members namely:—(a) Affiliated Organisations
      (b) Individual Members
      '(2) Affiliated Organisations shall consist of: (a) Trade Unions (b) Co-operative

---

1   [1977] 1 All ER 33, [1976] Ch 235

Societies . . . (c) Branches of those Socialist Societies affiliated to the Labour Party nationally. (d) Branches of other Organisations which, in the opinion of the National Executive Committee, have interests consistent with those of other affiliated organisations and which are affiliated to the Labour Party nationally. (e) The Trades Council. (f) Any other organisation or branch thereof which the National Executive Committee deems eligible for affiliation.

'(3) Individual Members shall be British subjects or citizens of Eire, or other persons resident in Great Britain for more than one year, who are not less than fifteen years of age and who subscribe to the conditions of membership.'

Clause IV prescribes the conditions of membership:

'(1) Each affiliated organisation must:—(a) Accept the programme, principles and policy of the Labour Party. (b) Agree to conform to the Constitution and Standing Orders of the Labour Party and the Rules of this Party.'

Each individual member must accept the same obligation and, if eligible, be a member of a trades union affiliated to the TUC.

Clause IX deals with management. By sub-cl (1) the management is put into the hands of a general committee of delegates elected by affiliated organisations, branches of individual members, women's sections and young socialist branches. Sub-clause (2) sets out the basis of representation. Sub-clauses (3) and (4) I must read in full:

'(3) The General Committee shall accept and make such changes in the Rules of this Party as may be agreed to by the Annual Party Conference or made by the National Executive Committee in accordance with the powers conferred upon it under Clause VIII (j) of the Party Constitution, and shall, further, subject to the approval in writing of the National Executive Committee, have power itself to make alterations, amendments or deletions in these Rules, provided that such changes do not contravene their spirit or intention as accepted by Annual Party Conferences or alter the objects, basis or conditions of affiliated and individual membership, or vary the procedure for the selection of Parliamentary Candidates (otherwise than is provided in the Rules of this Party) or effect a change in the relationship of Constituency Labour Parties with the Labour Party.

'(4) The General Committee shall, subject to the approval in writing of the National Executive Committee, have power either itself or to authorise the Executive Committee of this Party on its behalf (a) to buy freehold or leasehold land and to erect buildings thereon and/or freehold or leasehold premises and to borrow money on mortgage or otherwise on the security thereof; (b) to appoint trustees to hold any land and property so acquired for and on behalf of this Party; and (c) to define the powers of any trustees so appointed and to lay down the manner in which such power shall be exercised.'

Clause VIII(2)(j) of the Labour Party constitution reads as follows:

'To sanction, where local circumstances render it necessary, modifications in the rules laid down by the Annual Party Conference for the various classes of Party Organisations, provided that such modifications comply with the spirit and intention of the Annual Party Conference and do not alter the objects, basis or conditions of affiliated and individual membership, vary the procedure for the selection of Parliamentary Candidates (except as provided in the rules) or effect a change in the relationship of Constituency Labour Parties with the Labour Party.'

Thus, under cl IX(3) of the Chertsey and Walton CLP rules, the general committee are bound to change the rules to accord with changes '. . . agreed to by the Annual Party Conference'. The words I cite, '. . . as may be agreed to by the Annual Party Conference', must I think refer to the approval by the annual party conference of proposals made by

the National Executive Committee of the national Labour Party ('the NEC') under cl VIII
a (2)(*g*) of the party constitution, which reads as follows:

'(*g*) To propose to the Annual Party Conference such amendments to the
Constitution, Rules and Standing Orders as may be deemed desirable and to submit
to the Annual Party Conference or to any Special Party Conference, called in
accordance with the Standing Orders, such resolutions and declarations affecting the
Programme, Principles and Policy of the Party as in its view may be necessitated by
b political circumstances.'

Secondly, the general committee of the CLP must make any change prescribed by the
NEC in accordance with the powers conferred by cl VIII(2)(*j*) of the party constitution.
Lastly, the general committee of the CLP have power to change the rules of the CLP, but
only with the approval of the NEC, and provided that the changes do not contravene the
c spirit or intention of the annual party conference or alter the objects, basis or conditions
of affiliated and individual membership, or vary the procedure for the selection of
parliamentary candidates (otherwise than is provided in the rules of the party) or effect
a change in the relationship of constituency Labour parties with the national Labour
Party.

Clause XI of the Chertsey and Walton CLP rules is headed 'Affiliation Fees and
d Members' Contributions'. Under sub-cl (1): 'The affiliation fee payable by this Party to
the national Labour Party shall be at such rate as may be laid down by the Annual Party
Conference from time to time.' Affiliation fees and contributions to the CLP are payable
at the rate prescribed by sub-cl (2). In the case of individual members fees are payable to
the appropriate officer as determined by the CLP. The rules contain no provision as to
what is to happen to any property purchased under cl IX(4), or to any surplus of
e affiliation fees and members' fees in the event of the dissolution of the party. Subject to
any amendment to the rules approved by the annual party conference or made by the
NEC, or by the general committee of the CLP and approved by the NEC, such property
or moneys would prima facie be held in the resulting trust for the persons by whom they
were contributed.

Reading the gift in the will in the light of the rules governing the Chertsey and
f Walton CLP, it is in my judgment impossible to construe the gift as a gift made to the
members of the Chertsey and Walton CLP at the date of the testator's death with the
intention that it should belong to them as a collection of individuals, though in the
expectation that they and any other members subsequently admitted would ensure that
it was in fact used for what in broad terms has been labelled 'headquarters' purposes' of
the Chertsey and Walton CLP.

g I base this conclusion on two grounds. First, the members of the Chertsey and Walton
CLP do not control the property, given by subscription or otherwise, to the CLP. The
rules which govern the CLP are capable of being altered by an outside body which could
direct an alteration under which the general committee of the CLP would be bound to
transfer any property for the time being held for the benefit of the CLP to the national
Labour Party for national purposes. The members of the Chertsey and Walton CLP
h could not alter the rules so as to make the property bequeathed by the testator applicable
for some purpose other than that provided by the rules; nor could they direct that
property to be divided amongst themselves beneficially.

Brightman J observed in *Re Recher's Will Trusts*[1] that: 'It would astonish a layman to
be told there was a difficulty in his giving a legacy to an unincorporated non-charitable
society which he had or could have supported without trouble during his lifetime.' The
j answer to this apparent paradox is, it seems to me, that subscriptions by members of the
Chertsey and Walton CLP must be taken as made on terms that they will be applied by
the general committee in accordance with the rules for the time being, including any

---

1   [1971] 3 All ER 401 at 405, [1972] Ch 526 at 536

modifications imposed by the annual party conference or the NEC. In the event of the dissolution of the Chertsey and Walton CLP any remaining fund representing subscriptions would (as the rules now stand) be held on a resulting trust for the original subscribers. Thus although the members of the CLP may not be able themselves to alter the purposes for which a fund representing subscriptions is to be used or to alter the rules so as to make such a fund divisible amongst themselves the ultimate proprietary right of the original subscribers remains. There is, therefore, no perpetuity and no non-charitable purpose trust. But if that analysis of the terms on which subscriptions are held is correct, it is fatal to the argument that the gift in the testator's will should be construed as a gift to the members of the Chertsey and Walton CLP at the testator's death, subject to a direction not amounting to a trust that it be used for headquarters' purposes. Equally it is in my judgment impossible, in particular having regard to the gift over to the national Labour Party, to read the gift as a gift to the members of the national Labour Party at the testator's death, with a direction not amounting to a trust, that the national party permit it to be used by the Chertsey and Walton CLP for headquarters' purposes.

That first ground is of itself conclusive, but there is another ground which reinforces this conclusion. The gift is not in terms a gift to the Chertsey and Walton CLP, but to the Labour Party Property Committee, who are to hold the property for the benefit of, that is in trust for, the Chertsey headquarters of the Chertsey and Walton CLP. The fact that a gift is a gift to trustees and not in terms to an unincorporated association militates against construing it as a gift to the members of the association at the date when the gift takes effect, and against construing the words indicating the purposes for which the property is to be used as expressing the testator's intention or motive in making the gift and not as imposing any trust. This was, indeed, one of the considerations which led the Privy Council in *Leahy's* case[1] to hold that the gift '. . . upon trust for such Order of Nuns of the Catholic Church or the Christian Brothers as my Executors and Trustees should select' would, apart from the Australian equivalent of the Charitable Trusts (Validation) Act 1954, have been invalid.

I am, therefore, compelled to the conclusion that the gift of the testator's estate fails, and that his estate accordingly devolves as on intestacy. I will make the usual order that the costs of the plaintiffs as trustees, and the defendants on a common fund basis, be taxed and paid out of the estate in due course of administration.

Declaration accordingly.

Solicitors: *Cripps, Harries, Willis & Carter*, agents for *Clive Fisher & Co*, Addlestone (for the plaintiffs); *Milners, Curry & Gaskell* (for the first and second defendants); *Penman, Johnson & Ewins*, Watford (for the third defendant).

Jacqueline Metcalfe   Barrister.

---

1   [1959] 2 All ER 300, [1959] AC 457

Re Phelps (deceased)
Wells v Phelps and others

COURT OF APPEAL, CIVIL DIVISION
BUCKLEY, BRIDGE AND TEMPLEMAN LJJ
27th, 28th JUNE 1979

Intestacy – Appropriation by personal representatives – Surviving spouse – Matrimonial home – Right of surviving spouse to require appropriation of matrimonial home in or towards satisfaction of spouse's interest in intestate's estate – In or towards satisfaction of interest – Value of home greater than surviving spouse's absolute interest in estate – Whether right to require appropriation 'in or towards satisfaction of' interest giving right to require appropriation of home of greater value than interest – Administration of Estates Act 1925, s 41 – Intestates' Estates Act 1952, Sch 2, paras 1(1), 5(2).

A husband died intestate leaving a widow. At the date of his death they were both living in the house which was their matrimonial home. The house formed part of the deceased's residuary estate but its value was greater than that of the widow's absolute interest in the estate. The widow wanted the house transferred to her and was willing to pay the difference. Accordingly, she gave notice to the deceased's personal representatives requiring them, by the exercise of the power of appropriation conferred on them by s 41[a] of the Administration of Estates Act 1925, to appropriate the house to her in or towards satisfaction of her interest in the estate, pursuant to para 1(1)[b] of Sch 2 to the Intestates' Estates Act 1952. The question arose whether she could 'require' them to do so under para 1(1) of Sch 2. The judge[c] held that she could not do so, on the grounds that a surviving spouse only had the right under para 1(1) to require appropriation of the matrimonial home 'in or towards satisfaction of any absolute interest' if the value of his or her absolute interest in the intestate spouse's estate was equal to or exceeded the value of the matrimonial home, since 'in or towards satisfaction of' did not contemplate the satisfaction being greater in value than the interest. The widow appealed.

Held – The appeal would be allowed because para 1(1) of Sch 2 to the 1952 Act could not be construed in isolation but had to be read in conjunction with para 5(2)[d] of Sch 2 which extended the meaning of 'power of appropriation' in s 41 of the 1925 Act to include a transaction which was partly appropriation and partly sale. By so doing it widened the ambit of para 1(1) of Sch 2 and enabled a surviving spouse to require appropriation of the matrimonial home partly in satisfaction of his or her interest in the intestate spouse's estate and partly in return for the payment of money. It followed that the widow's notice to the deceased's personal representatives constituted a valid exercise of the right conferred on her by para 1(1) of Sch 2 (see p 375 f to p 376 a f and h to p 377 c e f, post).

Decision of Foster J [1978] 3 All ER 395 reversed.

Notes
For the right to require appropriation of the matrimonial home, see 17 Halsbury's Laws (4th Edn) para 1378.

For the Administration of Estates Act 1925, s 41, see 13 Halsbury's Statutes (3rd Edn) 66.

For the Intestates' Estates Act 1952, Sch 2, paras 1, 5, see ibid 130, 134.

---

a   Section 41, so far as material, is set out at p 374 g, post
b   Paragraph 1(1), so far as material, is set out at p 374 j to p 375 a, post
c   [1978] 3 All ER 395
d   Paragraph 5(2) is set out at p 375 e, post

Appeal

On 10th February 1971 Walter Murray Phelps ('the deceased') died intestate. On 1st *a*
March 1972 letters of administration were granted to the plaintiff, John Douglas Wells,
the first defendant, Amy Anne Phelps, the deceased's widow ('the widow'), and the
second defendant, Madeleine Claire Phelps, one of the deceased's daughters. The third
defendant, Jennifer Caroline Konopka, was another daughter of the deceased. On 15th
July 1974 the Official Solicitor was appointed judicial trustee of the estate. By an
amended summons, dated 1st November 1977, the Official Solicitor applied to the court *b*
for the determination, inter alia, of the question whether a notice dated 3rd June 1972
whereby the widow required the dwelling-house known as Broadway, Kenilworth Road,
Blackdown, Leamington Spa, to be appropriated in or towards satisfaction of her interests
in the deceased's estate constituted a valid exercise of the right conferred on her by s 5 of,
and para 1 of Sch 2 to, the Intestates' Estates Act 1952. On 28th April 1978 Foster J[1]
answered that question in the negative. The widow appealed. The respondents to the *c*
appeal were the second and third defendants.

Leolin Price QC and *Michael Hart* for the widow.
George Rink QC and *Peter Rawson* for the respondents.
R W Ham for the Official Solicitor.
The plaintiff did not appear.
d

TEMPLEMAN LJ delivered the first judgment at the invitation of Buckley LJ. This
is an appeal from a judgment of Foster J[1] and raises a short question of construction on
the Intestates' Estates Act 1952. The question is whether a surviving spouse of an
intestate can require the matrimonial home, which is more valuable than the absolute
interest of the spouse in the estate, to be appropriated partly in satisfaction of that interest
and partly in return for payment of the difference in value between the interest and the *e*
matrimonial home.

The intestate died on 10th February 1971. His widow is entitled to £8,750 under the
intestacy. The widow gave notice on 3rd June 1972 requiring appropriation of the
matrimonial home which was then, and now is, worth more than £8,750. If it is worth,
for example £12,000 on the relevant date, the widow requires the personal representative
to convey the house to her, partly in satisfaction of her interest, worth £8,750, in the *f*
estate, and partly in return for £3,250 which she will pay in cash.

By s 41(1) of the Administration of Estates Act 1925 which, by s 41(9) applies whether
the deceased died intestate or not, personal representatives were given a power of
appropriation 'in or towards satisfaction of any legacy bequeathed by the deceased, or of
any other interest or share in his property . . . as to the personal representative may seem
just and reasonable'. Thus the personal representative could make an appropriation in *g*
favour of a beneficiary, though only as the section subsequently provides, with his
consent. The personal representative could also in exercise of the statutory power of sale
conferred on him by s 33 of the Administration of Estates Act 1925, sell any property to
a beneficiary and, with his consent, set off against the purchase price any capital sum to
which the beneficiary was entitled from the estate. The beneficiary could not, however,
require the personal representative to exercise either the power of appropriation, or the *h*
power of sale, in his favour.

By s 5 of the Intestates' Estates Act 1952, which is entitled 'Rights of surviving spouse
as respects the matrimonial home', it was provided that Sch 2 to the Act shall 'have effect
for enabling the surviving husband or wife of a person dying intestate . . . to acquire the
matrimonial home'. Schedule 2 is also entitled 'Rights of surviving spouse as respects the
matrimonial home'. Paragraph 1(1) of Sch 2, so far as material, provides: *j*

> 'Subject to the provisions of this Schedule, where the residuary estate of the
> intestate comprises an interest in a dwelling-house in which the surviving husband

or wife was resident at the time of the intestate's death, the surviving husband or wife may require the personal representative, in exercise of the power conferred by section forty-one of [the 1925 Act] ... to appropriate the said interest in the dwelling-house in or towards satisfaction of any absolute interest of the surviving husband or wife in the real and personal estate of the intestate.'

In the present case it is conceded that the widow has an absolute interest in the estate amounting to £8,750 and that the widow could, and did, require the personal representatives to exercise the power of appropriation conferred on them by s 41 of the 1925 Act in or towards satisfaction of her interest. It is argued, and Foster J accepted, that a house which is worth £12,000 cannot be appropriated in or towards satisfaction of an absolute interest worth £8,750. The words 'in or towards satisfaction' are only appropriate when the value of the interest is equal to, or exceeds, the value of the dwelling-house. Those words are not apt to cover the case where the interest would be more than satisfied by the appropriation.

If the matter had rested solely on para 1(1) of Sch 2, I would have agreed with the learned judge, because para 1(1) only enables the widow to require the personal representatives to exercise their statutory power of appropriation and does not entitle her to require them to exercise a power which is partly an appropriation power and partly a sale power. The decision of the learned judge, however, gives no effect to para 5(2) of Sch 2 which, it seems to me, could only have been designed to meet, and does in fact meet, the present case. By para 5(2):

'The power of appropriation under section forty-one of [the 1925 Act] shall include power to appropriate an interest in a dwelling-house in which the surviving husband or wife was resident at the time of the intestate's death partly in satisfaction of an interest of the surviving husband or wife in the real and personal estate of the intestate and partly in return for a payment of money by the surviving husband or wife to the personal representative.'

The effect of para 5(2) is that for the purposes of Sch 2 a transaction which in essence is partly appropriation and partly sale becomes an appropriation, and Sch 2 must be read as if s 41 of the 1925 Act included this new hybrid power of appropriation. When a widow, pursuant to para 1(1) of Sch 2, requires the personal representatives to appropriate, in exercise of the power conferred by s 41, she is requiring them to exercise that power as enlarged by para 5(2). Where the dwelling-house and the widow's interests are equal in value, the personal representatives are required to appropriate in satisfaction of the widow's interest; where the dwelling-house is worth less than the widow's interest, they are required to appropriate towards satisfaction of the widow's interest; and where the dwelling-house is worth more than the widow's interest they are required to appropriate, in the words of para 5(2) 'partly in satisfaction' of the interest 'and partly in return for a payment of money'.

Counsel for the respondents, who appeared to support the judgment in the court below, submitted that para 5(2) conferred an additional power on the personal representatives, but did not enable the widow to require the personal representatives to exercise that power, because she could still only require them to appropriate 'in or towards' satisfaction of her interest in the estate, and those words still mean that she could not require them to make an appropriation that was neither 'in' nor 'towards' satisfaction, but partly in satisfaction and partly in return for a payment.

But the object of Sch 2 is to confer specified rights on the widow and such powers on the personal representatives as are necessary to enable them to give effect to any exercise by the widow of her rights. For the purposes of Sch 2 there was no point in conferring a power on the personal representatives unless the widow could require them to exercise that power. It is significant that para 5(2) does not merely confer a new power on the personal representatives; it directs that the power of appropriation under s 41 shall include the new power. In my judgment the object of that wording is to ensure that

when, pursuant to para 1(1) the widow requires the personal representatives to exercise
the power conferred by s 41, that requirement will include a duty to exercise where *a*
appropriate that power as extended by para 5(2).

With all respect to counsel for the respondents, the object of para 5(2) cannot have
been to confer a new power on the personal representatives without enabling the widow
to require them to exercise that power if necessary, because the personal representatives
already possess, under s 41, which confers a power of appropriation, and under s 33
which confers a power of sale, jurisdiction to effect a transaction which falls within para *b*
5(2). For example, in the present case if the widow's interest in the estate is worth
£8,750 and the house is worth £12,000, the personal representatives, without recourse
to para 5(2) could sell the house to the widow for £12,000 and, with her consent, set off
the sum of £8,750. They would thus, in the words of para 5(2), be appropriating the
dwelling-house partly in satisfaction of an interest of the widow in the estate of the
intestate, and partly in return for the payment of a sum of money, namely £3,250, by *c*
the widow.

The ingenuity of counsel for the respondents failed to persuade me that para 5(2)
serves any useful purpose at all if the widow cannot require the personal representatives
to exercise the new power which is included by that sub-paragraph in s 41 of the
Administration of Estates Act 1925.

Counsel for the respondents attempted to base an argument on para 5(1) which, for the *d*
purposes of Sch 2, partly abrogates the rule that a trustee cannot purchase trust property,
and also an argument on the fact that para 1(1) refers to an 'absolute interest' in the estate,
whereas para 5(2) refers to 'an interest' in the estate. With all respect to counsel for the
respondents, I am quite unable to discern any relevant relationship between para 5(1) and
(2), or any significant difference between para 1(1) and para 5(2) for the present
purposes. In short, counsel was unable to persuade me that para 5(2) is not wholly *e*
unnecessary unless it does enable the widow to require the personal representatives to
appropriate the dwelling-house to her if the circumstances so require, partly in
satisfaction of her interest in the estate of the intestate and partly in return for a payment
of money.

For the reasons which I have endeavoured to explain, I have reached the conclusion
that para 5(2) was intended to apply to the present circumstances and does apply to the *f*
present circumstances, and I would accordingly allow the appeal.

BRIDGE LJ. I was at first blush much attracted by the direct and simple approach of
the learned judge to the question of construction in this case. Read by itself, the
language of para 1(1) of Sch 2 to the Intestates' Estates Act 1952 clearly has the limited *g*
meaning that he ascribed to it. For some time I could see no good reason why any
extended meaning should be read into it by implication. But my eyes were opened by
the question raised by Templeman LJ in the course of argument as to the effect of para
5(2). If read independently of para 1(1), what does para 5(2) in practice empower a
personal representative to do which he could not already do by agreement with the
surviving spouse without the aid of that provision? To that question counsel for the *h*
respondents, was to my mind unable to provide any satisfactory answer.

It must follow, I think, that the only sensible purpose which can be ascribed to para
5(2) is to extend by implication the ambit of para 1(1) to enable the surviving spouse to
require appropriation of the matrimonial home partly in satisfaction of his or her
interest in the deceased spouse's estate and partly in return for a payment of money.

As counsel for the widow pointed out in reply, the implication is in a measure *j*
supported by the language of para 5(2), by which the extended power of appropriation
is to be 'included' in the power of appropriation under s 41 of the Administration of
Estates Act 1925, which is itself a power to appropriate 'in or towards the satisfaction of'
an interest.

Moreover, this construction seems more consonant with s 5 of the 1952 Act, which *a* declares the effect of Sch 2 to be for enabling the surviving spouse to acquire the matrimonial home.

At the end of the day, I am still left wondering why the draftsman did not spell out his purpose in plain language, as he could so easily have done by the addition of a very few words, instead of leaving it to be laboriously unearthed by the process of necessary implication. But for the reasons I have attempted to indicate, and for those given by Templeman LJ, I am fully persuaded that the implication is a necessary one, and
b accordingly I also would allow the appeal.

BUCKLEY LJ. I entirely agree with the judgment delivered by Templeman LJ. I only put the matter shortly in my own words out of respect for the learned judge, from whom we are differing.

Schedule 2 to the Intestates' Estates Act 1952 is enacted for the purpose of enabling the
c surviving husband or wife to acquire the matrimonial home (see s 5 of the Act); that is to say, for the purpose of enabling the husband or wife to achieve that end at his or her own option. This is, I think, emphasised by the fact that the marginal note to the section, and the cross-heading to the schedule both refer to 'rights of surviving spouse as respects the matrimonial home'. This applies to all the provisions of the schedule, so para 5(2) must, in my view, be read in a sense, and given an effect, which will contribute to that
d result. Merely extending existing powers of appropriation vested in personal representatives without enabling the husband or wife to require the exercise of those powers would not achieve this.

Moreover, as has been pointed out, the personal representatives could in any case achieve the objective of para 5(2) of Sch 2 by an exercise, not of their powers of appropriation under the Administration of Estates Act 1925, but of their powers of sale
e under s 33 of that Act. So, if para 5(2) were merely to have the effect of enlarging the personal representatives' powers of appropriation it would, in substance, achieve nothing.

Paragraph 5(2) has in my opinion the effect of widening the statutory power of appropriation conferred by s 41 of the 1925 Act for the purposes of para 1(1) of Sch 2, so that the last mentioned sub-paragraph must be read and given effect as referring to the s 41 powers as so enlarged.

f For the reasons so shortly expressed by myself and expressed in more detail by Templeman LJ in the judgment which he has delivered, I agree that this appeal succeeds.

Appeal allowed. Leave to appeal to the House of Lords refused.

Solicitors: *Bower, Cotton & Bower* (for the widow); *Farrer & Co* (for the first respondent);
g *Alexander Chart & Partners* (for the second respondent); *Official Solicitor.*

J H Fazan Esq   Barrister.

Montedison SpA v Icroma SpA
The Caspian Sea

a

QUEEN'S BENCH DIVISION
DONALDSON J
14th, 21st JUNE 1979

b

Shipping – Freight – Claim for freight – Freight payable on delivery – Cargo contaminated on delivery – Shipment of Bachaquero Crude oil – Special quality of Bachaquero crude that free from paraffin – Oil contaminated with paraffin on discharge – Whether 'the cargo' delivered – Whether contamination making description 'Bachaquero Crude' commercially inapplicable or merely qualifying that description.

c

The charterers chartered a vessel to carry a cargo of crude oil from Venezuela to Genoa. The terms of the charterparty provided that freight was payable on 'delivery of the cargo'. The oil shipped was Bachaquero Crude which had the special quality of being free from paraffin and therefore suitable for processing into high quality lubricating oils. The charterers took delivery of the oil at the port of discharge and consigned it to a refinery for processing. They alleged that on discharge the oil contained paraffin left *d* over from the residue of a previous oil cargo, and that the oil was unusable for processing into high quality lubricants. In arbitration proceedings the shipowners claimed payment of full freight. The charterers contended that 'the cargo' had not been delivered as required by the charterparty because the oil delivered was not merchantable as Bachaquero Crude, or alternatively was not identical commercially with the oil loaded, and therefore the shipowners were not entitled to payment. The shipowners contended *e* that a shipowner was entitled to freight unless the goods delivered were a total or constructive loss in insurance terms and worthless to the consignee, and that if a consignee took delivery of the goods he was obliged to pay freight whatever the state of the goods. The arbitrators stated their award in the form of a consultative case.

Held – (i) Where goods had been damaged or contaminated during shipment the test *f* whether there had been 'delivery of the cargo' so as to entitle the shipowner to payment of freight was whether on discharge an honest merchant would be forced to qualify the description which applied to the goods when shipped to such an extent that the description no longer applied, or whether he would merely qualify the cargo as goods of the description shipped but contaminated or damaged. If the qualification destroyed the description when shipped, the cargo had not been delivered and the shipowner was not *g* entitled to freight. The concept in insurance law of constructive total loss of goods was irrelevant. Thus it followed that the mere fact that on delivery the oil was not identical commercially with the oil loaded, or was not of merchantable quality within s 62(1A) of the Sale of Goods Act 1893, did not necessarily deprive the shipowners of the right to freight, nor did the fact that the charterers had taken delivery of the oil necessarily entitle the shipowners to be paid freight (see p 383 *g* to *j* and p 384 *a b*, post). *h*

(ii) The shipowners were entitled to freight if the oil delivered could, in commercial terms, be described as 'Bachaquero Crude'. In deciding that question the arbitrators would have to decide whether the description 'Bachaquero Crude' meant a paraffin-free crude oil (in which case the shipowners were not entitled to freight) or a crude oil from the Bachaquero region which in its natural state contained no paraffin (in which case the contamination of the oil by paraffin during shipment did not necessarily disentitle the *j* shipowners to freight). If they decided that it was the latter they had further to decide whether the oil delivered was merely contaminated Bachaquero Crude or whether the degree of contamination was such that the oil had ceased even to be that (in which case the shipowners were again not entitled to freight). The award would therefore be remitted to the arbitrators to make the appropriate further award (see p 384 *a* and *d* to *f*, post).

Dictum of Lord Esher MR in *Asfar & Co v Blundell* [1896] 1 QB at 127–128 applied.

a **Notes**

For the payment of freight, see 35 Halsbury's Laws (3rd Edn) 490–494, paras 705–710, and for cases on payment of freight where the cargo is delivered damaged, see 41 Digest (Repl) 571–572, 3502–3514.

Cases referred to in judgment

b *Aries Tanker Corpn v Total Transport Ltd, The Aries* [1977] 1 All ER 398, [1977] 1 WLR 185, [1977] 1 Lloyd's Rep 334, HL.

Asfar & Co v Blundell [1896] 1 QB 123, 65 LJQB 138, 73 LT 648, 8 Asp MLC 106, 1 Com Cas 185, CA, 41 Digest (Repl) 572, 3510.

Dakin v Oxley (1864) 15 CBNS 646, 13 LJCP 115, 10 LT 268, 10 Jur NS 655, 2 Mar LC 6, 143 ER 938, 41 Digest (Repl) 572, 3505.

c *Dickson v Buchanan* (1876) 13 Sc LR 401, 41 Digest (Repl) 572, *757.

Duthie v Hilton (1868) LR 4 CP 138, 38 LJCP 93, 19 LT 285, 3 Mar LC 166, 41 Digest (Repl) 561, 3388.

Garrett v Melhuish (1858) 33 LTOS 25, 4 Jur NS 943, 41 Digest (Repl) 572, 3508.

Shields v Davis (1815) 6 Taunt 65, 128 ER 957 41 Digest (Repl) 548, 3267.

d **Consultative case**

This was an award in the form of a consultative case stated pursuant to s 21 of the Arbitration Act 1950. By a voyage charterparty in the Tank Vessel form dated 21st November 1974, the claimants, Montedison SpA ('the owners'), chartered the Caspian Sea to the respondents, Icroma SpA ('the charterers'), for a voyage from Punta Cardon to Genoa, on terms and conditions as set out therein. Clause 18 of the charterparty *e* provided that any dispute arising thereunder should be settled by arbitration in London, each party appointing an arbitrator with power to the arbitrators to appoint a third arbitrator. Pursuant to s 9(1) of the Arbitration Act 1950 the reference to arbitration set out in cl 18 had effect as if it provided for the appointment of an umpire and not for the appointment of a third arbitrator. Disputes arose between the parties as a consequence of which the owners appointed Mr Donald Davies and the charterers appointed Mr *f* Cedric Barclay as arbitrators on their behalf respectively. The matters referred to their adjudication were: (1) A claim by the owners for freight in the sum of 58,046,030 Italian lira. (2) A counterclaim by the charterers for contamination of cargo in the sum of 172,380,294 Italian lira. The owners requested that a speedy award be made in respect of their claim for freight but this was opposed by the charterers who contended that the goods were unmerchantable on delivery thus denying the owners any immediate right *g* to freight. In the event, it was decided that the most expedient way of dealing with the matters in dispute was to obtain the court's ruling, by way of a consultative case, on a preliminary point as to whether or not the owners were entitled to payment of freight on the assumption that the goods were delivered in an unmerchantable state, leaving over an award in respect of the matters in dispute until the result of the court's decision. The relevant clauses of the charterparty, so far as material, read:

h

'1. That the vessel being tight, staunch, and strong, and in every way fitted for the voyage, and to be maintained in such condition during the voyage, perils of the sea excepted, shall, with all convenient despatch, sail and proceed to Punta Cardon as vessel completing account Dellepiane, loading ports rotation at Owners' option or so near thereunto as she may safely get (always afloat), and there load from the factors of the said Charterers a part cargo of 20,000 Tons five percent more or less in *j* Owners' option, one grade Crude Oil and/or Dirty Petroleum Products in bulk . . . and being so loaded shall therewith proceed (as ordered on signing Bills of Lading) direct to Genoa or so near thereunto as she may safely get (always afloat), and deliver the same on being paid Freight in accordance with the rate provided for by Worldscale 117.5 (one hundred and seventeen and one half) per ton of twenty cwts of Oil intake quantity.

'2. The Freight to be payable upon delivery of the Cargo in Cash, without discount, in Italian Lira at the rate of exchange Lira/Dollar ruling on the day of signing the Bills of Lading . . .

'13. This Contract shall be governed by the Laws of the flag of the vessel carrying the goods . . .

'16. The Captain is bound to keep the tanks, pipes and pumps of the Vessel always clean, but at the expense of the Charterers if they load in the tanks Oils of different nature to those previously shipped. The Vessel is not to be responsible for any consequences arising through Charterers shipping different kinds of oil. The Vessel is not to be accountable for leakage . . .

'23. Owners guarantee Vessel's last cargo consisted of Fuel Oil . . .

'25. Tank cleaning is to be effected on the reasonable basis of cargo quality to be loaded. Charterers advise that cargoes to be loaded are free of paraffins.'

The arbitrators found the following facts. The vessel proceeded to Punta Cardon and there loaded a quantity of 'Bachaquero Crude'. A bill of lading was issued for a quantity of 16,439·31 long tons net Bachaquero Crude, dated 8th December 1974. Being so loaded, the vessel proceeded via Puerto La Cruz to Genoa, where she arrived on or about 25th December 1974. The charterers there took delivery of the cargo discharged and consigned it to the Iplom refinery with whom they had a processing agreement. The owners issued a freight invoice based on the bill of lading quantity in the sum of 58,046,030 Italian lira, dated 2nd January 1975. The Caspian Sea was a British flag vessel, registered in Bermuda. The charterers alleged that the cargo which was delivered in Genoa was contaminated by the presence of paraffinic products by reason of the fact that residues of a previous cargo of low sulphur fuel oil had remained in the vessel's tanks before loading the charterers' cargo at Punta Cardon. They contended that the cargo which was delivered was unmerchantable as Bachaquero Crude or alternatively, was not identical commercially with the cargo loaded and that accordingly, no freight was payable under the charterparty. They further alleged that Bachaquero Crude was unusual in that it contained no paraffin and was therefore highly suitable for production of high quality/high value lubricating oils; that as a result of the contamination with paraffin products the oil could not be so used and they had a counterclaim for 172,380,294 Italian lira. The owners did not accept the charterers' arguments as to the cause, extent or effect of the alleged contamination. However, the owners submitted that even if the cargo delivered was unmerchantable as Bachaquero Crude or alternatively, not commercially identical with the cargo loaded, they would nevertheless be entitled to payment of freight in full without deduction, they having performed the carriage and having delivered the cargo. For the purposes of the consultative case, it was therefore to be assumed that the cargo which was delivered was in the condition alleged by the charterers. The question of law for the decision of the court was: 'Whether the owners are entitled to payment of freight in full without deductions on the assumption that the goods carried were delivered in a state which was unmerchantable as Bachaquero Crude and/or was not identical commercially with the cargo loaded.'

Jonathan Sumption for the owners.
Bernard Rix for the charterers.

Cur adv vult

21st June. **DONALDSON J** read the following judgment: The Caspian Sea was chartered to carry a part cargo of crude oil and/or dirty petroleum products from Punta Cardon to Genoa. Freight was payable 'upon delivery of the cargo'. The oil in fact shipped was 'Bachaquero Crude', a Venezuelan crude whose special value lies in the fact that it is free of paraffin and is therefore suitable for the production of lubricating oils of high quality and value. The charterers took delivery of the oil on discharge, but allege that what was discharged contained paraffinic products derived from the residues of a previous cargo of low sulphur fuel oil which had not been removed from the vessel's tanks before loading. I am asked to assume that the charterers' allegations are correct. In arbitration proceedings the owners claimed payment of the freight and the charterers counterclaimed damages for breach of contract. However, the owners contended that they were entitled to an immediate interim award covering the full amount of the freight, because a claim for damage to cargo cannot be set off against a claim for freight (*Aries Tanker Corpn v Total Transport Ltd*[1]). The charterers retorted that there was no *immediate* right to freight, because what was delivered was not merchantable as 'Bachaquero Crude' or alternatively was not identical commercially with the cargo loaded. This contention was unarguable and has rightly been abandoned by counsel for the charterers. The charterers' current contention is different. It is that in these circumstances there is no right to freight now or at any other time, because there was no 'delivery of the cargo' and accordingly no freight was ever earned.

In these circumstances, Mr Donald Davies and Mr Cedric Barclay, the arbitrators appointed by the parties, decided to state an award in the form of a consultative case asking the court to decide as a matter of law—

'Whether the owners are entitled to payment of freight in full without deductions on the assumption that the goods carried were delivered in a state which was unmerchantable as Bachaquero Crude and/or was not identical commercially with the cargo loaded.'

The object of this exercise was to obtain a speedy decision on the owners' right to freight. In this I fear that it has failed. The award was published on 9th January 1979, and the parties were given six weeks in which to set it down for argument. A period of 14 days might have been more appropriate and this is the period prescribed for equivalent proceedings under s 2(1) of the Arbitration Act 1979. In fact the award was set down within about four weeks, but another month elapsed before it was transferred to the commercial list. A date for hearing was fixed for April, but the parties asked that the date be vacated. Owing to unforeseen circumstances a new date could not be given until 14th June and even now the award has to go back to the arbitrators for further consideration.

I mention these matters solely in order that arbitrators may be aware that the attractions of the consultative case or of an application under s 2(1) of the Arbitration Act 1979 are often more apparent than real. Before resorting to either procedure, serious consideration should be given, in the words of s 2(2) of the 1979 Act, to whether 'the determination of the application might produce substantial savings in costs to the parties'. I fear that that has not been the result in the present case.

Counsel for the owners submits that the shipowner will be entitled to full freight unless the goods are a total or constructive total loss in insurance terms and that their identity must not only be changed, they must be worthless to the consignee. He also submits that whatever the state of the goods at the port of discharge, the consignee is obliged to pay the freight if he takes delivery of those goods.

Scrutton on Charterparties[2] states the law as follows:

'The shipowner will be entitled to full freight: (1) If he is ready to deliver in substance at the port of destination the goods loaded, though in a damaged condition. The freighter will not be entitled to make a deduction from the freight for the damage, but will have a separate cause of action or counterclaim for the damage, unless caused solely by excepted perils or by the vice of the goods themselves. The question is whether the substance delivered is identical commercially with the substance loaded, though it may have deteriorated in quality.'

---

1   [1977] 1 All ER 398, [1977] 1 WLR 185
2   18th Edn (1974), p 339

This statement of the law seems to me to be fully supported by the authorities and indeed to be the obvious conclusion apart from authority. The freight clause specifies *a* the circumstances in which freight becomes payable, namely 'upon delivery of the cargo'. If there is no delivery of anything or if what is delivered is not 'the cargo', no freight is payable. But the mere fact that goods are delivered in a damaged state does not necessarily, or even usually, involve the proposition that they are not 'the cargo'. The real problem is to determine the point at which the damage to, or transformation of, the goods which were shipped is such as to render them incapable of being any longer so *b* described.

The earliest case to which I have been referred is *Shields v Davis*[1]. Heath J said that '... the principle is, that if he [the cargo owner] has received any benefit whatever by the carriage, he cannot set up this defence'. However the point at issue was whether the mere fact that the goods had been damaged was a bar to the claim for freight and I think that this comment has to be read in that context. A similar case was *Garrett v Melhuish*[2], *c* in which payment of freight on a cargo of bricks was resisted on the ground that they were not delivered or alternatively were delivered damaged. It was certainly open to the cargo owner to have argued that the bricks were so damaged as no longer to be bricks, but this does not appear to have been done.

Next came *Dakin v Oxley*[3], in which the goods owner refused to take delivery of a cargo of damaged coal or to pay the freight. He adopted this attitude because the coal was *d* worth less than the freight. But he did not deny that the substance tendered was still coal, albeit damaged coal. Willes J, holding that the shipowners were entitled to the freight, said[4]:

'In both classes of cases, whether of loss of quantity or change in quality, the proper course seems to be the same, viz. to ascertain from the terms of the contract, construed by mercantile usage, if any, what was the thing for the carriage of which *e* freight was to be paid, and by the aid of a jury to determine whether that thing, or any and how much of it, has substantially arrived.'

Counsel for the owners seeks to support his argument by reference to a remark by Brett QC[5] as counsel, that if any part of the cargo is accepted, any claim for damage must be the subject matter of a cross-action. This may well be a correct statement of the law *f* in the context of that case because what was tendered for delivery was admittedly 'coal' or 'the cargo'. But it does not help in a case such as the present where that point is in issue and I see no reason in principle why a shipowner should be entitled to freight if he delivers something to the consignee which, although the latter's property, is not 'the cargo'. In such circumstances the shipowner has not performed the act for, and on the occasion of which, the freight was payable, namely delivery of 'the cargo'. *g*

Four years later *Duthie v Hilton*[6] was decided. There a cargo of cement in bags was submerged when the ship was scuttled to put out a fire. The cement solidified and was held no longer to be cement. It was not merely a case of the shipowners offering to deliver damaged cement. They could not deliver cement at all. Accordingly, the condition precedent to the right to receive the freight was not satisfied. This decision was followed in *Dickson v Buchanan*[7]. The cargo consisted of bundles of wire which *h* became so damaged that two-thirds were reduced to scrap iron and could no longer be considered as wire. The remaining one-third could, at great expense, be restored to a condition in which it could be described as wire, but even then could only be used for

1	(1815) 6 Taunt 65, 128 ER 957
2	(1858) 33 LTOS 25
3	(1864) 15 CBNS 646, 143 ER 938
4	15 CBNS 646 at 667, 143 ER 938 at 947
5	15 CBNS 646 at 655, 143 ER 938 at 942
6	(1868) LR 4 CP 138
7	(1876) 13 Sc LR 401

making small articles whereas the cargo as loaded was intended to be used for fencing.
a   Lord Shand in the Court of Session held that the wire was actually or constructively
totally lost. I do not think that this decision is authority for the proposition that the test
of when freight is payable depends on considerations of insurance law. It is simply a
decision that none of the goods could still be described as wire and that although part
could be put in a state in which it could be so described, this was not a practical
proposition from a commercial point of view.

b   The most recent, and in my view the most helpful, authority is *Asfar & Co v
Blundell*[1]. There a vessel carrying a cargo of dates was sunk during the voyage. She was
raised, but the dates were 'affected', to use a neutral term, by seawater and sewage.
Although the dates were unmerchantable as dates, and were not allowed to be landed in
London, a large proportion retained the appearance of dates and they had considerable
value abroad as the raw material for distillation into spirit. They were in fact transhipped
c   and sold for this purpose. The claim was brought on a policy insuring the freight and it
was held that the right to the freight had been lost. Lord Esher MR[2] put the matter in
this way:

   'There is a perfectly well known test which has for many years been applied to
   such cases as the present—that test is whether, as a matter of business, the nature of
   the thing has been altered. The nature of a thing is not necessarily altered because
d   the thing itself has been damaged; wheat or rice may be damaged, but may still
   remain the things dealt with as wheat or rice in business. But if the nature of the
   thing is altered, and it becomes for business purposes something else, so that it is not
   dealt with by business people as the thing which it originally was, the question of
   determination is whether the thing insured, the original article of commerce, has
   become a total loss. If it is so changed in its nature by the perils of the sea as to
e   become an unmerchantable thing, which no buyer would buy and no honest seller
   would sell, then there is a total loss.'

   Lopes LJ[3] held that the dates were totally lost and Kay LJ[4] held that whilst the
substance of the dates still remained, it was sufficient that there had been a total
destruction of their mercantile character.

f   The editors of Scrutton on Charterparties[5] have expressed doubt as to the correctness
of this decision, because the consignees took the cargo and sold it. With the greatest
respect, I do not share this doubt. The consignees took what was their property, but it
had been so damaged as to cease to be 'the cargo' and there was a total failure by the
shipowners to perform the contract for which the freight was payable, namely the
carriage and delivery of the cargo at the port of destination. But however that may be,
g   the decision is binding on me.

   I therefore turn to the question of law posed in the award. The mere fact that the oil
as delivered was not identical commercially with the cargo loaded does not, in my
judgment, deprive the owners of their right to freight. Undamaged or uncontaminated
goods can rarely be considered to be identical commercially with damaged or
contaminated goods, but it is well settled that damage or contamination is not, as such,
h   a bar to the right to freight. Nor do I accept the argument that the test is to be found in
the amended definition of 'merchantable quality' in s 62(1A) of the Sale of Goods Act
1893. Again I get no assistance by considering the law of insurance and the concept of
a constructive total loss of goods. I also reject the argument that the consignee having
accepted goods tendered by the shipowner, the shipowners necessarily are entitled to be
paid the freight.

j
_____

1   [1896] 1 QB 123
2   [1896] 1 QB 123 at 127–128
3   [1896] 1 QB 123 at 130
4   [1896] 1 QB 123 at 132
5   18th Edn (1974), p 340, footnote 64

The owners will be entitled to the freight if what they delivered could in commercial terms, bear a description which sensibly and accurately included the words 'Bachaquero Crude', eg 'Bachaquero Crude contaminated with paraffin or low sulphur oil residues'. The question is whether an honest merchant would be forced to qualify the description applicable to the goods on shipment to such an extent as to destroy it. If the qualification destroys the description, no freight has been earned because 'the cargo' has not been delivered. If the description is merely qualified, 'the cargo' has been delivered, albeit damaged or as the case may be contaminated. This, in my judgment, is what Lord Esher MR meant by the test of merchantability or of the nature of the goods being so altered as to become for business purposes something else.

I can best illustrate this by examples. If one takes a carboy of sulphuric acid and adds a limited quantity of water, an experiment which should only be conducted with extreme care and with knowledge of the likely consequences, the resulting liquid will still be sulphuric acid, albeit, dilute sulphuric acid. But if one adds enough water, the point will be reached at which the liquid is more properly described as water contaminated with acid than as dilute acid. This is the dividing line. Of course, some descriptions of goods are such that any damage or contamination contradicts the description, eg 'pure water' or 'sterile dressings'. The arbitrators will have to consider what is meant by the description 'Bachaquero Crude'. Does it mean a paraffin-free crude? If it does, 'Bachaquero Crude contaminated by paraffin' is a contradiction in terms and the owners will not be entitled to freight. Or does it mean 'a crude from the Bachaquero region which in its natural state contains no paraffin'? If so, there is no necessary contradiction in 'Bachaquero Crude contaminated by paraffin'. In that event, the fact of contamination will not of itself deprive the owners of their right to freight. However, the arbitrators would have to consider the degree of contamination. They would have to ask themselves the question: 'is the oil so contaminated that it has ceased to be even contaminated Bachaquero Crude?' If so, the right to freight has gone. No doubt a relevant factor will be the cost and practicability of extracting the paraffin, but there may well be other criteria. These are matters of fact which are for the arbitrators as the tribunal of fact.

The award will be remitted to the arbitrators in order that they may make such further award or awards as is appropriate in the light of this judgment.

Decision accordingly. Leave to appeal granted.

Solicitors: *Ince & Co* (for the owners); *Middleton Potts & Co* (for the charterers)

K Mydeen Esq   Barrister.

R v Inland Revenue Commissioners and others, ex parte Rossminster Ltd and others

QUEEN'S BENCH DIVISION

EVELEIGH LJ, PARK AND WOOLF JJ

30th, 31st JULY, 1st AUGUST 1979

COURT OF APPEAL, CIVIL DIVISION

LORD DENNING MR, BROWNE AND GOFF LJJ

13th, 14th, 15th, 16th AUGUST 1979

Income tax – Offence – Fraud – Suspected offence – Warrant to enter and seize documents – Validity – Warrant not specifying offence suspected but drawn in general terms of provision empowering issue of warrant – Proceedings for judicial review of warrant and seizure – Whether warrant ought to specify nature of suspected offence – Whether Revenue sole arbiter that reasonable belief documents required as evidence of an offence existed – Whether Revenue entitled to withhold grounds for seizure – Whether in proceedings for judicial review court entitled to make final declaration that seizure unlawful where action claiming damages for unlawful seizure pending – Taxes Management Act 1970, s 20c(1)(3) (as inserted by the Finance Act 1976, s 57(1), Sch 6) – RSC Ord 53, r 2(c).

In accordance with the provisions of s 20c[a] of the Taxes Management Act 1970 an officer of the Board of Inland Revenue laid information on oath before a circuit judge which satisfied the judge that there was reasonable ground for suspecting that an offence involving fraud in connection with tax had been committed and that incriminating documents would be found on the premises specified in the information. Those premises comprised the homes and business premises of the applicants. Accordingly the judge issued search warrants under s 20c(1). The warrants did not specify that any particular offence was suspected but simply stated, in the words of s 20c(1) and (3), that there was 'reasonable ground for suspecting that an offence involving fraud in connection with or in relation to tax has been committed and that evidence of it is to be found on the premises described [therein]', and authorised officers of the Revenue to enter those premises, search them and seize and remove 'any things whatsoever found there which [they had] reasonable cause to believe may be required as evidence for the purposes of proceedings in respect of such an offence'. In execution of the warrants the officers entered the specified premises and seized and removed numerous files, papers and documents of all kinds. There was evidence that the officers did not examine the bulk of the articles before seizing them, or did not examine them in enough detail to form an opinion on their evidential value. The applicants commenced an action in the Chancery Division against the Revenue claiming, inter alia, damages for wrongful interference with goods. Subsequently, in the Divisional Court of the Queen's Bench Division the applicants applied for judicial review of the seizure, under RSC Ord 53, and in those proceedings sought an order of certiorari to quash the warrants and a declaration that the seizure was unlawful and that the Revenue ought to return to the applicants all the articles seized, and all copies and notes taken of them. The Divisional Court dismissed the application for judicial review. The applicants appealed contending (1) that the warrants were invalid under s 20c(1) because they did not specify the particular offence involving fraud which was suspected and (2) that the seizure was unlawful because the articles taken were so numerous and inspection of the bulk of them so cursory that the officers could not at the time of the seizure have had reasonable grounds for believing they might be required as evidence of an offence, within s 20c(3). The Revenue contended (1) that it was sufficient if the warrants set out the wording of s 20c(1)(a)

---

a Section 20c, so far as material, is set out at p 398 *f* to *h*, post

because it defined a limited genus of offence within which there were only six species of offences[b], (2) that they were entitled at that stage to refuse to disclose the nature of the suspected offence because such a disclosure would be detrimental to their investigations and the conduct of any future criminal proceedings and (3) that they were the sole arbiters of whether there was reasonable cause to believe that the articles seized might be required as evidence, within s 20C(3), and were entitled to refuse to disclose the grounds for the seizure.

Held – The appeal would be allowed, the warrants quashed and a declaration in the terms claimed made for the following reasons—

(i) Since s 20C(1)(a) of the 1970 Act was in wide and general terms, it was insufficient to draw up a warrant in those terms, and a warrant issued thereunder had to specify the nature of the offence or offences which were suspected of having been committed. Accordingly, the warrants did not sufficiently specify the suspected offence and were invalid for want of particularity, and therefore the search and seizure were an illegal and excessive use of power because they were not validly authorised. It followed that the applicants were entitled to an order of certiorari to quash the warrants and to the declaration claimed (see p 401 g h, p 403 g to j, p 405 c d f g, p 407 e f, p 408 b and e to g and p 414 c d, post); dicta of Viscount Simon and of Lord Simonds in *Christie v Leachinsky* [1947] 1 All ER at 571, 575 applied.

(ii) Even if the warrants were valid the applicants were entitled to the declaration claimed because, on the true construction of s 20C(3), it was for the court to decide whether seizure under a warrant was lawful, ie whether the Revenue had reasonable cause to believe the articles seized might be required as evidence of an offence, and the Revenue were not entitled to refuse to disclose the grounds for the seizure. Accordingly, the Revenue should state the grounds for the seizure so that the court could determine whether their belief was reasonable. Since there was no such statement by the Revenue a strong prima facie case, which had not been displaced by the Revenue, had been raised by the applicants' evidence that the bulk of the articles had been seized without reasonable belief that they might be required as evidence of an offence and, as there were no means of distinguishing between the articles which had been properly seized and those improperly seized, the court would declare that the whole seizure was void and that all the articles seized, and copies taken, be returned to the applicants (see p 402 d, p 403 b c and g to j, p 405 f h j, p 406 h, p 407 b to f, p 409 g h, p 413 b f and p 414 c d, post); dictum of Lord Radcliffe in *Nakkuda Ali v M F de S Jayaratne* [1951] AC at 77 and *Ghani v Jones* [1969] 3 All ER 1700 applied.

(iii) In the circumstances, since the court could not make an interim declaration, and because it was just and convenient, within RSC Ord 53, r 2(c)[c], to grant immediate relief by way of final declaration where the rights of private individuals in respect of their property were involved, it was proper in the proceedings under Ord 53 to make a final declaration in the terms claimed, even though to make it would mean that the issue of the legality of the seizure in the action for damages would be finally determined between the parties on affidavit evidence (see p 402 e to j, p 407 e f, p 413 h j and p 414 b to d, post); *International General Electric Co of New York Ltd v Comrs of Customs and Excise* [1962] 2 All ER 398 applied.

Per Browne and Goff LJJ. The words 'such an offence' in s 20C(3) of the 1970 Act cover any of the offences within sub-s (1) of that section and justify retention of documents found disclosing an offence other than that on which the warrant is based (see p 406 a to d and p 408 f, post).

---

b   The offences are set out at p 400 j to p 401 a, post

c   Rule 2, so far as material, provides: 'An application for a declaration . . . may be made by way of an application for judicial review, and on such an application the Court may grant the declaration . . . claimed if it considers that, having regard to . . . (c) all the circumstances of the case, it would be just and convenient for the declaration . . . to be granted on an application for judicial review.'

Notes

a For the powers of an officer of the Commissioners of Inland Revenue to enter and search premises in a case in which there are reasonable grounds for suspecting that a tax fraud has been committed, see 23 Halsbury's Laws (4th Edn) para 1563.

For s 20C of the Taxes Management Act 1970 (as inserted by the Finance Act 1976, s 57(1), Sch 6), see 46 Halsbury's Statutes (3rd Edn) 1790.

Cases referred to in judgments

b *Chic Fashions (West Wales) Ltd v Jones* [1968] 1 All ER 229, [1968] 2 QB 299, [1968] 2 WLR 201, 132 JP 175, CA, 14(1) Digest (Reissue) 215, *1573*.

Christie v Leachinsky [1947] 1 All ER 567, [1947] AC 573, [1947] LJR 757, 176 LT 443, 111 JP 224, 45 LGR 201, HL, 14(1) Digest (Reissue) 206, *1491*.

Entick v Carrington (1765) 2 Wils 275, 19 State Tr 1029, 95 ER 807, 14(1) Digest (Reissue) 215, *1566*.

c *Ghani v Jones* [1969] 3 All ER 1700, [1970] 1 QB 693, [1969] 3 WLR 1158, 134 JP 166, CA, 11 Digest (Reissue) 745, *608*.

Huckle v Money (1763) 2 Wils 205, 95 ER 768, 17 Digest (Reissue) 219, *903*.

International General Electric Co of New York Ltd v Comrs of Customs and Excise [1962] 2 All ER 398, [1962] Ch 784, [1962] 3 WLR 20, [1962] RPC 235, CA, Digest (Cont Vol A) 457, *483a*.

d *Liversidge v Anderson* [1941] 3 All ER 338, [1942] AC 206, 110 LJKB 724, 166 LT 1, HL, 17 Digest (Reissue) 467, *28*.

Malone v Comr of Police of the Metropolis [1979] 1 All ER 256, [1978] 3 WLR 936, CA.

Nakkuda Ali v M F de S Jayaratne [1951] AC 66, PC, 8(2) Digest (Reissue) 811, *621*.

Padfield v Minister of Agriculture, Fisheries and Food [1968] 1 All ER 694, [1968] AC 997, [1968] 2 WLR 924, HL, Digest (Cont Vol C) 280, *1237a*.

e *R v Hudson* [1956] 1 All ER 814, [1956] 2 QB 252, [1956] 2 WLR 914, 120 JP 216, 36 Tax Cas 561, 40 Cr App R 55, CCA, 15 Digest (Reissue) 1392, *12,169*.

R v Secretary of State for the Home Department, ex parte Hosenball [1977] 3 All ER 452, [1977] 1 WLR 766, 141 JP 626, CA.

R v Wilkes (1763) 2 Wils 151, 19 State Tr 982, 95 ER 737, 32 Digest (Reissue) 337, *2811*.

f *Secretary of State for Education and Science v Metropolitan Borough of Tameside* [1976] 3 All ER 665, [1977] AC 1014, [1976] 3 WLR 641, 75 LGR 190, HL.

Wilover Nominees v Inland Revenue Comrs [1974] 3 All ER 496, [1974] 1 WLR 1342, [1974] STC 467, 49 Tax Cas 559, [1974] TR 367, CA, Digest (Cont Vol D) 485, *1565a*.

Cases also cited

American Cyanamid Co v Ethicon Ltd [1975] 1 All ER 504, [1975] AC 396, HL.

g *Butler v Board of Trade* [1970] 3 All ER 593, [1971] Ch 680.

D v National Society for the Prevention of Cruelty to Children [1977] 1 All ER 589, [1978] AC 171, HL.

Jeffrey v Black [1978] 1 All ER 555, [1978] QB 490, DC.

Norwest Holst Ltd v Secretary of State for Trade [1978] 3 All ER 280, [1978] Ch 201, CA.

Parry-Jones v Law Society [1968] 1 All ER 177, [1969] 1 Ch 1, CA.

h *R v Patel* (1973) 48 Tax Cas 647, CA.

Rogers v Secretary of State for the Home Department, Gaming Board for Great Britain v Rogers [1972] 2 All ER 1057, [1973] AC 388, HL.

Truman (Frank) Export Ltd v Metropolitan Police Comr [1977] 3 All ER 431, [1977] QB 952.

Application for judicial review

j By a notice of motion pursuant to RSC Ord 53, dated 18th July 1979, the applicants, Rossminster Ltd, A J R Financial Services Ltd, Ronald Anthony Plummer and Roy Clifford Tucker, applied for judicial review in the following forms: (1) an order of mandamus directed to the Inland Revenue Commissioners and their officers commanding them (a) to determine in accordance with law at certain listed premises whether anything they had found at those premises was something which they had reasonable cause to believe might be required as evidence for the purposes of proceedings in respect of an offence involving fraud in connection with or in relation to tax, (b) to remove nothing from the said premises unless they had so determined, (c) to provide to the applicants a list of each thing seized by them from the premises and (d) to afford reasonable access to the applicants to all documents relating to any business seized from the premises; (2) declarations prayed in proceedings commenced by the applicants in the Chancery Division by writ dated 16th July 1979 against the Inland Revenue Commissioners and one of their officers, Raymond Quinlan, and transferred to the Queen's Bench Division by an order dated 28th July 1979 (in which the applicants also claimed damages for wrongful interference with goods), namely a declaration that the defendants to that action were not at any material time entitled to remove and were bound to deliver up to the applicants all documents and other things, and all copies and extracts thereof, at the listed premises save those which the defendants had reasonable cause to believe and did believe might be required as evidence for the purpose of proceedings in respect of an offence involving fraud in connection with or in relation to tax; a declaration that the defendants were bound to provide the applicants with a list of all things seized by them from the listed premises and at all times were in breach of that duty and a declaration (a) that the documents seized related to the applicants' businesses, (b) that access to them was required for the continued conduct of the businesses, (c) that the defendants were bound to afford reasonable access to the documents and (d) that reasonable access could be afforded at two only of the listed premises: 1 Hanover Square and/or 19–24 St Georges Street, London W1; and (3) an order of certiorari to remove into the Queen's Bench Division and quash four warrants issued by his Honour Judge Leonard QC in the Central Criminal Court on 12th July 1979 by which he authorised Raymond Quinlan and other officers of the Board of Inland Revenue to enter the applicants' premises at the listed addresses and search them.

The grounds on which the relief was sought were that in executing the warrants to search the said premises (1) the officers of the Board seized and removed and were threatening to continue to seize and remove goods and documents from the premises which they had no reasonable cause to believe and/or did not believe might be required as evidence for the purpose of proceedings in respect of an offence involving fraud in connection with or in relation to tax, (2) the officers refused to provide any or any proper list of what they had removed, (3) the officers refused to give any access to the said documents which were required for the conduct of the applicants' businesses, (4) the judge erred in law and in fact in issuing the warrants in that he was not satisfied and there was no sufficient information to satisfy him that there was reasonable ground for suspecting that any particular person had at any particular time done any particular act to constitute an offence involving fraud in connection with or in relation to tax and (5) the warrants were illegal and void in that they did not state by whom and when there were reasonable grounds for suspecting an offence had been committed and the precise nature of and/or the particular acts constituting the offence. The facts are set out in the judgment of Eveleigh LJ.

Andrew J Bateson QC and *Michael Tugendhat* for the applicants.
Brian Davenport for the Crown.

EVELEIGH LJ. This application concerns the search for documents and the seizure of documents at four different premises, when the Revenue purported to act under s 20C of the Taxes Management Act 1970, as amended in 1976. They had obtained warrants relating to each of the premises, and as they are in the same form it is sufficient to read one of them. They were all obtained on the authority of his Honour Judge Leonard QC, sitting at the Central Criminal Court. The document is headed 'Search Warrant'. It is addressed to—

'RAYMOND QUINLAN, AND TO THE PERSONS NAMED IN THE FIRST SCHEDULE ANNEXED TO THIS WARRANT. Officers of the Board of Inland Revenue. Information on oath

a having been laid this day by Raymond Quinlan in accordance with the provisions
of Section 20C of the Taxes Management Act 1970 stating that there is reasonable
ground for suspecting that an offence involving fraud in connection with or in
relation to tax has been committed and that evidence of it is to be found on the
premises described in the second schedule annexed hereto. YOU ARE HEREBY
AUTHORISED to enter those premises, together with all or any of the officers of the
Board of Inland Revenue named in the first schedule hereto and together with such
b constables as you may require, if necessary by force, at any time within 14 days from
the time of issue of this Warrant, and search them; and on entering those premises
with this Warrant you may seize and remove any things whatsoever found there
which you have reasonable cause to believe may be required as evidence for the
purposes of proceedings in respect of such an offence.'

c   Application has been made to this court for certiorari to quash the warrant on the
ground that it was improperly issued, that the judge did not or could not have properly
exercised his discretion in relation to that, and that it is bad on the face of it, because it
lacks particularity. Application is also made for mandamus for a declaration and for
damages, all on the grounds of abuse of power by the Revenue.
     It is not necessary to state the precise relief claimed in the motion. Indeed, some of the
d matters in respect of which relief is prayed, for example access to the documents, has
been resolved by mutual agreement by the parties, but generally speaking what this
court is concerned with to decide is whether the documents were lawfully taken or not,
and whether the Revenue exceeded their power in seizing them.
     Section 20C of the Taxes Management Act 1970, in so far as it is relevant, reads as
follows:

e   '(1) If the appropriate judicial authority is satisfied on information on oath given
by an officer of the Board that—(a) there is reasonable ground for suspecting that an
offence involving any form of fraud in connection with, or in relation to, tax has
been committed and that evidence of it is to be found on premises specified in the
information . . . the authority may issue a warrant in writing authorising an officer
f of the Board to enter the premises, if necessary by force, at any time within 14 days
from the time of issue of the warrant, and search them.'

Subsection (3) reads:

g   'On entering the premises with a warrant under this section, the officer may seize
and remove any things whatsoever found there which he has reasonable cause to
believe may be required as evidence for the purposes of proceedings in respect of
such an offence as is mentioned in subsection (1) above.'

There then follow sub-ss (4) and (5) which respectively deal with the provision of a list
and access to the documents.
     It is contended on behalf of the applicants that the Revenue must specify a particular
h offence when applying for the warrant to the circuit judge who is the judicial authority
for the purposes of the section, and further that the warrant itself must prescribe that
offence, and that the warrant must specify the documents which are seizable or describe
them with some particularity which relates them to the offence. It is also contended that
sub-s (3) permits seizure only of documents that are limited to being evidence of the
j offence which it is said has to be specified when application is made for the warrant.
     It is further submitted that when the seizure is challenged, or alternatively if a prima
facie case of irregularity is shown, then it is incumbent on the Revenue to justify their
behaviour, and justification involves giving details of the offence and of the 'reasonable
cause' for the belief. So, it is said, justification involves stating the offence, stating the
belief, and the cause for it.

Finally, it is submitted in this case that should it be that after the documents have been seized those which are admitted to have been seized wrongfully are returned nonetheless the whole seizure is bad, and if all of the documents are returned no copies may be kept by the Revenue, because they will be copies that have been obtained as a result of a seizure which taken as a whole is itself bad.

The Revenue seek to answer those contentions by saying that all that is necessary is to satisfy the judge that there are grounds to suspect that some offence or other involving fraud against the Revenue has been committed. Further, they contend that on a proper construction of sub-s (3) the Revenue can seize anything which might be evidence of any offence of the kind referred to in sub-s (1).

It is further said that once the judge is satisfied of the grounds for suspicion there is no necessity to tell the applicant of the nature of the offence, and no necessity to tell the applicant what the grounds are. It has further been submitted on behalf of the Revenue that if they are called on to justify the seizure a bare assertion of the words in sub-s (3) is in law enough, namely it is enough to depose that they have reasonable cause to believe that the documents may be required as evidence for the purposes of proceedings etc.

It is said that a lack of detail is justified in this type of case because these are not criminal proceedings. They are preliminary stages, which may result in criminal proceedings, and to descend to detail would in all probability involve the disclosure of the names or name of the informants or an informant. It is further argued that s 20c(3) gives the officers who are conducting the search an unfettered discretion, as I understand the argument, that their assertion of a belief and reasonable cause is enough. This court was referred to the well known case of *R v Secretary of State for the Home Department, ex parte Hosenball*[1].

It is to be noted that the words of the Act with which that case was concerned are not the same as the words of the Taxes Management Act 1970, s 20c. Further, it was argued by counsel for the Revenue that in any event these affidavits were not as limited as his contentions could support, and that they did in fact disclose sufficient to answer the case that was raised against him.

I turn to consider the effect of s 20c. In doing so, it seems to me that the meaning of the two subsections with which we are concerned is to be obtained by reading the whole of the section, and that help on the construction of sub-s (1) is to be obtained from reading sub-s (3) and vice versa. Doing that, what does one find? Not that the court has to be satisfied that an offence has been committed by a particular person, but that there is reasonable ground for a suspicion, and that suspicion has to be that an offence has been committed, but the nature of the offence is not specified. It is widely described, namely one 'involving any form of fraud in connection with, or in relation to, tax'.

I do not regard that subsection as giving, as it were, by description a catalogue of offences. What it is doing is defining the nature of the suspicion which, if supported by reasonable ground for it, will entitle this application for the warrant to be made.

I then turn to sub-s (3). Again, the words used in sub-s (3) are general, if one reads them, relating back as they do to the words of sub-s (1). Subsection (3) does not say that they may seize and remove anything which the officer has reasonable cause to believe may be required as evidence for the offence for which application for the warrant was made, or any such specific words. The reference back to sub-s (1) is, in my opinion, quite general and not selective. What the evidence has to relate to is 'such offence as is mentioned in subsection (1)', in other words, an offence involving any form of fraud in connection with or in relation to tax.

There are many possible offences in the criminal calendar which will cover fraudulent activity, and in my opinion it is enough, on an application for a warrant, to show that there are grounds for suspecting fraud which would fall under the heading of one or other of the offences in the criminal calendar. Which particular offence might be selected would depend on the manner of the perpetration of the fraud, and as the whole

1   [1977] 3 All ER 452, [1977] 1 WLR 766

section is initiated by suspicion only I do not think that the legislature intended that
a particular offence to be named or specified at that stage. Therefore, it seems to me that
the Revenue in applying for a warrant of this nature must rely on a suspicion of fraud
against the Revenue which can come under the heading of some specific offence, but it
is not necessary for them to elect which one. In so far as sub-s (3) is concerned, I have said
enough to indicate that in my view it is not limited to any particular criminal offence,
provided it relates to that kind of offence as is specified in sub-s (1).

b   That being so, the next question arises as to the nature of the belief with which we are
concerned. On the one hand, it can be said that there must be a belief that the document
in question is evidence of a criminal offence, and that the 'may be required' relates only
to the chances of that document which is evidence being actually used in the
proceedings. That argument would of course necessitate 'reasonable cause' being shown
for a conclusion that the document or documents in question was or were evidence.

c   On the other hand, it is said at the other extreme that all that is necessary is that the
officer should believe that the documents seized might provide some evidence which
could be used, or might be required. Those are the extremes of the contentions here.

In deciding what is the correct approach I first of all conclude that the proceedings
referred to in sub-s (3) are criminal proceedings, and I understand that counsel for the
Revenue does not contest that. The evidence referred to will be evidence that is
d receivable in evidence in a court. That only brings us to the real nub of the problem.

Bearing in mind, as I say, that the whole section is based on suspicion, bearing in mind
that sub-s (3) is, as I read it, broadly drawn, bearing in mind that it may well be that no
specific offence has yet been determined on by the Revenue, I have come to the conclusion
that an officer is entitled to say: 'I believe that this document is one which could afford
evidence of an offence involving fraud', and consequently can reach the conclusion that
e it may be required as evidence of proceedings.

This approach will not, in my view, permit wild speculation. First of all, although the
subsection does not specifically say so, I think it is necessary that there should be a belief;
an actual belief should exist. The mere existence of the grounds for belief will not be
enough. Consequently, the officer is required to go through a mental process and is not
entitled to snatch documents willy-nilly. As I say, wild speculation as to the remote
f possibility of a document being used in evidence would not meet the test. One has to
read the statement of that which should be believed with the requirement that there
have to be reasonable grounds, and it follows that the belief must be based on those
reasonable grounds, so there must be reasonable grounds for the belief formed as to the
nature of the documents.

If it can be shown that the documents were seized in such a hurry, that no possible
consideration of their value could have been given, clearly it will not be possible, in my
g opinion, for the Revenue to claim the protection of sub-s (3). It may well be, depending
on the facts of each particular case, that an applicant need not put his case as high as that.

Then one has to consider what kind of evidence it is necessary to adduce before a court
to show the existence of that belief which satisfies the requirement for the exercise of the
seizure under sub-s (3), to what extent must the grounds be detailed, and who has to
h prove the existence of those grounds.

In approaching that question, it is important to bear in mind that we are not concerned
with a civil claim for the return of the documents. In such a case it might well be that
all the applicant has to do is to allege that the documents have been taken without his
permission. This would require a defence, and the defence might well read: 'The
documents were taken by an officer acting under a warrant, that officer having reasonable
j cause to believe,' etc, etc. In the pleading the particular grounds for the belief would not
have to be specified at that point, because looked at as a pleading there would be a defence
in law disclosed, but if the defendant were asked for further and better particulars of the
grounds of his belief I apprehend that he would have to give them, and those grounds for
belief would be investigated at the trial and would be treated in cross-examination.

But we are not concerned with a claim for the return of documents. We are concerned with an allegation of an abuse of executive power, so it is the abuse of power that has to be demonstrated to this court. I would not accept the argument, if I understand it rightly, that the Revenue should never descend to detail of their reasonable cause, because to do so would almost certainly mean revealing the name of an informer or other information which might be useful to a person who knows his affairs are about to be investigated. I do not think that the Revenue are entitled to claim such a wide privilege as that. It seems to me that what they have to disclose will depend on the case that is made against them. Consequently, each case will depend on its own facts and on its particular presentation.

That being my view of the law, what is the result in the present case? In so far as the warrant is concerned, we do not know what evidence was given on oath to the learned judge. What we do know is that it was sufficient to satisfy him that a warrant should issue. I see no grounds in this case whatsoever for concluding that he acted on any wrong principle. That conclusion I would have reached in any event, whatever had been my opinion as to the necessity for an offence to be specified. There simply is not the evidence in this case to enable this court to say that the learned judge exercised his discretion improperly.

The description of the documents in the warrant it is true is a wide one, and so too are the introductory words of the warrant. I do not regard that as any defect in the warrant. The warrant is the key to the opening of the door to a power that is granted by sub-s (3), and as sub-s (3) on the construction I have given it gives a wide power of seizure there can be no limited description of the documents, other than in the words of the subsection itself, in the warrant. For the warrant to limit the description in terms other than those which appear in it would take away the power which is granted under the Act by sub-s (3). When the officers enter and subsequently seize and remove, their power is derived from the subsection itself, albeit as I say, the warrant opens the way for the Revenue to invoke that subsection. I therefore see no ground for challenging the validity of the warrant.

Now I turn to consider the sufficiency of the affidavits for their purpose, and I specifically do not say 'for the purpose of establishing whether the Revenue had reasonable cause to believe'. I have to consider those affidavits as one does in proceedings for judicial review, as they are read in this court. That is the evidence on which this court has to proceed, and that is the evidence on which this court has to come to a conclusion whether or not there has been an abuse of the executive powers. At the end of the day the court has to ask itself that simple question.

Now, what are the facts as revealed in the affidavits? I will, of course, have to summarise those. It amounts to this, that on 13th July the Inland Revenue Special Investigations Section, supported by police officers, went to four different premises. They went to Nettlestead Place, near Maidstone, which is the home of Mr Tucker. He is a fellow of the Institute of Chartered Accountants, and he states that on the morning of Friday, 13th July, when he was in Guernsey on business, at 7.30 am he received a telephone call from his wife that the Inland Revenue had entered the house. The affidavit evidence is to the effect that there was a hurried collection of documents, and allegations are made to the effect that a number of documents were taken without examination, and that documents which were or which must be irrelevant to the purpose were taken. It was claimed that bank statements relating to students who lived at the house were taken. However, in an affidavit by the Revenue it is said that those bank statements were not taken. The envelopes containing them were opened but the statements were then left where they were.

It is alleged further that papers belonging to the deponent's brother were removed from the attic, the brother being a man who was in Venezuela. Furthermore, it is said the deponent's passport had been taken.

There is also an affidavit of a Mr Plummer. He is the managing director of Rossminster Ltd. He is a chartered accountant and a fellow of the Institute of Taxation. He says that Rossminster is a bank, incorporated in 1978 in England, being a subsidiary of Rossminster

Group Ltd. He says: 'Other companies which are or were controlled by the same persons
a as those controlling Rossminster have been involved in implementing legal tax avoidance
schemes. These have always been approved by counsel, but in a number of cases they
have been challenged in the courts.' The Rossminster Bank occasionally provides loans
in the ordinary course of its banking business to customers who require them in
connection with such schemes.

He then states that at 7 am on the morning of Friday, 13th July 1979, he was at home
b when an officer of the Revenue came to execute the warrant. He says:

'They went to my filing cabinet and removed a large number of files and made
a list of those which they proposed to take. I saw them look only at the names on
the files. I did not see them examining the contents. I asked to check the list and
I was not allowed to do so. Then they went to the safe and took building society
c passbooks, my children's passports and a number of cheque books belonging to my
children. Then they went to my bedroom where I had a suitcase containing things
I had intended to take to Guernsey. They removed a bundle of papers mostly
relating to my mother who lives in Guernsey and my personal affairs. They did not
read the papers. They then searched the house and took personal papers of my
wife. Two of the bundles they took included copies of financial newspapers and
d similar publications. I did not see them read any document before they took it.'

He then states that he went on to 1 Hanover Square, the premises of Rossminster Ltd,
and arrived at about 10 am. There were officers of the Inland Revenue and the police
there. He said he stayed until 12 noon, and during that time he saw that the officers
were removing large quantities of documents. 'I did not see any officer perusing any
e documents. The quantity of documents was so great that the officers could not have
perused them before removing them.' He produced also some lists of documents which
were given to a Mr Fuller, the office manager, by the officers conducting the search. He
said: '. . . the officers had cleared out the whole of my room, taking even my internal
telephone directory. Mr Coysh [who is also a director of Rossminster] had informed me
that he saw other rooms similarly cleared out.'

f The court has been invited to examine the list of documents in this case and to note the
times at the side of those lists, and has been invited to conclude from that, that there was
no time to examine the documents therein listed. In my opinion the contention that
there was no time to examine all of the documents therein listed is well founded. It does
not follow from that, that no documents were examined, and it does not necessarily
follow from that in my opinion, that the documents were seized willy-nilly. For
g example, the list contains a very large number of files which were seized over a period of
about two hours. It is quite clear that the contents of the files could not have been
inspected page by page, or looked at page by page, let alone read, but does it follow from
that, that no thought had been given to the nature of the documents that were being
seized?

Certainly the affidavit evidence of the applicants, and I have not referred to all of it,
h raises a case for an explanation by the Revenue. On the face of those affidavits it does
seem reasonable to infer a hurried search, where there would not have been an evaluation
of everything that was taken.

So one turns to see what is the explanation that has been given. Broadly, that
explanation can be summarised as follows: there was being conducted an investigation,
and as a result of that it was decided to ask for a warrant; that instructions were given to
j the officers concerned as to the type of documents they should look for, and that when
the documents were seized a great number of them were examined closely. Others were
not. It has been submitted in this court that the fact that a file is taken as a file does not
necessarily lead to the inference that it was taken without consideration or that it was not
permissible to take it, because it is said the file itself may tell a story, and consequently it
is a relevant document for the purpose of seizure.

Mr Quinlan, one of Her Majesty's inspectors of taxes, says this in reply to the affidavits of the applicants which he, Mr Quinlan, had read:

a

'I am a Senior Inspector of Taxes employed in the Inland Revenue Technical Division, Special Investigations Section. My duties include the investigation of the activities of what may be called the Rossminster Group of Companies and the many trusts, companies, partnerships and individuals with whom the Rossminster Group has a close relationship.'

b

Among those individuals are Mr Plummer and Mr Tucker. Among those companies are A J R Financial Services Ltd, whose premises (which I should say in parenthesis, are at George Street, adjacent to Hanover Square) were also searched, and in respect of which similar evidence was adduced by the applicant. He says:

'During the course of my investigations I reached the conclusion that I had ground for suspecting that offences involving a form of fraud in connection with or *c* in relation to tax had been committed and that evidence of them was to be found at (inter alia) the addresses set out in the Notices of Motion herein.'

He says that his team carried out the search and that they were instructed only to seize articles which they had reasonable cause to believe might be required for evidence for the purpose of proceedings in such offences. He stated that he was at the premises of 1 *d* Hanover Square almost the whole of the day of 13th July—

'and I verily believe that the said instructions were duly carried out. From time to time during the said search individual Revenue officers asked me whether certain material which they had found came into the said category and I would give a ruling. During the course of the day a great many documents were removed, but I verily believe that they all fell within my said instructions.'

e

He refers to Mr Plummer's affidavit, and to Mr Plummer's statement that Mr Coysh had said some officers only glanced at a few documents and did not read more than a handful. He said that is not an accurate description of what went on:

'For example, during the day I went through the 2 volume securities register page by page with the manager of Rossminster sitting beside me and selected only certain *f* objects in such register. I went through a very thick correspondence file of a Mr Glatt and released it all. I also went through all the incoming telex messages and the managers outgoing post, and released it all. I carried out a sample check of the ledger cards and made special arrangements with the manager to have them photocopied on the premises in order that the originals could remain. These are but examples of some of the detailed searching which I, and I verily believe, other *g* officers carried out on the day in question. But in a very great many instances files and bundles of documents were removed when their title or subject matter made it clear that their contents was such that the officers had reasonable cause to believe that they might be required as evidence for the purpose of proceedings . . .'

There is an affidavit from a Mr Ramage, an inspector of taxes. He went to 27 Radnor *h* Place, London, the premises of Mr Plummer, and he said he gave his team similar instructions to those which Mr Quinlan refers to. He said:

'Although Mr Plummer appeared to keep many business papers at his home it was in almost all cases possible to ascertain from the title of files or the subject matter of bundles or categories of documents whether they fell into the above description but where there was any doubt either I or one of the officers with me *j* went through the papers in further detail until we were satisfied that they either should or need not be seized.'

There are other affidavits to a similar effect.
There was put before this court on the third day of the hearing an affidavit from Mr

Dermit, an assistant director in the Inland Revenue Technical Division in charge of
a Special Investigations Section. Mr Dermit says:

> 'These enquiries are often extremely complicated. I verily believe that it would
> be greatly detrimental to and obstructive of enquiries of this nature to disclose at
> this stage the precise nature of the offences in respect of which proceedings may be
> taken and in which the documents seized may be required as evidence ... Such
> disclosure, in my view, would be harmful because, inter alia, it might reveal to
b those suspected of having committed offences not only that those persons have been
> identified by the Inland Revenue, but also the extent and nature of the information
> in the Revenue's possession concerning such offences ... I have carefully considered
> whether it is possible to say more about the nature of the detriment referred to or
> how it would arise, but in my opinion it would not be possible to do so without risk
> of thereby producing such detriment.'

c
As I have said already, in my view an affidavit of that nature will not always provide
an answer to the complaint. It depends on the nature of the complaint and the evidence
to support it. There may well be many cases where the court will itself require further
particulars of the cause for the belief that is asserted. It will entirely depend on the view
taken by the court of the evidence that is presented, or as it is presented before it.

d I turn to consider the nature of the contest in the present case and the issue before this
court. That issue, as I have said, is one of abuse of power and failure to follow the
procedure which would entitle the Revenue to exercise the power under sub-s (3). That
allegation of abuse of power rests on evidence of a hurried search, on evidence of failure
to inspect every document. It seems to me, looking at the evidence as a whole, that it
cannot be said that an officer could not have reasonable cause for his belief simply
because every document was not read. I am not saying that in proceedings of this kind
e it is necessary for the applicant to show that there could be no grounds for belief, in the
way that one meets that argument when one comes to consider whether there has been
an improper exercise of discretion or an improper finding by the justices on a case stated.
I simply say in this particular case that the evidence does not show that there could be no
proper cause. Of course, if the evidence did show that, the applicants' case would be
f strong.
What the applicants' evidence amounts to, as I say, is that not every document was
read, and not every document, as an individual document, was examined. Files were
taken as files. Then one had to look at those facts, bearing in mind the affidavits from the
Revenue. It seems to me that there can well be occasions when a glance at a document
will tell an investigating officer whether it is the kind of document that he is entitled to
g take. No one can expect that they should stay on the premises to read the words and the
details of every document.
Therefore, if one looks at the case in that light, is the inference to be drawn from all
this evidence that there was an abuse of power? I do not think that one can come to that
conclusion. In saying that, I am far from saying, as appeared to be submitted at one stage
in argument, that there would, as a result of such an approach, be a power in the Revenue
h to seize a whole mass of documents, unexamined, in the hope that one of them might
reveal some valuable evidential information. Indeed, one only has to apply the test to
such a situation to see that an argument like that by the Revenue is untenable. If they
are seeking one document to contain information, and they take 20, believing the
document to be one of the 20, it also follows that they should believe that 19 of the
documents are not permissible documents to seize. Consequently, in such a case, in my
j opinion it would be the duty of the officer concerned to search on the premises for the
document that he has in mind. If, on the other hand, the whole 20 documents were of
the type that fall within the description of documents that I have stated earlier in this
judgment, that would be another matter. He could take them all, but he would have to
have reasonable cause to believe that they all might be required as evidence for
proceedings.

As I have said, I do not find it possible to say in this case that there was an abuse of power. It is said that one should go further into the allegation of reasonable cause. One *a* should ask for details of that and, as I say, in some cases that may be necessary because the evidence adduced by the applicant may only be answerable by such detailed information coming from the Revenue, but that is not, as I see it, this case. The case that falls to be answered is not such a case. I therefore would refuse these applications.

May I just say this, however. It was also suggested in argument that, if some document were improperly seized, then as I have already stated the whole of the seizure was bad, *b* and even though documents improperly seized were returned, or if they were returned, the Revenue would not be entitled to retain copies of documents improperly seized. In so far as the documents returned are improperly seized, because they are not eligible documents, it is probably right to say that copies could not be retained. If, however, the documents that have been retained were documents that were of the class that could have been seized, but happen to have been improperly seized, for some reason or another (as *c* I say, it does not apply in this case) then in my opinion copies could (I say 'could') be retained. I am not, clearly, giving a judgment on any particular claim. I am merely stating that one cannot assert as a bald proposition that no copies could be retained in such a case. Indeed, I do not think counsel for the applicants was really going that far.

Generally speaking, it seems to me the position would be this: that if the document could have been seized lawfully, had the officer given consideration to the matter in the *d* proper way, then those documents which have now been returned could be made the subject of another search warrant and the Revenue could go in again and collect those very documents. It seems to me, therefore, that if the copies that are retained are copies of eligible documents, then copies may be kept even though those documents were obtained improperly in the first place.

There were proceedings in this matter in the Chancery Division. Those proceedings *e* were transferred to this court. I would emphasise that the judgment I have given, assuming it is concurred in by my brethren, would not be res judicata in so far as the proceedings in the Chancery Division, as I see them, but again I am in no position to influence a judge of the Chancery Division. I only say that because those proceedings have now been transferred to this court and have not been proceeded with any further.

f

PARK J. I agree.

WOOLF J. I agree.

Application refused.

g

N P Metcalfe Esq   Barrister.

Appeal
The applicants appealed to the Court of Appeal.

Andrew J Bateson QC and *Michael Tugendhat* for the applicants.   *h*
Brian Davenport for the Crown.

LORD DENNING MR. It was a military style operation. It was carried out by officers of the Inland Revenue in their war against tax frauds. Zero hour was fixed for 7 am on Friday, 13th July 1979. Everything was highly secret. The other side must not be forewarned. There was a briefing session beforehand. Some 70 officers or more of *j* the Inland Revenue attended. They were given detailed instructions. They were divided into teams each with a leader. Each team had an objective allotted to it. It was to search a particular house or office, marked, I expect, on a map: and to seize any incriminating documents found therein. Each team leader was on the day to be handed a search warrant authorising him and his team to enter the house or office. It would be *a* empowered to use force if need be. Each team was to be accompanied by a police officer. Sometimes more than one. The role of the police was presumably to be silent witnesses: or may be to let it be known that this was all done with the authority of the law: and that the householder had better not resist—or else!

Everything went according to plan. On Thursday, 12th July, Mr Quinlan, the senior inspector of the Inland Revenue, went to the Central Criminal Court: and put before a circuit judge, the Common Serjeant, the suspicions which the Revenue held. The circuit

b judge signed the warrants. The officers made photographs of the warrants, and distributed them to the team leaders. Then in the early morning of Friday, 13th July, the next day, each team started off at first light. Each reached its objective. Some in London. Others in the Home Counties. At 7 am there was a knock on each door. One was the home in Kensington of Mr Ronald Anthony Plummer, a chartered accountant. It was opened by his daughter aged 11. He came downstairs in his dressing-gown. The

c officers of the Inland Revenue were at the door accompanied by a detective inspector. The householder Mr Plummer put up no resistance. He let them in. They went to his filing cabinet and removed a large number of files. They went to the safe and took building society passbooks, his children's cheque books and passports. They took his daughter's school report. They went to his bedroom, opened a suitcase, and removed a bundle of papers belonging to his mother. They searched the house. They took personal

d papers of his wife.

Another house was the home near Maidstone of Mr Roy Clifford Tucker, a fellow of the Institute of Chartered Accountants. He was away on business in Guernsey. So his wife opened the door. The officers of the Inland Revenue produced the search warrant. She let them in. She did not know what to do. She telephoned her husband in Guernsey. She told him that they were going through the house taking all the

e documents they could find. They took envelopes addressed to students who were tenants. They went up to the attic and took papers stored there belonging to Mr Tucker's brother. They took Mr Tucker's passport.

The main attack was reserved for the offices at 1 Hanover Square of the Rossminster group of companies of which Mr Plummer and Mr Tucker were directors. They were let in by one of the employees. Many officers of the Inland Revenue went in

f accompanied by police officers. It was a big set of offices with many rooms full of files, papers and documents of all kinds. They took large quantities of them, pushed them into plastic bags, carried them down in the lift, and loaded them into a van. They carried them off to the offices of the Inland Revenue at Melbourne House in the Aldwych. Twelve van loads. They cleared out Mr Tucker's office completely: and other rooms too. They spent the whole day on it from 7 am until 6.30 at night. They did examine

g some of the documents carefully, but there were so many documents and so many files that they could not examine them all. They simply put a number on each file, included it in a list, and put it into the plastic bag. Against each file they noted the time they did it. It looks as if they averaged one file a minute. They did not stop at files. They took the shorthand notebooks of the typists; I do not suppose they could read them. They took some of the financial newspapers in a bundle. In one case the 'top half' of a drawer

h was taken in the first instalment and the balance of the drawer was taken in the second.

Another set of offices was next door in St George Street, I think along the same corridor. It was the office of A J R Financial Services Ltd. The director Mr Hallas was not there, of course, at 7 o'clock. He arrived at 9.10 am He found the officers of the Inland Revenue packing the company's files into bags for removal. He said that it amounted to several hundreds of documents. Police officers were in attendance there too.

j At no point did any of the householders make any resistance. They did the only thing open to them. They went off to their solicitors. They saw counsel. They acted very quickly. By the evening they had gone to a judge of the Chancery Division, Walton J, and asked for and obtained an injunction to stop any trespassing on the premises. They telephoned the injunction through to Hanover Square at about a quarter to six at night. The officers therefore brought the search and seizure to an end. They had, however, by this time practically completed it. So the injunction made very little difference. If the lawyers had had more time to think about it, they would have realised that it was not a case where an injunction would lie against the officers of the Revenue. They were officers of the Crown: and under s 31 of the Crown Proceedings Act 1947 no injunction would lie against the Crown or its officers. So the lawyers did not proceed with their claim for an injunction. They took further advice. Counsel advised them that there might be a remedy under a new procedure recently available. It is to restrain abuses of power under RSC Ord 53. Counsel advised that they might now apply for a declaration, a declaration which, if made, the Crown would be expected to obey. If the circumstances justified it, and if a declaration was made that the seizure was bad, that might be an efficient and expeditious remedy. Before that rule was enacted, the only thing to do would have been to submit to the seizure: to wait until everything had happened: and then to bring an action for damages. But under the new rule, there might be an expeditious remedy available by way of judicial review.

So end the facts. As far as my knowledge of history goes, there has been no search like it, and no seizure like it, in England since that Saturday, 30th April 1763, when the Secretary of State issued a general warrant by which he authorised the King's messengers to arrest John Wilkes and seize all his books and papers. They took everything, all his manuscripts and all papers whatsoever. His pocket-book filled up the mouth of the sack. He applied to the courts. Pratt CJ struck down the general warrant. You will find it all set out in *R v Wilkes*[1], *Huckle v Money*[2] and *Entick v Carrington*[3]. Pratt CJ said[4]:

> 'To enter a man's house by virtue of a nameless warrant, in order to procure evidence, is worse than the Spanish inquisition; a law under which no Englishman would wish to live an hour; it was a most daring public attack made upon the liberty of the subject.'

Now we have to see in this case whether this warrant was valid or not. It all depends of course on the statute. By the common law no search or seizure at any man's house can be made except for stolen goods. I set it all out in *Chic Fashions (West Wales) Ltd v Jones*[5]. Search and seizure is only authorised, and has been authorised, by many statutes in recent years. The one which concerns us was only passed in July 1976. It is a schedule to the Finance Act 1976. It is by s 20c[6]. As it is so important, I will read it in full:

> '(1) If the appropriate judicial authority [and he is defined as the circuit judge] is satisfied on information on oath given by an officer of the Board that—(a) there is reasonable ground for suspecting that an offence involving any form of fraud in connection with, or in relation to, tax has been committed and that evidence of it is to be found on premises specified in the information; and (b) in applying under this section, the officer acts with the approval of the Board given in relation to the particular case, the authority may issue a warrant in writing authorising an officer of the Board to enter the premises, if necessary by force, at any time within 14 days from the time of issue of the warrant, and search them . . .
>
> '(3) On entering the premises with a warrant under this section, the officer may seize and remove any things whatsoever found there which he has reasonable cause to believe may be required as evidence for the purposes of proceedings in respect of such an offence as is mentioned in subsection (1) above . . .'

That is the statute. It is under that statute that Mr Quinlan went to the appropriate judicial authority, in this case a circuit judge, the Common Sergeant of the City of

---

1   (1763) 2 Wils 151, 95 ER 737
2   (1763) 2 Wils 205, 95 ER 768
3   (1765) 2 Wils 275, 95 ER 807
4   2 Wils 205 at 207, 95 ER 768 at 769
5   [1968] 1 All ER 229, [1968] 2 QB 299
6   Ie section 20c of the Taxes Management Act 1970, as inserted by Sch 6 to the Finance Act 1976

London. I would much like to know the information which was given to the judge: the
a nature of the evidence which was put before him to found the suspicion, and the offence
of which the accused were suspected. I would also like to know why these private homes
were believed to hold incriminating material. But we have not been given any
information as to what the Common Sergeant was told. The Revenue take the view that
it would not be appropriate for us at this stage to know what were the grounds of their
suspicion. If this court were told them, it would follow equally that counsel for the
b applicants and his clients would be told them also. So we must remain in ignorance of
the information which was laid before the Common Sergeant. But I must say, and I
think it is right to say, that we should assume that there was laid before the Common
Sergeant material which did justify the view that there was reasonable ground for
suspecting that Mr Plummer, Mr Tucker, the Rossminster companies and the like had
been guilty of an offence involving some fraud on the Revenue: and also that
c incriminating documents would be found in these offices and homes.

Whilst I say that, I would like to emphasise that it is suspicion only. In our law every
man is presumed to be innocent until he is proved to be guilty. Suspicion is not by itself
enough to prove guilt. So I think we should proceed on the presumption that these were
innocent, or presumably innocent, men; and so far there was only a suspicion.

This brings me to the validity of the warrant, and indeed to consider the statute.

d *The validity of the warrant*

Beyond all doubt this search and seizure was unlawful unless it was authorised by
Parliament. As to the statute, we are not allowed to read Hansard; but you can. You can
find it if you turn up the debate[1]. The government of the day put forward the clause.
It was opposed by many as being a dangerous encroachment on individual freedom. It
was passed by a narrow majority.

e Many will ask: why has Parliament done this? Why have they allowed this search and
seizure by the Revenue officers? It did it here because the Board of Inland Revenue were
very worried by the devices used by some wicked people, such as those (and we often see
such cases in our courts) who keep two sets of books: one for themselves to use; the other
to be shown to the Revenue. Those who make out two invoices: one for the customer;
the other to be shown to the taxman. Those who enter into fictitious transactions and
f write them into their books as genuine. Those who show losses when they have in fact
made gains. In the tax evasion pool, there are some big fish who do not stop at tax
avoidance. They resort to frauds on a large scale. I can well see that if the legislation
were confined, or could be confined, to people of that sort, it would be supported by all
honest citizens. Those who defraud the Revenue in this way are parasites who suck out
the life-blood of our society. The trouble is that the legislation is drawn so widely that
g in some hands it might be an instrument of oppression. It may be said that 'honest
people need not fear: that it will never be used against them: that tax inspectors can be
trusted only to use it in the case of the big, bad frauds'. That is an attractive argument,
but I would reject it. Once great power is granted, there is a danger of it being abused.
Rather than risk such abuse, it is, as I see it, the duty of the courts so to construe the
statute as to see that it encroaches as little as possible on the liberties of the people of
h England.

The warrant and the challenge to it

The warrant is challenged on the ground that it does not specify any particular
offence. I must read it in full, because this was what was given to all the teams of
inspectors who went round:

j   'SEARCH WARRANT. TO: RAYMOND QUINLAN AND TO THE PERSONS NAMED IN THE
FIRST SCHEDULE ANNEXED TO THIS WARRANT
'Officers of the Board of Inland Revenue

---

1   911 HC Official Report, (5th Series) (17th May 1976), cols 981–1050; 915 ibid (15th July 1976),
cols 923–1006

'INFORMATION on oath having been laid this day by Raymond Quinlan in accordance with the provisions of Section 20c of the Taxes Management Act 1970 *a* stating that there is reasonable ground for suspecting that an offence involving fraud in connection with or in relation to tax has been committed and that evidence of it is to be found on the premises described in the second schedule annexed hereto.

'YOU ARE HEREBY AUTHORISED to enter those premises, together with all or any of the officers of the Board of Inland Revenue named in the first schedule hereto and together with such constables as you may require, if necessary by force, at any time *b* within 14 days from the time of issue of this Warrant, and search them; and on entering those premises with this Warrant you may seize and remove any things whatsoever found there which you have reasonable cause to believe may be required as evidence for the purposes of proceedings in respect of such an offence.

'DATED THIS 12th DAY OF JULY 1979 [signed by the circuit judge].'

c

Then in the first schedule there are a whole number of names, over 70 officers. And in the second schedule annexed to this particular warrant is the address 1 Hanover Square: and there would be similar warrants in respect of the other premises which were searched.

I come back to the challenge to the warrant. The challenge which is made here is that it does not specify any particular offence involving fraud. There may be 20 different *d* kinds of fraud, as someone suggested, and this warrant does not specify which one of them is suspected. Each of the deponents, in complaining to the court, complain of this. There is a paragraph which each of them makes in his affidavit:

'Despite requests by my Solicitor so to do, the Inland Revenue have refused to disclose the nature of the offence or offences they have in mind and neither I, nor I *e* verily believe my fellow directors, have the slightest idea what offence or offences they do have in mind, or even who is supposed to have committed it or them.'

That is acknowledged by the Revenue: and they give their justification for it in an affidavit which was put forward, I think at the request of the Divisional Court. It is an affidavit by Mr Dermit. He said: *f*

'In the course of my duties I am responsible for initiating and conducting many enquiries some of which may lead to proceedings for offences of fraud in relation to tax. These enquiries are often extremely complicated. I verily believe that it would be greatly detrimental to and obstructive of enquiries of this nature to disclose at this stage the precise nature of the offences in respect of which proceedings may be *g* taken and in which the documents seized may be required as evidence ... Such disclosure, in my view, would be harmful because, inter alia, it might reveal to those suspected of having committed offences not only that those persons have been identified by the Inland Revenue but also the extent and nature of the information in the Revenue's possession concerning such offences.'

h

So there it is. The justification is: 'We do not wish to tell more to those we suspect because we do not want them to know too much about what we intend to do. Otherwise they will be on their guard.'

Is this a just excuse? The words 'an offence involving any form of fraud in connection with, or in relation to, tax' are very wide words. We were taken by counsel for the *j* Revenue through a number of offences which might be comprised in them. There is no specific section in the Taxes Management Act 1970 itself. But there are a number of other offences which involve fraud. There is 'false accounting' under s 17 of the Theft Act 1968. There is 'evasion of liability by deception' in s 2 of the Theft Act 1978. There is perjury, forgery, conspiracy, and false statements relating to income tax. You will find

all those set out in Archbold[1]. They are all offences which involve fraud. But I myself
a   would not be prepared to limit it to those half dozen which counsel put before us. It
seems to me that these words 'fraud . . . in relation to tax' are so vague and so general that
it must be exceedingly difficult for the officers of the Inland Revenue themselves to
know what papers they can take or what they cannot take. Take an instance, for
example, which counsel for the Revenue put before us. They may say to themselves,
'This man must have been guilty of some fraud on the tax. His income is only £1,000
b   a year [let us say] and he is spending at a rate of £5,000 a year. He must be fiddling the
tax in some way. Let us see how he gets his money and what he spends it on'. That, as
we know in these courts, is the sort of evidence relied on by the Revenue when they are
charging a person with a tax fraud.

If such is the ground of suspicion, if such is the sort of evidence which points to fraud,
see how wide a scope it gives to the inspectors of the Inland Revenue. It enables them to
c   pick up all a man's papers, saying to themselves, 'This looks as though there may be
something useful in it. Let's take it'. The vice of a general warrant of this kind, which
does not specify any particular offence, is twofold. It gives no help to the officers when
they have to exercise it. It means also that they can roam wide and large, seizing and
taking pretty well all a man's documents and papers.

There is some assistance to be found in the cases. I refer to the law about arrest, when
d   a man is arrested under a warrant for an offence. It is then established by a decision of
the House of Lords that the warrant has to specify the particular offence with which the
man is charged: see *Christie v Leachinsky*[2]. I will read what Viscount Simon said[3]:

> 'If the arrest was authorised by magisterial warrant, or if proceedings were
> instituted by the issue of a summons, it is clear law that the warrant or summons
> must specify the offence . . . it is a principle involved in our ancient jurisprudence.
e   > Moreover, the warrant must be founded on information in writing and on oath and,
> except where a particular statute provides otherwise, the information and the
> warrant must particularise the offence charged.'

Lord Simonds put it more graphically when he said[4]:

> 'Arrested with or without a warrant, the subject is entitled to know why he is
f   > deprived of his freedom, if only in order that he may, without a moment's delay,
> take such steps as will enable him to regain it.'

So here. When the officers of the Inland Revenue come armed with a warrant to
search a man's home or his office, it seems to me that he is entitled to say, 'Of what
offence do you suspect me? You are claiming to enter my house and to seize my
g   papers.' And when they look at the papers and seize them, he should be able to say, 'Why
are you seizing these papers? Of what offence do you suspect me? What have these to
do with your case?' Unless he knows the particular offence charged, he cannot take steps
to secure himself or his property. So it seems to me, as a matter of construction of the
statute and therefore of the warrant, in pursuance of our traditional role to protect the
liberty of the individual, it is our duty to say that the warrant must particularise the
h   specific offence which is charged as being fraud on the tax.

If this be right, it follows necessarily that this warrant is bad. It should have specified
the particular offence of which the man is suspected. On this ground I would hold that
certiorari should go to quash the warrant.

---

1   Pleading, Evidence and Practice in Criminal Cases (40th Edn, 1979) §§ 1545–1552 (false
j   accounting), §§ 1599, 1599a, 1601, 1601a (evasion of liability by deception), §§ 3501–3522
(perjury), §§ 2140–2173 (forgery), §§ 4049–4088 (conspiracy), §§ 3547–3548, 3550 (false
statements relating to income tax)
2   [1947] 1 All ER 567, [1947] AC 573
3   [1947] 1 All ER 567 at 571, [1947] AC 573 at 585
4   [1947] 1 All ER 567 at 575, [1947] AC 573 at 592

If this be right, there is no need to go further. But I must go further in case it be
wrong. The warrant was issued under judicial authority. The circuit judge, the **a**
Common Sergeant of the City of London, issued it. But the seizure, the subsequent
conduct of the officers at Hanover Square and in the homes of these men, was not subject
to any judicial supervision. And as far as I know without any police check at all. The
police were there, but not doing anything except keeping the peace. The question is
whether or not that seizure came within the provisions of the statute, which I will repeat:
'. . . the officer may seize and remove any things whatsoever found there which he has **b**
reasonable cause to believe may be required as evidence . . .' Is he exempt from
supervision in that regard? Or is he the sole arbiter of 'which he has reasonable cause to
believe'? Surely not. In this regard I need only quote the words of Lord Radcliffe in
Nakkuda Ali v M F de S Jayaratne[1] on those very words 'reasonable cause to believe'. Lord
Radcliffe said:

> 'After all, words such as these are commonly found when a legislature or law- **c**
> making authority confers powers on a minister or official. However read, they
> must be intended to serve in some sense as a condition limiting the exercise of an
> otherwise arbitrary power. But if the question whether the condition has been
> satisfied is to be conclusively decided by the man who wields the power the value of
> the intended restraint is in effect nothing.'
>   **d**

So it cannot be that these officers are the people conclusively to decide whether there
is reasonable cause to believe. The courts must be able to exercise some supervision over
them. If the courts cannot do so, no one else can. Just see what these officers did here.
Council for the applicants went through the evidence of what they did. Minute by
minute. File after file. From their own lists. They could not possibly have had time to
examine all these documents or to come to a proper decision whether they were **e**
reasonably required as evidence. Instead of examining them on the premises, they
bundled them into plastic bags and took them off to Melbourne House. But, in fairness
to the Inland Revenue, I will read what Mr Quinlan said was done. The description
given by Mr Plummer's manager, he said—

> 'is not an accurate description of the way the search was carried out. For example, **f**
> during the day I went through the 2 volume securities register page by page with
> the manager of Rossminster sitting beside me and selected only certain objects in
> such register. I went through a very thick correspondence file of a Mr Glatt and
> released it all. I also went through all the incoming telex messages and the
> manager's outgoing post, and released it all. I carried out a sample check of the
> ledger cards and made special arrangements with the manager to have them
> photocopied on the premises in order that the originals could remain. These are but **g**
> examples of some of the detailed searching which I, and I verily believe, other
> officers carried out on the day in question. But in a very great many instances files
> and bundles of documents were removed when their title or subject matter made
> it clear that their contents were such that the officers had reasonable cause to believe
> that they might be required as evidence for the purpose of proceedings in respect of
> any such offences.'   **h**

Mr Quinlan tells us about the documents which he released. But he does not tell us
what documents he retained and on what ground and for what purpose, or which
particular fraud he had in mind. We are left to guess. I would ask, on what grounds did
these officers decide whether or not there was reasonable cause for believing that they
would be required in evidence? What about the shorthand notebooks, the diaries and all **j**
that kind of thing, would they be reasonably required? Counsel for the Revenue said
that at this stage the Revenue would not wish to go further than they had. They would

a   not tell us on what grounds they required these documents. At this stage, he said, it is not desirable. He emphasised 'at this stage', meaning, I suppose, not until after the criminal proceedings.

To my mind that is not a sufficient answer. It means that these officers would be exempt from any control by the courts or anyone else until after the criminal proceedings, if there are criminal proceedings, take place. It would mean that for all this time no one would have any control over the operations of the officers of the Inland
b   Revenue who are making this search and seizure. Nothing can be done even by the courts in case they have exceeded their powers. No one can control them.

On the question of seizure, counsel for the applicants has pointed to cogent reasons why it may be believed that the officers of the Inland Revenue misunderstood their powers, or exceeded them, or went too far. There is no way of deciding which documents were rightly taken, if they were rightly taken, and those which were wrongly taken, if
c   they were wrongly taken. In the absence of any possibility of dividing the good from the bad, it seems to me that this court has no option but to declare the whole seizure void, even at this stage.

The question was raised whether we could, under our new procedure, grant a declaration. I wish we could grant an interim declaration but it has been decided by this court that we cannot do so. That was decided in *International General Electric Co of New*
d   *York Ltd v Customs and Excise Comrs*[1]. All we can do is make a final declaration. So be it. If that be the only way, I would do it. This is a case where speed is of the essence. This is a case where the freedom of the individual is involved. It is a case where his right to his personal property is involved. It demands immediate remedy. It demands immediate decision. So I think we should decide it now, even on the affidavit evidence we have before us. On that evidence, it is a proper case under this new procedure (which
e   is now entrusted in our hands) in which to make a declaration.

It has this drawback. It means that in any subsequent proceedings or in a pending action the matter will be said to be finally adjudged. The Revenue may seek hereafter to say, 'We did reasonably require all these documents and we did not exceed our powers'. But the result of the declaration will be, and I think both counsel agree to this, that the matter is finally adjudged now. Justice demands that we should decide it quickly, as we
f   do, and give a decision now. I would hold that this seizure was bad and that the Revenue officers exceeded the powers given to them by the statute.

This brings me to the end. This case has given us much concern. No one would wish that any of those who defraud the Revenue should go free. They should be found out and brought to justice. But it is fundamental in our law that the means which are adopted to this end should be lawful means. A good end does not justify a bad means.
g   The means must not be such as to offend against the personal freedom, the privacy and the elemental rights of property. Every man is presumed to be innocent until he is found guilty. If his house is to be searched and his property seized on suspicion of an offence, it must be done by due process of law. And due process involves that there must be a valid warrant specifying the offence of which he is suspected: and the seizure is limited to those things authorised by the warrant. In this case, as I see it, the warrant was
h   invalid for want of particularity: and the search and seizure were not in accordance with anything which was authorised by the warrant. It was an illegal and excessive use of power.

I would therefore allow the appeal, quash the warrant, and make the declaration.

BROWNE LJ. I agree that this appeal should be allowed on the grounds stated by Lord
j   Denning MR, and that the results he has stated must follow.

I confess that I have found it difficult to approach this case without emotion, but I hope that I have not allowed my emotions to influence my decision. I bear in mind, of course,

---

1   [1962] 2 All ER 398, [1962] Ch 784

the vital importance of stopping tax frauds, but the events of this case are deeply
distasteful to my own old-fashioned, and perhaps now unfashionable, instincts. The *a*
knock on the door in the early morning. The entry of a posse of officials and police. The
ransacking of the premises and the clearing out of almost every document, down to
children's passports and cheque books. But putting all that on one side, as I hope I do, I
have no doubt that I am entitled, and bound, to remember the traditional right and duty
of the judges to protect individuals from abuse of power by the executive.

The powers given by s 20C of the Taxes Management Act 1970 (as inserted by the *b*
Finance Act 1976) are very wide and may involve very serious interference with what
would normally be the liberties of individuals. In my judgment, the section should be
construed strictly.

The procedure under s 20C has three stages. First, the application to the circuit judge;
secondly, the issue of the warrant by the circuit judge; and, thirdly, the execution of the
warrant by the Revenue. *c*

Stage 1. The application to the circuit judge

In stage 1, the application to the circuit judge, the circuit judge must be satisfied on
oath of three things. First, that there is reasonable ground for suspecting that an offence
involving any form of fraud in connection with or in relation to tax has been committed;
secondly, that there is reasonable ground for suspecting that evidence of it is to be found *d*
on premises specified in the information; and, thirdly, that the officer applying acts with
the approval of the Board given in relation to the particular case. No question as to the
third requirement arises in the present case.

Counsel for the Revenue accepted, as is obviously right, that the Revenue must put
before the circuit judge materials which satisfy him that there are reasonable grounds for
the suspicions referred to in the subsection. In this case we are not directly concerned *e*
with this stage of the procedure. In the applicants' original statement under RSC Ord 53,
they asked for certiorari to quash the warrants on the ground that there was no sufficient
evidence to satisfy the judge; but in this court counsel for the applicants could not and
did not persist in this part of the application because no information or evidence is
available to us about what material was before the circuit judge. But I think the
requirements which have to be fulfilled at this stage throw light on the construction of *f*
the provisions as to the later stages.

(a) Counsel for the Revenue told us that the offences to which this section relates are
not offences under the Tax Acts, which in England create no offences of fraud in
connection with or in relation to tax, but offences under the general criminal law. He
gave us a list of six common law or statutory offences of fraud to which he said the
suspicion could relate. They were s 17 of the Theft Act 1968 which deals with false *g*
accounting; s 2 of the Theft Act 1978 which deals with the evasion of liability by
deception; s 5 of the Perjury Act 1911; the common law offence of making a false
statement relating to income tax in an attempt to defraud the Revenue, which is dealt
with in Archbold[1]; conspiracy to defraud; and forgery.

The Revenue could no doubt apply to the circuit judge on the ground that they had
reasonable grounds to suspect that more than one offence had been committed. But *h*
there is no power to authorise search for evidence of tax avoidance, or even tax evasion,
not amounting to a criminal offence or of non-payment of tax. It seems to me that
before the Board can decide to apply for a warrant they must have made up their minds
as to at least the general nature of the offence or offences out of this comparatively small
category which they suspect, and that before the judge can be satisfied that there is
reasonable ground for suspecting that an offence has been committed he must be told at *j*
least the general nature of the suspected offence. As I understand it, counsel for the
Revenue accepted all this. This seems to me to dispose of any argument that it would be

---

1   40th Edn (1979) para 3547

impossible or difficult for the Revenue to specify the offence or offences in the warrant.

a   I will come back to this later.

(b) The suspicion must be that an offence *has been* committed; there is no power to authorise search for evidence that an offence *may be* committed in the future.

(c) The suspected evidence to be found on the specified premises must be evidence *of it*, that is, of the offence which is suspected to have been committed. It is not enough that there should be ground for suspecting that evidence of some other offence might be

b   found.

(d) As counsel for the applicants emphasised, the premises authorised to be searched need not be the premises of the person suspected of having committed the offence; they could be those of some perfectly innocent third party. Even if they are the premises of the suspected offender, the matter at this stage rests in suspicion only, and it may turn out that no offence has been committed.

c

Stage 2. The warrant

The warrant in this case, which Lord Denning MR has already read, simply follows the wording of the statute; and counsel for the Revenue submits that this is enough. In my judgment, it is not. I have come to the conclusion that the warrant must specify at least the general nature of the offence or offences which are suspected to have been committed

d   and the evidence to which the search relates. If the circuit judge has been satisfied that there are reasonable grounds for suspecting that more than one offence has been committed, the warrant can of course specify both or all of the offences. As I have said, the Revenue must already have made up their minds what offence or offences they suspect, and have satisfied the circuit judge that there are reasonable grounds for their suspicion. If the warrant does not show the nature of the offence, the occupier of the

e   premises being searched will not know what the Revenue are looking for and can keep no check on their activities; for example, to take a different type of case, if a search warrant was issued under the Firearms Act 1968 to search for firearms or ammunition, the occupier would know that the searchers were not entitled to search for documents, and could prevent them from doing so. What is more important, unless the offence is specified in the warrant it would be very difficult, if not impossible, for the court to

f   enquire under s 20C(3) whether the officers had reasonable cause to believe that a document may be required as evidence for the purposes of proceedings in respect of the offence in relation to which the warrant was granted. I am not going to try to define the degree of particularity which is required beyond saying that it must be enough for the two purposes I have mentioned. It is enough for the purposes of this appeal to say that I am satisfied that the warrants in this case did not sufficiently specify the offences.

g   The result is that in my judgment the warrants are bad on their face, and that an order of certiorari to quash them should go.

Stage 3. The execution of the warrants

In view of the importance of the question and the full arguments which were addressed to us, I must also deal with the position on the assumption, contrary to my view, that the

h   warrants were good.

As a matter of construction of s 20C(3), I have no doubt at all that it is for the court to decide whether an officer had reasonable cause to believe (see *Nakkuda Ali v M F de S Jayaratne*[1] from which Lord Denning MR has already quoted). It is not enough for an officer to swear that he had reasonable cause to believe: he must state the facts on which his belief was based so that the court can judge whether or not his belief was

j   reasonable. There was argument as to the meaning of the last words of the subsection, 'proceedings in respect of such an offence as is mentioned in subsection (1) above'. Does this mean *any* 'offence involving any form of fraud in connection with, or in relation to,

---

1   [1951] AC 66 at 76–77

tax', or is it limited to the particular offence or offences in relation to which the warrant was issued by the circuit judge? Because of the attitude taken up by the Revenue in refusing to disclose what offence they suspect, it is not necessary to decide that question in this case; but I am inclined to think that the effect of the subsection is to put the Revenue in a position analogous to the position of the police when executing a search warrant to search for stolen goods, as laid down in *Chic Fashions (West Wales) Ltd v Jones*[1] and *Ghani v Jones*[2]. In *Ghani v Jones*[3] Lord Denning MR said this:

'I would start by considering the law where police officers enter a man's house by virtue of a warrant, or arrest a man lawfully, with or without a warrant, for a serious offence. I take it to be settled law, without citing cases, that the officers are entitled to take any goods which they find in his possession or in his house which they reasonably believe to be material evidence in relation to the crime for which he is arrested or for which they enter. If in the course of their search they come on any other goods which show him to be implicated in some other crime, they may take them provided they act reasonably and detain them no longer than is necessary.'

Lord Denning MR then referred to two authorities. But in the present context it seems to me that the 'other crime' referred to in that passage must mean a crime falling within the definition of s 20c(1).

The attitude of the Revenue is that they refuse to disclose at this stage what offence or offences they suspected or what grounds they had for seizing the documents they did seize because such disclosure might be detrimental to their investigations and to the conduct of any criminal proceedings which may ensue and would or might involve disclosure, directly or indirectly, of the identity of informers. Counsel for the Revenue laid great stress on this last point and on the public interest privilege which requires the identity of informers to be protected. Like the Divisional Court, I am not impressed by the informer argument. The applicants are not asking for disclosure of the identity of informers (if there are any), and I cannot see why the disclosure of the nature of the offences and the grounds for belief in the relevance of documents need involve any such disclosure. Mr Dermit does not mention this point in his affidavit.

As I understand it, the Revenue's refusal to disclose 'at this stage' extends to the whole period until any ensuing criminal proceedings have been completed or it has been decided not to prosecute. They also say, as I understand it, that the court should not come to any decision by way of judicial review until the Revenue is prepared to disclose its evidence. As counsel for the applicants pointed out, the practical effect of the Revenue's contention, if it is right, would be to take away from the court any power to supervise the activities of the Revenue under s 20c(3). When any criminal proceedings are over or it has been decided not to prosecute, the things seized will presumably be returned anyway, but meanwhile their owners will have been deprived of them, probably for many months. As I have already said, the occupier of the premises searched and owners of the articles seized may be innocent of any offence and may not even have been the people suspected. It is true that they might in some cases have a right of action for damages, but in many cases damages would be a wholly inadequate remedy. I therefore reject the Revenue's contention that they have a right or privilege to refuse to disclose at this stage.

The application for judicial review must be dealt with on the evidence before the court. It is, of course, most unsatisfactory to have to reach a final decision which will amount to res judicata without full evidence from the respondents, the Revenue. If the respondents, the defendants in the action begun in the Chancery Division and transferred to the Queen's Bench Division, had not been the Crown, the problem could have been satisfactorily solved by making an interim injunction, leaving the substantive issues to

1   [1968] 1 All ER 229, [1968] 2 QB 299
2   [1969] 3 All ER 1700, [1970] 1 QB 693
3   [1969] 3 All ER 1700 at 1703, [1970] 1 QB 693 at 706

be fully explored and decided at the trial. But no injunction can be granted against the
Crown. Counsel for the applicants and for the Revenue agree that, most unfortunately,
I think, we cannot make an interim declaration; we were referred to *International General
Electric Co of New York Ltd v Customs and Excise Comrs*[1]. But if the Revenue decide not to
disclose the nature of the offences they suspect and the grounds for their belief that the
documents they seize may be required as evidence, they must take the consequences. I
entirely agree with what I understand Goff LJ is going to say about this aspect of the case.

Lord Denning MR has fully stated the facts and I do not think I need repeat them. On
the available evidence, the applicants have satisfied me that in respect of the bulk of the
documents seized the Revenue officers had no reasonable cause to believe *before* they
seized the documents that those documents may be required as evidence for the purposes
of proceedings for any relevant offence. The evidence on behalf of the applicants and the
lists prepared by the Revenue, especially as to the times of seizure, raise a strong prima
facie case that the great bulk of the documents were not examined at all, and certainly
not examined in enough detail to form any opinion about their evidential value. There
was evidence from the Revenue officers that some documents were examined in detail,
but even in respect of those documents the officers give no grounds for their belief as to
their relevance and merely assert that they had reasonable grounds for it. Even if the
Revenue did sufficiently examine some documents to have reasonable grounds for belief
that that particular document may be required as evidence, this is not a case where it is
possible to split up the documents seized and say that some were seized properly and
some were seized improperly. It is a case, as Lord Denning MR has said, of all or nothing.

Accordingly I agree with Lord Denning MR that the applicants have made out their
case, and that they are entitled to the two remedies Lord Denning MR has mentioned:
certiorari to quash the warrants and a declaration that the seizure was bad, and that the
Revenue must return the documents and all copies of them. We may wish to hear
counsel further about the detailed wording of the declaration.

GOFF LJ. Lord Denning MR has fully stated the facts of this case and I will not waste
time by repeating a recital of them, but will proceed at once to state in my own words the
reasons which lead me to concur with the conclusions Lord Denning MR and Browne LJ
have reached, which reasons do not, I think, conflict in any way with theirs which I also
adopt.

We do not know what was the evidence on oath on which the learned circuit judge
authorised the issue of the warrants in this case, and, therefore, in my judgment we
cannot consider whether it was sufficient, and we must I think proceed on the assumption
that it was and that he acted regularly.

The only way, if any, in which we could possibly arrive at a different conclusion on
that point, as it seems to me, would be on the ground that the warrant lacks sufficient
particularity, if that be right, and that we should infer, therefore, that the evidence on
which it was issued was similarly lacking. That approach, however, would make the
question whether the judge acted regularly in substance the same as the question what
form the warrant ought to take. I therefore proceed on the basis that the warrant was
regularly issued.

Then I turn to the question whether the warrant is good or bad on the face of it for
want of particularity. It is to be observed that the Taxes Management Act 1970 does not
specify any particular form, which can, therefore, only be gathered from the true
construction of s 20c(1) of the 1970 Act as amended which is quite general in its terms:
'. . . an offence involving any form of fraud in connection with, or in relation to, tax'.
The warrant simply uses these same words. The applicants say that that is not enough,
and there ought to be some definition or description of the suspected offence. In their
statement, filed pursuant to RSC Ord 53, r 3(2), they say that the warrants are illegal and

---

1   [1962] 2 All ER 398, [1962] Ch 784

void in that they do not state by whom and when there are reasonable grounds for
suspecting an offence has been committed and the precise nature of and/or the particular   *a*
acts constituting the offence. Counsel for the applicants was, however, I think forced to
concede that the case cannot be put as high as that. At all events, I do not accept that it
can. Bearing in mind that the warrant issues on suspicion and comes in the investigatory
stage, it seems to me that the Revenue cannot be expected to give, nor need the warrant
specify, the suspected offence with any degree of particularity, but I think it cannot be
right simply to copy the general words of the section into the warrant.   *b*

Counsel for the Revenue has pointed out (a) that those words define a genus and
exclude all criminal offences outside that genus; (b) that with one exception, and that
applicable only to Scotland, the Income Tax Acts do not create any criminal offences;
those have to be culled from the general law; and (c) that there are only six types of
offence within the genus. These may be shortly summarised as follows: (1) false
accounting within s 17 of the Theft Act 1968; (2) dishonestly obtaining exemption or   *c*
abatement of liability under s 2 of the Theft Act 1978; (3) perjury, which would include
false statements in tax returns; (4) common law cheating, and there is an actual instance
of that in a Revenue case in *R v Hudson*[1]; (5) conspiracy to defraud; and (6) forgery.

Counsel for the Revenue argues, therefore, that as the genus is thus limited, and the
different species within the genus may overlap and it may well be difficult to determine
before search within which category or categories the offence lies, and because the   *d*
Revenue must be entitled to specify more than one type of offence, it should be sufficient
in the warrant merely to state the whole genus.

On the other hand, in order to obtain the approval of the Board, which is a prerequisite
to the application to the circuit judge (see s 20c(1)(a) and (2)), and further to satisfy him
that there is reasonable ground for suspicion that an offence involving any form of fraud
in connection with or in relation to tax has been committed, and that there is evidence   *e*
of it at the premises sought to be searched, the Revenue must have sifted the matter to
a considerable degree, and in my judgment the warrant ought, therefore, to state on its
face that it relates to all or to some one or more, and, if so, which of the six species of
offence within the genus.

The words 'such an offence' in s 20c(3) would I think cover any of the offences within
sub-s (1) and justify retention of documents found disclosing an offence other than that   *f*
on which the warrant was based, but do not in my view justify the warrant being drawn
in entirely general terms. If the Revenue in any case are relying on what I have just said
to enable them to seize documents other than those in relation to the offence on which
the warrant was issued, it would be a condition that they must have been acting
reasonably.

In my judgment, therefore, the warrant was bad on its face and the applicants are   *g*
entitled to an order of certiorari to quash it, and it follows to a declaration that the
Revenue were not entitled to seize any of the documents which they took from any of
the premises and are bound to deliver them up together with all copies.

That is sufficient to dispose of the case, but I will consider how the matter stands on the
assumption that I am wrong in the conclusion I have so far reached.

Before doing so, however, I pause to say that it is not necessary to consider any question   *h*
of mandamus, since there is here no duty for the enforcement of which that remedy
could be made available. The sole question is whether the applicants are entitled to the
declarations I have mentioned notwithstanding the assumed validity of the warrant.

Counsel for the applicants submits that the evidence shows that there was really here
no search to find things, which the searchers might have reasonable grounds to believe
were evidence of a suspected offence or offences in respect of which the warrant was   *j*
obtained, but a general ransacking of the premises to see if evidence of some crime or

---

1   [1956] 1 All ER 814, [1956] 2 QB 252

other would show up, and he relies on the following passage in the judgment of Lord
Denning MR in *Ghani v Jones*[1]:

'The common law does not permit police officers, or anyone else, to ransack
anyone's house, or to search for papers or articles therein, or to search his person,
simply to see if he may have committed some crime or other. If police officers
should do so, they would be guilty of a trespass. Even if they should find something
incriminating against him, I should have thought that the court would not allow it
to be used in evidence against him, if the conduct of the police officers was so
oppressive that it would not be right to allow the Crown to rely on it.'

More specifically he says, first, that the documents taken were so numerous, and the
inspection of many of them so cursory, that with respect to a large proportion the
inspectors could not at the time of seizure have had reasonable grounds for believing that
they might be required as evidence of an offence, but only hoped that when compared
with others and diligently examined a case might be established.

Akin to this he says that the documents must be examined on the premises. There is
no power to remove them for examination elsewhere, since they can only be removed if
seized, and they cannot be seized until examined to see if there be reasonable grounds for
believing that they might be required as evidence. He argues that impracticability of
examination on the premises cannot give a right of removal for search elsewhere.

Against that, counsel for the Revenue, whilst he admits that the searchers must make
up their minds whilst on the premises that there are reasonable grounds for believing
that the documents removed may be required as evidence, and that reasonable grounds
for that belief must then and there exist, asserts that the Revenue may then seize all
documents as to which they have on reasonable grounds formed such belief and may
thereafter on their own premises or anywhere else analyse them, submit them to forensic
examination, and obtain expert advice, legal or otherwise, about them.

If, and when, as a result they ascertain that any are not required, then, as counsel for
the Revenue readily accepted, they must return them, but otherwise they are entitled to
keep them until the contemplated criminal proceedings have been launched and decided,
in support of which he relies on *Malone v Comr of Police of the Metropolis*[2] where the police
were held entitled to retain moneys seized under a search warrant until the end of the
criminal trial, although they had not been used in the committal proceedings; and, in
my judgment, if the documents were properly taken in the first instance, that would
follow.

In the end, as it seems to me, the position comes down to this. The applicants'
evidence does raise a strong prima facie case that counsel's submissions are right, so that
there was an abuse of power. Therefore, it is incumbent on the Revenue to justify the
seizure.

I should here observe that on the facts of this case there are no means of distinguishing
between documents properly seized and those not properly seized so as to enable the
court to separate them and to grant relief limited to the latter category. I say this so that
it may not be thought that my judgment is authority for the proposition that taking too
much necessarily invalidates the whole seizure. There may well be many cases in which
it will not.

This being so, the answer of the Revenue is twofold. (1) 'We are not at this stage
obliged to do more than swear that we did believe and had reasonable grounds to believe
that the documents we took might be required as evidence of an offence involving any
form of fraud in connection with or in relation to tax, because it would or might be
detrimental to our enquiries'; and in support of that in an affidavit put in on the last day
of the hearing before the Divisional Court Mr Dermit said:

---

1 [1969] 3 All ER 1700 at 1703, [1970] 1 QB 693 at 706–707
2 [1979] 1 All ER 256, [1978] 3 WLR 936

'I verily believe that it would be greatly detrimental to and obstructive of enquiries of this nature to disclose at this stage the precise nature of the offences in respect of which proceedings may be taken and in which the documents seized may be required as evidence . . . Such disclosure, in my view, would be harmful because, inter alia, it might reveal to those suspected of having committed offences not only that those persons have been identified by the Inland Revenue but also the extent and nature of the information in the Revenue's possession concerning such offences.'

Counsel for the Revenue also relied on *Wilover Nominees v Inland Revenue Comrs*[1], but that is I think distinguishable and posed a different problem.

(2) 'In any event, we did give sufficient evidence to show that we had reasonable grounds.' Here counsel for the Revenue relies in particular on the affidavit of Mr Quinlan from which I read the following extracts.

'Before the search warrants were executed all the teams were addressed in my presence by Mr W M Dermit, the Assistant Director in charge of the Special Investigations Section as to the principles and procedure to be followed in the search. Mr Dermit made it quite clear to all those involved that they were only to seize documents or articles which they had reasonable cause to believe might be required as evidence for the purpose of proceedings in respect to such offences. I had arranged with each team leader to give detailed instructions to his team in relation to the particular premises to be searched by them. In the case of my team I arranged for these instructions to be given by the said Mr Thomas and I verily believe that this was duly done. I have read the affidavit to be sworn herein by the said Mr Thomas and the instructions to which he there refers were as I had discussed with him in advance . . . From time to time during the said search individual Revenue officers asked me whether certain material which they had found came into the said category and I would give a ruling. During the course of the day a great many documents were removed but I verily believe that they all fell within my said instructions . . . during the day I went through the 2 volume securities register page by page with the manager of Rossminster sitting beside me and selected only certain objects in such register. I went through a very thick correspondence file of a Mr Glatt and released it all. I also went through all the incoming telex messages and the manager's outgoing post, and released it all. I carried out a sample check of the ledger cards and made special arrangements with the manager to have them photocopied on the premises in order that the originals could remain. These are but examples of some of the detailed searching which I, and I verily believe, other officers carried out on the day in question. But in a very great many instances files and bundles of documents were removed when their title or subject matter made it clear that their contents were such that the officers had reasonable cause to believe that they might be required as evidence for the purpose of proceedings in respect of any such offences . . . Consideration of the documents and other articles seized at the said premises of AJR Financial Services Limited and the homes of Mr Plummer and Mr Tucker reinforces my belief that none of the officers searching such premises seized material which he did not have reasonable cause to believe might be required for the aforesaid purposes.'

Counsel for the Revenue also referred us to the affidavit of Mr Thomas, from which I read the following short passage:

'When actually searching it was in almost all instances clear from the title to a file or the subject matter of a bundle of documents whether or not it should be seized. But during the course of the day I and my colleagues read through a large number

---

1   [1974] 3 All ER 496, [1974] 1 WLR 1342, [1974] STC 467

of documents in whole or in part in order to decide whether they should be seized or not.'

Then Mr Ramage in his affidavit said:

'Although Mr Plummer appeared to keep many business papers at his home it was in almost all cases possible to ascertain from the title of files or the subject matter of bundles or categories of documents whether they fell into the above description but where there was any doubt either I or one of the officers with me went through the papers in further detail until we were satisfied that they either should or need not be seized. I am quite satisfied in relation to each of the documents of which Mr Plummer makes specific mention in the said paragraph 5 that they did not fall within the above description and that I did have reasonable cause to believe that they might be required for the said purpose.'

Finally Mr Watt said:

'Mr Tucker did not appear to keep many business papers at his home and it was in all cases possible to ascertain from the title of files or the subject matter of bundles or categories of documents whether they fell into the above description. I did not have any difficulty in making up my mind in accordance with my instructions what I should and what I need not seize. I am quite satisfied in relation to each of the documents at Mr Tucker's house to which Mr Tucker makes specific mention in his said affidavit that they did fall within the above description and that I did have reasonable cause to believe that they might be required for the said purposes, with the exception of the bank statements belonging to student tenants to which Mr Tucker refers in paragraph 3 of his affidavit. These I examined but did not seize.'

In support of the first limb of this argument, counsel for the Revenue relies on the duty of the Board to detect and prosecute criminal dishonesty in evading taxes, and the dangers to their enquiries if they are called on to give reasons for their belief. It is, he submits, a case of balancing the public interest in the detection and punishment of crime and the necessity of protecting the rights of private individuals in respect of their property: see *Ghani v Jones*[1] where Lord Denning MR said:

'What is the principle underlying these instances? We have to consider, on the one hand, the freedom of the individual. His privacy and his possessions are not to be invaded except for the most compelling reasons. On the other hand, we have to consider the interest of society at large in finding out wrongdoers and repressing crime. Honest citizens should help the police and not hinder them in their efforts to track down criminals.'

I agree that this balancing problem does present itself, but in carrying out the exercise in this case there are, as it seems to me, three important considerations to bear in mind: (1) the general duty of the court to exercise surveillance over the exercise of executive power; (2) the extremely wide and general nature of the power conferred by s 20c and consequent danger of abuse; (3) the fact that it authorises the search of premises belonging to persons believed, or even known to be, entirely innocent and the seizure of the documents of such persons either on their own premises or elsewhere. If the documents of such persons can be taken and retained till after a decision has been reached to launch criminal proceedings against other people and until those proceedings have been heard, the consequences for the innocent party may be very serious indeed, if not totally ruinous.

1 [1969] 3 All ER 1700 at 1705, [1970] 1 QB 693 at 708

The importance of this duty of surveillance is in my judgment clearly borne out by *Ghani v Jones*[1] and the following authorities. First, in *Padfield v Minister of Agriculture, Fisheries and Food*[2] Lord Pearce said:

> 'I do not regard a Minister's failure or refusal to give any reasons as a sufficient exclusion of the court's surveillance. If all the prima facie reasons seem to point in favour of his taking a certain course to carry out the intentions of Parliament in respect of a power which it has given him in that regard, and he gives no reason whatever for taking a contrary course, the court may infer that he has no good reason and that he is not using the power given by Parliament to carry out its intentions.'

I am not overlooking the answer of counsel for the Revenue that such an inference should not be drawn where the party concerned gives the grounds on which he refuses to disclose his reasons, but that very argument defeats the court's right and duty to effect surveillance.

Secondly, a most important authority in this connection to which I would make reference is *Nakkuda Ali v M F de S Jayaratne*[3] where Lord Radcliffe delivering the judgment of the Board, after quoting *Liversidge v Anderson*[4] in the House of Lords, said:

> 'But the elaborate consideration which the majority of the House gave to the context and circumstances before adopting that construction itself shows that there is no general principle that such words are to be so understood; and the dissenting speech of Lord Atkin at least serves as a reminder of the many occasions when they have been treated as meaning "if there is in fact reasonable cause for A.B. so to believe". After all, words such as these are commonly found when a legislature or law-making authority confers powers on a minister or official. However read, they must be intended to serve in some sense as a condition limiting the exercise of an otherwise arbitrary power. But if the question whether the condition has been satisfied is to be conclusively decided by the man who wields the power the value of the intended restraint is in effect nothing. No doubt he must not exercise the power in bad faith: but the field in which this kind of question arises is such that the reservation for the case of bad faith is hardly more than a formality. Their Lordships therefore treat the words in reg. 62, "where the Controller has reasonable grounds to believe that any dealer is unfit to be allowed to continue as a dealer" as imposing a condition that there must in fact exist such reasonable grounds, known to the Controller, before he can validly exercise the power of cancellation.'

Finally, see per Lord Wilberforce in *Secretary of State for Education and Science v Metropolitan Borough of Tameside*[5]:

> 'The section is framed in a "subjective" form—if the Secretary of State "is satisfied". This form of section is quite well known, and at first sight might seem to exclude judicial review. Sections in this form may, no doubt, exclude judicial review on what is or has become a matter of pure judgment. But I do not think that they go further than that. If a judgment requires, before it can be made, the existence of some facts, then, although the evaluation of those facts is for the Secretary of State alone, the court must enquire whether those facts exist, and have been taken into account, whether the judgment has been made on a proper self direction as to those facts, whether the judgment has not been made on other facts

1   [1969] 3 All ER 1700, [1970] 1 QB 693
2   [1968] 1 All ER 694 at 714, [1968] AC 997 at 1053–1054
3   [1951] AC 66 at 77
4   [1941] 3 All ER 338, [1942] AC 206
5   [1976] 3 All ER 665 at 681–682, [1977] AC 1014 at 1047

which ought not to have been taken into account. If these requirements are not
met, then the exercise of judgment, however bona fide it may be, becomes capable
of challenge.'

Which way the balance lies is not wholly easy to determine, but I have in the end come
to a firm conclusion that the case is one in which the Revenue are required even at this
stage to state the grounds for their belief so that the court can determine whether they
are reasonable, and that, of course, they have failed to do.

In my judgment Mr Quinlan's affidavit and the other evidence on behalf of the
Revenue to which I have referred is not sufficient for these reasons. First, of course, it
goes only to some of the documents, and this is a case of all or nothing; secondly, except
possibly some items in the securities register and the ledger cards, it does not identify
which of the documents Mr Quinlan or any other searcher decided should be seized
because they might be required as evidence; and, thirdly, of course, and most important,
still these deponents do not state the grounds for their belief.

Counsel for the Revenue argued strenuously and persuasively that the various kinds
of documents taken might well be evidence for this or the other reason, and in particular
the children's cheque books, because one might want to see where money had gone, and
passports to show whether the holder had gone to some particular place at some particular
time. This line of argument, however, is insufficient in my judgment both because it is
hypothetical, and because much of it depends on assuming an offence has been
committed or appears to have been committed, but, of course, that has not been
shown. There is no evidence at all to show that the individuals and the companies whose
premises were searched, or any one or more of them, or anybody in particular is
suspected, much less proved to be guilty. As I have observed, the power of search given
by s 20c extends to perfectly innocent persons, and unless and until the Revenue adduce
evidence showing that they suspect this person or that, the question of reasonable
grounds must be decided on the assumption of innocence. If the Revenue's argument
were allowed to prevail, the court would be precluded from control not only at this very
moment but until after the conclusion of the criminal trial or the decision not to
prosecute, as the case may be.

For these reasons I would allow this appeal and make the declarations asked for, subject
to any observations by counsel as to the precise form in which they should go, even if the
warrant was good.

Before I close this judgment, I would like to add a few observations on a point which
did trouble me during the argument. The applicants commenced proceedings by an
ordinary writ action and moved for interlocutory relief which, but for the fact that the
respondents are in effect the Crown, could have been granted without prejudice to what
might be determined later at the trial. Because of that fact, however, such relief could
not be granted, and these proceedings by way of judicial review are the only means by
which the applicants can obtain expeditious relief, but then the order we make is a final
one and, as both parties agree, the declarations will make the issue of lawful or unlawful
seizure res judicata between the parties at the trial of the Chancery action, now
transferred to the Queen's Bench Division, leaving the Revenue with no answer to a
claim for damages, the only question being that of quantum.

I was concerned whether anything could or should be done to prevent the procedural
change having also this substantive effect. It was suggested that we should in the exercise
of our discretion refuse to make a declaration at all on the ground that it is not in all the
circumstances of the case just and convenient: see RSC Ord 53, r 2(c). In my judgment,
however, that cannot be right. We have heard and decided the case, and must grant
relief.

Then I considered whether it might be correct to qualify our declaration by a proviso
to the effect that it should be without prejudice to the issue of legality of the seizure at
the trial or perhaps more generally to any question of damages. I am satisfied, however,
that this is not open to the court, since it would inevitably make the declaration an

interlocutory or interim one, and that, it is well settled in this court, is not permissible, at all events against the Crown: see *International General Electric Co of New York Ltd v Comrs of Customs and Excise*[1]. I need only read part of the headnote of that case[2]:   **a**

'On appeal:—*Held*, that an order declaring the rights of parties must in its nature be a final order and (subject to appeal) be res judicata between the parties; and that in proceedings against the Crown it was not possible to obtain an order which corresponded to an interim injunction or an interim declaration which did not determine the rights of the parties but which was only intended to preserve the   **b** status quo.'

In my judgment, therefore, we must make a final declaration even though at a later stage the Revenue might otherwise have adduced further evidence to show reasonable grounds. This may perhaps be unfortunate for the Revenue, but they did know that the applicants were seeking a final order, and they elected to take their stand that they could   **c** not at this stage be required to give reasons.

I am comforted on this point also by the fact that if I am right on the question of the validity of the warrant, the question of interim or final order does not arise at all.

Be all that as it may, the conclusion that the applicants are on the evidence before us entitled to a final order by way of declaration, and that it is the duty of the court to make one, appears to me to be clear.   **d**

Appeal allowed. Order of certiorari to quash warrants. Declaration in terms agreed. Leave to appeal to the House of Lords granted.

Solicitors: *Roney, Vincent & Co* (for the applicants); *Solicitor of Inland Revenue.*

Sumra Green   Barrister.   e

---

1   [1962] 2 All ER 398, [1962] Ch 784
2   [1962] Ch 784 at 785

Re Cushla Ltd

CHANCERY DIVISION
VINELOTT J
28th FEBRUARY, 1st, 16th MARCH 1979

Bankruptcy – Proof – Set-off – Mutual credits, mutual debts or other mutual dealings – Claims arising otherwise than out of contract – Statutory debts due to Crown – Company in compulsory liquidation – Crown by mistake making payment to liquidator of company in respect of excess input value added tax without setting it off against debts due from company to Crown – Whether Crown entitled to set off statutory debts owed to it against input tax – Whether Crown's right of set-off ceased to apply when payment inadvertently made to liquidator – Bankruptcy Act 1914, s 31.

On 24th February 1975 an order was made for the compulsory winding-up of a company incorporated in the Isle of Man in 1972. At the date of the winding-up a balance of £4,055 was owed to the company by the Commissioners of Customs and Excise ('the commissioners') in respect of input tax for the period from 1st October 1973 to 1st September 1974, payable under s 3(2) of the Finance Act 1972. At the date of the winding-up petition the company's liabilities amounted to over £84,500 and the estimated deficiency in assets available to meet debts due to unsecured creditors amounted to approximately £80,000. The debts included £4,726 due to the Inland Revenue Commissioners and £951 due to the Department of Health and Social Security. A liquidator was appointed on 8th May 1975. On 10th September 1976 the commissioners by mistake sent to the liquidator a cheque for £3,651 in part settlement of the sum of £4,055 owed by them to the company in respect of input tax. Subsequently, the commissioners took the view that under s 31 of the Bankruptcy Act 1914 they were required to set off the debts owed by them to the company against the amounts owed by the company to the Inland Revenue Commissioners and the Department of Health and Social Security and they commenced proceedings to recover the sum of £3,651 which they had inadvertently paid to the liquidator. The liquidator applied to the court for an order that the commissioners repay the sum of £404 due from them to the company in respect of input tax, contending that s 31[a] of the Act did not require the commissioners to set off the input tax against the larger debts due from the company to the Inland Revenue Commissioners and the Department of Health and Social Security, and, that, even if it did, when the sum of £3,651 was paid to the company the section ceased to apply.

Held – The commissioners were entitled to recover the sum of £3,651 from the liquidator and were not bound to pay him the sum of £404 because—
  (i) On its true construction, s 31 of the 1914 Act applied to debts due to and from the Crown (see p 419 c to f and p 420 b to f, post); *Re D H Curtis (Builders) Ltd* [1978] 2 All ER 183 followed.
  (ii) As the provisions of s 31 were mandatory and prescribed the course to be followed in the administration of a bankrupt's estate, and could not therefore be excluded, the position immediately before the commencement of the winding-up was that the input tax due to the company from the commissioners fell to be set-off against the debt due from the company to the Inland Revenue Commissioners and the Department of Health

and Social Security. Accordingly the Crown was entitled to prove for and be paid a dividend on '. . . the balance of the account and no more', within s 31. It followed that the Crown was under no liability to pay anything to the liquidator, and was entitled to recover the sum of £3,651, being moneys paid under a mistake and therefore recoverable at law (see p 422 c d and p 423 a to c and f, post); dictum of Lord Wright in *Norwich Union Fire Insurance Society Ltd v Price Ltd* [1934] AC at 462 and *National Westminster Bank Ltd v Halesowen Presswork and Assemblies Ltd* [1972] 1 All ER 641 applied.

Notes

For the circumstances in which a right of set-off is available to a creditor, see 3 Halsbury's Laws (4th Edn) para 753, and for cases on mutual credit and set-off in bankruptcy, see 4 Digest (Reissue) 428–462, 3736–3974.

For the Bankruptcy Act 1914, s 31, see 3 Halsbury's Statutes (3rd Edn) 80.

Cases referred to in judgment

Attorney-General v Guy Motors Ltd [1928] 2 KB 78, 97 LJKB 421, 139 LT 311, 11 Digest (Reissue) 708, 360.

Curtis (D H) (Builders) Ltd, Re [1978] 2 All ER 183, [1978] Ch 162, [1978] 2 WLR 28.

Forster v Wilson (1843) 12 M & W 191, 13 LJ Ex 209, 152 ER 1165, 4 Digest (Reissue) 435, 3802.

James, Ex parte, re Condon (1874) LR 9 Ch App 609, [1874–80] All ER Rep 388, 43 LJ Bcy 107, 30 LT 773, LJJ, 5 Digest (Reissue) 881, 7298.

Laing (Liquidator of Inverdale Construction Co Ltd) v Lord Advocate 1973 SLT (Notes) 81.

National Westminster Bank Ltd v Halesowen Presswork and Assemblies Ltd [1972] 1 All ER 641, [1972] AC 785, [1972] 2 WLR 455, [1972] 1 Lloyd's Rep 101, Digest (Cont Vol D) 58, 1046a.

Norwich Union Fire Insurance Society Ltd v William H Price Ltd [1934] AC 455, [1934] All ER Rep 352, 103 LJPC 115, 151 LT 309, 29 Digest (Repl) 349, 2683.

Cases also cited

Bonham, Re, ex parte Postmaster-General (1879) 10 Ch D 595, CA.

British American Continental Bank v British Bank for Foreign Trade [1926] 1 KB 328, [1925] All ER Rep 486, CA.

City Equitable Fire Insurance Co Ltd, Re, (No 2) [1930] 2 Ch 293, [1930] All ER Rep 315, CA.

Clark (a bankrupt), Re, ex parte Trustee v Texaco Ltd [1975] 1 All ER 453, [1975] 1 WLR 559.

Gozzett, Re, ex parte Messenger & Co Ltd v Trustee [1936] 1 All ER 79, CA.

Naoroji v Chartered Bank of India (1868) LR 3 CP 444.

Rolls Razor Ltd v Cox [1967] 1 All ER 397, [1967] 1 QB 552, CA.

Thellusson, Re, ex parte Abdy [1919] 2 KB 735, [1918–19] All ER Rep 729, CA.

Thomas, Re, ex parte Woods and Forests Comrs (1888) 21 QBD 380, DC.

Town Investments Ltd v Department of the Environment [1977] 1 All ER 813, [1978] AC 359.

Tyler, Re, ex parte Official Receiver [1907] 1 KB 865, [1904–7] All ER Rep 181, CA.

Webb (H J) & Co (Smithfield, London) Ltd, Re [1922] 2 Ch 369.

Adjourned summonses

By an originating summons dated 10th July 1978, the Commissioners of Customs and Excise ('the commissioners') applied to the court seeking an order that Victor Ernest Grimwood, the liquidator of Cushla Ltd ('the company'), a company in compulsory liquidation, should repay to them the sum of £3,651, paid by the commissioners in error, on or about 10th September 1976, and had and received by him as such liquidator to the use of the commissioners. By an originating summons dated 2nd February 1979, the liquidator applied to the court seeking (1) a declaration that the commissioners were not entitled to set off the sum of £404 due from the commissioners to the company as value added tax repayable for the month of November 1973 against the claims of the Commissioners of Inland Revenue and the Department of Health and Social Security, and (2) an order that the commissioners repay the sum of £404 to the liquidator. Both

a   applications were heard together. The facts are set out in the judgment.

Peter Gibson for the commissioners.
M H K *Hamer* for the liquidator.

b

16th March. **VINELOTT J** read the following judgment: On 24th February 1975 an order was made for the compulsory winding-up of Cushla Ltd, a company which had been incorporated in the Isle of Man in 1972. On 8th May 1975 Victor Ernest Grimwood, a chartered accountant, was appointed liquidator of the company. The liabilities at the date of the winding-up petition amounted to over £84,000, and the estimated deficiency
c   in the assets available to meet the debts due to unsecured creditors is approximately £80,000.

The debts due to unsecured creditors include a balance of approximately £4,726 due to the Commissioners of the Inland Revenue (after deducting a preferential claim of £200) and a balance of £951 due to the Department of Health and Social Security. At the date of the winding-up there was a balance of £4,055·42 owed to the company by the
d   Commissioners of Customs and Excise ('the commissioners'), being input value added tax in respect of periods from 1st October 1973 to 1st September 1974, which is payable to the company under s 3(2) of the Finance Act 1972. In September 1976 a cheque for £3,651·28, part of this aggregate of £4,055·42, was sent to the company by the commissioners. It has been credited to the company's estate cash book with the Department of Trade. The circumstances of this payment are explained in an affidavit
e   of Dennis Cyril Pillin, a senior executive officer at the Value Added Tax Central Unit ('the VCU'), and paras 5 to 10 of his affidavit read as follows:

'5. Information relevant for the purposes of VAT to a registered person's VAT affairs is normally recorded in a computer which the Commissioners have installed at the VCU. Repayments of VAT are made by the Commissioners by means of the
f   said computer which, subject to the placing of an inhibitor as hereinafter mentioned, is programmed to send out a payable order to a registered person when a net credit in his favour is entered in the said computer in respect of the final period then recorded in the said computer. However when a registered person is a company which goes into liquidation, the Commissioners' practice is to record that fact in the said computer and to place therein an inhibitor with a view to preventing any payments being made to the Liquidator without clearance from the Commission-
g   ers. The purpose of the inhibitor is to give the Commissioners an opportunity to check whether any debts are owed to other Crown departments so that the Commissioners may give effect to the mandatory statutory requirements relating to set-off.

'6. On the 4th November 1975 it was recorded in the said computer that the
h   Liquidator had been appointed Liquidator of the Company and the said inhibitor was placed in the said computer.

'7. The Company prior to its winding up had failed to make VAT returns for the period 1st October 1973 to the 31st October 1973 or for any part of the period from 1st December 1973 to the date of its winding up. By letter dated 28th July 1976 the Liquidator sent to the VAT Machinery Division J ('the VMJ') at Bootle 11 VAT returns for the months of October and December 1973 and January to September
j   1974 (inclusive) showing a total sum of £3,651·28 (incorrectly added up by the Liquidator as £3,382·84) as VAT repayable by the Commissioners to the Company. On the 11th August 1976 the Liquidator sent to the VMJ four further VAT returns for the months of October, November and December 1974 and for the period the 1st January 1975 to the 23rd February 1975 (the day prior to the

commencement of the liquidation), showing no VAT due from or repayable to the Company in respect of those periods.

'8. The VAT returns sent by the Liquidator on the 28th July 1976 to the VMJ were sent on to the VCU but as the periods to which those returns related had elapsed so long before, the current computer files no longer recorded entries in respect of those periods. Accordingly the said credit of £3,651·28 was recorded on the 7th September 1976 on a period held in the computer used in insolvency cases for accounting periods where earlier periods are no longer recorded.

'9. It was not then appreciated that the action of entering a credit as aforesaid would have the effect of overriding the said inhibitor nor was it intended that it should have that effect. But it did have that effect and a payable order for the said sum of £3,651·28 was sent by the computer to the Liquidator on the 10th September 1976. The Liquidator by letter dated the 21st September 1976 acknowledged receipt of the said payable order but queried the amount.

'10. After payment of the said sum of £3,651·28 as aforesaid, it was ascertained by the Commissioners that the Company was at the date of its winding up and at the date of such repayment still remained indebted to the Commissioners of Inland Revenue in the sum of £4,925·99 (of which £200 was a preferential debt) and to the Department of Health and Social Security in the sum of £951·47. If the repayment had not been made in error in the circumstances aforesaid the Commissioners would have set-off the said credit of £3,651·28 against the said debts due to the Crown. A further amount of £404·14 due from the Commissioners as VAT repayable at the date of the Winding up Order in respect of the VAT Return furnished by the Company for the month of November 1973 has been set off against the said debts due to the Commissioners of Inland Revenue and the Department of Health and Social Security.'

In the first of the two applications now before me the commissioners ask for an order that the liquidator repay the sum of £3,651·28. In the second of the two applications, the liquidator asks for a declaration that the commissioners are not entitled to set off the sum of £404·14 payable in respect of November 1973 and for an order for payment of that sum to the liquidator. The aggregate of the sums due to the company in respect of input value added tax (that is, £4,055·42) is, of course, less than the aggregate (£5,677) due to the Commissioners of Inland Revenue and the Department of Health and Social Security.

These facts give rise to two main issues. The first is whether s 31 of the Bankruptcy Act 1914 requires that input value added tax be set off against the larger debts due to the Commissioners of Inland Revenue and the Department of Health and Social Security. If s 31 does not so require, then the liquidator is clearly not bound to repay the £3,651·28 accidentally paid to the company and is also entitled to be paid the outstanding balance of £404·14. The second issue is whether, if under s 31 the input value added tax initially fell to be set off against the larger debt due to the Commissioners of Inland Revenue and the Department of Health and Social Security, the provisions of s 31 ceased to apply when the sum of £3,651·28 was inadvertently paid to the company.

In *Re D H Curtis (Builders) Ltd*[1], a company in liquidation owed the Commissioners of Inland Revenue and the Department of Health and Social Security sums which exceeded in the aggregate a small balance of input value added tax which at the date of the liquidation was repayable to the company by the commissioners. Thus the first of the two questions which I have to answer was directly raised. The contention of the liquidator was that for over 80 years s 31 had been construed as confined to debts arising out of contract. Brightman J held that s 31 is not so confined and applies to debts arising by statute and due to and from different government departments. He pointed out[2] that

---

1   [1978] 2 All ER 183, [1978] Ch 162
2   [1978] 2 All ER 183 at 189, [1978] Ch 162 at 171–172

the liquidator's argument could lead to very startling consequences, which he illustrated
by the following example:

'Suppose that a trader owed to the Commissioners of Customs and Excise at the
end of one quarter the sum of £1,000 in respect of value added tax on his outputs.
Suppose at the end of the next quarter there was a balance in the trader's favour of
£1,000 in respect of value added tax laid on inputs. Suppose that the trader then
went bankrupt. Common sense would seem to suggest that the £1,000 owed by the
Commissioners should be set off against the £1,000 owed to the commissioners.
Neither debt arises out of contract. According to the submission made to me, the
Crown would be compelled to pay the £1,000 to the trustee in bankruptcy of the
trader and would be left to prove for the £1,000 due to it.'

This example was criticised by counsel for the liquidator who said that in the
circumstances envisaged by Brightman J the commissioners would have had the right
under s 3(2) of the Finance Act 1972 to deduct the output tax payable in the first quarter
from the input tax repayable in the second quarter. That criticism is, in my judgment,
misconceived. Section 3(2), read with s 3(1), provides that at the end of any prescribed
accounting period any balance of input tax, after deducting any output tax payable by
the trader, is to be repaid. But on bankruptcy or winding-up, a balance of input tax
arising in one prescribed accounting period can be set off against output tax due from the
trader in another prescribed accounting period, if at all, only under s 31 of the 1914 Act.

The decision of Brightman J in *Re D H Curtis (Builders) Ltd* [1] that s 31 is not limited to
mutual debts, mutual credits and mutual dealings arising out of contract was reached
after full argument and the judgment of Brightman J contains an exhaustive analysis of
all the authorities in England and elsewhere bearing on the construction of s 31 or
analagous sections in other jurisdictions. Although his decision is not strictly binding on
me, it is one which I should feel bound to follow unless I felt convinced that it was
vitiated by some oversight or error of reasoning. Far from feeling any such conviction,
I find the reasoning of Brightman J lucid and compelling.

Counsel for the liquidator in the course of his very full argument did not seek to
persuade me to take a contrary view, though he reserved his right to challenge the
decision of Brightman J in a higher court. He attacked the decision in *Curtis* [1] on a
different ground. He argued that I should not follow *Curtis* [1] because, he said, the real
question is whether, even if s 31 is given the wide construction placed on it by Brightman
J, it applies to debts due to and from the Crown, and in *Curtis* [1] that question was, he said,
not argued. He based his contention that s 31 does not apply to debts to and from the
Crown on two grounds. The first is that the history of s 31 and its predecessors in earlier
Bankruptcy Acts shows that s 31 (which is not expressly made binding on the Crown)
was not intended to apply to debts due to and from the Crown. The second is that such
debts are impliedly excluded by the limitation of s 31 to mutual debts, mutual credits
and mutual dealings.

In support of his first argument counsel for the liquidator relied on the fact that
originally, until restricted by statute, the Crown could claim priority for all its debts.
That absolute right of priority stemmed from the Royal prerogative. It was first cut
down by s 166 of the Bankruptcy Act 1849 which was repealed by the Bankruptcy Act
1883, s 166 of the 1849 Act being replaced first by s 40 of the 1883 Act and, when that
Act was repealed by the Bankruptcy Act 1914, by s 33 of the 1914 Act. It was not until
the coming into force of s 150 of the Bankruptcy Act 1883 that the Crown became bound
by the whole of the provisions of the Bankruptcy Acts. Counsel's argument for the
liquidator, as I understood it is shortly as follows. The Crown's absolute right of priority,
says counsel, was strictly an alternative to the right of set-off introduced by the
Bankruptcy Acts. Although the Crown's right of priority has now been restricted by the

---

1 [1978] 2 All ER 183, [1978] Ch 162

Bankruptcy Acts, those Acts do not specifically extend the right of set-off to debts due to
and from the Crown. And as the s 38 provisions of the 1883 Act (now s 31 of the 1914   *a*
Act) are not amongst those mentioned in s 150 of the 1883 Act (now s 151 of the 1914
Act) as being thereby made binding on the Crown, s 38 or s 31 (as the case may be) should
not, said counsel, be construed as impliedly conferring a right of set-off by and against the
Crown.

I have no hesitation in rejecting these submissions. I can see no reason why the
unrestricted priority for its debts originally enjoyed by the Crown should be taken as   *b*
inconsistent with the right of set-off. The machinery for enforcing the right of priority
was cumbersome and a set-off may in some cases have provided a simpler means
whereby the Crown could in effect secure payment of a debt due to it. But however that
may be, the Crown's right of priority has been restricted since before 1883. And if s 31
(or its predecessor s 38 of the 1883 Act) is construed in its proper context as part of a
group of sections dealing with proof, set-off and priority, it is in my judgment clear that   *c*
the section was intended to apply to debts due to and from the Crown. Section 30
prescribes what debts are to be provable in bankruptcy; s 31 provides for the taking of an
account where there have been mutual credits, mutual debts and other mutual dealings
and, as Brightman J observed in *Curtis*[1]: 'a natural assumption would be that s 31 is
intended to cover the same subject-matter as s 30'; s 33 gives priority to certain debts and
must, as I see it, apply to any balance due from the debtor to a person to whom priority   *d*
is given after striking a balance of account in accordance with s 31. Section 33 deals with
one of the matters (priority of debts) in respect of which 'Save as provided by the Act' the
provisions thereof are expressly made binding on the Crown. If the sections are read
together there is in my judgment nothing in them to found the inference that s 31 was
not intended to apply to debts due to and from the Crown. The provisions as to priority
were expressly made binding on the Crown because the Crown's prerogative right of   *e*
priority is limited by s 33; but that limited priority is not inconsistent with the
application of the provisions of s 31 which must be applied before the balance (if any) to
which this limited priority is afforded is ascertained.

Counsel's second argument for the liquidator is that there is no true mutuality
between Crown and subject in that prior to a bankruptcy or winding-up the subject
cannot set-off a debt due from the Crown against a debt due to the Crown. The rule that   *f*
the subject could not set off a debt claimed from the Crown against a debt due to the
Crown stems from the Crown's prerogative, and as Rowlatt J pointed out in *Attorney-
General v Guy Motors Ltd*[2]:

> '. . . at the back of the apparently hard rule that there can be no set-off in this case
> against the Crown there lies this fact, that the subject cannot make good a claim
> against the Crown except in a particular way [that is by petition of right], and my   *g*
> decision merely shows that he cannot get round that by refusing to pay a debt to the
> Crown and then asserting his claim by setting it off.'

Since 1947 right of set-off between the Crown and subject have been governed by the
Crown Proceedings Act 1947. Section 35(2), so far as material, reads as follows:

> 'Provision shall be made by rules of court and county court rules in respect of the   *h*
> following matters . . . (*g*) for providing:—(i) that a person shall not be entitled to
> avail himself of any set-off or counterclaim in any proceedings by the Crown for the
> recovery of taxes, duties or penalties, or to avail himself in proceedings of any other
> nature by the Crown of any set-off or counterclaim arising out of a right or claim to
> repayment in respect of taxes, duties or penalties; (ii) that a person shall not be   *j*
> entitled without leave of the court to avail himself of any set-off or counterclaim in
> any proceedings by the Crown if either the subject matter of the set-off or

---

1   [1978] 2 All ER 183 at 190, [1978] Ch 162 at 173
2   [1928] 2 KB 78 at 80

counterclaim does not relate to the Government department in the name of which
the proceedings are brought or the proceedings are brought in the name of the
Attorney-General; (iii) that the Crown, when sued in the name of a Government
department, shall not, without the leave of the court, be entitled to avail itself of any
set-off or counterclaim if the subject matter thereof does not relate to that
department; and (iv) that the Crown, when sued in the name of the Attorney-
General, shall not be entitled to avail itself of any set-off or counterclaim without the
leave of the court.'

Rules of court have been made in pursuance of the power conferred by s 35(2), and
RSC Ord 77, r 6, now provides that:

'(1) Notwithstanding Order 15, rule 2 and Order 18, rules 17 and 18, a person
may not in any proceedings by the Crown make any counterclaim or plead any set-
off if the proceedings are for the recovery of, or the counterclaim or set-off arises out
of a right or claim to repayment in respect of any taxes, duties or penalties.

'(2) Notwithstanding Order 15, rule 2 and Order 18, rules 17 and 18, no
counterclaim may be made, or set-off pleaded, without the leave of the Court, by the
Crown in proceedings against the Crown, or by any person in proceedings by the
Crown—(a) if the Crown is sued or sues in the name of a Government department,
and the subject-matter of the counterclaim or set-off does not relate to that
department; or (b) if the Crown is sued or sues in the name of the Attorney-General.'

Thus the rule that there can be no set-off of a debt due from the Crown is preserved to
the extent of claims by the Crown for taxes, duties or penalties. Counsel for the
liquidator, as I understand his argument, concedes that s 35(2), and RSC Ord 77, r 6,
govern rights of set-off and counterclaim in proceedings between the Crown and a
solvent litigant and that if, contrary to his first submission, s 31 applies to debts due to
and from the Crown the provisions of s 31 supersede the provisions of s 35(2) and RSC
Ord 77, r 6 after the commencement of a bankruptcy or winding-up. That concession
was, I think, rightly made. As Parke B pointed out in *Forster v Wilson*[1]:

'The right of set-off in bankruptcy does not appear to rest on the same principle
as the right of set-off between solvent parties. The latter is given by the statutes of
set-off (2 Geo. 2 c. 22, s. 13 and 8 Geo. 2 c. 24 s. 4) to prevent cross-actions; and if the
defendant could sue the plaintiff for a debt due to him not in his representative
character, he might set it off under these statutes in an action by a plaintiff suing in
his individual character also; though the plaintiff or defendant might claim their
respective debts as a trustee for a third person. If the debts were legal debts due to
each in his own right, it would be sufficient. But, under the bankrupt statutes, the
mutual credit clause has not been so construed. The object of this clause (originally
introduced in a temporary Act, 4 & 5 Anne c. 17, continued by 5 Geo. 2 c. 30 and
now re-enacted by the 6 Geo. 4 c. 16) is not to avoid cross-actions, for none would lie
against assignees, and one against the bankrupt would be unavailing, but to do
substantial justice between the parties, where a debt is really due from the bankrupt
to the debtor to his estate; and the Court of King's Bench, in construing this clause
. . . have held that it did not authorize a set-off, where the debt, though legally due
to the debtor from the bankrupt, was really due to him as trustee for another, and,
though recoverable in a cross action would not have been recoverable for his own
benefit.'

But, says counsel for the liquidator, to the extent that a subject could not before the
bankruptcy or winding-up set off a debt due to him from the Crown against a debt due
from him to the Crown, there are not mutual credits and debts within s 31.

---

1   (1843) 12 M & W 191 at 203–204, 152 ER 1165 at 1171

In my judgment this submission is also misconceived. It is trite law that for debts and credits to be mutual they must be between the same parties and in the same right and must be commensurable in the sense that at the time when s 31 falls to be applied both can be reduced to monetary terms. But I can see no ground in principle or authority for limiting the section to debts in respect of which, immediately before the bankruptcy or liquidation, the parties had the same rights and remedies. That submission is, it seems to me, inconsistent with counsel's concession that after a bankruptcy or liquidation rights of set-off are governed exclusively by s 31.

Counsel for the commissioners drew my attention to a passage in the current edition of Williams on Bankruptcy[1] where it is said:

'Notwithstanding that the Rules of the Supreme Court are not to apply "save as provided by these Rules," it presumed that the Rules, both of the Supreme Court (R.S.C., Ord. 77, r. 6) and of the county court (C.C.R., Ord. 46, r. 13) made under the Crown Proceedings Act 1947, s. 35, which provide for and limit the right of set-off against the Crown, must apply in bankruptcy proceedings, if that right of set-off is to be available to debtors.'

I can see no foundation for that presumption. The provisions of s 31 are mandatory and require a balance to be struck of debts due to and from the Crown. Rule 390 of the Bankruptcy Rules 1952[2] provides that: 'Save as provided by these Rules, the Rules of the Supreme Court shall not apply to any proceedings in bankruptcy.' I can see nothing in the rules which purports to import into bankruptcy proceedings the provisions of RSC Ord 77. It would be surprising if there were. The Rules of the Supreme Court govern proceedings in the High Court; see RSC Ord 1, r 2(1). Rule 2(2) provides that the rules are not to have effect 'in relation to proceedings of the kind specified in the first column of the following Table (being proceedings in respect of which rules may be made under the enactments specified in the second column of that Table).' The first item in the first column of the table is Bankruptcy Proceedings and in the second column the Bankruptcy Act 1914, s 132. There is in truth nothing in common between the Rules of the Supreme Court which regulate amongst other things set-off and counterclaim in proceedings in the High Court, and s 31 which governs substantive rights by requiring a balance of debts and credits to be struck in ascertaining claims against a bankrupt's property. Turning to r 227 of the Companies (Winding-Up) Rules 1949[3], this provides:

'In all proceedings in or before the Court, or any Judge, Registrar or Officer thereof, or over which the Court has jurisdiction under the Act and Rules, where no other provision is made by the Act or Rules, the practice, procedure and regulations shall, unless the Court otherwise in any special case directs, in the High Court be in accordance with the Rules of the Supreme Court and practice of the High Court . . . in proceedings for the administration of assets by the Court.'

However, 'other provision' is made by the Companies Act 1948, s 317. That section, in conjunction with r 390 of the Bankruptcy Rules, and RSC Ord 1, r 2(2) leave set-off of debts due to and from an insolvent company which is being wound up to be governed exclusively by s 31.

It appears from the decision of Lord Keith in *Laing v Lord Advocate*[4] that in Scotland the provisions of the 1947 Act do apply to set-off in bankruptcy. But in Scotland rules of set-off in bankruptcy are different, both in their origin and scope.

I turn therefore to the second issue. It was held by all their Lordships who heard the appeal in the House of Lords in *National Westminster Bank Ltd v Halesowen Presswork and*

---

1   18th Edn (1968), p 726
2   SI 1952 No 2113
3   SI 1949 No 330
4   1973 SLT (Notes) 81

Assemblies Ltd[1] that the provisions of s 31 cannot be waived or renounced by the creditor
a of a bankrupt and by a majority (Lord Cross dissenting) that the provisions of s 31 are
mandatory and prescribe the course to be followed in the administration of the
bankrupt's estate and cannot be excluded, even by a prior agreement between the
bankrupt and the creditor. Applying that latter principle to the present case, the position
immediately before the commencement of the winding-up was that the input value
added tax due to the company from the commissioners fell to be set-off against the debt
b due from the company to the Commissioners of Inland Revenue and the Department of
Health and Social Security, and the Crown was entitled to prove for and to be paid a
dividend on, and I cite from s 31, '. . . the balance of the account, and no more'. That
being so, the Crown was under no liability to pay anything to the liquidator, and the
payment made was made under a mistake which, in the words of Lord Wright in
Norwich Union Fire Insurance Society Ltd v William H Price Ltd[2], was of such a character as
c 'prevented there being that intention which the common law regards as essential to the
making of an agreement or the transfer of money or property'. The moneys mistakenly
paid are therefore recoverable at law by the Crown.

Counsel for the liquidator sought to draw a distinction between the waiver of a right
of set-off under s 31, which he accepted was not a legal possibility, and a payment which,
as he put it, operated as satisfaction of a debt. But in my judgment, if there was not and
d could not be a waiver or renunciation of a right of set-off, there was not and could not be
any debt to be satisfied.

I should add for completeness that if I had felt compelled to the conclusion that the
Crown had no right, legal or equitable, to recover moneys mistakenly paid to the
company, I would nonetheless have had jurisdiction to order, and would have ordered,
the liquidator to return those moneys to the commissioners. No doubt the jurisdiction
e to give such a direction to the liquidator as an officer of the court, which was first defined
in *Ex parte James*[3], is one to be applied only with the greatest caution. But a payment
made in the circumstances in which this payment was made, and which has directly
enriched the assets of the company, in my judgment falls clearly within that jurisdiction.
It would be shocking to the sense of propriety of any fair minded man that the liquidator
should retain these moneys for the benefit of the creditors generally.

f I propose, therefore, to make an order in the Crown's summons that the Crown is
entitled to recover; and in the liquidator's summons that the Crown is not bound to pay.

Orders accordingly.

Solicitors: *Solicitor for the Customs and Excise*; *Sharpe Pritchard & Co*, agents for *Whitehead*,
g *Monckton & Co*, Maidstone (for the liquidator).

Jacqueline Metcalfe   Barrister.

---

1   [1972] 1 All ER 641, [1972] AC 785
h 2   [1934] AC 455 at 462, [1934] All ER Rep 352 at 356
3   (1874) LR 9 Ch App 609, [1874–80] All ER Rep 388

Quazi v Quazi

COURT OF APPEAL, CIVIL DIVISION
ORR, ORMROD AND BROWNE LJJ
5th, 6th, 8th, 12th, 13th, 14th, 15th MARCH, 10th APRIL 1979

Divorce – Foreign decree – Recognition by English court – Basis of recognition – Divorce obtained by means of judicial or other proceedings – Test whether divorce so obtained – Muslim khula divorce obtained in Thailand – Subsequent talaq divorce obtained under Pakistan ordinance – Whether either obtained by 'judicial or other proceedings' – Recognition of Divorces and Legal Separations Act 1971, s 2(a).

Divorce – Foreign decree – Recognition by English court – Basis of recognition – Domicile – Divorce recognised by law of parties' domicile normally to be recognised in England – Muslim khula divorce obtained in Thailand – Parties domiciled in Thailand at time of divorce but nationals of Pakistan – Subsequent talaq divorce obtained by husband in Pakistan after acquiring English domicile – Whether khula divorce entitled to recognition – Whether valid according to law of Pakistan – Whether talaq divorce entitled to recognition – Recognition of Divorces and Legal Separations Act 1971, s 6.

The husband and wife, who were Muslims, were born in Hyderabad in India and were married there in November 1963. They were nationals of Pakistan. In January 1965 they went to live in Thailand and both acquired domiciles of choice there. On 22nd March 1968 in Thailand the parties went through a Muslim form of divorce known as making a khula which consisted of the wife making a written statement that she wished to end the marriage and the husband making a written statement that he accepted the position and that his wife's rights against him should cease. The parties continued to live under the same roof. In 1970 they moved to Malaya and severed their connections with Thailand. In February 1973 they moved to Pakistan. In March the husband came to England where he was joined by the child of the family and in August 1973 he bought a house in England. The rest of his family, other than the wife, joined him there. The husband's intention was to remain in England and enter employment. The husband, doubting the validity of the khula, went to Pakistan in 1974 and there pronounced, under the Pakistan Muslim Family Laws Ordinance 1961, a talaq divorce from the wife by formally repeating before witnesses the word 'talaq' three times. As required by the ordinance, the husband gave notice of pronouncement of the talaq to the appropriate authority. Under the ordinance failure to give notice was punishable by a fine or imprisonment. Moreover, the ordinance suspended the effect of the talaq for 90 days from the day notice was given, to enable the authority to perform its duty to constitute an arbitration council to bring about a reconciliation between the parties, and to enable the council to perform that function. During the suspension period the husband could revoke the talaq. However, the ordinance did not require the authority or the council to give a decision or issue a certificate making the divorce effective. The husband returned to England and in 1975 presented a petition for a declaration, pursuant to the Recognition of Divorces and Legal Separations Act 1971, that the marriage was lawfully dissolved by either the khula or the talaq. The judge granted the declaration. The talaq divorce, the judge held, had been 'obtained by means of judicial or other proceedings' in Pakistan and was 'effective under the law' of Pakistan and thus could be recognised under s 2[a] of the 1971 Act, while the khula, although not coming within the scope of 'judicial or other proceedings' for the purposes of s 2(a), had nevertheless been 'obtained in the country of the spouses' domicile' (ie Thailand) and was 'recognised as valid in that country' and could therefore be recognised at common law under the rules relating to jurisdiction based on domicile and preserved by s 6[b] of the 1971 Act. The wife appealed.

---

a Section 2, so far as material, is set out at p 429 *c*, post

Held – The appeal would be allowed for the following reasons—

a   (i) On the true construction of s 2(a) of the 1971 Act, the phrase 'obtained by means of judicial or other proceedings' was intended to limit the scope of foreign divorces that would be recognised in England as valid. A foreign divorce would only be recognised by English courts as having been obtained by judicial or other proceedings in another country if the state played some part in the divorce process, at least to the extent of being able to prevent dissolution of the marriage in a proper case. Although an extra-judicial
b   divorce was not necessarily excluded from recognition, a divorce which depended for its legal efficacy solely on the act of one or both parties to the marriage had not been obtained by judicial or other proceedings for the purposes of s 2(a) because even though the required formalities or procedures might have been complied with there had been nothing which could properly be regarded as 'proceedings' (see p 430 b to d and p 438 e f, post).

c   (ii) The talaq divorce obtained under the 1961 Pakistan ordinance was not a divorce by means of 'judicial or other proceedings' within s 2(a), despite the requirements of the ordinance, because the ordinance did not require any decision or certificate to make the divorce effective, and the divorce was obtained by the unilateral act of a husband over which, provided he gave the necessary notice, there was no state control. Furthermore, the khula divorce was not obtained by means of 'other proceedings' within s 2(a) because
d   it was an act purely inter partes, without state intervention. Accordingly both divorces failed to qualify for recognition (see p 430 h j, p 431 a f, p 432 c d f and p 438 e f, post); *R v Registrar General of Births, Deaths and Marriages, ex parte Minhas* [1976] 2 All ER 246 approved.

(iii) Neither the khula nor the talaq divorce qualified for recognition under the common law rules relating to jurisdiction based on domicile preserved by s 6 of the 1971
e   Act. At common law status depended primarily on the law of the parties' domicile and a party's status according to that law would be recognised by the English courts under s 6. Applying that principle to the khula divorce, the parties were domiciled in Thailand at the time it was obtained and it should therefore be recognised as valid in England, under s 6, if it was valid under Thai law. However, the evidence showed that under Thai law the validity of the khula depended on the law of the parties' nationality, ie on the law
f   of Pakistan, and that under Pakistan law the khula did not effectively dissolve the marriage. It followed that the khula divorce could not be recognised as valid under s 6. With regard to the talaq divorce, the husband was, on the evidence, domiciled in England by the time the talaq was obtained and it followed that it, also, could not be recognised as valid under s 6 (see p 433 g, 435 b, p 436 a and e to g, p 437 h and p 438 f, post); dicta of Lord Blackburn and of Lord Watson in *Harvey v Farnie* [1881–5] All ER
g   Rep 58, 60 and dictum of Lord Watson in *Le Mesurier v Le Mesurier* [1895–9] All ER Rep at 840 applied; *R v Hammersmith Superintendent Registrar of Marriages, ex parte Mir-Anwaruddin* [1916–17] All ER Rep 464 and *Russ (otherwise Geffers) v Russ* [1962] 3 All ER 193 considered.

Notes
h   For the recognition of overseas divorces, see 8 Halsbury's Laws (4th Edn) paras 484–485. For the Recognition of Divorces and Legal Separations Act 1971, ss 2, 6, see 41 Halsbury's Statutes (3rd Edn) 219, 221.

Cases referred to in judgment
Ali Nawaz Gardezi v Muhammad Yusuf PLD 1963 Supreme Court 51.
j   *Fahmida Bibi v Mukhtar Ahmad* PLD 1972 Lahore 694.

---

b   Section 6, so far as material, provides: 'This Act is without prejudice to the recognition of the validity of divorces and legal separations obtained outside the British Isles—(a) by virtue of any rule of law relating to divorces or legal separations obtained in the country of the spouses' domicile or obtained elsewhere and recognised as valid in that country . . .'

Harvey v Farnie (1882) 8 App Cas 43, [1881–5] All ER Rep 52, 52 LJP 33, 48 LT 273, 47 JP 308, HL, 11 Digest (Reissue) 545, *1193*.

Inamul Islam v Hussain Bano PLD 1976 Lahore 1466.

Joyce v Joyce and O'Hare [1979] 2 All ER 156, [1979] 2 WLR 770.

Le Mesurier v Le Mesurier [1895] AC 517, [1895–9] All ER Rep 836, 64 LJPC 97, 72 LT 873, 11 R 527, PC, 11 Digest (Reissue) 525, *1107*.

Muhammad Nawaz v Faiz Elahi PLD 1978 Lahore 328.

Mumtaz Mai v Ghulam Nabi PLD 1969 Baghdad-ul-Jadid 5.

Qureshi v Qureshi [1971] 1 All ER 325, [1972] Fam 172, [1971] 2 WLR 518, 27(2) Digest (Reissue) 1019, *8140*.

R v Hammersmith Superintendent Registrar of Marriages, ex parte Mir-Anwaruddin [1917] 1 KB 634, [1916–17] All ER Rep 464, 86 LJKB 210, 115 LT 882, 81 JP 49, 11 Digest (Reissue) 564, *1271*.

R v Registrar General of Births, Deaths and Marriages, ex parte Minhas [1976] 2 All ER 246, [1977] QB 1, [1976] 2 WLR 473, DC.

Russ (otherwise Geffers) v Russ (Russ (otherwise de Waele) intervening) [1962] 3 All ER 193, [1964] P 315, [1962] 2 WLR 930, 11, CA, Digest (Reissue) 565, *1273*.

Torok v Torok [1973] 3 All ER 101, [1973] 1 WLR 1066, Digest (Cont Vol D) 434, *7590a*.

Appeal

By a petition dated 18th June 1975 the petitioner, Mohammed Ameerudin Quazi ('the husband'), sought a declaration that his marriage to the respondent, Bilguis Hehan Begum Quazi ('the wife'), celebrated on 24th November 1963 at Aurangabad in India was lawfully dissolved by a khula made in Bangkok, Thailand, on 22nd March 1968, or alternatively by a talaq, pronounced three times before witnesses, made in Karachi, Pakistan in July 1974. By her answer the wife sought a decree of nullity, or alternatively a declaration that neither the khula nor the talaq was entitled to recognition by English courts as an overseas divorce, and in the further alternative, if the marriage had been dissolved by either the khula or the talaq, a declaration that she was entitled to the sum of 21,000 Indian rupees in respect of dower right. By a judgment given on 14th July 1978, Wood J held that the marriage was dissolved either by the khula in Bangkok or by the talaq pronounced in Karachi. The wife appealed. The facts are set out in the judgment of the court.

Joseph Jackson QC and *Peter Singer* for the wife.
Roger Titheridge QC and *Colin MacKay* for the husband.

Cur adv vult

10th April. **ORMROD LJ** read the following judgment of the court: This is an appeal by the appellant ('the wife') from an order made by Wood J on 14th July 1978 on a petition by the respondent ('the husband') praying for certain declarations relating to his matrimonial status. At the conclusion of a long and very careful analysis of the facts and the relevant law, the judge granted to the husband two declarations which are material to this appeal, namely: (a) that the marriage between the husband and the wife was dissolved by khula in Bangkok, Thailand, on 22nd March 1968, and (b) that, alternatively, the marriage was dissolved by talaq pronounced three times in Karachi in July 1974 and confirmed by the court of the VIIIth Senior Civil Judge First Class, Karachi on 18th February 1975.

This litigation has been going on since December 1974, and has occupied no less than 14 working days in the court below and seven days in this court. It has involved five experts in foreign law, three in Thai law, and two in Pakistani law, and a number of English lawyers. It has led to the expenditure, mostly out of the legal aid fund, of very large sums of money and to a disproportionate amount of intellectual effort to resolve

one practical question: is there jurisdiction in the English court to dissolve this marriage,
a and make consequential orders relating to the ownership or occupation of the house in
Wimbledon belonging to the husband in which the wife is, and has been, living with the
son of the marriage, since June 1974, and for their financial support? These heavy and
expensive labours have had to be undertaken because there is no statutory provision to
enable the courts in this country to deal with ancillary relief after divorce unless a decree
is granted in this country, notwithstanding that the persons concerned and the property
b are within the territorial jurisdiction. So it becomes necessary to investigate whether
there is a subsisting marriage which the courts can dissolve and thereafter exercise the
powers conferred by the Matrimonial Causes Act 1973. This involves long and
complicated enquiries into the validity of overseas divorces and their recognition in this
country. The costs of this case far exceed the value of the house in question and will fall
on the British public. The position urgently requires the attention of Parliament with
c a view to giving power to the court to deal, much more simply, with such situations. We
would draw attention to the judgment in *Torok v Torok*[1] in the hope that something will
now be done to avoid such situations in the future.

The facts
    The facts, in skeleton form, are as follows. Both parties were born in Aurangabad in
d the former state of Hyderabad. Both are Muslims. They married on 24th November
1963. They moved first to Dacca in East Pakistan in 1964, and then to Bangkok in
January 1965. The husband was an executive of a company operating jute mills. In
Bangkok, the marriage came under strain and on 22nd March 1968 they made a khula.
This is a form of divorce under Muslim law which is initiated by the wife and agreed to
by the husband. It consists of a written statement by the wife to the effect that she has
e come to the conclusion that she must put an end to her married life and live among her
relatives and only wants 'khula' from her husband, together with a written statement by
the husband accepting the position, and stating that all her rights against him as a wife
have ceased. However, they continued to live together under the same roof. In June
1970 they moved to Penang, where they continued to live, outwardly, as husband and
wife, though it is said that there were no sexual relations between them. In February
f 1973 the husband went to Karachi. The wife followed him to Karachi where they spent
one night in separate rooms in the house of a relative, thereafter living separately in
Karachi for a few weeks.
    In March 1973 the husband came to London where he has been ever since, though
travelling freely about the world from time to time. The son was sent to England in
April 1973 for his education. Other members of the husband's family joined them. In
g August 1973 the husband bought a house, 232 Durnsford Road, Wimbledon. On 7th
June 1974 the husband wrote to his wife in Karachi a letter referring to the khula which
he obviously thought was ineffective and saying that he was going to give her a
divorce. The wife's response was to come to London, where she arrived on 17th June
1974, and went to live at 232 Durnsford Road, presumably as an unwelcome guest. On
9th July the husband flew to Karachi, and on 12th July 1974 he pronounced the talaq, in
h writing before two witnesses, saying in effect 'I divorce you' three times. Notice of this
was sent to the wife at 232 Durnsford Road, Wimbledon, and at an address in Karachi.
Notice was also sent to the chairman of the union committee of the VIIIth Senior Civil
Judge in Karachi.
    Eventually the husband returned to England. He, the wife, and the boy, and some
other members of the family were still living at 232 Durnsford Road up to the time of
j the hearing in the court below.
    On 23rd December 1974 the wife presented a petition for divorce in this country.
This was subsequently stayed to give the husband an opportunity to present a petition

---

1   [1973] 3 All ER 101, [1973] 1 WLR 1066

himself, asking for a declaration that his marriage was lawfully dissolved either by the
khula in Bangkok on 22nd March 1968 or by the talaq in Karachi on 12th July 1974.   *a*

The appeal raises a difficult question of construction, arising out of the Recognition of
Divorces and Legal Separations Act 1971 as well as a multiplicity of questions of Pakistani
and Thai law. It is the first occasion on which the Court of Appeal has had to consider
and interpret this enactment, which was passed to simplify the English common law
rules relating to the recognition of foreign divorces. So far from simplifying the former
rules the effect of this Act and the later Domicile and Matrimonial Proceedings Act 1973   *b*
has been to create a series of new legal conundrums which are extremely difficult to
resolve. The resulting difficulties have been fully demonstrated by Dr North in his book
on The Private International Law of Matrimonial Causes in the British Isles and the
Republic of Ireland [1].

We think that the best way of approaching the problem is to begin by considering the
legislative history of the two Acts and the mischief at which each was directed. The 1971 *c*
Act ('the Recognition Act') was passed as a consequence of the Hague Convention on
Recognition of Divorces and Legal Separations 1968[2] to which Great Britain was a
signatory together with most of the European States and Israel, Turkey and the United
Arab Republic. This convention provided for the *mutual* recognition of divorces obtained
in the contracting states; see art 1. The Act, however, goes much further. It provides a
code of rules for recognition of overseas divorces generally. This is the source of some of *d*
the difficulties in interpretation and application. The effect of the rules contained in ss 2
to 5 of the Recognition Act is to extend recognition to a wide range of overseas divorces
and to enable persons domiciled, or habitually resident, in this country to obtain
recognition in this country for such divorces, while s 6, in its original form, preserved the
common law recognition rules for persons domiciled overseas. The primary object of
the Act was to reduce, as far as possible, the number of so-called 'limping marriages', but *e*
its effect was probably to enable significant numbers of persons domiciled or habitually
resident in this country to avoid taking divorce proceedings in England, and so to evade
the provisions of the Matrimonial Causes Act 1973 relating to financial provision and
property adjustment orders. No doubt it has had inconvenient consequences in other
areas of the law.

The 1973 Act ('the Domicile Act') was passed, primarily, to abolish the dependent   *f*
domicile of wives and to make consequential amendments to the common law rules
preserved by s 6 of the 1971 Act. But s 16 was obviously intended to control some of the
undesired effects, actual or potential, of the Recognition Act in respect of persons
domiciled or habitually resident here, by limiting the extent to which they can resort to
other countries to obtain their divorces. The section is difficult to construe, particularly
in relation to ss 2 to 5 of the 1971 Act. Its effect is to introduce special rules for divorces *g*
obtained in foreign countries where both the parties have been habitually resident in the
United Kingdom for one year immediately preceding the institution of the divorce
proceedings. In the result, the recognition rules applicable where the parties have been
habitually resident in this country for one year before the institution of the overseas
proceedings are narrower than those which apply to non-residents.

This dichotomy lies at the root of the problem of the recognition of divorces obtained *h*
in other countries. It is one thing to recognise the status, determined by his personal law,
of a person entering this country, or more or less loosely connected with it; it is another
to recognise that the status of a person habitually resident (or domiciled) in this country
whose personal law is English has been changed by a divorce obtained overseas. No
satisfactory solution of this dilemma has yet been found. Nonetheless, it accounts for
some of the well-known difficulties in reconciling apparently conflicting decisions in this *j*
branch of the law. For example, in *R v Hammersmith Superintendent Registrar of Marriages,*

1 (1978), ch 11
2 See Cmnd 4542, Law Com 34, app A

a *ex parte Mir-Anwaruddin*[1] ('the *Hammersmith* case) the status of the wife who was an English girl living in England was said to have been changed by means of a talaq divorce pronounced by her Muslim husband at an address in London; whereas in *Russ (otherwise Geffers) v Russ)*[2] the critical issue was whether the status of an English woman, habitually resident and domiciled in Egypt, had been changed by a talaq divorce pronounced by her Muslim husband in Egypt. With respect to the learned editors of Dicey and Morris's The Conflict of Laws[3], it is neither the grounds nor the method, but the consequences to *b* persons living in this country and to the public generally, which causes concern over foreign divorces.

It is against this background that we approach the construction of the relevant sections of the Recognition Act.

The Recognition Act (the 1971 Act)

c Section 3 provides that the validity of an overseas divorce shall be recognised if, at the date of the institution of the proceedings, either spouse was habitually resident in, or a national of, the country in which the divorce was obtained.

An overseas divorce is defined in s 2 as a divorce (i) 'obtained by means of judicial or other proceedings', and (ii) which is 'effective under the law of that country', that is, the country in which it was obtained.

d In the present case no question arises under s 3. It is conceded that both parties were habitually resident in Thailand at the date of the khula in March 1968; and both parties are, and were at all material times, admittedly, nationals of the State of Pakistan where the talaq was pronounced in July 1974. This part of the appeal depends on whether the khula and/or the talaq are divorces 'obtained by means of judicial or other proceedings' within the meaning of s 2(a) and, if either falls within this definition, whether it was *e* 'effective' under the law of Thailand or Pakistan as the case may be.

Judicial or other proceedings

There is no definition of 'proceedings' in the Act and little other material which throws any light on its meaning, except a number of references to 'the institution of proceedings' in other sections. The ordinary or natural meaning or meanings of the *f* word 'proceedings' standing by itself, without any adjectival description, are so general and imprecise that the dictionary definitions do not carry the matter any further. The phrase 'judicial proceedings' implies some form of adjudication and some kind of order of a court or of some other person or body acting in a judicial capacity. The word 'other' gives little indication of the draftsman's intention. The preamble to the Recognition Act mentions the Hague Convention of 1968 and states that the Act was passed with a view *g* to the ratification of the convention by the United Kingdom. Reference may, therefore, be made to the terms of the convention. Article 1 is in these terms:

> 'The present Convention shall apply to the recognition in one Contracting State of divorces and legal separations obtained in another Contracting State which follow judicial or other proceedings officially recognised in that State and which are legally effective there.'

h We have already drawn attention to the difference in the areas of application of the convention and of the Act. Article 1 poses a question which permits of a fairly simple answer. A divorce is entitled to recognition if it followed judicial or other proceedings officially recognised by the relevant contracting state. The Act, however, is not limited in its operation to the contracting states; its scope is quite general. Moreover, the *j* important words 'officially recognised in that State . . .' do not appear in s 2, and there is no alternative qualification to the words 'other proceedings'. This means that it is for this

---

1   [1917] 1 KB 634, [1916–17] All ER Rep 464
2   [1962] 3 All ER 193, [1964] P 315
3   8th Edn (1967) p 320

court itself to determine whether an overseas divorce has been obtained by means of 'judicial or other proceedings' within the section.

The inclusion of these words must be intended as a limitation on the scope of the section. If they were omitted, the only relevant question would be, 'Is the divorce effective under the relevant law?' Some forms of divorce must, therefore, be excluded, and the filter is the phrase 'judicial or other proceedings'. In our judgment, the phrase must be intended to exclude those divorces which depend for their legal efficacy solely on the act or acts of the parties to the marriage or of one of them. In such cases, although certain formalities or procedures have to be complied with, there is nothing which can properly be regarded as 'proceedings'. We think that, given the apposition of the words 'other proceedings' to the word 'judicial', 'proceedings' here means that the efficacy of the divorce depends in some way on the authority of the state expressed in a formal manner, as provided for by the law of the state. To put it in other words, the state or some official organisation recognised by the state must play some part in the divorce process at least to the extent that, in proper cases, it can prevent the wishes of the parties or one of them, as the case may be, from dissolving the marriage tie as of right. It, therefore, includes some 'extra-judicial' divorces, but, as it seems to us, it is impossible to be more precise. Individual examination by the court of the divorce process in each case seems to be unavoidable. In coming to this conclusion we have had to bear in mind the terms of s 6 of the Recognition Act, which enables those who are domiciled abroad to obtain recognition of divorces which, on this construction, are excluded from the operation of s 3. In these circumstances we do not think that reasons of policy require that an unduly liberal construction should be given to the phrase 'other proceedings', since those who are habitually resident in this country will have little difficulty in complying with our own jurisdictional rules, and those who are domiciled abroad can take advantage of s 6.

The Domicile Act (the 1973 Act)

Although s 16 of the Domicile Act does not apply in this case because the wife had not been habitually resident in the United Kingdom etc for one year at the date of the talaq in July 1974, it was referred to in the course of argument by both sides. Its terms cannot directly affect the construction of the earlier Act, though they must be borne in mind. Difficult though it may be to construe, we think that the intention of the section is clear. Section 16(1) excludes from recognition any divorce obtained in the United Kingdom, the Channel Islands and the Isle of Man otherwise than in a court of law. Section 16(2), which applies where both parties have been habitually resident in the United Kingdom etc for one year before the institution of the proceedings and are therefore within our own jurisdictional rules, excludes from recognition all foreign divorces except those which are entitled to recognition under s 3 of the Recognition Act, and those obtained in a court of law which are entitled to recognition under the common law rules as amended by the new s 6.

The khula and the talaq

The next question is whether the alleged divorce by khula or by talaq can be regarded as a divorce obtained by means of 'other proceedings' under s 2 of the Recognition Act.

The judge held that the khula could not be so regarded, but that the talaq fell within this description. We agree with his conclusion about the khula; it was an act purely inter partes and involved no intervention by the state in any form. Counsel for the husband formally submitted at the hearing of the appeal that the judge was wrong in his finding in this respect, but could not press the submission because, as he conceded, if his submission was right, para (a) of s 2 of the Recognition Act was surplusage.

The talaq requires more consideration. It was pronounced in Karachi by the husband. It consists of a formal repudiation of the marriage by the husband, by repeating the word 'talaq' three times before witnesses, or by writing it three times in the presence of two witnesses. This is the traditional or Koranic form and, in this respect, is indistinguishable from khula or mubarra, which are Muslim forms of divorce in which the wife plays an active role. So, for the same reasons, such a divorce cannot be said to be obtained by

a means of 'other proceedings' within s 2.

In Pakistan, however, and, as we understand it, in some other Muslim countries, the Koranic divorces have been modified by legislative enactments. In Pakistan the relevant law is to be found in the Muslim Family Laws Ordinance 1961 and in regulations made under it. The ordinance and the regulations are drafted in English and in a form or forms which look very familiar to the eyes of an English lawyer. The relevant section for

b present purposes is s 7, which reads thus:

'*Talaq*.—(1) Any man who wishes to divorce his wife shall, as soon as may be after the pronouncement of *talaq* in any form whatsoever, give the Chairman notice in writing of his having done so, and shall supply a copy thereof to the wife.

'(2) Whoever contravenes the provisions of subsection (1) shall be punishable with simple imprisonment for a term which may extend to one year or with fine

c which may extend to five thousand rupees or with both.

'(3) Save as provided in subsection (5), a *talaq* unless revoked earlier, expressly or otherwise, shall not be effective until the expiration of ninety days from the day on which notice under subsection (1) is delivered to the Chairman.

'(4) Within thirty days of the receipt of notice under subsection (1), the Chairman shall constitute an Arbitration Council for the purpose of bringing about a

d reconciliation between the parties, and the Arbitration Council shall take all steps necessary to bring about such reconciliation.'

The question then is whether the provisions of the ordinance, under which the talaq in this case was pronounced, are sufficient to bring it within s 2. This is a mixed question of law and fact to be determined by the English court with such assistance as the experts

e in Pakistani law can give. Section 7 of the ordinance makes three changes in the Koranic law, two of which are consequential to the first. It provides for the setting up of an arbitration council, the function of which is to explore the possibility of reconciliation. To enable the arbitration council to perform its function, the coming into effect of the talaq is suspended for a period of 90 days, and the husband is given power to revoke it during this period. In Koranic law the talaq effects an immediate change in status and

f cannot be revoked. In our judgment, these changes in the law are not sufficient to bring the talaq in the present case within the scope of s 2. On this point we respectfully agree with the judgment of Park J in the Divisional Court in *R v Registrar General of Births, Deaths and Marriages, ex parte Minhas*[1] and disagree with the conclusion reached by Wood J in the court below. He appears to have based his conclusion on two grounds, namely the reconciliation procedure and the fact that, as he put it, 'the final court order

g is also of an official nature and recognizes the divorce'. It is possible that he also had it in mind that there was some form of registration of these divorces.

At an earlier stage in his judgment, however, when considering whether the talaq in this case was legally effective under the law of Pakistan, he cited a valuable passage from the judgment of Sardar Mohammed Iqbal J in *Fahmida Bibi v Mukhtar Ahmad*[2] in 1972. The passage reads as follows:

h 'A divorce thus does not become effective unless the notice is served on the Chairman of the Union Committee or Council and ninety days expire from the date of receipt of the notice by him. The Chairman is required to bring about reconciliation between the parties for which purpose he is to give notice to them to nominate their representatives in order to constitute the Arbitration Council. If any of the parties fails to appear before him, he cannot enforce his attendance nor

j a default of appearance on the part of any of the parties can be visited with any penal consequence. The divorce, notwithstanding the conduct or attitude of any of the

---

1   [1976] 2 All ER 246, [1977] QB 1
2   PLD 1972 Lahore 694 at 695

parties, shall become effective after the expiry of ninety days unless the divorce is revoked earlier by the husband. In the event, the parties appear before the *a* Chairman and an Arbitration Council is constituted, but reconciliation does not succeed, the only thing the Council or Chairman may do, is to record in writing that reconciliation has failed. There is no other function which a Chairman or an Arbitration Council is competent to perform in this behalf. If reconciliation does not succeed or the husband does not revoke *talaq* before expiry of ninety days, it becomes automatically operative and effective. There is no provision either in the *b* Ordinance or the Rules requiring the Chairman or the Arbitration Council to give a decision or to issue a certificate to make the divorce effective. If the Chairman issued the certificate, it was not under any provision of law and had no legal effect.'

The judge added this comment of his own:

'It is thus clear so far as talaqs are concerned the Arbitration Council has no *c* function except to take steps to bring about reconciliation between the parties. Beyond this the Arbitration Council has really no effect.'

We respectfully agree with this observation which, in our judgment, makes it quite clear that a divorce obtained in this way is not obtained 'by means of judicial or other proceedings'. It is obtained by the unilateral act of the husband over which, provided he gives the necessary notices, there is no control. *d*

The above citation also shows that the judge was wrong in thinking that there was a 'final court order . . . of an official nature [which] recognizes the divorce'. It is true that a document was produced which is called an order and purports to have been made in the court of the VIIIth Senior Civil Judge, Karachi. A similar document was produced in *Qureshi v Qureshi*[1]. Both purport to be court orders, but it is clear from the judgment in the *Fahmida Bibi* case[2] that the chairman (now the civil judge) had no power to issue such *e* an order. The judge may also have been misled by references by counsel to 'registration', during the examination and cross-examination of the legal experts, but it is clear now that this was a misunderstanding by counsel.

In our judgment, therefore, neither the khula nor the talaq qualify for recognition under s 2(*a*). We shall have to consider later whether either was effective under the law of Thailand or Pakistan as the case may be. *f*

Recognition at common law: s 6 of the Recognition Act

We must now consider whether either 'divorce' is entitled to recognition under the common law rules which were preserved intact by s 6 of the Recognition Act in its original form, but are now subject to the modifications made by s 2 of the Domicile Act which substituted a new s 6. *g*

The Hammersmith case[3]

Counsel for the wife's first submission on this part of the case was that extra-judicial divorces of the type with which we are concerned are not recognised by the English courts. He argued that this court was bound by its previous decisions in the *Hammersmith* case[3] and *Russ v Russ*[4] to refuse recognition to a divorce obtained without any effective *h* intervention by a court of some kind. He contended that the *Hammersmith* case[3] was still good law, at least to this extent, and that Sir Jocelyn Simon P was wrong when he said in *Qureshi v Qureshi*[1] that the *Hammersmith* case[3] should not be followed. Counsel for the

j

---

1   [1971] 1 All ER 325, [1972] Fam 172
2   PLD 1972 Lahore 694
3   [1917] 1 KB 634, [1916–17] All ER Rep 464
4   [1962] 3 All ER 193, [1964] P 315

a   husband, on the contrary, submitted that Sir Jocelyn Simon P's view was right and ought to be supported by this court. We have come to the conclusion that circumstances have been so changed by legislation that the *Hammersmith* case[1], which, to quote the editors of Dicey and Morris's *The Conflict of Laws*[2] 'was distinguished out of existence by Scarman J and the Court of Appeal in *Russ v Russ*[3]', should now be regarded as a decision on its special facts. We, therefore, are in agreement with Sir Jocelyn Simon P on this point. All that the

b   *Hammersmith* case[1] actually decided was that the English courts would not recognise the dissolution of an English marriage between an English woman and a Muslim husband by means of a talaq pronounced by the husband in England. This proposition, though in a wide form, is now part of the statute law of this country as a result of s 16(1) of the Domicile Act 1973, with the consequence that the actual decision in *Qureshi v Qureshi*[4] is no longer good law and the last sentence of the passage, quoted by Sir Jocelyn Simon P[5]

c   from the 8th edition of Dicey and Morris's The Conflict of Laws[6], is now incorrect. It is only fair to the judges whose judgments in the *Hammersmith* case[1] have been so severely criticised to remember that they did not have the benefit of hearing proper adversary argument because the husband, Dr Mir-Anwaruddin, appeared throughout in person. Furthermore, the case for the Superintendent Registrar against the recognition of the divorce was put by the Solicitor-General on the narrow ground that divorce by talaq was

d   essentially a characteristic of a polygamous marriage and, therefore, had no application to an English monogamous marriage. Furthermore, the court was faced with a proposition that must have been very startling in 1917 and one which might still be startling to us today had not Parliament felt it necessary to intervene to exclude from recognition, by s 16(1), any divorce obtained in the United Kingdom, Channel Islands, and Isle of Man, otherwise than in a court of law.

e   No useful purpose will now be served by picking over the bones of the *Hammersmith* case[1], or of *Russ v Russ*[3], in the hope of finding some remnant of principle. In our judgment, we are free to return to the fundamental principle stated in *Harvey v Farnie*[7], in particular by Lord Blackburn[8] and by Lord Watson[9], and in *Le Mesurier v Le Mesurier*[10], again by Lord Watson, who said:

f   'When the jurisdiction of the Court is exercised according to the rules of international law, as in the case where the parties have their domicil within its forum, its decree dissolving their marriage ought to be respected by the tribunals of every civilized country.'

g   We think that this dictum was not intended to be confined to judicial divorces, but is to be understood as laying down the principle that status depends primarily on the law of the domicile and that, subject to any statutory restrictions and to the limited discretion of the court, that status should be recognised by the courts of this country.

h

1   [1917] 1 KB 634, [1916–17] All ER Rep 464
2   9th Edn (1973) p 327
3   [1962] 3 All ER 193, [1964] P 315
4   [1971] 1 All ER 325, [1972] Fam 172
j   5   [1971] 1 All ER 325 at 345, [1972] Fam 172 at 199
6   8th Edn (1967) pp 319–320
7   (1882) 8 App Cas 43, [1881–5] All ER Rep 52
8   8 App Cas 43 at 58, [1881–5] All ER Rep 52 at 58
9   8 App Cas 43 at 62, [1881–5] All ER Rep 52 at 60
10   [1895] AC 517 at 527, [1895–9] All ER Rep 836 at 840

Domicile

The next question is the domicile of the parties at the relevant time, which is the date *a* of the divorce under consideration. In circumstances such as exist in this case, this is always a difficult problem.

The domicile of origin of both husband and wife was the State of Hyderabad, since both were born in Aurangabad. The political upheavals and religious conflicts in India seem to have cut off the husband completely from his domicile of origin and, to a lesser extent, perhaps, the wife. As a result they have been moving about the world ever since *b* they left Aurangabad in 1964.

The judge came to the conclusion that in March 1968, at the time of the khula, both had acquired domiciles of choice in Thailand, largely on the evidence of the husband of his intentions at the time. Although their connection was tenuous, they owned no property there and lived in a house provided by the company, their connection with their domicile of origin was even more tenuous, so that it does not require very strong *c* evidence to establish a domicile of choice. Counsel for the wife did not seriously contest the judge's finding and we see no reason to differ from it. Consequently, the validity of the khula depends on the law of Thailand in the first place.

By the time of the talaq in July 1974 the position had completely changed. The parties had left Thailand for Penang in 1970 and severed all, or almost all, connection with Thailand, although the husband continued to pay annual visits to that country to keep *d* his residence permit alive. There was no evidence of any other connection. The judge, therefore, felt bound to hold that they had abandoned their domiciles of choice in Thailand. We think that that must be right, but it poses a difficult problem. Wood J could see no alternative but to fall back on the theoretical solution that, in the absence of another domicile of choice, the domiciles of origin revived. This produces a position which is so manifestly unreal and unsatisfactory that it can only be accepted in the last *e* resort. It means that both parties are domiciled in India, a country with which neither of them now has any connection at all. So far as the husband is concerned, the only other alternative is that, by July 1974, he had acquired a new domicile of choice in England. There is a considerable amount of evidence which supports this conclusion. On this aspect of the case, we decided to admit some further evidence from the Home Office and from the husband in explanation. *f*

The evidence as a whole shows that, from the time he was in Penang, the husband was planning to move to England with his children by his first marriage and his son Saleem, whom he wanted to be educated in this country. In June 1972, he obtained from the British High Commission in Kuala Lumpur a 'settlement' entry certificate for himself and was applying for a similar certificate for the other members of the family. In March 1973 he came to England by himself; in April 1973 the boy Saleem joined him in *g* England; in August 1973 he bought his house at 232 Durnsford Road, Wimbledon, and assembled his family, other than the wife, there. In a letter dated 12th April 1974 to the Home Office, he said in terms: 'I intend to reside in the United Kingdom and enter into Crown Service as an executive officer in the Department of Health and Social Security for which I have been selected by the Civil Service Commission.' In a letter dated 29th July 1974 he described himself as a 'resident of U.K.', and to emphasise the point added later *h* in the letter 'i.e. settled in U.K.'. Later in 1978 he was applying for British nationality and registration as a citizen of the United Kingdom and Colonies.

All this amounts to a strong case for his having acquired by July 1974 a domicile of choice in England. His oral evidence to us revealed him as a person of remarkable capacity for manipulating the rules relating to immigration and citizenship of this country to his own advantage. His reason for wanting to acquire British nationality and *j* UK citizenship was, he said, to enable him to live in Thailand or Pakistan, safe in the knowledge that should new political upheavals occur, he would always be able to take refuge here in England. We understand the feelings of a man who has been made into a wanderer on the face of the earth, but we must approach the issue of domicile realistically. The fact is that by July 1974 Mr Quazi had established a secure home here

a   at 232 Durnsford Road, Wimbledon, for himself and his family, the only house he has
ever actually owned, and was expressing the clearest intention to remain here indefinitely.
The only evidence to the contrary was the husband's own statement to the judge that
he was proposing to return to Pakistan as soon as the case was over. No evidence was
produced by him of any firm connection with any other country, or of his having any
business interests in any country; in fact, the whereabouts of his assets remains wholly
obscure.

b   In these circumstances, we find ourselves unable to accept the judge's finding that in
July 1974 the husband had reverted to his domicile of origin, now India. We feel bound
to hold that by that date he had acquired a domicile of choice in England. It follows that
under the common law rules this court should recognise the khula, if it was valid by Thai
law, but not the talaq, which was given when he was domiciled in this country.

c   *The validity of the khula*
The circumstances under which the khula came into existence in Bangkok in March
1968 were never satisfactorily explained in the evidence. The wife's case was that she was
induced to write out her part of the document by the use of force and threats. The judge
decisively rejected her evidence on this part of the case, holding that she was a wholly
unreliable and dishonest witness. There is no appeal from that finding, but it still leaves
d   the position between these parties in March 1968 in a state of obscurity. Notwithstanding
this alleged divorce, they continued to live together, outwardly at least, as husband and
wife. They went to Hong Kong together in 1969 for a trip. They moved together to
Penang and lived together until January 1972 when the husband moved out. It is said
that his motive for living this way was that the son Saleem was still under seven and
therefore, by Muslim law, still in the care of the mother. But a khula is a divorce
e   initiated by the wife and at no time had the wife ever shown any disposition to move
away; on the contrary, she joined the household in London in June 1974, when she was
obviously not welcomed. Moreover, the letters from the husband to the wife up to 1974
are very friendly and intimate, and indeed are written on the basis that they are going to
continue to live together. Furthermore, it is plain that in July 1974, when he pronounced
the talaq, he was extremely doubtful about the effectiveness of the khula of March 1968
f   as a divorce. We, however, must now consider that difficult question.
As it came into existence in Thailand, the legal validity of the khula depends in the
first place on Thai law. Unfortunately, the Thai lawyers who gave evidence disagreed
about its validity and about the proper test to be applied in Thai law. The evidence on
both sides is difficult to follow, perhaps because such problems rarely arise in connection
with family law. The judge must have had considerable difficulty in following this
g   evidence, but in the end he accepted the evidence of Mr Suavanari and Mr Chomgwilas,
as contained in affidavits filed on behalf of the husband, in preference to the evidence of
Mr Jaran, who gave oral evidence on behalf of the wife. As the judge put it in his
judgment, the difference between the two views boiled down to whether the appropriate
law to be applied was the Muslim law of Pakistan or the Muslim law of Thailand. The
husband's experts maintained the latter; the wife's expert the former, although he seems
h   to have confused the law applicable to Muslims in Pakistan with Muslim religious law in
Pakistan, a confusion for which Mr Jaran cannot be blamed, since he was careful to say
that he knew nothing about the law of Pakistan. The judge decided to accept the view
of the husband's experts, and concluded that the khula was a valid divorce by this test.
The judge and this court were provided with a copy of the Thai 'Act on Conflict of
Laws, B.E.2481', in what appears to be an official English translation. This is fortunate,
j   because the Act seems to be quite clear and easy to understand, in contrast to the evidence
of the experts. Under the heading 'Title V, Family', s 21 provides as follows: 'As regards
relationship between husband and wife, the law common to both spouses when they are
of the same nationality . . . shall govern.' Section 26 reads: 'Divorce by mutual consent
shall be valid if it is permitted by the respective law of nationality of both the husband
and the wife.' Under the heading 'Title II, Status and Capacity of Persons', s 10 provides:

'The capacity or incapacity of person is governed by the law of nationality of such person.' And under the heading 'Title I, General Provisions', s 6 provides: 'Whenever by application of the law of nationality, the local law, the communal law or the religious law, as the case may be, is to appply, such law shall govern.'

These provisions clearly indicate that the validity of the khula in the present case depends, according to Thai law, on the law of nationality; that is, the law of Pakistan. Section 6 however, seems to have caused confusion by its reference to 'religious law'. The husband's experts expressed their opinion in an affidavit dated 5th September 1977 thus:

> 'Section 6(e) of the Act on the Conflict of Laws says, "Whenever by application of the law of nationality, the local law, the communal law or the religious law, as the case may be, is to apply, such law shall govern". In Pakistan, where both the parties are Muslims, it is the Muslim law which is applied . . . Therefore, in this case by application of the law of nationality, it is the religious law which would govern which in this case is the Muslim law. Furthermore it is the established principle of private international law that the form in which this law is to be applied is the one locally in practice. Therefore in this particular case, due to the nationality of the parties, the application of Conflict of Laws makes them subject to Muslim Law of Thailand, under which a certificate of divorce has already been issued.'

The reference to the Muslim law of Thailand refers, according to Mr Jaran, to a special provision in Thai law relating to specific provinces of Thailand which are predominantly Muslim by religion and culture, for which special provision is made.

We find it impossible to accept the evidence of the husband's experts in this respect because their reasoning, in the passage which we have quoted at length, is based on an erroneous view of Pakistan law. The latter does not require that the religious law should be applied. The Muslim Family Laws Ordinance 1961 provides in s 1(2), that 'It [the ordinance] extends to the whole of Pakistan, and applies to all Muslim citizens of Pakistan, wherever they may be'. The law of nationality, therefore, requires that the provisions of this ordinance should be applied. In any event, to argue that the relevant law is the Muslim law of Thailand appears to be a clear non sequitur. Accordingly, we are unable, with respect, to accept Wood J's conclusion that the validity of the khula is established by Thai law. The certificate of divorce obtained by the husband in June 1976, referred to in the passage quoted above from the affidavit sworn by the husband's experts, does not carry the matter any further. We are confirmed in our opinion that the validity of the khula depends on the ordinance of 1961 by the admission in the husband's reply in regard to the khula signed in Bangkok in March 1968, that 'the Petitioner and the Respondent were bound by the provisions of the Muslim Family Laws Ordinance 1961'.

The validity of the khula in Pakistani law

We must now, therefore, consider whether the khula was effective in Pakistani law to dissolve the marriage. Once again there was a conflict at the trial between the expert witnesses, although at a preliminary conference between them, of which a signed minute was produced in evidence, it was agreed, inter alia, that 'The alleged khula form of divorce is not recognised in Pakistan'.

Dr Pearl, who gave evidence on behalf of the wife, is a lecturer in Islamic law at Cambridge and the author of a thesis entitled 'The inter personal conflict of laws in India and Pakistan'. Mr Qureshi, who gave evidence on behalf of the husband, is a member of the English Bar and has an LLB from Karachi University. He has never practised in Karachi. It was Dr Pearl's opinion that the provisions of the 1961 ordinance applied to the khula made in Bangkok. Mr Qureshi originally expressed the same opinion, but subsequently changed his mind. The judge, after examining for himself the provisions of the ordinance and a number of reported cases, came to the same conclusion as Mr Qureshi that the khula was not subject to the ordinance.

The validity of the khula in Pakistani law turns on the terms of s 8 of the ordinance,
a which reads as follows:

'Dissolution of marriage otherwise than by talaq. Where the right to divorce has
been duly delegated to the wife and she wishes to exercise her right, or where any
of the parties to a marriage wishes to dissolve the marriage otherwise than by talaq,
the provisions of section 7 (which requires notice to the Chairman for purposes of
reconciliation) shall, *mutatis mutandis* and so far as applicable, apply.'
b

The reference to divorce otherwise than by talaq can only refer to the forms of
consensual divorce, the khula and the mubarra, and the judicial form of khula which is
a divorce ordered by the court. Counsel for the husband submitted that the consensual
khula was not caught by s 8 because, first, there could be no point in insisting on the
parties going through the reconciliation procedure laid down by the ordinance if, as ex
c hypothesi is the case, they have agreed on divorce, and, secondly, the khula is irrevocable
under Muslim law and accordingly there was no room for reconciliation. Mr Qureshi
supported this argument in the course of his evidence.

The difficulty in which both experts found themselves arises from the absence of any
direct authority on the construction of s 8, so that both were, in effect, trying to predict
how the courts in Pakistan would decide if and when the point arose for decision. There
d was the added difficulty that Mr Qureshi had never dealt with a khula before, and Dr
Pearl had only seen one on two or three occasions. In the nature of things also, a
consensual divorce is unlikely to come before the court. There are, however, some useful
dicta to be found in some of the cases.

In the course of an elaborate judgment in *Ali Nawaz Gardezi v Muhammad Yusuf*[1] in
1963, in the Supreme Court, Rahman J observed that it would be idle to speculate what
e alternative forms of dissolution are contemplated by s 8 (which had recently come into
force), but he clearly did not rule out the possibility that khula and mubarra might come
within it. In *Mumtaz Mai v Ghulam Nabi*[2] in 1969, a case much relied on by the judge as
indicating that the section did not apply to khula types of divorce, Mushtaq Hussain J in
fact concluded his judgment by holding that 'reference to an Arbitration Council has
become a pre-condition for applying to a Family Court for dissolution of marriage on the
f ground of *Khula*'[3]. The khula there referred to was judicial khula, but earlier in his
judgment[4] he had used the words cited by Wood J:

'The question of reconciliation in the case of *Khula*' does not arise for how can a
wife who has a "fixed aversion" for her husband be reconciled with him.'

g *Muhammed Nawaz v Faiz Elahi*[5] in 1978, which was not cited to Wood J, takes the
matter much further. Muhammed Afzal Zullah J held that s 8 did apply to a consensual
khula notwithstanding the practical difficulties, which were increased rather than
diminished by his further conclusion that the terms of s 7(3), which permits revocation
of a talaq, did not apply in the case of a khula.

In this state of the law it is impossible for this court to be satisfied that the provisions
h of the 1961 ordinance did not apply to the khula of 12th March 1968. Since its
provisions are undoubtedly mandatory (see, for example, *Inamul Islam v Hussain Bano*[6],
and Dr Pearl's opinion), and extra-territorial (see Mr Qureshi's and Dr Pearl's opinions),
we must conclude that the husband has failed to prove that the khula of March 1968
effectively dissolved his marriage under the relevant law, namely the law of Pakistan.

j 1   PLD 1963 Supreme Court 51 at 75
2   PLD 1969 Baghdad-ul-Jadid 5
3   PLD 1969 Baghdad-ul-Jadid 5 at 10
4   PLD 1969 Baghdad-ul-Jadid 5 at 6
5   PLD 1978 Lahore 328
6   PLD 1976 Lahore 1466

Talaq

In view of our conclusion that the husband was domiciled in England at the date of the pronouncement of the talaq, it is unnecessary to decide whether the talaq complied with the requirements of the ordinance or not. We do, however, doubt whether the notice under s 7 was given to the right chairman, because we are not satisfied that the judge below was right to hold that on the relevant date the wife was 'residing' in Karachi. Habitual residence is not the test. At the relevant time the wife had no home of any kind in Karachi. She was actually living in London at the husband's house and obviously intending to remain there. This clearly appears from letters by the husband. The fact that she told a false story to the immigration authorities about coming to England for four months to escape the hot weather in Karachi means nothing, since it was admittedly a ruse to get into this country without alerting her husband. The alternatives under r 3 of the amended West Pakistan Rules under the 1961 ordinance do not apply because the parties have never resided together in West Pakistan and the husband was not 'permanently residing in West Pakistan'.

Public policy: s 8(2)(b)

The last matter raised in the notice of appeal is the question of public policy under s 8(2)(b) of the Recognition Act 1971. The implications of this subsection are far reaching, not least because of its association with art 10 of the convention, where it is equated with the French phrase 'ordre public', which is also found in the legislation of the European Economic Community. In view of our conclusions on the other aspects of the case, the question does not now arise for decision, and we prefer to express no opinion on it. We were referred to the recent decision of Lane J in *Joyce v Joyce and O'Hare*[1], which is another illustration of the lacuna in the powers of the court which has been opened up by the Recognition Act, and to which we have called attention at the beginning of this judgment. Whether s 8(2)(b) can properly be used to fill this lacuna is a matter which must be left for decision until it arises, when all its implications can be fully considered.

Our judgment, therefore, may be summarised in this way: (a) Neither the khula nor the talaq are divorces obtained by means of judicial or other proceedings within the meaning of s 2(a) of the Recognition of Divorces and Legal Separations Act 1971, and therefore are not entitled to recognition under s 3. (b) At the time of the khula the parties were domiciled in Thailand, but the husband has failed to prove that it was an effective or valid divorce by Thai law. (c) At the time of the talaq the husband (and probably the wife) was domiciled in England so that it cannot be recognised under s 6 as a valid divorce in this country. (d) Neither the khula nor the talaq is proved to be an effective and valid divorce by the law of Pakistan.

The wife, therefore, succeeds on this appeal, which must be allowed, and the husband's petition for a declaration is dismissed.

Appeal allowed; husband's petition dismissed. Leave to appeal to the House of Lords refused.

27th June. The Appeal Committee of the House of Lords (Lord Edmund-Davies, Lord Keith of Kinkel and Lord Scarman) allowed a petition by the husband for leave to appeal.

Solicitors: *Sowmans* (for the husband); *Sheratte Caleb & Co* (for the wife).

Avtar S Virdi Esq   Barrister.

---

1   [1979] 2 All ER 156, [1979] 2 WLR 770

a # Slater (Inspector of Taxes) v Richardson & Bottoms Ltd

CHANCERY DIVISION
OLIVER J
22nd JUNE 1979

b

Income tax – General Commissioners – Jurisdiction – Sub-contractors in the construction industry – Taxpayer company making payment to uncertified sub-contractors without deduction on account of income tax – Collector not exempting taxpayer company from liability to pay the amount that ought to have been deducted – Assessment made on taxpayer company in respect of the amount – Commissioners discharging assessment on ground that failure to deduct had arisen
c *through an error made in good faith – Whether commissioners had jurisdiction to discharge assessment – Finance Act 1971, ss 29, 30 – Taxes Management Act 1970, s 50(6) – Income Tax (Payments to Sub-Contractors in the Construction Industry) Regulations 1971 (SI 1971 No 1779), regs 6(3), 11(1).*

d In the year 1973–74 the taxpayer company made payments to two individual sub-contractors for construction work without making the deduction required by the Finance Act 1971, s 29[a]. The sub-contractors had produced exemption certificates under s 30[b] of the 1971 Act when first taken on, but these had expired by the time the payments were made. The collector of taxes then considered whether to make a direction under reg 6(3)[c] of the Income Tax (Payments to Sub-Contractors in the Construction Industry) Regulations 1971 exonerating the taxpayer company from liability in respect of the sum e it had failed to deduct. After due consideration, however, he declined to make such a direction. In May 1977 the inspector of taxes assessed the taxpayer company under reg 11(1)[d] of the 1971 regulations to recover from it the amount of the deduction it should have made. The taxpayer company appealed, contending, inter alia, that its error in not noticing that the sub-contractor's exemption certificates were not within date when the payments were made arose through lack of attention to clerical work on the part of the f foreman at the construction site and that accordingly the assessment should be discharged. The General Commissioners discharged the assessment on the ground that the taxpayer company had taken reasonable care to comply with the requirements of the law and that the failure to deduct had arisen through an error made in good faith. The Crown appealed.

g **Held** – There was nothing in the provisions of the 1971 Act or s 50(6)[e] of the Taxes Management Act 1970 which enabled the General Commissioners to arrogate to themselves the discretion to remit taxes which was conferred only on the collector of taxes, and it followed that the General Commissioners had no power to discharge the assessment made on the taxpayer company. The appeal would accordingly be allowed (see p 444 *f j* and p 445 *b c*, post).

h ## Notes

For the General Commissioners and their jurisdiction, see 23 Halsbury's Laws (4th Edn) paras 43, 1604.

For deductions from payments to sub-contractors in the construction industry, see ibid para 375.

j

a Section 29, so far as material, is set out at p 442 *b* to *g*, post
b Section 30, so far as material, is set out at p 442 *h*, post
c Regulation 6(3) is set out at p 443 *c*, post
d Regulation 11(1) is set out at p 443 *e f*, post
e Section 50(6) is set out at p 444 *h*, post

For the Taxes Management Act 1970, s 50, see 34 Halsbury's Statutes (3rd Edn) 1296.
For the Finance Act 1971, ss 29, 30, see ibid 1444, 1446.

From 6th April 1977, ss 29, 30 of the 1971 Act, and regs 6, 11 of the 1971 regulations, have been replaced by the Finance (No 2) Act 1975, ss 69, 70, and the Income Tax (Sub-Contractors in the Construction Industry) Regulations 1975, regs 7, 12, respectively.

Case referred to in judgment

Customs and Excise Comrs v J H Corbitt (Numismatists) Ltd [1979] STC 504, [1979] 3 WLR 291, CA.

Case stated

1. At a meeting of the General Commissioners of the Income Tax for the Division of Flitt in the County of Bedford held on 11th May 1977 at Luton, Richardson & Bottoms Ltd ('the taxpayer company') appealed against the following assessment made under reg 11(1) of the Income Tax (Payments to Sub-Contractors in the Construction Industry) Regulations 1971[1]: 1973–74—payments to sub-contractors—£3479·29.

2. The question for their decision was whether the taxpayer company was properly charged by the assessment in respect of sums required to be deducted from payments made to sub-contractors in the construction industry in the circumstances herein set out.

3. The commissioners' attention was directed to the provisions of Chapter II of the Finance Act 1971, ss 29 to 31, the Income Tax (Certification of Sub-Contractors in the Construction Industry) Regulations 1971[2] and the Income Tax (Payments to Sub-Contractors in the Construction Industry) Regulations 1971. It was not in dispute that the legislation applied to the circumstances of the case.

4. The following facts were admitted or proved in evidence before the commissioners: (a) During the year of assessment 1973–74 the taxpayer company made payments to sub-contractors for construction work from which it was required to deduct 30% unless the recipient sub-contractor was either a limited company or an individual holding a valid exemption certificate issued by an inspector of taxes. (b) Two individual sub-contractors to whom payments were made in full had produced exemption certificates in the names of Hayes and Dooley when first taken on. Hayes's certificate expired on 30th April 1973 and Dooley's on 19th November 1973 but the taxpayer company continued to make payments in full after the expiry dates as follows:

Hayes	Quarter ended July	1973	£285	£1312
	October	1973	1027	
Dooley	Quarter ended January	1974	621	£2167
	April	1974	1546	
				£3479

In January 1975 after a visit by Revenue officers to the taxpayer company it became clear that the certificates produced by Hayes and Dooley were certificates to which they were not entitled. (c) The taxpayer company was in a substantial way of business and carried out work at nine different sites. Site managers were responsible for ensuring that certificates produced to them were in order and these were the only two cases where the company had been found to be at fault out of total quarterly payments to sub-contractors which varied between £33,000 and £42,000. (d) Quarterly returns of payments made to sub-contractors had always been submitted by the taxpayer company timeously, ie within 14 days of the end of the quarter to which the return related. (e) The collector of taxes had considered whether to make a direction under reg 6(3) of the 1971 regulations exonerating the taxpayer company from liability. After due consideration, however, he had declined to make any such direction.

1   SI 1971 No 1779
2   SI 1971 No 1688

5. It was contended on behalf of the taxpayer company: (a) that Hayes and Dooley
a having produced initially exemption certificates, which prima facie appeared to be in
order, it was unreasonable to penalise the taxpayer company for actions of the two sub-
contractors who had deliberately embarked on a course of fraud on the Revenue; (b) that
the taxpayer company had genuinely endeavoured to fulfil its obligations under the new
legislation, about sub-contractors, brought in with effect from 5th April 1972 and the
error in not noticing that Hayes's and Dooley's exemption certificates were not within
b date when the payments set out in para 4(b) were made, really arose through lack of
attention to clerical work on site on the part of the foreman who was primarily a
building technician; (c) that the timely use by the Revenue of the information about
earlier payments to Hayes and Dooley might have given rise earlier to the question of
false certificates; (d) that the taxpayer company had adopted a practice of photocopying
exemption certificates once an employer's organisation had recommended that course as
c a means of combating the use of false certificates; (e) that the taxpayer company's error
in not noticing that Hayes's and Dooley's certificates had expired was made in good faith;
and (f) that the assessment made should be vacated.

6. It was contended on behalf of the Crown: (a) that s 29 of the Finance Act 1971
obliged a contractor to make the prescribed deduction from payments to which the
section applied and which he made to a sub-contractor unless that sub-contractor was a
d limited company or the lawful holder of a certificate under s 30 of the Act; (b) that since
no valid certificates were in force for either Hayes or Dooley when the payments here in
question were made to them, it followed that the taxpayer company should have made
the deduction prescribed by s 29 of the 1971 Act; (c) that since the deduction had not
been made, and since the collector had not made a direction under reg 6 of the 1971
Regulations, the inspector was entitled to make the assessment under appeal; (d) that the
e taxpayer company's failure to note the expiry dates on the certificates did not provide
them with any ground in law for objecting to the assessment; and (e) that the assessment
under appeal was therefore validly made in accordance with the regulations and should
be confirmed.

7. The commissioners who heard the appeal were of the opinion that the taxpayer
company had taken reasonable care to comply with the requirements of the new
f legislation and that the problem of non-deduction of tax had arisen through an error
made in good faith. Moreover, they felt that if it had been practical for earlier attention
to have been given to the taxpayer company's quarterly returns of payments made, it
might have been possible to prevent payments continuing to be made in full on the
certificates which turned out to be falsely used. In the circumstances the commissioners
considered that it would be wrong to penalise the taxpayer company for the loss which
g had as its origin the deceit of the sub-contractors concerned and but for which renewed
and valid certificates might have been in force. Accordingly, the commissioners held
that the appeal succeeded and discharged the assessment.

8. The Crown, immediately after that determination of the appeal, declared its
dissatisfaction therewith as being erroneous in point of law and in due course required
the commissioners to state a case for the opinion of the High Court pursuant to s 56 of
h the Taxes Management Act 1970.

9. The question of law for the opinion of the court was whether the decision set out
in para 7 was correct.

Brian Davenport for the Crown.
The taxpayer company was not represented.

j **OLIVER J.** This is an appeal on the case stated from the General Commissioners at
Luton. It is the Crown's appeal against the discharge by the General Commissioners of
an assessment made against the taxpayer company under the provisions of reg 11(1) of
the Income Tax (Payments to Sub-Contractors in the Construction Industry) Regulations
1971.

Before I go on to consider any of the relevant facts as they appear from the stated case, I ought I think to review the statutory provisions under which this assessment is made. *a*

The construction industry is one which, it is public knowledge, has for some time given rise to certain problems in the matter of the assessment and collection of tax and provisions were enacted to meet some of those problems, and in particular the provisions in force at the material time (that is, the time at which this particular appeal was concerned) were the provisions of the Finance Act 1971, ss 29 and 30. Section 29(1) sets the stage, as it were, for the application of the provisions and applies— *b*

> 'Where a contract relating to construction operations is not a contract of employment—but (*a*) one party to the contract is a sub-contractor (as defined in subsection (2) below); and (*b*) another party to the contract (in this section referred to as the contractor) either is a sub-contractor under another such contract relating to all or any of the construction operations or is a person to whom this paragraph applies.' *c*

Now it is not in dispute that the taxpayer company here was the contractor for the purposes of those provisions and that the two other persons with whom the case is concerned, and I shall have to refer to that later, were sub-contractors within the definition there set out.

The next relevant subsection for present purposes is s 29(4), which provides that: *d*

> 'On making a payment to which this section applies the contractor shall [and I pause to note that that is mandatory] deduct from it a sum equal to 30 per cent. [the figure at the material time] of so much of the payment as is not shown to represent the direct cost to any other person of materials used or to be used in carrying out construction operations to which the contract under which the payment is made relates; and the sum so deducted shall be paid to the Board and shall be treated for *e* the purposes of income tax—(*a*) as not diminishing the payment; but (*b*) as being income tax paid in respect of the profits or gains of the trade, profession or vocation of the person for whose work the contractor makes the payment.'

So there one sees the frame of the legislation; where you have a sub-contract in the construction industry, the main contractor is responsible for paying to the Revenue 30% *f* of so much of the amount due to the sub-contractor as is not shown to consist of the direct cost of materials used in the construction operations.

Then s 29(5) empowers the Board to make regulations. It is in these terms:

> 'The Board shall make regulations with respect to the collection and recovery, whether by assessment or otherwise, of sums required to be deducted from any payments under this section and for the giving of receipts by persons receiving the *g* payments to persons making them; and those regulations may include any matters with respect to which regulations may be made under section 204 (pay as you earn) of the Taxes Act.'

So far so good. Now s 30 provides for exemptions or exceptions from s 29, and as can be seen, they have a great materiality in this particular case. Section 30(1) provides: 'A *h* person is excepted from section 29 of this Act if a certificate under this section is in force—(*a*) in respect of him; or (*b*) in respect of a firm in which he is a partner . . .' I need not read the rest of the section because it is not a case in which a partnership is concerned. So the material point for examination here is whether in this case there was, so far as the sub-contractor is concerned, a certificate under s 30 in force at the material time. I need not, I think, read the rest of s 30, save perhaps to refer to the fact that the *j* Board has, under sub-s (7), the power to make regulations prescribing the period for which certificates are issued and providing for renewal, and so on.

Now the Board did, indeed, under the powers to which I have referred, make regulations, and those regulations are, or were at the material time at any rate, the Income Tax (Payments to Sub-Contractors in the Construction Industry) Regulations

1971. Regulation 4 requires certain forms to be completed and reg 6 requires the
a payment of the appropriate sums to the Collector. I had better read, I think, reg 6(1):

> 'Within 14 days of the end of every income tax month the contractor shall pay to
> the Collector all amounts which he was liable under the principal section to deduct
> from payments made by him during that income tax month.'

The principal section has been previously defined in the regulations as s 29 of the Finance
b Act 1971. Then there is a provision for giving receipts; and reg 6(3) is the critical
provision for present purposes, and it provides:

> 'If the amount which the contractor is liable to pay to the Collector under
> paragraph (1) of this Regulation exceeds the amount actually deducted by him from
> payments made during the relevant month but he satisfies the Collector that he
> took reasonable care to comply with the provisions of the principal section and of
c these Regulations and that either—(a) the under-deduction was due to an error
> made in good faith, or (b) in spite of such reasonable care as aforesaid, he had been
> led to the genuine belief that a payment made by him, which was one to which the
> principal section applies, was not or was not wholly such a payment; then the
> Collector may direct that the contractor shall not be liable to pay the said excess to
> the Collector.'
d
Finally I think I ought to refer to reg 11(1), which is the provision under which the
assessment in the instant case was made, and that provides:

> 'Where—(a) there is a dispute between a contractor and a sub-contractor as to the
> amount, if any, deductible by the contractor under the principal section from a
> payment to the sub-contractor or his nominee [that does not apply in the present
e case] or (b) the Inspector has reason to believe, as a result of an inspection under
> Regulation 10 or otherwise, that the amount which a contractor is liable to pay to
> the Collector under these Regulations is greater than the amount, if any, which he
> has so paid, or (c) the inspector for any other reason sees fit to do so; the Inspector
> may at his discretion make an assessment on the contractor in the amount which,
> according to the best of his judgment, the contractor is liable to pay under these
f Regulations, and all the provisions of the Income Tax Acts regarding appeals,
> collection and recovery shall apply as though it were an assessment to income tax,
> except that the amount charged by the assessment shall be due and payable fourteen
> days after the assessment is made.'

Now in the instant case the position is this. The taxpayer company is a company
g concerned in the construction industry and in the year of assessment 1973–74 it made
payments to sub-contractors for construction work from which it was required to deduct
the 30% provided in s 29. There were two sub-contractors going under the names of
Hayes and Dooley. Several payments were made by the taxpayer company. Those sub-
contractors were persons who held exemption certificates or produced exemption
certificates applying to Mr Hayes and Mr Dooley. I think there is some question as to
h whether they were the rightful holders of those certificates, but in the event that is not
really material to the present case. What is material is this, that the certificate issued in
the name of Hayes expired on 30th April 1973 and the certificate in the name of Mr
Dooley expired on 19th November 1973; but unfortunately this was not spotted by those
responsible for making the payments within the organisation of the taxpayer company
and payments continued to be made in full to those sub-contractors in respect of periods
j after the expiry of their certificates, when under the provisions of s 29 deductions should
have been made.

It should be said in fairness that the taxpayer company is in a substantial way of
business, as the General Commissioners found, and it carries on work at nine different
sites. The certificates had to be produced to the site managers. Indeed, out of all their
work only two cases were found in which the company had proved to be at fault,

although their quarterly payments to subcontractors amounted to very substantial sums, somewhere between £33,000 and £42,000. The case finds that the taxpayer company *a* had been punctilious in its making of quarterly payment returns and that the collector of taxes had considered, in relation to the circumstances of the instant case, whether he ought to make a direction under reg 6(3), to which I have referred, which enables him in certain circumstances to exonerate a company from that liability. For reasons which were good no doubt to him, and whether good or bad is not a matter for my judgment, he declined to make any such direction, and the inspector accordingly, under reg 11(1), *b* made an assessment.

The taxpayer company appealed to the General Commissioners against that assessment and the General Commissioners came to this conclusion: they, having heard the appeal, were of the opinion that the taxpayer company had taken reasonable care to comply with the requirements of the new legislation. The problem of non-deduction of tax had arisen from an error made in good faith. They went on: *c*

'Moreover, we felt that if it had been practical for earlier attention to have been given to the [taxpayer company's] quarterly returns of payments made it might have been possible to prevent payments continuing to be made in full on the certificates which turned out to be falsely used. In these circumstances we considered that it would be wrong to penalise the [taxpayer company] for the loss *d* which had as its origin the deceit of the sub-contractors concerned and but for which renewed and valid certificates might have been in force.'

Accordingly they held that the appeal succeeded and they discharged the assessment, and it is from that that the Crown now appeals.

The taxpayer company has not taken part in the appeal, has not turned up to resist it, *e* for reasons which I think have been explained in a letter to the registrar. It is, in any event, immaterial why they have not turned up. I have had the benefit of counsel's submissions on behalf of the Crown in which he has very fairly put the case and drawn my attention to all the material points which might be made in the taxpayer company's favour.

Having heard those submissions, I have no doubt whatever that this is a case in which *f* the appeal of the Crown must succeed, and for this reason: that it seems to me there is no power in the Statute, there is nothing in the provisions of the Finance Act 1971, nor indeed of the Taxes Management Act 1970, which enables, in my judgment, the General Commissioners to arrogate to themselves the discretion which is clearly conferred by the regulation to which I have referred on the collector of taxes.

The position is, of course, that the right to appeal arises under s 31 of the Taxes Management Act 1970, which provides that an appeal may be brought against any *g* assessment of tax by notice of appeal in writing given 30 days after the notice of assessment, and sub-s (4) of that section allows for the appeal to be made to the General Commissioners. The General Commissioners, when they entertain the appeal have their powers and duties prescribed by Part V of the 1970 Act, and s 50(6) there provides that:

h
'If, on an appeal, it appears to the majority of the Commissioners present at the hearing, by examination of the appellant on oath or affirmation, or by other lawful evidence, that the appellant is overcharged by any assessment, the assessment shall be reduced accordingly, but otherwise every such assessment shall stand good.'

There is nothing in those words, I think, which can possibly enable the General *j* Commissioners to discharge an assessment on the ground that the circumstances were such that the collector of taxes ought to have exercised a discretion which is placed on him to remit tax which is clearly payable under the provisions of the section.

Counsel for the Crown has very fairly drawn my attention to a case concerning value added tax, which was an appeal from a decision of Neill J to the Court of Appeal. It is the a case of the *Customs and Excise Comrs v J H Corbitt (Numismatists) Ltd*[1], in which the majority of the Court of Appeal held that on an appeal to the tribunal, the tribunal was empowered to consider matters which, under the statutory provisions, had been confided to the commissioners. But the wording of the sections was very different from the provisions which I have to consider, and in any event, there the position was that the persons exercising the discretion and the persons making the assessment, namely the commissioners, were the same. Here the discretion is clearly vested not in the inspector

b of taxes but in the collector of taxes, and I can find nothing in the statutory wording which enables or gives to the commissioners any power to review the collector's decision, nor any power in the inspector himself to review the collector's decision.

In these circumstances it seems to me that although I have the very greatest sympathy with the taxpayer company and the position in which it found itself as a result of having, in quite good faith, under-deducted, there is, I think, no answer to the Crown's claim and

c the appeal must be allowed and the decision of the General Commissioners reversed.

Appeal allowed. Case remitted to the commissioners to adjust the assessment in the light of the decision of the court. No order for costs.

Solicitor: *Solicitor of Inland Revenue.*

d   Rengan Krishnan Esq   Barrister.

Fothergill v Monarch Airlines Ltd

COURT OF APPEAL, CIVIL DIVISION

LORD DENNING MR, BROWNE AND GEOFFREY LANE LJJ

e 7th, 8th, 22nd JUNE, 31st JULY 1979

Carriage by air – Damage to baggage or cargo – Complaint to carrier within prescribed period after discovery of damage – Damage – Loss of articles from baggage – Whether loss of articles constituting 'damage' – Whether complaint to be made within prescribed period – Carriage by Air Act 1961, Sch 1, art 26(2) – Carriage by Air and Road Act 1979, s 2.

f *Statute – Construction – Convention given effect by legislation – Reference to travaux préparatoires – Text of convention incorporated in statute – Circumstances in which reference to travaux préparatoires permissible – Plain meaning of text of convention – Minutes of negotiations preceding convention showing that text to be understood in sense other than plain meaning – Whether resort to minutes permissible to override plain meaning of text – Carriage by Air Act*

g *1961, Sch 1, art 26(2).*

The plaintiff flew from Rome to Luton on an aircraft operated by the defendant airline. The carriage was 'international carriage', within art 1 of the Warsaw Convention, as amended at The Hague in 1955 and as set out in Sch 1 to the Carriage by Air Act 1961. The plaintiff's ticket incorporated a baggage check which, as required by art 4(1) of the convention, contained a provision stating: 'In case of damage to baggage . . .

h complaint must be made in writing to the carrier forthwith after discovery of the damage and, at the latest, within seven days from receipt.' When the plaintiff claimed his baggage he noticed that one side seam of his suitcase had been completely torn away. He reported it to an official of the airline and a 'property irregularity report' was completed which described the suitcase and, under the heading 'Nature of damage', stated: 'Side seam completely parted from case. Damage occurred on inbound flight.'

j More than seven days later, the plaintiff discovered that some articles were missing from the suitcase. He made a claim for £12 in respect of the damage to the suitcase and one for £16·50 in respect of the lost articles. The airline admitted liability as to the £12 but

1   [1979] STC 504, [1979] 3 WLR 291

rejected the claim for £16·50, contending that the loss of the articles constituted 'damage', within art 26(2)[a] of the convention, and the plaintiff had failed to give notice in writing   *a* of that damage within seven days from the date of receipt of the suitcase, as required by art 26(2) and (3). The airline supported their contention that the word 'damage' in art 26(2) included loss of contents by reference to the published minutes of the negotiations of the Hague Protocol in 1955 which disclosed that a proposal that the words 'or partial loss' should be inserted after 'damage' in art 26(2) of the convention had been withdrawn 'on the understanding that the word "damage" was to be understood as including partial   *b* loss'. The judge[b] upheld the plaintiff's claim on the ground that 'damage' in art 26(2) referred to physical injury to baggage and did not include loss of articles from a suitcase, but went on to decide that, had notice been required, the notice given by the plaintiff was insufficient since it merely related to the damage to the suitcase and made no reference to missing articles. The airline appealed, and, under RSC Ord 59, r 6(2), the plaintiff sought to uphold the judgment on the ground that the property irregularity report   *c* completed by him did constitute proper notice of the loss of the contents of the suitcase under art 26(2). Before the appeal was heard the Carriage by Air and Road Act 1979 was enacted. By s 2(1)[c] of that Act references to damage in art 26(2) were to be construed 'as including loss of part of the baggage' but, by s 2(2), that provision was not to apply to any loss occurring prior to the commencement of the Act on 4th April 1979. The plaintiff's loss having occurred before that date, his entitlement to claim remained in issue on   *d* appeal.

In both the court below and the Court of Appeal the question arose whether the court was entitled to have regard to travaux préparatoires in construing art 26(2), and if so, to what extent. The travaux préparatoires consisted, inter alia, of the minutes of 34 meetings of delegates at the conference at which the Hague Protocol was negotiated in 1955. The question whether the term 'damage' in art 26(2) included 'partial loss' was discussed at   *e* several of those meetings. The minutes were later published in Montreal, but not in the United Kingdom. In the Court of Appeal the question also arose whether the court ought to have regard to s 2(1) of the 1979 Act in construing art 26(2).

Held – The appeal would be dismissed for the following reasons –

(i) (Lord Denning MR dissenting) As a matter of ordinary English the term 'damage'   *f* used in art 26(2) of the Warsaw Convention referred to physical injury to baggage and did not extend to partial loss of the contents. (Per Geoffrey Lane LJ) In the absence of ambiguity it was unnecessary for the court to refer to the traveaux préparatoires of the 1955 Hague conference, but (per Browne and Geoffrey Lane LJJ) in any event the court would not have had regard to them because (a) air passengers from the United Kingdom could not be expected to be bound by the minutes of a conference which had never been   *g* published in the United Kingdom, (b) the ambit of enquiry as to what the delegates at the Hague conference thought art 26(2) was intended or understood to mean would be unlimited, and (c) (per Browne LJ) it would be contrary to authority for an English court to have regard to the delegates' direct statements or opinions as to the meaning of art 26(2) (see p 454 *e f*, p 456 *g* to p 457 *a f* to *h*, p 458 *a* to *d* and p 459 *c* and *f* to *j*, post); dicta of Lord Wilberforce, of Viscount Dilhorne and of Lord Salmon in *James Buchanan & Co*   *h* *Ltd v Babco Forwarding and Shipping (UK) Ltd* [1977] 3 All ER at 1052, 1056 and 1059, and of Shapiro J in *Schwimmer v Air France* (1976) 14 Avi at 17,467 applied; dicta of Lord Reid, of Lord Wilberforce and of Lord Diplock in *Black-Clawson International Ltd v Papierwerke Waldhof-Aschaffenburg AG* [1975] 1 All ER at 814, 828 and 835 applied.

(ii) (Lord Denning MR dissenting) The 1979 Act was to be disregarded in construing art 26(2) in cases of loss occurring before the Act came into force because to apply it to   *j* such loss would be to give s 2 retrospective effect which was contrary to the express provision of s 2(2) (see p 455 *h* to p 456 *a* and p 460 *c*, post).

---

a   Article 26, so far as material, is set out at p 449 *d e*, post
b   [1977] 3 All ER 616
c   Section 2, so far as material, is set out at p 452 *e f*, post

a (iii) (Per Lord Denning MR) Since 'damage' in art 26(2) included both physical damage and, since 4th April 1979, partial loss, a complaint was sufficient for the purposes of that article if it told the carrier that damage of some kind had happened to the baggage during transit. It followed that the plaintiff's complaint would have satisfied art 26(2) as it was now to be understood (see p 453 *c* to *f*, post).

Per Lord Denning MR. When the Parliament of the United Kingdom gives its authority to an international convention by incorporating it into the municipal law, the
b courts can have regard to the travaux préparatoires as an aid to its interpretation (see p 451 *b c*, post); dictum of Diplock LJ in *Post Office v Estuary Radio Ltd* [1967] 3 All ER at 684 applied.

Decision of Kerr J [1977] 3 All ER 616 affirmed.

Notes

c For time limits for complaints and claims of damage or delay to baggage or cargo, see 2 Halsbury's Laws (4th Edn) para 1395, and for cases on carriage of baggage and goods by air and liabilities of carriers, see 8(2) Digest (Reissue) 603–605, *29–37*.

For the interpretation of treaties, see 18 Halsbury's Laws (4th Edn) paras 1792–1794, for the construction of statutes giving effect to international agreements, see 36 Halsbury's Laws (3rd Edn) 394, para 592, and for cases on the subject, see 44 Digest (Repl)
d 228, *461–462*.

For the Carriage by Air Act 1961, Sch 1, see 2 Halsbury's Statutes (3rd Edn) 612.

Cases referred to in judgments

Black-Clawson International Ltd v Papierwerke Waldhof-Aschaffenburg AG [1975] 1 All ER
   810, [1975] AC 591, [1975] 2 WLR 513, [1975] 2 Lloyd's Rep 11, HL; *rvsg* [1974] 2 All
e   ER 611, [1974] QB 660, [1974] 2 WLR 789, [1974] 1 Lloyd's Rep 573, CA, Digest
   (Cont Vol D) 108, *1591a*.
Buchanan (James) & Co Ltd v Babco Forwarding and Shipping (UK) Ltd [1977] 3 All ER 1048,
   [1978] AC 141, [1977] 3 WLR 907, [1978] 1 Lloyd's Rep 119, HL.
Davis v Johnson [1978] 1 All ER 1132, [1979] AC 264, [1978] 2 WLR 553, HL.
Day v Trans-World Airlines (1975) 528 F 2d 31.
f *Escoigne Properties Ltd v Inland Revenue Comrs* [1958] 1 All ER 406, [1958] AC 549, [1958]
   2 WLR 336, 37 ATC 41, [1958] TR 37, HL, 9 Digest (Reissue) 739, *4400*.
London Borough of Ealing v Race Relations Board [1972] 1 All ER 105, [1972] AC 342, [1972]
   2 WLR 71, 136 JP 112, 70 LGR 219, HL, 2 Digest Reissue 316, *1783*.
Parke Davis & Co v British Overseas Airways Corpn (1958) 170 NYS 2d 385, [1958] US Av
   122.
g *Post Office v Estuary Radio Ltd* [1967] 3 All ER 663, [1968] 2 QB 740, [1967] 1 WLR 1396,
   [1967] 2 Lloyd's Rep 229, CA, Digest (Cont Vol C) 951, *40b*.
Schwimmer v Air France (1976) 14 Avi 17,466.
Stag Line Ltd v Foscolo Mango & Co Ltd [1932] AC 328, [1931] All ER Rep 666, 101 LJKB
   165, 146 LT 305, 18 Asp MLC 266, 37 Com Cas 54, HL, 41 Digest (Repl) 379, *1698*.

h **Appeal**

By a writ issued on 4th March 1976 the plaintiff, John Wesley Fothergill, brought an action against the defendants, Monarch Airlines Ltd, claiming (i) a declaration that under art 26 of the Warsaw Convention contained in Sch 1 to the Carriage by Air Act 1961 no complaint in respect of the partial loss of the contents of a suitcase belonging to the plaintiff which had been carried by the defendants by air was required and (ii) damages.
j On 17th March 1977 Kerr J[1] gave judgment for the plaintiff. The defendants appealed. By notice under RSC Ord 59, r 6(2), the plaintiff sought to uphold Kerr J's judgment on the additional ground that he had erred in holding that a property irregularity report completed by the plaintiff on 13th March 1975 did not constitute proper notice to the

1 [1977] 3 All ER 616, [1978] QB 108

defendants of the loss of contents of the plaintiff's suitcase under art 26(2) of the
convention. The facts are set out in the judgment of Lord Denning MR.   *a*

Christopher Staughton QC and *Richard Wood* for the plaintiff.
Marcus Edwards for the defendants.

Cur adv vult

b

31st July. The following judgments were read.

LORD DENNING MR. In March 1975 Mr Fothergill went for a holiday to Italy. He
insured his luggage through the tour operators called Cosmos. He returned on 13th
March 1975 by an aircraft of Monarch Airlines Ltd to London. When the luggage was   *c*
unloaded, he got his suitcase and found it was badly damaged. He went to the reception
desk and reported it. The lady filled in a form called the 'property irregularity report'.
She entered: 'damaged—One Navy S/C expanding'. Contents: 'P/E', that is, personal
effects. Then in a box headed 'Nature of Damage', she wrote: 'Side seam completely
parted from case. Damage occurred on inbound flight.'
     Mr Fothergill then went home to Colchester with his damaged suitcase. When he   *d*
opened it, he found that there were missing a shirt, a pair of sandals and a cardigan. He
did not write to Monarch Airlines. He wrote to the tour operators, who passed it on to
the insurance company. They sent back a claim form. The tour operators got Mr
Fothergill's answers and returned it on 11th April 1975.
     The claim form asked: 'State action taken to recover any lost articles.' The reply was:
'Apart from damage to suitcase, it was not known until a later date what articles had been   *e*
lost, but damaged suitcase was taken to Monarch Airlines' reception desk at Luton
Airport.' The claim form asked for particulars of the claim. The reply was that the
suitcase 'cannot be repaired' and the 'loss out of suitcase' of the shirt, sandals and
cardigan. The amount claimed was £12 for the suitcase and £16·50 for the contents,
totalling £28·50. Under the insurance Mr Fothergill had to bear himself the first
£2·50. So the insurance company paid him £26, and he accepted it in settlement.   *f*
     The insurance company then, by virtue of their right of subrogation, claimed from
Monarch Airlines. The airline accepted liability for the damage to the suitcase, £12, but
denied liability for the loss of the shirt, sandals or cardigan, which came to £16·50. The
reason for their denial was because they said that Monarch Airlines did not receive any
complaint of the loss of contents until 20th June 1975: whereas there was, under the
Warsaw Convention, a time limit of seven days. I expect this point is taken by the   *g*
insurers of Monarch Airlines. So the case is really a contest between two insurance
companies: those who insured Mr Fothergill's luggage and those who insured Monarch
Airlines for their liability in respect of it. The court can regard the matter quite
dispassionately, without taking into account any sympathy for Mr Fothergill: for he has
been satisfied.

h

The Warsaw Convention
     Now that carriage by air is universal and international, it is desirable that all countries
should have the same rules in regard to air transport. The first set of rules was agreed in
Warsaw in 1929. A convention was there agreed. In 1932 it was made law for the
United Kingdom by the Carriage by Air Act 1932. In 1955 there was a meeting at The
Hague at which amendments were agreed. This was known as 'The Warsaw Convention   *j*
as amended at The Hague, 1955'. It was made law for the United Kingdom by the
Carriage by Air Act 1961. That Act appended an English text and a French text: and said
that if there was any inconsistency between the two 'the text in French shall prevail'.
That is a funny sort of thing to tell us English lawyers. Some of us have no French.
Others have schoolboy French. None of us has sufficient knowledge of French to be able

to detect any inconsistency. I do not suppose that the members of Parliament were any
a more linguistically accomplished than we. So for the present I propose to go by the
English text.
   I will first set out the more important articles in the English text of the convention.

The convention
   Article 18(1):

b   'The carrier is liable for damage sustained in the event of the destruction or loss
     of, or damage to, any registered baggage or any cargo, if the occurrence which
     caused the damage so sustained took place during the carriage by air.'

   Article 22(2)(b):

c   'In the case of loss, damage or delay of part of registered baggage or cargo, or of
     any object contained therein, the weight to be taken into consideration in
     determining the amount to which the carrier's liability is limited shall be only the
     total weight of the package or packages concerned. Nevertheless, when the loss,
     damage or delay of a part of the registered baggage or cargo, or of an object
     contained therein, affects the value of other packages covered by the same baggage
     check or the same air waybill, the total weight of such package or packages shall also
d   be taken into consideration in determining the limit of liability.'

   Article 26(2):

     'In the case of damage, the person entitled to delivery must complain to the
     carrier forthwith after the discovery of the damage, and, at the latest, within seven
     days from the date of receipt in the case of baggage and fourteen days from the date
e   of receipt in the case of cargo . . .'

   Article 26(3):

     'Every complaint must be made in writing upon the document of carriage or by
     separate notice in writing despatched within the times aforesaid.'

f Article 29(1):

     'The right to damages shall be extinguished if an action is not brought within two
     years, reckoned from the date of arrival at the destination, or from the date on
     which the aircraft ought to have arrived, or from the date on which the carriage
     stopped.'

The issue of the case
g   The passenger admits that, in the case of *damage* to a suitcase, he has to make
   complaint in writing within seven days of the time he received it: but he says that in the
   case of *loss* of *part* of the contents (or *loss* of the whole suitcase) he need make no
   complaint and give no notice. It is sufficient if he brings an action within two years.
     The carrier says that *both* in the case of *damage* to the suitcase *and also* in the case of loss
h of *part* of the contents, the passenger must make complaint in writing within seven
   days. The carrier admits that in the case of the *whole* of the suitcase, there need be no
   complaint and no notice. It is sufficient if action is brought within two years.
     The issue depends on the meaning of 'damage' in art 26(2) of the convention. Is it
   confined to physical damage? Or does it include also 'loss of part of the contents'?

The meaning of 'damage'
j   I think that the word 'damage' in art 26(2) is ambiguous. It may be confined to
   physical damage or it may include loss of part of the contents.
     In other articles it is used variously. In art 18(1) I think 'loss of' means loss of the *whole*
   suitcase and 'damage' includes loss of part of the contents. In art 22(2)(b) 'damage' means
   physical damage only.

The meaning of 'avarie'

To my schoolboy French, the French text is also ambiguous. It says: 'En cas d'avarie', etc. The French dictionaries do not help to resolve the ambiguity. I doubt whether an interpreter could do any better than the dictionaries.

The minutes of the Hague conference of 1955

In 1955, when the Hague Protocol was negotiated, there was an important conference at The Hague, at which most countries of the world were represented. Mr Wilberforce appeared for the United Kingdom. He had just taken silk and was assisted by Mr Beaumont. There were 34 meetings. Minutes were kept. They were published by the International Civil Aviation Organisation in Montreal in 1956 in English, French and Spanish. Our very point on art 26(2) was discussed. Mr Wilberforce for the United Kingdom delegation proposed it should be amended so as to make it clear. He suggested that the opening words should be: 'In case of damage or partial loss of baggage or cargo'. Mr Beaumont (United Kingdom) said that the whole purpose of the United Kingdom's proposal was to incorporate certainty where at present uncertainty prevailed.

At a later meeting Mr Drion (Netherlands) proposed, seconded by Mr Sidenbladh (Sweden), the addition of the words 'or partial loss' after 'damage'. Mr Calkins (United States) said that it went without saying that 'damage' included 'partial loss'. He was opposed to the Netherlands' proposal. Mr Loaeza (Mexico), chairman of the drafting committee, speaking as the Mexican delegate, said that it was not necessary to insert the words 'or partial loss' after the word 'damage'. Messrs Drion (Netherlands) and Sidenbladh (Sweden) withdrew their proposal on the understanding that the word 'damage' was to be understood as including 'partial loss'.

Those minutes are most telling. But the judge thought they should have no weight[1]:

'. . . this material has come before this court mainly because the defendants' solicitors specialise in air law and have this publication available. It will not be readily available to a non-specialist lawyer, and no ordinary air passenger would have the slightest idea that it exists, nor be concerned if he or she knew.'

Here, I find myself differing from the judge. This convention is not a contract between passenger and carrier. Our strict rules about exemption clauses and limitation clauses (in money or time) do not apply to it. It is a convention which binds everyone affected by it, in all countries signatory to it, just as if it were a statute. It is no answer for passenger or carrier to say that he never agreed to it, or knew nothing of it, or had no notice of it. The only question is, what is the true interpretation of it? If the courts, in seeking its true interpretation, are entitled to have regard to these minutes as travaux préparatoires, then both passengers and carriers must abide by that true interpretation, even though they knew nothing of the minutes and had no means of knowing.

Is it permissible to have regard to the Hague minutes?

It is obvious that this convention should be interpreted in the same way, and given the same meaning, by the courts of each of the countries which signed it. If the courts of France and Germany could look at the Hague minutes so as to clear up an ambiguity or obscurity, so should we. To ensure this, the courts in England should have recourse to the same aids to interpretation as the courts of any other country which was a signatory to the convention. I ask the question, therefore, would the courts of France or Germany, or, I may add, of the Netherlands or Sweden or Mexico, have regard to the minutes of the Hague conference, so as to aid the interpretation of it?

To this question the answer is Yes. In giving this answer, I have read a valuable paper by Professor Dumon of the University of Brussels which he presented to the European Court at Luxembourg when I was there in 1976. He shows that, not only the International Court of Justice, but also the national courts of Germany, France, Italy,

---

1   [1977] 3 All ER 616 at 624, [1978] QB 108 at 119

a Luxembourg, the Netherlands, and Belgium all have recourse to travaux préparatoires in varying degrees. I have also read a valuable summary by Professor O'Connell (whose recent death we lament) in his book on International Law[1]. We were also referred to the decision of the United States Court of Appeals in 1975 in *Day v Trans-World Airlines*[2], where it was held that 'in interpreting a treaty, we may look at its legislative history'. The court looked at the minutes of a drafting committee so as to interpret the Warsaw Convention.

b As a result, I am prepared to say that when the Parliament of the United Kingdom gives its authority to an international convention, by incorporating it into our municipal law, then the courts of this country can have regard to the travaux préparatoires so as to aid them in the interpretation of it. This was in the mind of Diplock LJ when he said in *Post Office v Estuary Radio Ltd*[3] that light might be thrown 'by the travaux préparatoires of the Convention itself'. If the words are clear in themselves, there is little need to have recourse to the travaux préparatoires, though it can be done so as to confirm the

c meaning. But when there is any ambiguity or obscurity or anything that needs clearing up, then recourse can be had to the travaux préparatoires, so as to ascertain what was the meaning intended by the draftsmen and signatories of the convention. These travaux préparatoires can be used not only to see what was the mischief needing to be remedied, not only to see what was the purpose or object of the draftsmen, but also to find out what they really meant to convey by the words they used.

d As Professor O'Connell says[4] the problem is not whether resort to travaux préparatoires is permissible, that is conceded on all hands, but to strike a balance 'between the final text and the amorphous mass of documentation which goes under the name of *travaux préparatoires*'. In the case of a convention, I should think that in general only those papers or minutes should be included which record discussions between the various delegates to the convention, inter partes, as a result of which agreement was reached.

e Other material, such as the working papers of each delegation, on its own, or the private notes—memoranda—of those attending the conference, should usually be excluded. Professor Dumon quotes Professor Charles de Visscher as saying that 'a report drawn up by a committee at a diplomatic conference and approved by it usually carries considerable weight'; and Guggenheim as saying that 'the minutes of negotiations often contain

f declarations which, due to their clarity, are of prime importance in interpreting a treaty'.

Tried by these tests it seems to me that we can look at the minutes of the Hague meeting in 1955. On looking at them, it becomes clear that 'damage' in art 26(2) includes 'partial loss'.

Judicial decisions and text writers

g *Germany*

On 27th February 1973 the Berlin District Court decided a case where a passenger flew from Berlin to Istanbul. When he examined his cases, he found that there was lost out of them two suits, a lady's umbrella and a bottle of whisky. He failed because he had not given written notice within the time prescribed by art 26(2). The court said[5]:

h 'Since it is equally as difficult for the air carrier to determine the damages incurred by a partial loss of goods as it is to determine that incurred by actual damage to goods, the damages incurred by partial loss are covered by the protection included in Article 26 of the Warsaw Convention and are therefore equated with damages incurred by actual damage.'

j

1   2nd Edn (1970)
2   (1975) 528 F 2d 31 at 34
3   [1967] 3 All ER 663 at 684, [1968] 2 QB 740 at 761
4   2nd Edn (1970) vol 1, p 263
5   Case 435/72

United States
(1) *Parke Davis & Co v British Overseas Airways Corpn*[1]. In 1958 consignors sent by air
900 monkeys from India to Detroit by BOAC. On arrival 185 monkeys were missing.
The claim failed because it was not made until 47 days later. The point was taken about
partial loss. The judge of the New York City Court said[2]: 'There is no validity to the
claim by the plaintiff that this was a partial loss and not a damage claim.'
(2) *Schwimmer v Air France*[3]. Several cases of household goods were sent from Moscow
to New York. Seven were lost. It was argued that loss of a portion of a shipment
constitutes 'damage' under art 26(2). The judge of the New York City Court said: 'I
cannot agree. Damage is damage and loss is loss.'

Text writers
Professor Abrahams[4] of Frankfurt in 1960 and Dr Guldimann[5] of Zurich in 1965 say
that a broad interpretation is to be given to 'damage'. 'Partial loss and partial destruction
are both considered to be damage.' So the weight of judicial and academic opinion
clearly is in favour of interpreting 'damage' as including 'partial loss'.

The 1979 Act
It was on 17th March 1977 that Kerr J gave his decision in this case that 'damage' in art
26(2) did not include 'partial loss'. The defendants gave notice of appeal but unfortunately
the appeal has taken over two years to come on for hearing. Meanwhile those concerned
in these matters were so disturbed by Kerr J's decision that they approached the relevant
departments to get it reversed. As a result, this section[6] was included in the Carriage by
Air and Road Act 1979 which was passed on 4th April 1979:

> 'In Article 26(2) the references to damage shall be construed as including loss of
> part of the baggage or cargo in question and the reference to receipt of baggage or
> cargo shall, in relation to loss of part of it, be construed as receipt of the remainder
> of it.'

But there was this interesting addition: 'This section shall come into force at the passing
of this Act but shall not apply to loss which occurred before the passing of this Act.'
Seeing that the section is in force, we can look at it. It shows plainly what the
government thought was the meaning of art 26(2) of the convention. They realised that
it was their duty to implement it so as to be in conformity with all the other signatories.
It was therefore enacted that, for future losses, the courts of England were to construe art
26(2) by holding that 'damage' included 'partial loss'.
It is just as if the government said to Parliament: 'We think that Kerr J was wrong. He
ought not to have construed art 26(2) as he did. He ought to have held that "damage"
included "partial loss". But it would be contrary to principle for us to make this new
section retrospective. We will not deprive Mr Fothergill of the benefit of his judgment,
if Kerr J is held by the Court of Appeal to have been right. So we will provide that this
new section is not to apply to losses which occurred before the passing of the Act.'
So interpreted, the new section seems to me to be a declaration by Parliament of the
meaning of art 26(2), of the convention; the meaning which it was intended to have by
the signatories of the convention; the meaning which it was intended to have in 1929
and in 1956 when the convention and the amended convention were signed. It is
therefore to be considered as a declaratory Act, declaring what the true meaning of the

---

1   [1958] US Av 122
2   [1958] US Av 122 at 124
3   (1976) 14 Avi 17,466 at 17,467
4   Das Recht der Luftfahrt (1960)
5   Internationales Lufttransportrecht: Kommentar zu den Abkommen von Warschau 1929/55 und
    Guadalajara 1961 (1965)
6   Section 4A (1) inserted in the Carriage by Air Act 1961 by s 2(1) of the 1979 Act

convention was, and is, and is to be. As such it affords very great help to this court in deciding on the meaning of art 26(2). We can use the new Act, not so as to overrule Kerr J if he was right in his construction of art 26(2), but so as to show that he was wrong in his construction of it.

Summary of the appeal
The reasons taken together are overwhelming. Although the word 'damage' in art 26(2) is ambiguous or obscure, nevertheless the travaux préparatoires, the judicial decisions and the text writers, and the 1979 Act all lead to the conclusion that 'damage' in art 26(2) includes 'partial loss'.

The cross-appeal
Kerr J held that the complaint in the property irregularity report did not satisfy art 26(2) because it only referred to the damage to the suitcase and did not mention the loss of the shirt, sandals and cardigan. This raises an important point: what is sufficient 'complaint' to satisfy art 26(2)?
It has to be a complaint of 'damage' and damage includes both physical damage and partial loss. It seems to me that a complaint is sufficient if it tells the carrier that some damage of some kind has happened to the baggage during transit. The passenger need not go into details. It may be damage to the suitcase or loss of some of the contents. But, in any case, it is sufficient if he says: 'It has arrived damaged'. In many cases the passenger may not be able to specify the damage until later when he has inspected the suitcase more carefully. Meanwhile his initial complaint is sufficient to satisfy art 26(2).
Applied to this case, it seems to me (looking at the form) that the lady at the reception desk simply asked Mr Fothergill: 'What is the nature of the damage?' He replied: 'Here it is. Look at it. The side seam has completely parted from the case.' So she wrote it down. She did not ask him whether any of the contents were missing. If she had, he would probably have answered: 'I cannot tell now. I must wait till I get home.' On that presumed conversation, I think that Mr Fothergill's complaint was all that art 26(2) required of him.
So I would allow the cross-appeal.

Conclusion
The result is that Mr Fothergill retains his judgment for £28·50, but on grounds which are the reverse of those given by Kerr J.

BROWNE LJ. Lord Denning MR has stated the facts of this case and the relevant provisions of the Carriage by Air Act 1961 and I need not repeat them.
But for two points I should have little hesitation in dismissing this appeal; those two points are the 1979 Act and the 'travaux préparatoires'.
As to the other points:

1. *The construction of the English text of art 26(2)*
The judge rightly approached the construction of this statute, giving effect to an international convention, on the principle laid down by Lord Macmillan in *Stag Line Ltd v Foscolo, Mango & Co*[1] which Kerr J quotes in his judgment. Since Kerr J gave his judgment, the approach to the construction of statutes giving effect to international conventions has been considered by the House of Lords in *James Buchanan & Co Ltd v Babco Forwarding and Shipping (UK) Ltd*[2]. Lord Wilberforce said[3] (citing the *Stag Line* case[1]):

---

1   [1932] AC 328 at 350, [1931] All ER Rep 666 at 677
2   [1977] 3 All ER 1048, [1978] AC 141
3   [1977] 3 All ER 1048 at 1052, [1978] AC 141 at 152

'I think that the correct approach is to interpret the English text which after all is likely to be used by many others than British businessmen, in a normal manner, appropriate for the interpretation of an international convention, unconstrained by technical rules of English law, or by English legal precedent, but on broad principles of general acceptation.'

Viscount Dilhorne said[1]:

'In construing the terms of a convention it is proper and indeed right, in my opinion, to have regard to the fact that conventions are apt to be more loosely worded than Acts of Parliament. To construe a convention as strictly as an Act may indeed lead to a wrong interpretation being given to it. In construing a convention as in construing an Act where the language used is capable of two interpretations one must seek to give effect to the intentions of those who made it[2].'

Lord Salmon said[3]:

'No doubt these words are flexible and somewhat imprecise; but, especially as they appear in an international convention relating to commercial affairs, they should not be construed pedantically or rigidly but sensibly and broadly.'

The language of the Warsaw Convention, as originally enacted by the Carriage by Air Act 1932, and as re-enacted by the Carriage by Air Act 1961 with the amendments agreed at The Hague in 1955, is not always precise or consistent. In particular, as Kerr J pointed out, the word 'damage' is sometimes used to mean economic loss and sometimes to mean physical damage. In art 18(1) it is used three times, twice with the former meaning and once with the latter. Counsel for the defendants accepts that in art 26(2) it is used in the latter sense, but he says including partial physical loss.

Having regard to the statements as to the principles of interpretation which I have quoted above, I do not apply the English principles as to the interpretation of exemption clauses. But I agree with Kerr J that: 'As a matter of ordinary English the loss of articles from an undamaged suitcase would not be described as a case of "damage" in the sense of physical injury . . .' It can make no difference that the suitcase itself was damaged. Like the judge, I agree with Judge Shapiro that 'Damage is damage and loss is loss': see *Schwimmer v Air France*[4].

I do not find that other articles of the convention throw any light on the meaning of 'damage' in art 26(2). It was suggested that 'damage' there must include partial loss because the only provision imposing liability on the carrier in respect of partial loss was the word 'damage' in art 18(1), but I think the words 'loss of . . . *any* registered baggage' (my emphasis) are wide enought to include loss of the contents of registered baggage. The 'baggage' is not merely a suitcase but the suitcase and its contents. The same applies to arts 4(1)(c) and 8(c). Article 22(2)(b) is dealing with a special problem of the application of the money limit of the carrier's liability, and I do not think it helps on the meaning of 'damage' in other articles.

Nor am I impressed by the gloomy picture of counsel for the defendants of the dire consequences to air carriers if Kerr J's decision is right. It is now 50 years since the Warsaw Convention was signed, and so far as we know there have only been three disputed cases as to the meaning of this article before the present case. Counsel's arguments for the defendants seem to apply with equal force to personal injury to passengers (which might be quite slight), and to some extent to total loss of baggage or cargo, of neither of which is any 'complaint' required. For what it is worth, the carriers in this case seem to have thought that 'damage' in art 26(2) meant damage *to* baggage, as

---

1   [1977] 3 All ER 1048 at 1056, [1978] AC 141 at 157
2   See 4 Co Inst, p 330
3   [1977] 3 All ER 1048 at 1059, [1978] AC 141 at 160
4   (1976) 14 Avi 17,466 at 17,467

a Kerr J pointed out (see condition 7 on their ticket); their 'property irregularity report' makes no provision for reporting loss of contents.

Counsel for the defendants suggests that there may be difficulties in deciding in particular cases whether what has happened is damage or partial loss, eg if the handle of a suitcase is completely torn off and disappears, is that damage to the suitcase or loss of the handle? Or if the container of cargo is broken and some of the contents escapes? These problems will have to be solved when they arise.

b
2. The French text

Section 1(2) of the 1961 Act provides that: 'If there is any inconsistency between the text in English in Part I of the First Schedule to this Act and the text in French in Part II of that Schedule, the text in French shall prevail.'

The word which appears as 'damage' in art 26(2) of the English text is 'avarie' in the c French text. It is suggested on behalf of the defendants that, even if 'damage' in the English text does not include partial loss, 'avarie' does; there is therefore an inconsistency between the English and French texts and the French text must prevail.

It seems to me clear from the dictionaries which are before us, especially the Nouveau Dictionnaire de Droit et de Sciences Economiques[1] (which was not before Kerr J) that 'avarie' is a term of art in French law, possibly with different meanings in civil law and d maritime law. My knowledge of French is hopelessly inadequate to enable me to decide what 'avarie' means in the French language generally, in French law (civil or maritime) or in the context of the French text of this convention. I agree with counsel for the plaintiff that if the defendants wanted to rely on this point they should have called a French lawyer to give expert evidence. Without such evidence, I cannot attach any weight to it.

e
3. The foreign text writers and decisions

Of course I entirely accept (as does counsel for the plaintiff) what Lord Salmon said in the Buchanan case[2]: 'If a corpus of law had grown up overseas which laid down the meaning of art 23 [that in our case is art 26(2)], our courts would no doubt follow it for the sake of the uniformity which it is the object of the convention to establish.' But I also f agree with his next sentence: 'But no such corpus exists.' It would perhaps be surprising if it did. The Warsaw Convention applies almost all over the world, and the convention as amended at The Hague in 1955 nearly as widely, though the United States of America is not a party to the latter (see the Carriage by Air (Parties to Convention) Order 1977[3]). The parties include common law countries, civil law countries, and a large number of countries whose systems of law are derived from neither. All we have here are g expressions of opinion by two textbook writers, one German and one Swiss, who may be very eminent but about whose status and qualifications we have no information, and three decisions of courts of first instance, two of them conflicting. I find it quite impossible to regard this as 'a corpus of law'.

The 1979 Act

h I am afraid that in this I cannot agree with Lord Denning MR. There are two possible views about what the intention of Parliament was in enacting s 2 of that Act. It may have been declaring what the meaning of art 26(2) had always been in the 1961 Act (and in the 1932 Act before it), or it may have been amending the 1961 Act for the future. In spite of the contrary opinion of Lord Denning MR, I am clearly of the opinion that it is the latter. The long title of the Act is: 'An Act . . . to modify Article 26(2) . . .' and s 2(2) j expressly provides that 'This section . . . shall not apply to loss which occurred before the passing of this Act'. If we use the section, even indirectly, to establish that the decision

---

1   4th Edn (1974)
2   [1977] 3 All ER 1048 at 1060, [1978] AC 141 at 161
3   SI 1977 No 240

of Kerr J was wrong, we are giving it retrospective effect, contrary to the express
provision of s 2(2), and doing injustice to the plaintiff. I agree with counsel for the *a*
plaintiff that the only satisfactory solution is to put the 1979 Act on one side.

The travaux préparatoires

I think this is far the most difficult question in the case. The extent to which regard
can be had to 'preliminary works' in construing what may be called a 'purely' English
statute seems well-established. The court can have regard to reports of royal commissions, *b*
the Law Commission, committees and the like, leading up to the enactment of the Act,
to see what the 'mischief' was with which the Act was intended to deal, but it cannot take
into account direct statements of what the Act was intended or understood to mean; nor
can the courts look at Hansard: see, for example, *Black-Clawson International Ltd v
Papierwerke Waldhof-Aschaffenburg AG*[1] per Lord Reid, Lord Wilberforce, Lord Diplock,
and Lord Simon of Glaisdale (there was a complication in that case in that the document *c*
in question, the Greer Report[2] presented to Parliament, had annexed to it a draft bill,
which was enacted in substantially the same form, and a commentary, about the effect
of which there was some difference of opinion); see also *Davis v Johnson*[3] per Lord
Diplock, Viscount Dilhorne, Lord Salmon and Lord Scarman. In the *Black-Clawson* case[4]
Lord Reid said: 'Construction of the provisions of an Act is for the court and for no one
else.' Lord Wilberforce said[5]:
d

> 'In my opinion it is not proper or desirable to make use of such a document as a
> committee or commission report, or for that matter of anything reported as said in
> Parliament, or any official notes on clauses, for a direct statement of what a proposed
> enactment is to mean or of what the committee or commission thought it means:
> on this point I am in agreement with my noble and learned friend Lord Diplock
> ... it would be a degradation of [the constitutional] process if the courts were to be *e*
> merely a reflecting mirror of what some other interpretation agency might say ...
> It is sound enough to ascertain, if that can be done, the objectives of any particular
> measure, and the background of the enactment; but to take the opinion, whether
> of a Minister or an official or a committee, as to the intended meaning in particular
> applications of a clause or a phrase, would be a stunting of the law and not a healthy
> development.' *f*

Lord Diplock said[6]:

> 'It is for the court and no one else to decide what words in a statute mean. What
> the committee thought they meant is, in itself, irrelevant. Oral evidence by
> members of the committee as to their opinion of what the section meant would
> plainly be inadmissible. It does not become admissible by being reduced to writing.' *g*

I think it is implicit in these authorities that the material to which regard can be had
must be available to the public: see especially the *Black-Clawson* case[7] per Lord Reid and
Lord Simon of Glaisdale; *Davis v Johnson*[8] per Lord Diplock. The reason is that, as Lord
Reid said in the *Black-Clawson* case[4]: 'An Act is addressed to all the lieges and it would

h

1   [1975] 1 All ER 810 at 814–815, 828, 835, 841–842, [1975] AC 591 at 613–615, 629–630, 637,
    645–646
2   Report of the Foreign Judgments (Reciprocal Enforcement) Committee (1932) Cmd 4213
3   [1978] 1 All ER 1132 at 1141, 1147, 1153–1154, 1157–1158, [1979] AC 264 at 329–330, 337, 345,
    349–350
4   [1975] 1 All ER 810 at 814, [1975] AC 591 at 614
5   [1975] 1 All ER 810 at 828, [1975] AC 591 at 629–630
6   [1975] 1 All ER 810 at 835, [1975] AC 591 at 637
7   [1975] 1 All ER 810 at 814, 841–842, [1975] AC 591 at 614, 645–646
8   [1978] 1 All ER 1132 at 1141, [1979] AC 264 at 329–330

j

seem wrong to take into account anything which was not public knowledge at the time';

a and as Lord Simon of Glaisdale[1] said in the same case:

> '. . . in statutory construction, the court is not solely concerned with what the citizens, through their parliamentary representatives, meant to say; it is also concerned with the reasonable expectation of those citizens who are affected by the statute, and whose understanding of the meaning of what was said is therefore relevant.'

b

There are dicta which suggest that there might be a more liberal use of travaux préparatoires in the construction of a statute which is enacting an international convention, at any rate where the convention is accompanied by an official explanatory memorandum or commentary: see Diplock LJ in *Post Office v Estuary Radio Ltd*[2]; Lord Diplock in the *Black-Clawson* case[3]; Lord Diplock, and perhaps Lord Scarman, in *Davis v*

c *Johnson*[4], and Kerr J[5] in his judgment in the present case. But there is no authority justifying a fundamental departure from the principles applicable to the construction of purely English statutes.

I respectfully accept, of course, what Lord Denning MR has said about the use of travaux préparatoires in Western European countries. What the attitude of the courts of the other parties to the Warsaw Convention and the Hague Protocol all over the world

d would be I do not know. In *Day v Trans-World Airlines*[6] the United States Court of Appeals had regard to the minutes of the original drafting of the Warsaw Convention (not the Hague Protocol). The court also had regard to the Montreal Agreement of 1966, treating it as a part of the 'legislative history' of the treaty; this was not a statute or an international convention, but an agreement between airlines, approved by the United States Civil Aeronautics Board, which resulted in their filing with the Civil Aeronautics

e Board contracts by which they agreed to raise the Warsaw maximum limits of liability in respect of passengers and to waive the 'all necessary measures' defence (art 20). I think it is clear that in this country regard would not be had to this agreement. In *Escoigne Properties Ltd v Inland Revenue Comrs*[7] Lord Denning said: 'In this country we do not refer to the legislative history of an enactment as they do in the United States of America'; and in the *Black-Clawson* case[1] Lord Simon of Glaisdale said: '. . . experience in the United

f States has tended to show that scrutiny of the legislative proceedings is apt to be a disappointingly misleading and wasteful guide to the legislative intention.'

I am far from satisfied that the United Kingdom delegation at The Hague in 1955 thought that in art 26(2) of the original Warsaw Convention 'damage' included partial loss. The minutes of the 19th and 20th meetings suggest that they thought it did not, or at least that this was doubtful. Assuming that at the 33rd meeting all, or a majority,

g of the delegates thought it did, this was merely their opinion in 1955 about what the draftsmen of the Warsaw Convention had intended or thought in 1929 that it was to mean. In my judgment it would be contrary to the principles stated in the House of Lords to which I have referred for us to have regard to this opinion as to the meaning of the Warsaw Convention. These minutes were not part of the travaux préparatoires of the Warsaw Convention itself; even assuming that it was right in *Day v Trans-World*

h *Airlines*[6] to look at the minutes of the Warsaw meetings, this is quite different. It might be argued that this opinion was part of the travaux préparatoires of the Hague Protocol, because as a result of forming that opinion the delegates decided not to amend the

---

j   1   [1975] 1 All ER 810 at 842, [1975] AC 591 at 645
     2   [1967] 3 All ER 663 at 685, [1968] QB 740 at 760–761
     3   [1975] 1 All ER 810 at 838, [1975] AC 591 at 640–641
     4   [1978] 1 All ER 1132 at 1140–1141, 1157, [1979] AC 264 at 329, 350
     5   [1977] 3 All ER 616 at 622, [1978] QB 108 at 116
     6   (1975) 528 F 2d 31
     7   [1958] 1 All ER 406 at 414, [1958] AC 549 at 566

Warsaw Convention. But in my view it still remains merely their opinion of what the
Warsaw Convention was intended or understood by its draftsmen to mean.

I think this is enough reason to hold that we should not have regard to these minutes,
but there are two other considerations which I think support this conclusion. There is
no evidence that these minutes were ever published in this country. The defendants'
solicitors have a copy, perhaps because Major Beaumont, who was then their senior
partner, was one of the United Kingdom delegates. I suppose there may be a copy
somewhere in the pigeon-holes of Whitehall, and perhaps Lord Wilberforce has one.
Lord Denning MR views with equanimity the prospect that air passengers from this
country may be bound by travaux préparatoires of which they do not and cannot know
anything, but I confess I do not; it seems to me contrary to the opinions I have quoted as
to the need for the material to be available to the public (even if most people are unlikely
in fact to have seen it). Counsel for the plaintiff cited to us a very apposite passage from
Blackstone[1]. Further, as counsel for the plaintiff pointed out in the course of the
argument, if there is no need for publication it would be open to a party to call oral
evidence from someone who was present at the negotiation of the international
agreement to give evidence of what the delegates intended a provision in the agreement
to mean; it would then be open to the other party to call another witness to say that that
was not what was intended, and so on indefinitely. Apart from the other objections,
from the practical point of view of time and expense, which I understand has been one
of the factors which has influenced our courts in deciding what evidence should be
admissible in aid of the construction of statutes, this would be intolerable (see *London
Borough of Ealing v Race Relations Board*[2] per Lord Simon of Glaisdale; the *Black-Clawson*
case[3] per Lord Reid and Lord Simon of Glaisdale; *Davis v Johnson*[4] per Viscount Dilhorne,
quoting Lord Reid[5] in an earlier case). In my judgment we should not have regard to
these minutes.

I would dismiss this appeal. If I am right in this view, the respondents' notice does not
arise.

GEOFFREY LANE LJ (read by Browne LJ). The Carriage by Air Act 1961 made the
terms of the amended Warsaw Convention relating to air transport part of the law of this
country. In Part I of Sch 1 to the Act is printed the English text of the Warsaw
Convention with the amendments made in it by the Hague Protocol, and in Part II the
French text. Section 1(2) of the Act provides that if there is any inconsistency between
the text in English and the text in French the text in French shall prevail. We were
invited to find that there was indeed such an inconsistency, particularly in relation to art
26(2) of the convention. Our attention was drawn to French definitions of French legal
expressions in French dictionaries. Without the assistance of a bilingual expert in French
law I found myself unable to understand what if any inconsistency there might be.
Accordingly the problem becomes one of discovering the meaning of the English text as
it applies to the facts of this case.

What happened was this. The plaintiff and his wife went by air to Italy for a
holiday. The defendants were the carriers. On arrival back at Luton airport the plaintiff
noticed that one of the seams of his suitcase was torn away. He reported this to a
representative of the defendants who completed a Monarch Airlines Ltd Property
Irregularity Report. When he got home he realised that as well as the damage to the case
itself some of his personal effects had disappeared from inside. He had in fact insured his
baggage privately and he notified the insurers accordingly. The insurers passed the claim

1   1 Bl Com 45–46
2   [1972] 1 All ER 105 at 114, [1972] AC 342 at 361
3   [1975] 1 All ER 810 at 814, 842, [1975] AC 591 at 614, 645
4   [1978] 1 All ER 1132 at 1147, [1979] AC 264 at 337
5   *Beswick v Beswick* [1967] 2 All ER 1197 at 1202, [1968] AC 58 at 73–74

on to the defendants about four weeks after the aircraft had landed at Luton. The
insurers paid the plaintiff his claim in full less a £2·50 franchise under the policy. The
defendants admitted the claim of £12 for damage to the suitcase, but refused to pay the
£16·50 which represented the value of the missing effects. The reason for this refusal
was that notice of the claim to be effective should, they alleged, under the terms of the
convention have been given within seven days and it had not been. The plaintiff on the
other hand contends that the convention does not require notice to be given of partial
loss of the contents, and that accordingly his claim was only subject to the general time
limit of two years for instituting proceedings and should have been met.

Which of those two contentions is correct depends on the meaning of the word
'damage' in art 26(2) of the convention, which runs as follows:

'In the case of damage, the person entitled to delivery must complain to the
carrier forthwith after the discovery of the damage, and, at the latest, within seven
days from the date of receipt ...'

Taking it as a matter of first impression, it seems to me that the word as it stands there
can only mean damage in the sense of harm or physical injury to the baggage. It is not
apt to include partial loss of the contents. I am reinforced in that view by the 'property
irregularity report' used by the defendants themselves. This form is plainly intended to
ascertain whether the baggage is missing altogether or damaged in the sense of physically
harmed, and contains no clue that the passenger is required to give any information
about partial loss of any contents. The same applies to the tickets issued by the
defendants. Amongst the 'Conditions of Contract' printed on one of the forms of ticket
appears the following: '7. In case of damage to baggage moving on international
transportation complaint must be made to the carrier forthwith after discovery of
damage and at the latest within 7 days from receipt ...'

It is plain that the defendants themselves were reading art 26(2) in the way contended
for by the plaintiff and I think they were right.

Finally, no one contends that the word 'damage' in art 26(2) can mean economic
harm. This follows from the fact that no notice is required where baggage has been
totally destroyed or lost, although that would inevitably cause economic harm.
'Damage' therefore is confined to 'physical injury'. I do not see how 'physical injury'
in the ordinary meaning of words can comprise partial loss of contents.

That being so there is no room for invoking the contents of any travaux préparatoires
of the 1955 conference which considered the amendments to be made by the Hague
Protocol, because there is no true ambiguity about the words as they stand. I should have
been unhappy in any event to resort to this method of interpretation for two reasons.
First, because it would be difficult to limit the ambit of any such enquiry and, secondly,
because it would not be fair to the passenger or consignor. The plaintiff here was wise
enough to insure his baggage. Many passengers do not. They are entitled if they so wish
to rely on their rights against the carrier under the convention. They can only ascertain
those rights and any limitation on them by reading the terms of the convention. They
do not and could not know of the existence or content of the minutes and memoranda
of the 1955 Hague conference which have been shown to us. It seems to me quite wrong
that they should be adversely affected by statements made at that conference about the
meaning of art 26(2).

There may well be circumstances in which it is legitimate to have recourse to such
material to discover the meaning of international conventions, but where the terms of
the convention seek to regulate the contractual relationship between private individuals
or between private individuals and corporate bodies it must be rarely that such evidence
can properly be admissible. Accordingly I take the view that the judge was right in his
conclusion on this aspect of the case.

What has caused me concern, however, is s 2 of the Carriage by Air and Road Act 1979
which reads as follows:

'(1) In the Carriage by Air Act 1961, after section 4 there shall be inserted the following section—"4A. (1) In Article 26(2) the reference to damage shall be **a** construed as including loss of part of the baggage or cargo in question . . ."

'(2) This section shall come into force at the passing of this Act but shall not apply to loss which occurred before the passing of this Act.'

That enactment was passed after and clearly because of the decision of Kerr J.

It indicates the way in which Parliament itself interprets art 26(2), and therefore presumably the way in which Parliament always has interpreted that article. It is **b** tempting to say therefore that, despite the apparent meaning of 'damage', it should receive the meaning which the legislature always intended it to have and should include partial loss of baggage.

This would, however, be to apply the section to loss occurring before the 1979 Act which sub-s (2) expressly forbids. I would accordingly disregard this new provision so far as the present case is concerned. **c**

For these reasons I would dismiss this appeal. It is not necessary in those circumstances to decide the question raised by the respondents' cross-notice.

Appeal dismissed. No order on respondents' notice. Leave to appeal to the House of Lords.

Solicitors: *Gregory Rowcliffe & Co*, agents for *Wood McLellan & Williams*, Chatham (for the **d** plaintiff); *Beaumont & Son* (for the defendants).

Frances Rustin   Barrister.

R v B, R v A   **e**

COURT OF APPEAL, CRIMINAL DIVISION
LORD WIDGERY CJ, SHAW LJ AND MCNEILL J
2nd JULY 1979
                                                                               f
Criminal law – Criminal capacity – Child – Child between 10 and 14 – Rebuttable presumption that child between 10 and 14 incapable of committing crime – How presumption can be rebutted – Whether previous conviction, if relevant, admissible in evidence.

A boy aged 13 was arrested and charged with blackmail. At his trial he pleaded not guilty. As he was over 10 but under 14 at the date of the alleged offence there was a rebuttable presumption that he did not know the difference between right and wrong **g** and was therefore incapable of committing the crime. In order to rebut that presumption the prosecution sought to adduce evidence of his home background and his previous convictions. The judge ruled that the evidence was relevant and therefore admissible. The boy was convicted. He appealed, contending that the evidence of his previous convictions should not have been admitted.
                                                                               h
Held – The court could permit the prosecution to adduce any evidence to rebut the presumption that a child between the ages of 10 and 14 was incapable of committing the crime charged provided that the evidence was, in the opinion of the court, relevant to the issue of the child's capacity to know good from evil. It followed that, as the evidence of the boy's previous convictions was relevant to that issue, the appeal would be dismissed (see p 462 *d e* and p 463 *c* to *e*, post).   **j**

B v R (1960) 44 Cr App R 1 applied.

Notes
For the criminal capacity of children under 14 years of age, see 11 Halsbury's Laws (4th Edn) para 33, and for cases on the subject, see 14(1) Digest (Reissue) 65, *353–361*.

Cases referred to in judgment

a   *B v R* (1960) 44 Cr App R 1, DC.

F v Padwick [1959] Crim LR 439, [1959] The Times, 24th April, DC.

Appeals

The appellants appealed against their convictions at the Crown Court at Chester on 10th March 1978 before his Honour Judge David QC and a jury of the offence of blackmail.
b   The facts are set out in the judgment of the court.

Elgan Edwards for the appellants.
Martin Thomas QC for the Crown.

LORD WIDGERY CJ read the following judgment of the court: On 10th March 1978 at Chester Crown Court before his Honour Judge David QC, the appellants, who were
c   both 14 at the time, pleaded not guilty but were convicted of an offence of blackmail, a nasty offence committed against a man of 53 who was something of an eccentric. There were a number of these young boys who extracted money from him, and eventually a formal charge was brought against the two appellants today.

They were aged, as we have said, 14 at the time of trial and less when they committed the offence. So there arose a presumption that they could not be guilty of a criminal
d   offence as they lacked the ability to commit an offence. The position at common law is to be found in Archbold[1] where the sidenote is 'Children between 10 and 14', and it reads:

'At common law a child under fourteen years is presumed not to have reached the age of discretion and to be *doli incapax*; but this presumption may be rebutted by
e   strong and pregnant evidence of a mischievous discretion, expressed in the maxim *malitia supplet aetatem*; for the capacity to commit crime, do evil and contract guilt, is not so much measured by years and days as by the strength of the delinquent's understanding and judgment.'

In regard to each of these two boys, when their cases came up before the Chester Crown Court, the presumption was in their favour that they were not old enough to
f   commit a criminal offence. But the presumption is rebuttable and the whole argument in this case, both below and in this court, has been to what extent and by what means is it possible to rebut the presumption.

The judge listened to the argument and took a strong line on it. He took a strong line on the extent to which past convictions could properly be relied on as indicative of the malitia supplet aetatem which is necessary to rebut the presumption. What he said is
g   conveniently condensed in one page of foolscap and I will read it;

'The point that arises in this case is one of principle, and an important principle at that. Three of the defendants in the present case were under the age of 14 at the time of the incidents relied on by the Crown, and being under the age of 14 the common law requires the court to presume that these three defendants were
h   incapable of forming the necessary intent to make them guilty of the crime charged, and it is therefore on the prosecution to rebut it, if the prosecution is able to do so. And the prosecution must rebut it to the same degree of certainty as is required in any other aspect of criminal law. It seems to me that that being the case it must be open to the prosecution to call general evidence of the backgrounds of each of the defendants, evidence of the type of home that the youngster comes from, evidence
j   of the type of upbringing that he has had, evidence of any previous experiences that are relevant. The irony of the situation is this, that if such a defendant comes from a good home it could well tell against him in this situation, as it might be presumed by the court or jury that coming from a good home he had the necessary instruction

---

1   Pleading, Evidence and Practice in Criminal Cases (40th Edn 1979) para 29

and would know the difference between right and wrong in the criminal sense. On the other hand, coming from a bad home he might not have had that instruction, *a* and that might for the purposes of these proceedings be more advantageous to him. But, carrying the argument a stage further, it seems to be blindingly obvious that if a person charged with an offence of dishonesty has been before the juvenile court and there has been recorded a finding of guilt in respect of such a case, that must be relevant whether or not he knows the difference between right or wrong. Therefore I take the view that on this issue, where the burden of proof is on the *b* prosecution, the prosecution must be entitled to call general evidence of the backgrounds and character of the defendants concerned, provided that evidence is relevant to the issue "Did he know of the difference between right or wrong in the criminal sense?" And it must, in my view, include evidence of convictions, provided those are relevant. It does seem to me that a situation could arise where the prosecution might be seeking to prove findings of guilt which could really have *c* no bearing on this issue, and if that were the situation then one would without hesitation say that the prejudicial effect of such evidence would outweigh any possible beneficial value and that such evidence should be excluded. But that is not the situation which arises in this case.'

The judge in clear terms was taking the view that where the presumption applies the prosecution can seek to remove the effect of the presumption and to call evidence to that *d* effect. A moment's thought will make it clear that that is so. If the presumption is allowed to stand and the prosecution did not call evidence to rebut it, then, at the close of the prosecution case, there would be a ruling that there was no case to answer. It seems to us, as it seemed to the judge below, that to guard against that ridiculous result one must accept the fact that the prosecution can call relevant evidence which is relevant on the issue of the young man's capacity to know good from evil. *e*

There is not a great deal of authority on the point. Such as there is seems to be favourable to the argument adopted by the judge. One case of some relevance is *B v R*[1]. For present purposes it suffices to read the headnote only:

'A boy aged just under nine was charged at a juvenile court with housebreaking and larceny. Evidence was given before the justices, and again on appeal at quarter *f* sessions, that the boy came of a respectable family, had been properly brought up and was generally well behaved, apart from the matter wherewith he was charged. Held, that the evidence was sufficient to rebut the presumption of innocence which arose from the boy's age and to establish mens rea.'

So the character of the home background was brought in.

The other case, *F v Padwick*[2], was heard in the Divisional Court presided over by Lord *g* Parker CJ. The same question arose as to how the prosecution might rebut the presumption of innocence if it sought to do so. I will read the judgment, which is very short, first:

'The LORD CHIEF JUSTICE said that upon a submission by the defence that there was no evidence of a guilty mind the justices had decided to record a finding of guilt and *h* had remitted the boy to the Isle of Wight County Council as a fit person to look after him until he attained the age of 18. The question was whether there was the strong and pregnant evidence of a mischievous disposition which was required before the child could be convicted. The boy had taken the cash box, removed the money in it, and then thrown the box into a water tank, as he frankly admitted. He was arrested, charged, and released on bail. Six days later he took the fruit. On the first *j* occasion he had taken nothing but the cash box with the money, and had admitted "stealing" it. In his Lordship's judgment this was evidence from which the justices

---

1   (1960) 44 Cr App R 1
2   [1959] The Times, 24th April

a were entitled to hold that the presumption of innocence was rebutted. MR JUSTICE DONOVAN said that at first he had found it a difficult matter, but that he had come to the conclusion that there was evidence from which the justices were entitled to draw the conclusion which they had.'

In a sense the most interesting part of the report of this case comes from discussion during argument, which is in these terms. Counsel appearing for the boy submitted that 'all the evidence called by the prosecution was quite consistent with an innocent mind b when the body did the acts complained of'. Counsel for the prosecution said that 'having regard to the present state of education generally, it was very hard to suggest that the boy did not know that he was doing wrong'. Then Lord Parker CJ said: 'Before they rule in a case like this the justices should hear evidence of the boy's home background and all his circumstances. In a rotten home, what is more likely than that a child is brought up without knowledge of right and wrong?' Counsel: 'This would give information about c the child which might be highly prejudicial to him.' Donovan J: 'These matters are inevitably let in; it cannot be helped.' Salmon J said: 'It is most important to hear this evidence.'

The situation as we sit today to consider this appeal is this, that such authority that there is supports the view that on the issue of the presumption the prosecution can call any relevant evidence which is necessary to rebut the presumption. I stress the fact that d it should be relevant evidence, because the judge can stop any evidence which is not relevant to the issue of the boy's capacity to know evil. Assuming that the evidence is relevant it seems to us that the prosecution can adduce it.

It seems therefore that the judge's ruling in the case was right and we would dismiss the appeals.

e *Appeals dismissed.*

Solicitors: *Bowen Jones & Parry*, Wrexham (for the appellants); *Gwilym Hughes & Partners*, Wrexham (for the Crown).

Lea Josse   Barrister.
f

Puttick v Attorney-General and Puttick

FAMILY DIVISION

SIR GEORGE BAKER P

g 30th APRIL, 1st, 2nd, 3rd, 4th, 8th MAY 1979

Marriage – Validity – Declaration – Discretion to grant declaration – Marriage by licence – Misdescription of party – Husband and wife marrying by licence in England – Wife fraudulently impersonating another woman – Wife having German domicile of origin – Wife presenting petition to have marriage declared valid – Wife seeking declaration so as to claim status of British h subject and immunity from extradition – Whether marriage invalid by reason of misdescription – Whether wife domiciled in England when petition presented – Whether court having discretion to refuse decree – Marriage Act 1949, s 49 – Matrimonial Causes Act 1973, s 45(1)(5) – Domicile and Matrimonial Proceedings Act 1973, s 1.

The petitioner was a German national with a German domicile of origin. In 1971 she j was arrested in Germany and charged with a number of serious offences there. While on bail during her trial the petitioner absconded and, using the illegally obtained passport of another German national, came to England in August 1974 on a six month entry visa. The petitioner adopted the name and identity of the person described in the passport and lived at a series of temporary addresses. In October the petitioner met and formed a casual relationship with an English national and in January 1975, shortly before her entry visa was due to expire, married him. The marriage was by licence in a register office, the petitioner using the name in the passport and giving false particulars about herself in the notice of marriage. The certificate of marriage contained the same false particulars. Although the parties had sexual intercourse together before and after the marriage at no stage did they live together and by the end of 1975 the relationship had ended. Two days after the marriage the time limit on the petitioner's stay in England was removed by the Home Office on her husband's application. In July 1975 the petitioner applied for British citizenship giving the same false particulars as in the marriage application, but in December she withdrew her application because she was apprehensive that the Home Office might consult the German authorities. In August 1976 her husband left for India to join a religious sect. In September 1978 the petitioner was arrested under her real name and extradition proceedings were commenced against her. Part of her defence to those proceedings was that she had the right to be deemed a British subject by virtue of the 1975 marriage and was therefore immune from extradition[a]. In order to substantiate that defence the petitioner filed a petition in the Family Division pursuant to s 45(1)[b] of the Matrimonial Causes Act 1973, which provided that any person whose right to be deemed a British subject depended on the validity of a marriage 'may, if he is domiciled in England . . . apply by petition' for a declaration that the marriage was valid. The Attorney-General opposed the petition on the grounds (i) that, although a marriage by licence was not necessarily invalidated under s 49[c] of the Marriage Act 1949 by the assumption of a false name and description, it was invalidated where one of the parties impersonated a living and identifiable person, (ii) that the petitioner was not domiciled in England and was therefore not eligible to present a petition under s 45(1) of the Matrimonial Causes Act, and (iii) that under s 45(5)[d] of that Act the court had a discretion whether to make a decree on the petition and in the circumstances ought to exercise that discretion by refusing a decree in view of the petitioner's previous fraud and perjury.

Held – (i) In the case of a marriage by licence the misdescription of a party did not render the marriage void under s 49 of the 1949 Act. Accordingly, the petitioner's marriage was not void by reason of her assumption of a false name and description even though it was the name and identity of a living and identifiable person. The question whether the marriage was, at the suit of the husband, merely voidable did not arise since he had accepted it. It followed that the marriage was valid (see p 473 a, p 474 d to h and p 475 d, post); *Plummer v Plummer* [1916–17] All ER Rep 591 applied.

(ii) However, because of the abolition of a wife's dependent domicile by s 1[e] of the Domicile and Matrimonial Proceedings Act 1973 the petitioner could not obtain and had not obtained an English dependent domicile on marriage. Nor had she obtained an English domicile of choice, since her intention in residing in England was to avoid trial in Germany rather than to set up a permanent home in England. Moreover, the petitioner's illegal entry and residence barred her from acquiring an English domicile of choice. The petitioner had therefore not abandoned her German domicile of origin and was not domiciled in England and accordingly was not entitled to present a petition under s 45 of the Matrimonial Causes Act 1973 (see p 475 e f and j to p 476 d and p 477 d e, post).

(iii) In any event, by virtue of the power contained in s 45(5) of the Matrimonial Causes Act 1973 to make 'such decree as it thinks just', the court had a discretion not to make any decree at all if the circumstances so warranted. Because of the petitioner's fraud and

a   Under the extradition treaty in force between the United Kingdom and the Federal Republic of Germany the surrender of fugitive criminals from the state of which they were a national was prohibited (see the Federal Republic of Germany (Extradition) Order 1960, SI 1966 No 1375)

b   Section 45(1), so far as material, is set out at p 466 b, post

c   Section 49, so far as material, is set out at p 473 e, post

d   Section 45(5), so far as material, is set out at p 478 c, post

e   Section 1, so far as material, is set out at p 475 g to j, post

a criminal acts it would not be a just exercise of that discretion for the court to grant the decree sought, even if she had proved she had an English domicile. The petition would therefore be dismissed (see p 478 *d e* and p 480 *c d*, post).

Notes

For petition to establish validity of marriage, see 19 Halsbury's Laws (4th Edn) para 1333, and for cases on marriages celebrated under false names and descriptions, see 27(1) Digest
b (Reissue) 52–53, 342–349.

For the Matrimonial Causes Act 1973, s 45, see 43 Halsbury's Statutes (3rd Edn) 594.
For the Domicile and Matrimonial Proceedings Act 1973, s 1, see ibid 620.

Cases referred to in judgment

Aldrich v Attorney-General [1968] 1 All ER 345, [1968] P 281, [1968] 2 WLR 413, Digest (Cont Vol C) 43, *169a*.
c *Application under the Solicitors Act 1843, Re an* (1899) 80 LT 720, DC, 43 Digest (Repl) 39, *198*.
B v Attorney-General (B intervening) [1966] 2 All ER 145, [1967] 1 WLR 776, 32 Digest (Reissue) 22, *150*.
Boldrini v Boldrini and Martini [1932] P 9, [1931] All ER Rep 708, 101 LJP 4, 146 LT 121, CA, 2 Digest (Reissue) 188, *1129*.
d *Briggs v Briggs* (1880) LR 5 PD 163, 49 LJP 38, 42 LT 662, 11 Digest (Reissue) 532, *1136*.
Cockburn v Garnault (1792) cited in 1 Hag Con 435, 161 ER 608, 27(1) Digest (Reissue) 52, *342*.
Cope v Burt (falsely calling herself Cope) (1809) 1 Hag Con 434, 161 ER 608; *affd* (1811) 1 Phillim 224, 27(1) Digest (Reissue) 53, *345*.
Eneogiwe v Eneogiwe [1976] Court of Appeal Transcript 94.
e *Fitzwilliam v Attorney-General* [1951] The Times, 15th March.
Lane v Goodwin (1843) 4 QB 361, 3 Gal & Dav 610, 12 LJQB 157, 7 Jur 372, 114 ER 935, 23(1) Digest (Reissue) 50, *325*.
Plummer v Plummer [1917] P 163, [1916–17] All ER Rep 591, 86 LJP 145, 117 LT 321, CA, 27(1) Digest (Reissue) 55, *366*.
R v Lamb (1934) 150 LT 519, [1934] All ER Rep 540, 24 Cr App R 145, 30 Cox CC 91,
f CCA, 27(1) Digest (Reissue) 56, *367*.
R v Secretary of State for the Home Department, ex parte Hussain [1978] 2 All ER 423, [1978] 1 WLR 700.
R v Secretary of State for the Home Department (Governor of Horfield Prison), ex parte Sultan Mahmood [1978] Court of Appeal Transcript 541.
Rutter, Re, Donaldson v Rutter [1907] 2 Ch 592, 77 LJ Ch 34, 97 LT 883, 27(1) Digest
g (Reissue) 55, *365*.
Silver (orse Kraft) v Silver [1955] 2 All ER 614, [1955] 1 WLR 728, 27(1) Digest (Reissue) 30, *141*.
Stephens v Cuckfield Rural District Council [1960] 2 All ER 716, [1960] 2 QB 373, [1960] 3 WLR 248, 124 JP 420, 58 LGR 213, 11 P & CR 248, CA, 45 Digest (Repl) 357, *117*.
Winans v Attorney-General [1904] AC 287, [1904–7] All ER Rep 410, 73 LJKB 613, 90 LT
h 721, CA, 11 Digest (Reissue) 351, *47*.

Case also cited

Martin, Re, Loustalan v Loustalan [1900] P 211, CA.

Petition

j By a petition dated 15th January 1979 Astrid Huberta Isolde Marie Luise Hildegard Proll sought a declaration under s 45(1) of the Matrimonial Causes Act 1973 that the marriage she had entered into with the second respondent, Robin Esmond Scott Puttick, on 22nd January 1975 at Stepney Register Office was a valid and subsisting marriage. The Attorney-General was notified and joined as respondent to the petition as required by s 45(6) of the 1973 Act. The facts are set out in the judgment.

Barbara Calvert QC and *Owen Davies* for the petitioner.
Bernard Hargrove for the Attorney-General.
Bruce Blair for Robin Puttick.

SIR GEORGE BAKER P delivered the following judgment:

1. *The petition*

It is founded on s 45 of the Matrimonial Causes Act 1973, the relevant part of which reads as follows:

'(1) Any person who is a British subject, or whose right to be deemed a British subject depends wholly or in part . . . on the validity of any marriage, may, if he is domiciled in England and Wales or in Northern Ireland . . . apply by petition to the High Court for a decree declaring . . . that his own marriage was a valid marriage.'

The prayer of the petition seeks a declaration that the marriage celebrated on 22nd January 1975 between the petitioner and the second respondent may be declared a valid and subsisting marriage. In the petition it is said:

'At the said marriage the Petitioner falsely represented herself as having been born Senta Gretel Sauerbier and having been divorced from a previous marriage and gave other false particulars about herself which were required to be given by her for the said marriage.'

The first respondent, the Attorney-General, asked for further particulars of this paragraph. The first is whether there was any person entitled to the names of Senta Gretel Sauerbier and identifying such person. The answer to that is:

'The person entitled to the name Senta Gretel Sauerbier is a German national residing in West Berlin, in the Federal Republic of Germany. Her address is not known to the Petitioner but she is represented by lawyers acting on her behalf . . .'

Then she was asked whether it is alleged that at any other time, apart from the occasion of the marriage, the petitioner so represented herself in relation to having been divorced from a previous marriage, and she said that on no other occasion, apart from her marriage, had she represented herself as having been divorced from a previous marriage. That is not true. She was further asked what other false particulars she alleges she gave about herself and whether such false information was given knowingly. The answer is:

'Apart from the false particulars specifically set out in paragraph 4 of the Petition the Petitioner further falsely stated that she was at the time a student of sociology, that her father's name was Eric Schulz and that her father's occupation was that of a machine engineer, all the false particulars being related to the person entitled to the name Senta Gretel Sauerbier. All the said false information was given knowingly by the Petitioner.'

In her affidavit in support of the petition she says: 'These proceedings are brought by me in order to establish my entitlement to registration as a citizen of the United Kingdom and Colonies under s 6(2) of the British Nationality Act 1948.'

Appropriate action has been taken in accordance with the Matrimonial Causes Rules 1977[1], r 110, to notify and join the Attorney-General as is required by s 45(6) of the Matrimonial Causes Act 1973. By his answer the Attorney-General puts all the matters alleged in the petition in issue, and denies that the petitioner is entitled to the relief claimed or any relief.

For centuries it has been a fundamental legal principle in this country that no man can take advantage of his own wrong. That is to be found in Broom's Legal Maxims[2], citing

---

1 SI 1977 No 344
2 10th Edn (1939), p 191

a Coke on Littleton[1], that is, Lord Coke's Commentaries on The Laws of England by Littleton, published first around the year 1600. The quotation is in Latin: 'Nullus commodum capere potest de injuria sua propria'—'No man can take advantage of his own wrong'. Broom continues:

> 'It is a maxim of law, recognised and established, that no man shall take advantage of his own wrong; and this maxim, which is based on elementary principles, is fully recognised in Courts of law and of equity, and, indeed, admits of illustration from b every branch of legal procedure.'

It is closely allied to the maxim, ex dolo malo non oritur actio, that is, a right of action cannot arise out of fraud, and ex turpi causa non oritur actio, which in effect means the same thing.

c Coke's Commentary on Littleton[2] has through the centuries been accepted as defining the laws of England as they were at the turn of the 16th century. The latest edition refers to 'The Institutes of the Laws of England; or, a Commentary upon Littleton. Not the name of the author only, but of the law itself'. On the title page of Broom there is a quotation that 'Maxims are the condensed good sense of nations'.

It seemed to me at the start of this hearing that there was indeed a strong case on the pleadings for the court to reject out of hand as failing in limine a petition founded as it d is on fraud, perjury, false pretences and forgery. However, I thought it better to examine the facts and statute law, as this is a novel case. It is important to everybody and a decision is obviously urgent.

2. The facts and my findings

The petition is brought in the name of Anna Puttick. She states in her petition: 'The e Petitioner was born Astrid Huberta Isolde Marie Luise Hildegard Proll on the 29th day of May 1947 at Kassel, in the Federal Republic of Germany. The maiden name of her mother was Möller.' I have no reason to doubt that that is so, or to doubt that her domicile of origin is German, although that is not admitted by the Attorney-General.

I find that the woman who has appeared and given evidence as petitioner before this court is in fact Astrid Proll. In May 1971 she was arrested in Germany on criminal f offences including attempted murder and robbery. She does not admit these offences and has tendered what would amount in our procedure to a plea of not guilty. In September 1973 the trial began, and on 4th February 1974, an important date, the trial was adjourned because of her ill-health, and she was granted bail by the German authorities. Her evidence is that she remained in Germany for six weeks, which would take her to 1st April, although I do not, of course, seek to be exact as to dates. She then, g what we would colloquially call, 'jumped her bail'. She went first to Italy, having in her possession DM5,000, which were then DM5·52¾–5·53¾ to the pound, to give some idea of the amount in English money. But money alone, of course, was not enough: she had also a passport. Her evidence is that she bought it from another person for DM3,000, who in turn had bought it on the criminal market. The passport is in the name of Senta Gretel Sauerbier, born Schulz, in Bremen on 22nd June 1947, who had resided in h Hamburg. It gave the shape of her face and the colour of her eyes, and her height, and then said that she had no distinguishing marks. That would not quite coincide with the petitioner, who agrees that she had on her arm a tattoo of Mickey Mouse, which was subsequently removed in this country, of course under the national health scheme, and thereafter she could stand full inspection on the passport.

It was valid from 29th December 1972 (the date of issue) to 28th December 1977, and j was renewed in London on 19th November 1977. The photograph on the passport is a photograph of Astrid Proll, the petitioner. There is clearly a forgery because the photograph is partly covered by what appears to be the official stamp of Hamburg. The passport also contains a visa for the United States of America. The petitioner has said that

1 Co Litt 148 b

it is purely a coincidence that there is an American visa on the passport. I do not believe that, and for this reason (and this is why the date of the 4th February, and the eight weeks, is important) the visa is dated 10th April 1974, that is, ten days after the expiration of the eight weeks which the petitioner says she spent in Germany before going to Italy. The irresistible inference, having regard also to the facts that the petitioner's mother is in America, that the petitioner has been to America, she says, on three occasions, having on one occasion spent some months there and that she has been to school there, is that this visa, which was valid until 10th April 1975, was put on the passport after it came into the possession of the petitioner or her agent who was acquiring it for her on the criminal market.

Senta Sauerbier, who I will call hereafter Dr Sauerbier, has given evidence, and says that she is a physician, was married in April 1971 and divorced in June 1972. No divorce papers are now produced; the petitioner says they have been lost. There is no evidence of how the petitioner obtained the divorce papers. Dr Sauerbier was not a helpful witness. She said that she is now known as Schulz (her maiden name) and that she was married to Sauerbier. I was invited to give her the warning that she need not answer questions which she thought might incriminate her and I did so. She said that she had never met the petitioner, that it was not her photograph on the passport, but added: 'This passport appears to be an earlier passport of mine.' This was the first time that she had been in England. Then she refused to answer, as she was entitled to do, the question: 'What happened to the passport?' She was asked in cross-examination if she knew Astrid Proll, the lady in court. After a long pause she said that she did not, and then she said she did not wish to say whether she knew her or not. But I am satisfied, and find, that Dr Sauerbier (or Schultz) is not the woman who was concerned in the marriage of 22nd January 1975 alleged by the petitioner.

The purpose and intention of the petitioner, to quote her own words, is as follows: 'My intention was to get as far away from Germany as possible. I purchased a German passport to cross borders to work, and to identify myself because I could not use papers under my own name.' That has been the continuing purpose of the petitioner throughout. She left Italy after three months, that is, sometime in July, she says because there were too many German tourists and she was frightened of recognition. On 6th August she arrived in England as Senta Gretel Sauerbier. Her passport is stamped on arrival, with permission to stay for six months. She had with her, she says, something in the neighbourhood of £1,000, and received money to the extent of DM2,000 when she was here, so obviously some person knew how to find her. She did not work until after the marriage in January, and she stayed in various establishments, some of which are what we colloquially call 'squats'.

She was asked to give particulars of the places where she had resided, and she set out: 'To the best of her recollection the Petitioner took up the following residences in England and Wales . . .' and she has identified in her evidence which of these were 'squats', which were rented, and which belonged to a friend. It is clear beyond peradventure that these further particulars are in many respects inaccurate; the petitioner says 'imprecise', but I am afraid that they are a good deal worse than that. The first address at which she stayed, in Holland Park Avenue (she cannot remember exactly where) seems to have been arranged from Italy. The third address that she gives, 37 Belgrave Street, London E1, which she says was a 'squat', is not an address at which I think she ever lived at all. It was the address of Robin Puttick. As will appear, there are other inaccuracies. I appreciate that it may well be that she cannot remember exactly where she was, particularly as she says that she always used false addresses for documents and never put a true one unless she had to, in case she was found out.

In October 1974, that is, a couple of months after she arrived or a little more, she met the second respondent, Robin Esmond Scott Puttick (whom I will call Robin Puttick), at a birthday party given by a woman, Mrs Julia Mainwaring, who has appeared and given evidence. Her birthday was on 27th October and the party was probably about that time, in Julia Mainwaring's premises of which she was, and I think she still is, the tenant.

The evidence of Robin Puttick is given in an affidavit (and the weight to which I give all this will be apparent in due course): 'I met the Petitioner for the first time sometime in August/September 1974 . . .' Well, that is not the evidence before the court which is that it was towards the end of October:

'. . . when living in the same area as other squatters—37, Belgrave Street, London E1 and 10, Aston Street, London E14. I understood at that time that the Petitioner had an address in Hackney. We became acquainted with each other by moving in the same social circle, that is to say East London Squatters.'

He had a brother who lived in Aston Street but I do not accept that he lived there at all, or that she lived there, and they certainly did not live there together. His home was 37 Belgrave Street, so far as he had a home; and she was living, at the end of 1974, she says, 'in or about the summer of 1975' at 25 Marlborough Avenue, E8, which was her first 'squat'.

Her story is that he was a plumber and electrician and his practical work was important to her. She watched him at work, and sexual intercourse began between them in December 1974. In so far as there was sexual intercourse, I find that it was casual, infrequent and meaningless to her; but from her side with a purpose which she, in fact, achieved. She never moved in with him, or he with her, either before or after marriage, because, she said, it was very important for her to have her own place. She wanted to avoid people, and they always had separate addresses. That, I think, is true. Her permission to stay in England was due to end on 6th February 1975 at the expiration of the six months. She knew it would be dangerous to overstay, for if she was caught so doing attention would be drawn to her and questions asked. She was, I think, desperate to have her visa extended, preferably indefinitely. A way to achieve this was by marriage to an Englishman. So at about Christmas time she raised the question with Robin Puttick, who first knew her as Anna, and later, at the time of her marriage, as Senta Gretel Sauerbier.

Neither, so it is said, enquired about the background or family of the other. She says that she was not interested in his parents and made it quite clear to him that she did not want to be asked about her past, and he respected her wishes. He knew, however, that she was very interested in becoming a British national. That is apparent from his affidavit, where he says: 'The question of the Petitioner acquiring British nationality only arose after the marriage. The Petitioner seemed very interested in becoming a British national, but I did not realise the reason for this.' The inducements which she held out to him, namely that marriage would enable her to stay in the United Kingdom, so that their sexual relationship could continue, and that he would have a married man's tax allowance, prevailed. He discussed marriage with his friend Mrs Mainwaring, who was a sociologist. At first she did not agree, having regard to her own history, but changed her mind after meeting the petitioner once, and being 'pleased that they had established a relationship', whatever that means.

The petitioner appeared to me to be a clever witness and a persuasive woman. I am sure, and find, that the purpose of the marriage, and on her side the sole purpose, was to be able to remain in the United Kingdom and subsequently to obtain citizenship. Two of the witnesses to the ceremony, Gillian Lees and Monty Hurman, have said in evidence that they assumed it was a marriage of convenience, and some time has been devoted to that question. 'Marriage of convenience' is a popular, not a legal, description. All I need say is that this marriage lacked all the purposes and intentions of a genuine and generally accepted union, namely mutual love, support and comfort; cohabitation in the matrimonial home as husband and wife; a union for life and the production of children. But that is immaterial to the validity of the marriage: see *Silver (orse Kraft) v Silver*[1], although I think it is relevant when considering the question of domicile.

One of them telephoned the Stepney Register Office, and on 20th January 1975 they

1   [1955] 2 All ER 614, [1955] 1 WLR 728

went there together. She produced the passport and the divorce papers. A notice of marriage was completed and signed in the presence of the superintendent registrar by Robin Puttick, and confirmed by the signature (or alleged signature) of the petitioner. That signature is not unlike the one on the passport, but there is no evidence of who wrote the one on the passport. The application is a 'Notice of marriage by certificate and licence'. It gives the particulars of Robin Puttick and of Senta Gretel Sauerbier; she is 27 years. Well, that is right. Her previous marriage had been dissolved; she was a student of sociology. The place of residence in both instances is given as 10 Aston Street, E14; the period of residence 'more than a month' in each case. That was all untrue, and Robin Puttick must have realised that the residence and period of residence was false. Then he signed and she confirmed. There is a note on the first page, '22/1/75', which apparently was booked for the wedding. On the second page her father's name is given, and his occupation 'Engineer', and then 'P/P seen' (that must mean 'passport seen') and 'West German' and the number of the passport, which is the actual number of the Sauerbier passport, is given. Then there is mention of a divorce decree, in writing which I am not immediately able to decipher.

On the same day the superintendent registrar wrote to the Registrar General, as follows:

'Because of the urgency expressed by the parties concerned I send herewith a copy of notice of marriage taken here this morning for a proposed marriage by Licence at this Office between Robin Esmond Scott Puttick and Senta Gretel Sauerbier both resident in this District. Mrs Sauerbier has been previously married and submits her German Divorce Decree together with translation of the document. I will be glad to know that the decree is acceptable and that we may proceed with the marriage in due course.'

On 21st January a reply was received from the General Register Office saying, in effect, that the certificate and licence could be issued, and then a warning about the validity of the divorce, which does not arise.

It is not established that Robin Puttick knew that she was other than as described, although he knew that the residence columns were untrue.

On 22nd January Robin Puttick went to the register office and met there the petitioner, who had been driven to the register office by a girl, Jane Grant, whose house or squat, 25 Marlborough Avenue, she says she shared at that time. Monty Hurman, Julia Mainwaring and her small daughter, and Gillian Lees were present, and the parties were married. Of course, the same lies appear on the certificate as on the notice; that followed from the impersonation. There are two matters in relation to the ceremony which I have considered. There was a ring, a gold band. It was given to the petitioner, she says, by a friend two days, or shortly before, the ceremony. The friend was a male named Phil. She appeared very reluctant to reply to questions in cross-examination about the ring, but I have concluded that the only significance is that she wore it for but a short time only and gave it up, she says, because of her work.

The other matter is that Hurman never saw Robin Puttick with a beard; and Mrs Mainwaring did not think, according to her evidence, that he had one at the wedding. They both knew him well. The petitioner, on the other hand, when she identified Robin Puttick in recently taken photographs was asked, 'When you married him, did he look like that or are there any differences?' She answered: 'He has a longer beard now and longer hair.' 'Have you any doubts that it is him?' Answer, 'No'. Then I asked a question: 'He seems to have been clean-shaven at one time?' and I referred to an old passport of his which showed him to be clean-shaven. She was then asked by her counsel, 'Was he clean-shaven when you married him?' Answer, 'No, I have never known him without a beard'. However, I do not now think that that evidence goes to identity; it merely tends to show that the premarital relationship was both casual and infrequent.

I find that the two persons married on 22nd January were in fact the petitioner Astrid Proll and the second respondent Robin Puttick.

After the marriage they all went to a public house and then to a restaurant. I am not even satisfied that the two of them spent that night together at 10 Aston Street, or anywhere else.

The next event was that the husband went to the Home Office two days later, on 24th January, and had the time limit for her stay removed, because of her marriage to him. That, again, appears on the face of the passport.

Their relationship, such as it was, and I do not accept that it was anything like as close as she would have me believe, cooled rapidly. They never had a home, nor did he support her, even before she started work in the spring of 1975. She says that sexual intercourse continued until June or July 1975. Then, she says, it ceased at about the end of that year: 'We just drifted apart.' They were last seen together in the Lake District in the second week in August by Mrs Mainwaring, who was camping there. They called in on their way to Scotland. That is the only convincing evidence of their being together. He became increasingly interested in an Indian religious sect and, according to the petitioner, was already thinking of going to India by 28th May 1975. There was no suggestion that she should accompany him. He left for Poona, India on 5th August 1976. So, if Mrs Mainwaring is right about seeing them in the second week of August, it must have been 1975, and not 1976 as he says in his affidavit.

Late in the case Mrs Mainwaring, who was the second last witness, disclosed that he returned from India 18 months to two years ago, and then went back. The inference is that he never saw or attempted to find the petitioner.

Meanwhile, the petitioner made an application for British citizenship under s 6(2) of the British Nationality Act 1948, which reads as follows:

'Subject to the provisions of subsection (3) of this section, a woman who has been married to a citizen of the United Kingdom and Colonies shall be entitled, on making application therefor to the Secretary of State in the prescribed manner, and, if she is a British protected person or an alien, on taking an oath of allegiance in the form specified in the First Schedule to this Act, to be registered as a citizen of the United Kingdom and Colonies, whether or not she is of full age and capacity.'

Subsection (3) merely refers to a person who has renounced or been deprived of citizenship. The application, typed, signed, and declared by her to be true, before a solicitor empowered to administer oaths, repeats all the former lies. It is unnecessary for me to go through it in detail, because it sets out everything which identifies her as Sauerbier but, of course, giving the surname now of Puttick. It was consistent with the Sauerbier passport and produces a signature about which no evidence has been given, but it seems to be 'Senta Puttick'. It contains the same lies about her father and about the divorce. That was sent to the Home Office.

Had this fraud succeeded, the Secretary of State had power to deprive her of her citizenship under s 20 of the British Nationality Act 1948, which reads as follows:

'(2) Subject to the provisions of this section, the Secretary of State may by order deprive any such citizen of his citizenship if he is satisfied that the registration or certificate of naturalisation was obtained by means of fraud, false representation or the concealment of any material fact . . .

'(5) The Secretary of State shall not deprive a person of citizenship under this section unless he is satisfied that it is not conducive to the public good that that person should continue to be a citizen of the United Kingdom and Colonies.'

On 28th May 1975 Robin Puttick wrote to the Home Office:

'Thank you for your letter of 22/5/75. We enclose the £2, which was overlooked by my wife. We originally enclosed both of our passports, mine as proof of identity etc. If you think there likely to be a delay of more than 3–4 weeks before completing the application of my wife, can I (Robin Puttick) have my passport back, as I need it. [This was the time when she says he was contemplating going to India.] Ideally,

I should like my wife to come with me, so I'd like hers back as well. If you can't return it (and I understand you are very busy these days) please tell me how long it is likely to take.'

Then on 8th August (there had obviously been some further correspondence in between) she wrote:

'I regret this delay in responding to your letter of July the 10th. In that letter you asked that I take the oath of allegiance and submit it to you within a month. Family matters have made it very difficult for me to do so thus far, but I should be able to do this within the next month. I would like to apologise for any inconvenience this might cause your department and trust that if this raises any complications to my application you will let me know.'

The truth of the matter must be, I think, that she was apprehensive about being called on to take an oath of allegiance. Then, finally, on 10th December she writes:

'In response to your letter of the fourth November 1975, I have decided to cancel my application for registration as a citizen of the U.K. which I made July 10 1975. I apologise for the delay.'

She says, and I think this may well be right, that she withdrew her application because she was apprehensive that the Home Office might consult the German authorities.

She obtained work first with the Hackney Borough Council in the spring of 1975 and later, in 1977, as a fitter's mate, and then as a supervisor. She obtained work qualifications and various documents, including a union card and a driving licence, all in the name of and with the identity of Sauerbier, although in her married name of Puttick. How she came to obtain a driving licence, whether she took a test or what happened, has not been a matter of evidence but in any event the driving licence application must have given a false or an accommodation address, because that appears on her licence which has been produced.

On 15th September 1978 she was arrested as Astrid Proll. On 10th October 1978, after her arrest, she again applied for British citizenship under s 6(2) of the British Nationality Act 1948 in her true name and, so far as is known, with her true particulars. Section 20(2), which I have read, would therefore not apply. She sought a judicial review to compel the Home Secretary to act, but this was refused both by the Queen's Bench Divisional Court and by the Court of Appeal, who said, I am told, that the proper forum to decide the question of the validity of her marriage was the Family Division. She filed this petition on 15th January 1979. On 5th February 1979 the Chief Magistrate made an order for her extradition. On 15th February, that is to say ten days later, she applied for habeas corpus from the Queen's Bench Divisional Court who, I am told, adjourned her application pending this hearing.

The only other material fact is that on 19th March the senior registrar gave Robin Puttick leave to give his evidence on affidavit. This was supported by affidavits of the second respondent and his solicitor that he was unable to come to England, that there would be serious disruption of his religious way of life and to other members of the community in which he lives in Poona. There could also be obstacles to his return to India by the Government of India, and he would not come. The Attorney-General opposed the application and renewed his opposition before me on grounds which appeared to me to be sound. I refused to admit the second respondent's affidavit evidence unless it was clear that it was impossible for him to come. He has been given every opportunity to come, fare paid, since the start of this hearing; but the story now is that his guru will not allow him to come, and that he has undertaken by vow to live in the community. No mention has been made of his visit of 18 months or so ago. Finally I agreed to read his affidavits for what they are worth. Obviously there were many questions which the Attorney-General's counsel would wish to ask.

3. *The validity of the marriage*

a   This marriage is either valid or void. It cannot be voidable, as the husband accepts it and does not allege that he did not validly consent. I quote the words of s 11 of the Matrimonial Causes Act 1973:

'A marriage celebrated after 31st July 1971 shall be void on the following grounds only, that is to say—(a) . . . (iii) the parties have intermarried in disregard of certain requirements as to the formation of marriage . . .'

b   None of the other matters in para (a), (b), (c), or (d) is relevant. This was a marriage by certificate and licence, for which notice in the prescribed form must be given. Section 27(3) of the Marriage Act 1949 provides:

'A notice of marriage shall state the name and surname, marital status, occupation and place of residence of each of the persons to be married and the church or other
c   building in which the marriage is to be solemnized and . . . (b) in the case of a marriage intended to be solemnized by licence, shall state the period, not being less than fifteen days, during which one of the persons to be married has resided in the district in which notice of marriage is given.'

Section 32, which deals with marriage under certificate by licence, provides:

d   '(1) Where a marriage is intended to be solemnized on the authority of a certificate of a superintendent registrar by licence, the person by whom notice of marriage is given shall state in the notice that the marriage is intended to be solemnized by licence, and the notice shall not be suspended in the office of the superintendent registrar . . .'

Then follow various other requirements. Then further in s 45 there is provision for the
e   solemnisation of marriage in a register office, and how it is to be done. Finally, in s 49, void marriages:

'If any persons knowingly and wilfully intermarry under the provisions of this Part of this Act—(a) without having given due notice . . . (b) without a certificate for marriage having been duly issued . . . (c) without a licence having been so issued
f   [and various other instances which do not matter in this case] the marriage shall be void.'

A clear distinction has been recognised by the English courts between marriage by banns and marriage by licence. In the former a misdescription of a party renders the marriage void, because there had not been the required publicity. In the case of marriage by licence there is no such requirement and no such result follows, for the object of the
g   licence is not publicity but identity. In *Plummer v Plummer*[1] Lord Cozens-Hardy MR said:

'It was a marriage by licence and not a marriage by banns. There is a distinction as regards notice required to be given between a marriage by licence and a marriage by banns. In the case of the latter a wilful and fraudulent misstatement in the notice to the knowledge of both parties will invalidate marriage. But in the case of
h   a marriage by licence a licence can be obtained on payment of a certain sum of money, and after the application for it and before the marriage takes place no publicity is necessary, which seems to me to show that the principles which have been applied to marriages by banns or on notice without licence ought to have no application to a marriage by licence.'

j   Bankes LJ said[2]:

'It seems to me impossible to draw a distinction between a case where it is done fraudulently and a case where it may be said not to be done fraudulently. [Then he

---

1 [1917] P 163 at 168–169, [1916–17] All ER Rep 591 at 592
2 [1917] P 163 at 172, [1916–17] All ER Rep 591 at 594

cites from a decision of Swinfen Eady J in *Re Rutter, Donaldson v Rutter*[1] and
continues:] The conclusion I have come to is that there is no authority for saying *a*
that the giving of due notice requires anything more than the giving of notice in
due form of law, that is to say, in the form required by the statute, and that the
reasoning applicable to the publication of banns does not apply to the case of a
notice for a marriage given under s. 4 of the Marriage Act 1836.'

Finally, Warrington LJ, in this very strong Court of Appeal, said[2]:   *b*

'In my opinion, therefore, it comes to this that in the case of a marriage by licence,
which is the only case with which we here have to deal, although both parties may
make a false statement as to the names or the purpose of the notice and declaration,
yet the marriage will be valid, the consequence of giving the false notice being not
to invalidate the marriage, but to expose the parties to penalties of perjury.'

In that case the court approved the earlier decision and dicta of Swinfen Eady J in *Re*   *c*
Rutter, Donaldson v Rutter[1]. The distinction is to be found as long ago as 1809 in *Cope v
Burt*[3], and even then Sir William Scott considered that the point had been decided in
Cockburn v Garnault[4] in 1792, and in the Court of Arches in 1793. Then in 1934 the
Court of Criminal Appeal, presided over by Lord Hewart CJ (who had been counsel for
the Queen's Proctor in *Plummer v Plummer*[5]) sitting with Avery and Talbot JJ in *R v Lamb*[6],   *d*
did not call on counsel for the Crown to argue that the court was bound to follow *Re
Rutter*[1] and *Plummer v Plummer*[5]. It is consequently not surprising that counsel for the
Attorney-General conceded that I am bound to hold that the assumption of a false name
or description does not avoid the marriage, although I understand that he wishes to
reserve the point for argument elsewhere if necessary.

A distinction could be drawn if the person who gave notice was not the same individual   *e*
as the person who appeared at the ceremony. Such a marriage would, I think, be void.
See in *Lane v Goodwin*[7]:

'If fraud were practised, as if a licence given to one person were made use of by
another, it would, as is observed by Sir W. Scott in that case [*Cope v Burt*[3]) when
before the Consistory Court, be a fraud which would entirely vary the question.'

f
The Crown further submits that, whereas here it is not simply a matter of misdescription,
even fraudulent misdescription in the licence, but of impersonation by the complete
adoption of the name and identity of a living and identifiable person, namely Dr
Sauerbier, in order to obtain the status of a married woman, the marriage is invalid, at
least if Mr Puttick knew or was wilfully blind to the fact that the woman he was
purporting to marry was Astrid Proll. Such personation would strike at the roots of   *g*
registration and it could imperil the status of the person whose identity is assumed, that
is Dr Sauerbier, who would be recorded as having married in England. Great confusion
could be caused to any descendants of hers, especially after the death of the parties if it
happened before the discovery of the fraud. I cannot accept this argument, for which the
only support appears to be a submission made in *Lane v Goodwin*[8].

h

1   [1907] 2 Ch 592
2   [1917] P 163 at 174, [1916–17] All ER Rep 591 at 595
3   (1809) 1 Hag Con 434, 161 ER 608
4   (1792) cited in 1 Hag Con 435, 161 ER 608
5   [1917] P 163, [1916–17] All ER Rep 591
6   (1934) 150 LT 519, [1934] All ER Rep 540
7   (1843) 3 Gal & Dav 610 at 611
8   3 Gal & Dav 610

j

I am bound by authority. Defects in registration law cannot be cured by this court;
a nor can I find that Robin Puttick knew or was wilfully blind to the true identity of the
woman he married. Of course his evidence is as unsatisfactory as hers on this point, and
he says in his affidavit of 12th February:

'I did not know the Petitioner's true identity and knew very little of her
background. I did not know anything of the alleged offences for which she is being
extradited to West Germany. I did not know that she was Astrid Proll. I knew her
b as Senta Gretel Sauerbier. Basically, I simply knew the Petitioner as Anna.'

And in his other affidavit of 16th February he says:

'As I have stated in my affidavit of 12th February 1979, I did not know the
Petitioner was Astrid Proll. Throughout the time I knew her by the forename
"Anna" and believed her full name to be Senta Gretel Sauerbier. Only since her
c arrest in England have I found out through friends and newspapers that her real
name at the time of my marriage to her was Astrid Proll.'

Against this, of course, there was no cross-examination; and Monty Hurman, who saw
her only at the wedding, said that he thought from what Robin Puttick said that she was
a refugee, and he assumed she was from East Germany. Be that as it may, the evidence
d is insufficient for me to draw any inference against Robin Puttick, who does not oppose
the prayer of the petition.

My conclusion is that the marriage is valid.

4. *The husband's domicile and the wife's dependent domicile*

His domicile of origin is undoubtedly British. Much time has been spent in discussing
e whether the petitioner, as was the submission at the start, had a dependent domicile at
the relevant date, that is when she made this application, and whether he had abandoned
his domicile of origin, acquiring the domicile of choice in India. There is much to be
said for the view that he has, although the onus is on the Crown to prove it. But in my
opinion the question is now irrelevant as a woman no longer acquires the domicile of her
husband by virtue only of her marriage. Section 1 of the Domicile and Matrimonial
f Proceedings Act 1973 has a marginal note as follows: 'Abolition of wife's dependent
domicile.' The weight to be given to a marginal note was considered by the Court of
Appeal, whose judgment was delivered by Upjohn LJ, in *Stephens v Cuckfield Rural District
Council*[1]:

'While the marginal note to a section cannot control the language used in the
section, it is at least permissible to approach a consideration of its general purpose
g and the mischief at which it is aimed with the note in mind.'

The section reads:

'(1) Subject to subsection (2) below, the domicile of a married woman as at any
time after the coming into force of this section shall, instead of being the same as her
husband's by virtue only of marriage, be ascertained by reference to the same factors
h as in the case of any other individual capable of having an independent domicile
. . .'

Subsection (2) deals with cases where the married woman had the husband's domicile by
dependence at the coming into force of the Act:

'. . . she is to be treated as retaining that domicile (as a domicile of choice, if it is
j not also her domicile of origin) unless and until it is changed by acquisition or
revival of another domicile either on or after the coming into force of this section.'

Counsel for the petitioner argues that the 1973 Act was passed to enable a married

---

1   [1960] 2 All ER 716 at 720, [1960] 2 QB 373 at 383

woman to avoid taking a dependent domicile if she did not want it, but that she can still take it if she wishes, and so the petitioner can have, and has, a domicile dependent on the domicile of her husband, namely an English domicile. I cannot accept this construction of s 1. Test it in this way. There have been many cases where English girls have married servicemen, mostly American servicemen serving in this country. Indeed, divorce law was changed over the years in order to enable such women to bring proceedings based on residence in this country and not on domicile. The American serviceman (and I hope this is not defamatory of Americans, but it has happened) is posted back to America at the termination of his service here. He says that he will arrange for his wife with whom he has been living here since the marriage to come over in a week or two, and that is the last that is heard of him. In these circumstances the wife's domicile was and remained dependent on that of her husband, an American domicile, so she had and retained American domicile. But now, since the passing of this Act, her domicile on marriage is no longer automatically the domicile of her husband, and she cannot get an American domicile unless and until she goes to America, for domicile is acquired partly by intention and partly by residence; there must be both. I cannot construe s 1 as counsel for the petitioner suggests. Dependent domicile has been abolished and I find that this woman could not and did not obtain an English domicile on marriage.

Of course, a marriage as normally understood would be strong evidence that a woman has acquired the same domicile as her husband, for example, when a foreign woman comes here and marries an Englishman and they settle down as a married couple, have children and so on; but it is only one factor in her choice. Its compelling feature is that the woman sets up a home and lives with the husband. That is not so here. The example was suggested by counsel for the petitioner of two students marrying, the one studying at Bristol University and the other at Durham; they meet infrequently and do not get together to set up a home, at any rate during the time that they are at their studies. But the difference there is that these two intend to set up a home, to cohabit together as husband and wife. There is no evidence whatsoever in this case that the petitioner and Robin Puttick intended any such thing and, indeed, from the facts the inference, I think, must be the other way.

5. Wife's domicile of choice

Her case is, briefly, that she thinks that by marrying Robin Puttick she made a decision to stay here, that she had no intention of going back to Germany but intended to remain here and wanted to make it her permanent home. At the time of her application she had been here over four years. It is, of course, for her to prove that she has abandoned her German domicile of origin. The length of a person's residence, though material, is rarely decisive: see per Lord Macnaghten in *Winans v Attorney-General*[1]:

'Then it was said that the length of time during which Mr. Winans resided in this country leads to the inference that he must have become content to make this country his home. Length of time is of course a very important element in questions of domicil. An unconscious change may come over a man's mind. If the man goes about and mixes in society that is not an improbable result. But in the case of a person like Mr. Winans, who kept himself to himself and had little or no intercourse with his fellow men, it seems to me that at the end of any space of time, however long, his mind would probably be in the state it was at the beginning. When he came to this country he was a sojourner and a stranger, and he was, I think, a sojourner and a stranger in it when he died.'

Then evidence by a person himself of his or her intentions is treated with reserve, even where the truth of the evidence is undoubted. Here the petitioner's evidence is all suspect, if only because she is a woman who would tell any lie, use any deceit, to achieve her end, which is in short not to have to return to Germany. I cannot accept her evidence

---

1   [1904] AC 287 at 297–298, [1904–7] All ER Rep 410 at 416

unless it is supported, and in particular I cannot accept her evidence about her places of
residence here.

To put it colloquially, she was a woman on the run, and I think the true inference to
be drawn from the facts and circumstances is that, if at any time she had realised, not that
she was in danger, that was constant, but that detection and arrest was imminent, she
would have left England at once for a safer land, given the means to do so. Can anyone
doubt that at all times since her arrest she would, if she could, escape, and had she the
opportunity and means to do so, leave this country as quickly as possible? She is a
fugitive from justice, and her true intent has always been to avoid having to return to
Germany to face the trial. Her intention to remain in England, for whose laws she has
shown contempt, and for whose institutions and way of life she has never, so far as I
know, expressed any admiration, was a secondary intention forced on her only as
necessary to achieve her primary object.

The mere fact that a person is liable to be deported, for example, an alien subject to the
Aliens Order (see *Boldrini v Boldrini and Martini*[1]) does not of itself prevent acquisition of
a domicile of choice: but see *Briggs v Briggs*[2], where the respondent left the country
through fear of his creditors but did not acquire a domicile of choice in the United States
of America. The question is whether the person is in England primarily to avoid
detection, or is it primarily to set up home. She never set up home here, although she
resided and obtained work qualifications; but she did not want to go back to Germany,
her domicile of origin, because she did not want to surrender to her bail, to be tried. Her
primary purpose in living here was to avoid detection, and no abandonment of domicile
of origin has been proved. She agreed also in her evidence that she might have returned
to Germany if the charges against her were ever dropped. In my opinion she did not
acquire a domicile of choice in this country.

Another way of looking at her alleged domicile of choice is that it was unilateral. The
hosts, that is, the people of England as represented by the Crown, had no say in the
matter, for her residence beyond six months was achieved by lies and impersonation, and
fraud. Had the truth been known, she would never have been allowed to stay, so it was
not a free choice: see Rayden on Divorce[3]:

'Illegal entry and residence would clearly make the Court hostile to an assertion
that the illegal immigrant had thereby acquired a domicil of choice, but the Court
might take a different view, for example, where the time factor since the entry was
considerable or where possibly the immigrant genuinely did not appreciate that his
entry was illegal.'

Perhaps most important for this case is a passage in Dicey and Morris on the Conflict
of Laws[4]. The authors are dealing with the rule on acquisition of domicile of choice,
namely[5]: 'Every independent person can acquire a domicile of choice by the combination
of residence and intention of permanent or indefinite residence, but not otherwise.'
They say:

'It has been held that a domicile of choice cannot be acquired by illegal
residence. The reason for this rule is that a court cannot allow a person to acquire
a domicile in defiance of the law which that court itself administers. Thus a person
who is illegally resident in (for example) South Africa will not be regarded by the
courts of that country as domiciled there. In the same way, it is submitted that an
English court would hold that a person who was illegally resident in this country
could not thereby acquire an English domicile of choice.'

1   [1932] P 9, [1931] All ER Rep 708
2   (1880) LR 5 PD 163
3   13th Edn (1979) vol 1, p 61
4   9th Edn (1973), pp 96–97
5   Ibid, p 95, r 10

The cases cited in support of the proposition are all Dominion cases and none of them has been produced to this court. I accept this passage in Dicey, which supports the Crown's submission that a person cannot achieve status by fraud: see also *R v Secretary of State for the Home Department (Governor of Horfield Prison), ex parte Sultan Mahmood*[1] in the Court of Appeal. There Stephenson LJ, adopting the words of Lord Widgery CJ in the Divisional Court, said: 'A person who obtains some essential documents by fraud should not be allowed to enjoy a superior status on that account.' See also *R v Secretary of State for the Home Department, ex parte Hussain*[2]. There leave to enter was obtained by fraudulent production of an invalid passport. Such leave was held ineffective.

6. *Discretion*

Section 45(5) of the Matrimonial Causes Act 1973 is as follows:

'Applications to the High Court under the preceding provisions of this section may be included in the same petition, and on any application under the preceding provisions of this section the High Court or, as the case may be, the county court shall make such decree as it thinks just, and the decree shall be binding on Her Majesty and all other persons whatsoever, so however that the decree shall not prejudice any person—(*a*) if it is subsequently proved to have been obtained by fraud or collusion . . .'

The words 'shall make such decree as it thinks just' must, in my judgment, give the court a discretion not to make any decree if the circumstances warrant, even in a case in which domicile and a valid marriage are proved, in contrast with s 1(4) of the 1973 Act which provides:

'If the court is satisfied on the evidence of any such fact as is mentioned in subsection (2) above [that is, the facts which can be established to produce a divorce.] then, unless it is satisfied on all the evidence that the marriage has not broken down irretrievably, it shall . . . grant a decree of divorce.'

It does not contrast, in my view, with s 13(1) which is a specific provision for bars to relief where a marriage is voidable. The wording is:

'The court shall not, in proceedings instituted after 31st July 1971, grant a decree of nullity on the ground that a marriage is voidable if the respondent satisfies the court . . . (*b*) that it would be unjust to the respondent to grant a decree.'

Although s 45 stems from ss 21(*b*) and 188 of the Supreme Court of Judicature (Consolidation) Act 1925, through s 17 of the Matrimonial Causes Act 1950 and s 39 of the Matrimonial Causes Act 1965, the words in question do not seem ever to have been construed by a court, but a somewhat similar provision in s 24 of the Solicitors Act 1843, that any judge or the Master of the Rolls 'are hereby respectively authorised to make such Order in the Matter as may be just', was considered by the Divisional Court of the Queen's Bench Division in *Re an Application under the Solicitors Act 1843*[3]. Wills and Ridley JJ held that they were not bound to make any order for a practising certificate to be granted. Wills J said[4] that 'just' must mean 'that which is right and fitting with regard to the public interests'.

The petitioner argues that once the necessary facts are proved the only discretion the court has is to make a decree of validity or a decree of nullity, and that it could cause great difficulty and uncertainty and cost if a marriage was proved but a decree of validity refused, and it would cause hardship to 'a woman who has been married to a citizen of

---

1   [1978] Court of Appeal Transcript 541
2   [1978] 2 All ER 423, [1978] 1 WLR 700
3   (1899) 80 LT 720
4   80 LT 720 at 722

the United Kingdom who wants to apply', as does the petitioner, 'under s 6(2) of the
a British Nationality Act 1948'. This argument does not impress me, and there are several
answers to it.

(1) If, as here, the petitioner fails to prove domicile, the valid marriage will not result
in a declaration of validity, and the application must be dismissed: so much for the
'difficulty, uncertainty and cost argument'.

(2) I have always understood that s 45(1) enables the court to make a decree declaring
b a marriage valid but not a decree declaring a marriage invalid. Invalidity has to be
decreed, if at all, by proceedings under RSC Ord 15, r 16, which reads as follows:

> 'No action or other proceeding shall be open to objection on the ground that a
> merely declaratory judgment or order is sought thereby, and the Court may make
> binding declarations of right whether or not any consequential relief is or could be
> claimed.'

c This is inherent in the amendments to the Matrimonial Causes Rules made in 1976
following the decisions in the Court of Appeal in *Eneogwe v Eneogwe*[1], and of Ormrod J
in *Aldrich v Attorney-General*[2], which amendments are now to be found in the
Matrimonial Causes Rules 1977, rr 109 and 110. See also *B v Attorney-General (B
intervening)*[3], where Ormrod J said:

d > 'In the answer filed on behalf of the interveners there is a cross-prayer for a
> declaration that the petitioner is not the legitimate child of N.E.B., and it was by the
> consent of all parties, despite the fact that the petitioner is not proceeding with the
> allegation of his prayer, that I heard the evidence. I am still doubtful, very doubtful,
> whether there is jurisdiction in these circumstances to entertain the cross-prayer; I
> am doubtful, indeed, whether there is jurisdiction to entertain cross-prayers at all in
e > proceedings for a declaration of legitimacy. I suspect that the correct order in this
> situation is simply to dismiss the petition. That, in substance, is the order which
> was made in *Fitzwilliam* v. *A.-G.*[4], at which I have had the advantage of looking . . .'

I share that doubt.

(3) Rule 109 of the Matrimonial Causes Rules 1977, provides: '(1) Where . . . the only
f relief sought in any proceedings is a declaration with respect to a person's matrimonial
status, the proceedings shall be begun by petition.' It then sets out what the petition shall
state, and continues:

> '(3) Nothing in the foregoing provisions shall be construed—(a) as conferring any
> jurisdiction to make a declaration in circumstances in which the court could not
> otherwise make it, or (b) as affecting the power of the court to refuse to make a
g > declaration notwithstanding that it has jurisdiction to make it.'

It would be strange indeed if the court has discretion to refuse to make a declaration
affecting matrimonial status, in that it was unjust to make it, but not to refuse a
declaration of validity of marriage under s 45 in similar circumstances.

(4) I find myself unable to understand how s 45(4) can be brought within the
h petitioner's argument. That subsection reads:

> 'Any person who is domiciled in England and Wales or in Northern Ireland or
> claims any real or personal estate situate in England and Wales may apply to the
> High Court for a decree declaring his right to be deemed a British subject.'

(5) A decree subsequently proved to have been obtained by fraud or collusion shall not
j prejudice any person: that is s 45(5)(a) which I have already read. It cannot be the

---

1   [1976] Court of Appeal Transcript 94
2   [1968] 1 All ER 345, [1968] P 281
3   [1966] 2 All ER 145 at 145–146
4   [1951] The Times, 15th March

intention of the statute that a decree must be pronounced (to the permanent prejudice of the Crown) when, although there has been no fraud at the hearing, the whole history *a* is of fraud and perjury and the facts to found a decree have been brought about by criminal acts and offences and a fraudulent, deceitful course of conduct.

(6) In Halsbury's Laws of England[1], under the title Equity, appears this statement of the law, with which I entirely agree. 'Equity does not allow a statute to be made an instrument of fraud.'

It is unnecessary for me to repeat the Attorney-General's catalogue of evils which could *b* flow from the grant of this application. The applicant admits offences under s 3 of the Perjury Act 1911 by reason of what happened at the ceremony and by the description in the certificate. These offences carry a penalty of up to seven years' imprisonment. They are serious. She agrees that she attempted to obtain a certificate of naturalisation by deception. There are false statements contrary to s 28 of the British Nationality Act 1948. There is the forged passport, and offences under the Forgery Act 1913 in respect *c* of the use of that passport. She obtained entry by an offence against s 24(1)(a) of the Immigration Act 1971. She obtained a driving licence by deception.

I do not think it would be just, indeed, in my opinion it would be utterly unjust, to grant a decree, even if she had proved an English domicile, which she has not. Perhaps I am back where I began, with the maxim which I can now express as 'No woman can take advantage of her own wrong.' This court should not and cannot further the *d* criminal acts of this applicant and permit her to achieve an end by the course of conduct which she has pursued. The petition fails and is dismissed.

Petition dismissed.

Solicitors: *Seifert Sedley & Co* (for the petitioner); *Treasury Solicitor*; *Fisher Meredith* (for *e* Robin Puttick).

Georgina Chambers   Barrister.

---

1   16 Halsbury's Laws (4th Edn) para 1308

Vaughan-Neil v Inland Revenue Commissioners

CHANCERY DIVISION

OLIVER J

29th JUNE, 12th JULY 1979

Income tax – Surtax – Restrictive covenant – Consideration for restrictive covenant – Future employment – Undertaking in connection with the employment – Undertaking restricting employee's conduct or activities – Barrister undertaking to cease practice to take up employment – Employer paying him lump sum as an inducement for undertaking to cease practice – Whether payment in respect of 'an undertaking . . . the tenor or effect of which is to restrict him as to his conduct or activities' – Income and Corporation Taxes Act 1970, s 34.

The taxpayer was a barrister who had an extensive practice in the field of town planning law. In the course of his professional activities, the taxpayer had been engaged in a number of cases for W Ltd and in April 1972 that company approached him with an offer of employment carrying a salary of £15,000 per annum. As taking up the employment would have necessarily involved the taxpayer giving up his practice at the Bar, the company offered to pay him a sum of £40,000 as an inducement. The taxpayer decided to accept the offer and on 23rd May 1972 entered into a deed with the company. By that deed, to which a service agreement was annexed, the company covenanted to pay the taxpayer the sum of £40,000 as an inducement to him to give up his status as a practising barrister with the consequent loss of his established position and prospects of further distinction arising from his practice at the Bar, and the taxpayer covenanted that 'he will cease to practice at the Bar in order to enter into the service agreement'. Immediately after the execution of the deed the company paid the sum of £40,000 to the taxpayer. The taxpayer continued in practice until 31st July 1972 and then retired from practice. He joined the company in October 1972. The taxpayer was assessed to tax for the year 1972–73 in respect of the sum of £40,000 under s 34[a] of the Income and Corporation Taxes Act 1970 on the basis that the payment was one 'the tenor or effect of which is to restrict him as to his conduct or activities'. The Special Commissioners upheld the assessment. The taxpayer appealed, contending that, because he could not take up the employment without ceasing to practice, the covenant to cease practice was entirely otiose and mere surplusage, that the payment of £40,000 was, therefore, not in respect of the total or partial fulfilment of any undertaking within s 34, but in respect of the loss of status and loss of future professional advantage which were the inevitable concomitant of taking up the employment, and that, accordingly, s 34 did not apply.

Held – For the purposes of s 34 of the 1970 Act, an undertaking given by an individual in connection with the holding of an office or employment, the tenor or effect of which was to restrict him as to his conduct or activities, did not embrace the undertaking of the very duties which were inherent in and inseparable from the office or employment itself. Looking at the reality of the matter, the payment was an inducement to the taxpayer to accept the professional and social consequences which flowed from his taking up the proffered employment. In the circumstances the payment by the company was not one 'in respect of' a relevant undertaking, within s 34, by the taxpayer and accordingly did not fall to be taxed under that section. The appeal would therefore be allowed (see p 493 f to h, post).

Pritchard (Inspector of Taxes) v Arundale [1971] 3 All ER 1011 followed.

---

[a]   Section 34, so far as material, is set out at p 488 g to j, post.

Notes

For payments in respect of covenants in restraint of trade and their liability to tax in
excess of the basic rate, see 23 Halsbury's Laws (4th Edn) para 916.

For the Income and Corporation Taxes Act 1970, s 34, see 33 Halsbury's Statutes (3rd
Edn) 68.

For 1973–74 and subsequent years of assessment, s 34 has been amended by the
Finance Act 1971, Sch 6, para 15.

Cases referred to in judgment

Beak (Inspector of Taxes) v Robson [1943] 1 All ER 46, [1943] AC 352, 25 Tax Cas 33, 112
  LJKB 141, 169 LT 65, HL, 28(1) Digest (Reissue) 330, *1185*.
Hochstrasser (Inspector of Taxes) v Mayes [1959] 3 All ER 817, [1960] AC 376, [1960] 2
  WLR 63, 38 Tax Cas 673, 228 LT Jo 286, 38 ATC 360, [1959] TR 355, 53 R & IT, HL;
  affg [1958] 3 All ER 285, [1959] Ch 22, [1958] 3 WLR 215, 226 LT Jo 111, CA; *affg*
  [1958] 1 All ER 369, [1959] Ch 22, [1958] 2 WLR 982, 225 LT Jo 75, 28(1) Digest
  (Reissue) 326, *1164*.
Jarrold (Inspector of Taxes) v Boustead [1964] 3 All ER 76, [1964] 1 WLR 1357, 41 Tax Cas
  701, 43 ATC 209, [1964] TR 217, CA, 28(1) Digest (Reissue) 331, *1189*.
Pritchard (Inspector of Taxes) v Arundale [1971] 3 All ER 1011, [1972] Ch 229, [1971] 3
  WLR 877, 47 Tax Cas 680, 50 ATC 318, [1971] TR 277, Digest (Cont Vol D) 464,
  1226b.

Cases also cited

Drummond v Collins (Surveyor of Taxes) [1915] AC 1011, 6 Tax Cas 525, HL.
Mangin v Inland Revenue Comr [1971] 1 All ER 179, [1971] AC 739, PC.
Ormond Investment Co Ltd v Betts [1928] AC 143, [1928] All ER Rep 709, 13 Tax Cas 400,
  HL.
Vestey v Inland Revenue Comrs [1977] 3 All ER 1073, [1979] Ch 198, [1977] STC 414.
Westminster (Duke) v Inland Revenue Comrs [1936] AC 1, [1935] All ER Rep 259, 19 Tax
  Cas 490, HL.

Case stated

1. At a meeting of the Commissioners for the Special Purposes of the Income Tax Acts
held on 1st February 1978, the taxpayer, Edward Albert Vaughan-Neil, appealed against
an assessment to surtax for the year 1972–73 in the amount of £65,306.

2. Shortly stated the question for decision was whether the taxpayer was liable to
surtax under s 34 of the Income and Corporation Taxes Act 1970 in respect of the sum
of £40,000 received by him from George Wimpey & Co Ltd ('Wimpeys') in the
circumstances described below.

[Paragraph 3 named counsel appearing for the parties and para 4 listed the documents
proved or admitted before the commissioners.]

5. The following facts were admitted between the parties: (1) The taxpayer was called
to the Bar in 1951 having already qualified in civil engineering (MICE) and town
planning (MRTPI). (2) From being a senior inspector on the permanent staff of the
Ministry of Housing and Local Government (now the Department of the Environment)
holding public enquiries, he joined chambers (at the age of 43) at 2 Mitre Court Building,
Temple, on 7th April 1959. The chambers in question were well-known as specialising
in local government matters, particularly town-planning, rating and parliamentary
work. (3) The taxpayer soon developed a very large practice and for some years up to his
leaving the Bar, in 1972, was generally acknowledged to be the senior junior in the field
of town planning. (4) Apart from the variety of important cases in which the taxpayer
was involved, he was a member of the Bar Council's Special Committee on Development
Plans, and a member of the Planning Sub-Committee of the Bar Council's Committee on
Administrative Law. In 1967 he was nominated by the British government to advise the
government of Cyprus on the setting up of a system of law and administration for town

planning in the republic. This system was subsequently enacted into law. He was co-
opted on to a Civil Service Board for the appointment of inspectors. In 1970 he was asked
to advise the United Nations/government of Mauritius on town planning matters but
had to decline the request because of pressure of work. His standing at the Bar was such
that after he had left the Bar he was appointed by the Secretary of State to the Dobry
Committee on Development Control. (5) In 1972 with a standing based on the level of
practice indicated above and a seniority of 21 years after call to the Bar the taxpayer could
reasonably anticipate taking silk. His clerk had in fact asked him to consider making
application in 1971 but the taxpayer had decided to postpone the matter. Applications
for silk could not, of course, be made at any time, but only in the last months of the
calendar year. The status of silk, that is, Queen's Counsel, was a well-known distinction
in both the professional and social fields, and was the entrée to further advancement,
including election as a bencher of an Inn of Court, and judicial and administrative
appointments. The loss of those prospects had obviously to be taken specifically into
account by the taxpayer in assessing any offer of a job which would preclude his
continuing to practise at the Bar. The taxpayer received an invitation to take up such a
job from Wimpey's in April 1972. (6) The invitation came from Wimpeys Housing
Division and was conveyed by one of Wimpeys' solicitors, Mr Flegg, who knew the
taxpayer by reason of having instructed him frequently over a number of years on
matters affecting Wimpeys. The taxpayer agreed to discuss the matter but insisted on
speed and absolute confidentiality. The taxpayer insisted that there should be no
correspondence since he believed that that would lead to the possibility of a 'leak' which
could have a seriously damaging effect on his practice. Terms were therefore discussed
orally between the taxpayer and Mr Flegg, and it was agreed that there should be two
separate heads of payment (the amounts of which were also agreed) and that they should
be dealt with by separate documents which eventually took the form of the deeds dated
23rd May 1972 and 19th June 1972 hereinafter referred to. Mr Flegg reported back to
the taxpayer that Wimpeys Housing Division endorsed what he had agreed. Up to that
point of time discussions had been exclusively between Mr Flegg and the taxpayer, either
at the latter's home or elsewhere but never at the taxpayer's chambers nor on Wimpeys'
premises. However, at that stage a meeting, which was to be entirely confidential, was
arranged at Wimpeys' head office. The primary purpose of the meeting arose from the
fact that nobody in Wimpey's other than Mr Flegg had ever actually met the taxpayer,
only knowing him through reports of the cases which he conducted for Wimpeys.
Accordingly the object of the meeting was to make sure that as a person the taxpayer
would 'fit-in' in Wimpeys' organisation and, if so, to settle when the job would start and
after its initial duration. After that meeting the documents referred to above were
drafted, the drafts being largely based on text book precedents. Such matters as the
length of holidays, working hours etc which cropped up in the course of the drafting,
were settled on the telephone. In that period the taxpayer asked for his salary, which had
been agreed at £15,000 per annum, to be redistributed so that he received more in the
earlier years with a peak in the third year to maximise his pension entitlement. That
request was acceded to, and the figures which he suggested were inserted in the document
which became the deed dated 19th June 1972 hereinafter referred to. (7) The deed
executed on 23rd May 1972 provided for the payment to the taxpayer by Wimpeys of
the sum of £40,000, the sum in issue, and which was duly paid to the taxpayer on the
execution of the deed. The material parts of the deed read as follows:

'WHEREAS (A) [The taxpayer] a Barrister of some twenty one years seniority enjoys
an established position and status and prospects of further distinction arising from
his widespread and well-known practice at the Bar. (B) The Company desires [the
taxpayer] to enter into an agreement of service incompatible with the continuation
of his practice at the Bar. (C) The Company is willing to pay to [the taxpayer] the
sum of Forty thousand pounds (£40,000) as an inducement to him to give up his
status as a practising Barrister with the consequent loss of those advantages he now

enjoys and may reasonably anticipate as referred to in Recital A. Now THIS DEED WITNESSETH as follows: 1. The Company hereby covenants for the reasons and the purposes mentioned in the Recitals to this Deed to pay to [the taxpayer] the sum of Forty thousand pounds (£40,000) upon the execution hereof and [the taxpayer] hereby covenants that he will cease to practise at the Bar in order to enter into the service agreement hereinafter referred to. 2. Each of the parties hereto covenants with the other that to enter into a Service Agreement in the form of the draft document attached hereto (subject to such modifications as may be mutually agreed) not later than the Thirtieth day of September one thousand nine hundred and seventy two. IN WITNESS whereof the Company has caused its Common Seal to be hereunto affixed and [the taxpayer] has hereunto set his hand and seal the day and year first before written.'

(8) After the execution of this deed Wimpeys took out with the National Provident Institute an insurance policy for a sum of £57,500 on the taxpayer's life for the period 23rd May 1972 until 22nd October 1973, paying a premium of £652·90 therefor. (9) When the above-mentioned deed was executed there was attached to it the draft service agreement referred to in the deed. After the execution of the deed the draft service agreement was further considered but no questions arose necessitating any departure from the draft and accordingly the deed constituting the service agreement ('the service agreement'), was duly executed on 19th June 1972. The service agreement provided for the taxpayer to serve Wimpeys as Chief Town Planning Consultant for a term of five years from 20th October 1972 in the first instance. The material parts of the service agreement read as follows:

'4. During the continuance of this employment [the taxpayer] shall devote so much of his attention and abilities as is reasonably necessary for the proper performance of his duties hereunder and shall be prepared to travel within the United Kingdom on the relevant business of the Company but not so as to require the absence of [the taxpayer] from his Wimbledon office for more than two days in any one week . . .
'10. [The taxpayer] shall not without the express consent of the Company in writing either during the continuance of his said appointment hereunder or thereafter make use of or disclose for his own benefit or for or on behalf of any other person firm or company any trade secrets or confidential information obtained by him during his said appointment relating to the business of the Company.
'11. In performing his duties hereunder [the taxpayer] shall always give preference to the affairs and interests of the Company but subject thereto [the taxpayer] shall be free to act as a Consultant to persons or bodies other than the Company provided always that by so doing the interests of the Company are not likely to be interfered with or in any way adversely affected.'

(10) The taxpayer continued in practice without any intermission whatsoever until the end of the legal year on 31st July 1972. During the period after 23rd May 1972, his clients (including Wimpeys themselves) continued to send him papers at the Bar in the usual way, and to attend conferences with him in chambers. Wimpeys were well aware that his practice was continuing as usual and that they were having to fit in their appointments with those of other clients and his other Bar commitments. The relevant fees were of course paid to his clerk into chambers account. During that period the taxpayer appeared as counsel on ten days for Lyon's Development Group, on one day for Fairview Estates Ltd and on four separate one-day hearings for Wimpeys. His conferences and paperwork over the period related to many matters for many clients. (11) At the beginning of August 1972 the taxpayer went on holiday with his family returning in time to take up employment with Wimpeys on Monday 2nd October 1972. The taxpayer has continued to work for Wimpeys since that time, his employment with Wimpeys being governed initially by the service agreement; subsequently by the service

agreement as varied by the deed dated 14th January 1974, by which the five-year term
a of the service agreement which would have ended on 1st October 1977 was extended
until 19th October 1979 and the salary for the extended period was fixed at £17,500 per
annum with provision for indexation; and finally by the service agreement as varied by
the deed dated 10th August 1976, by which the scope of the taxpayer's service to
Wimpeys was enlarged as mentioned in cl 1 thereof; the period of the taxpayer's
employment by Wimpeys was extended until 31st October 1982; and his remuneration
b for the period from 1st November 1976 until 31st October 1982 was fixed at an annual
rate of £19,000 with provision for increase from 1st November 1977 onwards as therein
provided.

    6. It was contended on behalf of the taxpayer: (a) that the taxpayer was not on 23rd
May 1972, when he gave the covenant contained in the deed of that date and the sum of
£40,000 was paid to him, about to hold an employment with Wimpeys; (b) that the
c covenant was not given by the taxpayer in connection with his holding of the
employment with Wimpeys which he took up on 2nd October 1972; (c) that the tenor
or effect of the covenant was not to restrict the taxpayer as to his conduct or activities;
(d) that the sum of £40,000 was not paid to the taxpayer in respect either of the giving
of the covenant by him or of the total or partial fulfilment of the covenant by him; (e)
that the conditions of s 34(1)(a) and (b) of the Income and Corporation Taxes Act 1970
d were not satisfied in relation to the sum of £40,000; and (f) that accordingly the appeal
should be upheld and the assessment should be discharged.

    7. It was contended on behalf of the Crown: (1) that on 23rd May 1972 the taxpayer
was about to hold an employment with Wimpeys, (2) that in the deed of 23rd May 1972
the taxpayer gave an undertaking to Wimpeys, (3) that, on the facts, the undertaking was
a term of, or ancillary to, the entry of the taxpayer into the employment and was
e therefore given by the taxpayer in connection with his holding of the employment, (4)
that the tenor or effect of the undertaking was to prevent the taxpayer from practising
at the Bar and therefore to restrict him as to his conduct or activities, (5) that the sum of
£40,000 was paid to the taxpayer in respect of his giving that undertaking, (6) and
accordingly that the appeal should be dismissed and the assessment should be confirmed.

    [Paragraph 8 set out the cases[1] cited to the commissioners.]

f   9. The commissioners who heard the appeal, gave their decision orally as follows:

    'What we have to decide is a short point of construction involving clause 1 of the
Deed dated 23 May 1972 in the context of the rest of the deed and against the
background of the facts in the agreed statement.

    '[Counsel appearing for the taxpayer] has taken us carefully through the provisions
of section 34 Income and Corporations Taxes Act 1970 and extracted for us four
g conditions which need to be satisfied to enable the Crown to succeed. It has
emerged in the course of the argument that condition 4 is the most important as far
as [the taxpayer] is concerned but all the conditions are important from the Crown's
point of view.

    'We go first to condition 4 and have to decide whether the "sum" referred to in
section 34(1)(b), which in this case was £40,000, was paid to [the taxpayer] in respect
h of the giving by him of an undertaking. This takes us back to sub-clause (a) since
the payment has to be in connection with the holding of an office or employment.
[Counsel for the taxpayer] invites us to read clause 1 of the Deed dated 23 May 1972
having regard to the recitals, since Wimpey's covenant therein is made for the
reasons and purposes mentioned therein. The sum of £40,000 is paid for the giving
up of [the taxpayer's] status as a practising Barrister and not for the giving up of his
j practice. This is an extremely fine point but that is neither here nor there: the
question is whether that is a proper construction of this vital wording. [Counsel for
the Crown] meets this by asking for what was the sum of £40,000 paid if not for the

---

1   *Beak (Inspector of Taxes) v Robson* [1943] 1 All ER 46, [1943] AC 352, 25 Tax Cas 33, HL; *Jarrold*
  (Inspector of Taxes) v Boustead [1964] 3 All ER 76, [1964] 1 WLR 1357, 41 Tax Cas 701, CA

giving up of the practice. He says there is no need to bring in the recitals since under clause 1 the company pays £40,000 and [the taxpayer] gives up his practice. *a* He says both acts were "consideration". In our view the latter is the proper construction of the Deed and section 34(1)(b) is satisfied.

'We now come back to condition 1 and the words, "or is about to hold". [Counsel for the taxpayer] says the words import a degree of urgency and certainty which in this case are lacking or leave much to be desired. [Counsel for the Crown] argues that, "or is about to hold" means "will". He says there is no degree of urgency or *b* certainty: there is to be an office or employment in the forseeable future and the words are applicable to the present case without any strain. We agree with him and hold that condition 1 is thus far satisfied.

'Condition 2 is whether the undertaking is in connection with what is to happen. We have noted the careful argument of [counsel for the taxpayer] but it seems to us that the undertaking need be no more than ancillary—a prior rather *c* than a subsequent matter—with a causal connection. On that view condition 2 is also satisfied.

'Condition 3 is concerning tenor or effect. [Counsel's] argument is that the tenor or effect of [the taxpayer's] covenant contained in clause 1 of the Deed of 23 May 1972 was not to restrict him as to his conduct or activities but to put a stop to his professional activities altogether. It seems to us that, giving the words their ordinary *d* meaning, the undertaking was for the employment to be held, and the restriction was voluntarily undertaken by the employee himself. We can see no force in [counsel's] argument on this point. For those reasons we hold the appeal fails. There remains the possibility of agreement between the parties on section 34(1)(c) procedure, concerning which there was considerable discussion. Regarding the Schedule E appeals before the General Commissioners we have canvassed various *e* possible courses and feel we must leave the parties to proceed as they may be advised.

'The result is the appeal fails and the assessment is therefore confirmed in agreed figures.'

10. The taxpayer immediately after the determination of the appeal declared his dissatisfaction therewith as being erroneous in point of law and on 6th February 1978 *f* required the commissioners to state a case for the opinion of the High Court pursuant to the Taxes Management Act 1970, s 56.

11. The question of law for the opinion of the court was whether the decision was erroneous in point of law.

Martin Nourse QC for the taxpayer.   *g*
C H McCall for the Crown.

Cur adv vult

12th July. **OLIVER J** read the following judgment: This is a taxpayer's appeal from a *h* decision of the Special Commissioners dated 1st February 1978. The taxpayer was assessed to surtax for the year 1972–73 in the amount of £65,306, and the question raised by the appeal is whether he was rightly assessed in respect of a sum of £40,000 paid to him in the year 1972 by his present employers, George Wimpey & Co Ltd ('Wimpeys').

At the date of the relevant payment the taxpayer was 57 years of age. He had been called to the Bar in 1951, and had developed a very extensive practice in the field of town planning law in well-known chambers in the Temple specialising in work of that *j* nature. It is agreed that he was, and had been for some years prior to 1972, regarded as the senior junior counsel in this particular field, and was an obvious candidate for silk, for which his clerk had urged him to apply.

In the course of his professional activities the taxpayer had been engaged in a number of cases for Wimpeys, and in April 1972 that company, through one of its solicitors,

a approached him with a view to engaging his services as an employee of the company. After a number of confidential discussions it was agreed that he would join Wimpeys, but that, of course, involved necessarily his giving up practising at the Bar, both for practical and for professional reasons, for he could not, consistently with the Bar Council's code of professional conduct, both practise and hold an employment with Wimpeys involving his rendering, as an employee, those services which he had previously rendered

b in a professional capacity.

The decision was, therefore, one which involved the taxpayer's turning his back, effectively for good, on any further advancement in the professional field, by way, for instance, of taking silk, election to the bench of his Inn, or appointment to judicial or administrative office, for what was contemplated was a service agreement for five years and the taxpayer could not, practically, hope to return and resume practice at the end of

c that period, when he would be some 62 years of age. The stated case finds: 'The loss of these prospects had obviously to be taken specifically into account by the taxpayer in assessing any offer of a job which would preclude his continuing to practise at the Bar.'

Terms were discussed, and it was agreed that there should be two separate heads of payment which would be dealt with by separate documents. One was the payment of £40,000, with which this case is concerned. The other head of payment was the rate of

d salary, which was agreed at £15,000 per annum (subsequently redistributed over the period of five years in such a way as to increase the annual payment in the early years so as to maximise the taxpayer's pension entitlement). On 23rd May 1972 the parties entered into a deed, to which was annexed a form of service agreement which was ultimately executed without modification on 19th June 1972.

The deed was in the following terms (I omit the formal reference to the parties):

e   'Whereas (a) [the taxpayer] a Barrister of some twenty one years seniority enjoys an established position and status and prospects of further distinction arising from his widespread and well-known practice at the Bar. (b) The Company desires [the taxpayer] to enter into an agreement of service incompatible with the continuation of his practice at the Bar. (c) The Company is willing to pay to [the taxpayer] the sum of Forty thousand pounds (£40,000) as an inducement to him to give up his

f   status as a practising Barrister with the consequent loss of those advantages he now enjoys and may reasonably anticipate as referred to in Recital a. Now this deed witnesseth as follows: 1. The Company hereby covenants for the reasons and the purposes mentioned in the Recitals to this Deed to pay to [the taxpayer] the sum of Forty thousand pounds (£40,000) upon the execution hereof and [the taxpayer] hereby covenants that he will cease to practise at the Bar in order to enter into the

g   service agreement hereinafter referred to. 2. Each of the parties hereto covenants with the other ... to enter into a Service Agreement in the form of the draft document attached hereto (subject to such modifications as may be mutually agreed) not later than the Thirtieth day of September one thousand nine hundred and seventy two'

h and that deed was duly signed, sealed and delivered.

The material parts of the annexed service agreement, which was for a period of five years from 2nd October 1972 and described the office or employment as that of 'Chief Town Planning Consultant', are the following clauses:

     '4. During the continuance of this employment [the taxpayer] shall devote so much of his attention and abilities as is reasonably necessary for the proper performance of his duties hereunder and shall be prepared to travel within the

j   United Kingdom on the relevant business of the Company but not so as to require the absence of the Appointee from his Wimbledon office for more than two days in any one week ...

     '10. [The taxpayer] shall not without the express consent of the Company in writing either during the continuance of his said appointment hereunder or thereafter make use of or disclose for his own benefit or for or on behalf of any other person firm or company any trade secrets or confidential information obtained by him during his said appointment relating to the business of the Company.   *a*

'11. In performing his duties hereunder [the taxpayer] shall always give preference to the affairs and interests of the Company but subject thereto [the taxpayer] shall be free to act as a Consultant to persons and bodies other than the Company provided always that by so doing the interests of the Company are not likely to be interfered with or in any way adversely affected.'   *b*

Following the execution of these documents the taxpayer continued in practice at the Bar until 31st July 1972. His practice as a barrister ceased at that date, and after a vacation with his family he actually commenced work for Wimpeys on 2nd October 1972 and has continued in that employment ever since.

The deed of 23rd May 1972 provided for payment of the sum of £40,000 upon its execution, even though the taxpayer had not yet entered Wimpeys' employment, and it   *c* is not in dispute that the sum was then paid, the risk that the taxpayer might die before or shortly after taking up his employment being covered by an insurance policy on his life taken out by Wimpeys after the Deed had been executed. The Crown originally sought to charge the payment of the £40,000 to tax by an assessment under Sch E as an emolument of the taxpayer's office, and an appeal against that assessment is still formally pending before the General Commissioners. It is, however, not now contended by the   *d* Crown that the payment is one chargeable to tax under Sch E, and it is accepted by the Crown and the taxpayer for the purposes of this appeal that if the sum is not chargeable to tax under s 34 of the Income and Corporation Taxes Act 1970 (which is the point for decision on this appeal), it is not otherwise chargeable to tax.

That section is the successor section to s 26 of the Finance Act 1950 which was introduced as a result of the decision of the House of Lords in *Beak (Inspector of Taxes) v*   *e* *Robson*[1]. The general effect of that decision was that a payment in a service agreement specifically stated to be in consideration of the employee's entering into a covenant restraining competition by him after his employment had terminated escaped tax. No doubt the legislature considered that unless something were done to bring such payments within the revenue net this would open the door to a wholesale payment of tax-free emoluments.   *f*

Section 34 has since been amended, but at the dates relevant to the assessment in the instant case it read as follows:

'(1) Where—(a) an individual who holds, has held, or is about to hold, an office or employment gives in connection with his holding thereof an undertaking (whether absolute or qualified, and whether legally valid or not) the tenor or effect of which   *g* is to restrict him as to his conduct or activities, and (b) in respect of the giving of that undertaking by him, or of the total or partial fulfilment of that undertaking by him, any sum is paid either to him or to any other person, and (c) apart from this section, the sum paid would neither fall to be treated as income of any person for the purposes of income tax for any year of assessment nor fall to be taken into account as a receipt in computing, for the purpose of income tax for any year of assessment,   *h* the amount of any income of, or loss incurred by, any person, the same results shall follow in relation to surtax for the year of assessment in which the said sum is paid as would have followed if the said sum had been paid to the said individual (and not to any other person) as and for the net amount of an annual payment to which the said individual was entitled, being an annual payment chargeable to income tax from the gross amount of which income tax at the standard rate for that year had   *j* been duly deducted under section 52 or 53 of this Act . . .'

and then there is a proviso which I do not think I need read.

---

1   [1943] 1 All ER 46, [1943] AC 352, 25 Tax Cas 33

It will be seen that, in order to bring the section into operation at all, it is essential that
the sum paid should not be taxable under any other head of charge, and, as I have
mentioned, it is not in dispute for the purposes of this appeal that that condition is
satisfied. There are, however, four other essential conditions, the application of each of
which is disputed by the taxpayer. First, it applies only if the individual concerned
'holds, has held, or is about to hold, an office or employment', and it is submitted, albeit
faintly, that if (which is disputed) there was any relevant undertaking by the taxpayer,
then at the time when it was given he neither held nor had held any office or
employment, and that the holding of office was so far removed in time from the
undertaking that he could not be said to be 'about to hold' that office. The Special
Commissioners rejected that last submission, and in my judgment they were entirely
right to do so.

The second condition is that the undertaking should be given 'in connection with' the
holding of the office or employment. Now prima facie this would appear to involve no
more than that there should be a connection between the actual or prospective holding
of the office and the giving of the undertaking, and if that is right then there seems to
me, as there seemed to the Special Commissioners, to be little room for argument that
this condition was not fulfilled in the instant case. Counsel for the taxpayer however,
submits in effect, and this really forms part of a single submission which relates also to
the fulfilment of the third condition, that the words are used in an adjectival sense,
qualifying not the giving of the undertaking but the undertaking itself. To put it
another way, he submits that what the court has to look at is whether the nature of the
undertaking given is such that it can be described as an undertaking 'in connection with'
the holding of the office or employment. Thus read, he suggests, the section is dealing
only with the *Beak (Inspector of Taxes) v Robson*[1] type of undertaking; that is to say, the
conventional undertaking restraining the office-holder or employee from competing
after the termination of, or possibly during, his employment.

Now if it is right that the section is aimed only at that type of restriction, and whether
it is or not is something which I will consider in relation to counsel's submissions for the
taxpayer under the third condition, it seems to me that it cannot be because of the
adjectival quality in the words 'in connection with his holding thereof' for which counsel
for the taxpayer contends. As a matter simply of grammatical construction, it seems to
me that these words fulfil an adverbial function and qualify not the undertaking but the
giving of it. Counsel's construction involves treating them as if they were transposed in
the sentence in which they appear from their actual position to a position immediately
after the word 'undertaking', or possibly immediately after the parenthetical phrase
which follows it. I can see no grounds for such a transposition, and I agree with the
Special Commissioners that the second condition is also satisfied.

The third condition is one which gives rise to greater difficulty. It is an essential
feature of the application of the section that the undertaking, whether or not legally
enforceable, should be one 'the tenor or effect of which is to restrict' the individual who
gives it 'as to his conduct or activities'. On the face of it, those words are about as wide
as they can be. If I undertake to go to Brighton next Monday afternoon I cannot at the
same time attend a conference at Stoke-on-Trent, so that, to that extent, the effect of my
undertaking is to restrict my conduct or activity. But that can hardly be the meaning of
the section, for it is impossible to imagine an undertaking which does not restrict
conduct inconsistent with its fulfilment; and the reference in the section to the restrictive
tenor or effect of the undertaking would thus be otiose. The legislature must, therefore,
counsel for the taxpayer argues, have had some particular type of restriction in mind,
and, in order to see what it is, he submits that the court should look at the history of the
legislation and the mischief at which the section was aimed when it was introduced. So
viewed, he submits, the section is seen to be dealing only with what might be called the
'conventional' type of covenant in restraint of trade and not the sort of undertaking given

---

1   [1943] 1 All ER 46, [1943] AC 352, 25 Tax Cas 33

in the instant case, which was merely the expression of a necessary correlative consequence of the taxpayer's employment.

Counsel for the Crown, on the other hand, says that there is no room in a taxing statute for an equitable or lenient construction. He does not, I think, shrink from asserting that the section is deliberately widely worded so as to cover virtually every type of undertaking, but he submits that he does not need to go so far because, whatever type of undertaking is embraced by it, it plainly covers an undertaking by which the individual expressly contracts to refrain from a particular course of conduct or activity.

I find this submission persuasive. It is not, in my judgment, necessary to the decision of this case that I should seek to define or classify the types of undertaking embraced in the words 'the tenor or effect of which is to restrict him as to his conduct or activities'. It is sufficient in this case to say that, whatever those words mean, they appear to me plainly to cover a case in which the individual concerned expressly covenants that he will give up or refrain from a particular course of conduct which, at the time of the undertaking, he is pursuing. If a man contracts that he will cease to practise his profession, that must involve the consequence that he undertakes, after cessation, either permanently or temporarily, not to practise that profession, and I cannot construe that as anything but an undertaking restricting his future conduct.

It is the fourth condition which appears to me to be the critical one in the instant case. For a sum to be taxable under the section it must be a sum which is paid 'in respect' either of the giving of the undertaking or of its total or partial fulfilment. Counsel for the taxpayer submits that the sum of £40,000 paid by Wimpeys was quite plainly not paid in respect of the total or partial fulfilment of any undertaking. It was paid outright on the execution of the deed, and at that date the taxpayer had not ceased to practise, had not executed a service agreement and had not suffered any of the consequences which it was envisaged that he would suffer by entering Wimpeys' employment. Equally, he submits, the only undertaking by the taxpayer which can be extracted from the deed is the covenant by him in cl 1, and, whilst it appears in the same clause as the undertaking by Wimpeys to pay the sum, that sum was paid, as the deed itself states, not in respect of the undertaking but in respect of the matters which are set out in the recitals, which recitals are expressly incorporated by reference into the operative part of the deed.

The payment, counsel for the taxpayer submits, was in respect of the loss of status and loss of future professional advantage which were the inevitable concomitant of entering Wimpeys' employment. The covenant to cease practice was in fact entirely otiose and mere surplusage, because in fact the taxpayer could not take the employment without ceasing to practise. The loss of status and advantage therefore flowed not from the covenant but from the very fact of employment. This, he submits, becomes even clearer when the terms of the service agreement are looked at. The time which the taxpayer was obliged to devote to his duties and the nature of those duties do not of themselves make it impossible for him to continue to conduct a practice at the Bar if one ignores the barrister's code of professional conduct. What ruled out a continuation of practice was the very fact of entering into Wimpeys' service, and the covenant by the taxpayer in cl 1 was, therefore, not an undertaking sought by Wimpeys for the purpose of restricting the taxpayer's activities but simply the recognition of the consequence (expressed in recital (B)) that entry into the service agreement would have. So what the payment was 'in respect of' was the contemplated results of the employment which are summarised or described in recitals (A) and (C).

The position, therefore, counsel submits for the taxpayer, is no different from the position of the amateur footballer in *Jarrold (Inspector of Taxes) v Boustead*[1] or the chartered accountant in *Pritchard (Inspector of Taxes) v Arundale*[2]. Those cases were concerned with assessments to Sch E income tax, but counsel for the taxpayer submits

---

1 [1964] 3 All ER 76, [1964] 1 WLR 1357, 41 Tax Cas 701
2 [1971] 3 All ER 1011, [1972] Ch 229, 47 Tax Cas 680

a that they are of assistance in demonstrating what payments made in circumstances not dissimilar to those in the instant case were 'in respect of'. Just as, in the former case, the signing on with a professional club involved the permanent loss of amateur status, so here, he argues, the acceptance of the obligation to enter into the service agreement necessarily involved the taxpayer's doing that which followed from the moment that the service agreement took effect, that is to say, ceasing to practise as a barrister. An undertaking restricting activity must at least, he suggests, import the imposition of some

b restriction inter partes beyond that which is in itself inherent in the very relationship created by the holding of the office or employment. But here the covenant added nothing, and the result would have been exactly the same so far as both parties were concerned if it had been omitted altogether.

The answer of counsel for the Crown to this is that the court, in determining whether or not a particular payment is taxable, has to look not at what the parties might have

c done but at what they actually did. Here the taxpayer did in fact enter into a covenant with his future employer, and whether it had the slightest effect on what would have been the position in any event is entirely immaterial. The covenant is in the deed, and it cannot be treated as written out of it and ignored. With that, of course, I agree, but it does not really seem to me that it answers the crucial question: was the payment made 'in respect of' the undertaking? The deed does not say that it was. Counsel for the Crown

d has referred me to a number of dictionary definitions of the phrase 'in respect of', but I am not sure that in the construction of this section such delicate refinements of meaning are really of assistance.

Broadly, as it seems to me, in its context here the phrase means no more than 'for', and the question which has to be answered is: was the payment made to the taxpayer so made as the reward or recompense for the giving of the undertaking? To this counsel for the

e Crown would give an affirmative answer, simply because the covenant to cease practice appears in the same clause in the deed and is linked to the other party's obligation to pay by the word 'and'. If the payment was not for the covenant itself, then, he argues, it was for the matters referred to in recital (c), which were the anticipated consequences of the covenant and were thus the total fulfilment of the undertaking referred to in the section.

It does not seem to me that this latter submission really bears examination in the

f instant case. The payment was made on the execution of the deed and at a time when the taxpayer was still in practice and had not signed any service agreement. There was no provision for refund if he died or became incapable before the service agreement was signed, and it seems to me to be impossible rationally to say that the payment was for the total or partial fulfilment of that which was not then, and might never be, fulfilled.

I return, therefore, to what I conceive to be the principal point: was the payment made

g 'in respect of' or 'for' the giving of the undertaking in cl 1? I do not think it can be enough simply to look at the face of the deed and to treat the only reality of the transaction as that which emerges from the juxtaposition of the covenant for payment and the taxpayer's covenant to cease practice. *Pritchard (Inspector of Taxes) v Arundale*[1] was concerned with the not dissimilar question of whether a transfer of shares pursuant to a deed which provided for such a transfer 'in consideration of the taxpayer undertaking

h to serve the Company' was an emolument from his employment, a question which involved the consideration of whether it was (to use the words of Upjohn J in *Hochstrasser (Inspector of Taxes) v Mayes*[2]) a payment made 'in reference to the service the employee renders by virtue of his office'. That question (to quote again Upjohn J[3]) '. . . is a question to be answered in the light of the particular facts of every case'.

In his judgment Megarry J emphasised that the question was one of fact and, primarily,

j

---

1 [1971] 3 All ER 1011, [1972] Ch 221, 47 Tax Cas 680
2 [1958] 1 All ER 369 at 375, [1959] Ch 22 at 33, 38 Tax Cas 673 at 685
3 [1958] 1 All ER 369 at 374, [1959] Ch 22 at 33, 38 Tax Cas 673 at 685

of causal connection, and I do not think that the question of whether a payment is 'in respect of' the giving of an undertaking is on any different footing. He said this[1]:

'. . . whichever of these formulations is applied, and in whatever language, it seems to me that the question of fact must be resolved by looking at the whole of the relevant facts. Counsel for the Crown's sheet anchor was cl 2 of the agreement. This provided for Mr Lowe to transfer the shares to the taxpayer. "In consideration of [the taxpayer] undertaking to serve the company as aforesaid." This, said counsel for the Crown was conclusive: the consideration was made wholly referable to the contract to serve, and although extrinsic evidence was admissible to determine a doubtful meaning, it could not be used to contradict the express terms of the written agreement. His alternative submission was that even if evidence of the surrounding circumstances was admissible, the result would be the same. On these submissions a variety of points arose. The first, and on one view the most important, is that consideration and causation are by no means necessarily identical. Let me assume for one moment that no evidence is admissible to establish that there was a jot or tittle of consideration for the transfer save the taxpayer's undertaking to serve the company. That does not seem to me to answer the question whether or not the payment was made to the taxpayer in reference to, and as a reward for, services rendered by virtue of his office, or in return for acting as or being an employee. If the transfer had been made for no consideration at all, the reason for making it might still have been to reward the taxpayer for his services to the company, and so it might be taxable. Per contra, if the real reason for making the transfer had been not to reward him for his services, but to make him a free gift, or, as in the *Hochstrasser* case[2], to compensate him for some loss he had already suffered (which, being past consideration, could not be valuable consideration), then I cannot see that to make the agreement to transfer legally enforceable by expressing it to be in consideration of his undertaking to serve the company conclusively ousts the real reason for the transfer. The terms of the agreement are entitled to be given full weight, as part of the surrounding circumstances; but I do not think a contractual expression of consideration is conclusively determinative of causation.'

On this aspect of the matter he concluded[3]:

'In my judgment, the payments must be linked to the services not by mere words but by reality; and to this, contractual obligations may contribute, perhaps substantially, but they cannot pre-empt.'

In the instant case the Special Commissioners approached the question as one purely of construction of the deed. In their reasons for decision they said: 'This is an extremely fine point but that is neither here nor there: the question is whether that is a proper construction of this vital wording'. Certainly that was one question, but I do not, with respect, think that it was the only question. *Pritchard (Inspector of Taxes) v Arundale*[4] shows that the critical question is: what is the reality, and not simply, what does the deed say?

When that falls to be considered against the whole of the facts of the case the following are, it seems to me, the critical points. First, the fact was that the taxpayer had an assured position at the Bar and very bright prospects for the future, all of which must necessarily go and, as a practical matter, go for good if he took employment. Secondly, the reasons why Wimpeys were willing to make the payment and their purpose in making it are stated in the deed itself, and nothing in the background or in the facts found in the stated case leads to the conclusion that those statements are not perfectly accurate. The reason

---

1   [1971] 3 All ER 1011 at 1020–1021, [1972] Ch 229 at 238–239, 47 Tax Cas 680 at 687–688
2   [1959] 3 All ER 817, [1960] AC 376, 38 Tax Cas 673
3   [1971] 3 All ER 1011 at 1022, [1972] Ch 229 at 240, 47 Tax Cas 680 at 689
4   [1971] 3 All ER 1011, [1972] Ch 229, 47 Tax Cas 680

a
stated is the company's desire to employ the taxpayer, and the purpose is to provide him with an inducement to accept the relinquishment of his status and prospects which that employment necessarily involves.

Thirdly, if and so far as the terms of the deed alone are to be looked at, that purpose and that reason are repeated referentially in cl 1 of the deed, and there is no necessity to look further to see what the consideration for the payment was. Fourthly, there is nothing in cl 1 of the deed which expressly states or by necessary implication leads to the

b
conclusion that the covenant by the taxpayer was given as consideration for the payment, or that the payment was made as consideration for the covenant.

Fifthly, it is to be observed that the covenant is not simply a covenant to cease to practise at the Bar, which, if one is to look at the reality, could not be of the slightest materiality to Wimpeys. It is really fanciful to suggest that Wimpeys could have had any possible interest in the taxpayer's ceasing to practise apart from his entry into their

c
service. It is a covenant to cease practice for one purpose only, namely, 'in order to enter into the service agreement' and it is followed by an express mutual covenant by the parties to execute such an agreement. If that last-mentioned covenant is given effect to, and it is part and parcel of the same deed, then a covenant to cease to practise as a barrister in order to do what the covenantor is bound to do anyway adds nothing to it. It becomes merely a statement of a necessary and inevitable consequence of assuming the obligations

d
imposed by cl 2.

Of course, strictly speaking, it was not necessary for the taxpayer to cease to practise 'in order to enter into the service agreement', because, even after executing the agreement, he could, and, indeed, did, continue to practise until the employment under the agreement actually took effect. So the argument would run, his covenant imposed on him a restriction which was more than a necessary incident of his service. But that,

e
as it seems to me, is a two-edged argument, because if I am to look at the reality of what the payment was 'in respect of', and the principle of *Pritchard (Inspector of Taxes) v Arundale*[1] seems to me to be equally applicable to a question arising under s 34, then I cannot ignore that, to Wimpeys' knowledge, the taxpayer, having executed the service agreement, continued in practice (and, indeed, appeared as counsel for Wimpeys themselves) up to the date when his service under the agreement commenced.

f
In my judgment, the reality is as the deed states: the payment was to act as an inducement to the taxpayer to accept the professional and social consequences which flowed from his taking the preferred employment. Counsel for the Crown would argue, I think, that that means that it was a payment for entering into the service agreement, and that that is itself an undertaking restricting the taxpayer from any conduct or activity incompatible with the carrying out of the duties which he was engaged to perform, and therefore an undertaking caught by the section. But whatever restrictions

g
the section, on its true construction, is aimed at, I cannot read the expression 'an undertaking . . . the tenor or effect of which is to restrict him as to his conduct or activities' as embracing the simple undertaking of the very duties which are inherent in and inseparable from the office or employment itself.

I agree with the Special Commissioners that the point is a narrow one, but I do not

h
agree that it is simply a point of construction of the deed. The question is: does the Crown, in all the circumstances of the case, including the terms of the deed, demonstrate that the payment was one 'in respect of' a relevant undertaking by the taxpayer? In my judgment it does not, and the appeal must be allowed.

Appeal allowed.

j
Solicitors: *J Memery & Co* (for the taxpayer); *Solicitor of Inland Revenue*.

Rengan Krishnan Esq   Barrister.

---

1   [1971] 3 All ER 1011, [1972] Ch 229, 47 Tax Cas 680

B v B (mental health patient)

COURT OF APPEAL, CIVIL DIVISION
MEGAW, LAWTON AND BROWNE LJJ
26th JULY 1979

Mental health – Admission of patient to hospital – Admission for treatment – Application – Nearest relative – Consent to application – Unreasonable objection to application – Application for substitution of acting nearest relative – Evidence in support of application – Respondent to application required to be told substance of medical report – Whether communication of report to respondent's solicitor sufficient compliance with requirement – Whether non-compliance with statutory form of report vitiating proceedings – Mental Health Act 1959, s 52(3)(c) – CCR Ord 46, r 18(5).

In April 1979 Mrs B's daughter was admitted to hospital as a voluntary patient. While she was in hospital the mental welfare officer employed by the local health authority obtained an order under s 25 of the Mental Health Act 1959 for her compulsory admission to hospital and detention there for observation. The order expired on 8th May 1979. The doctor in charge of the daughter was of opinion that it was necessary to detain her in hospital for treatment and made out a report on the statutory form stating his reasons for thinking that she should remain in hospital. The mother, who was her 'nearest relative' within s 27[a] of the 1959 Act, refused to give her consent to an application under s 26[b] of that Act for the daughter's detention in hospital for treatment. Accordingly, the mental welfare officer applied for an order under s 52[c] of the 1959 Act that he be appointed to exercise the functions of the nearest relative of the daughter for the purpose of making the s 26 application on the ground that the mother had unreasonably objected, within s 52(3)(c), to an application for the daughter's admission to hospital for treatment under ss 26 and 27. For the purpose of s 26 a second medical examination of the daughter and a report were made by another doctor. At the hearing on 7th June 1979 of the s 52 application the solicitor acting for the local health authority produced the two medical reports and handed them to the mother's solicitor. The county court judge adjourned the application for a short time to give the mother's solicitor an opportunity of considering the reports. The mother's solicitor did not show the reports to the mother but told her that two doctors had recommended that her daughter be kept in hospital. Following the adjournment the county court judge ordered that the function of nearest relative be exercised by the local health authority. The mother appealed, contending (i) that the way that the county court judge had dealt with the medical reports did not comply with the requirement of the proviso to para (5) of CCR Ord 46, r 18[d], that the respondent be told 'the substance of any part of the report bearing on his fitness or conduct which the judge considers to be material to the manner in which the application should be dealt with', (ii) that the evidence tendered to the county court judge did not comply with s 26 or other statutory provisions in respect of the form and content of the medical reports and that the defects in the medical reports thereby vitiated the whole proceedings, and (iii) that for the purposes of making a s 52 application the mental health officer had to be in a position to make an immediate application under s 26.

Held – The appeal would be dismissed for the following reasons—
(i) The object of CCR Ord 46, r 18(5), was to give the respondent to an application

---

a   Section 27, so far as material, is set out at p 496 *e f*, post
b   Section 26, so far as material, is set out at p 496 *c*, post
c   Section 52, so far as material, is set out at p 496 *h j*, post
d   Rule 18(5) is set out at p 497 *e*, post

under s 52 of the 1959 Act an opportunity of knowing what was being alleged against
a him, and to comply with the requirement of the proviso to r 18(5), it was sufficient if a
report was handed to the respondent's legal adviser in circumstances where the legal
adviser could give advice and take instructions. It followed therefore that no objection
could be taken to the way that the reports had been dealt with at the county court
hearing (see p 498 *g* to *j*, p 499 *e j* and p 500 *a b g*, post).

b (ii) The object of an application under s 52 was to enable the provisions of s 26 of the
1959 Act to be brought into operation, and, until an application had been dealt with
under s 52, the mental welfare officer was not in a position to make an application under
s 26. It followed that if there were any defects for the purposes of s 26 in the form of the
medical reports tendered to the county court judge they were irrelevant for the purposes
of the s 52 application. The judge had to look at the reports for their medical content and
was not concerned with their statutory form; he could look at any evidence by any doctor
c for the purpose of making an order under s 52 dispensing with the consent of the nearest
relative for the purposes of an application under s 26 for compulsory admission and
detention of a patient for treatment in hospital. Accordingly, since the medical content
of the reports made it clear that the daughter did require compulsory admission and
detention in hospital, there was prima facie evidence before the county court judge on
which he could hold that the mother had been unreasonable in objecting to the making
d of an application under s 26 (see p 497 *g h*, p 499 *c* to *e* and *h j* and p 500 *a b g*, post).

Notes
For compulsory admission of patients to hospital for treatment, see 29 Halsbury's Laws
(3rd Edn) 504, para 953, for general provisions as to applications for admission for
observation or treatment, see ibid 515, para 974, and for appointment by the court of an
e acting nearest relative, see ibid 489, para 938.
   For the Mental Health Act 1959, ss 26, 27, 52, see 25 Halsbury's Statutes (3rd Edn) 63,
64, 90.

Appeal
This was an appeal by a mother against an order of his Honour Judge Forrester-Paton QC
f made on 7th June 1979 at the Whitby County Court sitting at Middlesbrough County
Court whereby he granted the application of a mental welfare officer that the functions
of the mother under Part IV of the Mental Health Act 1959 as nearest relative of her 24
year old daughter, a patient, should during the continuance in force of the order be
exercisable by the local health authority. The facts are set out in the judgment of Lawton
LJ.

g
Peter Duckworth for the mother.
William Gage for the mental welfare officer.

   LAWTON LJ delivered the first judgment at the request of Megaw LJ. This is an
appeal by Mrs B ('the mother') against an order made in the Whitby County Court,
h during a sitting at Middlesbrough County Court, by his Honour Judge Forrester-Paton
QC, whereby he ordered that the function of the nearest relative of the mother's daughter
should, during the continuance in force of the order, be exercisable by the local health
authority. The mother has submitted for a number of reasons that the order was
improperly made. The substance of her complaints, put before the court by her counsel,
really comes to this: before the respondent health authority could apply to the learned
j judge in the county court for an order in the terms which he granted, that authority
should have had 'all its tackle in order' (to adopt counsel's phrase) for the making of an
application under s 26 of the Mental Health Act 1959.
   It will be convenient if I start this judgment by referring to the relevant provisions of
the 1959 Act. That Act deals with mental disorders. The statutory definition of 'mental
disorder' is such as to include mental illness.˙ Under Part IV of the 1959 Act provision is

made for the 'compulsory admission to hospital and guardianship' (this case is not concerned with guardianship) of persons who are suffering from 'mental disorder' as *a* defined by the Act. Section 25 of the Act makes provision for the admission of patients for observation. No question arises in this case about the legality of an order made under s 25 for the admission of the daughter for observation.

Section 26 of the Act is concerned with compulsory admission for treatment. Before a patient may be admitted to hospital and detained for treatment, certain statutory provisions have to be complied with. It has to be shown that the patient is suffering from *b* mental disorder. It also has to be shown that the admission to and detention in hospital for treatment is necessary in the interests of the patient's health or safety or for the protection of other persons. Section 26 goes on in these terms, in sub-s (3):

> 'An application for admission for treatment shall be founded on the written recommendations in the prescribed form of two medical practitioners, including in each case a statement that in the opinion of the practitioner the conditions set out *c* in paragraphs (*a*) and (*b*) of subsection (2) of this section are complied with . . .'

Then the section goes on to provide what the recommendation 'shall include'. I do not think it necessary to deal with what the recommendation should include. The powers under s 26 depend on an application being made for the patient's admission to, and detention in, hospital for treatment. *d*

Section 27 of the Act says who can make an application. Subsection (1) provides as follows:

> 'Subject to the provisions of this section, an application for the admission of a patient for observation or for treatment may be made either by the nearest relative of the patient or by a mental welfare officer; and every such application shall be *e* addressed to the managers of the hospital to which admission is sought and shall specify the qualification of the applicant to make the application.'

Subsection (2) is as follows:

> 'An application for admission for treatment shall not be made by a mental welfare officer if the nearest relative of the patient has notified that officer, or the *f* local health authority by whom that officer is appointed, that he objects to the application being made . . .'

The mother notified the mental welfare officer that she objected to the application being made. It follows, therefore, that s 52 of the Act has to be considered, because s 52 gives jurisdiction to the county court to dispense with the consent of the nearest relative who is objecting to compulsory admission and detention for treatment. Subsection (1) *g* of s 52 provides as follows:

> 'The county court may, upon application made in accordance with the provisions of this section in respect of a patient, by order direct that the functions under this Part of this Act of the nearest relative of the patient shall, during the continuance in force of the order, be exercisable by the applicant, or by any other person specified *h* in the application, being a person who, in the opinion of the court, is a proper person to act as the patient's nearest relative and is willing to do so.'

Subsection (2) sets out who may make an application under s 52, and those who may make such an application include a mental welfare officer. Subsection (3) provides as follows: *j*

> 'An application for an order under this section may be made upon any of the following grounds, that is to say . . . (*c*) that the nearest relative of the patient unreasonably objects to the making of an application for admission for treatment . . . in respect of the patient . . .'

As I understand the structure of the 1959 Act in relation to the compulsory admission and detention for treatment of patients, it is this: once it becomes apparent that a particular person may require compulsory admission to and treatment in hospital, either the mental welfare officer or the nearest relative can consent to the making of an application. When an application is made, that application must comply with the provisions of s 26 of the Act. But before any question of complying with s 26 arises, the problem of consent has to be dealt with; and where (as in this case) the nearest relative objects, then the county court is empowered to make an order dispensing with the consent of the nearest relative.

That being the structure of the Act, the question now arises: on what evidence should the county court act when deciding whether the consent of the nearest relative should be dispensed with? The county court is not concerned with the making of an application under s 26: that is a matter for the appropriate authority. The county court judge is concerned with the question of dispensing with the consent of the nearest relative. The county court judge must have some evidence that compulsory admission to hospital and detention for treatment is necessary. What is that evidence to be?

The rule committee of the county court made provision for this problem. In 1960 a new order was added to the County Court Rules, namely Ord 46, r 18. This order was intended to settle the procedure for making applications to the county court under s 52 of the 1959 Act. Paragraph (5) of the rule provides as follows:

'On the hearing of the application the court may accept as *prima facie* evidence of the facts stated therein any report made by a medical practitioner and any report made in the course of his official duties by—(a) a probation officer, or (b) an officer of a local authority or of a voluntary organisation exercising statutory functions on behalf of a local authority, or (c) an officer of a hospital authority: Provided that the respondent shall be told the substance of any part of the report bearing on his fitness or conduct which the judge considers to be material to the manner in which the application should be dealt with.'

The following points arise with regard to that paragraph. First, the evidence is to be '*prima facie* evidence': the party opposing the application for dispensing with consent can call evidence in rebuttal. There is nothing conclusive about the evidence which is tendered in support of the application. Secondly, it is 'any report' which may be put in evidence, provided it is made by 'a medical practitioner' or is a report made by any other person specified in the rule. Paragraph (5) does not say that the report must be in any prescribed form. It does not say, as s 26 of the 1959 Act says, that the medical practitioner must be one who, in the words of s 28, is 'approved . . . by a local health authority', or (by a subsequent amendment) by the Secretary of State. It follows, therefore, that any evidence in a report made by a doctor can be looked at by the county court judge for the purposes of making an order dispensing with consent.

It is clear now, after we have had the benefit of counsel for the mental welfare officer's submissions, why this is so. Applications for compulsory admission to and detention in hospital for treatment often have to be made in an emergency. It is not always possible to obtain the opinions of medical practitioners approved by the Secretary of State or a local health authority. Therefore, *any* doctor can be called on for the purposes of supporting an application to dispense with consent in order to provide the necessary evidence for the county court. That is what happened in this case.

It is now necessary to set out the relevant facts. At the end of December 1978, the daughter became mentally ill. She had to be admitted to hospital. In February 1979, those in charge of her in that hospital (she was there as a voluntary patient) seem to have been of the opinion that she was well enough to be discharged to the care of her sister. On 4th April it was necessary to admit her to hospital again, still as a voluntary patient. For various reasons which it is not necessary to go into for the purposes of this judgment, the mental welfare officer employed by the local health authority, on 10th April thought it right to make an application for her compulsory admission to hospital and detention there for observation. Whether he obtained the consent of the mother we do not know; but no question arises with regard to the s 25 application. On 8th May the daughter's detention in hospital for observation came to an end, in the sense that she could no longer *a* be kept there compulsorily. But in the opinion of the doctor in charge of her, Dr Seymour-Shove, it was necessary to detain her in hospital for treatment. A few days before 8th May he had made out a report on a hospital statutory form known as Form 5A, setting out his reasons for thinking that she should remain in hospital. It was clear to those in charge of the daughter in the hospital that there was going to be difficulty about *b* getting the mother's consent to her being detained, the mother being her nearest relative. The mental welfare officer was authorised to make an application for compulsory admission and detention for treatment under s 26. As I have already recounted, for the purposes of s 26 examination by two doctors was necessary; and for the purposes of an application under s 26 the examination either had to be made by the doctors at the same time or within seven days of each other. A new doctor was called in *c* and he examined the daughter on 13th May, which was more than seven days after Dr Seymour-Shove had examined her.

The mental welfare officer, on or about 15th May, saw the mother and it was clear to him that the mother was not going to consent to her daughter being kept in hospital. As a result the mental welfare officer thought it necessary to apply to the county court for an order under s 52. The appropriate county court was Whitby County Court, but as *d* Whitby County Court only sits infrequently the application was in fact heard in the first place on 5th June at Scarborough County Court. At that time the mother was not legally represented. The judge seems to have thought that she should be given an opportunity of being legally represented, and he adjourned the mental welfare officer's application for hearing at a sitting of the Middlesbrough County Court on 7th June. On 7th June the mother was legally represented; her solicitor was in court to advise her and to conduct *e* the proceedings on her behalf. Up to 7th June the mother had not been shown either of the medical reports on which the mental welfare officer was basing his application for a s 26 order; but at the hearing on 7th June before his Honour Judge Forrester-Paton the solicitor acting for the local health authority produced the two reports made by Dr Seymour-Shove and the other psychiatrist and handed them to the solicitor representing the mother. Something seems to have been said to the judge, who suggested that the *f* solicitor representing the mother should have an opportunity of considering what was in the reports, and he adjourned the application for a short time. We have been told that the adjournment was for about five minutes. During that time, as appears from an affidavit which was produced today and which was put in with the consent of counsel appearing for the health authority, the solicitor acting for the mother did not show her the reports but told her that two doctors had recommended that her daughter should be *g* kept in hospital.

Complaint has been made to this court today that that way of dealing with the reports did not comply with the proviso to para (5) of CCR Ord 46, r 18. In my judgment it did comply with para (5) of that rule, and for this reason: it is clear that the object of para (5) is to give the respondent to a s 52 application an opportunity of knowing what is being alleged against him. The paragraph refers specifically to the 'part of the report bearing *h* on his fitness or conduct which the judge considers to be material in the manner in which the application should be dealt with'. If a report is handed to the legal adviser of the respondent to an application in circumstances where the legal adviser can give advice and take instructions, that seems to me to be enough to comply with the proviso to para (5). It follows that there is no substance in any complaint made about the way the reports were dealt with at the county court hearing.

I turn now to the way in which the mother, through her counsel, has put her case. *j* Counsel's submission was that before an application could be made to the county court under s 52 the applicant, in this case the mental welfare officer, had to have evidence which complied with the statutory provisions in s 26. He submitted that the evidence which was tendered to the judge did not comply with either s 26 or other statutory

provisions. He gave a number of reasons. One was that the medical examinations had
been more than seven days apart; that sufficient clinical detail was not set out in the
reports; that the reports did not specify, as s 26(3) says they should, why alternative
methods were not suitable for the patient. He also complained that, contrary to a
provision in the statutory rules governing the prescribed form of report, which are the
Mental Health (Hospital and Guardianship) Regulations 1960[1], s 4 of the 1959 Act had
not been printed on the Forms 5A used by the two psychiatrists. He said that these
defects in the medical reports before the county court judge vitiated the whole of the
proceedings, because it was reasonable for the mother to say that the provisions of the
1959 Act and in particular of s 26 had not been complied with. Indeed at one stage of his
argument counsel for the mother went so far as to suggest that if the reports put before
the county court judge did not comply with s 26 no valid application had been made to
the county court.

In my judgment, that puts the cart before the horse. The object of an application
under s 52 is to enable the provisions of s 26 to be brought into operation, and until an
application has been dealt with under s 52 the mental welfare officer is not in a position
to make an application under s 26. It follows, so it seems to me, that if there were any
defects for the purposes of s 26 in the form of the reports tendered to the county court
judge they were irrelevant for the purposes of the s 52 application. The county court
judge had to look at the reports for their medical content: he was not concerned with
their statutory form. The medical content of the two reports made it clear, in my
judgment, that the daughter did require compulsory admission to and detention for
treatment in hospital, and therefore the grounds put forward by the mother, through
her counsel, for objecting to the making of the s 52 application had no substance in them
and, on the evidence before the county court judge, she was unreasonable in objecting to
the making of an application under s 26.

Accordingly, I would dismiss the appeal.

BROWNE LJ. I agree that this appeal should be dismissed, for the reasons given by
Lawton LJ.

The crucial issue between the parties in this case seems to me to be this. Counsel for
the mother has said that for the purposes of s 52 an objection by a nearest relative cannot
be unreasonable unless at the time of the objection or at the time of the hearing the
mental welfare officer is in a position to make an immediate application under s 26.
That is, as counsel put it, that his tackle is in order for making such an application and,
in particular, that the medical recommendations are in the form which is proper for a
s 26 application. Counsel for the mental welfare officer, on the other hand, says that
what the court has to decide in a s 52 application is whether or not the nearest relative is
objecting unreasonably to the making of an application under s 26. The stage of making
a s 26 application has not yet been reached, and, he submits, whether or not the medical
reports are in the correct form to support a s 26 application if and when made is
irrelevant.

In my judgment there is no doubt that counsel for the mental welfare officer is right
in his submission. Lawton LJ has already stated the arguments in favour of this view,
and I need not repeat them. I am bound to say that it seems to me that, as a matter of
construction of the 1959 Act, counsel's submission is clearly right.

I agree also with Lawton LJ in what he said about the effect of CCR Ord 46, r 18(5).
The reports which were used in this case, even if they could be criticised on a s 26
application, were, on the s 52 application, '*prima facie* evidence of the facts stated therein'.
I also agree with Lawton LJ that the proviso to that rule was in this case complied with.

I express no opinion at all about the points raised by counsel for the mother as to the
form of these reports and whether or not they complied with the statutory requirements
applicable to a s 26 application. That question, it seems to me, is not before us in this

1   SI 1960 No 1241

appeal, though counsel for the mental welfare officer concedes that if this was a s 26 application these particular reports would not be in order because the examinations by the two doctors were more than seven days apart, contrary to s 28(1) of the 1959 Act.

For the reasons given by Lawton LJ, and the reasons I have tried to express myself, I entirely agree that this appeal should be dismissed.

MEGAW LJ. I agree with the conclusions expressed by Lawton and Browne LJJ, and with the reasons given by them for those conclusions.

I would add a word about the history of this matter before this court. It came before this court originally on Monday, 16th July 1979, when the mother appeared in person on a motion asking for leave to appeal out of time from the order made by Judge Forrester-Paton in the Middlesbrough County Court on 7th June. We did not on that occasion have the assistance of counsel instructed on behalf of the health authority. I make no criticism of that. On the hearing of the motion, the mother tried to put before us what were her complaints about the order that had been made. At her request, we looked at the bundle of correspondence which she had, including some of the documents which have been before us subsequently. We thought it right in the circumstances to adjourn the hearing of the application for leave to appeal out of time, and it was accordingly adjourned until the following Monday, 23rd July. On that occasion the mother had obtained legal representation. Counsel appeared on her behalf, instructed by solicitors who are not the solicitors who had represented her at the hearing in the Middlesbrough County Court. We also had the advantage on that occasion of counsel appearing instructed on behalf of the local health authority. All that we were concerned to deal with on that occasion was the question of leave to appeal. It was suggested then that it might well be that leave to appeal out of time was not required because it may be the matter was to be treated as being a final and not an interlocutory appeal. We granted leave to appeal if leave were necessary; and as it was obviously in the interests of all concerned that the appeal for which leave was thus given should be heard as as soon as possible we directed that it should be expedited, with the idea that it should be brought on in this court if possible today. I would like to pay tribute to counsel for the mother and the solicitors instructing him for the steps that they have taken urgently in that short period of time to enable the matter to be brought on today, and for the assistance that has been given to this court. In my view, counsel has said clearly and well everything that could possibly be said in support of this appeal. It is not through any fault of his or of his present instructing solicitors that the appeal in fact does not succeed.

I agree, as I say, with Lawton and Browne LJJ and with the reasons they have given why this appeal must be dismissed.

Appeal dismissed.

Solicitors: *Kenyon & Co*, Whitby (for the mother); *Colin Brown & Kidson*, Whitby (for the mental welfare officer).

Mary Rose Plummer   Barrister.

Grice v Needs and another

QUEEN'S BENCH DIVISION
LORD WIDGERY CJ AND LLOYD J
19th JUNE 1979

Value added tax – Penalty – Continuing penalty – Information laid before justices in respect of taxpayer's failure to make a return – Whether for calculating daily penalty taxpayer's failure continued to the date on which the information was laid or on which it was heard – Finance Act 1972, s 38(7) – Value Added Tax (General) Regulations 1975 (SI 1975 No 2204), reg 51.

On 9th March 1977 an information was laid before justices by the Customs and Excise Commissioners against the taxpayers that they, being registered for the purposes of value added tax as persons carrying on business in partnership, failed to comply with reg 51 of the Value Added Tax (General) Regulations 1975 by failing to furnish to the commissioners, not later than 31st January 1977, a return for the period from 1st June 1976 to 31st August 1976, contrary to the Finance Act 1972, s 38(7)[a]. The justices heard the information on 18th April 1977 and, having convicted the taxpayers, imposed against each of them a fine of £25. In addition they ordered each taxpayer to pay a penalty of £3 a day for the period from 31st January 1977 to the date on which the information was laid. The commissioners appealed contending that the taxpayers' failure to render a return had continued from 31st January 1977 to the date on which the information was heard and accordingly they were liable to a daily penalty of £10 in respect of each of the days until the date of hearing.

Held – There was no ground for the contention that the period over which the penalty imposed by s 38(7) of the 1972 Act of £10 for each day on which the failure continued stopped at the date the information was laid, since there was no link between the information and the penalty. By the time the matter came to be heard by the justices it would be known to all concerned that the default had continued until that date or, alternatively, had ceased at a known earlier date, so that the obligation up to the date of the hearing could be assessed with precision. The appeal would therefore be allowed, and the matter remitted to the justices for reconsideration of the sentence (see p 503 e to h, post).

Notes
For the duty to furnish returns for value added tax and for offences in connection with the furnishing of information, see 12 Halsbury's Laws (4th Edn) paras 952, 969.

For the Finance Act 1972, s 38, see 42 Halsbury's Statutes (3rd Edn) 195.

As from 1st January 1978 reg 51 of the Value Added Tax (General) Regulations 1975 has been replaced by reg 51 of the Value Added Tax (General) Regulations 1977 (SI 1977 No 1759).

Case cited
Airey v Smith [1907] 2 KB 273, DC.

Case stated
The Customs and Excise Commissioners appealed by way of case stated by the justices for the county of Warwick, acting in and for the petty sessional division of Nuneaton, in respect of their adjudication as a magistrates' court sitting at the Law Courts, Nuneaton, on 18th April 1977.

On 9th March 1977 an information was preferred by the commissioners against the

---

a   Section 38(7) is set out at p 502 j to p 503 a, post

taxpayers, Peter John Needs and Alfred George Davies Hale, that they, carrying on business at Anvil Precision Engineering Co, Nuneaton, being registered under the *a* Finance Act 1972 for the purposes of value added tax as persons carrying on a business in partnership, failed to comply with reg 51 of the Value Added Tax (General) Regulations 1975, as amended by reg 6 of the Value Added Tax (General) (Amendment) Regulations 1976, by failing to furnish to the Controller, Customs and Excise, Value Added Tax Central Unit, Southend-on-Sea, not later than 31st January 1977, a return for the period from 1st June 1976 to 31st August 1976 in the form prescribed by the said regulations, *b* contrary to s 38(7) of the Finance Act 1972. The justices heard the information on 18th April 1977. Both taxpayers attended at the hearing and pleas of guilty were tendered.

It was contended by the commissioners that the failure to render a return had continued from 31st January 1977 to 18th April 1977 and thus was punishable by a maximum penalty of £100 plus a daily penalty of £10 in respect of each of the continuing days. They did not quote any authority in support of that argument. The *c* taxpayers were not legally represented and made no representations. The justices were of the opinion that they should limit any such daily penalty to the period between 31st January 1977 and the date on which the information was laid, namely 9th March 1977 and that they should not impose any penalty in respect of any period after 9th March 1977 because they felt that an information should not relate to a continuing failure which had not then taken place. Accordingly they imposed fines against each taxpayer *d* of £25 and in addition ordered each taxpayer to pay a daily penalty of £3 for the relevant period of 36 days.

The question for the opinion of the High Court was whether the justices were right in law in limiting the period for the calculation of the daily penalty to the date on which the information was laid.

David Latham and *Valerie Pearlman* for the Crown.   *e*
The taxpayers did not appear.

LORD WIDGERY CJ. This is an appeal by case stated by justices for the County of Warwick acting in and for the petty sessional division of Nuneaton in respect of their adjudication as a magistrates' court sitting at the Law Courts, Nuneaton on 18th April *f* 1977.

On that date the justices had before them an information preferred by the appellant, who is an officer of Customs and Excise, alleging that the taxpayers, who were Anvil Precision Engineering Co, being registered under the Finance Act 1972 for the purposes of value added tax as persons carrying on a business in partnership failed to comply with reg 51 of the Value Added Tax (General) Regulations 1975 as amended by reg 6 of the *g* Value Added Tax (General) (Amendment) Regulations 1976 by failing to furnish to the Controller of Customs and Excise, Value Added Tax Central Unit, Southend-on-Sea not later than 31st January 1977 a return for the period from 1st June 1976 until 31st August 1976 in the form prescribed by the regulations.

What all that amounted to was that the taxpayers were carrying on business in circumstances which made them responsible for accounting for value added tax in *h* certain circumstances, and as part of that operation they were required to make a return disclosing how much they were prepared to account for. They committed the offence of failing to make the return as required, and they were prosecuted and perfectly properly convicted because they had broken the terms of the law in that regard.

When the question arose as to what the penalty might be and how much they might be fined in respect of this offence, one had to go and look at the terms of the statute under *j* which the obligation to make the return is created. It is the Finance Act 1972, and the relevant part is to be found in s 38(7). It says this:

'If any person fails to comply with any requirement imposed under section 34 or 35 of this Act or any regulations or rules made under this Part of this Act, he shall be liable to a penalty of £100 together with a penalty of £10 for each day on which the failure continues.'

It became necessary to work out what the maximum fine might be according to that formula because this is the subsection under which the taxpayers were prosecuted. There is no great difficulty about the penalty of £100. That can be put into the scale easily enough. When one comes to the second element of the penalty, which is a maximum of £10 for each day on which the failure continues, there again it was not too difficult to specify the initial date, the date on which the initial failure to produce the return was committed.

But what gave rise to some problem was, having ascertained the date on which the £10 a day fine began to accrue, one had to find another date on which it was to stop, in other words, a date beyond which the justices could not impose a penalty. A difference of opinion arose here because the Customs and Excise people said that the last day of the £10 a day was the date of the hearing, whereas it was contended by the taxpayers that the last day should be the date of the information.

We have got to decide which of those contentions is right. We have been taken by counsel for the commissioners into the legislation which lies behind this section, and we came out of it again as fast as we could because it was quite clear we were not going to gain any advantage by further researches there and the language is very uncomfortable and complicated.

I am quite satisfied that one has to go back to the section itself imposing the penalty. It is s 38 of the 1972 Act. Having done that, I think we must ask ourselves what the words of the subsection mean, given their ordinary meaning.

I do not think that it could possibly be right that the period over which the £10 a day accrues stops at the date of the information, because there is no link, as counsel for the commissioners submits, between the information and penalty. By the time the matter comes before the justices everybody knows at least that the default has continued up to that date, or, alternatively, knows an earlier date when it ceased, and the obligation up to the date of the hearing can be assessed with precision. That seems to me to be the intention of Parliament in this case.

I would, therefore, hold that in calculating the £10 a day penalty under s 38(7) the period ends with the date of the hearing, if it has not been terminated earlier with a compliance with the regulations.

LLOYD J. I agree. Counsel for the commissioners put the matter, if I may say so, very clearly when he said that the purpose of the information in a case such as this is to define the offence and not the penalty.

The language of s 38(7) of the Finance Act 1972 is, in my judgment, clear and the justices were wrong to confine their view to the period up to the date of the information.

The matter, therefore, will have to be remitted to the justices for reconsideration of the sentence. But I, for my part, would emphasise that they are not obliged to impose a penalty for the balance of the period at the same rate or indeed at any rate at all. The matter will be entirely for them.

Appeal allowed. Case remitted to justices.

Solicitors: *Solicitor for the Customs and Excise.*

Lea Josse   Barrister.

Old Grovebury Manor Farm Ltd v W Seymour Plant Sales & Hire Ltd and another (No 2)

COURT OF APPEAL, CIVIL DIVISION
LORD RUSSELL OF KILLOWEN AND BROWNE LJ
21st JUNE 1979

Landlord and tenant – Forfeiture of lease – Notice of breach – Persons to be served with notice – Assignment of lease – Assignment in breach of covenant not to assign without lessor's consent – Whether notice should be served on original lessee or on assignee – Law of Property Act 1925, s 146.

Where a lessee assigns the remainder of the term of his lease in breach of a covenant not to assign without the consent of the lessor, the assignment, though a breach of covenant, is an effective assignment, and any notice of forfeiture of the lease under s 146[a] of the Law of Property Act 1925 should be addressed to or served on the assignee, who is the person concerned to avoid forfeiture, and not on the original lessee, who, though liable to fulfil the covenants after assignment, is no longer the tenant or lessee of the lessor (see p 505 *e* and *g* to p 506 *b d e* and *j* to p 507 *a c* and *d*, post).

Notes

For the service of notice as a condition of re-entry, see 23 Halsbury's Laws (3rd Edn) 674–677, paras 1400–1402, and for cases on the subject, see 31(2) Digest (Reissue) 826–827, 6856–6862.

For the Law of Property Act 1925, s 146, see 27 Halsbury's Statutes (3rd Edn) 563.

Cases referred to in judgments

Church Comrs for England v Kanda [1957] 2 All ER 815, sub nom *Kanda v Church Comrs for England* [1958] 1 QB 332, [1957] 3 WLR 353, CA, 31(2) Digest (Reissue) 612, 4949.

Church Comrs for England v Ve-Ri-Best Manufacturing Co Ltd [1956] 3 All ER 777, [1957] 1 QB 238, [1956] 3 WLR 990, 31(2) Digest (Reissue) 831, 6887.

Cusack-Smith v Gold [1958] 2 All ER 361, [1958] 1 WLR 611, 31(2) Digest (Reissue) 631, 5153.

Dudley and District Benefit Building Society v Emerson [1949] 2 All ER 252, [1949] Ch 707, [1949] LJR 1441, CA, 31(2) Digest (Reissue) 978, 7865.

Cases also cited

Gentle v Faulkner [1900] 2 QB 267, CA.
Horsey Estate Ltd v Steiger [1899] 2 QB 79, [1895–9] All ER Rep 515, CA.
Regis Property Co Ltd v Dudley [1958] 3 All ER 491, [1959] AC 370, HL.
Scala House and District Property Co Ltd v Forbes [1973] 3 All ER 308, [1974] QB 575, CA.

---

[a] Section 146, so far as material, provides:

'(1) A right of re-entry or forfeiture under any proviso or stipulation in a lease for a breach of any covenant or condition in the lease shall not be enforceable, by action or otherwise, unless and until the lessor serves on the lessee a notice—(*a*) specifying the particular breach complained of; and (*b*) if the breach is capable of remedy, requiring the lessee to remedy the breach; and (*c*) in any case, requiring the lessee to make compensation in money for the breach; and the lessee fails, within a reasonable time thereafter, to remedy the breach, if it is capable of remedy, and to make reasonable compensation in money, to the satisfaction of the lessor, for the breach . . .

'(5) For the purposes of this section . . . "Lessee" includes an original or derivative under-lessee, and the persons deriving title under a lessee; also a grantee under any such grant as aforesaid and the persons deriving title under him . . .'

Interlocutory appeal

a The plaintiffs, Old Grovebury Manor Farm Ltd, appealed against the judgment of Walton J given on a preliminary issue at the trial of an action on 24th January 1979 whereby he decided that a notice under s 146 of the Law of Property Act 1925 should have been served on the first defendant, W Seymour Plant Sales & Hire Ltd, and not on the second defendant, James Brian Armstrong, the original lessee under a lease dated 3rd January 1975 of property known as Lee Cottage Motors, Leighton Buzzard Road,

b Billington in the county of Bedford, between the plaintiff and the second defendant, of which the second defendant assigned on 23rd September 1976 the remainder of his term to the first defendant. The facts are set out in the judgment of Lord Russell of Killowen.

Mark Myers QC and *Alaric Dalziel* for the plaintiffs.
John Waite QC and *Michael Kennedy* for the defendants.

c

LORD RUSSELL OF KILLOWEN. This is an interlocutory appeal from Walton J which raises a short point under s 146 of the Law of Property Act 1925. The plaintiffs granted a lease of certain business premises to the second defendant in 1975 for three years. Under that lease there was a covenant by the lessee, the second defendant, in a common form that he would not, inter alia, assign the term of the lease without the

d written consent of the lessor, that consent not to be unreasonably withheld in the case of a respectable and responsible tenant.

The point for the purposes of the preliminary question can be shortly stated. The second defendant, without the lessor's consent, on 23rd September 1976 executed an assignment of the remainder of the term to the first defendant. Although that was without the consent of the plaintiff, it is, in my judgment, perfectly plain that that assignment operated to vest the remainder of the term in the first defendant. The fact

e that it was done by the second defendant in breach of his covenant not to do it cannot in any way affect that situation as a matter of law. From 23rd September, therefore, the owner of the term, whose relationship by privity of estate with the plaintiff was one of lessor and lessee, became the first defendant.

A notice was served, the terms of which I need not refer to, on 1st October 1976,

f purporting to be a notice under s 146(1) of the 1925 Act. That section requires that before any proceedings are launched for forfeiting the term on the ground of breach of covenant such a notice should be served. That notice was served on the second defendant; and the one short point is whether it is correct to hold, as the learned judge held, that the notice should have been served on the first defendant, namely the assignee.

When you have a situation such as this where a lease is liable to be forfeited, s 146

g makes provision for a notice to be served before a writ is issued by the lessor asking for forfeiture. If at the end of the day in those proceedings forfeiture is ordered, or rather no relief from forfeiture is granted, then the term will have been terminated with effect from the issue of the writ (whether it is 'issue' or 'service' matters not in this case). The person who is interested and concerned whether the term should be forfeited or not is clearly the person to whom the term has been assigned; and, as I have said, and I agree

h with the learned judge, it is perfectly clear that this term was assigned to the first defendant; it ceased to be vested in the second defendant; it became vested in the first defendant.

The first defendant is the person who is concerned to avoid forfeiture; and, quite apart from the language used in s 146 itself, one would have expected the notice under s 146(1) to be addressed to the person who has that concern and not to the person (the original

j lessee) in whom the term is no longer vested. He remains, of course, liable to fulfil the covenants under the lease after the assignment, but he is no longer the tenant or lessee of the lessor. When we come to look at the use of the word 'lessee' in s 146, this seems to me to be undeniable. I will not read the section in detail, but sub-s (1) requires the notice to be served on 'the lessee'. Now the assignee is the person who is interested in getting the notice so that he can make up his mind what, if anything, he can do about avoiding the forfeiture. Under sub-s (2) the lessee may apply to the court for relief. Who is interested in that? The person who is interested in that is the assignee and not the original *a* lessee. When you come to sub-s (5), that provides under para (*b*) that 'lessee' includes the person deriving title under the lessee. It appears to me to be absolutely clear that an assignee in these circumstances is within the definition of 'lessee'. I am unable to fault the view of the learned judge that the notice in this case should have been addressed to and served on the first defendant; and it was not. He concluded as a preliminary point that therefore the issue of the writ was premature because no proper notice had been *b* served as required by s 146.

It is, I think, at the heart of the argument of counsel for the plaintiff that somehow this was not a valid assignment. He said, 'Well; it is effective and valid as between the assignor and assignee but not as between the lessor and the original lessee'. I am afraid that I am wholly unable to accept that. It is the fact, of course, that the assignment was in breach of covenant, but all that means is that there is an occasion offered to the lessor *c* to forfeit the lease and put an end to it. It is of the nature of the creation of a term of years that the owner of the term is capable of dealing with it as a piece of property. The only way that that can be prevented or hampered is by virtue of the common form clause that he covenants not to do it and there may be a forfeiture of the term if he does it. But I stress 'if he does it'; and unless he has effectively assigned the term to the assignee there has been no breach of the covenant not to assign. *d*

I am bound to say that, having listened, I hope carefully, to counsel's argument for the plaintiffs, there is at the core of his argument some suggestion in some shape or form that the assignment was imperfect. That I do not accept. The assignment was in breach of covenant, but it was an effective assignment notwithstanding the fact that the very transaction put the term at risk of forfeiture.

We were referred to one or two cases which did not appear to me to conclude the *e* matter, although three of them rather suggested to my mind that the judge was right in saying that it was the assignee to whom the notice should be addressed or on whom the notice should be served in one way or another and not the assignor. Without going into detail, we were referred to *Church Comrs for England v Kanda*[1]. That was, in fact, a breach of a repairing covenant and there was no vice in the assignment, and I use the word 'vice' in a very general way. But the general implication, I think, in that case was that if after *f* assignment there were a notice it should be served on the assignee. Similarly there was *Church Comrs for England v Ve-Ri-Best Manufacturing Co Ltd*[2] by Lord Goddard CJ; and also *Cusack-Smith v Gold*[3], a decision of Pilcher J in which he stated plainly that the person who has assigned is not entitled to receive a s 146 notice. Therefore the person on whom the notice should be served was the assignee. That was a case of a disrepair breach of covenant and not a case of an assignment in breach of covenant. But the tendency in all *g* those three cases is towards (although I do not think they are conclusive on the point) the view formed by Walton J, and which I prefer.

Another case which was referred to was *Dudley and District Benefit Building Society v Emerson*[4], but that, as was said by counsel for the plaintiffs, seems to be somewhat analogous and does not, I think, help him at all. That was a case of a lease by a mortgagor not binding on the paramount title of the mortgagee; and it was said[5], and I think *h* correctly said, that the mortgagor had not such an estate or interest as enabled him to grant the tenancy or the lease. Here there is no doubt at all that the second defendant had such an estate or interest as enabled him to assign the term. So I do not think that helps.

So in the end it seems to me that it is what one would expect from the general purpose of s 146, which was described as affording a cooling off period during which the person

j

1　[1957] 2 All ER 815, [1958] 1 QB 332
2　[1956] 3 All ER 777, [1957] 1 QB 238
3　[1958] 2 All ER 361, [1958] 1 WLR 611
4　[1949] 2 All ER 252, [1949] Ch 707
5　[1949] 2 All ER 252 at 255, [1949] Ch 707 at 714 per Evershed MR

a at risk of forfeiture can consider his position and see what offer he can make to prevent forfeiture; and also, from the details of the language, the definition of 'lessee', it seems to me really quite plain that the notice under sub-s (1) in this case was required to be served not on the second defendant but on the first defendant. In those circumstances, I am of opinion that this appeal has failed and should be dismissed.

What the ultimate outcome will be, of course, I do not know. It is taken as a preliminary point, and it may be, like so many preliminary points of law, that in the end b it will not have done very much good, because I should think it likely that the plaintiff can start again and in the end the only effect will be something to do with costs. Then the real nub of the battle, when one gets down to the real nub of the battle, ranges over a fairly wide field, as can be seen by anybody who has read the pleadings and the counterclaim in this matter. But for the time being I find myself only able to agree with the learned judge that the proceedings claiming forfeiture are premature because the c proper notice required by s 146 has not been served.

I would therefore dismiss the appeal.

BROWNE LJ. I agree that this appeal should be dismissed for the reasons given by Lord Russell. I agree so entirely with those reasons that I do not think there is anything that I can usefully add.

d
Appeal dismissed.

Solicitors: *Wilkins & Son*, Aylesbury (for the plaintiffs); *Neve, Son & Co*, Luton (for the defendants).

e
Frances Rustin   Barrister.

Prudential Assurance Co Ltd v Newman Industries Ltd and others

f
CHANCERY DIVISION
VINELOTT J
14th, 15th, 18th, 19th, 20th, 21st, 22nd, 25th, 26th, 27th, 28th JUNE 1979

Practice – Parties – Representative proceedings – Action in tort – Suit by minority shareholder g on behalf of itself and other shareholders – Shareholder seeking declaration of entitlement to damages for conspiracy against directors of company and seeking damages – Whether jurisdiction to entertain representative action where cause of action of each member of class a separate cause in tort for which proof of damage necessary – Whether court should exercise discretion to make representation order.

h A company ('Newman') proposed to acquire the assets of another company. Newman issued a circular to its shareholders, signed by the chairman, explaining the proposed transaction, and at a general meeting of Newman a majority of its shareholders passed a resolution approving the transaction. The plaintiff, a company which was a minority shareholder in Newman, voted against the resolution. It brought an action claiming, inter alia, damages for conspiracy against the defendants, the chairman and vice-j chairman, in respect of the transaction, alleging that the circular was tricky, misleading and contained statements which the defendants could not honestly have believed and further alleging misconduct on the part of the defendants as directors of Newman. The action as originally framed was in a form appropriate to a derivative action by the plaintiff as a minority shareholder in Newman claiming damages on behalf of Newman. It was also framed to entitle the plaintiff to bring a personal claim for damages against the defendants. The plaintiff proposed an amendment to the writ and statement of claim to enable it to bring a representative action on behalf of the shareholders of Newman at the date the resolution was passed, seeking (i) on behalf of such shareholders who had suffered damage as a result of the passing of the resolution, a declaration that they were entitled to damages for conspiracy from the defendants and (ii) damages on their behalf. The defendants contended that the court had no jurisdiction to entertain a representative action where the cause of action of each member of the class purported to be represented was a separate cause founded in tort in respect of which proof of damage was a necessary ingredient, or alternatively, if there was jurisdiction to order a representative action, the court in its discretion ought not to accede to the plaintiff's application to amend.

Held – (1) The court had jurisdiction to entertain a representative action by a plaintiff suing on behalf of a class where the cause of action of the plaintiff and each member of the class was alleged to be a separate cause of action in tort, provided that (i) an order for a representative action would not have the effect either of conferring on any member of the class a right he could not have claimed in a separate action, or of barring a defence which the defendant could have raised in such a separate action; for that reason, therefore, a plaintiff in his representative capacity would normally be able to obtain only declaratory relief; (ii) the members of the class shared an interest which was common to all of them; therefore, there had to be a common ingredient in the cause of action of each member (which was satisfied in the instant case); and (iii) the court was satisfied that it was for the benefit of the class that the plaintiff be permitted to sue in a representative capacity; therefore, the court had to be satisfied that the issues common to the members of the class would be decided after full discovery and in the light of all the evidence capable of being adduced in favour of the claim (see p 513 *f*, p 517 *g h* and p 520 *a* to *e*, post); *Taff Vale Railway Co v Amalgamated Society of Railway Servants* [1901] AC 426 applied; *Markt & Co Ltd v Knight Steamship Co* [1910] 2 KB 1021 and *Lord Churchill v Whetnall* (1918) 87 LJ Ch 524 distinguished; *J Bollinger v Costa Brava Wine Co Ltd (No 2)* [1961] 1 All ER 561 and *HP Bulmer and Showerings Ltd v J Bollinger SA* [1978] RPC 79 considered; dictum of Lindley LJ in *Temperton v Russell* [1893] 1 QB at 438 not followed.

(2) The court in the exercise of its discretion would allow the proposed amendments in principle, because (i) to allow the plaintiff to sue in a representative capacity would not enlarge the limitation period available to members of the class represented for they would still have to bring their own actions to establish damage within six years from the date when the cause of action accrued, and the only effect of an order in favour of the plaintiff in its representative capacity would be that the issues covered by that order would be res judicata between members of the class and the defendants; (ii) since allegations of misconduct and conspiracy on the part of the defendants had been made in the statement of claim as originally framed, to allow the plaintiff to amend the action to sue in a representative capacity would not add to the action numberless claims in fraud, but would merely allow a common element (ie the allegations of misconduct and conspiracy) in the causes of action of members of the class to be established in one representative action; and (iii) it was not a valid objection that, had the claim originally been formulated as a representative action, the defendants would have been able to adduce evidence that no member of the class had suffered damage, because the court could not make an order for damages in the representative action and accordingly the defendants would not have been entitled to adduce such evidence (see p 520 *g* to p 521 *e* and *h*, post).

Notes

For representative parties and when representative actions may be brought, see 7 Halsbury's Laws (4th Edn) paras 771–772, and for cases on representative proceedings in general, see 50 Digest (Repl) 465–470, 1603–1637.

Cases referred to in judgment

a   *Bedford (Duke) v Ellis* [1901] AC 1, [1900–3] All ER Rep 694, 70 LJ Ch 102, 83 LT 686, HL, 50 Digest (Repl) 466, *1605*.

Bollinger (J) v Costa Brava Wine Co Ltd [1959] 3 All ER 800, [1960] Ch 262, [1959] 3 WLR 966, [1960] RPC 16, 46 Digest (Repl) 227, *1485*.

Bollinger (J) v Costa Brava Wine Co Ltd (No 2) [1961] 1 All ER 561, [1961] 1 WLR 277, [1961] RPC 116, 46 Digest (Repl) 240, *1560*.

b   *Bulmer (HP) Ltd and Showerings Ltd v J Bollinger SA* [1978] RPC 79, CA.

Churchill (Lord) v Whetnall, Lord Aberconway v Whetnall (1918) 87 LJ Ch 524, 119 LT 34, 50 Digest (Repl) 469, *1634*.

Jones v Cory Brothers & Co Ltd, Thomas v Great Mountain Collieries Co (1921) 56 L Jo 302, 152 LT Jo 70, CA, 50 Digest (Repl) 466, *1609*.

Markt & Co Ltd v Knight Steamship Co Ltd, Sale & Frazar v Knight Steamship Co Ltd [1910]
c   2 KB 1021, 79 LJKB 939, 103 LT 369, 11 Asp MLC 460, CA, 50 Digest (Repl) 465, *1063*.

Taff Vale Railway Co v Amalgamated Society of Railway Servants [1901] AC 426, 70 LJKB 905, 85 LT 147, HL, 51 Digest (Repl) 753, *3362*.

Temperton v Russell [1893] 1 QB 435, 62 LJQB 300, 68 LT 425, CA, 50 Digest (Repl) 466, *1604*.

d

Application to amend writ and statement of claim

By a take-over transaction in 1975 the first defendant, Newman Industries Ltd ('Newman'), acquired substantially all the assets of the fourth defendant, Thomas Poole & Gladstone China Ltd ('TPG'), except its shareholding in Newman, and undertook certain liabilities of TPG, for a 'net' consideration (in addition to the liabilities assumed)
e   of £325,000. The second and third defendants, Alan Frank Bartlett and John Knox Laughton, were at all material times repectively chairman and chief executive of Newman and vice-chairman of Newman, and were also, respectively, chairman and vice-chairman of, and shareholders in, TPG. Because of their interest in TPG the agreement embodying the transaction was made conditional on the approval in general meeting of Newman and TPG. Furthermore, in accordance with Stock Exchange regulations and
f   practice a circular, signed by the second defendant, was issued by Newman to all its shareholders explaining and justifying the agreement. A resolution to approve the agreement was put to the vote at an extraordinary general meeting of Newman held on or about 29th July 1975. The plaintiff, the Prudential Assurance Co Ltd, a minority shareholder in Newman, opposed the resolution but on a poll it was approved. By a writ and statement of claim dated 9th January 1976 the plaintiff suing 'on behalf of themselves
g   and all the other shareholders' of Newman, other than the second defendant and TPG, alleged that the circular issued by Newman was tricky and misleading and contained statements which the second and third defendants could not honestly have believed to be true, and sought, against Newman and TPG, rescission of the agreement or alternatively damages in lieu of rescission, and against the second and third defendants (i) damages for breach of their fiduciary duty to Newman, and (ii) further or in the alternative, damages
h   for conspiracy. The plaintiff decided not to pursue the claim for rescission. On a summons taken out by the second and third defendants for an order that the question whether the plaintiff was entitled to maintain the action against them on the basis that it was a derivative one, ie one by a minority shareholder claiming relief on behalf of a company (Newman), be determined as a preliminary issue Vinelott J on 18th June 1979 held that a proper analysis of the statement of claim showed that the action against the
j   second and third defendants was not purely a derivative one but was also framed as a personal claim by the plaintiff for redress as a shareholder in Newman. Moreover, on a fair reading of the statement of claim the alleged conspiracy asserted was a conspiracy to injure each of the shareholders in Newman. Since it appeared to the court that the evidence on the personal claim would cover the same ground as the evidence on the derivative claim, the judge held that justice and convenience required that the evidence

be heard before the preliminary issue was determined, and dismissed the second and third defendants' application. The judgment left open whether the plaintiff could pursue its claim against the second and third defendants in a representative capacity, on behalf of the shareholders in Newman at the date of the resolution approving the take-over agreement, and if so whether the statement of claim required amendment. Subsequently the plaintiff sought to amend the writ and statement of claim in the action in order to pursue the claim for damages for conspiracy against the second and third defendants in a representative capacity on behalf of the shareholders in Newman at the date of the resolution. The second and third defendants contended that the court had no jurisdiction to make the amendments sought because the cause of action of each member of the class represented by the plaintiff was a separate cause in tort in which proof of damage was a necessary ingredient, or, alternatively, that if the court had jurisdiction it ought not in its discretion to allow the amendments. The amendments sought by the plaintiff are set out in the judgment.

Leonard Caplan QC, Peter Curry QC and *Philip Heslop* for the plaintiff.
Ian Edwards-Jones QC and *Robert Reid* for Newman.
Richard Scott QC, Alan Sebestyen and *Judith Jackson* for the second and third defendants.
David Lowe for TPG.

Cur adv vult

28th June. **VINELOTT J** read the following judgment: I have already given an interlocutory judgment at an earlier stage of these proceedings dismissing an application by the second and third defendants asking that there should be tried, as a preliminary issue, the question whether the plaintiff, as a minority shareholder in the first defendant, is entitled to bring a derivative action for the recovery by the first defendant of damages or equitable compensation from the second, third and fourth defendants. The facts relevant to the determination of the question now before me are sufficiently set out in that earlier judgment and I need not repeat them.

The question which I now have to decide arises out of an application by the plaintiff to amend the writ of summons and the statement of claim. The relevant amendments are as follows. In the title to the existing statement of claim the plaintiff is expressed to sue 'on behalf of [itself] and all the other shareholders of the First Defendant other than the Second and Fourth Defendants'. The relief prayed in the statement of claim includes a paragraph in these terms: '6. As against the Second and Third Defendants, Bartlett and Laughton—(i) damages for breach of duty and (ii) further or in the alternative damages for conspiracy.'

The proposed amendments, as modified in the course of argument, are as follows. First in the title to the proceedings the following words are substituted for those I have already cited:

'((i) in its personal capacity; and/or (ii) on behalf of [itself] and all the other shareholders of the First Defendant other than the Second and Fourth Defendants; and/or (iii) on behalf of all the shareholders of the First Defendant on 29th July 1975 who, like the Plaintiff, have suffered damage and are entitled to damages).'

Secondly, para 6 is expanded to read as follows:

'As against the Second and Third Defendants, Bartlett and Laughton: (i) [the plaintiff] in its personal capacity, as a shareholder in Newman [seeks the following]: (a) a declaration that the Plaintiff in its capacity as a shareholder in Newman is entitled to damages against the Defendants Bartlett and Laughton for conspiracy; and (b) damages for conspiracy (ii) [the plaintiff] in its personal capacity as a shareholder in Newman and on behalf of itself and all other shareholders in Newman who, like the plaintiff, have suffered damage, [seeks] a declaration that the

Plaintiff in its personal capacity as a shareholder in Newman and on behalf of itself and all other shareholders in Newman who like the Plaintiff have suffered damage are entitled to damages against the defendants Bartlett and Laughton for conspiracy; (iii) [the plaintiff] on behalf of itself and all other shareholders of the First Defendant other than the Second and Fourth Defendants, [seeks] damages . . . for conspiracy and/or breach of fiduciary duty.'

It is conceded by counsel for the plaintiff that the description of the capacity of the plaintiff in the title to the proceedings as originally framed, whilst leaving it open to the plaintiff to pursue a personal claim for damages for the tort of conspiracy against the second and third defendants, is in the form appropriate to a derivative action, that is, to an action by a minority shareholder claiming relief on behalf of a company. The purpose of the proposed amendment to the title to the proceedings is to found the declaration in para 6(ii) of the prayer to the statement of claim, that is, a declaration on behalf of shareholders of the first defendant as at the date on which the relevant resolution was passed that those who have suffered damage as a result of the passing of the resolution are entitled to recover damages from the second and third defendants for conspiracy.

The first objection made by counsel for the second and third defendants is that the court has no jurisdiction to make a representative order in a case where, as here, the cause of action of each member of the class is a separate cause of action founded on tort in which proof of damage is a necessary ingredient. Alternatively it is said that if the court has jurisdiction to entertain a representative action in such a case the application to amend the statement of claim should not be allowed in the present case at this stage of the proceedings.

Jurisdiction

RSC Ord 15, r 12(1) reads as follows:

'Where numerous persons have the same interest in any proceedings, not being such proceedings as are mentioned in Rule 13, the proceedings may be begun, and, unless the court otherwise orders, continued, by or against any one or more of them as representing all or as representing all except one or more of them.'

This current rule was introduced by the Rules of the Supreme Court (Revision) 1962[1]. It does not, as I see it, differ in any material respect from r 10 of the Rules of Procedure scheduled to the Supreme Court of Judicature Act 1873, which is in the following terms:

'Where there are numerous parties having the same interest in one action, one or more of such parties may sue or be sued, or may be authorised by the Court to defend in such action, on behalf or for the benefit of all parties so interested.'

That rule remained in force, as RSC Ord 16, r 9, until it was replaced by the current Ord 15, r 12(1).

Before the passing of the 1873 Act, the common law courts had no power to entertain an action by a representative plaintiff, or to entertain an action against a representative defendant. It was otherwise in the courts of Chancery. The position of the courts of Chancery was explained by Lord Macnaghten in *Duke of Bedford v Ellis*[2] in the following terms:

'The old rule in the Court of Chancery was very simple and perfectly well understood. Under the old practice the Court required the presence of all parties interested in the matter in suit, in order that a final end might be made of the controversy. But when the parties were so numerous that you never could "come at justice," to use an expression in one of the older cases, if everybody interested was made a party, the rule was not allowed to stand in the way. It was originally a rule

---

1 SI 1962 No 2145
2 [1901] AC 1 at 8, [1900–3] All ER Rep 694 at 697

of convenience: for the sake of convenience it was relaxed. Given a common interest and a common grievance, a representative suit was in order if the relief sought was in its nature beneficial to all whom the plaintiff proposed to represent.'

By the 1873 Act, s 16, the jurisdiction of the superior courts was transferred to the new High Court of Justice. Section 23 provided as follows:

'The jurisdiction by this Act transferred to the said High Court of Justice and the said Court of Appeal respectively shall be exercised (so far as regards procedure and practice) in the manner provided by this Act, or by such Rules and Orders of Court as may be made pursuant to this Act; and where no special provision is contained in this Act or in any such Rules or Orders of Court with reference thereto, it shall be exercised as nearly as may be in the same manner as the same might have been exercised by the respective Courts from which such jurisdiction shall have been transferred, or by any of such Courts.'

The purpose of r 10 was to make the jurisdiction and practice of the old Courts of Chancery permitting, in appropriate cases, proceedings to be commenced by representative plaintiffs or against representative defendants applicable to all proceedings in any division of the High Court. As some proceedings in the High Court would inevitably be proceedings which before the Act could only have been commenced in the common law courts the principles under which representative actions were permitted were necessarily extended into a new field where the principles would have to be applied by analogy to the cases in which actions by or against representative plaintiffs or defendants were permitted in the courts of Chancery. Consideration of the history of the rule thus militates against any narrow construction of it. It led Lord Lindley to say, in *Taff Vale Railway Co v Amalgamated Society of Railway Servants*[1]:

'The principle on which the rule is based forbids its restriction to cases for which an exact precedent can be found in the reports. The principle is as applicable to new cases as to old, and ought to be applied to the exigencies of modern life as occasion requires.'

Initially the courts construed RSC Ord 16, r 9 narrowly. In *Temperton v Russell*[2] an action was brought by a builder against defendants who were officials of various unions. They were sued 'as well on their own behalf as on behalf of and representing all the members of each of the said societies and joint committees to which they respectively belong'. The claim was for damages and an injunction. In the Court of Appeal, Lindley LJ, who delivered the judgment of the court, having cited RSC Ord 16, r 9, said this[3]:

'The question really turns on the meaning of the words "having the same interest in one cause or matter." This expression only extends, we think, to persons who have or claim some beneficial proprietary right, which they are asserting or defending in the cause or matter. The plaintiff in this case sues for damages, and the action, assuming it to lie at all, as to which we pronounce no opinion, is founded on tort. The old Court of Chancery had no jurisdiction to grant relief in such an action; and, although its rules as to parties to actions or suits maintainable in it have now to be applied in all Divisions in the High Court when exercising the old jurisdiction of the Court of Chancery, the rules ought not to be construed as creating a jurisdiction in one Division, which was never exercised by any court in the country before the rules were made.'

However, that passage was criticised by Lord Macnaghten in *Duke of Bedford v Ellis*[4] as imposing an unjustified restriction on RSC Ord 16, r 9, and was criticised by Lord

1   [1901] AC 426 at 443
2   [1893] 1 QB 435
3   [1893] 1 QB 435 at 438
4   [1901] AC 1, [1900–3] All ER Rep 694

a   Lindley himself in the *Taff Vale* case[1], where he said that 'the unfortunate observations made on that rule in *Temperton v. Russell*[2] have been happily corrected in this House in the *Duke of Bedford v. Ellis*[3] and in the course of the argument in the present case'.

In the *Taff Vale* case[4], as is well known, the House of Lords held that the effect of the Trade Union Acts 1871 and 1876 was by necessary implication to make a registered trade union liable to be sued in its registered name. That part of the decision of the House of Lords gave rise to political controversy, the echoes of which can be heard today. What

b   is often overlooked is that both Lord Macnaghten and Lord Lindley held that the question whether the Acts by implication made a union liable to be sued in its registered name was a question merely of form and not of substance, because apart from any implication of liability of a registered union to be sued in its registered name the plaintiff could have achieved substantially the same result by suing members who were genuinely representative, for instance, its executive committee, on behalf of themselves and the

c   other members of the union and that, in the words of Lord Lindley[1], '. . . an injunction and judgment for damages could be obtained in a proper case in an action so framed'. Lord Macnaghten explained the decision in *Temperton v Russell*[5] in these words:

d   '. . . *Temperton v. Russell*[2], as I said in *Duke of Bedford v. Ellis*[3], was an absurd case. The persons there selected as representatives of the various unions intended to be sued were selected in defiance of all rule and principle. They were not the managers of the union—they had no control over it or over its funds. They represented nobody but themselves. Their names seem to have been taken at random for the purpose, I suppose, of spreading a general sense of insecurity among the unions who ought to have been sued, if sued at all, either in their registered name, if that be permissible, or by their proper officers—the members of their executive committees

e   and their trustees.'

f   Thus the *Taff Vale* case[4] shows that the effect of RSC Ord 16, r 9 (and its predecessor) was to confer on the High Court of Justice jurisdiction to entertain a claim founded on a tort against a defendant as representative of a class. Counsel for the second and third defendants observed rightly that in that case the members of the union represented by the named defendants would have been jointly liable for conspiracy and that that decision, therefore, does not compel the conclusion that, when each of the members of a class purportedly represented by a plaintiff has a separate and not a joint cause of action in tort, an action can be brought by a representative on behalf of all the class. I shall

g   return to this point later in this judgment.

Between *Temperton v Russell*[2] and the *Taff Vale* case[4] the House of Lords also decided *Duke of Bedford v Ellis*[3]. In that case the respondents were plaintiffs in an action in which they sued as representing themselves and all other growers of fruit, flowers, vegetables, roots and herbs within the meaning of the Covent Garden Market Act 1828[6], a private Act of Parliament which gave certain preferential rights to stands in the market to

h   various classes of growers. The analysis of the claims in the speech of Lord Brampton shows that the first four plaintiffs claimed, as representing themselves and all other growers, to be entitled to preferential rights in respect of yearly cart stands; they claimed a declaration to that effect, and also injunctions and accounts, and repayment of excessive

j   1 [1901] AC 426 at 443
    2 [1893] 1 QB 435
    3 [1901] AC 1, [1900–3] All ER Rep 694
    4 [1901] AC 426
    5 [1893] 1 QB 435 at 439
    6 9 Geo 4 c cxiii

charges alleged to have been made by the duke. The fifth and sixth plaintiffs similarly claimed, as representing themselves and all other growers, to be entitled to preferential rights in relation to yearly pitching stands. They similarly claimed a declaration to that effect and an injunction and accounts and repayment of excessive charges. Lord Brampton thought that the claims, representative or personal, in respect of the yearly cart stands ought not to be permitted to be pursued in the same action as the claims, representative or personal, in respect of the yearly pitching stands. But he held that the separate causes of action of the first four plaintiffs in respect of the yearly cart stands on the one hand and the separate causes of action of the last two plaintiffs in respect of the yearly pitching stands on the other hand could properly be joined. None of the others of their Lordships who heard the appeal expressed an opinion whether the plaintiffs were properly joined as co-plaintiffs, save that Lord Halsbury LC expressed his concurrence with the speech of Lord Brampton. It is, however, necessary to bear in mind that there were these two questions in order to understand the vital passage in the speech of Lord Macnaghten. He said[1]:

'The Duke has applied by summons to stay the action on two grounds, which were mixed up in the argument, but which ought, I think, to be kept separate and distinct. The principal ground is that the plaintiffs are not entitled to sue in a representative character in defence of their alleged statutory rights. The other ground, which is a matter of very slight moment, is that they cannot join as co-plaintiffs in respect of their several grievances. The whole difficulty in the present case has arisen from confusing these two matters. They have really nothing to do with each other. If the persons named as plaintiffs are members of a class having a common interest, and if the alleged rights of the class are being denied or ignored, it does not matter in the least that the nominal plaintiffs may have been wronged or inconvenienced in their individual capacity. They are none the better for that and none the worse. They would be competent representatives of the class if they had never been near the Duke; they are not incompetent because they may have been turned out of the market. In considering whether a representative action is maintainable, you have to consider what is common to the class, not what differentiates the cases of individual members.'

What he is saying in this passage, as I understand it, is that in considering whether the action by the plaintiffs suing in a representative capacity for declarations that growers were entitled to preferential rights could be maintained, it was no objection that as between themselves (and, I would add, as between themselves and other members of the class on whose behalf they sued) they might have had separate causes of action for accounts and repayment of excessive charges previously imposed.

Counsel for the second and third defendants seeks to distinguish this decision on the ground that in *Duke of Bedford v Ellis*[2] the declaration sought by the plaintiffs in a representative capacity was a declaration as to the preferential rights of growers under the 1828 Act which, said counsel, could properly be asserted by any member of the class represented irrespective of whether he had suffered damage from interference with that right. By contrast, it is said, if the cause of action of each member of the class whom the plaintiff purports to represent is founded in tort and would, if established, be a separate cause of action and not a joint cause of action belonging to the class as a whole, no representative action can be brought; for the plaintiff can only obtain judgment as a representative plaintiff on behalf of a class every member of which is, by the judgment, shown to have a cause of action, and in the case postulated that would necessitate showing that each member of the class had suffered damage. Alternatively, it is said, no

---

1   [1901] AC 1 at 7, [1900–3] All ER Rep 694 at 696
2   [1901] AC 1, [1900–3] All ER Rep 694

representative action should be allowed if the effect of the judgment, or so much of it as
would be res judicata between the defendants and each and every member of the class
represented, might be to confer on a member of that class a right which he could not
otherwise have established against the defendant, or to deprive the defendant of a
defence on which he might otherwise have been entitled to rely.

In support of this argument counsel for the second and third defendants relied
primarily on two decisions. First, the decision of the Court of Appeal in *Markt v Knight
Steamship Co Ltd*[1] and secondly, *Lord Aberconway v Whetnall*[2], a decision of Eve J reported
with *Lord Churchill v Whetnall*[2].

The relevant facts in *Markt v Knight Steamship Co Ltd*[1], which was heard with *Sale &
Frazar v Knight Steamship Co Ltd*[1], are shortly as follows. The plaintiffs in the two actions,
and others, shipped goods on a general cargo ship for a voyage from New York to Japan
which was intercepted by a Russian cruiser on the suspicion that it was carrying
contraband and sunk. In both actions the plaintiffs were described as suing 'on behalf of
themselves and others owners of cargo lately laden on board'. In both writs the plaintiffs
claimed 'damages for breach of contract and duty in or about the carriage of goods by
sea'. By a letter written by the plaintiffs' solicitor on the day of issue of the writs it was
stated that the plaintiffs were suing on behalf of 44 other persons, firms or companies
named in the letter.

The representative claims as framed in the writs were clearly not maintainable if only
because the judgment would have been res judicata between the defendant and a shipper
of goods who had himself shipped contraband. It was proposed to meet this difficulty by
amending the writs so that the plaintiffs in the first action would be expressed to be
'Markt & Co., Limited, on behalf of themselves and all others the owners of cargo lately
on board the steamship *Knight Commander* not being shippers of goods which were
contraband of war' and so that the endorsement would ask for a declaration that the
defendants were liable to the plaintiffs and those on whose behalf they sued for breach of
contract and/or duty in and about the carriage of goods by sea.

Buckley LJ would have allowed the action to proceed in this amended form. The
majority, Vaughan Williams and Fletcher Moulton LJJ, took the view that the writs were
incapable of being amended so as to enable the plaintiffs to maintain representative
actions. It was pointed out by Vaughan Williams LJ[3]:

'There is nothing on the writ to shew that the bills of lading and the exceptions
therein were identical or that the goods the subject of the bill of lading were of the
same class either in kind or in relation to the rules of war, under which the same
article may be contraband or not according to its destination.'

And later[4]:

'These shippers no doubt have a common wrong in that their goods were lost by
the sinking of the *Knight Commander* by the Russian warship; but I see no common
right, or common purpose, in the case of these shippers who are not alleged to have
shipped to the same destinations. Moreover, it may be that there were contraband
goods on board which justified the Russian action—it may be that some of the
shippers knowingly shipped goods which were contraband of war. It may be that
some of the shippers were innocent of such shipping of contraband goods. All sorts
of facts and all sorts of exceptions may defeat the right of individual shippers. The
case of each shipper must to my mind depend upon its own merits.'

The same point was made by Fletcher Moulton LJ where he said[5]:

1   [1910] 2 KB 1021
2   (1918) 87 LJ Ch 524
3   [1910] 2 KB 1021 at 1026
4   [1910] 2 KB 1021 at 1029–1030
5   [1910] 2 KB 1021 at 1039–1040

'The counsel for the plaintiffs suggests that the people in the list are in similar circumstances, because they shipped goods under similar bills of lading in the same ship. Assuming, for the sake of argument, that that is so (although nothing of the kind appears on the record), each of these parties made a separate contract of shipment in respect of different goods entitling him to its performance by the defendants and to damages in case of non-performance. It may be that the claims are alike in nature, and that the litigation in respect of them will have much in common. But they are in no way connected: there is no common interest. Defences may exist against some of the shippers which do not exist against the others, such as estoppel, set-off, &c., so that no representative action can settle the rights of the individual members of the class.'

As I understand these passages the points that are there made are, first, that there was nothing in the writs which indicated that there was any common element in the contracts which could be the subject either of a declaration or any other order which would determine in favour of all members of the class represented an issue which would have to be determined in any action brought by a member of the class; and, secondly, that the form of the relief asked (namely in the amended writ, a declaration that the defendants were liable to every member of the class in damages) might have precluded the defendants from establishing in a subsequent action by a member of the class represented a defence (for instance, estoppel) which otherwise would have been available to him. This last point must, I think, have been the point which Fletcher Moulton LJ had in mind when he said in his judgment[1]:

'But the writs even as proposed to be amended fail to comply with Lord Macnaghten's interpretation of the rule in another and most essential particular. The relief sought is damages. Damages are personal only. To my mind no representative action can lie where the sole relief sought is damages, because they have to be proved separately in the case of each plaintiff, and therefore the possibility of representation ceases.'

The second case is *Lord Aberconway v Whetnall*[2] which was heard together with the action of *Lord Churchill v Whetnall*[2]. The defendant had been employed by Lord Churchill to keep a record of admissions to the Ascot Race Enclosure. Being in financial difficulties he sought to obtain subscriptions to a fund to his benefit and asked Lord Churchill for a testimonial. The summary of the facts in the report continues[2]:

'. . . Lord Churchill wrote that he wished the fund success and would personally contribute to it. The defendant then had the letter lithographed, and without Lord Churchill's knowledge or consent sent it out together with a circular stating that the fund had been opened and that holders of inclosure tickets might be glad to help. More than two hundred persons sent subscriptions, which together amounted to about 8ool.'

In the first of the two actions before Eve J Lord Churchill sought to recover books and documents containing lists of persons receiving invitations to the Royal Enclosure. In a second action Lord Aberconway and two others who had subscribed sought to recover (on behalf of themselves and all other subscribers) the return of all money subscribed on the ground that the subscriptions were induced by misrepresentation. In relation to this representative claim Eve J said[3]:

'Treating it, therefore, as an action to recover contributions on the ground that they were extracted from the donors by misrepresentation, the next question is, can

1 [1910] 2 KB 1021 at 1040–1041
2 (1918) 87 LJ Ch 524
3 87 LJ Ch 524 at 526

an action of such a nature be framed as this one is as a representative action within rule 9 of Order XVI.? The persons for whom the plaintiffs seek to constitute themselves the representatives are "the subscribers to the fund called the Whetnall Fund." This would include every one who subscribed, whether he received the circular containing the alleged misrepresentation or not, but assuming in favour of the plaintiffs that the description is equivalent to the subscribers to whom the circular was addressed, how can it be said that the recipients of that circular who became donors to the fund have a common interest and a common grievance, when the very existence of the grievance depends upon facts which may differ in each individual case? A dozen different reasons may have prompted favourable replies to the appeal, not one of which would have entitled the donor to a return of his contribution, if he had been a plaintiff in this action; and yet if the argument is sound that this is a proper representative action, such a one although he could not recover his money were he himself a plaintiff must still have his contribution returned to him because three other persons, who for this purpose I am content to assume can successfully maintain an action for the recovery of their money, have chosen to elect themselves as his representatives. The position is an impossible one. It may well be that all the contributors who claim to have their contributions returned could have joined in one action under rule 1 of Order XVI, but in such an action each individual would have to establish his own right to relief by proving the propositions I have already stated. This is really an attempt to obtain relief for over 200 individuals by proving the right of three of them thereto. Such an attempt cannot and ought not to succeed. This action, which, after all, is nothing more than an action to recover damages for misrepresentation, does not possess the essential conditions of a representative action, and in my opinion it is misconceived.'

Indeed in that case the claim by a plaintiff to sue in a representative capacity was absurd. The plaintiff could not, on behalf of all members of the class, claim to recover all subscriptions that had been made for it was an essential ingredient of the cause of action of any person seeking to recover that he had himself been deceived by a misrepresentation into making his subscription. This difficulty could not have been overcome by limiting the relief to a declaration that any subscriber who had been induced by a misrepresentation to contribute to the fund was entitled to recover because the declaration would have accomplished nothing. Each plaintiff would still have had to establish in separate proceedings that he had been so induced in order to rely on the judgment in the representative action.

These cases, in my judgment, establish two propositions. First, no order will be made in favour of a representative plaintiff if the order might in any circumstances have the effect of conferring on a member of the class represented a right which he could not have claimed in a separate action or of barring a defence which the defendant could have raised in such proceedings. Secondly, no order will be made in favour of a representative plaintiff unless there is some element common to the claims of all members of the class which he purports to represent. But these two cases do not, in my judgment, establish the wider proposition for which counsel for the second and third defendants contends, namely that the court has no jurisdiction in any circumstances to entertain an action by a plaintiff claiming to represent a class in cases where the cause of action of the plaintiff and of each member of the class is, or is alleged to be, a separate cause of action founded in tort.

But the matter does not rest there. Counsel for the second and third defendants very properly drew my attention to a decision of the Court of Appeal which is reported very briefly under the title *Jones v Cory Brothers & Co Ltd, Thomas v Great Mountain Collieries Co*[1]. As the title indicates, there were two actions before the Court of Appeal. In the first action five named plaintiffs sued on their own behalf, and on behalf of all other

---

1   (1921) 56 L Jo 302

underground and surface workmen employed at the colliery of Cory Brothers & Co Ltd
on three specified days in September 1919. They alleged that on those three days the
safety lamps in use at the colliery were not in accordance with statutory requirements,
that they were insufficient in number and were not properly examined, and that in
consequence the workmen justifiably refused to go to work and lost the wages they
would otherwise have been entitled to and were, therefore, entitled to damages. In the
second action the plaintiffs sued on behalf of themselves and on behalf of all other
underground and surface workmen at the colliery of Great Mountain Collieries Co
alleging that the defendants were in breach of their statutory duty in not having a
weighing machine to weigh the coal gotten as near the pit mouth as was reasonably
practicable. The claim seems to have been for damages founded on loss of wages which
were linked to production at the pit. It was argued as a preliminary point that the claims
could not be maintained as representative claims. It is reported[1]:

> 'In each action the claims of the plaintiffs were divisible under three heads: (1)
> The claims founded on common interest for declarations upon matters in which the
> classes represented were alleged to have a common interest; (2) claims for damages
> by the individual named plaintiffs; (3) claims for damages by the individual
> members of the classes represented.'

The judgment is very brief and is as follows[1]:

> 'THEIR LORDSHIPS (Scrutton, L.J., dissenting) allowed the appeal in part. Bankes
> and Atkin, L.JJ., held that the plaintiffs were entitled to sue in a representative
> capacity as regards claims that came within (1) and (2), but not as regards the claims
> for damages by the individual members of the classes represented. Leave was given
> to appeal. Scrutton, L.J. (dissenting), held that there was no common interest in the
> declarations sought sufficient to entitle the plaintiffs to sue in a representative
> capacity.'

It is difficult to relate this judgment to the claims in the action without seeing the
writs or statements of claim and counsel's researches in the Public Records Office have
failed to unearth these documents. However, their researches have revealed the order of
the Court of Appeal. It is only necessary to read the order made as regards the first
action. It reads as follows:

> 'It is ordered that this Appeal be allowed the Order of the Honourable Mr. Justice
> Lush dated the 4th day of March 1921 whereby the court decided the points of law
> raised in paragraph 12 of the Defence herein in favour of the Defendants be set aside
> and this Court doth decide the points of Law so raised in favour of the Plaintiffs
> except as follows. Claims of the first named Plaintiffs to be confined to claim for the
> declaration and mandatory order numbered 1, 2, and 3 in the Statement of Claim
> and for an enquiry as to damages sustained by the named Plaintiffs, the declaration
> and enquiry as to damages claimed by the second named Plaintiffs to be struck out
> with general liberty to all parties to amend as they may be advised.'

It is, I think, apparent from the report, together with the order, that the Court of
Appeal held that the action could be maintained as a representative action if confined to
declarations that the safety lamps in use in the colliery were not in accordance with
statutory requirements, that they were insufficient in number and not properly
examined, and that in consequence on the three specified days the workmen were
justified in refusing to go to work. The claim for a mandatory order may have been a
claim for an order compelling the defendant company to comply with the statutory
requirements in the future. Such declarations would leave it open to any workman
employed at the colliery on the specified date or any of them to sue and to rely on the
declaration as res judicata, and to recover damages on establishing that he refused to go

---

1   (1921) 56 L Jo 302 at 303

to work by reason of the breach of statutory duty by the employer. A declaration that

a every workman employed at the colliery on the specified dates was entitled to damages would have infringed the first of the two propositions I have stated, because it might have been open to the defendant in separate proceedings to establish that his failure to attend work was not the consequence of the breach of statutory duty, but was due, for instance, to illness.

The researches of counsel have not unearthed any other case in which the power of the

b court to entertain a representative action founded on separate causes of action in tort in each member of the class represented has been argued. However, there are two cases where such actions have been permitted. In the well known Spanish champagne case of *J Bollinger v Costa Brava Wine Co Ltd (No 2)*[1] an action was brought by the 12 leading champagne houses on behalf of themselves and all other persons producing champagne in the Champagne area of France, claiming injunctions restraining the defendants from

c applying the trade description 'champagne' to wine produced in Spain and passing it off as champagne. An injunction was granted in those terms. At first sight this case invites the observation that the class represented had a joint cause of action in tort. However, in the more recent case of *H P Bulmer Ltd and Showerings Ltd v J Bollinger S A*[2] the plaintiffs, manufacturers of Babycham, sued for a declaration that they were entitled to use the description 'champagne cider' and 'champagne perry' for their products. They joined

d two champagne houses as representatives of the class of producers of champagne in the Champagne district of France. The defendants counterclaimed in their representative capacity, alleging passing-off and claiming injunctions. Buckley LJ in a long and careful analysis of the decision of Danckwerts J in *J Bollinger v Costa Brava Wine Co Ltd*[3] said this[4]:

> '[Counsel] in this court has disclaimed any intention of suggesting that
e Danckwerts, J.'s decision in that case was wrong in any respect. Having heard no argument to the contrary, I propose for present purposes to assume (without deciding) that the decision was correct. [Counsel] has contended that Danckwerts, J. proceeded upon the basis that the Champagne Houses were entitled to a joint goodwill in respect of the word "Champagne". Since all the Champagne Houses were plaintiffs in person or by representation in the Spanish Champagne Case, it was not necessary for Danckwerts, J. to decide whether their right of action was a joint
f or a several one, but the point was clearly raised in argument before him and it seems to me that he did accept that each Champagne House had a separate goodwill in the word "Champagne". He said[5]: "In my view, it ought not to matter that the persons truly entitled to describe their goods by the name and description are a class producing goods in a certain locality, and not merely one individual. The description is part of their goodwill and a right of property." This language seems
g to me to be consistent only with the view that each Champagne House was entitled to goodwill in the word "Champagne" which constituted part of that House's own goodwill in its business. Upon this view of the matter the position of the Champagne Houses does not appear to me to differ in principle from the position of B and C selling "XYZ sauce" in my fictitious example. The ability of any one
h Champagne House to describe its product as Champagne is of value to it not in relation to the Champagne market but in relation to the wider wine market distinguishing their products from other wines.'

Thus these two cases are cases where injunctions have been granted to plaintiffs suing in a representative capacity on behalf of a class each member of which has a separate as well as a joint cause of action in tort.

j _____

1   [1961] 1 All ER 561, [1961] 1 WLR 277
2   [1978] RPC 79
3   [1959] 3 All ER 800, [1960] Ch 262
4   [1978] RPC 79 at 98
5   [1959] 3 All ER 800 at 811, [1960] Ch 262 at 284

In summary, in my judgment, it is clear on authority and principle that a representative action can be brought by a plaintiff, suing on behalf of himself and all other members of a class, each member of which, including the plaintiff, is alleged to have a separate cause of action in tort, provided that three conditions are satisfied. The first I have already stated. No order can properly be made in such a representative action if the effect might in any circumstances be to confer a right of action on a member of the class represented who would not otherwise have been able to assert such a right in separate proceedings, or to bar a defence which might otherwise have been available to the defendant in such a separate action. Normally, therefore, if not invariably the only relief that will be capable of being obtained by the plaintiff in his representative capacity will be declaratory relief, though, of course, he may join with it a personal claim for damages. It is not clear how far the grant of injunctive relief is consistent with this principle in that for any member of the class represented to establish a right to injunctive relief in separate proceedings he would have to show a present apprehension of injury and might be faced with a defence of laches or acquiesence. Injunctions were, of course, granted in the Spanish Champagne[1] and Babycham[2] cases, but that may have been justifiable in the particular circumstances of those cases on the ground that there was both a joint and several cause of action in tort.

The second condition is that there must be an 'interest' shared by all members of the class. In relation to a representative action in which it is claimed that every member of the class has a separate cause of action in tort, this condition requires, as I see it, that there must be a common ingredient in the cause of action of each member of the class. In the present case that requirement is clearly satisfied. It was not satisfied in Markt[3] or in Lord Aberconway v Whetnall[4]. The third and related condition is that the court must be satisfied that it is for the benefit of the class that the plaintiff be permitted to sue in a representative capacity. The court must, therefore, be satisfied that the issues common to every member of the class will be decided after full discovery and in the light of all the evidence capable of being adduced in favour of the claim. For unless this condition is satisfied it would be wrong (as Fletcher Moulton LJ remarked in Markt[5]) to permit the representative plaintiff 'to conduct litigation on behalf of another without his leave and yet so as to bind him'.

Discretion

I turn, therefore, to the question of discretion. Counsel for the second and third defendants urged that the amendment should not be allowed, because if it were allowed the period of limitation available to the class represented would be enlarged from six to 12 years and possibly for longer if time stopped running from the date of the issue of the writ. In my judgment the answer to that argument is that given by counsel for the plaintiff, namely that the Limitation Act 1939 will continue to operate in the same way as it would have operated if no order had been made in the representative action. Any member of the class will have to bring his own action to establish damage within six years from the date when the cause of action accrued. The only effect of an order in favour of the plaintiff in its representative capacity will be that the issues covered by that order will be res judicata. Then it is said that the effect of allowing the action to proceed will be to add numberless claims founded on fraud and that the court should therefore be slow to admit the amendment as it always is slow to allow an amendment alleging fraud. In my judgment, that submission is misconceived. Allegations of misconduct on the part of the individual defendants as directors and of conspiracy are made in the

1   [1961] 1 All ER 561, [1961] 1 WLR 277
2   [1978] RPC 79
3   [1910] 2 KB 1021
4   (1918) 87 LJ Ch 524
5   [1910] 2 KB 1021 at 1040

statement of claim. The effect of allowing the plaintiff to sue in a representative capacity

a is that if those allegations are proved any member of the class will be entitled to rely on the judgment as res judicata. The amendment, therefore, does not add causes of action. It allows a common element in the causes of action of all members of the class to be established in one representative action.

Next, it is said that if the claim had been originally formulated as a representative claim the defendants might have wished to adduce evidence that no member of the class

b has suffered damage. That objection is, in my judgment, also misconceived. The court cannot in a representative action make an order for damages, though, of course, the plaintiff in its own non-representative capacity will be entitled to pursue its claim for damages. It would be as wrong to permit the defendants to adduce evidence that other members of the class represented, who are not actually parties, have not suffered damage, as it would be to allow the representative action to proceed as a claim for damages on

c behalf of all members of the class.

Lastly, it is said, the plaintiff cannot be allowed to pursue two representative claims, one on behalf of the present shareholders and one on behalf of the shareholders at the date of the resolution. That objection is, in my judgment, founded on the form and not the substantial effect of the amendment. The derivative claim is framed in the conventional way as a claim on behalf of all the shareholders in the defendant company,

d except the second and third defendants. But the claim is in effect a claim for recovery of damages or equitable compensation by Newman, the first defendant. If it succeeds the plaintiff may not wish to pursue its claim for damages for conspiracy. But I can see no reason why that claim, whether alternative or cumulative should not be pursued in the representative capacity, at least to the extent of the issues that would be raised in an action for damages for conspiracy by any member of the class represented.

e
The form of the amendment

As drafted the order which the plaintiff seeks in its representative capacity is for a declaration that the plaintiff in its personal capacity as a shareholder in Newman and on behalf of itself and all other shareholders in Newman who like the plaintiff have suffered damage are entitled to damages against the defendants, Bartlett and Laughton, for

f conspiracy. The practical effect of such a declaration would, it seems to me, be no greater and no less than the effect of declarations, first, that the circular was tricky and misleading; secondly that the individual defendants conspired to procure its circulation in order to procure the passing of the relevant resolution; and thirdly, that in so doing they conspired either to injure the plaintiff and the other shareholders at that date or to commit an unlawful act, or to induce a breach by Newman of its contractual duty to the

g shareholders. It would, I think, be better that those declarations, which constitute the common element of any claim by any member of the class for damages for conspiracy, should be so spelt out. Further, I can see no reason for defining the class of shareholders of Newman at 29th July 1975 as persons 'who like the plaintiff have suffered damage and are entitled to damages'. The words I have cited appear to me to be unnecessary and undesirable. The members of the class who share a common interest in obtaining the

h declarations I have outlined are shareholders other than the second and fourth defendants as at 29th July. A person coming within that class will be entitled to rely on the declarations as res judicata, but will still have to establish damage in a separate action.

I therefore propose to allow the amendments in principle, but to invite counsel for the plaintiff to consider their form in the light of the judgment I have just given.

j *Amendments allowed.*

Solicitors: *C F Whitehorn* (for the plaintiff); *Simmons & Simmons* (for Newman and the second and third defendants); *Clifford Turner & Co* (for TPG).

Jacqueline Metcalfe   Barrister.

Barclays Bank Ltd v W J Simms Son & Cooke (Southern) Ltd and another

a

QUEEN'S BENCH DIVISION
ROBERT GOFF J
21st, 22nd, 23rd, 26th, 27th, 28th, 29th, 30th MARCH, 2nd, 24th APRIL 1979

b

Mistake – Mistake of fact – Money paid under mistake of fact – Recovery – Bank – Cheque stopped by drawer – Cheque paid by bank due to oversight – Whether bank intended payee to have money at all events – Whether payment made for valuable consideration – Whether payee changing his position – Whether money recoverable from payee – Whether payee can invoke defence that he had been deprived of opportunity of giving notice of dishonour – Bills of Exchange Act 1882, s 50(2)(c).

c

On 12th September 1977 a customer of Barclays Bank who owed £24,000 to a building company drew a cheque in favour of the building company for that amount. On 13th September, the building company's bankers, National Westminster Bank, appointed a receiver of the building company under the terms of a mortgage debenture granted to them. On 14th September Barclays' customer learned of the appointment and on 15th September telephoned Barclays instructing them to stop payment of the cheque. Barclays immediately prepared that instruction for their computer, which was programmed accordingly. The customer subsequently confirmed its instructions in writing. The cheque reached the receiver in the ordinary course of post. Being unaware of the instructions to stop payment on the cheque, he paid it into National Westminster with a direction that it be specially cleared. On 16th September, due to a mistake by an employee who had overlooked the stop instruction, Barclays paid the cheque. Barclays subsequently demanded repayment of the cheque from the receiver but he refused to repay. Barclays thereupon brought an action against the building company and the receiver claiming repayment of the £24,000 as money paid under a mistake of fact. The defendants contended that Barclays were not entitled to recover the money because (i) there had been no mistake of fact between Barclays and the defendants or either of them, or alternatively that any mistake or misapprehension of fact was confined to Barclays; (ii) the money had been paid by Barclays and received by the building company in discharge of an obligation owed to the company or alternatively under the cheque; and (iii) Barclays had failed to give notice of their claim on the day the cheque was paid so that the defendants had a good defence to the claim on the established principle that they had been deprived of the opportunity of giving notice of dishonour on that day and so were deemed to have changed their position.

d

e

f

g

Held – (1) Where a person paid money to another under a mistake of fact which caused him to make the payment, he was prima facie entitled to recover it as money paid under a mistake of fact. His claim might however fail if (i) the payer had intended that the payee should have the money at all events (irrespective of whether the fact was true or false) or was deemed in law to have so intended; (ii) the payment had been made for good consideration, and in particular if the money had been paid to discharge, and did discharge, a debt owed to the payee (or a principal on whose behalf he was authorised to receive payment) by the payer or by a third party by whom he had been authorised to discharge the debt, or (iii) the payee had changed his position in good faith or was deemed in law to have done so. However, his claim would not fail merely because the mistake had not been 'as between' the payer and the payee or because the mistake had not induced the payer to believe that he was liable to pay the money to the payee or his principal (see p 531 *b c*, p 532 *f g*, p 534 *f* to *h* and p 535 *e* to p 536 *e*, post); dictum of Parke B in *Kelly v Solari* [1835–42] All ER Rep at 322, *Aiken v Short* [1843–60] All ER Rep 425, *Kleinwort, Sons & Co v Dunlop Rubber Co* (1907) 97 LT 263, *Kerrison v Glyn, Mills,*

h

j

Currie & Co [1911–13] All ER Rep 417 and *R E Jones Ltd v Waring & Gillow Ltd* [1926] All
ER Rep 36, applied; dictum of Erle CJ in *Chambers v Miller* (1862) 13 CBNS at 133
a explained; *Colonial Bank v Exchange Bank of Yarmouth, Nova Scotia* (1885) 11 App Cas 84
and *Morgan v Ashcroft* [1937] 3 All ER 92 considered; dictum of Bramwell B in *Aiken v
Short* [1843–60] All ER Rep at 427 and *Barclay & Co Ltd v Malcolm & Co* (1925) 133 LT
512 not followed.

b (2) Where a bank paid, under a mistake of fact, a cheque drawn on it by one of its
customers, it was prima facie entitled to recover payment from the payee if it had acted
without mandate (eg if it had overlooked a notice of countermand given by a customer)
unless the payee had changed his position in good faith or was deemed in law to have
done so (see p 539 *f* to *j* and p 540 *a b* and *d*, post); *Chambers v Miller* (1862) 13 CBNS 125
and *Pollard v Bank of England* (1871) LR 6 QB 623 distinguished.

(3) It was a prerequisite to the application of the defence that the defendant had been
c deprived of the opportunity of giving notice of dishonour and was therefore deemed to
have changed his position that the defendant was under a duty to give notice of
dishonour. However, since s 50(2)(c)[a] of the Bills of Exchange Act 1882 provided that
notice of dishonour was dispensed with, as regards the drawer, where the drawer
countermanded payment, the payee could not invoke that defence in the case of a simple
unendorsed cheque, payment of which had been countermanded by the drawer (see
d p 541 *d* and p 542 *b* to *d*, post); *Imperial Bank of Canada v Bank of Hamilton* [1903] AC 49
applied; *Cocks v Masterman* [1824–34] All ER Rep 431 distinguished.

(4) Barclays were entitled to succeed in their claim because (i) their mistake in
overlooking the drawer's instructions to stop payment of the cheque had caused them to
pay the cheque, (ii) they had acted without mandate since the drawer had countermanded
payment, and so the payment was not effective to discharge the drawer's obligation on
e the cheque and as a result the payee had given no consideration for the payment, and (iii)
there was no evidence of any actual change of position on the part of either of the
defendants and, as notice of dishonour was not required in the circumstances, the payee
was not deemed to have changed his position by reason of the lapse of time in giving
notification of the error and claiming repayment (see p 542 *e* to *g*, post).

Notes
f For the recovery of money paid under a mistake of fact, see 26 Halsbury's Laws (3rd Edn)
921–922, paras 1711–1714, and for cases on the subject, see 35 Digest (Repl) 158–166,
475–527.
For the Bills of Exchange Act 1882, s 50, see 3 Halsbury's Statutes (3rd Edn) 216.

Cases referred to in judgment
g *Aiken v Short* (1856) 1 H & N 210, [1843–60] All ER Rep 425, 25 LJ Ex 321, 27 LTOS 188,
156 ER 1180, 35 Digest (Repl) 159, 481.
Barclay & Co Ltd v Malcolm & Co (1925) 133 LT 512, 35 Digest (Repl) 161, 491.
Chambers v Miller (1862) 13 CBNS 125, 1 New Rep 95, 32 LJCP 30, 7 LT 856, 9 Jur NS
626, 143 ER 50, 35 Digest (Repl) 161, 489.
Cocks v Masterman (1829) 9 B & C 902, [1824–34] All ER Rep 431, Dan & Ll 329, 4 Man
h & Ry KB 676, 8 LJOSKB 77, 109 ER 335, 3 Digest (Reissue) 643, 4019.
Colonial Bank v Exchange Bank of Yarmouth, Nova Scotia (1885) 11 App Cas 84, 55 LJPC 14,
54 LT 256, PC, 3 Digest (Reissue) 569, 3664.
Diplock's Estate, Re, Diplock v Wintle [1948] 2 All ER 318, sub nom *Re Diplock, Diplock v
Wintle* [1948] Ch 465, [1948] LJR 1670, CA; *affd* sub nom *Ministry of Health v Simpson*
[1950] 2 All ER 1137, [1951] AC 251, HL, 8(1) Digest (Reissue) 416, 1481.
j *Fibrosa Spolka Akcyjna v Fairbairn Lawson Combe Barbour Ltd* [1942] All ER 122, [1943] AC
32, 111 LJKB 433, 167 LT 101, HL, 12 Digest (Reissue) 495, 3470.
Imperial Bank of Canada v Bank of Hamilton [1903] AC 49, 72 LJPC 1, 87 LT 457, PC, 35
Digest (Repl) 165, 519.

---

a   Section 50(2), so far as material, is set out at p 542 *c*, post

Jones (RE) Ltd v Waring & Gillow Ltd [1926] AC 670, [1926] All ER Rep 36, 95 LJKB 913,
   135 LT 548, 32 Com Cas 8, HL; *rvsg* [1925] 2 KB 612, CA, 35 Digest (Repl) 161, 492. *a*
Kelly v Solari (1841) 9 M & W 54, [1835–42] All ER Rep 320, 11 LJ Ex 10, 6 Jur 107, 152
   ER 24, 35 Digest (Repl) 164, 512.
Kerrison v Glyn, Mills, Currie & Co (1911) 81 LJKB 465, [1911–13] All ER Rep 417, 105
   LT 721, HL; *rvsg* (1910) 15 Com Cas 241, CA, 3 Digest (Reissue) 555, 3600.
Kleinwort, Sons & Co v Dunlop Rubber Co (1907) 97 LT 263, HL, 3 Digest (Reissue) 569,
   3666. *b*
Larner v London County Council [1949] 1 All ER 964, [1949] 2 KB 683, [1949] LJR 1363,
   113 JP 300, 47 LGR 533, CA, 35 Digest (Repl) 170, 558.
London and River Plate Bank v Bank of Liverpool [1896] 1 QB 7, [1895–9] All ER Rep 1005,
   65 LJQB 80, 73 LT 473, 1 Com Cas 170, 6 Digest (Reissue) 100, 770.
Morgan v Ashcroft [1937] 3 All ER 92, [1938] 1 KB 49, 106 LJKB 544, 157 LT 87, CA, 35
   Digest (Repl) 159, 484. *c*
National Westminster Bank Ltd v Barclays Bank International Ltd [1974] 3 All ER 834, [1975]
   QB 654, [1975] 2 WLR 12, [1974] 2 Lloyd's Rep 506, 3 Digest (Reissue) 637, 3998.
Norwich Union Fire Insurance Society Ltd v William H Price Ltd [1934] AC 455, [1934]
   All ER Rep 352, 103 LJPC 115, 151 LT 309, 40 Com Cas 132, 49 Ll L Rep 55, PC,
   29 Digest (Repl) 349, 2683.
Pollard v Bank of England (1871) LR 6 QB 623, 40 LJQB 233, 3 Digest (Reissue) 634, 3980. *d*
Porter v Latec Finance (Qld) Pty Ltd (1964) 111 CLR 177, 38 ALJR 184.
Price v Neal (1762) 3 Burr 1354, 1 Wm Bl 390, 96 ER 221, 6 Digest (Reissue) 98, 763.
Sinclair v Brougham [1914] AC 398, [1914–15] All ER Rep 622, 83 LJ Ch 465, HL, 3
   Digest (Reissue) 543, 3545.
Thomas v Houston Corbett & Co [1961] NZLR 151, CA.
United Australia Ltd v Barclays Bank Ltd [1940] 4 All ER 20, [1941] AC 1, 109 LJKB 919, *e*
   46 Com Cas 1, HL, 3 Digest (Reissue) 607, 3842.
Ward & Co v Wallis [1900] 1 KB 675, 69 LJQB 423, 82 LT 261, 35 Digest (Repl) 171, 565.
Weld Blundell v Synott [1940] 2 All ER 580, [1940] 2 KB 107, 109 LJKB 684, 163 LT 39,
   45 Com Cas 218, 35 Digest (Reissue) 162, 497.

Action *f*

By a writ issued on 5th December 1977 the plaintiffs, Barclays Bank Ltd ('Barclays'),
brought an action against the defendants, W J Simms Son & Cooke (Southern) Ltd ('the
company') and William Sowman ('the receiver'), claiming £24,000 as money paid under
mistake of fact. The facts are set out in the judgment.

David Hunter QC and *Peter Cresswell* for Barclays.
Edward Evans Lombe QC and *Michael Crystal* for the defendants. *g*

Cur adv vult

24th April. **ROBERT GOFF J** read the following judgment: This case raises for
decision the question whether a bank, which overlooks its customer's instructions to stop *h*
payment of a cheque and in consequence pays the cheque on presentation, can recover
the money from the payee as having been paid under a mistake of fact. The point is one
on which there is no decision in this country; and it is a point, I was told, of considerable
importance to bankers, not only because it is an everyday hazard that customer's
instructions may be overlooked, but because modern technology, rather than eliminating
the risk, has if anything increased it.
   The matter comes before the court on agreed facts, which I now propose to set out in *j*
this judgment.
   On 10th June 1971 W J Simms Son & Cooke (Southern) Ltd (which I shall call 'the
company') granted to National Westminster Bank Ltd (which I shall call 'National
Westminster') a mortgage debenture which provided, inter alia, as follows:

a
'2. The Company as beneficial owner . . . (v) charges by way of floating security its undertaking and all its other property, assets and rights whatsoever and wheresoever present or future . . .

'7. At any time after this security shall have become enforceable [National Westminster] may by writing . . . appoint any person . . . to be a Receiver of the property hereby charged . . . Any Receiver so appointed shall be the agent of the Company and the Company shall be solely responsible for his acts or defaults and for

b
his remuneration and any Receiver so appointed shall have power: (i) to take possession of, collect and get in the property hereby charged and for that purpose to take any proceedings in the name of the Company or otherwise . . . (v) to do all such other acts and things he may consider necessary or desirable for the realisation of any of the property hereby charged.

c
'8. All monies received by any Receiver shall be applied by him in the following order: (i) in payment of the costs charges and expenses of and incidental to the appointment of the Receiver and the exercise of all or any of his powers and of all outgoings paid by him (ii) in payment of remuneration to the Receiver at such rates as may be agreed between him and the Bank at or at any time after his appointment (iii) in or towards satisfaction of the amount owing on this security (iv) the surplus (if any) shall be paid to the Company or other person entitled to it.'

d
The mortgage debenture was registered pursuant to s 95 of the Companies Act 1948 on 24th June 1971.

On 21st June 1976 the company entered into a contract in the RIBA standard form of building contract, 1963 edition, with the Royal British Legion Housing Association Ltd (which I shall call 'the association') to perform certain works for the association at Borstal Road, Rochester, Kent, for the total sum of £699,024. Clause 25 of the building contract

e
provided:

'. . . (2) In the event of the Contractor . . . having . . . a receiver or manager of his business or undertaking duly appointed, or possession taken, by or on behalf of the holders of any debentures secured by a floating charge, of any property comprised in or subject to the floating charge, the employment of the Contractor under this Contract shall be forthwith automatically determined but the said employment

f
may be reinstated and continued if the Employer and the Contractor [or] his . . . receiver or manager . . . shall so agree.

'(3) In the event of the employment of the Contractor being determined as aforesaid and so long as it has not been reinstated and continued, the following shall be the respective rights and duties of the Employer and Contractor:— (a) The

g
Employer may employ and pay other persons to carry out and complete the Works . . . (b) The . . . Employer may pay any supplier or sub-contractor for any materials or goods delivered or works executed for the purposes of this Contract (whether before or after the date of determination) in so far as the price thereof has not already been paid by the Contractor. The Employer's rights under this paragraph are in addition to his rights to pay nominated sub-contractors as provided in clause

h
27(c) of these Conditions and payments made under this paragraph may be deducted from any sum due or to become due to the Contractor . . . (d) The Contractor shall allow or pay to the Employer in the manner hereinafter appearing the amount of any direct loss and/or damage caused to the Employer by the determination. Until after completion of the Works under paragraph (a) of this sub-clause the Employer shall not be bound by any provision of this Contract to make any further payment

j
to the Contractor, but upon such completion and the verification within a reasonable time of the accounts therefor the Architects shall certify the amount of expenses properly incurred by the Employer and the amount of any direct loss and/or damage caused to the Employer by the determination and, if such amounts when added to the monies paid to the Contractor before the date of determination exceed the total amount which would have been payable on due completion in accordance

with this Contract, the difference shall be a debt payable to the Employer by the Contractor; and if the said amounts when added to the said monies be less than the said total amount, the difference shall be a debt payable by the Employer to the Contractor.'

On 2nd September 1977 Messrs Michael Aukett Associates, architects under the building contract, issued an interim certificate based on a valuation of works performed at 25th August 1977, certifying that £24,000 was payable under the building contract by the association to the company.

At all material times the association has been a customer of the plaintiffs, Barclays Bank Ltd (which I shall call 'Barclays'), at their branch at 78 Victoria Street, London SW1 (which I shall call 'the branch').

On Monday, 12th September 1977, the association drew a cheque (which I shall call 'the cheque') for £24,000 on its account with Barclays at the branch in favour of the company in payment of the interim certificate. At all material times there were sufficient funds in the account to meet the cheque. On Tuesday, 13th September 1977, pursuant to the terms of the mortgage debenture, National Westminster appointed Mr William Sowman, a chartered accountant, to be receiver of the undertaking, property and assets of the company. On Thursday, 15th September 1977, at 9.20 am, the association telephoned the branch and instructed Barclays to stop payment on the cheque. The branch immediately prepared that instruction for the computer which was then programmed accordingly. On the morning of Friday, 16th September 1977, a member of the branch staff checked the computer amendment applied report to ensure that the stop details had been recorded correctly. The association subsequently confirmed its telephone instructions in writing to Barclays. The cheque was received by Mr Sowman in the ordinary course of post and his assistant paid in the cheque at the Waddon branch of National Westminster with a direction that the cheque be specially cleared. It is not suggested that in giving such instruction for special clearance or at any time prior to the cheque being specially cleared, Mr Sowman, or his assistant or the company, was aware of the instructions given by the association to Barclays on Thursday, 15th September 1977.

Late on Thursday, 15th September, or early on Friday, 16th September 1977, a special presentation from the Waddon branch of National Westminster was received by the branch enclosing the cheque. Details of its presentation were recorded in the branch register on Friday, 16th September 1977, and the cheque was paid by the branch that day due to a mistake by the paying official at the branch who overlooked the stop instruction. A credit for National Westminster's special presentation account was sent to National Westminster in the branch credit transfers that evening. The cheque was rejected by Barclays' computer on Monday, 19th September 1977, the next business day, and was placed to the debit of the computer's suspense account for the work of 16th September 1977. The cheque was subsequently filed with the association's vouchers and its omission from the association's statement was discovered at Barclays' central accounting unit on Monday, 19th September 1977. On 27th September 1977 Barclays' head office telephoned the branch to state that there was an outstanding item for £24,000. The branch then telephoned the association to establish the reason for payment being countermanded. The association have since confirmed to Barclays (i) that they heard of the receiver's appointment on about 14th September 1977 and (ii) that they decided to stop the cheque in the belief that they were entitled so to act under the building contract.

Barclays subsequently demanded repayment of the cheque from Mr Sowman, who declined to make such repayment. Correspondence ensued between Barclays and its solicitors and Mr Sowman and his solicitors. The bank subsequently commenced proceedings claiming repayment of the £24,000 from the company and/or Mr Sowman as moneys paid under a mistake of fact. Mr Sowman has at all times since December 1977 held £24,000 in a separate account pending a decision in these proceedings.

a
In the receivership there is likely to be a deficiency as regards the preferential creditors. There will certainly be a substantial deficiency in the receivership for National Westminster, the mortgage debenture holder.

In the action as constituted, the plaintiffs, Barclays, claimed to be entitled to recover the money from the first defendants, the company, and the second defendant, the receiver as money paid under a mistake of fact. Pleadings were served. In the defence, apart from certain non-admissions of fact (which were subsequently resolved in the

b
agreed facts), the substantial point taken by the defendants was that Barclays were not entitled to recover because there was no mistake of fact between Barclays and the defendants or either of them, or alternatively that any mistake or misapprehension of fact was confined to Barclays. This point went to the nature of the mistake necessary to ground recovery, the matter to which the greater part of the argument in the case was devoted; and the defendants' argument on this point was (as will be seen) the subject of

c
some development. However, in the course of argument other points were raised by the defendants. These were as follows: (i) the money was irrecoverable from either defendant, because it was paid by Barclays and received by the company in discharge of the association's obligation to the company under the building contract or alternatively under the cheque; (ii) since Barclays failed to give notice of their claim on the day when the cheque was paid, they were unable (on the principle in *Cocks v Masterman*[1] and other

d
cases) to recover the money; (iii) in any event, no action lay against the receiver (iv) it was at one time submitted that the effect of the crystallisation of the floating charge was that Barclays could only succeed in their claim if they could establish that the money was impressed with a trust in their favour, and this, it was submitted, on the authority of *Re Diplock's Estate*[2] and other cases, Barclays could not establish. This submission provoked the response by Barclays that the money was indeed impressed with such a trust, and

e
would not therefore go as a windfall to the company's creditors; alternatively that Barclays would if necessary seek leave to join as defendants National Westminster, as the immediate recipients of the payment. In the outcome the point was not pursued by the defendants; and it was recognised by them that, since the action was intended to be in the nature of a test case to ascertain whether money paid in the circumstances of the present case was recoverable, Barclays' action should not fail for want of parties and that, on

f
Barclays not proceeding further against the receiver, the receiver would procure payment of any sum found due by the judgment.

I propose to deal with the matter as follows. I shall first consider the principles on which money is recoverable on the ground that it has been paid under a mistake of fact. Next, I shall consider the application of those principles to a case where a bank has paid, under a mistake of fact, a cheque drawn on it by a customer. Third, I shall consider

g
how far the defence in *Cocks v Masterman*[1] is available to defeat a claim brought by a bank which has paid a cheque under a mistake of fact. Lastly, I shall consider the application of these principles to the present case.

1 *The principles on which money is recoverable on the ground that it has been paid under a mistake of fact*

h
Nearly 40 years ago, Asquith J stated that 'it is notoriously difficult to reconcile all the cases dealing with payment of moneys under a mistake of fact' (see *Weld Blundell v Synott*[3]). This is indeed true, and it does not make easy the task of the trial judge, whose duty it is both to search for guiding principles among the authorities, and to pay due regard to those authorities by which he is bound. I have, however, come to the conclusion that it is possible for me, even in this field, to achieve both these apparently

j
irreconcilable objectives. The key to the problem lies, in my judgment, in a careful reading of the earliest and most fundamental authorities, and in giving full effect to

---

1   (1829) 9 B & C 902, [1824–34] All ER Rep 431
2   [1948] 2 All ER 318, [1948] All ER Rep 465
3   [1940] 2 All ER 580 at 583, [1940] 2 KB 107 at 112

certain decisions of the House of Lords. It is necessary therefore for me to review the leading authorities.

I shall go straight to three early cases, the first of which provided the basis of the modern law on this topic. That is *Kelly v Solari*[1]. The action was brought by the plaintiff, as one of the directors of Argus Life Assurance Co, to recover from the defendant a sum of money alleged to have been paid to her under a mistake of fact. The evidence was that the money had been paid to her, as executrix of her deceased husband, on a policy on the life of her husband, in entire forgetfulness that the assured had by mistake allowed the policy to lapse by reason of the non-payment of the premium. At the trial, Lord Abinger CB directed a nonsuit, expressing the opinion that if the directors had had knowledge, or the means of knowledge, of the policy having lapsed, the plaintiff could not recover; but he reserved leave to the plaintiff to move to enter a verdict for him for the amount claimed. The plaintiff obtained a rule nisi accordingly, or for a new trial; and the Court of Exchequer made the rule absolute for a new trial. The principal issue in the case was therefore whether negligence on the part of the plaintiff precluded recovery; it was held that it did not, a conclusion that has stood ever since. For present purposes, however, the case is important for a statement of principle by Parke B in the following terms[2]:

'I think that where money is paid to another under the influence of a mistake, that is, upon the supposition that a specific fact is true, which would entitle the other to the money, but which fact is untrue, and the money would not have been paid if it had been known to the payer that the fact was untrue, an action will lie to recover it back and it is against conscience to retain it ... If, indeed, the money is intentionally paid, without reference to the truth or falsehood of the fact, the plaintiff meaning to waive all inquiry into it, and that the person receiving shall have the money at all events, whether the fact be true or false, the latter is certainly entitled to retain it; but if it is paid under the impression of the truth of a fact which is untrue, it may, generally speaking, be recovered back, however careless the party paying may have been, in omitting to use due diligence to inquire into the fact.'

Rolfe B said[3]:

'Wherever [money] is paid under a mistake of fact, and the party would not have paid it if the fact had been known to him, it cannot be otherwise than unconscientious to retain it.'

The case was concerned with a payment made with the intention of discharging a supposed liability of the plaintiff to the defendant. It is no doubt for that reason that the first part of Parke B's statement of principle was directed to such a case; although it is to be observed that, in the context of such a case, Parke B did not place any restriction on the nature of the mistake which would ground recovery. But it would not, in my judgment, be right to infer that Parke B was stating that money paid under a mistake of fact was only recoverable in cases where the plaintiff's mistake led him to believe that he was under a liability to the defendant to pay the money to him. There is nothing to indicate that the first part of his statement of principle was intended so to restrict the right of recovery; indeed later in his judgment he stated the principle of recovery in broader terms, as did Rolfe B, which appears to indicate that it is sufficient to ground recovery that the plaintiff's mistake has caused him to make the payment.

The second of these three cases is *Aiken v Short*[4]. The plaintiffs were bankers. The bank was the transferee from one Carter of an inheritance to which Carter was supposedly entitled. The plaintiffs paid £226 16s 6d (£200 plus interest) to the defendant in discharge of a debt owed by Carter to the defendant, which was secured by an equitable

1 (1841) 9 M & W 54, [1835–42] All ER Rep 320
2 9 M & W 54 at 58–59, [1835–42] All ER Rep 320 at 322
3 9 M & W 54 at 59, [1835–42] All ER Rep 320 at 322
4 (1856) 1 H & N 210, [1843–60] All ER Rep 425

a
mortgage on Carter's supposed inheritance. It transpired that Carter had no inheritance; and the plaintiffs claimed to recover the money from the defendant as having been paid under a mistake of fact. It was held by the Court of Exchequer that the money was in those circumstances irrecoverable. It is a crucial fact in the case that, the payment having been authorised by Carter, it was effective to discharge the debt which was in fact owed by Carter to the defendant; the defendant therefore gave consideration for the payment which was, for that reason irrecoverable. This was the basis of the decision of both

b
Pollock CB and Platt B; it seems likely, from interventions in the argument, that Martin B (who was absent when judgment was given) would have decided the case on the same basis. Pollock CB said[1]:

'The Bank had paid the money in one sense without any consideration, but the defendant had a perfect right to receive the money from Carter, and the bankers paid for him . . . The money was, in fact, paid by the Bank, as agents of Carter.'

c
Platt B said[2]:

'Carter referred [the defendant] to the Bank, who paid the debt, and the bond was satisfied. The money which the defendant got from her debtor was actually due to her, and there can be no obligation to refund it.'

d
The case is, however, remembered principally for an obiter dictum of Bramwell B. He said[2]:

'In order to entitle a person to recover back money paid under a mistake of fact, the mistake must be as to a fact which, if true, would make the person paying liable to pay the money; not where, if true, it would merely make it desirable that he should pay the money.'

e
He recognised that the bankers were under no antecedent obligation to pay the money[2]: they 'were at liberty to pay or not, as they pleased'; and, having 'voluntarily parted with their money to purchase that which the defendant had to sell', they were unable to recover. It appears from a rather fuller report[3] that Bramwell B did not necessarily regard his statement of principle as comprehensive. But, strictly construed,

f
it appears to restrict the right of recovery more narrowly than did Parke B in *Kelly v Solari*[4]. It purports to exclude recovery in cases where the plaintiff's mistake did not lead him to believe that he was liable to pay the money to the defendant; and it appears in particular to exclude recovery in a case where the plaintiff had paid the money to the defendant in the mistaken belief, not that he was liable to the defendant to pay it, but that he was under an obligation to a third party to pay it to the defendant, even when the payment did not discharge a debt owing to the defendant who therefore gave no

g
consideration for it. Subsequent decisions of the House of Lords show that so restricted a statement of the principle of recovery does not represent the law.

The third of the early cases to which I must refer is *Chambers v Miller*[5], not because it sheds any particular light on this branch of the law, but because its effect has been misrepresented in certain textbooks, and in particular a dictum of Erle CJ has frequently

h
been cited out of context and so misunderstood. The case was not concerned with recovery of money paid under a mistake of fact, but with an action for assault and false imprisonment. The plaintiff was a clerk, who presented for payment at the defendant's bank a cheque held by his employers, drawn on the bank by one of their customers. The cashier, overlooking the fact that the customer's account was insufficient to meet the cheque, received it and placed the amount in cash on the counter. The plaintiff counted

j
1   (1856) 1 H & N 210 at 214, [1843–60] All ER Rep 425 at 427
2   1 H & N 210 at 215, [1843–60] All ER Rep 425 at 427
3   25 LJ Ex 321 at 324
4   (1841) 9 M & W 54, [1835–42] All ER Rep 320
5   (1862) 13 CBNS 125

the money, and was counting it a second time when the cashier, realising his mistake, returned and said that the cheque could not be paid. The plaintiff put the money in his *a* pocket, whereupon the cashier detained him, under threat of being given into custody on a charge of theft; he was so detained until he handed over the money, when he was given back the cheque uncancelled. The cheque was subsequently presented to the drawer and paid by him. The crucial question in the case was whether, in these circumstances, the property in the money had passed to the bearer of the cheque. All the members of the court held that it had, and a rule nisi to enter a verdict for the defendant *b* was accordingly discharged.

It was part of the defendant's argument that the money was recoverable, as having been paid under a mistake of fact. However that was, as at least two members of the court recognised (see per Williams and Byles JJ[1]) irrelevant to the question whether the property had passed; indeed, where an action is brought to recover money paid under a mistake of fact, property will almost invariably have passed to the defendant, the effect *c* of the action, if successful, being simply to impose on the defendant a personal obligation to repay the money. Furthermore, the kind of mistake that will ground recovery is, as Parke B's statement of the law in *Kelly v Solari*[2] shows, far wider than the kind of mistake which will vitiate an intention to transfer property. The court was satisfied in *Chambers v Miller*[3] that the cashier's mistake did not prevent the property in the money from passing. It was in the context of considering that question that Erle CJ referred to the *d* mistake as being[4] 'not as between [the cashier] and the bearer of the cheque, but as between him and the customer'. This dictum has, however, been taken out of its context and it has subsequently been suggested on its authority that no action will lie to recover money paid under a mistake of fact, unless the mistake was 'as between' the payer and the payee, in the sense that both parties were suffering under the same mistake. *Chambers v Miller*[3] provides, in my judgment, no basis for any such proposition, which was later to *e* be authoritatively rejected by the House of Lords.

Such are the early cases most frequently cited on this topic. I propose to go next to three cases in the House of Lords, in which the law on this subject was authoritatively established; but before I do so, I will first refer to a decision of the Privy Council, which was later to be relied on in one of the cases in the House of Lords. This is *Colonial Bank v Exchange Bank of Yarmouth, Nova Scotia*[5]. A firm called B Rogers & Son was in business *f* in Yarmouth, Nova Scotia. They instructed agents in Antigua to remit certain funds to the Halifax branch of the Bank of British North America. The agents paid the funds into the plaintiff bank, and gave them 'rather ambiguous instructions' for their remittance in favour of the Bank of British North America, which omitted any reference to that bank's branch in Halifax. The plaintiff bank then gave instructions to New York agents to carry out the instructions so received by them from B Rogers & Son's agents. The New York *g* agents proceeded to put the New York branch of the Bank of British North America in funds, but gave them instructions in terms which erroneously required payment 'for account Yarmouth Bank, credit of Rogers'. The Bank of British North America had no branch in Yarmouth, but considered that the proper way of remitting funds to Yarmouth was to pay them to the defendant bank, with whom they had arrangements. This they did, paying the money to the defendant bank, 'credit of Rogers'. It so happened that *h* Rogers was a customer of the defendant bank, and was considerably in their debt at the time, and so they put the money to the credit of Rogers, and to the debit of the Bank of British North America. On the following day the Bank of British North America in New York, having been advised by Rogers of the mistake, called for the repayment of the

j

1　(1862) 13 CBNS 125 at 135, 136–137
2　(1841) 9 M & W 54, [1835–42] All ER Rep 320
3　13 CBNS 125
4　13 CBNS 125 at 133
5　(1885) 11 App Cas 84

money from the defendant bank; this was refused on the ground that the credit had been
a 'used', which meant that it had been placed in the defendant bank's books in reduction
of Rogers's indebtedness to them. It was held that the plaintiff bank were entitled to
recover the money from the defendant bank. The principal question in the case was
whether the plaintiff bank had a sufficient interest to proceed direct against the defendant
bank for the money. But for present purposes, the decision is of interest because the
plaintiff bank did not suffer under a mistake which led them to believe that they were
b under any liability to the defendants to pay the money to them; indeed nobody, in the
whole chain of parties, believed that they were under any such liability. The decision is
therefore clearly contrary to the view, founded on Bramwell B's dictum in *Aiken v Short*[1],
that to ground recovery, a mistake of fact must fall within any such restrictive category;
indeed there is nothing in the advice of the Board in this case, which was delivered by
Lord Hobhouse, to suggest that there is any limitation to be placed on the category of
c mistake necessary to ground recovery, other than that it must have caused the payment.
   I come then to the three cases in the House of Lords. The first is *Kleinwort, Sons & Co
v Dunlop Rubber Co*[2]. A firm called Messrs Kramrisch were rubber merchants, who were
financed both by the appellants, Messrs Kleinworts, and by another merchant bank,
Messrs Brandts. Kramrisch supplied the respondents, the Dunlop Rubber Co, with a
quantity of rubber, directing them to pay the price to Brandts, who had an equitable
d mortgage on it. The respondents mistakenly paid it to the appellants, who received it in
good faith. Messrs Kramrisch failed and the respondents were subsequently held liable
to pay the money to Messrs Brandts. They claimed to recover from the appellants the
money they had mistakenly paid to them. It was held that they were entitled to recover
it as having been paid under a mistake of fact. The main question in the case was
whether the appellants could rely on the defence of change of position; but that plea was
e conclusively negatived by the answers of the jury at the trial. For present purposes, the
interest of the case lies in two matters. First, there was no question of the respondents
mistakenly believing that they were under any liability to the appellants to pay the
money to them. Second, Lord Loreburn LC stated the principle of recovery in very
broad terms. He said[3]:

f   '. . . it is indisputable that, if money is paid under a mistake of fact and is
       redemanded from the person who received it before his position has been altered to
       his disadvantage, the money must be repaid in whatever character it was received.'

   The second of these cases is *Kerrison v Glyn, Mills, Currie & Co*[4]. The appellant paid a
sum of money to the respondents, for the account of a New York bank called Kessler &
Co, in anticipation of a liability to recoup Kessler & Co for advances made by them to a
g mining company in Mexico in which the appellant was interested. Unknown to the
appellant or the respondents, Kessler & Co were insolvent at the time of the payment.
The money was not paid over by the respondents to Kessler & Co; but since Kessler & Co
were indebted to them, the respondents claimed to be entitled to retain the money and
declined to refund it to the appellant. It was held that the appellant was entitled to
recover the money from the respondents. Two questions arose in the case. First,
h whether the arrangements between the appellant and Kessler & Co were such that he was
indebted to Kessler & Co in the sum of money; it was held by the House of Lords
(differing from the Court of Appeal[5] on this point) that he was not, and that the money
was paid only in anticipation of a future liability. Had the appellant been so indebted,
it was recognised by the House of Lords that the money would have been paid in
discharge of an existing debt and would have been irrecoverable, despite the fact that the

j
——
 1   (1856) 1 H & N 210 at 215, [1843–60] All ER Rep 425 at 427
 2   (1907) 97 LT 263
 3   97 LT 263 at 264
 4   (1911) 81 LJKB 465, [1911–13] All ER Rep 417
 5   (1910) 15 Com Cas 241

appellant had paid it under the misapprehension that Kessler & Co were solvent. Lord Atkinson, who delivered the leading speech, said[1]:

> '[The appellant] lodged the money in the belief that Kessler & Co. were a living commercial entity able to carry on their business as theretofore, that they were in a position to honour and would honour the drafts of the Bote Mining Co. up to the sum which he, in anticipation, sent to recoup them for their repeated advances. Kessler & Co. had, in fact, ceased to be in that position.'

The second question was whether the fact that the respondents were bankers enabled them to resist the appellant's claim, on the ground that money once paid into a bank ceases altogether to be the money of the payer. That was held to be irrelevant.

This decision, too, is therefore inconsistent with the proposition that the only mistake which will ground recovery is a mistake which leads the payer to believe that he is liable to the payee to pay it to him. But the case is also of interest for present purposes because of statements in the speeches of their Lordships relating to the type of mistake which will ground recovery. These are in very broad terms. Lord Atkinson said[1]:

> 'I cannot doubt but that on general principles, [the appellant] would be entitled to recover back money paid in ignorance of these vital matters as money paid in mistake of fact.'

Lord Shaw said[2]:

> 'The money was paid . . . under the mistake in fact—which was material, and was indeed the only reason for payment—that Kessler & Co. could perform their obligations.'

Lord Mersey said[3] that the facts brought the case directly within the terms of the judgment of Lord Loreburn LC in *Kleinwort, Sons & Co v Dunlop Rubber Co*[4], and then quoted the passage[5] from that judgment which I have set out above. He went on to dismiss an attempt by the respondents 'to take the case out of this plain and simple rule of law'. It is to be observed that Lord Loreburn LC was a member of the Judicial Committee in *Kerrison's* case[6], and concurred, as did the Earl of Halsbury.

It thus appears that, provided the plaintiff's mistake is 'vital' or 'material', which I understand to mean that the mistake caused the plaintiff to pay the money, the money is prima facie recoverable; but that if the payment discharged an existing debt owing to the payee (or to a principal on whose behalf the payee is authorised to receive the payment) it is irrecoverable. Such a conclusion is, if I may say so with respect, entirely consistent with the decision in *Aiken v Short*[7], though not with the dictum of Bramwell B[8] in that case.

The third decision of the House of Lords to which I must refer is *R E Jones Ltd v Waring & Gillow Ltd*[9]. The facts of the case are complicated and somewhat unclear, due in part to the curious way in which they were found, since they appear to have been taken by the trial judge from the opening speech of the plaintiff's counsel. In summary, a rogue named Bodenham obtained from the respondents furniture and other effects to a value

---

1   (1911) 81 LJKB 465 at 470, [1911–13] All ER Rep 417 at 422
2   81 LJKB 465 at 471, [1911–13] All ER Rep 417 at 423
3   81 LJKB 465 at 472, [1911–13] All ER Rep 417 at 424
4   (1907) 97 LT 263
5   97 LT 263 at 264
6   81 LJKB 465, [1911–13] All ER Rep 417
7   (1856) 1 H & N 210, [1843–60] All ER Rep 425
8   1 H & N 210 at 215, [1843–60] All ER Rep 425 at 427
9   [1926] AC 670, [1926] All ER Rep 36

of over £13,000 on hire-purchase terms, under which the down payment was to be

a £5,000. It appears that Bodenham defaulted in making the down payment, and that the respondents then repossessed the goods. Bodenham then approached the appellants, informing them that he represented a firm of motor manufacturers called International Motors who had control of a car called the Roma, and he persuaded the appellants to accept an appointment as agents for the sale of the car in certain parts of this country, one term of the agency being the payment of a deposit of £5,000 (£10 for each of 500

b cars). Bodenham told the appellants that the people who were financing the thing and who were the principals behind him in the matter were the respondents, and that the deposit might be paid to them. The appellants then made out two cheques payable to the order of the respondents, one for £2,000 and one for £3,000, and handed them to Bodenham; he handed them to the respondents, who received them from him in respect of his deposit under the hire-purchase agreement. The respondents' accountant observed

c that the cheques bore the signature of only one director; he then arranged with the appellants to exchange them for one cheque for £5,000, duly signed. This exchange was effected in good faith, nothing being said about the nature of the transaction. The cheque for £5,000 was cashed by the respondents, who then restored to Bodenham the furniture they had seized, and let him have some more. Subsequently, the fraud came to light, and it transpired that there was no International Motors and no Roma car. The

d respondents resumed possession of the furniture. The appellants claimed repayment of the sum of £5,000 from the respondents.

The trial judge gave judgment for the appellants; but his judgment was reversed by the Court of Appeal[1]. The reasons given by the members of the court vary; but for present purposes the significant judgment is that of Pollock MR. He held that the appellants' claim to recover the money as paid under a mistake of fact must fail, because

e the mistake was not a mistake *as between* the appellants and the respondents. He referred to the dicta of Parke B in *Kelly v Solari*[2] and of Bramwell B in *Aiken v Short*[3]; he also referred to the decision in *Chambers v Miller*[4] and to the dictum of Erle CJ in that case[5]. Pollock MR concluded[6]:

f
> 'The plaintiffs and the defendants were each of them under misapprehension— different misapprehensions—and different mistakes of fact. It appears to me, therefore, that it is not possible for the plaintiffs to recover the money as having been paid under a mistake of fact.'

The House of Lords[7] were however unanimous in concluding that the appellants' mistake of fact was sufficient to ground recovery, although a minority considered that the respondents had a good defence to the claim because they had changed their position

g in good faith. The House accordingly allowed the appeal. For present purposes, I am only concerned with the nature of the mistake which will ground recovery. Viscount Cave LC (with whose speech Lord Atkinson agreed) stated the principle in very broad terms, which show that he considered it sufficient for the plaintiff to show that he suffered under a mistake of fact which caused the payment. He said[8]:

h
> 'The plaintiffs were told by Bodenham that he represented a firm called International Motors which was about to be formed into a company, that the firm had control of a car called the "Roma" car which he described as an existing car, and

1 [1925] 2 KB 612
2 (1841) 9 M & W 54 at 58, [1835–42] All ER Rep 320 at 322
j 3 (1856) 1 H & N 210 at 215
4 (1862) 13 CBNS 125
5 32 LJCP 30 at 32; cf 13 CBNS 125 at 133
6 [1925] 2 KB 612 at 632
7 [1926] AC 670, [1926] All ER Rep 36
8 [1926] AC 670 at 679–680, [1926] All ER Rep 36 at 39

that the defendants were financing the firm and were the principals behind him and behind International Motors in the matter. Believing these statements to be true, the plaintiffs entered into an agreement which bound them to pay a deposit of 5,000l. on 500 Roma cars; and still believing them to be true, and that the respondents as the nominees of International Motors could give a good receipt for the 5,000l., they paid that sum to the respondents. In fact the statements were untrue from beginning to end; and the money was, therefore, paid under a mistake of fact induced by the false statements of a third party and, apart from special circumstances, could be recovered. As to the general principle, it is sufficient to refer to the well known case of *Kelly* v. *Solari*[1], and to the more recent decisions in *Colonial Bank* v. *Exchange Bank of Yarmouth, Nova Scotia*[2] and *Kerrison* v. *Glyn, Mills, Currie & Co*.[3]'

It is significant that Viscount Cave LC did not consider it necessary to identify the precise capacity in which the appellants supposed that the respondents received the money; it was enough for him that the appellants supposed that the respondents were 'nominees' of International Motors who could give a good receipt for the money, a purely neutral term. It follows that he did not regard it as necessary that the appellants should have supposed that they were liable to the respondents to pay the money to them, as is borne out by his citation of the *Colonial Bank* case[2] and of *Kerrison's* case[3]. It is scarcely surprising that Lord Atkinson, who delivered the leading speech in *Kerrison's* case[3], agreed with Viscount Cave LC on this aspect of the case. Lord Shaw also agreed with Viscount Cave LC that the money was paid under a mistake of fact. He concluded[4] that it seemed quite clear that the appellants would never have parted with the money if they had had any knowledge of the real truth, and that the money was recoverable. It appears from his statement of the facts that he did not consider that the appellants mistakenly believed that they were liable to the respondents to pay the money to them. Lord Sumner[5] stated the facts in terms which show that he considered that the appellants supposed that, in paying the money, they were discharging an obligation to International Motors, not an obligation to the respondents. Lord Carson, in agreeing with Viscount Cave LC that the money was paid under a mistake of fact, cited and relied on both the dictum of Parke B and the very broad dictum of Rolfe B in *Kelly v Solari*[6], of which at least the latter requires only that the plaintiff's mistake should have caused him to pay the money.

I wish to make three comments on the decision of the House of Lords in *R E Jones Ltd v Waring & Gillow Ltd*[7]. First, the House of Lords must have rejected the view, expressed by Pollock MR[8], that to ground recovery the mistake must have been 'as between' payer and payee, in the sense of having been a mistake shared by both parties. Second, it is implicit in the speeches of all their Lordships that it is not a prerequisite of recovery that the plaintiff must have mistakenly believed that he was liable to the defendant to pay the money to him. Third, as I understand their Lordships' speeches, in particular the speech of Viscount Cave LC (with which Lord Atkinson agreed) and the speeches of Lord Shaw and Lord Carson, it is sufficient to ground recovery that the plaintiff's mistake should have caused him to pay the money to the payee.

I should add, with great respect, that the reasoning, if not the decision, of Roche J in *Barclay & Co Ltd v Malcolm & Co*[9] cannot in my judgment be reconciled with the decision

1   (1841) 9 M & W 54, [1835–42] All ER Rep 320
2   (1885) 11 App Cas 84
3   (1911) 81 LJKB 465, [1911–13] All ER Rep 417
4   [1926] AC 670 at 686, [1926] All ER Rep 36 at 43
5   [1926] AC 670 at 691–692, [1926] All ER Rep 36 at 45
6   9 M & W 54 at 58–59, [1835–42] All ER Rep 320 at 322
7   [1926] AC 670, [1926] All ER Rep 36
8   [1925] 2 KB 612 at 632
9   (1925) 133 LT 512

of the House of Lords in *R E Jones Ltd v Waring & Gillow Ltd*[1]. It is striking that *Barclay*

a *& Co Ltd v Malcolm & Co*[2] was argued and decided between the decisions of the Court of Appeal[3] and the House of Lords[1] in *R E Jones Ltd v Waring & Gillow Ltd*. Moreover, leading counsel for the plaintiffs in *Barclay & Co Ltd v Malcolm & Co*[2] had appeared for the respondents in *R E Jones Ltd v Waring & Gillow Ltd*[3] before the Court of Appeal only three months earlier. The decision of the Court of Appeal in the latter case is not mentioned in the report of *Barclay & Co Ltd v Malcolm & Co*[2]; but that case is very briefly

b reported in the Law Times Reports, and it is inconceivable that so recent an authority, in which counsel had appeared, was not cited to Roche J. In *Barclay & Co Ltd v Malcolm & Co*[2], the plaintiff bank had mistakenly paid the same sum twice to the defendants, in the belief that a confirming letter from another bank constituted a second set of instructions. Roche J held that the money was not recoverable. The first and principal ground on which he so held was expressed by him in the following words[4]:

c   'It is not contrary to good conscience that the defendants should be allowed to keep the money in question. The mistake was in no way due to them. The mistake which was made concerned only the plaintiffs and the Warsaw Bank by whom the plaintiffs were instructed, and it was not a mistake with regard to the liability of one person to pay or the right of another person to receive. The nearest authority appears to be *Chambers* v. *Miller*[5]. In my view, the first point gives a good defence

d to the action.'

Such reasoning is, in my judgment, inconsistent with the ratio decidendi of the decision of the House of Lords in *R E Jones Ltd v Waring & Gillow Ltd*[1].

From this formidable line of authority certain simple principles can, in my judgment, be deduced.

e   1. If a person pays money to another under a mistake of fact which causes him to make the payment, he is prima facie entitled to recover it as money paid under a mistake of fact.

2. His claim may however fail if: (a) the payer intends that the payee shall have the money at all events, whether the fact be true or false, or is deemed in law so to intend; (b) the payment is made for good consideration, in particular if the money is paid to

f discharge, and does discharge, a debt owed to the payee (or a principal on whose behalf he is authorised to receive the payment) by the payer or by a third party by whom he is authorised to discharge the debt; (c) the payee has changed his position in good faith, or is deemed in law to have done so.

To these simple propositions, I append the following footnotes: (a) *Proposition 1*. This is founded on the speeches in the three cases in the House of Lords, to which I have

g referred. It is also consistent with the opinion expressed by Turner J in *Thomas v Houston Corbett & Co*[6]. Of course, if the money was due under a contract between the payer and the payee, there can be no recovery on this ground unless the contract itself is held void for mistake (as in *Norwich Union Fire Insurance Society Ltd v William H Price Ltd*[7]) or is rescinded by the plaintiff.

(b) *Proposition 2(a)*. This is founded on the dictum of Parke B in *Kelly v Solari*[8]. I have

h felt it necessary to add the words 'or is deemed in law so to intend' to accommodate the

---

1   [1926] AC 670, [1926] All ER Rep 36
2   (1925) 133 LT 512
j 3   [1925] 2 KB 612
4   133 LT 512 at 513
5   (1862) 13 CBNS 125
6   [1969] NZLR 151 at 167
7   [1934] AC 455, [1934] All ER Rep 352
8   (1841) 9 M & W 54 at 58, [1835–42] All ER Rep 320 at 322

decision of the Court of Appeal in *Morgan v Ashcroft*[1], a case strongly relied on by the
defendants in the present case, the effect of which I shall have to consider later in this
judgment.

(c) *Proposition 2(b)*. This is founded on the decision in *Aiken v Short*[2], and on dicta in
Kerrison's case[3]. However, even if the payee has given consideration for the payment, for
example by accepting the payment in discharge of a debt owed to him by a third party
on whose behalf the payer is authorised to discharge it, that transaction may itself be set
aside (and so provide no defence to the claim) if the payer's mistake was induced by the
payee, or possibly even where the payee, being aware of the payer's mistake, did not
receive the money in good faith: cf *Ward & Co v Wallis*[4] per Kennedy J.

(d) *Proposition 2(c)*. This is founded on the statement of principle of Lord Loreburn
LC in *Kleinwort, Sons & Co v Dunlop Rubber Co*[5]. I have deliberately stated this defence
in broad terms, making no reference to the question whether it is dependent on a breach
of duty by the plaintiff or a representation by him independent of the payment, because
these matters do not arise for decision in the present case. I have, however, referred to
the possibility that the defendant may be deemed in law to have changed his position,
because of a line of authorities concerned with negotiable instruments which I shall have
to consider later in this judgment, of which the leading case is *Cocks v Masterman*[6].

(e) I have ignored, in stating the principle of recovery, defences of general application
in the law of restitution, for example where public policy precludes restitution.

(f) The following propositions are inconsistent with the simple principle of recovery
established in the authorities: (i) that to ground recovery, the mistake must have induced
the payer to believe that he was liable to pay the money to the payee or his principal; (ii)
that to ground recovery, the mistake must have been 'as between' the payer and the
payee. Rejection of this test has led to its reformulation (notably by Asquith J in *Weld
Blundell v Synott*[7] and by Windeyer J in *Porter v Latec Finance (Qld) Pty Ltd*[8]) in terms
which in my judgment mean no more than that the mistake must have caused the
payment.

In the case before me, counsel submitted on behalf of the defendants that I could not
proceed on the basis of the simple principles I have stated, because I was precluded from
so doing by binding authority, viz the decision of the Court of Appeal in *Morgan v
Ashcroft*[1]. That case came on appeal from the county court. The respondent was a
bookmaker, with whom the appellant was in the habit of making bets. The respondent
claimed that his clerk mistakenly credited the appellant twice over with a sum of
£24 2s 1d, and claimed to recover that sum from the appellant as having been paid
under a mistake of fact. The county court judge held that the respondent was entitled
to recover the money. The Court of Appeal allowed the appeal, holding that the money
was not recoverable. The first ground of the court's decision was that, in order to
ascertain whether there had been an overpayment, it would be necessary for the court to
examine the state of account between the parties, and that the court could not do, by
reason of the Gaming Act 1845. However the court also held that the money was in any
event not recoverable as having been paid under a mistake of fact. Counsel relied in
particular on a passage in the judgment of Greene MR, in which he stated[9]:

'. . . a person who intends to make a voluntary payment, and thinks that he is

---

1　[1937] 3 All ER 92, [1938] 1 KB 49
2　(1856) 1 H & N 210, [1843–60] All ER Rep 425
3　(1911) 81 LJKB 465, [1911–13] All ER Rep 417
4　[1900] 1 KB 675 at 678–679
5　(1907) 97 LT 263
6　(1829) 9 B & C 902, [1824–34] All ER Rep 431
7　[1940] 2 All ER 580, [1940] 2 KB 107
8　(1964) 111 CLR 177 at 204
9　[1937] 3 All ER 92 at 98, [1938] 1 KB 49 at 66

a   making one kind of voluntary payment, whereas, upon the true facts, he is making another kind of voluntary payment, does not make the payment under a mistake of fact which can be described as fundamental or basic.'

That passage counsel for the defendants identified as being the crucial passage in Greene MR's judgment on this point; and he submitted further that the expression 'voluntary payment' must here be understood as a payment made without legal obligation, so that, generally speaking, a person who makes a payment without the intention of discharging
b   a legal obligation cannot recover the money from the payee although it has been paid under a mistake of fact, except possibly in circumstances where the mistake can be described as fundamental, for example where the mistake is as to the identity of the payee.

It is legitimate to observe the consequences of counsel's submission. If he is right, money would be irrecoverable in the following, by no means far-fetched, situations
c   (i) A man, forgetting that he has already paid his subscription to the National Trust, pays it a second time. (ii) A substantial charity uses a computer for the purpose of distributing small benefactions. The computer runs mad, and pays one beneficiary the same gift one hundred times over. (iii) A shipowner and a charterer enter into a sterling charterparty for a period of years. Sterling depreciates against other currencies; and the charterer decides, to maintain the goodwill of the shipowner but without obligation, to increase
d   the monthly hire payments. Owing to a mistake in his office, the increase in one monthly hire payment is paid twice over. (iv) A Lloyd's syndicate gets into financial difficulties. To maintain the reputation of Lloyd's, other underwriting syndicates decide to make gifts of money to assist the syndicate in difficulties. Due to a mistake, one syndicate makes its gift twice over.

It would not be difficult to construct other examples. The consequences of counsel's
e   submission are therefore so far-reaching that it is necessary to examine the ratio decidendi of this part of the decision in *Morgan v Ashcroft*[1] to ascertain whether it produces the result for which counsel contends. Only two judges sat to hear the appeal in *Morgan v Ashcroft*[1]: Greene MR and Scott LJ. Furthermore, there are considerable differences between their two judgments on this part of the case. First, there was a difference in the basic philosophy expounded by the two judges. Greene MR favoured the so-called
f   'implied contract' theory as the basis of recovery of money paid under a mistake of fact. Citing a well-known dictum of Lord Sumner from *Sinclair v Brougham*[2] he rejected the principle of unjust enrichment and stated that the claim was based on an imputed promise to repay[3]. Scott LJ adopted a less restricted view. While accepting that the moral principle of unjust enrichment had been rejected as a universal or complete legal touchstone whereby to test the cause of action, he referred to passages from the works of
g   eminent jurists and concluded that his citations emphasised[4]—

'the importance of trying to find some common positive principles upon which these causes of action called "implied contracts" can be said to rest, and which will not altogether exclude that of unjust enrichment embodied in those citations.'

Scott LJ's approach has been amply vindicated by subsequent developments in the law,
h   as is shown in particular by authoritative statements of principle in the House of Lords by Lord Atkin in *United Australia Ltd v Barclays Bank Ltd*[5] and by Lord Wright in *Fibrosa Spolka Akcyjna v Fairbairn Lawson Combe Barbour Ltd*[6].

How far Greene MR's narrower philosophic approach affected his analysis in *Morgan*

---

j   1   [1937] 3 All ER 92, [1938] 1 KB 49
     2   [1914] AC 398 at 452, [1914–15] All ER Rep 622 at 648
     3   [1937] 3 All ER 92 at 96, [1938] 1 KB 49 at 62
     4   [1937] 3 All ER 92 at 104, [1938] 1 KB 49 at 76
     5   [1940] 4 All ER 20 at 36–37, [1941] AC 1 at 28–29
     6   [1942] 2 All ER 122 at 135–136, [1943] AC 32 at 61

v Ashcroft[1] is difficult to tell; but there was a further difference between him and Scott LJ in their view of the nature of the mistake which will ground recovery of money paid under a mistake of fact. Again, Greene MR adopted a more restricted view. He founded himself on the dictum of Bramwell B in *Aiken v Short*[2], which he accepted as an authoritative statement of the law 'so far as regards the class of mistake with which he was dealing', ie in 'cases where the only mistake is as to the nature of the transaction'[3]. From that dictum he deduced the conclusion on which counsel for the defendants relied before me, viz that if a person thinks that he is making one kind of voluntary payment, whereas on the true facts he is making another kind of voluntary payment, his mistake is not fundamental or basic and therefore cannot ground recovery[4]. Scott LJ, on the other hand, was not prepared to accept Bramwell B's dictum as authoritative; in particular, he referred to *Kerrison's* case[5] and said that the decision of the House of Lords in that case seemed to him[6]—

'conclusive that the rule as stated in *Aiken* v. *Short*[7] cannot be regarded as final and exhaustive in the sense that no mistake, which does not induce in the mind of the payer a belief that payment will discharge or reduce his liability, can ground an action for money had and received.'

In these circumstances it is by no means easy to determine the ratio decidendi of this part of the case. It may well be found in the opinion of both judges than an overpayment of betting debts by a bookmaker is not made under a mistake of fact sufficiently fundamental to ground recovery, apparently on the basis that the payment is in any event intended to be a purely voluntary gift, because 'the law prevents the plaintiff from saying that he intended anything but a present' (per Scott LJ[8]) and the plaintiff is therefore deemed in law to intend that the payee shall be entitled to retain the money in any event.

That the ratio decidendi is not to be found in the passage from Greene MR's judgment on which counsel relied is shown by the fact that the subsequent decision of the Court of Appeal in *Larner v London County Council*[9] is, in my judgment, inconsistent with that passage. In that case, the London County Council had resolved to pay all their employees who went to the war the difference between their war service pay and their civil pay until further order. Mr Larner was an ambulance driver employed by the council, who was called up in 1942. As a result of his failure to keep the council accurately informed about changes in his war service pay, the council overpaid the difference. In contending that the overpayment was irrecoverable, Mr Larner's counsel relied on the dictum of Bramwell B in *Aiken v Short*[2]. The Court of Appeal, however, held that the money was recoverable. Denning LJ[10], who delivered the judgment of the court, declined to follow that dictum, because the 'dictum, as Scott, L.J., pointed out in *Morgan* v. *Ashcroft*[6], cannot be regarded as an exhaustive statement of the law'. He pointed out that the council[10]—

'made a promise to the men which they were in honour bound to fulfil. The payments made under that promise were not mere gratuities. They were made as a matter of duty . . .'

---

1   [1937] 3 All ER 92, [1938] 1 KB 49
2   (1856) 1 H & N 210 at 215, [1843–60] All ER Rep 425 at 427
3   [1937] 3 All ER 92 at 98, 99, [1938] 1 KB 49 at 66
4   [1937] 3 All ER 92 at 98–99, [1938] 1 KB 49 at 65–67
5   (1911) 81 LJKB 465, [1911–13] All ER Rep 417
6   [1937] 3 All ER 92 at 103, [1938] 1 KB 49 at 73–74
7   (1856) 1 H & N 210, [1843–60] All ER Rep 425
8   [1937] 3 All ER 92 at 105, [1938] 1 KB 49 at 77
9   [1949] 1 All ER 964, [1949] 2 KB 683
10   [1949] 1 All ER 964 at 966, [1949] 2 KB 683 at 688

a but he went on to state that it was irrelevant that the council's promise was unsupported by consideration or unenforceable by action. It was enough that the council would never have paid the money to Mr Larner had they known the true facts. It is doubtful if the decision in *Larner v London County Council*[1] is one of which Greene MR would have approved; but, if I may say so with respect, it is entirely consistent with the principles of recovery established in the earlier decisions of the House of Lords to which I have referred. Accordingly it is those principles which I intend to apply in the present case.

b 2 *Where a bank pays a cheque drawn on it by a customer of the bank, in what circumstances may the bank recover the payment from the payee on the ground that it was paid under a mistake of fact?*

It is a basic obligation owed by a bank to its customer that it will honour on presentation cheques drawn by the customer on the bank, provided that there are c sufficient funds in the customer's account to meet the cheque, or the bank has agreed to provide the customer with overdraft facilities sufficient to meet the cheque. Where the bank honours such a cheque, it acts within its mandate, with the result that the bank is entitled to debit the customer's account with the amount of the cheque, and further that the bank's payment is effective to discharge the obligation of the customer to the payee on the cheque, because the bank has paid the cheque with the authority of the customer.

d In other circumstances, the bank is under no obligation to honour its customer's cheques. If, however, a customer draws a cheque on the bank without funds in his account or agreed overdraft facilities sufficient to meet it, the cheque on presentation constitutes a request to the bank to provide overdraft facilities sufficient to meet the cheque. The bank has an option whether or not to comply with that request. If it declines to do so, it acts entirely within its rights and no legal consequences follow as e between the bank and its customer. If, however, the bank pays the cheque, it accepts the request and the payment has the same legal consequences as if the payment had been made pursuant to previously agreed overdraft facilities; the payment is made within the bank's mandate, and in particular the bank is entitled to debit the customer's account, and the bank's payment discharges the customer's obligation to the payee on the cheque.

In other cases, however, a bank which pays a cheque drawn or purported to be drawn f by its customer pays without mandate. A bank does so if, for example, it overlooks or ignores notice of its customer's death, or if it pays a cheque bearing the forged signature of its customer as drawer; but, more important for present purposes, a bank will pay without mandate if it overlooks or ignores notice of countermand of the customer who has drawn the cheque. In such cases the bank, if it pays the cheque, pays without mandate from its customer; and, unless the customer is able to and does ratify the g payment, the bank cannot debit the customer's account, nor will its payment be effective to discharge the obligation (if any) of the customer on the cheque, because the bank had no authority to discharge such obligation.

It is against the background of these principles, which were not in dispute before me, that I have to consider the position of a bank which pays a cheque under a mistake of fact. In such a case, the crucial question is, in my judgment, whether the payment was h with or without mandate. The two typical situations, which exemplify payment with or without mandate, arise first where the bank pays in the mistaken belief that there are sufficient funds or overdraft facilities to meet the cheque and second where the bank overlooks notice of countermand given by the customer. In each case, there is a mistake by the bank which causes the bank to make the payment. But in the first case the effect of the bank's payment is to accept the customer's request for overdraft facilities; the j payment is therefore within the bank's mandate, with the result that not only is the bank entitled to have recourse to its customer, but the customer's obligation to the payee is discharged. It follows that the payee has given consideration for the payment, with the consequence that, although the payment has been caused by the bank's mistake, the

1   [1949] 1 All ER 964, [1949] 2 KB 683

money is irrecoverable from the payee unless the transaction of payment is itself set
aside. Although the bank is unable to recover the money, it has a right of recourse to its   *a*
customer. In the second case, however, the bank's payment is without mandate. The
bank has no recourse to its customer, and the debt of the customer to the payee on the
cheque is not discharged. Prima facie, the bank is entitled to recover the money from
the payee, unless the payee has changed his position in good faith, or is deemed in law to
have done so.

It is relevant to observe that if, in *Chambers v Miller*[1], the action had, instead of being   *b*
a claim by the bearer for damages for false imprisonment, taken the form of a claim by
the paying bank for recovery of the money as having been paid under a mistake of fact,
that claim would, on the foregoing analysis, have failed, because the mistake of the bank
in that case was a mistaken belief that there were sufficient funds in the customer's
account to meet the cheque. Similarly in *Pollard v Bank of England*[2], where a bank paid
a bill of exchange accepted by one of their customers payable at the bank, in ignorance   *c*
of the fact that the balance of the credit of the acceptors at the bank was insufficient to
meet the bill and indeed that the acceptors had, in the general sense, stopped payment
(and so were unable to pay their debts when they fell due), the bank was held to be unable
to recover from the payee the money so paid: see per Blackburn J[3], who delivered the
judgment of the court. In both these cases, the bank acted within its mandate; but
where the bank's mistake relates not to sufficiency of funds in its customer's account, but   *d*
arises from ignorance or oversight of a notice of countermand, the bank acts without
mandate, and the money is in my judgment prima facie recoverable.

3 *If a bank pays a cheque under a mistake of fact, in what circumstance has
the payee a good defence to the bank's claim to recover the money, on the
principle in Cocks v Masterman*[4]*?*

The authorities on this topic have recently been analysed by Kerr J in *National*   *e*
Westminster Bank Ltd v Barclays Bank International Ltd[5], an analysis which I gratefully
adopt and which makes it unnecessary for me to burden this judgment with a full
analysis of the authorities. The case before Kerr J was concerned with a claim by the
plaintiff bank to recover from the defendant bank a sum paid by it on a forged cheque
presented by the defendant bank on behalf of a customer for special collection, which the   *f*
plaintiff bank had paid to the defendant bank in ignorance of the forgery, and the
defendant bank had then credited to its customer's account. A principal question in the
case was whether the plaintiff bank was estopped from claiming repayment by a
representation, in honouring the cheque, that the cheque was genuine. Kerr J, in
holding that the bank made no such representation and was not so estopped, considered
the line of cases, commencing with the decision of Lord Mansfield CJ in *Price v Neal*[6], in
which payments of bills of exchange which contained forged signatures had been held   *g*
irrecoverable on a number of grounds. The early cases on the topic culminated in the
leading case of *Cocks v Masterman*[4]. In that case the plaintiff bankers paid a bill, which
purported to have been accepted by their customer, in ignorance of the fact that the
acceptance was forged, a fact they did not discover until the day after payment. It was
held by the Court of King's Bench that they could not recover the money from the   *h*
defendants, the holders' bankers. Bayley J, who delivered the judgment of the court,
said[7]:

---

1   (1862) 13 CBNS 125
2   (1871) LR 6 QB 623   *j*
3   LR 6 QB 623 at 631
4   (1829) 9 B & C 902, [1824–34] All ER Rep 431
5   [1974] 3 All ER 834, [1975] QB 654
6   (1762) 3 Burr 1355
7   9 B & C 902 at 908–909, [1824–34] All ER Rep 431 at 433

a '. . . we are all of opinion that the holder of a bill is entitled to know, on the day when it becomes due, whether it is an honoured or dishonoured bill, and that, if he receive the money and is suffered to retain it during the whole of that day, the parties who paid it cannot recover it back. The holder, indeed, is not bound by law (if the bill be dishonoured by the acceptor) to take any steps against the other parties to the bill till the day after it is dishonoured. But he is entitled so to do, if he thinks fit, and the parties who pay the bill ought not by their negligence to deprive the
b holder of any right or privilege. If we were to hold that the plaintiffs were entitled to recover, it would be in effect saying that the plaintiffs might deprive the holder of a bill of his right to take steps against the parties to the bill on the day when it becomes due.'

The principle to be derived from this case is probably that, if the plaintiff fails to give notice on the day of payment that the bill contained a forged signature and that the
c money, having been paid in ignorance of that fact, is being claimed back, the defendant is deprived of the opportunity of giving notice of dishonour on the day when the bill falls due, and so is deemed to have changed his position and has a good defence to the claim on that ground. But, whatever the precise basis of the defence, it is clearly founded on the need for the defendant to give notice of dishonour; and it can therefore have no application where notice of dishonour is not required. Thus in *Imperial Bank of Canada*
d *v Bank of Hamilton*[1] it was held by the Privy Council that the defence had no application to an unendorsed cheque in which the amount of the cheque had been fraudulently increased by the drawer after it had been certified. The cheque was regarded as a total forgery, and not as a negotiable instrument at all. Lord Lindley, who delivered the advice of the Board, said[2]:

e 'The cheque for the larger amount was a simple forgery; and Bauer, the drawer and forger, was not entitled to any notice of its dishonour by non-payment. There were no indorsers to whom notice of dishonour had to be given. The law as to the necessity of giving notice of dishonour has therefore no application. The rule laid down in *Cocks v. Masterman*[3], and recently reasserted in even wider language by Mathew J. in *London and River Plate Bank* v. *Bank of Liverpool*[4], has reference to
f negotiable instruments, on the dishonour of which notice has to be given to some one, namely, to some drawer or indorser, who would be discharged from liability unless such notice were given in proper time. Their Lordships are not aware of any authority for applying so stringent a rule to any other cases. Assuming it to be as stringent as is alleged in such cases as those above described, their Lordships are not prepared to extend it to other cases where notice of the mistake is given in reasonable
g time, and no loss has been occasioned by the delay in giving it.'

Likewise, in *National Westminster Bank Ltd v Barclays Bank International Ltd*[5], Kerr J held that the defence had no application in the case which he had to consider of a wholly forged cheque, which was also not a negotiable instrument at all.

In a passage in Paget's Law of Banking[6], which was relied on by counsel for the defendants in the present case, it is suggested that the law as expounded by Lord Lindley
h in the *Imperial Bank of Canada* case[1] is open to criticism, on the ground that if a bill is paid and the money is thereafter reclaimed no dishonour takes place until the money is reclaimed and therefore no notice of dishonour can be given until then, from which it follows that it is hard to conceive of any case of payment by mistake where the

j   1   [1903] AC 49
    2   [1903] AC 49 at 58
    3   (1829) 9 B & C 902, [1824-34] All ER Rep 431
    4   [1896] 1 QB 7, [1895-9] All ER Rep 1005
    5   [1974] 3 All ER 834, [1975] QB 654
    6   8th Edn (1972), pp 377-378

opportunity of giving notice of dishonour is lost. I am unable to accept this criticism.
If the money is recovered, then the bill will not have been paid on the due date or at all,   *a*
for the payment will not have discharged the debt due on the bill. It follows that, in such
a case, the bill is in fact dishonoured on the day it falls due, and as Bayley J in *Cocks v
Masterman*[1] and Lord Lindley in the *Imperial Bank of Canada* case[2] both contemplated,
unless notice of the plaintiff's claim is given on that date, the opportunity of the
defendant to give notice of dishonour on that day is lost. Like Lord Lindley in the
Imperial Bank of Canada case[2], I can find nothing inconsistent with this conclusion in the   *b*
decision of Mathew J in *London and River Plate Bank v Bank of Liverpool*[3].

It is therefore a prerequisite to the application of the defence that the defendant should
be under a duty to give notice of dishonour. The provisions regarding notice of
dishonour in the Bills of Exchange Act 1882 are contained in ss 48 to 50 of the Act. In
s 50(2) are set out the circumstances in which notice of dishonour is dispensed with. For
present purposes, the relevant provision is contained in s 50(2)(c), which provides (inter   *c*
alia) that 'Notice of dishonour is dispensed with . . . (c) As regards the drawer . . . where
the drawer has countermanded payment'. It follows that in the case of a simple
unendorsed cheque, payment of which is countermanded by the drawer, notice of
dishonour is not required; and in such a case, the payee cannot invoke the defence
established in *Cocks v Masterman*[1].

It is to be observed that, in the *Imperial Bank of Canada* case[4], Lord Lindley described   *d*
the rule laid down in *Cocks v Masterman*[1] as a stringent rule. It is not merely stringent,
but very technical. It is possible that if, in due course, full recognition is accorded to the
defence of change of position there will be no further need for any such stringent rule
and the law can be reformulated on a more rational and less technical basis. Whether the
law will hereafter develop in this way remains to be seen.

e

4 *Application of the foregoing principles to the present case*

In the light of the above principles, it is plain that in the present case Barclays are
entitled to succeed in their claim. First, it is clear that the mistake of the bank, in
overlooking the drawer's instruction to stop payment of the cheque, caused the bank to
pay the cheque. Second, since the drawer had in fact countermanded payment, the bank
were acting without mandate and so the payment was not effective to discharge the   *f*
drawer's obligation on the cheque; from this it follows that the payee gave no
consideration for the payment, and the claim cannot be defeated on that ground. Third,
there is no evidence of any actual change of position on the part of either of the
defendants or on the part of National Westminster; and, since notice of dishonour is not
required in a case such as this, the payee is not deemed to have changed his position by
reason of lapse of time in notifying them of Barclays' error and claiming repayment.   *g*

I must confess that I am happy to be able to reach the conclusion that the money is
recoverable by Barclays. If the bank had not failed to overlook its customer's instructions,
the cheque would have been returned by it marked 'Orders not to pay', and there would
have followed a perfectly bona fide dispute between the association and the receiver on
the question, arising on the terms of the building contract, whether the association was
entitled to stop the cheque, which ought to be the real dispute in the case. If Barclays had   *h*
been unable to recover the money, not only would that dispute not have been ventilated
and resolved on its merits but, in the absence of ratification by the association, Barclays
would have had no recourse to the association. Indeed, if under the terms of the building
contract the money had not been due to the company, non-recovery by Barclays would
have meant quite simply a windfall for the preferred creditors of the company at

j

1   (1829) 9 B & C 902, [1824–34] All ER Rep 431
2   [1903] AC 49
3   [1896] 1 QB 7, [1895–9] All ER Rep 1005
4   [1903] AC 49 at 57

Barclays' expense. As however I have held that the money is recoverable, the situation
a is as it should have been; nobody is harmed, and the true dispute between the association
and the receiver can be resolved on its merits.

I have, however, to consider the identity of the party against whom Barclays are
entitled to judgment. As at present advised I am reluctant to enter judgment against the
company without further argument. I say that because the argument before me was
concentrated on the right of recovery generally, and there was not fully canvassed before
b me the question whether, assuming that National Westminster received the payment as
agent for the company, an action will lie against its principal to whom Barclays had
neither paid the money nor done anything equivalent to payment. I will be glad,
therefore, to hear submissions from counsel as to how the parties wish the matter to be
taken from here.

[There followed a discussion with counsel, in the course of which the defendants by
c their counsel conceded that, for the purposes of the case before the court, the receipt of
the money by National Westminster, as collecting banker or agent of the company, was
a sufficient receipt of the money by the company to entitle Barclays to judgment for the
sum so paid as against the company.]

Judgment for Barclays against the company for £26,451·38 being £24,000 together with
d *£2,451·38 by way of interest. Action against the receiver dismissed.*

Solicitors: *Durrant Piesse* (for Barclays); *Harvey, Ingram,* Leicester (for the defendants).

K Mydeen Esq   Barrister.

Note
Ollett v Bristol Aerojet Ltd

QUEEN'S BENCH DIVISION AT BRISTOL
ACKNER J
17th OCTOBER 1978

Practice – Evidence – Expert evidence – Disclosure to other parties – Substance of evidence in form of written report – RSC Ord 38, r 38(1).

ACKNER J, after giving judgment for the plaintiff on the issue of liability in a personal injuries action, said: Before leaving this case I would like to make two observations with regard to expert reports, and I would be grateful if a copy of this part of my judgment be sent to the registrars of Bristol and Bath. I shall also communicate with the Chief Master of the Supreme Court because, in this case, the order made is not an order made by a registrar in this area. It is one that was made in London. Its terms are, however, those that are currently in operation in Bristol.

The first point I make is this. There has been in the past some suggestion that, when an order is made under RSC Ord 38, r 38(1)[1], that the *substance* of the experts' reports be exchanged, then that order is satisfied by the experts merely setting out factual descriptions of the machine and the alleged circumstances in which the accident happened and leaving out any conclusions as to the defects in the machine, the system of work or other relevant opinion evidence. This seems to me to be a total misconception of the ordinary meaning of the word 'substance'. It is also a misconception of the function of an expert. An expert, unlike other witnesses, is allowed, because of his special qualifications and/or experience, to give *opinion* evidence. It is for his opinion evidence that he is called, not for a factual description of the machine or the circumstances of the accident, although that is often necessary in order to explain and/or justify his conclusions. When the substance of the expert's report is to be provided, that means precisely what it says, both the substance of the factual description of the machine and /or the circumstances of the accident and his expert opinion in relation to that accident, which is the very justification for calling him.

Secondly, there appears to be a tendency to make orders which do not involve any obligation to disclose experts' reports, other than medical reports. It is true that the court has to be satisfied that it is desirable for experts' reports to be exchanged but, as the Supreme Court Practice[2] indicates, the court will ordinarily make such an order.

The whole purpose of Ord 38 is, in relation to expert evidence, to save expense by dispensing with the calling of experts when there is in reality no real dispute and, where there is a dispute, by avoiding parties being taken by surprise as to the true nature of the dispute and thereby being obliged to seek adjournments.

This case was the simplest of industrial accidents, without the slightest justification for the withholding of experts' reports. It was exactly the sort of case where exchange of experts' reports would have highlighted the only potential issue. The exchange, if it had been ordered, as should have been the case, would have resulted in the amendment sought at the trial causing no surprise to the defendants, and probably it would have resulted in the action not being fought. I trust that in future registrars will in practice ordinarily make an order for the exchange of experts' reports.

Mary Rose Plummer Barrister.

---

1   Rule 38(1), so far as material, provides: '. . . the Court may, if satisfied that it is desirable to do so, direct that the substance of any expert evidence which is to be adduced by any party be disclosed in the form of a written report or reports to such other parties and within such period as the Court may specify.'

2   (1976) vol 1, para 38/37–39/6, p 604; see now (1979) vol 1, para 38/37–39/6, p 626

a R v Hull Prison Board of Visitors, ex parte St Germain and others (No 2)

QUEEN'S BENCH DIVISION
LORD WIDGERY CJ, GEOFFREY LANE LJ AND ACKNER J
22nd, 23rd, 24th, 25th MAY, 15th JUNE 1979

b

Natural justice – Prison board of visitors – Exercise of disciplinary powers – Procedure – Duty of board to give fair hearing to prisoner charged with disciplinary offence – Extent of board's duty – Prisoner's right to be heard himself and to call witnesses – Chairman's power to limit right to call witnesses – Whether board bound by technical rules of evidence – Prison Act 1952, s 47(2) – Prison Rules 1964 (SI 1964 No 388), r 49(2).

c

In 1976 a riot broke out among the prisoners at a prison and serious damage was done to it. It was decided not to take criminal proceedings against the prisoners but to deal with them under the prison disciplinary procedure. They were accordingly charged with disciplinary offences under the Prison Rules 1964, which were made under s 47(2)[a] of the Prison Act 1952, and brought before the prison's board of visitors. Rule 49(2)[b] of the d rules provided that at such an inquiry the prisoner should be given a full opportunity of hearing what was alleged against him and of presenting his own case. The procedure laid down in the rules for such an inquiry was explained in a booklet which was given to each of the accused prisoners prior to the hearing. The booklet stated, inter alia, that if a prisoner wanted to call witnesses he had to ask the chairman for permission to do so and tell him who the witnesses were and what he thought their evidence would prove. The e booklet further stated that if the board thought the witnesses might be able to give useful evidence it would hear them and after it had done so it would ask the prisoner if he wanted to add anything further about the case and that he could then comment on all the evidence and point out anything that he thought was in his favour. The prison governor was present at the hearing before the board of visitors. He had in front of him a dossier containing the prison officers' accounts of the part played by the accused in the f riot. From time to time during the hearing the governor gave the board information from the dossier. Eight of the accused ('the applicants') were found guilty and awarded punishments which involved substantial loss of privileges. They each applied for an order of certiorari to quash the findings of the board on the grounds that they had not been given a proper opportunity of presenting their cases in accordance with r 49(2) and that the board had failed to observe the rules of natural justice in that it had, inter alia, g refused to allow them to call witnesses in support of their cases and had admitted and then acted on statements made during the hearing by the governor which were based on reports by prison officers who had not given oral evidence.

Held – (i) Section 47(2) of the 1952 Act and r 49(2) of the 1964 rules were merely declaratory of the basic rule of natural justice that every party to a controversy had a right h to a fair hearing, i e that he had to be told what evidence had been given and what statements had been made affecting him and he then had to be afforded a fair opportunity to correct or contradict them. In the case of a person charged with a serious disciplinary offence under the 1964 rules not only had he the right to be heard himself but he also had the right to call any evidence which was likely to assist in establishing vital facts in issue (see p 548 *f g* and p 552 *a b*, post); dictum of Lord Denning in *Kanda v Government of the* j *Federation of Malaya* [1962] AC at 337–338 and *General Medical Council v Spackman* [1943] 2 All ER 337 applied; dictum of Lord Loreburn LC in *Board of Education v Rice* [1911–13] All ER Rep at 38 considered.

---

a Section 47(2) is set out at p 548 e, post
b Rule 49(2) is set out at p 548 f, post

(ii) There was nothing in the board's procedure to which any objection could properly be taken. The discretion given to the chairman to refuse to allow a prisoner to call *a* witnesses was a necessary part of any procedure for dealing with alleged offences against discipline by prisoners but it was to be exercised reasonably, in good faith and on proper grounds. Thus it would not be proper to refuse to allow a prisoner to call a witness merely on the ground that it would cause considerable administrative inconvenience. The chairman could, however, limit the number of witnesses where he had good reason to believe that the prisoner, by requesting the attendance of a large number of witnesses, *b* was attempting to render the hearing of the charge virtually impracticable or where he thought it was unnecessary for all the witnesses to be called to establish the point at issue (see p 549 *g* and *j* to p 550 *e*, post).

(iii) The board was not bound by the technical rules of evidence which applied in courts in criminal cases. It could admit hearsay evidence but its right to do so was subject to the overriding obligation to provide the accused with a fair hearing. Depending on *c* the facts of the particular case and the nature of the hearsay evidence provided, the obligation to give the accused a fair hearing might require the board not only to inform the accused of the evidence but also to give him a sufficient opportunity to deal with it, which could involve the cross-examination of witnesses whose evidence was initially before the board in the form of hearsay. Where a prisoner wished to dispute hearsay evidence, and for that purpose to question a witness, the board should, if there were *d* insuperable or very grave difficulties in arranging for the witness's attendance, refuse to admit the evidence, or, if it had already come to its notice, expressly dismiss it from its consideration (see p 552 *e* and *h* to p 553 *e*, post); dicta of Viscount Simon LC in *General Medical Council v Spackman* [1943] 2 All ER at 338, of Lord Jenkins in *University of Ceylon v Fernando* [1960] 1 All ER at 637 and of Diplock LJ in *R v Deputy Industrial Injuries Comr, ex parte Moore* [1965] 1 All ER at 93 applied.

e

(iv) On the evidence the board's findings should be quashed in respect of one of the charges on the ground that the applicant had been improperly refused permission to call witnesses, and in respect of some of the remaining charges because of the manner in which the board had handled the hearsay evidence. Orders for certiorari would be granted accordingly in those cases. The other applications for orders of certiorari would be refused (see p 554 *b c* and *f* to *j*, post).

f

Notes

For the rules of natural justice and a disciplinary board, see 30 Halsbury's Laws (3rd Edn) 718, para 1368, and for cases on the subject, see 38 Digest (Repl) 102–103, 732–736.

For the scope of the rule against hearsay evidence in criminal proceedings, see 11 Halsbury's Laws (4th Edn) para 438, and for cases on the subject, see 14(2) Digest *g* (Reissue) 596–598, 4841–4862.

For the Prison Act 1952, s 47, see 25 Halsbury's Statutes (3rd Edn) 851.

For the Prison Rules 1964, r 49, see 18 Halsbury's Statutory Instruments (3rd Reissue) 25.

Cases referred to in judgment

h

Board of Education v Rice [1911] AC 179, [1911–13] All ER Rep 36, 80 LJKB 796, 104 LT 689, 75 JP 393, 9 LGR 652, HL; *affg* sub nom *R v Board of Education* [1910] 2 KB 165, CA, 19 Digest (Repl) 630, 206.

De Verteuil v Knaggs [1918] AC 557, 87 LJPC 128, sub nom *De Verteuil v Acting Governor of Trinidad* 118 LT 738, PC, 8(2) Digest (Reissue) 667, 50.

General Medical Council v Spackman [1943] 2 All ER 337, [1943] AC 627, 112 LJKB 529, *j* 169 LT 226, HL, 33 Digest (Repl) 520, 27.

Kanda v Government of the Federation of Malaya [1962] AC 322, [1962] 2 WLR 1153, PC, 37 Digest (Repl) 189, *8.

R v Deputy Industrial Injuries Comr, ex parte Moore [1965] 1 All ER 81, [1965] 1 QB 456, [1965] 2 WLR 89, CA, Digest (Cont Vol B) 542, 4589a.

a *R v Fulham, Hammersmith & Kensington Rent Tribunal, ex parte Zerek* [1951] 1 All ER 482, [1951] 2 KB 1, 115 JP 132, 49 LGR 275, DC, 31(2) Digest (Reissue) 1044, 8238.

R v Hull Prison Board of Visitors, ex parte St Germain [1979] 1 All ER 701, [1979] 2 WLR 42, CA; *rvsg* [1978] 2 All ER 198, [1978] QB 678, [1978] 2 WLR 598, 66 Cr App R 141, DC.

R v Local Government Board, ex parte Arlidge [1914] 1 KB 160, 83 LJKB 86, 109 LT 651, 78 JP 25, 11 LGR 1186, CA; *rvsd sub nom Local Government Board v Arlidge* [1915] AC

b 120, [1914–15] All ER Rep 1, 84 LJKB 72, 111 LT 905, 79 JP 97, 12 LGR 1109, HL, 18 Digest (Reissue) 159, *1298*.

R v Turnbull [1976] 3 All ER 549, [1977] QB 224, [1976] 3 WLR 445, 140 JP 648, 63 Cr App R 132, CA, 14(2) Digest (Reissue) 489, *4038*.

Ridge v Baldwin [1963] 2 All ER 66, [1964] AC 40, [1962] 2 WLR 935, 127 JP 295, 61 LGR 369, HL, 37 Digest (Repl) 195, *32*.

c *University of Ceylon v Fernando* [1960] 1 All ER 631, [1960] 1 WLR 223, PC, 19 Digest (Repl) 655, **362*.

Wiseman v Borneman [1969] 3 All ER 275, [1971] AC 297, 45 Tax Cas 540, [1969] 3 WLR 706, [1969] TR 279, 48 ATC 278, HL, 28(1) Digest (Reissue) 493, *1760*.

Cases also cited

d *Breen v Amalgamated Engineering Union* [1971] 1 All ER 1148, [1971] 2 QB 175, CA.

Daemar v Hall [1978] 2 NZLR 594.

Enderby Town Football Club Ltd v Football Association Ltd [1971] 1 All ER 215, [1971] 1 Ch 591, CA.

Lee v Showmen's Guild of Great Britain [1952] 1 All ER 1175, [1952] 2 QB 329, CA.

MacLean v Workers' Union [1929] 1 Ch 602, [1929] All ER Rep 468.

e *Norman and Moran v National Docks Labour Board* [1957] 1 Lloyd's Rep 455, CA.

Motion for certiorari

Ronald St Germain, Michael Reed, Keith Saxton, Kenneth Anderson, James Joseph Pike, Peter Rajah and Geoffrey Dennis Cotterill each applied by way of motion for an order of certiorari to bring up and quash decisions of the board of visitors of Hull Prison whereby

f they were held to be guilty of certain charges in respect of offences against discipline and punishments were imposed on them involving the loss of various privileges. The case is reported only on the rules of natural justice in so far as they relate to adjudications by a prison board of visitors and on the extent to which the technical rules of evidence can be dispensed with by such a board. The facts are set out in the judgment of the court. At the same time the court heard an application by Raymond David Rosa for an order of

g certiorari to bring up and quash a decision of the Board of Visitors of Wandsworth Prison whereby it held that he was guilty of the offence of assaulting a prison warder and imposed on him 90 days' loss of remission. That case turned on its own facts and is not set out in the report.

Andrew Collins for the applicants St Germain, Saxton and Rosa.

h *Peter Thornton* for the applicants Reed, Anderson, Pike and Rajah.

J B Gateshill for the applicant Cotterill.

Alan Campbell QC, Nicolas Bratza and *Robert Owen* for the prison visitors.

Cur adv vult

j 15th June. **GEOFFREY LANE LJ** read the following judgment of the court: These are seven motions for orders of certiorari against the board of visitors of Hull prison and one application for a similar order directed to the board of visitors of Wandsworth prison.

All these matters, except the Wandsworth case which can be dealt with separately, arose out of a riot which took place at Hull Prison from 31st August to 2nd September

1976. Serious damage was done to the prison which made it largely uninhabitable. The inmates or most of them were dispersed to other prisons.

It was decided not to take criminal proceedings against the rioters but to deal with them internally under the prison disciplinary procedure. For reasons which will become apparent when the statute and regulations are examined, the task of adjudicating on the various allegations fell on representatives of the board of visitors of Hull prison. Three such representatives were selected, two of whom were justices of the peace. Some idea of the size of their task can be gained from the fact that proceedings were taken against 185 of the 310 inmates of the prison and that the total number of individual charges was over 500. The hearings took place at a number of different prisons, the board of visitors moving on from one prison to another as the hearings were completed. Whatever other criticisms may have been levelled at the board of visitors, no one could fail to admire their industry and application and no one could fail to applaud the way in which the proceedings were recorded and documented.

The adjudication took place on various dates during November and December 1976. Applications for judicial review of the findings were made during the early part of 1977. The matter first came before the Divisional Court on 5th December 1977 when the contention of the board of visitors that the court had no jurisdiction to entertain the application was upheld. On 3rd October 1978 the Court of Appeal reversed that decision on the grounds that the board of visitors, when adjudicating on disciplinary charges, were performing a judicial, and not merely an administrative, act, that they had a duty to act judicially and that their decisions were in principle subject to judicial review by way of certiorari (see *R v Hull Prison Board of Visitors, ex parte St Germain*[1]).

We turn now to the statutory provisions and regulations so far as they are material. Section 47 of the Prison Act 1952 provides that the Secretary of State may make rules for the regulation and management, inter alia, of prisons and for the discipline and control of persons required to be detained therein. Subsection (2) provides: 'Rules made under this section shall make provision for ensuring that a person who is charged with any offence under the rules shall be given a proper opportunity of presenting his case.'

The rules at the material time are contained in the Prison Rules 1964[2]. Rule 49 is headed 'Rights of prisoners charged'. Rule 49(2) provides: 'At any inquiry into a charge against a prisoner he shall be given a full opportunity of hearing what is alleged against him and of presenting his own case.'

In our judgment the statutory obligation to make the rules, and r 49(2) in particular, are merely declaratory of one of the basic rules of natural justice, namely that every party to the controversy has a right to a fair hearing. He must know what evidence has been given and what statements have been made affecting him; and then he must be given a fair opportunity to correct or contradict them (per Lord Denning in *Kanda v Government of the Federation of Malaya*[3]).

Rule 50 deals with the powers of prison governors to make awards for offences against discipline. In respect of graver offences as defined by r 51, the governor shall, unless he dismisses the charge, forthwith inform the Secretary of State and shall, unless otherwise directed by him, refer the charge to the board of visitors. Rule 52 provides that where a prisoner is charged with mutiny or incitement to mutiny or doing gross personal violence to an officer, then, where such a charge is referred to a board of visitors, the chairman shall summon a special meeting of which not more than five nor fewer than three members, at least two being justices of the peace, shall be present. The board thus constituted shall enquire into the charge and, if they find the offence proved, shall make one or more of the awards listed in r 51(4). If they make an award of forfeiture of remission, the period forfeited may not exceed 180 days. Rule 56 provides that the Secretary of State may remit a disciplinary award or mitigate it either by reducing it or

1   [1979] 1 All ER 701, [1979] 2 WLR 42
2   SI 1964 No 388
3   [1962] AC 322 at 337–338

by substituting another award which is, in his opinion, less severe. He is not given any power to quash the adjudication.

A document entitled 'Explanation of the procedure at adjudications by board of visitors'[1] is provided to every prisoner accused of a disciplinary offence who is to appear before a board of visitors. It sets out the procedure which follows essentially that which would occur in any magistrates' court on summary trial. These paragraphs of this explanation are relevant and we quote from them:

> '(5) When a witness has given his evidence you will be told that you may question him if you wish. You may then ask the witness any questions which you think may help your case. Remember just to ask questions and not to argue with the witness. If you want to dispute something he has said you should either ask him another question or explain your point to the Chairman who will help you . . .
>
> '(7) If you want to call witnesses ask the Chairman for permission to do so. Tell him who they are and what you think their evidence will prove. If the Board think that the witnesses may be able to give useful evidence they will hear them. After they have been heard the Board will ask you if you want to say anything further about the case, and you may then comment on all the evidence and point out anything that you think is in your favour.
>
> '(8) If you have pleaded not guilty, but in the end are found guilty, you will be given an opportunity, before punishment is imposed, of giving any reasons why you think you should be dealt with leniently.'

Megaw LJ in his judgment in *R v Hull Prison Board of Visitors, ex parte St Germain*[2] referred to the submissions of counsel that proceedings of boards of visitors for offences against discipline are 'subject to judicial review, at any rate where the allegations are of breaches of the procedure laid down in the Prison Rules and/or rules of fairness and natural justice'. He said[2]:

> 'I think that is too widely stated. It is certainly not any breach of any procedural rule which would justify or require interference by the courts. Such interference, in my judgment, would only be required, and would only be justified, if there were some failure to act fairly, having regard to all relevant circumstances, and such unfairness could reasonably be regarded as having caused a substantial, as distinct from a trivial or merely technical, injustice which was capable of remedy.'

He further pointed out that which has been frequently stated recently, that it would be fallacious to assume that the requirements of natural justice in one sphere are necessarily identical in a different sphere. In our judgment there is nothing in the procedure as detailed in the written explanation to which any objection can properly be taken.

We turn now to the way in which the case has been presented on behalf of the applicants. Broadly speaking each applicant complains that he was not given a 'proper opportunity of presenting his case', and that the board of visitors failed to observe the elementary rules of fair play or natural justice and that accordingly the findings should be quashed. In particular there are four specific complaints: (1) that the board of visitors refused to allow the applicants to call witnesses in support of their cases; (2) that they admitted and acted on statements made during the hearing by the governor which were based on reports from prison officers who did not give oral evidence; (3) that the chairman of the board of visitors insisted on questions by the applicants in cross-examination being channelled through him; and (4) that the applicants were not allowed to speak in mitigation after a finding of guilt.

Counsel accepted that it was perfectly proper for a chairman to insist that all questions were put through him where he was of the view that otherwise arguments would break

---

1 An extract of the Report of the Working Party on Adjudication Procedures in Prisons (Home Office, 1975)
2 [1979] 1 All ER 701 at 713, [1979] 2 WLR 42 at 57

out between the prisoner and the witness, which would make the proceedings difficult
to control. There was some suggestion that the chairman should have no discretion to
disallow the calling of a witness whose attendance is requested by the prisoner. This
suggestion was largely withdrawn in the course of argument and we do not think it had
any validity. Those who appear before the board of visitors on charges are, ex hypothesi,
those who are serving sentences in prison. Many of such offenders might well seek to
render the adjudications by the board of visitors quite impossible if they had the same
liberty to conduct their own defences as they would have in an ordinary criminal trial.
In our judgment the chairman's discretion is necessary as part of a proper procedure for
dealing with alleged offences against discipline by prisoners.

However, that discretion has to be exercised reasonably, in good faith and on proper
grounds. It would clearly be wrong if, as has been alleged in one instance before us, the
basis for refusal to allow a prisoner to call witnesses was that the chairman considered that
there was ample evidence against the accused. It would equally be an improper exercise
of the discretion if the refusal was based on an erroneous understanding of the prisoner's
defence, for example, that an alibi did not cover the material time or day, whereas in
truth and in fact it did.

A more serious question was raised whether the discretion could be validly exercised
where it was based on considerable administrative inconvenience being caused if the
request to call a witness or witnesses was permitted. Clearly in the proper exercise of his
discretion a chairman may limit the number of witnesses, either on the basis that he has
good reason for considering that the total number sought to be called is an attempt by the
prisoner to render the hearing of the charge virtually impracticable or where quite
simply it would be quite unnecessary to call so many witnesses to establish the point at
issue. But mere administrative difficulties, simpliciter, are not in our view enough.
Convenience and justice are often not on speaking terms (see per Lord Atkin in *General
Medical Council v Spackman*[1]).

At the outset of his submissions counsel for the board of visitors urged that there was
no obligation at all on the board to allow any witnesses to be called. He said, and to this
extent we accept his submission, that the written explanation of the procedure at
adjudications by boards of visitors has no statutory force. He based his submission on the
bald proposition that although natural justice imposes an obligation to hear the party
accused, it does not involve any obligation to hear any witnesses whom he wishes to call.

He based his submission essentially on Lord Loreburn LC's well-known speech in the
House of Lords in *Board of Education v Rice*[2] where the following passage appears:

'Comparatively recent statutes have extended, if they have not originated, the
practice of imposing upon departments or officers of State the duty of deciding or
determining questions of various kinds. In the present instance, as in many others,
what comes for determination is sometimes a matter to be settled by discretion,
involving no law. It will, I suppose, usually be of an administrative kind; but
sometimes it will involve matter of law as well as matter of fact, or even depend
upon matter of law alone. In such cases the Board of Education will have to
ascertain the law and also to ascertain the facts. I need not add that in doing either
they must act in good faith and fairly listen to both sides, for that is a duty lying
upon every one who decides anything. But I do not think they are bound to treat
such a question as though it were a trial. They have no power to administer an oath,
and need not examine witnesses. They can obtain information in any way they
think best, always giving a fair opportunity to those who are parties in the
controversy for correcting or contradicting any relevant statement prejudicial to
their view.'

---

1   [1943] 2 All ER 337 at 341, [1943] AC 627 at 638
2   [1911] AC 179 at 182, [1911–13] All ER Rep 36 at 38

a
Counsel for the board of visitors relies on, in particular, the phrase 'need not examine witnesses'.

Lord Atkin in his speech in *General Medical Council v Spackman*[1] said in terms that he would demur to any suggestion that the words of Lord Loreburn LC offer a complete guide to the General Medical Council on whom there was a statutory obligation to make 'due inquiry' under s 29 of the Medical Act 1858 into an allegation of infamous conduct in a professional respect by a registered medical practitioner. He said[1]: '. . . it is not

b
correct that "they need not examine witnesses." They must examine witnesses if tendered, and their own rules rightly provide for this.'

Viscount Simon LC, in his speech, said[2]:

c
'Unless Parliament otherwise enacts, the duty of considering the defence of a party accused, before pronouncing the accused to be rightly adjudged guilty, rests on any tribunal, whether strictly judicial or not, which is given the duty of investigating his behaviour and taking disciplinary action against him. The form in which this duty is discharged—e.g., whether by hearing evidence *viva voce* or otherwise—is for the rules of the tribunal to decide. What matters is that the accused should not be condemned without being first given a fair chance of exculpation.'

d
In our view a fair chance of exculpation cannot in many cases by given without hearing the accused's witnesses, e g in a case of an alibi defence.

Lord Wright in his speech[3] initially observed that the obligation to comply with the rules of natural justice aptly described what the council had to do: to make 'due inquiry'. While accepting that 'contrary to natural justice' is an expression 'sadly lacking in precision' (see Hamilton LJ in *R v Local Government Board, ex parte Arlidge*[4]), he

e
emphasised that the essential requirement was that the tribunal should be impartial and that the medical practitioner who is impugned should be given a full and fair opportunity of being heard. Later[5] he stated that the doctor proceeded against must be entitled to call evidence, either his own or that of other witnesses, to controvert the charge. In commenting on the council's rules (which had not been invoked in the case) which provided that the practitioner would be called on to state his case and produce the

f
evidence in support of it, he said in terms that the rules satisfied 'the essential requirements of justice and fair play'.

Counsel for the board of visitors argues that *General Medical Council v Spackman*[6] is in a special category of its own, because the very rules of the General Medical Council provided in terms as part of its procedure that the practitioner would be called on by the president to state his case and produce the evidence in support of it. However, as we have

g
already pointed out, the speech of Lord Wright makes it clear that these domestic rules were merely declaratory of the rules of natural justice.

It was in fact 25 years earlier, in *De Verteuil v Knaggs*[7] that the Privy Council stated:

h
'Their Lordships are of opinion that in making such an inquiry there is, apart from special circumstances, a duty of giving to any person against whom the complaint is made a fair opportunity to make any relevant statement which he may desire to bring forward and a fair opportunity to correct or controvert any relevant statement brought forward to his prejudice.'

These words were quoted with approval in the Privy Council in *University of Ceylon v*

j
1   [1943] 2 All ER 337 at 341, [1943] AC 627 at 638
2   [1943] 2 All ER 337 at 340, [1943] AC 627 at 635–636
3   [1943] 2 All ER 337 at 342, [1943] AC 627 at 640
4   [1914] 1 KB 160 at 199, [1914–15] All ER Rep 1 at 20
5   [1943] 2 All ER 337 at 345, [1943] AC 627 at 645
6   [1943] 2 All ER 337, [1943] AC 627
7   [1918] AC 557 at 560

Fernando[1]. They imply, in our view, that the right to be heard will include, in appropriate cases, the right to call evidence. It would in our judgment be wrong to attempt an exhaustive definition as to what are appropriate cases, but they must include proceedings whose function is to establish the guilt or innocence of a person charged with serious misconduct. In the instant cases, what was being considered was alleged serious disciplinary offences, which, if established, could and did result in a very substantial loss of liberty. In such a situation it would be a mockery to say that an accused had been 'given a proper opportunity of presenting his case' (s 47(2) of the Prison Act 1952) or 'a full opportunity . . . of presenting his own case' (r 49(2) of the Prison Rules 1964), if he had been denied the opportunity of calling evidence which was likely to assist in establishing the vital facts at issue.

For completeness we should deal with a further submission of counsel for the board of visitors, namely that, since in many of the decided cases there were frequent references to a domestic tribunal being the master of its own procedure, the rules of natural justice can have no relevance to matters of procedure. This, in our judgment, is a fundamental misconception. The rules of natural justice are a compendious reference to those rules of procedure which the common law requires persons who exercise quasi-judicial functions to observe (*R v Deputy Industrial Injuries Comr, ex parte Moore*[2]). Natural justice requires that the procedure before any tribunal which is acting judicially shall be fair in all the circumstances. For a long time the courts have without objection from Parliament supplemented procedure laid down in legislation where they have found that to be necessary for this purpose (see *Wiseman v Borneman*[3] per Lord Reid).

So much for the calling of witnesses. We now turn to the suggestion that hearsay evidence is not permissible in a hearing before a board of visitors.

It is of course common ground that the board of visitors must base their decisions on evidence. But must such evidence be restricted to that which would be admissible in a criminal court of law? Viscount Simon LC, in *General Medical Council v Spackman*[4], considered there was no such restriction. That was also clearly the view of the Privy Council in *University of Ceylon v Fernando*[5].

The matter was dealt with in more detail by Diplock LJ in *R v Deputy Industrial Injuries Comr, ex parte Moore*[6] as follows:

'. . . these technical rules of evidence, however, form no part of the rules of natural justice. The requirement that a person exercising quasi-judicial functions must base his decision on evidence means no more than that it must be based on material which tends logically to show the existence or non-existence of facts relevant to the issue to be determined, or to show the likelihood or unlikelihood of the occurrence of some future event the occurrence of which would be relevant. It means that he must not spin a coin or consult an astrologer; but he may take into account any material which, as a matter of reason, has some probative value in the sense mentioned above. If it is capable of having any probative value, the weight to be attached to it is a matter for the person to whom Parliament has entrusted the responsibility of deciding the issue. The supervisory jurisdiction of the High Court does not entitle it to usurp this responsibility and to substitute its own view for his.'

However, it is clear that the entitlement of the board of visitors to admit hearsay evidence is subject to the overriding obligation to provide the accused with a fair hearing. Depending on the facts of the particular case and the nature of the hearsay evidence provided to the board of visitors, the obligation to give the accused a fair chance to exculpate himself, or a fair opportunity to controvert the charge, to quote the phrases

1   [1960] 1 All ER 631 at 638, [1960] 1 WLR 223 at 232
2   [1965] 1 All ER 81 at 93, [1965] 1 QB 456 at 487
3   [1969] 3 All ER 275 at 277, [1971] AC 297 at 308
4   [1943] 2 All ER 337 at 338, [1943] AC 627 at 634
5   [1960] 1 All ER 631 at 639, [1960] 1 WLR 223 at 234
6   [1965] 1 All ER 81 at 94, [1965] 1 QB 456 at 488

used in the cases cited above, or a proper or full opportunity of presenting his case, to
quote the language of s 47 or r 49, may oblige the board of visitors not only to inform the
a accused of the hearsay evidence but also to give the accused a sufficient opportunity to
deal with that evidence. Again, depending on the nature of that evidence and the
particular circumstances of the case, a sufficient opportunity to deal with the hearsay
evidence may well involve the cross-examination of the witness whose evidence is
initially before the board in the form of hearsay.

b We again take by way of example the case in which the defence is an alibi. The
prisoner contends that he was not the man identified on the roof. He, the prisoner, was
at the material time elsewhere. In short the prisoner has been mistakenly identified.
The evidence of identification given by way of hearsay may be of the 'fleeting glance'
type as exemplified by the well-known case of *R v Turnbull*[1]. The prisoner may well wish
to elicit by way of questions all manner of detail, eg the poorness of the light, the state
of confusion, the brevity of the observation, the absence of any contemporaneous record,
c etc, all designed to show the unreliability of the witness. To deprive him of the
opportunity of cross-examination would be tantamount to depriving him of a fair
hearing.

We appreciate that there may well be occasions when the burden of calling the witness
whose hearsay evidence is readily available may impose a near impossible burden on the
d board. However, it has not been suggested that hearsay evidence should be resorted to
in the total absence of any firsthand evidence. In the instant cases hearsay evidence was
only resorted to to supplement the firsthand evidence and this is the usual practice.
Accordingly where a prisoner desires to dispute the hearsay evidence and for this purpose
to question the witness, and where there are insuperable or very grave difficulties in
arranging for his attendance, the board should refuse to admit that evidence, or, if it has
already come to their notice, should expressly dismiss it from their consideration.

e Our view that a fair hearing may well involve providing to the accused an opportunity
to question the witness whose evidence is proffered in a hearsay form is supported by the
report of a Home Office Working Party on Adjudication Procedures in Prisons published
in 1975. It consisted of representative members of the boards of visitors, officers of the
prison department and members of the prison service, and their terms of reference were:

f   'To review the arrangements for the hearing by Governors and Boards of Visitors
of disciplinary charges against inmates of Prison Department establishments and to
make recommendations.'

In notes to paras 16 and 17 the following is stated: 'Generally, hearsay evidence by the
reporting officer should not be admitted unless it is supported by first-hand evidence.'
Then it deals with limited circumstances in which it may be appropriate, in particular
g the case of the accused prisoner pleading guilty. It then continues:

'If the reporting officer or other witness is not available to give evidence in person,
the situation should be explained to the prisoner, and it should be left to him to
decide whether the hearing should proceed with just the witness's written evidence,
and in the knowledge that he would not be able to question the officer on his
h   evidence; or whether the hearing should be postponed until the officer returns to
duty, however long that may be eg an officer could be off duty sick for some time.'

We now turn to consider the effects of those conclusions on the individual applications
which are before us.

So far as the refusal to allow the applicants to call witnesses is concerned, this presents
little difficulty, except in the case of Cotterill. All the other cases are covered by the
j statement in the affidavit of the chairman of the board of visitors to the following effect:

'Furthermore and in any event, we took the view that the calling of witnesses
would be of limited value unless it was clear that the witnesses would be of real
value in a specific case. If it had ever been apparent to us that it was essential to the

---

1   [1976] 3 All ER 549, [1977] QB 224

course of justice that a witness be called, I would have allowed a prisoner to do so, if necessary by adjourning the adjudication.'

Generally speaking, where there is a conflict of evidence as to a point on which the dispute turns, the court will decline to interfere (see *R v Fulham, Hammersmith and Kensington Rent Tribunal, ex parte Zerek*[1]). Since we have had to decide this matter on affidavit evidence without the benefit of cross-examination, we are obliged to take the facts where they are in issue as they are deposed to on behalf of the board of visitors. By applying the test which the chairman describes, the board was acting with obvious fairness. No room for criticism in this aspect remains.

In the case of Cotterill, however, it is clear from the record of the proceedings that the test was wrongly applied on the third charge against him and the finding of guilt on this charge must be quashed.

There remains to consider the more difficult problem of what may for convenience be called the hearsay evidence.

After the disturbances had subsided all the prison officers involved submitted written reports of their observations, naming such prisoners as they had seen taking part in the riot. A dossier was then prepared in respect of each prisoner so named, the dossier containing the reports of the various officers who said they had observed him. These dossiers were before the governor of Hull prison who was of course present at the hearings.

The governor explains in his affidavit, and it can be seen from the record of the proceedings, that from time to time, at the tacit or express invitation of the chairman, the governor would give to the board of visitors information which he derived from the dossiers. To take one example: the applicant Saxton faced a number of charges, one of which was under r 47(10) of the 1964 rules, the particulars being that he had been seen on 'A' wing roof filling bottles with floor polish. The suggestion was that these were to be used as incendiary bombs. Evidence was given by Officer Wooldridge that he had seen through binoculars Saxton and another man, Duffy, filling the bottles. Saxton said he knew nothing about it. The chairman asked him: 'Are all the officers wrong?' whereupon the governor said this: 'Six out of 14 sightings say he was the first man onto the roof—others suggest it was Saxton who carried the bed to smash the windows to get on the roof.' Then the chairman said: 'Case proven.'

It is clear that no opportunity was given to the applicant to examine the evidence to which the governor was referring. He was not told the names of the officers who had allegedly seen him at the material time and place, or from what positions they had observed him. He was not given the opportunity, so far as one can ascertain, to make any comment on what the governor had said.

It seems to us that this constituted a serious departure from the principle enunciated by Lord Denning in *Kanda v Government of the Federation of Malaya*[2] and the other cases already cited. The prisoner was not told what evidence had been given or what statements had been made affecting him, nor was he given a fair opportunity to correct or contradict them.

That the hearsay evidence carried weight with the board of visitors is clear from a passage in the record of the hearing of one of the charges against the applicant Anderson. It was a charge of looting on which he was found guilty. It is now conceded that there was no evidence on which a finding of guilt could properly have been based and that finding must be quashed. It seems to us that in the way this hearsay evidence was handled there was a departure from the rule of fairness and that that departure could reasonably be regarded as having caused what Megaw LJ describes as[3] 'a substantial, as distinct from a trivial or merely technical, injustice'.

We confess it is with some reluctance that we come to this conclusion, because there is inevitably a feeling that the board of visitors may have reached the right result

1   [1951] 1 All ER 482, [1951] 2 KB 1
2   [1962] AC 322 at 337–338
3   *R v Hull Prison Board of Visitors* [1979] 1 All ER 701 at 713, [1979] 2 WLR 42 at 57

a   ultimately in spite of the irregularities. These men were prisoners. Some of them were dangerous. Most of them were difficult. All of them were no doubt to some extent untrustworthy. But they faced (and received) severe punishment and they were entitled to a fuller hearing than that which they in fact received.

Lord Morris of Borth-y-Gest in *Ridge v Baldwin*[1] said:

b
> 'It is well established that the essential requirements of natural justice at least include that before someone is condemned he is to have an opportunity of defending himself and in order that he may do so that he is to be made aware of the charges or allegations or suggestions which he has to meet; see *Kanda v Government of The Federation of Malaya*[2]. My lords, here is something which is basic to our system: the importance of upholding it far transcends the significance of any particular case.'

Lord Morris continued[3]:

c
> 'My lords, it was submitted to your lordships that the decision of the watch committee should be upheld as having been the only reasonable decision. I consider this to be an entirely erroneous submission. Since no charges have been formulated it is impossible to assess their weight or the weight of the answering evidence of the appellant and others. When the appellant was in the witness-box in the present action he was questioned as to what witnesses he would have wished to call in order
d   to deal with the "Leach" and the "Page" matters. As charges in respect of those matters were not formulated, I cannot think that it was appropriate to elicit the names of certain witnesses whom the appellant might have decided to call and then without hearing or being able to hear such witnesses to seek to discount their value and effectiveness and then to seek to draw a vague and artificial conclusion that if matters had been regularly done and if the appellant had been heard and if his
e   witnesses had been heard a result adverse to him would have followed. All the defects and all the unfairness of the original irregularity are inherent in any such approach.'

It should be noted that in so far as we are quashing any findings of guilt for lack of procedural fairness, the charges remain capable of being the subject of a fresh investigation before a differently constituted board of visitors, should this be considered
f   appropriate.

There is no need to set out in detail how the hearsay evidence was adduced or handled in each case.

[His Lordship then dealt with each case in turn and held that five findings of guilt in respect of Reed, three findings of guilt in respect of Cotterill and Saxton, two findings of guilt in respect of Rajah and St Germain and one finding of guilt in respect of Anderson
g   should be quashed. His Lordship then considered the application by Raymond David Rosa and after stating the facts held that there was no fault in the way in which the Wandsworth Prison Board of Visitors had handled the matter and that therefore there was no possible ground for an order of certiorari.]

Orders accordingly.

h   Solicitors: *Gamlens*, agents for *George E Baker & Co*, Guildford (for the applicant St Germain); *Bindman & Partners* (for the applicant Saxton); *Neilson & Co* (for the applicant Rosa); *Sharpe Pritchard & Co*, agents for *Philip Hamer & Co*, Hull (for the applicant Reed); *Douglas-Mann & Co*, agents for *Patterson, Glenton, Stracey*, South Shields (for the applicants Anderson and Pike); *Hilary Kitchin* (for the applicant Rajah); *Turner, Peacock* (for the applicant Cotterill); *Treasury Solicitor*.

j
N P Metcalfe Esq   Barrister.

---

1   [1963] 2 All ER 66 at 102, [1964] AC 40 at 113–114
2   [1962] AC 322
3   [1963] 2 All ER 66 at 110–111, [1964] AC 40 at 126–127

Re Southard & Co Ltd

a

COURT OF APPEAL, CIVIL DIVISION
BUCKLEY, BRIDGE AND TEMPLEMAN LJJ
25th, 26th, 27th JUNE 1979

Company – Compulsory winding-up – Winding-up order – Court's discretion to make winding-up order – Voluntary liquidation in progress – Petitioning and supporting creditors members of *b* *same group of companies as company in liquidation and having majority in value of debts – Opposing creditors independent of group and greater in number but having minority in value of debts – Whether nature of petitioning and supporting creditors' debts relevant in depriving petitioning creditor of prima facie right to winding-up order – Whether court having unfettered discretion or bound to accede to views of creditors having majority in value of debts – Companies* *c* *Act 1948, s 346(1)(2).*

A subsidiary company in a group of companies owed money to both the parent and an associated company of the group. In September 1978 the parent company ('the petitioning creditor') initiated the voluntary liquidation of the debtor company and attempted to secure the appointment of its nominee, an accountant employed by the group, as the voluntary liquidator. The debtor company passed a resolution appointing *d* as the voluntary liquidators two accountants of integrity unconnected with the group. On 11th October the petitioning creditor presented a petition for the compulsory winding-up of the debtor company. This was supported by the associated company ('the supporting creditor') to whom money was owed. The petitioning creditor also took steps to prevent the voluntary liquidators acting in the voluntary liquidation. At the date of the hearing of the petition the debtor company was unable to pay its debts and was *e* indebted to the petitioning and supporting creditors in the aggregate sum of £21,488. The reasons put forward by the petitioning and supporting creditors in favour of a compulsory winding-up as opposed to the continuation of the voluntary liquidation were that it would more quickly realise the assets of the debtor company and would be more economical. The independent creditors of the company, to whom the company *f* was indebted in aggregate in the lesser sum of £13,226, opposed the petition on the ground that investigation of the company's affairs under the voluntary liquidation would be more effective. The judge[a] took the view that the voluntary liquidation should continue and dismissed the petition. In reaching his decision he took into consideration (i) that the reasons put forward for a compulsory winding-up lacked substance, (ii) that the view of the petitioning and supporting creditors should not be decisive because of *g* their relationship to the debtor company, (iii) that all the independent creditors wished to continue with the voluntary liquidation and (iv) that the petitioning creditor itself had initiated the voluntary liquidation. The petitioning and supporting creditors appealed against the dismissal of the petition, contending that an unpaid creditor in respect of an undisputed debt was prima facie entitled as of right to a winding-up order, and that if there was a diversity of views among the creditors whether there should be a compulsory *h* winding-up the court's discretion under s 346[b] of the Companies Act 1948 was fettered and, unless there were exceptional circumstances, it had to give effect to the views of the majority in value where they were seeking a compulsory winding-up.

Held – On the true construction of s 346(1) of the 1948 Act the court had an unfettered discretion whether to make a compulsory winding-up order on a petition by an *j*

---

a [1979] 1 All ER 582
b Section 346, so far as material, provides:
  '(1) The court may, as to all matters relating to the winding up of a company, have regard to the wishes of the creditors ... of the company ...
  '(2) In the case of creditors, regard shall be had to the value of each creditor's debt ...'

undisputed creditor, notwithstanding that in certain situations the court could
a confidently be expected to exercise that discretion in a particular way because justice so
required. Accordingly, although the views of the majority of creditors in value was a
factor to be taken into account under s 346(2), it was not the decisive factor if they were
seeking a compulsory winding-up order, and the court was required to take into account
all considerations relevant to the interests of the other creditors. In the circumstances the
judge had been justified in taking into account the considerations he had, and in
b particular whether, having regard to the relationship between the petitioning creditor,
the supporting creditor and the debtor company, the interests of the independent
creditors would be better served by continuing the voluntary liquidation, and he had not
left out of account any relevant matter. It followed that the judge had properly exercised
his discretion, and, the appeal would therefore be dismissed (see p 561 *c* and *h* to p 562
g, p 563 *e* to p 564 *e*, p 565 *a* to *c*, p 566 *b* and p 567 *a* to *c*, post).
c   Re P & J Macrae Ltd [1961] 1 All ER 302 followed.
Dictum of Lord Cranworth in *Bowes v Directors of Hope Life Insurance and Guarantee Co*
(1865) 11 HL Cas at 402 explained.
Decision of Brightman J [1979] 1 All ER 582 affirmed.

Notes

d For creditors' wishes and the value of their debts in relation to a winding-up, see 7
Halsbury's Laws (4th Edn) para 1033, and for cases on the subject, see 10 Digest (Reissue)
945–948, 5531–5553.
For the Companies Act 1948, s 346, see 5 Halsbury's Statutes (3rd Edn) 369.

Cases referred to in judgments

Bowes v Directors of Hope Life Insurance and Guarantee Co (1865) 11 HL Cas 389, 11 ER
e   1383, sub nom *Bowes v Hope Mutual Life Assurance Co* 35 LJ Ch 574, 12 LT 680, 11 Jur
NS 643, HL, 10 Digest (Reissue) 932, 5429.
Chapel House Colliery Co, Re (1883) 24 Ch D 259, 52 LJ Ch 934, 49 LT 575, CA, 10 Digest
(Reissue) 946, 5538.
Evans v Bartlam [1937] 2 All ER 646, [1937] AC 473, 106 LJKB 568, 157 LT 311, HL, 50
Digest (Repl) 401, 1113.
f *Gardner v Jay* (1885) 29 Ch D 50, 54 LJ Ch 762, 52 LT 395, CA, 51 Digest (Repl) 791,
3489.
Langley Mill Steel and Iron Works Co, Re (1871) LR 12 Eq 26, LJ Ch 13, 24 LT 382, 10
Digest (Reissue) 945, 5535.
Macrae (P & J) Ltd, Re [1961] 1 All ER 302, [1961] 1 WLR 229, CA, 10 Digest (Reissue)
1121, 6932.
g *Swain (JD) Ltd, Re* [1965] 2 All ER 761, [1965] 1 WLR 909, CA, 10 Digest (Reissue) 946,
5542.

Cases also cited

ABC Coupler and Engineering Co, Re [1961] 1 All ER 354, [1961] 1 WLR 243.
Crigglestone Coal Co Ltd, Re [1906] 2 Ch 327, [1904–7] All ER Rep 894, CA.
h *Home Remedies Ltd, Re* [1942] 2 All ER 552, [1943] Ch 1.
Millward (James) & Co Ltd, Re [1940] 1 All ER 347, [1940] Ch 333, CA.
Smith and Fawcett Ltd, Re [1942] 1 All ER 542, [1942] Ch 304, CA.
Vuma Ltd, Re [1960] 3 All ER 629, [1960] 1 WLR 1283, CA.

Appeal

j This was an appeal by Seton Trust Ltd ('the petitioning creditor') and Scandic Credit &
Commerce Ltd ('the supporting creditor') against the judgment of Brightman J[1] given on
23rd November 1978 whereby he dismissed the petitioning creditor's petition, presented
on 18th October 1978, for the compulsory winding-up of Southard & Co Ltd ('the

---

company'). The grounds of the appeal were (inter alia) that (1) the judge erred in law in holding that he had a discretion to refuse a compulsory winding-up order in the circumstances of the case, namely that the company was insolvent and unable to pay its debts, and the debts of those supporting the petition vastly exceeded the debts of the opposing creditors and had not been paid or satisfied; (2) if there was such a discretion it was exercisable only in exceptional circumstances which did not exist in the present case; (3) if there was such a discretion, it was exercisable to deprive a majority in value of unpaid creditors of their right ex debito justitiae to a winding-up order only where the opposing minority in value of the creditors adduced positive or compelling reasons for denying that the company be wound up, and no such reasons had been adduced; (4) the judge erred in regarding the fact that the majority in value of the creditors supporting the petition were closely connected with the company as a reason for discounting their right to a compulsory winding-up order. The facts are set out in the judgment of Buckley LJ.

Jeremiah Harman QC and *Simon Berry* for the petitioning and supporting creditors.
John Lindsay for the opposing creditors.

BUCKLEY LJ. This is an appeal from an order of Brightman J[1] refusing to make an order for the compulsory winding-up of a company called Southard & Co Ltd, which I shall call 'the company'. The company is the wholly owned subsidiary of the petitioning creditor, Seton Trust Ltd, which is itself a subsidiary of a company called Seton Securities Ltd. There was one supporting creditor, Scandic Credit & Commerce Ltd, a company which I shall call 'Scandic' for short. That is a subsidiary of a company called Ramor Investments Ltd, which is the subsidiary of a company called Seton Investments Ltd, which is a subsidiary of Seton Securities Ltd. So the supporting creditor was in the same group of companies and a sub-subsidiary of Seton Securities Ltd, of which the petitioning creditor and the company were also members.

The company carried on a business as wine merchants, and in May 1978 it was heavily indebted to its bankers, who were then the National Westminster Bank. The indebtedness to the bank then exceeded £175,000.

On or about 24th May 1978 that indebtedness was paid off by Barclays Bank Ltd who took a debenture from the company which was a debenture in a normal bank form, securing payment on demand of all moneys due from time to time from the company to the bank by a floating charge on the undertaking of the company. That debenture was guaranteed by Seton Trust Ltd.

On 18th September, at an extraordinary general meeting of the company, the shareholders (that is to say, in effect, Seton Trust Ltd) passed a resolution for the voluntary liquidation of the company. No declaration of solvency was made and accordingly the winding-up so set on foot was a creditors' voluntary winding-up.

Thereafter there was some confusion about the proper procedure to be followed, and the proper procedure was not in fact followed. What happened was that the shareholders' nominee for the office of voluntary liquidator of the company, a Mr Stevens, who was in fact an accountant employed by Ramor Investments Ltd, a company in the group that I have already mentioned, convened a meeting of creditors. The meeting should have been convened by the board, but no point is now taken about that incorrect procedure. The meeting was held on 10th October; it was a tumultuous meeting. Before the meeting took place, Seton Trust Ltd had assigned to 24 assignees £600-worth in each case of the company's indebtedness to Seton Trust Ltd in order to secure a majority in number at the meeting. That was clearly a device for that purpose, but I dare say it is the kind of device which is frequently employed; at any rate, it was employed in this case. It seems to have engendered a good deal of indignation. As I say, the meeting was a tumultuous meeting; Mr Stevens resigned from his position as shareholders' nominee

---

1   [1979] 1 All ER 582, [1979] 1 WLR 546

for the office of voluntary liquidator and the meeting passed, or purported to pass, a
resolution appointing two gentlemen, a Mr Curtis and a Mr Auger, to be voluntary
liquidators. They are two professional accountants, members of well-known firms of
accountants, and are both of them experienced in liquidation work. No criticism is
made of their independence, integrity or ability.

On the next day, Seton Trust Ltd presented a petition for the compulsory winding-up
of the company. One can only suppose that that was prompted by the fact that they had
been unsuccessful in getting their own nominee, Mr Stevens, into the chair as voluntary
liquidator of the company.

On 13th October, Seton Trust Ltd, being as I have said guarantors of Barclays Bank's
debenture, paid a sum of upwards of £175,000 to Barclays Bank in discharge of that
obligation and took a transfer of the debenture; and on that very same day, in exercise of
the power of appointing a receiver contained in that debenture, they appointed Mr
Stevens to be the receiver of the company.

On 18th October Seton Trust Ltd launched a motion to restrain Messrs Curtis and
Auger from acting as voluntary liquidators. When that matter initially came before the
court undertakings were given by those two gentlemen that they would not act as
voluntary liquidators pending an adjournment of the motion.

On 24th October an opposing creditor, Gilbey Vintners Ltd, a trade creditor of the
company, launched a motion for confirmation of Messrs Curtis and Auger in the office
of voluntary liquidators. Those two motions eventually came on for hearing together;
that is, Seton Trust Ltd's motion of 18th October 1978 and Gilbey Vintners Ltd's motion
of 24th October 1978. They were heard by Mr Robert Wright QC, sitting as a deputy
judge of the Chancery Division, who, on 6th November, dismissed Seton Trust Ltd's
motion and confirmed Messrs Curtis and Auger in their office as voluntary liquidators.

On the next day an ex parte application was made by Seton Trust Ltd to the Court of
Appeal for an injunction restraining the voluntary liquidators from acting in that
capacity and a temporary injunction was granted; but on 13th November, when the
matter came before this court inter partes, the injunction was not continued and from
that time forward the deputy judge's order confirming Messrs Curtis and Auger in their
office as voluntary liquidators has been in effective operation.

The winding-up petition first came before the court on 13th November when it was
stood over for further evidence; it came on for effective hearing on 21st November, and
on 23rd November Brightman J dismissed the petition and it is from that order that the
present appeal comes.

The position as regards supporting and opposing creditors at that hearing was this: the
petitioning creditor, that is to say Seton Trust Ltd, claims to be an unsecured creditor in
the sum of £47,140. It also claims to be a creditor in respect of the debenture debt.
Seton Trust Ltd valued its security (that is to say, the whole of the assets and undertaking
of the company) at £150,000, leaving a balance of £25,348 of the debenture debt
unsecured; so that the total debts claimed to be due by the company to the petitioner as
unsecured debts amounted to £72,488; but the petition was supported by Scandic,
claiming to be a creditor in the sum of £49,000, so that the total indebtedness on that
side was £121,488. No other creditor supported the petition. There were eight opposing
creditors admitted to the list before the court, for an aggregate amount of £13,266. The
judge disregarded one very small debt due to an employee of the company named
Beetley for £66, because he thought that that was in all probability a preferential debt;
and he to some extent discounted the debts of two other employees because some part of
their debt was likely to be preferential. So the amount of opposing indebtedness which
the judge took into account as being debts due to opposing creditors was somewhere
between £12,000 and £13,000, very much less in amount than the debts of the petitioner
and the supporting creditor taken together.

The petitioner and the supporting creditor appeal. They base their appeal on the
contention that where a petition for a compulsory winding-up is brought by a creditor
who has an undisputed debt, that creditor is prima facie entitled, ex debito justitiae, to

a winding-up order, and that, where there is a diversity of view amongst the creditors of the company whether a winding-up order should or should not be made, the court should have regard, pursuant to s 346 of the Companies Act 1948, to the value of the debts on either side and should pay attention to, and give effect to, the views of the majority in value.

It is a well recognised fact that, if a creditor petitions for the winding-up of a company and he is a creditor in respect of a debt which is not disputed by the company, as between himself and the company he has what has in many of the cases been referred to as a right ex debito justitiae to a winding-up order. But of course his interest is not the only interest which the court must take into account. The court must take into account the position with regard to the other creditors of the company; indeed, it may have to take into account the position of the members of, or the contributors to, the company. The petitioning creditor and the creditors of the company who are in equal degree with the petitioner have in some cases been described as having a class interest in this respect, but counsel for the petitioning and supporting creditors says that it is not right to describe it as a class interest, because they are not truly a class; each of them has an individual right of a similar kind and the court has to pay regard to the views and the wishes of all the persons who are creditors of the company in the same degree as the petitioner. That position is recognised by s 346(1) of the 1948 Act, which provides that the court may, and the word used is 'may', as to all matters relating to the winding-up of the company have regard to the wishes of the creditors or contributories of the company as proved to it by any sufficient evidence. Then the section goes on to say how the court may discover what those wishes are if it needs to do so; and 346(2) provides that in the case of creditors regard shall, and the word used is 'shall', be had to the value of each creditor's debt. If the majority want the company wound up, or if they want it wound up compulsorily rather than voluntarily, the court should, counsel suggests, make the order. If they want the company not to be wound up compulsorily and give satisfactory reasons the court should, having regard to their wishes, not make the order, notwithstanding that the petitioner and it may be other creditors, but not a majority in value, wish that the company should be wound up compulsorily. If there are conflicting views put forward by the creditors, the court should no doubt have regard to the value of their debts. That is what s 346 requires, but counsel submits that if a majority want a company wound up their wishes should, and I think he says must, prevail, except perhaps in very exceptional circumstances, of which no examples are to be found in the reports. If on the other hand the majority want the voluntary winding-up to continue, they must put forward adequate reasons to the court, which could be weighed against whatever reasons in favour of a compulsory winding-up are put forward by the petitioning creditor and any supporting creditors.

The classic statement on this subject is to be found in what was said by Lord Cranworth in *Bowes v Directors of Hope Life Insurance and Guarantee Co*[1]:

'. . . it is not a discretionary matter with the Court when a debt is established, and not satisfied, to say whether the company shall be wound up or not; that is to say, if there be a valid debt established, valid both at law and in equity. One does not like to say positively that no case could occur in which it would be right to refuse it; but, ordinarily speaking [and I stress those words], it is the duty of the Court to direct the winding up.'

It is perfectly true that Lord Cranworth in that passage does say that it is not a discretionary matter with the court, but the closing words of the passage make it clear, I think, that he was not saying that the jurisdiction is not discretionary; what he was saying was that where the debt is established and not satisfied and there are no exceptional circumstances, the creditor is entitled to expect the court to exercise its jurisdiction in the way of making a winding-up order.

---

1   (1865) 11 HL Cas 389 at 402, 11 ER 1383 at 1389

Counsel for the opposing creditors has said that three questions arise on this appeal.
First, had the judge an unfettered discretion? to which he suggests that the correct
answer is Yes; secondly, if so, what test should this court apply before upsetting
Brightman J's exercise of his discretion? and he suggests that the correct answer to that
question is that we should not interfere with the judge's decision unless he has clearly
gone wrong in principle or has clearly reached a wrong conclusion; thirdly, there is the
question whether on the particular facts of this case the judge's decision should be
disturbed.

Counsel for the opposing creditors accepts that an unpaid petitioning creditor in
respect of an undisputed debt is entitled to expect the court to exercise its discretion in
his favour in the absence of special circumstances. Both s 222 of the 1948 Act, which is
the section conferring the jurisdiction to wind up the company compulsorily, and
s 346(1) are expressed in permissive language; in each case the verb used is 'may'. In
every case, counsel for the opposing creditor submits, the court has an unfettered
discretion, and in my judgment that is the true view of the situation.

This matter was discussed in *Re P & J Macrae Ltd*[1], a decision of this court. Counsel for
the petitioning and supporting creditors submits that a reading of the judgment shows
that Upjohn LJ approached the problem from a rather different standpoint from that
adopted by Ormerod and Willmer LJJ. In my judgment that is not the case. I think that
all three members of the court regarded the question of jurisdiction in the same light.
Upjohn LJ came to a different conclusion from that of Ormerod and Willmer LJJ on the
question of whether the county court judge, whose decision in that case was under
appeal, had exercised his discretion in a proper way having regard to the circumstances
of that case. Upjohn LJ puts the matter thus[2]:

'That the court has a complete discretion was recognised as long ago as 1871 when
MALINS, V.-C., in *Re Langley Mill Steel & Iron Works Co.*[3], put the matter in a nutshell
in reference to the corresponding s. 91 of the Companies Act, 1862.'

That, I may say, was the section which now is replaced by s 346 of the 1948 Act. Then
he cites from the judgment of Malins V-C in that case[4]:

'I am of opinion that the court has, under that section, complete discretion in all
cases of winding-up, and must exercise that discretion with reference to all the
surrounding circumstances.'

Then Upjohn LJ goes on to draw attention to the fact that s 222 of the 1948 Act itself
confers by its language a discretionary jurisdiction, and he goes on to say[5]:

'... although an undoubted creditor is as a general rule entitled to an order ex
debito justitiae, there may be special cases where, apart altogether from the wishes
of creditors generally, the court may not think fit to make an order: see for an
example *Re Chapel House Colliery Co.*[6]'

The ground on which in *Re Chapel House Colliery Co*[6] the court did not think fit to
make an order was that it seemed that no advantage could be obtained by the making of
an order because the company was without any assets; but since that case was decided the
law on that matter has been altered and now, by s 225(1) of the 1948 Act, it is provided
that the court should not refuse to make a winding-up order on the ground only that the
assets of the company have been mortgaged to an amount equal to, or in excess of, those
assets or that the company has no assets. So the particular ground on which the court in

1   [1961] 1 All ER 302, [1961] 1 WLR 229
2   [1961] 1 All ER 302 at 309, [1961] 1 WLR 229 at 237
3   (1871) LR 12 Eq 26
4   LR 12 Eq 26 at 29
5   [1961] 1 All ER 302 at 309, [1961] 1 WLR 229 at 238
6   (1883) 24 Ch D 259

Re Chapel House Colliery Co[1] declined to make an order would not be one that would any longer be a proper ground for refusing to make an order. But that does not, I think, alter ***a*** the position that the jurisdiction is a discretionary jurisdiction. It is not inconsistent with this that in particular types of situation the court should be expected confidently to exercise that discretion in a particular way. This does not import that the discretion is fettered but that to a judicial mind a particular pattern of facts will indicate that justice requires the exercise of discretion in a particular fashion.

Counsel for the opposing creditors has referred us to *Gardner v Jay*[2] where Bowen LJ ***b*** expresses the view that where a judicial discretion is concerned it is mistaken to attempt to lay down rules for its exercise. That, if I may say so with humility about an observation of so clear-minded a judge as Bowen LJ, is obviously right. Any other approach contradicts the existence of the discretion. Where a discretion is conferred on the court, no judge can fetter any other judge in a later case in the exercise of it; so no judge, or court, can lay down rules binding others in the exercise of the discretion. ***c***

The right of an unpaid creditor in respect of an undisputed debt to a winding-up order is a right only as between himself and the company: see what was said by Baggallay LJ in the *Chapel House Colliery* case[3]. It does not entitle him to insist on a winding-up order if such an order would be inimical to the interests of others who are in the same position as his own. In the present case the attitudes of Seton Trust Ltd and Scandic on the one hand and the opposing creditors on the other were in conflict. Consequently it was ***d*** incumbent on Brightman J to decide which view should be accepted. In doing so, he was bound in accordance with s 346 of the 1948 Act to have regard to the values of the debts on each side, but in my view this does not mean that he was bound slavishly to adopt the wish of the majority in value. The disparity in value was one of the matters to which he was bound to have regard.

Counsel for the opposing creditors has suggested a number of other circumstances to ***e*** which the judge was also bound to pay attention: first, that the petitioner was the beneficial owner of all the shares of the company and the supporting creditor was a company in the same group and controlled, through, no doubt, a chain of companies and of directors, by the same ultimate parent company. Consequently the views and wishes of the petitioner and of the supporting creditor were likely to be, or it was at least possible that they would be, influenced by matters which do not affect trade creditors and other ***f*** outside creditors of the company. Where a creditor has, or may have, reasons for wishing a particular course which are distinct from those considerations which are common to the general body of creditors, of which he is one, the court may have to consider, and I think should consider, what weight should be given to those reasons having regard to that particular relationship between the petitioner and the company.

Another matter which is relevant to be taken into consideration in the present case is ***g*** the fact that the petitioner is also a debenture holder, holding a debenture which, if it is valid, will, on the valuation which has been put on the security by the petitioner himself, be more than enough to absorb all the assets of the company. That debenture was created less than 12 months before the commencement of the winding-up and so is vulnerable under s 322 of the 1948 Act. That is a matter which, it is common ground, is one which requires to be investigated in the winding-up of this company. It is also one ***h*** which, in my view, the judge had to take into account, and properly took into account, in considering how similar to the position of the outside creditors the petitioner's position was, or rather, perhaps I should say, how dissimilar the petitioner's position was from the position of the outside creditors. Then there is the circumstance that in the present case the affairs of the company and all its books and records are at the present time under the control or in the possession of the receiver appointed by the petitioner; ***j*** and counsel for the opposing creditors calls attention to the fact that where the petitioner is the sole beneficial owner of the company there is really no opportunity at the stage of

1   (1883) 24 Ch D 259
2   (1885) 29 Ch D 50 at 58
3   (1883) 24 Ch D 259 at 266

petition to investigate the indebtedness of the company to the petitioner. In the present
a case, he says, the petitioner's debt has not been clearly established, and there may be cross-
claims by the company against the petitioner; there may be other inter-company claims
and obligations; the position is one which needs investigation before the amount of the
indebtedness of the company to the petitioner can be clearly ascertained; and there is the
rather marked characteristic of this case, which is unlike most cases of petitions for
compulsory winding-up, that the petitioner initially sought a voluntary winding-up and
b would presumably have been perfectly content to continue on that course had it not been
for the outcome of the meeting of 10th October.

In the course of his judgment[1] the judge set out the circumstances which he
particularly bore in mind in considering whether or not to make a winding-up order.
The first was that the only reasons put forward by the petitioning and supporting
creditors for preferring a compulsory winding-up to a voluntary winding-up was that in
c a compulsory winding-up the assets of the company would be realised more expeditiously
and more economically than in a voluntary winding-up. In this court counsel for the
petitioning creditor has admitted that he cannot really say that a compulsory winding-up
would be more expeditious than a voluntary winding-up, and the judge took the view
that there was really no substance in the other reason, the suggestion that a compulsory
winding-up would be more economical than a voluntary winding-up; he said that he was
d not impressed by that suggestion and, I confess, neither am I.

His second numbered paragraph refers to the family relationship of the company to
the petitioning creditor and to Scandic; the judge said that in those circumstances the
wishes of the petitioner and the supporting creditor did not carry with him weight
commensurate with the size of the alleged indebtedness; and he said that he thought that
the petitioning creditor was, at least prima facie, morally responsible for the company
e having become so gravely insolvent as it had. In those circumstances he said that he did
not consider that the views of the petitioning creditor and Scandic ought to carry decisive
weight. In my judgment that was a perfectly reasonable and permissible approach by
the judge to that aspect of the matter. It does not mean that he is not having regard to
the value of those creditors' debts; he is having regard to how persuasive the views
expressed by those creditors should be in view of their special position in relation to the
f company, particularly the special position of the petitioner.

The third matter taken into account by the judge was that the independent creditors
(that is to say, those creditors who had not any family link with the company) all wanted
the voluntary liquidation to continue, and he said that he had to bear in mind that seven
totally independent creditors wanted the voluntary liquidation to continue, compared
with two, what he called domestic creditors, who wished, on slender grounds in his view,
g for a compulsory liquidation.

Fourthly, the judge took into consideration the feature which, I have said, is rather
striking, that the petitioning creditor initially put the company into voluntary
liquidation. I myself certainly regard it as a significant and important feature in the case
that that was so and that the petitioning creditor was apparently originally content that
the company should be wound up voluntarily but that they now desire a compulsory
h winding-up for reasons which seem to me, as they did to the judge, to be insubstantial.

On the other hand, the reasons put forward by the opposing creditors seem to me to
be strong reasons for thinking that the company should be wound up by a liquidator or
liquidators who are truly and entirely independent. Of course, that would be the case if
the Official Receiver were the liquidator. On the other hand, it would equally be so if
Messrs Curtis and Auger are the liquidators. There seem to me to be no strong reasons
j for preferring the Official Receiver; on the contrary there are some reasons for preferring
voluntary liquidators, because I think the judge's fear that the Official Receiver might be
inhibited by lack of funds from carrying out a possibly expensive investigation of the
company's affairs is not altogether without foundation or unreal; and there is here a

---

1   [1979] 1 All ER 582 at 587, [1979] 1 WLR 546 at 552

voluntary liquidation on foot which will result in the affairs of the company being fully and properly investigated, as I am satisfied the voluntary liquidators intend should be the case, and which will result in the company's being eventually dissolved. *a*

In this court, in any appeal from the exercise of a discretionary jurisdiction, we must always bear in mind that although the appeal is a rehearing this court ought not to exercise its own discretion but should address itself to considering whether the judge at first instance exercised his discretion in accordance with proper principles, or whether he exercised it wrongly. In this connection our attention was drawn to *Re J D Swain Ltd*[1] and *b* to *Evans v Bartlam*[2], and particularly to the remarks of Lord Wright[3].

In my judgment the petitioning and supporting creditors have not established that Brightman J was clearly wrong in refusing a winding-up order. There appear to me to be grounds on which he could properly have reached that conclusion, and in these circumstances I do not consider that we should disturb his decision. I would dismiss this appeal. *c*

BRIDGE LJ. I am in full agreement with the judgment delivered by Buckley LJ; I add only a few words of my own.

In the course of the argument at various points I thought that it had been conceded on behalf of the petitioning and supporting creditors that the judgment appealed against was one given in the exercise of an essentially discretionary jurisdiction. At the end of *d* the day I am left in some uncertainty whether any relevant concession was made in that regard, and, if so, as to its nature and extent. But independently of any concession, it seems to me clear on reading s 346 of the Companies Act 1948 that that section does confer an essentially discretionary jurisdiction; if the point were in any way in doubt, the doubt would, to my mind, be completely resolved by the decision of this court to which Buckley LJ has referred, *Re P & J Macrae Ltd*[4]. *e*

I also think it came near to being common ground, or, if not common ground really beyond dispute, that the facts of this case were wholly exceptional, if not indeed unique. The story has been fully recounted in the judgment Buckley LJ has delivered, and I only draw attention, very briefly, to some of the salient features which seem to me of particular significance.

The petitioning creditor and the supporting creditor are respectively the parent and an *f* associated company of the debtor company. It was the petitioning creditor who initiated the voluntary liquidation which it now so violently opposes. Only when it failed, unexpectedly, to secure the appointment of its own nominee as liquidator did it execute a volte-face and seek simultaneously to oust the professional liquidators appointed by the independent creditors and to secure the order for the winding-up by the court. The reasons given by the petitioning creditor in evidence for that change of face are to my *g* mind totally unconvincing.

The independent minority opposing creditors, on the other hand, make what seems to me to be a convincing case for their belief that the investigation of the company's affairs by the voluntary liquidators, whose integrity and competence have never been in question, need be no more expensive, and may indeed by more effective, than an investigation, if any were undertaken, by the Official Receiver. *h*

Against that background and the background of the other facts set out in Buckley LJ's judgment, I find it difficult to see how much assistance is to be derived from authorities which lay down general guidelines for the exercise of the court's discretion under s 346 of the 1948 Act in the ordinary case. Certainly those guidelines are to be borne in mind, but in my judgment they cannot be invoked as necessarily leading to a particular conclusion in a case so unusual as this case is. *j*

1 [1965] 2 All ER 761, [1965] 1 WLR 909
2 [1937] 2 All ER 646, [1937] AC 473
3 [1937] 2 All ER 646 at 654, [1937] AC 473 at 486
4 [1961] 1 All ER 302, [1961] 1 WLR 229

To my mind, one proposition is clear in principle and is not refuted by any authority
a to which we have been referred. The proposition is this: in a dispute between creditors
with reference to a proposed compulsory winding-up, the voice of the majority in value
is certainly a factor to be considered; but whether that voice is raised in opposition to, or
in support of, the making of a compulsory winding-up order, it cannot per se, and
independently of other considerations, be decisive of the issue. To hold otherwise would
be to impose a wholly unwarranted fetter on the discretion which the statute confers.

b   Having reached that conclusion, I am of the opinion that the judge was amply justified
in taking into account all the considerations he did in reaching his discretionary
conclusion, and I cannot see that he left any relevant matter out of account, or erred in
principle in any way. That being so, we could only reverse his decision if we were
convinced that he was clearly wrong. So far from being so convinced, I am persuaded
that on the same evidence and arguments I would have reached the same conclusion.

c   I too would dismiss the appeal.

TEMPLEMAN LJ. English company law possesses some curious features, which may
generate curious results. A parent company may spawn a number of subsidiary
companies, all controlled directly or indirectly by the shareholders of the parent
company. If one of the subsidiary companies, to change the metaphor, turns out to be
d the runt of the litter and declines into insolvency to the dismay of its creditors, the parent
company and the other subsidiary companies may prosper to the joy of the shareholders
without any liability for the debts of the insolvent subsidiary. It is not surprising that,
when a subsidiary company collapses, the unsecured creditors wish the finances of the
company and its relationship with other members of the group to be narrowly examined,
to ensure that no assets of the subsidiary company have leaked away, that no liabilities of
e the subsidiary company ought to be laid at the door of other members of the group, and
that no indemnity from or right of action against any other company, or against any
individual, is by some mischance overlooked.

     The anxiety of the creditors will be increased where, as in the present case, all the assets
of the subsidiary company are claimed by another member of the group in right of a
debenture.

f   The present appeal concerns the Seton group of companies, a group which includes
Seton Trust Ltd and Scandic Credit & Commerce Ltd, who claim to be creditors of a third
company, Southard & Co Ltd, now insolvent. The outside creditors of Southard, that is
to say, creditors who have no interest in the group, ask that Southard be wound up by the
present liquidators in the voluntary winding-up, two professional men of acknowledged
expertise, integrity and independence, in whom the outside creditors have confidence.
g There are cogent reasons why the outside creditors seek the reassurance of an investigation
by the present liquidators, who have expressed their willingness to carry it out. First,
Seton Trust made improper attempts to ensure that an employee of the group was
appointed liquidator. I say 'improper' because of the clear conflict of interest between
Seton Trust asserting its debenture and possibly having to defend its management of
Southard which resulted in insolvency on the one hand and the outside creditors on the
h other hand. Secondly, Seton Trust has persisted in litigation designed to ensure that the
two liquidators appointed by the outside creditors should not be allowed to wind up
Southard. Thirdly, Seton Trust sought and obtained injunctions which, until the matter
reached this court inter partes, prohibited the two liquidators from acting. Fourthly, as
soon as Seton Trust failed to secure the appointment of its employee as liquidator, it took
an assignment of a debenture and appointed that very same employee as receiver and he,
j of course, took charge of all the assets and books of Southard. Seton Trust explained
some of its conduct and its actions as being due to ineptitude; that explanation is neither
reassuring nor convincing. Fifthly, Seton Trust, who was converted to the virtues of a
compulsory winding-up only after it had failed to appoint its own employee of the group
as a voluntary liquidator, has only put forward arguments of speed and cost which, in the
light of the evidence, are wholly unconvincing. Sixthly, if Seton Trust has rightly valued

its debenture, and if the debenture is valid, it does not matter to it whether the company is wound up voluntarily or compulsorily; the motives for this appeal are wholly unexplained. Finally, Brightman J, whose experience in the Companies Court is unrivalled, thought that in the present circumstances the voluntary liquidation ought to go on and that, without making any criticism of the Official Receiver, whose hands are tied by the multitude of cases which he must investigate, and by the duty which he owes of protecting public funds, it would be better if the present liquidators in the voluntary winding-up, having regard to their evidence, were allowed to continue.

In my judgment these reasons establish an overwhelming case for allowing the independent creditors to have the reassurance of an investigation by their liquidators, which they now seek.

Counsel for the petitioning and supporting creditors did his best to make palatable the inedible. His main submission, however, was that the court only has a fettered discretion and should not, or cannot, deny a majority when the majority are seeking, and not opposing, the ordinary remedy of an unpaid creditor, namely a winding-up by the court.

Both counsel referred to all the relevant authorities, which begin with *Bowes v Directors of Hope Life Insurance and Guarantee Co*[1], and end with *Re J D Swain Ltd*[2]. The guidance is summed up in extracts from the judgment of Upjohn LJ in *Re P & J Macrae Ltd*[3]:

'Where a creditor has proved his case against the company to a winding-up order ex debito justitiae, but other creditors of the company have expressed conflicting views as to the desirability of winding it up, the judge has conferred on him a discretion by the Companies Act, 1948, s. 346(1), which, leaving out immaterial words provides: "The court may . . . have regard to the wishes of the creditors ... as proved to it by any sufficient evidence . . ." The discretion is permissive and not mandatory, and is in terms complete and unfettered. However, it is a discretion which must be exercised judicially, and the court is not entitled arbitrarily to disregard the wishes of the creditors as proved to it. . . . statute has conferred a complete and unfettered judicial discretion on the court, and, where the statute has seen fit to do so, a judicial or text-book gloss on the terms of the discretion are apt to mislead if they are treated as a complete statement of the law. Reported cases can only be quoted as examples of the way in which in the past judges have thought fit to exercise the discretion, and judicial discretion cannot fetter or limit the discretion conferred by statute or even create a binding rule or practice . . . the power to make a winding-up order is by the very terms of s. 222 of the Companies Act, 1948, itself discretionary, and, although an undoubted creditor is as a general rule entitled to an order ex debito justitiae, there may be special cases where, apart altogether from the wishes of creditors generally, the court may not think fit to make an order . . . Although the statute provides that it is the wishes of the creditors to which the court may have regard, it is quite clear that, as the statute gives a complete discretion, the weight to be given to those wishes in determining whether a winding-up order ought to be made varies according to the number and value of the creditors expressing wishes, and the nature and quality of their debts. . . . the weight to be given to the wishes of the opposing creditors must necessarily depend on all the circumstances of the case but, other things being equal, will increase in the mind of the judge as the majority of opposing creditors increases. . . . when weighing all the circumstances in deciding whether to wind up the company, the voice of the creditors must either ultimately be for or against, and that is in the ordinary case determined by the majority; but the power of the voice must necessarily depend on all the circumstances. . . . When the judge has decided what weight, if any, he is

---

1 (1865) 11 HL Cas 389, 11 ER 1383
2 [1965] 2 All ER 761, [1965] 1 WLR 909
3 [1961] 1 All ER 302 at 308–311, [1961] 1 WLR 229 at 237–240

going to give to the wishes of the majority of creditors, he balances that together with all the other relevant circumstances in evidence before him in order to see whether in the end it is proper that a winding-up order should be made.'

I would only add that where the choice before the court is between a compulsory winding-up and a voluntary winding-up, the judge, after hearing the reasons of the majority and the reasons advanced by the minority, must decide whether the interests of the unsecured creditors, and in particular the interests of the independent outside creditors, and thus the interests of the public, are likely to be better served by making a compulsory winding-up order or not.

Applying those principles to the present circumstances, I agree that this appeal should be dismissed, and I accept and gratefully adopt the reasons also advanced by Buckley and Bridge LJJ.

Appeal dismissed. Leave to appeal to House of Lords refused.

Solicitors: *Janners* (for the petitioning and supporting creditors); *Evan Davies* (for the creditors).

J H Fazan Esq   Barrister.

Fawke v Viscount Chelsea

COURT OF APPEAL, CIVIL DIVISION
STEPHENSON, GOFF AND BRANDON LJJ
25th, 26th, 29th JANUARY, 23rd FEBRUARY 1979

Landlord and tenant – Rent – Business premises – Interim rent – Application by landlord for determination of rent during continuance of tenancy – Determination of interim rent – Determination of rent for new tenancy – Factors to be taken into consideration – State of disrepair of premises – Power of court to award differential rent – Landlord and Tenant Act 1954, ss 24A (as inserted by the Law of Property Act 1969, s 3(1)), 34.

The tenant was granted a lease of certain business premises for a term expiring on 30th May 1975. On the expiry of the term the tenancy continued by virtue of s 24 of the Landlord and Tenant Act 1954. On 3rd December the landlord served a notice terminating the tenancy on 7th June 1976. The tenant served a counter-notice stating that he was not willing to give up possession and on 29th March 1976 applied for a new tenancy. On 7th April the landlord served notice objecting to the terms of the new tenancy proposed by the tenant and applied to the county court to determine an interim rent under s 24A[a] of the 1954 Act while the existing tenancy continued by virtue of s 24. Under the terms of the tenancy the landlord was subject to a full repairing covenant in respect of the exterior of the premises. The parties' valuers failed to agree a figure for the rent, the landlord's valuer proposing £4,350 per annum for the interim rent and the tenant's valuer £3,000. By the time the case came on for hearing in March 1978 it had been discovered that the premises were infected with dry rot due to many years of neglect of the exterior and that, as a result, extensive external repairs and interior work were necessary to eradicate the rot and replace the ruined woodwork, and further, that it would be about a year before the work was completed. At the hearing the tenant's valuer changed his figure for the interim rent to £1,000 per annum and proposed that the rent should remain payable at that rate under the new lease until completion of the necessary works of repair and restoration. The judge refused to take into account the state of repair of the premises and held that he had no jurisdiction (i) under s 24A to award a differential rent (ie one which varied according to the state of repair of the premises) in respect of the interim period, or (ii) under s 34[b] to award a differential rent in respect of the new lease, and that, as the landlord was subject to a full repairing covenant, the tenant's proper remedy was to claim damages for breach of covenant. He determined an interim rent of £3,450 per annum and a rent for the new lease of £3,950 per annum with no period of reduced rent while the works were carried out. The tenant appealed.

Held – (1) In assessing what would be a reasonable rent under s 24A of the 1954 Act for a tenant to pay while the existing tenancy continued by virtue of s 24 of that Act, the court could have regard to the state of repair of the premises, take into account what was known at the date of the hearing as to the actual condition of the premises at the commencement of the interim period, and (Goff LJ dubitante) determine a differential interim rent if that was justified (see p 574 c to f h, p 575 b c f, p 576 a b, p 577 f g, p 578 f to h and p 579 e to g, post).

(2) Furthermore, on the true construction of s 34 of the 1954 Act the court could also determine a differential rent in respect of a new tenancy. Whether it should do so depended on the evidence in the particular case (see p 574 j to p 575 a, p 577 f, p 578 b to d h and p 579 d and f g, post).

---

a Section 24A is set out at p 572 c to f, post
b Section 34, so far as material, is set out at p 572 g h, post

a (3) Since the judge had erred in disregarding the state of repair of the premises and holding that he had no jurisdiction to determine a differential rent under either s 24A or s 34, the appeal would be allowed and the question of the interim rent and the question whether, in the event of the repair works not being completed by the commencement of the new lease, the rent should be reduced or suspended until the completion of the works, and if so by how much, would be remitted to the county court judge (see p 576 a b, p 577 d to f and p 579 f g, post).

b   Per Brandon and Stephenson LJJ. The cases in which the evidence may support a differential rent on the basis of the state of disrepair are likely to be limited to those in which the state of disrepair at the commencement of the new tenancy, or the commencement of the period of the interim rent, is of a very serious character (see p 578 h j and p 579 f g, post).

c **Notes**
For the rent payable under a new tenancy of business premises, see 23 Halsbury's Laws (3rd Edn) 898, para 1725, and for cases on the subject, see 31(2) Digest (Reissue) 957–959, 7767–7772.
For applications to determine an interim rent, see Supplement to 23 Halsbury's Laws (3rd Edn) para 1714A.

d For the Landlord and Tenant Act 1954, ss 24A, 34, see 18 Halsbury's Statutes (3rd Edn) 559, 573.

Cases referred to in judgments
English Exporters (London) Ltd v Eldonwall Ltd [1973] 1 All ER 726, [1973] Ch 415, [1973] 2 WLR 435, 31(2) Digest (Reissue) 958, 7771.
Regis Property Co Ltd v Lewis & Peat Ltd [1970] 3 All ER 227, [1970] Ch 695, [1970] 3 e WLR 361, 21 P & CR 761, [1970] RVR 805, 31(2) Digest (Reissue) 958, 7770.

Appeal
On 7th April 1976 the Hon Charles Gerald John Cadogan, Viscount Chelsea ('the landlord') applied to the county court for an order determining what rent it was reasonable for Leslie Arthur Fawke ('the tenant') to pay for certain business premises on f the first and second floors of 27 Sloane Square, London SW1, whilst the tenancy was continued by virtue of s 24 of the Landlord and Tenant Act 1954. On 15th March 1978 at West London County Court his Honour Judge Corcoran determined an interim rent of £3,450 per annum for the period whilst the tenancy continued by virtue of s 24 and a rent of £3,950 per annum for the new lease and held that there should be no period of reduced rent whilst agreed works of rot eradication and reinstatement were carried out g to the premises. The tenant appealed against his decision. The facts are set out in the judgment of Goff LJ.

Patrick Ground for the tenant.
William Poulton for the landlord.

Cur adv vult

h

23rd February. The following judgments were read.

GOFF LJ (delivering the first judgment at the invitation of Stephenson LJ). This is an appeal from a judgment given on 15th March 1978 by his Honour Judge Corcoran in the j West London County Court, whereby he determined an interim rent under s 24A of the Landlord and Tenant Act 1954, and the rent and terms for a new lease of offices on the first and second floors of 27 Sloane Square, London SW1.
The applicant for a new tenancy under Part II of the 1954 Act was the tenant, who is a solicitor and carries on his practice at the demised premises. The landlord, did not oppose the grant of a new tenancy but objected to the terms proposed by the tenant and

applied to the court for an order determining the rent which it would be reasonable for
him to pay while his tenancy continued by virtue of s 24 of the 1954 Act, what is called *a*
in RSC Ord 97, r 9A, and in the cases, though not in the Act itself or in the County Court
Rules, 'an interim rent'. The learned judge determined an interim rent of £3,450, and
a new rent of £3,950.

The tenant held the premises under a sub-underlease dated 2nd November 1970 ('the
tenancy') from a company called Soletanche Ltd for a term of two years certain and
thereafter from year to year until 30th May 1975 at a rent of £2,750 per annum. The *b*
landlord acquired the freehold on 24th June 1975, on the falling in of the most superior
head lease, subject only so far as the demised premises are concerned to and with the
benefit of the tenancy, all other relevant underleases having determined.

There was a dispute between the parties whether the landlord was subject to any
covenant to repair. The learned judge held that he was, and by a respondent's notice the
landlord sought to reverse that finding. Briefly the point is that in the grant of the *c*
tenancy, Soletanche Ltd covenanted to perform the lessee's covenants, which included a
full repairing covenant, contained in their underlease, being that immediately superior
to the tenancy, and the landlord contends that the liability of Soletanche Ltd under that
covenant ceased when the underlease to Soletanche Ltd expired, as it did on 7th June
1975. I need not develop this any further because counsel for the landlord has conceded,
for the purposes of these proceedings only, that we shall proceed on the basis that under *d*
the terms of the tenancy the landlord is subject to a full repairing covenant concerning
the structure of the whole building including the demised premises. On the other hand,
under the tenancy, the tenant covenanted to keep the interior of the demised premises
(but excluding all load bearing walls, roofs and floor joists) and the sewers, drains and
walls thereof in good and tenantable repair and condition.

The tenancy continued, of course, after the contractual expiry date, 30th May 1975, by *e*
virtue of s 24 of the 1954 Act, and on 3rd December 1975 the landlord served notice to
determine it on 7th June 1976. On 23rd January 1976 the tenant served a counter-notice
stating that he would not be willing to give up possession, and on 29th March 1976 he
applied for a new tenancy, which he proposed should be for 14 years from 7th June 1976
at the rent of £3,600 per annum, and on other terms as stated in his notice. On 7th April
1976 the landlord served notice objecting to the proposed terms and asking the court to *f*
determine an interim rent under s 24A.

The expert witnesses for the two parties put forward competing figures, and the judge
made the assessments I have already mentioned. The major battle, however, turned on
the fact that the building, including that part of it which constituted the demised
premises, became infested with dry rot due to many years neglect of the exterior, so that
not only was it necessary for extensive external repairs to be carried out, but also very *g*
substantial internal work to eradicate the rot and replace ruined woodwork. This it was
clear would cause great inconvenience to the tenant, and indeed whilst work was being
carried out within the demised premises he might not be able to use them at all except
for storage. There had been two serious floodings in September 1975 due to a blocked
drainpipe, but having regard to the lapse of time these had probably not caused or
resulted in dry rot. *h*

Mr St John, who gave evidence for the tenant, and Mr Fraser-Mitchell, who gave
evidence for the landlord, met at the premises in June 1976 and endeavoured to agree
figures. Mr St John proposed £3,000 per annum for the interim rent, and Mr Fraser-
Mitchell £4,350. Mr St John made a report at that time which shows that he had not
made or had the benefit of any survey, but that because of the damp in the premises he
took account of the possibility of dry rot, although as far as can be seen he did not know *j*
whether or not it then in fact existed.

I read the following passages from his report:

'(7) We were not instructed to make a structural or other survey of the building
and we did not do so. In view of the water and damp penetration which has

occurred and is occurring (to which we shall presently refer again) and the age of the building, the Landlord would be well advised to check on the possibility of rot and to take remedial steps to prevent further damage to the structure . . .'

'(10) We observed that rainwater from the roof discharges into the main sewer and if the downpipe is blocked, flooding is caused into the rear room on the second Floor and Telephone room on the first Floor. Also, the cladding tiles to the exterior cause stoppage in downpipe backflow of water into the third Floor and this backflow of water pours through the ceiling into the rear rooms second and first Floors.'

'(11) At the time of our inspection, the skylight at the top of the building was open to the skies and water was coming in therefrom.'

The judge himself viewed the demised premises as he said in his judgment:

'On Tuesday 21st February 1977 at the request of both counsel I had a view of the premises at 27 Sloane Square. I am entitled to take into account my own impression on a view of the premises as it is a part of the evidence in the case on which I can rely. Of course, when considering my impressions, I take full account of all the oral evidence I have heard and particularly the evidence given by the expert witnesses.'

The judge also found:

'After the inconvenience and disturbance to the two rear rooms caused by the flooding, [the tenant] carried on his solicitor's practice over this period without complaint and had full use of all the rooms. The interior decorations were damaged to the extent already indicated. I saw the premises and, discounting the exploratory work done in January 1978 to assess the extent of the dry rot discovered shortly before and some damage to the decorations caused by comparatively recent penetration of water, [the tenant's] premises were in a reasonable state.'

In November 1977 dry rot was found in areas around the central light well extending from the fourth floor down to sill level of the windows to the well on the first floor which was due, as the judge found, to seepage of water for a long period from a defective gutter. Notwithstanding the exploratory work done in January 1978, it appears that some further dry rot may still be discovered because Mr Keen, an expert in the eradication of dry rot and the cure of all forms of dampness in buildings whose evidence the judge accepted, said: 'The damp areas are areas of potential dry rot as they dry out. After an area affected by damp begins to dry out it takes from six to twelve months before it can be ascertained whether or not dry rot is present.'

Then the judge said this:

'He [McKeen] said that he would not be able to commence the job having regard to present commitments until the end of April 1978; it would take two to three months to complete the work of eradication; then before redecoration could commence one month would have to elapse for the plastering to dry out. That would mean that redecoration could not commence at the earliest before the end of August 1978, and that is on the basis that no further extensive areas of dry rot were discovered during the remedial work. At the expiration of six months from now further exploratory work could begin to ascertain whether there was dry rot in those damp areas already referred to as conducive to dry rot. Those areas are not extensive and if dry rot was not found they would be replastered and could be redecorated four weeks later. If dry rot was found, the work of eradication would not take very long. It would be early December 1978 before [the tenant] could expect to have his premises fully redecorated. The exterior work necessary to be done would be completed in the main before Mr Keen commenced work.'

Work did not commence as early as anticipated and we understand that much remains to be done. The parties sought leave to adduce further evidence about this, but we did

not think it necessary to go into precise details. It was common ground that it would
seem likely to be completed before the new lease will commence.

a

At the trial Mr St John resiled from his figure of £3,000 for the interim rent. He went
so far as to say that the premises were unlettable, and he proposed an interim rent of
£1,000 per annum, and further that the rent should remain payable at that rate under
the new lease until completion of the necessary works of repair and restoration. At that
time it was apprehended that the new lease would commence before then. The learned
judge rejected this contention and he determined an interim rent of £3,450 per annum

b

and a rent for the new lease of £3,950 with no period of reduced rent whilst agreed
works of rot eradication and reinstatement were carried out.

The tenant now appeals asking for an order substituting an interim rent of £1,000 per
annum or such other figure as the court should think fit for the period of the tenancy
covered by s 24A and for any further period used for the carrying out of the said remedial
and reinstatement work. Included, or intended to be included, in this notice of motion

c

is a challenge to the new rent also.

I must now read s 24A and the material parts of s 34 of the 1954 Act. Section 24A says:

'(1) The landlord of a tenancy to which this Part of this Act applies may,—(a) if he
has given notice under section 25 of this Act to terminate the tenancy; or (b) if the
tenant has made a request for a new tenancy in accordance with section 26 of this
Act; apply to the court to determine a rent which it would be reasonable for the

d

tenant to pay while the tenancy continues by virtue of section 24 of this Act, and the
court may determine a rent accordingly.

'(2) A rent determined in proceedings under this section shall be deemed to be
the rent payable under the tenancy from the date on which the proceedings were
commenced or the date specified in the landlord's notice or the tenant's request,
whichever is the later.

e

'(3) In determining a rent under this section the court shall have regard to the
rent payable under the terms of the tenancy, but otherwise subsections (1) and (2)
of section 34 of this Act shall apply to the determination as they would apply to the
determination of a rent under that section if a new tenancy from year to year of the
whole of the property comprised in the tenancy were granted to the tenant by order
of the court.'

f

Then s 34 says:

'(1) The rent payable under a tenancy granted by order of the court under this
Part of this Act shall be such as may be agreed between the landlord and the tenant
or as, in default of such agreement, may be determined by the court to be that at
which, having regard to the terms of the tenancy (other than those relating to rent),

g

the holding might reasonably be expected to be let in the open market by a willing
lessor, there being disregarded—(a) any effect on rent of the fact that the tenant has
or his predecessors in title have been in occupation of the holding, (b) any goodwill
attached to the holding by reason of the carrying on thereat of the business of the
tenant (whether by him or by a predecessor of his in that business) . . .

'(3) Where the rent is determined by the court the court may, if it thinks fit,

h

further determine that the terms of the tenancy shall include such provision for
varying the rent as may be specified in the determination.'

Section 24A of the 1954 Act (as inserted by s 3(1) of the Law of Property Act 1969) is,
as has been stated by Stamp J in *Regis Property Co Ltd v Lewis & Peat Ltd*[1] and by Megarry
J in *English Exporters (London) Ltd v Eldonwall Ltd*[2], extremely difficult to construe and

j

apply because it is not easy to reconcile sub-s (1) with sub-s (3) or to see the true
relationship between the opening words of sub-s (3), requiring regard to be had to the

1   [1970] 3 All ER 227, [1970] Ch 695
2   [1973] 1 All ER 726, [1973] Ch 415

rent payable under the tenancy, and the later part of the section, incorporating sub-ss (1) and (2) of s 34 by reference, because the very general expression 'shall have regard to' necessarily imports a large degree of uncertainty, and finally because, as Megarry J said in *English Exporters (London) Ltd v Eldonwall Ltd*[1]—

'I would only add that the process of applying s 34 to a hypothetical yearly tenancy is one that, at least under present conditions, may often have an air of unreality about it that would puzzle the most expert of valuers.'

In the *Regis Property Co* case[2] Stamp J construed the words 'shall have regard to the rent payable under the terms of the tenancy' as merely amending s 34(1), as applied to the determination of an interim rent under s 24A, by in effect striking out the words 'other than those relating to rent' and substituting 'including those relating to rent'. So he held there was only one operation to be performed under sub-s (3), that is to say the assessment of the rent as a matter of market value in accordance with s 34 as so, in effect, amended and, of course, on the basis of a yearly tenancy. He held that one could have regard to the rent under the existing tenancy if, but only if, it had evidential value for the purposes of ascertaining the market value, and he considered that but for the opening words of sub-s (3) it could not have been regarded at all, because of the words of exclusion in that sub-section.

Once the valuation exercise has been performed, however, in his view the matter is at an end and the figure arrived at cannot be modified either by the provision in sub-s (1) that the landlord may 'apply to the court to determine a rent which it would be reasonable for the tenant to pay' or by the direction in sub-s (3) to have regard to the rent. That is to say he rejected what was described as the cushion argument.

Megarry J, taking a different view, accepted that argument. According to him the direction to have regard to the rent and the reference to s 34 are two separate things, so that one must first provisionally determine the interim rent in accordance with the terms of s 34 but, of course, as if the court were ordering not a term of years but a yearly tenancy, and then review that against the actual rent payable under the current tenancy in the light of the direction in sub-s (1) that the rent is to be reasonable. Megarry J considered that Stamp J was wrong in thinking that unless his construction were adopted one could not refer to the existing rent even in the examples given by him where it would have evidentiary value.

In the result, therefore, both agreed, though for different reasons, that the court and the expert witnesses appearing before it may, and should, have regard to the existing rent if it has evidentiary value, but the difference between them lies in Stamp J's view that, apart from that, it is irrelevant and the matter ends with the valuation, whereas in Megarry J's view it then has in any event to be considered in order to determine whether it is reasonable to adopt the valuation without modification.

Unfortunately no argument was addressed to us as to which of these views we should adopt, or whether, indeed, neither affords the correct solution to the problems posed by s 24A, as both parties were prepared to accept Megarry J's decision. We must, therefore, proceed on that basis, and this case cannot be regarded as a binding decision on this particular question of construction, but I must say that, as at present advised, I prefer the reasoning and decision of Megarry J. With all respect to Stamp J I think he fell into error, because he overlooked the fact that there are two tenancies and two rents involved, not one. The rent to which the court is directed to have regard under sub-s (3) is the rent payable under the contractual tenancy, which is continuing by virtue of the 1954 Act, but when one applies s 34 to the determination of an interim rent, as directed by s 24(3), one is considering a new hypothetical yearly tenancy, and one can no more consider the rent appropriate to such a tenancy when determining that rent than one can consider the rent under a new tenancy when determining that rent.

1   [1973] 1 All ER 726 at 740, [1973] Ch 415 at 430
2   [1970] 3 All ER 227, [1970] Ch 695

I should also make some observations about the question of time, Megarry J's fourth point[1]. It is possible to argue, as counsel did, that the valuation for the purposes of s 24A *a* must be made as at the date of the hearing, or at least of the application to determine an interim rent, because the section applies s 34 as if the court were granting a new tenancy, albeit a yearly one, and, of course, when finally determining the matter by ordering a new lease under s 34 the court must of necessity consider the position at the date of the hearing, or at all events the latest date at which evidence is available. However, the reasons given by Megarry J appear to me to be compelling, and I agree that the values to *b* be applied should be those existing when the interim period begins to run, which having regard to s 24A(2) is not necessarily the same date as that on which the contractual tenancy expires.

In my judgment the valuation should be made not, as was argued by the tenant on what knowledge of the state of the premises at the commencement of the interim period a reasonable prospective tenant properly advised and having such survey, if any, as might *c* be reasonable would or should have discovered, for that imports a large measure of uncertainty, nor yet on the actual knowledge of the actual parties, for that is subjective whilst the test ought to be objective, but on all that is known at the date of the hearing as to the condition the premises were actually in at the commencement of that interim period. I do not see anything in s 24A which requires the court, in determining what rent it is reasonable for the tenant to pay, albeit by reference to a hypothetical letting, to *d* shut its eyes to known facts.

Before considering the evidence in this case and the judge's findings, there are certain other questions of construction to be decided.

First, has the court jurisdiction under s 24A to award a rent which is not to come into operation until repairs have been effected or is to be increased when they are, or which commences at once but is later to become subject to a moratorium, or reduction for a *e* certain period?

I have had the advantage of reading the judgment which Brandon LJ proposes to deliver, and with which I understand Stephenson LJ agrees, and they take the view that it has. The question is I think a very difficult one, and I confess with all respect to them that I have some hesitation in accepting their views on this point, notwithstanding the referential incorporation of s 34(1) and (2) in s 24A. It seems to me that the words 'a rent *f* which it would be reasonable for the tenant to pay while the tenancy continues by virtue of section 24 of this Act' in sub-s (1), and the words in sub-s (2) 'shall be deemed to be the rent payable under the tenancy from the date' etc may well be too strong to admit of such a construction, especially so when one remembers that s 24A is conferring a power to substitute an interim rent for the contractual rent, which otherwise would continue uninterruptedly until a new lease be ordered or refused, and that in the absence of a *g* provision in that behalf in the contractual tenancy the tenant holding over under ss 24 and 64 would not be entitled to any reduction or suspension of rent during repairs. I am, however, not prepared to dissent on this point and content myself with expressing my doubts.

The next question of construction which was argued, although in the events which have happened it is probably now academic, is whether the court has any such power *h* when determining a rent under s 34 for a new tenancy. Here in my view the answer is free from doubt. I am satisfied that s 34(3) authorises nothing more than the inclusion of a rent review clause; but what of sub-s (1)? The judge thought that he could not make any such order because this would be 'not a variation of the determined rent for the new tenancy, but the determination of two rents'. With all respect I do not agree. If supported by evidence that this would be the manner in which 'the holding might reasonably be expected to be let in the open market by a willing lessor' I see no reason why the court should not determine a rent increasing by fixed amounts at specified times. By the same token the court has, in my judgment, power to provide that the rent

---

1   [1973] 1 All ER 726 at 741, [1973] Ch 415 at 431

shall not commence, or shall be at a less rate, until repairs are effected, or shall cease to be
a   payable or be reduced as from the time, albeit later than the commencement of the new
lease, when they are in fact started and until completed. This does not in any way
conflict with sub-s (3) or render that subsection otiose, because under a rent review clause
the court would not itself be determining the rent but delegating that function.

The next question is how the valuers should regard want of repair and breaches of
covenant, when assessing an interim rent, and it seems to me they should consider what
b   would be a reasonable rent for the tenant to pay from the date for commencement of that
rent as a yearly tenant, having regard to the actual condition and state of the premises at
that date, and having regard to the terms of the contractual tenancy so far as applicable
to a yearly tenancy. This will mean that the hypothetical tenant will have the benefit of
any covenant to repair on the part of the landlord and the burden of any on the part of
the tenant, or there may be no covenant to repair on either side.
c   The learned judge said:

'A term of the hypothetical yearly tenancy obliged the landlord to well and
substantially repair, maintain and keep the premises in good and substantial repair
and condition. In determining the interim rent the court must have regard (inter
alia) to that term. Likewise the court must have regard to the tenant's covenant to
d   decorate the premises. When the state or condition of the premises is regulated by
such terms, in my judgment, lack of repair or want of decoration albeit a lack of
repair, is not an element which the court should take into account in assessing
interim rent because the landlord by the term of the tenancy is under an obligation
to effect necessary repairs and if he does not the tenant has the right to enforce the
covenant to repair against the landlord and claim damages. This is the correct
e   procedure for dealing with lack of repair to the premises and consequential damage
suffered by the tenant.'

He was, of course, right to take into account the landlord's and tenant's covenants to
repair, but with respect in my judgment not to treat the lack of repair as an element not
to be taken into account in assessing interim rent, on the ground that the tenant will have
f   an action for damages or indeed for any other reason. The valuation being on the basis
of a new yearly tenancy it must in my view be assumed that these covenants will be duly
performed. There can at this stage be no question of breach.

The fixing of an interim rent will not, however, affect the right of either party to sue
the other for any breach of the repairing covenants in the contractual tenancy, which
may have already occurred or may subsequently occur, save that, in assessing damages
for diminution in value with respect to any period after the determination of the
g   contractual tenancy, credit must be given for the amount by which the interim rent was
reduced on account of the want of repair from what it would have been if the premises
had been in the state of repair required by the covenants. This may be considerably less
than the actual diminution in value during the period of breach, since the valuation
postulates prompt repair. The fixing of an interim rent would also not affect a claim by
h   the tenant for damages for extra disturbance on the ground that the landlord's failure to
repair after notice had made more extensive repairs necessary.

In cases where the interim rent so determined is less than the contractual rent the
court must then consider whether, in the light of its duty to have regard to the rent
payable under the terms of the existing tenancy, it should increase the interim rent up
or near to that rent, or should, in the exercise of its discretion, refuse to determine an
j   interim rent at all, which would leave the contractual rent payable. In determining these
matters the court will, of course, bear in mind that s 24A is a section obviously designed
by Parliament to improve the landlord's position, as is shown, if in no other way, by the
fact that he alone can apply under it; and certainly where the low valuation is due to
breaches by the landlord of his repairing covenants it would I think have to be a very
special case in which the court would determine an interim rent less than the contractual

rent. Different considerations will apply if the low valuation is due to a fall in property values.

With these principles in mind I turn to consider the facts of this particular case. The basic rent determined for the new lease is not challenged in the notice of appeal but, as I have said, it was argued below and before us that the low figure of £1,000 should be continued for the new lease until all necessary repairs have been effected, and as I have already indicated in my judgment, the judge was wrong in holding that he had no jurisdiction to order that. This point has, however, been overtaken by events since this appeal has postponed the date when the new lease will come into force so that as far as can be seen, I gather, the repairs will all be finished before then. Thus the question now affects the interim rent only. It is, therefore, strictly unnecessary to say anything more about the rent for the new lease. I will just add this, however, Mr Fraser-Mitchell gave evidence in cross-examination as follows: 'If repairs are necessary the estate company's policy is to allow a rent-free period for the tenant to do the repair. Having regard to the evidence heard it would be a period of three or four months—three months would be fair.'

There seems to be some confusion here since in the present case it would be for the landlord to do the repairs, but overlooking that point, this passage affords some evidence which might have supported a postponement of the rent under the new lease, although the company's policy is subjective and does not necessarily reflect objectively what a willing lessor might be expected to do.

However, the judge did make an allowance for the want of repair in a different way, for he said:

'In my judgment, having regard to all the circumstances and background and to the fact that it will be many months yet before [the tenant] can settle down to quiet enjoyment of his holding owing to the works of reparation and redecoration which must be carried out, I consider that it will be right for the rent review to take place at the expiration of seven years.'

I would, therefore, not interfere with the rent determined by the judge for the new lease even if it is open to the tenant to challenge this having regard to the terms of the notice of motion, and I turn to consider the problem in relation to the interim rent.

As I have said, the evidence of Mr Fraser-Mitchell is some, but by itself quite insufficient, evidence to justify a differential rent and in any case the evidence does not show what the actual state of affairs was in June 1976. Mr Hitchin in his report dated 16th December 1977 says: 'Dry rot is a dangerous fungus and grows swiftly—the quicker work is done the less likelihood there is of any additional work being necessary', so that the position may well have worsened substantially between June 1976 and November 1977, and still more so by January 1978.

If a differential provision pending or during repairs is to be ordered it will be necessary to have further evidence on the lines which will be indicated by Brandon LJ to establish clearly that on the actual facts in June 1976 this would have been the only, or at least a probable, basis for a yearly letting.

Apart from this, the question is whether the judge was correct in fixing a rent of £3,450 against Mr St John's figure of £3,000 and Mr Fraser-Mitchell's figure of £4,350 when they met in June 1976.

The figure of £1,000 which Mr St John put forward at the trial was based mainly at any rate on the fact that dry rot was discovered in November 1977, and the judge quoted from Mr St John's evidence and commented thereon as follows:

'He further said: "I have considered the interim rent pursuant to s 24A" and "in the period from 7th June 1976 with the knowledge I have now (a) the premises are not lettable, (b) in June 1976 the premises were not readily lettable, (c) the landlord would be lucky to let them at £1,000 per annum, (d) had I been advising a prospective tenant I would have advised him not to touch the premises having regard to the possibility of rot." . . . I think it is important to note in this connection a that he also says that while the work of reparation is being carried out [the tenant's] premises will not be usable by [the tenant] for office purposes, but only as storage and his valuation of the premises for storage only is £1,000 per annum, ie the same figure he now gives for interim rent over a period when [the tenant] was using the premises for carrying on his practice without complaint and in premises, which, on the evidence, I have found were in a reasonable state.'

b I do not think the judge was entitled to take into account the fact that in the events which happened the tenant was in fact able to carry on his practice in reasonable comfort, since that became known only after the relevant date, as at which the valuation has to be made, but he was entitled and bound to take into account the condition in which, assisted by a view, he found the premises to have been at the commencement of the interim period.

c I think also in (d) quoted from Mr St John's evidence he was purporting to consider the position as it appeared in June 1976 and not relying on subsequent facts because he speaks of 'the possibility of rot', but the judge was quite right in taking a general view that his evidence was coloured by the information obtained in November 1977 that there was not merely a possibility of dry rot but actual dry rot.

With respect, the judge also erred as I have said in disregarding the state of repair when determining the interim rent. Mr Fraser-Mitchell committed the same error, as he too d made no allowance for the state of repair of the premises and the tenant's decorations.

In the circumstances, for my part, I cannot regard the judge's determination of an interim rent as entirely satisfactory. It may be in view of what counsel told us during the hearing that the questions of principle having been resolved they will be able to agree to accept or modify the judge's determination of £3,450, with or without a differential provision pending or during repairs, in which case we could, by consent, order e accordingly, but failing that I would, for my part, refer this part of the case back to him for rehearing with liberty to either party to adduce further evidence.

BRANDON LJ (read by Stephenson LJ). I agree in general with the judgment of Goff LJ. There is, however, one question in respect of which he has expressed doubts. That f question is whether the court has power, not only when determining the rent of a new tenancy under s 34(1) of the 1954 Act, but also when determining an interim rent under s 24A, to determine what I shall for convenience call a differential rent, by which I mean a rent which varies from time to time during the period of the tenancy according to the situation with regard to the state of repair of the premises. Although I have found the question a difficult one, I do not in the end share the doubts which Goff LJ has expressed, g and I shall accordingly set out my views on the matter and the reasons on which they are based.

I consider, first, the power of the court when determining under s 34(1) the rent payable under a new tenancy. The rent to be determined is the rent at which, having regard to the terms of the new tenancy other than those relating to rent, the holding might reasonably be expected to be let in the open market by a willing lessor, in other h words the market rent. It is clear that the market rent of premises may in general be affected not only by the terms of the tenancy concerning the obligations of the lessor and lessee in relation to repair but also by the actual state of repair of the premises at the commencement of the tenancy.

To take an extreme example: let it be supposed, first, that under the terms of the tenancy it is the obligation of the lessor to put the premises into repair; secondly, that the j premises are, at the commencement of the tenancy, so seriously out of repair, by reason of previous fire or flood, that they are of only partial use to the lessee; thirdly, that an appreciable period must necessarily elapse before the lessor can begin to perform his obligation of putting the premises into repair; and, fourthly, that, while the lessor is performing that obligation, the disturbance will be such that the premises will be virtually of no use to the lessee at all. In those circumstances it may well be that the market rent of the premises, which would be appropriate after they had been put into repair, would be appreciably reduced during the period which would necessarily elapse before the work of putting them into repair was begun, and even more reduced during the further period while such work was being carried out.

Similar considerations would, as it seems to me, apply if the premises were seriously out of repair at the commencement of the tenancy, not by reason of previous fire or flood, but by reason of the failure of the lessor or the lessee or both to perform their previous obligations to repair. The cause or causes of the premises being out of repair are not, for this purpose, significant; the fact that they are out of repair, for whatever cause or causes, is so.

On the footing that the market rent of premises in general may be affected by the situation with regard to their state of repair in the manner which I have described, the questions whether and how the market rent of the premises concerned in any particular case are so affected must depend on the evidence in that case. If the evidence showed that the market rent would be a rent which varied during the period of the tenancy according to whether the premises (a) remained out of repair, (b) were in the course of being put into repair and (c) had been put into repair, then it seems to me that the court, applying the principle of determination prescribed by s 34(1), not only would have power to determine, but would be obliged to determine, a differential rent accordingly. If, on the other hand, the evidence showed that the market rent, though affected in amount by the present and future situation with regard to state of repair, would nevertheless be a normal fixed rent over the whole period of the tenancy, then the court's duty would be to determine a fixed rent in accordance with that evidence.

I consider, second, the power of the court when determining under s 24A an interim rent payable during the continuation of a pre-existing tenancy. The rent which the court has to determine in this case, subject always to its additional duty to have regard to the rent payable under the pre-existing tenancy, is the rent at which the holding might reasonably be let, having regard to the terms of such tenancy other than those relating to rent, from year to year in the open market by a willing lessor, in other words the market rent on a year to year basis. Here again it seems to me, for the same reasons as those discussed above in relation to s 34(1), that the market rent may in general be affected by the situation with regard to the state of repair of the premises at the date when the interim rent is to commence, and that the questions whether and how the market rent of the premises concerned in any particular case are so affected must depend on the evidence in that case. So, if the evidence showed that the market rent would be a differential rent in the sense in which I have used that expression, then the court would have both the power and the duty to determine a differential rent accordingly. On the other hand, if the evidence showed that the market rent, though affected in amount by the present and future situation with regard to state of repair, would nevertheless be a normal fixed rent, the duty of the court would be to determine a fixed interim rent.

In what I have said so far I have been considering whether the court has power to determine a differential rent first under s 34(1) and secondly under s 24A, and I have concluded that it has power to do so in either case if the evidence warrants it. I should not, however, wish to encourage the view that this is a power which the court should exercise at all frequently. The cases in which the evidence may support a differential rent on the basis of the situation with regard to state of repair are likely, in my view, to be limited to cases in which the state of disrepair at the commencement of the new tenancy, or the commencement of the period of interim rent, is of a very serious character. In any other case it seems to me that the evidence will be very unlikely to do so.

A further question could in theory arise whether, in a case where the situation with regard to the state of repair was such that the premises would, in effect, be worthless to a lessee for a certain period, the court would have power to determine a nil rent for that period. That question does not, however, arise for decision in the present case for, although the tenant's valuer gave evidence that the premises were, in their original state of disrepair, incapable of being let at all, the judge did not accept that evidence. In these a circumstances, I should prefer to reserve this further question until there is a case in which the facts found make a decision on it necessary.

There is one other matter which I would mention. It might be thought that, because a rent determined under s 24A is an interim rent, it can only be applicable for a short time, and ought therefore to be in every case a fixed rent rather than a differential one. In practice, however, the period for which such a rent may be applicable, having regard to the provisions of ss 25(1) and 64(2), may well be of considerable length (by which I
b mean up to two or even three years), either because of delay in the trial of the proceedings in the county court, or because of prolongation of the proceedings by one or more appeals, or both. It would be wrong, therefore, to approach the interpretation of s 24A on the basis that the period for which a rent determined under it will apply is bound to be short, and to construe the section as not giving the court power to determine a differential rent in a proper case on that account.

c **STEPHENSON LJ.** I have had the advantage of considering in draft the judgments of Goff and Brandon LJJ. I have had many doubts in the course of the case, but of one thing I feel reasonably certain: namely that Parliament in enacting s 34 in 1954 and in amending s 34 and enacting s 24A in 1969 never considered the problem raised by this appeal: the impact of disrepair in the property comprised in a tenancy on the court's
d power to determine a rent under either section.

I agree with both Goff and Brandon LJJ that on its true construction s 34 as amended authorises, by sub-s (3), what has been called a variable rent, that is a provision for the parties varying the rent by a rent review clause, and, by sub-s (1), what Brandon LJ has termed a differential rent; that is a provision by the court varying the rent payable at different periods during the term of the new tenancy. But I long shared Goff LJ's doubts
e whether s 24A, on its true construction, permitted a differential interim rent. However, the reasoning of Brandon LJ has resolved those doubts and driven me to his conclusion that, if the court has the power to give effect to disrepair of the property during the new tenancy and to determine a differential new rent, there is nothing in the language or the purpose of s 24A which prevents the court from giving effect to the disrepair of the premises while the current tenancy continues and 'differentiating' the interim rent in a
f case where the evidence justifies it.

The cases in which the court could fix a differential interim rent must, I would think, be extremely rare, even where the period when interim rent is payable is prolonged by the operation of s 64. But like Brandon LJ, with whose judgment I am in complete agreement, I would not like to rule out the possibility of admitting expert evidence which could lead the court to take the exceptional course of determining a differential
g interim rent.

On all other points I am in agreement with the judgment of Goff LJ.

Appeal allowed. Question of interim rent and question whether in the event of works of repair not being completed by commencement of new lease there be some and, if so, what provision for suspension or reduction of rent until completion of works of repair remitted to county court judge.

h Solicitors: *Leslie A Fawke*; *Lee & Pembertons* (for the landlord).

Elizabeth Hindmarsh   Barrister.

Ross v Caunters (a firm)

CHANCERY DIVISION

SIR ROBERT MEGARRY V-C

12th, 13th, 14th, 15th, 16th MARCH, 15th JUNE 1979

Solicitor – Negligence – Duty – Will – Instructions to draw up will conferring benefit on identified beneficiary – Solicitor failing to warn testator that attestation by beneficiary's spouse would invalidate gift – Beneficiary's husband attesting will – Solicitor failing to notice attestation by him – Gift to beneficiary void – Whether solicitor owing duty of care to beneficiary – Whether solicitor liable in negligence to beneficiary – Whether fact that loss purely financial precluding claim in negligence – Whether beneficiary entitled to damages for legal expenses of investigating claim up to date of issue of writ.

The testator instructed solicitors to draw up his will to include gifts of chattels and a share of his residuary estate to the plaintiff, who was his sister-in-law. The solicitors drew up the will accordingly, naming the plaintiff and giving her address in the will. The testator requested the solicitors to send the will to him at the plaintiff's home, where he was staying, to be signed and attested. The solicitors sent the will to the testator with a covering letter giving instructions on executing it but failed to warn him that under s 15 of the Wills Act 1837 attestation of the will by a beneficiary's spouse would invalidate a gift to the beneficiary. The plaintiff's husband attested the will which was then returned to the solicitors who failed to notice that he had attested it. The testator died two years later, and nine months after that the solicitors informed the plaintiff that the gifts to her under the will were void because her husband had attested the will. The plaintiff brought an action against the solicitors claiming damages in negligence for the loss of the gifts under the will, and for her legal expenses in investigating her claim up to the date of issue of the writ. The plaintiff alleged that the solicitors were negligent in failing (i) to warn the testator about the consequences of s 15, (ii) on the return of the will, to check that it had been executed in conformity with the 1837 Act, (iii) to observe that the plaintiff's husband was an attesting witness, and (iv) to draw that fact to the testator's attention so that he could re-execute the will or make a new and valid will. The solicitors admitted negligence but denied that they were liable to the plaintiff, contending (i) that a solicitor was liable only to his client and then only in contract and not in tort, and could not, therefore, be liable in tort to a third party, (ii) that for reasons of policy a solicitor ought not to be liable in negligence to anyone except his client, and (iii) that in any event the plaintiff had no cause of action in negligence because the damage suffered was purely financial. The solicitors further contended that if damages were recoverable they ought not to include any sum in respect of the plaintiff's legal expenses prior to the issue of the writ, although they might be recoverable as costs in the action.

Held – The solicitors were liable to the plaintiff for the following reasons—

(1) A solicitor who was instructed by his client to carry out a transaction to confer a benefit on an identified third party owed a duty to that third party to use proper care in carrying out the instructions because (i) it was not inconsistent with the solicitor's liability to his client for him to be held liable in tort to the third party, having regard to the fact that the solicitor could be liable for negligence to his client both in contract and in tort, (ii) there was a sufficient degree of proximity between a solicitor and an identified third party for whose benefit the solicitor was instructed to carry out a transaction for it to be within the solicitor's reasonable contemplation that his acts or omissions in carrying out the instructions would be likely to injure the third party, and (iii) there were no reasons of policy for holding that a solicitor should not be liable in negligence to the third party, for the limited duty owed to him of using proper care in carrying out the client's instructions differed from the wider duty owed to the client of doing for the client all that the solicitor could properly do, and far from conflicting with or diluting the duty to

the client was likely to strengthen it (see p 587 *b c* and *e* to p 588 *b g h*, p 589 *d e*, p 591 *g*
a *h*, p 599 *b c g h* and p 600 *a b*, post); *Donoghue v Stevenson* [1932] All ER Rep 1, *Ministry of Housing and Local Government v Sharp* [1970] 1 All ER 1009 and *Midland Bank Trust Co Ltd v Hett, Stubbs & Kemp (a firm)* [1978] 3 All ER 571 applied; dicta of Lord Campbell LC and of Lord Cranworth in *Robertson v Fleming* (1861) 4 Macq at 177, 184–185 and *Groom v Crocker* [1938] 2 All ER 394 not followed.

(2) The fact that the plaintiff's claim in negligence was for purely financial loss, and
b not for injury to the person or property, did not preclude her claim, for, having regard to the high degree of proximity between her and the solicitors arising from the fact that they knew of her and also knew that their negligence would be likely to cause her financial loss, the plaintiff was entitled to recover the financial loss she had suffered by their negligence. Judgment would therefore be entered for the plaintiff for damages to be assessed (see p 596 *d e*, p 598 *b c* and p 600 *a to e*, post); *Donoghue v Stevenson* [1932] All
c ER Rep 1 and *Ministry of Housing and Local Government v Sharp* [1970] 1 All ER 1009 applied.

(3) The plaintiff's legal expenses of investigating her claim up to the date of the issue of the writ could not, however, be recovered as damages but only as costs, so far as they properly ranked as such (see p 601 *b* to *d*, post); *Cockburn v Edwards* (1881) 18 Ch D 449 and dictum of Lord Hanworth MR in *Pêcheries Ostendaises (SA) v Merchants' Marine*
d *Insurance Co* [1928] All ER Rep at 176 applied.

Notes

For a solicitor's duty towards his clients, see 36 Halsbury's Laws (3rd Edn) 95, 99, 102, paras 131, 135, 138, and for cases on the subject, see 43 Digest (Repl) 97–98, 106–108, 831–862, 953–979.

e **Cases referred to in judgment**

Anns v London Borough of Merton [1977] 2 All ER 492, 191 JP 526, sub nom *Anns v Merton London Borough Council* [1978] AC 728, [1977] 2 WLR 1024, 75 LGR 555, HL.
Batty v Metropolitan Property Realizations Ltd [1978] 2 All ER 445, [1978] QB 554, [1978] 2 WLR 500, CA.
Biakanja v Irving (1958) 320 P 2d 16.
f *Caltex Oil (Australia) Pty Ltd v Dredge Willemstad* (1976) 136 CLR 529.
Candler v Crane Christmas & Co [1951] 1 All ER 426, [1951] 2 KB 164, CA, 36(1) Digest (Reissue) 22, 75.
Cattle v Stockton Waterworks Co (1875) LR 10 QB 453, [1874–80] All ER Rep 220, 44 LJQB 139, 33 LT 475, 30 JP Jo 791, 36(1) Digest (Reissue) 306, 1232.
Clark v Kirby-Smith [1964] 2 All ER 835, [1964] Ch 506, [1964] 3 WLR 239, [1964] 2
g Lloyd's Rep 172, Digest (Cont Vol B), 1049a.
Cockburn v Edwards (1881) 18 Ch D 449, 51 LJ Ch 46, 45 LT 500, CA, 43 Digest (Repl) 92, 795.
Cook v S [1967] 1 All ER 299, sub nom *Cook v Swinfen* [1967] 1 WLR 457, CA, Digest (Cont Vol C) 898, 894a.
Davis Contractors Ltd v Fareham Urban District Council [1956] 2 All ER 145, [1956] AC 696,
h [1956] 3 WLR 37, 54 LGR 289, HL, 7 Digest (Reissue) 368, 2356.
Donoghue (or McAlister) v Stevenson [1932] AC 562, [1932] All ER Rep 1, 101 LJPC 119, 37 Com Cas 350, 1932 SC (HL) 31, 1932 SLT 317, HL, 36(1) Digest (Reissue) 144, 562.
Dutton v Bognor Regis United Building Co Ltd [1972] 1 All ER 462, 136 JP 201, [1972] 1 Lloyd's Rep 227, sub nom *Dutton v Bognor Regis Urban District Council* [1972] 1 QB 373, [1972] 2 WLR 299, 70 LGR 57, CA, 36(1) Digest (Reissue) 30, 98.
j *Esso Petroleum Co Ltd v Mardon* [1975] 1 All ER 203, [1976] QB 801, [1975] 2 WLR 147, 36(1) Digest (Reissue) 31, 99.
Fish v Kelly (1864) 17 CBNS 194, 144 ER 78, 43 Digest (Repl) 117, 1054.
Glanzer v Shepard (1922) 135 NE 275.
Groom v Crocker [1938] 2 All ER 394, [1939] 1 KB 194, 108 LJKB 296, 158 LT 477, 60 Ll L Rep 393, CA, 43 Digest (Repl) 117, 1058.

Hedley Byrne & Co Ltd v Heller & Partners Ltd [1963] 2 All ER 575, [1964] AC 465, [1963]
    3 WLR 101, [1963] 1 Lloyd's Rep 485, HL, 36(1) Digest (Reissue) 24, 84.

Heywood v Wellers (a firm) [1976] 1 All ER 300, [1976] QB 446, [1976] 2 WLR 101, [1976]
    2 Lloyd's Rep 88, CA.

Home Office v Dorset Yacht Co Ltd [1970] 2 All ER 294, [1970] AC 1004, [1970] 2 WLR
    1140, [1970] 1 Lloyd's Rep 453, 36(1) Digest (Reissue) 27, 93.

Lucas v Hamm (1961) 11 Cal Rep 727; *on appeal* 364 P 2d 685.

Midland Bank Trust Co Ltd v Hett, Stubbs & Kemp (a firm) [1978] 3 All ER 571, [1979] Ch
    304, [1978] 3 WLR 167.

Ministry of Housing and Local Government v Sharp [1970] 1 All ER 1009, [1970] 2 QB 223,
    [1970] 2 WLR 802, 68 LGR 187, 21 P & CR 166, CA; *rvsg in part* [1969] 3 All ER 225,
    [1970] 2 QB 223, [1969] 3 WLR 1020, 20 P & CR 1100, 36(1) Digest (Reissue) 49, 157.

Mutual Life & Citizens' Assurance Co Ltd v Evatt [1971] 1 All ER 150, [1971] AC 793,
    [1971] 2 WLR 23, [1970] 2 Lloyd's Rep 441, [1971] ALR 235, PC, 36(1) Digest
    (Reissue) 28, 95.

Pêcheries Ostendaises (SA) v Merchants' Marine Insurance Co [1928] 1 KB 750, [1928] All ER
    Rep 174, 97 LJKB 445, 138 LT 532, 17 Asp MLC 404, CA, 18 Digest (Reissue) 69, 483.

Rivtow Marine Ltd v Washington Iron Works (1972) 26 DLR 559; *on appeal* (1973) 40
    DLR(3d) 530, [1974] SCR 1189, 36(1) Digest (Reissue) 337, *2779.

Robertson v Fleming (1861) 4 Macq 167, HL, 43 Digest (Repl) 116, 1053.

SCM (United Kingdom) Ltd v W J Whittall & Son Ltd [1970] 3 All ER 245, [1971] 1 QB 337,
    [1970] 3 WLR 694, CA, 36(1) Digest (Reissue) 28, 94.

Société Anonyme de Remorquage à Hélice v Bennetts [1911] 1 KB 243, 80 LJKB 228, 16 Com
    Cas 24, 42 Digest (Repl) 939, 7301.

Spartan Steel & Alloys Ltd v Martin & Co (Contractors) Ltd [1972] 3 All ER 557, [1973] QB
    27, [1972] 3 WLR 502, CA, 17 Digest (Reissue) 149, 403.

Ultramares Corpn v Touche (1931) 174 NE 441.

Weller & Co v Foot and Mouth Research Institute [1965] 3 All ER 560, [1966] 1 QB 569,
    [1965] 3 WLR 1082, [1965] 2 Lloyd's Rep 414, 36(1) Digest (Reissue) 45, 143.

Whittingham v Crease & Co [1978] 5 WWR 45.

Action

By a writ dated 16th November 1977 the plaintiff, Mrs Eileen Maud Ross, a beneficiary
under a will made in 1974, claimed against the defendants, Caunters, of Liskeard,
Cornwall, a firm of solicitors employed by William Hayward Stokes Philp ('the testator')
in drawing up the will, damages for negligence and breach of duty in (i) failing to warn
or inform the testator as to the consequences of s 15 of the Wills Act 1837, (ii) failing to
check whether the will had been duly executed in conformity with the Wills Act 1837,
(iii) failing to observe that one of the attesting witnesses was the plaintiff's husband and
thereby the disposition in her favour was rendered void under the 1837 Act, and (iv)
failing to draw the testator's attention to that fact. The facts are set out in the judgment.

John Cherryman for the plaintiff.
Peter St J H Langan for the defendants.

Cur adv vult

15th June.   **SIR ROBERT MEGARRY V-C** read the following judgment: In this
case, the facts are simple and undisputed, and the point of law that it raises is short; yet
it has taken five days to argue, and over 30 authorities, from both sides of the Atlantic,
have very properly been cited, some at considerable length. In broad terms, the question
is whether solicitors who prepare a will are liable to a beneficiary under it if, through
their negligence, the gift to the beneficiary is void. The solicitors are liable, of course, to
the testator or his estate for a breach of the duty that they owed to him, though as he has

suffered no financial loss it seems that his estate could recover no more than nominal damages. Yet it is said that however careless the solicitors were, they owed no duty to the beneficiary, and so they cannot be liable to her.

If this is right, the result is striking. The only person who has a valid claim has suffered no loss, and the only person who has suffered a loss has no valid claim. However grave the negligence, and however great the loss, the solicitors would be under no liability to pay substantial damages to anyone. No doubt they would be liable to the testator if the mistake was discovered in his lifetime, though in that case the damages would, I think, be merely for the cost of making a new and valid will, or otherwise putting matters right. But the real question is whether the solicitors are under any liability to the disappointed beneficiary. On behalf of the plaintiff in this case counsel says Yes, and on behalf of the defendant solicitors counsel says No.

The plaintiff is the sister of the testator's third wife, who died in 1972. Under a will made for the testator by the solicitors in 1970 the testator left his whole estate to his wife, but provided that if she predeceased him, the plaintiff should take certain chattels and 2/20ths of the residue. After the death of his wife in 1972, the solicitors made another will for the testator, under which the plaintiff was given certain chattels and 5/20ths of the residue. In March 1974 the testator wished to have certain alterations and additions made to his 1972 will, and sent the solicitors a letter with a note of the proposed changes. In April he wrote to them asking for the redrafted will which, he said, he would have witnessed and returned promptly to the solicitors. He added, 'Am I right in thinking that beneficiaries may not be witnesses?' Without answering this question, the solicitors then sent the testator a draft of the new will, with certain questions, and after these had been dealt with, the will reached its final form. This is the will in question in this case. In it, the plaintiff was again given certain chattels and 5/20ths of the residue, though as the total number of twentieths given came to 21, the gift would take effect as a gift of five twenty-first parts of the residue. As in the two previous wills, the plaintiff's address was correctly stated as being 26 St Stephen's Avenue, Ealing, London, W13. The testator, I may say, lived at Liskeard in Cornwall, and the solicitors have their office there.

The 1970 and 1972 wills had both been witnessed by solicitors' clerks employed by the defendants. However, on 2nd June 1974, when the testator had made the final revisions to the draft will, he returned the revised draft to the solicitors, saying that he was about to go and stay with his in-laws at Ealing for three weeks. The letter asked the solicitors to send the final document and duplicate to 'c/o, J Ross Esq., St. Stephen's Avenue, Ealing, London, W13 8ES', and added 'I will have it signed and witnessed there'. Ten days later the solicitors sent the will to the testator at Ealing as he had requested, with a covering letter giving instructions as to executing the will. These said that the will must first be dated by the testator 'on the first page (in words) and signed by you at the foot or end in the presence of two independent witnesses (ie not somebody benefiting under the Will), who should sign their respective names and their addresses and occupations as indicated in pencil. Please then return the Will to me in the enclosed envelope.'

Three weeks later, on 3rd July 1974, the testator executed the will in the presence of two witnesses. The first of these signed as 'I. Ross, 26 St. Stephen's Avenue, West Ealing, London W.13, Accountant'. Mr Isaac Ross is the plaintiff's husband. Soon after signing the will, the testator must have returned it to the solicitors; for a week after the date of execution the solicitors wrote to him at his home in Liskeard, thanking him for returning the will signed by him 'and duly witnessed'. Nearly a fortnight later the testator wrote to the solicitors, expressing his thanks for their work in preparing his will, and commenting with gratitude on the modesty of their charges.

Some two years later, on 5th March 1976, the testator died. Nearly nine months later, the solicitors wrote to the plaintiff, referring to 'a possible difficulty' in connection with the witnessing of the 1974 will, and enclosing a copy of the Wills Act 1837, s 15. For present purposes, the spacious language of this section may be summarised by saying that it provides that if an attesting witness of a will is a beneficiary under it 'or the wife or husband of such person', any gift by the will to that beneficiary is void. As Mr Ross, who attested the will, was and is the husband of the plaintiff, she can take no benefit under the will.

The negligence alleged against the solicitors may be put under four heads, which to some extent overlap. These are, first, the failure to inform or warn the testator properly about s 15; second, the failure, on the return of the will, to check whether it had been duly executed in conformity with the Act; third, the failure to observe that an attesting witness was the plaintiff's husband, so that the gifts to her would be void; and fourth, the failure to draw this to the testator's attention. It is alleged that if his attention had been drawn to it, he would have re-executed the will before different attesting witnesses, or would have made a new and valid will in the same terms. The solicitors have not attempted to quibble or make fine distinctions, but with commendable frankness have by their defence admitted all these allegations, subject to the overriding contention that their obligation to take reasonable care in and about the making of the 1974 will was owed to the testator, and to him alone, and that they owed no duty of care to the plaintiff.

The foundation of the defence is a case in the House of Lords, *Robertson v Fleming*[1]. In this, Lord Cranworth, Lord Wensleydale and Lord Chelmsford, with Lord Campbell LC dissenting, allowed an appeal from the Second Division of the Court of Session. What had to be decided was whether there should be a new trial on the ground that one of the issues which the Second Division had directed to be tried had failed to raise the true question of fact to be decided; and in the end this turned on the meaning of the phrase 'for behoof of' in the issue. Lord Campbell LC's view was that it meant 'by the authority of'; but the majority held that it meant 'for the benefit of'. Thus stated, the decision seems to be of little relevance to what is before me; but such prominence on solicitors' negligence as the case has attained has been achieved by a series of dicta which occupy most of the headnote.

On this point, no difference appears between Lord Campbell LC and the other law lords. Lord Campbell LC said[2] that the duty alleged in that case could be established—

'. . . only by showing privity of contract between the parties. I never had any doubt of the unsoundness of the doctrine, unnecessarily (and I must say unwisely) contended for by the Respondent's Counsel, that A. employing B., a professional lawyer, to do any act for the benefit of C., A. having to pay B., and there being no intercourse of any sort between B. and C.,—if through the gross negligence or ignorance of B. in transacting the business, C. loses the benefit intended for him by A., C. may maintain an action against B., and recover damages for the loss sustained. If this were law a disappointed legatee might sue the solicitor employed by a testator to make a will in favour of a stranger, whom the solicitor never saw or before heard of, if the will were void for not being properly signed and attested. I am clearly of opinion that this is not the law of Scotland, nor of England, and it can hardly be the law of any country where jurisprudence has been cultivated as a science.'

Lord Cranworth said[3]:

'The doctrine contended for at the bar, that where A. employs B., a professional man, to do some act professionally, under which, when done, C. would derive a benefit, if, then, B. is guilty of negligence towards his employer, so that C. loses the contemplated benefit, B. is, as a matter of course, responsible to C., is evidently untenable. Such a doctrine would, as is pointed out by my noble friend, lead to the result, that a disappointed legatee might sue the testator's solicitor for negligence in not causing the will to be duly signed and attested, though he might be an entire stranger both to the solicitor and the testator.'

---

1   (1861) 4 Macq 167
2   4 Macq 167 at 177
3   4 Macq 167 at 184–185

a I think that Lord Cranworth's view[1] was that on this point there was no difference between the law of Scotland and the law of England. Lord Wensleydale[2], who spoke third, plainly concurred with the two preceding speeches on this point; and although Lord Chelmsford[3] was not so explicit, I think that he was of the same mind. I have described what was said on the point before me as being dicta, and I think that Lord Cranworth[4] would have agreed. However, it is arguable that the dicta were of the ratio; and even if they were not, they are plainly of high authority.

b *Robertson v Fleming*[5] was, of course, decided nearly 120 years ago, and some 70 years before *Donoghue v Stevenson*[6]. Today, negligence has long been established as an independent tort and not merely a constituent element in certain other torts. Further, it is difficult today to see the logic in the proposition that if A employs B to do an act for the benefit of C, the existence of B's contractual duty to A to do the act with proper care negates any possible duty of B towards C, since B has no contract with C. Why should

c the existence of a contractual duty to A preclude the existence of any non-contractual duty to others? If one examines the facts of the case before me to discover whether the three-fold elements of the tort of negligence exist, a simple answer would be on the following lines. First, the solicitors owed a duty of care to the plaintiff since she was someone within their direct contemplation as a person so closely and directly affected by their acts and omissions in carrying out their client's instructions to provide her with a

d share of his residue that they could reasonably foresee that she would be likely to be injured by those acts or omissions. Second, there has undoubtedly been a breach of that duty of care; and third, the plaintiff has clearly suffered loss as a direct result of that breach of duty. Accordingly, in the absence of anything to indicate the contrary, the plaintiff's claim should succeed. Such an answer, however, would be far too simple for the volume of case law that has arisen on the subject. It could, no doubt, be called an

e answer of artless Chancery simplicity; and so in due course I must turn to the authorities.

The six propositions of counsel for the defendants may, I think, be conveniently ranged under three main heads. First, he said that the authorities had established that a solicitor could not be liable in negligence in relation to his professional work to anyone save his client, and that his liability to his client was only in contract, and not in tort. This latter proposition strongly suggested that there could be no liability to third parties

f in tort, for if the solicitor was not liable in tort even to his own client, it would be remarkable to hold him liable in tort to third parties. These propositions, counsel said, were not affected by the decision of the House of Lords in *Hedley Byrne & Co Ltd v Heller & Partners Ltd*[7], a decision that I shall cite simply as *Hedley Byrne*. The only effect of this decision was that as between solicitors and their clients, like everybody else, there could be a liability for financial loss resulting from reliance on a negligent misrepresentation

g of fact, whether written or spoken, if the person making the representation has some special skill and he knows, or ought to know, that the other party is relying on that skill. If a case fell within these narrow limits, then the solicitor could be liable to his client in tort. But the limits did not include statements or opinions on law, or advice, whether on law or fact, or acts, or omissions: only statements or opinions on fact were within them. Apart from that, *Hedley Byrne*[7] had made no difference to the law as

h regards solicitors' negligence.

Counsel's second main head was that if a claim was made in negligence for financial or economic loss alone, with no claim for damage to property or the person, then apart

---

j 1 See (1861) 4 Macq 167 at 189, 197
2 See 4 Macq 167 at 199–200
3 See 4 Macq 167 at 209–210
4 See 4 Macq 167 at 189
5 4 Macq 167
6 [1932] AC 562, [1932] All ER Rep 1
7 [1963] 2 All ER 575, [1964] AC 465

from the narrow category of cases falling within the *Hedley Byrne*[1] principle, it must fail: for with that one qualification there was no cause of action in negligence for mere economic loss. Counsel's third main head was based on policy. There were reasons of policy, he said, which pointed against holding a solicitor liable in negligence to any save clients of his; per contra, there were no reasons of policy which could justify any extension of his liability to persons such as the plaintiff in the present case.

On the first point, counsel for the defendants relied on *Robertson v Fleming*[2], which I have already cited, and also on *Fish v Kelly*[3]. There, an attorney was held not liable for negligently mis-stating the contents of a deed to an enquirer who was not a client of his. However, Erle CJ[4] referred to the occasion as being one in which the parties met 'casually', and to the conversation as being 'casual'. Counsel was disposed to question whether the occasion and the conversation were correctly so described: but whether or not this was so, the law was laid down on that footing. Further, in cases of high authority the decision is treated as having been made on that basis: see e g *Hedley Byrne*[5], per Lord Hodson and Lord Pearce; *Mutual Life and Citizens' Assurance Co Ltd v Evatt*[6], per Lord Diplock, speaking for the majority. See also *Glanzer v Shepard*[7], per Cardozo J ('a 'casual response made in mere friendliness or courtesy'). In the old days it was proverbial that a gratuitous opinion expressed by counsel in response to enquiries from his instructing solicitor while they were walking back from Westminster Hall to Lincoln's Inn was worth no more than the fee paid for it; and in *Fish v Kelly*[8] Byles J said that if such actions could be maintained 'it would be extremely hazardous for an attorney to venture to give an opinion on any point of law in the course of a journey by railway'. I do not think that *Fish v Kelly*[3] assists the defendants. In any case, counsel for the defendants accepted that, like *Robertson v Fleming*[2], the case might well be affected by 19th century ideas about contract and about negligence not being a separate tort; and he placed his main reliance on a solicitor's liability to his client as being in contract alone, apart from the limited *Hedley Byrne*[1] liability that counsel accepted.

The mainstay of counsel's contention for the defendants on this point was, of course, the decision of the Court of Appeal in *Groom v Crocker*[9], holding that a solicitor's duty to his client is contractual and not tortious. Counsel met the contention that this position had been altered by *Hedley Byrne*[1] by pointing to three cases decided since *Hedley Byrne*[1] which all supported the view that the solicitor's liability to his client was still contractual and not tortious: these were *Clark v Kirby-Smith*[10], *Cook v S*[11] and *Heywood v Wellers*[12]. *Clark v Kirby-Smith*[10] is directly in point. There, Plowman J[13] refused to accept the argument that *Hedley Byrne*[1] was an authority 'for saying that the liability of a solicitor to his client for negligence is a liability in tort'. In *Cook v S*[14] Lord Denning MR, with the concurrence of Danckwerts and Winn LJJ, said: 'An action against a solicitor is always one for breach of contract, as was held in *Groom v Crocker*[9]. However, *Hedley Byrne*[1] does not seem to have been cited. In the third case, *Heywood v Wellers*[12], there similarly appears to have been no mention of *Hedley Byrne*[1]. James LJ[15] said that it was 'well

---

1   [1963] 2 All ER 575, [1964] AC 465
2   (1861) 4 Macq 167
3   (1864) 17 CBNS 194, 144 ER 78
4   17 CBNS 194 at 205, 206, 144 ER 78 at 83
5   [1963] 2 All ER 575 at 598, 617, [1964] AC 465 at 510, 539
6   [1971] 1 All ER 150 at 158, [1971] AC 793 at 806
7   (1922) 135 NE 275 at 276
8   17 CBNS 194 at 207, 144 ER 78 at 83
9   [1938] 2 All ER 394, [1939] 1 KB 194
10   [1964] 2 All ER 835, [1964] Ch 506
11   [1967] 1 All ER 299, [1967] 1 WLR 457
12   [1976] 1 All ER 300, [1976] QB 446
13   [1964] 2 All ER 835 at 837, [1964] Ch 506 at 510
14   [1967] 1 All ER 299 at 302, [1967] 1 WLR 457 at 461
15   [1976] 1 All ER 300 at 308, [1976] QB 446 at 461

a   known and settled law that an action by a client against a solicitor alleging negligence in the conduct of the client's affairs is an action for breach of contract: *Groom v Crocker*[1]. Lord Denning MR[2], however, said that *Groom v Crocker*[1] and *Cook v S*[3] 'may have to be reconsidered'; and within three months, in *Esso Petroleum Co Ltd v Mardon*[4], he had plainly rejected *Groom v Crocker*[1] and *Clark v Kirby-Smith*[5] (and, by implication, *Cook v S*[3]) as being inconsistent with other decisions of high authority that had not been cited.

     The latest authority on this point is *Midland Bank Trust Co Ltd v Hett, Stubbs & Kemp*[6].
b   In this, Oliver J considered and discussed the authorities that I have mentioned, with a number of others, and came to the conclusion that the doctrine associated with *Groom v Crocker*[1] was not law. A solicitor's liability to his client for negligence is not confined to liability in contract, to the exclusion of liability in tort: the client may base his claim on tort, irrespective of contract. I have read and re-read the discussion of both the authorities and the principles, extending over nearly 30 pages of the report, and I have been quite unable to find anything in counsel's contentions for the defendants to impugn the
c   judge's survey or his conclusions. I would, indeed, express my most respectful concurrence in an exhaustive and convincing discussion of a complex subject. I may say that *Batty v Metropolitan Property Realizations Ltd*[7], which the judge mentioned[8] but did not rely on, as only an uncorrected transcript was before him, seems to me to provide some support for his conclusions on this issue, different though the facts were.

d   From this, it follows that I reject part of counsel's first main contention. Let me for the moment leave on one side the narrow liability that he said *Hedley Byrne*[9] established. That apart, it cannot be contended that to hold a solicitor liable to a third party for the tort of negligence would be inconsistent with a solicitor's immunity in tort towards his client, for there is no such immunity, and so there can be no such inconsistency. With that ground of objection removed, the question is whether a solicitor owes a duty of care
e   to a beneficiary under a will that he makes for a client, and, if so, on what basis that duty rests. This is, of course, the central core of the case.

     In considering this, three features of the case before me seem to stand out. First, there is the close degree of proximity of the plaintiff to the defendants. There is no question of whether the defendants could fairly have been expected to contemplate the plaintiff as a person likely to be affected by any lack of care on their part, or whether they ought
f   to have done so: there is no 'ought' about the case. This is not a case where the only nexus between the plaintiff and the defendants is that the plaintiff was the ultimate recipient of a dangerous chattel or negligent mis-statement which the defendants had put into circulation. The plaintiff was named and identified in the will that the defendants drafted for the testator. Their contemplation of the plaintiff was actual, nominate and direct. It was contemplation by contract, though of course the contract was with a third party, the testator.
g   Second, this proximity of the plaintiff to the defendants was a product of the duty of care owed by the defendants to the testator: it was in no way casual or accidental or unforeseen. The defendants accepted a duty towards the testator to take reasonable care that the will would, inter alia, carry a share of residue from the testator's estate to the plaintiff. In all that they did (or failed to do) in relation to the will, the solicitors were
h   bound by the duty of care towards the testator that they had accepted; and that duty included a duty to confer a benefit on the plaintiff. When a solicitor undertakes to a client to carry through a transaction which will confer a benefit on a third party, it seems

---

1   [1938] 2 All ER 394, [1939] 1 KB 194
2   [1976] 1 All ER 300 at 306, [1976] QB 446 at 459
j   3   [1967] 1 All ER 299, [1967] 1 WLR 457
4   [1975] 1 All ER 203, [1976] QB 801
5   [1964] 2 All ER 835, [1964] Ch 506
6   [1978] 3 All ER 571, [1979] Ch 384
7   [1978] 2 All ER 445, [1978] QB 554
8   [1978] 3 All ER 571 at 610, [1979] Ch 384 at 433
9   [1963] 2 All ER 575, [1964] AC 465

to me that the duty to act with due care which binds the solicitor to his client is one which may readily be extended to the third party who is intended to benefit.

Third, to hold that the defendants were under a duty of care towards the plaintiff would raise no spectre of imposing on the defendants an uncertain and unlimited liability. The liability would be to one person alone, the plaintiff. The amount would be limited to the value of the share of residue intended for the plaintiff. There would be no question of widespread or repeated liability, as might arise from some published misstatement on which large numbers might rely, to their detriment. There would be no possibility of the defendants being exposed, in the well-known expression of Cardozo CJ, 'to a liability in an indeterminate amount for an indeterminate time to an indeterminate class': see *Ultramares Corpn v Touche*[1]. Instead, there would be a finite obligation to a finite number of persons, in this case one.

With these considerations in mind, I return to *Donoghue v Stevenson*[2]. That was a case which, in *Home Office v Dorset Yacht Co Ltd*[3], Lord Reid said might be regarded as a milestone—

'. . . and the well-known passage in Lord Atkin's speech[4] should I think be regarded as a statement of principle. It is not to be treated as if it were a statutory definition. It will require qualification in new circumstances. But I think that the time has come when we can and should say that it ought to apply unless there is some justification or valid explanation for its exclusion.'

This statement commanded unanimous approval in *Anns v Merton London Borough Council*[5]. Lord Wilberforce[6] referred to *Donoghue v Stevenson*[2], *Hedley Byrne*[7] and the *Dorset Yacht* case[8], and said that—

'. . . the position has now been reached that in order to establish that a duty of care arises in a particular situation, it is not necessary to bring the facts of that situation within those of previous situations in which a duty of care has been held to exist. Rather the question has to be approached in two stages. First one has to ask whether, as between the alleged wrongdoer and the person who has suffered damage there is a sufficient relationship of proximity or neighbourhood such that, in the reasonable contemplation of the former, carelessness on his part may be likely to cause damage to the latter, in which case a prima facie duty of care arises. Secondly, if the first question is answered affirmatively, it is necessary to consider whether there are any considerations which ought to negative, or to reduce or limit the scope of the duty or the class of person to whom it is owed or the damages to which a breach of it may give rise (see the *Dorset Yacht* case[9], per Lord Reid).'

Lord Salmon's speech plainly adopts the same views, and the other members of the House simply concurred with Lord Wilberforce.

If one approaches the present case in the manner indicated by Lord Wilberforce, I can see only one answer to the question that has to be asked at the first stage. Prima facie a duty of care was owed by the defendants to the plaintiff because it was obvious that carelessness on their part would be likely to cause damage to her. As for the second stage, I shall have to consider in due course the reasons of policy on which counsel for the defendants relied, under his third main head, as excluding liability in this case. At this

1 (1931) 174 NE 441 at 444
2 [1932] AC 562, [1932] All ER Rep 1
3 [1970] 2 All ER 294 at 297, [1970] AC 1004 at 1027
4 [1932] AC 562 at 580, [1932] All ER Rep 1 at 11
5 [1977] 2 All ER 492, [1978] AC 728
6 [1977] 2 All ER 492 at 498, [1978] AC 728 at 751–752
7 [1963] 2 All ER 575, [1964] AC 465
8 [1970] 2 All ER 294, [1970] AC 1004
9 [1970] 2 All ER 294 at 297–298, [1970] AC 1004 at 1027

stage I do not think that I need do more than refer to certain instances mentioned by
Lord Reid and Lord Wilberforce. In the *Dorset Yacht* case[1] the former gave as examples
the acts of traders whose competition injures their trade rivals; various acts which
landowners may do even though they injure their neighbours; and the absence of any
obligation by one person to go to the aid of another person, with whom he has not put
himself into any relationship, if that other person or his property is in distress. Lord
Wilberforce, in the *Anns* case[2], gave as instances the *Hedley Byrne* case[3], 'where the class of
potential plaintiffs was reduced to those shown to have relied upon the correctness of
statements made', and *Weller & Co v Foot and Mouth Disease Research Institute*[4], where
liability for an escape of foot and mouth disease was held to exist towards cattle owners
in the district but not towards auctioneers whose business was injured by the closure of
the local cattle markets. Lord Wilberforce also cited two cases about 'economic loss',
where the nature of the recoverable damages was limited. To these cases I shall return
when I consider counsel for the defendants' second main head: they are *SCM (United
Kingdom) Ltd v W J Whittall & Son Ltd*[5] and *Spartan Steel & Alloys Ltd v Martin & Co
(Contractors) Ltd*[6].

At this stage, and without prejudice to counsel's contentions on policy which I shall
consider under his third head, I can see nothing in this case which suggests that the scope
of the prima facie duty of care ought to be negatived or reduced or limited. Indeed, the
close degree of proximity of the defendants to the plaintiff, and the restricted ambit of
the liability, seem to me to point in the opposite direction. Furthermore, the fact that
the defendants were under a duty of care towards the testator to see that the share of
residue was carried to the plaintiff negatives any possibility of the defendants having
some independent right, such as exists between competing traders, to inflict an injury on
the plaintiff. The testator, the plaintiff and the defendants were all 'on the same side', as
it were.

Certain transatlantic cases were cited. In *Biakanja v Irving*[7] the Supreme Court of
California considered the case of a notary public who prepared a will for his client. The
client signed it in the presence of the notary who thereupon signed it and affixed his
notarial seal. Some time later the notary procured two other persons to sign it. Neither
had been present when the testator signed; they did not sign it in each other's presence;
and the testator did not acknowledge his signature in their presence. The notary's brave
theory was that 'Anybody knows a will which bore a notarial seal was a valid will', and
required no witnesses. The will, of course, was invalid, and the universal legatee sued the
notary for damages for negligence. The court unanimously held him liable, despite the
absence of privity of contract.

The judgment of the court was delivered by Gibson CJ. He said[8] that the determination
whether a defendant would be held liable to someone with whom he was not in privity
was a matter of policy, and involved the balancing of various factors. He then gave six
instances. They were the extent to which the transaction was intended to affect the
plaintiff; the foreseeability of harm to him; the degree of certainty of the plaintiff
suffering injury; the closeness of the connection between the defendant's conduct and
the plaintiff's injury; the moral blameworthiness of the defendant's conduct; and the
policy of preventing future harm. He added that 'the end and aim' of the transaction was

1   [1970] 2 All ER 294 at 297, [1970] AC 1004 at 1027
2   [1977] 2 All ER 492 at 498–499, [1978] AC 728 at 752
3   [1963] 2 All ER 575, [1964] AC 465
4   [1965] 3 All ER 560, [1966] 1 QB 569
5   [1970] 3 All ER 245, [1971] QB 337
6   [1972] 3 All ER 557, [1973] QB 27
7   (1958) 320 P 2d 16
8   320 P 2d 16 at 19

to provide for the testator's estate to pass to the plaintiff (citing *Glanzer v Shepard¹*), and
that the defendant must have known from the terms of the will that if it was not
properly executed the plaintiff would 'suffer the very loss which occurred'.   *a*

To this, I would add two quotations from the *Dorset Yacht* case², the case of Home
Office liability for damage done to a yacht by escaping Borstal boys. Lord Morris of
Borth-y-Gest³ doubted—

> '. . . whether it is necessary to say, in cases where the court is asked whether in a
> particular situation a duty existed, that the court is called on to make a decision as   *b*
> to policy. Policy need not be invoked where reason and good sense will at once
> point the way. If the test whether in some particular situation a duty of care arises
> may in some cases have to be whether it is fair and reasonable that it should so arise
> the court must not shrink from being the arbiter. As Lord Radcliffe said in his
> speech in *Davis Contractors Ltd v Fareham Urban District Council⁴*, the court is "the
> spokesman of the fair and reasonable man".'   *c*

Lord Pearson⁵ said that to some extent—

> '. . . the decision in this case must be a matter of impression and instinctive
> judgment as to what is fair and just. It seems to me that this case ought to, and does,
> come within the *Donoghue v Stevenson⁶* principle unless there is some sufficient
> reason for not applying the principle to this case.'   *d*

Whatever may be the position about describing the relevant considerations as matters of
'policy', I find it difficult to envisage a fair and reasonable man, seeking to do what is fair
and just, who would reach the conclusion that it was right to hold that solicitors whose
carelessness deprives an intended beneficiary of the share of a testator's estate that was
destined for that beneficiary should be immune from any action by that beneficiary, and   *e*
should have no liability save for nominal damages due to the testator's estate.

Some three years after *Biakanja v Irving⁷* had been decided it was applied in another
case. In *Lucas v Hamm⁸* an attorney had made a will for a testator which contained a
provision which infringed the rule against perpetuities. The intended beneficiaries who
were defeated by the rule then sued the attorney for negligence. On a demurrer, the
claim failed at first instance but succeeded before the District Court of Appeal, which   *f*
applied *Biakanja v Irving⁷*: the lack of privity between the plaintiffs and the defendant was
held to be no bar to the claim. On a further appeal, the Supreme Court of California held
that this view was correct: see *Lucas v Hamm⁹*. The decision at first instance in favour of
the attorney was, however, restored, on the ground that the rule against perpetuities is
so complex that neither in contract nor in tort was an attorney in California liable for
negligence if he made a mistake of the type in question when making a will for a   *g*
client. On this latter point I need make no comment. I will only add that these two
Californian cases are not entirely strangers to England: see the Law Quarterly Review¹⁰,
where there is some account of parallel developments in the law of negligence in
America and England. Furthermore, both decisions have that especial authority which
flows from Traynor J being a party to them.

h

---

1   (1922) 135 NE 275
2   [1970] 2 All ER 294, [1970] AC 1004
3   [1970] 2 All ER 294 at 307–308, [1970] AC 1004 at 1039
4   [1956] 2 All ER 145 at 160, [1956] AC 696 at 728
5   [1970] 2 All ER 294 at 321, [1970] AC 1004 at 1054   *j*
6   [1932] AC 562 at 580, [1932] All ER Rep 1 at 11
7   (1958) 320 P 2d 16
8   (1961) 11 Cal Rep 727
9   (1961) 364 P 2d 685
10 (1965) 81 LQR 478

The other transatlantic decision that I should mention was in the British Columbia
a Supreme Court. In *Whittingham v Crease & Co*[1] a solicitor had drawn up a will under
which the plaintiff was the residuary beneficiary. The plaintiff and his wife were present
when the testator executed the will, and the solicitor pressed the wife to sign it as a
witness, despite enquiries whether the wife of a beneficiary ought to be a witness. In the
end, the wife yielded to the solicitor's explanation that it was all right for her to sign as
she was not mentioned in the will, and so she signed as a witness. When it was
b discovered that this invalidated the gift to the plaintiff, he sued the solicitor's firm for
negligence. Aikens J held that the solicitor was liable. The essence of his decision, I
think, was that *Donoghue v Stevenson*[2], and *Hedley Byrne*[3], as applied in Canada, had set the
court free from the restrictions of the *Robertson v Fleming*[4] line of cases, and allowed the
plaintiff to sue the defendants for negligence on the ground that they owed him a duty
of care.

c   One feature of the case that I should mention is this. It will be remembered that in
Hedley Byrne[3] the liability of the bankers (had there been no disclaimer of responsibility)
depended on the advertising agents having acted in reliance on the references given by
the bankers, coupled with the fact that the bankers knew or ought to have known of that
reliance. Where a testamentary gift fails by reason of the negligence of the solicitor who
prepares the will, there will often be no reliance at all, as where the beneficiary knows
d nothing of the intended gift until after the testator's death. In other cases there will be
no more than a passive reliance: the beneficiary knows of the making of the will and the
gift to him, and does nothing, relying on the solicitor to have seen to it that the will is
effective, or simply assuming this.

The Canadian case fell into the latter category. The judge held that the solicitor had
made an implied representation that the will would be effective and that the plaintiff had
e passively relied on this, without doing anything on the strength of it. The judge said[5]
that he had found no case in which the *Hedley Byrne*[3] principle had been applied where
the plaintiff had not acted on the representation and the immediate cause of the loss had
been the defendant's own act (I correct an obvious slip in the report). Despite this lack
of authority, there were two interlinked reasons why the plaintiff should succeed: I
summarise them in my own words. First, there was no need for the plaintiff to act on
f the implied representation in order to attract the loss which befell him. Second, the
solicitor could reasonably foresee that his negligence would, by itself, cause the very loss
that in fact occurred, without the plaintiff doing any act. The chain of causation was
complete without any such act.

It seems to me that these reasons apply with equal force to a case in the first category
mentioned above, namely, those in which there is no reliance at all by the beneficiary,
g whether active or passive. If a solicitor negligently fails to secure the due execution of a
will, I can see no rational ground for distinguishing between those who knew that a will
in their favour was being made and passively relied on the solicitor's skill or his implicit
representation of the due execution of the will, and those who knew nothing of the
making of the will and relied on nothing. In each case, once it is held that the solicitor
owes a duty of care to the beneficiaries, the loss to them is directly caused by the solicitor's
h breach of that duty, and reliance by the plaintiff is irrelevant. If the duty of care is
imposed on what I may call pure *Donoghue v Stevenson*[2] principles, and the loss occurs
without being dependent on any reliance by the plaintiff, then I cannot see how the
presence or absence of reliance by the plaintiff can affect liability: see, for instance, *Dutton*

j
1   [1978] 5 WWR 45
2   [1932] AC 562, [1932] All ER Rep 1
3   [1963] 2 All ER 575, [1964] AC 465
4   (1861) 4 Macq 167
5   [1978] 5 WWR 45 at 69

v Bognor Regis United Building Co Ltd[1]. On the other hand, in many cases reliance is
essential to liability: if the defendant negligently makes an untrue statement but the loss
to the plaintiff occurs without his having relied on that statement, plainly the defendant
has in no way caused the loss.

Hedley Byrne[2] is important, of course, as opening the door to the recovery of damages
for negligence to at least some cases where the negligence has caused purely financial loss,
without any injury to person or property: to that I shall come under the second main
head of counsel for the defendants. But for present purposes its importance is that the
House of Lords rejected pure *Donoghue v Stevenson*[3] principles as forming the basis of
liability for negligent mis-statements and instead based liability on the plaintiff having
trusted the defendant to exercise due care in giving information on a matter in which the
defendant had a special skill, and knew or ought to have known of the plaintiff's reliance
on his skill and judgment. In this type of case, reliance forms part of the test of liability,
as well as part of the chain of causation: and the effect of such a test of liability is to
confine the extent of liability far more closely than would an application of pure
Donoghue v Stevenson[3] principles. If liability for negligently putting into circulation some
innocent misrepresentation were to be imposed on the same basis as negligently putting
into circulation some dangerous chattel, the resulting liability might be for enormous
sums to a great multiplicity of plaintiffs. One way of preventing any such liability being
imposed is to make the test of liability more strict: and that was the way adopted in
Hedley Byrne[2]. But that does not affect those cases in which the principles of *Donoghue v
Stevenson*[3] apply. If I am right in thinking that the case before me falls within those
principles, then there is no need to consider questions of reliance.

In the case before me, I do not think that there was anything which could fairly be
called any reliance by the plaintiff on any statement by the defendants. The acts of
negligence alleged (and accepted) are all expressed as being failures by the defendants:
their failures were failures to inform or warn the testator and failures to check or
observe. It is accepted that if the defendants had warned the testator of the invalidity of
his gifts to the plaintiff, the testator would have re-executed the will, or would have made
a valid new will in the same terms; but there is no allegation of any acts of reliance on the
defendants by the plaintiff, or of any knowledge by the defendants that the plaintiff was
relying on them. There is thus no question of bringing the case directly within the
Hedley Byrne[2] decision as to the basis of liability, with the reliance on an implied
representation that played so large a part in *Whittingham v Crease & Co*[4]. I would
respectfully agree with the decision in that case, and accept that the reasoning there is one
means of reaching the right result. But that does not preclude me from reaching a
similar result by somewhat different reasoning in a case in which there has been no
reliance on any representation, either express or implied.

I have delayed too long any further reference to counsel's contentions for the
defendants about the limited effect of *Hedley Byrne*[2] in this sphere. Broadly, it was that
that decision was narrowly confined to negligent statements of fact, or opinions on
matters of fact, and had no application to statements or opinions on matters of law, or to
advice, whether on law or on fact. Thus confined, it had no effect on the doctrine of
Groom v Crocker[5]. I have already expressed my views on this latter point, and I shall not
repeat them. As to the ambit of *Hedley Byrne*[2], I can only say that I was unable to see what
magic there was about law that would remove it from the sphere of *Hedley Byrne*[3], or, for
that matter, why all advice should be outside it. Counsel for the defendants was very

---

1   [1972] 1 All ER 462 at 489, [1972] 1 QB 373 at 413
2   [1963] 2 All ER 575, [1964] AC 465
3   [1932] AC 562, [1932] All ER Rep 1
4   [1978] 5 WWR 45
5   [1938] 2 All ER 394, [1939] 1 KB 194

patient with me when I attempted to ascertain why it was that *Hedley Byrne*[1] was so
circumscribed in its operation; but at the end of the day I was left without any cogent
a reason for this limitation, and without any authority. Indeed, the view of Oliver J was
that the decision applied to representations and statements of fact, opinion or advice: see
Midland Bank Trust Co Ltd v Hett, Stubbs & Kemp[2].

In any event, on the view of the present case that I take, I do not think that it matters
much whether the scope of *Hedley Byrne*[1] in this respect is narrow or wide: for, as I have
b indicated, my view is that the true basis of liability flows directly from *Donoghue v
Stevenson*[3] and not via *Hedley Byrne*[1]. I think that the main object of counsel's strenuous
contentions for the defendants on this point was to establish that a solicitor's liability was
limited to a contractual and not tortious general liability for negligence, coupled with a
narrow *Hedley Byrne*[1] liability in tort for negligent mis-statements or opinions on fact
alone. Once it is decided that there is a general liability in tort for negligence, the ambit
c of the *Hedley Byrne*[1] liability becomes of little moment, save in respect of liability for
economic loss; and to this I shall turn in a moment. Before I do so, however, I should say
that an important authority on this first main head is *Ministry of Housing and Local
Government v Sharp*[4]. This, however, is more conveniently considered under the head to
which I am about to turn, and I shall therefore postpone any discussion of it.

The second main head of counsel for the defendants was that apart from cases within
d *Hedley Byrne*[1], a claim in negligence for financial or economic loss alone was bound to
fail; for with that one exception there is no cause of action in negligence for such loss.
The present case, of course, is plainly one in which the plaintiff's loss is purely
financial. Neither person nor property nor anything else has been injured: the loss is
simply that the plaintiff will not receive a gift of money and chattels as a result of the
defendants' negligence. No loss could be more purely and exclusively financial. Does
e that preclude recovery unless the case can be brought within *Hedley Byrne*[1]?

There are at least two ways in which *Hedley Byrne*[1] may be regarded. First, it may be
regarded as establishing a special category of case in which alone, by way of exception
from the general rule, purely financial loss may be recovered in an action for
negligence. Second, it may alternatively be regarded as establishing that there is no
longer any general rule (if there ever was one) that purely financial loss is irrecoverable
f in negligence. Instead, such loss may be recovered in those classes of case in which there
are no sufficient grounds for denying recovery, and in particular no danger of exposing
the defendant to a degree of liability that is unreasonable in its extent.

Cattle v Stockton Waterworks Co[5] heads the line of cases which deny recovery for pure
financial loss; and counsel for the defendants relied on this and on *Société Anonyme de
Remorquage à Hélice v Bennetts*[6]. These cases were decided, of course, before *Hedley Byrne*[1],
g and counsel understandably put greater weight on subsequent cases. One was *Weller &
Co v Foot and Mouth Disease Research Institute*[7], which I have already cited. There, the
claim that failed was the auctioneers' claim. They were not within the contemplation of
the defendants, and so far as their loss (which was purely financial) was a consequence of
injuries to cattle dealers, it was mere consequential damage, and not direct. As I read the
judgment, Widgery J[8] was adopting the views of Lord Devlin in *Hedley Byrne*[1], and
h saying that a claim in negligence for purely financial loss which fails will not do so
merely because the claim is purely financial, though it may do so if there is no breach of
a duty of care which suffices to support the claim.

---

1 [1963] 2 All ER 575, [1964] AC 465
2 [1978] 3 All ER 571 at 595, [1979] Ch 384 at 416
j 3 [1932] AC 562, [1932] All ER Rep 1
4 [1970] 1 All ER 1009, [1970] 2 QB 223
5 (1875) LR 10 QB 453, [1874–80] All ER Rep 220
6 [1911] 1 KB 243
7 [1965] 3 All ER 560, [1966] 1 QB 569
8 [1965] 3 All ER 560 at 569–570, [1966] 1 QB 569 at 586–587

Then there are two cases relating to the negligent interruption of the electricity supply
to factories. In *SCM (United Kingdom) Ltd v W J Whittall & Son Ltd*[1], the interruption
caused damage to materials and machines in the plaintiff's typewriter factory, and a
consequent loss of production. On a preliminary issue, the Court of Appeal held that the
plaintiffs could recover both for the physical damage and the consequent loss of
production, even though it was a purely financial loss. In *Spartan Steel & Alloys Ltd v
Martin & Co (Contractors) Ltd*[2], the plaintiffs were manufacturers of stainless steel alloys.
The interruption of the electricity supply had two results. One was that metal that was
molten at the time of the interruption had to be decanted to avoid injury to the furnaces,
and the other was that four other melts that could have been carried out, if there had
been no interruption, could not be executed. A divided Court of Appeal held that the
plaintiffs were entitled to recover both the depreciation in value of the molten metal that
had to be decanted and also the loss of profit from the sale of that metal, but nothing for
the loss of profit on the melts that could not be made.

I would not embark on the task of analysing these cases and the differing reasons for
the decisions unless I were driven to it; and I do not think that I am. They do not deny
that in some circumstances purely financial loss may be recoverable in negligence, but
they do not resolve the circumstances in which they are recoverable. Some are cases
which show that where there is physical injury, the damages may include sums for any
direct financial losses. In a number of cases a possible explanation is that the financial loss
that was held to be irrecoverable was a loss that was consequential or at one remove from
the primary loss: and the financial loss was said to be too remote. In the *Cattle* case[3], the
injury was the flooding of A's land, and the claim that failed was the plaintiff's claim for
the monetary loss that this caused him in carrying out his contract to do work on A's
land. In the *Remorquage* case[4] the injury was the sinking of a vessel in tow, and the claim
that failed was the tug owner's loss of profit on the tow. In the *Weller* case[5] the
auctioneers' losses were plainly consequential. In the *Spartan* case[2] the injury was to the
molten metal, and the claim that failed was in respect of the unmelted metal waiting to
make a profit. In some of these cases the financial loss stood on its own, and in others it
was directly connected with physical damage.

The subject is one of great difficulty, especially for a mere Chancery judge adrift on the
limitless seas of the common law, and I do not propose to spend more time on it. When
Lord Denning MR can utter the cry of despair to be found in the *Spartan Steel* case[6], it is
not for me to struggle on: for I can gratefully turn to *Ministry of Housing and Local
Government v Sharp*[7]. Of the various points in the case I need consider only one. That is
the claim by the plaintiff Ministry against the local authority whose clerk had negligently
failed to mention in the certificate given in response to a local land charge search made
by an intending purchaser that the Ministry had a charge on the land in question. The
purchaser had accordingly taken the land free from the charge, and the Ministry then
sued the local authority for the value of the charge that had been lost. The claim was
thus a claim for pure financial loss, without any injury to person or property; and it
succeeded.

Now if the case had been one in which the plaintiff had made the search and had relied
on the search certificate, as the local authority must have expected him to, thereby
suffering loss, then the case would have fallen within *Hedley Byrne*[8]; and in that case, of
course, it is clear that pure financial loss is recoverable. But that was not the case. The
plaintiff Ministry made no search, saw no certificate of search and placed no reliance on

1   [1970] 3 All ER 245, [1971] QB 337
2   [1972] 3 All ER 557, [1973] QB 27
3   (1875) LR 10 QB 453
4   [1911] 1 KB 243
5   [1965] 3 All ER 560, [1966] 1 QB 569
6   [1972] 3 All ER 557 at 562, [1973] QB 27 at 37
7   [1970] 1 All ER 1009, [1970] 2 QB 223
8   [1963] 2 All ER 575, [1964] AC 465

any statement by the local authority; it was the purchaser who did these things. The case
was thus far from being a plain *Hedley Byrne* case[1]. The points whether there was liability

a for pure financial loss as opposed to physical injury, and whether *Hedley Byrne*[1] was
applicable to a case where no representation was made to the plaintiff, were plainly
taken[2]. I shall take *Hedley Byrne*[1] first: somewhat different views on it were taken by the
three members of the court.

Lord Denning MR[3] stated that the case fell four square within his dissenting judgment
b in *Candler v Crane, Christmas & Co*[4] which the House of Lords had approved in *Hedley
Byrne*[1]. The clerk for whose negligence the local authority was liable owed a duty of care
at common law to anyone whom he knew or ought to have known might be injured if
he made a mistake. The clerk owed that duty not only to the purchaser who made the
search, but also 'to any person who he knows, or ought to know, will be injuriously
affected by a mistake, such as the incumbrancer here'[5].

On the other hand Salmon LJ[6] appears to rest his decision on *Donoghue v Stevenson*[7]
c rather than *Hedley Byrne*[1]. He said that the clerk (and certainly the local authority) must
or should have known that unless the search was conducted and the certificate prepared
with reasonable care, any incumbrancer whose charge was carelessly omitted from the
certificate would lose it and be likely to suffer damage:

d   'In my view, this factor certainly creates as close a degree of proximity between
      the council and the incumbrancer as existed between the appellant and respondent
      in *Donoghue v Stevenson*[7] . . . It is true that in *Donoghue v Stevenson*[7] it was physical
      injury that was to be foreseen as a result of the failure to take reasonable care
      whereas in the present case it is financial loss. But this no longer matters, and it is
      now well established that, quite apart from any contractual or fiduciary relationship,
      a man may owe a duty of care in what he writes or says just as much as in what he
e   does: see *Hedley Byrne & Co Ltd v Heller & Partners Ltd*[1]. No doubt in our criminal
      law, injury to the person is or should be regarded as more serious than damage to
      property and punished accordingly. So far, however, as the law of negligence
      relating to civil actions is concerned, the existence of a duty to take reasonable care
      no longer depends on whether it is physical injury or financial loss which can
      reasonably be foreseen as a result of a failure to take such care.'

f Cross LJ was the third member of the court; and on this point he expressed considerable
doubt, in the end reaching the conclusion that he was not prepared to dissent[8]. I have not
been able to find anything in this part of his judgment which provides any real assistance
on what is before me.

What seems plain is that the Court of Appeal held that the action lay in negligence for
g pure financial loss, namely, the loss of a monetary charge on the land. The case was one
in which no statement or representation of any kind had been made to the plaintiff, and
so of course there was no question of the plaintiff having placed any reliance on any
statement or representation, or having done anything in such reliance. The plaintiff was
passive throughout, and ignorant of the clerk's negligence. The local authority was held
liable because the clerk (or the local authority) knew or ought to have known that the
h plaintiff was likely to be injuriously affected by the careless omission of any mention of
the plaintiff's incumbrance from the certificate.

On the facts of the present case, I do not think that it matters much whether that result
is reached by extending the *Hedley Byrne*[1] principle to such cases, as Lord Denning MR

j
1 [1963] 2 All ER 575, [1964] AC 465
2 [1969] 3 All ER 225 at 238, 240, [1970] 2 QB 223 at 241, 243, 254
3 [1970] 1 All ER 1009 at 1018, [1970] 2 QB 223 at 268
4 [1951] 1 All ER 426 at 433–436, [1951] 2 KB 164 at 179–185
5 [1970] 1 All ER 1009 at 1019, [1970] 2 QB 223 at 268–269
6 [1970] 1 All ER 1009 at 1026–1027, [1970] 2 QB 223 at 278
7 [1932] AC 562, [1932] All ER Rep 1
8 [1970] 1 All ER 1009 at 1038, [1970] 2 QB 223 at 291

did, or whether it is reached by determining liability on *Donoghue v Stevenson*[1] principles, and then using *Hedley Byrne*[2] to extend those principles to cases of pure financial loss, as **a** I think was done by Salmon LJ. In view of what Denning LJ said in *Candler v Crane, Christmas & Co*[3] about the persons to whom the duty of care is owed, I find some difficulty in seeing how the principles stated in that judgment apply to someone to whom no statement will be made or shown but who will be injured by a negligent statement being acted on by some third party. With great respect and considerable hesitation, I would prefer the approach of Salmon LJ, though I am happy not be required **b** to decide anything on the point.

It seems to me that the *Sharp* case[4] is conclusive of the point before me. Indeed, it seems to me that despite the factual differences between that case and the case before me, they are closely similar in principle. Let me take P as the plaintiff in each case, D as the defendant (ignoring any distinction between the clerk and the local authority in the *Sharp* case[4]) and X as the third party, the purchaser in the *Sharp* case[4] and the testator in **c** the case before me. I will take five points. First, D was guilty of negligent omissions in his dealings with X: he failed to discover the land charge or failed to include it in the certificate that he gave to the purchaser, or he failed to warn the testator about attestation by a beneficiary's spouse, warning him only about attestation by a beneficiary ('not somebody benefiting under the will'). Second, X acted on the negligent omission but suffered no loss. Third, by acting in this way X caused financial loss to P: P's charge **d** became void against the purchaser, and P's legacy was invalidated. Fourth, D contemplated, or ought to have contemplated, that his negligent omissions would injure P, an identified or identifiable person. Fifth, there was no possible liability for an indeterminate amount to an indeterminate number of persons. The *Sharp* case[4] accordingly seems to me, particularly when read in the context of the other cases that I have cited, to provide ample authority both for holding that the defendants are liable to **e** the plaintiff in negligence, and for holding that the fact that the claim is for purely financial loss is no bar to that liability.

On the latter point I think that I should refer to two overseas cases that were not discussed in argument. One is *Rivtow Marine Ltd v Washington Iron Works*[5]. That was a case of purely financial loss. In British Columbia the plaintiff had chartered a log barge which was fitted with two cranes. The manufacturers and distributors of those cranes **f** were not in any contractual relationship with the plaintiff: see the facts as stated in the court below[6]. In the busiest part of the logging season the plaintiff discovered dangerous defects in the cranes, and the barge had to be taken out of service for repairs. The manufacturers and distributors had become aware of these defects in this type of crane many months earlier, and they also knew that the plaintiff was using the cranes for the logging work to which they were in fact put. Nevertheless, the manufacturers and **g** distributors had negligently failed to warn the plaintiff of the defects in the cranes at an earlier time, when withdrawing the cranes from service for repairs could have been carried out during a slack season, and so with much less loss. The Supreme Court of Canada unanimously held that the additional loss of earnings resulting from the repairs having to be effected during the busy season instead of a slack season was recoverable in tort, even though it was purely monetary. Two of the nine judges would, in addition, **h** have awarded the cost of effecting the repairs: but they were alone in this. The court relied on *Hedley Byrne*[2] for the sole purpose of demonstrating that liability in negligence

j

1 [1932] AC 562, [1932] All ER Rep 1
2 [1963] 2 All ER 575, [1964] AC 465
3 [1951] 1 All ER 426 at 434, [1951] 2 KB 164 at 180–181
4 [1970] 1 All ER 1009, [1970] 2 QB 223
5 (1973) 40 DLR (3d) 530
6 (1972) 26 DLR (3d) 559 at 560

'is not limited to physical damage but extends also to economic loss': see per Ritchie J[1].

a   I do not think that the view of the majority was that in every case (as distinct from the facts of the case before the court) all financial loss was always recoverable: certainly that was not the view of Laskin J in his minority judgment, with which Hall J concurred.

The other case is *Caltex Oil (Australia) Pty Ltd v Dredge Willemstad*[2]. The essential facts were that the dredger negligently injured a pipeline belonging to an oil refining company. Caltex delivered its crude oil to the refining company, and the company

b   delivered the refined oil products to Caltex through the pipeline. While the pipeline was being repaired, Caltex suffered the loss of having to obtain delivery of the refined oil products by more expensive means than the pipeline; and for this loss Caltex successfully sued the dredger. The importance of the decision of the High Court of Australia was that all five judges, while holding that the loss was recoverable despite being purely financial, sought to do what the majority in the *Rivtow Marine* case[3] did not do, namely, to

c   determine what limits there should be to the right to recover for pure economic loss. Jacobs J[4] evolved a basis of physical propinquity which seems to be closely related to the particular facts of the case: the financial loss was recoverable because the duty of care was based on Caltex having crude and processed oil products in close proximity to where the dredger was working. The other judgments are, I think, of greater assistance in the present case. Stephen J[5] put matters somewhat generally on the need for a sufficient

d   degree of proximity between the tortious act and the resultant detriment. Murphy J[6] took the view that all economic loss should be recoverable unless there were sufficient reasons of public policy to limit recovery. The views of Gibbs J[7] and Mason J[8] had much in common. The question was whether the defendant knew or ought to have known that the plaintiff individually (and not merely as a member of an indeterminate or unascertained class) would be likely to suffer financial loss as a result of the negligence.

e   The headnote attributes this view to Stephen J as well, and it may be that this is a consequence of the views that he expressed. The judgments as a whole are (if I may respectfully say so) characteristically thorough in the examination of the authorities and academic writings on the subject, and in their discussion of principle. The case is plainly a terminus a quo for any further investigation of the subject.

Before saying anything more about these tests of liability, I should say this. Apart

f   from *Hedley Byrne*[9], the standard generally adopted in negligence cases is to impose liability on the general *Donoghue v Stevenson*[10] basis of reasonable foreseeability. In *Hedley Byrne*[9] that basis was rejected for negligent mis-statements, and instead a more restrictive test of special skill, reliance and so on was applied. The *Sharp* case[11] (and also, I think, *Dutton v Bognor Regis United Building Co Ltd*[12]) may be said to have applied *Hedley Byrne*[9] in admitting liability for purely financial loss without accepting its concomitant

g   restrictive test of liability. If the general *Donoghue v Stevenson*[10] basis is applied at large to cases of purely financial loss, the problems of indeterminate liability are bound to occur. Cases of negligent mis-statements already have the restrictive test of liability that was laid down in *Hedley Byrne*[9]. For other cases the question is what modification or form of application of the *Donoghue v Stevenson*[10] basis must be applied in order to meet

h

1   (1973) 40 DLR (3d) 530 at 546
2   (1976) 136 CLR 529
3   40 DLR (3d) 530
4   136 CLR 529 at 604
5   136 CLR 529 at 575–576
6   136 CLR 529 at 606
7   136 CLR 529 at 555
8   136 CLR 529 at 593
9   [1963] 2 All ER 575, [1964] AC 465
10   [1932] AC 562, [1932] All ER Rep 1
11   [1970] 1 All ER 1009, [1970] 2 QB 223
12   [1972] 1 All ER 462, [1972] 1 QB 373

these problems. One possibility is on the lines advanced by Murphy J in the *Caltex* case[1]: all financial loss flowing from the negligence is to be admitted, unless there are sufficient grounds for excluding it. Another possibility is to follow Stephen J and admit only those losses with a sufficient degree of proximity to the negligence. Both tests are clearly far from precise, and leave much room for argument. The views of Gibbs and Mason JJ are less open to this objection: the plaintiff can recover only if the defendant knew or ought to have known that the negligence would be likely to injure the plaintiff individually, and not merely as a member of an indeterminate or unascertained class.

This is far from exhausting the possible tests, quite apart from that proposed by Jacobs J, which is plainly inapposite to the facts of this case. However, I do not think that I need explore the matter further. Whichever test is applied, the facts of the present case seem to me to satisfy it. I can see no reason for excluding liability. There is clearly a high degree of proximity between the negligence and the loss. Plainly the defendants not only actually knew of the plaintiff individually (without any 'or ought to have known'), but also knew that the negligence would be likely to cause her financial loss. Indeed, I find it difficult to envisage any test based on *Donoghue v Stevenson*[2] that would be stringent enough to exclude the plaintiff. In my judgment, both on authority and on principle the plaintiff ought to recover her financial loss. I am content, indeed happy, to leave it to other courts in other cases on other facts to evolve the test or tests that have to be applied. In some cases there may be not much more than the 'feel' of the case to point to the answer. But enough decisions in enough cases must sooner or later make possible the inductive process of laying down a test or tests by which all may be guided. I shall indulge in no feats of prophecy beyond saying that whatever is evolved will be wide enough to allow the plaintiff in the present case to succeed.

Before I leave this part of the case, I must refer to a subsidiary point under this head. Counsel for the defendants bravely contended that in this case the plaintiff had suffered no financial loss. Nothing of hers had been taken away or destroyed; she had merely failed to get something extra. All that she had lost was a mere spes. The point, he said, was devoid of authority; and I am not surprised. I accept, of course, that a testator may at any time change his will, and that while he lives no beneficiary under his current will can have more than a spes. But his death changes all that. In this case, but for the negligence of the defendants, the plaintiff would have received a share of the residue of an ascertainable amount; and that amount is no mere spes. It is, indeed, the amount of the plaintiff's loss. I do not think that the expression 'loss' can be confined to deprivation. To me, a failure to receive an assured benefit is a loss. If a gift in transit to a donee is destroyed or stolen, I think both English usage and common sense would accept that the donee had suffered a loss, even if the property had not passed. In saying that I do not forget *Dutton v Bognor Regis United Building Co Ltd*[3]. In my judgment, there is nothing in this point.

With that, I turn to the third main head of counsel for the defendants. This is concerned with reasons of policy. These reasons, he said, not only pointed against holding a solicitor liable in negligence to anyone save his clients, but also failed to support any extension of his liability to those who are not his clients, such as the plaintiff in the present case. Under the first limb of this, the main contention was that the primary duty of a solicitor was to his client, and that to impose on a solicitor a duty to third parties would be to dilute the solicitor's duty to his client; and that would be undesirable. Counsel for the defendants took as an example a solicitor who is preparing a will for a rich man with a wife, an ex-wife and issue of both marriages. In discussing the will, questions between the two families would be likely to arise, and it would be undesirable for the solicitor to have to look over his shoulder in such cases of possible conflict by

1   (1976) 136 CLR 529
2   [1932] AC 562, [1932] All ER Rep 1
3   [1972] 1 All ER 462, [1972] 1 QB 373

imposing on him any duty of care to others than his client. When asked how this view could apply to a case such as the case before me, where there was no possibility of any conflict, and the testator's object was to give a share of residue to the plaintiff, a gift which the plaintiff would gladly receive, counsel was obliged to contend that the rule for cases where there is a possible conflict must also govern cases where there is none.

This argument seems to me to confuse duties which differ in their nature. In broad terms, a solicitor's duty to his client is to do for him all that he properly can, with, of course, proper care and attention. Subject to giving due weight to the adverb 'properly', that duty is a paramount duty. The solicitor owes no such duty to those who are not his clients. He is no guardian of their interests. What he does for his client may be hostile and injurious to their interests; and sometimes the greater the injuries the better he will have served his client. The duty owed by a solicitor to a third party is entirely different. There is no trace of a wide and general duty to do all that properly can be done for him. Instead, in a case such as the present, there is merely a duty, owed to him as well as the client, to use proper care in carrying out the client's instructions for conferring the benefit on the third party. If it is to be held that there is a duty that is wider than that, that will have to be determined in some other case. The duty that I hold to exist in the present case, far from diluting the solicitor's duty to his client, marches with it, and, if anything, strengthens it. I therefore reject the first limb of this contention.

The second limb of the argument was even more tenuous. Counsel for the defendant stressed that there had been no physical injury, and no financial loss consequent on physical injury, and that all the plaintiff had suffered was a failure to receive the testator's bounty. Such a plaintiff, it was said, was not deserving of the protection that would be given by a right to sue in negligence. I need only say that I have already discussed the considerations that were relied on under this head, and I propose to say nothing further about them. In any case, I do not think it is right to pose the question as being whether there are sufficient grounds for 'extending' a solicitor's liability in this way. The position is not that under the relevant principles of law a solicitor's liability does not reach so far, and so it must be asked whether it should be extended. Instead, in my view the principles do carry a solicitor's liability that far, and so the only question is that posed by the first limb, namely, whether there are sufficient grounds for restricting that liability. I have already dealt with the first limb, and I can see no cogency in the second. I therefore reject it as well.

That, I think, disposes of the issues before me. It may be of assistance if I summarise my main conclusions:

(1) Despite the dicta in *Robertson v Fleming*[1], and what was said in *Groom v Crocker*[2], and other cases in that line, there is no longer any rule that a solicitor who is negligent in his professional work can be liable only to his client in contract; he may be liable both to his client and to others for the tort of negligence.

(2) The basis of the solicitor's liability to others is either an extension of the *Hedley Byrne*[3] principle or, more probably, a direct application of the principle of *Donoghue v Stevenson*[4].

(3) A solicitor who is instructed by his client to carry out a transaction that will confer a benefit on an identified third party owes a duty of care towards that third party in carrying out that transaction, in that the third party is a person within his direct contemplation as someone who is likely to be so closely and directly affected by his acts or omissions that he can reasonably foresee that the third party is likely to be injured by those acts or omissions.

1   (1861) 4 Macq 167
2   [1938] 2 All ER 394, [1939] 1 KB 194
3   [1963] 2 All ER 575, [1964] AC 465
4   [1932] AC 562, [1932] All ER Rep 1

(4) The mere fact that the loss to such a third party caused by the negligence is purely financial, and is in no way a physical injury to person or property, is no bar to the claim against the solicitor.

(5) In such circumstances there are no considerations which suffice to negative or limit the scope of the solicitor's duty to the beneficiary.

From what I have said, it follows that the plaintiff's claim succeeds, and she is entitled to damages against the defendants for the loss of the benefits that the 1974 will would have carried to her but for the negligence of the defendants. That loss consists of the value of the chattels specifically bequeathed to her and also the share of the residue. As I have said, though stated in the will to be 5/20ths, this would have taken effect as five twenty-first parts. The statement of claim also claims the legal expenses of investigating the plaintiff's claim up to the date of the issue of the writ, estimated at £250. Little was said about this claim, and at present I doubt whether any sum is recoverable under this head. If an order for costs is made in favour of the plaintiff, then some of these legal expenses of investigation may fall within that order as being 'costs of or incidental to' these proceedings, and so of course could not be claimed as damages. I propose to make no order under this head until I have heard any submissions that counsel may wish to make on the point; and it may be convenient to do this as part of any submissions that are made on costs. At the same time I will hear what counsel have to say about the plaintiff's claim to interest under the Law Reform (Miscellaneous Provisions) Act 1934. It may be that the amount of damages in respect of the loss of benefits under the will can be agreed between counsel; if not, I will hear them on this also. Subject to these outstanding matters, judgment will be entered for the plaintiff.

[His Lordship heard counsel on the point and gave judgment as follows:] I have now heard argument on the point that I reserved for further argument at the end of my judgment this morning, namely, whether the plaintiff can recover anything under a head of damages which is particularised as being 'legal expenses of investigating the Plaintiff's claim up to the date of the issue of the Writ herein—estimated £250'. Counsel for the plaintiff's says that these expenses were a consequence of the defendants' negligence, and so they should be recoverable as damages in the ordinary way. Counsel for the defendants, on the other hand, says that nothing should be recovered under this head in the form of damages, though it may well be that some, if not all, of the items under this head can be recovered in the form of costs, an order for the payment of costs by the defendants to the plaintiff having been made. The short point then is whether these legal expenses of investigating the claim can be recovered as damages in any event, or whether only so much of them as survives after taxation can be recovered in the form of costs.

The relevant rule of court is RSC Ord 62, r 2(4). This refers to s 50 of the Supreme Court of Judicature (Consolidation) Act 1925, under which the court has a discretion as to 'the costs of and incidental to all proceedings in the Supreme Court'. The expression 'incidental to' is plainly of some width. Counsel for the defendants has put before me the decision of the Court of Appeal in *Pêcheries Ostendaises (SA) v Merchants' Marine Insurance Co*[1]. This dealt with the question, among other things, whether a taxing master had power to decide whether costs that had been incurred before the action was brought were necessary or proper for the attainment of justice and, if they were, to allow them. The Court of Appeal unanimously held that the taxing master had this power. I think the most material passage in the case for the present purpose is a passage in the judgment of Lord Hanworth MR[2]. What he said there was that it appeared to him—

'... that there is power in the Master to allow costs incurred before action brought, and that if the costs are in respect of materials ultimately proving of use

---

1   [1928] 1 KB 750, [1928] All ER Rep 174
2   [1928] 1 KB 750 at 757, cf [1928] All ER Rep 174 at 176

a and service in the action, the Master has a discretion to allow these costs, which he probably will exercise in favour of the party incurring them, because they have been made use of during the course of the action.'

It also seems to me that there is ample authority for saying that a successful plaintiff cannot obtain, in the guise of damages, any costs which, on a party and party taxation of costs, are disallowed by the taxing master. It is not enough for the plaintiff to claim that such costs were incurred by him as a result of the defendant's negligence. I think that *b* this is sufficiently established by *Cockburn v Edwards*[1]. I am saying nothing about damages which fall outside the particular form in which they are claimed in this case, namely, the legal expenses of investigating the plaintiff's claim up to the date of the issue of the writ. It seems to me that both on authority and on principle those legal expenses can be recovered by the plaintiff only as costs, and not in the form of damages. In so far as the plaintiff can persuade the taxing master that the items incurred should be allowed *c* as costs on a party and party taxation, then the plaintiff can recover them; but so far as they are not allowed by the taxing master, then I think that they cannot be recovered in the shape of damages.

Accordingly, on the enquiry as to damages which counsel agree should be ordered, no head of damage for the legal expenses of investigating the plaintiff's claim up to the date of the issue of the writ will be allowable as damages. The claim for interest has been *d* agreed.

Judgment for the plaintiff.

Solicitors: *Vickers & Co* (for the plaintiff); *Bond Pearce & Co* (for the defendants).

e   Hazel Hartman Barrister.

---

1   (1881) 18 Ch D 449

Practice Direction

COMPANIES COURT

Practice – Companies Court – Chambers – Postal transactions – Companies (Winding-up) Rules 1949 (SI 1949 No 330) – RSC Ord 102.

1. These directions apply to proceedings in chambers in the High Court in London *b* under the Companies (Winding-up) Rules 1949 and under RSC Ord 102. They are made with a view to enabling certain formal business in the chambers of the companies court registrar in London to be transacted by post when this is more expeditious, economical or convenient. They will be reviewed from time to time and, in the light of practical experience, may be varied, extended or withdrawn as seen fit. Parties may nevertheless continue to transact such business by personal attendance if they so wish.   *c*

2. In these directions, 'Ord 102' means Ord 102 of the Rules of the Supreme Court, 'the Winding-up Rules' means the Companies (Winding-up) Rules 1949, and 'the registrar' means the registrar and the companies court registrar as defined in the Winding-up Rules and Ord 102 respectively.

3. The classes of business which may be transacted by post subject to the general and *d* specific provisions of this Practice Direction are set out in the schedule hereto.

4. *General directions*
   (1) The use of postal facilities is at the risk of the solicitor or party concerned who should have regard to any material time limits prescribed and should enclose all necessary papers.
   (2) Applications for the conduct of business by post must be made by a letter signed *e* by or on behalf of the solicitor for a party or by the party if he is acting in person (a) specifying precisely what the court is being asked to do, (b) enclosing any requisite documents, and (c) enclosing an adequately stamped envelope of adequate size properly addressed to the sender for the return of any relevant documents to him.
   (3) The letter of application together with any requisite documents must be posted in *f* a prepaid envelope properly addressed to—

>   The High Court of Justice
>   Companies Court
>   Registrar's Chambers: Room 312
>   Thomas More Building
>   Royal Courts of Justice
>   Strand   *g*
>   London WC2A 2LL

If any deficiency is found in or among the necessary documents, a note marked 'Please call' will be sent to the solicitors or litigant in person but the deficiency will not be specified. It will not be possible to enter into correspondence concerning deficiencies.
   (4) Applications will be treated as having been made at the date and time of the actual *h* receipt of the requisite documents in the registrar's chambers and for this purpose the date and time of despatch will be disregarded.
   (5) If an acknowledgment of the receipt of papers is required they must be accompanied by a list setting out the papers in question, sent with a stamped and addressed envelope. The court will not accept responsibility for papers which are alleged to have been sent to it unless an acknowledgment is produced.
   (6) The documents required for the conduct of any business by post will include all *j* those documents which would have been required had the business been conducted by personal attendance.
   (7) Any application by post which does not comply with the relevant rules or with this direction will be rejected and, in any other case, the court may exercise its power to

decline to deal with a postal application. If any application is rejected the party making
a the application will be notified by post and he should then conduct the business in
question by personal attendance in the ordinary way.

(8) It is emphasised that any party applying for the issue of proceedings by post will
be responsible for the service of all documents requiring to be served under the rules in
the same way as if the proceedings had been issued on personal attendance and that the
costs of any adjournment occasioned by non-service of any necessary documents are
b likely to be awarded against the party responsible.

(9) On making any application by post the proper amount of any court fees payable
must be enclosed together with a stamped addressed envelope. Any cheque or other
draft should be made payable to HM Paymaster-General.

5. *Particular classes of business*

(1) *The presentation of petitions*
c (a) *Winding-up petitions and petitions under s 210 of the Companies Act 1948* A
typed copy and at least two additional copies (not carbons) certified by the petitioner or
his solicitor to be true copies of the typed copy of the petition should be sent to the court.
To facilitate the verification of petitions within the time limit imposed by the Winding-
up Rules the court will generally accept and file affidavits sworn within seven days before
receipt of the petition at the registrar's chambers and sent with the petition.
d (b) *Petitions to confirm reduction of capital or to sanction schemes of arrangement* A
typed copy of the petition and one other copy (not a carbon) certified by the petitioner's
solicitor to be a true copy of the typed copy should be sent to the court together with the
appropriate fee and a stamped addressed envelope.

(2) *The issue of summonses and applications for the restoration or adjournment of summonses*
In dealing with any postal application for the issue of a summons not being an
e originating summons requiring an appearance, the proper officer of the court will
allocate an appropriate time and date for the first hearing and will seal and return one
copy of the summons for service, if necessary. Any specific requests for a particular date
will be considered by the proper officer but there can be no guarantee that they can be
met. Generally speaking the first available appointment will be allotted having regard
to any time needed for service of the summons, for swearing and filing evidence and for
f completion of any other necessary formalities. Counsels' appointments at 12 o'clock will
not be allotted unless specifically requested.

Applications for the restoration or adjournment of summonses will be dealt with in
similar manner.

An originating summons requiring an appearance will be sealed and returned to the
sender for service.
g (3) *The issue of notices of motion*
A typed copy and two additional copies of the notice of motion should be sent to the
court together with the appropriate fee payable (if any) and a stamped addressed
envelope. The typed copy *must* be signed by the applicant personally or by his
solicitors. The proper officer will appoint the date for hearing the motion allowing
sufficient time for service if necessary and will seal and return one copy of the notice to
h the sender.

6. *Drawing up of orders*
In future, subject to the exception mentioned below, all orders, whether made by the
judge or registrar, and whether made in court or in chambers, will, unless otherwise
directed, be drafted in the chambers of the registrar. It is therefore of the utmost
importance that solicitors should ensure that all documents required to enable such
j orders to be drawn expeditiously (eg briefs, copy charges etc) are lodged in chambers as
soon as possible after the matter has been heard, particularly in cases where limitations
as to time are involved. In the case of any order other than a winding-up order, a copy
of the draft order will be sent to the solicitors for the parties, together with an
appointment to settle the same. Should the parties be in agreement with the form of the

order as drafted they may return the same marked 'approved' and the order will be engrossed in that form and the appointment to settle vacated. If any variation in the form of order is desired by any party he must notify all other parties of the variation desired and thereafter all parties must attend on the appointment to settle and discuss the matter with the appropriate official.

The exceptions referred to above are (a) orders by the registrar on the application of the Official Receiver or for which the Treasury Solicitor is responsible under the existing practice, (b) orders of the registrar or the judge in relation to reductions of capital, share premium account or capital redemption reserve fund or in relation to schemes of arrangement under ss 206 to 208 of the 1948 Act.

7. This Practice Direction will come into effect on 15th October 1979.

THE SCHEDULE

(1) The presentation of petitions under Ord 102 and the Winding-up Rules.

(2) The issue of summonses under Ord 102 and the Winding-up Rules.

(3) The issue of notices of motion under Ord 102 and the Winding-up Rules.

(4) The issue of third party notices (where leave to issue such notice has been granted) and notices under r 68 of the Winding-up Rules.

(5) The filing and lodging of affidavits, exhibits and other documents required to be filed or lodged.

(6) Entry of appearances.

(7) The issue of notices of appointments for the hearing of originating summonses to which an appearance is required.

(8) Fixing appointments for the restoration of adjourned summonses.

(9) Drawing up orders.

(10) The issue of certificates of taxation.

(11) The adjournment of summonses by consent.

(12) Notification that proceedings have been disposed of.

By the direction of the Vice-Chancellor.

15th October 1979

R v Smith (Stanley)

a

COURT OF APPEAL, CRIMINAL DIVISION

GEOFFREY LANE LJ, SWANWICK AND WATERHOUSE JJ

2nd JULY 1979

b
Criminal law – Murder – Defence of automatism – Defendant examined by psychiatrists in prison before trial to determine mental condition – Defendant making statements to psychiatrists inconsistent with subsequent plea of automatism – Defendant not pleading insanity or diminished responsibility – Judge allowing Crown to cross-examine defendant on statements and call doctors to give evidence in rebuttal of plea of automatism – Whether cross-examination and admission of evidence properly allowed – Whether statements to psychiatrists inadmissible because made in confidence – Whether jury entitled to help from expert when plea of automatism raised – Whether

c
unfair to admit psychiatrists' evidence – Whether evidence admissible if statements to psychiatrists contrary to judges' rules.

d
The applicant, a butcher, was asleep in his room in a house when another occupant, a man, came into the room. Noises from the room were heard and a third occupant went to the room and found the man lying on the floor with stab wounds and the applicant standing over him with a butcher's knife in his hand. The man died from his wounds. While he was in prison awaiting trial for murder, the applicant was examined by two psychiatrists to determine his mental condition, and made certain statements to them. Those statements were inconsistent with the defence of automatism which he subsequently pleaded, namely that he killed the man while asleep. The psychiatrists reported that the applicant's responsibility for the killing was substantially impaired.

e
The defendant did not, however, plead insanity or diminished responsibility. The Crown sought leave to cross-examine the applicant on his statements to the psychiatrists to show that the defence of automatism was an afterthought and little regard should be paid to it. The judge allowed the cross-examination, in the course of which the applicant gave evidence of the killing which was consistent with his plea of automatism. The

f
judge then allowed the Crown to call the psychiatrists to give evidence in rebuttal of the plea, and they gave evidence that the applicant's account that the killing happened while he was asleep was not physically possible. The applicant was convicted of murder. He applied for leave to appeal against the conviction on the grounds that the judge had erred in allowing the cross-examination and in allowing the psychiatrists to give evidence rebutting the plea of automatism. The applicant contended (i) that in the absence of a plea of insanity or diminished responsibility the statements to the psychiatrists were, as

g
a matter of law, inadmissible, because they were made in confidence in a doctor/patient relationship, (ii) that as a matter of discretion the psychiatrists' evidence should not have been admitted, because the issue whether the killing was done in a state of automatism was for the jury to decide in the light of their own experience, without medical assistance, and the psychiatrists' evidence was irrelevant to that issue, (iii) that in any event it was unfair to admit the psychiatrists' reports in evidence because the applicant had submitted

h
to the medical examination on the basis that the medical reports would be used in court only if he pleaded insanity or diminished responsibility, and (iv) that the statements to the psychiatrists were inadmissible because they were made in breach of the judges' rules.

j
Held – The application would be dismissed for the following reasons—

(i) The psychiatrists' reports could not be regarded as confidential since the rules governing examination of prisoners in prison provided for submission of reports of a prisoner's medical condition to the Director of Public Prosecutions and for the supply by him of copies of the report to the defence. The reports were not, therefore, inadmissible as a matter of law (see p 610 f, post); *R v Howard* (1957) 42 Cr App R 23 explained.

(ii) Automatism was an abnormal medical condition, which was not within an ordinary juryman's experience, and a jury were therefore entitled to expert help when *a* automatism was pleaded. It followed that the jury were entitled to the benefit of the psychiatrists' evidence in deciding whether the applicant had committed the killing in a state of automatism. Accordingly, the judge had been justified in admitting that evidence (see p 611 *d e* and p 612 *a h*, post); dicta of Devlin J in *Hill v Baxter* [1958] 1 All ER at 197 and of Roskill LJ in *R v Chard* (1972) 56 Cr App R at 270 applied.

(iii) Assuming that a judge was entitled to exclude evidence if he thought it had been *b* gathered unfairly or illegally, it had not been unfair to use the psychiatrists' reports in evidence, even though the applicant had not pleaded insanity or diminished responsibility, because the applicant had known that the reports would be used at the trial in relation to any abnormality in his mental condition, and automatism was an abnormal mental condition (see p 612 *e f*, post); *R v Payne* [1963] 1 All ER 848 distinguished.

c

(iv) Even if the statements to the psychiatrists had been made in breach of the judges' rules, which was doubtful, they were nevertheless admissible because the jury were entitled to expert help on the plea of automatism (see p 612 *h* to p 613 *b*, post).

Notes

For automatism, see 11 Halsbury's Laws (4th Edn) para 6, and for cases on the subject, see 14(1) Digest (Reissue) 14–16, 31–35. *d*

For admissibility of medical evidence, see 11 Halsbury's Laws (4th Edn) para 445.

For the judges' rules in relation to written statements made after caution, see ibid para 423.

For the trial judge's discretion to exclude evidence where its admission would operate unfairly against the defendant, see ibid para 364.

Cases referred to in judgment

e

D v National Society for the Prevention of Cruelty to Children [1977] 1 All ER 589, [1978] AC 171, [1977] 2 WLR 201, 76 LGR 5, HL; *affg* [1976] 2 All ER 993, [1978] AC 171, [1976] 3 WLR 76, CA.

Hill v Baxter [1958] 1 All ER 193, [1958] 1 QB 277, [1958] 2 WLR 76, 122 JP 134, 42 Cr App R 51, 56 LGR 117, DC, 45 Digest (Repl) 35, *119*.

R v Chard (1972) 56 Cr App R 268, CA.

f

R v Howard (1957) 42 Cr App R 23, CCA, 14 (2) Digest (Reissue) 470, *3914*.

R v Payne [1963] 1 All ER 848, [1963] 1 WLR 637, 127 JP 230, 47 Cr App R 122, CCA, 45 Digest (Repl) 115, *391*.

R v Sang [1979] 2 All ER 46, [1979] 2 WLR 439, CA; *affd* [1979] 2 All ER 1222, [1979] 3 WLR 263, HL.

R v Turner [1975] 1 All ER 70, [1975] QB 834, [1975] 2 WLR 56, 60 Cr App R 86, CA, *g* Digest (Cont Vol D) 328, *5771a*.

Case also cited

Bratty v Attorney-General for Northern Ireland [1961] 3 All ER 523, [1963] AC 386, HL.

Application for leave to appeal

On 12th July 1978 at the Central Criminal Court, before Griffiths J and a jury, the *h* applicant, Stanley Ivan Smith, was convicted by a majority verdict of murder and sentenced to life imprisonment. He applied for leave to appeal against the conviction. The grounds of the application were that the judge erred in ruling (i) that counsel for the Crown be allowed to cross-examine him on the statements he had made to two psychiatrists who had examined him before the trial in prison to enable them to prepare reports on his medical condition, sanity and fitness to plead and on the question of *j* diminished responsibility, (ii) that Crown counsel should be allowed to call the psychiatrists to give evidence in rebuttal of the applicant's evidence in cross-examination in order to express their opinion that neither the statements made to them by the applicant whilst in prison nor his evidence at the trial were consistent with his defence of automatism whilst asleep and (iii) that the verdict was against the weight of the a evidence and was unsafe and unsatisfactory. The facts are set out in the judgment of the court.

Louis Blom-Cooper QC and David Altaras for the applicant.
Michael Hill QC and Graham Boal for the Crown.

GEOFFREY LANE LJ delivered the following judgment of the court: On 12th July 1978 at the Central Criminal Court the applicant was convicted by a majority of ten to two of the murder of a man called Bob Montgomery and was accordingly sentenced to life imprisonment. He now applies for leave to appeal against that conviction.

The murder took place on 8th February 1978 and the facts which gave rise to the charge can be dealt with quite shortly. Mr Montgomery, the victim of the murder, occupied some rooms in a house in Garratt Lane, London SW18 with his wife. There were a number of other people sleeping in the house, one of whom was the applicant. Another was the sister of Mrs Montgomery, a Miss Nore, and a youth named James Craig.

Earlier in the evening of the day in question, that is 8th February, there had been some sort of altercation between the applicant and Mrs Montgomery. It does not matter what it was about but there had been words between them. Later that evening Bob Montgomery came back having spent the evening drinking and there was no doubt even for a man of his capacity, which was apparently startling, he had had a good deal more to drink than was good for him. It seems that Mrs Montgomery told him of the altercation which had taken place earlier in the evening with the applicant. As a result of that he expressed his intention of going upstairs 'to sort the applicant out'.

That he did. He went up to the room where the applicant was asleep and he went into the room. From downstairs there was then heard the noise of a quarrel or a squabble or a fight taking place. In short, one of the other people in the house went up to the bedroom. The door was half open. There was only very feeble light in the room and there on the floor was Bob Montgomery lying on his back and the applicant standing just inside the door with a knife in his hand. It was a butcher's knife. The applicant legitimately had it with him because it was his own personal possession as a butcher and he habitually kept the knife with him in case it might be stolen. What had undoubtedly happened in that room was that the applicant had plunged his knife into Montgomery's body on a very large number of occasions. Suffice it to say that having muttered a few words Mr Montgomery died of shock and haemorrhage due to the stab wounds of which there were some 26 about his face and body.

Police arrived very soon afterwards. They asked the applicant what had happened. He said: 'I was in bed asleep. Someone burst into my room. I think it was Bob. I just grabbed my knife and stabbed him.' He was then taken to the police station. All the precautions with regard to cautioning him were properly taken and, there, in the police station, he was put in a cell accompanied by a young officer called Pc McDonald to whom he made a similar remark as to what had happened and, finally, in a written statement to the police very much the same sort of thing was said. That was in brief the case.

The three defences which were run at the trial were these: first of all there was automatism, namely that this man was, so to speak, sleepwalking when he did what undoubtedly his hand did and, accordingly, he was not accountable for what he had done, secondly, there was self-defence and, thirdly, provocation. It is obvious it could have been no easy task to run those three defences before the jury. Strangely, the one defence which would undoubtedly have succeeded was never run at all and that was the defence of diminished responsibility. This will emerge in one moment almost as the basis of the application.

The applicant had been examined by two doctors who are both highly qualified psychiatrists, one a Dr Rollin and the other a Dr Shepherd. Each had examined him on two separate occasions and, although to begin with they were in some doubt as to what his mental condition at the time of the examination might have been, when further facts

came to light and when they re-examined him for a second time they were unanimously
of the view that the applicant's responsibility for his actions was substantially impaired.
Had the defence of diminished responsibility been run it would have been supported by
those two doctors and would undoubtedly have succeeded. But, of course, it is a
defendant's option whether he runs that defence or not, and the applicant chose not to.

The emergence of the suggested defence of automatism came somewhat late in the
day and it was really only when the applicant himself gave evidence that anyone for
certain could have said that defence was being run. In fairness to those representing him,
it had been intimated by them to the Crown that such a defence was on the cards but that
is as far as it went. Now, when the Crown realised that this was a defence which was in
fact being propounded on behalf of the applicant, they sought leave to cross-examine
him as to certain remarks he had made to Dr Rollin and, less importantly, to Dr
Shepherd. These were remarks which indicated his then account of what had happened
at the scene of the death of Montgomery. The reason for putting those questions was
that the Crown desired to demonstrate that the defence of automatism was a recently
thought of idea and that it was not in the applicant's mind at the time when he was being
interviewed by the doctor and, accordingly, it was something to which little attention
should be paid. The judge allowed those questions to be put and, in due course, he
allowed the doctors to be called in order to give their views as to the defence of
automatism. In effect, they said two things: first of all, that the answers given to the
police and to them in the interviews and examinations were not consistent with
automatism. They were in court when the applicant gave evidence. That was by leave
of the judge. The evidence he gave to the jury was quite different from what he had told
the police or the doctors and was consistent, on the face of it, with automatism. But,
what the doctors said about that evidence which they had heard him give was that his
account of the facts which he had given in evidence to the jury was not physically
possible. I will read one short passage from the summing-up:

> 'In the first place we just cannot accept that you are going to stay asleep for so long
> when a man is trying to strangle you and you are delivering a whole series of blows
> all over his body and face with a knife. [I interpolate here to say that this is the
> judge's précis of what the doctors were saying to the jury. It goes on:] We just
> cannot accept it, but if we think that you are so deeply asleep that this is a
> conceivable state of affairs, then you are not going to come to very quickly so that
> you are awake for the end of the sequence and, indeed, awake with a knife in your
> hand. As one of them put it, you can't have it both ways. You are either so
> extraordinarily deeply asleep it would take you up to half an hour to come round,
> or the more likely thing were if some drunken man comes barging into your small
> bedroom at night it wakes you up. Well, there it is but that was the way they were
> putting the matter. There it is.'

That is the only passage I need read from the direction.

I now turn to the grounds of appeal. They run as follows: first, it is said that the judge
erred in ruling that counsel for the Crown should be allowed to cross-examine the
applicant on the statements he made to each of the psychiatrists. Secondly, it is said the
judge erred in ruling that counsel for the Crown should be allowed to call the psychiatrists
in rebuttal to express their opinions that neither (a) statements made to them by the
applicant whilst at Brixton prison nor (b) the evidence given by him at his trial were
consistent with his defence of automatism while asleep.

Counsel for the applicant, who argued the application before us with his usual clarity
and with commendable skill, puts the argument in this way: first, he submits that before
a witness can be cross-examined as to a previous inconsistent statement made by him
under s 4 of Mr Denman's Act[1], it must be shown that that statement is admissible. Put
in another way, it must be shown the statement is not inadmissible for reasons other than

---

1   The Criminal Procedure Act 1865

that it is hearsay. I do not think anyone would quarrel with that initial proposition. As
a he points out correctly, the statements which are in question in the present case are the
statements made to the doctors. Those statements were put to the applicant in cross-
examination and he admitted he had made them to those doctors. Counsel for the
applicant submits they were not admissible for a variety of reasons. His primary reason
is that they were as a matter of law not admissible because the statements were made
under what he describes as 'the seal of confidence' in the doctor/patient relationship.
b That relationship, he says, is in form this: the doctor is invited to examine the prisoner
as an independent expert who will provide information for the use of the court, if it is
required, on the man's mental condition. Counsel submits that in those circumstances
it is a confidential report which as a matter of law cannot be adduced in evidence unless
the defendant himself lets it in by raising the question of insanity or diminished
responsibility. Counsel for the applicant bases that argument on two decisions. First,
c the decision of the House of Lords in *D v National Society for the Prevention of Cruelty to
Children*[1]. That was a civil action and although, of course, the matters which are there are
binding so far as civil actions are concerned, it seems to us that those rules may have little
application in the criminal context with which we are now dealing. Let me just read for
the purposes of this judgment the headnote[2]:

d   '*Held*, allowing the appeal . . . that a similar immunity from disclosure of their
      identity in civil proceedings should be extended to those who gave information
      about neglect or ill-treatment of children to a local authority or the N.S.P.C.C. to
      that which the law allowed to police informers, viz., that the identity of the
      informer might not be disclosed, whether by discovery, interrogatories, or questions
      at trial, the public interests served by preserving the anonymity of both classes of
      informants being analogous . . . Confidentiality does not of itself provide a ground
e   of non-disclosure of the nature of the information or the identity of the informant
      if either of those matters would assist the court to ascertain relevant facts, nor is it
      the basis of all privilege from disclosure of documents or information in legal
      proceedings.'

Counsel for the applicant directed our attention to a passage of the judgment of Lord
f Denning MR in the Court of Appeal. He dissented in the Court of Appeal but as their
Lordships in the House of Lords reversed the decision of the Court of Appeal, it is
suggested that the dictum of Lord Denning MR may have more effect than otherwise
would be the case. We do not find that dictum helpful. What that case decided and no
more was that informers, whether they be informers to the police or to the National
Society for the Prevention of Cruelty to Children or otherwise, are in a special category
g so far as the protection from discovery of their identity is concerned. It seems to us that
the case is not helpful so far as the problem with which we are faced here is concerned.
The next case is the decision in 1958 of *R v Howard*[3]. It is a slightly odd report. The
headnote does not seem precisely to reflect the contents of the judgment which was the
judgment of Lord Goddard CJ[3]:

h   'It is undesirable that the report of a psychiatrist who has examined a prisoner in
      custody should be given over to the prosecution or the defence unless a question of
      insanity is raised. Where no such question is raised, it is not proper for counsel to
      use such a report for the purpose of examination or cross-examination.'

The passage to which counsel particularly referred reads as follows[4]:

      'It is not for this court to say whether psychiatrists are to examine persons in

j _____

1   [1977] 1 All ER 589, [1978] AC 171
2   [1978] AC 171 at 172
3   (1957) 42 Cr App R 23
4   42 Cr App R 23 at 26–27

prison or not; that is a matter for the Secretary of State and the Regulations. But what we do say is if an attempt is made to use a psychiatrist's report by reading from it to a prisoner, that would not be a proper thing to do. If, in the opinion of the prosecution or in the opinion of the defence the psychiatrist can give material evidence, the psychiatrist must be called and then the question can be decided whether, if he is called by the prosecution to prove an admission made by the prisoner, a statement can properly be given in evidence or whether it might have been given under the seal of confidence or in consequence of a question which would violate the Judges' Rules. In the opinion of the court it would be very much better if psychiatrists' reports were regarded as confidential and were not given to the prosecution or the defence unless the question of insanity is raised and the evidence is material. We cannot find anything wrong was done here with regard to the psychiatrist's report.'

There it is. The appeal in that case was dismissed. It is not altogether clear, perhaps, on what basis that took place, but the fact remains that events have overtaken that decision because if one turns to the rules which govern the examination of prisoners (in this case, medically) in prison[1], one finds r 28(1) which was apparently amended in 1962 which was, in time, after the decision in R v Howard[2]:

'A report will be submitted to the Director of Public Prosecutions of the mental condition of the prisoner as soon as possible after his committal for trial, as it is the general practice of the Director to supply copies of such reports to the defence who may require time for enquiries.'

We are told that what in fact happens is that five copies of these reports are made. The court's administrator gets those five copies and it is his job to distribute them. Generally speaking, the prosecution get a copy, the defence get a copy; it is sent almost invariably without any request from them but it is certainly sent to them immediately if a request is made. The other copies are, of course, available for the judge and the court file. But in these days, and, certainly, since the defence of diminished responsibility became available, it seems to us that the practice which was adumbrated in R v Howard[2] no longer holds good. It seems to us there is no foundation for the primary submission of counsel for the applicant that this examination was under a seal of confidentiality and no warrant for the suggestion that there is some rule of law which makes these reports in the circumstances which we have here inadmissible as a matter of law.

The next point he made is this: as a matter of discretion these reports should not be admitted. In effect, he says this: that in order to be admissible at all the reports must be relevant; that is to say, relevant to some issue which the jury have to determine. He submits that, since there was no question of insanity or diminished responsibility, automatism or not was a matter which could and should be decided by the jury in the light of their own experience and they should not be assisted by medical or expert evidence as to the state of mind of the applicant. That being so, he suggests the doctors' evidence was irrelevant and, on that basis, should not have been admitted.

Here, again, he cites a number of authorities. First was the decision of this court in R v Chard[3]:

'Where no issue of insanity, diminished responsibility or mental illness has arisen and it is conceded on the medical evidence that the defendant is entirely normal, it is not permissible to call a medical witness to state how, in his opinion, the defendant's mind operated at the time of the alleged crime with regard to the question of intent.'

---

1 Home Office Instructions: Prisons Standing Orders 8A (unconvicted prisoners charged with murder)
2 (1957) 42 Cr App R 23
3 (1972) 56 Cr App R 268

He referred to a passage in Roskill LJ's judgment[1]:

a   '[Counsel for the defendant] was unable to cite any authority in support of that proposition, not altogether surprisingly, for with the greatest respect to his argument, it seems to this Court his submission, if accepted, would involve the Court admitting medical evidence in every case not where there was an issue, for example, of insanity or diminished responsibility but where the sole issue which the jury had to consider, as happens in scores of different kinds of cases, was the question

b   of intent . . . one purpose of jury trials is to bring into the jury box a body of men and women who are able to judge ordinary day-to-day questions by their own standards, that is, the standards in the eyes of the law of theoretically ordinary reasonable men and women. That is something which they are well able by their ordinary experience to judge for themselves. Where the matters in issue go outside that experience and they are invited to deal with someone supposedly abnormal, for

c   example, supposedly suffering from insanity or diminished responsibility, then plainly in such a case they are entitled to the benefit of expert evidence.'

There is a further decision very much to the same effect which we do not find it necessary to cite in detail. I mention it simply for the purpose of completeness. That is *R v Turner*[2].

d   So, the question seems to be whether or not the applicant exhibited the type of abnormality in relation to automatism that would render it proper and, indeed, desirable for the jury to have expert help in reaching their conclusion. It seems to us without the benefit of authority that that is clearly the case. This type of automatism, sleepwalking, call it what you like, is not something, we think, which is within the realm of the ordinary juryman's experience. It is something on which, speaking for ourselves as

e   judges, we should like help were we to have to decide it and we do not see why a jury should be deprived of that type of help. We are assisted to that view by a passage in the judgment of Devlin J in *Hill v Baxter*[3].

Before coming to that passage, it is worthwhile just examining what the facts of that case were. The charge was one of dangerous driving and what Mr Baxter who was the alleged driver of the motor car had done was to drive across a road junction at fast speed

f   and come into collision with a car being driven at right angles to his own. Mr Baxter then carried on for a short distance and the car then overturned. A police constable came to the scene and found Mr Baxter in a dazed condition and took him to the hospital. In short, what Mr Baxter alleged at the trial was that he was not conscious of what he was doing. He was driving as an automaton and, accordingly, in the strict meaning of the word, he could not have been said to have been driving at all. Despite counsel for the

g   applicant's endeavours to distinguish that case from the present one, that is precisely, it seems to us, what the applicant here himself is saying. He is saying that, although there is no doubt that the hand which held the knife which inflicted the 26 stab wounds on Mr Montgomery was his, his mind did not go with the act and, ergo, in law it could not be said to be his act. What Devlin J said about this matter was[3]:

h   'I agree that the conclusion which this court has reached does not mean that the justices have acted in any way perversely. We have been told that the chairman of the justices was a medical man and it may be he felt able to draw inferences from the evidence which are not apparent to a layman. But judges of all kinds sit as laymen and not as experts and verdicts of all kinds must be given according to the evidence. I do not doubt that there are genuine cases of automatism and the like, but I do not see how laymen can safely attempt without the help of some medical

j   or scientific evidence to distinguish the genuine from the fraudulent.'

---

1   (1972) 56 Cr App R 268 at 270
2   [1975] 1 All ER 70, [1975] QB 834
3   [1958] 1 All ER 193 at 197, [1958] 1 QB 277 at 285

Accordingly, it seems to us this was a case where the jury were entitled to have the
benefit of medical evidence and the judge was right on that basis at any rate to admit the
evidence in question as he did. *a*

The next point taken by counsel for the applicant is that, in any event, it was unfair to
allow this evidence to be used. Now, we are making the assumption without by any
means deciding the matter or even suggesting it may be correct, we are making the
assumption that a judge is entitled to exclude evidence if he thinks it has been gathered
unfairly or illegally. That is a question which, we are told, is at the moment under *b*
consideration by the House of Lords in a case called *R v Sang*[1]. But, on the assumption
that there is that discretion, ought it to be exercised in favour of the applicant in the
present case? It is suggested the applicant submitted himself to a medical examination
on the basis that the results would be made available to the court and the jury only if he
raised the defence of insanity or diminished responsibility. Accordingly, when the
evidence was given on the defence of automatism being raised that was, so to speak, a *c*
breach of confidence and was a dirty trick and the court should have prevented that
evidence from being given. The authority for that proposition is another decision of this
court in *R v Payne*[2]. That was a case where the appellant had been taken to a police
station on suspicion that he was unfit to drive a motor car by reason of the drink that he
had taken. He was asked if he was prepared to be examined by a doctor and he was told
it was no part of the doctor's duty to examine him in order to give an opinion as to his *d*
unfitness to drive. On that basis the defendant consented to be examined and, then, at
the trial the doctor gave evidence he was unfit to drive by reason of the drink he had
consumed. The court there quashed the conviction on the basis that the judge in his
discretion should not have allowed that evidence to have been given.

This is a case of doubtful validity and may, as a result of the House of Lord's opinion
in *R v Sang*[1], be overruled. However that may be it seems to us that the circumstances *e*
there were entirely different. The evidence was given on a basis which the defendant
had been promised it would not be given. Here, the applicant knew that the medical
evidence from the psychiatrists, if it were given at all, would be given in relation to any
abnormality in his mental condition and that is exactly what happened. True the mental
condition was not one of insanity or of diminished responsibility but it was one of
automatism and that seems to us to be a sufficiently abnormal mental condition to *f*
prevent the evidence from having any taint of unfairness.

The next two points which counsel for the applicant makes are these: he says, first the
statements made to the psychiatrists were in breach of the judges' rules. Secondly, he
says it was not sufficiently demonstrated that the statements were made voluntarily by
the applicant to the doctors. Now, the difficulty there is this, that this particular point
was not taken at the trial below. If it had been, the judge in the absence of the jury *g*
would have had to determine whether the judges' rules had been broken and whether it
had been shown by the Crown the statements had been made voluntarily by the
applicant. Doing the best we can, we have tried to gauge what would have happened if
such an enquiry had been made. It seems to us quite clear that any decision on that
matter would have gone against the applicant. First, there is, as far as we can see, no
evidence at all that the statements were other than voluntary. Secondly, so far as the *h*
judges' rules are concerned, we very much doubt whether there was any breach of them
but it does seem to us that this was plainly a case where the statements would nevertheless
have been admitted despite any such breach. The fundamental question, it seems to us,
is really that of automatism, a mental condition on which the jury is entitled to have
expert help.

If so, and it seems to us that is the case, the rest follows: the doctors can give evidence *j*
as to their opinions. They can give evidence as to the facts on which those opinions are
based and one of those facts may be what they were told by the applicant whom they
examined. If that is right, it follows the applicant himself is entitled to be able to say

---

1   [1979] 2 All ER 1222, [1979] 3 WLR 263
2   [1963] 1 All ER 848, [1963] 1 WLR 637

whether or not he admits that he did tell the doctors those things. Although we think
that point (a) which should have been decided first was decided second and point (b)
which should have been decided second was decided first, these considerations
nevertheless hold good. For those reasons it seems to us the submissions of counsel for
the applicant do not succeed and, accordingly, this application is dismissed.

We grant leave to appeal, treating the hearing as the appeal. The appeal is dismissed.

Appeal dismissed.

*6th July. The court refused leave to appeal to the House of Lords but certified under s 33(2) of the
Criminal Appeal Act 1968 that the following points of law of general public importance were
involved in the decision: (a) whether things said by a prisoner in custody on a charge of murder
to a psychiatrist preparing a report for the court of trial are admissible when neither insanity nor
diminished responsibility is in issue; (b) whether, when the defendant alleges that he committed the
act constituting an indictable offence while he was asleep, any issue is thereby raised before the jury
on which expert psychiatric testimony can be admitted.*

*11th October. The Appeal Committee of the House of Lords (Lord Diplock, Lord Fraser of
Tullybelton and Lord Russell of Killowen) refused leave to appeal.*

Solicitors: *Registrar of Criminal Appeals*; *Director of Public Prosecutions*.

Howard Roberts Esq   Barrister.

Practice Direction

COMPANIES COURT

*Practice – Companies Court – Chief clerk – Applications and orders – Exercise of functions by
chief clerk – Hearing of applications by and adjournment to registrar.*

1. It has been decided that the chief clerk of the Companies Court may assist the
registrar in the hearing of the following applications and making orders thereon: (a)
applications by the Official Receiver to consider reports of first meetings of creditors and
contributories, to dispense with the submission of statements of affairs and to extend the
time for holding first meetings of creditors and contributories; (b) applications to extend
the time for filing affidavits verifying winding-up petitions; (c) applications to extend
the date of hearing of winding-up petitions; (d) applications for leave to amend
proceedings; and (e) applications for substituted service within the jurisdiction by post
only.

2. The evidence (if any) in support of any such application must be lodged in Room
312, Thomas More Building, and will be considered by the chief clerk who will deal
provisionally with the application. The registrar will initial the note of any order made
before the order takes effect.

3. The chief clerk may also without reference to the registrar (a) give leave to file
affidavits notwithstanding any irregularity in their form, and (b) sign certificates of
attendances in chambers for the purpose of taxation of costs.

4. Any party may require the application to be heard by the registrar instead of the
chief clerk; and when an application has been heard by the chief clerk any party
dissatisfied with the chief clerk's decision may thereupon require the matter to be
adjourned to the registrar who will consider it afresh.

5. Nothing in this Practice Direction will prevent the registrar from dealing with any
of the matters listed above if it is more appropriate or convenient for him to do so.

By the direction of the Vice-Chancellor.

15th October 1979

N W L Ltd v Woods
N W L Ltd v Nelson and another

HOUSE OF LORDS

LORD DIPLOCK, LORD FRASER OF TULLYBELTON AND LORD SCARMAN

25th, 26th JULY, 25th OCTOBER 1979

Trade dispute – Acts done in contemplation or furtherance of trade dispute – Meaning of trade dispute – Dispute between shipowners and union – Attempts by union to induce port workers in England and elsewhere to break their contracts of employment and withdraw services from ship unless owners agreeing with union terms and conditions of employment of crew – Policy of union to compel owners by industrial action to employ crews on standard terms at union rates – Ship's crew not in dispute with owners – Whether dispute between owners and union a trade dispute – Whether acts done in contemplation or furtherance of trade dispute – Trade Union and Labour Relations Act 1974, ss 13(1) (as amended by the Trade Union and Labour Relations (Amendment) Act 1976, s 3(2)), 29(1).

Injunction – Interlocutory – Trade dispute – Claim by party against whom injunction sought that he had acted in contemplation or furtherance of trade dispute – Likelihood of that party's succeeding at trial of action in establishing defence to action – Matters to be considered by court before granting injunction – Weight to be given by court to likelihood of defendants establishing at trial that action in contemplation or furtherance of dispute connected with terms and conditions of employment – Trade Union and Labour Relations Act 1974, ss 13(1) (as amended by the Trade Union and Labour Relations (Amendment) Act 1976, s 3(2)), 17(2) (as amended by the Employment Protection Act 1975, s 125, Sch 16, Part III, para 6).

A Hong Kong company with a Swedish controlling interest owned a vessel sailing under a flag of convenience. The vessel was engaged by the plaintiffs on chartered voyages worldwide and was manned by a Hong Kong crew who were paid relatively low wages by European standards. In June 1979, when the vessel arrived at Redcar to discharge its cargo, W, a representative of the International Transport Federation ('ITF'), an international federation of trade unions representing transport workers in 85 countries whose policy was to compel owners of vessels sailing under flags of convenience to employ officers and seamen on standard terms and at ITF rates of wages, attempted to persuade the port workers at Redcar to 'black' the vessel unless the shipowners signed an agreement with ITF that they would enter into articles with the crew on the standard ITF terms. The crew were content with their existing articles and were not in dispute with the owners. The owners issued a writ ('the first action') against W seeking an injunction to restrain the blacking, and pending the trial of the action applied for an interlocutory injunction in the terms of the writ. An interlocutory injunction was granted by the judge but it was discharged by the Court of Appeal. The owners appealed to the House of Lords. Meanwhile, although ITF's further attempts to black the vessel at Redcar failed, the owners were concerned that the vessel might be blacked elsewhere. Accordingly they brought an action ('the second action') against N and L, two other officials of ITF, seeking an injunction similar to that sought in the first action and also an interlocutory injunction pending the trial of the action. The judge's refusal to grant an interlocutory injunction was upheld by the Court of Appeal. The owners appealed to the House of Lords. The two appeals were consolidated. The questions for consideration of the House were (i) whether the dispute between the shipowners and the union officials was a 'trade dispute', within s 29(1)[a] of the Trade Union and Labour Relations Act 1974, (ii) if it was, whether the officials' demands and actions were 'in contemplation or furtherance of a trade dispute', within s 13(1)[b] of that

---

a   Section 29(1), is set out at p 620 f to h, post
b   Section 13(1) is set out at p 620 c d, post

Act, and (iii) what effect s 17(2)[c] of that Act had on applications for interlocutory
injunctions in such cases.

Held – (i) For the purposes of s 29 of the 1974 Act, ITF were, by virtue of s 29(4),
'workers' notwithstanding that they were an international federation of trade unions,
and since the dispute between ITF and the shipowners was therefore a dispute between
'employers and workers' in connection with 'terms and conditions of employment' it
followed that it was a 'trade dispute' within s 29(1)(a). In so far as the Hong Kong crew
supported the shipowners in their resistance to ITF's demands the dispute might also
have qualified as a dispute between 'workers and workers' within sub-s (1) (see p 621 *f* to
h, p 631 *a b* and p 626 *g h*, post).

(ii) For the purposes of s 13(1) of the 1974 Act, the making and maintaining of threats
of blacking and the attempts by W to induce the port workers at Redcar to adopt such a
course were acts done 'in furtherance of a trade dispute' between ITF and the shipowners
connected with the terms and conditions of employment of existing and future crews of
the owners' ship, and the fact that the ultimate object of ITF's campaign of blacking
vessels sailing under flags of convenience was to drive flags of convenience off the seas did
not prevent the immediate dispute between ITF and the shipowners from being a
dispute connected with the terms and conditions of employment of workers who were
or might become members of the ship's crew, since the predominant subject-matter of
the dispute was irrelevant: all that was required was that there was a genuine connection
between the subject-matter of the dispute and the matters listed in s 29(1). However,
since one of the main commercial attractions of registering vessels under flags of
convenience was to facilitate the use of cheap labour to crew them, the ultimate object
of ITF's campaign was in fact connected with the terms and conditions of employment
of seamen. Furthermore, a dispute did not cease to be a dispute connected with the
terms and conditions of employment merely because the demands made by the union
on the employer regarding terms and conditions of employment were unreasonable or
commercially impracticable. Nor did it matter that the demand was made and the
dispute pursued with more than one object in mind, and that of those objects the
predominant one was not the improvement of the terms and conditions of employment
of those workers to whom the demand related (see p 621 *h* to p 622 *e*, p 624 *a* to *d*, p 626
g h and p 631 *c* to *g* and *h* to p 632 *a e f*, post); *Conway v Wade* [1908–10] All ER Rep 344
explained; *Star Sea Transport Corpn v Slater, The Camilla M* [1979] 1 Lloyd's Rep 26
overruled.

(iii) In exercising its discretion whether to grant an interlocutory injunction pending
the trial of an action, when the respondent claimed that he was acting in contemplation
or furtherance of a trade dispute and accordingly was immune from liability for tort by
virtue of s 13 of the 1974 Act, the degree of likelihood of the defendant's succeeding in
establishing that defence, to which the court was required to have regard by s 17(2) of
that Act, was only one of the factors to be taken into consideration by the court, whether
(per Lord Diplock and Lord Fraser of Tullybelton) as one of the elements of the balance
of convenience or (per Lord Scarman) as a separate factor, the relative weight of which
might vary with the circumstances of the case. An injunction would ordinarily be
refused in cases where the defendant had shown that it was more likely than not that the
defence of statutory immunity would succeed, although where the consequences to the
plaintiff or others might be disastrous if an injunction were not granted a high degree of
probability that the defence of statutory immunity would succeed would have to be
established before the injunction would be refused. Since W, N and L had a virtual
certainty of establishing the defence of statutory immunity, the appeals would be
dismissed (p 624 *j* to p 625 *a*, p 626 *e* to *h*, p 627 *h* to p 628 *b*, p 629 *e* and p 633 *b* to p 634
a, post).

---

c   Section 17(2) is set out at p 621 *e*, post

Notes

For the legal liability of trade unions, see Supplement to 38 Halsbury's Laws (3rd Edn) para 677B.3.

For the Trade Union and Labour Relations Act 1974, s 13(1) (as substituted by the Trade Union and Labour Relations (Amendment) Act 1976, s 3(2)), see 46 Halsbury's Statutes (3rd Edn) 1941, for s 17(2) (as inserted by the Employment Protection Act 1975, s 125, Sch 16, Part III, para 6), see 45 ibid 2438, and for s 29(1) of the 1974 Act see 44 ibid 1779.

Cases referred to in opinions

American Cyanamid Co v Ethicon Ltd [1975] 1 All ER 504, [1975] AC 396, [1975] 2 WLR 316, [1975] RPC 513, HL, Digest (Cont Vol D) 536, *152a*.

Attorney-General v HRH Prince Ernest Augustus of Hanover [1957] 1 All ER 49, [1957] AC 436, [1957] 2 WLR 1, HL, 44 Digest (Repl) 241, *647*.

British Broadcasting Corpn v Hearn [1978] 1 All ER 111, [1977] 1 WLR 1004, CA.

Chill Foods (Scotland) Ltd v Cool Foods Ltd [1977] RPC 522, 1977 SLT 38.

Conway v Wade [1909] AC 506, [1908–10] All ER Rep 344, 78 LJKB 1025, 101 LT 248, HL, 45 Digest (Repl) 572, *1436*.

Edinburgh Magistrates v Edinburgh etc Railway Co (1847) 19 Scot Jur 421.

Free Church of Scotland (General Assembly) v Johnston (1905) 7 F (Ct of Sess) 517.

Huntley v Thornton [1957] 1 All ER 234, [1957] 1 WLR 321, 45 Digest (Repl) 565, *1396*.

Star Sea Transport Corpn v Slater, The Camilla M [1979] 1 Lloyd's Rep 26, CA.

Stratford (JT) & Son Ltd v Lindley [1964] 3 All ER 102, [1965] AC 269, [1964] 3 WLR 541, [1964] 2 Lloyd's Rep 133, HL, 45 Digest (Repl) 563, *1389*.

Interlocutory appeals

By a writ issued on 18th June 1979 the plaintiffs, N W L Ltd ('the shipowners'), a company incorporated in Hong Kong in which the controlling interest was Swedish, brought an action ('the first action') seeking an injunction restraining the defendant, James Woods, an official of the International Transport Workers Federation ('ITF'), from seeking to interfere with the lawful discharge of the shipowners' vessel mv Nawala at Redcar or elsewhere or from sailing from such port thereafter, and/or interfering with discharging operations, tugs, pilots or other necessary services to the vessel, and/or causing or encouraging stevedores and/or employees of tug operators and/or pilots and/or other persons to break their contracts of employment by refusing to render those services. By a summons issued on the same day the shipowners claimed an interlocutory injunction pending the trial of the action in the terms of the writ. On 19th June 1979 Donaldson J granted the shipowners an injunction ordering 'that the defendant, his servants or agents be restrained from issuing instructions to and/or encouraging stevedores and/or tug operators and/or their employees and/or pilots or others concerned with the discharge and/or free passage and operation of the mv Nawala to break their contracts of employment or otherwise howsoever interfere with such discharge, free passage or operation'. The defendant appealed and on 21st June 1979 the Court of Appeal (Lord Salmon and Stephenson LJ) allowed the appeal and discharged the injunction, giving their reasons for so doing on 29th June. The shipowners appealed to the House of Lords with leave of the Court of Appeal.

The injunction having been discharged by the Court of Appeal on 21st June the ITF attempted to 'black' the shipowners vessel at Redcar but failed in their attempts because the port workers' union were opposed to the blacking. Being concerned that ITF would black their vessel elsewhere the shipowners brought an action ('the second action') against two other ITF officials, John Nelson and Brian Laughton, seeking an injunction in the terms of that granted by Donaldson J in the first action and also sought an interlocutory injunction pending the trial of the action. On 26th June Donaldson J refused their application and on 3rd July the Court of Appeal (Lord Denning MR, Waller and Eveleigh LJJ) affirmed his decision. The shipowners appealed to the House of Lords *a* with leave of the Court of Appeal. The two appeals were consolidated. The facts are set out in the opinion of Lord Diplock.

Roger Buckley QC, Christopher Clarke and *Timothy Charlton* for the shipowners.
Cyril W F Newman and *M Gair* for the defendants.

At the conclusion of the argument their Lordships dismissed the appeals stating that they would give their reasons for judgment later.

b 25th October. The following opinions were delivered.

LORD DIPLOCK. My Lords, in these consolidated appeals the plaintiffs ('the shipowners'), a Hong Kong company all of whose shares are beneficially owned in Sweden, seek to prevent officials of the International Transport Workers' Federation ('ITF') from inducing port workers in England and elsewhere to 'black' their vessel, the
c Nawala.

In an endeavour to stop the blacking before the damage had been done, they applied in each of the actions for interlocutory injunctions. In the first action, against the defendant Woods, Donaldson J granted an interlocutory injunction, thinking that the judgment of the Court of Appeal in *Star Sea Transport Corpn v Slater, The Camilla M*[1] compelled him to do so. This injunction was discharged by a Court of Appeal consisting
d of Lord Salmon and Stephenson LJ. In the subsequent action against the defendants Nelson and Laughton, Donaldson J refused the shipowners' application and his refusal was upheld by a Court of Appeal consisting of Lord Denning MR, Waller and Eveleigh LJJ. Against these two decisions of the Court of Appeal that the shipowners are not entitled to interlocutory injunctions, these appeals (now consolidated) have been brought to your Lordships' House by leave of the Court of Appeal.

e The cases arise out of the threat by ITF that industrial action will be taken against the Nawala unless the shipowners conform to ITF's requirements as to the wages and conditions of employment of the members of its crew. ITF, which has its headquarters in London, is an international federation of national trade unions, in 85 different countries, representing transport workers of all kinds, including seamen. As is well known in shipping circles and to the commercial judges, it has a policy as respects vessels
f which sail under what it describes as 'flags of convenience', an expression which it uses with a much extended meaning as covering all vessels that are registered in a country which is not the domicile of the beneficial owner of the vessel. That policy is described in detail in the judgment of the Court of Appeal in the action against Woods, and is placed in its worldwide perspective in the judgment of Donaldson J in the action against Nelson and Laughton. It may be summarised as follows.

g ITF endeavours to exert such 'industrial muscle' as its affiliated national unions are prepared to exercise at its behest in order to compel the owners of vessels sailing under flags of convenience (in this extended sense) to employ their officers and seamen on terms of standard articles prepared by ITF and providing for wages at rates said to be the middle rates paid to ships' crews under collective agreements negotiated by national trade unions for ships on their national registries in European countries outside the
h communist bloc. An alternative way of buying off industrial action inspired by ITF is to change the vessel's flag by transferring its registry to that of the country of domicile of its beneficial owner, whereupon he will be obliged to negotiate terms of employment and wages of crews with the national seamen's union affiliated to the ITF. The ultimate aim is to abolish throughout the world the use by shipowners of flags of convenience as ITF defines them.

j Your Lordships are in no way concerned with the economic wisdom or the moral justification of this policy. The evidence in the instant appeals confirms what the evidence in *The Camilla M*[1] suggested, that the policy does not command the approbation of seamen and their national trade unions in those countries of Asia which have

1 [1979] 1 Lloyd's Rep 26

traditionally formed the recruiting grounds for many thousands of seamen eager to serve under articles that provide for wages which, although much lower than those demanded by their European, North American and Australasian counterparts, are, nevertheless, much higher than anything that they could hope to earn in land-based work in their own countries. Their competitiveness as candidates for manning the merchant navies of the world depends on their cheapness. Their natural fear, as indicated by the evidence, is that if the competitiveness is reduced by forcing shipowners who employ them to pay to them wages at the middle rate paid to European seamen, their chances of sea-faring employment will be very much reduced. This readily accounts for the attitude taken up by the Indian crew in *The Camilla M*[1] and by the Hong Kong crew in the instant case.

The history of the Nawala which led to her selection as a target of ITF's campaign against flags of convenience and the way in which that campaign has been carried on against her up to 3rd July 1979 are set out in such vivid detail in the judgment of Lord Denning MR[2] delivered on that date, that, rather than repeat it in less readable style, I recommend reference to it direct and will restrict myself to stating in summary form such facts as are essential in order to identify the questions of law which fall to be decided by your Lordships. The Nawala did not, however, remain stationary while the lawyers were arguing about her; nor has she done so between 3rd July 1979 and the hearing in the Appellate Committee of the shipowners' appeal to this House. A further chapter to Lord Denning's saga of the Nawala must also be recounted briefly.

The Nawala is a large bulk-carrier with a capacity of more than 120,000 tonnes dwt. She was built in Germany in 1974 for Scandinavian shipowners and entered on the Norwegian registry. She was manned by a Norwegian crew at rates of wages that had been negotiated by their national trade union and are among the highest current in European countries. When the slump in the freight market came she was trading under the Norwegian flag but at a loss. Her owners were unable to meet the mortgage payments and sold her to buyers based in Sweden, who for the purpose of transferring her to the Hong Kong registry formed a Hong Kong company of whose shares a Swedish company was beneficial owner. The Hong Kong company became the nominal owner of the vessel, and a Hong Kong crew was engaged at very much lower wages to take the place of the Norwegian crew. It was not necessary for the Nawala to visit Hong Kong in order to effect the change of flag or to engage the Hong Kong crew. The crew was engaged there by an agency that was officially licensed in the colony to do so. The crew signed their articles there and were flown to Hamburg where they joined the vessel.

The Nawala, under her new flag and manned by her new and much lower paid crew, was engaged by her new owners on chartered voyages world-wide. Early in 1979 she had berthed at Redcar with a cargo of Australian iron ore for British Steel. A representative of ITF boarded her and demanded of the master that he sign on behalf of the shipowners an agreement with ITF that they would enter into articles with the crew on standard ITF terms. The demand was refused. When she arrived at Redcar on her next consecutive voyage with a similar cargo on 15th June 1979, Mr Woods, who was an official of both ITF and the English National Seamen's Union, repeated the demand and said that if it were not complied with the Nawala would be 'blacked' by the port workers. He, and later Mr Nelson and Mr Laughton, attempted to persuade port workers who belonged to other unions affiliated to ITF to refuse to allow her to enter her berth, to unload her if she got there or to let her leave it. In the result these attempts, when they were resumed after the interlocutory injunction granted by Donaldson J had been lifted by Lord Salmon and Stephenson LJ on 21st June 1979, were unsuccessful because they were resisted by the trade unions to which the port workers belonged. So the Nawala succeeded in unloading her cargo and sailed away from Redcar to Narvik to load a cargo of Norwegian iron ore for carriage to the Netherlands.

She was off Narvik waiting for a berth when the shipowners' appeal against the refusal

---

1   [1979] 1 Lloyd's Rep 26
2   [1979] IRLR 321

of Donaldson J of an interlocutory injunction against the defendants Nelson and
Laughton was heard by the Court of Appeal, and ITF had, by telegrams despatched from
London and a personal visit by the defendant Nelson, persuaded the national trade union
there, the Scandinavian Transport Workers' Federation, to black her. On that very day,
3rd July 1979, a judge of the appropriate court of first instance in Narvik stayed the
shipowners' application to prevent the Norwegian blacking, apparently to await the final
determination of the English litigation; but on 12th July the stay was removed by an
appellate court and the case remitted to the judge at Narvik for further consideration.
On 19th July 1979 he granted the shipowners a temporary injunction against the
blacking of the Nawala at Narvik. She proceeded to her loading berth, loaded a full cargo
and left on 22nd July bound for Ijmuiden in the Netherlands. The stop press news,
received on 26th July, the last day of the hearing before this House, was that the Dutch
trade unions, of which port workers at Ijmuiden were members, were threatening to
black the Nawala there. If she is not prevented from carrying out the future voyages for
which she is already fixed she will be returning to discharge a cargo of iron ore at a port
in England, but not until the autumn of this year.

The interlocutory injunction which the shipowners seek against all three defendants
is in the terms of that granted by Donaldson J against the defendant Woods, but
discharged by the Court of Appeal, viz an injunction against:

'Issuing instructions to and/or encouraging stevedores and/or tug operators and/or
their employees and/or pilots or others concerned with the discharge and/or free
passage and operation of the M.V. Nawala to break their contracts of employment
or otherwise howsoever interfere with such discharge, free passage or operation.'

My Lords, these words are not restricted to prohibiting instructions or encouragement
given within the jurisdiction to parties to contracts of employment made and to be
performed within the jurisdiction. Questions of great nicety in private international law
might arise if it were sought to enforce this injunction in respect of instructions or
encouragement of port workers employed in Narvik to 'black' the Nawala there or of
port workers anywhere else outside the jurisdiction of the English court. The possible
significance of such jurisdictional problems appears to have been overlooked by the
Court of Appeal in *The Camilla M*[1] where the port at which the blacking of the vessel was
enjoined was Glasgow, a place outside the jurisdiction of the English courts.

However, I do not think it necessary for your Lordships to enter on a consideration of
these questions now. The jurisdiction of an English court to entertain, against a
defendant on whom its process can be served within the jurisdiction, an action for an
allegedly wrongful act committed *outside* the jurisdiction is dependent on the act being
not only unlawful in the place where it was committed but also being one which, had it
been committed in England, would have amounted to a tort in English law. So, if what
the defendants in the instant case did at Redcar had succeeded in procuring the blacking
of the Nawala there, but even then would not have constituted a tortious act in English
law, an English court would have no jurisdiction to entertain an action based on similar
conduct by the defendants at Narvik, and a fortiori would have no jurisdiction to
entertain a quia timet action to restrain it.

I understand your Lordships to be of the opinion, which I also share, that even if the
defendants had succeeded in inducing port workers at Redcar to break their contracts of
employment and to black the Nawala, they would not have committed any tort in
English law, because their conduct was excused by s 13 of the Trade Union and Labour
Relations Act 1974, as amended by s 3(2) of the Trade Union and Labour Relations
(Amendment) Act 1976. So any similar conduct outside England cannot be the subject-
matter of any action, quia timet or otherwise, which English courts have jurisdiction to
entertain.

I turn then to the crucial question in this appeal which, since it relates to an application

---

1   [1979] 1 Lloyd's Rep 26

for an interlocutory injunction, not a final one, I take it to be this: have the defendants shown on the evidence such a likelihood of establishing that what they did or threatened to do at Redcar was done or threatened in contemplation or furtherance of a trade dispute, as would justify the court in exercising its discretion in favour of refusing the injunction sought?

The relevant sections of the 1974 Act are s 13 which confers the immunity for acts done in contemplation or furtherance of trade disputes, s 29 which says what is meant by a trade dispute, s 17 which imposes restrictions on the grant of interlocutory injunctions and s 28 which makes it clear that a federation of trade unions such as ITF is itself a trade union within the meaning of the Act. The first three of these sections deserve to be reproduced in full:

'13. *Acts in contemplation or furtherance of trade disputes.* (1) An act done by a person in contemplation or furtherance of a trade dispute shall not be actionable in tort on the ground only—(a) that it induces another person to break a contract or interferes or induces any other person to interfere with its performance; or (b) that it consists in his threatening that a contract (whether one to which he is a party or not) will be broken or its performance interfered with, or that he will induce another person to break a contract or to interfere with its performance.

'(2) For the avoidance of doubt it is hereby declared that an act done by a person in contemplation or furtherance of a trade dispute is not actionable in tort on the ground only that it is an interference with the trade, business or employment of another person, or with the right of another person to dispose of his capital or his labour as he wills.

'(3) For the avoidance of doubt it is hereby declared that—(a) an act which by reason of subsection (1) or (2) above is itself not actionable; (b) a breach of contract in contemplation or furtherance of a trade dispute; shall not be regarded as the doing of an unlawful act or as the use of unlawful means for the purposes of establishing liability in tort.

'(4) An agreement or combination by two or more persons to do or procure the doing of any act in contemplation or furtherance of a trade dispute shall not be actionable in tort if the act is one which, if done without any such agreement or combination, would not be actionable in tort.'

'29. *Meaning of trade dispute.* (1) In this Act "trade dispute" means a dispute between employers and workers, or between workers and workers, which is connected with one or more of the following, that is to say—(a) terms and conditions of employment, or the physical conditions in which any workers are required to work; (b) engagement or non-engagement, or termination or suspension of employment or the duties of employment, of one or more workers; (c) allocation of work or the duties of employment as between workers or groups of workers; (d) matters of discipline; (e) the membership or non-membership of a trade union on the part of a worker; (f) facilities for officials of trade unions; and (g) machinery for negotiation or consultation, and other procedures, relating to any of the foregoing matters, including the recognition by employers or employers' associations of the right of a trade union to represent workers in any such negotiation or consultation or in the carrying out of such procedures.

'(2) A dispute between a Minister of the Crown and any workers shall, notwithstanding that he is not the employer of those workers, be treated for the purposes of this Act as a dispute between an employer and those workers if the dispute relates—(a) to matters which have been referred for consideration by a joint body on which, by virtue of any provision made by or under any enactment, that Minister is represented; or (b) to matters which cannot be settled without that Minister exercising a power conferred on him by or under an enactment.

'(3) There is a trade dispute for the purposes of this Act even though it relates to matters occurring outside Great Britain.

'(4) A dispute to which a trade union or employers' association is a party shall be
treated for the purposes of this Act as a dispute to which workers or, as the case may
be, employers are parties.

'(5) An act, threat or demand done or made by one person or organisation against
another which, if resisted, would have led to a trade dispute with that other, shall,
notwithstanding that because that other submits to the act or threat or accedes to the
demand no dispute arises, be treated for the purposes of this Act as being done or
made in contemplation of a trade dispute with that other.

'(6) In this section—"employment" includes any relationship whereby one person
personally does work or performs services for another; "worker" in relation to a
dispute to which an employer is a party, includes any worker even if not employed
by that employer.'

'17. *Restriction on grant of ex parte injunctions and interdicts.* (1) Where an
application for an injunction or interdict is made to a court in the absence of the
party against whom the injunction or inderdict is sought or any representative of
his and that party claims, or in the opinion of the court would be likely to claim,
that he acted in contemplation or furtherance of a trade dispute, the court shall not
grant the injunction or interdict unless satisfied that all steps which in the
circumstances were reasonable have been taken with a view to securing that notice
of the application and an opportunity of being heard with respect to the application
have been given to that party.

'(2) It is hereby declared for the avoidance of doubt that where an application is
made to a court, pending the trial of an action, for an interlocutory injunction and
the party against whom the injunction is sought claims that he acted in
contemplation or furtherance of a trade dispute, the court shall, in exercising its
discretion whether or not to grant the injunction, have regard to the likelihood of
that party's succeeding at the trial of the action in establishing the matter or matters
which would, under any provision of section 13, 14(2) or 15 above, afford a defence
to the action.

'(3) Subsection (2) above shall not extend to Scotland.'

A 'trade dispute' is defined in s 29(1) by reference (a) to the parties to it and (b) to the
subject-matter with which it is connected. That in the instant case there was a dispute
between ITF and the shipowners at the time that the threats of blacking the Nawala at
Redcar were made is too plain for argument and sub-s (4) makes it clear that ITF qualifies
as 'workers' for the purpose of making it a 'dispute between employers and workers'
within the meaning of sub-s (1). What ITF were demanding and the shipowners were
resisting was that the crew employed on the Nawala should be employed at ITF rates of
wages under articles in ITF standard terms. That this is not a dispute in connection with
terms and conditions of employment seems to me to be simply unarguable. The fact
that the Hong Kong crew were content with their existing articles and were not in
dispute with the shipowners as to their own terms or conditions of employment is not,
in my view, material. To the extent that they supported the shipowners in their
resistance to ITF's demand the dispute may also have qualified as a dispute 'between
workers and workers' within the meaning of sub-s (1).

The next question is whether the threats of blacking and the attempts by the
defendants to induce port workers at Redcar to adopt this course were 'acts done in
contemplation or furtherance of that dispute' within the meaning of s 13(1). Here again,
but for the judgments in *The Camilla M*[1], I should have thought the contrary to be
unarguable. It is accepted by both sides that ITF would have withdrawn its threat to have
the Nawala blacked, and its attempts to persuade port workers to break their contracts
with their employers by doing so, if the shipowners had signed on either the existing

---

[1]   [1979] 1 Lloyd's Rep 26

crew or a fresh crew under articles in ITF's standard form at ITF's rates of wages and had
agreed to pay the existing crew the difference between their actual wages and wages at *a*
ITF rates from the date of their engagements to the date of signing their new articles. So
in any sensible meaning of the words, the making and maintenance of the threats and
the attempts was done 'in furtherance' of a dispute between ITF and the shipowners that
was connected with the terms and conditions of employment of existing and future
crews of the Nawala. Such was the view of all five members of the Court of Appeal by
whom the appeals in these two cases have been heard; but in order to give effect to that *b*
view it was necessary for them to distinguish the case from that of *The Camilla M*[1], an
embarrassment by which your Lordships are not affected.

It was submitted on behalf of the shipowners in the instant cases, as it had been in *The
Camilla M*[1], that the real object of ITF is to drive 'flags of convenience' (as they define
them) off the seas, so that every vessel is entered on the registry of the nation to which its
beneficial owner belongs; and that, it is suggested, is a political object and not what Lord *c*
Denning MR in *The Camilla M*[1] described as 'a legitimate trade object'. It may well be
that this is indeed the ultimate object of ITF's campaign of blacking vessels sailing under
flags of convenience unless their crews are engaged on ITF standard articles at ITF rates
of wages; but this, in my view, would not prevent the immediate dispute between ITF
and the shipowners in which the interlocutory injunctions are sought from being a
dispute connected with the terms and conditions of employment of those workers who *d*
were or might become members of the Nawala's crew. Furthermore in a case originating
in the commercial court it would be carrying judicial anchoretism too far if this House
were to feign ignorance of the fact that, apart from fiscal advantages, one of the main
commercial attractions of registering vessels under flags of convenience is that it
facilitates the use of cheap labour to man them. So even the ultimate object of ITF's
campaign is connected with the terms and conditions of employment of seamen. *e*

The facts in *The Camilla M*[1] differed from those in the instant case only to the extent
that the owners of the vessel, which sailed under the Liberian flag but was beneficially
owned by Greek nationals, had taken some unsuccessful steps to buy off the blacking by
the time the case reached the Court of Appeal. When the blacking had started she had
an Indian crew signed on under articles approved by the National Union of Seafarers of
India ('NUSI') of which the crew were members. NUSI was at that time affiliated to *f*
ITF. Under the threat of continued blacking, the owner of the Camilla M agreed with
ITF that the crew of the vessel should be engaged on new articles in ITF's standard form
at ITF rates of wages and that the members of the existing crew, whether re-engaged or
not, should be paid the difference between the actual wages paid to them and ITF rates
of wages from the commencement of their existing articles. The Indian crew of the
Camilla M with the backing of NUSI refused to enter into new articles, fearing, no doubt, *g*
that when their current engagement finished they would have little chance of re-
employment in competition with European seamen at the greatly increased rates of
pay. The owners discharged the Indian crew. To replace them they recruited in Piraeus
a Greek crew on the terms of standard Greek articles, the terms of which differed from
the ITF standard terms but were not, it was said, substantially less advantageous to the
crew members. ITF refused to accept this as sufficient compliance with what the owners *h*
had agreed to do; they insisted that any new crew should be engaged on ITF standard
terms. The newly-recruited Greek crew preferred the Greek articles on which they had
been engaged and refused to substitute ITF standard terms for them. So to comply with
ITF's requirements and thus obtain a lifting of the blacking, the owners, if the newly-
engaged Greek crew had persisted in their refusal to change to the ITF standard form of
articles, would have had to discharge that crew and to recruit yet another crew of seamen *j*
willing to sail under ITF standard articles.

1   [1979] 1 Lloyd's Rep 26

a The Court of Appeal (Lord Denning MR, Stephenson and Brandon LJJ) thought this to be an unreasonable demand which was not made with the interests of those who were actually members of the crew of the Camilla M in mind but was motivated exclusively or, at least, predominantly by ITF's dislike of flags of convenience. Lord Denning MR based his decision on his interpretation of the expression 'in contemplation or furtherance' of a trade dispute in s 13. He took the view that, having regard to the attitudes adopted first by the Indian and later by the Greek crew, what ITF persisted in demanding was

b virtually impossible of performance by the owners, and that it could be inferred from this that ITF was acting 'for some extraneous motive and not for any legitimate trade object'. This in his view prevented what they were doing from being acts done in furtherance of a trade dispute. Brandon LJ was of opinion that where there could be said to be two subject-matters of a dispute one of which did, and the other did not, fall within one of the descriptions in paras (a) to (g) of s 29(1), the dispute was not a trade dispute

c unless the predominant subject-matter fell within those paragraphs; and similar considerations as to what was the predominant object sought to be attained applied in deciding whether acts that were done with more than one object in mind were done in furtherance of a trade dispute or not.

        As authority for these propositions reliance was placed on the decision of this House in *Conway v Wade*[1], a case decided shortly after the passing of the Trade Disputes Act

d 1906. The definition of a trade dispute in that Act was much less extensive than in the 1974 Act and in particular a trade union itself could not be a party to one. The defendant Wade was a trade union official and not a workman, and the jury, by whom such cases were then tried, found that the only dispute was between Wade and the plaintiff Conway whom Wade was trying to get sacked from his employment to punish him for non-payment of a union fine, and that there was no dispute existing or contemplated between

e Conway and his fellow workers at the factory. On these findings it is not surprising that it was held that what Wade had done was not in contemplation of a trade dispute but in furtherance of his own dispute with Conway about the unpaid fine, a dispute in which, incidentally, he did not even have the support of the trade union of which he was only a subordinate official. It is not surprising either that in the course of the speeches Wade should have been referred to as an intermeddler and as a mischief-maker. But, since the

f amendments to the definition of trade disputes, trade unions acting through their officials can with impunity intermeddle with relationships between employers and workers and may initiate their own dispute with an employer as to the terms and conditions of employment even where, to use Lord Atkinson's phrase, 'perfect peace prevailed in the factory or establishment'. It would, in my view, be unwise to treat what was said 70 years ago by members of this House in *Conway v Wade*[1] as still

g authoritative. The modern legislation reflects the change of Parliamentary attitude towards trade unions whether one likes the change or not; in interpreting the legislation the judges must take account of it.

        My Lords, I would accept that there may be cases where strikes are called or refusals to perform contracts of employment in some particular respect are ordered by trade unions for political reasons that are unconnected with any of the subject-matters described in

h s 13(1). *British Broadcasting Corpn v Hearn*[2] provides an example of this. Union officials threatened that their members would refuse to allow the BBC to televise the cup final in such a way that it could be seen by viewers in South Africa. This was not a dispute connected with the terms and conditions of employment; but it could readily have been turned into one by a demand by the union that the contracts of employment of

j

---

1   [1909] AC 506, [1908–10] All ER Rep 344
2   [1978] 1 All ER 111, [1977] 1 WLR 1004

employees of the BBC should be amended to incorporate a term that they should not be obliged to take any part in the transmission of sporting events to South Africa.

My Lords, if a demand on an employer by the union is about terms and conditions of employment the fact that it appears to the court to be unreasonable because compliance with it is so difficult as to be commercially impracticable or will bankrupt the employer or drive him out of business does not prevent its being a dispute connected with terms and conditions of employment. Immunity under s 13 is not forfeited by being stubborn or pig-headed. Neither, in my view, does it matter that the demand is made and the dispute pursued with more than one object in mind and that of those objects the predominant one is not the improvement of the terms and conditions of employment of those workers to whom the demand relates. Even if the predominant object were to bring down the fabric of the present economic system by raising wages to unrealistic levels, or to drive Asian seamen from the seas except when they serve in ships beneficially owned by nationals of their own countries, this would not, in my view, make it any less a dispute connected with terms and conditions of employment and thus a trade dispute, if the actual demand that is resisted by the employer is as to the terms and conditions on which his workers are to be employed. The threat of industrial action if the demand is not met is nonetheless an act done in furtherance of that trade dispute. I do not regard *The Camilla M*[14] as distinguishable from the instant case. In my view it should be treated as overruled.

I turn next to the effect of s 17(2) on applications for interlocutory injunctions in cases of this kind. The nature and goals of industrial action, the virtual immunity from liability for tort conferred on trade unions by s 14, and the immunity from liability for the tort of wrongfully inducing breaches of contract conferred on all persons by s 13 where this is done in connection with a trade dispute are three factors which, in combination, would make the balance of convenience come down heavily in favour of granting an interlocutory injunction if the usual criteria were alone applied.

In the normal case of threatened industrial action against an employer, the damage that he will sustain if the action is carried out is likely to be large, difficult to assess in money and may well be irreparable. Furthermore damage is likely to be caused to customers of the employer's business who are not parties to the action, and to the public at large. On the other hand the defendant is not the trade union but an individual officer of the union who, although he is acting on its behalf, can be sued in his personal capacity only. In that personal capacity he will suffer virtually no damage if the injunction is granted, whereas if it is not granted and the action against him ultimately succeeds it is most improbable that damages on the scale that are likely to be awarded against him will prove to be recoverable from him. Again, to grant the injunction will maintain the status quo until the trial; and this too is a factor which in evenly-balanced cases generally operates in favour of granting an interlocutory injunction. So on the face of the proceedings in an action of this kind the balance of convenience as to the grant of an interlocutory injunction would appear to be heavily weighted in favour of the employer.

To take this view, however, would be to blind oneself to the practical realities (1) that the real dispute is not between the employer and the nominal defendant but between the employer and the trade union that is threatening industrial action, (2) that the threat of 'blacking' or other industrial action is being used as a bargaining counter in negotiations either existing or anticipated to obtain agreement by the employer to do whatever it is the union requires of him, (3) that it is the nature of industrial action that it can be promoted effectively only so long as it is possible to strike while the iron is still hot; once postponed it is unlikely that it can be revived, and (4) that, in consequence of these three characteristics, the grant or refusal of an interlocutory injunction generally disposes finally of the action; in practice actions of this type seldom if ever come to actual trial.

Subsection (2) of s 17 which is said to be passed 'for the avoidance of doubt' and does not apply to Scotland appears to me to be intended as a reminder addressed by Parliament

---

1   [1979] 1 Lloyd's Rep 26

to English judges that where industrial action is threatened that is prima facie tortious
because it induces a breach of contract they should, in exercising their discretion whether
or not to grant an interlocutory injunction, put into the balance of convenience in favour
of the defendant those countervailing practical realities and, in particular, that the grant
of an injunction is tantamount to giving final judgment against the defendant.

The subsection, it is to be noted, does not expressly enjoin the judge to have regard to
the likelihood of success in establishing any other defence than a statutory immunity
created by the Act although there may well be other defences to alleged wrongful
inducement of breach of contract, such as denial of inducement or that what was sought
to be induced would not constitute a breach, or justification of the inducement on other
grounds than the existence of a trade dispute. So the subsection is selective; it applies to
one only out of several possible defences and, consequently, only to those actions which,
since they are connected with trade disputes, involve the practical realities which I have
mentioned.

My Lords, when properly understood, there is in my view nothing in the decision of
this House in *American Cyanamid Co v Ethicon Ltd*[1] to suggest that in considering whether
or not to grant an interlocutory injunction the judge ought not to give full weight to all
the practical realities of the situation to which the injunction will apply. *American
Cyanamid Co v Ethicon Ltd*[1], which enjoins the judge on an application for an interlocutory
injunction to direct his attention to the balance of convenience as soon as he has satisfied
himself that there is a serious question to be tried, was not dealing with a case in which
the grant or refusal of an injunction at that stage would, in effect, dispose of the action
finally in favour of whichever party was successful in the application, because there
would be nothing left on which it was in the unsuccessful party's interest to proceed to
trial. By the time the trial came on the industrial dispute, if there were one, in
furtherance of which the acts sought to be restrained were threatened or done, would be
likely to have been settled and it would not be in the employer's interest to exacerbate
relations with his workmen by continuing the proceedings against the individual
defendants none of whom would be capable financially of meeting a substantial claim for
damages. Nor, if an interlocutory injunction had been granted against them, would it
be worthwhile for the individual defendants to take steps to obtain a final judgment in
their favour, since any damages that they could claim in respect of personal pecuniary
loss caused to them by the grant of the injunction and which they could recover under
the employer's undertaking on damages would be very small.

Cases of this kind are exceptional, but when they do occur they bring into the balance
of convenience an important additional element. In assessing whether what is
compendiously called the balance of convenience lies in granting or refusing interlocutory
injunctions in actions between parties of undoubted solvency the judge is engaged in
weighing the respective risks that injustice may result from his deciding one way rather
than the other at a stage when the evidence is incomplete. On the one hand there is the
risk that if the interlocutory injunction is refused but the plaintiff succeeds in establishing
at the trial his legal right for the protection of which the injunction had been sought he
may in the meantime have suffered harm and inconvenience for which an award of
money can provide no adequate recompense. On the other hand there is the risk that if
the interlocutory injunction is granted but the plaintiff fails at the trial the defendant
may in the meantime have suffered harm and inconvenience which is similarly
irrecompensable. The nature and degree of harm and inconvenience that are likely to be
sustained in these two events to the defendant and the plaintiff respectively in
consequence of the grant or the refusal of the injunction are generally sufficiently
disproportionate to bring down, by themselves, the balance on one side or the other; and
this is what I understand to be the thrust of the decision of this House in *American*

---

1   [1975] 1 All ER 504, [1975] AC 396

Cyanamid Co v Ethicon Ltd[1]. Where, however, the grant or refusal of the interlocutory injunction will have the practical effect of putting an end to the action because the harm that will have been already caused to the losing party by its grant or its refusal is complete and of a kind for which money cannot constitute any worthwhile recompense, the degree of likelihood that the plaintiff would have succeeded in establishing his right to an injunction if the action had gone to trial is a factor to be brought into the balance by the judge in weighing the risks that injustice may result from his deciding the application one way rather than the other.

The characteristics of the type of action to which s 17 applies have already been discussed. They are unique; and, whether it was strictly necessary to do so or not, it was clearly prudent of the draftsman of the section to state expressly that in considering whether or not to grant an interlocutory injunction the court should have regard to the likelihood of the defendant's succeeding in establishing that what he did or threatened was done or threatened in contemplation or furtherance of a trade dispute.

My Lords, counsel for the defendants have invited this House to say that because it is singled out for special mention it is an 'overriding' or a 'paramount' factor against granting the injunction once it appears to the judge that the defence of statutory immunity is more likely to succeed than not. I do not think that your Lordships should give your approval to the use of either of these or any other adjective to define the weight to be given to this factor by the judge, particularly as the subsection does not apply to Scotland where, as my noble and learned friend, Lord Fraser of Tullybelton, explains, it would be but one of several factors to be taken into consideration whose relative weight might vary with the circumstances of the case. Parliament cannot be taken to have intended that radically different criteria should be applied by English and Scots courts. The degree of likelihood of success of the special defence under s 13 beyond its being slightly more probable than not is clearly relevant; so is the degree of irrecoverable damage likely to be sustained by the employer, his customers and the general public if the injunction is refused and the defence ultimately fails. Judges would, I think, be respecting the intention of Parliament in making this change in the law in 1975[2], if in the normal way the injunction were refused in cases where the defendant had shown that it was more likely than not that he would succeed in his defence of statutory immunity; but this does not mean that there may not be cases where the consequences to the employer or to third parties or the public and perhaps the nation itself, may be so disastrous that the injunction ought to be refused, unless there is a high degree of probability that the defence will succeed.

My Lords, the instant case presents no problem. On the evidence before the court at each stage of these proceedings, the defendants have a virtual certainty of establishing their defence of statutory immunity.

I would dismiss these appeals.

LORD FRASER OF TULLYBELTON. My Lords, I agree with my noble and learned friend, Lord Diplock, whose speech I have had the advantage of reading in draft, that the defendants would almost certainly succeed in showing that the dispute between the parties to this appeal is a 'trade dispute', and that the threatened action of blacking the Nawala at Redcar would have been 'in contemplation or furtherance of that dispute'. I agree with him also that *The Camilla M*[3] was wrongly decided and should be overruled.

I turn to consider the effect to be given to s 17(2) of the Trade Union and Labour Relations Act 1974. Subsection (2) was inserted into s 17 of the 1974 Act by the Employment Protection Act 1975. Section 17 as a whole is concerned with interlocutory injunctions in cases that may or do come within the 1974 Act. I note in passing that the marginal note to s 17 ('Restriction on grant of ex parte injunctions and interdicts'), which

---

1 [1975] 1 All ER 504, [1975] AC 396
2 See the Employment Protection Act 1975, s 125, Sch 16, Part III, para 6
3 [1979] 1 Lloyd's Rep 26

was apt when the section contained only what is now sub-s (1), is inappropriate or at least
a inadequate for the section as expanded by sub-s (2). It could not therefore throw any
light on the meaning of sub-s (2) even if it were permissible to refer to it as an aid to
construction.

Subsection (1) is relevant to the construction of sub-s (2) only to this extent, that it
demonstrates the importance attached by Parliament to giving the respondent an
opportunity of putting forward the defence that he was acting in contemplation or
b furtherance of a trade dispute. The court is therefore charged that it 'shall not' grant an
ex parte injunction against a party who claims, or would be likely to claim, that he was
so acting, unless the court is satisfied that all reasonable steps have been taken to give him
an opportunity of being heard. No doubt the reason why such a provision was considered
necessary is that in nearly every case to which the subsection applies the balance of
convenience (apart from this defence) will be in favour of granting an interim
c injunction. The dispute will generally be causing disruption of the employer's business
with consequent loss to him and probably also to other persons (employers and workers)
who have no direct connection with the dispute. It will also in some cases cause
inconvenience to the public as a whole. But the grant or refusal of an interlocutory
injunction is almost always decisive in such cases because the dispute is usually settled
one way or another before there is time for the action to proceed to trial. It might
d therefore be thought to be unfair to the parties (in practice trade unions) who would be
likely to claim that they were acting in contemplation or furtherance of a trade dispute
if interlocutory injunctions were granted purely by reference to the balance of
convenience without regard to that defence, as they might be in England on one view of
the decision in *American Cyanamid Co v Ethicon Ltd*[1]; in practice there would hardly ever
be an opportunity for putting forward the defence. It is probably significant that
e sub-s (2) was inserted by the 1975 Act which received the royal assent on 12th November
1975, a few months after the *American Cyanamid*[1] decision (given on 5th February 1975):
see the opinion of Lord Denning MR in *The Camilla M*[2].

Considerations of that sort explain the reason for adding sub-s (2) to s 17. But counsel
for the defendants relied on these considerations for the further purpose of supporting an
argument as to the effect of the subsection. The argument as I understood it was that if
f the court, in exercising its discretion whether or not to grant an interlocutory injunction,
reached the view that the respondent was more likely than not to succeed at the trial of
the action in establishing a defence that he was acting in contemplation or furtherance
of a trade dispute it should regard that as being for practical purposes a conclusive reason
for not granting an interlocutory injunction. That reason was to be accorded overriding
or paramount importance, except perhaps if there was some exceptionally powerful
g reason of public safety in favour of granting an interlocutory injunction. The argument
went so far as to say that, provided the court was satisfied that the trade dispute defence
was more likely than not to be established, the degree of likelihood was irrelevant. So it
would make no difference whether the court considered the defence was almost certain
to be established or that the balance was narrowly in favour of its being established.

My Lords, I reject that contention. What sub-s (2) of s 17 provides is that the court in
h exercising its discretion is to 'have regard to' the likelihood of this defence being
established at the trial. It does not provide that the court is to have regard to that matter
to the exclusion of other matters, nor that it is to be treated as of overriding or paramount
importance or given any other special legal status. No doubt the likelihood of successfully
establishing the defence would be treated by the court as a matter of importance, and in
a case where the court considered that the respondent would probably be entitled to rely
j on the defence, it might be slow to grant an interlocutory injunction which would in
practice exclude the defence. But that would be a matter for the court to decide in the

---

1   [1975] 1 All ER 504, [1975] AC 396
2   [1979] 1 Lloyd's Rep 26 at 31

circumstances of each particular case. The word 'likelihood' is a word of degree and the weight to be given to the likelihood of establishing the defence will vary according to the degree of the likelihood. If the court considers that the respondent is virtually certain to establish the trade dispute defence, it will naturally give more weight to this factor than if it considers the prospect of successfully establishing the defence is doubtful. In my opinion therefore the effect of sub-s (2) of s 17 is that the court, in exercising its discretion, should have regard to the balance of convenience including the likelihood (and the degree of likelihood) of the respondent's succeeding in establishing the defence of trade dispute, and then come to a decision on the whole matter.

I have reached that opinion on the words of sub-s (2) itself, but my opinion is fortified by sub-s (3) which provides that 'subsection (2) above shall not extend to Scotland'. No explanation was suggested by counsel on either side as to why Parliament should have enacted that sub-s (2) was not to apply to Scotland, and at first sight it seems surprising. The policy to which the Act gives effect would seem to be equally applicable to Scotland and England. The Act as a whole applies to both countries, and presumably for that reason sub-s (1) refers expressly to 'injunction or interdict'. The reason why sub-s (2) is declared not to apply to Scotland must be, I think, that Parliament regarded it as unnecessary for Scotland because it would merely give effect to the existing Scots law. The relevant difference between English law on interlocutory injunctions and Scots law on the very similar remedy of interim interdict can be appreciated by reference to the decision of this House in *American Cyanamid Co v Ethicon Ltd*[1], a decision which does not apply to Scotland. In that case this House laid down that the court in exercising its discretion as to granting or refusing an interlocutory injunction ought not to weigh up the relative strengths of the parties' cases on the evidence (necessarily incomplete) available at the interlocutory stage. Lord Diplock, with whose speech the other four noble and learned Lords agreed, said[2]:

'The court no doubt must be satisfied that the claim is not frivolous or vexatious; in other words, that there is a serious question to be tried. It is no part of the court's function at this stage of the litigation to try to resolve conflicts of evidence on affidavit as to facts on which the claims of either party may ultimately depend nor to decide difficult questions of law which call for detailed argument and mature considerations. These are matters to be dealt with at the trial.'

In Scotland the practice is otherwise, and the court is in use to have regard to the relative strength of the cases put forward in averment and argument by each party at the interlocutory stage as one of the many factors that may go to make up the balance of convenience. That is certainly in accordance with my own experience as Lord Ordinary, and I believe the practice of other judges in the Court of Session was the same. Whether the likelihood of success should be regarded as one of the elements of the balance of convenience or as a separate matter seems to me an academic question of no real importance, but my inclination is in favour of the former alternative. It seems to make good sense; if the pursuer or petitioner appears very likely to succeed at the end of the day, it will tend to be convenient to grant interim interdict and thus prevent the defender or respondent from infringing his rights, but if the defender or respondent appears very likely to succeed at the end of the day it will tend to be convenient to refuse interim interdict because an interim interdict would probably only delay the exercise of the defender's legal activities. Reported cases on this matter are not easy to find, because applications for interim interdict are usually disposed of quickly without full opinions being given, but the view of the law that I have expressed is I think vouched by some authority. In *General Assembly of the Free Church of Scotland v Johnston*[3] the Lord Ordinary (Lord Pearson), whose opinion was approved by the Second Division on appeal, said:

1 [1975] 1 All ER 504, [1975] AC 396
2 [1975] 1 All ER 504 at 510, [1975] AC 396 at 407
3 (1905) 7 F (Ct of Sess) 517 at 522

'Of course on this question of interim interdict, I can only deal with the matter provisionally; but it is certainly according to the practice of the Court in such cases to consider how the rights of parties appear on a prima facie aspect.'

In *Edinburgh Magistrates v Edinburgh etc Railway Co*[1] Lord Justice-Clerk Hope said that, in a case where the respondent relied on an asserted right—

'there surely can be no better ground for an interim interdict than that the court, which is itself to decide the question of right, think that question so difficult, and the onus of establishing the power claimed *so weighty against the respondent*, that, in their opinion, until he obtains judgment he ought not to be allowed to interfere with the interests, or rights and privileges of others, although in regard to property to which he has a title.' (Emphasis mine.)

As an example of the modern practice, though without any full statement of principle, I refer to *Chill Foods (Scotland) Ltd v Cool Foods Ltd*[2] where in the first petition the Lord Ordinary (Lord Maxwell) refused interim interdict because the petitioner's case was based on averments that there was a contract between the parties, but he was unable to produce any document setting out the contract, and the existence of the contract was denied by the respondent.

While the courts in Scotland would have regard to the likelihood of the respondent's succeeding in establishing the trade dispute defence, I would not expect them to accord any special priority to the defence beyond what it might seem to deserve in the circumstances of a particular case. That is exactly the effect that sub-s (2) of s 17 is, in my opinion, intended to produce and does produce in England.

In the present case, having regard to the likelihood that the defendants would succeed in establishing a defence under s 13 of the 1974 Act, I would dismiss the appeals.

LORD SCARMAN. My Lords, it cannot be doubted that a dispute exists between the appellant shipowners, who are plaintiffs in the two suits, and the International Transport Workers' Federation, the union of which the respondents are officers. Nor is it open to doubt that the threat to 'black' the plaintiffs' ship Nawala at Redcar and later at Narvik and the efforts made by the union to persuade workers at the two ports to implement the threat were acts done in furtherance of the dispute.

These two appeals raise two questions on the interpretation of the Trade Union and Labour Relations Act 1974, as amended by the Employment Protection Act 1975. The first question arises under s 29(1) of the 1974 Act. When and in what circumstances is a dispute between an employer and a trade union not a 'trade dispute'? The answer seems simple and conclusive: when it falls outside the definition contained in the subsection. But, if counsel for the shipowners is correct, the subsection is not conclusive. He relies on the case law for the proposition that a dispute, which on the face of it appears to be within the subsection, may prove on investigation to be outside it. The second question arises on s 17(2) of the 1974 Act. On an application for an interlocutory injunction against a party who claims to have a defence that he acted in contemplation or furtherance of a trade dispute, what measure of regard are the courts to have to 'the likelihood' of his establishing the defence at the trial? The answer to this question is not to be found in the subsection which, by its silence, leaves it to the courts.

My Lords, in construing these two subsections I consider it to be of vital importance to determine the correct judicial approach to the two Acts. As Viscount Simonds said in *Attorney-General v HRH Prince Ernest Augustus of Hanover*[3]:

'... words, and particularly general words, cannot be read in isolation; their colour and content are derived from their context. So it is that I conceive it to be my

1   (1847) 19 Scot Jur 421 at 426
2   1977 SLT 38 at 39
3   [1957] 1 All ER 49 at 53, [1957] AC 436 at 461

right and duty to examine every word of a statute in its context, and I use context in its widest sense, which I have already indicated as including not only other *a* enacting provisions of the same statute, but its preamble, the existing state of the law, other statutes in pari materia, and the mischief which I can, by those and other legitimate means, discern that the statute was intended to remedy.'

It is wrong to attempt to construe any section or subsection of these Acts without reference to their legislative purpose. And it is also necessary to have regard to the history of the statute law and the case law since 1906 for a full understanding of them. *b* This history I would summarise as a shifting pattern of Parliamentary assertions and judicial responses, a legal point counterpoint which has been more productive of excitement than of harmony. The judges have been, understandably, reluctant to abandon common law and equitable principles, unless unambiguously told to do so by statute. Parliament has created ambiguity not through any lack of drafting skill but by its own changes of mind. So far as the 1974 Act is concerned, the legislative purpose is *c* clear: to sweep away not only the structure of industrial relations created by the Industrial Relations Act 1971, which it was passed to repeal, but also the restraints of judicial review which the courts have been fashioning one way or another since the enactment of the Trade Disputes Act 1906. The court of inquiry into the Grunwick affair (of which I was chairman) put it correctly, I continue to think, when it said[1]:
d

> 'The policy [of the statutes] is to exclude "trade disputes" . . . from judicial review by the courts . . . There is substituted for judicial review of trade disputes an advisory, conciliation and arbitration process with ACAS as the statutory body to operate it.'

This policy (or legislative purpose, a phrase which causes fewer judicial tremors) is achieved by those sections of the 1974 Act which impose restrictions on legal liability and *e* legal proceedings (ss 13 to 17), by the wide meaning given to 'trade dispute' by s 29, and by the establishment of the Advisory, Conciliation and Arbitration Service by Part I of the 1975 Act (now consolidated into the Employment Protection (Consolidation) Act 1978). Briefly put, the law now is back to what Parliament had intended when it enacted the 1906 Act, but stronger and clearer than it was then. An act done in contemplation or furtherance of a trade dispute is not actionable in tort on the ground only that it *f* induces a breach of contract or interferes with the performance of a contract or with another person's trade, business or employment: see s 13. Trade unions and employers' associations are not liable in tort for acts done in contemplation or furtherance of a trade dispute: see s 14. And restrictions are placed by s 17 on the grant of interlocutory injunctions against parties claiming, or likely to claim, that they were acting in contemplation or furtherance of a trade dispute.
g
Against that background I look first to the meaning given to 'trade dispute' by s 29 of the 1974 Act. It is, basically, the meaning given by the 1906 Act but widened and clarified to undo the effect of some intervening judicial decisions, doubts and dicta. Subsection (1) retains the basic structure of s 5(3) of the 1906 Act: 'trade dispute' means 'a dispute between employers and workers, or between workers and workers, which is connected with one or more of' the seven matters specified in the subsection. In its *h* specification, the subsection amplifies and clarifies the provisions of the 1906 Act, and in particular makes express what might well be thought to have been implicit in the 1906 Act, that disputes over trade union matters (e g membership, negotiation and consultation procedures and recognition) are trade disputes. Subsection (3) provides that 'there is a trade dispute . . . even though it relates to matters occurring outside Great Britain', and sub-s (4) makes clear that a dispute to which a trade union or employers' association is a *j*

---

1   Cmnd 6922, para 58

party is to be treated as a dispute to which workers or, as the case may be, employers are parties. Subsection (5) makes sure that instant submission by one party or the other does not enable one to claim that the act or threat causing him to submit is not something done in contemplation of a trade dispute, and sub-s (6) provides that the term 'worker' in relation to a dispute with an employer includes 'any worker even if not employed by that employer'.

In the present case, therefore, it is of no moment that the union, of whom the respondents are officials, is an international federation of trade unions ('ITF'), or that, since the Nawala left Redcar, the dispute relates to matters occurring outside Great Britain, or that none (if that be so) of the crew is a member of any union affiliated to ITF. The dispute is within the subsection if it is between the shipowners and the union or between the members of the crew of the ship and the union, provided only that it is connected with one or more of the matters set forth in the subsection.

The dispute is, on its face, connected with the terms and conditions of employment not only of the crew of the Nawala but of all seafarers, many of whom are members by affiliation of the union. The union objects to the practice of shipowners making use of 'flags of convenience' to secure cheap labour on their ships. The evidence certainly suggests that the union also has other objections to 'flag of convenience' ships. But, unless one gives words whatever meaning one chooses (and judges, unlike Humpty-Dumpty, are not permitted this freedom), the dispute is connected with the terms and conditions of the employment of workers (including the crew of the Nawala) in the shipping industry. It is, therefore, apparently covered by para (a) of sub-s (1). The shipowners concede this much. Their case is, however, that the dispute is not really about the terms and conditions of employment of this particular crew at all but part and parcel of a campaign being waged all over the world by the ITF against 'flags of convenience'. The 'predominant motive' of the union, it is said, is political, not industrial. They rely on Conway v Wade[1] and The Camilla M[2] for the proposition that an extraneous motive, if it be the predominant motive, will prevent a dispute from being a trade dispute even though it appears to fall within the subsection.

I totally reject the legal foundation of this case. If there be a conflict between the decision of this House in Conway v Wade[1] and the language of the subsection constructed in the light of the purpose (or policy) of the legislation, I have no doubt that it would be the duty of this House to reject Conway v Wade[1]. If the decision of the Court of Appeal in The Camilla M[2] is (as I believe) inconsistent with the subsection, it is wrong and must be overruled.

All that the subsection requires is that the dispute be connected with one or more of the matters it mentions. If it be connected, it is a trade dispute, and it is immaterial whether the dispute also relates to other matters or has an extraneous, e g political or personal, motive. The connection is all that has to be shown.

Does it follow that Conway v Wade[1] must now be treated as wrongly decided? I confess that I find it a difficult case to understand. Section 5(3) of the 1906 Act was basically the same as s 29(1) of the 1974 Act: all it required was that a dispute be connected with one or more of the matters it mentioned. On the face of it, the dispute in the case was so connected. But the facts were very special. The jury found as a fact that it was a case of personal animosity or grudge, and nothing else, as also was Huntley v Thornton[3] decided by Harman J. No connection was, therefore, proved in either case.

The continuing importance of Conway v Wade[1] is that it remains good authority for the proposition that the connection required by the subsection must be a genuine one,

1   [1909] AC 506, [1908–10] All ER Rep 344
2   [1979] 1 Lloyd's Rep 26
3   [1957] 1 All ER 234, [1957] 1 WLR 321

and not a sham. The mere pretext, or 'specious cover', of a trade dispute will not do: see *J T Stratford & Son Ltd v Lindley*[1] per Lord Pearce.

But *The Camilla M*[2] was, in my view, wrongly decided. My noble and learned friend, Lord Diplock, has analysed the decision, and I agree with the analysis. The basis error, which is to be found in all three judgments of the Court of Appeal, is in the proposition, which the court accepted (conveniently summarised in the headnote[2]), that 'not every dispute connected with terms or conditions of employment . . . was necessarily a trade dispute' and that 'some limitation of those statutory words was necessary'. The legislative purpose of the Act is such that no limitation on the ordinary meaning of the simple English words used by the statute is permissible. The fallacy of the Court of Appeal is clearly exposed by one passage in the judgment of Brandon LJ[3]:

'As regards the subject matter of the dispute, there are two possibilities. There may be a case where a dispute is ostensibly connected with a subject matter which would make it a trade dispute but is in fact and in reality connected with some wholly different subject matter. The other possibility is that the dispute is connected with both subject matters, but the predominant subject matter with which the dispute is connected is the second rather than the first. Neither of those cases, as I understand the authorities, is one of a trade dispute.'

Ostensible connection is, as Brandon LJ says, not enough to make a dispute a trade dispute: see *Conway v Wade*[4]. If the connection is only 'ostensible', there is no connection. But predominance of subject-matter is an irrelevance, provided always there is a real connection between the dispute and one or other of the matters mentioned in the subsection. A dispute may be political or personal in character and yet be connected with, for example, the terms and conditions of employment of workers; such a dispute would be within the subsection. It is only if the alleged connection is a pretext or cover for another dispute which is in no way connected with any of the matters mentioned in the subsection that it is possible to hold that the dispute is not a trade dispute. The facts in *British Broadcasting Corpn v Hearn*[5] illustrate the sort of case in which there may be no connection, an objection by workers to 'apartheid' leading to a decision to 'black' the transmission to South Africa of the television showing of the Cup Final.

A study of the case law is, however, only of secondary importance. Judicial decision cannot impose limitations on the language of Parliament where it is clear from the words, context and policy of the statute that no limitation was intended. The Court of Appeal erred in *The Camilla M*[2] in holding that it was necessary to place 'some limitation' on the words of s 29(1). None is needed: none was intended by Parliament.

I turn now to consider s 17(2) of the 1974 Act. The subsection was not part of the Act when it became law in 1974. In 1975 your Lordships' House decided *American Cyanimid Co v Ethicon Ltd*[6]. The effect of the decision was that, provided a plaintiff could show that there was a serious question to be tried, he could obtain an interim injunction if he could show that the balance of convenience tilted his way. The decision had a fateful significance for trade unions engaged in trade disputes. An employer would in most cases have no difficulty in showing that action to disrupt his business contemplated or

---

1   [1964] 3 All ER 102 at 114, [1965] AC 269 at 335
2   [1979] 1 Lloyd's Rep 26
3   [1979] 1 Lloyd's Rep 26 at 35
4   [1909] AC 506, [1908–10] All ER Rep 344
5   [1978] 1 All ER 111, [1977] 1 WLR 1004
6   [1975] 1 All ER 504, [1975] AC 396

undertaken by members of the union with which he was in dispute would cause him
serious, even catastrophic, loss. On a balance of convenience, he would ordinarily have
a little difficulty in showing that the status quo should be preserved until full investigation
at trial. Yet, if this argument should prevail, the trade union's bargaining counter would
disappear. Its power to bring instant and real pressure on the employer would be
denied. Section 17(2) was introduced by the 1975 Act after the *Cyanimid*[1] decision. As
Lord Denning MR observed in *The Camilla M*[2], it restores the old law, so far as the
b defence of acts done in contemplation or furtherance of a trade dispute are concerned.
The court must under the subsection have regard to the likelihood of this defence being
established before deciding whether or not to grant an interlocutory injunction.

The measure of the regard is the critical question. Before answering it, I think it is
necessary to analyse what the law now requires of a court before it grants an interim
injunction in the case of an alleged trade dispute.

c My view of the law continues to be that which I expressed in *British Broadcasting Corpn
v Hearn*[3]. There are three stages. First, has the plaintiff shown 'a serious question to be
tried'? I will assume that in the present case the shipowners have shown that there is.
Certainly, but for s 13 of the Act, they would have a good cause of action in tort against
the respondents. Secondly, has he shown that the balance of convenience lies with
him? Almost invariably it will lie with the employer. Bearing in mind the immense
d losses a shipowner will suffer if his ship is 'blacked', I do not doubt that in the present case
this balance tilts strongly in favour of the shipowners. Thirdly, is there a likelihood of
the union establishing a defence under s 13 (the relevant section in these appeals), or
s 14(2) or s 15 of the Act?

Both of my noble and learned friends treat the likelihood as an element to be weighed
in the balance of convenience. Though the difference may be no more than semantic, I
e do not. I see it as a separate factor to which regard is to be had. Counsel for the
defendants submitted that it must be treated as an overriding or paramount factor; in
other words, if established (even on no more than a balance of probabilities), it precludes
the issue of an injunction. But the subsection does not say so; and I would not fetter the
residual discretion left to the courts by an epithet which Parliament could have used but
did not. Nevertheless the question remains: if the likelihood is no more than a
f probability, is the court to pay the regard to it that it would if it were a practical
certainty? The legislative purpose, or policy, of the Act provides the answer. If there is
a trade dispute, the policy of the legislation is immunity, or (as the case may be)
restriction of civil liability, for acts done in contemplation or furtherance of the
dispute. There is to be, outside the criminal courts, no judicial review of such acts. The
existence of so sweeping a legislative purpose leads me to conclude that, if there is a
g likelihood as distinct from a mere possibility of a party showing that he acted in
contemplation or furtherance of a trade dispute, no interlocutory injunction should
ordinarily be issued. A balance of probabilities will suffice in most cases for the court to
refuse it. I do not rule out the possibility that the consequences to the plaintiff (or others)
may be so serious that the court feels it necessary to grant the injunction, for the
subsection does leave a residual discretion with the court. But it would, indeed, be a rare
h case in which a court, having concluded that there was a real likelihood of the defence
succeeding, granted the injunction.

In the instant two appeals, however, these difficulties do not arise. I consider it a
practical certainty, on the evidence made available to the House, that, whatever be the
other reasons for its campaign against flags of convenience, the union is engaged in a
dispute with this shipowner which is connected with the terms and conditions of
j employment of workers on their ship and in the shipping industry generally. It is very

---

1   [1975] 1 All ER 504, [1975] AC 396
2   [1979] 1 Lloyd's Rep 26 at 31
3   [1978] 1 All ER 111, [1977] 1 WLR 1004

unlikely that this connection is a sham. I would, therefore, dismiss in each case the shipowners' appeal against the refusal of the Court of Appeal to allow the issue of an *a* interlocutory injunction.

Appeals dismissed.

Solicitors: *Holman, Fenwick & Willan* (for the shipowners); *Clifford-Turner* (for the defendants).   *b*

Mary Rose Plummer   Barrister.

Chorley Borough Council v   *c* Barratt Developments (North West) Ltd

CHANCERY DIVISION AT MANCHESTER
BLACKETT-ORD V-C SITTING AS A JUDGE OF THE HIGH COURT
6th, 7th MARCH 1979
     d

Housing – Fitness of property for human habitation – Back-to-back houses intended for working classes – Back-to-back houses – Working classes – Company building blocks of four one-bedroomed houses – Houses built back to back as well as side by side – Each house having two outside walls with windows and two interior party walls – Houses sold inexpensively to variety of purchasers – Whether houses 'back-to-back houses' – Whether houses 'intended for working classes' – Whether construction prohibited – Housing Act 1957, s 5(1).   *e*

A company were developing a large estate with different types of housing including two blocks of four one-bedroomed houses. Each house in the block had two outside walls with windows and two interior party walls so that the houses were back to back as well as being side by side. This design had been widely acclaimed and the company had built many such houses. They were inexpensive according to current prices, being intended *f* for sale at under £10,000 each. The evidence showed that those purchasing the houses came from varied occupations, including a lady doctor, a nurse and a professional ice-skater. The local authority brought an action against the company alleging that the houses were 'back-to-back houses intended to be used as dwellings for the working classes' and therefore prohibited by s 5(1)[a] of the Housing Act 1957. In support of this claim the authority contended that because the houses were relatively inexpensive they *g* were intended for lower income groups and thus 'the working classes'.

Held – The action would be dismissed for the following reasons—
    (i) The expression 'back-to-back houses' in s 5(1) of the 1957 Act was not a term of art but was used in a popular and general sense to mean terraces of houses where all the houses, except those at the end of the terrace, had three inside walls and only one outside *h* wall. Whether dwellings were back-to-back houses was a question of fact, and since the houses being constructed by the company did not fall within the popular and general meaning of back-to-back houses they were not prohibited by s 5 (see p 638 *h* to p 639 *a*, post); dictum of Lord Dundas in *Murrayfield Real Estate Co v Edinburgh Magistrates* 1912 SC at 222 and *White v St Marylebone Borough Council* [1915] 3 KB 249 applied.
    (ii) Even if the houses were 'back-to-back houses', the company did not have the *j* necessary intention, either actual or imputed, to erect them 'for the working classes', contrary to s 5, since, on the evidence, it had no intention of selling the houses to any

---

a   Section 5(1), so far as material, is set out at p 636 *b*, post

particular income group but sold them to purchasers who tended to be single people or
a couples without children rather than people with low incomes (see p 640 *b* to *g*, post).

Notes

For prohibition of construction of back-to-back houses, see 22 Halsbury's Laws (4th Edn)
para 573, and for the meaning of 'working classes', see ibid para 402.

For the Housing Act 1957, s 5, see 16 Halsbury's Statutes (3rd Edn) 118.

b

Cases referred to in judgment

Belcher v Reading Corpn [1949] 2 All ER 969, [1950] Ch 380, 114 JP 21, 48 LGR 71, 26
Digest (Repl) 704, *141*.

Crow v Davis (1903) 89 LT 407, 67 JP 319, DC, 38 Digest (Repl) 252, *615*.

Crow v Davis (No 2) (1904) 91 LT 88, 68 JP 447, 2 LGR 1034, DC, 38 Digest (Repl) 252,
c   *616*.

Green (H E) & Sons v Minister of Health (No 2) [1947] 2 All ER 469, [1948] 1 KB 34, [1948]
LJR 1, 111 JP 590, 26 Digest (Repl) 701, *117*.

Guinness Trust (London Fund) v Green [1955] 2 All ER 871, [1955] 1 WLR 872, CA, Digest
(Cont Vol A) 1071, 7590a.

Murrayfield Real Estate Co v Edinburgh Magistrates 1912 SC 217, 49 Sc LR 148, 36 Digest
d   (Repl) 681, **1*.

White v St Marylebone Borough Council [1915] 3 KB 249, 84 LJKB 2142, 113 LT 447, 79 JP
350, 13 LGR 977, 26 Digest (Repl) 681, *6*.

Cases also cited

Campbell College, Belfast (Governors) v Valuation Comr for Northern Ireland [1964] 2 All ER
e   705, [1964] 1 WLR 912, HL.

Devonport Corpn v Tozer [1902] 2 Ch 182, 71 LJ Ch 754; *affd* [1903] 1 Ch 759, CA.

Sanders' Will Trusts, Re, Public Trustee v McLaren [1954] 1 All ER 667, [1954] Ch 265.

Stafford Borough Council v Elkenford Ltd [1977] 2 All ER 519, [1977] 1 WLR 324, CA.

Action

f By an originating summons issued on 21st September 1978 the plaintiff, the Chorley
Borough Council, claimed against the defendant, Barratt Developments (North West)
Ltd ('the company'), (i) a declaration that the construction or proposed construction by
the company of two blocks of four houses of the 'Mayfair' type at Astley Park, Chorley,
being back-to-back houses, was unlawful and in breach of s 5 of the Housing Act 1957,
(ii) injunctions to restrain the company by themselves, their servants or agents or
g otherwise howsoever from commencing, or continuing with, the construction of any of
the houses, (iii) an order that the company forthwith pull down and demolish and
remove so much of the houses as had already been constructed, and (iv) an injunction
restraining the company by themselves, their servants or agents or otherwise howsoever,
from constructing houses of the 'Mayfair' type anywhere within the borough council's
area. The facts are set out in the judgment.

h
Charles Cross for the borough council.
Roy Vandermeer QC and *Michael Harrison* for the company.

BLACKETT-ORD V-C. The facts of this case are not in dispute. The defendant,
Barratt Developments (North West) Ltd ('the company'), has a large residential
j development at Astley Park, near Chorley, and under the New Towns Act 1965, the
planning authority is the Central Lancashire New Town Development Corporation. The
estate is in the course of development, and on it the company is building two blocks, each
of four dwellings consisting of, on the ground floor, a livingroom and fitted kitchen and,
on the first floor, one bedroom with a fitted bathroom, access to the first floor being
reached by a sort of skeleton spiral staircase in the back of the living room. This design

has been much admired for what it is, and indeed has won a prize.   The outside of each
block looks to the uninstructed like a pair of semi-detached houses, and each dwelling in   *a*
the block has two outside walls with windows in them and, of course, two interior party
walls.   So it can be said that as well as being side by side, these dwellings are also back to
back.   They are all semi-semi-detached.
       But s 5 of the Housing Act 1957, so far as material, says:

       '(1) . . . it shall not be lawful to erect any back-to-back houses intended to be used
       as dwellings for the working classes, and any such house shall, for the purposes of   *b*
       this Act, be deemed to be unfit for habitation . . .'

And then there is a proviso, which does not apply in this case, because it is directed to
flats; but which is relevant to this extent, that it says that where it does apply, the
operation of the section is excluded if the local medical officer of health certifies that
ventilation of all habitable rooms is satisfactory.   *c*
       Building regulation approval was given for the structures in question on 3rd February
1978 by the plaintiff, Chorley Borough Council ('the borough council').   But this was not
a matter of discretion: the approval has to be given if the regulations are met, and it is not
disputed that they were.   And at about the same time, the company wrote to the
borough council asking it to confirm that if planning permission were granted, the
borough council would not seek to take any action under s 5, and received a reply   *d*
refusing any assurance.
       The borough council disapproves of these buildings.   If it had been the planning
authority, I have little doubt that planning permission would not have been granted.
But it is not the planning authority; and planning permission was granted on 25th May
1978.
       The borough council went carefully into the question of these houses, and the relevant   *e*
committee appointed a sub-committee which went and inspected similar dwellings
which had been built by the company somewhere else.   The reasons given by the sub-
committee for disapproving these houses are stated by Mr Kelly, the chief environmental
health officer, in his second affidavit in these proceedings, to which I now refer.   He says
this in para 4 of his affidavit of 5th March 1979:

       'The Members of the Sub-Committee, together with various Officers of [the   *f*
       borough council] including myself inspected the development at Congleton on
       10th March 1978.   During and after the visit discussions took place and in same
       various views were expressed by the Members.   The first was that the erection of
       this type of "back-to-back" housing in the rapidly developing area of [the borough
       council] was a retrograde step on principle notwithstanding that the houses are
       more adequately ventilated than the types of back-to-back houses erected in the area   *g*
       of [the borough council] in the 19th Century.   The second was that the development
       of this type of house was likely to cause problems in future years due to the possible
       financial inability of some owners to obtain larger accommodation should they
       require it, for example, if a married couple had children.   It was considered that this
       type of property would be attractive due to its price to persons in the lower income
       groups who might find their expenditure increased, for example, if a married   *h*
       couple had children whilst their income might reduce, for example if the wife had
       to stop working due to the aforesaid fact.   The third was that the rooms were small
       and that the external door opened directly into the living room and that this was
       unsatisfactory.'

       The report of the sub-committee was accepted by the committee and, apparently, by   *j*
the borough council and these reasons or observations which I have read out are the only
reasons which appear in evidence for the borough council's opposition to the erection of
this sort of house.   And I would say briefly of them that the first one I find rather vague;
and the second and third objections are really matters of planning, which is not the
province of the borough council.

The company has gone ahead with building at its own risk, I think knowing
a substantially from the beginning that when the not over-speedy procedures of the
borough council came into operation action was likely; and indeed, the originating
summons in this matter was issued on 21st September 1978. By it the borough council
seek, first, a declaration that the construction or proposed construction by the company
of the two blocks of four houses of the 'Mayfair' type ('Mayfair' is the name given to these
dwellings) at Astley Park, Chorley, being back-to-back houses, is unlawful and in breach
b of s 5 of the Housing Act 1957. Then, secondly, an injunction to restrain the company,
first, from commencing the construction (that I think has been overtaken by events) and
from continuing with construction; and a mandatory order requiring the company to
pull down so much of the houses as has been constructed. And, finally, an injunction
restraining the company from constructing houses of the 'Mayfair' type anywhere within
the area of the borough council.

c So the primary question for the court is whether the development which I have
described, these blocks of four 'Mayfair' houses, is prohibited by s 5 of the Housing Act
1957. This section was not then new. It derives initially from the Housing, Town
Planning etc Act 1909, s 43, and it was re-enacted as s 22 in Part II of the Housing Act
1936. The Housing Act 1936 contained a Part V dealing with the housing of the
working classes. But the expression 'working classes' has fallen into desuetude, and Part
d V, so far as it refers to those classes, has been repealed and not re-enacted. I understand
that s 5 of the 1957 Act is the sole surviving reference to 'working classes' in this
legislation; and, with no material amendment, it is s 43 of the 1909 Act. It is clear from
the proviso to which I referred that the principal mischief at which the section was aimed
was bad ventilation; and that is not criticised by the borough council in the present case.

I should, I think, interpolate this: I said that if the borough council had been the
e planning authority it is fairly clear that it would not have granted planning permission.
I should add that that might not have been the end of the story, because in evidence there
are two decisions of inspectors after inquiries relating to similar houses in which planning
permission was granted on appeal.

In construing s 5 of the 1957 Act, proper effect must, of course, be given to the words
used in the light of any authority. But the mischief at which it is aimed, this matter of
f ventilation, is one which now can be dealt with in other ways, under planning legislation
and, I suppose, building regulations; so that the section is to that extent anachronistic, as
is also its reference to the working classes. In construing it, the first question, I think, is,
what is the meaning of the expression 'back-to-back houses'? There are two authorities
dealing with this point to some extent: first, a Scottish case, *Murrayfield Real Estate Co v
Edinburgh Magistrates*[1] in 1911, and I think it was an appeal to the Court of Session from
g an inferior court. The case concerned tenements in Edinburgh, that is to say, what we
would now call 'flats'. And the court below decided that these were not 'back-to-back
houses' because they were not what in England would be regarded as back-to-back
houses. It appears from the petition of appeal that it had been said[2]:

'It appears that back-to-back houses in England are built in terraces, and the
h buildings have a solid party wall running parallel to two terraces, and the houses are
built on each side of this party wall, one set of houses facing one terrace and the
other set facing the other. In such houses, the means of ventilation is from the front
of the house except in the case of the houses at the end of the terraces, where there
is ventilation on the front and one side.'

And that, I venture to think, corresponds with what was well known in this area as the
j form that back-to-back housing took. But the Court of Session took a wider view. Lord
Dundas says of the tenements in question[3]:

---

1   1912 SC 217
2   49 Sc LR 148 at 149
3   1912 SC 217 at 222

'These houses may, I should think, be back-to-back houses within the meaning of
the Act, although they do not correspond precisely to what are known in England   *a*
as back-to-back houses. I do not think the phrase is a technical one; it appears to me
to be used in the Act in a popular and general sense. I apprehend that if it had been
intended to have a definite and restricted meaning, it would have been specially so
defined by the [1909] Act.'

Lord Guthrie said[1], referring to s 43 of the 1909 Act: *b*

'It is quite clear from the first proviso that the object of the Act was to secure
effective ventilation of the habitable rooms in every tenement. Back-to-back houses,
if one may attempt a definition, are houses facing opposite ways and with one
common back wall. I am not prepared to say that there might not be houses which
would correspond to that definition but which still would not be back-to-back
houses within the meaning of section 43.'   *c*

And there is an English case, *White v St Marylebone Borough Council*[2], heard on a case stated
by the Divisional Court of the King's Bench Division. That was a case where flats for
chauffeurs had been erected over garages back to back, but approximately one-third of
the back wall of each flat gave on to a ventilation shaft, so that the position was that two-
thirds of the wall was a party or common wall and one-third gave on to the ventilation   *d*
shaft. Lord Reading CJ[3] said:

'Sect. 43 of the Act of 1909 prohibits the erection of "back-to-back houses"
intended to be used as dwellings for the working classes. The object of the section
was to provide that with regard to any dwelling-houses to be erected in future—that
is after the passing of the Act—no houses should be built back to back if it was
intended that they should be used by the working classes, and what Parliamant had   *e*
in mind, as appears quite clearly from the language of the section and having regard
to the whole scope of the Act, was to ensure that there should be proper ventilation
in the houses of the working classes, and that the means that the Legislature adopted
for this purpose was to enact that they should not be built back to back. Now in the
present case there is no doubt on the statement of the facts that two-thirds of the
back of each pair of these houses was back to back, that is to say that there was a   *f*
common back as regards two-thirds to the two houses, and as regards one-third
which was occupied by their air shaft the houses were not back to back, and the
question therefore resolves itself into this: Where it is shown that two-thirds of the
space at the back of a house is back to back and one-third is not, is it open to the Local
Government Board to conclude that the dwelling-houses so constructed are "back-
to-back houses"? In my opinion, it is open to the Local Government Board to come   *g*
to that conclusion. I do not mean for one moment to decide the question of fact;
that is for the Local Government Board to decide upon the evidence before them;
but, as a matter of law, it certainly is open to them to come to that conclusion if they
think fit. Equally, it is open to them if they think fit to say that these are not "back-
to-back houses" upon the view that one-third of the space is open in the sense which
I have described. The real test is whether substantially these houses so constructed   *h*
are "back-to-back houses". The question of fact is not for us to decide . . .'

So the question is one of fact. And I accept the observation of Lord Dundas[4] that in the
legislation the expression 'back-to-back houses' is not used in a technical sense or as a term
of art, but in a popular and general sense. In that sense, 'back-to-back houses' means, in
my judgment, terraces of back-to-back houses, where all the houses except the end ones

1   1912 SC 217 at 223
2   [1915] 3 KB 249
3   [1915] 3 KB 249 at 256–257
4   1912 SC 217 at 222

have three inside walls and only one outside wall.   Those terraces and the houses
a constituting them are nothing at all like the dwellings being constructed by the company
in the present case, and I decline to hold that they are 'back-to-back' within the meaning
of the 1957 Act.

But if I am wrong about this, it is necessary, and I think proper, that I should go on to
consider the expression 'intended to be used as dwellings for the working classes'.   I
observe in passing that the Act says 'for the working classes', not 'by the working classes',
b which perhaps contains a hint of paternalism: someone says, 'This is for you': houses have
been provided *for* the working classes, as against being bought *by* the working class or
anybody else.   But be that as it may, I have to construe the phrase in the 1957 Act.   And
there has been a good deal of discussion about the meaning today to be given to the
expression 'working classes'.   I was referred to *H E Green & Sons v Minister of Health
(No 2)*[1], in which Denning J said the expression was quite inappropriate today and that
c at that time, apparently, social distinctions had been abolished.   But he nevertheless went
on to try to give some meaning to the expression by reference to a definition in the
schedule to what was then the 1936 Act, which was inserted for quite other purposes, and
the case itself was concerned with the power of a local authority under Part V of the 1936
Act to acquire any land as a site for the erection of houses for the working classes.   It was
held that that meant in that context 'houses of a type suitable for occupation by the
d working classes', and I do not find it of assistance in the present case.   It was followed by
Romer J in *Belcher v Reading Corpn*[2].   But, again, that was not a decision on the provision
which I have to try to construe, and I do not find it very helpful.

But I should refer to *Guinness Trust (London Fund) v Green*[3], a decision of the Court of
Appeal, where the point was whether the Guinness Trust, which was providing what I
may be forgiven for calling 'working class housing' in London, was a housing trust
e within the meaning of the 1936 Act, so that its tenants were not protected by the Rent
Restriction Acts.   The trust deed of about 1890 referred to a fund which had been set up
for 'the amelioration of the condition of the poorer classes of the working population of
London', and the question was whether its funds were being devoted to the provision of
houses for persons the majority of whom were in fact members of the working classes.
In that case, Denning LJ said[4]:

f
'Some years ago in *Green & Sons v. Minister of Health (No. 2)*[5] . . . I said that the
phrase "working classes" was quite inappropriate to modern conditions.   Fifty years
ago the phrase was well understood to mean people who worked with their hands,
whether on the land or on the railways or in the mines.   Such people in those days
earned wages which on the whole were much less than the rest of the community.
Nowadays the phrase is quite inapplicable.   People who work on the land or in
g factories often earn more than people who work in offices or shops.   Craftsmen earn
as much as or more than clergymen or teachers.   Yet we still have to apply the test
whether a house is provided for the working classes.   The only way to do it, I think,
is to ask whether the house is provided for people in the lower income range, or in
other words for people whose circumstances are such that they are deserving of
support from a charitable institution in their housing needs.   Applying this test, I
h am quite satisfied that the Guinness Trust does provide houses for such people.   The
majority of them do fall within the lower income group, and they are deserving of
support by this charitable institution.'

So I think there Denning LJ is for the purposes of the case saying that 'the working
classes' as an expression means 'the lower income groups'.

j _____

1   [1947] 2 All ER 469, [1948] 1 KB 34
2   [1949] 2 All ER 969, [1950] Ch 380
3   [1955] 2 All ER 871, [1955] 1 WLR 872
4   [1955] 2 All ER 871 at 873, [1955] 1 WLR 872 at 875
5   [1947] 2 All ER 469 at 471, [1948] 1 KB 34 at 38

Basing himself on this, counsel for the borough council says that these are inexpensive houses as houses go nowadays; and that is not to be denied. They still sell, apparently, or would sell for under £10,000, though, of course, the price is rising, I daresay, daily or at least frequently. Secondly, it follows, he says, that these houses are likely to be bought by relatively poor people; that is to say, by the working classes. And from these two obvious facts, he says, the court must imply an intention on the part of the company to commit a breach of s 5.

The company, on the other hand, says in its evidence that it has no intention of selling to any particular income group. Naturally enough, one-bedroomed houses are bought by single people or couples without children who may, of course, be seeking a first rung on the housing ladder. They say they have built a considerable number of these houses over the country, and 60% of them have been bought by single people. Anyway, they say, if you look at what happened in this case, you see that when the first of the two blocks was nearing completion they sold or accepted reservations for the four dwellings in it, and the purchasers were a lady doctor, a professional ice-skater, a personnel officer and a nursing sister; and those, they say, are not members of the working classes. And they also put in evidence a list of the occupations of the purchasers of these properties over the country, which certainly shows a great variety of occupations and again does not support the view that the initial purchasers, at any rate, are necessarily or at all likely to be members of what could be called 'the working classes', if that expression is to be given any meaning.

The estate where these properties are being developed is a large one of different types of housing, the biggest, I think, being four-bedroomed detached, and there are a number of varieties down to the smallest ones, which are the 'Mayfair'. It is not a working class area where a house or a building is being erected clearly divided so as to be only suitable in practice for the lodgings of the poor, as was the case in *Crow v Davis*[1], to which I was referred.

These houses now in question are not in such an area and of such construction that the court should infer that they are intended for the poor as distinct from the single, and no intention therefore to breach s 5 can in my judgment be imputed to the company. And as regards their actual intention, I am satisfied again that it is not their intention to erect these houses to be used as dwellings for the working classes. I do not propose to attempt a definition of the modern meaning of 'working classes', but I think that the borough council has not made out that it is entitled to the declaration sought, and the originating summons is therefore dismissed with costs.

Summons dismissed.

Solicitors: *A Marshall* (for the borough council); *Cohen & Co*, Stockton-on-Tees (for the company).

M Denise Chorlton   Barrister.

---

1   (1903) 89 LT 407; (1904) 91 LT 88

R v Dytham

a

COURT OF APPEAL, CRIMINAL DIVISION
LORD WIDGERY CJ, SHAW LJ AND MCNEILL J
9th, 18th JULY 1979

b *Criminal law – Misbehaviour in public office – Common law offence – Ingredients of offence – Police constable charged with wilful neglect to carry out his duty by omitting to take steps to preserve the peace and protect a man being violently assaulted and arrest his assailants – Whether offence constituted by matters charged – Whether corruption or fraud a necessary element of offence.*

c The appellant, a police constable, was on duty in uniform at about 1 am near a club when a man was ejected from the club and then violently assaulted by a number of men who beat and kicked him tó death. The appellant took no steps to intervene in the assault and when it was over merely drove away. He was charged in an indictment with misconduct whilst acting as an officer of justice in that he deliberately failed to carry out his duty as a police constable by wilfully omitting to take any steps to preserve the peace or to protect the man or to arrest or otherwise bring to justice his assailants. At the trial he *d* objected to the indictment on the ground that it did not disclose an offence known to the law. The trial judge ruled against the objection and the trial proceeded. The jury returned a verdict of guilty and the appellant was convicted. He appealed against the conviction on the ground that the trial judge erred in ruling that the indictment disclosed an offence known to law. The appellant conceded that at common law there existed an offence of misconduct in a public office, but contended that mere non-feasance *e* by a person in the discharge of his duty as the holder of a public office was insufficient to constitute the offence and there had to be a malfeasance or, at least, a misfeasance involving corruption or fraud.

Held – A public officer who wilfully and without reasonable excuse or justification *f* neglected to perform any duty he was bound to perform by common law or statute was indictable for the common law offence of misconduct in a public office. The element of culpability required was not restricted to corruption or dishonesty, although it had to be such that the conduct impugned was calculated to injure the public interest and called for condemnation and punishment. Whether there was such conduct was a matter for the jury on the evidence. Since the indictment alleged deliberate and wilful neglect by the appellant to perform his duty as a police constable, it disclosed an offence of *g* misconduct in a public office. It followed that the judge's ruling had been correct and that the appeal would be dismissed (see p 644 *g* to *j*, post).

R v Wyat (1705) 1 Salk 380 applied.
Dictum of Widgery J in *R v Llewellyn-Jones* (1966) 51 Cr App R at 6–7 considered.

h **Notes**
For neglect of duty by a public officer, see 11 Halsbury's Laws (4th Edn) para 932, and for cases on the subject, see 15 Digest (Reissue) 943–944, 8107–8149.

Cases referred to in judgment
j *R v Bembridge* (1783) 3 Doug KB 327, 22 State Tr 1, 99 ER 679, 15 Digest (Reissue) 940, 8087.
R v Llewellyn-Jones and Lougher (1966) 51 Cr App R 4; *affd* [1967] 3 All ER 225, [1968] 1 QB 429, [1967] 3 WLR 1298, 51 Cr App R 204, CA, 15 Digest (Reissue) 940, 8096.
R v Quinn, R v Bloom [1961] 3 All ER 88, [1962] 2 QB 245, [1961] 3 WLR 611, 125 JP 565, 45 Cr App R 279, CCA, 15 Digest (Reissue) 1054, 9077.

R v Wyat (1705) 1 Salk 380, Fortes Rep 127, 2 Ld Raym 1189, 91 ER 331, sub nom *R v Wiat* [1705] 11 Mod Rep 53, 15 Digest (Reissue) 944, 8138.

Cases also cited

Crouther's Case (1599) Cro Eliz 654, 78 ER 893.
Fentiman, Ex parte (1834) 2 Ad & El 127, 111 ER 49.
R v Borran (1820) 3 B & Ald 432, [1814–23] All ER Rep 775.
R v Davie (1781) 2 Doug KB 588, 99 ER 371.
R v Williams and Davis (1762) 3 Burr 1317, 97 ER 851.

Appeal

On 9th November 1978 in the Crown Court at Liverpool before Neill J and a jury the appellant, Philip Thomas Dytham, a police constable, was convicted on indictment of misconduct whilst acting as an officer of justice in that on 18th March 1977, being present and a witness to a criminal offence, namely a violent assault on one Peter Malcolm Stubbs by three others, he deliberately failed to carry out his duty as a police constable by wilfully omitting to take any step to preserve the peace, to protect Mr Stubbs or to arrest or otherwise bring to justice Mr Stubbs's assailants. The appellant was fined £150 payable within four months and in default was sentenced to three months' imprisonment. He was also ordered to pay £50 towards the legally aided costs of his defence. He appealed against the conviction on the ground that on a demurrer to the indictment pleaded by his counsel on the ground that the indictment did not disclose an offence known to the law, the trial judge erred in ruling that the indictment did disclose an offence known to the law. The facts are set out in the judgment of the court.

Gerard Wright QC and *David Maddison* for the appellant.
T P Russell QC and *H H Andrew* for the Crown.

Cur adv vult

18th July. **LORD WIDGERY CJ** read the following judgment of the court prepared by Shaw LJ: The appellant was a police constable in Lancashire. On 17th March 1977 at about one o'clock in the morning he was on duty in uniform and was standing by a hot dog stall in Duke Street, St Helens. A Mr Wincke was inside the stall and a Mr Sothern was by it. Some thirty yards away was the entrance to Cindy's Club. A man named Stubbs was ejected from the club by a bouncer. A fight ensued in which a number of men joined. There arose cries and screams and other indications of great violence. Mr Stubbs became the object of a murderous assault. He was beaten and kicked to death in the gutter outside the club. All this was audible and visible to the three men at the hot dog stall. At no stage did the appellant make any move to intervene or any attempt to quell the disturbance or to stop the attack on the victim. When the hubbub had died down he adjusted his helmet and drove away. According to the other two at the hot dog stall, he said that he was due off and was going off.

His conduct was brought to the notice of the police authority. As a result he appeared on 10th October 1978 in the Crown Court at Liverpool to answer an indictment which was in these terms:

'... the charge against you is one of misconduct of an officer of justice, in that you ... misconducted yourself whilst acting as an officer of justice in that you being present and a witness to a criminal offence namely a violent assault upon one ... Stubbs by three others deliberately failed to carry out your duty as a police constable by wilfully omitting to take any steps to preserve the Queen's Peace or to protect the person of the said ... Stubbs or to arrest or otherwise bring to justice [his] assailants.'

On arraignment the appellant pleaded not guilty and the trial was adjourned to 7th November. On that day before the jury was empanelled counsel for the appellant took an objection to the indictment by way of demurrer. The burden of that objection was

that the indictment as laid disclosed no offence known to the law. Neill J ruled against
a the objection and the trial proceeded. The defence on the facts was that the appellant had
observed nothing more than that a man was turned out of the club. It was common
ground that in that situation his duty would not have required him to take any action.
The jury were directed that the crucial question for their consideration was whether the
appellant had seen the attack on the victim. If he had they could find him guilty of the
offence charged in the indictment. The jury did return a verdict of guilty. Hence this
b appeal which is confined to the matters of law raised by the demurrer pleaded at the
court of trial.

At the outset of his submissions in this court counsel for the appellant conceded two
matters. The first was that a police constable is a public officer. The second was that
there does exist at common law an offence of misconduct in a public office.

From that point the argument was within narrow limits though it ran deep into
c constitutional and jurisprudential history. The effect of it was that not every failure to
discharge a duty which devolved on a person as the holder of a public office gave rise to
the common law offence of misconduct in that office. As counsel for the appellant put
it, non-feasance was not enough. There must be a malfeasance or at least a misfeasance
involving an element of corruption. In support of this contention a number of cases
were cited from 18th and 19th century reports. It is the fact that in nearly all of them
d the misconduct asserted involved some corrupt taint; but this appears to have been an
accident of circumstance and not a necessary incident of the offence. Misconduct in a
public office is more vividly exhibited where dishonesty is revealed as part of the
dereliction of duty. Indeed in some cases the conduct impugned cannot be shown to
have been misconduct unless it was done with a corrupt or oblique motive. This was the
position for example in R v Bembridge[1] and also in the modern case of R v Llewellyn-Jones
e and Lougher[2]. There the registrar of a county court was charged in a count which alleged
that he had made an order in relation to funds under his control 'in the expectation that
he would gain personal advantage from the making of such order'. On a motion to
quash the count as disclosing no offence known to the law I, as trial judge in the course
of my ruling, made the following pronouncement[3]:

f 'The authorities to which I have been referred show that there is a variety of ways
in which the holder of a public office may be indicted under this principle for
misconduct or misbehaviour. It is clear that a culpable failure to exercise a public
duty may, because the duty is a public one, lay the defaulter open to indictment for
criminal offences, whereas, had he been working for a private employer, his default
would have been no more than a civil liability. Even so, it is not easy to lay down
with precision the exact limits of the kind of misconduct or misbehaviour which
g can result in an indictment under this rule. I have formed a clear view, but stated
in hypothetical terms, that if the registrar of a county court when exercising his
power to order payment out of court of money held on behalf of a beneficiary were
to make an order in expectation of some personal benefit which he hoped to obtain
and in circumstances where, had it not been for the personal benefit, he would not
have made the order, that would be an example of misconduct in a public duty
h sufficient to come within this rule. The reason why I feel that that would come
within the rule is because in that hypothetical case a public officer would be
distorting the course of justice to meet his own personal ends and, in my opinion,
it would be sufficient to justify a conviction if it could be shown that he had made
such an order with intent to obtain personal benefit for himself and in circumstances
in which there were no grounds for supposing that he would not have made the
j order but for his personal interest and expectation. On the other hand, I have

---

1   (1783) 3 Doug KB 327, 99 ER 679
2   (1967) 51 Cr App R 4
3   51 Cr App R 4 at 6–7

reached an equally clear view that it is not enough to bring a county court registrar within the principle merely to show that, when making an order which was within his power and which he could make for perfectly proper motives, he knew that by a side wind, as it were, he was going to gain some personal benefit. The mere fact that he knows of his personal interest is, in my view, a very good ground for his declining to exercise jurisdiction and for his arranging for someone else, such as the judge, to make an order for him. Everyone in judicial office knows how unwise it is to deal with a case in which personal interests are raised, but I would not be prepared to say that it would be misconduct for this purpose for a registrar to make a decision which did affect his personal interests, merely because he knew that his interests were so involved, if the decision was made honestly and in a genuine belief that it was a proper exercise of his jurisdiction so far as the beneficiaries and other persons concerned came into it. When one looks at the terms of count 1 as it now stands, it seems to me that it alleges no more than knowledge on the part of the defendant that his personal interest was involved. For the reasons I have given, it is not enough to disclose an offence known to the law and, if the matter rested there, that count and others to which similar considerations apply would have to be quashed. On the other hand, it is not difficult to amend count 1 so as to introduce the vital element to which I have already referred and I am satisfied that such an amendment can be made without injustice in the circumstances of this case.'

So also in R v Wyat[1], a case tried in 1705 it was held that 'where an officer [in that case a constable] neglects a duty incumbent on him either by common law or statute, he is for his fault indictable'. Counsel for the appellant contended that this was too wide a statement of principle since it omitted any reference to corruption or fraud; but in Stephen's Digest of the Criminal Law[2] are to be found these words:

'Every public officer commits a misdemeanour who wilfully neglects to perform any duty which he is bound either by common law or by statute to perform provided that the discharge of such duty is not attended with greater danger than a man of ordinary firmness and activity may be expected to encounter.'

In support of this proposition R v Wyat[1] is cited as well as R v Bembridge[3], a judgment of Lord Mansfield. The neglect must be wilful and not merely inadvertent; and it must be culpable in the sense that it is without reasonable excuse or justification.

In the present case it was not suggested that the appellant could not have summoned or sought assistance to help the victim or to arrest his assailants. The charge as framed left this answer open to him. Not surprisingly he did not seek to avail himself of it, for the facts spoke strongly against any such answer. The allegation made was not of mere non-feasance but of deliberate failure and wilful neglect. This involves an element of culpability which is not restricted to corruption or dishonesty but which must be of such a degree that the misconduct impugned is calculated to injure the public interest so as to call for condemnation and punishment. Whether such a situation is revealed by the evidence is a matter that a jury has to decide. It puts no heavier burden on them than when in more familiar contexts they are called on to consider whether driving is dangerous or a publication is obscene or a place of public resort is a disorderly house: see R v Quinn, R v Bloom[4].

The judge's ruling was correct. The appeal is dismissed.

———————————

1　(1705) 1 Salk 380, 91 ER 331
2　9th Edn (1950) p 114–115, art 145
3　(1783) 3 Doug KB 327, 99 ER 679
4　[1961] 3 All ER 88 at 91, [1962] 2 QB 245 at 255

Appeal dismissed.

a   *24th July. The court refused to certify under s 33(2) of the Criminal Appeal Act 1968 that a point of law of general public importance was involved in the decision.*

Solicitors: *Mace & Jones,* Huyton (for the appellant); *Director of Public Prosecutions.*

Lea Josse   Barrister.

b

Jessel v Jessel

COURT OF APPEAL, CIVIL DIVISION
c   LORD DENNING MR, BROWNE AND GEOFFREY LANE LJJ
6th JUNE 1979

Divorce – Financial provision – Jurisdiction to vary order incorporating terms agreed between spouses – Order for periodical payments 'until further order' – Order containing agreement by wife to accept payments in settlement of all her claims to periodical payments and undertaking by
d   *her not to apply to increase husband's liability – Subsequent application by wife to vary periodical payments – Whether order a final order or a continuing order capable of variation or discharge – Matrimonial Causes Act 1973, s 31(1) (2) (b).*

The husband and wife separated in 1971. The agreement which they reached on the financial arrangements between them was, with the court's consent, embodied in
e   minutes of order which provided that the husband would pay the wife periodical payments, during their joint lives or until her marriage or 'until further order', of £2,400 per annum to be reduced to £1,200 per annum in certain events. By para 2 of the minutes the wife agreed to 'accept the periodical payments order . . . in settlement of all her claims to periodical payments' and undertook 'not to apply to increase the [husband's] liability'. On 12th December 1973 a formal order was drawn up
f   incorporating the terms of the minutes. In 1978 the wife applied to the court to vary the periodical payments payable under the order on the ground that the parties' circumstances had changed since the order of 12th December. The husband contended that by reason of the provisions in para 2 the court had no jurisdiction to alter the periodical payments and could not entertain the wife's application. The registrar held that there was jurisdiction to entertain her application. The husband appealed to a judge who held, on
g   authority[a], that the court had no jurisdiction to entertain the wife's application because the provisions in para 2 of the minutes meant that the order for periodical payments was not a continuing order capable of variation or discharge under s 31[b] of the Matrimonial Causes Act 1973. He therefore struck out the application. The wife appealed.

Held – The order for periodical payments of 12th December 1973, being for indefinite
h   payments 'until further order', was a continuing order and was not, despite the provisions in para 2 of the minutes, a final or 'once and for all' order. The court therefore retained jurisdiction, under s 31(1) and (2)(b) of the 1973 Act, to vary, discharge or suspend any provision of the order. Moreover, it was against public policy that the maintenance agreement contained in the order should be unalterable. It followed that as para 2 of the minutes was a provision of the periodical payments order, para 2 was capable of being
j   varied or discharged under s 31(1), and did not prevent the court from entertaining the wife's application to vary the periodical payments. Accordingly, the court had

_____

a   *Minton v Minton* [1979] 1 All ER 79, HL
b   Section 31, so far as material, is set out at p 650 g h, post

jurisdiction to entertain the application, and the appeal would be allowed (see p 648 *b c* and *e* to *g*, p 649 *a* to *f h j*, p 650 *a* to *h* and p 651 *c*, post).

Minton v Minton [1979] 1 All ER 79 distinguished.

Notes

For waiver of claims for financial provision, see 13 Halsbury's Laws (4th Edn) para 1158, and for variation of orders, see ibid para 1168.

For the Matrimonial Causes Act 1973, s 31, see 43 Halsbury's Statutes (3rd Edn) 576.

Cases referred to in judgments

Bennett v Bennett (1934) 103 LJP 38, 150 LT 460, 27(2) Digest (Reissue) 813, 6539.
Hall v Hall [1915] P 105, 84 LJP 93, 113 LT 58, CA, 27(2) Digest (Reissue) 842, 6700.
Hyman v Hyman [1929] AC 601, [1929] All ER Rep 245, 98 LJP 81, 141 LT 329, 93 JP 209, 27 LGR 379, HL, 27(1) Digest (Reissue) 274, 2030.
Minton v Minton [1979] 1 All ER 79, [1979] 2 WLR 31, HL.
Turk v Turk, Dufty v Dufty [1931] P 116, [1931] All ER Rep 505, 100 LJP 90, 145 LT 331; subsequent proceedings (1932) 147 LT 18, 27(2) Digest (Reissue) 841, 6690.

Cases also cited

Dean v Dean [1978] 3 All ER 758, [1978] Fam 161.
de Lasala v de Lasala [1979] 2 All ER 1146, [1979] 3 WLR 390, PC.
L v L [1961] 3 All ER 834, [1962] P 101, CA.
Tulip v Tulip [1951] 2 All ER 91, [1951] P 378, CA.
Wright v Wright [1970] 3 All ER 209, [1970] 1 WLR 1219, CA.

Appeal

This was an appeal by Philippa Brigid Jessel ('the wife') from an order of Bush J made on 16th February 1979 whereby he allowed the appeal of Toby Francis Henry Jessel ('the husband') from the order of Mr Registrar Bayne-Powell made on 13th July 1978 dismissing the wife's application for a variation of the periodical payments payable to her by the husband under an order made on 12th December 1973. The facts are set out in the judgment of Lord Denning MR.

Anthony Temple for the wife.
Matthew Thorpe for the husband.

LORD DENNING MR. Mr and Mrs Jessel married on 29th July 1967. They had a daughter Sarah who was born on 6th November 1970. Unfortunately there were unhappy differences between the husband and wife. They separated in October 1971. There followed unsuccessful discussions between their respective solicitors regarding a possible reconciliation. Eventually the parties were divorced in December 1973. Very sadly, the little girl was killed in an accident about a year later.

The action before us today concerns the provision of periodical payments for the wife, Mrs Jessel. Soon after the parties separated, their respective solicitors negotiated as to the financial arrangements to be made. On 24th February 1972 the husband's solicitors wrote a letter to the wife's solicitors setting out the various terms of the financial arrangements. The matrimonial home, which had been in joint names, was to be vested in the husband only, but he was to make a financial provision by way of a lump sum. It was to enable the wife to be provided with a flat, which she has occupied ever since. Furthermore, and I need not pause on them now, there were provisions for maintenance in regard to the child of the marriage. But so far as the wife was concerned, there was an unusual provision as to her periodical payments; and that is what comes into question here. It was agreed that, so long as Mr Jessel was a member of Parliament, there should be periodical payments amounting to £2,400 a year. But if he ceased to be a member of Parliament, it should be half that sum, £1,200 a year. But I ought to say that in that

letter there was a clause which said that Mrs Jessel (the wife) would not make any further
a claims against her husband or apply for any further periodical payments or anything of
that kind. In other words, she was to have no claim against him other than the
provisions which I have recited.

I pause at once to say that that clause was void under the statutes on that behalf. The
statute in its present state is the Matrimonial Causes Act 1973, s 34(1) of which provides:

'If a maintenance agreement includes a provision purporting to restrict any right
b   to apply to a court for an order containing financial arrangements, then—(a) that
provision shall be void . . .'

Therefore, so far as that clause in the agreement restricted the right of Mrs Jessel to come
to the court, it was void.

I will say no more about that agreement. It has ceased to exist. It was subject to the
c approval of the court, and it has been replaced by documents which were approved by
the court.

In July 1972 a deputy circuit judge expressed an opinion that the agreement was
reasonable and fair. Thereafter minutes of order were drawn up by the solicitors on each
side, and approved. They were embodied in an order. Paragraph 2 of the minutes of the
order says:

d   'The Petitioner [that is the wife] shall accept the periodical payments Order from
date of decree absolute made in settlement of all her claims to periodical payments
and hereby undertakes not to apply to increase the Respondent's [that is the
husband's] liability.'

Then followed this provision in the minutes of order:

e   'AND IT IS FURTHER ORDERED that the Respondent [that is the husband] do pay or
cause to be paid to the Petitioner for herself by way of periodical payments during
joint lives or until the Petitioner's remarriage or until further Order the sum of
£2,400 per annum less tax such sum to be reduced to £1,200 per annum less tax
should the Respondent cease to be a Member of Parliament and whilst he should
cease to be a Member of Parliament the above sum to be payable monthly as from
f   the date on which this decree nisi shall be made absolute.'

Those are the important terms of the minutes. They were initialled and consented to
by the solicitors for the parties. Then on the formal order of 12th December 1973 it was
ordered that those minutes of order should be made a rule of court. This was the formal
order which was drawn up on 12th December 1973:

g   'AND it is further ordered that the Respondent [that is, the husband] do pay or
cause to be paid to the Petitioner [that is the wife] for herself periodical payments
during their joint lives or until the Petitioner shall remarry or until further order at
the rate of £2,400 per annum less tax to be reduced to £1,200 per annum less tax
should the Respondent cease to be a Member of Parliament . . . AND it is further
ordered that the Minutes of Order . . . be made a rule of Court.'

h
In February 1978 Mrs Jessel applied for a variation of the terms of that order with
regard to the periodical payments. She said that the situation had changed much in the
intervening five or six years. The husband by his lawyers applied to dismiss her
application on the ground that the court had no jurisdiction to alter it. The matter came
before the registrar. He refused to dismiss her application. He held that the court had
j jurisdiction to entertain the wife's application and go into the case.

There was an appeal to a judge of the High Court. The case was held over pending a
decision of the House of Lords: see Minton v Minton[1]. The judge was so influenced by the
decision of the House of Lords that he felt that the court had no jurisdiction to give Mrs

Jessel any further sum for periodical payments. So he struck out the wife's application. She appeals to this court.

To my mind *Minton v Minton*[1] has no application to the present case. It does not apply to an order for periodical payments. *Minton v Minton*[1] only applies when there is a genuine final order which contains no continuing order for periodical payments, as for instance when the wife has applied for periodical payments and her application has been dismissed, or, as in *Minton v Minton*[1], a nominal order for periodical payments came to an end. *Minton v Minton*[1] must be confined to such a situation. It has no application whatsoever to the present case.

In this case, on the very face of the order there is a continuing provision for periodical payments to go on indefinitely 'until further order', either in the sum of £2,400 a year as long as he is a member of Parliament or £1,200 a year if he should no longer be a member of Parliament. It comes within the qualification which Lord Scarman mentioned[2]:

'Once an application has been dealt with on its merits, the court has no future jurisdiction [now this is the important qualification] save where there is a continuing order capable of variation or discharge under s 31 of the 1973 Act.'

Section 31(1) provides:

'Where the court has made an order to which this section applies, then, subject to the provisions of this section, the court shall have power to vary or discharge the order or to suspend *any provision thereof* temporarily and to revive the operation of any provision so suspended.'

Subsection (2) provides: 'This section applies to the following orders, that is to say . . . (b) any periodical payments order . . .' So to my mind it is as plain as can be that *Minton v Minton*[1] does not apply. Section 31 does apply. The court has power to vary or discharge this order which has been made.

To this I would add the words of the second paragraph of the order that periodical payments were to be paid during the joint lives of the husband and wife or until the wife remarried 'or until further order'. Those words 'or until further order' are of much importance. There are many cases to show this. I need not go through them all. I will just mention their names: *Hall v Hall*[3], *Turk v Turk*[4] and *Bennett v Bennett*[5]. It is as plain as can be that the words 'or until further order' keep the position alive so that an application can be made at any time for a further order to vary the periodical payments upwards or downwards as the situation changes in regard to them.

Counsel for the husband sought to avoid those words by saying, 'Oh, yes; that is quite an important order to put in for the protection of the husband'. He put this instance: 'Suppose the wife formed an association with a rich man and lived with him without actually going through a form of marriage, would the husband not then be entitled to come and ask for a variation of the periodical payments downwards?' Counsel said that in that case the husband could come and ask for the payments to be reduced. But the wife, he said, could not take advantage of the words 'until further order'. She could not come and ask for the payments to be increased. He relied on the provision in para 2 of the minutes of order which ran:

'The Petitioner shall accept the periodical payments Order from date of decree absolute made in settlement of all her claims to periodical payments and hereby undertakes not to apply to increase the Respondent's liability.'

1   [1979] 1 All ER 79, [1979] 2 WLR 31
2   [1979] 1 All ER 79 at 87, [1979] 2 WLR 31 at 41
3   [1915] P 105
4   [1931] P 116, [1931] All ER Rep 505
5   (1934) 103 LJP 38

He said that, despite the words 'or until further order', the wife had shut herself out by
a that provision.

To my mind there is one short simple answer to that argument. Section 31 gives the
court power to vary or discharge the order or to suspend *any provision* of the order for
periodical payments. That provision (by which the wife agreed not to apply to increase
the husband's liability) was a provision of the order for periodical payments. So the court
can vary, discharge or suspend that provision. In a case of this kind, it can and should say
b that the provision no longer operates against the wife. It does not exclude the court from
hearing her claim. The court does have jurisdiction to order a variation in the periodical
payments.

So it seems to me that in this particular case the registrar was right and the court does
have jurisdiction to entertain the wife's claim for a variation of the periodical payments
order. She is not to be shut out by the terms of the agreement or of the order which
c made it a rule of court. It was said many, many years ago in *Hyman v Hyman*[1] that it
would be contrary to public policy that a wife, who should be helped to be maintained
by her husband, should be fettered by agreements made at an earlier time without
knowledge of what the future might hold. It is wrong as a matter of public policy that
those agreements should be made binding unalterably on her. The only situation in
which such agreements are binding is as in *Minton v Minton*[2] where the House of Lords
d held that there was a countervailing principle, what they called 'the principle of a clean
break'. I have no doubt that there are situations such as were envisaged there, where the
parties make a 'once and for all' provision in the shape of a house, or whatever it may be,
for the wife, with no provision for continuing payments at all. There is a clean break
between the parties and there is nothing to be revived. That is one principle which
Minton v Minton[2] exemplifies. But when there is a provision for periodical payments like
e this which are certainly not 'once and for all', it seems to me that the court retains
complete jurisdiction to consider any further application made by the wife, having
regard to the whole of the history. The court has jurisdiction to deal with it.

I would allow the appeal and allow the wife's claim to go forward to be considered on
the merits.

f **BROWNE LJ.** I agree that this appeal should be allowed for the reasons given by Lord
Denning MR. Counsel for the husband accepts that as contractual terms para 9(c) of the
letter of 24th February 1972 and para 2 of the draft minutes of order are void. This of
course follows inevitably from *Hyman v Hyman*[1], to which Lord Denning MR referred,
and subsequent authorities to the same effect, and now from s 34 of the 1973 Act.

Counsel also accepts that the order of Mr Stogdon, sitting as a deputy circuit judge, on
g 18th July 1972 under s 7 of the Divorce Reform Act 1969 does nothing to validate the
contractual provisions of the letter of 24th February 1972. But he submits that the order
of Mr Kidner, sitting as a deputy circuit judge, on 12th December 1973 does validate
para 2 of the minutes of order which was thereby made a rule of court.

I do not find it necessary to decide whether this last submission is right. I doubt
whether it is, but assuming that para 2 of the minute should be treated as validated by
h the order of 12th December, I am clearly of opinion that the court still has jurisdiction
to consider Mrs Jessel's application to vary. I entirely agree with Lord Denning MR that
this is not a genuinely final order, or a once and for all order. It provided for continuing
periodical payments to continue indefinitely unless certain events happened, one of
which was until further order.

It seems to me that this case is exactly within s 31 of the 1973 Act. Section 31(2)
j provides: 'This section applies to the following orders, that is to say . . . (b) any periodical

---

1 [1929] AC 601, [1929] All ER Rep 245
2 [1979] 1 All ER 79, [1979] 2 WLR 31

payments order . . .' That being so, the section clearly does apply to this order; and, by
virtue of s 31(1), which Lord Denning MR has already read and which I need not read
again, the court has power to vary or discharge the order or suspend any provision
thereof temporarily, and so on.

The fact that in this case s 31 applies makes it entirely distinguishable from *Minton v
Minton*[1] in which s 31 had not and could not have any application; and counsel for the
husband rightly accepted that *Minton v Minton*[1] was a case where in substance the wife's
application had been dismissed and was so treated by the House of Lords.

In my judgment, the court has jurisdiction to consider Mrs Jessel's application to vary;
and, of course, we are not in any way concerned with what the result may be of the
consideration of that application on the merits.

GEOFFREY LANE LJ. In deference to the judge from whose views we are differing,
I desire to add a word or two of my own. It seems to me, first of all, that the judge did
not have all the assistance given to him which we have been lucky enough to receive in
this court. Before him the wife appeared in person; and, although no doubt she did her
best, we have had the advantage of hearing her counsel's argument on the points, which
have been of great assistance.

In this case there was a continuing periodical payment by the husband to the wife.
Consequently the decision of the House of Lords in *Minton v Minton*[1] has no effect. As
Lord Scarman said[2]:

'Once an application has been dealt with on its merits, the court has no future
jurisdiction save where there is a continuing order capable of variation or discharge
under s 31 of the 1973 Act,'

and he went on to deal with what he called 'the principle of the clean break'. But in this
case there was ex hypothesi no clean break (whatever that expression may mean) because
there were continuing payments by the husband to the wife which, like it or not,
operated as a continuing link. In those circumstances, s 31 of the 1973 Act plainly
applies. It reads as follows:

'(1) Where the court has made an order to which this section applies, then, subject
to the provisions of this section, the court shall have power to vary or discharge the
order or to suspend any provision thereof temporarily and to revive the operation
of any provision so suspended.

'(2) This section applies to the following orders, that is to say—(a) any order for
maintenance pending suit and any interim order for maintenance; (b) any periodical
payments order . . .'

Those provisions give the court power to vary the order and any provisions of it, and
confer jurisdiction on the court in this case.

This is not a case where there has been any dismissal of the wife's application. It is not
a case where there has been anything which could remotely be described as equivalent
to a dismissal as there was in *Minton v Minton*[1]. Therefore s 31 applies in full force. That
is enough to decide the case in favour of the wife and to justify the allowing of the
appeal. But I would add this. I very much doubt whether the minutes of order which
are before us are capable of having the effect for which counsel for the husband
contends. The passage which is material reads as follows, and the wording is important:

'2. The Petitioner shall accept the periodical payments Order from date of decree
absolute made in settlement of all her claims to periodical payments and hereby

---

1   [1979] 1 All ER 79, [1979] 2 WLR 31
2   [1979] 1 All ER 79 at 87, [1979] 2 WLR 31 at 41

a undertakes not to apply to increase the Respondent's liability. 3. The above
   agreements shall be made a Rule of Court.'

If one turns to s 34 of the 1973 Act, one finds this:

'(1) If a maintenance agreement includes a provision purporting to restrict any
right to apply to a court for an order containing financial arrangements then—(a)
that provision shall be void . . .'

b It is stated in the minute of the court that there has been such an agreement; and s 34
makes that agreement void. I find it extremely difficult to believe that embodying that
into a minute of the court or a minute of order makes valid something which was
previously by statute void.

However, I prefer not to base my conclusion on that reason, but simply on the ground
of the applicability of s 31. I too have come to the conclusion that the court has
c jurisdiction in this case. For those reasons I would also allow the appeal.

Appeal allowed. Case remitted to judge or registrar on merits.

Solicitors: *Edwin Coe & Calder Woods* (for the wife); *Bischoff & Co* (for the husband).

d   Frances Rustin   Barrister.

O'Brien (Inspector of Taxes) v Benson's   *a*
Hosiery (Holdings) Ltd

HOUSE OF LORDS

LORD DIPLOCK, VISCOUNT DILHORNE, LORD SIMON OF GLAISDALE, LORD FRASER OF TULLYBELTON
AND LORD RUSSELL OF KILLOWEN

2nd, 3rd JULY, 25th OCTOBER 1979   *b*

Capital gains tax – Disposal of assets – Assets – Employer's rights under service agreement with employee – Payment to company by employee to secure release from service agreement – Whether release of company's rights under service agreement a disposal of 'assets' – Whether company assessable to corporation tax in respect of payment by employee – Finance Act 1965, s 22(1)(3)(c).   *c*

By a service contract dated 23rd September 1968 a company appointed B its sales and merchandise director for a period of seven years at a salary of £4,000 per annum. Early in 1970 B asked to be released from the contract and by an agreement dated 2nd April 1970 the company, in consideration of the payment to it of £50,000 by B, released him from his obligations under the contract. The company was assessed to corporation tax in *d* respect of the receipt of the £50,000 on the basis that its rights under the service agreement were assets, within s 22(1)[a] of the Finance Act 1965, and that the release of those rights in return for consideration received was a disposal of assets under s 22(3)(c) of the 1965 Act. The Special Commissioners determined that the company's rights under the service agreement were not assets within s 22(1) and discharged the assessments. On appeal to the High Court, Fox J[b] reversed that decision, holding that an *e* employer's rights under a service agreement were assets within s 22(1), notwithstanding that they were non-assignable, since they were beneficial contractual rights under s 22(3)(c) and as such were assets within s 22(1). The Court of Appeal[c] allowed an appeal by the company, holding that the company's rights to the services of B under the service contract were not an asset within s 22(1) since such an asset consisted of property for which a market value could be ascertained and a right to personal services under a *f* contract of service, not being assignable, could not have a market value. The Crown appealed to the House of Lords.

Held – To contend that the rights of an employer under a contract of service were not property or an asset because they could not be turned to account by transfer or assignment to another was to give a restricted interpretation of the scheme of the imposition of *g* capital gains tax which the language of the legislation did not permit. If an employer was able to exact from an employee a substantial sum as a term of releasing him from his obligations to serve, the rights of the employer bore quite sufficiently the mark of an asset of the employer, within s 22(1) and (3)(c) of the 1965 Act, as something he could turn to account, notwithstanding that his ability to do so was by a type of disposal limited by its nature. It was erroneous to deduce from the language of s 22(4) of the Act, which *h* for certain purposes introduced the concept of market value, that there was a principle of general application for the purposes of capital gains tax that an asset had to have a market value. It followed that the sum of £50,000 paid by B to secure his release from the contract constituted a chargeable gain in the hands of the company. The appeal would therefore be allowed (see p 653 *h j*, p 654 *a b* and p 655 *h* to p 656 *c* and *f*, post).   *j*

Decision of the Court of Appeal [1978] 3 All ER 1057 reversed.

---

a   Section 22, so far as material, is set out at p 655 *a* to *c*, post
b   [1977] 3 All ER 352, [1977] STC 262
c   [1978] 3 All ER 1057, [1978] STC 549

Notes

a For chargeable assets for the purposes of capital gains, see 5 Halsbury's Laws (4th Edn) para 68, and for capital sums derived from assets where no assets are acquired, see ibid para 39.

For the Finance Act 1965, s 22, see 34 Halsbury's Statutes (3rd Edn) 877.

With effect from 6th April 1979 s 22(1) and (3) of the 1965 Act has been replaced by ss 19(1) and 20(1) of the Capital Gains Tax Act 1979.

b

Cases referred to in opinions

Bailey v Thurston & Co Ltd [1903] 1 KB 137, [1900–3] All ER Rep 818, 72 LJKB 36, 88 LT 43, CA, 5 Digest (Reissue) 998, *7992.*

Inland Revenue Comrs v Crossman, Inland Revenue Comrs v Mann [1936] 1 All ER 762, [1937] AC 26, sub nom *Re Crossman, Re Paulin* 105 LJKB 450, 154 LT 570, HL, 21 *c* Digest (Repl) 56, *219.*

Nokes v Doncaster Amalgamated Collieries Ltd [1940] 3 All ER 549, [1940] AC 1014, 109 LJKB 865, 163 LT 343, HL, 10 Digest (Reissue) 1229, *7728.*

Sutton v Dorf [1932] 2 KB 304, [1932] All ER Rep 70, 101 LJKB 536, 47 LT 171, 96 JP 259, 30 LGR 312, 5 Digest (Reissue) 1003, *8038.*

d ## Cases also cited

Aberdeen Construction Group Ltd v Inland Revenue Comrs [1978] 1 All ER 962, [1978] AC 885, [1978] STC 127, HL.

Inland Revenue Comrs v Montgomery [1975] 1 All ER 664, [1975] Ch 266, [1975] STC 182.

Appeal

e The Crown appealed against the decision of the Court of Appeal[1] (Buckley, Bridge LJJ and Sir David Cairns) given on 12th May 1978 whereby it reversed the decision of Fox J[2] allowing the Crown's appeal by way of case stated[3] against the decision of the Commissioners for the Special Purposes of the Income Tax Acts who, on 24th October 1975, allowed an appeal against the assessment to corporation tax of a payment of £50,000 made pursuant to an agreement dated 2nd April 1970 between Robert Solomon *f* Behar and the taxpayer, Benson's Hosiery (Holdings) Ltd, in consideration of the release by the taxpayer of Mr Behar from a service agreement dated 23rd September 1968 under which Mr Behar was appointed the taxpayer's sales and merchandise director for seven years. The facts are set out in the opinion of Lord Russell of Killowen.

Michael Nolan QC and *Brian Davenport* for the Crown.
g *D C Potter QC* and *Andrew Thornhill* for the taxpayer.

Their Lordships took time for consideration.

25th October. The following opinions were delivered.

h **LORD DIPLOCK.** My Lords, I have had the advantage of reading in draft the speech of my noble and learned friend, Lord Russell of Killowen. I agree with it and, for the reasons stated by him, I think this appeal should be allowed.

VISCOUNT DILHORNE. My Lords, I have had the advantage of reading in draft the speech of my noble and learned friend, Lord Russell of Killowen. I agree with it and *j* have nothing to add. For the reasons stated by him, I think this appeal should be allowed.

---

1   [1978] 3 All ER 1057, [1979] Ch 152, [1978] STC 549
2   [1977] 3 All ER 352, [1977] Ch 348, [1977] STC 262
3   The case is set out at [1977] 3 All ER 353–359

LORD SIMON OF GLAISDALE. My Lords, I have had the privilege of reading in draft the speech about to be delivered by my noble and learned friend, Lord Russell of Killowen. I agree with it; and for the reasons which he gives I would allow the appeal and concur in the order which he proposes.

LORD FRASER OF TULLYBELTON. My Lords, I have had the advantage of reading in draft the speech prepared by my noble and learned friend, Lord Russell of Killowen. I agree with its reasoning and conclusions, and I also would allow this appeal.

LORD RUSSELL OF KILLOWEN. My Lords, In September 1968 the respondent company ('the taxpayer') entered into a written agreement with a Mr Behar under which Mr Behar agreed to serve the taxpayer as sales and merchandise director in exchange for an annual remuneration for a period of seven years. In April 1970 by a further written agreement the taxpayer released Mr Behar from any obligation further to serve the taxpayer in consideration of payment by Mr Behar to the taxpayer of £50,000. The question in this appeal is whether that sum (subject perhaps to some deduction) is to be brought into the computation of the taxpayer's profits for corporation tax; and that question in turn depends on whether it was a capital gain accruing to the taxpayer on the disposal of an asset within that part of the Finance Act 1965 that introduced capital gains tax. Hereunder the primary question is whether the right of the taxpayer under the contract to require the personal service of Mr Behar was an 'asset' within the 1965 Act.

Before turning to the language of the statute I will summarise the facts and the two agreements involved. In 1968 a company called Benson's Hosiery Ltd ('Hosiery') was carrying on a business of selling hosiery through thitherto unexploited outlets, such as shops not usually associated with such goods. Mr Behar owned 25% of Hosiery's issued share capital, had been for some years its sales and merchandise director, and had pioneered and exploited with conspicuous success their novel method of hosiery marketing. The taxpayer (a holding company) in 1968 acquired the issued share capital of Hosiery in exchange for shares in the taxpayer. At the same time it acquired the issued share capital of another company, South Coast Warehousemen Ltd. It was in those circumstances that the taxpayer entered into a service agreement with Mr Behar, who, it will have been observed, became a shareholder in the taxpayer. By that service agreement Mr Behar was appointed sales and merchandise director of the taxpayer for seven years at a salary of £4,000 per annum. There was no provision for commission or bonus, though it appears that some bonus was paid. Thereunder Mr Behar was required to perform the duties assigned to him by the board of the taxpayer including rendering services to any subsidiary of the taxpayer; these services would no doubt be within the scope of a sales and merchandise director. His major function was to find and maintain sales outlets, and this function he performed with 'conspicuous success'. In March 1970 Mr Behar sought release from his service contract. I suppose, my Lords, that he considered that his services were undervalued in the service contract, even with bonuses, and wished to be at liberty to earn more elsewhere. Of course, if he simply walked out he might have been liable for considerable damages for breach of contract. It is perhaps for question whether, in the circumstance that the taxpayer was only a holding company and could not assert direct damages in trade from his possible defection, such damages could embrace decline in profitability of its shares in the subsidiaries. In the result the agreement of 1970 in express terms required the payment by Mr Behar of £50,000 in consideration of his release from the service contract. It also imposed limitations on Mr Behar's ability to sell his shareholding in the taxpayer, which I do not consider relevant to detail. The £50,000 in the taxpayer's accounts was deducted from the figure of goodwill, which had been built up from the excess cost to the taxpayer of the acquisition of the shares in subsidiaries over their book value net assets; I do not think that point assists in solution of the present appeal.

With that display of the essential facts I turn now to the relevant statutory provisions in order to examine whether there has been here a capital gain on the disposal of an

asset. Section 19 of the 1965 Act is the charging section. It imposes a charge to the tax
a in respect of 'chargeable gains computed in accordance with this Act and accruing to a
person on the disposal of assets'.

Section 22(1) provides that 'all forms of property' shall be relevantly 'assets' including
'(a) options, debts and incorporeal property generally, and . . . (c) any form of property
created by the person disposing of it, or otherwise coming to be owned without being
acquired'. Section 22(3) is of importance. That relevantly provides as follows:

b   '. . . there is . . . a disposal of assets by their owner where any capital sum is
      derived from assets notwithstanding that no asset is acquired by the person paying
      the capital sum, and this subsection applies in particular to—(a) capital sums
      received by way of compensation for any kind of damage or injury to assets or for
      the loss, destruction or dissipation of assets or for any depreciation or risk of
      depreciation of an asset . . . (c) capital sums received in return for forfeiture or
c   surrender of rights, or for refraining from exercising rights . . .'

I should make it clear at this stage that it is not disputed by the taxpayer that the
receipt of £50,000 involves a capital sum. The battle ground lies in s 22(3)(c) of the 1965
Act. The question is whether (notwithstanding that as a result of the 1970 agreement Mr
Behar acquired no asset by paying £50,000) the capital sum was received by the taxpayer
d in return for surrender of its rights under the service agreement or for refraining from
exercising its rights under the service agreement.

My Lords, at first glance I find it difficult to see why the rights of the taxpayer under
the contract of service was not an 'asset' of the taxpayer within the unrestricted language
of ss 19 and 22 of the 1965 Act. The Court of Appeal in deciding this case in favour of
the taxpayer (and reversing Fox J) relied greatly on the reasons for the decision of this
e House in *Nokes v Doncaster Amalgamated Collieries Ltd*[1]. The question there was whether
on the occasion of the approval by the court under the Companies Act 1929 of a scheme
for the amalgamation of companies an employee's contract of service was automatically
transferred to the new entity, the statutory language stating the relevant effect, on
existing contracts and rights, of the order approving the amalgamation being of a width
amply sufficient, prima facie, to embrace contracts of employment. This House however
f declined, despite the width of that language, to include within it contracts of
employment; the reason was that to do so would breach a fundamental principle of the
law that such contracts were not *assignable,* and that something more particular was
needed than mere generality of language (however widely expressed) if such a breach of
principle was to be accepted as being intended by Parliament.

My Lords, I do not accept that that decision affords guidance to a decision under the
g capital gains tax legislation which deals not merely with assignments but with
disposals. To treat the events which took place in the instant case as coming within the
wide generality of the language of ss 19 and 22, and in particular of s 22(3)(c), cannot be
regarded as breaching any fundamental principle of the law that a contract of personal
service is not assignable. Similarly I derive no guidance from the cases in bankruptcy law
of *Bailey v Thurston & Co Ltd*[2], which decided that rights under a contract of personal
h service did not vest in the trustee in bankruptcy, and *Sutton v Dorf*[3], which similarly
decided in the case of a statutory tenancy.

It was contended for the taxpayer that the rights of an employer under a contract of
service were not 'property' or an 'asset' of the employer, because they cannot be turned
to account by transfer or assignment to another. But in my opinion this contention
supposes a restricted view of the scheme of the imposition of the capital gains tax which
j the statutory language does not permit. If, as here, the employer is able to exact from the
employee a substantial sum as a term of releasing him from his obligations to serve, the

1   [1940] 1 All ER 549, [1940] AC 1014
2   [1903] 2 KB 137, [1900–3] All ER Rep 818
3   [1932] 3 KB 304, [1932] All ER Rep 70

rights of the employer appear to me to bear quite sufficiently the mark of an asset of the employer, something which he can turn to account, notwithstanding that his ability to turn it to account is by a type of disposal limited by the nature of the asset. In this connection I would also refer to the provisions of s 22(3)(a) which appear to me apt to cover a case where damages are recovered by an employer from a third party for wrongful procurement of breach by the employee of his contract of service.

Reliance was placed by the taxpayer and the Court of Appeal on the provisions of ss 22(4) and 44(1) of the 1965 Act which in certain circumstances introduce the concept of a market value, the contention being that the rights of the employer under the contract of service being non-transferable they could have no market value. In my opinion it is erroneous to deduce from s 22(4), the language of which has no direct application to the present case, a principle of general application for the purposes of capital gains tax that an asset must have a market value. This appears to me to be a preferable answer to the alternative contention of the Crown of analogy with the estate duty cases such as *Inland Revenue Comrs v Crossman*[1] in which a market value could be found notwithstanding restrictions on transfer of shares in a private company. It appears to me that there is a distinction to be drawn between a case in which the asset has the essential character of transferability but subject to restrictions imposed by the contract contained in the articles of association and the asset in the instant case which lacks that essential character.

The Court of Appeal I think placed some reliance on the provisions of the statute relating to part disposals. While I can envisage that problems may arise in the application of such provisions I can find nothing in them to lead me to conclude that the decision of Fox J was erroneous.

The final point taken for the taxpayer was that in truth the £50,000 payment was derived from the taxpayer's shareholding in its subsidiary companies. This submission was rejected by both Fox J and the Court of Appeal and I am content to say that I agree with them.

Accordingly, my Lords, I would allow this appeal and restore the order of Fox J. Having regard to the terms on which leave to appeal was given by the Court of Appeal there will be no order for costs here and the order for the costs of the appeal to the Court of Appeal shall stand.

Appeal allowed. No order for costs; order for costs in Court of Appeal to stand.

Solicitors: *Solicitor of Inland Revenue; Howard, Kennedy & Rossi* (for the taxpayer).

Rengan Krishnan Esq   Barrister.

---

1   [1936] 1 All ER 762, [1937] AC 26

Rank Xerox Ltd v Lane (Inspector of Taxes)

HOUSE OF LORDS
LORD WILBERFORCE, VISCOUNT DILHORNE, LORD SALMON, LORD RUSSELL OF KILLOWEN AND
LORD KEITH OF KINKEL
10th, 11th JULY, 25th OCTOBER 1979

Capital gains tax – Exemptions and reliefs – Disposal of right to annual payments due under personal covenant not secured on property – Due under a covenant – Obligations to make payments created by undertaking embodied in document executed under seal – Obligations enforceable as contract debt apart from agreement under seal – Whether payments 'due under a covenant' – Finance Act 1965, Sch 7, para 12(c).

In 1956 an American corporation ('Xerox') and two other companies agreed to exploit jointly throughout the world (outside Canada, the USA and certain other territories associated with the USA) the reproduction process known as xerography and for that purpose to form an English company ('the taxpayer company') through which the business of exploitation would be carried out. In 1957, after the taxpayer company had been incorporated, Xerox granted it an exclusive licence to use the patents etc relating to the process throughout the world except in Canada and the USA. In 1964, by an agreement between the taxpayer company and Xerox, the taxpayer company surrendered to Xerox its rights in respect of the exploitation of xerography in Central and South America. In consideration of that Xerox agreed to pay the taxpayer company a royalty of 5% of net sales in those areas. In 1967 a similar agreement was entered into between the taxpayer company and Xerox in respect of the British West Indies. Both the 1964 and 1967 agreements were executed by Xerox under seal. In 1969 the taxpayer company passed a resolution to pay its shareholders a dividend of £8,400,000 by distributing in specie its rights to receive payments from Xerox under the 1964 and 1967 agreements. In assessing the taxpayer company to corporation tax, the Crown claimed that, for the purpose of Part III of the Finance Act 1965, the distribution represented the disposal of an asset and that accordingly the gain arising from the disposal was liable to corporation tax in the hands of the taxpayer company. The taxpayer company appealed contending that the payments by Xerox represented 'annual payments . . . due under a covenant' within para 12(c)[a] of Sch 7 to the 1965 Act and that accordingly the taxpayer company's distribution of its rights to those payments to its shareholders did not give rise to a chargeable gain. The Special Commissioners held that the Xerox payments were 'annual payments' within para 12(c) but dismissed the appeal on the ground that they were not payments 'due under a covenant' within para 12(c) because the right to those payments would have been enforceable as a contract debt even if the agreements had not been executed by Xerox under seal. The taxpayer company appealed. Slade J held[b] that the Xerox payments were payments 'due under a covenant' within para 12(c) but dismissed the appeal on the ground that they were not 'annual payments'. The taxpayer company appealed to the Court of Appeal[c] which allowed the appeal on the grounds that the Xerox payments were (i) 'annual payments' within para 12(c), and (ii) were payments 'due under a covenant' because the word 'covenant' in para 12(c) meant a promise in a document executed by the promisor under seal and once, as in the present case, the promise had been embodied in a deed executed by the payer, then, notwithstanding any valuable consideration given for the promise, the debt arising on the promise was due as a specialty debt and not as a simple contract debt. The Crown appealed contending, inter alia, that the meaning given to the word 'covenant' in para 12(c) by the Court of Appeal

---

a   Paragraph 12, so far as material, is set out at p 659 c d, post
b   [1977] 3 All ER 593, [1977] STC 285
c   [1978] 2 All ER 1124, [1978] STC 449

was wrong because it was based on technical rules of English law which had no application in Scotland and it would result in the legislation having a different effect in England from that in Scotland.

Held – The word 'covenant' in para 12(*c*) of Sch 7 to the 1965 Act could not be construed in isolation but was to be interpreted in the context of the whole phrase 'annual payments which are due under a covenant made by any person'. On the true construction of that phrase, para 12(*c*) applied only in those cases where there was a gratuitous promise to make annual payments and the promise was enforceable only because of the form in which it was evidenced, ie in England in a document under seal. It did not cover bilateral agreements, such as that between the taxpayer company and Xerox, in which the payments were the consideration for an obligation undertaken by the payee and the presence of the seal added nothing to the obligation to make the payments. It followed that the taxpayer company's disposal of its rights to receive the payments from Xerox under the 1964 and 1967 agreements could not come within the exemption conferred by para 12(*c*). The appeal would therefore be allowed (see p 660 *a b*, p 661 *d e*, p 663 *b* to *e h*, p 664 *h j*, p 665 *d* to *f* and p 666 *b* to *e*, post).

Per Curiam. In applying para 12(*c*) in Scotland, it would be a suitable analogy to construe the phrase as limited to cases where the gratuitous nature of the undertaking to pay required it to be evidenced by the writ or oath of the undertaker (see p 661 *d e*, p 663 *f g*, p 665 *b d e* and p 666 *d*, post).

Decision of the Court of Appeal [1978] 2 All ER 1124 reversed.

Notes

For capital gains tax in relation to disposal of a right to annual payments due under deeds of covenant, see 5 Halsbury's Laws (4th Edn) para 81.

For the Finance Act 1965, Sch 7, para 12, see 34 Halsbury's Statutes (3rd Edn) 956.

With effect from 6th April 1979 para 12 of Sch 7 to the 1965 Act was replaced by the Capital Gains Tax Act 1979, s 144.

Cases referred to in opinions

Baird's Trustees v Lord Advocate (1888) 15 R (Ct of Sess) 682, 25 Sc LR 533, 28(1) Digest (Reissue) 485, *1230.

Canadian Eagle Oil Co Ltd v R, Selection Trust Ltd v Devitt [1945] 2 All ER 499, [1946] AC 119, 27 Tax Cas 205, 114 LJKB 451, 173 LT 234, HL, 28(1) Digest (Reissue) 299, 1026.

Cape Brandy Syndicate v Inland Revenue Comrs [1921] 1 KB 64, 12 Tax Cas 358; affd [1921] 2 KB 403, 12 Tax Cas 358, 90 LJKB 461, 125 LT 108, CA, 28(1) Digest (Reissue) 586, 2172.

Comrs for Special Purposes of Income Tax v Pemsel [1891] AC 531, [1891–4] All ER Rep 28, 3 Tax Cas 53, 61 LJQB 265, 65 LT 621, 55 JP 805, HL, 8(1) Digest (Reissue) 236, 1.

Comrs for the General Purposes of Income Tax for the City of London v Gibbs [1942] 1 All ER 415, [1942] AC 402, 111 LJKB 301, 166 LT 345, sub nom R v Income Tax General Comrs for City of London, ex parte Gibbs 24 Tax Cas 221, HL, 28(1) Digest (Reissue) 391, 1439.

Lord Advocate v Anna, Countess of Moray [1905] AC 531, 74 LJPC 122, 93 LT 569, HL, 21 Digest (Reissue) 88, 401.

Mangin v Inland Revenue Comr [1971] 1 All ER 179, [1971] AC 739, [1971] 2 WLR 39, [1970] TR 249, PC, 28(1) Digest (Reissue) 543, *1322.

Stephenson v Higginson (1851) 3 HL Cas 638, 10 ER 252, HL, 44 Digest (Repl) 218, 340.

Appeal

This was an appeal by the Crown against a decision of the Court of Appeal[1] (Buckley and Bridge LJJ and Sir David Cairns) dated 12th May 1978 allowing an appeal by Rank Xerox Ltd ('the taxpayer company') against a decision of Slade J[2], dated 9th March 1977,

---

1   [1978] 2 All ER 1124, [1979] Ch 113, [1978] STC 449
2   [1977] 3 All ER 593, [1978] Ch 1, [1977] STC 285

whereby, on a case stated by the Commissioners for the Special Purposes of the Income
a Tax Acts, he dismissed an appeal by the taxpayer company against a decision of the
Special Commissioners dismissing an appeal by the taxpayer company against an
assessment to corporation tax for the accounting period of 12 months to 30th June 1970
in the sum of £49,100,000. The facts are set out in the opinion of Lord Russell of
Killowen.

b D C Potter QC, J A D Hope QC and C H McCall for the Crown.
Michael Nolan QC, John Murray QC and Andrew Thornhill for the taxpayer company.

Their Lordships took time for consideration.

25th October. The following opinions were delivered.

c
LORD WILBERFORCE. My Lords, this appeal is concerned with the capital gains
tax. It turns on Sch 7, para 12, to the Finance Act 1965 which provides:

'No chargeable gain shall accrue to any person on the disposal of a right to, or to
any part of . . . (c) annual payments which are due under a covenant made by any
person and which are not secured on any property.'

d
The payments which were, admittedly, disposed of by the taxpayer company arose out
of two agreements made in 1964 and 1967 by which, in consideration of the assignment
by the taxpayer company to a US company, now called Xerox Corpn, of certain patents,
other rights, goodwill and know-how in defined territories, Xerox agreed to make the
payments. The relevant clause in the agreement of 1964 read as follows:

e
'4. In consideration of the premises, Xerox shall pay or cause to be paid to [the
taxpayer company] a royalty of 5% of Net Sales in the Western Hemisphere with the
exception of the United States of America, its territories and possessions, and
Canada.'

The agreement of 1967 contained a clause in similar terms. Each of these agreements
f was executed by Xerox under seal. So it is contended that the payments satisfy the words
'annual payments which are due under a covenant', so that capital gains tax is not
chargeable. The Court of Appeal[1] (reversing Slade J[2]) has so decided.

My Lords, there can surely be no doubt that to bring the payments which arose to the
taxpayer company under the agreements of 1964 and 1967 within the exemption
conferred by Sch 7, para 12(c), is paradoxical. If the signature of Xerox to these
g agreements had not been under seal, the taxpayer company's liability to capital gains tax
in respect of the payments could not have been disputed. To make their liability depend
on a circumstance so inessential and immaterial as the affixing, or absence, of a seal is
arbitrary in the extreme. As a matter of substance it is impossible to detect any reason
of fiscal policy why the affixing of a seal to an agreement should have any relevance to the
imposition of the tax.

h   Now the intention of Parliament, in taxation matters, may sometimes be inscrutable
or obscure, but we should hardly attribute to it so great a degree of arbitrariness as the
decision of the Court of Appeal involves. If any reasonable meaning can be found for the
words in question which would avoid this, that meaning should be accepted. And I do
not have great difficulty in finding one. It can be accepted that the primary meaning of
'covenant' is a promise by deed. As a secondary meaning the word may be applied to any
j promise or stipulation, whether under seal or not (Stroud's Judicial Dictionary[3], s v
'covenant'). It can equally be accepted that in a statute, including a taxing statute, a word

---

1   [1978] 2 All ER 1124, [1979] Ch 113, [1978] STC 449
2   [1977] 3 All ER 593, [1978] Ch 1, [1977] STC 285
3   4th Edn (1971)

should be given its primary meaning unless something in the context, or in the history of the enactment, or the reasons for the enactment, indicates otherwise. But what has to be interpreted is not merely the word 'covenant', but the whole phrase 'annual payments which are due under a covenant made by any person'. As a matter purely of grammar the words 'due under' and 'made by any person' suggest to me a unilateral promise which is enforceable in spite of the absence of consideration. They are not apt to refer to bilateral agreement in which the annual payments are consideration for some obligation undertaken by the payee.

There is a further argument which supports what is so far a tentative interpretation. It has become for at least 50 years a well-known practice for individuals to promise to make annual payments to their dependants or to charities. These transactions have acquired in both popular and legal parlance the description 'annual payments under covenant', or 'seven year covenants'. Charities when appealing for money invariably invite supporters to enter into a covenant, meaning a voluntary promise to pay, for a period. And this practice, and its nomenclature, has been recognised by fiscal legislation. I shall not trace this historically; it is sufficient to refer to the codifying Income and Corporation Taxes Act 1970.

Annual payments under covenant are dealt with by s 434 which, effectively, lays down the seven year rule. The relevant wording is:

'(1) Any income which, by virtue or in consequence of any disposition made . . . by any person . . . for a period which cannot exceed six years . . .
'(2) . . . "disposition" includes any trust, covenant, agreement or arrangement.'

So if one reads 'covenant' into s 434(1) in place of 'disposition' the enactment becomes 'any income which, by virtue or in consequence of any covenant made . . . by any person', language which is very close to the phrase in Sch 7, para 12(c), which, as it appeared in the Income Tax Act 1952, the draftsmen of the latter must have had in mind. The word 'covenant' again appears in s 441(1) in the definition of 'settlement'. Similarly in s 445, we find references to annual payments payable by virtue or in consequence of any provision of the settlement, the latter word again including 'covenant' (s 454(3)). By contrast s 457 refers to annual payments made under a partnership agreement, being payments made under a liability incurred for full consideration, clearly treated as a different case. So 'covenant' in this part of the Act has a clear and special meaning, corresponding to practice, of a unilateral and voluntary enforceable promise as distinguished from an 'agreement' supported by consideration. Counsel for the Crown, whose experience in these matters is very great, was only able to point to one place in the 1970 Act where 'covenant' has a different meaning, namely to s 34. There, the marginal note refers to restrictive 'covenants' but the text of the section refers to 'undertaking', confirming, to my mind, that 'covenant' in the Act bears a special sense not extending to an obligation under a bilateral agreement. Assuming, therefore, that the word 'covenant' is to be interpreted as necessarily involving a seal, the manner in which it is used in the income tax legislation, conforming to practice, would suggest that it should be understood as referring only to unilateral promises of a voluntary character. This might, it is true, exclude promises to make annual payments contained in a marriage settlement or a separation or divorce agreement, but such cases are unlikely to involve capital gains tax. If this is right, that would exclude the contractual and bilateral agreement in the present case.

There are two further points which deserve mention. First, it was said for the Crown that a distinction is to be made in the legislation, specifically in the Finance Act 1965, between annual payments and royalties or other sums in respect of the user of a patent. The payments in the present case were, it is said, of the latter character, and so for this reason, not within para 12(c). In the view which I take of the meaning of para 12(c) it is not necessary to decide this point.

Secondly, since the Finance Act 1965, as all Finance Acts, is a United Kingdom statute, applicable to Scotland as well as to England and Wales, it was argued that it should be given an interpretation which would produce a similar effect in both parts of the Kingdom. This is certainly in accordance with principle and with authority (see *Lord Advocate v Anna, Countess of Moray*[1], *Comrs for the General Purposes of Income Tax for the City of London v Gibbs*[2]). In Scotland no distinction is made between contracts under seal, which are valid without consideration, and other contracts which require consideration, though for purposes of proof gratuitous may differ from onerous obligations.

My Lords, this type of problem received attention in *Comrs for Special Purposes of Income Tax v Pemsel*[3] in connection with the word 'charitable' and was the subject of observations by more than one of their Lordships. It was pointed out by Lord Macnaghten that statutes which apply to Scotland as well as to England may be divided into three classes: first those which avoid the use of legal terms, second, those in which an English expression is followed by its Scottish counterpart. In the third, in which the Income Tax Acts may be included, the drafting is English with perhaps some Scottish phrases casually thrown in. In such cases, he said, you must take the meaning of legal expressions from the country to which they belong, and in any case arising in the sister country you must apply the statute in an analogous or corresponding sense. I think that this is the right course here. 'Covenant' should be given its English meaning in England, viz, of a promise under seal; in Scotland, the phrase should be understood as referring to enforceable gratuitous promises. We were indeed told that promises in favour of charities, though made simply in writing, may be referred to as covenants. There is therefore no difficulty in construing Sch 7, para 12(c), so as in either part of the Kingdom to exclude the agreements in question.

I would allow the appeal.

VISCOUNT DILHORNE. My Lords, I have had the advantage of reading in draft the speeches of my noble friends, Lord Wilberforce and Lord Russell of Killowen. I agree with them and there is nothing that I can usefully add. For the reasons they state, I would allow the appeal.

LORD SALMON. My Lords, since 1956 the taxpayer company has done a great deal of business with a US company now named Xerox Corpn. In 1964 the taxpayer company entered into a written contract, governed by English law, with Xerox Corpn which contained two clauses of importance to this appeal. They read as follows:

> '1. [The taxpayer company] hereby sells, assigns and transfers to Xerox its entire right, title and interest in all property, rights and assets in the Western Hemisphere [as defined] . . . including, without limitation, its goodwill, technical information, know-how, trade secrets, customer lists, patents . . .
>
> '4. In consideration of the premises, Xerox shall pay or cause to be paid to the taxpayer company a royalty of 5% of Net Sales in the Western Hemisphere with the exception of the USA . . . and Canada . . .'

In 1967 a similar contract was entered into between the same parties relating to sales in what was then the British West Indies. Both these contracts were typical commercial contracts. Each of them however happened to be executed by Xerox under seal. The contracts would, of course, have been equally effective had they not been executed by either party under seal. On 11th December 1969 the taxpayer company passed a resolution to pay its shareholders a dividend of £8·4 million by distributing in specie its rights to receive annual payments under cl 4 of the 1964 and 1967 contracts. An assessment to corporation tax in respect of the distribution to which I have referred was made against the taxpayer company for the accounting period of 12 months to 30th June 1970. This assessment was made because corporation tax falls to be charged on profits of

---

1 [1905] AC 531
2 [1942] 1 All ER 415, [1942] AC 402
3 [1891] AC 531, [1891–4] All ER Rep 28

the taxpayer and profits for this purpose include chargeable gains which for all purposes relevant to the present case fall to be computed in accordance with the principles applicable for capital gains tax: see ss 238(1) and (4)(a) and 265 of the Income and Corporation Taxes Act 1970.

Schedule 7, para 12(c), to the Finance Act 1965 provides:

'No chargeable gain shall accrue to any person on the disposal of a right to, or to any part of . . . (c) annual payments which are due under a covenant made by any person and which are not secured on any property.'

The taxpayer company contended that no chargeable gain can have accrued to them on their disposal of their right to what they argue are 'annual payments due under a covenant'. The Special Commissioners did not accept this argument. They found in favour of the Crown on the ground (a) that a chargeable gain had accrued to the taxpayer company on their disposal of their right to the annual payments due under the written agreements of 1964 and 1967 whether or not they had been executed under seal and (b) that para 12(c) of Sch 7 refers only to a right to annual payments made not by a bilateral agreement but by a personal voluntary disposition of income by a deed of covenant.

Slade J, who did not agree with the reasons relied on by the Special Commissioners, nevertheless dismissed the appeal on the ground that the taxpayer company could not show that the rights disposed of by the distribution in 1969 were rights to 'annual payments' within the meaning of those words in para 12(c) of Sch 7. The Court of Appeal reversed the decision of Slade J because they disagreed both with the reasons given by him and those given by the Special Commissioners in favour of the Crown. The Crown now appeals to your Lordships' House.

The result of this appeal must depend on whether or not para 12(c) of Sch 7, on its true construction, applies to contracts such as those of 1964 and 1967 to which I have referred. If para 12(c) does apply to such contracts, it follows that should such contracts happen to be executed under seal by the party liable to make the annual payments, the disposal by the other party of the right to annual payments due under the contracts would escape tax, sometimes, as in the present case, running into millions of pounds. If, on the other hand, the contracts had no seal on them, having been signed in the ordinary way by each party, tax would be payable on the disposal of the rights to annual payments. This result is obviously absurd for whether or not it has a seal on it makes no difference whatsoever to the effect or enforceability of the contract. Why should tax be payable if the contract is a simple contract but not payable if the contract is executed under seal? No reason has been or could be advanced to justify the view that Parliament could have intended that its legislation should have such a bizarre result. It has been submitted, however, that whatever the intention of Parliament may have been, the only possible meaning of para 12(c) is that the presence of a seal on the contract exempts the taxpayer from payment of the tax which would otherwise be exigible. The rules of interpretation to be applied in the construction of taxing statutes were summarised by Lord Donovan in delivering the majority judgment of the Privy Council in *Mangin v Inland Revenue Comr*[1]:

'First, the words are to be given their ordinary meaning . . . Secondly, ". . . one has to look merely at what is clearly said. There is no room for any intendment. There is no equity about a tax. There is no presumption as to tax. Nothing is to be read in, nothing is to be implied. One can only look fairly at the language used." (Per Rowlatt J in *Cape Brandy Syndicate v Inland Revenue Comrs*[2], approved by Viscount Simon LC in *Canadian Eagle Oil Co Ltd v Regem*[3].) Thirdly, the object of the construction of a statute being to ascertain the will of the legislature it may be presumed that neither injustice nor absurdity was intended. If therefore a literal

---

1 [1971] 1 All ER 179 at 182, [1971] AC 739 at 746
2 [1921] 1 KB 64 at 71
3 [1945] 2 All ER 499 at 507, [1946] AC 119 at 140

interpretation would produce such a result, and the language admits of an
interpretation which would avoid it, then such an interpretation may be adopted.'

The primary meaning of 'covenant' is a promise by deed. I recognise that, therefore,
the words 'due under a covenant' could in some contexts be interpreted as 'due under any
promise by deed'. This interpretation would however lead to the absurd result which I
have indicated if applied in the context of para 12(c).

This appeal does not turn on the interpretation only of the words 'due under a
covenant' but on the interpretation of the words 'annual payments which are due under
a covenant made by any person'. These words are, in my view, singularly inept to cover
annual payments under bilateral agreements such as the agreements with which we are
concerned. If that had been the intention of the legislature, nothing would have been
more natural or easier than to have said 'annual payments due under an agreement'. It
seems inconceivable to me that the legislature intended to and did lay down (as, in effect,
the taxpayer company contends) that no chargeable gain should accrue to any person on
the disposal of a right to annual payments due under a business or indeed any agreement,
if but only if the agreement was executed under seal. There is no fiscal or any other
reason for making the taxpayer's liability to tax dependent on whether or not the
relevant agreement had a seal on it. It would be utterly ridiculous to make liability to tax
depend on the existence of a seal.

For these reasons the language of para 12(c) of Sch 7 is, in my opinion, wholly
inconsistent with the meaning which the taxpayer company seeks to attribute to it. In
my view, it refers only to a unilateral promise made by deed which is therefore
enforceable in spite of the absence of consideration; and the paragraph certainly has
nothing whatsoever to do with business or any other bilateral agreements.

There exists and has existed for upwards of 50 years a well-known and widespread
practice by which charities of all kinds, 'family' and dependants have been supported by
annual payments under deeds of covenant over specified periods. Paragraph 12(c) was,
to my mind, designed to relieve beneficiaries under such covenants from any liability to
tax on disposal of any of their rights to annual payments due under such covenants
provided the annual payments were not secured on any property. Annual payments to
charity were most unlikely to be so secured, although annual payments to 'family' might
be.

The Finance Act 1965 like all Finance Acts applies to the whole of the United
Kingdom. It was, I think, agreed by counsel on each side that in Scotland there is no such
thing as a promise under seal, but there exist enforceable gratuitous promises in writing;
and these when made in favour of charities, 'family' or dependants, are, in Scotland, also
commonly referred to as covenants. Paragraph 12(c) would accordingly be construed
alike in both parts of the United Kingdom.

Having regard to the conclusion at which I have arrived in relation to the true
interpretation of para 12(c) of Sch 7, it is unnecessary to express any opinion on the point
as to whether the royalties payable under cl 4 of the contracts of 1964 and 1967 are
'annual payments' within the meaning of those words in para 12(c).

My Lords, for the reasons I have stated, I would allow the appeal with costs here and
in the Court of Appeal.

LORD RUSSELL OF KILLOWEN. My Lords, this case raises a question on the
liability of the taxpayer company to corporation tax on its profits. For that purpose its
profits include what are chargeable gains for the purpose of capital gains tax. The
taxpayer company contends that the particular sums in question fall within para 12(c) of
Sch 7 to the Finance Act 1965, which provides:

'No chargeable gain shall accrue to any person on the disposal of a right to, or to
any part of . . . (c) annual payments which are due under a covenant made by any
person and which are not secured on any property.'

Two questions were and are raised for decision. First: whether the relevant payments, the right to which was disposed of, were 'annual payments'. Second: whether they were 'due under a covenant made by any person'.

Slade J held that they were due under a covenant, but that they were not annual payments, and so decided against the taxpayer. The Court of Appeal reversed Slade J holding in favour of the taxpayer that they were both 'annual payments' and 'due under a covenant'. The Special Commissioners had concluded against the taxpayer that though they were annual payments they were not due under a covenant.

In 1956 an agreement was entered into between three companies, one of which was Xerox Corpn, for the joint exploitation throughout the world (exclusive of Canada, the USA, and certain other countries associated with the USA) of a reproduction process known as Xerography; to incorporate for this purpose an English limited company, in fact the taxpayer company, through which the business of such exploitation would be carried on; and to participate in the profits of the taxpayer on the basis there set out. Xerox Corpn agreed that it would transfer to the taxpayer company when formed all its relevant patents, patent applications, and licences then or thereafter owned in respect of the territory to be exploited: and the agreement scheduled a large number of such patents, applications and licences. In 1957 Xerox entered into a licence agreement with the taxpayer accordingly, though this took the form of exclusive licences and sub-licences rather than assignments.

In 1964 by an agreement between Xerox and the taxpayer company, the latter (in effect) sold, assigned and transferred to Xerox all its rights in all property, rights and assets in Central and South America including its know-how, patents, trade marks and so forth, thus surrendering to Xerox its rights to continue the exploitation of Xerography in that area. In consideration of that Xerox agreed to pay 'a royalty of 5% of Net Sales' (including hirings) of Xerographic machines, equipment, apparatus, paper and supplies in that area. In 1967 a similar agreement was entered into between the taxpayer company and Xerox in respect of the British West Indies. These two agreements were executed by Xerox by the affixing of its corporate seal.

In 1969 the taxpayer company resolved to pay to its shareholders a dividend of £8·4 million to be satisfied by distribution in specie of its rights to receive payments from Xerox under the 1964 and 1967 agreements. This was clearly a disposal giving rise to a chargeable gain, unless within para 12(c) of Sch 7 it was a disposal of a right to annual payments due under a covenant.

I consider first whether the payments due from Xerox to the taxpayer company can be within the phrase 'due under a covenant made by any person' in that paragraph. I ask myself first why Parliament should have elected to single out for special treatment a commercial bargain such as was made in 1964 (and 1967) if, and only if, the person who undertook to make the payments happens to affix his or its seal to the agreement. Indeed, if the taxpayer company is right, it need not be affixed to the agreement; by the simple expedient of a subsequent agreement under seal to carry out the terms of the original bargain (not under seal) a case could be steered into this paragraph shortly before a proposed disposal. There is, it is true, a difference in point of limitation period between action on a speciality and one on simple contract. But I apprehend that an action based on the agreement by Xerox to pay the 5% royalty could not be defective for failure to plead that it was under seal. In my opinion 'due under a covenant' is fairly to be construed as something narrower in scope than 'due under an agreement' would have been. I construe the phrase as meaning due by reason of the fact that the promise is under seal, because of the existence of the seal. If the presence of the seal adds nothing to the obligation to make the annual payments, I do not consider that the payments were 'due under a covenant made by a person'. This construction is in my view legitimate as avoiding the wholly capricious outcome of exclusion or non-exclusion from chargeable gain depending on the chance of an unnecessary seal.

It is of course true to say that this construction of the phrase narrows its application to cases of other than for valuable consideration, whether in favour of charity or individuals,

the latter most commonly being in favour of members of the covenantor's family. It is
a also true to say that covenants in favour of charity would not be expected to be secured
on property. But 'family' covenants might well be so secured; and this exclusion from
the exemption is presumably because the disposal would involve the disposal of the
security.

Argument on the Scots law was addressed to this House, and it appears that the English
concept of a seal as constituting a covenant has no place in that law. But I decline to
b deduce from that fact that 'due under a covenant' is to be read as 'due under an
agreement'. Rather would I venture to suggest that in applying para 12(c) in Scotland it
would be a suitable analogy to construe the phrase as limited to cases where the gratuitous
nature of the undertaking to pay requires it to be evidenced by the writ of the undertaker.

If that view of the scope of the phrase 'due under a covenant by a person' is correct, it
suffices to decide this appeal in favour of the Crown, and to allow it. The alternative
c contention for the Crown was that these payments were not annual payments because
they were royalties in respect of the user of patents. I need not rehearse the closely
reasoned arguments in support of that submission. In the end I was not convinced that,
assuming the payments agreed to be made by Xerox were such royalties, that would be
inconsistent with their being also annual payments.

Accordingly I would allow the appeal with costs here and in the Court of Appeal, and
d restore the order of Slade J which remitted the case to the special commissioners for
adjustment of the assessment.

LORD KEITH OF KINKEL. My Lords, I agree with the speeches of my noble and
learned friends, Lord Wilberforce and Lord Russell of Killowen, which I have had the
opportunity of reading in draft.
e The appeal is concerned with the proper construction of the words 'annual payments
which are due under a covenant made by any person and which are not secured on any
property', which appear in para 12(c) of Sch 7 to the Finance Act 1965. In my opinion it
is clear that the type of transaction intended to be indicated by the expression 'covenant
made by any person' is a unilateral binding obligation entered into without consideration,
the binding character of which, under English law, depends on the affixing of a seal, and
f not any sort of agreement whatever which happens to have a seal affixed to it.

Counsel for the Crown sought to reinforce his case by reference to the position under
the law of Scotland, where the presence or absence of a seal is irrelevant to the binding
force of any obligation. It was argued that para 12(c), being a fiscal enactment, must be
construed so as to make the incidence of taxation the same both in England and in
Scotland, and that if it were interpreted in an English case as meaning that the mere
g affixing of seal was to be the critical factor attracting the application of the paragraph, the
same rule must apply to Scotland, which in view of the irrelevant nature of a seal there
was absurd. It followed that such an interpretation must be incorrect. For the taxpayer
company, on the other hand, it was argued that a recognised secondary meaning of
'covenant' in English law was 'agreement', and that this was the meaning of the word in
Scots law. The adoption of this meaning would produce a result which was consistent
h with both English and Scots law and which was favourable to their case.

In my opinion reference to the law of Scotland is not of assistance for the purpose of
construing para 12(c) in its application to the present case, which arises in England. The
use of technical terms of English law is commonly found in fiscal legislation applicable
to all parts of the United Kingdom. The correct approach to such terms was settled by
the decision of this House in *Comrs for Special Purposes of Income Tax v Pemsel*[1]. Lord
j Macnaghten[2] thus explained the position:

---

1 [1891] AC 531, [1891–4] All ER Rep 28
2 [1891] AC 531 at 580, [1891–4] All ER Rep 28 at 54

'. . . you must take the meaning of legal expressions from the law of the country to which they properly belong, and in any case arising in the sister country you **a** must apply the statute in an analogous or corresponding sense, so as to make the operation and effect of the statute the same in both countries . . . In construing Acts of Parliament, it is a general rule, not without authority in this House (*Stephenson* v. *Higginson*[1]) that words must be taken in their legal sense unless a contrary intention appears. Is a contrary intention shewn merely by the circumstance that the legal meaning of the words used belongs more properly, or even exclusively, to the **b** jurisprudence of one part of Great Britain? Agreeing with Lord Hardwicke [in his well-known letter to Lord Kames] rather than with the Court of Session [in *Baird's Trustees v Lord Advocate*[2]], I am disposed to answer that question in the negative.'

I think it is clear that in para 12(c) 'covenant' is to be read in its technical English legal meaning of a document under seal. But a proper construction of all the relevant words in their context leads to the conclusion that the type of transaction pointed to by the **c** paragraph is that which I have described above. That conclusion having been reached in a case arising in England, there would be no difficulty, following the course mapped out by Lord Macnaghten, in arriving at a consistent result in a comparable Scottish case. The substance of the type of transaction covered by the paragraph is that it is a unilateral binding obligation. The form of such an obligation differs in England and in Scotland. In England it must be under seal, in Scotland no particular formality is required, but **d** proof of the obligation is limited to the writ or oath of the granter. Through thus reasoning by analogy the application of the paragraph may be made the same in both countries. The use of the word 'covenant' to describe an agreement of any sort is archaic in Scottish legal terminology. But in the context of annual payments the word is commonly applied, no doubt under English influence, to the familiar seven year unilateral obligation in favour of relatives or charities, which often is, but need not **e** necessarily be, in probative form.

My Lords, I would allow the appeal.

Appeal allowed.

Solicitors: *Solicitor of Inland Revenue*; *Linklaters & Paines* (for the taxpayer company).   **f**

Christine Ivamy   Barrister.

1 (1851) 3 HL Cas 38, 10 ER 252
2 (1888) 15 R (Ct of Sess) 682

a
Myerson v Martin

COURT OF APPEAL, CIVIL DIVISION
LORD DENNING MR, WALLER AND EVELEIGH LJJ
25th, 26th JUNE 1979

b
Practice – Service – Substituted service – Substituted service within jurisdiction – Defendant outside jurisdiction at date of issue of writ – Defendant subsequently within the jurisdiction – Personal service of writ impracticable – Whether order for substituted service could be made – RSC Ord 65, r 4(1).

c
In 1976 the plaintiff, who was resident in Jersey, was committed to prison there on an ex parte application by the defendant, another Jersey resident, and others who claimed that the plaintiff owed them money. The plaintiff denied the debt but had no opportunity of disputing the allegation in Jersey. On his release from prison he left Jersey and came to England where, on 14th April 1977, he initiated legal proceedings by writ for service within the jurisdiction against the defendant in respect of the wrongs alleged to have been done to him in Jersey. Although the defendant was resident outside the jurisdiction, he was a director of a company which had its head office in England and frequently came

d
to England on the company's business. He was not in England on 14th April, when the writ was issued, but came to England shortly afterwards for a week. During that period and on subsequent occasions when the defendant was in England the process server tried unsuccessfully to serve him personally with the writ. The plaintiff eventually applied for, and obtained, an order under RSC Ord 65, r 4[a], for substituted service of the writ. The defendant received the writ, but having received it he applied to have the order for

e
substituted service, and the service effected thereunder, set aside as being improper. His contention that an order for substituted service could not be made unless at the time of the issue of the writ the defendant was within the jurisdiction and personal service could in law have been effected on him on that date was upheld and the order and substituted service were set aside. The plaintiff appealed, contending that the court had a wide discretion, under r 4(1), to make an order for substituted service in a case where personal

f
service was impracticable, and that in the circumstances that discretion should be exercised in his favour as the defendant had come within the jurisdiction after the issue of the writ and it had proved impracticable to serve it on him personally.

g
Held – In order to determine whether the court had jurisdiction under RSC Ord 65, r 4(1), to make an order for substituted service of a writ, the court had to look at the circumstances existing at the time the writ was issued. If the defendant was at that time outside the jurisdiction and the plaintiff in ignorance of the fact issued a writ for service within the jurisdiction he would have to wait for the defendant to come within the jurisdiction and serve him personally there; there could not be substituted service in such a case. If the defendant was within the jurisdiction at the time the writ was issued and the plaintiff issued a writ for service there, he could obtain an order for substituted

h
service even if the defendant had left the jurisdiction since the issue of the writ. However if the defendant was outside the jurisdiction at the time the writ was issued and the plaintiff was aware of the fact either the plaintiff could issue the writ for service within the jurisdiction and wait for the defendant to return to be served personally (and in such a case substituted service could not be ordered) or, if his claim came within RSC Ord 11, r 1, apply for leave to serve the writ out of the jurisdiction. Since the defendant had not

j
been in England on 14th April 1977 when the plaintiff had issued the writ the court had no jurisdiction to order substituted service. The appeal would therefore be dismissed (see p 670 c, p 671 b to g and p 672 c to j, post).

---

a   Rule 4, so far as material, is set out at p 669 h, post

Fry v Moore [1886–90] All ER Rep 309, *Trent Cycle Co Ltd v Beattie* (1899) 15 TLR 176, *Porter v Freudenberg* [1914–15] All ER Rep 918 and *Laurie v Carroll* (1958) 98 CLR 310 followed.

Per Eveleigh LJ. The court should not exercise its jurisdiction under RSC Ord 65, r 4, to order substituted service where the effect would be to add another cause of action to those listed in RSC Ord 11 (see p 672 *h*, post).

Notes

For the circumstances when substituted service may be ordered, see 30 Halsbury's Laws (3rd Edn) 321, para 385, and for cases on the subject, see 50 Digest (Repl) 326–3331, 558–591.

Cases referred to in judgments

Field v Bennett (1886) 56 LJQB 89, 50 Digest (Reissue) 328, 571.
Fry v Moore (1889) 23 QBD 395, [1886–90] All ER Rep 309, 58 LJQB 382, 61 LT 545, CA, 50 Digest (Reissue) 329, 578.
Laurie v Carroll (1958) 98 CLR 310 (Aust HC).
Porter v Freudenberg, Kreglinger v Samuel and Rosenfeld, Re Merten's Patents [1915] 1 KB 857, [1914–15] All ER Rep 918, 84 LJKB 1001, 112 LT 313, 20 Com Cas 189, 32 RPC 109, CA, 50 Digest (Reissue) 326, 558.
Trent Cycle Co Ltd v Beattie (1899) 15 TLR 176, CA, 50 Digest (Reissue) 329, 584.

Cases also cited

Boys v Chaplin [1968] 1 All ER 283, [1968] 2 QB 1, CA; *affd* [1969] 2 All ER 1085, [1971] AC 356, HL.
Colt Industries Inc v Sarlie [1966] 1 All ER 673, [1966] 1 WLR 440, CA.
Hillyard v Smyth (1887) 36 WR 7.
Jay v Budd [1898] 1 QB 12, CA.
Maharanee of Baroda v Wildenstein [1972] 2 All ER 689, [1972] 2 QB 283, CA.
Urquhart, Re, ex parte Urquhart (1890) 24 QBD 723, CA.
Watkins v North American Land & Timber Co Ltd (1904) 20 TLR 534, HL.
Wilding v Bean [1891] 1 QB 100, [1886–90] All ER Rep 1026, CA.

Interlocutory appeal

Geoffrey Myerson, the plaintiff in an action against the first defendant, Richard Haig Martin ('the defendant'), and nine other defendants, appealed against an order of Boreham J, dated 10th November 1978, dismissing his appeal against an order of Master Creightmore, dated 25th May 1978, setting aside (i) an order, dated 23rd January 1978, for substituted service of the writ on the defendant and (ii) the service effected pursuant to that order. The facts are set out in the judgment of Lord Denning MR.

Steven Gee for the plaintiff.
Wilfred Getz for the defendant.

LORD DENNING MR. The principal parties to this case are Mr Geoffrey Myerson and Mr Richard Haig Martin. Mr Myerson is a solicitor of the Supreme Court who practises at 13 Harley Street, London. Mr Martin is also a solicitor of the Supreme Court who practises at 41 Marina Court, St Helier, Jersey. At the time when the troubles arose between them, they were both resident in Jersey. They were not within the jurisdiction of this court. The trouble arose because, in the course of very complicated dealings, Mr Myerson seems to have given to some parties a promissory note for the sum of £15,750 with interest. Mr Myerson says that the note was conditional and could be avoided for misrepresentation and the like. I need not go into all the details, except to say that a crucial matter arose in October 1976. Mr Martin, with others and in particular some assignees of the promissory note, took proceedings in Jersey (such proceedings are not

known in England) for an 'ordre provisoire' from the Royal Court of Justice of the Island
a of Jersey. The result of that, so far as one can ascertain, was that it was tried ex parte
without Mr Myerson being heard at all; and he was imprisoned in La Moye Prison in
Jersey on 1st November 1976. There was nothing against him except that these people
said that he owed them money. That very special procedure seems to me to be very much
out of date; but it is still extant in the island of Jersey. A man can be cast into prison on
a disputed debt without being heard.

b Mr Myerson was very upset about this. With the help of his future wife, whilst he was
in prison, he entered into negotiations for his release. As a result of those negotiations,
he was allowed to leave the prison on executing several documents. He says that they
were extracted from him by duress.

After executing the documents, Mr Myerson left Jersey and came to England. He
sought to start legal proceedings by writ against Mr Martin and other people. He accused
c them of conspiracy against him and other wrongs which had been done to him in the
island of Jersey. In the ordinary way, if he wanted to sue these people in Jersey, he would
have to get leave to serve a writ out of the jurisdiction under RSC Ord 11, r 1.

But Mr Myerson did not want to take those proceedings. It is doubtful whether he
would ever have got leave to serve out because all these transactions took place in
Jersey. So on 14th April 1977 Mr Myerson, being resident in England, issued a writ
d against Mr Martin and the other defendants not for service out of the jurisdiction, and
this is important, but for service within the jurisdiction.

That writ has never been personally served on Mr Martin. Mr Myerson wishes to
make substituted service on him although he is not in this country. On 14th April 1977
Mr Martin was not in England. As far as we know, he was in Jersey on that date. He was
not within the jurisdiction of this court at the time the writ was issued. That is an
e important matter which I must stress at the moment.

Nevertheless, although Mr Martin was not here on that date, he is obviously a
gentleman who goes to and fro from Jersey to England. He is a director of an important
public company in England called the Myson Group Ltd, which has its head office at
Ongar in Essex, and which has its showrooms at 25 St James's Street in London. Mr
Martin frequently comes to England for monthly meetings of the directors of that
f company. Over the last four or five years he has attended 41 out of 58 board meetings:
and he often visits the group's showrooms at 25 St James's Street. There was a board
meeting on the date when the writ was issued, 14th April 1977, but Mr Martin was not
in England on that date. But he did come to England shortly afterwards on 27th April
1977 and stayed until 3rd May 1977. During that time the process server tried to serve
him personally with the writ. He made arrangements with a lady who was working in
g the showroom to try and fix a time when he would be available for service. But all those
arrangements came to nothing. It turned out that it was impracticable to serve him
personally on that visit to England and on subsequent visits. In some way Mr Martin
managed to avoid the process servers. They did not find it practicable to serve him on
any of his visits to England.

In those circumstances, Mr Myerson applied for substituted service on Mr Martin. RSC
h Ord 65, r 4(1) provides:

'If, in the case of any document which by virtue of any provision of these rules is
required to be served personally on any person, it appears to the Court that it is
impracticable for any reason to serve that document personally on that person, the
Court may make an order for substituted service of that document.'

j So an application was made for substituted service. On 23rd January 1978 an order was
made for substituted service to be made on Mr Martin at 25 St James's Street, the group's
showrooms, which he often visits. It was to be made by letter addressed to 25 St James's
Street. We do not know whether it was given to him there or sent over to Jersey. But
at all events he received it. Having received it, he applied to set aside that service as being

improper. That is the question in this case. Is it a case where substituted service was permissible on Mr Martin?
    a

We have been referred to many cases on the subject. It is clear that the courts have to draw a dividing line between cases which are appropriate for service within the jurisdiction (which do not require the leave of the court) and those for service out of the jurisdiction (where the leave of the court is required). On this point for many years the courts have followed some dicta in *Fry v Moore*[1]. Mr Moore had previously lived at Woodbridge in Suffolk, but, before the writ was issued, he had gone to Canada and *b* remained in Canada thereafter. I put aside the point of waiver on which the case turned. I will only read the principle as stated by Lindley LJ[2]:

> '. . . there are certain principles which govern the rules, and in *Field* v. *Bennett*[3] the Queen's Bench Division laid down the principle that, if a writ could not be served personally at the time when it is issued, there cannot be substituted service. That is a sound principle.'
>   *c*

Lopes LJ[4] said words to the same effect. Note the words 'if a writ could not be served personally at the time when it is issued'. Those words make *the time of issue* crucial.

Next there was an authoritative statement in *Porter v Freudenberg*[5]. That was a case about alien enemies. A special court of seven members of this court was constituted. In a reserved judgment delivered by Lord Reading CJ the court said:
    d

> 'The general rule is that an order for substituted service of writ of summons within the jurisdiction cannot be made in any case in which, at the time of the issue of the writ, there could not be *at law* a good personal service of the writ because the defendant is not within the jurisdiction.'

Note the words 'at the time of the issue of the writ'. Those cases have been followed in *e* the Supreme Court Practice. I will read a note to RSC Ord 65, r 4[6]:

> 'If, at the time of the issue of a writ for service within the jurisdiction, there could at law have been personal service of it upon the defendant sought to be served, but circumstances prevented such service being made, then substituted service of such writ may be allowed . . . But if at the time of issue personal service of such writ could not at law have been made, then . . . substituted service cannot be ordered *f* [citing *Fry v Moore*[1]].'

Counsel for the plaintiff in his excellent argument relied on *Trent Cycle Co Ltd v Beattie*[7]. The defendant Mr Beattie was an Irishman ordinarily resident in Ireland. Counsel for the plaintiff suggested to us that Mr Beattie might have been out of England at the time of the issue of the writ; and that he was going to and fro, staying at the Hotel *g* Metropole in London. It seems, however, that he was in England at the time the writ was issued. The Annual Practice of 1900[8] said of that case:

> 'In the *Trent Cycle Co.* v. *Beattie*[7] . . . an action was brought against B., a domiciled Irishman, for breach of contract made and to be performed in England . . . The writ was an ordinary one for service within the jurisdiction, and was issued when defendant was in London, staying at an hotel.'
>   *h*

---

1 (1889) 23 QBD 395, [1886–90] All ER rep 309
2 (1889) 23 QBD 395 at 397–398; cf [1886–90] All ER Rep 309 at 310
3 (1886) 56 LJQB 89   *j*
4 (1889) 23 QBD 395 at 399, [1886–90] All ER Rep 309 at 311
5 [1915] 1 KB 857 at 887, [1914–15] All ER Rep 918 at 933
6 (1979) vol 1, p 1100, para 65/4/4
7 (1899) 15 TLR 176
8 Vol 1, p 63

It was held that because he was staying at an hotel here, an order for substituted service
a could be made. That interpretation was confirmed by Dixon CJ in Australia in *Laurie v
Carroll*[1]. He said:

> 'That view was applied afterwards in a case where the writ having been issued
> *during the presence in England* of the defendant, a domiciled Irishman visiting London
> frequently, it could not be served because he successfully evaded service and
> *b*   returned to Ireland.' (My emphasis.)

The same view was taken in Dicey and Morris on the Conflict of Laws[2].

The weight of authority is overwhelming that one should look at the time when the
writ was issued. If the defendant was in fact outside the jurisdiction at the time the writ
was issued, and the plaintiff in ignorance of it issued a writ for service *within* the
jurisdiction, then the plaintiff must wait until the defendant comes back *within* the
c jurisdiction and serve him personally on his return. There cannot be substituted service
on the defendant.

If the defendant was in fact *within* the jurisdiction at the time the writ was issued, and
the plaintiff issues a writ for service *within* the jurisdiction, the plaintiff can get an order
for substituted service on him, even if he has gone overseas since the issue of the writ.

If the defendant was in fact *outside* the jurisdiction at the time the writ was issued, and
d the plaintiff knows it, the plaintiff can take his choice and issue a writ for service *within*
the jurisdiction, but in that case he has to wait his opportunity and hope that the
defendant will return to England and be served personally. There cannot be substituted
service.

Otherwise if the defendant was in fact outside the jurisdiction when the writ was
issued, and is likely to remain outside, the proper course for the plaintiff is to apply for
e leave to serve out of the jurisdiction, in which case he can only get it if the case comes
within RSC Ord 11.

In the present case Mr Martin was *outside* the jurisdiction at the time the writ was
issued. There cannot therefore be substituted service. The only course for the plaintiff
is to try to serve him personally when he comes here. Or, alternatively, apply for leave
to issue a writ for service out of the jurisdiction, and get leave if he brings the case within
f RSC Ord 11.

I would therefore dismiss the appeal.

WALLER LJ. I agree. RSC Ord 65, r 4(1) says:

g
> 'If, in the case of any document which by virtue of any provision of these rules is
> required to be served personally on any person, it appears to the Court that it is
> impracticable for any reason to serve that document personally on that person, the
> Court may make an order for substituted service of the document.'

The cases and textbooks indicate that the general rule is that which Lord Denning MR
h has quoted from *Porter v Freudenberg*[3].

Counsel on behalf of the plaintiff (the appellant), in a very interesting and persuasive
argument, sought to submit to this court that those propositions were wrong and were
founded on a misunderstanding of certain of the cases, and he supported his argument
by referring to the various reports of *Fry v Moore*[4] where the judgments of their
j Lordships are differently reported in a particular which is vital to this particular case; and

1   (1958) 98 CLR 310 at 327
2   9th Edn (1973) pp 158–161
3   [1915] 1 KB 857, [1914–15] All ER Rep 918
4   Ie (1889) 58 LJQB 382, 61 LT 545, 37 WR 565.

he submitted that *Trent Cycle Co Ltd v Beattie*[1], when you look at the actual words of the report, was in favour of his submissions about the law. He relied on the word 'may' in the rule as showing that the court has a wide discretion, and a discretion which he submitted should be exercised in his favour in this case with a view of the law different from that which has been stated in the Supreme Court Practice at any rate for nearly 80 years.

On the other hand, counsel for the defendant (the respondent) submitted that the authorities which supported that proposition, and he relied particularly on *Porter v Freudenberg*[2], a decision of a court of seven judges of this court, and on *Laurie v Carroll*[3], a decision of Dixon CJ in Australia, affirmed not only that it was the law, but that it was the correct law; and he submitted that the law was properly stated, because to view it in any other way would be in conflict with the carefully and fully drawn rule of RSC Ord 11, ie r 1, dealing with the service of writs out of the jurisdiction.

I agree with counsel for the plaintiff that the rule gives a discretion, but in my view it would be impossible for this court to say, in view of the strength of those authorities, that the discretion is not sufficiently circumscribed to avoid the conflict between RSC Ord 65, r 4 and Ord 11, r 1. But, as Lord Denning MR has said, that does not mean that the discretion has entirely vanished, and there may well be cases where an application may be made relating to somebody who may be briefly outside the jurisdiction at the time of the issue of the writ, but who is nevertheless domiciled within the jurisdiction, and wholly resident within the jurisdiction, when there would be no conflict between the provisions of Ord 65, r 4, and Ord 11, r 1, and where it might be perfectly proper for the court to exercise its discretion in favour of allowing substituted service. That would cover the extreme example which was put in the course of argument of a man who was temporarily absent for two or three days from the country and a writ being issued on one of those days, when all the rest of the time he was residing within this country.

As I say, I found the argument of counsel for the plaintiff very attractive and persuasive but not sufficiently persuasive for me to say that the authorities of the last 90 years were wrong.

EVELEIGH LJ. I do not think that *Fry v Moore*[4] and the other authorities referred to the court compel me to hold that there can never be substituted service where the defendant is out of the jurisdiction at the time of the issue of the writ, no matter who the defendant is or where he lives. I would accept that no substituted service is permissible in a case where personal service has never been possible; but, once it becomes possible, as by the presence of the defendant after the writ has been issued, I am inclined to think that the court has power to order substituted service.

In approaching this problem I think it is necessary to distinguish between the extent of the court's jurisdiction and how and when it will be exercised. The procedure for its exercise is laid down in the rules of court. Therefore, when considering the exercise of jurisdiction under RSC Ord 65, r 4, the court should have regard to other relevant rules. RSC Ord 11 is one such. It provides that the court may permit service of process outside the jurisdiction, but only in a limited number of cases listed in that order. When the defendant is abroad and the case is outside the court's jurisdiction under Ord 11, I do not think that the court should exercise its discretion under Ord 65, r 4, to order substituted service where the effect would be to add yet another cause of action to those listed in Ord 11. So, even if the court were to have jurisdiction under Ord 65, r 4, I do not think that this case is a proper case in which to exercise it.

I agree that this appeal should be dismissed.

1   (1899) 15 TLR 176
2   [1915] 1 KB 857, [1914–15] All ER Rep 918
3   (1958) 98 CLR 310
4   (1889) 23 QBD 395, [1886–90] All ER Rep 309

Appeal dismissed. Leave to appeal the House of Lords refused.

a Solicitors: *Geoffrey Myerson & Co* (for the plaintiff); *Ashurst, Morris, Crisp & Co* (for the defendant).

Sumra Green Barrister.

b

Science Research Council v Nassé
BL Cars Ltd (formerly Leyland Cars) v Vyas

c HOUSE OF LORDS

LORD WILBERFORCE, LORD SALMON, LORD EDMUND-DAVIES, LORD FRASER OF TULLYBELTON AND
LORD SCARMAN

5th, 6th, 7th, 11th, 12th, 13th, 14th, 18th JUNE, 1st NOVEMBER 1979

Industrial tribunal – Procedure – Discovery – Confidential documents – Complaint of
discrimination in employment – Discovery of confidential reports and references on employees
d and applicants for employment – Principles applicable in ordering discovery – Whether discovery
at tribunal's discretion – Whether tribunal's discretion to order discovery same as discretion to
order discovery in county court – Whether general order for discovery of all reports or references
on employees should be made – Whether tribunal under a duty to inspect documents before
ordering discovery – Industrial Tribunals (Labour Relations) Regulations 1974 (SI 1974 No
e 1386), Sch, r 4(1)(b) – CCR Ord 14, r 2(2).

In the first case the complainant, a clerical officer employed by the Science Research
Council, made a complaint to an industrial tribunal that the council had discriminated
against her in selecting two other clerical officers, but not her, to be interviewed for
promotion. The complainant alleged that she had been discriminated against on the
f ground of her trade union activities, contrary to s 53(1) of the Employment Protection
Act 1975, and because she was a married woman, contrary to s 6 of the Sex Discrimination
Act 1975. Each year a confidential report was made on every employee by his or her
immediate superior giving a detailed assessment of the employee's performance during
the year and his or her suitability for promotion. The reports were studied by a local
review board which analysed and commented on them and then made recommendations
for promotion. Before the industrial tribunal hearing took place the complainant
g applied, under r 4(1)[a] of the rules of procedure[b] for industrial tribunals, for discovery of
the annual confidential reports on the two officers who were selected for interview and
herself and the relevant extracts from the minutes of the local review board. The council
were willing to disclose the reports on the complainant herself but declined to disclose
the reports on the other two officers or the extracts from the minutes dealing with
them. The industrial tribunal made an order, under r 4(1)(b), for discovery of the
h documents sought without having inspected them. The council appealed to the
Employment Appeal Tribunal which affirmed the industrial tribunal's decision. The
council appealed to the Court of Appeal[c] which held that in exceptional cases an industrial
tribunal could order the disclosure of confidential documents which had been sought to
be withheld on the ground of public interest immunity, if the chairman after inspecting
the documents he decided that it was essential in the interests of justice that the
j confidence should be overridden. The court allowed the council's appeal and set aside

---

a Rule 4(1), so far as material, is set out at p 693 *g*, post
b Industrial Tribunal (Labour Relations) Regulations 1974, Sch
c [1978] 3 All ER 1196, [1979] QB 144

the order for discovery on the ground that disclosure of the documents was not necessary for fairly disposing of the appeal. The complainant appealed to the House of Lords.   *a*

In the second case the complainant, who was of Asian origin and was employed by Leyland Cars at one of their works, made a complaint to an industrial tribunal that Leyland had discriminated against him by refusing his application to transfer to another department of the works where posts had been advertised. The complainant alleged that he had been discriminated against because of his colour, contrary to s 4(2)(*b*) of the Race Relations Act 1974, and that after an interview by a panel two white employees whose   *b* qualifications were inferior to his own had been selected for the advertised posts. The complainant was dissatisfied with the answers given by Leyland to interrogatories put to them under the Race Relations Act 1976 and applied for further particulars of documents relating to the employees who had applied for transfer to the advertised posts. Leyland were willing to disclose certain information but not the service records, personal history forms or personal assessment records of the other employees, or the reports of the   *c* members of the interviewing panel. The complainant's application to an industrial tribunal, under r 4(1) of the rules of procedure, for discovery of that information was refused. The complainant appealed to the Employment Appeal Tribunal which, following its decision in the first case, allowed the appeal and ordered discovery of the information without the chairman having seen the documents. Leyland appealed to the Court of Appeal[d]. On the hearing of the appeal they gave evidence that disclosure of   *d* confidential information about employees would constitute a gross breach of faith and would be likely to damage industrial relations and impair the efficiency of their promotion procedures, which were similar to those of many industrial concerns. They contended that the withholding of such confidential information was protected by public interest immunity and disclosure should never be made unless the person supplying the information was willing to allow disclosure. The Court of Appeal allowed   *e* Leyland's appeal and set aside the order for discovery on the ground that discovery of the confidential information relating to the successful employees was not necessary. The complainant appealed to the House of Lords.

Held – (i) Whether discovery of confidential assessments, references, reports or other documents relating to an employee or applicant for employment should be ordered in proceedings before an industrial tribunal arising out of discrimination in employment   *f* was always a question of discretion for the court under r 4(1)(*b*) of the rules of procedure because such confidential documents were not protected from disclosure on the ground of public interest immunity. In exercising that discretion, which was the same as the county court's discretion under CCR Ord 14, r 2(2), an industrial tribunal should not order discovery unless it was necessary either for disposing fairly of the proceedings or for saving costs, and when exercising that discretion, in relation to confidential documents,   *g* it should in the interests of justice have regard to (a) the fact that the documents were confidential and that to order disclosure would involve a breach of confidence and (b) the extent to which the interest of third parties would be affected by disclosure. Furthermore, although relevance was a necessary ingredient, the tribunal was not bound to order discovery of all documents which were relevant if, for example, the information could be obtained from other sources. If however discovery was necessary for fairly disposing   *h* of the proceedings discovery must be ordered notwithstanding the documents' confidentiality. In deciding whether discovery was necessary for that reason the tribunal should first inspect the documents and consider whether justice could be done by special measures, such as covering up confidential but irrelevant parts of the documents, substituting anonymous references for specific names, or, in rare cases, a hearing in camera (see p 679 *g* to p 680 *d*, p 684 *b c* and *e* to p 685 *a* and *f* to *h*, p 686 *a b h*, p 687 *b*   *j* to *d*, p 689 *b* to *f*, p 690 *a b*, p 693 *b*, p 695 *f* to *j*, p 696 *g h*, p 697 *c d* and p 698 *b d* to *f* and *j* to p 699 *d*, post), dictum of Arnold J in *British Railways Board v Natarajan* [1979] 2 All ER at 799 approved.

---

d   [1978] 3 All ER 1196

(ii) The Court of Appeal had rightly held that discovery should not have been ordered in either of the two cases without the respective tribunals first inspecting the documents. Accordingly the appeals would be dismissed and the cases remitted to the tribunals so that the chairmen could examine those documents claimed to be confidential before deciding which, if any, should be disclosed and inspected and whether any irrelevant parts of the disclosed documents should be covered up (see p 682 *e* to *h*, p 685 *h* to p 686 *b*, p 689 *h*, p 690 *b c*, p 697 *a* to *d*, and p 699 *d e*, post).

approved.

Decision of the Court of Appeal [1978] 3 All ER 1196 affirmed.

Notes

For discovery of documents in proceedings before industrial tribunals, see 16 Halsbury's Laws (4th Edn) para 1018, and for the rules of procedure which apply to the proceedings, see ibid paras 1014–1028.

For discovery of documents in the country court, see 10 ibid paras 287, 288.

For withholding documents on the gound that disclosure would be injurious to the public interest, see 13 ibid paras 86–91, and for cases on the subject, see 18 Digest (Reissue) 154–160, 1265–1301.

Cases referred to in opinions

Argyll (Duke of) v Duchess of Argyll 1962 SC (HL) 88, 27(1) Digest (Reissue) 418, *1647.

Attorney-General v Clough [1963] 1 All ER 420, [1963] 1 QB 773, [1963] 2 WLR 343, 22 Digest (Reissue) 459, 4587.

Attorney-General v Mulholland, Attorney-General v Foster [1963] 1 All ER 767, [1963] 2 QB 477, [1963] 2 WLR 658, CA, 22 Digest (Reissue) 459, 4588.

Attorney-General v North Metropolitan Tramways Co [1892] 3 Ch 70, 61 LJ Ch 693, 67 LT 283; affd (1895) 72 LT 340, CA, 18 Digest (Reissue) 12, 51.

British Railways Board v Natarajan, Natarajan v British Railways Board [1979] 2 All ER 794, [1979] ICR 326, EAT.

Conway v Rimmer [1968] 1 All ER 874, [1968] AC 910, [1968] 2 WLR 998, HL, rvsg [1967] 2 All ER 1260, [1967] 1 WLR 1031, CA, 18 Digest (Reissue) 155, 1273

Crompton (Alfred) Amusement Machines Ltd v Customs and Excise Comrs (No 2) [1973] 2 All ER 1169, [1974] AC 405, [1973] 3 WLR 268, HL, 18 Digest (Reissue) 102, 756.

D v National Society for the Prevention of Cruelty to Children [1977] 1 All ER 589, [1978] AC 171, [1977] 2 WLR 201, HL.

Duncan v Cammell Laird & Co Ltd [1942] 1 All ER 587, [1942] AC 624, 111 LJKB 406, 166 LT 366, HL, 18 Digest (Reissue) 155, 1272.

Grosvenor Hotel, London, Re, (No 2), [1964] 3 All ER 354, [1965] Ch 1210, [1964] 3 WLR 992, CA, 18 Digest (Reissue) 157, 1279.

Hopkinson v Lord Burghley (1867) LR 2 Ch App 447, 36 LJ Ch 504, LJJ, 18 Digest (Reissue) 148, 1193.

McIvor v Southern Heath and Social Services Board [1978] 2 All ER 625, [1978] 1 WLR 757, HL.

North British Railway Co v Garroway (1893) 20 R (Ct of Sess) 397.

Oxford v Department of Health and Social Security [1977] ICR 884, EAT.

Rogers v Secretary of State for the Home Department, Gaming Board for Great Britain v Rogers [1972] 2 All ER 1057, [1973] AC 388, [1972] 3 WLR 279, 136 JP 574, HL, 22 Digest (Reissue) 461, 4600.

Stone v Charrington & Co Ltd (15th February 1977) unreported, EAT.

Interlocutory appeals

Science Research Council v Nassé

The employee, Joan Marguerite Nassé, a clerical officer employed by the Science Research Council ('the SRC') at their Appleton laboratory, complained to an industrial tribunal that the SRC, in not selecting her for an interview with a view to promotion to executive officer, had discriminated against her because of her trade union activities and because she was a married woman, contrary to s 53(1) of the Employment Protection Act 1975 and s 6 of the Sex Discrimination Act 1975, respectively. The SRC filed an answer denying discrimination. Mrs Nassé applied by letter dated 8th May 1977, pursuant to r 4(1)(b) of the rules of procedure contained in the schedule to the Industrial (Labour Relations) Regulations 1974 for an order requiring the SRC to disclose the annual confidential reports for the years 1975 and 1976 relating to herself and the two clerical officers who were selected for interview for promotion (later extended in the case of one of the officers to 1974) and the minutes of the local review board. The SRC opposed the application so far as disclosure of the confidential reports relating to the two clerical officers and the extracts from the minutes dealing with those officers was concerned. On 23rd November 1977 an industrial tribunal sitting in London (chairman Mr Oliver Lodge) ordered inspection of all documents in respect of which the application was made. The SRC appealed to the Employment Appeal Tribunal (Bristow J, Mrs A L T Taylor and Mr R Thomas) which, on 20th March 1978, dismissed the appeal and ordered the SRC to disclose the confidential reports for 1975 and 1976 on the two clerical officers who were selected for interview and the minutes of the local review board relating to the decision to select those officers for interview and not to select Mrs Nassé. On 26th July 1978 the Court of Appeal[1] (Lord Denning MR, Lawton and Browne LJJ) allowed an appeal by the SRC and refused Mrs Nassé's application for discovery. Mrs Nassé appealed to the House of Lords pursuant to leave of the House granted on 19th October 1978. The facts are set out in the opinion of Lord Wilberforce.

BL Cars Ltd (formerly Leyland Cars) v Vyas

The employee, Nat Vinu Vyas, who was employed by Leyland Cars (now BL Cars Ltd) at their Cowley works, complained to an industrial tribunal that Leyland Cars had discriminated against him on the grounds of race, colour, ethnic or national origin, contrary to s 4(2)(b) of the Race Relations Act 1976, in refusing his application for transfer to another department at the Cowley works and in accepting the applications for transfer of two other employees. The Commission for Racial Equality supported his complaint. Leyland Cars denied discrimination. By letter dated 15th February 1978, the commission applied to the secretary of the industrial tribunals, under r 4(1) of the rules of procedure contained in the schedule to the Industrial Tribunals (Labour Relations) Regulations 1974, for disclosure by Leyland Cars of specified information. Leyland Cars disclosed some of that information but refused to disclose details of the employment and service records of the persons apart from Mr Vyas who were interviewed for transfer to the other department, and the completed interview report forms returned by each member of the interview panel in relation to those persons and Mr Vyas. By letter dated 14th March the chairman of the tribunals refused to make an order for further and better particulars of the withheld documents. The commission on behalf of Mr Vyas appealed to the Employment Appeal Tribunal (Phillips J, Mr A J Nicol and Mr J M Wood) which, on 28th April, allowed the appeal, following their decision in *Science Research Council v Nassé*[2], and ordered discovery of the withheld documents. On 26th July 1978 the Court of Appeal[1] (Lord Denning MR, Lawton and Browne LJJ) allowed an appeal by Leyland Cars. Mr Vyas appealed to the House of Lords with leave of the House granted on 19th October 1978. The facts are set out in the opinion of Lord Wilberforce.

Raymond Kidwell QC and *Frederic Reynold* for Mrs Nassé.
T H Bingham QC, Peter Gibson and *David Blunt* for the SRC.

---

1   [1978] 3 All ER 1196, [1979] QB 144
2   [1978] ICR 777

Anthony Lester QC[1] and *Frederic Reynold* for Mr Vyas.

a *Robert Alexander QC* and *Michael Howard* for BL Cars Ltd.

Their Lordships took time for consideration.

1st November. The following opinions were delivered.

b **LORD WILBERFORCE.** My Lords, Mrs Nassé and Mr Vyas, who are the two appellants in these conjoined appeals, have complained to industrial tribunals of discrimination against them by their employers.

Mrs Nassé was employed as a clerical officer by the Science Research Council ('SRC') a body incorporated by Royal Charter. She sought, unsuccessfully, promotion to the grade of executive officer and complained, originally, that she had been discriminated against
c on the ground of her activities in her trade union. Later she added a complaint of discrimination under the Sex Discrimination Act 1975.

Mr Vyas was employed as a methods analyst by Leyland Cars (now BL Cars Ltd) ('Leyland'). He sought, unsuccessfully, a level transfer to another division in the company, and complained of discrimination on racial grounds: he is of Asian origin.

Each appeal raises the question whether and to what extent a complainant under the
d Employment Protection Act 1975, or the Sex Discrimination Act 1975 or the Race Relations Act 1976, may obtain discovery and inspection of documents, and, in particular, whether she or he is entitled to see confidential assessments, references, reports or other documents relating to the complainant and to other persons, particularly those persons who have been perferred to the complainant. In each case the employer has been willing to produce for inspection a certain amount of material. But in each case
e it objects to the disclosure of matters revealed in confidence on the ground, broadly, that this would involve a breach of the confidence under which the material came into existence, and would undermine the whole system and structure of promotion and employer management.

The appeals call for a decision on principles applicable generally to complaints of discrimination, but in the end these particular cases have to be decided, so I think it
f advisable to say something more about them before attempting generalisations. Mrs Nassé, as had other employees of the SRC, had made on her an annual confidential report. This form of report, commonly used in the public service, is made by the employee's immediate superior, by an officer senior to the reporting officer, and by the next senior officer to the latter. These reports to some extent involve an assessment of personal qualities and are confidential in the sense that those signing them know that
g they will not be shown to the person reported on. They are also confidential in the sense that the person reported on knows that the contents of the report will only be used or disclosed for the purpose of monitoring his performance. However, the person reported on may ask to be told of some of the information given in the report.

The reports on Mrs Nassé, in accordance with the usual procedure, were considered by a local review board together with reports on other employees. The local review board
h made notes from the reports and then made recommendations to the director of the laboratory where she was employed as to clerical officers to be put forward for promotion. After endorsement by the director, the recommendations were forwarded to a central review board. Mrs Nassé was not recommended for promotion: the only officer who was recommended in 1976 was a Mr Roberts. The central review board decided to call for interview Mr Roberts and a Miss Richardson, but not Mrs Nassé. Ultimately Mr Roberts
j and Miss Richardson were promoted.

---

1 Lester QC, as a special concession from the House and with the consent of opposing counsel, was granted permission, after he had presented his arguments on behalf of Mr Vyas, to present arguments on behalf of the Equal Opportunities Commission and the Commission for Racial Equality

The documents which Mrs Nassé, by letter to the industrial tribunal, requested should be supplied to her were (a) the annual confidential reports on Mr Roberts, Miss *a* Richardson and herself for 1975 and 1976 (later extended in the case of Mr Roberts to 1974) and (b) the minutes of the local review board. The SRC furnished her with copies of the report on herself but refused her other requests. After a hearing on 23rd November 1977 the industrial tribunal granted Mrs Nassé's application and this decision (with a small variation) was upheld by the Employment Appeal Tribunal on 20th March 1978. On appeal by the SRC to the Court of Appeal, that court allowed the appeal and refused *b* Mrs Nassé's application.

Mr Vyas applied in October 1977 for a level transfer to a position in respect of which his employer had advertised two vacancies. Three other persons applied for the vacancies and they, together with Mr Vyas, were interviewed. Mr Vyas was unsuccessful. After he had made his complaint to an industrial tribunal an application was made (inter alia) for an order requiring the employer to disclose details of the employment record of the *c* other persons interviewed, their service records, personal history forms, personal assessment records and details of commendations, if any, together with their application forms for the post advertised. He also asked for disclosure of the completed interview report forms returned by each member of the interview panel in relation to each person interviewed. Certain other information requested was supplied to the complainant, but the employer objected to disclosing the matters referred to. As to the latter, the chairman *d* of the industrial tribunal refused the application, but it was allowed on appeal by the Employment Appeal Tribunal, with an indication that in doing so the tribunal felt constrained to follow its decision in Mrs Nassé's case. On appeal to the Court of Appeal, an affidavit was admitted at a late stage from the employer's staff director stating that disclosure of such documents would lead to an inhibition of freedom and candour in reporting and an inhibition on the part of employees when applying for jobs or *e* promotion. It was further stated that such disclosure would constitute a breach of faith which would be likely to lead to industrial unrest and diminution of the effectiveness of selection procedures. The Court of Appeal allowed the employer's appeal.

On the appeals coming before your Lordships very extensive arguments were heard ranging widely over many areas of substantive and procedural law, with references to American cases under the Civil Rights Act 1964 and to the European Convention of *f* Human Rights[1], art 6. Since I regard our task in this House to be at most to establish rules which can be applied by industrial tribunals (and analogously by county courts in discrimination cases), I shall summarise the statutory background and then state the conclusions to which I have come before developing certain supporting arguments.

There are three statutes dealing with discrimination: in these appeals we are concerned with all of them. I shall refer only to such provisions as are essentially relevant. The *g* Employment Protection Act 1975, ss 53 to 56, deals with action taken against an employee for the purpose of penalising him for being a member of an independent trade union, or of preventing or deterring him from taking part in the activities of an independent trade union. Complaints go to an industrial tribunal where the employer has the burden of showing that the purpose for which the action was taken was not such as has been mentioned (see s 55(1)(b)). Complaints of discrimination in employment *h* under the Sex Discrimination Act 1975 or the Race Relations Act 1976 also go to an industrial tribunal, but in these cases the burden of proof is on the employee. Discrimination in other matters (eg as to education or housing) go to a county court and are to be dealt with 'as any other claim in tort' (see ss 66(1) and 57(1) of these Acts respectively).

In cases under the Sex Discrimination Act 1975 and the Race Relations Act 1976 the *j* necessary information and material to support or refute a claim will rarely be in the possession of the employee, but, on the contrary, is likely to be in the possession of the employer. Discrimination, at least in promotion cases, involves an allegation that,

---

1   Rome, 4th November 1950; TS 71 (1953); Cmd 8969

a although the unselected complainant is as well qualified as the person selected, or indeed better qualified, he was not chosen, an allegation which almost necessarily involves a careful comparison of qualifications and an enquiry into the selection process. The employer is likely to have information on these matters. So, in order to ensure its production, each of the Acts contains a powerful inquisitorial procedure enabling the statutory commissions set up under each Act to obtain information. They may conduct a 'formal investigation' and in the course of it require any person to give oral information *b* and produce documents; there is however the limitation that a person cannot be required to give information, or produce documents, which he could not be compelled to give in evidence or produce in civil proceedings before the High Court. If an individual considers that he may have been discriminated against, the relevant commission may assist him (by advice or 'legal aid') and may help him to question the employer by means of a questionnaire. If the employer refuses to answer, or if his answer appears evasive or *c* equivocal, inferences adverse to him may be drawn. Furthermore, industrial tribunals have powers, of their own motion, to ask for particulars of the grounds on which a person relies and of any facts or contentions relevant thereto. These provisions may appear Draconian (they did so to some extent to Lord Denning MR) but for my part I do not find it necessary to characterise them. The powers have been conferred by Parliament on statutory bodies as part of the machinery for eliminating discrimination in situations *d* where the parties are of unequal strength: no instance was given to us of an oppressive use of them and we should presume that they will be reasonably used for the purpose for which they were given. The relevant point to be made is that, by reason of these powers, employees and the tribunals have the means, before any question of discovery arises, to obtain a great deal of information which may assist the employees' case, and indeed by conferring them Parliament has shown that its policy is that they should have every *e* chance to lay before the tribunal or the court all material that may be relevant to a discrimination claim.

That brings me to the question of discovery (in which I include inspection) as to which the situation, as I see it, is formally simple. By a number of cross-references between regulations[1], the County Court Rules and the Rules of the Supreme Court the position is reached that the tribunal, or the county court, has a general discretion to order discovery, *f* coupled with the qualification that 'discovery *shall not* be ordered if and so far as the court is of opinion that it is not necessary either for disposing fairly of the proceedings or for saving costs' (CCR Ord 14, r 2(2); emphasis mine). These provisions, applied as they have been since their introduction, are sufficient to provide a solution for the issues in these appeals. These are, broadly, two. First, is there in relation to confidential documents, or any relevant class of confidential documents, any *immunity* from disclosure? Second, if *g* not, how should the tribunal exercise its discretion as to discovery in relation to confidential documents in this field? (Here and elsewhere I use the word 'tribunal' so as to include, where appropriate, a county court.)

On these points my conclusions are as follows:

(1) There is no principle of public interest immunity, as that expression was developed from *Conway v Rimmer*[2], protecting such confidential documents as these with which *h* these appeals are concerned. That such an immunity exists, or ought to be declared by this House to exist, was the main contention of Leyland. It was not argued for by the SRC; indeed that body argued against it.

(2) There is no principle in English law by which documents are protected from discovery by reason of confidentiality alone. But there is no reason why, in the exercise of its discretion to order discovery, the tribunal should not have regard to the fact that *j* documents are confidential, and that to order disclosure would involve a breach of confidence. In the employment field, the tribunal may have regard to the sensitivity of

---

1   Ie the Industrial Tribunals (Labour Relations) Regulations 1974 (SI 1974 No 1386), as amended by the Industrial Tribunals (Labour Relations) (Amendment) Regulations 1978 (SI 1978 No 991)
2   [1968] 1 All ER 874, [1968] AC 910

particular types of confidential information, to the extent to which the interests of third parties (including other employees on which confidential reports have been made, as well as persons reporting) may be affected by disclosure, to the interest which both employees and employers may have in preserving the confidentiality of personal reports, and to any wider interest which may be seen to exist in preserving the confidentiality of systems of personal assessments.

(3) As a corollary to the above, it should be added that relevance alone, though a necessary ingredient, does not provide an automatically sufficient test for ordering discovery. The tribunal always has a discretion. That relevance alone is enough was, in my belief, the position ultimately taken by counsel for Mrs Nassé thus entitling the complainant to discovery subject only to protective measures (sealing up etc). This I am unable to accept.

(4) The ultimate test in discrimination (as in other) proceedings is whether discovery is necessary for disposing fairly of the proceedings. If it is, then discovery must be ordered notwithstanding confidentiality. But where the court is impressed with the need to preserve confidentiality in a particular case, it will consider carefully whether the necessary information has been or can be obtained by other means, not involving a breach of confidence.

(5) In order to reach a conclusion whether discovery is necessary notwithstanding confidentiality the tribunal should inspect the documents. It will naturally consider whether justice can be done by special measures such as 'covering up', substituting anonymous references for specific names, or, in rare cases, hearing in camera.

(6) The procedure by which this process is to be carried out is one for tribunals to work out in a manner which will avoid delay and unnecessary applications. I shall not say more on this aspect of the matter than that the decisions of the Employment Appeal Tribunal in *Stone v Charrington & Co Ltd*[1] per Phillips J, *Oxford v Department of Health and Social Security*[2] per Phillips J and *British Railways Board v Natarajan*[3] per Arnold J, well indicate the lines of a satisfactory procedure, which must of course be flexible.

(7) The above conclusions are essentially in agreement with those of the Court of Appeal[4]. I venture to think however that the formula suggested, namely:

'The industrial tribunals should not order or permit the disclosure of reports or references that have been given and received in confidence except in the very rare cases where, after inspection of a particular document, the chairman decides that it is essential in the interests of justice that the confidence should be overridden: and then only subject to such conditions as to the divulging of its as he shall think fit to impose, both for the protection of the maker of the document and the subject of it.'

may be rather too rigid. For myself I prefer to rest such rule as can be stated on the discretion of the court.

To these conclusions I will now add some supporting arguments. I make these briefly since a large part of the ground is familiar, and to deal fully with all the contentions we have heard would require treatment disproportionate to the case. In the end the issue between the parties, apart from the claim to public interest immunity, is a narrow one.

1. I reject the contention of public interest immunity basically on three grounds. First there is no acceptable analogy, still less any precedent, on which such a claim could be admitted. The area in which the immunity is claimed is essentially one of private right even though interest beyond those of the particular employer concerned may be involved. Secondly, to admit such a claim in this field would conflict with the clear public interest accepted and emphasised by Parliament in the Sex Discrimination Act 1975 and the Race Relations Act 1976 that the fullest information should be before the

---

1 (15th February 1977) unreported
2 [1977] ICR 884 at 887
3 [1979] 2 All ER 794
4 See [1978] 3 All ER 1196 at 1208, [1979] QB 144 at 173 per Lord Denning MR

tribunals. Thirdly, to admit such a claim would produce most undesirable results in
a   excluding classes of documents altogether from use in the proceedings, since documents
covered by immunity on grounds of public interest not only may but must be withheld.

2. No authority is needed for the negative proposition that confidentiality alone is no
ground for protection; see, however, *Alfred Crompton Amusement Machines Ltd v Customs
and Excise Comrs (No 2)*[1].

English law as to discovery is extremely far reaching; parties can be compelled to
b   produce their private diaries; confidences, except between lawyer and client, may have
to be broken however intimate they may be. But there are many examples of cases
where the courts have recognised that confidences, particularly those of third persons,
ought, if possible, in the interests of justice, to be respected. See, for recent examples,
Attorney-General v Mulholland[2] and *Attorney-General v Clough*[3] and compare *Attorney-
General v North Metropolitan Tramways Co*[4]. This principle was accepted by this House in
c   *D v National Society for Prevention of Cruelty to Children*[5]. Employment cases, and indeed
all cases involving selection, involve a wide dimension of confidentiality, affecting other
candidates or applicants, who may be numerous, and a number of reporting officers and
selection bodies. No court attempting to administer these Acts can fail to give weight to
this, though it is not, as above stated, the only element. It is sometimes said that in
taking this element into account, the court has to perform a balancing process. The
d   metaphor is one well worn in the law, but I doubt if it is more than a rough metaphor.
Balancing can only take place between commensurables. But here the process is to
consider fairly the strength and value of the interest in preserving confidentiality and the
damage which may be caused by breaking it; then to consider whether the objective, to
dispose fairly of the case, can be achieved without doing so, and only in a last resort to
order discovery, subject if need be to protective measures. This is a more complex
e   process than merely using the scales: it is an exercise in judicial judgment.

3. It was justly pointed out by counsel for Mr Vyas, also representing the commissions,
that Parliament in enacting the two discrimination Acts, and also in the field of
employment protection, undoubtedly had in mind that considerations of confidentiality
might arise, and indeed legislated as to this matter. Thus, in the Industrial Relations Act
1971, while employers were obliged to disclose certain information to employees, or to
f   trade union representatives (ss 56, 57), there was a specific provision relieving employers
of their obligation as regards 'information which has been communicated to the
employer in confidence, or which the employer has otherwise obtained in consequence
of the confidence reposed in him by another person' (s 158(1)). That same Act contained
provision regarding discovery in industrial tribunals similar to those which apply in the
present cases (Sch 6, para 2(d)) without any reference to confidential matters. On the
g   repeal of the Industrial Relations Act 1971 these provisions were carried forward into the
Trade Union and Labour Relations Act 1974 which extended the powers of industrial
tribunals (Sch 1, Part III, para 16) with a similar reference to confidential matters as had
been made in s 158 above (Sch 1, Part III, para 21(5)), power being given to sit in private
to protect confidentiality. So the policy of this Act was to allow discovery and inspection
in industrial tribunals on the same basis as would be allowed in county courts with
h   specified safeguards for confidentiality. The Employment Protection Act 1975 contained
similar provisions regarding disclosure and confidential information to those contained
in the (repealed) Industrial Relations Act 1971, ss 56 and 158, but gave no immunity as
regards such information in proceedings in industrial tribunals under Part II of that
Act. These repeated enactments show, it was said, a deliberate abstention by Parliament
from introducing any immunity for confidential information into proceedings before

j
1   [1973] 2 All ER 1169, [1974] AC 405
2   [1963] 1 All ER 767, [1963] 2 QB 477
3   [1963] 1 All ER 420, [1963] 1 QB 773
4   [1892] 3 Ch 70
5   [1977] 1 All ER 589, [1978] AC 171

industrial tribunals, although Parliament had to hand the necessary language for so doing.

My Lords, I recognise the force of all this but I do not think that it leads to the conclusion which is sought to be drawn from it. The fact that Parliament has conferred a specific degree of immunity on confidential information required to be disclosed in particular circumstances is not inconsistent with a legislative intention that industrial tribunals should have the same power, in their discretion, to refuse or limit discovery where confidential information is concerned. This power is not one to confer immunity: it is simply the ordinary discretionary power which is enjoyed by the High Court and by county courts. By equating the powers of the tribunals to those of the courts, Parliament has, in my opinion, indicated in a clear enough way that those limitations on the granting of discovery which the courts have long accepted should apply to tribunals, and the granting of the much wider immunity in other cases does not, in my understanding, negate this.

4. The European Convention on Human Rights[1]. The point here is a very short one. Article 6(1) of the Convention guarantees the right to a fair hearing: Mr Vyas relies on this as requiring total disclosure of all information relevant to the case, confidential or not. But this is a fallacy, because the whole aim and object of those carefully worked out provisions of English law which regulate the right to discovery and inspection of documents is precisely to achieve a fair hearing. That is the standard of our law and it is unnecessary to have resort to the Convention to establish it.

It remains to dispose of the actual appeals. In Mrs Nassé's case, discovery was sought of a whole range of documents as specified above, claimed by the employer to be confidential. The chairman of the industrial tribunal ordered accordingly without inspecting the documents. The Court of Appeal held that this was wrong and that discovery should only be ordered if, after inspection, the tribunal considered discovery to be necessary in order to dispose fairly of the proceedings. In my opinion, the Court of Appeal was right, and the appeal must be dismissed. This does not prevent Mrs Nassé, if she goes on with her case, from requesting the tribunal to look at the requested documents and ordering, subject if necessary to safeguards, discovery and inspection of such of them as are necessary for fair disposal of the case. In Mr Vyas's case the situation is similar. The Employment Appeal Tribunal ordered that he should be allowed to inspect all the documents to which I have referred (as listed in a letter dated 15th February 1978) regardless of confidentiality. The Court of Appeal held that this was wrong and I agree with them. The order of the Employment Appeal Tribunal was correctly set aside, and the appeal must be dismissed. However some of the documents may well be necessary for disposing fairly of the case. If it goes on, the industrial tribunal should consider, at the time and in the manner which it considers most suitable, which, if any, of the requested documents should be disclosed and produced in order to enable the proceedings to be fairly disposed of.

I would dismiss the appeals and order each appellant to pay the respective respondents' costs in this House.

LORD SALMON. My Lords, my noble and learned friend, Lord Wilberforce, has lucidly stated all the material facts, the relevant provisions of the three statutes and the rules and orders with which these two appeals are concerned. I will not repeat but gratefully adopt them.

The question which these appeals raises is of great importance: what rights has an employee, complaining of unlawful discrimination, to obtain an order against his employer for the production of documents which contain confidential information? 'Complaints' include all who complain of and seek redress for unlawful discrimination on account of their sex, race or trade union activities. Such discrimination is treated as a tort in England and as a breach of statutory duty in Scotland.

---

1 Rome, 4th November 1950; TS 71 (1953); Cmd 8969

It is plain from the Industrial Tribunals (Labour Relations) Regulations 1974 that
a Parliament did not intend to deprive the person against whom such discrimination is
alleged to have been committed, of any of the facilities enjoyed by the ordinary plaintiff
suing for damages for tort. One of the most useful of these facilities is the right in certain
circumstances to obtain an order for discovery and inspection of documents. This right
is of particular importance in cases of alleged discrimination such as the present for it is
the employer alone who will ordinarily be in possession of the documents likely to throw
b light on the question as to whether or not the employer has unlawfully discriminated
against the complainant. I do not think that the importance to the complainant of his
right to claim an order for inspection of the relevant documents is diminished by the
statutory machinery which exists to allow the complainant and indeed the industrial
tribunal to question the employer and at an early stage to obtain answers relating to
whether the employer has unlawfully discriminated against his employee. It is, no
c doubt, possible that the answers, if reliable, might establish or negative the alleged
unlawful discrimination and therefore make inspection of any documents unnecessary.
On the other hand, there is the danger that the answers may be exiguous or unreliable
and misleading. The only way of testing the accuracy of the employer's answers may
often be by comparing them with the reports and records in their possession. The
statutory machinery for obtaining early information from the employers was not, in my
d view, intended to be a substitute for, but an addition to the complainant's rights to
discovery and inspection of documents.

It is plain from the facts of the present case that there is, particularly in large
enterprises, an elaborate system for making and filing written reports and records in
relation to each employee, and that these reports are of special importance when it comes
to decide which of the employees applying for promotion or transfer shall be interviewed
e by the panel which selects the applicants for promotion or transfer. Suppose that one of
the candidates who happened to be black had excellent written records and reports but
failed to obtain the promotion or transfer for which he had applied, whilst two other
candidates who happened to be white did obtain promotion or transfer although their
records and reports were far below those of the black man; this could well be regarded
as establishing, at any rate, a strong prima facie case of race discrimination. But without
f discovery and inspection of the relevant documents, the truth could not have been found
nor justice done.

The argument advanced with great skill and relied on almost exclusively by counsel
for British Leyland was that the following documents which Mr Vyas required to be
produced enjoyed public interest immunity:

g '3. Details of the employment record of the persons mentioned in (1) and (2)
above; their service records whilst in the employment of the respondents, ie length
of service, positions held, promotions, job classification according to grades, personal
history forms, personal assessment records and details of commendations (if any)
etc. together with their application forms for the post advertised, and applied for by
the applicant . . .

h '6. The completed interview report forms returned by each and every member
of the interview panel in relation to every person, including the applicant,
interviewed for the afore-mentioned post in the services division of the respondents.'

I cannot agree that the production of such documents could have the dire effect which
has been suggested, and of which there is certainly no real evidence. I cannot accept the
proposition that those whose duty it was to write reports about a candidate and his
j record, suitability for promotion etc would lack in candour because the reports, or some
of them, might possibly sometimes see the light of day. This proposition bears a striking
resemblance to that which was accepted as sound for upwards of 20 years after the obiter
dicta pronounced by Viscount Simon LC in *Duncan v Cammell Laird & Co Ltd*[1]. This

1   [1942] 1 All ER 587, [1942] AC 624

proposition was however held to be unsound in *Re Grosvenor Hotel, London (No 2)*[1], and generally accepted as unsound during the three years following that decision. The obiter dicta in *Duncan v Cammell Laird & Co Ltd*[2] was then temporarily revivified by a majority decision of the Court of Appeal in *Conway v Rimmer*[3], but was finally put to rest when that majority decision was reversed in your Lordships' House[4]. No more than I accept the proposition relating to candour, do I accept the proposition that employees anxious for promotion or transfer would be inhibited from making the necessary applications if they knew that their application forms and the written decisions relating to them might also sometimes be allowed to see the light of day.

I do not consider that an order to produce for the employees' inspection such documents as those to which I have referred could be contrary to public interest; nor do any such documents bear any resemblance to the kind of documents which are normally accepted as immune from production in the public interest. I therefore consider that the main argument relied on by British Leyland (but rejected by the Science Research Council in the second appeal) must fail.

The next question that arises is whether and to what extent the fact that the documents concerned are considered to be confidential affects the complainant's right to discovery and inspection. In most cases, whether before the High Court, the county court or an industrial tribunal, there has been discovery of documents with no claim to privilege or immunity from production; and the documents are normally produced for inspection as a matter of course. This however does not always apply to cases in which the documents which one of the parties wishes to inspect have come into the hands of the other party in confidence. It has long been established, however, that no documents which have been acquired in confidence can for that reason be privileged from production or inspection. This point was not challenged by counsel for the Science Research Council or British Leyland; and no doubt this also explains why counsel for British Leyland relied almost entirely on public interest immunity.

Since confidential documents are not privileged from inspection and public interest immunity fails, the tribunal, which for this purpose is in the same position as the High Court and the county court, may order discovery (which includes inspection) of any such documents as it thinks fit, with this proviso: discovery shall not be ordered if and so far as the court [or tribunal] is of opinion that it is not necessary either for disposing fairly of the proceedings or for saving costs.

If the tribunal is satisfied that it is necessary to order certain documents to be disclosed and inspected in order fairly to dispose of the proceedings, then, in my opinion, the law requires that such an order should be made; and the fact that the documents are confidential is irrelevant.

The law has always recognised that it is of the greatest importance from the point of view of public policy that proceedings in the courts or before tribunals shall be fairly disposed of. This, no doubt, is why the law has never accorded privilege against discovery and inspection to confidential documents which are necessary for fairly disposing of the proceedings. What does 'necessary' in this context mean? It, of course, includes the case where the party applying for an order for discovery and inspection of certain documents could not possibly succeed in the proceedings unless he obtained the order; but it is not confined to such cases. Suppose, for example, a man had a slim chance of success without inspection of documents but a very strong chance of success with inspection, surely the proceedings could not be regarded as being fairly disposed of, were he to be denied inspection.

I, of course, recognise that the tribunal, like the courts, has a discretion in the exercise of its power to order discovery. It would, however, in my view, be a wholly wrongful

1   [1964] 3 All ER 354, [1965] Ch 1210 at 1233
2   [1942] 1 All ER 587, [1942] AC 624
3   [1967] 2 All ER 1260, [1967] 1 WLR 1031, CA
4   [1968] 1 All ER 874, [1968] AC 910

exercise of discretion, were an order for discovery and inspection to be refused because
a of the court's or the tribunal's natural aversion to the disclosure of confidential documents
notwithstanding that the proceedings might not be fairly disposed of without them.

I cannot accept the view that the courts have recognised that there are circumstances
in which the confidentiality of documents should be so respected that their production
should be refused even if by doing so the proceedings might not be fairly disposed of.
Rogers v Secretary of State for the Home Department[1] and *D v National Society for the*
b *Prevention of Cruelty to Children*[2] have been relied on for support of this view but they do
not appear to me to have anything to do with it. In the first case, an application had been
made to the Gaming Board to issue a certificate consenting to an applicant applying to
the licensing authority for a licence to carry on a gaming club. An anonymous letter had
been received by the Gaming Board strongly suggesting that the applicant was not fit to
have such a licence issued to him. The applicant applied to be shown this letter. The
c Gaming Board refused to disclose it. Your Lordships decided that it would have been
contrary to the public interest for such a letter (the contents of which could have revealed
the identity of its writer) to be disclosed. To disclose it might have discouraged others
from communicating to the Board what they knew about applicants for fear of libel
actions, their safety and maybe their lives. It was of the greatest public importance for
the Board to obtain every scrap of information it could in respect of anyone proposing to
d apply for a licence to carry on a gaming club. The basis of your Lordships' decision had
little to do with respect for confidentiality, but a great deal to do with the danger of
eliminating the Board's sources of information.

D v National Society for the Prevention of Cruelty to Children[2] had equally little to do with
respect for confidentiality. Cruelty to children is a most serious and fairly common
social evil. The society for its prevention has done much successful work, a large
e proportion of which was made possible by the information received by the society. Your
Lordships held that it was in the public interest that the identity of the society's informers
should not be revealed for much the same reason as the identity of police informers is not
revealed. If it were, informers would cease to inform. The result would be strongly
against public interest for in the one case little children would suffer and in the other case
crime would increase.

f My Lords, I cannot agree that industrial tribunals should approach cases such as these
relating to confidential documents with any preconceived notion that discovery should
not be ordered 'except in very rare cases' and only in the last resort. I think that these
cases should be approached with a completely open mind. The question being 'is
discovery necessary for fairly disposing of these proceedings?', if the answer to that
question is in the affirmative, as I venture to think it often may be, then discovery should
g be ordered notwithstanding the documents' confidentiality. The irrelevant parts of the
documents should, of course, be effectively covered up.

In my view, it would be impossible for a tribunal to decide whether the disclosure of
confidential documents was necessary for fairly disposing of the proceedings, without
examining the documents. I think that in *Science Research Council v Nassé*[3] the appeal
tribunal did not examine the documents and said 'disclosure of the documents . . . is
h . . . necessary in order that the industrial tribunal may be in a position to do justice not
only to [Mrs Nassé] but to [the Council] . . .' because it overlooked the fact that the
council might not wish to make use of the documents even if they were in its favour.

My Lords, I would dismiss both appeals and remit the two cases to the tribunal so that
the chairman may now examine the documents which are claimed to be confidential and
decide which (if any) of them should be disclosed and inspected, and order any irrelevant
j parts of the disclosed documents to be covered up. I consider that especially as there has

---

1   [1972] 2 All ER 1057, [1973] AC 388
2   [1977] 1 All ER 589, [1978] AC 171
3   [1978] ICR 777 at 780

already been such a long delay, it may well be desirable that the question of discovery should be resolved as soon as possible, so that if it is resolved in favour of the complainants, *a* inspection may take place well in advance of the hearing.

LORD EDMUND-DAVIES. My Lords, I respectfully agree with the reasons for dismissing these consolidated appeals advanced in the speech of my noble and learned friend, Lord Wilberforce, which I have had the advantage of reading in draft, and also with the order which he proposes. What follows should therefore be regarded as simply *b* enlarging on some of the topics involved which are of particular interest and importance.

The principal issue raised is as to the manner in which the discretionary powers conferred on industrial tribunals to order discovery and inspection of documents should be exercised in cases of alleged discrimination in the employment field, where the complainant seeks access to confidential assessments and other documents relating to his fellow-employees. The appeals also indirectly concern the powers conferred on county *c* courts in cases of alleged sex or racial discrimination outside the employment field, under Part III of both the Sex Discrimination Act 1975 and the Race Relations Act 1976. The relevant facts are related in the speeches of others of your Lordships and I shall not repeat them.

1. *Public interest immunity* *d*
   I deal first with the plea (advanced only on behalf of the employers of Mr Vyas, but disclaimed and indeed criticised by the Science Research Council) that such confidential documents are protected by public interest immunity. It was rightly rejected by a majority of the Court of Appeal Browne LJ saying[1]:

   'I am most impressed by the disadvantages of the disclosure of such [confidential] information ... But I have come to the conclusion that I cannot hold that the *e* disclosure of this information is prohibited by "public interest privilege". It is now established that this "privilege" is not confined to government departments or other organs of the central government, but it has so far been confined to bodies exercising statutory duties or functions. Further, it has so far been confined to cases analogous to the "police informer" immunity (*Rogers v Secretary of State for the Home Department*[2] and the *NSPCC* case[3]. If it extends to the present cases, it would mean *f* that an employer who wished to rely on some such confidential report (presumably with the consent of the author) would not be able to do so: counsel for Leyland Cars said that Leyland Cars would accept this, and would rather lose a case than disclose confidential information, but other employers ... might take a different view. Further, if such a "public interest privilege" applies, the commission [for Racial Equality] would not be entitled to require such information in their inquisitorial *g* role (see the Sex Discrimination Act 1975, s 59(3), and the Race Relations Act 1976, s 50(3)). And if there was a duty not to disclose such documents in discrimination proceedings it would also apply in ordinary litigation.'

To hold that public interest immunity applied here would mean that, whatever the attitude of the parties concerned, it could never be waived and would indeed have to be raised by the chairman or judge himself if not taken by the parties or by the Crown (see *h* *Rogers v Secretary of State for the Home Department*[2]). The manifest intention of Parliament could thereby become substantially frustrated. I therefore concur in holding that this plea of immunity should be rejected.

2. *Protection of confidentiality*
   Counsel for the appellants went so far as to submit that the confidential nature of the *j* documents here in question is totally irrelevant to the matter of discovery, and that the

1 [1978] 3 All ER 1196 at 1213, [1979] QB 144 at 180
2 [1972] 2 All ER 1057, [1973] AC 388
3 [1977] 1 All ER 589, [1978] AC 171 at 203

tribunal or court should therefore wholly ignore the protests of third parties against the
a disclosure of information furnished by them in the belief that neither it nor its sources
would ever be revealed. Reliance for that submission was placed on cases ranging from
Hopkinson v Lord Burghley[1] in 1867 to *McIvor v Southern Health and Social Services Board*[2] in
1978; and the Industrial Relations Act 1971, s 158(1), and the Employment Protection
Act 1975, s 18, were adverted to as illustrating Parliament's ability to provide express
safeguards for the preservation of confidences when it thinks this is desirable. But for
b myself I am wholly unable to spell out from the absence of corresponding statutory
provisions applicable to the present cases the conclusion that confidentiality is an
irrelevance. It is true that it cannot *of itself* ensure protection from disclosure (see *Alfred
Crompton Amusement Machines Ltd v Customs and Excise Comrs (No 2)*[3]; *D v National Society
for Prevention of Cruelty to Children*[4]), but confidentiality may nevertheless properly play
a potent part in the way in which a tribunal or court exercises its discretion in the matter
c of discovery.

There was ample evidence supporting the view expressed by the Court of Appeal that
the disclosure to inspection of confidential reports could well create upsets and unrest
which would have a general deleterious effect. And a court, mindful of that risk, may
understandably, and properly, think it right to scrutinise with particular care a request
for their inspection. That is not to say, however, that the fear of possible unrest should
d deter the court from ordering discovery where the demands of justice clearly require it,
but it serves to counsel caution in such cases.

3. *Rules governing discovery*

As the heading to Mrs Nassé's first letter showed, her original complaint related solely
to 'Discrimination for Trade Union Activities', and this was adhered to throughout until,
e in her originating application three months later, she added for the first time,
'Discrimination against me because I am a married person'. I mention this because there
is an important difference between the Employment Protection Act 1975 and the Sex
Discrimination Act 1975 in that if an employee complains to an industrial tribunal of
penalisation because of participation in trade union activities, s 55(1) of the former Act
(now s 25 of the Employment Protection (Consolidation) Act 1978) imposes on the
f employer the burden of establishing the contrary. But no corresponding provision is
contained in the latter Act, or in the Race Relations Act 1976 on which Mr Vyas relies.

Mrs Nassé's employers expressly conceded the relevance to her complaint of the
withheld documents. That concession, in combination with the aforementioned
statutory provision in her favour, formed the basis of her counsel's submission that she
was entitled as of right to the interlocutory relief sought. For, so he submitted, as no one
g suggested that her case was frivolous or vexatious, the interest of others (not being parties
to the litigation) in having their confidences preserved had to be ignored. And, he added,
the single fact that she had never even been interviewed for the appointment she sought
showed that she had been eliminated solely on the basis of her documents and those of
the other aspirants, and this established the great importance to her of obtaining
discovery. Indeed she had testified to the industrial tribunal that they were 'all the
h evidence I can produce' and had added that she had 'no case without them'.

My Lords, I have referred to the facts of Mrs Nassé's case in a little detail because they
are, as I think, helpful in considering the proper approach in this matter of discovery.
Counsel for both apellants stoutly submitted that in such circumstances a general order
for production and inspection of all relevant documents should forthwith be made. As
to that, it has to be said in the first place that acceptance of the submission would involve
j

1   (1867) LR 2 Ch App 447
2   [1978] 2 All ER 625, [1978] 1 WLR 757
3   [1973] 2 All ER 1169, [1974] AC 405
4   [1977] 1 All ER 589, [1978] AC 171

departure from the settled practice of industrial tribunals, regarding which Phillips J in *Stone v Charrington & Co Ltd*[1] made the following wise observations, based on his great experience of the practical operation of the relevant legislation: *a*

> 'Industrial tribunals were set up with the purpose of operating cheaply, quickly and informally, and as far as possible therefore it is desirable that the formalities of the regular courts should be avoided. To introduce a formal system of discovery and inspection, interlocutories, and so on, might in the abstract produce more perfect justice, but it would be at such great cost in time, money and manpower that *b* the whole machine would grind to a halt ... Occasionally it becomes necessary for adjournments to be granted so that unforeseen problems can be considered in the light of additional documents and enquiries, or further particulars. No doubt that is sometimes inconvenient and is not an ideal solution, but it is the only alternative to an elaborate structure of interlocutory proceedings ... We should certainly not discourage ... making orders for *particular* discovery, and so on, in cases where to *c* do so is really necessary to ensure the fair trial of the application. But it would be absurd to do so as a matter of routine in every case.'

The second thing to be said about the apellants' submission that they are entitled as of right to general discovery is that it is unacceptable whenever (as here) disclosure is resisted; and this even though a party is in the ordinary way permitted to inspect relevant *d* documents listed by his opponent as being in his possession, custody or power. Indeed, the rules governing discovery in cases arising under these three statutes are no different in nature from those governing discovery in the general run of cases: see, for example, *Attorney-General v North Metropolitan Tramways Co*[2]. Industrial tribunals are regulated by r 4(1)(*b*) of the schedule to the Industrial Tribunal Rules 1974, entitling them to 'grant ... such discovery or inspection of documents as might be granted by a county court', *e* while the latter court, whether dealing with Sex Discrimination Act or Race Relations Act cases or indeed any other kind of litigation shall not make an order for inspection of documents 'if and so far as the court is of opinion that it is not necessary either for disposing fairly of the proceedings or for saving costs' (CCR Ord 14, r 2(2)). In a similar manner, complaints of discrimination *outside* the employment field are required to be dealt with in England 'in like manner as any other claim in tort', and in Scotland as in *f* 'any other claim ... in reparation for breach of statutory duty' (see the Sex Discrimination Act 1975, s 66(1), and the Race Relations Act 1976, s. 57(1)).

So an industrial tribunal or county court needs to be satisfied not only of the relevance of documents, but also that inspection of them, and *each* of them, is 'necessary' for achieving one or both of the purposes indicated. Admissions already made by the party against whom inspection is sought may have rendered discovery unnecessary, or (as *g* counsel for Mr Vyas conceded) the probative value of documents may clearly be so slight as to render unjustifiable an order for their inspection. Or the very nature of the documents, their dates, or other features may indicate that they are unlikely to prove 'necessary'. Again, a request for inspection of a great mass of documents, without any attempt at selection, could well be regarded as oppressive. Or resort to the various procedures under the statutes (described as 'inquisitorial' and 'litigious' by Lord Denning *h* MR[3]) may have yielded as much information as any documents would be likely to do; and, although counsel for Mr Vyas disputed the relevance of such procedures to the matter in hand, I see no reason why a tribunal, being naturally reluctant to order discovery of confidential documents if this could properly be avoided, should not first resort to the implementation of such procedures. But, on the other hand, the aforementioned statutory provision in favour of employees created by the Employment *j* Protection Act 1975, s 55(1) seems irrelevant; for, although it would operate to preclude

---

1   (15th February 1977) unreported
2   [1892] 3 Ch 70; *affd* (1895) 72 LT 340
3   [1978] 3 All ER 1196 at 1205 and 1207, [1979] QB 144 at 170, 171 and 172

a successful submission by the employer of 'no case to answer', inspection of his
documents might nevertheless be essential for the effective cross-examination of his
witnesses and to counter submissions presented on his behalf.

But what if, having heeded all proper considerations, the tribunal or county court
judge remains in doubt about the necessity, and therefore the propriety, of ordering
discovery? Resort may then be had to their statutory power to inspect the withheld
documents for themselves, Lord Denning MR[1] putting the matter in this way:

> 'The industrial tribunals should not order or permit the disclosure of reports or
> references that have been given and received in confidence *except in the very rare
> cases* where, *after* inspection of a *particular* document, the chairman decides that it
> is essential in the interests of justice that the confidence should be overridden; and
> then only subject to such conditions as to the divulging of it as he shall think fit to
> impose, both for the protection of the maker of the document and the subject of
> it. He might, for instance, limit the sight of it to counsel and solicitors on their
> undertaking that it should go no further.' (Emphasis mine.)

With respect, however, I would omit the reference to 'very rare cases', for this could
convey to some the mistaken notion that a tribunal or judge should approach the
problem from the viewpoint that he is being asked to sanction something which, on the
face of it, is unwarrantable and that he should seek all means of avoiding it. But, as
Lawton LJ[2] said, the matter is largely one of emphasis, and I am with him when he
added:

> 'In my judgment, when balancing the interest of the applicant against the
> desirability of preserving confidentiality, the judge or chairman must remember
> that Parliament has created new causes of action which it has enacted are to be tried
> like actions in tort. If amongst the defendant's documents there are some (albeit
> confidential ones) which will help the applicant to prove his case, he is entitled to see
> them: the statutory Rules of Procedure and County Court Rules say so.'

4. Conclusion

I studiously refrain from further comment on the facts of these two cases lest I appear
to advert, however unintentionally, to their prospects of success, a consideration which
has no relevance where no one suggests the claims are frivolous or vexatious. But what
is directly in point is that in the case of Mrs Nassé the industrial tribunal (upheld on
appeal) granted her originating application on her ipse dixit that the withheld documents
were necessary for the establishment of her claim, while in the later case of Mr Vyas the
Employment Appeal Tribunal (presided over by Phillips J) with manifest reluctance
reversed the industrial tribunal's refusal of discovery, on the ground that to depart from
the recent decision in *Science Research Council v Nassé*[3] 'would only cause confusion were
we at this stage to take a different line from that which has been taken previously'.

While the reluctance of Phillips J is understandable, the outcome in both cases was, in
my judgment, unacceptable. For neither the tribunals nor the Employment Appeal
Tribunals were possessed of sufficient knowledge to entitle them to decide as they did,
and whether any of the documents sought were 'necessary for disposing fairly of the
proceedings or for saving costs' must for them have been still a matter of mere
guesswork. That being the position, the proper course was that described by Arnold J in
British Railways Board v Natarajan[4]:

> 'We think that before deciding whether an examination is necessary, the judge or
> chairman of the tribunal . . . or the appellate court . . . must decide whether there
> is a prima facie prospect of relevance of the confidential material to an issue which
> arises in the litigation; put another way, whether it is reasonable to expect that there

---

1   [1978] 3 All ER 1196 at 1208, [1979] QB 144 at 173
2   [1978] 3 All ER 1196 at 1211, [1979] QB 144 at 177
3   [1978] ICR 777
4   [1979] 2 All ER 794 at 799

is any real likelihood of such relevance emerging from the examination. If there is not, we do not think that the exercise of examination is necessary or should take place.'

Whether a tribunal or court should decide that they themselves should inspect must always depend on the particular facts and issues, thought it is difficult to see how they can ever properly conclude that discovery *is* 'necessary' without such inspection. But where a court inspection is decided on, there can be no hard-and-fast rule as to *when* it should take place. As Arnold J said further in *Natarajan's* case[1]:

'... it is, we think, a matter of convenience in each case whether the examination should take place at the interlocutory stage of discovery or immediately the matter arises at the trial. We can conceive that there would be many cases in which, having regard to the probable way in which the material, if found relevant, would have to be treated, that it would be essential for the decision to be made at the interlocutory stage of discovery. But there are also cases where, having regard to the way in which the material would have to be dealt with, such an early examination would not be necessary. That is a matter which we think must be decided in relation to each case in which the point is relevant.'

The Court of Appeal rightly held that discovery should not have been ordered in either of these two cases without the respective industrial tribunals or the apellate courts first inspecting the withheld documents. That unfortunately not having been done, it follows that both appeals should be dismissed. The cases should be remitted to the respective industrial tribunals, so that they may consider afresh the matter of discovery in the light of the observations of your Lordships' House.

LORD FRASER OF TULLYBELTON. My Lords, these appeals raise questions of much practical importance about the powers of industrial tribunals and county courts to order discovery and inspection of confidential documents in proceedings by persons complaining of discrimination on the ground of sex, race, or trade union activities, contrary to the recent Acts making such discrimination unlawful. The first question is whether confidential documents relating to persons other than the complainers are covered by public interest immunity, with the result that tribunals and courts cannot order them to be disclosed. If the answer to that question is that the documents are not immune from disclosure in such proceedings, a second question arises as to the circumstances in which tribunals (or county courts) should order them to be disclosed.

In one appeal the apellant and claimant is a married woman, Mrs Nassé, who was employed by the Science Research Council ('SRC') as a clerical officer at their Appleton laboratory. In 1977 two other clerical officers, one a man and the other a woman, who was then single but has since married, were interviewed for promotion, although they were both junior to Mrs Nassé in terms of service and in her view their claims to promotion were no better than hers. Mrs Nassé was not called for interview at that time. The appellant complainer in the other appeal is Mr Vyas who was employed by BL Cars Ltd ('BL') as a senior supplies analyst. Mr Vyas is of Asian origin. He applied for transfer to one of the vacancies in the same grade as the job that he held at that time. He was not selected for transfer but two other men, one of whom was of a lower grade than he was, were transferred to the job for which he had applied.

In both appeals the complainers allege, and invite an industrial tribunal to infer, that the reason why they were not selected for interview (in Mrs Nassé's case) or for transfer (in Mr Vyas's, case) must have been unlawful discrimination by the employers. Mrs Nassé complained that the SRC had penalised her for her militant behaviour as chairman of the local sub-branch of a trade union, and had also discriminated against her because she was a married woman, and that they had thereby acted contrary to s 53 of the Employment Protection Act 1975, and s 6 of the Sex Discrimination Act 1975. Mr

1   [1979] 2 All ER 794 at 799

Vyas's complaint was that BL had discriminated against him because of his racial origin,
a contrary to s 4(2)(*b*) of the Race Relations Act 1976. The common feature of both cases
which is relevant for present purposes is that the allegations involve comparison between
the complainers' qualifications and those of other employees with whom they were in
competition for promotion or transfer. The argument for both complainers, in its
simplest form, is that all records and reports bearing on the qualifications of the appellants
themselves and of their fellow employees who were preferred to them must be relevant
b for the purpose of such comparison and therefore that production and inspection of all
these records and reports should be ordered as of course and in advance of the hearing by
the industrial tribunal. The arguments for the two apellants on the principles which
should be applied did not, in the end, raise substantially different issues, and they can I
think be considered together.

The employers (respondents in the appeals) presented quite separate arguments. BL
c contended that the documents which are the subject of dispute fall within a class of
documents which is protected from disclosure by what was known formerly as Crown
privilege, now as public interest immunity. The SRC did not rely on public interest
immunity, and indeed they supported the complainers in arguing against it, but they
argued that the documents should not be ordered to be produced unless they were not
only relevant, but necessary for the fair disposal of the case. The point at issue between
d the SRC and the complainers came down eventually to this: there being no immunity
for the documents, is the discretionary power of a tribunal to refuse to order their
production excluded if they are relevant (as the appellants contended) or only if they are
not merely relevant but necessary for fairly disposing of the proceedings (as the SRC
contended)? To put it the other way round, is the tribunal *bound* to order discovery and
inspection of all documents that are relevant, or only of those that are necessary for fairly
e disposing of the proceedings?

The first question is whether the documents in question are protected by public
interest immunity. The disputed documents in Mr Vyas's appeal are the following.
(1) The employment records of all the employees who were interviewed for the position
for which Mr Vyas unsuccessfully applied. These records would include records of the
employee's service, positions occupied, promotions, personal history forms, personal
f assessment records, details of commendations and other such matters. (2) The completed
interview report forms returned by each and every member of the interview panel who
interviewed Mr Vyas and the other applicants for transfer. In Mrs Nassé's appeal the
disputed documents are the annual confidential reports for the years 1975 and 1976 of
the two clerical officers who were selected to appear before the interview panel when she
was not, and the minutes of the local review board of meetings at which it considered the
g annual confidential reports for 1976 of the clerical officers employed at the Appleton
laboratory. In both cases the confidential reports relating to the complainers themselves
have been disclosed to them, along with certain other information for which they
asked. The appeals are concerned entirely with confidential reports on fellow
employees. It is apparent that the fellow employees who were the subject of the reports
might well object to their being disclosed, and in Mrs Nassé's case one of them has done
h so.

Both employers rightly accepted that the reports were not entitled to immunity from
disclosure merely because they were confidential. The law on this matter was stated in
Alfred Crompton Amusement Machines v Customs and Excise Comrs (No 2)[1] by Lord Cross of
Chelsea who said:

j   '"Confidentiality" is not a separate head of privilege, but it may be a very material
consideration to bear in mind when privilege is claimed on the ground of public
interest. What the court has to do is to weigh on the one hand the considerations
which suggest that it is in the public interest that the documents in question should

---

1   [1973] 2 All ER 1169 at 1184, [1974] AC 405 at 433

be disclosed and on the other hand those which suggest that it is in the public interest that they should not be disclosed and to balance one against the other.'

The considerations that were urged on behalf of BL as showing that it would not be in the public interest for the documents concerned in Mr Vyas's case to be disclosed may be summarised, not I hope unfairly, as follows. (They would apply equally to Mrs Nassé's case). First, it was said that disclosure of confidential reports such as are in question here would inhibit candour by senior employees in reporting on the suitability of subordinate employees for promotion and would also inhibit employees from applying for promotion. Secondly it was said that disclosure would be a breach of faith with the authors of the reports and with the subjects of the reports, that it would be likely to have an adverse effect on industrial relations, and might well lead to industrial unrest. These arguments were supported by an affidavit from BL's staff director. In Mrs Nassé's case, although the SRC were not claiming immunity from disclosure, there were affidavits from one of the employees who was interviewed in preference to Mrs Nassé objecting strongly to disclosure of his own confidential reports and there was a more general objection from the staff side of the SRC Whitley Council to disclosure of all such reports. The public interest was said to be involved because of the importance of having a proper system for making decisions to employ and promote persons in industry in order to secure efficiency, and because of the risk that such a system could not be maintained unless complete candour could be ensured for those responsible for operating it.

The argument based on the need for candour in reporting echoes the argument which was presented in *Conway v Rimmer*[1] and I do not think that it has any greater weight now than it had then. The objections by and on behalf of employees other than the complainers to having their confidential reports disclosed, readily understandable as they are, do not create a public interest against disclosure. They are based on a private interest which must yield, in accordance with well-established principles, to the greater public interest that is deemed to exist in ascertaining the truth in order to do justice between the parties to litigation. I am not satisfied that disclosure of the contents of confidential reports of the kind in question here would have serious consequences on the efficiency of British industry. In any event, the possibility of industrial unrest is not a sufficient reason for the courts to fail to give full effect to the intentions of Parliament; the courts cannot refuse to apply the law between litigants because of threats by third parties. Much reliance was placed in argument on a passage in the speech of Lord Hailsham of St Marylebone in *D v National Society for the Prevention of Cruelty to Children*[2] as follows:

'The categories of public interest are not closed, and must alter from time to time whether by restriction or extension as social conditions and social legislation develop.'

Speaking for myself I fully accept that proposition, but any extension can only be made by adding new categories analogous to those already existing, just as in that case immunity was extended to a new category of informers to the NSPCC by analogy with informers to the police who were already entitled to immunity. There is no analogy between the suggested public interest in the present cases and the kinds of public interest that have so far been held to justify immunity from disclosure. Such public interest as there is in withholding the documents from disclosure is not enough to justify the creation of a new head of immunity for a whole class of documents.

Two other considerations point against immunity. One is that in some cases immunity would make it impossible for an employee to enforce his rights under the Acts. The confidential information is almost always in the possession of the employer, and, in cases where discrimination cannot be inferred from the bare fact that someone other than the complainer has been selected for preferment, it may be of vital importance

---

1 [1968] 1 All ER 874, [1968] AC 910
2 [1977] 1 All ER 589 at 605, [1978] AC 171 at 230

to the complainer to have access to the reports on the preferred individual. This is
a particularly true where the complaint is based on discrimination on grounds of race or
sex, because in those cases the onus of proof is on the complainer. But even where the
complaint is of discrimination for trade union activities, and the onus is on the employer,
disclosure may be essential in order to do justice between the parties.

The second consideration is that, if public interest immunity applied, it could not be
waived either by the employer alone, or by the employer with the consents of the
individual who is the subject of a report and of the person who made it. That would be
b inconvenient, and, in my opinion, quite unnecessarily restrictive.

For these reasons I think that the confidential reports in question here are not protected
by public interest immunity.

I pass now to consider the circumstances in which production ought to be ordered by
a tribunal. For this purpose it is necessary to look first at the three statutes under which
c the appeals arise: the Sex Discrimination Act 1975, the Race Relations Act 1976, and the
Employment Protection Act 1975 (the relevant part of which is now superseded by the
Employment Protection (Consolidation) Act 1978). The effect of these Acts, so far as
material for present purposes, was to create new statutory duties including duties
imposed on employers to refrain from discriminating against employees (in which term
I include applicants for employment) on the grounds of their sex, race, or trade union
d activities. It conferred corresponding statutory rights on employees. Claims by persons
that their rights have been infringed in fields other than the employment field 'may be
made the subject of civil proceedings in like manner as *any other claim in tort* or (in
Scotland) in reparation for breach of statutory duty' (see the Sex Discrimination Act 1975,
s 66(1) and Race Relations Act 1976, s 57(1); emphasis mine), the proceedings being
brought in the county court or the sheriff court. Where the complaint arises in the
e employment field it may be presented to an industrial tribunal (see the Sex Discrimination
Act 1975, s 63, and the Race Relations Act 1976, s 54) but the subsequent proceedings are
essentially of the same nature as proceedings for discrimination in other fields. So are
proceedings under s 54 of the Employment Protection Act 1975 following on a complaint
of discrimination for trade union activity. Accordingly we are concerned with
proceedings for tort, or breach of statutory duty, and the ordinary rules with regard to
f discovery and inspection of documents in such proceedings should apply unless there are
express provisions in the statutes, or other special reasons, to the contrary.

As regards express provisions, those applicable to the present appeals are found mainly
in the Industrial Tribunals (Labour Relations) Regulations 1974[1] amended in minor
respects in 1978. By r 4 in the schedule to the 1974 regulations it is provided as follows:

g
> '(1) . . . a tribunal may on the application of a party to the proceedings . . . made
> either by notice to the Secretary of the Tribunals or at the hearing of the originating
> application . . . (b) grant to the person . . . making the application such discovery or
> inspection of documents as might be granted by a county court . . . and may appoint
> the time at or within which or the place at which any act required in pursuance of
> this Rule is to be done.'

h The discovery and inspection that might be granted by a county court is regulated by
rules of court, including CCR Ord 14, r 2 which provides that the court may order
discovery to be made of such documents as it thinks fit and adds:

> '. . . but discovery shall not be ordered if and so far as the court is of opinion that
> it is not necessary either for disposing fairly of the proceedings or for saving costs.'

j So far, therefore, from there being express provision that the ordinary rules for discovery
are not to apply, the ordinary rules are in effect incorporated into the rules for industrial
tribunals.

Are there then special reasons why the ordinary rules should be applied in a way

---

1   SI 1974 No 1386 as amended by SI 1978 No 991

different from that in which they are applied by the county court? Some reasons were
suggested. Counsel for the appellants, who argued that all relevant information should *a*
be disclosed, relied on provisions in the statutes restricting the obligations of respondents
to disclose information for certain purposes, not including proceedings in respect of the
tort of discrimination. Thus in the Employment Protection Act 1975, s 17 imposes on
an employer an obligation, for the purposes of collective bargaining with a trade union,
to make very extensive disclosure of information to the trade union representatives. But
s 18, which limits the obligation, provides that no employer shall 'by virtue of section 17 *b*
above' be required to disclose, inter alia, '(c) Any information which has been
communicated to the employer in confidence . . .' The provisions of ss 17 and 18 are
derived from the Industrial Relations Act 1971 (repealed and partly re-enacted by the
Trade Union and Labour Relations Act 1974). Section 17 corresponds to s 56 of the 1971
Act. Section 22 of the 1971 Act created a civil right in employees not to be unfairly
dismissed. Section 158 of the 1971 Act is in terms almost identical with those of s 18 of *c*
the 1975 Act, and it gave employers immunity only against the obligations of disclosure
arising 'by virtue of section 56' (or s 57 which required large employers to disclose
information to their employees). The argument, as I understood it, was that Parliament
had had in mind the need to protect employers from an obligation to disclose confidential
information where the obligation arose 'by virtue of' s 17 of the 1975 Act or ss 56 and 57
of the 1971 Act, but had not thought it appropriate to give protection from such *d*
obligation arising from other sources such as s 22 of the 1971 Act or the general law
applicable to proceedings for tort under the 1975 Act. The only protection that
Parliament considered appropriate for confidential information in proceedings before an
industrial tribunal was the power given to tribunals to sit in private: see para 3 of Sch 6
to the 1971 Act (repeated in para 21 of Sch 1 to the 1974 Act) and r 6(1)(b) of the 1974
rules for industrial tribunals, to which I have already referred. A similar point arises *e*
under the Sex Discrimination Act 1975 where s 61(1) provides that information given to
the Equal Opportunities Commission in connection with a formal investigation shall not
be disclosed by the commission except in certain events which include on the orders of
a court (para (a)) and for the purpose of civil proceedings to which the commission is a
party (para (f)). Section 61(3) of the Act directs the commission in preparing its report
to exclude so far as consistent with their duty, any matter which relates to the private *f*
affairs of any individual or business interests of any person 'where the publication of that
matter might, in the opinion of the commission, prejudicially affect that 'individual or
person'. These provisions also show that Parliament did not think it necessary to give
any special immunity against disclosure of confidential information except in the case of
a formal investigation. There are exactly similar provisions in the Race Relations Act
1976. The argument seems to me quite correct so far as it goes, but the conclusion to *g*
which it leads is that Parliament, having made no special provisions for discovery in
proceedings before an industrial tribunal, must be presumed to have intended that (as
the 1974 rules say) discovery should be 'such as might be granted by a county court',
neither more nor less.

    Several arguments were adduced on behalf of the respondents with a view to showing
that discovery in proceedings under these statues should be more restricted than in civil *h*
proceedings. One was that adequate other means have been specially provided by the
statutes for enabling complainers to obtain information, and that there is therefore no
need for the ordinary rules of discovery to be applied in their full rigour. A statutory
power of interrogation ('the questionnaire procedure') is provided by s 74 of the Sex
Discrimination Act 1975 with a view to helping an aggrieved person to decide whether
to institute proceedings. The respondent is bound to answer the questionnaire and the *j*
court may draw an adverse inference if it considers his replies to be evasive or equivocal.
A further provision is that by s 75 of the Act the Equal Opportunities Commission may
give assistance to a complainer both in the form of advice and of financial aid. Moreover
the Equal Opportunities Commission has power under s 57 to conduct a formal
investigation for any purpose connected with carrying out its statutory duties, and to

require any person to furnish under s 59 written and oral information and to produce
a documents. No doubt the use of these procedures, especially the questionnaire
procedure, will often make extensive discovery of documents unnecessary, but I do not
think it will do so in all cases. Some respondents may be less responsible than the
respondents in the present appeals and it would not be right that there should be no
means of verifying their replies to the questionnaire by reference to their own records.
Even where frank replies to the questionnaires are made, they may be of less use in
b revealing the respondent's reasons than his actual records and reports. It is not so much
that the reports are likely to contain positive statements of discrimination on grounds of
sex or race or trade union activity, as that they may, by their silence as to any particular
merits of an employee who has been promoted, lead to an inference that the only reason
for his being promoted in preference to the complainer must have been that the
employer had discriminated against the complainer. As regards the formal investigations,
c these will be directed to the 'strategic' object of ascertaining the practice in a firm or a
whole industry, and the commission is directed not to disclose information received in
connection with a formal investigation except under certain conditions, one of which is
that publication must be in the form of a summary or other general statement which
does not identify any person to whom the information relates: Sex Discrimination Act
1975, s 61(1)(c). Such a summary would be of little use to complainers such as the
d present apellants who rely on comparisons with particular persons in order to prove their
complaint.
   Another suggested reason why discovery in proceedings under the statutes should be
more restricted than in ordinary civil proceedings was that disclosure of personal
particulars about an employee (such as the successful candidate for promotion) would be
more objectionable when made to a colleague beside whom he would have to continue
e working than it would be when made by a party to an ordinary litigation who would not
usually have a continuing relationship with the opposing party. A hearing in private
(which may be ordered by a tribunal for the purpose of hearing evidence of information
communicated to the witness in confidence: see r 6(1)(b) in the schedule to the 1974
rules) provides no solution of this difficulty, because it does not avoid disclosure to the
complainer, who is a fellow employee. There is force in this argument, but it should be
f possible, by the use of the ordinary rules of discovery, to protect an employee from any
embarrassing disclosure which is not absolutely necessary for disposal of the case.
Discovery of confidential reports sought by one party and objected to by the other should
not be ordered when the same information can be obtained from other sources which are
not confidential or which do not contain sensitive material. The court or tribunal always
has a discretion to refuse to order discovery where it would operate oppressively:
g oppression could occur if the quantity of documents involved is large or if the
information is private and could be otained in another way without infringing privacy:
see *Attorney-General v North Metropolitan Tramways Co*[1]. Where discovery of confidential
reports has to be ordered in spite of objections, every effort should be made to avoid
disclosing sensitive information by covering up any parts of the documents disclosure of
which is not essential. But where disclosure is necessary then in my opinion it must be
h made and personal privacy must be sacrificed in the interest of justice.
   Where the holder of reports or other documents objects to producing them on the
ground that they have been written on the basis that they will be confidential or when
they contain sensitive private particulars about third parties, it will be the duty of the
judge or of an appropriate officer of the court to read them and decide whether disclosure
of the contents is necessary for the fair disposal of the case, or for saving expense. On a
j procedural level, we heard some argument about the stage at which discovery ought to
be ordered in proceedings before an industrial tribunal. The respondents contended that
discovery and inspection should not normally be made until the hearing. The appellants
contended that it should normally be made at the interlocutory stage. Rule 4(1) (quoted

1   [1892] 3 Ch 70

above) certainly contemplates disclosure at the interlocutory stage as a possibility; but it
does not seem to indicate that it is to be the normal practice. I can see arguments tending   *a*
in both directions. In favour of early disclosure, there is the fact that there will be cases
where discovery should satisfy a complainer that his complaint is unfounded and that
proceedings ought to be dropped at once without further expenditure of time and
money. Moreover if the number of documents to be discovered is large, then discovery
at the hearing will almost certainly cause delay. On the other hand the procedure before
an industrial tribunal is less formal than in court, the pleadings are exiguous; and   *b*
hearings often take place very shortly after proceedings have been instituted. These are
all factors tending to suggest that interlocutory procedure relating to discovery should be
avoided if possible: see *Stone v Charrington & Co Ltd*[1] in the Employment Appeal Tribunal
per Phillips J. The solution seems to me very much a matter for the industrial tribunals
and the Employment Appeal Tribunal to work out in the light of experience; the
practice probably ought to be flexible and to have regard to such matters as the nature of   *c*
the case and the volume of documents involved. I agree entirely with the observations
on this matter of Arnold J in *British Railways Board v Natarajan*[2].

We were reminded during the argument that the statutes under which these appeals
arise apply not only to England but also to Scotland (though not to Northern Ireland) and
our attention was called to The Industrial Tribunals (Labour Relations) (Scotland)
Regulations 1974[3] which regulates the procedure of tribunals in Scotland by rules which   *d*
are almost exactly the same mutatis mutandis as the rules for tribunals in England. The
effect is to apply the sheriff court rules as to granting commission and diligence for
recovery of documents. If there had been anything in Scots law or practice on this matter
which seemed to make the kind of approach that I have suggested unsuitable for
application in Scotland, I would have reconsidered my view. But I do not think there
is. It seems that confidentiality (in the sense of immunity) is rather more extensive in   *e*
Scotland where it applies to a private diary (see *Duke of Argyll v Duchess of Argyll*[4]) than in
England, but I do not think there is any difference in the extent of immunity relevant to
the question raised here. The court in Scotland will exercise its discretion to refuse to
order a third party to produce private documents containing relevant information if the
information has been (or, I think, can be) obtained from other sources which do not
involve disclosing private information (see *North British Railway Co v Garroway*[5]). The   *f*
Scottish system of having excerpts taken from books and records by a commissioner,
appointed as an officer of the court, would make it easy in a case where disclosure is to be
dealt with at the interlocutory stage, to avoid disclosing personal particulars about third
parties, unless their disclosure is essential. Accordingly I do not see any reason why the
views I have expressed in these appeals should not be conveniently applicable by a
tribunal sitting in Scotland.   *g*

The result is that I agree substantially with the principle stated in the Court of Appeal
by Lord Denning MR[6] and approved by Browne LJ (which has been quoted by my noble
and learned friend, Lord Wilberforce) except that I would omit from it the words 'in the
very rare cases'. I doubt whether the cases in which the chairman of an industrial
tribunal will decide that disclosure of confidential reports is necessary will be very rare,
and I do not think it would be right to suggest that the chairman should approach   *h*
consideration of any particular case with a presumption against disclosure.

I come back at last to the instant appeals. In Mrs Nassé's case the chairman of the
industrial tribunal ordered discovery of the documents in question without having seen
them, and his decision was upheld by the Employment Appeal Tribunal. In Mr Vyas's

---

1   (15th February 1977) unreported   *j*
2   [1979] 2 All ER 794 at 799
3   SI 1974 No 1387
4   1962 SC (HL) 88
5   (1893) 20 R (Ct of Sess) 397
6   [1978] 3 All ER 1196 at 1208, [1979] QB 144 at 173

case the chairman of the industrial tribunal refused to order discovery and his decision
a was reversed by the Employment Appeal Tribunal. In my opinion the latter tribunal
erred in both cases in ordering discovery, in spite of objections by the respondents,
without the chairman of the respective industrial tribunals having seen the documents.
I agree with the Court of Appeal that both cases should go back to an industrial tribunal
so that the chairman can look at the documents now. He may be able to decide,
immediately after reading them, whether it is essential that they should be produced in
b whole or in part, or he may think it better to defer a decision in one or other case, or in
both cases, until the hearing. The reason why I think the chairman should look at the
documents now is that the long delay, which has already occurred by reason of the
appeals, has prevented the complaints from being disposed of rapidly and informally,
and has therefore removed one of the main objections to dealing with the discovery at
the interlocutory stage.
c   I would dismiss both appeals and make an order in the terms proposed by my noble
and learned friend, Lord Wilberforce.

LORD SCARMAN. My Lords, I also would dismiss both appeals. I would respectfully
adopt the reasoning and the conclusion of my noble and learned friend, Lord Fraser of
Tullybelton, subject only to the observations which I now make, on these appeals.
d   The confidential nature of a document does not, by itself, confer 'public interest
immunity' from disclosure. The confidential nature of a document or of evidence is no
ground for a refusal to disclose the document or to give the evidence, if the court requires
it: see *Alfred Crompton Amusement Machines Ltd v Customs and Excise Comrs (No 2)*[1] and
Attorney-General v Clough[2].
      For myself, I regret the passing of the currently rejected term 'Crown privilege'. It at
e least emphasised the very restricted area of public interest immunity. As was pointed
out by counsel who presented most helpful submissions on behalf of the two statutory
bodies as well as specifically for the appellant, Mr Vyas, the immunity exists to protect
from disclosure only information the secrecy of which is essential to the proper working
of the government of the state. Defence, foreign relations, the inner workings of
government at the highest levels where ministers and their advisers are formulating
f national policy, and the prosecution process in its pre-trial stage are the sensitive areas
where the Crown must have the immunity if the government of the nation is to be
effectually carried on. We are in the realm of public law, not private right. The very
special case of *D v National Society for the Prevention of Cruelty to Children*[3] is not to be seen
as a departure from this well established principle. Immunity from disclosure existed in
that case because the House recognised the special position of the NSPCC in the
g enforcement process of the provisions of the Children Act 1969, a position which the
House saw as comparable with that of a prosecuting authority in criminal proceedings.
But I would not, with respect, go as far as my noble and learned friend, Lord Hailsham[4],
when he said in that case 'The categories of public interest are not closed'; nor can I agree
with the dictum of my noble and learned friend, Lord Edmund-Davies[5], that, where a
confidential relationship exists and disclosure would be in breach of some ethical or social
h value involving the public interest, the court may uphold a refusal to disclose relevant
evidence, if, on balance, the public interest would be better served by excluding it.
      I do not find anything in *Conway v Rimmer*[6] or the cases therein cited which would
extend public interest immunity in this way. On the contrary, the theme of Lord Reid's
speech[7] is that the immunity arises only if 'disclosure would involve a danger of real

j 1   [1973] 2 All ER 1169, [1974] AC 405
  2   [1963] 1 All ER 420, [1963] 1 QB 773
  3   [1977] 1 All ER 589, [1978] AC 171
  4   [1977] 1 All ER 589 at 605, [1978] AC 171 at 230
  5   [1977] 1 All ER 589 at 618, [1978] AC 171 at 245
  6   [1968] 1 All ER 874, [1968] AC 910
  7   [1968] 1 All ER 874 at 879, [1968] AC 910 at 939

prejudice to the national interest'. The public interest protected by the immunity is that 'harm shall not be done to the nation or the public service by disclosure' (see per Lord *a* Reid[1]). Whatever may be true generally of the categories of public interest, the 'public interest immunity', which prevents documents from being produced or evidence from being given, is restricted, and is not, in my judgment, to be extended either by demanding ministers or by the courts. And, though I agree with my noble and learned friend, Lord Edmund-Davies, in believing that a court may refuse to order production of a confidental document if it takes the view that justice does not require its production, *b* I do not see the process of decision as a balancing act. If the document is necessary for fairly disposing of the case, it must be produced, notwithstanding its confidentiality. Only if the document should be protected by public interest immunity, will there be a balancing act. And then the balance will be not between 'ethical or social' values of a confidential relationship involving the public interest and the document's relevance in the litigation, but between the public interest represented by the state and its public *c* service, ie the executive government, and the public interest in the administration of justice: see per Lord Reid[1]. Thus my emphasis would be different from that of my noble and learned friends. 'Public interest immunity' is, in my judgment, restricted to what must be kept secret for the protection of government at the highest levels and in the truly sensitive areas of executive responsibility.

The submission, therefore, of the respondents in the Vyas case that confidential reports *d* on other employees, and particularly on those who succeeded where the applicant failed, are immune from disclosure must be rejected. The question, then, becomes one of the exercise of the court's discretion.

It does not follow that, because we are outside the field of public interest immunity, the confidential nature of documents is to be disregarded by the court in the exercise of its discretionary power to order discovery of documents. *e*

Under the modern practice, discovery is to be ordered in the High Court, the county court, and in an industrial tribunal whenever necessary for fairly disposing of the case or saving costs: see RSC Ord 24, rr 3, 5 and 8; CCR, Ord 14, r 2(2); the Industrial Tribunals (Labour Relations) Regulations 1974, r 4 of the schedule, as amended.

In most, but not all, High Court litigation discovery is 'automatic': see RSC Ord 24, r 2. But the right to object to production of documents as unnecessary remains available *f* to the party who has to make the discovery. In an industrial tribunal (as also in a county court) discovery is not automatic. An order has to be made by the tribunal in the proceedings. An industrial tribunal (but not, I think, a county court) may make an order not only on a party's application, but by its own motion. And the tribunal (or court) may make either a general order or one limited to specific documents or classes of documents.

How should the discretion of an industrial tribunal (or a county court) be exercised in *g* a discrimination case? Counsel for the appellant Mrs Nassé submitted that in all such cases all relevant documents should be disclosed: in other words, that a general order should be made. And counsel for the appellant Mr Vyas supported this submission. Counsel for Mrs Nassé further submitted that the confidential nature of a document, if relevant, was no ground for refusing to order its disclosure. Counsel for Mr Vyas, while stoutly rejecting any suggestion of public interest immunity, did not go so far. He *h* accepted that the court has a discretion but argued for general orders in discrimination cases on the reasonable ground that the very nature of such cases requires a comparison of the qualifications and circumstances of the disappointed applicant with those who were successful where he failed or who were in competition with him. In my judgment, however, both submissions are too wide. The criterion is not relevance alone, nor are general orders for discovery appropriate in this class of litigation. The true test, as *j* formulated by the rules of court, is whether discovery is necessary either to save costs or for the fair disposal of the case. Where speed and cheapness of legal process are essential, as they are in county courts and industrial tribunals, general orders should ordinarily be

1   [1968] 1 All ER 874 at 880, [1968] AC 910 at 940

a avoided. And where, as will be frequent in this class of litigation, confidential records about other people are relevant, the court must honour the confidence to this extent: that it will not order production unless the interest of justice requires that they be disclosed. No hard and fast rules can be laid down: but I agree with others of your Lordships in thinking that the Employment Appeal Tribunal gave very useful guidance on the appropriate practice in *British Railways Board v Natarajan*[1]: see the judgment delivered by Arnold J.

b To conclude, I recognise the importance of discovery in discrimination cases. There is no special law protecting confidential documents in such cases. It is for that reason that I have avoided discussing the new 'statutory torts' or the investigating powers of the statutory bodies. We are concerned with the litigation of private citizens seeking redress for private wrongs. The only complicating factor is the confidential nature of relevant documents in the possession of the party from whom redress is sought. The production *c* of some of these may be necessary for doing justice to the applicant's case. If production is necessary, they must be produced. The factor of confidence however militates against general orders for discovery and does impose on the tribunal the duty of satisfying itself, by inspection if need be, that justice requires disclosure. Ordinarily, therefore, a tribunal will itself examine documents which are confidential before it orders their disclosure.

I agree therefore that the two appeals should be dismissed. It will be for the industrial *d* tribunal in each case to decide whether, and to what extent, discovery should be ordered. I would expect that the tribunal would decide to inspect the documents for which confidence is claimed and determine whether any, and if so, which, should be produced. The inspection should be before the hearing takes place, so that the applicant may consider any that are produced. But the tribunal retains the power to order the production of further documents at a later stage (including at the hearing itself) if in its *e* judgment it becomes necessary to do so in the interests of justice.

Appeals dismissed.

Solicitors: *Lawford & Co* (for Mrs Nassé); *Treasury Solicitor* (for the SRC); *Bindman & Partners* (for Mr Vyas); *R P A Coles* (for BL Cars Ltd).

f
Mary Rose Plummer   Barrister.

---

1   [1979] 2 All ER 794 at 799

Burmah Oil Co Ltd v Bank of England (Attorney-General intervening)

HOUSE OF LORDS

LORD WILBERFORCE, LORD SALMON, LORD EDMUND-DAVIES, LORD KEITH OF KINKEL AND LORD SCARMAN

25th, 26th, 28th JUNE, 2nd, 3rd, 4th JULY, 1st NOVEMBER 1979

Discovery – Privilege – Production contrary to public interest – Class of documents – Documents relating to government policy – Information given in confidence by businessmen to government – Documents relating to decision that Bank of England should give financial help to major private undertaking – Financial help necessary in national interest to save undertaking from liquidation – Certificate of Chief Secretary to Treasury claiming privilege in public interest on ground documents within class of documents relating to government policy – Whether claim to privilege valid.

Burmah Oil Co Ltd ('Burmah') owned some 80 million shares in British Petroleum Co Ltd ('BP'). In the middle of 1974 the stock was worth £6 per share. Burmah also had important interests in the North Sea oilfields. It had borrowed large sums, which included dollar borrowings, to finance various enterprises. By December 1974 Burmah was in financial difficulties and at the same time the value of BP stock fell to £2·30 per share. In consequence Burmah's creditors became entitled to require immediate payment of their loans and it appeared they might be entitled to force Burmah into liquidation. It was in the national interest that Burmah be kept afloat, for default on its dollar borrowings would seriously affect the pound sterling, and its financial collapse would seriously affect the government's North Sea oil policy. The Bank of England ('the Bank') requested Burmah not to obtain foreign financial support because that was against the national interest, but to wait and see what the Bank could do. The Bank gave Burmah temporary credit while the situation was sorted out, in return for a charge over the BP holding. By the beginning of January 1975 Burmah was advised that it needed financial assistance of £225 million. On 10th January the Bank suggested that Burmah should sell its BP holding to the Bank at the current market quoted price and that any subsequent profit on resale of the holding should be divided between the Bank and Burmah. Over the next 11 days negotiations took place between Burmah on the one hand and the Treasury, the Department of Energy and the Bank on the other. On 22nd January the Bank told Burmah that the government was not prepared to accept a profit-sharing formula if the BP stock was resold, and that the price to be paid would be £2·30 per share, although by then BP stock was quoted at £2·68 per share. By an agreement dated 23rd January, the Bank agreed to purchase the BP stock at £2·30 per share and to provide a stand-by facility of £75 million and Burmah agreed to transfer to the government 51% of its interest in the North Sea oilfields. Burmah alleged that it had no choice but to accept those terms. The value of BP stock continued to rise. Burmah brought an action against the Bank seeking to set aside the sale of the stock on the grounds, inter alia, that the sale was unconscionable, inequitable and unreasonable, was in breach of the Bank's duty of fair dealing and was at an undervalue.

The Bank's list of documents in the litigation included documents which disclosed the part played by the government in the transaction and the advice received by the government. At the request of the Crown the Bank objected to discovery of 62 of those documents. The certificate given by the Chief Secretary to the Treasury claiming privilege from production for the documents stated that he had formed the opinion that their production would be injurious to the public interest because it was 'necessary for the proper functioning of the public service' that they be withheld. The certificate divided the documents into three classes. Category A consisted of memoranda of meetings attended by Ministers and category B memoranda of meetings at which a government officials but not Ministers were present. The certificate claimed privilege for the documents in those categories on the ground that they fell within 'the class of documents' relating to formulation of government policy on important economic matters. Category C consisted of commercial or financial information communicated in confidence to the government or to the Bank, in its capacity as the government's adviser, by businessmen. The certificate claimed privilege for the documents in that category on the ground of the public interest in protecting the confidentiality of the documents. The certificate gave particulars of the considerations to which the government had had regard in formulating the policies in question, and the subject-matter of those policies. The judge dismissed Burmah's application for discovery of the documents covered by the certificate and his decision was upheld by the Court of Appeal[a]. Burmah appealed to the House of Lords and during argument it became apparent that only ten of the documents might assist Burmah on the central issue of whether the Bank's conduct had been unconscionable. Burmah accordingly asked for production of the ten documents, all of which fell within categories A and B.

Held – (i) There was no rule of law that a claim by the Crown on the grounds of public interest for immunity from production of a class of documents of a high level of public importance was conclusive. If it was likely, or was reasonably probable or (per Lord Wilberforce) a strong positive case was made out, that the documents in question contained matter which was material to the issues arising in the case and if on consideration of the ministerial certificate claiming immunity there was a doubt whether the balance of the public interest lay against disclosure (and not merely where it was established that the certificate was probably inaccurate), the court had a discretion to review the Crown's claim that the withholding of documents was necessary for the proper functioning of the public service. In reviewing the Crown's claim to privilege in such a case the court had to balance the competing interests of preventing harm to the state or the public service by disclosure and preventing frustration of the administration of justice by withholding disclosure, and could inspect the documents concerned privately in order to determine where the balance of public interest lay (see p 708 *e* to *g*, p 711 *b d*, p 715 *b* to p 716 *a*, p 719 *b h*, p 721 *f* to *h*, p 725 *c* to *h*, p 726 *a j*, p 727 *a b*, p 731 *d* to *g*, p 732 *c d*, p 733 *a* to *g*, p 734 *a* to *d* and p 735 *d e*, post); dicta of Lord Blanesburgh in *Robinson v State of South Australia (No 2)* [1931] All ER Rep at 337–338 and of Lord Reid and of Lord Upjohn in *Conway v Rimmer* [1968] 1 All ER at 888, 915–916 applied; *Nixon v USA* (1975) 418 US 683 and dictum of Gibbs ACJ in *Sankey v Whitlam* (1978) 21 ALR at 529–530 adopted; dicta of Lord Reid in *Conway v Rimmer* [1968] 1 All ER at 880, 888 doubted.

g (ii) (Lord Wilberforce dissenting) Burmah's action was not concerned with the policy reasons for rescuing it but with the separate issue of whether the Bank had acted unconscionably in obliging Burmah to sell its BP stock to the Bank on terms dictated to Burmah, and it would reinforce Burmah's action if it were able to prove that the Bank itself considered those terms unconscionable. Since the ten documents in issue were likely to reveal both the Bank's attitude to the terms of the sale of the BP stock (which in view of the Bank's known advocacy of a profit-sharing scheme was likely to be that the final terms were unconscionable and that the Bank had expressed that view to the government) and since if that were the case the documents would be material 'necessary . . . for disposing fairly of the cause', within RSC Ord 24, r 13(1), and since the disclosure of the Bank's attitude would not be prejudicial to state policy, the court would inspect the documents before deciding whether to override the Crown's objections to their disclosure. However, on inspection, it was clear that the documents did not in fact contain material necessary for disposing fairly of the case and in those circumstances the Crown's objection to their production would be upheld. Accordingly (Lord Wilberforce concurring) the appeal would be dismissed (see p 711 *h*, p 713 *h j*, p 714 *e* to *h*, p 715 *d*, p 716 *a b*, p 718 *h* to p 719 *a* and *d* to *f*, p 722 *a* to *d*, p 726 *e* to *j*, p 727 *c* to *e*, p 731 *g* to *j*, p 734 *c* and p 735 *g h*, post).

Decision of Court of Appeal [1979] 2 All ER 461 affirmed on other grounds.

Notes

For withholding documents from production on the ground that disclosure would be injurious to the public interest, see 13 Halsbury's Laws (4th Edn) paras 86–91, and for cases on the subject see 18 Digest (Reissue) 154–160, 1265–1301.

Cases referred to in opinions

Barty-King v Ministry of Defence [1979] 2 All ER 80, [1979] STC 218.

Chappell v The Times Newspapers Ltd [1975]1 WLR 482; *affd* [1975] 2 All ER 233, [1975] 1 WLR 482, CA, Digest (Cont Vol D) 540, 702b.

Compagnie Financière et Commerciale du Pacifique v Peruvian Guano Co (1882) 11 QBD 55, CA.

Conway v Rimmer [1968] 1 All ER 874, [1968] AC 910, [1968] 2 WLR 998, HL; *subsequent proceedings* [1968] 2 All ER 304, [1968] 2 WLR 1535, HL, 18 Digest (Reissue) 155, 1273.

Crompton (Alfred) Amusement Machines Ltd v Comrs of Customs and Excise (No 2) [1973] 2 All ER 1169, [1974] AC 405, [1973] 3 WLR 268, HL, 18 Digest (Reissue) 102, 756.

D v National Society for the Prevention of Cruelty to Children [1977] 1 All ER 589, [1978] AC 171, [1977] 2 WLR 201, HL.

Duncan v Cammell Laird & Co Ltd [1942] 1 All ER 587, [1942] AC 624, 111 LJKB 406, 166 LT 366, HL, 18 Digest (Reissue) 155, 1272.

Glasgow City Corpn v Central Land Board 1956 SC (HL) 1, HL.

Grosvenor Hotel, London, Re, (No 2) [1964] 3 All ER 354, [1965] Ch 1210, [1964] 3 WLR 992, CA, 18 Digest (Reissue) 157, 1279.

Nixon v USA (1975) 418 US 683.

North Ocean Shipping Co v Hyundai Construction Co Ltd [1978] 3 All ER 1170, [1979] 1 Lloyd's Rep 89.

Occidental Worldwide Investment Corpn v Skibs A/S Avanti, the Siboen and the Sibotre [1976] 1 Lloyd's Rep 293.

Pao On v Lau Yiu Long p 65, ante, [1979] 3 WLR 435, PC.

Robinson v State of South Australia (No 2) [1931] AC 704, [1931] All ER·Rep 333, 100 LJPC 183, 145 LT 408, PC, 18 Digest (Reissue) 171, *689.

Rogers v Secretary of State for the Home Department, Gaming Board for Great Britain v Rogers [1972] 2 All ER 1057, [1973] AC 388, [1972] 3 WLR 279, 136 JP 574, HL, Digest (Cont Vol D) 267, 2835c.

Sankey v Whitlam (1978) 21 ALR 505, 53 ALJR 11.

Science Research Council v Nassé p 673, ante, HL; *affg* [1978] 3 All ER 1196, [1979] QB 144, [1978] 3 WLR 754, CA.

Smith v East India Co (1841) 1 Ph 50, 11 LJ Ch 71, 6 Jur 1, 41 ER 550, LC, 18 Digest (Reissue) 159, 1293.

Tito v Waddell (3rd March 1975) unreported.

United States v Bethlehem Steel Corpn (1942) 315 US 289.

United States v Reynolds (1953) 345 US 1.

Wadeer v East India Co (1856) 8 De GM & G 182, 27 LTOS 30, 2 Jur NS 407, 44 ER 360, LJJ, 18 Digest (Reissue) 159, 1288.

Westminster Airways Ltd v Kuwait Oil Co Ltd [1950] 2 All ER 596, [1951] 1 KB 134, CA, 18 Digest (Reissue) 119, 923.

Appeal

By writ dated 6th October 1976 and a statement of claim served on 20th October 1976 the plaintiffs, Burmah Oil Co Ltd ('Burmah'), claimed a declaration that the sale and transfer by Burmah of its holding of 77,817,507 ordinary stock units in British Petroleum

Co Ltd ('BP') to the Bank of England ('the Bank') pursuant to an agreement dated 23rd
a January 1975, at the price of £178,980,266·10, was unconscionable, inequitable and
unreasonable, that it was procured by the Bank acting in breach of its duty of fair dealing
and taking an unfair and unconscionable advantage of Burmah, that it wrongfully
purported to render nugatory Burmah's right to redeem, and that it involved the Bank
obtaining an improper collateral advantage in connection with the taking of security. In
support of that claim Burmah relied on the alleged inequality of bargaining power of the
b Bank and Burmah, the advantage taken by the Bank of Burmah's temporary financial
predicament, the sale of the BP stock at an undervalue, the absence of profit sharing, the
delay by the Bank in stating its proposals, the failure of the Bank to provide guidelines
for sale to third parties, Burmah's inability to seek assistance elsewhere, the Bank's duty
owed to Burmah of fair dealing, and the loss of dividend income from the BP stock. In
addition Burmah sought an order that the Bank cause the BP stock to be transferred back
c to Burmah against payment back by Burmah of the price (paid by the Bank), less any
dividends or other moneys received by the Bank or its nominees in respect of the stock,
an enquiry as to damages, such accounts, directions and enquiries and other declarations
as might be necessary or expedient, and further or other relief. The Bank denied
Burmah's claim.

By a summons dated 15th March 1978 Burmah sought an order that the Bank produce
d for inspection 62 documents enumerated in the Bank's list of documents served on 21st
December 1977, which the Bank at the direction of the Attorney-General, intervening
on behalf of the Crown, objected to produce on the ground that the documents belonged
to classes of documents the production of which would be injurious to the public
interest. Burmah also asked the court to look at those documents to see whether they fell
within those classes. On the summons the Bank took no part in the hearing and the
e issues raised were between Burmah and the Attorney-General. On 28th July 1978 Foster
J dismissed Burmah's application for discovery, but gave leave to appeal. Burmah's
appeal to the Court of Appeal[1] (Bridge and Templeman LJJ, Lord Denning MR
dissenting) was dismissed on 19th January 1979. Burmah appealed to the House of
Lords. The facts are set out in the opinions of Lord Wilberforce and Lord Scarman.

f *Leonard Hoffman QC* and *J M Chadwick* for Burmah.
Donald Rattee QC and *Andrew Smith* for the Bank.
Samuel Silkin QC and *Peter Gibson* for the Attorney-General.

Their Lordships took time for consideration.

g 1st November. The following opinions were delivered.

LORD WILBERFORCE. My Lords, in this action the appellant, the Burmah Oil Co
Ltd ('Burmah'), is suing the Governor and Company of the Bank of England ('the Bank')
for relief in respect of the sale to the Bank by Burmah in 1975 of 77,817,507 ordinary
stock units of £1 each of the British Petroleum Co Ltd ('BP') at a price of approximately
£179 million. Burmah claims, in brief, that this price represented a substantial
h undervalue of the stock and that the bargain was unconscionable, inequitable and
unreasonable. It is important to understand that this action, and these issues, arise
exclusively between Burmah and the Bank.

The present appeal arises out of an application by Burmah for production of 62
documents listed in the list of documents served by the Bank. The Bank on the
instructions of the Crown have objected to produce these on the ground that they belong
j to classes of documents production of which would be injurious to the public interest.
They have put forward a certificate dated 18th October 1977 signed by the Chief
Secretary to the Treasury supporting this objection. On the interlocutory hearing of the
objection in the High Court Her Majesty's Attorney-General intervened in order to argue

1 [1979] 2 All ER 461, [1979] 1 WLR 473

the case in support of it, and it was upheld by Foster J. On appeal by Burmah to the Court of Appeal, the Attorney-General took a similar course, and that court[1], by majority, *a* affirmed the judge. On a further appeal to this House, the Attorney-General was joined as a respondent and as such argued the case against production; the Bank, as in the High Court and in the Court of Appeal, took no part in the argument. But, I repeat, the only defendant in the action is the Bank.

My Lords, in an interlocutory matter involving a large element of discretion, which has been concurrently decided by both courts below, I apprehend that your Lordships *b* should be reluctant to intervene and indeed should only do so if of opinion that some different principle of law from that accepted below ought to be applied. On the view which I take of the case, it is not one for a different exercise of the court's discretion, indeed I regard it as a straightforward one, more so than is usually found in this class of case. I shall deal with the suggestion that some extension or change in the existing law ought to be made.
c
The starting point in the discussion must be the certificate of the Chief Secretary. This is a lengthy and detailed document to which justice cannot be done without setting it out in full. It is perfectly clear that this document represents the result of careful and responsible consideration, that the Minister has read and applied his mind to each of the documents, that, to adopt language used by the courts in other cases, the Minister has not merely repeated a mechanical formula, that the certificate is not 'amorphous' or of a *d* blanket character, but is specific and motivated. Further, the Minister has not contented himself with a general assertion that production would be injurious to the public interest, he has stated very fully the reasons why this would in his opinion be so, in summary that they concern discussions at a very high level, as to one category at ministerial level, and as to another the highest official level, as to the formulation of government policy. He has not even contented himself with a general reference to *e* government policy. He has specified this as concerned with (i) the possible effect of a collapse of Burmah on the pound sterling, on other British companies with large overseas borrowings, on the government's North Sea oil policy, and the future production of North Sea oil and correspondingly on the expectation which might be aroused on the part of other private borrowers if Burmah were to receive assistance, (ii) the international and other consequences of a sale of the BP stock to the Bank (which would bring the *f* government shareholding up to 70%), and (iii) possible further financial support to Burmah after January 1975 having regard to the possible consequences of a financial collapse by Burmah.

It is apparent that these identified matters of policy were of the highest national and political importance and that they called for formulation of policy at the highest governmental levels, including the Cabinet, involving directly several Ministers in the *g* Treasury, the Department of Energy and the Paymaster-General, and, in the first two mentioned departments, handled by the Permanent Under Secretary of State.

Omitting some formal passages, the certificate is as follows:

'3. I have personally read and carefully considered all the documents listed in the Schedule and I have formed the opinion that their production would be injurious to the public interest for the reasons hereinafter set out. *h*

'4. The documents listed in the Schedule fall within three categories described below. There is or are shown in the Schedule against each document listed the appropriate category or, where a document falls within more than one category, the appropriate categories. The three categories are as follows:—

'CATEGORY A

'These consist of communications between, to and from Ministers (including *j* Ministers' Personal Secretaries acting on behalf of Ministers) and minutes and briefs for Ministers and memoranda of meetings attended by Ministers. All such documents relate to the formulation of the policy of the Government—

---

1 [1979] 2 All ER 461, [1979] 1 WLR 473

'(a) in face of the financial difficulties of the Burmah Oil Company Limited (hereinafter called "Burmah") in December 1974 and January 1975, and having regard especially to: (i) the likely effect of the default of Burmah in respect of a large dollar loan upon:— (a) The £ Sterling (b) Other British companies with large overseas borrowings: (ii) the possible effect of a financial collapse by Burmah upon the Government's North Sea oil policy and upon the future production of North Sea oil; (iii) the expectations which would be aroused on the part of other private borrowers defaulting on dollar debts if Burmah were to receive assistance;

'(b) in consequence of the measures taken in response to Burmah's said financial difficulties and in particular as to what was to be done with the B.P. Stock sold by Burmah to the Bank in January 1975 having regard especially to the international consequences of a sale by the Bank of that Stock;

'(c) in connection with the giving of further support to Burmah after January 1975, having regard particularly to the international consequences of a financial collapse by Burmah and the effect of such a collapse on the Government's North Sea oil policy.

'CATEGORY B

'These consist of communications between, to and from senior officials of the Department of Energy, of the Treasury and of the Bank including memoranda of meetings of and discussions between such officials, and drafts prepared by such officials (including drafts of minutes and briefs comprised in Category A), all such communications and drafts relating to the formulation of one or more aspects of the policy described in Category A.

'CATEGORY C

'These consist of memoranda of telephone conversations and meetings between senior representatives of major companies and other businessmen on the one hand and a Minister or senior officials of government departments and of the Bank on the other and memoranda of meetings of such officials and briefs for Ministers and drafts of such briefs, all recording or otherwise referring to commercial or financial information communicated in confidence by such company representatives and businessmen.

'5. Many of the documents listed in the Schedule though in the possession, custody or power of the Bank, were not brought into existence by the Bank or addressed to the Bank. The Bank occupies a unique position in relation to the Government. Though distinct from the Government, it is the principal banker to the Government and, inter alia, performs the function of advising the Government in the field of economic and financial affairs. The Bank is frequently consulted by the Government, particularly when policy decisions in that field fall to be taken. Through the Governor, Deputy Governor and other of its officials it often takes part together with officers of the Treasury and other Government departments in the process of briefing and advising Ministers. To assist the Bank in the performance of its functions it is supplied by the Government with many confidential documents. In addition the Bank brings into existence and itself receives documents in the course of its participation in the process of the formulation of Government policy. These are as much a part of the decision-making process as the internal documents of Government departments relating to the formulation of policy.

'6. It is, in my opinion, necessary for the proper functioning of the public service that the documents in Category A and Category B should be withheld from production. They are all documents falling within the class of documents relating to the formulation of Government policy. Such policy was decided at a very high level, involving as it did matters of major economic importance to the United Kingdom. The documents in question cannot properly be described as routine documents. Those in Category A are all documents passing at a very high level, including communications intended for the guidance and recording the views of the Prime Minister or recording discussions at a very high level. The documents in Category B though passing at a lower level or recording discussions at a lower level, nevertheless all relate to the policy decisions to be taken at a higher level. Decisions made by Ministers are frequently preceded by detailed discussion within and between Government departments (and in appropriate cases, of which the present is one, within the Bank and between the Bank and Government departments) and by consideration of the various possibilities open to Ministers. It is out of such discussion and consideration that the advice to be tendered to Ministers is often formulated (frequently, initially, in the form of drafts of documents intended for the consideration and approval of Ministers) and the decisions of Ministers are often reflected in departmental documents passing at a lower level. This is true of the present case. More generally, it would, in my view, be against the public interest that documents revealing the process of providing for Ministers honest and candid advice on matters of high level policy should be subject to disclosure. In this connection, I would respectfully agree with the reasoning of Lord Reid in *Conway v Rimmer*[1], to whose remarks my attention has been drawn, as regards the effect on the inner workings of the government machine of the public disclosure of documents concerned with policy.

'7. It is further, in my opinion, necessary for the proper functioning of the public service that the documents in Category C should be withheld from production. All the documents in this Category record or otherwise refer to commercial or financial information communicated by businessmen outside Government (including senior officers of other oil companies) in confidence to Ministers or senior officials in Government departments or to the Bank in its capacity as adviser to the Government. Again they cannot be called routine documents. It is of very great importance to the government that it should receive information from those in business which is or may be relevant to the Government's management of the country's financial and economic affairs. The giving of such information is facilitated by the knowledge that it will be treated by the Government or the Bank, in its said capacity, as entirely confidential. Sometimes the Government itself takes the initiative in asking for the information; at other times the information is volunteered by outside sources. There are examples of each in the documents of this Category. If the documents in this Category were produced, those supplying the information could be seriously embarrassed. In my opinion once it was known that what was imparted in confidence might be revealed publicly there would be a grave danger that such information would cease to be as readily forthcoming as it now is. I have no doubt but that this would be detrimental to the public interest.

'8. I understand that oral evidence may be given in these proceedings. If oral evidence were sought to be given of the contents of any of the documents to the production of which I have in this certificate objected, I would wish to object to such evidence on the same grounds as those hereinbefore set out in relation to the documents in question.'

There followed a schedule listing 62 documents and specifying into which category or categories they fell. The documents in category C do not call for separate consideration.

The claim to 'public interest immunity' in respect of these documents is clearly what has come under a rough but accepted categorisation to be known as a 'class' claim, not a 'contents' claim, the distinction between them being that with a class claim it is immaterial whether the disclosure of the particular contents of particular documents would be injurious to the public interest (the point being that it is the maintenance of the immunity of the class from disclosure in litigation that is important), whereas in a contents claim the protection is claimed for particular contents in a particular document. A claim remains a class claim even though something may be known about the contents; it remains a class claim even if parts of documents are revealed and part

---

1   [1968] 1 All ER 874 at 888, [1968] AC 910 at 952

disclosed. Burmah did not, I think, dispute this. And, the claim being a class claim, I
a must state with emphasis that there is not the slightest ground for doubting that the
documents in question fall within the class described; indeed the descriptions themselves
and references in disclosed documents make it clear that they do. So this is not one of
those cases, which anyway are exceptional, where the court feels it necessary to look at
the documents in order to verify that fact. We start with a strong and well-fortified basis
for an immunity claim.

b   I now deal with the two main arguments used by Burmah. The first is to seek to make
a distinction between a decision to allow the Bank to buy the BP stock and a decision as
to price: the first, it is said, may be 'policy', the second is something less than policy. I
have to reject this distinction. The whole course of negotiation of which, as I shall
explain, we know a great deal, shows that these two matters were indissolubly linked as
part of one decision. It is indeed inconceivable that any responsible Minister or civil
c servant would regard the only matter of policy to be decided to be the purchase of the
stock in principle and would leave over the matter of price as one merely of 'nuts and
bolts'.

The second argument is perhaps more plausible. It is to say that, whatever may have
been the need to protect governmental policy from disclosure at the time (1975) all is
now past history: the decision has been made; the sale has gone through; Burmah has
d been saved from collapse. So what is the public interest in keeping up the protective
screen?

I think that there are several answers to this. The first (and easiest) is that all is not past
history, at least we do not know that it is. Government policy as to supporting private
firms in danger of collapse, as to ownership of BP stock, as to the development of North
Sea oil, is on-going policy; the documents are not yet for the Public Record Office. They
e are not, to use a phrase picked out of Lord Reid's speech in *Conway v Rimmer*[1] of purely
historical interest. Secondly the grounds on which public interest immunity is claimed
for this class of document are, no doubt within limits, independent of time. One such
ground is the need for candour in communication between those concerned with policy
making. It seems now rather fashionable to decry this, but if as a ground it may at one
time have been exaggerated, it has now, in my opinion, received an excessive dose of cold
f water. I am certainly not prepared, against the view of the Minister, to discount the
need, in the formation of such very controversial policy as that with which we are here
involved, for frank and uninhibited advice from the Bank to the government, from and
between civil servants and between Ministers. It does not require much imagination to
suppose that some of those concerned took different views as to the right policy and
expressed them. The documents indeed show that they did. To remove protection from
g revelation in court in this case at least could well deter frank and full expression in similar
cases in the future.

Another such ground is to protect from inspection by possible critics the inner
working of government while forming important governmental policy. I do not believe
that scepticism has invaded this, or that it is for the courts to assume the role of advocates
for open government. If, as I believe, this is a valid ground for protection, it must
h continue to operate beyond the time span of a particular episode. Concretely, to reveal
what advice was *then* sought and given and the mechanism for seeking and considering
such advice might well make the process of government more difficult *now*. On this
point too I am certainly not prepared to be wiser than the Minister. So I think that the
'time factor' argument must fail.

The basis for an immunity claim, then, having been laid, it is next necessary to
j consider whether there is any other element of public interest telling in favour of
production. The interest of the proper and fair administration of justice falls under this
description. It is hardly necessary to state that the mere fact that the documents are or
may be 'relevant' to the issues, within the extended meaning of relevance in relation to

---

1   [1968] 1 All ER 874 at 888, [1968] AC 910 at 952

discovery, is not material. The question of privilege or immunity only arises in relation to 'relevant' documents and itself depends on other considerations, viz whether *a* production of these documents (admittedly relevant) is necessary for the due administration of justice. In considering how these two elements are to be weighed one against the other, the proper starting point must be the decision of this House in *Conway v Rimmer*[1]. That case established the law in line with that thought to exist in Scotland, and it is also well in line with Commonwealth authority: see *Sankey v Whitlam*[2], and *Robinson v State of South Australia (No 2)*[3]. The latter case, strongly relied on by Lord *b* Denning MR in the Court of Appeal, does not in my view lay down any principle diverging from or extending beyond *Conway v Rimmer*[1] and was indeed absorbed in that case. Of course *Conway v Rimmer*[1], as the speeches of their Lordships show, does not profess to cover every case, nor has it frozen the law, but it does provide a solid basis for progress as regards the point now under discussion.

It may well be arguable whether, when one is faced with a claim for immunity from *c* production on 'public interest' grounds, and when the relevant public interest is shown to be of a high, or the highest, level of importance, that fact is of itself conclusive, and nothing which relates to the interest in the administration of justice can prevail against it. As Lord Pearce said in *Conway v Rimmer*[4] 'obviously production would never be ordered of fairly wide classes of documents at a high level' (and see *Rogers v Secretary of State for the Home Department*[5] per Lord Salmon). In the words of May J in *Barty-King v* *d* *Ministry of Defence*[6] (which was concerned with internal thinking and policy at a high civil service level) it is not even necessary to bring out the scales. Counsel for the Attorney-General did not contend for any such rigorous proposition, ie that a high level public interest can never, in any circumstances, be outweighed. In this I think that he was in line with the middle of the road position taken by Lord Reid in *Conway v Rimmer*[1] and also with the median views of the members of the High Court of Australia in *Sankey* *e* *v Whitlam*[2]: see particularly the judgment of Gibbs ACJ. I am therefore quite prepared to deal with this case on the basis that the courts may, in a suitable case, decide that a high level governmental public interest must give way to the interests of the administration of justice.

But it must be clear what this involves. A claim for public interest immunity having been made, on manifestly solid grounds, it is necessary for those who seek to overcome *f* it to demonstrate the existence of a counteracting interest calling for disclosure of particular documents. When this is demonstrated, but only then, may the court proceed to a balancing process. In *Conway v Rimmer*[1] itself it was known that there were in existence probationary reports on the plaintiff as to which an obviously strong argument could be made that their disclosure was necessary if the plaintiff's claim were to have any hope of succeeding (in the end they turned out to be far from helpful to him), so the *g* court had something very definite to go on which it could put into the scales against the (minor) public interest of not revealing routine reports. So, too, in *Sankey v Whitlam*[2] the High Court thought it scarcely credible that the documents in question would not reveal factual material as to Commonwealth borrowing. But the present case is quite different. There is not, and I firmly assert this, the slightest ground, apart from pure speculation, for supposing that there is any document in existence, among those which *h* it is sought to withhold, or anything in a document which could outweigh the public interest claim for immunity. I make this assertion good under two heads.

1. A very full and careful disclosure has been made of all documents bearing on negotiations between Burmah and the Bank leading to the sale of the stock. As was said

---

1 [1968] 1 All ER 874, [1968] AC 910
2 (1978) 21 ALR 505
3 [1931] AC 704, [1931] All ER Rep 333
4 [1968] 1 All ER 874 at 910, [1968] AC 910 at 987
5 [1972] 2 All ER 1057 at 1070–1071, [1973] AC 388 at 412
6 [1979] 2 All ER 80

by Templeman LJ[1], '. . . very great care has been taken to conceal the minimum and to

a produce consistently with the public interest every document which is relevant to the action'. Thus, disclosure has been made of all documents relating to occasions and discussions at which representatives of Burmah were present. Disclosure has been made of all factual reports of meetings with Burmah and of Burmah's statements to the Bank and vice versa. There is a mass of these documents which your Lordships have read and carefully considered. What are withheld are documents, or in some cases parts of

b documents, recording discussions either between the Bank and the government or public officials, or internally within the government or the civil service, when Burmah was not present. Since the proceedings are between Burmah and the Bank, there must be a strong argument for believing that the dividing line has been correctly drawn, that what is necessary to Burmah's case has been disclosed, and that what has not been disclosed cannot help Burmah's case. However, I shall explore this further in relation to

c the actual issues.

2. The exact nature of Burmah's claim against the Bank is not very clear, but I need not, indeed should not, analyse it for present purposes. I must not be taken as holding that there is any support for it in law, or the contrary: the claim must at this stage be treated as valid. There are very detailed pleadings in which issues of fact and also matters of evidence are stated. The basic claim is that the sale of the BP stock at the price of

d £179 million ought to be reopened. For this four grounds are stated, namely that the sale—

'(a) was unconscionable, inequitable and unreasonable; (b) was procured by the Bank acting in breach of its duty of fair dealing and taking an unfair and unconscionable advantage of Burmah; (c) wrongfully purported to render nugatory

e Burmah's right to redeem; (d) involved the Bank obtaining an improper collateral advantage in connection with the taking of security.'

In support of these Burmah relies on nine points—

'(1) the inequality of bargaining power of the Bank and Burmah; (2) the advantage taken by the Bank of Burmah's temporary financial predicament; (3) the

f sale of the BP Stock at an undervalue; (4) the absence of profit sharing; (5) the delay by the Bank in stating its proposals; (6) the failure of the Bank to provide guidelines for sale to third parties; (7) the inability of Burmah to seek assistance elsewhere; (8) the duty of the Bank referred to in paragraph 4 above [ie a 'duty of fair dealing']; (9) the loss of dividend income from the BP Stock.'

g Now it is clear from this presentation of the case that the success or failure of Burmah's claim must rest on the objective nature of the bargain, the negotiations between Burmah and the Bank, the relevant circumstances or bargaining power of the parties and any pressure which the Bank may be shown to have exercised on Burmah. As to these matters, much is common ground and is admitted on the pleadings: the mass of documents disclosed provides part of what is necessary to make good the remainder; part

h may depend on oral evidence given by representatives of Burmah, representatives of the Bank and by representatives of the important financial institutions which were advising Burmah in the negotiations. How then can anything said between the Bank and the government or its officials help to resolve these issues? Whether the Bank acted at the behest of the government or not seems to me (with all respect to some views expressed in the Court of Appeal) irrelevant. After a lengthy and thorough argument I was only

j able to perceive two as to which a case of any kind could be made. The first relates to issue (4) above: the absence of profit sharing. The fact here was that the Bank, at one time in the negotiations, had suggested that the sale of the BP stock should involve an

---

1   [1979] 2 All ER 461 at 476, [1979] 1 WLR 473 at 495

agreement that if (as might have seemed likely) the value of the stock were to rise, Burmah should share in the profit. It is clear already from disclosed documents (i) that *a* the Bank thought that a profit sharing term would be fair, (ii) that the Bank, and later Burmah itself, so represented to the government, (iii) that the government refused to agree; all this is as plain as can be from the documents. I cannot see therefore that any document passing between the Bank and the government, or recording any discussion between the Bank and the government, or internally to the government could assist Burmah's case. If any such reference at all were made in any such document to profit *b* sharing (a matter of pure speculation) why should it be in terms different from what the Bank had said to Burmah? If it were in the same terms it would add nothing to this case. The second relates to the general allegation that the sale was unconscionable. In my opinion establishment of this must depend on the objective facts as indicated above. But Burmah submits otherwise. Their claim is rather remarkable. It is 'very likely', to use their own words, that some of the withheld documents (they specify 18 out *c* of the 62) may record a statement by a representative of the Bank to the government, or at some meeting, that in the opinion of the Bank the sale, on terms fixed by the Government was 'unfair', even, in forensic hyperbole, 'grossly unfair' and that this would greatly assist Burmah's case.

My Lords, I am willing to leave aside the question whether, on the pleaded issues, such a statement, made as it would have been in the course of fluid discussions, would assist *d* Burmah to prove its case which, as I have said, depends on objective considerations and on action between Burmah and the Bank. For, in my opinion, the claim is on its face totally unjustified. The phrase 'very like' is a pure ipse dixit of Burmah and unsupported by any evidence; there is nothing anywhere which affords the slightest support for it; any finding that such a statement exists is 'very likely', 'likely' or 'not unlikely', or as to its possible terms, can not judicially be made. That such a document may exist, and what *e* it may contain, is the purest speculation.

This brings me to the issue of inspection. For now it is said, 'Well, let us look at the documents and see; to do so cannot do any harm. If there is nothing there no damage will be done; if there is, we can weigh its importance'. As presented (and to be fair to Burmah's very able counsel such a submission occupied a far from prominent place in their argument) this may appear to have some attraction. But, with all respect to those *f* who think otherwise, I am firmly of opinion that we should not yield to this siren song. The existing state of the authorities is against it; and no good case can be made for changing the law. Indeed, to do so would not in my opinion be progress.

As to authority. Before *Conway v Rimmer*[1], although the court had power to inspect any document, the question whether to exercise it was treated as one for the discretion of the judge, who, it was said, should normally accept the affidavit claiming the *g* immunity: see *Westminster Airways Ltd v Kuwait Oil Co Ltd*[2]. In *Re Grosvenor Hotel, London (No 2)*[3] a number of conflicting opinions were expressed as to both the law and the facts. I think that the Court of Appeal regarded the objection of the Minister as defective and considered therefore that the documents could be inspected for the court to form its own opinion as to the public interest. In *Conway v Rimmer*[4] itself it was said that the power should be exercised 'sparingly' (per Lord Morris of Borth-y-Gest), and then only if *h* there are reasons to doubt the accuracy of the certificate or the cogency of the Minister's reasons. Inspection should be by way of 'final check'[5]. Or, as Lord Upjohn put it, inspection should be made if the judge 'feels any doubt about the reason for [the document's] inclusion as a class document'[6]. In *Alfred Crompton Amusement Machines Ltd*

---

1   [1968] 1 All ER 874, [1968] AC 910
2   [1950] 2 All ER 596, [1951] 1 KB 134
3   [1964] 3 All ER 354, [1965] Ch 1210
4   [1968] 1 All ER 874 at 900, [1968] AC 910 at 971
5   [1968] 1 All ER 874 at 889, [1968] AC 910 at 953
6   [1968] 1 All ER 874 at 916, [1968] AC 910 at 995

j

v .Customs and Excise Comrs (No 2)[1] this House upheld the claim to public interest immunity without inspecting the documents, although that course had been taken by the Court of Appeal. In first instance cases, the judges have treated the power to inspect as an exceptional one, to be rarely used; in two instances they sought and obtained the Crown's consent to inspect selected documents: in *Tito v Waddell*[2] and *Barty-King v Ministry of Defence*[3]. This is inconsistent with the recognition of a general right or duty to inspect.

As to principle, I cannot think that it is desirable that the court should assume the task of inspection except in rare instances where a strong positive case is made out, certainly not on a bare unsupported assertion by the party seeking production that something to help him may be found, or on some unsupported, viz speculative, hunch of its own. In the first place it is necessary to draw a reasonably clear line between the responsibility of Ministers on the one hand, and those of the courts on the other. Each has its proper contribution to make towards solution of the problem where the public interest lies; judicial review is not a 'bonum in se', it is a part, and a valuable one, of democratic government in which other responsibilities coexist. Existing cases, from *Conway v Rimmer*[4] onwards, have drawn this line carefully and suitably. It is for the Minister to define the public interest and the grounds on which he considers that production would affect it. Similarly, the court, responsible for the administration of justice, should, before it decides that the Minister's view must give way, have something positive or identifiable to put into the scales. To override the Minister's opinion by 'amorphous' phrases, or unsupported contentions, would be to do precisely what the courts will not countenance in the actions of Ministers. Secondly, decisions on grounds of public interest privilege fall to be made at first instance, by judges or masters in chambers. They should be able to make these decisions according to simple rules; these are provided by the law as it stands. To invite a general procedure of inspection is to embark the courts on a dangerous course; they have not in general the time or the experience to carry out in every case a careful inspection of documents and thereafter a weighing process. The results of such a process may, indeed are, likely to be variable from court to court and from case to case. This case provides an example of opposite conclusions come to on identical materials[5]. This inevitable uncertainty is not likely to do credit to the administration of justice and is bound to encourage appeals.

In the end, I regard this as a plain case: of public interest immunity properly claimed on grounds of high policy on the one hand in terms which cannot be called in question; of nothing of any substance to put in the scale on the other. I return to the point that both courts below have refused to exercise a discretionary power to order production of these documents, or to inspect them. Their decision can only be reversed if they erred in law. To say that they erred in law in not inspecting the documents involves the proposition that there is a duty, either in all cases or at least in such a case as this, to inspect. In my opinion it is not the law, and ought not to be the law that there is any such duty. In saying this, and in the previous discussion, I have done no more than adopt, with greater prolixity, the completely convincing judgment of Bridge LJ (with whom in substance Foster J and Templeman LJ agreed) in the Court of Appeal.

I would dismiss the appeal.

LORD SALMON. My Lords, in December 1974 the Burmah Oil Co Ltd (which I shall refer to as 'Burmah') was facing ruin and needed massive financial assistance to survive. Burmah had borrowed £54 million on loan stock in England and $650 million loans in the USA to finance its business. In the normal course, the maturity date for these loans

1   [1973] 2 All ER 1169, [1974] AC 405
2   (3rd March 1975) unreported
3   [1979] 2 All ER 80
4   [1968] 1 All ER 874, [1968] AC 910
5   See *Chappell v Times Newspapers Ltd* [1975] 1 WLR 482 at 493 per Megarry J

would have been 1991–96. Towards the end of 1974 there had been a very serious
slump, one of the worst since 1929. Having regard to factors I need not recite, Burmah's *a*
creditors could have become entitled to require immediate repayment of the loans.
There was a great risk that unless somebody came to Burmah's rescue, Burmah would be
forced into liquidation and a receiver and manager would be appointed. This would
have put in jeopardy all Burmah's assets which included their most important interests
in the North Sea oil fields.

When towards the end of December 1974, the Bank of England (which I shall call 'the *b*
Bank') and the government heard of the alarming debacle facing Burmah, which, unless
avoided, could do serious harm to sterling and other important national interests, it was
decided to come to Burmah's rescue.

According to Burmah, it might well have been possible for it to obtain the necessary
financial support from abroad. This support, however, might have had conditions
attached to it which would have seriously prejudiced the national economy; so the Bank *c*
asked Burmah not to look for help abroad until it had discovered what help the Bank
could offer. Between 23rd December 1974 and 23rd January 1975, there were constant
negotiations between Burmah, the Bank, the Treasury and the Department of Energy.

Burmah's most valuable assets were about 78 million stock units in the British
Petroleum Co Ltd (which I shall call 'BP'). By 31st December 1974, outline proposals had
been provisionally agreed between Burmah and the Bank to the effect that the Bank *d*
should produce the necessary cash and guarantees to save Burmah, and Burmah should
mortgage its 78 million stock unit in BP to the Bank and transfer 51% of its interest in
the North Sea oil fields to the government for a price to be negotiated later. The market
value of the BP stock units had been about £6 per unit in July 1974 but, owing to the
slump, had fallen to below £2 towards the end of December 1974.

By 10th January 1975 it had become apparent that the position of Burmah was even *e*
more precarious and that even more help was needed to save it than had previously been
anticipated. On about 10th January the Bank told Burmah that the previously suggested
mortgage of Burmah's BP stock would not meet the situation and suggested that Burmah
should sell its BP stock to the Bank at its current market price and that any profit made
by the Bank out of this transaction should be shared between the Bank and Burmah. At
this time, Burmah thought that the BP stock units were likely to recover to the price they *f*
had commanded in July 1974.

According to Burmah, five days went by before it learned from the Bank that the
government did not agree to any profit sharing scheme with Burmah. Seven days later,
on 22nd January, the Governor and the Deputy Governor of the Bank told Burmah that
it was and always had been their view that a profit sharing scheme between Burmah and
the Bank was reasonable and should be arranged, but that the government would not *g*
agree to any such scheme. It was made plain to Burmah that the government was not
prepared to rescue Burmah unless its BP stock units were sold to the Bank at £2·30 per
unit, ie 38p below the then rising market price and without a profit sharing scheme of
any kind between the Bank and Burmah.

Burmah had no choice but to accept these terms. The selling price amounted to about
£179 million. By July 1975 the market price per unit had recovered to about £5·50. *h*
Accordingly the stock which had been bought by the Bank only a few months previously
for about £179 million was already again worth about £480 million in July 1975.

In the present action, Burmah claims against the Bank that the purchase of the BP
stock at the price of £179 million should be reopened mainly on the grounds that the
purchase was '(a) unconscionable, inequitable and unreasonable; and (b) procured by
the Bank acting in breach of its duty of fair dealing and taking an unfair and *j*
unconscionable advantage of Burmah'.

My Lords, it has been conceded, but only for the purpose of this appeal, that Burmah
has a good cause of action if it can establish its allegations against the Bank.

The present appeal is however concerned only with discovery of documents. The
Bank disclosed a very long list of documents but never itself objected to producing any

a
of them for inspection by Burmah. The government, however, objected to the
production of 62 of these documents on the ground of public interest immunity. On the
interlocutory hearing at first instance, Her Majesty's Attorney-General successfully
intervened to support the objection to the production of the 62 documents in question.
On the unsuccessful appeal by Burmah to the Court of Appeal the Attorney-General took
a similar course; and on appeal to this House the then Attorney-General was joined as a
respondent and counsel appearing for him argued the case against production. The

b
Bank, in this House, as in both the courts below, took no part in the argument.

I am in no way criticising the very full and carefully prepared certificate of the Chief
Secretary to the Treasury clearly explaining why in his view it would be contrary to the
public interest if any part of the classes of documents were to be produced for inspection
which he has listed in his certificate under categories A, B and C. The Chief Secretary's
certificate is set out verbatim in the speech of my noble and learned friend Lord

c
Wilberforce, and I will not repeat it. I shall recite only—

'CATEGORY A

'These consist of communications between, to and from Ministers (including
Ministers' Personal Secretaries acting on behalf of Ministers) and minutes and briefs
for Ministers and memoranda of meetings attended by Ministers. All such
documents relate to the formulation of the policy of the Government—

d
'(a) in face of the financial difficulties of the Burmah Oil Company Limited
(hereinafter called "Burmah") in December 1974 and January 1975, and having
regard especially to: (i) the likely effect of the default of Burmah in respect of a large
dollar loan upon: (a) The £ Sterling (b) Other British companies with large overseas
borrowings: (ii) the possible effect of a financial collapse by Burmah upon the
Government's North Sea oil policy and upon the future production of North Sea oil;

e
(iii) the expectations which would be aroused on the part of other private borrowers
defaulting on dollar debts if Burmah were to receive assistance;

'(b) in consequence of the measures taken in response to Burmah's said financial
difficulties and in particular as to what was to be done with the B.P. Stock sold by
Burmah to the Bank in January 1975 having regard especially to the international
consequences of a sale by the Bank of that Stock;

f
'(c) in connection with the giving of further support to Burmah after January
1975, having regard particularly to the international consequences of a financial
collapse by Burmah and the effect of such a collapse on the Government's North Sea
oil policy.'

g
Category B consists of recorded communications between senior officials relating to
the formulation of one or more of the aspects of government policy described in category
A.

Category C consists of recorded communications made in confidence by important
companies or businessmen to Ministers or senior officials in relation to commercial or
financial information. In my view, the classes of documents in categories A and B should
be treated alike. The class of documents in category C seems to me to be irrelevant and

h
could, in any event, be protected from production on the principles laid down in *Rogers
v Secretary of State for the Home Department*[1] and *D v National Society for the Prevention of
Cruelty to Children*[2].

In my opinion, this case has nothing whatever to do with whether the Bank was right
or wrong in deciding to rescue Burmah from the disaster which faced it, still less with the
reasons which prompted the Bank to arrive at this decision. I entirely agree that the

j
reasons for rescuing Burmah were of the highest national and political importance and
that such parts of the documents in categories A and B (if any) which dealt with these
reasons were immune from production and irrelevant.

1   [1972] 2 All ER 1057, [1973] AC 388
2   [1977] 1 All ER 589, [1978] AC 171

It is common ground that the Bank decided to rescue Burmah. There is no issue as to why it did so. The only issues of fact are whether the Bank's insistence on buying *a* Burmah's BP stock units below the market price and with no profit sharing scheme of any kind was 'unconscionable, inequitable and unreasonable' and whether this transaction was 'procured by the Bank acting in breach of its duty of fair dealing and taking an unfair and unconscionable advantage of Burmah'.

When the decision was taken that Burmah should be saved, it must have been obvious to the Bank and to the government that this rescue operation might involve the *b* expenditure of a great deal of money. In these circumstances, I find it difficult to imagine how £179 million would have been paid to Burmah for their BP stock units unless it had been confidently expected that this stock might well rise to a price yielding a surplus well above £179 million which would more than cover the expense of the rescue operation. In other words, apparently the Bank considered that the stock might well rise to a value which would leave a substantial residue after debiting it with the cost *c* of the rescue operation. This residue is probably what, in all the circumstances, the Bank thought it would be fair to share with Burmah, in proportions to be discussed, and strongly advised the government to accept this profit sharing as fair. This, I think, is also the kind of profit sharing which my noble and learned friend, Lord Wilberforce, considered might be shown to be fair, objectively, by the documents already released for inspection.　　　　　　　　　　　　　　　　　　　　　　　　　　　　　　　　　　*d*

What is not fair is, I suppose, unfair; and there may be a very fine line or a chasm dividing the fair from the unfair. If the Bank took what they believed to be an unfair advantage of Burmah, this might point to the chasm rather than to the fine line. If the chasm exists, this could point to unconscionable conduct by the Bank for which it would be responsible, even although it may have been ordered so to behave by the government, and was incapable of disobeying such an order. Whether unconscionable conduct of this *e* kind would carry any legal liability can be decided only at the trial of the action. Whether the Bank's conduct was unconscionable may well, in the long run, depend on objective tests alone. If, however, during the Bank's discussions with the government immediately prior to the conclusion of the agreement for the purchase of the BP stock, the Bank had said anything to suggest that in its view the terms of the purchase insisted on by the government was unconscionable, this would strongly support Burmah's *f* assertion that those terms were indeed unconscionable. The known fact that the Bank had already stated, in effect, that the terms were unfair and unreasonable suggests that it may well be that it stated that the terms were also unconscionable. If the Bank did so, it would be strong evidence to support Burmah's case on the facts. No one can tell without looking at the documents referring to the discussions between the Bank and the government what was said by the Bank at these discussions. I recognise also that these *g* documents may not necessarily record everything that was said.

Nevertheless, in the circumstances to which I have referred, I certainly consider, and I understand that the majority of your Lordships also consider, that ten out of the 62 documents which the Attorney-General does not wish to be produced should be examined by your Lordships to see whether they may contain evidence 'necessary for disposing fairly' of the instant action. These ten documents cover the period from 10th *h* to 28th January 1975 and are numbered 16, 20, 21, 22, 24, 34, 26, 32, 35 and 36 in Burmah's case. The Attorney-General contends that these documents belong to a class of documents which must be immune from inspection because the immunity is 'necessary for the proper functioning of the public service'. There are, no doubt, classes of documents which are immune from production because their production would imperil the safety of the state or diplomatic relations, and also classes of documents such as *j* Cabinet minutes and others whose immunity from production is considered necessary for the proper functioning of the public service.

I would agree that the documents disclosed in this case might be included amongst the latter classes of documents to the extent which they related to the reasons which persuaded the government and the Bank, in the national interest, to rescue Burmah from

the debacle with which it was faced in January 1975. In such circumstances, the lapse of
time since 1975 on which Burmah relies would, in my opinion, in no way affect the
immunity.

The instant case, however, as I have already indicated, is in no way concerned with the
reasons for the decision to save Burmah. It is solely concerned with the question whether
the Bank acted unconscionably when it, in effect, made Burmah sell its BP stock units on
the terms dictated by the government. If these terms were unconscionable, the fact that
the Bank was obliged by the government to insist on them would not, I think, release the
Bank from responsibility for what it did, nor would it reflect any credit on the
government.

Had any of the ten documents which I have mentioned (a) referred to the reasons why
Burmah had been saved from ruin in the national interest, and (b) contained evidence
that the terms on which Burmah was obliged to sell its BP stock units were
unconscionable, then in my opinion the documents should have been produced for
inspection but with everything under (a) completely covered up.

I entirely agree that the final decision whether or not the national interest made it
necessary for Burmah to be saved from ruin was certainly a most important piece of
policy making which probably required many delicate and secret factors to be
considered. The terms on which Burmah was to be obliged to sell its BP stock units to
the Bank, however, seem to me to have little to do with policy making in the ordinary
sense of that term but only with the making of a hard and perhaps questionable business
bargain. A very strong Board of the Privy Council in *Robinson v State of South Australia
(No 2)*[1] said:

'In view of the increasing extension of State activities into the spheres of trading
business and commerce, and of the claim of privilege in relation to liabilities arising
therefrom now apparently freely put forward, [Turner LJ's] observations [in *Wadeer
v East India Co*[2]] stand on record to remind the Courts that, while they must duly
safeguard genuine public interests they must see to it that the scope of the admitted
privilege is not, in such litigation, extended. Particularly must it be remembered
in this connection that the fact that production of the documents might in the
particular litigation prejudice the Crown's own case or assist that of the other side is
no such "plain overruling principle of public interest" as to justify any claim of
privilege. The zealous champion of Crown rights may frequently be tempted to
take the opposite view, particularly in cases where the claim against the Crown
seems to him to be harsh or unfair. But such an opposite view is without
justification. In truth the fact that the documents, if produced, might have any
such effect upon the fortunes of the litigation is of itself a compelling reason for
their production—one only to be overborne by the gravest considerations of State
policy or security.'

Robinson's case[3], as Lord Denning MR[4] pointed out in the Court of Appeal, was
commended in *Conway v Rimmer*[5] by my noble and learned friends, Lord Morris of
Borth-y-Gest, Lord Hodson and Lord Pearce. *Robinson's* case[3] also laid down that in a case
in what used to be called Crown privilege but which is now referred to as public interest
immunity the courts might in a proper case inspect the documents privately and decide
whether or not they should be produced. This was also approved in *Conway v Rimmer*[6]
by my noble and learned friends, Lord Hodson and Lord Pearce, where the latter said[7]:

1   [1931] AC 704 at 715–716, [1931] All ER Rep 333 at 337–338
2   (1856) 8 De GM & G 182 at 189, 44 ER 360 at 363
3   [1931] AC 704, [1931] All ER Rep 333
4   [1979] 2 All ER 461 at 469, [1979] 1 WLR 473 at 487
5   [1968] 1 All ER 874 at 900, 905, 908, [1968] AC 910 at 970, 979, 983
6   [1968] 1 All ER 874, [1968] AC 910
7   [1968] 1 All ER 874 at 908, [1968] AC 910 at 983

'The court has always had an inherent power to inspect and order the production *a* of a document or classes of documents if in its view the documents, to quote MARTIN, B.'s words[1], "may be made public without prejudice to the public service".'

My Lords, I have privately inspected the ten documents to which I have referred. In my opinion, none of them throws much, if any, light on what is necessary for fairly disposing of this case; and I would accordingly dismiss the appeal.

b

LORD EDMUND-DAVIES. My Lords, whatever doubts may or may not assail one, this House is required to deal with this interlocutory appeal on the basis (a) that the plaintiffs, Burmah Oil Co Ltd ('Burmah'), have a good cause of action, and (b) that the likelihood or otherwise of their succeeding in their claim is at present irrelevant.

Expressed in the broadest terms, the action, brought against the Bank of England alone, is for a declaration and ancillary relief in respect of an agreement entered into by *c* the parties on 23rd January 1975. Its most important term for present purposes was that Burmah undertook to sell to the Bank its largest single asset, consisting of 77,817,507 ordinary stock units of £1 each of the British Petroleum Co Ltd ('the BP stock') for £178,980,266, this representing a price of £2·30 for each unit. Burmah seeks to set aside the agreement on several grounds, the chief being that it was unconscionable, inequitable and unreasonable. *d*

The appeal relates solely to the discovery of documents. It is common ground that the government played an active part in the negotiations leading up to and culminating in the agreement, and the documents held by the Bank naturally include a number which reveal something of the important role played by the government. The existence of such documents has been disclosed in a long list prepared by the Bank, but on the instructions of the government they have resisted production of 62 of their number. In his certificate *e* the Chief Secretary to the Treasury says that he has read and carefully considered all of them and has formed the opinion that their production would be injurious to the public interest. He divides them into categories A, B and C, which he describes in the following terms:

'CATEGORY A   *f*

'These consist of communications between, to and from Ministers (including Ministers' Personal Secretaries acting on behalf of Ministers) and minutes and briefs for Ministers and memoranda of meetings attended by Ministers. All such documents relate to the formulation of the policy of the Government ... [The Minister thereafter sets out various aspects of Government policy in relation to the financial difficulties of Burmah.] *g*

'CATEGORY B

'These consist of communications between, to and from senior officials of the Department of Energy, of the Treasury, and of the Bank, including memoranda of meetings of and discussions between such officials, and drafts prepared by such officials (including drafts of minutes and briefs comprised in Category A), all such *h* communications and drafts relating to the formulation of one or more aspects of the policy described in Category A.

'CATEGORY C

'These consist of memoranda of telephone conversations and meetings between senior representatives of major companies and other businessmen, on the one hand, *j* and a Minister or senior officials of Government departments and of the Bank on the other and memoranda of meetings of such officials and briefs for Ministers and drafts of such briefs, all recording or otherwise referring to commercial or financial

---

1 See *Beatson v Shene* (1860) 5 H & N 838 at 854, [1843–60] All ER Rep 882 at 885

information communicated in confidence by such company representatives and
a businessmen.'

In explanation of the government's opposition to the disclosure of documents falling
within these categories, the Chief Secretary stated:

> 'It is, in my opinion, necessary for the proper functioning of the public service
> that the documents in Category A and Category B should be withheld from
> *b* production. They are all documents falling within the class of documents relating
> to the formulation of Government policy. Such policy was decided at a very high
> level, involving as it did matters of major economic importance to the United
> Kingdom . . .
>
> 'It is, further, in my opinion, necessary for the proper functioning of the public
> service that the documents in Category C should be withheld from production. All
> *c* the documents in this Category record or otherwise refer to commercial or financial
> information communicated by businessmen outside Government (including senior
> officers of other oil companies) in confidence to Ministers or senior officials in
> Government departments or to the Bank in its capacity as adviser to the Government
> . . . If the documents in this Category were produced, those supplying the
> information could be seriously embarrassed. In my opinion, once it was known
> *d* that what was imparted in confidence might be revealed publicly there would be a
> grave danger that such information would cease to be as readily forthcoming as it
> now is. I have no doubt that this would be detrimental to the public interest.'

My Lords, let me say at once that, in the light particularly of the decision of this House
in *D v National Society for the Prevention of Cruelty to Children*[1], I am not satisfied that the
claim made in respect of category C documents could be maintained. But, having regard
e to the conclusion I have arrived at regarding the outcome of this interlocutory appeal, the
validity of that particular claim need not now be discussed.

The wording of the claim advanced has obviously been chosen in the light of certain
observations of this House in *Conway v Rimmer*[2]. It is a 'class' claim, in contradistinction
to a 'contents' claim. In other words, the Chief Secretary avers that all 62 documents
belong to a *class* of documents which by their very nature ought to be withheld, and this
f regardless of whether there is anything in the contents of any or all of them the
disclosure of which would be against public interest. For a class claim may legitimately
be advanced even in respect of documents having *no* contents which it would prejudice
the public interest to disclose. A 'contents' claim, on the other hand, is self-explanatory,
and in *Conway v Rimmer*[3] Lord Reid said:

> *g* 'It does not appear that any serious difficulties have been or are likely to arise with
> regard to [a "contents" claim]. However wide the power of the court may be held
> to be, cases would be very rare in which it could be proper to question the view of
> the responsible Minister that it would be contrary to the public interest to make
> public the contents of a particular document.'

Even then, however, as Lord Reid added, the question might arise of selecting for
h disclosure *parts* of a document the subject of a 'contents' claim.

A party to litigation who seeks, as here, to withhold from disclosure to the other party
documents which, being included in their list or affidavit of documents, are ex concessis
relevant to the litigation has, as this House made clear in *Conway v Rimmer*[2] and *Rogers
v Secretary of State for the Home Department*[4] per Lord Reid, a heavy burden of proof. But
j it is not contended by Burmah that the Chief Secretary has failed to establish a good

1   [1977] 1 All ER 589, [1978] AC 171
2   [1968] 1 All ER 874, [1968] AC 910
3   [1968] 1 All ER 874 at 882, [1968] AC 910 at 943
4   [1972] 2 All ER 1057 at 1060, [1973] AC 388 at 400

prima facie case for withholding all the listed documents. Indeed, it does not stop there, for Burmah (which nevertheless seeks to inspect 18 of them) accepts that it is now for *a* them in their turn to establish that those 18 documents are 'very likely to contain evidence which is highly material' to the issues arising in the case. And they must go further, for the court has no power to order disclosure unless it is 'of opinion that the order is necessary either for disposing fairly of the cause or matter or for saving costs' (see RSC Ord 24, r 13(1)). By no means all relevant documents satisfy such a test.

Indeed, many documents may be of merely vestigial importance, and therefore not *b* the proper subject-matter of an order for disclosure. But it is by no means unknown in litigation, and perhaps understandable, to ask for more documents than one hopes to get. And that, in my view, has happened in this case. It is not necessary for me to relate the events leading up to the 'December agreement' arrived at between the parties by Burmah's letter to the Bank dated 3rd January 1975, accepting certain 'outline proposals' advanced by the latter on 31st December. It should be sufficient to state that the *c* agreement effected an equitable charge to the Bank of Burmah's BP stock, that it provided that in the event of a sale of such stock Burmah would be consulted beforehand, and that the proceeds of sale would have benefited Burmah by being applied in full discharge of its liability to the Bank. But, for the purposes of this interlocutory appeal, based on the alleged unconscionability not of the December agreement but of the later agreement concluded on 23rd January 1975, I should have thought that no question of *d* disclosure could properly arise in relation to any document earlier than about 10th January 1975, and I proceed to deal with the appeal on that basis.

Summarising the later events, Burmah's case is that on 10th January the Bank expressed the view that the only solution of their financial problems was for them to sell their BP stock to the Bank at the current quoted price and on terms that Burmah would share in any profit enuring on the Bank's resale of the BP stock. And, as the appeal *e* proceeded before this House, it became Burmah's case that not until 15th January did it learn from the Bank that the government was opposed to any sharing of profit made on the resale, and that not until 22nd January did the Bank inform Burmah that (a) the government had decided that the price to be paid by the Bank for the BP stock was a mere £2·30 per ordinary stock unit, (b) the government was not prepared to accept any profit-sharing formula, and (c) subject to (a) and (b), the government agreed to the Bank *f* buying Burmah's BP stock.

Burmah asserts that, despite its protests against the unconscionability of these terms, they were in due course obliged to accept them, as by that time they had no other course open to them. In their defence the Bank expressly admit (a) that on 22nd January their Governor and Deputy Governor told Burmah that they remained of the view that profit-sharing was reasonable and that they had done their best to represent this view to the *g* government, and further (b) that the quoted price of BP ordinary stock units had been rising since 14th January. But they deny the unconscionability which is at the root of the plaintiff's claim, and the object of the discovery now sought from them is to destroy that denial.

My Lords, I have already indicated that Burmah have asked for too much. But it was urged by the Attorney-General that, so expansive were the numerous admissions made *h* in the Bank's defence and so liberal had the Bank been in supplying documents that Burmah had all the material necessary for the presentation of their case. I do not think that is right. In the face of the Bank's umbrella denial of any inequality of bargaining power, the sale of BP stock at an undervalue, and all other forms of unconscionable conduct on their part, it could, as I think, prove a valuable reinforcement of Burmah's case if they could establish by means of some of the withheld documents that the Bank *j* had itself committed themselves to the view that the terms finally presented to Burmah were tainted by those unconscionable features of which Burmah complained.

What are the probabilities of such documentary support being in existence? Is it merely pure conjecture? If so, applying Burmah's's own test, production should be refused. But in my judgment, there is more to it than that. It is, at the very least, 'on the

cards' that, in the light of the Bank's known support and advocacy of profit-sharing, they
a expressed their unequivocal dislike when the government expressed determination to
impose its final terms on Burmah. It was, I think an over simplification for the Attorney-
General to submit that the only issue is whether the January agreement was in fact
inequitable, and not whether the Bank regarded it as inequitable. For if, faced by
government obduracy despite its strong representations, the Bank insisted on the
proposed contractual terms, an arguable foundation for Burmah's allegations of
b unconscionability against the Bank itself could be laid. Then is all this merely 'on the
cards', simply a 'fishing expedition'? If that is all there is to it, discovery should be
refused. But in my judgment the existence of such documentary material is likely. And
that, in my judgment, is sufficient. For although, as the noble and learned Lord, Lord
Wilberforce, has pointed out, it was *known* in *Conway v Rimmer*[1] that there were in
existence probationary reports on the plaintiff, positive knowledge of that sort is not, in
c my view, a sine qua non before discovery may be ordered. Nevertheless, as I have already
indicated, I think it is very unlikely to have come into existence before 10th January
1975 and (if it exists at all) it will probably be found in the ten documents numbered 16,
20, 21, 22, 24, 34, 26, 32, 35 and 36 in Burmah's case.

And so, as I see it, the position is reached that, on the one hand, Burmah seek disclosure
of ten documents which may well contain material 'necessary . . . for disposing fairly of
d the cause or matter or for saving costs', while, on the other hand, the Attorney-General
by his intervention asserts that the withholding of these ten documents (two in category
A and eight in category B) is 'necessary for the proper functioning of the public service'.
In these circumstances, the balancing exercise with which the courts of this country have
become increasingly familiar since *Conway v Rimmer*[1] is called for, and if Burmah are to
succeed the scales must come down decisively in their favour (see *Alfred Crompton*
e *Amusement Machines Ltd v Customs and Excise Comrs (No 2)*[2], per Lord Cross).

Despite the strong claims advanced by the Chief Secretary, none of the ten documents
belongs to those categories (such as Cabinet decisions and papers) hitherto largely
regarded as totally immune from production. And acceptance of that claim does not
necessarily preclude disclosure. For, as Lord Radcliffe said in *Glasgow Corpn v Central*
Lands Board[3]:
f
'The power reserved to the Court is . . . a power to order production even though
the public interest is to some extent affected prejudicially . . . The interests of
government, for which the Minister should speak with full authority, do not
exhaust the public interest. Another aspect of that interest is seen in the need that
impartial justice should be done in the Courts of law, not least between citizen and
Crown and that a litigant who has a case to maintain should not be deprived of the
g means of its proper presentation by anything less than a weighty public reason. It
does not seem to me unreasonable to expect that the Court would be better qualified
than the Minister to measure the importance of such principles in application to the
particular case that is before it.'

My Lords, it follows, as I think, that the Attorney-General was wrong in submitting
h that, if Burmah are to succeed in this interlocutory appeal, they must establish that the
Chief Secretary's certificate is probably inaccurate. On the contrary, disclosure may well
be ordered even though its accuracy is not impugned, for the Minister's view is one-sided
and may be correct as far as it goes but is yet not to be regarded as decisive of the matter
of disclosure. For, as Lord Reid said in *Conway v Rimmer*[4]:

j
'The Minister who withholds production of a "class" document has no duty to

1   [1968] 1 All ER 874, [1968] AC 910
2   [1973] 2 All ER 1169 at 1185, [1974] AC 405 at 434
3   1956 SC (HL) 1 at 18–19
4   [1968] 1 All ER 874 at 882, [1968] AC 910 at 943

consider the degree of public interest involved in a particular case by frustrating in that way the due administration of justice. If it is in the public interest in his view to withhold documents of that class, then it matters not whether the result of withholding a document is merely to deprive a litigant of some evidence on a minor issue in a case of little importance or, on the other hand is to make it impossible to do justice at all in a case of the greatest importance.'

There is a further feature in this case which it would be pusillanimous to ignore. It consists in the fact that this is not one of those cases where the complete detachment of the party resisting disclosure is beyond doubt. It is true that the government is not a party to these proceedings, but it would be unrealistic to think that the conduct of government's servants and advisers nowise enters into this case. Not only is it the fact that the Bank, left to its own devices, would have complied in full with Burmah's request for discovery, but its only opponent (through the intervention of the Attorney-General) is the government, whose own role must inevitably and inescapably be scrutinised and may be subjected to criticism. Accordingly, since not only justice itself but also the *appearance* of justice is of considerable importance, the balancing exercise is bound to be affected to some degree where the party objecting to discovery is not a wholly detached observer of events in which it was in no way involved. It cannot realistically be thought that the government is wholly devoid of interest in the outcome of these proceedings. On the contrary, it has a very real and lively interest, for were Burmah to succeed it could only be on the basis that the Bank behaved unconscionably, and the evidence indicates that the Bank was acting throughout in accordance with government instructions. This fact renders apposite certain observations of Lord Blanesburgh, who said in *Robinson v State of South Australia (No 2)*[1]:

'In view of the increasing extension of State activities into the spheres of trading business and commerce, and of the claim of privilege in relation to liabilities arising therefrom now apparently freely put forward, [Turner LJ's] observations [in *Wadeer v East India Co*[2]] stand on record to remind the Courts that, while they must duly safeguard genuine public interests they must see to it that the scope of the admitted privilege is not, in such litigation, extended. Particularly must it be remembered in this connection that the fact that the production of the documents might in the particular litigation prejudice the Crown's own case or assist that of the other side is no such "plain overruling principle of public interest" as to justify any claim of privilege. The zealous champion of Crown rights may frequently be tempted to take the opposite view, particularly in cases where the claim against the Crown seems to him to be harsh or unfair. But such an opposite view is without justification. In truth the fact that the documents, if produced, might have any such effect upon the fortunes of the litigation is of itself a compelling reason for their production—one only to be overborne by the gravest considerations of State policy or security.'

My Lords, I should add that, on the state of the available material, I have difficulty in regarding it as conceivably prejudicial to state policy were it revealed by such discovery of documents as I have earlier referred to that the Bank themselves regarded as unconscionable the terms dictated by the government before the January agreement could be concluded. That the government might well be considerably embarrassed by the revelation is readily understandable, but that is without relevance to this interlocutory appeal.

Yet, when all this is said and done and even accepting that the withheld documents are likely to contain material supportive of the allegation of unconscionability, this House is at present completely in the dark as to the cogency of such material. For example, does it clearly and substantially support the allegation, or only to an insignificant degree?

---

1   [1931] AC 704 at 715–716, [1931] All ER Rep 333 at 337–338
2   (1856) 8 De GM & G 182 at 189, 44 ER 360 at 363

Unless its evidentiary value is clear and cogent, the balancing exercise may well lead to
a the conclusion that the public interest would best be served by upholding the Chief
Secretary's objection to disclosure. On the other hand, if the material provides strong
and striking support of Burmah's claim, the court may conclude that, when this is set
against such prejudice to the public interest as is likely to arise were any disclosure made
in late 1979 regarding even high-policy commercial negotiations conducted in January
1975, the interests of justice demand that disclosure (complete or partial) should be
b ordered. A judge conducting the balancing exercise needs to know, in the words of Lord
Pearce in *Conway v Rimmer*[1]:

> '... whether the documents in question are of much or little weight in the
> litigation, whether their absence will result in a complete or partial denial of justice
> to one or other of the parties or perhaps to both, and what is the importance of the
> particular litigation to the parties and the public. All these are matters which
> *c* should be considered if the court is to decide where the public interest lies.'

No judge can profitably embark on such a balancing exercise without himself seeing
the disputed documents. May he take a peep? In *Conway v Rimmer*[2] Lord Reid said:

> 'It appears to me that, if the Minister's reasons are such that a judge can properly
> weigh them, he must on the other hand consider what is the probable importance
> *d* in the case before him of the documents or other evidence sought to be withheld.
> If he decides that on balance the documents probably ought to be produced, I think
> that it would generally be best that he should see them before ordering production
> ... I can see nothing wrong in the judge seeing documents without their being
> shown to the parties ... If on reading the document he ... thinks that it ought to
> be produced he will order its production. It is important, however, that the Minister
> *e* should have a right to appeal before the document is produced.'

Lord Upjohn said[3]:

> '... if privilege is claimed for a document on the ground of "class" the judge, if
> he feels any doubt about the reason for its inclusion as a class document, should not
> hesitate to call for its production for his private inspection, and to order and limit its
> *f* production if he thinks fit.'

But it has been suggested that the position is otherwise where the 'class' claim is not
challenged. I see no reason why this should be so, once it is postulated that the withheld
'class' documents are 'likely' to contain material substantially useful to the party seeking
discovery. That qualification is necessary, for what is no more than a 'fishing expedition'
g ought not to be advanced by the judge's having a peep to see whether they contain an
attractive catch. But, provided such reservation is rigidly adhered to, a judicial peep
seems to be justifiable in both cases and may, indeed, prove vital in each if the judge is
to be enabled to arrive at a just conclusion in the matter of discovery. Indeed though not
so intended, the further observations of Lord Upjohn in *Conway v Rimmer*[4] seem to be
entirely apposite to both cases. He said:

h
> 'There is a lis between A and B; the Crown may be A or B or, as in this case, a third
> party ... but when the judge demands to see the documents for which privilege is
> claimed he is not considering that lis but quite a different lis, that is whether the
> public interest in withholding the document outweighs the public interest that all
> relevant documents not otherwise privileged should be disclosed in litigation. The
> judge's duty is to decide that lis; if he decides it in favour of disclosure, cadit
j

---

1   [1968] 1 All ER 874 at 911, [1968] AC 910 at 987
2   [1968] 1 All ER 874 at 888–889, [1968] AC 910 at 953
3   [1968] 1 All ER 874 at 915–916, [1968] AC 910 at 995
4   [1968] 1 All ER 874 at 916, [1968] AC 910 at 995

quaestio; if he decides it in favour of non-disclosure he banishes its contents from his mind for the purposes of the main lis.'

    In my judgment, such material as is presently available leads me to the conclusion that this Appellate Committee of your Lordships' House should now privately inspect the ten documents earlier referred to. What they contain remains to be seen. All three members of the Court of Appeal themselves inspected certain documents and expressed widely varying conclusions as to their materiality, but your Lordships have no knowledge of which of the 62 listed documents they inspected, and, even if you had, it is still for your Lordships to form your own views regarding the ten documents earlier specified. If the conclusion is that they contain nothing of any significance, this appeal should be dismissed. But if, on the other hand, material evidence comes to light, your Lordships will be called on to adjudicate whether, in balancing the competing public interests, disclosure of any of the ten documents or any parts of them should be ordered. The final disposal of this appeal must await and will depend on the nature of that adjudication.

    My Lords, it was some days after I had completed and passed for typing the foregoing observations that I privately inspected the ten documents earlier referred to. Having done so, in my judgment disclosure of none of them can be described as 'necessary either for disposing fairly of the cause or matter or for saving costs'. It follows that I would uphold in its entirety the objection to production advanced by the Chief Secretary to the Treasury and dismiss this interlocutory appeal.

LORD KEITH OF KINKEL. My Lords, this appeal is concerned with the legal topic known formerly as Crown privilege and now as public interest immunity. The topic embraces those rules of law which are applicable for the purpose of determining whether a litigant is entitled to the discovery of documents claimed to be relevant to his case, the production of which is resisted by the Crown on the ground that it would be detrimental to the public interest, that ground being vouched by a Ministerial certificate.

    The matter was last considered comprehensively by this House in *Conway v Rimmer*[1]. It was there held, contrary to certain dicta in *Duncan v Cammell Laird & Co*[2], that a Minister's certificate was not conclusive, but that it was a proper function of the court to weigh against each other the aspect of public interest appearing from the reasons stated in the certificate and the public interest that the administration of justice should not be frustrated. This result was regarded as being in line with the law of Scotland as affirmed in *Glasgow Corpn v Central Land Board*[3], and also with that of most Commonwealth countries on the lines expounded in *Robinson v State of South Australia (No 2)*[4] and that of the United States as appearing from *United States v Reynolds*[5].

    Having held that the Minister's certificate was not conclusive and laid down the principle that the decision for or against discovery was to be reached by the balancing process described, the House had to go on to consider whether discovery was appropriate in the circumstances of the case before it. The documents sought to be produced were reports of a routine character relating to the plaintiff during his period of probation as a police constable, and by their nature were of extreme importance to the proper disposal of his action for malicious prosecution against his former superintendent. The House had no difficulty in deciding that prima facie they ought to be produced, but thought it proper, before so ordering, to inspect the documents in order to make sure that there was nothing in their contents the disclosure of which would prejudice the public interest. For this purpose it was necessary to enter to some extent on a general consideration of the

---

1   [1968] 1 All ER 874, [1968] AC 910
2   [1942] 1 All ER 587, [1942] AC 624
3   1956 SC (HL) 1
4   [1931] AC 704, [1931] All ER Rep 333
5   (1953) 345 US 1

type of circumstances under which discovery might correctly be ordered despite Crown
a objection backed by a Ministerial certificate. But in my opinion no definitive body of
binding rules universally applicable to future cases in the field is to be gathered from the
speeches delivered, and the sound development of the law now requires that it be
examined afresh. As was said by Lord Upjohn[1], '. . . in this field the courts are entitled
from time to time to make a reappraisal in relation to particular documents of just what
it is that the public interest demands in shielding them from production'.

b It is convenient to start with the points of distinction between what are commonly
called 'class' and 'contents' claims to immunity. In *Conway v Rimmer*[2] Lord Reid said:

'A Minister's certificate may be given on one or other of two grounds: either
because it would be against the public interest to disclose the contents of the
particular document or documents in question, or because the document belongs to
a class of documents which ought to be withheld whether or not there is anything
c in the particular document in question disclosure of which would be against the
public interest. It does not appear that any serious difficulties have arisen or are
likely to arise with regard to the first class. However wide the power of the court
may be held to be, cases would be very rare in which it could be proper to question
the view of the responsible Minister that it would be contrary to the public interest
to make public the contents of a particular document. A question might arise
d whether it would be possible to separate those parts of a document of which
disclosure would be innocuous from those parts which ought not to be made public,
but I need not pursue that question now. In the present case your lordships are
directly concerned with the second class of documents.'

Lord Hodson[3] in the same case said that he did not regard the classification which
places all documents under the heading either of contents or of class as being wholly
e satisfactory. I agree with him. What really matters is the specific ground of public
interest on which the Ministerial objection is based, and it scarcely needs to be said that
the more clearly this ground is stated the easier will be the task of the court in weighing
it against the public interest in the administration of justice. The weight of a contents
claim is capable of being very readily measured. Obvious instances are documents
f relating to defence of the realm or relations with other states. It might be said that such
documents constitute a class defined by reference to the nature of their contents. But I
would prefer to regard the claim in regard to such a document as being in substance a
contents claim, in relation to which Lord Upjohn said in *Conway v Rimmer*[4]:

'A claim made by a Minister on the basis that the disclosure of the contents would
be prejudicial to the public interest must receive the greatest weight; but even here
g I am of opinion that the Minister should go as far as he properly can without
prejudicing the public interest in saying why the contents require protection. In
such cases it would be rare indeed for the court to overrule the Minister, but it has
the legal power to do so, first inspecting the document itself and then ordering its
production.'

h Claims to immunity on class grounds stand in a different category because the reasons
of public interest on which they are based may appear to some minds debatable or even
nebulous. In *Duncan v Cammell Laird & Co*[5] Lord Simon referred to cases 'where the
practice of keeping a class of documents secret is necessary for the proper functioning of
the public service'. These words have been seized on as convenient for inclusion in many
a Ministerial certificate, including the one under consideration in the present case. But
j they inevitably stimulate the query 'Why is the concealment necessary for that purpose?'

1   [1968] 1 All ER 874 at 913, [1968] AC 910 at 991–992
2   [1968] 1 All ER 874 at 882, [1968] AC 910 at 943–944
3   [1968] 1 All ER 874 at 905, [1968] AC 910 at 979
4   [1968] 1 All ER 874 at 914, [1968] AC 910 at 993
5   [1942] 1 All ER 587 at 595, [1942] AC 624 at 642

and unless it is answered there is nothing tangible to put in the balance against the public interest in the proper administration of justice.

Over a considerable period it was maintained, not without success, that the prospect of the disclosure in litigation of correspondence or other communications within government departments would inhibit a desirable degree of candour in the making of such documents, with results detrimental to the proper functioning of the public service. As mentioned by Lord Reid in *Conway v Rimmer*[1] the fashion for this was set by Lord Lyndhurst LC through the reasons, possibly oblique, which he gave for refusing production of communications between the directors of the East India Company and the Board of Control in *Smith v East India Co*[2]. This contention must now be treated as having little weight, if any. In *Conway v Rimmer*[3] Lord Morris of Borth-y-Gest referred to it as being of doubtful validity. Lord Hodson[4] thought it impossible at the present day to justify the doctrine in its widest term. Lord Pearce[5] considered that a general blanket protection of wide class led to a complete lack of common sense. Lord Upjohn[6] expressed himself as finding it difficult to justify the doctrine 'when those in other walks of life which give rise to equally important matters of confidence in relation to security and personnel matters as in the public service can claim no such privilege'. The notion that any competent and conscientious public servant would be inhibited at all in the candour of his writings by consideration of the off-chance that they might have to be produced in a litigation is in my opinion grotesque. To represent that the possibility of it might significantly impair the public service is even more so. Nowadays the state in multifarious manifestations impinges closely on the lives and activities of individual citizens. Where this has involved a citizen in litigation with the state or one of its agencies, the candour argument is an utterly insubstantial ground for denying him access to relevant documents. I would add that the candour doctrine stands in a different category from that aspect of public interest which in appropriate circumstances may require that the sources and nature of information confidentially tendered should be withheld from disclosure. *Rogers v Secretary of State for the Home Department*[7] and *D v National Society for the Prevention of Cruelty to Children*[8] are cases in points on that matter.

I turn to what was clearly regarded in *Conway v Rimmer*[9] as the really important reason for protecting from disclosure certain categories of documents on a class basis. It was thus expressed by Lord Reid[10]:

'I do not doubt that there are certain classes of documents which ought not to be disclosed whatever their contents may be. Virtually everyone agrees that cabinet minutes and the like ought not to be disclosed until such time as they are only of historical interest; but I do not think that many people would give as the reason that premature disclosure would prevent candour in the cabinet. To my mind the most important reason is that such disclosure would create or fan ill-informed or captious public or political criticism. The business of government is difficult enough as it is, and no government could contemplate with equanimity the inner workings of the government machine being exposed to the gaze of those ready to criticise without adequate knowledge of the background and perhaps with some axe to grind. And that must, in my view, also apply to all documents concerned with policy making within departments including it may be minutes and the like by quite junior

---

1 [1968] 1 All ER 874 at 882–883, [1968] AC 910 at 944
2 (1841) 1 Ph 50, 41 ER 550
3 [1968] 1 All ER 874 at 891, [1968] AC 910 at 957
4 [1968] 1 All ER 874 at 904, [1968] AC 910 at 976
5 [1968] 1 All ER 874 at 910, [1968] AC 910 at 986
6 [1968] 1 All ER 874 at 916, [1968] AC 910 at 995
7 [1972] 2 All ER 1057, [1973] AC 388
8 [1977] 1 All ER 589, [1978] AC 171
9 [1968] 1 All ER 874, [1968] AC 910
10 [1968] 1 All ER 874 at 888, [1968] AC 910 at 952

a officials and correspondence with outside bodies. Further, it may be that deliberations about a particular case require protection as much as deliberations about policy. I do not think that it is possible to limit such documents by any definition . . .'

Lord Hodson[1] referred to classes of documents which from their very character ought to be withheld from production, such as Cabinet minutes, dispatches from ambassadors abroad and minutes of discussions between heads of departments. Lord Pearce[2] said that *b* obviously production would never be considered of fairly wide classes of documents of a high level such as Cabinet correspondence, letters or reports on appointments to office of importance and the like. Lord Upjohn[3] spoke to similar effect, saying that the reason for the privilege was that it would be wrong and entirely inimical to the proper functioning of the public service if the public were to learn of these high level communications, however innocent of prejudice to the state the actual contents of any *c* particular document might be, and that this was obvious.

In my opinion, it would be going too far to lay down that no document in any particular one of the categories mentioned should ever in any circumstances be ordered to be produced, and indeed I did not understand counsel for the Attorney-General to pitch his submission that high before this House. Something must turn on the nature of the subject-matter, the persons who dealt with it, and the manner in which they did *d* so. In so far as a matter of government policy is concerned, it may be relevant to know the extent to which the policy remains unfulfilled, so that its success might be prejudiced by disclosure of the considerations which led to it. In that context the time element enters into the equation. Details of an affair which is stale and no longer of topical significance might be capable of disclosure without risk of damage to the public interest. The Ministerial certificate should offer all practicable assistance on these *e* aspects. But the nature of the litigation and the apparent importance to it of the documents in question may in extreme cases demand production even of the most sensitive communications at the highest level. Such a case might fortunately be unlikely to arise in this country, but in circumstances such as those of *Sankey v Whitlam*[4] or *Nixon v USA*[5], to which reference is made in the speech of my noble and learned friend Lord Scarman, I do not doubt that the principles there expounded would fall to be applied. *f* There can be discerned in modern times a trend towards more open governmental methods than were prevalent in the past. No doubt it is for Parliament and not for courts of law to say how far that trend should go. The courts are, however, concerned with the consideration that it is in the public interest that justice should be done and should be publicly recognised as having been done. This may demand, though no doubt only in a very limited number of cases, that the inner workings of government should be *g* exposed to public gaze, and there may be some who would regard this as likely to lead, not to captious or ill-informed criticism, but to criticism calculated to improve the nature of that working as affecting the individual citizen. I think that considerations of that nature were present in the mind of Lord Denning MR when delivering his dissenting judgment in the Court of Appeal[6] in this case, and in my opinion they correctly reflect what the trend of the law should be.
h There are cases where a consideration of the terms of the Ministerial certificate and of the nature of the issues in the case before it as revealed by the pleadings, taken with the description of the documents sought to be recovered, will make it clear to the court that the balance of public interest lies against disclosure. In other cases the position will be the reverse. But there may be situations where grave doubt arises, and the court feels

j 1 [1968] 1 All ER 874 at 901, [1968] AC 910 at 973
2 [1968] 1 All ER 874 at 911, [1968] AC 910 at 987
3 [1968] 1 All ER 874 at 914, [1968] AC 910 at 993
4 (1978) 21 ALR 505
5 (1975) 481 US 683
6 [1979] 2 All ER 461 at 465–471, [1979] 1 WLR 473 at 481–489

that it cannot properly decide on which side the balance falls without privately inspecting the documents. In my opinion the present is such a case. Those of your Lordships who *a* have already spoken have set out comprehensively the circumstances of the case, the nature and the claimed grounds of the cause of action on which Burmah found and the terms of the Ministerial certificate. I need not rehearse these matters. Burmah maintains that the bargain struck between it and the Bank of England on 23rd January 1975, whereby, inter alia, the latter acquired Burmah's holding of BP stock at a very low price, was an unconscionable one, impetrated by abuse of the Bank's superior bargaining *b* power, and that it should therefore be set aside. The particular aspect of the bargain which Burmah claims to have been unconscionable was that it made no provision for it participating in any gain which might accrue from a future rise in the value of the BP stock units. The Bank in relation to the transaction acted in substance as an agency of the government and was able to offer only the terms which the government required it to offer. It is common ground that the Governor and Deputy Governor of the Bank *c* favoured an arrangement whereby Burmah would participate in any future profit on the BP stock units, but that the government were not prepared to agree to this. Naturally there were meetings and discussions about this matter between representatives of the government departments concerned and of the Bank of England. The list of 62 documents discovery of which was originally sought by Burmah is now reduced to ten. These all relate to such meetings and discussions between 10th and 22nd January 1975. *d* The Secretary of State for Energy and the Paymaster-General were present at one of these meetings. The Deputy Governor of the Bank of England was present at all of them. Certain of them constituted a follow-on of meetings for the earlier part of which representatives of Burmah had been present.

The ten documents in question are certified by the Minister as relating to the formulation of the policy of the government in face of Burmah's financial difficulties in *e* the light of certain considerations which he sets out. Two of them involve Ministers, the remainder senior officials of various government departments. There are of course a substantial number of documents among the other 52 which are similarly certified. While it must be accepted that the ten documents have to do with the formulation of policy, I consider it to be a proper inference that they are not concerned solely with that. Having regard to the timing and the context, they must clearly deal to some extent *f* with the application of policy, with the expression by the Deputy Governor of the Bank of the Bank's views about what would be reasonable terms for any agreement to be entered into with Burmah, and with the instructions ultimately given to the Bank by the governmental representatives. It has to be kept in mind that the court need not order disclosure of the whole terms of any particular document. Parts of it relating to any politically sensitive aspects of the formulation of policy may be withheld from disclosure, *g* while disclosing other parts of evidential importance in the litigation. Having carefully considered all the circumstances, I have come to the conclusion that a reasonable probability exists of finding the documents in question to contain a record of the views of the responsible officials of the Bank of England expressed in such terms as to lend substantial support to the contention that the bargain eventually concluded with Burmah was unconscionable. I do not agree that the issue of unconscionability is to be treated *h* entirely objectively. If it were to be proved, for example, that the Deputy Governor of the Bank strongly protested that the terms of the bargain were unconscionable but was overborne by the government, that would, in my view, be important evidence in Burmah's favour. There can be no doubt that the court has power to inspect the documents privately. This was clearly laid down in *Conway v Rimmer*[1]. I do not consider that exercise of such power, in cases responsibly regarded by the court as doubtful, can *j* be treated as itself detrimental to the public interest. Indeed, I am of opinion that it is calculated to promote the public interest, by adding to public confidence in the administration of justice. Whatever the merits of the present action, there can be no

---

1   [1968] 1 All ER 874, [1968] AC 910

doubt that the numerous shareholders of Burmah suffered a grievous blow as a result of
a the transaction which is the subject of it. Whether they might have suffered worse had
the transaction not been entered into is neither here nor there. They might not
unreasonably feel a sense of grievance were the court not even to inspect the documents
privately to operate the balancing exercise which it is the court's duty to carry through.
Such considerations were in the mind of Walton J in *Tito v Waddell*[1] when he asked and
obtained the consent of counsel for the Crown to his inspection of certain documents, lest
b the Banaban Islanders might feel that they had received less than justice. In my opinion
he could and might appropriately have inspected the documents without any such
consent. Apprehension has on occasion been expressed lest the power of inspection
might be irresponsibly exercised, perhaps by one of the lower courts. As a safeguard
against this, an appeal should always be available, as indicated in *Conway v Rimmer*[2] by
Lord Reid.
c   For these reasons I am in agreement with the majority of your Lordships that this is
a proper case for the court to require the ten documents in question to be made available
for private inspection. I do not consider that the discretion to order or refuse production
of the documents was capable of being exercised soundly and with due regard to
principle in the absence of such inspection. Accordingly I see no difficulty in differing
from Foster J and the majority of the Court of Appeal.
d   Having inspected the documents, I agree with the majority of your Lordships, though
with some hesitation, that none of them contains matter of such evidential value as to
make an order for their disclosure, in all the circumstances, necessary for disposing fairly
of the case.
     It follows that I would dismiss the appeal.

e
LORD SCARMAN. My Lords, at the beginning of his long and careful argument,
counsel on behalf of the Attorney-General reminded the House that this is an
interlocutory appeal from a decision of the Court of Appeal refusing (by a majority) to
interfere with decisions reached by Foster J in the exercise of his discretion. Of course,
he was correct. But it would be wrong to infer either that the appeal lacks importance
f because it is interlocutory or that no question of law arises because on questions as to
discovery of documents the judge exercises his discretion. The truth is that the appeal
raises a question of law of great importance. Your Lordships are asked to determine the
respective spheres of the executive and the judiciary where the issue is whether
documents for which 'public interest immunity' is claimed are to be withheld from
disclosure in litigation to which they are relevant. More specifically, the House has to
g decide whether *Conway v Rimmer*[3] is definitive of the law, i e sets limits statute-wise to the
power of the court, or is an illustration on its particular facts of a broader principle of
judicial review.
     Others of your Lordships have already told the story of Burmah's disaster. Briefly,
Burmah was in appalling financial trouble at the end of 1974. The company was on the
brink of default in respect of £54,627,900 8½% unsecured loan stock. By the trust deed
h which constituted the stock, Burmah was liable to repay the whole if the trustees were
to declare that the undischarged borrowings by Burmah and its United Kingdom wholly-
owned subsidiaries exceeded the total of their share capital plus capital and revenue
reserves. Such a declaration was believed to be imminent. Some informed observers
believed that the undischarged debt already exceeded Burmah's capital and reserves.
This spectre of insolvency arose from the misfortunes, and perhaps the mistakes, of
j 1974. In order to extend its North American operations Burmah had in January and July
1974 arranged loan facilities up to $650 million with some 30 banks, mostly overseas.

1   (3rd March 1975) unreported
2   [1968] 1 All ER 874 at 914, [1968] AC 910 at 993
3   [1968] 1 All ER 874, [1968] AC 910

Burmah had drawn some $625 million on those facilities. In the event of default under any of the dollar loan agreements, or of any other indebtedness becoming prematurely *a* due by reason of default (eg under the trust deed, to which I have already referred), Burmah had to repay all the dollar loans. Burmah was also seriously at risk of default under arrangements it had made for financing the construction or chartering of tankers. The company's two financial advisers, Flemings and Barings, saw no way out of these difficulties for Burmah, unaided. And aid could only come from the market (including the big oil companies and the financial institutions of the City of London) or *b* the British government. In any negotiation for financial help Burmah had two assets of special importance: the BP stock and a substantial interest in two North Sea oilfields, 'Thistle' and 'Ninian'. Burmah owned some 20% of the ordinary stock of BP; but at the end of 1974 the market value of this stock had fallen very low, much lower, in fact, than its 'asset value'. The stock was, however, unencumbered. It was, therefore, a source of confidence to Burmah's unsecured creditors and available to Burmah in any financial *c* negotiation the company might be advised to undertake. The two oilfields were assets of great potential value, but in 1974, required heavy development expenditure.

Clearly much else was at stake besides the loss of shareholders' capital if Burmah were to be forced by insolvency into liquidation. Failure by a large British company to meet its dollar obligations and the disruptive effect of the company's failure on the exploitation of North Sea oil would be matters of national importance. Burmah's financial advisers, *d* therefore, approached the Bank of England ('the Bank'). The Bank immediately informed the government.

The litigation which gives rise to the question which the House now has to decide is concerned with the negotiations between Burmah, the Bank and the government, which began at the very end of December 1974 and ended on 23rd January 1975, when Burmah agreed to sell the BP stock to the Bank at a price of £2·30 a stock unit. It is Burmah's case *e* that the Bank, under instructions from the government, took an unconscionable advantage of Burmah's weakness by insisting on a price which, while reflecting the current market depression, was a gross undervalue, and without offering Burmah, as the Governor and Deputy Governor thought it would have been reasonable to do, a share in any profit on a resale of the stock by the Bank. All expected the market price to recover; and, indeed, its recovery began in January 1975. By July 1975 the price had risen *f* appreciably; and by July 1978 it was over £8 a unit.

There were two phases of the negotiation. The first ended with the 'December agreement' (made on 31st December 1974 and confirmed in writing by Burmah on the 3rd January 1975). The relevant terms were that the Bank would guarantee the dollar loans for 12 months and would cover the repayment of the unsecured loan stock by subscribing in cash at par a new £54 million loan stock; in consideration of this *g* assistance, Burmah was to transfer to the Bank by way of security, with full power of sale, the BP stock, and agreed to the transfer, whenever required by the government, of 51% of its interest in the oilfields of the continental shelf. Burmah also agreed to the appointment of Peat, Marwick, Mitchell & Co to report on its finances.

One obvious consequence of the December agreement was that Burmah lost the power to dispose of the BP stock as it thought fit. The stock was charged to the Bank, *h* who had full powers of sale. The power of disposal of this vital asset had, therefore, passed from Burmah to the Bank. A not so obvious, but very serious, consequence was that the agreement did nothing to prevent default under either the loan stock trust deed or the dollar loan agreements. The December agreement offered a cure after default; but it was prevention of default which alone could save Burmah. A third consequence was that the confidence of Burmah's unsecured creditors was profoundly shaken by the loss, *j* as they saw it, of the BP stock without any compensating benefit being offered to them.

The second phase of the negotiations began on 10th January 1975, by which time Barings had become aware of the dangerous implications of the December agreement for Burmah. Burmah put forward a proposal which would not commit the company to a sale of the BP stock. But the Bank, reflecting the views of the government and, in effect, *a* acting on the instructions of the government, rejected it. Cash, which was what Burmah needed to avoid default on its borrowings, was on offer only for a sale of the stock at a price determined by the government; and that price, £2·30 per unit, was very low indeed. Burmah, having lost the right to dispose of the stock without the Bank's consent and having no chance of raising money elsewhere in the time available, were in no position to resist. The government, in the revealing words of the Attorney-General's written case, 'had decided that the price to be paid for the BP Stock should be £2·30 per

b unit, the Government was not prepared to accept any profit-sharing formula and subject thereto the Government agreed to the Bank purchasing the BP Stock from Burmah'.

Burmah pleaded with the Bank. The Governor and Deputy Governor were sympathetic; but the government was adamant and the Bank was not prepared to commit itself to any terms other than those acceptable to the government. At a meeting on 22nd January 1975 the Governor and Deputy Governor said that they remained of the

c view that the suggestion of a profit-sharing arrangement was reasonable and that they had done what they could to represent this view to the government. Later the same day HM Paymaster-General told the representatives of Burmah that it was not possible for the government to improve the terms of sale.

On 23rd January 1975 Burmah accepted the terms proposed by the government and the Bank. The acceptance constituted the 'January agreement' which took the place of

d the December agreement. Burmah now agreed with the Bank (so far as relevant) that (i) the Bank would purchase the BP stock at £2·30 per unit for a cash sum of £178,980,266·10, (ii) the Bank would guarantee Burmah's dollar borrowings up to $650 million and (iii) the Bank would provide a stand-by facility of £75 million. The BP stock was transferred to the Bank on the same day. Shortly afterwards Barings wrote a letter to the Bank protesting against the terms of sale.

e A feature of the negotiations was the participation of the government. The Permanent Secretary to the Department of Energy and senior officials of the Treasury took a prominent part. When at their very end, 22nd January 1975 (Burmah then being within eight days of a catastrophic default on its obligations), Burmah protested at the terms being offered, the Deputy Governor said the Bank would not object to Burmah having direct discussions with the Paymaster-General who was handling the matter for the

f government; and later on the same day it was the Paymaster-General who in answer to Burmah's representations replied that it was not possible to improve the terms of the sale. The role of the Bank is clear: whatever the opinion of the Governor or Deputy Governor as to the fairness of the terms on offer, the Bank was not prepared to negotiate terms of sale other than those acceptable to the government. The government's attitude created the pressure (whether reasonable or not); the Bank exerted it on Burmah by

g refusing to modify the government's terms.

By a writ, issued on 6th October 1976, Burmah claimed against the Bank an order that it cause 77,817,507 ordinary stock units of £1 each of the British Petroleum Co Ltd ('the BP stock') to be transferred back to Burmah against repayment of the purchase price of £178,980,266·10. To succeed, Burmah has to make good one or more of the allegations contained in para 53 of its statement of claim. Burmah alleges that the sale of the BP

h stock to the Bank (a) was unconscionable, inequitable and unreasonable, or (b) was procured by the Bank acting in breach of its duty of fair dealing and taking an unfair and unconscionable advantage of Burmah, (c) by its terms, wrongfully purported to render nugatory Burmah's right to redeem, and (d) involved the Bank in obtaining an improper collateral advantage in connection with the taking of security.

Counsel for Burmah provided a brief but helpful analysis of the cause of action. He

j described it as one 'not yet fully developed in English law'. In its narrow formulation his case is based on, or analogous to, the mortgagor's equity of redemption: the Bank, having a charge on the BP stock, rendered Burmah's right of redemption nugatory, it is said, by forcing Burmah to sell on unreasonable terms. In its broadest formulation his case is one of 'economic duress', as developed in the case law of the United States of America. This development is said to spring from equitable principles established and recognised by the

English Courts of Chancery, and to have a common law, or Admiralty, analogue in the
law of salvage at sea. He relies on *United States v Bethlehem Steel Corpn*[1] (in particular the
concurring opinion of Murphy J[2] and the discussion of the English and American case
law in the dissenting opinion of Frankfurter J[3]).

Despite its boldness, the cause of action is to be assumed for the purpose of this appeal
to be one recognised by English law. No application has been made to strike out the
statement of claim; nor, in my opinion, could such an application succeed. Indeed, there
are indications in the modern case law that economic duress in a commercial setting may
well constitute a good cause of action: see *The Siboen*[4] (Kerr J), *North Ocean Shipping Co Ltd
v Hyundai Construction Co Ltd*[5] (Mocatta J) and the Privy Council decision, *Pao On v Lau Yiu
Long*[6].

The Bank has pleaded fully to the statement of claim, admitting much but denying
specifically the allegations of unfair pressure, unconscionability and abuse of its
bargaining power. On 21st December 1977 the Bank served on Burmah its list of
documents. Full discovery was given of all minutes or notes of meetings at which
Burmah was represented. But in Part III of Sch 1 to the list the Bank described and
enumerated 62 documents which it objected to produce on the ground that they 'belong
to classes of documents, the production of which would be injurious to the public
interest'. Burmah issued a summons for production of the 62 documents, which after
considering a certificate of objection given by the Chief Secretary to the Treasury Foster
J dismissed. On 19th January 1979 the Court of Appeal[7] (Bridge and Templeman LJJ,
Lord Denning MR dissenting) dismissed Burmah's appeal, but gave leave to appeal. The
judge and the Court of Appeal allowed the Attorney-General to intervene. In your
Lordships' House the Attorney-General has been made a party to the appeal. In the event
the case against production of the documents has been argued at all stages by counsel for
the Attorney-General, the Bank being content to abide by whatever order is ultimately
made.

In his certificate, dated 18th October 1977, the Chief Secretary to the Treasury
recognises that the 62 documents, disclosure of which Burmah seeks, relate to the
matters in question in this action. He expresses the opinion that their production would
be injurious to the public interest. The reason given for his opinion is that it is necessary
for the proper functioning of the public service that production of the documents should
be withheld. His objection is what has become known as a 'class' objection. The Chief
Secretary grounds his opinion not on the contents but on the class of the documents. He
places them in three classes: categories A, B and C. The documents in categories A and
B relate to the formulation of government policy. Category C is a class of documents
which refer to commercial or financial information communicated by businessmen in
confidence to Ministers or senior officials of the government or to the Bank in its capacity
as adviser to the government. None of the 62 documents, he says, can be called
'routine'. He makes clear that, if it were sought to give oral evidence of the contents of
any of the documents, the government would object.

The appeal, as it turns out, concerns only categories A and B. In its written case
Burmah concedes that of the 62 listed documents only 18 are likely to contain evidence
highly material to the issues in the action. These 18 documents are in categories A and
B, which relate to the formulation of government policy. During argument it became
clear that only ten of the 18 could contain information likely to assist on the critical issue:
the Bank's conduct of the negotiations of the terms of sale of the BP stock in the sensitive
areas of price and a possible profit-sharing formula. The question for the House is,

1   (1942) 315 US 289
2   315 US 289 at 311
3   315 US 289 at 325
4   [1976] 1 Lloyd's Rep 293
5   [1978] 3 All ER 1170
6   Page 65, ante
7   [1979] 2 All ER 461, [1979] 1 WLR 473

therefore, whether these ten documents, which cover discussions and communications
a between the Bank and the government during the second phase of the negotiations, ie
the negotiation of the January agreement, are to be withheld from production.

Although in the High Court discovery of documents is automatic in most civil
litigation, this is no more than a convenient practice ordered and regulated by rules of
court: see RSC Ord 24, and the recent decision of this House in *Science Research Council v
Nassé*[1]. Discovery of documents remains, ultimately, a matter for the discretion of the
b court. It is a discretion governed by two general rules of law. The first is that discovery
is not to be ordered unless necessary for fairly disposing of the case or for saving costs:
RSC Ord 24.

The second is that only documents in a party's possession and control which relate to
the matters in issue are required to be disclosed, but all such documents, subject to
certain exceptions, are to be disclosed, whether or not admissible in evidence. Public
c interest immunity is, of course, an exception. The case law has given an extended
meaning to the qualifying clause 'which relate to the matters in issue'. It embraces not
only documents directly relevant but also documents which may well lead to a relevant
train of enquiry: see *Compagnie Financière Commerciale du Pacifique v Peruvian Guano Co*[2].
This extended meaning is a vital part of the law of discovery, enabling justice to be done
where one party knows the facts and possesses the documents and the other does not.

d Foster J based his decision on the view which he formed that production of the
documents for which immunity is claimed would not materially assist Burmah's case at
trial. He was, I think, right, when faced with the public interest immunity objection to
disclosure, to ask himself whether production could be said to be necessary for fairly
disposing of the case. For, if it be shown that production was not necessary, it becomes
unnecessary to balance the interest of justice against the interest of the public service to
e which the Minister refers in his certificate. But the judge formed his view without
himself inspecting the documents. It is said, and this view commended itself to the
majority of the Court of Appeal, that the Bank has given very full discovery of the
documents directly relevant to the critical issue in the action, namely the conduct by the
Bank of the negotiations with Burmah, that Burmah knows as much about this issue as
does the Bank, and that it can be fully investigated and decided on the documents
f disclosed and the evidence available to Burmah without recourse to documents noting or
recording the private discussions between the Bank and the government. On this view,
Burmah's attempt to see these documents is no more than a fishing expedition.

I totally reject this view of the case. First, as a matter of law, the documents for which
immunity is claimed relate to the issues in the action and, according to the *Peruvian
Guano*[2] formulation, may well assist towards a fair disposal of the case. It is unthinkable
g that in the absence of a public immunity objection and without a judicial inspection of
the documents disclosure would have been refused. Secondly, common sense must be
allowed to creep into the picture. Burmah's case is not merely that the Bank exerted
pressure: it is that the Bank acted unreasonably, abusing its power and taking an
unconscionable advantage of the weakness of Burmah. On these questions the withheld
documents may be very revealing. This is not 'pure speculation'. The government was
h creating the pressure; the Bank was exerting it on the government's instructions. Is a
court to assume that such documents will not assist towards an understanding of the
nature of the pressure exerted? The assumption seems to me as unreal as the proverbial
folly of attempting to understand Hamlet without reference to his position as the Prince
of Denmark. I do not understand how a court could properly reach the judge's
conclusion without inspecting the documents; and this he refused to do. The judge in
j my opinion wrongly exercised his discretion when he refused to inspect unless public
policy (of which public interest immunity is a manifestation) required him to refuse.

1 Page 673, ante
2 (1882) 11 QBD 55

It becomes necessary, therefore, to analyse closely the public interest immunity objection made by the Minister and to determine the correct approach of the court to a situation in which there may be a clash of two interests, that of the public service and that of justice.

In *Conway v Rimmer*[1] this House had to consider two questions. They were formulated by Lord Reid[2] in these terms:

'... first, whether the court is to have any right to question the finality of a Minister's certificate and, secondly, if it has such a right, how and in what circumstances that right is to be exercised and made effective.'

The House answered the first question, but did not, in my judgment, provide, nor was it required to provide, a complete answer to the second.

As I read the speeches in *Conway v Rimmer*[1] the House answered the first question by establishing the principle of judicial review. The Minister's certificate is not final. The immunity is a rule of law; its scope is a question of law; and its applicability to the facts of a particular case is for the court, not the Minister, to determine. The statement of Viscount Kilmuir LC of 6th June 1956 (all that is relevant is quoted in *Conway v Rimmer*[3]) that 'the Minister's certificate on affidavit setting out the ground of the claim must in England be accepted by the court' is no longer a correct statement of the law. Whether *Conway v Rimmer*[1] be seen as a development of or a departure from previous English case law is a matter of no importance. What is important is that it aligned English law with the law of Scotland and of the Commonwealth. It is the heir apparent not of *Duncan v Cammell Laird & Co*[4] but of *Robinson v State of South Australia (No 2)*[5] and of *Glasgow Corpn v Central Land Board*[6].

Having established the principle of judicial review, the House had in *Conway v Rimmer*[1] a simple case on the facts to decide. The question was whether routine reports, albeit of a confidential character, on a former probationary police constable should in the interests of justice be disclosed in an action brought by him against his former superintendent in which he claimed damages for alleged malicious prosecution. There was a public interest in the confidentiality of such reports, but the Home Secretary, in his affidavit objecting to production on the ground of injury to the public interest, did not go so far as to say that it was necessary for the proper functioning of the public service to withhold production. On the other hand, the reports might be of critical importance in the litigation. Granted the existence of judicial review, here was a justiciable issue of no great difficulty. The House decided itself to inspect the documents, and, having done so, ordered production.

In reaching its decision the House did indicate what it considered to be the correct approach to the clash of interests which arises whenever there is a question of public interest immunity. The approach is to be found stated in two passages of Lord Reid's speech[7]. The essence of the matter is a weighing, on balance, of the two public interests, that of the nation or the public service in non-disclosure and that of justice in the production of the documents. A good working, but not logically perfect, distinction is recognised between the contents and the classes of documents. If a Minister of the Crown asserts that to disclose the contents of a document would, or might, do the nation or the public service a grave injury, the court will be slow to question his opinion or to allow any interest, even that of justice, to prevail over it. Unless there can be shown to exist some factor suggesting either a lack of good faith (which is not likely) or an error of

---

1 [1968] 1 All ER 874, [1968] AC 910
2 [1968] 1 All ER 874 at 882, [1968] AC 910 at 943
3 [1968] AC 910 at 922
4 [1942] 1 All ER 587, [1942] AC 624
5 [1931] AC 704, [1931] All ER Rep 333
6 1956 SC (HL) 1
7 [1968] 1 All ER 874 at 880, 888, [1968] AC 910 at 940, 952

_a_ judgment or an error of law on the Minister's part, the court should not (the House held) even go so far as itself to inspect the document. In this sense, the Minister's assertion may be said to be conclusive. It is, however, for the judge to determine whether the Minister's opinion is to be treated as conclusive. I do not understand the House to have denied that even in 'contents' cases the court retains its power to inspect or to balance the injury to the public service against the risk of injustice, before reaching its decision.

_b_ In 'class' cases the House clearly considered the Minister's certificate to be more likely to be open to challenge. Undoubtedly, however, the House thought that there were certain classes of documents which ought not to be disclosed however harmless the disclosure of their contents might be, and however important their disclosure might be in the interests of justice. Cabinet minutes were cited as an example. But the point did not arise for decision. For the documents in _Conway v Rimmer_[1], though confidential, were 'routine', in no way concerned with the inner working of the government at a high
_c_ level; and their production might well be indispensable to the doing of justice in the litigation.

The point does arise in the present case. The documents are 'high level'. They are concerned with the formulation of policy. They are part of the inner working of the government machine. They contain information which the court knows does relate to matters in issue in the action, and which may, on inspection, prove to be highly
_d_ material. In such circumstances the Minister may well be right in his view that the public service would be injured by disclosure. But is the court bound by his view that it is _necessary_ for the proper functioning of the public service that they be withheld from production? And, if non-disclosure is necessary for that purpose, is the court bound to hold that the interest in the proper functioning of the public service is to prevail over the requirements of justice?

_e_ If the answer to these two questions is to be in the affirmative as Lord Reid appears to suggest in _Conway v Rimmer_[1], I think the law reverts to the statement of Viscount Kilmuir LC. A properly-drawn Minister's certificate, which is a bona fide expression of his opinion, becomes final. But the advance made in the law by _Conway v Rimmer_[1] was that the certificate is not final. I think, therefore, that it would now be inconsistent with principle to hold that the court may not, even in a case like the present, review the
_f_ certificate and balance the public interest of government to which alone it refers, against the public interest of justice, which is the concern of the court.

I do not therefore accept that there are any classes of documents which, however harmless their contents and however strong the requirement of justice, may never be disclosed until they are only of historical interest. In this respect I think there may well be a difference between a 'class' objection and a 'contents' objection, though the residual
_g_ power to inspect and to order disclosure must remain in both instances. A Cabinet minute, it is said, must be withheld from production. Documents relating to the formulation of policy at a high level are also to be withheld. But is the secrecy of the 'inner workings of the government machine' so vital a public interest that it must prevail over even the most imperative demands of justice? If the contents of a document concern the national safety, affect diplomatic relations or relate to some state secret of
_h_ high importance, I can understand an affirmative answer. But if they do not (and it is not claimed in this case that they do), what is so important about secret government that it must be protected even at the price of injustice in our courts?

The reasons given for protecting the secrecy of government at the level of policy-making are two. The first is the need for candour in the advice offered to Ministers; the second is that disclosure 'would create or fan ill-informed or captious public or political
_j_ criticism'. Lord Reid in _Conway v Rimmer_[2] thought the second 'the most important reason'. Indeed, he was inclined to discount the candour argument.

---

1   [1968] 1 All ER 874, [1968] AC 910
2   [1968] 1 All ER 874 at 888, [1968] AC 910 at 952

I think both reasons are factors legitimately to be put into the balance which has to be struck between the public interest in the proper functioning of the public service (ie the *a* executive arm of government) and the public interest in the administration of justice. Sometimes the public service reasons will be decisive of the issue; but they should never prevent the court from weighing them against the injury which would be suffered in the administration of justice if the document was not to be disclosed. And the likely injury to the cause of justice must also be assessed and weighed. Its weight will vary according to the nature of the proceedings in which disclosure is sought, the relevance of the *b* documents and the degree of likelihood that the document will be of importance in the litigation. In striking the balance, the court may always, if it thinks it necessary, itself inspect the documents.

Inspection by the court is, I accept, a power to be exercised only if the court is in doubt, after considering the certificate, the issues in the case and the relevance of the documents whose disclosure is sought. Where documents are relevant (as in this case they are), I *c* would think a pure 'class' objection would by itself seldom quieten judicial doubts, particularly if, as here, a substantial case can be made for saying that disclosure is needed in the interest of justice.

I am fortified in the opinion which I have expressed by the trend towards inspection and disclosure to be found both in the United States and in Commonwealth countries. Of course, the United States have a written constitution and a Bill of Rights. Nevertheless *d* both derive from the common law and British political philosophy. Mutatis mutandis, I would adopt the principle accepted by the Supreme Court in *Nixon v USA*[1] which is summarised as follows:

'Neither the doctrine of separation of powers, nor the need for confidentiality of high level communications, without more, can sustain an absolute unqualified presidential privilege of immunity from judicial process under all circumstances; *e* although the President's need for complete candor and objectivity from advisers calls for great deference from the courts, nevertheless when the privilege depends solely on the broad, undifferentiated claim of public interest in the confidentiality of such conversations, a confrontation with other values arises; absent a claim of need to protect military, diplomatic or sensitive national security secrets, it is difficult to accept the argument that even the very important interest in *f* confidentiality of Presidential communications is significantly diminished by production of such material for in camera inspection with all the protection that a United States District Court will be obliged to provide.'

In Australia the High Court had to consider the problem in a recent case where the facts were, admittedly, exceptional. In *Sankey v Whitlam*[2] the plaintiff sought declarations *g* that certain papers and documents, to which the magistrate in criminal proceedings instituted by the plaintiff against the defendants had accorded privilege, should be produced. The offences alleged against Mr Whitlam, a former Prime Minister, and others were serious: conspiracies to act unlawfully in the conduct of official business. Gibbs ACJ dealt with the issue of Crown privilege as follows[3]:

'For these reasons I consider that although there is a class of documents whose *h* members are entitled to protection from disclosure irrespective of their contents, the protection is not absolute, and it does not endure for ever. The fundamental and governing principle is that documents in the class may be withheld from production only when this is necessary in the public interest. In a particular case the court must balance the general desirability that documents of that kind should not be disclosed against the need to produce them in the interests of justice. The court will of course *j*

---

1   (1975) 418 US 683, summarised in 41 L Ed 2d at 1046
2   (1978) 21 ALR 505
3   21 ALR 505 at 529–530

a   examine the question with especial care, giving full weight to the reasons for preserving the secrecy of documents of this class, but it will not treat all such documents as entitled to the same measure of protection—the extent of protection required will depend to some extent on the general subject matter with which the documents are concerned. If a strong case has been made out for the production of the documents, and the court concludes that their disclosure would not really be detrimental to the public interest, an order for production will be made. In view of

b   the danger to which the indiscriminate disclosure of documents of this class might give rise, it is desirable that the government concerned, Commonwealth or State, should have an opportunity to intervene and be heard before any order for disclosure is made. Moreover, no such order should be enforced until the government concerned has had an opportunity to appeal against it, or test its correctness by some other process, if it wishes to do so (cf *Conway v Rimmer*[1]).'

c   Both *Nixon's* case[2] and *Sankey v Whitlam*[3] are far closer to the Scottish and Commonwealth stream of authority than to the English. In the *Glasgow Corpn* case[4] Lord Simonds said that 'there always has been and is now in the law of Scotland an inherent power of the court to override the Crown's objection to produce documents on the ground that it would injure the public interest to do so'.

d   In *Robinson v State of South Australia (No 2)*[5] the Privy Council reminded the Supreme Court of South Australia of the existence of this power. The power must be exercised judicially, and all due weight must be given to the objections of the Crown; that is all.

Something was made in argument about the risk to the nation or the public service of an error at first instance. Injury to the public interest, perhaps even very serious injury, could be done by production of documents which should be immune from disclosure before an appellate court could correct the error. This risk is inherent in the principle of

e   judicial review. The House in *Conway v Rimmer*[6] recognised its existence, but, nevertheless, established the principle as part of our law. Gibbs ACJ also mentioned it in *Sankey v Whitlam*[3]. I would respectfully agree with Lord Reid's observations on the point in *Conway v Rimmer*[7]: 'It is important that the Minister should have a right to appeal before the document is produced.'

f   In cases where the Crown is not a party, as in the present case, the court should ensure that the Attorney-General has the opportunity to intervene before disclosure is ordered.

For these reasons I was one of a majority of your Lordships who thought it necessary to inspect the ten documents. Having done so, I have no doubt that they are relevant and, but for the immunity claim, would have to be disclosed, but their significance is not such as to override the public service objections to their production. Burmah will not suffer injustice by their non-disclosure, while their disclosure would be, in the opinion

g   of the responsible Minister, injurious to the public service. I would, therefore, dismiss the appeal.

By way of tail-piece I mention the strange affair of the edited documents. The Bank, claiming immunity for part, but not the whole, of certain documents, covered up the parts to the disclosure of which it objected. Burmah's advisers were able to penetrate the cover and read their contents. They did not tell their client what they had seen. Should

h   they now be disclosed, the cover having been blown? The issue evaporated because it became clear in argument that Burmah were ultimately fighting to see only the ten documents, which a majority of your Lordships has now inspected. But the accident of

j 1 [1968] 1 All ER 874 at 888–889, [1968] AC 910 at 953
    2 (1975) 418 US 683
    3 (1978) 21 ALR 505
    4 1956 SC (HL) 1 at 11
    5 [1931] AC 704, [1931] All ER Rep 333
    6 [1968] 1 All ER 874, [1968] AC 910
    7 [1968] 1 All ER 874 at 889, [1968] AC 910 at 953

an insufficient cover cannot weaken the objection of public interest immunity. Even if
the parties allow discovery, the court must take the objection of its own motion; and this *a*
may have to be done even before the Crown intervenes. There was a difference of
opinion as to the importance of the covered up parts. But in view of the course taken by
the parties in argument in this House the question does not arise. Burmah's advisers
acted with propriety in the handling of the incident.

Appeal dismissed.   *b*

Solicitors: *Allen & Overy* (for Burmah); *Freshfields* (for the Bank); *Treasury Solicitor.*

Mary Rose Plummer   Barrister.

Bocardo SA v S & M Hotels Ltd and another

COURT OF APPEAL, CIVIL DIVISION
MEGAW, LAWTON AND BROWNE LJJ
9th, 10th, 11th, 31st JULY 1979

Landlord and tenant – Covenant against assignment without consent – Consent not to be unreasonably withheld – Express provision in lease for consent not to be unreasonably withheld – Covenant that tenant, if wishing to assign, should first offer to surrender lease – Validity of covenant – Landlord and Tenant Act 1927, s 19(1).

The first defendants, a company, were the tenants of a flat under a lease granted to them by the predecessors in title of the plaintiffs ('the landlords') for a term of six years from 25th December 1973. The second defendant was a director of the company and occupied the flat as their sub-tenant or licensee. The lease contained in cl 2(j) a covenant by the tenant 'Not to assign the whole of the flat without the previous consent in writing of the Landlord such consent not to be unreasonably withheld in the case of a respectable and responsible assignee . . .' The covenant was subject to a proviso that if the tenant desired to assign the whole of the flat he 'shall first by irrevocable notice in writing to the Landlord offer to surrender this lease by deed absolutely without any consideration . . . and the Landlord may within twenty-one days of the service of such notice upon it accept such offer', and, further, that if the tenant assigned without first making the offer to surrender 'he shall be deemed to have made it and the Landlord shall be entitled to accept it within seven days of becoming aware of the said assignment or parting with possession . . .' The lease also included a covenant entitling the landlord to re-enter thus determining the lease if the tenant entered into liquidation. On 16th May 1977 a winding-up order of the tenant company was made and the landlords brought proceedings for possession claiming forfeiture of the lease. The tenants applied for relief against forfeiture and for a declaration that, by virtue of s 19(1)[a] of the Landlord and Tenant Act 1927, the proviso to cl 2(j) was void and that in the event of the tenants applying to the landlords for a licence to assign or underlet the flat to a respectable and responsible person the landlords were not entitled to refuse such licence by reason only that the tenants had not first offered to surrender the lease. The master refused the tenants relief from forfeiture or the declaration sought and on appeal his decision was upheld by the judge. The tenants appealed. They conceded that if the clause was valid they could not obtain relief against forfeiture.

Held – Since s 19(1) of the 1927 Act did not purport to prevent or limit the freedom of contract of the parties to agree in a lease to forbid altogether assignments by the tenant, but merely provided that where by the terms of the lease the landlord's consent was required to an assignment a term was to be implied that his consent was not to be unreasonably withheld, there were no reasons of policy for invalidating a covenant which in effect prohibited assignment unless a condition precedent, ie the offer and refusal of a surrender, had been fulfilled, particularly since the form of such a covenant had stood and been acted on for more than 20 years and moreover had been approved by the High Court of Australia. It followed therefore that the proviso to cl 2(j) of the lease was valid and the appeal would be dismissed (see p 741 *b d* to *f*, p 743 *c* to *h*, p 745 *b c g h* and p 746 *a b*, post).

Adler v Upper Grosvenor Street Investment Ltd [1957] 1 All ER 229 applied.
Creer v P & O Lines of Australia Pty Ltd (1971) 45 ALJR 697 adopted.

---

a   Section 19(1), so far as material, is set out at p 740 *c*, post

Notes

For unreasonable withholding of consent by a landlord to assignment of a lease, see 23   *a*
Halsbury's Laws (3rd Edn) 633, para 1338, and for cases on the subject, see 31(2) Digest
(Reissue) 693–698, 5673–5702.

For the Landlord and Tenant Act 1927, s 19, see 18 Halsbury's Statutes (3rd Edn) 464.

Cases referred to in judgments

Adler v Upper Grosvenor Street Investment Ltd [1957] 1 All ER 229, [1957] 1 WLR 227,   *b*
 31(2) Digest (Reissue) 689, 5659.

Bates v Donaldson [1896] 2 QB 241, [1895–9] All ER Rep 170, 65 LJQB 578, 74 LT 751,
 60 JP 596, CA, 31(2) Digest (Reissue) 693, 5680.

Creer v P & O Lines of Australia Pty Ltd (1971) 45 ALJR 697, [1972] ALR 226, H Ct of
 Aust.

Gibbs and Houlder Bros & Co Ltd's Lease, Re, Houlder Bros & Co Ltd v Gibbs [1925] 1 Ch 575,   *c*
 [1925] All ER Rep 128, 94 LJ Ch 312, 133 LT 322, CA, 31(2) Digest (Reissue) 694,
 5682.

Greene v Church Commissioners for England [1974] 3 All ER 609, [1974] Ch 467, [1974] 3
 WLR 349, 29 P & CR 285, CA, Digest (Cont Vol D) 754, 925ab.

Kirkness (Inspector of Taxes) v John Hudson & Co Ltd [1955] 2 All ER 345, [1955] AC 696,
 [1955] 2 WLR 1135, [1955] TR 145, 34 ATC 142, 48 R & IT 352, sub nom *John Hudson*   *d*
 & Co Ltd v Kirkness, 36 Tax Cas 28, HL, 44 Digest (Repl) 255, 801.

Property and Bloodstock Ltd v Emerton, Bush v Property and Bloodstock Ltd [1967] 3 All ER
 321, [1968] Ch 94, [1967] 3 WLR 973, CA, Digest (Cont Vol C) 718, 2598a.

Smith's Lease, Re, Smith v Richards [1951] 1 All ER 346, 31(2) Digest (Reissue) 696, 5691.

Woolworth (FW) & Co Ltd v Lambert [1936] 2 All ER 1523, [1937] Ch 37, 106 LJ Ch 15,
 155 LT 236, CA, 31(1) Digest (Reissue) 404, 3224.   *e*

Cases also cited

Balfour v Kensington Gardens Mansions Ltd (1932) 49 TLR 29.

Creery v Summersell and Flowerdew & Co Ltd, Flowerdew & Co Ltd v Summersell (Third   *f*
 Party) [1949] Ch 751.

Joseph v Joseph [1966] 3 All ER 486, [1967] Ch 78, CA.

Plymouth Corpn v Harvey [1971] 1 All ER 623, [1971] 1 WLR 549.

West Layton Ltd v Ford [1979] 2 All ER 657, [1979] 3 WLR 14, CA.

                          g

Appeal

The first defendants, S & M Hotels Ltd ('the tenants'), appealed against an order made by
Chapman J in chambers on 17th May 1978 dismissing their appeal against an order made
by Master Waldman on 17th March 1978 whereby he refused their application for relief
against forfeiture of a lease of a flat which the plaintiffs, Bocardo SA ('the landlords'), were
seeking to enforce and upheld the validity of a clause in the lease which required the   *h*
tenants to make an offer to surrender the lease to the landlords in the event of the tenants
desiring to assign the lease. The event which gave rise to the forfeiture thus entitling the
landlord to re-enter and determine the lease occurred on 16th May 1977 when an order
winding up the tenant company was made. The liquidator of the company wished to
assign the lease to the second defendant, Sidney Winton, a director of the company and
guarantor of the company's obligations under the lease who occupied the flat as their sub-   *j*
tenant or licensee. The second defendant did not appeal. The facts are set out in the
judgment of Megaw LJ.

Benjamin Levy for the tenants.
Derek Wood QC and *Jonathan Gaunt* for the landlords.

Cur adv vult

a

31st July. The following judgments were read.

MEGAW LJ. This is an appeal from an order of Chapman J in chambers, dismissing an appeal from an order of Master Waldman. The master and the judge refused to order that the first defendants, S & M Hotels Ltd ('the tenants'), should be relieved against

b forfeiture of a lease, which forfeiture the plaintiffs, Bocardo SA ('the landlords'), who are a Liechtenstein company, were seeking to enforce. The judge, as I understand it, and this is not a criticism of him, gave no reasons except that he regarded the case as indistinguishable from *Adler v Upper Grosvenor Street Investment Ltd*[1]. That was a decision of Hilbery J. Chapman J saw no reason why he should not follow that decision. Of course, the decision was not binding on him or on us. But its persuasive authority has

c been greatly increased by the fact that it has been approved and followed by the High Court of Australia[2], in a case arising on a New South Wales enactment which, so far as is relevant for this purpose, is in identical terms with s 19(1) of the Landlord and Tenant Act 1927. Hilbery J's decision was concerned with s 19(1). The present case depends on s 19(1).

The facts, so far as they are relevant for this appeal, are short and simple and not in

d dispute. The issue of law, once one has perused s 19(1) of the 1927 Act and struggled through the verbosity of cl 2(j) of the lease in the present case, is also capable of being very shortly stated. The answer is not simple, because each of the two answers, contradictory of one another, suggested respectively by the opposing parties, can be criticised, and has been criticised by counsel, as being inconsistent with common sense or the reasoning of decided cases. Yet we have to choose between the two suggested answers.

e First, the facts. The landlords were the owners of flat 48, 60 Park Lane, Mayfair (I dare say they own other property as well). They are assignees from the original lessors of the relevant lease. The tenants are (subject to the forfeiture now in question) tenants of flat 48, under a lease for a term of six years from 25th December 1973. The lease included a covenant entitling the landlords to re-enter, thus determining the lease, if the tenants should enter into liquidation. On 16th May 1977 a winding-up order of the tenant

f company was made. A notice under s 146 of the Law of Property Act 1925 was served on the tenants on 25th June. On 18th July the landlords issued a writ claiming possession. On 5th August the tenants made application for relief against forfeiture. They also, by a later amendment suggested by Master Waldman, asked, both in their application and in a counterclaim, for a declaration that a certain portion of the lease, contained in cl 2(j) thereof, was void. It is the issue raised as to that declaration which is

g the issue in this appeal.

Mr Sidney Winton, who was named as the second defendant in the action, is, in theory, not concerned in this appeal. In reality, he is intimately concerned; for, if this appeal is decided against the tenants, Mr Winton will lose any right to continue in occupation of flat 48, where he has been living for many years. He was a director of the tenant company and occupied the flat as their sub-tenant or licensee. The lease is not

h within the Rent Act. Mr Winton was made a defendant because he was a guarantor of the tenant company's obligations under the lease. No question, however, arises in this appeal as to any failure or inability to pay the proper rent, whatever it may be. (There are other proceedings, of no relevance to the issue in this appeal, as to the proper amount of the rent.)

It is agreed between the parties that, if the tenants fail in their attack on the legal

j validity of certain of the provisions of cl 2(j) of the lease, then they cannot obtain relief against forfeiture. If, on the other hand, they are right in their submission that those provisions are invalid because of s 19(1) of the Landlord and Tenant Act 1927, and cases

---

1   [1957] 1 All ER 229, [1957] 1 WLR 227
2   In *Creer v P & O Lines of Australia Pty Ltd* (1971) 45 ALJR 697

decided with regard thereto, then the landlords would still be entitled to consider whether it would be reasonable for them to refuse consent to the assignment by the *a* tenants of the remainder of the lease to Mr Winton. If the landlords were to refuse consent, the tenants could then have the question of reasonableness determined by the courts. So, in one sense, this appeal is on a preliminary issue; but there seems to me to be no good reason why we should refuse to decide the preliminary issue. It is, I think, wrongly listed as a final appeal. But that does not now matter. The issue, as I say, depends on the provisions of s 19(1) of the Landlord and Tenant Act 1927 and their *b* application to the terms set out in cl 2(j) of the lease.

I shall set out the relevant words of s 19(1). I should however mention that, while the present case is concerned with assignment, the subsection applies also to 'underletting, charging or parting with possession'. Section 19(1) provides:

'In all leases . . . containing a covenant condition or agreement against assigning . . . demised premises . . . without licence or consent, such covenant condition or *c* agreement shall, notwithstanding any express provision to the contrary, be deemed to be subject—(*a*) to a proviso to the effect that such licence or consent is not to be unreasonably withheld . . .'

It is better that, despite its length, I should set out cl 2(j) of the lease in full. It reads:

'(i) Not to assign part only of the flat or charge or underlet or take in paying guests *d* or share or (subject to the provisions of paragraph (ii) of this sub-clause) part with possession of the whole or any part of the flat

'(ii) Not to assign the whole of the flat without the previous consent in writing of the Landlord such consent not to be unreasonably withheld in the case of a respectable and responsible assignee but the Landlord shall not be required to consent to an assignment to a Limited Company unless two directors thereof (being *e* persons acceptable to the Landlord in its absolute discretion) join in the licence or the assignment as sureties for the company and jointly and severally covenant with the Landlord to pay the rents reserved by and other sums of money made payable by this Lease and any damages accruing to the Landlord by reason of the failure of the company to observe and perform the Tenant's covenants and conditions herein contained *f*

'PROVIDED ALWAYS that every licence for an assignment relating to the flat shall if required by the Landlord contain a covenant by the assignee directly with the Landlord to observe and perform the covenants and conditions in this Lease contained AND FURTHER PROVIDED ALWAYS that if the Tenant desires to assign the whole of the flat as aforesaid he shall first by irrevocable notice in writing to the Landlord offer to surrender this Lease by deed absolutely without any consideration *g* on the next subsequent quarter day or if that be within twenty-eight days of the said notice then upon the second subsequent quarter day (such surrender to be prepared by the Landlord's Solicitors at the Tenant's expense) and the Landlord may within twenty-one days of the service of such notice upon it accept such offer such acceptance to be in writing and without prejudice to all rights and remedies of the Landlord in respect of rent or breach of covenants If the said offer is not accepted *h* by the Landlord or on its behalf within the said twenty-one days it shall be deemed to have been rejected and if the Tenant assigns or parts with possession of the flat without first making the said offer to surrender he shall be deemed to have made it and the Landlord shall be entitled to accept it within seven days of becoming aware of the said assignment or parting with possession in breach of this covenant.'

The only other provision of the lease to which I need refer is cl 6, which entitles the *j* tenants, on one month's notice, to terminate the lease on 24th December 1976, that is, half-way through the term provided in the habendum. No corresponding right of shortening the habendum term at their will is given to the landlords.

We have had interesting and elaborate argument by counsel on either side, analysing

s 19(1), with cross-references to sub-ss (2) and (3) and to other statutory provisions
a including s 127 of the Rent Act 1977; analysing in detail the words of cl 2(j); and
discussing numerous decided cases, before and after 1927. I hope that it will not be
regarded as being in any way disrespectful of those powerfully reasoned submissions if
I do not specifically set them all out in expressing my conclusion.

What was s 19(1) of the 1927 Act intended to achieve? I think, in the end, that it must
be taken to have had a very limited objective. Apart from legislation, a landlord and a
b tenant had freedom of contract, in agreeing the terms of their lease, to permit or to limit
or to abrogate the right of either or both of them to assign their respective interests.
Section 19(1) did not purport to destroy that freedom of contract of the parties to agree
to forbid assignment by the tenant. That proposition is accepted by both parties before
us, though counsel were unable to identify any decided case to that effect, such as Hilbery
J appears to have had in mind in his judgment in *Adler's* case[1], when he says: 'It is clear
c and has been decided . . .' Neither of the parties before us asks us to give effect to the
doubts on that point expressed by Danckwerts LJ in *Property and Bloodstock Ltd v
Emerton*[2]. It is hard to see how the words of s 19(1), 'In all leases . . . containing a covenant
. . . against assigning . . . demised premises . . . without licence or consent', could fairly
be construed as applying to leases which contain a simple covenant against assigning,
with no reference whatever to 'without licence or consent'. I do not pursue that question
d because it is accepted before us that s 19(1) has no application where there is a prohibition
of assignment.

It follows that the deemed proviso, 'such consent is not to be unreasonably withheld',
applies only if and to the extent that the covenant or agreement in the lease, by its terms,
provides for assignment with consent. Such a provision would, in strict law, be
meaningless or ineffective, unless it were to have implied in it some such term as 'such
e consent not to be unreasonably withheld'. For if the landlord was entitled to refuse
consent at his own entirely unrestricted discretion, the provision for assignment with
consent would add nothing to, and subtract nothing from, the effect in law of the
contract as it would be without those words being included. For a contracting party is
entirely free to agree to a variation of the contract at the request of the other party. That
applies equally where, as here, the variation of the contract would constitute a novation.
f It seems to me to follow that the effect of s 19(1) of the 1927 Act, on its true analysis, was
merely to make statutory an implied term which must already have been implied, if the
express words were to have any sensible purpose.

The nature of the implied term has in some degree been expounded by decisions of the
courts subsequent to the 1927 Act. Such cases as *Re Smith's Lease, Smith v Richards*[3], a
decision of Roxburgh J, hold that as a result of s 19(1) the parties cannot by the terms of
g their contract abrogate the right and duty of the court, in the event of a dispute as to the
reasonableness of the withholding of consent where consent is required by the terms of
the lease, to decide by an objective standard whether or not the refusal is reasonable.
Thus, if the parties by their contract purport to say that in such and such circumstances
the landlord may withhold his consent, that term of the contract is invalid and is to be
disregarded. The court itself decides whether in the circumstances which actually existed
h the refusal of consent is reasonable.

In *Re Smith's Lease*[3] the provision of the contract which Roxburgh J held to be invalid
in the light of s 19(1) was a term which provided expressly that a refusal of consent 'shall
not be deemed to be an unreasonable withholding of consent . . .' and then the clause
went on to provide, as not being unreasonable, an elaborate formulation of a transaction
in which the landlord, when he gave his refusal, offered to the tenant to accept surrender
j of the tenancy. If that decision be right, the distinction between it and the present case

---

1   [1957] 1 WLR 227 at 230; cf [1957] 1 All ER 229 at 231
2   [1967] 3 All ER 321 at 330, [1968] Ch 94 at 119–120
3   [1951] 1 All ER 346

depends, not in any way on the realities of what would be achieved by the respective provisions of the leases, but simply on the fact that a different verbal formula is used. *a* That is not a satisfactory distinction.

After the decision in *Re Smith's Lease*[1], a different formula was evolved which it was hoped, at least by those who evolved it, would produce a different legal result. That new formula was tested in *Adler's* case[2], and Hilbery J held, distinguishing *Re Smith's Lease*[1], that the new formula achieved its object. Although the wording is in various respects different, there is, in my view, no material difference from the point of view of legal *b* effect, between the *Adler*[2] formula and the formula used in the present lease, in cl 2(j)(ii) and the second of the two provisos. If anything, the *Adler*[2] formula was more vulnerable than the present formula, because, after the words 'such consent', it contained the parenthesis which the opening words of cl 2(j)(ii) do not contain, '(subject as hereinafter provided)'. The *Adler*[2] formula avoided the inclusion of any provision as to deeming anything not to be unreasonable. It stipulated, by a proviso, that before the tenant *c* applied for consent to assign (literally, it said before he 'desired' to assign), he should make an offer to the landlord to surrender the lease. If the offer of surrender were accepted, the question of consent to assignment would not arise. If it were refused, then the tenant would, if he wished, make his application to assign; and, if the landlord were to refuse to consent, the tenant could invite the court to apply the objective test of reasonableness under s 19(1) of the 1927 Act. *d*

As I have said, the distinction between the *Adler*[2] formula and *Re Smith's Lease*[1] formula is semantic. The practical result is the same. If the latter is not permissible or effective in the light of s 19(1), why should the former escape the ban?

On the other hand, if one is to assume, as for the reasons which I have given it seems to me right for us to assume, that s 19(1) does not prevent or limit freedom of contract to ban assignments altogether by agreement in the lease, why should the subsection be *e* treated as having the effect of preventing, or limiting freedom of contract to ban, assignments during a part of the lease? Counsel for the landlords, I think rightly, submitted that the courts could not treat s 19(1) as invalidating a contractual proviso that no assignment should be made, that no question of assignment by consent should arise, during, say, the first, or the last, seven years of a 14 year lease. Why, then, as a matter of policy or practical sense or logic should the courts hold that s 19(1) invalidates a proviso *f* that, before the tenant's right of assignment with consent shall arise, a condition precedent shall be fulfilled, namely, the tenant's obligation first to offer a surrender? If by agreement an assignment by consent can be precluded altogether, what logical reason or policy can be invoked to preclude a limited right of the tenant to assign with consent; the limitation being that the landlord, if he wishes, can insist on a surrender?

In *Adler's* case[2], as I have said, Hilbery J upheld the new formula. Thereafter, so far as *g* counsel's researches go, there was no criticism or adverse comment on that decision or its reasoning in any reported, or, so far as is known, any unreported, case until 1974. The decision has been cited by textbook writers, almost without criticism. The *Adler*[2] formula, no doubt with variation, has been set out in widely used books of forms and precedents. It has, we are told, I have no doubt correctly, been used in thousands of leases, agreed between landlords and tenants. So far as is known this present case is one *h* of only two cases in which the *Adler*[2] decision and reasoning have been challenged in the courts of this country. The other challenge was in *Greene v Church Comrs for England*[3]. Although the s 19(1) question had been raised in the county court from which that appeal was brought, it had not been there decided, because another issue, under the Land Charges Act 1972, decided in favour of the tenant, rendered a decision on the s 19(1) issue *j*

---

1   [1951] 1 All ER 346
2   [1957] 1 All ER 229, [1957] 1 WLR 227
3   [1974] 3 All ER 609, [1974] Ch 467

unnecessary. So, also, when the appeal in *Greene*[1] came to this court, the decision of his

a Honour Judge Leslie in the county court was upheld by this court. (Counsel for the landlords in this case relies on the decision in that case on that issue as supporting his submissions in the present case. He may be right, but I do not find it necessary to go into that submission. That particular point clearly cannot have been argued in *Greene's* case[1].) However, in *Greene's* case[1], there were observations by members of the court, obiter, expressing doubt as to the correctness of *Adler*[2]: see per Lord Denning MR[3] and

b Sir Eric Sachs[4].

What does seem clear is that the members of the court who expressed those dicta of doubt as to *Adler*[2] in *Greene's* case[1] did not have the advantage, which we have had, of having had cited the judgments given in the High Court of Australia in *Creer v P & O Lines of Australia Pty Ltd*[5]. That case involved, directly and indistinguishably, the correctness of Hilbery J's decision in *Adler*[2]. The case arose on s 133B(1) of the

c Conveyancing Act 1919–1969 (New South Wales). The statutory terms are identical with s 19(1). The High Court, with closely reasoned judgments by Barwick CJ, Menzies and Windeyer JJ, approved and followed *Adler*[2].

I would do the same. In the balance of conflicting arguments, I reach that conclusion substantially for three reasons. First, the respect due to the decision of the High Court of Australia, and to the reasoning of the judgments therein; secondly (as is, indeed, a

d ground which clearly strongly influenced Menzies J in that case), the fact that the *Adler*[2] decision has stood, and has been acted on, for so many years; and thirdly (a ground which makes me feel able to place much greater reliance on the second ground than I should otherwise have done), the fact that I cannot see any good argument of policy for interfering, more than is essentially required by the words of the statute or by binding authority, with freedom of contract in respect of an agreement between the parties that

e the landlord should be entitled to the option of requiring a surrender of the lease, where the tenant desires to be freed from his obligation under the lease, bearing in mind that the legislature did not in 1927 consider, and has not since considered, that policy requires infringement of freedom of contract between a potential landlord and a potential tenant validly and effectively to agree that there shall be no right of assignment at all, however reasonable the tenant's subsequent desire to assign might be.

f It is contended further for the tenants that, even if *Adler*[2] be right, cl 2(j) is materially different from the *Adler*[2] clause. The chief ground for that submission is that the last few lines of the second proviso to cl 2(j)(ii) do not make provision for anything that could be called a condition precedent to the tenant's right to such consent for an assignment, but make provision for what is to happen after the stage to which the preceding provisions of the proviso relate. I do not know what the effect, if any, in law of these last few lines

g of the proviso would be. I doubt if they would have any effect. But if and in so far as they might be thought to be inconsistent with what is required by s 19(1), they would, as I understand the authorities, simply fall to be ignored. They would not, as it were, carry through their infection into the rest of the clause, so as to invalidate the rest of the proviso.

I would dismiss the appeal.

h **LAWTON LJ.** At common law there were no fetters on what a landlord could put in a lease, if his tenant agreed, to restrain or control its assignment. He might insert a covenant prohibiting assignment; or he might give the tenant a right to assign with his consent; or he might allow the tenant to assign with his consent, undertaking that his consent would not be unreasonably withheld; or he might omit any covenant against

j assignment.

1   [1974] 3 All ER 609, [1974] Ch 467
2   [1957] 1 All ER 229, [1957] 1 WLR 227
3   [1974] 3 All ER 609 at 613–614, [1974] Ch 467 at 477
4   [1974] 3 All ER 609 at 615, [1974] Ch 467 at 479
5   (1971) 45 ALJR 697

In 1927 Parliament, by the Landlord and Tenant Act of that year, provided for the payment of compensation for improvements and goodwill to the tenants of premises   *a* used for business purposes, or the grant of new leases, and for the amendment of the law of landlord and tenant: see the long title to that Act. Part I dealt with compensation for improvements and goodwill, Part II with amendments of the law. Three topics were dealt with in Part II: provisions as to covenants to repair, 'provisions as to covenants not to assign etc. without licence or consent' (I quote from the marginal note to s 19), and apportionment of rents.   *b*

What was the intention of Parliament in enacting s 19 in the terms it did? Was it intended to confer a jurisdiction on courts to relieve lessees from covenants or to modify them? In *F W Woolworth & Co Ltd v Lambert*[1] Greene LJ referred to this question in relation to s 19(2) which was concerned with covenants against the making of improvements without licence or consent and answered it in these terms: 'It is a statutory addition to the terms of a particular type of covenant, and the proviso which the   *c* subsection mentions is to be read into the covenant.' The same can be said about the proviso mentioned in sub-s (1) with which this appeal is concerned. This being so, the landlords submit that there is nothing in s 19(1) which fetters a landlord's right, save in the terms of the proviso, to insert in a lease a covenant requiring his tenant to act in a specified way before asking for consent to assign and making his acting in that way a condition precedent to his acquiring any right to assign. This is what the landlords say   *d* they have done in the second proviso to cl 2(j)(ii) of the lease under consideration in this appeal. They rely on the decision of Hilbery J in *Adler v Upper Grosvenor Street Investment Ltd*[2], a case in which there was a proviso in broadly similar terms to the one with which we are concerned. The judge decided that a tenant's right to assign under this kind of proviso only arises when his landlord refuses the proffered surrender[3].

The decision in *Adler's* case[2] does not seem to have surprised conveyancers, and   *e* although, as counsel informed us, it was discussed in articles in specialist legal journals, there was virtually no criticism of it. This form of covenant found its way into a number of precedent books (see for example Prideaux's Precedents in Conveyancing[4]). The probabilities are, as counsel for the tenants accepted, that this kind of proviso is now to be found in many leases.

The decision of the High Court of Australia in *Creer v P & O Lines of Australia Pty Ltd*[5]   *f* shows that this form of proviso was in use in the Commonwealth. That distinguished court had to consider its effect having regard to Australian legislation in much the same terms of s 19(1) of the Landlord and Tenant Act 1927. Two members of that court, Barwick CJ and Windeyer J, decided that *Adler's* case[2] had been rightly decided. Menzies J was not as certain about the correctness of that decision as his brethren, but decided in the end to accept it. For my part I found the reasoning of Barwick CJ and Windeyer J   *g* most convincing.

As Megaw LJ has pointed out in his judgment, the *Adler*[2] form of proviso was queried obiter in *Greene v Church Comrs for England*[6]. I adopt his comments on that case.

The history of the *Adler*[2] form of proviso has had an odd twist which was made by the Rent Act 1977. Section 127(1) of that Act excluded the statutory prohibition on premiums on grants of protected tenancies when a tenancy was both a long tenancy   *h* within the meaning of Part I of the Landlord and Tenant Act 1954 and a protected tenancy, provided the conditions specified in sub-s (2) were fulfilled. The third of those conditions, which is set out in para (c), was that assignment or underletting was precluded by the terms of the tenancy—

  j

---

1 [1936] 2 All ER 1523 at 1542, [1937] Ch 37 at 60
2 [1957] 1 All ER 229, [1957] 1 WLR 227
3 See [1957] 1 All ER 229 at 231, [1957] 1 WLR 227 at 230
4 25th Edn (1966), vol 2, p 321
5 (1971) 45 ALJR 697
6 [1974] 3 All ER 609, [1974] Ch 467

'and, if it is subject to any consent, there is neither a term excluding section 144 of the Law of Property Act 1925 ... nor a term requiring in connection with a request for consent the making of an offer to surrender the tenancy.'

Parliament in 1977 seems to have assumed that the *Adler*[1] form of covenant was valid. This assumption does not make it valid; but it is a statutory reflection of what is in the precedent books.

I am satisfied that the judgment of Hilbery J in *Adler*[1] was correct, for the reasons given by Barwick CJ and Windeyer J in the High Court of Australia in *Creer's* case[2]. As I can find no significant difference between the *Adler*[1] form of proviso and that under consideration in this case, I would dismiss the appeal.

BROWNE LJ (read by Lawton LJ). I have found this a very difficult case, but in the end I agree that the appeal should be dismissed.

According to the law as it stood immediately before the passing of the 1927 Act (which the draftsmen must be assumed to have had in mind), a lease could validly contain a covenant absolutely prohibiting assignment or subletting; on the other hand, if there was a covenant not to assign or sublet without the landlord's consent, such consent not to be unreasonably withheld, the wish of the landlord to regain possession for himself was not a reasonable ground for refusing consent: see *Bates v Donaldson*[3]; *Re Gibbs and Houlder Bros & Co Ltd's Lease, Houlder Bros & Co Ltd v Gibbs*[4]. As Megaw LJ has said, neither party asked us to give effect to the doubts of Danckwerts LJ to which he has referred, and I accept that s 19(1) of the 1927 Act does not affect an absolute covenant against assignment. The primary purpose of s 19(1) seems to be to add a statutory proviso to a covenant not to assign without consent. The problem in this case is its application where there is already in the lease a contractual proviso that consent is not to be unreasonably withheld in the case of a respectable and responsible assignee, followed by further provisions which, if valid, limit the tenant's liberty to assign. I think that a possible view of the effect of s 19(1) is that the lease must be read as if it simply contained the statutory proviso, 'Such licence or consent is not to be unreasonably withheld', and no more, and what follows must be disregarded. If so, on the law as it stood in 1927, a refusal of consent on the ground that the landlord wanted possession for himself would be unreasonable. Further, as Megaw LJ has said, the practical object and effect of the clause which was held invalid in *Re Smith's Lease*[5] and the clause which was held valid in *Adler*[1] by the High Court of Australia in *Creer v P & O Lines of Australia Pty*[2] was the same (ie to give the benefit of any increase in the value of the lease to the landlord and not the tenant), and the difference between the clauses was simply that the object and purpose was wrapped up in a different verbal formula. For these reasons I have shared the doubts expressed (obiter) by Lord Denning MR and Sir Eric Sachs in *Greene v Church Comrs for England*[6] and by Menzies J in *Creer v P & O Lines of Australia Pty Ltd*[7].

But after a good deal of hesitation I have come to the conclusion that this appeal should be dismissed, for the three reasons given by Megaw LJ. I will not try to paraphrase them or repeat them at length. In substance they are: 1. The respect due to the decision of the High Court of Australia. 2. The fact that *Adler*[1] has stood for more than 20 years and has, we are told by counsel for the landlords, been acted on in thousands of leases, without criticism except in *Greene's* case[8] (which was followed by a guarded note in the Law

---

1   [1957] 1 All ER 229, [1957] 1 WLR 227
2   (1971) 45 ALJR 697
3   [1896] 2 QB 241, [1895–9] All ER Rep 170
4   [1925] 1 Ch 575, [1925] All ER Rep 128
5   [1951] 1 All ER 346
6   [1974] 3 All ER 609 at 614 and 616, respectively, [1974] Ch 467 at 477 and 479–480, respectively
7   45 ALJR 697 at 699
8   [1974] 3 All ER 609, [1974] Ch 467

Quarterly Review[1]) and by Menzies J. As Windeyer J pointed out in *Creer's* case[2], it had previously been noted, with apparent approval, by Mr Megarry (as he then was) in the *a* Law Quarterly Review[3], and counsel for the landlords provided us with a number of extracts from textbooks and precedent books which generally treat it as good law. 3. Since Parliament has not thought it necessary or desirable to prohibit or limit absolute covenants against assignment, I cannot discern any policy reason for invalidating a covenant which in effect prohibits assignment unless a condition precedent has been fulfilled, namely the offer and refusal of a surrender. I was impressed by the analogy of *b* an absolute covenant against assignment during (say) the first seven years or the last seven years of a 14 year lease.

I would only add that I cannot myself rely on the argument based on s 127 of the Rent Act 1977: see *Kirkness (Inspector of Taxes) v John Hudson & Co Ltd*[4], especially per Lord Reid.

c

Appeal dismissed.

Solicitors: *Davidson, Doughty & Co* (for the tenants); *Freshfields* (for the landlords).

Mary Rose Plummer   Barrister.

d

1   (1975) 91 LQR 3
2   (1971) 45 ALJR 697 at 699
3   (1957) 73 LQR 157
4   [1955] 2 All ER 345 esp at 365–366, [1955] AC 696 esp at 735

London Borough of Enfield v Local Government Boundary Commission for England and another

HOUSE OF LORDS

LORD DIPLOCK, VISCOUNT DILHORNE, LORD SALMON, LORD FRASER OF TULLYBELTON AND LORD SCARMAN

15th OCTOBER, 8th NOVEMBER 1979

Local government – Electoral arrangements – Proposal for change of arrangements – Objection by local authority – Commission required to observe rules laid down for considering electoral arrangements – Failure to observe rule to achieve electoral equality between wards – Commission rejecting scheme based on electoral equality and adopting scheme not based on electoral equality – Scheme adopted by commission in interests of effective and convenient local government – Whether proposals valid – Whether commission required to comply with rules – Whether interests of effective and convenient local government an overriding consideration – Local Government Act 1972, s 47(1), Sch 11, para 3(2)(a).

The Local Government Boundary Commission for England, in making proposals under s 47(1)[a] of the Local Government Act 1972 for changes in the electoral arrangements of a local government area, were required by s 78(2)[b] of the Act to comply, so far as reasonably practicable, with the rules set out in Sch 11 to the Act. In making proposals for electoral changes in a London borough the commission adopted a scheme put forward by a local political party that there should be 66 councillors and 33 wards in the borough, and rejected the scheme put forward by the borough council for 70 councillors and 35 wards. The council's scheme was reasonably practicable, and provided, as nearly as possible, for electoral equality, ie equal weight for each vote throughout the borough, whereas the scheme adopted by the commission did not provide for electoral equality to that degree. The council applied for a declaration that the commission's proposals were invalid because it had failed to comply with the requirement, in para 3(2)(a)[c] of Sch 11, that the proposed electoral arrangements should provide 'as nearly as may be' for electoral equality. The judge[d] granted the declaration on the ground that the requirement in para 3(2)(a) was mandatory and the failure to comply with it invalidated the proposals. The commission appealed to the Court of Appeal[e] which allowed the appeal and upheld the proposals holding that the rules in Sch 11 were subsidiary to the overriding provisions in s 47(1) which required that the proposed changes should appear to the commission to be desirable in the interests of effective and convenient local government, and accordingly the commission were entitled to take the view in making the proposals that it was in the interests of effective and convenient government of the borough to have 66 councillors and 33 wards. The council appealed to the House of Lords contending that in determining the appropriate number of councillors, para 3(2) must have priority over s 47(1), and if the provision of a larger number of councillors than was required for the effective and convenient government of the borough would produce more nearly the result that the vote of every elector in the borough was of equal weight, the commission were required by the 1972 Act to propose that number.

Held – Although para 3(2) of Sch 11 to the 1972 Act required electoral equality to take priority in the fixing of boundaries and in relation to local ties, there was no

---

a   Section 47(1), so far as material, is set out at p 748 *j* to p 749 *d*, post
b   Section 78(2) is set out at p 749 *f*, post
c   Paragraph 3(2), so far as material, is set out at p 750 *j* to p 751 *a*, post
d   [1978] 2 All ER 1073
e   [1979] 1 All ER 950

corresponding provision in the Act requiring electoral equality to take priority in the fixing of the number of councillors; any contention that there was such a provision *a* ignored the fact that under s 47 of the Act the only proposals which the commission were authorised to make were proposals for changes which appeared desirable in the interests of effective and convenient local government. Accordingly, having decided on the appropriate number of councillors required for effective and convenient local government, it was then the duty of the commission to give effect so far as was reasonably practicable to the requirements of para 3(2) and then as nearly as possible to *b* secure electoral equality. The appeal would therefore be dismissed (see p 748 *g* and p 751 *d* to *j*, post).

Decision of the Court of Appeal [1979] 1 All ER 950 affirmed.

Notes

For changes in English local government areas, see Supplement to 24 Halsbury's Laws *c* (3rd Edn) para 778A.

For the Local Government Act 1972, s 47 and Sch 11, para 3, see 42 Halsbury's Statutes (3rd Edn) 887, 1147.

Appeal

The plaintiffs, the London Borough of Enfield, appealed against the decision of the Court *d* of Appeal[1] (Lord Denning MR, Eveleigh LJ and Sir David Cairns) dated 27th July 1978 allowing an appeal by the first defendants, the Local Government Boundary Commission for England, from the judgment of Bristow J[2] given on 25th January 1978 whereby he granted the borough a declaration that the commission when considering electoral arrangements for the borough had failed to comply with s 78 of and Sch 11 to the Local Government Act 1972 and that in consequence the report and proposals submitted by *e* the commission to the second defendant, the Secretary of State for the Home Department, were invalid. The Secretary of State took no part in the proceedings before the House. The facts are set out in the opinion of Viscount Dilhorne.

J Newey QC and *M Howard* for the borough.
Michael Mann QC and *N Bratza* for the commission.   *f*

Their Lordships took time for consideration.

8th November. The following opinions were delivered.

LORD DIPLOCK. My Lords, I have had the advantage of reading in draft the speech *g* of my noble and learned friend, Viscount Dilhorne. I agree with it and, for the reasons stated by him, I think this appeal should be dismissed.

VISCOUNT DILHORNE. My Lords, this appeal will decide whether the council of the Borough of Enfield should have 70 members or only 66. It arises in this way. The borough council consisted of ten aldermen and 60 councillors. Then the office of *h* alderman was abolished by the Local Government Act 1972 with effect, in the case of London boroughs, from 1977 (s 8(1) and Sch 2). That Act by s 46 established a Local Government Boundary commission for England and s 47 of that Act, so far as material, reads as follows:

'(1) ... the English Commission may in consequence of a review conducted by them or a district council under this Part of this Act make proposals to the Secretary *j* of State for effecting changes appearing to the Commission desirable in the interests

1   [1979] 1 All ER 950
2   [1978] 2 All ER 1073

of effective and convenient local government by any of the following means or any combination of those means . . . (*a*) the alteration of a local government area: (*b*) the constitution of a new local government area of any description outside Greater London by the amalgamation of two or more such areas of the like description or by the aggregation of parts of such areas of the like description or by the separation of part of such an area of the like description; (*c*) the abolition of a principal area of any description outside Greater London and its distribution among other areas of the like description; (*d*) the conversion of a metropolitan into a non-metropolitan county or of a non-metropolitan into a metropolitan county and in consequence thereof the conversion of a metropolitan into a non-metropolitan district or of a non-metropolitan into a metropolitan district within the county; (*e*) the constitution of a new London borough by the amalgamation of two of more London boroughs or by the aggregation of parts of London boroughs or by the separation of parts of a London borough; (*f*) the abolition of a London borough and the distribution of its area among other London boroughs; (*g*) the constitution of a new parish by— (i) the establishment of any area which is not a parish or part of one as a parish; or (ii) the aggregation of the whole or any part of any such area with one or more parishes or parts of parishes; (*h*) the abolition of a parish with or without the distribution of its area among other parishes; (*i*) a change of electoral arrangements for any local government area which is either consequential on any change in local government areas proposed under the foregoing paragraphs or is a change (hereafter in this Part of this Act referred to as a substantive change) which is independent of any change in local government areas so proposed . . .'

'Electoral arrangements' are defined by s 78, which reads as follows:

'(1) In this Part of this Act—"electoral arrangements" means—(*a*) in relation to a principal area, the number of councillors of the council for that area, the number and boundaries of the electoral areas into which that area is for the time being divided for the purpose of the election of councillors, the number of councillors to be elected for any electoral area in that principal area and the name of any electoral area . . .

'(2) In considering the electoral arrangements for local government areas for the purposes of this Part of this Act, the Secretary of State, each of the Commissions and every district council shall so far as is reasonably practicable comply with the rules set out in Schedule 11 to this Act.'

The local government commission carried out a review of the electoral arrangements of the borough of Enfield for the purpose of considering whether or not to make proposals for a 'substantive change' in those electoral arrangements, and it is clear beyond doubt that a substantive change in the electoral arrangements could only be proposed by the commission if they considered it desirable in the interests of efficient and convenient local government. The borough council were invited to prepare a draft scheme of representation for the commission's consideration. They were asked to obey the rules set out in Sch 11 and the guidelines set out in a letter of 10th June 1975 from the commission as to the size of the council and other matters. That letter contained the following passage:

'Following the consultations with the London Boroughs Association and the political parties, the Commission have decided that a range of council sizes of 50–70 councillors should apply throughout Greater London. In choosing the future number of councillors, your Council should have regard to the size and responsibilities of the authority . . . they [the commission] can see no justification in London for councils of more than 70 members.'

After consultation with local interests, the borough council submitted a scheme for 70 councillors. Other alternative schemes were submitted and the commission considered that an alternative scheme for 66 councillors offered the best standard for representation for the borough and decided to adopt it as a basis for their draft proposals.

The borough council objected to these draft proposals on three grounds: (1) that the proposed council was not large enough, (2) that natural boundaries had not been used and (3) that community ties had been broken. Others consulted accepted the commission's proposals in principle.

The commission decided that they needed further information to reach a conclusion and Mr Slocombe was appointed as an assistant commissioner by the Secretary of State for that purpose. He held a meeting at Enfield on 30th and 31st May 1977 at which a considerable number of persons were present and a variety of views were expressed. From his report it appears that Mr W D Day, chief executive and town clerk for the council, put forward the case for the borough council. He withdrew the council's original scheme, asked that a revised scheme should be considered and indicated that he would later submit further amendments to secure even greater electoral equality. He dealt with the council's case in three sections: size of council, councillors per ward and boundaries and areas of wards. As to the size of councils, he said the council's policy since 1972 had been that there should be 70 councillors and he put forward a variety of grounds for that conclusion, one of them being that the majority party on the council should have a majority on each committee and that this could be better achieved with a larger council. The Labour group on the council disagreed. Their representative said that there was no need for 70 members and that 66 was perfectly adequate. The Edmonton Constituency Labour Party and the Southgate Labour Party agreed that there should be 66. So did the Edmonton Conservative and Unionist Association and the Liberal Central Committee for the borough. Councillor Young, however, the leader of the council, said that the council had consistently maintained the view that 70 was the proper number and that there was a real need for that number.

The assistant commissioner in his report to the commission said:

'There is a solid weight of evidence against 70. I consider that the maximum figure in the guide lines should be used sparingly and I think it is too many for Enfield. I cannot believe that the Committee Structure cannot quickly be adapted to a Council of 66, which is only about a 5% reduction. My view is that 66 is the right number and this figure forms the basis of most of the other schemes prepared by the political parties . . . I now reject the Council's proposals for a Council of 70 members elected from 35 wards. In doing this I make it clear that I do so because of the decision I have made about the size of the Council and not on the grounds of electoral equality. The Council's scheme cannot be faulted on an electoral ratio basis—in this respect it is almost perfect.'

The commission concluded that the assistant commissioner's recommendations should be accepted and on 23rd September 1977 they submitted their report to the Secretary of State. There is no indication to be found in the report of the commission or in that of the assistant commissioner that it was ever suggested to them on behalf of the borough council that they had failed to comply with the provisions of the Act. The borough council's case was, as I have indicated, that 70 councillors were required for the government of the borough.

The contention that they had failed to comply with the Act appears first to have been made in the statement of claim endorsed on the writ issued on 3rd November 1977 after the commission had reported. It was then alleged that there had been non-compliance with the rules set out in Sch 11 of the Act and a declaration was sought that in consequence of that failure the commission's report was invalid. The rule which it was said had not been complied with was para 3 in that schedule which, so far as material, reads as follows:

'(2) Having regard to any change in the number or distribution of the local government electors of the district or borough likely to take place within the period of five years immediately following the consideration—(a) the ratio of the number of local electors to the number of councillors to be elected shall be, as nearly as may be, the same in every ward of the district or borough . . .

'(3) Subject to paragraph (2) above, in considering the electoral arrangements . . . regard shall be had to—(a) the desirability of fixing boundaries which are and will remain easily identifiable; and (b) any local ties which would be broken by the fixing of any particular boundary.'

Bristow J[1] held that the object of this rule was to get as near as possible to 'one voter one vote of equal weight'. He held that the commission had picked a 66 councillor scheme which was significantly inferior to the council's 70 councillor scheme in providing electoral equality and that the electoral equality given priority by para 3(2) applied as much to the selection of the appropriate number of councillors as to the selection of the number of councillors per ward and to the drawing of the ward boundaries and he granted a declaration.

The Court of Appeal[2] (Lord Denning MR, Eveleigh LJ and Sir David Cairns) allowed the appeal from his decision and in this House the borough council again contended that in determining the appropriate number of councillors, para 3(2) must have priority, that is to say, that if the provision of a larger number of councillors than is required for the effective and convenient government of a borough will produce more nearly the result that the vote of every elector in the borough is of equal weight, the commission is required by the Act to propose that number.

My Lords, that is a contention with which I cannot agree. While para 3(2) makes it clear that electoral equality is to take priority in the fixing of boundaries and in relation to local ties, there is no corresponding provision in the Act giving it priority in the fixing of the number of councillors. Indeed, I would regard it as very odd if there was. The contention ignores the fact that under s 47 the only proposals which the commission are authorised to make are proposals for changes which appear desirable in the interests of effective and convenient local government. The section gives it power to put forward proposals which can be effected in a wide variety of purposes but all the proposals they put forward must be with that object and not just to secure as nearly as may be electoral equality.

Having decided on the appropriate number of councillors required for effective and convenient local government, it is then the duty of the commission to give effect so far as is reasonably practicable to the requirements of para 3(2) and then as nearly as may be secure electoral equality; but to say that that must take priority over what is required for such government is, in my view, to misconstrue the Act.

It follows that in my opinion this appeal should be dismissed and that the costs of this litigation to decide whether the borough should have four more councillors than the commission proposes, should be borne by the borough council.

LORD SALMON. My Lords, for reasons stated by my noble and learned friend, Viscount Dilhorne, I would dismiss the appeal.

LORD FRASER OF TULLYBELTON. My Lords, I have had the advantage of reading in draft the speech of my noble and learned friend, Viscount Dilhorne. I agree with it and for reasons stated in it I agree that this appeal should be dismissed.

LORD SCARMAN. My Lords, I have had the advantage of reading in draft the speech of my noble and learned friend, Viscount Dilhorne. I agree with it and, for the reasons stated by him, I think this appeal should be dismissed.

---

1   [1978] 2 All ER 1073
2   [1979] 1 All ER 950

Appeal dismissed.

Solicitors: *Sharpe, Pritchard & Co,* agents for *Wilfred D Day,* Enfield (for the borough); *a*
Treasury Solicitor.

Mary Rose Plummer   Barrister.

b

MEPC Ltd v Christian-Edwards and others

HOUSE OF LORDS
LORD WILBERFORCE, VISCOUNT DILHORNE, LORD SALMON, LORD RUSSELL OF KILLOWEN AND
LORD KEITH OF KINKEL   *c*
12th, 16th, 17th JULY, 8th NOVEMBER 1979

*Sale of land – Title – Vendor's obligation to prove – Presumption of fact affecting title – When
court entitled to make presumption – Will of testator dying in 1911 giving son option to purchase
property – Deed of family arrangement made in 1912 reciting contract for sale of property to son
at stated sum – Further deed made in 1930 reciting that contract for sale not yet performed and d
performance suspended by consent of all interested parties – Recital not making clear whether
suspension to be indefinite – Contract not remaining in existence – Son dying in 1942 without
completing contract – Trustees in 1973 entering into contract for sale of property to purchasers
– Whether trustees showing good title – Whether court entitled to presume abandonment of 1912
contract.*

e
The testator owned the freehold of business premises in partnership with his son. The
testator died in 1911 and by his will directed that if the son did not exercise an option to
purchase the property given to him by the will, the trustees of the estate should grant
him a lease and subject thereto should hold the property on trust for sale. Prior to 1912
the trustees granted the son a lease of the premises for 21 years expiring in 1932. In a deed
of family arrangement made in 1912 it was recited that the trustees had agreed to sell the *f*
property to the son for £23,750. That recital referred to a written contract for the sale of
the property to him entered into since the grant of the lease. A subsequent family deed,
made in 1930, referred to the contract for sale and stated that it had not been completed
and that, by consent of all interested parties, it had been 'suspended'. The terms of the
suspension were unknown. In 1933 the son was granted a second lease of the premises
for 21 years subject to an agreement to carry out repairs. The second lease and the
agreement did not mention the contract for sale. Thereafter the contract was not *g*
mentioned in subsequent deeds regarding the estate, including a deed of appointment of
new trustees of the estate made in 1936 which contained meticulous recitals as to the
administration of the estate up to that date and which referred to the 1912 deed. The son
died in 1942. Neither the grant of representation to his estate nor the contract for sale
to him could be traced. In 1973 the trustees of the estate, acting under the trust for sale *h*
in the will, entered into a contract with the purchasers for the sale of the premises to
them for £710,000. On examination of the title the purchasers discovered (from the
recital in the 1912 deed) the incumbrance on the title created by the contract for sale to
the son. Accordingly, they took out a vendor and purchaser summons to determine
whether the trustees had shown a good title. They contended that the title shown should
not be forced on them because it was not clearly established that the contract for sale to
the son had ever been abandoned or that, if a representative of the son's estate were to *j*
turn up, specific performance of the contract would not be ordered. Goulding J*a* held

---

a   [1978] 1 All ER 295

that the trustees had not shown a good title because specific performance might be
a obtainable to enforce the contract with the son. On the trustees' appeal, the Court of
Appeal[b] held that a good title had been shown. The purchasers appealed to the House of
Lords.

Held – Where the question whether a good title was shown depended on a conclusion
or inference as to a fact it was the court's duty, unless there were exceptional
b circumstances, to decide the question of title as between the vendor and the purchaser
even though a third person who was not a party to the action would not be bound by the
decision. Where, therefore, the facts and circumstances of a case were so compelling that
the court could conclude beyond reasonable doubt that the purchaser would not be at
risk of a successful assertion against him of an incumbrance on the title, the court ought
to declare that a good title had been shown and ought not to be deterred from so deciding
c by the mere possibility that the purchaser might be involved in future litigation by a
claimant to the incumbrance who was not bound by the court's decision. Since it was
beyond reasonable doubt that the contract for sale to the son had been abandoned before
1936, and that no representative of his could, at the time of the contract of sale with the
purchasers in 1973, have established against them a case for specific performance of the
contract, it followed that a good title had been shown. The appeal would accordingly be
d dismissed (see p 754 a b and p 757 g to p 758 c and g to j, post).

Dictum of Lord Cozens-Hardy MR in *Smith v Colbourne* [1914–15] All ER Rep at 802
and *Johnson v Clarke* [1928] Ch 847 applied.

Per Curiam. The rules regarding the circumstances in which land may be registered
without notice of an incumbrance should be the same as the rules laid down for showing
a good marketable title (see p 754 a b and p 758 e to j, post).

e Decision of the Court of Appeal [1978] 3 All ER 795 affirmed.

Notes

For the vendor's obligation to make a marketable title, see 34 Halsbury's Laws (3rd Edn)
271, para 443, for presumptions as to title, see ibid 284, para 467, note (f), and for cases
on the duty to make title, see 40 Digest (Repl) 146–164, 1115–1272.

f **Cases referred to in opinion**

Johnson v Clarke [1928] Ch 847, 97 LJ Ch 337, 139 LT 552, 44 Digest (Repl) 75, 603.
Smith v Colbourne [1914] 2 Ch 533, [1914–15] All ER Rep 800, 84 LJ Ch 112, 111 LT 927,
    44 Digest (Repl) 88, 718.

Appeal

g This was an appeal by the plaintiffs, MEPC Ltd ('the appellants'), by leave of the Court of
Appeal, from an order of the Court of Appeal[1] (Stephenson, Orr and Goff LJJ) dated 9th
May 1978 discharging an order of Goulding J[2] dated 17th May 1977, and declaring (inter
alia) that a good title had been shown by the defendants, Thomas Guy Christian-Edwards,
Jessie Marie Wyles and Margaret Hornby ('the respondents'), to freehold property known
h as 8 Storey's Gate, London, SW1, in accordance with a contract dated 10th April 1973
made between Thomas Guy Christian-Edwards and others of the one part and the
appellants of the other part for the sale of the property to the appellants. The facts are set
out in the opinion of Lord Russell of Killowen.

Jonathan Parker QC and *Timothy Lloyd* for the appellants.
j *G B H Dillon QC* and *E W H Christie* for the respondents.

---

b   [1978] 3 All ER 795
1   [1978] 3 All ER 795, [1978] Ch 281
2   [1978] 1 All ER 295, [1977] 1 WLR 1328

LORD WILBERFORCE. My Lords, I have had the advantage of reading in draft the speech of my noble and learned friend, Lord Russell of Killowen. I agree with it and that *a* the appeal should be dismissed.

VISCOUNT DILHORNE. My Lords, I have had the advantage of reading in draft the speech of my noble and learned friend, Lord Russell of Killowen. I agree with it and that the appeal should be dismissed.

b

LORD SALMON. My Lords, I have had the advantage of reading in draft the speech of my noble and learned friend, Lord Russell of Killowen. I agree with it, and accordingly I would dismiss the appeal.

LORD RUSSELL OF KILLOWEN. My Lords, this is in some respects a curious case. The question was raised on a vendor and purchaser summons whether the *c* respondents as trustees of the estate of W P Metchim who died on 14th December 1911, had made out a title to property under a contract for its sale to the appellants sufficient to entitle them to enforce the contract against the appellants. Goulding J[1] decided that they had not. The Court of Appeal[2] decided the contrary. The crucial factor concerns a missing contract made in 1912 for the sale by the then trustees of the same property to Percy Bridgman Metchim, son of the deceased, for some £23,000. The contract at *d* present in dispute was entered into in April 1973 and was for the sale of the property, 8 Storey's Gate, Westminster, a commercial property, for the sum of £710,000.

The testator carried on a printing business at the property, of which he owned the freehold, in partnership with his son Percy under a partnership deed dated 25th April 1905 which was current at the testator's death, Percy being entitled to one-eighth share, and credited with a sum of £3,000 on capital account: the partnership was treated as a *e* tenant of the testator of the property at a rent of £850 yearly exclusive of rates and taxes, with liability to repair and insure. The will gave Percy an option to purchase the property at a valuation, which he did not exercise. Instead the trustees at some date prior to 1st July 1912 granted to Percy a lease of the property for 21 years and 11 days from 14th December 1911 (the testator's death) at a rent fixed by a valuer of £950 a year. This lease was no doubt pursuant to the provision in the testator's will that a lease should be *f* granted to Percy should he wish to have one for whatever term he should wish. The will imposed a trust for sale of the property after the granting of such lease. The beneficial interests in the property and the proceeds of its sale were given to the daughters.

On 1st July 1912 a deed of family arrangement was executed by the widow, three sons, W P (or Douglas), Percy and Ralph, and four daughters, Maud Whitley-Wilson, Henrietta Blackwood (wife of W B Blackwood), Beatrice, Violet Wyles (wife of J W Wyles), J W *g* Wyles and W B Blackwood. In this deed appears a recital that the trustees 'have agreed with the said Percy . . . for the sale to him at the sum of £23,750 of [the property] for all the interest therein of the said testator and subject to and with the benefit of the said Lease': this was the lease to Percy already mentioned due to expire on 25th December 1932. I have no doubt that this recital refers to a contract in writing for sale, entered into since the lease. So far as the business was concerned it was agreed that the will and a *h* codicil should take effect as giving it to Percy with a two-thirds interest and Ralph with a one-third interest, with effect from the testator's death. It appears that Percy and Ralph entered into a partnership agreement accordingly.

No further mention of the contract for sale to Percy appears until a deed dated 11th February 1930, and thereafter it is sunk without trace. That was a deed of covenant by Henrietta Blackwood and Violet Wyles of a yearly sum in favour of the daughter of a *j* deceased sister. It recited the lease to Percy already mentioned and that 'since the grant of such Lease the Trustees agreed with . . . Percy . . . for the sale to him of [the property]

---

1   [1978] 1 All ER 295, [1977] 1 WLR 1328
2   [1978] 3 All ER 795, [1978] Ch 281

at the price of £23,750 subject to the said Lease but such purchase has not yet been
a completed and by consent of all parties interested the performance thereof has been
suspended'. The covenant was to pay to the niece while living 'and the sale of [the
property] shall be incomplete' out of the covenantors' share of the rents from the
property £80 yearly: 'and if and when during the life of [the niece] the sale of the said
premises shall be duly completed' the covenant was to purchase out of the covenantors'
shares of the proceeds of sale a life annuity of the same amount for the niece. I would
b expect this deed to have been prepared by the family solicitors: and one of the
covenantors was the wife of J W Wyles who was one of the trustees.

The lease to Percy having expired on 25th December 1932, a further lease to him of
the property was executed on 19th January 1933 from 25th December 1932 at a rent of
£1,300 rising to £1,400 for a term of 21 years breakable by Percy at seven and 14
years. This was granted pursuant to an agreement therefor dated 16th February 1932
c conditional on Percy carrying out before 25th December 1932 a schedule of works of
repair to the property, including rewiring the whole for electricity and external repairs
to comply with the tenant's obligations under the existing lease. There is no trace of any
reference in either of these documents to the fact that Percy was entitled by contract to
buy the freehold for £23,000 odd. It may be remarked that while it was not at all
unusual to find a full repairing lease followed by a contract with the lessee for the
d acquisition of the freehold, a full repairing lease for up to 21 years to a person entitled by
contract to buy the freehold is certainly unusual. But there is the matter of suspension
of performance of the contract for sale, the terms of which suspension are not
discoverable. I would say that if there was abandonment of the contract for sale this
would be its most likely occasion.

I observe here that there is some evidence that the increased rent was not exacted
e owing to poor business: which suggests that Percy was in no financial position to buy the
freehold.

The next fact, in the pursuit of a conclusion whether the sale contract was abandoned,
is an appointment of additional trustees on 18th March 1936. The existing trustees were
Ralph and J W Wyles. They appointed J L Wyles (son of J W Wyles) and J Colin
Christian-Edwards to be trustees of the estate with them. The new trustees were of
f course, as to one, related to the family: the other was a member of the firm of solicitors
to the trust. The Wyles family were surveyors. It would be important to the new
trustees to know, and be told on the record of their appointment, whether there was in
existence (albeit suspended as to performance) a contract for the sale of the property at
£23,750: and it will be observed that Ralph (an existing trustee) was indirectly interested
in the property as a partner with Percy in the business carried on thereon. But there was
g no reference to the contract of sale to Percy. There was a detailed and meticulous recital
of (a) the will of the testator, (b) the codicil thereto, (c) the death of the testator, (d) the
family history, (e) the lack of exercise by Percy of the option to purchase, (f) the first loan
to Percy, (g) the deed of family arrangement of 1912, (h) various other matters of detail
in the history of the family and the trust. But there was no mention at all of any contract
for sale of the freehold of the property to Percy, though the second lease to Percy was
h recited. Finally the deed recited that the property held by the trustees consisted
(relevantly) of the property, subject to the second lease, but not to anything else. It is true
that for the mere description of the legal estate vested in the trustees and the legal interest
to which it was subject, a reference to the contract of sale to Percy would be out of
place. But if the draftsman and the existing trustees who would have executed the
contract for sale to Percy had thought for a moment that the contract for sale, which was
j referred to in their recited deed of family arrangement, was still alive, the deed of
appointment would surely have mentioned it as a warning to the new trustees who were
after all to become trustees for sale of the property.

But this is by no means the only instance of an occasion when the contract with Percy
dropped out of sight.

In 1937 J W Wyles (one of the trustees) valued Henrietta Blackwood's interest in the

property for estate duty on her death at £5,250: her interest was three-eighths subject to
the annuity to the niece of £40. No mention was made of any existing contract for sale   *a*
of the freehold to Percy.

Departing momentarily from chronological order a similar point is to be noted in
connection with the death of Violet Wyles. Colin Christian-Edwards (a trustee and
member of the firm of the trust's solicitors) wrote to her son J L Wyles (also a trustee) in
October 1960 on the subject of the estate duty paid on her death in 1955. He referred to
a then existing lease which I mention later. He made no reference to any then subsisting   *b*
contract of sale to Percy (who had in fact died in 1942). He reported that the value of the
property was agreed with the district valuer at £45,000 throwing up a figure of £30,000
in respect of Mrs Wyles's interest. The agreed valuation of the property is of course quite
inconsistent with the continuance in existence of the contract to sell to Percy for £23,750.

To return to chronology. In December 1933 a company was formed to take over the
printers' business from the partnership of Percy and Ralph, the partners being the   *c*
shareholders. Whether the then existing lease was assigned to that company does not
appear. Percy died in 1942. It is thought that he left two children. No grant of
representation to his estate has been traced: nor have his children. In December 1947
Ralph died. What happened to Percy's shareholding in the company does not appear.
The company appears to have been regarded as the tenants under the second lease to
Percy. At some date prior to 1954 some people called Madley acquired the company.   *d*
On 25th March 1954 the trustees demised the property to the company for a term of 21
years from 25th December 1953 at a yearly rent of £3,000 breakable by the lessee at
seven or 14 years with a probably ineffective option to extend for a further 21 years at a
rent to be agreed. The sale to the appellants was expressed to be subject to that lease. The
lessor trustees were J W Wyles, J L Wyles and Colin Christian-Edwards. J W Wyles
would have been a party to the agreement to sell for £23,750 to Percy.   *e*

With regard to the document of the contract of sale to Percy it has disappeared.
Thomas Guy Christian-Edwards in 1919 joined the firm of solicitors who acted for the
trustees of the testator's will throughout, becoming a partner in 1934. A partner, Charles
Edwards, dealt with the trust business until October 1957: and thereafter Colin Christian-
Edwards (trustee) in 1936 until his death in 1966. T G Christian-Edwards deposed that
he had searched the records of his present firm (with which Edwards & Co amalgamated)   *f*
and found no trace of the sale agreement to Percy other than the two mentions in 1912
and 1930. There had been wartime destruction in 1940 of all documents in the office of
Edwards & Son including those relating to this trust. But the firm had also a safe deposit
in Winchester House, EC2: 'As a general rule all bills and trust instruments and papers
of importance were kept in this safe deposit box, the contents of which were
preserved'. And it is to be observed that in 1936 (the appointment of new trustees) there   *g*
would have been no question of the contract for sale to Percy being overlooked owing to
wartime destruction.

In the above circumstances the contention of the appellants is simply stated. Here is
clear evidence that there was in 1912 created an incumbrance on the title in the form of
a contract to sell to Percy: of that the appellants have notice: it is not clearly established
that the contract was ever abandoned, or that if a representative of Percy turned up with   *h*
the contract of sale having obtained a grant to his estate specific performance would not
be ordered: and this is especially so since there is evidence in the 1930 document that
performance of the contract was suspended on terms unknown. The title should not be
forced on the purchaser in those circumstances, even if it was thought that on balance of
possibilities there had been abandonment or that specific performance would not be
granted. The proper course would have been for the vendor to clear the matter up in   *j*
proceedings against someone appointed to represent Percy's estate. Mr Creasey, a deputy
managing director of the appellants, a chartered surveyor with 25 years experience in the
field of property investment and development, contended in his affidavit that the
situation that was revealed would lead to difficulties in the financing arrangements of the
company (who proposed to develop the site with other property), tending to deter an

institutional lender from accepting the property as security, and perhaps leading to
further difficulty in disposing of completed properties after development.

Johnson v Clarke[1] was a decision of Maugham J forcing a title on a purchaser in a
vendors' action for specific performance of a contract to sell a freehold. The question
whether the occupant was more than a tenant from year to year depended on the
construction and effect of a document signed by one of the vendor trustees for sale
in favour of the occupant. This involved a question of law. The point was taken that
good title had not been made because a decision that, notwithstanding the document,
the occupant was not more than a yearly tenant would not bind the occupant,
and the purchaser might be exposed to an adverse claim by, and perhaps litigation
with, the occupant. Maugham J held, on authority, that according to the modern
practice the old rule had been changed, and that subject to an exception which he later
mentioned the court was nevertheless bound, except in very special circumstances, to
decide a point of that sort, and to decide on the evidence at the hearing whether the
objection to title is good or bad. The exception was when a question arose on the
construction of a will when a doubtful matter could be readily decided so as to bind all
parties concerned on an originating summons. On the authorities Maugham J held that
it was not the right thing to compel the vendors to start an action against the occupant
to determine whether the document had any validity. He qualified the duty of the court
to decide the point of the occupant's rights under the document by the phrase[2] 'unless
there is going to emerge . . . some very great or serious difficulty with regard to the
document in question'. On the evidence Maugham J[3] concluded that the occupant 'will
have no reasonable chance of success in an action against the purchaser', and that the
document did not create an incumbrance on the property. I repeat that the decision in
that case was on a question of law involving the construction of the document and the
powers of a single executor. In his judgment Maugham J adverted to the comment of
Lord Cozens-Hardy MR in *Smith v Colbourne*[4]:

> 'Lastly it was urged that the title is too doubtful to be forced upon a purchaser.
> The Courts have in modern times not listened with favour to such a defence. It is
> the duty of the Court, unless in very exceptional circumstances, to decide the rights
> between the vendor and the purchaser, even though a third person not a party to the
> action will not be bound by the decision.'

To the same effect was the judgment of Swinfen Eady LJ[5]. That case also involved a
decision on points of law.

These two cases were concerned with a decision of the court on a question of law. But
in my opinion their principle is to be applied also when the question whether a
sufficiently good title has been shown depends on a conclusion or inference as to fact: and
this appears from the statement of the law in Fry on Specific Performance[6], and the
authorities there cited. So that a mere possibility that a claimant to an incumbrance, not
bound by the decision of the court in proceedings to which he was not a party, will
involve the purchaser in future litigation will not, in an appropriate case, deter the court
from determining that the title is good against the purchaser on a view of the facts before
it. Lord Hardwicke LC said[7] the court 'must govern itself by a moral certainty, for it is
impossible in the nature of things, there should be a mathematical certainty of a good
title'. I am not sure that the instant case can be fitted into the principle enunciated in
some cases (and in Fry) that a test is whether it would be the duty of a judge, where the

---

1 [1928] Ch 847
2 [1928] Ch 847 at 856
3 [1928] Ch 847 at 859
4 [1914] 2 Ch 533 at 541, [1914–15] All ER Rep 800 at 802
5 [1914] 2 Ch 533 at 544, [1914–15] All ER Rep 800 at 804
6 6th Edn (1921), paras 889–891
7 See *Lyddall v Weston* (1739) 2 Atk 19 at 20, 26 ER 409

title depends on a presumption of fact, to direct the jury to find in favour of the fact: in which case I suppose a contrary view by the jury could be regarded as perverse. In my opinion if the facts and circumstances of a case are so compelling to the mind of the court that the court concludes beyond reasonable doubt that the purchaser will not be at risk of a successful assertion against him of the incumbrance, the court should declare in favour of a good title shown.

In the instant case, apart from the reference in the deed of 1930 to the performance of the contract for sale being suspended, there can I think be no shadow of doubt that the purchaser cannot be at such risk. Everything from the second lease in 1933 onwards points in great or less degree, and particularly the 1936 appointment of new trustees, to abandonment of the contract, and in any event to the impossibility of a representative of Percy obtaining specific performance of it in 1973. Goulding J I think founded his view on the reference to suspension of performance of the contract, and the fact that the terms of the suspension are unknown. But if the term of the suspension was during the life of Percy, he died more than 30 years before the contract with the appellants. If the term of the suspension was indefinite the agreement would have infringed the perpetuity rule. Goulding J speculated that there might have been a carefully drawn document in some way avoiding the impact of the perpetuity rule. I think with respect that that is too fanciful a theory, and should be ignored as a possibility: as a conjecture I think it not permissible.

One final point was raised. The land is in a compulsory registration area, so that the appellants will be obliged to apply for registration. It was said that the title ought not to be forced on the purchaser because the registrar might decide to enter the supposed contract of 1912 on the register as an incumbrance and so would place on the purchaser the burden of having it removed. Your Lordships heard an interesting argument from junior counsel for the appellants on the law and practice of registration but, with respect to him, I remain unconvinced that this particular factor makes any difference to the case. No separate criteria have been defined in the Land Registration Act 1925, or in the rules, as to the circumstances in which land may be registered without notice of an incumbrance, so there is no reason in my opinion why the court should depart from the rules which it has laid down, as I have tried to show above, for dealing with situations such as the present. It would be illogical moreover if different rules were to apply according as land comes to be included in a compulsory area, as it may do at any time, or remains outside. It would, finally, be inconceivable that in a case where a vendor has been held by the Court of Appeal and by this House to have shown a good marketable title the Chief Land Registrar should hold that he has shown something less, or, if he should do so, why the vendor under an open contract should be held by the court not to have shown such a title. I would reject this argument.

Accordingly I am of opinion beyond reasonable doubt on the facts (a) that there was abandonment of the contract of sale to Percy before 1936 (and probably in connection with the second lease to Percy in 1932/33) and (b) additionally that no representative of Percy could at the time of the contract for sale to the appellants have established a case for specific performance against the appellants. I therefore agree that good title is shown and would dismiss the appeal with costs.

LORD KEITH OF KINKEL. My Lords, I have had the benefit of reading in draft the speech prepared by my noble and learned friend Lord Russell of Killowen. I agree with it, and for the reasons which he gives I would dismiss the appeal.

Appeal dismissed.

Solicitors: *Simmons & Simmons* (for the appellants); *Monro Pennyfather & Co* (for the respondents).

Wendy Shockett   Barrister.

a # R v Greater Birmingham Supplementary Benefit Appeal Tribunal, ex parte Khan

QUEEN'S BENCH DIVISION
LORD WIDGERY CJ, SHAW LJ AND LLOYD J
28th JUNE 1979

b

Supplementary benefit – Calculation of benefit – Reduction of amount of supplementary allowance – Claim for unemployment benefit not yet determined – Right to reduce allowance where commission of opinion applicant would be disqualified from receiving unemployment benefit – Failure of commission to form opinion whether applicant would be so disqualified – Whether reduction in allowance validly made – Supplementary Benefits Act 1976, Sch 1, para 9.

c

The applicant left his employment and then registered, under s 5 of the Supplementary Benefits Act 1976, for work and applied for a supplementary allowance and unemployment benefit. By the time his supplementary allowance application came before the Supplementary Benefits Commission, his claim for unemployment benefit had been suspended by the Department of Employment, pending enquiries into whether *d* he had contributed to his own unemployment. The commission calculated the amount of supplementary allowance which would normally be payable to him and then, purporting to act under para 9*ᵃ* of Sch 1 to the 1976 Act, deducted 40%. Under para 9(1)(*b*) and (2)(*b*) an applicant's supplementary allowance could be reduced by 40% if, in the opinion of the commission, he would, if his claim for unemployment benefit had been determined, be disqualified for unemployment benefit by virtue of s 20(1)*ᵇ* of the *e* Social Security Act 1975 (which concerned disqualification by reason of conduct resulting in unemployment). The applicant appealed to a supplementary benefit appeal tribunal against the deduction but the tribunal dismissed his appeal, giving as their reasons that the allowance had been correctly calculated in accordance with the 1976 Act and on the available evidence the deduction under para 9 had been correctly applied. The applicant's solicitor then wrote to the clerk of the tribunal saying that the tribunal appeared to have *f* made no finding on the question whether the applicant had contributed to his own unemployment. He asked the clerk to enquire of the tribunal, inter alia, whether they had in fact considered the matter. In reply the tribunal stated that they had not been in a position to decide to what extent, if any, the applicant had contributed to his own unemployment. The applicant applied for an order of certiorari to quash the tribunal's decision on the ground that the tribunal could not make a deduction of 40% under para *g* 9 unless they had first formed an opinion whether the applicant would have been disqualified from receiving unemployment benefit if his claim to that benefit had been determined. The tribunal contended that it would be very difficult for it to form any such opinion because they did not have the machinery for making extensive enquiries.

Held – Although it might be very difficult for a supplementary benefit appeal tribunal *h* to form an opinion whether an applicant would have been disqualified from receiving unemployment benefit if his claim had been determined, they nonetheless were required to do so before they could make a deduction under para 9 of Sch 1 to the 1976 Act of 40% of the supplementary allowance that would otherwise have been payable to the applicant. Since the evidence showed that the tribunal had not formed their own opinion on the applicant's case and had therefore erred in deducting 40%, and since the *j* error was apparent on the face of their letter and so on the face of the record, an order of certiorari would be granted (see p 761 *j* and p 762 *f* to p 763 *b*, post).

---

a   Paragraph 9, so far as material, is set out at p 761, post
b   Section 20(1), so far as material, is set out at p 761 *g*, post

Notes

For calculating social security benefits, see Supplement to 27 Halsbury's Laws (3rd Edn) *a* para 947A.

For the Social Security Act 1975, s 20, see 45 Halsbury's Statutes (3rd Edn) 1100.

For the Supplementary Benefits Act 1976, s 5 and Sch 1, para 9, see 46 ibid 1050, 1079.

Motion for certiorari

On 11th January 1977 the applicant, Zaman Khan, left the employment of D P Millar *b* & Sons Ltd. He then registered for employment under s 5 of the Supplementary Benefits Act 1976 and applied for a supplementary allowance and unemployment benefit. By the time his supplementary allowance application came before the Supplementary Benefits Commission, his claim for unemployment benefit had been suspended by the Department of Employment pending enquiries into whether he had contributed to his own unemployment. The commission calculated the amount of supplementary *c* allowance which would normally be payable to him and then made a deduction of 40% under para 9 of Sch 1 to the 1976 Act. The applicant appealed against the deduction. On 16th March 1977 the Greater Birmingham Supplementary Benefit Appeal Tribunal dismissed the appeal. By notice of motion, dated 12th July 1977, the applicant applied for an order of certiorari to remove the tribunal's decision into the High Court for the purpose of its being quashed. The facts are set out in the judgment of Lloyd J. *d*

Lord Gifford for the applicant.
Simon Brown for the commission.

LLOYD J delivered the first judgment at the invitation of Lord Widgery CJ. This is an *e* application by Mr Zaman Khan for an order of certiorari to quash a decision of the Greater Birmingham Supplementary Benefit Appeal Tribunal made on 16th March, 1977. The question, in a nutshell, is whether the tribunal erred in law in deducting 40% from the amount of the applicant's supplementary benefit under para 9 of Sch 1 to the Supplementary Benefits Act 1976, and, if so, whether that error appears on the face of the record. *f*

The facts of the case can be stated in a sentence or two. Until 11th January 1977 the applicant was employed by a company called D P Millar & Sons Ltd, and had been so employed for a period of about 12 years. I need not go into the circumstances in which that employment ceased. It is said that he was laid off from his old job with the company, that he was offered a new job which he tried for a period of about four weeks, but he found that he could not earn so much money in the new job, and, therefore, he *g* asked for his old job back. This was refused. That led to his leaving the employment of his old employers on 11th January and on 12th January (the very next day) he registered for employment under s 5 of the Supplementary Benefits Act 1976 and applied on the same day for supplementary benefit. That application was considered by the Supplementary Benefits Commission on 17th January.

Meanwhile, on 14th January he had received from his old employers four weeks' *h* wages in lieu of notice. The commission decided that the applicant had sufficient to meet his requirements until 14th February 1977. There was an appeal from that decision, but that is not a matter with which this court is now concerned.

The applicant has another string to his bow. He claims that the commission were in error in the way they arrived at the rate for supplementary benefit for the period subsequent to 14th February 1977. What the commission had done was to make a *i* calculation of the applicant's requirements, as they were obliged to do under the Act, and that calculation produced a figure of £16·41 a week. They then made a calculation of the applicant's resources, which were nil. Instead of subtracting the one from the other, they made a deduction of 40% from the applicant's normal requirements and so arrived at a figure of £11·36. In doing that they purported to act under para 9 of Sch 1 of the 1976

Act. They applied what has come to be known as 'the 40% rule'. In fact the sum which
a they deducted has now been made up so that there will be no financial consequences of
our decision today one way or the other. In one sense, therefore, it could be said that the
present case is academic. But both counsel invited us to deal with this case as a matter of
principle. They said that it involved a point of practical importance on which our
guidance was sought. Moreover, as both counsel pointed out, it is difficult to think that
there could ever be a case on this point which would have financial consequences at the
b time when it came to be dealt with by this court.

There was then an appeal from the decision of the commission on grounds set out in
a letter of 2nd March 1977. That appeal came before the Greater Birmingham Appeal
Tribunal on 16th March 1977, who upheld the decision of the commission. It is that
decision which is challenged now in this court by counsel for the applicant.

At this stage it is convenient to have in mind the terms of para 9 of Sch 1. I will read
c only what is relevant for present purposes. Paragraph 9(1) provides:

'If a person's right to a supplementary allowance is subject to the condition of
registration for employment under section 5 of this Act, then, in relation to any
period during which—(*a*) he is disqualified for receiving unemployment benefit
under the Social Security Act 1975 by virtue of section 20(1) of that Act
(disqualification by reference to conduct resulting in unemployment or conducing
d to its continuance); or (*b*) he is not so disqualified, but the circumstances are as
mentioned in sub-paragraph (2) below; this Part of this Schedule shall have effect,
as regards the determination of the amount of any supplementary allowance to
which he is entitled, as if the amount specified in the entry in paragraph 7 or 8 of
this Schedule which relates to his requirements . . . were reduced by a sum equal
to—(i) 40 per cent of the amount so specified . . .'
e
Then para 9(2) reads:

'The circumstances referred to in sub-paragraph (1)(*b*) above are that the person
concerned—(*a*) has not made a claim for unemployment benefit; or (*b*) has made
such a claim, but the claim has not yet been determined; or (*c*) has had such a claim
disallowed otherwise than by reason of his being disqualified as mentioned in sub-
f paragraph (1)(*a*) above; but in the opinion of the Commission he would be so
disqualified if he were to make such a claim, or if his claim had been determined,
or if it had not been disallowed for a different reason.'

The circumstances in which a claim for unemployment benefit can be disallowed are set
out in s 20 of the Social Security Act 1975, and again I will read only what is relevant for
g present purposes. It provides:

'(1) A person shall be disqualified for receiving unemployment benefit for such
period not exceeding 6 weeks as may be determined in accordance with sections 97
to 104 of this Act . . . if—(*a*) he has lost his employment as an employed earner
through his misconduct, or has voluntarily left such employment without just
h cause . . .'

Returning to para 9 of Sch 1 to the 1976 Act, we are not here concerned with para 9(1)(*a*).
We are concerned with para 9(1)(*b*), and so with sub-para (2) of para 9, and in particular
with sub-para (2)(*b*) which provides for the circumstances in which the applicant has
made a claim, that is to say a claim for unemployment benefit and the claim has not yet
j been determined. Counsel's submission for the applicant in relation to that sub-
paragraph is simplicity itself. He says that the tribunal could not make a deduction
under sub-para (2) without forming an opinion whether the applicant would have been
disqualified from receiving unemployment benefit if the claim had been determined,
which it had not. In my judgment, that submission is, on the language of the sub-
paragraph, plainly correct. Indeed it was conceded to be correct by counsel for the

commission on behalf of the tribunal. One then turns to the decision of the tribunal to see how the matter stands. Their reasons are set out very briefly. They say this:

> 'The allowance has been correctly calculated in accordance with the Supplementary Benefits Act, 1976. On the evidence available to them, the Tribunal felt that the deduction under Paragraph 9 of Schedule 1 of the Supplementary Benefits Act, 1976 had been correctly applied.'

If the matter had rested there, there would have been no material on which this court could have said that there was any error of law on the face of the record. But the matter does not rest there, because the applicant's solicitors wrote to the clerk to the supplementary benefit appeal tribunal on 23rd March 1977 as follows:

> 'We refer to the hearing of the above case and to the reasons supplied by the Tribunal for their decision. On a careful study of the findings and reasons, we note that the Tribunal appear not to have made any finding on the question which was argued before them by counsel that they should consider whether the [applicant] had contributed to his dismissal. In the circumstances, would you ask the Tribunal to indicate, by way of expansion of the reasons already supplied, whether they would answer the following questions: (a) Did the Tribunal consider that they were bound by a decision of the Insurance Officer? (b) If so, what was the decision by which they considered themselves bound? (c) If the answer to (a) is no, did the Tribunal consider whether the [applicant] had contributed to his own unemployment? (d) If the Tribunal did not consider Question (c) why not; (e) If the Tribunal did consider Question (c), what was their conclusion, and on what evidence did they base it?'

The answer from the tribunal was as follows:

> 'I have received your letter dated 23 March via the local office of the DHSS ... Your letter was shown to the Chairman of the Tribunal and her comment was as follows (a) The Tribunal did not consider that they were bound by the decision of the Insurance Officer. (b) [and this is the important paragraph] The Tribunal were not in a position to decide to what extent, if any, [the applicant] had contributed to his own unemployment.'

If the tribunal were not, as appears from what is said in that letter, in a position to decide to what extent, if any, the applicant had contributed to his own unemployment, they were not in a position to form any opinion whether he would have been disqualified if his claim had been dealt with. If they formed no opinion as to that, then they were not entitled to deduct the 40%.

Counsel for the commission argued that it would be very difficult for the tribunal to form an opinion on the matter. They did not have the means for making extensive inquiries. They did not have machinery for that purpose. That may very well be so. But it does not mean, in my judgment, that they can simply wash their hands of the matter or, to use a phrase used by Watkins J in a recent judgment, 'abdicate all responsibility'. They must, it seems to me, do the best they can. The Act, in plain terms, requires them to form an opinion before deducting 40%. That in this case they have not done, and on those grounds it seems to me that the tribunal have fallen into error.

There then remains the question whether that error is one which is apparent on the face of the record. The answer to that question must again be yes. We are not confined to the decision itself. We can look at the subsequent letter explaining and expanding the tribunal's reasons for their decision. The error is apparent on the face of that letter.

For those reasons, in my judgment, this decision cannot stand and the application for certiorari succeeds.

SHAW LJ. I agree.

LORD WIDGERY CJ. I also agree. I think it quite clear that, however difficult the
a task may prove to be, a tribunal which is faced with a question of making an assessment
under the so-called 40% rule must do its best to achieve a result. Further, in pursuing its
best in this context, it should not regard itself as being bound strictly to the rules of
evidence as they are applied in a court of law. It is open to the tribunal in this particular
type of case to take into account all the circumstances, so far as they are probative, so far
as they help to conclude proof of the truth in the individual case. I would expect in this
b type of case that tribunals should draw considerable strength from evidence which
would not strictly be relevant in a court of law.

I agree that certiorari should go.

Order of certiorari.

c Solicitors: *Alan Robinson,* Birmingham (for the applicant); *Solicitor to the Department of
Health and Social Security.*

Sumra Green   Barrister.

---

d Raineri v Miles and another (Wiejski and another, third parties)

COURT OF APPEAL, CIVIL DIVISION
BUCKLEY, BRIDGE AND TEMPLEMAN LJJ
21st, 22nd JUNE, 6th JULY 1979

e
*Sale of land – Notice to complete – Failure of vendor to complete on date fixed for completion –
Vendor completing within reasonable time after service on him of notice to complete – Effect of
notice to complete on contractual date for completion – Failure of third party to complete contract
resulting in defendant being in breach of contract with plaintiff – Time not essence of contract
between third party and defendant – Defendant liable in damages to plaintiff – Defendant
f claiming indemnity from third party – Whether third party in breach where contract completed
in reasonable time of date of completion if time not essence – Whether service of notice to complete
depriving defendant of any remedy accruing to him on original failure of third party to complete
– Whether third party liable to indemnify defendant against claim by plaintiff – Law of Property
Act 1925, s 41 – Law Society's Conditions of Sale (1973 Revision), condition 19.*

g By a contract incorporating the Law Society's Conditions of Sale (1973 Revision) the third
parties agreed to sell a house to the defendants. The contract provided that the purchase
should be completed on or before 12th July 1977, when vacant possession was to be given
to the defendants. At the same time the defendants agreed to sell the house in which
they were then living to the plaintiff, that contract also providing for completion with
vacant possession on 12th July. In neither case was the time for completion expressed to
h be of the essence of the contract. On 11th July the defendants were told that the third
parties could not complete their contract with them on the following day. The
defendants immediately informed the plaintiff's solicitors, but the plaintiff himself had
already vacated his previous house and was on the road with his furniture intending to
take possession of his new house. In consequence of the third parties' failure to complete
their contract with the defendants on 12th July, the defendants were prevented from
j giving the plaintiff vacant possession and could not complete their contract with him on
that day in accordance with its terms On 13th July the defendants, being then able,
ready and willing to complete their contract with the third parties, gave them notice,
pursuant to condition 19^a of the conditions of sale, to complete the contract by 11th

---

a Condition 19, so far as material, is set out at p 770 *d* to *f,* post

August. The contract between the defendants and the third parties was duly completed on that day. The defendants' contract with the plaintiff was also completed on that day and the plaintiff was let into possession. Between 12th July and 11th August the plaintiff incurred expense in providing himself and his family with living accommodation for which he recovered damages from the defendants. The defendants served the third parties with a third party notice claiming indemnity against the plaintiff's claim on the ground of the third parties' failure to give vacant possession on or before 12th July. The judge dismissed the third party proceedings. On an appeal by the defendants the third parties contended that, where time was not of the essence, the contract only required completion on the date fixed for completion or within a reasonable time thereafter and that, since they had completed in a reasonable time, they had not committed a breach of the contract and so were not liable in damages for the delay. They further contended that the effect of the notice to complete was to substitute for 12th July a new date for completion and that they had fulfilled the contract as so varied.

Held – (i) A term in a contract providing that it was to be completed on a named day could not, in the absence of a clear context, be construed as meaning that it was to be completed on some later date; although the effect of the term might be modified by equitable rules, the meaning of its language could not. The effect of s 41[b] of the Law of Property Act 1925 was not to negative the existence of a breach of contract where one had occurred but merely in certain circumstances to bar any assertion that the breach amounted to a repudiation of the contract. It followed that, by failing to complete with vacant possession on 12th July, the third parties committed, both at law and in equity, a breach of their contract with the defendants; but, although that breach could not have been relied on by the defendants as a ground for avoiding an action for specific performance, it afforded no ground for construing the contract otherwise than in accordance with its clear terms (see p 769 e g h, p 770 a to c, p 771 e f, p 773 e to g and p 774 d, post); dicta of Fry LJ in *Howe v Smith* [1881–5] All ER Rep at 209 and of Lord Parker of Waddington in *Stickney v Keeble* [1914–15] All ER Rep at 81 applied; *Woods v Mackenzie Hill Ltd* [1975] 2 All ER 170 explained; *Babacomp Ltd v Rightside Properties Ltd* [1974] 1 All ER 142 distinguished; *Smith v Hamilton* [1950] 2 All ER 928 disapproved.

(ii) The service under condition 19 of a notice to complete, which presupposed that the contract had not been completed on the contractual date, made new rights and remedies available to the party serving the notice in the event of the party served failing to comply with it. However, there was nothing in the terms of the condition which had the effect of discharging any accrued right or cause of action vested in the party serving the notice. It followed that the defendants had not been deprived of any cause of action in damages against the third parties which had accrued to them before they served the notice to complete. The appeal would accordingly be allowed (see p 770 j to p 771 b and d to f and p 773 f j to p 774 a c d, post).

Notes

For the date of completion of a contract for the sale of land, see 34 Halsbury's Laws (3rd Edn) 256, para 426, and for cases on the subject, see 40 Digest (Repl) 116–121, 905–949.

For the Law of Property Act 1925, s 41, see 27 Halsbury's Statutes (3rd Edn) 405.

Cases referred to in judgments

Babacomp Ltd v Rightside Properties Ltd [1973] 3 All ER 873, 26 P & CR 102; *affd* [1974] 1 All ER 142, 26 P & CR 526, CA, Digest (Cont Vol D) 798, 944a.

Bennett v Stone [1902] 1 Ch 226; *affd* [1903] 1 Ch 509, 72 LJ Ch 240, 88 LT 35, CA, 40 Digest (Repl) 130, 997.

---

b Section 41 provides: 'Stipulations in a contract, as to time or otherwise, which according to rules of equity are not deemed to be or to have become of the essence of the contract, are also construed and have effect at law in accordance with the same rules.'

Howe v Smith (1884) 27 Ch D 89, [1881–5] All ER Rep 201, 53 LJ Ch 1055, 50 LT 573, 48
a   JP 773, CA, 40 Digest (Repl) 24, *2027.*

Jaques v Millar (1877) 6 Ch D 153, 37 LT 151, 42 JP 20, 44 Digest (Repl) 155, *1346.*

Jones v Gardiner [1902] 1 Ch 191, 71 LJ Ch 93, 86 LT 74, 40 Digest (Repl) 290, *2431.*

Lock v Bell [1931] 1 Ch 35, [1930] All ER Rep 635, 100 LJ Ch 22, 144 LT 108, 40 Digest
(Repl) 117, *909.*

Phillips v Lamdin [1949] 1 All ER 770, [1949] 2 KB 33, [1949] LJR 1293, 40 Digest (Repl)
b   381, *3058.*

Smith v Hamilton [1950] 2 All ER 928, [1951] Ch 174, 40 Digest (Repl) 242, *2042.*

Stickney v Keeble [1915] AC 386, [1914–15] All ER Rep 73, 84 LJ Ch 259, 112 LT 664, HL,
40 Digest (Repl) 120, *942.*

Tilley v Thomas (1867) LR 3 Ch App 61, 17 LT 422, 32 JP 180, LJJ, 40 Digest (Repl) 118,
924.

c   *Woods v Mackenzie Hill Ltd* [1975] 2 All ER 170, [1975] 1 WLR 613, 29 P & CR 306,
Digest (Cont Vol D) 799, *944b.*

Cases also cited

Hargraves Transport Ltd v Lynch [1969] 1 All ER 455, [1969] 1 WLR 215.

Johnson v Agnew [1978] 3 All ER 314, [1978] Ch 176, CA.

d   *Quadrangle Development and Construction Co Ltd v Jenner* [1974] 1 All ER 729, [1974] 1
WLR 68, CA.

*United Scientific Holdings Ltd v Burnley Borough Council, Cheapside Land Development Co Ltd
v Messels Service Co* [1977] 2 All ER 62, [1978] AC 904, HL.

Appeal

e   By order of Master Chamberlain dated 14th April 1978 summary judgment was given
for the plaintiff, Carlo Raineri, against the defendants, Gruffydd Royston Miles and Beryl
Miles, in an action in which the plaintiff claimed, inter alia, damages for expense
occasioned to him by the failure of the defendants to complete, on the date provided
therein, an agreement in writing made on 14th June 1977 between the plaintiff and the
defendants for the sale of freehold property at 36 Kingfield Road, Ealing, London. By
f   a third party notice the defendants sought from the third parties, Zygmunt Wiejski and
Matilda Wiejski, indemnity against the plaintiff's claim on the ground of the failure of
the third parties to give up the freehold of 19 New Inn Lane, Burpham, Guildford,
Surrey with vacant possession on or before 12th July 1977 in accordance with an
agreement in writing made on 14th June 1977 between the third parties and the
defendants. On 19th October 1978 Whitford J dismissed the third party proceedings.
The defendants appealed against Whitford J's decision. The facts are set out in the
g   judgment of Buckley LJ.

Alan Steinfeld for the defendants.
John H Weeks for the third parties.
The plaintiff did not appear.

h

Cur adv vult

6th July. The following judgments were read.

BUCKLEY LJ. This case raises a point of general interest on the law of the sale of
j   land. It seems, surprisingly, to be devoid of direct judicial authority. If one party to a
contract for the sale of land fails to complete the contract on the stipulated completion
date for reasons unconnected with making or accepting a good title to the land or other
conveyancing reasons, the other party being then able, ready and willing to complete,
whereby the innocent party suffers damage, and if the innocent party thereafter serves
a notice to complete the contract within a stipulated reasonable time and the party in

default does complete the contract within that time, can the innocent party recover the damage he has suffered by reason of the original default?

By a contract dated 14th June 1977 the third parties in this action agreed to sell a freehold residential house in Guildford to the defendants for £25,500. The contract incorporated the Law Society's Conditions of Sale 1973, with the exclusion of conditions 6(1) and 16(4). It provided that the purchase should be completed on or before 12th July 1977, when vacant possession should be given to the purchasers.

The defendants, also on 14th June 1977, entered into a contract for the sale by them to the plaintiff of the house in Ealing in which they were then living. That contract also stipulated that the transaction should be completed on 12th July 1977, with vacant possession on completion.

In neither case was the time for completion expressed to be of the essence of the contract.

The third parties had contracted to buy another house. For this purpose they apparently needed to raise £30,000 which they proposed to do by way of two mortgages of that other house, each for £15,000. One of the lenders, however, proved at a very late stage to be unwilling to lend more than £10,000 with the result that the third parties were £5,000 short of the amount necessary to complete their purchase.

Late on Monday 11th July the defendants' solicitors were told that the third parties could not complete their contract with the defendants on the following day. They immediately informed the plaintiff's solicitors, but the plaintiff himself had already vacated his previous house, which was in Warrington, and was on the road to London with his furniture, intending to take possession of the house in Ealing on the following day, 12th July.

In consequence of the third parties' failure to complete their contract with the defendants on 12th July, the defendants were prevented from giving the plaintiff vacant possession of the house at Ealing and so could not complete their contract with the plaintiff on that day in accordance with its terms.

On 13th July the defendants, being then able, ready and willing to complete the contract, gave the third parties notice pursuant to condition 19 of the Law Society's General Conditions of Sale to complete their contract within 28 days. The third parties' financial difficulties were resolved in time to enable them to vacate the house in Guildford and complete their contract with the defendants on 11th August. The defendants' contract with the plaintiff was completed on the same day and the plaintiff was let into possession of the Ealing house. Between 12th July and 11th August the plaintiff had necessarily incurred expense in providing himself and his family with living accommodation. He sued the defendants in damages and recovered summary judgment for damages to be certified on enquiry. The defendants served the third parties with a third party notice claiming indemnity against the plaintiff's claim on the ground of the failure of the third parties to give vacant possession of the house at Guildford on or before 12th July. The third party proceedings came before Whitford J who, on 19th October 1978, dismissed them. The defendants appeal from that decision.

It was common ground before Whitford J that, if the third parties were in breach of their contract by reason of their failure to complete on 12th July 1977, they were liable to indemnify the defendants against their liability to the plaintiff. The third parties' case here and below has been that they were never in breach of their contract. They contend that on the true construction of that contract they were only bound to complete on 12th July or within a reasonable time thereafter. Consequently there could be no breach until a reasonable time after 12th July had elapsed. They further submit that the effect of the notice to complete was to substitute for 12th July a new date for completion, and that they fulfilled the contract as so varied. The judge reached his conclusion on the following ground stated at the end of his judgment:

'I have come to the conclusion that, accepting, as on the authorities I think I ought to accept, that notwithstanding the fact that a failure to meet an original date for

completion may not constitute a breach sufficient to bring an agreement to an end
it may nonetheless in appropriate circumstances amount to what could be described
as a partial breach giving rise to a good claim in damages, it does in fact only do so
if the failure arose from some unreasonable action or inaction on the side of the
person who failed. The claim can only be good if it can be established that a person
in default had not acted reasonably in doing what they in fact did. It was not
suggested before me that any such case could be made out against the third parties
on the facts and in the result I have come to the conclusion that the defendants are
not entitled to the relief which they seek against the third parties.'

It will be convenient to deal first with the point of construction. On this counsel for
the third parties relied on three authorities, *Babacomp Ltd v Rightside Properties Ltd*[1],
Woods v Mackenzie Hill Ltd[2] and *Smith v Hamilton*[3]. In the first of these cases, the
purchasers, having given a notice to complete which was held to have made time of the
essence of the contract, and with which the vendors had not complied, sued for return of
their deposit and damages. They were successful. The original time for completion in
that case was 60 days after 12th July 1972, which was the date of the contract. On 31st
October 1972 the purchasers wrote the letter which is set out in the judgment[4]. Goff J
held this letter to be a sufficient notice to make time of the essence pursuant to the
contract. The judge, having held that the purchasers' case did not there depend on
repudiation by the vendor, said[5]:

'As time was originally not of the essence, there was no breach of contract either
at law or in equity at the expiration of the 60 days, but provided proper steps were
taken to make time of the essence, then the defendants' failure to perform on the
date so made essential would be a breach of contract at law and in equity.'

He then cited a passage from Williams on Vendor and Purchaser[6], which includes the
following:

'It follows that, except where time is of the essence of the stipulation, a breach of
contract is only committed in the case of unreasonable delay in the performance of
any act agreed to be done. For example, where time is not essential, a party failing
to complete a sale of land on the day fixed therefor by the agreement does not then
commit a breach of contract either in equity or at law; it is only on failure to
complete within a reasonable time after that date that the contract is broken.'

The plaintiffs' right to relief in that action did not depend on whether there had been a
breach of contract at the expiration of the 60 day period. Once it had been decided that
the letter of 31st October 1972 was an effective notice to complete for the purposes of the
contract, the plaintiffs' right to relief flowed from the undoubted breach of contract
involved in the vendors' not completing in accordance with that notice. Consequently
the passage which I have read from the judgment was, in my opinion, obiter.

In *Woods v Mackenzie Hill Ltd*[2] the vendors sued for specific performance of a contract
of sale of land. The contractual date for completion was 30th September 1974, but the
contract was not then completed. Two of the three vendors purported to give a notice
to complete pursuant to the contract, but this was invalid. On 8th November 1974 the
vendors issued a writ claiming specific performance. Megarry J held that the service of
a notice to complete was not a condition precedent for the enforcement of the contract

1 [1973] 3 All ER 873
2 [1975] 2 All ER 170, [1975] 1 WLR 613
3 [1950] 2 All ER 928, [1951] Ch 174
4 [1973] 3 All ER 873 at 874
5 [1973] 3 All ER 873 at 875
6 4th Edn (1936) vol 2, p 991

and that, since more than a reasonable time for completion had elapsed, the plaintiffs
were entitled to specific performance. In one paragraph Megarry J[1] twice refers to the
contractual obligation of the parties 'to complete on the date fixed for completion or
within a reasonable time thereafter'. He was not concerned with the question whether
a breach of contract had occurred on 30th September 1974, but with whether the delay
after that date had been so great as to amount to an unreasonable delay justifying a decree
of specific performance without any notice to complete having been served.

In *Smith v Hamilton*[2] a purchaser sued for the return of her deposit and the vendor
counterclaimed for a declaration that the deposit was forfeited. By the terms of the
contract completion with vacant possession was fixed for 4th April 1949. The purchaser
was unable to complete on that date. By a letter dated 5th April 1949 the vendor agreed
to an extension of the time to complete in terms which were held not to have made time
of the essence of the contract. On 4th May 1949 the purchaser was in a position to
complete but the vendor had in the meantime, but after the end of the agreed extension,
sold the property elsewhere. The contract incorporated the following condition 25 from
the National Conditions of Sale:

> 'If the purchaser shall neglect or fail to complete his purchase according to these
> conditions, his deposit shall thereupon be forfeited (unless the court otherwise
> directs) to the vendor . . . and the vendor may, with or without notice or without
> previously tendering a conveyance, re-sell the property at such time, and in such
> manner and subject to such conditions as he shall think fit.'

Harman J held that the vendor's rights under the contract were governed by that
condition, and that the true construction of the special condition fixing the date for
completion was that the purchaser should complete on the day fixed or within a
reasonable time thereafter; but that such a time had not elapsed and the remedies given
by condition 25 did not become available until the purchaser had, by her delay, deprived
herself of the right to specific performance, which would not be so at the end of only 14
days after the date fixed for completion. He therefore held that the purchaser was
entitled to the return of her deposit.

In all three of these cases the judges used language capable of giving colour to the third
parties' contention in the present case, but only in *Smith v Hamilton*[2] can it be said that the
relevant remarks formed part of the ratio decidendi. As I understand Harman J's
judgment, he was saying that the special condition in that case which required
completion on 4th April 1949 should be construed as requiring completion on that date
or within a reasonable time thereafter with the consequence that the rights of forfeiture
and resale under condition 25 of the National Conditions could not accrue until the
purchaser had failed to complete within a reasonable time after 4th April.

The authority cited in Williams on Vendor and Purchaser[3] for the proposition that it
is only on failure to complete within a reasonable time after the date contractually fixed
for completion that the contract is broken is *Howe v Smith*[4]. In that case a contract for sale
provided that the purchase should be completed on a day named and that if the purchaser
should fail to comply with the agreement the vendor should be at liberty to resell and to
recover any deficiency in price as liquidated damages. The purchaser was not ready with
his purchase money on the date fixed for completion, and after repeated delays on the
purchaser's part the vendor resold the property. The purchaser brought an action for
specific performance. Kay J, who was affirmed in this court, held that the purchaser had
lost his right to enforce specific performance by reason of his delay. In the Court of
Appeal the purchaser was allowed to raise an additional claim to repayment of his

---

1 [1975] 2 All ER 170 at 172, [1975] 1 WLR 613 at 615–616
2 [1950] 2 All ER 928, [1951] Ch 174
3 4th Edn (1936) vol 2, p 991
4 (1884) 27 Ch D 89, [1881–5] All ER Rep 201

deposit. The judgments in this court were mainly concerned with the nature of a deposit and the rights of the parties in it. The court decided that the purchaser had by his delay not only debarred himself from any right to seek specific performance, but had repudiated the contract. In these circumstances the purchaser was held not to be entitled to the return of his deposit. In my judgment, the case is no authority for the proposition in support of which it is cited in Williams.

At common law a term of a contract stipulating when the contract should be performed was always regarded as an essential term of the contract, but, as Lord Parker pointed out in *Stickney v Keeble*[1], in contracts for the sale of land equity, having a concurrent jurisdiction, did not look on the stipulation as to time in precisely the same light. Where it could do so without injustice to the contracting parties it decreed specific performance notwithstanding failure to observe the time fixed by the contract for completion, and as an incident of specific performance relieve the party in default by restraining proceedings at law based on such failure (see also per Lord Loreburn and Lord Atkinson[2]). Since the statutory fusion of law and equity in 1873 it has been enacted (by the Supreme Court of Judicature Act 1873, s 25(7), now re-enacted in slightly different language in the Law of Property Act 1925, s 41) that stipulations of a contract, as to time or otherwise, which according to rules of equity are not deemed to be or to have become of the essence of the contract are also to be construed and have effect at law in accordance with the same rules. The third parties rely on s 41 on the point of construction. But, as was pointed out by Lord Cairns and Rolt LJJ in *Tilley v Thomas*[3], the construction of a contract must be the same in equity as in a court of law (see also *Stickney v Keeble*[4] per Lord Atkinson and Lord Parker, and *Lock v Bell*[5] per Maugham J). A clause which provides in terms that the contract shall be completed on a named day cannot, in the absence of a clear context, be construed as meaning that it shall be completed on some later day. Its effect may be modified by equitable rules, but the meaning of the language cannot be.

In equity a party to a contract who is seeking equitable relief was not barred merely by an earlier failure on his part to comply precisely with a completion date. So long as a court of equity would have disregarded a failure to comply with a time stipulation for the purpose of granting the equitable remedy of specific performance, it would have restrained an action at law based on that failure. In considering whether to restrain an action at law the Court of Chancery took cognizance of everything which had happened up to the date of the decree restraining the action at law. Since the fusion of law and equity the High Court is to have regard to all those events and is to grant or withhold the common law remedy of damages for breach of contract on the principles which would have actuated the Court of Chancery in permitting or restraining proceedings at law (see *Stickney v Keeble*[6] per Lord Parker). This is, in my opinion, the whole effect of the Law of Property Act 1925, s 41, relevant to this case. It does not negative the existence of a breach of contract where one has occurred, but in certain circumstances it bars any assertion that the breach has amounted to a repudiation of the contract. Thus, if a purchaser has failed to complete on the contractual completion date, he may still recover damages which he has suffered by reason of some default by the vendor if he was ready and willing to complete within a reasonable time after that date (see *Howe v Smith*[7] per Fry LJ). This is not because the purchaser committed no breach of contract in failing to complete on the fixed date, but because equity would not allow the vendor to rely on that breach in the circumstances.

1   [1915] AC 386 at 415, [1914–15] All ER Rep 73 at 80–81
2   [1915] AC 386 at 400, 401, [1914–15] All ER Rep 73 at 77, 78
3   (1867) LR 3 Ch App 61 at 69
4   [1915] AC 386 at 402, 417, [1914–15] All ER Rep 73 at 78, 81
5   [1931] 1 Ch 35 at 43, [1930] All ER Rep 635 at 637
6   [1915] AC 386 at 417, [1914–15] All ER Rep 73 at 81
7   (1884) 27 Ch D 89 at 103, [1881–5] All ER Rep 201 at 209

In the present case the third parties undoubtedly committed a breach of their contract with the defendants in the contemplation of the common law by failing to complete *a* with vacant possession on 12th July 1977. It was also, in my judgment, a breach of the contract as it would be construed in equity, since the contract would fall to be construed in precisely the same way in equity as at law. Had the third parties had occasion to sue for specific performance of the contract, the defendants could very probably not have relied on that breach as a ground for avoiding an order for specific performance; but the third parties, being the parties in default, never had occasion to seek equitable relief. *b* None of this, in my judgment, affords any ground for construing the contract otherwise than in accordance with its clear terms. In my judgment, Harman J, whose attention was not drawn in *Smith v Hamilton*[1] to either *Tilley v Thomas*[2] or *Stickney v Keeble*[3], was mistaken in accepting the argument in *Smith v Hamilton*[1] that the condition fixing the completion date at 4th April 1949 should be construed as though it required completion on that date or within a reasonable time thereafter. *c*

For these reasons in my judgment the third parties fail on the question of construction.

The next question is the effect on the rights and obligations of the parties of the service of a notice to complete under condition 19 of the Law Society's General Conditions of Sale, cll (2) and (3) of which provide as follows:

> '(2) If the sale shall not be completed on the date fixed for completion either party *d* may on that date or at any time thereafter (unless the contract shall first have been rescinded or become void) give to the other party notice in writing to complete the transaction in accordance with this condition but such notice shall only be effective if the party giving the same at the time the notice is sent is either ready, able and willing to complete or is not so ready, able and willing by reason of the default or omission of the other party to the contract.
>
> '(3) Upon service of an effective notice pursuant to the preceding clause it shall be *e* an express term to the contract that the party to whom the notice is given shall complete the transaction within twenty-eight days after the day of service of the notice (excluding the day of service) and in respect of such period time shall be of the essence of the contract but without prejudice to any intermediate right of rescission by either party.' *f*

Clause (4) of the condition states what shall be the consequences of failure by a purchaser to comply with such a notice and cl (5) what shall be the consequences of failure by a vendor.

The third parties contend that on the service of a notice pursuant to this condition the contract is varied by the substitution of the date for completion stipulated in the notice for the original contractual date fixed for completion, thus eliminating the latter and *g* substituting a new term of the contract that the contract shall be completed on the date specified in the notice. If the party on whom the notice is served completes the sale on or before the new date for completion, the third parties submit that there has been no breach of contract, for the contract has been completed in accordance with the substituted term. True, condition 19(3) preserves any intermediate right to rescission by either party, but no subsisting right of action based on failure to complete on or before the date *h* originally fixed for completion is preserved. If the contract is completed within the time permitted by the notice, there has in the event been no breach of the contract. So runs the argument.

In my judgment this is not the true effect of the condition. The service of a notice under the condition, which presupposes that the sale has not been completed on the contractual date, makes new rights and remedies available to the party who serves the *j*

---

1   [1950] 2 All ER 928, [1951] Ch 174
2   (1867) LR 3 Ch App 61
3   [1915] AC 386, [1914–15] All ER Rep 73

notice in the event of the party served failing to comply with it. There is nothing in its
a terms which has the effect of discharging any accrued right or cause of action vested in
the party who serves the notice. In other words, as counsel for the defendants submitted,
the service of a notice under condition 19 gives the party serving the notice additional
rights and remedies, but does not detract from pre-existing rights or remedies.
Accordingly, in my judgment, the service of the notice to complete in the present case
did not deprive the defendants of any cause of action in damages which may have
b accrued to them before the service of the notice by reason of the failure to complete the
contract on 12th July 1977.

There is, of course, a distinction to be drawn between a breach of contract of so grave
a character as to constitute a repudiation of the contract by the defaulting party and a
breach of contract which will sound only in damages without amounting to a
repudiation; but with deference to Whitford J I do not think that there can be such a
c thing as a 'partial' breach, unless the expression be used to describe a breach of part only
of a contract. An alleged breach of a contract must either be or not be a breach. If it is
a breach, the fact that the offending party asserts that he acted reasonably cannot make
it any less a breach. At law a failure to complete punctually in accordance with a time
stipulation is a fundamental breach amounting to repudiation, but not so in equity if the
time stipulation is not of the essence of the contract. At law every breach of contract
d sounds in damages, but in some circumstances already referred to equity will not permit
the injured party to pursue that remedy. For reasons which I have already given I do not
think that equity can in the present case shield the third parties from liability for their
breach in failing to complete on 12th July 1977. Since it is conceded that, if the third
parties are liable in damages, the measure is that which is necessary to indemnify the
defendants against their liability to the plaintiff, I have reached a different conclusion
e from that of the judge.

For these reasons I would allow this appeal.

BRIDGE LJ. I agree, both with the judgment of Buckley LJ and with that to be
delivered by Templeman LJ which I have had the advantage of reading in draft. For the
reasons given in those judgments, I too would allow the appeal.
f

TEMPLEMAN LJ. A contract for the sale of a dwelling-house provided for completion
on 12th July 1977. The vendors, the third parties, did not complete until 11th August
because they could not raise enough money to complete the purchase of their new
dwelling-house. The third parties now dispute their liability to the defendants, the
purchasers, for damages arising out of the delay.
g The question is whether a vendor of land under a contract which does not make time
of the essence, who fails to complete on the contractual date for completion, is liable for
damages for the delay.

Where time is not of the essence, a breach of contract as to time will not entitle the
aggrieved party to treat the contract as at an end or constitute a bar to specific performance
at the suit of the party in default, unless there has been unreasonable delay or there are
h other circumstances which render specific performance unfair.

Thus in *Stickney v Keeble*[1] the effect of a breach of contract as to time was explained by
Lord Parker of Waddington as follows:

'. . . in a contract for the sale and purchase of real estate, the time fixed by the
parties for completion has at law always been regarded as essential. In other words,
courts of law have always held the parties to their bargain in this respect, with the
j result that if the vendor is unable to make title by the day fixed for completion, the
purchaser can treat the contract as at an end and recover his deposit with interest and
the cost of investigating the title. In such cases, however, equity having a concurrent

---

1   [1915] AC 386 at 415–416, [1914–15] All ER Rep 73 at 80–81

jurisdiction did not look upon the stipulations as to time in precisely the same light. Where it could do so without injustice to the contracting parties it decreed *a* specific performance notwithstanding failure to observe the time fixed by the contract for completion, and as an incident of specific performance relieved the party in default by restraining proceedings at law based on such failure. This is really all that is meant by and involved in the maxim that in equity the time fixed for completion is not of the essence of the contract, but this maxim never had any application to cases in which the stipulation as to time could not be disregarded *b* without injustice to the parties, when, for example, the parties, for reasons best known to themselves, had stipulated that the time fixed shall be essential, or where there was something in the nature of the property or the surrounding circumstances which would render it inequitable to treat it as a non-essential term of the contract. It should be observed, too, that it was only for the purposes of granting specific performance that equity in this class of case interfered with the remedy at law.'   *c*

Likewise, Harman J in *Smith v Hamilton*[1] said:

'... the equitable view which ... has prevailed for a long time in the case of real estate, is that the court looks to the substance of the matter, and will not allow the existence of dates to alter the general view that the contract is to be performed if it is just and equitable to do so, notwithstanding that time may be overrun in certain *d* respects.'

It appears that equity intervenes to prevent a breach of contract which sounds in damages from being exploited by a vendor so as to recover, or by a purchaser so as to repudiate, the equitable interest in land created by the contract. But there is no justification for the intervention of equity to relieve either vendor or purchaser from liability for damages which he has caused by his breach of contract in failing to complete *e* on the contractual date for completion.

In *Jaques v Millar*[2] damages were awarded against a vendor in addition to specific performance in respect of delay caused by his refusal to carry out a contract. The measure of damages was held to be such damages as may reasonably be said to have arisen naturally from the delay or which may reasonably be supposed to have been in the contemplation of the parties.   *f*

In *Jones v Gardiner*[3] damages for delay were awarded because—

'... a very considerable part of the delay which has occurred in carrying out the contract (after making full allowance for the time which may fairly be considered to have been due to difficulties in making out title, and to a controversy as to the form of the conveyance) has arisen entirely from the default of the vendor—default, *g* that is, in doing what he could reasonably and fairly have done had he been duly careful to fulfil his contract.'

In *Phillips v Lamdin*[4] Croom-Johnson J held that damages for delay can be awarded against the vendor where a contract is completed or enforced, where time is not of the essence and where the delay has been caused by default of the vendor and not by want of, or defect in, title or conveyancing difficulties.   *h*

In the present appeal counsel for the third parties relied on dicta in two authorities and passages in textbooks in support of a submission that where time is not of the essence the contract only requires completion on the date fixed for completion or within a reasonable time thereafter; the vendors having completed in a reasonable time in the present case, have not committed a breach of contract and are therefore not liable in damages for the delay.   *j*

---

1   [1951] Ch 174 at 179, [1950] 2 All ER 928 at 932
2   (1877) 6 Ch D 153
3   [1902] 1 Ch 191 at 195
4   [1949] 1 All ER 770, [1949] 2 KB 33

a

In *Smith v Hamilton*[1] the contract provided a date for completion and authorised the vendor to forfeit the deposit and resell 'if the purchaser shall neglect or fail to complete his purchase according to these conditions'. The purchaser failed to complete on the contractual date and the vendor then purported to forfeit the deposit and treat the contract as at an end. Harman J held that time was not of the essence and had never become of the essence. The right to forfeit and resell never became exercisable because the purchaser had not by excessive delay or other circumstances deprived himself of the

b

equitable remedy of specific performance. In reaching that conclusion, the correctness of which is not in question, the judge expressed the view that because time was not of the essence the contract must be construed as a contract for completion on the day fixed 'or within a reasonable time thereafter'.

In *Babacomp Ltd v Rightside Properties Ltd*[2] the validity of a notice making time of the essence was upheld and the correctness of that decision is not in question. In the course

c

of his judgment Goff J quoted a passage from Williams on Vendor and Purchaser[3] which correctly advised that a notice making time of the essence must (in the absence of special conditions governing the sale) allow a reasonable time for compliance. But the reason proffered for this advice was that—

d

> '. . . where time is not essential a party failing to complete a sale of land on the day fixed therefor by the agreement does not then commit a breach of contract either in equity or at law; it is only on failure to complete within a reasonable time after that date that the contract is broken.'

e

That proposition and similar statements in other textbooks are relevant where the court is considering whether a contract in respect of which time is not of the essence is still subsisting. In deciding whether specific performance should be awarded notwithstanding delay, it may be helpful to treat the contract as though it had expressly provided for completion on a fixed date or within a reasonable time thereafter.

f

But if in truth the contract provides for completion on a fixed day there is no warrant for any implication and it is not the task of equity to amend or rewrite the contract. Where time is not of the essence a breach of contract with regard to completion is not a bar to specific performance unless unreasonable delay or other circumstances renders specific performance unfair. But equity does not need to expunge a breach of contract in order to award specific performance and has no need to deprive, and no warrant to deprive, the party aggrieved by the breach of a claim for damages which the aggrieved party has suffered by reason of the breach. Equity only modifies those consequences of a breach which prevent specific performance, consequences which would otherwise be out of all proportion to the damage suffered as a result of the breach.

g

Counsel for the third parties relied in the alternative on s 41 of the Law of Property Act 1925. That provision only preserved the priority and did not alter the nature of the rules of equity.

Counsel for the third parties also relied on condition 19 of the Law Society's General Conditions of Sale (1973), which were incorporated in the contract under discussion. The condition allows a notice to complete to be served, and by condition 19(3), thereupon

h

'it shall be an express term of the contract that the party to whom the notice is given shall complete the transaction within twenty-eight days after the day of service of the notice . . . and in respect of such period time shall be of the essence . . .' Counsel submitted that this power when exercised substituted a new and later date of completion for the date originally agreed. But a notice to complete can only be served, in the words of condition 19(2), 'If the sale shall not be completed on the date fixed for completion'. Condition 19

j

creates a second date for completion. As regards that date time is expressly made of the essence. As regards the first date fixed by the contract if the vendor or purchaser is in

1   [1950] 2 All ER 928, [1951] Ch 174

2   [1973] 3 All ER 873

3   4th Edn (1936) vol 2, p 991

breach of contract damages are payable. Of course, if a reasonable offer to complete is made before the second date arrives it will be the duty of the aggrieved party to mitigate *a* damages by using his best endeavours to accept earlier completion.

Finally counsel for the third parties submitted, as Whitford J had held, that the vendors in the present case are absolved from liability because they were not guilty of wilful default. For present purposes the definition of wilful default contained in *Bennett v Stone*[1] is appropriate, namely:

> 'The result of the authorities, I think, is this: that by the word "wilful" is meant *b* the vendor, being a free agent and in a position to do either one of two acts, chooses to do the one and not to do the other; and that "default" includes the case where the vendor, owing to the purchaser the duty to act reasonably in all matters relating to completion, does an act in breach of that duty.'

In the present case the vendors had a choice between completion or breaking the *c* contract. They chose to break their contract and thereby to inflict damages on the purchasers. For those damages the vendors are liable. In a good many cases a short delay will not cause damage and if sufficient advance warning is given a purchaser will be able to mitigate or prevent any damage and is under a duty to do so. But where, as in the instant case, damage cannot be avoided, a vendor who chooses not to complete must take the consequences. *d*

For these reasons, and for the reasons expressed by Buckley LJ, I too would allow the appeal.

Appeal allowed. Leave to appeal to House of Lords refused .

Solicitors: *Collyer, Bristow & Co*, agents for *Barlows and Wells & Philpot*, Guildford (for the *e* defendants); *Waterhouse & Co*, agents for *Hart, Brown & Co*, Guildford (for the third parties).

J H Fazan Esq   Barrister.

---

1   [1902] 1 Ch 226 at 232–233 *f*

a # Inland Revenue Commissioners v Plummer

HOUSE OF LORDS

LORD WILBERFORCE, VISCOUNT DILHORNE, LORD DIPLOCK, LORD FRASER OF TULLYBELTON AND LORD KEITH OF KINKEL

19th, 20th, 21st JUNE, 1st NOVEMBER 1979

b

Income tax – Settlement – Meaning – Element of bounty – Bona fide commercial transaction – Tax avoidance scheme – Transaction part of scheme – Disposition for valuable and sufficient consideration – Sale of annuity by surtax payer to charitable company in return for capital sum – Transaction involving no element of bounty on either side – Whether 'disposition' or 'settlement' – Income and Corporation Taxes Act 1970, ss 434(1), 454(3), 457(1).

c

Income tax – Annual payment – Payments out of profits etc already taxed – Tax avoidance scheme – Sale of annuity by surtax payer to charitable company in return for capital – Capital sum invested by payer in promissory notes and payments met out of proceeds of notes – Whether 'annuity or other annual payment' – Whether payment in reality repayments of capital – Whether payment out of profits or gains already taxed – Income and Corporation Taxes Act 1970, s 52(1).

d

The taxpayer, an employee of Slater Walker Ltd ('SW'), decided to participate in a tax saving scheme devised by brokers to reduce his liability to surtax. The scheme involved the taxpayer entering into an agreement with a charity ('HOVAS') whereby in consideration of the sum of £2,480 (called the 'purchase price') paid by HOVAS (described as 'the annuitant') the taxpayer agreed to pay HOVAS, for a period of five years

e

or during the remainder of his life (whichever was the shorter), an 'annuity' at such a rate as should after deduction of income tax at the standard rate for the time being be equal to £500 per annum. HOVAS intended to recover from the Revenue the difference between £500 per annum and its grossed up equivalent before deduction of tax, so that the only sum payable by the taxpayer under the agreement was £500 per annum. His total liability under the agreement was therefore £2,500. HOVAS insured the taxpayer's

f

life to cover the event of his death before the payments were made. Although the agreement referred to the £2,480 as the purchase price, it was a term of the scheme that that sum was to be spent on the purchase of promissory notes of a value equal to the total of the annual payments to be made, ie £2,500, and that the notes should be lodged with HOVAS as security for the payments. Accordingly, before the £2,480 was credited to his account with SW, the taxpayer instructed SW to pay £2,500 to another company ('OCC'),

g

which was in the same group of companies as SW, in return for promissory notes of that value, and the notes were then lodged with HOVAS. When a payment of £500 fell to be made to HOVAS under the agreement, SW paid it under a standing order, debiting the taxpayer's account with the amount of the payment and allowing the account to be overdrawn for that purpose. Immediately on the payment to HOVAS, a promissory note to the value of £500 was released to SW and met by OCC, and the taxpayer's account

h

was credited with the proceeds of the note. OCC agreed to pay interest on the promissory notes. The taxpayer claimed that the annual payments to HOVAS were deductible in computing his income for surtax purposes because they were an 'annuity or other annual payment' within s 52(1)[d] of the Income and Corporation Taxes Act 1970. That claim succeeded before the Special Commissioners and, on appeals by the Crown, also succeeded before Walton J[b] and the Court of Appeal[c]. The Crown appealed to the House of Lords,

j

contending (i) that the annual payments were not an 'annuity or annual payment' within

---

a   Section 52(1), so far as material, is set out at p 780 *a*, post

b   [1977] 3 All ER 1009

c   [1978] 3 All ER 513

s 52(1), and the taxpayer was not, therefore, entitled to deduct from them tax at the
standard rate because, although the payments were called an 'annuity' in the agreement,   *a*
they were in fact payments of a capital nature since they were repayments to HOVAS of
its own capital of £2,480 which had remained in existence in the form of the promissory
notes and had been repaid to HOVAS in that form, (ii) that if the annual payments were
an annuity or other annual payment within s 52(1), they were not paid 'wholly out of
profits or gains bought into charge to income tax' within s 52(1) because, although the
taxpayer had sufficient taxed income in the years in question to cover the payments, in   *b*
fact they were paid out of the moneys provided by the promissory notes which were not
taxed income, or were paid out of the overdraft provided by SW which was fed by the
proceeds of the notes, (iii) that, if however the annual payments were income payments
wholly payable out of the taxpayer's chargeable profits or gains, he was not entitled to
deduct them from his income for the purposes of surtax because the payments were
deemed to be his income under s 434(1)^d of the 1970 Act since they were payable by   *c*
virtue of a disposition not made for 'valuable and sufficient consideration', and (iv) that,
alternatively, the payments were to be treated as the taxpayer's income under s 457(1)^e
of the Act because they were income arising under a 'settlement' within s 457(1) which,
by s 454(3)^f of the Act, included an 'agreement', for the word 'agreement' included all
transactions that were not bona fide commercial transactions, and thus included the
present agreement since it was made solely to avoid tax. The taxpayer contended that a   *d*
'settlement' within s 457(1) included only those agreements in which there was an element
of bounty and did not include the present transaction.

Held (Viscount Dilhorne and Lord Diplock dissenting) – The appeal would be dismissed
for the following reasons—
  (i) (Per Lord Wilberforce, Lord Fraser of Tullybelton and Lord Keith of Kinkel, Viscount   *e*
Dilhorne dissenting) The general rule that an annuity purchased with capital was income
in the hands of the recipient applied to the transaction because having regard to the legal
form of the documents comprising the transaction, which could not be disregarded, it was
clear that the nature of the transaction was a covenant to make annual payments to HOVAS
in return for a capital sum, and was not merely the repayment to HOVAS of the capital
sum of £2,480 it had paid. There was no identity between the amount paid by HOVAS   *f*
and the payments they received back since the £2,480 had become the taxpayer's property
when paid by HOVAS, and the rights of HOVAS in the promissory notes in which it was
invested were rights of security only. Moreover, although the notes were the source of the
annual payments, that was a matter of convenience only and the taxpayer could have
chosen to make the payments from some other source. It followed that in the hands of
HOVAS the payments were income, and were payments of an 'annuity or other annual   *g*
payment' within s 52(1) of the 1970 Act (see p 780 d and f to p 781 a, p 793 h to p 794 d f
to h and p 796 b, post); *Sothern-Smith v Clancy* [1941] 1 All ER 111 applied.
  (ii) (Per Lord Wilberforce, Lord Fraser of Tullybelton and Lord Keith of Kinkel,
Viscount Dilhorne concurring) The annual payments were to be treated as having been
made 'wholly out of profits or gains brought into charge' to tax within s 52(1), even
though the source of the payments was not the taxpayer's taxed income but the moneys   *h*
provided by the promissory notes, for the significant factor in considering whether an
individual was entitled to the benefit of deductions under s 52(1) was not the actual
source out of which the payments in question were made but the status of the notional
account between the individual and the Revenue in the tax year in question; if in that
notional account the amount of any payments made by the individual was equal to or
less than his taxed income, he was entitled to claim the benefit of s 52(1). It followed that   *j*
as the manner in which the taxpayer had chosen to provide the annual payments to

---

d   Section 434(1) is set out at p 789 e, post
e   Section 457(1), so far as material, is set out at p 787 h, post
f   Section 454(3), so far as material, is set out at p 787 j, post

a HOVAS, ie from the proceeds of the promissory notes, was irrelevant, and as the very nature of the scheme involved an intention to make the payments out of the taxpayer's income, the taxpayer had done nothing to preclude him from claiming the benefit of s 52(1) (see p 781 c d h j, p 791 e, p 794 h and p 796 b, post); *Allchin (Inspector of Taxes) v Coulthard* [1943] 2 All ER 352 and *Chancery Lane Safe Deposit and Offices Co Ltd v Inland Revenue Comrs* [1966] 1 All ER 1 applied; *Fenton's Trustee v Inland Revenue Comrs* [1936] 1 All ER 116 disapproved.

b (iii) (Per Lord Wilberforce, Viscount Dilhorne, Lord Fraser of Tullybelton and Lord Keith of Kinkel) The annual payments were dispositions which were made for 'valuable and sufficient consideration' within s 434(1) of the 1970 Act, for the money actually paid by the taxpayer to HOVAS amounted only to £2,500, and the £2,480 he received from HOVAS was sufficient consideration for that sum. Moreover, the intended fiscal consequences of the transaction, ie that the taxpayer would be able to deduct the annual c payments from his income for surtax purposes and to make the payments subject to deduction of tax at the standard rate, were elements to be taken into account in determining whether the consideration was sufficient. It followed that s 434(1) was not applicable and that the payments were not deemed thereunder to be treated as the taxpayer's income (see p 782 a b, p 789 g h, p 794 h and p 796 b, post).

d (iv) Furthermore (Viscount Dilhorne and Lord Diplock dissenting), the annual payments did not fall to be treated as the taxpayer's income under s 457(1) of the 1970 Act, because the term 'settlement' in s 454(3) of the Act applied only to transactions which included an element of bounty and not to all transactions that were not bona fide transactions. Since there was no element of bounty in the transaction between the taxpayer and HOVAS and it was a bona fide commercial transaction, it was not a 'settlement' within s 457(1) (see p 783 g to p 784 a, p 795 c d h and p 796 b, post); *Bulmer* e *v Inland Revenue Comrs* [1966] 3 All ER 801 approved.

Decision of the Court of Appeal [1978] 3 All ER 513 affirmed.

Notes

For annuities or other annual payments payable out of profits or gains brought into charge to income tax, see 23 Halsbury's Laws (4th Edn) para 586, and for cases on the subject, see 28(1) Digest (Reissue) 258–267, 829–866.

f For dispositions for a period which cannot exceed six years, see 23 Halsbury's Laws (4th Edn) paras 1422–1424.

For the treatment of income arising under a settlement as the income of the settlor for excess liability, see ibid paras 1457–1460.

For the meaning of 'settlement' for the purposes of income tax, see ibid paras 1425, 1436 and for cases on the subject, see 28(1) Digest (Reissue) 430–434, 1553–1565.

g For the Income and Corporation Taxes Act 1970, ss 52, 434, 454, 457, see 33 Halsbury's Statutes (3rd Edn) 87, 562, 584, 587.

Cases referred to in opinions

Allchin (Inspector of Taxes) v Coulthard [1943] 2 All ER 352, [1943] AC 607, 112 LJKB 539, 107 JP 191, 41 LGR 207, sub nom *Allchin (Inspector of Taxes) v South Shields County Borough* 25 Tax Cas 445, 169 LT 238, HL; *affg* [1942] 2 All ER 39, [1942] 2 KB 228, 25 h Tax Cas 445, 111 LJKB 609, CA, 28(1) Digest (Reissue) 287, 964.

Bulmer v Inland Revenue Comrs [1966] 3 All ER 801, [1967] Ch 145, [1966] 3 WLR 672, 44 Tax Cas 1, 45 ATC 293, [1966] TR 257, 28(1) Digest (Reissue) 433, 1561.

Central London Railway Co v Inland Revenue Comrs, London Electric Railway Co v Inland Revenue Comrs, Metropolitan Railway Co v Inland Revenue Comrs [1937] AC 77, 20 Tax Cas 102, 105 LJKB 513, 155 LT 66, HL, 28(1) Digest (Reissue) 272, 898.

j *Chamberlain v Inland Revenue Comrs* [1943] 2 All ER 200, 25 Tax Cas 317, HL, 28(1) Digest (Reissue) 430, 1555.

Chancery Lane Safe Deposit and Offices Co Ltd v Inland Revenue Comrs [1966] 1 All ER 1, [1966] AC 85, [1966] 2 WLR 251, 43 Tax Cas 83, 44 ATC 450, [1965] TR 433, HL, 28(1) Digest (Reissue) 278, 924.

Copeman (Inspector of Taxes) v Coleman [1939] 3 All ER 224, [1939] 2 KB 484, 22 Tax Cas
594, 108 LJKB 813, 28(1) Digest (Reissue) 423, 1532.

FA & AB Ltd v Lupton (Inspector of Taxes) [1971] 3 All ER 948, [1972] AC 634, [1971] 3 *a*
WLR 670, 47 Tax Cas 580, 50 ATC 326, [1971] TR 285, HL, Digest (Cont Vol D) 441,
207.

Fenton's Trustee v Inland Revenue Comrs [1936] 1 All ER 116, [1936] 2 KB 59, 21 Tax Cas
626, 105 LJKB 394, 154 LT 343, CA; affd sub nom Paton (Fenton's Trustee) v Inland
Revenue Comrs [1938] 1 All ER 786, [1938] AC 341, 21 Tax Cas 626, 107 LJKB 354, 158 *b*
LT 426, HL, 28(1) Digest (Reissue) 286, 958.

Foley (Lady) v Fletcher (1858) 3 H & N 769, [1843–60] All ER Rep 952, 28 LJ Ex 100, 33
LTOS 11, 22 JP 819, 5 Jur NS 342, 157 ER 678, 28(1) Digest (Reissue) 256, 822.

Hood-Barrs v Inland Revenue Comrs [1946] 2 All ER 768, 27 Tax Cas 385, 176 LT 283, CA,
28(1) Digest (Reissue) 422, 1531.

Inland Revenue Comrs v Church Comrs for England [1975] 3 All ER 614, [1975] 1 WLR *c*
1383, [1975] STC 546, [1975] TR 141, CA; affd [1976] 2 All ER 1037, [1977] AC 329,
[1976] 3 WLR 214, [1976] STC 339, [1976] TR 187, HL.

Inland Revenue Comrs v Duke of Westminster [1936] AC 1, [1935] All ER Rep 259, 19 Tax
Cas 490, 104 LJKB 383, 153 LT 223, HL, 28(1) Digest (Reissue) 507, 1845.

Inland Revenue Comrs v Goodwin, Inland Revenue Comrs v Baggley [1975] 1 All ER 708,
[1975] 1 WLR 640, [1975] STC 173, 50 Tax Cas 583, CA; affd [1976] 1 All ER 481, *d*
[1976] 1 WLR 191, [1976] STC 28, 50 Tax Cas 583, HL.

Inland Revenue Comrs v Leiner (1964) 41 Tax Cas 589, [1964] TR 63, 43 ATC 56, 28(1)
Digest (Reissue) 433, 1560.

Perrin v Dickson (Inspector of Taxes) [1929] 2 KB 85, 14 Tax Cas 608; affd [1930] 1 KB 107,
[1929] All ER Rep 685, 14 Tax Cas 608, 98 LJKB 683, 142 LT 29, CA, 28(1) Digest
(Reissue) 258, 836.

Sothern-Smith v Clancy (Inspector of Taxes) [1941] 1 All ER 111, [1941] 1 KB 276, 24 Tax *e*
Cas 1, 110 LJKB 189, 164 LT 210, CA, 28(1) Digest (Reissue) 259, 838.

Thomas v Marshall (Inspector of Taxes) [1953] 1 All ER 1102, [1953] AC 543, [1953] 2
WLR 944, 34 Tax Cas 178, 32 ATC 128, [1953] TR 141, 46 R & IT 295, HL, 28(1)
Digest (Reissue) 423, 1584.

Cases also cited
f

Bishop (Inspector of Taxes) v Finsbury Securities Ltd [1966] 3 All ER 105, [1966] 1 WLR
1402, 43 Tax Cas, HL.

Campbell (Trustees of Davies's Educational Trust) v Inland Revenue Comrs [1968] 3 All ER
588, [1970] AC 77, 45 Tax Cas 427, HL.

Chinn v Collins (Inspector of Taxes) [1979] 2 All ER 529, [1979] 2 WLR 411, [1979] STC *g*
332, CA.

Crossland (Inspector of Taxes) v Hawkins [1961] 2 All ER 812, [1961] Ch 537, 39 Tax Cas
493, CA.

Inland Revenue Comrs v Frere [1964] 3 All ER 796, [1965] AC 402, 42 Tax Cas 125, HL.

Appeal
h

This was an appeal by the Crown from an order of the Court of Appeal[1] (Buckley and
Bridge LJJ and Foster J) dated 5th May 1978 dismissing an appeal by the Crown from an
order of Walton J[2] dated 1st July 1977 whereby he dismissed the Crown's appeal by way
of case stated against a determination of the Commissioners for the Special Purposes of
the Income Tax Acts allowing an appeal by the taxpayer, Ronald Anthony Plummer,
against assessments to surtax for 1970–71 in the sum of £3,485, for 1971–72 in the sum *j*
of £3,476 and for 1972–73 in the sum of £4,165, and discharging the assessments for

1   [1978] 3 All ER 513, [1979] Ch 63, [1978] STC 517
2   [1977] 3 All ER 1009, [1977] 1 WLR 1227, [1977] STC 440

1970–71 and 1971–72 and reducing the assessment for 1972–73 to £3,349. The facts are
a set out in the opinion of Viscount Dilhorne.

G B H Dillon QC, Patrick Medd QC, Peter Gibson and *Brian Davenport* for the Crown.
Michael Nolan QC, Robert Alexander QC, and *David C Milne* for the taxpayer.

Their Lordships took time for consideration.

b
1st November. The following opinions were delivered.

LORD WILBERFORCE. My Lords, this case arises out of a 'tax saving scheme'
devised by a firm of insurance and investment brokers. They sent out to a number of
persons thought likely to be interested, under the heading 'Most Confidential', details of
c what they called a 'capital income plan'. The general nature of this was to enable
taxpayers paying income tax at a high marginal rate to turn some of this income into
capital, while, conversely, enabling a non income-taxpayer (viz a charity) to convert some
capital into income. Operations of this general description are quite common, and legal;
indeed many investors in annuities or in insurance policies do just this in the normal
d course of prudent investment. This particular operation is perhaps an extreme case.
    The plan now involved was explained by the brokers in great detail, and its intended
accomplishment set out, with timetables, in almost military precision. This (as I
ventured to suggest in *Inland Revenue Comrs v Church Comrs for England*[1]) entitles and
requires us to look at the plan as a whole. It does not entitle us to disregard the legal form
and nature of the transactions carried out. It was not suggested that any part of the plan
e as executed was a sham; indeed the Special Commissioners found to the contrary. It is
entitled to a fair, if not a particularly benevolent, analysis.
    The taxpayer decided to enter into the plan in a modest way. By an annuity agreement
made on 15th March 1971 with Home and Overseas Voluntary Aid Services Ltd
('HOVAS'), a body with charitable status, he agreed, in consideration of £2,480 paid by
HOVAS, to pay HOVAS for five years, or the lesser duration of his life, an annual sum of
f such an amount as after deduction of income tax at the standard rate for the time being
would equal £500. This amounted in fact to £851·06. HOVAS paid £2,480 to an
account which the taxpayer had opened shortly before, with a credit of £40, with Slater
Walker Ltd. The taxpayer had instructed Slater Walker Ltd when they received the
£2,480 to pay £15 to the brokers as their fee and to pay £2,500 to Old Change Court
(Investments) Ltd ('OCC'), a company in the Slater Walker group, in exchange for five
g promissory notes of £500 each. These notes were then to be lodged with HOVAS as
security for payment of the annual sums, and were to be released as the taxpayer paid the
latter. OCC agreed to pay interest at 6½% on the amounts of the notes. There were
further arrangements involving the borrowing by HOVAS of the money they needed in
order to pay the capital sum, and insurance of the taxpayer's life which I need not detail:
they are neutral as regards the issues under consideration. What happened thereafter
h was that the taxpayer, by means of a standing order on Slater Walker Ltd, paid the annual
sums to HOVAS on overdraft, which was liquidated a few days later by the release of a
promissory note. The taxpayer signed each year and sent to HOVAS the usual certificate
as to deduction of tax and HOVAS applied for the repayment of this tax. But this part
of the plan miscarried: the Inland Revenue refused to make the refund and on appeal to
the Special Commissioners their refusal was upheld. HOVAS has not taken the matter
j further. Then the taxpayer claimed to deduct the amount of each payment as an
'annuity or other annual payment' in computing his total income for surtax purposes.
This claim has succeeded before the Special Commissioners and in both courts below.
    In the courts the plan has been subjected to a four-way attack.

---

1   [1976] 2 All ER 1037, [1977] AC 329, [1976] STC 339

i. The first is based on the terms of s 52 of the Income and Corporation Taxes Act 1970 which opens with the words '(1) Where any annuity or other annual payment charged with tax under Case III of Schedule D . . .' then the maker of the payment is entitled to deduct tax at the standard rate.

It is common ground that these words cover, and cover only, payments having the character of income and do not cover capital payments even if made annually. The argument for the Crown was that the payments of £500 per annum made by the taxpayer were in reality capital payments and not payments having the character of income. In the courts below this argument took the form of a contention that the £2,480 was paid to the taxpayer by way of loan, and that the 'annuity' payments were nothing other than repayments of this loan. This argument having been rejected (rightly in my opinion) in both courts, the Crown presented a reconstructed form. This, as I understood it, was that the payments represented nothing but a repayment to HOVAS of its own capital. While it may be true that an annuity bought for a capital sum has the character of income, and while there was such an annuity in this case, it was said that the concomitant arrangements, in particular the arrangements for security, changed the character of the payments. The capital sum of £2,480 paid by HOVAS remained in existence in the form of promissory notes, and it was this sum, in that form, which was paid back to HOVAS. HOVAS instead of receiving an annuity was simply receiving back its own capital in instalments.

My Lords, if it were possible to disregard the legal form of the documents and to look behind them for an underlying substance, there would be attractions beyond those of ingenuity in this argument. But I do not find it possible to do this. The classic analysis of this type of transaction is the judgment of Greene MR in *Sothern-Smith v Clancy (Inspector of Taxes)*[1]. There, on the facts, there was a strong case for saying that the annuitant or the annuitant plus the named recipient was simply receiving his capital back. But the Court of Appeal would not have this. Greene MR thought that there could be much to be said for regarding a purchase of an annuity for a term of years as being one for purchase of instalments consisting mainly of capital and partly of interest, but did not feel himself at liberty to adopt any such principle[2]:

'I feel bound to regard the purchase of an annuity of the kind to which I have referred as the purchase of an income, and the whole of the income so purchased as a profit or gain notwithstanding the way in which the payments are calculated.'

If this is the general rule, is there anything in the present case which causes it not to apply? In my opinion there is not. The £2,480 when paid became the property of the taxpayer. It remained his property none the less though he invested it, plus £20, in promissory notes and deposited them by way of security. He became entitled to release of a portion of it each year as he paid the annuity, each portion coming to him with interest: at the end of the five years he had received the whole, with interest. During the five years the taxpayer had a right, a limited one it is true, to select the manner in which the money should be invested.

Looked at from the other side, HOVAS's right was to receive an annual sum under covenant. If the taxpayer did not pay, they could sue him on his covenant. There was no identity between the amount they paid and that which they might receive back. In the first place the sums they were entitled to were the gross amount of the 'annuity' which, assuming that the value remained unchanged, would be five times £851·06, ie £4,255·30 subject, or not, to tax at the standard rate. In the second place, if the taxpayer died during the five years they would receive from the taxpayer only those annuity payments which he made during his life. (In addition they would recover something on the insurance policy they took out.) Such rights as they might have over the promissory notes were rights by way of security only. In short, unless we are prepared to disregard

---

1   [1941] 1 All ER 111, [1941] KB 276, 24 Tax Cas 1
2   [1941] 1 All ER 111 at 117, [1941] KB 276 at 285, 24 Tax Cas 1 at 7

the legal structure of these transactions, their nature is clear: a covenant, for a capital
sum, to make annual payments, coupled with security arrangements for the payments.
But no attack was made on the transactions as a sham and we must accept the
consequences of them.

2. The second argument arises also out of s 52(1)(c) which, if the payer of an annual
sum is to be entitled to deduct and retain income tax on it, requires the annual payments
to be payable wholly out of profits or gains brought in to charge to income tax. It is not
disputed that the taxpayer had in each relevant year sufficient taxed income to cover the
payments. What is said is that the taxpayer in fact made the payments out of the moneys
provided by the promissory notes, which were not taxed income, or, if this is not
accurate, out of an overdraft provided by Slater Walker which was fed by the proceeds of
the promissory notes. My Lords, on the authorities which have dealt with this difficult
branch of income tax law, the position as regards this taxpayer is clear. The general rule,
in the case of an individual at least, is that what is significant, when one is considering the
application of the statutory rule, is not the actual source out of which the money is paid,
nor even the way in which the taxpayer for his own purposes keeps his accounts, if
indeed he keeps any, but the status of a notional account between himself and the
Revenue. He is entitled, in respect of any tax year, to set down on one side his taxed
income and on the other the amount of the annual payments he had made and if the
latter is equal to or less than the former, to claim the benefit of the section.

To this general rule some exceptions have recently been introduced and explained at
length in this House: see *Central London Railway Co v Inland Revenue Comrs*[1] and *Chancery
Lane Safe Deposit and Offices Co Ltd v Inland Revenue Comrs*[2]. Very briefly and summarily
these apply so that the taxpayer cannot claim the benefit of the section, (inter alia) if he
had treated the payments in accounts in such a way as to produce consequences
inconsistent with their being treated as income. The above two cases are both cases of
corporations, which are limited by law and by their own 'vires' as to the preparation of
their accounts and their treatment of income in a way in which individuals are not
limited. Whether an individual by his conduct may prevent himself from preparing his
notional account with the Revenue has not, I think, been the subject of reliable
decision. *Fenton's Trustee v Inland Revenue Comrs*[3] is sometimes relied on by the Crown
as an authority on this point, and though not invoked in the courts below, was deployed
in this House: I hope that this may be for the last time. The appeal was made to the
judgment of Romer LJ, and that of Lord Wright MR was to the same effect, that if a
payment of interest is made out of money borrowed for the purpose of paying it, and is
then added to the amount of the capital borrowed, the taxpayer is to be treated as having
made an election which precludes him from taking the benefit of the section (then s 36
of the Income Tax Act 1918). But, in my opinion, the judgments of Lord Wright MR
and Romer LJ in that case, from which Greene LJ dissented, can no longer be considered
to state the law. Greene LJ restated his opinion (which in any event I would find
unanswerable) in *Allchin (Inspector of Taxes) v Coulthard*[4] and that judgment in turn was
approved by this House[5] and again in the *Chancery Lane* case[2]: it has now become
established doctrine. On this view of the law, the position is clear. The taxpayer here did
nothing (even assuming that he could have done anything) to prevent himself from
claiming the benefit of the section. On the contrary, the whole nature of the plan
involved him in an intention to make the payments out of income and if he had drawn
up any accounts he would have shown them as so paid. The manner in which he chose
to provide the cash, itself open to modification at any time, is completely irrelevant. In
my opinion this argument fails.

1   [1937] AC 77, 20 Tax Cas 102
2   [1966] 1 All ER 1, [1966] AC 85, 43 Tax Cas 83
3   [1936] 1 All ER 116, [1936] 2 KB 59, 21 Tax Cas 626
4   [1942] 2 All ER 39, [1942] 2 KB 228, 25 Tax Cas 445
5   [1943] 2 All ER 352, [1943] AC 607, 25 Tax Cas 445

3. This argument arises under s 434(1) of the Income and Corporation Taxes Act 1970 which in the case of payments made for a period which cannot exceed six years deems income to be the income of the payer unless made for valuable and sufficient consideration. On this point the Special Commissioners were in favour of the Crown. But Walton J in his judgment effectively demonstrated, in my opinion, that they had fallen into error on the mathematics and, further, that there was no ground for holding that the consideration for the payments was not valuable and sufficient. The Court of Appeal agreed and I do not find it necessary to do more than to accept their reasoning.

4. The final argument for the Crown arises under s 457 of the Income and Corporation Taxes Act 1970:

> '(1) Where, during the life of the settlor, income arising under a settlement made on or after 7th April 1965 is, under the settlement and in the events that occur, payable to or applicable for the benefit of any person other than the settlor, then, unless, under the settlement and in the said events, the income either [and then there is a whole list of matters, none of which applies here], the income shall be treated for the purposes of surtax as the income of the settlor and not as the income of any other person . . .'

The applicable definition of a 'settlement' is to be found in s 454(3); it is 'any disposition, trust, covenant, agreement or arrangement'. It is not disputed that if the agreement in this case (of 15th March 1971) was a 'settlement' within this definition, s 457 would apply and the income, ie the annuity payments, would be treated as the income of the settlor, ie of the taxpayer and not as the income of any other person.

This raises a question of some difficulty and general importance. Are the words of the definition to be given the full unrestricted meaning which apparently they have, or is some limitation to be read into them, and if so what limitation? If given the full unrestricted meaning, the section would clearly cover the present agreement, and would also cover a large number of ordinary commercial transactions.

My Lords, it seems to me to be clear that it is not possible to read into the definition an exception in favour of commercial transactions whether with or without the epithet 'ordinary' or 'bona fide'. To do so would be legislation not interpretation; if Parliament had intended such an exception it could and must have expressed it.

But it still becomes necessary to enquire what is the scope of the words 'settlement' and 'settlor' and of the words which are included in 'settlement' in the context in which they appear. If it appears, on the one hand, that a completely literal reading of the relevant words would so widely extend the reach of the section that no agreement of whatever character fell outside it, but that, on the other hand, a legislative purpose can be discerned of a more limited character which Parliament can reasonably be supposed to have intended, and that the words used fairly admit of such a meaning as to give effect to that purpose, it would be legitimate, indeed necessary, for the courts to adopt such a meaning.

Part XVI of the 1970 Act, which includes ss 434 to 459 is headed 'Settlements'. It includes a number of provisions which have been enacted at different times, the general effect of which is to cause income of which a person has disposed in various ways to be treated, in spite of the disposition, as the income of the disponor. These had been successively enacted (inter alia) in the Finance Acts of 1922, 1936, 1938 and 1946 with increasing severity. Chapter I of Part XVI is headed 'Dispositions for Short Periods'; exempting dispositions for valuable and sufficient consideration, it treats dispositions of income for a period which cannot exceed six years as the income of the disponor. Chapter II deals with settlements on children, the general purpose being to prevent (ie to tax if they are made) dispositions the effect of which is to spread income among the children of a settlor. This chapter has its own definition of 'settlement' as 'any disposition, trust, covenant, agreement, arrangement or transfer of assets'. Chapter III deals with revocable settlements, settlements in which a settlor retains an interest and capital payments made to a settlor or his spouse, the effect of which is to tax income from which a settlor, or his wife, may benefit as the settlor's income. The definition of 'settlement'

(s 454(3)) is that which I have quoted as applicable in the present case. Lastly Chapter IV,
a headed 'Surtax Liability of Settlors in Certain Cases' contains (briefly) a broad sweeping-
up provision for taxing any income of a settlement except income from property of
which the settlor has divested himself absolutely by the settlement. The definition of
'settlement' (s 459) is that which I have quoted.

My Lords, it can, I think, fairly be seen that all of these provisions, in Part XVI, have
a common character. They are designed to bring within the net of taxation dispositions
b of various kinds, in favour of a settlor's spouse, or children, or of charities; cases, in
popular terminology, in which a taxpayer gives away a portion of his income, or of his
assets, to such persons, or for such periods, or subject to such conditions, that Parliament
considers it right to continue to treat such income, or income of the assets, as still the
settlor's income. These sections, in other words, though drafted in wide, and increasingly
wider language, are nevertheless dealing with a limited field, one far narrower than the
c field of the totality of dispositions, or arrangements, or agreements, which a man may
make in the course of his life. Is there then any common description which can be
applied to this?

The courts which, inevitably, have had to face this problem, have selected the element
of 'bounty' as a necessary common characteristic of all the 'settlements' which Parliament
had in mind. The decisions are tentative, but all point in this direction. The first clear
d indication of this was given by Lord Macmillan in *Chamberlain v Inland Revenue Comrs*[1].
Dealing with a case arising under the predecessor of s 447 of the 1970 Act he said that he
agreed that the settlement or arrangement—

> 'must be one whereby the settlor charges certain property of his with rights in
> favour of others . . . it must confer the income of the comprised property on others,
> for it is this income so given to others that is to be treated as, nevertheless, the
e > income of the settlor.'

I do not think that this passage is affected by the observations of Lord Greene MR in
Hood-Barrs v Inland Revenue Comrs[2]. In *Inland Revenue Comrs v Leiner*[3], Plowman J said
that it was common ground, ie accepted by the Crown, that 'it is implicit in the
fasciculus of Sections of which [Chapter II of Part XVI of the 1970 Act] forms a part that
f some element of bounty is necessary to make the Sections apply . . .' and this point was
made explicit by Pennycuick J in *Bulmer v Inland Revenue Comrs*[4]. Dealing with a case
under the predecessor of Chapter III of Part XVI of the 1970 Act he followed the previous
cases in holding that a sufficient context existed for a restriction in the scope of the
definition and that he accepted the 'element of bounty' test.

My Lords, I think that in so doing the judge was well within the limits of permissible
g interpretation, and that with the 'element of bounty' test we have a definition which is
in agreement with the intention of Parliament as revealed through the whole miniature
code of Chapter XVI. I would compare with this the reasons of this House in *Thomas v
Marshall (Inspector of Taxes)*[5]. In that case the contention was that the word 'settlement'
did not extend to an outright gift. Their Lordships rejected this, holding that the
intention was clearly to enlarge the meaning of settlement so as to include gifts.
h Enlargement in one direction and restriction in another are both part of a balanced
process of judicial interpretation directed towards implementing but not exceeding the
general legislative purpose.

My Lords, there cannot be any doubt that in this case no element of bounty existed.
The Special Commissioners indeed said that they regarded the transaction as a bona fide

j

1 [1943] 2 All ER 200 at 204, 25 Tax Cas 317 at 331
2 [1946] 2 All ER 768, 27 Tax Cas 385
3 (1964) 41 Tax Cas 589 at 596
4 [1966] 3 All ER 801, [1967] Ch 145, 44 Tax Cas 1
5 [1953] 1 All ER 1102, [1953] AC 543, 34 Tax Cas 178

commercial transaction without any element of bounty. The taxpayer therefore succeeds
on this point. *a*

One final point: the familiar argument was used that Parliament can never have
intended to exempt from the taxing provisions an arrangement solely designed to obtain
fiscal advantages. But this is not the question, nor is a canon of interpretation of this kind
an admissible, or indeed a workable canon. The question is whether a certain series of
transactions in a certain legal form do or do not fall within the taxing words. If they do
not, and if Parliament dislikes the consequence, it can change the law, as in fact it has *b*
done since the scheme in question was operated. The subject is entitled to be judged
under the law as it stood at the relevant time.

I would dismiss the appeal.

VISCOUNT DILHORNE. My Lords, in this appeal we are concerned with an
ingenious, complicated and well thought out scheme which had two objects, first, as the
Special Commissioners found, to reduce the surtax liability of payers of a high rate of *c*
surtax, and secondly, to build up a tax free fund in a company called Home and Overseas
Voluntary Aid Services Ltd ('HOVAS') by that company securing payment by the Inland
Revenue of sums equivalent to those deducted by the individual participants in the
scheme on their making annual payments to HOVAS.

It was, to adapt the words of Lord Donovan in *Lupton v FA & AB Ltd*[1], a scheme to *d*
avoid the payment of tax by those who participated and to raid the Treasury using the
technicalities of revenue law as the necessary weapon.

It was called the 'capital income plan' and details of it were sent in a letter marked
'Most Confidential' to a number of people by S Cardale & Co Ltd ('Cardale'), insurance
and investment brokers.

Although in some minor respects there were departures from the scheme in the case
of the taxpayer, as the letter states very clearly what was involved, I propose to cite its *e*
relevant parts. It reads as follows:—

'MOST CONFIDENTIAL

'CAPITAL INCOME PLAN

'1. SITUATION
'Mr. X has a taxable income of £30,000 a year. The following example assumes *f*
that, in addition to Income Tax at the standard rate, the top £14,694 of this income
suffers surtax @ 10/- in the £: i.e. £7,347.

'2. INVESTMENT PLAN
'(a) A Charity purchases an Annuity from Mr. X at a Purchase Price of say
£44,800. The exact Purchase Price will depend on his age and health. *g*
'(b) In return, Mr. X agrees to pay the Charity five net annual payments of
£9,000 (i.e. a gross sum of £14,694 before deduction of Income Tax @ 7/9 in the
£).
'(c) The Charity requires a guarantee that Mr. X will make his annual payments
as agreed. To effect this, with the £44,800 received from the Charity, Mr. X
purchases Promissory Notes for a total value of £45,000 from a reputable Finance *h*
Company. The difference between the Purchase Price (£44,800) and the cost of the
Promissory Notes (£45,000) must be found by Mr. X: i.e. £200. The Promissory
Notes are payable over the five years—£9,000 each year on the same day each
year. These notes are accepted by the Charity by way of guarantee. Further
security is required as the total value of security must be worth a minimum of 110%
of the net Unpaid Annuities (not including the first Annuity payment). *j*

'3. OPERATION
'(a) On the day Mr. X signs his Annuity Agreement, he is required to take the

---

1 [1971] 3 All ER 948 at 963, [1972] AC 634 at 657, 47 Tax Cas 580 at 629

following action:—

1. Open a Deposit Account with a Merchant Bank and deposit say £15 in this account. 2. Pay stamp duty of £73 to the Inland Revenue based on the gross amount of the annual payment. 3. Pay an amount equal to 5% of the Purchase Price (£2,240) by way of initial charge. 4. On receipt of the Purchase Price (£44,800), purchase Promissory Notes for £45,000 which are lodged with the Charity. The Promissory Notes will earn interest at 6½% per annum. 5. Deposit Short Dated Gilt Edged Securities equivalent in value to 10% (a minimum of 15% in the case of acceptable equities) of four net annual payments 10% × (4 × £9,000) = £3,600.

'(b) Twenty eight days after receiving the Purchase Price, Mr. X makes his first payment of £9,000 to the Charity which releases the same amount to him from the Promissory Notes a day later. Overdraft facilities will be available for this one day.

'(c) The Promissory Notes are repaid to Mr. X as he pays his future annual payments. At the same time, any security surplus to the requirments of the Charity is available for release to Mr. X.

'(d) If Mr. X should die at any time before making his final payment, no further payment is due. All remaining Promissory Notes are converted into cash at par and this is released to his Estate with any interest due together with all additional security.

'4. RESULT

'(a) The gross equivalent of the £9,000 a year is £14,694. Mr. X deducts this latter sum each year in computing his total income for Surtax. With Surtax at 10/- in the £ his annual saving is £7,347.

'(b) On the basis that Mr. X survives the five years and fulfils all his commitments, his estimated final position is:—

COST		BENEFIT	
Initial Charge	£2,240	Surtax Saving	
		(5 × £7,347)	£36,735
Cash	200	Net Interest	
Stamp Duty	73	(Promissory Notes)	683
	£2,513		£37,418

'His profit on the transaction is thus £34,905 FREE OF TAX.'

This so-called profit is, it will be appreciated, the amount of tax Mr X will avoid less the cost of participating in the scheme.

The charity concerned was HOVAS, a company incorporated on 30th December 1970 with an authorised share capital of £10 and at all material times an issued share capital of 10 shares of £1 each. It was registered as a charity.

On 10th March 1971 HOVAS borrowed from a company called Baldrene Ltd £1,430,000 with interest at 12%. At that time bank rate stood at 6½%. Baldrene was a company in the Slater Walker group and the taxpayer was one of its directors. At all material times he was employed as taxation manager by Slater Walker Ltd, and he acted in that capacity for the whole of the Slater Walker group. One of his duties was to ensure the efficient working of the capital income plan. HOVAS held itself out as prepared to buy annuities on terms attractive to payers of a high rate of surtax, the money borrowed from Baldrene being available for the purpose.

The taxpayer decided to participate in the scheme and on the 9th March 1971 Cardale wrote to him telling him that HOVAS had agreed to purchase an annuity from him and that their charge for negotiating the contract would be 5% of the purchase price of the annuity. Later they reduced this to £15.

On 11th March HOVAS wrote to the taxpayer telling him that they would accept as security for the payment of the net annuity payments outstanding of £2,500, promissory notes to that value and a cheque for £300 to be used for the purchase of Midland Bank

Ltd ordinary stock. The next day the taxpayer wrote to Slater Walker Ltd asking them to open an account in his name and enclosing a cheque for £40 for the credit of his *a* account. He told them that on 15th March they would receive a cheque for £2,480 from HOVAS, which they did, and that it was to be credited to his account and that as soon as it was received, they were to pay £15 to Cardale and £2,500 to Old Change Court (Investments) Ltd ('OCC') and for that sum that company, also one of the Slater Walker group, would issue to him ten promissory notes payable to bearer which they were to lodge with HOVAS as security for the due performance of his obligations under the *b* annuity agreement. He told them that as his obligations under that agreement were fulfilled, a proportion of the security given by him would be released and that if at any time when a release of any promissory note was made to them his account was overdrawn, they were to present the note as soon as possible to OCC and to credit the sums paid by OCC to his account.

    The same day, 12th March, he gave Slater Walker Ltd a standing order for the *c* payment of £500 to HOVAS on the 29th March 1971 and annually on that date up to and including 19th March 1975 or until the order was cancelled.

    On 15th March the annuity agreement was entered into. Under it in consideration for the payment of £2,480 by HOVAS he undertook to pay that company for five years or during the remainder of his life, whichever should be the shorter, an annuity 'at such rate as shall after deduction of income tax at the standard rate for the time being in force be *d* equal to £500 per annum . . .' He also warranted to HOVAS that statements made by him to the Royal Insurance Co for the purpose of enabling HOVAS to insure his life were true and that he had made full disclosure of all material information and he agreed to indemnify them should that not prove to be the case and they suffered loss or damage in consequence. HOVAS insured his life until 16th April 1975 for a premium of £16·97.

    On 15th March the taxpayer also wrote to HOVAS saying that he had authorised Slater *e* Walker to deposit with them ten promissory notes of the value of £2,500. HOVAS in turn lodged the notes with Baldrene as part security for the money they had borrowed from that company. OCC agreed to pay 6½% interest less tax on the outstanding notes and the taxpayer assigned that interest to HOVAS to hold as security for the fulfilment of his obligations.

    The same day he sent to Slater Walker Nominees a cheque for £300 and asked HOVAS *f* to purchase with that sum equities acceptable to them as security. He also sent five forms which he had signed but not completed to Slater Walker Ltd and asked them to complete them as the annual payments were made and to send each completed form to HOVAS. Each form would then show the sum alleged to have been deducted on the payment of each £500.

    It will be noted that under the arrangement made by the taxpayer there were minor *g* departures from the capital income plan outlined in Cardale's letter, the most important of them being the insurance of the taxpayer's life for five years by HOVAS. Five annual payments amounting in total to £2,500 were to be paid to HOVAS in return for the payment by them of £2,480, the difference between the two figures presumably being to make provision for the payment by the taxpayer of the life insurance premium.

    The effect of these operations was that this part of the money borrowed by HOVAS *h* from Baldrene never passed out of the control of the Slater Walker group. It was a term of the arrangements made by the taxpayer with HOVAS that on receipt of the purchase price, it would be used with the addition of £20 to buy promissory notes of a total value of £2,500 from OCC. It was a stipulation in the capital income plan that the purchase money should be applied in the purchase of promissory notes. £2,500 was so used and the notes were lodged with HOVAS and by them with Baldrene as part security for the *j* loan from Baldrene to HOVAS. It may be that the taxpayer could have bought the notes with other moneys but that would have been a departure from the capital income plan and his arrangements with HOVAS.

    When the time came for payment of an annual payment, it was paid out of his account with Slater Walker Ltd and the temporary overdraft that created would be discharged by a the release by Baldrene to HOVAS and by them to Slater Walker Ltd of promissory notes to the value of £500 which were presented for payment by Slater Walker to OCC and paid.

The cost to the taxpayer was consequently the £15 paid to Cardale, the £20 to cover the payment of the insurance premium on his life and a small amount of interest on the overdrafts. If the scheme worked, he would as a result be relieved of a considerable liability for surtax.

b The cost to HOVAS was the interest at 12% payable to Baldrene. If they succeeded in obtaining a refund from the Revenue of the amount deducted by the taxpayer from the annual payments, they would, the Special Commissioners found, receive a return the equivalent of compound interest at the rate of some 36% on their outlay, assuming no undue delay in repayment of tax or 27% assuming a delay of one year; and at the end of the five years they would have received back the £2,480 credited to the taxpayer and

c £20.

On various dates between its incorporation on 30th December 1970 and the 30th March 1971 HOVAS entered into similar transactions with 40 individuals. HOVAS's income and expenditure account for the period 30th December 1970 to 5th April 1972 showed an income of £954,982·45 of which £919,461·65 represented 'annuities (gross)' and their expenditure during that period showed that they had spent on 'charitable work'

d £19·55.

In these circumstances it is hardly surprising that the Crown should challenge the taxpayer's right to deduct tax from the annual payments of £500 and HOVAS's right to obtain payment from them of the amount deducted. Before the Special Commissioners, Walton J and the Court of Appeal, they were not successful. They, however, succeeded in resisting HOVAS's claim for a refund on the ground that that company had not

e applied its income for charitable purposes only. From the Special Commissioners' decision HOVAS has not appealed.

The Crown contended: (1) that the payments to HOVAS were not payments of an annuity or other annual payment, with the consequence that the taxpayer was not entitled to deduct therefrom tax at the standard rate; (2) that the sums were not payable by him out of profits or gains brought into charge to income tax; (3) that s 434 of the

f Income and Corporation Taxes Act 1970 applies as the payments were not made for valuable and sufficient consideration; and (4) that s 457 of that Act applies with the consequence that for the purposes of surtax the payments were to be treated as the income of the taxpayer.

It will, I think, be convenient to consider the fourth contention first.

g *Does s 457 apply?*

So far as material s 457 reads as follows:

'(1) Where, during the life of the settlor, income arising under a settlement made on or after 7th April 1965 is, under the settlement and in the events that occur, payable to or applicable for the benefit of any person other than the settlor, then, unless, under the settlement and in the said events, the income ... (e) is income

h which, by virtue of some provision of the Income Tax Acts not contained in this Chapter, is to be treated for the purposes of those Acts as income of the settlor, the income shall be treated for the purposes of surtax as the income of the settlor and not as the income of any other person ...'

This section is the first section of Chapter IV of the Act, headed 'Surtax Liability of

j Settlors in Certain Cases' and s 459 of this chapter states that 'In this Chapter ... "settlement" and "settlor" have the meanings assigned to them for the puposes of Chapter III' by s. 454. Section 454(3) provides that '"settlement" includes any disposition, trust, covenant, agreement or arrangement, and "settlor", in relation to a settlement, means any person by whom the settlement was made'. This definition of 'settlement' and 'settlor' is the same as that in s 41(4)(b) of the Finance Act 1938 and corresponds with that

in s 21(9)(b) of the Finance Act 1936 save that in the latter Act the definition includes the
words 'transfers of assets'.

    In *Chamberlain v Inland Revenue Comrs*[1] Lord Macmillan accepted the view that 'the
statutory expansion of the term "settlement" [in s 41], which includes an "arrangement,"
justifies and, indeed, requires a broad application' and then added: 'but a settlement or
arrangement to come within the statute must still be of the type which the language of
the section contemplates.'

    These observations were considered by Lord Greene MR in *Hood-Barrs v Inland Revenue
Comrs*[2]. He rejected the argument that Lord Macmillan had meant that to come within
the statute a settlement or arrangement must be of the type which the word 'settlement'
in the section contemplated. He thought that Lord Macmillan's proposition said no
more than what was obvious, namely: 'You never construe a word in a statute, whether
it be in the body of the statute or in an interpretation clause, without reference to the
context in which it appears'. In *Bulmer v Inland Revenue Comrs*[3] Pennycuick J said that
unless one implied some restriction to the width of the definition, it 'represents as odd a
provision as one would anywhere find in a taxing statute'.

    It cannot, in my opinion, be right for the courts to amend the definition by adding
words to it limiting its scope. That would be legislating. On the other hand, it is open
to the courts when considering particular transactions and whether they come within the
definition, to conclude that Parliament cannot have intended that they should be treated
as doing so; and to decide, if that conclusion is reached, that they do not. There must be
a number of cases in which it cannot have been the intention of Parliament that income
transferred to another pursuant to an agreement or arrangement should nevertheless
continue to be treated as the income of the transferor. In *Copeman (Inspector of Taxes) v
Coleman*[4] Lawrence J held that there was a disposition or an arrangement in the nature of
a disposition coming within s 21 of the Finance Act 1936. In the course of his judgment
he said that what had been done was not a bona fide commercial transaction. In *Inland
Revenue Comrs v Leiner*[5] it was common ground that it was implicit in Chapter II of the
Income Tax Act 1952 dealing with 'Settlements on Children' that some element of
bounty was necessary to make the sections in the chapter apply and that a bona fide
commercial transaction would be excluded from them. For this latter proposition
Copeman (Inspector of Taxes) v Coleman[4] was cited. In *Bulmer v Inland Revenue Comrs*[6]
Pennycuick J followed what was said in these two cases. He held that the transaction he
had to consider was a bona fide commercial transaction and that there was no element of
bounty and so he allowed the taxpayer's appeal.

    My Lords, if Parliament had intended that the definition in s 454(3) should only apply
to a settlement, disposition, trust, covenant, agreement or arrangement in which there
was an element of bounty, that could easily have been stated. Similarly if Parliament
intended that despite the width of the definition, bona fide commercial transactions
should be excluded that also could easily have been stated. For my part I decline to
construe the definition as if it contained these words. It may well be that in a great many
cases there will be an element of bounty but to hold, when Parliament has not so enacted,
that s 457 only applies when there is a element of bounty may be to restrict its operation
far beyond Parliament's intention, and the width of the definition is a clear indication
that its scope was intended to be wide. What exactly is comprehended in the phrase
culled from Lawrence J's judgment 'a bona fide commercial transaction', I do not
know. Bona fide means, I suppose, that it was not a sham. A wide variety of transactions

---

1 [1943] 2 All ER 200 at 204, 25 Tax Cas 317 at 331
2 [1946] 2 All ER 768 at 774, 27 Tax Cas 385 at 402
3 [1966] 3 All ER 801 at 810–811, [1967] Ch 145 at 165, 44 Tax Cas 1 at 29
4 [1939] 3 All ER 224, [1939] 2 KB 484, 22 Tax Cas 594
5 (1964) 41 Tax Cas 589, [1964] 41 Tax Cas 589
6 [1966] 3 All ER 801, [1967] Ch 145, 44 Tax Cas 1

a may be called commercial transactions. As Russell LJ said in *Inland Revenue Comrs v Goodwin*[1] 'there can be a bona fide commercial transaction with the obtaining of a tax advantage as *a* main object' (emphasis mine).

My Lords, the Income and Corporation Taxes Act 1970 must be construed like any other Act and in my opinion the right approach to construing s 457 and the definition is to consider first, whether in its ordinary natural meaning the language of these provisions applies to the matters under consideration; and then, if it does, to consider whether or not Parliament can have intended that the transactions in question should come within their scope.

In the present case counsel for the taxpayer conceded in the Court of Appeal that s 457 applied apart from the decision in *Bulmer v Inland Revenue Comrs*[2]. I do not, for the reasons I have stated, consider that decision prevents the section from applying. That there are some who carry on the business of devising schemes for tax avoidance is well known. Their activities may well be described as commercial. The question to be decided is whether Parliament can have intended that the arrangement of which *the* main object was the obtaining of tax advantages should be outside the operation of s 457. In my opinion the answer is in the negative and so the answer to the question 'Does section 457 apply?' is Yes, if the payments of £500 a year are to be regarded as income, a subject to which I shall return later.

I now turn to the Crown's third contention.

Does s 434 apply?

Section 434 reads as follows:

> '(1) Any income which, by virtue or in consequence of any disposition made, directly or indirectly, by any person (other than a disposition made for valuable and sufficient consideration), is payable to or applicable for the benefit of any other person for a period which cannot exceed six years shall be deemed for all purposes of the Income Tax Acts to be the income of the person, if living, by whom the disposition was made, and not to be the income of any other person.
>
> '(2) In this Chapter, unless the context otherwise requires, "disposition" includes any trust, covenant, agreement or arrangement.'

While in my opinion a court can conclude that a disposition, trust, covenant, agreement or arrangement which prima facie is one to which the section applies, is not one to which Parliament can have intended it to apply, as I see no grounds for such a conclusion in this case, the section applies unless the disposition, agreement or arrangement was made for valuable and sufficient consideration.

The Special Commissioners were not satisfied that it was, saying that the taxpayer was to receive £2,480 in return for gross payments before deduction of tax of some £4,255 over five years. Walton J and the Court of Appeal did not agree. I agree with them. HOVAS in return for £2,480 were to receive in the five years £2,500 in circumstances in which they hoped to recover from the Revenue the difference between the grossed up equivalent of £500 before deduction of income tax at the standard rate, ie in March 1971 £351·06. The only money which notionally or actually would be paid by the taxpayer over the five years was £2,500 and for that he had £2,480 credited to his bank account. If the payments of £500 are properly to be regarded as income payable to HOVAS, a question to which I shall come later, the arrangement or agreement to pay those sums was in my opinion made for valuable and sufficient consideration.

The answer, therefore, to this question is in my view that s 434 does not apply.

I now turn to the Crown's first two contentions which can conveniently be considered together.

1 [1975] 1 All ER 708 at 714, [1975] 1 WLR 640 at 647, [1975] STC 173 at 179
2 [1966] 3 All ER 801, [1967] Ch 145, 44 Tax Cas 1

Were the payments to HOVAS payments of an annuity or other annual payment coming within s 52 of the 1970 Act, and if so, were they payable wholly out of profits or gains brought into charge to income tax?

If the answers to these questions are in the affirmative, then the section provides that no assessment to income tax, other than surtax, is to be made on the recipient of the annuity or annual payment and that the payer is entitled to deduct and retain a sum representing the amount of income tax thereon at the standard rate.

Section 52 begins as follows: '(1) Where any annuity or other annual payment charged with tax under Case III of Schedule D . . . is payable wholly out of profits or gains brought into charge to income tax . . .'

Payments charged with income tax under Case III are payments of income. Profits or gains brought into charge to income tax must also be income. So is it the case that the payments of £500 were income in the hands of HOVAS and were payable wholly out of income of the taxpayer?

The £2,480 paid into the taxpayer's bank account was clearly a payment of a capital nature. The difference between that and the value of the promissory notes bought was obviously to secure that the taxpayer paid for the insurance of his life. Did HOVAS thereby secure an income for themselves for five years or was each payment a repayment of part of the capital they had expended? In considering this question one is entitled to have regard to all the arrangements made and not only to the document called the annuity agreement: see *Inland Revenue Comrs v Church Comrs for England*[1] per Lord Wilberforce and per Lord Morris of Borth-y-Gest, where the latter said[2]:

'If a receipt of money might be of an income nature or might be of a capital nature or might be partly the one and partly the other then in the search for the truth and reality all established facts should in my view be brought into survey.'

See also *Perrin v Dickson (Inspector of Taxes)*[3].

Although in the annuity agreement the £2,480 was referred to as the purchase price of the annuity, it was a term of the capital income plan in which the taxpayer was engaging that the price paid for the annuity should be spent on the purchase of promissory notes of a value equal to the total of the annual payments to be made; and before the £2,480 had been credited to his account, the taxpayer had instructed his bankers, Slater Walker Ltd, to pay £2,500 to OCC for notes of that value.

When a payment of £500 fell to be made to HOVAS, Slater Walker paid it, debiting his account with the amount and allowing his account to be overdrawn for a day or two for the purpose. Immediately on payment to HOVAS, Baldrene released notes to the value of £500 to HOVAS, presumably, though the case stated does not say so, on payment to them of £500 in part repayment of their loan to HOVAS, and HOVAS released the notes to Slater Walker. They were then met by OCC and the taxpayer's account was credited with £500.

Throughout the whole operation the £2,480 and the notes of the value of £2,500 remained under the control of the Slater Walker group and HOVAS. It was never a sum of which the taxpayer was free to dispose as he might wish. It was his duty as taxation manager of Slater Walker Ltd to ensure the efficient working of the capital income plan. If anyone had sought to spend the sum received from HOVAS on anything other than the purchase of promissory notes from OCC, one wonders whether he would have been allowed to do so.

It was at one time contended by the Crown that the payments made to HOVAS were in repayment of a loan by them to the taxpayer. This contention was rejected, I think rightly. The £2,480 went with an additional £20 immediately on its being credited to his bank account to OCC.

1 [1976] 2 All ER 1037 at 1044, [1977] AC 329 at 344, [1976] STC 339 at 346
2 [1976] 2 All ER 1037 at 1047, [1977] AC 329 at 348, [1976] STC 339 at 349
3 [1930] 1 KB 107, [1929] All ER Rep 685, 14 Tax Cas 608

In *Perrin v Dickson (Inspector of Taxes)*[1] Rowlatt J, whose judgment was affirmed on
a appeal[2], said: 'The substance of the present transaction is that the appellant does not really
adventure his capital at all.   Under the terms of the policy the capital is in any event to
be returned to him.'

So here in my view the substance of the capital income plan did not involve HOVAS
or any member of the Slater Walker Group in adventuring their capital at all by the
making of payments to individuals in return for five annual payments totalling the same
b amount.   The £2,480 credited to the taxpayer's account was part of the sum loaned by
Baldrene to HOVAS.   It had to be paid with an additional £20 to OCC and then on £500
being debited to the taxpayer's account by Slater Walker Ltd, on presentation of
promissory notes, OCC paid £500 into the taxpayer's account with Slater Walker and
were to continue to do so until the whole £2,500 had been repaid.   In the circumstances
I am unable to regard each payment of £500 as anything other than repayment by OCC
c of part of the £2,500 paid to that company, and to adapt Rowlatt J's sentence, one can say
that under the terms of the capital income plan the capital sum provided initially by
Baldrene and then by HOVAS was in any event to be returned to them.

The Special Commissioners thought that it was a fair description of the transactions to
say that it was a bona fide commercial transaction without any element of bounty.   That
it had no element of bounty is clear.   Attaching that label to it does not in my view
d exclude the operation of s 457.   I would agree that that is a fair description if it is one that
can properly be applied to a scheme operated by the Slater Walker group, no doubt as
part of their business, solely designed to secure without their adventuring any capital the
obtaining of tax advantages.

In my view the payments of £500 emanating from OCC were payments of capital and
the fact that one or two days before they were made, the sums were paid to HOVAS by
e overdrawing the taxpayer's bank account was a mere matter of machinery which does
not disguise the true character of the operation.

If, contrary to my view, the sums of £500 were income in the hands of HOVAS I see
no reason to conclude that they were not payable out of profits or gains brought into
charge.

For these reasons this appeal should in my opinion be allowed.   It follows from what
f I have said that the taxpayer was not entitled to deduct tax at the standard rate from the
gross payments.   His taxable profits or gains remain unaffected by the payments.   If, on
the other hand, the payments were income and not out of income which formed part of
his profits or gains, they are by virtue of s 457 to be treated for the purposes of surtax as
his income.

LORD DIPLOCK. My Lords, I have had the advantage of reading in draft the speeches
g of my noble and learned friends, Lord Wilberforce and Viscount Dilhorne.   Of the four
grounds on which the Crown has sought the reversal of the judgment of the Court of
Appeal I propose to examine only that one which Lord Wilberforce deals with last and
Viscount Dilhorne first: the application of s 457 of the Income and Corporation Taxes
Act 1970, to a transaction whose avowed and only purpose was the avoidance of surtax.

It is common ground between my noble and learned friends that on a literal
h interpretation of what, according to s 454, is to be understood as included in the
expression 'settlement', the transaction would fall within it.   It is likewise common
ground that Parliament must have intended some narrower construction than this to be
placed on the word 'settlement' in the context of s 457; for, unless it is, it is difficult to
think of any transaction in consequence of it in which income paid by one person to
another that would not fall within the section.   The competing views are, on the one
j hand, that the context in which the word 'settlement' appears in Part XVI of the Act
shows a parliamentary intention to *exclude* from its meaning bona fide business
transactions only, and, on the other hand, that it shows an intention to *include* only
transactions in which there is an element of bounty.

---

1   [1929] 2 KB 85 at 88, cf 14 Tax Cas 608 at 614
2   [1930] 1 KB 107, [1929] All ER Rep 685, 14 Tax Cas 608

My Lords, I do not find either of these limitations on the meaning of the word easy to justify on the language of the section itself or of Part XVI of the Act considered as a whole. In the section itself the draftsman has thought it necessary, by para (*a*) of sub-s (1) and by sub-ss (2) to (4), to exclude expressly from the operation of the section particular kinds of transactions in which there is clearly no element of bounty and which would also merit the description of bona fide business transactions. If one considers also the other sections in this Part of the Act in which the expressions 'settlement' or 'disposition' (to which a similar unrestricted meaning is assigned in s 434) appear there is nothing there that calls for a more restricted meaning to be given to either of those words than is ascribed to them by ss 454 and 434 respectively, since the nature of the particular transaction to which each of those other sections in Part XIV apply is limited by the description in the section of the legal effects of the transaction.

So it seems to me that in order to reach a conclusion whether in addition to those transactions which are expressly excluded from s 457 by sub-sections (1) to (4) any other kinds of transaction whereby income is paid by one person to another were intended to be excluded from its operation, it is necessary to apply to this part of the Act a purposive construction and to ask oneself the question in relation to the particular kind of transaction which is under consideration: 'Can Parliament really have intended to tax this particular kind of transaction by the wide words that the draftsman has used?' If the only sensible answer to that question is, No, the words of the Act should be understood as inapplicable to the transaction.

That question when asked about a transaction which not only falls within the literal meaning of the words used in the section but has no other object than to enable the settlor to avoid a liability to surtax on his income which he would otherwise be obliged to pay, so far from inviting the answer No, invites the answer: 'Whatever kind of transaction Parliament may have intended to exclude it cannot have been this one'.

The earlier sections in Part XVI of the Act deal with the liability of the settlor to income tax as well as surtax on income payable to persons other than himself. Section 457 deals with his liability to surtax alone. As respects this element of tax, it is a sweeping-up section dealing, as sub-s (1)(*e*) makes clear, with surtax on income from settlements that do not comprise transactions of any of the particular kinds described in those earlier sections. That Parliament cannot have intended to sweep into its maw every transaction, even though entered into in the ordinary course of business, if it resulted in income being paid by one person to another, would seem self-evident; but as between giving to it a purposive construction which involves excluding bona fide business transactions and one which involves excluding transactions in which there is no element of bounty, it does not seem to me to be correct to distinguish between these rival views by describing the former as involving judicial legislation and the latter as consisting of judicial construction only.

For my part, in agreement with Viscount Dilhorne, I too, for the reasons that he gives, prefer the former; but even assuming that the latter be correct, it seems to me that on the face of the document under which annual payments were made the transaction under consideration did involve an element of bounty. If one is to disregard the underlying realities of the whole tax avoidance scheme in which that document played an essential part and recognise only the legal obligations which it imposed on the parties to it, the taxpayer undertook an obligation to pay to HOVAS in return for a payment of £2,480, five sums of £851 each over a period of just over four years or a total sum of £4,255. This, as it seems to me, involves a substantial element of bounty. The fact that if he chooses to pay the sum out of his own profits or gains brought into tax, he can discharge his obligation in part by assuming (under s 52 of the Act) the liability of the payee to pay income tax at the standard rate on it and so, in the case of a charity such as HOVAS, transfer to the Revenue the ultimate burden of the element of bounty is a matter which the blinkers that the court, by *Inland Revenue Comrs v Duke of Westminster*[1] and cases that have followed it, is enjoined to wear in revenue cases, compels it to ignore.

---

1 [1936] AC 1, [1935] All ER Rep 259, 19 Tax Cas 490

For these reasons I would allow this appeal.

a **LORD FRASER OF TULLYBELTON.** My Lords, the details of the complicated tax avoidance scheme with which this appeal is concerned have already been described by my noble and learned friends Lord Wilberforce and Viscount Dilhorne, and I need not repeat what they have said. The questions that arise for decision are four. (1) Were the five annual payments made by the taxpayer to HOVAS payments of 'an annuity or other annual payment charged with tax under Case III of Schedule D' within s 52(1) of the

b Income and Corporation Taxes Act 1970? (2) Were they 'payable wholly out of profits or gains brought into charge to income tax' within the meaning of that subsection? (3) Were the payments made otherwise than for valuable and sufficient consideration in the sense of s 434 of that Act? (4) Were the payments income arising under a 'settlement' within s 457 and the definition in s 454(3), applied by s 459(1) of that Act?

1. On the first question the contention of the Crown was that the five sums of £500

c each paid to HOVAS, notwithstanding that they were called payments of an annuity, were in reality of a capital nature. The name given to payments by the parties to the transaction is of course not conclusive as to their true nature and in considering whether they are of an income or of a capital character the court is entitled to have regard not only to the contractual documents, but to all the facts which are relevant for determination of the question: see *Inland Revenue Comrs v Church Comrs for England*[1]. In the Court of

d Appeal[2] the Crown argued that the purchase price of £2,480 paid by HOVAS should be regarded as a loan and that the 'annuity' payments were truly instalments of capital in repayment of the loan. This argument was rejected by Buckley LJ on two grounds, with both of which I agree, and it was not repeated in your Lordships' House. The argument for the Crown here was that they did not have to attach any particular label to the payments and that it was enough for them if they could show that the payments were of a capital

e nature. It is of course true that purchase of an annuity always consists of paying out capital and receiving back in exchange money which, in a general sense, represents, at least in part, the capital purchase price. But it is accepted that in principle the whole annuity is income in the hands of the recipient: (see *Sothern-Smith v Clancy (Inspector of Taxes)*[3]) and I did not understand that counsel for the Crown disputed that that was the general rule. It continues to be so notwithstanding the statutory provisions for taxation of purchased life annuities

f originating in the Finance Act 1956, s 27. The argument for the Crown sought to distinguish the present transaction from a normal purchase of an annuity in various respects so as to take it out of the general rule. *Perrin v Dickson (Inspector of Taxes)*[4] was cited as an example of a case which escaped the general rule partly because of the method of calculating the payments to be made in that case, and partly because of a term in the contract whereby in the event of the pupose for which the policy was effected failing either

g wholly or partly the assurance company was to repay to the taxpayer the whole or part as the case might be of the money paid by him. (In *Inland Revenue Comrs v Church Comrs for England*[5] I was guilty of inaccuracy in referring to *Perrin v Dickson (Inspector of Taxes)*[4] as a case where there had been a pre-existing relation of debtor and creditor between the parties.) The argument in the present case was that the obligation of the taxpayer, like that of the company in *Perrin v Dickson (Inspector of Taxes)*[4] was simply to repay the money paid

h by the annuitant and that that money had never 'ceased to exist' so as to satisfy the test stated by Watson B in *Lady Foley v Fletcher*[6]: '. . . an annuity means where an income is purchased with a sum of money, and the capital has gone and has ceased to exist, the principal having been converted into an annuity.'

---

j
1 [1976] 2 All ER 1037, [1977] AC 329, [1976] STC 339
2 [1975] 3 All ER 614, [1975] 1 WLR 1383, [1975] STC 546
3 [1941] 1 All ER 111, [1941] 1 KB 276, 24 Tax Cas 1
4 [1930] 1 KB 107, [1929] All ER Rep 685, 14 Tax Cas 608
5 [1976] 2 All ER 1037 at 1055, [1977] AC 329 at 356, [1976] STC 339 at 357
6 (1858) 3 H & N 769 at 784, [1843–60] All ER Rep 952 at 961

I cannot accept that contention. The transaction in the present case was exceptional in respect that the annuity payer was a private individual and not an established insurance company, and for that reason security for the payments was required. It was the provisions made for securing the payments that afforded the principal basis for the Crown's argument on this part of the case. The argument was that the purchase price of £2,480 was never handed over to the fund and was simply paid back to HOVAS by instalments. It is true that the taxpayer never had unfettered control of the money. But that was only because it was earmarked from the beginning as security for his obligation to pay the annuity, and the investments which were acceptable as security were stipulated by HOVAS. The money belonged to the taxpayer, and with the agreement of HOVAS he could have changed the way in which it was invested. It was actually invested (along with a further £20 provided by the taxpayer from his own resources) in promissory notes issued by Old Change Court (Investments) Ltd. That was in accordance with the suggestion in the scheme for the capital income plan. But it might have been invested in short term gilt edged securities, as HOVAS explained in their letter of 11th March 1971 to the taxpayer. Subsequently on 26th July 1971 the taxpayer wrote to HOVAS asking them to accept British Transport stock 1968/73 in place of the promissory notes and HOVAS agreed to do so. For some unexplained reason, the change was not made. But the taxpayer was the owner of the money and if it had been invested in a security which had either appreciated or depreciated in value, any profit or loss would have accrued to him.

Apart from the limit imposed on the taxpayer's freedom to use the money, another unusual feature of the scheme was that HOVAS insured the life of the taxpayer for annually reducing amounts to cover the possibility that he might die before he had paid all five sums of £500. This life assurance was not part of the contractual arrangement between HOVAS and the taxpayer, though its existence is one of the facts which can properly be taken into consideration for the purpose of determining whether the annuity payments were truly of an income character. It was argued for the Crown that the life assurance was effected by HOVAS to safeguard its capital and that its existence showed that the capital was not being risked. In my opinion the fact that HOVAS chose to insure the taxpayer's life is completely neutral for this purpose. The life policy would have provided the appropriate number of annual sums of £500 in the event of the taxpayer dying before he had paid all the five sums that he had contracted to pay, but I cannot see that it throws any light on the question of whether these sums were income or capital in the hands of HOVAS. Once they were received by HOVAS it was free to use them in any way it thought fit. They were not instalments of the price of any property sold by HOVAS nor were they stamped in any way as capital in its hands.

In practice, of course, the £2,500 invested in promissory notes was the obvious source from which the annuity payments were to be made, but it was only a matter of convenience and if the taxpayer had chosen to make all or any of the payments from some other source, he was free to do so. For example, if he had wished to save the small amount of interest on the overdraft which he incurred between the date of paying the annuity and receiving the proceeds of promissory notes repaid, he could have paid the annuity out of any other funds that he might have had available.

1. In these circumstances I am of the opinion that the payments of annuity were income in the hands of HOVAS and I therefore answer the first question in the affirmative.

2. and 3. On these questions I have nothing to add to what my noble and learned friend Lord Wilberforce has already said.

4. The answer to this question turns on the meaning to be given to the word 'settlement' in s 457 of the Income and Corporation Taxes Act 1970. The meaning is defined in s 454(3) (applied by s 459) thus: '"settlement" includes any disposition, trust, covenant, agreement or arrangement.'

The contract between the taxpayer and HOVAS was not a settlement in the ordinary sense of that word, but it was an agreement and it is therefore within the extended meaning of settlement if the extended meaning is read literally. But if it were read literally it would include a large number of business agreements and would produce results so

inconvenient and surprising as to lead to a strong presumption that they cannot have been
intended. The courts have therefore recognised that some limit must be placed on the
width of the words, and the need for some limit was accepted by both parties to this
appeal. The limit must be fixed by some rule capable of general application. I do not
think it is enough for the court simply to decide the case on the view that Parliament could
never have intended this transaction to escape taxation; a decision on that ground would
approach too closely to arbitrariness.

The argument on this part of the appeal was about what was the proper rule to apply.
The Crown contended that the definition in s 454(3) applied to all transactions that did not
have a bona fide commercial reason, and that it applied to the present transaction, the sole
reason for which was to avoid tax. The taxpayer contended that the definition applied only
to transactions which included an element of bounty. In many cases the two contentions
might lead to the same result, but not in the present case. In my opinion the true rule is
that the definition applies only where there is an element of bounty. One reason is that the
commercial transaction test seems to go too far; many transactions which would be
generally regarded as perfectly legitimate forms of investment, are entered into solely, or
at least predominantly, for tax reasons, and I think it would be wrong to suggest that they
might be taxable for that reason alone. But the main reason in favour of the bounty test
is that the word 'settlement', even allowing for its extended definition in s 454(3), seems to
me to be used throughout Part XVI of the Act with a flavour of donation or bounty. I agree
with the observations of my noble and leaned friend Lord Wilberforce that the various
provisions in Part XVI, to which he has referred, have a common characteristic of bounty.
I would add that the same characteristic seems to apply to the first three exceptions to
s 457(1) itself. Section 457(1) provides that:

> 'Where, during the life of the settlor, income arising under a settlement . . . is,
> under the settlement . . . payable to . . . any person other than the settlor, then,
> unless, under the settlement . . . the income either [and there follow five exceptions],
> the income shall be treated for the purposes of surtax as the income of the settlor and
> not as the income of any other person.'

The first exception in para (a) is for (in effect) a pension to a former member of a
partnership or his widow or dependants 'being payments made under a liability incurred
for full consideration'. Gratuitous payments to such persons are not excepted from the
subsection. Secondly, by para (b) (which incorporates sub-s (2)) there is a corresponding
exception for (in effect) pensions paid by an individual who has acquired a business to a
former owner or partner in the business or to the widow or dependants of such persons,
and again the exception is limited by a provision, 'being payments made under a liability
incurred for full consideration'. Thirdly, para (c) makes an exception for income arising
under a settlement in favour of a former spouse of the settlor, or in favour of a spouse
living apart from the settlor under a separation order of a court or under a separation
agreement or when the separation is likely to be permanent. There is no express
requirement in para (c) for full consideration, as that would clearly be inappropriate, but
it is reasonable to assume that payments in the circumstances mentioned in this
paragraph would usually be motivated by obligation, legal or moral, rather than by
bounty. The other two exceptions in s 457(1) are not relevant to this question, but the
three to which I have referred seem to reinforce the argument that in the context of Part
XVI the word 'settlement' 'is used in the limited sense of settlements containing an
element of bounty'.

This view of the Act receives some support from the speech of Lord Macmillan in
Chamberlain v Inland Revenue Comrs[1] in a passage which, as Lord Greene MR pointed out
in *Hood-Barrs v Inland Revenue Comrs*[2] draws attention to the importance of the statutory
context. The bounty test was accepted without argument in *Inland Revenue Comrs v*

---

1 [1943] 2 All ER 200 at 204, 25 Tax Cas 317 at 331
2 [1946] 2 All ER 768 at 774, 27 Tax Cas 385 at 402

Leiner.[1] In *Bulmer v Inland Revenue Comrs*[2] it was applied by Pennycuick J, but he evidently thought that in the circumstances of that case there was no material difference between the bounty test and the commercial transaction test and did not have to decide between them.

I would dismiss the appeal.

LORD KEITH OF KINKEL. My Lords, I have had the advantage of reading in draft the speech prepared by my noble and learned friend, Lord Wilberforce. My own views on all the points argued in this appeal accord so closely with those which he has there expressed that no purpose would be served by my adding anything. I too would dismiss the appeal.

Appeal dismissed

Solicitors: *Solicitor of Inland Revenue*; *Roney Vincent & Co* (for the taxpayer).

Wendy Shockett   Barrister.

---

1 (1964) 41 Tax Cas 589
2 [1966] 3 All ER 801 at 811, [1967] Ch 145 at 166, 44 Tax Cas 1 at 29

Customs and Excise Commissioners v Royal Exchange Theatre Trust

QUEEN'S BENCH DIVISION

NEILL J

3rd, 17th JULY 1979

Value added tax – Supply of goods or services – Supply in course of a business – Assignment of lease – Trust set up to advance public education by promoting the arts of drama, ballet etc – Trust fund raised by appeals to the public not involving taxable supplies – Trustees obtaining lease of land on which to build a theatre and then assigning the lease to charitable company incorporated by them – Whether assignment of lease a supply in the course of business carried on by trustees – Finance Act 1972, s 2(2).

The trustees under a trust set up for the purposes of advancing public education by promoting and improving the arts of drama, ballet, opera, music and the cinema were directed to incorporate a company registerable as a charity, to endeavour to obtain for the company at their expense a lease of part of a building with sufficient floor space to erect a theatre thereon and to raise funds to pay for the erection of the theatre. The trust deed provided that once the theatre had been completed and the company had been incorporated the trustees were to make a gift of the theatre to the company on certain terms. In due course the trustees raised substantial sums of money by appealing to the public for funds. The great majority of the sums raised did not involve any taxable supplies. The trustees then incorporated a company, acquired a lease of a building for a term of 25 years and, having completed a theatre therein, assigned the lease to the company. The trustees' claim that the assignment of the lease was a supply in the course of a business within s 2(2)[a] of the Finance Act 1972 was upheld by a value added tax tribunal. The Crown appealed.

Held – Although the word 'business' in s 2 of the 1972 Act was to be given a wide meaning and could not be exhaustively defined, it was necessary, when determining whether the activities of a taxable person constituted a business carried on by him, to look at the nature of the activities in question as a whole and not merely the efficiency with which they were undertaken. Notwithstanding that many of the attributes of business were present in the trustees' activities, the great majority of the sums were raised by appeals to the public which did not involve any taxable supplies and the activities culminated in a disposition by the trustees by way of a gift. In the absence of any monetary consideration moving from the company or of any commercial element in the trustees' activities, those activities could not be regarded as business activities. It followed that the assignment of the lease to the company did not constitute a supply in the course of a business carried on by the trustees within s 2. The appeal would therefore be allowed (see p 801 *d* and p 802 *b* to *e* and *g* to p 803 *a*, post).

Dictum of Lord Emslie in *Customs and Excise Comrs v Morrison's Academy Boarding Houses Association* [1978] STC at 5–6 followed.

Notes

For the charge of value added tax, see 12 Halsbury's Laws (4th Edn) para 870.

For the Finance Act 1972, s 2, see 42 Halsbury's Statutes (3rd Edn) 164.

Section 2 of the 1972 Act was substituted by the Finance Act 1977, Sch 6, para 1, with effect from 1st January 1978.

---

a   Section 2(2), so far as material, provides: 'Tax on the supply of goods or services shall be charged only where . . . (*b*) the goods or services are supplied by a taxable person in the course of a business carried on by him . . .'

Cases referred to in judgment

Customs and Excise Comrs v Morrison's Academy Boarding Houses Association [1978] STC 1, CS.

National Water Council v Customs and Excise Comrs [1979] STC 157.

Rael-Brook Ltd v Minister of Housing and Local Government [1967] 1 All ER 262, [1967] 2 QB 65, [1967] 2 WLR 604, 131 JP 237, 65 LGR 239, 18 P & CR 290, DC, Digest (Cont Vol C) 961, 3ol.

Town Investments Ltd v Department of the Environment [1977] 1 All ER 813, [1978] AC 359, [1977] 2 WLR 450, 34 P & CR 48, [1977] RVR 76, HL.

Cases also cited

Church of Scientology of California v Customs and Excise Comrs [1979] STC 297.

Inland Revenue Comrs v Marine Steam Turbine Co Ltd [1920] 1 KB 193, 12 Tax Cas 174.

Appeal

By a notice of motion dated 14th August 1978, the Crown appealed against the decision of a value added tax tribunal sitting in Manchester (chairman Mr P A Ferns), whereby the tribunal held, allowing the appeal by the respondent, Robert David Hillyer Scott, on behalf of the trustees of the Royal Exchange Theatre Trust, that the assignment of the benefit of a lease together with a theatre situate in the hall of the Royal Exchange, Manchester, by the trustees to a charitable company was a supply made in the course of a business carried on by the trustees. The facts are set out in the judgment.

Simon D Brown for the Crown.
Stephen Oliver for the trustees.

Cur adv vult

July 17th. **NEILL J** read the following judgment: This is an appeal by the Commissioners of Customs and Excise against a decision of a value added tax tribunal sitting in Manchester on 23rd, 24th and 25th March 1977. The decision is dated 24th July 1978. By its decision the tribunal allowed an appeal by the respondent, who had appealed to the tribunal on behalf of the trustees of the Royal Exchange Theatre Trust. I shall refer to the respondent to the present appeal as 'the trust'.

In 1977 the trust assigned to Royal Exchange Theatre Trustees Ltd ('the landlord company') the benefit of a lease of part of the Royal Exchange building in Manchester. The question for determination in the present appeal is whether the assignment of that lease was, for the purposes of value added tax, a supply in the course of a business carried on by the trust.

The facts are set out in the decision of the tribunal. I can summarise them quite shortly.

The present Manchester Royal Exchange was opened in October 1921, at a time when Manchester still dominated the world trade in cotton. In 1940 the building was badly damaged by fire, but much of the damaged structure was rebuilt and the restored building was opened in November 1953. After a short burst of activity following the 1939–45 war, however, the Lancashire cotton industry and with it the size of the membership of the Manchester Royal Exchange suffered a steady decline. On 31st December 1968 the Exchange ceased to function. Soon after its closure as an 'Exchange' the building passed into the hands of the Prudential Assurance Co Ltd. The Prudential recognised the potentialities of the considerable office accommodation as a property investment. In addition to the office accommodation, however, the building included a very large hall, some three-quarters of an acre in extent. A hall of this size presented a difficult letting problem.

Meanwhile, in the summer of 1968, that is, a few months before the Exchange in Manchester closed, a newly formed professional theatre company had just begun to rehearse its first production in London. The theatre company was called the 69 Theatre a Co Ltd. In due course the theatre company came to Manchester. It had a very successful season at the University Theatre, and following that success the company decided to seek a permanent home in Manchester. At one time the theatre company was minded to look for a site on which to build a conventional theatre, but the cost of such a scheme would have been very high. A committee of local industrialists and philanthropists was formed to help solve the problems of the theatre company. It was this committee which saw the possibilities of the large hall at the Royal Exchange.

b The trust was set up by a trust deed dated 1st September 1972. The trustees were seven in number. Six of the trustees were eminent men in the north-west of England including the then Lord Mayor of Manchester. The seventh trustee was the chairman of the 69 Theatre Co Ltd. I should read the recital and some of the clauses of the trust deed. The recital provided:

c 'WHEREAS the Trustees are about to make an Appeal for contributions to a fund . . . for the purpose of the advancement of education by causing the operation of a theatre or theatres in the Manchester area.'

Clause 2 was in the following terms:

d 'THE Trustees shall apply the Trust Fund for the purposes of advancing public education by promoting and improving the arts of drama ballet opera music and the cinema or any of them and of stimulating public appreciation of such arts or any of them and generally in the cultivation and improvement of public taste in the said arts or any of them by means inter alia of the erection of and endowment of a theatre or theatres in the Manchester area.'

Clause 3 provided:

e 'IN furtherance of the said purposes the Trustees shall in so far as it may be practicable (a) cause the incorporation of a non-profit distributing company limited by guarantee and registerable as a charity with members and directors nominated by the 69 Theatre Company Limited and approved by the Trustees such approval not being unreasonably withheld to any person who appears to be willing to support and further the objects of the said company (b) endeavour to obtain for such f company at their expense the grant of a lease . . . of part of the Royal Exchange Manchester including in particular sufficient space on the floor of the Exchange to erect a theatre . . . (c) to raise sufficient funds to pay for the erection of the theatre and to expend such sums on the said erection.'

Clause 4 provided:

g 'IN the event of the Trustees enabling the incorporation of the said company (hereinafter called "the Landlord Company") and erecting the Theatre they shall give the Theatre to the Landlord Company upon terms which shall include (a) the obligation for the Landlord Company to license the initial use of the theatre to the 69 Theatre Company Limited (b) allow the licensee of the Theatre to use it on such terms as to payment and otherwise as it thinks fit (c) insofar as they think fit endow h the Landlord Company with any funds donated to the Trustees which they have not expended in erecting the Theatre.'

Pausing there, it will be seen (a) that the trust was set up to obtain funds from donations by the public to finance the construction of a theatre in Manchester, (b) that the primary intention was to construct a theatre in the hall area of the Royal Exchange, (c) that when j the theatre had been constructed it was to be given to a new charitable company (described in the deed as the 'Landlord Company') on terms that the landlord company was to license the initial use of the theatre to the theatre company.

It is not necessary for me to refer in detail to all the remaining clauses of the trust deed. I mention only the following provisions. (1) By cl 5 the trustees were empowered to use any part of the trust fund for the maintenance and repair of the theatre. (2) By

other clauses the trustees were given borrowing powers and wide powers of
investment. They were also given power to maintain bank accounts. (3) Clause 14
contained provisions relating to the meetings and proceedings of the trustees. By cl
14 (e) it was provided: 'The Trustees shall keep a Minute Book of their proceedings and
proper books of account and sections 8 and 32 of the Charities Act 1960 in relation to the
accounts of the charity shall be duly observed.'

In due course the trust commenced its operations. Appeals for funds were made to the
public and very substantial amounts were received both from companies and
individuals. Architects and contractors were engaged and the construction of a theatre
inside the Royal Exchange building began. On 31st January 1973 the company which
had been described in the trust deed as the landlord company was duly incorporated.
The original name of that company was Exchange Theatre Trustees (Manchester) Ltd.
Later in September 1975 its name was changed to Royal Exchange Theatre Trustees
Ltd. By a lease dated 30th March 1974 the Prudential demised to the trust parts of the
Royal Exchange building for the term of 25 years. The lease contained a covenant
against assignment but this was subject to the proviso that no breach should be occasioned
by an assignment to the landlord company or by a subletting to the theatre company.
The theatre was completed and was ready for transfer to the landlord company by 12th
August 1976. In fact, as I understand the matter, the assignment was not executed until
June 1977, that is after the hearing before the tribunal, but this delay has no relevance to
the present appeal.

It is quite clear from the decision and from the documents which I have seen that the
building of this new theatre was a remarkable undertaking and that the trustees and all
those concerned in the project must have devoted countless hours to ensuring that the
project was a success. The question which I have to decide, however, is whether the
assignment of the lease to the landlord company in June 1977 was a supply made by the
trust in the course of a business carried on by the trust. In answering that question I
cannot allow myself to be influenced by any feeling of admiration for the way in which
this project was conceived and carried out.

Starting in the autumn of 1973 there was correspondence between the commissioners
and the trust in which the trust was seeking registration for the purposes of value added
tax. The object of seeking registration was to enable the trust to recover input tax
charged to the trust on supplies made in connection with its projected building
operations. On 8th April 1975 the trust submitted a formal application. The application
was accepted and the trust was registered from 3rd May 1974. In the following months,
however, the commissioners examined the trust's position again and came to the
conclusion that in accepting the registration they had made a mistake. By letters dated
22nd March and 9th April 1976 the commissioners informed Mr Scott on behalf of the
trust that the trust would be deregistered.

By a notice of appeal dated 10th May 1976 the trust appealed to the value added tax
tribunal. At that stage it was an appeal under the provisions of s 40(1)(a) of the Finance
Act 1972 against a decision of the commissioners with respect to the cancellation of a
registration. Before the appeal came on for hearing, however, in March 1977 the
commissioners had cause to modify their opinion again. They decided that some of the
fund-raising activities of the trust constituted taxable supplies. Thus on 8th June 1975
the trust had arranged a theatrical entertainment for which the public had been charged
for admission. The decision contained in the letters of 22nd March and 9th April 1976
was withdrawn and a new decision was substituted by a letter dated 8th February 1977.
In this letter the commissioners stated that the earlier registration would be valid
provided the tribunal decided (1) that the assignment to the landlord company
constituted a 'supply', (2) that that supply was made in the course of a business carried on
by the trust, (3) that that supply was a taxable supply, being a grant of a major interest
by a person constructing a building and therefore eligible for zero-rating under item 1
of Group 8 of Sch 4 to the 1972 Act.

When the appeal came before the tribunal on 23rd March 1977 the questions for

determination by the tribunal were therefore very different from those raised in the
original appeal. At the request of the parties and with the approval of the tribunal,
however, the tribunal proceeded to deal with the issues formulated in the letter of 8th
February 1977.

I am not concerned with all the matters canvassed before the tribunal. In particular
it is not necessary for me to consider whether the theatre was a building within the
meaning of item 1 in Group 8 of Sch 4 to the 1972 Act. That point is now conceded by
the commissioners. As I have already indicated, the only point for my determination is
whether the assignment of the lease to the landlord company was a supply in the course
of a business carried on by the trust.

Counsel who appeared on behalf of the Crown in this court submitted that the
assignment did not constitute a supply in the course of a business carried on by the
trust. He accepted that it was legitimate to have regard to the activities of the trust
throughout the period of its existence, but he contended that these activities looked at
collectively did not amount to the carrying on of a business. It was true that in the course
of raising funds the trust had engaged in some business activities, for example when
offering entertainment to the public for reward. But, said counsel, the mere fact that the
raising of funds may involve from time to time the carrying on of some business
activities does not mean that the fund-raising itself is a business activity. The raising of
money by an appeal to the public is not per se a business activity, nor is the disposition
of the funds when raised such an activity. In order to characterise an activity as a business
activity it is necessary to find some commercial element in it. Counsel emphasised that
the assignment to the landlord company was a disposition by way of gift and that it
lacked any commercial element or flavour.

Counsel on behalf of the trust on the other hand contended that the tribunal had
reached the right decision. He relied on the constitution of the trust and on the duties
imposed on and carried out by the trustees over a period of years. He drew my attention
to the trust deed which he likened to the memorandum of a company. Clause 3 of the
trust deed, he suggested, imposed on the trustees duties of a business nature. In the
course of his argument he defined the business as being that of implementing the
undertaking given to the public to raise funds, to utilise them in the building of this
theatre inside the Royal Exchange and then to transfer the completed building for use by
the theatre company.

These then in outline were the arguments.

I should turn first to the definition of 'business' in Part I of the 1972 Act. Section 45
(as originally enacted) was in these terms:

'(1) In this Part of this Act "business" includes any trade, profession or vocation;
and (a) the provision by the Independant Broadcasting Authority of broadcasting
services; and (b) the provision by a club or by an association to which this paragraph
applies of the facilities available to its members; and (c) the provision by an
organisation to which this paragraph applies of the advantages of membership; and
(d) the admission, for a consideration, of persons to any premises; shall be deemed
to be the carrying on of a business.'

The section was considered by the Inner House of the Court of Session in *Customs and
Excise Comrs v Morrison's Academy Boarding Houses Association*[1]. Lord Emslie, the Lord
President, said[2]:

'The answer is to be found by looking at the whole activities carried on by the
association to see if those activities constitute a "business" within the meaning of
Part I of the 1972 Act. It has been said already that the word "business" is not
exhaustively or precisely defined for the purposes of this part of the 1972 Act. The

1   [1978] STC 1
2   [1978] STC 1 at 5–6

definition in s 45(1) is, however, not unhelpful for, by providing that "business" includes any trade, profession or vocation, a clear hint is given that a wide meaning is intended, and I observe that nowhere in Part I of the 1972 Act is there any use of the word "commerce" or "profit" in association with the word "business", or otherwise . . . The tax is, after all, not a tax on profit or income but on taxable supplies by taxable persons . . .'

I respectfully agree that a wide meaning is to be given to the word 'business' in s 2 of the 1972 Act. Moreover, there is great force in the submission of counsel for the trustees that if one looks at the constitution of the trust and at the activities of the trustees, many of the attributes of a business seem to be present. In this context I bear in mind the definitions to which I referred in my judgment in the *National Water Council v Customs and Excise Comrs*[1]. The work of the trust between 1972 and 1976 was clearly 'a serious undertaking earnestly pursued', to adopt the words of Widgery J in *Rael-Brook Ltd v Minister of Housing and Local Government*[2]. Further, it was capable of coming within the definition given by Lord Kilbrandon in *Town Investments Ltd v Department of the Environment*[3]: 'a serious occupation, not necessarily confined to commercial or profit-making undertakings.' But if one looks at the activities of the trustees as a whole, one is faced with two striking facts: (a) that the great majority of the sums raised by the trustees were raised by appeals to the public which did not involve any taxable supplies; and (b) that the activities culminated in a disposition by the trustees by way of gift.

There is no doubt that gifts may be made in the course of a business; indeed there is a specific provision in s 5(2) of the 1972 Act to include the making of a gift within the scope of the supply of goods. But I am unable to accept that in the context of the 1972 Act the word 'business' is to be construed so widely as to embrace the activities of these trustees who raised money from the public mainly by means of appeals and then handed over the fruits of their work as a gift to the landlord company. I regard the complete absence of any monetary consideration moving from the landlord company as a matter of great importance. In the *Morrison Academy* case[4] Lord Emslie gave this guidance on the construction of s 2(2) of the 1972 Act:

'In my opinion it will never be possible or desirable to define exhaustively "business" within the meaning of s 2(2)(*b*). What one must do is to discover what are the activities of the taxable person in course of which taxable supplies are made. If these activities are, as in this case, predominantly concerned with the making of taxable supplies to consumers for a consideration it seems to me to require no straining of the language of s 2(2)(*b*) of the 1972 Act to enable one to conclude that the taxable person is in the "business" of making taxable supplies, and that taxable supplies which he makes are supplies made in the course of carrying on that business . . .'

I accept that the word 'business' cannot be exhaustively defined within the meaning of s 2 of the 1972 Act, but I would underline the words 'for a consideration' in the passage I have cited.

In reaching this conclusion I have not overlooked the line of reasoning which led the tribunal to come to a different conclusion. I take the view, however, that the fact that the commissioners recognised some of the activities of the trustees as business activities does not affect the question of how all the activities looked at collectively are to be classified. The trustees no doubt carried on their affairs with great skill and in a 'business-like' manner. But so might a private philanthropist. It is the nature of the activities and not

---

1   [1979] STC 164
2   [1967] 1 All ER 262 at 266, [1967] 2 QB 65 at 76
3   [1977] 1 All ER 813 at 835, [1978] AC 359 at 402
4   [1978] STC 1 at 6

the efficiency with which they are undertaken which is the determining factor. Looking
a at the activities of these trustees as a whole it seems to me that they lacked any commercial
element at all and that they cannot properly be regarded as business activities.
Accordingly, I do not consider that the assignment to the landlord company in June 1977
constituted a supply in the course of a business carried on by the trust.

For these reasons I allow this appeal.

b *Appeal allowed. No order for costs. Leave to appeal to the Court of Appeal granted.*

Solicitors: *Solicitor for the Customs and Excise*; *Addleshaw, Sons & Latham,* Manchester (for
the trustees).

Evelyn M C Budd   Barrister.

c

Royco Homes Ltd v Southern Water
d # Authority

HOUSE OF LORDS
LORD WILBERFORCE, VISCOUNT DILHORNE, LORD SALMON, LORD RUSSELL OF KILLOWEN AND
LORD KEITH OF KINKEL
5th, 9th JULY, 8th NOVEMBER 1979

e
*Water supply – Supply of water for domestic purposes – Duty of undertakers to provide domestic
supply to new buildings – Duty on requisition by owner of land on which buildings to be erected
– Power of water authority to require owner to make contribution to cost of laying necessary
mains – Necessary mains – Point from which necessary mains to start – Request by landowner for
supply of water to new houses – No existing mains on site – Nearest distribution main to site too
f small to convey quantity of water required – Wider main capable of supplying water further
away from site – Request to landowner by water authority for contribution to cost of laying new
main from wider main to site – Whether proposed new main a 'necessary main' – Whether
'necessary main' must start from nearest existing main – Water Act 1945, s 37.*

A company owned a site near Sittingbourne in Kent which it proposed to develop for
g residential purposes. They obtained outline planning permission for the erection of 700
houses on it and detailed planning permission for 204 of them. There were no existing
water mains on the site. They required the local water authority to provide, under
s 37(1)[a] of the Water Act 1945, a domestic water supply to the houses. The nearest
distribution main to the site was a 4 inch main in a nearby avenue, Middletune Avenue,
which was too small to carry the quantity of water needed for the houses and was in any
h event already fully committed to satisfying the existing requirements of consumers.
Other distribution mains a little further from the site were also fully committed. Some
distance from the site there was a 10 inch main in Key Street which carried sufficient
water to supply the houses and which was not fully committed. The water authority
proposed, in response to the company's request, to lay an 8 inch main, which was the
smallest stock size main capable of supplying 700 houses, from the main in Key Street to
j the company's site. It was to run for part of the way under a main road and be 3·5 km
in length. For the provision of the new main the water authority required the company
to enter into an undertaking in accordance with s 37(1)(a) of the 1945 Act and to deposit,
under s 37(1)(b), £115,000 as security for the payment of the annual sums falling due

───────────────────────────────

a   Section 37 is set out at p 809 *h* to p 810 *g*, post

under the undertaking. There happened to be road works in progress at the time on the
main road and the water authority, in order to save greater expense in the future, at the a
same time laid one kilometre's length of the new main under the road. In respect of that
work the company paid to the water authority, under protest, £16,000 in part satisfaction
of the required deposit of £115,000. The company brought an action against the water
authority claiming a declaration that the authority was not legally entitled to demand
any deposit and guarantee of revenue in respect of the proposed new main from Key
Street to the boundary of the company's site, and that the company were entitled to b
repayment of the £16,000 with interest. The company contended (i) that the proposed
new main was not a 'necessary main' within the meaning of s 37(1), (ii) that the starting
point for a 'necessary main' within s 37(1) had to be the nearest point to the site to which
water was already being brought by a main (which was the 4 inch main in Middletune
Avenue), (iii) that the cost of bringing that main up to sufficient capacity had to be met
not by the company but by the general body of ratepayers, and (iv) that the company's c
contribution should be limited to the cost of providing a main from Middletune Avenue
to the site and providing any on-site distribution mains. The water authority submitted
that it would be uneconomic and contrary to sensible water engineering practice for the
new main to start from Middletune Avenue.

Held – (i) The starting point for any new main necessary for the connection of a d
proposed development to a water supply did not have to be the nearest point to the
proposed development at which there was an existing main. The point at which the new
main had to start was where, in accordance with sound water engineering practice, the
new main could in the circumstances be fed with sufficient water to meet the particular
purposes for which it was required (see p 805 c, p 807 a to d, p 809 b to e, p 811 f to h and
p 814 d to h, post); *Cherwell District Council v Thames Water Authority* [1975] 1 All ER 763 e
distinguished.
   (ii) Whether a main was 'necessary' was a question of fact, and on the evidence, from
a sound water engineering point of view, there was no point nearer than the main in Key
Street selected by the water authority from which the additional quantity of water
required for the purposes of the proposed development could be provided. The proposed
new main was therefore a 'necessary main' within s 37(1) of the 1945 Act and the water f
authority was entitled to recover the appropriate amount from the company under
s 37(1)(*a*) and to require a deposit under s 37(1)(*b*) (see p 805 c, p 807 a to d, p 809 b f g, and
p 814 h, post).
   Per Curiam. The principle that the cost of improvements or additions to an existing
distribution system cannot be laid to the charge of site developers applies only to
improvements or additions executed on sections of the system short of the point at which g
any new main necessary for the connection of the proposed new development takes its
departure (see p 805 c, p 807 d and p 814 a b, post).

Notes
For the duty of statutory water undertakers to provide a domestic water supply for new
buildings, see 39 Halsbury's Laws (3rd Edn) 402, para 618. h
   For the Water Act 1945, s 37 see 39 Halsbury's Statutes (3rd Edn) 108.

Case referred to in opinions
Cherwell District Council v Thames Water Authority [1975] 1 All ER 763, [1975] 1 WLR
   448, 139 JP 441, 73 LGR 227, [1975] RVR 232, HL, Digest (Cont Vol D) 1017, 49*a*.
                                                                                 j

Appeal
Royco Homes Ltd appealed against the part of the judgment of Forbes J, dated 9th June
1978, whereby he refused to grant them a declaration that the respondents, the Southern
Water Authority, were not entitled to require a financial contribution or deposit in

a respect of a water main which the water authority proposed to construct from Key Street, Sittingbourne, Kent, to the appellants' Milton Church Farm Housing Estate. Forbes J granted the appellants a certificate under s 12 of the Administration of Justice Act 1969 for leave to present a petition of appeal to the House of Lords. Leave to appeal was granted on 24th July 1978. The facts are set out in the opinion of Lord Keith of Kinkel.

b *John Drinkwater QC* and *Barry Payton* for the appellants.
Conrad Dehn QC and *W D Ainger* for the water authority.

Their Lordships took time for consideration.

8th November. The following opinions were delivered.

c

LORD WILBERFORCE. My Lords, I have had the benefit of reading in advance the speeches prepared by my noble and learned friends, Viscount Dilhorne and Lord Keith of Kinkel. I agree with them and would dismiss the appeal.

d **VISCOUNT DILHORNE.** My Lords, the appellants own the Milton Church Farm Estate near Sittingbourne in Kent. They have obtained outline planning permission for the erection of 700 houses on that estate and detailed planning permission for 204 houses. By letter dated 7th June 1976 they required the Southern Water Authority to supply water for domestic purposes for the 204 houses they proposed to erect on their land.

e Section 37 of the Water Act 1945 as amended and so far as material reads as follows:

'(1) Where an owner of land proposes to erect thereon buildings for which a supply of water for domestic purposes will be needed, he may require any water authority within whose limits of supply that land is situated to construct any necessary service reservoirs, to lay the necessary mains to such point or points as will enable the buildings to be connected thereto at a reasonable cost and to bring water f to that point or those points, and thereupon the water authority shall, subject as hereinafter provided, comply with that requisition: Provided that the water authority before complying with a requisition under this subsection—(a) may require the owner to undertake to pay in respect of each year a sum amounting to one-eighth of the expense of providing and constructing the necessary service reservoirs and providing and laying the necessary mains (less any amounts received g by the water authority in respect of water supplied, whether for domestic or non-domestic purposes, in that year from those mains) until the aggregate amount of water charges as are stated by the water authority to be payable for a supply of water for domestic purposes payable annually in respect of the buildings when erected and in respect of any other premises connected with the said mains at the rates for the time being charged by the water authority equals or exceeds such sum as aforesaid h or until the expiration of a period of twelve years, whichever first occurs; and (b) except where the owner is a local or public authority, may also require him to deposit with the water authority as security for payment of the said annual sums, such sum, not exceeding the total expense of constructing the service reservoirs and providing and laying the mains, as the water authority may require . . .'

j   In April 1976 in response to an enquiry by the appellants, the water authority told them that to supply water to the 700 houses, they proposed to lay a 200 mm main from Key Street on the A2 road, which would go for some part of its way along the A249 road and would be some 3·5 km in length. Key Street was the nearest point to the appellants' site at which there was a main carrying water available and sufficient to supply the appellants' houses.

For the provision of the new main the water authority required the appellants to enter
into an undertaking in accordance with para (a) of s 37(1) and to deposit £115,000 as **a**
security for the payment of the annual sums falling due under the undertaking. At the
time there were road works on part of the A249 and it was suggested that the appellants
should deposit £16,500 to enable the main to be laid along that stretch of road before the
road works were completed and so avoid some expense. Under protest the appellants
deposited £16,000. On 9th August they commenced this action, claiming, inter alia,
declarations that the water authority could not lawfully demand a contribution from **b**
them in respect of the proposed main from Key Street and that the appellants were
entitled to repayment of the £16,000.

The appellants contend that they can only be required to give an undertaking under
s 37 and to provide a deposit in relation to the provision of a main from the nearest point
to their site to which water is brought by a main. There is a network of distribution
mains on all sides of the appellants' site but with the exception of a 10 inch main to the **c**
north of the site, all these mains were of smaller size than any main which would be
required to convey the quantity of water needed for the proposed development, and the
distribution network is for all practical purposes committed to present demands. The 10
inch main and also an 18 inch main which carries water to the Isle of Sheppey and which
runs along Sheppey Way are also fully committed to satisfy the existing requirements of
consumers. The distribution mains in the network vary in size from 6 inches to 3 **d**
inches.

So the appellants' contention is that under s 37 they can only be required to give an
undertaking and to provide security in relation to a main which cannot, save at the
expense of other consumers, supply an adequate amount of water to the houses they
propose to build. If the development of their site renders the existing mains inadequate,
then they say the cost of laying larger mains must be met by the water authority and they **e**
cannot be required to give any such undertaking or to make a deposit in relation thereto.

In support of their contentions, the appellants seek to rely on some observations made
by Lord Diplock in the course of his speech in *Cherwell District Council v Thames Water
Authority*[1] with which I and the other members of the House agreed. That was a very
different case from this. There the question was whether the Cherwell District Council
could be required to contribute to the cost of laying a trunk main to carry water from the **f**
Thames near Woodstock to a service reservoir at Banbury to supplement the supply of
water to that reservoir from the river Cherwell for the benefit of consumers in the
Banbury area. The council were proposing to build dwellings on two sites and did not
dispute their liability under s 37 in respect of the new distribution mains which would
be necessary to bring water to the immediate vicinity of their sites.

In the present case no question arises as to a trunk main and in the *Cherwell* case[1] no **g**
question arose as to the place from which a 'necessary' main should start. 'Necessary',
Lord Diplock said, was 'the keyword' in s 37 and he said that the section presupposed that
there were no existing mains bringing water to points at which it would be practicable
at reasonable cost to connect the proposed buildings to those mains by means of service
pipes.

In the present case although there are distribution mains in the vicinity of the **h**
appellants' site, it was not suggested that there were any mains bringing water to points
at which it would be practicable at reasonable cost to connect the proposed buildings to
those mains by service pipes. It was common ground that a new main was necessary.
The dispute was as to the point on the supply system from which that main should
start. As my noble and learned friend pointed out, under the Water Act 1945 if there
was a distribution main to which it was practicable to connect buildings by service pipes, **j**
the owner or occupier could not be required to contribute to the cost of replacing the

_____

1 [1975] 1 All ER 763, [1975] 1 WLR 448

existing main by one of greater capacity to meet the additional demand resulting from
a the connection of the buildings to them.   Whether or not a main is 'necessary' is a
question of fact.   It is necessary if it is required to bring water to 'such point or points as
will enable the buildings to be connected thereto at a reasonable cost' by service pipes.
And the question now to be decided is the point from which a necessary main must
start.   The appellants' contention is that such a main is only necessary if it starts from a
near existing main even though that main is of such small capacity as to be unable to
b supply the quantity of water required for the buildings.
I see nothing in the Act to require acceptance of this contention.   In my view a
necessary main is one which will carry the quantity of water required to the point or
points to which it is practicable at reasonable cost to connect the buildings by service
pipes.   If there was a point nearer than Key Street from which the additional quantity of
water required for the proposed buildings could be provided, then the appellants would
c be entitled to say that it was not necessary for the new main to be laid from Key Street
and that they were being asked to contribute to the cost of a main that was longer than
was necessary.   In this case there is no such evidence and in my view, for the reasons
stated, the appellants' claim should be dismissed.

LORD SALMON.   My Lords, I agree for the reasons stated in the speeches of my noble
d and learned friends, Viscount Dilhorne and Lord Keith of Kinkel, that this appeal should
be dismissed.

LORD RUSSELL OF KILLOWEN.   My Lords, the contention of the appellant
developer in this case is that while it is financially liable to the Southern Water Authority
in respect of distribution mains on its site, it is not thus liable in respect of distribution
e mains off its site save from a point at which an existing water main is nearest to the site;
any other distribution main which is required by the exigencies of the situation and
common sense water engineering practice, if the houses on the development site are to
have an adequate supply of water for domestic purposes, is not, it is contended, a
'necessary water main'.
The facts of this case and the relevant statutory provisions are fully set out in the
f opinion of my noble and learned friend Lord Keith of Kinkel, and I need not repeat
them.   I say at once that I am in agreement with his conclusions, and with the judgment
of Forbes J.   It was frankly agreed by counsel for the appellants that he was not able to
support his case by reference to the statutory provisions alone.   His contentions were
based on certain expressions contained in the speech of Lord Diplock in *Cherwell District
Council v Thames Water Authority*[1], a speech with which the rest of their Lordships
g expressed simple agreement.
As has been stated by my noble and learned friend Lord Keith of Kinkel the actual
ratio decidendi (that the then appellants could not be required to contribute to the
particular main) is to be found in the report of that case[2]: and that was that the particular
main was not a 'necessary main' because its purpose was not only to produce an adequate
water supply for the proposed development but also (and indeed in greater measure) for
h a much wider area.   With that decision on that ground I would, my Lords, have no
possible quarrel.   But it is not applicable to the present case where the purpose of the
main in question is, and is no more than, to supply the proposed 700 house
development.   (For I agree that the excess capacity involved in the only standard size
suitable for the development cannot be a defect in the argument that this is a 'necessary
main'.)
j Based however on some comments in the *Cherwell* case[2] it was contended, in effect,
that there could be no necessary main starting otherwise than from a point where there

---

1   [1975] 1 All ER 763, [1975] 1 WLR 448
2   [1975] 1 All ER 763 at 771, [1975] 1 WLR 448 at 457

was already a main nearest to the development site. In this case it is a 4 inch main in Middletune Avenue. This would be quite useless as a source of supply to the proposed *a* development, this main and other mains in the general vicinity of the development site being already fully committed. The appellants contend however that the water authority cannot require the appellants to contribute to the cost of bringing the nearest main up to a sufficient capacity, and that such contribution must be limited to the cost of off-site mains from that nearest point, as well as of course any on-site distribution mains. My Lords, I find no support for this contention in the speech of Lord Diplock. *b*

Lord Diplock summarises the statutory provisions in this manner. He deals first with the case of existing buildings for which a domestic water supply is required. In such a case, if those premises are reachable by a *service pipe* (pipes leading from a main to an individual building) from an existing main the owner of that building can demand connection with that main, paying only the cost of the service pipe. He points out that 'main' is a pipe laid for giving a general supply of water, as distinct from a service pipe *c* to particular premises; and it is to be noted that this is a reference to service pipes from a main in a highway or street on which the existing premises abut. He then states that in such case the owner cannot be required to make any contribution to the original cost of the main in question; nor can he be required to contribute to any expense that may be involved in improving or replacing the main so as to produce an adequate supply of water even if inadequacy results from the very connection of the new premises. *d*

Lord Diplock next deals with existing premises which cannot be connected with an existing main by service pipes. In such a case the owners can require that necessary mains be laid. Such must be laid if the annual water rates of the requiring owners will amount to one-eighth of the cost of provision of such necessary mains; and if they do not, the local authority may pay the difference for 12 years.

Lord Diplock next deals with cases where there are no existing premises, but a *e* development is proposed. Originally such development could not be carried out without assurance of a domestic water supply. Under the statute the developer may require the laying of the 'necessary mains' to points that will enable connection to the proposed buildings at reasonable cost, ie by service pipe. In those circumstances payment is required of the developer.

I now quote Lord Diplock[1]: *f*

> 'The section pre-supposes, first, that there are no existing mains bringing water to points at which it would be practicable at reasonable cost to connect the proposed buildings to those mains by service pipes. If there were, there would be no need for any requisition. Once the building was erected the owner would be entitled to require the connection to be made under cl 30, without any liability to contribute to the cost previously incurred by the undertakers in laying the existing mains or to *g* the cost of replacing them by mains of greater capacity to meet the additional demand resulting from the connection of the newly erected building to them. Secondly, the section pre-supposes that there will be a supply of water in bulk capable of being brought to the new mains by the undertakers, which if it is not already available to them it is their duty to procure without demanding from the *h* requisitioner any contribution to the cost of doing so. So the "necessary mains" with which the section deals are confined to new mains to be laid by the undertakers in a street or other place where there are no existing distribution mains and to start from a point to which a supply of water is already being brought in existing works belonging to the undertaker; and the answer to the question: "Necessary for what?" is: necessary in order to convey the water from that starting point to points at which *j* it would be practicable to connect the proposed buildings to those mains by service pipes, and for no other purpose.'

---

1   [1975] 1 All ER 763 at 769–770, [1975] 1 WLR 448 at 455

It is to be observed that nothing whatever is said there as to *where* the starting point in
a the system of the 'necessary main' is to be. The case of an existing building within
'service pipe' distance of an existing main (the first dealt with by Lord Diplock) is quite
different, and does not throw light on the present question, which is whether a necessary
main must start at a point where there is the nearest existing main, however contrary to
sensible water engineering practice and economics such as a proposition would be.

In agreeing that this appeal should be dismissed I would accept the summary of
b Forbes J in his judgment:

> 'I can summarise my conclusions in this way: (a) A necessary main (or service
> reservoir) is one which can be said to be necessary for the purpose of conveying
> water from the existing distribution system to the developer's site and, within it, to
> points suitable for giving individual supplies. (b) The point on the existing
c > distribution system from which the new main takes its departure is not ineluctably
> the nearest point on that system to the developer's site; it is the point from which,
> in accordance with proper water engineering practice, it is possible to charge the
> main with sufficient water to supply the proposed development. In this connection,
> it should be remembered that the appropriate point may be one on a trunk main,
> and the "necessary" works may, therefore, include a trunk main from this point to
d > a service reservoir as well as the reservoir itself and the distribution main from there
> on to and within the site. (c) The size and the route of the main must be such as are
> necessary for that purpose also and not for any other, subject to this, that the size
> may take into account the needs of potential customers along the route of the
> pipe. (d) The fact that once the main is laid the water in it may be used for some
> purpose other than supplying the developer's site does not of itself mean that the
e > main is not a necessary main; what governs the matter is the purpose for which the
> main is laid, and not the purpose for which the water in it may subsequently be
> used. (e) So long as a main is bona fide laid in accordance with the principles set out
> in (a), (b) and (c) above, no theoretical re-arrangement (however ingenious) either of
> the existing distribution system or of the new works, can serve to vitiate that
> purpose, except, presumably, if it can be shown, on the *Wednesbury*[1] principle, that
f > no reasonable water undertaking could have adopted the original solution.'
> Applying these principles to the circumstances of the Milton site, I conclude that the
> main proposed by the defendants is a necessary main within the meaning of s 37(1)
> and that the defendants are entitled to recover the appropriate amounts from the
> plaintiffs under proviso (*a*) to that subsection, and to require the deposit under
> proviso (*b*) to be made.'

g Accordingly I would dismiss the appeal.

LORD KEITH OF KINKEL. My Lords, this appeal comes directly before the House,
pursuant to s 12 of the Administration of Justice Act 1969, from a judgment of Forbes J
dated 9th June 1978.

The appeal is concerned with the proper construction of s 37 of the Water Act 1945
h which, as amended by s 46 of the Housing Act 1949 and s 11 of and Sch 8, para 53 to the
Water Act 1973, provides:

> '*Duty of water authority to provide domestic supply for new buildings* (1) Where an
> owner of land proposes to erect thereon buildings for which a supply of water for
> domestic purposes will be needed, he may require any water authority within
j > whose limits of supply that land is situated to construct any necessary service
> reservoirs, to lay the necessary mains to such point or points as will enable the
> buildings to be connected thereto at a reasonable cost and to bring water to that

---

1   *Associated Provincial Picture Houses Ltd v Wednesbury Corpn* [1947] 2 All ER 680, [1948] 1 KB 223,
CA

point or those points, and thereupon the water authority shall, subject as hereinafter provided, comply with that requisition: Provided that the water authority before *a* complying with a requisition under this subsection—(*a*) may require the owner to undertake to pay in respect of each year a sum amounting to one-eighth of the expense of providing and constructing the necessary service reservoirs and providing and laying the necessary mains (less any amounts received by the water authority in respect of water supplied, whether for domestic or non-domestic purposes, in that year from those mains) until the aggregate amount of water charges as are stated by *b* the water authority to be payable for a supply of water for domestic purposes payable annually in respect of the buildings when erected and in respect of any other premises connected with the said mains at the rates for the time being charged by the water authority equals or exceeds such sum as aforesaid or until the expiration of a period of twelve years, whichever first occurs; and (*b*) except where the owner is a local or public authority, may also require him to deposit with the water *c* authority as security for payment of the said annual sums, such sum, not exceeding the total expense of constructing the service reservoirs and providing and laying the mains, as the water authority may require.

'(2) The water authority shall pay interest at the prescribed rate or, if no rate is prescribed, at four per cent per annum on any sum in their hands by virtue of a requirement under paragraph (*b*) of the proviso to the last foregoing subsection, and *d* shall, on the request of the owner of the land, appropriate out of that sum any amount due under the undertaking referred to in paragraph (*a*) of the said proviso and shall, when the said undertaking is finally discharged, repay to the owner any sum remaining in their hands as aforesaid.

'(3) Any question arising under subsection (1) of this section as to the point or points to which mains must be taken in order to enable buildings to be connected *e* thereto at a reasonable cost shall, in default of agreement, be determined by the Minister.

'(4) If the water authority, after receipt of a requisition under subsection (1) of this section and after tender to them of any undertaking or deposit which they may require in accordance with that subsection, do not before the expiration of three months (or, where a question has, before that time, been referred to the Minister *f* under the last foregoing subsection, before the expiration of three months from the date when the Minister notifies the water authority of his decision, if that period expires later) comply with the requisition, they shall, unless they show that the failure was due to unavoidable accident or other unavoidable cause, be guilty of an offence against this Act.'

The relevant facts, as found by Forbes J, are as follows. The appellants are developers *g* of land for residential purposes. They own and propose to develop for those purposes a substantial site near Sittingbourne in Kent, known as the Milton Church Farm Estate. The site is capable of accommodating 2,200 houses, and the appellants have so far received outline planning permission for the erection of 700 houses, and detailed planning permission for the erection of 204 of those. The respondents are the statutory *h* water authority within whose limits of supply the site lies. By letter dated 7th June 1976 the appellants required the water authority to provide a domestic water supply to the 204 houses, but it was common ground that this requisition was to be taken as applying to the whole of the 700 houses for which the appellants had outline planning permission. The existing position as regards water supply was that there were no mains actually on the site. The nearest distribution main to the site was in Middletune Avenue at a point *j* to the south of it. This was a 4 inch main. There were in the locality other small distribution mains somewhat further away and certain larger mains further away still. All these mains were fully committed. Well to the south side of the site, however, was a 10 inch main laid under the east/west A2 Dover to London road. This main was not fully committed. The water authority proposed, in response to the appellants'

requisition, to construct a new 8 inch distribution main connected to the 10 inch main
a under the A2 road at a point (known as Key Street) near the junction of the latter with
the A249 road running north-east to the Isle of Sheppey. The proposed new main was
to follow the A249 for some distance and then turn eastwards into the appellants' site.
Its total length was to be about 3·5 kilometres. The total number of houses capable of
being supplied by this new 8 inch main was 950. The next smaller stock size of main,
however, would not have sufficient capacity to supply as many as 700 houses, while the
b cost of manufacturing a special size of main capable of supplying precisely 700 houses
would be prohibitive. The water authority required from the appellants, in terms of
s 37(1)(*b*) of the 1945 Act, a deposit of £115,000 in respect of the construction of the new
main. There happened to be road works in progress at the time on the A249, and the
water authority took the opportunity, in order to save greater expense in the future, of
laying about one kilometre's length of the new main under the road. In respect of this
c work the appellants paid to the water authority under protest the sum of £16,000 in part
satisfaction of the required deposit of £115,000.

By the present action the appellants seek a declaration that the water authority is not
entitled in law to demand any deposit and guarantee of revenue in respect of the
proposed main from Key Street to the boundary of the appellants' site, and that the
appellants are entitled to repayment of the sum of £16,000 with interest. By the
d judgment under appeal Forbes J refused the declarations so sought and dismissed the
action in relation thereto. It is to be mentioned that by the action the appellants also
sought certain declarations related to another site owned by them within the water
authority's limits of supply. These declarations were granted by Forbes J, and the water
authority does not seek to disturb the part of his judgment concerned with that aspect of
the case.

e The appellants accept responsibility in respect of distribution mains within the
boundaries of their site, but they maintain that they cannot lawfully be required to give
any undertaking or pay any deposit in respect of the proposed new main between Key
Street and the site boundary, on the ground that it is not a 'necessary' main within the
meaning of s 37(1). Their argument, in effect, is that no main outside the boundaries of
the site can be a 'necessary' main other than one which runs to the site from the nearest
f point where there is an existing distribution main. The particular point which they pick
on here is the location of the 4 inch distribution main in Middletune Avenue. That main
is, of course, fully committed, and its capacity is in any event far too small for the purpose
of delivering an adequate supply of water for the appellants' development. But the
appellants say that it is up to the water authority, at the expense of the general body of
ratepayers, to carry out all such extensions and improvements of the existing system as
g may be necessary to secure that a sufficient supply of water is available at the point
indicated. This is on the face of it an absurd proposition, involving as it does that the
water authority might be required to carry out works that were completely uneconomic
and quite contrary to sound water engineering practice. The appellants argue, however,
that this result is compelled by the decision of this House in *Cherwell District Council v
Thames Water Authority*[1], and the reasons for that decision contained in the speech of Lord
h Diplock, concurred in by all the other Lords of Appeal who were party to the decision.

In my opinion the decision, properly understood, does not support the appellants'
proposition. The facts were that the appellant council proposed to build houses on two
sites in Banbury, where there were no existing water mains. The water supply at
Banbury was obtained from a service reservoir into which water was pumped from the
river Cherwell. The supply was becoming inadequate, and the proposed new houses
j would exacerbate the situation. To supplement the supply the respondent water
authority proposed to extract water from the Thames at Woodstock and convey it by a
new 27 inch trunk main to the existing service at Banbury. In response to an enquiry
from the appellant council as to the amount which they would be required to undertake

1 [1975] 1 All ER 763, [1975] 1 WLR 448

to pay under s 37(1) in respect of the supply of water for the proposed housing
development, the water authority quoted a figure which comprised the cost of new *a*
mains in the immediate vicinity of the site and also a very small contribution towards the
cost of the new 27 inch trunk main. The matter at issue was the appellant council's
liability in respect of the latter element. The case had become unnecessarily complicated
in the lower courts through counsel for the parties agreeing that the issue turned on the
answer to a hypothetical question as to whether a trunk main was capable in law of being
a 'necessary main' within the meaning of s 37(1), but there is no need to go into that *b*
aspect. The House decided that the appellant council was not liable for any contribution
towards the cost of the new trunk main, on the ground that, since it was not provided
solely for the purpose of conveying water to points at which the new houses could be
connected up by means of service pipes, it was not a 'necessary main'. The ultimate ratio
of the case is to be found in the following part of the speech of Lord Diplock[1]:

> 'In the instant case it is common ground that the 27 inch trunk main, when *c*
> completed, would serve to supply water to the general body of consumers of water
> for domestic purposes as well as to the proposed new buildings that were the subject
> of the contemplated requisition. How small a part the necessity to supply water to
> these buildings played in creating the need to provide the new trunk main is
> indicated by the minute proportion of the total cost of it that the board thought it
> equitable to ascribe to the council as requisitioners in respect of those buildings. *d*
> That the 27 inch trunk main would serve such other purposes as well, in my view,
> precludes it being a "necessary main" within the meaning of s 37 of the Water Act
> 1945.'

In the course of arriving at this ratio Lord Diplock made a number of general
observations about s 37, certain parts of which, as they were strongly founded on by *e*
counsel for the appellants in the present case, it is necessary to quote in full[2]:

> '"Mains" is, by virtue of its definition in the 1945 Act, a generic term which
> prima facie includes trunk mains as well as distribution mains, unless the context in
> which it appears makes it clear that it was used in some more restricted meaning.
> In s 37 (as also in cl 29) the only express restriction on its generality is that the mains
> must be "necessary". This is, in my view, the key-word in the section for the *f*
> purposes of deciding the actual question raised by the originating summons. It
> poses immediately the question: "Necessary for what?" The section pre-supposes,
> first, that there are no existing mains bringing water to points at which it would be
> practicable at reasonable cost to connect the proposed buildings to those mains by
> service pipes. If there were, there would be no need for any requisition. Once the
> building was erected the owner would be entitled to require the connection to be *g*
> made under cl 30, without any liability to contribute to the cost previously incurred
> by the undertakers in laying the existing mains or to the cost of replacing them by
> mains of greater capacity to meet the additional demand resulting from the
> connection of the newly erected building to them. Secondly, the section pre-
> supposes that there will be a supply of water in bulk capable of being brought to the
> new mains by the undertakers, which if it is not already available to them it is their *h*
> duty to procure without demanding from the requisitioner any contribution to the
> cost of doing so. So the "necessary mains" with which the section deals are confined
> to new mains to be laid by the undertakers in a street or other place where there are
> no existing distribution mains and to start from a point to which a supply of water
> is already being brought in existing works belonging to the undertaker; and the
> answer to the question: "Necessary for what?" is: necessary in order to convey the *j*
> water from that starting point to points at which it would be practible to connect

---

1   [1975] 1 All ER 763 at 771, [1975] 1 WLR 448 at 457
2   [1975] 1 All ER 763 at 769–770, [1975] 1 WLR 448 at 455–456

the proposed buildings to those mains by service pipes, and for no other purpose.
The section contemplates that as well as "necessary mains" there may be "necessary
service reservoirs" to be constructed. Ex hypothesi these must lie between the
starting point to which a supply of water is already being brought in existing works
belonging to the undertakers and the new distribution mains to which the proposed
new buildings will be connected. The new main which will carry water from that
starting point to the service reservoir may well fall within the definition of "trunk
main", and if the new trunk main and the new service reservoir will serve no other
purpose than to convey water from that starting point to the new distribution main
or mains to which the proposed buildings in respect of which the requisition has
been made will be connected it would, in my view, fall within the expression
"necessary mains". For in the context of s 37 I would construe "necessary" as
applicable to new mains and service reservoirs provided for that purpose only and
not to mains or reservoirs which will also serve some other purpose of the
undertakers in connection with the supply of water to existing consumers or to
potential new customers whose water will not be brought to them through the new
distribution main or mains. To ascribe any wider meaning to the word "necessary"
where it appears in s 37—or, in a similar context, in cl 29—would, in my view,
conflict with the general scheme of the 1945 Act for allocating the cost of works
between the proceeds of the annual water rate payable by the general body of
consumers of water for domestic purposes and charges additional to the water rate
imposed on particular consumers. Once works have been constructed by the
undertakers which bring a supply of water to an existing distribution main, the cost
of additions or improvements to any of those works lying between the ultimate
source of the supply and service pipes connected with that main which are needed
to meet increased demand for water must be provided for out of the proceeds of the
annual water rate or loans serviced out of the proceeds of that rate. No additional
charge may be imposed on the individual consumers who benefit from particular
additions or improvements, even where they are new consumers whose exercise of
their right under cl 30 to have their premises connected to an existing main has
caused the increased demand. The 1945 Act thus appears to accept as a general
principle that new consumers as well as old are entitled to the benefit of additions
and improvements to existing works rendered necessary by increased demand for
water for domestic purposes which they themselves have caused; and that they
cannot be required to make any individual contribution to the cost of those additions
or improvements beyond what is payable by them by way of the annual water rate
in common with consumers who may derive no such benefit. It would seem to
conflict with that principle that an exception should be made in respect of additions
or improvements to works lying between the ultimate source of supply and the
point to which water had already been brought by the undertakers, merely because
the supply to the new consumer involved, in addition to the laying of service pipes,
the laying of a new distribution main beyond that point to a point in the vicinity of
the premises for which the water was required.'

In my opinion it is clear that Lord Diplock did not have present to his mind, anywhere
in the course of this passage, the kind of situation which prevails here, where the water
authority have already brought to a point quite close to the proposed development a
distribution main of small capacity, carrying a limited supply of water for existing
buildings in the immediate vicinity, and where the extension of that main so as to serve
the proposed development would be impracticable, or at least uneconomic and contrary
to sound water engineering practice. The passage must be read secundum subjectam
materiam, namely a situation where the water authority proposed to execute, and charge
the requisitioner with part of the cost of, works intended to enhance and improve the
general supply of water in the broad locality within which the proposed development
lay. It is true that one of the cases which Lord Diplock had in contemplation was that

where the need for an enhanced or improved supply was brought about entirely by the
requirements of the proposed development. But even so, the principle that the cost of *a*
improvements or additions to the system cannot be laid to the charge of the developers
applies only, on Lord Diplock's analysis, to improvements or additions executed on
sections of the system short of the point at which any new main necessary for the
connection of the proposed development takes its departure. The present appeal is
concerned with the question what is the appropriate starting point of a new main laid
solely for the purpose of supplying the new development, and the related question *b*
whether the choice by the water authority of a particular starting point for such a main
can have the effect of eliding the developers' liability in respect of it. These questions
were not in issue in the *Cherwell* case[1], and it would, in my opinion, be a mistake to
regard anything in Lord Diplock's speech as being directed to their resolution, or as
imposing any necessary restriction upon the range of the search for the correct answers.

It is evident that any 'necessary main' must start from a point where water is available *c*
to be led into it. So much was pointed out by Lord Diplock in the *Cherwell* case[2] in the
course of the passage quoted. But what, if any, are the other essential characteristics of
the starting point? Is it enough that there should be a certain limited supply of water
there, albeit quite insufficient to charge the new main, or is it right to postulate that the
existing supply of water at the point in question should be adequate for that purpose?
Neither answer would, in my view, necessarily be correct in all circumstances. I am of *d*
opinion that the necessary starting point is to be determined in the light of sound water
engineering practice. In some instances that might indicate that the necessary starting
point lay somewhere on an existing main of adequate capacity. But in others it might
involve replacing an existing main of inadequate capacity with a larger one, and
connecting the new main to the replacement at a suitable point. In that event no part of
the cost of the replacement main could, under the decision in the *Cherwell* case[1], lawfully *e*
be charged to the requisitioner. But there are no sound grounds whatever for the view
that the necessary starting point must invariably be the nearest point to the proposed
development at which there is an existing supply of water in an existing main, however
limited.

At this stage there is to be noted an argument for the water authority to the effect that
the matter of the necessary starting point for the new main is entirely for the judgment *f*
of the water authority, acting reasonably and in good faith. In my opinion this argument
is to be rejected. In this context the question is one to be decided by the court, in the
event of dispute, in the light of evidence led about sound water engineering practice.

On the facts of this case, as found by Forbes J, there can be no doubt that the starting
point selected by the water authority for the proposed new main was the correct one
from the point of view of sound water engineering practice, and that it did not, in all the *g*
circumstances, have the effect of depriving the main of the character of a 'necessary
main'. The main would be laid with the sole purpose of supplying the domestic water
requirements of the appellants' proposed development, and at the end of the day it was
not maintained that its superfluity of capacity for that purpose involved in the
circumstances that it was larger than it need be.

For these reasons I am of the opinion that the judgment of Forbes J was correct and *h*
soundly reasoned, and that the appeal should be dismissed.

Appeal dismissed.

Solicitors: *Harold Benjamin & Collins* (for the appellants); *Barlow, Lyde & Gilbert* (for the
water authority).   *i*

Christine Ivamy   Barrister.

---

1 [1975] 1 All ER 763, [1975] 1 WLR 448
2 [1975] 1 All ER 763 at 770, [1975] 1 WLR 448 at 455

a

Re Coventry (deceased)

COURT OF APPEAL, CIVIL DIVISION
BUCKLEY, GEOFFREY LANE AND GOFF LJJ
17th, 18th JULY 1979

b *Family provision – Son – Reasonable provision for maintenance – Father dying intestate – Application by adult son – Adult son returning to live at home – Wife leaving home soon after – Son living rent-free in house but doing all domestic work – Deceased dying intestate leaving estate consisting of house worth some £7,000 – Wife entitled under intestacy to whole of estate – Wife then aged 74 and living on pension in council house – Son then aged 46 and earning £52 per week – Whether son's blood relationship and necessitous circumstances entitling him to reasonable*
c *financial provision out of estate for his maintenance – Whether events subsequent to hearing to be taken into account on appeal – Inheritance (Provision for Family and Dependants) Act 1975, ss 1, 2(1), 3(5).*

The deceased and his wife were married in 1927 and acquired a house. The wife's contributions to the household entitled her to a one-third interest in the house. A son,
d the only child of the marriage, was born in 1931. In 1957 he returned to live at home and shortly after the wife left the home for good. Thereafter the deceased contributed nothing to the wife's support. From 1957 to 1961 the son, who was in full-time employment, did the domestic work under an arrangement whereby he lived rent-free in the house but paid for the food and for a time the gas, electricity and water. In 1961 the son married and, until the marriage broke up in 1975, he and his wife and their three
e children lived rent-free in the house with the son's wife taking over the domestic duties. In 1976 the deceased died intestate leaving an estate consisting solely of his two-thirds interest in the house, worth some £7,000. The deceased's wife, who was entitled under the intestacy to the whole of the estate, was then aged 74 and living on a pension in a council flat. The son was aged 46 and earning about £52 per week after tax, out of which he was required to pay £12 per week maintenance. He had little capital and
f would have to find alternative accommodation if required to move out of the house. The judge[a] dismissed the son's application under s 1[b] of the Inheritance (Provision for Family and Dependants) Act 1975 for provision out of the estate for reasonable maintenance, holding that, as the deceased was not under a moral obligation to maintain the son, it was not unreasonable that the son should not receive anything out of the estate. The son appealed. On the appeal he contended that the court could have regard
g under s 3(5)[c] to events subsequent to the hearing, namely that his financial position had worsened since then because he had had to leave the house and had bought a caravan on mortgage and had incurred hire-purchase commitments to furnish it, but he did not adduce evidence of those facts.

Held – (i) Under s 2(1)[d] of the 1975 Act there were two stages in considering an
h application for relief out of a deceased's estate, namely whether the provisions governing the disposal of the estate (either under a will or an intestacy or a combination of both) had failed to make reasonable financial provision for the applicant, and if so whether the court in its discretion ought to exercise its powers under the Act to order further provision for the applicant. Whether reasonable financial provision had been made for the applicant under the provisions governing the disposal of the estate was a question of
j fact to be determined by the judge making a value judgment (or qualitative decision)

---

a [1979] 2 All ER 408
b Section 1, so far as material, is set out at p 819 *d*, post
c Section 3(5) is set out at p 820 *h*, post
d Section 2(1), so far as material, is set out at p 820 *a b*, post

whether in the circumstances, looked at objectively, it was unreasonable that the provisions governing the estate did not provide for the applicant, and not merely by *a* deciding whether the deceased had acted unreasonably or unfairly in leaving his estate as he had. Such a value judgment ought not to be disturbed on appeal unless the judge of first instance had clearly erred in principle. In the instant case, the judge had properly directed himself, and had not erred in principle by failing to take account of any relevant circumstance or by paying attention to anything to which he ought not. Furthermore he had correctly concluded (a) that there was no special circumstance such as a moral *b* obligation on the deceased to provide for the son which made the provision, or lack of it, under the intestacy unreasonable and (b) that the mere fact that the son found himself in necessitous circumstances was not by itself sufficient to establish his claim. It followed that the appeal would be dismissed (see p 821 *j* to p 822 *a* and *f* to *j*, p 823 *c f g*, p 825 *d e*, p 826 *c d g h*, p 827 *e* to *g* and p 828 *b* to *f* and *h*, post).

(ii) The court was not entitled to have regard to the events subsequent to the hearing, *c* for under s 3(5) of the 1975 Act it could have regard only to facts 'known to the court', and therefore could have regard only to facts which had been properly proved to the court (see p 825 *a b e*, p 826 *d e g h* and p 828 *h*, post).

Per Curiam. (i) What is proper 'maintenance' depends on all the facts and circumstances of the case being considered; but, although it does not mean just enough to enable an applicant to get by on, neither does it mean anything which may be regarded as *d* reasonably desirable for the applicant's general benefit or welfare (see p 819 *h* to p 820 *a*, p 825 *e*, p 826 *g h* and p 828 *h*, post).

(ii) Where the estate is small, appeals under the 1975 Act should be discouraged because they tend to dissipate the estate in costs (see p 820 *j* to p 821 *a*, p 825 *e j*, p 826 *g h* and p 828 *g*, post).

Decision of Oliver J [1979] 2 All ER 408 affirmed. *e*

Notes

For matters to which the court is to have regard on an application for financial provision from a deceased's estate, see 17 Halsbury's Laws (4th Edn) para 1337.

For the Inheritance (Provision for Family and Dependants) Act 1975, ss 1, 2, 3, see 45 Halsbury's Statutes (3rd Edn) 496, 498, 501.

f

Cases referred to in judgments

Christie (deceased), Re, Christie v Keeble [1979] 1 All ER 546, [1979] Ch 168, [1979] 2 WLR 106.

Duranceau, Re [1952] 3 DLR 714.

E (deceased), Re, E v E [1966] 2 All ER 44, [1966] 1 WLR 709, Digest (Cont Vol B) 290, 9760a.

Gregory (deceased), Re, Gregory v Goodenough [1971] 1 All ER 497, [1970] 1 WLR 1455, *g* CA, Digest (Cont Vol D) 336, 9736b.

Millward v Shenton [1972] 2 All ER 1025, [1972] 1 WLR 711, CA, Digest (Cont Vol D) 335, 9756a.

Cases also cited

Borthwick, Re, Borthwick v Beauvais [1948] 2 All ER 635, [1948] Ch 645, CA. *h*

Ducksbury (deceased), Re, Ducksbury v Ducksbury [1966] 2 All ER 374, [1966] 1 WLR 1226.

F (a minor), Re [1976] Fam 238, [1976] 1 All ER 417, CA.

Little, Re [1953] 4 DLR 846.

Milliken, Re [1966] NI 68.

Styler, Re, Styler v Griffith [1942] 2 All ER 201, [1942] Ch 387.

Appeal *j*

Albert Edward Coventry ('the applicant') appealed against the judgment of Oliver J[1] given on 9th November 1978 dismissing his application for an order against the respondent, Blanche Elizabeth Coventry, his mother and the widow of the deceased,

1 [1979] 2 All ER 408, [1979] 2 WLR 853

Albert James Coventry, and the person beneficially entitled to the deceased's estate under
a an intestacy, that he be granted relief out of the deceased's estate under the Inheritance
(Provision for Family and Dependants) Act 1975. The grounds of the appeal were that
the judge misdirected himself in that (1) he took the view that financial provision for the
applicant was conditional on the existence of a moral obligation on the deceased to make
financial provision for him, (2) he took the view that no such obligation existed, (3) he
placed an unduly restrictive construction on the words 'for his maintenance' in s 1(2)(b)
b of the 1975 Act, (4) he erroneously considered that the applicant was not in need of
provision for his maintenance, (5) he failed to attach any or sufficient weight to the
matters to which the court was directed to have regard in s 3(1)(a), (c), (d), (e) and (g) of
the Act, (6) he attached excessive weight to the respondent's financial needs in the
foreseeable future and to the deceased's obligations and responsibilities towards her, (7)
he failed to distinguish those cases where the deceased had left a will or expressed
c otherwise an unequivocal intention, (8) he failed to consider exercising the power
conferred by s 2(1)(d) of the Act and (9) he placed undue restriction on the wide powers
conferred on the court by the Act. The facts are set out in the judgment of Goff LJ.

A B Hollis QC and *Michael Stephen* for the applicant.
Michael Hutchinson QC and *Giles Harrap* for the respondent.

d
GOFF LJ delivered the first judgment at the invitation of Buckley LJ. This is an appeal
from a judgment given by Oliver J[1] on 9th November 1978 and entered on 20th
December, whereby he dismissed a claim by the applicant for relief under the Inheritance
(Provision for Family and Dependants) Act 1975 out of the estate of his deceased father.
The matter was originally heard by Master Gowers, who awarded the applicant the sum
e of £2,000. The applicant was not satisfied with that figure, and at his request the matter
was adjourned to the judge and, as I have indicated, it came before Oliver J. The parties
agreed to accept the master's findings of fact.
     The applicant is the only son of the deceased. It is an unhappy feature of this type of
litigation that in this case the respondent is his mother, the widow of the deceased, who
died on 10th June 1976, letters of administration being granted to her on 29th November
f 1976.
     It is important to observe that the estate is a small one. Indeed, the net estate is
confined to the value of the house and is really less than that since it is obvious that costs
have been incurred, some of which must come out of that property.
     The house was purchased many years ago, in 1935, for the sum of £560, but it is now
agreed, owing to inflation, that it is worth £12,000. It has been established that the
g widow, by reason of her contribution to the expenses of the household in the years when
she and the deceased were living together, is entitled in her own right to a one-third
beneficial interest in the house. Of course, in considering the questions which arise in
this case, one has to bear in mind that she, therefore, has that capital sum, which will in
due course, subject to costs, become available as capital in her hands. But one must at the
same time keep clear that that is in no sense a share received by her out of the deceased's
h estate. It was her own at all material times.
     The deceased and the respondent were married on 26th December 1927. The
applicant was born nearly four years later and is now aged 48. The age of the respondent
is 76. In 1950 the applicant joined the Royal Navy. He completed his engagement of
seven years, by which time he had expectations of becoming a chief petty officer. In
1957 he returned home, but left again almost immediately because, he says, of bickering
j between his parents. After a few months, however, he returned to the house, and he
lived there for the rest of the lifetime of the deceased and for some time thereafter, when
he was forced to leave as the result of an ejection order obtained by the respondent.

1   [1979] 2 All ER 408, [1979] 2 WLR 853

The judge said[1]:

'The deceased was aged 58 in 1957 and was unaccustomed to looking after *a* himself and the [applicant] says that, because of this, he concluded that he ought to stay at home, rather than re-engaging for service in the navy. This is not accepted by the [respondent] and the master made no finding about it; but whatever the [applicant's] motives may have been he did not, in fact, re-enlist in the navy but continued for the next 19 years to live with [the deceased].'

b

Very soon after the second return of the applicant to the home, the respondent left. She never returned and there was really no further contact between her on the one hand, and the deceased and the applicant on the other. She applied that same year, 1957, to the magistrates' court at Stratford for maintenance, but her application was dismissed. We do not know what evidence was given. Master Gowers thought that the position had not been much investigated, and he attached little significance to the failure of that *c* application. There is no finding that the deceased and the applicant, or either of them, in fact drove the respondent out of the house, but the master did find that they 'ganged up on her' and caused her misery which, I think, is a not unimportant circumstance of this case.

During this long separation, no money was paid by the deceased to the respondent. He did not provide her with support in any way and she made no further application *d* against him. She has, during that long time, supported herself in one way or another and is now living in part on her pension and in part on social security payments.

For some four years the applicant ran the home, discharging all the domestic duties, cooking, washing up, shopping and so forth. He paid for food for himself and the deceased and on occasions (I think on frequent occasions) he paid for the gas and electricity, and he paid the water rate, although those burdens were sometimes borne by *e* the deceased, who paid the mortgage instalments due on the house and paid the general rates. The applicant lived in the house rent free.

In 1961 he married. His wife came to live in the house as well, and after that she carried out the duties previously carried out by her husband (the applicant) and she bought food for the family, including the deceased, again at the applicant's expense. They had three children who also of course lived in the house. Unhappily, in 1975 the *f* marriage broke up and the wife left the home, taking the children with her. They were later divorced, and the children remained with her. After the wife left, the applicant carried on as he had done before his marriage.

It seems that the deceased was reluctant to, and certainly did not, spend any material sums on proper maintenance of the house. There is evidence that the applicant suggested borrowing about £2,000 on mortgage for this purpose but the deceased would not trust *g* him, or would not let him have the deeds for this purpose. Some repairs and decorations were effected, but over this long period they were trifling in the extreme, and the house is of such a deteriorated character that it is not now lettable and, of course, that failure to maintain the property in which the deceased and the applicant and his wife and family were living has depreciated the value of the respondent's one-third share.

The respondent and the applicant are in modest circumstances, and the applicant is in *h* some financial difficulties occasioned by the debts which he has incurred. He owes arrears of maintenance and costs. He says that the total is £400 including costs, but his divorced wife contends that the figure is about £600. He is also liable on a judgment for mesne profits in respect of his stay in the house since the death of the deceased. He says that he is a self-employed chauffeur. I confess that I do not altogether understand what that means, but according to the explanation given to us by counsel I gather that he *j* drives someone else's car for his own profit, having made some kind of agreement for sharing profits or paying remuneration to the owner of the car. The judge found that his average take-home pay was £52 a week, out of which there falls to be deducted a total of

---

1   [1979] 2 All ER 408 at 411, [1979] 2 WLR 853 at 857

a £12 per week for the maintenance of the three children, and expenditure on food and electricity, leaving a balance of £21·70 per week. He had, at one stage at all events, a capital sum of £200 or thereabouts, described as 'savings', but which was in fact an income tax rebate which he received after a period of unemployment. On those figures he was on the right side, but it is said that in truth there is a deficit and that his weekly earnings do not meet his expenses. That is largely, if not exclusively, due (i) to the fact that he has purchased, on mortgage, a caravan in which to live, and he has to service the b loan, and (ii) also to hire purchase payments made in respect of furniture. I shall come back presently to a consideration of the comparative needs of the applicant and the respondent.

I should now refer to some provisions in the 1975 Act. In his judgment the judge set out all the relevant provisions of the Act, and I do not think I need recite them in the same detail that he adopted. The preamble says that it is—

c   'An Act to make fresh provision for empowering the court to make orders for the making out of the estate of a deceased person of provision for the spouse, former spouse, child, child of the family or dependant of that person; and for matters connected therewith.'

Some argument turned on the use of the expression 'fresh provision'.

d   Then, by s 1(1):

'Where after the commencement of this Act a person dies domiciled in England and Wales and is survived by any of the following persons . . . (c) a child of the deceased . . . that person may apply to the court for an order under section 2 of this Act on the ground that the disposition of the deceased's estate effected by his will or the law relating to intestacy, or the combination of his will and that law, is not such e   as to make reasonable financial provision for the applicant.'

Subsection (2) defines the expression 'reasonable financial provision'. The judge pointed out, and in my judgment rightly, the distinction between para (a) of sub-s (2), which deals with an application by a husband or a wife, where the definition is 'such financial provision as it would be reasonable in all the circumstances of the case f for a husband or wife to receive, whether or not that provision is required for his or her maintenance', and the case of any other application (under para (b) of sub-s (2)), where the words mean 'such financial provision as it would be reasonable in all the circumstances of the case for the applicant to receive for his maintenance'. So that whatever be the precise meaning of the word 'maintenance' (and I do not think it necessary to attempt any precise definition) it is clear that it is a word of somewhat limited meaning in its g application to any person qualified to apply, other than a husband or a wife.

There have been a number of cases under the Inheritance (Family Provision) Act 1938, previously in force, and also some cases from sister jurisdictions, which have dealt with the meaning of 'maintenance'. In particular, in this country there is Re E[1], in which Stamp J said that the purpose was not to keep a person above the breadline, but to provide reasonable maintenance in all the circumstances. If I may say so with respect, 'breadline' h there would be more accurately described as 'subsistence level'. Then there was a case in this court, Millward v Shenton[2]. I think I need only refer to one of the overseas reports, Re Duranceau[3], where in somewhat poetic language, the court said that the question is: 'Is the provision sufficient to enable the dependent to live neither luxuriously nor miserably, but decently and comfortably according to his or her station in life?'

What is proper maintenance must in all cases depend on all the facts and circumstances j of the particular case being considered at the time, but I think it is clear on the one hand that one must not put too limited a meaning on it; it does not mean just enough to

1   [1966] 2 All ER 44, [1966] 1 WLR 709
2   [1972] 2 All ER 1025, [1972] 1 WLR 711
3   [1952] 3 DLR 714 at 720

enable a person to get by, on the other hand, it does not mean anything which may be regarded as reasonably desirable for his general benefit or welfare.

Returning to the 1975 Act, s 2(1) provides as follows:

'Subject to the provisions of this Act, where an application is made for an order under this section, the court may, if it is satisfied that the disposition of the deceased's estate effected by his will or the law relating to intestacy, or the combination of his will and that law, is not such as to make reasonable financial provision for the applicant [and that of course has to be read in the light of the definition to which I have referred], make any one or more of the following orders . . .'

and then are set out various types of provision which the court may direct to be made. Then, s 3(1) provides:

'Where an application is made for an order under section 2 of this Act, the court shall, in determining whether the disposition of the deceased's estate effected by his will or the law relating to intestacy, or the combination of his will and that law, is such as to make reasonable financial provision for the applicant and, if the court considers that reasonable financial provision has not been made, in determining whether and in what manner it shall exercise its powers under that section, have regard to the following matters, that is to say—[and then they are set out, under seven separate heads, the last of which is a general one:] (g) any other matter, including the conduct of the applicant or any other person, which in the circumstances of the case the court may consider relevant.'

In his judgment the judge set that section out in full.

Then I must read s 3(3), since much argument turned on it. It provides as follows:

'Without prejudice to the generality of paragraph (g) of subsection (1) above, where an application for an order under section 2 of this Act is made by virtue of section 1(1)(c) [which is this case] or 1(1)(d) of this Act, the court shall, in addition to the matters specifically mentioned in paragraphs (a) to (f) of that subsection, have regard to the manner in which the applicant was being or in which he might expect to be educated or trained, and where the application is made by virtue of section 1(1)(d) [which is not this case] the court shall also have regard—(a) to whether the deceased had assumed any responsibility for the applicant's maintenance and, if so, to the extent to which and the basis upon which the deceased assumed that responsibility and to the length of time for which the deceased discharged that responsibility; (b) to whether in assuming and discharging that responsibility the deceased did so knowing that the applicant was not his own child; (c) to the liability of any other person to maintain the applicant.'

Section 3(5) provides:

'In considering the matters to which the court is required to have regard under this section, the court shall take into account the facts as known to the court at the date of the hearing.'

Section 3(6) provides:

'In considering the financial resources of any person for the purposes of this section the court shall take into account his earning capacity and in considering the financial needs of any person for the purposes of this section the court shall take into account his financial obligations and responsibilities.'

I think that covers all that is relevant in the Act.

Before turning to consideration of the judgment, and the criticisms which have been levelled against it, I have to make two preliminary observations. The first is that it has been said, and I would adopt the proposition, that applications in small estates should be

discouraged, because the costs tend to become wholly disproportionate to the end in
a   view, although, of course that does not mean that an application cannot be made in a
small estate, nor that when made it should not be duly considered on its merits. My
second observation is that at times the argument came near to saying that what the court
had to consider was how the available assets could be fairly divided. That, of course, is
not the position under the Act, and is not what the court has to decide.

   The judge directed himself as follows[1]:

b   'So these matters have to be considered at two stages, first, in determining the
       reasonableness of such provision, if any, as has been made by the deceased for the
       applicant's maintenance and, secondly, in determining the extent to which the
       court should exercise its powers under the 1975 Act if, but only if, it is satisfied that
       reasonable provision for the applicant's maintenance has not been made.'

c   In my judgment, in so saying the judge was perfectly correctly giving effect to the
provisions of s 2(1) of the 1975 Act. There are these two stages and, as will appear, the
applicant failed before the judge because he failed to get over the first hurdle. He failed
to satisfy the judge that the provisions failed to make reasonable financial provision for
him.

   The second part of that composite problem is clearly a question of discretion, but I
d   think the first is not. It is a question of fact, but it is a value judgment, or a qualitative
decision, which I think ought not to be interfered with by us unless we are satisfied that
it was plainly wrong.

   In my view, having observed the dual nature of the problem, the judge then based his
approach correctly in the view that he took of the changes effected by the new Act. In
his judgment he says[2]:

e   '. . . I do not think that it can have been the intention of the legislature that the
       body of case law built up under the 1938 Act should be put on one side and
       ignored. The 1975 Act may have been one to make "fresh" provision but it forms
       part of a continuum and the introduction of an expanded class of potential applicants
       does not of itself point to the adoption of any different approach to the exercise of
f   the discretion, which remains restricted to "reasonable provision for maintenance".
       At the same time, I have to bear in mind that, in relation to all applications under
       the 1975 Act, s 3 now lays down an expanded list of guidelines to which the court
       is directed to have regard both in relation to the question of whether it shall exercise
       its discretion at all and in relation to the extent to which, if it does so, that discretion
       is to be exercised. I think, in these circumstances, that I ought not to approach this
       application with any preconceived notion that there is some especially heavy burden
g   on a male applicant of full age beyond that which must, as a practical matter,
       necessarily exist when a person who applies to be maintained by somebody else is
       already capable of adequately maintaining himself.'

   But it was said that in three ways the judge fell into error. Those three ways were as
follows. First, he placed too restrictive a meaning on the word 'maintenance'. Secondly,
h   he in effect made a moral obligation a pre-condition of such an application succeeding,
and it was said that although in the cases there were a number of references to moral
obligation, they were all cases of wills, and it was submitted that the position was very
different in cases of intestacy. The third criticism was that the judge had found that
there was no moral obligation, whereas it was submitted that in fact there was.

   I reject the second of those criticisms at once. The judge nowhere said that a moral
j   obligation was a prerequisite of an application under s 1(1)(c); nor did he mean any such
thing. It is true that he said a moral obligation was required, but in my view that was on

1   [1979] 2 All ER 408 at 413, [1979] 2 WLR 853 at 860
2   [1979] 2 All ER 408 at 417, [1979] 2 WLR 853 at 864

the facts of this particular case, because he found nothing else sufficient to produce unreasonableness. He made this clear, I think, in numerous places in his judgment but *a* I shall refer to two in particular. First he said[1]:

'It cannot be enough to say, "Here is a son of the deceased, he is in necessitous circumstances, there is property of the deceased which could be made available to assist him but which is not available if the deceased's dispositions stand; therefore those dispositions do not make reasonable provision for the applicant." There must, *b* as it seems to me, be established some sort of moral claim by the applicant to be maintained by the deceased or at the expense of his estate beyond the mere fact of a blood relationship, some reason why it can be said that, in the circumstances, it is unreasonable that no or no greater provision was in fact made.'

He picks that up very clearly when he comes to the end of his judgment. He says[2]: *c*

'In my judgment the [applicant's] claim substantially rests on two limbs only, that is to say, (a) that he is a son of the deceased with whom it might be thought that there would be a bond of natural affection, and (b) that although he is in employment and capable of maintaining himself his circumstances leave him little or no margin for expenditure on anything other than the necessities of life. I have every sympathy for any [applicant] who, on relatively slender earnings, has to meet *d* a steadily rising cost of living, but, as I have said, I cannot regard the 1975 Act as one which entitles the court to interfere with a deceased person's dispositions simply because a qualified applicant feels in need of financial assistance. I cannot in this case find any circumstances which satisfy me that it is an unreasonable result of the intestacy laws that no provision is made for the [applicant's] maintenance and in my judgment the application must fail.'

e

Counsel for the applicant argued in his reply that the judge had found as a fact that the applicant was in need of maintenance, because at best his circumstances were near the subsistence level, and possibly below, and that, therefore, the judge should have found that the provisions were unreasonable; but in my judgment that does not follow. The question is not whether it might have been reasonable for the deceased to assist his son, the applicant, but whether in all the circumstances, looked at objectively, it is *f* unreasonable that the effective provisions governing the estate did not do so.

As part of this second objection, it was submitted that the question of moral obligation had only been raised in will cases, and that there was a difference between will cases where the testator has stated his wishes, and intestacies where he has not. As I see it, that is not an entirely correct dichotomy in any event, because a deceased person may have deliberately chosen to be intestate, and the provisions provided by the legislature to cover *g* the case where there is no will, or an incomplete will, may be as much the wishes of the deceased as those which he has expressed in a will. In my judgment, the problem must be exactly the same whether one is dealing with a will or an intestacy, or with a combination of both. The question is whether the operative dispositions make, or fail to make, reasonable provision in all the circumstances. Indeed, I think any view expressed by a deceased person that he wishes a particular person to benefit will generally be of *h* little significance, because the question is not subjective but objective. An express reason for rejecting the applicant is a different matter and may be very relevant to the problem. However, that does not arise in this case and so, for my part, the second of the three criticisms is one which I think cannot be adopted.

In pursuing his argument on the second criticism, junior counsel for the applicant relied on the passage in the judgment in which the judge said[3]: *j*

---

1   [1979] 2 All ER 408 at 418, [1979] 2 WLR 853 at 865
2   [1979] 2 All ER 408 at 420–421, [1979] 2 WLR 853 at 868
3   [1979] 2 All ER 408 at 418, [1979] 2 WLR 853 at 864–865

a
'Subject to the court's powers under the 1975 Act and to fiscal demands, an Englishman still remains at liberty at his death to dispose of his own property in whatever way he pleases [which, of course, at first blush relates only to a will, but the judge went on:] or, if he chooses to do so, to leave that disposition to be regulated by the laws of intestate succession. [So the judge had both in mind. Then he said:] In order to enable the court to interfere with and reform those dispositions [that is to say, dispositions by the will or on the intestacy or on a combination of both] it

b
must, in my judgment, be shown, not that the deceased acted unreasonably, but that, looked at objectively, his disposition or lack of disposition produces an unreasonable result in that it does not make any or any greater provision for the applicant . . .'

So far as the third point is concerned, I cannot accept the submission that there was in fact a moral obligation. Indeed, the judge, reviewing all the facts, found the balance the

c
other way. He said[1]:

'Counsel for the [applicant] submits that a moral obligation in the deceased was created in this way. Because, he suggests, the [applicant] elected to stay at home and go out to work instead of re-enlisting in the Royal Navy (which he says he did because his father was not accustomed to looking after himself) the [applicant] gave

d
up a career which might have led to his promotion and to his receiving an early pension on his retirement. Moreover, by the arrangement which was made, while the [applicant] and his wife lived at the house, they were encouraged not to do what they might otherwise have done, that is to say, to acquire a house for themselves. There was thus, counsel submits, a moral obligation cast on the deceased to ensure that after his death a home would be provided for his son . . . Indeed the [applicant], in his own evidence, agrees that he did indeed look for other accommodation but he

e
does not seek to suggest that he was prevented from providing a home for himself or that the arrangement by which he enjoyed rent-free accommodation for himself and his family was not one which was at least as much to his advantage as it was to the advantage of the deceased. No doubt it could be thought that reasonable family affection might have prompted the father to make some provision for a son who, although earning an adequate living, was clearly not well-to-do; but there is no

f
question of the [applicant] having given up work and disabled himself from earning an adequate living in order to devote himself to his father and I cannot see anything in the history of the relationship between them which could be said to impose any sort of moral duty on the father to provide for his son's maintenance, either during his lifetime or after his death.'

g
That reasoning commends itself to me and I would accept it.

Then the judge went on to review the position of the respondent and the view which had rather impressed itself on the master's mind, that taking on intestacy was rather a windfall. The judge continued[2]:

'So far as the [respondent] is concerned the master was, I think, rather influenced

h
by the fact that the deceased's intestacy brought her a windfall. Even assuming that to be so, this does not, in my judgment, involve as a corollary that some provision ought, in reason, to have been made for a son of full age to whom the deceased owed no obligation of or responsibility for maintenance. But in fact the "windfall", as it seems to me, was one to which the [respondent] can show some colour of entitlement and such obligations as the deceased may have had were, I should have

j
thought, rather towards her than towards his son. After living with him for 30 years she was induced to leave by the joint conduct of the deceased and the [applicant], abandoning a matrimonial home in which she had already acquired a

---
1 [1979] 2 All ER 408 at 419–420, [1979] 2 WLR 853 at 866–867
2 [1979] 2 All ER 408 at 420, [1979] 2 WLR 853 at 867

substantial interest. She received from the deceased no maintenance at all at any
time thereafter and no recompense for the continued use of her property which was   *a*
enjoyed by the deceased and the [applicant] to her total exclusion for the next 19
years. And indeed the fact that the estate and the [respondent's] share in the
property is not substantially larger than it is in fact is due to the continued failure
by the deceased and the [applicant] between them, to keep the property in a
reasonable state . . .'

So that it really all comes down to the first criticism, that the judge adopted too   *b*
stringent a test of maintenance. But I do not think he did, because, as counsel for the
respondent has pointed out, he accepted the wider principles laid down in Re E[1] and
Millward v Shenton[2]. I agree that that is the effect of what the judge said, although he
then went on to reject the very wide meaning of maintenance which he conceived junior
counsel for the applicant to be putting forward, and also to criticise Re Christie, Christie v
Keeble[3]. I think that that case may well have gone too far, though it was a strong case and   *c*
one fully appreciates and sympathises with the deputy judge's desire to give effect to
what appeared to be the clear wishes of the testator. But in any event, as I have already
pointed out, the decision at the end of the day did not go on whether the applicant was
in need of maintenance but on whether he could show that it was unreasonable that the
intestacy provisions that were applicable did not provide for him.

I confess that what has weighed on my mind at certain stages of the argument has been   *d*
whether the judge adequately and correctly weighed, as s 3(1) of the 1975 Act required
him to do, by para (*a*), the financial resources and financial needs which the applicant has
or is likely to have in the foreseeable future; and by para (*c*), the financial resources and
financial needs which any beneficiary of the estate of the deceased has or is likely to have
in the foreseeable future, which I think is the only criticism which could possibly stand
up. But, having carefully considered it, and having listened to all the argument, I am   *e*
satisfied that even in that regard there is nothing to suggest that the judge did not apply
the correct principles (certainly, throughout his judgment, he deals with the financial
position of both of the parties) or to suggest that he incorrectly evaluated them or arrived
at a wrong conclusion on them.

Anything which the widow receives will of course be subject to the inroads of costs.
No doubt, when her capital interests are realised, the social security payments may be   *f*
reduced, but only because she will then have an income, and she has capital to meet an
emergency. One must not lose sight of the fact that she is an elderly lady of 76.

The applicant's position appears to be very difficult, but it is right to observe that the
judge said that he was bound to say that he treated the figures put before him with
considerable reserve, and he added[4]:
                                                                                       g
'They assume that the [applicant] when he leaves [the house], (and it is, as I
understand it, common ground that the property is in a condition in which it is no
longer habitable with comfort in the absence of major repair work) [and I interpose
in the quotation to say that he has of course now left] will not be housed by the local
authority pursuant to its statutory duties and that he will be obliged to seek a
furnished flat in the private sector at a rent equal to, possibly, three-quarters of his   *h*
available income. His own evidence is that he has not even enquired about the cost
of a single furnished room. I am prepared to assume, however, in the [applicant's]
favour that the necessity to provide accommodation for himself will leave him a
considerably smaller margin for living expenses than he enjoys at the moment. A
gross wage of £66 a week in present conditions is not, perhaps, quite on the
breadline, but it is not far above it.'   *j*

---

1 [1966] 2 All ER 44, [1966] 1 WLR 709
2 [1972] 2 All ER 1025, [1972] 1 WLR 711
3 [1979] 1 All ER 546, [1979] Ch 168
4 [1979] 2 All ER 408 at 419, [1979] 2 WLR 853 at 866

Counsel on his behalf has argued that his position is now much worse, because he has had
a to borrow money to buy a caravan and he has hire purchase commitments in respect of
furniture; and they suggest that he should surely have enough, say £5,000, to pay off the
mortgage.

Reliance was placed on s 3(5) of the 1975 Act as entitling us to have regard to these
subsequent events, and I think the true meaning of that section must be that the court
is required to have regard to the facts known to it at the date of the hearing, and not
b merely any further knowledge that the court may have acquired about the facts as they
were. But it is 'facts known to the court', and therefore, anything of this sort should be
properly proved and if it is not it is open to some criticism.

Counsel for the respondent said that this could only properly be taken into account if
further evidence were adduced as to the local authority's attitude and why, if there be a
reason, he has not taken furnished lodgings instead of committing himself to buying a
c caravan. I do not think that those later facts show that the judge erred, but in any event,
as I have already indicated, his decision was not that the applicant was not in need of
maintenance, but that on the facts of the case he was not in a position to show that
intestate disposition failed to make reasonable provision for his maintenance.

In my judgment the judge did consider all the relevant facts, and did properly pose for
himself the problem he had to answer, namely, the dual question under s 2(1) of the
d 1975 Act. For my part I do not consider that this is a case in which it would be right for
us to interfere with the judge's conclusion, even were I minded to do so, which I am not.

The only other observation I would wish to make is that the judge was criticised
because he referred to the provisions in s 3(3) relating to the manner in which an
applicant was being, or in which he might be expected to be, educated or trained. Those
considerations are not directly applicable to the case and it is submitted that they are
e irrelevant. But I consider that the judge was entitled to have that in mind in his overall
consideration of the whole problem.

For these reasons I would dismiss the appeal.

GEOFFREY LANE LJ. I agree.
f The questions to be answered by the judge were these. First of all, did the statutory
provisions relating to intestacy operate in this particular case so as not to make reasonable
financial provision for the applicant son; secondly, if they did so operate (that is to say, if
there was no reasonable provision), should the court in its discretion exercise its power
to order some provision to be made; and, thirdly, if so, in what manner should that
provision be ordered?

g Since the applicant received nothing from the estate on his father's death intestate, in
effect the first question becomes this: was it reasonable in all the circumstances that he
should receive no provision from his father's estate?

The judge reserved his judgment. The result was a meticulous and painstaking
examination of all the relevant facts of the case, and a conclusion that in the circumstances
the contentions on behalf of the applicant must fail; that it was reasonable for this son to
h receive nothing and for the mother, who is the respondent, to receive whatever was left
after all this litigation had been paid for.

Now whatever the rights and wrongs of this matter may be, it seems to me that this
was par excellence a case in which the decision of the judge should stand as to what is
reasonable and what is not reasonable, unless it is clearly shown that he has gone wrong
on a point of law, or in some way has misapplied the facts of the case to the law.
j Particularly in the case of small estates such as this one, appeals like this to this court are
strongly to be discouraged. It has been said before, in particular in the passage to which
our attention has been drawn, by Fenton Atkinson LJ in *Re Gregory (deceased)*[1]. I regard

---

1 [1971] 1 All ER 497 at 503, [1970] 1 WLR 1455 at 1462

it as little short of disastrous that the applicant was advised to contest the master's order in this case.

There have been three principal criticisms levelled at the judge's decision, with which Goff LJ has already dealt, and I respectfully agree with his conclusions on those three matters.

It was the fourth matter that principally caused me, like Goff LJ, concern in this case; that was the undoubted fact that, on the evidence before the judge, the applicant's financial position was stringent. The judge held it to be so, and he described it in this way[1]:

> 'If, therefore, financial need were the sole criterion, then I think that undoubtedly it exists although its stringency may have been to some extent the [applicant's] own responsibility. But the mere fact that the [applicant] finds himself in necessitous circumstances cannot, in my judgment, by itself render it unreasonable that no provision has, in the events which have happened, been made for his maintenance out of the deceased's estate.'

I respectfully agree with that approach by the judge. He is asking himself the right question and he is applying his mind to that question and not to the irrelevant question, namely in all circumstances, was what happened reasonable? That is not the problem.

In every case, inevitably, it is going to be a matter of degree, but I am bound to say that the evidence of the applicant's means and outgoings, as the judge himself pointed out, had several unsatisfactory features about it. As I say, the judge deals with that.

What is perfectly clear to me is that this court has to view the situation as it existed at the time of the hearing before the judge, and not as it exists today. We are not concerned with events which may have happened since the judge delivered his judgment. There are obvious reasons for that. First of all the allegation is not supported by any affidavit; it is not capable of being checked, and one is bound to say that it may even be self-serving, although I do not suggest that that is the case here.

It seems to me in the end that the degree of stringency and the degree of need in the applicant did not justify the judge in coming to the conclusion that the applicant's contentions were correct. The judge set the matter out in a passage[2] which Goff LJ has already read and which there is no need for me to repeat. There is no doubt at all that the widow herself is far from financially affluent; for years she has had to pinch and scrape, but she has managed to keep a pound or so on the right side of the line. Life has not been much fun for her. I am inclined to agree with the judge that in so far as the balance of obligation exists at all it is, if anything, slightly in her favour. In the end, to my mind the judge struck a balance and reached a conclusion which I find it impossible to fault; indeed, it is the conclusion which I would myself have reached on these facts.

I too would dismiss the appeal.

BUCKLEY LJ. I agree with both the judgments which have been delivered. I only add some observations of my own because we are told that this is the first case under the Inheritance (Provision for Family and Dependants) Act 1975 to have reached this court, and also out of deference to the arguments which have been presented to us by counsel for the applicant.

The present application could not have been made before the commencement of the 1975 Act, because the applicant is a son of the deceased who is of full age, in employment and able to provide for himself. A relation of the deceased in such a position could never have made an application under the earlier Act, the Inheritance (Family Provision) Act 1938.

Those who can now invoke the jurisdiction of the court under the 1975 Act are in effect divided into two classes by s 1(2), because para (a) of sub-s (2) says that in the case

---

1 [1979] 2 All ER 408 at 419, [1979] 2 WLR 853 at 866
2 [1979] 2 All ER 408 at 418, [1979] 2 WLR 853 at 865

of a husband or a wife of the deceased 'reasonable financial provision' shall mean such
a financial provision as it would be reasonable in all the circumstances of the case for a
husband or wife to receive, whether or not that provision is required for his or her
maintenance. Paragraph (*b*) says that in the case of any other application, 'reasonable
financial provision' shall mean such financial provision as it would be reasonable in all
the circumstances of the case for the applicant to receive for his maintenance.

   The judge has been criticised by counsel for the applicant in the present case on the
b ground that it is said that he took too restricted a view of what is meant in that subsection
by the word 'maintenance'. But the judge clearly did not take the view that 'maintenance'
in that context means merely the provision of the bare necessities of life for the applicant,
for he said[1]:

   'Counsel for the [applicant] has to face the initial hurdle that the court still has to
   be satisfied that the deceased did not make reasonable provison for the *maintenance*
c   of the applicant, but, as he points out, maintenance does not mean mere subsistence
   . . .'

and then he mentioned two earlier decisions[2]. It has been common ground between
counsel in this court that 'maintenance' in this context does not relate merely to
subsistence, but must have a more generous construction than that.

d   I would venture to suggest that perhaps s 1(2)(*b*) might, in order to explain the
interpretation that I would be inclined to put on it, be paraphrased somewhat in this
way: 'In the case of any other application made by virtue of sub-s (1) above, "reasonable
financial provision" means such financial provision as would be reasonable in all the
circumstances of the case to enable the applicant to maintain himself in a manner
suitable to those circumstances.'

e   But the measure of the relief which can be granted under the 1975 Act only becomes
of any significance if a case is first made out for relief at all; and, in order to achieve that,
the applicant has to satisfy the court that the disposition of the deceased's estate effected
by his will, or the law relating to intestacy or a combination of his will and that law, is
not such as to make reasonable financial provision for the applicant; that is s 1(1) of the
1975 Act.

f   Was it, or was it not, reasonable in the circumstances of the present case that the
deceased made no financial provison for the applicant. That was the actual position. If
that was not unreasonable, the present application could not succeed and the present
appeal cannot succeed. The judge is said to have treated the existence of a moral
obligation as a condition precedent to the exercise of this jurisdiction, a moral obligation
resting on the deceased to make some provision for the applicant. On a correct reading
g of the judge's judgment, I do not think that he did so.

   His approach was that where an applicant is an adult male in employment, and so
capable of earning his own living, some special circumstance is required to make a failure
on the part of the deceased to make some financial provision for the applicant
unreasonable.

   The judge said[3]:

h
   'An application in such circumstances [he is referring to the character of the
   applicant in the present case] would not have been possible at all before 1st April
   1976 but the 1975 Act now enables a child of the deceased to apply for provision
   even though that child is male, of full age, and suffering from no disability.
   Nevertheless, applications under the 1975 Act for maintenance by able-bodied and
j   comparatively young men in employment and able to maintain themselves must be

---

1 [1979] 2 All ER 408 at 414, [1979] 2 WLR 853 at 861
2 *Re E (deceased)* [1966] 2 All ER 44 at 48, [1966] 1 WLR 709 at 715; *Millward v Shenton* [1972] 2 All
   ER 1025 at 1027, [1972] 1 WLR 711 at 715
3 [1979] 2 All ER 408 at 410, [1979] 2 WLR 853 at 856

relatively rare and need, I should have thought, to be approached with a degree of circumspection.'   *a*

Later on he said[1]:

'It seems to me, however, that in regarding the circumstances and in applying the guidelines set out in s 3, it always has to be borne in mind that the 1975 Act, so far as it relates to applicants other than spouses, is an Act whose purpose is limited to the provision of reasonable maintenance. It is not the purpose of the Act to provide legacies or rewards for meritorious conduct. Subject to the court's powers under the *b* 1975 Act and to fiscal demands, an Englishman still remains at liberty at his death to dispose of his own property in whatever way he pleases or, if he chooses to do so, to leave that disposition to be regulated by the laws of intestate succession. In order to enable the court to interfere with and reform those dispositions it must, in my judgment, be shown, not that the deceased acted unreasonably, but that, looked at objectively, his disposition or lack of disposition produces an unreasonable result in *c* that it does not make any or any greater provision for the applicant and that means, in the case of an applicant other than a spouse, for that applicant's maintenance.'

In my judgment the judge there correctly states the problem, and I think he states the appropriate test to be applied. He went on to make the observations[2] which Goff LJ read in the course of his judgment and which I shall not reread, which make it clear to my *d* mind that the judge was referring there to a moral claim as a special circumstance without which, on the facts of the present case, he could find no ground for making any provision for the applicant under the 1975 Act.

The decision which falls to be made by a court in a case of this kind is essentially a qualitative decision; that is to say, the decision whether the disposition which the deceased has made, if any, is such as to make reasonable financial provision for the *e* applicant. It is a qualitative decision, or what is sometimes called a 'value judgment'. A decision of that kind is one which is particularly difficult to disturb on appeal, unless the judge of first instance has clearly proceeded on some error of principle. There is no indication that I can find in the judge's judgment that he failed to take account of anything of which he ought to have taken account, or that he paid attention to anything to which he ought not to have paid attention, or that he erred in principle in any way. *f*

I do not propose to go through the circumstances of the case, and the way in which the judge regarded them, in any detail; they will be found in the reports of his judgment[3], and Goff LJ has dealt with them in the course of the judgment which he has delivered. I would associate myself with what has been said by Goff and Lane LJJ about the inadvisability of appeals in this jurisdiction where the estate is a small one. The only consequence of excessive litigation in such a case is to dissipate the whole estate in costs *g* and leave nothing for those who have or want to assert claims on the deceased's estate.

In the present case it so happens that the applicant would have been much better advised to have been content with what he would have got under the order that was proposed to be made by the master. But he did not do so, and the costs which have resulted must be very considerable, very considerable indeed in relation to the value of this comparatively very small estate.   *h*

For the reasons which have been given by Goff and Lane LJJ in the judgments which they have delivered, and for the few additional reasons which I have endeavoured to express in my own judgment, I agree that this appeal fails and must be dismissed.

Appeal dismissed.

Solicitors: *K E Davis & Sons*, Hayes (for the applicant); *E D C Lord & Co*, Southall (for the *j* respondent).

J H Fazan Esq   Barrister.

---

1 [1979] 2 All ER 408 at 417–418, [1979] 2 WLR 853 at 864–865
2 [1979] 2 All ER 408 at 418, [1979] 2 WLR 853 at 865
3 [1979] 2 All ER 408, [1979] 2 WLR 853

Knole Park Golf Club v Chief Superintendent, Kent County Constabulary

a

QUEEN'S BENCH DIVISION
EVELEIGH LJ AND WOOLF J
20th JULY 1979

b

Licensing – Permitted hours – Special order of exemption for special occasion – Special occasion – Registered club – Sporting club – Annual sporting occasions held by club – Whether 'special occasions' – Whether event held by club itself on club premises could be a 'special occasion' – Licensing Act 1964, s 74(4).

c The secretary of a golf club which was a registered club under the Licensing Act 1964 applied to justices for special orders of exemption under s 74(4)[a] of the Act to extend the permitted drinking hours in the club on certain annual sporting occasions organised by the club. They included the past captains' dinner, the annual invitation meeting when the club invited friends from other clubs, the club summer dance and the captain's prize competition. The justices refused the applications on the ground that the occasions in *d* question were not 'special occasions' within s 74(4) since they were held by the club itself on its own premises and were not events external to the club. The club appealed.

Held – In relation to an application for a special order of exemption under s 74(4) of the 1964 Act it was not essential that there was some event completely external to the applicant in order for there to be a special occasion. Each case depended on its own facts, *e* and in many cases it could well be that the licence holder was himself creating his own occasion for the purposes of the licensed business, so that it was not a special occasion within s 74(4). However the occasions in respect of which the club had sought orders of exemption were not special occasions for the purpose of the licensed business. Each was a special occasion created by a sporting club, which as a result of holding that special sporting activity had sought an extension of drinking hours. Had the club booked a *f* hotel for the event it was quite clear that the justices would have treated it as a special occasion, and it would be illogical not to grant an order of exemption merely because the club had its own licensed facilities. It followed that the appeal would be allowed (see p 831 *e* to p 832 *e*, post).

Dictum of Widgery J in *Lemon v Sargent* [1971] 3 All ER at 937 applied.

g **Notes**

For special orders of exemption, see 26 Halsbury's Laws (4th Edn) para 339, and for cases on the subject, see 30 Digest (Reissue) 83–85, 625–641.

For the Licensing Act 1964, s 74, see 17 Halsbury's Statutes (3rd Edn) 1134.

Cases referred to in judgments

h *Lemon v Sargent* (1967) [1971] 3 All ER 936, [1972] 1 WLR 72, DC, 30 Digest (Reissue) 84, 634.

R v Llanidloes (Lower) Justices, ex parte Thorogood [1971] 3 All ER 932, [1972] 1 WLR 68, DC, 30 Digest (Reissue) 84, 635.

Case stated

j This was an appeal by Knole Park Golf Club by way of case stated from a decision of the

---

a   Section 74(4), so far as material, provides: 'Justices of the peace may . . . (b) on an application by the secretary of a club registered in respect of any premises, make an order (in this Act referred to as a special order of exemption) adding such hours as may be specified in the order to the permitted hours in those premises on such special occasion or occasions as may be so specified.'

Sevenoaks licensing justices on 13th March 1979 refusing applications in respect of 13th
May, 8th, 17th, 24th June, 7th July and 1st September 1979 for special orders of   *a*
exemption under s 74(4) of the Licensing Act 1964. The facts are set out in the judgment
of Eveleigh LJ.

Andrew Patience for the club.
F J M Marr-Johnson for the respondent.

EVELEIGH LJ. This is an appeal by way of case stated from the decision of the   *b*
Sevenoaks justices who refused applications for various special exemptions from
permitted hours pursuant to s 74(4)(*b*) of the Licensing Act 1964. These applications
were made by the Knole Park Golf Club ('the club'), which was and is a registered club.

The applications were as follows: first, for Sunday, 13th May 1979, from 8 pm to
11 pm for what was called the Martin Cup prize giving. This is the club's major 36-hole   *c*
competition of the year. It is open to all members, though the numbers are limited.
Members playing in this competition qualify for the club championship. The event is
held on a Sunday because many members work on Saturday. Play usually finishes
between 7.30 to 8.00 pm. There are usually about 100 members present, and wives and
families join the members.

The second event was on Friday, 8th June 1979 from 10.30 pm to 11.30 pm for the   *d*
committee and past captains' dinner. On that occasion the committee of the club would
entertain the past captains to a golfing afternoon and dinner in the evening. There are
guests invited on that occasion, many of whom live some distance away. That is an
annual occasion.

On Sunday, 17th June 1979 from 8 pm to 11 pm an invitation meeting was to be
held. That is the normal annual meeting that most golf clubs have, and on that occasion   *e*
members invite friends from other clubs. It is held on a Sunday because many of the
participants work on a Saturday. In the evening there is prize giving. About half of the
participants are guests, many of whom travel from outside Kent for the occasion.

The fourth application related to Sunday, 24th June 1979 from 8 pm to 11 pm. That
occasion was said to be the highlight of the captain's year of office, as it is with all golf
clubs. The captain's prize is played for over the Saturday and Sunday, and on the evening   *f*
of the second day the members' wives and families join the captain. The captain pays for
the competition, and it is said that is the most special event of the captain's year.

The fifth application was for Saturday, 7th July 1979 from 10.30 pm to 1.30 am. This
was the club's summer dance. The club has three major social occasions each year, the
summer, winter and Christmas or New Year's Eve dances. They are attended by
members, friends and guests. On that occasion a buffet supper is provided with music   *g*
and dancing. The premises have been altered specifically to accommodate these
functions.

The sixth application related to Saturday, 1st September 1979 from 10.30 pm to
midnight. This was the Kent Cob open meeting. This is the principal amateur meeting
in South East England. Contestants may come from anywhere, even from Scotland. It
has been held for some 50 years and always has been held at the Knole Club.   *h*

In considering these applications the justices said that they would have granted them
all had they not felt obliged by law to refuse. Their obligation to refuse stemmed from
decisions of this court, in particular *Lemon v Sargent*[1]. The justices referred to words of
Lord Parker CJ where he said[2]:

　　'I am quite satisfied that a dance cannot be turned into a special occasion for the
　　purposes of the Licensing Acts merely because the organiser chooses to give the   *j*
　　dance, and it is wholly unconnected with any special event in the locality. I am also

---

1　[1971] 3 All ER 936, [1972] 1 WLR 72
2　[1971] 3 All ER 936 at 937, [1972] 1 WLR 72 at 73

a   clear that the degree of repetition here, the frequency, also prevents these from being special occasions.'

In that case the applicant was the licensee of a public hotel which for some 16 years had organised dances for the benefit not merely of residents in the hotel but all members of the public on Wednesday and Saturday of each week. The frequency of the occasions is quite clear, and one can fully understand that that of itself would have prevented these occasions from being special. But also, be it noted, the dances were organised in *b*   connection with the licensee's licensed activities.

In *R v Llanidloes (Lower) Justices, ex parte Thorogood*[1] application was made by the holder of a justices' on-licence for exemption for one hour in respect of each of six Saturdays. Each occasion was a football match played on their home ground by the local team, and the requirement was for facilities for refreshment for players and officials. The licence was granted by the justices. In that case Lord Widgery CJ said[2]:
c

'As counsel for the applicant points out, the present application was not subject to the first of those vices; there was an occasion quite independent of the activity of the licensee, the occasion being the football match which was held on each of the days to which the application related. So far as that ground is concerned, the present case does not disclose comparable circumstances,'

d   that is to say comparable to those in *Lemon v Sargent*[3].

In *Lemon v Sargent*[4] Widgery J said:

'I agree, and would add only in regard to dances that there may, I would think, be occasions when a local cricket or sports club or something of that kind, wishes to organise an annual dance and hold it in the hotel. I would have thought that that *e*   was a special occasion, or might be so, within the meaning of the Licensing Act 1964, although the day in question had no significance other than the fact that it was booked by the club organising the dance.'

The justices in the present case had regarded it as essential that there should be some external event, external completely to the club itself in order for there to be a special occasion. It has been said many times in these cases that the court will not attempt a *f*   specific definition of 'special occasion' but should leave it to the justices on the facts of each case to determine that question for themselves. That does not mean, however, that, if the justices have taken a wrong restricted view of the wording, this court will not interfere.

As I say, in this present case the justices seemed to regard it as an insuperable difficulty that it was the club itself that was holding the sporting event and the club itself was *g*   applying for the extension of hours, and that prevented the occasion from being a special occasion. Let it be said that in this case no question of frequency preventing it from being a special occasion has arisen.

On this rather difficult matter I have come to the conclusion that the justices did misdirect themselves in dealing with the application. Each case must depend on its own facts, and no doubt there will be many cases in which it is said that the licence holder is *h*   himself creating his own occasion, and for that reason the occasion is not a special one within the meaning of the 1964 Act.

In the present case, however, it cannot, in my view, be said that a licensee was creating a special occasion for the purpose of the licensed business. There was a special occasion created by a sporting club, which as a result of holding that special sporting activity asked for an extension of drinking hours. Had they booked a hotel for the event, I think that
j

1   [1971] 3 All ER 932, [1972] 1 WLR 68
2   [1971] 3 All ER 932 at 935, [1972] 1 WLR 68 at 71
3   [1971] 3 All ER 936, [1972] 1 WLR 72
4   [1971] 3 All ER 936 at 937, [1972] 1 WLR 72 at 73

it would have been quite clear that the justices in this case would have treated the occasions as special occasions, because then it would have been unconnected with the *a* activity of the applicant, namely the licensee of the hotel. It seems to be wholly illogical that a licence could be granted in that case, the occasion being special, and not granted in the present case when in fact it is exactly the same occasion that has to be considered.

In looking at each case I see that they are special sporting occasions organised by a sporting club. That sporting club happens to have its own licensed facilities. In its role as a licensee, albeit a registered club, it is applying for an extension of hours. I, therefore, *b* for those reasons would allow this appeal.

There remains the question: what is to be done? There is only one event, namely 1st September yet to be held. From the statement of the justices in the stated case it is quite clear that, had they not felt themselves bound by the restriction which they considered was imposed by *Lemon v Sargent*[1], they would have granted these applications. Therefore, I myself would allow this appeal and at the same time grant the extension asked for. *c*

WOOLF J. I agree and would just add a few words. Widgery J in *Lemon v Sargent*[2] in the passage quoted by Eveleigh LJ referred to occasions of a local sports club or something of that kind, organising an annual dance and holding it in a hotel, and he thought that would be a special occasion. Nowadays many clubs of the sort that Widgery J had in mind are registered clubs, entitled to hold functions themselves where alcoholic liquor *d* is provided. The fact that they hold them on their own premises does not prevent them being local occasions. A local cricket club dance is a local occasion, whether it be held at the club or at a hotel.

I would adopt and agree with what Eveleigh LJ has said about the importance of looking at the facts of the matter and deciding on the facts in relation to that particular organisation whether or not it is a special occasion. As long as the justices look at the facts *e* and come to their own conclusions whether or not it is a special occasion, I apprehend they will not get into too many difficulties.

Appeal allowed.

Solicitors: *Vallis & Struthers*, Sevenoaks (for the club); *Sharpe, Pritchard & Co* (for the *f* respondent).

N P Metcalfe Esq   Barrister.

---

1   [1971] 3 All ER 936, [1972] 1 WLR 72   *g*
2   [1971] 3 All ER 936 at 937, [1972] 1 WLR 72 at 73

Ministry of Defence v Jeremiah

a

COURT OF APPEAL, CIVIL DIVISION
LORD DENNING MR, BRANDON AND BRIGHTMAN LJJ
3rd, 4th, 5th, 19th OCTOBER 1979

b
Employment – Discrimination against a man – Act of discrimination – Men volunteering for overtime required to work in unpleasant conditions whereas women volunteering for overtime not required to work there – Women objecting to dirty conditions and to wearing protective clothing and taking showers – Whether unlawful discrimination against male employee – Whether men subjected to a 'detriment' by compulsory working in unpleasant conditions when volunteering for overtime – Whether any 'detriment' occurring removed by extra pay – Whether arrangements made in the interests of safety, good administration and chivalrous treatment of women could be
c *unlawful discrimination – Sex Discrimination Act 1975, ss 1(1)(a), 2(1), 6(2)(b).*

At an ordnance factory where they employed both men and women examiners the Ministry of Defence ('the employers') operated a practice whereby men examiners who volunteered for overtime were periodically required to work their overtime in the shops where colour-bursting shells were made. Women examiners who volunteered for
d overtime were not required to work in those shops because the working conditions were dusty and dirty (because of the dyes used) and they objected to wearing protective clothing and taking showers when they finished working. There were no separate facilities for protective clothing and showers for the women. Men examiners who worked in the colour-bursting shops were paid extra to compensate for the dirty conditions. A male examiner complained to an industrial tribunal that the practice
e amounted to unlawful discrimination against him on the ground of his sex, contrary to the Sex Discrimination Act 1975, because it subjected him to a 'detriment' within s 6(2)(b)[a] (read with s 2(1)[b]) of the Act to which the women examiners were not subjected. The tribunal decided that the practice was unlawful because the requirement that the men work in less pleasant working conditions in the colour-bursting shops compared with other shops in the factory meant that they were subjected to a
f 'detriment'. The tribunal therefore declared the practice to be unlawful, and that decision was affirmed by the Employment Appeal Tribunal. The employers appealed contending, inter alia, (i) that since men examiners received extra pay for working in the colour-bursting shops it was not a 'detriment' for them to work there, (ii) that the arrangement that the women should not be required to work in the shops, being made in the interests of safety and good administration, did not constitute unlawful
g discrimination even if it favoured one sex more than the other, and (iii) that there was no evidence that in treating the men examiners differently the employers were acting adversely or in a hostile manner to their interests.

Held – The appeal would be dismissed for the following reasons—
     (1) Because the men examiners were required to work in the colour-bursting shops
h when volunteering for overtime and women were not, the men were treated less favourably than the women and accordingly were discriminated against by the employers contrary to s 1(1)(a)[c] of the 1975 Act, read with s 2(1). Furthermore that discrimination amounted to a 'detriment' within s 6(2)(b) of the Act, and was thus unlawful, because—
     (i) (per Lord Denning MR and Brightman LJ) if the women examiners who
j volunteered for overtime had been required to work in the shops, and not the men, there

_____

b Section 2(1), so far as material, provides: 'Section 1, and the provisions of Parts II . . . relating to sex discrimination against women are to be read as applying equally to the treatment of men . . .'
c Section 1(1), so far as material, is set out at p 836 b, post

would have been unlawful discrimination against the women and it followed that as the
1975 Act required equality of treatment for men and women, the practice of requiring *a*
the men to work in the shops, but not the women, was unlawful discrimination against
the men (see p 836 *c* to *e*, p 840 *h j* and p 841 *a c* and *e f*, post);

(ii) (per Brandon LJ) the test of whether the men examiners had been subjected to a
detriment was whether they had been put under a disadvantage by comparison with the
women examiners; that was a question of fact for the industrial tribunal which they had
answered in the affirmative and there was no ground to interfere with their decision. *b*
The facts that the women objected to working in the shops and that no facilities existed
for them to work there were irrelevant (see p 837 *h j*, p 839 *c d* and p 840 *d e*, post.)

(2) The fact that the men examiners were paid extra for working in the colour-
bursting shops did not remove the detriment because (per Lord Denning MR and
Brightman LJ) the employers could not buy the right to discriminate against the men
and (per Brandon LJ) the extra payment was a fact relevant to the question whether there *c*
was detriment and had been taken into account by the industrial tribunal in reaching the
conclusion that detriment existed (see p 836 *e* to *g*, p 839 *e* to *g* and p 841 *f*, post).

Per Lord Denning MR. The fact that arrangements have been made in the interests
of safety, good administration and the chivalrous treatment of women should no longer
be relied on as a defence to a complaint of unlawful discrimination (see p 837 *a b*, post);
Peake v Automotive Products Ltd [1978] 1 All ER 106 disapproved in part. *d*

Per Brandon LJ. It is not right to interpret the concept of unlawful discrimination
under the 1975 Act by reference to a consideration whether the employer is acting
adversely or in a hostile manner to the interests of his employees (see p 840 *c d*, post);
dictum of Shaw LJ in *Peake v Automotive Products Ltd* [1978] 1 All ER at 110 considered.

Per Brightman LJ. A 'detriment' within s 6(2)(*b*) exists if in all the circumstances
a reasonable employee would or might take the view that there is a detriment (see *e*
p 841 *d e*, post).

Notes

For sex discrimination generally and for discrimination against employees, see 16
Halsbury's Laws (4th Edn) paras 771:2 and 771:5.

For the Sex Discrimination Act 1975, ss 1, 2 and 6, see 45 Halsbury's Statutes (3rd Edn) *f*
227, 229.

Cases referred to in judgments

Dixon v British Broadcasting Corpn [1979] 2 All ER 112, [1979] QB 546, [1979] 2 WLR
647, [1979] ICR 281, CA.
Peake v Automotive Products Ltd [1978] 1 All ER 106, [1978] QB 233, [1977] 3 WLR 853, *g*
[1977] ICR 968, CA.
Rosenfeld v Southern Pacific Co (1971) 444 F 2d 1219.

Cases also cited

Clay Cross (Quarry Services) Ltd v Fletcher [1979] 1 All ER 474, [1978] 1 WLR 1429, CA.
Greig v Community Industry [1979] ICR 365, EAT. *h*
Griggs v Duke Power Co (1971) 91 S Ct 849, 401 US 424.
Miliangos v George Frank (Textiles) Ltd [1975] 3 All ER 701, [1976] AC 443, HL.
Price v Civil Service Commission [1978] 1 All ER 1228, [1977] 1 WLR 1417, EAT.
Shields v E Coomes (Holdings) Ltd [1979] 1 All ER 456, [1978] 1 WLR 1408, CA.

Appeal

j

The employers, the Ministry of Defence ('the Ministry'), appealed against that part of a
decision of the Employment Appeal Tribunal (Slynn J, Mrs A L T Taylor and Mr D A C
Lambert) dated 31st July 1978 dismissing their appeal against a decision of an industrial
tribunal (chairman Sir Martin Edwards) sitting at Cardiff on 30th November 1977
declaring that the Ministry were guilty of an act of unlawful discrimination, contrary to

s 6(2)(*b*) of the Sex Discrimination Act 1975, against a male employee, Mr R E Jeremiah,
a by compelling him when volunteering for overtime to work in colour-bursting shell
shops in which female employees were not required to work. The facts are set out in the
judgment of Lord Denning MR.

Anthony Boswood for the Ministry.
Anthony Lester QC and *Patrick Curran* for Mr Jeremiah.

b   *Cur adv vult*

19th October. The following judgments were read.

LORD DENNING MR. A woman's hair is her crowning glory, so it is said. She does
not like it disturbed: especially when she has just had a 'hair-do'. The women at an
ordnance factory in Wales are no exception. They do not want to work in a part of the
c factory, called a 'shop', which ruins their 'hair-do'.

The shop here is one which turns out 'colour-bursting' shells. These are shells which
are used by artillery on practice shoots. When they burst, they explode into red or
orange colours, so that the gunners can see whether they are on target or not. The work
in the shop is dusty and dirty, because they use red or orange dyes. There are only two
or three men working in the shop. A couple doing the actual process, and an examiner
d to make the necessary inspections. Before starting work the men have to strip off their
ordinary clothes and put on protective clothing. After the day's work, they have to have
showers before putting on their ordinary clothes. They do this in their overtime. They
finish work in the shop at 4.00 pm. They are allowed overtime pay for the next three-
quarters of an hour, even though they get dressed in a quarter of an hour and go off.
They also get 4p extra pay for every hour they work in the shop. It is called 'obnoxious
e pay', not because the pay is obnoxious, but because it is compensation for working in
dirty conditions.

Now Mr Jeremiah was an examiner in the ordnance factory. He worked in various
shops, but occasionally he had to do a stint in the colour-bursting shop. He complains
now under the Sex Discrimination Act 1975. He says that men are required to work in
the colour-bursting shop and that women are not; and that this is unfair discrimination
f against the men.

Hitherto, the work in the colour-bursting shop has been regarded as men's work. The
men are required to do it in this way: if they volunteer to do overtime, then they must
do their stint in the colour-bursting shop. It does not come round very often, because
there is not much need for colour-bursting shells. But it is compulsory for those who
volunteer for overtime. But no women are required to work in the colour-bursting
g shop. Even if a woman volunteers to do overtime, she is not required to work in the
colour-bursting shop. It is not regarded as women's work. There is no good reason why
women should not do it. The actual work is just as suitable for women as for men. They
could be provided with protective clothing, just as the men. Showers could be arranged
for them, just as the men. Those facilities are available in other parts of the factory. But
the women simply do not want to work in the colour-bursting shop. The manager said
h they had several reasons. One was the daily shower and its effect on their hair. Another
was personal embarrassment.

Now, Mr Jeremiah has little regard for chivalry or for the women's hair-dos. He is a
modern man. He says that there should be equality between the sexes. *Either* the
women should be required to do their stint (in the colour-bursting shop), just like the
men. *Or* the men should not be required to do it any more than the women.

j Before I consider the law, I would ask this simple question. Suppose the position were
reversed. Suppose that the *women* (who volunteer for overtime) were required to work
in the colour-bursting shop, and that the men were not. At once everyone would say
that there was discrimination against the women. Now if that be the case, the Sex
Discrimination Act 1975 comes in like a lion. It commands us to treat men and women
just the same. It says that wherever 'woman' is used in the Act, we are to read 'man', and

vice versa: see s 2 of the Act. Equality is the order of the day. In both directions. For both sexes.

a

Now I turn to the Act. Section 1(1)(*a*) says that:

'A person discriminates against a woman . . . if . . . (*a*) on the ground of her sex he treats her less favourably than he treats or would treat a man.'

Reading 'man' for 'woman' etc, it is plain that the Ministry of Defence here discriminated against Mr Jeremiah. They required him to work in the dirty shop. They treated him *b* less favourably than they treated a woman; and they did it on the ground of his sex, because he was a man.

Section 6(2)(*b*) says:

'It is unlawful for a person, in the case of a woman employed by him at an establishment in Great Britain, to discriminate against her . . . (*b*) by dismissing her, or subjecting her to any other detriment.'

c

In this section the critical word is 'detriment'. Now I must say that I think it is a detriment for Mr Jeremiah to be required to work in the colour-bursting shop, when women are not. Test it by the converse. If a woman was so required, it would obviously be a detriment to her, to have to work in dirty and dusty conditions when she did not wish to do so. Likewise with a man. What is sauce for the goose is sauce for the gander, *d* nowadays.

But it is said that any 'detriment' is removed by the payment of 4p an hour for working in the colour-bursting shop. By that money, Mr Jeremiah is compensated for the dirty and dusty work. So, it is said then, he is not subjected to any detriment. I do not accept this argument. The 'obnoxious pay' of 4p an hour is made solely because it is compensation for the dirty work. If the women were required to do the work, they *e* would get it just the same. It is not paid because of the difference in the sexes. It is, therefore, quite irrelevant. If it were paid because of the difference in the sexes, it would be unlawful under s 77(1) of the Act. An employer cannot buy a right to discriminate by making an extra payment to the men. If he could, it would drive a gaping hole in the statute. All the men would pass through it.

Section 7 does not apply in this case. It is confined to cases where a person *applies* for *f* a job or for promotion, transfer or training. It does not apply to *existing* employees who are suffering a detriment.

In order to illustrate the impact of s 7, I may say that if the Ministry of Defence were to *offer* a man a post as examiner on the terms that he would do a stint in the colour-bursting shop, and the Ministry would not offer it to a woman on those terms, that would be unlawful. It would not come within the exceptions in s 7: because this is not *g* a case where being a man is a 'genuine occupational qualification' for the job: see *Rosenfeld v Southern Pacific Co*[1]. So that fits in with my interpretation of s 6.

I should mention s 8(5). It affords no answer, seeing that the difference between the men's contract and the women's contract is due to the difference of sex.

Next, the Ministry relies on *Peake v Automotive Products Ltd*[2]. The women there were allowed to go off work five minutes before the men, for reasons of safety to avoid the *h* rush. Turning to that case again, I think we were under a disadvantage, because Mr Peake appeared in person; and we were not referred to some of the relevant parts of the statute. There were two grounds for the decision. Now on reconsideration, I think the only sound ground was that the discrimination was de minimis. Counsel for Mr Jeremiah told us that on a petition to the House of Lords, they refused leave to appeal for that very reason. They thought that the decision was correct on the de minimis *j* ground. In these circumstances, the other ground (about chivalry and administrative

---

1 (1971) 444 F 2d 1219
2 [1978] 1 All ER 106, [1978] QB 233

practice) should no longer be relied on. We can dispense with it just as we did in *Dixon*
a *v British Broadcasting Corpn*[1].

Some question arose about the remedies. There should be a declaration that Mr
Jeremiah has the right not to be discriminated against by the Ministry of Defence (see
s 65(1)(a)) but I would not make any specific recommendation under s 65(1)(c). It will be
the duty of the Ministry to find out their own means of eliminating the discrimination.
It can be done by requiring all women (who volunteer for overtime) to do their stint in
b the colour-bursting shop; or by making it voluntary both for men and women; or any
other way acceptable to all concerned. This accords with the decision of the Employment
Appeal Tribunal. I would dismiss the appeal accordingly.

BRANDON LJ. The appellants ('the Ministry') employ both men and women as grade
one examiners at their explosives factory at Glascoed in South Wales. This case raises the
c question whether they have been discriminating unlawfully against the men in that
employment.

On the findings of the industrial tribunal to which the respondent, Mr Jeremiah,
complained, there was a difference in the way in which men examiners on the one hand,
and women examiners on the other, were treated for the purposes of overtime.

The difference was this. Men examiners who volunteered for overtime were required
d to work from time to time in the colour-bursting shops, whether they wished to do so or
not. By contrast women examiners who volunteered for overtime were never required
to work in such shops. Indeed, it would not have been practicable for women examiners
to work in the colour-bursting shops even if they had wished to do so (which they did
not), for no separate facilities in the form of protective clothing and showering were
provided for them.

e The industrial tribunal found that the Ministry, by treating men examiners differently
from women examiners in this respect, committed an act of unlawful discrimination
against Mr Jeremiah under the Sex Discrimination Act 1975. The Employment Appeal
Tribunal affirmed that part of the industrial tribunal's decision. The question on this
appeal is whether the Employment Appeal Tribunal was right to do so.

The provisions of the Act directly relevant are those contained in ss 1(1)(a), 2(1) and
f 6(2)(b). The effect of these provisions, taken together, is that the difference of treatment
concerned constituted unlawful discrimination if it meant that men examiners were
subjected to some detriment by comparison with women examiners, so that the
treatment of the former was in this respect less favourable than the treatment of the
latter.

I do not regard the expression 'subjecting to any other detriment', as used in s 6(2)(b),
g as meaning anything more than 'putting under a disadvantage'. The question which
arose in this case can therefore be simplified to this: did the difference in treatment
referred to above put the men examiners under a disadvantage by comparison with the
women examiners?

That was, in my opinion, a question of fact rather than law, and as such fell to be
answered by the industrial tribunal on the material before it. Unfortunately, as I shall
h explain later, part of the material before the industrial tribunal on which it answered that
question was agreed subsequently before the Employment Appeal Tribunal to have been
incorrect. The case as it fell to be considered by the Employment Appeal Tribunal was
therefore to that extent a different case from that originally before the industrial tribunal.

Before the industrial tribunal two aspects of the requirement that men examiners
should work in the colour-bursting shops were investigated. One aspect was the dirty
j nature of the work involved. The other aspect, on which a good deal of stress, if not the
main stress, appears to have been laid by Mr Jeremiah at that stage, was the adverse
financial consequences of having to work in such shops.

---

1   [1979] 2 All ER 112, [1979] QB 546

With regard to the first aspect, the industrial tribunal found, in para 7 of their reasons, that the work in the colour-bursting shops was dirty work in that red and orange dyes were used which created dust, and it was necessary for workers and examiners in such shops to wear protective clothing and to take a shower at the end of the day's work.

With regard to the second aspect, the industrial tribunal found, again in para 7 of their reasons, that those working in the colour-bursting shops received obnoxious pay at the rate of 4p an hour. It was further agreed between the parties, as appears from para 10 of the reasons, that men examiners who worked in the colour-bursting shops thereby had less opportunity of earning at the higher rate applicable to lead rate shops, rather than at the lower rate applicable to non-lead rate shops; and that the reduction in their earnings in this respect would be reflected adversely in the amounts of their gratuities and pensions on retirement. It further appears to have been admitted by the Ministry that the obnoxious money payments received by men examiners working in the colour-bursting shops would not be reflected beneficially in the amounts of their gratuities and pensions.

On these facts, as found, agreed or admitted, the industrial tribunal concluded, in para 13 of their reasons, that the examiners were subjected to a detriment on two grounds. The first ground was that work in the colour-bursting shops was less pleasant work than work in some other shops, although there were other shops where obnoxious payments were made. The second ground was that for men only to be engaged in such shops was to their financial prejudice.

On the basis of their conclusion that men examiners were subjected to a detriment on these two grounds, the industrial tribunal decided that the Ministry had discriminated unlawfully against Mr Jeremiah under s 6(2)(b) of the 1975 Act.

On the hearing of the Ministry's appeal to the Employment Appeal Tribunal, the factual basis on which the industrial tribunal had proceeded was in part displaced by an agreement between the parties (see the judgment of the Employment Appeal Tribunal[1]). It was agreed, firstly, that obnoxious payments received by men examiners for working in the colour-bursting shops did in fact fall to be taken into account in calculating their pensions and gratuities; and, secondly, that Mr Jeremiah had never in fact lost any opportunity of earning at the higher rate applicable to lead rate shops as a result of having to work in the colour-bursting shops. The Employment Appeal Tribunal further held that there was no evidence to suggest that the situation in this respect would change in the future.

The result of all this was that the second ground for the industrial tribunal's conclusion that men examiners were subjected to a detriment, namely that having to work in the colour-bursting shops caused them financial prejudice, in effect disappeared. That left the conclusion supported, and supported only, by the first ground, namely that the work in the colour-bursting shops was less pleasant than that in some other shops, although there were other shops where obnoxious payments were made.

It appeared to me at one stage of the argument that this change in the factual basis on which the industrial tribunal had proceeded made it necessary, in order to do justice, for the case to be remitted for reconsideration by that tribunal. I formed this opinion because it seemed to be very arguable that the industrial tribunal's conclusion that there was a detriment was not founded on each of the two grounds relied on separately, but on both those grounds taken together, so that, if only the first ground had existed without the second, the conclusion might not have been the same. On further reflection, however, I have been persuaded that the two grounds were separate and independent, so that the displacement of the second ground does not itself make a remission necessary. This seems to have been the approach adopted by the Employment Appeal Tribunal, and, despite the earlier doubts which I have indicated, I think in the end that it was the correct approach.

---

1   [1978] ICR 984 at 987

On the footing that the conclusion that there was a detriment depends on the industrial
tribunal's first ground alone, four main grounds of appeal were developed before us.

The first main ground of appeal was that there were various facts and circumstances
which, singly or together, made the decision that there was unlawful discrimination
wrong in law. The facts and circumstances relied on were these. First, that the women
examiners objected to working in the colour-bursting shops; secondly, that facilities did
not exist for women to work in the colour bursting shops; thirdly, that to require
women to work in the colour-bursting shops would be unreasonable and likely to lead
to industrial unrest; fourthly, that there was no evidence that any men examiners other
than Mr Jeremiah objected to the difference of treatment. I am not at all sure that the
fourth of these matters was in accordance with the evidence. Be that as it may, I am of
opinion that, on the proper construction of the 1975 Act, none of these facts and
circumstances was relevant to the issue which the industrial tribunal had to decide,
namely whether, as a result of the difference in treatment, the men examiners were
subjected to a detriment.

The second main ground of appeal was that, since men examiners, when they worked
in the colour-bursting shops, received obnoxious payments negotiated by their union on
their behalf, the conclusion that having to work in such shops was a detriment could not
be justified.

In answer to this argument, it was contended for Mr Jeremiah that the fact that such
payments were received was irrelevant to the question whether there was a detriment or
not, and should therefore be disregarded. I do not accept this contention. It seems to me
that, in answering the question whether having to work in the colour-bursting shops was
a detriment or not, the industrial tribunal was not only entitled, but bound, to take into
account all the surrounding circumstances, including particularly the circumstances that
these payments were received.

Assuming that to be the correct principle, however, it seems to me that the Ministry's
argument still fails on another ground. That is that the industrial tribunal was fully
aware of the payments and clearly took them into account in reaching its conclusion that
there was a detriment to men examiners in that the work in the colour-bursting shops
was less pleasant than in some other shops. That was a conclusion of fact to which they
were entitled to come on the material before them, and, subject to one point, I do not see
how it can be successfully challenged on appeal.

The one point is that the industrial tribunal proceeded on the basis that the obnoxious
payments would not be taken into account in the calculation of gratuities and pensions
on retirement, whereas it was agreed before the Employment Appeal Tribunal that they
would be so taken into account. Here again, if it were reasonable to suppose that this
relatively minor distinction might have led the industrial tribunal to a different
conclusion on the issue of detriment, it would, strictly speaking, be necessary to remit
the case for reconsideration to that tribunal. In my opinion, however, it is not reasonable
to suppose that this distinction would have led the industrial tribunal to a different
conclusion on that issue. There is accordingly no substance in the point.

The third main ground of appeal was that the case was governed by the principle said
to have been laid down by this court in *Peake v Automotive Products Ltd*[1]. In that case it
was held that a difference between the treatment of men and women with regard to time
of ceasing work (a difference which was of five minutes only) did not constitute unlawful
discrimination against the men. There were two grounds for the decision. The first
ground was that arrangements made in the interest of safety and good administration
did not constitute unlawful discrimination even if they were more favourable to workers
of one sex that to those of the other. The second ground was that the difference of
treatment was in any case de minimis.

It was argued for Mr Jeremiah that, in so far as that case was decided on the first
ground as distinct from the second, it was decided per incuriam and should not be

---

1   [1978] 1 All ER 106, [1978] QB 233

followed. I do not find it necessary to express any opinion one way or the other on this
contention, because it seems to me that, even assuming that the first ground of decision   *a*
was correct and is binding on this court, it has no application to the facts of this case.
There is no finding by the industrial tribunal that the difference in treatment here in
question arose out of arrangements made in the interests of safety or good administration;
nor, so far as I can see, was there any evidence on which such a finding could possibly
have been made.

The fourth main ground of appeal was that there was no evidence that the Ministry,   *b*
in treating men and women examiners differently as regards working in the colour-
bursting shops, were acting in any way inherently adverse or hostile to the interests of
the men. This ground is based on the language used by Shaw LJ in his judgment in *Peake
v Automotive Products Ltd*[1]. With respect to Shaw LJ, who was the only member of the
court to express himself in that way, I am not persuaded that it is right to interpret the
concept of unlawful discrimination under the Act of 1975 in quite as forceful a way as   *c*
he did in that judgment. I think, as I indicated earlier, that the sole question to be
answered in this case was whether the men examiners were put under a disadvantage by
comparison with the women examiners. That was a question of fact; it was answered by
the industrial tribunal in the affirmative; and I can see nothing wrong in law with that
answer.

For the reasons which I have given, subject to a variation in the terms of the declaration   *d*
made which may have to be considered further, I would dismiss the appeal.

BRIGHTMAN LJ. It is obviously reasonable that women, who are more concerned
with, and devote more time and attention to, their personal appearance than men,
should not be required by their employer to work in the atmosphere of the place so
graphically described as the colour-bursting shop; and should not have to scrub   *e*
themselves down under a shower and reset their hair before leaving the factory premises
at the end of the day's work. The evidence suggests that women might not volunteer for
overtime at all if this would necessitate their doing a compulsory stint in the colour-
bursting shop.

Whether a woman would be allowed to work in the colour-bursting shop if she so
wished, and would then be given the necessary cleaning facilities, is not clear on the   *f*
evidence. The point has not yet arisen, and the answer is irrelevant to the decision in this
case.

The question is whether the employer's solicitude towards female workers is unlawful
under the Sex Discrimination Act 1975. I think it is. The case turns on the meaning of
ss 1(1) and 6(2)(b) of the Act. Under s 1, read with s 2, an employer discriminates against
his male employee if 'he treats [him] less favourably than he treats [his female employee]   *g*
on the ground of [his] sex', that is to say, because he is a man and not a woman. Under
s 6(2), read with s 2, it is unlawful for an employer to discriminate against his male
employee by 'subjecting [him] to [a] detriment' not imposed on a female employee.

The effect of the work practice relating to the colour-bursting shop is that an overtime
volunteer is periodically directed there willy-nilly if that person is a man, but not if that
person is a woman. The colour-bursting shop is not a nice place in which to work. The   *h*
atmosphere is obnoxious. *His* treatment is therefore less favourable than *her* treatment.
He is therefore subjected to a detriment, as the industrial tribunal found. There was
ample evidence to support that finding.

I do not say that the mere deprivation of choice for one sex, or some other
differentiation in their treatment, is necessarily unlawful discrimination. The deprivation
of choice, or differentiation, in the sort of case we are considering, must be associated   *j*
with a detriment. It is possible to imagine a case where one sex has a choice but the other
does not, yet there is nevertheless no detriment to the latter sex, that is to say, no

1   [1978] 1 All ER 106 at 110, [1978] QB 233 at 240

unlawful discrimination. Railway carriages used to have compartments marked 'Ladies
only'. A lady had a choice of travelling in an ordinary compartment or in a 'Ladies only'
compartment. A man had no such choice. In such a case a court would conclude that
there was no sensible detriment to the men flowing from the absence of choice. A
similar case might arise on factory premises where there might be two canteens with
equal amenities, one canteen for men and women and the other for women only. A
court would conclude, other things being equal, that there was no unlawful
discrimination, though the ladies had a choice where they ate, and the men did not.

   In deciding whether or not there is a detriment to a worker who complains, the court
must in my opinion take all the circumstances into account. To take an example from
the facts of the present case, if (a) a male worker is under a duty to work in the colour-
bursting shop one day a fortnight and is compensated with a dirty work payment of 4p
an hour and consequential pay-related pension benefits, and (b) a female worker has no
such duty, and (c) a male worker complains, there is clearly discrimination based on
sex. The question before the tribunal in my view would be whether a reasonable male
worker would or might take the view that there was a detriment. I say, 'would or
might', because tastes differ. Some male workers might take the view that the 4p an
hour bonus, with consequent increase in pension rights, made the dirty work well worth
while, and not therefore detrimental to their interests. Other male workers might take
the view that it was not worth while, that it was to their detriment. It would be
unrealistic to expect a tribunal to decide which group of workers were correct in their
assessment. I think a detriment exists if a reasonable worker would or might take the
view that the duty was in all the circumstances to his detriment. It may be said that, on
this interpretation of the Act, both a male worker and a female worker might complain
about the same discrimination and that both might be right. I see no anomaly in such
a result. The purpose of the legislation is to secure equal treatment of the sexes so far as
appropriate.

   I should add that I agree with what Lord Denning MR has said with regard to the extra
payment for work in the colour-bursting shop in the present case; an employer cannot
lawfully buy the right to discriminate by making an extra payment.

   I would dismiss the appeal.

*Appeal dismissed. Declaration in form set out in judgment of Lord Denning MR. Leave to appeal
to the House of Lords refused.*

Solicitors: *Treasury Solicitor ; Derek James & Vaux*, Newport, Gwent (for Mr Jeremiah).

Sumra Green   Barrister.

Smiths Ltd v Middleton   a

CHANCERY DIVISION AT MANCHESTER

BLACKETT-ORD V-C SITTING AS A JUDGE OF THE HIGH COURT

31st JULY, 1st AUGUST 1978

Company – Receiver – Appointment by debenture holder – Duty to company – Duty to account
– Whether receiver under duty to company to provide full accounts of company's affairs – b
Whether duty limited to providing abstracts of accounts – Companies Act 1948, s 372(2).

A company executed a debenture in favour of a bank to secure an overdraft. By cl 4 of
the debenture the bank was given power to appoint a receiver and manager who was to
be deemed the company's agent. The bank called in the overdraft and under the
debenture appointed the defendant as receiver, in which capacity he continued to act c
until the debt to the bank was discharged and his receivership was terminated. The
company thereafter continued in business. In accordance with s 372(2)ᵃ of the Companies
Act 1948, the defendant prepared two abstracts of his receipts and payments for the
period he was receiver and sent them to the company. The company was dissatisfied
with the figures supplied in the abstracts and required more information for the purpose
of producing its audited accounts. The defendant refused to elaborate on the figures in d
the abstracts on the ground that he had done all that was required of him under
s 372(2). The company brought proceedings against him claiming, inter alia, an account
of receipts and payments during his receivership, and an account of the calculation of his
remuneration, or in the alternative, a general account. The registrar adjourned the
proceedings to the judge for determination of a preliminary issue whether the defendant
was under a duty to account to the company in more detail than was required by e
s 372(2). The defendant contended that where a borrower was a company under a
debenture governed by the Companies Acts the company had no equitable right to call
on the receiver, as its agent, to account to it because the duty, under s 12 of the
Companies Act 1976, imposed on the directors of the company (who remained in office)
to keep accounts, taken with the receiver's duty under s 372(2), replaced any equitable
right the company might have to call on the receiver to account. The defendant further f
contended that that was confirmed by the fact that where a receiver failed to make the
returns required by s 372(2), the summary remedy provided by s 375ᵇ of the 1948 Act
was available not to the company but to a member or creditor of the company or to the
registrar of companies.

Held – A receiver appointed under a debenture providing for him to be the agent of the g
debtor company, in practice ran the company on behalf of its directors and was, therefore,
answerable to the company for the conduct of its affairs. That being so, the receiver was
under a duty to keep full accounts (ie fuller than the abstracts of receipts and payments
required under s 372(2) of the 1948 Act) and to produce those accounts to the company
when required to do so. In order to enforce that right the company required a remedy
beyond that provided by s 375 of the 1948 Act. The receiver would therefore be treated h

---

a   Section 372(2), so far as material, is set out at p 844 g h, post
b   Section 375, so far as material, provides:
      '(1) If any receiver or manager of the property of a company—(a) having made default in filing,
      delivering or making any return, account or other document, or in giving any notice, which a
      receiver or manager is by law required to file, deliver, make or give . . . the court may, on an j
      application made for the purpose, make an order directing the receiver or manager, as the case may
      be, to make good the default within such time as may be specified in the order.
      '(2) In the case of any such default as is mentioned in paragraph (a) of the foregoing subsection,
      an application . . . may be made by any member or creditor of the company or by the registrar of
      companies . . .'

as an accounting party to the company. The issue would be decided accordingly (see
a p 846 *d* to p 847 *a* and *d* to *g*, post).
Dicta of Jenkins LJ in *Re B Johnson & Co (Builders) Ltd* [1955] 2 All ER at 790 and of
Phillimore J in *R v Board of Trade, ex parte St Martin Preserving Co Ltd* [1964] 2 All ER at
566 applied.

Notes
b For a receiver's obligation to give information, see 7 Halsbury's Laws (4th Edn) para 904.
For the Companies Act 1948, s 372, see 5 Halsbury's Statutes (3rd Edn) 384.

Cases referred to in judgment
Johnson (B) & Co (Builders) Ltd, Re [1955] 2 All ER 775, [1955] Ch 634, [1955] 3 WLR 269,
CA, 10 Digest (Reissue) 891, 5172.
c *R v Board of Trade, ex parte St Martin Preserving Co Ltd* [1964] 2 All ER 561, [1965] 1 QB
603, [1964] 3 WLR 262, DC, 9 Digest (Reissue) 649, 3899.

Cases also cited
Ashworth v Lord (1887) 3 Ch D 545.
Cuckmere Brick Co Ltd v Mutual Finance Ltd, Mutual Finance Ltd v Cuckmere Brick Co Ltd
d [1971] 2 All ER 633, [1971] Ch 949, CA.
Leicester Permanent Building Society v Butt [1943] 2 All ER 523, [1943] Ch 308.

Adjourned summons
By an originating summons issued on 10th January 1978 the plaintiffs, Smiths Ltd ('the
company') claimed against the defendant, Trevor Carrick Middleton, formerly receiver
e of the company under a debenture to Lloyd's Bank Ltd dated 21st April 1950, an account
of all receipts from sales and debtors in respect of the sum of £586,405·32 in the abstract
of payments and receipts for the period 16th January 1976 to 15th January 1977 filed by
the defendant with the Registrar of Companies pursuant to his statutory duty under
s 372(2) of the Companies Act 1948 in respect of his receivership; an inquiry to identify
certain other items or an account of how they were made up, including an account of
f how the claim by the defendant for fees in respect of professional services rendered were
calculated; alternatively, a general account for the whole of the defendant's receivership
of the company, and delivery to the company of all books, working papers,
correspondence and other documents or paper writings in the possession or control of the
defendant relating to his receivership and in particular certain specified documents; and
in the further alternative, inspection of the said documents. On 23rd May 1978 Mr
g Registrar Morris Jones, at Liverpool, adjourned the summons to the judge to hear and
determine a preliminary issue between the parties, whether the defendant was an
accounting party to the company. The facts are set out in judgment.

J Maurice Price QC and *J D Newton* for the company.
Michael Turner QC and *I J Dawson* for the defendant.

h
Cur adv vult

1st August. **BLACKETT-ORD V-C** delivered the following judgment: The plaintiff
company was incorporated in 1912 and carried on business for many years as a retailer
of furniture and similar goods. In 1950 it executed a debenture in favour of Lloyds Bank
j Ltd to secure an overdraft, which was in usual bank terms, and which charged the
goodwill and the uncalled capital of the company and the undertaking and all other
property and assets of the company, creating over the latter a floating charge in the usual
way. By cl 4 the bank was given power to appoint a receiver and manager, who again
was to have usual powers to take possession, carry on managing the business and so forth,
including a power to sell the undertaking and—

'To do all such other acts and things as may be considered to be incidental or
conducive to any of the matters or powers aforesaid and which he or they lawfully *a*
may or can do as Agent or Agents for the Company.'

The latter part of cl 4, after the enumeration of the specific powers, is in these terms:

'All money received by such Receiver or Receivers shall be applied first in
payment of his or their remuneration and the costs of realization; secondly in
providing for the matters specified in the first three paragraphs of sub-section 8 of *b*
section 109 of the Law of Property Act 1925 and for the purposes aforesaid; and
thirdly in or towards satisfaction of the money and liabilities hereby secured and all
the foregoing provisions shall take effect as and by way of variation and extension
of the provisions of sections 99 to 109 inclusive of the said Act which provisions so
varied and extended shall be regarded as incorporated therein. Any Receiver or
Receivers so appointed shall be deemed to be the Agent or Agents of the Company *c*
and the Company shall be solely responsible for his or their acts or defaults and for
his or their remuneration.'

In January 1976 the bank called in the overdraft debt, which amounted to about
£290,000, and a day or two later, on 16th January, appointed the defendant, Mr
Middleton, a principal of the well-known firm of accountants Coopers & Lybrand, to be *d*
receiver under the debenture. He continued as such until 8th February 1977, when he
ceased to act, the receivership being terminated and the bank paid off. The debenture
was formally discharged by vacating receipt of 22nd February 1977.

There had been some internal reorganisation of the company, and it continued to
function thereafter as a holding company with, I understand, one or more trading or
property-owning subsidiaries. But, from the layman's point of view, it was back in *e*
business.

Section 372 of the Companies Act 1948 is one of the sections dealing with the
appointment of a receiver and manager where the borrower is a company within the
Act. That section is headed: 'Provisions as to information where receiver or manager
appointed'. The first two subsections as drawn relate to a receiver appointed by the court,
but sub-s (3) makes them applicable to a receiver appointed under an instrument, as in *f*
the present case, with consequential amendments. Section 372(1) provides that the
receiver has to give notice to the company of his appointment in a prescribed form and
that the company within 14 days is to submit to the receiver a statement of affairs, again
in a prescribed form, on which the receiver can then comment and which is registered
by the registrar of companies. It goes on the file. Such a statement of affairs was
produced by the company, though late, and not until September 1976.

Then s 372(2) provides that the receiver has, after the expiration of every period of 12 *g*
months from the date of his appointment, to send to the Registrar of Companies, to the
trustees for the debenture holders, to the company and to the debenture holders 'an
abstract in the prescribed form showing his receipts and payments during that period of
twelve months' or until he ceases to act. In consequence of that provision, the defendant
has prepared two abstracts of receipts and payments, one for the only whole year during *h*
which he acted, from 16th January 1976 to 15th January 1977, and the second one from
16th January 1977 until he ceased to act on 8th February. Having prepared those
documents and sent them to the various recipients named in the section, including, of
course, the company, he says that he has done all that he is required to do by way of
accounting to the company; he has fulfilled his statutory obligation; that, he says, is all
that he is required to do; and he has declined to elaborate on the figures contained in *j*
these abstracts.

The company is dissatisfied with the figures which have been supplied, or rather seek
to have them further explained. Simply by way of example, in the first and main
abstract, the receiver, under the heading of 'Receipts', states: 'Total receipts from sales and
debtors: £586,405·22'. That, I understand is all the information about the receipts from

sales and debtors that the receiver considers he is bound to supply to the company. The
a company is dissatisfied, as I said, and says in particular that its auditors require more
information than this before audited and unqualified accounts can be produced. There
is a further point, that a subsidiary has been sold at a price calculated by reference to the
tax losses of the company, and it says there is insufficient information available to enable
these losses, and thus the sale price, to be ascertained.

And so the present proceedings by way of originating summons were issued on 10th
b January 1978, whereby the company seeks detailed relief, broadly under the following
heads: first, an account of receipts and payments; secondly, an account of how the
remuneration charged by the defendant has been calculated (it is simply in the abstract
a lump sum of £30,000 odd), or in the alternative, a general account from the receiver.
Then the company seeks delivery up of all books and papers or, alternatively, inspection.

The summons came before Mr Registrar Morris Jones at Liverpool on 23rd May 1978,
c and he, amongst other things, adjourned the summons to me to hear the issue between
the parties as to whether the defendant is an accounting party to the company, a
fundamental point and a point of law arising on the facts which I have briefly mentioned.

Counsel for the defendant conceded that if the case was one of what he called 'an
ordinary mortgage', the position would be untenable. The matter is dealt with in a few
lines in Kerr on Receivers[1] under the heading of 'Liability to the mortgagor'. It says:
d 'The mortgagor can maintain an action for an account against the receiver as his agent',
and for that proposition, which is unchallenged, a case[2] is quoted which I need not refer
to. I understand this to mean the ordinary case of the application of the statutory powers
under s 101 of the Law of Property Act 1925. Under sub-s (1)(iii) of that section, a
mortgagee is given the power when mortgage money has become due to appoint a
receiver; and sub-s (3) provides:

e   'The provisions of this Act relating to the foregoing powers, comprised either in
this section, or in any other section regulating the exercise of those powers, may be
varied or extended by the mortgage deed, and, as so varied or extended, shall, as far
as may be, operate in the like manner and with all the like incidents, effects and
consequences, as if such variations or extensions were contained in this Act.'

f It will be remembered that the debenture in the present case does in fact vary and extend
the statutory powers.

I take it then that it is conceded that where that power of appointment has been
exercised normally, the receiver is accountable to the mortgagor. I should refer to s 109
of the 1925 Act, which is one of the sections incorporated, with amendments, in the
debenture. It is headed: 'Appointment, powers, remuneration and duties of receiver'.
g Sub-section (2) provides:

        'A receiver appointed under the powers conferred by this Act, or any enactment
replaced by this Act, shall be deemed to be the agent of the mortgagor; and the
mortgagor shall be solely responsible for the receiver's acts or defaults unless the
mortgage deed otherwise provides.'

h It will be recalled that in the present case, far from otherwise providing, the mortgage
deed expressly says the same thing. Then s 109 refers to powers, and in sub-s (8) lays
down the order of application of moneys received by the receiver, an order which is
varied in the debenture, as I have found. Subsection (8) reads:

        'Subject to the provisions of this Act as to the application of insurance money, the
receiver shall apply all money received by him as follows, namely [then there is the
j list of priorities]; and shall pay the residue, if any, of the money received by him to
the person who, but for the possession of the receiver, would have been entitled to

---

1   15th Edn (1978) p 292
2   *Jefferys v Dickson* (1886) LR 1 Ch 183 at 190

receive the income of which he is appointed receiver, or who is otherwise entitled to the mortgaged property.'

So under s 109, I think there are at least two good reasons why the receiver is accountable to the mortgagor, the first being that he is the mortgagor's agent, a peculiar sort of agent of course, but nevertheless an agent, and an agent is prima facie an accountable party; and, secondly, because it must be deduced from the passage which I have last read, where the receiver is directed to pay the residue to the person entitled, that he must have kept an account so as to be able to know and demonstrate to others, particularly presumably to the mortgagor, what the residue is. This much, I think, is conceded.

But counsel for the defendant says that where the borrower is a company and the mortgage is therefore a debenture governed by the Companies Act 1948 and subsequent legislation, the position is different, for two reasons. First, he says, because the directors of the company remain in office and remain under their duty to keep accounts under what was s 147 of the Companies Act 1948 and is now s 12 of the Companies Act 1976; and, secondly, because the duty imposed by s 372(2) of the 1948 Act about abstracts of receipts and payments is a statutory duty and, taken with the duty of the directors to keep accounts, provides all that the company is entitled to. And he says this is confirmed by the fact that s 375 of the 1948 Act provides a summary remedy in the case of a receiver or manager failing to make proper returns or deliver the accounts or other documents which is given, not to the company, but to any member or creditor of the company or the Registrar of Companies. He says that these statutory rights are intended to replace any equitable right that the company might otherwise have had to call on its agent to account. He referred to, first, Re B Johnson & Co (Builders) Ltd[1] for various dicta, mainly about debentures, showing that when a receiver is appointed, and if he is a receiver and manager, he manages for the benefit primarily of the debenture holder. That was a case concerned with the question of whether a receiver and manager was an officer of the company for the purpose of misfeasance proceedings under s 333 of the 1948 Act, and was not directly in point. But although Evershed MR[2] pointed out that the power to appoint a receiver and manager and its subsequent exercise were intended to benefit and protect the mortgagee, that is not in my judgment inconsistent with the mortgagor having a right to an account. Indeed Jenkins LJ said[3]:

'. . . whereas a receiver and manager for debenture-holders is a person appointed by the debenture-holders to whom the company has given powers of management pursuant to the contract of loan constituted by the debenture and as a condition of obtaining the loan, to enable him to preserve and realise the assets comprised in the security for the benefit of the debenture-holders. The company gets the loan on terms that the lenders shall be entitled, for the purpose of making their security effective, to appoint a receiver with powers of sale and of management pending sale, and with full discretion as to the exercise and mode of exercising those powers. The primary duty of the receiver is to the debenture-holders and not to the company. He is receiver and manager of the property of the company for the debenture-holders, not manager of the company. The company is entitled to any surplus assets remaining after the debenture debt has been discharged, *and is entitled to proper accounts.*'

I emphasise those last words.

In the present case, perhaps unusually, the whole undertaking of the company has not been sold; the company has not gone into liquidation; it has pulled through. But this cannot, in my judgment, affect the liability of the receiver to account to the company for

1 [1955] 2 All ER 775, [1955] Ch 634
2 [1955] 2 All ER 775 at 779, [1955] Ch 634 at 644–645
3 [1955] 2 All ER 775 at 790, [1955] Ch 634 at 661–662

the assets remaining after the debt has been discharged, and this involves him producing

a proper accounts.

I think the same thing really is stated in a slightly different way in the other case which counsel for the defendant referred to, *R v Board of Trade, ex parte St Martin Preserving Co Ltd*[1], where Phillimore J said:

> 'There is clear authority for the proposition that, where a receiver and manager is appointed by the court, his function as manager confers a duty on him to preserve
> *b* the goodwill and property of the company, both in the interests of the mortgagee and of the mortgagor. [And he then refers to authorities.] If this is true for a manager appointed by the court, is it to be said that a manager appointed by a debenture holder to act as the agent of the company has no similar obligation? As previously stated, the fact that an action of the receiver and manager may be primarily designed to serve the interests of the debenture holder and to that extent
> *c* be his affair, does not, in my judgment, prevent it being an affair of the company, whose future may depend on such action carried out in its name. If he is the agent provided for in the debenture, why should he not be answerable for his conduct of "its affairs"?'

There, I think, one has the concept of the receiver being answerable to the company

d which, in my judgment, must mean keeping proper accounts. And if that is the duty of the receiver and therefore the right of the company, the company must have a remedy apart from s 375. During the receivership, the keeping of accounts obviously requires co-operation between the company and the receiver, because although the directors are still, I think, liable technically under s 147 of the 1948 Act and its successor[2], clearly they may have to get the necessary information from the receiver. He is to a very large extent

e running the company on the directors' behalf. I appreciate he is not managing the business strictly for the company, but he is the receiver of the property of the company, and the practicalities are that he is largely running the company on the directors' behalf, and it may, not necessarily will, be practically impossible for the directors to keep within their technical obligations without his assistance. He has a statutory obligation to produce these yearly abstracts of receipts and payments, and these in a long receivership

f can be complementary to the annual accounts of a company. But the documents required under s 372 are only abstracts, and that must mean, I think, that there are fuller accounts in the background. There would be accounts which the receiver, as the company's agent, is bound to keep and to produce to the company when required.

In my judgment, therefore, on the preliminary issue, the defendant is an accounting party to the company.

g

Order accordingly. Leave to appeal refused.

Solicitors: *Wilson Cowie & Dillon*, Liverpool (for the company); *Robert Muckle, Son & Hall*, Newcastle upon Tyne (for the defendant).

h   Mary Rose Plummer   Barrister.

---

1   [1964] 2 All ER 561 at 566, [1965] 1 QB 603 at 614
2   Section 12 of the Companies Act 1976

Stile Hall Properties Ltd v Gooch   *a*

COURT OF APPEAL, CIVIL DIVISION

DANCKWERTS, DAVIES AND EDMUND DAVIES LJJ

4th JULY 1968

Landlord and tenant – Business premises – Application for new tenancy – Request by tenant for
new tenancy – Request specifying date for commencement of new tenancy – Tenant not applying   *b*
to court for new tenancy within prescribed period – Tenant serving second request for new
tenancy two days before current tenancy due to terminate by virtue of first request – Second
request specifying later date for commencement of new tenancy than that in first request – Tenant
purporting to withdraw first request – Whether tenancy automatically determined immediately
before date specified in first request – Whether tenant entitled to withdraw valid request for a new
tenancy and serve fresh request specifying later commencement date – Landlord and Tenant Act   *c*
1954, ss 26(5), 29(3).

The tenant under a lease of business premises expiring on 6th January 1967 served on the
landlords on 20th March 1967 a notice under s 26ᵃ of the Landlord and Tenant Act 1954
requesting a new tenancy from 29th September. By virtue of s 26(5) the effect of the
notice was to continue the current tenancy until 28th September 1967. The tenant did   *d*
not however apply to the court for a new tenancy within four months as prescribed by
s 29(3)ᵇ of the 1954 Act. On 26th September, two days before the current tenancy (as
extended) would have terminated under s 26(5), the tenant served a second request for
a new tenancy specifying 24th June 1968 as the commencement date of the tenancy and
purported to withdraw the first request. The landlord brought proceedings against the   *e*
tenant claiming possession of the premises on the ground that the tenancy had
terminated on 28th September 1967 by virtue of the first request. The county court
judge made an order for possession and the tenant appealed.

Held – Where a tenant made a valid request for a new tenancy under s 26 of the 1954
Act specifying the date on which the tenancy was to commence then by virtue of s 26(5)   *f*
his current tenancy automatically terminated immediately before that date unless he
applied to the court for a new tenancy within the period prescribed by s 29(3) of that Act,
since the effect of the request by the tenant was to fix the date for the termination of the
current tenancy by reference to the date on which the new tenancy was to commence.
It followed that if a tenant failed to apply to the court within the prescribed period, he
lost his right to a new tenancy under the 1954 Act, because it would frustrate the scheme   *g*
of the Act if a tenant could serve successive requests for a new tenancy which prolonged
the current tenancy. Since the tenant had failed to apply to the court for a new tenancy
within the prescribed period from the date of the first request, the current tenancy had
terminated on 28th September 1967, and the landlords were accordingly entitled to
possession. The appeal would therefore be dismissed (see p 851 *a* to *j* and p 852 *a* to *f*,
post).   *h*

Notes

For a request for new tenancy of business premises, see 23 Halsbury's Laws (3rd Edn)
890, para 1712, for a tenant's right to apply to court for new tenancy, see ibid 891, para
1714, and for cases on the subject, see 31(2) Digest (Reissue) 949–955, 7742–7762.

For the Landlord and Tenant Act 1954, ss 26, 29, see 18 Halsbury's Statutes (3rd Edn)   *j*
561, 564.

---

a   Section 26, so far as material, is set out at p 850 *g* to *j*, post
b   Section 29(3) is set out at p 850 *d*, post

Appeal

a Mrs Mary Elizabeth Gooch ('the tenant') appealed against a judgment of his Honour Judge Sir Shirley Worthington-Evans given at Brentford County Court on 10th January 1968 whereby he made an order for possession of business premises at 1 Stile Hall Parade, Chiswick in favour of Stile Hall Properties Ltd ('the landlords') and awarded them mesne profits. The case is reported because of its significance in *Polyviou v Seeley*[1] The facts are set out in the judgment of Danckwerts LJ.

b
Christopher Beaumont for the tenant.
George Avgherinos for the landlords.

DANCKWERTS LJ. This is an appeal from a judgment of Sir Shirley Worthington-Evans, the county court judge at Brentford, on 10th January 1968. The appellant ('the
c tenant') was a tenant of the respondents ('the landlords') under a lease dated 21st March 1960 for seven years from 7th January 1960. The tenant has herself been there in this lock-up shop and basement since 1956. The rent was £225 a year, rising to £250 a year for the last four years.

I will refer to the first notice which is in the form required for an application under the Landlord and Tenant Act 1954. It was by the tenant in respect of 1 Stile Hall Parade,
d Chiswick, the shop where she carries on business. It requests the landlords to grant a new tenancy commencing on 29th September 1967:

'I propose that the property to be comprised in the new tenancy should be the lock up shop known as No. 1 Stile Hall Parade, Chiswick [and so on]. My proposals as to the rent to be payable under the new tenancy and as to the other terms of the new tenancy are £250 per annum and otherwise upon the terms of the present
e   Lease dated the 21st March 1960.'

Then there is a reference to s 26 of the 1954 Act. The date of that is 9th September 1966. That was invalid, because the period for the commencement of the tenancy was more than 12 months ahead.

Then a second notice in the statutory form was served by the tenant dated 20th March
f 1967. That was in respect of the same premises, proposing that the date for commencement of the new tenancy be 29th September 1967. The terms were again the same: £250 per annum for rent on the terms of the present lease dated 21st March 1960, for a period of 14 years from 29th September 1967.

Then the landlords suggested £400 a year. The result of that was a letter of 21st April 1967 on behalf of the tenant:

g   'With reference to your clients offer of a new Lease for seven years from the 25th March at £400 per annum subject to their paying your costs of approximately £22, Mrs Gooch feels that the rent is excessive and considers a rental of £300 per annum at most as advised by her Surveyor and also that any new Lease should not commence before the 29th September next.'

h The next letter is on 8th September 1967 from the landlords:

'We refer to the Notice served by your Client under the Landlord & Tenant Act 1954 dated 20th March, 1967 and expiring on the 29th September, 1967. As proceedings have not been commenced within the statutory four months, we therefore assume that your client will be vacating on the due date and will you please take your Client's instructions in regard to her vacation and for arrangements
j   to be made for our Clients' Surveyor to attend the premises and prepare a schedule of dilapidations.'

Subsequently the landlords' solicitors wrote:

---

1   Page 853, post

'We are in receipt of your letter of 13th September, upon which we have taken our Clients' instructions. In view of the subsequent correspondence that occurred *a* since our clients' offer, they inform us that they are not agreeable to reopening negotiations and wish your Client to vacate on 29th September in accordance with the Notice which you served on her behalf.'

On 26th September, 1967, the tenant's solicitors wrote to the landlords' solicitors:

'We enclose Tenant's request for a new tenancy of the above property. This is in *b* place of our client's earlier request dated 20th March 1967, which was withdrawn by our letter to Messrs. Palmer Paletz & Mark dated 21st April, 1967.'

The date of that letter is 26th September, two days before the expiration of the period ending on 28th September 1967. That proposed notice is in the statutory form and it appears to accept the landlords' proposed £400 per annum for the rent, for the terms of *c* the present lease and for a period of 14 years. Therefore there was an attempt by the tenant to withdraw her second notice, which was perfectly valid, and substitute a fresh one after the period of four months mentioned in s 29 had expired.
Section 29(3) provides as follows:

'No application under subsection (1) of section twenty-four of this Act shall be *d* entertained unless it is made not less than two nor more than four months after the giving of the landlord's notice under section twenty-five of this Act or, as the case may be, after the making of the tenant's request for a new tenancy.'

That period had, of course, expired by the time of the last request, and it is necessary to look at other provisions of the Act to see what is the effect of that.   *e*
Section 24(1) provides:

'A tenancy to which this Part of this Act applies shall not come to an end unless terminated in accordance with the provisions of this Part of this Act; and, subject to the provisions of section twenty-nine of this Act [we will have to refer to that] the tenant under such a tenancy may apply to the court for a new tenancy.'   *f*

The result of that is that after the expiration of the old lease, which expired in January 1968, the tenant's lease continued by s 24, subject to the provisions of the Act. There is a provision in s 25 for the termination of the tenancy by the landlord, with which I need not trouble further, because the landlord did nothing in respect of that provision.
The material provisions are found in s 26 as follows: *g*

'(3) A tenant's request for a new tenancy shall not have effect unless it is made by notice in the prescribed form given to the landlord and sets out the tenant's proposals as to the property to be comprised in the new tenancy (being either the whole or part of the property comprised in the current tenancy), as to the rent to be payable under the new tenancy and as to the other terms of the new tenancy.   *h*
'(4) A tenant's request for a new tenancy shall not be made if the landlord has already given notice under the last foregoing section to terminate the current tenancy, or if the tenant has already given notice to quit or notice under the next following section; and no such notice shall be given by the landlord or the tenant after the making by the tenant of a request for a new tenancy.
'(5) Where the tenant makes a request for a new tenancy in accordance with the *j* foregoing provisions of this section, the current tenancy shall, subject to the provisions of subsection (2) of section thirty-six of this Act [which are not material for the present purpose] and the provisions of Part IV of this Act as to the interim continuation of tenancies, terminate immediately before the date specified in the request for the beginning of the new tenancy.'

Therefore the effect of that was that when the tenant served her second notice it had
a the effect of determining the tenancy continued under s 24 on 28th September 1967, the
day immediately before, that is to say, the date she was asking for a new lease.

The only other thing to which I need refer is the passage in Woodfall on Landlord and
Tenant[1], in which it is observed:

b 'It is important to observe that if the tenant fails to make this application to the
court, irrespective of whether the landlord has served a notice of intention to
oppose, the current tenancy ends immediately before the date specified by the
tenant in his request for the commencement of the new tenancy and the tenant
loses his right to a new tenancy and indeed all his rights under the Act.'

Apparently there is no case which deals with the observation in Woodfall, and so far
as we have been informed no textbook or other book of that kind has commented on it
c in any way. It seems to me that the observation is plainly right. The effect of what the
tenant did was that, by her request, she fixed the date of the termination of the continued
tenancy that the Act conferred on her by s 24, by reference to the date when she was
asking for a new lease, and accordingly automatically, under the provisions of s 26, the
continued tenancy came to an end. That was the end of the matter, unless she had
followed it up within two or four months as required by s 29 by an application to the
d appropriate court. She made no such application and accordingly the tenancy determined
on 28th September 1967, and that is the end of the matter.

It seems to me that the county court judge plainly reached the right conclusion, and
this appeal must fail.

DAVIES LJ. I agree. After the first abortive attempt in September 1966 to make a
e request under the 1954 Act for a new tenancy, an attempt which was abortive because it
proposed a date for the commencement of the new tenancy more than 12 months ahead,
a perfectly valid request was made on 20th March 1967 for a tenancy commencing on
29th September. The effect of that request would be, under s 26(5) of the Act, to
terminate the current tenancy on 28th September 1967. Of course, if the tenant had
applied within the statutory period of four months the interim provisions for the
f continuation of the tenancy would have come into effect. But she did not. And
therefore once the four months had expired the tenancy was due to come to an end on
28th September.

Speaking for myself, I agree with the observations by the learned editor of Woodfall
which have been read by Danckwerts LJ. It would seem to me, as counsel for the
landlords suggests, to cut right across the intent of the Act if a tenant, such as the present
g tenant, having given a perfectly valid notice and having failed to take the necessary
follow-up step to apply to the court for a new lease, could a couple of days before the
statutory expiration of the tenancy serve (as was attempted to be done in the present case)
another notice for 24th June 1968, which would, under the statute, continue the tenancy
to 23rd June 1968, and then, I suppose, on 21st June serve another one, and so on and on
and on ad infinitum. The landlord would never know where he stood. The statute, as
h we all know, is an invasion of the landlord's right, for perfectly proper and sound reasons;
but it must be construed strictly in accordance with its terms, and I can see nothing
whatsoever in it that would permit the procedure that was adopted by the tenant in the
present case.

I entirely agree with Danckwerts LJ that this appeal, bravely as it is sought to be
supported by counsel on behalf of the tenant, is quite hopeless and should be dismissed.

j
EDMUND DAVIES LJ. Counsel for the landlords has rightly said that when one has
a statute of this kind which, albeit not a codification of the law, sets out to provide a
comprehensive scheme dealing with the position of landlords and tenants of premises

---

1   26th Edn (1960), vol 1, p 1410

coming within the Act, those who assert that either the landlord or the tenant has rights over and above and independent of that statutory scheme are confronted by a formidable task.

In the present case counsel for the tenant has had to struggle with a really impossible task and he has failed, despite his efforts, to discharge it. The suggestion put forward that it is open to the tenant, without the concurrence of the landlord, to withdraw his request for a new tenancy is one which would cut entirely across the statutory scheme. The Act vests radical rights in the tenant of business premises. It also recognises that the landlord also has certain rights and must be protected against exploitation and against harassment. If what is suggested here were indeed the position and the tenant could go on indefinitely serving the landlord with fresh requests, it appears to me that a quite impossible situation would result. The tenant having served an entirely valid request on 20th March 1967, it had certain legal consequences. If she did nothing more, s 26(5) came into operation and would operate to terminate that tenancy immediately before the date specified in the request for the beginning of the new tenancy, in this case on 28th September 1967. In order that the tenant should prevent that event occurring it was up to her, pursuant to s 29(3), to make an application to the court for a new tenancy, that application being made not less than two nor more than four months after the making of the tenant's request to the landlords for a new tenancy. This tenant never proceeded under s 29(3), and accordingly the landlords perfectly properly sent her solicitor a letter on 8th September 1967, in which they said: 'As proceedings have not been commenced within the statutory four months, we therefore assume that your Client will be vacating on the due date'. The result of that was, very belatedly, to evoke from the tenant the purported further request of 26th September, to which reference has already been made.

In my judgment that clearly will not do. The whole scheme would be frustrated were such a request to have any validity. I have no doubt, any more than Danckwerts and Davies LJJ have, that the learned editor of Woodfall has perfectly correctly expounded the effect of the Act, and particularly of the operation of s 26(5) and s 29(3), in the passage which has already been cited.

For those reasons I have no hesitation, with respect, in agreeing with Danckwerts and Davies LJJ that this appeal should be dismissed.

Appeal dismissed. Order for possession within 28 days.

Solicitors: *Bond & Banbury* (for the tenant); *Palmer, Paletz & Mark* (for the landlords).

Mary Rose Plummer   Barrister.

Polyviou v Seeley

COURT OF APPEAL, CIVIL DIVISION
MEGAW AND BROWNE LJJ
13th JULY 1979

Landlord and tenant – Business premises – Application for new tenancy – Request by tenant for new tenancy – Request specifying date for commencement of new tenancy – Tenant not applying to court for new tenancy within prescribed period – Tenant serving second request for new tenancy – Second request specifying same date for commencement as in first request – Tenant applying to court for new tenancy on basis of second request – Whether second request valid – Whether tenant entitled to serve second request where valid request already served – Whether application based on second request valid – Landlord and Tenant Act 1954, ss 26(5), 29(3).

On 11th August 1978 the tenant of business premises under a lease expiring on 15th July 1979 made a valid request to the landlord for a new tenancy, under s 26[a] of the Landlord and Tenant Act 1954, requesting a tenancy for three years commencing on 16th July 1979. On 5th September the landlord served a counter-notice stating that he would oppose the grant of a new tenancy on various grounds. The tenant did not apply to the court for a new tenancy under s 24(1)[b] of the 1954 Act, within the four months prescribed by s 29(3)[c] of that Act. On 12th January 1979 the tenant purported to make a second request to the landlord for a new tenancy of the premises, again requesting a three year term to run from 16th July 1979, i e from the same date as was specified in the first request. By a letter dated 26th January the landlord replied, contending that the second request was invalid because the previous request could not be withdrawn without his consent. On 15th March 1979 the tenant applied to the court for a new tenancy, basing his application on the second request. The county court judge held that the second request was invalid because of the existence of the first request, and refused the application. The tenant appealed, contending that the second request was a valid request because it specified the same date for commencement of the new tenancy as was specified in the first request, and not a later date.

Held – Once a tenant had made a valid request for a new tenancy specifying the commencement date of the new tenancy, he could not withdraw it and serve a fresh request at a later date, because, once a valid request had been served, s 26(5) of the 1954 Act operated to determine the current tenancy immediately before the date specified for commencement of the new tenancy unless the tenant, within the time prescribed by s 29(3) of that Act, applied to the court for a new tenancy. Since the tenant had failed to apply to the court within the prescribed time, he had lost the right to apply to the court for a new tenancy and could not withdraw the first request and make a second request in order to apply to the court within the time which would be the prescribed time were the second request valid. It followed that the appeal would be dismissed (see p 858 c e and g to p 859 a, post).

Stile Hall Properties Ltd v Gooch p 848, ante, applied.

Notes

For a request for a new tenancy of business premises, see 23 Halsbury's Laws (3rd Edn) 890, para 1712, for the tenant's right to apply to court for new tenancy, see ibid 891, para 1714, and for cases on the subject, see 31(2) Digest (Reissue) 949–955, 7742–7762.

For the Landlord and Tenant Act 1954, ss 24, 26, 29, see 18 Halsbury's Statutes (3rd Edn) 557, 561, 564.

---

a   Section 26, so far as material, is set out at p 855 *b c*, post
b   Section 24(1) is set out at p 855 *a b*, post.
c   Section 29(3) is set out at p 855 *d e*, post

Case referred to in judgment
Stile Hall Properties Ltd v Gooch p 848, ante.

a

Appeal
This was an appeal by Polyvious Polyviou ('the tenant') from an order by his Honour
Judge Hutton made on 1st May 1979 in the Bristol County Court whereby he held on a
preliminary point that the tenant's request for a new tenancy of premises known as Le *b*
Chalut Restaurant, St Paul's Road, Bristol, made to George Andrew Seeley ('the landlord')
pursuant to the Landlord and Tenant Act 1954, was not a valid request and that an
application to the court based on it for a new tenancy of the premises was also invalid.
The facts are set out in the judgment of Browne LJ.

Roderick Denyer for the tenant.   *c*
James Wigmore for the landlord.

BROWNE LJ delivered the first judgment at the request of Megaw LJ. This is an
appeal from a decision of his Honour Judge Hutton given at the Bristol County Court on *d*
1st May 1979. He gave judgment for the respondent landlord on a preliminary point
arising under the Landlord and Tenant Act 1954. The appellant is the tenant (and I shall
so call him); and the landlord is the respondent in this court. His Honour Judge Hutton
held that the tenant's application for a new tenancy under that Act was out of time and
invalid, and that his request for a new tenancy on which the application to the court was
based was not a valid request. The result of that decision on the preliminary point is that *e*
the tenant has lost his right to apply for a new tenancy under the 1954 Act.
    The history of this case is as follows. By a lease dated 4th March 1977 for three years
from 16th July 1976, the present landlord granted to a Mr Serrat a lease for three years
of the premises with which we are concerned, which are premises in St Paul's Road,
Bristol, which were and are used as a restaurant. By an assignment and other operations
that lease became vested first in the present tenant and his brother and later in the tenant *f*
himself alone. In those premises the tenant carried on, and carries on, the business of a
restaurant. That tenancy, being for three years from 16th July 1976, would expire on
15th July 1979.
    On 11th August 1978 the tenant made a request for a new tenancy pursuant to the
1954 Act. It asks for a new tenancy commencing on 16th July 1979; and it asks for a
fresh tenancy of, again, three years. On 5th September the landlord served a counter- *g*
notice to that, setting out various grounds on which he stated that he proposed to oppose
any application to the court for the grant of that new tenancy. Nothing more happened
about that request. No application was made to the court within the time limited by the
Act, which would have been between 11th October 1978 and 11th December 1978.
However, on 12th January 1979 the tenant made, or purported to make, a further
request for a new tenancy. It relates to these premises, the Le Chalut Restaurant, St Paul's *h*
Road, and it again asks for a new tenancy beginning on the same day as that specified in
the first request, that is, 16th July 1979. It again asks for a fresh term of three years. In
reply to that, by letter dated 26th January, the landlord took the point that this request
was invalid because of the previous request, and also repeated in the alternative the same
grounds as those set out in his previous counter-notice, saying that he would object to the
grant of a new tenancy.
    The application to the court for a new tenancy, based on that request, was dated 15th *j*
March 1979; and it was a preliminary point in respect of that application which came
before his Honour Judge Hutton on 1st May. It sets out the history as I have stated it.
It does not refer to the first request for a new tenancy and is based on the request of 12th
January 1979.

The relevant provisions of the Landlord and Tenant Act 1954 are as follows:

a   '24.—(1) A tenancy to which this Part of this Act applies shall not come to an end unless terminated in accordance with the provisions of this Part of this Act; and, subject to the provisions of section twenty-nine of this Act, the tenant under such a tenancy may apply to the court for a new tenancy . . . (b) if the tenant has made a request for a new tenancy in accordance with section twenty-six of this Act . . .

b   '26 . . . (2) A tenant's request for a new tenancy shall be for a tenancy beginning with such date, not more than twelve nor less than six months after the making of the request, as may be specified therein . . .

'(3) A tenant's request for a new tenancy shall not have effect unless it is made by notice in the prescribed form given to the landlord and sets out the tenant's proposals [It is accepted, I think, that in this case both the requests which were made were made in the prescribed form.]

c   '(5) Where the tenant makes a request for a new tenancy in accordance with the foregoing provisions of this section, the current tenancy shall [subject to certain other provisions as to the interim continuation of tenancies] terminate immediately before the date specified in the request for the beginning of the new tenancy.'

Then sub-s (6) provides for a counter-notice by the landlord.

d   Section 29 (3) provides:

'No application under sub-section (1) of section twenty-four of this Act shall be entertained unless it is made not less than two nor more than four months after the giving of the landlord's notice under section twenty-five of this Act or, as the case may be, after the making of the tenant's request for a new tenancy.'

e   It was because of that section, as I have said, that the application to the court, if it had been made as a result of the first request of 11th August 1978 would have had to be made between 11th October and 11th December 1978.

The county court judge based his decision on the view that this case was indistinguishable from an earlier decision of this court in *Stile Hall Properties Ltd v Gooch*[1]. The judge was supplied, and we have been supplied, with a transcript of the judgment of this court in that case, which consisted of Danckwerts, Davies and Edmund *f* Davies LJJ. The facts in that case, as they appear from the judgment, are these. The appellant, Mrs Gooch, was the tenant of property in Brentford under a lease dated 21st March 1960 for seven years from 7th January 1960. So that that lease would have expired on 6th January 1967. The tenant first gave a notice on 9th September 1966, but that notice was invalid because the date specified for the commencement of the new lease was more than 12 months after the date of the notice and was therefore invalid under the *g* provisions of the Act which I have read. Then a second notice was served, dated 20th March 1967. That proposed that the date of commencement of the new tenancy should be 29th September 1967, and that the lease should be for 14 years. Nothing was done under that notice by way of making an application to the court. On 8th September 1967 the landlords wrote and said: 'As proceedings have not been commenced within the statutory four months, we therefore assume that your client will be vacating on the due *h* date'. As a result of that, on 26th September 1967, that being only two or three days before the termination of the tenancy by virtue of the previous notice, the tenant's solicitors wrote to the landlord's solicitors:

'We enclose tenant's request for a new tenancy of the above property. This is in place of our client's earlier request dated 20th March 1967, which was withdrawn *j* by our letter . . . dated 21st April 1967.'

That enclosed a notice which was in the statutory form and which specified 24th June 1968 as the date for the commencement of the new tenancy, that being, of course, about

---

1   Page 848, ante

nine months later than the date which had been specified in the previous request for a
new tenancy.   *a*
Danckwerts LJ said[1]:

> 'Therefore there was an attempt by the tenant to withdraw her second notice,
> which was perfectly valid, and substitute a fresh one after the period of four months
> mentioned in s 29 had expired.'

Danckwerts LJ then went through the relevant provisions of the Act, and said[2]:   *b*

> 'The only other thing to which I need refer is the passage in Woodfall on Landlord
> and Tenant[3], in which it is observed: "It is important to observe that if the tenant
> fails to make this application to the court, irrespective of whether the landlord has
> served a notice of intention to oppose, the current tenancy ends immediately before
> the date specified by the tenant in his request for the commencement of the new
> tenancy and the tenant loses his right to a new tenancy and indeed all his rights   *c*
> under the Act." Apparently there is no case which deals with the observation in
> Woodfall, and so far as we have been informed no textbook or other book of that
> kind has commented on it in any way. It seems to me that the observation is plainly
> right. The effect of what the tenant did was that, by her request, she fixed the date
> of the termination of the continued tenancy that the Act conferred on her by s 24,
> by reference to the date when she was asking for a new lease, and accordingly   *d*
> automatically, under the provisions of s 26, the continued tenancy came to an end.
> That was the end of the matter, unless she had followed it up within two or four
> months as required by s 29 by an application to the appropriate court. She made no
> such application and accordingly the tenancy determined on 28th September 1967,
> and that is the end of the matter.'

Davies LJ referred to the request of March 1967, and said[2]:   *e*

> 'The effect of that request would be, under s 26(5) of the Act, to terminate the
> current tenancy on 28th September 1967. Of course, if the tenant had applied
> within the statutory period of four months the interim provisions for the
> continuation of the tenancy would have come into effect. But she did not. And
> therefore once the four months had expired the tenancy was due to come to an end   *f*
> on 28th September. Speaking for myself, I agree with the observations by the
> learned editor of Woodfall which have been read by Danckwerts LJ. It would seem
> to me, as counsel for the landlords suggests, to cut right across the intent of the Act
> if a tenant, such as the present tenant, having given a perfectly valid notice and
> having failed to take the necessary follow-up step to apply to the court for a new
> lease, could a couple of days before the statutory expiration of the tenancy serve (as   *g*
> was attempted to be done in the present case) another notice for 24th June 1968,
> which would, under the statute, continue the tenancy to 23rd June 1968, and then,
> I suppose, on 21st June serve another one, and so on and on and on ad infinitum.'

Pausing there, it is that last sentence on which counsel for the tenant particularly relies;
and I will come back to that later. Davies LJ[2] went on: *h*

> 'The landlord would never know where he stood. The statute, as we all know, is
> an invasion of the landlord's right, for perfectly proper and sound reasons; but it
> must be construed strictly in accordance with its terms, and I can see nothing
> whatsoever in it that would permit the procedure that was adopted by the tenant in

                                                                              j

---

1   See p 850, ante
2   See p 851, ante
3   26th Edn (1960), vol 1, ch 23, p 1410, para 2780. See now 28th Edn (1978), vol 2, ch 22, p 2395,
    para 2–0680

the present case. I entirely agree with Danckwerts LJ that this appeal, bravely as it
is sought to be supported by counsel on behalf of the tenant, is quite hopeless and
should be dismissed.'

Edmund Davies LJ said[1]:

'In the present case counsel for the tenant has had to struggle with a really
impossible task and he has failed, despite his efforts, to discharge it. The suggestion
put forward that it is open to the tenant, without the concurrence of the landlord,
to withdraw his request for a new tenancy is one which would cut entirely across the
statutory scheme. The Act vests radical rights in the tenant of business premises.
It also recognises that the landlord also has certain rights and must be protected
against exploitation and against harassment. If what is suggested here were indeed
the position and the tenant could go on indefinitely serving the landlord with fresh
requests, it appears to me that a quite impossible situation would result. The tenant
having served an entirely valid request on 20th March 1967, it had certain legal
consequences. If she did nothing more, s 26(5) came into operation and would
operate to terminate that tenancy immediately before the date specified in the
request for the beginning of the new tenancy, in this case on 28th September
1967. In order that the tenant should prevent that event occurring it was up to her,
pursuant to s 29(3), to make an application to the court for a new tenancy, that
application being made not less than two nor more than four months after the
making of the tenant's request to the landlords for a new tenancy. This tenant
never proceeded under s 29(3), and accordingly the landlords perfectly properly sent
her a letter on 8th September 1967, in which they said [that they assumed that as no
application had been made the tenant would be giving up possession]. The result
of that was, very belatedly, to evoke from the tenant the purported further request
of 26th September, to which reference has already been made. In my judgment
that clearly will not do. The whole scheme would be frustrated were such a request
to have any validity. I have no doubt, any more than Danckwerts and Davies LJJ
have, that the learned editor of Woodfall has perfectly correctly expounded the
effect of the Act, and particularly of the operation of s 26(5) and s 29(3), in the
passage which has already been cited.'

All three of their Lordships, accordingly, had no hesitation in dismissing the appeal.

When this matter came before his Honour Judge Hutton, he set out the facts in his
judgment and referred to the relevant provisions of the Act, and to the applications. He
went on:

'Counsel [who appeared for the landlord there, as he has here] has submitted that
it was only possible for the tenant to make one request. That once a request is made
the procedure starts working. The clock starts running and cannot be stopped and
started again by a further request.'

He then referred to the *Stile Hall* case[2] and said: 'That case is similar to this one in all
respects except one.' Then he referred to the judgments of Danckwerts and Edmund
Davies LJJ and quoted the passages which I have already quoted, including the quotation
from Woodfall. He went on:

'That case is distinguished by counsel for the tenant. In the *Stile Hall* case[2], he
says, the final request used a different date for the start of a new tenancy, a later
date. So there was there a complete lack of merit on behalf of the tenant who was
simply stalling for more time. Counsel for the tenant submits that here the same

---

1   See p 852, ante
2   Page 848, ante

date is requested, so no hardship could be alleged and the landlord is being purely
technical and lacking in merit. He further says that the Act in itself does not   *a*
provide that no further request can be made. I reject the submissions by the
tenant. The *Stile Hall* case[1] sets out the law not only on the facts of that case but
generally, and the findings in that case apply equally here. Merit has no relevance
to the decisions. The landlord is entitled to rely on the provisions of the Act, as set
out by the court in *Stile Hall*[1]. Therefore the tenant's application is invalid as being
out of time following the original request.'   *b*

Counsel for the tenant in this court has sought valiantly to distinguish the *Stile Hall*
case[1], on the same ground as that on which he relied before the judge, that is, that the
ground of the decision in the *Stile Hall* case[1] was that the second request specified a date
for the commencement of the new tenancy which was different from and later than that
specified in the first request; whereas here the second request specified the same date.

It seems to me that the ratio of the *Stile Hall* case[1] was this. By virtue of s 26(5) the *c*
existing tenancy terminates immediately before the date specified in the request for a
new tenancy, unless the tenant within the time specified by s 29(3) makes an application
to the court. If he does make an application, the tenancy continues till three months
after the final disposal of the proceedings: see s 64. But if the tenant does not make such
an application, the tenancy automatically comes to an end on that date. If the tenant fails
to make an application within the proper time, he cannot withdraw the first request and *d*
make another. In the *Stile Hall* case[1] the court was obviously impressed by the hardship
to the landlord if the tenant could go on serving successive notices and so continuing the
tenancy ad infinitum. Here, of course, the tenant is not trying to do any such thing. It
is true that the particular hardship to the landlord which impressed this court in the *Stile
Hall* case[1] would not arise in this case. But I find it impossible to distinguish this case
from *Stile Hall*[1] on the ground put forward by counsel for the tenant.   *e*

I have already read s 29(3) and I need not read it in full again; but it provides that no
application under sub-s (1) of s 24 of the Act 'shall be entertained' unless it is made within
the specified time. Counsel for the tenant accepts that the first request was a valid
request and that it had one of the consequences laid down; that is, the consequence of
terminating the tenancy on 15th July 1979. He does not explicitly ask to withdraw that
request, but in substance I think that is really what he does ask; that is, that the request *f*
should be treated as withdrawn so as to allow the application based on the second request
to be made. In *Stile Hall*[1] this court held that the first notice could not be withdrawn. If
counsel for the tenant's submission were right, I can see no reason why a tenant should
not specify a later date in his second request than the date specified in his first request.
It seems to me that in principle this case is indistinguishable from the *Stile Hall* case[1]. It
seems to me that the case is exactly covered by the passage from the judgment of *g*
Danckwerts LJ[2] which I have already read. I do not think I need read it again; it is the
passage which begins 'The effect of what the tenant did was that, by her request, she fixed
the date of the termination of the continued tenancy' and ends with the words 'and that
is the end of the matter'.

In spite of counsel for the tenant's very brave attempt to distinguish *Stile Hall*[1], it seems
to me that it is quite impossible to distinguish that case from this; that decision is *h*
binding on this court; and accordingly this appeal must, in my judgment, be dismissed.

MEGAW LJ. I agree with the order proposed by Browne LJ, for the reasons given by
him.

Counsel for the tenant, with, if I may say so, proper and admirable economy of words, *j*

---

1   Page 848, ante
2   See p 851, ante

a has put forward his submission that there is a material distinction between the ratio decidendi of the decision of this court in the *Stile Hall* case[1] and the present case. In my judgment there is no such material distinction.

The only other thing that I should add, in case it might be of relevance in certain other contexts, is that the solicitors who have represented the tenant on the hearing of the preliminary issue in the county court and again on the appeal in this court are not the same as the solicitors who apparently, as agents for the appellant in this appeal, put *b* forward notices of 11th August 1978 and 12th January 1979 and the formal application for a new tenancy of 15th March 1979.

Appeal dismissed. Leave to appeal to the House of Lords refused.

Solicitors: *Church, Adams, Tatham & Co*, agents for *Leaman, Sparks & Co*, Bristol (for the *c* tenant); *Donald Bennett & Legat*, Bristol (for the landlord).

Mary Rose Plummer   Barrister.

d
Practice Direction
FAMILY DIVISION

Probate – Practice – Documents – Testamentary documents – Fiat copies – Photographic facsimiles.

e To assist in the preparation of fiat copies of testamentary documents, it has been decided that, subject to the registrar's discretion, as an alternative to typewritten engrossments, facsimile copies produced by photography may be used in the following circumstances:
  1. where a complete page or pages are to be excluded,
  2. where words on the same page below the testator's signature can be excluded by *f* masking out, and
  3. where the original has been altered but not re-executed or republished and there exists a photocopy of the original executed document.

This extended practice will apply in the district probate registries and sub-registries as well as in the Principal Registry.

g   R L BAYNE-POWELL
8th November 1979   Senior Registrar.

---

1   Page 848, ante

Lothbury Investment Corporation Ltd v Inland Revenue Commissioners

a

CHANCERY DIVISION
GOULDING J
2nd, 3rd, 4th JULY 1979

b

Income tax – Close company – Apportionment of income – Apportionment for surtax – Undistributed income – Manner of apportionment – Apportionment of income on basis of interest in winding-up – Special Commissioners' jurisdiction to review the decision – Income and Corporation Taxes Act 1970, s 296(5)(10).

The taxpayer company was a non-trading close company. For the year ended 31st March *c* 1971, the Board of Inland Revenue made apportionments of its income for surtax purposes among the participators of the company. The apportionment was made by reference to the participators' interests in the event of a winding-up under s 296(5)[a] of the Income and Corporation Taxes Act 1970, rather than, as was normal, by reference to the participators' interests in income under s 296(4) of that Act. The taxpayer company appealed contending, inter alia, (a) that on the merits the Board's decision to invoke *d* s 296(5) was not justified, (b) that under s 296(10) the Special Commissioners had power to review the merits of the Board's decision and (c) that in the exercise of those powers the Special Commissioners should substitute whatever decision they thought proper. The Special Commissioners upheld the apportionment, holding that the review contemplated by sub-s (10) was limited to cases where it seemed to them that the Board had exceeded their powers and not genuinely exercised their discretion. They further held that the *e* case before them was not such a case and that, in any event, in the circumstances and in the light of the evidence before them, it was proper for the Board to have made the apportionment on a 'winding-up interest' basis rather than on the 'interest in income' basis. The taxpayer company appealed.

Held – On an appeal against apportionment of income of a close company amongst its *f* participators on the basis of their respective interests in the assets of the company in the event of a winding-up of the company, the Special Commissioners had, under s 296(10) of the 1970 Act, a right and a duty to form their own view of the whole matter and, if necessary, substitute their decision for that of the Board if persuaded on any ground that the decision of the Board was wrong. However, on the facts before the Special Commissioners and, having regard to the unfettered quality of the power given to the *g* Board by s 296(5), it could not be said that the Board had acted outside their powers in deciding to apportion the income of the company on the basis of the participators' interest in the event of a winding-up, and accordingly the Special Commissioners had not erred in law in affirming the Board's decision. The appeal would therefore be dismissed (p 870 *j* to p 871 *b*, p 873 *j*, p 874 *a b* and p 875 *b c*, post).

Penang and General Investment Trust Ltd v Inland Revenue Comrs [1943] 1 All ER 514 *h* followed.

Notes

For the apportionment of a close company's income, see 23 Halsbury's Laws (4th Edn) paras 1211–1234.

For the Income and Corporation Taxes Act 1970, s 296, see 33 Halsbury's Statutes (3rd *j* Edn) 403.

In relation to accounting periods ending after 5th April 1973, s 296(5) and (10) was replaced by the Finance Act 1972, Sch 16, paras 4(2), 16(3).

---

a Section 296, so far as material, is set out at p 867 *e* to p 868 *b*, post

Cases referred to in judgment

a *Associated Provincial Pictures Houses Ltd v Wednesbury Corpn* [1947] 2 All ER 680, [1948]
1 KB 223, [1948] LJR 190, 177 LT 641, 112 JP 55, CA, 45 Digest (Repl) 215, *189*.

Penang and General Investment Trust Ltd v Inland Revenue Comrs [1943] 1 All ER 514,
[1943] AC 486, 25 Tax Cas 219, 112 LJKB 356, 169 LT 93, HL; *affg* [1942] 1 All ER
290, [1942] 1 KB 420, 25 Tax Cas 219, CA, 28(1) Digest (Reissue) 415, *1509*.

Robinson v Minister of Town and Country Planning, Re City of Plymouth (City Centre)
b *Declaratory Order 1946* [1947] 1 All ER 851, [1947] KB 702, [1947] LJR 1285, 177 LT
375, 111 JP 378, 45 LGR 497, CA, 45 Digest (Repl) 366, *158*.

Sagnata Investments Ltd v Norwich Corpn [1971] 2 All ER 1441, [1971] QB 614, [1971] 3
WLR 133, 69 LGR 471, CA, Digest (Cont Vol D) 358, *316ae*.

Stepney Borough Council v Joffe [1949] 1 All ER 256, [1949] 1 KB 599, [1949] LJR 561, 113
JP 124, 47 LGR 189, DC, 26 Digest (Repl) 483, *1694*.

c

Cases also cited

Central and District Properties Ltd v Inland Revenue Comrs [1966] 2 All ER 433, [1966] 1
WLR 1015, HL.

Comr of Stamp Duties of New South Wales v Pearse [1954] 1 All ER 19, [1954] AC 91, PC.

Essex v Inland Revenue Comrs [1979] STC 525.

d *Evans v Bartlam* [1937] 2 All ER 646, [1937] AC 473, HL.

Inland Revenue Comrs v Fred's Securities Co [1939] 3 All ER 241, [1939] 2 KB 734, 22 Tax
Cas 445.

Wilover Nominees Ltd v Inland Revenue Comrs [1974] 3 All ER 496, [1974] 1 WLR 1342,
[1974] STC 467, CA.

e

Case stated

1. At a meeting of the Commissioners for the Special Purposes of the Income Tax Acts
held on 21st, 22nd March and 5th April 1977 Lothbury Investment Corpn Ltd ('the
taxpayer company') appealed against apportionments of its income for surtax purposes
made under s 78 of the Finance Act 1965 and s 259 of the Income Tax Act 1952, for the
f accounting period ended 31st March 1970 and under ss 296 and 298 of the Income and
Corporation Taxes Act 1970, for the accounting period ended 31st March 1971 among
participators (as defined in Sch 18 to the 1965 Act and s 303 of the 1970 Act). Particulars
of the apportionments were as follows:

	Period ended 31st March 1970 £	Period ended 31st March 1971 £
g		
Preference shareholders	26,361	40,093
Mr Isidore Ostrer ('Isidore')	16,681	23,304
Mr Maurice Ostrer ('Maurice')	6,484	8,504
Mrs S Castlemount ('Mrs		
h Castlemount')	1,022	1,555
Balance	1	1
	50,549	73,457

2. In making the apportionments the Commissioners of Inland Revenue ('the Board')
j proceeded under s 78(5) of the 1965 Act and s 259(1) of the 1952 Act for the period ended
31st March 1970 and under s 296(5) of the 1970 Act for the period ended 31st March
1971, thus attributing to each participator in the taxpayer company an interest
corresponding to his interest in the assets of the taxpayer company available for
distribution among them in the event of a winding-up. The main question for decision
was whether the commissioners had jurisdiction to review the Board's choice of this

method of apportionment instead of the more usual method of apportionment by
reference to the participators' interests in income. The statutory provisions applicable to **a**
the taxpayer company's accounting period ended 31st March 1970 were re-enacted, on
consolidation, in the 1970 Act, and the case was argued before the commissioners by
reference to the period ended 31st March 1971, to which the 1970 Act applied, on the
understanding that a decision in principle for that period would apply also to the period
ended 31st March 1970.

[Paragraph 3 listed the documents proved or admitted before the commissioners.] **b**

4. The following facts were admitted between the parties: (1) The taxpayer company
was incorporated on 25th August 1919. At all material times it was, for the purposes of
ss 296 and 298 of the 1970 Act (and for the purposes of statutory provisions thereby
reproduced on consolidation) a close company which was not a trading company. (2)
Throughout both relevant accounting periods the issued share capital of the taxpayer
company fell into two classes, held as follows: **c**

Ordinary shares (of £1 each)	
Isidore	111,613
Maurice	73,387
Total	185,000

d

6% preference shares (of £1 each)	
Trustees of a family settlement	
dated 30th November 1960 made	
by Isidore	400,000
Trustees of a family settlement	
dated 30th November 1960 made	
by Maurice	266,667
Sundry individuals	106,500
Total	773,167

e

(3) Also throughout the two relevant accounting periods the taxpayer company owed **f**
the following debts to 'loan creditors' as defined in s 303(7) of the 1970 Act (and in the
provisions thereby re-enacted on consolidation): to Isidore, £200,000, and to Mrs
Castlemount, £30,000. Mrs Castlemount was the sister of Isidore and Maurice. She died
on 9th September 1971 and left the whole of her estate to Maurice. (4) The ordinary
shares had been in issue for many years. The preference shares were issued for full
consideration in 1960 in two ways, as follows: (a) 94,630 in exchange for 473,150 shares **g**
in Illingworth Morris & Co Ltd ('IMCL') acquired from Isidore and Maurice. £94,630
was the market value at the time the IMCL shares were acquired. (b) 678,537 in
consideration of £678,537 in cash, made up as follows: Isidore's Settlement, £400,000;
Maurice's Settlement, £266,667; Maurice and Isidore, £11,870. The £678,537 was then
applied by the taxpayer company in purchasing from Isidore and Maurice a holding of **h**
IMCL shares at the current market value. Isidore and Maurice immediately disposed of
the 106,500 preference shares subscribed for by them as mentioned in (a) and (b) above,
and they did not thereafter own any preference shares in the taxpayer company. (5) In
1960 when the preference shares were issued 6% was a normal rate for preference
dividends. The preference dividends were paid in full for both the relevant accounting
periods. No dividend was paid on the ordinary shares for the accounting period ended **j**
31st March 1970 but a dividend of £16,650 gross was paid for the period ended 31st
March 1971. (6) The loan of £200,000 to the taxpayer company from Isidore was made
on 1st October 1966 to enable the taxpayer company to reduce a bank overdraft incurred
mainly in 1964 to provide funds for the taxpayer company to take up a rights issue made
by IMCL. Interest was paid on the loan at 6½% per annum for the three months to

December 1966 but throughout the two accounting periods concerned in the appeal no
a interest was paid. The revenue accounts for both years contain a deduction for 'Loan
Interest (less £13,000 waived . . .)'. In their letter of 8th March 1972 the taxpayer
company's auditors stated that Isidore waived the whole of the interest on the loan. The
£13,000 referred to was the interest which would have been payable if Isidore had
charged interest at 6½% for the year. The loan was repaid on 12th June 1973. The
arrangements concerning the loan were, however, always a matter of informal
b agreement. There was no written contract. (7) The loan of £30,000 to the taxpayer
company from Mrs Castlemount was made on 20th December 1967. Interest was paid
at the rate of 7% per annum until 30th June 1970 and thereafter at the rate of 10½% per
annum until 30th June 1972. The loan was repaid to Mrs Castlemount's estate as
follows:

c
3rd November 1972	£8,000
22nd December 1972	£10,000
31st December 1973	£10,000
26th November 1974	£2,000

The arrangements concerning the loan were a matter of informal agreement and there
d was no written loan contract. (8) The taxpayer company had at all material times been
an investment company. Throughout the two relevant accounting periods its main
investments were its holdings of IMCL shares, particulars of which were given in the
notes to the accounts. In those accounting periods it waived certain of the dividends
which it might otherwise have received on its IMCL shares. Details of the waivers also
appear in the notes to the accounts. (9) The waiving or non-charging by Isidore of
interest on his loan to the taxpayer company and the waiving by the taxpayer company
e of dividends on its IMCL holding were related in the sense that the taxpayer company
decided on the size of its dividend waivers in the knowledge that it would not have to
provide for interest on the loan. In both of the accounting years to which the appeal
related the dividends waived substantially exceeded the interest which would have been
payable on the loan if it had been charged at 6½% (the rate at which interest was charged
f for the first three months of the loan's existence in 1966). If interest had been charged
on the loan the dividend waivers by the taxpayer company would have been smaller, so
that the taxpayer company would still have had sufficient income to pay the full
dividends on its preference shares. (10) For the period ended 31st March 1971 the
taxpayer company's investment income amounted to £73,768 and the 'required standard'
as defined in s 290 of the 1970 Act was £73,457, representing franked investment
income of £73,546 less the excess (£89) of the sum of management expenses and interest
g paid over the sum of chargeable gains and unfranked investment income. (11) After
giving the matter due consideration the Board saw reason to apportion the taxpayer
company's income for the two relevant accounting periods under ss 296 and 298 of the
1970 Act and they thought it proper to make such apportionments by reference to
s 296(5). The commissioners were informed that it had been stated on behalf of the
h Board that the prime reason for the apportionments was the existence of the interest-free
loans. However, they were informed by Mr A L L Alexander, who appeared on behalf
of the Board, that the Board's action in making apportionments on this basis was justified
because Isidore was prepared to forgo interest due on his loan the taxpayer company
could afford to take less by way of dividend from IMCL, thus swelling the funds of IMCL
and improving the market value of its shares and so indirectly benefiting the shareholders
j in the taxpayer company.
    5. It was contended on behalf of the taxpayer company: (1) that there was no
appropriate case for apportionment under s 298(2) of the 1970 Act; (2) that, if such
apportionment was appropriate, (a) the amount which the Board sought to apportion was
excessive and should be reduced by reference to management expenses and yearly
interest paid by the taxpayer company, two alternative bases of reduction being put

forward; (b) the Special Commissioners who heard the appeal had jurisdiction under s
296(10) of the 1970 Act to review the Board's decision to apportion by reference to s   *a*
296(5) and to substitute whatever decision we thought proper; (c) on the merits the
Board's decision to invoke s 296(5) was not justified because (i) in general the sort of case
in which apportionment under s 296(5) was proper was where (usually, but not
necessarily, as part of an avoidance scheme) the income of an investment company was
artificially diverted from those who might be regarded as the true beneficial owners, (ii)
the present was not such a case; none of the participators in the taxpayer company   *b*
received more than a proper return on his capital, and also, if one looked through the
taxpayer company's corporate personality, none of the income which in fact went to
preference shareholders would have gone to Isidore or Maurice, (iii) it produced an unfair
result, and in particular it was inappropriate to 're-allocate' income which had been
actually distributed to preference shareholders, (iv) the waivers by the taxpayer company
of dividends from IMCL provided no justification for the apportionments; an   *c*
apportionment related to the income which a close company in fact received, and where
that income was distributed in a natural and straightforward way an apportionment of
it could not be justified by reference to different income which the close company might
have received but in fact did not receive, (v) the Board's real complaint was not against
any misdistribution of the taxpayer company's income but rather against the under-
distribution of IMCL's income; it was entirely wrong to seek to remedy that complaint   *d*
by an apportionment made on the taxpayer company as opposed to IMCL; (d) that, if
apportionment by reference to s 296(5) had to stand in principle, then in calculating the
amount to be apportioned to each participator a discount should be allowed from the
quoted value of the taxpayer company's shares in IMCL to allow for the effect of
marketing a holding of that magnitude.

6. It was contended on behalf of the Crown: (1) that it was appropriate to make the   *e*
apportionment by reference to s 298(2) and s 296(5) of the 1970 Act; (2) that *Penang and
General Investment Trust Ltd v Inland Revenue Comrs*[1] was authority for regarding the
Board as having an unfettered discretion to apportion by reference to participators'
interests in the event of a winding-up; (3) that s 296(10), being a re-enactment on
consolidation of provisions of more general application in Sch 4 to the Income Tax
Management Act 1964, which reflected the change in functions of the Special   *f*
Commissioners from a mixture of administrative and judicial functions to an almost
exclusively judicial function, did not confer on the commissioners jurisdiction to review
the merits of the Board's decision to invoke s 296(5); (4) that the commissioners were
only empowered to interfere with the exercise of the Board's discretion if it were to
appear to them on the evidence that the Board had failed to consider the matter or had
exercised their discretion in an oppressive fashion; (5) that if, contrary to the submissions   *g*
made on behalf of the Crown, the commissioners had power to review the merits of their
decision to invoke s 296(5) they should find that the decision was proper: Isidore, by
forgoing interest had enabled the taxpayer company to take less by dividends from IMCL
with the result that the assets of the taxpayer company (in which Isidore was a major
shareholder) were correspondingly increased thereby increasing the value of Isidore's
stake in IMCL; (6) that the word 'income' in s 298(2) must be read literally and there was   *h*
no justification for reducing by reference to management expenses and interest paid by
the taxpayer company the amount to be apportioned; (7) that in calculating the amount
to be apportioned under s 296(5) to each participator there were no grounds for allowing
any discount from the quoted value of the taxpayer company's shares in IMCL. The
specific valuation of those shares at middle market price in the relevant balance sheets
had been approved by the taxpayer company's auditors and no evidence had been   *j*
adduced to support the taxpayer company's contention that a lower value should have
been adopted for the purposes of apportionment under s 296(5).

---

1   [1943] 1 All ER 514, [1943] AC 486, 25 Tax Cas 219

[Paragraph 7 listed the cases[1] cited to the commissioners.]

a   8. The commissioners who heard the appeal took time to consider their decision and gave it in writing on 2nd May 1977 as follows:

'1. The matter was argued before us in relation to the year ended 31 March 1971, it being agreed that our decision on that year would govern the preceding year also, and accordingly we make reference to that year only.

b   '2. The apportionment was made under section 298(2), which provides that there may be apportioned, if the Board see reason for it, the whole of [the taxpayer company's] income up to the amount of the required standard, and it was contended that this was not an appropriate case for a section 298(2) apportionment at all. The question of invoking this subsection rests with the Board, and we cannot interfere with their action in so doing; even if we could, we would have been quite unable to say there was no reason for it, as the income of [the taxpayer company] exceeded the

c   distribution made and also exceeded the standard.

'3. The amount apportioned. The section authorises apportionment of "the whole of" an investment company's "income . . . up to the amount of the required standard". The argument concerned management expenses, which are deductible in computing "total profits" (section 304) and yearly interest, which is allowed as a deduction against total profits in computing corporation tax chargeable (section

d   248, where it is included as a "charge on income"). What we have to look at is the "income" of an investment company—up to the amount of the standard. The income (as distinct from what one might call the net result) of an investment company, can in this context only mean the income coming from its investments. This was £73,768; it exceeded the required standard (the computation of which takes care, in its own way, of management expenses and interest) and accordingly

e   the apportionment is limited to the amount of the standard. In our opinion the amount apportioned is correct.

'4. The apportionment under appeal apportions the income, by reference to section 296(4) and (5). Under subsection (4) the apportionment has to be made "according to the respective interests in the company in question of the participators". It appeared to be common ground that the normal apportionment

f   hereunder will be according to the respective interests of the participators in income. Subsection (5) provides that in determining the respective interests "the Board may if it seems proper to them to do so" make the apportionment on the basis of winding-up interests. The apportionment under appeal was made on the subsection (5) basis, and the questions are first, whether we have jurisdiction to interfere with that, and second, if we have such jurisdiction, whether we should

g   ourselves apportion the income in a different way. The question as to jurisdiction arises from subsection (10). The history of this provision was shown to us, and the Crown suggested that it was placed in section 296 of the 1970 Act, which is a consolidation Act, as a result of the similar provision (of more general application) in Schedule 4 to the Income Tax Management Act 1964, and that in relation to

h   section 296(5), it does not give us jurisdiction to "review" the Board's decision to invoke subsection (5).

'5. Subsection (5) says "the Board may if it seems proper to them to do so"; this, in the plainest of terms, gives the Board a discretion. If we had a case where it appeared that the Board had exceeded their powers or had not genuinely exercised their discretion at all, we would think it right to set it aside. But this is not such a

j
1   *Congreve v Home Office* [1976] 1 All ER 697, [1976] QB 629, CA; *Craigengillan Estates Co Ltd v Inland Revenue Comrs* [1975] STC 233, CS; *FPH Finance Trust Ltd v Inland Revenue Comrs* [1945] 1 All ER 492, [1946] AC 38, 28 Tax Cas 209, HL; *Liversidge v Anderson* [1941] 3 All ER 338, [1942] AC 206, HL; *Penang and General Investment Trust Ltd v Inland Revenue Comrs* [1943] 1 All ER 514, [1943] AC 486, 25 Tax Cas 219, HL.

case; the Board have told us, in outline, why it was thought proper to use subsection
(5) and they clearly did not exceed their powers and genuinely exercised their *a*
discretion.

'6. We have looked at the other sections of the Act where a provision similar to
subsection (10) and with the same history appears, and two things strike us. First,
this is the only such provision which, it could be suggested, may give jurisdiction
to review a plain discretion. We notice in particular that section 298(6) does not
relate to 298(2); we can see no reason why the Act should provide for a review of the *b*
Board's discretion in section 296(5), while not providing a similar review in relation
to section 298(2)—the provision which is at the very root of the apportionment in
this case. Second, the other similar provisions can only, we think, involve us in a
review of the sort of issues which any judicial body will find familiar; for example,
section 298(6) and 299(7) would involve us in the ascertainment, measuring and
weighing of powers, rights and interests—matters perfectly capable of judicial *c*
ascertainment.

'7. In the present case the Board have told us the reasons why it seemed proper
to them to use subsection (5). Their reasons appear to us to be relevant, and proper
to be taken into account. But [the taxpayer company] puts forward a number of
considerations which, it is contended, should on an objective view be taken to point
to the conclusion that the proper course would have been not to invoke the *d*
subsection. Assuming we thought that, on balance, we ourselves would have
considered that [the taxpayer company's] view of the matter should prevail, then
does subsection (10) enable us to substitute our own discretion for that of the
Board? That, as we see it, is the radical question. We find it difficult; the Board are
entrusted with the care and management of the tax, and the Board's discretions
must, we apprehend, be exercised with that function in mind; our discretion (if we *e*
have any) can only be judicial—the two things are different, as we know nothing of
the general scene in which the Board has to make its decisions. If subsection (5) said
"the Board, or the Special Commissioners on appeal may . . ." then our function
would be clear; what it says is "the Board may . . ." and "the Commissioners have
jurisdiction to review . . ." Giving the matter the best consideration we can, our
conclusion is that the review contemplated by subsection (10) is limited to the sort *f*
of review we have indicated in paragraph (5) above, ie where it might seem to us
that the Board have exceeded their powers and not genuinely exercised their
discretion, and as we have there said, this is not such a case. To our minds there is
nothing in the judgment in the *Penang* case[1] inconsistent with this conclusion.

'8. In any event (ie if the conclusions we have expressed in paragraph 7 above had
been different) it seems to us in the light of all the circumstances and evidence *g*
before us, including the Board's intention to make an adjustment to tax already
borne, that it is proper in the present case to make the apportionment on the
"winding-up interest" basis, rather than on the "interest-in-income" basis.

'9. For the foregoing reasons we uphold the apportionment in principle. There
remains only a question of the value to be attached to [the taxpayer company's]
holding in [IMCL]; in all the circumstances we think that the parties should have a *h*
further opportunity of considering this, and accordingly we leave it for further
discussion between them, and we adjourn the appeal for this purpose.'

9. On 23rd January 1978 the taxpayer company's solicitors wrote requesting the
commissioners to state a case for the opinion of the High Court in principle. The Board
supported the request. Although there was no express provision in the Taxes
Management Act 1970 enabling a case to be stated in principle only, the practice of doing *j*
so in suitable circumstances received some support from Rowlatt J in his judgment in
MacLaine & Co v Eccott (Inspector of Taxes)[2].

---

1 [1943] 1 All ER 514, [1943] AC 486, 25 Tax Cas 219
2 (1924) 10 Tax Cas 481 at 550

10. The question of law for the opinion of the court was whether the commissioners'
a decision was correct.

Andrew Park QC and *D G Goldberg* for the taxpayer company.
Patrick Medd QC and *Michael Hart* for the Crown.

GOULDING J. This is an appeal by Lothbury Investment Corpn Ltd ('the taxpayer
b company') from a decision of the Special Commissioners. Before the Special
Commissioners the taxpayer company appealed against apportionments of its income to
named participators for surtax purposes in respect of two accounting periods, the first
being the year ended 31st March 1970 and the second following year, ended 31st March
1971.

The material legislation under which the apportionment was made for the second
c accounting period is to be found in ss 296 and 298 of the Income and Corporation Taxes
Act 1970. The earlier period fell to be dealt with under legislation previously in force
which was re-enacted and consolidated in the 1970 Act. Before the Special Commissioners
it was accepted that the passing of the consolidation Act did not materially alter the
relevant law, and the case was argued by reference to the later accounting period, to
which the 1970 Act applied, on the understanding that a decision in principle for that
d period would apply also to the preceding period. The same course has been followed
before me, although I shall in the course of this judgment have to refer to one part of the
unconsolidated legislation.

Before I go further I shall read certain parts of the Act 1970 namely parts of the two
sections to which I have already referred and of another section which contains a
definition. Section 296, so far as material, provides:

e
'(1) Subject to the provisions of this section, the income of a close company for any
accounting period may, for the purposes of surtax, be apportioned by the Board
among the participators, and any amount apportioned to a close company, whether
originally or by one or more sub-apportionments under this provision, may be
further apportioned among the participators in that company . . .

f   '(3) Subject to subsection (2) above and (in the case of non-trading companies) to
section 298(2) below—(a) an apportionment shall not be made under this section of
a company's income for an accounting period unless an assessment is made on the
company under section 289 above in respect of a shortfall in its distributions for that
period, and (b) the amount apportioned shall be the amount of the shortfall taken
into account in making that assessment (and for this purpose a set-off of a surplus of
franked investment income under section 289(3) above shall not be taken as
g   reducing the amount of the shortfall), and an assessment under the said section 289,
when it becomes final and conclusive, shall also be final and conclusive for the
purposes of this subsection.

'(4) Subject to subsection (5) below and (in the case of non-trading companies) to
section 298 below, any apportionment under this section, including any sub-
h   apportionment of an amount directly or indirectly apportioned to a company, shall
be made according to the respective interests in the company in question of the
participators.

'(5) In determining for the purposes of subsection (4) above the respective interests
of the participators, the Board may if it seems proper to them to do so attribute to
each participator an interest corresponding to his interest in the assets of the
j   company available for distribution among the participators in the event of a winding
up . . .

'(8) A company which is aggrieved by any notice of apportionment under this
section shall be entitled to appeal to the Special Commissioners on giving notice to
an officer of the Board within thirty days after the date of the notice; and subject to
that an apportionment under this section shall be final and conclusive.

'(9) If a company fails or refuses, on being required to do so by the Board, to furnish a statement of its income for any accounting period apportionable under *a* this section, or renders a statement with which the Board are not satisfied, the Board may make an estimate of that income to the best of their judgment.

'(10) On an appeal to the Special Commissioners, the Commissioners shall have jurisdiction to review any relevant decision taken by the Board under subsection (5) or subsection (9) above.'

Then, in s 298 I will read part of the first three subsections: *b*

'(1) The provisions of this section and section 299 below apply in relation to a close company which is not a trading company, and in those provisions such a company is referred to as a "non-trading company".

'(2) There may be apportioned under section 296 above, if the Board see reason for it, the whole of a non-trading company's income for an accounting period up to *c* the amount of the required standard (notwithstanding that there has been no shortfall in distributions for that period), together with any addition to be made under subsection (2) of that section, but with such reduction, if any, as may be just in respect of distributions made for the period to persons other than participators and associates of participators . . .

'(3) Where an apportionment is made by virtue of subsection (2) above, an *d* individual shall not be charged to surtax on an amount treated in consequence of the apportionment or any sub-apportionment as being his income except in so far as it exceeds the amount which, apart from the apportionment, falls in respect of distributions made by the company in the accounting period to be included in the statement of total income to be made by him for the purposes of surtax.'

It is common ground that the taxpayer company in the present case is a close company *e* for the purposes of the 1970 Act and is also a non-trading company. I need not therefore consider the definitions of those terms. Nor is it necessary to consider how the figure defined as 'the required standard' is arrived at. I should, however, read the opening part of s 303(1) of the Act to show, so far as necessary, what is meant by a 'participator'. It begins: *f*

'For the purposes of this Chapter, a "participator" is, in relation to any company, a person having a share or interest in the capital or income of the company, and, without prejudice to the generality of the preceding words, includes—(*a*) any person who possesses, or is entitled to acquire, share capital or voting rights in the company, (*b*) any loan creditor of the company . . .'

and the subsection adds other categories of participators to which I need not now refer. *g* It is my intention, for brevity, to cite subsections of s 296 simply by their own numbers as subsections, without mentioning the section itself.

Before leaving the text of the 1970 Act it is convenient to go back for a moment to sub-ss (4) and (5). It will be observed that, while sub-s (4) requires an apportionment to be made according to the respective interests in the company in question of the participators, *h* it contains no further directions showing exactly what interests are meant or how they are to be arrived at. It is common ground, however, that, in general, the apportionment is made on the basis of interests in income, with no doubt modification according to other relevant considerations in special cases. Thus, sub-s (5), which empowers the Board to attribute interests on the footing of a winding-up, gives authority to make a departure in suitable cases from what would otherwise be the normal basis. I may also say at this *j* point that, whatever may have happened before the Special Commissioners, there has been no attack in this court on the decision of the Board to apply s 298(2) to the taxpayer company in respect of the two accounting periods with which I am concerned.

I will now summarise the facts as they appear from the case stated by the Special Commissioners. Having decided to make apportionments on the taxpayer company in

respect of the two accounting periods, the Board further, in purported exercise of their
a power under sub-s (5), decided to attribute to each participator an interest corresponding
to his interest in the assets of the taxpayer company available for distribution among
them in the event of a winding-up. The state of the company at all material times was
as follows. Its issued capital consisted of 773,167 6% redeemable cumulative preference
shares of £1 each, and of 185,000 ordinary shares of £1 each. The preference shares were
held by a number of persons with whose identity I am not concerned. The ordinary
b shares were held, as to 111,613 thereof, by Mr Isidore Ostrer ('Isidore') and, as to the
remainder, by Mr Maurice Ostrer ('Maurice'). There were also two relevant loan
creditors: Isidore, who had lent the company £200,000, and his sister, Mrs Castlemount,
who had lent £30,000.

Taking the apportionment for the second accounting period, the one that the Special
Commissioners selected as the subject of argument, the effect of what was done was to
c attribute to the preference shareholders a fraction of the total sum to be apportioned
considerably less than the preference dividends actually payable and paid. Conversely,
the ordinary shareholders, Isidore and Maurice, received in apportionment more than
the ordinary dividend actually paid for the accounting period ended 31st March 1971.
There was also a substantial sum attributed to Isidore in respect of his loan, although
during both the periods in question he informally agreed with the taxpayer company to
d receive no interest thereon. Finally, the sum apportioned to Mrs Castlemount was in
excess of the interest paid to her for the year in question at the rate of 10½% per annum.
I have abstained from stating actual figures because 'the required standard' under the Act
did not, owing to facts that I need not describe, agree with the actual amount of the
company's income available for distribution and in fact distributed.

Now the main asset of the taxpayer company at all material times was its holding of
e shares in a public company known as Illingworth Morris & Co Ltd ('IMCL'). The shares
in that company, so it appears, have a quotation on the Stock Exchange. During each of
the accounting periods in question the taxpayer company waived certain of the dividends
which it might otherwise have received on its shares in IMCL, and the Special
Commissioners state that the waiving or non-charging by Isidore of interest on his loan
to the taxpayer company and the waiving by the taxpayer company of dividends on its
f holding in IMCL were related in the sense that the taxpayer company—

> 'decided upon the size of its dividend waivers in the knowledge that it would not
> have to provide for interest on the loan. In both of the accounting years . . . the
> dividends waived substantially exceeded the interest which would have been
> payable on the loan if it had been charged at 6½% (the rate at which interest was
g > charged for the first 3 months of the loan's existence in 1966). If interest had been
> charged on the loan [and this is a point, I may say, on which counsel for the taxpayer
> company laid great weight] the dividend waivers by [the taxpayer company] would
> have been smaller, so that [the taxpayer company] would still have had sufficient
> income to pay the full dividends on its preference shares.'

h That summary of the facts, which are more fully stated by the Special Commissioners
in the case, does not result from any contest of evidence before them. The whole of the
facts, as I understand the proceedings below, were agreed, and the argument proceeded
on that footing.

The decision of the Special Commissioners was very largely concerned with the extent
of their jurisdiction under sub-s (10) to review the Board's decision under sub-s (5) to
j apportion income by reference to the interests of the participators on a winding-up. The
Special Commissioners said:

> 'The main question for our decision was whether we had jurisdiction to review
> the Board's choice of this method of apportionment instead of the more usual
> method of apportionment by reference to the participators' interests in income . . .

does subsection (10) enable us to substitute our own discretion for that of the Board? That, as we see it, is the radical question.'

Their conclusion was in these terms:

'Giving the matter the best consideration we can, our conclusion is that the review contemplated by subsection (10) is limited to the sort of review we have indicated in paragraph (5) above, ie where it might seem to us that the Board have exceeded their powers and not genuinely exercised their discretion, and as we have there said, this is not such a case.'

In the para (5) to which they there refer, the Special Commissioners said:

'If we had a case where it appeared that the Board had exceeded their powers or had not genuinely exercised their discretion at all, we would think it right to set it aside. But this is not such a case; the Board have told us, in outline, why it was thought proper to use subsection (5) and they clearly did not exceed their powers and genuinely exercised their discretion.'

The debate on jurisdiction has been renewed on this appeal to the High Court. Counsel for the taxpayer company contend that sub-s (10) requires the Special Commissioners to hear and determine the whole question of the basis of apportionment and fairly decide it according to their own judgment, substituting, if necessary, their opinion for that of the Board. The submission for the Crown is that the appellate tribunal's power of review given by sub-s (10) is restricted by the rules that in general limit a court's jurisdiction in this country to review the decision of a ministerial officer performing a statutory duty. Counsel for the Crown cited the classical statements of those limits by Lord Greene MR in *Robinson v Minister of Town and Country Planning, re City of Plymouth (City Centre) Declaratory Order 1946*[1] and in *Associated Provincial Picture Houses Ltd v Wednesbury Corpn*[2].

In my judgment, those authorities are of little help in relation to the present problem. The *Plymouth* case[1] was brought before the court under the narrow provisions of s 16 of the Town and Country Planning Act 1944, the *Wednesbury* case[2] by an ordinary action for a declaration. In neither case was there available any statutory provision for appeal or review conferred in general terms. Here, I think, I have to construe sub-s (10) in its context without preconceptions drawn from general constitutional law.

The following points, in my view, are important. First, a decision by the Board to apply sub-s (5) is an act of administration performed without any obligation to consult the company in question. So far as I know, the company has no statutory right to make representations before the Board's decision is arrived at. Secondly, the decision may, and in many cases does, materially affect the company's liability to tax. Thirdly, sub-s (10) operates in the context of an appeal under sub-s (8), at which appeal the Special Commissioners must hear any relevant evidence and listen to any relevant arguments that may be tendered. Fourthly, on such an appeal the basis of apportionment is an integral element in the apportionment to be considered, just as much as the amount of the apportionable income, the identity of the participators and the numerical ratio of apportionments between them. Fifthly, sub-s (10) expressly gives jurisdiction to review the Board's decision, clearly intending to confer powers which might otherwise be absent or doubtful, and does not itself contain any limiting words. Sixthly, having regard to the language of sub-s (5), namely the words 'the Board may if it seems proper to them to do so', the right to a review would be of slight value if the Crown's argument were upheld.

In those circumstances, I am of opinion that the Special Commissioners have a right and a duty to form their own view of the whole matter and substitute it, if necessary, for

---

1   [1947] 1 All ER 851, [1947] KB 702
2   [1947] 2 All ER 680, [1948] 1 KB 223

that of the Board, paying full regard to the fact of the Board's decision as that of the
a authoritative and highly experienced body which they are, but not hesitating to set it
aside if persuaded on any ground that it was wrong. In other words, on an appeal the
winding-up basis of apportionment is not to be applied if it seems improper to the Special
Commissioners to do so. Their situation is in my judgment not unlike that of the
metropolitan magistrate in *Stepney Borough Council v Joffe*[1], an authority referred to with
approval by Edmund Davies LJ in *Sagnata Investments Ltd v Norwich Corpn*[2].

b   I have arrived at my conclusion in the context of the 1970 Act alone. It is to my mind
strengthened by the legislative history of sub-s (10). The subsection is one of a number
scattered about the 1970 Act, all derived from a common source, namely para (3) of Sch
4 to the Income Tax Management Act 1964. That Act, among other reforms of
management, transferred to the inspectors of taxes and to the Board of Inland Revenue
various functions of an administrative rather than a judicial character formerly vested in
c General Commissioners and Special Commissioners. They are set out in Sch 4 to the
1964 Act. The passage in question contains three numbered paragraphs under the
heading, 'Translation of references to Commissioners', and reads:

'(1) For references to the General Commissioners or the Special Commissioners
(or to both, and however expressed) in the enactments listed in the Table set out at
d   the end of this paragraph there shall be substituted—(a) in the enactments in Part
I of the Table, references to the Board, (b) in the enactments in Part II of the Table,
references to the Board or, for the purpose of charging tax at the standard rate, an
inspector, and (c) in the enactments in Part III of the Table, references to an
inspector.
'(2) The Board may delegate any of the functions conferred on them by this
e   paragraph to an officer of the Board.
'(3) On an appeal to the General Commissioners or Special Commissioners, the
Commissioners shall have jurisdiction to review any relevant decision taken by an
inspector or the Board in exercise of the functions transferred to the inspector or the
Board by this Schedule.'

f   There follows a table in three parts containing numerous references to provisions of
the Income Tax Acts, and respectively headed 'Functions transferred to Board', 'Functions
transferred to Board or inspector' and 'Functions transferred to inspector'. All those
functions, of course, were previously exercised by General or Special Commissioners, or
both.
      The inference I draw from that schedule is that, inasmuch as the transferred functions,
g or some of them, might be held to be not purely administrative but also to include an
element of quasi-judicial determination, the taxpayer, in those cases where the subject-
matter gave a right of appeal to General or Special Commissioners, could if he wanted it,
by means of an appeal, still obtain a decision of the commissioners themselves. That
consideration, if well founded, tells in favour of an unrestricted jurisdiction in the appeal
commissioners to review.
h   The 1964 Act is plainly relevant to this appeal in relation to the accounting period
ending on 31st March 1970, for it was then in force. Whether, in relation to the second
period, which ended on 31st March 1971, it ought to influence my interpretation of the
1970 consolidating Act may be arguable. However, as I have already said, I reached the
same conclusion in the first place by reference to the consolidating Act alone.
      Thus I think the Special Commissioners took too restricted a view of their jurisdiction
j over the decisions of the Board under sub-s (5). Reading the whole of the case stated, the
question of jurisdiction seems to have bulked so very large in their consideration that,
had either party desired it, I might have been persuaded to remit the matter to them for

1   [1949] 1 All ER 256, [1949] 1 KB 599
2   [1971] 2 All ER 1441, [1971] QB 614

reconsideration in the light of this court's view of their powers. However, neither party *a* wants me to take that course, and it is true that the Special Commissioners expressed, though concisely, an opinion on the merits of the case and showed how they would have decided if they had taken a more liberal view of their jurisdiction. The taxpayer company contends that such alternative decision by the Special Commissioners is erroneous in point of law, and therefore ought to be overruled by this court.

The decision by the Special Commissioners on this second point is as follows. It occurs, I should say, in para 8 of their written decision, and that is preceded by para 7, *b* where they stated the conclusion on jurisdiction that I read earlier. In para 8 they say this:

'In any event (ie if the conclusions we have expressed in paragraph 7 above had been different) it seems to us in the light of all the circumstances and evidence before us, including the Board's intention to make an adjustment to tax already *c* borne, that it is proper in the present case to make the apportionment on the "winding-up interest" basis, rather than on the "interest-in-income" basis.'

I ought also to refer to the grounds that were before the Special Commissioners as those which had actuated the Board. They say:

'We were informed that in a letter which was not exhibited to us it had been *d* stated on behalf of the Board that the prime reason for the apportionments was the existence of the interest-free loans. However, we were informed by Mr A L L Alexander, who appeared on behalf of the Inland Revenue, that the Board's action in making apportionments on this basis was justified as follows. Because Isidore was prepared to forgo interest due on his loan [the taxpayer company] could afford to take less by way of dividend from IMCL, thus swelling the funds of IMCL and *e* improving the market value of its shares and so indirectly benefiting the shareholders in the [taxpayer company].'

On that, I should comment that there was no evidence before the Special Commissioners of the alleged improvement in market value of shares in IMCL, and it is denied by the taxpayer company. *f*

The Special Commissioners also said, in relation to what I have just read: 'In the present case the Board have told us the reasons why it seemed proper to them to use subsection (5). Their reasons appear to us to be relevant, and proper to be taken into account.'

That, I think, is all I can find as to the view of the Special Commissioners had they come to a wider conclusion regarding their jurisdiction. The question for me, as it *g* seems, is whether there is any error of law in that part of the Special Commissioners' determination, and that, in turn, depends, I think, on whether it could be proper on the agreed facts for the Board to come to their original decision.

There is one authority that has been cited to me which touches on the ambit of the Board's power under sub-s (5). It is *Penang and General Investment Trust Ltd v Inland Revenue Comrs*[1]. It was heard on appeal from the Special Commissioners by Macnaghten J[2] *h* and then went on appeal from him to the Court of Appeal[3] and finally to the House of Lords[1]. It concerned the provision, then in force in the Finance Act 1937, now represented by sub-s (5). The judgment of the Court of Appeal was delivered by Clauson LJ, and was that of Lord Greene MR, Clauson LJ himself and du Parcq LJ. In that judgment I find this[4]:

j

1　[1943] 1 All ER 514, [1943] AC 486, 25 Tax Cas 219
2　25 Tax Cas 219
3　[1942] 1 All ER 290, [1942] 1 KB 420, 25 Tax Cas 219
4　[1942] 1 All ER 290 at 293, [1942] 1 KB 420 at 433, 25 Tax Cas 219 at 235

'We do not propose to burden this judgment by going through the subsequent
legislation in detail, but it is necessary to note that, by virtue of the Finance Act,
1937, s. 14(3), the commissioners are given power, in determining the respective
interests of the members for the purpose of apportioning income, to attribute to
each member an interest corresponding to his interest in the assets of the company
available for distribution among the members in the event of a winding up. It was
suggested in argument before us that this power was one which must be read as
subject to some implied limitation and was other than a power given by the
legislature to the commissioners without control or fetter. We do not appreciate
what implied fetter or limitation is suggested. In our opinion, the power thus given
to them is quite unfettered.'

That part of the judgment was summarised at the very end of the decision by the
sentence[1]: 'We have already expressed our opinion that the discretion left to them in this
matter by the Act is wholly unfettered.'

Counsel for the taxpayer company suggested that those observations of the Court of
Appeal were no longer to be taken at their face value. In support of that contention it
was said, first of all, that they were inconsistent with the way in which Lord Romer dealt
with the matter when the *Penang* case[2] was decided by the House of Lords. At the end
of his speech Lord Romer said this:

'The only other question to be decided is whether, having given such a direction,
the Special Commissioners properly exercised their discretion in making the
consequential apportionment among the members under sect. 14(3) of the 1937
Act, instead of in accordance with the members' interests in the company's
income. As to this I have little to say.'

Then Lord Romer looked at the facts shortly and observed that the decision to act under
the subsection had certainly prejudiced a certain individual appellant in the case. Having
come to that conclusion, he went on[3]: 'But I am not prepared to deduce from these
circumstances that the commissioners have not properly exercised their discretion.' He
then pointed out that the individual appellant in question was a taxpayer who had
exercised much ingenuity in finding lawful ways of diminishing his liability to surtax,
and concluded[3]:

'If Sir John sees no impropriety in exercising for this purpose the powers of
managing his affairs that are allowed to him by the laws of the country, it does not
lie in his mouth to accuse the Special Commissioners of impropriety if they choose
to exercise the powers given to them by these same laws in such a way as to defeat
Sir John's object, and procure for the national revenue as large an amount from surtax as is possible in the circumstances.'

Lord Romer's words, to my mind, if carefully considered, rather emphasise than
qualify the lack of any legal restriction on the ambit of what were then the Special
Commissioners' powers. I am sure he did not think, or mean to suggest, that the lawful,
though to him unattractive, actions of the taxpayer in question created any estoppel or
similar inhibition of legal rights as between him and the Crown. On the contrary, Lord
Romer accepted that the Special Commissioners acted in the interests of the national
revenue to get as large an amount of surtax as possible, and was content to look no
further. Accordingly, what he said seems to me perfectly consistent with what was said
in the Court of Appeal, that the discretion is unfettered. It is of course nonetheless a
discretion that has to be exercised in a manner proper to public officers, not a mere power
of capricious or arbitrary decision.

1   [1942] 1 All ER 290 at 294, [1942] 1 KB 420 at 436, 25 Tax Cas 219 at 237
2   [1943] 1 All ER 514 at 521, [1943] AC 486 at 505, 25 Tax Cas 219 at 247
3   [1943] 1 All ER 514 at 522, [1943] AC 486 at 506, 25 Tax Cas 219 at 248

The other reason why it was suggested by counsel that the Court of Appeal's judgment in the *Penang* case[1] was no longer a proper guide was that the Income Tax Management *a*
Act 1964, to which I have already referred, gave the Special Commissioners power to review the Board's exercise of discretion. That does not seem to me to affect the matter in principle. All it means, assuming my decision on the first point is right, is that first of all the Board's discretion is unfettered and then, if there is an appeal and an opportunity, therefore, of review by the Special Commissioners, the discretion of the Special Commissioners is unfettered.   *b*

Now I must examine the taxpayer company's arguments as to the validity of the Board's decision in the present case, and I must do so, I think, having regard to the grounds stated by the Board's advocate before the Special Commissioners below. I have already read them, and I will not take time to read them again. What is said by counsel for the taxpayer company is that the Board erred by taking into consideration something that was improper, because irrelevant to the exercise of their discretion. That argument *c*
would still be open to them, I think, even if the Special Commissioners' jurisdiction were somewhat more restricted than I have held it to be. It can only be proper to apply sub-s (5), counsel submit, to counteract either a retention of income by the close company in question or a diversion of that company's income from a participator who might otherwise have received it to some other person.

It may be proper, it is said, to invoke sub-s (5) if one or other of two conditions is *d*
satisfied: either that one or more participators have received more than a proper return on their capital interest in the company, or that the members of a particular class of participators have received disproportionate returns instead of being treated pari passu. Counsel said that, subject possibly to some very special exceptions, it could not be proper to use sub-s (5) where neither of those conditions was fulfilled.

Here, however, they argue that the taxpayer company's income was fully distributed, *e*
and there was no artificiality and no contrivance in the mode of distribution. It is the apportionment which is anomalous, by attributing to others a part of the income lawfully payable and in fact paid to the preference shareholders; and that introduces, it is submitted, a measure of double taxation, only to be counteracted, if at all, by an adjustment for which there is no statutory authority. It was also anomalous to apportion additional income to Mrs Castlemount over and above the full interest that she was *f*
entitled to receive, and did receive, on her loan to the taxpayer company; and equally so was the treatment of Isidore and Maurice.

The true basis of the Board's action, as revealed by their confessed reasoning, was the retention of undistributed income in IMCL which resulted from Isidore's waiver of his right to interest and the connected waiver of dividend rights by the taxpayer company. If IMCL is a close company, then, it is submitted, the Crown has its remedy in *g*
apportionment and sub-apportionment of that company's income; but if, as seems to be the case, it is not a close company, then, so it is contended, it is quite wrong to invoke sub-s (5) against the taxpayer company, which has fully distributed its own income. Had Isidore held shares directly in IMCL, it would have been impossible, unless that were a close company, for the Crown to counteract any surtax-saving effect of a waiver of dividend rights by him. It cannot be proper to take advantage, counsel continue, of what *h*
in this context is the merely accidental interposition of the taxpayer company in order to produce a different consequence. The justification for apportionment on a winding-up basis must have reference to the income being apportioned, and not to other income or circumstances. Therefore, the argument concludes, the Board exceeded their powers in making the apportionment under scrutiny and the Special Commissioners erred in law in affirming it.   *j*

There is force in that line of argument once you accept the major premise limiting the motives on which the Board may act under sub-s (5). But it seems to me that if I

---

1   [1942] 1 All ER 290, [1942] 1 KB 420, 25 Tax Cas 219

formulate any such limit I shall in effect be amending the Act, for Parliament most
a carefully and evidently refrained from imposing bounds. The words 'if it seems proper
to them to do so' make that clear. Of course, there are cases imaginable in which the
court would have to say that the purported decision had not in truth and in law seemed
proper to the Board at all. If the step had been procured by corruption of an officer of the
Board, that would be so; if the Board had acted in order to punish a company for lawful
resistance to some policy of the government in no way connected with taxation, there
b would no doubt be an arguable case. But here it is conceded that the Board genuinely
considered the facts and made their purported decision in good faith. It does not matter
whether I like the decision or not.

Having regard to the unfettered quality of the power given to the Board by sub-s (5),
I am unable on the agreed facts to hold that they went outside it. Accordingly, the
Special Commissioners did not err in law in upholding them. I should make it clear that,
c unlike the Special Commissioners, I do not myself regard the promise of some extra-
statutory remission of tax as a matter which should influence my decision.

On those grounds I must dismiss the appeal, without prejudice to the pending
adjournment of the case before the Special Commissioners.

Appeal dismissed.

d
Solicitors: *Courts & Co* (for the taxpayer company); *Solicitor of Inland Revenue.*

Rengan Krishnan Esq   Barrister.

London & Clydeside Estates Ltd v Aberdeen District Council and another

a

HOUSE OF LORDS

LORD HAILSHAM OF ST MARYLEBONE LC, LORD WILBERFORCE, LORD FRASER OF TULLYBELTON, LORD RUSSELL OF KILLOWEN AND LORD KEITH OF KINKEL

2nd, 3rd OCTOBER, 8th NOVEMBER 1979

b

Compulsory purchase – Compensation – Certificate of alternative development – Validity – Duty of local planning authority to include in certificate statement of rights of appeal – Rights of appeal not stated in certificate – Whether certificate invalid – Whether certificate should be set aside – Land Compensation (Scotland) Act 1963, ss 25(4), 26 – Town and Country Planning (General Development) (Scotland) Order 1959 (SI 1959 No 1361), arts 3(2)(3), 4(1).

c

A company owned three areas of land in Scotstoun, Aberdeenshire, which the local authority proposed to acquire compulsorily for educational purposes. On 9th September 1974 the company applied to the local authority (as the local planning authority) for a certificate of alternative development under s 25[a] of the Land Compensation (Scotland) *d* Act 1963 and submitted that an appropriate class of development for the three areas of land would be residential with associated commercial purposes. The local planning authority were required, by s 25(4), to issue to the applicant, not earlier than 21 days after the date of service of the application, a certificate stating that in their opinion either planning permission for development of one or more classes therein specified might reasonably be expected to be granted or planning permission could not reasonably be *e* expected to be granted for any development other than that proposed to be carried out by the acquiring authority. The certificate governed the amount of compensation which would be payable for the compulsory acquisition of the land. By virtue of art 3(2)[b] of the Town and Country Planning (General Development) (Scotland) Order 1959 the certificate was, subject to the provisions of s 26(4)[c] of the 1963 Act, required to be issued by the local planning authority within two months of the date of receipt of the application under *f* s 25. On 22nd October 1974, ie within the two month period prescribed by art 3(2), the local planning authority issued a certificate in the terms of s 25(4)(b) but omitted to include, as required by art 3(3) of the 1959 order, a statement in writing of the rights of appeal given by s 26 of the 1963 Act and by the order. The company received the certificate on 24th October 1974. On 9th January 1975, by a letter to the Secretary of State, it sought to appeal against the certificate on its merits. The Secretary of State held *g* that he had no jurisdiction to entertain the application because it was outside the time limit prescribed by art 4(1)[d] of the order, which was one month from the date of receipt of the certificate. He adhered to that decision despite a further letter from the company complaining that the certificate was defective by reason of the omission of the statement of the rights of appeal. The company brought an action seeking to have the certificate set aside and a new certificate complying with the requirements of the 1963 Act and the *h* 1959 order issued. The local planning authority contended that the requirement in art 3(3) of the order to include a statement of the rights of appeal was directory only and the certificate was not invalidated by the omission of the statement, and that even if the certificate was vitiated by the omission the position was the same as if no certificate had been issued within the prescribed time, that accordingly a certificate in the terms of s 25(4)(b) was deemed to have been issued by virtue of s 26(4) and that as a result of s 26(4) *j*

---

a Section 25, so far as material, is set out at p 888 *g*, post
b Article 3, so far as material, is set out at p 890 *j*, post
c Section 26(4) is set out at p 890 *e f*, post
d Article 4(1) is set out at p 891 *a*, post

a and arts 3 and 4 of the order the company had lost any right of appeal by not appealing to the Secretary of State within one month of the expiry of the period of two months from the local authority's receipt of the company's application for a certificate. They further contended that the company had not been misled by the omission and that that was the reason for the appeal against the certificate being late.

b **Held** – (i) The certificate of 22nd October 1974 was invalid because (a) the requirement in art 3(3) of the 1959 order to include a statement in writing of the rights of appeal to the Secretary of State was mandatory and the local authority had not complied with it, (b) it was not possible to treat the certificate as consisting of two parts (one part being the actual certificate and the other being the statement of the rights of appeal), which were capable of being severed from one another, because both parts were required by the order and were of substantial importance so that the omission of either part was therefore fatal *c* to the validity of the whole, (c) it was irrelevant for the purpose of determining the validity of the certificate whether the company was in fact misled by the local planning authority's failure to include the statement of the rights of appeal and whether it was as a result of that that its appeal was out of time (see p 880 *h* to p 881 *b*, p 882 *j* to p 883 *a j*, p 884 *c*, p 886 *e* to p 887 *a f g*, p 889 *j*, p 892 *g* to *j*, p 893 *d* to *f* and p 895 *e*, post); *Brayhead (Ascot) Ltd v Berkshire County Council* [1964] 1 All ER 149 and *Agricultural,* *d* *Horticultural and Forestry Industry Training Board v Kent* [1970] 1 All ER 304 considered.

(ii) Section 26(4) of the 1963 Act had no application because the issue by a local planning authority of a certificate vitiated by failure to comply with a mandatory requirement was not the same thing as the failure by that authority to issue any certificate at all because an invalid certificate under s 25 of the Act was not a complete nullity: it had some legal effect unless and until it was set aside; it might, for example, *e* be the proper subject of a timeous appeal to the Secretary of State (see p 881 *c* and *g* to p 882 *a*, p 884 *c*, p 886 *j*, p 889 *j* and p 893 *j* to p 894 *d*, post); *Calvin v Carr* [1979] 2 All ER 440 applied.

(iii) The certificate would be set aside because (a) on the true construction of ss 25 and 26 of the 1963 Act and art 3 of the 1959 order, the local planning authority's duty to issue a valid certificate did not cease at the end of the two month period prescribed by art 3(2); *f* their obligation to issue a valid certificate was a continuing one and they could be required to issue such a certificate outside that period, and (b) in the circumstances the issue of a fresh certificate was the appropriate remedy (see p 884 *a* to *c*, p 888 *a d e*, p 889 *b* to *j* and p 894 *e* to *j*, post).

Per Curiam. The use of terms such as 'void' and 'voidable' in relation to the effect of non-compliance by a statutory authority with the statutory requirements affecting the *g* discharge of one of its functions may be helpful in argument but is misleading in effect if relied on to show that the courts in deciding the consequences of a defect in the exercise of power are necessarily bound to fit the facts of a particular case into rigid legal categories. The use of such rigid classifications should not be encouraged in the field of administrative law and in the domain where the courts apply a supervisory jurisdiction over the acts of subordinate authority purporting to exercise statutory powers (see p 883 *h* *c g h*, p 884 *c*, p 889 *j* and p 894 *b*, post).

Notes

For the failure to comply with procedural requirements in the purported exercise of a statutory power, see 1 Halsbury's Laws (4th Edn) para 25.

Sections 25 and 26 of the Land Compensation (Scotland) Act 1963 correspond to ss 17 *j* and 18 of the Land Compensation Act 1961. For ss 17 and 18 of the 1961 Act, see 6 Halsbury's Statutes (3rd Edn) 257, 260.

Articles 3 and 4 of the Town and Country Planning (General Development) (Scotland) Order 1959 correspond to arts 3 and 4 of the Land Compensation Development Order 1974. For arts 3 and 4 of the 1974 order, see 21 Halsbury's Statutory Instruments (Third Reissue) 222.

Cases referred to in opinions

Agricultural, Horticultural and Forestry Industry Training Board v Kent [1970] 1 All ER 304, *a*
[1970] 2 QB 19, [1970] 2 WLR 426, CA, Digest (Cont Vol C) 982, 37j.

Brayhead (Ascot) Ltd v Berkshire County Council [1964] 1 All ER 149, [1964] 2 QB 303,
[1964] 2 WLR 507, 128 JP 167, 62 LGR 162, 15 P & CR 423, DC, 45 Digest (Repl) 348,
81.

Calvin v Carr [1979] 2 All ER 440, [1979] 2 WLR 755, PC.

Edwick v Sunbury-on-Thames Urban District Council [1961] 3 All ER 10, [1962] 1 QB 229, *b*
[1961] 3 WLR 553, 125 JP 551, 59 LGR 428, 12 P & CR 355, 45 Digest (Repl) 347, 78.

James v Secretary of State for Wales (formerly Minister of Housing and Local Government)
[1966] 3 All ER 964, [1968] AC 409, [1967] 1 WLR 171, 131 JP 122, 65 LGR 171, 18
P & CR 165, HL; on appeal from [1965] 3 All ER 602, [1966] 1 WLR 135, 130 JP 11,
CA, Digest (Cont Vol B) 689, 3oc.

London Ballast Co Ltd v Buckinghamshire County Council (1966) 65 LGR 227, 18 P & CR 446, *c*
Digest (Cont Vol C) 968, 55ab.

Maitland, Petitioner 1961 SC 291.

Rae v Davidson 1954 SC 361, 2 Digest (Reissue) 16, *39.

Rayner v Stepney Corpn [1911] 2 Ch 312, 80 LJ Ch 678, 105 LT 362, 75 JP 468, 10 LGR
307, 28(2) Digest (Reissue) 993, 244.

d

Appeal and cross-appeal

By a summons, dated 16th April 1975, the appellants, London and Clydeside Estates Ltd
(formerly London and Clydeside Properties Ltd), raised an action against the respondents,
Aberdeen District Council, concluding (i) for reduction of a purported certificate of
alternative development issued to the appellants on 22nd October 1974 by the
respondents' predecessors, Aberdeen County Council, under s 25(4) of the Land *e*
Compensation (Scotland) Act 1963 in respect of three areas of ground at Scotstoun,
Bridge of Don, Aberdeenshire, (ii) for declarator that the respondents were bound, on an
application of the appellants dated 9th September 1974, to issue an amended certificate
of alternative development in respect of the three areas of land in terms of Part IV of the
1963 Act, and (iii) for decree ordaining the respondents to issue such a certificate in terms
of Part IV of the Act within two months after the date of the decree. The Secretary of *f*
State for Scotland was called as second defender for any interest that he might have. The
case came before the Lord Ordinary (Lord Dunpark) on procedure roll and on 24th
February 1977 he delivered an opinion in which he expressed the view that the certificate
of 22nd October 1974 was invalid on the ground that it contained no statement in
writing of the appellants' rights of appeal, contrary to art 3(3) of the Town and Country
Planning (General Development) (Scotland) Order 1959. Instead of granting decree of *g*
reduction and declarator as concluded for, he made a finding that the appellants' letter to
the Secretary of State dated 9th January 1975 was a valid notice of appeal against the
certificate and expressed the hope that the Secretary of State would take his finding as
equivalent to a decree of declarator that the appellants' notice of appeal was timeous and
valid in the circumstances. At that stage the Secretary of State had lodged no defences.
The respondents reclaimed against the Lord Ordinary's interlocutor and were allowed to *h*
amend their pleadings by adding a conclusion (conclusion 3) for declarator that their
letter of 9th January 1975 was a timeous and valid notice of appeal with which the
Secretary of State was bound to deal. The Secretary of State then lodged defences and the
case was remitted by the Second Division of the Court of Session to the Lord Ordinary to
consider it further. At a further hearing the Lord Ordinary was persuaded, after hearing
argument for the Secretary of State, to depart from his earlier finding that the appellants *j*
had given valid notice of appeal. By an interlocutor dated 15th June 1978 he (i) refused
to grant decree of declarator in terms of conclusion 3 and dismissed the action so far as
directed against the Secretary of State, (ii) granted decree of reduction of the certificate in
the terms of the appellants' first conclusion, and (iii) on the basis of a concession by
counsel for the respondents, granted decree of declarator in terms of the second

conclusion, ie that the respondents were bound to issue a fresh certificate within two
months of the date of the decree. The respondents reclaimed and the reclaiming motion
was heard by the Second Division (the Lord Justice-Clerk (Lord Wheatley), Lord Kissen
and Lord Robertson). Counsel for the respondents withdrew the concession that decree
in terms of the second conclusion must necessarily follow from decree in terms of the
first and also contended that the certificate of 22nd October 1974 was valid on the ground
that the provisions of art 3(3) of the 1959 order were directory only. By interlocutor
dated 26th January 1979 the Second Division (i) affirmed the Lord Ordinary's decision
that the certificate was invalid and should be reduced but (ii) refused as incompetent
decree in terms of the second conclusion ordaining the respondents to issue an amended
certificate. The appellants appealed against the second part of the Second Division's
interlocutor. The respondents cross-appealed against the first part of the interlocutor.
The facts are set out in the opinion of Lord Hailsham of St Marylebone LC.

A M Morison QC and *A G C McGregor* (both of the Scottish Bar) for the appellants.
M S R Bruce QC and *J A Cameron* (both of the Scottish Bar) for the respondents.

Their Lordships took time for consideration.

8th November. The following opinions were delivered.

LORD HAILSHAM OF ST MARYLEBONE LC. My Lords, my task in this case
is rendered considerably lighter by reason of the fact that I have had the advantage of
reading in draft the opinions prepared by my noble and learned friends, Lord Fraser of
Tullybelton and Lord Keith of Kinkel. With them I agree, and accordingly I am of the
opinion that this appeal should succeed, the cross-appeal be dismissed, and that the
appellants should be allowed their expenses throughout these proceedings, including
those of the proceedings before your Lordships' House, other than the expenses relating
to the joinder of the second defender as to which it is not now sought to disturb the order
of the Second Division of the Court of Session. Nevertheless I wish to frame my own
reasons for coming to this conclusion.

It will be logical to deal first with the cross-appeal which seeks to reverse the
interlocutors to the extent to which the pursuers succeeded below. These interlocutors
were in the terms of the first conclusion of the pursuers' summons in these proceedings,
which sought the reduction of a purported certificate by the respondents. The appeal
itself is confined to the contention that the Second Division of the Court of Session were
wrong to refuse the second conclusion in the appellants' summons after sustaining their
contention that they were entitled to succeed on the first (which is the subject of the
cross-appeal).

The proceedings relate to three areas of ground at Scotstoun, Bridge of Don, which the
respondents or their predecessors desire to acquire for educational purposes.

On 9th September 1974 the appellants applied through their architects to the
respondents' predecessor authority for a certificate of alternative development pursuant
to s 25 of the Land Compensation (Scotland) Act 1963. The form of this certificate
necessarily affects the amount of compensation payable for the acquisition, and, although
this does not appear directly from the record, we were told that, independently of these
proceedings, a reference to the Lands Tribunal following an agreement for sale has duly
taken place and has resulted in an award in an alternative form on each of two alternative
bases.

On 22nd October 1974, and in response to the appellants' application, the respondents'
predecessors issued what purported to be the appropriate certificate. But this purported
certificate was admittedly defective (to use a neutral word) because, contrary to the terms
of art 3(3) of the Town and Country Planning (General Development) (Scotland) Order
1959[1], which is admitted to apply to the case, it did not 'include a statement in writing
. . . of the rights of appeal to the Secretary of State . . .' These rights under the relevant

---

1   SI 1959 No 1361

terms of art 4(1) of the order provided for notice of appeal to be given within one month
from the date of receipt of the certificate.

In the events which happened, the appellants purported after the expiry of the time *a*
limit of one month to intimate an appeal to the Secretary of State. This they did by letter
dated 9th January 1975. But by letter dated 15th January 1975, the Secretary of State
declined to accept this letter as a valid appeal on the grounds that it was out of time, and
adhered to this decision despite a further letter on behalf of the appellants complaining
in effect of the defective character of the respondents' certificate. *b*

The outcome was the raising on 16th April 1975 of the present proceedings in which
the appellants concluded (1) for a reduction of the purported certificate of 22nd October
1974, and (2) for a declarator that the respondents were bound to issue an amended, or,
more properly, a fresh, certificate complying with art 3(3) of the order, and a decree
ordaining the respondents to issue such a certificate within two months of the decree.
These are the only two conclusions still alive in the proceedings before your Lordships. *c*
There was a third and alternative conclusion, now no longer effective, which resulted
from a provisional view framed by the Lord Ordinary in the course of the proceedings
before him. The Lord Ordinary had at first been disposed to consider that the Secretary
of State was wrong to decline jurisdiction to hear the attempted appeal, but changed his
mind on hearing argument for the Secretary of State who had been joined by amendment
for the purposes. No point on this abortive solution remains to be decided on this appeal, *d*
the appellants expressly refraining from pursuing the argument as to expenses raised in
their case to your Lordships' House.

In the event, the appellants succeeded in their first conclusion (for the reduction of the
purported certificate) both before the Lord Ordinary and the Second Division, and this
result forms the subject of the respondents' cross-appeal. But before the Second Division
the appellants failed in their claim to the decree concluded for in their second claim for *e*
relief (the subject of the appeal itself) on the ground, as the Second Division held, that to
ordain in accordance with the second conclusion would be 'flying in the face' of art 3(2)
of the development order. This provided that the time within which the relevant
certificate was to be issued by the respondents was to be 'the period of two months from
the date of receipt' of the relevant application, and from this the Second Division were of
opinion that the respondents had no remaining power to issue a certificate in the form *f*
required by the second conclusion of the appellants' summons. In passing, I should
remark that the point was a novel one before the Second Division, the respondents
having conceded before the Lord Ordinary that the two conclusions stood or fell together,
and having withdrawn this concession on the reclaiming motion in the Second Division.

It will be convenient to deal with the points raised in what I conceive to be their logical
order rather than the order in which they were argued by the respective counsel. *g*

On this basis, the first question for consideration is the consequence of what was
admitted to be a defect in the purported certificate of 22nd October 1974, namely the
failure by the predecessors of the respondents to include in the certificate information in
writing as to the appellants' rights of appeal to the Secretary of State. Was this
requirement, which has the authority of Parliament behind it, mandatory or was it in
some sense directory only? I have no doubt that it was mandatory, and that the failure *h*
to include this information was fatal to the certificate. In the course of argument counsel
for the respondents candidly conceded that the only purpose of the requirement was to
inform the applicant of his rights of appeal, including the time limit within which they
should be exercised. The present appellants aver that they were misled by this defect and
that it was as a result of this that their appeal was out of time. The averment has never
been put to the proof, and one of the respondents' alternative arguments was that, in the *j*
event of otherwise total failure, the appellants should be put to the proof of this. But in
my view this argument is without foundation. The validity of the certificate itself is in
question, and if, as I believe, the requirement is mandatory the certificate falls
independently of whether the appellants were in fact misled. I find it impossible to
accept that a requirement by an instrument of statutory force designed for the very

purpose of compelling a public authority to inform the subject of his legal rights can be

a treated as simply regulatory if the requirement is not complied with. If I required authority for this proposition I would refer to *Agricultural, Horticultural and Forestry Industry Training Board v Kent*[1], *Rayner v Stepney Corpn*[2] and *Brayhead (Ascot) Ltd v Berkshire County Council*[3] notwithstanding that it relied on *Edwick v Sunbury-on-Thames Urban District Council*[4] which was disapproved in *James v Secretary of State for Wales*[5], which was decided on an argument irrelevant to the present appeal. However I am

b content to assert a general principle to the effect that where Parliament prescribes that an authority with compulsory powers should inform the subject of his right to question those powers, prima facie the requirement must be treated as mandatory. For the reasons which follow, however, this does not dispose the matter in the appellants' favour.

If the requirement that the subject should be informed of his legal rights was mandatory, what follows? The respondents attempted, as I thought, at one time, to

c argue that it thereupon became a nullity, and that therefore a decree of reduction was inappropriate because there was nothing on which it could operate. But I do not accept this argument. The certificate was effective until it was struck down by a competent authority (cf *Brayhead (Ascot) Ltd v Berkshire County Council*[3] and *James v Secretary of State for Wales*[5]). In the course of argument I ventured to draw attention to the passage of the opinion of the Judicial Committee in *Calvin v Carr*[6] in which Lord Wilberforce says of

d a contention that a decision of the stewards of the Australian Jockey Club was void for breach of natural justice:

'This argument led necessarily into the difficult area of what is void and what is voidable, as to which some confusion exists in the authorities. Their Lordships' opinion would be, if it became necessary to fix on one or other of these expressions,

e that a decision made contrary to natural justice is void, but that, until it is so declared by a competent body or court, it may have some effect, or existence, in law. This condition might be better expressed by saying that the decision is invalid or vitiated. In the present context, where the question is whether an appeal lies, the impugned decision cannot be considered as totally void, in the sense of being legally non-existent. So to hold would be wholly unreal.'

f

The subject-matter of that case was wholly different from the present, but my opinion is that the thinking behind it is applicable. The certificate was vitiated in the sense that it failed to comply with a mandatory requirement. But the subject could not safely disregard it as not having been issued. Had he done so, he might well have fallen into the very trap of losing his right to complain of the vitiating factor which has caught other

g subjects in the reported decisions, and, in my view, he was not only wise but bound to seek a decree of reduction or some other appropriate remedy striking down the offending certificate.

A similar line of reasoning disposes of the next contention of the respondents, also rejected in the Second Division, to the effect that, if the certificate is vitiated, the position is the same as if no certificate had been issued and that s 26(4) of the Land Compensation

h (Scotland) Act 1963 then operates in such a way that, no certificate having been issued under s 25, the preceding provisions of the section as to appeals should apply at the expiry of the prescribed period 'as if' the local planning authority had issued a certificate 'containing such a statement as is mentioned in' s 25(4)(*b*) of the Act. The effect of this

j   1   [1970] 1 All ER 304, [1970] 2 QB 19
2   [1911] 2 Ch 312
3   [1964] 1 All ER 149, [1964] 2 QB 303
4   [1961] 3 All ER 10, [1962] 1 QB 229
5   [1966] 3 All ER 964, [1968] AC 409
6   [1979] 2 All ER 440 at 445–446, [1979] 2 WLR 755 at 763

read with arts 3 and 4 of the order would have put the appellants out of time for appeal on the expiry of one month after the expiry of the period prescribed (two months) for the due issue of the certificate by the respondents. The fallacy in this argument lies in the assumption (for it is no more) that the issue by an authority of a certificate vitiated by failure to comply with a mandatory requirement is the same thing as the failure by that authority to issue any purported certificate at all.

The respondents were at pains to argue that the issue by the authority of a certificate vitiated for want of compliance with a mandatory requirement was a casus omissus from the Act and that, in this context, the law of Scotland (unlike the law of England) afforded no remedy at all unless it be by the invocation of the jurisdiction peculiar to Scottish law, which goes by the imposing name of 'nobile officium'. I was utterly unpersuaded by this argument or that there was any difference between Scottish and English law in this respect, and my want of belief is reinforced by what my two learned and noble friends, Lord Fraser of Tullybelton and Lord Keith of Kinkel, have to say about the more arcane aspects of nobile officium. In my opinion, in both jurisdictions the law is the same. The first task is to construe the statute, and ask the question whether the duty in question is mandatory or directory. If it be mandatory, the second task is to ask what remedy is available for non-compliance. If the statute specifies the remedy, well and good. If it is silent, the ordinary remedies available in each jurisdiction, e g proceedings for declaration or prerogative order in England, summons for declarator or reduction in Scotland, should be pursued as appropriate. There is no room for a casus omissus in either case. Counsel for the appellants called in aid of this part of the case the authority of *Maitland, Petitioner*[1], but I do not think authority is required for a proposition to my mind so evident on general principle.

More persuasive, in some way, was the argument for the respondents that it was an odd sort of statute which first provided that an applicant should look at the Act in order to ascertain his right under s 25 (now amended and printed as a Keeling schedule in Sch 9 to the Community Land Act 1975) to make an application and then, if no certificate were forthcoming, look at s 26(4) of the Act and the order in order to note and exercise his right of appeal, but, as regards a purported certificate failing to apprise him of his rights of appeal (which by that time one would have supposed him to know), that he should be in the position to rely on the invalidity of the certificate in the way he now seeks to do. That there is a certain paradox in this I do not deny. But I do not think we are entitled to play fast and loose with statutory requirements designed to inform the subject as to his legal rights against an authority possessed of compulsory powers. There would be an even greater paradox in allowing an acquiring or planning authority first to flout such a requirement and then be heard to say that its non-compliance had no effect on the validity of its legal documents. I do not think that prescriptions for the benefit of the subject are so to be disregarded.

At this stage I should notice a contention on the part of the respondents, which, though, as will be seen, I partly agree with it, does not seem to me to be relevant to the disposal of the cross-appeal. The contention was that in the categorisation of statutory requirements into 'mandatory' and 'directory' there was a subdivision of the category 'directory' into two classes composed (i) of those directory requirements 'substantial compliance' with which satisfied the requirement to the point at which a minor defect of trivial irregularity could be ignored by the court and (ii) of those requirements so purely regulatory in character that failure to comply could in no circumstances affect the validity of what was done. The contention of the respondents was that, even on the assumption against themselves that the requirement of the order that the certificate should include a notification of the appellants' rights to appeal to the Secretary of State, the rest of the certificate was so exactly in accordance with the provisions of the order that the remaining defect could be safely ignored. I do not consider that this argument assists the respondents in the present appeal. I have already held that the requirement relating

---

1   1961 SC 291

to notification of the appellants' rights of appeal was mandatory and not directory in

a either sense contended for by the respondents. But on the assumption that I am wrong about this, a total failure to comply with a significant part of a requirement cannot in any circumstances be regarded as 'substantial compliance' with the total requirement in such a way as to bring the respondents' contention into effect.

Nevertheless I wish to examine the contention itself. In this appeal we are in the field of the rapidly developing jurisprudence of administrative law, and we are considering

b the effect of non compliance by a statutory authority with the statutory requirements affecting the discharge of one of its functions. In the reported decisions there is much language presupposing the existence of stark categories such as 'mandatory' and 'directory', 'void' and 'voidable', a 'nullity', and 'purely regulatory'. Such language is useful; indeed, in the course of this opinion I have used some of it myself. But I wish to say that I am not at all clear that the language itself may not be misleading in so far as it

c may be supposed to present a court with the necessity of fitting a particular case into one or other of mutually exclusive and starkly contrasted compartments, compartments which in some cases (e g 'void' and 'voidable') are borrowed from the language of contract or status, and are not easily fitted to the requirements of administrative law.

When Parliament lays down a statutory requirement for the exercise of legal authority it expects its authority to be obeyed down to the minutest detail. But what the courts

d have to decide in a particular case is the legal consequence of non compliance on the rights of the subject viewed in the light of a concrete state of facts and a continuing chain of events. It may be that what the courts are faced with is not so much a stark choice of alternatives but a spectrum of possibilities in which one compartment or description fades gradually into another. At one end of this spectrum there may be cases in which a fundamental obligation may have been so outrageously and flagrantly ignored or

e defied that the subject may safely ignore what has been done and treat it as having no legal consequences on himself. In such a case if the defaulting authority seeks to rely on its action it may be that the subject is entitled to use the defect in procedure simply as a shield or defence without having taken any positive action of his own. At the other end of the spectrum the defect in procedure may be so nugatory or trivial that the authority can safely proceed without remedial action, confident that, if the subject is so misguided

f as to rely on the fault, the courts will decline to listen to his complaint. But in a very great number of cases, it may be in a majority of them, it may be necessary for a subject, in order to safeguard himself, to go to the court for declaration of his rights, the grant of which may well be discretionary, and by the like token it may be wise for an authority (as it certainly would have been here) to do everything in its power to remedy the fault in its procedure so as not to deprive the subject of his due or themselves of their power

g to act. In such cases, though language like 'mandatory', 'directory', 'void', 'voidable', 'nullity' and so forth may be helpful in argument, it may be misleading in effect if relied on to show that the courts, in deciding the consequences of a defect in the exercise of power, are necessarily bound to fit the facts of a particular case and a developing chain of events into rigid legal categories or to stretch or cramp them on a bed of Procrustes invented by lawyers for the purposes of convenient exposition. As I have said, the case

h does not really arise here, since we are in the presence of total non compliance with a requirement which I have held to be mandatory. Nevertheless I do not wish to be understood in the field of administrative law and in the domain where the courts apply a supervisory jurisdiction over the acts of subordinate authority purporting to exercise statutory powers, to encourage the use of rigid legal classifications. The jurisdiction is inherently discretionary and the court is frequently in the presence of differences of

j degree which merge almost imperceptibly into differences of kind.

There was only one other argument for the respondents on their cross-appeal that I need notice. This was that the requirement not complied with was separable from the rest of the requirements as to the certificate. I do not read it as such. It was an integral part of the requirement that the certificate should 'include' a written notification of the rights of appeal.

Once the cross-appeal is disposed of, I do not find much difficulty in stating my reasons
for allowing the appeal. In my view the Second Division only refused the second *a*
conclusion of the summons because in their view of art 3(2) of the order the respondents
had no power to issue the new certificate demanded. Again, I do not so read the order.
The duty under s 25 is a continuing duty. The fact that art 3(2) of the order is not
complied with in time does not put an end to the obligation of the authority to
comply. That this is so is apparent from a construction of s 25 (as amended) in the light
of s 26 which expressly allows the parties to agree an extension of time, which would not *b*
be possible if an extension of time was ultra vires the authority.

In my view, therefore, the appeal succeeds, and the cross-appeal fails with the results
indicated in the first paragraphs of this opinion.

LORD WILBERFORCE. My Lords, I have had the benefit of reading in advance the
opinions of the noble and learned Lord on the Woolsack and my noble and learned *c*
friend, Lord Keith of Kinkel. I agree with them and with the conclusions proposed.

LORD FRASER OF TULLYBELTON. My Lords, this appeal raises the question
whether a certificate of alternative development issued by a local planning authority
which was defective in form is valid or invalid and, if invalid, what remedy is available
to the party who applied for it. The defect was that the certificate did not include a *d*
statement of the appellants' rights of appeal to the Secretary of State as required by the
relevant statutory instrument. The appellants (pursuers in the action), on whose behalf
the certificate was applied for by their architects, maintain that the defective certificate
is invalid. The respondents, who are the local planning authority, maintain that the
requirement that the certificate shall include a statement on the rights of appeal is not
mandatory but only directory, and that the failure to comply with it does not affect the *e*
validity of the certificate that was issued. The action has two conclusions still alive, apart
from one for expenses. The first conclusion is for reduction of the defective certificate.
The second is for decree of declarator that the respondents are bound to issue a fresh
certificate (sc in proper form) and for decree ordaining the respondents to issue such a
certificate within two months after the date of decree. The Lord Ordinary, Lord
Dunpark, granted decree in terms of both conclusions. The Second Division granted *f*
decree of reduction, but refused decree in terms of the second conclusion. The
respondents have cross-appealed against the interlocutor of the Second Division, in so far
as it granted decree of reduction, and their cross-appeal is opposed by the appellants.

All the facts, which, in my opinion, are relevant are agreed. There is a dispute on one
matter of fact but, for reasons to be mentioned later, I do not consider that the matter is
material. The appellants are the owners of three areas of ground at Scotstoun, Bridge of *g*
Don, Aberdeenshire, which Aberdeen County Council, who were then the education
authority, proposed to acquire compulsorily for educational purposes. On 9th September
1974 a firm of chartered architects applied on behalf of the appellants to Aberdeen
County Council (in their capacity as local planning authority) for a certificate of
alternative development under s 25 of the Land Compensation (Scotland) Act 1963. The
respondents are the statutory successors of Aberdeen County Council as local planning *h*
authority. A certificate of alternative development governs the amount of compensation
payable to the appellants for the compulsory acquisition of their land. The application
specified 'residential with associated commercial purposes' as a class of development
which appeared to the appellants to be appropriate for these areas of land. If the local
planning authority had issued a certificate that planning permission for that purpose
might reasonably have been expected to be granted, compensation would have been *j*
assessed on the assumption that it would have been granted: see s 23(5). (The assumption
has been changed by the Community Land Act 1975, Sch 10, para 5, but the change does
not affect this appeal.) On 22nd October 1974 Aberdeen County Council issued a
certificate stating that 'in the opinion of the local planning authority ... planning
permission could not reasonably be expected to be granted for any development other

than that proposed to be carried out by the acquiring authority' (which may conveniently
a be called a 'negative certificate') and stating the reason for that opinion. But the certificate
did not include any statement of the rights of appeal to the Secretary of State as it should
have done in order to comply with the Town and Country Planning (General
Development) (Scotland) Order 1959, art 3(3), which provides as follows:

> 'If a local planning authority issue a certificate otherwise than for the class or
> classes of development specified in the application made to them, or contrary to
b > representations in writing made to them by a party directly concerned, they shall in
> that certificate include a statement in writing of their reasons for so doing and of the
> rights of appeal to the Secretary of State given by section 6 and this order.'

The reference to s 6 is to a section of the Town and Country Planning (Scotland) Act 1959
which was repealed and superseded by s 26 of the Land Compensation (Scotland) Act
c 1963. The order was continued in force under s 47(1) of the 1963 Act.
The certificate was received by the appellants' architects on 24th October 1974. On
9th January 1975 the appellants' solicitors wrote to the Scottish Development Department
intimating an appeal against the certificate on its merits, on grounds stated in the
letter. The intimation was of course more than one month (actually about two and a half
months) after the receipt of the certificate and was therefore out of time under art 4(1)
d of the regulations which provides: 'The time for giving notice of an appeal under section
6 shall be the period of one month from the date of receipt of the certificate . . .' On 15th
January 1975 the Scottish Development Department replied stating that notice of appeal
had to be given within one month and that the Secretary of State had no power to extend
the period. They added: 'As the certificate against which you wish to appeal was issued
on 22nd October 1974, the Secretary of State regrets that he is unable to accept your letter
e as a valid appeal.' On 10th February 1975 the appellants' solicitors wrote again to the
Scottish Development Department saying that the purported certificate had omitted to
advise their clients of their rights of appeal to the Secretary of State and that it was
therefore defective as a certificate. They requested that, rather than adopting the
cumbersome and expensive procedure of insisting on a fresh certificate, to be followed
by an appeal, the Secretary of State should allow the notice of appeal in their letter of 9th
f January to stand. On 6th March 1975 the Scottish Development Department replied
that 'the Secretary of State has no power to accept a late appeal' and suggested that the
appellants take up the matter with the county council. The solicitors then wrote to the
county clerk on 14th March 1975 pointing out the defect in the certificate and asking for
a 'certificate in proper form' to be issued as soon as possible. The county council refused
to issue a fresh certificate and on 16th April 1975 the appellants raised this action
g concluding for reduction and declarator. Aberdeen County Council were called as the
first defenders (now succeeded by the present appellants). The Secretary of State for
Scotland was called as second defender for any interest he might have.
The action came before Lord Dunpark as Lord Ordinary in procedure roll for the first
time in January 1977 and by interlocutor dated 24th February 1977 (not 24th January
1977 as stated in the interlocutor sheet in appendix 1) he found in favour of the
h appellants. His Lordship, in a laudable attempt to short circuit procedure, made a
finding that 'The notice of appeal given by letter dated 9th January 1975 [from the
appellants' solicitors to the second named defender] was a valid notice of appeal'. In his
opinion the Lord Ordinary expressed the hope that the Secretary of State would take his
finding as equivalent to a decree of declarator that the appellants' notice of appeal was
timeous and valid in the circumstances and stated that he would certainly have granted
j decree to that effect if there had been a conclusion for it. At that stage the Secretary of
State had not lodged defences. Aberdeen County Council reclaimed against the Lord
Ordinary's interlocutor of 24th February 1977 and the appellants amended the closed
record by adding a conclusion for declarator in the terms which the Lord Ordinary had
said he would have upheld. The Secretary of State then lodged defences and the case was
remitted by the Second Division to the Lord Ordinary to consider it further.

At a further hearing the Lord Ordinary was persuaded by counsel for the Secretary of
State that his finding made on 24th February 1977 was wrong and on 15th June 1978 he   *a*
refused to grant decree of declarator in terms of the third conclusion (the one that had
been added by amendment) and dismissed the action so far as directed against the
Secretary of State. That part of his decision has been accepted by all parties and his
original finding was not supported by any party before the Second Division. The Lord
Ordinary granted decree of reduction in terms of the first conclusion. He also granted
decree of declarator and ordaining the defenders to issue an amended certificate in terms   *b*
of the second conclusion; in this part of his interlocutor the Lord Ordinary proceeded on
a concession made by senior counsel then appearing for the respondents to the effect that
if decree in terms of the first conclusion was granted then decree in terms of the second
conclusion should follow. That concession was withdrawn when the case came before
the Second Division. The question of whether or not the concession was rightly made is
now in substance the question raised in this appeal. The Second Division upheld the   *c*
Lord Ordinary's interlocutor in granting decree of reduction, but they recalled the
interlocutor in so far as it granted decree in terms of the second conclusion. They held
that the time limit for issuing a certificate of alternative development had expired and
that decree in terms of the second conclusion would be incompetent. The result is that
matters are left in a state which is clearly unsatisfactory. The defective certificate has
been reduced, but nothing has been put in its place, and no order has been pronounced   *d*
requiring the respondents to issue a fresh or amended certificate. Their Lordships of the
Second Division evidently recognised that the position was unsatisfactory and in their
opinion they said[1]: 'It may be, and on this we express no view, that the pursuers have
some other remedy against the first defenders for issuing the certificate which has now
to be reduced.' But they gave no indication of what other remedy there might be.

It will be convenient to consider first the cross-appeal, that is, the respondents' appeal   *e*
against the decree reducing the certificate of 22nd October 1974. Logically the first
point to consider is whether the provision in art 3(3) of the 1959 order to the effect that
the local planning authority 'shall in that certificate include a statement in writing of
. . . the rights of appeal' is mandatory or not. I do not think that literal compliance with
the provision is mandatory; for example, if a statement of the rights of appeal had not
been 'included' in the certificate but had been sent with it in a separate sheet, that would   *f*
in my opinion have been substantial compliance and would have been sufficient. But
here there was no compliance at all with the provision. The purpose of the statement
required by art 3(3) clearly is to inform the applicant first that he has a right of appeal and
secondly of the time in which the right has to be exercised. These are matters of
importance to an applicant and Parliament, acting through the Secretary of State, has
considered their importance to be such that they ought to be expressly brought to the   *g*
notice of an applicant. Failure to do so cannot in my opinion be treated as if it were a
mere technicality or a procedural irregularity which might be overlooked. The omission
in this case was similar to, but more serious than, the omission of the address for the
service of a notice of appeal which was held by the Court of Appeal to invalidate an
assessment notice in *Agricultural, Horticultural and Forestry Industry Training Board v
Kent*[2]. It was much more serious than the omission in *Rae v Davidson*[3], which was   *h*
described by the Lord Justice Clerk as 'the merest technicality', but which was held
nevertheless to invalidate a notice to remove from a farm because the statutory
requirements for such a notice had not been exactly complied with. I agree with both
those decisions, and I have no doubt that the effect of the omission in this case was to
make the certificate invalid in the sense that it cannot stand, if challenged by the
appellants. It is not a complete nullity (for example it could have been appealed against   *j*
by an appeal taken timeously) and it exists until it is reduced, or set aside in some way.

1   1979 SLT 221 at 227
2   [1970] 1 All ER 304, [1970] 2 QB 19
3   1954 SC 361

I do not think it is possible to treat the certificate as consisting of two parts, capable of
a being severed from one another, one part being the actual certificate and the other being
the statement of the rights of appeal. Both parts are required by the order and both are
of substantial importance. The omission of either part is therefore fatal to the validity of
the whole.

Counsel for the respondents argued that there were three reasons why the inclusion of
a statement of rights of appeal to the Secretary of State was not mandatory. The first was
b that the notice was not of great assistance to the applicant, because receipt of the
certificate would not be the first he knew of the matter. He must have applied for the
certificate, and therefore he must already have read the 1959 order. I agree that he must
have read the order, but in my opinion that does not mean that a statement of these
rights of appeal, even if it is only a reminder of what he had already read, is not of value
to him. The second reason was that the obligation to include the statement was imposed
c only by the 1959 order and not by the statute itself, whereas the scheme of the legislation
was for all the essential requirements of the certificate to be laid down in the Act itself.
In my opinion it is not possible to distinguish in this way between essential and non-
essential requirements: any such distinction must depend on the importance of the
particular requirements and not on the machinery by which they are specified. The
third reason was the only one that is in my opinion entitled to some weight. It was based
d on the provisions of s 26(4) of the Act to the effect that if, at the expiry of the period of
two months within which the certificate is to be issued, no certificate has in fact been
issued, the provisions for appeal shall apply as if a negative certificate had been issued, i e
the applicant can appeal within one further month. In circumstances where that
provision has to be applied, the applicant ex hypothesi would not have the benefit of a
statement of his rights of appeal but he would have to discover them for himself. How
e then, it was asked rhetorically, could the inclusion of such a statement in a certificate,
when one was issued, be essential? I see the force of the argument but in my opinion it
cannot prevail against the express provision in the order made under the authority of
Parliament.

The appellants have averred that, as a result of the failure of the county council to
comply with art 3(3), they did not appreciate that notice of appeal required to be given
f within one month of receipt of the certificate and that that was the reason for the appeal
being out of time. These averments are denied by the respondents and their counsel
argued that in the event of the appeal succeeding otherwise they should be remitted for
proof before the Lord Ordinary. In my opinion that is unnecessary and the averments
themselves are irrelevant. The validity of the certificate is not in my opinion dependent
on whether the appellants were actually prejudiced by it or not. This is the single
g disputed matter of fact to which I referred above.

The next question is whether reduction of the certificate is the appropriate remedy in
the circumstances. Counsel for the respondents argued that whatever the appropriate
remedy might be, it certainly was not reduction, because, he said, the nobile officium of
the Court of Session was available to provide for what was a casus improvisus. The
argument as I understood it was that a casus improvisus arose in this way. It is now too
h late for the appellants to make a fresh or amended application for a certificate because a
reference has been made to the Lands Tribunal for Scotland (which has replaced the
official arbiter) to assess compensation: see s 25(2) of the 1963 Act. We were told that the
Lands Tribunal had, at the request of both parties, made alternative assessments on
different assumptions. I agree that it is too late for a fresh application. It is also too late,
so it is said, for the respondents to issue a fresh or amended certificate because a certificate
j has to be issued within two months from the date of application (unless the period is
extended by agreement) and after the expiry of the two months' period the local
planning authority is functus and cannot issue a certificate. A complete impasse
therefore arises comparable to that which existed in *Maitland, Petitioner*[1] when a licensing

1   1961 SC 291

court could not be reconvened to pronounce an order that it had omitted to make per incuriam. The Court of Session resolved the impasse by an exercise of its nobile officium. For reasons that I shall explain, I do not agree that it is too late for the respondents to issue a proper certificate, but, even assuming that it is, I am of opinion that the argument is misconceived. The fact that Parliament has not provided for the legal consequences to follow from a failure to carry out the statutory procedure does not give rise to a casus improvisus. The consequences of such failure have to be ascertained according to the general rules of law. They may include a right to recover damages, or to have a document reduced, or to obtain a decree of declarator or some other redress but there is no impasse of the kind that has hitherto been regarded as suitable for solution by an exercise of the nobile officium. That is an exceptional power and the court 'does not view with favour its indefinite extension': see McClaren on Court of Session Practice[1]. Its proper use as the Lord President pointed out in *Maitland, Petitioner*[2] is 'to enable justice to be done where, per incuriam, some *formal step* [my italics] has been omitted' but it cannot be invoked 'even by agreement of all parties interested, to enable the court to supplement the statutory procedure by what would, in effect, be an amendment of a statute'. The proposal that the nobile officium should be invoked in the present case to extend the period either for issuing the certificate or for appealing against the certificate assumes that whichever period is to be extended is one which has been fixed by the statute or the order and which has expired. Otherwise no extension would be necessary. But an exercise of the power for such a purpose would be in order to get round the Act or the order and thus in effect to amend it. That would not be a proper exercise of the power.

I am therefore of opinion that the Lord Ordinary and the Second Division were well founded in granting decree of reduction of the defective certificate, and I would dismiss the cross-appeal.

Turning now to the original appeal, the question is whether the issue of a fresh or amended certificate of alternative development now, more than five years after the application made on 9th September 1974, would be contrary to the provisions of the 1963 Act and the 1959 order. The second conclusion in its original form was for a 'fresh' conclusion, but for some reason it was amended while the case was before the Second Division by substituting 'amended' for 'fresh'. I do not regard the difference as important, but I consider that 'fresh' is the more appropriate word and I would allow an amendment to restore it to the second conclusion. The provision of the Act which is directly relevant to this question is in s 25(4), as follows:

> 'Where an application is made to the local planning authority for a certificate under this section in respect of an interest in land, the local planning authority shall, not earlier than twenty-one days after the date [on which a copy of the application has been or will be served on the other party] issue to the applicant a certificate stating that, in the opinion of the local planning authority in respect of the land in question, either . . .'

Then follow two alternatives, the second of which is a negative certificate such as the purported certificate issued in this case.

Two points in s 25(4) are important for the present purpose. First, it imposes a duty on the local planning authority to issue a certificate under the section when application is made for one. Second, it prescribes a date 'not earlier' on which a certificate is to be issued. The reason, no doubt, is to allow time for the opposing party to make representations to the authority. But neither in s 25(4) nor elsewhere in the Act itself is any date prescribed after which a certificate may not be issued. The Act does provide for a time to be prescribed by a 'development order' within which a certificate is to be issued (see s 28(*b*): 'for prescribing the manner in which notices of appeals under section 26 of

1　(1916) p 101
2　1961 SC 291

this Act are to be given, and the time for giving any such notice'). A 'development order'
a is defined by s 45(1) to mean an order under s 11(1) of the Town and Country Planning
(Scotland) Act 1947 and it therefore includes the 1959 order. The time for the issue of
a certificate of alternative development is prescribed by art 3(2) of the 1959 order, which
is as follows:

'The time within which a certificate is to be issued by a local planning authority
shall, subject to the provisions of subsection (4) of [s 25 of the 1963 Act], be the
b period of two months from the date of receipt of such an application by them.'

It was argued for the respondents that the effect of art 3(2) was to fix a maximum
period of two months (subject to extension by agreement under s 26(4) of the Act) for
issuing a certificate and that after the end of that period no certificate could lawfully be
issued. The issue of a certificate after that would be, in the words of the Second Division,
c 'in the teeth of the statutory provisions'. I am unable to accept that submission. One
starts with the fact that the local planning authority is under a duty to issue a certificate:
see s 25(4). The purpose of art 3(2) is in my opinion to direct the local planning authority
to perform its duty within the period of two months (unless extended by agreement) and
that is a provision primarily in the interests of the party who has applied for the
certificate. But it seems to me wrong and, if I may say so without disrespect to those who
d think otherwise, almost perverse, to read art 3(2) as implying that if the local planning
authority can stall and avoid performing its duty for two months, the duty is then to fly
off altogether. Yet that would be the result of the respondents' argument. On the
contrary, I am of opinion that the local planning authority remains under a continuing
duty to issue a valid certificate even though it may have failed to do so within two
months. Mere delay cannot absolve it from its duty. The expiry of the two months'
e period from receipt of the application is not, on any view, an absolute bar to issue of a
certificate because the period can be extended by agreement: see s 26(4). Moreover, and
this is a point of importance, an extension can be agreed on 'at any time'. In my opinion
those words mean at any time either during the period of two months or after the end
of the period, and they are a positive indication that the power and duty of the local
planning authority to issue a certificate do not cease at the end of the period. The
f subsequent provision of s 26(4) to the effect that if no certificate has been issued by the
local planning authority within the two-month period the provisions relating to appeal
shall apply 'as if' a negative certificate had been issued gives the applicant a right of
appeal, but it does not include or imply a provision that if the applicant does not avail
himself of his right of appeal, the certificate cannot be issued after the end of the two-
month period. In my opinion, therefore, the Second Division was in error in thinking
g that it would be incompetent for them now to ordain the respondents to issue a fresh or
amended certificate; but for their having taken that view, I think they would have
pronounced decree in terms of the second conclusion.

I would allow the appeal, recall the interlocutor of the Second Division dated 26th
January 1979 so far as it refused to grant decree in terms of the second conclusion of the
summons, sustain the second and third pleas in law for the appellants, and refuse the
h respondents' cross-appeal. The appellants should have the costs of the appeal in this
House and their expenses in the Court of Session except that, as counsel for the appellants
conceded, they are not entitled to relief against the respondents for the expenses for
which the appellants have been found liable to the second defender.

LORD RUSSELL OF KILLOWEN. My Lords, I have had the advantage of reading
j in draft the opinion to be delivered by my noble and learned friend, Lord Keith of
Kinkel. I agree with it and with the order proposed by him.

LORD KEITH OF KINKEL. My Lords, in 1974 Aberdeen County Council, the
respondents' predecessors as local authority for the area in question, were proposing to
acquire for educational purposes three sites owned by the appellants at Scotstoun, Bridge

of Don. Aberdeen County Council were an authority possessing powers of compulsory
purchase. On 9th September 1974 a firm of architects acting for the appellants applied *a*
to the council in its capacity as local planning authority for a certificate of alternative
development under the provisions of s 25 of the Land Compensation (Scotland) Act
1963. It is unnecessary to go into the details of these provisions. Their effect, in outline,
is that where an authority possessing compulsory purchase powers proposes to acquire an
interest in land, either the authority or the owner of the interest may (except in certain
cases which do no include the present one) apply to the local planning authority for what *b*
may conveniently be called a certificate of appropriate alternative development. The
application is to be served on the other party, and by sub-s (4) the local planning authority
is required, not earlier than 21 days after the date of service, to issue to the applicant a
certificate stating that, in the opinion of that authority, either (a) planning permission for
development of one or more classes therein specified might reasonably be expected to be
granted, or (b) planning permission could not reasonably be expected to be granted for *c*
any development other than that proposed to be carried out by the acquiring authority.
    By virtue of ss 22(4) and 23(5) of the Act, the terms of a certificate issued under s 25
may affect very materially the amount of compensation to be paid for acquisition of the
relevant interest in land. So s 26 provides for an appeal to the Secretary of State for
Scotland against such a certificate by the person entitled to the relevant interest in land
or by the acquiring authority. The Secretary of State is required on appeal to him to *d*
consider the matter de novo, and, if either party so desires, to afford the parties and also
the local planning authority an opportunity of appearing and being heard before a
person appointed by him. Subsection (4) is of some materiality and must be quoted in
full:

> 'Where an application is made for a certificate under section 25 of this Act, and at *e*
> the expiry of the time prescribed by a development order for the issue thereof (or,
> if an extended period is at any time agreed upon in writing by the parties directly
> concerned and the local planning authority, at the end of that period) no certificate
> has been issued by the local planning authority in accordance with that section, the
> preceding provisions of this section shall apply as if the local planning authority had
> issued such a certificate containing such a statement as is mentioned in subsection *f*
> (4)(b) of that section.'

    Section 28 of the Act deals with the making by development order of provisions
regulating, inter alia, the making of applications under s 25 and appeals under s 26, in
particular prescribing the time within which a certificate is required to be issued under
the former section and the time for giving notice of appeal under the latter. Prior to the *g*
coming into force of the 1963 Act, the Secretary of State for Scotland had made, under
the corresponding powers contained in the Town and Country Planning (Scotland) Act
1959, the Town and Country Planning (General Development) (Scotland) Order 1959.
It was common ground that this fell to be treated at the material time as having been
made by virtue of the powers of the 1963 Act. The provisions of the order relevant for
present purposes, read with the substitution of appropriate references to the 1963 Act for *h*
references to the 1959 Act, are as follows:

> '3 . . . (2) The time within which a certificate is to be issued by a local planning
> authority shall, subject to the provisions of [s 25(4)], be the period of two months
> from the date of receipt of such an application by them.
>   '(3) If a local planning authority issue a certificate otherwise than for the class or *j*
> classes of development specified in the application made to them, or contrary to
> representations in writing made to them by a party directly concerned, they shall in
> that certificate include a statement in writing of their reasons for so doing and of the
> rights of appeal to the Secretary of State given by [s 26] and this order . . .

a
'4.—(1) The time for giving notice of an appeal under [s 26] shall be the period of one month from the date of receipt of the certificate or of the expiry of the time or extended period mentioned in subsection (4) of that section, as the case may be . . .'

b
To resume the factual narrative, it is to be observed that in the appellants' application of 9th September 1974 it was represented that an appropriate class of development for the land in question would be residential with associated commercial purposes. On 22nd October 1974 the respondents issued to the appellants a certificate, in effect under s 25(4)(b) of the 1963 Act, stating that, in their opinion as local planning authority, planning permission could not reasonably be expected to be granted in respect of the land for any development other than that proposed to be carried out by themselves as acquiring authority, i e development for school purposes. The certificate was contained

c
in a letter from the deputy town clerk, which went on to give the reasons for which the respondents' planning committee took that view, but which omitted to comply with the requirement of art 3(3) of the 1959 order that a certificate under s 25(4)(b) of the 1963 Act should include also a statement in writing of the rights of appeal given by s 26 of the Act and by the order. On 9th January 1975 the appellants by letter to the Secretary of State for Scotland sought to appeal to him against the certificate. This was, of course,

d
outside the time limit of one month prescribed by art 4(1) of the 1959 order. The appellants in their pleadings aver that they did not appreciate that notice of appeal had to be given within that period by reason that the certificate omitted the requisite statement of their rights of appeal, but the respondents dispute this. In the result, the Secretary of State refused to entertain any appeal on the ground that it was out of time and he therefore had no power to do so. The appellants' solicitors on 14th March 1975 called on the respondents to issue a certificate in proper form, but they refused to do so.

e
Accordingly the appellants, on 16th April 1975, raised the present action against the respondents concluding, first, for reduction of the purported certificate dated 22nd October 1974, and second (as the conclusion was amended in the Inner House) for declarator that the respondents were bound, on the appellants' application of 9th September 1974, to issue an amended certificate in respect of the land in question and decree ordaining them to do so within two months of such decree. The Secretary of State

f
was called as second defender for any interest which he might have.
The case came before the Lord Ordinary (Lord Dunpark) on procedure roll, and on 24th February 1977 he delivered an opinion in which he expressed the view that the certificate of 22nd October 1974 was invalid by reason that it contained no statement in writing of the appellants' rights of appeal such as was required by art 3(3) of the 1959 order. Instead, however, of granting decree of reduction and declarator as concluded for,

g
he made a finding that the appellants' letter to the Secretary of State dated 9th January 1975 was a valid notice of appeal against the certificate 'in the belief', as he put it, 'that the Secretary of State will now accept it as such and arrange to hear the appeal'. The respondents reclaimed, and in the course of the proceedings before the Inner House the appellants proposed to amend their pleadings by adding a conclusion for declarator that

h
their letter of 9th January 1975 was a timeous and valid notice of appeal with which the Secretary of State was bound to deal. This amendment was allowed and the Secretary of State thereupon lodged defences. The Lord Ordinary's interlocutor of 24th February 1977 was then recalled and the case was remitted back to him to proceed as accords. In due course there was a further procedure roll debate before Lord Dunpark, as a result of which he was persuaded, having heard argument for the Secretary of State, to depart

j
from his earlier finding that the appellants had given valid notice of appeal. Accordingly he issued an interlocutor dated 15th June 1978 granting decree of reduction of the certificate in terms of the appellants' first conclusion and also, on the basis of a concession by counsel for the respondents that this must necessarily follow, decree of declarator in terms of the second conclusion, that the respondents were bound to issue a fresh certificate within two months of the date of decree. The action so far as directed against

the Secretary of State was dismissed as irrelevant, and that matter has since been allowed
to rest, the Secretary of State taking no further part in the proceedings.

The respondents reclaimed, and the reclaiming motion was heard by the Second
Division (the Lord Justice-Clerk (Lord Wheatley), Lord Kissen and Lord Robertson).
Counsel for the respondents withdrew the concession that decree in terms of the second
conclusion must necessarily follow from decree in terms of the first, and also argued for
the validity of the certificate dated 22nd October 1974 on the ground that the provisions
of art 3(3) of the 1959 order were not mandatory but only directory. By interlocutor
dated 26th January 1979, which is that now appealed from, the Second Division affirmed
the Lord Ordinary's decision that the certificate was invalid and should be reduced, but
refused as incompetent decree in terms of the second conclusion ordaining the
respondents to issue an amended certificate. Their ground for so refusing was thus stated
in the opinion of the court[1]:

'The procedure called for in the second conclusion would involve ignoring the
specific statutory requirements regulating the issue of a certificate, and issuing an
order of court ordaining the first defenders contrary to their wishes to do something
for which there is not only no statutory authority but which would be directly in
the teeth of the statutory provisions.'

The appellants by their appeal to this House seek reversal of that part of the Second
Division's interlocutor which refused decree in terms of the second conclusion. The
respondents not only resist that but by their cross-appeal attack that part of the
interlocutor which granted decree in terms of the first conclusion.

It is logical in the circumstances to consider first whether the Lord Ordinary and their
Lordships of the Second Division were right in granting decree of reduction of the
certificate dated 22nd October 1974. It was argued for the respondents initially that the
notice as to rights of appeal required by art 3(3) of the 1959 order was something
severable from the certificate itself. The certificate, so it was maintained, constituted a
decision of the local planning authority which had a force and validity of its own
unaffected by any failure to give the statutorily required notice about rights of appeal.
Reference was made to the decision of the Court of Appeal in *Brayhead (Ascot) Ltd v
Berkshire County Council*[2], where it was held that the failure of a local planning authority,
when granting planning permission subject to a condition, to give reasons in writing for
the imposition of the condition as required by art 5(9) of the Town and Country
Planning General Development Order 1950[3] did not render the condition void. This
was on the ground, as stated by Winn J[4], that while the requirement was mandatory in
the sense that compliance with it could be enforced by mandamus, non-compliance did
not render the condition void because that result was not required for the effective
achievement of the purposes of the statute under which the requirement was imposed,
and not intended by Parliament on a proper construction of that statute. In my opinion
the argument is not assisted by the case referred to and is unsound. Article 3(3) of the
1959 order specifically states that any certificate issued under s 25(4)(*b*) of the Act 'shall
include' a statement in writing of rights of appeal. This is entirely contrary to any idea
of severability, and the provision is clearly necessary for effectively achieving the obvious
purpose that the applicant receiving the certificate should know what his rights are. The
consequences of failure to inform him of these rights may be irretrievable, unlike the
consequences of failure to state reasons in writing, which can always be put right at a
later date without anything more serious than some inconvenience.

Then it was contended that art 3(3) was not intended to be mandatory or imperative,
but merely directory and procedural in effect. It was said that any applicant for a
certificate of appropriate alternative development must have read the 1959 order for the

---

1   1979 SLT 221 at 227
2   [1964] 1 All ER 149, [1964] 2 QB 303
3   SI 1950 No 728
4   [1964] 1 All ER 149 at 153–154, [1964] 2 QB 303 at 313–314

purpose of finding out how to make application.   Reliance was also placed on the
circumstance that, in cases where s 26(5) of the 1963 Act operated so as to give the
applicant a right of appeal by reason of the planning authority's failure to issue a
certificate timeously, no machinery was provided whereby the applicant might have
notice of that right of appeal.   It was pointed out that such machinery was provided in
Sch 2 to the Town and Country Planning General Development Order 1950 in relation
to the analogous statutory provisions regarding appeals against deemed refusal of
planning permission (though curiously enough not in the corresponding Scottish order[1]),
by way of the form there prescribed for acknowledgment by local planning authorities
of applications for planning permission.

The word 'shall' used in art 3(3) is normally to be interpreted as connoting a mandatory
provision, meaning that what is thereby enjoined is not merely desired to be done but
must be done.   In many instances failure to obtemper a mandatory provision has the
consequence that the proceedings with which the failure is connected are rendered
invalid.   But that is not necessarily so.   As is shown by *Brayhead (Ascot) Ltd v Berkshire
County Council*[2] something may turn on the importance of the provision in relation to the
statutory purpose which the provision is directed to achieving, and whether any
opportunity exists of later putting right the failure.   I have no doubt that in the present
case the provision under consideration is intended to be mandatory and is of such a
character that failure to comply with it renders the certificate invalid.   Where Parliament,
albeit through subordinate legislation, has enacted that a person is to be informed of the
rights of appeal conferred on him by statute in relation to a particular subject-matter
whereby his rights may be very materially affected, it will not do to say that failure to
comply with the enactment has no legal result whatever.   The matter is of great
importance and has been shown to have been so regarded by Parliament.   Failure to
comply may deprive the person concerned of his rights of appeal with no opportunity of
rectifying the situation.   While it is indeed curious that no provision is made for
acquainting an applicant for a certificate with his rights of appeal where no certificate is
issued within the prescribed time, I regard that omission as inadvertent, and not as
serving in any way to indicate an intention that the provisions of art 3(3) about
notification of rights of appeal should be merely directory.   I note that authority in
favour of the view that a provision of this nature is mandatory in the sense that failure
to comply renders the proceedings invalid is to be found in *Agricultural, Horticultural and
Forestry Industry Training Board v Kent*[3].   That was a decision of the Court of Appeal on
art 4(3) of the Industrial Training Levy (Agricultural, Horticultural and Forestry) Order
1967[4], whereby any notice of assessment to a levy made under s 4 of the Industrial
Training Act 1964 was required to state the appropriate address for service of notice of
appeal against the levy.   Failure to comply with this requirement was held to invalidate
the notice of assessment.

The final argument for the respondents on this branch of the case turned on the terms
of s 26(4) of the 1963 Act, which I have quoted above.   That enactment gives a right of
appeal where the local authority fails to issue a certificate within the prescribed time, on
the basis that a certificate in terms of s 25(4)(*b*) is deemed to have been issued.   In the
event, so the argument ran, that the certificate actually issued in this case is held to have
been invalid, the situation is the same as if no certificate had been issued.   Therefore
s 26(4) applies, under which no question of notification of rights of appeal arises.   The
appellants should have appealed to the Secretary of State within one month of the expiry
of the period of two months from the receipt by the respondents of the appellants'
application for a certificate.   They did not do so, and therefore they have lost any right of
appeal.   In my opinion this argument also is unsound.   In the first place it is to be

---

1   SI 1950 No 942
2   [1964] 1 All ER 119, [1964] 2 QB 303
3   [1970] 1 All ER 304, [1970] 2 QB 19
4   SI 1967 No 1747

observed that the argument is elided if decree is to be granted not only reducing the certificate actually issued but also ordaining the respondents to issue a new certificate in proper form. It is not an argument in favour of the validity of the certificate issued.   *a* Indeed, it requires that the certificate should have been totally void ab initio and that the respondents should be treated as having done nothing at all in response to the appellants' application. That would, in my opinion, be totally unrealistic. The respondents did issue a certificate, but it contained a defect enabling it to be successfully attacked as invalid. I do not consider that s 26(4) applies to that situation. It applies where after the expiry of the time prescribed 'no certificate has been issued'. Here a certificate was issued   *b* which, though defective, was not a complete nullity. In this context use of the expressions 'void' and 'voidable', which have a recognised significance and importance in certain fields of the law of contract, is to be avoided as inappropriate and apt to confuse. A decision or other act of a more or less formal character may be invalid and subject to being so declared in court of law, and yet have some legal effect or existence prior to such declaration. In particular, it may be capable of being submitted to an appeal (cf *Calvin v*   *c* *Carr*[1] per Lord Wilberforce). In my opinion the certificate issued in the present case was of that character. It had some legal effect unless and until reduced, and in particular it might, in my view, have been the proper subject of a timeous appeal to the Secretary of State.

It follows that in my opinion the Lord Ordinary and the Second Division were right in granting decree of reduction of the certificate, and it is necessary to consider next   *d* whether the Second Division was right to refuse decree in terms of the second conclusion.

The view taken in the Second Division was, as I have already mentioned, that the respondents had no power to issue a certificate after the expiry of two months from the date of receipt of the appellants' application, that it would be 'in the teeth of the statutory provisions' to ordain them to do so, and that the second conclusion was therefore incompetent. But art 3(2) of the 1959 order, while laying down that the time within   *e* which a certificate is to be issued shall be the two months' period, does not expressly forbid the issue of a certificate after the expiry of that period. Nor, in my opinion, does it do so by necessary implication. It cannot reasonably be considered necessary for the achievement of the purposes of the 1963 Act that the two months' time limit should be strictly adhered to, or that failure to do so might have irretrievable consequences. Therefore I would regard this provision as clearly having not a mandatory but a directory   *f* character, designed to secure reasonable expedition on the part of the local planning authority. It is easy to envisage that an application for a certificate might call for elucidation or further information than was at first available, with the result that strict adherence to the time limit was impossible or at least not conducive to the satisfactory disposal of the application, and might be departed from without any prejudice to anyone. Such considerations make it quite unreasonable to regard the provision as   *g* mandatory. I think that further support for the view that it is not is to be gathered from that part of s 26(4) of the Act which indicates that the parties concerned and the planning authority may 'at any time' agree on an extended period, of whatever duration, for the issue of a certificate. This also serves to show that the obligation to issue a certificate which is laid on the local planning authority by s 25(4) is a continuing one. I see no sound grounds for supposing that this obligation is not to be capable of enforcement by   *h* appropriate legal proceedings, where these are necessary in order to vindicate the rights of an applicant. It is true that s 26(4) provides a means whereby, if the local planning authority is guilty of delay in issuing a certificate, the applicant can in effect short-circuit the authority and go straight to the Secretary of State. But this remedy appears to be an optional one, and its existence does not, in my view, lead properly to the inference that the authority's statutory duty to issue a certificate can in no circumstances be enforced by   *j* legal proceedings.

---

1   [1979] 2 All ER 440 at 445, [1979] 2 WLR 755 at 763

In support of the proposition that the issue of a certificate outside the statutorily prescribed periods is not ultra vires the local planning authority, counsel for the appellants founded on *James v Minister of Housing and Local Government*[1] and *London Ballast Co Ltd v Buckinghamshire County Council*[2]. In each of these cases a point arose regarding the validity of a conditional planning permission granted after the expiry of the period statutorily prescribed for doing so. It is unnecessary to examine the cases in detail. It is sufficient to say that in each of them opinions were expressed to the effect that a planning permission so granted was not necessarily voidable, but that it might be so in certain circumstances. That appears to me to be an unexceptionable statement of the law.

The argument for the respondents on this branch of the case, in its main thrust, was concerned with the contention that the remedy sought by the appellants was inappropriate. It was suggested that recourse might be had to the nobile officium of the court. I regard that suggestion as entirely misplaced. The nobile officium does not exist to deal with matters of disputed right. Its chief object is to provide a means of rectifying obvious errors or omissions, principally of an administrative character, which cannot be dealt with in any other way. The present case is concerned with the appellants' right, disputed by the respondents, to require the latter to issue to them a certificate under s 25(4) of the 1963 Act which is in proper form. That is a matter appropriate to be dealt with by the ordinary processes of law, and which does not in any respect concern the nobile officium. The argument for the respondents did not, in my opinion, come to grips at all with the appellants' contentions on this matter of disputed right, let alone counter them successfully. These contentions must therefore prevail.

It remains to notice a submission for the respondents that the appellants should be put to proof of their averment that they were unaware of the time limit for appealing to the Secretary of State and this was the reason why their appeal was late. I reject that submission. The invalidity of the certificate derives from a defect of general application, and nothing turns on the state of the appellants' knowledge.

My Lords, for these reasons I would allow the appeal and dismiss the cross-appeal. Counsel for the appellants asked leave to further amend the second conclusion of the summons by substituing the word 'fresh' for the word 'amended' before the word 'certificate', and such leave should be granted. Subject to that, the appropriate order would be to recall the interlocutor of the Second Division dated 26th January 1979 in so far as it refused decree in terms of the second conclusion of the summons, and quoad that conclusion as amended to sustain the second and third pleas in law for the pursuer and to grant decree in terms thereof. The respondents will be liable to the appellants for costs in this House and also for all expenses in the Court of Session, apart from those for which the appellants were found liable to the second respondent by interlocutor of the Lord Ordinary dated 15th June 1978.

Appeal allowed; cross-appeal dismissed.

Solicitors: *Stephenson Harwood*, agents for *Biggart, Baillie & Gifford*, WS, Edinburgh (for the appellants); *Martin & Co*, agents for *Shepherd & Wedderburn*, WS, Edinburgh (for the respondents).

Christine Ivamy   Barrister.

1   [1965] 3 All ER 602, [1966] 1 WLR 135, CA; *on appeal* [1966] 3 All ER 964, [1968] AC 409, HL
2   (1966) 65 LGR 227

Practice Direction

FAMILY DIVISION

a

Divorce – Costs – Taxation – Bill of costs – Simplified procedure – Division of bill into parts – Work done in High Court and divorce county court.

In the Practice Direction of 11th April 1979[1] on the new practice on taxation it was laid *b* down that bills must be divided into parts to show, inter alia, the work done in the High Court and the divorce county court.

There appears to be some degree of misunderstanding about the method of setting out the work in the two courts and the object of this note is to clarify this method.

Where work is begun in the county court and transferred to the High Court (or, rarely, vice versa) items 10(*a*) and 10(*b*) relating to that work must be set out at the end of that *c* part of the bill. In any subsequent transfer between the High Court and the county court the same procedure will apply.

The Family Division has not been asked to approve any form of bill and will not accept as correct any form of bill that does not conform with the Practice Direction of 11th April 1979[1] as explained in the present Practice Direction.

d

R L BAYNE-POWELL
12th November 1979   Senior Registrar.

1   [1979] 2 All ER 150

Quazi v Quazi

a

HOUSE OF LORDS

LORD DIPLOCK, VISCOUNT DILHORNE, LORD SALMON, LORD FRASER OF TULLYBELTON AND LORD SCARMAN

17th 18th OCTOBER, 22nd NOVEMBER 1979

b *Divorce – Foreign decree – Recognition by English court – Basis of recognition – Divorce obtained by means of judicial or other proceedings – Test whether divorce so obtained – Talaq divorce obtained under Pakistan ordinance – Whether obtained by 'judicial or other proceedings' – Recognition of Divorces and Legal Separations Act 1971, s 2(a).*

The husband and the wife were both born in India and were married there in 1963.
c Both were Pakistani nationals and Muslims. After the marriage they resided in a number of places in the Far East but in February 1973 they moved to Pakistan. The marriage was not a happy one and in March 1973 the husband left Pakistan and came to England where he bought a house. The wife continued to reside in Pakistan. In June 1974 the wife came to England on a temporary visit and lived separately from the husband in his house. In July 1974 the husband went to Pakistan and there pronounced
d under the Pakistan Muslim Family Laws Ordinance 1961 a talaq divorce from the wife by formally repeating before witnesses the word 'talaq' three times. As required by the ordinance the husband gave notice of the pronouncement of the talaq to a public authority and supplied a copy of the notice to the wife. Under the ordinance failure to comply with this requirement was punishable by a fine or imprisonment. Moreover, the ordinance suspended the effect of the talaq for 90 days from the day the notice was
e given to the authority, to enable the authority to constitute an arbitration council for the purpose of bringing about a reconciliation between the parties. There was no sanction to compel a party to take part in conciliation proceedings and if, as in the instant case, the husband chose not to do so, then, subject to his having given the required notice, divorce by talaq was still obtainable by the husband's unilateral act, and the divorce could not be prevented from taking effect automatically after the expiration of 90 days. During the
f suspension period the husband could revoke the talaq. The ordinance did not require the authority or the council to give a decision or issue a certificate making the divorce effective. The husband returned to England and in 1975 presented a petition for a declaration, pursuant to the Recognition of Divorces and Legal Separations Act 1971, that the marriage was lawfully dissolved, inter alia, by the talaq. The judge granted the declaration. He held that the talaq divorce had been obtained by means of 'judicial or
g other proceedings' in Pakistan and was 'effective under the law' of Pakistan and thus could be recognised as valid under s 2*ᵃ* of the 1971 Act. The Court of Appeal*ᵇ* reversed his decision. On appeal by the husband to the House of Lords the issue was whether the talaq divorce was obtained by 'other proceedings' within the meaning of s 2(a) of the 1971 Act and was effective under the law of Pakistan. The wife contended that the words 'other proceedings' must mean proceedings which, by application of the ejusdem generis
h rule, were quasi judicial.

Held – (i) The expression 'other proceedings' in the phrase 'by means of judicial or other proceedings' in s 2 of the 1971 Act could not be read as referring only to 'other quasi judicial proceedings' by means of applying the ejusdem generis rule, because that rule applied to limit the generality of the term 'other' only where it was preceded by a list of
j two or more expressions having specific meanings and common characteristics from which a common genus could be identified. Accordingly, having regard to the policy of

---

a Section 2 is set out at p 900 *f*, post
b Page 424, ante

the 1971 Act as a whole and the purpose for which it was enacted, the words 'or other proceedings' in s 2(*a*) included all proceedings for divorce, other than judicial proceedings, *a* which were legally effective in the country where they were taken (see p 902 *f* to p 903 *b*, p 904 *b*, p 906 *d e*, p 908 *e* and *j* to p 909 *a* and p 916 *d*, post).

(ii) The talaq divorce obtained under the 1961 Pakistan ordinance followed the acts of pronouncing a talaq and giving of notice to the authority and the wife, which though not judicial in character fell within the description of 'other proceedings' in s 2(*a*), for they were acts officially recognised by the law of Pakistan as leading to an effective divorce, *b* and without which divorce by talaq could never become effective in that country. It followed therefore that the husband was entitled to a declaration that the marriage had lawfully been dissolved by the talaq (see p 903 *e f*, p 904 *a b f*, p 906 *f g*, p 907 *e*, p 911 *b* to *e h j*, p 917 *g* to *j* and p 918 *b c* and *g*, post).

Per Viscount Dilhorne and Lord Scarman. The law should be altered to enable a resident in the United Kingdom whose divorce or legal separation abroad has been *c* recognised here as valid to claim a property adjustment or other financial order under the Matrimonial Causes Act 1973 (see p 904 *f* and p 912 *g h*, post).

Decision of the Court of Appeal reversed.

Notes

For the recognition of overseas divorces, see 8 Halsbury's Laws (4th Edn) paras 484, 485. *d*

For the Recognition of Divorces and Legal Separations Act, s 2, see 41 Halsbury's Statutes (3rd Edn) 219.

Cases referred to in opinions

Ali Nawaz Gardezi v Muhammed Yusuf PLD 1963 Supreme Court 51.
Fahmida Bibi v Mukhtar Ahmad PLD 1972 Lahore 694.
Jatoi v Jatoi PLD 1967 Supreme Court 580. *e*
Post Office v Estuary Radio Ltd [1967] 3 All ER 663, [1968] 2 QB 740, [1967] 1 WLR 1396, [1967] 2 Lloyd's Rep 299, CA, Digest (Cont Vol C) 951, 40*a*.
Qureshi v Qureshi [1971] 1 All ER 325, [1972] Fam 173, [1971] 2 WLR 518, 27(2) Digest (Reissue) 1019, 8140.
R v Registrar General of Births, Deaths and Marriages, ex parte Minhas [1976] 2 All ER 246, [1977] QB 1, [1976] 2 WLR 473, DC. *f*
Rands v Oldroyd [1958] 3 All ER 344, [1959] 1 QB 204, [1958] 3 WLR 583, 123 JP 1, 56 LGR 429, DC, 33 Digest (Repl) 9, 25.
Salomon v Customs and Excise Comrs [1966] 3 All ER 871, [1967] 2 QB 116, [1966] 3 WLR 1223, CA, Digest (Cont Vol B) 621, 77*a*.

Appeal *g*

By a petition dated 18th June 1975 the petitioner, Mohammed Ameerudin Quazi ('the husband'), sought a declaration that his marriage to the respondent, Bilquis Jehan Begum Quazi ('the wife'), celebrated on 24th November 1963 at Aurangabad in India was lawfully dissolved by a khula made in Bangkok, Thailand, on 22nd March 1968, or alternatively by a talaq, pronounced three times before witnesses, made in Karachi, Pakistan in July 1974. By her answer the wife sought a decree of nullity, or alternatively *h* a declaration that neither the khula nor the talaq was entitled to recognition by English courts as an overseas divorce, and in the further alternative, if the marriage had been dissolved by either the khula or the talaq, a declaration that she was entitled to the sum of 21,000 Indian rupees in respect of dower right. By a judgment given on 14th July 1978, Wood J held that the marriage was dissolved either by the khula in Bangkok or by the talaq pronounced in Karachi. On 10th April 1979 the Court of Appeal[1] (Orr, *j* Ormrod and Browne LJJ) reversed that decision. The husband appealed to the House of Lords pursuant to leave of the House granted on 27th June 1979. The facts are set out in the opinion of Lord Scarman.

---

1 Page 424, ante

Roger Titheridge QC and *Colin Mackay* for the husband.
a *Joseph Jackson QC* and *Peter Singer* for the wife.

Their Lordships took time for consideration.

22nd November. The following opinions were delivered.

LORD DIPLOCK. My Lords, so far as the parties to the proceedings are concerned all
b that is at stake in this appeal is the wife's right under the Matrimonial Causes Act 1973
to claim some share in a small house in Wimbledon which the husband bought in 1973
for £3,000 with money that he says he borrowed from a friend. Both parties are of
Pakistan nationality and of the Muslim faith. They were both born in India and married
there in 1963. The wife's right to make a claim under the Act depends on whether or not
that Indian marriage was still subsisting on 23rd December 1974 when she instituted
c divorce proceedings against the husband in England.
       The husband claimed that the marriage had been dissolved either (1) by khula (a
consensual form of Muslim divorce) entered into in March 1968 in accordance with the
law of Thailand, in which country it is common ground that the parties were domiciled
at that time; or alternatively (2) by talaq (a form of Muslim divorce obtainable at the will
of the husband alone) pronounced by the husband in Karachi on 30th July 1974, and
d taking effect under the law of Pakistan 90 days thereafter, ie 28th November 1974, and
so before the wife's proceedings for divorce in England had been started.
       The issue whether the Indian marriage between the parties was still subsisting came
before Wood J in the Family Division of the High Court, where it took 14 days to try.
The judge held that the khula had been effective to dissolve the marriage under Thai law
in 1968; but, since the expert evidence of Thai law had been conflicting he also held that
e if, contrary to his own view, the Indian marriage was still subsisting in July 1974 it was
effectively dissolved not later than 28th November 1974 by the talaq pronounced in
Pakistan and the steps that had been taken thereafter in Pakistan and in England to make
it effective.
       The Court of Appeal[1] (Orr, Ormrod and Browne LJJ), after a hearing which lasted
seven days, reversed this judgment, holding that neither the khula nor the talaq was
f entitled to recognition as valid either under ss 2 and 3 of the Recognition of Divorces and
Legal Separations Act 1971 ('the Recognition Act'), or under the common law rules
which s 6 of the Recognition Act preserves.
       My Lords, to dispose of this appeal it is sufficient if the husband succeeds in showing
that either of the foreign divorces that he relies on in the alternative as having dissolved
his marriage to the wife, is entitled to recognition by the English courts. The validity of
g a divorce by talaq obtained by a Pakistani national in accordance with Pakistani law raises
a question as to the true construction of the Recognition Act and its application to talaqs
obtained in Pakistan. This is of general importance in view of the number of Pakistani
nationals who are settled in the United Kingdom either accompanied or unaccompanied
by their wives. On the other hand, the validity of a divorce by khula entered into in
Thailand by Pakistani nationals who are domiciled there, is not a question that is very
h likely to require consideration by an English court in any subsequent case. It depends on
the domestic law of Thailand, the Thai rules of conflict of laws, the application by the
Thai courts of the doctrine of renvoi, and under that doctrine, the applicability of the
Muslim Family Laws Ordinance 1961 of Pakistan to consensual divorces. These are
questions of fact to be decided by an English court on expert evidence of the foreign law
concerned. In the instant case the expert evidence on these matters was inadequate,
j conflicting and confusing and any decision of the Court of Appeal or of this House that
was based on that evidence would be valueless as a precedent in any subsequent case
between other parties even in the unlikely event that the circumstances were similar.

---

1   Page 424, ante

It was for this reason that it was decided to hear the argument in this House restricted in the first instance to the question of the validity of the divorce by talaq under the *a* Recognition Act. At the conclusion of this argument your Lordships were all of the opinion, which I also share, that even if the marriage were still subsisting on 30th July 1973, it was effectively dissolved on 28th November 1974, by a divorce by talaq that is entitled to recognition under ss 2 and 3 of the Recognition Act. So in order to avoid unnecessary prolongation of a costly hearing in a case which has been throughout conducted entirely on legal aid, this House has limited its consideration to the only *b* question that is of general importance, the validity of the Pakistani talaq, and has decided the appeal on that point alone.

The preamble to the Recognition Act makes it plain that its principal, though not its only, purpose was to enable the United Kingdom to give effect in its domestic law to the Hague Convention on the Recognition of Divorces and Legal Separations of 1970[1] ('the Recognition Convention'). The mischief that the convention was designed to cure was *c* that of 'limping marriages', that is, marriages that were recognised in some jurisdictions as having been validly dissolved, but in other jurisdictions as still subsisting. The cause of these discrepancies in the recognition of foreign divorces by the courts of different states was that some states under their rules of conflict of laws treated the nationality of the parties as the sole ground of jurisdiction in matters of divorce, others treated as the only ground of jurisdiction 'domicile' in the strict sense in which that concept plays a part *d* in English common law, and yet others 'domicile' in the looser sense, in which that term is used in civil law as meaning habitual residence. The solution adopted by the Recognition Convention was to require all contracting states to recognise as valid grounds of jurisdiction in matters of divorce and legal separation all three concepts, nationality, domicile and habitual residence. Article 16, however, left them at liberty to apply rules of law *more* favourable to the recognition of foreign divorces than those called for by the *e* convention.

The sections of the Recognition Act that are relevant to the recognition of the divorce by talaq in the instant case are ss 2 and 3. They read as follows:

'2. Sections 3 to 5 of this Act shall have effect, subject to section 8 of this Act, as respects the recognition in Great Britain of the validity of overseas divorces and legal separations, that is to say, divorces and legal separations which—(*a*) have been *f* obtained by means of judicial or other proceedings in any country outside the British Isles; and (*b*) are effective under the law of that country.

'3.—(1) The validity of an overseas divorce or legal separation shall be recognised if, at the date of the institution of the proceedings in the country in which it was obtained—(*a*) either spouse was habitually resident in that country; or (*b*) either spouse was a national of that country.   *g*

'(2) In relation to a country the law of which uses the concept of domicile as a ground of jurisdiction in matters of divorce or legal separation, subsection (1)(*a*) of this section shall have effect as if the reference to habitual residence included a reference to domicile within the meaning of that law.

'(3) In relation to a country comprising territories in which different systems of law are in force in matters of divorce or legal separation, the foregoing provisions of *h* this section (except those relating to nationality) shall have effect as if each territory were a separate country.'

It is not disputed that both spouses in the instant case have at all relevant times been nationals of Pakistan; nor is it disputed that if the procedural requirements of the Muslim Family Laws Ordinance 1961 of Pakistan were complied with the divorce would *j* be effective under the law of that country, though there is a dispute of fact (to which I will have to revert later) as to whether one of those requirements was satisfied. This leaves as the only question of law arising under the Recognition Act: was the divorce by

---

1   1st June 1970; TS 123 (1975); Cmnd 6248

talaq 'obtained by means of judicial or other proceedings' which took place in Pakistan,
a within the meaning of that phrase as used in s 2?

One must therefore first look to see what it was that was done in Pakistan which
resulted in the divorce by talaq being effective there. The concept of divorce by talaq
under the classic religious law of Islam is one with which English courts have become
familiar. It is effected by the husband solemnly pronouncing the word 'talaq' either once
or thrice in the presence of witnesses. Neither the presence of the wife nor even any
b notice to her is required by the classic religious law of Islam. The absence of any
requirement of notice or publicity in this classic or 'bare' form of talaq, has led certain
Muslim states, of which Pakistan is one, to pass legislation requiring additional formalities
to be complied with in order to make a bare talaq effective to dissolve the marriage. The
relevant law in Pakistan is to be found in ss 1 and 7 of the Muslim Family Laws
Ordinance 1961, and is in the following terms:

c   '1 ... (2) It [sc the ordinance] extends to the whole of Pakistan, and applies to all
Muslim citizens of Pakistan, wherever they may be ...

'7. *Talaq*—(1) Any man who wishes to divorce his wife shall, as soon as may be
after the pronouncement of *talaq* in any form whatsoever, give the Chairman notice
in writing of his having done so, and shall supply a copy thereof to the wife.

d   '(2) Whoever contravenes the provisions of subsection (1) shall be punishable
with simple imprisonment for a term which may extend to one year or with [a] fine
which may extend to five thousand rupees or with both.

'(3) Save as provided in subsection (5), a *talaq* unless revoked earlier, expressly or
otherwise, shall not be effective until the expiration of ninety days from the day on
which notice under subsection (1) is delivered to the Chairman.

e   '(4) Within thirty days of the receipt of notice under subsection (1), the Chairman
shall constitute an Arbitration Council for the purpose of bringing about a
reconciliation between the parties, and the Arbitration Council shall take all steps
necessary to bring about such reconciliation.

'(5) If the wife be pregnant at the time *talaq* is pronounced *talaq* shall not be
effective until the period mentioned in subsection (2) or the pregnancy, whichever
be later, ends.

f   '(6) Nothing shall debar a wife whose marriage has been terminated by *talaq*
effective under this section from remarrying the same husband, without an
intervening marriage with a third person, unless such termination is for the third
time so effective.'

The 'Chairman' referred to in this section is the chairman of the union council, an
g administrative, not judicial, body, although the chairman in the instant case happened
to be a judge. Rules made under the ordinance provide, inter alia, which union council
shall have jurisdiction in the case of notice of talaq, and lay down the procedure to be
followed by the arbitration council constituted under s 7(4).

The relevant rules are:

h   '3. The Union Council which shall have jurisdiction in the matter for purposes
of clause (*d*) of section 2, shall be as follows, namely ... (*b*) in the case of a notice of
talaq under subsection (1) of section 7, it shall be the Union Council of the Union
or Town where the wife in relation to whom *talaq* has been pronounced was
residing at the time of pronouncement of *talaq*: Provided that if at the time of
pronouncement of *talaq* such wife was not residing in any part of West Pakistan, the
j Union Council that shall have jurisdiction shall be—(i) in case such wife was at any
time residing with the person pronouncing the *talaq* in any part of West Pakistan,
the Union Council of the Union or Town where such wife so last resided with such
person; and (ii) in any other case, the Union Council of the Union or Town where
the person pronouncing the *talaq* is permanently residing in West Pakistan ...

'6.—(1) Within 7 days of receiving an application under subsection (2) of section

6 or under subsection (1) of section 9 or a notice under subsection (1) of section 7, the
Chairman shall, by order in writing, call upon each of the parties to nominate his or *a*
her representative and each such party shall, within seven days of receiving the
order, nominate in writing a representative and deliver the nomination to the
Chairman or send it to him by registered post: Provided that where a party on
whom the order is to be served is residing outside Pakistan, the order may be served
on such party through the Consular Officer of Pakistan in or for the country where
such party is residing.'   *b*

It appears to be the practice, though it is not required by the rules, for the chairman
of the union council at the request of either of the spouses after the 90 days have expired
without the talaq having been revoked, to issue a document recording that the procedure
laid down in the ordinance and rules has been followed and that the talaq dissolving the
marriage is confirmed.

Although the ordinance is primarily procedural the evidence shows that it does *c*
involve at least two substantive changes in the classic religious law of Islam. Whereas
under the classic religious law the talaq once pronounced takes effect immediately and
is irrevocable, under the ordinance (i) it cannot take effect until at least 90 days after it has
been pronounced or even longer if notice is not delivered promptly to the chairman of
the union council; and (ii) until it does take effect it can be revoked. If notice is not given *d*
to the chairman at all it would appear that the talaq never does take effect.

There is nothing to compel either spouse to take part in conciliation proceedings
before the arbitration council. If, as happened in the instant case, the husband chooses
not to do so, then, subject to his having given the required notice of talaq to the chairman
of the union council and supplied a copy to his wife, divorce by talaq is still obtainable
at the husband's will alone, and no authority in Pakistan, whether judicial or *e*
administrative, has any power to prevent its taking effect automatically the moment that
the 90 day period expires. It was the absence of such power that led the Court of Appeal
to hold that the procedure for which the ordinance and rules provide does not make a
divorce by talaq obtained in Pakistan a divorce that has 'been obtained by means of
judicial or other proceedings' within the meaning of s 2 of the Recognition Act.

It was not the husband's case that the divorce by talaq was obtained in Pakistan by *f*
proceedings that were 'judicial'; it is the reference in the section to 'other proceedings' on
which he relied. The argument for the wife is that these words, which on the face of
them would include *any* proceedings that were not judicial, are to be read as limited to
proceedings that are quasi judicial, by application of the ejusdem generis rule. This
involves reading 'other' as if it meant 'similar' and, as it seems to me, is based on a
misunderstanding of that well-known rule of construction that is regrettably common.
As the Latin words of the label attached to it suggest the rule applies to cut down the *g*
generality of the expression 'other' only where it is preceded by a list of two or more
expressions having more specific meanings and sharing some common characteristics
from which it is possible to recognise them as being species belonging to a single genus
and to identify what the essential characteristics of that genus are. The presumption
then is that the draftsman's mind was directed only to that genus and that he did not, by *h*
his addition of the word 'other' to the list, intend to stray beyond its boundaries, but
merely to bring within the ambit of the enacting words those species which complete the
genus but have been omitted from the preceding list either inadvertently or in the
interests of brevity. Where, however, as in s 2 of the Recognition Act, the word 'other'
as descriptive of proceedings is preceded by one expression only that has a more specific
meaning, viz 'judicial', there is no room for the application of any ejusdem generis rule; *j*
for unless the draftsman has indicated at the very least two different species to which the
enacting words apply there is no material on which to base an inference that there was
some particular genus of proceedings to which alone his mind was directed when he used
the word 'other', which on the face of it, would embrace all proceedings that were *not*
judicial, irrespective of how much or little they resembled judicial proceedings.

The fact that the ejusdem generis rule is not applicable does not, however, necessarily
a mean that where the expression 'other' appears in a statute preceded by only one
expression of greater specificity its generality may not be cut down if to give it its wide
prima facie meaning would lead to results that would be contrary to the manifest policy
of the Act looked at as a whole, or would conflict with the evident purpose for which it
was enacted.

    In the instant case, however, this does not help the respondent wife; it helps the
b appellant husband. The purpose for which the Recognition Act was passed is declared by
the preamble to be with a view to the ratification by the United Kingdom of the
Recognition Convention and for other purposes. Where Parliament passes an Act
amending the domestic law of the United Kingdom in order to enable this country to
ratify an international treaty and thereby assume towards other states that are parties to
the treaty an obligation in international law to observe its terms, it is a legitimate aid to
c the construction of any provisions of the Act that are ambiguous or vague to have
recourse to the terms of the treaty in order to see what was the obligation in international
law that Parliament intended that this country should be enabled to assume. The
ambiguity or obscurity is to be resolved in favour of that meaning that is consistent with
the provisions of the treaty: see *Salomon v Customs and Excise Comrs*[1] and *Post Office v
Estuary Radio Ltd*[2].

d   Article 1 of the Recognition Convention provides that it shall apply to the 'recognition
in one Contracting State of divorces and legal separations obtained in another Contracting
State which follow judicial or other proceedings officially recognised in that State and
which are legally effective there'.

    It is rightly conceded on behalf of the wife that the divorce by talaq which was
obtained in Pakistan followed on acts which though not judicial do fall within the
e description 'other proceedings officially recognised' in that country. The pronouncement
of the talaq was required by law to be notified to a public authority, the chairman of the
union council; he in turn was required by law to constitute an arbitration council for the
purposes of conciliation and to invite each spouse to nominate a representative. These
are 'proceedings'; none the less so because in the event neither spouse elects to take
advantage of the opportunity for conciliation which the arbitration council presents.
f They are proceedings that are not merely officially recognised but are also enforced by
penal sanctions under the Muslim Family Laws Ordinance 1961. Without such
proceedings the divorce by talaq never becomes effective. The proceedings come first,
the divorce follows them 90 days after they have been commenced.

    My Lords, the presumption is that the draftsman of the Recognition Act, by his use of
the phrase 'obtained by means of judicial or other proceedings in any country outside the
g British Isles', intended to provide for the recognition of all divorces to which the
Recognition Convention applies, for to fail to do so would be a breach of that convention
by this country. The ordinary meaning of the phrase he used is amply wide enough to
cover at least them. It may even have been intended to cover more, since art 17 permits
contracting states to be more favourable to the recognition of foreign divorces than is
needed to comply with the provisions of the convention. This, however, is not a matter
h that arises for decision in the present appeal. It suffices for this House to hold that the
phrase must have been intended to embrace divorces by talaq obtained in Pakistan under
the provisions of the Muslim Family Laws Ordinance 1961.

    It remains to notice a subsidiary argument advanced for the wife; that the notice of
pronouncement of the talaq was given to the chairman of a union council on whom
jurisdiction was not conferred under rule. This depended on whether the wife was
j 'residing' in Karachi when the talaq was pronounced on 30th July 1973. She was
physically present in London on that date, but the judge was entitled on the evidence to

---

1   [1966] 3 All ER 871, [1967] 2 QB 116
2   [1967] 3 All ER 663, [1968] 2 QB 740

find, as he did, that this was but a temporary absence from Karachi, which continued to
be her place of residence.
a

For these reasons I would allow the appeal. Since it has not been necessary to consider
the validity of the alleged divorce by khula, the declarations made by Wood J relating to
it and to the divorce by talaq respectively are inappropriate and his order should be varied
by replacing them by a single declaration 'that the said marriage [sc the Indian marriage]
had been dissolved on or before 28th November 1974'.

b

VISCOUNT DILHORNE. My Lords, as my noble and learned friends, Lord Diplock
and Lord Scarman, have dealt so fully with this case in their speeches which I have seen
in draft, and with which I agree, I desire only to make a few observations.

Counsel for the wife sought to contend that the ejusdem generis rule should be applied
in the construction of the words 'judicial or other proceedings' in s 2(*a*) of the Recognition
of Divorces and Legal Separation Act 1971. In my opinion this rule does not apply for c
there is no genus. The 'other proceedings' must be proceedings which are not judicial.
I think that is clear.

In the course of the argument it was sought to attach importance to the difference of
language between that in the Convention on the Recognition of Divorces and Legal
Separations[1] and that in this Act, which had as its main object amendment of the law so
as to enable the United Kingdom to ratify the convention. d

Article 1 of the convention stated that it should apply to the recognition of divorces
and legal separations 'obtained . . . which follow judicial or other proceedings officially
recognised in that state and which are legally effective there'. Section 2 of the Act
provides for recognition of the validity of overseas divorces and legal separations which
'(*a*) have been obtained by means of judicial or other proceedings in any country outside
the British Isles; and (*b*) are effective under the law of that country'. The Act does not e
contain the words 'officially recognised in that state'. In my opinion the probable reason
for their omission is that the draftsman thought the inclusion of those words unnecessary,
for a divorce and legal separation legally effective in a foreign country must surely be one
that is officially recognised there.

Finally, I would like to give my wholehearted support to my noble and learned friend
Lord Scarman's suggestion that the law should be altered so that a resident in the United f
Kingdom whose divorce or legal separation abroad is recognised here as valid should not
be debarred from the protection afforded by the Matrimonial Causes Act 1973 by the fact
that a divorce or legal separation was not granted in our courts.

I would allow the appeal.

LORD SALMON. My Lords, the husband and the wife are Muslims and were born in g
Hyderabad, then a princely state, which in 1948 was incorporated in India. On 2nd
November 1963 they were married to each other in India. They each became a Pakistani
national, the husband in 1958 and the wife in 1964. They have retained their Pakistani
nationality ever since. After the marriage the parties resided in a number of places in the
East. The marriage was not a happy one. In February and March 1973 they were both
residing in Karachi; but, during that period, they spent only one day and one night h
together in the same house. The wife was still residing in Karachi in June 1974. In
March 1973 the husband left Karachi and came to London where he bought a house in
Wimbledon. On 17th June 1974 the wife flew to London from Karachi on a return
ticket valid only for four months and turned up at the husband's house unannounced at
midnight. She lived separately from the husband in his house and refused to accept the
'true role of a Muslim wife'. The learned trial judge in the Family Division, Wood J, held j
that she was an untruthful witness and also that she had deliberately misled the
immigration authorities in order to gain admission to the United Kingdom. He came to

---

1   1st June 1970; TS 123 (1975); Cmnd 6248

the conclusion, on abundant evidence, that in July 1974 her true place of residence was
_a_ Karachi and that she then intended to remain in the United Kingdom only on a
temporary visit until her return to Karachi.

Early in June the husband flew to Karachi and on 12th of that month pronounced
talaq before witnesses in Karachi by saying 'I divorce you' three times.

The Muslim Family Laws Ordinance 1961 (as amended) is of great importance in
relation to the effect of talaq in Pakistan. Section 2(_d_) of the ordinance provides that
_b_ 'Union Council' means 'the Union Council of the Town . . . having jurisdiction in the
area concerned.' Section 7 of the ordinance, so far as relevant, reads:

> '_Talaq_—(1) Any man who wishes to divorce his wife shall, as soon as may be after
> the pronouncement of _talaq_ in any form whatsoever, give the Chairman [of the
> Union Council having jurisdiction in the area concerned] notice in writing of his
> having done so, and shall supply a copy thereof to the wife.
_c_
> '(2) Whoever contravenes the provisions of subsection 1 shall be punishable with
> simple imprisonment for a term which may extend to one year or with [a] fine
> which may extend to five thousand rupees or with both.
>
> '(3) . . . a _talaq_ unless revoked earlier, expressly or otherwise, shall not be effective
> until the expiration of 90 days from the day on which notice under subsection (1)
_d_ > is delivered to the Chairman.
>
> '(4) Within thirty days of the receipt of notice under subsection (1), the Chairman
> shall constitute an Arbitration Council for the purpose of bringing about a
> reconciliation between the parties, and the Arbitration Council shall take all steps
> necessary to bring about such reconciliation . . .'

_e_ Rule 3 of the rules (as amended) made under the 1961 ordinance reads, so far as
relevant, as follows:

> 'The Union Council which shall have jurisdiction in the matter . . . shall be as
> follows, namely; . . . (_b_) in the case of notice of _talaq_ under subsection (1) of section
> 7, it shall be the Union Council . . . of the Town where the wife in relation to whom
> _talaq_ has been pronounced was residing at the time of the pronouncement of _talaq_:
_f_ > Provided that if at the time of pronouncement of _talaq_ such wife was not residing
> in any part of West Pakistan, the Union Council that shall have jurisdiction shall be
> (i) in case such wife was at any time residing with the person pronouncing the _talaq_
> in any part of West Pakistan, the Union Council of the Union or Town where such
> wife so last resided with such person; and (ii) in any other case, the Union Council
> of the Union or Town where the person pronouncing the _talaq_ is permanently
_g_ > residing in West Pakistan . . .'

From a so-called court order dated 18th February 1975 it is plain that the eighth senior
civil judge of Karachi was the chairman of the Karachi Union Council and that a written
notice of talaq was received by him from the husband on 30th July 1974, and that a copy
of that notice was promptly sent to and received by the wife whose solicitor wrote to the
_h_ chairman and asked for the matter to be postponed. When, however, 90 days had
elapsed since the notice of talaq had been received by the chairman and the wife, the talaq
had become effective and could not be revoked. It follows that the parties were thereby
divorced according to the law of Pakistan.

I recognise that it is well-settled law in Pakistan that no court order can make a talaq
effective or revoke it. The fact that the chairman of the Karachi Union Council on whom
_j_ the notice under s 7(1) of the 1961 ordinance was served happened to be a judge is
irrelevant, and so is the so-called court order itself. Nevertheless it is equally clear that,
because of Wood J's finding that in July 1974 when the talaq was pronounced the wife
was living temporarily in England but that Karachi was then her place of residence, the
divorce between the parties would be recognised as valid in Pakistan by reason of r 3
which I have recited. It is therefore unnecessary to consider whether the fact that the

parties resided together for one day and night in Karachi during February 1974 would
have brought the case within proviso (1) of r 3.   *a*
   The only question that remains is whether the divorce in Pakistan was obtained by
'judicial or other proceedings' within the meaning of those words in s 2 of the
Recognition of Divorces and Legal Separations Act 1971, which reads as follows:

> 'Sections 3 to 5 of this Act shall have effect, subject to section 8 of this Act, as
> respects the recognition in Great Britain of the validity of overseas divorces and legal
> separations, that is to say, divorces and legal separations which—(a) have been *b*
> obtained by means of judicial or other proceedings in any country outside the
> British Isles; and (b) are effective under the law of that country.'

Section 3 of the 1971 Act, so far as relevant, reads:

> '(1) The validity of an overseas divorce or legal separation shall be recognised if,
> at the date of the institution of the proceedings in the country in which it was *c*
> obtained . . . (b) either spouse was a national of that country . . .'

   It is impossible in the United Kingdom, but not in Pakistan, to obtain divorce by any
proceedings other than judicial proceedings. It must have been well known when the
1971 Act was passed that there were many countries in the world such as, for example,
India and Pakistan, where divorce was obtainable by proceedings such as talaq which *d*
bore no resemblance to judicial proceedings. I do not think that there can be any cogent
reason for construing the words 'other proceedings' as ejusdem generis with 'judicial
proceedings' and therefore meaning 'quasi judicial proceedings'. On the contrary, the
words 'other proceedings' cover a very wide field in their context and can only mean 'any
proceedings other than judicial proceedings'. I therefore construe s 2 as applying,
amongst other things, to overseas divorces obtained by proceedings other than judicial *e*
proceedings if such divorces are effective under the law of the country in which they are
obtained.
   The argument that there was nothing which could properly be described as
'proceedings' in relation to the divorce with which this appeal is concerned seems to me
to be untenable. Section 7 of the 1971 Act lays down plainly the proceeding which the
husband must take in order to make talaq legally effective to obtain a divorce in *f*
Pakistan. The obligation of the husband under s 7(1) of the Muslim Family Laws
Ordinance of 1961 is to give notice of talaq to the chairman of the relevant union
promptly after its pronouncement. This seems to me to oblige the husband to take a
proceeding of crucial importance, for if he fails to take this proceeding he is liable to be
sentenced to a term of imprisonment of up to one year or fined up to 5,000 rupees or
both. Moreover, talaq is of no effect until the expiration of 90 days from the day on *g*
which notice of it is delivered to the chairman. If the husband fails to take the proceeding
of giving notice of talaq in accordance with s 7(1), the talaq is not effective to constitute
a divorce under the law of Pakistan.
   For my part, I do not place very much importance on the preamble to the 1971 Act,
which so far as relevant, reads:

> 'Whereas a Convention on the recognition of divorces and legal separations was *h*
> opened for signature at the Hague on 1st June 1970 and was signed on behalf of the
> United Kingdom on that date: And whereas with a view to the ratification by the
> United Kingdom of that Convention, *and for other purposes,* it is expedient to amend
> the law relating to the recognition of divorces and legal separations.' (Emphasis
> mine.)

The convention opens as follows: *j*

> 'The States signatory to the present Convention, desiring to facilitate the
> recognition of divorces and legal separations obtained in their respective territories,
> Have resolved to conclude a Convention to this effect, and have agreed on the
> following provisions—

'Article 1

a   'The present Convention shall apply to the recognition in one Contracting State of divorces and legal separations obtained in another Contracting State which follow judicial or other proceedings officially recognised in that State and which are legally effective there . . .'

There are six signatories to this convention in addition to the United Kingdom. We do not know whether a divorce can be obtained in any of these six signatory states other b   than by judicial proceedings and officially recognised and legally effective if obtained by other proceedings. If it can be, the preamble to the 1971 Act would certainly support my construction of s 2 of the Act.

Even if a divorce cannot be obtained in any of the signatory states save by judicial proceedings, the preamble to the 1971 Act would not conflict with my construction of s 7. The words 'and for other purposes' in the preamble show that the purpose of the Act c   was not solely to facilitate the recognition in the United Kingdom of overseas divorces obtained in the territories of the states signatory to the convention.

Moreover, it may well be that when the convention was registered, it was considered that amongst the states which would sign and ratify it, there might be some, like Pakistan, in which divorces and legal separations were officially recognised and legally effective although they had not been obtained by judicial proceedings.

d   Having regard to the opinion I have formed about s 2 of the 1971 Act, it is unnecessary to deal with the arguments in relation to s 6 of that Act. Nor is it necessary to express any view about the extremely difficult questions relating to domicile. The expert evidence relating to the validity of a divorce by khula in Thailand was inadequate, conflicting and confusing; and the decision of the learned trial judge on that issue cannot be regarded as a precedent. As far as s 8 of the 1971 Act is concerned, I can find no ground whatever to e   support the allegation that to recognise talaq as a divorce would be contrary to public policy in the circumstances of this case.

My Lords, for these reasons I would allow the appeal from the decision of the Court of Appeal and substitute for the two declarations made by the learned trial judge a single declaration that the marriage between the parties has been lawfully dissolved by talaq.

f   **LORD FRASER OF TULLYBELTON.** My Lords, for the reasons explained by my noble and learned friend, Lord Diplock, the single issue which falls to be decided in this appeal is whether a talaq divorce of the respondent wife, obtained by the appellant husband in Karachi, Pakistan, in 1974, should be recognised by the English courts as valid. Both parties are Muslims born in Hyderabad, India, and the marriage took place in India in 1963. Both parties are nationals of Pakistan and they have been so since at g   least 1969. That is clear and undisputed, although there is room for controversy as to the countries in which they were respectively domiciled and habitually resident in 1974. It is also clear that all the events (to use a neutral word) which are said by the husband to be 'proceedings' by which the divorce was obtained, occurred in 1974, at a time when both parties were nationals of Pakistan. It follows that in terms of s 3(1)(b) of the Recognition of Divorces and Legal Separations Act 1971 the validity of the divorce must be recognised h   by the English courts if it satisfies the other relevant provisions of the Act.

Sections 2 and 3(1) of the Act provide as follows:

'2. Sections 3 to 5 of this Act shall have effect, subject to section 8 of this Act, as respects the recognition in Great Britain of the validity of overseas divorces and legal separations, that is to say, divorces and legal separations which—(a) have been j   obtained by means of judicial or other proceedings in any country outside the British Isles; and (b) are effective under the law of that country.

'3.—(1) The validity of an overseas divorce or legal separation shall be recognised if, at the date of the institution of the proceedings in the country in which it was obtained—(a) either spouse was habitually resident in that country; or (b) either spouse was a national of that country . . .'

The divorce was not obtained by means of judicial proceedings and the principal
question is whether it was obtained by 'other proceedings' in the sense in which those *a*
words are used in s 2(*a*). One of the purposes of the 1971 Act, as set out in the preamble,
was to amend the law relating to the recognition of divorces and legal separations, and
accordingly, I do not find it necessary to consider in any detail what the former law on
the matter was. It is enough to notice that in *Qureshi v Qureshi*[1], which was decided in
October 1970, about nine months before the 1971 Act received the Royal Assent, Simon
P held, after a full review of the authorities, that a talaq divorce obtained in England by *b*
a husband domiciled in Pakistan should be recognised by the English courts. He said[2]:

> 'In my view, therefore, the fact that there has been no judicial intervention or
> even presence is irrelevant if the purported divorce is effective by the law of the
> domicile to terminate the marriage in question, and it should be recognised as such,
> unless the result would be offensive to the conscience of the English court ... The
> talaq was valid according to the law of the domicile and ... there is no rule of *c*
> English law which precludes its recognition by reason of its non-forensic
> character ...'

We have heard some argument as to whether that was a correct statement of the law,
but even if there were room for doubt as to its correctness (and I do not suggest that there
is) I think that when Parliament passed the 1971 Act it must have proceeded on the view *d*
that such a recent and authoritative statement was correct. Accordingly, there is no
reason, arising from the former law, why the words 'other proceedings' in s 2 should not
have been intended to have a meaning wide enough to include non-forensic or non-
judicial proceedings.

Coming to the Act itself the words 'other proceedings' in s 2(*a*) must mean proceedings
that are not judicial, otherwise they would add nothing to what has gone before, and I see *e*
no indication in the section that they are to be limited to quasi-judicial proceedings. The
words occur also in art 1 of the Hague Convention of 1970 on the Recognition of
Divorces and Legal Separations[3], and, as the 1971 Act was passed with a view, inter alia,
to the ratification of the convention, it is legitimate to look at it as an aid to construing
the Act. Article 1 of the convention provides that it is to apply to the recognition of
divorces etc obtained in another contracting state which follow 'judicial or other *f*
proceedings *officially recognised in that state* and which are legally effective there'. The
words I have italicised do not appear in s 2 of the Act, probably because they were
considered to be unnecessary; proceedings cannot be legally effective unless they are
officially recognised. But they do in my opinion emphasise that the only limitation on
the nature of other proceedings to which the convention and the Act are intended to
apply is that they shall be legally effective in the country where they are taken. If they *g*
are to be proceedings at all, they must of course have some regular definite form, but
anything that can properly be regarded as proceedings will qualify so long as it is legally
effective. The Court of Appeal held that the words 'other proceedings' in s 2 were used
in a much more limited sense and that their effect was that—

> 'the state or some official organisation recognised by the state must play some part *h*
> in the divorce process at least to the extent that, in proper cases, it can prevent the
> wishes of the parties, or one of them, as the case may be, from dissolving the
> marriage tie as of right'.

That restricted meaning was not supported in the argument by counsel for the wife in
this House and it appears to me, with respect, to be unjustified. I would agree with *j*

---

1   [1971] 1 All ER 325, [1972] Fam 173
2   [1971] 1 All ER 325 at 345, [1972] Fam 173 at 199
3   1st June 1970; TS 123 (1975); Cmnd 6248

a Wood J that the words of s 2 'cover a divorce or judicial separation which is finally recognised after some form of procedure. I would also take the view that the recognition should be an official recognition.'

It therefore becomes necessary to enquire whether the divorce in this case was obtained by means of any 'proceedings' in the sense that I have mentioned. Under classical Muslim law all that a husband had to do in order to divorce his wife was to pronounce talaq before witnesses three times either orally or in writing and the divorce was immediately

b effective. But modern legislation in Pakistan has imposed further requirements in addition to the mere pronouncement of talaq. The Pakistan Muslim Family Laws Ordinance of 1961 provides in s 7 as follows:

'7. *Talaq*—(1) Any man who wishes to divorce his wife shall, as soon as may be after the pronouncement of *talaq* in any form whatsoever, give the Chairman notice in writing of his having done so, and shall supply a copy thereof to the wife.

c '(2) Whoever contravenes the provisions of subsection (1) shall be punishable with simple imprisonment for a term which may extend to one year or with [a] fine which may extend to five thousand rupees or with both.

'(3) Save as provided in subsection (5), a *talaq* unless revoked earlier, expressly or otherwise, shall not be effective until the expiration of ninety days from the day on which notice under subsection (1) is delivered to the Chairman.

d '(4) Within thirty days of the receipt of notice under subsection (1), the Chairman shall constitute an Arbitration Council for the purpose of bringing about a reconciliation between the parties, and the Arbitration Council shall take all steps necessary to bring about such reconciliation.'

e Subsection (5) has no application to the facts of this case. The reference to 'the Chairman' must now be read as a reference to the civil judge having the appropriate jurisdiction. Rules have been made in West Pakistan providing for jurisdiction for arbitration purposes and providing further that proceedings before an arbitration council shall be held in camera and shall be conducted as expeditiously as possible. I must quote the following rule:

f '6.—(1) Within seven days of receiving . . . a notice under subsection (1) of section 7, the Chairman shall, by order in writing, call upon each of the parties to nominate his or her representative, and each such party shall, within seven days of receiving the order, nominate in writing a representative and deliver the nomination to the Chairman or send it to him by registered post . . .'

g The husband duly complied with s 7(1) of the ordinance by giving notice in writing to the civil judge (subject to a question to which I shall refer later as to whether notice was given to the appropriate judge) and by supplying a copy to the wife. The divorce would therefore (subject to that question being answered in the husband's favour) be effective under the law of Pakistan, and would satisfy s 2(b) of the 1971 Act.

One result of s 7(3) of the ordinance is that a talaq is not effective until the 90 days allowed for arbitration have expired. Another is that talaq has ceased to be a purely

h private unilateral act by the husband. The object and effect of s 7 was explained by S A Rahman J in *Ali Nawaz Gardezi v Muhammad Yusuf*[1] as follows:

'But here it is obvious that the object of section 7 is to prevent hasty dissolution of marriages by *talaq*, pronounced by the husband, unilaterally, without an attempt being made to prevent disruption of the matrimonial status. If the husband himself thinks better of the pronouncement of *talaq* and abstains from giving a notice to the

j Chairman, he should perhaps be deemed, in view of section 7, to have revoked the pronouncement and that would be to the advantage of the wife. Subsection (3) of this section precludes the *talaq* from being effective as such, for a certain period and

---

1   PLD 1963 Supreme Court 51 at 75, para 39

within that period, consequently, it could not be said that the marital status of the
parties had in any way been changed. They would still in law continue to be *a*
husband and wife.'

Unfortunately that case was not brought to the notice of the Divisional Court in *R v
Registrar General of Births, Deaths and Marriages, ex parte Minhas*[1], where the husband had
pronounced talaq in England and had then served notice on the chairman and sent a copy
to the wife. Park J, who delivered the judgment of the court, said that the effect of the
Family Laws Ordinance was merely that the talaq was revocable within 90 days from the *b*
date on which notice was sent to the chairman, and that 'subject to that, the marriage was
brought to an end immediately on the pronouncement of the talaq'. That was evidently
based on a misunderstanding of the ordinance.

A further explanation of the effect of the ordinance was given in Pakistan by S A
Rahman J in *Jatoi v Jatoi*[2], who delivered the judgment of the majority of the Supreme
Court. He said: *c*

'A pertinent factor to note in this context is that divorce by *talaq* is now regulated
in Pakistan by the procedure prescribed in the Muslim Family Laws Ordinance, so
that it no longer remains a purely private unilateral act of the husband. The matter
does go before a public authority before it receives finality.'

It is apparently the practice for the civil judge to issue a formal document, generally *d*
referred to as a certificate or as an order, narrating that the procedure under the ordinance
has been observed and stating whether the arbitration proceedings have been successful
or not. In the present case such a document, which is headed 'Order' was issued on 18th
February 1975, narrating that the husband had divorced his wife, that notice of talaq was
received but that the parties did not nominate their representatives. It concludes with
the sentence: 'The *talaq* as such stands confirmed after expiry of ninety days since the *e*
notice was received by this court, and the matter stands disposed of.' It is signed by the
VIIIth Senior Civil Judge, Karachi. The exact legal status of this document is not clear to
me. Notwithstanding the imperative terms of the rules, there is no sanction to compel
a party to nominate a representative and the civil judge has no power to compel
attendance, or to prevent the talaq coming into effect after the expiration of 90 days.
Moreover, if the spouses are reconciled and the husband revokes the talaq within the 90 *f*
days, the parties continue in law to be husband and wife but they are not obliged to
inform the civil judge. Consequently a certificate or order may be issued in terms like
those in the present order but it may be entirely misleading. All this is explained in
Fahmida Bibi v Mukhtar Ahmad[3], where the court said:

'There is no provision either in the Ordinance or the rules requiring the Chairman *g*
or the Arbitration Council to give a decision or to issue a certificate to make the
divorce effective. If the Chairman issued the certificate, it was not under any
provision of law and had no legal effect.'

In the present case, *Fahmida Bibi v Mukhtar Ahmad*[4] was cited by Wood J who added the
comment:
                                                                                         h
'It is thus clear so far as *talaqs* are concerned the Arbitration Council has no
function except to take steps to bring about reconciliation between the parties.
Beyond this the Arbitration Council has really no effect.'

The Court of Appeal expressed their agreement with that observation, which they
said[5]—
                                                                                         j

1   [1976] 2 All ER 246, [1977] QB 1
2   PLD 1967 Supreme Court 580 at 605–606
3   PLD 1972 Lahore 694 at 697
4   PLD 1972 Lahore 694
5   See p 432, ante

a 'makes it quite clear that a divorce obtained in this way is not obtained "by means of judicial or other proceedings". It is obtained by the unilateral act of the husband over which, provided he gives the necessary notices, there is no control.'

I respectfully agree that there is no control over the husband provided he gives the necessary notice but I am unable to agree with the court's conclusion. I treat the order as having no legal effect, in accordance with the statement quoted from *Fahmida Bibi v* *Mukhtar Ahmad*[1], but even without the order I am of the opinion that the talaq and the

b notice to the civil judge, a copy of which has to be sent to the wife, taken together are 'proceedings' within the sense of s 2 of the 1971 Act. The proceedings are instituted by the talaq itself, which forms part of them. That must be so having regard to the provision in s 3(1) of the Act that the tempus inspiciendum for habitual residence and nationality is the date of the institution of the proceedings. The subsequent notice to the civil judge may or may not lead to arbitration proceedings actually taking place, but it at

c least gives an opportunity to the wife to make her views known to the arbitration council and it also invests the divorce with a certain formality which is essential in Pakistan to its effectiveness. I express no opinion whether a bare talaq pronounced in some country where, unlike Pakistan, it would be effective without any further procedure, should be recognised under the Recognition Act of 1971 as a valid divorce.

d As the talaq is not effective in terms of s 7(3) of the Pakistan ordinance until the expiration of 90 days from the date on which notice is declared to the chairman, the giving of notice is an essential step to obtain a divorce. In these circumstances it is, in my opinion, proper to regard the divorce as being 'obtained by means of' proceedings which include the procedure under the ordinance.

My conclusion on this matter is reinforced by a consideration of the Domicile and Matrimonial Proceedings Act 1973. Section 16(1) of the 1973 Act provides as follows:

e
'No proceeding in the United Kingdom, the Channel Islands or the Isle of Man shall be regarded as validly dissolving a marriage unless instituted in the courts of law of one of those countries.'

That provision seems clearly intended to reverse the decision in *Qureshi v Qureshi*[2] but

f it would be ineffective for that purpose unless the word 'proceeding' applies to the talaq which was the form of divorce in that case. The implication is that a talaq is a proceeding in the sense of the 1973 Act. That Act is in my opinion relevant to the construction of the 1971 Act, because it amended the 1971 Act, into which it inserted a substituted s 6, and s 16 of the 1973 Act refers to the substitution. The fact that the word 'proceeding' is used in the singular throughout s 16 is not in my opinion of any particular significance. It seems to be used in the same sense as 'proceedings' in the plural in the

g 1971 Act. Thus in sub-s (2) of s 16, which is to apply notwithstanding anything in s 6 of the 1971 Act 'as substituted by section 2 of this Act', the word is used in the singular, and in the substituted s 6 in the plural.

On the question whether notice was given to the appropriate civil judge, I agree with the opinion expressed by my noble and learned friend, Lord Diplock, that it was.

h Accordingly it is effective by the law of Pakistan and comes within s 2(b) of the 1971 Act. I see no reason to think that the judge exercised his discretion under s 8 on any wrong principle.

I would allow the appeal.

LORD SCARMAN. My Lords, I also would allow the appeal.

j On 18th June 1975, Mohammed Ameerudin Quazi, whom I shall call the husband, presented a petition in which he sought a declaration that his marriage with Bilquis Jehan Begum Quazi, whom I shall call the wife, had been lawfully dissolved either by a

---

1 PLD 1972 Lahore 694 at 697
2 [1971] 1 All ER 325, [1972] Fam 173

khula agreed between the parties at the instance of the wife in Bangkok on 22nd March 1968 or by a talaq pronounced by the husband in Karachi in July 1974. The wife by her answer sought a declaration that neither the khula nor the talaq was entitled to recognition under English law. She raised a number of factual defences and cross-prayed for the repayment of her zar-e-meher (a dowry) if the husband should succeed in establishing a dissolution. The judge negatived her factual defences and rejected the cross-prayer for dowry. He found as a fact that it had been repaid. He made the declaration sought by the husband, but his decision was reversed on appeal. The husband now appeals to this House.

The only issue which remains is whether either the khula or the talaq is to be recognised in the United Kingdom as a valid overseas divorce. It is, at the end of the day, a short point on the construction of s 2 of the Recognition of Divorces and Legal Separations Act 1971. But in order to reach it the courts have had to make their way through some difficult country. Indeed, had it not been for the excellent work done by the courts below in explaining and analysing the various foreign laws with which the case is concerned, the House could not have dealt with the case as swiftly as has fortunately proved possible. For there was no short cut to the decisive point. The labyrinth had to be negotiated; and at public expense.

As Wood J said at the beginning of his long and careful judgment, 'the real reason behind all this litigation is financial. The petitioner's only known asset . . . is a house at 232 Durnsford Road, London, SW19'. Both parties want it; this suit will, in effect, determine whether the husband has an exclusive right to it or the wife can claim an interest in it.

A small house, it has generated an immense lawsuit embracing the laws of India, Pakistan and Thailand and requiring our courts to consider the family law of Islam as recognised and applied in the legal systems of those countries. By a quaint but eminently sensible subterfuge our law treats issues of foreign law as questions of fact. The parties have, therefore, placed before the courts a voluminous quantity of expert evidence on the issues of foreign law which arise in the case. The digestion and analysis of this material presented the trial judge and the Court of Appeal with some formidable problems. It is no criticism of them, indeed, it is a tribute to their painstaking investigation of laws with which they are not familiar, that the case occupied the judge for some 15 days, and the Court of Appeal for eight days.

This complex, laborious, and expensive lawsuit has been almost totally financed from public funds. Legal aid alone has made it possible; and the costs borne by the public are out of all proportion to the modest prize at stake. While it is legitimate to take pride in our legal system which assures to the poor the same right of access to our courts for the resolution of their disputes as is enjoyed at their own expense by the wealthy (indeed, only the wealthy and the poor can find the finance for such a dispute as this) one must ask oneself whether there are not better and cheaper ways of doing justice. I agree with the Court of Appeal that the reform needed is one whereby a resident in the United Kingdom whose overseas divorce (or legal separation) is recognised by our law as valid, should be able, like one who has obtained a divorce or separation in this country, to claim a property adjustment or other financial order under the Matrimonial Causes Act 1973. In expressing the hope that the problem may be referred to the two Law Commissions, I would comment that such a reform should achieve not only a greater measure of justice for first-generation immigrant families but a considerable saving for the legal aid fund. The incentive to challenge the foreign divorce would have gone: and the court could deal with the property and financial problems of the parties on their merits.

The history of the marriage

The critical facts of the married life are as follows. Both the husband and the wife are Muslims and were born in India. They were married according to the rites of Islam at Aurangabad on 24th November 1963. It was the husband's second marriage, his first having been disolved by talaq. Before the marriage the husband lived and worked in

East Pakistan, where he took Pakistani nationality and acquired a domicile of choice in
a Pakistan. His domicile of origin had been Indian. After the marriage the husband took
employment in Bangkok where he acquired a domicile of choice in Thailand. The wife,
who followed him to Bangkok, where they set up home, also became a national of
Pakistan (the evidence is not clear whether in 1965 or 1969). They have a son, Salim,
who was born in 1964.

   They were not happy in Bangkok. The wife sought and obtained the husband's
b consent to a divorce, and on 22nd March 1968 a 'khula' was written, signed, and
witnessed. A khula is a form of divorce according to Islamic religious law where it is the
wife who proposes the divorce and the husband who agrees to it. To be effective
according to the internal law of Thailand it has to be in writing and witnessed, as this
khula was. Despite the khula, they continued to live under the same roof, but there was
no sexual intercourse. They maintained the outward appearance of marriage. Their
c cohabitation, however, in no way diminished the effect of the khula.

   In June 1970 they moved to Penang. In December 1971 Salim reached the age of
seven, when by Islamic law he would live with his father, if his parents were separated.
So, in January 1972 the husband moved into a separate house, intending that Salim
should live with him.

   In 1972 the husband felt it necessary to 'rethink' his life, as the judge put it. In
d February 1973 he left Penang. He visited Bangkok, and then spent a few weeks in
Karachi. In March 1973 he came to London where he intended that Salim and his son
by his first marriage should be educated. In August 1973 he bought 232 Durnsford
Road.

   The wife also left Penang not long after the husband. She went to Karachi where she
remained until June 1974. On 17th June 1974 the wife arrived in London
e unannounced. She had with her a return ticket to Karachi, but no visa or other entry
permit. The judge thought her visit was tactical, associated with her matrimonial
difficulties. Her arrival was unwelcome to the husband and led to discussions about their
future. They could not agree, and he made it clear to her that he wanted an effective and
publicly recognised divorce. He doubted whether the khula was effective; and
knowledge of its existence was confined to a very few people.

f   Accordingly on 9th July he went with Salim to Karachi, where after consulting
lawyers he pronounced talaq three times in a document bearing the date 12th July
1974. Notice was given to the wife by sending a copy to her address in Karachi and to
232 Durnsford Road, where she had been living since her arrival in London. Notice was
also given to the VIIIth Senior Civil Judge, First Class, Karachi. The wife also received
notice that the civil judge proposed to hold an arbitration council on 30th August 1974,
g or alternatively 9th November 1974. She was invited to take part and to nominate a
representative. Undoubtedly all these notices were received, seen, and understood by
her. Indeed she consulted solicitors in London, who wrote to the Karachi judge seeking
a stay of the arbitration proceedings. In December 1974 she presented to the English
court a petition for divorce on the ground of her husband's unreasonable behaviour.
Proceedings on her petition have been stayed pending a decision in the husband's suit.

h   Finally there was an issue as to whether the husband had acquired a domicile of choice
in England. The trial judge held that he had abandoned his Thai domicile of choice but
had 'certainly not formed the intention to continue to live in England'. He held that his
Indian domicile of origin had revived. The Court of Appeal disagreed holding that the
husband had acquired a domicile of choice in England. On the view of the case which
I have formed it is unnecessary to resolve this difference of opinion. Suffice it to say that
j on the judge's findings of fact there are formidable difficulties in sustaining the opinion
of the Court of Appeal.

The English law
   The recognition of overseas divorces is now regulated by the Recognition of Divorces
and Legal Separations Act 1971, as amended by the Domicile and Matrimonial

Proceedings Act 1973. The common law survives only to the extent that certain overseas divorces which are not covered by the statutory code may be recognised pursuant to 'common law rules' if the domiciliary requirements set out in s 6 of the 1971 Act, as amended, are met. In other words, the scope of the law is now set by the statute. In certain circumstances it may be extended by virtue of the 'common law rules', but not restricted.

The scope of the statutory code is to be determined by reference to the language of the statute and its legislative purpose. Section 2 of the 1971 Act is the critical provision. It specifies the divorces and separations to which the code contained in ss 3 to 5 applies. It is in these terms:

> 'Sections 3 to 5 of this Act shall have effect, subject to section 8 of this Act, as respects the recognition in Great Britain of the validity of overseas divorces and legal separations, that is to say, divorces and legal separations which—(a) have been obtained by means of judicial or other proceedings in any country outside the British Isles; and (b) are effective under the law of that country.'

Section 6, which extends the scope of the code to certain divorces and legal separations if they qualify for recognition under common law rules, does not touch the present case. Apart from s 2, the only directly relevant provision is s 3(1) which specifies the grounds for recognition. It is in these terms:

> 'The validity of an overseas divorce or legal separation shall be recognised if, at the date of the institution of the proceedings in the country in which it was obtained— (a) either spouse was habitually resident in that country; or (b) either spouse was a national of that country.'

At the date of the khula both husband and wife were habitually resident in Thailand, the country in which it was obtained. At the date of the talaq both husband and wife were nationals of Pakistan, the country in which it was obtained, and the wife, on the findings of the judge which in my opinion were well justified, was also habitually resident in that country. The requirement of s 3(1) was therefore met.

Section 2 of the 1971 Act specifies the divorces to which recognition is to be given once the requirements of s 3 have been met. The question for your Lordships' House is, therefore, whether the khula or, if not the khula, the talaq, is a divorce 'obtained by means of judicial or other proceedings in any country outside the British Isles' and is effective under the law of the country where it was obtained.

It is conceded in respect of both the khula and the talaq that neither of them was obtained 'by means of judicial proceedings'. The issue is whether either was obtained by 'other proceedings', and was effective under the law of the country in which it was obtained.

Counsel for the wife submitted that the term 'other proceedings' in the context of s 2 refers only to quasi-judicial proceedings. He contended that the term should not be construed as extending the common law of recognition, and that, notwithstanding the decision to the contrary of Simon P in *Qureshi v Qureshi*[1], the pre-existing common law did not recognise foreign divorces unless obtained in judicial or quasi-judicial proceedings; and he also relied on the ejusdem generis rule of interpretation. Counsel for the husband submitted that the words 'other proceedings' were general and covered any acts, whether of the parties or by the state, which were recognised by the law of the country where they were done as being effective under the law of that country to obtain a divorce. Basic to his submission is the view that the word 'proceedings' is used in the section not as a term of art but in its general sense of actions or conduct of any sort by any person or body of persons. In his submission the one limitation on its generality is that the proceedings must be recognised by the state as steps without which a divorce would not be legally effective. If necessary, he was prepared to submit that the pre-existing

---

1   [1971] 1 All ER 325, [1972] Fam 173

common law of recognition extended to non-judicial proceedings, as Simon P held in
a *Qureshi v Qureshi*.[1]

When the statute is examined in detail, the view that the common law is no guide to
the true interpretation of s 2 of the 1971 Act is reinforced. The Act, as its long title
declares, was 'to amend the law relating to the recognition of divorces and legal
separations'. One of the purposes for which it was enacted was, as its preamble recites,
the 'ratification by the United Kingdom' of the Hague Convention dated 1st June 1970
b on the Recognition of Divorces and Legal Separations[2] (it was ratified by the United
Kingdom on 21st May 1974, and entered into force on 24th August 1975). The true
mete-wand for determining the meaning of the code of recognition introduced by the
1971 Act is, therefore, not the common law but the Hague Convention (in both its
authentic texts, French and English).

Counsel for the wife, with his usual and engaging candour, conceded that, if reference
c be made to the convention for the purpose of interpreting the statute, he was in great
difficulties. I would go further and simply say 'Cadit quaestio'. The language of art 1 in
its English text (and the French is even clearer) puts the issue beyond doubt. Recognition
is to be accorded, subject to the terms of the convention, to divorces (and legal separations)
obtained in a contracting state 'which follow judicial or other proceedings officially
recognised in that State and which are legally effective there'. Had the convention been
d intended to be limited to proceedings of a state authority culminating in a state decision
(judicial, quasi judicial, or administrative), the one word 'official' would have served the
purpose. But the term used is 'proceedings officially recognised in that State'. The
language is apt to include proceedings by persons other than the state, which the state
officially recognises as steps leading to effective divorce. The convention's formulation
is such that it cannot be limited by the ejusdem generis rule or any other restrictive rule
e of interpretation to proceedings of the state. If the proceedings which precede the
obtaining of the divorce are officially recognised and the divorce thereby obtained is
legally effective in the state where it is obtained, art 1 provides that the convention
applies. The only requirement is a proceeding, or proceedings (for there is no magic in
the singular or the plural), officially recognised resulting in a divorce which is effective
under the country's law. The convention, of course, applies only to contracting states;
f and neither Thailand nor Pakistan are contracting states. No matter; for there is no
inconsistency in applying to all overseas divorces and legal separations the rules which
contracting states have bound themselves to apply among themselves.

But the overall purpose of the convention is as important as the language of art 1. The
states signatory to the convention 'desiring to facilitate the recognition of divorces and
legal separations obtained in their respective territories have resolved to conclude a
g convention to this effect'. And art 17 provides that the convention shall not prevent the
application of rules of law more favourable to recognition (incidently, this authorises the
common law extension in s 6 of the 1971 Act).

A legislative purpose of the 1971 Act being to enable the convention to be ratified by
the United Kingdom, there is no room for the sort of restriction for which counsel for the
wife contends, whether it be based on the pre-existing common law or on an ejusdem
h generis interpretation of the phrase 'other proceedings' in s 2 of the Act. Nor, for the
same reasons, is it possible to restrict the meaning of those words, as the Court of Appeal
did, to proceedings in which 'the state or some official organisation recognised by the
state must play some part in the divorce process at least to the extent that, in proper cases,
it can prevent the wishes of the parties or one of them, as the case may be, from
dissolving the marriage tie as of right'. No hint of any such restriction appears in the
j convention or the Act; nor is any such restriction to be implied, if not expressly stated,
in a convention or statute the purpose of which is to facilitate the recognition of divorces

---

1 [1971] 1 All ER 325, [1972] Fam 173
2 TS 123 (1975); Cmnd 6248

and legal separations. Nor did counsel for the wife seek to support the Court of Appeal's interpretation. I would add the comment that it would have been strange if the United Kingdom, so shortly after the enactment for England and Wales of the Divorce Reform Act 1969, should have enacted any such restriction as a condition of recognition of overseas divorces.

While, on the view I have formed as to the correct judicial approach to the statute it is unnecessary to examine what was the pre-existing common law, the point was raised in argument. It was not, however, fully developed. As at present advised, I see no reason to doubt the correctness of *Qureshi v Qureshi*[1]. However, both counsel for the wife's submission and the Court of Appeal's interpretation really stand or fall by the weight to be attached to the ejusdem generis rule. It is, at best, a very secondary guide to the meaning of a statute. The all-important matter is to consider the purpose of the statute: see *Rands v Oldroyd*.[2]

If the legislative purpose of a statute is such that a statutory series should be read ejusdem generis, so be it; the rule is helpful. But, if it is not, the rule is more likely to defeat than to fulfil the purpose of the statute. The rule, like many other rules of statutory interpretation, is a useful servant but a bad master.

For these reasons I construe s 2 as applying to any divorce which has been obtained by means of any proceeding, i e any act or acts, officially recognised as leading to divorce in the country where the divorce was obtained, and which itself is recognised by the law of the country as an effective divorce. Specifically, 'other proceedings' will include an act or sequence of acts other than a proceeding instituted in a court of law, as, indeed, Parliament must have thought when enacting s 16 of the Domicile and Matrimonial Proceedings Act 1973: see in particular sub-s (2) of the section.

It remains to consider two questions. Was the khula in Thailand, or the talaq in Pakistan 'obtained by means of' officially recognised proceedings in the respective country? If either was, was it an effective divorce under the law of the country where it was obtained?

The khula

Under Thai law the khula had to be in writing and witnessed by two persons. This khula was. It, therefore, complied with s 1498 of the Thai Civil Code. If this were all, it would be clear, in my judgment, that the khula was obtained by means of an officially recognised proceeding (i e the signing and witnessing of the instrument) and was effective under Thai law. However, the parties were not Thai nationals. They were Pakistan nationals, and s 26 of the Civil Code provides that 'Divorce by mutual consent shall be valid if it is permitted by the respective law of nationality of both the husband and the wife'. The expert witnesses, the trial judge, and the Court of Appeal were, if I may respectfully say so, thrown into disarray by this provision. The trial judge held that, notwithstanding the section, the divorce was valid in Thailand (as it undoubtedly did) it complied with s 1498 of the Civil Code. The Court of Appeal gave an exclusive interpretation to s 26, holding that to be valid in Thailand the khula had to be recognised in Pakistan, which it would not be because it failed to comply with the Pakistan Muslim Family Laws Ordinance. I refrain from entering this controversy. It suffices that the obscurities of the expert evidence were such that, in my judgment, the husband cannot be said to have proved the existence of a khula effective under the law of Thailand. He fails, therefore, to establish that the khula of 22nd March 1968 is entitled to recognition under English law.

The talaq

By the law of Islam a man may divorce his wife by pronouncing talaq three times. But

---

1   [1971] 1 All ER 325, [1972] Fam 173
2   [1958] 3 All ER 344, [1959] 1 QB 204

in Pakistan (as in many Muslim countries) divorce by talaq is subject to safeguarding
a   provisions of the civil law. In Pakistan, it is subject to the Muslim Family Laws
Ordinance 1961. The ordinance modifies certain aspects of the substantive family law of
Islam as well as requiring certain procedural steps to be taken with regard to marriage
and divorce. Where it makes specific provision, it overrides even the classic law of Islam:
for s 3(1) provides that the ordinance 'shall have the effect notwithstanding any law,
custom or usage'. Section 7 deals with talaq, and is, so far as material, in these terms:

b   'Talaq—(1) Any man who wishes to divorce his wife shall, as soon as may be after
the pronouncement of talaq in any form whatsoever, give the Chairman notice in
writing of his having done so, and shall supply a copy thereof to the wife . . .
'(3) Save as provided in subsection (5), a talaq unless revoked earlier, expressly or
otherwise, shall not be effective until the expiration of ninety days from the day on
which notice under subsection (1) is delivered to the Chairman.
c   '(4) Within thirty days of the receipt of notice under subsection (1), the Chairman
shall constitute an Arbitration Council for the purpose of bringing about a
reconciliation between the parties, and the Arbitration Council shall take all steps
necessary to bring about such reconciliation.
'(5) If the wife be pregnant at the time talaq is pronounced talaq shall not be
effective until the period mentioned in subsection (2) or the pregnancy, whichever
d   be later, ends.'

By the rules made under the ordinance the chairman is the chairman of the union
council or committee having jurisdiction in the area or town where the wife was residing
at the time of the pronouncement of the talaq. An arbitration council is defined in the
ordinance as a body consisting of the chairman and the parties' representatives.
e   The husband pronounced his talaq in writing on 12th July 1974, sent copies of it to the
wife and to the chairman of the union or town (Karachi) where the wife resided
immediately before she left for London in June 1974. The wife was well aware of the
proceedings and had a full opportunity to attend and to send a representative to the
arbitration council which the chairman convened; but she declined to do so. On 18th
February 1975, the civil judge as chairman of the union committee issued an 'order'
f   which concluded with these words: 'The talaq . . . stands confirmed after expiry of ninety
days since the notice was received by this Court'.
Certain features of this course of action are not in dispute. The talaq became effective
under the law of Pakistan 90 days after service of the notice on the chairman, unless
revoked earlier expressly or otherwise. No 'order' was required: and the status of the
'order' issued in this case is obscure. The steps prescribed by the ordinance as necessary
g   to make the talaq effective were neither judicial nor 'quasi judicial'. If a husband is set
on divorce and takes, as this husband did, the steps prescribed, the divorce cannot be
prevented from becoming in due course effective.
On the view that I have formed as to the meaning of s 2 of the 1971 Act, the
pronouncement of talaq, the notices to the chairman and the wife, though not judicial
in character, were 'other proceedings' as that term is used in the section: for they were
h   acts officially recognised by the law of Pakistan as leading to an effective divorce. The
divorce became under Pakistan law effective not, as under the classic Islamic law, on
pronouncement of talaq but on the expiry of 90 days, unless revoked, from the notice in
writing to the chairman of the union committee. That this is the law of Pakistan brooks
of no doubt. It is put succinctly by S A Rahman J in Ali Nawaz Gardezi v Muhammad
Yusuf[1]:

j   'Subsection 3 of this section precludes the talaq from being effective, as such, for
a certain period and within that period, consequently, it could not be said that the

---

1   PLD 1963 Supreme Court 51 at 75, para 39

marital status of the parties had in any way been changed. They would still in law
continue to be husband and wife.'   *a*

In the later case of *Jatoi v Jatoi*[1] the same judge, with whom the majority of the Supreme
Court agreed, said:

'... divorce by *talaq* is now regulated in Pakistan by the procedure prescribed in
the ... Ordinance, so that it no longer remains a purely private unilateral act of the
husband. The matter does go before a public authority before it receives finality.'   *b*

Under the law of Pakistan, therefore, talaq is the institution of proceedings officially
recognised as leading to divorce and becomes an effective divorce only after the
completion of the proceedings and the expiry of a period laid down by statute. The
proceedings in this case were, therefore, officially recognised, and led to a divorce legally
effective in Pakistan. Further, the trial judge was correct in holding that the effective
divorce was obtained *by means of* these proceedings; for without them there would have   *c*
been no effective divorce.

There is, however, a technical point. Was notice of the talaq given to the correct union
council (or committee) chairman? If it was not, the submission is that the requirements
of the ordinance were not met and the talaq was ineffective. Whether the submission be
right or wrong, I am satisfied that the trial judge was justified in holding on the evidence
that the wife, although physically in London, was resident in Karachi when talaq was   *d*
pronounced. She had resided there for more than a year when in June 1974 she went,
unannounced and with a return ticket to Karachi in her bag, to see the husband in
London. She went because she had received her husband's letter of 7th June in which he
had made it clear that he wanted a divorce and was coming to Karachi to get it. She
anticipated him by turning up in London, where they had their unhappy discussions
about their family difficulties without him being persuaded that a reconciliation was   *e*
possible. I think the judge was right to treat her as a visitor in London and a resident of
Karachi. And, if she was so resident, notice was given to the correct chairman.

Finally, there is the question of discretion. Section 8(2) of the 1971 Act provides that
recognition of the validity of a divorce or legal separation obtained outside the British
Isles may be refused 'if, and only if ... (*b*) its recognition would manifestly be contrary
to public policy'. The trial judge considered that the facts of the case did not justify him   *f*
in refusing recognition. It was a matter for his discretion; he considered all the facts, and
fell into no error of law. Even if I might have exercised the discretion differently, it
would be wrong to interfere; but, in truth, I think he was right.

For these reasons I would allow the appeal and restore with one modification the order
of Wood J. Since I am not satisfied as to the validity of the khula, I would limit the
declaration of dissolution to the talaq.   *g*

Appeal allowed.

Solicitors: *Sowmans* (for the husband); *Sheratte, Caleb & Co* (for the wife).

                                        Mary Rose Plummer   Barrister.   *h*

---

1   PLD 1967 Supreme Court 580 at 605

a

Re Bond Worth Ltd

CHANCERY DIVISION

SLADE J

7th, 8th, 12th, 13th, 14th, 15th, 18th, 19th, 20th, 21st, 22nd DECEMBER 1978, 15th, 16th, 17th, 18th JANUARY, 12th FEBRUARY 1979

b

Sale of goods – Passing of property – Vendor retaining property in goods – Equitable charge – Floating charge – Goods supplied on credit terms – Contract reserving 'equitable and beneficial ownership' in goods to vendor until full payment made – Purchaser free to use goods as he pleased in ordinary course of his business – Purchaser becoming insolvent – Whether vendor's retention of title creating a trust or merely an equitable charge – Whether charge a floating charge – Whether charge 'created by' vendor or purchaser – Whether charge void against other creditors for want of registration – Companies Act 1948, s 95(1).

c

The sellers supplied synthetic fibre on credit terms to the buyers who used it in the manufacture of carpets. The fibre was supplied by separate deliveries each of which was a separate contract. The contracts stipulated that the risk in the fibre passed to the buyers

d

on delivery but 'the equitable and beneficial ownership' of the fibre was to 'remain' with the sellers until full payment had been made for the fibre delivered or until prior resale in which case the seller's beneficial entitlement was to attach to the proceeds of sale, and further, if the fibre became a constituent of, or was converted into, other products the sellers were to have equitable and beneficial ownership in those products or the proceeds of resale thereof. In the buyers' manufacturing process the fibre was spun into yarn with

e

other fibre and the yarn was then processed and woven into carpets. In the course of this process the fibre supplied by the sellers became an inseparable component of both the yarn and the carpets. The buyers became insolvent and receivers were appointed by a debenture holder. On the date when the receivers were appointed the buyers owed the sellers £587,397 in respect of 29 unpaid deliveries of fibre. The buyers held very little raw fibre at that date but they were holding substantial stocks of yarn and finished

f

carpets. The yarn held consisted of fibre supplied by the sellers (some of which was paid for and some of which was not), reprocessed fibre owned by the buyers, and yarn purchased from a subsidiary of the buyers. It was impossible to separate the unpaid fibre from the yarn and carpets held or to determine accurately the proportion of unpaid fibre therein. The buyers claimed that, by virtue of the retention of title clause in the contracts, they were entitled to trace their fibre into the stocks of yarn and carpets held or the proceeds of sale of carpets in which it had been used. The receivers took out a

g

summons seeking the directions of the court whether the sellers had an interest or charge over fibre held by the buyers in the form of raw fibre, fibre processed either with or without other products owned by the buyers or other suppliers, fibre incorporated into carpets, or over the proceeds of sale thereof. The receivers contended that the only rights conferred on the sellers by the retention of title clause were those under a floating charge which was void as against other creditors, under s 95(1)[a] of the Companies Act 1948, for

h

want of registration. The sellers contended that their position was that of beneficiary under a trust, or, alternatively, if no more than a charge securing payment of the purchase price had been created, it had not been 'created' by the buyers but by the sellers by reserving it to themselves and therefore did not come within the scope of s 95.

j

Held – (i) The contracts between the buyers and the sellers for the delivery of the fibre were primarily contracts for the sale of goods under which the property and risk in the goods passed on delivery to the buyers who were at liberty to resell them or use them for their manufacturing purposes, subject however to the intention of the parties that the

---

a   Section 95, so far as material, is set out at p 955 *h j* and p 956 *b c*, post

sellers should retain rights of equitable and beneficial ownership until payment was made. Having regard to the substance of the transactions, as appearing from the whole *a*
of the retention of title clause, the characteristics of the transactions were that the buyers were entitled to redeem the sellers' interest of property remaining in the fibre by paying the money owing, and if the sellers exercised their power of resale any surplus belonged to the buyers and not the sellers, while any deficiency had to be made good by the buyers. Therefore on the true construction of the retention of title clause, the rights conferred on the sellers were merely by way of an equitable charge over the fibre *b*
supplied (or the products of which it was a constituent or proceeds of sale thereof), since the buyers' equity of redemption was inconsistent with the existence of a trust under which the entire beneficial interest in the fibre or products or proceeds of sale remained in the sellers (see p 936 *e* to *g* and *j* to p 937 *d* and p 938 *h* to p 939 *b* and *f* to *j*, post); dicta of Lord Hanworth MR, of Lawrence LJ and of Romer LJ in *Re George Inglefield Ltd* [1932] All ER Rep at 251, 254 and 256–257 applied.   *c*

(ii) On the true construction of the contract, the equitable charge in favour of the sellers was created by the buyers by way of an implied grant back to the sellers after the whole of the property in the fibre had first passed to the buyers, and not by the sellers reserving or excepting to themselves an interest out of the property passing to the buyers. Furthermore, having regard to the buyers' implied authority and freedom to use the fibre as they pleased for their own purposes and benefit in the course of their *d*
business, the charge could only be construed as a floating charge and not as a specific charge over specific assets, and was in fact a floating charge since it was a shifting charge against fluctuating assets which the buyers were free to deal with in the ordinary course of their business (see p 945 *c d f*, p 953 *d* to *g* and p 955 *d*, post); *Coburn v Collins* (1887) 35 Ch D 373, dicta of Lord Herschell LC in *McEntire v Crossley Brothers Ltd* [1895–9] All ER at 832, 833, of Romer LJ in *Re Yorkshire Woolcombers' Association Ltd* [1903] 2 Ch at *e*
295 and of Lord Macnaghten in *Illingworth v Houldsworth* [1904] AC at 358 applied; *McEntire v Crossley Brothers Ltd* [1895–9] All ER Rep 829 and *Re Connolly Brothers Ltd* [1912] 2 Ch 25 distinguished.

(iii) Since the charge was 'a floating charge on the . . . property' of the buyers, which had been 'created' by them and which had not been registered, it was void under s 95(1) of the 1948 Act against their creditors (see p 956 *e f* and p 957 *e* and *h* to p 958 *a*, post); *f*
Aluminium Industrie Vaassen BV v Romalpa Aluminium Ltd [1976] 2 All ER 552 distinguished.

Notes
For the right to follow and recover assets or the money into which they have been *g*
converted, see 16 Halsbury's Laws (4th Edn) para 1460.

For the Companies Act 1948, s 95, see 5 Halsbury's Statutes (3rd Edn) 189.

Cases referred to in judgment
Aluminium Industrie Vaassen BV v Romalpa Aluminium Ltd [1976] 2 All ER 552, [1976] 1 WLR 676, [1976] 1 Lloyd's Rep 443, CA.   *h*
Barker (George) (Transport) Ltd v Eynon [1974] 1 All ER 900, [1974] 1 WLR 462, [1974] 1 Lloyd's Rep, CA, Digest (Cont Vol D) 607, 298a.
Borden (UK) Ltd v Scottish Timber Products Ltd [1978] The Times, 15th November.
Capital Finance Co Ltd v Stokes, re Cityfield Properties Ltd [1968] 3 All ER 625, [1969] 1 Ch 261, [1968] 1 WLR 899, 19 P & CR 791, CA, 32 Digest (Reissue) 433, 3444.
Coburn v Collins (1887) 35 Ch D 373, 56 LJ Ch 504, 56 LT 431, 7 Digest (Reissue) 13, 57. *j*
Connolly Brothers Ltd, Re (No 2), Wood v Co [1912] 2 Ch 25, 81 LJ Ch 517, 106 LT 738, 19 Mans 259, CA, 10 Digest (Reissue) 840, 4845.
Diplock's Estate, Re, Diplock v Wintle [1948] 2 All ER 318, [1948] Ch 465, CA; *affd* sub nom *Ministry of Health v Simpson* [1950] 2 All ER 1137, [1951] AC 251, HL, 47 Digest (Repl) 532, 4825.

a *Evans v Rival Granite Quarries Ltd* [1910] 2 KB 979, 79 LJKB 970, 18 Mans 64, CA, 10 Digest (Reissue) 817, 4717.

Evans (J) & Son (Portsmouth) Ltd v Andrea Merzario Ltd [1975] 1 Lloyd's Rep 162; *rvsd* [1976] 2 All ER 930, [1976] 1 WLR 1078, [1976] 2 Lloyd's Rep 165, CA.

Foley v Hill (1848) 2 HL Cas 28, [1843–60] All ER Rep 16, 9 ER 1002, HL, 20 Digest (Repl) 286, 289.

b *Hallett's Estate, Re, Knatchbull v Hallett* (1880) 13 Ch D 696, [1874–80] All ER Rep 793, 49 LJ Ch 415, 42 LT 421, CA, 1 Digest (Repl) 655, 2278.

Henry v Hammond [1913] 2 KB 515, 82 LJKB 575, 108 LT 729, 1 Digest (Repl) 530, 1065.

Illingworth v Houldsworth [1904] AC 355, 73 LJ Ch 739, 91 LT 602, 12 Mans 141, HL; *affg* sub nom *Re Yorkshire Woolcombers' Association Ltd, Houldsworth v Yorkshire Woolcombers' Association Ltd* [1903] 2 Ch 284, 72 LJ Ch 635, 88 LT 811, 10 Mans 276, CA, 10 Digest (Reissue) 815, 4709.

c *Inglefield (George) Ltd, Re* [1933] Ch 1, [1932] All ER Rep 244, 101 LJ Ch 360, 147 LT 411, [1931] B & CR 220, CA, 10 Digest (Reissue) 864, 4978.

London and Cheshire Insurance Co Ltd v Laplagrene Property Co Ltd [1971] 1 All ER 766, [1971] Ch 499, [1971] 2 WLR 257, 22 P & CR 108, Digest (Cont Vol D) 759, 933d.

McEntire v Crossley Brothers Ltd [1895] AC 457, [1895–9] All ER Rep 829, 64 LJPC 129, 72 LT 731, 2 Mans 334, 11 R 207, HL, 39 Digest (Repl) 595, 1128.

d *Nevill, Re, ex parte White* (1871) LR 6 Ch App 397, 40 LJ Bcy 73, 24 LT 45, LJJ, *on appeal* sub nom *Towle & Co v White* (1873) 29 LT 78, HL, 39 Digest (Repl) 625, 1370.

Security Trust Co v Royal Bank of Canada [1976] 1 All ER 381, [1976] AC 503, [1976] 2 WLR 437, PC.

Sinclair v Brougham [1914] AC 398, [1914–15] All ER Rep 622, 83 LJ Ch 465, 111 LT 1, HL, 12 Digest (Reissue) 666, 4804.

e *South Australian Insurance Co v Randell* (1869) LR 3 PC 101, 6 Moo PCCNS 341, 22 LT 843, 16 ER 755, PC, 39 Digest (Repl) 447, 28.

Stucley, Re, Stucley v Kekewich [1906] 1 Ch 67, [1904–7] All ER Rep 281, 75 LJ Ch 58, 93 LT 718, CA, 32 Digest (Repl) 332, 609.

Transport and General Credit Corpn Ltd v Morgan [1939] 2 All ER 17, [1939] Ch 531, 108 LJ Ch 179, 160 LT 380, 35 Digest (Repl) 233, 336.

f *Wait, Re* [1927] 1 Ch 606, [1926] All ER Rep 433, 96 LJ Ch 179, 136 LT 552, [1927] B & CR 140, CA, 39 Digest (Repl) 821, 2836.

Wallis & Simmonds (Builders) Ltd, Re [1974] 1 All ER 561, [1974] 1 WLR 391, 28 P & CR 37, [1974] 1 Lloyd's Rep 272, 10 Digest (Reissue) 866, 4986.

Wheatley v Silkstone and Haigh Moor Coal Co (1885) 29 Ch D 715, 54 LJ Ch 778, 52 LT 978, 10 Digest (Reissue) 816, 4710.

g

Cases also cited

Abigail v Lapin [1934] AC 491, [1934] All ER Rep 720, PC.

Alsop's Patent, Re [1906] 1 Ch 85, CA.

Automatic Bottle Makers Ltd, Re [1926] Ch 412, [1926] All ER Rep 618, CA.

h *Barclay's Bank Ltd v Quistclose Investments Ltd* [1968] 3 All ER 651, [1970] AC 567, HL.

Barnhart v Greenshields (1853) 9 Moo PCC 18, 14 ER 204, PC.

Birmingham, Re, Savage v Stannard [1958] 2 All ER 397, [1959] Ch 523.

Brantom v Griffits (1877) 2 CPD 212, CA.

Brunton v Electrical Engineering Corpn [1892] 1 Ch 434.

Capell v Winter [1907] 2 Ch 376.

j *Car and Universal Finance Co Ltd v Caldwell* [1964] 1 All ER 290, [1965] 1 QB 525, CA.

Cardiff Savings Bank, Re, Marquis of Bate's Case [1892] 2 Ch 100.

Carritt v Real and Personal Advance Co (1889) 42 Ch D 263.

Castell & Brown Ltd, Re [1898] 1 Ch 315.

Cave v Cave (1880) 15 Ch D 639

Clayton's Case (1816) 1 Mer 572, [1814–23] All ER Rep 1.

Decro-Wall International SA v Practitioners in Marketing Ltd [1971] 2 All ER 216, [1971] 1
   WLR 361, CA.   *a*
Dempsey v Traders' Finance Corpn Ltd [1933] NZLR 1258.
Dilworth v Stamp Comrs [1899] AC 99, PC.
Dublin City Distillery Ltd v Doherty [1914] AC 823, HL.
Eaglesfield v Marquis of Londonderry (1875) 4 Ch D 693, CA.
Eastern Distributors Ltd v Goldring [1957] 2 All ER 525, [1957] 2 QB 600, CA.
Edwards v Edwards (1876) 2 Ch D 291, CA.   *b*
English & Scottish Mercantile Investment Co Ltd v Brunton [1892] 2 QB 700, CA.
Gallaher Ltd v British Road Services Ltd [1974] 2 Lloyd's Rep 440.
Governments Stock and other Securities Investment Co v Manila Railway Co [1897] AC 81, HL.
Grey v Inland Revenue Comrs [1959] 3 All ER 603, [1960] AC 1, HL.
Hamilton Young & Co, Re, ex parte Carter [1905] 2 KB 772, CA.
Hancock v Smith (1889) 41 Ch D 456, [1886–90] All ER Rep 306, CA.   *c*
Harris v Truman (1882) 9 QBD 264, CA.
Helby v Matthews [1895] AC 471, [1895–9] All ER Rep 821, HL.
Kelly & Co v Kellond (1888) 20 QBD 569, CA.
Kent and Sussex Sawmills Ltd, Re [1946] 2 All ER 638, [1947] Ch 177.
King v Greig [1931] VLR 413.
Ladenburg & Co v Goodwin, Ferreira & Co Ltd [1912] 3 KB 275.   *d*
Lloyd's Bank Ltd v Swiss Bankverein (1913) 108 LT 143, CA.
Lyons, ex parte, Re Lyons (1872) LR 7 Ch App 494.
Mackay, ex parte, ex parte Brown, Re Jeavons (1873) LR 8 Ch App 643.
National Provincial Bank of England Ltd v United Electric Theatres Ltd [1916] 1 Ch 132.
Oatway, Re [1903] 2 Ch 356.
Official Assignee, Madras v Bhat (1933) 60 LR Ind App 203.   *e*
Powles v Page (1846) 3 CB 16, 136 ER 7.
Reis, Re, ex parte Clough [1904] 2 KB 769, CA.
Rice v Rice (1854) 2 Drew 73, 61 ER 646.
Rimmer v Webster [1902] 2 Ch 163.
Rother Iron Works Ltd v Canterbury Precision Engineers Ltd [1973] 1 All ER 394, [1974] QB
   1, CA.   *f*
Sewell v Burdick (1884) 10 App Cas 74, HL.
Shropshire Union Railways and Canal Co v R (1875) LR 7 HL 499.
Siebe Gorman & Co Ltd v Barclays Bank Ltd [1979] 2 Lloyd's Rep 142.
Standard Manufacturing Co, Re [1891] 1 Ch 627, [1891–4] All ER Rep 1212, CA.
Standard Rotary Machine Co Ltd, Re (1906) 95 LT 829.
Steele, Re, ex parte Conning (1873) LR 16 Eq 414.   *g*
Stoneleigh Finance Ltd v Phillips [1965] 1 All ER 513, [1965] 2 QB 537, CA.
Stratton's Deed of Disclaimer, Re [1957] 2 All ER 594, [1958] Ch 42, CA.
Tailby v Official Receiver (1888) 13 App Cas 523, [1886–90] All ER Rep 486, HL.
Taylor v Plumer (1815) 3 M & S 562, 105 ER 721.
Thomas v Kelly (1888) 13 App Cas 506, [1886–90] All ER Rep 431, HL.
Tilley's Will Trusts, Re [1967] 2 All ER 303, [1967] Ch 1179.   *h*
Valletort Sanitary Steam Laundry Co Ltd, Re [1903] 2 Ch 654.
Vandervell v Inland Revenue Comrs [1967] 1 All ER 1, [1967] 2 AC 291, HL.
West of England and South Wales District Bank, Re, ex parte Dale & Co (1879) 11 Ch D 772.
Wilson v Kelland [1910] 2 Ch 306.
Worcester Works Finance Co Ltd v Cooden Engineering Co Ltd [1971] 3 All ER 708, [1972]
   1 QB 182, CA.   *j*

Originating summons

The applicants, Christopher Morris and Anthony Raymond Houghton, the receivers of
Bond Worth Ltd appointed by the fifth respondent, Alliance Assurance Co Ltd, sought

by an originating summons[1] dated 21st December 1977 the determination of the court
a on the question whether the first respondent, Monsanto Ltd, the sellers under 29
contracts of sale concluded with Bond Worth Ltd for the sale and delivery of Acrilan
fibre, had by an amendment to the conditions of sale notified to Bond Worth Ltd by
letter on 30th June 1976 and effective from 1st July 1976 effectively retained an interest
or charge over Acrilan supplied by Monsanto Ltd to Bond Worth Ltd between 1st July
1976 and 16th August 1976, the date when the second respondent, George Alan Milnes,
b was appointed receiver of Bond Worth Ltd by the third respondent, National Westminster
Bank Ltd. Mr Milnes was replaced as receiver by Messrs Morris and Houghton on 25th
August 1976. The summons further sought the determination of the ownership of
Acrilan fibre transferred to the fourth respondent, Carpets of Worth Ltd (formerly
known as Glixcroft Ltd) under an agreement dated 19th August 1977, the priority (if
any) of Monsanto Ltd's interest or charge over other creditors of Bond Worth Ltd,
c whether all or any of the receivers were accountable to Monsanto Ltd in respect of any
part of the Acrilan and if so to what extent. The facts are set out in the judgment.

Jeremiah Harman QC and *Murray Pickering* for the applicants and Carpets of Worth Ltd.
Raymond Sears QC and *John McDonnell* for Monsanto Ltd.
A R Barrowclough QC and *Elizabeth Gloster* for Mr Milnes.
d *R A Morritt QC* and *Peter Scott QC* for National Westminster Bank Ltd.
Judith Jackson for Alliance Assurance Co Ltd.

Cur adv vult

12th February. **SLADE J** read the following judgment: In form, this is an application
e for directions made by Mr C Morris and Mr A R Houghton ('the applicants'), as receivers
of the property of Bond Worth Ltd ('Bond Worth'), under s 369(1) of the Companies Act
1948. They were appointed as such receivers on 25th August 1977. The first respondent
to the summons is Monsanto Ltd ('Monsanto'). The second is Mr G A Milnes who had
been appointed as such receiver by the third respondent, National Westminster Bank Ltd
('the bank') on 16th August 1977 and acted as such until the appointment of the
f applicants. The fourth respondent is a company which is now called Carpets of Worth
Ltd, but was formerly called Glixcroft Carpets Ltd ('Glixcroft'). The fifth respondent is
Alliance Assurance Co Ltd ('Alliance').
    In substance the application raises questions as to the construction and legal effect of
a clause whereby a supplier of Bond Worth, Monsanto, in selling raw fibre to Bond
Worth and transferring to it the legal property therein, purported to retain, until
g payment in full for the material, what was described in the clause as 'equitable and
beneficial ownership', not only of the fibre itself but also of other products produced
from it and of the respective proceeds of sale thereof.
    As the evidence shows, clauses purporting to reserve proprietary rights of one kind or
another to a vendor on the sale of goods are now in quite common use in this country.
Indeed the validity of one such clause was recently recognised by a decision of the Court
h of Appeal in *Aluminium Industrie Vaassen BV v Romalpa Aluminium Ltd*[2]. This case has led
to the frequent use in practice of the phrase '*Romalpa* clauses' or some similar description
to refer generically to clauses of this nature. They may, however, take a wide variety of
forms. As will appear, the *Romalpa* case[2] itself concerned the construction and effect of
one which was materially different from that in question in the present case, if only
because it reserved legal, as well as beneficial, ownership to the vendor. Accordingly,
j only limited guidance can be derived from it for the purpose of the present case which,

---

1 The questions to which the summons sought answers are, so far as material, set out at p 931 *f* to
    p 932 *b*, post
2 [1976] 2 All ER 552, [1976] 1 WLR 676

while likewise raising important points of principle, will likewise fall to be decided on its particular facts.

　　a

The parties to this summons have filed a very large amount of evidence, consisting in all of nearly 800 pages of affidavits and exhibits. There has, however, been no cross-examination on the affidavits and the facts are substantially not in dispute. I will therefore set out only those which appear to me material for the purpose of determining those questions which, in the event, fall to be answered or of understanding the general background to those questions.

　　b

Bond Worth is a company which at all material times up to August 1977 carried on the business of manufacturing and selling carpets. The principal premises used by it for these purposes appear to have been a spinning factory at Stroud in Gloucestershire and two factories at Stourport and Kidderminster in Worcestershire, used for dyeing processes.

By a trust deed dated 22nd April 1966 ('the 1966 trust deed') made between Bond *c* Worth's parent company, Thomas Bond Worth & Sons Ltd and certain of its subsidiaries including Bond Worth and Alliance as trustees, Bond Worth (together with other members of the group) charged by way of floating charge in favour of Alliance its undertaking and all its property and assets, both present and future, to secure an issue of £1,200,000 7¼% debenture stock 1986–91 of Thomas Bond Worth & Sons Ltd. By cl 7 power was reserved to each of the charging companies (subject to certain restrictions *d* contained in cl 8) from time to time to create or permit to subsist in favour of bankers a floating charge or charges on the mortgaged premises owned by it or any part thereof, ranking pari passu in point of security with the floating charge created by the 1966 trust deed or from time to time to increase the maximum amount for which any charge then stood as continuing security, for the purpose of securing indebtedness and liabilities to bankers. Clause 10(c) contained certain provisions restricting the rights of each of the *e* charging companies to change its business or dispose of its assets without the written consent of Alliance. Clause 10(D) contained certain provisions restricting the rights of members of the charging group to transfer their assets to a non-charging subsidiary. By cl 10(H) the parent company agreed to procure that the aggregate amount for the time being outstanding of all borrowed moneys of it and all its United Kingdom subsidiaries would not exceed certain defined limits.

　　f

Clause 11 of the 1966 trust deed provided that the security thereby constituted should become enforceable in any of a number of stated events, of which one, set out in para 11(C), was as follows:

> 'If any incumbrancer shall take possession or a receiver shall be appointed of the mortgaged premises or any part thereof and such taking possession or appointment as the case may be shall be certified in writing by the Trustees to be in their opinion *g* prejudicial to the security hereby constituted.'

Clause 23 provided, inter alia, that at any time after the security thereby constituted should have become enforceable Alliance might at its discretion appoint in writing a receiver of the mortgaged premises.

The name of Bond Worth's parent company was later changed to its present name, *h* Bond Worth Holdings Ltd.

By a debenture dated 17th May 1972 ('the 1972 debenture') Bond Worth charged in favour of the bank by way of floating security its undertaking and all its other property assets and rights, present or future, by way of continuing security for the discharge on demand of (inter alia) all present or future indebtedness of Bond Worth to the bank on any account. Clause 2 provided that the security thereby created should rank pari passu *j* with the floating charge created by the 1966 trust deed 'to the extent from time to time agreed in writing by the bank with the Trustees pursuant to the provisions of the Trust Deed'. It appears that no such written agreement between the bank and Alliance has ever been concluded. Clause 4(a) of the 1972 debenture provided that Bond Worth should not be at liberty without the bank's written consent to create any mortgage or

charge ranking in priority to or pari passu with the floating charge thereby created.
a Clause 6 provided (inter alia) that the security should immediately become enforceable
at any time after notice demanding payment of any moneys thereby secured should have
been served by the bank on Bond Worth. Clause 7 provided that at any time after the
security had become enforceable the bank might appoint any person or persons to be a
receiver of the property thereby charged.

   The 1966 trust deed and 1972 debenture were duly registered pursuant to s 95 of the
b Companies Act 1948.

   The fibre principally used by Bond Worth for its carpet manufacturing processes has
been that produced by Monsanto and sold under the trade name 'Acrilan'. For several
years before the appointment of Mr Milnes as receiver, Monsanto had been supplying
Bond Worth with Acrilan fibre under a purchasing account. The present dispute stems
from the fact that substantial quantities of fibre delivered by Monsanto on and after 15th
c March 1977 have not yet been paid for by Bond Worth, which has found itself in
financial difficulties.

   Though it will be necessary later in this judgment to examine in greater detail the
procedure by which contracts for the sale and purchase of Acrilan were concluded
between the parties, it was briefly as follows. Bond Worth's orders were submitted in
writing on printed order forms. They were then acknowledged by Monsanto in writing
d on a series of printed confirmation notes, but on a piecemeal basis, so that each
confirmation note would relate to less than the full quantity ordered and, correspondingly,
two or more confirmation notes would have to be sent before the full quantity ordered
was covered.

   It appears that each confirmation note was accompanied by a set of Monsanto's
standard conditions of sale, which had been in use since 1974 or thereabouts and were
e used by it during the period from March to July 1977, the material period for present
purposes.

   These conditions of sale contained provisions dealing with a number of matters such
as price variation, buyer's credit, freight, taxes and duties, warranties, limitation of
liability etc. They further contained in para 2 a provision headed 'Quantity-Shipments',
of which the first sentence read: 'The seller may deliver an excess or deficiency of up to
f 10% of the quantity of goods ordered and buyer shall pay for the quantity of goods
delivered by seller.' Paragraph 10 of the conditions of sale read as follows:

   'The validity, interpretation and performance of this contract shall be governed
   and constructed [sic] in accordance with the laws of the country of incorporation of
   the seller. This contract constitutes the full understanding of the parties and a
   complete and exclusive statement of the terms of their agreement. Except as
g provided in section 1 hereof, no conditions, understanding or agreement
   purpotrating [sic] to modify or vary the terms of this contract shall be binding
   unless hereafter made in writing and signed by the party to be bound and no
   modifications shall be effected by the acknowledgement or acceptance of purchase
   order or shipment instruction forms containing terms or conditions at variance or
   in addition to those set forth herein. No waiver by either seller or buyer with
h respect to any breach or default or of any right or remedy, and no course of dealing,
   shall be deemed to constitute a continuing waiver of any further breach or default
   or of any other right or remedy, unless such waiver be expressed in writing signed
   by the party to be bound.'

   The conditions of sale, however, contained no provision expressly reserving to
j Monsanto any legal or beneficial property or interest in the goods pending payment of
the full purchase price.

   On the face of them the conditions of sale would appear to contain a complete and
exhaustive catalogue of the conditions applicable to contracts for the supply and delivery
of Acrilan fibre by Monsanto to Bond Worth. However, the situation is complicated by
the fact that on 30th June 1976, some months before the commencement of the period

of delivery with which this case is primarily concerned, Mr J E Day, the credit manager
of Monsanto had written a letter addressed to Bond Worth in the following terms: *a*

'Dear Sirs:

Change in Conditions of Sale

'Would you please note that with effect from July 1, 1976, we are amending our
standard terms of contract insofar as all future business will be conducted on normal
terms and conditions of sale, except that the following Clause shall be incorporated
into any contract to the exclusion of any conflicting provisions in our standard *b*
terms as presently appears on our confirmation of orders.

'(a) The risk in the goods passes to the buyer upon delivery, but equitable and
beneficial ownership shall remain with us until full payment has been received
(each order being considered as a whole), or until prior resale, in which case our
beneficial entitlement shall attach to the proceeds of resale or to the claim for such
proceeds.   *c*

'(b) Should the goods become constituents of or be converted into other products
while subject to our equitable and beneficial ownership we shall have the equitable
and beneficial ownership in such other products as if they were solely and simply
the goods and accordingly sub-clause (a) shall as appropriate apply to such other
products.

'We would appreciate your acknowledgement that this clause now applies to *d*
future deliveries to your goodselves by signing the attached copy letter and
returning it to us.'

In accordance with the request contained in the final paragraph of the letter of 30th
June 1976, Mr F B Morton, the company secretary of Bond Worth, signed the copy and
returned it to Monsanto.   *e*

The evidence of Mr Loveridge, the secretary of Monsanto, is that if Bond Worth had
refused to sign this letter, Monsanto would without doubt have withheld further supplies
of Acrilan fibre until it was signed. He further states that, since Monsanto received the
signed copy back from Bond Worth, Monsanto has always regarded the 'retention of title
clause' as set out in and incorporated in every contract for the purchase by Bond Worth
of Acrilan fibre since July 1976. I have no reason to doubt the accuracy of any of this *f*
evidence. Monsanto contends that it is effectively so incorporated.

In an affidavit sworn on 19th June 1978, Mr Milnes gave reasons for submitting that,
as a matter of law, the retention of title clause does not apply to and is not incorporated
in any of the contracts of sale of Acrilan made between Monsanto and Bond Worth,
whether as a result of the letter of 30th June 1976 or otherwise. Mr Loveridge's
unchallenged evidence is that, before the statement in this affidavit, no suggestion that *g*
the clause had not been incorporated had ever been made to Monsanto by anyone on
behalf of Bond Worth.

Though the greater part of the Acrilan ordered by Bond Worth from Monsanto was
delivered to its spinning factory, part of it was delivered to a company called O'Brien Bros
(Spinners) Ltd (which I will call 'O'Brien'), which is an associated company of Bond
Worth, incorporated in Ireland. Under arrangements that had been continuing since *h*
about 1970, Bond Worth would arrange for the purchase of all the production materials
(including Acrilan) that O'Brien required from English sources. Before the appointment
of receivers in August 1977, O'Brien would, each week, telephone to Bond Worth with
an order of Acrilan. Bond Worth would then place the order with Monsanto. The
Acrilan required by O'Brien was therefore included in the Bond Worth order to
Monsanto. Pursuant to the Bond Worth order, Monsanto would deliver that Acrilan *j*
required by Bond Worth to Stroud and that required by O'Brien to O'Brien in Cork. It
would, however, send confirmation notes and invoices to Bond Worth alone, both in
respect of Acrilan delivered to Bond Worth and in respect of that delivered to O'Brien.
Bond Worth in turn would invoice O'Brien for the Acrilan supplied by Monsanto and
delivered direct to O'Brien, at the price charged by Monsanto.

Before Bond Worth was put into receivership, it was ordering about 20,000 lbs of
a Acrilan for O'Brien each week. O'Brien would then spin the Acrilan and sell about half
of the yarn so spun to Bond Worth, for which it would invoice Bond Worth
accordingly. The carpets manufactured by Bond Worth were thus woven with a mixture
of yarn supplied by O'Brien and yarn spun directly by Bond Worth from Acrilan
purchased from Monsanto. The remaining amount of yarn spun from the Acrilan
purchased by O'Brien from Bond Worth was sold to a subsidiary company of O'Brien,
b also incorporated in Ireland.

The sums due from O'Brien in respect of the Acrilan purchased from Bond Worth
were set against the sums due from Bond Worth in respect of the yarn purchased from
O'Brien. As a result of these inter-company transactions, O'Brien was one of the larger
debtors of Bond Worth when Bond Worth went into receivership on 16th August
1977. Of the sum of £587,397·49 due to Monsanto at this time, £103,938·08
c represented money due in respect of Acrilan procured by Bond Worth for O'Brien.

The production director of Bond Worth, Mr Robin Axford, has sworn an affidavit
describing the carpet manufacturing processes of Bond Worth. From this the following
facts emerge. Acrilan was purchased from Monsanto and delivered to Bond Worth's
spinning factory at Stroud for conversion into spun yarn. Bond Worth purchased three
different types of Acrilan fibre from Monsanto, respectively known as 'semi-dull lustre',
d 'bright lustre' and 'mid-lustre'. These three types of fibre, together with the reprocessed
fibre referred to hereafter, were blended together, in various combinations and
proportions, to produce two types of yarn, respectively known as 'white yarn' and 'grey
yarn'. The white yarn was made up solely of the three different types of raw Acrilan
fibre. The grey yarn was made of a mixture containing reprocessed fibre as well as raw
fibre. The reprocessed fibre was the result of recycling waste dyed Acrilan white yarn,
e originally spun at Stroud and further processed at the Stourport and Kidderminster
factories of Bond Worth. All reprocessed fibre used by Bond Worth was obtained in this
way and none was purchased or acquired from other sources. During the years 1972 to
1978, of 100,000 lbs of Acrilan yarn spun each week at Stroud, 75,000 lbs was white yarn
obtained from Acrilan and 25,000 lbs was grey yarn. In addition about 10,000 lbs of
white yarn was acquired each week from O'Brien. Of the total weight of 110,000 lbs of
f spun yarn used each week, about 25,000 lbs was grey yarn.

The reprocessed fibre comprised in the grey yarn might represent Acrilan that had
been purchased from Monsanto many months previously. The proportion of reprocessed
fibre in yarn and carpet in stock was about 3·64% of the total quantity. Once fibres have
been blended into yarn, either white or grey, there is no commercial method of
separating them again and restoring the original constituents. When the fibre had been
g blended into yarn in the proper proportions, whether white yarn or grey yarn, it was fed
into a machine and sprayed with oil (the property of Bond Worth) to prevent fibre
damage in spinning. The mixture of fibre and oil then passed to another machine,
which converted the fibre into a white slubbing, depending on whether white yarn or
grey yarn was being processed. The slubbing was then transferred to spinning frames,
where it was twisted to form a single thread of yarn, which in turn was itself further
h processed on a doubling machine, where two strands of single thread were twisted
together to form one double thread. The yarn after doubling was then reeled to form a
hank of about 1¼ lbs in weight. Several hanks were then tied together to form a
bundle. The bundles were then placed loosely in a vehicle for transport to the Stourport
and Kidderminster dye houses.

On delivery they were first placed into a hank dyeing machine to be dyed into the
j particular shade required. During the dyeing process, most of the spinning lubricant
was scoured from the yarn. Having been dyed and dried, the individual hanks were
wound on to plastic conical centres to form cones of lengths of yarn of a single colour.
The cones of various coloured yarns were then subjected to 'setting', which was a process
whereby they were placed in a vertical creel in a colour sequence determined by reference
to the carpet design. The ends of yarn from the cones were then fed forward to a

machine, which rolled the ends side by side on to a metal spool, which contained the pile
yarn necessary to form one row of pile in each repeat of the carpet design. Thus for each *a*
pattern a larger number of metal spools had to be wound with pile yarn.

The spools after setting were placed in a container and transported to the weaving shed
for threading. This was a process whereby the individual loose ends of the strands of
yarn rolled on the spool were drawn through individual tubes of what was known as a
tube frame. The tube frames were attached to the endless chain of a spool or loom. The
yarn was then woven into the carpet backing threads contained in the loom. None of the *b*
backing threads themselves was supplied by Monsanto.

After the carpet had been woven, it was inspected and any apparent faults were
corrected. It then passed to the backing machine, where it was steamed (to burst the pile
and give an even surface) and a latex compound was applied to its back. It was then
dried, sheared, further inspected and rolled up ready to be sent to potential customers.

As at 16th August 1977, therefore, the yarn in stock held by Bond Worth comprised *c*
yarn in various stages of the carpet making process, namely (a) undyed yarn, (b) dyed
yarn, (c) goods in process and (d) finished carpet stocks.

Mr Axford states that of the total weight of the spun yarn, 0·74% represented Bond
Worth material, in the form of the oil with which it had been sprayed. His evidence,
however, is that it is impossible to state exactly what proportion of the weight of dyed
spun yarn comprised Monsanto raw Acrilan. As one reason among others, he points out *d*
that at least a part of the weight is attributable to dyestuffs and chemicals owned by Bond
Worth.

Mr Axford's further evidence (also unchallenged) is that at any point of time a
substantial, but not accurately ascertainable, proportion of the dyed yarn in stock (in
hank, on cone and on spool) represented Acrilan fibre which had been delivered to Bond
Worth more than six months previously. This was because stocks were not used *e*
according to a predetermined policy. More often than not, the last yarn to go into the
stores was the first to be taken out, since less handling and movement of yarn was
involved. The spun undyed yarn and the dyed yarn that were in store in mid-August
1977 were likely to be the oldest material, rather than that which had been most recently
delivered. Dyed yarn in hanks might lie around for four or five months or more, and
even after it had been wound on to a spool, it might remain in that state for as long as six *f*
to eight weeks.

A number of material points emerged from Mr Axford's and other evidence, which
has not been challenged by Monsanto. First, as at the date when Mr Milnes was
appointed receiver, a substantial proportion of Bond Worth's dyed yarn then in stock
(representing Acrilan that had been delivered to it before 15th March 1977) had in fact
been paid for by it. Secondly, this proportion is not capable of being accurately *g*
ascertained. Thirdly, it would be impossible to identify either the particular batches of
Acrilan fibre which according to the terms of the retention of title clause remain in
Monsanto's 'equitable and beneficial ownership' or the proceeds of sale or other products
to which, according to those terms, such 'ownership' has attached.

On 18th July 1969 a first supplemental trust deed, supplemental to the 1966 trust
deed, was executed; its provisions are not material for present purposes. On 30th June *h*
1977 a second supplemental trust deed was executed. This recited that a breach of the
limit imposed by cl 10(H) of the 1966 trust deed had occurred and that consequently the
security had become enforceable. It further recited that, at a meeting of the debenture
stockholders, they had agreed to the waiver of the breach in consideration of Bond Worth
Holdings Ltd agreeing the amendments to the 1966 trust deed thereby effected. The
second supplemental trust deed then effected a number of such amendments, one of *j*
which was to amend cl 7 of the 1966 trust deed by providing that the power thereby
reserved to each of the charging companies to create or permit to subsist or to increase the
maximum amount secured by pari passu bank charges should be suspended until 1st
July 1979.

On 10th August 1977 the bank appointed Mr F S McWhirter and Mr W F Ratford,

who I think were both partners in Peat, Marwick, Mitchell & Co ('Peat Marwick') to be
a receivers of Bond Worth Holdings Ltd, the holding company of Bond Worth. On 15th
and 16th August a meeting took place between representatives of Peat Marwick, Alliance
and the bank at which discussion took place about the various courses of action open to
Alliance and in particular whether it should appoint a receiver of its own. This
discussion, however, was inconclusive.

On 16th August 1977 the bank served on Bond Worth notice demanding payment of
b moneys secured by the 1972 debenture. At this date the amount owing by Bond Worth
to the bank on its current bank account alone amounted to about £1·1 million. It owed
about a further £1 million in wages and salaries and had liabilities of over £12 million
as guarantor. On the same day Mr Milnes (a chartered accountant and a partner in Peat
Marwick) was appointed to be receiver and manager of the undertaking property and
assets of Bond Worth by the bank, pursuant to cl 7 of the 1972 debenture. Also that same
c day he went into possession of Bond Worth as receiver and manager. He himself went
at once to its head office in Stourport, while on the next day other members of his staff
travelled to its factories at Stroud and Kidderminster. With effect from the evening of
16th August 1977 he assumed total responsibility for the management of Bond Worth's
business of carpet manufacturing and selling, which I will henceforth call 'the business'.

As at 16th August 1977 Acrilan fibre representing the subject matter of 29 contracts
d made between Bond Worth and Monsanto at various dates between March and July 1977
was still unpaid for. Monsanto's last delivery of Acrilan fibre to Bond Worth, pursuant
to such contracts, was effected on or about 20th July 1977. The amount owed to
Monsanto by Bond Worth in respect of these contracts is and has at all material times
been £587,397·49, of which £103,938·08 represents moneys due in respect of Acrilan
procured by Bond Worth for O'Brien. Later in this judgment I shall have to examine in
e greater detail the manner in which these contracts were concluded; however, I think it
is common ground that they were 29 in number.

On 23rd July 1977 Bond Worth's factory at Stroud closed down for a fortnight's
holiday and no further delivery was made until supplies were resumed in the name of
Glixcroft on 19th August 1977. On the basis of a rough estimate that the amount due
to Monsanto from Bond Worth at 16th August 1977 was £592,000 and assuming a strict
f 'first in first out' basis of stock handling, Mr Milnes prepared an approximate estimate
showing that the debt was represented as to £111,000 by untreated Acrilan held by Bond
Worth, as to £282,000 by undyed and dyed yarn and work in progress so held, as to
£163,000 by finished carpet stock so held, and as to the remaining £36,000 by no such
assets. Mr Milnes, however, added the qualification to his estimate that it was
'questionable' whether the strict 'first in first out' basis of stock handling was applicable
g for all stages of stock handling, and Mr Axford's evidence shows that it is not. The
estimate is therefore of only very limited assistance.

On 11th August 1977 Monsanto had sent a telex to Mr McWhirter drawing his
attention to the fact that since 1st July 1976 all goods sold by Monsanto to Bond Worth
had been subject to 'retention of title'. On 17th August 1977 Mr Milnes received from
Monsanto a telex and a letter in very similar terms; enclosed with the letter was a copy
h of Monsanto's letter to Bond Worth of 30th June 1976, which had contained the retention
of title clause.

Also on 17th August 1977 a meeting took place between Mr Milnes and representatives
of Bond Worth and of Monsanto, at which Mr Milnes informed Monsanto's representative
of his intention to 'hive down' the business, with effect from the close of business on 16th
August 1977, and to hive off certain of the assets of Bond Worth to a newly formed
j subsidiary of Bond Worth. The subsidiary was Glixcroft, the fourth respondent to this
summons, which was a wholly-owned subsidiary of Bond Worth. Believing that it was
not legally possible to sell to Glixcroft goods which were subject to retention of title, Mr
Milnes stated in the course of this meeting that he would transfer to Glixcroft all goods
used in the business excluding those subject to retention of title. It was, nevertheless,
always his intention, as the representatives of Monsanto at the meeting appear to have

understood, that the Acrilan supplied to Bond Worth by Monsanto would be used in the business for the manufacture of carpets by Glixcroft, which would thereafter be carrying *a* on the business.

At that time Bond Worth had very little untreated Acrilan in stock, though no actual stocktaking of Bond Worth's assets was made when Mr Milnes went into possession or during the time within which he continued in possession. Accordingly it was agreed at the meeting that Monsanto would supply Glixcroft with about £40,000 worth of Acrilan, being the amount required for about one week's production of carpets. Terms were *b* agreed in relation to the mode of payment. It was, however, also agreed that payments for such Acrilan were not to be set off against the amounts owing by Bond Worth to Monsanto in respect of goods supplied before the commencement of Mr Milnes's receivership. There was no question of Glixcroft assuming any of the liabilities of Bond Worth. Deliveries were made pursuant to this agreement on 19th August 1977 and during the following week. *c*

On 19th August 1977 a hiving down agreement (which I will call 'the hive-down agreement') was signed whereby Bond Worth, acting by Mr Milnes as its receiver, agreed to sell and Glixcroft agreed to purchase as a going concern as at and with effect from the close of business on 16th August 1977, and free from all liens, charges and incumbrances, the goodwill, undertaking and all other property and assets of Bond Worth employed in connection with the business, but excluding a number of stated categories of assets which *d* were listed in cl 1 of the agreement. Among the categories so excluded were 'goods supplied to the vendor under retention of title'. Clause 2(A) provided (inter alia) that Bond Worth should continue to be responsible for all debts payable by and claims outstanding against it or any of its assets as at the close of business at 16th August 1977. Clause 4(C) provided (inter alia) that in any case where the consent of any person not a party to the agreement was required to the transfer of any asset thereby agreed to be sold *e* the sale of such asset should be conditional on such consent. Alliance, however, as appears from an affidavit sworn on its behalf by Mr L C Howes on 8th December 1978, accepts that the agreement is binding on it.

Mr Milnes sent circular letters on 18th and 19th August 1977 to customers and suppliers of the business informing them of his appointment as receiver and manager of Bond Worth and of the hiving down of the business to Glixcroft. With effect on and *f* from 17th August the business was carried on in the name of Glixcroft under the registered business name of 'Carpets of Worth'. All purchase orders, sales invoices, delivery notes and other documentation relating to the day-to-day conduct of the business on or after that date were issued by Glixcroft, trading under that business name.

The Acrilan which had been delivered to Bond Worth by Monsanto before Mr Milnes's receivership, and which was at the date of his appointment in various stages of *g* manufacture, was used by Glixcroft after that date in the manufacture of carpets. Acrilan which had been delivered by Monsanto before his appointment was not at any stage of manufacture kept separate from Acrilan supplied to Glixcroft by Monsanto after Mr Milnes's appointment or from Acrilan supplied from any other source. It has not, I think, been suggested on behalf of Monsanto or any other party to these proceedings that this failure to segregate involved any impropriety. *h*

Following a meeting with the bank on 23rd August 1977, Alliance decided to make its own appointment of receivers, namely the applicants. On 24th August 1977 Mr L C Howes, the assistant manager of the trustee department of Alliance, signed the certificate required by cl 11(C) of the 1966 trust deed, certifying that the appointment by the bank of receivers of Bond Worth Holdings Ltd was prejudicial to the security constituted by the 1966 trust deed. On 25th August 1977 Alliance appointed the applicants as joint *j* receivers of Bond Worth Holdings Ltd, Bond Worth and the other charging subsidiaries under the 1966 trust deed.

That same day they took over from Mr Milnes the management of the business. He and his staff moved out of possession within the course of the next few days and since a that time he has had no detailed knowledge of or involvement with the business, though I think his appointment as receiver has not been revoked by the bank.

As at 25th August 1977 it appeared to the applicants that all of the Acrilan previously owned by Bond Worth had been sold or otherwise transferred to Glixcroft. There was not and never had been any entry or other reference in the books of Bond Worth to stocks of Acrilan or goods made from Acrilan withheld from the sale of assets under the hive-down agreement and remaining in the possession, control or disposition of Bond

b Worth. Furthermore no such stocks of goods existed physically, in the sense that there were no Acrilan or goods made from Acrilan separately marked, stored or otherwise set apart from the other assets of Bond Worth which were sold to Glixcroft. The Acrilan and Acrilan-derived products so transferred to Glixcroft were all used and disposed of by Glixcroft in the normal course of its business, being the continuation of the business previously carried on by Bond Worth. It appears that these facts have always been

c known to and accepted by Monsanto. As long ago as the meeting of 17th August 1977, the intention to hive down Bond Worth's business was made known to Monsanto. As supplies of Acrilan have been made since only to Glixcroft, it must have been fully apparent that Bond Worth had retained no carpet manufacturing or marketing facilities at all. The Acrilan in question was disposed of to Glixcroft along with the other assets of Bond Worth at their full book value to Bond Worth.

d Broadly, the contentions of Monsanto have been and are that, by virtue of the retention of title clause, all the Acrilan fibre comprised in the 29 contracts, to the extent that it remains unpaid for (about £587,000), remains in the equitable and beneficial ownership of Monsanto with the exception of any fibre which may have been resold by or on behalf of Bond Worth. In the case of any such last-mentioned fibre, it claims that its beneficial entitlement has attached to the proceeds of resale or to the claim for such proceeds. It

e claims a wide variety of remedies to enforce the rights thus asserted, principally by way of tracing.

Claims such as these led to the issue by the applicants of the summons now before the court on 21st December 1977.

The re-amended summons defines the retention of title clause as 'the clause'. It also defines the term 'the Acrilan' as meaning the goods which had been supplied by

f Monsanto to Bond Worth after 1st July 1976, but before the appointment of a receiver of Bond Worth on 16th August 1977, which had not been paid for as at the latter date.

Paragraph 1 of the re-amended summons then asks whether, in the events which have occurred, Monsanto by virtue of the clause had, on the appointment of a receiver of Bond Worth on 16th August 1977, an interest or charge over—

g '(i) Acrilan then held by Bond Worth in any or all of the following categories: (a) Acrilan in the condition in which it was supplied and delivered to Bond Worth; (b) Acrilan processed or in the course of process by or on behalf of Bond Worth either (i) with, or (ii) without the mixing or combining with other products not owned by Monsanto but owned by Bond Worth or by a third party supplier at the time of such mixing or combining; or (c) Acrilan processed as in (b) above and incorporated in carpets and/(ii) the proceeds of resale of the Acrilan in any or all of the above

h categories.'

Paragraph 2 of the re-amended summons asks whether by virtue of the hive-down agreement or otherwise there was transferred to Glixcroft (and if so when) the legal and/or beneficial ownership of the Acrilan then held by Bond Worth in any or all of a number of certain stated categories which are set out in sub-paras (a), (b) and (c). These

j sub-paragraphs respectively follow the form of the corresponding sub-paragraphs of para 1(i). Paragraph 3 asks whether in the events which have occurred Monsanto had on or after 19th August 1977 and if so still has any and if so what interest in or charge over a number of specified categories of assets. Paragraph 4 asks whether and if so the extent to which the proceeds of sale of the business, undertaking and assets of Bond Worth or

Glixcroft can and should be apportioned between certain items specified in para 3 for the
purpose of satisfying any claim of Monsanto. Paragraph 5 asks whether Monsanto's *a*
interest or charge referred to in questions 1 and 3 had and if so still have priority over any
and if so which of the creditors of Bond Worth. Paragraph 6 asks whether (a) Mr Milnes,
(b) the applicants or (c) all of them are accountable or liable to Monsanto in respect of any
and if so what part of the Acrilan. Paragraph 7 contains a general prayer for such further
directions or declarations as the court thinks just. Paragraph 8 relates to costs.

The legal issues   *b*
   Though other subsidiary questions have arisen, I think that substantially seven
questions of law have been argued before me: (a) By what manner and at what dates were
the 29 relevant contracts respectively concluded? (b) Has the retention of title clause
been incorporated in such contracts? (c) If so, is the clause capable of having any, and if
so what, legal effect? (d) If the clause is capable of having legal effect, is it registrable
under s 95 of the Companies Act 1948? (e) Has there been transferred to Glixcroft, either *c*
by virtue of the hive-down agreement or otherwise, any interest in the Acrilan held by
Bond Worth at 19th August 1977 and falling within any of the categories referred to in
para 2 of the summons? (f) On the assumption that the retention of the title clause has
been incorporated in the 29 contracts and is capable of having legal effect, but is not
registrable, what remedies (if any) should be afforded to Monsanto? (g) On the same
assumption, is Monsanto's claim entitled to priority over either or both of the floating *d*
charges of Alliance and the bank?

Question (a)
   [In answer to question (a) his Lordship summarised the evidence relating to the
manner in which the 29 contracts were concluded and then stated:] I therefore conclude
that each of the 29 contracts was concluded when, but not until, the Acrilan referred to *e*
in it was actually delivered to and accepted by Bond Worth (or O'Brien, as the case might
be).

Question (b)
   It is now necessary to consider the terms of the contracts concluded between Bond
Worth and Monsanto in this manner and, in particular, whether or not they incorporated *f*
the retention of title clause.
   Monsanto's letter of 30th June 1976, according to its terms, had constituted a
notification to Bond Worth that it was amending its standard terms of contract—

      'insofar as all future business will be conducted on normal terms and conditions
      of sale except that [the retention of title clause] shall be incorporated into any
      contract to the exclusion of any conflicting provisions in our standard terms as *g*
      presently appears on our confirmation of orders.'

   The letter ended by requesting Bond Worth to acknowledge that the retention of title
clause applied to future deliveries to Bond Worth by signing and returning the attached
copy letter. The attached copy letter was duly signed by Bond Worth's company secretary
and returned to Monsanto.   *h*
   On the face of it, two points seem to me clear in relation to this correspondence. First,
Monsanto thereby proposed and Bond Worth thereby agreed that notwithstanding any
conflicting provisions appearing in Monsanto's printed standard conditions of sale (such
as condition 10 in particular) the retention of title clause should be deemed to be
incorporated in any future contract for the sale and purchase of any goods which might
thereafter be delivered by Monsanto to Bond Worth. Secondly, both parties must be *j*
taken to have intended that the agreement thus concluded should have legal effect. (And
indeed counsel for the applicants and counsel for Alliance have not invited me to find
that it was not legally binding.) In these circumstances my initial reaction to this
correspondence is to give effect to the agreement embodied in it, unless there is some
compelling reason to the contrary.

This initial reaction derives some support from the decision of the Court of Appeal in
a *J Evans & Sons (Portsmouth) Ltd v Andrea Merzario Ltd*[1]. In that case, the plaintiffs had for
many years arranged the carriage of certain machines to England under contracts with
the defendants, who were forwarding agents. The contracts were in printed standard
form and included conditions, which gave the defendants complete freedom as to means
in handling and transportation of the machines and, with certain exceptions, exempted
them from liability for loss of or damage to them. Until 1967, the defendants always
b arranged for the transport of the machines to England in crates or trailers, since they
were liable to rust. In late 1967, the defendants proposed to change their system to
packing and transporting the machines in containers. Their general manager in England
at that time, Mr Spano, gave the plaintiffs' traffic agent, Mr Leonard, an oral assurance
that for the future the machines shipped in containers would be carried under deck. In
reliance on this oral promise, the plaintiffs accepted the proposed change and agreed the
c terms, but they did not include any written provisions about carrying goods in containers
under deck. About a year later, in October 1968, the defendants loaded one of the
plaintiffs' machines, packed in a container, on deck. It fell overboard and was a total
loss. The plaintiffs brought an action claiming damages. The defendants denied liability,
relying on an exemption in their printed conditions of carriage. Their plea was upheld
by Kerr J[2]. The Court of Appeal allowed an appeal by the plaintiffs from his decision.
d Lord Denning MR said[3]:

'. . . it seems to me plain that Mr Spano gave an oral promise or assurance that the
goods in this new container traffic would be carried under deck. He made the
promise in order to induce Mr Leonard to agree to the goods being carried in
containers. On the faith of it, Mr Leonard accepted the quotations and gave orders
for transport. In those circumstances the promise was binding. There was a breach
e of that promise and the forwarding agents are liable—unless they can rely on the
printed conditions.'

Lord Denning MR[4] then proceeded to hold that the defendants could not rely on such
conditions because they were repugnant to the express oral promise or representation.
Roskill LJ[5] said that the defendants gave a promise that the containers would be
f shipped under deck, which plainly amounted to an enforceable contractual promise. He
continued:

'In those circumstances it seems to me that this contract was this: "If we continue
to give you our business, you will ensure that those goods in containers are shipped
under deck"; and the defendants agreed that this would be so. Thus there was a
breach of that contract by the defendants when this container was shipped on deck.'
g
On this basis Roskill LJ[6] concluded that none of the exemption clauses could be
applied, because the promise that no container would be shipped on deck had to be
treated as overriding any exempting conditions.
Geoffrey Lane LJ agreed that the effect of the relevant conversation was to produce a
binding obligation on the defendants to ensure that the plaintiffs' machinery in
h containers would be carried under deck. He said[7]:

'This was not a collateral contract in the sense of an oral agreement varying the
terms of a written contract. It was a new express term which was to be included

---

j 1 [1976] 2 All ER 930, [1976] 1 WLR 1078
   2 [1975] 1 Lloyd's Rep 162
   3 [1976] 2 All ER 930 at 933, [1976] 1 WLR 1078 at 1081
   4 [1976] 2 All ER 930 at 933, [1976] 1 WLR 1078 at 1082
   5 [1976] 2 All ER 930 at 935, [1976] 1 WLR 1078 at 1083
   6 [1976] 2 All ER 930 at 935, [1976] 1 WLR 1078 at 1084
   7 [1976] 2 All ER 930 at 936, [1976] 1 WLR 1078 at 1084

thereafter in the contracts between the plaintiffs and the defendants for the carriage of machinery from Italy.'

He too thought that the printed trading conditions could not override this new express term.

There are some obvious similarities between the facts of the Evans case[1] and those of the present case. However, counsel for Mr Milnes, whose argument in this context was adopted by counsel for the bank, submitted that the former decision is distinguishable on its facts, and that in the present case the retention of title clause has not been effectively incorporated in the 29 relevant contracts. The Evans case[1], he pointed out, was one where a supplier of services had standard terms of contract which limited his liability. The supplier then made to a particular customer a promise which, if of a contractual nature, would increase his responsibilities and liabilities to this customer under later contracts. It was a kind of promise which no one would have expected to be included in standard conditions of sale. The only substantial question before the Court of Appeal, counsel for Mr Milnes submitted, was whether the promise was intended to have legal contractual effect; once this question was decided in the affirmative, it was obvious that it would override the standard conditions of sale. The present case, according to his analysis, is quite different. Here, the suppliers did not make a promise to a particular customer. Instead, they were seeking to introduce a new term into their standard conditions of sale, in so far as they related to one customer, Bond Worth. They set about it, he submitted, in a misleading manner. The wording of their letter to Bond Worth of 30th June 1976 suggested that Monsanto's standard terms of contract were to be amended in relation to all Monsanto's customers, by the incorporation of the retention of title clause in a revised printed version of such standard conditions. Bond Worth, counsel for Mr Milnes submitted, could have anticipated that Monsanto would require a reasonable time within which to obtain the consents of its principal customers, before the revised version of its printed standard conditions would be produced, but likewise could have anticipated that, after the expiration of a reasonable time (which he designated as two or three months), the revised printed version would be produced. In the event, many more than three months went by without Monsanto producing any kind of revised printed version of its standard conditions. Instead, it continued to attach to all its confirmation notes a copy of its standard conditions of sale in their original form, including (inter alia) the inconsistent condition 10. In these circumstances, it was submitted, the time came two or three months after the letter of 30th June 1976 when Bond Worth was entitled to assume that any subsequent contractual arrangements between it and Monsanto would be exclusively on the basis of the printed standard conditions of sale presented to it by Monsanto and on no other basis. The crucial distinction between the present case and the Evans case[1], it was said, was that in that case the promise given to the customer was clearly intended to apply to all subsequent contracts between the two parties until notice to the contrary, while in the present case the contractual arrangements embodied in the letter of 30th June 1976 as signed by Bond Worth had no such indeterminate duration.

I accept that Bond Worth, on reading the letter, could have derived the impression that a new version of its standard conditions of sale was to be produced by Monsanto for general use with its customers. In contrast, Mr Loveridge's evidence suggests that the retention of title clause was in fact only introduced by Monsanto in the case of certain customers whose credit-worthiness was doubtful. I also think that counsel for Mr Milnes was justified in his observation that the course adopted by Monsanto had at least one unsatisfactory feature in the sense that, even if the correspondence of June 1976 achieved the legal result desired by it, namely that of incorporating the retention of title clause in all subsequent contracts between Monsanto and Bond Worth, it was inherently probable that such incorporation would or might not come to the notice of all persons closely

concerned with Bond Worth's affairs, such as its auditors and bankers. Nevertheless I feel
a unable to accept his principal submission in this context. By necessary implication, he
accepts that in any contracts resulting from the delivery of Acrilan fibre to Bond Worth
during the two or three months immediately following 30th June 1976 the retention of
title clause would have been incorporated, notwithstanding the inconsistent provisions
in the standard conditions of sale attached to the relevant confirmation notes by
Monsanto. Thus far the contrary seems to me more or less unarguable, bearing in mind
b that the letter of 30th June 1976 was a formal document, clearly intended to bring about
a change in the subsequent legal relations between the parties and by its express terms
plainly envisaged that, at least for a period of time, Monsanto would continue to present
to Bond Worth standard conditions of sale which in part would conflict with the
retention of title clause, but that such clause should, as a matter of law, nevertheless be
deemed to be incorporated in any subsequent contracts between them. In my
c judgment, however, it is impossible to imply any kind of limitation in this arrangement
to the effect that it should only operate for a 'reasonable' period of time, be it two or three
months or any other period. If Bond Worth had wished to terminate the arrangements
embodied in the correspondence of June 1976, either because Monsanto had failed to
produce a revised version of its standard conditions of sale or for any other reason, it
could have terminated them by notice to Monsanto. Monsanto's reaction would
d doubtless have been to decline to supply further Acrilan to Bond Worth. In default of
such notice, I think that Monsanto was entitled to assume that the arrangements agreed
to by Bond Worth in this correspondence continued; it has not been suggested that Bond
Worth's company secretary did not have the requisite authority to bind Bond Worth to
them.

   Though there are certain points of distinction to be drawn between the facts of the
e present case and the *Evans* case[1], on my interpretation of them they contain one crucial
common feature. The relevant agreement on the part of Bond Worth, evidenced by the
signature of its company secretary, like the relevant promise in the *Evans* case[1], was
intended to be legally binding and was intended to apply to all subsequent relevant
transactions between the two parties, notwithstanding any conflicting provisions in the
relevant standard conditions of sale, until determined by notice to the contrary. The
f present case, however, is a stronger one, in the sense that the relevant agreement on the
part of Bond Worth, unlike the relevant promise in the *Evans* case[1], was made in or
evidenced by a formal written document. I can see no sufficient reason why legal effect
should not be given to this agreement.

   In my judgment, the proper way to look at the matter is this. On each and every
occasion when Bond Worth and Monsanto entered into one of the 29 relevant contracts,
g by necessary implication they tacitly incorporated the arrangements embodied in the
correspondence of June 1976, notwithstanding the continued presentation by Monsanto
of conflicting standard conditions of sale in an unchanged form. Each of such contracts
was concluded partly in writing and partly by conduct of the parties. The effect was the
same as if the retention of title clause had been expressly incorporated in the printed
standard conditions presented by Monsanto to Bond Worth.

h In this present context, however, I would add this observation. For several years
before June 1976, Monsanto had been supplying Acrilan to Bond Worth on terms which
incorporated nothing equivalent to the retention of title clause. Such terms had left
Bond Worth entirely free to deal with the Acrilan supplied as absolute owners, whether
by way of use for manufacture, resale or in any other way. It has not been submitted on
behalf of Monsanto that the introduction of the retention of title clause placed Bond
j Worth under any express or implied contractual obligation to segregate Acrilan, supplied
subject to the clause, from its earlier existing stock of Acrilan or to segregate any products
into which it might be converted or of which it might become a constituent from other

1   [1976] 2 All ER 930, [1976] 1 WLR 1078

products. As I understand the position, it has been accepted on behalf of Monsanto that the clause left Bond Worth free to deal with the Acrilan supplied, at least in the ordinary course of business, whether in the processes of manufacture or by way of resale, and did not even oblige it to keep any particular records. It is therefore not surprising to find on the evidence that for practical purposes the introduction of the retention of title clause appears to have caused no alteration whatever in the manner in which Bond Worth carried on its business and dealt with the Acrilan supplied to it by Monsanto. As counsel for Monsanto pointed out several times in the course of argument, the purpose of the clause was clearly to provide Monsanto with security in respect of the unpaid purchase price; no other purpose was suggested. Correspondingly, so long as Bond Worth remained apparently good for the money, the retention of title clause seems for practical purposes to have been forgotten by both the interested parties.

Question (c)

It is now necessary to determine the true construction, nature and effect of the relevant contracts on the footing, as I have decided, that the retention of title clause was incorporated in each of them. There being no suggestion that the documents in evidence do not contain a true record of the transactions entered into between the parties, the court must discover the substance of the contracts from the language of the documents themselves. As Lord Watson said in *McEntire v Crossley Brothers Ltd*[1]:

'... it is entirely beyond the function of a Court to discard the plain meaning of any term in the agreement unless there can be found within its four corners other language and other stipulations which necessarily deprive such term of its primary significance.'

Approaching the matter in this way, I turn to consider the relevant contracts. In my judgment at least the following points are fairly clear.

(1) They were absolute contracts for the sale of goods within the meaning of s 1(2) of the Sale of Goods Act 1893, though this is not to say that they did not comprise other features in addition.

(2) The legal title or property in the Acrilan fibre comprised in any one of the contracts passed to Bond Worth when the fibre was delivered to Bond Worth (see r 1 in s 18 of the 1893 Act). In using the term 'property' in this context I refer to the general property in the goods (which is the definition given to the word in s 62(1) of the 1893 Act) and not merely a special property, such as that possessed by a bailee.

(3) The risk in the goods likewise passed to Bond Worth on delivery. This followed not only from s 20 of the 1893 Act, but also from the opening words of para (a) of the retention of title clause. Thus if, after delivery, the goods had been stolen or destroyed before Bond Worth had had the opportunity to use them in any way, Bond Worth would nevertheless have had to pay the full purchase price for them.

(4) Though para (a) of the retention of title clause provided that 'equitable and beneficial ownership' in the goods would remain with Monsanto until full payment for the whole amount of the relevant order had been received or until prior resale, it was manifestly not the intention to confer on or reserve to Monsanto all the rights which would normally be enjoyed by a sui juris person, having the sole beneficial title to property, as against the trustee holding the legal title. Counsel for Monsanto, expressly conceded and affirmed that Monsanto would not, by virtue of its so called 'equitable and beneficial ownership', have had the right to call for redelivery of the goods, at any rate so long as Bond Worth was not in default under its payments. Bond Worth, on the other hand, was to have far-reaching rights even before payment to deal with the goods, which would not normally be possessed by a trustee holding the legal title therein on behalf of one sole, sui juris beneficiary.

(5) Even during the period before full payment had been received by Monsanto and

---

1   [1895] AC 457 at 467, [1895–9] All ER Rep 829 at 834

notwithstanding the provisions relating to 'equitable and beneficial ownership', Bond
Worth were to be at liberty to sell all or any part of the goods and to transfer the property
therein to a purchaser. The words 'until prior resale', in para (a) of the retention of title
clause, render the implication of such authority to resell inevitable. They go far beyond
the provisions of s 25(1) of the Sale of Goods Act 1893 which empower a buyer of goods
in possession after sale in some circumstances, even without the authority of his vendor,
to resell and pass a good title to a purchaser on a resale, but confer no authority on him
to effect such resale, as between him and his vendor.

b
    (6) The parties nevertheless intended that if Bond Worth were to resell all or any part
of the goods at a time when Monsanto had not yet been paid the full price due under the
order Monsanto's 'equitable and beneficial ownership', whatever that meant, would
attach to the proceeds of sale or to the claim for such proceeds.
    (7) Even during the period before full payment had been received by Monsanto and
notwithstanding the provisions relating to 'equitable and beneficial ownership', Bond
Worth were to be at liberty to use the goods for the purposes of manufacture. The words
'should the goods become constituents of or be converted into other products while
subject to our equitable and beneficial ownership', which are to be found in para (a) of
the retention of title clause, render inevitable the implication of this authority given to
Bond Worth.
    (8) The parties nevertheless intended that if, by virtue of such last-mentioned use, the
goods should become constituents of or be converted into other products, the retention
of title clause should attach to such other products as if they had been the original subject
matter of the sale. In other words, they intended that (a) until Monsanto had received
full payment of the whole amount due in respect of the original order or until such other
products were sold, Monsanto would be entitled to the 'equitable and beneficial
ownership' of such other products in the same sense as it was entitled to such ownership
of the goods originally delivered under the order; (b) even during the period before full
payment had been received by Monsanto, Bond Worth were nevertheless to be at liberty
to sell all or any part of such products and to transfer the property therein to a purchaser;
(c) if, however, Bond Worth were to resell all or any part of such products at a time when
Monsanto had not yet been paid the full price due under the original order, Monsanto's
'equitable and beneficial ownership' would attach to the proceeds of sale or to the claim
for such proceeds.
    Thus far, the position would seem to me reasonably clear. The real difficulty arises
concerning the meaning and legal effect (if any) of the provisions in the retention of title
clause concerning 'equitable and beneficial ownership'. If the contracts embody
something more than a mere sale, what is this additional feature? What is the nature of
the relationship beyond a mere vendor–purchaser relationship between Monsanto and
Bond Worth that comes into existence by virtue of the provisions relating to 'equitable
and beneficial ownership'?
    In the *Romalpa* case[1], to which I shall have to refer in greater detail later, it was
expressly admitted that the retention of title clause had the effect of making the
defendants *bailees* of the relevant goods while in their possession until all money owing
had been paid (see per Mocatta J[2]). On the different facts of the present case, however,
there can be no question of a bailor–bailee relationship, since it is common ground that
the property in the Acrilan fibre passed to Bond Worth at latest when it was delivered,
while it is of the essence of a bailment that the general property in the goods concerned
remains in the bailor, while only a special property passes to the bailee, which entitles
him to exercise certain possessory remedies. Nor can the relationship be one of agency,
since the documents contain no suggestion that Bond Worth is to be regarded as an agent
and the rights which by necessary implication are given to it deal with the goods on its
own behalf are quite inconsistent with a principal–agent relationship.

---

1   [1976] 2 All ER 552, [1976] 1 WLR 676
2   [1976] 2 All ER 552 at 555, [1976] 1 WLR 676 at 680

In these circumstances, I think it plain that, if the retention of title clause operated to create any effective rights at all for the benefit of Monsanto, such rights can only have *a* been rights either (i) by way of a trust under which Monsanto was the sole beneficiary or (ii) by way of a trust under which Monsanto had a charge in equity over the relevant assets to secure payment of the unpaid purchase price. No possible third alternative has occurred to me.

Counsel, in contending for the first of these two alternatives on behalf of Monsanto, submitted that the retention of title clause, in the context of each of the relevant *b* contracts, had the effect of creating a trust, under which the legal title to the Acrilan fibre delivered to it passed to Bond Worth, but the entire beneficial interest therein remained in Monsanto, until it was paid in full for all the goods comprised in the relevant order from Bond Worth. The terms of the trust, he accepted, were such that Bond Worth would have the right to sell the Acrilan even before it had made full payment; but in such event, he submitted, the trust would be transferred and attach to the proceeds of *c* sale, until payment in full had been made. It was not in the least inconsistent with the existence of a trust that Bond Worth should be given the authority to sell the Acrilan before payment since, even in the absence of an express authority so to do, it would have had the power to pass the property in the goods to a third party during this interim period under s 25 of the Sale of Goods Act 1893. The ordinary law of trusts, he submitted, would itself produce the result that the proceeds of Acrilan sold during this *d* period would themselves be held in trust for Monsanto as sole beneficiary, unless and until the relevant payment was made in full. Furthermore, he accepted and affirmed that the terms of the trust were such that, even during this interim period, Bond Worth would be at liberty to use the Acrilan for the purposes of manufacture and thus to mix it with other goods of which it was the absolute owner, but only, in his submission, on terms that the products of which the Acrilan thus became a constituent, or into which *e* it was converted, would themselves be held by Bond Worth in trust for Monsanto as sole beneficiary, unless and until the relevant payment was made in full. The retention of title clause, he submitted, may be an unusual one, but there is no good reason why effect should not be given to it in accordance with the express terms of the agreement into which the parties entered. Since they have chosen to adopt a clause which expressly leaves the entire 'equitable and beneficial ownership' with Monsanto until a specified *f* event occurs, the court in his submission is entitled and bound to give effect to that clause according to its terms (see, for example, the passage from Lord Watson's speech in *McEntire v Crossley Brothers Ltd*[1] already cited). The mere fact that it might be necessary for a court of equity to grant a remedy by way of equitable charge as the only effective means of enabling Monsanto to enforce its rights under the clause does not of itself, it was contended, convert Monsanto's full equitable and beneficial ownership into a right by *g* way of a mere mortgage or charge; right and remedy must not be confused.

I readily accept that the court is not entitled to discard the plain ordinary meaning of the phrase 'equitable and beneficial ownership' unless there can be found in the relevant contracts other language and stipulations which necessarily deprive it of its ordinary meaning. The court, however, is entitled and indeed bound to look at the substance of the transactions as appearing from the wording of the *whole* of the retention of title *h* clause, and indeed the other provisions of the relevant contracts of sale, for the purpose of deciding whether the essence of the transactions which the clause embodied was on the one hand a bare trust or on the other hand a trust by way of equitable mortgage or charge (see *Re George Inglefield Ltd*[2] per Lord Hanworth MR, per Lawrence LJ and per Romer LJ). Counsel for Monsanto accepted, as I think he had to accept, that the whole purpose of the retention of title clause was to afford Monsanto security for the payment *j* of the purchase price under each relevant order. I have come to the clear conclusion that

---

1　[1895] AC 457 at 467, [1895–9] All ER Rep 829 at 834
2　[1933] Ch 1 at 17, 23, 27, [1932] All ER Rep 244 at 251, 254, 256

if, contrary to the submissions of other counsel, the clause operated so as to give any
legally enforceable rights at all to Monsanto, such rights must necessarily have been
rights by way of mortgage or charge. In my judgment, any contract which, by way of
security for the payment of a debt, confers an interest in property defeasible or
destructible on payment of such debt, or appropriates such property for the discharge of
the debt, must necessarily be regarded as creating a mortgage or charge, as the case may
be. The existence of the equity of redemption is quite inconsistent with the existence of
a bare trustee–beneficiary relationship.

The fact that all the characteristics of a mortgage or charge are to be found present in
the retention of title clause is borne out by a passage from the judgment of Romer LJ in
Re George Inglefield Ltd[1]. There he summarised the essential characteristics of a mortgage
as follows:

> 'In a transaction of sale the vendor is not entitled to get back the subject-matter
> of the sale by returning to the purchaser the money that has passed between them.
> In the case of a mortgage or charge, the mortgagor is entitled, until he has been
> foreclosed, to get back the subject-matter of the mortgage or charge by returning to
> the mortgagee the money that has passed between them. The second essential
> difference is that if the mortgagee realizes the subject-matter of the mortgage for a
> sum more than sufficient to repay him, with interest and the costs, the money that
> has passed between him and the mortgagor he has to account to the mortgagor for
> the surplus. If the purchaser sells the subject-matter of the purchase, and realizes a
> profit, of course he has not got to account to the vendor for the profit. Thirdly, if
> the mortgagee realizes the mortgage property for a sum that is insufficient to repay
> him the money that he has paid to the mortgagor, together with interest and costs,
> then the mortgagee is entitled to recover from the mortgagor the balance of the
> money, either because there is a covenant by the mortgagor to repay the money
> advanced by the mortgagee, or because of the existence of the simple contract debt
> which is created by the mere fact of the advance having been made.'

Mutatis mutandis all these three features of a charge are present in this case. Bond Worth
was entitled to redeem the charge in favour of Monsanto by paying to it the outstanding
debt due under the relevant order. If Monsanto, in exercise of the rights conferred on it
by the retention of title clause, were to compel a sale of the relevant assets for a sum more
than sufficient to pay this debt, the parties' intention was surely that Bond Worth, rather
than Monsanto, would be entitled to receive the surplus. In contrast, if such last-
mentioned sale were to produce a sum less than the outstanding debt, they surely
intended that Monsanto would remain entitled to recover the balance from Bond Worth
as a simple contract debt.

Thus in my judgment there are to be found within the retention of title clause itself
other language and stipulations which necessarily deprive the phrase 'equitable and
beneficial ownership' of its primary meaning. In my judgment, the clause, when
properly construed, purported to create equitable charges in favour of Monsanto over
four separate categories of assets, namely: (a) the raw Acrilan which was the original
subject-matter of the original sale; (b) the proceeds of sale of any such raw Acrilan which
might be sold; (c) any products of which any part of the raw Acrilan might become a
constituent or into which it might be converted; (d) the proceeds of sale of any such
products which might be sold. I shall for brevity, from time to time hereafter, refer
respectively to these four categories as the first, second, third and fourth categories of
charged assets.

Subject to the provisions of the Bills of Sale Acts (which generally do not apply to
instruments charging the property of a company), I can see nothing in principle to
prevent a vendor and a purchaser of specific ascertained chattels from expressly agreeing

---

1 [1933] Ch 1 at 27–28, [1932] All ER Rep 244 at 256–257

that the vendor shall have a mortgage or charge over such chattels to secure the payment of the unpaid purchase price, in addition to or in substitution for any lien which may be *a* conferred on him by the Sale of Goods Act 1893. Section 55 of that Act specifically provides that where any right would arise under a contract for the sale of goods by implication of law it may be negatived or varied by express agreement. As Atkin LJ said in *Re Wait*[1]:

> 'The rules for transfer of property as between seller and buyer, performance of the contract, rights of the unpaid seller against the goods, unpaid sellers' lien, remedies *b* of the seller, remedies of the buyer, appear to be complete and exclusive statements of the legal relations both in law and equity. They have, of course, no relevance when one is considering rights, legal or equitable, which may come into existence dehors the contract for sale. A seller or a purchaser may, of course, create any equity he pleases by way of charge, equitable assignment or any other dealing with or disposition of goods, the subject-matter of sale; and he may, of course, create such *c* an equity as one of the terms expressed in the contract of sale.'

Thus in my judgment, in principle, subject to the provisions of the Bills of Sale Acts, a person may create an effective equitable charge over chattels by declaring that he holds them in trust for a creditor by way of security for the payment of a specified debt. Likewise he can for good consideration create an effective equitable charge over chattels *d* of a specified category to be acquired by him in the future, or over future book debts, in such manner that the charge will attach to chattels when acquired, or to the book debts when they arise. All these things can in my judgment be done by the chargor declaring himself a trustee of the relevant assets for the purposes of the security (compare *Re Yorkshire Woolcombers Association Ltd*[2] per Farwell J).

In the present context, therefore, the relevant questions are whether or not the *e* retention of title clause operated to confer on Monsanto rights by way of equitable charge (which I think are the only rights it can have conferred on it) and if so in what manner. A brief reference to terminology perhaps may be helpful at this stage. I have used the description 'charge' rather than 'mortgage' for these reasons. The technical difference between a 'mortgage' or 'charge', though in practice the phrases are often used interchangeably, is that a mortgage involves a conveyance of property subject to a right *f* of redemption, whereas a charge conveys nothing and merely gives the chargee certain rights over the property as security for the loan (see Megarry and Wade's Law of Real Property[3]). Technically therefore it seems to me the rights (if any) of Monsanto under the retention of title clause fall to be regarded as rights by way of charge rather than mortgage, if it is proper to regard such rights as being no more than rights by way of security. This particular technical distinction, however, is of no practical significance in *g* the present case, since the expression 'charge' in the context of s 95 of the Companies Act 1948 is defined by s 95(10) as including 'mortgage'.

I have used the word 'equitable' to describe the charge (if any) created by the retention of title clause, since it must be of an equitable rather than of a legal nature, inasmuch as the legal property in the relevant goods passed to Bond Worth and has never been transferred back to Monsanto. I have used the phrase 'charge' rather than the word 'lien', *h* because, though the word 'lien' is sometimes used in practice to describe a right which arises by way of express contractual agreement of the interested parties, it is more commonly used, in a narrower sense, to refer to a right arising by operation of law. Liens in this narrower sense may arise by virtue of statute, common law or equity. An unpaid vendor of goods, so long as he retains possession of them, will have a statutory lien on them to secure payment of the purchase price, by virtue of ss 41 and 42 of the Sale of *j* Goods Act 1893. However, no reliance has been or could be placed by Monsanto on any

---

1 [1927] 1 Ch 606 at 636, [1926] All ER Rep 433 at 446
2 [1903] 2 Ch 284 at 288
3 4th Edn (1975) p 887

such statutory lien in the present case, since it has not retained possession of any part of
a the relevant goods. For similar reasons there can be no question here of any common
law lien, since, where such a lien arises at all, it consists of the right to retain possession
of another's property until a debt is paid. An equitable lien is of a rather different nature,
which is described by the editors of Megarry and Wade's Law of Real Property as
follows[1]:

> 'An equitable lien is not dependent upon continued possession of the property
> *b*   and in this respect resembles a mortgage . . . But it differs from a mortgage (*inter
> alia*) in that a mortgage is intentionally created by contract whereas an equitable lien
> arises automatically under some doctrine of equity. Thus a vendor of land has an
> equitable lien on it until the full purchase price is paid, even if he has conveyed the
> land to the purchaser and put him into possession. This lien gives him no right to
> possession of the land, but enables him to apply to the court for a declaration of
> *c*   charge and for an order for sale of the land, under which he will be paid the money
> due . . . An equitable lien is therefore a species of equitable charge arising by
> implication of law.'

It appears from the decision of the Court of Appeal in *Re Stucley*[2] that the court may
in some circumstances be prepared to find that an unpaid vendor has an equitable lien
d even on a sale of personal property, if the contract is such that the court would order
specific performance of it (see per Vaughan Williams LJ, per Stirling LJ and per Cozens-
Hardy LJ[3]). Simonds J, however, in *Transport and General Credit Corpn Ltd v Morgan*[4]
suggested that it would be inconsistent with what he regarded as 'an exhaustive statement
of the law in the Sale of Goods Act 1893' to say that 'in the case of an ordinary commercial
article under a commercial agreement there can be any other vendor's lien than that
e possessory lien which the statute itself provides'.

In the present case, however, it is unnecessary to decide whether, in the absence of the
retention of title clause, the court would have been prepared to infer that Monsanto, so
long as the purchase price had not been paid for in full, had an equitable lien over the
Acrilan fibre delivered to Bond Worth. On the present facts there is in my judgment no
room for implying any vendor's lien arising by operation of law, after completion of the
f purchase, bearing in mind the express agreement of the parties in the terms embodied
in the retention of title clause, which was designed to secure payment of the full purchase
price (compare *Capital Finance Co Ltd v Stokes*[5] per Harman LJ). And indeed no lien
arising by operation of law has been relied on by Monsanto. If the clause operated to
confer any legally enforceable rights at all on Monsanto, these can only in my judgment
have been rights by way of *express* contractual charge.

g Counsel for Monsanto, who was concerned to argue that the charges (if any) involved
in the present case should not be treated as having been 'created' by Bond Worth for the
purpose of s 95(1) of the Companies Act 1948, submitted in effect that there are two
alternative methods by which, on a sale, a charge can be created in favour of the vendor
to secure the purchase price. It may be created by means of a grant back in favour of the
vendor as was done in *Capital Finance Co Ltd v Stokes*[6]. Alternatively, he suggested, it may
h be created by the vendor reserving or excepting to himself a charge over the relevant
property and simply disposing of the equity of redemption. The latter, he submitted, if
a charge was created at all, was precisely what happened in the present case. The terms
of the retention of title clause themselves, he suggested, made it plain that the 'equitable

---

j   1   4th Edn (1975) p 886
      2   [1906] 1 Ch 67, [1904–7] All ER Rep 281
      3   [1906] 1 Ch 67 at 75–76, 79–80, 84, [1904–7] All ER Rep 281 at 283–284, 285–286, 288
      4   [1939] 2 All ER 17 at 25, [1939] Ch 531 at 546
      5   [1968] 3 All ER 625 at 630, [1969] 1 Ch 261 at 280
      6   [1968] 3 All ER 625, [1969] 1 Ch 261

and beneficial ownership' of the goods was to 'remain' in Monsanto until it had been paid in full for the relevant order and correspondingly that no part of the beneficial ownership, beyond at most a mere equity of redemption, passed to Bond Worth on the sale, even for a moment of time.

In this context he relied particularly on the decision of the Court of Appeal in *Re Connolly Brothers Ltd (No 2)*[1]. In that case, a company had issued debentures creating a floating charge on all its present and future property, one of the conditions of the debenture being that the company should not be at liberty to create any other mortgage or charge in priority to the debenture. Subsequently, it wanted to purchase certain property, but had not the necessary money and applied to a Mrs O'Reilly to lend it the sum of £1,000. It agreed to give her a charge on the property to secure this loan. She advanced the money on these terms. The company then concluded a contract to buy the property from the owner (who was not Mrs O'Reilly) for £1,100 and paid a deposit of £150. Mrs O'Reilly duly gave the company a cheque for £1,000, which was paid into its banking account. It then drew a cheque for £950, which was cashed, the cash being paid over to the vendor. A week later, the company executed in favour of Mrs O'Reilly a memorandum of equitable charge on the property, for the express purpose of securing the £1,000 debt. The question then arose whether the security acquired by her took priority over the debentures. The Court of Appeal held that it did, on the grounds that, before the purchase was completed, a contract had been concluded between her and the company under the terms of which, on completion of the purchase, she was to have a first charge and the company was only to get the property subject thereto. Accordingly, as Cozens-Hardy MR[2] said, '. . . all the company in equity obtained was the equity of redemption in the property subject to Mrs. O'Reilly's charge of 1,000l'.

Correspondingly, it was submitted on behalf of Monsanto in the present case, even if, contrary to its primary submission, the retention of title clause operated to confer on it a mere charge, this was a charge created by Monsanto in favour of itself, by way of exception out of the entirety of the beneficial interest in the property; Bond Worth, it was suggested, never acquired in equity, even for a moment in time, more than the equity of redemption in the Acrilan, subject to Monsanto's interest by way of charge.

Though this argument has some superficial attraction, I do not think that the *Connolly*[1] decision, when properly analysed, is of any assistance to Monsanto. As will have appeared, that was a case where A, the purchaser of the relevant property from B, had, before completion, entered into a contract, for good consideration, to grant a charge over the property in favour of C. Accordingly, the very moment that A acquired the legal estate in the property, A held it in trust to give effect in equity to C's rights, by virtue of the pre-existing contract between A and C. In the face of this contract, it could not therefore have been successfully claimed that the purchaser A, even for a moment, acquired more than an equity of redemption in the property (though it may be observed that the relevant charge, even in that case, was undeniably created by A rather than the vendor, B). The case did not even touch the question whether it would have been conceptually possible for the vendor B to except to himself a mortgage in such manner that the subject-matter of the sale, as between A and B, was a mere equity of redemption, so that the transaction involved no express or implied grant back by A in favour of B. Notwithstanding the arrangements made between A and C, the transaction as between A and B in the *Connolly* case[1] remain throughout one for the sale of the entire legal and beneficial interest in the property. This case was, as Harman LJ pointed out in *Capital Finance Co Ltd v Stokes*[3], merely one where the Court of Appeal was considering equitable priorities.

A concept familiar to conveyancers is that, on a grant of land, it is possible for the grantor to except out of that which is granted something which is actually in existence

1   [1912] 2 Ch 25
2   [1912] 2 Ch 25 at 31
3   [1968] 3 All ER 625 at 628, [1969] 1 Ch 261 at 277

at the time of the grant, such as mines and minerals. The effect of such exception is not
a to include in the grant that which is excepted; and, correspondingly, it will take effect
even though the grantee has not executed the relevant instrument. However, no
authority has been cited which satisfies me that, on the transfer of the legal property in
land or chattels, it is competent to a vendor expressly to except from the grant in favour
of himself an equitable mortgage or charge thereon to secure the unpaid purchase price
(in addition to or in substitution for any lien which may arise by operation of law) in such
b manner that the exception will take effect without any express or implied grant back of
a mortgage or charge in the vendor's favour by the purchaser. In my judgment, as a
matter of conveyancing in the case of land, the proper course is to follow that actually
adopted by the conveyancers in *Capital Finance Co Ltd v Stokes*¹ and described by Harman
LJ² as 'the ordinary conveyancing practice'; this is for the documentation to contain an
express grant of the entire legal and beneficial title, followed by an immediate grant back
c of the requisite mortgage or charge. In the case of either land or personal property, an
express or implied grant back in favour of the original grantor is in my judgment
required to create such mortgage or charge. If the court is satisfied that both parties to
a transaction of sale have contracted that the vendor shall have defined rights by way of
mortgage or charge over the subject-matter of the sale, no doubt it will be prepared to
imply the necessary grant back of such rights by the purchaser, even though inappropriate
d words, for example words by way of purported exception, may have been used; equity
will regard as done that which ought to be done. This does not, however, remove the
theoretical necessity of a grant back.

Support for the view that in such a case an express or implied grant back of rights by
the purchaser to the vendor is in principle necessary is to be found in the decision in
*Coburn v Collins*³, as explained by Lord Herschell LC in *McEntire v Crossley Brothers Ltd*⁴.
e In the former case, Kekewich J had specifically to consider whether the provisions of a
particular contract of sale imported the grant back of a charge, over the property sold, by
the purchaser to the vendor or merely a sale of the property subject to a charge. The case
concerned the effect of an agreement approved by the court and made between a Mr
Coburn and a Mr Abraham, who were the trustees of a will of a testator, whose estate
included a wine and spirit business. Clause 1 of the agreement provided that in
f consideration of payments to be made by Abraham, Coburn agreed to sell the business
and the goodwill thereof and also 'all the stock-in-trade, utensils, plant, implements,
office furniture, and effects now in and upon the said business premises, and also the
book-debts of the said business, for the sum of £10,329 18s.' By cl 2 Abraham agreed to
effect the purchase for the said sum and to pay for the same with interest from a specified
date. Clause 3 provided, inter alia, that Abraham should pay all the outstanding debts
g and liabilities due and owing by the business on that date and that Coburn and Abraham,
as such trustees, 'shall have and be entitled to a lien or charge upon the said business and
effects hereby agreed to be sold for the said sum of £10,329 18s., or for so much thereof
as shall be from time to time remaining unpaid . . .' The question arose whether cl 3 of
the agreement operated as a bill of sale falling within s 4 of the Bills of Sale Act 1878 and
was thus void against Abraham's trustee in bankruptcy for lack of registration. It was
h submitted⁵ that the agreement did not fall within the Act, on the grounds that the real
nature of the transaction was not a regrant but a sale by trustees to one of themselves,
with an overriding lien or charge in favour of the trust as one of the terms of the
contract. Kekewich J rejected this argument. He said⁶:

j 1 [1968] 3 All ER 625, [1969] 1 Ch 261
2 [1968] 3 All ER 625 at 628, [1969] 1 Ch 261 at 277
3 (1887) 35 Ch D 373
4 [1895] AC 457 at 466, [1895–9] All ER Rep 829 at 833
5 35 Ch D 373 at 377–378 *arguendo*
6 35 Ch D 373 at 382

'I think the proper construction of the agreement read as a whole (and I think it must be read as a whole) is that there was an absolute out and out sale to *John Abraham* of the whole property, and that then, by an independent clause, *John Abraham* charges what is due from him, the purchase-money and interest, on the thing purchased, so as to give the trustees, the vendors, including himself, some security for the purchase-money over and above that which is contained in the earlier part of the agreement.'

In *McEntire v Crossley Brothers Ltd*[1] a written agreement for the hire of an engine provided for the hirer to pay rent for it by instalments amounting in all to £240. It was provided that on payment in full the agreement should be at an end and the engine should become the lessee's property, but it contained an express provision that until payment in full it should remain the sole and absolute property of the owners and lessors. The lessee paid the first instalment and the engine was placed on his premises. While it was still there, he became bankrupt, at a time when some instalments were still outstanding. An attempt was made on behalf of his assignees in bankruptcy to obtain possession of the engine, on the grounds that the true nature of the transaction was that of sale and purchase, with the vendor having a charge on the engine for the unpaid purchase money, and that since such charge was not registered as a bill of sale, it was invalid. The House of Lords rejected this argument, the essence of their reasoning being that summarised by Lord Herschell LC in the following passage[2]:

'Here the parties have in terms expressed their intention, and said that the property shall not pass till the full purchase-money is paid. I know of no reason to prevent that being a perfectly lawful agreement. If that was really the intention of the parties, I known of no rule or principle of law which prevents its being given effect to.'

Counsel for Monsanto relied on this and other similar passages in other speeches in this case in support of his contention that full effect should be given to the expressed intention of the parties that 'equitable and beneficial ownership' in the Acrilan should *'remain'* in the vendor until payment. Lord Herschell LC went on to say this[2]:

'I quite agree that if, although the parties have inserted a provision to that effect, they have shewn in other parts of the agreement, by the language they have used or the provisions they have made, that they intended the property to pass, you must look at the transaction as a whole; and it might be necessary to hold that the property has passed, although the parties have said that their intention was that it should not, because they have provided that it shall. No doubt any provisions which were inconsistent with the intention that the property should not pass would be given effect to in preference to a mere expression of intention in words—that is a proposition which I should not dispute for a moment; and if the appellants could have pointed here to any provisions in this deed inconsistent with the intention that the property should remain in the vendors, I think they might very likely have succeeded, notwithstanding that the parties had in terms said what their intention was.'

Later in his speech Lord Herschell LC distinguished the case of *Coburn v Collins*[3], on which reliance had been placed. He said this[4]:

'That was an agreement for the sale of a business the price of which was to be paid at a future time. There was no agreement between the parties in that case that the

1 [1895] AC 457, [1895–9] All ER Rep 829
2 [1895] AC 457 at 463, [1895–9] All ER Rep 829 at 832
3 (1887) 35 Ch D 373
4 [1895] AC 457 at 466, [1895–9] All ER Rep 829 at 833

property should not pass at once. There were none of the stipulations which one finds here as to the use of that which was the subject of the agreement to sell. In this case the intending purchaser cannot sell, assign, sub-let or even remove from one building to another, this gas-engine, the property of which is supposed to be in him; in *Coburn* v. *Collins*[1] it was the sale of a business which the purchaser was intending to continue, he selling the stock-in-trade—two contracts of a very different nature. In the next place, there, in terms, the vendors were to have a lien or charge until the full price was paid—a lien or charge implying that the property had passed to others, for a man does not have a lien on his own property or a charge either. Therefore, in that case there were provisions in the agreement which pointed to the intention being that the substance of the transaction was a sale in which the property passed with a security, eo instanti, given by the purchaser to the vendor.'

Applying similar reasoning, I conclude that the proper manner of construing the retention of title clause, together with all the other relevant provisions of the contracts of sale read as a whole, is to regard them as effecting a sale in which the entire property in the Acrilan passes to Bond Worth followed by a security, eo instanti, given back by Bond Worth to the vendor, Monsanto.

In my judgment, therefore, Bond Worth rather than Monsanto must be regarded as creator of the relevant charges in relation to the first category of charged assets. A fortiori it must be so regarded in relation to the second, third and fourth categories, since the third and fourth categories, at least, might include or represent (inter alia) property of which Monsanto had never at any time been the owner (eg materials belonging to Bond Worth, other than Acrilan, with which Acrilan had been mixed). Charges over these categories could not possibly have been created except by grant made by Bond Worth. This, in my judgment, would be a powerful reason in itself for concluding that Bond Worth should be treated as having been the grantor and creator of the charges over all the categories of assets comprised in the retention of title clause even if, contrary to my view, it had been theoretically possible for charges on the first and second categories to have been created without the need for any express or implied grant by Bond Worth.

Up to this point, therefore, my prima facie conclusion is that the effect of the incorporation of the retention of title clause in each of the 29 contracts, concluded by the acceptance by Bond Worth of Acrilan, when delivered to it, was to give rise to the creation by it in favour of Monsanto of equitable charges over such Acrilan and the other three related categories of charged assets, by way of implied grant in favour of Monsanto.

Counsel for the applicants and counsel for the bank, however, each made strong attacks on the essential validity of the retention of title clause, on grounds which have not yet been mentioned. They submitted in effect that, while in principle it may be possible, subject to the provisions of the Bills of Sales Acts, for a purchaser of chattels to declare himself a trustee thereof for the purpose of a charge in favour of the vendor to secure the purchase price, no such trust and charge, having any legal effect, exist at all on the facts of the present case. For, it was pointed out, the contracts of sales in the present case have special features of crucial importance. They do not embody chattels which are, by their very nature, likely to retain their identity (such as, for example, a grand piano). Nor do they impose any obligation on the purhaser to keep them safely and to preserve their identity, for the better safeguarding of the vendor's security. No express obligation was imposed on Bond Worth by the clause to keep the unpaid-for raw Acrilan separate from its other stores of raw Acrilan; and it is not suggested by Monsanto that the introduction of this clause in June 1976 placed Bond Worth under any implied obligation of this nature. On the contrary, Bond Worth was free to deal with the unpaid for fibre, together with the other products and book debts referred to in the clause, just as if they were its own property. Without committing any breach of the alleged trust, it could mix the raw fibre with its other goods, sell it on such terms as to price and otherwise as it pleased,

---

1   (1887) 35 Ch D 373

spin it into yarn and use it for all the purposes of its carpet manufacture. Likewise, without committing any such breach, it could deal with the book debts, to which the *a* clause purported to attach, for its own purposes and for its own benefit. These facts, which were not disputed by Monsanto in argument, led to two separate allied lines of attack on the validity of the retention of title clause.

First, for the creation of a valid trust, three 'certainties' are necessary. There must be certainty of words, in the sense that the words used must indicate the intention to create a trust. There must be certainty of subject-matter, in the sense that the property to be *b* held on trust must be certain. And there must be certainty of objects, in the sense that the objects or persons intended to benefit under the trust must be certain (see Snell on Equity[1]). In the present case, it was submitted, in view of the unfettered rights of Bond Worth to deal with the Acrilan, the subject-matter of the alleged trust would, as a matter of fact, necessarily be incapable of ascertainment and this inevitably invalidated the alleged trust ab initio, since the second of the three certainties would not be present. *c*

If, as counsel for Monsanto submitted, the clause had imposed or purported to impose the trust on the raw Acrilan which was the original subject-matter of the sale, even after it had become a constituent of or had been converted into other products, I would have seen considerable force in the attack based on uncertainty. For as soon as either of these things has happened, the raw Acrilan will have lost its original identity; correspondingly there will no longer be any identifiable subject-matter to which the trust can be said to *d* attach. In my judgment, however, the wording of the clause on its true construction indicates that, as soon as either of these two things happens to a particular batch of raw Acrilan, the trust set out in para (a) will cease to apply to such batch and instead the trust set out in para (b) will at once attach to the relevant product of which such batch has become a constituent or into which it has been converted. It seems clear that the word 'products' in para (b) as a matter of construction comprehends, inter alia, the relevant *e* Acrilan fibre itself, and I can see no reason for supposing that the same batch of fibre would have been intended to be subject simultaneously to trusts under both para (a) and para (b).

This being the interpretation which I place on the retention of title clause, I do not think that the attack based on alleged uncertainty of subject-matter succeeds. There is, in my judgment, all the difference between a purported trust affecting subject-matter *f* which from the beginning is ex hypothesi bound to be incapable of ascertainment, and one, such as the present, affecting subject-matter which, while it may prove difficult or even in some events impossible to ascertain in practice, is not from the beginning ex hypothesi bound to be so incapable.

For these reasons I do not accept the uncertainty point as invalidating the alleged trusts ab initio, though I say this without prejudice to any question of the availability or *g* unavailability of effective remedies for its enforcement.

A second, allied line of attack was made on the validity of the alleged trusts. It is quite inconsistent with the concept of a trust or fiduciary relationship, it was submitted, that Bond Worth should be free to use the Acrilan fibre and other categories of assets subject to the retention of title clause for the purposes of its own business and manufacturing processes, in the manner which I have described. Four authorities, in particular, were *h* relied on in this context.

In Re Nevill, ex parte White[2] a firm of cotton manufacturers, Towle & Co, was in the habit of selling goods to one Nevill. The course of dealing between the parties was that the goods were accompanied by a price list. Nevill disposed of the goods on what terms he pleased and did not pay for them unless he disposed of them. At the end of each month, he sent the firm an account of sales of goods which he had actually made. Then *j* after the lapse of another month, he paid in cash for the amount of the goods so sold,

---

1   27th Edn (1973), pp 111–115
2   (1871) LR 6 Ch App 397

according to the value shown in the price list, without regard to the prices which he
himself received. Though Nevill received all the goods on his private account, he was a
partner in a firm called Nevill & Co into whose general account he paid the moneys
received from his sales and through which he made his payments to Towle & Co. He
kept with Nevill & Co an account of moneys paid in and drawn out by him in respect of
moneys unconnected with the partnership. This account included many items
unconnected with the goods of Towle & Co. Nevill & Co having executed a deed of
arrangement with their creditors, Towle & Co sought to prove against the joint estate for
the amount showing to Nevill's credit with his firm, on the grounds that the same arose
from trust moneys belonging in equity to Towle & Co and that they had been improperly
placed by Nevill in the hands of his firm. The Court of Appeal rejected this submission
on the grounds that the relationship between Towle & Co and Nevill was not, as claimed,
a fiduciary relationship. The grounds for this decision adequately appear from the
following passage from the judgment of James LJ[1]:

> 'It does not appear that he ever was expected to return any particular contract, or
> the names of the persons with whom he had dealt. He pursued his own course in
> dealing with the goods, and frequently before sale he manipulated them to a very
> considerable extent by pressing, dyeing and otherwise altering their character,
> changing them as much as wheat would be changed by being turned into flour; and
> he sold them on what terms he pleased as to price and length of credit. No question
> appears ever to have been raised as to whether he was entitled to do this; we must
> take it that he did not commit any breach of duty in so doing. That is quite
> inconsistent with the notion that he was acting in a fiduciary character in respect of
> those goods. If he was entitled to alter them, to manipulate them, to sell them at
> any price that he thought fit after they had been so manipulated, and was still only
> liable to pay for them at a price fixed beforehand, without any reference to the price
> at which he had sold them or to anything else than the fact of his having sold them
> in a certain month, it seems to me impossible to say that the produce of the goods
> so sold was the money of the consignors or that the relation of vendor and purchaser
> existed between *Towle & Co.* and the different persons to whom he sold the goods.'

By analogy in the present case, it was forcibly pointed out, Bond Worth was never
expected to render to Monsanto any account of what it did with the Acrilan. It could
pursue its own course in dealing with it. It could sell it on what terms it pleased as to
price and otherwise. It could use it, and did regularly use it, for the purposes of
manufacture. If it happened that it were to use it for such purposes in a wasteful or
inefficient manner, Monsanto would apparently have had no grounds of complaint. All
this, it was submitted, was quite inconsistent with the existence of any kind of trustee–
beneficiary relationship between Bond Worth and Monsanto, whether by way of
mortgage security or otherwise.

Reference was also made in this context to the decision of the House of Lords in *Foley
v Hill*[2]. There it was held that the relation between a banker and customer, who pays
money into the bank, is the ordinary relationship of debtor and creditor, with an added
obligation arising out of the custom of bankers to honour the customers' drafts, and that
it is not of a fiduciary character. Lord Cottenham LC[3] rejected a suggested analogy
between the position of a banker and customer on the one hand and that between a
principal and an agent selling goods on his behalf on the other. The goods, he pointed
out, remain the goods of the owner or principal until the sale takes place and the moment
the money is received it remains the property of the principal. The agent obtains no
interest himself in the subject-matter beyond his remuneration; he is dealing throughout

---

1   (1871) LR 6 Ch App 397 at 400
2   (1848) 2 HL Cas 28, [1843–60] All ER Rep 16
3   2 HL Cas 28 at 35–36, [1843–60] All ER Rep 16 at 19

for another and, though not a trustee in the strict sense, is a quasi-trustee for the particular transaction, which is why the courts have assumed jurisdiction. Lord *a* Cottenham LC[1] then contrasted the position of banker and customer:

> 'Money, when paid into a bank, ceases altogether to be the money of the principal ... it is then the money of the banker, who is bound to return an equivalent by paying a similar sum to that deposited with him when he is asked for it. The money paid into the banker's is known by the principal to be placed there for the *b* purpose of being under the control of the banker; it is then the banker's money; he is known to deal with it as his own; he makes what profit of it he can, which profit he retains to himself, paying back only the principal, according to the custom of bankers in some places, or the principal and a small rate of interest, according to the custom of bankers in other places. The money placed in the custody of the banker is, to all intents and purposes, the money of the banker, to do with it as he pleases; *c* he is guilty of no breach of trust in employing it; he is not answerable to the principal if he puts it into jeopardy, if he engages in a hazardous speculation; he is not bound to keep it or deal with it as the property of his principal, but he is of course answerable for the amount, because he has contracted, having received that money, to repay to the principal, when demanded, a sum equivalent to that paid into his hands.' *d*

It was submitted that similar reasons to those which prevented Lord Cottenham LC from holding that a fiduciary relationship exists as between banker and customer would prevent such a relationship from existing between Bond Worth and Monsanto in the present case. Another decision relied on by counsel for the applicants and counsel for the bank was *South Australian Insurance Co v Randell*[2] ('*Randell's* case'). In that case corn had *e* been deposited by farmers with a miller to be stored and used as part of the current consumable stock of the miller's trade. He was at liberty to and did mix it with other corn deposited for the like purpose, subject to the right of the farmers to claim at any time an equal quantity of corn of the like quality, without reference to any specific bulk from which it was to be taken, or in lieu thereof the market price of any equal quantity, on the day on which the demand was made. A fire occurred at the mill, destroying the stock in it. The miller's insurers disputed a claim for the amount of the loss, substantially *f* on the grounds that the corn belonged not to the miller, but to the farmers, being the subject of a mere bailment. The Privy Council rejected the insurers' submission, on the grounds that where there is a delivery of property on a contract for an equivalent in money, or some other valuable commodity, and not for the return of the identical subject-matter in its original form or an altered form, this is a sale and not a bailment. The Board, having in its judgment cited the passage from the speech of Lord Cottenham *g* LC in *Foley v Hill*[1] already cited in this present judgment, continued as follows[3]:

> 'An indelible incident of trust property is that a Trustee can never make use of it for his own benefit. An incident of property, that is in bailment, is that the Bailor may require its restoration. This right of recalling the deposit is relied on by Lord *Cottenham*, as a test to try the principle on which the fiduciary relation was sought *h* to be maintained. But in this case, no right seems to exist on the part of the Depositor to get back either his identical wheat, or a share of the specific bulk in which his wheat was mixed with his consent; there is no such right on the one side, while, on the other, there is the power in the Miller of doing what he liked with the wheat after it became part of his current stock. This is an inverted order of right

j

---

1   (1848) 2 HL Cas 28 at 36–37, [1843–60] All ER Rep 16 at 19
2   (1869) LR 3 PC 101
3   LR 3 PC 101 at 110

that is wholly inconsistent with the relation of Trustee and *cestui que trust* that is contended for in this case.'

A similar principle, relating to the case of money, was stated by Channell J in *Henry v Hammond*[1] as follows:

'It is clear that if the terms upon which the person receives the money are that he is bound to keep it separate, either in a bank or elsewhere, and to hand that money to be so kept as a separate fund to the person entitled to it, then he is a trustee of that money and must hand it over to the person who is his cestui que trust. If on the other hand he is not bound to keep the money separate, but is entitled to mix it with his own money and deal with it as he pleases, and when called upon to hand over an equivalent sum of money, then, in my opinion, he is not a trustee of the money, but merely a debtor.'

Subject to the recent decision of the Court of Appeal in the *Romalpa* case[2], these four last-mentioned authorities seem to me clear authority for the proposition that, where an alleged trustee has the right to mix tangible assets or moneys with his own other assets or moneys and to deal with them as he pleases, this is incompatible with the existence of a *presently* subsisting fiduciary relationship in regard to such particular assets or moneys. It is, however, necessary to consider whether any qualification needs to be placed on that proposition in the light of the *Romalpa* case[2], the facts of which are as follows.

Between September 1973 and 1974, the plaintiffs ('AIV') had sold to the defendant company aluminium foil, some of which the defendant resold to third parties. Clause 13 of the plaintiffs' general selling terms and conditions substantially contained two limbs. The first limb, which embodied a provision for reservation of title in respect of the original material delivered, was in the following form[3]:

'The ownership of the material to be delivered by A.I.V. will only be transferred to purchaser when he has met all that is owing to A.I.V., no matter on what grounds. Until the date of payment, purchaser, if A.I.V. so desires, is required to store this material in such a way that it is clearly the property of A.I.V.'

The second limb of the clause read as follows[3]:

'A.I.V. and purchaser agree that, if purchaser should make (a) new object(s) from the material, mixes this material with (an) other object(s) or if this material in any way whatsoever becomes a constituent of (an) other object(s) A.I.V. will be given the ownership of this (these) new object(s) as surety of the full payment of what purchaser owes A.I.V. To this end A.I.V. and purchaser now agree that the ownership of the article(s) in question, whether finished or not, are to be transferred to A.I.V. and that this transfer of ownership will be considered to have taken place through and at the moment of the single operation or event by which the material is converted into (a) new object(s), or is mixed with or becomes a constituent of (an) other object(s). Until the moment of full payment of what purchaser owes A.I.V. purchaser shall keep the object(s) in question for A.I.V. in his capacity of fiduciary owner and, if required, shall store this (these) object(s) in such a way that it (they) can be recognized as such. Nevertheless, purchaser will be entitled to sell these objects to a third party within the framework of the normal carrying on of his business and to deliver them on condition that—if A.I.V. so requires—purchaser, as long as he has not fully discharged his debt to A.I.V. shall hand over to A.I.V. the claims he has against his buyer emanating from this transaction.'

1　[1913] 2 KB 515 at 521
2　[1976] 2 All ER 552, [1976] 1 WLR 676
3　[1976] 2 All ER 552 at 554, [1976] 1 WLR 676 at 679

On 1st November 1974, by which time the defendant was in financial difficulties, a
receiver of its assets was appointed. At that date it owed the plaintiffs £122,239. After *a*
his appointment the receiver certified that a certain quantity of aluminium foil was
actually held by him which had originated in deliveries to the defendant by the plaintiffs
and that £35,152 was held in an account in his name, which represented the proceeds of
sale of aluminium foil supplied by the plaintiffs to the defendant and then sold by the
latter to third parties. The plaintiffs sought a declaration that this latter quantity of foil
was theirs and an order for its delivery up. They further sought a declaration that they *b*
had a charge to the extent of £35,152 on the moneys in the receiver's account, basing
their claim on a right to trace, on the principle established in *Re Hallett's Estate*[1]. Mocatta
J granted the plaintiffs these two forms of relief. On appeal, the first question that fell to
be decided was whether Mocatta J had been right in deciding that cl 13 of the plaintiffs'
general selling terms and conditions applied to the relevant contracts of sale. The Court
of Appeal held that he was. From this it necessarily followed that the plaintiffs were *c*
entitled to recover the relevant foil still in the receiver's hands and that the appeal under
this head failed. The court then proceeded to consider whether the plaintiffs were
entitled to trace and recover the £35,152 standing in the receiver's account, on the basis
of the principle laid down by Jessel MR in *Hallett's* case[1].

In this context, Roskill LJ[2] said that the 'critical question' was whether there was a
fiduciary relationship between the plaintiffs and the defendant which entitled the *d*
plaintiffs so to claim this sum. The defendant had denied that there was such a
relationship, submitting that the bargain between them did no more than create the
ordinary contractual relationship of buyer and seller, which left the sellers with their
ordinary contractual remedy, as unsecured creditors, but no additional proprietary
remedy.

It is clear from the judgments that the Court of Appeal regarded the answer to this *e*
submission as turning on the nature and extent of the defendant's right to sell the
unmanufactured foil in its possession during the period before it had been fully paid
for. It was common ground that a power of sale during the period that any money
remained owing to the plaintiffs had to be implied in the first part of cl 13; the question
was on what terms. The defendant contended that there ought to be implied an
unfettered power to sell and apply the proceeds of sale for its own purposes. The *f*
plaintiffs contended that there ought solely to be implied a limited power, entitling the
defendant to sell only on the footing that it would hold the proceeds of sale in trust for
them until all the defendant's indebtedness to them on any contract was discharged. The
Court of Appeal preferred the latter argument. It regarded the obvious purpose of the
first limb of cl 13 as being to give the requisite security to the plaintiffs and this purpose
could only be achieved by implying into the first limb of the clause not only the power *g*
to sell but also the power to account for the proceeds of sale. It followed that there was
a sufficient fiduciary relationship between the parties to enable this obligation to be
enforced (see per Roskill LJ, per Goff LJ and per Megaw LJ[3]).

All three judgments seem to have accepted that there was no conceptual difficulty in
the proposition that, as between itself and its sub-purchasers, the defendant sold as
principal, but that as between itself and the plaintiffs, those goods which it was selling *h*
within its implied authority from the plaintiffs were the plaintiffs' goods, which it was
selling as agent for the plaintiffs, to whom it remained fully accountable. Roskill LJ
expressly said so and continued[4]:

'If an agent lawfully sells his principal's goods, he stands in a fiduciary relationship
to his principal and remains accountable to his principal for those goods and their
                                                                                        j

1 (1880) 13 Ch D 696, [1874–80] All ER Rep 793
2 [1976] 2 All ER 552 at 561, [1976] 1 WLR 676 at 687
3 [1976] 2 All ER 552 at 564, 566, 566, [1976] 1 WLR 676 at 690, 692–693, 694
4 [1976] 2 All ER 552 at 563–564, [1976] 1 WLR 676 at 690

proceeds. A bailee is in like position in relation to his bailor's goods. What, then,
a   is there here to relieve the defendants from their obligation to account to the
plaintiffs for those goods of the plaintiffs which they lawfully sell to sub-
purchasers? The fact that they so sold them as principals does not, as I think, affect
their relationship with the plaintiffs; nor, as at present advised, do I think—contrary
to argument of counsel for the defendant—that the sub-purchasers could on this
analysis have sued the plaintiffs on the sub-contracts as undisclosed principals for,
b   say, breach of warranty of quality.'

The facts of the *Romalpa* case[1] have this much in common with those of the present
case: in each instance the relevant clause, by necessary implication, left the purchaser at
liberty both to sell the relevant goods and to use them unrestrictedly for the purposes of
manufacture, at least in the ordinary course of business. For the purposes of my present
decision, therefore, it is perhaps unfortunate that the decisions in *Re Nevill, ex parte*
c   *White*[2], *Foley v Hill*[3] and *Randell's* case[4] do not appear to have been cited in argument
before either court in the *Romalpa* case[1]. If they had been cited, the judgments of those
courts would no doubt have explained specifically why the principles exemplified in
these three earlier decisions presented no obstacle to the crucial conclusion that at all
material times, up to and including sale, a presently subsisting fiduciary relationship
existed between vendor and purchaser in regard to the goods or their proceeds.
d   The reasons for this conclusion, however, are not in my judgment hard to seek. In the
Romalpa case[1], unlike the present, the full legal ownership of the material sold was
expressly reserved by the relevant clause to the vendors, until the purchasers had paid all
that was owing to the vendors. In these circumstances the court was not prevented (as
it would be prevented in the present case) from finding a bailor–bailee relationship
between the parties by any previous finding that the property in the goods had passed to
e   the purchasers. In fact, as had already been stated, the defendants in the *Romalpa* case[1]
expressly admitted that the clause had the effect of making it a bailee of the goods, while
in its possession, until all money owing had been paid. This was a concession of crucial
importance, the like of which has not of course been made here; it may well have been
influenced by the fact that in that case the relevant clause placed the purchaser under an
express obligation to store the material, if so required by the plaintiffs, in such a way that
f   it was clearly the plaintiffs' property. Similarly, it was there expressly agreed that, if the
purchaser should make new objects from the material or mix it with other objects or it
should become a constituent part of new objects, the purchaser should, if required, store
such objects in such a way that they could be recognised as such. Furthermore, there was
in that case no difficulty in ascertaining the moneys (if any) in respect of which the
defendant was liable to account. The receiver received the relevant moneys after he had
g   entered into his receivership from sales made by the defendant to sub-purchasers before
that date. He duly kept them separate and they never became mixed with other moneys
(see per Roskill LJ[5]). Further light as to the intentions of the parties was thrown in that
case by the second limb of the relevant clause, which expressly described the purchaser
as keeping the objects there referred to 'in his capacity of fiduciary owner' until the
moment of full payment.
h   In the face of the many special features of the *Romalpa* case[1] to which I have referred
but which are not present in the case before me, it is scarcely surprising, if I may

j
1   [1976] 2 All ER 552, [1976] 1 WLR 676
2   (1871) LR 6 Ch App 397
3   (1848) 2 HL Cas 28, [1843–60] All ER Rep 16
4   (1869) LR 3 PC 101
5   [1976] 2 All ER 552 at 561, [1976] 1 WLR 676 at 687

respectfully say so, that the courts in that case found little difficulty in importing to the
first part of the relevant clause 'not only the power to sell but also the obligation to *a*
account in accordance with the normal fiduciary relationship of principal and agent,
bailor and bailee' (see per Roskill LJ[1]).

However, as Goff LJ commented, the part of the *Romalpa* case[2] now under discussion
ultimately resolved itself to a short question of construction of the relevant clause. In the
end, I think, the decision only provides very limited assistance or guidance on the facts
of the present case.   *b*

It was, however, recently followed by his Honour Judge Rubin QC in *Borden (UK) Ltd*
v Scottish Timber Products Ltd[3]. In that case the plaintiff ('Borden') had supplied resin
to the first defendant, the purchaser, on standard conditions which stated, inter alia:

> 'Property in goods supplied hereunder will pass to the customer when: (a) the
> goods the subject of the contract; and (b) all other goods the subject of any other
> contract between the Company and the customer which, at the time of payment of *c*
> the full price of the goods sold under the contract, have been delivered to the
> customer but not paid for in full, have been paid for in full.'

The judge considered that on the facts it was essential to imply into the contract of sale
a licence to use the resin in the usual course of manufacture before it was paid for. Resin
was delivered to the purchaser under conditions containing this provision between 14th *d*
February 1977 and the subsequent date when the second defendant was appointed
receiver, but not all of it had been paid for. Three issues fell to be decided. The first was
whether Borden had any proprietary interest at common law in any chipboard
manufactured by the purchaser, using resin supplied by Borden. This question was
answered in the negative and has no relevance here. The second issue was what right (if
any) Borden had to trace its resin into the proceeds of sale of the manufactured goods. *e*
Judge Rubin held that the purchaser received the resin (which under the clause remained
the property of Borden) as bailee for Borden and that for this reason a fiduciary
relationship was created. Following the reasoning of the *Romalpa* decision[4], he held that,
once it was accepted that initially the purchaser received resin as a bailee and that a
fiduciary relationship arose, then the tracing remedies illustrated by *Hallett's* case[5] must
apply, unless there was to be implied into the contract not only the power in the *f*
purchaser to use the resin in manufacture, but also a further power to hold any goods so
manufactured to its own account. He rejected its contention that the use of the resin in
the process of manufacture put an end to the right to trace, as being inconsistent with the
Hallett[5] principle as applied in the *Romalpa* case[4], and held that Borden was entitled to
trace its resin into chipboard manufactured therefrom or into the proceeds of sale
thereof, to the extent of the contract price of the resin. Thirdly, Judge Rubin held that *g*
the right to trace given by *Hallett's* case[5] was not a charge falling within s 95 of the
Companies Act 1948 and that, even if it were, it was not created by the company, so that
it was not void against the company's creditors for lack of registration.

An interesting feature of the *Borden*[3] decision is that it extended the reasoning of the
Romalpa[4] decision not only to goods which were resold by the defaulting purchaser, but
also to goods which had been mixed with other goods to produce a new product. In this *h*

---

1 [1976] 2 All ER 552 at 564, [1976] 1 WLR 676 at 690   *j*
2 [1976] 2 All ER 552 at 565, [1976] 1 WLR 676 at 691
3 [1978] The Times, 15th November. Subsequent to the decision reported herein *Borden's* case was
   reversed by the Court of Appeal: see p 961, post
4 [1976] 2 All ER 552, [1976] 1 WLR 676
5 (1880) 13 Ch D 696, [1874–80] All ER Rep 793

sense, therefore, the facts were closer to those of the present case than those of the

a Romalpa case[1]. Furthermore, the tracing remedy was afforded, even though both parties had implicitly agreed that the goods would be so used at the time when the contract was made. The effect of the decision was to take that part of the proceeds of sale of the purchaser's products which represented the value of the goods outside the reach of the general body of the purchaser's creditors.

In my judgment, however, the facts of the *Borden* case[2], like those of the *Romalpa* case[1]

b itself, are distinguishable from those of the present in at least three crucial respects. First, there the relevant clause had the effect that neither the legal property in the goods nor any part of the beneficial ownership therein passed to the purchaser until full payment of the purchase price. Secondly, and as a result, the existence of a bailor–bailee relationship was legally possible and was expressly found or admitted; the whole of Judge Rubin's judgment was clearly founded on the essential premise of such relationship.

c Thirdly, in the *Borden* case[2], in contrast with the present, the possibility did not exist that the purchaser (to whom the legal property had never passed) held the goods either as bare trustee for the vendor or as trustee for the purpose of giving effect to a charge in favour of the vendor.

It follows that the *Romalpa*[1] and *Borden*[2] decisions themselves provide no answer to the attack made on the validity of the retention of title clause in the present case by reference

d to *Re Nevill, ex parte White*[3], *Foley v Hill*[4], *Randell's* case[5] and *Henry v Hammond*[6]. In my judgment, there can be no answer to this attack in so far as it relates to the particular interpretation of the retention of title clause, which counsel for Monsanto has invited me to adopt. The implicit authority and freedom of Bond Worth to employ the relevant raw materials, products and other moneys as it pleased and for its own purposes during the subsistence of the operation of the retention of title clause were in my judgment quite incompatible with the existence of a relationship of Bond Worth as trustee and Monsanto

e as beneficiary solely and absolutely entitled to such assets, which is the relationship asserted.

I have, however, already indicated that this is not my own view of the effect (if any) of the retention of title clause when properly construed, but that such effect (if any) is a declaration of trust by Bond Worth in respect of the relevant assets by way of equitable

f charge to secure repayment of the moneys from time to time owing in respect of the relevant order. Does the authority and freedom of Bond Worth, to which I have last referred, by itself negative the existence of a valid trust by way of equitable charge? In my judgment, in so far as it might be suggested that the clause operated to create in this manner an immediate *specific* charge, the answer to this question must be Yes. It is in my judgment quite incompatible with the existence of an effective trust by way of specific charge in equity over specific assets that the alleged trustee should be free to use them as

g he pleases for his own benefit in the course of his own business.

There is, however, one type of charge (and I think one type only) which, by its very nature, leaves a company at liberty to deal with the assets charged in the ordinary course of its business, without regard to the charge, until stopped by a winding-up or by the appointment of a receiver or the happening of some other agreed event. I refer to what

h is commonly known as a 'floating charge' (see for example *Wheatley v Silkstone & Haigh*

j 1 [1976] 2 All ER 552, [1976] 1 WLR 676
2 [1978] The Times, 15th November; since reversed; see p 961, post
3 (1871) LR 6 Ch App 397
4 (1848) 2 HL Cas 28, [1843–60] All ER Rep 16
5 (1869) LR 3 PC 101
6 [1913] 2 KB 515

Moor Coal Co[1] per North J and *George Barker Ltd v Eynon*[2] per Edmund Davies LJ). Such a charge remains unattached to any particular property and leaves the company with a ***a*** licence to deal with, and even sell, the assets falling within its ambit in the ordinary course of business, as if the charge had not been given, until it is stopped by one or other of the events to which I have referred, when it is said to 'crystallise'; it then becomes effectively fixed to the assets within its scope.

Romer LJ in *Re Yorkshire Woolcombers' Association Ltd*[3] gave the following description of a floating charge: ***b***

'I certainly do not intend to attempt to give an exact definition of the term "floating charge", nor am I prepared to say that there will not be a floating charge within the meaning of the [Companies Act 1900], which does not contain all of the three characteristics that I am about to mention, but I certainly think that if a charge has the three characteristics that I am about to mention, it is a floating charge. (1.) If it is a charge on a class of assets of a company present and future; (2.) if that class is ***c*** one which, in the ordinary course of the business of the company, would be changing from time to time; and (3.) if you find that by the charge it is contemplated that, until some future step is taken by or on behalf of those interested in the charge, the company may carry on its business in the ordinary way as far as concerns the particular class of assets I am dealing with.'
d
This description of a floating charge shows that it need not extend to all the assets of the company. It may cover assets merely of a specified category or categories. The third characteristic mentioned by Romer LJ is clearly present in relation to each of the four categories of charged assets in the present case; it was clearly contemplated that until some future step was taken by or on behalf of Monsanto, Bond Worth might carry on its business in the ordinary way in relation to each of these four categories. The second ***e*** characteristic mentioned by him is likewise clearly present at least in relation to each of the second, third and fourth categories of charged assets; these are ex hypothesi classes of assets which in the ordinary course of business will be changing from time to time.

This much could be said against the existence of floating charges in the present case. As regards the first characteristic mentioned by Romer LJ, the charge on the first category of charged assets is exclusively a charge on present assets of the company, while ***f*** the charges on the other three categories of charged assets are exclusively charges on future assets of the company. If the charges are looked at separately, they do not comprise classes of mixed present and future assets. Furthermore, the second characteristic mentioned by him is present in relation to the first category of charged assets (the raw fibre) only in the sense that the assets comprised in this category may diminish by being used for the purposes of manufacture or sale; they cannot be ***g*** increased. I do not, however, think that these points of possible distinction prevent all or any of the four relevant charges from being floating charges within the ordinary meaning of legal terminology. Romer LJ himself disclaimed any intention of saying that there could not be a floating charge within the meaning of the Companies Acts which did not contain all the three characteristics that he mentioned.

The critical distinction in my judgment is that between a specific charge on the one ***h*** hand and a floating charge on the other. Vaughan Williams LJ pointed out in the *Yorkshire Woolcombers'* case[4] that it is quite inconsistent with the nature of a specific charge, though not of a floating charge, that the mortgagor is at liberty to deal with the relevant property as he pleases. He said:

'I do not think that for a "specific security" you need have a security of a subject- ·
matter which is then in existence. I mean by "then" at the time of the execution of ***j***

1　(1885) 29 Ch D 715 at 723–724
2　[1974] 1 All ER 900 at 905, [1974] 1 WLR 462 at 467
3　[1903] 2 Ch 284 at 295
4　[1903] 2 Ch 284 at 294

a
the security; but what you do require to make a specific security is that the security, whenever it has once come into existence, and been identified or appropriated as a security, shall never thereafter at the will of the mortgagor cease to be a security. If at the will of the mortgagor, he can dispose of it and prevent its being any longer a security, although something else may be substituted more or less for it, that is not a "specific security".'

b
When that case went on appeal to the House of Lords, under the name *Illingworth v Houldsworth*[1], Lord Macnaghten drew the distinction between a specific charge and a floating charge in the following terms[2]:

c
'A specific charge, I think, is one that without more fastens on ascertained and definite property or property capable of being ascertained and defined; a floating charge, on the other hand, is ambulatory and shifting in its nature, hovering over and so to speak floating with the property which it is intended to affect until some event occurs or some act is done which causes it to settle and fasten on the subject of the charge within its reach and grasp.'

d
In the present case, in my judgment, the respective charges on each of the four categories of charged assets were ambulatory and shifting in their nature, and were intended to hover over them until the happening of an event which caused them to crystallise. The assets comprised in each of the four categories were of a fluctuating class, albeit in the case of the first category liable to fluctuate only by diminution. Until a crystallising event occurred, it was clearly not intended that any restriction should be placed on Bond Worth to deal with them in the ordinary course of its business.

e
Accordingly in the end I answer question (c) above by saying that in my judgment the effect of the retention of title clause was to create floating equitable charges over the four categories of charged assets, for the purpose of securing payment of the purchase prices due under the relevant orders, and to constitute Bond Worth a trustee of such assets for the purpose of such security, but for no other purpose. The mere likelihood that evidentiary difficulties would in the event have presented Monsanto with formidable, if not insuperable, obstacles in obtaining effective remedies by way of enforcement of such charges did not, in my judgment, render them void ab initio. Nor in my judgment were

f
they rendered void ab initio by the somewhat misleading and inadequate form of their drafting, which purported to disguise what was in essence a floating charge as a bare trust and failed to specify either the rights of the chargee or the events which would cause the charge to crystallise. I can, however, see no footing on which Monsanto can have obtained, by virtue of the clause, proprietary rights of a nature known to the law, save by way of equitable floating charge.

g

Question (d)
I now turn to consider whether the charges created under the retention of title clause were registrable under s 95 of the Companies Act 1948. Section 95(1), so far as material for present purposes, provides:

h
'Subject to the provisions of this Part of this Act, every charge created after the fixed date by a company registered in England and being a charge to which this section applies shall, so far as any security on the company's property or undertaking is conferred thereby, be void against the liquidator and any creditor of the company, unless the prescribed particulars of the charge together with the instrument, if any, by which the charge is created or evidenced, are delivered to or received by the

j
registrar of companies for registration in manner required by this Act within twenty-one days after the date of its creation . . .'

1   [1904] AC 355
2   [1904] AC 355 at 358

It is common ground that particulars of the relevant contracts have never been delivered to the registrar of companies for registration under the section and accordingly that if, contrary to Monsanto's submission, the rights (if any) conferred on Monsanto by the retention of title clause constituted 'charges' which were 'created by' Bond Worth, in each case within the meaning of s 95(1), such charges must be void against the bank and Alliance and any other creditors of Bond Worth.

Section 95(2) then lists in nine separate paragraphs the charges to which the section applies. Only three of these paragraphs have been referred to in the course of argument, these three being as follows:

> '. . . (c) a charge created or evidenced by an instrument which, if executed by an individual, would require registration as a bill of sale . . . (e) a charge on book debts of the company; (f) a floating charge on the undertaking or property of the company . . .'

Section 95(10) defines the expression 'the fixed date' as meaning, in relation to the charges specified in paras (a) to (f) inclusive of sub-s (2), 1st July 1908. It also defines the word 'charge' as including mortgage.

As the wording of s 95(1) itself indicates, two conditions have to be satisfied if the subsection is to apply in a particular case. First, the charge must be a charge to which s 95 applies. Pausing at this point, it is common ground that s 95(2) contains an exhaustive list of the categories of charge to which s 95 applies. Secondly, the relevant charge must be one that was 'created' by the company.

In the context of s 95 two principal questions have thus fallen to be argued. (1) Did the relevant charge or charges in the present case fall within any of the categories specified in s 95(2)? (2) If so, were they 'created' by Bond Worth?

As to the first of these two questions, it has been submitted in opposition to Monsanto that the charge or charges arising as a result of the retention of title clause fell within one or more of paras (c), (e) and (f) of s 95(2). I need not consider the arguments which have been presented in relation to paras (c) and (e), because it follows more or less inevitably from my earlier conclusions that each of the respective charges, on all four categories of charged assets, was in my judgment a 'floating charge on . . . property of the company' within the meaning of s 95(2)(f). The judgment of Romer LJ in the Yorkshire Woolcombers' case[1], which concerned the meaning of the equivalent words 'floating charge on the undertaking or property of the company' contained in s 14(1)(d) of the Companies Act 1900 shows that a charge may fall within the statutory definition, even though it does not comprise the entire undertaking and property of the company. It also shows that in considering whether a charge is a floating charge within the statutory definition the court must deal with it as a question of substance to be answered according to the particular facts of the case. Approaching the matter in this way, I am driven to the conclusion that all the relevant charges are floating charges on property of Bond Worth within the statutory definition.

It remains to be considered whether such charges were 'created' by Bond Worth within the meaning of s 95(1) of the 1948 Act. It was submitted on behalf of Monsanto that, even if, contrary to its primary submission, charges had been created by virtue of the retention of title clause, they were 'created' by Monsanto rather than Bond Worth. It was accordingly submitted that on this footing the case would fall within s 97(1), rather than s 95(1), of that Act. Section 97(1), omitting an immaterial proviso, is in the following terms:

> 'Where a company registered in England acquires any property which is subject to a charge of any such kind as would, if it had been created by the company after the acquisition of the property, have been required to be registered under this Part of this Act, the company shall cause the prescribed particulars of the charge, together

---

1   [1903] 2 Ch 284 at 294–295

a with a copy (certified in the prescribed manner to be a correct copy) of the instrument, if any, by which the charge was created or is evidenced, to be delivered to the registrar of companies for registration in manner required by this Act within twenty-one days after the date on which the acquisition is completed . . .'

Though s 97 contains provisions for fines, if default is made in complying with it, it (unlike s 95) contains no provision for invalidating an unregistered charge as against the liquidator or creditors of the company. It was submitted on behalf of Monsanto that, if *b* charges existed at all, Bond Worth had 'acquired' the raw Acrilan 'subject to' such charges within the meaning of s 97(1) and that s 95(1) had no application.

There was interesting argument as to the relationship between the two subsections, by reference to such cases as *Re Connolly Brothers Ltd (No 2)*[1], *Capital Finance Co Ltd v Stokes*[2] and *Security Trust Co v Royal Bank of Canada*[3]. Difficult questions might have arisen as to the interrelation between the two subsections, if I had accepted Monsanto's submission *c* that its charge (if any) over the raw Acrilan arose merely because such interest had been excepted from the grant made by it, in favour of Bond Worth, and that Bond Worth had merely acquired an equity of redemption. The phrase 'which is subject to a charge' appearing in s 97(1) at first sight appears apt to refer only to a charge already in existence before the relevant acquisition, and accordingly not to a charge created simultaneously with such acquisition. This appears to have been the view of the Privy Council in *d* *Security Trust Co v Royal Bank of Canada*[3]. Accordingly, if Monsanto's last-mentioned submission had been correct, it might well have followed that the relevant charges were registrable neither under s 95(1) (because it could not have been said that they had been created by Bond Worth) nor under s 97(1).

However, I need pursue these matters no further. Having held that the relevant charges arose by way of grant back by Bond Worth in favour of Monsanto, I think it must *e* follow that they were 'created' by Bond Worth for the purpose of s 95. This case is distinguishable from the *Romalpa* case[4] in this present context. Notwithstanding the provision for assignment of certain book debts in the relevant clause in that case, Mocatta J[5] in the court of first instance held briefly that s 95(1) had no application, because the property in the foil never passed to the defendants, with the result that the proceeds of the sub-sales belonged in equity to the plaintiffs. The point was not even *f* touched on in the judgments in the Court of Appeal. I do not therefore think that the decision is of any help in the present context, where, in my view, it cannot on any footing be said that the relevant Acrilan or other products or book debts belonged wholly in equity to Monsanto. The *Borden*[6] decision is likewise of no assistance, because the charge which Judge Rubin there held not to be registrable was simply the charge afforded by the court by way of equitable remedy and not a charge created by express agreement of the *g* parties. There is authority for the proposition that a charge which arises merely by operation of law is not registrable under s 95 (see e g *London and Cheshire Insurance Co Ltd v Laplagrene Property Co Ltd*[7], a case relating to an unpaid vendor's lien). The latter decision may be contrasted with *Re Wallis & Simmonds (Builders) Ltd*[8], in which it was held that an equitable charge on land arising from a deposit of title deeds, although created as a result of a presumption of law, was contractual in nature and was therefore *h* registrable under s 95.

Prescribed particulars of the relevant charges in the present case were never delivered

---

1 [1912] 2 Ch 25
2 [1968] 3 All ER 625, [1969] 1 Ch 261
j 3 [1976] 1 All ER 381, [1976] AC 503
4 [1976] 2 All ER 552, [1976] 1 WLR 676
5 [1976] 2 All ER 552 at 557, [1976] 1 WLR 676 at 683
6 [1978] The Times, 15th November; since reversed; see p 961, post
7 [1971] 1 All ER 766, [1971] Ch 499
8 [1974] 1 All ER 561, [1974] 1 WLR 391

to the registrar of companies in accordance with s 95(1). In my judgment, the charges must be void against any creditor of Bond Worth, but without prejudice to the contractual obligation of Bond Worth for repayment of the moneys thereby secured.   *a*

Questions (e), (f) and (g)

In the light of my answers to the earlier questions, questions (f) and (g) above do not arise and, as I understand the position, no answer to question (e) can be required, now that Monsanto is no longer concerned with the effect of the hive-down agreement. With one exception, therefore, I shall not prolong this judgment by making obiter observations   *b* on these remaining questions. There is a mass of factual documentary evidence, which would be relevant if they fell to be argued before a higher court, but it is all to be found in the affidavits and exhibits already in evidence, on which, as I have said, there has been no cross-examination.

I should, however, quite briefly, canvass question (f) above, relating to the remedies   *c* (if any) that would have been available to Monsanto, if it had succeeded on the earlier issues. For this could be thought to throw some light on my answer to question (c), relating to the essential nature of Monsanto's rights. Counsel for Monsanto submitted that, on the evidence, it was a reasonable inference that by far the greater part of the Acrilan actually in the hands of Bond Worth on 16th August 1977 represented material which had been supplied by Monsanto to Bond Worth after 1st July 1976, but before the   *d* appointment of a receiver on 16th August 1977. Nevertheless, he accepted that it is not possible to identify what Acrilan in the hands of Bond Worth on that last date represented such material. In other words, he accepted that the 'Acrilan' as defined by the summons is not and never now can be ascertainable. Accordingly, though he invited me to answer questions 1, 2 and 3 of the summons by making declarations in the sense most favourable to Monsanto, he accepted, by necessary inference, that these declarations would by   *e* themselves be rather barren relief so far as Monsanto was concerned.

In these circumstances, in reliance on such decisions as *Re Hallett's Estate*[1], *Re Diplock*[2] and *Sinclair v Brougham*[3], counsel for Monsanto sought a wide variety of further declarations of equitable charge (which he spelt out in detail) by way of tracing into specified categories of mixed assets now held or previously held by Bond Worth or by Glixcroft or by the successive receivers. He further gave notice that, if I were to decide   *f* in his favour on the earlier points, he would apply for an enquiry whether any proceeds of sale of Acrilan, as defined by the summons, were on 16th August 1977 comprised in moneys held on behalf of Bond Worth by any other companies in its group; an application which some other counsel intimated that they would probably oppose. Counsel for Monsanto further submitted that the receivers would be personally accountable to Monsanto in respect of any moneys received by them, over which   *g* Monsanto was, as at the date when they received them, entitled to the equitable charge so declared. He accepted that if declarations were made in the form requested, they might, as a matter of fact, comprise within their ambit moneys, raw Acrilan, yarn, carpets and other assets which on no possible footing could have been comprised within the ambit of the wording of the retention of title clause. He submitted, however, that right and remedy must not be confused and that, if the grant of such relief were the only   *h* way of vindicating Monsanto's proprietary rights, the court could and should grant relief of this nature.

Even if I had decided that the charges conferred on Monsanto by virtue of the retention of title clause were not registrable under s 95 of the Companies Act 1948, and therefore not as such void against creditors of Bond Worth, I would have felt great difficulty in granting any relief of the nature sought, for these reasons.   *j*

Monsanto has not submitted that Bond Worth did anything wrong or acted in any

1   (1880) 13 Ch D 696, [1874–80] All ER Rep 793
2   [1948] 2 All ER 318, [1948] Ch 465
3   [1914] AC 398, [1914–15] All ER Rep 622

breach of any duty to it in dealing with the assets comprised in the floating charges in the
_a manner in which it did deal with them before 16th August 1977, for example by mixing
the raw fibre with its other stocks of raw fibre, by converting the fibre into yarn and the
yarn into carpets, by mixing the carpets so made with other carpets and by paying
proceeds of sale of such carpets into its account with the bank, so as to reduce the amount
of its overdraft. (It was expressly accepted by counsel for Monsanto that all moneys paid
into Bond Worth's account with the bank were paid into an overdrawn account and had
_b the effect of simply extinguishing pro tanto Bond Worth's indebtedness to the bank.)

So long as a floating security has not crystallised, the company which has granted such
a security may in the ordinary course of business deal with the assets comprised in it as
if the security had not been granted, save only in so far as the conditions of the document
creating such security expressly prohibit such dealing. Any such unprohibited dealing
with a particular asset will bind the mortgagee as against the company and other persons
_c dealing with the company, provided only that the dealing is completed before the charge
ceases to be a floating charge; the reason is that the mortgage has given the company
licence to use all the property comprised in the charge for the purpose of its business until
the licence comes to an end on crystallisation (see, generally, *Evans v Rival Granite
Quarries Ltd*[1], particularly per Buckley LJ). In substance, therefore, the relief sought by
Monsanto in the present case amounts to a claim for relief to be granted as if the relevant
_d charges had prohibited Bond Worth from dealing with the assets comprised in them for
the general purposes of its business or alternatively as if Bond Worth had granted to
Monsanto a floating charge over *all* its stocks whatsoever of raw Acrilan, yarn, carpets and
book debts arising from carpet sales. These, however, were not rights or restrictions to
which Bond Worth ever agreed and I could see no sufficient grounds in equity for
dealing with the matter as if it had so agreed, particularly if this would operate to the
_e prejudice of other creditors of Bond Worth.

On these narrow grounds, if the point arose, I would not myself be disposed to grant
Monsanto the equitable relief by way of tracing which it seeks. I leave open a very
important wider question which has been substantially canvassed in argument before
me. This is the question whether it is ever open to an alleged beneficiary, by virtue of an
alleged beneficial interest or charge in equity, to seek remedies by way of declaration of
_f equitable charge on a mixed fund of assets, when he cannot affirmatively prove that this
particular fund contains or represents any of the assets affected by the trust and when his
claim is not founded on any alleged breach of trust which is said to have caused the assets,
in which his interest originally subsisted, to lose their identity.

Conclusions

_g At the end of his helpful final speech, counsel for Monsanto submitted that one of the
principal complaints against Monsanto had effectively been that the doctrine of reputed
ownership, which is applicable in bankruptcy, does not apply in the case of companies.
Under the Bankruptcy Acts, goods which are in the possession, order or disposition of a
bankrupt in his trade or business by the consent and permission of the true owner, under
such circumstances that he is the reputed owner thereof, vest in his trustee in bankruptcy
_h free from any third party rights. This doctrine would have been likely to apply to the
purchaser of the Acrilan in the present case if it had been an individual who had
subsequently gone bankrupt, but cannot apply to the corporate Bond Worth. Counsel
for Monsanto submitted that it would be wrong for the court to attempt to remedy this
possible gap in company law by ascribing to the retention of title clause some form of
registrable charge.

_j As will have appeared, however, I have viewed the matter rather differently. Quite
apart from the matter of registration, it has seemed to me clear that, if the retention of
title clause has operated to confer any rights in equity at all on Monsanto, such rights can

---

1   [1910] 2 KB 979 at 1000

only have been by way of equitable floating charge created by Bond Worth to secure
payment of the purchase price. It is, I think, a fair inference that the retention of title
clause was never intended to be invoked by Monsanto, unless and until Bond Worth *a*
proved to be in financial difficulties. Bond Worth would doubtless have declined to
agree to the creation of an immediate specific charge on the relevant assets, since such
charge would ex hypothesi have prevented it from dealing with them as absolute owner
in the ordinary course of its business. In all the circumstances of this case, if there be a
justifiable ground of complaint against Monsanto, I think it is that it has attempted to *b*
procure the creation in its own favour of what are in substance floating charges over
several classes of present and future assets in Bond Worth's possession and control,
without giving other creditors of the company the opportunity to acquire notice of such
charges by registration under s 95(1) of the Companies Act 1948.

Subject to any further submissions by counsel, I propose to answer question 1 of the
summons and every part thereof in the negative sense. I do not propose to answer
question 2. Though the Acrilan, as defined by the summons, is incapable of *c*
identification, this question would have required an answer if Monsanto had had an
enforceable charge. As things are, however, the question has become, I think, of solely
academic significance. I propose to answer question 3 of the summons and every part
thereof in the negative sense. In the light of my answers to the earlier questions,
questions 4 and 5 do not arise. I propose to answer question 6 and every part thereof in *d*
the negative sense.

Order accordingly.

Soliticors: *Markby's* (for the applicants, Carpets of Worth Ltd and Alliance Assurance Co
Ltd); *Samuel Tonkin & Co* (for Monsanto); *Stephenson Harwood* (for Mr Milnes); *Wilde Sapte* *e*
& Co (for National Westminster Bank Ltd).

Tokunbo Williams   Barrister.

Borden (UK) Ltd v Scottish Timber Products Ltd and another

COURT OF APPEAL, CIVIL DIVISION

BUCKLEY, BRIDGE AND TEMPLEMAN LJJ

4th, 5th, 6th, 9th, 10th JULY 1979

Sale of goods – Passing of property – Vendor retaining property in goods – Goods supplied on credit terms – Contract reserving property in goods to vendor after delivery – Property reserved to vendor until full payment made for goods and all other goods supplied – Vendor supplying resin used by buyers in manufacture of chipboard – Resin becoming inseparable component of chipboard – Purchaser becoming insolvent – Whether vendor having charge on chipboard manufactured from resin or on proceeds of sale of chipboard – Whether fiduciary relationship existing between vendor and purchaser – Whether vendor entitled to trace and recover debt from proceeds of sale of chipboard – Whether any charge arising would be void – Companies Act 1948, s 95.

The sellers supplied resin to the buyers on credit terms under a contract which provided that the property in goods supplied was to pass to the buyers when full payment had been made for those goods and all other goods supplied up to the date of payment. As the sellers well knew, the buyers used the resin as an ingredient in the manufacture of chipboard within two days of it being supplied, the resin thereafter becoming an inseparable component of the chipboard. The buyers became insolvent, and a compulsory winding-up order was made. The sellers, who were owed £318,321 and who would otherwise have been ordinary unsecured creditors, claimed against the receiver of the buyers that under the reservation of title clause any chipboard which had been manufactured using resin supplied by them was charged with the amount owing, and that they were entitled to trace their resin into any chipboard manufactured from it or the proceeds of sale of such chipboard. On the trial of a preliminary issue the judge held (i) that the reservation of title clause had the effect in law of charging any chipboard manufactured by the buyers to the extent that it consisted of resin supplied by the buyers with the amount owing to the sellers, (ii) that all moneys and other property representing any such chipboard were similarly charged, and (iii) that the charge resulting from the reservation of title condition was not one to which s 95ᵃ of the Companies Act 1948 had any application. The grounds on which the judge held that the sellers were entitled to a tracing remedy were that the buyers had received the resin as bailees and that the resulting fiduciary relationship entitled the sellers to trace. The buyers appealed.

Held – The appeal would be allowed for the following reasons—

(i) Once the buyers had used the resin in the manufacture of chipboard the resin ceased to exist as resin and there was nothing which the sellers could trace. The effect of the reservation of title clause in the contract was merely to reserve to the sellers the property in the resin so long as it remained unused; and on the resin's ceasing to exist when it was incorporated in the chipboard the seller's title to the resin also ceased to exist. Futhermore, there was no express agreement and no ground to imply an

---

a Section 95, so far as material, provides:

'(1) . . . every charge created . . . by a company registered in England and being a charge to which this section applies shall, so far as any security on the company's property or undertaking is conferred thereby, be void against the liquidator and any creditor of the company, unless the prescribed particulars of the charge together with the instrument, if any, by which the charge is created or evidenced, are delivered to or received by the registrar of companies for registration . . .

'(2) This section applies to the following charges . . . (c) a charge created or evidenced by an instrument which, if executed by an individual, would require registration as a bill of sale . . . (f) a floating charge on the undertaking or property of the company . . .'

agreement in the contract that the buyers were to provide substituted security for the resin used in the chipboard (see p 966 *a b*, p 968 *e f*, p 971 *e*, p 973 *a* to *c* and p 974 *a* to *h*, post).

(ii) In any event, there did not exist between the buyers and the sellers the necessary fiduciary relationship in regard to the chipboard to entitle the sellers to trace the resin supplied by them into the chipboard manufactured from it, or into the proceeds of sale of such chipboard, because the resin was supplied under a contract of sale and purchase by which the buyers received the resin for themselves as purchasers and were free to use it in the manufacture of chipboard. The buyers did not receive the resin in any fiduciary capacity or (per Bridge LJ) as bailees, since by delivering the resin knowing it would be used before it was paid for the sellers had no right to call for its return and it was never intended by the parties that it should be recovered in its original or its altered form (see p 965 *g h*, p 968 *f*, p 970 *e f*, p 972 *j* to p 973 *a* and p 974 *a*, post); dictum of Jessel MR in *Re Hallett's Estate, Knatchbull v Hallett* [1874–80] All ER Rep at 796–797 applied; *Aluminium Industrie Vaassen BV v Romalpa Aluminium Ltd* [1976] 2 All ER 552 distinguished.

(iii) (Per Buckley and Templeman LJJ) Even if the sellers had acquired an interest or share in the chipboard it would have been by way of an unregistered charge attached to the chipboard or the proceeds of sale thereof and as such void under s 95*a* of the 1948 Act as against the liquidator and other creditors for want of registration (see p 973 *d* to *g* and p 974 *h* to p 975 *b*, post).

Per Bridge LJ. Quaere whether a tracing remedy can ever apply where there has been a mixture of heterogeneous goods in a manufacturing process wherein the original goods lose their character and what emerges is a wholly new product. Quaere further, if the remedy were available in such cases, how the proportion of the value of the manufactured product which the tracer could claim as property attributable to his ingredient could be quantified (see p 970 *h* and p 971 *b*, post).

Notes

For the right to follow and recover assets or the money into which they have been converted, see 16 Halsbury's Laws (4th Edn) para 1460.

For the Companies Act 1948, s 95, see 5 Halsbury's Statutes (3rd Edn) 189.

Cases referred to in judgment

Aluminium Industrie Vaassen BV v Romalpa Aluminium Ltd [1976] 2 All ER 552, [1976] 1 WLR 676, [1976] Lloyd's Rep 443, CA.

Bond Worth Ltd, Re p 919, ante, [1979] 3 WLR 629.

Business Computers Ltd v Anglo-African Leasing Ltd [1977] 2 All ER 741, [1977] 1 WLR 578.

Hallett's Estate, Re, Knatchbull v Hallett (1880) 13 Ch D 696, [1874–80] All ER Rep 793, 49 LJ Ch 415, 42 LT 421, CA, 47 Digest (Repl) 537, 4854.

South Australian Insurance Co v Randell (1869) LR 3 PC 101, 6 Moo PCCNS 341, 22 LT 843, 16 ER 755, PC, 39 Digest (Repl) 447, 28.

Seymour v Brown (1821) 19 Johns 44.

Cases also cited

Diplock's Estate, Re, Diplock v Wintle [1948] 2 All ER 318, [1948] Ch 465, CA; *affd* sub nom *Ministry of Helath v Simpson* [1950] 2 All ER 1137, [1951] AC 251, HL.

Foley v Hill (1844) 1 Ph 399, 41 ER 683, HL.

Henry v Hammond [1913] 2 KB 515, DC.

Hussey v Palmer [1972] 3 All ER 744, [1972] 1 WLR 1286, CA.

London and Cheshire Insurance Co Ltd v Laplagrene Property Co Ltd [1971] 1 All ER 766, [1971] Ch 499.

Manley v Sartori [1927] 1 Ch 157, [1926] All ER Rep 661.

Tilley's Will Trusts, Re, Burgin v Croad [1967] 2 All ER 303, [1967] 2 Ch 1179.

Wallis & Simmonds (Builders) Ltd, Re [1974] 1 All ER 561, [1974] 1 WLR 391.

Appeal

a The defendants, Scottish Timber Products Ltd ('the buyers') and its receiver, William McNicol Brownlie, appealed against the decision of his Honour Judge Rubin QC, sitting as a judge of the High Court on 15th November 1978 on the trial of a preliminary issue that the plaintiffs, Borden (UK) Ltd ('the sellers'), were entitled to trace any resin supplied to the buyers after 14th February 1977 into any chipboard manufactured from the resin or into the proceeds of sale of such chipboard. The facts are set out in the judgment of
b Bridge LJ.

Richard Southwell QC and *Mark Potter* for the buyers and the Official Receiver.
W J Mowbray QC and *Charles Purle* for the sellers.

BRIDGE LJ delivered the first judgment at the invitation of Buckley LJ. This is an
c appeal from a judgment of his Honour Judge Rubin QC sitting as a judge of the Chancery Division, given on 15th November 1978 on the trial of certain preliminary issues of law pursuant to an order of Master Cholmondeley Clarke made on 6th July 1978. We have heard arguments on the essential points of the appeal at some length; that is no criticism whatever of counsel, as the arguments have been extremely helpful, but in my judgment the points that we have to decide are, in the end, really rather short
d ones and I hope it will not be thought that I am in any way being discourteous to counsel if I endeavour to deal with them shortly in this judgment.

For the purpose of the preliminary issues of law which were ordered to be tried, certain facts were agreed between the parties. So far as material to the only points remaining for decision by this court, the agreed facts can be very shortly stated.

The plaintiffs ('the sellers') are the manufacturers of a product called urea-formaldehyde
e chipboard resin. Over a period of some four years up to September 1977 they were the main, but not the exclusive, suppliers of that product to the first defendants ('the buyers') for use by the buyers in the manufacture of chipboard. The buyers had a storage capacity for the resin which they needed, which was only sufficient at most to keep them supplied for two days' production in their factory. Accordingly, when their factory was working in the ordinary way it was inevitable that the resin supply would be used in the
f manufacture within two days of delivery. This circumstance was well known to the sellers, and it is really essential to the main issue arising in this appeal that one should infer from those circumstances that the contract clearly permitted the use of the resin in the manufacturing process before it had been paid for, the resin being sold on credit terms.

In the course of the manufacturing process the resin was mixed with certain hardeners
g and wax emulsion, to form something which is referred to as a 'glue mix'. This process of mixture was essentially irreversible in the sense that, once mixed, the resin as such could no longer be recovered. The glue mix was then blended with various grades of wood chippings and finally pressed together to form the end product, the chipboard.

On 16th September 1977 a receiver and manager of the buyers' undertaking was appointed by debenture holders; the receiver is the second defendant in the
h proceedings. The buyers have subsequently gone into compulsory liquidation pursuant to an order made on 25th June 1979, and are now continuing to defend this action by leave of the Official Receiver as provisional liquidator.

The sellers claim that as at 16th September 1977, when the receiver was appointed, the sum of £318,321·27 net was due to them from the buyers for resin supplied since 1st June 1977. They further claim that since 14th February 1977 all sales of resin to the
j buyers have been made pursuant to an express contractual condition in the following terms:

> '2. RISK AND PROPERTY. Goods supplied by the company shall be at the purchaser's risk immediately on delivery to the purchaser or into custody on the purchaser's behalf (whichever is the sooner) and the purchaser should therefore be insured

accordingly. Property in goods supplied hereunder will pass to the customer when:
(a) the goods the subject of this contract; and (b) all other goods the subject of any
other contract between the Company and the customer which, at the time of
payment of the full price of the goods sold under this contract, have been delivered
to the customer but not paid for in full, have been paid for in full.'

There is an issue on the pleadings whether that was indeed an effective term of the
contract between the parties.

It is further pleaded by the sellers in their statement of claim, reading only so much as
is relevant to the issues which we now have to decide, that:

'In the premises . . . any chipboard . . . manufactured or fabricated with any of the
said resin [that is, the sellers' resin] . . . is charged [to the extent that it consists of any
of the said resin] with payment to the Plaintiff of £318,321·27 . . . further or
alternatively, all monies and other property representing any of the . . . chipboard
. . . or any of the proceeds of sale or other disposal thereof are charged to the extent
that they represent the said resin with the payment to the Plaintiff of £318,321·27.'

In the relief claimed in the statement of claim appropriate declarations are claimed,
pursuant to those pleaded rights.

Master Cholmondeley Clarke's order required the decision of the following points of
law, namely:

'(a) Whether upon the facts pleaded in the Amended Statement of Claim the
Condition pleaded in paragraph 5 thereof [that is the alleged condition 2 of the
contract] has the result in law [and here again I read only so much as is material to
the points we have to decide] . . . (ii) that any chipboard . . . is charged . . . [to the
extent that it consists of any of the said resin] with the payment to the Plaintiff of
£318,321·27; and/or (iii) that all monies and other property representing any of the
said . . . chipboard . . . or any of the proceeds of sale or other disposal thereof are
charged to the extent that they represent the said resin with the payment to the
Plaintiff of £318,321·27. (b) Whether any charge resulting from such Condition
was and is void by reason of Section 95 of the Companies Act 1948 . . .'

I should say that there was a further plea included in the sellers' statement of claim to
be entitled to the ownership, in part, of the chipboard. That also was the subject of one
of the questions of law raised as a preliminary issue; that was decided by the judge against
the sellers and no cross-appeal was raised with regard to that, so we may take it that it is
not in dispute that the title to the manufactured chipboard is the title of the buyers.

The judge answered questions (a) (ii) and (iii) affirmatively in favour of the sellers, and
question (b) negatively in favour of the sellers, the material part of the order being that:

'. . . THIS COURT DOTH DECLARE that the Plaintiffs are entitled to trace any of their
resin supplied after 14th February 1977 the title to which had not passed to the
Defendants Scottish Timber Products Limited under Clause 2 of the Plaintiffs'
standard conditions in the Pleadings mentioned into any chipboard manufactured
from such resin or into the proceeds of sale of such chipboard but so that the
Plaintiffs cannot recover a sum in excess of the contract price of such resin AND THIS
COURT DOTH DECLARE that the exercise of such a tracing remedy is not a charge
created by the company to which Section 95 of the Companies Act 1948 has any
application.'

It is common ground, I think, that that form of order, which purports to declare
finally the rights of the parties, would in any event require some modification, since
what the judge was called on to do was to decide preliminary issues of law on certain
assumptions of fact which had not yet been proved; but nothing turns on that.

The essence of the judge's reasoning in arriving at the conclusion that the sellers were
a entitled to a tracing remedy, which was the first issue for consideration, is stated in the
judgment in a few sentences. The judge said:

> 'It seemed to me clear from an early stage in the argument that the buyers
> received resin which remained the property of the sellers as a bailee for the sellers
> and accordingly a fiduciary relationship was created . . . The defendants argued that
> the tracing remedy does not extend where there is a use in manufacture to the
b > manufactured product and its proceeds of sale. In my judgment unless the fiduciary
> relationship was brought to an end by the use in manufacture, or it is possible to
> imply a further term into the contract that the buyers would be entitled to deal with
> the chipboard on its own account, there is no reason why the tracing remedy should
> not extend both to the chipboard and its proceeds of sale.'

c   In my judgment the first question which arises for our decision is whether there was
a fiduciary relationship here between the buyers and the sellers in the nature of the
relationship of bailee and bailor. As I have already said, it is common ground that the
buyers were at liberty to use the resin which had not been paid for in the manufacture
of chipboard, so that before the resin was paid for, the result was that it ceased to exist as
such. Is that consistent with the relationship of the parties being that of bailor and
d bailee?
    The judge, in deciding that question, did not, I think, have the advantage, as we have
had, of being referred to the decision of the Privy Council in *South Australian Insurance Co
v Randell*[1]. Sir Joseph Napier, giving the advice of the Board, said this:

> 'A bailment on trust implies, that there is reserved to the Bailor the right to claim
> a redelivery of the property deposited in bailment . . . The law seems to be concisely
e > and accurately stated by Sir William Jones in the passages cited by Mr. Mellish from
> his treatise on Bailments[2]. Wherever there is a delivery of property on a contract for
> an equivalent in money or some other valuable commodity, and not for the return
> of his identical subject matter in its original or an altered form, this is a transfer of
> property for value—it is a sale and not a bailment. Chancellor *Kent* in his
> Commentaries[3] where he refers to the case of *Seymour* v. *Brown*[4], of which he
f > disapproves in common with Mr. Justice *Story*, adopts the test, whether the identical
> subject mattet was to be restored either as it stood or in an altered form; or whether
> a different thing was to be given for it as an equivalent; for in the latter case it was
> a sale, and not a bailment. This is the true and settled doctrine according to his
> opinion.'

g   I can well appreciate that in the present circumstances, if the buyers repudiated the
contract, or became insolvent, before the resin had been paid for, the buyers might then
have become a bailee of any resin which at that time remained unused. But so long as
the business transacted between these parties continued in the ordinary way and resin
was delivered for use in the manufacturing process at a time before it could have been
paid for, in circumstances in which the sellers clearly had no right to call for its return or
h to object to its use in the manufacture of chipboard, and where it was never intended that
the resin should be recovered, either in its original or in its altered form at all, it seems
to me quite impossible to say that this was a contract of bailment. The contract was
essentially one of sale and purchase, subject only to the reservation of title clause,
whatever its effect may have been.
    Now what was the effect of that clause? Looked at in principle, and independently of
j authority, I find it difficult to see how the clause was apt to create any fiduciary

---

1   (1869) LR 3 PC 101 at 108–109
2   3rd Edn pp 64, 102
3   Kent's Commentaries on American Law (11th Edn), vol 2, § 589, p 781
4   (1821) 19 Johns 44

relationship. I am much attracted by the view which was canvassed in argument that the effect of condition 2 was such that the beneficial interest in the resin passed to the buyers, who were to be entirely free to use it for their own purposes in the manufacture of chipboard, and that all that was retained by the sellers was the bare legal title to the resin so long as the resin existed, held as security for the unpaid price of that resin and of any other resin which the sellers had supplied. But I am quite content to assume that this is wrong and to suppose that up to the moment when the resin was used in manufacture it was held by the buyers in trust for the sellers in the same sense in which a bailee or a factor or an agent holds goods in trust for his bailor or his principal. If that was the position, then there is no doubt that as soon as the resin was used in the manufacturing process it ceased to exist as resin, and accordingly the title to the resin simply disappeared. So much is accepted by counsel for the sellers.

The contract contains no express stipulation conferring on the sellers any rights over the chipboard and counsel for the sellers has repeatedly disclaimed any intention to argue for an implied term in the contract that any rights over the chipboard should be conferred on the sellers. He nevertheless argues that the tracing remedy arises from the mixture of the sellers' resin with the buyers' other materials in the manufacture of chipboard, so that an appropriate proportion of the chipboard now represents the sellers' security for moneys due to them as the unpaid price of all the resin delivered. In my judgment, the crux of the whole case is whether this argument can be sustained.

It is conceded that there is no previous authority which establishes that the tracing remedy can be exercised where there has been an admixture of the goods of A with the goods of B in such a way that they both lose their identity and result in the production of goods of an entirely different kind; but it is urged that the availability of such a remedy is supported by the application by analogy of principles derived from the decided cases.

The main authority relied on by the judge in reaching his conclusion, and by counsel in his argument for the sellers is the decision of this court in the case of *Aluminium Industrie Vaassen BV v Romalpa Aluminium Ltd*[1]. The plaintiffs in that case sold aluminium foil to the defendants. The defendants went into liquidation, owing the plaintiffs over £122,000 and the receiver certified that £35,152 was held in an account in his name with the defendants' bankers, representing the proceeds of sale of aluminium foil supplied by the plaintiffs, which the defendants had sold to third parties. The plaintiffs, who had a reservation of title clause in their conditions of sale, claimed to be entitled to trace the aluminium foil into the proceeds of sale, and that claim was upheld by Mocatta J at first instance and by this court on appeal. The particular condition of the contract which applied is set out in full in the judgment of Mocatta J[2]:

'The ownership of the material to be delivered by A.I.V. [ie the plaintiffs] will only be transferred to purchaser when he has met all that is owing to A.I.V., no matter on what grounds. Until the date of payment, purchaser, if A.I.V. so desires, is required to store this material in such a way that it is clearly the property of A.I.V. A.I.V. and purchaser agree that, if purchaser should make (a) new object(s) from the material, mixes this material with (an) other object(s) or if this material in any way whatsoever becomes a constituent of (an) other object(s) A.I.V. will be given the ownership of this (these) new objects(s) as surety of the full payment of what purchaser owes A.I.V. To this end A.I.V. and purchaser now agree that the ownership of the article(s) in question, whether finished or not, are to be transferred to A.I.V. and that this transfer of ownership will be considered to have taken place through and at the moment of the single operation or event by which the material is converted into (a) new object(s), or is mixed with or becomes a constituent of (an) other object(s). Until the moment of full payment of what purchaser owes A.I.V. purchaser shall keep the object(s) in question for A.I.V. in his capacity of fiduciary

1   [1976] 2 All ER 552, [1976] 1 WLR 676
2   [1976] 2 All ER 552 at 554, [1976] 1 WLR 676 at 679

a
owner and, if required, shall store this (these) object(s) in such a way that it (they) can be recognized as such. Nevertheless, purchaser will be entitled to sell these objects to a third party within the framework of the normal carrying on of his business and to deliver them on condition that—if A.I.V. so requires—purchaser, as long as he has not fully discharged his debt to A.I.V. shall hand over to A.I.V. the claims he has against his buyer emanating from this transaction.'

b
The condition is expressed in very curious language because it is a translation from the Dutch, which was the original language of the contract. Mocatta J held that that clause showed an intention to create a fiduciary relationship between the parties and that the plaintiffs were entitled to follow the proceeds of the sub-sales; he reached that conclusion in the application of the principles of the decision in *Re Hallett's Estate*[1].

In the Court of Appeal the essence of the reasoning of their Lordships can be collected from some quite short passages, first from the leading judgment of Roskill LJ where he

c
says[2]:

'The crucial facts to my mind are two: first, that the defendants were selling goods which the plaintiffs owned at all material times; and secondly, that cl 13 as a whole is obviously designed to protect the plaintiffs, in the event of later insolvency, against the consequences of having parted with possession of, though not with legal title to, these goods before payment was received, 75 days' credit being allowed.

d
When, therefore, one is considering what, if any, additional implication has to be made to the undoubted implied power of sale in the first part of cl 13, one must ask what, if any additional implication is necessary to make effective the obvious purpose of giving the requisite security to the plaintiffs? One is, I think, entitled to look at the second part of cl 13 to answer this; for it would be strange if the first part were to afford no relevant security when the second part is, as I think, elaborately

e
drawn to give such security in relation to manufactured or mixed goods. I see no difficulty in the contractual concept that, as between the defendants and their sub-purchasers, the defendants sold as principals, but that, as between themselves and the plaintiffs, those goods which they were selling as principals within their implied authority from the plaintiffs were the plaintiffs' goods which they were selling as agents for the plaintiffs to whom they remained fully accountable. If an agent

f
lawfully sells his principal's goods, he stands in a fiduciary relationship to his principal and remains accountable to his principal for those goods and their proceeds. A bailee is in like position in relation to his bailor's goods. What, then, is there here to relieve the defendants from their obligation to account to the plaintiffs for those goods of the plaintiffs which they lawfully sell to sub-purchasers?'

g
Then Roskill LJ went on, a little later[3]:

'It seems to me clear . . . that to give effect to what I regard as the obvious purpose of cl 13 one must imply into the first part of the clause not only the power to sell but also the obligation to account in accordance with the normal fiduciary relationship of principal and agent, bailor and bailee. Accordingly, like the judge I find no

h
difficulty in holding that the principles in *Re Hallett's Estate*[1] . . . are of immediate application, and I think that the plaintiffs are entitled to trace these proceeds of sale and to recover them, as the learned judge has held by his judgment.'

Goff LJ said[4]:

'In my judgment the second part of the case comes down to a short question of
j
construction. It is common ground that a power of sale during the period that any

1   (1880) 13 Ch D 696, [1874–80] All ER Rep 793
2   [1976] 2 All ER 552 at 563–564, [1976] 1 WLR 676 at 689–690
3   [1976] 2 All ER 552 at 564, [1976] 1 WLR 676 at 690
4   [1976] 2 All ER 552 at 565, [1976] 1 WLR 676 at 691

money remains owing to the plaintiffs must be implied; but the question is on what terms.'

Then, at the end of his judgment, he said[1]:

'In short, my conclusion is that the power of sale to be implied where none has been expressed must be so qualified as not to defeat the intention clearly shown by cl 13 as a whole, including the latter part, which only emphasises this. It follows that there was, as Roskill LJ says, a sufficient fiduciary relationship between the parties, and this is indeed expressly contemplated in the reference to a fiduciary owner in the second part of cl 13. The implied power must, therefore, in my judgment be a power to sell, not for the defendants' own account, but for the account of the plaintiffs unless and until all moneys owing be paid.'

Megaw LJ, still more succinctly, said[2]:

'The power of sale to be implied in the first part of cl 13, where none has been expressed, must be such as not to defeat the intention shown by cl 13. It is not a power to sell for the defendants' own account, but it is a power to sell for the account of the plaintiffs.'

It seems to me that there are certain very clear distinctions between that case and this. First, it was conceded throughout in that case that the defendants were bailees of the aluminium foil for the plaintiffs; secondly, on the facts on which the decision turned there had been no admixture of the foil with any other material; if there had been, it would have been covered by the express terms of the second part of condition 13, but all that was in issue was a claim to trace the foil into the proceeds of sale of the foil. Thirdly, the clause turned on the construction of the particular clause and on what was to be implied in the first part of the clause as to the terms on which the defendants were entitled to sell aluminium foil. Here, by contrast, first, as I have said, in my judgment there clearly was no bailment of the resin; secondly, there was an admixture of the goods of the sellers with other materials of the buyers, producing a wholly new substance. Thirdly, we are not here concerned with any sale of the resin; it is not suggested by either party that the terms of sale here contemplated that the buyers should be at liberty to sell the resin as such; all that was contemplated was that they should be at liberty to use it in their own process of manufacture.

But to my mind the most important distinction is that the essence of the decision in *Romalpa*[3] was that on the facts found or admitted Romalpa were selling the plaintiffs' material, the aluminium foil, as agents for the plaintiffs. It seems to me quite impossible to say here that in using the sellers' resin in their own manufacturing process to manufacture their own chipboard, the buyers could possibly be described as acting in any sense as agents for the sellers. I do not in any way question the correctness of the decision in the case of *Romalpa*[3], but for my own part I really do not find that it throws any significant light on the questions which we have to decide.

The only argument derived from the consideration of *Romalpa*[3] which is worthy of attention is that it is said here, as it was said in *Romalpa*[3], that the intention of the clause under consideration must have been to give the sellers an effective security as unpaid vendor for the purchase price of any resin, and their security would not be effective unless the tracing remedy claimed on behalf of the sellers is an effective remedy. For my part, I am wholly unimpressed by that argument. I accept that in stipulating for condition 2 in their conditions of sale, it was a pious hope on the part of the sellers that they were creating for themselves an effective security for the payment of any unpaid

---

1 [1976] 2 All ER 552 at 566, [1976] 1 WLR 676 at 693
2 [1976] 2 All ER 552 at 568, [1976] 1 WLR 676 at 694
3 [1976] 2 All ER 552, [1976] 1 WLR 676

a purchase price due to them at any time; but the mere fact that they hoped that that would be so and intended that it should be so, is quite insufficient to carry the day if the language they used in relation to the agreed facts and the legal relationship which they created, whatever it may have been, is insufficient to make their intention an effective one.

b I come to what, to my mind, is really the heart of the matter: can the tracing remedy here claimed be supported in the application by analogy of the well-known principles of tracing expounded so clearly in the judgment of Jessel MR *Re Hallett's Estate*[1]? Jessel MR said:

c 'The modern doctrine of Equity as regards property disposed of by persons in a fiduciary position is a very clear and well-established doctrine. You can, if the sale was rightful, take the proceeds of the sale, if you can identify them. If the sale was wrongful, you can still take the proceeds of the sale, in a sense adopting the sale for the purpose of taking the proceeds, if you can identify them. There is no distinction, therefore, between a rightful and a wrongful disposition of the property, so far as regards the right of the beneficial owner to follow the proceeds. But it very often happens that you cannot identify the proceeds. The proceeds may have been invested together with money belonging to the person in a fiduciary position, in a purchase. He may have bought land with it, for instance, or he may have bought chattels with it. Now, what is the position of the beneficial owner as regards such purchases? I will, first of all, take his position when the purchase is clearly made with what I will call, for shortness, the trust money, although it is not confined, as I will shew presently, to express trusts. In that case, according to the now well-established doctrine of Equity, the beneficial owner has a right to elect either to take the property purchased, or to hold it as a security for the amount of the trust money laid out in the purchase; or, as we generally express it, he is entitled at his election either to take the property, or to have a charge on the property for the amount of the trust money. But in the second case, where a trustee has mixed the money with his own, there is this distinction, that the *cestui que trust*, or beneficial owner, can no longer elect to take the property, because it is no longer bought with the trust-money simply and purely, but with a mixed fund. He is, however, still entitled to a charge on the property purchased, for the amount of the trust-money laid out in the purchase; and that charge is quite independent of the fact of the amount laid out by the trustee. The moment you get a substantial portion of it furnished by the trustee, using the word "trustee" in the sense I have mentioned, as including all persons in a fiduciary relation, the right to the charge follows. That is the modern doctrine of Equity. Has it ever been suggested, until very recently, that there is any distinction between an express trustee, or an agent, or a bailee, or a collector of rents, or anybody else in a fiduciary position? I have never heard, until quite recently, such a distinction suggested. It cannot, as far as I am aware (and since this Court sat last to hear this case, I have taken the trouble to look for authority), be found in any reported case even suggested, except in the recent decision[2] of Mr. Justice Fry, to which I shall draw attention presently. It can have no foundation in principle, because the beneficial ownership is the same, wherever the legal ownership may be. If you have goods bargained and sold to a man upon trust to sell and hand over the net proceeds to another, that other is the beneficial owner; but if instead of being bargained and sold, so as to vest the legal ownership in the trustee, they are deposited with him to sell as agent, so that the legal ownership remains in the beneficial owner, can it be supposed, in a Court of Equity, that the rights of the beneficial owner are different, he being entire beneficial owner in both cases? I say on principle it is impossible to imagine there can be any difference. In practice we know there is no difference, because the moment you get into a Court of Equity,

---

1   (1880) 13 Ch D 696 at 708–711, [1874–80] All ER Rep 793 at 796–797
2   *Re West of England and South Wales District Bank, ex parte Dale & Co* (1879) 11 Ch D 772

where a principal can sue an agent as well as a *cestui que trust* can sue a trustee, no
such distinction was ever suggested, as far as I am aware. Therefore, the moment *a*
you establish the fiduciary relation, the modern rules of Equity, as regards following
trust money, apply . . . Now that being the established doctrine of Equity on this
point, I will take the case of the pure bailee. If the bailee sells the goods bailed, the
bailor can in Equity follow the proceeds, and can follow the proceeds wherever they
can be distinguished, either being actually kept separate, or being mixed up with
other moneys. I have only to advert to one other point, and that is this—supposing, *b*
instead of being invested in the purchase of land or goods, the moneys were simply
mixed with other moneys of the trustee, using the term again in its full sense as
including every person in a fiduciary relation, does it make any difference according
to the modern doctrine of Equity? I say none. It would be very remarkable if it
were to do so. Supposing the trust money was 1000 sovereigns, and the trustee put
them into a bag, and by mistake, or accident, or otherwise, dropped a sovereign of *c*
his own into the bag. Could anybody suppose that a Judge in Equity would find any
difficulty in saying that the *cestui que trust* has a right to take 1000 sovereigns out of
that bag? I do not like to call it a charge of 1000 sovereigns on the 1001 sovereigns,
but that is the effect of it. I have no doubt of it. It would make no difference if,
instead of one sovereign, it was another 1000 sovereigns; but if instead of putting
it into his bag, or after putting it into his bag, he carries the bag to his bankers, what *d*
then? According to law, the bankers are his debtors for the total amount; but if you
lend the trust money to a third person, you can follow it.'

What are the salient features of the doctrine that Jessel MR there expounds? First, it
will be observed that in all cases the party entitled to trace is referred to as the beneficial
owner of the property, be it money or goods, which the 'trustee', in the broad sense in *e*
which Jessel MR uses that word, including all fiduciary relationships, has disposed of. In
the instant case, even if I assume that so long as the resin remained resin the beneficial
ownership of the resin remained in the sellers, I do not see how the concept of the
beneficial ownership remaining in the sellers after use in manufacture can here possibly
be reconciled with the liberty which the sellers gave to the buyers to use that resin in the
manufacturing process for the buyers' benefit, producing their own chipboard and in the *f*
process destroying the very existence of the resin.

Secondly, the doctrine expounded by Jessel MR contemplates the tracing of goods into
money and money into goods. In the latter case it matters not that the moneys represent
a mixed fund of which a part only is impressed with the relevant trust. The cestui qui
trust has a charge on the mixed fund or the property into which it has passed for the
amount of the trust moneys. It is at the heart of counsel's argument for the sellers to *g*
submit that the same applies to a mixture of goods with goods, relying in particular on
Jessel MR's illustration of the mixed bag of sovereigns. Now I can well see the force of
that argument if the goods mixed are all of a homogeneous character. Supposing I
deposit a ton of my corn with a corn factor as bailee, who does not store it separately but
mixes it with corn of his own. This, I apprehend, would leave unaffected my rights as
bailor, including the right to trace. But a mixture of heterogeneous goods in a *h*
manufacturing process wherein the original goods lose their character and what emerges
is a wholly new product is in my judgment something entirely different.

Some extreme examples were canvassed in argument. Suppose cattle cake is sold to a
farmer, or fuel to a steel manufacturer, in each case with a reservation of title clause, but
on terms which permit the farmer to feed the cattle cake to his herd and the steelmaker
to fuel his furnaces, before paying the purchase price. Counsel for the sellers concedes *j*
that in these cases the seller cannot trace into the cattle or the steel. He says that the
difference is that the goods have been consumed. But once this concession is made, I find
it impossible to draw an intelligible line of distinction in principle which would give the
sellers a right to trace the resin into the chipboard in the instant case. What has happened
in the manufacturing process is much more akin to the process of consumption than to

any simple process of admixture of goods. To put the point in another way, if the contribution that the resin has made to the chipboard gives rise to a tracing remedy, I find it difficult to see any good reason why, in the steelmaking example, the essential contribution made by the fuel to the steel manufacturing process should not do likewise.

These are the principal considerations which have led me to the conclusion that the sellers are not entitled to the tracing remedy which they claim. But I am fortified in that conclusion by the further consideration that if the remedy were available in such cases, a most intractible problem could, and in many cases would, arise in quantifying the proportion of the value of the manufactured product which the tracer could claim as properly attributable to his ingredient. In the instant case, a breakdown of the actual costings of chipboard over a period of seven months to 29th July 1977 has been agreed, attributing 17% of the total cost to the cost of resin, subject to a reservation with respect to wastage and overusage. But one can well see that in many cases where the cost of materials and labour involved in a particular production process were constantly fluctuating it might be quite impossible to assign a proportion of the total cost properly attributable to one particular ingredient with any certainty at all.

The lesson to be learned from these conclusions is a simple one. If a seller of goods to a manufacturer, who knows that his goods are to be used in the manufacturing process before they are paid for, wishes to reserve to himself an effective security for the payment of the price, he cannot rely on a simple reservation of title clause such as that relied on by the sellers. If he wishes to acquire rights over the finished product, he can only do so by express contractual stipulation. We have seen an elaborate, and presumably effective, example of such a stipulation in *Romalpa*[1]. An attempt to acquire rights over the finished product by a stipulation which proved ineffective for want of registration under s 95 of the Companies Act 1948 is to be seen in the decision of Slade J in *Re Bond Worth Ltd*[2], to which in the course of argument we were helpfully referred.

For the reasons that I have attempted to explain, I would allow this appeal and set aside the judge's order. I would answer questions (a)(ii) and (iii) set out in Master Cholmondeley Clarke's order in the negative; in the light of those answers, in my judgment question (b), as to the effect of s 95, does not arise, and I would express no opinion about it.

TEMPLEMAN LJ. Unsecured creditors rank after preferential creditors, mortgagees and the holders of floating charges and they receive a raw deal: see *Business Computers Ltd v Anglo-African Leasing Ltd*[3]. It is not therefore surprising that this court looked with sympathy on an invention designed to provide some protection for one class of unsecured creditors, namely unpaid sellers of goods (see *Aluminium Industrie Vaassen BV v Romalpa Aluminium Ltd*[1], known as the *Romalpa* case), although there is no logical reason why this class of creditor should be favoured as against other creditors such as the suppliers of consumables and services.

The present appeal seeks to extend the *Romalpa* case[1] by combining an idea culled from the Dutch civil law (see the *Romalpa* case[4]) and the English principles of equity, so as to produce a new super-equitable trace, having the same effect as a charge, but superior to a charge, in that it is immune from the requirements of registration.

For the purposes of this appeal, it must be assumed that the sellers, from time to time, sold and delivered to the buyers quantities of resin subject to a retention of title condition, which provided that the 'property in goods supplied' would only pass to the buyers when payment in full had been made for the goods supplied and for all other goods supplied before the date of such payment in full. There was nothing in any contract between the sellers and the buyers which precluded the buyers from using the resin immediately

1   [1976] 2 All ER 552, [1976] 1 WLR 676
2   Page 919, ante
3   [1977] 2 All ER 741, [1977] 1 WLR 578
4   [1976] 2 All ER 552 at 558, [1976] 1 WLR 676 at 684

after delivery and before any payment. The buyers incorporated the resin supplied in the manufacture of chipboard. The resin became an inseparable component, or ingredient, of the chipboard. The property in the chipboard vested in the buyers. There was nothing in any contract which precluded the buyers from selling that chipboard, receiving the purchase price and employing the proceeds of sale in their business.

The sellers claim that the retention of title condition operated on each supply of resin after 14th February 1977 and that the buyers owe the sellers £318,321·27 for resin sold and delivered by various contracts incorporating the retention of title condition after 1st June 1977. The sellers plead that all chipboard manufactured with resin wholly or partly supplied by the sellers since 14th February 1977, to the extent that the chipboard consists of the sellers' resin, is charged with payment to the sellers of £318,321·27. The sellers plead that all proceeds of sale of chipboard and all property representing proceeds of sale of chipboard to the extent that the proceeds of sale represent, or are attributable to, resin supplied by the sellers, are likewise charged with payment to the sellers of that sum. The buyers are insolvent; a receiver has been appointed and a compulsory winding-up order has been made. The buyers, it is pleaded, were under a fiduciary duty to keep separate from their other assets a proper proportion, estimated to be 12%, of the proceeds of sale of chipboard. Apart from the uncertainties involved in this casual estimate, the sellers accept that the buyers used and mixed resin other than the sellers' resin in the manufacture of the buyers' chipboard.

No one knows at this stage whether the price of resin fluctuated from time to time, or whether the other ingredients, costs of labour, overheads and profit margins involved in the manufacture and sale of chipboard, fluctuated to a corresponding degree. No one knows how the buyers, going about their business, no doubt blissfully unconscious of any fiduciary duty, employed the proceeds of sale of chipboard. They may have paid part to discharge their debt to the sellers; they may have paid the money into their bank in reduction of an overdraft; they may have paid their taxes; they may have bought and consumed other goods and paid other creditors. No one knows whether the proceeds of sale of chipboard could now be traced with any degree of certainty and what the results would be.

The sellers seek to surmount these difficulties by an enquiry of what has become of the resin and of what property now represents resin. The sellers seek to simplify matters in their own favour by an injunction which would place the buyers' receiver in danger of committal to prison, unless, to be safe, he set aside the arbitrary proportion of 12% of everything the buyers received and everything which he receives which may, by any stretch of imagination, be derived directly or indirectly from the buyers' chipboard, at any rate until he has amassed the sum of £318,321. At some distant date, when the court has unearthed the unearthable, traced the untraceable and calculated the incalculable, there will emerge the sum which it is said belongs to the sellers in equity, a sum which is immune from the claims of Crown and mortgagee, debenture holder and creditor, a sum secured to the sellers by a simple retention of title clause, which referred only to resin but was pregnant with all the consequences alleged in the statement of claim and hidden from the gaze of all other persons who dealt with the buyers.

On behalf of the sellers it was submitted that the retention of title condition, which reserved to the sellers the property in the resin, imposed on the buyers fiduciary duties and enables the sellers to trace the resin through all its transformations. In my judgment, when resin was sold and delivered the property in the resin could be retained by the sellers, and was retained, only as security for the payment of the purchase price and other debts incurred, and to be incurred, by the buyers to the sellers in respect of supplies of resin. If the buyers repudiated one contract the sellers could accept that repudiation and recover possession of the resin. If the sellers did not accept repudiation, or if the buyers failed to make payment due under any other contract, the sellers could enforce their security by selling the resin, for which purpose they had reserved the title to themselves. When resin was sold and delivered, the buyers admittedly took possession subject to the title and right of the sellers; but the buyers did not receive the resin in any

fiduciary capacity, but for themselves as purchasers. They could not sell and make title
to the resin, because the title had been retained by the sellers. But the buyers were free
to employ the resin in the manufacture of chipboard.

When the resin was incorporated in the chipboard, the resin ceased to exist, the sellers'
title to the resin became meaningless and the sellers' security vanished. There was no
provision in the contract for the buyers to provide substituted or additional security.
The chipboard belonged to the buyers.

We were not invited to imply in the contract between the sellers and the buyers an
agreement by the buyers to furnish substituted security in the form of an interest in the
chipboard; we were invited to allow the sellers to trace their vanished resin to the
chipboard and thence to the proceeds of sale of chipboard and property representing
those proceeds of sale. I agree that in a commercial contract of this nature no agreement
should be implied for the furnishing of additional security. In the absence of any
implied or express agreement to provide substitutional security, equity has nothing to
trace: the resin and the title and the security disappeared without trace. I am in any
event unwilling to imply a term or invoke the aid of equity to produce a result which
other creditors of the buyers might justifiably regard as a fraudulent preference.

For good measure, it seems to me that if the sellers have any interest or share in
chipboard or proceeds of sale of chipboard, or property representing proceeds of sale of
chipboard, they fall foul of s 95 of the Companies Act 1948. Any such interest or share
must have been agreed to be granted by the buyers when they bought and accepted
delivery of resin on the terms of the retention of title condition. Any such interest or
share must have been created by the buyers when they employed the resin in the
manufacture of chipboard. Any such interest or share must have been agreed to be
granted and must have been created as security and only as security for the payment of
the debts incurred and to be incurred by the buyers to the sellers in respect of the supply
of resin. Those debts were charged on the interest or share granted and created by the
buyers. If tracing is permissible, the charge attached to the chipboard, when chipboard
was manufactured, then attached to the proceeds of sale when the chipboard was sold,
and finally attached to any property representing those proceeds of sale of chipboard. If
the buyers created a charge on chipboard, such a charge is void against the liquidator and
creditors of the buyers under s 95, which makes void against the company or its creditors
an unregistered charge created or evidenced by an instrument which, if executed by an
individual, would require registration as a bill of sale. If the interest floated from the
chipboard to proceeds of sale and onwards, so floated the charge, and s 95 makes void any
unregistered floating charge on the undertaking or property of the company.

It was said that a floating charge of this nature has not so far been comprised in any
authority on s 95; the fact that this is the first authority does not seem to me to be any
drawback.

We were much pressed with the *Romalpa* case[1], in which buyers were entitled to sell
goods supplied by unpaid sellers, but only as agents for the sellers, who retained the
property in the goods pending payment. On the construction of a contract described by
Roskill LJ in refusing leave to appeal to the House of Lords as 'a rather simple contract,
not altogether happily expressed in the English language, but [which] could not govern
any other case', the court implied an obligation on the buyers to account as bailees and
held that the sellers were entitled to trace the proceeds of sale. Section 95 was not argued;
it does not appear whether the buyers were in liquidation, and in any event the argument
was probably not put forward because the retention of title in the sellers' goods was
thought not to be the creation of a charge by the buyers. In the present case the buyers
did not manufacture or sell chipboard, or perform any other function as agents for the
sellers, and any charge on the buyers' chipboard and other property of the buyers must
necessarily have been created by the buyers and be void.

In the result, I agree that the appeal must be allowed.

---

1   [1976] 2 All ER 552, [1976] 1 WLR 676

BUCKLEY LJ. I agree that this appeal should be allowed.

We are concerned here with resin sold under the terms of the condition which has *a* been referred to by Bridge LJ in the course of his judgment, and manufactured into chipboard. Under the terms of that condition the legal property in the resin initially remained in the sellers. I do not find it necessary to pause to consider whether, during the continuance of that state of affairs, the defendants were properly to be regarded as bailees of the resin or not.

It is common ground that it was the common intention of the parties that the buyers *b* should be at liberty to use the resin in the manufacture of chipboard. After they had so used the resin there could, in my opinion, be no property in the resin distinct from the property in the chipboard produced by the process. The manufacture had amalgamated the resin and the other ingredients into a new product by an irreversible process and the resin, as resin, could not be recovered for any purpose; for all practical purposes it had ceased to exist and the ownership in that resin must also have ceased to exist. *c*

The condition does not expressly deal with any property in the chipboard, or create any equitable charge on the chipboard, produced by the manufacture. If any term is to be implied, that must be a term which is necessary to give the contract business efficacy, but it must also be a term which the court can see unambiguously to be a term which the parties would have inserted into their contract had they thought it appropriate to express it. If no such term can be identified, then the court may have to conclude that the *d* contract was inept to achieve any valuable, practical result in that respect.

Is it possible here to imply any term giving the sellers a proprietary interest in the chipboard manufactured by the buyers, or giving the plaintiffs an equitable charge on that chipboard?

Common ownership of the chipboard at law is not asserted by the buyers; so the sellers must either have the entire ownership of the chipboard, which is not suggested, or they *e* must have some equitable interest in the chipboard or an equitable charge of some kind on the chipboard. For my part, I find it quite impossible to spell out of this condition any provision properly to be implied to that effect.

It was impossible for the sellers to reserve any property in the manufactured chipboard, because they never had any property in it; the property in that product originates in the buyers when the chipboard is manufactured. Any interest which the sellers might have *f* had in the chipboard must have arisen either by transfer of ownership or by some constructive trust or equitable charge, and, as I say, I find it impossible to spell out of this condition anything of that nature.

Counsel for the sellers, in a very valiant argument, has contended that he can achieve his end by relying on the doctrine of tracing. But in my judgment it is a fundamental feature of the doctrine of tracing that the property to be traced can be identified at every *g* stage of its journey through life, and that it can be identified as property to which a fiduciary obligation still attaches in favour of the person who traces it.

In the present case, in the circumstances that I have described of the resin losing its identity in the chipboard, I find it impossible to hold that the resin can be traced into the chipboard, or to any other form of property into which the chipboard might at any time be converted. Accordingly, it seems to me that the doctrine of tracing is inapplicable to *h* a case such as this.

If it were possible to arrive at the conclusion on the facts of this case that the sellers acquired an equitable charge of some kind on the chipboard, I should have thought that the case would fall within s 95(2)(c) of the Companies Act 1948, which is the paragraph which relates to a charge 'created or evidenced by an instrument which, if executed by an individual, would require registration as a bill of sale'. I would not myself have *j* thought that in the circumstances of this case there could be said to be a floating charge, for the charge, if it arises at all, arises when a particular parcel of the sellers' resin is incorporated in a particular batch of the buyers' chipboard, and the charge must then arise either immediately or, possibly, in futuro in respect of that particular batch of chipboard, and I would have thought that it must be a specific charge on that specific *a* parcel of chipboard and not a charge on the chipboard produced by the defendants from time to time. Consequently, it does not seem to me that it could have the character of a floating charge. But that it would be a charge arising from a contract entered into between the parties, and therefore a charge created by the parties, I would think to be the position if such a charge arises at all, for it is a charge which must flow, and flow exclusively, from the fact that the parties entered into a contract containing this particular condition reserving the property in the resin.

b But, for the reasons I gave earlier in my judgment, in my opinion one does not reach s 95 in this case, because the plaintiffs acquired no interest of any kind in the chipboard. For these reasons I also agree that this appeal should be allowed.

Appeal allowed. Leave to appeal to the House of Lords refused.

c Solicitors: *Coward Chance* (for the buyers); *Lovell, White & King* (for the sellers); *Cameron, Kemm, Nordon* (for the Official Receiver).

J H Fazan Esq   Barrister.

Vestey v Inland Revenue Commissioners (Nos 1 and 2)

HOUSE OF LORDS

LORD WILBERFORCE, VISCOUNT DILHORNE, LORD SALMON, LORD EDMUND-DAVIES, LORD KEITH OF KINKEL

23rd, 24th, 25th, 26th, 30th JULY, 22nd NOVEMBER 1979

Income tax – Avoidance – Transfer of assets abroad – Persons liable to tax – Individuals ordinarily resident in United Kingdom – Discretionary trust – Beneficiaries – Power to enjoy income of person resident or domiciled overseas – Receipt by United Kingdom resident of capital sum payment of which connected with transfer of assets abroad – Transfer of assets to trustees abroad – Trustees holding assets on discretionary trusts – Trustees accumulating income and paying sums to selected appointees from class of beneficiaries – Beneficiaries 'ordinarily resident in United Kingdom' – Whether liability to tax attaching to any appointee ordinarily resident in United Kingdom – Whether liability limited to person ordinarily resident in United Kingdom who transferred assets – Whether appointees liable to tax – Income Tax Act 1952, s 412.

By a settlement dated 25th March 1942 and governed by the law of Northern Ireland, the settlors, Sir Edmund Vestey ('Edmund') and Lord Vestey ('Samuel'), transferred certain overseas property to trustees outside the United Kingdom to hold on discretionary trusts for the benefit of Edmund's and Samuel's descendants. The settlement provided that the trustees were to invest the income received from the trust property so as to form a capital fund. The income of the capital fund was to be divided by the trustees into two halves, ie Edmund's fund and Samuel's fund, which were to be held on trust for Edmund's and Samuel's descendants respectively. Both funds were to be invested by the trustees, who were, on the direction of persons designated as 'Edmund's manager' and 'Samuel's manager', to accumulate the income and invest it, and the resulting income and accumulation of income were to form part of the capital of Edmund's fund and of Samuel's fund respectively. Each manager had power under the settlement to direct the trustees to appropriate or realise or raise any part of the capital of his fund and to pay or apply it in such manner as he 'shall think proper' for the benefit of descendants connected with his fund and, with the consent of the manager of the other fund, for his own benefit. On 26th March 1942 the trustees leased the trust property to a company and the rent received was accumulated and invested by the trustees so as to form a capital fund. The income produced from the capital fund was then divided equally between Edmund's fund and Samuel's fund, and in turn the income of the two funds was accumulated by the direction of Edmund's and Samuel's managers. Between 1962 and 1966, under the powers contained in the settlement, appointments from capital were made in favour of beneficiaries each year so that by 1966 six out of the 29 potential beneficiaries alive in 1963 had received payments of varying amounts from the funds. The class of potential beneficiaries was liable to increase in any given year and in fact did so at various times after 1963. In 1970 the Crown assessed the six appointees to tax for the years 1963–64 to 1968–69 by assessing each appointee, for the years he or she was resident in the United Kingdom, in respect of a proportion of the total income of the trustees in each year in which any appointment was made regardless of whether the appointee in fact received any payment that year or in any year before or after that year. The proportion of the trustees' income decided on by the Crown for assessment was that proportion which the capital sum received by the appointee bore to the total income for each year, and not merely to the income of the trustees in the year of payment. This method of assessment had the result in one case that a beneficiary who received a single capital payment, of £100,000 in 1966, was assessed to income tax and surtax on a total of £274,121 over the six years. On the Crown's method of assessment each appointee could have been liable *a*   to assessment on the whole of the trustees' income, but the Crown voluntarily restricted the assessments so that the total amount of the trustees' income was apportioned between the appointees. In two separate appeals by the beneficiaries the Crown justified these assessments under s 412[a] of the Income Tax Act 1952 on the basis that each beneficiary, being an 'individual ordinarily resident in the United Kingdom', had avoided tax as a result of a transfer of assets abroad resulting in the transfer of income to a person abroad, and was thus liable to tax because as 'such an individual' either (i) he had received a capital

b   sum the payment of which was connected with the transfer of assets and accordingly had become liable to tax on the trustees' income by the operation of s 412(2), or (ii) he had rights by which he had power to enjoy the trustees' income and accordingly was liable to tax on that income by the operation of s 412(1). The Special Commissioners upheld the assessments in both appeals. Walton J[b] allowed the beneficiaries' appeals in both cases, although he rejected their overriding contention that, because the words 'such an

c   individual' in s 412(1) and (2) were restricted to the person originally transferring the assets, s 412 did not apply at all, holding on authority[c] that those words referred only to an individual ordinarily resident in the United Kingdom. The Crown appealed against Walton J's decisions to the House of Lords.

Held – The appeals would be dismissed for the following reasons—

d   (i) Having regard to the arbitrary, unconstitutional and potentially unjust results which could follow if s 412 of the 1952 Act were given an extended meaning which embraced all persons, born or unborn, who in any way might benefit from assets transferred abroad by others, s 412 was to be construed, as the natural meaning of the words used in the section in fact permitted and notwithstanding previous House of Lords authority to the contrary, on the basis that Parliament in enacting the section intended

e   it to have the limited effect of penalising only those persons who transferred assets abroad to avoid tax and did not intend it to refer to beneficiaries under a discretionary trust resulting from such a transfer. Accordingly, on the natural and intended meaning of s 412 'such an individual' who was liable to tax under s 412(1) in respect of a power to enjoy any income of a person resident or domiciled abroad or under s 412(2) in respect of the receipt of a capital sum connected with the transfer of assets abroad referred only

f   to an individual ordinarily resident in the United Kingdom who sought to avoid his own or his spouse's liability to tax by the transfer of assets abroad while continuing to reside in the United Kingdom (see p 986 *h* to p 987 *a e* and *g* to p 988 *a*, p 989 *a b f* to *h*, p 993 *h* to p 994 *c*, p 996 *e*, p 998 *e*, p 1003 *h* to p 1004 *c* and *f* to *h* and p 1005 *a b*, post); *Congreve v Inland Revenue Comrs* [1948] 1 All ER 948 overruled.

(ii) In any event, the Revenue's levying of tax on, and apportioning of liability among, the appointees who had received payments from the funds by the exercise of a self-

g   asserted administrative discretion in the absence of any statutory basis on which the tax could be assessed or levied was unconstitutional since it offended the principle that a citizen could not be taxed unless he was designated in clear terms by a taxing Act as a taxpayer and the amount of his liability was clearly defined. The assessments therefore failed in the case of discretionary beneficiaries (see p 984 *h* to p 985 *e*, p 986 *a*, p 989 *g h*, p 994 *f* to *h*, p 998 *e*, p 1003 *h*, p 1004 *b* and p 1005 *b*, post).

h   Decisions of Walton J [1977] 3 All ER 1073 and [1979] 2 All ER 225 affirmed on other grounds.

Notes

For avoidance of tax by means of the transfer of assets abroad by individuals, see 23 Halsbury's Laws (4th Edn) paras 1479–1487, and for cases on the subject, see 28(1) Digest

j   (Reissue) 439–445, 1579–1592.

---

a   Section 412, so far as material, is set out at p 991 *b* to *f*, post.

b   [1977] 3 All ER 1073, [1977] STC 414; [1979] 2 All ER 225, [1978] STC 567

c   *Congreve v Inland Revenue Comrs* [1948] 1 All ER 948, HL, *Bambridge v Inland Revenue Comrs* [1955] 3 All ER 812, HL

For the Income Tax Act 1952, s 412, see 31 Halsbury's Statutes (2nd Edn) 390.

For the Finance Act 1969, s 33, see 49 ibid 764.

a

For 1970–71 and subsequent years of assessment, s 412 of the 1952 Act has been replaced by the Income and Corporation Taxes Act 1970, s 478.

Cases referred to in opinions

Absalom v Talbot (Inspector of Taxes) [1943] 1 All ER 589, 26 Tax Cas 166, CA; *rvsd* [1944] 1 All ER 642, [1944] AC 204, 26 Tax Cas 166, 113 LJ Ch 369, 171 LT 53, HL, 28(1) Digest (Reissue) 86, *258*.

b

Bambridge v Inland Revenue Comrs [1955] 3 All ER 812, [1955] 1 WLR 1329, 36 Tax Cas 313, [1955] TR 295, 48 R & IT 814, 34 ATC 181, HL; *affg* [1954] 3 All ER 682, [1954] 1 WLR 1460, 36 Tax Cas 313, CA, [1954] TR 375, 48 R & IT 63, 33 ATC 393, CA; *rvsg in part* [1954] 3 All ER 86, [1954] 1 WLR 1265, 36 Tax Cas 313, [1954] TR 255, 47 R & IT 466, 33 ATC 267, 28(1) Digest (Reissue) 440, *1582*.

c

Bates v Inland Revenue Comrs [1967] 1 All ER 84, [1968] AC 483, [1967] 2 WLR 60, 44 Tax Cas 225, [1966] TR 369, HL; *affg* [1965] 3 All ER 64, [1965] 1 WLR 1133, [1965] TR 189, 44 Tax Cas 225, CA, 28(1) Digest (Reissue) 429, *1552*.

Chetwode (Lord) v Inland Revenue Comrs [1977] 1 All ER 638, [1977] 1 WLR 248, [1977] STC 64, [1977] TR 11, HL; *rvsg* [1976] 1 All ER 641, [1976] 1 WLR 310, CA.

Cleary v Inland Revenue Comrs [1967] 2 All ER 48, [1968] AC 766, [1967] WLR 1271, [1967] TR 57, 46 ATC 51, 44 Tax Cas 399, HL, 28(1) Digest (Reissue) 489, *1753*.

d

Congreve v Inland Revenue Comrs [1948] 1 All ER 948, 30 Tax Cas 163, [1948] LJR 1229, 27 ATC 102, 41 R & IT 319, HL; *affg* [1947] 1 All ER 168, 30 Tax Cas 163, CA; *rvsg* [1946] 2 All ER 170, 30 Tax Cas 163, 28(1) Digest (Reissue) 443, *1590*.

Corbett's Executrices v Inland Revenue Comrs [1943] 2 All ER 218, 25 Tax Cas 305, 169 LT 166, CA, 28(1) Digest (Reissue) 443, *1589*.

e

Drummond v Collins (Inspector of Taxes) [1915] AC 1011, 6 Tax Cas 525, 84 LJKB 1690, 113 LT 665, HL, 28(1) Digest (Repl) 302, *1039*.

FS Securities v Inland Revenue Comrs [1963] 3 All ER 229, [1963] 1 WLR 1223, 41 Tax Cas 666, CA; *rvsd* [1964] 2 All ER 691, [1965] AC 631, [1964] 1 WLR 742, 41 Tax Cas 666, [1964] TR 171, 43 ATC 156, HL, 28(1) Digest (Reissue) 400, *1468*.

Gartside v Inland Revenue Comrs [1968] 1 All ER 121, [1968] AC 553, [1968] 2 WLR 277, [1967] TR 309, 46 ATC 323, HL, Digest (Cont Vol C) 326, *74a*.

f

Herbert (Lord) v Inland Revenue Comrs [1943] 1 All ER 336, [1943] 1 KB 288, 25 Tax Cas 93, 112 LJKB 369, 108 LT 379, 28(1) Digest (Reissue) 428, *1547*.

Howard de Walden (Lord) v Inland Revenue Comrs [1942] 1 All ER 287, [1942] 1 KB 389, 25 Tax Cas 121, 111 LJKB 273, CA, 28(1) Digest (Reissue) 442, *1586*.

Inland Revenue Comrs v Frere [1964] 3 All ER 796, [1965] AC 402, [1964] 3 WLR 1193, 42 Tax Cas 125, [1964] TR 333, 43 ATC 308, HL, 28(1) Digest (Reissue) 521, *1902*.

g

Inland Revenue Comrs v Hinchy [1960] 1 All ER 505, [1960] AC 748, [1960] 2 WLR 448, 38 Tax Cas 625, [1960] TR 33, 39 ATC 13, 53 R & IT 188, HL, 28(1) Digest (Reissue) 579, *2159*.

Inland Revenue Comrs v Korner [1969] 1 All ER 679, [1969] 1 WLR 554, 45 Tax Cas 287, [1969] TR 33, 48 ATC 29, HL, 28(1) Digest (Reissue) 235, *726*.

h

Jones v Secretary of State for Social Services [1972] 1 All ER 145, [1972] AC 944, [1972] 2 WLR 210, HL, Digest (Cont Vol D) 683, *4585b*.

Latilla v Inland Revenue Comrs [1943] 1 All ER 265, [1943] AC 377, 112 LJKB 158, 168 LT 411, 25 Tax Cas 107, HL; *affg* [1942] 1 All ER 214, [1942] 1 KB 299, 25 Tax Cas 107, CA, 28(1) Digest (Reissue) 442, *1587*.

Minister of Social Security v Amalgamated Engineering Union [1967] 1 All ER 210, [1967] 1 AC 725, [1967] 2 WLR 516, Digest (Cont Vol C) 704, *4585a*.

j

Philippi v Inland Revenue Comrs [1971] 3 All ER 61, [1971] 1 WLR 1272, 47 Tax Cas 75, [1971] TR 167, 50 ATC 37, CA, Digest (Cont Vol D) 487, *1579b*.

Vestey's (Lord) Executors v Inland Revenue Comrs [1949] 1 All ER 1108, 31 Tax Cas 1, [1949] TR 149, 42 R & IT 314, 325, HL, 28(1) Digest (Reissue) 443, *1591*.

Cases also cited

a   *Canadian Eagle Oil Co Ltd v R* [1945] 2 All ER 499, [1946] AC 119, 27 Tax Cas 205, HL.
Dickinson (Inspector of Taxes) v Abel [1969] 1 All ER 484, [1969] 1 WLR 295, 45 Tax Cas 353.
Luke v Inland Revenue Comrs [1963] 1 All ER 655, [1963] AC 557, 40 Tax Cas 630, HL
Ramsden v Inland Revenue Comrs (1957) 37 Tax Cas 619.
Sassoon v Inland Revenue Comrs (1943) 25 Tax Cas 154, CA.
b   *Stanley v Inland Revenue Comrs* [1944] 1 All ER 230, [1944] 1 KB 255, 26 Tax Cas 12, CA.

Appeals and cross-appeals

These were appeals by the Crown direct to the House of Lords under Part II of the Administration of Justice Act 1969 against two decisions of Walton J in respect of assessments to tax made between the years 1962–63 to 1967–68 on the respondents, Ronald Arthur Vestey, Edmund Hoyle Vestey, James Gladstone Payne, John Richard *c*   Baddeley, Lord Vestey, and Mark William Vestey ('the taxpayers'), who were beneficiaries under discretionary trusts settled by Baron Vestey deceased and Sir Edmund Vestey Bt. In the first decision[1] Walton J allowed the taxpayers' appeals by way of case stated[2] against the decision of the Special Commissioners given on 20th March 1974 dismissing their appeals against their assessment to tax, under s 412(2) of the Income Tax Act 1952, on *d*   sums received by them from the trustees of the discretionary trusts. Walton J referred the case back to the Special Commissioners to consider and decide on the Crown's alternative contention that the assessments could be supported under s 412(1) of the 1952 Act. On 11th January 1978 the Special Commissioners upheld that contention and dismissed the taxpayers' appeals. The taxpayers appealed by way of case stated[3] to Walton J who in the second decision[4] allowed their appeal in respect of the Crown's alternative contention but decided that the assessments should stand to the extent that *e*   the taxpayers fell to be assessed in the year in which sums from the trusts were received. The taxpayers cross-appealed against this latter finding. The facts are summarised in the opinion of Lord Wilberforce.

D C Potter QC, James Holroyd Pearce QC and *Alastair G Wilson* for the taxpayers.
Michael Nolan QC, Peter Gibson and *Brian Davenport* for the Crown.

f   Their Lordships took time for consideration.

22nd November. The following opinions were delivered.

LORD WILBERFORCE. My Lords, these are six appeals and cross-appeals from two decisions of Walton J[5]. They come direct to this House under Part II of the Administration of Justice Act 1969. They are concerned with assessments for income tax and surtax *g*   made on the six respondents for the years 1963–64, 1964–65, 1965–66, 1966–67 and 1968–69 (except that no assessments were made on Lord Vestey for 1964–65 and 1965–66 and no assessment was made on M W Vestey for 1966–67). The assessments were made under s 412 of the Income Tax Act 1952 (now incorporated in s 478 of the Income and Corporation Taxes Act 1970) which is concerned with the transfer of assets abroad. The original sources of these sections were the Finance Act 1936, s 18, and the Finance *h*   Act 1938, s 28. The assessments for 1968–69 are additionally made under the Finance Act 1969, s 33. The sums involved are very large, and important and difficult questions arise for decision.

The origin of the matter is a settlement made on 25th March 1942 by the second Baron Vestey and his uncle, Sir Edmund Hoyle Vestey Bt, as settlors. These persons were

j   1   [1977] 3 All ER 1073, [1979] Ch 177, [1977] STC 414
    2   The case stated is set out at [1977] 3 All ER 1075–1084
    3   The case stated is set out at [1979] 2 All ER 227–232
    4   [1979] 2 All ER 225, [1979] Ch 198, [1978] STC 567
    5   [1977] 3 All ER 1073, [1979] Ch 177, [1977] STC 414; [1979] 2 All ER 225, [1979] Ch 198, [1978] STC 567

the heads of two Vestey families, to one or other of which the taxpayers belong. The
taxpayers transferred no assets and had no hand in the settlement; they, together with a *a*
number of other persons, are potential beneficiaries under it.

By the settlement the settlors conveyed certain very valuable properties outside the
United Kingdom to trustees resident outside the United Kingdom to hold on the trusts
of the settlement.

There is no doubt that this was a transfer of assets by virtue of which income became
payable to persons resident out of the United Kingdom (viz the trustees) so as potentially *b*
to bring s 412 into operation. However, it is important to notice that neither of the
settlors had any rights, nor at any time received any sum, so as to make themselves liable
to be charged with tax under either s 412(1) or s 412(2). The claim is, and is only, against
beneficiaries under the settlement.

The trusts of the settlement are elaborate and are fully set out in the case stated[1]. I
think that the following summary is sufficient to enable the contentions of the Crown *c*
to be understood.

1   The trustees were obliged during a period called 'the prescribed term', which, unless
extended will expire in 1984, to accumulate the income of the trust property by
investment so as to form a capital fund, called the 'rental fund'. Advantage was taken, in
this connection, of the law of Northern Ireland, under which the settlement was made,
which does not include the Thellusson Act[2], which would have limited the period of *d*
accumulation. After the end of the prescribed term the rental fund was to be divided
into two equal parts, Edmund's fund and Samuel's fund, and held on the trusts declared
concerning these funds. During the prescribed term the income of the rental fund was
to be divided into two equal parts which were to be held on the trusts which would be
applicable to Edmund's fund and Samuel's fund if already in possession.

2   Subject to the above provisions the trust property was to be held for the son of Sir *e*
Edmund, the respondent Ronald Arthur Vestey, and the son of the second Lord Vestey,
W H Vestey in equal shares.

3   During a period defined by reference to the law against perpetuities, designed to last
until AD 2030, and called 'the specified period', a person designated as Edmund's manager
(who in fact was at all material times the respondent Ronald Arthur Vestey) had power
to direct the accumulation of the income of Edmund's fund. Edmund's manager did in *f*
fact so direct.

4   Subject as aforesaid Edmund's manager had power during the specified period to
appoint the income of Edmund's fund between a class including Ronald Arthur Vestey
and his issue and other persons. Subject thereto the income was to be held on protective
trusts for (inter alia) the issue of Ronald Arthur Vestey per stirpes.

5   Trusts were declared of Edmund's fund to take effect after the end of the specified *g*
period.

6   (This is the material provision as regards these appeals.) Edmund's manager had
power during the specified period to direct the trustees to pay or apply capital of
Edmund's fund to or for the benefit of Ronald Arthur Vestey or his issue, or failing this,
the issue of Sir Edmund, but Edmund's manager could only exercise this power in
favour of himself jointly with Samuel's manager or the trustees. *h*

7   Similar trusts mutatis mutandis to those referred to under paras 4 to 6 above were
declared as regards Samuel's fund, there being designated a person to act as Samuel's
manager. He also directed accumulation.

8   There were cross-remainders applicable to Edmund's fund and Samuel's fund in the
event of failure of the trusts applicable to them respectively.

9   Finally there was (cl 14) a wide power given to Edmund's manager and Samuel's *j*
manager during the specified period to revoke the trusts, powers or provisions of the

---

1   See [1979] 3 All ER 1073, at 1090–1093, [1977] STC 414 at 431–434
2   Accumulations Act 1800

a settlement and to reconstitute the same, but not so as to confer any interest on either of the settlors.

Thus, in the most summary form, the income from the transferred properties was to be accumulated in three stages. First it was to be accumulated so as to form the rental fund. Secondly the income of the rental fund was to be accumulated so as to form (i) Edmund's fund and (ii) Samuel's fund. Thirdly the income of (i) Edmund's fund and (ii) Samuel's fund was to be accumulated, and it was out of these accumulations that the

b relevant capital payments were made.

It is next necessary to ascertain who were (i) the potential and (ii) the actual beneficiaries who either had rights by virtue of which they had power to enjoy income of the settlement (s 412(1)) or might receive capital payments under paras 6 and 7 above (s 412(2)).

The *potential* beneficiaries in 1963–64 were (a) 16 members of the Vestey family on Sir

c Edmund Vestey's side, (b) 12 members of the Vestey family on Samuel Vestey's side. In 1963–64 two more persons became members of class (a), making 18; and one of class (b), making 13, and these remained the relevant numbers through 1966–67. Each class was, of course, susceptible of increase in any subsequent year, and has in fact been so increased.

The *actual* beneficiaries were the taxpayers to whom capital payments were made. I shall set these out not only against the individual recipients but also under each relevant

d year of assessment; I do this because, as I think it important to emphasise, it is each assessment on each separate beneficiary in each separate year that has to be justified (or attacked). The combination in this case of a number of years of assessment on a number of beneficiaries, however convenient for the Crown, or for argument, is liable to confuse the legal issues. The dates mentioned are the dates when the sums were appointed: it does not appear whether they were paid on the same dates or later.

e The payments were:

Beneficiary	Date(s)	Amount
	Edmund's Fund	
R A Vestey	29th October 1962	£215,000
	18th November 1964	£150,000
E H Vestey	1st January 1963	£700,000
	18th November 1966	£220,000
Mrs Payne	2nd May 1966	£100,000
Mrs Baddeley	2nd May 1966	£100,000
	Samuel's Fund	
Baron Vestey	9th July 1962	£123,000
	1st January 1963	£800,000
M W Vestey (through his mother)	1st January 1963	£200,000

and, arranged according to date:

Tax year	Dates	Beneficiary	Amount
1962–63	9th July 1962	Baron Vestey	£123,000
	29th October 1962	R A Vestey	£215,000
	1st January 1963	E H Vestey	£700,000
	1st January 1963	Baron Vestey	£800,000
	1st January 1963	M W Vestey	£200,000
1963–64	——	——	——
1964–65	18th November 1964	R A Vestey	£150,000
1965–66	——	——	——
1966–67	2nd May 1966	Mrs Payne	£100,000
	2nd May 1966	Mrs Baddeley	£100,000
1967–68	[No evidence of any payments]		

On these figures, the Commissioners of Inland Revenue have made the assessments now in question. The assessments were first made in 1970, ie subsequent to all the *a* payments of capital sums in issue in these appeals. The commissioners then appear to have looked back at six years of assessment, and to have assessed each beneficiary in respect of a proportion of the total income of the trustees in each year (allowance being made for periods when he was resident outside the United Kingdom), irrespective of whether that beneficiary received any payment in that year, or in any year prior to or subsequent to that year. The proportion decided on was that which the capital sum(s) *b* received by each beneficiary bore to the total income of the trustees for *each* year, ie not to the income of the trustees in the year of payment. The resultant figures for 1963–64 to 1966–67 are set out in the case for the respondents; for convenience I reproduce them in an appendix[1].

There are many remarkable features about these figures. I shall comment on some later. They can be highlighted by reference to the cases of Mrs Payne and Mrs *c* Baddeley. Though these beneficiaries received nothing until 1966–67, in which year each received £100,000, they (in fact their husbands) have been assessed for a proportion of the trustees' income in each relevant year, starting with 1963–64, totalling (in each case) £274,121·97. It is the Crown's claim that they could have been assessed for many times that amount.

The Crown's claim, on these figures, was based first on s 412(2) of the 1952 Act, on the *d* grounds that each beneficiary received a capital sum of the character described, and secondly on s 412(1), on the ground that each beneficiary had rights by virtue of which he had power to enjoy income of the trustees. Whichever subsection applied, the Crown claimed to be entitled to tax each beneficiary on the whole of the trustees' income, but they limited their actual claim to a proportion fixed as described above. The taxpayers dispute each of these claims, and additionally, as an overriding contention, submit that *e* s 412 does not apply at all to a case where (as here) the transfer of assets was not made by any of them, but by other persons (viz the original settlors).

The learned judge (Walton J) considered that he was precluded from accepting the overriding contention by the decision of this House in *Congreve v Inland Revenue Comrs*[2] and by that of the Court of Appeal in *Bambridge v Inland Revenue Comrs*[3]. On the particular arguments, he rejected the Crown's claim under s 412(2), holding that each *f* taxpayer's liability was limited to tax in respect of the actual sum(s) received by him in any particular year of assessment. As to s 412(1), he held that, before the subsection was amended by the Finance Act 1969, s 33, the Crown's claim failed because no beneficiary had *any rights* by virtue of which he had power to enjoy income; as to the last year, to which the amended subsection applied (deleting any reference to 'rights'), the claim failed because what the beneficiaries had power to enjoy was not income but capital, viz *g* accumulations of income which had been capitalised.

All of these contentions (and others involving subsidiary but important points) are in issue in these appeals, and the House is invited if necessary to depart from its previous decision in *Congreve*[2] and to overrule the Court of Appeal's decision in *Bambridge*[3]. Since, if it were to do so, that would dispose of all the appeals in the taxpayers' favour, it would appear to be logical and economical to consider this question first. *h*

I find myself unable immediately to take this course. A decision whether *Congreve*[2] should be followed cannot be made until it is seen what the consequences of following the case would be, and this involves consideration of the meaning of the two subsections of s 412 and of the judge's decisions with regard to them. These, on the view which I take, need not be lengthy. I make it clear that the following analysis only applies on the assumption that *Congreve*[2] is correct. *j*

I take first s 412(2). If this subsection could be limited in the way suggested by the

___

1   See pp 1006–1007, post
2   [1948] 1 All ER 948, 30 Tax Cas 163
3   [1954] 3 All ER 682, [1954] 1 WLR 1460, 36 Tax Cas 313

judge, a result would be produced that would be intelligible, workable, certain and, from

a some points of view, not unjust. The taxpayer receiving a capital sum, assuming that the trustees had income in that year, would pay tax on it as income; assessment on this basis would be clear and mandatory, and lacking in any element of arbitrariness or discretion. I have sympathy with the judge's efforts to achieve this result.

However, I regret that I am unable to accept the suggested limitation. The judge achieved it by means of what he (justly) described as a bold emendation through the

b insertion of words. I transcribe the subsection as emended[1], the inserted words being italicised:

> 'Where, whether before or after any such transfer, such an individual receives or is entitled to receive any capital sum the payment whereof is in any way connected with the transfer or any associated operation, *to the extent to which it comprises* any income which, by virtue or in consequence of the transfer, either alone or in
> **c** conjunction with associated operations, has become the income of a person resident or domiciled out of the United Kingdom *it* shall, whether it would or would not have been chargeable to income tax apart from the provisions of this section, be deemed to be the income of that individual for all the purposes of this Act.'

My Lords, it is not necessary to enter on objections of a detailed character to this

d emendation though some are formidable. For inspection of it unanswerably shows that the process involved is not one of construction, even one of strained construction, but is one of rewriting the enactment. The subsection says in the clearest terms that 'any income' of the foreign resident etc is to be deemed the income of the recipient of the capital sum. To say that what is to be deemed the recipient's income is not 'any income' but a portion of that income equal to the capital sum received, would be a totally

e different fiscal approach, one which Parliament might certainly have taken, but which it has manifestly avoided in this instance.

Certain other suggestions were made by leading counsel for the taxpayers as to the manner in which the subsection might be cut down. These had the merit of being less radical than the judge's emendation, but the defect of being ineffective. I do not pursue them for the reason, which I find overwhelming, that the subsection is clear beyond

f doubt in its terms. It is 'any income' of the foreign transferees which is deemed to be the income of the recipient of a capital sum, indeed of each and every recipient of any capital sum, small or large, whenever received. From these words there is no escape.

I pass to sub-s (1), still on the assumption that *Congreve*[1] is correct. It is the Crown's contention that each and every one of the potential beneficiaries (viz 13–14 as to one fund and 16–18 as to the other, making 29–32 in all) had rights by virtue of which they

g had power to enjoy income etc. They accept, and indeed maintain, that at least each *actual* recipient, having such rights, can be assessed in respect of any income of the foreign transferees; inferentially they must accept, for there is no basis for any distinction, that each *potential* recipient (each of the 29–32 persons) can be so assessed, and this in respect of each year in which he has the rights etc. They submit that the subsection, coupled with *Congreve*[1], compels this.

h My Lords, I do not agree, in this particular case, that any of the taxpayers had 'rights by virtue of which they had power to enjoy'. On this point, in my opinion, the judge was clearly right: they were simply members of a discretionary class to which income, or capital, might in the discretion of other persons become available. To hold that as such they had any rights of the character described would be inconsistent with much authority and with principle (see, inter alia, *Gartside v Inland Revenue Comrs*[2] per Lord Reid and

j *Vestey's Executors v Inland Revenue Comrs*[3]).

---

1   [1948] 1 All ER 948, 30 Tax Cas 163
2   [1968] 1 All ER 121 at 127, [1968] AC 553 at 606
3   [1949] 1 All ER 1108, 31 Tax Cas 1

However (and this is what is relevant when it becomes necessary to consider *Congreve*[1])   *a*
there might well be situations in which numerous persons, beneficiaries under a trust,
might justly be considered to have 'rights etc'; and moreover, since the deletion of the
reference to 'rights etc' by the Finance Act 1969, s 33, all actual and potential beneficiaries
(viz all 29–32) under this settlement may have 'power to enjoy' within one or more of the
definitions of that expression contained in sub-s (5). More generally, and apart from the
provisions of this particular settlement, there may be cases in which some beneficiaries
have 'power to enjoy' within one paragraph of sub-s (5) and other beneficiaries have   *b*
'power to enjoy' within other paragraphs. The total of the cases may be very large. On
the Crown's contention each and every one of such beneficiaries if resident in the United
Kingdom is liable to income and surtax in respect of the whole income of the trustees.

On this broad analysis of the two subsections how then is an assessment to
income/surtax to be made? The subsections give no indication than that 'that income'
(sub-s (1)) or 'any income' (sub-s (2)), ie any income of the foreign trustees, is to be   *c*
deemed the income of an individual; they give no guidance or indication whatever as to
what is to be done if there is more than one individual to whom either subsection may
apply.

The contention of the Crown is that in such cases they have a discretion which enables
them to assess one or more or all of the individuals in such sums as they think fit; the
only limitation on this discretion is, they say, that the total income (of the foreign   *d*
trustees) may not be assessed more than once. This is a remarkable contention. Let us
consider first some of the practical consequences, if it is correct.

(1) It is open to the Revenue to select one or more of the beneficiaries to tax and to pass
over the others. (2) It is open to the Revenue to apportion the tax between several
beneficiaries according to any method they think fit, and this without any possibility of
appeal, none being provided for. (3) The liability of individual beneficiaries may depend   *e*
on when the Revenue chooses to make its assessment. Thus, if assessments had been
made in 1962–63, or in 1963–64, the income of those years would have been apportioned
between selected beneficiaries. On the Revenue's method, these would have been the
recipients of capital sums in 1962–63. This having been done, the income of those years
could not subsequently have been apportioned to other beneficiaries. But by deferring
assessments until after 1966–67, the Revenue has been able to impose liability in respect   *f*
of the income of 1963–64 on fresh entrants, viz Mrs Payne and Mrs Baddeley, who
received capital sums in 1966. How does this square with the principle that income tax
is an annual tax, that a taxpayer is entitled to know what tax is claimed against him? In
principle a taxpayer who has made a completely correct return is entitled to be taxed on
the basis of it and not to have his liability determined by the choice of the Revenue when
to make its assessment. I repeat what I have already said, that the question is not as to the   *g*
correctness of the overall assessments on all the respondents in all the selected years, but
as to the correctness of, eg, the assessment on Mrs Payne in respect of 1963–64. (4) The
Revenue is entitled to continue the process of discretionary assessment so long as the
settlement endures. It may adhere to its present system, or change it; it may take into
account changes in facts (eg the appearance of new entrants into the class, or new
recipients) or it may not. No beneficiary has any means of challenging its decisions.   *h*

These are some of the consequences, in this case, and applied to these beneficiaries, of
the Crown's contention; they are frightening enough. But there are more fundamental
objections, in principle, to the whole proposition.

Taxes are imposed on subjects by Parliament. A citizen cannot be taxed unless he is
designated in clear terms by a taxing Act as a taxpayer, and the amount of his liability is
clearly defined.   *j*

A proposition that whether a subject is to be taxed or not, or that, if he is, the amount
of his liability is to be decided (even though within a limit) by an administrative body,
represents a radical departure from constitutional principle. It may be that the Revenue

---

1   [1948] 1 All ER 948, 30 Tax Cas 163

a   could persuade Parliament to enact such a proposition in such terms that the courts would have to give effect to it; but unless it has done so, the courts, acting on constitutional principles, not only should not, but cannot validate it.

The Crown's contentions to the contrary, however moderate and persuasive their presentation by leading counsel, fail to support the proposition.

The Crown says that the income tax legislation gives the commissioners a general administrative discretion as to the execution of the Acts, and it refers to particular

b   instances, of which one is s 115(2) of the Income and Corporation Taxes Act 1970 (power to decide period of assessment). The judge described the comparison of such limited discretions with that now contended for as 'laughable'. Less genially I agree. More generally, they say that s 412 imposes a liability on each and every beneficiary for tax in respect of the whole income of the foreign transferees; that there is no duty on the commissioners to collect the whole of this from any one beneficiary, that they are

c   entitled, so long as they do not exceed the total, to collect from selected beneficiaries an amount decided on by themselves.

My Lords, I must reject this proposition. When Parliament imposes a tax, it is the duty of the commissioners to assess and levy it on and from those who are liable by law. Of course they may, indeed should, act with administrative common sense. To expend a large amount of taxpayers' money in collecting, or attempting to collect, small

d   sums would be an exercise in futility; and no one is going to complain if they bring humanity to bear in hard cases. I accept also that they cannot, in the absence of clear power, tax any given income more than once. But all of this falls far short of saying that so long as they do not exceed a maximum they can decide that beneficiary A is to bear so much tax and no more, or that beneficiary B is to bear no tax.

This would be taxation by self asserted administrative discretion and not by law. As

e   the judge well said[1], 'One should be taxed by law, and not be untaxed by concession.' The fact in the present case is that Parliament has laid down no basis on which tax can be apportioned where there are numerous discretionary beneficiaries.

This was clearly seen by the Special Commissioners. They say in the supplemental case stated on 27th January 1978[2]:

f   'Apportionment of the "deemed" income according to the quantum of the respective beneficial interests has much to commend it, but (as we noticed in paragraph 12 of our original decision) section 412 does not so provide. We recognise that apportionment may be impossible in the case of some of the discretionary beneficiaries whose expectancy may be insignificant. Various methods of apportionment were canvassed before us, the merits of each differing according to the circumstances. In our view, in default of a method prescribed by the section,

g   and we can find none, it is for the Board in exercise of their powers in the execution of the Acts to decide on the appropriate apportionment.'

It is interesting to compare this passage, and what Parliament has *not* done in the present context, with what it *has* done in another. There is power, as is well known, to apportion for purposes of surtax (or higher rates of income tax) income of 'close companies' to shareholders, or 'participators', including in some cases persons entitled to

h   secure that income or assets will be applied for their benefit. But, here, Parliament has expressly conferred the power to apportion, has laid down principles according to which the apportionment is to be made, has defined the period for which assessments are to be made, and has allowed for appeals; all this in a detailed and precise manner (see Income and Corporation Taxes Act 1970, s 296ff, derived from the Finance Act 1965 and the

j   Finance Act 1972, Sch 16). The contrast between this legislation and the present is striking.

The commissioners have, I gladly accept, done their best to devise a system which is

---

1   [1977] 3 All ER 1073 at 1098, [1979] Ch 177 at 197, [1977] STC 414 at 439

2   [1979] 2 All ER 225 at 230, [1978] STC 567 at 572

workable and reasonably fair. But whatever system they might devise lacks any legal basis. I must regard this case therefore as one in which Parliament has attempted to *a* impose a tax, but in which it has failed, in the case of discretionary beneficiaries, to lay down any basis on which it can be assessed or levied. In the absence of any such basis the tax must fail. That this must be the result was correctly perceived by Macnaghten J in *Lord Herbert v Inland Revenue Comrs*[1] a decision based on the Finance Act 1938, s 38. The learned judge there used these words:

'It seems to me fantastic to suppose that Parliament has conferred upon inspectors *b* of taxes, or even upon the Special Commissioners, the right to decide at their own will and pleasure which of several persons should be liable to income tax or surtax as the case might be.'

My Lords, this brings me to *Congreve*[2] itself. Can a decision which involves the consequences which I have described be acceptable? I must say at once that I cannot *c* accept leading counsel for the taxpayers' argument that the proposition, that s 412 applies to cases where the person sought to be taxed was not himself or herself a transferor, was not a ratio decidendi of that case. He certainly gets some support for the proposition that the case was decided on a different ground from the headnote to the report in the All England Law Reports[3]:

'An individual can, within the meaning of s. 18 of the Finance Act, 1936, be said *d* to acquire rights "by means of" a transfer of assets though the transfer is effected neither by the individual nor by his agent, but by a company, the whole or greater part of the share capital of which is held by or on behalf of that individual.'

However, that is the limit of his comfort for the headnote is certainly incomplete. It is clear, on consideration of the facts, elaborate it is true but susceptible of analysis, and *e* from the judgments, that it was argued that Mrs Congreve could not be taxed in respect of assets transferred by her father. The judgments in the Court of Appeal[4] and in this House[2] unambiguously reject this contention and the fact that they accepted an alternative argument to the effect that in any case Mrs Congreve had organised or engineered transfers by her father does not prevent their rejection of the contention from being a ratio decidendi. Indeed not only was it a ratio, it was the main ratio. It was *f* followed, as such, in the subsequent cases of *Bambridge*[5] and *Philippi v Inland Revenue Comrs*[6]. So the issue cannot be avoided whether this ratio is correct.

The result of the preceeding argument is that, if *Congreve*[2] is correct in this respect, a result is produced, in the case of discretionary trusts, which is arbitrary, unjust, and in my opinion unconstitutional. That must cast doubt on the decision. For it is a well accepted principle that if one interpretation of an Act of Parliament produces such a *g* result, but another avoids it, the latter is to be preferred.

There are undoubtedly two possible interpretations of s 412 of the 1952 Act, particularly having regard to the preamble. The first is to regard it as having a limited effect; to be directed against persons who transfer assets abroad; who by means of such transfers avoid tax, and who yet manage when resident in the United Kingdom to obtain or to be in a position to obtain benefits from those assets. For myself I regard this as *h* being the natural meaning of the section. This avoids all the difficulties discussed above. No difficulty arises from cases of multiple transferors. The second is to give the

---

1   [1943] 1 All ER 336 at 338, [1943] 1 KB 288 at 291, 25 Tax Cas 93 at 99   *j*
2   [1948] 1 All ER 948, 30 Tax Cas 163
3   [1948] 1 All ER 948
4   [1947] 1 All ER 168, 30 Tax Cas 163
5   [1955] 3 All ER 812, [1955] 1 WLR 1329, 36 Tax Cas 313
6   [1971] 3 All ER 61, [1971] 1 WLR 1272, 47 Tax Cas 75

a   whole section an extended meaning, so as to embrace all persons, born or unborn, who in any way may benefit from assets transferred abroad by others. This is or follows from the *Congreve*[1] interpretation. This I regard as a possible but less natural meaning of the section.

Apart from linguistic considerations there are other arguments. I mention two. 1. One much used by the Crown is that the section is a penal section. But this cuts both ways. In a case such as *Lord Howard de Walden v Inland Revenue Comrs*[2] this argument has *b*   much force. The transferor in that case, who derived a comparatively small benefit from the tranferred assets, was taxed in respect of the whole income. It was an entirely valid argument, lucidly explained by Lord Greene MR, in support of so severe a liability, to say that the section was penal and meant to deter transfers abroad. In such a context his metaphor of burnt fingers is completely apposite. But the argument turns the other way when so Draconian a tax ('astonishingly severe' were leading counsel for the Crown's *c*   words) is sought to be imposed on persons who had no hand in the transfer, who may never benefit from it, who cannot escape from it, who remain under liability so long as they live or the settlement lasts. In relation to such persons equity and principle suggest that Parliament intended no such thing, or at least cannot be assumed from the veiled language used to have intended any such thing. To penalise is one thing, to visit the sins of the transferor on future generations is quite another. 2. There is the reference to *d*   avoiding tax; prevention of avoidance is the stated objective. But there may be many cases, of which this is one, in which no tax is avoided by the person sought to be charged. If this settlement had been made in England with English trustees, not a penny of tax could, at the relevant time, have been levied on any of the beneficiaries. The settlement would be a classic accumulating settlement with power to pay capital sums, accepted at the time as not attracting any tax. This seems to show that the mischief at *e*   which the section was directed was a more limited one.

My Lords, these and other arguments, together with the linguistic, persuade me that the better interpretation of the section is not that accepted in *Congreve*[1] but is one limiting its operation and charging effect to the transferors of assets.

We now have to face the fact that this House decided otherwise, unanimously, and affirming the Court of Appeal[3]. That was 30 years ago; the decision has been followed *f*   in reported cases (*Bambridge*[4] and *Philippi*[5]) and no doubt many persons have been taxed on the basis of it, without resistance. I have reflected with anxiety whether this House ought, within the principles which should guide the exercise of the power taken in 1966, to depart from it. I bear in mind that the decision was one of interpretation of a taxing Act; that the interpretation accepted was, I say with all respect, a tenable one; that this House ought not to sanction attempts to obtain reversals of decisions deliberately reached *g*   however attractive to their successors another view may appear to be.

But on the other side, and this must be a rare situation, it can now be seen, as it certainly was not seen in 1949, that the consequences of the interpretation then accepted must lead, in relation to a large class of settlements and in particular where sub-s (2) might be invoked (it was not considered in *Congreve*[1]) to a situation involving results which are arbitrary, potentially unjust, and fundamentally unconstitutional. If these *h*   had been seen in 1949 (within the ambit of proper argument they could not reasonably have been seen) I cannot believe that the eminent Lords who decided the case would have been willing to ascribe to Parliament an intention to produce such results. The alternative which is supported by the language is to suppose that the section was intended by Parliament as a limited section, attacking, with penal consequences, those who

j

1   [1948] 1 All ER 948, 30 Tax Cas 163
2   [1942] 1 All ER 287, [1942] 1 KB 389, 25 Tax Cas 121
3   [1947] 1 All ER 168, 30 Tax Cas 163
4   [1955] 3 All ER 812, [1955] 1 WLR 1329, 36 Tax Cas 313
5   [1971] 3 All ER 61, [1971] 1 WLR 1272, 47 Tax Cas 75

removed assets abroad so as to gain tax advantages while residing in the United Kingdom *a* and not a section representing such a departure from principle, yet without any prescribed mechanism to operate it, as the alternative can now be seen to involve.

It may be said, and I believe that some of your Lordships share this opinion, that to limit the section so as to relate only to transferors of assets is to emasculate it, or to open up a wide gap in its application. But is this so? Let us consider some of the earlier pronouncements as to its purpose. In *Inland Revenue Comrs v Barclays Bank Ltd*[1] Lord Greene MR after quoting the preamble said: *b*

> 'It is notorious that before the passing of this legislation [ie the Finance Act 1936, s 18] individuals who were minded to enjoy their income without bearing any appropriate burden of British taxation were able to do so by transferring assets productive of income to a non-resident person or company by whom the income was retained abroad, so as not to incur taxation in England. The money representing the income was then by means of one or other of several well-known expedients, *c* transferred to England as capital.'

He affirmed this statement of the purpose of the section in *Lord Howard de Walden v Inland Revenue Comrs*.[2] Macnaghten J[3] at first instance had given his analysis of the section which brings out very clearly that it must be the transferor who acquires rights (cf also Kanga and Palkhivala on Income Tax[4] on the corresponding Indian section). *d*

The pronouncements of Lord Greene MR were made in December 1941, ie just before the settlement was executed.

When *Latilla v Inland Revenue Comrs*[5] came before this House Viscount Simon LC opened his speech with these words:

> 'My Lords, of recent years much ingenuity has been expended in certain quarters in attempting to devise methods of disposition of income by which those who were *e* prepared to adopt them might enjoy the benefits of residence in this country while receiving the equivalent of such income without sharing in the appropriate burden of British taxation. Judicial *dicta* may be cited which point out that, however elaborate and artificial such methods may be, those who adopt them are "entitled" to do so. There is, of course, no doubt that they are within their legal rights, but that is no reason why their efforts, or those of the professional gentlemen who assist *f* them in the matter, should be regarded as a commendable exercise of ingenuity or as a discharge of the duties of good citizenship. On the contrary, one result of such methods, if they succeed, is, of course, to increase *pro tanto* the load of tax on the shoulders of the great body of good citizens who do not desire, or do not know how, to adopt these manoeuvres. Another consequence is that the legislature has made amendments to our income tax code which aim at nullifying the effectiveness of *g* such schemes.'

So we have a clear, identifiable and substantial mischief against which the section, as I would now construe it, was certainly directed. Then are we to suppose that the section must also have been directed against cases where a person transfers assets abroad for the benefit of a child or grandchild; and is it incredible that Parliament should not have *h* covered that case?

My Lords, to extend so penal a section so as to catch future generations is not merely something which logically follows from penalising transferors themselves, but is something which appears to me to introduce a new dimension, indeed an innovation, in our tax law. Are we to deduce from an evident intention to tax (and penalise) transferors

j

---

1 [1942] 1 All ER 214 at 216, [1942] 1 KB 299 at 303, 25 Tax Cas 107 at 115
2 [1942] 1 All ER 287, [1942] 1 KB 389, 25 Tax Cas 121
3 (1941) 25 Tax Cas 121 at 128–129
4 7th Edn (1976) p 725
5 [1943] 1 All ER 265 at 266, [1943] AC 377 at 381, 25 Tax Cas 107 at 117

of assets one is to visit their offence on their children, or their grandchildren? Surely
a such an extension, which would certainly have attracted debate, if not criticism, in
Parliament, would have been spelled out and not left to be deduced from such cryptic
words as have been used. I find in the section, if directed at transferors, and benefits
taken by them, an ample and powerful anti-avoidance instrument and I feel not only no
need, but a great reluctance, in view of the wording used, to extend it against any
beneficiary, child or grandchild, or descendant.

b   I recognise that there is always the possibility of 'overkill'. Parliament itself may not
have consciously intended to go beyond the transferor, yet words may have been used
which are so wide as to do so. Such cases exist in modern fiscal legislation (cf *Cleary v
Inland Revenue Comrs*[1]). But then I think that the courts, if they are satisfied that the
words used, on one interpretation, go so far as to create extreme injustices and departure
from fiscal propriety, are well entitled to take another interpretation which does not do
c this. And in this case, the other interpretation can be found without straining words or
writing anything in.

My Lords, the discretion conferred by the practice direction of 1966[2] is a general
one. We should exercise it sparingly and try to keep it governed by stated principles.
But the fact that the circumstances of one particular case cannot be brought precisely
within the formulae used in others of a different character should not be fatal to its
d exercise, or the discretion would become ossified. I regard this case as one where a
previous decision has been given on facts of a particular type without consideration being
given (and there is no shred of criticism in saying this) to the possible consequences in a
wider type of situation. Of course it is generally true that when a decision of principle
is given, the fact that those who gave it did not have every possible situation in mind does
not prevent the decision being applied to new and unforeseen facts. The doctrine of
e precedent and the interest of certainty require that it should be. But if, as I believe to be
the case here, extension of a limited decision to totally different situations involves a new
dimension which itself embraces administrative and constitutional difficulties of a high
degree, I think that this House ought to use its discretion to refuse the extension. The
only choice is then between overruling the previous decision so far as the principal ratio
is concerned or confining it to its, or similar, facts.

f   My Lords, we have not, I hope, in recent years become so habituated to fiscal severities
or to 'overkill' sections as to be insensitive to those proprieties which were so eloquently
stressed by Walton J in his judgments. It is respect for these and for the fabric of our fiscal
law which persuade me that *Congreve*[3], as to its principal ratio and the following cases,
should be departed from or overruled and the section interpreted as applying only where
the person sought to be charged made, or, maybe, was associated with, the transfer. If
g your Lordships do not follow me so far, then, in view of the consequences which would
result from the extension of *Congreve*[3] into a case where there are discretionary
beneficiaries, I would hold that it cannot be applied to such a case, that no method for
levying the tax in such cases has been prescribed by Parliament, that this gap cannot be
filled by administrative decision and that the tax and the assessments of it fail.

I would dismiss the appeals and allow the cross-appeals.

h

VISCOUNT DILHORNE. My Lords, in these consolidated appeals the taxpayer
Ronald Arthur Vestey is the son of Sir Edmund Vestey Bt. The taxpayer Edmund Hoyle
Vestey is Ronald's son and the taxpayers J R Baddeley and James C Payne are Ronald's
sons-in-law. The taxpayers Lord Vestey and Mark William Vestey are great grandsons of
the first Lord Vestey. By a settlement dated 25th March 1942 Sir Edmund Vestey and
j the first Lord Vestey conveyed a large number of properties outside the United Kingdom
to trustees and on 26th March 1942 the trustees leased the trust property to Union Cold

---

1   [1967] 2 All ER 48, [1968] AC 766, 44 Tax Cas 399
2   *Note* [1966] 3 All ER 77, [1966] 1 WLR 1234
3   [1948] 1 All ER 948, 30 Tax Cas 163

Storage Ltd for 21 years at an annual rent of £960,000. By a further lease dated 10th April 1963 the trust property was again leased to that company at that rent. The trustees *a* of the settlement, who have at all times been resident out of the United Kingdom, also held all the shares in three companies, in two as subscribers for their shares and in the third, the Commercial Insurance Corpn Ltd, by purchasing the shares.

Under the settlement the trustees were to receive the income of the properties conveyed to them and of property representing the same during a prescribed period and to invest it so as to form a capital fund, called the rental fund. During the prescribed *b* term the income of the rental fund was to be divided into two moieties and held on the trusts applicable to what were called Edmund's fund and Samuel's fund. From and after the end of the prescribed term the trustees were able to divide the rental fund into two moieties, Edmund's fund and Samuel's fund, and hold them on the trusts declared with regard thereto.

The settlement provided that the trustees might be directed by 'Edmund's manager' *c* who was the respondent, Ronald Arthur Vestey, to accumulate for such period or periods, within the period specified in the deed, the whole or any part of the income of Edmund's fund and that, subject to the power of accumulation and to other provisions of the deed, the trustees should hold the income on trust for Ronald Arthur Vestey and his issue or, if no issue of his should be living, for the issue of Sir Edmund Vestey in such amounts or shares as Edmund's manager might direct. Similar provisions were made *d* with regard to Samuel's fund and Samuel's manager was, until his death in 1944, William Howarth Vestey, the grandson of the first Lord Vestey. He was followed as Samuel's manager by Mr Brown and then in 1966 the third Lord Vestey was appointed to that office. On 30th August 1942 Samuel's manager directed the trustees to accumulate the whole of the income of Samuel's fund by investing it. On 14th September 1942 a similar direction was given by Edmund's manager in relation to the *e* income of Edmund's fund.

The settlement gave Edmund's manager power within the specified period to direct the trustees to appropriate and realise capital and to pay it to Ronald Arthur Vestey and his issue and in default to the issue of Sir Edmund Vestey in such shares and in such manner as Edmund's manager might direct. A similar power to direct the trustees to distribute capital as he might direct among the issue of the first Lord Vestey was given *f* to Samuel's manager.

In the exercise of these powers the trustees were directed to distribute and did distribute between the taxpayers Ronald Arthur Vestey, Edmund Hoyle Vestey, Lord Vestey and Mark Vestey and also Mrs Payne and Mrs Baddeley, daughters of Ronald Arthur Vestey, the sum of £2,608,000 on various dates between October 1962 and November 1966. *g*

The Revenue then raised assessments on the six respondents. It is not necessary to state in detail the amount of each assessment. Two examples will suffice. Ronald Arthur Vestey received a total of £365,000 from the trustees, £215,000 on 29th October 1962 and £150,000 on 18th November 1964. He was consequently assessed to income tax and surtax for the years 1963–64, 1964–65, 1965–66 and 1966–67 amounting to £888,500. Mr Baddeley, as the husband of Mrs Baddeley who received £100,000 on 2nd May 1966, *h* was in consequence of that assessed to tax for 1963–64 in the sum of £62,088·71, for 1964–65 in the sum of £64,818·14, in 1965–66 in the sum of £84,667·75. In none of those years had Mrs Baddeley received anything from the trustees. For 1966–67 Mr Baddeley was assessed in the sum of £62,547·35. So in consequence of the receipt by his wife of £100,000 in 1966, he was assessed to tax in the sum of £274,121·95.

The taxpayers appealed from these assessments to the Special Commissioners without *j* success. They then appealed to the High Court[1] and Walton J allowed their appeals and remitted the cases to the Special Commissioners for them to consider whether the assessments were justified under s 412(1) of the Income Tax Act 1952. They had been

---

1   [1977] 3 All ER 1073, [1979] Ch 177, [1977] STC 414

made under s 412(2). The Special Commissioners concluded that the assessments were
justified under s 412(1) and the taxpayers' appeal from that decision was heard by Walton
J[1] who allowed their appeals. The Crown now appeal direct to this House from Walton
J's decision by virtue of s 12 of the Administration of Justice Act 1969.

Section 412 commences with what has been called a preamble. That and what is
contained in sub-s (1) of that section was first enacted by the Finance Act 1936, s 18.
Subsection (2) was added by the Finance Act 1938, s 28. These parts of s 412 read as
follows:

> 'For the purpose of preventing the avoiding by individuals ordinarily resident in
> the United Kingdom of liability to income tax by means of transfers of assets by
> virtue or in consequence whereof, either alone or in conjunction with associated
> operations, income becomes payable to persons resident or domiciled out of the
> United Kingdom, it is hereby enacted as follows:

> '(1) Where such an individual has by means of any such transfer, either alone or
> in conjunction with associated operations, acquired any rights by virtue of which he
> has, within the meaning of this section, power to enjoy, whether forthwith or in the
> future, any income of a person resident or domiciled out of the United Kingdom
> which, if it were income of that individual received by him in the United Kingdom,
> would be chargeable to income tax by deduction or otherwise, that income shall,
> whether it would or would not have been chargeable to income tax apart from the
> provisions of this section, be deemed to be income of that individual for all the
> purposes of this Act.

> '(2) Where, whether before or after any such transfer, such an individual receives
> or is entitled to receive any capital sum the payment whereof is in any way
> connected with the transfer or any associated operation, any income which, by
> virtue or in consequence of the transfer, either alone or in conjunction with
> associated operations, has become the income of a person resident or domiciled out
> of the United Kingdom shall, whether it would or would not have been chargeable
> to income tax apart from the provisions of this section, be deemed to be the income
> of that individual for all the purposes of this Act.'

The taxpayers contended that these provisions only applied where the taxpayer assessed
had made the transfer of assets by virtue or in consequence of which income became
payable to a person resident or domiciled out of the United Kingdom or where he had
caused such a transfer to be made. This argument was put forward without success in
Congreve v Inland Revenue Comrs[2]. The respondents now contend that that decision of
this House should be distinguished and, alternatively, if it cannot be distinguished,
should now be reviewed and not followed.

The facts of that case were very complicated. It will suffice to say that Mr Glasgow, Mrs
Congreve's father, had prior to the enactment of the Finance Act 1936 transferred assets
to a foreign company. Mrs Congreve had done so too and it was not disputed that she
had acquired rights by virtue of which she had power to enjoy income payable to a
number of foreign companies. Lord Simonds in his speech with which the other
members of the House agreed, posed the question[3]—

> 'whether the transfer of assets, on which either alone or in conjunction with
> associated operations the liability is founded, must be (as the taxpayers contend) a
> transfer effected by Mrs. Congreve or her agent or may be (as the Crown contends)
> effected by anyone, father, friend or company in which she has an interest great or
> small, so long as the result is reached that she has power to enjoy the relevant
> income.'

1 [1979] 2 All ER 225, [1979] Ch 198, [1978] STC 567
2 [1948] 1 All ER 948, 30 Tax Cas 163
3 [1948] 1 All ER 948 at 951–952, 30 Tax Cas 163 at 203

Lord Simonds said[1] that he did not know what better words could have been used in the section if the legislature intended to define its purpose as covering a transfer of assets by A by means of which B avoided liability to tax. He regarded the language of the section as plain and said[2]:

'If there has been such a transfer as is mentioned in the introductory words, and if an individual has by means of such transfer (either alone or in conjunction with associated operations) acquired the rights referred to in the section, then the prescribed consequences follow.'

This was, in my view, clearly the ratio decidendi of the House in this case. It was also the ratio decidendi of the Court of Appeal where the judgment of the court was given by Cohen LJ[3]. Both this House and the Court of Appeal clearly rejected the contention that the section only applied to the individual who had by himself or through an agent made such a trasfer.

I can see no ground for distinguishing that case from this, so unless the House is prepared to hold that that case was wrongly decided, the taxpayers must in my opinion succeed on this issue.

Cohen LJ, with whose judgment Lord Simonds agreed on all points, treated the words 'such an individual' in sub-ss (1) and (2) as meaning an individual ordinarily resident in the United Kingdom. Their meaning does not appear to have been debated in the House. A possible meaning appears to me an individual ordinarily resident who has sought to avoid liability to income tax by means of a transfer of assets abroad. If that was their meaning, then the scope of s 412 is limited. If on the other hand, the words just mean an individual ordinarily resident in the United Kingdom, the decision of this House in *Congreve*[4] was I think right.

Lord Simonds in the course of his speech did not refer to sub-s (8) of s 412. It states, inter alia: 'For the purposes of this section—(a) a reference to an individual shall be deemed to include the wife or husband of the individual . . .''

These words have considerable significance and importance if 'such an individual' means an individual ordinarily resident in the United Kingdom who has sought to avoid income tax by the transfer of assets abroad. If the decision in *Congreve*[4] is right, it is not easy to attach significance to them. Counsel for the Crown suggested that they might have been inserted to cover a case where a husband and wife jointly but not separately had control of a company. I find it difficult to accept that this provision was inserted by Parliament to meet that situation. I think it is much more likely that they were inserted to secure that the wife or the husband of the transferor was brought within the scope of the section and I consequently regard this provision as an indication that by 'such an individual' is meant an individual who has sought to avoid tax by the transfer of assets abroad.

In *Congreve*[4] the House did not have to consider, and, so far as one can see, did not when construing the section consider, the operation of sub-ss (1) and (2) when there was more than one individual who had acquired rights giving power to enjoy income of a person resident or domiciled abroad, and more than one individual had received or was entitled to receive a capital sum connected with the transfer of assets abroad. Walton J[5], when considering sub-s (2), said that if its provisions were taken literally the income of the person resident or domiciled abroad was to be deemed without limit of time to be the income of each individual who received or was entitled to receive such a capital sum 'so

---

1 [1948] 1 All ER 948 at 952, 30 Tax Cas 163 at 204
2 [1948] 1 All ER 948 at 953, 30 Tax Cas 163 at 205
3 [1947] 1 All ER 168, 30 Tax Cas 163
4 [1948] 1 All ER 948, 30 Tax Cas 163
5 [1977] 3 All ER 1073 at 1088, [1979] Ch 177 at 184 [1977] STC 414 at 429

that the Crown is, at the end of the day, entitled to multiple tax, the multiplier being the
number of different appointments made'.

a

He refused to believe that Parliament can ever have so intended, and relying on a
passage from Lord Loreburn LC's speech in *Drummond v Collins*[1] he thought he was
entitled to treat sub-s (2) as so amended as to secure that the individual who received or
was entitled to receive the capital sum was taxable only to the extent to which the capital
sum comprised income which by virtue of a transfer of assets had become the income of
a foreigner. Such a radical alteration of the plain language of this part of the subsection

b

is one that in my opinion can only be made by Parliament. Counsel for the taxpayers
suggested another amendment of the subsection. If made, I am not at all sure that it
would work as he desired but again such an alteration as he proposed could in my view
be made by Parliament alone.

In *Inland Revenue Comrs v Hinchy*[2] where the Crown contended that Mr Hinchy was

c

liable under s 25(3) of the Income Tax Act 1952 to pay a penalty of treble the whole tax
with which he ought to be charged for the relevant year for failing to disclose in his
return the receipt of £32 19s 9d in interest, Lord Reid gave instances of that penalty
being 'grossly and extravagantly disproportionate to the offences' and said:

> 'Difficulties and extravagant results of this kind caused DIPLOCK, J., and the Court
> of Appeal to search for an interpretation which would yield a more just result.

d

> What we must look for is the intention of Parliament, and I also find it difficult to
> believe that Parliament ever really intended the consequences which flow from the
> Crown's contention. But we can only take the intention of Parliament from the
> words which they have used in the Act and, therefore, the question is whether these
> words are capable of a more limited construction. If not, then we must apply them
> as they stand, however unreasonable or unjust the consequences, and however

e

> strongly we may suspect that this was not the real intention of Parliament.'

He concluded that the words were not capable of a more limited construction.

My Lords, I see no escape from the conclusion, if *Congreve*[3] was rightly decided, that
each individual who receives or is entitled to receive a capital sum of the character
referred to in sub-s (2) must be deemed to have the income of the foreigner with the
result, as Walton J[4] said, 'that the Crown is, at the end of the day, entitled to multiple tax'.

f

If *Congreve*[3] is right, sub-s (1) would produce the same result if a number of individuals
had acquired rights giving them power to enjoy a part of the income of a foreigner.

I share Walton J's view that Parliament cannot have intended that a person, who might
be unborn at the time of the transfer of assets, should be chargeable to tax on the whole
of the income of the foreigner if he acquired rights giving him power to enjoy part of
that income or received or was entitled to receive a capital sum coming within sub-s (2)

g

and without limit of time or that the Revenue should be able to recover multiple tax if
there were a number of such individuals.

None of these consequences would arise if the persons deemed to have the income of
the non-resident were the individuals who had sought to avoid income tax and, by virtue
of s 412(8) (*a*), his wife or her husband. It would not be unjust that they should be
chargeable to income tax on the income enjoyed by the non-resident in consequence of

h

the indvidual's transfer of assets abroad to avoid tax. Further, the omission to make any
provision in the section when, if *Congreve*[3] is right, a number of individuals have to be
deemed to have the income of the non-resident is, I think, very significant.

The choice lies between the section having a limited application, applying only to the
individual who has sought to avoid income tax and his or her spouse and a wide

j

---

1 [1915] AC 1011 at 1017, 6 Tax Cas 525 at 538–539
2 [1960] 1 All ER 505 at 512, [1960] AC 748 at 767, 38 Tax Cas 625 at 652
3 [1948] 1 All ER 948, 30 Tax Cas 163
4 [1977] 3 All ER 1073 at 1088, [1979] Ch 177 at 184, [1977] STC 414 at 429

application to all individuals who have the rights bringing them within sub-s (1) or who have received a capital sum within sub-s (2), however innocent of tax avoidance an individual might be and without regard to the amount which he might have power to enjoy or which he has received or is entitled to receive as a capital sum. *a*

The limited application would leave, it is said, 'a yawning gap'. Persons who transfer assets abroad may do so for the benefit of their families and not for their own benefit. With this construction their descendants would not come within the section. Gaps when they are found in our tax laws are usually speedily filled. The wider application is productive of such manifest injustices that in my view Parliament cannot have intended it. *b*

I have therefore come to the conclusion that the decision in *Congreve*[1] on this question was wrong, though the actual decision of the case can be upheld on the alternative ground stated by Cohen LJ[2] in his judgment.

The Crown has not in this case sought to assess each taxpayer on the whole of the income of the non-resident trustees. They have apportioned each year that income in proportion to the capital sum received by each individual between October 1962 and November 1966, so, if the Crown is right, the extent of Mr Baddeley's liability to tax depended on the amounts received by the others. In its case the Crown says that it has always been their practice to apportion the income between the individuals concerned in what seems the most appropriate manner. Although an individual has the right to appeal against an assessment made on him, this right is worthless if the amount of his assessment depends solely on the discretion of the Revenue: *d*

'This practice [it was said] may be justified either on the ground that the section does impose multiple liability, but that the [Revenue] are not required as a matter of law and ought not as a matter of proper administration, to recover tax on the income more that once or on the ground that the [Revenue] are not entitled to tax the same income more than once.' *e*

In the course of his judgment in relation to sub-s (1) Walton J[3] said that the Crown had submitted that—

'if the conditions of the section were satisfied, then the taxpayer was chargeable in respect of the whole of the income of the non-resident . . . and that nonetheless because there might also be somebody else who was in precisely the same situation.' *f*

This, if the decision in *Congreve*[1] was right, must be so. Has the Revenue then any right or power to mitigate the gross injustice that results? I think not. The section is mandatory. It says that the income of the non-resident 'shall . . . be deemed to be income of that individual for all the purposes of the Act'. The income of each individual to whom the section applies must be deemed to include the income of the non-resident. There is no question of the income of any induvidual being taxed more than once. *g*

On this view the consequences to each individual may be even worse than they are to the respondents in this case and in my opinion the Revenue has no power to override the clear provisions of this section.

I now turn to the question whether, if as I think the decision of this House in *Congreve*[1] was wrong, it should not now be followed. That case decided 31 years ago. It was followed and not questioned in *Bambridge v Inland Revenue Comrs*[4] and it does not appear to have been questioned in any subsequent case. *h*

In *Jones v Secretary of State for Social Services*[5] the decision of this House in *Minister of*

---

1   [1948] 1 All ER 948, 30 Tax Cas 163
2   [1947] 1 All ER 168, 30 Tax Cas 163
3   [1979] 2 All ER 225 at 241, [1979] Ch 198 at 213, [1978] STC 567 at 583
4   [1954] 3 All ER 682, [1954] 1 WLR 1460, 36 Tax Cas 313, CA; *affd* [1955] 3 All ER 812, [1955] 1 WLR 1329, HL
5   [1972] 1 All ER 145, [1972] AC 944

j

Social Security v Amalgamated Engineering Union ('*Dowling's* case')[1] was challenged and the
question whether it should be overruled was considered by a committee of seven, four
a   of whom came to the conclusion that the case had been wrongly decided but four of
whom held that it should not be overruled, my noble and learned friends, Lord
Wilberforce and Lord Diplock, and I thinking that it should be. Lord Reid said that in
his opinion[2]—

b
'the typical case for reconsidering an old decision is where some broad issue is
involved, and that it should only be in rare cases that we should reconsider questions
of construction of statutes or other documents. In very many cases it cannot be said
positively that one construction is right and the other wrong. Construction so often
depends on weighing one consideration against another. Much may depend on
one's approach. If more attention is paid to meticulous examination of the language
used in the statute the result may be different from that reached by paying more
c   attention to the apparent object of the statute so as to adopt that meaning of the
words under consideration which best accord with it. Holding these views, I am
firmly of opinion that *Dowling's* case[1] ought not to be reconsidered. No broad issue
of justice or public policy is involved nor is any question of legal principle. The
issue is simply the proper construction of complicated provisions in a statute. There
must be a large number of decisions of this House of this character. Possibly some
d   of your Lordships may think the decision in *Dowling's* case[1] more wrong than most
of them. But a decision to reconsider *Dowling's* case[1] would I think encourage those
who would like to see others of such decisions reversed to think that litigation for
that purpose might be worthwhile and would have a rather far-reaching tendency
to impair existing certainty.'

Lord Morris of Borth-y-Gest[3] thought it wholly inappropriate not to treat *Dowling's*
e   case[1] as a binding authority. 'It was', he said, 'essentially a decision which involved
questions of construction of the statutory provisions.'

Lord Pearson[4] pointed out that in *Dowling's* case[1] there were conflicting views and that
each of them was tenable, and said:

'If a tenable view taken by a majority in the first appeal could be overruled by a
f   majority preferring another tenable view in a second appeal, then the original
tenable view could be restored by a majority preferring it in a third appeal. Finality
of decision would be utterly lost.'

Lord Simon of Glaisdale[5], while thinking the decision in *Dowling's* case[1] wrong,
thought that it would be wrong to depart from it for a number of reasons, one of which
was that—

g
'A variation of view on a matter of statutory construction—so much a matter of
impression—would, I should have thought, rarely provide a suitable occasion, by
itself, that is to say, for it would be different if it were convincingly shown that a
previous construction, clearly demonstrated to be wrong, was causing administrative
difficulties or individual injustice.'

h   My Lords, it is clear that our power to depart from previous decisions is one that
should rarely be exercised. None of their Lordships in *Jones's* case[6] said that it should
never be exercised in relation to the construction of a statute but the passages from the

---

j   1   [1967] 1 All ER 210, [1967] 1 AC 725
2   [1972] 1 All ER 145 at 149, [1972] AC 944 at 966
3   [1972] 1 All ER 145 at 155, [1972] AC 944 at 973
4   [1972] 1 All ER 145 at 174, [1972] AC 944 at 996–997
5   [1972] 1 All ER 145 at 196, [1972] AC 944 at 1024
6   [1972] 1 All ER 145, [1972] AC 944

speeches which I have cited indicate that in such cases it should be exercised very rarely
indeed. Here the choice is not between a literal construction and what is now not *a*
infrequently called a purposive construction. Here, as Walton J showed, the construction
placed on the section in *Congreve*[1] can be productive of very great injustice to persons like
Mr Baddeley and many others. I would myself be reluctant to assert that any decision of
this House on a question of law was not a tenable view and when this House has
reconsidered a previous decision there is always the possibility, remote though I think it
is, that in a further appeal the first decision would be restored. Indeed where a decision *b*
on construction has been reconsidered, I would have thought that the possibility of this
House reconsidering it again very remote indeed.

Is this one of those very rare cases in which it would be right to depart from the
construction placed on the subsection in *Congreve*[1]? At one time I thought not and that
it should be left to the legislature to remedy the injustice but on further consideration I
have come to the conclusion that it is. *c*

There is no indication in the judgments in the *Congreve* case[1] or in the speech of Lord
Simonds that in the course of that litigation any consideration was given to s 412(8)(*a*) or
to the fact that the construction this House accepted meant that the income of the non-
resident was to be deemed the income of as many individuals as had rights giving them
power to enjoy any income of the non-resident or as had received any capital sum,
however small, coming within sub-s (2). If these matters had been adverted to, it is, I *d*
think, inconceivable that Lord Simonds would not have referred to them in his speech.
It is these matters which have led me to think that the decision in *Congreve*[1] was wrong,
and if these matters had been brought to the attention of the House in that case it might
well be that a different conclusion would then have been reached.

In my opinion the decision in *Congreve v Inland Revenue Comrs*.[1] should be overruled
with the consequence that none of the assessments in the present case should be upheld. *e*

If, however, a majority of your Lordships take a different view and hold that, despite
the injustice that can ensue, that decision should be followed, in my view the assessments
made on Mr Baddeley for the years 1963–64, 1964–65 and 1965–66 should in any event
be discharged. While the income of the non-resident trustees would be deemed to be
income of his wife on her receipt of the £100,000 on 2nd May 1966 in that and
subsequent financial years, I see nothing in sub-s (2) which gives it retroactive effect. It *f*
does not provide that the income of the non-resident in any year before a person receives
or is entitled to receive it is to be deemed that person's income. Assessments totalling
£449,782 were made on him for those three years. Mr Payne is in the same position as
Mr Baddeley as his wife received £100,000 on the same date and in my view the
assessments made on him for those years should also be discharged.

Leading counsel for the taxpayers contended that the capital sums received were not *g*
within sub-s (4) associated operations as those sums originated from the accumulations
of income derived from accumulations of income made by the trustees. That subsection
is in very wide terms and reads as follows:

> 'For the purposes of this section, "an associated operation" means, in relation to
> any transfer, an operation of any kind effected by any person in relation to any of the
> assets transferred or any assets representing, whether directly or indirectly, any of *h*
> the assets transferred, or to the income arising for any such assets, or to any assets
> representing, whether directly or indirectly, the accumulations of income arising
> from any such assets.'

This submission was rejected by Walton J and I think rightly for the reasons he gives.
I would, however, point out that whether or not the distribution of capital was an *j*

---

1   [1948] 1 All ER 948, 30 Tax Cas 163

a   associated operation, a capital sum which comes within sub-s (2) is one which is 'in any way connected with the transfer or any associated operation . . .'

In my opinion the capital sums in this case were clearly so connected.

Leading counsel for the taxpayers also contended that the income of the three companies in which the non-resident trustees held all the shares was not to be regarded as the income of the non-resident trustees. The Crown conceded that the income of the Commercial Insurance Corpn Ltd was not to be treated as the income of the trustees as *b*   they had purchased all the shares but I see no ground for not treating the income of the two companies, the shares in which were subscribed for by the trustees, as part of their income.

Leading counsel for the taxpayers did not pursue the point he took in relation to the Hon Mark Vestey before Walton J and on which he failed.

I now turn, on the basis that the *Congreve*[1] decision is followed, to the Crown's *c*   alternative claim under sub-s (1). Section 412 was amended by s 33 of the Finance Act 1969 to read as follows:

> '(1) Where by virtue or in consequence of any such transfer, either alone or in conjunction with associated operations, such an individual has, within the meaning of this section, power to enjoy . . .'

d   The effect of this amendment was to make it unnecessary for the Revenue to establish that the individual had acquired any rights. It sufficed, to bring him within the subsection, to establish that he had 'power to enjoy'.

Leading counsel contended that no rights giving a power to enjoy had been acquired and that there was no power to enjoy. Walton J[2] held, again in my opinion rightly, that 'none of these discretionary beneficiaries had any "right" to anything at all which could *e*   possibly bring the subsection into play prior to the Finance Act 1969'.

I need not repeat the reasons he gave for that conclusion with which I agree. Before the second hearing before him assessments for the year 1968–69 were added to those under consideration at the first hearing by agreement between the parties in order to obtain a decision on the effect of the amendment of s 412.

'Power to enjoy' is given a very wide meaning by sub-s (5). So far as material that *f*   subsection reads as follows:

> 'An individual shall, for the purposes of this section, be deemed to have power to enjoy income of a person resident or domiciled out of the United Kingdom if . . . (c) the individual receives or is entitled to receive, at any time, any benefit provided or to be provided out of that income or out of moneys which are or will be available for the purpose by reason of the effect or successive effects of the associated *g*   operations on that income and on any assets which directly or indirectly represent that income; or (d) the individual has power, by means of the exercise of any power of appointment or power of revocation or otherwise, to obtain for himself, whether with or without the consent of any other person, the beneficial enjoyment of the income, or may, in the event of the exercise of any power vested in any other person, become entitled to the beneficial enjoyment of the income . . .'

h

Subsection (8)(c) provides that 'benefit' includes a payment of any kind.

I can see no ground for holding that the capital sums received were not provided 'out of [the] income [of the trustees] or out of moneys . . . available' for that purpose by reason of the effect or successive effects of the associated operations; nor do I see any ground for holding that when Edmund's manager and Samuel's manager exercised the power vested *j*   in them of directing the trustees to make the capital payments, the recipients of the capital sums did not become entitled to the beneficial enjoyment of the income. In my view paras (c) and (d) apply.

---

1   [1948] 1 All ER 948, 30 Tax Cas 163
2   [1979] 2 All ER 225 at 236, [1979] Ch 198 at 206, [1978] STC 567 at 577

So, in my opinion, if the *Congreve*[1] decision is followed, the assessment for the years 1963–64, 1964–65, 1965–66 and 1966–67 cannot be sustained under sub-s (1) but the *a* assessments for 1968–69 can be sustained under that subsection as amended. It is common ground that an individual cannot be assessed under sub-s (1) and also under sub-s (2) though the assessments made under s 412 may be justified under either subsection.

My Lords, in this complicated case at least one thing is clear and that is the urgent need for the reconsideration by Parliament of the terms of s 412 as amended (now re-enacted *b* by s 478 of the Income and Corporation Taxes Act 1970). If the conclusion I have reached as to the construction of the section is accepted, then there is indeed a gap to be filled for then the section only applies to the individual who has sought to avoid tax and to his or her spouse and others who may benefit from the tax avoidance will not be penalised even though they participated in the tax avoidance. I need not dilate on the injustice which may be suffered by a number of individuals if the *Congreve*[1] construction *c* is applied. They would not I think have grounds for complaint if they were only assessed to tax on the sums they received or were entitled to receive or had power to enjoy, though a distinction might be drawn between those who participated in the tax avoidance and those who did not. The former category might continue to be liable to be assessed to tax on the whole income of the non-resident.

Consideration of the penalty provisions in s 25 of the Income Tax Act 1952 in *Inland* *d* *Revenue Comrs v Hinchy*[2] led to the law being changed in the next Finance Act. I hope that in consequence of the light now thrown on s 412, that section may equally speedily be amended. In my opinion it certainly should be.

For the reasons I have stated, in my view the appeals should be dismissed with costs and the cross-appeals allowed with costs.

e

LORD SALMON. My Lords, I agree so completely with everything stated in the luminous speech of my noble and learned friend, Lord Wilberforce, that I find it impossible to add anything. I would dismiss the appeals and allow the cross appeals.

LORD EDMUND-DAVIES. My Lords, these appeals and cross-appeals arise from assessments to income tax and surtax made on each of the taxpayers under s 412 of the *f* Income Tax Act 1952, which contained provisions formerly in s 18 of the Finance Act 1936. They were some (but not all) of the potential beneficiaries under a discretionary settlement of 25th March 1942, the nature of which has been helpfully summarised in the speeches of my noble and learned friends, Lord Wilberforce and Viscount Dilhorne. The assessments were made on the basis that s 412 deemed the income of the non-resident trustees of that settlement to be the income of *each* respondent for all the *g* purposes of the Income Tax Acts. None of the respondents was, either directly or indirectly, a settlor of the settlement. The primary point of substance is whether the Commissioners of Inland Revenue can, as they assert, apply s 412 to a person or persons other than the individual who made the transfer contemplated by the settlement. The point can best be dealt with by asking two questions. (1) Was *Congreve v Inland Revenue Comrs*[1] correctly decided by this House? (2) Even if it was wrong, should your Lordships *h* nevertheless follow it?

By way of a preface, reference should first be had to the earlier decision in *Lord Howard de Walden v Inland Revenue Comrs*[3], which, like *Congreve*[1], turned on s 18 of the Finance Act 1936, but which, unlike *Congreve*[1] and the instant case, related only to the liability to tax of the actual transferor of assets to foreign companies and did not deal with the

j

1 [1948] 1 All ER 948, 30 Tax Cas 163
2 [1960] 1 All ER 505, [1960] AC 748, 38 Tax Cas 625
3 [1942] 1 All ER 287, [1942] 1 KB 389, 25 Tax Cas 121

position of later beneficiaries under the settlement. Upholding Macnaghten J's finding[1]

a that such a transferor was liable to be assessed to income tax and surtax, Lord Greene MR said in his extempore judgment[2]:

> 'If, as it seems to us, the language of the section clearly does not limit the income of the non-resident, in respect of which the taxpayer is charged, to the actual benefit which he draws from the income of the non-resident—a construction, be it observed, which would largely defeat the expressed purpose of the section—it is
> b illegitimate to force upon that language a strained construction merely because it may otherwise lead to a result which to some minds may appear to be unjust. However ... we are not prepared to say that it is necessarily as unjust as [the taxpayer's counsel] contends. The section is a penal one, and, whatever its consequences may be, they are intended to be an effective deterrent to practices which the legislature considers to be against the public interest. For years a battle
> c of manoeuvre has been waged between the legislature and those who are minded to throw the burden of taxation off their own shoulders on to those of their fellow-subjects ... It scarcely lies in the mouth of *the taxpayer who plays with fire to complain of burnt fingers*.' (Emphasis mine.)

And, again speaking of the transferor himself, Lord Greene MR added[3]: '... the father
d will be taxed on the companies' income *because he is the "person against whom the deterrent action of the section is directed."*' (Emphasis mine.)

The actual decision in *Lord Howard de Walden Inland Revenue Comrs*[4] turned on the *amount* of the assessments appealed against, which were based on the view that the *whole* income of the foreign companies were, under s 18 of the 1936 Act, to be deemed to be the transferor's income for the purposes of the Income Tax Acts. Notwithstanding that
e the transferor himself received and enjoyed far less, the Court of Appeal held that the whole income was to be deemed his, since the companies' income was traceable to the assets he had transferred. The decision has been criticised, notably by Buckley LJ who described it in *Lord Chetwode v Inland Revenue Comrs*[5] as 'extremely harsh' and expressed difficulty in accepting that the construction of s 18 had received adequate consideration. And in the instant case Walton J regarded it as 'wrong', but added[6]:

f
> 'I do not see how I can escape the straitjacket ... Standing *Lord Howard de Walden v Inland Revenue Comrs*[4], my own fundamental conception of the rule of law is deeply offended. The only alternative is for the Crown to tax all who could possibly under any circumstances be recipients of any sliver of income on the whole of that income; a suggestion equally as offensive. Being bound by that case I am, unhappily, in no position to right a clearly perceived wrong.'

g
But, although I confess to entertaining considerable sympathy with those views, we are not presently concerned to determine the correctness of the *Lord Howard de Walden*[4] decision. Right or wrong, its present importance lies in the fact that it was within the framework of that case that *Congreve* was considered, both the Court of Appeal[7] and the House of Lords[8] citing it with apparent approval. The primary holding in the latter case
h was that s 18 of the 1936 Act applied if the transfer was procured by the taxpayer, even

---

1   (1941) 25 Tax Cas 121
2   [1942] 1 All ER 287 at 289, [1942] 1 KB 389 at 396–397, 25 Tax Cas 121 at 134
j 3   [1942] 1 All ER 287 at 290, [1942] 1 KB 389 at 398, 25 Tax Cas 121 at 134–135
4   [1942] 1 All ER 287, [1942] 1 KB 389, 25 Tax Cas 121
5   [1976] 1 All ER 641 at 657, [1976] 1 WLR 310 at 328, [1976] STC 43 at 70
6   [1979] 2 All ER 225 at 243–244, [1979] Ch 198 at 215–217, [1978] STC 567 at 584–586
7   [1947] 1 All ER 168, 30 Tax Cas 163
8   [1948] 1 All ER 948, 30 Tax Cas 163

though not actually executed by him. So far, so good. But more important for present
purposes was the further holding that s 18 was *not* directed solely against such a taxpayer, *a*
Cohen LJ saying[1]:

> 'We do not think the words "by means of" [in the preamble to s 412] connote
> activity by the individual concerned ... [The words] are fully satisfied if the
> avoidance of tax is effected through the instrumentality of the transfer by whosoever
> it is executed.'

Any doubt as to the ambit of those words was removed in the House of Lords, Lord *b*
Simonds saying[2]:

> 'My Lords, on this question I agree at all points with the unanimous judgment of
> the Court of Appeal which was delivered by Cohen, L.J. The preamble or
> introductory words of the section which state its purpose do not, in my view, assist
> the contention, which was developed on its operative words, that the avoidance by *c*
> an individual of liability to tax must be achieved by means of a transfer of assets
> effected by that individual. They are, on the contrary, in the widest possible terms,
> and I do not know what better words could be used if the legislature intended to
> define its purpose as covering a transfer of assets by A, by means of which B avoided
> liability to tax ... If there has been such a transfer as is mentioned in the
> introductory words, and if an individual has by means of such transfer (either alone *d*
> or in conjunction with associated operations) acquired the rights referred to in the
> section, then the prescribed consequences follow.'

Your Lordships were invited to hold that these passages were merely obiter dicta and,
as such, need not now be applied. But it is an invitation that, for my part, I find it
impossible to accept. On the contrary, they appear to me to contain the true ratio *e*
decidendi of both courts. There is accordingly no escape from the problem of whether
it can and should now be departed from, and this is particularly so when regard is had to
its application by this House in such later cases as *Bambridge*[3] and *Philippi*[4].

My Lords, the correctness of the general proposition enunciated in *Congreve*[5] can be
tested by applying it to facts which, while markedly different from those which were
there being considered, may (as the Crown contends) nevertheless be regarded as falling *f*
completely within its ambit. Although *Congreve*[5] dealt with the tax liability of a single
beneficiary of a settlement giving rise to the transfer of assets abroad, the Crown submits
it applies with full force to the instant case of multiple beneficiaries, none of whom
played any part in the transfer. The astounding consequences of assessing some (but not
all) of them in accordance with that submission were condemned in understandably
strong language by Walton J, and they have been closely considered in the speeches of my *g*
noble and learned friends, Lord Wilberforce and Viscount Dilhorne. So startling and
unattractive do I find them that I gladly abstain from covering the same ground.
Instead, I content myself with recalling that learned counsel for the Crown informed
your Lordships at one stage, 'We accept that the result of applying *Congreve*[5] to the
taxpayers here may be disastrous', while, at another stage, he submitted that a strict
application of s 412 would have entitled them to assess a single beneficiary on the basis *h*
of the *total* income of the settlement in the year of apportionment of the capital sums,
and this regardless of the amount of benefit actually received by him. The commissioners
never went as far as to do that, but one solitary example should serve to illustrate the
breathtaking implications of even a modified application of their basic contention. In

j

1   [1947] 1 All ER 168 at 172, 30 Tax Cas 163 at 196
2   [1948] 1 All ER 948 at 952–953, 30 Tax Cas 163 at 204–205
3   [1955] 3 All ER 812, [1955] 1 WLR 1329, 36 Tax Cas 313
4   [1971] 3 All ER 61, [1971] 1 WLR 1272, 47 Tax Cas 75
5   [1948] 1 All ER 948, 30 Tax Cas 163

1966–67 Mrs Baddeley, one of the beneficiaries, received a capital sum of £100,000 from Edmund's fund; as a result, her husband was assessed in the following amounts of surtax and income tax:

	Income tax £	Surtax £
1963–64 (nothing received)	20,013·71	40,075·00
1964–65 (nothing received)	21,100·14	43,718·00
1965–66 (nothing received)	22,777·91	61,889·85
1966–67 (£100,000 received)	21,416·86	41,130·50

In the result, arising out of the receipt of one capital sum of £100,000, Mr Baddeley suffered a claim of £274,121·97. And that is not the end of the story, for the Crown contended that, even so, they had exercised a 'dispensing' power in claiming no more, since by strict entitlement they could have assessed the Baddeleys on the basis the whole trust income of some millions of pounds.

My Lords, such boldness has no connection with Lord Greene MR's[1] view that a taxpayer who plays with fire has no right to complain if his fingers get burnt. The truth is that the strict application of Congreve[2] to the facts of the present case leads to such extraordinary conclusions that the commissioners have found themselves compelled to temper the wind to the (comparatively) shorn lamb. This procedure has been attacked as highly questionable, but, invoking the provision in s 5(2) of the Income Tax Act 1952, that they 'may do all such acts as may be deemed necessary and expedient for raising, collecting, receiving and accounting for the [income] tax *in the like and as full and ample a manner* as they are authorised to do with relation to any other duties under their care and management' the commissioners' claim to exercise dispensing powers and to make 'extra-statutory concessions' in suitable cases. They submit that they have done no more than exercise those powers in the instant case 'by apportioning the estimated "foreign income" for each year . . . in the proportions in which the appointees had benefited, in the aggregate, by actually receiving accumulated income'. Indeed, they added that in the present case they have done no more than their predecessors did in *Corbett's Executrices v Inland Revenue Comrs*[3] and in *Bambridge*[4], and that 'sub silentio such apportionments were approved by the court in both cases'.

My Lords, it is surely high time to consider the basis of this claim by the executive to make such extra-statutory concessions. It is, of course, well known that published lists of concessions have existed for many years. The first was in 1944, though in practice they have existed in one form or another for a much longer period. But, beneficent and relatively harmless though such concessions may have been in most cases, it is difficult to reconcile them with the view expressed by Lord Loreburn LC in *Drummond v Collins*[5] that—

'Lord Cairns long ago said that "if the person sought to be taxed comes within the letter of the law, he must be taxed". And though there have been cases in which the letter of the law has been disregarded in view of other statutory language, I think it can be only in case of necessity. It must be a necessary interpretation.'

It has recently been pointed out in an article[6] to which I am considerably indebted that Sir Stafford Cripps said in 1947 that they had come into existence 'without any particular legal authority under any Act of Parliament, but by the Inland Revenue under my

1 In *Lord Howard de Walden v Inland Revenue Comrs* [1942] 1 All ER 287 at 289, [1942] 1 KB 389 at 397, 25 Tax Cas 121 at 134
2 [1948] 1 All ER 948, 30 Tax Cas 163
3 [1943] 2 All ER 218, 25 Tax Cas 305
4 [1955] 3 All ER 812, [1955] 1 WLR 1329, 36 Tax Cas 313
5 [1915] AC 1011 at 1018, 6 Tax Cas 525 at 539
6 'Extra Statutory Concessions' by David W Williams [1979] British Tax Review 137 at 140

authority'[1]. And, despite the reliance sometimes placed on the Income and Corporation Taxes Act 1970, s 115(2), the Taxes Management Act 1970, s 1, and the Inland Revenue Regulation Act 1890, s 1, the fact is that there exists *no* statutory support for the assessment procedure adopted in the present case. And, even were there some statutory or other basis for the published list of concessions, Walton J[2] made the important point that—

> 'they do represent a *published* code, which applies indifferently to all those who fall, or who can bring themselves within, its scope. What is claimed by the Crown now is something radically different. There is *no* published code, and no necessity for the treatment of all those who are in consimili casu alike. In one case the Crown can remit one-third, in another one-half, and in yet another case the whole, of the tax properly payable, at its own sweet will and pleasure. If this is indeed so, we are back to the days of the Star Chamber. Again, I want to make it crystal clear that nobody is suggesting that the Crown has, or indeed ever would, so utilise the powers which it claims to bring about unjust results . . . The root of the evil is that it claims it has, in fact, the right to do so.' (Emphasis mine.)

Judicial comment regarding extra-statutory concessions has been mixed. Speaking 'in no spirit of criticism' Donovan LJ observed in *FS Securities v Inland Revenue Comrs*[3] that 'This is a difficult code to administer, and practical considerations no doubt justify at times some departure from strict law for the common convenience of the revenue and the taxpayer'. Even Lord Upjohn spoke with two voices. In 1966 he said in *Bates v Inland Revenue Comrs*[4]:

> '. . . the Commissioners of Inland Revenue realising the monstrous result of giving effect to the true construction of the section, have in fact worked out what they consider to be an equitable way of operating it which seems to them to result in a fair system of taxation. I am quite unable to understand on what principle they can properly do so . . .'

Yet in the following year he said in *Inland Revenue Comrs v Korner*[5] of an unpublished concession: 'This practice is very old, works great justice between the Crown and the subject, and I trust will never be disturbed.' Among the critics was Lord Radcliffe, who 'never understood the procedure of extra-statutory concessions in the case of a body to whom at least the door of Parliament is opened every year for adjustment of the tax code' (*Inland Revenue Comrs v Frere*[6]), and in another another case Lord Wilberforce, in rejecting a concession, observed that 'administrative moderation . . . is . . . no real substitute for legislative clarity and precision' (*Bates v Inland Revenue Comrs*[7]). And, my Lords, it should above all be remembered that none other than the Bill of Rights declared[8]:

> 'That the pretended power of suspending of laws or the execution of laws by regall authority without consent of Parlyament is illegall. That the pretended power of dispensing with laws or the execution of laws by regall authoritie as it hath been assumed and exercised of late is illegall.'

Wholly in line with such authoritative declarations were the observations of Scott LJ in *Absalom v Talbot*[9] that:

---

1   446 HC Official Reprint (5th series) col 2266
2   [1979] 2 All ER 225 at 234, [1979] Ch 198 at 204, [1979] STC 567 at 575–576
3   [1963] 3 All ER 229 at 234, [1963] 1 WLR 1223 at 1233, 41 Tax Cas 666 at 683
4   [1967] 1 All ER 84 at 96, [1968] AC 483 at 516, 44 Tax Cas 225 at 268
5   [1969] 1 All ER 679 at 686, [1969] 1 WLR 554 at 558, 45 Tax Cas 287 at 297
6   [1964] 3 All ER 796 at 806, [1965] AC 402 at 429, 42 Tax Cas 125 at 154
7   [1967] 1 All ER 84 at 100, [1968] AC 483 at 521, 44 Tax Cas 225 at 272
8   1 Will & Mar sess 2 c 2 (1688)
9   [1943] 1 All ER 589 at 598, 26 Tax Cas 166 at 181

'No judicial countenance can or ought to be given in matters of taxation to any system of extra-legal concessions. Amongst other reasons, it exposes revenue officials to temptation, which is wrong, even in the case of a service like the Inland Revenue, characterised by a wonderfully high sense of honour. *The fact that such extra-legal concessions have to be made to avoid unjust hardships is conclusive that there is something wrong with the legislation.*' (Emphasis mine.)

But the alternative explanation, my Lords, may in the instant case be that the fault lies not in s 412 of the Income Tax Acts 1952, but in the way in which it (like its forerunner, s 18 of the Finance Act 1936) has been interpreted. In my judgment, the words 'such an individual' appearing in sub-ss (1) and (2) hark back to the opening words of the preamble, namely to individuals whose purpose is the avoidance of liability to tax, and do *not* refer simply to any individual 'ordinarily resident in the United Kingdom'. Indeed, as the noble and learned Lord, Viscount Dilhorne, has observed, if the latter, restricted interpretation is to be adopted it is not easy to see why sub-s (8) of s 412 provided that 'For the purposes of this section—(a) a reference to an individual shall be deemed to include the wife or husband of the individual . . .' As was submitted in the taxpayers' case: 'Section 412(8)(a) has a positive and important function if the [taxpayers] . . . are correct; but otherwise it is superfluous.' And, indeed, Walton J[1] had himself expressed the view that 'the provisions of sub-s (8)(a) . . . do not otherwise make good sense . . .' It follows that in my judgment the extension of s 412 by the judgment of this House in *Congreve*[2] to beneficiaries wholly disconnected with the original transferor or transferors was erroneous.

Even so, my Lords, ought we now to depart from it? It has stood for 30 years and, as previously observed, it has been followed in this House. But if it be permitted to stand, we have the deplorable situation that the Commissioners of Inland Revenue can capriciously select which of several beneficiaries they are going to tax, and may equally capriciously decide the basis on which they are going to be assessed. And it is said that all this is perfectly lawful even though the afflicted taxpayer has *no* means of challenging his assessment. Viscount Dilhorne has analysed in some detail the circumstances in which this House, by a majority, refused in *Jones v Secretary of State for Social Services*[3] to overrule a five-year-old decision, Lord Reid saying[4]:

'. . . I am firmly of opinion that *Dowling's* case[5] ought not to be reconsidered. No broad issue of justice or public policy is involved nor is any question of legal principle. The issue is simply the proper construction of complicated provisions in a statute. There must be a large number of decisions of this House of this character.'

I have also in mind the earlier observation of Lord Reid[4] that 'it should only be in rare cases that we should reconsider questions of construction of statutes or other documents', and, like others of your Lordships, I was minded at one time to conclude that, despite the strong adverse view I had formed about the decision in *Congreve*[2], this House ought not now to overrule it. But there can be no absolute veto against overruling decisions turning on the construction of statutes or other documents, or, indeed, any other type of decision. We can now see the startling and unacceptable consequences of *Congreve*[2] when applied to circumstances never contemplated when that case was being considered. So remarkable are they, and so disturbing are the unconstitutional devices now resorted to by the Commissioners of Inland Revenue, that I am forced to the

1   [1977] 3 All ER 1073 at 1087, [1979] Ch 177 at 183, [1977] STC 414 at 428
2   [1948] 1 All ER 948, 30 Tax Cas 163
3   [1972] 1 All ER 145, [1972] AC 944
4   [1972] 1 All ER 145 at 149, [1972] AC 944 at 966
5   [1967] 1 All ER 210, [1967] 1 AC 725

conclusion that the interests, not only of the taxpayers but of the public at large alike, demand that the claim of the executive in this matter be challenged and rejected. The Crown takes its stand on *Congreve*[1] and claims that while that decision remains the devices the commissioners have resorted to may continue. My Lords, they must not, and I judge that in these circumstances the Crown itself leaves us with no alternative but to overrule *Congreve*[1]. I accordingly concur in dismissing the appeals and allowing the cross-appeals.

LORD KEITH OF KINKEL. My Lords, I agree with the views expressed in the speeches of my noble and learned friends, Lord Wilberforce and Viscount Dilhorne, which I have had the opportunity of considering in draft.

The important issues in these appeals are whether the principal ground for the decision of this House in *Congreve v Inland Revenue Comrs*[1] was erroneous, and, if so, whether the decision, in so far as it proceeded on that ground, should now be departed from.

The ground in question consisted in a clear ruling on the proper construction of s 412 of the Income Tax Act 1952, and was thus stated by Lord Simonds[2]:

'The preamble or introductory words of the section which state its purpose do not, in my view, assist the contention, which was developed on its operative words, that the avoidance by an individual of liability to tax must be achieved by means of a transfer of assets effected by that individual. They are, on the contrary, in the widest possible terms, and I do not know what better words could be used if the legislature intended to define its purpose as covering a transfer of assets by A, by means of which B avoided liability to tax.'

In the result, transfers of assets by the taxpayer's father were held to involve her in liability under the section. The House also accepted an argument that in any event certain transfers had been organised or brought about by the taxpayer herself, but this ground, though capable of supporting the correctness of the actual decision on liability to tax, was plainly a subsidiary one.

I have arrived at the firm opinion that the principal ground of decision in *Congreve*[1] was indeed erroneous. I consider that the natural and intended meaning of the words 'such an individual' in s 412(1) is that they indicate not merely an individual ordinarily resident in the United Kingdom, but an individual so resident who has sought to avoid liability to income tax by means of such transfers of assets as are mentioned in the preamble. Further, this meaning gives a sensible content, which would otherwise be lacking, to the provision in sub-s (8)(a) that reference to an individual shall be deemed to include the husband or wife of the individual. Finally, the consequences which follow from attributing the wider meaning to the words, when that meaning is applied to a numerous class of beneficiaries under a discretionary trust, are so dramatically unjust, as the facts of the present case illustrate, that I cannot think it to have been intended by Parliament. These consequences have been examined in depth in the speeches of my noble and learned friends, and need no repetition.

So it is necessary to consider whether this is one of these rare cases where it would be proper for this House, acting under the practice direction of 1966[3], to depart from one of its own previous decisions. In my opinion it is. The decision was one on a matter of statutory construction. It turned on a view which was a tenable one, regarded from the purely linguistic angle, although no attempt was made in the speech of Lord Simonds to account for the presence in s 412 of sub-s (8)(a), which may not have been drawn to their

---

1   [1948] 1 All ER 948, 30 Tax Cas 163
2   [1948] 1 All ER 948 at 952, 30 Tax Cas 163 at 204
3   *Note* [1966] 3 All ER 77, [1966] 1 WLR 1234

Lordships' attention. But the implications of that view, as now revealed in the instant
a   appeals, were not present to the minds of their Lordships. A consideration of these
implications must, in my opinion, lead to the conclusion that the view taken is not
tenable, and would not have been so regarded at the time had their Lordships had the
opportunity of such consideration. For the reasons fully developed in the speeches of my
noble and learned friends, these implications are of the greatest importance from the
point of view of constitutional propriety and the proper administration of revenue law.
b   In my opinion they involve broad issues of justice and public policy, such as were
mentioned by Lord Reid in *Jones v Secretary of State for Social Services*[1], the character of
which makes it not only proper but necessary to depart from the earlier decision.

Accordingly, I too would dismiss the appeals and allow the cross-appeals.

Appeals dismissed. Cross-appeals allowed.

c   Solicitors: *Speechly, Bircham & Co* (for the taxpayers); *Solicitor of Inland Revenue.*

Rengan Krishnan Esq   Barrister.

d   _____

1   [1972] 1 All ER 145 at 149, [1972] AC 944 at 966

APPENDIX TO LORD WILBERFORCE'S OPINION

AGREED FIGURES FOR INCOME TAX AND SURTAX 1963–64 TO 1966–67

	1963–64				1964	
	Income tax		*Surtax*		*Income tax*	
	Share of gross amount £	Assessed £	Share of gross amount £	Assessed £	Share of gross amount £	Assessed £
BENEFICIARIES OF EDMUND'S FUND						
Mr Ronald Arthur Vestey	193,623	193,623	307,147	307,147	203,894	203,894
Mr Edmund Hoyle Vestey	488,037	488,037	774,180	774,180	513,925	513,925
Mrs Jane McLean Baddeley assessed on her husband Mr J R Baddeley	53,047	53,047	84,150	84,150	55,861	55,861
Mrs Margaret Payne assessed on her husband Mr J G Payne	53,047	53,047	84,150	84,150	55,861	55,861
Total number of potential beneficiaries of Edmund's fund alive at any time during year	(16)					
BENEFICIARIES OF SAMUEL'S FUND						
Samuel, 3rd Lord Vestey	489,628		776,704		515,601	
Reduced because of non-residence for part year		461,535		748,611		
Eliminated because of non-residence for whole year					—	
Hon Mark William Vestey	106,095	106,095	168,300	168,300	111,723	111,723
Reduced because of non-residence for part year						
Eliminated because of non-residence for whole year						
Total number of potential beneficiaries of Samuel's fund alive at any time during year	(13)					
TOTAL GROSS AMOUNT	1,383,477	1,355,384	2,194,631	2,166,538	1,456,865	941,264

INCLUSIVE ON BASIS OF LIABILITY ON WHOLE OF TRUSTEE'S INCOME

| -65 | | 1965–66 | | | | 1966–67 | | | |
| Surtax | | Income tax | | Surtax | | Income tax | | Surtax | |
Share of gross amount £	Assessed £	Share of gross amount £	Assessed £	Share of gross amount £	Assessed £	Share of gross amount £	Assessed £	Share of gross amount £	Assessed £
319,143	319,143	207,176	207,176	410,721	410,721	196,416	196,416	300,252	300,252
804,415	804,415	522,197	522,197	1,035,243	1,035,243	495,077	495,077	756,801	756,801
87,436	87,436	56,761	56,761	112,527	112,527	53,813	53,813	82,261	82,261
87,436	87,436	56,761	56,761	112,527	112,527	53,813	53,813	82,261	82,261
(18)				(18)				(18)	
807,038		523,900		1,038,619		496,691		759,269	
							360,611		623,189
	—		—		—				
174,873	174,873	113,521		225,053		107,625		164,522	
			77,754		189,286				
							—		—
(14)				(14)				(14)	
2,280,341	1,473,303	1,480,316	920,649	2,934,690	1,860,304	1,403,435	1,159,730	2,145,366	1,844,764

Allen v Gulf Oil Refining Ltd

COURT OF APPEAL, CIVIL DIVISION

LORD DENNING MR AND CUMMING-BRUCE LJ

17th, 18th, 21st, 22nd MAY, 27th JUNE 1979

Nuisance – Defence – Statutory authority – Action for damages for nuisance arising out of construction and operation of oil refinery – Statute authorising oil company to acquire land compulsorily for construction of oil refinery – Oil company authorised to construct certain works and to construct and use certain subsidiary works in connection with refinery – Whether oil company able to rely on defence of statutory authority in action for nuisance – Gulf Oil Refining Act 1965 (c xxiv), ss 5, 15, 16.

By the Gulf Oil Refining Act 1965, an oil company ('Gulf Oil') were authorised to construct certain works in connection with an oil refinery they intended to establish at Milford Haven. Section 5 gave them power compulsorily to acquire land near Milford Haven 'for the purposes of [works authorised by s 15 of the Act] or for the construction of an oil refinery'. Section 15 authorised the construction of certain jetties and a branch railway line outside the boundary of the land. Section 16(1) authorised Gulf Oil to 'construct .... and use' for the purposes of or in connection with the works authorised by s 15 certain subsidiary works, including, inter alia, railways, sidings etc. Section 16(3) provided for Gulf Oil to make reasonable compensation for any damage caused by the exercise of the power conferred by s 16(1). In 1967 Gulf Oil built a large oil refinery on the land referred to in the Act and which they had compulsorily acquired for the purpose, and constructed various jetties and railways in connection with it. The plaintiff, who lived in the near neighbourhood of the refinery, brought an action for damages or compensation against Gulf Oil, alleging that the operation of the refinery was a nuisance or alternatively that Gulf Oil were guilty of negligence in the method of construction and operation of the refinery. Gulf Oil resisted the claim by the plea of statutory authority. On a preliminary issue the judge ordered that Gulf Oil could rely on the 1965 Act as having authorised the construction and operation of the oil refinery. The plaintiff appealed.

Held – The appeal would be allowed for the following reasons—

(i) (Per Lord Denning MR) In relation to the branch line of railway outside the boundary of the compulsorily acquired land, Gulf Oil were liable under the common law for the escape of sparks or for any nuisance due to the use of locomotive engines on that line since s 15 of the 1965 Act merely authorised the construction of the line but did not contain any provision which expressly authorised the use on it of such engines. In relation to the subsidiary works inside the boundary however, Gulf Oil were not liable in nuisance under the common law since s 16(1) of the 1965 Act authorised not only the construction of those works but also their use with engines, pumps, machinery etc. However by virtue of s 16(3), they were expressly liable to make reasonable compensation for any damage caused by the exercise of those powers. By interpreting s 5 of the 1965 Act in the light of the interpretation of ss 15 and 16 it was apparent that, since Gulf Oil were authorised by s 5 to acquire lands 'for the construction of a refinery' and not for the use of a refinery, there was no statutory authority for them to use the refinery in such a way as to commit a nuisance or to let dangerous things escape so as to do damage, and therefore those living nearby retained their common law remedy (see p 1014 c to f and h to p 1015 d and p 1016 g, post); *Jones v Festiniog Railway Co* (1868) LR 3 QB 733 applied; *R v Pease* [1824–34] All ER Rep 579, *Vaughan v Taff Vale Railway Co* [1843–60] All ER Rep 474, *Hammersmith and City Railway Co v Brand* [1861–73] All ER Rep 60 and *London, Brighton and South Coast Railway Co v Truman* [1881–5] All ER Rep considered.

(ii) (Per Cumming-Bruce LJ) Although in enacting the 1965 Act Parliament had

granted Gulf Oil the power to acquire land on which to construct an unspecified refinery
a (which was not included in the works authorised by the Act to be constructed), there was
nothing in the Act which led to the inference that Parliament intended in s 5(1) to grant
them power to construct a particular specified refinery or to use it, and there was no
existing precedent of a statute granting compulsory powers for acquisition of land for a
purpose which had been held to have conferred statutory authority to construct and use
the thing built on the land simply as an inference of legislative intention to be collected
b from the grant of power compulsorily to acquire the land. Although Gulf Oil retained
the liberty to build on their land such refinery as they wished, subject only to the
granting of planning permission, they created nuisance at their peril. If the plaintiff
could establish that she had suffered damage through nuisance, and that there was a
threat that the nuisance would continue, it would be for the trial judge to decide the
remedy. So far as any of the nuisances alleged were proved to be caused by the railway,
c sidings or other subsidiary works which Gulf Oil were empowered to construct by
s 16(1), the plaintiff might have a right to compensation under s 16(3) but, as a necessary
corollary, no right of action in nuisance for such damage (see p 1023 *h* to p 1024 *c* and *f*
g, post); dicta of Lord Chelmsford in *Hammersmith and City Railway Co v Brand* [1861–73]
All ER Rep at 65 and of Lord Watson in *Metropolitan Asylum District Managers v Hill*
[1881–5] All ER Rep at 545 considered.
d   Per Lord Denning MR. Where, under modern statutes, private undertakers seek
statutory authority to construct and operate an installation which might cause damage
to people living in the neighbourhood, it should not be assumed that Parliament intends
that those people should be without redress for any such damage. Just as in principle
property should not be taken compulsorily except on proper compensation being paid
for it, so also in principle property should not be damaged compulsorily except on proper
e compensation being made for the damage done whether the undertakers use due
diligence or not. In the absence of provision to the contrary modern statutes should be
so construed that persons living in the neighbourhood retain their rights at common law
and that it is no defence for the undertakers to plead statutory authority so as to excuse
them from any liability (see p 1016 *a* to *d*, post).

f **Notes**
For the defence of statutory authority in actions for nuisance and negligence, see 30
Halsbury's Laws (3rd Edn) 690–696, paras 1330–1337, and for cases on the subject, see
38 Digest (Repl) 13, 34–41, 49, *173–212*.

Cases referred to in judgments
g *Baines v Baker* (1752) Amb 158, 27 ER 105, sub nom *Anon* 3 Atk 750, LC, 36(1) Digest
     (Reissue) 479, *580*.
Emsley v North Eastern Railway Co [1896] 1 Ch 418, 65 LJ Ch 385, 74 LT 113, 60 JP 182,
     CA, 38 Digest (Repl) 304, *95*.
Geddis v Proprietors of Bann Reservoir (1878) 3 App Cas 430, HL.
Hammersmith and City Railway Co v Brand (1869) LR 4 HL 171, [1861–73] All ER Rep 60,
h   38 LJQB 265, 21 LT 238, 34 JP 36, HL; *rvsg* (1867) LR 2 QB 223, Ex Ch, 38 Digest
     (Repl) 15, *59*.
Jones v Festiniog Railway Co (1868) LR 3 QB 733, 9 B & S 835, 37 LJQB 214, 18 LT 902,
     32 JP 693, 38 Digest (Repl) 400, *613*.
Leeds Industrial Co-operative Society Ltd v Slack [1924] AC 851, [1924] All ER Rep 259, 93
     LJ Ch 436, 131 LT 710, HL; *rvsg* [1923] 1 Ch 431, CA; *subsequent proceedings* [1924] 2
j   Ch 475, CA, 28(2) Digest (Reissue) 1012, *396*.
London, Brighton and South Coast Railway Co v Truman (1885) 11 App Cas 45, [1881–5] All
     ER Rep 134, 55 LJ Ch 354, 54 LT 250, 50 JP 388, HL; *rvsg* (1885) 29 Ch D 89, CA, 38
     Digest (Repl) 41, *212*.
Manchester Corpn v Farnworth [1930] AC 171, [1929] All ER Rep 90, 99 LJKB 83, 94 JP
     62, 27 LGR 709, 142 LT 145, HL, 38 Digest (Repl) 38, *193*.

Metropolitan Asylum District Managers v Hill (1881) 6 App Cas 193, [1881–5] All ER Rep
536, 50 LJQB 353, 44 LT 653, 45 JP 664, HL, 36(1) Digest (Reissue) 520, 887.   *a*

Pyx Granite Co Ltd v Ministry of Housing and Local Government [1959] 3 All ER 1, [1960] AC
260, [1959] 3 WLR 346, 123 JP 429, 58 LGR 1, 10 P & CR 319, HL, 45 Digest (Repl)
336, 37.

R v Pease (1832) 4 B & Ad 30, [1824–34] All ER Rep 579, 1 Nev & MKB 690, 1 Nev &
MMC 535, 2 LJMC 26, 110 ER 366, 38 Digest (Repl) 39, 205.

Sturges v Bridgman (1879) 11 Ch D 852, 48 LJ Ch 785, 41 LT 219, 43 JP 716, CA, 36(1)   *b*
Digest (Reissue) 407, 32.

Vaughan v Taff Vale Railway Co (1860) 5 H & N 679, [1843–60] All ER Rep 474, 29 LJ Ex
247, 2 LT 394, 24 JP 453, 6 Jur NS 899, 157 ER 1351, Ex Ch, 38 Digest (Repl) 13, 54.

Cases also cited

Attorney-General v HRH Prince Ernest Augustus of Hanover [1957] 1 All ER 49, [1957] AC
436, HL.   *c*

British Railways Board v Pickin [1974] 1 All ER 609, [1974] AC 765, HL.

Canadian Pacific Railway Co v Parke [1899] AC 535, PC.

Clowes v Staffordshire Potteries Waterworks Co (1872) 8 Ch App 125, LJJ.

Goldberg & Son Ltd v Liverpool Corpn (1900) 82 LT 362, CA.

Interlocutory appeal   *d*

By writ issued on 13th February 1975 in the Haverfordwest District Registry and
amended pursuant to an order of the district registrar dated 22nd May 1975, the
plaintiff, Elsie May Allen, the occupier of premises at 20 Alban Crescent in the village of
Waterston commenced an action against the defendants, Gulf Oil Refining Ltd ('Gulf
Oil'), for the nuisance alleged to be caused by the operation of an oil refinery constructed
by Gulf Oil in 1967 at Waterston, near Milford Haven in the County of Dyfed. By a   *e*
statement of claim served on 19th February 1975 and amended pursuant to an order of
the district registrar dated 10th June 1976 the plaintiff alleged nuisance, the particulars
of which were noxious odours, vibration, offensive noise levels, excessive flames from
burning waste gases, causing consequent ill-health, and fear of an explosion. Further and
in the alternative, the plaintiff alleged negligence in the construction and/or operation of
the refinery and claimed that by reason of nuisance and negligence, she and her family   *f*
had sustained personal injury, damage and expense. The plaintiff claimed an injunction
that Gulf Oil forthwith desist from the acts of nuisance and negligence, and damages. By
their defence served on 19th April 1975 and re-served as amended on 1st October 1976
Gulf Oil denied nuisance, negligence, personal injury, loss or damage, and further or in
the alternative pleaded that if any of the matters referred to in the statement of claim
otherwise constituted a nuisance, the construction and operation of the refinery were and   *g*
continued to be authorised by the Gulf Oil Refining Act 1965 and they relied on the
defence of statutory authority. On the summons for directions the plaintiff sought an
order for determination of a preliminary point of law before trial of the action on the
question whether Gulf Oil could rely on the defence of statutory authority. On 29th
November 1976 the district registrar granted the order. Gulf Oil appealed against the
registrar's order and on 23rd May 1977, Kerr J in chambers dismissed Gulf Oil's appeal,   *h*
but on an undertaking being given by the plaintiff's counsel that if Gulf Oil were held to
be entitled to rely on the defence of statutory authority the plaintiff would not proceed
with the allegation of negligence, varied the registrar's order by ordering that the
question 'Can the defendant rely on the Gulf Oil Refining Act 1965 as having authorised
the construction and operation of an oil refinery at Waterston, Milford Haven in the
County of Dyfed?' be tried as a preliminary issue. On 4th May 1978 May J tried the   *j*
preliminary issue and gave judgment for Gulf Oil. The plaintiff appealed. The facts are
set out in the judgment of Lord Denning MR.

John Davies QC and *Gordon Langley* for the plaintiff.
Charles Sparrow QC and *Francis Ferris* for Gulf Oil.

Cur adv vult

a 27th June. The following judgments were read.

LORD DENNING MR. Milford Haven is a fine harbour. Twenty years ago the big oil companies saw that it was a very suitable site for their oil refineries. It had deep water which big modern tankers could navigate. It had open land ashore where the refineries **b** could be built. One company after another got statutory powers to build a refinery there. In 1957 Esso got a private Act of Parliament. In 1962 Regent Oil. In 1965 Gulf Oil. In 1971 Amoco. Each of these great oil companies have established refineries on the shores of Milford Haven.

We are here concerned with the inhabitants of Waterston. That is a small village about half a mile inland. Gulf Oil have built a huge refinery stretching right from the **c** shore to the very doors of the villagers of Waterston. The Methodist chapel lies in the very access way to the refinery. Gulf Oil have built their operational plant so close to the village that it towers above the houses. They have sited the tank farm some distance away. The villagers say that ever since the refinery was built in 1967 they have suffered from the noxious odours emitted by it, such as sulphur dioxide, which makes them feel sick; they have had vibration and a continuous roaring with occasional high-pitched **d** noises; there have been flames from burning waste gases; and they live in fear of explosions. Beyond all doubt their complaints are so genuine that at common law the householders would have a cause of action for nuisance. Fifty or sixty of them have brought actions for damages or compensation against Gulf Oil. One of them has been taken as a test action. In the statement of claim the plaintiff alleged that the operation of the refinery was a nuisance or alternatively that Gulf Oil were guilty of negligence in the **e** method of construction and operation of the refinery. Gulf Oil resist the claim by the plea of statutory authority. This is how they put it in their defence:

'. . . the Defendant will say that the construction and operation of the said refinery were and are authorised by the Gulf Oil Refining Act 1965 and the Defendant will rely upon the defence of statutory authority.'

f On these pleadings there has been raised a preliminary point of law. It is this:

'Can the defendant rely on the Gulf Oil Refining Act, 1965, as having authorised the construction and operation of an oil refinery at Waterston, Milford Haven in the County of Dyfed?'

That question, as it stands, seems to me to be useless, because it does nothing to resolve **g** the issues in the action. Even if the Act did authorise the construction and operation of the refinery, the plaintiff could still complain that Gulf Oil were guilty of negligence, in that they did not do what was reasonable to prevent the damage: see the well-known statement by Lord Blackburn in *Geddis v Proprietors of Bann Reservoir*[1].

Some light is thrown on the question by an undertaking which was given to the judge. It was in these terms:

h
'AND UPON Counsel for the plaintiff undertaking . . . that, in the event of its being decided by way of preliminary issue that the defendant is not entitled to rely on a plea of statutory authority as a defence in this action, they will not proceed with the allegation of negligence . . .'

j In view of that undertaking, I take it that if the answer to the point of law is, No, the plaintiff will rely on the allegation of nuisance but not on the allegation of negligence. If the answer to the point of law is Yes, the undertaking does not apply. The plaintiff will still in theory be able to rely on the allegation of negligence. We were told, however, by

---

1   (1878) 3 App Cas 430 at 456

counsel that the plaintiff would not then rely on the allegation of negligence because it
would give rise to much difficulty and expense, especially as the plaintiff is legally aided. *a*
   In the course of the discussion before us, the preliminary issue broadened into this
debate: to what extent is statutory authority a defence to the claim in the action on the
assumption that Gulf Oil were not negligent and did all that was reasonable to prevent
damage to the plaintiff, but nevertheless in spite of their efforts their operations did cause
damage to the plaintiff? The issue was put in graphic form by Cumming-Bruce LJ.
Suppose there was an explosion (as recently took place in Bantry Bay) without negligence, *b*
and people were killed and injured and houses destroyed. Would statutory authority be
a defence to the claim?
   Counsel for Gulf Oil hesitated about the answer. But he realised that logically, if his
contention were right, Gulf Oil would not be liable to pay a penny in compensation.
   The issue depends on the true interpretation of the statute under which Gulf Oil
constructed the refinery. May J below held that Gulf Oil were entitled to rely on the *c*
1965 Act as having authorised the construction and operation of the oil refinery; and on
this account they were not liable in the absence of negligence. The plaintiff appeals to
this court.

The 19th century cases
   All the cases on statutory authority go back to the first days of railways. They start *d*
with *R v Pease*[1]. Edward Pease was a Quaker. In 1821 he promoted a private Act of
Parliament, the Stockton and Darlington Railway Act[2], so as to make a railway from the
river Tees at Stockton to a colliery at Wilton. He intended only to use horses to draw the
coal wagons along the railway. He appointed George Stephenson to be the engineer to
the railway company. Now George was a genius. He persuaded Edward Pease to let him
try locomotives on the railway. So in 1824 the cautious old Quaker promoted another *e*
private Act[3] so as to make it lawful for the railway company to 'employ and use'
locomotives to pull wagons along the railway. Note those words 'employ and use'.
George Stephenson built his steam engine. On 27th September 1825 the first train did
the journey from Stockton. There was tremendous opposition to this new revolution.
It was said that the engine would burn and shatter people to fragments. It would set
their houses on fire and poison the milk. The railway ran alongside a public highway. *f*
Those on foot were frightened. Horses shied. Carts overturned. So great were the
complaints that Edward Pease was indicted for a public nuisance. It was tried at the York
Assizes in 1832 before Parke J. The jury found a special verdict setting out the facts. In
it they found that the locomotive engines were of the best known construction and were
used with due care and diligence. The law was argued before the Court of King's
Bench[4]. They held that Edward Pease was justified by the Act and was not guilty of a *g*
nuisance. The reason given was that—

   'the words of the clause in question clearly give to the company the unqualified
   authority *to use* the engines . . . The Legislature . . . must be *presumed to have known*
   that the railroad would be adjacent for a mile to the public highway, and
   consequently that travellers upon the highway would be in all probability
   incommoded by the passage of locomotive engines along the railroad.' (My *h*
   emphasis.)

That decision was highly beneficial. It opened the way to the railway age. G M
Trevelyan[5] says that 'railways were England's gift to the world'.

j

1   (1832) 4 B & Ad 30, [1824–34] All ER Rep 579
2   1 & 2 Geo 4 c lxiv
3   4 Geo 4 c xxxiii
4   4 B & Ad 30 at 40–41, cf [1824–34] All ER Rep 579 at 581, per Parke J
5   English Social History (3rd Edn, 1946), p 531

a   Put in legal terms, the decision turned on the true construction of the second private Act. When passing that Act, Parliament must be *presumed* to have known that the use of locomotive engines, even with all due care, would cause a nuisance and cause damage to innocent people. Nevertheless Parliament *expressly* authorised that use and that damage without providing for any compensation in respect of it.

b   That decision was followed in 1860 in *Vaughan v Taff Vale Railway Co*[1]. Sparks from an engine set fire to a wood and destroyed eight acres of it. This was exceedingly hard on the landowner. Here was a new invention shooting out fire and destroying his property. He sued for damages but Blackburn J said[2]:

c   '. . . *Rex* v. *Pease*[3] has settled that when the legislature has sanctioned the *use* of a locomotive engine, there is no liability for injury caused by *using* it, so long as every precaution is taken consistent with its use.' (My emphasis.)

d   But eight years later there was a 'sparks' case in which a railway company were held liable in damages. It was in *Jones v Festiniog Railway Co*[4]. Sparks from an engine set fire to a haystack and it was burnt down. The railway company proved that they had taken all reasonable precautions to prevent the emission of sparks. But they were held liable. It was because the private Act[5] did not *expressly* authorise the *use* of locomotive engines. Blackburn J[6] distinguished *Vaughan v Taff Vale Railway Co*[1] by saying that therein 'the legislature has *expressly* authorized *the use* of locomotive engines', but that 'in the present Act, there is nothing amounting to *express* authority' (my emphasis).

e   That case was decided on 26th June 1868. A week later six judges were summoned to the House of Lords to give their opinion on another railway case, *Hammersmith and City Railway Co v Brand*[7]. It was not a 'sparks' case but a 'vibration' case. The decisions in *R v Pease*[3] and *Vaughan v Taff Vale Railway Co*[1] were challenged, but were upheld on the ground that in those cases the *use* of the locomotives was *expressly* authorised by the statute. Section 86 of the Railway Clauses Consolidation Act 1845 gave the railway companies *express* authority to *employ and use* locomotive engines and contained no provision for compensation for damage occasioned by the use. In view of that *express* authority Lord Chelmsford said[8]:

f   '. . . it must be taken that power is given to cause that vibration without liability to an action. The right given to *use* the locomotive would otherwise be nugatory, as each time a train passed upon the line and shook the houses in the neighbourhood actions might be brought by their owners, which would soon put a stop to the use of the railway.' (My emphasis.)

g

Blackburn J[9] (whose opinion was approved by the House) confirmed the correctness of *Jones v Festiniog Railway Co*[4] saying that in that case the general words in the Act 'did not contain any *express* authority to *use* locomotive power' and that this omission 'left the company at liberty, no doubt, to use locomotives, but on the common law terms, that they must keep in the fire at their own peril' (my emphasis).

h

---

1   (1860) 5 H & N 679, [1843–60] All ER Rep 474
2   5 H & N 679 at 688, cf [1843–60] All ER Rep 474 at 477
3   (1832) 4 B & Ad 30, [1824–34] All ER Rep 579
4   (1868) LR 3 QB 733
5   2 Wm 4 c xlviii
6   LR 3 QB 733 at 737
7   (1869) LR 4 HL 171, [1861–73] All ER Rep 60
8   LR 4 HL 171 at 202, [1861–73] All ER Rep 60 at 65
9   LR 4 HL 171 at 199

The principle thus established was applied in *London, Brighton and South Coast Railway Co v Truman*[1]. The London and Brighton Railway Co had a yard at Croydon which they turned to use for cattle pens. A neighbouring owner complained of noise and nuisance. But as the use of the yard was 'expressly authorised' by the statute for the keeping of cattle, the neighbour lost his case.

So the law was settled in regard to railways. If the private Act *expressly* authorised the *use* of locomotives, or *use* for cattle pens, or any other specific use, without providing compensation for damage, and all due diligence was used, the railway company were not liable. The reason was because if an action for nuisance had been permitted it would mean that any adjoining owner could, by legal action, bring the railway to a standstill; and that would have been intolerable for the public at large. But if the private Act did not *expressly* authorise the *use* of locomotives or other specific purpose the railway company were liable for any damage done by the use of them.

Application to this statute

(i) *The outside branch line.* Those cases are very much in point here. The Gulf Oil Refining Act 1965[2] empowered Gulf Oil to acquire a big area of land compulsorily on which to build a refinery, and also to make subsidiary works such as lines of railway within that area up to their boundary. But outwards from their land the Act also authorised the *construction* of a branch line of railway 2½ miles long so as to connect up with the main line. But the Act did not contain any provision which *expressly* authorised the *use* of that branch line by locomotive engines. Indeed in s 3(1)(b) it specifically excluded s 86 of the Railways Clauses Consolidation Act 1845 which was the basis of *Hammersmith and City Railway Co v Brand*[3]. So in regard to this branch line of 2½ miles of railway Gulf Oil were liable for any escape of sparks or any nuisance due to the use of locomotive engines. It is governed by *Jones v Festiniog Railway Co*[4].

(ii) *The inside subsidiary lines.* Inside their land, Gulf Oil were authorised to construct subsidiary works such as lines of railway so as to connect up with that branch line. Now in regard to these subsidiary works the Act expressly authorised not only their *construction*, but also their *use* with engines, pumps, machinery and so forth (see s 16(1)(a)). In regard to these subsidiary works, the statute expressly provided for compensation. Section 16(3) says:

'In the exercise of the powers conferred by this section the Company shall cause as little detriment and inconvenience as the circumstances permit to any person and shall make reasonable compensation for any damage caused by the exercise of such powers.'

(iii) *Conclusion.* So we have this illuminating comparison: in s 15 (which authorised the *construction* of main works) there is no provision for compensation for damage done to people in the neighbourhood, but in s 16 which allowed the *construction* and *use* of subsidiary works, there is a provision for compensation. This shows that the draftsman had before him the principle of the railway cases of the 19th century. Parliament gave express statutory authority for the *construction* of the works specified in s 15 but did not give any statutory authority for the *use* of them, or at any rate no statutory authority for the *use* of them so as to be a nuisance. As a result, those living in the neighbourhood retained, therefore, the common law right of action for nuisance or the escape of dangerous things. But in s 16 Parliament gave express statutory authority not only for the *construction* of the subsidiary works but also for the *use* of them. That statutory authority, if it stopped there, would have exempted Gulf Oil from liability so long as

1 (1885) 11 App Cas 45 at 54, [1881–5] All ER Rep 134 at 138, per Lord Selborne
2 1965 c xxiv
3 (1869) LR 4 HL 171, [1861–73] All ER Rep 60
4 (1868) LR 3 QB 733

they exercised due diligence, as in *R v Pease*[1] and *Vaughan v Taff Vale Railway Co*[2]. That
a would have been very hard on those living in the neighbourhood. So Parliament in
s 16(3) inserted a provision for compensation for any damage done.

That is the explanation of s 16(3) as compared with s 15. It was necessary to provide
for compensation in s 16(3); but it was not necessary in s 15, because the common law
was available in case there was a nuisance.

b

Application to the refinery
This interpretation of ss 15 and 16 throws much light on the rest of the statute. In s 5
there are words which authorise Gulf Oil to acquire lands 'for the construction of a
refinery in the parish of Llanstadwell'. But there are no words authorising them to
operate or *use* the refinery so as to be a nuisance. Section 5 says, significantly, 'for the
c *construction* of a refinery', not for the *use* of it. It follows that there is no statutory
authority for Gulf Oil to *use* the refinery in such a way as to commit a nuisance or to let
dangerous things escape so as to do damage. Those living nearby are left to their
common law remedies.

The reason why Gulf Oil did not need statutory authority to use or operate the
refinery, and did not get it, was given by Lindley LJ in *Emsley v North Eastern Railway*
d *Co*[3]:

'A statutory power is, I apprehend, a power conferred by statute to do something
which could not be lawfully done without it. A statute is not wanted to enable even
a company to build on land which is its own if the company has capital properly
applicable to the purpose.'

e   So a statute is not wanted to enable the oil company to operate an oil refinery on land
which it owns. If it does operate it, it does so by reason of its common law right to do
what it likes with its own and, so long as it does not commit a nuisance.

Parallel statutes
It is interesting to look at parallel statutes dealing with oil installations. In the Pipe-
f lines Act 1962 there are provisions authorising the *construction* of pipe-lines (see ss 8, 11,
12) together with an *express* provision in s 69 that: 'nothing in this Act or in a compulsory
rights order shall exonerate a person from any action or other proceedings for nuisance.'

In the Petroleum and Submarine Pipe-lines Act 1975 there are provisions authorising
the *construction* of a refinery (see s 34) together with an express provision in s 48(3) that
'... nothing in this Act ... derogates from any right of action or other remedy (whether
g civil or criminal) in proceedings instituted otherwise than under this Act'.

Those provisions are clearly inserted ex abundanti cautela. They make it clear that
when Parliament authorises the *construction* of an oil installation (saying nothing about
the use or operation of it) Parliament does not thereby intend that those living in the
neighbourhood should be damaged by it or suffer any nuisance from it; or, at any rate,
if they are, they have their common law rights of action in respect of it.
h

Planning
The 1965 Act did not exempt Gulf Oil from the necessity of getting planning
permission: see s 55. Gulf Oil were granted permission on 3rd February 1965 and made
the arrangements required by the Pembrokeshire County Council. But that cannot
j exempt them from liability for nuisance or the escape of dangerous things.

---

1 (1832) 4 B & Ad 30, [1824–34] All ER Rep 579
2 (1860) 5 H & N 679, [1843–60] All ER Rep 474
3 [1896] 1 Ch 418 at 428

General principles

I have considered this case on the construction of the statute, according the principles   *a*
laid down in the railway cases of the 19th century. But I venture to suggest that modern
statutes should be construed on a new principle. Wherever private undertakers seek
statutory authority to construct and operate an installation which may cause damage to
people living in the neighbourhood, it should not be assumed that Parliament intended
that damage should be done to innocent people without redress. Just as in principle
property should not be taken compulsorily except on proper compensation being paid   *b*
for it, so also in principle property should not be damaged compulsorily except on proper
compensation being made for the damage done. No matter whether the undertakers use
due diligence or not, they ought not to be allowed, for their own profit, to damage
innocent people or property without paying compensation. They ought to provide for
it as part of the legitimate expenses of their operation, either as initial capital cost or out
of the subsequent revenue. *Vaughan v Taff Vale Railway Co*[1] exposes the injustice of the   *c*
Victorian rule. A landowner had a wood of eight acres before the railway came. The
railway company got a private bill and built the railway. Sparks from an engine burnt
down the wood. He was denied any compensation at all. To avoid such injustice, I
would suggest that, in the absence of any provision in the statute for compensation, the
proper construction of a modern statute should be that any person living in the
neighbourhood retains his action at common law; and that it is no defence for the   *d*
promoters to plead the statute. Statutory authority may enable the promoters to make
the installation and operate it but it does not excuse them from paying compensation for
injury done to those living in the neighbourhood.

I realise that there is a difficulty about an injunction. No court would wish to grant
an injunction to stop a great enterprise and render it useless. But that difficulty is easily
overcome. By means of Lord Cairns's Act[2] the court can award damages to cover past or   *e*
future injury in lieu of an injunction: see *Leeds Industrial Co-operative Society Ltd v Slack*[3].

So in this case I would hold that if there should be an explosion at this refinery the
company are bound to compensate those who are killed or injured or whose property is
damaged; and it is no answer for the company to say, 'We are sorry. We were very
careful. We used all the latest safety precautions. But yet it happened'. Justice demands
that, despite those protestations, compensation should be paid by the company to those   *f*
who suffered by the operations.

This is not a case of an explosion. But the principle is the same. It is damage done to
the occupiers of houses by noxious odours, vibration and noise. Compensation should
be paid to the owners and present occupiers of the houses on the lines of the compensation
for 'injurious affection' in lieu of an injunction. But this should not cover damage such
as would be caused by an explosion. That should be the subject of separate compensation.   *g*

I would therefore allow the appeal and answer the question, 'No'.

CUMMING-BRUCE LJ.

The pleadings

By her statement of claim the plaintiff alleges that in or about 1967 Gulf Oil   *h*
constructed an oil refinery at Waterston, near Milford Haven, and have since occupied
and operated that refinery. She alleges that the operation of the refinery has caused
nuisance to her in the occupation of her premises at 20 Alban Crescent, Waterston. The
nuisances complained of are noxious odours, vibration, substantial levels of noise which
are offensive, and offensive flames from burning waste gases. She gave further and better
particulars of those complaints: *j*

---

1   (1860) 5 H & N 679, [1843–60] All ER Rep 474
2   Chancery Amendment Act 1858
3   [1924] AC 851, [1924] All ER Rep 259

a
'(B) i. Noxious odours began in or about the year 1967. The Plaintiff is unable to specify precisely each and every occasion on which such odours emanated from such refinery, but the Plaintiff's case is that on frequent occasion after the commencement of operations at the said refinery such odours emanated and continued to emanate. ii. The Plaintiff cannot give these particulars in full detail. The Defendants have the best knowledge of gases and similar products emanating from their refinery. The Plaintiff's case is that he/she (and members of the family) felt sick in consequence of inhaling noxious odours, such as: sulphur dioxide; sulphides; mercaptans; light hydro-carbons and other oil based compounds . . .

b
(C) i. The vibrations began in or about the year 1967, and have continued thereafter. ii. The vibrations constitute a nuisance in that they interfere with the reasonable enjoyment by the Plaintiff of her premises and further interfere with the Plaintiff's reasonable enjoyment of her daily life. iii. The Plaintiff makes no complaint of structural damage in respect of vibrations.

c
(D) i. Offensive noise levels began in or about the year 1967 and have continued subsequently. ii. Levels in excess of the criteria of the Wilson Report[1]; in particular, levels exceeding background noise level 36 dBA have been measured . . . iv. The Plaintiff and other residents in the locality. v. The best description which the Plaintiff can give is that it is a continuous roaring with occasional high-pitched noises caused by steam escaping; workshop and train-shunting noises.'

d
She further and in the alternative alleged negligence. She alleged that by reason of the nuisance and negligence she and her family sustained personal injury, damage and expense. She complained that her health was affected, and that she and her family live in fear of explosion at the refinery. The way in which her own health and that of her grown-up grandson were affected was by nausea, headaches, breathlessness and coughs; her fear of explosion was due to her knowledge of the occurrence of several medium-sized explosions and numerous minor explosions at the refinery, and to her belief that explosions have occurred at other refineries and chemical plants carrying out processes similar to Gulf Oil's processes.

e

The plaintiff claimed an injunction that Gulf Oil forthwith desist from the acts of nuisance or negligence, and damages. The injunction sought is particularised in the further and better particulars.

f
It is to be observed that the nuisances alleged do not in terms include the fact or the threat of explosions causing injury to the plaintiff or damage to the land she occupies. Though, if the facts justified it, such an allegation might be made by amendment, the preliminary point falls for answer on the issues now raised by the pleadings, and in 1881 in *Metropolitan Asylum District Managers v Hill*[2] Lord Blackburn affirmed, as undoubtedly the law, Lord Hardwicke LC's decision in *Baines v Baker*[3] that loss arising from the fears of mankind though in themselves reasonable would not create a nuisance at law. I only advert to this matter of detail because for the reasons I give below I find some difficulty in appreciating the scope of the question which has been ordered to be determined as a preliminary point.

g

h
Gulf Oil by their amended defence admitted construction of the refinery in 1967, and occupation and operation thereof ever since. They denied nuisance, negligence, personal injury, loss and damage. By para 3 they pleaded:

'. . . if . . . any of the matters referred to in the Statement of Claim would otherwise constitute a nuisance the Defendant will say that the construction and

j
_____

1   Noise: Final Report of the Committee on the Problem of Noise (chairman: Sir Alan Wilson FRS) (1963) Cmnd 2056
2   (1881) 6 App Cas 193 at 206, [1881–5] All ER Rep 536 at 542
3   (1752) Amb 158, 27 ER 105

operation of the said refinery were and are authorised by the Gulf Oil Refining Act 1965 and the Defendant will rely upon the defence of statutory authority.'

On the summons for directions the plaintiff sought an order for determination of a preliminary point of law before any evidence was called in the action. The registrar made such an order and defined the question as follows:

'Can the Defendants, on the true construction of the Gulf Oil Refining Act 1965, rely on the Defence of Statutory Authority to excuse them from liability for nuisance, if any, resulting from the construction and operation of the Refinery?'

Gulf Oil appealed against the registrar's order that the point of law should be determined as a preliminary point. Kerr J affirmed the order for determination of a preliminary question of law, but having received the undertaking recited by Lord Denning MR, ordered that the point of law to be decided is:

'Can the defendant rely on the Gulf Oil Refining Act, 1965, as having authorised the construction and operation of an oil refinery at Waterston, Milford Haven in the County of Dyfed?'

Doubtless the learned judge revised the question into that form because what Parliament has directed cannot be complained of by the subject as a wrong, whatever the consequence, so that there was an inherent contradiction in the form of the question originally defined. But there is a practical difficulty in answering the question which arises from the character of the nuisances alleged in the statement of claim. The plaintiff disclaims any allegation of structural damage in respect of vibration, so that no physical damage to land or anything growing on it is alleged. In respect of this kind of nuisance, the character of the neighbourhood and the surrounding circumstances are not matters to be taken into consideration. But where the nuisance alleged is 'the personal inconvenience and interference with one's enjoyment, one's quiet, anything that discomposes or injuriously affects the senses or the nerves', there is no absolute standard to be applied. It is always a question of degree whether the interference with comfort or convenience is sufficiently serious to constitute a nuisance, and in that connection the character of the neighbourhood must be taken into account. As Thesiger LJ put it in *Sturges v Bridgman*[1]:

'... whether anything is a nuisance or not is a question to be determined, not merely by an abstract consideration of the thing itself, but in reference to its circumstances; what would be a nuisance in *Belgrave Square* would not necessarily be so in *Bermondsey*; and where a locality is devoted to a particular trade or manufacture carried on by the traders or manufacturers in a particular and established manner not constituting a public nuisance, Judges and juries would be justified in finding ... that the trade or manufacture so carried on in that locality is not a private or actionable wrong.'

So in the instant case, if as a matter of interpretation of the Act it is clear that the intention of Parliament was to change the immediate environment of the village of Waterston by the construction on the specified site immediately beside the village of a great oil refinery with jetties appropriate to the berthing of large tankers bringing in vast quantities of crude oil, and a railway to carry the products of the refinery away overland, it would follow that Parliament has authorised a dramatic change in the neighbourhood of the village. Thereafter a complaint of nuisance by interference with the enjoyment of life in the village would on any view have to show such a degree of interference with enjoyment as exceeded such levels of noise and impurity of air as are inevitable in a neighbourhood in which oil refinery business is to be regarded as the norm. This perhaps difficult question of fact is not the same as the question whether the refinery has

---

1   (1879) 11 Ch D 852 at 865

been constructed and operated with due regard to the application of such mechanical and
a chemical and chemical devices as will minimise interference with the lives of the inhabitants of the
village, ie the question of negligence in the special sense in which breach of the duty of
care is described in this context. So if it is right to hold as a matter of construction of the
Act that it was not the intention of Parliament to grant Gulf Oil a licence to invade the
common law rights of the inhabitants by subjecting them to any degree of interference
with their comfort and convenience by noise, vibration or air pollution, there will still
b remain the question whether the complaints of the plaintiff are such as to constitute a
nuisance having regard to the changed character of the environment which Parliament
has authorised.

The Act

I turn to the question of construction, which, as May J appreciated, could not be
c answered without a careful examination of the cases in which the words of various
statutes have been examined in order to ascertain what exactly Parliament did authorise,
and in which guidance is given on the approach to the problem.

In the Gulf Oil Refining Act 1965 statutory authority was sought by the promoters
and granted by Parliament for the exercise of the powers set out in Parts II and III of the
Act. As a drafting convenience the term 'the authorised works' were defined as 'the
d works authorised by Section 15 (Power to construct works)'. Part II is on its face
concerned only with the compulsory acquisition of the lands delineated on the deposited
plans and described in the deposited book of reference. Section 5(1) provides:

'Subject to the provisions of this Act, the Company may enter upon, take and use
such of the lands . . . as it may require for the purposes of the authorised works or
for the construction of a refinery in the parish of Llanstadwell . . . or for purposes
e ancillary thereto or connected therewith.'

Plan 3 shows by a broken line the boundaries of the lands to be acquired. The jetties
(works 1, 2 and 3) are to be constructed on the navigable waters of Milford Haven. A
single track railway is to be constructed along the line shown and lands acquired therefor
within the limits of deviation marked on the plan. Plan 4 shows in larger scale the lands
f to be acquired for the construction of the refinery and for the jetties. Plan 5 shows
dimensions and section of the jetties. Plans 6 and 7 show dimensions and levels of the
railway (work 4). The plans show no particulars of the refinery for which the lands
within the boundary were compulsorily acquired.

Section 7(1) provides:

'The Company may, instead of acquiring any land that it is authorised to acquire
g compulsorily under this Act, acquire compulsorily such easements and rights over
or in the land as it may require for the purpose of constructing, using, maintaining,
renewing or removing the works authorised by this Act or for the purpose of
obtaining access to the works or for the purpose of doing any other thing necessary
in connection with the works or for the construction of a refinery.'

h In this subsection the draftsman has followed the same technique as in s 5(1). In that
subsection lands may be taken and used as the company may require *for the purposes of the
authorised works or for the construction of a refinery* or for purposes ancillary thereto or
connected therewith. So in s 7(1) easements may be acquired compulsorily as the
company may require for the purpose of *constructing or using* the works authorised by the
Act, or for the purpose of doing any other thing *necessary in connection with the works* or
j for *the construction of the refinery.* For some reason no power is expressly granted to
acquire easements required for the use or maintenance of the refinery, unless, as is a
possible construction of the words, 'the works authorised by this Act' are not limited to
the 'authorised works' as defined in s 4. But if that was the intention, it is a little difficult
to see why in the last line of the subsection the draftsman uses language suggesting that
'the works' are something different from 'the construction of a refinery'.

When one turns of Part III, s 15(1) grants the powers to construct works 1, 2, 3 and 4. The first three works are constructions over the foreshore and sea bed, and are defined in s 4(1) as 'the pier'. The 'pier undertaking' is defined 'as the undertaking of the Company in connection with the pier as from time to time authorised'.

Section 15(2) provides:

'The Company may ... hold and use as part of the pier undertaking so much of the foreshore and bed of the sea as is situate within the limits of deviation ... and is required for or in connection with the said works.'

By s 16 there is the usual power to construct and use subsidiary works as described, including railways, tramways, junctions, sidings, turntables etc as may be necessary or convenient for or in connection with or subsidiary to the authorised works. By s 16(3) it is provided:

'In the exercise of the powers conferred by this section the Company shall cause as little detriment and inconvenience as the circumstances permit to any person and shall make reasonable compensation for any damage caused by the exercise of such powers.'

This is the only provision expressly imposing an obligation for compensation for damage and granting a right to any person to compensation for damage in terms which suggest that the right to compensation is wider in its scope than compensation for injurious affection to occupiers who qualify for that kind of compensation. The section is in the conventional form of sections providing for subsidiary works and interference with statutory undertakers or public utilities; and although I appreciate the force of the reasoning of Lord Denning MR on the contrast between ss 15 and 16, I am not confident that the provisions of s 16 throw great light on the intention of Parliament in Part II of the Act.

There follow in Part III provisions designed to enable Gulf Oil from time to time to deepen, dredge, scour and improve the bed and foreshore of the sea, provisions to prevent danger to navigation, and powers to sell or lease the pier undertaking on such terms and conditions as may be approved by the Minister. In Part IV Gulf Oil are granted jurisdiction as a pier authority, given power to make byelaws for the pier, and a bundle of sections provide protection for various public bodies and undertakers including compensation for damage or loss sustained by such undertakers.

Section 55 is important. It preserves the powers exercisable under the Town and Country Planning Act 1962 and any restrictions or powers thereby imposed or conferred in relation to land shall apply and may be exercised in relation to any land notwithstanding that the development thereof is or may be authorised or regulated by the Act. This in effect preserves the power of the planning authority (and the Minister) in respect of the proposed change of use of the land from existing agricultural use to industrial use. It affords an additional safeguard to the neighbourhood and its inhabitants to be exercised by the planning authority. But in connection with this case the section may be regarded as neutral, because the planning authority has no jurisdiction to authorise nuisance save (if at all) in so far as it has statutory power to permit the change of the character of a neighbourhood in relation to the comfort and convenience of the inhabitants. At the date of the enactment of the Gulf Oil Refining Act 1965 in fact, outline planning consent had been given. But I agree with May J that as the parliamentary history of the Act is outside the purview of this court it is wrong to draw any inference from that fact.

Contention of the parties

The rival contentions of the parties on the construction of the 1965 Act may be concisely summarised. Counsel for the plaintiff submitted that there is a clear distinction in the Act between the effect of the operative words in Part II and the effect of the operative words in Part III. Part II is concerned only with the grant of power to acquire lands and easements from the owners and occupiers stated in the book of reference.

There is in Part II no express authority granted to do anything on the land once

a compulsorily acquired, though the only use of the land permitted to the acquiring company is to use the lands for the purposes of the authorised works (defined as the pier and the railway) or for the construction of a refinery. Gulf Oil needed statutory authority to build the pier as it was an obstruction to the Milford Haven harbour, which is a harbour at common law regulated by the Harbours, Docks, and Piers Clauses Act 1847; and the Crown had its rights over the foreshore. And they needed statutory authority to

b run the railway, which was work 4, if only to protect themselves from nuisance. But in respect of the refinery, all that the promoters sought from Parliament was acquisition of the land on which to construct it. They sought no express statutory authority in respect of its construction or its use, and though the preamble recited that the plans showing the lands which may be taken *or used* compulsorily under the powers of this Act for the purposes thereof, counsel submitted that the preamble could not add to the powers

c granted by the operative words of the Act, and could only aid construction where there is a real doubt as to the intention to be collected from the operative words. The promoters sought no authority from Parliament in respect of the refinery save acquisition of the land for its construction. That explains the absence of any particulars or description of the refinery in the deposited plans. So as a matter of construction, authority was neither sought nor granted as to the kind of refinery to be constructed or as to the

d conditions or consequences of its operation. That explained the conspicuous absence of any provision for compensation for the inhabitants of the village immediately alongside the refinery whose common law rights would be invaded if the operation of the refinery constituted a nuisance to their use or enjoyment of their land.

Counsel for Gulf Oil submitted that this was a misunderstanding of the Act as drafted. By s 5 Parliament authorised the exercise of compulsory powers in favour of

e Gulf Oil for the construction of an oil refinery on the specified lands. Having granted Gulf Oil power to acquire the land for the single object of the construction of an oil refinery thereon, it was clearly the intention of Parliament that its authority was granted for the construction and the operation of that refinery. No particulars of the refinery to be constructed were required to be given to Parliament in the deposited plans, but the fact that Parliament granted the power to acquire the lands compulsorily led inescapably

f to the inference that having decided that Gulf Oil had proved a public need for another oil refinery Parliament authorised its construction and operation without requiring any safeguard other than such conditions as the planning authority had the power to impose in respect of the development of land.

Counsel for Gulf Oil threw out the challenge that there is no case in the books where it has been held that Parliament authorised the construction of a specific thing in a

g specific place but also held that an action would lie for the inevitable consequence of the operation of the works authorised to be constructed. The legislative intention to be collected from s 5 was that Parliament was satisfied that it was in the public interest to authorise such oil refinery as Gulf Oil intended to construct subject only to the consent of the planning authority. It would be extraordinary to impute to Parliament an authority to the promoters to construct the works without a collateral authority to use

h them. If there is any doubt about the intention to authorise the operation of the refinery, it is removed by the recitals of the preamble. The legislature accepted (i) that in order to meet the increasing public demand for the company's products it was essential that further facilities for the importation of crude oil and petroleum products and for their refinement should be made available in the United Kingdom, (ii) that Gulf Oil intended to establish a refinery in the parish of Llanstadwell, (iii) that it was expedient

j in the public interest that Gulf Oil should be empowered to construct the works authorised by the Act, and (iv) that it was expedient that Gulf Oil be empowered to acquire lands as in the Act provided. Counsel for Gulf Oil submitted that the relevant question of construction was: what did Parliament intend to take place on this site? and that this question is distinguishable from the question: what are the legal consequences of that which Parliament has intended to occur?

The defence of statutory authority to an action for nuisance developed in the railway age. The line of cases beginning with *R v Pease*[1], followed by *Vaughan v Taff Vale Railway Co*[2], *Jones v Festiniog Railway Co*[3], *Hammersmith and City Railway Co v Brand*[4] and *London, Brighton and South Coast Railway Co v Truman*[5], establish that where the use of a railway is expressly authorised by statute no action for nuisance will lie. The law is declared by Blackburn J[6] in *Hammersmith and City Railway Co v Brand*[4], and by Lord Chelmsford[7] in the passage quoted by May J:

'. . . we do not expect to find words in an Act of Parliament expressly authorizing an individual or a company to commit nuisance or do damage to a neighbour. The 86th section gives power to the company to use and employ locomotive engines, and if such locomotives cannot possibly be used without occasioning vibration and consequent injury to neighbouring houses . . . it must be taken that power is given to cause that vibration without liability to an action. The right given to use the locomotive would otherwise be nugatory . . .'

Throughout the railway cases there is the common foundation of fact that locomotive power could not be used on a railway without emission of sparks and vibration so that the authority to use the engines must carry with it their necessary consequences.

This principle has since been consistently applied outside the railway context. I need not in this judgment do more than cite the most relevant authorities as they have been reviewed by May J: *Geddis v Proprietors of Bann Reservoir*[8], *Metropolitan Asylums District Managers v Hill*[9] and *Manchester Corpn v Farnworth*[10]. In all those cases on the facts it was inevitable that nuisance would be a necessary consequence of the thing constructed and operated. On the other hand, it has not been stated in any case as the law that the defence will only apply when it is shown that the legislature must have known at the time that the statute was passed that the consequence of the authorised act must be to injure others. So I accept the submission of counsel for Gulf Oil that the relevant question of construction in this case is simply, did the Act authorise the use of this refinery on this site? Answering that question in the affirmative, he relies strongly on a statement of the law by Lord Watson in *Metropolitan Asylum District Managers v Hill*[11] when he said:

'The judgment of this House in *The Hammersmith Railway Company v. Brand*[4] determines that where Parliament has given express powers to construct certain buildings or works according to plans and specifications, upon a particular site, and for a specific purpose, the use of these works or buildings, in the manner contemplated and sanctioned by the Act, cannot, except in so far as negligent, be restrained by injunction, although such use may constitute a nuisance at common law; and that no compensation is due in respect of injury to private rights, unless the Act provides for such compensation being made. Accordingly the respondents did not dispute that if the Appellants or the Local Government Board had been, by the *Metropolitan Poor Act*, 1867, expressly empowered to build the identical hospital which they have erected at *Hampstead*, upon the very site which it now occupies, and that with a view to its being used for the treatment of patients suffering from

1   (1832) 4 B & Ad 30, [1824–34] All ER Rep 579
2   (1860) 5 H & N 679, [1843–60] All ER Rep 474
3   (1868) LR 3 QB 733
4   (1869) LR 4 HL 171, [1861–73] All ER Rep 60
5   (1885) 11 App Cas 45, [1881–5] All ER Rep 134
6   LR 4 HL 171 at 196
7   LR 4 HL 171 at 202, [1861–73] All ER Rep 60 at 65
8   (1878) 3 App Cas 430
9   (1881) 6 App Cas 193, [1881–5] All ER Rep 536
10 [1930] AC 171, [1929] All ER Rep 90
11 6 App Cas 193 at 211–212, [1881–5] All ER Rep 536 at 545

small-pox, the respondents would not be entitled to the judgment which they have obtained. The Appellants do not assert that express power or authority to that effect has been given by the Act either to themselves or to the Board; but they contend that, having regard to the nature of the public duties laid upon them, and the necessities of the case, it must, on a fair construction of the Act, be held that the Legislature did intend them to exercise, and authorize them to exercise, such power and authority under the direction and control of the Poor Law Board. I see no reason to doubt that, wherever it can be shewn to be matter of plain and necessary implication from the language of a statute, that the Legislature did intend to confer the specific powers above referred to, the result in law will be precisely the same as if these powers had been given in express terms. And I am disposed to hold that if the Legislature, without specifying either plan or site, were to prescribe by statute that a public body shall, within certain defined limits, provide hospital accommodation for a class or classes of persons labouring under infectious disease, no injunction could issue against the use of an hospital established in pursuance of the Act, provided that it were either apparent or proved to the satisfaction of the Court that the directions of the Act could not be complied with at all, without creating a nuisance. In that case, the necessary result of that which they have directed to be done must presumably have been in the view of the Legislature at the time when the Act was passed.'

It is to be observed that in his summary of the decision in the *Hammersmith Railway* case[1] Lord Watson carefully and accurately refers to the grant of express powers to construct certain buildings or works according to plans and specifications on a particular site, and for a specific purpose; and further I observe that in that case the railway company had statutory authority not only to make a railway but also, by virtue of the incorporation of s 86 of the Railway Clauses Consolidation Act 1845, 'to use and employ locomotive engines and other moving power'. I cannot discover from the report of *Manchester Corpn v Farnworth*[2] that Lord Dunedin was conscious of declaring the law in any different sense to the declaration of Lord Watson, although his more concise formulation omits reference to the important qualification made by Lord Watson, 'according to plans and specifications'. And in *Metropolitan Asylums District Managers v Hill*[3] the case proceeded on the basis that whatever the particulars or specification of the hospital it was likely to be a potential source of infectious disease in whatever locality it was built and used.

Against this history of judicial construction of earlier statutes, I approach the attempt to determine the intention of Parliament as expressed in the Gulf Oil Refining Act 1965. The structure of the Act, with its division into four parts, all introduced by a preamble, I have already described. There is an obvious contrast between the draftsman's technique in Part II granting powers for acquisition of lands delineated on the plans and his technique in Part III granting power to construct works. Works 1, 2, 3 and 4 are specifically described in s 15(1). The plans of the works show their outline, their sections, and levels. In Part II the lands to be acquired are delineated on plans 3 and 4. There is no description of the refinery intended to be constructed, no particulars of its dimensions or engineering or chemical functions or capacity. The promoters appear to have deliberately decided not to include the refinery in Part III among the works which they sought power to construct, or if they did seek such power it has not been granted. In my view there is nothing in the words of the preamble which leads to the inference that Parliament intended in s 5(1) to grant power to construct a particular specified refinery as compared merely to a grant of power to acquire lands on which to construct an unspecified refinery which was not included in the works authorised by Part III.

1   (1869) LR 4 HL 171, [1861–73] All ER Rep 60
2   [1930] AC 171, [1929] All ER Rep 90
3   (1881) 6 App Cas 193, [1881–5] All ER Rep 536

No case was cited at the bar of a statute which granted compulsory powers for acquisition of land for a purpose, and which had been held to have conferred statutory **a** authority to construct and use the thing built on the land simply as an inference of legislative intention to be collected from the grant of compulsory powers for acquisition of land. I accept that the verb 'authorised' in this context carries the meaning proposed by Lord Jenkins in *Pyx Granite Co Ltd v Ministry of Housing and Local Government*[1]. So I conclude that May J reached a wrong conclusion. I do not find in this Act any statutory authority to construct or build or use this refinery. The promoters retained the liberty **b** to build on their land such refinery as they wished, subject only to planning permission. They create nuisance at their peril. If the plaintiff establishes that she has suffered damage through nuisance, and that there is a threat that the nuisance will continue, it will be for the trial judge to decide on the remedy.

I stated earlier in this judgment some anxiety about the difficulty that I felt in answering the question ordered to be tried as a preliminary question. There has been no **c** evidence and for the purpose of the question the facts alleged in the statement of claim are assumed to be correct. It does not of course follow that the refinery on this site has caused or does cause a nuisance. The impact on the residents of adjoining houses of an oil refinery built on a square mile of land may vary greatly according to the particular specification and operation of the works constructed on the site. It does seem to me to be clear that by granting compulsory powers of acquisition of the land delineated on plan **d** 3, together with powers to construct the works specified in Part III of the Act, Parliament intended and authorised this agricultural land to be developed on a change of use to use for the purpose of an oil refinery subject to the controls of the planning authority. This is a different issue to the question whether Parliament gave authority to construct the particular refinery that has been built. But for the reasons stated earlier in this judgment, the trial of the allegations of the particular kind of nuisances alleged in the statement of **e** claim may involve a nice enquiry into questions of the kind of inconvenience and loss of enjoyment that anyone living in such an industrial environment must be expected to put up with.

I would finally add that in so far as any of the nuisances alleged are proved to be caused by the railway, the sidings or other contraptions on the site which have been built as subsidiary works pursuant to s 16 of the 1965 Act, the plaintiff may have a right to **f** compensation under s 16(3), and by a necessary corollary has no right of action in nuisance for such damage.

For those reasons I agree with Lord Denning MR that the appeal should be allowed.

Appeal allowed. Leave to appeal to the House of Lords granted.

g

Solicitors: *Price & Kelway*, Milford Haven (for the plaintiff); *Cartwrights*, Bristol (for Gulf Oil).

Sumra Green   Barrister.

h

1   [1959] 3 All ER 1 at 22, [1960] AC 260 at 311–312

Chase Manhattan Bank NA v Israel-British Bank (London) Ltd

CHANCERY DIVISION

GOULDING J

30th APRIL, 1st, 2nd, 3rd, 4th, 8th, 9th, 10th, 11th, 14th, 15th, 16th, 17th, 18th, 21st, 22nd, 23rd, 24th MAY, 5th, 6th, 7th, 11th, 12th, 13th, 14th, 15th, 18th, 19th, 20th JUNE, 16th JULY 1979

Mistake – Mistake of fact – Money paid under mistake of fact – Equitable right to trace money paid under mistake of fact – Basis of right – American company paying sum into New York bank for the account of an English company – Payment made as a result of a factual mistake by employee of American company – English company insolvent and compulsory winding-up order made in respect of it – Action brought against English company by American company to trace and recover sum paid – Whether American company entitled to trace and recover sum paid – Whether winding-up of English company affecting right of American company to trace and recover sum paid.

On 2nd July 1974 the plaintiff, a New York bank, was instructed to pay $US2,000,687·50 to M Ltd, another New York bank, for the account of the defendant, a bank in England. On 3rd July the plaintiff duly made the payment through the New York clearing house system. Later that day by mistake because of a clerical error it made a second payment of the same amount through the clearing house system to M Ltd for the account of the defendant. On 2nd August the defendant petitioned the English High Court to be wound up compulsorily. On 2nd December a winding-up order was made. The defendant was insolvent and the plaintiff could not hope to recover the whole of the $US2,000,687·50 paid by mistake on 3rd July if it proved as a creditor in the winding-up. The plaintiff brought an action in England against the defendant claiming, inter alia, a declaration that on 3rd July 1974 the defendant became a trustee for the plaintiff of the sum of $US2,000,687·50. It contended that it was entitled in equity to trace and recover that sum. At the trial it was common ground that the legal effects of the mistaken payment had in the first instance to be determined in accordance with the law of the State of New York as the lex causae but that the procedural rights and remedies had to be ascertained by the law of England as the lex fori. The defendant contended that the plaintiff was not entitled in equity to trace and recover the mistaken payment because (i) the equitable right of a person who paid money by mistake to trace and claim it was not part of the substantive law of the State of New York but merely the result of its remedial or procedural law, (ii) under English law the equitable right of tracing depended on the existence of an initial fiduciary relationship arising from some consensual arrangement and that was lacking in the instant case, and (iii) in any event, irrespective of what rights or remedies the plaintiff might have had before the commencement of the winding-up on 2nd August 1974, all the defendant's property had been held since that date on a statutory trust requiring its application in discharge of the defendant's liabilities under the winding-up, so that the plaintiff's only surviving right was to prove as a creditor in the winding-up.

Held – The plaintiff was entitled in equity to trace the mistaken payment and to recover what currently represented the $US2,000,687·50 because (i) under English law it had the right to do so since a person who paid money to another under a mistake of fact retained an equitable property in it and the conscience of the payee was subjected to a fiduciary duty to respect that continuing proprietary interest, (ii) on the evidence, the plaintiff had a similar right which was also founded on a continuing proprietary interest under the law of the State of New York, and (iii) as a result, under whichever system of law the plaintiff's title was founded, the assets, if any, in the defendant's hands properly representing the plaintiff's money at the commencement of the winding-up did not belong to the defendant beneficially and had never formed part of its property subject to *a* the statutory trust under the winding-up. The declaration would accordingly be granted and an enquiry ordered into what had become of the $US2,000,687·50 paid by mistake and what assets, if any, in the possession or power of the defendant currently represented that sum or any part thereof (see p 1031 *f*, p 1032 *e f*, p 1033 *c* and *g* to p 1034 *a* and p 1039 *h* to p 1040 *d*, post).

Newton v Porter (1877) 69 NY 133, Re Berry (1906) 147 F 208, dictum of Lord Haldane *b* LC in *Sinclair v Broughton* [1914–15] All ER Rep at 632 and *Simonds v Simonds* (1978) 408 NYS 2d 359 applied; *Re Diplock's Estate* [1948] 2 All ER 318 explained; *Oakes v Turquand* [1862–73] All ER Rep 738 and *Tennent v City of Glasgow Bank* (1879) 4 App Cas 615 distinguished.

Notes
 c

For principle of following assets, see 16 Halsbury's Laws (4th Edn) para 1460, and for cases on the subject, see 35 Digest (Repl) 182–183, 2–10.

Cases referred to in judgment

American Sugar Refining Co v Fancher (1895) 40 NE 206, 145 NY 552. *d*
Beatty v Guggenheim Exploration Co (1919) 225 NY 380.
Berry, Re (1906) 147 F 208.
Chaplin v Boys [1969] 2 All ER 1085, [1971] AC 356, [1969] 3 WLR 322, [1969] 2 Lloyd's Rep 487, HL, 11 Digest (Reissue) 496, 951.
Colorado, The [1923] P 102, [1923] All ER Rep 531, 92 LJP 100, 128 LT 759, 16 Asp MLC 145, CA, 11 Digest (Reissue) 631, 1684. *e*
Diplock's Estate, Re, Diplock v Wintle [1948] 2 All ER 318, [1948] Ch 465, [1948] LJR 1670, CA; *affd sub nom Ministry of Health v Simpson* [1950] 2 All ER 1137, [1951] AC 251, HL, 47 Digest (Repl) 532, 4825.
Hallett's Estate, Re, Knatchbull v Hallett (1880) 13 Ch D 696, [1874–80] All ER Rep 793, 49 LJ Ch 415, 42 LT 421, CA, 47 Digest (Repl) 537, 4854.
Healy v Comr of Internal Revenue (1952) 345 US 278. *f*
Knight Newspapers Inc v Comr of Internal Revenue (1944) 143 F 2d 1007.
National Bank v Insurance Co (1880) 104 US 54.
Newton v Porter (1877) 69 NY 133.
Oakes v Turquand and Harding, Peek v Turquand and Harding, Re Overend, Gurney & Co (1867) LR 2 HL 325, [1861–73] All ER Rep 738, 36 LJ Ch 949, 16 LT 808, 31 JP 195, HL; *affd sub nom Re Overend, Gurney & Co, ex parte Oakes and Peek* LR 3 Eq 576, 9 *g* Digest (Reissue) 263, 1554.
Oriental Inland Steam Co, Re, ex parte Scinde Railway Co (1874) LR 9 Ch App 557, 43 LJ Ch 699, 31 LT 5, LJJ, 10 Digest (Reissue) 978, 5894.
Simonds v Simonds (1978) 408 NYS 2d 359.
Sinclair v Brougham [1914] AC 398, [1914–15] All ER Rep 622, 83 LJ Ch 465, 111 LT 1, HL, *varying sub nom Re Birkbeck Permanent Building Society* [1912] 2 Ch 183, CA, 35 *h* Digest (Repl) 182, 8.
Tebin v Moldock (1963) 241 NYS 2d 629, *modified on appeal* (1964) 200 NE 2d 216.
Tennent v City of Glasgow Bank (1879) 4 App Cas 615, 40 LT 694, HL, 9 Digest (Reissue) 264, 1563.

Cases also cited
 j

Acrux, The [1965] 2 All ER 323, [1965] P 391.
Aluminium Industrial Vaassen BV v Romalpa Aluminium Ltd [1976] 2 All ER 552, [1976] 1 WLR 676, CA.
American Surety Co of New York v Wrightson (1910) 103 LT 663.
Anjopa Paper and Board Manufacturing Co, Re (1967) 269 F Supp 241.

Arab Bank Ltd v Barclays Bank (Dominion, Colonial and Overseas) [1954] 2 All ER 226, [1954]
a   AC 495; *affg* [1953] 2 All ER 263, [1953] 2 QB 527, CA.
Ayerst v C & K (Contractors) Ltd [1975] 2 All ER 537, [1976] AC 167, HL.
Baschet v London Illustrated Standard Co [1900] 1 Ch 73.
Brown v Father Divine (1940) 18 NYS 2d 544.
Butler v Attwood (1966) 369 F 2d 811.
Coane v American Distilling Co (1948) 298 NY 197.
b   *Cohn, Re* [1944] 1 Ch 5.
De la Vega v Vianna (1830) 1 B & Ad 284, 109 ER 792.
Don v Lippman (1837) 5 Cl & Fin 1, 7 ER 303, HL.
Dysart (Earl) v Hammerton & Co [1914] 1 Ch 822, CA; *rvsd* [1916] 1 AC 57, HL.
Falk v Hoffman (1922) 135 NE 243.
Foreman v Foreman (1929) 251 NY 239.
c   *Früling v Schroeder* (1835) 2 Bing NC 77, 132 ER 31.
Fuld (deceased), In the estate of, (No 3), Hartley v Fuld [1965] 3 All ER 776, [1968] P 675.
Fur & Wool Trading Co Ltd v George I Fox Inc (1927) 245 NY 215.
Giblin v McMullen (1868) LR 2 PC 317, PC.
Gissing v Gissing [1970] 2 All ER 780, [1971] AC 886, HL.
Hoyt v Wright (1932) 261 NYS 131.
d   *ITT Co Development Corpn v Barton* (1978) 457 F Supp 224.
Industrial Export & Import Corpn v Hongkong & Shanghai Banking Corpn (1947) 77 NYS 2d
541.
International Refugee Organization v Maryland Drydock Co (1949) 179 F 2d 284.
Kloebe, Re, Kannreuther v Geiselbrecht (1884) 28 Ch D 175.
Kountze Bros, Re (1935) 79 F 2d 98.
e   *Lamb v Schiefner* (1908) 114 NYS 34.
Latham v Father Divine (1949) 85 NE 2d 168.
Lawrence v American National Bank (1873) 54 NY 432.
Lightfoot v Davis (1910) 91 NE 582.
M'Bain v Wallace & Co (1881) 6 App Cas 588.
McGrath v Hilding (1977) 394 NYS 2d 603.
f   *Maldonado (deceased), Re, State of Spain v Treasury Solicitor* [1953] 2 All ER 1579, [1954]
P 223, CA.
Melbourn, Ex parte, re Melbourn (1870) LR 6 Ch App 64.
Moses v Macferlan (1760) 2 Burr 1005, 97 ER 676.
National Benefit Association, Re (1947) 29 NW 2d 81.
Pardo v Bingham (1868) LR 6 Eq 485.
g   *Reading v Attorney-General* [1951] 1 All ER 617, [1951] AC 507, HL.
Roberts v Ely (1889) 113 NY 128.
Robinson v Robinson and Lane (1858) 1 Sw & Tr 362, 164 ER 767.
Sandiford, Re, (No 2), Italo-Canadian Corpn Ltd v Sandiford [1935] Ch 681, [1935] All ER
Rep 364.
Scott v Freedom Development Corpn (1961) 219 NYS 2d 494.
h   *Simonds v Simonds* (1977) 396 NYS 2d 547.
Suidair International Airways Ltd (in liquidation), Re [1950] 2 All ER 920, [1951] Ch 165.
Tagus, The [1903] P 44.
Tervaete, The [1922] P 259, [1922] All ER Rep 387, CA.
Thellusson, Re, ex parte Abdy [1919] 2 KB 735, [1918–19] All ER Rep 729.
Thurburn v Steward (1871) LR 3 PC 478, PC.
j   *Trieseler v Helmbacher* (1943) 168 SW 2d 1030.
Tyler, Re, ex parte Official Receiver [1907] 1 KB 865, [1904–7] All ER Rep 181, CA.
Watkins v Gorlick (1958) 323 P 2d 649.
Watson, Re, Guardians of Stamford Union v Bartlett [1899] 1 Ch 72.
Wiggzell, Re, ex parte Hart [1921] 2 KB 835.
Zigurds, The [1932] P 113, CA; *affd* [1934] AC 209, [1933] All ER Rep 717, HL.

Action

The plaintiff, the Chase Manhattan Bank NA, brought an action against the defendant, *a* Israel-British Bank (London) Ltd, seeking by a re-amended statement of claim (i) a declaration that on 3rd July 1974 the defendant became trustee for the plaintiff of the sum of $US2,000,687·50 paid by mistake through the New York clearing house system to Mellon Bank International in New York for the account of the defendant, and (ii) such accounts, enquiries and directions as might be necessary or expedient for the purpose of ascertaining what property currently represented that sum or any part thereof. In its *b* defence, as re-amended, the defendant, inter alia, denied (i) that it became a trustee for the plaintiff either on 3rd July 1974 or on any date of $US2,000,687·50 or any other sum, or (ii) that the plaintiff was entitled either to the relief claimed or to any relief. The facts are set out in the judgment.

J M Chadwick and *M N Keenan* for the plaintiff.   *c*
W F Stubbs QC and *Robin Potts* for the defendant.

Cur adv vult

16th July. **GOULDING J** read the following judgment: This action concerns a sum of *d* money paid by mistake. In July 1974 the plaintiff, Chase Manhattan Bank NA, and the defendant, Israel-British Bank (London) Ltd, were carrying on business as bankers, the plaintiff in New York and the defendant in London. On or before 2nd July an Italian bank instructed the plaintiff to pay $US2,000,687·50 to Mellon Bank International, another bank in New York, for the defendant's account. The plaintiff duly made that payment through the New York clearing house system on 3rd July. Later on the same *e* day, 3rd July, the plaintiff made a further payment of the same amount, also through the clearing system, to the same recipient, Mellon Bank International, again for the account of the defendant. This second payment purported to be made on the instructions of a bank in Hong Kong. But no such instructions had been given, and the second payment was a pure mistake. Its original cause was a clerical error made by a servant of the plaintiff earlier on 3rd July. That error however was discovered in good time by another *f* servant of the plaintiff, who gave instructions to correct it. His instructions were executed only in part by his fellow employees, and their failure was the proximate cause of the mistaken payment.

It is unnecessary for me to go into the facts further, for they are not in dispute. There was an issue on the pleadings as to the order in which the two payments to Mellon Bank International were made, but the defendant admitted by counsel, on the first day of the *g* trial, that, as contended by the plaintiff, the correct payment preceded the mistaken one.

There was a further issue as to the defendant's knowledge of the mistake. On my view of the matter, it is not necessary to determine the point, but I think it right to do so in case it becomes important in an appellate court, or otherwise in subsequent proceedings between the parties. I have heard on this issue the evidence of Miss Hilliard, an employee of Mellon Bank International, and of Mr Blaik, employed at the material time by the *h* defendant. Both were honest and careful witnesses. Neither professed to have any specific recollection of the relevant communications that took place almost five years ago. Each accordingly spoke from a knowledge of his or her business practices and experience, and from a general recollection of the time in question, which was distinguished by disturbance and uncertainty in international banking circles. In case of difference I prefer Miss Hilliard's testimony, mainly because, as Mr Blaik repeatedly *j* pointed out, the time was one of much confusion for him, with the defendant's parent company and some of the defendant's banking correspondents in trouble, and the defendant's own failure only a few days away. Miss Hilliard too was busier than usual, but in conditions far less disturbing to the regular performance of her work than those which affected Mr Blaik. In the result, I am satisfied on a balance of probabilities that on 5th July 1974 the defendant learned of the mistaken payment, and either knew it was a *a* mistake, or was put fully on enquiry by facts that should have indicated it might be a mistake.

On 2nd August 1974, the defendant presented a petition to the English High Court, praying to be wound up by the court. Counsel for the plaintiff said in opening that the plaintiff did not discover the mistake until after that event, but the fact has not been pleaded or proved, nor has the defendant either admitted or denied it. It formed no part of the plaintiff's case as argued before me. A winding-up order was made on the *b* defendant's petition on 2nd December 1974. Meanwhile, on 23rd September, the defendant had also filed its bankruptcy petition in New York. On 3rd August 1976, with the leave of the Companies Court, the plaintiff began the present action, in which it seeks to trace and to recover in equity the sum which it paid by mistake in 1974.

Since the commencement of the action the plaintiff has proved, and has received a dividend or dividends, in the winding-up proceedings. The joint liquidators of the *c* defendant questioned the plaintiff's right to prove during the pendency of the tracing claim, but on 5th April 1977 Oliver J directed them to admit the plaintiff's proof. He held that the plaintiff had a claim against the defendant for money had and received, but that there was nothing to preclude it from asserting also a proprietary claim over specific assets should it be possible to trace them. The defendant is insolvent and the plaintiff cannot hope to recover the whole of its loss by way of dividends in the winding-up. *d* Hence the importance to the plaintiff of the present action.

The debate at the trial has been concerned with three main subjects, the law of the State of New York as to the recovery of money paid under a mistake of fact, the law of England on the same topic, and the resolution of any conflict of laws which may arise if the two systems differ. It is common ground that the legal effects of the mistaken payment must in the first instance be determined in accordance with New York law as *e* the lex causae. It is also common ground that procedural rights and remedies must be ascertained by the law of England as the lex fori. There is, however, disagreement as to the relevant provisions of each system of law and there is also acute controversy over the application to the present case of the distinction between substantive and procedural law.

The plaintiff's claim, viewed in the first place without reference to *any* system of positive law, raises problems to which the answers, if not always difficult, are at any rate *f* not obvious. If one party P pays money to another party D by reason of a factual mistake, either common to both parties or made by P alone, few conscientious persons would doubt that D ought to return it. But suppose that D is, or becomes, insolvent before repayment is made, so that P comes into competition with D's general creditors, what then? If the money can still be traced, either in its original form or through successive conversions, and is found among D's remaining assets, ought not P to be able to claim it, *g* or what represents it, as his own? If he ought, and if in a particular case the money has been blended with other assets and is represented by a mixed fund, no longer as valuable as the sum total of its original constituents, what priorities or equalities should govern the distribution of the mixed fund? If the money can no longer be traced, either separate or in mixture, should P have any priority over ordinary creditors of D? In any of these cases, does it make any difference whether the mistake was inevitable, or was caused by *h* P's carelessness, or was contributed to by some fault, short of dishonesty, on the part of D?

At this stage I am asked to take only one step forward, and to answer the initial question of principle, whether the plaintiff is entitled in equity to trace the mistaken payment and to recover what now properly represents the money. The subsequent history of the payment and the rules for ascertaining what now represents it have not *j* been proved or debated before me. They will have to be established in further proceedings if the plaintiff can clear the first hurdle today.

The initial question in the action appears not to be the subject of reported judicial decision in England. Let me read a few lines from Goff and Jones on Restitution[1]. The authors say:

---

1   2nd Edn (1978), p 89

'Whether a person who has paid money under a mistake of fact should be granted a restitutionary proprietary claim can arise in a number of contexts. It will be most *a* important when the payee is insolvent and the payer seeks to gain priority over the payee's general creditors. The English courts have never had to consider this question. But in the United States it has arisen on a few occasions. A leading case is *Re Berry*[1].'

That was a case decided in 1906 in the Circuit Court of Appeals of the Second Circuit. I shall read a passage from the judgment of the court, delivered by Coxe J[2]:   *b*

'Stripped of all complications and entanglements we have this naked fact that Raborg & Manice by mistake paid Berry & Co. $1,500, which they did not owe and which Berry & Co. could not have retained without losing the respect of every honorable business man. It is conceded on all hands that had not insolvency and bankruptcy intervened Raborg & Manice could have recovered the money on an *c* implied assumpsit in the event that Berry & Co. declined to return it after knowledge of the facts—a highly improbable contingency. Of course such an action would lie. On no possible theory could the retention of the money by Berry & Co. be justified; it was paid to them and received by them under mistake, both parties believing that Raborg & Manice owed the amount. If $1,500 had been placed in a package by Raborg & Manice and delivered to a messenger with *d* instructions to deposit it in their bank, and the messenger, by mistake, had delivered it to Berry & Co., it will hardly be pretended that the latter would acquire any title to the money, and yet the actual transaction in legal effect gave them no better right. It is urged that to compel restitution now will work injustice to the general creditors of the bankrupts, but this contention loses sight of the fact that the money in dispute never belonged to the bankrupts, and their creditors, upon broad *e* principles of equity, have no more right to it than if the transaction of November 25th had never taken place. If the trustees succeed on this appeal the creditors will receive $1,500, the equitable title to which was never in the bankrupts. There can be no doubt of the fact that the payment to Berry & Co. was a mistake and that by reason of the mistake the trustees have in their possession $1,500 which, otherwise, they would not have. The proposition that Raborg & Manice, who have done no *f* wrong, shall be deprived of their property and that it shall be divided among creditors to whom it does not fairly belong, is not one that appeals to the conscience of a court of equity. The rule invoked by the District Court is well stated by Judge Story.'

Coxe J then read a passage from Story on Equity Jurisprudence[3]. He omitted certain sentences, and I think the extract will be clearer if I read the whole passage: *g*

'1255. One of the most common cases in which a Court of Equity acts upon the ground of implied trusts *in invitum*, is where a party has received money which he cannot conscientiously withhold from another party. It has been well remarked, that the receiving of money which consistently with conscience cannot be retained is, in Equity, sufficient to raise a trust in favour of the party for whom or on whose *h* account it was received. This is the governing principle in all such cases. And therefore, whenever any controversy arises, the true question is, not whether money has been received by a party of which he could not have compelled the payment, but whether he can now, with a safe conscience, *ex æquo et bono*, retain it. Illustrations of this doctrine are familiar in cases of money paid by accident, or mistake, or fraud. And the difference between the payment of money under a *j*

---

1   (1906) 147 F 208
2   147 F 208 at 210
3   2nd Edn (1839) paras 1255, 1256

a mistake of fact, and a payment under a mistake of law, in its operation upon the conscience of the party, presents the equitable qualifications of the doctrine in a striking manner.

'1256. It is true that Courts of Law now entertain jurisdiction in many cases of this sort where formerly the remedy was solely in Equity; as for example, in an action of assumpsit for money had and received, where the money cannot conscientiously be withheld by the party; following out the rule of the Civil Law; b *Quod condictio indebiti non datur ultra, quam locupletior factus est, qui accepit.* But this does not oust the general jurisdiction of Courts of Equity over the subject-matter, which had for many ages before been in full exercise, although it renders a resort to them for relief less common, as well as less necessary, than it formerly was. Still, however, there are many cases of this sort where it is indispensable to resort to Courts of Equity for adequate relief, and especially where the transactions are c complicated, and a discovery from the defendant is requisite.'

Coxe J, after citing two reported cases[1], added this[2]:

'When the money was paid under a plain mistake of fact equity impressed upon it a constructive trust which followed it through the bank and into the hands of the trustees.'

d The effect of the American case law, developed in a number of different states, as well as in the federal jurisdiction, is summarised as follows in Professor A W Scott's important book on Trusts[3]:

'Similarly where chattels are conveyed or money is paid by mistake, so that the person making the conveyance or payment is entitled to restitution, the transferee or payee holds the chattels or money upon a constructive trust. In such a case, it is e true, the remedy at law for the value of the chattels or for the amount of money paid may be an adequate remedy, in which case a court of equity will not ordinarily give specific restitution. If the chattels are of a unique character, however, or if the person to whom the chattels are conveyed or to whom the money is paid is insolvent, the remedy at law is not adequate and a court of equity will enforce the f constructive trust by decreeing specific restitution. The beneficial interest remains in the person who conveyed the chattel or who paid the money, since the conveyance or payment was made under a mistake.'

In my opinion, on the evidence that I have heard, to which I shall have to return later, the foregoing passages correctly represent the law of the State of New York. I believe they are also in accord with the general principles of equity as applied in England, and in the g absence of direct English authority I should wish to follow them.

Counsel for the defendant contends that I am not at liberty to do so, because of the judgment of the Court of Appeal in *Re Diplock's Estate*[4], explaining and developing the earlier decision of the House of Lords in *Sinclair v Brougham*[5]. *Re Diplock's Estate*[4] itself went to the House of Lords, sub nom *Ministry of Health v Simpson*[6], but the appeal did not relate to the question which is material in the present litigation. Counsel for the h defendant says that, as stated in Snell on Equity[7], there is no equitable right to trace

---

1   *National Bank v Insurance Co* (1880) 104 US 54, *American Sugar Refining Co v Fancher* (1895) 40 NE 206
j 2   (1906) 147 F 208 at 211
3   3rd Edn (1967) vol 5, p 3428
4   [1948] 2 All ER 318, [1948] Ch 465
5   [1914] AC 398, [1914–15] All ER Rep 622
6   [1950] 2 All ER 1137, [1951] AC 251
7   27th Edn (1973), p 289

property unless some initial fiduciary relationship exists, the right being founded on the existence of a beneficial owner with an equitable proprietary interest in property in the hands of a trustee or other fiduciary agent. Counsel says further that the essential fiduciary relationship must initially arise from some consensual arrangement.

The facts and decisions in *Sinclair v Brougham*[1] and in *Re Diplock's Estate*[2] are well known and I shall not take time to recite them. I summarise my view of the *Diplock*[2] judgment as follows. 1. The Court of Appeal's interpretation of *Sinclair v Brougham*[1] was an essential part of their decision and is binding on me. 2. The court thought[3] that the majority of the House of Lords in *Sinclair v Brougham*[1] had not accepted Lord Dunedin's opinion in that case, and themselves rejected it. 3. The court (as stated in Snell[4]) held[5] that an initial fiduciary relationship is a necessary foundation of the equitable right of tracing. 4. They also held[6] that the relationship between the building society directors and depositors in *Sinclair v Brougham*[1] was a sufficient fiduciary relationship for the purpose. The latter passage reads[7]:

> '. . . a sufficient fiduciary relationship was found to exist between the depositors and the directors by reason of the fact that the purposes for which the depositors had handed their money to the directors were by law incapable of fulfilment.'

It is founded, I think, on the observations of Lord Parker in *Sinclair v Brougham*[1].

This fourth point shows that the fund to be traced need not (as was the case in *Re Diplock's Estate*[2] itself) have been the subject of fiduciary obligations before it got into the wrong hands. It is enough that, as in *Sinclair v Brougham*[1], the payment into wrong hands itself gave rise to a fiduciary relationship. The same point also throws considerable doubt on counsel's submission for the defendants that the necessary fiduciary relationship must originate in a consensual transaction. It was not the intention of the depositors or of the directors in *Sinclair v Brougham*[1] to create any relationship at all between the depositors and the directors as principals. Their object, which unfortunately disregarded the statutory limitations of the building society's powers, was to establish contractual relationships between the depositors and the society. In the circumstances, however, the depositors retained an equitable property in the funds they parted with, and fiduciary relationships arose between them and the directors. In the same way, I would suppose, a person who pays money to another under a factual mistake retains an equitable property in it and the conscience of that other is subjected to a fiduciary duty to respect his proprietary right.

I am fortified in my opinion by the speech in *Sinclair v Brougham*[1] of Lord Haldane LC, who, unlike Lord Dunedin, was not suspected of heresy in *Re Diplock's Estate*[2]. Lord Haldane LC[8] (who spoke for Lord Atkinson as well as himself) includes money paid under mistake of fact among the cases where money could be followed at common law, and he proceeds[9] to the auxiliary tracing remedy, available (as he said) wherever money was held to belong in equity to the plaintiff, without making any relevant exception.

---

1 [1914] AC 398, [1914–15] All ER Rep 622
2 [1948] 2 All ER 318, [1948] Ch 465
3 [1948] 2 All ER 318 at 358–359, [1948] Ch 465 at 543
4 27th Edn (1973), p 289
5 [1948] 2 All ER 318 at 347, [1948] Ch 465 at 521
6 [1948] 2 All ER 318 at 351, 357, [1948] Ch 465 at 529, 540
7 [1948] 2 All ER 318 at 357, [1948] Ch 465 at 540–541
8 [1914] AC 398 at 419–420, [1914–15] All ER Rep 622 at 632
9 [1914] AC 398 at 421, [1914–15] All ER Rep 622 at 632

Thus my problem over Re Diplock's Estate[1] is in the end this: can I adopt into English
a equity the passage I have quoted from Professor Scott without making the forbidden
transition to the opinion of Lord Dunedin? I have carefully considered the passages in
Re Diplock's Estate[1] where that opinion is criticised. In the end I believe that the whole
subject of the Court of Appeal's condemnation was the suggestion that the tracing
remedy could be applied wherever the defendant could be shown to have got an unjust
enrichment, a superfluity as Lord Dunedin called it. The court[2] insisted on the more
b precise test of a continuing right of property recognised in equity or of what I think to
be its concomitant, a fiduciary or quasi-fiduciary relationship. At the same time they
recognised that exactly what relationships were sufficient for the purpose, had not yet
been precisely laid down[3].

Thus, in the belief that the point is not expressly covered by English authority and that
Re Diplock's Estate[1] does not conclude it by necessary implication, I hold that the equitable
c remedy of tracing is in principle available, on the ground of continuing proprietary
interest, to a party who has paid money under a mistake of fact. On that prime question,
I see no relevant difference between the law of England and the law of New York and
there is no conflict of laws to be resolved.

It is important, however, to make clear the limits of what I have just said. I do not say,
and I do not imply, that on the facts and figures of any particular case the courts of
d England and of New York, when tracing in equity a sum paid by mistake, will necessarily
apply the same tracing rules or arrive at the same final result. For example, in Re Berry[4],
an extract from which I have read, the American court applied the rule in Re Hallett's
Estate[5] for the purpose of identifying the claimant's money in the bankrupts' bank
account. Counsel for the defendant, when discussing Re Berry[4] before me, has argued
that if, contrary to his contention, an English court allowed tracing at all on the facts of
e that case, it would apply a different rule. I decline to answer any question of that sort
until actually raised on ascertained facts.

I must, however, in order to decide the case, deal with a more radical submission on
the part of counsel for the defendant. He says that, whatever rights or remedies the
plaintiff may have had against the defendant before 2nd August 1974, all the defendant's
property has since that date been held on a statutory trust requiring its application in
f discharge of the defendant's liabilities in accordance with the provisions of the Companies
Acts, on the principle of Re Oriental Inland Steam Co[6]. Therefore, the argument continues,
the only surviving right of the plaintiff is to prove as a creditor in the winding-up
pursuant to the statutory provisions in that behalf.

The answer, in my judgment, is short and simple. It is common ground that if (as I
have decided) there is a right in English law to trace money paid by mistake, it rests on
g a persistent equitable proprietary interest. Moreover, as I have already indicated, the
right to trace given by New York law is, in my judgment, on the evidence, likewise
founded on such a proprietary interest: see my quotations from Re Berry[4], from Story,
and from Professor Scott. If I am right, therefore, under whichever law the plaintiff's
title ought to be founded, the assets (if any) in the defendant's hands properly representing
the plaintiff's money at the commencement of the winding-up, did not belong to the
h defendant beneficially and never formed part of its property subject to the statutory

j 1   [1948] 2 All ER 318, [1948] Ch 465
2   [1948] 2 All ER 318 at 346–347, [1948] Ch 465 at 520
3   [1948] 2 All ER 318 at 357, [1948] Ch 465 at 540
4   (1906) 147 F 208
5   (1880) 13 Ch D 696, [1874–80] All ER Rep 793
6   (1874) LR 9 Ch App 557

trust. I do not think that *Oakes v Turquand*[1] and *Tennent v City of Glasgow Bank*[2] contain anything inconsistent with that conclusion. They simply show that a contributory induced to take shares by fraud may not rescind his contract to the detriment of the company's creditors when it is in liquidation. There may, of course, be special cases where the conduct or inaction of a party who has paid money by mistake similarly makes it inequitable for him to recover it to the prejudice of third parties, but nothing in the facts pleaded and proved in the present case discloses any such situation.

In an alternative submission, likewise going to the root of the plaintiff's claim, counsel for the defendant argued that, by not pleading and proving in greater detail the operations of the clearing house inter-bank payment system in New York, the plaintiff had failed to identify any chose in action or other particular subject of property to which the plaintiff's alleged equitable interest could attach and from which tracing could begin. I cannot accept that contention. A payment, and a mistake, are alleged in terms by para 2 of the re-amended statement of claim and plainly admitted by para 2 of the re-amended defence; and when equitable rights are in question, the court does not encourage fine distinctions founded on the technicalities of financial machinery.

What I have said is enough to show that the plaintiff must succeed at this stage in the action, but in case the matter goes further I ought to express my findings on New York law in greater detail than I did at the outset of my judgment. The issue between the parties on that subject is stated in the pleadings as follows. Paragraph 4 of the re-amended statement of claim alleges:

'Under the law of the State of New York money paid by mistake is held by the payee upon trust for the person by whom the payment is made. In the circumstances hereinbefore described the respective rights of the Plaintiff and the Defendant . . . are to be determined in accordance with the law of the State of New York. Accordingly, on 3rd July 1974 the Defendant became trustee of the said sum for the Plaintiff.'

That allegation is answered by paras 7 to 11 of the re-amended defence in these terms:

'7. There is a principle of the law of New York State to the effect that where a sum of money is paid by mistake the payee thereof becomes obliged to repay an equivalent sum to the person by whom such payment is made. This principle, on its true characterization, forms part of the substantive law of New York State, and is a principle of substantive law for the purposes of English law as the *lex fori*.

'8. There is a further principle of the law of New York State to the effect that a sum of money which is paid by mistake should be deemed to be received by the payee as constructive trustee for the person by whom the payment is made when this provides, and for the purpose of providing, such person with a remedy of tracing such money into another asset. This further principle, on its true characterization, does not form part of the substantive law of New York State, and is not a principle of substantive law for the purposes of English law as the *lex fori*. Instead this further principle forms a part of the law of New York State which is concerned with remedies; is intended by the law of the said State to afford to the person by whom the payment is made a specific remedy for the enforcement of the obligation referred to in paragraph 7 hereof; and for the purposes of English law, as the *lex fori*, is in essence a principle of remedial and/or procedural law.

'9. Save as aforesaid the Defendant makes no admission as to the allegation contained in the first sentence of paragraph 4 of the Re-Amended Statement of Claim.

'10. The Defendant denies each and every allegation contained in the second sentence of paragraph 4 of the Re-Amended Statement of Claim, and will contend that the rights of the Plaintiff against the Defendant in respect of the payment of the

1   (1867) LR 2 HL 325, [1861–73] All ER Rep 738
2   (1879) 4 App Cas 615

sum of U.S. $2,000,687·50 which is referred to in such second sentence are to be determined in all respects in accordance with English law.

'11. In the alternative to paragraph 10 hereof the rights of the Plaintiff in respect of the said payment are to be determined in accordance with such principles of the law of New York State as, on their proper characterization, form part of the substantive law of the said State, and are principles of substantive law for the purposes of English law as the *lex fori*; but the remedies and procedures available to the Plaintiff for the enforcement of such rights (as so determined) are to be determined by English law as the *lex fori*. In the premises the further principle of the law of New York State which is set forth in paragraph 8 hereof is in any event wholly irrelevant for the purposes of this action.'

The issue is thus whether the equitable right of a person who pays money by mistake to trace and claim such money under the law of New York is conferred by substantive law or is of a merely procedural character.

The elucidation of the issue has led to a protracted investigation of the relevant American law. I say 'American law', not merely 'New York law', because it appears from the evidence that the law regarding mistake, fraud, and unjust enrichment has developed on similar lines in the different states of the union, and likewise in the federal courts. Accordingly judicial decisions in any of those jurisdictions are cited as persuasive authority in the courts of the others.

The evidence of American law which has been placed before me falls into three parts: first a large body of judicial decisions in various courts and of textbooks and magazine articles by learned writers; secondly, the viva voce evidence of Professor G E Palmer, called on behalf of the defendant; and thirdly the viva voce evidence of Mr E T Patrikis, called on behalf of the plaintiff. I may say at once that I have obtained little assistance from the last element. Mr Patrikis is a member of the Bar of the State of New York and of the Bar of the Federal District Court for the Southern District of New York and is employed by the Federal Reserve Bank of New York as its deputy general counsel. He was an entirely honest and careful witness and one of independent opinions, but he had not the learning or experience in this special branch of the law to answer Professor Palmer adequately on his own ground. The professor on the other hand is an academic lawyer of long experience who has specialised in the law of restitution and unjust enrichment. He has taught and written extensively on those subjects and in particular is the author of a recent textbook on the law of restitution in four volumes[1]. Thus he was able to give full explanations, and express his own considered opinions, of the written authorities that were placed before me in a manner that Mr Patrikis could not rival.

However, Professor Palmer's evidence has failed to persuade me that the defendant's view is correct. On a consideration of the written material, I am clearly of the opinion that on the whole it supports the plaintiff's rather than the defendant's case.

Now, I have to find, on a balance of probabilities, how a court of the State of New York would at the present time decide the question of New York law raised by the pleadings. It is obvious that Professor Palmer with his own learning and experience acquired in the United States is more likely than I am to answer that question correctly. On the other hand, considering that Mr Patrikis, though with less adequate qualifications, clearly disagreed with the professor's conclusions, I am, I think, bound to apply my own mind to the American law and to weigh the authority of the professor's opinions against my own impression of the written material. I proceed therefore to state my conclusions on the evidence.

In the first place, I have been referred to no American case which gives a direct and conscious answer to the question posed by the pleadings. Counsel for the defendants sought to find such a decision in the opinion of the Appellate Division of the New York Supreme Court in *Tebin v Moldock*[2], a case that in England would be called one of secret

1   Law of Restitution (1978)
2   (1963) 241 NYS 2d 629

trust. In my judgment, however, the court was there concerned not so much with the character of the claimant's interest as with the limits of the court's power to fashion a   *a* remedy to protect it. Professor Palmer did not attach any great importance to *Tebin v Moldock*[1], and the authority of the appellate division's opinion is in any case weakened by the short but reasoned judgment of the Court of Appeals[2] which materially altered their decree.

Secondly, it is easy to collect an anthology of divergent and apparently contradictory passages from the judicial or academic pronouncements of American jurists made alio   *b* intuitu. For example, Professor A W Scott, in an article where he is contrasting constructive trusts with express trusts, says this[3]:

'In other words, as Professor Pound has pointed out[4], a constructive trust, unlike an express trust, is a remedial and not a substantive institution. The court does not give relief because a constructive trust has been created; but the court gives relief because otherwise the defendant would be unjustly enriched; and because the court   *c* gives this relief it declares that the defendant is chargeable as a constructive trustee.'

The same Professor Scott, in his work on Trusts[5] which I have already cited, in a section explaining at what time a constructive trust arises says:

'The beneficial interest in the property is from the beginning in the person who has been wronged. The constructive trust arises from the situation in which he is   *d* entitled to the remedy of restitution, and it arises as soon as that situation is created. For this reason, the person who is wronged is entitled to specific restitution from the wrongdoer even though the wrongdoer becomes insolvent before suit is brought, and he is entitled to specific restitution from a person to whom the wrongdoer has transferred the property, if the transferee is not a bona fide purchaser, even though the transfer is made before suit is brought for restitution. It would   *e* seem that there is no foundation whatever for the notion that a constructive trust does not arise until it is decreed by a court. It arises when the duty to make restitution arises, not when that duty is subsequently enforced.'

I will take another example from tax cases in the federal courts. In *Knight Newspapers v Comr of Internal Revenue*[6] the Circuit Court of Appeals of the Sixth Circuit held that a   *f* purported dividend, credited in a company's books to a stockholder's account, but afterwards found to be illegally declared, and cancelled by the company, was never part of the stockholder's taxable income. The court said[7]:

'Under the foregoing circumstances, it should be held that the receipt of the dividend gave rise to a constructive trust and petitioner thereby became a constructive trustee of the dividend. The effect, of course, of such a determination   *g* is that petitioner never became the owner of the dividend and, hence, did not receive the income for which it has been taxed.'

Contrast this with *Healy v Comr of Internal Revenue*[8] where the Supreme Court of the United States held that excessive salaries paid to officers of corporations were fully taxable in the year of receipt, any adjustments falling to be made in a later year, after the revenue   *h* authorities had determined them to exceed reasonable compensation. Vinson CJ, delivering the opinion of the court, said[9]:

1   (1963) 241 NYS 2d 629
2   (1964) 200 NY 2d 216
3   (1955) 71 LQR 39 at 41
4   The Progress of the Law, (1920) 33 Harv LR 420–421
5   3rd Edn (1967) vol 5, p 3421
6   (1944) 143 F 2d 1007
7   143 F 2d 1007 at 1011
8   (1952) 345 US 278
9   345 US 278 at 282–283

'A constructive trust is a fiction imposed as an equitable device for achieving
a justice. It lacks the attributes of a true trust, and is not based on any intention of the
parties. Even though it has a retroactive existence in legal fiction, fiction cannot
change the "readily realizable economic value" and practical "use and benefit"
which these taxpayers enjoyed during a prior annual accounting period, antecedent
to the declaration of the constructive trust.'

I see no purpose in multiplying such illustrative passages, for I do not believe they are
b helpful to the solution of the problem raised by the pleadings. Within the municipal
confines of a single legal system, right and remedy are indissolubly connected and
correlated, each contributing in historical dialogue to the development of the other, and
save in very special circumstances it is as idle to ask whether the court vindicates the
suitor's substantive right or gives the suitor a procedural remedy, as to ask whether
thought is a mental or a cerebral process. In fact the court does both things by one and
c the same act.

Thirdly, the relevant municipal law of New York is not, in my view, in serious doubt.
I find it, shortly stated in my own words, to be as follows. (i) If one party P transfers
property to another party D by reason of a mistake of fact, P has in general a right to
recover it and D a duty to restore it. (ii) P in general has a right to sue in equity for an
order that D return the property, or its traceable proceeds, to P. Sometimes this requires
d actual retransfer by D; sometimes the court can use the alternative remedy of
reformation, ie rectification of instruments, to produce the same result. P is said to
retain an equitable title to the property notwithstanding it may have been legally
transferred to D, and D is treated as a constructive trustee thereof. (iii) In many cases P
has also a common law right of action in quasi-contract to recover damages in respect of
his loss. (iv) The court will not, in its equitable jurisdiction, order specific restitution
e under (ii) above where common law damages under (iii) furnish adequate relief. (v)
Accordingly where the property in question is money, equitable relief is not available to
restore the sum paid by mistake if the payee D is solvent. But when D is insolvent P is
entitled to a decree in equity for the purpose of tracing the money paid and recovering
it or the property representing it. (vi) Modern analysis concentrates attention less on the
protection of P than on preventing the unjust enrichment of D, thus bringing the law of
f mistake into a broad jurisprudence of restitutionary rights and remedies.

Fourthly, there is in my opinion no doubt that historically, the tracing remedy in the
State of New York is founded on the existence of an equitable property in the plaintiff,
in respect of which the court treats the defendant as a trustee. That, to my mind, appears
clearly from *Newton v Porter*[1] decided by the Court of Appeals in 1877. Professor Palmer,
in his evidence, described it as one of the most important decisions in the 19th century,
g in which the New York Court of Appeals really divorced constructive trust from express
trust. For myself I cannot find from the authorities as a whole that the shift of emphasis
to the unjust enrichment of the defendant has in any way altered the law stated in
Newton v Porter[1]. Unjust enrichment cannot be a complete cause of action in itself, for
(short of the law giving an action to a common informer) it does not identify the
plaintiff.

h A century after hearing *Newton v Porter*[1], the Court of Appeals of New York in 1978
decided *Simonds v Simonds*[2]. The opinion of Breitel CJ, wherein his six colleagues
concurred, is remarkable in marrying the old and the new approach without feeling any
inconsistency between them. I regard this as an important judgment, not only because
it is so recent, not only because it is a decision of the highest appellate court in the State
of New York itself, but also because (although not concerned with mistake) it gives a full
j view of the doctrine of constructive trust as part of the law of restitution.

Breitel CJ began his opinion by stating that the plaintiff, who was the first wife of a
deceased person, sought to impress a constructive trust on the proceeds of policies on his

1   (1877) 69 NY 133
2   (1978) 408 NYS 2d 359

life which had been paid to his second wife and her daughter as nominated
beneficiaries. The plaintiff asserted an equitable interest arising out of a provision in her   *a*
separation agreement with the decedent, and had succeeded in the court of first
instance. She had also succeeded before the Appellate Division. The opinion continues
as follows[1]:

> 'The separation agreement required the husband to maintain in effect, with the
> wife as beneficiary to the extent of $7,000, existing life insurance policies or, if the
> policies were to be canceled or to lapse, insurance policies of equal value. The issue   *b*
> is whether that provision entitles the first wife to impress a constructive trust on
> proceeds of insurance policies subsequently issued, despite the husband's failure to
> name her as the beneficiary on any substitute policies once the original life insurance
> policies had lapsed. There should be an affirmance. The separation agreement
> vested in the first wife an equitable right in the then existing policies. Decedent's
> substitution of policies could not deprive the first wife of her equitable interest,   *c*
> which was then transferred to the new policies. Since the proceeds of the substituted
> policies have been paid to decedent's second wife, whose interest in the policies is
> subordinate to plaintiff's, a constructive trust may be imposed.'

Having thus concisely stated the court's decision, Breitel CJ reviewed the facts in detail,
referred to the historical origins of equity, and remarked that[2]: 'Whatever the legal rights   *d*
between insurer and insured, the separation agreement vested in the first wife an
equitable interest in the insurance policies then in force.' After referring to authority for
the proposition that mere substitution of policies, or even substitution of insurance
companies, did not defeat such an equitable interest, he seems to have felt some difficulty
over the particular facts of the case, and said this[2]:

> 'For a certainty, the first wife's equitable interest would be easier to trace if the   *e*
> new policies were quid pro quo replacements for the original policies. The record
> does not reveal whether this was so. But inability to trace plaintiff's equitable rights
> precisely should not require that they not be recognised, much as in the instance of
> damages difficult to prove.'

He found the solution of the difficulty in the general rule that equity regards as done that   *f*
which should have been done and said[3]:

> 'Due to the husband's failure to do what he should have done, the first wife
> acquired not only a right at law to sue his estate for breach of contract, a right now
> worthless, but also an equitable right in the policies, a right which, upon the
> husband's death, attached to the proceeds ... And, since the first wife was entitled
> to $7,000 of the insurance proceeds at the time of the husband's death, she is no less   *g*
> entitled because the proceeds have already been converted by being paid,
> erroneously, to the named beneficiaries ... Her remedy is imposition of a
> constructive trust.'

So far, it will have been observed, the opinion proceeds on the classical foundation of
a persistent equitable interest in the plaintiff, but now, after the mention of constructive   *h*
trust as a remedy, it goes on to cite passages approved of by Professor Palmer, namely the
saying of Cardozo J in *Beatty v Guggenheim Exploration Co*[4] that: 'A constructive trust is the
formula through which the conscience of equity finds expression', and Professor Scott's
remark in his book on Trusts[5], that a party is not compelled to convey property because

j

---

1   (1978) 408 NYS 2d 359 at 360–361
2   408 NYS 2d 359 at 362
3   408 NYS 2d 359 at 363
4   (1919) 225 NY 380 at 386
5   3rd Edn (1967), p 3413

a   he is a constructive trustee, it is because he can be compelled to convey it that he is a constructive trustee. After emphasising the breadth and flexibility of the doctrine of constructive trusts, Breitel CJ says[1]:

> 'It is agreed that the purpose of the constructive trust is prevention of unjust enrichment ... Unjust enrichment, however, does not require the performance of any wrongful act by the one enriched.'

b   and concludes that the unjust enrichment in the instant case was manifest.

This authoritative judgment seems to me to confirm the view I have formed on the American material as a whole, that the plaintiff is right in alleging that the defendant became a trustee for the plaintiff of the sum paid by mistake and that the plaintiff's equitable interest as cestui que trust was given (so far as the distinction has any meaning within the confines of New York law itself) by a rule of substantive law and is not the *c*   mere result of a remedial or procedural rule. Ought I to reject that conclusion in deference to the opinion of Professor Palmer? I think not. I do not doubt that his view of the law, and his criticisms of Professor Scott, are sincere and of long standing, but his evidence has failed to convince me that he is right.

I take some comfort from finding my own opinion expressed in the American Law Institute's Restatement of the Law of Restitution[2]. The passage is part of a commentary *d*   on a proposition stated in the following terms[3]:

> 'Where the owner of property transfers it as a result of a mistake of such a character that he is entitled to restitution, the transferee holds the property upon a constructive trust for him.'

On this the commentary[4] points out that a court of equity will not decree specific *e*   restitution where the remedy at law is adequate, and continues[2]:

> 'The refusal to decree specific restitution, however, does not mean that the transferee does not hold the property transferred to him by mistake upon a constructive trust for the transferor; it does not mean that the transferee holds the property free of trust or that the transferor has no beneficial interest in the property. On the contrary, where property is transferred under a mistake entitling *f*   the transferor to restitution, the transferor retains the beneficial interest in the property, and a holding that where the legal remedy is adequate he cannot have specific restitution is merely procedural. If the transferee is insolvent, the transferor is entitled to specific restitution, even though the property is of such a character that were he not insolvent the remedy at law would be adequate and the transferor would not be entitled to specific restitution. This is true not only where the *g*   transferee was insolvent at the time the transfer was made to him, but also where he subsequently becomes insolvent.'

Little evidence has been adduced to show how a court in New York would classify or characterise for the purposes of private international law those provisions of its own law which have been under scrutiny in this case. It is not necessary for me to make a finding *h*   on the point, and I do not feel I have the materials to make one de bene esse.

I have on the other hand heard a good deal of argument, and I have been referred to a number of authorities, regarding the characterisation of the same provisions of New York law by an English court. It is unnecessary, and therefore undesirable, for me to express any opinion on that question. I have held, after examining *Re Diplock's Estate*[5], that under English municipal law a party who pays money under a mistake of fact may

j

---

1   (1978) 408 NYS 2d 359 at 364
2   (1937), pp 664–665
3   (1937), p 661
4   (1937), p 664
5   [1948] 2 All ER 318, [1948] Ch 465

claim to trace it in equity, and that this right depends on a continuing right of property recognised in equity. I have found, on the evidence presented by the parties, that a similar right to trace is conferred by New York municipal law, and that there too the party paying by mistake retains a beneficial interest in the assets. No doubt the two systems of law in this field are not in all respects identical, but if my conclusions are right no conflict has arisen between them in the present case, and there is no occasion to draw a line, on either side of the Atlantic, between provisions that belong to substantive law and provisions that belong to adjective law. The difficulties of defining the distinction and of applying it in various legal contexts appear in several well-known authorities, e g in the judgment of Atkin LJ in *The Colorado*[1], and in the speech of Lord Pearson in *Chaplin v Boys*[2]. It would be wrong for me, merely in recognition of counsels' industry, for which I am nonetheless grateful, to make observations obiter on so important a subject.

Subject to any discussion of the wording, I will declare that on 3rd July 1974 the defendant became trustee for the plaintiff of the sum mentioned in para 4 of the re-amended statement of claim, and I will direct an enquiry as to what has become of that sum, and what assets (if any) in the possession or power of the defendant, now represent the said sum or any part thereof or any interest or income thereof. The further consideration of the action will be adjourned and the parties are to be at liberty to apply as they may be advised.

Order accordingly.

Solicitors: *Allen & Overy* (for the plaintiff); *Cameron, Kemm, Nordon* (for the defendant).

Evelyn M C Budd   Barrister.

---

1   [1923] P 102 at 110–112, [1923] All ER Rep 531 at 535–536
2   [1969] 2 All ER 1085 at 1106, [1971] AC 356 at 394–395

Reel v Holder and another

QUEEN'S BENCH DIVISION

FORBES J

19th, 20th MARCH, 2nd APRIL 1979

Estoppel – Representation – Existing fact – Representation by members of unincorporated association – Representation that rules of association changed – International athletics association – Members consisting of associations controlling athletics in their countries – Rules providing for only one member for each 'country' to be affiliated to international association – Association controlling athletics in mainland China elected – Subsequently association controlling athletics in Taiwan elected – Taiwan remaining member of international association for 22 years – International association resolving to recognise mainland association as sole body controlling athletics on mainland and in Taiwan – Taiwan association claiming declarations that decision invalid and that it remained a member of the international association – Whether 'country' in rules meaning a politically recognised nation or merely a geographical area – Whether international association estopped from asserting that decision to elect Taiwan association invalid.

The IAAF, the international body controlling athletics, was an unincorporated association with officers, a council and a congress which met biennially. Rule 1 of its rules stated that the IAAF was to comprise duly elected 'national' governing associations or federations which controlled athletics, and that only one member for each 'country' could be affiliated to the IAAF. At the 1954 congress of the IAAF the body controlling athletics on the Chinese mainland ('the mainland body') was accepted as a member of the IAAF. At the same time the congress extended an invitation to the body controlling athletics in Formosa (subsequently Taiwan) ('the Taiwan body') to apply for membership of the IAAF. The governments of mainland China and Taiwan each claimed to be the legitimate government of the whole of China and that China included both the mainland and Taiwan. In 1956 the Taiwan body was elected a member of the IAAF but certain IAAF members dissented from its election. In 1958 the mainland body resigned from the IAAF because of the election of the Taiwan body. The Taiwan body remained a member of the IAAF for 22 years, regularly paying its subscription, and engaging in competition with other members, without any steps being taken to challenge its membership by the dissenting members of the IAAF. At the 1978 congress of the IAAF the council circulated a resolution to the congress recommending re-affiliation of the mainland body and that it should be the only representative for China in the IAAF, on the grounds that the United Nations considered that the political boundaries of mainland China included Taiwan and that the mainland body had given a guarantee to the IAAF that Taiwan athletes would be allowed to compete in international competitions under the jurisdiction of the mainland body. The congress, by a majority, passed the resolution and thus accepted the mainland body as the body representing athletics both in mainland China and in Taiwan. The result of that resolution was to exclude the Taiwan body from membership of the IAAF. The plaintiff, who was a representative of the Taiwan body, brought an action against representatives of the IAAF as defendants, seeking (inter alia) declarations that the resolution passed in 1978 was void and of no effect and that the Taiwan body remained a member of the IAAF. The plaintiff contended that the term 'country' in the IAAF rules embraced Taiwan, and that the defendants were estopped from denying that Taiwan was a country within r 1 since the IAAF had treated the Taiwan body as a member for 22 years. The defendants contended that the 'country' concerned was 'China' which embraced both the mainland and Taiwan, and that therefore the election in 1956 of the Taiwan body was invalid under r 1 since there was already an elected member for the country of China, ie the mainland body. They further contended that the rules of a club or unincorporated association such as the IAAF could not, unless the rules expressly provided for amendment, be changed unless every

member of the association agreed to change them, and that an association could not be
estopped by the conduct of its members in acquiescing in a decision taken contrary to the   *a*
association's rules (as was the decision to accept the Taiwan body as a member of the IAAF
although Taiwan was not a 'country') from subsequently asserting that the decision was
invalid under those rules.

Held – The declarations would be granted for the following reasons—.

(i) In construing the word 'country' in r 1 of the IAAF rules, which constituted the
contract between the members of the IAAF, the court had to place itself in the   *b*
surrounding circumstances in which the contract was formed, namely that the IAAF was
intended to govern the affairs of an international association dedicated to promoting
friendly competition in athletics between the inhabitants of various countries. Rule 1
had clearly been introduced to prevent or resolve a situation where the identity of a
country was not in dispute but there were two or more rival associations within the
country claiming they were in control of its athletics. Accordingly, 'country' in the   *c*
context of r 1 was not to be equated with a nation in the political sense but meant a
geographically defined area in which there existed an association which was in control of
athletics within that area and which was not subservient to, or controlled by, some other
association covering a wider area. Since the mainland body was not in control of athletics
in Taiwan, but only in mainland China, and both Taiwan and mainland China were
separate geographical areas, each could properly be described as a 'country' within r 1.   *d*
It followed that the purported resolution of 5th October 1978 was not in accordance with
the IAAF rules and that the Taiwan body had been wrongly excluded from membership
of the IAAF (see p 1050 *f* to *h* and p 1051 *d* to p 1052 *a*, post); dictum of Lord Wilberforce
in *Reardon Smith Line Ltd v Hansen-Tangen* [1976] 3 All ER at 575 applied.

(ii) An unincorporated association could be estopped, by the conduct of all its
members, from asserting that a decision it had taken contary to its rules was not valid.   *e*
If, therefore, 'country' was to be construed as excluding Taiwan, then, since for 22 years
the Taiwan body had been regarded by all the members of the IAAF, other than the
dissenting members, as a member of the IAAF, there was an estoppel by representation
of an existing fact (ie that the decision to accept the Taiwan body as a member was a valid
decision) whereby the IAAF was estopped from asserting that that decision was invalid
under the rules. Moreover, since the dissenting IAAF members had, by their failure to   *f*
challenge the validity of the election of the Taiwan body, themselves represented to the
plaintiff and to the non-dissenting IAAF members that the Taiwan body was a duly
elected member, the defendants could not rely on the dissenting members as indicating
that not all the members had made the representation. Alternatively, the representation
of fact made by the members' conduct in electing the Taiwan body was that the word
'country' in the rules was to be used in a way which permitted inclusion of both   *g*
mainland China and Taiwan as 'countries' so that the members' conduct estopped the
IAAF from asserting that a different meaning was to be given to the word 'country' (see
p 1055 *a b* and *e* to *h*, post); *Harington v Sendall* [1903] 1 Ch 921 and *Re Tobacco Trade
Benevolent Association, Baron Sinclair v Finlay* [1958] 3 All ER 353 explained.

Notes   *h*
For estoppel by conduct, and inaction amounting to a representation, see 16 Halsbury's
Laws (4th Edn) paras 1609, 1618, and for cases on the subject, see 21 Digest (Repl) 411–
412, 1310–1322.

Cases referred to in judgement
Alan (W J) & Co Ltd v El Nasr Export & Import Co [1972] 2 All ER 127, [1972] 2 QB 189,   *j*
     [1972] 2 WLR 800, [1972] 1 Lloyd's Rep 313, CA, Digest (Cont Vol D) 124, 4170a.
Central London Property Trust Ltd v High Trees House Ltd (1946) [1956] 1 All ER 256,
     [1947] KB 130, [1947] LJR 77, 175 LT 332, 31(1) Digest (Reissue) 447, 3933.
Harington v Sendall [1903] 1 Ch 921, 72 LJ Ch 396, 88 LT 323, 8(2) Digest (Reissue) 615,
     22.

Hughes v Metropolitan Railway Co (1877) 2 App Cas 439, [1874–80] All ER Rep 187, 46
LJQB 583, 36 LT 932, 42 JP 421, HL, 21 Digest (Repl) 392, *1221*.
Partenreederei MS Karen Oltmann v Scarsdale Shipping Co Ltd, The Karen Oltmann [1976] 2
Lloyd's Rep 708.
Prenn v Simmonds [1971] 3 All ER 237, [1971] 1 WLR 1381, HL, 17 Digest (Reissue) 359,
1264.
Reardon Smith Line Ltd v Hansen-Tangen, Hansen-Tangen v Sanko Steamship Co [1976] 3 All
ER 570, [1976] 1 WLR 989, [1976] 2 Lloyd's Rep 621, HL.
Tobacco Trade Benevolent Association, Re, Baron Sinclair v Finlay [1958] 3 All ER 353, [1958]
1 WLR 1113, 8(1) Digest (Reissue) 429, *1684*.
Utica City National Bank v Gunn (1918) 118 NE 607.

Action

By an originating summons dated 25th January 1979 the plaintiff, Cheng Chi Reel,
secretary-general of the Republic of China Track and Field Association ('ROCTFA'), suing
on behalf of herself and as representing the members of ROCTFA, sought against the
defendants, Frederick W Holder and Adriaan Paulen, the honorary treasurer and
president respectively of the International Amateur Athletic Federation ('IAAF'), sued on
behalf of themselves and as representing the members of the IAAF, declarations (1) that
ROCTFA were and remained members of the IAAF, (2) that ROCTFA were and remained
entitled to all the rights and privileges of membership of the IAAF and (3) that the
resolution dated 5th October 1978 of the congress of IAAF, in so far as it purported to
deprive or had the effect of depriving ROCTFA of membership or alternatively of the
rights and privileges of membership of the IAAF, was void and of no effect. The plaintiff
also sought an injunction restraining the defendants whether by themselves, their
servants, their agents or otherwise from doing any act pursuant to or in consequence of
the resolution of 5th October 1978 in so far as any such act was inconsistent with
ROCTFA being a member of the IAAF and entitled to all the rights and privileges of such
membership. The facts are set out in the judgment.

Robert Alexander QC, Brian Davenport and *Jeremy Cooke* for the plaintiff.
Richard Yorke QC and *John G C Phillips* for the defendants.

Cur adv vult

2nd April. **FORBES J** delivered the following judgment: This is a representative action
in which the plaintiff, Mrs Cheng Chi Reel, sues as secretary general of the Republic of
China Track and Field Association ('ROCTFA'), and on behalf of that association, sues Mr
Holder and Mr Paulen, who are respectively honorary treasurer and president of the
International Amateur Athletic Federation ('IAAF'), as representing that federation.

The IAAF is an international body which controls the sport of athletics. It is an
unincorporated association whose bureau or office is in Putney. I shall have to consider
some of its rules later but broadly its members comprise those national associations
which control within their respective countries the athletes of those countries. The
federation has certain officers, a council and a congress, the latter meeting biennially and
being attended by not more than three delegates from each member.

The ROCTFA is an organisation which, there appears to be no conflict, actually
controls the athletes within an area which includes Taiwan and certain adjacent islands.
This association claims that it is a member of the IAAF and that the latter body has
wrongfully deprived the association of the rights and privileges of membership of the
federation. It will be necessary shortly to consider both the political and the athletic
history of this part of the world.

The IAAF was founded in 1912. In 1914 a body called the China National Amateur
Athletic Federation ('CNAAF') was established as the controlling body for athletes in

what may be called mainland China, and shortly thereafter the CNAAF became a member of the International Federation. At that time what was then called the Island of *a* Formosa was part of Japan though the Chinese laid claim to it as part of China. After the end of the 1939–45 war Formosa was ceded to China. After the end of that war, too, there was an internal conflict in China between what were known as the Chinese Nationalists under Generalissimo Chiang Kai-shek and the Chinese Communists under Chairman Mao Tse Tung. In 1949 the forces of Chairman Mao prevailed and the supporters of Chiang Kai-shek withdrew to Formosa and established a government on *b* that island, while a Communist régime was established in mainland China. Each government claims to be the legitimate government of the whole of China which, in the view of each government, includes both the mainland and Formosa (which has now been renamed Taiwan). A state of war exists between the two governments, though neither recognises the other as a government at all. Taiwan is regularly shelled from the mainland by the forces of the Communist government and the government of Taiwan *c* has passed laws which make it a penal offence to associate with persons owing allegiance to the Communist régime on the mainland. The government on the mainland is called the People's Republic of China and the government in Taiwan is called the Republic of China.

In 1954 a body known as the All China Athletic Association ('ACAA') controlled all the athletes on the Chinese mainland. That body applied for membership of the International *d* Federation and their application was considered and accepted by the congress at their meeting on 23rd and 24th August 1954. It is clear from the minutes of that congress that the ACAA claimed that they were already members, presumably because they stood in the shoes of the CNAAF, but that this claim was rejected and they were elected as new members. At the same time an invitation was extended to Formosa to apply for membership. I should read the relevant part of the minute: *e*

'The application for membership of the All China Athletic Association was considered by the Congress. Mr. N. Kalinin (U.S.S.R.) supported the application which had previously been discussed at Helsinki and asked that there be taken into account the development since that time in athletics in China and the fact that the International Olympic Committee had recognised the National Olympic Committee of that country. *f*

'The President stated that this application was in a very different category from that of the previous application. The control of all athletes on the Chinese mainland was in Peking and he felt that the All China Athletic Association should be admitted to membership. If they were accepted, the way would be clear for them to compete in the next Olympic Games as the I.O.C. had already recognised them at their meeting in Athens. *g*

'The President stated that it had been pointed out by the Honorary Secretary that the All China Athletic Association had claimed that they had been in continual membership but that was not so. Although the offices were still in Peking, the personnel of our former members was in Formosa and he suggested that if the present application were approved, they be elected as new members.

'It was unanimously agreed that the All China Athletic Association be accepted as *h* a newly affiliated member of the Federation and that they would be placed in Group "B".

'It was also agreed that if Formosa wished to apply for membership this would be given consideration.'

On 9th November 1954 the honorary secretary/treasurer of the International *j* Federation wrote to the president of the CNAAF in Taiwan passing on that invitation;

'Dear Mr. Gunsum Hoh,

'With reference to our correspondence culminating in my letter to you of 2nd April 1954, I must advise you that the application of the All China Athletic

Association for membership of the I.A.A.F. was considered at the Congress in
August this year and that association was accepted as a new member.

'At the same time it was agreed that an application for membership from the
controlling body of athletics in Formosa would receive consideration.

'It is and has always been the earnest desire of the I.A.A.F. that all athletes
irrespective of race, creed or political belief should have the opportunity to represent
their country and I sincerely hope that we may receive from your Formosa
association an application for membership which will permit the participation in
the Olympic Games and continental championships of your athletes. I accordingly
enclose a form of application for membership.

'You will recall that Mr. Holt received from you the sum of £20, which is being
held in a suspense account by us. Will you be good enough to give me your
instructions as to its disposal.'

That is apparently a reference to what I might describe as a tender of the membership fee
by the CNAAF on the basis that they were still in continuing membership.

On 26th May 1956 CNAAF applied for membership on the standard application
form. The form contains various printed portions together with blanks for the applicant
to complete appropriately. Two of the questions and the applicant's answers were as
follows: 'Does the Association/Federation control amateur athletics in . . .' and there is
then a blank filled as follows: 'The Republic of China which at present actually controls
and has jurisdiction over Taiwan, Penghue, Kinmen, Matzu and other islands.' The next
question reads: 'Are there any other existing amateur associations or federations, if so,
please name them?' And the answer reads: 'This is the governing body to which several
associations are attached such as Taiwan, Penghue, Kinmen, Matzu amateur athletic
associations.' This application was accepted by the 1956 congress which was held at
Melbourne during the Olympic Games there. The minutes read:

'Application for Affiliation—Taiwan.

'The President informed Congress that as competitors from this country were
already in Melbourne awaiting the decision of this Congress he suggested that this
item should be taken at this point in the agenda so that if the decision were
favourable, they would be given the opportunity to compete.

'The President said that he himself wished to support this application for
affiliation in the same way as he had done for other countries. The young people
from a country with a population of 18,000,000 were involved and any question of
politics should be left out of any discussion the aim in view was to bring as many
young athletes as possible into the family group of the Federation. It was impossible
for the athletic association in Peking to organise athletic matches for the Taiwan
athletes as there was no communication between the two countries and he therefore
moved from the Chair that this application be accepted.

'The delegate from the Athletic Association of the People's Republic of China
opposed the application on the grounds that Taiwan was part of China and,
therefore, came within their jurisdiction.

'The Hon. Secretary stated that he felt that this was a matter upon which the
Congress should take an extremely practical view. The present situation was that
Taiwan was recognised by some countries and not by others, but we could not get
away from the fact that millions of people were being deprived of the opportunity
for participation in international sport. He thought that we must make a reasonable
approach to the present day situation and affiliate this country.

'The delegate from Greece supported this view.

'The delegates from the U.S.S.R., Czechoslovakia and Roumania supported the
A.A. of the People's Republic of China in their opposition.

'On a vote being taken it was agreed, with only four dissentients, that the
application of the China National Amateur Athletic Federation be accepted on the
understanding that they would compete and be known as "Taiwan".'

In 1958 the ACAA, by then renamed the Athletic Association of the People's Republic of China ('AAPROC'), resigned from the International Federation. The contemporary documents are perhaps important and I should read them. The following is a letter from the secretary of the AAPROC, dated 19th August 1958, to the honorary secretary/treasurer of the International Federation:

'Dear Sir,

'In protest to the unlawful recognition of the so-called "China National Amateur Athletic Federation" in Taiwan by the International Amateur Athletic Federation, which constitutes a gross violation of I.A.A.F.'s Constitution, the Athletic Association of the People's Republic of China hereby declares that it has decided to withdraw from the I.A.A.F. Now, we are sending you the official Statement of the Athletic Association of the People's Republic of China.'

There then follows a printed 'Statement of the Athletic Association of the People's Republic of China on its withdrawal from the International Amateur Athletic Federation' dated 'August 19, 1958, Peking':

'Disregarding the protests of the Athletic Association of the People's Republic of China, the International Amateur Athletic Federation, under the manipulation of a few people with ulterior motives, persists in creating a situation of "two Chinas" in the Federation. The Athletic Association of the People's Republic of China absolutely cannot tolerate the continuance of this situation and hereby officially declares its withdrawal from the I.A.A.F.

'Originally China was represented in the I.A.A.F. by the "China National Amateur Athletic Federation." Following the founding of the People's Republic of China, the former "China National Amateur Athletic Federation" was reorganised into the present All-China Athletic Federation. Since then, the "China National Amateur Athletic Federation" has become a historical name and the All-China Athletic Federation is the sole legal national sports organisation in our country. On April 3, 1952, the All-China Athletic Federation wrote to inform the I.A.A.F. of this change and asked for continued recognition of the All-China Athletic Federation as its member. But this proper request was unreasonably shelved. On November 21, 1953, the All-China Athletic Federation again cabled the I.A.A.F. asking it to solve speedily the question of continued recognition of the All-China Athletic Federation. But it was not till the 19th Congress of the I.A.A.F. held in Berne, Switzerland, in August 1954 that the question of membership of the All-China Athletic Federation was solved (The All-China Athletic Federation's track and field section was later reorganised into the Athletic Association of the People's Republic of China).

'According to the stipulation of article I of the I.A.A.F. Constitution, which reads: "only one member for each country can be affiliated", the I.A.A.F. has no right to recognise any Chinese sports organisation as its member other than the Athletic Association of the People's Republic of China which is the sole supreme national athletic organisation in China. However, under the manipulation of some people with ulterior motives, the I.A.A.F., in violation of its own Constitution, admitted at its Congress in November 1956, the so called "China National Amateur Athletic Federation" in Taiwan. The Athletic Association of the People's Republic of China had lodged protests against this, but the I.A.A.F. brazenly ignored our protests.

'This action on the part of the I.A.A.F. is closely related with the hostile policy of the U.S. imperialists towards the Chinese people. The U.S. imperialists and their followers are not reconciled to the Chinese people's victory and the tremendous development of the People's Republic of China in the past few years. Failing to blot out the existence of the mighty People's Republic of China, they have resorted to all sorts of means to create "two Chinas" on the international scene in an attempt thereby to weaken the ever-growing influence of our country and to legalise the U.S.

occupation of China's territory of Taiwan. The above-mentioned line followed by the I.A.A.F. suits exactly the U.S. scheme of creating "two Chinas". This is absolutely intolerable to the Chinese people. There is only one China in the world and that is the People's Republic of China. The Chinese people will not allow a situation of "two Chinas" to arise in any international organisation, conference or occasion. The Chinese people are determined to liberate Taiwan, and this is not to be obstructed by any force.

'We know that quite a number of gentlemen in the I.A.A.F. are just-minded. They have contributed to the upholding of the spirit and prestige of the I.A.A.F. constitution. The Athletic Association of the People's Republic of China is willing to cooperate with them and has in the past made its utmost efforts to do so. But the Athletic Association of the People's Republic of China cannot tolerate the I.A.A.F. to be turned, under the control of a few people, into a tool serving the reactionary policy of the U.S. imperialists, nor will they tolerate a situation of "two Chinas" in the I.A.A.F. Only when the I.A.A.F. really lives up to the spirit of its Constitution and cancels the membership of the so-called sports organisation in Taiwan, can we consider resuming cooperation with it.'

The reply from the honorary secretary/treasurer of the International Federation was as follows, dated 8th September 1958:

'I acknowledge your letter of 19th August, 1958, advising me of the resignation of the Athletic Association of the People's Republic of China from membership of the International Amateur Athletic Federation and enclosing a printed statement by your Association. This arrived after the close of the Congress Meeting in Stockholm so could not be reported to the delegates present.

'I do not propose to comment on the allegations set out in this statement except to point out that no question of "two Chinas" exists in our membership. The two countries are clearly named in our list of members as "China" and "Taiwan", the election to membership of the latter being approved by an overwhelming majority at the full Congress of the I.A.A.F. at Melbourne in 1956, subject to the provision that the athletes from that country should only compete internationally as "Taiwan". Incidentally this ruling was insisted upon at the recent Asian Games competitions where in athletics "Taiwan" and not "China" took part.

'The I.A.A.F. recognises clearly your Association as the controlling body for all athletics on the mainland, and the existing member in Taiwan has been limited to representing that country as "Taiwan" and not "China" as they have complete control of the young people there. There has been no political interference with the I.A.A.F. whatever and such would not be permitted in any case.

'What I have written is factual and no doubt is well understood by you.

'My greatest concern however is that for avowed political reasons your association is by its present action debarring your many fine athletes from taking part in international competition for I have no alternative but to advise all our member countries of your resignation from the I.A.A.F. and that in consequence your athletes are no longer eligible to enter into competition abroad. I do earnestly hope that you will give most serious consideration to this aspect as I assure you that all member federations of the I.A.A.F. will deplore this intrusion of politics into the sphere of amateur athletics where, I am sure we all agree, it should most certainly have no place.

'As I trust that what I have now written in all sincerity will receive the full consideration of your association, and in view of the very drastic consequences of your resignation upon your athletes, I propose to defer circulating the advice of your resignation to our member countries until the end of the year in the hope that I may learn from you that you have reconsidered your position.'

Apparently no communication was received before the end of the year from AAPROC.

CNAAF changed its name to Republic of China Track and Field Association ('ROCTFA') and in 1970 the congress of the International Federation approved the 'application by the member for Taiwan to compete in international competitions in future under the name of the Republic of China Track and Field Association'.

In 1978 a further congress of the International Federation was held in Puerto Rico on 5th and 6th October. The agenda for their meeting contained only two matters of relevance to this case. The first is that although affiliations or applications for affiliation were reported from other countries no application for affiliation was noted from AAPROC. The second is that there was a resolution tabled to change the name of the Republic of China to Taiwan. On the morning of 5th October, however, a resolution from the council was circulated to congress in the following terms:

'In connection with the request for affiliation of the Athletic Association of the People's Republic of China and 1. having considered I.A.A.F. Rule 4 with particular reference to political boundaries; and 2. having heard from the United Nations that the political boundaries of the People's Republic of China include the island of Taiwan; and 3. having received a guarantee that Taiwan athletes may compete in international competitions under I.A.A.F. Rules, under the jurisdiction of the Athletic Association of the People's Republic of China the Council recommends the re-affiliation of the People's Republic of China as the only representative in the I.A.A.F. for China.'

With it was circulated a letter from AAPROC:

'We have enclosed herewith our membership application form and the Constitution of our Association and we would like to make the following explanations concerning our application:

'1. According to Article 4 of the Constitution of the I.A.A.F. that only one member may be affiliated for each country and be recognised by the I.A.A.F. as the only national governing body for all amateur athletics in each country, the I.A.A.F. at its 1954 Congress accepted our Association as the sole member representing whole China. Therefore it was illegal for the I.A.A.F. to admit subsequently in 1956 a so-called "Republic of China Athletic Association" as its member. There is only one China in the world, that is the People's Republic of China and Taiwan is a province of China. The Athletic Association of the People's Republic of China is the sole legitimate body governing athletics on the entire territory of China. Only she is entitled to represent China in the I.A.A.F.

'2. Our application for membership in the I.A.A.F. will be effective only after the I.A.A.F. has re-established the situation as in 1954 when the I.A.A.F. only recognised our Association as the sole legitimate organisation representing whole China, without the appearance of "two Chinas" or "one China, one Taiwan".

'3. The Chinese Government, the Chinese people and our Association are most concerned about participation in international and domestic competitions by the sportsmen and athletes from our Taiwan Province. The All-China Sports Federation has duly informed the sports associations and sportsmen from Taiwan to participate in the First National Games in 1959, the Second National Games in 1965, the Third National Games in 1975, the Seventh Asian Games in 1974 and the Eighth Asian Games in 1978. Our Association has provided all kinds of conveniences for the sportsmen of Taiwan origin to come to take part in the Games or in the National Selection Trials and has guaranteed their complete freedom in coming and leaving.'

The council's resolution had been passed by ten votes to nine and when the matter was put to the vote in congress it was passed by 200 votes to 153 and the result is shown thus in the minutes:

a
'The Athletic Association of the People's Republic of China was, therefore, accepted as an I.A.A.F. Member, to have jurisdiction also over that Territory where athletics was at present governed by the existing I.A.A.F. member in Taiwan.'

It will thus be seen that the effect of the decision of congress was to exclude ROCTFA from membership of the International Federation, the area of Taiwan being represented on the International Federation for the future by AAPROC.

b
ROCTFA as represented by the plaintiff, now comes to this court by originating summons asking for relief by way of declarations and an injunction. Broadly the declarations sought are that the resolution of congress on 5th October 1978 was void and of no effect and that ROCTFA remains a member of the International Federation; and the injunction they seek would restrain the federation from acting in any way inconsistent with ROCTFA's continued membership.

c
I should now turn to the rules. These have been amended from time to time but at the time of the election of ROCTFA in 1956 were those which had been current at least since 1953. There is a short interpretation section which defines a member of the federation as a 'National Governing Association or Federation.' I should read r 1 in full. It states:

d
'(1) The title shall be the International Amateur Athletic Federation; it shall comprise duly elected national governing associations or federations for the control of amateur track and field athletics, cross-country, running and walking; and it agrees to abide by the rules and regulations of the I.A.A.F. Only one member for each country can be affiliated. (2) The jurisdiction of members of the Federation shall be limited to the political boundaries of the country they represent.'

Rule 2 might also be important:

e
'The objects of the Federation shall be: (1) To establish friendly and loyal co-operation between all Members for the benefit of amateur athletics throughout the world. (2) To compile rules and regulations governing international competitions for men and women in amateur athletics. (3) To ensure that all contests between the Members of the Federation, including continental championships, regional championships and all other international competitions, shall be held under the

f
laws and the rules of competition of the Federation. (4) To affiliate national governing associations and federations.'

There are three subsequent paragraphs to this rule which are for the present purposes irrelevant. There are other references sprinkled throughout the rules to 'international' competition and to 'national' governing bodies. The constitutional rules at this time might only be changed by 51% of the total voting power of the IAAF or two-thirds of the

g
voting power present, whichever was the lesser: see r 4(6).

The contention of the defendants is that the election of ROCTFA in 1956 was invalid (they actually used the term ultra vires) because the rules provide that there can only be one member for each country and that the geographical area of Taiwan is not a separate country but part of the country of China which embraces both the mainland and

h
Taiwan.

Counsel for the plaintiff makes five main submissions which I can abbreviate as follows. (1) There is no doctrine of ultra vires which is applicable to unincorporated associations such as the International Federation. Such a doctrine has its place in the law of statutory corporations or companies which have been incorporated on the basis of their memorandum and articles of association. But an unincorporated association

j
depends for its powers on the consent of its members and the relationship between the association and individual members is purely contractual. (2) On the ordinary construction of the rules the term 'country' must have a meaning which permits the inclusion of the area of Taiwan within its definition. (3) In deciding what the term 'country' means it is permissible to consider whether the parties to the contract have themselves given their 'own dictionary meaning' to the term (see per Kerr J in

Partenreederei MS Karen Oltmann v Scarsdale Shipping Co Ltd, The Karen Oltmann[1]) and here
by conduct and in documents they have given such a meaning to the term as will serve   *a*
to include Taiwan. (4) If not originally a member because they did not fall within the
meaning of the term 'country' the rules have been altered to provide for representation
for a 'country or territory'; Taiwan certainly must fall within the meaning of 'territory',
if it is not included within the term 'country', and as the amendment was made well
before 1978 the International Federation has, by treating ROCTFA as a member until
that date, by conduct created a contract that it should be a member. (5) The defendants   *b*
are now estopped from denying that Taiwan is a country within the meaning of the rules
since all the classical elements of estoppel are present and the International Federation has
treated ROCTFA as a member for 22 years.

   In answer, counsel for the defendants submits that the whole of these arguments
proceeds on a fundamental fallacy. Because it is an unincorporated association the
International Federation has no existence in law. The contract is between one member   *c*
and all the other members, and the law of unincorporated associations is, says counsel,
part of the law of agency. The persons who originally form the club (because it is in the
context of clubs that these problems usually arise and the federation is in no different
position) contract one with another on the basis of the original rules which have been
agreed. If those rules do not expressly provide for their amendment then they remain
immutable and can only be changed if every member agrees. Even a unanimous   *d*
decision at a meeting to change the rules is of no effect unless all the members are in fact
present and voting. It is never possible, he says, to infer unanimity from a situation in
which some members have always objected, and the fact that such objecting members
have taken no action and have not resigned cannot in any way estop them from asserting,
at any suitable time, that a purported rule change is of no effect because it was not given
universal assent. What governs the position of a club is not the ultra vires rule but the   *e*
rules governing the authority of agents.

   Thus, so runs the argument, if 'China' is a country which embraces both the mainland
and Taiwan (and both AAPROC and ROCTFA maintain that it is), then as AAPROC was
elected in 1954 the election of ROCTFA in 1956 must have been invalid under the rules
since there was already a member for 'China'; and the fact that ROCTFA was treated as
a member from 1956 to 1978 cannot validate the invalid election since there were never   *f*
fewer than four members of the International Federation who maintained that the
election was in fact invalid.

   As the first difference between the parties is over the definition of the word 'country'
in the rules the first step should be to determine how that word should be defined. I am
reminded by counsel for the plaintiff that in construing terms in a contract such as this
the court must 'place itself in thought in the same factual matrix' as were the parties (per   *g*
Lord Wilberforce *Reardon Smith Line Ltd v Hansen-Tangen*[2]) or, as Cardozo J put it in *Utica
City National Bank v Gunn*[3] (quoted with approval by Lord Wilberforce in *Prenn v
Simmonds*[4]) surrounding circumstances may 'stamp upon a contract a popular or looser
meaning' than the strict legal meaning. The contract one here has to construe has as its
surrounding circumstances that it was intended to govern the affairs of an international
association dedicated to promoting and controlling friendly competition in athletic   *h*
games between the inhabitants of various countries of the world. The term 'country'
would not appear to be one which has a particular significance in international law. The
Foreign Office letter which is an exhibit in this case, makes the point neatly:

   'Her Majesty's Government do not, and have never regarded Taiwan as a State.
   Nor do we regard the Chinese Nationalist authorities in Taiwan as a Government   *j*

1   [1976] 2 Lloyd's Rep 708 at 712
2   [1976] 3 All ER 570 at 575, [1976] 1 WLR 989 at 997
3   (1918) 118 NE 607 at 608
4   [1971] 3 All ER 237 at 240, [1971] 1 WLR 1381 at 1384

and have not done so since 1950, when we ceased to recognise them as the Government of China.'

And later, when dealing with a possible government statement: 'Any statement would have to be in terms of "governments" and "States" rather than "countries".' No one suggests that this case falls to be determined on any question of national or international recognition by the government so that the fact that neither Her Majesty's Government, nor for that matter the United Nations, recognises the existence of Taiwan as a separate national entity does not assist. When I say 'no one suggests', I mean neither counsel in this case, though it is noteworthy that in the passage from the minutes which I have read it appears that that may have been one of the matters which were considered by the Federation's congress when passing the offending resolution ('offending' in the sense that it offends ROCTFA). Further, I am ready to accept, as appears to be the fact, that the government on the mainland and the authorities in Taiwan each regard themselves as the legitimate government for the whole of the State of China (which includes Taiwan). I am further ready to accept that any athlete who owed allegiance to the one authority or the other would take a similar view: it would probably be treasonable if he (or she) did not. But I do not think that either the meaning of the term 'country' or the identity of a country, once defined, can conclusively be deduced from the attitudes, or aspirations, of these respective authorities or even of the athletes themselves. The word must be given its ordinary meaning, having regard to the 'factual matrix' in which it was formed. I should find it surprising if the ordinary person did not regard Scotland and Wales as being examples of countries; in doing so they would not be considering the existence, or absence, of a separate government, nor the desire, or lack of it, of any of the inhabitants of either area to achieve the position of belonging to a separate state. If the ordinary person was asked whether, in the context of international sport, Scotland and Wales were separate countries I think he would say, 'Of course'. The slightly more sophisticated respondent might add: 'But it might depend on whether there is some special definition of "country" in the rules.' Scotland and Wales are regarded for both Association and Rugby Union football as separate countries; for international yacht racing they are not. No doubt discrepancies of this kind could be multiplied. This must all depend on whether the rules of the appropriate international body allows for representation of 'countries' and whether if so there is some form of words which gives to the term 'country' a meaning other than the ordinary one. Despite reference to 'international' competition and to 'national' authorities in the IAAF rules, I see no warrant for equating 'country' with 'nation', for the terms 'international' and 'national' are not insisting on nationhood in the sense of political independence or ethnic origin. The significant part of r 1 seems to me to be that the bodies to be elected must be those in 'control of amateur track and field athletics' in the countries which they represent. The sentence in r 1(1), 'Only one member for each country can be affiliated', was never, in my view, intended to regulate differences caused by rival political claims to sovereignty; it was clearly introduced to prevent, or compose, a situation where, although the identity of the country was not in dispute, there were two or more rival associations within the country claiming that they were in control of the athletes situated there. There is one thing which is abundantly clear on the facts, and is indeed unchallenged (and I disregard aspirations): AAPROC is not in control of the athletes in Taiwan and ROCTFA is not in control of the athletes on the mainland.

I would thus explain the term 'country' as covering some area in which there exists an association or federation which is in control of amateur track and field athletics within that area and such association or federation is not subservient to or itself controlled by some other association or federation covering a wider area. No doubt there might be cases in which the area covered by such an association is so clearly to be regarded as only part of a country that no ordinary person would apply the term to it, in which case it would not be a separate country. But here we have two areas, one containing a population of 19,000,000 people, the other about 900,000,000, not in fact under political or governmental control from any other area, and each with an association which is in fact in control of track and field athletics within its area, and each is an area recognisable as a separate geographical entity readily defined or definable. I conclude that each area can properly be described as a country within the meaning of the IAAF rules. If that is so the purported resolution of 5th October 1978 was not in accordance with the rules and ROCTFA have been wrongly excluded from membership.

If this is wrong it then becomes necessary to consider the rival arguments about the standing in law of the IAAF as an unincorporated association. Counsel for the defendants, as I understand it, accepts that the ultra vires rule does not apply; the term was used in the defendants' affidavits, I suppose, as an expression inexactly describing the want of authority of an agent. But counsel's main submission is that, if 'country' is defined so as to exclude ROCTFA (and for this argument one must assume it is), then the members present at the congress in 1956 and voting in favour of the election of ROCTFA were acting without authority, and that no amount of subsequent conduct, either by ROCTFA or any other member of the International Federation, can validly change that position, unless it can be shown that all the members treated ROCTFA as validly elected. His authorities for the proposition that no amount of conduct serves to validate an act done without authority are *Re Tobacco Trade Benevolent Association*[1], and a proposition in Halsbury's Laws of England[2] which is said to be supported by *Harington v Sendall*[3]. The proposition is in these terms:

> 'Thus where the rules of such a club contain no express provision for their amendment or alteration, but have been altered from time to time in general meeting, and the members have acquiesced in the alterations, a member who declines to pay an increased subscription which has been resolved upon in general meeting, and who is posted in default, is entitled to an injunction restraining the committee from excluding him from the privileges of the club, *although he has himself acquiesced in some of the previous alterations*, and the reasonableness or otherwise of the alteration objected to is immaterial.' (Emphasis mine.)

It is on the words I have emphasised that counsel relies. *Harington v Sendall*[3] was concerned with certain members of the Oxford and Cambridge University Club who objected to the fact that the membership subscription had been raised from eight guineas to nine. The plaintiff, one of the dissentient members, had been elected in 1886 and the rules at that time had no provision for amendment. He objected that the resolution to raise the subscription was invalid, refused to pay more than eight guineas and, when posted as a defaulter, brought the action for an injunction against the club. Joyce J had no difficulty in finding that, as there was no provision for altering the rules, the purported alteration, even by a majority, was initially invalid as such an alteration required the assent of all. This is clearly right and I do not understand counsel for the plaintiff to seek to challenge it. But then one of the club's arguments before Joyce J as recorded was that[4]—

> 'the plaintiff, never having objected to any previous exercise of the power of the general meeting to alter the rules, is precluded by acquiescence from raising any objection in the present instance.'

Joyce J dealt with that argument thus[5]:

> 'Again, it is said that the plaintiff has acquiesced in certain alterations in the rules having during his time been made by general meetings. Such alterations appear to

1   [1958] 3 All ER 353, [1958] 1 WLR 1113
2   6 Halsbury's Laws (4th Edn) para 221
3   [1903] 1 Ch 921
4   [1903] 1 Ch 921 at 925
5   [1903] 1 Ch 921 at 927

me to have been altogether of a minor character, and it may have been with perfect
unanimity of opinion among the members. Because the plaintiff instituted no
action for an injunction in these trifling matters, when neither he nor any one else
objected, I cannot hold him to be precluded from insisting upon his right when a
case arises in which his pecuniary interests are directly and materially affected.'

Now this passage is not at all authority for the very wide proposition in Halsbury's
Laws of England. It seems clear that Joyce J was concentrating on the trivial nature of the
alterations acquiesced in by the plaintiff and that if the matters had been of substance he
would or might have considered a failure to take proceedings for an injunction as fatal
to the plaintiff's claim; such proceedings would, of course, have had to be prompt
because of the equitable doctrine of laches.

What of the *Tobacco Trade* case[1]? That was a case where the rule which was objected
to was a new rule giving the association, which was a charity, power to widen the range
of its permitted investments. The main point in the case was thus whether an alteration
to the rules permitting a charity to do that which, without a valid rule permitting it,
would be statutorily illegal, could be said to be a valid alteration although no express
power to make such an alteration was contained in the rules. The suggestion was that
the members of the unincorporated body had for so long assumed that such a power
existed that it ought now to be considered as existing. Harman J put it in this way[2]:

'The present summons starts by asking the court the question whether that was
a valid alteration. In my opinion, it plainly was not. This body started with no
power to alter its rules, and such a body cannot alter its rules by its own motion
except possibly by the concurrence of every member of the body. There never was
any pretence that anything of that sort was obtained here. In 1860, those who had
control of this body thought they could alter their rules as they pleased. The
alteration made in 1871 did not purport to confer a power of alteration, but to curb
a power of alteration which was presumed to exist. In my judgment it did not exist
and, therefore, the new rule adopted in 1871 is a mere nullity. It is said that the rule
has been so long acted on and must have been so well known to those who
subscribed and those who gave legacies over so many years, that it ought now to be
considered as a rule of the association. In my judgment that is not so. Those in
control wrongly assumed that there was power to alter when there was no power to
alter and, therefore, the alterations have always been invalid alterations. If that is
awkward for the association, they have an easy remedy in their hands. They can go
to the Charity Commission and get a proper scheme setting their house in order.
I do not suppose any harm has been done, but a charity, unless empowered by its
rules, cannot go outside investments authorised by law.'

That case seems to me to be quite different from the present one. It involved a charity
whose powers were statutorily limited unless a decision valid under the rules was taken;
and the argument was not that the decision itself had been long acquiesced in; it was that
the power to alter the rules had long been assumed. There must it seems to me be a
fundamental distinction between the proposition that continued acquiescence in rule
alterations results in the creation of a power to alter rules where no such power existed,
and the proposition that continued acquiescence in a decision taken without conforming
with the rules validates that particular decision. Both propositions can be said to depend
on either estoppel or waiver.

To take estoppel first, until *Central London Property Trust Ltd v High Trees House Ltd*[3] it
was generally assumed that to found estoppel there had to be a representation of an
existing fact. Where, as here, estoppel by conduct is relied on, the existing fact about

---

1   [1958] 3 All ER 353, [1958] 1 WLR 1113
2   [1958] 3 All ER 353 at 355, [1958] 1 WLR 1113 at 1115
3   (1946) [1956] 1 All ER 256, [1947] KB 130

which the representation is being made is that the decision already taken is regarded as a valid one; it is not a representation that any future decision taken in the same circumstances will be regarded as a valid one. The distinction between the two propositions earlier set out is then plain; the latter is concerned with representations of existing fact and the former with statements or promises as to future intention. On the old understanding of the doctrine therefore, the latter would be covered by estoppel while the former would not. The doctrine of 'promissory estoppel' was first enunciated by Lord Cairns LC in *Hughes v Metropolitan Railway Co*[1] and 'rescued from oblivion' by the *High Trees case*[2] (per Lord Denning MR in *W J Alan & Co v El Nasr Export & Import Co*[3]). The doctrine was expressed in this way by Lord Cairns LC[4]:

> '. . . it is the first principle upon which all Courts of Equity proceed, that if parties who have entered into definite and distinct terms involving certain legal results— certain penalties or legal forfeiture—afterwards by their own act or with their own consent enter upon a course of negotiation which has the effect of leading one of the parties to suppose that the strict rights arising under the contract will not be enforced, or will be kept in suspense, or held in abeyance, the person who otherwise might have enforced those rights will not be allowed to enforce them where it would be inequitable having regard to the dealings which have thus taken place between the parties.'

As Lord Denning MR pointed out in the *El Nasr* case[5]: 'The principle is much wider than waiver itself; but waiver is a good instance of its application.' And Lord Denning MR went on[6]:

> 'The principle of waiver is simply this: If one party, by his conduct, leads another to believe that the strict rights arising under the contract will not be insisted on, intending that the other should act on that belief, and he does act on it, then the first party will not afterwards be allowed to insist on the strict legal rights when it would be inequitable for him to do so . . . There may be no consideration moving from him who benefits by the waiver. There may be no detriment to him by acting on it. There may be nothing in writing. Nevertheless, the one who waives his strict rights cannot afterwards insist on them. His strict rights are at any rate suspended so long as the waiver lasts. He may on occasion be able to revert to his strict legal rights for the future by giving reasonable notice in that behalf, or otherwise making it plain by his conduct that he will thereafter insist upon them . . . But there are cases where no withdrawal is possible. It may be too late to withdraw; or it cannot be done without injustice to the other party. In that event he is bound by his waiver. He will not be allowed to revert to his strict legal rights. He can only enforce them subject to the waiver he has made.'

It is to be noted that despite the eminence of the advocates involved and the erudition of the judge who decided it no mention is made from first to last in the *Tobacco Trade* case[7] of any principle of promissory estoppel or waiver, nor was *Hughes v Metropolitan Railway Co*[1] or the *High Trees* case[2] referred to in argument or judgment. In any event, these two principles formed a rapidly developing part of our law. The most that can be said for the *Tobacco Trade* case[7] (and even at the highest in counsel for the defendants'

1 (1877) 2 App Cas 439, [1874–80] All ER Rep 187
2 (1946) [1956] 1 All ER 256, [1947] KB 130
3 [1972] 2 All ER 127 at 139, [1972] 2 QB 189 at 212
4 2 App Cas 439 at 448, [1874–80] All ER Rep 187 at 191
5 [1972] 2 All ER 127 at 139–140, [1972] 2 QB 189 at 212
6 [1972] 2 All ER 127 at 140, [1972] 2 QB 189 at 213
7 [1958] 3 All ER 353, [1958] 1 WLR 1113

favour for *Harington v Sendall*[1]) is that they are authorities for the proposition that

a previous alterations of rules, where no power exists to alter them, even if acquiesced in for long periods, cannot prevent a member of a club from maintaining that a fresh attempt to alter them is invalid. Even that proposition, it seems to me, may require modification in the light of the developing recognition of the principles of promissory estoppel and waiver to which I have referred. But it is clear to me that neither case is saying that there is a principle in the law of unincorporated associations that there can be

b no estoppel by the conduct of members where that conduct amounts to a representation that a decision taken, albeit without authority, is a valid decision. The conduct, to found estoppel, will of course have to be the conduct of all.

If estoppel by conduct can therefore be found applicable to the case of members of an unincorporated association the question is then whether in this case the conduct of all the members can be said to have the effect of estopping the federation from denying the

c continuing membership of ROCTFA.

ROCTFA was elected in 1956. There were certain members opposed to its election but they did nothing to challenge that election in the courts as they could have done. For 22 years ROCTFA regarded itself as a member of the federation as did the officers and all the other members except those opposed to their election. ROCTFA paid its subscription regularly and engaged in international competitions with other members. Had any

d determined effort been made by the dissentient voices to challenge the election it may well be that a decision to alter the rules could have been taken in accordance with the then existing rule which required a majority of 51% of the total voting power present or two-thirds of the voting power present *whichever was the less.* The present rule requires the vote to be *both* two-thirds of the votes cast *and* at least one-half of the total voting power.

e In the circumstances, and on the basis of estoppel by representation as to existing fact, I am satisfied that it is too late for the federation, and that means all its members, to seek to say that the election of ROCTFA was invalid under the rules. The defendants cannot rely on the dissent of some members as indicating that all the members, and therefore the federation itself, are not bound, since those dissenting members themselves by their conduct in failing to challenge, by proper process, the validity of the election of ROCTFA

f over a period as long as 22 years, have represented, not only to the plaintiff but to all the non-dissentient members as well, that ROCTFA was in fact a duly elected member. I should come to the same conclusion if it were necessary to apply the principles of waiver, if, that is, the two principles of waiver and estoppel can be said in the present circumstances to fall to be separately considered.

There is another way of putting the estoppel point: that is that the representation of

g fact made by the conduct of the members was that the term 'country' in the rules was used in such a way as to embrace within its ambit both AAPROC and ROCTFA. In this way the members could be said by their conduct to be estopped from asserting that 'their own dictionary meaning' of the word 'country' could be taken to have any other significance. I think that this view of the matter would also be right for the same reasons.

h Finally, there is the mysterious affair of the membership of CNAAF. This body, it will be remembered, was elected as the member for 'China' at some time around the war of 1914–18 or shortly thereafter. It has never been expelled. ROCTFA certainly claims to be that same organisation. A similar claim was made by AAPROC, when it originally applied for membership, but was rejected by the federation. It would be interesting to know whether any Chinese athletes competed in the 1948 Olympic Games in London or

j the 1952 Games in Helsinki. If they did so it could only be on the basis that CNAAF was still regarded as a member at those dates. The argument that there is only one 'country' of China under the rules would then be a difficult one for the federation to sustain since

---

1   [1903] 1 Ch 921

they elected AAPROC to membership in 1954 without expelling CNAAF. However, since evidence about this matter seems sparse or non-existent and since there are already better reasons for deciding that ROCTFA is still a member I shall not pursue what remains an interesting speculation. *a*

For these reasons I think that there should be judgment for the plaintiff that ROCTFA remains a member of the International Federation and that it is entitled to the rights and privileges of membership. Counsel for the plaintiff also asks for an injunction. Counsel for the defendants resists this, saying that the president and honorary treasurer, the two *b* senior officers of the federation, have been in court throughout the argument, are honourable men, and there is no likelihood that the federation will not give effect to the declarations. The two officers, who are of course the titular defendants, in fact took the view in the debate which resulted in the effective expulsion of ROCTFA, that ROCTFA was validly elected. It is apparent that I think they were right. They were, however, unable to persuade the members to adopt the course they advocated. I do not know *c* whether the court's declarations would carry any more weight with this international body, most of whose members are not susceptible to the court's jurisdiction. I understand that there is an important meeting of the International Federation shortly and that there is no realistic prospect of ROCTFA being able to compete in any international contest before that date. In the circumstances I think it would be wrong, because it might complicate a delicate situation, to grant the injunction at this stage. *d* That will not prevent the plaintiff coming back to the court to ask for the injunction if there is evidence that the declaratory order of the court is in danger of being flouted.

I should end with one further word of warning. My ruling that ROCTFA was validly elected does not mean, as I see it, that the election of AAPROC is invalid. Whether the matter is decided on the meaning of the word 'country' in the rules, or on the doctrines of estoppel or waiver, the position is in my view that in the events which have occurred *e* neither the application of the rules nor the conduct of the members can have any other result than that both AAPROC and ROCTFA can be and are members simultaneously, and the declarations I am making must not be construed as effecting any other result. As I read the third declaration prayed, it would in no way impeach the validity of that part of the resolution of 5th October 1978 which declared that AAPROC was elected to membership of the federation. *f*

Declarations accordingly. Liberty to apply for injunction.

Solicitors: *Herbert Smith & Co* (for the plaintiff); *Linklaters & Paines* (for the defendants).

K Mydeen Esq   Barrister. *g*

End of Volume 3